The Martin-Gay Student Success Program

Each Martin-Gay product is motivated by Elayn's firm belief that every student can succeed. This Student Success Program is designed to help students review and retain basic algebra concepts <u>and</u> gain the study skills necessary for success in all levels of mathematics!

Options to support a variety of classroom environments!

MyMathLab® for School

The Student Organizer includes selected examples from the text and videos. It was written to help students achieve organized course notes and examples.

New Student Success Tips
My new 3-4 minute video segments on study skills are daily reminders to renew organizational and study habits.

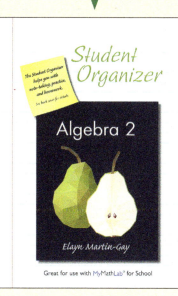

Martin-Gay Interactive Lecture Series Contains:

- Video Lecture Series
- Student Success Tips Videos
- Chapter Test Prep Videos

Algebra 2

Elayn Martin-Gay

PEARSON

Boston Columbus Hoboken Indianapolis New York San Francisco
Amsterdam Cape Town Dubai London Madrid Milan Munich Paris Montréal Toronto
Delhi Mexico City São Paulo Sydney Hong Kong Seoul Singapore Taipei Tokyo

Editorial Director, Mathematics: *Christine Hoag*
Editor-in-Chief: *Michael Hirsch*
Acquisitions Editor: *Mary Beckwith*
Project Manager: *Christine Whitlock*
Project Team Lead: *Peter Silvia*
Assistant Editor: *Matthew Summers*
Editorial Assistant: *Megan Tripp*
Executive Development Editor: *Dawn Nuttall*
Program Team Lead: *Karen Wernholm*
Program Manager: *Patty Bergin*
Cover Design: *Tamara Newnam*
Program Design Lead: *Heather Scott*
Director, Course Production: *Ruth Berry*

Executive Content Manager, MathXL: *Rebecca Williams*
Senior Content Developer, TestGen: *John Flanagan*
Media Producer: *Shana Siegmund/Marielle Guiney*
Executive Marketing Manager: *Jaclyn Flynn*
Director of Marketing, Mathematics: *Roxanne McCarley*
Senior Marketing Manager: *Rachel Ross*
Marketing Assistant: *Kelly Cross*
Senior Author Support/Technology Specialist: *Joe Vetere*
Senior Procurement Specialist: *Carol Melville*
Interior Design, Production Management, Answer Art, and Composition: *Integra Software Services Pvt. Ltd.*
Text Art: *Scientific Illustrators*
Cover Image: *Natalia NK/Shutterstock*

Acknowledgments of third party content appear on pages P1–P3, which constitutes an extension of this copyright page.

PEARSON, ALWAYS LEARNING, and MYMATHLAB are exclusive trademarks in the U.S. and/or other countries owned by Pearson Education, Inc. or its affiliates.

Unless otherwise indicated herein, any third-party trademarks that may appear in this work are the property of their respective owners and any references to third-party trademarks, logos or other trade dress are for demonstrative or descriptive purposes only. Such references are not intended to imply any sponsorship, endorsement, authorization, or promotion of Pearson's products by the owners of such marks, or any relationship between the owner and Pearson Education, Inc. or its affiliates, authors, licensees or distributors.

Library of Congress Cataloging-in-Publication Data
Martin-Gay, K. Elayn, 1955-
  Algebra 2 / Elayn Martin-Gay, University of New Orleans.—1st edition.
    pages cm
  ISBN 0-13-409388-7 (alk. paper)
1. Mathematics—Textbooks. 2. Mathematics—Study and teaching (Secondary) I. Title.
II. Title: Algebra two.
  QA135.6.M3656 2016
  512.9—dc 3   2015004963

Copyright © 2016 Pearson Education, Inc. or its affiliates. All Rights Reserved. Printed in the United States of America. This publication is protected by copyright, and permission should be obtained from the publisher prior to any prohibited reproduction, storage in a retrieval system, or transmission in any form or by any means, electronic, mechanical, photocopying, recording, or otherwise. For information regarding permissions, request forms and the appropriate contacts within the Pearson Education Global Rights & Permissions department, please visit www.pearsoned.com/permissions/.

24 2022

www.pearsonschool.com

ISBN-10: 0-13-409388-7 (Student Edition)
ISBN-13: 978-0-13-409388-8

Contents

CHAPTER 1 Real Numbers and Algebraic Expressions 1

- 1.1 Tips for Success in Mathematics 2
- 1.2 Algebraic Expressions and Sets of Numbers 7
- 1.3 Operations on Real Numbers 17
  Integrated Review: Algebraic Expressions and Operations on Whole Numbers 29
- 1.4 Properties of Real Numbers 30

CHAPTER 2 Equations, Inequalities, and Problem Solving 46

- 2.1 Linear Equations in One Variable 47
- 2.2 An Introduction to Problem Solving 55
- 2.3 Formulas and Problem Solving 67
- 2.4 Linear Inequalities and Problem Solving 74
  Integrated Review: Linear Equations and Inequalities 85
- 2.5 Compound Inequalities 85
- 2.6 Absolute Value Equations 92
- 2.7 Absolute Value Inequalities 97

CHAPTER 3 Graphs and Functions 108

- 3.1 Graphing Equations 109
- 3.2 Introduction to Functions 120
- 3.3 Graphing Linear Functions 136
- 3.4 The Slope of a Line 145
- 3.5 Equations of Lines 157
  Integrated Review: Linear Equations in Two Variables 167
- 3.6 Graphing Piecewise-Defined Functions and Shifting and Reflecting Graphs of Functions 168
- 3.7 Graphing Linear Inequalities 176
  Extension: Stretching and Compressing Graphs of Absolute Value Functions 181

CHAPTER 4 Systems of Equations 195

- 4.1 Solving Systems of Linear Equations in Two Variables 196
- 4.2 Solving Systems of Linear Equations in Three Variables 207
- 4.3 Systems of Linear Equations and Problem Solving 214
  Integrated Review: Systems of Linear Equations 226
- 4.4 Solving Systems of Equations by Matrices 227
- 4.5 Systems of Linear Inequalities 233
- 4.6 Linear Programming 236

CHAPTER 5 More Work with Matrices 250

- 5.1 Matrix Operations and Solving Matrix Equations 251
- 5.2 Multiplying Matrices and Solving Applications 257
  Integrated Review: Operations on Matrices 266
- 5.3 Solving Systems of Equations Using Determinants 266
- 5.4 Multiplicative Inverses of Matrices 272
- 5.5 Matrix Equations 277

CHAPTER 6 Exponents, Polynomials, and Polynomial Functions 286

- 6.1 Exponents and Scientific Notation 287
- 6.2 More Work with Exponents and Scientific Notation 296
- 6.3 Polynomials and Polynomial Functions 302
- 6.4 Multiplying Polynomials 314
- 6.5 The Greatest Common Factor and Factoring by Grouping 322
- 6.6 Factoring Trinomials 328
- 6.7 Factoring by Special Products 337
  Integrated Review: Operations on Polynomials and Factoring Strategies 343
- 6.8 Solving Equations by Factoring and Problem Solving 347
  Extension: Even and Odd Power Functions and End Behavior 359

CHAPTER 7 Rational Expressions 370

- 7.1 Rational Functions and Multiplying and Dividing Rational Expressions 371
- 7.2 Adding and Subtracting Rational Expressions 383

- 7.3 Simplifying Complex Fractions 391
- 7.4 Dividing Polynomials: Long Division and Synthetic Division 398
- 7.5 Solving Equations Containing Rational Expressions 409
  Integrated Review: Expressions and Equations Containing Rational Expressions 416
- 7.6 Rational Equations and Problem Solving 418
- 7.7 Variation and Problem Solving 426

CHAPTER 8 Rational Exponents, Radicals, and Complex Numbers 441

- 8.1 Radicals and Radical Functions 442
- 8.2 Rational Exponents 450
- 8.3 Simplifying Radical Expressions 457
- 8.4 Adding, Subtracting, and Multiplying Radical Expressions 466
- 8.5 Rationalizing Denominators and Numerators of Radical Expressions 471
  Integrated Review: Radicals and Rational Exponents 478
- 8.6 Radical Equations and Problem Solving 479
- 8.7 Complex Numbers 489
- 8.8 Standard Deviation 496

CHAPTER 9 Quadratic and Higher Degree Equations and Functions 513

- 9.1 Solving Quadratic Equations by Completing the Square 514
- 9.2 Solving Quadratic Equations by the Quadratic Formula 523
- 9.3 Solving Equations by Using Quadratic Methods 533
  Integrated Review: Summary on Solving Quadratic Equations 542
- 9.4 Zeros of Polynomial Functions 543
- 9.5 The Fundamental Theorem of Algebra 548
- 9.6 Nonlinear Inequalities in One Variable 552

CHAPTER 10 Exponential and Logarithmic Functions 564

- 10.1 The Algebra of Functions; Composite Functions 565
- 10.2 Inverse Functions 570
- 10.3 Exponential Functions 581

10.4 Logarithmic Functions 589
10.5 Properties of Logarithms 597
Integrated Review: Functions and Properties of Logarithms 602
10.6 Common Logarithms, Natural Logarithms, and Change of Base 603
10.7 Exponential and Logarithmic Equations and Applications 608

CHAPTER 11 Graphing Quadratic Functions, Rational Functions, and Conic Sections 622

11.1 Quadratic Functions and Their Graphs 623
11.2 Further Graphing of Quadratic Functions 631
11.3 Graphing Rational Functions by Transformations 638
11.4 Further Graphing of Rational Functions 644
11.5 The Parabola and the Circle 653
11.6 The Ellipse and the Hyperbola 662
Integrated Review: Review of Conic Sections Only 669
11.7 Solving Nonlinear Systems of Equations 670
11.8 Nonlinear Inequalities and Systems of Inequalities 675

CHAPTER 12 Sequences, Series, and the Binomial Theorem 687

12.1 Sequences 688
12.2 Arithmetic and Geometric Sequences 692
12.3 Series 699
Integrated Review: Sequences and Series 703
12.4 Partial Sums of Arithmetic and Geometric Sequences 704
12.5 The Binomial Theorem 711
Extension: Inductive and Deductive Reasoning 715

CHAPTER 13 Counting Methods and Probability Theory 728

13.1 The Fundamental Counting Principle 729
13.2 Permutations 734
13.3 Combinations 740
13.4 Fundamentals of Probability 746
Integrated Review 754

13.5 Probability with the Fundamental Counting Principle, Permutations, and Combinations 755
13.6 Events Involving *Not* and *Or*; Odds 760
13.7 Events Involving *And*; Conditional Probability 770
13.8 The Normal Distribution 779
Extension: Expected Value 783

CHAPTER 14 Trigonometric Functions 794

14.1 Angles and Radian Measure 795
14.2 Right Triangle Trigonometry 810
14.3 Trigonometric Functions of Any Angle 826
14.4 Trigonometric Functions of Real Numbers; Periodic Functions 838
Integrated Review: Angles and Right Triangles 846
14.5 Graphs of Sine and Cosine Functions 847
14.6 Graph of the Tangent Function 867
14.7 Inverse Trigonometric Functions 873
14.8 Applications of Trigonometric Functions 887

CHAPTER 15 Trigonometric Identities, Equations, and Applications 904

15.1 Verifying Trigonometric Identities 905
15.2 Sum and Difference Formulas 915
15.3 Double-Angle and Half-Angle Formulas 925
Integrated Review: What You Know 933
15.4 Trigonometric Equations 934
15.5 The Law of Sines 947
15.6 The Law of Cosines 959

Appendices

Appendix A 972

A.1 Geometric Figures and Formulas 972
A.2 Trigonometric Formulas 973
A.3 Table of Percent, Decimal, and Fraction Equivalents 975

Appendix B: Surveys and Margins of Error 976

Appendix C: Practice Final Exam 980

Answers to Selected Exercises A1 • Index I1 • Photo Credits P1

Preface

Algebra 2 was written to provide a solid foundation in algebra for students who might not have previous experience in algebra. Specific care was taken to make sure students have the most up-to-date relevant text preparation for their next mathematics course or for nonmathematical courses that require an understanding of algebraic fundamentals. I have tried to achieve this by writing a user-friendly text that is keyed to objectives and contains many worked-out examples and illustrations. As suggested by AMATYC and the NCTM Standards (plus Addenda), real-life and real-data applications, data interpretation, conceptual understanding, problem solving, writing, cooperative learning, appropriate use of technology, mental mathematics, number sense, estimation, critical thinking, and geometric concepts are emphasized and integrated throughout the book.

What's in this text?

- **The Martin-Gay Program** and MyMathLab® for School actively encourage students to use the text, video program, and Student Organizer as an integrated learning system.
- **The Student Organizer** guides students through the 3 main components of studying effectively—notetaking, practice, and homework.
    - The Organizer includes before-class preparation exercises, notetaking pages in a 2-column format for use in class, and examples paired with exercises for practice for each section. Includes an outline and questions for use with the Student Success Tip Videos.

    It is 3-hole-punched. Available in loose-leaf, notebook-ready format and in MyMathLab for School.

- **Student Success Tips Videos** are 3- to 5-minute video segments designed to be daily reminders to students to continue practicing and maintaining good organizational and study habits. They are organized in three categories and are available in MyMathLab for School and the Interactive Lecture Series. The categories are:

    1. Success Tips that apply to any course such as Time Management.
    2. Success Tips that apply to any mathematics course. One example is based on understanding that mathematics is a course that requires homework to be completed in a timely fashion.
    3. Section- or Content-specific Success Tips to help students avoid common mistakes or to better understand concepts that often prove challenging. One example of this type of tip is how to apply the order of operations to simplify an expression.

- **Interactive Lecture Series**, featuring your text author (Elayn Martin-Gay), provides students with active learning at their own pace. The videos are available in MyMathLab for School and offer the following resources and more:

    A complete lecture for each section of the text highlights key examples and exercises from the text. "Pop-ups" reinforce key terms, definitions, and concepts.

    An interface with menu navigation features allows students to quickly find and focus on the examples and exercises they need to review.

    Student Success Tips Videos.

- **The Interactive Lecture Series** also includes the following resources for test prep:

    The Chapter Test Prep Videos help students during their most teachable moment—when they are preparing for a test. This innovation provides step-by-step solutions for the exercises found in each Chapter Test. The chapter test prep videos are also available on YouTube™. The videos are captioned in English and Spanish.

- **The Martin-Gay MyMathLab** course includes extensive exercise coverage and a comprehensive video program. There are section lecture videos for every section, which students can also access at the specific objective level; Student Success Tips Videos; and watch clips at the exercise level to help students while doing homework.

Key Pedagogical Features

Chapters Chapters are divided into Sections. Below is an overview of a Section, then an Exercise Set, then the End-of-Chapter features.

Sections Each section begins with a list of Objectives. These objectives are also repeated at the place of discussion within the section. When applicable, under the list of objectives there is a list of new Vocabulary words. Throughout the section, each new vocabulary word is highlighted at place of definition.

Examples Detailed, step-by-step examples are available throughout each section. Many examples reflect real life and include illustrations. Additional instructional support is provided in the annotated examples.

Practice Exercises Throughout the text, each worked-out example has a parallel Practice exercise. These invite students to be actively involved in the learning process. Students should try each Practice exercise after finishing the corresponding example. Learning by doing will help students grasp ideas before moving on to other concepts. All answers to the Practice exercises are provided at the back of the text.

Helpful Hints Helpful Hints contain practical advice on applying mathematical concepts. Strategically placed where students are most likely to need immediate reinforcement, Helpful Hints help students avoid common trouble areas and mistakes.

Exercise Sets The exercise sets have been carefully written with a special focus on making sure that even- and odd-numbered exercises are paired and that they contain real-life applications and illustrations. In addition, many types of exercises were included to help students obtain a full conceptual knowledge of the section's topics. These types of exercises are labeled and include: Multiple Choice, Complete the Table, Multiple Steps, Sketch, Construction, Fill in the Blank, Complete the Proof, Proof, Coordinate Geometry, and Find the Error.

Overall, the exercises in an exercise set are written starting with less difficult ones and then increasing in difficulty. This allows students to gain confidence while working the earlier exercises. To help achieve this, the exercises at the beginning of a section are keyed to previously worked examples. If applicable, a section of Mixed Practice exercises are included. The odd answers to these exercises are found at the end of this text.

Vocabulary and Readiness Check These questions are immediately prior to a section's exercise set. These exercises quickly check a student's understanding of new vocabulary words. Also, the readiness exercises center on a student's understanding of a concept that is necessary in order to continue to the exercise set. The odd answers to these exercises are in the back of this text.

Applications Real-world and real-data application exercises occur in almost every exercise set and show the relevance of mathematics and geometry and help students gradually and continuously develop their problem-solving skills.

Concept Extensions These exercises are found toward the end of every exercise set, but before the Review and Preview exercises (described below). Concept Extension exercises require students to take the concepts from that section a step further by combining them with concepts learned in previous sections or by combining several concepts from the current section.

Writing Exercises These exercises occur in almost every exercise set and require students to provide a written response to explain concepts or justify their thinking.

Review and Preview Exercises These exercises occur at the end of each exercise set (except in Chapter 1) and are keyed to earlier sections. They review concepts learned earlier in the text that will be needed in the next section or chapter.

Exercise Set Resource Icons Located at the opening of each exercise set, these icons remind students of the resources available for extra practice and support:

MyMathLab® for School

See Student Resources descriptions on page xiv for details on the individual resources available.

End-of-Chapter The following features can be found at the end of each chapter. They are meant to give students an overall view of the chapter and thus help them have an understanding of how the concepts of a chapter fit together. All answers to these features below are found at the end of this text.

Mixed Practice Exercises In the section exercise sets, these exercises require students to determine the problem type and strategy needed to solve it just as they would need to do on a test.

Vocabulary Check This feature provides an opportunity for students to become more familiar with the use of mathematical terms as they strengthen their verbal skills. These appear at the end of each chapter before the Chapter Review.

Chapter Review The end of every chapter contains a comprehensive review of topics introduced in the chapter. The Chapter Review offers exercises keyed to every section in the chapter, as well as Mixed Review exercises that are not keyed to sections.

Chapter Test and Chapter Test Prep Videos The Chapter Test is structured to include those problems that involve common student errors. The **Chapter Test Prep Videos** give students instant access to a step-by-step video solution of each exercise in the Chapter Test.

Chapter Standardized Test After each Chapter Test, there is a standardized test. These chapter standardized tests are written to help students prepare for standardized tests in the future. They are multiple choice tests and cover the material presented in the associated chapter.

Instructor and Student Resources

INSTRUCTOR RESOURCES

Many of the teacher supplements are available electronically, at no charge, to qualified adopters on the Instructor Resource Center (IRC). To obtain IRC access, you must first register and set up a user name and password. To register, visit **PearsonSchool.com/access_request.** You will be required to complete a brief, one-time registration subject to verification of educator status. Upon verification, access information and instructions will be sent via email.

After you receive your confirmation, go to **pearsonhighered.com** and choose **Support** from the top right navigation, then select **Educator.** Enter the ISBN of your student edition in the search box. Once you locate your program select the *Resources* tab to preview a list of available online resources.

MyMathLab® for School (available for purchase; access code required)

MyMathLab for School is a text-specific, easily customizable, online course that integrates interactive multimedia instruction with textbook content. MyMathLab for School gives you the tools you need to deliver all or a portion of your course online.

MyMathLab for School features include:

- Interactive eText, including highlighting and note taking tools, and links to videos and exercises
- Rich and flexible course management, communication, and teacher support tools
- Online homework and assessment, and personalized study plans
- Complete multimedia library to enhance learning
- All teacher resources in one convenient location

For more information, visit **www.mymathlabforschool.com** or contact your Pearson Account General Manager.

Instructor's Solutions Manual (Available for download from the IRC)

TestGen® (Available for download from the IRC)

Instructor-to-Instructor Videos—available in the Instructor Resources section of the MyMathLab for School course.

MathXL® for School (access code required)

MathXL for School is a powerful online homework, tutorial, and assessment supplement that aligns to Pearson Education's textbooks in mathematics or statistics. With MathXL for School, teachers can:

- Create, edit, and assign auto-graded online homework and tests correlated at the objective level to the textbook
- Utilize automatic grading to rapidly assess student understanding
- Track both student and group performance in an online gradebook
- Prepare students for high-stakes testing, including aligning assignments to state standards, where available
- Deliver quality, effective instruction regardless of experience level

With MathXL for School, students can:

- Do their homework and receive immediate feedback
- Get self-paced assistance on problems in a variety of ways (guided solutions, step-by-step examples, video clips, animations)
- Have a large number of practice problems to choose from, helping them master a topic
- Receive personalized study plans and homework based on test results

For more information and to purchase student access codes after the first year, visit our Web site at www.mathxlforschool.com, or contact your Pearson Account General Manager.

STUDENT RESOURCES

The following resources are available for purchase and in MyMathLab for School:

Interactive Lecture Series Videos	Student Organizer	Student Solutions Manual
Provides students with active learning at their pace. The videos offer: • A complete lecture for each text section. The interface allows easy navigation to examples and exercises students need to review. • Interactive Concept Check exercises • Student Success Tips Videos • Chapter Test Prep Videos	Guides students through the 3 main components of studying effectively—notetaking, practice, and homework. • The Organizer includes before-class preparation exercises, notetaking pages in a 2-column format for use in class, and examples paired with exercises for practice for each section. Includes an outline and questions for use with the Student Success Tip Videos. It is 3-hole-punched. Available in loose-leaf, notebook-ready format and in MyMathLab.	Provides completely worked-out solutions to the odd-numbered section exercises; all exercises in the Integrated Reviews, Chapter Reviews, Chapter Tests, and Cumulative Reviews

ABOUT THE AUTHOR

Elayn Martin-Gay has taught mathematics at the University of New Orleans for more than 25 years. Her numerous teaching awards include the local University Alumni Association's Award for Excellence in Teaching, and Outstanding Developmental Educator at University of New Orleans, presented by the Louisiana Association of Developmental Educators.

Prior to writing textbooks, Elayn Martin-Gay developed an acclaimed series of lecture videos to support developmental mathematics students in their quest for success. These highly successful videos originally served as the foundation material for her texts. Today, the videos are specific to each book in the Martin-Gay series. The author has also created Chapter Test Prep Videos to help students during their most "teachable moment"—as they prepare for a test—along with Instructor-to-Instructor videos that provide teaching tips, hints, and suggestions for each developmental mathematics course, including basic mathematics, prealgebra, beginning algebra, and intermediate algebra.

Elayn is the author of 12 published textbooks as well as multimedia, interactive mathematics, all specializing in developmental mathematics courses. She has also published series in Algebra 1 and Geometry. She has participated as an author across the broadest range of educational materials: textbooks, videos, tutorial software, and courseware. This provides an opportunity of various combinations for an integrated teaching and learning package offering great consistency for the student.

CHAPTER

1 Real Numbers and Algebraic Expressions

- **1.1** Tips for Success in Mathematics
- **1.2** Algebraic Expressions and Sets of Numbers
- **1.3** Operations on Real Numbers

  Integrated Review— Algebraic Expressions and Operations on Whole Numbers

- **1.4** Properties of Real Numbers

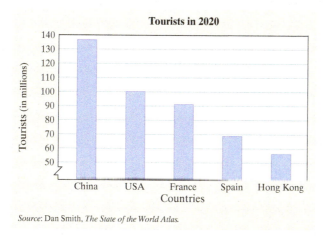

Source: Dan Smith, *The State of the World Atlas*.

Tourism is vital for many countries because income is generated by the consumption of goods and services by tourists. In addition, there is the opportunity for employment in these service industries.

In this chapter, we review operations on real numbers and the corresponding algebraic expressions. Also, we read bar graphs such as the one above on tourism.

1.1 TIPS FOR SUCCESS IN MATHEMATICS

OBJECTIVES

1. Get ready for this course.
2. Understand some general tips for success.
3. Understand how to use the resources provided in MyMathLab and Math XL.
4. Get help as soon as you need it.
5. Learn how to prepare for and take an exam.
6. Develop good time management.

Before reading this section, remember that your instructor is your best source for information. Please see your instructor for any additional help or information.

OBJECTIVE 1 ▶ Getting ready for this course. Now that you have decided to take this course, remember that a *positive attitude* will make all the difference in the world. Your belief that you can succeed is just as important as your commitment to this course. Make sure you are ready for this course by having the time and positive attitude that it takes to succeed.

Next, make sure you have scheduled your math course at a time that will give you the best chance for success. For example, if you are also working, you may want to check with your employer to make sure that your work hours will not conflict with your course schedule. Also, schedule your class during a time of day when you are more attentive and do your best work.

This online course is different than traditional math courses that you have taken in the past. You will work exercises and complete homework online. Because of this, it is your responsibility to keep a written notebook or journal of your work. You will need this documentation of your work when it comes to studying for a quiz, exam or test.

On the day of your first class period, double-check your schedule and allow yourself plenty of time to arrive. Make sure you bring a notebook or binder, paper, and a pencil or some other writing instrument. If you are required to have a lab manual, graph paper, calculator, or some other supply, bring these with you, also.

OBJECTIVE 2 ▶ General tips for success. Below are some general tips that will increase your chance for success in a mathematics class. Many of these tips will also help you in other courses you may be taking.

Note: Many tips have to do with the specifics of this online course and will be listed in Objective 3.

Exchange names and phone numbers with at least one other person in class. This contact person can be a great help if you miss an assignment or want to discuss math concepts or exercises that you find difficult.

Choose to attend all class periods and be on time. If possible, sit near the front of the classroom. This way, you will see and hear the presentation better. It may also be easier for you to participate in classroom activities.

Do your homework. You've probably heard the phrase "practice makes perfect" in relation to music and sports. It also applies to mathematics. You will find that the more time you spend solving math exercises, the easier the process becomes. In this online course, homework can be submitted as many times as you like. This means you can work and re-work those exercises that you struggle with until you master them. It is a good idea to work through all homework exercises twice before the submission deadline. Also, be sure to schedule enough time to complete your assignments before the due date assigned by your teacher.

Check your work. Checking work is the same for an online course as it is with a traditional course. This is why it is imperative that you work each exercise on paper before submitting the answer. If it's on paper, you can go back, check your work, and follow your steps to ensure the answer is correct, or find any mistakes and correct them. If you can't find your mistake or if you have any questions, make sure you talk to your teacher.

Learn from your mistakes and be patient with yourself. Everyone, even your instructor, makes mistakes. (That definitely includes me—Elayn Martin-Gay.) Use your errors to learn and to become a better math student. The key is finding and understanding your errors.

Was your mistake a careless one, or did you make it because you can't read your own math writing? If so, try to work more slowly or write more neatly and make a conscious effort to carefully check your work.

Did you make a mistake because you don't understand a concept? Take the time to review the concept or ask questions to better understand it.

Did you skip too many steps? Skipping steps or trying to do too many steps mentally may lead to preventable mistakes.

Know how to get help if you need it. It's always a good idea to ask for help whenever there is something that you don't understand. One great advantage about doing homework in MathXL is that there is built-in "help" whenever you need it. Should you get a wrong answer, a box will appear and offer you hints for working the exercise correctly. Again, this is why it is so important to keep a record of all your work on paper so you can go back and follow the suggestions. You will have three attempts to get each exercise correct before it is marked wrong. **Remember:** Even though you are working online, your teacher is your most valuable resource for answering questions. Having a written journal of neatly worked exercises helps your teacher identify mistakes on an exercise or about a concept in general.

Organize your class materials, including homework assignments, graded quizzes and tests, and notes from your class or lab. All of these items will be valuable references throughout your course, especially when studying for upcoming tests or your final exam. Make sure you can locate these materials when you need them. An excellent way to do this is by using the Organizer, which is reviewed in Objective 3.

Read your ebook or watch the section lecture videos before class. Your course ebook is available through MyMathLab. Use this online text just as you would a printed textbook. Read the assigned section(s), then write down any questions you may have. You will then be prepared to ask any questions in class the next day. Also, familiarizing yourself with the material before class will help you understand it much more readily when it is presented. There is also a reading assessment homework if assigned by your teacher.

Lecture videos, approximately 20 minutes in length, are available for every section of your ebook. These videos are specific to the material in the ebook and are presented by the ebook author, Elayn Martin-Gay. Watching a section video before class is another way to familiarize yourself with the material. Write down any questions you may have so that you can ask them in class. Watching a section video after class is also an excellent way to review concepts that are difficult for you.

Don't be afraid to ask questions. Teachers are not mind readers. Many times they do not know a concept is unclear until a student asks a question. You are not the only person in class with questions. Other students are normally grateful that someone has spoken up.

Turn in assignments on time. Always be aware of the schedule of assignments and due dates set by your teacher. Do not wait until the last minute to submit your work online. It is a good idea to submit your assignments 6–8 hours before the submission deadline to ensure some "cushion" time in case you have technology trouble.

When assignments are turned in online, it is extremely important for you to keep a copy of your written work. You will find it helpful to organize this work in a 3-ring binder. This way, you can refer to your written work to ask questions and to use it later to study for tests. (See the Organizer in Objective 3.)

OBJECTIVE 3 ▶ Understanding how to use the resources provided in MathXL and MyMathLab. There are many helpful resources available to you through MathXL and MyMathLab. It is important that you understand these resources and know when to use them. Let's start with the resources that are available within MathXL to help you successfully complete and master the exercises in your assigned homework. When working your homework assignments, you will find the following buttons listed on the right hand side of the screen.

- **Help Me Solve This**—Select this resource to get guided, step-by-step help for the exercise you are working. Once you have reached the correct answer (through the help feature) you must work an additional exercise of the same type before you receive credit for having worked it correctly.

- **View an Example**—Select this resource to view a correctly worked example similar to the exercise you are working on. After viewing the example, you can go back to your original exercise and complete it on your own.
- **Textbook**—Select this resource to go to the section of the ebook where you can find exercises similar to the one you are working on.
- **Video**—Select this resource to view a video clip of Elayn Martin-Gay (your ebook author) working an exercise similar to the one you need help with. **Not all exercises have an accompanying video clip. This button will not be listed if no video clip is available.
- **Ask My Instructor**—Select this resource to send an email to your teacher that will include the exercise that you are unsure of.

Let's now take a moment to go over a few of the features available in MyMathLab to help you prepare for class, review outside class, organize, improve your study skills, and succeed.

- **Ebook and Videos**—You can choose to read the ebook and/or watch the videos for every section of the text. The ebook includes worked examples, helpful hints, practice exercises, and section exercises for every text section. Read the material actively, and make a note of any questions you have so that you can then ask them in class.

  There are lecture **videos,** approximately 20 minutes in length, for every ebook section. Watch these videos to prepare for class, to review after class, or to help you catch up if you miss class. The videos are presented by your ebook author, Elayn Martin-Gay, so all material covered in the videos is consistent with the coverage in your ebook. Make a note of any questions you have after watching the videos so that you can ask your instructor. Your instructor may assign watching the videos as homework to prepare for class.

- **Organizer**—This is a special resource designed to help you prepare for class, take notes, practice exercise solving, and organize your homework and tests. The Organizer is intended to be placed in a 3-ring binder, and it is divided into the following segments for each ebook section:

  Before Class—directs you to read specific material in the ebook and answer questions.

  During Class—provides an organized, 2 column, in-class note taking format for you to write key examples and concepts presented in the lesson. In the **Class Notes/Examples** column, write down any examples (line-by-line) demonstrated by your instructor, seen as an example in MyMathLab, or in the Lecture Videos. In the **Your Own Notes** column, annotate the examples with your personal notes that you do not want to forget. Insert additional pages as needed.

  Practice—provides you with worked examples paired with matching **Your Turn** exercises for each text section. Read the **Review this Example** to make sure you understand the work. Then, complete the matched **Your Turn** exercise. **Complete the Example** exercises provide you with guided practice by completing part of the solution and asking you to fill in specific steps.

  After this page, insert your completed, written work for each exercise on your MathXL homework assignment.

  This Organizer is available in MyMathLab and in print.

OBJECTIVE 4 ▶ Getting help. If you have trouble completing assignments or understanding the mathematics, get help as soon as you need it! This tip is presented as an objective on its own because it is so important. In mathematics, usually the material presented in one section builds on your understanding of the previous section. This means that if you don't understand the concepts covered during a class period, there is a good chance that you will not understand the concepts covered during the next class period. If this happens to you, get help as soon as you can.

Where can you get help? Many suggestions have been made in the section on where to get help, and now it is up to you to do it. Try your instructor, a tutoring center, or a math lab, or you may want to form a study group with fellow classmates. If you do decide to see your instructor or go to a tutoring center, make sure that you have a neat notebook and are ready with your questions.

OBJECTIVE 5 ▶ Preparing for and taking an exam. Make sure that you allow yourself plenty of time to prepare for a test. If you think that you are a little "math anxious," it may be that you are not preparing for a test in a way that will ensure success. The way that you prepare for a test in mathematics is important. To prepare for a test,

1. Review your previous homework assignments. You may also want to rework some of them.
2. Review any notes from class and section-level quizzes you have taken. (If this is a final exam, also review chapter tests you have taken.)
3. Practice working out exercises by completing the Chapter Review found at the end of each chapter.
4. Since homework exercises are online, you may easily work new homework exercises. If you open an already submitted homework assignment, you can get new exercises by clicking "similar exercise." This will generate new exercises similar to the homework exercises you have already submitted. You can then work and rework exercises until you fully understand them. *Don't stop here!*
5. It is important that you place yourself in conditions similar to test conditions to find out how you will perform. In other words, as soon as you feel that you know the material, try taking some sample tests.

   In your ebook, there are two forms of chapter tests at the end of each chapter. One form is an open response test form and the second is a standardized test form. You can use these two tests as practice tests. Do not use your notes or any other help when completing these tests. Check your answers by using the answer section in the ebook. There are also exact video clip solutions to the open response practice test form. Finally, identify any concepts that you do not understand and consult your teacher.
6. Get a good night's sleep before the exam.
7. On the day of the actual test, allow yourself plenty of time to arrive at your exam location.

When taking your test,

1. Read the directions on the test carefully.
2. Read each problem carefully as you take the test. Make sure that you answer the question asked.
3. Pace yourself by first completing the problems you are most confident with. Then work toward the problems you are least confident with. Watch your time so you do not spend too much time on one particular problem.
4. If you have time, check your work and answers.
5. Do not turn your test in early. If you have extra time, spend it double-checking your work.

OBJECTIVE 6 ▶ Managing your time. As a student, you know the demands that classes, homework, work, and family place on your time. Some days you probably wonder how you'll ever get everything done. One key to managing your time is developing a schedule. Here are some hints for making a schedule:

1. Make a list of all of your weekly commitments for the term. Include classes, work, regular meetings, extracurricular activities, etc.
2. Next, estimate the time needed for each item on the list. Also make a note of how often you will need to do each item. Don't forget to include time estimates for reading, studying, and homework you do outside of your classes. You may want to ask your instructor for help estimating the time needed.
3. In the following exercise set, you are asked to block out a typical week on the schedule grid given. Start with items with fixed time slots like classes and work.
4. Next, include the items on your list with flexible time slots. Think carefully about how best to schedule some items such as study time.
5. Don't fill up every time slot on the schedule. Remember that you need to allow time for eating, sleeping, and relaxing! You should also allow a little extra time in case some items take longer than planned.
6. If you find that your weekly schedule is too full for you to handle, you may need to make some changes in your workload, classload, or in other areas of your life. If you work, you may want to talk to your advisor, manager or supervisor, or someone in your school's counseling center for help with such decisions.

1.1 EXERCISE SET

1. How many times is it suggested that you work through homework exercises before the submission deadline?
2. How does the "Help Me Solve This" feature work?
3. Why is it important that you write your step-by-step solutions to homework exercises and keep a hard copy of all work submitted online?
4. How many times are you allowed to submit homework online?
5. How can the lecture videos for each section help you in this course? When is the best time to use them?
6. In the homework assignments, how many attempts do you get to correct an exercise before it is marked incorrect?
7. If the "View an Example" feature is used, is it necessary to work an additional exercise before continuing the assignment?
8. How does reading the ebook section before class help you prepare for class?
9. Do all homework exercises in MathXL come with an accompanying video clip solution?
10. How can you use MathXL to contact your teacher about an exercise you don't understand?
11. When are your homework assignments due?
12. How much "cushion" time is recommended before your deadline when submitting homework online?
13. Is it still OK to ask your teacher for help even though this is an online course?
14. Name two ways you can prepare for any chapter tests.
15. If you are absent, name two ways you can review the material you missed.
16. List the resources available to help you in MyMathLab. Which of these resources do you think will be most helpful to you?
17. Are you allowed to use a calculator in this class?
18. Review objective 6 and fill in the schedule grid below.
19. Study your completed grid from Exercise 18. Decide whether you have the time necessary to successfully complete this course and any others you are registered for.

	Monday	*Tuesday*	*Wednesday*	*Thursday*	*Friday*	*Saturday*	*Sunday*
4:00 A.M.							
5:00 A.M.							
6:00 A.M.							
7:00 A.M.							
8:00 A.M.							
9:00 A.M.							
10:00 A.M.							
11:00 A.M.							
12:00 P.M.							
1:00 P.M.							
2:00 P.M.							
3:00 P.M.							
4:00 P.M.							
5:00 P.M.							
6:00 P.M.							
7:00 P.M.							
8:00 P.M.							
9:00 P.M.							
10:00 P.M.							
11:00 P.M.							
Midnight							
1:00 A.M.							
2:00 A.M.							
3:00 A.M.							

1.2 ALGEBRAIC EXPRESSIONS AND SETS OF NUMBERS

OBJECTIVES

1. Identify and evaluate algebraic expressions.
2. Identify natural numbers, whole numbers, integers, and rational and irrational real numbers.
3. Find the absolute value of a number.
4. Find the opposite of a number.
5. Write phrases as algebraic expressions.

OBJECTIVE 1 ▶ Evaluating algebraic expressions. Recall that letters that represent numbers are called **variables**. An **algebraic expression** is formed by numbers and variables connected by the operations of addition, subtraction, multiplication, division, raising to powers, and/or taking roots. For example,

$$2x + 3, \quad \frac{x+5}{6} - \frac{z^2}{y^2}, \quad \text{and} \quad \sqrt{y} - 1.6$$

are algebraic expressions or, more simply, expressions.

Algebraic expressions occur often during problem solving. For example, the B747-400 aircraft costs $8443 per hour to operate. (*Source: The World Almanac*) The algebraic expression $8443t$

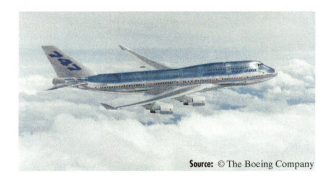

Source: © The Boeing Company

gives the total cost to operate the aircraft for t hours. To find the cost to operate the aircraft for 5.2 hours, for example, we replace the variable t with 5.2 and perform the indicated operation. This process is called **evaluating** an expression, and the result is called the **value** of the expression for the given replacement value.

In our example, when $t = 5.2$ hours,

$$8443t = 8443(5.2) = 43{,}903.60$$

Thus, it costs \$43,903.60 to operate the B747-400 aircraft for 5.2 hours.

> **Helpful Hint**
> Recall that $8443t$ means $8443 \cdot t$.

EXAMPLE 1 Finding the Area of a Tile

The research department of a flooring company is considering a new flooring design that contains parallelograms. The area of a parallelogram with base b and height h is bh. Find the area of a parallelogram with base 10 centimeters and height 8.2 centimeters.

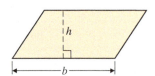

Solution We replace b with 10 and h with 8.2 in the algebraic expression bh.

$$bh = 10 \cdot 8.2 = 82$$

The area is 82 square centimeters.

PRACTICE 1 The tile edging for a bathroom is in the shape of a triangle. The area of a triangle with base b and height h is $A = \frac{1}{2}bh$. Find the area of the tile if the base measures 3.5 cm and the height measures 8 cm.

Algebraic expressions simplify to different values depending on replacement values. (Order of operations is needed for simplifying many expressions. We fully review this in Section 1.3.)

EXAMPLE 2 Evaluate: $3x - y$ when $x = 15$ and $y = 4$.

Solution We replace x with 15 and y with 4 in the expression.

$$3x - y = 3 \cdot 15 - 4 = 45 - 4 = 41$$

PRACTICE 2 Evaluate $2p - q$ when $p = 17$ and $q = 3$.

Section 1.2 Algebraic Expressions and Sets of Numbers   9

When evaluating an expression to solve a problem, we often need to think about the kind of number that is appropriate for the solution. For example, if we are asked to determine the maximum number of parking spaces for a parking lot to be constructed, an answer of $98\frac{1}{10}$ is not appropriate because $\frac{1}{10}$ of a parking space is not realistic.

OBJECTIVE 2 ▶ **Identifying common sets of numbers.** Let's review some common sets of numbers and their graphs on a number line. To construct a number line, we draw a line and label a point 0 with which we associate the number 0. This point is called the **origin.** Choose a point to the right of 0 and label it 1. The distance from 0 to 1 is called the **unit distance** and can be used to locate more points. The **positive numbers** lie to the right of the origin, and the **negative numbers** lie to the left of the origin. The number 0 is neither positive nor negative.

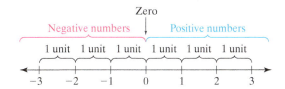

Concept Check ✓

Use the definitions of positive numbers, negative numbers, and zero to describe the meaning of *nonnegative numbers.*

A number is **graphed** on a number line by shading the point on the number line that corresponds to the number. Some common sets of numbers and their graphs include:

Natural numbers: $\{1, 2, 3, \ldots\}$

Whole numbers: $\{0, 1, 2, 3, \ldots\}$

Integers: $\{\ldots, -3, -2, -1, 0, 1, 2, 3, \ldots\}$

The symbol ... is used in each set above. This symbol, consisting of three dots, is called an **ellipsis** and means to continue in the same pattern.

The members of a set are called its **elements.** When the elements of a set are listed, such as those displayed in the previous paragraph, the set is written in **roster** form. A set can also be written in **set builder notation,** which describes the members of a set but does not list them. The following set is written in set builder notation.

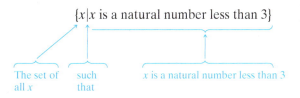

Answer to Concept Check:
a number that is 0 or positive

▶ **Helpful Hint**
Use { } or ∅ to write the empty set. {∅} is **not** the empty set because it has one element: ∅.

This same set written in roster form is $\{1, 2\}$.

A set that contains *no* elements is called the **empty set** (or **null set**) symbolized by { } or ∅. The set

$\{x | x \text{ is a month with 32 days}\}$ is ∅ or { }

because no month has 32 days. The set has no elements.

EXAMPLE 3 List the elements in each set.

a. $\{x \mid x \text{ is a natural number greater than } 100\}$

b. $\{x \mid x \text{ is a whole number between 1 and 6}\}$

Solution

a. $\{101, 102, 103, \ldots\}$ b. $\{2, 3, 4, 5\}$

PRACTICE 3 List the elements in each set.

a. $\{x \mid x \text{ is a whole number between 5 and 10}\}$

b. $\{x \mid x \text{ is a natural number greater than } 40\}$

The symbol $\in$ is used to denote that an element is in a particular set. The symbol $\in$ is read as "is an element of." For example, the true statement

3 is an element of $\{1, 2, 3, 4, 5\}$

can be written in symbols as

$$3 \in \{1, 2, 3, 4, 5\}$$

The symbol $\notin$ is read as "is not an element of." In symbols, we write the true statement "p is not an element of $\{a, 5, g, j, q\}$" as

$$p \notin \{a, 5, g, j, q\}$$

EXAMPLE 4 Determine whether each statement is true or false.

a. $3 \in \{x \mid x \text{ is a natural number}\}$ b. $7 \notin \{1, 2, 3\}$

Solution

a. True, since 3 is a natural number and therefore an element of the set.

b. True, since 7 is not an element of the set $\{1, 2, 3\}$.

PRACTICE 4 Determine whether each statement is true or false.

a. $7 \in \{x \mid x \text{ is a natural number}\}$ b. $6 \notin \{1, 3, 5, 7\}$

We can use set builder notation to describe three other common sets of numbers.

Identifying Numbers

Real Numbers: $\{x \mid x \text{ corresponds to a point on the number line}\}$

$\longleftarrow\!\!\!\!\!\!\underset{0}{|}\!\!\!\!\!\!\longrightarrow$

Rational numbers: $\left\{\dfrac{a}{b} \,\middle|\, a \text{ and } b \text{ are integers and } b \neq 0\right\}$

Irrational numbers: $\{x \mid x \text{ is a real number and } x \text{ is not a rational number}\}$

▶ **Helpful Hint**
Notice from the definition that all real numbers are either rational or irrational.

Every rational number can be written as a decimal that either repeats or terminates. For example,

Rational Numbers

$$\frac{1}{2} = 0.5 \qquad \frac{5}{4} = 1.25$$

$$\frac{2}{3} = 0.6666666\ldots = 0.\overline{6} \qquad \frac{1}{11} = 0.090909\ldots = 0.\overline{09}$$

An irrational number written as a decimal neither terminates nor repeats. For example, π and $\sqrt{2}$ are irrational numbers. Their decimal form neither terminates nor repeats. Decimal approximations of each are below:

Irrational Numbers

$$\pi \approx 3.141592\ldots \qquad \sqrt{2} \approx 1.414213\ldots$$

Notice that every integer is also a rational number since each integer can be written as the quotient of itself and 1:

$$3 = \frac{3}{1}, \quad 0 = \frac{0}{1}, \quad -8 = \frac{-8}{1}$$

Not every rational number, however, is an integer. The rational number $\frac{2}{3}$, for example, is not an integer. Some square roots are rational numbers and some are irrational numbers. For example, $\sqrt{2}$, $\sqrt{3}$ and $\sqrt{7}$ are irrational numbers while $\sqrt{25}$ is a rational number because $\sqrt{25} = 5 = \frac{5}{1}$. The set of rational numbers together with the set of irrational numbers make up the set of real numbers. To help you make the distinction between rational and irrational numbers, here are a few examples of each.

	Real Numbers	
	Rational Numbers	**Irrational Numbers** (Decimal Form Neither Terminates Nor Repeats)
Numbers	**Equivalent Quotient of Integers, $\frac{a}{b}$** (Decimal Form Terminates or Repeats)	
$-\frac{2}{3}$	$\frac{-2}{3}$ or $\frac{2}{-3}$	$\sqrt{5}$
$\sqrt{36}$	$\frac{6}{1}$	$\frac{\sqrt{6}}{7}$
5	$\frac{5}{1}$	$-\sqrt{13}$
0	$\frac{0}{1}$	π
1.2	$\frac{12}{10}$	$\frac{2}{\sqrt{3}}$
$3\frac{7}{8}$	$\frac{31}{8}$	

Some rational and irrational numbers are graphed below.

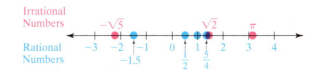

Earlier we mentioned that every integer is also a rational number. In other words, all the elements of the set of integers are also elements of the set of rational numbers. When this happens, we say that the set of integers, set Z, is a subset of the set of rational numbers, set Q. In symbols,

$$Z \subseteq Q$$

is a subset of

The natural numbers, whole numbers, integers, rational numbers, and irrational numbers are each a subset of the set of real numbers. The relationships among these sets of numbers are shown in the following diagram.

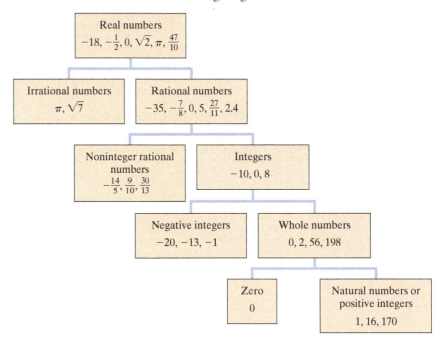

EXAMPLE 5 Determine whether the following statements are true or false.

a. 3 is a real number.

b. $\dfrac{1}{5}$ is an irrational number.

c. Every rational number is an integer.

d. $\{1, 5\} \subseteq \{2, 3, 4, 5\}$

Solution

a. True. Every whole number is a real number.

b. False. The number $\dfrac{1}{5}$ is a rational number, since it is in the form $\dfrac{a}{b}$ with a and b integers and $b \neq 0$.

c. False. The number $\dfrac{2}{3}$, for example, is a rational number, but it is not an integer.

d. False. Since the element 1 in the first set is not an element of the second set.

PRACTICE 5 Determine whether the following statements are true or false.

a. -5 is a real number.

b. $\sqrt{8}$ is a rational number.

c. Every whole number is a rational number.

d. $\{2, 4\} \subset \{1, 3, 4, 7\}$

OBJECTIVE 3 ▶ Finding the absolute value of a number. The number line can also be used to visualize distance, which leads to the concept of absolute value. The **absolute**

value of a real number a, written as $|a|$, is the distance between a and 0 on the number line. Since distance is always positive or zero, $|a|$ is always positive or zero.

Using the number line, we see that

$$|4| = 4 \quad \text{and also} \quad |-4| = 4$$

Why? Because both 4 and -4 are a distance of 4 units from 0.

An equivalent definition of the absolute value of a real number a is given next.

Absolute Value

The absolute value of a, written as $|a|$, is

$$|a| = \begin{cases} a & \text{if } a \text{ is 0 or a positive number} \\ -a & \text{if } a \text{ is a negative number} \end{cases}$$

↑
the opposite of

EXAMPLE 6 Find each absolute value.

a. $|3|$ **b.** $\left|-\dfrac{1}{7}\right|$ **c.** $-|2.7|$ **d.** $-|-8|$ **e.** $|0|$

Solution

a. $|3| = 3$ since 3 is located 3 units from 0 on the number line.

b. $\left|-\dfrac{1}{7}\right| = \dfrac{1}{7}$ since $-\dfrac{1}{7}$ is $\dfrac{1}{7}$ units from 0 on the number line.

c. $-|2.7| = -2.7$. The negative sign outside the absolute value bars means to take the opposite of the absolute value of 2.7.

d. $-|-8| = -8$. Since $|-8|$ is 8, $-|-8| = -8$.

e. $|0| = 0$ since 0 is located 0 units from 0 on the number line.

PRACTICE 6 Find each absolute value.

a. $|4|$ **b.** $\left|-\dfrac{1}{2}\right|$ **c.** $|1|$ **d.** $-|6.8|$ **e.** $-|-4|$

Concept Check ✓

Explain how you know that $|14| = -14$ is a false statement.

OBJECTIVE 4 ▶ Finding the opposite of a number. The number line can also help us visualize opposites. Two numbers that are the same distance from 0 on the number line but are on opposite sides of 0 are called **opposites**.

See the definition illustrated on the number lines below.

> **Helpful Hint**
> The opposite of 0 is 0.

Answer to Concept Check:
$|14| = 14$ since the absolute value of a number is the distance between the number and 0 and distance cannot be negative.

The opposite of 6.5 is -6.5.

The opposite of $\dfrac{2}{3}$ is $-\dfrac{2}{3}$.

The opposite of -4 is 4.

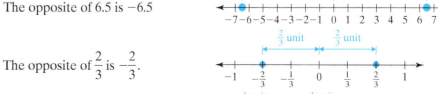

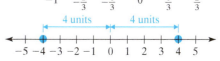

> **Opposite**
> The opposite of a number a is the number $-a$.

Above we state that the opposite of a number a is $-a$. This means that the opposite of -4 is $-(-4)$. But from the number line above, the opposite of -4 is 4. This means that $-(-4) = 4$, and in general, we have the following property.

> **Double Negative Property**
> For every real number a, $-(-a) = a$.

EXAMPLE 7 Write the opposite of each number.

a. 8   **b.** $\dfrac{1}{5}$ **c.** -9.6

Solution

a. The opposite of 8 is -8.

b. The opposite of $\dfrac{1}{5}$ is $-\dfrac{1}{5}$.

c. The opposite of -9.6 is $-(-9.6) = 9.6$.

PRACTICE 7 Write the opposite of each number.

a. 5.4   **b.** $-\dfrac{3}{5}$ **c.** 18

OBJECTIVE 5 ▶ Writing phrases as algebraic expressions. Often, solving problems involves translating a phrase to an algebraic expression. The following is a partial list of key words and phrases and their usual direct translations.

Selected Key Words/Phrases and Their Translations			
Addition	Subtraction	Multiplication	Division
sum	difference of	product	quotient
plus	minus	times	divide
added to	subtracted from	multiply	into
more than	less than	twice	ratio
increased by	decreased by	of	
total	less		

EXAMPLE 8 Translate each phrase to an algebraic expression. Use the variable x to represent each unknown number.

a. Eight times a number
b. Three more than eight times a number
c. The quotient of a number and -7
d. One and six-tenths subtracted from twice a number
e. Six less than a number
f. Twice the sum of four and a number

Section 1.2 Algebraic Expressions and Sets of Numbers   15

Solution

a. $8 \cdot x$ or $8x$
b. $8x + 3$
c. $x \div -7$ or $\dfrac{x}{-7}$
d. $2x - 1.6$ or $2x - 1\dfrac{6}{10}$
e. $x - 6$
f. $2(4 + x)$

PRACTICE 8 Translate each phrase to an algebraic expression. Use the variable x to represent the unknown number.

a. The product of 3 and a number
b. Five less than twice a number
c. Three and five-eighths more than a number
d. The quotient of a number and 2
e. Fourteen subtracted from a number
f. Five times the sum of a number and ten

VOCABULARY & READINESS CHECK

Word Bank. Use the choices below to fill in each blank. Not all choices will be used.

whole numbers	integers	rational number	a
natural numbers	value	irrational number	$-a$
absolute value	expression	variables	

1. Letters that represent numbers are called _____.
2. Finding the _____ of an expression means evaluating the expression.
3. The _____ of a number is that number's distance from 0 on the number line.
4. A(n) _____ is formed by numbers and variables connected by operations such as addition, subtraction, multiplication, division, raising to powers, and/or taking roots.
5. The _____ are $\{1, 2, 3, \ldots\}$.
6. The _____ are $\{0, 1, 2, 3, \ldots\}$.
7. The _____ are $\{\ldots -3, -2, -1, 0, 1, 2, 3, \ldots\}$.
8. The number $\sqrt{5}$ is a(n) _____.
9. The number $\dfrac{5}{7}$ is a(n) _____.
10. The opposite of a is _____.

1.2 EXERCISE SET

Find the value of each algebraic expression at the given replacement values. See Examples 1 and 2.

1. $5x$ when $x = 7$
2. $3y$ when $y = 45$
3. $9.8z$ when $z = 3.1$
4. $7.1a$ when $a = 1.5$
5. ab when $a = \dfrac{1}{2}$ and $b = \dfrac{3}{4}$
6. yz when $y = \dfrac{2}{3}$ and $z = \dfrac{1}{5}$
7. $3x + y$ when $x = 6$ and $y = 4$
8. $2a - b$ when $a = 12$ and $b = 7$

9. The aircraft B737-400 flies an average speed of 400 miles per hour.

The expression $400t$ gives the distance traveled by the aircraft in t hours. Find the distance traveled by the B737-400 in 5 hours.

10. The algebraic expression $1.5x$ gives the total length of shelf space needed in inches for x encyclopedias. Find the length of shelf space needed for a set of 30 encyclopedias.

11. Employees at Wal-Mart constantly reorganize and reshelve merchandise. In doing so, they calculate floor space needed for displays. The algebraic expression $l \cdot w$ gives the floor space needed in square units for a display that measures length l units and width w units. Calculate the floor space needed for a display whose length is 5.1 feet and whose width is 4 feet.

12. The algebraic expression $\dfrac{x}{5}$ can be used to calculate the distance in miles that you are from a flash of lightning, where x is the number of seconds between the time you see a flash of lightning and the time you hear the thunder. Calculate the distance that you are from the flash of lightning if you hear the thunder 2 seconds after you see the lightning.

13. The B737-400 aircraft costs $2948 dollars per hour to operate. The algebraic expression $2948t$ gives the total cost to operate the aircraft for t hours. Find the total cost to operate the B737-400 for 3.6 hours.

14. Flying the SR-71A jet, Capt. Elden W. Joersz, USAF, set a record speed of 2193.16 miles per hour. At this speed, the algebraic expression $2193.16t$ gives the total distance flown in t hours. Find the distance flown by the SR-71A in 1.7 hours.

List the elements in each set. See Example 3.

15. $\{x \mid x \text{ is a natural number less than } 6\}$
16. $\{x \mid x \text{ is a natural number greater than } 6\}$
17. $\{x \mid x \text{ is a natural number between 10 and 17}\}$
18. $\{x \mid x \text{ is an odd natural number}\}$
19. $\{x \mid x \text{ is a whole number that is not a natural number}\}$
20. $\{x \mid x \text{ is a natural number less than } 1\}$
21. $\{x \mid x \text{ is an even whole number less than } 9\}$
22. $\{x \mid x \text{ is an odd whole number less than } 9\}$

Graph each set on a number line.

23. $\{0, 2, 4, 6\}$
24. $\{-1, -2, -3\}$
25. $\left\{\dfrac{1}{2}, \dfrac{2}{3}\right\}$
26. $\{1, 3, 5, 7\}$
27. $\{-2, -6, -10\}$
28. $\left\{\dfrac{1}{4}, \dfrac{1}{3}\right\}$

29. In your own words, explain why the empty set is a subset of every set.
30. In your own words, explain why every set is a subset of itself.

List the elements of the set $\left\{3, 0, \sqrt{7}, \sqrt{36}, \dfrac{2}{5}, -134\right\}$ *that are also elements of the given set. See Example 4.*

31. Whole numbers
32. Integers
33. Natural numbers
34. Rational numbers
35. Irrational numbers
36. Real numbers

Place $\in$ or $\notin$ in the space provided to make each statement true. See Example 4.

37. $-11 \quad \{x \mid x \text{ is an integer}\}$
38. $0 \quad \{x \mid x \text{ is a positive integer}\}$
39. $-6 \quad \{2, 4, 6, \ldots\}$
40. $12 \quad \{1, 2, 3, \ldots\}$
41. $12 \quad \{1, 3, 5, \ldots\}$
42. $0 \quad \{1, 2, 3, \ldots\}$
43. $\dfrac{1}{2} \quad \{x \mid x \text{ is an irrational number}\}$
44. $0 \quad \{x \mid x \text{ is a natural number}\}$

True or False. *Determine whether each statement is true or false. See Examples 4 and 5. Use the following sets of numbers.*

$$N = \text{set of natural numbers}$$
$$Z = \text{set of integers}$$
$$I = \text{set of irrational numbers}$$
$$Q = \text{set of rational numbers}$$
$$\mathbb{R} = \text{set of real numbers}$$

45. $Z \subseteq \mathbb{R}$
46. $\mathbb{R} \subseteq N$
47. $-1 \in Z$
48. $\dfrac{1}{2} \in Q$
49. $0 \in N$
50. $Z \subseteq Q$
51. $\sqrt{5} \notin I$
52. $\pi \notin \mathbb{R}$
53. $N \subseteq Z$
54. $I \subseteq N$
55. $\mathbb{R} \subseteq Q$
56. $N \subseteq Q$

57. In your own words, explain why every natural number is also a rational number but not every rational number is a natural number.
58. In your own words, explain why every irrational number is a real number but not every real number is an irrational number.

Find each absolute value. See Example 6.

59. $-|2|$
60. $|8|$
61. $|-4|$
62. $|-6|$
63. $|0|$
64. $|-1|$
65. $-|3|$
66. $-|-11|$

67. Explain why $-(-2)$ and $-|-2|$ simplify to different numbers.

68. The boxed definition of absolute value states that $|a| = -a$ if a is a negative number. Explain why $|a|$ is always nonnegative, even though $|a| = -a$ for negative values of a.

Write the opposite of each number. See Example 7.

69. -6.2
70. -7.8
71. $\dfrac{4}{7}$
72. $\dfrac{9}{5}$
73. $-\dfrac{2}{3}$
74. $-\dfrac{14}{3}$
75. 0
76. 10.3

Write each phrase as an algebraic expression. Use the variable x to represent each unknown number. See Example 8.

77. Twice a number.
78. Six times a number.
79. Five more than twice a number.
80. One more than six times a number.
81. Ten less than a number.
82. A number minus seven.
83. The sum of a number and two.
84. The difference of twenty-five and a number.
85. A number divided by eleven.
86. The quotient of a number and thirteen.
87. Twelve, minus three times a number.
88. Four, subtracted from three times a number.
89. A number plus two and three-tenths.
90. Fifteen and seven-tenths plus a number.
91. A number less than one and one-third.
92. Two and three-fourths less than a number.
93. The quotient of five and the difference of four and a number.
94. The quotient of four and the sum of a number and one.
95. Twice the sum of a number and three.
96. Eight times the difference of a number and nine.

CONCEPT EXTENSIONS

Complete a Table. *Use the bar graph below to complete the given table by estimating the millions of tourists predicted for each country. (Use whole numbers.)*

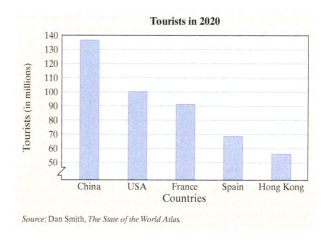

Source: Dan Smith, *The State of the World Atlas.*

97. China	
98. France	
99. Spain	
100. Hong Kong	

101. In your own words, explain why every natural number is also a rational number but not every rational number is a natural number.

102. In your own words, explain why every irrational number is a real number but not every real number is an irrational number.

1.3 OPERATIONS ON REAL NUMBERS

OBJECTIVES

1. Add and subtract real numbers.
2. Multiply and divide real numbers.
3. Evaluate expressions containing exponents.
4. Find roots of numbers.
5. Use the order of operations.
6. Evaluate algebraic expressions.

OBJECTIVE 1 ▶ Adding and subtracting real numbers. When solving problems, we often have to add real numbers. For example, if the New Orleans Saints lose 5 yards in one play, then lose another 7 yards in the next play, their total loss may be described by $-5 + (-7)$.

The addition of two real numbers may be summarized by the following.

Adding Real Numbers

1. To add two numbers with the *same sign*, add their absolute values and attach their common sign.
2. To add two numbers with *different signs*, subtract the smaller absolute value from the larger absolute value and attach the sign of the number with the larger absolute value.

18 CHAPTER 1 Real Numbers and Algebraic Expressions

For example, to add $-5 + (-7)$, first add their absolute values.

$$|-5| = 5, |-7| = 7, \text{ and } 5 + 7 = 12$$

Next, attach their common negative sign.

$$-5 + (-7) = -12$$

(This represents a total loss of 12 yards for the New Orleans Saints in the example above.)
To find $(-4) + 3$, first subtract their absolute values.

$$|-4| = 4, |3| = 3, \text{ and } 4 - 3 = 1$$

Next, attach the sign of the number with the larger absolute value.

$$(-4) + 3 = -1$$

EXAMPLE 1 Add.

a. $-3 + (-11)$ b. $3 + (-7)$ c. $-10 + 15$

d. $-8.3 + (-1.9)$ e. $-\dfrac{2}{3} + \dfrac{3}{7}$

Solution

a. $-3 + (-11) = -(3 + 11) = -14$ b. $3 + (-7) = -4$

c. $-10 + 15 = 5$ d. $-8.3 + (-1.9) = -10.2$

e. $-\dfrac{2}{3} + \dfrac{3}{7} = -\dfrac{14}{21} + \dfrac{9}{21} = -\dfrac{5}{21}$

PRACTICE 1 Add.

a. $-6 + (-2)$ b. $5 + (-8)$ c. $-4 + 9$

d. $(-3.2) + (-4.9)$ e. $-\dfrac{3}{5} + \dfrac{2}{3}$

Subtraction of two real numbers may be defined in terms of addition.

> **Subtracting Real Numbers**
> If a and b are real numbers,
> $$a - b = a + (-b)$$

In other words, to subtract a real number, we add its opposite.

EXAMPLE 2 Subtract.

a. $2 - 8$ b. $-8 - (-1)$ c. $-11 - 5$ d. $10.7 - (-9.8)$

e. $\dfrac{2}{3} - \dfrac{1}{2}$ f. $1 - 0.06$ g. Subtract 7 from 4.

Solution   Add the opposite   Add the opposite

a. $2 - 8 = 2 + (-8) = -6$ b. $-8 - (-1) = -8 + (1) = -7$

c. $-11 - 5 = -11 + (-5) = -16$ d. $10.7 - (-9.8) = 10.7 + 9.8 = 20.5$

Section 1.3 Operations on Real Numbers 19

e. $\dfrac{2}{3} - \dfrac{1}{2} = \dfrac{2 \cdot 2}{3 \cdot 2} - \dfrac{1 \cdot 3}{2 \cdot 3} = \dfrac{4}{6} + \left(-\dfrac{3}{6}\right) = \dfrac{1}{6}$

f. $1 - 0.06 = 1 + (-0.06) = 0.94$ g. $4 - 7 = 4 + (-7) = -3$

PRACTICE 2 Subtract.

a. $3 - 11$ b. $-6 - (-3)$ c. $-7 - 5$ d. $4.2 - (-3.5)$

e. $\dfrac{5}{7} - \dfrac{1}{3}$ f. $3 - 1.2$ g. Subtract 9 from 2.

To add or subtract three or more real numbers, add or subtract from left to right.

EXAMPLE 3 Simplify the following expressions.

a. $11 + 2 - 7$ b. $-5 - 4 + 2$

Solution

a. $11 + 2 - 7 = 13 - 7 = 6$ b. $-5 - 4 + 2 = -9 + 2 = -7$

PRACTICE 3 Simplify the following expressions.

a. $13 + 5 - 6$ b. $-6 - 2 + 4$

OBJECTIVE 2 ▶ Multiplying and dividing real numbers. In order to discover sign patterns when you multiply real numbers, recall that multiplication by a positive integer is the same as repeated addition. For example,

$$3(2) = 2 + 2 + 2 = 6$$
$$3(-2) = (-2) + (-2) + (-2) = -6$$

Notice here that $3(-2) = -6$. This illustrates that the product of two numbers with different signs is negative. We summarize sign patterns for multiplying any two real numbers as follows.

Multiplying Two Real Numbers
The product of two numbers with the *same* sign is positive.
The product of two numbers with *different* signs is negative.

Also recall that the product of zero and any real number is zero.

$$0 \cdot a = 0$$

Product Property of 0
$0 \cdot a = 0$ Also $a \cdot 0 = 0$

EXAMPLE 4 Multiply.

a. $(-8)(-1)$ b. $-2\left(\dfrac{1}{6}\right)$ c. $-1.2(0.3)$ d. $0(-11)$

e. $\dfrac{1}{5}\left(-\dfrac{10}{11}\right)$ f. $(7)(1)(-2)(-3)$ g. $8(-2)(0)$

Solution

a. Since the signs of the two numbers are the same, the product is positive. Thus $(-8)(-1) = +8$, or 8.

b. Since the signs of the two numbers are different or unlike, the product is negative. Thus $-2\left(\dfrac{1}{6}\right) = -\dfrac{2}{6} = -\dfrac{1}{3}$.

c. $-1.2(0.3) = -0.36$

d. $0(-11) = 0$

e. $\dfrac{1}{5}\left(-\dfrac{10}{11}\right) = -\dfrac{10}{55} = -\dfrac{2}{11}$

f. To multiply three or more real numbers, you may multiply from left to right.
$$(7)(1)(-2)(-3) = 7(-2)(-3)$$
$$= -14(-3)$$
$$= 42$$

g. Since zero is a factor, the product is zero.
$$(8)(-2)(0) = 0$$

PRACTICE 4 Multiply.

a. $(-5)(3)$ **b.** $(-7)\left(-\dfrac{1}{14}\right)$ **c.** $5.1(-2)$ **d.** $14(0)$

e. $\left(-\dfrac{1}{4}\right)\left(\dfrac{8}{13}\right)$ **f.** $6(-1)(-2)(3)$ **g.** $5(-2.3)$

> ▶ **Helpful Hint**
>
> The following sign patterns may be helpful when we are multiplying.
>
> 1. An odd number of negative factors gives a negative product.
> 2. An even number of negative factors gives a positive product.

Recall that $\dfrac{8}{4} = 2$ because $2 \cdot 4 = 8$. Likewise, $\dfrac{8}{-4} = -2$ because $(-2)(-4) = 8$. Also, $\dfrac{-8}{4} = -2$ because $(-2)4 = -8$, and $\dfrac{-8}{-4} = 2$ because $2(-4) = -8$. From these examples, we can see that the sign patterns for division are the same as for multiplication.

> **Dividing Two Real Numbers**
>
> The quotient of two numbers with the *same* sign is positive.
> The quotient of two numbers with *different* signs is negative.

Also recall that division by a nonzero real number b is the same as multiplication by $\dfrac{1}{b}$. In other words,
$$\dfrac{a}{b} = a \cdot \dfrac{1}{b}$$

This means that to simplify $\dfrac{a}{b}$, we can divide by b or multiply by $\dfrac{1}{b}$. The nonzero numbers b and $\dfrac{1}{b}$ are called **reciprocals**. Notice that b *must* be a nonzero number. We do not define division by 0. For example, $5 \div 0$, or $\dfrac{5}{0}$, is undefined. To see why, recall that if $5 \div 0 = n$, a number, then $n \cdot 0 = 5$. This is not possible since $n \cdot 0 = 0$ for any number n, and never 5. Thus far we have learned that we cannot divide 5 or any other nonzero number by 0.

Can we divide 0 by 0? By the same reasoning, if $0 \div 0 = n$, a number, then $n \cdot 0 = 0$. This is true for any number n so that the quotient $0 \div 0$ would not be a single number. To avoid this, we say that

> Division by 0 is undefined.

EXAMPLE 5 Divide.

a. $\dfrac{20}{-4}$ **b.** $\dfrac{-9}{-3}$ **c.** $-\dfrac{3}{8} \div 3$ **d.** $\dfrac{-40}{10}$ **e.** $\dfrac{-1}{10} \div \dfrac{-2}{5}$ **f.** $\dfrac{8}{0}$

Solution

a. Since the signs are different or unlike, the quotient is negative and $\dfrac{20}{-4} = -5$.

b. Since the signs are the same, the quotient is positive and $\dfrac{-9}{-3} = 3$.

c. $-\dfrac{3}{8} \div 3 = -\dfrac{3}{8} \cdot \dfrac{1}{3} = -\dfrac{1}{8}$ **d.** $\dfrac{-40}{10} = -4$

e. $\dfrac{-1}{10} \div \dfrac{-2}{5} = -\dfrac{1}{10} \cdot -\dfrac{5}{2} = \dfrac{1}{4}$ **f.** $\dfrac{8}{0}$ is undefined.

PRACTICE 5 Divide.

a. $\dfrac{-16}{8}$ **b.** $\dfrac{-15}{-3}$ **c.** $-\dfrac{2}{3} \div 4$

d. $\dfrac{54}{-9}$ **e.** $-\dfrac{1}{12} \div \left(-\dfrac{3}{4}\right)$ **f.** $\dfrac{0}{-7}$

With sign rules for division, we can understand why the positioning of the negative sign in a fraction does not change the value of the fraction. For example,

$$\dfrac{-12}{3} = -4, \quad \dfrac{12}{-3} = -4, \quad \text{and} \quad -\dfrac{12}{3} = -4$$

Since all the fractions equal -4, we can say that

$$\dfrac{-12}{3} = \dfrac{12}{-3} = -\dfrac{12}{3}$$

In general, the following holds true.

> If a and b are real numbers and $b \neq 0$, then $\dfrac{a}{-b} = \dfrac{-a}{b} = -\dfrac{a}{b}$.

OBJECTIVE 3 ▶ Evaluating expressions containing exponents. Recall that when two numbers are multiplied, they are called **factors**. For example, in $3 \cdot 5 = 15$, the 3 and 5 are called factors.

A natural number *exponent* is a shorthand notation for repeated multiplication of the same factor. This repeated factor is called the **base**, and the number of times it is used as a factor is indicated by the **exponent**. For example,

$$4^3 = 4 \cdot 4 \cdot 4 = 64$$

base ↑ ↑ exponent; 4 is a factor 3 times.

> **Exponents**
> If a is a real number and n is a natural number, then the **nth power of a, or a raised to the nth power**, written as a^n, is the product of n factors, each of which is a.
>
> $$a^n = \underbrace{a \cdot a \cdot a \cdot \,\cdots\, \cdot a}_{a \text{ is a factor } n \text{ times.}}$$
>
> where the arrow points to n as the exponent and to a as the base.

It is not necessary to write an exponent of 1. For example, 3 is assumed to be 3^1.

EXAMPLE 6 Evaluate each expression.

a. 3^2 b. $\left(\dfrac{1}{2}\right)^4$ c. -5^2

d. $(-5)^2$ e. -5^3 f. $(-5)^3$

Solution

a. $3^2 = 3 \cdot 3 = 9$ b. $\left(\dfrac{1}{2}\right)^4 = \left(\dfrac{1}{2}\right)\left(\dfrac{1}{2}\right)\left(\dfrac{1}{2}\right)\left(\dfrac{1}{2}\right) = \dfrac{1}{16}$

c. $-5^2 = -(5 \cdot 5) = -25$ d. $(-5)^2 = (-5)(-5) = 25$

e. $-5^3 = -(5 \cdot 5 \cdot 5) = -125$ f. $(-5)^3 = (-5)(-5)(-5) = -125$

PRACTICE 6 Evaluate each expression.

a. 2^3 b. $\left(\dfrac{1}{3}\right)^2$ c. -6^2

d. $(-6)^2$ e. -4^3 f. $(-4)^3$

> ▶ **Helpful Hint**
> Be very careful when simplifying expressions such as -5^2 and $(-5)^2$.
>
> $-5^2 = -(5 \cdot 5) = -25$ and $(-5)^2 = (-5)(-5) = 25$
>
> Without parentheses, the base to square is 5, not -5.

OBJECTIVE 4 ▶ **Finding roots of numbers.** The opposite of squaring a number is taking the **square root** of a number. For example, since the square of 4, or 4^2, is 16, we say that a square root of 16 is 4. The notation $\sqrt{a}$ is used to denote the **positive**, or **principal, square root** of a nonnegative number a. We then have in symbols that $\sqrt{16} = 4$. The negative square root of 16 is written $-\sqrt{16} = -4$. The square root of a negative number, such as $\sqrt{-16}$ is not a real number. Why? There is no real number, that when squared gives a negative number.

EXAMPLE 7 Find the square roots.

a. $\sqrt{9}$ b. $\sqrt{25}$ c. $\sqrt{\dfrac{1}{4}}$ d. $-\sqrt{36}$ e. $\sqrt{-36}$

Solution

a. $\sqrt{9} = 3$ since 3 is positive and $3^2 = 9$. b. $\sqrt{25} = 5$ since $5^2 = 25$.

c. $\sqrt{\dfrac{1}{4}} = \dfrac{1}{2}$ since $\left(\dfrac{1}{2}\right)^2 = \dfrac{1}{4}$. d. $-\sqrt{36} = -6$

e. $\sqrt{-36}$ is not a real number.

Section 1.3 Operations on Real Numbers   23

PRACTICE 7   Find the square roots.

a. $\sqrt{49}$ b. $\sqrt{\dfrac{1}{16}}$ c. $-\sqrt{64}$ d. $\sqrt{-64}$ e. $\sqrt{100}$

We can find roots other than square roots. Since 2 cubed, written as 2^3, is 8, we say that the **cube root** of 8 is 2. This is written as

$$\sqrt[3]{8} = 2.$$

Also, since $3^4 = 81$ and 3 is positive,

$$\sqrt[4]{81} = 3.$$

EXAMPLE 8   Find the roots.

a. $\sqrt[3]{27}$ b. $\sqrt[5]{1}$ c. $\sqrt[4]{16}$

Solution

a. $\sqrt[3]{27} = 3$ since $3^3 = 27$.
b. $\sqrt[5]{1} = 1$ since $1^5 = 1$.
c. $\sqrt[4]{16} = 2$ since 2 is positive and $2^4 = 16$.

PRACTICE 8   Find the roots.

a. $\sqrt[3]{64}$ b. $\sqrt[5]{-1}$ c. $\sqrt[4]{10{,}000}$

Of course, as mentioned in Section 1.2, not all roots simplify to rational numbers. We study radicals further in Chapter 8.

OBJECTIVE 5 ▶ Using the order of operations. Expressions containing more than one operation are written to follow a particular agreed-upon **order of operations.** For example, when we write $3 + 2 \cdot 10$, we mean to multiply first, and then add.

> **Order of Operations**
> Simplify expressions using the order that follows. If grouping symbols such as parentheses are present, simplify expressions within those first, starting with the innermost set. If fraction bars are present, simplify the numerator and denominator separately.
>
> 1. Evaluate exponential expressions, roots, or absolute values in order from left to right.
> 2. Multiply or divide in order from left to right.
> 3. Add or subtract in order from left to right.

EXAMPLE 9   Simplify.

a. $20 \div 2 \cdot 10$ b. $1 + 2(1 - 4)^2$ c. $\dfrac{|-2|^3 + 1}{-7 - \sqrt{4}}$

Solution

a. Be careful! Here, we multiply or divide in order from left to right. Thus, divide, then multiply.

$$20 \div 2 \cdot 10 = 10 \cdot 10 = 100$$

b. Remember order of operations so that you are *not* tempted to add 1 and 2 first.

$$1 + 2(1 - 4)^2 = 1 + 2(-3)^2 \quad \text{Simplify inside grouping symbols first.}$$
$$= 1 + 2(9) \quad \text{Write } (-3)^2 \text{ as 9.}$$
$$= 1 + 18 \quad \text{Multiply.}$$
$$= 19 \quad \text{Add.}$$

c. Simplify the numerator and the denominator separately; then divide.

$$\frac{|-2|^3 + 1}{-7 - \sqrt{4}} = \frac{2^3 + 1}{-7 - 2} \quad \text{Write } |-2| \text{ as 2 and } \sqrt{4} \text{ as 2.}$$
$$= \frac{8 + 1}{-9} \quad \text{Write } 2^3 \text{ as 8.}$$
$$= \frac{9}{-9} = -1 \quad \text{Simplify the numerator, then divide.}$$

PRACTICE 9 Simplify.

a. $14 - 3 \cdot 4$ **b.** $3(5 - 8)^2$ **c.** $\dfrac{|-5|^2 + 4}{\sqrt{4} - 3}$

Besides parentheses, other symbols used for grouping expressions are brackets [ ] and braces { }. These other grouping symbols are commonly used when we group expressions that already contain parentheses.

EXAMPLE 10 Simplify: $3 - [(4 - 6) + 2(5 - 9)]$

Solution
$$3 - [(4 - 6) + 2(5 - 9)] = 3 - [-2 + 2(-4)] \quad \text{Simplify within the innermost sets of parentheses.}$$
$$= 3 - [-2 + (-8)]$$
$$= 3 - [-10]$$
$$= 13$$

> **Helpful Hint**
> When grouping symbols occur within grouping symbols, remember to perform operations on the innermost set first.

PRACTICE 10 Simplify: $5 - [(3 - 5) + 6(2 - 4)]$.

EXAMPLE 11 Simplify: $\dfrac{-5\sqrt{30 - 5} + (-2)^2}{4^2 + |7 - 10|}$

Solution Here, the fraction bar, radical sign, and absolute value bars serve as grouping symbols. Thus, we simplify within the radical sign and absolute value bars first, remembering to calculate above and below the fraction bar separately.

$$\frac{-5\sqrt{30 - 5} + (-2)^2}{4^2 + |7 - 10|} = \frac{-5\sqrt{25} + (-2)^2}{4^2 + |-3|} = \frac{-5 \cdot 5 + 4}{16 + 3} = \frac{-25 + 4}{16 + 3}$$
$$= \frac{-21}{19} \text{ or } -\frac{21}{19}$$

PRACTICE 11 Simplify: $\dfrac{-2\sqrt{12 + 4} - (-3)^2}{6^2 + |1 - 9|}$

Concept Check

True or false? If two different people use the order of operations to simplify a numerical expression and neither makes a calculation error, it is not possible that they each obtain a different result. Explain.

OBJECTIVE 6 ▸ Evaluating algebraic expressions. Recall from Section 1.2 that an algebraic expression is formed by numbers and variables connected by the operations of addition, subtraction, multiplication, division, raising to powers, and/or taking roots. Also, if numbers are substituted for the variables in an algebraic expression and the operations performed, the result is called **the value of the expression** for the given replacement values. This entire process is called **evaluating an expression.**

EXAMPLE 12 Evaluate each expression when $x = 4$ and $y = -3$.

a. $3x - 7y$ **b.** $-2y^2$ **c.** $\dfrac{\sqrt{x}}{y} - \dfrac{y}{x}$

Solution For each expression, replace x with 4 and y with -3.

a. $3x - 7y = 3 \cdot 4 - 7(-3)$ Let $x = 4$ and $y = -3$.
$= 12 - (-21)$ Multiply.
$= 12 + 21$ Write as an addition.
$= 33$ Add.

b. $-2y^2 = -2(-3)^2$ Let $y = -3$.
$= -2(9)$ Write $(-3)^2$ as 9.
$= -18$ Multiply.

▸ **Helpful Hint**
In $-2(-3)^2$, the exponent 2 goes with the base of -3 only.

c. $\dfrac{\sqrt{x}}{y} - \dfrac{y}{x} = \dfrac{\sqrt{4}}{-3} - \dfrac{-3}{4}$

$= -\dfrac{2}{3} + \dfrac{3}{4}$ Write $\sqrt{4}$ as 2.

$= -\dfrac{2}{3} \cdot \dfrac{4}{4} + \dfrac{3}{4} \cdot \dfrac{3}{3}$ The LCD is 12.

$= -\dfrac{8}{12} + \dfrac{9}{12}$ Write each fraction with a denominator of 12.

$= \dfrac{1}{12}$ Add.

Answer to Concept Check:
true; answers may vary

PRACTICE 12 Evaluate each expression when $x = 16$ and $y = -5$

a. $2x - 7y$ **b.** $-4y^2$ **c.** $\dfrac{\sqrt{x}}{y} - \dfrac{y}{x}$

Sometimes variables such as x_1 and x_2 will be used in this book. The small 1 and 2 are called **subscripts.** The variable x_1 can be read as "x sub 1," and the variable x_2 can be read as "x sub 2." The important thing to remember is that they are two different variables. For example, if $x_1 = -5$ and $x_2 = 7$, then

$$x_1 - x_2 = -5 - 7 = -12.$$

EXAMPLE 13 The algebraic expression $\dfrac{5(x-32)}{9}$ represents the equivalent temperature in degrees Celsius when x is the temperature in degrees Fahrenheit. Complete the following table by evaluating this expression at the given values of x.

Degrees Fahrenheit	x	-4	10	32
Degrees Celsius	$\dfrac{5(x-32)}{9}$			

Solution To complete the table, evaluate $\dfrac{5(x-32)}{9}$ at each given replacement value.

When $x = -4$,
$$\dfrac{5(x-32)}{9} = \dfrac{5(-4-32)}{9} = \dfrac{5(-36)}{9} = -20$$

When $x = 10$,
$$\dfrac{5(x-32)}{9} = \dfrac{5(10-32)}{9} = \dfrac{5(-22)}{9} = -\dfrac{110}{9}$$

When $x = 32$,
$$\dfrac{5(x-32)}{9} = \dfrac{5(32-32)}{9} = \dfrac{5 \cdot 0}{9} = 0$$

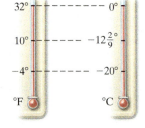

The completed table is

Degrees Fahrenheit	x	-4	10	32
Degrees Celsius	$\dfrac{5(x-32)}{9}$	-20	$-\dfrac{110}{9}$	0

Thus, $-4°$F is equivalent to $-20°$C, $10°$F is equivalent to $-\dfrac{110°}{9}$C, and $32°$F is equivalent to $0°$C.

PRACTICE 13 The algebraic expression $\dfrac{9}{5}x + 32$ represents the equivalent temperature in degrees Fahrenheit when x is the temperature in degrees Celsius. Complete the following table by evaluating this expression at the given values of x.

Degrees Celsius	x	-5	10	25
Degrees Fahrenheit	$\dfrac{9}{5}x + 32$			

Section 1.3 Operations on Real Numbers 27

VOCABULARY & READINESS CHECK

Multiple Choice. Choose the fraction(s) equivalent to the given fraction. (There may sometimes be more than one correct choice.)

1. $-\dfrac{1}{7}$ a. $\dfrac{-1}{-7}$ b. $\dfrac{-1}{7}$ c. $\dfrac{1}{-7}$ d. $\dfrac{1}{7}$

2. $\dfrac{-x}{y}$ a. $\dfrac{x}{-y}$ b. $-\dfrac{x}{y}$ c. $\dfrac{x}{y}$ d. $\dfrac{-x}{-y}$

3. $\dfrac{5}{-(x+y)}$ a. $\dfrac{5}{(x+y)}$ b. $\dfrac{-5}{(x+y)}$ c. $\dfrac{-5}{-(x+y)}$ d. $-\dfrac{5}{(x+y)}$

4. $-\dfrac{(y+z)}{3y}$ a. $\dfrac{-(y+z)}{3y}$ b. $\dfrac{-(y+z)}{-3y}$ c. $\dfrac{(y+z)}{3y}$ d. $\dfrac{(y+z)}{-3y}$

5. $\dfrac{-9x}{-2y}$ a. $\dfrac{-9x}{2y}$ b. $\dfrac{9x}{2y}$ c. $\dfrac{9x}{-2y}$ d. $-\dfrac{9x}{2y}$

6. $\dfrac{-a}{-b}$ a. $\dfrac{a}{b}$ b. $\dfrac{a}{-b}$ c. $\dfrac{-a}{b}$ d. $-\dfrac{a}{b}$

Word Bank. Use the choices below to fill in each blank. Some choices may be used more than once and some used not at all.

| exponent | undefined | base | 1 | $\dfrac{-a}{-b}$ | $\dfrac{a}{b}$ |
| square root | reciprocal | 0 | 9 | $\dfrac{-a}{b}$ | $\dfrac{a}{-b}$ |

7. $0 \cdot a = $ _____.

8. $\dfrac{0}{4}$ simplifies to _____ while $\dfrac{4}{0}$ is _____.

9. The _____ of the nonzero number b is $\dfrac{1}{b}$.

10. The fraction $-\dfrac{a}{b} = $ _____ = _____.

11. A(n) _____ is a shorthand notation for repeated multiplication of the same number.

12. In $(-5)^2$, the 2 is the _____ and the -5 is the _____.

13. The opposite of squaring a number is taking the _____ of a number.

14. Using order of operations, $9 \div 3 \cdot 3 = $ _____.

1.3 EXERCISE SET

Add or subtract as indicated. See Examples 1 through 3

1. $-3 + 8$
2. $12 + (-7)$
3. $-14 + (-10)$
4. $-5 + (-9)$
5. $-4.3 - 6.7$
6. $-8.2 - (-6.6)$
7. $13 - 17$
8. $15 - (-1)$
9. $\dfrac{11}{15} - \left(-\dfrac{3}{5}\right)$
10. $\dfrac{7}{10} - \dfrac{4}{5}$
11. $19 - 10 - 11$
12. $-13 - 4 + 9$
13. $-\dfrac{4}{5} - \left(-\dfrac{3}{10}\right)$
14. $-\dfrac{5}{2} - \left(-\dfrac{2}{3}\right)$
15. Subtract 14 from 8.
16. Subtract 9 from -3.

Multiply or divide as indicated. See Examples 4 and 5.

17. $-5 \cdot 12$
18. $-3 \cdot 8$
19. $-17 \cdot 0$
20. $-5 \cdot 0$
21. $\dfrac{0}{-2}$
22. $\dfrac{-2}{0}$
23. $\dfrac{-9}{3}$
24. $\dfrac{-20}{5}$
25. $\dfrac{-12}{-4}$
26. $\dfrac{-36}{-6}$
27. $3\left(-\dfrac{1}{18}\right)$
28. $5\left(-\dfrac{1}{50}\right)$
29. $(-0.7)(-0.8)$
30. $(-0.9)(-0.5)$
31. $9.1 \div (-1.3)$
32. $22.5 \div (-2.5)$
33. $-4(-2)(-1)$
34. $-5(-3)(-2)$

Evaluate each expression. See Example 6.

35. -7^2
36. $(-7)^2$
37. $(-6)^2$
38. -6^2
39. $(-2)^3$
40. -2^3

41. $\left(-\dfrac{1}{3}\right)^3$

42. $\left(-\dfrac{1}{2}\right)^4$

Find the following roots. See Examples 7 and 8.

43. $\sqrt{49}$

44. $\sqrt{81}$

45. $-\sqrt{\dfrac{4}{9}}$

46. $-\sqrt{\dfrac{4}{25}}$

47. $\sqrt[3]{64}$

48. $\sqrt[5]{32}$

49. $\sqrt[4]{81}$

50. $\sqrt[3]{1}$

51. $\sqrt{-100}$

52. $\sqrt{-25}$

MIXED PRACTICE

Simplify each expression. See Examples 1 through 11.

53. $3(5-7)^4$

54. $7(3-8)^2$

55. $-3^2 + 2^3$

56. $-5^2 - 2^4$

57. $\dfrac{3.1 - (-1.4)}{-0.5}$

58. $\dfrac{4.2 - (-8.2)}{-0.4}$

59. $(-3)^2 + 2^3$

60. $(-15)^2 - 2^4$

61. $-8 \div 4 \cdot 2$

62. $-20 \div 5 \cdot 4$

63. $-8\left(-\dfrac{3}{4}\right) - 8$

64. $-10\left(-\dfrac{2}{5}\right) - 10$

65. $2 - [(7-6) + (9-19)]$

66. $8 - [(4-7) + (8-1)]$

67. $\dfrac{(-9+6)(-1^2)}{-2-2}$

68. $\dfrac{(-1-2)(-3^2)}{-6-3}$

69. $(\sqrt[3]{8})(-4) - (\sqrt{9})(-5)$

70. $(\sqrt[3]{27})(-5) - (\sqrt{25})(-3)$

71. $25 - [(3-5) + (14-18)]^2$

72. $10 - [(4-5)^2 + (12-14)]^4$

73. $\dfrac{(3-\sqrt{9}) - (-5-1.3)}{-3}$

74. $\dfrac{-\sqrt{16} - (6-2.4)}{-2}$

75. $\dfrac{|3-9| - |-5|}{-3}$

76. $\dfrac{|-14| - |2-7|}{-15}$

77. $\dfrac{3(-2+1)}{5} - \dfrac{-7(2-4)}{1-(-2)}$

78. $\dfrac{-1-2}{2(-3)+10} - \dfrac{2(-5)}{-1(8)+1}$

79. $\dfrac{\tfrac{1}{3} \cdot 9 - 7}{3 + \tfrac{1}{2} \cdot 4}$

80. $\dfrac{\tfrac{1}{5} \cdot 20 - 6}{10 + \tfrac{1}{4} \cdot 12}$

81. $3\{-2 + 5[1 - 2(-2+5)]\}$

82. $2\{-1 + 3[7 - 4(-10+12)]\}$

83. $\dfrac{-4\sqrt{80+1} + (-4)^2}{3^3 + |-2(3)|}$

84. $\dfrac{(-2)^4 + 3\sqrt{120-20}}{4^3 + |5(-1)|}$

Evaluate each expression when $x = 9$ and $y = -2$. See Example 12.

85. $9x - 6y$

86. $4x - 10y$

87. $-3y^2$

88. $-7y^2$

89. $\dfrac{\sqrt{x}}{y} - \dfrac{y}{x}$

90. $\dfrac{y}{2x} - \dfrac{\sqrt{x}}{3y}$

91. $\dfrac{3 + 2|x - y|}{x + 2y}$

92. $\dfrac{5 + 2|y - x|}{x + 6y}$

93. $\dfrac{y^3 + \sqrt{x-5}}{|4x - y|}$

94. $\dfrac{y^2 + \sqrt{x+7}}{|3x - y|}$

Multiple Steps. See Example 13.

95. The algebraic expression $8 + 2y$ represents the perimeter of a rectangle with width 4 and length y.

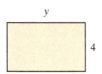

a. Complete the table that follows by evaluating this expression at the given values of y.

Length	y	5	7	10	100
Perimeter	$8 + 2y$				

b. Use the results of the table in part **a** to answer the following question. As the width of a rectangle remains the same and the length increases, does the perimeter increase or decrease? Explain how you arrived at your answer.

96. The algebraic expression πr^2 represents the area of a circle with radius r.

a. Complete the table below by evaluating this expression at given values of r. (Use 3.14 for π.)

Radius	r	2	3	7	10
Area	πr^2				

b. As the radius of a circle increases, (see the table) does its area increase or decrease? Explain your answer.

97. The algebraic expression $\dfrac{100x + 5000}{x}$ represents the cost per bookshelf (in dollars) of producing x bookshelves.

a. Complete the table below.

Number of Bookshelves	x	10	100	1000
Cost per Bookshelf	$\dfrac{100x + 5000}{x}$			

b. As the number of bookshelves manufactured increases, (see the table) does the cost per bookshelf increase or decrease? Why do you think that this is so?

98. If c is degrees Celsius, the algebraic expression $1.8c + 32$ represents the equivalent temperature in degrees Fahrenheit.

a. Complete the table below.

Degrees Celsius	c	-10	0	50
Degrees Fahrenheit	$1.8c + 32$			

b. As degrees Celsius increase (see the table), do degrees Fahrenheit increase or decrease?

CONCEPT EXTENSIONS

Find the value of the expression when $x_1 = 2$, $x_2 = 4$, $y_1 = -3$, $y_2 = 2$.

99. $\dfrac{y_2 - y_1}{x_2 - x_1}$

100. $\sqrt{(x_2 - x_1)^2 + (y_2 - y_1)^2}$

Each circle below represents a whole, or 1. Determine the unknown fractional part of each circle.

101.

102.

Counter Example. *Determine whether each statement is true or false. If false, provide a counter example. (A counter example is a specific example of the falsity of a statement.)*

Let x and y be positive numbers; let z be a negative number.
Example: $x - y$ always simplifies to a positive number.
False. Counter Example: $7 - 10$ simplifies to a negative number, -3.

103. $x + y$ always simplifies to a positive number.

104. $x \cdot y$ always simplifies to a positive number.

105. $xz + y$ always simplifies to a negative number.

106. $\dfrac{x}{y} + z$ always simplifies to a negative number.

107. x^2 is always greater than z^2.

108. z^2 always simplifies to a positive number.

109. Most of Mauna Kea, a volcano on Hawaii, lies below sea level. If this volcano begins at 5998 meters below sea level and then rises 10,203 meters, find the height of the volcano above sea level.

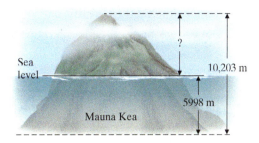

110. The highest point on land on Earth is the top of Mt. Everest in the Himalayas, at an elevation of 29,028 feet above sea level. The lowest point on land is the Dead Sea, between Israel and Jordan, at 1319 feet below sea level. Find the difference in elevations.

Insert parentheses so that each expression simplifies to the given number.

111. $2 + 7 \cdot 1 + 3$; 36

112. $6 - 5 \cdot 2 + 2$; -6

113. Explain why -3^2 and $(-3)^2$ simplify to different numbers.

114. Explain why -3^3 and $(-3)^3$ simplify to the same number.

Use a calculator to approximate each square root. Round answers to four decimal places.

115. $\sqrt{10}$

116. $\sqrt{273}$

117. $\sqrt{7.9}$

118. $\sqrt{19.6}$

INTEGRATED REVIEW — ALGEBRAIC EXPRESSIONS AND OPERATIONS ON WHOLE NUMBERS

Sections 1.2–1.3

Find the value of each expression when $x = -1$, $y = 3$, and $z = -4$.

1. z^2

2. $-z^2$

3. $\dfrac{4x - z}{2y}$

4. $x(y - 2z)$

Perform indicated operations.

5. $-7 - (-2)$

6. $\dfrac{9}{10} - \dfrac{11}{12}$

7. $\dfrac{-13}{2 - 2}$

8. $(1.2)^2 - (2.1)^2$

9. $\sqrt{64} - \sqrt[3]{64}$

10. $-5^2 - (-5)^2$

11. $9 + 2[(8 - 10)^2 + (-3)^2]$

12. $8 - 6[\sqrt[3]{8}\,(-2) + \sqrt{4}(-5)]$

30 CHAPTER 1 Real Numbers and Algebraic Expressions

For Exercises 13 and 14, write each phrase as an algebraic expression. Use x to represent each unknown number.

13. Subtract twice a number from −15.
14. Five more than three times a number.
15. Name the whole number that is not a natural number.
16. True or false: A real number is either a rational number or an irrational number, but never both.

1.4 PROPERTIES OF REAL NUMBERS

OBJECTIVES
1. Use operation and order symbols to write mathematical sentences.
2. Identify identity numbers and inverses.
3. Identify and use the commutative, associative, and distributive properties.
4. Write algebraic expressions.
5. Simplify algebraic expressions.

OBJECTIVE 1 ▶ Using symbols to write mathematical sentences. In Section 1.2, we used the symbol = to mean "is equal to." All of the following key words and phrases also imply equality.

Equality			
equals	is/was	represents	is the same as
gives	yields	amounts to	is equal to

EXAMPLES Write each sentence as an equation.

1. The sum of x and 5 is 20.

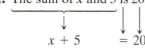

$$x + 5 = 20$$

2. Two times the sum of 3 and y amounts to 4.

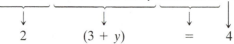

$$2 \cdot (3 + y) = 4$$

3. The difference of 8 and x is the same as the product of 2 and x.

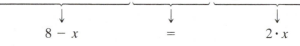

$$8 - x = 2 \cdot x$$

4. The quotient of z and 9 amounts to 9 plus z.

$$z \div 9 = 9 + z$$

or $\dfrac{z}{9} = 9 + z$

PRACTICES
1–4 Write each sentence using mathematical symbols.

1. The product of −4 and x is 20.
2. Three times the difference of z and 3 equals 9.
3. The sum of x and 5 is the same as 3 less than twice x.
4. The sum of y and 2 is 4 more than the quotient of z and 8.

If we want to write in symbols that two numbers are not equal, we can use the symbol ≠, which means "**is not equal to.**" For example,

$$3 \neq 2$$

Graphing two numbers on a number line gives us a way to compare two numbers. For two real numbers *a* and *b*, we say *a* **is less than** *b* if on the number line *a* lies to the left of b. Also, if b is to the right of a on the number line, then **b is greater than a.** The symbol $<$ means "**is less than.**" Since a is less than b, we write

$$a < b$$

> **Helpful Hint**
> Notice that if $a < b$, then $b > a$.
> For example, since $-1 < 7$, then $7 > -1$.

The symbol $>$ means "**is greater than.**" Since b is greater than a, we write

$$b > a$$

EXAMPLE 5 Insert $<$, $>$, or $=$ between each pair of numbers to form a true statement.

a. -1 $\quad$ -2 $\qquad$ b. $\dfrac{12}{4}$ $\quad$ 3 $\qquad$ c. -5 $\quad$ 0 $\qquad$ d. -3.5 $\quad$ -3.05

Solution

a. $-1 > -2$ since -1 lies to the right of -2 on the number line.

b. $\dfrac{12}{4} = 3$.

c. $-5 < 0$ since -5 lies to the left of 0 on the number line.

d. $-3.5 < -3.05$ since -3.5 lies to the left of -3.05 on the number line.

PRACTICE 5 Insert $<$, $>$, or $=$ between each pair of numbers to form a true statement.

a. -6 $\quad$ -5 $\qquad$ b. $\dfrac{24}{3}$ $\quad$ 8 $\qquad$ c. 0 $\quad$ -7 $\qquad$ d. 2.76 $\quad$ 2.67

> **Helpful Hint**
> When inserting the $>$ or $<$ symbol, think of the symbols as arrowheads that "point" toward the smaller number when the statement is true.

In addition to $<$ and $>$, there are the inequality symbols $\leq$ and $\geq$. The symbol

$$\leq \text{ means "\textbf{is less than or equal to}"}$$

and the symbol

$$\geq \text{ means "\textbf{is greater than or equal to}"}$$

For example, the following are true statements.

$$10 \leq 10 \quad \text{since} \quad 10 = 10$$
$$-8 \leq 13 \quad \text{since} \quad -8 < 13$$
$$-5 \geq -5 \quad \text{since} \quad -5 = -5$$
$$-7 \geq -9 \quad \text{since} \quad -7 > -9$$

EXAMPLE 6 Write each sentence using mathematical symbols.

a. The sum of 5 and y is greater than or equal to 7.
b. 11 is not equal to z.
c. 20 is less than the difference of 5 and twice x.

Solution

a. $5 + y \geq 7$ b. $11 \neq z$ c. $20 < 5 - 2x$

PRACTICE 6 Write each sentence using mathematical symbols.

a. The difference of x and 3 is less than or equal to 5.
b. y is not equal to -4.
c. Two is less than the sum of 4 and one-half z.

OBJECTIVE 2 ▶ Identifying identities and inverses. Of all the real numbers, two of them stand out as extraordinary: 0 and 1. Zero is the only number that when *added* to any real number, the result is the same real number. Zero is thus called the **additive identity.** Also, one is the only number that when *multiplied* by any real number, the result is the same real number. One is thus called the **multiplicative identity.**

	Addition	Multiplication
Identity Properties	The additive identity is 0. $a + 0 = 0 + a = a$	The multiplicative identity is 1. $a \cdot 1 = 1 \cdot a = a$

In Section 1.2, we learned that a and $-a$ are opposites.

Another name for opposite is **additive inverse.** For example, the additive inverse of 3 is -3. Notice that the sum of a number and its opposite is always 0.

In Section 1.3, we learned that, for a nonzero number, b and $\frac{1}{b}$ are reciprocals.

Another name for reciprocal is **multiplicative inverse.** For example, the multiplicative inverse of $-\frac{2}{3}$ is $-\frac{3}{2}$. Notice that the product of a number and its reciprocal is always 1.

	Opposite or Additive Inverse	*Reciprocal or Multiplicative Inverse*
Inverse Properties	For each number a, there is a unique number $-a$ called the **additive inverse** or **opposite** of a such that $a + (-a) = (-a) + a = 0$	For each nonzero a, there is a unique number $\frac{1}{a}$ called the **multiplicative inverse** or **reciprocal** of a such that $a \cdot \frac{1}{a} = \frac{1}{a} \cdot a = 1$

EXAMPLE 7 Write the additive inverse, or opposite, of each.

a. 4   b. $\frac{3}{7}$ c. -11.2

Solution

a. The opposite of 4 is -4.
b. The opposite of $\frac{3}{7}$ is $-\frac{3}{7}$.
c. The opposite of -11.2 is $-(-11.2) = 11.2$.

PRACTICE 7 Write the additive inverse, or opposite of each.

a. -7 b. 4.7   c. $-\frac{3}{8}$

Section 1.4 Properties of Real Numbers 33

EXAMPLE 8 Write the multiplicative inverse, or reciprocal, of each.

a. 11   **b.** −9   **c.** $\dfrac{7}{4}$

Solution

a. The reciprocal of 11 is $\dfrac{1}{11}$.

b. The reciprocal of −9 is $-\dfrac{1}{9}$.

c. The reciprocal of $\dfrac{7}{4}$ is $\dfrac{4}{7}$ because $\dfrac{7}{4} \cdot \dfrac{4}{7} = 1$.

PRACTICE 8 Write the multiplicative inverse, or reciprocal, of each.

a. $-\dfrac{5}{3}$ **b.** 14   **c.** −2

> ▶ **Helpful Hint**
> The number 0 has no reciprocal. Why? There is no number that when multiplied by 0 gives a product of 1.

Concept Check ✓

Can a number's additive inverse and multiplicative inverse ever be the same? Explain.

OBJECTIVE 3 ▶ **Using the commutative, associative, and distributive properties.** In addition to these special real numbers, all real numbers have certain properties that allow us to write equivalent expressions—that is, expressions that have the same value. These properties will be especially useful in Chapter 2 when we solve equations.

The **commutative properties** state that the order in which two real numbers are added or multiplied does not affect their sum or product.

> **Commutative Properties**
> For real numbers a and b,
>
> Addition: $a + b = b + a$
> Multiplication: $a \cdot b = b \cdot a$

The **associative properties** state that regrouping numbers that are added or multiplied does not affect their sum or product.

> **Associative Properties**
> For real numbers a, b, and c,
>
> Addition: $(a + b) + c = a + (b + c)$
> Multiplication: $(a \cdot b) \cdot c = a \cdot (b \cdot c)$

EXAMPLE 9 Use the commutative property of addition to write an expression equivalent to $7x + 5$.

Solution $7x + 5 = 5 + 7x$.

PRACTICE 9 Use the commutative property of addition to write an expression equivalent to $8 + 13x$.

Answer to Concept Check:
no; answers may vary

EXAMPLE 10 Use the associative property of multiplication to write an expression equivalent to $4 \cdot (9y)$. Then simplify this equivalent expression.

Solution $\qquad 4 \cdot (9y) = (4 \cdot 9)y = 36y.$

PRACTICE 10 Use the associative property of multiplication to write an expression equivalent to $3 \cdot (11b)$. Then simplify the equivalent expression.

The **distributive property** states that multiplication distributes over addition.

Distributive Property

For real numbers a, b, and c,

$$a(b + c) = ab + ac$$

EXAMPLE 11 Use the distributive property to multiply.

a. $3(2x + y)$ **b.** $-(3x - 1)$ **c.** $0.7a(b - 2)$

Solution

a. $3(2x + y) = 3 \cdot 2x + 3 \cdot y$ Apply the distributive property.
$\qquad\qquad\qquad = 6x + 3y$ Apply the associative property of multiplication.

b. Recall that $-(3x - 1)$ means $-1(3x - 1)$.

$$-1(3x - 1) = -1(3x) + (-1)(-1)$$
$$= -3x + 1$$

c. $0.7a(b - 2) = 0.7a \cdot b - 0.7a \cdot 2 = 0.7ab - 1.4a$

PRACTICE 11 Use the distributive property to multiply.

a. $4(x + 5y)$ **b.** $-(3 - 2z)$ **c.** $0.3x(y - 3)$

Concept Check ✓

Is the statement below true? Why or why not?

$$6(2a)(3b) = 6(2a) \cdot 6(3b)$$

OBJECTIVE 4 ▶ Writing algebraic expressions. As mentioned earlier, an important step in problem solving is to be able to write algebraic expressions from word phrases. Sometimes this involves a direct translation, but often an indicated operation is not directly stated but rather implied.

EXAMPLE 12 Write each as an algebraic expression.

a. A vending machine contains x quarters. Write an expression for the *value* of the quarters.

b. The number of grams of fat in x pieces of bread if each piece of bread contains 2 grams of fat.

c. The cost of x desks if each desk costs $156.

d. Sales tax on a purchase of x dollars if the tax rate is 9%.

Each of these examples implies finding a product.

Answer to Concept Check:
no; $6(2a)(3b) = 12a(3b) = 36ab$

Solution

a. The value of the quarters is found by multiplying the value of a quarter (0.25 dollar) by the number of quarters.

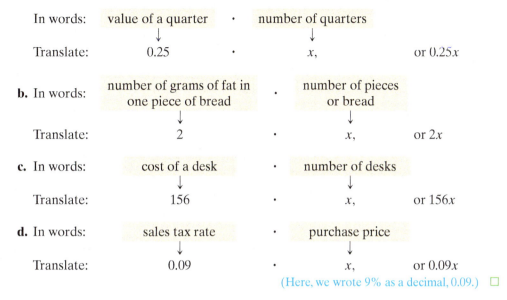

(Here, we wrote 9% as a decimal, 0.09.)

PRACTICE 12 Write each as an algebraic expression.

a. A parking meter contains x dimes. Write an expression for the value of the dimes.
b. The grams of carbohydrates in y cookies if each cookie has 26 g of carbohydrates.
c. The cost of z birthday cards if each birthday card costs $1.75.
d. The amount of money you save on a new cell phone costing t dollars if it has a 15% discount.

Two or more unknown numbers in a problem may sometimes be related. If so, try letting a variable represent one unknown number and then represent the other unknown number or numbers as expressions containing the same variable.

EXAMPLE 13 Write each as an algebraic expression.

a. Two numbers have a sum of 20. If one number is x, represent the other number as an expression in x.
b. The older sister is 8 years older than her younger sister. If the age of the younger sister is x, represent the age of the older sister as an expression in x.
c. Two angles are complementary if the sum of their measures is 90°. If the measure of one angle is x degrees, represent the measure of the other angle as an expression in x.
d. If x is the first of two consecutive integers, represent the second integer as an expression in x.

Solution

a. If two numbers have a sum of 20 and one number is x, the other number is "the rest of 20."

In words:	twenty	minus	x
	↓	↓	↓
Translate:	20	−	x

b. The older sister's age is

In words: eight years   added to   younger sister's age

Translate: 8   +   x

c. In words: ninety   minus   x

Translate: 90   −   x

d. The next consecutive integer is always one more than the previous integer.

In words: the first integer   plus   one

Translate: x   +   1

PRACTICE 13 Write each as an algebraic expression.

a. Two numbers have a sum of 16. If one number is x, represent the other number as an expression in x.

b. Two angles are supplementary if the sum of their measures is 180°. If the measure of one angle is x degrees, represent the measure of the other angle as an expression in x.

c. If x is the first of two consecutive even integers, represent the next even integer as an expression in x.

d. One brother is 9 years younger than another brother. If the age of the younger brother is x, represent the age of the older brother as an expression in x.

OBJECTIVE 5 ▶ Simplifying algebraic expressions. Often, an expression may be **simplified** by removing grouping symbols and combining any like terms. The **terms** of an expression are the addends of the expression. For example, in the expression $3x^2 + 4x$, the terms are $3x^2$ and $4x$.

Expression	*Terms*
$-2x + y$	$-2x, y$
$3x^2 - \dfrac{y}{5} + 7$	$3x^2, -\dfrac{y}{5}, 7$

Terms with the same variable(s) raised to the same power are called **like terms.** We can add or subtract like terms by using the distributive property. This process is called **combining like terms.**

EXAMPLE 14 Use the distributive property to simplify each expression.

a. $3x - 5x + 4$ **b.** $7yz + yz$ **c.** $4z + 6.1$

Solution

a. $3x - 5x + 4 = (3 - 5)x + 4$ Apply the distributive property.
$= -2x + 4$

b. $7yz + yz = (7 + 1)yz = 8yz$

c. $4z + 6.1$ cannot be simplified further since $4z$ and 6.1 are not like terms.

PRACTICE 14 Use the distributive property to simplify.

a. $6ab - ab$ **b.** $4x - 5 + 6x$ **c.** $17p - 9$

Let's continue to use properties of real numbers to simplify expressions. Recall that the distributive property can also be used to multiply. For example,

$$-2(x + 3) = -2(x) + (-2)(3) = -2x - 6$$

The associative and commutative properties may sometimes be needed to rearrange and group like terms when we simplify expressions.

$$-7x^2 + 5 + 3x^2 - 2 = -7x^2 + 3x^2 + 5 - 2$$
$$= (-7 + 3)x^2 + (5 - 2)$$
$$= -4x^2 + 3$$

EXAMPLE 15 Simplify each expression.

a. $3xy - 2xy + 5 - 7 + xy$ **b.** $7x^2 + 3 - 5(x^2 - 4)$

c. $(2.1x - 5.6) - (-x - 5.3)$ **d.** $\frac{1}{2}(4a - 6b) - \frac{1}{3}(9a + 12b - 1) + \frac{1}{4}$

Solution

a. $3xy - 2xy + 5 - 7 + xy = 3xy - 2xy + xy + 5 - 7$ Apply the commutative property.
$$= (3 - 2 + 1)xy + (5 - 7)$$ Apply the distributive property.
$$= 2xy - 2$$ Simplify.

b. $7x^2 + 3 - 5(x^2 - 4) = 7x^2 + 3 - 5x^2 + 20$ Apply the distributive property.
$$= 2x^2 + 23$$ Simplify.

c. Think of $-(-x - 5.3)$ as $-1(-x - 5.3)$ and use the distributive property.
$$(2.1x - 5.6) - 1(-x - 5.3) = 2.1x - 5.6 + 1x + 5.3$$
$$= 3.1x - 0.3$$ Combine like terms.

d. $\frac{1}{2}(4a - 6b) - \frac{1}{3}(9a + 12b - 1) + \frac{1}{4}$

$$= 2a - 3b - 3a - 4b + \frac{1}{3} + \frac{1}{4}$$ Use the distributive property.

$$= -a - 7b + \frac{7}{12}$$ Combine like terms.

PRACTICE 15 Simplify each expression.

a. $5pq - 2pq - 11 - 4pq + 18$ **b.** $3x^2 + 7 - 2(x^2 - 6)$

c. $(3.7x + 2.5) - (-2.1x - 1.3)$

d. $\frac{1}{5}(15c - 25d) - \frac{1}{2}(8c + 6d + 1) + \frac{3}{4}$

Concept Check ✓

Find and correct the error in the following

$$x - 4(x - 5) = x - 4x - 20$$
$$= -3x - 20$$

Answer to Concept Check:
$x - 4(x - 5) = x - 4x + 20$
$= -3x + 20$

CHAPTER 1 Real Numbers and Algebraic Expressions

VOCABULARY & READINESS CHECK

Complete a Table. *Complete the table by filling in the symbols.*

	Symbol	Meaning		Symbol	Meaning
1.		is less than	2.		is greater than
3.		is not equal to	4.		is equal to
5.		is greater than or equal to	6.		is less than or equal to

Word Bank. *Use the choices below to fill in each blank. Not all choices will be used.*

like   terms   distributive $-a$ commutative

unlike   combining   associative $\frac{1}{a}$

7. The opposite of nonzero number *a* is _____.
8. The reciprocal of nonzero number *a* is _____.
9. The _____ property has to do with "order."
10. The _____ property has to do with "grouping."
11. $a(b + c) = ab + ac$ illustrates the _____ property.
12. Terms with the same variable(s) raised to the same powers are called _____ terms.
13. The _____ of an expression are the addends of the expression.
14. The process of adding or subtracting like terms is called _____ like terms.

1.4 EXERCISE SET

MIXED PRACTICE

Write each sentence using mathematical symbols. See Examples 1 through 4 and 6 through 8.

1. The sum of 10 and *x* is -12.
2. The difference of *y* and 3 amounts to 12.
3. Twice *x*, plus 5, is the same as -14.
4. Three more than the product of 4 and *c* is 7.
5. The quotient of *n* and 5 is 4 times *n*.
6. The quotient of 8 and *y* is 3 more than *y*.
7. The difference of *z* and one-half is the same as the product of *z* and one-half.
8. Five added to one-fourth *q* is the same as 4 more than *q*.
9. The product of 7 and *x* is less than or equal to -21.
10. 10 subtracted from the reciprocal of *x* is greater than 0.
11. Twice the difference of *x* and 6 is greater than the reciprocal of 11.
12. Four times the sum of 5 and *x* is not equal to the opposite of 15.
13. Twice the difference of *x* and 6 is -27.
14. 5 times the sum of 6 and *y* is -35.

Insert $<$, $>$, or $=$ between each pair of numbers to form a true statement. See Example 5.

15. -16 -17
16. -14 -24
17. 7.4 7.40
18. $\frac{7}{2}$ $\frac{35}{10}$
19. $\frac{7}{11}$ $\frac{9}{11}$
20. $\frac{9}{20}$ $\frac{3}{20}$
21. $\frac{1}{2}$ $\frac{5}{8}$
22. $\frac{3}{4}$ $\frac{7}{8}$
23. -7.9 -7.09
24. -13.07 -13.7

Complete a Table. *Fill in the chart. See Example 7 and 8.*

	Number	Opposite	Reciprocal
25.	5		
26.	7		
27.		8	
28.			$-\frac{1}{4}$
29.	$-\frac{1}{7}$		
30.	$\frac{1}{11}$		
31.	0		
32.	1		
33.			$\frac{8}{7}$
34.		$\frac{23}{5}$	

35. Name the only real number that has no reciprocal, and explain why this is so.

36. Name the only real number that is its own opposite, and explain why this is so.

Use a commutative property to write an equivalent expression. See Example 9.

37. $7x + y$
38. $3a + 2b$
39. $z \cdot w$
40. $r \cdot s$
41. $\dfrac{1}{3} \cdot \dfrac{x}{5}$
42. $\dfrac{x}{2} \cdot \dfrac{9}{10}$

43. Is subtraction commutative? Explain why or why not.
44. Is division commutative? Explain why or why not.

Use an associative property to write an equivalent expression. See Example 10.

45. $5 \cdot (7x)$
46. $3 \cdot (10z)$
47. $(x + 1.2) + y$
48. $5q + (2r + s)$
49. $(14z) \cdot y$
50. $(9.2x) \cdot y$

51. Evaluate $12 - (5 - 3)$ and $(12 - 5) - 3$. Use these two expressions and discuss whether subtraction is associative.

52. Evaluate $24 \div (6 \div 3)$ and $(24 \div 6) \div 3$. Use these two expressions and discuss whether division is associative.

Use the distributive property to find the product. See Example 11.

53. $3(x + 5)$
54. $7(y + 2)$
55. $-(2a + b)$
56. $-(c + 7d)$
57. $2(6x + 5y + 2z)$
58. $5(3a + b + 9c)$
59. $-4(x - 2y + 7)$
60. $-10(2a - 3b - 4)$
61. $0.5x(6y - 3)$
62. $1.2m(9n - 4)$

Fill in the Blank. *Complete the statement to illustrate the given property.*

63. $3x + 6 = $ _____ Commutative property of addition
64. $8 + 0 = $ _____ Additive identity property
65. $\dfrac{2}{3} + \left(-\dfrac{2}{3}\right) = $ ____ Additive inverse property
66. $4(x + 3) = $ _____ Distributive property
67. $7 \cdot 1 = $ _____ Multiplicative identity property
68. $0 \cdot (-5.4) = $ ____ Multiplication property of zero
69. $10(2y) = $ _____ Associative property
70. $9y + (x + 3z) = $ _____ Associative property

71. To demonstrate the distributive property geometrically, represent the area of the larger rectangle in two ways: First as length a times width $b + c$, and second as the sum of the areas of the smaller rectangles.

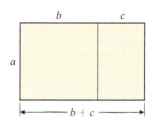

Write each of the following as an algebraic expression. See Examples 12 and 13.

72. Write an expression for the amount of money (in dollars) in n nickels.
73. Write an expression for the amount of money (in dollars) in d dimes.
74. Two numbers have a sum of 25. If one number is x, represent the other number as an expression in x.
75. Two numbers have a sum of 112. If one number is x, represent the other number as an expression in x.
76. Two angles are supplementary if the sum of their measures is 180°. If the measure of one angle is x degrees, represent the measure of the other angle as an expression in x.
77. If the measure of an angle is $5x$ degrees, represent the measure of its complement as an expression in x.
78. The cost of x compact discs if each compact disc costs $6.49.
79. The cost of y books if each book costs $35.61.
80. If x is an odd integer, represent the next odd integer as an expression in x.
81. If $2x$ is an even integer, represent the next even integer as an expression in x.

MIXED PRACTICE

Simplify each expression. See Examples 11, 14, and 15.

82. $-9 + 4x + 18 - 10x$
83. $5y - 14 + 7y - 20y$
84. $5k - (3k - 10)$
85. $-11c - (4 - 2c)$
86. $(3x + 4) - (6x - 1)$
87. $(8 - 5y) - (4 + 3y)$
88. $3(xy - 2) + xy + 15 - x^2$
89. $-4(yz + 3) - 7yz + 1 + y^2$
90. $-(n + 5) + (5n - 3)$
91. $-(8 - t) + (2t - 6)$
92. $4(6n^2 - 3) - 3(8n^2 + 4)$
93. $5(2z^3 - 6) + 10(3 - z^3)$
94. $3x - 2(x - 5) + x$
95. $7n + 3(2n - 6) - 2$
96. $1.5x + 2.3 - 0.7x - 5.9$
97. $6.3y - 9.7 + 2.2y - 11.1$

98. $\frac{3}{4}b - \frac{1}{2} + \frac{1}{6}b - \frac{2}{3}$

99. $\frac{7}{8}a - \frac{11}{12} - \frac{1}{2}a + \frac{5}{6}$

100. $2(3x + 7)$
101. $4(5y + 12)$
102. $\frac{1}{4}(8x - 4) - \frac{1}{5}(20x - 6y)$
103. $\frac{1}{2}(10x - 2) - \frac{1}{6}(60x - 5y)$
104. $\frac{1}{6}(24a - 18b) - \frac{1}{7}(7a - 21b - 2) - \frac{1}{5}$
105. $\frac{1}{3}(6x - 33y) - \frac{1}{8}(24x - 40y + 1) - \frac{1}{3}$

CONCEPT EXTENSIONS

In each statement, a property of real numbers has been incorrectly applied. Correct the right-hand side of each statement. See the second Concept Check in this section.

106. $3(x + 4) = 3x + 4$
107. $5(7y) = (5 \cdot 7)(5 \cdot y)$

Simplify each expression.

108. $8.1z + 7.3(z + 5.2) - 6.85$
109. $6.5y - 4.4(1.8x - 3.3) + 10.95$
110. **Multiple Choice.** Choose the expression that simplifies to $3x - y$.
   a. $-(2x - 5y) + 5x + 4y$ b. $2(x - y) + x$
   c. $3(x - y) + 2y$
111. **Multiple Choice.** Choose the correct translation for "Twice the difference of a number and 6 equals the sum of 5 times the number and -3."
   a. $2x - 6 = 5(x + (-3))$ b. $2(x - 6) = 5x + (-3)$
   c. $2(6 - x) = 5x + (-3)$ d. $2x - 6 = 5x + (-3)$
112. Do figures with the same surface area always have the same volume? To see, take two $8\frac{1}{2}$-by-11-inch sheets of paper and construct two cylinders using the following figures as a

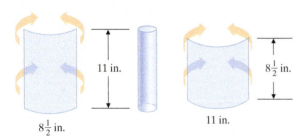

Cylinder 1   Cylinder 2

guide. Working with a partner, measure the height and the radius of each resulting cylinder and use the expression $\pi r^2 h$ to approximate each volume to the nearest tenth of a cubic inch. Explain your results.

113. Use the same idea as in Exercise 112, work with a partner, and discover whether two rectangles with the same perimeter always have the same area. Explain your results.

Read a Graph. *The following graph is called a broken-line graph, or simply a line graph. To find the population over 65 for a particular year, read the height of the corresponding point. To read the height, follow the point horizontally to the left until you reach the vertical axis. Use this graph to answer Exercises 114 through 119.*

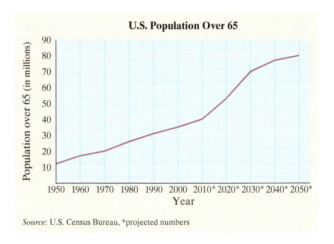

Source: U.S. Census Bureau, *projected numbers

114. Estimate the population over 65 in the year 1970.
115. Estimate the predicted population over 65 in the year 2050.
116. Estimate the predicted population over 65 in the year 2030.
117. Estimate the population over 65 in the year 2000.
118. Is the population over 65 increasing as time passes or decreasing? Explain how you arrived at your answer.
119. The percent of Americans over 65 in 1950 was 8.1%. The percent of Americans over 65 in 2050 is expected to be 2.5 times the percent over 65 in 1950. Estimate the percent of Americans expected to be over age 65 in 2050.

CHAPTER 1 VOCABULARY CHECK

Fill in each blank with one of the words or phrases listed below.

distributive   real   reciprocals   absolute value   opposite   associative
inequality   commutative   whole   algebraic expression   exponent   variable

1. A(n) _____ is formed by numbers and variables connected by the operations of addition, subtraction, multiplication, division, raising to powers, and/or taking roots.
2. The _____ of a number a is $-a$.
3. $3(x - 6) = 3x - 18$ by the _____ property.
4. The _____ of a number is the distance between that number and 0 on the number line.
5. A(n) _____ is a shorthand notation for repeated multiplication of the same factor.
6. A letter that represents a number is called a _____.
7. The symbols $<$ and $>$ are called _____ symbols.
8. If a is not 0, then a and $\frac{1}{a}$ are called _____.
9. $A + B = B + A$ by the _____ property.
10. $(A + B) + C = A + (B + C)$ by the _____ property.
11. The numbers $0, 1, 2, 3, \ldots$ are called _____ numbers.
12. If a number corresponds to a point on the number line, we know that number is a _____ number.

CHAPTER 1 REVIEW

(1.2) Find the value of each algebraic expression at the given replacement values.

1. $7x$ when $x = 3$
2. st when $s = 1.6$ and $t = 5$
3. The hummingbird has an average wing speed of 90 beats per second. The expression $90t$ gives the number of wing beats in t seconds. Calculate the number of wing beats in *1 hour* for the hummingbird.

List the elements in each set.

4. $\{x \mid x \text{ is an odd integer between } -2 \text{ and } 4\}$
5. $\{x \mid x \text{ is an even integer between } -3 \text{ and } 7\}$
6. $\{x \mid x \text{ is a negative whole number}\}$
7. $\{x \mid x \text{ is a natural number that is not a rational number}\}$
8. $\{x \mid x \text{ is a whole number greater than } 5\}$
9. $\{x \mid x \text{ is an integer less than } 3\}$

Determine whether each statement is true or false if $A = \{6, 10, 12\}$, $B = \{5, 9, 11\}$, $C = \{\ldots, -3, -2, -1, 0, 1, 2, 3, \ldots\}$, $D = \{2, 4, 6, \ldots, 16\}$ $E = \{x \mid x \text{ is a rational number}\}$, $F = \{\ \}$, $G = \{x \mid x \text{ is an irrational number}\}$, *and* $H = \{x \mid x \text{ is a real number}\}$.

10. $10 \in D$
11. $B \in 9$
12. $\sqrt{169} \notin G$
13. $0 \notin F$
14. $\pi \in E$
15. $\pi \in H$
16. $\sqrt{4} \in G$
17. $-9 \in E$
18. $A \subseteq D$
19. $C \nsubseteq B$
20. $C \nsubseteq E$
21. $F \subseteq H$
22. $B \subseteq B$
23. $D \subseteq C$
24. $C \subseteq H$
25. $G \subseteq H$
26. $\{5\} \in B$
27. $\{5\} \subseteq B$

List the elements of the set $\left\{5, -\frac{2}{3}, \frac{8}{2}, \sqrt{9}, 0.3, \sqrt{7}, 1\frac{5}{8}, -1, \pi\right\}$ *that are also elements of each given set.*

28. Whole numbers
29. Natural numbers
30. Rational numbers

31. Irrational numbers
32. Real numbers
33. Integers

Find the opposite.

34. $-\dfrac{3}{4}$
35. 0.6
36. 0
37. 1

Find the reciprocal.

38. $-\dfrac{3}{4}$
39. 0.6
40. 0
41. 1

(1.3) *Simplify.*

42. $-7 + 3$
43. $-10 + (-25)$
44. $5(-0.4)$
45. $(-3.1)(-0.1)$
46. $-7 - (-15)$
47. $9 - (-4.3)$
48. $(-6)(-4)(0)(-3)$
49. $(-12)(0)(-1)(-5)$
50. $(-24) \div 0$
51. $0 \div (-45)$
52. $(-36) \div (-9)$
53. $60 \div (-12)$
54. $\left(-\dfrac{4}{5}\right) - \left(-\dfrac{2}{3}\right)$
55. $\left(\dfrac{5}{4}\right) - \left(-2\dfrac{3}{4}\right)$

56. Determine the unknown fractional part.

Simplify.

57. $-5 + 7 - 3 - (-10)$
58. $8 - (-3) + (-4) + 6$
59. $3(4-5)^4$
60. $6(7-10)^2$
61. $\left(-\dfrac{8}{15}\right) \cdot \left(-\dfrac{2}{3}\right)^2$
62. $\left(-\dfrac{3}{4}\right)^2 \cdot \left(-\dfrac{10}{21}\right)$
63. $\dfrac{-\dfrac{6}{15}}{\dfrac{8}{25}}$
64. $\dfrac{\dfrac{4}{9}}{-\dfrac{8}{45}}$
65. $-\dfrac{3}{8} + 3(2) \div 6$
66. $5(-2) - (-3) - \dfrac{1}{6} + \dfrac{2}{3}$
67. $|2^3 - 3^2| - |5 - 7|$
68. $|5^2 - 2^2| + |9 \div (-3)|$
69. $(2^3 - 3^2) - (5 - 7)$
70. $(5^2 - 2^4) + [9 \div (-3)]$
71. $\dfrac{(8-10)^3 - (-4)^2}{2 + 8(2) \div 4}$
72. $\dfrac{(2+4)^2 + (-1)^5}{12 \div 2 \cdot 3 - 3}$
73. $\dfrac{(4-9) + 4 - 9}{10 - 12 \div 4 \cdot 8}$
74. $\dfrac{3 - 7 - (7-3)}{15 + 30 \div 6 \cdot 2}$

75. $\dfrac{\sqrt{25}}{4 + 3 \cdot 7}$
76. $\dfrac{\sqrt{64}}{24 - 8 \cdot 2}$

Find the value of each expression when $x = 0$, $y = 3$, and $z = -2$.

77. $x^2 - y^2 + z^2$
78. $\dfrac{5x + z}{2y}$
79. $\dfrac{-7y - 3z}{-3}$
80. $(x - y + z)^2$

△ 81. The algebraic expression $2\pi r$ represents the circumference of (distance around) a circle of radius r.

a. Complete the table below by evaluating the expression at given values of r. (Use 3.14 for π)

Radius	r	1	10	100
Circumference	$2\pi r$			

b. As the radius of a circle increases, does the circumference of the circle increase or decrease?

(1.4) *Simplify each expression.*

82. $5xy - 7xy + 3 - 2 + xy$
83. $4x + 10x - 19x + 10 - 19$
84. $6x^2 + 2 - 4(x^2 + 1)$
85. $-7(2x^2 - 1) - x^2 - 1$
86. $(3.2x - 1.5) - (4.3x - 1.2)$
87. $(7.6x + 4.7) - (1.9x + 3.6)$

Write each statement using mathematical symbols.

88. Twelve is the product of x and negative 4.
89. The sum of n and twice n is negative fifteen.
90. Four times the sum of y and three is -1.
91. The difference of t and five, multiplied by six is four.
92. Seven subtracted from z is six.
93. Ten less than the product of x and nine is five.
94. The difference of x and 5 is at least 12.
95. The opposite of four is less than the product of y and seven.
96. Two-thirds is not equal to twice the sum of n and one-fourth.
97. The sum of t and six is not more than negative twelve.

Name the property illustrated.

98. $(M + 5) + P = M + (5 + P)$

99. $5(3x - 4) = 15x - 20$

100. $(-4) + 4 = 0$

101. $(3 + x) + 7 = 7 + (3 + x)$

102. $(XY)Z = (YZ)X$

103. $\left(-\frac{3}{5}\right) \cdot \left(-\frac{5}{3}\right) = 1$

104. $T \cdot 0 = 0$

105. $(ab)c = a(bc)$

106. $A + 0 = A$

107. $8 \cdot 1 = 8$

Complete the equation using the given property.

108. $5x - 15z =$ _____ Distributive property

109. $(7 + y) + (3 + x) =$ _____ Commutative property

110. $0 =$ ____ Additive inverse property

111. $1 =$ ____ Multiplicative inverse property

112. $[(3.4)(0.7)]5 =$ _____ Associative property

113. $7 =$ _____ Additive identity property

Insert $<$, $>$, or $=$ to make each statement true.

114. -9 ____ -12

115. 0 ____ -6

116. -3 ____ -1

117. 7 ____ $|-7|$

118. -5 ____ $-(-5)$

119. $-(-2)$ ____ -2

MIXED REVIEW

Complete the table.

	Number	Opposite of Number	Reciprocal of Number
120.	$-\frac{3}{4}$		
121.		-5	

Simplify. If necessary, write answers with positive exponents only.

122. $-2\left(5x + \frac{1}{2}\right) + 7.1$

123. $\sqrt{36} \div 2 \cdot 3$

124. $-\frac{7}{11} - \left(-\frac{1}{11}\right)$

125. $10 - (-1) + (-2) + 6$

126. $\left(-\frac{2}{3}\right)^3 \div \frac{10}{9}$

127. $\dfrac{(3 - 5)^2 + (-1)^3}{1 + 2(3 - (-1))^2}$

128. $\frac{1}{3}(9x - 3y) - (4x - 1) + 4y$

129. The following bar graph shows the U.S. life expectancy at birth for females born in the years shown. Use the graph to fill in the table below by calculating the *increase* in life expectancy of each five-year period shown. (*Source:* Centers for Disease Control)

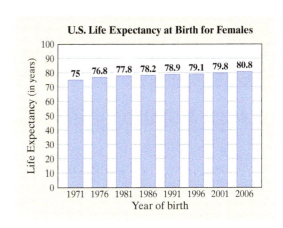

U.S. Life Expectancy at Birth for Females

Year	Increase in Life Expectancy (in Years) from 5 Years Earlier
1976	
1981	
1986	
1991	
1996	
2001	
2006	

CHAPTER 1 TEST

Remember to use the Chapter Test Prep Videos to see the fully worked-out solutions to any of the exercises you want to review.

Determine whether each statement is true or false.

1. $-2.3 > -2.33$
2. $-6^2 = (-6)^2$
3. $-5 - 8 = -(5 - 8)$
4. $(-2)(-3)(0) = \dfrac{-4}{0}$
5. All natural numbers are integers.
6. All rational numbers are integers.

Simplify.

7. $5 - 12 \div 3(2)$
8. $5^2 - 3^4$
9. $(4 - 9)^3 - |-4 - 6|^2$
10. $12 + \{6 - [5 - 2(-5)]\}$
11. $\dfrac{6(7 - 9)^3 + (-2)}{(-2)(-5)(-5)}$
12. $\dfrac{(4 - \sqrt{16}) - (-7 - 20)}{-2(1 - 4)^2}$

Evaluate each expression when $q = 4$, $r = -2$, and $t = 1$.

13. $q^2 - r^2$
14. $\dfrac{5t - 3q}{3r - 1}$

15. The algebraic expression $5.75x$ represents the total cost for x adults to attend the theater.
    a. Complete the table that follows.
    b. As the number of adults increases does the total cost increase or decrease?

Adults	x	1	3	10	20
Total Cost	$5.75x$				

Write each statement using mathematical symbols.

16. Twice the sum of x and five is 30.
17. The square of the difference of six and y, divided by seven, is less than -2.
18. The product of nine and z, divided by the absolute value of -12, is not equal to 10.
19. Three times the quotient of n and five is the opposite of n.
20. Twenty is equal to 6 subtracted from twice x.
21. Negative two is equal to x divided by the sum of x and five.

Name each property illustrated.

22. $6(x - 4) = 6x - 24$
23. $(4 + x) + z = 4 + (x + z)$
24. $(-7) + 7 = 0$
25. $(-18)(0) = 0$
26. Write an expression for the total amount of money (in dollars) in n nickels and d dimes.

Simplify each expression.

27. $-2(3x + 7)$
28. $\dfrac{1}{3}a - \dfrac{3}{8} + \dfrac{1}{6}a - \dfrac{3}{4}$
29. $4y + 10 - 2(y + 10)$
30. $(8.3x - 2.9) - (9.6x - 4.8)$

CHAPTER 1 STANDARDIZED TEST

Multiple Choice. *Choose the one alternative that best completes the statement or answers the question. Determine whether the statement is true or false.*

1. $-3.9 > -3.99$
   a. True b. False
2. $-3^3 = (-3)^3$
   a. True b. False
3. $-5 + 4 = -(-5 - 4)$
   a. True b. False
4. $(6)(0)(-5) = \dfrac{0}{8}$
   a. True b. False
5. All whole numbers are integers.
   a. True b. False
6. All irrational numbers are rational numbers.
   a. True b. False

Simplify.

7. $9(4) - 21 \div 3$
   a. 0 b. 29 c. 43 d. 5

8. $7^3 - (-8)^2$
   a. -43 b. 279 c. 407 d. 37
9. $(3 - 7)^3 - |-4 - 5|^2$
   a. -145 b. 17 c. -17 d. -65
10. $(8)(7) + \{15 \div [8 - (3 + 2)]\}$
    a. 63 b. 60 c. 62 d. 61
11. $\dfrac{5^2 + (12 - 3)^2}{12 \div 4 - (1 + 1)}$
    a. 28 b. 106 c. 160 d. 1130
12. $\dfrac{-2(5^2) - 5(9 - 4)}{-5(3 - 8) \div (-5)}$
    a. 23 b. -23 c. 15 d. -15

Evaluate the expression for the given replacement values.

13. $s^3 + t^2$ when $s = 4$ and $t = 5$.
    a. 74 b. 89 c. 37 d. 22
14. $\dfrac{y - 8x}{5x - xz}$ when $x = -1$, $y = 3$, and $z = -3$.
    a. $\dfrac{5}{8}$ b. $\dfrac{5}{2}$ c. $-\dfrac{11}{8}$ d. $-\dfrac{21}{8}$

Solve.

15. The algebraic expression $6.5x$ represents the total cost for x adults to attend the theater.

    a. Complete the table that follows.

x	1	3	10	20
$6.5x$				

    b. As the number of adults increases, does the total cost increase or decrease?

    i.

x	1	3	10	20
$6.5x$	6.5	19.5	32.5	65

    ii.

x	1	3	10	20
$6.5x$	6.5	19.5	65	130

    iii.

x	1	3	10	20
$6.5x$	6.5	19.5	65	130

    iv.

x	1	3	10	20
$6.5x$	7.5	9.5	16.5	26.5

Write the statement using mathematical symbols.

16. 50 is equal to two plus the product of twenty and x.
    a. $50 = (2 + 20)x$ **b.** $50 = 2 \cdot (x + 20)$
    c. $50 = 2 + 20x$ **d.** $50 = (2 + x) \cdot 20$

17. Sixty is seventeen subtracted from the product of six and y.
    a. $60 = 6y - 17$ **b.** $60 = 6(y - 17)$
    c. $60 = (6 - 17) \cdot y$ **d.** $60 = 17 - 6y$

18. The square of the sum of x and fourteen, divided by three, is greater than -20.
    a. $\dfrac{(x+14)^2}{3} > -20$ **b.** $\dfrac{x^2+14}{3} > -20$
    c. $\dfrac{x^2}{3} + 14 < -20$ **d.** $\left(\dfrac{x+14}{3}\right)^2 > -20$

19. The quotient of z and six, subtracted from the absolute value of -40 is not equal to fourteen.
    a. $|-40| - \dfrac{z}{6} \neq 14$ **b.** $\dfrac{z}{6} - |-40| \neq 14$
    c. $\dfrac{z}{|-40| - 6} \neq 14$ **d.** $|-40| - \dfrac{6}{z} \neq 14$

20. The opposite of n is six times the difference of eighteen and n.
    a. $\dfrac{1}{n} = 6(18 - n)$ **b.** $-n = 6(18 - n)$
    c. $-n = 6(18) - n$ **d.** $-n = 6(n - 18)$

21. Negative two is equal to x divided by the difference of ten and x.

    a. $-2 = \dfrac{x}{x = -10}$ **b.** $-2 = \dfrac{x}{10 - x}$
    c. $-2 = \dfrac{x}{10} - x$ **d.** $-2 - x = \dfrac{x}{10}$

Name the property illustrated by the statement.

22. $-3(x + 8) = -3x - 24$
    a. distributive property
    b. associative property of multiplication
    c. commutative property of multiplication
    d. commutative property of addition

23. $11 \cdot (18 \cdot 13) = (11 \cdot 18) \cdot 13$
    a. commutative property of multiplication
    b. associative property of multiplication
    c. associative property of addition
    d. distributive property

24. $\dfrac{1}{9}(9) = 1$
    a. multiplicative identity property
    b. associative property of multiplication
    c. distributive property
    d. multiplicative inverse property

25. $-5 + 0 = -5$
    a. additive identity property
    b. distributive property
    c. additive inverse property
    d. commutative property of addition

Solve.

26. Write an expression for the total cost (in dollars) of Sam's purchase if he buys x candies costing 46 cents each and y bars of chocolate costing $2.40 each.
    a. $0.46x + 2.40y$ **b.** $(0.46 + x) \cdot (2.40 + y)$
    c. $46x + 2.40y$ **d.** $2.86(x + y)$

Simplify the expression.

27. $-3(3x - 6)$
    a. $-9x + 18$ **b.** $-9x - 18$ **c.** $9x + 18$
    d. $-9x - 6$

28. $\dfrac{3}{4}x + \dfrac{1}{6} + \dfrac{1}{2}x + \dfrac{4}{5}$
    a. $\dfrac{5}{4}x - \dfrac{19}{30}$ **b.** $-\dfrac{1}{4}x - \dfrac{19}{30}$ **c.** $\dfrac{5}{4}x + \dfrac{29}{30}$
    d. $-\dfrac{1}{4}x + \dfrac{29}{30}$

29. $-6a - 2 - 12(a - 5)$
    a. $-18a + 3$ **b.** $-18a + 58$ **c.** $18a + 58$
    d. $18a + 3$

30. $(3.6y - 7.6) - (8.7y - 3.5)$
    a. $-5.1y - 11.1$ **b.** $12.3y - 4.1$ **c.** $-5.1y - 4.1$
    d. $12.3y - 11.1$

CHAPTER

2　Equations, Inequalities, and Problem Solving

- **2.1** Linear Equations in One Variable
- **2.2** An Introduction to Problem Solving
- **2.3** Formulas and Problem Solving
- **2.4** Linear Inequalities and Problem Solving

    Integrated Review—Linear Equations and Inequalities

- **2.5** Compound Inequalities
- **2.6** Absolute Value Equations
- **2.7** Absolute Value Inequalities

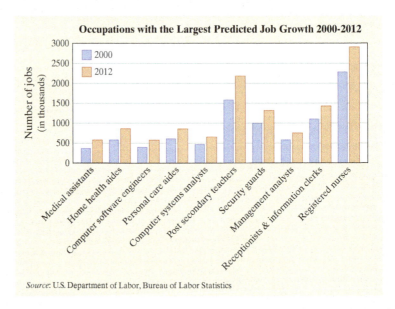

Source: U.S. Department of Labor, Bureau of Labor Statistics

The federal Bureau of Labor Statistics (BLS) has issued its projections for job growth in the United States between 2000 and 2012. In this chapter, we solve various types of equations, inequalities, and applications, including finding the actual increase in the number of some jobs as well as the percent increase in the number of jobs.

2.1 LINEAR EQUATIONS IN ONE VARIABLE

OBJECTIVES

1. Solve linear equations using properties of equality.
2. Solve linear equations that can be simplified by combining like terms.
3. Solve linear equations containing fractions or decimals.
4. Recognize identities and equations with no solution.

OBJECTIVE 1 ▶ Solving linear equations using properties of equality. Linear equations model many real-life problems. For example, we can use a linear equation to calculate the increase in the percent of households with digital cameras.

With the help of your computer, digital cameras allow you to see your pictures and make copies immediately, send them in e-mail, or use them on a Web page. Current projected percentage of households with these cameras is shown in the graph below.

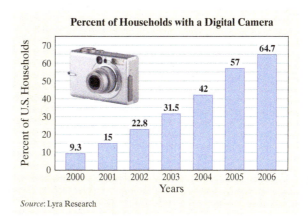

Source: Lyra Research

To find the increase in percent of households from 2005 to 2006, for example, we can use the equation below:

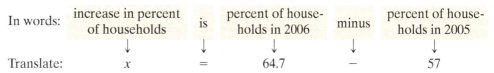

Since our variable x (increase in percent of households) is by itself on one side of the equation, we can find the value of x by simplifying the right side.

$$x = 7.7$$

The increase in the households with digital cameras from 2005 to 2006 is 7.7%.

The **equation** $x = 64.7 - 57$, like every other equation, is a statement that two expressions are equal. Oftentimes, the unknown variable is not by itself on one side of the equation. In these cases, we will use properties of equality to write equivalent equations so that a solution may be found. This is called **solving the equation.** In this section, we concentrate on solving equations such as this one, called **linear equations** in one variable. Linear equations are also called **first-degree equations** since the exponent on the variable is 1.

Linear Equations in One Variable

$$3x = -15 \qquad 7 - y = 3y \qquad 4n - 9n + 6 = 0 \qquad z = -2$$

Linear Equations in One Variable

A linear equation in one variable is an equation that can be written in the form

$$ax + b = c$$

where a, b, and c are real numbers and $a \neq 0$.

When a variable in an equation is replaced by a number and the resulting equation is true, then that number is called a **solution** of the equation. For example, 1 is a solution of the equation $3x + 4 = 7$, since $3(1) + 4 = 7$ is a true statement. But 2 is not a solution of this equation, since $3(2) + 4 = 7$ is not a true statement. The **solution set** of an equation is the set of solutions of the equation. For example, the solution set of $3x + 4 = 7$ is $\{1\}$.

To **solve an equation** is to find the solution set of an equation. Equations with the same solution set are called **equivalent equations.** For example,

$$3x + 4 = 7 \quad 3x = 3 \quad x = 1$$

are equivalent equations because they all have the same solution set, namely $\{1\}$. To solve an equation in x, we start with the given equation and write a series of simpler equivalent equations until we obtain an equation of the form

$$x = \text{number}$$

Two important properties are used to write equivalent equations.

The Addition and Multiplication Properties of Equality

If $a, b,$ and $c,$ are real numbers, then

$a = b$ and $a + c = b + c$ are equivalent equations.
Also, $a = b$ and $ac = bc$ are equivalent equations as long as $c \neq 0$.

The **addition property of equality** guarantees that the same number may be added to both sides of an equation, and the result is an equivalent equation. The **multiplication property of equality** guarantees that both sides of an equation may be multiplied by the same nonzero number, and the result is an equivalent equation. Because we define subtraction in terms of addition ($a - b = a + (-b)$), and division in terms of multiplication $\left(\dfrac{a}{b} = a \cdot \dfrac{1}{b}\right)$, these properties also guarantee that we may *subtract* the same number from both sides of an equation, or *divide* both sides of an equation by the same nonzero number and the result is an equivalent equation.

For example, to solve $2x + 5 = 9$, use the addition and multiplication properties of equality to isolate x—that is, to write an equivalent equation of the form

$$x = \text{number}$$

We will do this in the next example.

EXAMPLE 1 Solve for x: $2x + 5 = 9$.

Solution First, use the addition property of equality and subtract 5 from both sides. We do this so that our only variable term, $2x$, is by itself on one side of the equation.

$$2x + 5 = 9$$
$$2x + 5 - 5 = 9 - 5 \quad \text{Subtract 5 from both sides.}$$
$$2x = 4 \quad \text{Simplify.}$$

Now that the variable term is isolated, we can finish solving for x by using the multiplication property of equality and dividing both sides by 2.

$$\dfrac{2x}{2} = \dfrac{4}{2} \quad \text{Divide both sides by 2.}$$
$$x = 2 \quad \text{Simplify.}$$

Check: To see that 2 is the solution, replace x in the original equation with 2.

$$2x + 5 = 9 \quad \text{Original equation}$$
$$2(2) + 5 \stackrel{?}{=} 9 \quad \text{Let } x = 2.$$
$$4 + 5 \stackrel{?}{=} 9$$
$$9 = 9 \quad \text{True}$$

Since we arrive at a true statement, 2 is the solution or the solution set is $\{2\}$.

PRACTICE
1 Solve for x: $3x + 7 = 22$.

Section 2.1 Linear Equations in One Variable   49

EXAMPLE 2   Solve: $0.6 = 2 - 3.5c$.

Solution   We use both the addition property and the multiplication property of equality.

$$0.6 = 2 - 3.5c$$
$$0.6 - 2 = 2 - 3.5c - 2 \quad \text{Subtract 2 from both sides.}$$
$$-1.4 = -3.5c \quad \text{Simplify. The variable term is now isolated.}$$
$$\frac{-1.4}{-3.5} = \frac{-3.5c}{-3.5} \quad \text{Divide both sides by } -3.5.$$
$$0.4 = c \quad \text{Simplify } \frac{-1.4}{-3.5}.$$

> **Helpful Hint**
>
> Don't forget that
>
> $0.4 = c$ and $c = 0.4$ are equivalent equations.
>
> We may solve an equation so that the variable is alone on either side of the equation.

Check:

$$0.6 = 2 - 3.5c$$
$$0.6 \stackrel{?}{=} 2 - 3.5(0.4) \quad \text{Replace } c \text{ with } 0.4.$$
$$0.6 \stackrel{?}{=} 2 - 1.4 \quad \text{Multiply.}$$
$$0.6 = 0.6 \quad \text{True}$$

The solution is 0.4.

PRACTICE 2   Solve: $2.5 = 3 - 2.5t$.

OBJECTIVE 2 ▶ Solving linear equations that can be simplified by combining like terms.
Often, an equation can be simplified by removing any grouping symbols and combining any like terms.

EXAMPLE 3   Solve: $-4x - 1 + 5x = 9x + 3 - 7x$.

Solution   First we simplify both sides of this equation by combining like terms. Then, let's get variable terms on the same side of the equation by using the addition property of equality to subtract $2x$ from both sides. Next, we use this same property to add 1 to both sides of the equation.

$$-4x - 1 + 5x = 9x + 3 - 7x$$
$$x - 1 = 2x + 3 \quad \text{Combine like terms.}$$
$$x - 1 - 2x = 2x + 3 - 2x \quad \text{Subtract } 2x \text{ from both sides.}$$
$$-x - 1 = 3 \quad \text{Simplify.}$$
$$-x - 1 + 1 = 3 + 1 \quad \text{Add 1 to both sides.}$$
$$-x = 4 \quad \text{Simplify.}$$

Notice that this equation is not solved for x since we have $-x$ or $-1x$, not x. To solve for x, we divide both sides by -1.

$$\frac{-x}{-1} = \frac{4}{-1} \quad \text{Divide both sides by } -1.$$
$$x = -4 \quad \text{Simplify.}$$

Check to see that the solution is -4.

PRACTICE 3   Solve: $-8x - 4 + 6x = 5x + 11 - 4x$.

If an equation contains parentheses, use the distributive property to remove them.

CHAPTER 2 Equations, Inequalities, and Problem Solving

EXAMPLE 4 Solve: $2(x - 3) = 5x - 9$.

Solution First, use the distributive property.

$$2(x - 3) = 5x - 9$$
$$2x - 6 = 5x - 9 \quad \text{Use the distributive property.}$$

Next, get variable terms on the same side of the equation by subtracting $5x$ from both sides.

$$2x - 6 - 5x = 5x - 9 - 5x \quad \text{Subtract } 5x \text{ from both sides.}$$
$$-3x - 6 = -9 \quad \text{Simplify.}$$
$$-3x - 6 + 6 = -9 + 6 \quad \text{Add 6 to both sides.}$$
$$-3x = -3 \quad \text{Simplify.}$$
$$\frac{-3x}{-3} = \frac{-3}{-3} \quad \text{Divide both sides by } -3.$$
$$x = 1$$

Let $x = 1$ in the original equation to see that 1 is the solution.

PRACTICE 4 Solve: $3(x - 5) = 6x - 3$.

OBJECTIVE 3 ▶ Solving linear equations containing fractions or decimals. If an equation contains fractions, we first clear the equation of fractions by multiplying both sides of the equation by the *least common denominator* (LCD) of all fractions in the equation.

EXAMPLE 5 Solve for y: $\frac{y}{3} - \frac{y}{4} = \frac{1}{6}$.

Solution First, clear the equation of fractions by multiplying both sides of the equation by 12, the LCD of denominators 3, 4, and 6.

$$\frac{y}{3} - \frac{y}{4} = \frac{1}{6}$$
$$12\left(\frac{y}{3} - \frac{y}{4}\right) = 12\left(\frac{1}{6}\right) \quad \text{Multiply both sides by the LCD 12.}$$
$$12\left(\frac{y}{3}\right) - 12\left(\frac{y}{4}\right) = 2 \quad \text{Apply the distributive property.}$$
$$4y - 3y = 2 \quad \text{Simplify.}$$
$$y = 2 \quad \text{Simplify.}$$

Check: To check, let $y = 2$ in the original equation.

$$\frac{y}{3} - \frac{y}{4} = \frac{1}{6} \quad \text{Original equation.}$$
$$\frac{2}{3} - \frac{2}{4} \stackrel{?}{=} \frac{1}{6} \quad \text{Let } y = 2.$$
$$\frac{8}{12} - \frac{6}{12} \stackrel{?}{=} \frac{1}{6} \quad \text{Write fractions with the LCD.}$$
$$\frac{2}{12} \stackrel{?}{=} \frac{1}{6} \quad \text{Subtract.}$$
$$\frac{1}{6} = \frac{1}{6} \quad \text{Simplify.}$$

This is a true statement, so the solution is 2.

PRACTICE 5 Solve for y: $\frac{y}{2} - \frac{y}{5} = \frac{1}{4}$.

Section 2.1 Linear Equations in One Variable 51

As a general guideline, the following steps may be used to solve a linear equation in one variable.

> **Solving a Linear Equation in One Variable**
> **STEP 1.** Clear the equation of fractions by multiplying both sides of the equation by the least common denominator (LCD) of all denominators in the equation.
> **STEP 2.** Use the distributive property to remove grouping symbols such as parentheses.
> **STEP 3.** Combine like terms on each side of the equation.
> **STEP 4.** Use the addition property of equality to rewrite the equation as an equivalent equation with variable terms on one side and numbers on the other side.
> **STEP 5.** Use the multiplication property of equality to isolate the variable.
> **STEP 6.** Check the proposed solution in the original equation.

EXAMPLE 6 Solve for x: $\dfrac{x+5}{2} + \dfrac{1}{2} = 2x - \dfrac{x-3}{8}$.

Solution Multiply both sides of the equation by 8, the LCD of 2 and 8.

▶ **Helpful Hint**
When we multiply both sides of an equation by a number, the distributive property tells us that each term of the equation is multiplied by the number.

$8\left(\dfrac{x+5}{2} + \dfrac{1}{2}\right) = 8\left(2x - \dfrac{x-3}{8}\right)$ Multiply both sides by 8.

$8\left(\dfrac{x+5}{2}\right) + 8 \cdot \dfrac{1}{2} = 8 \cdot 2x - 8\left(\dfrac{x-3}{8}\right)$ Apply the distributive property.

$4(x+5) + 4 = 16x - (x-3)$ Simplify.

$4x + 20 + 4 = 16x - x + 3$ Use the distributive property to remove parentheses.

$4x + 24 = 15x + 3$ Combine like terms.

$-11x + 24 = 3$ Subtract $15x$ from both sides.

$-11x = -21$ Subtract 24 from both sides.

$\dfrac{-11x}{-11} = \dfrac{-21}{-11}$ Divide both sides by -11.

$x = \dfrac{21}{11}$ Simplify.

Check: To check, verify that replacing x with $\dfrac{21}{11}$ makes the original equation true. The solution is $\dfrac{21}{11}$. □

PRACTICE 6 Solve for x: $x - \dfrac{x-2}{12} = \dfrac{x+3}{4} + \dfrac{1}{4}$.

If an equation contains decimals, you may want to first clear the equation of decimals.

EXAMPLE 7 Solve: $0.3x + 0.1 = 0.27x - 0.02$.

Solution To clear this equation of decimals, we multiply both sides of the equation by 100. Recall that multiplying a number by 100 moves its decimal point two places to the right.

$100(0.3x + 0.1) = 100(0.27x - 0.02)$

$100(0.3x) + 100(0.1) = 100(0.27x) - 100(0.02)$ Use the distributive property.

$$30x + 10 = 27x - 2 \quad \text{Multiply.}$$
$$30x - 27x = -2 - 10 \quad \text{Subtract } 27x \text{ and } 10 \text{ from both sides.}$$
$$3x = -12 \quad \text{Simplify.}$$
$$\frac{3x}{3} = \frac{-12}{3} \quad \text{Divide both sides by 3.}$$
$$x = -4 \quad \text{Simplify.}$$

Check to see that the solution is -4.

PRACTICE 7 Solve: $0.15x - 0.03 = 0.2x + 0.12$.

Concept Check ✓

Explain what is wrong with the following:

$$3x - 5 = 16$$
$$3x = 11$$
$$\frac{3x}{3} = \frac{11}{3}$$
$$x = \frac{11}{3}$$

OBJECTIVE 4 ▶ Recognizing identities and equations with no solution. So far, each linear equation that we have solved has had a single solution. A linear equation in one variable that has exactly one solution is called a **conditional equation.** We will now look at two other types of equations: contradictions and identities.

An equation in one variable that has no solution is called a **contradiction,** and an equation in one variable that has every number (for which the equation is defined) as a solution is called an **identity.** For review: A linear equation in one variable with

No solution	Is a	Contradiction
Every real number as a solution (as long as the equation is defined)	Is an	Identity

The next examples show how to recognize contradictions and identities.

EXAMPLE 8 Solve for x: $3x + 5 = 3(x + 2)$.

Solution First, use the distributive property and remove parentheses.

$$3x + 5 = 3(x + 2)$$
$$3x + 5 = 3x + 6 \quad \text{Apply the distributive property.}$$
$$3x + 5 - 3x = 3x + 6 - 3x \quad \text{Subtract } 3x \text{ from both sides.}$$
$$5 = 6$$

The equation $5 = 6$ is a false statement no matter what value the variable x might have. Thus, the original equation has no solution. This equation is a contradiction.

PRACTICE 8 Solve for x: $4x - 3 = 4(x + 5)$.

▶ **Helpful Hint**

A solution set of $\{0\}$ and a solution set of $\{\ \}$ are not the same. The solution set $\{0\}$ means 1 solution, 0. The solution set $\{\ \}$ means *no* solution.

Answer to Concept Check:
$$3x - 5 = 16$$
$$3x = 21$$
$$x = 7$$
Therefore, the correct solution is 7.

EXAMPLE 9 Solve for x: $6x - 4 = 2 + 6(x - 1)$.

Solution First, use the distributive property and remove parentheses.

$6x - 4 = 6(x - 1)$

$6x - 4 = 2 + 6x - 6$ Apply the distributive property.

$6x - 4 = 6x - 4$ Combine like terms.

At this point we might notice that both sides of the equation are the same, so replacing x by any real number gives a true statement. Thus the solution set of this equation is the set of real numbers, and the equation is an identity. Continuing to "solve" $6x - 4 = 6x - 4$, we eventually arrive at the same conclusion.

$6x - 4 + 4 = 6x - 4 + 4$ Add 4 to both sides.

$6x = 6x$ Simplify.

$6x - 6x = 6x - 6x$ Subtract $6x$ from both sides.

$0 = 0$ Simplify.

Since $0 = 0$ is a true statement for every value of x, all real numbers are solutions. The solution set is the set of all real numbers, or $\mathbb{R}$, and the equation is called an identity.

PRACTICE 9 Solve for x: $5x - 2 = 3 + 5(x - 1)$.

> **Helpful Hint**
> For linear equations, *any* false statement such as $5 = 6, 0 = 1$, or $-2 = 2$ informs us that the original equation has no solution. Also, *any* true statement such as $0 = 0, 2 = 2$, or $-5 = -5$ informs us that the original equation is an identity.

VOCABULARY & READINESS CHECK

Word Bank. *Use the choices below to fill in the blanks. Not all choices will be used.*

multiplication   value   like
addition   solution   equivalent

1. Equations with the same solution set are called _____ equations.
2. A value for the variable in an equation that makes the equation a true statement is called a _____ of the equation.
3. By the _____ property of equality, $y = -3$ and $y - 7 = -3 - 7$ are equivalent equations.
4. By the _____ property of equality, $2y = -3$ and $\frac{2y}{2} = \frac{-3}{2}$ are equivalent equations.

Fill in the Blank. *Identify each as an equation or an expression.*

5. $\frac{1}{3}x - 5$ _____
6. $2(x - 3) = 7$ _____
7. $\frac{5}{9}x + \frac{1}{3} = \frac{2}{9} - x$ _____
8. $\frac{5}{9}x + \frac{1}{3} - \frac{2}{9} - x$ _____

Decision Making. *By inspection, decide which equations have no solution and which equations have all real numbers as solutions.*

9. $2x + 3 = 2x + 3$
10. $2x + 1 = 2x + 3$
11. $5x - 2 = 5x - 7$
12. $5x - 3 = 5x - 3$

2.1 EXERCISE SET

Solve each equation and check. See Examples 1 and 2.

1. $-5x = -30$
2. $-2x = 18$
3. $-10 = x + 12$
4. $-25 = y + 30$
5. $x - 2.8 = 1.9$
6. $y - 8.6 = -6.3$
7. $5x - 4 = 26 + 2x$
8. $5y - 3 = 11 + 3y$
9. $-4.1 - 7z = 3.6$
10. $10.3 - 6x = -2.3$
11. $5y + 12 = 2y - 3$
12. $4x + 14 = 6x + 8$

Solve each equation and check. See Examples 3 and 4.

13. $3x - 4 - 5x = x + 4 + x$
14. $13x - 15x + 8 = 4x + 2 - 24$
15. $8x - 5x + 3 = x - 7 + 10$
16. $6 + 3x + x = -x + 8 - 26 + 24$
17. $5x + 12 = 2(2x + 7)$
18. $2(4x + 3) = 7x + 5$
19. $3(x - 6) = 5x$
20. $6x = 4(x - 5)$
21. $-2(5y - 1) - y = -4(y - 3)$
22. $-4(3n - 2) - n = -11(n - 1)$

Solve each equation and check. See Examples 5 through 7.

23. $\dfrac{x}{2} + \dfrac{x}{3} = \dfrac{3}{4}$
24. $\dfrac{x}{2} + \dfrac{x}{5} = \dfrac{5}{4}$
25. $\dfrac{3t}{4} - \dfrac{t}{2} = 1$
26. $\dfrac{4r}{5} - \dfrac{r}{10} = 7$
27. $\dfrac{n-3}{4} + \dfrac{n+5}{7} = \dfrac{5}{14}$
28. $\dfrac{2+h}{9} + \dfrac{h-1}{3} = \dfrac{1}{3}$
29. $0.6x - 10 = 1.4x - 14$
30. $0.3x + 2.4 = 0.1x + 4$
31. $\dfrac{3x-1}{9} + x = \dfrac{3x+1}{3} + 4$
32. $\dfrac{2z+7}{8} - 2 = z + \dfrac{z-1}{2}$
33. $1.5(4 - x) = 1.3(2 - x)$
34. $2.4(2x + 3) = -0.1(2x + 3)$

Solve each equation. See Examples 8 and 9.

35. $4(n + 3) = 2(6 + 2n)$
36. $6(4n + 4) = 8(3 + 3n)$
37. $3(x + 1) + 5 = 3x + 2$
38. $4(x + 2) + 4 = 4x - 8$
39. $2(x - 8) + x = 3(x - 6) + 2$
40. $5(x - 4) + x = 6(x - 2) - 8$
41. $4(x + 5) = 3(x - 4) + x$
42. $9(x - 2) = 8(x - 3) + x$

MIXED PRACTICE

Solve each equation. See Examples 1 through 9.

43. $\dfrac{3}{8} + \dfrac{b}{3} = \dfrac{5}{12}$
44. $\dfrac{a}{2} + \dfrac{7}{4} = 5$
45. $x - 10 = -6x - 10$
46. $4x - 7 = 2x - 7$
47. $5(x - 2) + 2x = 7(x + 4) - 38$
48. $3x + 2(x + 4) = 5(x + 1) + 3$
49. $y + 0.2 = 0.6(y + 3)$
50. $-(w + 0.2) = 0.3(4 - w)$
51. $\dfrac{1}{4}(a + 2) = \dfrac{1}{6}(5 - a)$
52. $\dfrac{1}{3}(8 + 2c) = \dfrac{1}{5}(3c - 5)$
53. $2y + 5(y - 4) = 4y - 2(y - 10)$
54. $9c - 3(6 - 5c) = c - 2(3c + 9)$
55. $6x - 2(x - 3) = 4(x + 1) + 4$
56. $10x - 2(x + 4) = 8(x - 2) + 6$
57. $\dfrac{m-4}{3} - \dfrac{3m-1}{5} = 1$
58. $\dfrac{n+1}{8} - \dfrac{2-n}{3} = \dfrac{5}{6}$
59. $8x - 12 - 3x = 9x - 7$
60. $10y - 18 - 4y = 12y - 13$
61. $-(3x - 5) - (2x - 6) + 1 = -5(x - 1) - (3x + 2) + 3$
62. $-4(2x - 3) - (10x + 7) - 2 = -(12x - 5) - (4x + 9) - 1$
63. $\dfrac{1}{3}(y + 4) + 6 = \dfrac{1}{4}(3y - 1) - 2$
64. $\dfrac{1}{5}(2y - 1) - 2 = \dfrac{1}{2}(3y - 5) + 3$
65. $2[7 - 5(1 - n)] + 8n = -16 + 3[6(n + 1) - 3n]$
66. $3[8 - 4(n - 2)] + 5n = -20 + 2[5(1 - n) - 6n]$

REVIEW AND PREVIEW

Translate each phrase into an expression. Use the variable x to represent each unknown number. See Section 1.2.

67. The quotient of 8 and a number
68. The sum of 8 and a number
69. The product of 8 and a number
70. The difference of 8 and a number
71. Five subtracted from twice a number
72. Two more than three times a number

CONCEPT EXTENSIONS

Find the error for each proposed solution. Then correct the proposed solution. See the Concept Check in this section.

73. $2x + 19 = 13$
    $2x = 32$
    $\dfrac{2x}{2} = \dfrac{32}{2}$
    $x = 16$

74. $-3(x - 4) = 10$
    $-3x - 12 = 10$
    $-3x = 22$
    $\dfrac{-3x}{-3} = \dfrac{22}{-3}$
    $x = -\dfrac{22}{3}$

75. ~~$9x + 1.6 = 4x + 0.4$
    $5x = 1.2$
    $\dfrac{5x}{5} = \dfrac{1.2}{5}$
    $x = 0.24$~~

76. ~~$\dfrac{x}{3} + 7 = \dfrac{5x}{3}$
    $x + 7 = 5x$
    $7 = 4x$
    $\dfrac{7}{4} = \dfrac{4x}{4}$
    $\dfrac{7}{2} = x$~~

77. **Multiple Steps.**
    a. Simplify the expression $4(x + 1) + 1$.
    b. Solve the equation $4(x + 1) + 1 = -7$.
    c. Explain the difference between solving an equation for a variable and simplifying an expression.

78. Explain why the multiplication property of equality does not include multiplying both sides of an equation by 0. (*Hint:* Write down a false statement and then multiply both sides by 0. Is the result true or false? What does this mean?)

79. In your own words, explain why the equation $x + 7 = x + 6$ has no solution while the solution set of the equation $x + 7 = x + 7$ contains all real numbers.

80. In your own words, explain why the equation $x = -x$ has one solution—namely, 0—while the solution set of the equation $x = x$ is all real numbers.

Find the value of K such that the equations are equivalent.

81. $3.2x + 4 = 5.4x - 7$
    $3.2x = 5.4x + K$

82. $-7.6y - 10 = -1.1y + 12$
    $-7.6y = -1.1y + K$

83. $\dfrac{7}{11}x + 9 = \dfrac{3}{11}x - 14$
    $\dfrac{7}{11}x = \dfrac{3}{11}x + K$

84. $\dfrac{x}{6} + 4 = \dfrac{x}{3}$
    $x + K = 2x$

85. Write a linear equation in x whose only solution is 5.
86. Write an equation in x that has no solution.

Solve the following.

87. $x(x - 6) + 7 = x(x + 1)$
88. $7x^2 + 2x - 3 = 6x(x + 4) + x^2$
89. $3x(x + 5) - 12 = 3x^2 + 10x + 3$
90. $x(x + 1) + 16 = x(x + 5)$

Solve and check.

91. $2.569x = -12.48534$
92. $-9.112y = -47.537304$
93. $2.86z - 8.1258 = -3.75$
94. $1.25x - 20.175 = -8.15$

2.2 AN INTRODUCTION TO PROBLEM SOLVING

OBJECTIVES

1. Write algebraic expressions that can be simplified.
2. Apply the steps for problem solving.

OBJECTIVE 1 ▶ Writing and simplifying algebraic expressions. In order to prepare for problem solving, we practice writing algebraic expressions that can be simplified.

Our first example involves consecutive integers and perimeter. Recall that *consecutive integers* are integers that follow one another in order. Study the examples of consecutive, even, and odd integers and their representations.

Consecutive Integers: *Consecutive Even Integers:*   *Consecutive Odd Integers:*

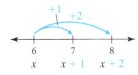 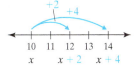 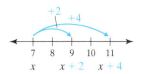

EXAMPLE 1 Write the following as algebraic expressions. Then simplify.

a. The sum of three consecutive integers, if x is the first consecutive integer.

b. The perimeter of the triangle with sides of length x, $5x$, and $6x - 3$.

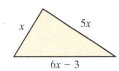

Solution

a. Recall that if x is the first integer, then the next consecutive integer is 1 more, or $x + 1$ and the next consecutive integer is 1 more than $x + 1$, or $x + 2$.

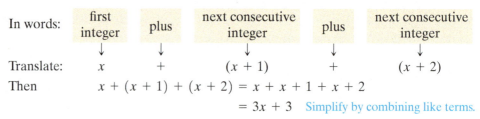

Then
$$x + (x + 1) + (x + 2) = x + x + 1 + x + 2$$
$$= 3x + 3 \quad \text{Simplify by combining like terms.}$$

b. The perimeter of a triangle is the sum of the lengths of the sides.

In words:	side	+	side	+	side
	↓		↓		↓
Translate:	x	+	$5x$	+	$(6x - 3)$

Then
$$x + 5x + (6x - 3) = x + 5x + 6x - 3$$
$$= 12x - 3 \quad \text{Simplify.} \quad \square$$

PRACTICE 1 Write the following algebraic expressions. Then simplify.

a. The sum of three consecutive odd integers, if x is the first consecutive odd integer

b. The perimeter of a trapezoid with bases x and $2x$, and sides of $x + 2$ and $2x - 3$

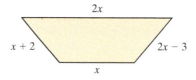

EXAMPLE 2 The three busiest airports in the United States are in Chicago, Atlanta, and Los Angeles. The airport in Atlanta has 13.3 million more arrivals and departures than the Los Angeles airport. The Chicago airport has 1.3 million more arrivals and departures than the Los Angeles airport. Write the sum of the arrivals and departures from these three cities as a simplified algebraic expression. Let x be the number of arrivals and departures at the Los Angeles airport. (*Source:* U.S. Department of Transportation)

Solution If $x =$ millions of arrivals and departures at the Los Angeles airport, then

$x + 13.3 =$ millions of arrivals and departures at the Atlanta airport and
$x + 1.3 =$ millions of arrivals and departures at the Chicago airport.

Since we want their sum, we have

In words:	arrivals and departures at Los Angeles	+	arrivals and departures at Atlanta	+	arrivals and departures at Chicago
	↓		↓		↓
Translate:	x	+	$(x + 13.3)$	+	$(x + 1.3)$

Then
$$x + (x + 13.3) + (x + 1.3) = x + x + 13.3 + x + 1.3$$
$$= 3x + 14.6 \quad \text{Combine like terms.}$$

In Exercise 57, we will find the actual number of arrivals and departures at these airports. $\quad \square$

PRACTICE 2 The three busiest airports in Europe are in London, England; Paris, France; and Frankfurt, Germany. The airport in London has 15.7 million more arrivals and departures than the Frankfurt airport. The Paris airport has 1.6 million more arrivals and departures than the Frankfurt airport. Write the sum of the arrivals and departures from these three cities as a simplified algebraic expression. Let x be the number of arrivals and departures at the Frankfurt airport. (*Source:* Association of European Airlines)

> ▶ **Helpful Hint**
> You may want to begin this section by studying key words and phrases and their translations in Sections 1.2 Objective 5 and 1.4 Objective 4.

OBJECTIVE 2 ▶ Applying steps for problem solving. Our main purpose for studying algebra is to solve problems. The following problem-solving strategy will be used throughout this text and may also be used to solve real-life problems that occur outside the mathematics classroom.

> **General Strategy for Problem Solving**
> 1. UNDERSTAND the problem. During this step, become comfortable with the problem. Some ways of doing this are:
>   Read and reread the problem.
>   Propose a solution and check. Pay careful attention to how you check your proposed solution. This will help when writing an equation to model the problem.
>   Construct a drawing.
>   **Choose a variable to represent the unknown.** (Very important part)
> 2. TRANSLATE the problem into an equation.
> 3. SOLVE the equation.
> 4. INTERPRET the results: *Check* the proposed solution in the stated problem and *state* your conclusion.

Let's review this strategy by solving a problem involving unknown numbers.

EXAMPLE 3 Finding Unknown Numbers

Find three numbers such that the second number is 3 more than twice the first number, and the third number is four times the first number. The sum of the three numbers is 164.

Solution

1. UNDERSTAND the problem. First let's read and reread the problem and then propose a solution. For example, if the first number is 25, then the second number is 3 more than twice 25, or 53. The third number is four times 25, or 100. The sum of 25, 53, and 100 is 178, not the required sum, but we have gained some valuable information about the problem. First, we know that the first number is less than 25 since our guess led to a sum greater than the required sum. Also, we have gained some information as to how to model the problem.

   Next let's assign a variable and use this variable to represent any other unknown quantities. If we let

   > ▶ **Helpful Hint**
   > The purpose of guessing a solution is not to guess correctly but to gain confidence and to help understand the problem and how to model it.

   x = the first number, then
   $2x + 3$ = the second number
   　　　↑　↑
   　　　3 more than
   　twice the second number
   $4x$ = the third number

2. TRANSLATE the problem into an equation. To do so, we use the fact that the sum of the numbers is 164. First let's write this relationship in words and then translate to an equation.

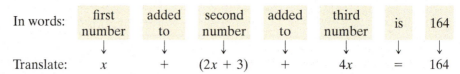

3. SOLVE the equation.

$$x + (2x + 3) + 4x = 164$$
$$x + 2x + 4x + 3 = 164 \quad \text{Remove parentheses.}$$
$$7x + 3 = 164 \quad \text{Combine like terms.}$$
$$7x = 161 \quad \text{Subtract 3 from both sides.}$$
$$x = 23 \quad \text{Divide both sides by 7.}$$

4. INTERPRET. Here, we *check* our work and *state* the solution. Recall that if the first number $x = 23$, then the second number $2x + 3 = 2 \cdot 23 + 3 = 49$ and the third number $4x = 4 \cdot 23 = 92$.

Check: Is the second number 3 more than twice the first number? Yes, since 3 more than twice 23 is $46 + 3$, or 49. Also, their sum, $23 + 49 + 92 = 164$, is the required sum.

State: The three numbers are 23, 49, and 92.

PRACTICE 3 Find three numbers such that the second number is 8 less than triple the first number, the third number is five times the first number, and the sum of the three numbers is 118.

Many of today's rates and statistics are given as percents. Interest rates, tax rates, nutrition labeling, and percent of households in a given category are just a few examples. Before we practice solving problems containing percents, let's briefly take a moment and review the meaning of percent and how to find a percent of a number.

The word *percent* means "per hundred," and the symbol % is used to denote percent. This means that 23% is 23 per hundred, or $\frac{23}{100}$. Also,

$$41\% = \frac{41}{100} = 0.41$$

To find a percent of a number, we multiply.

$$16\% \text{ of } 25 = 16\% \cdot 25 = 0.16 \cdot 25 = 4$$

Thus, 16% of 25 is 4.

Study the table below. It will help you become more familiar with finding percents.

Percent	Meaning/Shortcut	Example
50%	$\frac{1}{2}$ or half of a number	50% of 60 is 30.
25%	$\frac{1}{4}$ or a quarter of a number	25% of 60 is 15.
10%	0.1 or $\frac{1}{10}$ of a number (move the decimal point 1 place to the left)	10% of 60 is 6.0 or 6.
1%	0.01 or $\frac{1}{100}$ of a number (move the decimal point 2 places to the left)	1% of 60 is 0.60 or 0.6.
100%	1 or all of a number	100% of 60 is 60.
200%	2 or double a number	200% of 60 is 120.

Concept Check ✓

Suppose you are finding **112%** of a number x. Which of the following is a correct description of the result? Explain.

a. The result is less than x. **b.** The result is equal to x. **c.** The result is greater than x.

Next, we solve a problem containing a percent.

EXAMPLE 4 Finding the Original Price of a Computer

Suppose that a computer store just announced an 8% decrease in the price of a particular computer model. If this computer sells for $2162 after the decrease, find the original price of this computer.

Solution

1. **UNDERSTAND.** Read and reread the problem. Recall that a percent decrease means a percent of the original price. Let's guess that the original price of the computer is $2500. The amount of decrease is then 8% of $2500, or $(0.08)(\$2500) = \$200$. This means that the new price of the computer is the original price minus the decrease, or $2500 − $200 = $2300. Our guess is incorrect, but we now have an idea of how to model this problem. In our model, we will let x = the original price of the computer.

2. **TRANSLATE.**

In words:	original price of computer	minus	8% of original price	is	new price
	↓	↓	↓	↓	↓
Translate:	x	−	$0.08x$	=	2162

3. **SOLVE** the equation.

   $$x - 0.08x = 2162$$
   $$0.92x = 2162 \qquad \text{Combine like terms.}$$
   $$x = \frac{2162}{0.92} = 2350 \qquad \text{Divide both sides by 0.92.}$$

4. **INTERPRET.**

   Check: If the original price of the computer was $2350, the new price is

   $$\$2350 - (0.08)(\$2350) = \$2350 - \$188$$
   $$= \$2162 \qquad \text{The given new price}$$

   State: The original price of the computer was $2350. □

   PRACTICE 4 At the end of the season, the cost of a snowboard was reduced by 40%. If the snowboard sells for $270 after the decrease, find the original price of the board.

⚠ EXAMPLE 5 Finding the Lengths of a Triangle's Sides

A pennant in the shape of an isosceles triangle is to be constructed for the Slidell High School Athletic Club and sold at a fund-raiser. The company manufacturing the pennant charges according to perimeter, and the athletic club has determined that a perimeter of 149 centimeters should make a nice profit. If each equal side of the triangle is twice the length of the third side, increased by 12 centimeters, find the lengths of the sides of the triangular pennant.

Answer to Concept Check:
c; the result is greater than x

Solution

1. **UNDERSTAND.** Read and reread the problem. Recall that the perimeter of a triangle is the distance around. Let's guess that the third side of the triangular pennant is 20 centimeters. This means that each equal side is twice 20 centimeters, increased by 12 centimeters, or $2(20) + 12 = 52$ centimeters.

This gives a perimeter of $20 + 52 + 52 = 124$ centimeters. Our guess is incorrect, but we now have a better understanding of how to model this problem.

Now we let the third side of the triangle $= x$

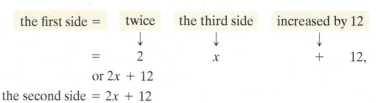

the second side $= 2x + 12$

2. **TRANSLATE.**

In words: first side + second side + third side = 149

Translate: $(2x + 12) + (2x + 12) + x = 149$

3. **SOLVE** the equation.

$$(2x + 12) + (2x + 12) + x = 149$$
$$2x + 12 + 2x + 12 + x = 149 \quad \text{Remove parentheses.}$$
$$5x + 24 = 149 \quad \text{Combine like terms.}$$
$$5x = 125 \quad \text{Subtract 24 from both sides.}$$
$$x = 25 \quad \text{Divide both sides by 5.}$$

4. **INTERPRET.** If the third side is 25 centimeters, then the first side is $2(25) + 12 = 62$ centimeters and the second side is 62 centimeters also.

Check: The first and second sides are each twice 25 centimeters increased by 12 centimeters or 62 centimeters. Also, the perimeter is $25 + 62 + 62 = 149$ centimeters, the required perimeter.

State: The lengths of the sides of the triangle are 25 centimeters, 62 centimeters, and 62 centimeters. □

PRACTICE

5 For its 40th anniversary, North Campus Community College is placing rectangular banners on all the light poles on campus. The perimeter of these banners is 160 inches. If the longer side of each banner is 16″ less than double the width, find the dimensions of the banners.

EXAMPLE 6 Finding Consecutive Integers

Kelsey Ohleger was helping her friend Benji Burnstine study for an algebra exam. Kelsey told Benji that her three latest art history quiz scores are three consecutive even integers whose sum is 264. Help Benji find the scores.

Solution

1. **UNDERSTAND.** Read and reread the problem. Since we are looking for consecutive even integers, let

   x = the first integer. Then
   $x + 2$ = the second consecutive even integer
   $x + 4$ = the third consecutive even integer.

2. **TRANSLATE.**

In words:	first integer	+	second even integer	+	third even integer	=	264
Translate:	x	+	$(x + 2)$	+	$(x + 4)$	=	264

3. **SOLVE.**

   $x + (x + 2) + (x + 4) = 264$
   $3x + 6 = 264$ Combine like terms.
   $3x = 258$ Subtract 6 from both sides.
   $x = 86$ Divide both sides by 3.

4. **INTERPRET.** If $x = 86$, then $x + 2 = 86 + 2$ or 88, and $x + 4 = 86 + 4$ or 90.

   Check: The numbers 86, 88, and 90 are three consecutive even integers. Their sum is 264, the required sum.

   State: Kelsey's art history quiz scores are 86, 88, and 90.

PRACTICE 6 Find three consecutive odd integers whose sum is 81.

VOCABULARY & READINESS CHECK

Fill in the Blank. *Fill in each blank with* <, >, *or* =. *(Assume that the unknown number is a positive number.)*

1. 130% of a number _____ the number.
2. 70% of a number _____ the number.
3. 100% of a number _____ the number.
4. 200% of a number _____ the number.

Complete a Table. *Complete the table. The first row has been completed for you.*

	First Integer	All Described Integers
Three consecutive integers	18	18, 19, 20
5. Four consecutive integers	31	
6. Three consecutive odd integers	31	
7. Three consecutive even integers	18	
8. Four consecutive even integers	92	
9. Three consecutive integers	y	
10. Three consecutive even integers	z (z is even)	
11. Four consecutive integers	p	
12. Three consecutive odd integers	s (s is odd)	

2.2 EXERCISE SET

Write the following as algebraic expressions. Then simplify. See Examples 1 and 2.

1. The perimeter of the square with side length y.

2. The perimeter of the rectangle with length x and width $x - 5$.

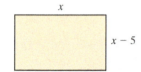

3. The sum of three consecutive integers if the first is z.

4. The sum of three consecutive odd integers if the first integer is x.

5. The total amount of money (in cents) in x nickels, $(x + 3)$ dimes, and $2x$ quarters. (*Hint:* the value of a nickel is 5 cents, the value of a dime is 10 cents, and the value of a quarter is 25 cents)

6. The total amount of money (in cents) in y quarters, $7y$ dimes, and $(2y - 1)$ nickels. (Use the hint for Exercise 5.)

7. A piece of land along Bayou Liberty is to be fenced and subdivided as shown so that each rectangle has the same dimensions. Express the total amount of fencing needed as an algebraic expression in x.

8. A flooded piece of land near the Mississippi River in New Orleans is to be surveyed and divided into 4 rectangles of equal dimension. Express the total amount of fencing needed as an algebraic expression in x.

9. Write the perimeter of the floor plan shown as an algebraic expression in x.

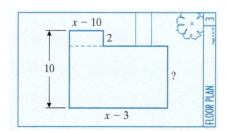

10. Write the perimeter of the floor plan shown as an algebraic expression in x.

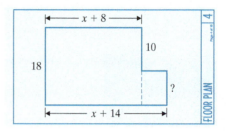

Solve. See Example 3.

11. Four times the difference of a number and 2 is the same as 2 increased by four times the number plus twice the number. Find the number.

12. Twice the sum of a number and 3 is the same as five times the number minus 1 minus four times the number. Find the number.

13. A second number is five times a first number. A third number is 100 more than the first number. If the sum of the three numbers is 415, find the numbers.

14. A second number is 6 less than a first number. A third number is twice the first number. If the sum of the three numbers is 306, find the numbers.

Solve. See Example 4.

15. The United States consists of 2271 million acres of land. Approximately 29% of this land is federally owned. Find the number of acres that are not federally owned. (*Source:* U.S. General Services Administration)

16. The state of Nevada contains the most federally owned acres of land in the United States. If 90% of the state's 70 million acres of land is federally owned, find the number of acres that are not federally owned. (*Source:* U.S. General Services Administration)

17. In 2006, a total of 2748 earthquakes occurred in the United States. Of these, 85.3% were minor tremors with magnitudes of 3.9 or less on the Richter scale. How many minor earthquakes occurred in the United States in 2006? Round to

the nearest whole number. (*Source:* U.S. Geological Survey National Earthquake Information Center)

18. Of the 958 tornadoes that occurred in the United States during 2006, 25.5% occurred during the month of April. How many tornadoes occurred during April 2006? Round to the nearest whole. (*Source:* Storm Prediction Center)

19. In a recent survey, 15% of online shoppers in the United States say that they prefer to do business only with large, well-known retailers. In a group of 1500 online shoppers, how many are willing to do business with any size retailers? (*Source:* Inc.com)

20. In 2006, the restaurant and food service industry employed 9.1% of the total employees in the state of California. In 2006, California had approximately 17,029,300 employed workers. How many people worked in the restaurant and food service industry in California? Round to the nearest whole number. (*Source:* California Employment Development Center.)

Read a Graph. *The following graph is called a circle graph or a pie chart. The circle represents a whole, or in this case, 100%. This particular graph shows the number of minutes per day that people use e-mail at work. Use this graph to answer Exercises 21 through 24.*

21. What percent of e-mail users at work spend less than 15 minutes on e-mail per day?
22. Among e-mail users at work, what is the most common time spent on e-mail per day?
23. If it were estimated that a large company has 5957 employees, how many of these would you expect to be using e-mail more than 3 hours per day? Round to the nearest whole employee.
24. If it were estimated that a medium size company has 278 employees, how many of these would you expect to be using e-mail between 2 and 3 hours per day? Round to the nearest whole employee.
25. In 2006, the population of Canada was 31.6 million. This represented an increase in population of 5.4% since 2001. What was the population of Canada in 2001? (Round to the nearest hundredth of a million.) (*Source:* Statistics Canada)
26. In 2006, the cost of an average hotel room per night was $96.73. This was an increase of 6.8% over the average cost in 2005. Find the average hotel room cost in 2005. (*Source:* Smith Travel Research)

Use the diagrams to find the unknown measures of angles or lengths of sides. Recall that the sum of the angle measures of a triangle is 180°. See Example 5.

27.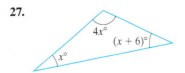

28.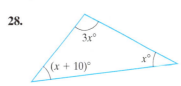

29.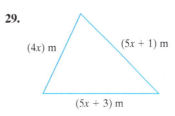

   Perimeter is 102 meters.

30.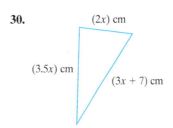

   Perimeter is 75 centimeters.

31.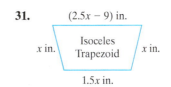

   Perimeter is 99 inches.

32.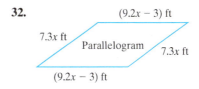

   Perimeter is 324 feet.

Solve. See Example 6.

33. The sum of three consecutive integers is 228. Find the integers.
34. The sum of three consecutive odd integers is 327. Find the integers.
35. The zip codes of three Nevada locations—Fallon, Fernley, and Gardnerville Ranchos—are three consecutive even integers. If twice the first integer added to the third is 268,222, find each zip code.

36. During a recent year, the average SAT scores in math for the states of Alabama, Louisiana, and Michigan were 3 consecutive integers. If the sum of the first integer, second integer, and three times the third integer is 2637, find each score.

MIXED PRACTICE

Solve. See Examples 1 through 6. Many companies and government agencies predict the growth or decline of occupations. The following data are based on information from the U.S. Department of Labor. Notice that the first table is in increase in number of jobs (in thousands) and the second table is in percent increase in number of jobs.

37. Read a Table. Use the table to find the actual number of jobs for each occupation.

Occupation	Increase in Number of Jobs (in thousands) from 2000 to 2012
Security guards	$2x - 51$
Home health aides	$\frac{3}{2}x + 3$
Computer systems analysts	x
Total	780 thousand

38. Read a Table. Use the table to find the actual percent increase in number of jobs for each occupation.

Occupation	Precent Increase in Number of Jobs from 2000 to 2012
Computer software engineers	$\frac{3}{2}x + 1$
Management analysts	x
Receptionist and information clerks	$x - 1$
Total	105%

39. The occupations of postsecondary teachers, registered nurses, and medical assistants are among the ten with the largest growth from 2000 to 2012. (See the Chapter 2 opener.) The number of postsecondary teacher jobs will grow 173 thousand more than twice the number of medical assistant jobs. The number of registered nurse jobs will grow 22 thousand less than three times the number of medical assistant jobs. If the total growth of these three jobs is predicted to be 1441 thousand, find the predicted growth of each job.

40. The occupations of telephone operators, fishers, and sewing machine operators are among the ten with the largest job decline from 2000 to 2012, according to the U.S. Department of Labor. The number of telephone operators will decline 8 thousand more than twice the number of fishers. The number of sewing machine operators will decline 1 thousand less than 10 times the number of telephone operators. If the total decline of these three jobs is predicted to be 137 thousand, find the predicted decline of each job.

41. America West Airlines has 3 models of Boeing aircraft in their fleet. The 737-300 contains 21 more seats than the 737-200. The 757-200 contains 36 less seats than twice the number of seats in the 737-200. Find the number of seats for each aircraft if the total number of seats for the 3 models is 437. (*Source:* America West Airlines)

42. The new governor of California makes $27,500 more than the governor of New York, and $120,724 more than the governor of Alaska. If the sum of these 3 salaries is $471,276, find the salary of each governor. (*Source:* State Web sites)

43. A new fax machine was recently purchased for an office in Hopedale for $464.40 including tax. If the tax rate in Hopedale is 8%, find the price of the fax machine before tax.

44. A premedical student at a local university was complaining that she had just paid $158.60 for her human anatomy book, including tax. Find the price of the book before taxes if the tax rate at this university is 9%.

45. In 2006, the population of South Africa was 44.2 million people. From 2006 to 2050, South Africa's population is expected to decrease by 5.6%. Find the expected population of South Africa in 2050. Round to the nearest tenth of a million. (*Source:* Population Reference Bureau)

46. In 2006, the population of Morocco was 33.2 million. This represented an increase in population of 1.5% from a year earlier. What was the population of Morocco in 2005? Round to the nearest tenth of a million. (*Source:* Population Reference Bureau)

Recall that two angles are complements of each other if their sum is 90°. Two angles are supplements of each other if their sum is 180°. Find the measure of each angle.

47. One angle is three times its supplement increased by 20°. Find the measures of the two supplementary angles.

48. One angle is twice its complement increased by 30°. Find the measure of the two complementary angles.

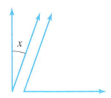

Recall that the sum of the angle measures of a triangle is 180°.

49. Find the measures of the angles of a triangle if the measure of one angle is twice the measure of a second angle and the third angle measures 3 times the second angle decreased by 12.

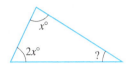

50. Find the angles of an isoceles triangle whose two base angles are equal and whose third angle is 10° less than three times a base angle.

51. Two frames are needed with the same perimeter: one frame in the shape of a square and one in the shape of an equilateral triangle. Each side of the triangle is 6 centimeters longer than each side of the square. Find the dimensions of each frame. (An equilateral triangle has sides that are the same length.)

52. Two frames are needed with the same perimeter: one frame in the shape of a square and one in the shape of a regular pentagon. Each side of the square is 7 inches longer than each side of the pentagon. Find the dimensions of each frame. (A regular polygon has sides that are the same length.)

53. The sum of the first and third of three consecutive even integers is 156. Find the three even integers.

54. The sum of the second and fourth of four consecutive integers is 110. Find the four integers.

55. The perimeter of the triangle in Example 1b in this section is 483 feet. Find the length of each side.

56. The perimeter of the trapezoid in Practice 1b in this section is 110 meters. Find the lengths of its sides and bases.

57. The airports in Chicago, Atlanta, and Los Angeles have a total of 197.6 million annual arrivals and departures. Use this information and Example 2 in this section to find the number from each individual airport.

58. The airports in London, Paris, and Frankfurt have a total of 173.9 million annual arrivals and departures. Use this information and Practice 2 in this section to find the number from each airport.

59. Incandescent, fluorescent, and halogen bulbs are lasting longer today than ever before. On average, the number of bulb hours for a fluorescent bulb is 25 times the number of bulb hours for a halogen bulb. The number of bulb hours for an incandescent bulb is 2,500 less than the halogen bulb. If the total number of bulb hours for the three types of bulbs is 105,500, find the number of bulb hours for each type. (*Source: Popular Science Magazine*)

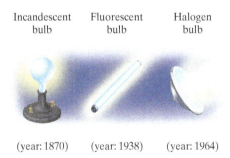

60. The three tallest hospitals in the world are Guy's Tower in London, Queen Mary Hospital in Hong Kong, and Galter Pavilion in Chicago. These buildings have a total height of 1320 feet. Guy's Tower is 67 feet taller than Galter Pavilion and the Queen Mary Hospital is 47 feet taller than Galter Pavilion. Find the heights of the three hospitals.

61. The official manual for traffic signs is the *Manual on Uniform Traffic Control Devices* published by the Government Printing Office. The rectangular sign below has a length 12 inches more than twice its height. If the perimeter of the sign is 312 inches, find its dimensions.

62. INVESCO Field at Mile High, home to the Denver Broncos, has 11,675 more seats than Heinz Field, home to the Pittsburgh Steelers. Together, these two stadiums can seat a total of 140,575 NFL fans. How many seats does each stadium have? (*Sources:* Denver Broncos, Pittsburgh Steelers)

63. In 2004, sales in the athletic footwear market in the United States were $4.7 billion. (*Source:* NPD Group)
    a. There was a 5% increase in the athletic footwear sales from 2004 to 2006. Find the total sales for the athletic footwear market in 2006. (Round to the nearest tenth of a billion.)
    b. Twenty-five percent of the sales of footwear were running shoes. Find the amount of money spent on running shoes in 2006. (Round to the nearest hundredth of a billion.)

64. The number of deaths caused by tornadoes decreased 59.2% from the 1950s to the 1990s. There were 579 deaths from tornadoes in the 1990s. (*Source:* National Weather Service)
    a. Find the number of deaths caused by tornadoes in the 1950s. Round to the nearest whole number.
    b. In your own words, explain why you think that the number of tornado-related deaths has decreased so much since the 1950s.

65. China, the United States, and Russia are the countries with the most cellular subscribers in the world. Together, the three countries have 34.8% of the world's cellular subscribers. If the percent of world subscribers in China is 3.1 less than 4 times the percent of world subscribers in Russia, and the percent of world subscribers in the United States is 4.3% more than the percent of world subscribers in Russia, find the percent of world subscribers for each country. (*Source:* Computer Industry of America)

66. In 2006, 74.2 million tax returns were filed electronically (on-line filing, professional electronic filing, and TeleFile). This represents a 108.8% increase over the year 2005. How many income tax returns were filed electronically in 2005? Round to the nearest tenth of a million. (*Source:* IRS)

67. The popularity of the Harry Potter series of books is an unmatched phenomenon among readers of all ages. To satisfy their desires for Harry Potter adventures, author J. K. Rowling increased the number of pages in the later books of the Harry Potter adventures. The final adventure of the series, *Harry Potter and the Deathly Hallows*, boasts 784 pages in its hardcover edition. This is a 154% increase over the number of pages in the first Harry Potter adventure. How many pages are in *Harry Potter and the Sorcerer's Stone*? (Round to the nearest whole page) (*Source:* Amazon.com)

68. During the 2006 Major League Baseball season, the number of home runs hit by Alfonso Soriano of the Washington Nationals, Lance Berkman of the Houston Astros, and Jermaine Dye of the Chicago White Sox were three consecutive integers. Of these three players, Soriano hit the most home runs and Dye hit the least. The total number of home runs hit by these three players over the course of the season was 135. How many home runs did each player hit during the 2006 season? (*Source:* Major League Baseball)

69. During the 2006 Winter Olympic Games in Torino, Italy, the total number of gold medals won by Germany, Canada, and the United States were three consecutive odd integers. Of these three countries, Germany won the most gold medals and Canada won the fewest. If the sum of the first integer, twice the second integer, and four times the third integer is 69, find the number of gold medals won by each country. (*Source:* Sports Illustrated Almanac)

REVIEW AND PREVIEW

Find the value of each expression for the given values. See Section 1.3.

70. $4ab - 3bc$; $a = -5$, $b = -8$, and $c = 2$
71. $ab + 6bc$; $a = 0$, $b = -1$, and $c = 9$
72. $n^2 - m^2$; $n = -3$ and $m = -8$
73. $2n^2 + 3m^2$; $n = -2$ and $m = 7$
74. $P + PRT$; $P = 3000$, $R = 0.0325$, and $T = 2$
75. $\frac{1}{3}lwh$; $l = 37.8$, $w = 5.6$, and $h = 7.9$

CONCEPT EXTENSIONS

76. For Exercise 38, the percents have a sum of 105%. Is this possible? Why or why not?
77. In your own words, explain the differences in the tables for Exercises 37 and 38.
78. Choose five occupations from the chapter opener graph and define these occupations.
79. Find an angle such that its supplement is equal to twice its complement increased by 50°.

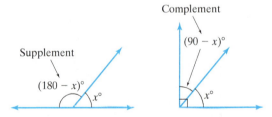

80. Newsprint is either discarded or recycled. Americans recycle about 27% of all newsprint, but an amount of newsprint equivalent to 30 million trees is discarded every year. About how many trees' worth of newsprint is *recycled* in the United States each year? (*Source:* The Earth Works Group)

81. The average annual number of cigarettes smoked by an American adult continues to decline. For the years 1997–2006, the equation $y = -49.4x + 1756.8$ approximates this data. Here, x is the number of years since 1997 and y is the average annual number of cigarettes smoked. (*Source:* Centers for Disease Control)
    a. If this trend continues, find the year in which the average annual number of cigarettes smoked is 0. To do this, let $y = 0$ and solve for x.
    b. Predict the average annual number of cigarettes smoked by an American adult in 2012. To do so, let $x = 15$ (since $2012 - 1997 = 15$) and find y.

c. Use the result of part b to predict the average *daily* number of cigarettes smoked by an American adult in 2012. Round to the nearest whole cigarette. Do you think this number represents the average daily number of cigarettes smoked by an adult smoker? Why or why not?

To break even in a manufacturing business, income or revenue R must equal the cost of production C. Use this information to answer Exercises 82 through 85.

82. The cost C to produce x number of skateboards is $C = 100 + 20x$. The skateboards are sold wholesale for $24 each, so revenue R is given by $R = 24x$. Find how many skateboards the manufacturer needs to produce and sell to break even. (*Hint:* Set the cost expression equal to the revenue expression and solve for x.)

83. The revenue R from selling x number of computer boards is given by $R = 60x$, and the cost C of producing them is given by $C = 50x + 5000$. Find how many boards must be sold to break even. Find how much money is needed to produce the break-even number of boards.

84. In your own words, explain what happens if a company makes and sells fewer products than the break-even number.

85. In your own words, explain what happens if more products than the break-even number are made and sold.

86. In 2006, 74.2 million tax returns were filed electronically. From 2007 to 2011, the average annual increase in electronic filing is projected to be 4.2% of each previous year. If this holds true, what will the number of electronic tax returns be for the next 5 years? Round to the nearest tenth of a million. (*Source:* IRS)

2.3 FORMULAS AND PROBLEM SOLVING

OBJECTIVES

1. Solve a formula for a specified variable.
2. Use formulas to solve problems.

OBJECTIVE 1 ▶ Solving a formula for a specified variable. Solving problems that we encounter in the real world sometimes requires us to express relationships among measured quantities. An equation that describes a known relationship among quantities, such as distance, time, volume, weight, money, and gravity is called a **formula**. Some examples of formulas are

Formula	Meaning
$I = PRT$	Interest = principal · rate · time
$A = lw$	Area of a rectangle = length · width
$d = rt$	Distance = rate · time
$C = 2\pi r$	Circumference of a circle = 2 · π · radius
$V = lwh$	Volume of a rectangular solid = length · width · height

Other formulas are listed in the front cover of this text. Notice that the formula for the volume of a rectangular solid $V = lwh$ is solved for V since V is by itself on one side of the equation with no V's on the other side of the equation. Suppose that the volume of a rectangular solid is known as well as its width and its length, and we wish to find its height. One way to find its height is to begin by solving the **formula** $V = lwh$ for h.

  EXAMPLE 1 Solve: $V = lwh$ for h.

Solution To solve $V = lwh$ for h, isolate h on one side of the equation. To do so, divide both sides of the equation by lw.

$$V = lwh$$
$$\frac{V}{lw} = \frac{lwh}{lw} \quad \text{Divide both sides by } lw.$$
$$\frac{V}{lw} = h \quad \text{Simplify.}$$

Then to find the height of a rectangular solid, divide the volume by the product of its length and its width.

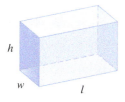

PRACTICE
1 Solve: $I = Prt$ for t.

The following steps may be used to solve formulas and equations in general for a specified variable.

> **Solving Equations for a Specified Variable**
> **STEP 1.** Clear the equation of fractions by multiplying each side of the equation by the least common denominator.
> **STEP 2.** Use the distributive property to remove grouping symbols such as parentheses.
> **STEP 3.** Combine like terms on each side of the equation.
> **STEP 4.** Use the addition property of equality to rewrite the equation as an equivalent equation with terms containing the specified variable on one side and all other terms on the other side.
> **STEP 5.** Use the distributive property and the multiplication property of equality to isolate the specified variable.

EXAMPLE 2 Solve: $3y - 2x = 7$ for y.

Solution This is a linear equation in two variables. Often an equation such as this is solved for y in order to reveal some properties about the graph of this equation, which we will learn more about in Chapter 3. Since there are no fractions or grouping symbols, we begin with Step 4 and isolate the term containing the specified variable y by adding $2x$ to both sides of the equation.

$$3y - 2x = 7$$
$$3y - 2x + 2x = 7 + 2x \quad \text{Add } 2x \text{ to both sides.}$$
$$3y = 7 + 2x$$

To solve for y, divide both sides by 3.

$$\frac{3y}{3} = \frac{7 + 2x}{3} \quad \text{Divide both sides by 3.}$$
$$y = \frac{2x + 7}{3} \quad \text{or} \quad y = \frac{2x}{3} + \frac{7}{3}$$

PRACTICE 2 Solve: $7x - 2y = 5$ for y.

EXAMPLE 3 Solve: $A = \frac{1}{2}(B + b)h$ for b.

Solution Since this formula for finding the area of a trapezoid contains fractions, we begin by multiplying both sides of the equation by the LCD 2.

$$A = \frac{1}{2}(B + b)h$$
$$2 \cdot A = 2 \cdot \frac{1}{2}(B + b)h \quad \text{Multiply both sides by 2.}$$
$$2A = (B + b)h \quad \text{Simplify.}$$

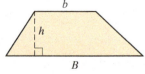

> **Helpful Hint**
> Remember that we may isolate the specified variable on either side of the equation.

Next, use the distributive property and remove parentheses.

$$2A = (B + b)h$$
$$2A = Bh + bh \quad \text{Apply the distributive property.}$$
$$2A - Bh = bh \quad \text{Isolate the term containing } b \text{ by subtracting } Bh \text{ from both sides.}$$
$$\frac{2A - Bh}{h} = \frac{bh}{h} \quad \text{Divide both sides by } h.$$
$$\frac{2A - Bh}{h} = b, \quad \text{or} \quad b = \frac{2A - Bh}{h}$$

PRACTICE 3 Solve: $A = P + Prt$ for r.

OBJECTIVE 2 ▶ Using formulas to solve problems. In this section, we also solve problems that can be modeled by known formulas. We use the same problem-solving steps that were introduced in the previous section.

Formulas are very useful in problem solving. For example, the compound interest formula

$$A = P\left(1 + \frac{r}{n}\right)^{nt}$$

is used by banks to compute the amount A in an account that pays compound interest. The variable P represents the principal or amount invested in the account, r is the annual rate of interest, t is the time in years, and n is the number of times compounded per year.

EXAMPLE 4 Finding the Amount in a Savings Account

Karen Estes just received an inheritance of $10,000 and plans to place all the money in a savings account that pays 5% compounded quarterly to help her son go to college in 3 years. How much money will be in the account in 3 years?

Solution

1. UNDERSTAND. Read and reread the problem. The appropriate formula needed to solve this problem is the compound interest formula

$$A = P\left(1 + \frac{r}{n}\right)^{nt}$$

Make sure that you understand the meaning of all the variables in this formula.

A = amount in the account after t years
P = principal or amount invested
t = time in years
r = annual rate of interest
n = number of times compounded per year

2. TRANSLATE. Use the compound interest formula and let $P = \$10,000$, $r = 5\% = 0.05$, $t = 3$ years, and $n = 4$ since the account is compounded quarterly, or 4 times a year.

Formula: $A = P\left(1 + \frac{r}{n}\right)^{nt}$

Substitute: $A = 10,000\left(1 + \frac{0.05}{4}\right)^{4 \cdot 3}$

3. SOLVE. We simplify the right side of the equation.

$$A = 10{,}000\left(1 + \frac{0.05}{4}\right)^{4 \cdot 3}$$

$A = 10{,}000(1.0125)^{12}$ Simplify $1 + \frac{0.05}{4}$ and write $4 \cdot 3$ as 12.

$A \approx 10{,}000(1.160754518)$ Approximate $(1.0125)^{12}$.

$A \approx 11{,}607.55$ Multiply and round to two decimal places.

4. INTERPRET.

Check: Repeat your calculations to make sure that no error was made. Notice that $11,607.55 is a reasonable amount to have in the account after 3 years.

State: In 3 years, the account will contain $11,607.55.

PRACTICE 4 Russ placed $8000 into his credit union account paying 6% compounded semi-annually (twice a year). How much will be in Russ's account in 4 years?

Graphing Calculator Explorations

To solve Example 4, we approximated the expression

$$10{,}000\left(1 + \frac{0.05}{4}\right)^{4 \cdot 3}.$$

Use the keystrokes shown in the accompanying calculator screen to evaluate this expression using a graphing calculator. Notice the use of parentheses.

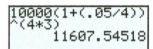

EXAMPLE 5 Finding Cycling Time

The fastest average speed by a cyclist across the continental United States is 15.4 mph, by Pete Penseyres. If he traveled a total distance of about 3107.5 miles at this speed, find his time cycling. Write the time in days, hours, and minutes. (*Source: The Guinness Book of World Records*)

Solution

1. UNDERSTAND. Read and reread the problem. The appropriate formula needed is the distance formula

$$d = rt \quad \text{where}$$
$$d = \text{distance traveled} \quad r = \text{rate} \quad \text{and} \quad t = \text{time}$$

2. TRANSLATE. Use the distance formula and let $d = 3107.5$ miles and $r = 15.4$ mph.

Check: $d = rt$

State: $3107.5 = 15.4t$

3. SOLVE.

$$\frac{3107.5}{15.4} = \frac{15.4t}{15.4} \quad \text{Divide both sides by 15.4.}$$

$$201.79 \approx t$$

The time is approximately 201.79 hours. Since there are 24 hours in a day, we divide 201.79 by 24 and find that the time is approximately 8.41 days. Now, let's convert the decimal part of 8.41 days back to hours. To do this, multiply 0.41 by 24 and the result is 9.84 hours. Next, we convert the decimal part of 9.84 hours to minutes by multiplying by 60 since there are 60 minutes in an hour. We have $0.84 \cdot 60 \approx 50$ minutes rounded to the nearest whole. The time is then approximately

8 days, 9 hours, 50 minutes.

4. INTERPRET.

Check: Repeat your calculations to make sure that an error was not made.

State: Pete Penseyres's cycling time was approximately 8 days, 9 hours, 50 minutes. □

PRACTICE 5 Nearly 4800 cyclists from 36 U.S. states and 6 countries recently rode in the Pan-Massachusetts Challenge recently to raise money for cancer research and treatment. If the riders of a certain team traveled their 192-mile route at an average speed of 7.5 miles per hour, find the time they spent cycling. Write the answer in hours and minutes.

2.3 EXERCISE SET

Solve each equation for the specified variable. See Examples 1–3.

1. $D = rt$; for t
2. $W = gh$; for g
3. $I = PRT$; for R
4. $V = lwh$; for l
5. $9x - 4y = 16$; for y
6. $2x + 3y = 17$; for y
7. $P = 2L + 2W$; for W
8. $A = 3M - 2N$; for N
9. $J = AC - 3$; for A
10. $y = mx + b$; for x
11. $W = gh - 3gt^2$; for g
12. $A = Prt + P$; for P
13. $T = C(2 + AB)$; for B
14. $A = 5H(b + B)$; for b
15. $C = 2\pi r$; for r
16. $S = 2\pi r^2 + 2\pi rh$; for h
17. $E = I(r + R)$; for r
18. $A = P(1 + rt)$; for t
19. $s = \dfrac{n}{2}(a + L)$; for L
20. $C = \dfrac{5}{9}(F - 32)$; for F
21. $N = 3st^4 - 5sv$; for v
22. $L = a + (n - 1)d$; for d
23. $S = 2LW + 2LH + 2WH$; for H
24. $T = 3vs - 4ws + 5vw$; for v

In this exercise set, round all dollar amounts to two decimal places. Solve. See Example 4.

25. **Complete a Table.** Complete the table and find the balance A if $3500 is invested at an annual percentage rate of 3% for 10 years and compounded n times a year.

n	1	2	4	12	365
A					

26. **Complete a Table.** Complete the table and find the balance A if $5000 is invested at an annual percentage rate of 6% for 15 years and compounded n times a year.

n	1	2	4	12	365
A					

27. A principal of $6000 is invested in an account paying an annual percentage rate of 4%. Find the amount in the account after 5 years if the account is compounded
    a. semiannually
    b. quarterly
    c. monthly

28. A principal of $25,000 is invested in an account paying an annual percentage rate of 5%. Find the amount in the account after 2 years if the account is compounded
    a. semiannually
    b. quarterly
    c. monthly

MIXED PRACTICE

Solve. See Examples 4 and 5.

29. The day's high temperature in Phoenix, Arizona, was recorded as 104°F. Write 104°F as degrees Celsius. [Use the formula $C = \dfrac{5}{9}(F - 32)$]

30. The annual low temperature in Nome, Alaska, was recorded as −15°C. Write −15°C as degrees Fahrenheit. [Use the formula $F = \dfrac{9}{5}C + 32$]

31. Omaha, Nebraska, is about 90 miles from Lincoln, Nebraska. Irania must go to the law library in Lincoln to get a document for the law firm she works for. Find how long it takes her to drive round-trip if she averages 50 mph.

32. It took the Selby family $5\frac{1}{2}$ hours round-trip to drive from their house to their beach house 154 miles away. Find their average speed.

△ 33. A package of floor tiles contains 24 one-foot-square tiles. Find how many packages should be bought to cover a square ballroom floor whose side measures 64 feet.

△ 34. One-foot-square ceiling tiles are sold in packages of 50. Find how many packages must be bought for a rectangular ceiling 18 feet by 12 feet.

△ 35. If the area of a triangular kite is 18 square feet and its base is 4 feet, find the height of the kite.

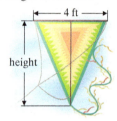

36. Bryan, Eric, Mandy, and Melissa would like to go to Disneyland in 3 years. Their total cost should be $4500. If each invests $1000 in a savings account paying 5.5% interest, compounded semiannually, will they have enough in 3 years?

△ 37. A gallon of latex paint can cover 500 square feet. Find how many gallon containers of paint should be bought to paint two coats on each wall of a rectangular room whose dimensions are 14 feet by 16 feet (assume 8-foot ceilings).

△ 38. A gallon of enamel paint can cover 300 square feet. Find how many gallon containers of paint should be bought to paint three coats on a wall measuring 21 feet by 8 feet.

△ 39. A portion of the external tank of the Space Shuttle *Endeavour* is a liquid hydrogen tank. If the ends of the tank are hemispheres, find the volume of the tank. To do so, answer parts **a** through **c**.

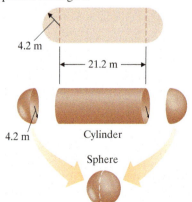

a. Find the volume of the cylinder shown. Round to 2 decimal places.
b. Find the volume of the sphere shown. Round to 2 decimal places.
c. Add the results of parts **a** and **b**. This sum is the approximate volume of the tank.

△ 40. In 1945, Arthur C. Clarke, a scientist and science-fiction writer, predicted that an artificial satellite placed at a height of 22,248 miles directly above the equator would orbit the globe at the same speed with which the Earth was rotating. This belt along the equator is known as the Clarke belt. Use the formula for circumference of a circle and find the "length" of the Clarke belt. (*Hint:* Recall that the radius of the Earth is approximately 4000 miles. Round to the nearest whole mile.)

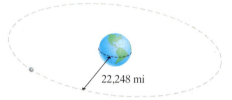

41. Amelia Earhart was the first woman to fly solo nonstop coast to coast, setting the women's nonstop transcontinental speed record. She traveled 2447.8 miles in 19 hours 5 minutes. Find the average speed of her flight in miles per hour. (Change 19 hours 5 minutes into hours and use the formula $d = rt$.) Round to the nearest tenth of a mile per hour.

△ 42. The Space Shuttle *Endeavour* has a cargo bay that is in the shape of a cylinder whose length is 18.3 meters and whose diameter is 4.6 meters. Find its volume.

△ 43. The deepest hole in the ocean floor is beneath the Pacific Ocean and is called Hole 504B. It is located off the coast of Ecuador. Scientists are drilling it to learn more about the Earth's history. Currently, the hole is in the shape of a cylinder whose volume is approximately 3800 cubic feet and whose length is 1.3 miles. Find the radius of the hole to the nearest hundredth of a foot. (*Hint:* Make sure the same units of measurement are used.)

44. The deepest man-made hole is called the Kola Superdeep Borehole. It is approximately 8 miles deep and is located near a small Russian town in the Arctic Circle. If it takes 7.5 hours to remove the drill from the bottom of the hole, find the rate that the drill can be retrieved in feet per second. Round to the nearest tenth. (*Hint:* Write 8 miles as feet, 7.5 hours as seconds, then use the formula $d = rt$.)

△ 45. Eartha is the world's largest globe. It is located at the headquarters of DeLorme, a mapmaking company in Yarmouth, Maine. Eartha is 41.125 feet in diameter. Find its exact circumference (distance around) and then approximate its circumference using 3.14 for π. (*Source:* DeLorme)

△ 46. Eartha is in the shape of a sphere. Its radius is about 20.6 feet. Approximate its volume to the nearest cubic foot. (*Source:* DeLorme)

47. Find *how much interest* $10,000 earns in 2 years in a certificate of deposit paying 8.5% interest compounded quarterly.

48. Find how long it takes Mark to drive 135 miles on I-10 if he merges onto I-10 at 10 a.m. and drives nonstop with his cruise control set on 60 mph.

The calorie count of a serving of food can be computed based on its composition of carbohydrate, fat, and protein. The calorie count C for a serving of food can be computed using the formula $C = 4h + 9f + 4p$, where h is the number of grams of carbohydrate contained in the serving, f is the number of grams of fat contained in the serving, and p is the number of grams of protein contained in the serving.

49. Solve this formula for f, the number of grams of fat contained in a serving of food.

50. Solve this formula for h, the number of grams of carbohydrate contained in a serving of food.

51. A serving of cashews contains 14 grams of fat, 7 grams of carbohydrate, and 6 grams of protein. How many calories are in this serving of cashews?

52. A serving of chocolate candies contains 9 grams of fat, 30 grams of carbohydrate, and 2 grams of protein. How many calories are in this serving of chocolate candies?

53. A serving of raisins contains 130 calories and 31 grams of carbohydrate. If raisins are a fat-free food, how much protein is provided by this serving of raisins?

54. A serving of yogurt contains 120 calories, 21 grams of carbohydrate, and 5 grams of protein. How much fat is provided by this serving of yogurt? Round to the nearest tenth of a gram.

REVIEW AND PREVIEW

Determine which numbers in the set $\{-3, -2, -1, 0, 1, 2, 3\}$ are solutions of each inequality. See Sections 1.3 and 2.1.

55. $x < 0$
56. $x > 1$
57. $x + 5 \leq 6$
58. $x - 3 \geq -7$
59. In your own words, explain what real numbers are solutions of $x < 0$.
60. In your own words, explain what real numbers are solutions of $x > 1$.

CONCEPT EXTENSIONS

61. **Complete a Table.** Solar system distances are so great that units other than miles or kilometers are often used. For example, the astronomical unit (AU) is the average distance between Earth and the Sun, or 92,900,000 miles. Use this information to convert each planet's distance in miles from the Sun to astronomical units. Round to three decimal places. (*Source:* National Space Science Data Center)

Planet	Miles from the Sun	AU from the Sun	Planet	Miles from the Sun	AU from the Sun
Mercury	36 million		Saturn	886.1 million	
Venus	67.2 million		Uranus	1783 million	
Earth	92.9 million		Neptune	2793 million	
Mars	141.5 million		Pluto	3670 million	
Jupiter	483.3 million				

62. An orbit such as Clarke's belt in Exercise 40 is called a geostationary orbit. In your own words, why do you think that communications satellites are placed in geostationary orbits?

63. How much do you think it costs each American to build a space shuttle? Write down your estimate. The space shuttle *Endeavour* was completed in 1992 and cost approximately $1.7 billion. If the population of the United States in 1992 was 250 million, find the cost per person to build the *Endeavour*. How close was your estimate?

64. If you are investing money in a savings account paying a rate of r, which account should you choose—an account compounded 4 times a year or 12 times a year? Explain your choice.

65. To borrow money at a rate of r, which loan plan should you choose—one compounding 4 times a year or 12 times a year? Explain your choice.

66. The Drake Equation is a formula used to estimate the number of technological civilizations that might exist in our own Milky Way Galaxy. The Drake Equation is given as $N = R^* \times f_p \times n_e \times f_l \times f_i \times f_c \times L$. Solve the Drake Equation for the variable n_e. (*Note:* Descriptions of the meaning of each variable in this equation, as well as Drake Equation calculators, exist online. For more information, try doing a Web search on "Drake Equation.")

67. On April 1, 1985, *Sports Illustrated* published an April Fool's story by writer George Plimpton. He wrote that the New York Mets had discovered a man who could throw a 168-miles-per-hour fast ball. If the distance from the pitcher's mound to the plate is 60.5 feet, how long would it take for a ball thrown at that rate to travel that distance? (*Hint:* Write the rate 168 miles per hour in feet per second. Then use the formula $d = r \cdot t$.)

$$168 \text{ miles per hour} = \frac{168 \text{ miles}}{1 \text{ hour}}$$
$$= \frac{\_\text{feet}}{\_\text{seconds}}$$
$$= \frac{\_\text{feet}}{1 \text{ second}}$$
$$= \_\text{feet per second}$$

*The measure of the chance or likelihood of an event occurring is its **probability**. A formula basic to the study of probability is the* *formula for the probability of an event when all the outcomes are equally likely. This formula is*

$$\text{Probability of an event} = \frac{\text{number of ways that the event can occur}}{\text{number of possible outcomes}}$$

For example, to find the probability that a single spin on the spinner will result in red, notice first that the spinner is divided into 8 parts, so there are 8 possible outcomes. Next, notice that there is only one sector of the spinner colored red, so the number of ways that the spinner can land on red is 1. Then this probability denoted by P(red) is

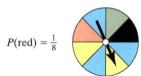

$P(\text{red}) = \frac{1}{8}$

Find each probability in simplest form.

68. *P*(green)

69. *P*(yellow)

70. *P*(black)

71. *P*(blue)

72. *P*(green or blue)

73. *P*(black or yellow)

74. *P*(red, green, or black)

75. *P*(yellow, blue, or black)

76. *P*(white)

77. *P*(red, yellow, green, blue, or black)

78. From the previous probability formula, what do you think is always the probability of an event that is impossible occuring?

79. What do you think is always the probability of an event that is sure to occur?

2.4 LINEAR INEQUALITIES AND PROBLEM SOLVING

OBJECTIVES

1. Graph inequalities.
2. Solve linear inequalities using the addition property of inequality.
3. Solve linear inequalities using the multiplication and the addition properties of inequality.
4. Solve problems that can be modeled by linear inequalities.

Relationships among measurable quantities are not always described by equations. For example, suppose that a salesperson earns a base of $600 per month plus a commission of 20% of sales. Suppose we want to find the minimum amount of sales needed to receive a total income of *at least* $1500 per month. Here, the phrase "at least" implies that an income of $1500 *or more* is acceptable. In symbols, we can write

$$\text{income} \geq 1500$$

This is an example of an inequality, and we will solve this problem in Example 8.

A **linear inequality** is similar to a linear equation except that the equality symbol is replaced with an inequality symbol, such as $<$, $>$, $\leq$, or $\geq$.

Linear Inequalities in One Variable

$3x + 5 \geq 4$ — is greater than or equal to

$2y < 0$ — is less than

$3(x - 4) > 5x$ — is greater than

$\dfrac{x}{3} \leq 5$ — is less than or equal to

Linear Inequality in One Variable

A linear inequality in one variable is an inequality that can be written in the form

$$ax + b < c$$

where a, b, and c are real numbers and $a \neq 0$.

In this section, when we make definitions, state properties, or list steps about an inequality containing the symbol $<$, we mean that the definition, property, or steps apply to inequalities containing the symbols $>$, $\leq$ and $\geq$ also.

OBJECTIVE 1 ▶ Graphing inequalities. A **solution** of an inequality is a value of the variable that makes the inequality a true statement. The **solution set** of an inequality is the set of all solutions.

Section 2.4 Linear Inequalities and Problem Solving 75

The inequality $x > 2$ has a solution set of

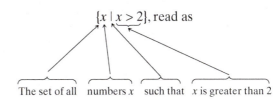

In this text, we will simply write the solutions as $x > 2$.

Since the solutions of $x > 2$ are all numbers greater than 2, the graph of $x > 2$ is an interval on a number line. For the inequalities $<$ or $>$, we use an open dot and for $\leq$ or $\geq$, we use a solid dot.

The graph of $x > 2$ and $x \leq -3$ are below.

Other inequalities and their graphs are shown on the next table. Pay careful attention to the last two inequalities and graphs, called **compound inequalities.**

Inequality	Graph
$x < a$	← ○————→ a
$x > a$	← ○————→ a
$x \leq a$	← ————●→ a
$x \geq a$	← ●————→ a
$a < x < b$	← ○—○ → a b
$a \leq x \leq b$	← ●—● → a b
$a < x \leq b$	← ○—● → a b
$a \leq x < b$	← ●—○ → a b

The last two rows are labeled: Compound inequalities

EXAMPLE 1 Graph each on a number line.

a. $x \geq 2$ **b.** $x < -1$ **c.** $0.5 < x \leq 3$

Solution

a. ← ●————→ −2 −1 0 1 2 3 4

b. ← ———○ —→ −3 −2 −1 0 1 2 3

c. ← ○————● → −1 0 0.5 1 2 3 4 5

PRACTICE 1 Graph each on a number line.

a. $x < 3.5$

b. $x \geq -3$

c. $-1 \leq x < 4$

OBJECTIVE 2 ▶ **Solving linear inequalities using the addition property.** We will use interval notation to write solutions of linear inequalities. To solve a linear inequality, we use a process similar to the one used to solve a linear equation. We use properties of inequalities to write equivalent inequalities until the variable is isolated.

> **Addition Property of Inequality**
> If a, b, and c are real numbers, then
> $$a < b \quad \text{and} \quad a + c < b + c$$
> are equivalent inequalities.

In other words, we may add the same real number to both sides of an inequality and the resulting inequality will have the same solution set. This property also allows us to subtract the same real number from both sides.

EXAMPLE 2 Solve: $x - 2 < 5$. Graph the solutions.

Solution
$$x - 2 < 5$$
$$x - 2 + 2 < 5 + 2 \quad \text{Add 2 to both sides.}$$
$$x < 7 \quad \text{Simplify.}$$

The solutions are all numbers less than 7, or $x < 7$. The graph of the solutions are

PRACTICE 2 Solve: $x + 5 > 9$. Graph the solutions.

> ▶ **Helpful Hint**
> In Example 2, the solutions are $x < 7$. This means that *all* numbers less than 7 are solutions. For example, 6.9, 0, $-\pi$, 1, and -56.7 are solutions, just to name a few. To see this, replace x in $x - 2 < 5$ with each of these numbers and see that the result is a true inequality.

EXAMPLE 3 Solve: $3x + 4 \geq 2x - 6$. Graph the solutions.

Solution
$$3x + 4 \geq 2x - 6$$
$$3x + 4 - 2x \geq 2x - 6 - 2x \quad \text{Subtract } 2x \text{ from both sides.}$$
$$x + 4 \geq -6 \quad \text{Combine like terms.}$$
$$x + 4 - 4 \geq -6 - 4 \quad \text{Subtract 4 from both sides.}$$
$$x \geq -10 \quad \text{Simplify.}$$

The solutions are all numbers greater than or equal to -10, or $x \geq -10$. The graph of the solutions are

PRACTICE 3 Solve: $8x + 21 \leq 2x - 3$. Graph the solutions.

OBJECTIVE 3 ▶ **Solving linear inequalities using the multiplication and addition properties.** Next, we introduce and use the multiplication property of inequality to

Section 2.4 Linear Inequalities and Problem Solving 77

solve linear inequalities. To understand this property, let's start with the true statement $-3 < 7$ and multiply both sides by 2.

$$-3 < 7$$
$$-3(2) < 7(2) \quad \text{Multiply by 2.}$$
$$-6 < 14 \quad \text{True}$$

The statement remains true.

Notice what happens if both sides of $-3 < 7$ are multiplied by -2.

$$-3 < 7$$
$$-3(-2) < 7(-2) \quad \text{Multiply by } -2.$$
$$6 < -14 \quad \text{False}$$

The inequality $6 < -14$ is a false statement. However, **if the direction of the inequality sign is reversed,** the result is true.

$$6 > -14 \quad \text{True}$$

These examples suggest the following property.

Multiplication Property of Inequality

If a, b, and c are real numbers and c is **positive,** then

$$a < b \quad \text{and} \quad ac < bc$$

are equivalent inequalities.

If a, b, and c are real numbers and c is **negative,** then

$$a < b \quad \text{and} \quad ac > bc$$

are equivalent inequalities.

In other words, we may multiply both sides of an inequality by the same positive real number and the result is an equivalent inequality.

We may also multiply both sides of an inequality by the same **negative number** and **reverse the direction of the inequality symbol,** and the result is an equivalent inequality. The multiplication property holds for division also, since division is defined in terms of multiplication.

> **Helpful Hint**
> Whenever both sides of an inequality are multiplied or divided by a negative number, the direction of the inequality symbol **must be** reversed to form an equivalent inequality.

EXAMPLE 4 Solve and graph the solutions.

a. $\dfrac{1}{4}x \le \dfrac{3}{8}$ **b.** $-2.3x < 6.9$

Solution

> **Helpful Hint**
> The inequality symbol is the same since we are multiplying by a *positive* number.

a.
$$\frac{1}{4}x \le \frac{3}{8}$$
$$4 \cdot \frac{1}{4}x \le 4 \cdot \frac{3}{8} \quad \text{Multiply both sides by 4.}$$
$$x \le \frac{3}{2} \quad \text{Simplify.}$$

78 CHAPTER 2 Equations, Inequalities, and Problem Solving

The graph of the solutions are

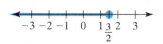

b.
$$-2.3x < 6.9$$
$$\frac{-2.3x}{-2.3} > \frac{6.9}{-2.3}$$ Divide both sides by -2.3 and reverse the inequality symbol.
$$x > -3$$ Simplify.

> **Helpful Hint**
> The inequality symbol is *reversed* since we divided by a *negative* number.

The graph of the solutions are

PRACTICE 4 Solve and graph the solutions.

a. $\dfrac{2}{5}x \geq \dfrac{4}{15}$

b. $-2.4x < 9.6$

Concept Check ✓

In which of the following inequalities must the inequality symbol be reversed during the solution process?

a. $-2x > 7$
b. $2x - 3 > 10$
c. $-x + 4 + 3x < 7$
d. $-x + 4 < 5$

To solve linear inequalities in general, we follow steps similar to those for solving linear equations.

Solving a Linear Inequality in One Variable

STEP 1. Clear the inequality of fractions by multiplying both sides of the inequality by the least common denominator (LCD) of all fractions in the inequality.

STEP 2. Use the distributive property to remove grouping symbols such as parentheses.

STEP 3. Combine like terms on each side of the inequality.

STEP 4. Use the addition property of inequality to write the inequality as an equivalent inequality with variable terms on one side and numbers on the other side.

STEP 5. Use the multiplication property of inequality to isolate the variable.

EXAMPLE 5 Solve: $-(x - 3) + 2 \leq 3(2x - 5) + x$.

Solution
$$-(x - 3) + 2 \leq 3(2x - 5) + x$$
$$-x + 3 + 2 \leq 6x - 15 + x \quad \text{Apply the distributive property.}$$
$$5 - x \leq 7x - 15 \quad \text{Combine like terms.}$$
$$5 - x + x \leq 7x - 15 + x \quad \text{Add } x \text{ to both sides.}$$
$$5 \leq 8x - 15 \quad \text{Combine like terms.}$$

Answer to Concept Check:
a, d

Section 2.4 Linear Inequalities and Problem Solving 79

> **Helpful Hint**
> Don't forget that $\frac{5}{2} \leq x$ means the same as $x \geq \frac{5}{2}$.

$$5 + 15 \leq 8x - 15 + 15 \quad \text{Add 15 to both sides.}$$
$$20 \leq 8x \quad \text{Combine like terms.}$$
$$\frac{20}{8} \leq \frac{8x}{8} \quad \text{Divide both sides by 8.}$$
$$\frac{5}{2} \leq x, \text{ or } x \geq \frac{5}{2} \quad \text{Simplify.}$$

The graph is

PRACTICE 5 Solve: $-(4x + 6) \leq 2(5x + 9) + 2x$.

EXAMPLE 6 Solve: $\frac{2}{5}(x - 6) \geq x - 1$.

Solution
$$\frac{2}{5}(x - 6) \geq x - 1$$
$$5\left[\frac{2}{5}(x - 6)\right] \geq 5(x - 1) \quad \text{Multiply both sides by 5 to eliminate fractions.}$$
$$2(x - 6) \geq 5(x - 1)$$
$$2x - 12 \geq 5x - 5 \quad \text{Apply the distributive property.}$$
$$-3x - 12 \geq -5 \quad \text{Subtract } 5x \text{ from both sides.}$$
$$-3x \geq 7 \quad \text{Add 12 to both sides.}$$
$$\frac{-3x}{-3} \leq \frac{7}{-3} \quad \text{Divide both sides by } -3 \text{ and reverse the inequality symbol.}$$
$$x \leq -\frac{7}{3} \quad \text{Simplify.}$$

The graph is

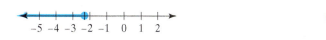

PRACTICE 6 Solve: $\frac{3}{5}(x - 3) \geq x - 7$.

EXAMPLE 7 Solve: $2(x + 3) > 2x + 1$.

Solution
$$2(x + 3) > 2x + 1$$
$$2x + 6 > 2x + 1 \quad \text{Distribute on the left side.}$$
$$2x + 6 - 2x > 2x + 1 - 2x \quad \text{Subtract } 2x \text{ from both sides.}$$
$$6 > 1 \quad \text{Simplify.}$$

$6 > 1$ is a true statement for all values of x, so this inequality and the original inequality are true for all numbers. All real numbers are solutions. The graph is

PRACTICE 7 Solve: $4(x - 2) < 4x + 5$.

OBJECTIVE 4 ▶ Solving problems modeled by linear inequalities. Application problems containing words such as "at least," "at most," "between," "no more than," and "no less than" usually indicate that an inequality be solved instead of an equation. In solving applications involving linear inequalities, we use the same procedure as when we solved applications involving linear equations.

EXAMPLE 8 Calculating Income with Commission

A salesperson earns $600 per month plus a commission of 20% of sales. Find the minimum amount of sales needed to receive a total income of at least $1500 per month.

Solution

1. UNDERSTAND. Read and reread the problem. Let x = amount of sales.
2. TRANSLATE. As stated in the beginning of this section, we want the income to be greater than or equal to $1500. To write an inequality, notice that the salesperson's income consists of $600 plus a commission (20% of sales).

   In words: 600   +   commission (20% of sales)   ≥   1500

   Translate: 600   + $0.20x$ ≥   1500

3. SOLVE the inequality for x.

$$600 + 0.20x \geq 1500$$
$$600 + 0.20x - 600 \geq 1500 - 600$$
$$0.20x \geq 900$$
$$x \geq 4500$$

4. INTERPRET.

Check: The income for sales of $4500 is

$$600 + 0.20(4500), \text{ or } 1500.$$

Thus, if sales are greater than or equal to $4500, income is greater than or equal to $1500.

State: The minimum amount of sales needed for the salesperson to earn at least $1500 per month is $4500 per month.

PRACTICE 8 A salesperson earns $900 a month plus a commission of 15% of sales. Find the minimum amount of sales needed to receive a total income of at least $2400 per month.

EXAMPLE 9 Finding the Annual Consumption

In the United States, the annual consumption of cigarettes is declining. The consumption c in billions of cigarettes per year since the year 1990 can be approximated by the formula

$$c = -9.2t + 527.33$$

where t is the number of years after 1990. Use this formula to predict the years that the consumption of cigarettes will be less than 200 billion per year.

Solution

1. **UNDERSTAND.** Read and reread the problem. To become familiar with the given formula, let's find the cigarette consumption after 20 years, which would be the year 1990 + 20, or 2010. To do so, we substitute 20 for t in the given formula.

$$c = -9.2(20) + 527.33 = 343.33$$

Thus, in 2010, we predict cigarette consumption to be about 343.3 billion.

Variables have already been assigned in the given formula. For review, they are
c = the annual consumption of cigarettes in the United States in billions of cigarettes

t = the number of years after 1990

2. **TRANSLATE.** We are looking for the years that the consumption of cigarettes c is less than 200. Since we are finding years t, we substitute the expression in the formula given for c, or

$$-9.2t + 527.33 < 200$$

3. **SOLVE** the inequality.

$$-9.2t + 527.33 < 200$$
$$-9.2t < -327.33$$
$$t > \text{approximately } 35.58$$

4. **INTERPRET.**

Check: Substitute a number greater than 35.58 and see that c is less than 200.

State: The annual consumption of cigarettes will be less than 200 billion more than 35.58 years after 1990, or in approximately $36 + 1990 = 2026$.

PRACTICE 9 Use the formula given in Example 9 to predict when the consumption of cigarettes will be less than 250 billion per year.

VOCABULARY & READINESS CHECK

Multiple Choice. *Match each graph with the inequality that describes it.*

1.
   a. $x > -5$ b. $x \geq -5$
   c. $x < -5$ d. $x \leq -5$

2.
   a. $x \leq -11$ b. $x > -11$
   c. $x \geq -11$ d. $x < -11$

3.
   a. $\frac{7}{4} \leq x < -2.5$ b. $-2.5 < x \leq \frac{7}{4}$
   c. $-2.5 \leq x < \frac{7}{4}$ d. $\frac{7}{4} < x < -2.5$

4.
   a. $-\frac{10}{3} \leq x < 0.2$ b. $0.2 < x \leq \frac{-10}{3}$
   c. $-\frac{10}{3} < x \leq 0.2$ d. $0.2 \leq x < \frac{-10}{3}$

Decision Making. *Each inequality below is solved by dividing both sides by the coefficient of x. In which inequality will the inequality symbol be reversed during this solution process?*

5. $3x > -14$
6. $-3x \leq 14$
7. $-3x < -14$
8. $-x \geq 23$

2.4 EXERCISE SET

Graph the solutions of each inequality. See Example 1.

1. $x < -3$
2. $x > 5$
3. $x \geq 0.3$
4. $x < -0.2$
5. $-7 \leq x$
6. $-7 \geq x$
7. $-2 < x < 5$
8. $-5 \leq x \leq -1$
9. $5 \geq x > -1$
10. $-3 > x \geq -7$

Solve. Graph the solutions. See Examples 2 through 4.

11. $x - 7 \geq -9$
12. $x + 2 \leq -1$
13. $7x < 6x + 1$
14. $11x < 10x + 5$
15. $8x - 7 \leq 7x - 5$
16. $7x - 1 \geq 6x - 1$
17. $\frac{3}{4}x \geq 6$
18. $\frac{5}{6}x \geq 5$
19. $5x < -23.5$
20. $4x > -11.2$
21. $-3x \geq 9$
22. $-4x \geq 8$

Solve. See Examples 5 through 7.

23. $-2x + 7 \geq 9$
24. $8 - 5x \leq 23$
25. $15 + 2x \geq 4x - 7$
26. $20 + x < 6x - 15$
27. $4(2x + 1) > 4$
28. $6(2 - 3x) \geq 12$
29. $3(x - 5) < 2(2x - 1)$
30. $5(x + 4) \leq 4(2x + 3)$
31. $\frac{5x + 1}{7} - \frac{2x - 6}{4} \geq -4$
32. $\frac{1 - 2x}{3} + \frac{3x + 7}{7} > 1$
33. $-3(2x - 1) < -4[2 + 3(x + 2)]$
34. $-2(4x + 2) > -5[1 + 2(x - 1)]$

MIXED PRACTICE

Solve. See Examples 1 through 7.

35. $x + 9 < 3$
36. $x - 9 < -12$
37. $-x < -4$
38. $-x > -2$
39. $-7x \leq 3.5$
40. $-6x \leq 4.2$
41. $\frac{1}{2} + \frac{2}{3} \geq \frac{x}{6}$
42. $\frac{3}{4} - \frac{2}{3} \geq \frac{x}{6}$
43. $-5x + 4 \leq -4(x - 1)$
44. $-6x + 2 < -3(x + 4)$
45. $\frac{3}{4}(x - 7) \geq x + 2$
46. $\frac{4}{5}(x + 1) \leq x + 1$
47. $0.8x + 0.6x \geq 4.2$
48. $0.7x - x > 0.45$
49. $4(x - 6) + 2x - 4 \geq 3(x - 7) + 10x$
50. $7(2x + 3) + 4x \leq 7 + 5(3x - 4) + x$
51. $14 - (5x - 6) \geq -6(x + 1) - 5$
52. $13y - (9y + 2) \leq 5(y - 6) + 10$
53. $\frac{1}{2}(3x - 4) \leq \frac{3}{4}(x - 6) + 1$
54. $\frac{2}{3}(x + 3) < \frac{1}{6}(2x - 8) + 2$
55. $\frac{-x + 2}{2} - \frac{1 - 5x}{8} < -1$
56. $\frac{3 - 4x}{6} - \frac{1 - 2x}{12} \leq -2$
57. $\frac{x + 5}{5} - \frac{3 + x}{8} \geq -\frac{3}{10}$
58. $\frac{x - 4}{2} - \frac{x - 2}{3} > \frac{5}{6}$
59. $\frac{x + 3}{12} + \frac{x - 5}{15} < \frac{2}{3}$
60. $\frac{3x + 2}{18} - \frac{1 + 2x}{6} \leq -\frac{1}{2}$
61. $0.4(4x - 3) < 1.2(x + 2)$
62. $0.2(8x - 2) < 1.2(x - 3)$
63. $\frac{2}{5}x - \frac{1}{4} \leq \frac{3}{10}x - \frac{4}{5}$
64. $\frac{7}{12}x - \frac{1}{3} \leq \frac{3}{8}x - \frac{5}{6}$
65. $4(x - 1) \geq 4x - 8$
66. $3x + 1 < 3(x - 2)$
67. $7x < 7(x - 2)$
68. $8(x + 3) \leq 7(x + 5) + x$

Multiple Steps. *Solve. See Examples 8 and 9.*

69. Shureka Washburn has scores of 72, 67, 82, and 79 on her algebra tests.

    a. Use an inequality to find the scores she must make on the final exam to pass the course with an average of 77 or higher, given that the final exam counts as two tests.

b. In your own words, explain the meaning of your answer to part a.

70. In a Winter Olympics 5000-meter speed-skating event, Hans Holden scored times of 6.85, 7.04, and 6.92 minutes on his first three trials.

   a. Use an inequality to find the times he can score on his last trial so that his average time is under 7.0 minutes.

   b. In your own words, explain the meaning of your answer to part a.

Multiple Steps. *Solve. See Examples 8 and 9. For Exercises 71 through 76,* **a.** *answer with an inequality, and* **b.** *in your own words, explain the meaning of your answer to part a.*

71. A small plane's maximum takeoff weight is 2000 pounds or less. Six passengers weigh an average of 160 pounds each. Use an inequality to find the luggage and cargo weights the plane can carry.

72. A shopping mall parking garage charges $1 for the first half-hour and 60 cents for each additional half-hour. Use an inequality to find how long you can park if you have only $4.00 in cash.

73. A clerk must use the elevator to move boxes of paper. The elevator's maximum weight limit is 1500 pounds. If each box of paper weighs 66 pounds and the clerk weighs 147 pounds, use an inequality to find the number of whole boxes she can move on the elevator at one time.

74. To mail an envelope first class, the U.S. Post Office charges 41 cents for the first ounce and 17 cents per ounce for each additional ounce. Use an inequality to find the number of whole ounces that can be mailed for no more than $2.50.

75. Northeast Telephone Company offers two billing plans for local calls.

   Plan 1: $25 per month for unlimited calls

   Plan 2: $13 per month plus $0.06 per call

   Use an inequality to find the number of monthly calls for which plan 1 is more economical than plan 2.

76. A car rental company offers two subcompact rental plans.

   Plan A: $36 per day and unlimited mileage

   Plan B: $24 per day plus $0.15 per mile

   Use an inequality to find the number of daily miles for which plan A is more economical than plan B.

77. At room temperature, glass used in windows actually has some properties of a liquid. It has a very slow, viscous flow. (Viscosity is the property of a fluid that resists internal flow. For example, lemonade flows more easily than fudge syrup. Fudge syrup has a higher viscosity than lemonade.) Glass does not become a true liquid until temperatures are greater than or equal to 500°C. Find the Fahrenheit temperatures for which glass is a liquid. (Use the formula $F = \frac{9}{5}C + 32$.)

78. Stibnite is a silvery white mineral with a metallic luster. It is one of the few minerals that melts easily in a match flame or at temperatures of approximately 977°F or greater. Find the Celsius temperatures for which stibnite melts. [Use the formula $C = \frac{5}{9}(F - 32)$.]

79. Although beginning salaries vary greatly according to your field of study, the equation

$$s = 651.2t + 28{,}472$$

can be used to approximate and to predict average beginning salaries for candidates with bachelor's degrees. The variable s is the starting salary and t is the number of years after 1990.

   a. Approximate when beginning salaries for candidates will be greater than $42,000.

   b. Determine the year you plan to graduate from college. Use this year to find the corresponding value of t and approximate your beginning salary.

80. **Multiple Steps.**

   a. Use the formula in Example 9 to estimate the years that the consumption of cigarettes will be less than 50 billion per year.

   b. Use your answer to part a to describe the limitations of your answer.

Read a Graph. *The average consumption per person per year of whole milk w in gallons can be approximated by the equation*

$$y = -0.19t + 7.6$$

where t is the number of years after 2000. The average consumption of nonfat milk s per person per year can be approximated by the equation

$$y = -0.07t + 3.5$$

where t is the number of years after 2000. The consumption of whole milk is shown on the graph in red and the consumption of nonfat milk is shown on the graph in blue. Use this information to answer Exercises 81–88.

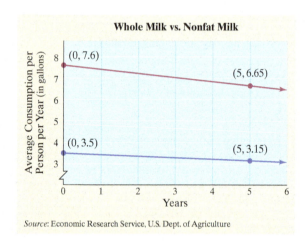

Source: Economic Research Service, U.S. Dept. of Agriculture

81. Is the consumption of whole milk increasing or decreasing over time? Explain how you arrived at your answer.

82. Is the consumption of nonfat milk increasing or decreasing over time? Explain how you arrived at your answer.

83. Predict the consumption of whole milk in the year 2010. (*Hint:* Find the value of *t* that corresponds to the year 2010.)

84. Predict the consumption of nonfat milk in the year 2010. (*Hint:* Find the value of *t* that corresponds to the year 2010.)

85. Determine when the consumption of whole milk will be less than 6 gallons per person per year.

86. Determine when the consumption of nonfat milk will be less than 3 gallons per person per year.

87. For 2000 through 2005 the consumption of whole milk was greater than the consumption of nonfat milk. Explain how this can be determined from the graph.

88. How will the two lines in the graph appear if the consumption of whole milk is the same as the consumption of nonfat milk?

REVIEW AND PREVIEW

List or describe the integers that make both inequalities true. See Section 1.4.

89. $x < 5$ and $x > 1$
90. $x \geq 0$ and $x \leq 7$
91. $x \geq -2$ and $x \geq 2$
92. $x < 6$ and $x < -5$

Solve each equation for x. See Section 2.1.

93. $2x - 6 = 4$
94. $3x - 12 = 3$
95. $-x + 7 = 5x - 6$
96. $-5x - 4 = -x - 4$

CONCEPT EXTENSIONS

Complete a Table. *Each row of the table shows three equivalent ways of describing an interval. Complete this table by filling in the equivalent descriptions. The first row has been completed for you.*

	Inequality	Graph
	$x < -3$	←───○───→ at −3
97.		←───●───→ at 2
98.		←───○───→ at −4
99.	$x < 0$	
100.	$x \leq 5$	
101.	$-2 < x \leq 1.5$	
102.	$-3.7 \leq x < 4$	

103. Solve: $2x - 3 = 5$.

104. Solve: $2x - 3 < 5$.

105. Solve: $2x - 3 > 5$.

106. Read the equations and inequalities for Exercises 103, 104, and 105 and their solutions. In your own words, write down your thoughts.

107. When graphing the solutions of an inequality, explain how you know whether to use an open or closed dot/circle.

108. Explain how solving a linear inequality is similar to solving a linear equation.

109. Explain how solving a linear inequality is different from solving a linear equation.

INTEGRATED REVIEW LINEAR EQUATIONS AND INEQUALITIES

Sections 2.1– 2.4

Solve each equation or inequality.

1. $-4x = 20$
2. $-4x < 20$
3. $\dfrac{3x}{4} \geq 2$
4. $5x + 3 \geq 2 + 4x$
5. $6(y - 4) = 3(y - 8)$
6. $-4x \leq \dfrac{2}{5}$
7. $-3x \geq \dfrac{1}{2}$
8. $5(y + 4) = 4(y + 5)$
9. $7x < 7(x - 2)$
10. $\dfrac{-5x + 11}{2} \leq 7$
11. $-5x + 1.5 = -19.5$
12. $-5x + 4 = -26$
13. $5 + 2x - x = -x + 3 - 14$
14. $12x + 14 < 11x - 2$
15. $\dfrac{x}{5} - \dfrac{x}{4} = \dfrac{x - 2}{2}$
16. $12x - 12 = 8(x - 1)$
17. $2(x - 3) > 70$
18. $-3x - 4.7 = 11.8$
19. $-2(b - 4) - (3b - 1) = 5b + 3$
20. $8(x + 3) < 7(x + 5) + x$
21. $\dfrac{3t + 1}{8} = \dfrac{5 + 2t}{7} + 2$
22. $4(x - 6) - x = 8(x - 3) - 5x$
23. $\dfrac{x}{6} + \dfrac{3x - 2}{2} < \dfrac{2}{3}$
24. $\dfrac{y}{3} + \dfrac{y}{5} = \dfrac{y + 3}{10}$
25. $5(x - 6) + 2x > 3(2x - 1) - 4$
26. $14(x - 1) - 7x \leq 2(3x - 6) + 4$
27. $\dfrac{1}{4}(3x + 2) - x \geq \dfrac{3}{8}(x - 5) + 2$
28. $\dfrac{1}{3}(x - 10) - 4x > \dfrac{5}{6}(2x + 1) - 1$

2.5 COMPOUND INEQUALITIES

OBJECTIVES

1. Find the intersection of two sets.
2. Solve compound inequalities containing **and**.
3. Find the union of two sets.
4. Solve compound inequalities containing **or**.

Two inequalities joined by the words **and** or **or** are called **compound inequalities.**

Compound Inequalities

$x + 3 < 8$ and $x > 2$

$\dfrac{2x}{3} \geq 5$ or $-x + 10 < 7$

OBJECTIVE 1 ▶ Finding the intersection of two sets. The solution set of a compound inequality formed by the word **and** is the **intersection** of the solution sets of the two inequalities. We use the symbol ∩ to represent "intersection."

Intersection of Two Sets

The intersection of two sets, A and B, is the set of all elements common to both sets. A intersect B is denoted by

$A \cap B$

EXAMPLE 1 If $A = \{x \mid x \text{ is an even number greater than 0 and less than 10}\}$ and $B = \{3, 4, 5, 6\}$, find $A \cap B$.

Solution Let's list the elements in set A.

$$A = \{2, 4, 6, 8\}$$

The numbers 4 and 6 are in sets A and B. The intersection is $\{4, 6\}$.

PRACTICE 1 If $A = \{x \mid x$ is an odd number greater than 0 and less than 10$\}$ and $B = \{1, 2, 3, 4\}$, find $A \cap B$.

OBJECTIVE 2 ▶ Solving compound inequalities containing "and." A value is a solution of a compound inequality formed by the word **and** if it is a solution of *both* inequalities. For example, the solution set of the compound inequality $x \leq 5$ and $x \geq 3$ contains all values of x that make the inequality $x \leq 5$ a true statement **and** the inequality $x \geq 3$ a true statement. The first graph shown below is the graph of $x \leq 5$, the second graph is the graph of $x \geq 3$, and the third graph shows the intersection of the two graphs. The third graph is the graph of $x \leq 5$ **and** $x \geq 3$.

$x \leq 5$

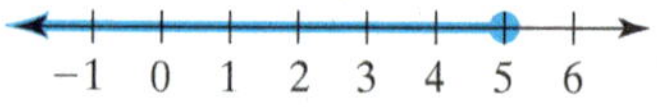

$x \geq 3$

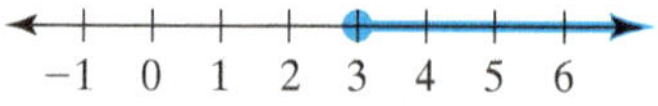

$x \leq 5$ and $x \geq 3$, also written as $3 \leq x \leq 5$ (see below)

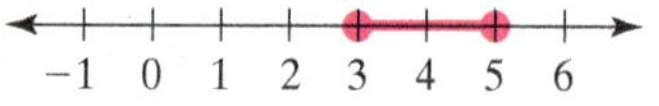

Since $x \geq 3$ is the same as $3 \leq x$, the compound inequality $3 \leq x$ and $x \leq 5$ can be written in a more compact form as $3 \leq x \leq 5$. This inequality includes all numbers that are greater than or equal to 3 and at the same time less than or equal to 5.

When possible, we will write compound inequalities in a compact form.

▶ **Helpful Hint**
Don't forget that some compound inequalities containing "and" can be written in a more compact form.

Compound Inequality	Compact Form
$2 \leq x$ and $x \leq 6$	$2 \leq x \leq 6$

Graph:

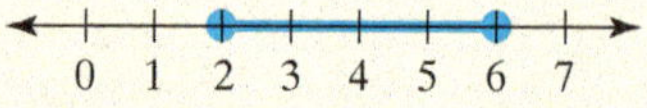

EXAMPLE 2 Solve: $x - 7 < 2$ and $2x + 1 < 9$.

Solution First we solve each inequality separately.

$$x - 7 < 2 \quad \text{and} \quad 2x + 1 < 9$$
$$x < 9 \quad \text{and} \quad 2x < 8$$
$$x < 9 \quad \text{and} \quad x < 4$$

Now we can graph the two inequalities on two number lines and find their intersection. Their intersection is shown on the third number line.

$x < 9$

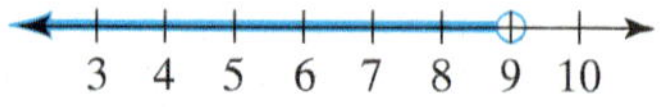

$x < 4$

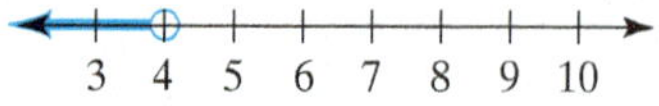

$x < 9$ and $x < 4$, also written as

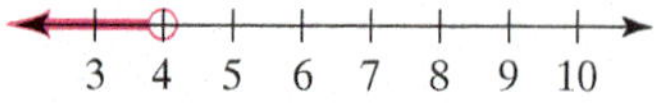

$x < 4$

As we see from the last number line, the solutions are all numbers less than 4, written as $x < 4$.

PRACTICE 2 Solve: $x + 3 < 8$ and $2x - 1 < 3$.

Section 2.5 Compound Inequalities 87

EXAMPLE 3 Solve: $2x \geq 0$ and $4x - 1 \leq -9$.

Solution First we solve each inequalities separately.

$$2x \geq 0 \quad \text{and} \quad 4x - 1 \leq -9$$
$$x \geq 0 \quad \text{and} \quad 4x \leq -8$$
$$x \geq 0 \quad \text{and} \quad x \leq -2$$

Now we can graph the two inequalities and find their intersection.

$x \geq 0$

$x \leq -2$

$x \geq 0$ and $x \leq -2$, which is no solution

There is no number that is greater than or equal to 0 *and* less than or equal to -2. The answer is no solution.

PRACTICE 3 Solve: $4x \leq 0$ and $3x + 2 > 8$.

> **Helpful Hint**
> Example 3 shows that some compound inequalities have no solution. Also, some have all real numbers as solutions.

To solve a compound inequality written in a compact form, such as $2 < 4 - x < 7$, we get x alone in the "middle part." Since a compound inequality is really two inequalities in one statement, we must perform the same operations on all three parts of the inequality.

EXAMPLE 4 Solve: $2 < 4 - x < 7$.

Solution To get x alone, we first subtract 4 from all three parts.

$$2 < 4 - x < 7$$
$$2 - 4 < 4 - x - 4 < 7 - 4 \quad \text{Subtract 4 from all three parts.}$$
$$-2 < -x < 3 \quad \text{Simplify.}$$
$$\frac{-2}{-1} > \frac{-x}{-1} > \frac{3}{-1} \quad \text{Divide all three parts by } -1 \text{ and reverse the inequality symbols.}$$
$$2 > x > -3$$

> **Helpful Hint**
> Don't forget to reverse both inequality symbols.

This is equivalent to $-3 < x < 2$.
The graph is shown.

PRACTICE 4 Solve: $3 < 5 - x < 9$.

EXAMPLE 5 Solve: $-1 \leq \frac{2x}{3} + 5 \leq 2$.

Solution First, clear the inequality of fractions by multiplying all three parts by the LCD of 3.

$$-1 \leq \frac{2x}{3} + 5 \leq 2$$

88 CHAPTER 2 Equations, Inequalities, and Problem Solving

$$3(-1) \leq 3\left(\frac{2x}{3} + 5\right) \leq 3(2) \quad \text{Multiply all three parts by the LCD of 3.}$$
$$-3 \leq 2x + 15 \leq 6 \quad \text{Use the distributive property and multiply.}$$
$$-3 - 15 \leq 2x + 15 - 15 \leq 6 - 15 \quad \text{Subtract 15 from all three parts.}$$
$$-18 \leq 2x \leq -9 \quad \text{Simplify.}$$
$$\frac{-18}{2} \leq \frac{2x}{2} \leq \frac{-9}{2} \quad \text{Divide all three parts by 2.}$$
$$-9 \leq x \leq -\frac{9}{2} \quad \text{Simplify.}$$

The graph of the solutions are shown.

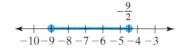

PRACTICE 5 Solve: $-4 \leq \frac{x}{2} - 1 \leq 3$.

OBJECTIVE 3 ▶ Finding the union of two sets. The solution set of a compound inequality formed by the word **or** is the **union** of the solution sets of the two inequalities. We use the symbol $\cup$ to denote "union."

▶ **Helpful Hint**
The word "either" in this definition means "one or the other or both."

Union of Two Sets

The **union** of two sets, A and B, is the set of elements that belong to *either* of the sets. A union B is denoted by

EXAMPLE 6 If $A = \{x | x \text{ is an even number greater than 0 and less than 10}\}$ and $B = \{3, 4, 5, 6\}$. Find $A \cup B$.

Solution Recall from Example 1 that $A = \{2, 4, 6, 8\}$. The numbers that are in either set or both sets are $\{2, 3, 4, 5, 6, 8\}$. This set is the union. □

PRACTICE 6 If $A = \{x | x \text{ is an odd number greater than 0 and less than 10}\}$ and $B = \{2, 3, 4, 5, 6\}$. Find $A \cup B$.

OBJECTIVE 4 ▶ Solving compound inequalities containing "or." A value is a solution of a compound inequality formed by the word **or** if it is a solution of **either** inequality. For example, the solution set of the compound inequality $x \leq 1$ **or** $x \geq 3$ contains all numbers that make the inequality $x \leq 1$ a true statement **or** the inequality $x \geq 3$ a true statement.

$x \leq 1$

$x \geq 3$

$x \leq 1 \text{ or } x \geq 3$

As we see from the last number line, there is no more compact way to write the solutions. They are all numbers, x, such that $x \leq 1$ or $x \geq 3$.

EXAMPLE 7 Solve: $5x - 3 \leq 10$ or $x + 1 \geq 5$.

Solution First we solve each inequality separately.

$$5x - 3 \leq 10 \quad \text{or} \quad x + 1 \geq 5$$
$$5x \leq 13 \quad \text{or} \quad x \geq 4$$
$$x \leq \frac{13}{5} \quad \text{or} \quad x \geq 4$$

Now we can graph each inequality and find their union.

$x \leq \dfrac{13}{5}$

$x \geq 4$

$x \leq \dfrac{13}{5}$ or $x \geq 4$

The solutions are $x \leq \dfrac{13}{5}$ or $x \geq 4$.

PRACTICE 7 Solve: $8x + 5 \leq 8$ or $x - 1 \geq 2$.

EXAMPLE 8 Solve: $-2x - 5 < -3$ or $6x < 0$.

Solution First we solve each inequality separately.

$$-2x - 5 < -3 \quad \text{or} \quad 6x < 0$$
$$-2x < 2 \quad \text{or} \quad x < 0$$
$$x > -1 \quad \text{or} \quad x < 0$$

Now we can graph each inequality and find their union.

$x > -1$

$x < 0$

$x > -1$ or $x < 0$,
also written as
all real numbers

The solutions are all real numbers.

PRACTICE 8 Solve: $-3x - 2 > -8$ or $5x > 0$.

Concept Check ✓

Which of the following is *not* a correct way to represent all numbers between -3 and 5?

a. $-3 < x < 5$
b. $-3 < x$ or $x < 5$
c. $x > -3$ and $x < 5$

Answer to Concept Check:
b is not correct

CHAPTER 2 Equations, Inequalities, and Problem Solving

VOCABULARY & READINESS CHECK

Word Bank. *Use the choices below to fill in each blank. Some choices may be used more than once.*

or   ∪   ∅

and   ∩   compound

1. Two inequalities joined by the words "and" or "or" are called _____ inequalities.
2. The word _____ means intersection.
3. The word _____ means union.
4. The symbol _____ represents intersection.
5. The symbol _____ represents union.
6. The symbol _____ is the empty set.
7. The inequality $-2 \leq x < 1$ means $-2 \leq x$ _____ $x < 1$.
8. $\{x \mid x < 0 \text{ and } x > 0\} =$ _____.

2.5 EXERCISE SET

MIXED PRACTICE

If $A = \{x \mid x \text{ is an even integer}\}$, $B = \{x \mid x \text{ is an odd integer}\}$, $C = \{2, 3, 4, 5\}$, and $D = \{4, 5, 6, 7\}$, list the elements of each set. See Examples 1 and 6.

1. $C \cup D$
2. $C \cap D$
3. $A \cap D$
4. $A \cup D$
5. $A \cup B$
6. $A \cap B$
7. $B \cap D$
8. $B \cup D$
9. $B \cup C$
10. $B \cap C$
11. $A \cap C$
12. $A \cup C$

Solve each compound inequality. Graph the solutions. See Examples 2 and 3.

13. $x < 1$ and $x > -3$
14. $x \leq 0$ and $x \geq -2$
15. $x \leq -3$ and $x \geq -2$
16. $x < 2$ and $x > 4$
17. $x < -1$ and $x < 1$
18. $x \geq -4$ and $x > 1$

Solve each compound inequality. See Examples 2 and 3.

19. $x + 1 \geq 7$ and $3x - 1 \geq 5$
20. $x + 2 \geq 3$ and $5x - 1 \geq 9$
21. $4x + 2 \leq -10$ and $2x \leq 0$
22. $2x + 4 > 0$ and $4x > 0$
23. $-2x < -8$ and $x - 5 < 5$
24. $-7x \leq -21$ and $x - 20 \leq -15$

Solve each compound inequality. See Examples 4 and 5.

25. $5 < x - 6 < 11$
26. $-2 \leq x + 3 \leq 0$
27. $-2 \leq 3x - 5 \leq 7$
28. $1 < 4 + 2x < 7$
29. $1 \leq \frac{2}{3}x + 3 \leq 4$
30. $-2 < \frac{1}{2}x - 5 < 1$
31. $-5 \leq \frac{-3x + 1}{4} \leq 2$
32. $-4 \leq \frac{-2x + 5}{3} \leq 1$

Solve each compound inequality. Graph the solutions. See Examples 7 and 8.

33. $x < 4$ or $x < 5$
34. $x \geq -2$ or $x \leq 2$
35. $x \leq -4$ or $x \geq 1$
36. $x < 0$ or $x < 1$
37. $x > 0$ or $x < 3$
38. $x \geq -3$ or $x \leq -4$

Solve each compound inequality. See Examples 7 and 8.

39. $-2x \leq -4$ or $5x - 20 \geq 5$
40. $-5x \leq 10$ or $3x - 5 \geq 1$
41. $x + 4 < 0$ or $6x > -12$
42. $x + 9 < 0$ or $4x > -12$
43. $3(x - 1) < 12$ or $x + 7 > 10$
44. $5(x - 1) \geq -5$ or $5 - x \leq 11$

MIXED PRACTICE

Solve each compound inequality. See Examples 1 through 8.

45. $x < \frac{2}{3}$ and $x > -\frac{1}{2}$
46. $x < \frac{5}{7}$ and $x < 1$
47. $x < \frac{2}{3}$ or $x > -\frac{1}{2}$
48. $x < \frac{5}{7}$ or $x < 1$
49. $0 \leq 2x - 3 \leq 9$
50. $3 < 5x + 1 < 11$
51. $\frac{1}{2} < x - \frac{3}{4} < 2$
52. $\frac{2}{3} < x + \frac{1}{2} < 4$
53. $x + 3 \geq 3$ and $x + 3 \leq 2$
54. $2x - 1 \geq 3$ and $-x > 2$

55. $3x \geq 5$ or $-\dfrac{5}{8}x - 6 > 1$

56. $\dfrac{3}{8}x + 1 \leq 0$ or $-2x < -4$

57. $0 < \dfrac{5 - 2x}{3} < 5$

58. $-2 < \dfrac{-2x - 1}{3} < 2$

59. $-6 < 3(x - 2) \leq 8$

60. $-5 < 2(x + 4) < 8$

61. $-x + 5 > 6$ and $1 + 2x \leq -5$

62. $5x \leq 0$ and $-x + 5 < 8$

63. $3x + 2 \leq 5$ or $7x > 29$

64. $-x < 7$ or $3x + 1 < -20$

65. $5 - x > 7$ and $2x + 3 \geq 13$

66. $-2x < -6$ or $1 - x > -2$

67. $-\dfrac{1}{2} \leq \dfrac{4x - 1}{6} < \dfrac{5}{6}$

68. $-\dfrac{1}{2} \leq \dfrac{3x - 1}{10} < \dfrac{1}{2}$

69. $\dfrac{1}{15} < \dfrac{8 - 3x}{15} < \dfrac{4}{5}$

70. $-\dfrac{1}{4} < \dfrac{6 - x}{12} < -\dfrac{1}{6}$

71. $0.3 < 0.2x - 0.9 < 1.5$

72. $-0.7 \leq 0.4x + 0.8 < 0.5$

REVIEW AND PREVIEW

Evaluate the following. See Sections 1.2 and 1.3.

73. $|-7| - |19|$

74. $|-7 - 19|$

75. $-(-6) - |-10|$

76. $|-4| - (-4) + |-20|$

Find by inspection all values for x that make each equation true.

77. $|x| = 7$

78. $|x| = 5$

79. $|x| = 0$

80. $|x| = -2$

CONCEPT EXTENSIONS

Read a Graph. *Use the graph to answer Exercises 81 and 82.*

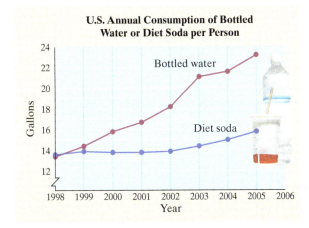

U.S. Annual Consumption of Bottled Water or Diet Soda per Person

81. For what years was the consumption of bottled water greater than 20 gallons per person *and* the consumption of diet soda greater than 14 gallons per person?

82. For what years was the consumption of bottled water less than 15 gallons per person *or* the consumption of diet soda greater than 14 gallons per person?

The formula for converting Fahrenheit temperatures to Celsius temperatures is $C = \dfrac{5}{9}(F - 32)$. Use this formula for Exercises 83 and 84.

83. During a recent year, the temperatures in Chicago ranged from $-29°$ to $35°C$. Use a compound inequality to convert these temperatures to Fahrenheit temperatures.

84. In Oslo, the average temperature ranges from $-10°$ to $18°$ Celsius. Use a compound inequality to convert these temperatures to the Fahrenheit scale.

Solve.

85. Christian D'Angelo has scores of 68, 65, 75, and 78 on his algebra tests. Use a compound inequality to find the scores he can make on his final exam to receive a C in the course. The final exam counts as two tests, and a C is received if the final course average is from 70 to 79.

86. Wendy Wood has scores of 80, 90, 82, and 75 on her chemistry tests. Use a compound inequality to find the range of scores she can make on her final exam to receive a B in the course. The final exam counts as two tests, and a B is received if the final course average is from 80 to 89.

*Solve each compound inequality for x. See the example below. To solve $x - 6 < 3x < 2x + 5$, notice that this inequality contains a variable not only in the middle, but also on the left and the right. When this occurs, we solve by rewriting the inequality using the word **and**.*

$$x - 6 < 3x \quad \text{and} \quad 3x < 2x + 5$$
$$-6 < 2x \quad \text{and} \quad x < 5$$
$$-3 < x$$
$$x > -3 \quad \text{and} \quad x < 5$$

$-3 < x < 5$

87. $2x - 3 < 3x + 1 < 4x - 5$

88. $x + 3 < 2x + 1 < 4x + 6$

89. $-3(x - 2) \leq 3 - 2x \leq 10 - 3x$

90. $7x - 1 \leq 7 + 5x \leq 3(1 + 2x)$

91. $5x - 8 < 2(2 + x) < -2(1 + 2x)$

92. $1 + 2x < 3(2 + x) < 1 + 4x$

2.6 ABSOLUTE VALUE EQUATIONS

OBJECTIVE
1. Solve absolute value equations.

OBJECTIVE 1 ▶ **Solving absolute equations.** In Chapter 1, we defined the absolute value of a number as its distance from 0 on a number line.

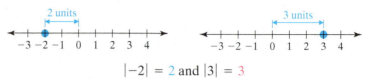

$|-2| = 2$ and $|3| = 3$

In this section, we concentrate on solving equations containing the absolute value of a variable or a variable expression. Examples of absolute value equations are

$$|x| = 3 \qquad -5 = |2y + 7| \qquad |z - 6.7| = |3z + 1.2|$$

Since distance and absolute value are so closely related, absolute value equations and inequalities (see Section 2.7) are extremely useful in solving distance-type problems, such as calculating the possible error in a measurement.

For the absolute value equation $|x| = 3$, its solution set will contain all numbers whose distance from 0 is 3 units. Two numbers are 3 units away from 0 on the number line: 3 and -3.

Thus, the solution set of the equation $|x| = 3$ is $\{3, -3\}$. This suggests the following:

Solving Equations of the Form $|X| = a$

If a is a positive number, then $|X| = a$ is equivalent to $X = a$ or $X = -a$.

EXAMPLE 1 Solve: $|p| = 2$.

Solution Since 2 is positive, $|p| = 2$ is equivalent to $p = 2$ or $p = -2$.

To check, let $p = 2$ and then $p = -2$ in the original equation.

$\|p\| = 2$	Original equation	$\|p\| = 2$	Original equation
$\|2\| = 2$	Let $p = 2$.	$\|-2\| = 2$	Let $p = -2$.
$2 = 2$	True	$2 = 2$	True

The solutions are 2 and -2 or the solution set is $\{2, -2\}$.

PRACTICE 1 Solve: $|q| = 7$.

If the expression inside the absolute value bars is more complicated than a single variable, we can still apply the absolute value property.

▶ **Helpful Hint**

For the equation $|X| = a$ in the box above, X can be a single variable or a variable expression.

EXAMPLE 2 Solve: $|5w + 3| = 7$.

Solution Here the expression inside the absolute value bars is $5w + 3$. If we think of the expression $5w + 3$ as X in the absolute value property, we see that $|X| = 7$ is equivalent to

$$X = 7 \quad \text{or} \quad X = -7$$

Then substitute $5w + 3$ for X, and we have

$$5w + 3 = 7 \quad \text{or} \quad 5w + 3 = -7$$

Solve these two equations for w.

$$5w + 3 = 7 \quad \text{or} \quad 5w + 3 = -7$$
$$5w = 4 \quad \text{or} \quad 5w = -10$$
$$w = \frac{4}{5} \quad \text{or} \quad w = -2$$

Check: To check, let $w = -2$ and then $w = \frac{4}{5}$ in the original equation.

Let $w = -2$ Let $w = \frac{4}{5}$

$|5(-2) + 3| = 7$ $\left|5\left(\frac{4}{5}\right) + 3\right| = 7$

$|-10 + 3| = 7$ $|4 + 3| = 7$

$|-7| = 7$ $|7| = 7$

$7 = 7$ True $7 = 7$ True

Both solutions check, and the solutions are -2 and $\frac{4}{5}$.

PRACTICE 2 Solve: $|2x - 3| = 5$.

EXAMPLE 3 Solve: $\left|\frac{x}{2} - 1\right| = 11$.

Solution $\left|\frac{x}{2} - 1\right| = 11$ is equivalent to

$$\frac{x}{2} - 1 = 11 \quad \text{or} \quad \frac{x}{2} - 1 = -11$$
$$2\left(\frac{x}{2} - 1\right) = 2(11) \quad \text{or} \quad 2\left(\frac{x}{2} - 1\right) = 2(-11) \quad \text{Clear fractions.}$$
$$x - 2 = 22 \quad \text{or} \quad x - 2 = -22 \quad \text{Apply the distributive property.}$$
$$x = 24 \quad \text{or} \quad x = -20$$

The solutions are 24 and -20.

PRACTICE 3 Solve: $\left|\frac{x}{5} + 1\right| = 15$.

To apply the absolute value rule, first make sure that the absolute value expression is isolated.

> ▶ **Helpful Hint**
>
> If the equation has a single absolute value expression containing variables, isolate the absolute value expression first.

EXAMPLE 4 Solve: $|2x| + 5 = 7$.

Solution We want the absolute value expression alone on one side of the equation, so begin by subtracting 5 from both sides. Then apply the absolute value property.

$$|2x| + 5 = 7$$
$$|2x| = 2 \qquad \text{Subtract 5 from both sides.}$$
$$2x = 2 \quad \text{or} \quad 2x = -2$$
$$x = 1 \quad \text{or} \quad x = -1$$

The solutions are -1 and 1.

PRACTICE 4 Solve: $|3x| + 8 = 14$.

EXAMPLE 5 Solve: $|y| = 0$.

Solution We are looking for all numbers whose distance from 0 is zero units. The only number is 0. The solution is 0.

PRACTICE 5 Solve: $|z| = 0$.

The next two examples illustrate a special case for absolute value equations. This special case occurs when an isolated absolute value is equal to a negative number.

EXAMPLE 6 Solve: $2|x| + 25 = 23$.

Solution First, isolate the absolute value.

$$2|x| + 25 = 23$$
$$2|x| = -2 \qquad \text{Subtract 25 from both sides.}$$
$$|x| = -1 \qquad \text{Divide both sides by 2.}$$

The absolute value of a number is never negative, so this equation has no solution.

PRACTICE 6 Solve: $3|z| + 9 = 7$.

EXAMPLE 7 Solve: $\left|\dfrac{3x + 1}{2}\right| = -2$.

Solution Again, the absolute value of any expression is never negative, so no solution exists. This equation has no solution.

PRACTICE 7 Solve: $\left|\dfrac{5x + 3}{4}\right| = -8$.

Given two absolute value expressions, we might ask, when are the absolute values of two expressions equal? To see the answer, notice that

$$|2| = |2|, \quad |-2| = |-2|, \quad |-2| = |2|, \quad \text{and} \quad |2| = |-2|$$

$\qquad\qquad$ same $\qquad$ same $\qquad$ opposites $\qquad$ opposites

Two absolute value expressions are equal when the expressions inside the absolute value bars are equal to or are opposites of each other.

Section 2.6 Absolute Value Equations 95

EXAMPLE 8 Solve: $|3x + 2| = |5x - 8|$.

Solution This equation is true if the expressions inside the absolute value bars are equal to or are opposites of each other.

$$3x + 2 = 5x - 8 \quad \text{or} \quad 3x + 2 = -(5x - 8)$$

Next, solve each equation.

$$3x + 2 = 5x - 8 \quad \text{or} \quad 3x + 2 = -5x + 8$$
$$-2x + 2 = -8 \quad \text{or} \quad 8x + 2 = 8$$
$$-2x = -10 \quad \text{or} \quad 8x = 6$$
$$x = 5 \quad \text{or} \quad x = \frac{3}{4}$$

The solutions are $\frac{3}{4}$ and 5.

PRACTICE 8 Solve: $|2x + 4| = |3x - 1|$.

EXAMPLE 9 Solve: $|x - 3| = |5 - x|$.

Solution
$$x - 3 = 5 - x \quad \text{or} \quad x - 3 = -(5 - x)$$
$$2x - 3 = 5 \quad \text{or} \quad x - 3 = -5 + x$$
$$2x = 8 \quad \text{or} \quad x - 3 - x = -5 + x - x$$
$$x = 4 \quad \text{or} \quad -3 = -5 \quad \text{False}$$

Recall from Section 2.1 that when an equation simplifies to a false statement, the equation has no solution. Thus, the only solution for the original absolute value equation is 4.

PRACTICE 9 Solve: $|x - 2| = |8 - x|$.

Concept Check ✓

True or false? Absolute value equations always have two solutions. Explain your answer.

The following box summarizes the methods shown for solving absolute value equations.

Absolute Value Equations

$|X| = a$
- If a is positive, then solve $X = a$ or $X = -a$.
- If a is 0, solve $X = 0$.
- If a is negative, the equation $|X| = a$ has no solution.

$|X| = |Y|$ Solve $X = Y$ or $X = -Y$.

Answer to Concept Check:
false; answers may vary

VOCABULARY & READINESS CHECK

Matching. *Match each absolute value equation with an equivalent statement.*

1. $|x - 2| = 5$
2. $|x - 2| = 0$
3. $|x - 2| = |x + 3|$
4. $|x + 3| = 5$
5. $|x + 3| = -5$

A. $x - 2 = 0$
B. $x - 2 = x + 3$ or $x - 2 = -(x + 3)$
C. $x - 2 = 5$ or $x - 2 = -5$
D. $\emptyset$
E. $x + 3 = 5$ or $x + 3 = -5$

2.6 EXERCISE SET

Solve each absolute value equation. See Examples 1 through 7.

1. $|x| = 7$
2. $|y| = 15$
3. $|3x| = 12.6$
4. $|6n| = 12.6$
5. $|2x - 5| = 9$
6. $|6 + 2n| = 4$
7. $\left|\dfrac{x}{2} - 3\right| = 1$
8. $\left|\dfrac{n}{3} + 2\right| = 4$
9. $|z| + 4 = 9$
10. $|x| + 1 = 3$
11. $|3x| + 5 = 14$
12. $|2x| - 6 = 4$
13. $|2x| = 0$
14. $|7z| = 0$
15. $|4n + 1| + 10 = 4$
16. $|3z - 2| + 8 = 1$
17. $|5x - 1| = 0$
18. $|3y + 2| = 0$

19. Write an absolute value equation representing all numbers x whose distance from 0 is 5 units.
20. Write an absolute value equation representing all numbers x whose distance from 0 is 2 units.

Solve. See Examples 8 and 9.

21. $|5x - 7| = |3x + 11|$
22. $|9y + 1| = |6y + 4|$
23. $|z + 8| = |z - 3|$
24. $|2x - 5| = |2x + 5|$

25. Describe how solving an absolute value equation such as $|2x - 1| = 3$ is similar to solving an absolute value equation such as $|2x - 1| = |x - 5|$.
26. Describe how solving an absolute value equation such as $|2x - 1| = 3$ is different from solving an absolute value equation such as $|2x - 1| = |x - 5|$.

MIXED PRACTICE

Solve each absolute value equation. See Examples 1 through 9.

27. $|x| = 4$
28. $|x| = 1$
29. $|y| = 0$
30. $|y| = 8$
31. $|z| = -2$
32. $|y| = -9$
33. $|7 - 3x| = 7$
34. $|4m + 5| = 5$
35. $|6x| - 1 = 11$
36. $|7z| + 1 = 22$
37. $|4p| = -8$
38. $|5m| = -10$
39. $|x - 3| + 3 = 7$
40. $|x + 4| - 4 = 1$
41. $\left|\dfrac{z}{4} + 5\right| = -7$
42. $\left|\dfrac{c}{5} - 1\right| = -2$
43. $|9v - 3| = -8$
44. $|1 - 3b| = -7$
45. $|8n + 1| = 0$
46. $|5x - 2| = 0$
47. $|1 + 6c| - 7 = -3$
48. $|2 + 3m| - 9 = -7$
49. $|5x + 1| = 11$
50. $|8 - 6c| = 1$
51. $|4x - 2| = |-10|$
52. $|3x + 5| = |-4|$
53. $|5x + 1| = |4x - 7|$
54. $|3 + 6n| = |4n + 11|$
55. $|6 + 2x| = -|-7|$
56. $|4 - 5y| = -|-3|$
57. $|2x - 6| = |10 - 2x|$
58. $|4n + 5| = |4n + 3|$
59. $\left|\dfrac{2x - 5}{3}\right| = 7$
60. $\left|\dfrac{1 + 3n}{4}\right| = 4$
61. $2 + |5n| = 17$
62. $8 + |4m| = 24$
63. $\left|\dfrac{2x - 1}{3}\right| = |-5|$
64. $\left|\dfrac{5x + 2}{2}\right| = |-6|$
65. $|2y - 3| = |9 - 4y|$
66. $|5z - 1| = |7 - z|$
67. $\left|\dfrac{3n + 2}{8}\right| = |-1|$
68. $\left|\dfrac{2r - 6}{5}\right| = |-2|$
69. $|x + 4| = |7 - x|$
70. $|8 - y| = |y + 2|$
71. $\left|\dfrac{8c - 7}{3}\right| = -|-5|$
72. $\left|\dfrac{5d + 1}{6}\right| = -|-9|$

73. Explain why some absolute value equations have two solutions.
74. Explain why some absolute value equations have one solution.

REVIEW AND PREVIEW

Read a Graph. *The circle graph shows the U.S. cheese consumption for 2005. Use this graph to answer Exercises 75–77. See Section 2.2. (Source: National Agriculture Statistics Service, USDA)*

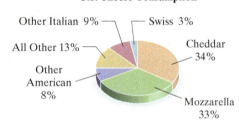

U.S. Cheese Consumption

75. What percent of cheese consumption came from chedder cheese?
76. A circle contains 360°. Find the number of degrees in the 3% sector for swiss cheese.
77. If a family consumed 120 pounds of cheese in 2005, find the amount of mozzarella we might expect they consumed.

List five integer solutions of each inequality. See Sections 1.2 through 1.4.

78. $|x| \leq 3$
79. $|x| \geq -2$
80. $|y| > -10$
81. $|y| < 0$

CONCEPT EXTENSIONS

82. Write an absolute value equation representing all numbers x whose distance from 1 is 5 units.
83. Write an absolute value equation representing all numbers x whose distance from 7 is 2 units.

Write each as an equivalent absolute value.

84. $x = 6$ or $x = -6$
85. $2x - 1 = 4$ or $2x - 1 = -4$
86. $x - 2 = 3x - 4$ or $x - 2 = -(3x - 4)$
87. For what value(s) of c will an absolute value equation of the form $|ax + b| = c$ have
    a. one solution?
    b. no solution?
    c. two solutions?

2.7 ABSOLUTE VALUE INEQUALITIES

OBJECTIVES

1. Solve absolute value inequalities of the form $|x| < a$.
2. Solve absolute value inequalities of the form $|x| > a$.

OBJECTIVE 1 ▶ **Solving absolute value inequalities of the form $|x| < a$.** The solution set of an absolute value inequality such as $|x| < 2$ contains all numbers whose distance from 0 is less than 2 units, as shown below.

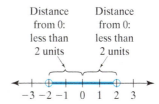

The solutions are $-2 < x < 2$.

EXAMPLE 1 Solve: $|x| \leq 3$.

Solution The solution set of this inequality contains all numbers whose distance from 0 is less than or equal to 3. Thus 3, −3, and all numbers between 3 and −3 are in the solution set.

The solutions are $-3 \leq x \leq 3$.

PRACTICE 1 Solve: $|x| < 2$ and graph the solutions.

In general, we have the following.

Solving Absolute Value Inequalities of the Form $|X| < a$

If a is a positive number, then $|X| < a$ is equivalent to $-a < X < a$.

This property also holds true for the inequality symbol $\leq$.

EXAMPLE 2 Solve for m: $|m - 6| < 2$.

Solution Replace X with $m - 6$ and a with 2 in the preceding property, and we see that

$$|m - 6| < 2 \text{ is equivalent to } -2 < m - 6 < 2$$

Solve this compound inequality for m by adding 6 to all three parts.

$$-2 < m - 6 < 2$$
$$-2 + 6 < m - 6 + 6 < 2 + 6 \quad \text{Add 6 to all three parts.}$$
$$4 < m < 8 \quad \text{Simplify.}$$

The graph is shown.

PRACTICE 2 Solve for b: $|b + 1| < 3$. Graph the solutions.

> ▶ **Helpful Hint**
> Before using an absolute value inequality property, isolate the absolute value expression on one side of the inequality.

EXAMPLE 3 Solve for x: $|5x + 1| + 1 \leq 10$.

Solution First, isolate the absolute value expression by subtracting 1 from both sides.

$$|5x + 1| + 1 \leq 10$$
$$|5x + 1| \leq 10 - 1 \quad \text{Subtract 1 from both sides.}$$
$$|5x + 1| \leq 9 \quad \text{Simplify.}$$

Since 9 is positive, we apply the absolute value property for $|X| \leq a$.

$$-9 \leq 5x + 1 \leq 9$$
$$-9 - 1 \leq 5x + 1 - 1 \leq 9 - 1 \quad \text{Subtract 1 from all three parts.}$$
$$-10 \leq 5x \leq 8 \quad \text{Simplify.}$$
$$-2 \leq x \leq \frac{8}{5} \quad \text{Divide all three parts by 5.}$$

The solutions are -2, $\frac{8}{5}$, and all numbers between these two. The graph is shown above. □

PRACTICE 3 Solve for x: $|3x - 2| + 5 \leq 9$. Graph the solutions.

EXAMPLE 4 Solve for x: 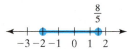.

Solution The absolute value of a number is always nonnegative and can never be less than -13. Thus this absolute value inequality has no solution. □

PRACTICE 4 Solve for x: $\left|3x + \frac{5}{8}\right| < -4$.

OBJECTIVE 2 ▶ Solving absolute value inequalities of the form $|x| > a$. Let us now solve an absolute value inequality of the form $|X| > a$, such as $|x| \geq 3$. The solution set contains all numbers whose distance from 0 is 3 or more units. Thus the graph of the solution set contains 3 and all points to the right of 3 on the number line or -3 and all points to the left of -3 on the number line.

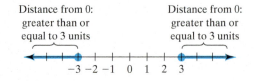

The solutions are $x \leq -3$ or $x \geq 3$. In general, we have the following.

> **Solving Absolute Value Inequalities of the Form $|X| > a$**
> If a is a positive number, then $|X| > a$ is equivalent to $X < -a$ or $X > a$.

This property also holds true for the inequality symbol $\geq$.

EXAMPLE 5 Solve for y: $|y - 3| > 7$.

Solution Since 7 is positive, we apply the property for $|X| > a$.

$|y - 3| > 7$ is equivalent to $y - 3 < -7$ or $y - 3 > 7$

Next, solve the compound inequality.

$$y - 3 < -7 \quad \text{or} \quad y - 3 > 7$$
$$y - 3 + 3 < -7 + 3 \quad \text{or} \quad y - 3 + 3 > 7 + 3 \quad \text{Add 3 to both sides.}$$
$$y < -4 \quad \text{or} \quad y > 10 \quad \text{Simplify.}$$

The solutions are all numbers x such that $y < -4$ or $y > 10$. The graph is shown.

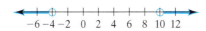

PRACTICE 5 Solve for y: $|y + 4| \geq 6$.

Examples 6 and 8 illustrate special cases of absolute value inequalities. These special cases occur when an isolated absolute value expression is less than, less than or equal to, greater than, or greater than or equal to a negative number or 0.

EXAMPLE 6 Solve: $|2x + 9| + 5 > 3$.

Solution First isolate the absolute value expression by subtracting 5 from both sides.

$$|2x + 9| + 5 > 3$$
$$|2x + 9| + 5 - 5 > 3 - 5 \quad \text{Subtract 5 from both sides.}$$
$$|2x + 9| > -2 \quad \text{Simplify.}$$

The absolute value of any number is always nonnegative and thus is always greater than -2. This inequality and the original inequality are true for all values of x. The solutions are all real numbers. The graph is shown.

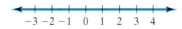

PRACTICE 6 Solve: $|4x + 3| + 5 > 3$. Graph the solutions.

Answer to Concept Check:
All real numbers are solutions since the absolute value is always nonnegative

Concept Check ✓

Without taking any solution steps, how do you know that the absolute value inequality $|3x - 2| > -9$ has a solution? What is its solution?

EXAMPLE 7 Solve: $\left|\dfrac{x}{3} - 1\right| - 7 \geq -5$.

Solution First, isolate the absolute value expression by adding 7 to both sides.

$$\left|\dfrac{x}{3} - 1\right| - 7 \geq -5$$

$$\left|\dfrac{x}{3} - 1\right| - 7 + 7 \geq -5 + 7 \quad \text{Add 7 to both sides.}$$

$$\left|\dfrac{x}{3} - 1\right| \geq 2 \quad \text{Simplify.}$$

Next, write the absolute value inequality as an equivalent compound inequality and solve.

$$\dfrac{x}{3} - 1 \leq -2 \quad \text{or} \quad \dfrac{x}{3} - 1 \geq 2$$

$$3\left(\dfrac{x}{3} - 1\right) \leq 3(-2) \quad \text{or} \quad 3\left(\dfrac{x}{3} - 1\right) \geq 3(2) \quad \text{Clear the inequalities of fractions.}$$

$$x - 3 \leq -6 \quad \text{or} \quad x - 3 \geq 6 \quad \text{Apply the distributive property.}$$

$$x \leq -3 \quad \text{or} \quad x \geq 9 \quad \text{Add 3 to both sides.}$$

The solutions are $x \leq -3$ or $x \geq 9$, and the graph is shown.

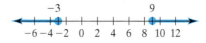

PRACTICE 7 Solve: $\left|\dfrac{x}{2} - 3\right| - 5 > -2$. Graph the solutions.

EXAMPLE 8 Solve for x: $\left|\dfrac{2(x + 1)}{3}\right| \leq 0$.

Solution Recall that "$\leq$" means "less than or equal to." The absolute value of any expression will never be less than 0, but it may be equal to 0. Thus, to solve $\left|\dfrac{2(x + 1)}{3}\right| \leq 0$ we solve $\left|\dfrac{2(x + 1)}{3}\right| = 0$

$$\dfrac{2(x + 1)}{3} = 0$$

$$3\left[\dfrac{2(x + 1)}{3}\right] = 3(0) \quad \text{Clear the equation of fractions.}$$

$$2x + 2 = 0 \quad \text{Apply the distributive property.}$$

$$2x = -2 \quad \text{Subtract 2 from both sides.}$$

$$x = -1 \quad \text{Divide both sides by 2.}$$

The solution is -1.

PRACTICE 8 Solve for x: $\left|\dfrac{3(x - 2)}{5}\right| \leq 0$.

The following box summarizes the types of absolute value equations and inequalities.

Solving Absolute Value Equations and Inequalities with $a > 0$

Algebraic Solution	Solution Graph
$\|X\| = a$ is equivalent to $X = a$ or $X = -a$.	
$\|X\| < a$ is equivalent to $-a < X < a$.	
$\|X\| > a$ is equivalent to $X < -a$ or $X > a$.	

VOCABULARY & READINESS CHECK

Matching. *Match each absolute value statement with an equivalent statement.*

1. $|2x + 1| = 3$
2. $|2x + 1| \leq 3$
3. $|2x + 1| < 3$
4. $|2x + 1| \geq 3$
5. $|2x + 1| > 3$

A. $2x + 1 > 3$ or $2x + 1 < -3$
B. $2x + 1 \geq 3$ or $2x + 1 \leq -3$
C. $-3 < 2x + 1 < 3$
D. $2x + 1 = 3$ or $2x + 1 = -3$
E. $-3 \leq 2x + 1 \leq 3$

2.7 EXERCISE SET

Solve each inequality. Then graph the solutions. See Examples 1 through 4.

1. $|x| \leq 4$
2. $|x| < 6$
3. $|x - 3| < 2$
4. $|y - 7| \leq 5$
5. $|x + 3| < 2$
6. $|x + 4| < 6$
7. $|2x + 7| \leq 13$
8. $|5x - 3| \leq 18$
9. $|x| + 7 \leq 12$
10. $|x| + 6 \leq 7$
11. $|3x - 1| < -5$
12. $|8x - 3| < -2$
13. $|x - 6| - 7 < -1$
14. $|z + 2| - 7 < -3$

Solve each inequality. Graph the solutions. See Examples 5 through 7.

15. $|x| > 3$
16. $|y| \geq 4$
17. $|x + 10| \geq 14$
18. $|x - 9| \geq 2$
19. $|x| + 2 > 6$
20. $|x| - 1 > 3$
21. $|5x| > -4$
22. $|4x - 11| > -1$
23. $|6x - 8| + 3 > 7$
24. $|10 + 3x| + 1 > 2$

Solve each inequality. Graph the solutions. See Example 8.

25. $|x| \leq 0$
26. $|x| \geq 0$
27. $|8x + 3| > 0$
28. $|5x - 6| < 0$

MIXED PRACTICE

Solve each inequality. Graph the solutions. See Examples 1 through 8.

29. $|x| \leq 2$
30. $|z| < 8$
31. $|y| > 1$
32. $|x| \geq 10$
33. $|x - 3| < 8$
34. $|-3 + x| \leq 10$
35. $|0.6x - 3| > 0.6$
36. $|1 + 0.3x| \geq 0.1$
37. $5 + |x| \leq 2$
38. $8 + |x| < 1$
39. $|x| > -4$
40. $|x| \leq -7$
41. $|2x - 7| \leq 11$
42. $|5x + 2| < 8$
43. $|x + 5| + 2 \geq 8$
44. $|-1 + x| - 6 > 2$
45. $|x| > 0$
46. $|x| < 0$
47. $9 + |x| > 7$
48. $5 + |x| \geq 4$
49. $6 + |4x - 1| \leq 9$
50. $-3 + |5x - 2| \leq 4$
51. $\left|\dfrac{2}{3}x + 1\right| > 1$
52. $\left|\dfrac{3}{4}x - 1\right| \geq 2$
53. $|5x + 3| < -6$
54. $|4 + 9x| \geq -6$
55. $\left|\dfrac{8x - 3}{4}\right| \leq 0$
56. $\left|\dfrac{5x + 6}{2}\right| \leq 0$
57. $|1 + 3x| + 4 < 5$
58. $|7x - 3| - 1 \leq 10$
59. $\left|\dfrac{x + 6}{3}\right| > 2$
60. $\left|\dfrac{7 + x}{2}\right| \geq 4$
61. $-15 + |2x - 7| \leq -6$

62. $-9 + |3 + 4x| < -4$
63. $\left|2x + \dfrac{3}{4}\right| - 7 \le -2$
64. $\left|\dfrac{3}{5} + 4x\right| - 6 < -1$

MIXED PRACTICE

Solve each equation or inequality for x. (Sections 2.6, 2.7)

65. $|2x - 3| < 7$
66. $|2x - 3| > 7$
67. $|2x - 3| = 7$
68. $|5 - 6x| = 29$
69. $|x - 5| \ge 12$
70. $|x + 4| \ge 20$
71. $|9 + 4x| = 0$
72. $|9 + 4x| \ge 0$
73. $|2x + 1| + 4 < 7$
74. $8 + |5x - 3| \ge 11$
75. $|3x - 5| + 4 = 5$
76. $|5x - 3| + 2 = 4$
77. $|x + 11| = -1$
78. $|4x - 4| = -3$
79. $\left|\dfrac{2x - 1}{3}\right| = 6$
80. $\left|\dfrac{6 - x}{4}\right| = 5$
81. $\left|\dfrac{3x - 5}{6}\right| > 5$
82. $\left|\dfrac{4x - 7}{5}\right| < 2$

REVIEW AND PREVIEW

Recall the formula:

$$\text{Probability of an event} = \dfrac{\text{number of ways that the event can occur}}{\text{number of possible outcomes}}$$

Find the probability of rolling each number on a single toss of a die. (Recall that a die is a cube with each of its six sides containing 1, 2, 3, 4, 5, and 6 black dots, respectively.) See Section 2.3.

83. $P(\text{rolling a 2})$
84. $P(\text{rolling a 5})$
85. $P(\text{rolling a 7})$
86. $P(\text{rolling a 0})$
87. $P(\text{rolling a 1 or 3})$
88. $P(\text{rolling a 1, 2, 3, 4, 5, or 6})$

Consider the equation $3x - 4y = 12$. For each value of x or y given, find the corresponding value of the other variable that makes the statement true. See Section 2.3.

89. If $x = 2$, find y
90. If $y = -1$, find x
91. If $y = -3$, find x
92. If $x = 4$, find y

CONCEPT EXTENSIONS

93. Write an absolute value inequality representing all numbers x whose distance from 0 is less than 7 units.
94. Write an absolute value inequality representing all numbers x whose distance from 0 is greater than 4 units.
95. Write $-5 \le x \le 5$ as an equivalent inequality containing an absolute value.
96. Write $x > 1$ or $x < -1$ as an equivalent inequality containing an absolute value.
97. Describe how solving $|x - 3| = 5$ is different from solving $|x - 3| < 5$.
98. Describe how solving $|x + 4| = 0$ is similar to solving $|x + 4| \le 0$.

The expression $|x_T - x|$ is defined to be the absolute error in x, where x_T is the true value of a quantity and x is the measured value or value as stored in a computer.

99. If the true value of a quantity is 3.5 and the absolute error must be less than 0.05, find the acceptable measured values.
100. If the true value of a quantity is 0.2 and the approximate value stored in a computer is $\dfrac{51}{256}$, find the absolute error.

CHAPTER 2 VOCABULARY CHECK

Fill in each blank with one of the words or phrases listed below.

contradiction   linear inequality in one variable   compound inequality   solution
absolute value   consecutive integers   identity   union
formula   linear equation in one variable   intersection

1. The statement "$x < 5$ or $x > 7$" is called a(n) _____.
2. An equation in one variable that has no solution is called a(n) _____.
3. The _____ of two sets is the set of all elements common to both sets.
4. The _____ of two sets is the set of all elements that belong to either of the sets.
5. An equation in one variable that has every number (for which the equation is defined) as a solution is called a(n) _____.

6. The equation $d = rt$ is also called a(n) _____.
7. A number's distance from 0 is called its _____.
8. When a variable in an equation is replaced by a number and the resulting equation is true, then that number is called a(n) _____ of the equation.
9. The integers 17, 18, 19 are examples of _____.
10. The statement $5x - 0.2 < 7$ is an example of a(n) _____.
11. The statement $5x - 0.2 = 7$ is an example of a(n) _____.

CHAPTER 2 REVIEW

(2.1) Solve each linear equation.

1. $4(x - 5) = 2x - 14$
2. $x + 7 = -2(x + 8)$
3. $3(2y - 1) = -8(6 + y)$
4. $-(z + 12) = 5(2z - 1)$
5. $n - (8 + 4n) = 2(3n - 4)$
6. $4(9v + 2) = 6(1 + 6v) - 10$
7. $0.3(x - 2) = 1.2$
8. $1.5 = 0.2(c - 0.3)$
9. $-4(2 - 3x) = 2(3x - 4) + 6x$
10. $6(m - 1) + 3(2 - m) = 0$
11. $6 - 3(2g + 4) - 4g = 5(1 - 2g)$
12. $20 - 5(p + 1) + 3p = -(2p - 15)$
13. $\dfrac{x}{3} - 4 = x - 2$
14. $\dfrac{9}{4}y = \dfrac{2}{3}y$
15. $\dfrac{3n}{8} - 1 = 3 + \dfrac{n}{6}$
16. $\dfrac{z}{6} + 1 = \dfrac{z}{2} + 2$
17. $\dfrac{y}{4} - \dfrac{y}{2} = -8$
18. $\dfrac{2x}{3} - \dfrac{8}{3} = x$
19. $\dfrac{b - 2}{3} = \dfrac{b + 2}{5}$
20. $\dfrac{2t - 1}{3} = \dfrac{3t + 2}{15}$
21. $\dfrac{2(t + 1)}{3} = \dfrac{2(t - 1)}{3}$
22. $\dfrac{3a - 3}{6} = \dfrac{4a + 1}{15} + 2$

(2.2) Solve.

23. Twice the difference of a number and 3 is the same as 1 added to three times the number. Find the number.
24. One number is 5 more than another number. If the sum of the numbers is 285, find the numbers.
25. Find 40% of 130.
26. Find 1.5% of 8.
27. In 2000, a record number of music CDs were sold by manufacturers in the United States. By 2005, this number had decreased to 705.4 million music CDs. If this represented a decrease of 25%, find the number of music CDs sold by U.S. manufacturers in 2000. (*Source:* Recording Industry Association of America.)
28. Find four consecutive integers such that twice the first subtracted from the sum of the other three integers is 16.
29. Determine whether there are two consecutive odd integers such that 5 times the first exceeds 3 times the second by 54.
30. The length of a rectangular playing field is 5 meters less than twice its width. If 230 meters of fencing goes around the field, find the dimensions of the field.

31. A car rental company charges $19.95 per day for a compact car plus 12 cents per mile for every mile over 100 miles driven per day. If Mr. Woo's bill for 2 days use is $46.86, find how many miles he drove.
32. The cost C of producing x number of scientific calculators is given by $C = 4.50x + 3000$ and the revenue R from selling them is given by $R = 16.50x$. Find the number of calculators that must be sold to break even. (Recall that to break even, revenue = cost.)

(2.3) Solve each equation for the specified variable.

△ 33. $V = LWH$ for W
△ 34. $C = 2\pi r$ for r
35. $5x - 4y = -12$ for y
36. $5x - 4y = -12$ for x
37. $y - y_1 = m(x - x_1)$ for m
38. $y - y_1 = m(x - x_1)$ for x
39. $E = I(R + r)$ for r
40. $S = vt + gt^2$ for g
41. $T = gr + gvt$ for g
42. $I = Prt + P$ for P

43. A principal of $3000 is invested in an account paying an annual percentage rate of 3%. Find the amount (to the nearest cent) in the account after 7 years if the amount is compounded
   a. semiannually.
   b. weekly.

44. The high temperature in Slidell, Louisiana, one day was 90° Fahrenheit. Convert this temperature to degrees Celsius.

△ 45. Angie Applegate has a photograph for which the length is 2 inches longer than the width. If she increases each dimension by 4 inches, the area is increased by 88 square inches. Find the original dimensions.

△ 46. One-square-foot floor tiles come 24 to a package. Find how many packages are needed to cover a rectangular floor 18 feet by 21 feet.

(2.4) Solve each linear inequality.

47. $3(x - 5) > -(x + 3)$
48. $-2(x + 7) \geq 3(x + 2)$
49. $4x - (5 + 2x) < 3x - 1$
50. $3(x - 8) < 7x + 2(5 - x)$
51. $24 \geq 6x - 2(3x - 5) + 2x$
52. $\dfrac{x}{3} + \dfrac{1}{2} > \dfrac{2}{3}$
53. $x + \dfrac{3}{4} < -\dfrac{x}{2} + \dfrac{9}{4}$
54. $\dfrac{x - 5}{2} \leq \dfrac{3}{8}(2x + 6)$

Solve.

55. George Boros can pay his housekeeper $15 per week to do his laundry, or he can have the laundromat do it at a cost of 50 cents per pound for the first 10 pounds and 40 cents for each additional pound. Use an inequality to find the weight at which it is more economical to use the housekeeper than the laundromat.

56. Ceramic firing temperatures usually range from 500° to 1000° Fahrenheit. Use a compound inequality to convert this range to the Celsius scale. Round to the nearest degree.

57. In the Olympic gymnastics competition, Nana must average a score of 9.65 to win the silver medal. Seven of the eight judges have reported scores of 9.5, 9.7, 9.9, 9.7, 9.7, 9.6, and 9.5. Use an inequality to find the minimum score that Nana must receive from the last judge to win the silver medal.

58. Carol would like to pay cash for a car when she graduates from college and estimates that she can afford a car that costs between $4000 and $8000. She has saved $500 so far and plans to earn the rest of the money by working the next two summers. If Carol plans to save the same amount each summer, use a compound inequality to find the range of money she must save each summer to buy the car.

(2.5) Solve each inequality.

59. $1 \leq 4x - 7 \leq 3$
60. $-2 \leq 8 + 5x < -1$
61. $-3 < 4(2x - 1) < 12$
62. $-6 < x - (3 - 4x) < -3$
63. $\dfrac{1}{6} < \dfrac{4x - 3}{3} \leq \dfrac{4}{5}$
64. $x \leq 2$ and $x > -5$
65. $3x - 5 > 6$ or $-x < -5$

(2.6) Solve each absolute value equation.

66. $|x - 7| = 9$
67. $|8 - x| = 3$
68. $|2x + 9| = 9$
69. $|-3x + 4| = 7$
70. $|3x - 2| + 6 = 10$
71. $5 + |6x + 1| = 5$
72. $-5 = |4x - 3|$
73. $|5 - 6x| + 8 = 3$
74. $-8 = |x - 3| - 10$
75. $\left|\dfrac{3x - 7}{4}\right| = 2$
76. $|6x + 1| = |15 + 4x|$

(2.7) Solve each absolute value inequality. Graph the solutions.

77. $|5x - 1| < 9$
78. $|6 + 4x| \geq 10$
79. $|3x| - 8 > 1$
80. $9 + |5x| < 24$
81. $|6x - 5| \leq -1$
82. $\left|3x + \dfrac{2}{5}\right| \geq 4$
83. $\left|\dfrac{x}{3} + 6\right| - 8 > -5$
84. $\left|\dfrac{4(x - 1)}{7}\right| + 10 < 2$

MIXED REVIEW

Solve.

85. $\dfrac{x - 2}{5} + \dfrac{x + 2}{2} = \dfrac{x + 4}{3}$
86. $\dfrac{2z - 3}{4} - \dfrac{4 - z}{2} = \dfrac{z + 1}{3}$

87. China, the United States, and France are predicted to be the top tourist destinations by 2020. In this year, the United States is predicted to have 9 million more tourists than France, and China is predicted to have 44 million more tourists than France. If the total number of tourists predicted for these three countries is 332 million, find the number predicted for each country in 2020.

△ 88. $A = \dfrac{h}{2}(B + b)$ for B

△ 89. $V = \dfrac{1}{3}\pi r^2 h$ for h

△ 90. Determine which container holds more ice cream, an 8 inch × 5 inch × 3 inch box or a cylinder with radius of 3 inches and height of 6 inches.

91. Erasmos Gonzalez left Los Angeles at 11 a.m. and drove nonstop to San Diego, 130 miles away. If he arrived at 1:15 p.m., find his average speed, rounded to the nearest mile per hour.

Solve.

92. $48 + x \geq 5(2x + 4) - 2x$

93. $\dfrac{3(x - 2)}{5} > \dfrac{-5(x - 2)}{3}$

94. $0 \leq \dfrac{2(3x + 4)}{5} \leq 3$

95. $x \leq 2$ or $x > -5$

96. $-2x \leq 6$ and $-2x + 3 < -7$

97. $|7x| - 26 = -5$

98. $\left|\dfrac{9 - 2x}{5}\right| = -3$

99. $|x - 3| = |7 + 2x|$

100. $|6x - 5| \geq -1$

101. $\left|\dfrac{4x - 3}{5}\right| < 1$

CHAPTER 2 TEST

Remember to use the Chapter Test Prep Videos to see the fully worked-out solutions to any of the exercises you want to review.

Solve each equation.

1. $8x + 14 = 5x + 44$
2. $9(x + 2) = 5[11 - 2(2 - x) + 3]$
3. $3(y - 4) + y = 2(6 + 2y)$
4. $7n - 6 + n = 2(4n - 3)$
5. $\dfrac{7w}{4} + 5 = \dfrac{3w}{10} + 1$
6. $\dfrac{z + 7}{9} + 1 = \dfrac{2z + 1}{6}$
7. $|6x - 5| - 3 = -2$
8. $|8 - 2t| = -6$
9. $|2x - 3| = |4x + 5|$
10. $|x - 5| = |x + 2|$

Solve each equation for the specified variable.

11. $3x - 4y = 8$ for y
12. $S = gt^2 + gvt$ for g
13. $F = \dfrac{9}{5}C + 32$ for C

Solve each inequality.

14. $3(2x - 7) - 4x > -(x + 6)$
15. $\dfrac{3x - 2}{3} - \dfrac{5x + 1}{4} \geq 0$
16. $-3 < 2(x - 3) \leq 4$
17. $|3x + 1| > 5$
18. $|x - 5| - 4 < -2$
19. $x \geq 5$ and $x \geq 4$
20. $x \geq 5$ or $x \geq 4$
21. $-1 \leq \dfrac{2x - 5}{3} < 2$
22. $6x + 1 > 5x + 4$ or $1 - x > -4$
23. Find 12% of 80.
24. In 2014, the number of people employed as network systems and data communications analysts is expected to be 357,000 in the United States. This represents a 55% increase over the number of people employed in these fields in 2004. Find the number of network systems and data communications analysts employed in 2004. (*Source:* Bureau of Labor Statistics.)
25. A circular dog pen has a circumference of 78.5 feet. Approximate π by 3.14 and estimate how many hunting dogs could be safely kept in the pen if each dog needs at least 60 square feet of room.
26. The company that makes Photoray sunglasses figures that the cost C to make x number of sunglasses weekly is given by $C = 3910 + 2.8x$, and the weekly revenue R is given by $R = 7.4x$. Use an inequality to find the number of sunglasses that must be made and sold to make a profit. (Revenue must exceed cost in order to make a profit.)
27. Find the amount of money in an account after 10 years if a principal of $2500 is invested at 3.5% interest compounded quarterly. (Round to the nearest cent.)
28. The most populous city in the United States is New York, although it is only the third most populous city in the world. Tokyo is the most populous city in the world. Second place is held by Seoul, Korea. Seoul's population is 1.3 million more than New York's, and Tokyo's is 10.2 million less than twice the population of New York. If the sum of the populations of these three cities is 78.3 million, find the population of each city.

CHAPTER 2 STANDARDIZED TEST

Multiple Choice. *Choose the one alternative that best completes the statement or answers the question.*

Solve the equation.

1. $10x + 18 = 4x + 48$
   a. 8 b. -5 c. 5 d. -8

2. $-[8x + (7x + 9)] = 3 - (2x + 5)$
   a. -1 b. $\frac{1}{13}$ c. 7 d. $-\frac{7}{13}$

3. $6(x - 2) - 6 = 8x - 2(x - 7)$
   a. -20 b. no solution c. 8
   d. all real numbers

4. $12(x + 1) = 2(6x + 1) + 10$
   a. 0 b. no solution c. all real numbers
   d. 6

5. $\frac{7x}{10} + \frac{8}{5} = \frac{3x}{5}$
   a. 22 b. 16 c. -22 d. -16

6. $\frac{3x - 2}{9} + x = \frac{3x + 2}{3} + 3$
   a. $-\frac{11}{5}$ b. 7 c. $\frac{35}{3}$ d. $-\frac{31}{3}$

7. $|8x + 6| + 9 = 14$
   a. $\frac{1}{8}, \frac{11}{8}$ b. $-\frac{1}{8}, -\frac{11}{8}$ c. no solution
   d. $-\frac{1}{6}, -\frac{11}{6}$

8. $|8x + 3| + 14 = 8$
   a. $\frac{3}{8}, -\frac{9}{8}$ b. $-\frac{3}{8}, \frac{9}{8}$ c. $1, -3$ d. no solution

9. $|-7x + 8| = |7 - 5x|$
   a. $\frac{1}{2}, -\frac{5}{4}$ b. $\frac{1}{2}$ c. $\frac{1}{2}, \frac{5}{4}$ d. no solution

10. $|x + 2| = |4 - x|$
    a. no solution b. 1 c. -1 d. 2

Solve the equation for the specified variable.

11. $2x - 3y = 5$ for y
    a. $y = \frac{5 - 2x}{3}$ b. $y = 2x - 5$ c. $y = \frac{2x + 5}{3}$
    d. $y = \frac{2x - 5}{3}$

12. $F = pq^2 + prq$ for p
    a. $p = \frac{q^2 + rq}{F}$ b. $p = F - p - rq$ c. $p = \frac{F}{q^3 r}$
    d. $p = \frac{F}{q^2 + rq}$

13. $S = 2\pi rh + 2\pi r^2$ for h
    a. $h = \frac{S - 2\pi r^2}{2\pi r}$ b. $h = S - r$
    c. $h = 2\pi(S - r)$ d. $h = \frac{S}{2\pi r} - 1$

Solve the inequality.

14. $4(4x - 2) + 5 \leq 14x - 1$
    a. $x \leq 1$ b. $x \geq -1$ c. $x \leq 1$
    d. none of these

15. $\frac{5x + 1}{8} - \frac{1 + 3x}{4} \leq -\frac{1}{2}$
    a. $x \geq -3$ b. $x \geq 3$ c. $x \leq 3$
    d. none of these

16. $-1 \leq 4(x - 1) < 6$
    a. $\frac{3}{4} < x \leq \frac{5}{2}$ b. $\frac{3}{4} \leq x < \frac{5}{2}$
    c. $0 \leq x < \frac{7}{4}$ d. $0 < x \leq \frac{7}{4}$

17. $|2k + 3| \geq 2$
    a. $k \leq -\frac{5}{2}$ or $k \geq -\frac{1}{2}$ b. $-\frac{5}{2} < k < -\frac{1}{2}$
    c. $k \geq -\frac{1}{2}$ d. $-\frac{5}{2} \leq k \leq -\frac{1}{2}$

18. $|x - 8| + 5 \leq 14$
    a. $-1 < x < 17$ b. $-1 \leq x \leq 14$
    c. no solution d. $-1 \leq x \leq 17$

19. $x \leq 2$ and $x \leq -3$
    a. $-3 \leq x \leq 2$ b. $x \geq -3$ c. $x \leq -3$ or $x \geq 2$
    d. $x \leq -3$

20. $x < 3$ or $x < 8$
    a. $x < 8$ b. $x > 3$ c. $3 < x < 8$
    d. $x < 3$ or $x > 8$

21. $0 \leq \frac{2x + 3}{2} < 3$
    a. $-\frac{3}{2} < x < \frac{3}{2}$ b. $-\frac{3}{2} \leq x < \frac{3}{2}$
    c. $-\frac{3}{2} < x \leq \frac{3}{2}$ d. none of these

22. $-3x + 1 \geq 7$ or $4x + 3 \geq -13$
    a. $x \geq -4$ b. $x \geq -2$ c. all real numbers
    d. $-4 \leq x \leq -2$

Solve the problem.

23. Find 16% of 43.
    a. 688 b. 68.8 c. 6.88 d. 0.688

24. The population of a town increased by 60% in 5 years. If the population is currently 39,000, find the population of this town 5 years ago. (Round to the nearest whole number, if necessary.)

　a. 23,400　**b.** 15,600　**c.** 65,000　**d.** 24,375

25. You have a cylindrical cooking pot whose radius is 6 inches and whose height is 7 inches. How many full cans of soup will fit into the pot if each can holds 20 cubic inches of soup? (Use 3.14 as an approximation for π.)

　a. 39 cans of soup　**b.** 40 cans of soup

　c. 13 cans of soup　**d.** 12 cans of soup

26. The cost C to produce x number of tennis rackets is $C = 150 + 25x$. The tennis rackets are sold wholesale for $30 each, so revenue R is given by $R = 30x$. Find how many tennis rackets the manufacturer needs to produce and sell to break even.

　a. 30 tennis rackets　**b.** 25 tennis rackets

　c. 15 tennis rackets　**d.** 35 tennis rackets

27. A principal of $12,000 is invested in an account paying an annual interest rate of 12%. Use the formula $A = P\left(1 + \dfrac{r}{n}\right)^{nt}$ to find the amount in the account after 4 years if the account is compounded quarterly.

　a. $19,256.48　**b.** $18,695.61　**c.** $7256.48

　d. $18,882.23

28. The three most prominent buildings in a city, Washington Center, Lincoln Galleria, and Jefferson Square Tower, have a total height of 1800 feet. Find the height of each building if Jefferson Square Tower is three times as tall as Lincoln Galleria and Washington Center is 450 feet taller than Lincoln Galleria.

　a. Washington Center: 720 feet

　　Lincoln Galleria: 270 feet

　　Jefferson Square Tower: 810 feet

　b. Washington Center: 450 feet

　　Lincoln Galleria: 00 feet

　　Jefferson Square Tower: 1350 feet

　c. Washington Center: 00 feet

　　Lincoln Galleria: 00 feet

　　Jefferson Square Tower: 1800 feet

　d. Washington Center: 570 feet

　　Lincoln Galleria: 190 feet

　　Jefferson Square Tower: 1040 feet

CHAPTER

Graphs and Functions

- **3.1** Graphing Equations
- **3.2** Introduction to Functions
- **3.3** Graphing Linear Functions
- **3.4** The Slope of a Line
- **3.5** Equations of Lines

  Integrated Review—Linear Equations in Two Variables

- **3.6** Graphing Piecewise-Defined Functions and Shifting and Reflecting Graphs of Functions
- **3.7** Graphing Linear Inequalities

  Extension: Stretching and Compressing Graphs of Absolute Value Functions.

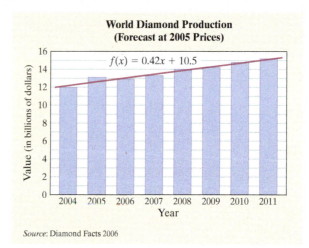

Source: Diamond Facts 2006

Over the past few years, strong consumer demand for diamonds has caused the industry to increase production. The function $f(x) = 0.42x + 10.5$ approximates the data above where $f(x)$ is world diamond production value (in billions of dollars) and where x is the number of years past 2000. In this chapter, we will use this linear equation to predict diamond production.

3.1 GRAPHING EQUATIONS

OBJECTIVES

1. Plot ordered pairs.
2. Determine whether an ordered pair of numbers is a solution to an equation in two variables.
3. Graph linear equations.
4. Graph nonlinear equations.

OBJECTIVE 1 ▶ Plotting ordered pairs. Graphs are widely used today in newspapers, magazines, and all forms of newsletters. A few examples of graphs are shown here.

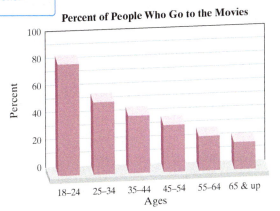

Source: TELENATION/Market Facts, Inc.

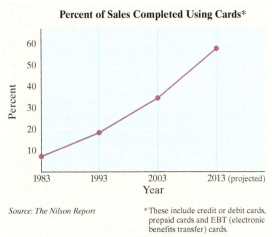

Source: The Nilson Report

*These include credit or debit cards, prepaid cards and EBT (electronic benefits transfer) cards.

To review how to read these graphs, we review their origin—the rectangular coordinate system. One way to locate points on a plane is by using a **rectangular coordinate system,** which is also called a **Cartesian coordinate system** after its inventor, René Descartes (1596–1650).

A rectangular coordinate system consists of two number lines that intersect at right angles at their 0 coordinates. We position these axes on paper such that one number line is horizontal and the other number line is then vertical. The horizontal number line is called the *x*-axis (or the axis of the **abscissa**), and the vertical number line is called the *y*-axis (or the axis of the **ordinate**). The point of intersection of these axes is named the **origin.**

Notice in the left figure below that the axes divide the plane into four regions. These regions are called **quadrants.** The top-right region is quadrant I. Quadrants II, III, and IV are numbered counterclockwise from the first quadrant as shown. The *x*-axis and the *y*-axis are not in any quadrant.

Each point in the plane can be located, or **plotted,** or graphed by describing its position in terms of distances along each axis from the origin. An **ordered pair,** represented by the notation (x, y), records these distances.

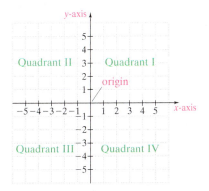
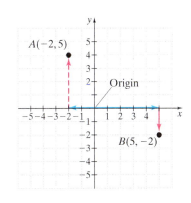

For example, the location of point A in the figure on the right on the previous page is described as 2 units to the left of the origin along the x-axis and 5 units upward parallel to the y-axis. Thus, we identify point A with the ordered pair (−2, 5). Notice that the order of these numbers is *critical*. The x-value −2 is called the **x-coordinate** and is associated with the x-axis. The y-value 5 is called the **y-coordinate** and is associated with the y-axis.

Compare the location of point A with the location of point B, which corresponds to the ordered pair (5, −2). Can you see that the order of the coordinates of an ordered pair matters? Also, two ordered pairs are considered equal and correspond to the same point if and only if their x-coordinates are equal and their y-coordinates are equal.

Keep in mind that **each ordered pair corresponds to exactly one point in the real plane and that each point in the plane corresponds to exactly one ordered pair.** Thus, we may refer to the ordered pair (x, y) as the point (x, y).

EXAMPLE 1 Plot each ordered pair on a Cartesian coordinate system and name the quadrant or axis in which the point is located.

a. $(2, -1)$ **b.** $(0, 5)$ **c.** $(-3, 5)$ **d.** $(-2, 0)$ **e.** $\left(-\frac{1}{2}, -4\right)$ **f.** $(1.5, 1.5)$

Solution The six points are graphed as shown.

a. $(2, -1)$ lies in quadrant IV.

b. $(0, 5)$ is on the y-axis.

c. $(-3, 5)$ lies in quadrant II.

d. $(-2, 0)$ is on the x-axis.

e. $\left(-\frac{1}{2}, -4\right)$ is in quadrant III.

f. $(1.5, 1.5)$ is in quadrant I.

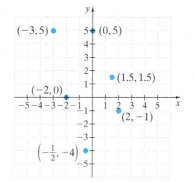

PRACTICE 1 Plot each ordered pair on a Cartesian coordinate system and name the quadrant or axis in which the point is located.

a. $(3, -4)$ **b.** $(0, -2)$ **c.** $(-2, 4)$ **d.** $(4, 0)$ **e.** $\left(-1\frac{1}{2}, -2\right)$ **f.** $(2.5, 3.5)$

Notice that the y-coordinate of any point on the x-axis is 0. For example, the point with coordinates (−2, 0) lies on the x-axis. Also, the x-coordinate of any point on the y-axis is 0. For example, the point with coordinates (0, 5) lies on the y-axis. These points that lie on the axes do not lie in any quadrants.

Concept Check ✓

Which of the following correctly describes the location of the point (3, −6) in a rectangular coordinate system?

a. 3 units to the left of the y-axis and 6 units above the x-axis

b. 3 units above the x-axis and 6 units to the left of the y-axis

c. 3 units to the right of the y-axis and 6 units below the x-axis

d. 3 units below the x-axis and 6 units to the right of the y-axis

Answer to Concept Check: c

Many types of real-world data occur in pairs. The graph below was shown at the beginning of this section. Notice the paired data (2013, 57) and the corresponding plotted point, both in blue.

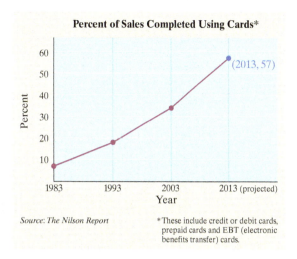

This paired data point, (2013, 57), means that in the year 2013, it is predicted that 57% of sales will be completed using some type of card (credit, debit, etc.).

OBJECTIVE 2 ▶ Determining whether an ordered pair is a solution. Solutions of equations in two variables consist of two numbers that form a true statement when substituted into the equation. A convenient notation for writing these numbers is as ordered pairs. A solution of an equation containing the variables x and y is written as a pair of numbers in the order (x, y). If the equation contains other variables, we will write ordered pair solutions in alphabetical order.

EXAMPLE 2 Determine whether $(0, -12)$, $(1, 9)$, and $(2, -6)$ are solutions of the equation $3x - y = 12$.

Solution To check each ordered pair, replace x with the x-coordinate and y with the y-coordinate and see whether a true statement results.

Let $x = 0$ and $y = -12$. Let $x = 1$ and $y = 9$. Let $x = 2$ and $y = -6$.
$$3x - y = 12$$
$$3(0) - (-12) \stackrel{?}{=} 12$$
$$0 + 12 \stackrel{?}{=} 12$$
$$12 = 12 \quad \text{True}$$

$$3x - y = 12$$
$$3(1) - 9 \stackrel{?}{=} 12$$
$$3 - 9 \stackrel{?}{=} 12$$
$$-6 = 12 \quad \text{False}$$

$$3x - y = 12$$
$$3(2) - (-6) \stackrel{?}{=} 12$$
$$6 + 6 \stackrel{?}{=} 12$$
$$12 = 12 \quad \text{True}$$

Thus, $(1, 9)$ is not a solution of $3x - y = 12$, but both $(0, -12)$ and $(2, -6)$ are solutions. □

PRACTICE 2 Determine whether $(1, 4)$, $(0, 6)$, and $(3, -4)$ are solutions of the equation $4x + y = 8$.

OBJECTIVE 3 ▶ Graphing linear equations. The equation $3x - y = 12$, from Example 2, actually has an infinite number of ordered pair solutions. Since it is impossible to list all solutions, we visualize them by graphing.

A few more ordered pairs that satisfy $3x - y = 12$ are $(4, 0)$, $(3, -3)$, $(5, 3)$, and $(1, -9)$. These ordered pair solutions along with the ordered pair solutions from Example 2 are plotted on the following graph. The graph of $3x - y = 12$ is the single line containing these points. Every ordered pair solution of the equation corresponds to a point on this line, and every point on this line corresponds to an ordered pair solution.

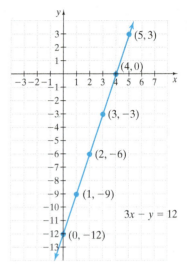

x	y	$3x - y = 12$
5	3	$3 \cdot 5 - 3 = 12$
4	0	$3 \cdot 4 - 0 = 12$
3	-3	$3 \cdot 3 - (-3) = 12$
2	-6	$3 \cdot 2 - (-6) = 12$
1	-9	$3 \cdot 1 - (-9) = 12$
0	-12	$3 \cdot 0 - (-12) = 12$

The equation $3x - y = 12$ is called a linear equation in two variables, and **the graph of every linear equation in two variables is a line.**

Linear Equation in Two Variables

A linear equation in two variables is an equation that can be written in the form

$$Ax + By = C$$

where A and B are not both 0. This form is called **standard form.**

Some examples of equations in standard form:

$$3x - y = 12$$
$$-2.1x + 5.6y = 0$$

> **Helpful Hint**
> Remember: A linear equation is written in standard form when all of the variable terms are on one side of the equation and the constant is on the other side.

Many real-life applications are modeled by linear equations. Suppose you have a part-time job at a store that sells office products.

Your pay is $3000 plus 20% or $\frac{1}{5}$ of the price of the products you sell. If we let *x* represent products sold and *y* represent monthly salary, the linear equation that models your salary is

$$y = 3000 + \frac{1}{5}x$$

(Although this equation is not written in standard form, it is a linear equation. To see this, subtract $\frac{1}{5}x$ from both sides.)

Some ordered pair solutions of this equation are below.

Products Sold	x	0	1000	2000	3000	4000	10,000
Monthly Salary	y	3000	3200	3400	3600	3800	5000

For example, we say that the ordered pair (1000, 3200) is a solution of the equation $y = 3000 + \frac{1}{5}x$ because when x is replaced with 1000 and y is replaced with 3200, a true statement results.

$$y = 3000 + \frac{1}{5}x$$

$$3200 \stackrel{?}{=} 3000 + \frac{1}{5}(1000) \quad \text{Let } x = 1000 \text{ and } y = 3200.$$

$$3200 \stackrel{?}{=} 3000 + 200$$

$$3200 = 3200 \quad \text{True}$$

A portion of the graph of $y = 3000 + \frac{1}{5}x$ is shown in the next example.

Since we assume that the smallest amount of product sold is none, or 0, then x must be greater than or equal to 0. Therefore, only the part of the graph that lies in Quadrant I is shown. Notice that the graph gives a visual picture of the correspondence between products sold and salary.

> **Helpful Hint**
> A line contains an infinite number of points and each point corresponds to an ordered pair that is a solution of its corresponding equation.

EXAMPLE 3 Use the graph of $y = 3000 + \frac{1}{5}x$ to answer the following questions.

a. If the salesperson has $8000 of products sold for a particular month, what is the salary for that month?

b. If the salesperson wants to make more than $5000 per month, what must be the total amount of products sold?

Solution

a. Since x is products sold, find 8000 along the x-axis and move vertically up until you reach a point on the line. From this point on the line, move horizontally to the left until you reach the y-axis. Its value on the y-axis is 4600, which means if $8000 worth of products is sold, the salary for the month is $4600.

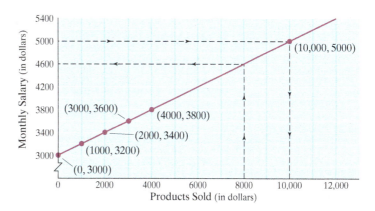

b. Since y is monthly salary, find 5000 along the y-axis and move horizontally to the right until you reach a point on the line. Either read the corresponding x-value from the labeled ordered pair, or move vertically downward until you reach the x-axis. The corresponding x-value is 10,000. This means that $10,000 worth of products sold gives a salary of $5000 for the month. For the salary to be greater than $5000, products sold must be greater than $10,000.

PRACTICE 3 Use the graph in Example 3 to answer the following questions.

a. If the salesperson has $6000 of products sold for a particular month, what is the salary for that month?

b. If the salesperson wants to make more than $4800 per month, what must be the total amount of products sold?

Recall from geometry that a line is determined by two points. This means that to graph a linear equation in two variables, just two solutions are needed. We will find a third solution, just to check our work. To find ordered pair solutions of linear equations in two variables, we can choose an *x*-value and find its corresponding *y*-value, or we can choose a *y*-value and find its corresponding *x*-value. The number 0 is often a convenient value to choose for *x* and also for *y*.

EXAMPLE 4 Graph the equation $y = -2x + 3$.

Solution This is a linear equation. (In standard form it is $2x + y = 3$.) Find three ordered pair solutions, and plot the ordered pairs. The line through the plotted points is the graph. Since the equation is solved for *y*, let's choose three *x*-values. We'll choose 0, 2, and then −1 for *x* to find our three ordered pair solutions.

Let $x = 0$	Let $x = 2$	Let $x = -1$
$y = -2x + 3$	$y = -2x + 3$	$y = -2x + 3$
$y = -2 \cdot 0 + 3$	$y = -2 \cdot 2 + 3$	$y = -2(-1) + 3$
$y = 3$ Simplify.	$y = -1$ Simplify.	$y = 5$ Simplify.

The three ordered pairs $(0, 3)$, $(2, -1)$ and $(-1, 5)$ are listed in the table and the graph is shown.

x	y
0	3
2	−1
−1	5

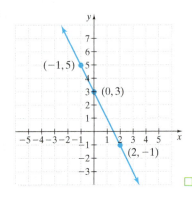

PRACTICE 4 Graph the equation $y = -3x - 2$.

Notice that the graph crosses the *y*-axis at the point $(0, 3)$. This point is called the **y-intercept.** (You may sometimes see just the number 3 called the *y*-intercept.) This graph also crosses the *x*-axis at the point $\left(\frac{3}{2}, 0\right)$. This point is called the **x-intercept.** (You may also see just the number $\frac{3}{2}$ called the *x*-intercept.)

Since every point on the *y*-axis has an *x*-value of 0, we can find the *y*-intercept of a graph by letting $x = 0$ and solving for *y*. Also, every point on the *x*-axis has a *y*-value of 0. To find the *x*-intercept, we let $y = 0$ and solve for *x*.

> **Finding x- and y-Intercepts**
>
> To find an *x*-intercept, let $y = 0$ and solve for *x*.
> To find a *y*-intercept, let $x = 0$ and solve for *y*.

We will study intercepts further in Section 3.3.

Section 3.1 Graphing Equations 115

EXAMPLE 5 Graph the linear equation $y = \frac{1}{3}x$.

Solution To graph, we find ordered pair solutions, plot the ordered pairs, and draw a line through the plotted points. We will choose x-values and substitute in the equation. To avoid fractions, we choose x-values that are multiples of 3. To find the y-intercept, we let $x = 0$.

> **Helpful Hint**
> Notice that by using multiples of 3 for x, we avoid fractions.

$$y = \frac{1}{3}x$$

If $x = 0$, then $y = \frac{1}{3}(0)$, or 0.

If $x = 6$, then $y = \frac{1}{3}(6)$, or 2.

If $x = -3$, then $y = \frac{1}{3}(-3)$, or -1.

x	y
0	0
6	2
-3	-1

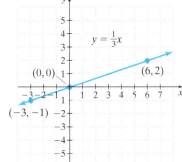

> **Helpful Hint**
> Since the equation $y = \frac{1}{3}x$ is solved for y, we choose x-values for finding points. This way, we simply need to evaluate an expression to find the y-value, as shown.

This graph crosses the x-axis at $(0, 0)$ and the y-axis at $(0, 0)$. This means that the x-intercept is $(0, 0)$ and that the y-intercept is $(0, 0)$.

PRACTICE 5 Graph the linear equation $y = -\frac{1}{2}x$.

OBJECTIVE 4 ▶ Graphing nonlinear equations. Not all equations in two variables are linear equations, and not all graphs of equations in two variables are lines.

EXAMPLE 6 Graph $y = x^2$.

Solution This equation is not linear because the x^2 term does not allow us to write it in the form $Ax + By = C$. Its graph is not a line. We begin by finding ordered pair solutions. Because this graph is solved for y, we choose x-values and find corresponding y-values.

If $x = -3$, then $y = (-3)^2$, or 9.
If $x = -2$, then $y = (-2)^2$, or 4.
If $x = -1$, then $y = (-1)^2$, or 1.
If $x = 0$, then $y = 0^2$, or 0.
If $x = 1$, then $y = 1^2$, or 1.
If $x = 2$, then $y = 2^2$, or 4.
If $x = 3$, then $y = 3^2$, or 9.

x	y
-3	9
-2	4
-1	1
0	0
1	1
2	4
3	9

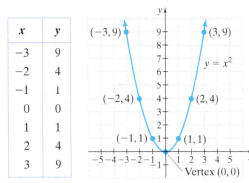

Study the table a moment and look for patterns. Notice that the ordered pair solution $(0, 0)$ contains the smallest y-value because any other x-value squared will give a positive result. This means that the point $(0, 0)$ will be the lowest point on the graph. Also notice that all other y-values correspond to two different x-values. For example, $3^2 = 9$ and also $(-3)^2 = 9$. This means that the graph will be a mirror image of itself across the y-axis. Connect the plotted points with a smooth curve to sketch the graph.

This curve is given a special name, a parabola. We will study more about parabolas in later chapters.

PRACTICE 6 Graph $y = 2x^2$.

EXAMPLE 7 Graph the equation $y = |x|$.

Solution This is not a linear equation since it cannot be written in the form $Ax + By = C$. Its graph is not a line. Because we do not know the shape of this graph, we find many ordered pair solutions. We will choose x-values and substitute to find corresponding y-values.

If $x = -3$, then $y = |-3|$, or 3.
If $x = -2$, then $y = |-2|$, or 2.
If $x = -1$, then $y = |-1|$, or 1.
If $x = 0$, then $y = |0|$, or 0.
If $x = 1$, then $y = |1|$, or 1.
If $x = 2$, then $y = |2|$, or 2.
If $x = 3$, then $y = |3|$, or 3.

x	y
-3	3
-2	2
-1	1
0	0
1	1
2	2
3	3

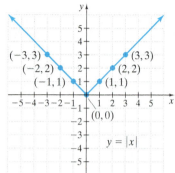

Again, study the table of values for a moment and notice any patterns.
From the plotted ordered pairs, we see that the graph of this absolute value equation is V-shaped.

PRACTICE 7 Graph $y = -|x|$.

Graphing Calculator Explorations

In this section, we begin a study of graphing calculators and graphing software packages for computers. These graphers use the same point plotting technique that we introduced in this section. The advantage of this graphing technology is, of course, that graphing calculators and computers can find and plot ordered pair solutions much faster than we can. Note, however, that the features described in these boxes may not be available on all graphing calculators.

The rectangular screen where a portion of the rectangular coordinate system is displayed is called a **window**. We call it a **standard window** for graphing when both the x- and y-axes display coordinates between -10 and 10. This information is often displayed in the window menu on a graphing calculator as

Xmin = -10
Xmax = 10
  Xscl = 1 The scale on the x-axis is one unit per tick mark.
Ymin = -10
Ymax = 10
  Yscl = 1 The scale on the y-axis is one unit per tick mark.

To use a graphing calculator to graph the equation $y = -5x + 4$, press the $\boxed{Y=}$ key and enter the keystrokes

↑

(Check your owner's manual to make sure the "negative" key is pressed here and not the "subtraction" key.)

The top row should now read $Y_1 = -5x + 4$. Next press the GRAPH key, and the display should look like this:

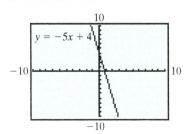

Use a standard window and graph the following equations. (Unless otherwise stated, we will use a standard window when graphing.)

1. $y = -3.2x + 7.9$
2. $y = -x + 5.85$
3. $y = \frac{1}{4}x - \frac{2}{3}$
4. $y = \frac{2}{3}x - \frac{1}{5}$
5. $y = |x - 3| + 2$
6. $y = |x + 1| - 1$
7. $y = x^2 + 3$
8. $y = (x + 3)^2$

VOCABULARY & READINESS CHECK

Read a Graph. *Determine the coordinates of each point on the graph.*

1. Point A
2. Point B
3. Point C
4. Point D
5. Point E
6. Point F
7. Point G
8. Point H

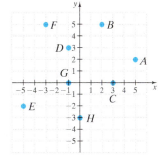

Decision Making. *Without graphing, visualize the location of each point. Then give its location by quadrant or x- or y-axis.*

9. $(2, 3)$
10. $(0, 5)$
11. $(-2, 7)$
12. $(-3, 0)$
13. $(-1, -4)$
14. $(4, -2)$
15. $(0, -100)$
16. $(10, 30)$
17. $(-10, -30)$
18. $(0, 0)$
19. $(-87, 0)$
20. $(-42, 17)$

3.1 EXERCISE SET

Plot each point and name the quadrant or axis in which the point lies. See Example 1.

1. $(3, 2)$
2. $(2, -1)$
3. $(-5, 3)$
4. $(-3, -1)$
5. $\left(5\frac{1}{2}, -4\right)$
6. $\left(-2, 6\frac{1}{3}\right)$
7. $(0, 3.5)$
8. $(-5.2, 0)$
9. $(-2, -4)$
10. $(-4.2, 0)$

Given that x is a positive number and that y is a positive number, determine the quadrant or axis in which each point lies. See Example 1.

11. $(x, -y)$
12. $(-x, y)$
13. $(x, 0)$
14. $(0, -y)$
15. $(-x, -y)$
16. $(0, 0)$

Determine whether each ordered pair is a solution of the given equation. See Example 2.

17. $y = 3x - 5; (0, 5), (-1, -8)$
18. $y = -2x + 7; (1, 5), (-2, 3)$
19. $-6x + 5y = -6; (1, 0), \left(2, \dfrac{6}{5}\right)$
20. $5x - 3y = 9; (0, 3), \left(\dfrac{12}{5}, -1\right)$
21. $y = 2x^2; (1, 2), (3, 18)$
22. $y = 2|x|; (-1, 2), (0, 2)$
23. $y = x^3; (2, 8), (3, 9)$
24. $y = x^4; (-1, 1), (2, 16)$
25. $y = \sqrt{x} + 2; (1, 3), (4, 4)$
26. $y = \sqrt[3]{x} - 4; (1, -3), (8, 6)$

MIXED PRACTICE

Determine whether each equation is linear or not. Then graph the equation by finding and plotting ordered-pair solutions. See Examples 3 through 7.

27. $x + y = 3$
28. $y - x = 8$
29. $y = 4x$
30. $y = 6x$
31. $y = 4x - 2$
32. $y = 6x - 5$
33. $y = |x| + 3$
34. $y = |x| + 2$
35. $2x - y = 5$
36. $4x - y = 7$
37. $y = 2x^2$
38. $y = 3x^2$
39. $y = x^2 - 3$
40. $y = x^2 + 3$
41. $y = -2x$
42. $y = -3x$
43. $y = -2x + 3$
44. $y = -3x + 2$
45. $y = |x + 2|$
46. $y = |x - 1|$
47. $y = x^3$
    (*Hint:* Let $x = -3, -2, -1, 0, 1, 2$.)
48. $y = x^3 - 2$
    (*Hint:* Let $x = -3, -2, -1, 0, 1, 2$.)
49. $y = -|x|$
50. $y = -x^2$
51. $y = \dfrac{1}{3}x - 1$
52. $y = \dfrac{1}{2}x - 3$
53. $y = -\dfrac{3}{2}x + 1$
54. $y = -\dfrac{2}{3}x + 1$

REVIEW AND PREVIEW

Solve the following equations. See Section 2.1.

55. $3(x - 2) + 5x = 6x - 16$
56. $5 + 7(x + 1) = 12 + 10x$
57. $3x + \dfrac{2}{5} = \dfrac{1}{10}$
58. $\dfrac{1}{6} + 2x = \dfrac{2}{3}$

Solve the following inequalities. See Section 2.4.

59. $3x \le -15$
60. $-3x > 18$
61. $2x - 5 > 4x + 3$
62. $9x + 8 \le 6x - 4$

CONCEPT EXTENSIONS

Multiple Choice. *See the Concept Check in this section.*

63. Which correctly describes the location of the point $(-1, 5.3)$ in a rectangular coordinate system?
    a. 1 unit to the right of the y-axis and 5.3 units above the x-axis
    b. 1 unit to the left of the y-axis and 5.3 units above the x-axis
    c. 1 unit to the left of the y-axis and 5.3 units below the x-axis
    d. 1 unit to the right of the y-axis and 5.3 units below the x-axis

64. Which correctly describes the location of the point $\left(0, -\dfrac{3}{4}\right)$ in a rectangular coordinate system?
    a. on the x-axis and $\dfrac{3}{4}$ unit to the left of the y-axis
    b. on the x-axis and $\dfrac{3}{4}$ unit to the right of the y-axis
    c. on the y-axis and $\dfrac{3}{4}$ unit above the x-axis
    d. on the y-axis and $\dfrac{3}{4}$ unit below the x-axis

Matching. *For Exercises 65 through 68, match each description with the graph that best illustrates it.*

65. Moe worked 40 hours per week until the fall semester started. He quit and didn't work again until he worked 60 hours a week during the holiday season starting mid-December.

66. Kawana worked 40 hours a week for her father during the summer. She slowly cut back her hours to not working at all during the fall semester. During the holiday season in December, she started working again and increased her hours to 60 hours per week.

67. Wendy worked from July through February, never quitting. She worked between 10 and 30 hours per week.

68. Bartholomew worked from July through February. The rest of the time, he worked between 10 and 40 hours per week. During the holiday season between mid-November and the beginning of January, he worked 40 hours per week.

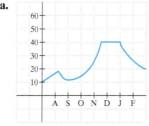
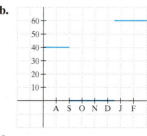
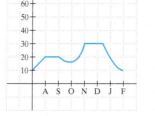
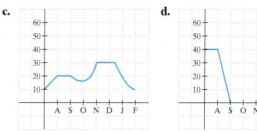

Read a Graph. *The graph below shows first-class postal rates and the years it increased. Use this graph for Exercises 69 through 72.*

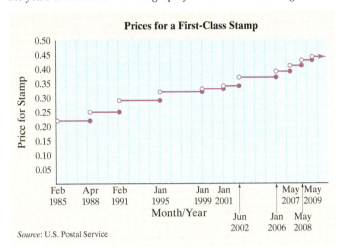

Source: U.S. Postal Service

69. What was the first year that the price for a first-class stamp rose above $0.25?

70. What was the first year that the price for a first-class stamp rose above $0.30?

71. Why do you think that this graph is shaped the way it is?

72. The U.S. Postal Service issued first-class stamps as far back as 1885. The cost for a first-class stamp then was $0.02. By how much had it increased by 2007?

73. Graph $y = x^2 - 4x + 7$. Let $x = 0, 1, 2, 3, 4$ to generate ordered pair solutions.

74. Graph $y = x^2 + 2x + 3$. Let $x = -3, -2, -1, 0, 1$ to generate ordered pair solutions.

75. **Multiple Steps.** The perimeter y of a rectangle whose width is a constant 3 inches and whose length is x inches is given by the equation

$$y = 2x + 6$$

  a. Draw a graph of this equation.
  b. Read from the graph the perimeter y of a rectangle whose length x is 4 inches.

76. **Multiple Steps.** The distance y traveled in a train moving at a constant speed of 50 miles per hour is given by the equation

$$y = 50x$$

where x is the time in hours traveled.

  a. Draw a graph of this equation.
  b. Read from the graph the distance y traveled after 6 hours.

Read a Graph. *For income tax purposes, Jason Verges, owner of Copy Services, uses a method called* **straight-line depreciation** *to show the loss in value of a copy machine he recently purchased. Jason assumes that he can use the machine for 7 years. The following graph shows the value of the machine over the years. Use this graph to answer Exercises 77 through 82.*

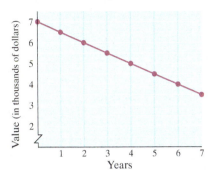

77. What was the purchase price of the copy machine?

78. What is the depreciated value of the machine in 7 years?

79. What loss in value occurred during the first year?

80. What loss in value occurred during the second year?

81. Why do you think that this method of depreciating is called straight-line depreciation?

82. Why is the line tilted downward?

83. On the same set of axes, graph $y = 2x$, $y = 2x - 5$, and $y = 2x + 5$. What patterns do you see in these graphs?

84. On the same set of axes, graph $y = 2x$, $y = x$, and $y = -2x$. Describe the differences and similarities in these graphs.

85. Explain why we generally use three points to graph a line, when only two points are needed.

Write each statement as an equation in two variables. Then graph each equation.

86. The y-value is 5 more than three times the x-value.

87. The y-value is -3 decreased by twice the x-value.

88. The y-value is 2 more than the square of the x-value.

89. The y-value is 5 decreased by the square of the x-value.

Use a graphing calculator to verify the graphs of the following exercises.

90. Exercise 39
91. Exercise 40
92. Exercise 47
93. Exercise 48

3.2 INTRODUCTION TO FUNCTIONS

OBJECTIVES

1. Define relation, domain, and range.
2. Identify functions.
3. Use the vertical line test for functions.
4. Find the domain and range of a function.
5. Use function notation.

OBJECTIVE 1 ▶ Defining relation, domain, and range. Recall our example from the last section about products sold and monthly salary. We modeled the data given by the equation $y = 3000 + \frac{1}{5}x$. This equation describes a relationship between x-values and y-values. For example, if $x = 1000$, then this equation describes how to find the y-value related to $x = 1000$. In words, the equation $y = 3000 + \frac{1}{5}x$ says that 3000 plus $\frac{1}{5}$ of the x-value gives the corresponding y-value. The x-value of 1000 corresponds to the y-value of $3000 + \frac{1}{5} \cdot 1000 = 3200$ for this equation, and we have the ordered pair (1000, 3200).

There are other ways of describing relations or correspondences between two numbers or, in general, a first set (sometimes called the set of *inputs*) and a second set (sometimes called the set of *outputs*). For example,

First Set: Input	— Correspondence →	Second Set: Output
People in a certain city	— Each person's age →	The set of nonnegative integers

A few examples of ordered pairs from this relation might be (Ana, 4); (Bob, 36); (Trey, 21); and so on.

Below are just a few other ways of describing relations between two sets and the ordered pairs that they generate.

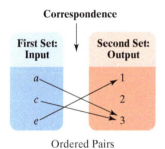

Ordered Pairs
$(a, 3), (c, 3), (e, 1)$

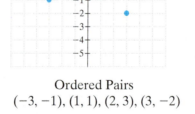

Ordered Pairs
$(-3, -1), (1, 1), (2, 3), (3, -2)$

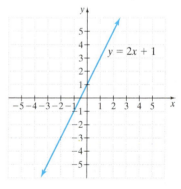

Some Ordered Pairs
$(1, 3), (0, 1)$, and so on

Relation, Domain, and Range

A **relation** is a set of ordered pairs.
The **domain** of the relation is the set of all first components of the ordered pairs.
The **range** of the relation is the set of all second components of the ordered pairs.

For example, the domain for our relation above is $\{a, c, e\}$ and the range is $\{1, 3\}$. Notice that the range does not include the element 2 of the second set. This is because no element of the first set is assigned to this element. If a relation is defined in terms of *x*- and *y*-values, we will agree that the domain corresponds to *x*-values and that the range corresponds to *y*-values that have *x*-values assigned to them.

> **Helpful Hint**
> Remember that the range only includes elements that are paired with domain values. For the correspondence below, the range is $\{a\}$.

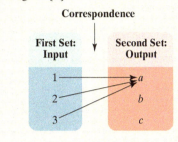

EXAMPLE 1 Determine the domain and range of each relation.

a. $\{(2, 3), (2, 4), (0, -1), (3, -1)\}$

b.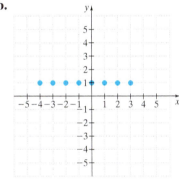

c.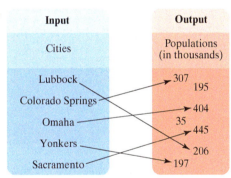

Solution

a. The domain is the set of all first coordinates of the ordered pairs, $\{2, 0, 3\}$. The range is the set of all second coordinates, $\{3, 4, -1\}$.

b. Ordered pairs are not listed here, but are given in graph form. The relation is $\{(-4, 1), (-3, 1), (-2, 1), (-1, 1), (0, 1), (1, 1), (2, 1), (3, 1)\}$. The domain is $\{-4, -3, -2, -1, 0, 1, 2, 3\}$. The range is $\{1\}$.

c. The domain is the set of inputs, {Lubbock, Colorado Springs, Omaha, Yonkers, Sacramento}. The range is the numbers in the set of outputs that correspond to elements in the set of inputs {307, 404, 445, 206, 197}.

> **Helpful Hint**
> Domain or range elements that occur more than once need only to be listed once.

PRACTICE 1 Determine the domain and range of each relation.

a. {(4, 1)(4, −3)(5, −2)(5, 6)}

b.

c.

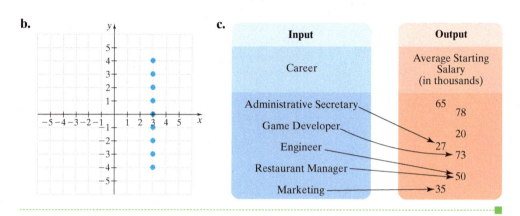

OBJECTIVE 2 ▶ Identifying functions.
Now we consider a special kind of relation called a function.

> **Function**
> A **function** is a relation in which each first component in the ordered pairs corresponds to *exactly* one second component.

> ▶ **Helpful Hint**
> A function is a special type of relation, so all functions are relations, but not all relations are functions.

EXAMPLE 2 Which of the following relations are also functions?

a. {(−2, 5), (2, 7), (−3, 5), (9, 9)}

b.

c. Input — People in a certain city Correspondence — Each person's age Output — The set of nonnegative integers

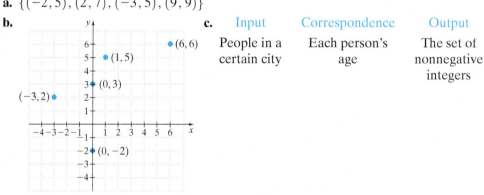

Solution

a. Although the ordered pairs (−2, 5) and (−3, 5) have the same *y*-value, each *x*-value is assigned to only one *y*-value, so this set of ordered pairs is a function.

b. The *x*-value 0 is assigned to two *y*-values, −2 and 3, in this graph so this relation does not define a function.

c. This relation is a function because although two different people may have the same age, each person has only one age. This means that each element in the first set is assigned to only one element in the second set.

PRACTICE
2 Which of the following relations are also functions?

a. $\{(3, 1), (-3, -4), (8, 5), (9, 1)\}$

b.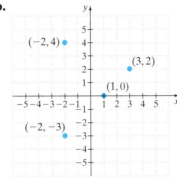

c.
Input	Correspondence	Output
People in a certain city	Birth date (day of month)	Set of nonnegative integers

Concept Check ✓

Explain why a function can contain both the ordered pairs $(1, 3)$ and $(2, 3)$ but not both $(3, 1)$ and $(3, 2)$.

We will call an equation such as $y = 2x + 1$ a **relation** since this equation defines a set of ordered pair solutions.

EXAMPLE 3 Is the relation $y = 2x + 1$ also a function?*

Solution The relation $y = 2x + 1$ is a function if each x-value corresponds to just one y-value. For each x-value substituted in the equation $y = 2x + 1$, the multiplication and addition performed on each gives a single result, so only one y-value will be associated with each x-value. Thus, $y = 2x + 1$ is a function.

*For further discussion including the graph, see Objective 3.

PRACTICE
3 Is the relation $y = -3x + 5$ also a function?

EXAMPLE 4 Is the relation $x = y^2$ also a function?*

Solution In $x = y^2$, if $y = 3$, then $x = 9$. Also, if $y = -3$, then $x = 9$. In other words, we have the ordered pairs $(9, 3)$ and $(9, -3)$. Since the x-value 9 corresponds to two y-values, 3 and -3, $x = y^2$ is not a function.

*For further discussion including the graph, see Objective 3.

PRACTICE
4 Is the relation $y = -x^2$ also a function?

Answer to Concept Check:
Two different ordered pairs can have the same y-value, but not the same x-value in a function.

OBJECTIVE 3 ▶ **Using the vertical line test.** As we have seen so far, not all relations are functions. Consider the graphs of $y = 2x + 1$ and $x = y^2$ shown next. For the graph of $y = 2x + 1$, notice that each x-value corresponds to only one y-value. Recall from Example 3 that $y = 2x + 1$ is a function.

124 CHAPTER 3 Graphs and Functions

Graph of Example 3:
$y = 2x + 1$

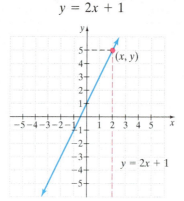

Graph of Example 4:
$x = y^2$

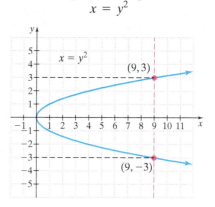

For the graph of $x = y^2$ the x-value 9, for example, corresponds to two y-values, 3 and -3, as shown by the vertical line. Recall from Example 4 that $x = y^2$ is not a function.

Graphs can be used to help determine whether a relation is also a function by the following vertical line test.

> **Vertical Line Test**
> If no vertical line can be drawn so that it intersects a graph more than once, the graph is the graph of a function.

EXAMPLE 5 Which of the following graphs are graphs of functions?

a.
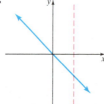

b.
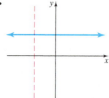

c.
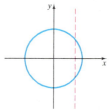

Solution

Yes, this is the graph of a function since no vertical line will intersect this graph more than once.

Yes, this is the graph of a function.

No, this is not the graph of a function. Note that vertical lines can be drawn that intersect the graph in two points.

d.
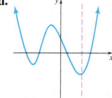

e.
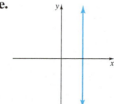

Solution

Yes, this is the graph of a function.

No, this is not the graph of a function. A vertical line can be drawn that intersects this line at every point.

Section 3.2 Introduction to Functions 125

PRACTICE
5 Which of the following graphs are graphs of functions?

a. 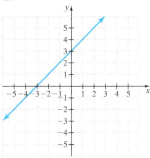 b. 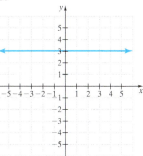 c.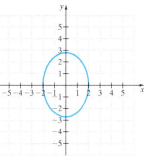

d. 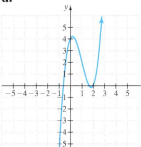 e.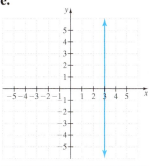

Recall that the graph of a linear equation in two variables is a line, and a line that is not vertical will pass the vertical line test. Thus, **all linear equations are functions except those whose graph is a vertical line.**

Concept Check ✓

Determine which equations represent functions. Explain your answer.

a. $y = |x|$ **b.** $y = x^2$ **c.** $x + y = 6$

OBJECTIVE 4 ▶ **Finding the domain and range of a function.** Next, we practice finding the domain and range of a relation from its graph.

EXAMPLE 6 Find the domain and range of each relation. Determine whether the relation is also a function.

a. 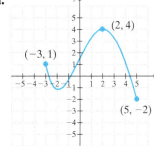 b.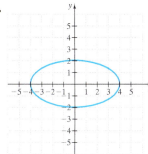

c. 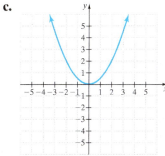 d.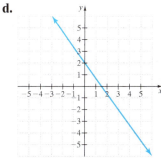

Answer to Concept Check: a, b, c

126 CHAPTER 3 Graphs and Functions

Solution By the vertical line test, graphs **a, c,** and **d** are graphs of functions. The domain is the set of values of x and the range is the set of values of y. We read these values from each graph.

> **Helpful Hint**
> In Example 6, Part **a**, notice that the graph contains the endpoints $(-3, 1)$ and $(5, -2)$ whereas the graphs in Parts **c** and **d** contain arrows that indicate that they continue forever.

a.

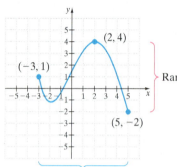

Range: The y-values graphed are from -2 to 4, or $-2 \leq y \leq 4$

Domain: The x-values graphed are from -3 to 5, or $-3 \leq x \leq 5$

b.

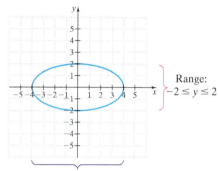

Range: $-2 \leq y \leq 2$

Domain: $-4 \leq x \leq 4$

c.

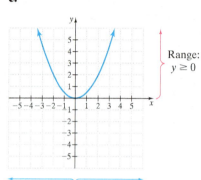

Range: $y \geq 0$

Domain: all real numbers

d.

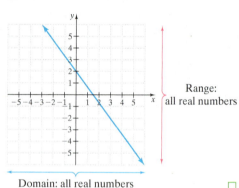

Range: all real numbers

Domain: all real numbers

PRACTICE 6 Find the domain and range of each relation. Determine whether each relation is also a function.

a.

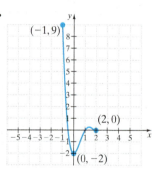

b.

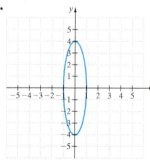

c.

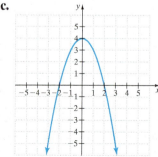

d.

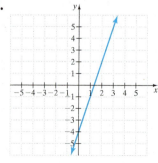

OBJECTIVE 5 ▶ Using function notation. Many times letters such as f, g, and h are used to name functions.

> **Function Notation**
>
> To denote that y is a function of x, we can write
>
> $$y = \underbrace{f(x)}_{\text{Function Notation}} \quad \text{(Read ``}f\text{ of }x\text{.'')}$$
>
> This notation means that **y is a function of x** or that y *depends on* x. For this reason, y is called the **dependent variable** and x the **independent variable.**

For example, to use function notation with the function $y = 4x + 3$, we write $f(x) = 4x + 3$. The notation $f(1)$ means to replace x with 1 and find the resulting y or function value. Since

$$f(x) = 4x + 3$$

then

$$f(1) = 4(1) + 3 = 7$$

This means that when $x = 1$, y or $f(x) = 7$. The corresponding ordered pair is $(1, 7)$. Here, the input is 1 and the output is $f(1)$ or 7. Now let's find $f(2)$, $f(0)$, and $f(-1)$.

$$\begin{aligned} f(x) &= 4x + 3 \\ f(2) &= 4(2) + 3 \\ &= 8 + 3 \\ &= 11 \end{aligned} \qquad \begin{aligned} f(x) &= 4x + 3 \\ f(0) &= 4(0) + 3 \\ &= 0 + 3 \\ &= 3 \end{aligned} \qquad \begin{aligned} f(x) &= 4(x) + 3 \\ f(-1) &= 4(-1) + 3 \\ &= -4 + 3 \\ &= -1 \end{aligned}$$

Ordered Pairs:

$(2, 11)$ $\qquad\qquad (0, 3) \qquad\qquad (-1, -1)$

> ▶ **Helpful Hint**
> Make sure you remember that $f(2) = 11$ corresponds to the ordered pair $(2, 11)$.

> ▶ **Helpful Hint**
> Note that $f(x)$ is a special symbol in mathematics used to denote a function. The symbol $f(x)$ is read "f of x." It does *not* mean $f \cdot x$ (f times x).

EXAMPLE 7 If $f(x) = 7x^2 - 3x + 1$ and $g(x) = 3x - 2$, find the following.

a. $f(1)$ **b.** $g(1)$ **c.** $f(-2)$ **d.** $g(0)$

Solution

a. Substitute 1 for x in $f(x) = 7x^2 - 3x + 1$ and simplify.

$f(x) = 7x^2 - 3x + 1$
$f(1) = 7(1)^2 - 3(1) + 1 = 5$

b. $g(x) = 3x - 2$
$g(1) = 3(1) - 2 = 1$

c. $f(x) = 7x^2 - 3x + 1$
$f(-2) = 7(-2)^2 - 3(-2) + 1 = 35$

d. $g(x) = 3x - 2$
$g(0) = 3(0) - 2 = -2$

PRACTICE 7 If $f(x) = 3x - 2$ and $g(x) = 5x^2 + 2x - 1$, find the following.

a. $f(1)$ **b.** $g(1)$ **c.** $f(0)$ **d.** $g(-2)$

128 CHAPTER 3 Graphs and Functions

Concept Check ✓

Suppose $y = f(x)$ and we are told that $f(3) = 9$. Which is not true?

a. When $x = 3$, $y = 9$.
b. A possible function is $f(x) = x^2$.
c. A point on the graph of the function is $(3, 9)$.
d. A possible function is $f(x) = 2x + 4$.

If it helps, think of a function, f, as a machine that has been programmed with a certain correspondence or rule. An input value (a member of the domain) is then fed into the machine, the machine does the correspondence or rule and the result is the output (a member of the range).

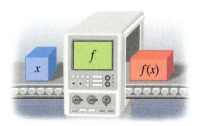 

EXAMPLE 8 Given the graphs of the functions f and g, find each function value by inspecting the graphs.

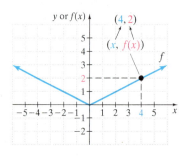 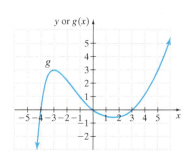

a. $f(4)$ b. $f(-2)$ c. $g(5)$ d. $g(0)$
e. Find all x-values such that $f(x) = 1$.
f. Find all x-values such that $g(x) = 0$.

Solution

a. To find $f(4)$, find the y-value when $x = 4$. We see from the graph that when $x = 4$, y or $f(x) = 2$. Thus, $f(4) = 2$.
b. $f(-2) = 1$ from the ordered pair $(-2, 1)$.
c. $g(5) = 3$ from the ordered pair $(5, 3)$.
d. $g(0) = 0$ from the ordered pair $(0, 0)$.
e. To find x-values such that $f(x) = 1$, we are looking for any ordered pairs on the graph of f whose $f(x)$ or y-value is 1. They are $(2, 1)$ and $(-2, 1)$. Thus $f(2) = 1$ and $f(-2) = 1$. The x-values are 2 and -2.
f. Find ordered pairs on the graph of g whose $g(x)$ or y-value is 0. They are $(3, 0)$ $(0, 0)$ and $(-4, 0)$. Thus $g(3) = 0$, $g(0) = 0$, and $g(-4) = 0$. The x-values are 3, 0, and -4.

Answer to Concept Check: d

PRACTICE 8 Given the graphs of the functions f and g, find each function value by inspecting the graphs.

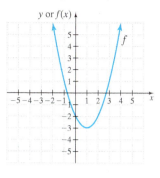
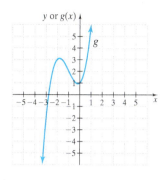

a. $f(1)$ **b.** $f(0)$ **c.** $g(-2)$ **d.** $g(0)$

e. Find all x-values such that $f(x) = 1$.

f. Find all x-values such that $g(x) = -2$.

Many types of real-world paired data form functions. The broken-line graph below shows the research and development spending by the Pharmaceutical Manufacturers Association.

EXAMPLE 9 The following graph shows the research and development expenditures by the Pharmaceutical Manufacturers Association as a function of time.

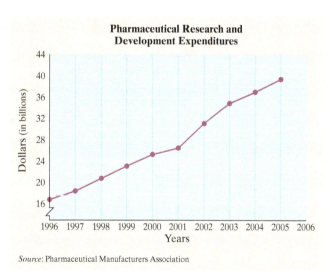

Source: Pharmaceutical Manufacturers Association

a. Approximate the money spent on research and development in 2002.

b. In 1958, research and development expenditures were $200 million. Find the increase in expenditures from 1958 to 2004.

Solution

a. Find the year 2002 and move upward until you reach the graph. From the point on the graph move horizontally, to the left, until the other axis is reached. In 2002, approximately $31 billion was spent.

b. In 2004, approximately $37 billion, or $37,000 million was spent. The increase in spending from 1958 to 2004 is $37,000 - $200 = $36,800 million or $36.8 billion.

PRACTICE 9 Use the graph in Example 9 and approximate the money spent in 2003.

Notice that the graph in Example 9 is the graph of a function since for each year there is only one total amount of money spent by the Pharmaceutical Manufacturers Association on research and development. Also notice that the graph resembles the graph of a line. Often, businesses depend on equations that "closely fit" data-defined functions like this one in order to model the data and predict future trends. For example, by a method called **least squares,** the function $f(x) = 2.602x - 5178$ approximates the data shown. For this function, x is the year and $f(x)$ is total money spent. Its graph and the actual data function are shown next.

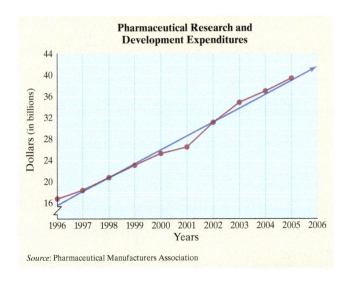

Source: Pharmaceutical Manufacturers Association

EXAMPLE 10 Use the function $f(x) = 2.602x - 5178$ to predict the amount of money that will be spent by the Pharmaceutical Manufacturers Association on research and development in 2014.

Solution To predict the amount of money that will be spent in the year 2014 we use $f(x) = 2.602x - 5178$ and find $f(2014)$.

$$f(x) = 2.602x - 5178$$
$$f(2014) = 2.602(2014) - 5178$$
$$= 62.428$$

We predict that in the year 2014, $62.428 billion dollars will be spent on research and development by the Pharmaceutical Manufacturers Association.

PRACTICE
10 Use $f(x) = 2.602x - 5178$ to approximate the money spent in 2012.

Graphing Calculator Explorations

It is possible to use a graphing calculator to sketch the graph of more than one equation on the same set of axes. For example, graph the functions $f(x) = x^2$ and $g(x) = x^2 + 4$ on the same set of axes.

To graph on the same set of axes, press the $\boxed{Y =}$ key and enter the equations on the first two lines.

$$Y_1 = x^2$$
$$Y_2 = x^2 + 4$$

Then press the GRAPH key as usual. The screen should look like this.

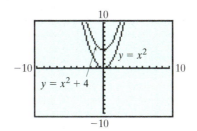

Notice that the graph of y or $g(x) = x^2 + 4$ is the graph of $y = x^2$ moved 4 units upward.

Graph each pair of functions on the same set of axes. Describe the similarities and differences in their graphs.

1. $f(x) = |x|$
   $g(x) = |x| + 1$
2. $f(x) = x^2$
   $h(x) = x^2 - 5$
3. $f(x) = x$
   $H(x) = x - 6$
4. $f(x) = |x|$
   $G(x) = |x| + 3$
5. $f(x) = -x^2$
   $F(x) = -x^2 + 7$
6. $f(x) = x$
   $F(x) = x + 2$

VOCABULARY & READINESS CHECK

Word Bank. *Use the choices below to fill in each blank. Some choices may not be used. These exercises have to do with functions and the rectangular coordinate system (Sections 3.1 and 3.2)*

| x | domain | vertical | relation | (1.7, −2) | line | parabola |
| y | range | horizontal | function | (−2, 1.7) | origin | V-shaped |

1. The intersection of the x-axis and y-axis is a point, called the _____.
2. To find an x-intercept, let _____ = 0 and solve for _____.
3. To find a y-intercept, let _____ = 0 and solve for _____.
4. The graph of $Ax + By = C$, where A and B are not both 0 is a _____.
5. The graph of $y = |x|$ looks _____.
6. The graph of $y = x^2$ is a _____.
7. A _____ is a set of ordered pairs.
8. The _____ of a relation is the set of all second components of the ordered pairs.
9. The _____ of a relation is the set of all first components of the ordered pairs.
10. A _____ is a relation in which each first component in the ordered pairs corresponds to *exactly* one second component.
11. By the vertical line test, all linear equations are functions except those whose graphs are _____ lines.
12. If $f(-2) = 1.7$, the corresponding ordered pair is _____.

3.2 EXERCISE SET

Find the domain and the range of each relation. Also determine whether the relation is a function. See Examples 1 and 2.

1. $\{(-1, 7), (0, 6), (-2, 2), (5, 6)\}$

2. $\{(4, 9), (-4, 9), (2, 3), (10, -5)\}$

3. $\{(-2, 4), (6, 4), (-2, -3), (-7, -8)\}$

4. $\{(6, 6), (5, 6), (5, -2), (7, 6)\}$

5. $\{(1, 1), (1, 2), (1, 3), (1, 4)\}$

6. $\{(1, 1), (2, 1), (3, 1), (4, 1)\}$

7. $\left\{\left(\dfrac{3}{2}, \dfrac{1}{2}\right), \left(1\dfrac{1}{2}, -7\right), \left(0, \dfrac{4}{5}\right)\right\}$

8. $\{(\pi, 0), (0, \pi), (-2, 4), (4, -2)\}$

9. $\{(-3, -3), (0, 0), (3, 3)\}$

10. $\left\{\left(\dfrac{1}{2}, \dfrac{1}{4}\right), \left(0, \dfrac{7}{8}\right), (0.5, \pi)\right\}$

11.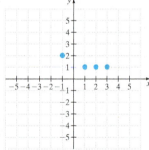

12.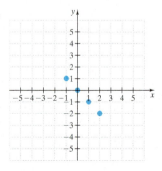

13.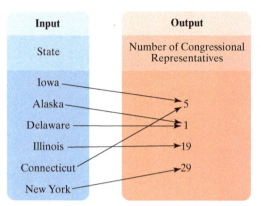

14.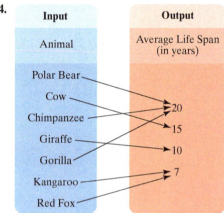

15.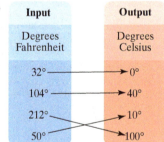

16.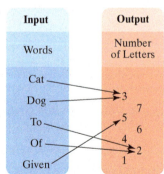

17.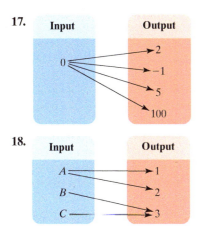

18.

In Exercises 19 through 22, determine whether the relation is a function. See Example 2.

	First Set: Input	Correspondence	Second Set: Output
19.	Class of algebra students	Final grade average	non negative numbers
20.	People who live in Cincinnati, Ohio	Birth date	days of the year
21.	blue, green, brown	Eye color	People who live in Cincinnati, Ohio
22.	Whole numbers from 0 to 4	Number of children	50 Women in a water aerobics class

Use the vertical line test to determine whether each graph is the graph of a function. See Example 5.

23. 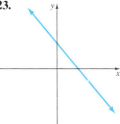   **24.**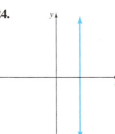

25.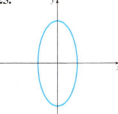

26.

27. 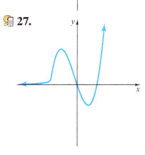   **28.**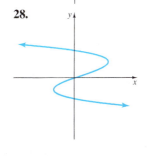

Find the domain and the range of each relation. Use the vertical line test to determine whether each graph is the graph of a function. See Example 6.

29. 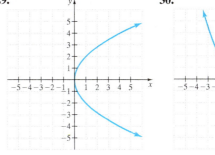   **30.**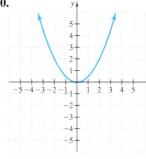

31. 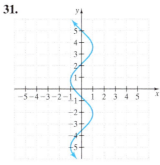   **32.**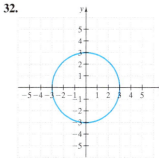

33. 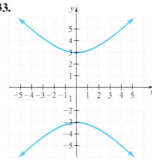   **34.**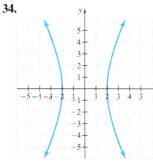

35. 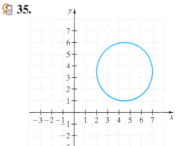   **36.**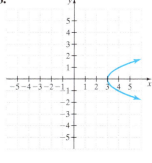

37. 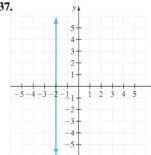 **38.**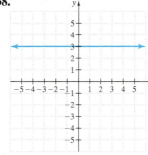

64. $g(x) = -\dfrac{1}{3}x$;
   a. $g(0)$ **b.** $g(-1)$ **c.** $g(3)$

65. $g(x) = 2x^2 + 4$;
   a. $g(-11)$ **b.** $g(-1)$ **c.** $g\left(\dfrac{1}{2}\right)$

66. $h(x) = -x^2$;
   a. $h(-5)$ **b.** $h\left(-\dfrac{1}{3}\right)$ **c.** $h\left(\dfrac{1}{3}\right)$

67. $f(x) = -5$;
   a. $f(2)$ **b.** $f(0)$ **c.** $f(606)$

68. $h(x) = 7$;
   a. $h(7)$ **b.** $h(542)$ **c.** $h\left(-\dfrac{3}{4}\right)$

69. $f(x) = 1.3x^2 - 2.6x + 5.1$
   a. $f(2)$ **b.** $f(-2)$ **c.** $f(3.1)$

70. $g(x) = 2.7x^2 + 6.8x - 10.2$
   a. $g(1)$ **b.** $g(-5)$ **c.** $g(7.2)$

39. 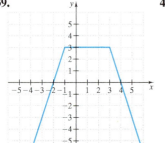 **40.**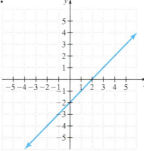

Read a Graph. *Use the graph of the functions below to answer Exercises 71 through 82. See Example 8.*

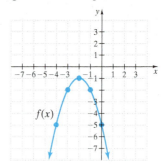

41. In your own words define **(a)** function; **(b)** domain; **(c)** range.

42. Explain the vertical line test and how it is used.

71. If $f(1) = -10$, write the corresponding ordered pair.

72. If $f(-5) = -10$, write the corresponding ordered pair.

MIXED PRACTICE

Decide whether each is a function. See Examples 3 through 6.

43. $y = x + 1$ **44.** $y = x - 1$
45. $x = 2y^2$ **46.** $y = x^2$
47. $y - x = 7$ **48.** $2x - 3y = 9$
49. $y = \dfrac{1}{x}$ **50.** $y = \dfrac{1}{x - 3}$
51. $y = 5x - 12$ **52.** $y = \dfrac{1}{2}x + 4$
53. $x = y^2$ **54.** $x = |y|$

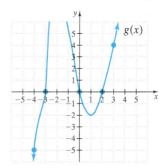

If $f(x) = 3x + 3$, $g(x) = 4x^2 - 6x + 3$, and $h(x) = 5x^2 - 7$, find the following. See Example 7.

55. $f(4)$ **56.** $f(-1)$
57. $h(-3)$ **58.** $h(0)$
59. $g(2)$ **60.** $g(1)$
61. $g(0)$ **62.** $h(-2)$

73. If $g(4) = 56$, write the corresponding ordered pair.
74. If $g(-2) = 8$, write the corresponding ordered pair.
75. Find $f(-1)$.
76. Find $f(-2)$.
77. Find $g(2)$.
78. Find $g(-4)$.
79. Find all values of x such that $f(x) = -5$.
80. Find all values of x such that $f(x) = -2$.
81. Find all positive values of x such that $g(x) = 4$.
82. Find all values of x such that $g(x) = 0$.

Given the following functions, find the indicated values. See Example 7.

63. $f(x) = \dfrac{1}{2}x$;
   a. $f(0)$ **b.** $f(2)$ **c.** $f(-2)$

83. What is the greatest number of x-intercepts that a function may have? Explain your answer.
84. What is the greatest number of y-intercepts that a function may have? Explain your answer.

Read a Graph. *Use the graph in Example 9 to answer the following. Also see Example 10.*

85. a. Use the graph to approximate the money spent on research and development in 1996.
    b. Recall that the function $f(x) = 2.602x - 5178$ approximates the graph in Example 9. Use this equation to approximate the money spent on research and development in 1996.
86. a. Use the graph to approximate the money spent on research and development in 1999.
    b. Use the function $f(x) = 2.602x - 5178$ to approximate the money spent on research and development in 1999.

The function $f(x) = 0.42x + 10.5$, can be used to predict diamond production. For this function, x is the number of years after 2000, and $f(x)$ is the value (in billions of dollars) of the years diamond production. (See the Chapter 3 opener.)

87. Use the function in the directions above to predict diamond production in 2012.
88. Use the function in the directions above to predict diamond production in 2015.
89. Since $y = x + 7$ describes a function, rewrite the equation using function notation.
90. In your own words, explain how to find the domain of a function given its graph.

The function $A(r) = \pi r^2$ may be used to find the area of a circle if we are given its radius.

91. Find the area of a circle whose radius is 5 centimeters. (Do not approximate π.)
92. Find the area of a circular garden whose radius is 8 feet. (Do not approximate π.)

The function $V(x) = x^3$ may be used to find the volume of a cube if we are given the length x of a side.

93. Find the volume of a cube whose side is 14 inches.
94. Find the volume of a die whose side is 1.7 centimeters.

Forensic scientists use the following functions to find the height of a woman if they are given the height of her femur bone f or her tibia bone t in centimeters.

$$H(f) = 2.59f + 47.24$$
$$H(t) = 2.72t + 61.28$$

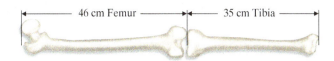

95. Find the height of a woman whose femur measures 46 centimeters.
96. Find the height of a woman whose tibia measures 35 centimeters.

The dosage in milligrams D of Ivermectin, a heartworm preventive, for a dog who weighs x pounds is given by

$$D(x) = \frac{136}{25}x$$

97. Find the proper dosage for a dog that weighs 30 pounds.
98. Find the proper dosage for a dog that weighs 50 pounds.
99. The per capita consumption (in pounds) of all poultry in the United States is approximated by the function $C(x) = 2.28x + 94.86$, where x is the number of years since 2001. (*Source:* Based on actual and estimated data from the Economic Research Service, U.S. Department of Agriculture)
    a. Find and interpret $C(5)$.
    b. Estimate the per capita consumption of all poultry in the United States in 2007.
100. The average length of U.S. hospital stays has been decreasing, following the equation $y = -0.09x + 8.02$ where x is the number of years since 1970. (*Source:* National Center for Health Statistics)

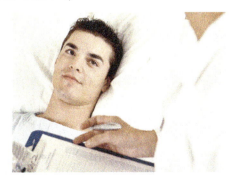

   a. What was the length of the average hospital stay in 1995?
   b. If this trend continues, what will the average length be in 2011?

REVIEW AND PREVIEW

Complete a Table. *Complete the given table and use the table to graph the linear equation. See Section 3.1.*

101. $x - y = -5$

x	0		1
y		0	

102. $2x + 3y = 10$

x	0		
y		0	2

103. $7x + 4y = 8$

x	0	
y		0	-1

104. $5y - x = -15$

x	0		-2
y		0	

105. $y = 6x$

x	0		-1
y		0	

106. $y = -2x$

x	0		-2
y		0	

△ **107.** Is it possible to find the perimeter of the following geometric figure? If so, find the perimeter.

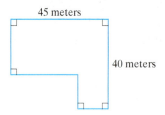

45 meters

40 meters

CONCEPT EXTENSIONS

True or False. *For Exercises 108 through 111, suppose that $y = f(x)$ and it is true that $f(7) = 50$. Determine whether each is true or false. See the second Concept Check in this section.*

108. An ordered-pair solution of the function is (7, 50).

109. When x is 50, y is 7.

110. A possible function is $f(x) = x^2 + 1$.

111. A possible function is $f(x) = 10x - 20$.

Given the following functions, find the indicated values.

112. $f(x) = 2x + 7$;
    a. $f(2)$ **b.** $f(a)$

113. $g(x) = -3x + 12$;
    a. $g(s)$ **b.** $g(r)$

114. $h(x) = x^2 + 7$;
    a. $h(3)$ **b.** $h(a)$

115. $f(x) = x^2 - 12$;
    a. $f(12)$ **b.** $f(a)$

✎ **116.** Describe a function whose domain is the set of people in your hometown.

✎ **117.** Describe a function whose domain is the set of people in your algebra class.

3.3 GRAPHING LINEAR FUNCTIONS

OBJECTIVES

1. Graph linear functions.
2. Graph linear functions by finding intercepts.
3. Graph vertical and horizontal lines.

OBJECTIVE 1 ▶ Graphing linear functions. In this section, we identify and graph linear functions. By the vertical line test, we know that all linear equations except those whose graphs are vertical lines are functions. For example, we know from Section 3.1 that $y = 2x$ is a linear equation in two variables. Its graph is shown.

x	y = 2x
1	2
0	0
-1	-2

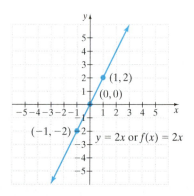

Because this graph passes the vertical line test, we know that $y = 2x$ is a function. If we want to emphasize that this equation describes a function, we may write $y = 2x$ as $f(x) = 2x$.

Section 3.3 Graphing Linear Functions 137

EXAMPLE 1 Graph $g(x) = 2x + 1$. Compare this graph with the graph of $f(x) = 2x$.

Solution To graph $g(x) = 2x + 1$, find three ordered pair solutions.

x	$f(x) = 2x$	$g(x) = 2x + 1$
0	0	1
−1	−2	−1
1	2	3

(add 1)

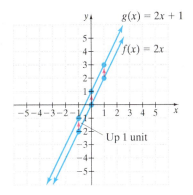

Notice that y-values for the graph of $g(x) = 2x + 1$ are obtained by adding 1 to each y-value of each corresponding point of the graph of $f(x) = 2x$. The graph of $g(x) = 2x + 1$ is the same as the graph of $f(x) = 2x$ shifted upward 1 unit.

PRACTICE 1 Graph $g(x) = 4x - 3$ and $f(x) = 4x$ on the same axes.

In general, a **linear function** is a function that can be written in the form $f(x) = mx + b$. For example, $g(x) = 2x + 1$ is in this form, with $m = 2$ and $b = 1$.

EXAMPLE 2 Graph the linear functions $f(x) = -3x$ and $g(x) = -3x - 6$ on the same set of axes.

Solution To graph $f(x)$ and $g(x)$, find ordered pair solutions.

x	$f(x) = -3x$	$g(x) = -3x - 6$
0	0	−6
1	−3	−9
−1	3	−3
−2	6	0

(subtract 6)

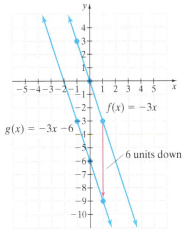

Each y-value for the graph of $g(x) = -3x - 6$ is obtained by subtracting 6 from the y-value of the corresponding point of the graph of $f(x) = -3x$. The graph of $g(x) = -3x - 6$ is the same as the graph of $f(x) = -3x$ shifted down 6 units.

PRACTICE 2 Graph the linear functions $f(x) = -2x$ and $g(x) = -2x + 5$ on the same set of axes.

OBJECTIVE 2 ▶ **Graphing linear functions using intercepts.** Notice that the y-intercept of the graph of $g(x) = -3x - 6$ in the preceding figure is $(0, -6)$. In general, if a linear function is written in the form $f(x) = mx + b$ or $y = mx + b$, the y-intercept is $(0, b)$. This is because if x is 0, then $f(x) = mx + b$ becomes $f(0) = m \cdot 0 + b = b$, and we have the ordered pair solution $(0, b)$. We will study this form more in the next section.

EXAMPLE 3 Find the y-intercept of the graph of each equation.

a. $f(x) = \frac{1}{2}x + \frac{3}{7}$ **b.** $y = -2.5x - 3.2$

Solution

a. The y-intercept of $f(x) = \frac{1}{2}x + \frac{3}{7}$ is $\left(0, \frac{3}{7}\right)$.

b. The y-intercept of $y = -2.5x - 3.2$ is $(0, -3.2)$.

PRACTICE 3 Find the y-intercept of the graph of each equation.

a. $f(x) = \frac{3}{4}x - \frac{2}{5}$ **b.** $y = 2.6x + 4.1$

In general, to find the y-intercept of the graph of an equation not in the form $y = mx + b$, let $x = 0$ since any point on the y-axis has an x-coordinate of 0. To find the x-intercept of a line, let $y = 0$ or $f(x) = 0$ since any point on the x-axis has a y-coordinate of 0.

> **Finding x- and y-Intercepts**
> To find an x-intercept, let $y = 0$ or $f(x) = 0$ and solve for x.
> To find a y-intercept, let $x = 0$ and solve for y.

Intercepts are usually easy to find and plot since one coordinate is 0.

EXAMPLE 4 Find the intercepts and graph: $3x + 4y = -12$.

Solution To find the y-intercept, we let $x = 0$ and solve for y. To find the x-intercept, we let $y = 0$ and solve for x. Let's let $x = 0$, $y = 0$, and then let $x = 2$ to find a third point as a check.

Let $x = 0$.
$3x + 4y = -12$
$3 \cdot 0 + 4y = -12$
$4y = -12$
$y = -3$

$(0, -3)$

Let $y = 0$.
$3x + 4y = -12$
$3x + 4 \cdot 0 = -12$
$3x = -12$
$x = -4$

$(-4, 0)$

Let $x = 2$.
$3x + 4y = -12$
$3 \cdot 2 + 4y = -12$
$6 + 4y = -12$
$4y = -18$
$y = -\frac{18}{4} = -4\frac{1}{2}$

$\left(2, -4\frac{1}{2}\right)$

The ordered pairs are on the table below. The graph of $3x + 4y = -12$ is the line drawn through these points, as shown.

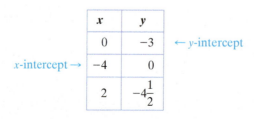
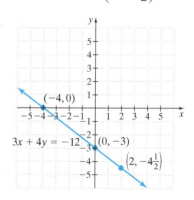

PRACTICE 4 Find the intercepts and graph: $4x - 5y = -20$.

Notice that the equation $3x + 4y = -12$ describes a linear function—"linear" because its graph is a line and "function" because the graph passes the vertical line test.

If we want to emphasize that the equation $3x + 4y = -12$ from Example 4 describes a function, first solve the equation for y.

$$3x + 4y = -12$$
$$4y = -3x - 12 \quad \text{Subtract } x \text{ from both sides.}$$
$$\frac{4y}{4} = \frac{-3x}{4} - \frac{12}{4} \quad \text{Divide both sides by } -3.$$
$$y = -\frac{3}{4}x - 3 \quad \text{Simplify.}$$

Next, let

$$y = f(x).$$
$$f(x) = -\frac{3}{4}x - 3$$

> **Helpful Hint**
> Any linear equation that describes a function can be written using function notation. To do so,
> 1. solve the equation for y and then
> 2. replace y with $f(x)$, as we did above.

EXAMPLE 5 Graph $x = -2y$ by plotting intercepts.

Solution Let $y = 0$ to find the x-intercept and $x = 0$ to find the y-intercept.

If $y = 0$ then   If $x = 0$ then
$x = -2(0)$ or $0 = -2y$ or
$x = 0$ $0 = y$
$(0, 0)$ $(0, 0)$

Ordered pairs Both the x-intercept and y-intercept are $(0, 0)$. This happens when the graph passes through the origin. Since two points are needed to determine a line, we must find at least one more ordered pair that satisfies $x = -2y$. Let $y = -1$ to find a second ordered pair solution and let $y = 1$ as a check point.

If $y = -1$ then   If $y = 1$ then
$x = -2(-1)$ or $x = -2(1)$ or
$x = 2$ $x = -2$

The ordered pairs are $(0, 0)$, $(2, -1)$, and $(-2, 1)$. Plot these points to graph $x = -2y$.

x	y
0	0
2	-1
-2	1

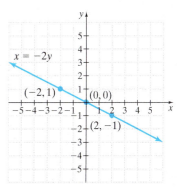

PRACTICE 5 Graph $y = -3x$ by plotting intercepts.

OBJECTIVE 3 ▶ **Graphing vertical and horizontal lines.** The equations $x = c$ and $y = c$, where c is a real number constant, are both linear equations in two variables. Why? Because $x = c$ can be written as $x + 0y = c$ and $y = c$ can be written as $0x + y = c$. We graph these two special linear equations below.

EXAMPLE 6   Graph $x = 2$.

Solution   The equation $x = 2$ can be written as $x + 0y = 2$. For any y-value chosen, notice that x is 2. No other value for x satisfies $x + 0y = 2$. Any ordered pair whose x-coordinate is 2 is a solution to $x + 0y = 2$ because 2 added to 0 times any value of y is $2 + 0$, or 2. We will use the ordered pairs $(2, 3), (2, 0)$ and $(2, -3)$ to graph $x = 2$.

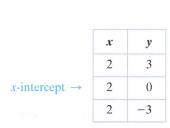

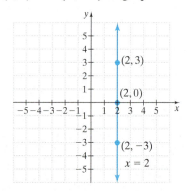

The graph is a vertical line with x-intercept $(2, 0)$. Notice that this graph is not the graph of a function, and it has no y-intercept because x is never 0.

PRACTICE 6   Graph $x = -4$.

EXAMPLE 7   Graph $y = -3$.

Solution   The equation $y = -3$ can be written as $0x + y = -3$. For any x-value chosen, y is -3. If we choose 4, 0, and -2 as x-values, the ordered pair solutions are $(4, -3), (0, -3)$, and $(-2, -3)$. We will use these ordered pairs to graph $y = -3$.

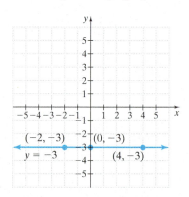

The graph is a horizontal line with y-intercept $(0, -3)$ and no x-intercept. Notice that this graph is the graph of a function.

PRACTICE 7   Graph $y = 4$.

From Examples 6 and 7, we have the following generalization.

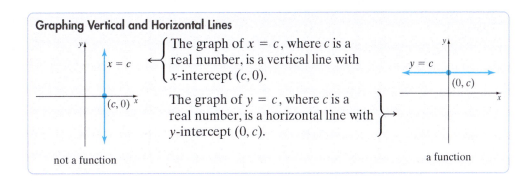

not a function   a function

Graphing Calculator Explorations

You may have noticed by now that to use the $\boxed{Y=}$ key on a graphing calculator to graph an equation, the equation must be solved for y.

Graph each function by first solving the function for y.

1. $x = 3.5y$
2. $-2.7y = x$
3. $5.78x + 2.31y = 10.98$
4. $-7.22x + 3.89y = 12.57$
5. $y - |x| = 3.78$
6. $3y - 5x^2 = 6x - 4$
7. $y - 5.6x^2 = 7.7x + 1.5$
8. $y + 2.6|x| = -3.2$

VOCABULARY & READINESS CHECK

Word Bank. *Use the choices below to fill in each blank. Some choices may be used more than once and some not at all.*

| horizontal | y | (c, 0) | (b, 0) | (m, 0) | linear |
| vertical | x | (0, c) | (0, b) | (0, m) | f(x) |

1. A _____ function can be written in the form $f(x) = mx + b$.
2. In the form $f(x) = mx + b$, the y-intercept is _____.
3. The graph of $x = c$ is a _____ line with x-intercept _____.
4. The graph of $y = c$ is a _____ line with y-intercept _____.
5. To find an x-intercept, let ____ = 0 or _____ = 0 and solve for ____.
6. To find a y-intercept, let _____ = 0 and solve for _____.

3.3 EXERCISE SET

Graph each linear function. See Examples 1 and 2.

1. $f(x) = -2x$
2. $f(x) = 2x$
3. $f(x) = -2x + 3$
4. $f(x) = 2x + 6$
5. $f(x) = \frac{1}{2}x$
6. $f(x) = \frac{1}{3}x$
7. $f(x) = \frac{1}{2}x - 4$
8. $f(x) = \frac{1}{3}x - 2$

Matching. *The graph of $f(x) = 5x$ follows. Use this graph to match each linear function with its graph. See Examples 1 through 3.*

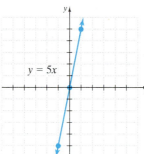

A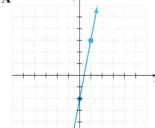
B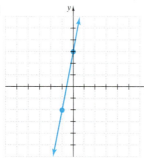
C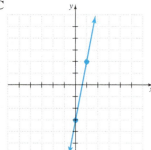
D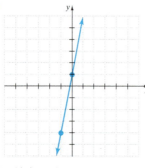

9. $f(x) = 5x - 3$
10. $f(x) = 5x - 2$
11. $f(x) = 5x + 1$
12. $f(x) = 5x + 3$

Graph each linear function by finding x- and y-intercepts. Then write each equation using function notation. See Examples 4 and 5.

13. $x - y = 3$
14. $x - y = -4$
15. $x = 5y$
16. $2x = y$
17. $-x + 2y = 6$
18. $x - 2y = -8$
19. $2x - 4y = 8$
20. $2x + 3y = 6$
21. In your own words, explain how to find x- and y-intercepts.
22. Explain why it is a good idea to use three points to graph a linear equation.

Graph each linear equation. See Examples 6 and 7.

23. $x = -1$
24. $y = 5$
25. $y = 0$
26. $x = 0$
27. $y + 7 = 0$
28. $x - 3 = 0$

Matching. *Match each equation below with its graph.*

A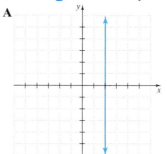
B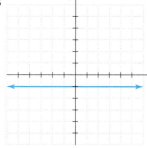
C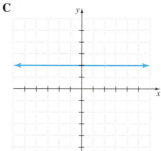
D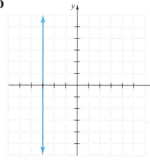

29. $y = 2$
30. $x = -3$
31. $x - 2 = 0$
32. $y + 1 = 0$
33. Discuss whether a vertical line ever has a y-intercept.
34. Discuss whether a horizontal line ever has an x-intercept.

MIXED PRACTICE

Graph each linear equation. See Examples 1 through 7.

35. $x + 2y = 8$
36. $x - 3y = 3$
37. $3x + 5y = 7$
38. $3x - 2y = 5$
39. $x + 8y = 8$
40. $x - 3y = 9$

41. $5 = 6x - y$
42. $4 = x - 3y$
43. $-x + 10y = 11$
44. $-x + 9 = -y$
45. $y = \dfrac{3}{2}$
46. $x = \dfrac{3}{2}$
47. $2x + 3y = 6$
48. $4x + y = 5$
49. $x + 3 = 0$
50. $y - 6 = 0$
51. $f(x) = \dfrac{3}{4}x + 2$
52. $f(x) = \dfrac{4}{3}x + 2$
53. $f(x) = x$
54. $f(x) = -x$
55. $f(x) = \dfrac{1}{2}x$
56. $f(x) = -2x$
57. $f(x) = 4x - \dfrac{1}{3}$
58. $f(x) = -3x + \dfrac{3}{4}$
59. $x = -3$
60. $f(x) = 3$

REVIEW AND PREVIEW

Solve the following. See Sections 2.6 and 2.7.

61. $|x - 3| = 6$
62. $|x + 2| < 4$
63. $|2x + 5| > 3$
64. $|5x| = 10$
65. $|3x - 4| \leq 2$
66. $|7x - 2| \geq 5$

Simplify. See Section 1.3.

67. $\dfrac{-6 - 3}{2 - 8}$
68. $\dfrac{4 - 5}{-1 - 0}$
69. $\dfrac{-8 - (-2)}{-3 - (-2)}$
70. $\dfrac{12 - 3}{10 - 9}$
71. $\dfrac{0 - 6}{5 - 0}$
72. $\dfrac{2 - 2}{3 - 5}$

CONCEPT EXTENSIONS

Multiple Steps. *Solve.*

73. Broyhill Furniture found that it takes 2 hours to manufacture each table for one of its special dining room sets. Each chair takes 3 hours to manufacture. A total of 1500 hours is available to produce tables and chairs of this style. The linear equation that models this situation is $2x + 3y = 1500$, where x represents the number of tables produced and y the number of chairs produced.

   a. Complete the ordered pair solution (0,) of this equation. Describe the manufacturing situation this solution corresponds to.

   b. Complete the ordered pair solution (, 0) for this equation. Describe the manufacturing situation this solution corresponds to.

   c. If 50 tables are produced, find the greatest number of chairs the company can make.

74. While manufacturing two different camera models, Kodak found that the basic model costs $55 to produce, whereas the deluxe model costs $75. The weekly budget for these two models is limited to $33,000 in production costs. The linear equation that models this situation is $55x + 75y = 33,000$, where x represents the number of basic models and y the number of deluxe models.

   a. Complete the ordered pair solution (0,) of this equation. Describe the manufacturing situation this solution corresponds to.

   b. Complete the ordered pair solution (, 0) of this equation. Describe the manufacturing situation this solution corresponds to.

   c. If 350 deluxe models are produced, find the greatest number of basic models that can be made in one week.

75. The cost of renting a car for a day is given by the linear function $C(x) = 0.2x + 24$, where $C(x)$ is in dollars and x is the number of miles driven.

   a. Find the cost of driving the car 200 miles.

   b. Graph $C(x) = 0.2x + 24$.

   c. How can you tell from the graph of $C(x)$ that as the number of miles driven increases, the total cost increases also?

76. The cost of renting a piece of machinery is given by the linear function $C(x) = 4x + 10$, where $C(x)$ is in dollars and x is given in hours.

   a. Find the cost of renting the piece of machinery for 8 hours.

   b. Graph $C(x) = 4x + 10$.

   c. How can you tell from the graph of $C(x)$ that as the number of hours increases, the total cost increases also?

77. The yearly cost of tuition (in-state) and required fees for attending a public two-year college full time can be estimated by the linear function $f(x) = 107.3x + 1245.62$, where x is the number of years after 2000 and $f(x)$ is the total cost. (*Source:* U.S. National Center for Education Statistics)

   a. Use this function to approximate the yearly cost of attending a two-year college in the year 2015. [*Hint:* Find $f(15)$.]

   b. Use the given function to predict in what year the yearly cost of tuition and required fees will exceed $2500. [*Hint:* Let $f(x) = 2500$, solve for x, then round your solution up to the next whole year.

   c. Use this function to approximate the yearly cost of attending a two-year college in the present year. If you attend a two-year college, is this amount greater than or less than the amount that is currently charged by the college you attend?

78. The yearly cost of tuition (in-state) and required fees for attending a public four-year college full time can be estimated by the linear function $f(x) = 291.5x + 2944.05$, where x is the number of years after 2000 and $f(x)$ is the total cost in dollars. (*Source:* U.S. National Center for Education Statistics)

   a. Use this function to approximate the yearly cost of attending a four-year college in the year 2015. [*Hint:* Find $f(15)$.]

   b. Use the given function to predict in what year the yearly cost of tuition and required fees will exceed $6000. [*Hint:* Let $f(x) = 6000$, solve for x, then round your solution up to the next whole year.]

   c. Use this function to approximate the yearly cost of attending a four-year college in the present year. If you attend a four-year college, is this amount greater than or less than the amount that is currently charged by the college you attend?

Use a graphing calculator to verify the results of each exercise.

79. Exercise 9   **80.** Exercise 10

81. Exercise 17   **82.** Exercise 18

83. The graph of $f(x)$ or $y = -4x$ is given below. Without actually graphing, describe the shape and location of

   a. $y = -4x + 2$ **b.** $y = -4x - 5$

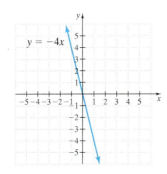

It is true that for any function $f(x)$, the graph of $f(x) + K$ is the same as the graph of $f(x)$ shifted K units up if K is positive and $|K|$ units down if K is negative. (We study this further in Section 3.7.)

The graph of $y = |x|$ is

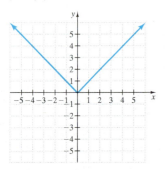

Matching. Without actually graphing, match each equation with its graph.

a. $y = |x| - 1$

b. $y = |x| + 1$

c. $y = |x| - 3$

d. $y = |x| + 3$

84.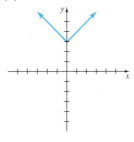

85.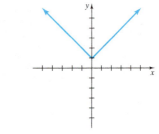

86.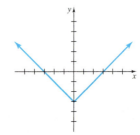

87.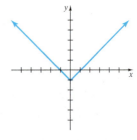

3.4 THE SLOPE OF A LINE

OBJECTIVES

1. Find the slope of a line given two points on the line.
2. Find the slope of a line given the equation of a line.
3. Interpret the slope-intercept form in an application.
4. Find the slopes of horizontal and vertical lines.
5. Compare the slopes of parallel and perpendicular lines.

OBJECTIVE 1 ▶ Finding slope given two points. You may have noticed by now that different lines often tilt differently. It is very important in many fields to be able to measure and compare the tilt, or **slope**, of lines. For example, a wheelchair ramp with a slope of $\frac{1}{12}$ means that the ramp rises 1 foot for every 12 horizontal feet. A road with a slope or grade of 11% $\left(\text{or } \frac{11}{100}\right)$ means that the road rises 11 feet for every 100 horizontal feet.

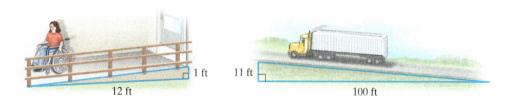

We measure the slope of a line as a ratio of **vertical change** to **horizontal change**. Slope is usually designated by the letter m.

Suppose that we want to measure the slope of the following line.

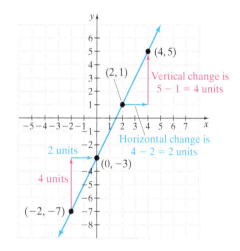

The vertical change between *both* pairs of points on the line is 4 units per horizontal change of 2 units. Then

$$\text{slope } m = \frac{\text{change in } y \text{ (vertical change)}}{\text{change in } x \text{ (horizontal change)}} = \frac{4}{2} = 2$$

We can also think of slope as a **rate of change** between points. A slope of 2 or $\frac{2}{1}$ means that between pairs of points on the line, the rate of change is a vertical change of 2 units per horizontal change of 1 unit.

Consider the line in the box on the next page, which passes through the points (x_1, y_1) and (x_2, y_2). (The notation x_1 is read "x-sub-one.") The vertical change, or *rise*, between these points is the difference of the y-coordinates: $y_2 - y_1$. The horizontal change, or *run*, between the points is the difference of the x-coordinates: $x_2 - x_1$.

Slope of a Line

Given a line passing through points (x_1, y_1) and (x_2, y_2) the **slope** m of the line is

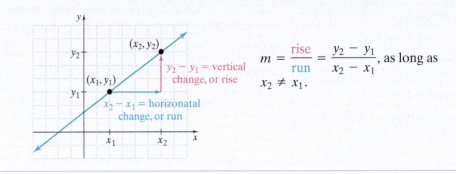

$$m = \frac{\text{rise}}{\text{run}} = \frac{y_2 - y_1}{x_2 - x_1}, \text{ as long as } x_2 \neq x_1.$$

Concept Check ✓

In the definition of slope, we state that $x_2 \neq x_1$. Explain why.

EXAMPLE 1 Find the slope of the line containing the points $(0, 3)$ and $(2, 5)$. Graph the line.

Solution We use the slope formula. It does not matter which point we call (x_1, y_1) and which point we call (x_2, y_2). We'll let $(x_1, y_1) = (0, 3)$ and $(x_2, y_2) = (2, 5)$.

$$m = \frac{y_2 - y_1}{x_2 - x_1}$$

$$= \frac{5 - 3}{2 - 0} = \frac{2}{2} = 1$$

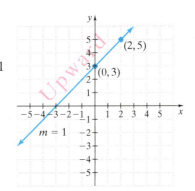

Notice in this example that the slope is *positive* and that the graph of the line containing $(0, 3)$ and $(2, 5)$ moves *upward*, or increases, as we go from left to right. □

PRACTICE

1 Find the slope of the line containing the points $(4, 0)$ and $(-2, 3)$. Graph the line.

▶ **Helpful Hint**

The slope of a line is the same no matter which 2 points of a line you choose to calculate slope. The line in Example 1 also contains the point $(-3, 0)$. Below, we calculate the slope of the line using $(0, 3)$ as (x_1, y_1) and $(-3, 0)$ as (x_2, y_2).

$$m = \frac{y_2 - y_1}{x_2 - x_1} = \frac{0 - 3}{-3 - 0} = \frac{-3}{-3} = 1 \quad \text{Same slope as found in Example 1.}$$

Answer to Concept Check:
So that the denominator is not 0

EXAMPLE 2 Find the slope of the line containing the points $(5, -4)$ and $(-3, 3)$. Graph the line.

Solution We use the slope formula, and let $(x_1, y_1) = (5, -4)$ and $(x_2, y_2) = (-3, 3)$.

$$m = \frac{y_2 - y_1}{x_2 - x_1}$$
$$= \frac{3 - (-4)}{-3 - 5} = \frac{7}{-8} = -\frac{7}{8}$$

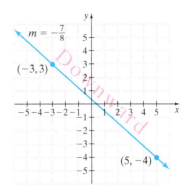

Notice in this example that the slope is negative and that the graph of the line through $(5, -4)$ and $(-3, 3)$ moves downward, or decreases, as we go from left to right.

> **Helpful Hint**
> When we are trying to find the slope of a line through two given points, it makes no difference which given point is called (x_1, y_1) and which is called (x_2, y_2). Once an x-coordinate is called x_1, however, make sure its corresponding y-coordinate is called y_1.

PRACTICE 2 Find the slope of the line containing the points $(-5, -4)$ and $(5, 2)$. Graph the line.

Concept Check ✓
Find and correct the error in the following calculation of slope of the line containing the points $(12, 2)$ and $(4, 7)$.

$$m = \frac{12 - 4}{2 - 7} = \frac{8}{-5} = -\frac{8}{5}$$

OBJECTIVE 2 ▶ Finding slope given an equation. As we have seen, the slope of a line is defined by two points on the line. Thus, if we know the equation of a line, we can find its slope.

EXAMPLE 3 Find the slope of the line whose equation is $f(x) = \frac{2}{3}x + 4$.

Solution Two points are needed on the line defined by $f(x) = \frac{2}{3}x + 4$ or $y = \frac{2}{3}x + 4$ to find its slope. We will use intercepts as our two points.

If $x = 0$, then
$$y = \frac{2}{3} \cdot 0 + 4$$
$$y = 4$$

If $y = 0$, then
$$0 = \frac{2}{3}x + 4$$
$$-4 = \frac{2}{3}x \quad \text{Subtract 4.}$$
$$\frac{3}{2}(-4) = \frac{3}{2} \cdot \frac{2}{3}x \quad \text{Multiply by } \frac{3}{2}.$$
$$-6 = x$$

Use the points $(0, 4)$ and $(-6, 0)$ to find the slope. Let (x_1, y_1) be $(0, 4)$ and (x_2, y_2) be $(-6, 0)$. Then

$$m = \frac{y_2 - y_1}{x_2 - x_1} = \frac{0 - 4}{-6 - 0} = \frac{-4}{-6} = \frac{2}{3}$$

Answer to Concept Check:
$m = \frac{2 - 7}{12 - 4} = \frac{-5}{8} = -\frac{5}{8}$

PRACTICE 3 Find the slope of the line whose equation is $f(x) = -4x + 6$.

Analyzing the results of Example 3, you may notice a striking pattern:

The slope of $y = \frac{2}{3}x + 4$ is $\frac{2}{3}$, the same as the coefficient of x.

Also, the y-intercept is $(0, 4)$, as expected.

When a linear equation is written in the form $f(x) = mx + b$ or $y = mx + b$, m is the slope of the line and $(0, b)$ is its y-intercept. The form $y = mx + b$ is appropriately called the **slope–intercept form.**

> **Slope–Intercept Form**
>
> When a linear equation in two variables is written in slope–intercept form,
>
> $$y = mx + b$$
>
> where slope is m and y-intercept is $(0, b)$,
>
> then m is the slope of the line and $(0, b)$ is the y-intercept of the line.

EXAMPLE 4 Find the slope and the y-intercept of the line $3x - 4y = 4$.

Solution We write the equation in slope–intercept form by solving for y.

$$3x - 4y = 4$$
$$-4y = -3x + 4 \quad \text{Subtract } 3x \text{ from both sides.}$$
$$\frac{-4y}{-4} = \frac{-3x}{-4} + \frac{4}{-4} \quad \text{Divide both sides by } -4.$$
$$y = \frac{3}{4}x - 1 \quad \text{Simplify.}$$

The coefficient of x, $\frac{3}{4}$, is the slope, and the y-intercept is $(0, -1)$.

PRACTICE 4 Find the slope and the y-intercept of the line $2x - 3y = 9$.

OBJECTIVE 3 ▶ Interpreting slope-intercept form. On the following page is the graph of one-day ticket prices at Disney World for the years shown.

Notice that the graph resembles the graph of a line. Recall that businesses often depend on equations that "closely fit" graphs like this one to model the data and to predict future trends. By the **least squares** method, the linear function $f(x) = 2.7x + 38.64$ approximates the data shown, where x is the number of years since 1996 and y is the ticket price for that year.

> ▶ **Helpful Hint**
>
> The notation $0 \leftrightarrow 1996$ below the graph on the next page means that the number 0 corresponds to the year 1996, 1 corresponds to the year 1997, and so on.

Price of Adult One-Day Pass at Disney World

$f(x) = 2.7x + 38.64$

Year
$0 \leftrightarrow 1996$

Source: The Walt Disney Company

EXAMPLE 5 Predicting Future Prices

The adult one-day pass price $f(x)$ for Disney World is given by

$$f(x) = 2.7x + 38.64$$

where x is the number of years since 1996

a. Use this equation to predict the ticket price for the year 2010.
b. What does the slope of this equation mean?
c. What does the y-intercept of this equation mean?

Solution

a. To predict the price of a pass in 2010, we need to find $f(14)$. (Since year 1996 corresponds to $x = 0$, year 2010 corresponds to $x = 14$.)

$$f(x) = 2.7x + 38.64$$
$$f(14) = 2.7(14) + 38.64 \quad \text{Let } x = 14.$$
$$= 76.44$$

We predict that in the year 2010 the price of an adult one-day pass to Disney World will be about $76.44.

b. The slope of $f(x) = 2.7x + 38.64$ is 2.7. We can think of this number as $\dfrac{\text{rise}}{\text{run}}$ or $\dfrac{2.7}{1}$. This means that the ticket price increases on the average by $2.70 every 1 year.

c. The y-intercept of $f(x) = 2.7x + 38.64$ is $(0, 38.64)$.
  ↑ ↑
  year price

This means that at year 0, or 1996, the ticket price was about $38.64.

PRACTICE 5 Use the equation from Example 5 to predict the ticket price for the year 2012.

OBJECTIVE 4 ▶ Finding slopes of horizontal and vertical lines. Next we find the slopes of two special types of lines: vertical lines and horizontal lines.

EXAMPLE 6 Find the slope of the line $x = -5$.

Solution Recall that the graph of $x = -5$ is a vertical line with x-intercept $(-5, 0)$. To find the slope, we find two ordered pair solutions of $x = -5$. Of course, solutions of $x = -5$ must have an x-value of -5. We will let $(x_1, y_1) = (-5, 0)$ and $(x_2, y_2) = (-5, 4)$.

Then

$$m = \frac{y_2 - y_1}{x_2 - x_1}$$
$$= \frac{4 - 0}{-5 - (-5)}$$
$$= \frac{4}{0}$$

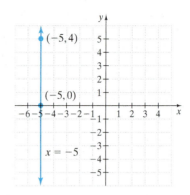

Since $\frac{4}{0}$ is undefined, we say that the slope of the vertical line $x = -5$ is undefined.

PRACTICE 6 Find the slope of the line $x = 4$.

EXAMPLE 7 Find the slope of the line $y = 2$.

Solution Recall that the graph of $y = 2$ is a horizontal line with y-intercept $(0, 2)$. To find the slope, we find two points on the line, such as $(0, 2)$ and $(1, 2)$, and use these points to find the slope.

$$m = \frac{2 - 2}{1 - 0}$$
$$= \frac{0}{1}$$
$$= 0$$

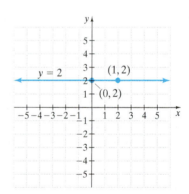

The slope of the horizontal line $y = 2$ is 0.

PRACTICE 7 Find the slope of the line $y = -3$.

From the previous two examples, we have the following generalization.

> The slope of any vertical line is undefined.
> The slope of any horizontal line is 0.

> **▶ Helpful Hint**
> Slope of 0 and undefined slope are not the same. Vertical lines have undefined slope, whereas horizontal lines have slope of 0.

The following four graphs summarize the overall appearance of lines with positive, negative, zero, or undefined slopes.

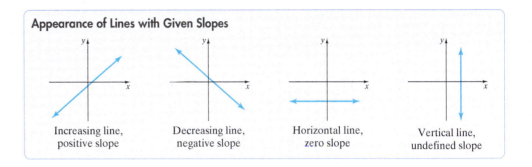

Appearance of Lines with Given Slopes

Increasing line, positive slope | Decreasing line, negative slope | Horizontal line, zero slope | Vertical line, undefined slope

The appearance of a line can give us further information about its slope.

The graphs of $y = \frac{1}{2}x + 1$ and $y = 5x + 1$ are shown to the right. Recall that the graph of $y = \frac{1}{2}x + 1$ has a slope of $\frac{1}{2}$ and that the graph of $y = 5x + 1$ has a slope of 5.

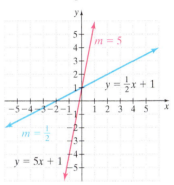

Notice that the line with the slope of 5 is steeper than the line with the slope of $\frac{1}{2}$. This is true in general for positive slopes.

> For a line with positive slope m, as m increases, the line becomes steeper.

To see why this is so, compare the slopes from above.
$\frac{1}{2}$ means a vertical change of 1 unit per horizontal change of 2 units
5 or $\frac{10}{2}$ means a vertical change of 10 units per horizontal change of 2 units

For larger positive slopes, the vertical change is greater for the same horizontal change. Thus, larger positive slopes mean steeper lines.

OBJECTIVE 5 ▶ Comparing slopes of parallel and perpendicular lines. Slopes of lines can help us determine whether lines are parallel. Parallel lines are distinct lines with the same steepness, so it follows that they have the same slope.

Parallel Lines

Two nonvertical lines are parallel if they have the same slope and different y-intercepts.

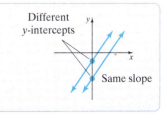

How do the slopes of perpendicular lines compare? (Two lines intersecting at right angles are called **perpendicular lines**.) Suppose that a line has a slope of $\frac{a}{b}$. If the line is rotated 90°, the rise and run are now switched, except that the run is now negative. This means that the new slope is $-\frac{b}{a}$. Notice that

$$\left(\frac{a}{b}\right)\cdot\left(-\frac{b}{a}\right) = -1$$

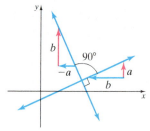

This is how we tell whether two lines are perpendicular.

> **Perpendicular Lines**
> Two nonvertical lines are perpendicular if the product of their slopes is -1.

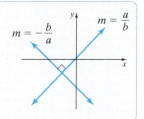

In other words, two nonvertical lines are perpendicular if the slope of one is the negative reciprocal of the slope of the other.

EXAMPLE 8 Are the following pairs of lines parallel, perpendicular, or neither?

a. $3x + 7y = 4$
$6x + 14y = 7$

b. $-x + 3y = 2$
$2x + 6y = 5$

Solution Find the slope of each line by solving each equation for y.

a.
$$3x + 7y = 4 \qquad\qquad 6x + 14y = 7$$
$$7y = -3x + 4 \qquad\qquad 14y = -6x + 7$$
$$\frac{7y}{7} = \frac{-3x}{7} + \frac{4}{7} \qquad \frac{14y}{14} = \frac{-6x}{14} + \frac{7}{14}$$
$$y = -\frac{3}{7}x + \frac{4}{7} \qquad\qquad y = -\frac{3}{7}x + \frac{1}{2}$$

slope y-intercept   slope y-intercept
$\left(0, \frac{4}{7}\right)$ $\left(0, \frac{1}{2}\right)$

The slopes of both lines are $-\frac{3}{7}$.

The y-intercepts are different, so the lines are not the same. Therefore, the lines are parallel.

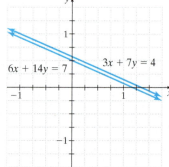

b.
$$-x + 3y = 2 \qquad\qquad 2x + 6y = 5$$
$$3y = x + 2 \qquad\qquad 6y = -2x + 5$$
$$\frac{3y}{3} = \frac{x}{3} + \frac{2}{3} \qquad \frac{6y}{6} = \frac{-2x}{6} + \frac{5}{6}$$
$$y = \frac{1}{3}x + \frac{2}{3} \qquad\qquad y = -\frac{1}{3}x + \frac{5}{6}$$

slope y-intercept   slope y-intercept
$\left(0, \frac{2}{3}\right)$ $\left(0, \frac{5}{6}\right)$

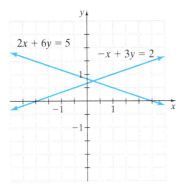

Answer to Concept Check:
y-intercepts are different

The slopes are not the same and their product is not -1. $\left[\left(\frac{1}{3}\right) \cdot \left(-\frac{1}{3}\right) = -\frac{1}{9}\right]$

Therefore, the lines are neither parallel nor perpendicular.

PRACTICE 8 Are the following pairs of lines parallel, perpendicular, or neither?

a. $x - 2y = 3$
$2x + y = 3$

b. $4x - 3y = 2$
$-8x + 6y = -6$

Concept Check

What is *different* about the equations of two parallel lines?

Graphing Calculator Explorations

Many graphing calculators have a TRACE feature. This feature allows you to trace along a graph and see the corresponding x- and y-coordinates appear on the screen. Use this feature for the following exercises.

Graph each function and then use the TRACE feature to complete each ordered pair solution. (Many times the tracer will not show an exact x- or y-value asked for. In each case, trace as closely as you can to the given x- or y-coordinate and approximate the other, unknown coordinate to one decimal place.)

1. $y = 2.3x + 6.7$
   $x = 5.1, y = ?$
2. $y = -4.8x + 2.9$
   $x = -1.8, y = ?$
3. $y = -5.9x - 1.6$
   $x = ?, y = 7.2$
4. $y = 0.4x - 8.6$
   $x = ?, y = -4.4$
5. $y = x^2 + 5.2x - 3.3$
   $x = 2.3, y = ?$
   $x = ?, y = 36$
   (There will be two answers here.)
6. $y = 5x^2 - 6.2x - 8.3$
   $x = 3.2, y = ?$
   $x = ?, y = 12$
   (There will be two answers here.)

VOCABULARY & READINESS CHECK

Word Bank. *Use the choices below to fill in each blank. Some choices may be used more than once and some not at all.*

| horizontal | the same | -1 | y-intercepts | $(0, b)$ | slope |
| vertical | different | m | x-intercepts | $(b, 0)$ | slope-intercept |

1. The measure of the steepness or tilt of a line is called _____.
2. The slope of a line through two points is measured by the ratio of _____ change to _____ change.
3. If a linear equation is in the form $y = mx + b$, or $f(x) = mx + b$, the slope of the line is _____ and the y-intercept is _____.
4. The form $y = mx + b$ or $f(x) = mx + b$ is the _____ form.
5. The slope of a _____ line is 0.
6. The slope of a _____ line is undefined.
7. Two non-vertical perpendicular lines have slopes whose product is _____.
8. Two non-vertical lines are parallel if they have _____ slope and different _____.

Decision Making. *Decide whether a line with the given slope slants upward or downward from left to right, or is horizontal or vertical.*

9. $m = \frac{7}{6}$
10. $m = -3$
11. $m = 0$
12. m is undefined

3.4 EXERCISE SET

Find the slope of the line that goes through the given points. See Examples 1 and 2.

1. $(3, 2), (8, 11)$
2. $(1, 6), (7, 11)$
3. $(3, 1), (1, 8)$
4. $(2, 9), (6, 4)$
5. $(-2, 8), (4, 3)$
6. $(3, 7), (-2, 11)$
7. $(-2, -6), (4, -4)$
8. $(-3, -4), (-1, 6)$
9. $(-3, -1), (-12, 11)$
10. $(3, -1), (-6, 5)$
11. $(-2, 5), (3, 5)$
12. $(4, 2), (4, 0)$
13. $(-1, 1), (-1, -5)$
14. $(-2, -5), (3, -5)$
15. $(0, 6), (-3, 0)$
16. $(5, 2), (0, 5)$
17. $(-1, 2), (-3, 4)$
18. $(3, -2), (-1, -6)$

Decision Making. *Two lines are graphed on each set of axes. Decide whether l_1 or l_2 has the greater slope. See the boxed material on page 151.*

19.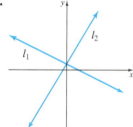
20.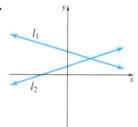
21.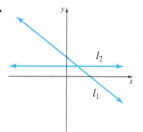
22.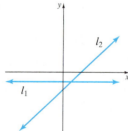
23.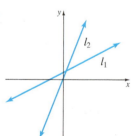
24.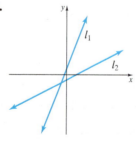

Find the slope and the y-intercept of each line. See Examples 3 and 4.

25. $f(x) = 5x - 2$
26. $f(x) = -2x + 6$
27. $2x + y = 7$
28. $-5x + y = 10$
29. $2x - 3y = 10$
30. $-3x - 4y = 6$
31. $f(x) = \dfrac{1}{2}x$
32. $f(x) = -\dfrac{1}{4}x$

Matching. *Match each graph with its equation. See Examples 1 and 2.*

A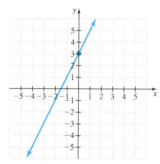
B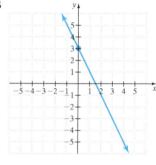
C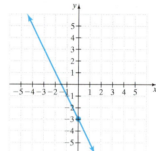
D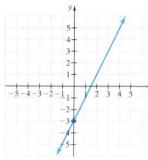

33. $f(x) = 2x + 3$
34. $f(x) = 2x - 3$
35. $f(x) = -2x + 3$
36. $f(x) = -2x - 3$

Find the slope of each line. See Examples 6 and 7.

37. $x = 1$
38. $y = -2$
39. $y = -3$
40. $x = 4$
41. $x + 2 = 0$
42. $y - 7 = 0$

43. Explain how merely looking at a line can tell us whether its slope is negative, positive, undefined, or zero.
44. Explain why the graph of $y = b$ is a horizontal line.

MIXED PRACTICE

Find the slope and the y-intercept of each line. See Examples 3 through 7.

45. $f(x) = -x + 5$
46. $f(x) = x + 2$
47. $-6x + 5y = 30$
48. $4x - 7y = 28$
49. $3x + 9 = y$
50. $2y - 7 = x$
51. $y = 4$
52. $x = 7$
53. $f(x) = 7x$
54. $f(x) = \dfrac{1}{7}x$
55. $6 + y = 0$
56. $x - 7 = 0$
57. $2 - x = 3$
58. $2y + 4 = -7$

Determine whether the lines are parallel, perpendicular, or neither. See Example 8.

59. $f(x) = -3x + 6$
$g(x) = 3x + 5$

60. $f(x) = 5x - 6$
$g(x) = 5x + 2$

61. $-4x + 2y = 5$
$2x - y = 7$

62. $2x - y = -10$
$2x + 4y = 2$

63. $-2x + 3y = 1$
$3x + 2y = 12$

64. $x + 4y = 7$
$2x - 5y = 0$

65. Explain whether two lines, both with positive slopes, can be perpendicular.

66. Explain why it is reasonable that nonvertical parallel lines have the same slope.

Use the points shown on the graphs to determine the slope of each line. See Examples 1 and 2.

67.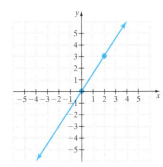

68.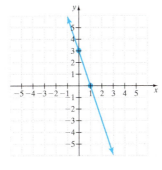

69.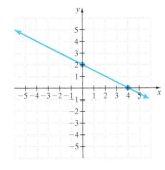

70.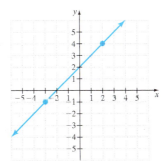

Find each slope. See Examples 1 and 2.

71. Find the pitch, or slope, of the roof shown.

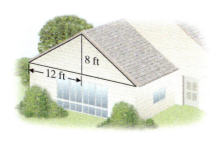

72. Upon takeoff, a Delta Airlines jet climbs to 3 miles as it passes over 25 miles of land below it. Find the slope of its climb.

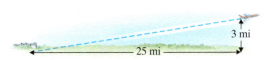

73. Driving down Bald Mountain in Wyoming, Bob Dean finds that he descends 1600 feet in elevation by the time he is 2.5 miles (horizontally) away from the high point on the mountain road. Find the slope of his descent rounded to two decimal places (1 mile = 5280 feet).

74. Find the grade, or slope, of the road shown.

Mutiple Steps. *Solve. See Example 5.*

75. The annual average income y of an American man over 25 with an associate's degree is approximated by the linear equation $y = 694.9x + 43,884.9$, where x is the number of years after 2000. (*Source:* Based on data from the U.S. Bureau of the Census).

a. Predict the average income of an American man with an associate's degree in 2009.

b. Find and interpret the slope of the equation.

c. Find and interpret the y-intercept of the equation.

76. The annual average income of an American woman over 25 with a bachelor's degree is given by the linear equation $y = 1059.6x + 36,827.4$, where x is the number of years after 2000. (*Source:* Based on data from the U.S. Bureau of the Census).

a. Find the average income of an American woman with a bachelor's degree in 2009.

b. Find and interpret the slope of the equation.

c. Find and interpret the y-intercept of the equation.

77. With wireless Internet (WiFi) gaining popularity, the number of public wireless Internet access points (in thousands) is projected to grow from 2003 to 2008 according to the equation

$$-66x + 2y = 84$$

where x is the number of years after 2003.

a. Find the slope and y-intercept of the linear equation.

b. What does the slope mean in this context?

c. What does the y-intercept mean in this context?

78. One of the faster growing occupations over the next few years is expected to be nursing. The number of people y in thousands employed in nursing in the United States can be estimated by the linear equation $-266x + 10y = 27{,}409$, where x is the number of years after 2000. (*Source:* Based on data from American Nurses Association)

a. Find the slope and y-intercept of the linear equation.

b. What does the slope mean in this context?

c. What does the y-intercept mean in this context?

79. In an earlier section, it was given that the yearly cost of tuition and required fees for attending a public four-year college full-time can be estimated by the linear function

$$f(x) = 291.5x + 2944.05$$

where x is the number of years after 2000 and $f(x)$ is the total cost. (*Source:* U.S. National Center for Education Statistics)

a. Find and interpret the slope of this equation.

b. Find and interpret the y-intercept of this equation.

80. In an earlier section, it was given that the yearly cost of tuition and required fees for attending a public two-year college full-time can be estimated by the linear function

$$f(x) = 107.3x + 1245.62$$

where x is the number of years after 2000 and $f(x)$ is the total cost. (*Source:* U.S. National Center for Education Statistics)

a. Find and interpret the slope of this equation.

b. Find and interpret the y-intercept of this equation.

REVIEW AND PREVIEW

Simplify and solve for y. See Section 2.3.

81. $y - 2 = 5(x + 6)$
82. $y - 0 = -3[x - (-10)]$
83. $y - (-1) = 2(x - 0)$
84. $y - 9 = -8[x - (-4)]$

CONCEPT EXTENSIONS

Each slope calculation is incorrect. Find the error and correct the calculation. See the Concept Check in this section.

85. $(-2, 6)$ and $(7, -14)$

$$m = \frac{-14 - 6}{7 - 2} = \frac{-20}{5} = -4$$

86. $(-1, 4)$ and $(-3, 9)$

$$m = \frac{9 - 4}{-3 - 1} = \frac{5}{-4} \text{ or } -\frac{5}{4}$$

87. $(-8, -10)$ and $(-11, -5)$

$$m = \frac{-10 - 5}{-8 - 11} = \frac{-15}{-19} = \frac{15}{19}$$

88. $(0, -4)$ and $(-6, -6)$

$$m = \frac{0 - (-6)}{-4 - (-6)} = \frac{6}{2} = 3$$

89. Find the slope of a line parallel to the line $f(x) = -\frac{7}{2}x - 6$.

△ 90. Find the slope of a line parallel to the line $f(x) = x$.

△ 91. Find the slope of a line perpendicular to the line

$$f(x) = -\frac{7}{2}x - 6.$$

△ 92. Find the slope of a line perpendicular to the line $f(x) = x$.

△ 93. Find the slope of a line parallel to the line $5x - 2y = 6$.

△ 94. Find the slope of a line parallel to the line $-3x + 4y = 10$.

△ 95. Find the slope of a line perpendicular to the line $5x - 2y = 6$.

96. **Multiple Steps.** Each line below has negative slope.

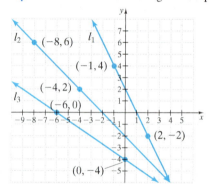

a. Find the slope of each line.

b. Use the result of Part **a** to fill in the blank. For lines with negative slopes, the steeper line has the _____ (greater/lesser) slope.

97. **Read a Graph.** The following graph shows the altitude of a seagull in flight over a time period of 30 seconds.

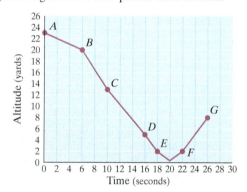

a. Find the coordinates of point B.

b. Find the coordinates of point C.

c. Find the rate of change of altitude between points B and C. (Recall that the rate of change between points is the slope between points. This rate of change will be in yards per second.)

d. Find the rate of change of altitude (in yards per second) between points *F* and *G*.

98. Professional plumbers suggest that a sewer pipe should be sloped 0.25 inch for every foot. Find the recommended slope for a sewer pipe. (*Source: Rules of Thumb* by Tom Parker, 1983, Houghton Mifflin Company)

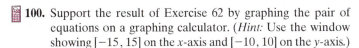99. Support the result of Exercise 61 by graphing the pair of equations on a graphing calculator.

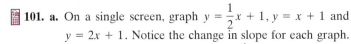100. Support the result of Exercise 62 by graphing the pair of equations on a graphing calculator. (*Hint:* Use the window showing $[-15, 15]$ on the *x*-axis and $[-10, 10]$ on the *y*-axis.)

101. a. On a single screen, graph $y = \frac{1}{2}x + 1$, $y = x + 1$ and $y = 2x + 1$. Notice the change in slope for each graph.

b. On a single screen, graph $y = -\frac{1}{2}x + 1$, $y = -x + 1$ and $y = -2x + 1$. Notice the change in slope for each graph.

c. Determine whether the following statement is true or false for slope *m* of a given line. As $|m|$ becomes greater, the line becomes steeper.

3.5 EQUATIONS OF LINES

OBJECTIVES

1 Use the slope-intercept form to write the equation of a line.

2 Graph a line using its slope and *y*-intercept.

3 Use the point-slope form to write the equation of a line.

4 Write equations of vertical and horizontal lines.

5 Find equations of parallel and perpendicular lines.

OBJECTIVE 1 ▶ Using slope-intercept form to write equations of lines. In the last section, we learned that the slope–intercept form of a linear equation is $y = mx + b$. When a linear equation is written in this form, the slope of the line is the same as the coefficient *m* of *x*. Also, the *y*-intercept of the line is $(0, b)$. For example, the slope of the line defined by $y = 2x + 3$ is, 2, and its *y*-intercept is $(0, 3)$.

We may also use the slope–intercept form to write the equation of a line given its slope and *y*-intercept. The equation of a line is a linear equation in 2 variables that, if graphed, would produce the line described.

EXAMPLE 1 Write an equation of the line with *y*-intercept $(0, -3)$ and slope of $\frac{1}{4}$.

Solution We want to write a linear equation in 2 variables that describes the line with *y*-intercept $(0, -3)$ and has a slope of $\frac{1}{4}$. We are given the slope and the *y*-intercept. Let $m = \frac{1}{4}$ and $b = -3$, and write the equation in slope-intercept form, $y = mx + b$.

$$y = mx + b$$
$$y = \frac{1}{4}x + (-3) \quad \text{Let } m = \frac{1}{4} \text{ and } b = -3.$$
$$y = \frac{1}{4}x - 3 \quad \text{Simplify.}$$

PRACTICE 1 Write an equation of the line with *y*-intercept $(0, 4)$ and slope of $-\frac{3}{4}$.

Concept Check ✓

What is wrong with the following equation of a line with *y*-intercept $(0, 4)$ and slope 2?

$$y = 4x + 2$$

Answer to Concept Check:
y-intercept and slope were switched, should be $y = 2x + 4$

OBJECTIVE 2 ▶ Graph a line using slope and *y*-intercept. Given the slope and *y*-intercept of a line, we may graph the line as well as write its equation. Let's graph the line from Example 1.

EXAMPLE 2 Graph $y = \frac{1}{4}x - 3$.

Solution Recall that the slope of the graph of $y = \frac{1}{4}x - 3$ is $\frac{1}{4}$ and the y-intercept is $(0, -3)$. To graph the line, we first plot the y-intercept $(0, -3)$. To find another point on the line, we recall that slope is $\frac{\text{rise}}{\text{run}} = \frac{1}{4}$. Another point may then be plotted by starting at $(0, -3)$, rising 1 unit up, and then running 4 units to the right. We are now at the point $(4, -2)$. The graph is the line through these two points.

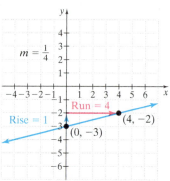

Notice that the line does have a y-intercept of $(0, -3)$ and a slope of $\frac{1}{4}$.

PRACTICE 2 Graph $y = \frac{3}{4}x + 2$.

EXAMPLE 3 Graph $2x + 3y = 12$.

Solution First, we solve the equation for y to write it in slope–intercept form. In slope–intercept form, the equation is $y = -\frac{2}{3}x + 4$. Next we plot the y-intercept $(0, 4)$. To find another point on the line, we use the slope $-\frac{2}{3}$, which can be written as $\frac{\text{rise}}{\text{run}} = \frac{-2}{3}$. We start at $(0, 4)$ and move down 2 units since the numerator of the slope is -2; then we move 3 units to the right since the denominator of the slope is 3. We arrive at the point $(3, 2)$. The line through these points is the graph, shown below to the left.

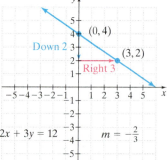 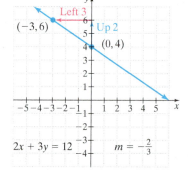

The slope $\frac{-2}{3}$ can also be written as $\frac{2}{-3}$, so to find another point in Example 3 we could start at $(0, 4)$ and move up 2 units and then 3 units to the left. We would arrive at the point $(-3, 6)$. The line through $(-3, 6)$ and $(0, 4)$ is the same line as shown previously through $(3, 2)$ and $(0, 4)$. See the graph above to the right.

PRACTICE 3 Graph $x + 2y = 6$.

Section 3.5 Equations of Lines **159**

OBJECTIVE 3 ▶ Using point-slope form to write equations of lines. When the slope of a line and a point on the line are known, the equation of the line can also be found. To do this, use the slope formula to write the slope of a line that passes through points (x_1, y_1) and (x, y). We have

$$m = \frac{y - y_1}{x - x_1}$$

Multiply both sides of this equation by $x - x_1$ to obtain

$$y - y_1 = m(x - x_1)$$

This form is called the **point–slope form** of the equation of a line.

Point-Slope Form of the Equation of a Line

The **point-slope form** of the equation of a line is

$$y - y_1 = m(x - x_1)$$

where m is the slope of the line and (x_1, y_1) is a point on the line.

EXAMPLE 4 Find an equation of the line with slope -3 containing the point $(1, -5)$. Write the equation in slope–intercept form $y = mx + b$.

Solution Because we know the slope and a point of the line, we use the point–slope form with $m = -3$ and $(x_1, y_1) = (1, -5)$.

$$y - y_1 = m(x - x_1) \quad \text{Point-slope form}$$
$$y - (-5) = -3(x - 1) \quad \text{Let } m = -3 \text{ and } (x_1, y_1) = (1, -5).$$
$$y + 5 = -3x + 3 \quad \text{Apply the distributive property.}$$
$$y = -3x - 2 \quad \text{Write in slope-intercept form.}$$

In slope–intercept form, the equation is $y = -3x - 2$.

PRACTICE

4 Find an equation of the line with slope -4 containing the point $(-2, 5)$. Write the equation in slope-intercept form $y = mx + b$.

▶ **Helpful Hint**

Remember, "slope-intercept form" means the equation is "solved for y."

EXAMPLE 5 Find an equation of the line through points $(4, 0)$ and $(-4, -5)$. Write the equation using function notation.

Solution First, find the slope of the line.

$$m = \frac{-5 - 0}{-4 - 4} = \frac{-5}{-8} = \frac{5}{8}$$

Next, make use of the point–slope form. Replace (x_1, y_1) by either $(4, 0)$ or $(-4, -5)$ in the point–slope equation. We will choose the point $(4, 0)$. The line through $(4, 0)$ with slope $\frac{5}{8}$ is

$$y - y_1 = m(x - x_1) \quad \text{Point-slope form.}$$
$$y - 0 = \frac{5}{8}(x - 4) \quad \text{Let } m = \frac{5}{8} \text{ and } (x_1, y_1) = (4, 0).$$
$$8y = 5(x - 4) \quad \text{Multiply both sides by 8.}$$
$$8y = 5x - 20 \quad \text{Apply the distributive property.}$$

To write the equation using function notation, we solve for y, then replace y with $f(x)$.

$$8y = 5x - 20$$
$$y = \frac{5}{8}x - \frac{20}{8} \quad \text{Divide both sides by 8.}$$
$$f(x) = \frac{5}{8}x - \frac{5}{2} \quad \text{Write using function notation.}$$

PRACTICE 5 Find an equation of the line through points $(-1, 2)$ and $(2, 0)$. Write the equation using function notation.

> **Helpful Hint**
> If two points of a line are given, either one may be used with the point-slope form to write an equation of the line.

EXAMPLE 6 Find an equation of the line graphed. Write the equation in standard form.

Solution First, find the slope of the line by identifying the coordinates of the noted points on the graph.

The points have coordinates $(-1, 2)$ and $(3, 5)$.

$$m = \frac{5 - 2}{3 - (-1)} = \frac{3}{4}$$

Next, use the point-slope form. We will choose $(3, 5)$ for (x_1, y_1), although it makes no difference which point we choose. The line through $(3, 5)$ with slope $\frac{3}{4}$ is

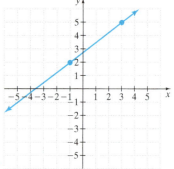

$$y - y_1 = m(x - x_1) \quad \text{Point-slope form}$$
$$y - 5 = \frac{3}{4}(x - 3) \quad \text{Let } m = \frac{3}{4} \text{ and } (x_1, y_1) = (3, 5).$$
$$4(y - 5) = 3(x - 3) \quad \text{Multiply both sides by 4.}$$
$$4y - 20 = 3x - 9 \quad \text{Apply the distributive property.}$$

To write the equation in standard form, move x- and y-terms to one side of the equation and any numbers (constants) to the other side.

$$4y - 20 = 3x - 9$$
$$-3x + 4y = 11 \quad \text{Subtract } 3x \text{ from both sides and add 20 to both sides.}$$

The equation of the graphed line is $-3x + 4y = 11$.

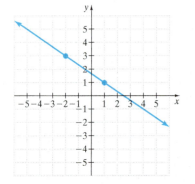

PRACTICE 6 Find an equation of the line graphed. Write the equation in standard form.

The point–slope form of an equation is very useful for solving real-world problems.

EXAMPLE 7 Predicting Sales

Southern Star Realty is an established real estate company that has enjoyed constant growth in sales since 2000. In 2002 the company sold 200 houses, and in 2007 the company sold 275 houses. Use these figures to predict the number of houses this company will sell in the year 2016.

Solution

1. UNDERSTAND. Read and reread the problem. Then let

   x = the number of years after 2000 and

   y = the number of houses sold in the year corresponding to x.

   The information provided then gives the ordered pairs (2, 200) and (7, 275). To better visualize the sales of Southern Star Realty, we graph the linear equation that passes through the points (2, 200) and (7, 275).

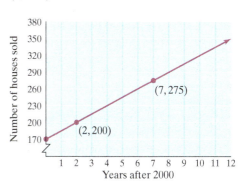

2. TRANSLATE. We write a linear equation that passes through the points (2, 200) and (7, 275). To do so, we first find the slope of the line.

$$m = \frac{275 - 200}{7 - 2} = \frac{75}{5} = 15$$

Then, using the point–slope form and the point (2, 200) to write the equation, we have

$$y - y_1 = m(x - x_1)$$
$$y - 200 = 15(x - 2) \quad \text{Let } m = 15 \text{ and } (x_1, y_1) = (2, 200).$$
$$y - 200 = 15x - 30 \quad \text{Multiply.}$$
$$y = 15x + 170 \quad \text{Add 200 to both sides.}$$

3. SOLVE. To predict the number of houses sold in the year 2016, we use $y = 15x + 170$ and complete the ordered pair (16,   ), since $2016 - 2000 = 16$.

$$y = 15(16) + 170 \quad \text{Let } x = 16.$$
$$y = 410$$

4. INTERPRET.

Check: Verify that the point (16, 410) is a point on the line graphed in step 1.

State: Southern Star Realty should expect to sell 410 houses in the year 2016.

PRACTICE 7

Southwest Florida, including Fort Myers and Cape Coral, has been a growing real estate market in past years. In 2002, there were 7513 house sales in the area, and in 2006, there were 9198 house sales. Use these figures to predict the number of house sales there will be in 2014.

OBJECTIVE 4 ▶ Writing equations of vertical and horizontal lines. A few special types of linear equations are linear equations whose graphs are vertical and horizontal lines.

EXAMPLE 8 Find an equation of the horizontal line containing the point $(2, 3)$.

Solution Recall that a horizontal line has an equation of the form $y = b$. Since the line contains the point $(2, 3)$, the equation is $y = 3$, as shown to the right.

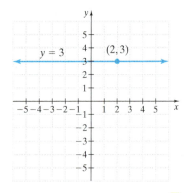

PRACTICE 8 Find the equation of the horizontal line containing the point $(6, -2)$.

EXAMPLE 9 Find an equation of the line containing the point $(2, 3)$ with undefined slope.

Solution Since the line has undefined slope, the line must be vertical. A vertical line has an equation of the form $x = c$. Since the line contains the point $(2, 3)$, the equation is $x = 2$, as shown to the right.

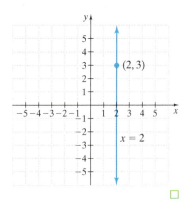

PRACTICE 9 Find an equation of the line containing the point $(6, -2)$ with undefined slope.

OBJECTIVE 5 ▶ Finding equations of parallel and perpendicular lines. Next, we find equations of parallel and perpendicular lines.

EXAMPLE 10 Find an equation of the line containing the point $(4, 4)$ and parallel to the line $2x + 3y = -6$. Write the equation in standard form.

Solution Because the line we want to find is *parallel* to the line $2x + 3y = -6$, the two lines must have equal slopes. Find the slope of $2x + 3y = -6$ by writing it in the form $y = mx + b$. In other words, solve the equation for y.

$$2x + 3y = -6$$
$$3y = -2x - 6 \quad \text{Subtract } 2x \text{ from both sides.}$$
$$y = \frac{-2x}{3} - \frac{6}{3} \quad \text{Divide by 3.}$$
$$y = -\frac{2}{3}x - 2 \quad \text{Write in slope-intercept form.}$$

The slope of this line is $-\frac{2}{3}$. Thus, a line parallel to this line will also have a slope of $-\frac{2}{3}$. The equation we are asked to find describes a line containing the point (4, 4) with a slope of $-\frac{2}{3}$. We use the point-slope form.

$$y - y_1 = m(x - x_1)$$
$$y - 4 = -\frac{2}{3}(x - 4) \quad \text{Let } m = -\frac{2}{3}, x_1 = 4, \text{ and } y_1 = 4.$$
$$3(y - 4) = -2(x - 4) \quad \text{Multiply both sides by 3.}$$
$$3y - 12 = -2x + 8 \quad \text{Apply the distributive property.}$$
$$2x + 3y = 20 \quad \text{Write in standard form.}$$

> **Helpful Hint**
> Multiply both sides of the equation $2x + 3y = 20$ by -1 and it becomes $-2x - 3y = -20$. Both equations are in standard form, and their graphs are the same line.

PRACTICE 10 Find an equation of the line containing the point (8, −3) and parallel to the line $3x + 4y = 1$. Write the equation in standard form.

EXAMPLE 11 Write a function that describes the line containing the point (4, 4) and is perpendicular to the line $2x + 3y = -6$.

Solution In the previous example, we found that the slope of the line $2x + 3y = -6$ is $-\frac{2}{3}$. A line perpendicular to this line will have a slope that is the negative reciprocal of $-\frac{2}{3}$, or $\frac{3}{2}$. From the point-slope equation, we have

$$y - y_1 = m(x - x_1)$$
$$y - 4 = \frac{3}{2}(x - 4) \quad \text{Let } x_1 = 4, y_1 = 4 \text{ and } m = \frac{3}{2}.$$
$$2(y - 4) = 3(x - 4) \quad \text{Multiply both sides by 2.}$$
$$2y - 8 = 3x - 12 \quad \text{Apply the distributive property.}$$
$$2y = 3x - 4 \quad \text{Add 8 to both sides.}$$
$$y = \frac{3}{2}x - 2 \quad \text{Divide both sides by 2.}$$
$$f(x) = \frac{3}{2}x - 2 \quad \text{Write using function notation.}$$

PRACTICE 11 Write a function that describes the line containing the point (8, −3) and is perpendicular to the line $3x + 4y = 1$.

> **Forms of Linear Equations**
>
> $Ax + By = C$ **Standard form** of a linear equation
> A and B are not both 0.
>
> $y = mx + b$ **Slope–intercept form** of a linear equation
> The slope is m, and the y-intercept is $(0, b)$.
>
> $y - y_1 = m(x - x_1)$ **Point–slope form** of a linear equation
> The slope is m, and (x_1, y_1) is a point on the line.
>
> $y = c$ **Horizontal line**
> The slope is 0, and the y-intercept is $(0, c)$.
>
> $x = c$ **Vertical line**
> The slope is undefined and the x-intercept is $(c, 0)$.
>
> **Parallel and Perpendicular Lines**
> Nonvertical parallel lines have the same slope. The product of the slopes of two nonvertical perpendicular lines is -1.

164 CHAPTER 3 Graphs and Functions

VOCABULARY & READINESS CHECK

State the slope and the y-intercept of each line with the given equation.

1. $y = -4x + 12$
2. $y = \frac{2}{3}x - \frac{7}{2}$
3. $y = 5x$
4. $y = -x$
5. $y = \frac{1}{2}x + 6$
6. $y = -\frac{2}{3}x + 5$

Decision Making. Decide whether the lines are parallel, perpendicular, or neither.

7. $y = 12x + 6$
   $y = 12x - 2$
8. $y = -5x + 8$
   $y = -5x - 8$
9. $y = -9x + 3$
   $y = \frac{3}{2}x - 7$
10. $y = 2x - 12$
    $y = \frac{1}{2}x - 6$

3.5 EXERCISE SET

Use the slope-intercept form of the linear equation to write the equation of each line with the given slope and y-intercept. See Example 1.

1. Slope -1; y-intercept $(0, 1)$
2. Slope $\frac{1}{2}$; y-intercept $(0, -6)$
3. Slope 2; y-intercept $\left(0, \frac{3}{4}\right)$
4. Slope -3; y-intercept $\left(0, -\frac{1}{5}\right)$
5. Slope $\frac{2}{7}$; y-intercept $(0, 0)$
6. Slope $-\frac{4}{5}$; y-intercept $(0, 0)$

Graph each linear equation. See Examples 2 and 3.

7. $y = 5x - 2$
8. $y = 2x + 1$
9. $4x + y = 7$
10. $3x + y = 9$
11. $-3x + 2y = 3$
12. $-2x + 5y = -16$

Find an equation of the line with the given slope and containing the given point. Write the equation in slope-intercept form. See Example 4.

13. Slope 3; through $(1, 2)$
14. Slope 4; through $(5, 1)$
15. Slope -2; through $(1, -3)$
16. Slope -4; through $(2, -4)$
17. Slope $\frac{1}{2}$; through $(-6, 2)$
18. Slope $\frac{2}{3}$; through $(-9, 4)$
19. Slope $-\frac{9}{10}$; through $(-3, 0)$
20. Slope $-\frac{1}{5}$; through $(4, -6)$

Find an equation of the line passing through the given points. Use function notation to write the equation. See Example 5.

21. $(2, 0), (4, 6)$
22. $(3, 0), (7, 8)$
23. $(-2, 5), (-6, 13)$
24. $(7, -4), (2, 6)$
25. $(-2, -4), (-4, -3)$
26. $(-9, -2), (-3, 10)$
27. $(-3, -8), (-6, -9)$
28. $(8, -3), (4, -8)$
29. $\left(\frac{3}{5}, \frac{4}{10}\right)$ and $\left(-\frac{1}{5}, \frac{7}{10}\right)$
30. $\left(\frac{1}{2}, -\frac{1}{4}\right)$ and $\left(\frac{3}{2}, \frac{3}{4}\right)$

Find an equation of each line graphed. Write the equation in standard form. See Example 6.

31.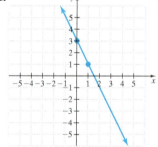
32.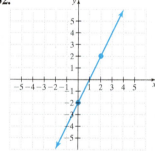

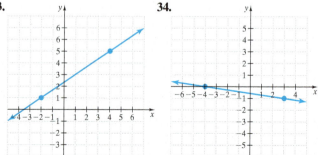

33.
34.

Read a Graph. *Use the graph of the following function f(x) to find each value.*

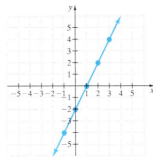

35. $f(0)$
36. $f(-1)$
37. $f(2)$
38. $f(1)$
39. Find x such that $f(x) = -6$.
40. Find x such that $f(x) = 4$.

Write an equation of each line. See Examples 8 and 9.

41. Slope 0; through $(-2, -4)$
42. Horizontal; through $(-3, 1)$
43. Vertical; through $(4, 7)$
44. Vertical; through $(2, 6)$
45. Horizontal; through $(0, 5)$
46. Undefined slope; through $(0, 5)$

Find an equation of each line. Write the equation using function notation. See Examples 10 and 11.

47. Through $(3, 8)$; parallel to $f(x) = 4x - 2$
48. Through $(1, 5)$; parallel to $f(x) = 3x - 4$
49. Through $(2, -5)$; perpendicular to $3y = x - 6$
50. Through $(-4, 8)$; perpendicular to $2x - 3y = 1$
51. Through $(-2, -3)$; parallel to $3x + 2y = 5$
52. Through $(-2, -3)$; perpendicular to $3x + 2y = 5$

MIXED PRACTICE

Find the equation of each line. Write the equation in standard form unless indicated otherwise. See Examples 1, 4, 5 and 8 through 11.

53. Slope 2; through $(-2, 3)$
54. Slope 3; through $(-4, 2)$
55. Through $(1, 6)$ and $(5, 2)$; use function notation.
56. Through $(2, 9)$ and $(8, 6)$
57. With slope $-\frac{1}{2}$; y-intercept 11
58. With slope -4; y-intercept $\frac{2}{9}$; use function notation.
59. Through $(-7, -4)$ and $(0, -6)$
60. Through $(2, -8)$ and $(-4, -3)$
61. Slope $-\frac{4}{3}$; through $(-5, 0)$
62. Slope $-\frac{3}{5}$; through $(4, -1)$
63. Vertical line; through $(-2, -10)$
64. Horizontal line; through $(1, 0)$
65. Through $(6, -2)$; parallel to the line $2x + 4y = 9$
66. Through $(8, -3)$; parallel to the line $6x + 2y = 5$
67. Slope 0; through $(-9, 12)$
68. Undefined slope; through $(10, -8)$
69. Through $(6, 1)$; parallel to the line $8x - y = 9$
70. Through $(3, 5)$; perpendicular to the line $2x - y = 8$
71. Through $(5, -6)$; perpendicular to $y = 9$
72. Through $(-3, -5)$; parallel to $y = 9$
73. Through $(2, -8)$ and $(-6, -5)$; use function notation.
74. Through $(-4, -2)$ and $(-6, 5)$; use function notation.

Multiple Steps. *Solve. See Example 7.*

75. Del Monte Fruit Company recently released a new applesauce. By the end of its first year, profits on this product amounted to $30,000. The anticipated profit for the end of the fourth year is $66,000. The ratio of change in time to change in profit is constant. Let x be years and P be profit.
    a. Write a linear function $P(x)$ that expresses profit as a function of time.
    b. Use this function to predict the company's profit at the end of the seventh year.
    c. Predict when the profit should reach $126,000.

76. The value of a computer bought in 2003 depreciates, or decreases, as time passes. Two years after the computer was bought, it was worth $2000; 4 years after it was bought, it was worth $800.
    a. If this relationship between number of years past 2003 and value of computer is linear, write an equation describing this relationship. [Use ordered pairs of the form (years past 2003, value of computer).]
    b. Use this equation to estimate the value of the computer in the year 2008.

77. The Pool Fun Company has learned that, by pricing a newly released Fun Noodle at $3, sales will reach 10,000 Fun Noodles per day during the summer. Raising the price to $5 will cause the sales to fall to 8000 Fun Noodles per day.
    a. Assume that the relationship between sales price and number of Fun Noodles sold is linear and write an equation describing this relationship.
    b. Predict the daily sales of Fun Noodles if the price is $3.50.

78. The value of a building bought in 1990 appreciates, or increases, as time passes. Seven years after the building was bought, it was worth $165,000; 12 years after it was bought, it was worth $180,000.
    a. If this relationship between number of years past 1990 and value of building is linear, write an equation describing this relationship. [Use ordered pairs of the form (years past 1990, value of building).]
    b. Use this equation to estimate the value of the building in the year 2010.

79. In 2006, the median price of an existing home in the United States was approximately $222,000. In 2001, the median price of an existing home was $150,900. Let y be the median price of an existing home in the year x, where $x = 0$ represents 2001. (*Source:* National Association of REALTORS®)
    a. Write a linear equation that models the median existing home price in terms of the year x. [*Hint:* The line must pass through the points $(0, 150{,}900)$ and $(5, 222{,}000)$.]

b. Use this equation to predict the median existing home price for the year 2010.

c. Interpret the slope of the equation found in part **a**.

80. The number of births (in thousands) in the United States in 2000 was 4060. The number of births (in thousands) in the United States in 2004 was 4116. Let y be the number of births (in thousands) in the year x, where $x = 0$ represents 2000. (*Source:* National Center for Health Statistics)

   a. Write a linear equation that models the number of births (in thousands) in terms of the year x. (See hint for Exercise 79a.)

   b. Use this equation to predict the number of births in the United States for the year 2013.

   c. Interpret the slope of the equation in part a.

81. The number of people employed in the United States as medical assistants was 387 thousand in 2004. By the year 2014, this number is expected to rise to 589 thousand. Let y be the number of medical assistants (in thousands) employed in the United States in the year x, where $x = 0$ represents 2004. (*Source:* Bureau of Labor Statistics)

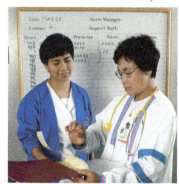

   a. Write a linear equation that models the number of people (in thousands) employed as medical assistants in the year x. (See hint for Exercise 79a.)

   b. Use this equation to estimate the number of people who will be employed as medical assistants in the year 2013.

82. The number of people employed in the United States as systems analysts was 487 thousand in 2004. By the year 2014, this number is expected to rise to 640 thousand. Let y be the number of systems analysts (in thousands) employed in the United States in the year x, where $x = 0$ represents 2004. (*Source:* Bureau of Labor Statistics)

   a. Write a linear equation that models the number of people (in thousands) employed as systems analysts in the year x. (See hint for Exercise 79a.)

   b. Use this equation to estimate the number of people who will be employed as systems analysts in the year 2012.

REVIEW AND PREVIEW

Solve. See Section 2.4.

83. $2x - 7 \leq 21$

84. $-3x + 1 > 0$

85. $5(x - 2) \geq 3(x - 1)$

86. $-2(x + 1) \leq -x + 10$

87. $\dfrac{x}{2} + \dfrac{1}{4} < \dfrac{1}{8}$

88. $\dfrac{x}{5} - \dfrac{3}{10} \geq \dfrac{x}{2} - 1$

CONCEPT EXTENSIONS

True or False. *Answer true or false.*

89. A vertical line is always perpendicular to a horizontal line.

90. A vertical line is always parallel to a vertical line.

Example:

Find an equation of the perpendicular bisector of the line segment whose endpoints are (2, 6) and (0, −2).

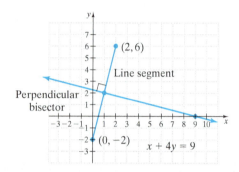

Solution:

A perpendicular bisector is a line that contains the midpoint of the given segment and is perpendicular to the segment.

Step 1: The midpoint of the segment with endpoints (2, 6) and (0, −2) is (1, 2).

Step 2: The slope of the segment containing points (2, 6) and (0, −2) is 4.

Step 3: A line perpendicular to this line segment will have slope of $-\dfrac{1}{4}$.

Step 4: The equation of the line through the midpoint (1, 2) with a slope of $-\dfrac{1}{4}$ will be the equation of the perpendicular bisector. This equation in standard form is $x + 4y = 9$.

Find an equation of the perpendicular bisector of the line segment whose endpoints are given. See the previous example.

△ **91.** $(3, -1); (-5, 1)$

△ **92.** $(-6, -3); (-8, -1)$

△ **93.** $(-2, 6); (-22, -4)$

△ **94.** $(5, 8); (7, 2)$

△ **95.** $(2, 3); (-4, 7)$

△ **96.** $(-6, 8); (-4, -2)$

97. Describe how to check to see if the graph of $2x - 4y = 7$ passes through the points $(1.4, -1.05)$ and $(0, -1.75)$. Then follow your directions and check these points.

Use a graphing calculator with a TRACE feature to see the results of each exercise.

98. Exercise 56; graph the equation and verify that it passes through (2, 9) and (8, 6).

99. Exercise 55; graph the function and verify that it passes through $(1, 6)$ and $(5, 2)$.

100. Exercise 62; graph the equation. See that it has a negative slope and passes through $(4, -1)$.

101. Exercise 61; graph the equation. See that it has a negative slope and passes through $(-5, 0)$.

102. Exercise 48: Graph the equation and verify that it passes through $(1, 5)$ and is parallel to $y = 3x - 4$.

103. Exercise 47: Graph the equation and verify that it passes through $(3, 8)$ and is parallel to $y = 4x - 2$.

INTEGRATED REVIEW LINEAR EQUATIONS IN TWO VARIABLES

Sections 3.1–3.5

Below is a review of equations of lines.

Forms of Linear Equations

$Ax + By = C$	**Standard form** of a linear equation A and B are not both 0.
$y = mx + b$	**Slope-intercept form** of a linear equation. The slope is m, and the y-intercept is $(0, b)$.
$y - y_1 = m(x - x_1)$	**Point-slope form** of a linear equation. The slope is m, and (x_1, y_1) is a point on the line.
$y = c$	**Horizontal line** The slope is 0, and the y-intercept is $(0, c)$.
$x = c$	**Vertical line** The slope is undefined and the x-intercept is $(c, 0)$.

Parallel and Perpendicular Lines

Nonvertical parallel lines have the same slope. The product of the slopes of two nonvertical perpendicular lines is -1.

Graph each linear equation.

1. $y = -2x$ **2.** $3x - 2y = 6$ **3.** $x = -3$ **4.** $y = 1.5$

Find the slope of the line containing each pair of points.

5. $(-2, -5), (3, -5)$ **6.** $(5, 2), (0, 5)$

Find the slope and y-intercept of each line.

7. $y = 3x - 5$ **8.** $5x - 2y = 7$

Determine whether each pair of lines is parallel, perpendicular, or neither.

9. $y = 8x - 6$
$y = 8x + 6$

10. $y = \frac{2}{3}x + 1$
$2y + 3x = 1$

Find the equation of each line. Write the equation in the form $x = a$, $y = b$, or $y = mx + b$. For Exercises 14 through 17, write the equation in the form $f(x) = mx + b$.

11. Through $(1, 6)$ and $(5, 2)$

12. Vertical line; through $(-2, -10)$

13. Horizontal line; through $(1, 0)$

14. Through $(2, -9)$ and $(-6, -5)$

15. Through $(-2, 4)$ with slope -5

16. Slope -4; y-intercept $\left(0, \dfrac{1}{3}\right)$

17. Slope $\dfrac{1}{2}$; y-intercept $(0, -1)$

18. Through $\left(\dfrac{1}{2}, 0\right)$ with slope 3

19. Through $(-1, -5)$; parallel to $3x - y = 5$

20. Through $(0, 4)$; perpendicular to $4x - 5y = 10$

21. Through $(2, -3)$; perpendicular to $4x + y = \dfrac{2}{3}$

22. Through $(-1, 0)$; parallel to $5x + 2y = 2$

23. Undefined slope; through $(-1, 3)$

24. $m = 0$; through $(-1, 3)$

3.6 GRAPHING PIECEWISE-DEFINED FUNCTIONS AND SHIFTING AND REFLECTING GRAPHS OF FUNCTIONS

OBJECTIVES

1. Graph piecewise-defined functions.
2. Vertical and horizontal shifts.
3. Reflect graphs.

OBJECTIVE 1 ▶ Graphing piecewise-defined functions. Throughout Chapter 3, we have graphed functions. There are many special functions. In this objective, we study functions defined by two or more expressions. The expression used to complete the function varies with, and depends upon the value of x. Before we actually graph these piecewise-defined functions, let's practice finding function values.

EXAMPLE 1 Evaluate $f(2), f(-6)$, and $f(0)$ for the function

$$f(x) = \begin{cases} 2x + 3 & \text{if } x \leq 0 \\ -x - 1 & \text{if } x > 0 \end{cases}$$

Then write your results in ordered-pair form.

Solution Take a moment and study this function. It is a single function defined by two expressions depending on the value of x. From above, if $x \leq 0$, use $f(x) = 2x + 3$. If $x > 0$, use $f(x) = -x - 1$. Thus

$f(2) = -(2) - 1$
$ = -3$ since $2 > 0$
$f(2) = -3$
Ordered pairs: $(2, -3)$

$f(-6) = 2(-6) + 3$
$ = -9$ since $-6 \leq 0$
$f(-6) = -9$
$(-6, -9)$

$f(0) = 2(0) + 3$
$ = 3$ since $0 \leq 0$
$f(0) = 3$
$(0, 3)$

PRACTICE 1 Evaluate $f(4), f(-2)$, and $f(0)$ for the function

$$f(x) = \begin{cases} -4x - 2 & \text{if } x \leq 0 \\ x + 1 & \text{if } x > 0 \end{cases}.$$

Now, let's graph a piecewise-defined function.

Section 3.6 Graphing Piecewise-Defined Functions and Shifting and Reflecting Graphs of Functions   169

EXAMPLE 2   Graph $f(x) = \begin{cases} 2x + 3 & \text{if } x \leq 0 \\ -x - 1 & \text{if } x > 0 \end{cases}$

Solution   Let's graph each piece.

If $x \leq 0$,   If $x > 0$,
$f(x) = 2x + 3$ $f(x) = -x - 1$

Values ≤ 0:

x	$f(x) = 2x + 3$
0	3 Closed circle
-1	1
-2	-1

Values > 0:

x	$f(x) = -x - 1$
1	-2
2	-3
3	-4

The graph of the first part of $f(x)$ listed will look like a ray with a closed-circle endpoint at $(0, 3)$. The graph of the second part of $f(x)$ listed will look like a ray with an open-circle endpoint. To find the exact location of the open-circle endpoint, use $f(x) = -x - 1$ and find $f(0)$. Since $f(0) = -0 - 1 = -1$, we graph the second table and place an open circle at $(0, -1)$.

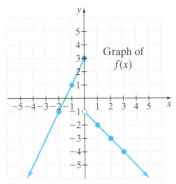

Graph of $f(x)$

Notice that this graph is the graph of a function because it passes the vertical line test. The domain of this function is all real numbers and the range is $y \leq 3$.   □

PRACTICE 2   Graph

$$f(x) = \begin{cases} -4x - 2 & \text{if } x \leq 0 \\ x + 1 & \text{if } x > 0 \end{cases}$$

OBJECTIVE 2 ▶ **Vertical and horizontal shifting.**

Review of Common Graphs

We now take common graphs and learn how more complicated graphs are actually formed by shifting and reflecting these common graphs. These shifts and reflections are called transformations, and it is possible to combine transformations. A knowledge of these transformations will help you simplify future graphs.

Let's begin with a review of the graphs of four common functions. Many of these functions we graphed in earlier sections.

First, let's graph the linear function $f(x) = x$, or $y = x$. Ordered-pair solutions of this graph consist of ordered pairs whose x- and y-values are the same.

x	y or $f(x) = x$
-3	-3
0	0
1	1
4	4

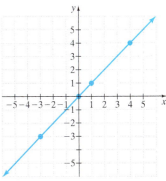

Next, **let's graph the nonlinear function** $f(x) = x^2$ **or** $y = x^2$.

This equation is not linear because the x^2 term does not allow us to write it in the form $Ax + By = C$. Its graph is not a line. We begin by finding ordered pair solutions. Because this graph is solved for $f(x)$, or y, we choose x-values and find corresponding $f(x)$, or y-values.

If $x = -3$, then $y = (-3)^2$, or 9.
If $x = -2$, then $y = (-2)^2$, or 4.
If $x = -1$, then $y = (-1)^2$, or 1.
If $x = 0$, then $y = 0^2$, or 0.
If $x = 1$, then $y = 1^2$, or 1.
If $x = 2$, then $y = 2^2$, or 4.
If $x = 3$, then $y = 3^2$, or 9.

x	$f(x)$ or y
-3	9
-2	4
-1	1
0	0
1	1
2	4
3	9

Study the table for a moment and look for patterns. Notice that the ordered pair solution $(0, 0)$ contains the smallest y-value because any other x-value squared will give a positive result. This means that the point $(0, 0)$ will be the lowest point on the graph. Also notice that all other y-values correspond to two different x-values. For example, $3^2 = 9$ and also $(-3)^2 = 9$. This means that the graph will be a mirror image of itself across the y-axis. Connect the plotted points with a smooth curve to sketch its graph.

This curve is given a special name, a **parabola**. We will study more about parabolas in later chapters.

Next, **let's graph another nonlinear function** $f(x) = |x|$ **or** $y = |x|$.

This is not a linear equation since it cannot be written in the form $Ax + By = C$. Its graph is not a line. Because we do not know the shape of this graph, we find many ordered pair solutions. We will choose x-values and substitute to find corresponding y-values.

If $x = -3$, then $y = |-3|$, or 3.
If $x = -2$, then $y = |-2|$, or 2.
If $x = -1$, then $y = |-1|$, or 1.
If $x = 0$, then $y = |0|$, or 0.
If $x = 1$, then $y = |1|$, or 1.
If $x = 2$, then $y = |2|$, or 2.
If $x = 3$, then $y = |3|$, or 3.

x	y
-3	3
-2	2
-1	1
0	0
1	1
2	2
3	3

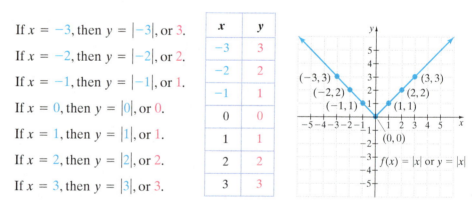

Again, study the table of values for a moment and notice any patterns.

From the plotted ordered pairs, we see that the graph of this absolute value equation is V-shaped.

Finally, a fourth common function, $f(x) = \sqrt{x}$ or $y = \sqrt{x}$. For this graph, you need to recall basic facts about square roots and use your calculator to approximate some square roots to help locate points. Recall also that the square root of a negative number is not a real number, so be careful when finding your domain.

Now **let's graph the square root function** $f(x) = \sqrt{x}$, **or** $y = \sqrt{x}$.

To graph, we identify the domain, evaluate the function for several values of x, plot the resulting points, and connect the points with a smooth curve. Since $\sqrt{x}$ represents the nonnegative square root of x, the domain of this function is the set of all nonnegative numbers, $x \geq 0$. We have approximated $\sqrt{3}$ below to help us locate the point corresponding to $(3, \sqrt{3})$.

If $x = 0$, then $y = \sqrt{0}$, or 0.

If $x = 1$, then $y = \sqrt{1}$, or 1.

If $x = 3$, then $y = \sqrt{3}$, or 1.7.

If $x = 4$, then $y = \sqrt{4}$, or 2.

If $x = 9$, then $y = \sqrt{9}$, or 3.

x	$f(x) = \sqrt{x}$
0	0
1	1
3	$\sqrt{3} \approx 1.7$
4	2
9	3

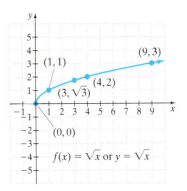

Notice that the graph of this function passes the vertical line test, as expected.

Below is a summary of our four common graphs. Take a moment and study these graphs. Your success in the rest of this section depends on your knowledge of these graphs.

Common Graphs

$f(x) = x$

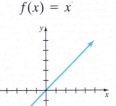

$f(x) = x^2$

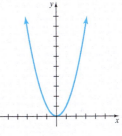

$f(x) = \sqrt{x}$

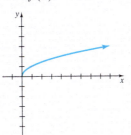

$f(x) = |x|$

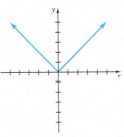

Your knowledge of the slope-intercept form, $f(x) = mx + b$, will help you understand simple shifting of transformations such as vertical shifts. For example, what is the difference between the graphs of $f(x) = x$ and $g(x) = x + 3$?

$f(x) = x$
slope, $m = 1$
y-intercept is $(0, 0)$

$g(x) = x + 3$
slope, $m = 1$
y-intercept is $(0, 3)$

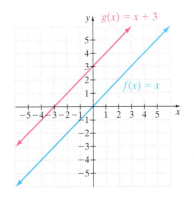

172 CHAPTER 3 Graphs and Functions

Notice that the graph of $g(x) = x + 3$ is the same as the graph of $f(x) = x$, but moved **upward 3 units**. This is an example of a **vertical shift** and is true for graphs in general.

> **Vertical Shifts (Upward and Downward)**
> Let k be a Positive Number
>
> | Graph of | Same As | Moved |
> |---|---|---|
> | $g(x) = f(x) + k$ | $f(x)$ | k units upward |
> | $g(x) = f(x) - k$ | $f(x)$ | k units downward |

EXAMPLES 3–4 Without plotting points, sketch the graph of each pair of functions on the same set of axes.

3. $f(x) = x^2$ and $g(x) = x^2 + 2$ **4.** $f(x) = \sqrt{x}$ and $g(x) = \sqrt{x} - 3$

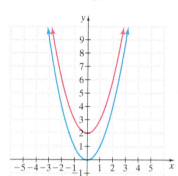
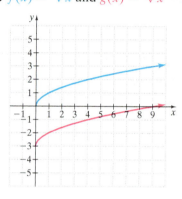

PRACTICES
3–4 Without plotting points, sketch the graphs of each pair of functions on the same set of axes.

3. $f(x) = x^2$ and $g(x) = x^2 - 3$ **4.** $f(x) = \sqrt{x}$ and $g(x) = \sqrt{x} + 1$

A horizontal shift to the left or right may be slightly more difficult to understand. Let's graph $g(x) = |x - 2|$ and compare it with $f(x) = |x|$.

EXAMPLE 5 Sketch the graphs of $f(x) = |x|$ and $g(x) = |x - 2|$ on the same set of axes.

Solution Study the table to the left to understand the placement of both graphs.

x	$f(x) = |x|$	$g(x) = |x - 2|$
-3	3	5
-2	2	4
-1	1	3
0	0	2
1	1	1
2	2	0
3	3	1

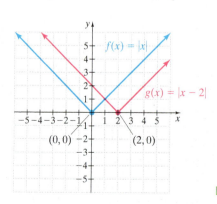

PRACTICE
5 Sketch the graphs of $f(x) = |x|$ and $g(x) = |x - 3|$ on the same set of axes.

Section 3.6 Graphing Piecewise-Defined Functions and Shifting and Reflecting Graphs of Functions 173

The graph of $g(x) = |x - 2|$ is the same as the graph of $f(x) = |x|$, but moved 2 units to the right. This is an example of a **horizontal shift** and is true for graphs in general.

Horizontal Shift (To the Left or Right)
Let **h** be a Positive Number

Graph of	Same as	Moved
$g(x) = f(x - h)$	$f(x)$	h units to the right
$g(x) = f(x + h)$	$f(x)$	h units to the left

> **Helpful Hint**
> Notice that $f(x - h)$ corresponds to a shift to the right and $f(x + h)$ corresponds to a shift to the left.

Vertical and horizontal shifts can be combined.

EXAMPLE 6 Sketch the graphs of $f(x) = x^2$ and $g(x) = (x - 2)^2 + 1$ on the same set of axes.

Solution The graph of $g(x)$ is the same as the graph of $f(x)$ shifted 2 units to the right and 1 unit up.

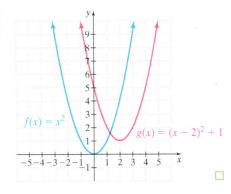

PRACTICE 6 Sketch the graphs of $f(x) = |x|$ and $g(x) = |x - 2| + 3$ on the same set of axes.

OBJECTIVE 3 ▶ Reflecting graphs. Another type of transformation is called a **reflection**. In this section, we will study reflections (mirror images) about the x-axis only. For example, take a moment and study these two graphs. The graph of $g(x) = -x^2$ can be verified, as usual, by plotting points.

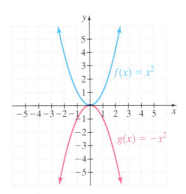

Reflection about the x-axis
The graph of $g(x) = -f(x)$ is the graph of $f(x)$ reflected about the x-axis.

EXAMPLE 7 Sketch the graph of $h(x) = -|x - 3| + 2$.

Solution The graph of $h(x) = -|x - 3| + 2$ is the same as the graph of $f(x) = |x|$ reflected about the x-axis, then moved three units to the right and two units upward.

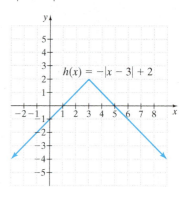

PRACTICE 7 Sketch the graph of $h(x) = -(x + 2)^2 - 1$.

There are other transformations, such as stretching that won't be covered in this section. For a review of this transformation, see the Extension at the end of this chapter.

VOCABULARY & READINESS CHECK

Matching. *Match each equation with its graph.*

1. $y = \sqrt{x}$
   A
2. $y = x^2$
   B
3. $y = x$
   C
4. $y = |x|$
   D

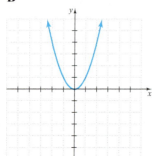
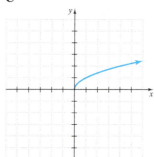
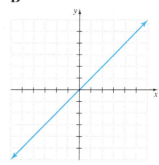

3.6 EXERCISE SET

Graph each piecewise-defined function. See Examples 1 and 2.

1. $f(x) = \begin{cases} 2x & \text{if } x < 0 \\ x + 1 & \text{if } x \geq 0 \end{cases}$

2. $f(x) = \begin{cases} 3x & \text{if } x < 0 \\ x + 2 & \text{if } x \geq 0 \end{cases}$

3. $f(x) = \begin{cases} 4x + 5 & \text{if } x \leq 0 \\ \frac{1}{4}x + 2 & \text{if } x > 0 \end{cases}$

4. $f(x) = \begin{cases} 5x + 4 & \text{if } x \leq 0 \\ \frac{1}{3}x - 1 & \text{if } x > 0 \end{cases}$

5. $g(x) = \begin{cases} -x & \text{if } x \leq 1 \\ 2x + 1 & \text{if } x > 1 \end{cases}$

6. $g(x) = \begin{cases} 3x - 1 & \text{if } x \leq 2 \\ -x & \text{if } x > 2 \end{cases}$

7. $f(x) = \begin{cases} 5 & \text{if } x < -2 \\ 3 & \text{if } x \geq -2 \end{cases}$

8. $f(x) = \begin{cases} 4 & \text{if } x < -3 \\ -2 & \text{if } x \geq -3 \end{cases}$

MIXED PRACTICE

(Sections 3.2, 3.6) Graph each piecewise-defined function. Use the graph to determine the domain and range of the function. See Examples 1 and 2.

9. $f(x) = \begin{cases} -2x & \text{if } x \leq 0 \\ 2x + 1 & \text{if } x > 0 \end{cases}$

Section 3.6 Graphing Piecewise-Defined Functions and Shifting and Reflecting Graphs of Functions 175

10. $g(x) = \begin{cases} -3x & \text{if } x \leq 0 \\ 3x + 2 & \text{if } x > 0 \end{cases}$

11. $h(x) = \begin{cases} 5x - 5 & \text{if } x < 2 \\ -x + 3 & \text{if } x \geq 2 \end{cases}$

12. $f(x) = \begin{cases} 4x - 4 & \text{if } x < 2 \\ -x + 1 & \text{if } x \geq 2 \end{cases}$

13. $f(x) = \begin{cases} x + 3 & \text{if } x < -1 \\ -2x + 4 & \text{if } x \geq -1 \end{cases}$

14. $h(x) = \begin{cases} x + 2 & \text{if } x < 1 \\ 2x + 1 & \text{if } x \geq 1 \end{cases}$

15. $g(x) = \begin{cases} -2 & \text{if } x \leq 0 \\ -4 & \text{if } x \geq 1 \end{cases}$

16. $f(x) = \begin{cases} -1 & \text{if } x \leq 0 \\ -3 & \text{if } x \geq 2 \end{cases}$

MIXED PRACTICE

Sketch the graph of function. See Examples 3 through 6.

17. $f(x) = |x| + 3$
18. $f(x) = |x| - 2$
19. $f(x) = \sqrt{x} - 2$
20. $f(x) = \sqrt{x} + 3$
21. $f(x) = |x - 4|$
22. $f(x) = |x + 3|$
23. $f(x) = \sqrt{x + 2}$
24. $f(x) = \sqrt{x - 2}$
25. $y = (x - 4)^2$
26. $y = (x + 4)^2$
27. $f(x) = x^2 + 4$
28. $f(x) = x^2 - 4$
29. $f(x) = \sqrt{x - 2} + 3$
30. $f(x) = \sqrt{x - 1} + 3$
31. $f(x) = |x - 1| + 5$
32. $f(x) = |x - 3| + 2$
33. $f(x) = \sqrt{x + 1} + 1$
34. $f(x) = \sqrt{x + 3} + 2$
35. $f(x) = |x + 3| - 1$
36. $f(x) = |x + 1| - 4$
37. $g(x) = (x - 1)^2 - 1$
38. $h(x) = (x + 2)^2 + 2$
39. $f(x) = (x + 3)^2 - 2$
40. $f(x) = (x + 2)^2 + 4$

Sketch the graph of each function. See Examples 3 through 7.

41. $f(x) = -(x - 1)^2$
42. $g(x) = -(x + 2)^2$
43. $h(x) = -\sqrt{x} + 3$
44. $f(x) = -\sqrt{x + 3}$
45. $h(x) = -|x + 2| + 3$
46. $g(x) = -|x + 1| + 1$
47. $f(x) = (x - 3) + 2$
48. $f(x) = (x - 1) + 4$

REVIEW AND PREVIEW

Match each equation with its graph. See Section 3.3.

49. $y = -1$
50. $x = -1$
51. $x = 3$
52. $y = 3$

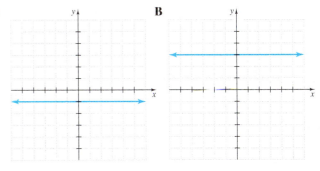

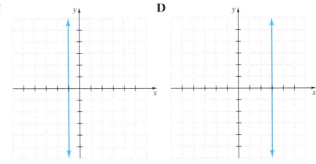

CONCEPT EXTENSIONS

53. Draw a graph whose domain is $x \leq 5$ and whose range is $y \geq 2$.

54. In your own words, describe how to graph a piecewise-defined function.

55. Graph: $f(x) = \begin{cases} \frac{1}{2}x & \text{if } x \leq 0 \\ x + 1 & \text{if } 0 < x \leq 2 \\ 2x - 1 & \text{if } x > 2 \end{cases}$

56. Graph: $f(x) = \begin{cases} -\frac{1}{3}x & \text{if } x \leq 0 \\ x + 2 & \text{if } 0 < x \leq 4 \\ 3x - 4 & \text{if } x > 4 \end{cases}$

Write the domain and range of the following exercises.

57. Exercise 29
58. Exercise 30
59. Exercise 45
60. Exercise 46

Without graphing, find the domain of each function.

61. $f(x) = 5\sqrt{x - 20} + 1$

62. $g(x) = -3\sqrt{x + 5}$

63. $h(x) = 5|x - 20| + 1$

64. $f(x) = -3|x + 5.7|$

65. $g(x) = 9 - \sqrt{x + 103}$

66. $h(x) = \sqrt{x - 17} - 3$

Sketch the graph of each piecewise-defined function. Write the domain and range of each function.

67. $f(x) = \begin{cases} |x| & \text{if } x \leq 0 \\ x^2 & \text{if } x > 0 \end{cases}$

68. $f(x) = \begin{cases} x^2 & \text{if } x < 0 \\ \sqrt{x} & \text{if } x \geq 0 \end{cases}$

69. $g(x) = \begin{cases} |x - 2| & \text{if } x < 0 \\ -x^2 & \text{if } x \geq 0 \end{cases}$

70. $g(x) = \begin{cases} -|x + 1| - 1 & \text{if } x < -2 \\ \sqrt{x + 2} - 4 & \text{if } x \geq -2 \end{cases}$

3.7 GRAPHING LINEAR INEQUALITIES

OBJECTIVES

1. Graph linear inequalities.
2. Graph the intersection or union of two linear inequalities.

OBJECTIVE 1 ▶ Graphing linear inequalities. Recall that the graph of a linear equation in two variables is the graph of all ordered pairs that satisfy the equation, and we determined that the graph is a line. Here we graph **linear inequalities** in two variables; that is, we graph all the ordered pairs that satisfy the inequality.

If the equal sign in a linear equation in two variables is replaced with an inequality symbol, the result is a linear inequality in two variables.

Examples of Linear Inequalities in Two Variables

$$3x + 5y \geq 6 \qquad 2x - 4y < -3$$
$$4x > 2 \qquad y \leq 5$$

To graph the linear inequality $x + y < 3$, for example, we first graph the related **boundary** equation $x + y = 3$. The resulting boundary line contains all ordered pairs the sum of whose coordinates is 3. This line separates the plane into two **half-planes.** All points "above" the boundary line $x + y = 3$ have coordinates that satisfy the inequality $x + y > 3$, and all points "below" the line have coordinates that satisfy the inequality $x + y < 3$.

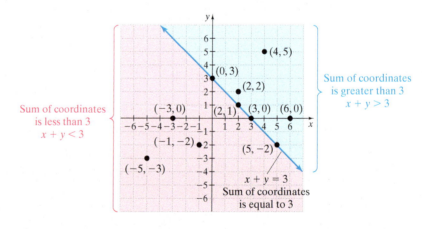

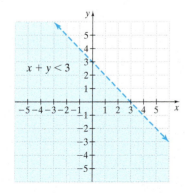

The graph, or **solution region,** for $x + y < 3$, then, is the half-plane below the boundary line and is shown shaded in the graph on the left. The boundary line is shown dashed since it is not a part of the solution region. These ordered pairs on this line satisfy $x + y = 3$ and not $x + y < 3$.

The following steps may be used to graph linear inequalities in two variables.

> **Graphing a Linear Inequality in Two Variables**
>
> **STEP 1.** Graph the boundary line found by replacing the inequality sign with an equal sign. If the inequality sign is $<$ or $>$, graph a dashed line indicating that points on the line are not solutions of the inequality. If the inequality sign is $\leq$ or $\geq$, graph a solid line indicating that points on the line are solutions of the inequality.
>
> **STEP 2.** Choose a **test point not on the boundary line** and substitute the coordinates of this test point into the **original inequality.**
>
> **STEP 3.** If a true statement is obtained in Step 2, shade the half-plane that contains the test point. If a false statement is obtained, shade the half-plane that does not contain the test point.

EXAMPLE 1   Graph $2x - y < 6$.

Solution   First, the boundary line for this inequality is the graph of $2x - y = 6$. Graph a dashed boundary line because the inequality symbol is $<$. Next, choose a test point on either side of the boundary line. The point $(0, 0)$ is not on the boundary line, so we use this point. Replacing x with 0 and y with 0 in the *original inequality* $2x - y < 6$ leads to the following:

$$2x - y < 6$$
$$2(0) - 0 < 6 \quad \text{Let } x = 0 \text{ and } y = 0.$$
$$0 < 6 \quad \text{True}$$

Because $(0, 0)$ satisfies the inequality, so does every point on the same side of the boundary line as $(0, 0)$. Shade the half-plane that contains $(0, 0)$. The half-plane graph of the inequality is shown at the right.

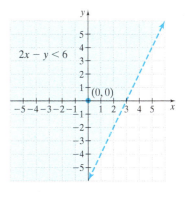

Every point in the shaded half-plane satisfies the original inequality. Notice that the inequality $2x - y < 6$ does not describe a function since its graph does not pass the vertical line test. □

PRACTICE
1   Graph $3x + y < 8$.

In general, linear inequalities of the form $Ax + By \leq C$, where A and B are not both 0, do not describe functions.

EXAMPLE 2   Graph $3x \geq y$.

Solution   First, graph the boundary line $3x = y$. Graph a solid boundary line because the inequality symbol is $\geq$. Test a point not on the boundary line to determine which half-plane contains points that satisfy the inequality. We choose $(0, 1)$ as our test point.

$$3x \geq y$$
$$3(0) \geq 1 \quad \text{Let } x = 0 \text{ and } y = 1.$$
$$0 \geq 1 \quad \text{False}$$

This point does not satisfy the inequality, so the correct half-plane is on the opposite side of the boundary line from (0, 1). The graph of $3x \geq y$ is the boundary line together with the shaded region shown.

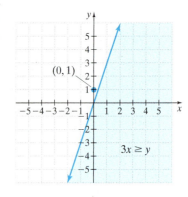

PRACTICE 2 Graph $x \geq 3y$.

Concept Check ✓

If a point on the boundary line is included in the solution of an inequality in two variables, should the graph of the boundary line be solid or dashed?

OBJECTIVE 2 ▶ Graphing intersections or unions of linear inequalities. The intersection and the union of linear inequalities can also be graphed, as shown in the next two examples.

EXAMPLE 3 Graph the intersection of $x \geq 1$ and $y \geq 2x - 1$.

Solution Graph each inequality. The intersection of the two graphs is all points common to both regions, as shown by the dark pink shading in the third graph.

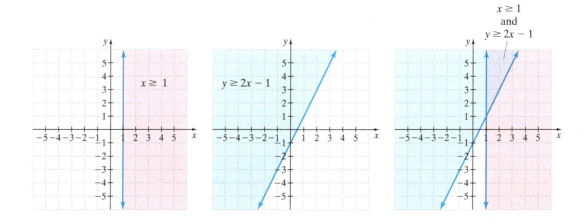

Answer to Concept Check:
Solid

PRACTICE 3 Graph the intersection of $x \leq 3$ and $y \leq x - 2$.

Section 3.7 Graphing Linear Inequalities   179

EXAMPLE 4 Graph the union of $x + \frac{1}{2}y \geq -4$ or $y \leq -2$.

Solution Graph each inequality. The union of the two inequalities is both shaded regions, including the solid boundary lines shown in the third graph.

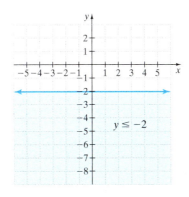
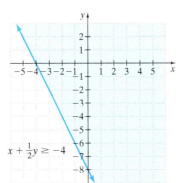
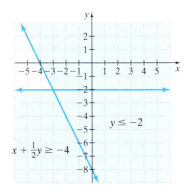

PRACTICE 4 Graph the union of $2x - 3y \leq -2$ or $y \geq 1$.

3.7 EXERCISE SET

Graph each inequality. See Examples 1 and 2.

1. $x < 2$
2. $x > -3$
3. $x - y \geq 7$
4. $3x + y \leq 1$
5. $3x + y > 6$
6. $2x + y > 2$
7. $y \leq -2x$
8. $y \leq 3x$
9. $2x + 4y \geq 8$
10. $2x + 6y < 12$
11. $5x + 3y > -15$
12. $2x + 5y < -20$

13. Explain when a dashed boundary line should be used in the graph of an inequality.

14. Explain why, after the boundary line is sketched, we test a point on either side of this boundary in the original inequality.

Graph each union or intersection. See Examples 3 and 4.

15. The intersection of $x \geq 3$ and $y \leq -2$
16. The union of $x \geq 3$ or $y \leq -2$
17. The union of $x \leq -2$ or $y \geq 4$
18. The intersection of $x \leq -2$ and $y \geq 4$
19. The intersection of $x - y < 3$ and $x > 4$
20. The intersection of $2x > y$ and $y > x + 2$
21. The union of $x + y \leq 3$ or $x - y \geq 5$
22. The union of $x - y \leq 3$ or $x + y > -1$

MIXED PRACTICE

Graph each inequality.

23. $y \geq -2$
24. $y \leq 4$
25. $x - 6y < 12$
26. $x - 4y < 8$
27. $x > 5$
28. $y \geq -2$
29. $-2x + y \leq 4$
30. $-3x + y \leq 9$
31. $x - 3y < 0$
32. $x + 2y > 0$
33. $3x - 2y \leq 12$
34. $2x - 3y \leq 9$
35. The union of $x - y > 2$ or $y < 5$
36. The union of $x - y < 3$ or $x > 4$
37. The intersection of $x + y \leq 1$ and $y \leq -1$
38. The intersection of $y \geq x$ and $2x - 4y \geq 6$
39. The union of $2x + y > 4$ or $x \geq 1$
40. The union of $3x + y < 9$ or $y \leq 2$
41. The intersection of $x \geq -2$ and $x \leq 1$
42. The intersection of $x \geq -4$ and $x \leq 3$
43. The union of $x + y \leq 0$ or $3x - 6y \geq 12$
44. The intersection of $x + y \leq 0$ and $3x - 6y \geq 12$
45. The intersection of $2x - y > 3$ and $x > 0$
46. The union of $2x - y > 3$ or $x > 0$

180 CHAPTER 3 Graphs and Functions

Matching. *Match each inequality with its graph.*

47. $y \leq 2x + 3$ **48.** $y < 2x + 3$

49. $y > 2x + 3$ **50.** $y \geq 2x + 3$

A B
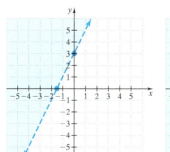
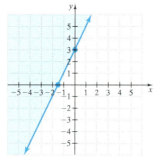

C D

Decision Making. *Write the inequality whose graph is given.*

51. **52.**
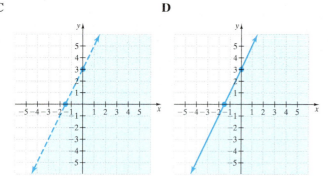

53. **54.**
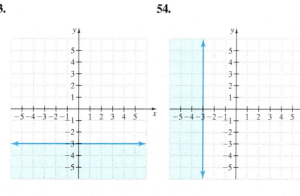

55. **56.**
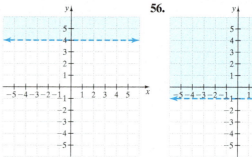

57. **58.**
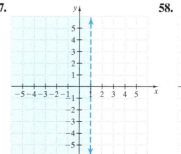
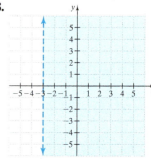

REVIEW AND PREVIEW

Evaluate each expression. See Sections 1.3 and 1.4.

59. 2^3 **60.** 3^2 **61.** -5^2

62. $(-5)^2$ **63.** $(-2)^4$ **64.** -2^4

65. $\left(\dfrac{3}{5}\right)^3$ **66.** $\left(\dfrac{2}{7}\right)^2$

Find the domain and the range of each relation. Determine whether the relation is also a function. See Section 3.2.

67.
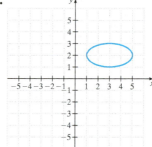

68.
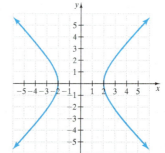

CONCEPT EXTENSIONS

Solve.

69. Rheem Abo-Zahrah decides that she will study at most 20 hours every week and that she must work at least 10 hours every week. Let x represent the hours studying and y represent the hours working. Write two inequalities that model this situation and graph their intersection.

70. The movie and TV critic for the *New York Times* spends between 2 and 6 hours daily reviewing movies and fewer than 5 hours reviewing TV shows. Let x represent the hours watching movies and y represent the time spent watching TV. Write two inequalities that model this situation and graph their intersection.

71. Chris-Craft manufactures boats out of Fiberglas and wood. Fiberglas hulls require 2 hours work, whereas wood hulls require 4 hours work. Employees work at most 40 hours a week. The following inequalities model these restrictions, where x represents the number of Fiberglas hulls produced and y represents the number of wood hulls produced.

$$\begin{cases} x \geq 0 \\ y \geq 0 \\ 2x + 4y \leq 40 \end{cases}$$

Graph the intersection of these inequalities.

EXTENSION: STRETCHING AND COMPRESSING GRAPHS OF ABSOLUTE VALUE FUNCTIONS

In Section 3.6, we learned to shift and reflect graphs of common functions: $f(x) = x$, $f(x) = x^2$, $f(x) = |x|$ and $f(x) = \sqrt{x}$. Since other common functions are studied throughout this text, in this Extension we concentrate on the absolute value function.

Recall that the graph of $h(x) = -|x - 1| + 2$, for example, is the same as the graph of $f(x) = |x|$ reflected about the x-axis, moved 1 unit to the right and 2 units upward. In other words,

$$h(x) = -|x - 1| + 2$$

opens downward $(1, 2)$ location of vertex of V-shape

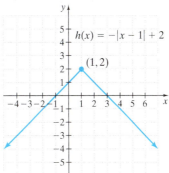

Let's now study the graphs of a few other absolute value functions.

EXAMPLE 1   Graph $h(x) = 2|x|$, and $g(x) = \frac{1}{2}|x|$.

Solution Let's find and plot ordered-pair solutions for the functions.

x	$h(x)$	$g(x)$
-2	4	1
-1	2	$\frac{1}{2}$
0	0	0
1	2	$\frac{1}{2}$
2	4	2

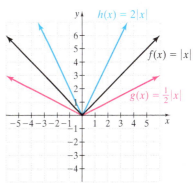

Notice that the graph of $h(x) = 2|x|$ is narrower than the graph of $f(x) = |x|$ and the graph of $g(x) = \frac{1}{2}|x|$ is wider than the graph of $f(x) = |x|$.

PRACTICE 1 Graph $h(x) = -3|x|$ and $g(x) = -\frac{1}{3}|x|$.

In general, for the absolute function, we have the following

> **The Graph of the Absolute Value Function**
> The graph of $f(x) = a|x - h| + k$
> - Has vertex (h, k) and is V-shaped.
> - Opens up if $a > 0$ and down if $a < 0$.
> - If $|a| < 1$, the graph is wider than the graph of $y = |x|$.
> - If $|a| > 1$, the graph is narrower than the graph of $y = |x|$.

EXAMPLE 2 Graph $f(x) = -\frac{1}{3}|x + 2| + 4$.

Solution Let's write this function in the form $f(x) = a|x - h| + k$. For our function, we have $f(x) = -\frac{1}{3}|x - (-2)| + 4$. Thus,

- vertex is $(-2, 4)$
- since $a < 0$, V-shape opens down
- since $|a| = \left|-\frac{1}{3}\right| = \frac{1}{3} < 1$, the graph is wider than $y = |x|$

We will also find and plot ordered-pair solutions.

If $x = -5, f(-5) = -\frac{1}{3}|-5 + 2| + 4$, or 3

If $x = 1, f(1) = -\frac{1}{3}|1 + 2| + 4$, or 3

If $x = 3, f(3) = -\frac{1}{3}|3 + 2| + 4$, or $\frac{7}{3}$, or $2\frac{1}{3}$

x	$f(x)$
-5	3
1	3
3	$2\frac{1}{3}$

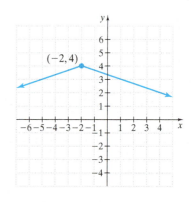

PRACTICE 2 Graph $f(x) = 4|x - 2| - 3$

EXAMPLE 3 Write an equation of the absolute value function graphed.

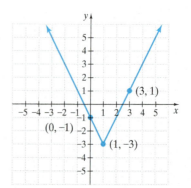

Solution The vertex is $(1,-3)$. For the absolute value function $f(x)$ or $y = a|x - h| + k$, we have $h = 1$ and $k = -3$. Thus,

$$y = a|x - 1| + (-3) \text{ or } y = a|x - 1| - 3.$$

To find the value of a, use the equation above and substitute the coordinates of *any* other given point. We will substitute $(0, -1)$ into the equation and solve for a.

$y = a\|x - 1\| - 3$	
$-1 = a\|0 - 1\| - 3$	Let $x = 0$ and $y = -1$.
$-1 = a\|-1\| - 3$	Simplify.
$-1 = 1a - 3$	Write $\|-1\|$ as 1.
$2 = a$	Add 3 to both sides.

The equation of the graph is $y = 2|x - 1| - 3$.

PRACTICE 3 Write an equation of the absolute value function graphed.

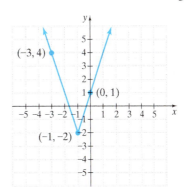

CHAPTER 3 EXTENSION | EXERCISE SET

Sketch the graph of each function. Label the vertex of the V-shape.

1. $f(x) = 3|x|$
2. $f(x) = 5|x|$
3. $f(x) = \frac{1}{4}|x|$
4. $f(x) = \frac{1}{3}|x|$
5. $g(x) = 2|x| + 3$
6. $g(x) = 3|x| + 2$
7. $h(x) = -\frac{1}{2}|x|$
8. $h(x) = -\frac{1}{3}|x|$
9. $f(x) = 4|x - 1|$
10. $f(x) = 3|x - 2|$
11. $g(x) = -\frac{1}{3}|x| - 2$
12. $g(x) = -\frac{1}{2}|x| - 3$
13. $f(x) = -2|x - 3| + 4$
14. $f(x) = -3|x - 1| + 5$
15. $f(x) = \frac{2}{3}|x + 2| - 5$
16. $f(x) = \frac{3}{4}|x + 1| - 4$

For exercises 17–24, write an equation of each absolute value function graph.

17.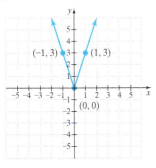

18.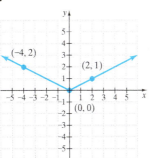

19.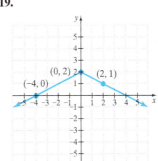

20.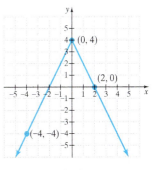

184 CHAPTER 3 Graphs and Functions

21. 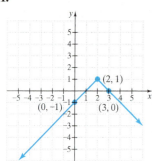 22. 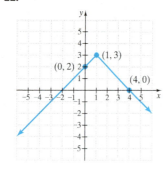 23. 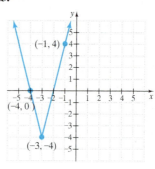 24.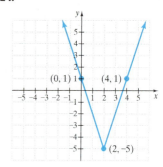

CHAPTER 3 VOCABULARY CHECK

Fill in each blank with one of the words or phrases listed below.

relation	standard	slope–intercept	range	point–slope
line	slope	x	parallel	perpendicular
function	domain	y	linear function	linear inequality

1. A _____ is a set of ordered pairs.
2. The graph of every linear equation in two variables is a _____.
3. The statement $-x + 2y > 0$ is called a _____ in two variables.
4. _____ form of linear equation in two variables is $Ax + By = C$.
5. The _____ of a relation is the set of all second components of the ordered pairs of the relation.
6. _____ lines have the same slope and different y-intercepts.
7. _____ form of a linear equation in two variables is $y = mx + b$.
8. A _____ is a relation in which each first component in the ordered pairs corresponds to exactly one second component.
9. In the equation $y = 4x - 2$, the coefficient of x is the _____ of its corresponding graph.
10. Two lines are _____ if the product of their slopes is -1.
11. To find the x-intercept of a linear equation, let _____ $= 0$ and solve for the other variable.
12. The _____ of a relation is the set of all first components of the ordered pairs of the relation.
13. A _____ is a function that can be written in the form $f(x) = mx + b$.
14. To find the y-intercept of a linear equation, let _____ $= 0$ and solve for the other variable.
15. The equation $y - 8 = -5(x + 1)$ is written in _____ form.

CHAPTER 3 REVIEW

(3.1) Plot the points and name the quadrant or axis in which each point lies.

1. $A(2, -1), B(-2, 1), C(0, 3), D(-3, -5)$
2. $A(-3, 4), B(4, -3), C(-2, 0), D(-4, 1)$

Determine whether each ordered pair is a solution to the given equation.

3. $7x - 8y = 56; (0, 56), (8, 0)$
4. $-2x + 5y = 10; (-5, 0), (1, 1)$
5. $x = 13; (13, 5), (13, 13)$
6. $y = 2; (7, 2), (2, 7)$

Determine whether each equation is linear or not. Then graph the equation.

7. $y = 3x$
8. $y = 5x$
9. $3x - y = 4$
10. $x - 3y = 2$
11. $y = |x| + 4$
12. $y = x^2 + 4$
13. $y = -\frac{1}{2}x + 2$
14. $y = -x + 5$
15. $y = 2x - 1$
16. $y = \frac{1}{3}x + 1$
17. $y = -1.36x$
18. $y = 2.1x + 5.9$

(3.2) Find the domain and range of each relation. Also determine whether the relation is a function.

19. $\left\{\left(-\frac{1}{2}, \frac{3}{4}\right), (6, 0.75), (0, -12), (25, 25)\right\}$

20. $\left\{\left(\frac{3}{4}, -\frac{1}{2}\right), (0.75, 6), (-12, 0), (25, 25)\right\}$

21.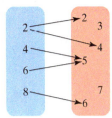

22.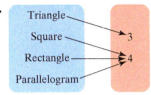

23.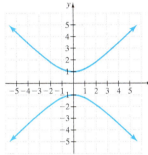

24.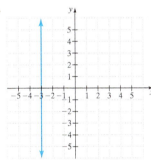

25.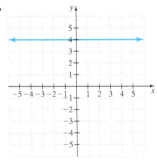

26.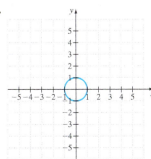

If $f(x) = x - 5$, $g(x) = -3x$, and $h(x) = 2x^2 - 6x + 1$, find the following.

27. $f(2)$
28. $g(0)$
29. $g(-6)$
30. $h(-1)$
31. $h(1)$
32. $f(5)$

The function $J(x) = 2.54x$ may be used to calculate the weight of an object on Jupiter J given its weight on Earth x.

33. If a person weighs 150 pounds on Earth, find the equivalent weight on Jupiter.
34. A 2000-pound probe on Earth weighs how many pounds on Jupiter?

Use the graph of the function below to answer exercises 35 through 38.

35. Find $f(-1)$.
36. Find $f(1)$.
37. Find all values of x such that $f(x) = 1$.
38. Find all values of x such that $f(x) = -1$.

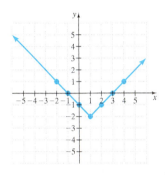

(3.3) Graph each linear function.

39. $f(x) = x$
40. $f(x) = -\dfrac{1}{3}x$
41. $g(x) = 4x - 1$

The graph of $f(x) = 3x$ is sketched below. For exercises 42–45, use this graph to match each linear function with its graph.

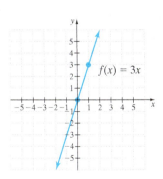

42. $f(x) = 3x + 1$
43. $f(x) = 3x - 2$
44. $f(x) = 3x + 2$
45. $f(x) = 3x - 5$

(continued next page)

A 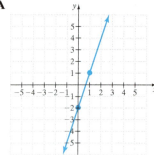 **B**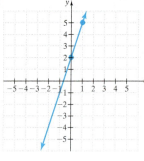

C 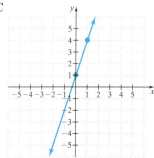 **D**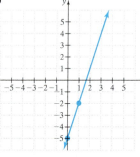

Graph each linear equation by finding intercepts if possible.

46. $4x + 5y = 20$ **47.** $3x - 2y = -9$
48. $4x - y = 3$ **49.** $2x + 6y = 9$
50. $y = 5$ **51.** $x = -2$

Graph each linear equation.

52. $x - 2 = 0$ **53.** $y + 3 = 0$

54. The cost C, in dollars, of renting a minivan for a day is given by the linear function $C(x) = 0.3x + 42$, where x is number of miles driven.
   a. Find the cost of renting the minivan for a day and driving it 150 miles.
   b. Graph $C(x) = 0.3x + 42$.

(3.4) Find the slope of the line through each pair of points.

55. $(2, 8)$ and $(6, -4)$ **56.** $(-3, 9)$ and $(5, 13)$
57. $(-7, -4)$ and $(-3, 6)$ **58.** $(7, -2)$ and $(-5, 7)$

Find the slope and y-intercept of each line.

59. $6x - 15y = 20$

60. $4x + 14y = 21$

Find the slope of each line.

61. $y - 3 = 0$ **62.** $x = -5$

Two lines are graphed on each set of axes. Decide whether l_1 or l_2 has the greater slope.

63. 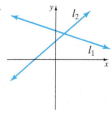 **64.**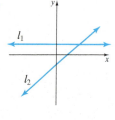

65. 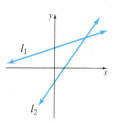 **66.**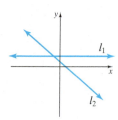

67. Recall from Exercise 54, that the cost C, in dollars, of renting a minivan for a day is given by the linear equation $y = 0.3x + 42$, where x is number of miles driven.
   a. Find and interpret the slope of this equation.
   b. Find and interpret the y-intercept of this equation.

Decide whether the lines are parallel, perpendicular, or neither.

△ **68.** $f(x) = -2x + 6$ △ **69.** $-x + 3y = 2$
$g(x) = 2x - 1$ $6x - 18y = 3$

(3.5) Graph each linear equation using the slope and y-intercept.

70. $y = -x + 1$ **71.** $y = 4x - 3$
72. $3x - y = 6$ **73.** $y = -5x$

Find an equation of the line satisfying the given conditions.

74. Horizontal; through $(3, -1)$
75. Vertical; through $(-2, -4)$
△ **76.** Parallel to the line $x = 6$; through $(-4, -3)$
77. Slope 0; through $(2, 5)$

Find the standard form equation of each line satisfying the given conditions.

78. Through $(-3, 5)$; slope 3
79. Slope 2; through $(5, -2)$
80. Through $(-6, -1)$ and $(-4, -2)$
81. Through $(-5, 3)$ and $(-4, -8)$
△ **82.** Through $(-2, 3)$; perpendicular to $x = 4$
△ **83.** Through $(-2, -5)$; parallel to $y = 8$

Find the equation of each line satisfying the given conditions. Write each equation using function notation.

84. Slope $-\frac{2}{3}$; y-intercept $(0, 4)$
85. Slope -1; y-intercept $(0, -2)$
△ **86.** Through $(2, -6)$; parallel to $6x + 3y = 5$
△ **87.** Through $(-4, -2)$; parallel to $3x + 2y = 8$
△ **88.** Through $(-6, -1)$; perpendicular to $4x + 3y = 5$
△ **89.** Through $(-4, 5)$; perpendicular to $2x - 3y = 6$

90. In 2005, the percent of U.S. drivers wearing seat belts was 82%. The number of drivers wearing seat belts in 2000 was 71%. Let y be the number of drivers wearing seat belts in the year x, where $x = 0$ represents 2000. (*Source:* Strategis Group for Personal Communications Asso.)

a. Write a linear equation that models the percent of U.S. drivers wearing seat belts in terms of the year x. [*Hint:* Write 2 ordered pairs of the form (years past 2000, percent of drivers).]

b. IUse this equation to predict the number of U.S. drivers wearing seat belts in the year 2009. (Round to the nearest percent.)

91. In 1998, the number of people (in millions) reporting arthritis was 43. The number of people (in millions) predicted to be reporting arthritis in 2020 is 60. Let y be the number of people (in millions) reporting arthritis in the year x, where $x = 0$ represents 1998. (*Source:* Arthritis Foundation)

a. Write a linear equation that models the number of people (in millions) reporting arthritis in terms of the year x (See the hint for Exercise 90.)

b. Use this equation to predict the number of people reporting arthritis in 2010. (Round to the nearest million.)

(3.6) Graph each function.

92. $f(x) = \begin{cases} -3x & \text{if } x < 0 \\ x - 3 & \text{if } x \geq 0 \end{cases}$

93. $g(x) = \begin{cases} -\dfrac{1}{5}x & \text{if } x \leq -1 \\ -4x + 2 & \text{if } x > -1 \end{cases}$

Graph each function.

94. $y = \sqrt{x} - 4$
95. $f(x) = \sqrt{x - 4}$
96. $g(x) = |x - 2| - 2$
97. $h(x) = -(x + 3)^2 - 1$

(3.7) Graph each linear inequality.

98. $3x + y > 4$
99. $\dfrac{1}{2}x - y < 2$
100. $5x - 2y \leq 9$
101. $3y \geq x$
102. $y < 1$
103. $x > -2$

104. Graph the union of $y > 2x + 3$ or $x \leq -3$.
105. Graph the intersection of $2x < 3y + 8$ and $y \geq -2$.

MIXED REVIEW

Graph each linear equation or inequality.

106. $3x - 2y = -9$
107. $x = -4y$
108. $3y \geq x$

Write an equation of the line satisfying each set of conditions. If possible, write the equation in the form $y = mx + b$.

109. Vertical; through $\left(-7, -\dfrac{1}{2}\right)$

110. Slope 0; through $\left(-4, \dfrac{9}{2}\right)$

111. Slope $\dfrac{3}{4}$; through $(-8, -4)$

112. Through $(-3, 8)$ and $(-2, 3)$

113. Through $(-6, 1)$; parallel to $y = -\dfrac{3}{2}x + 11$

114. Through $(-5, 7)$; perpendicular to $5x - 4y = 10$

Graph each piecewise-defined function.

115. $f(x) = \begin{cases} x - 2 & \text{if } x \leq 0 \\ -\dfrac{x}{3} & \text{if } x \geq 3 \end{cases}$

116. $g(x) = \begin{cases} 4x - 3 & \text{if } x \leq 1 \\ 2x & \text{if } x > 1 \end{cases}$

Graph each function.

117. $f(x) = \sqrt{x - 2}$
118. $f(x) = |x + 1| - 3$

CHAPTER 3 TEST

Remember to use the Chapter Test Prep Videos to see the fully worked-out solutions to any of the exercises you want to review.

1. Plot the points, and name the quadrant or axis in which each is located: $A(6, -2)$, $B(4, 0)$, $C(-1, 6)$.

Graph each line.

2. $2x - 3y = -6$
3. $4x + 6y = 7$
4. $f(x) = \dfrac{2}{3}x$
5. $y = -3$

6. Find the slope of the line that passes through $(5, -8)$ and $(-7, 10)$.

7. Find the slope and the y-intercept of the line $3x + 12y = 8$.

Graph each nonlinear function. Suggested x-values have been given for ordered pair solutions.

8. $f(x) = (x - 1)^2$ Let $x = -2, -1, 0, 1, 2, 3, 4$

9. $g(x) = |x| + 2$ Let $x = -3, -2, -1, 0, 1, 2, 3$

Find an equation of each line satisfying the given conditions. Write Exercises 10–14 in standard form. Write Exercises 15–17 using function notation.

10. Horizontal; through $(2, -8)$

11. Vertical; through $(-4, -3)$

12. Perpendicular to $x = 5$; through $(3, -2)$

13. Through $(4, -1)$; slope -3

14. Through $(0, -2)$; slope 5

15. Through $(4, -2)$ and $(6, -3)$

 16. Through $(-1, 2)$; perpendicular to $3x - y = 4$

 17. Parallel to $2y + x = 3$; through $(3, -2)$

 18. Line L_1 has the equation $2x - 5y = 8$. Line L_2 passes through the points $(1, 4)$ and $(-1, -1)$. Determine whether these lines are parallel lines, perpendicular lines, or neither.

Graph each inequality.

19. $x \leq -4$ **20.** $2x - y > 5$

21. The intersection of $2x + 4y < 6$ and $y \leq -4$

Find the domain and range of each relation. Also determine whether the relation is a function.

22.

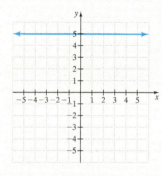

23.

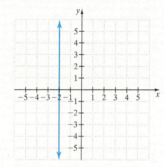

24.

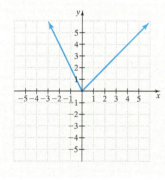

25.

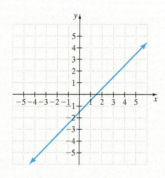

26. The average yearly earnings for high school graduates age 18 and older is given by the linear function

$$f(x) = 1031x + 25{,}193$$

where x is the number of years since 2000 that a person graduated. (*Source:* U.S. Census Bureau)

a. Find the average earnings in 2000 for high school graduates.

b. Find the average earnings for high school graduates in the year 2007.

c. Predict the first whole year that the average earnings for high school graduates will be greater than $40,000.

d. Find and interpret the slope of this equation.

e. Find and interpret the y-intercept of this equation.

Graph each function. For Exercises 27 and 29, state the domain and the range of the function.

27. $f(x) = \begin{cases} -\dfrac{1}{2}x & \text{if } x \leq 0 \\ 2x - 3 & \text{if } x > 0 \end{cases}$

28. $f(x) = (x - 4)^2$

29. $g(x) = -|x + 2| - 1$

30. $h(x) = \sqrt{x} - 1$

CHAPTER 3 STANDARDIZED TEST

Multiple Choice. *Choose the one alternative that best completes the statement or answers the question. Plot the points and name the quadrant or axis in which each is located.*

1. $A(4, -2)$, $B(-6, 0)$, $C(-2, 6)$

   a. **A:** quadrant II
      B: y-axis
      C: quadrant I

   b. **A:** quadrant IV
      B: x-axis
      C: quadrant II

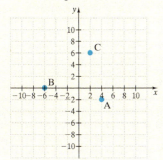

   c. **A:** quadrant II
      B: y-axis
      C: quadrant I

   d. **A:** quadrant IV
      B: x-axis
      C: quadrant II

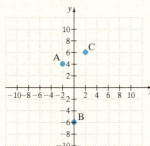 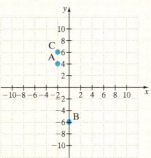

Graph the line.

2. $3x - 5y = 15$

   a. 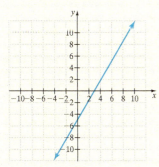   b.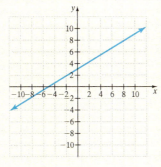

   c. 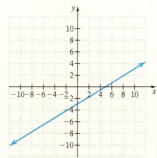   d.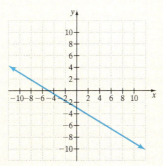

3. $9x - 3y = -6$

   a. 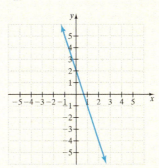   b.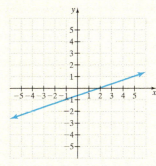

   c. 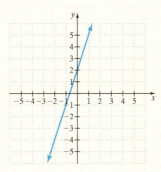   d.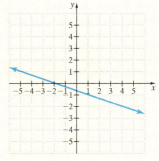

4. $f(x) = \dfrac{4}{5}x - 4$

   a. 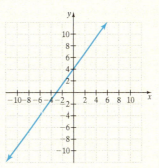   b.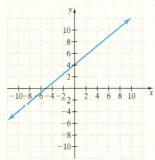

   c. 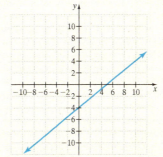   d.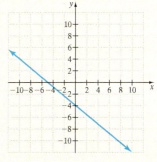

5. $x = 2$

a.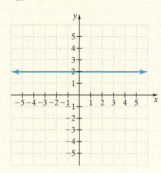
b.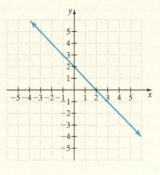
c.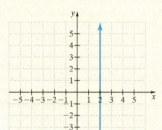
d.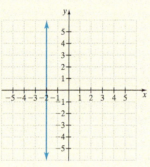

Solve.

6. Find the slope of the line that passes through $(9, -3)$ and $(2, -6)$.
  a. $\dfrac{3}{2}$
  b. $\dfrac{7}{3}$
  c. $\dfrac{3}{7}$
  d. $\dfrac{2}{3}$

7. Find the slope and the y-intercept of the line $8x - 10y = 80$.
  a. $m = \dfrac{5}{4}; b = 10$
  b. $m = \dfrac{4}{5}; b = -8$
  c. $m = 8; b = 80$
  d. $m = \dfrac{4}{5}; b = 8$

Graph the nonlinear function. Suggested x-values have been given for ordered pair solutions.

8. $f(x) = x^2 - 5$ Let $x = -3, -2, -1, 0, 1, 2, 3$

a.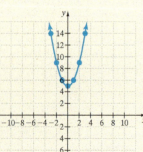
b.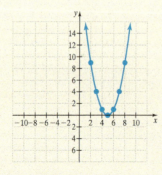
c.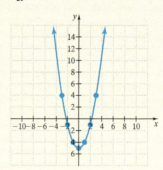
d.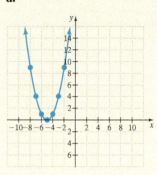

9. $f(x) = -|x| + 3$ Let $x = -3, -2, -1, 0, 1, 2, 3$

a.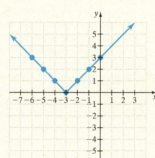
b.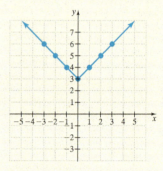
c.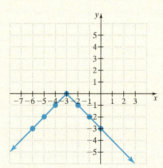
d.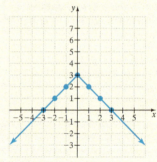

Find an equation of the line satisfying the given conditions.

10. Horizontal; through $(9, 5)$
  a. $y = 9$
  b. $x = 9$
  c. $y = 5$
  d. $x = 5$

11. Vertical; through $(7, 4)$
  a. $x = 4$
  b. $y = 7$
  c. $y = 4$
  d. $x = 7$

12. Perpendicular to $y = 8$; through $(2, 1)$
  a. $x = 2$
  b. $y = 1$
  c. $y = 2$
  d. $x = 1$

Find an equation of the line satisfying the given conditions. Write the equation in standard form.

13. Slope 4; through $(-2, -3)$
  a. $4x - y = 5$
  b. $x + 4y = -5$
  c. $-4x + y = 5$
  d. $x - 4y = 5$

14. Slope $-\dfrac{9}{11}$; through $\left(0, \dfrac{30}{11}\right)$

    a. $11x + 9y = 30$ **b.** $11x - 9y = 30$
    c. $-9x + 11y = 30$ **d.** $9x + 11y = 30$

Find an equation of the line satisfying the given conditions. Write the equation using function notation.

15. Through $(-21, 7)$ and $(-15, 5)$

    a. $f(x) = -3x$ **b.** $f(x) = \dfrac{1}{3}x$
    c. $f(x) = -3x - 1$ **d.** $f(x) = -\dfrac{1}{3}x$

16. Through $(-5, -1)$; perpendicular to $x - 5y = 5$

    a. $f(x) = -5x - 26$ **b.** $f(x) = -\dfrac{1}{5}x - 2$
    c. $f(x) = -5x - 24$ **d.** $f(x) = \dfrac{1}{5}x - 2$

17. Through $(-5, 5)$; parallel to $2x - 5y = -7$

    a. $f(x) = \dfrac{2}{5}x + 7$ **b.** $f(x) = -\dfrac{2}{5}x + 3$
    c. $f(x) = -\dfrac{5}{2}x + 7$ **d.** $f(x) = \dfrac{5}{2}x + 7$

Solve the problem.

18. Line L_1 has the equation $3x - 6y = 1$. Line L_2 passes through the points $(1,2)$ and $(2,4)$. Determine whether these lines are parallel, perpendicular, or neither.

    a. Parallel   **b.** Perpendicular   **c.** Neither

Graph the inequality.

19. $y \geq -5$

a.
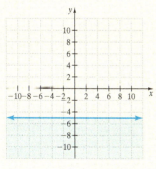

b.
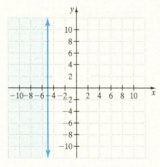

c.
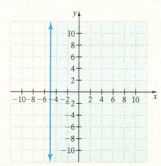

d.
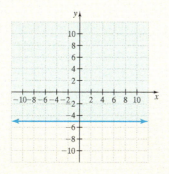

20. $4x + y > 6$

a.
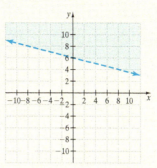

b.
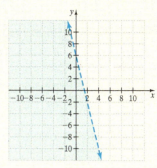

c.
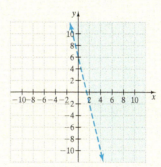

d.
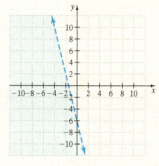

21. The intersection of $x \geq 1$ and $-x + 3y < 6$

a.
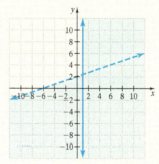

b.
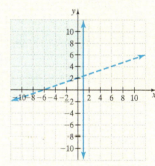

c.
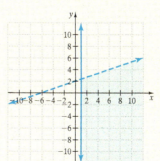

d.
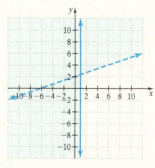

Find the domain and range of the relation. Also determine whether the relation is a function.

22.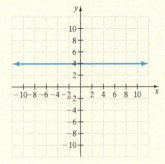

   a. domain: {4}; range: all real numbers; not a function
   b. domain: all real numbers; range: {4}; function
   c. domain: all real numbers; range: {4}; not a function
   d. domain: {4}; range: all real numbers; function

23.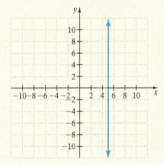

   a. domain: all real numbers; range: {5}; function
   b. domain: {5}; range: all real numbers; function
   c. domain: {5}; range: all real numbers; not a function
   d. domain: all real numbers; range: {5}; not a function

24.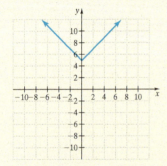

   a. domain: all real numbers; range: $y \geq 5$; function
   b. domain: all real numbers; range: $y \leq 5$; function
   c. domain: all real numbers; range: $y \geq 5$; not a function
   d. domain: $x \geq 5$; range: all real numbers; not a function

25.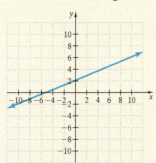

   a. domain: all real numbers; range: all real numbers; function
   b. domain: all real numbers; range: $y > 0$; not a function
   c. domain: all real numbers; range: all real numbers; not a function
   d. domain: $x > 0$; range: $y > 0$; function

Solve the problem.

26. Sales for a small clothing company can be modeled by the linear function $S(x) = 4112x + 61{,}483$, where x is the number of years since 2000 and $S(x)$ is in dollars. Find the sales in 2000.

   a. $4112
   b. $0
   c. $61,483
   d. $65,595

27. Sales for a small clothing company can be modeled by the linear function $S(x) = 3210x + 49{,}134$, where x is the number of years since 2000 and $S(x)$ is in dollars. Find the sales in 2006.

   a. $65,184
   b. $298,014
   c. $314,064
   d. $68,394

28. Sales for a small clothing company can be modeled by the linear function $S(x) = 4600x + 60{,}300$, where x is the number of years since 2000 and $S(x)$ is in dollars. Predict the first year that sales will exceed $111,000 during that year.

   a. 2009
   b. 2010
   c. 2011
   d. 2013

29. When a tow truck is called, the cost of the service is given by the linear function $y = 2x + 65$, where y is in dollars and x is the number of miles the car is towed. Find and interpret the slope and y-intercept of the linear equation.

   a. $m = 65$; The number of miles the car is towed increases 65 miles for every dollar spent on the service. $b = 2$; The tow truck will tow the car 2 miles for no cost.
   b. $m = 2$; The cost of the service increases $2 every mile the car is towed. $b = 65$; The cost of the service is $65 if the car is not towed.
   c. $m = 65$; The cost of the service increases $65 every mile the car is towed. $b = 2$; The cost of the service is $2 if the car is not towed.
   d. $m = 2$; The number of miles the car is towed increases 2 miles for every dollar spent on the service. $b = 65$; The tow truck will tow the car 65 miles for no cost.

Graph the function. State the domain and range of the function.

30. $f(x) = \begin{cases} 5x + 1 & \text{if } x \leq 0 \\ \dfrac{1}{3}x - 6 & \text{if } x > 0 \end{cases}$

(continued next page)

a. domain: all real numbers; range: all real numbers

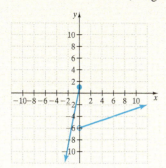

b. domain: all real numbers; range: $y > -6$

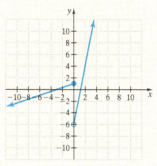

c. domain: all real numbers; range: $y > -6$

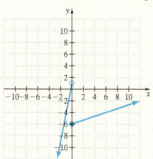

d. domain: $x < 0$ or $x > 0$; range: all real numbers

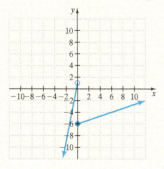

31. $f(x) = x^2 + 2$

a. domain: all real numbers; range: $y \geq 0$

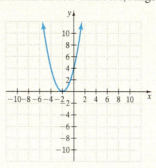

b. domain: all real numbers; range: $y \geq -2$

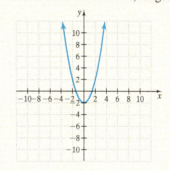

c. domain: all real numbers; range: $y \geq 0$

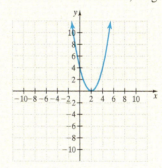

d. domain: all real numbers; range: $y \geq 2$

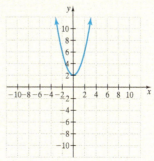

32. $f(x) = -|x - 2|$

a. domain: all real numbers; range: $y \leq 0$

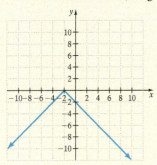

b. domain: all real numbers; range: $y \leq 0$

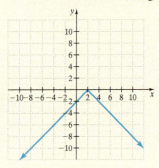

c. domain: all real numbers; range: all real numbers

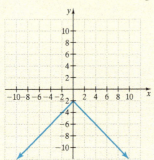

d. domain: all real numbers; range: $y \geq 0$

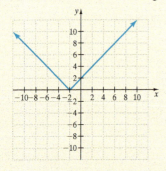

33. $f(x) = \sqrt{x + 1} - 1$

a. domain: $x \geq 1$; range: $y \geq 1$

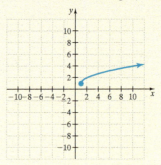

b. domain: $x \geq -1$; range: $y \geq -1$

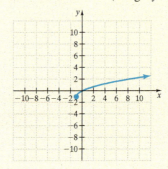

c. domain: $x \leq -1$; range: $y \geq 1$

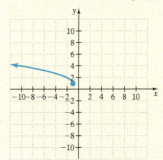

d. domain: $x \leq 1$; range: $y \geq -1$

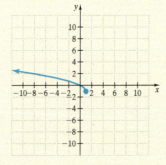

CHAPTER

4 Systems of Equations

- **4.1** Solving Systems of Linear Equations in Two Variables
- **4.2** Solving Systems of Linear Equations in Three Variables
- **4.3** Systems of Linear Equations and Problem Solving

Integrated Review—Systems of Linear Equations

- **4.4** Solving Systems of Equations by Matrices
- **4.5** Systems of Linear Inequalities
- **4.6** Linear Programming

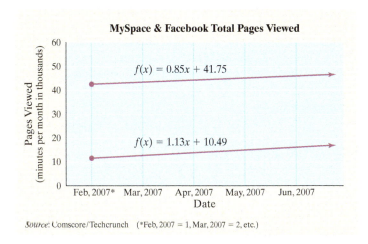

MySpace and Facebook are both popular social networking Web sites. Each function graphed above represents the pages view for each site. In this chapter, we use the functions graphed to form and solve a system of equations. Two or more equations in two or more variables are called a **system of equations.**

4.1 SOLVING SYSTEMS OF LINEAR EQUATIONS IN TWO VARIABLES

OBJECTIVES

1. Determine whether an ordered pair is a solution of a system of two linear equations.
2. Solve a system by graphing.
3. Solve a system by substitution.
4. Solve a system by elimination.

An important problem that often occurs in the fields of business and economics concerns the concepts of revenue and cost. For example, suppose that a small manufacturing company begins to manufacture and sell compact disc storage units. The revenue of a company is the company's income from selling these units, and the cost is the amount of money that a company spends to manufacture these units. The following coordinate system shows the graphs of revenue and cost for the storage units.

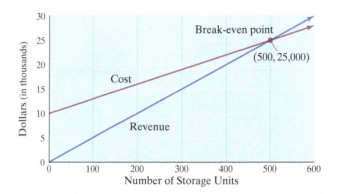

These lines intersect at the point (500, 25,000). This means that when 500 storage units are manufactured and sold, both cost and revenue are $25,000. In business, this point of intersection is called the **break-even point.** Notice that for x-values (units sold) less than 500, the cost graph is above the revenue graph, meaning that cost of manufacturing is greater than revenue, and so the company is losing money. For x-values (units sold) greater than 500, the revenue graph is above the cost graph, meaning that revenue is greater than cost, and so the company is making money.

Recall from Chapter 3 that each line is a graph of some linear equation in two variables. Both equations together form a **system of equations.** The common point of intersection is called the **solution of the system.** Some examples of systems of linear equations in two variables are

Systems of Linear Equations in Two Variables

$$\begin{cases} x - 2y = -7 \\ 3x + y = 0 \end{cases} \qquad \begin{cases} x = 5 \\ x + \dfrac{y}{2} = 9 \end{cases} \qquad \begin{cases} x - 3 = 2y + 6 \\ y = 1 \end{cases}$$

OBJECTIVE 1 ▶ Determining whether an ordered pair is a solution. Recall that a solution of an equation in two variables is an ordered pair (x, y) that makes the equation true. A **solution of a system** of two equations in two variables is an ordered pair (x, y) that makes both equations true.

EXAMPLE 1 Determine whether the given ordered pair is a solution of the system.

a. $\begin{cases} -x + y = 2 \\ 2x - y = -3 \end{cases}$ $(-1, 1)$ **b.** $\begin{cases} 5x + 3y = -1 \\ x - y = 1 \end{cases}$ $(-2, 3)$

Solution

a. We replace x with -1 and y with 1 in each equation.

$$-x + y = 2 \quad \text{First equation} \qquad\qquad 2x - y = -3 \quad \text{Second equation}$$
$$-(-1) + (1) \stackrel{?}{=} 2 \quad \text{Let } x = -1 \text{ and } y = 1. \qquad 2(-1) - (1) \stackrel{?}{=} -3 \quad \text{Let } x = -1 \text{ and } y = 1.$$
$$1 + 1 \stackrel{?}{=} 2 \qquad\qquad\qquad\qquad\qquad -2 - 1 \stackrel{?}{=} -3$$
$$2 = 2 \quad \text{True} \qquad\qquad\qquad\qquad -3 = -3 \quad \text{True}$$

Since $(-1, 1)$ makes *both* equations true, it is a solution. Using set notation, the solution set is $\{(-1, 1)\}$.

b. We replace x with -2 and y with 3 in each equation.

$5x + 3y = -1$ First equation $x - y = 1$ Second equation

$5(-2) + 3(3) \stackrel{?}{=} -1$ Let $x = -2$ and $y = 3$. $(-2) - (3) \stackrel{?}{=} 1$ Let $x = -2$ and $y = 3$.

$-10 + 9 \stackrel{?}{=} -1$ $-5 = 1$ False

$-1 = -1$ True

Since the ordered pair $(-2, 3)$ does not make *both* equations true, it is not a solution of the system.

PRACTICE 1   Determine whether the given ordered pair is a solution of the system.

a. $\begin{cases} -x - 4y = 1 \\ 2x + y = 5 \end{cases}$ $(3, -1)$ **b.** $\begin{cases} 4x + y = -4 \\ -x + 3y = 8 \end{cases}$ $(-2, 4)$

> ▶ **Helpful Hint**
>
> Reading values from graphs may not be accurate. Until a proposed solution is checked in both equations of the system, we can only assume that we have *estimated* a solution.

OBJECTIVE 2 ▶ **Solving a system by graphing.** We can *estimate* the solutions of a system by graphing each equation on the same coordinate system and estimating the coordinates of any point of intersection.

EXAMPLE 2   Solve each system by graphing. If the system has just one solution, estimate the solution.

a. $\begin{cases} x + y = 2 \\ 3x - y = -2 \end{cases}$ **b.** $\begin{cases} x - 2y = 4 \\ x = 2y \end{cases}$ **c.** $\begin{cases} 2x + 4y = 10 \\ x + 2y = 5 \end{cases}$

Solution   Since the graph of a linear equation in two variables is a line, graphing two such equations yields two lines in a plane.

a. $\begin{cases} x + y = 2 \\ 3x - y = -2 \end{cases}$

These lines intersect at one point as shown in the figure to the right. The coordinates of the point of intersection appear to be $(0, 2)$. Check this estimated solution by replacing x with 0 and y with 2 in **both** equations.

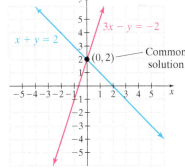

$x + y = 2$ First equation $3x - y = -2$ Second equation

$0 + 2 \stackrel{?}{=} 2$ Let $x = 0$ and $y = 2$. $3 \cdot 0 - 2 \stackrel{?}{=} -2$ Let $x = 0$ and $y = 2$.

$2 = 2$ True $-2 = -2$ True

The ordered pair $(0, 2)$ does satisfy both equations. We conclude therefore that $(0, 2)$ is the solution of the system. A system that has at least one solution, such as this one, is said to be **consistent**.

198 CHAPTER 4 Systems of Equations

b. $\begin{cases} x - 2y = 4 \\ x = 2y \end{cases}$

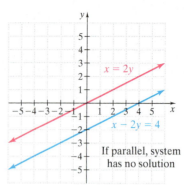

If parallel, system has no solution

The lines appear to be parallel. To be sure, write each equation in point–slope form, $y = mx + b$.

$x - 2y = 4$	First equation	$x = 2y$	Second equation
$-2y = -x + 4$	Subtract x from both sides.	$\frac{1}{2}x = y$	Divide both sides by 2.
$y = \frac{1}{2}x - 2$	Divide both sides by -2.	$y = \frac{1}{2}x$	

> **Helpful Hint**
> - If a system of equations has *at least one solution*, the system is *consistent*.
> - If a system of equations has *no solution*, the system is *inconsistent*.

The graphs of these equations have the same slope, $\frac{1}{2}$, but different y-intercepts, so we have confirmed that these lines are parallel. Therefore, the system has no solution since the equations have no common solution (there are no intersection points). A system that has no solution is said to be **inconsistent**.

c. $\begin{cases} 2x + 4y = 10 \\ x + 2y = 5 \end{cases}$

> **Helpful Hint**
> - If the graphs of two equations *differ*, they are *independent* equations.
> - If the graphs of two equations are the *same*, they are *dependent* equations.

The graph of each equation appears to be in the same line. To confirm this, notice that if both sides of the second equation are multiplied by 2, the result is the first equation. This means that the equations have identical solutions. Any ordered pair solution of one equation satisfies the other equation also. Thus, these equations are said to be **dependent equations** and there are an infinite number of solutions to this system.

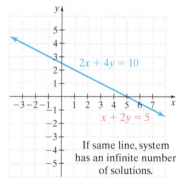

If same line, system has an infinite number of solutions.

> **Helpful Hint**
> The solution set of the system in part c is $\{(x, y) | x + 2y = 5\}$ or, equivalently, $\{(x, y) | 2x + 4y = 10\}$ since the lines describe identical ordered pairs. Written this way, the solution set is read "the set of all ordered pairs (x, y), such that $2x + 4y = 10$."

PRACTICE
2 Solve each system by graphing. If the system has just one solution, estimate the solution.

a. $\begin{cases} 3x - 2y = 4 \\ -9x + 6y = -12 \end{cases}$ b. $\begin{cases} y = 5x \\ 2x + y = 7 \end{cases}$ c. $\begin{cases} y = \frac{3}{4}x + 1 \\ 3x - 4y = 12 \end{cases}$

Concept Check ✓

The equations in the system are dependent and the system has an infinite number of solutions. Which ordered pairs below are solutions?

$\begin{cases} -x + 3y = 4 \\ 2x + 8 = 6y \end{cases}$

Answer to Concept Check: b, c   a. $(4, 0)$ b. $(-4, 0)$ c. $(-1, 1)$

We can summarize the information discovered in Example 2 as follows.

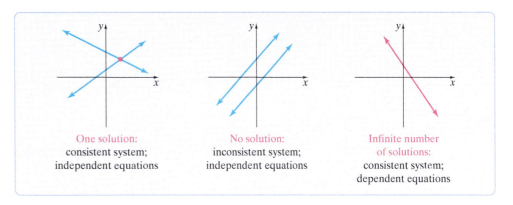

One solution:
consistent system;
independent equations

No solution:
inconsistent system;
independent equations

Infinite number
of solutions:
consistent system;
dependent equations

Concept Check ✓

How can you tell just by looking at the following system that it has no solution?

$$\begin{cases} y = 3x + 5 \\ y = 3x - 7 \end{cases}$$

How can you tell just by looking at the following system that it has infinitely many solutions?

$$\begin{cases} x + y = 5 \\ 2x + 2y = 10 \end{cases}$$

OBJECTIVE 3 ▶ **Solving a system by substitution.** Graphing the equations of a system by hand is often a good method of finding approximate solutions of a system, but it is not a reliable method of finding exact solutions of a system. We turn instead to two algebraic methods of solving systems. We use the first method, the **substitution method,** to solve the system

$$\begin{cases} 2x + 4y = -6 & \text{First equation} \\ x = 2y - 5 & \text{Second equation} \end{cases}$$

EXAMPLE 3 Use the substitution method to solve the system.

$$\begin{cases} 2x + 4y = -6 & \text{First equation} \\ x = 2y - 5 & \text{Second equation} \end{cases}$$

Solution In the second equation, we are told that x is equal to $2y - 5$. Since they are equal, we can *substitute* $2y - 5$ for x in the first equation. This will give us an equation in one variable, which we can solve for y.

$$2x + 4y = -6 \quad \text{First equation}$$
$$2(2y - 5) + 4y = -6 \quad \text{Substitute } 2y - 5 \text{ for } x.$$
$$4y - 10 + 4y = -6$$
$$8y = 4$$
$$y = \frac{4}{8} = \frac{1}{2} \quad \text{Solve for } y.$$

The y-coordinate of the solution is $\frac{1}{2}$. To find the x-coordinate, we replace y with $\frac{1}{2}$ in the second equation,

$$x = 2y - 5.$$
$$x = 2y - 5$$
$$x = 2\left(\frac{1}{2}\right) - 5 = 1 - 5 = -4$$

Answer to Concept Check:
answers may vary

The ordered pair solution is $\left(-4, \dfrac{1}{2}\right)$. Check to see that $\left(-4, \dfrac{1}{2}\right)$ satisfies both equations of the system. □

PRACTICE 3 Use the substitution method to solve the system.
$$\begin{cases} y = 4x + 7 \\ 2x + y = 4 \end{cases}$$

Solving a System of Two Equations Using the Substitution Method

STEP 1. Solve one of the equations for one of its variables.

STEP 2. Substitute the expression for the variable found in Step 1 into the other equation.

STEP 3. Find the value of one variable by solving the equation from Step 2.

STEP 4. Find the value of the other variable by substituting the value found in Step 3 into the equation from Step 1.

STEP 5. Check the ordered pair solution in *both* original equations.

EXAMPLE 4 Use the substitution method to solve the system.
$$\begin{cases} -\dfrac{x}{6} + \dfrac{y}{2} = \dfrac{1}{2} \\ \dfrac{x}{3} - \dfrac{y}{6} = -\dfrac{3}{4} \end{cases}$$

Solution First we multiply each equation by its least common denominator to clear the system of fractions. We multiply the first equation by 6 and the second equation by 12.

$$\begin{cases} 6\left(-\dfrac{x}{6} + \dfrac{y}{2}\right) = 6\left(\dfrac{1}{2}\right) \\ 12\left(\dfrac{x}{3} - \dfrac{y}{6}\right) = 12\left(-\dfrac{3}{4}\right) \end{cases} \text{ simplifies to } \begin{cases} -x + 3y = 3 & \text{First equation} \\ 4x - 2y = -9 & \text{Second equation} \end{cases}$$

> **Helpful Hint**
> To avoid tedious fractions, solve for a variable whose coefficient is 1 or −1, if possible.

To use the substitution method, we now solve the first equation for x.

$$-x + 3y = 3 \quad \text{First equation}$$
$$3y - 3 = x \quad \text{Solve for } x.$$

Next we replace x with $3y - 3$ in the second equation.

$$4x - 2y = -9 \quad \text{Second equation}$$
$$4(3y - 3) - 2y = -9$$
$$12y - 12 - 2y = -9$$
$$10y = 3$$
$$y = \dfrac{3}{10} \quad \text{Solve for } y.$$

To find the corresponding x-coordinate, we replace y with $\dfrac{3}{10}$ in the equation $x = 3y - 3$. Then

$$x = 3\left(\dfrac{3}{10}\right) - 3 = \dfrac{9}{10} - 3 = \dfrac{9}{10} - \dfrac{30}{10} = -\dfrac{21}{10}$$

Section 4.1 Solving Systems of Linear Equations in Two Variables 201

The ordered pair solution is $\left(-\dfrac{21}{10}, \dfrac{3}{10}\right)$. Check to see that this solution satisfies both original equations.

PRACTICE 4 Use the substitution method to solve the system.

$$\begin{cases} -\dfrac{x}{3} + \dfrac{y}{4} = \dfrac{1}{2} \\ \dfrac{x}{4} - \dfrac{y}{2} = -\dfrac{1}{4} \end{cases}$$

> **Helpful Hint**
> If a system of equations contains equations with fractions, first clear the equations of fractions.

OBJECTIVE 4 ▶ Solving a system by elimination. The **elimination method**, or **addition method**, is a second algebraic technique for solving systems of equations. For this method, we rely on a version of the addition property of equality, which states that "equals added to equals are equal."

$$\text{If } A = B \text{ and } C = D \text{ then } A + C = B + D.$$

EXAMPLE 5 Use the elimination method to solve the system.

$$\begin{cases} x - 5y = -12 & \text{First equation} \\ -x + y = 4 & \text{Second equation} \end{cases}$$

Solution Since the left side of each equation is equal to the right side, we add equal quantities by adding the left sides of the equations and the right sides of the equations. This sum gives us an equation in one variable, y, which we can solve for y.

$$\begin{array}{ll} x - 5y = -12 & \text{First equation} \\ \underline{-x + y = 4} & \text{Second equation} \\ -4y = -8 & \text{Add.} \\ y = 2 & \text{Solve for } y. \end{array}$$

The y-coordinate of the solution is 2. To find the corresponding x-coordinate, we replace y with 2 in either original equation of the system. Let's use the second equation.

$$\begin{array}{ll} -x + y = 4 & \text{Second equation} \\ -x + 2 = 4 & \text{Let } y = 2. \\ -x = 2 \\ x = -2 \end{array}$$

The ordered pair solution is $(-2, 2)$. Check to see that $(-2, 2)$ satisfies both equations of the system.

PRACTICE 5 Use the elimination method to solve the system.

$$\begin{cases} 3x - y = 5 \\ 5x + y = 11 \end{cases}$$

The steps below summarize the elimination method.

> **Solving a System of Two Linear Equations Using the Elimination Method**
> **STEP 1.** Rewrite each equation in standard form, $Ax + By = C$.
> **STEP 2.** If necessary, multiply one or both equations by some nonzero number so that the coefficients of a variable are opposites of each other.
> **STEP 3.** Add the equations.
> **STEP 4.** Find the value of one variable by solving the equation from Step 3.
> **STEP 5.** Find the value of the second variable by substituting the value found in Step 4 into either original equation.
> **STEP 6.** Check the proposed ordered pair solution in *both* original equations.

EXAMPLE 6 Use the elimination method to solve the system.

$$\begin{cases} 3x - 2y = 10 \\ 4x - 3y = 15 \end{cases}$$

Solution If we add the two equations, the sum will still be an equation in two variables. Notice, however, that we can eliminate y when the equations are added if we multiply both sides of the first equation by 3 and both sides of the second equation by -2. Then

$$\begin{cases} 3(3x - 2y) = 3(10) \\ -2(4x - 3y) = -2(15) \end{cases} \quad \text{simplifies to} \quad \begin{cases} 9x - 6y = 30 \\ -8x + 6y = -30 \end{cases}$$

Next we add the left sides and add the right sides.

$$\begin{array}{r} 9x - 6y = 30 \\ -8x + 6y = -30 \\ \hline x = 0 \end{array}$$

To find y, we let $x = 0$ in either equation of the system.

$$3x - 2y = 10 \quad \text{First equation}$$
$$3(0) - 2y = 10 \quad \text{Let } x = 0.$$
$$-2y = 10$$
$$y = -5$$

The ordered pair solution is $(0, -5)$. Check to see that $(0, -5)$ satisfies both equations of the system.

PRACTICE 6 Use the elimination method to solve the system.

$$\begin{cases} 3x - 2y = -6 \\ 4x + 5y = -8 \end{cases}$$

Section 4.1 Solving Systems of Linear Equations in Two Variables   203

EXAMPLE 7   Use the elimination method to solve the system.

$$\begin{cases} 3x + \dfrac{y}{2} = 2 \\ 6x + y = 5 \end{cases}$$

Solution   If we multiply both sides of the first equation by -2, the coefficients of x in the two equations will be opposites. Then

$$\begin{cases} -2\left(3x + \dfrac{y}{2}\right) = -2(2) \\ 6x + y = 5 \end{cases} \quad \text{simplifies to} \quad \begin{cases} -6x - y = -4 \\ 6x + y = 5 \end{cases}$$

Now we can add the left sides and add the right sides.

$$\begin{aligned} -6x - y &= -4 \\ \underline{6x + y} &= \underline{5} \\ 0 &= 1 \quad \text{False} \end{aligned}$$

The resulting equation, $0 = 1$, is false for all values of y or x. Thus, the system has no solution.

This system is inconsistent, and the graphs of the equations are parallel lines.   □

PRACTICE
7   Use the elimination method to solve the system.

$$\begin{cases} 8x + y = 6 \\ 2x + \dfrac{y}{4} = -2 \end{cases}$$

EXAMPLE 8   Use the elimination method to solve the system.

$$\begin{cases} -5x - 3y = 9 \\ 10x + 6y = -18 \end{cases}$$

Solution   To eliminate x when the equations are added, we multiply both sides of the first equation by 2. Then

$$\begin{cases} 2(-5x - 3y) = 2(9) \\ 10x + 6y = -18 \end{cases} \quad \text{simplifies to} \quad \begin{cases} -10x - 6y = 18 \\ 10x + 6y = -18 \end{cases}$$

Next we add the equations.

$$\begin{aligned} -10x - 6y &= 18 \\ \underline{10x + 6y} &= \underline{-18} \\ 0 &= 0 \end{aligned}$$

The resulting equation, $0 = 0$, is true for all possible values of y or x. Notice in the original system that if both sides of the first equation are multiplied by -2, the result is the second equation. This means that the two equations are equivalent. They have the same solution set and there are an infinite number of solutions.   □

PRACTICE
8   Use the elimination method to solve the system.

$$\begin{cases} -3x + 2y = -1 \\ 9x - 6y = 3 \end{cases}$$

> **Helpful Hint**
>
> Remember that not all ordered pairs are solutions of the system in Example 8. Only the infinite number of ordered pairs that satisfy $-5x - 3y = 9$ or equivalently $10x + 6y = -18$.

Graphing Calculator Explorations

A graphing calculator may be used to approximate solutions of systems of equations by graphing each equation on the same set of axes and approximating any points of intersection. For example, approximate the solution of the system

$$\begin{cases} y = -2.6x + 5.6 \\ y = 4.3x - 4.9 \end{cases}$$

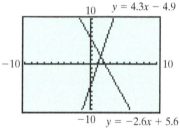

First use a standard window and graph both equations on a single screen.

The two lines intersect. To approximate the point of intersection, trace to the point of intersection and use an Intersect feature of the graphing calculator or a Zoom In feature.

Using either method, we find that the approximate point of intersection is (1.52, 1.64).

Solve each system of equations. Approximate the solutions to two decimal places.

1. $y = -1.65x + 3.65$
   $y = 4.56x - 9.44$

2. $y = 7.61x + 3.48$
   $y = -1.26x - 6.43$

3. $2.33x - 4.72y = 10.61$
   $5.86x + 6.22y = -8.89$

4. $-7.89x - 5.68y = 3.26$
   $-3.65x + 4.98y = 11.77$

VOCABULARY & READINESS CHECK

Matching. *Match each graph with the solution of the corresponding system.*

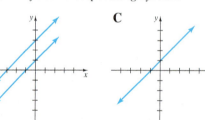 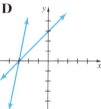

1. no solution
2. Infinite number of solutions
3. $(1, -2)$
4. $(-3, 0)$

4.1 EXERCISE SET

Determine whether each given ordered pair is a solution of each system. See Example 1.

1. $\begin{cases} x - y = 3 \\ 2x - 4y = 8 \end{cases}$ $(2, -1)$

2. $\begin{cases} x - y = -4 \\ 2x + 10y = 4 \end{cases}$ $(-3, 1)$

3. $\begin{cases} 2x - 3y = -9 \\ 4x + 2y = -2 \end{cases}$ $(3, 5)$

4. $\begin{cases} 2x - 5y = -2 \\ 3x + 4y = 4 \end{cases}$ $(4, 2)$

5. $\begin{cases} 3x + 7y = -19 \\ -6x = 5y + 8 \end{cases}$ $\left(\dfrac{2}{3}, -3\right)$

6. $\begin{cases} 4x + 5y = -7 \\ -8x = 3y - 1 \end{cases}$ $\left(\dfrac{3}{4}, -2\right)$

Solve each system by graphing. See Example 2.

7. $\begin{cases} x + y = 1 \\ x - 2y = 4 \end{cases}$

8. $\begin{cases} 2x - y = 8 \\ x + 3y = 11 \end{cases}$

Section 4.1 Solving Systems of Linear Equations in Two Variables 205

9. $\begin{cases} 2y - 4x = 0 \\ x + 2y = 5 \end{cases}$
10. $\begin{cases} 4x - y = 6 \\ x - y = 0 \end{cases}$
11. $\begin{cases} 3x - y = 4 \\ 6x - 2y = 4 \end{cases}$
12. $\begin{cases} -x + 3y = 6 \\ 3x - 9y = 9 \end{cases}$

13. Can a system consisting of two linear equations have exactly two solutions? Explain why or why not.

14. Suppose the graph of the equations in a system of two equations in two variables consists of a circle and a line. Discuss the possible number of solutions for this system.

Solve each system of equations by the substitution method. See Examples 3 and 4.

15. $\begin{cases} x + y = 10 \\ y = 4x \end{cases}$
16. $\begin{cases} 5x + 2y = -17 \\ x = 3y \end{cases}$
17. $\begin{cases} 4x - y = 9 \\ 2x + 3y = -27 \end{cases}$
18. $\begin{cases} 3x - y = 6 \\ -4x + 2y = -8 \end{cases}$
19. $\begin{cases} \frac{1}{2}x + \frac{3}{4}y = -\frac{1}{4} \\ \frac{3}{4}x - \frac{1}{4}y = 1 \end{cases}$
20. $\begin{cases} \frac{2}{5}x + \frac{1}{5}y = -1 \\ x + \frac{2}{5}y = -\frac{8}{5} \end{cases}$
21. $\begin{cases} \frac{x}{3} + y = \frac{4}{3} \\ -x + 2y = 11 \end{cases}$
22. $\begin{cases} \frac{x}{8} - \frac{y}{2} = 1 \\ \frac{x}{3} - y = 2 \end{cases}$

Solve each system of equations by the elimination method. See Examples 5 through 8.

23. $\begin{cases} -x + 2y = 0 \\ x + 2y = 5 \end{cases}$
24. $\begin{cases} -2x + 3y = 0 \\ 2x + 6y = 3 \end{cases}$
25. $\begin{cases} 5x + 2y = 1 \\ x - 3y = 7 \end{cases}$
26. $\begin{cases} 6x - y = -5 \\ 4x - 2y = 6 \end{cases}$
27. $\begin{cases} \frac{3}{4}x + \frac{5}{2}y = 11 \\ \frac{1}{16}x - \frac{3}{4}y = -1 \end{cases}$
28. $\begin{cases} \frac{2}{3}x + \frac{1}{4}y = -\frac{3}{2} \\ \frac{1}{2}x - \frac{1}{4}y = -2 \end{cases}$
29. $\begin{cases} 3x - 5y = 11 \\ 2x - 6y = 2 \end{cases}$
30. $\begin{cases} 6x - 3y = -3 \\ 4x + 5y = -9 \end{cases}$
31. $\begin{cases} x - 2y = 4 \\ 2x - 4y = 4 \end{cases}$
32. $\begin{cases} -x + 3y = 6 \\ 3x - 9y = 9 \end{cases}$
33. $\begin{cases} 3x + y = 1 \\ 2y = 2 - 6x \end{cases}$
34. $\begin{cases} y = 2x - 5 \\ 8x - 4y = 20 \end{cases}$

MIXED PRACTICE

Solve each system of equations.

35. $\begin{cases} 2x + 5y = 8 \\ 6x + y = 10 \end{cases}$
36. $\begin{cases} x - 4y = -5 \\ -3x - 8y = 0 \end{cases}$
37. $\begin{cases} x + y = 1 \\ x - 2y = 4 \end{cases}$
38. $\begin{cases} 2x - y = 8 \\ x + 3y = 11 \end{cases}$
39. $\begin{cases} \frac{1}{3}x + y = \frac{4}{3} \\ -\frac{1}{4}x - \frac{1}{2}y = -\frac{1}{4} \end{cases}$
40. $\begin{cases} \frac{3}{4}x - \frac{1}{2}y = -\frac{1}{2} \\ x + y = -\frac{3}{2} \end{cases}$
41. $\begin{cases} 2x + 6y = 8 \\ 3x + 9y = 12 \end{cases}$
42. $\begin{cases} x = 3y - 1 \\ 2x - 6y = -2 \end{cases}$
43. $\begin{cases} 4x + 2y = 5 \\ 2x + y = -1 \end{cases}$
44. $\begin{cases} 3x + 6y = 15 \\ 2x + 4y = 3 \end{cases}$
45. $\begin{cases} 10y - 2x = 1 \\ 5y = 4 - 6x \end{cases}$
46. $\begin{cases} 3x + 4y = 0 \\ 7x = 3y \end{cases}$
47. $\begin{cases} 5x - 2y = 27 \\ -3x + 5y = 18 \end{cases}$
48. $\begin{cases} 3x + 4y = 2 \\ 2x + 5y = -1 \end{cases}$
49. $\begin{cases} x = 3y + 2 \\ 5x - 15y = 10 \end{cases}$
50. $\begin{cases} y = \frac{1}{7}x + 3 \\ x - 7y = -21 \end{cases}$
51. $\begin{cases} 2x - y = -1 \\ y = -2x \end{cases}$
52. $\begin{cases} x = \frac{1}{5}y \\ x - y = -4 \end{cases}$
53. $\begin{cases} 2x = 6 \\ y = 5 - x \end{cases}$
54. $\begin{cases} x = 3y + 4 \\ -y = 5 \end{cases}$
55. $\begin{cases} \frac{x+5}{2} = \frac{6-4y}{3} \\ \frac{3x}{5} = \frac{21-7y}{10} \end{cases}$
56. $\begin{cases} \frac{y}{5} = \frac{8-x}{2} \\ x = \frac{2y-8}{3} \end{cases}$
57. $\begin{cases} 4x - 7y = 7 \\ 12x - 21y = 24 \end{cases}$
58. $\begin{cases} 2x - 5y = 12 \\ -4x + 10y = 20 \end{cases}$
59. $\begin{cases} \frac{2}{3}x - \frac{3}{4}y = -1 \\ -\frac{1}{6}x + \frac{3}{8}y = 1 \end{cases}$
60. $\begin{cases} \frac{1}{2}x - \frac{1}{3}y = -3 \\ \frac{1}{8}x + \frac{1}{6}y = 0 \end{cases}$
61. $\begin{cases} 0.7x - 0.2y = -1.6 \\ 0.2x - y = -1.4 \end{cases}$
62. $\begin{cases} -0.7x + 0.6y = 1.3 \\ 0.5x - 0.3y = -0.8 \end{cases}$
63. $\begin{cases} 4x - 1.5y = 10.2 \\ 2x + 7.8y = -25.68 \end{cases}$
64. $\begin{cases} x - 3y = -5.3 \\ 6.3x + 6y = 3.96 \end{cases}$

REVIEW AND PREVIEW

Determine whether the given replacement values make each equation true or false. See Section 1.3.

65. $3x - 4y + 2z = 5$; $x = 1, y = 2,$ and $z = 5$
66. $x + 2y - z = 7$; $x = 2, y = -3,$ and $z = 3$
67. $-x - 5y + 3z = 15$; $x = 0, y = -1,$ and $z = 5$
68. $-4x + y - 8z = 4$; $x = 1, y = 0,$ and $z = -1$

Add the equations. See Section 4.1.

69. $\begin{array}{l} 3x + 2y - 5z = 10 \\ -3x + 4y + z = 15 \end{array}$
70. $\begin{array}{l} x + 4y - 5z = 20 \\ 2x - 4y - 2z = -17 \end{array}$

206 CHAPTER 4 Systems of Equations

71. $10x + 5y + 6z = 14$
$-9x + 5y - 6z = -12$

72. $-9x - 8y - z = 31$
$9x + 4y - z = 12$

CONCEPT EXTENSIONS

Read a Graph. *The concept of supply and demand is used often in business. In general, as the unit price of a commodity increases, the demand for that commodity decreases. Also, as a commodity's unit price increases, the manufacturer normally increases the supply. The point where supply is equal to demand is called the equilibrium point. The following shows the graph of a demand equation and the graph of a supply equation for previously rented DVDs. The x-axis represents the number of DVDs in thousands, and the y-axis represents the cost of a DVD. Use this graph to answer Exercises 73 through 76.*

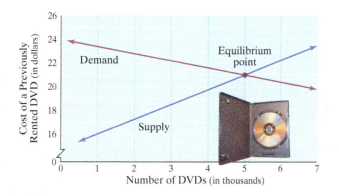

73. Find the number of DVDs and the price per DVD when supply equals demand.

74. When x is between 3 and 4, is supply greater than demand or is demand greater than supply?

75. When x is greater than 7, is supply greater than demand or is demand greater than supply?

76. For what x-values are the y-values corresponding to the supply equation greater than the y-values corresponding to the demand equation?

Read a Graph. *The revenue equation for a certain brand of toothpaste is $y = 2.5x$, where x is the number of tubes of toothpaste sold and y is the total income for selling x tubes. The cost equation is $y = 0.9x + 3000$, where x is the number of tubes of toothpaste manufactured and y is the cost of producing x tubes. The following set of axes shows the graph of the cost and revenue equations. Use this graph for Exercises 77 through 82.*

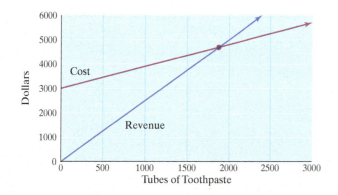

77. Find the coordinates of the point of intersection, or break-even point, by solving the system
$$\begin{cases} y = 2.5x \\ y = 0.9x + 3000 \end{cases}$$

78. Explain the meaning of the ordered pair point of intersection.

79. If the company sells 2000 tubes of toothpaste, does the company make money or lose money?

80. If the company sells 1000 tubes of toothpaste, does the company make money or lose money?

81. For what x-values will the company make a profit? (*Hint:* For what x-values is the revenue graph "higher" than the cost graph?)

82. For what x-values will the company lose money? (*Hint:* For what x-values is the revenue graph "lower" than the cost graph?)

83. Write a system of two linear equations in x and y that has the ordered pair solution $(2, 5)$.

84. Which method would you use to solve the system?
$$\begin{cases} 5x - 2y = 6 \\ 2x + 3y = 5 \end{cases}$$
Explain your choice.

85. Multiple Steps. The amount y of red meat consumed per person in the United States (in pounds) in the year x can be modeled by the linear equation $y = -0.3x + 113$. The amount y of all poultry consumed per person in the United States (in pounds) in the year x can be modeled by the linear equation $y = x + 68$. In both models, $x = 0$ represents the year 2000. (*Source:* Based on data and forecasts from the Economic Research Service, U.S. Department of Agriculture)

  a. What does the slope of each equation tell you about the patterns of red meat and poultry consumption in the United States?

  b. Solve this system of equations. (Round your final results to the nearest whole numbers.)

  c. Explain the meaning of your answer to part (b).

86. Multiple Steps. The number of books (in thousands) in the University of Texas libraries y for the years 2002 through 2005 can be modeled by the linear equation $y = 230x + 8146$. For the same time period, the number of books (in thousands) in the Columbia University libraries can be modeled by $y = 611x + 7378$, where x is the number of years since 2002. (*Source:* Association of Research Libraries)

  a. What does the slope of each equation tell you about the pattern of books in these two university libraries?

  b. Solve this system of equations. (Round your results to the nearest whole number.)

  c. Explain the meaning of your answer to part (b).

Solve each system. To do so you may want to let $a = \dfrac{1}{x}$ (if x is in the denominator) and let $b = \dfrac{1}{y}$ (if y is in the denominator.)

87. $\begin{cases} \dfrac{1}{x} + y = 12 \\ \dfrac{3}{x} - y = 4 \end{cases}$

88. $\begin{cases} x + \dfrac{2}{y} = 7 \\ 3x + \dfrac{3}{y} = 6 \end{cases}$

89. $\begin{cases} \dfrac{1}{x} + \dfrac{1}{y} = 5 \\ \dfrac{1}{x} - \dfrac{1}{y} = 1 \end{cases}$

90. $\begin{cases} \dfrac{2}{x} + \dfrac{3}{y} = 5 \\ \dfrac{5}{x} - \dfrac{3}{y} = 2 \end{cases}$

93. $\begin{cases} \dfrac{2}{x} - \dfrac{4}{y} = 5 \\ \dfrac{1}{x} - \dfrac{2}{y} = \dfrac{3}{2} \end{cases}$

91. $\begin{cases} \dfrac{2}{x} + \dfrac{3}{y} = -1 \\ \dfrac{3}{x} - \dfrac{2}{y} = 18 \end{cases}$

92. $\begin{cases} \dfrac{3}{x} - \dfrac{2}{y} = -18 \\ \dfrac{2}{x} + \dfrac{3}{y} = 1 \end{cases}$

94. $\begin{cases} \dfrac{5}{x} + \dfrac{7}{y} = 1 \\ -\dfrac{10}{x} - \dfrac{14}{y} = 0 \end{cases}$

4.2 SOLVING SYSTEMS OF LINEAR EQUATIONS IN THREE VARIABLES

OBJECTIVE

1 Solve a system of three linear equations in three variables.

In this section, the algebraic methods of solving systems of two linear equations in two variables are extended to systems of three linear equations in three variables. We call the equation $3x - y + z = -15$, for example, a **linear equation in three variables** since there are three variables and each variable is raised only to the power 1. A solution of this equation is an **ordered triple** (x, y, z) that makes the equation a true statement. For example, the ordered triple $(2, 0, -21)$ is a solution of $3x - y + z = -15$ since replacing x with 2, y with 0, and z with -21 yields the true statement $3(2) - 0 + (-21) = -15$. The graph of this equation is a plane in three-dimensional space, just as the graph of a linear equation in two variables is a line in two-dimensional space.

Although we will not discuss the techniques for graphing equations in three variables, visualizing the possible patterns of intersecting planes gives us insight into the possible patterns of solutions of a system of three three-variable linear equations. There are four possible patterns.

1. Three planes have a single point in common. This point represents the single solution of the system. This system is **consistent.**

2. Three planes intersect at no point common to all three. This system has no solution. A few ways that this can occur are shown. This system is **inconsistent.**

3. Three planes intersect at all the points of a single line. The system has infinitely many solutions. This system is **consistent.**

4. Three planes coincide at all points on the plane. The system is consistent, and the equations are **dependent.**

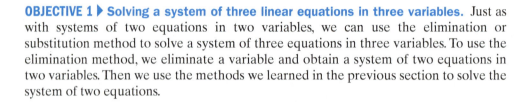

OBJECTIVE 1 ▶ **Solving a system of three linear equations in three variables.** Just as with systems of two equations in two variables, we can use the elimination or substitution method to solve a system of three equations in three variables. To use the elimination method, we eliminate a variable and obtain a system of two equations in two variables. Then we use the methods we learned in the previous section to solve the system of two equations.

EXAMPLE 1 Solve the system.

$$\begin{cases} 3x - y + z = -15 & \text{Equation (1)} \\ x + 2y - z = 1 & \text{Equation (2)} \\ 2x + 3y - 2z = 0 & \text{Equation (3)} \end{cases}$$

Solution Add equations (1) and (2) to eliminate z.

$$\begin{aligned} 3x - y + z &= -15 \\ \underline{x + 2y - z = 1} \\ 4x + y &= -14 \quad \text{Equation (4)} \end{aligned}$$

Next, add two *other* equations and *eliminate z again*. To do so, multiply both sides of equation (1) by 2 and add this resulting equation to equation (3). Then

$$\begin{cases} 2(3x - y + z) = 2(-15) \\ 2x + 3y - 2z = 0 \end{cases} \text{simplifies to} \begin{cases} 6x - 2y + 2z = -30 \\ \underline{2x + 3y - 2z = 0} \\ 8x + y = -30 \end{cases} \text{Equation (5)}$$

▶ **Helpful Hint**
Don't forget to add two other equations besides equations (1) and (2) *and* to **eliminate the same variable.**

Now solve equations (4) and (5) for x and y. To solve by elimination, multiply both sides of equation (4) by -1 and add this resulting equation to equation (5). Then

$$\begin{cases} -1(4x + y) = -1(-14) \\ 8x + y = -30 \end{cases} \text{simplifies to} \begin{cases} -4x - y = 14 \\ \underline{8x + y = -30} \\ 4x = -16 \quad \text{Add the equations.} \\ x = -4 \quad \text{Solve for } x. \end{cases}$$

Replace x with -4 in equation (4) or (5).

$$\begin{aligned} 4x + y &= -14 & \text{Equation (4)} \\ 4(-4) + y &= -14 & \text{Let } x = -4. \\ y &= 2 & \text{Solve for } y. \end{aligned}$$

Finally, replace x with -4 and y with 2 in equation (1), (2), or (3).

$$\begin{aligned} x + 2y - z &= 1 & \text{Equation (2)} \\ -4 + 2(2) - z &= 1 & \text{Let } x = -4 \text{ and } y = 2. \\ -4 + 4 - z &= 1 \\ -z &= 1 \\ z &= -1 \end{aligned}$$

The solution is $(-4, 2, -1)$. To check, let $x = -4$, $y = 2$, and $z = -1$ in all three original equations of the system.

Equation (1)	*Equation (2)*	*Equation (3)*
$3x - y + z = -15$	$x + 2y - z = 1$	$2x + 3y - 2z = 0$
$3(-4) - 2 + (-1) \stackrel{?}{=} -15$	$-4 + 2(2) - (-1) \stackrel{?}{=} 1$	$2(-4) + 3(2) - 2(-1) \stackrel{?}{=} 0$
$-12 - 2 - 1 \stackrel{?}{=} -15$	$-4 + 4 + 1 \stackrel{?}{=} 1$	$-8 + 6 + 2 \stackrel{?}{=} 0$
$-15 = -15$	$1 = 1$	$0 = 0$
True	True	True

All three statements are true, so the solution is $(-4, 2, -1)$.

PRACTICE 1 Solve the system. $\begin{cases} 3x + 2y - z = 0 \\ x - y + 5z = 2 \\ 2x + 3y + 3z = 7 \end{cases}$

EXAMPLE 2 Solve the system.

$$\begin{cases} 2x - 4y + 8z = 2 & (1) \\ -x - 3y + z = 11 & (2) \\ x - 2y + 4z = 0 & (3) \end{cases}$$

Solution Add equations (2) and (3) to eliminate x, and the new equation is

$$-5y + 5z = 11 \quad (4)$$

To eliminate x again, multiply both sides of equation (2) by 2, and add the resulting equation to equation (1). Then

$$\begin{cases} 2x - 4y + 8z = 2 \\ 2(-x - 3y + z) = 2(11) \end{cases} \quad \text{simplifies to} \quad \begin{cases} 2x - 4y + 8z = 2 \\ \underline{-2x - 6y + 2z = 22} \\ -10y + 10z = 24 \quad (5) \end{cases}$$

Next, solve for y and z using equations (4) and (5). Multiply both sides of equation (4) by -2, and add the resulting equation to equation (5).

$$\begin{cases} -2(-5y + 5z) = -2(11) \\ -10y + 10z = 24 \end{cases} \quad \text{simplifies to} \quad \begin{cases} 10y - 10z = -22 \\ \underline{-10y + 10z = 24} \\ 0 = 2 \quad \text{False} \end{cases}$$

Since the statement is false, this system is inconsistent and has no solution.

PRACTICE 2 Solve the system. $\begin{cases} 6x - 3y + 12z = 4 \\ -6x + 4y - 2z = 7 \\ -2x + y - 4z = 3 \end{cases}$

The elimination method is summarized next.

> **Solving a System of Three Linear Equations by the Elimination Method**
>
> **STEP 1.** Write each equation in standard form $Ax + By + Cz = D$.
>
> **STEP 2.** Choose a pair of equations and use the equations to eliminate a variable.
>
> **STEP 3.** Choose any **other** pair of equations and eliminate the **same variable** as in Step 2.
>
> **STEP 4.** Two equations in two variables should be obtained from Step 2 and Step 3. Use methods from Section 4.1 to solve this system for both variables.
>
> **STEP 5.** To solve for the third variable, substitute the values of the variables found in Step 4 into any of the original equations containing the third variable.
>
> **STEP 6.** Check the ordered triple solution in *all three* original equations.

> **Helpful Hint**
> Make sure you read closely and follow Step 3.

Concept Check ✓

In the system

$$\begin{cases} x + y + z = 6 & \text{Equation (1)} \\ 2x - y + z = 3 & \text{Equation (2)} \\ x + 2y + 3z = 14 & \text{Equation (3)} \end{cases}$$

equations (1) and (2) are used to eliminate y. Which action could be used to best finish solving? Why?

a. Use (1) and (2) to eliminate z. **b.** Use (2) and (3) to eliminate y.
c. Use (1) and (3) to eliminate x.

EXAMPLE 3 Solve the system.

$$\begin{cases} 2x + 4y = 1 & (1) \\ 4x - 4z = -1 & (2) \\ y - 4z = -3 & (3) \end{cases}$$

Solution Notice that equation (2) has no term containing the variable y. Let us eliminate y using equations (1) and (3). Multiply both sides of equation (3) by -4, and add the resulting equation to equation (1). Then

$$\begin{cases} 2x + 4y = 1 \\ -4(y - 4z) = -4(-3) \end{cases} \text{ simplifies to } \begin{cases} 2x + 4y = 1 \\ -4y + 16z = 12 \\ \hline 2x + 16z = 13 \end{cases} \quad (4)$$

Next, solve for z using equations (4) and (2). Multiply both sides of equation (4) by -2 and add the resulting equation to equation (2).

$$\begin{cases} -2(2x + 16z) = -2(13) \\ 4x - 4z = -1 \end{cases} \text{ simplifies to } \begin{cases} -4x - 32z = -26 \\ 4x - 4z = -1 \\ \hline -36z = -27 \end{cases}$$

$$z = \frac{3}{4}$$

Replace z with $\frac{3}{4}$ in equation (3) and solve for y.

$$y - 4\left(\frac{3}{4}\right) = -3 \quad \text{Let } z = \frac{3}{4} \text{ in equation (3).}$$

Answer to Concept Check: b

$$y - 3 = -3$$
$$y = 0$$

Replace y with 0 in equation (1) and solve for x.

$$2x + 4(0) = 1$$
$$2x = 1$$
$$x = \frac{1}{2}$$

The solution is $\left(\frac{1}{2}, 0, \frac{3}{4}\right)$. Check to see that this solution satisfies all three equations of the system.

PRACTICE 3 Solve the system. $\begin{cases} 3x + 4y = 0 \\ 9x - 4z = 6 \\ -2y + 7z = 1 \end{cases}$

EXAMPLE 4 Solve the system.

$$\begin{cases} x - 5y - 2z = 6 & (1) \\ -2x + 10y + 4z = -12 & (2) \\ \frac{1}{2}x - \frac{5}{2}y - z = 3 & (3) \end{cases}$$

Solution Multiply both sides of equation (3) by 2 to eliminate fractions, and multiply both sides of equation (2) by $-\frac{1}{2}$ so that the coefficient of x is 1. The resulting system is then

$$\begin{cases} x - 5y - 2z = 6 & (1) \\ x - 5y - 2z = 6 & \text{Multiply (2) by } -\frac{1}{2}. \\ x - 5y - 2z = 6 & \text{Multiply (3) by 2.} \end{cases}$$

All three equations are identical, and therefore equations (1), (2), and (3) are all equivalent. There are infinitely many solutions of this system. The equations are dependent.

PRACTICE 4 Solve the system. $\begin{cases} 2x + y - 3z = 6 \\ x + \frac{1}{2}y - \frac{3}{2}z = 3 \\ -4x - 2y + 6z = -12 \end{cases}$

As mentioned earlier, we can also use the substitution method to solve a system of linear equations in three variables.

EXAMPLE 5 Solve the system:

$$\begin{cases} x - 4y - 5z = 35 & (1) \\ x - 3y = 0 & (2) \\ -y + z = -55 & (3) \end{cases}$$

Solution Notice in equations (2) and (3) that a variable is missing. Also notice that both equations contain the variable y. Let's use the substitution method by solving equation (2) for x and equation (3) for z and substituting the results in equation (1).

$$x - 3y = 0 \quad (2)$$
$$x = 3y \quad \text{Solve equation (2) for } x.$$
$$-y + z = -55 \quad (3)$$
$$z = y - 55 \quad \text{Solve equation (3) for } z.$$

Now substitute $3y$ for x and $y - 55$ for z in equation (1).

$$x - 4y - 5z = 35 \quad (1)$$

> **Helpful Hint**
> Do not forget to distribute.

$$3y - 4y - 5(y - 55) = 35 \quad \text{Let } x = 3y \text{ and } z = y - 55.$$
$$3y - 4y - 5y + 275 = 35 \quad \text{Use the distributive law and multiply.}$$
$$-6y + 275 = 35 \quad \text{Combine like terms.}$$
$$-6y = -240 \quad \text{Subtract 275 from both sides.}$$
$$y = 40 \quad \text{Solve.}$$

To find x, recall that $x = 3y$ and substitute 40 for y. Then $x = 3y$ becomes $x = 3 \cdot 40 = 120$. To find z, recall that $z = y - 55$ and substitute 40 for y, also. Then $z = y - 55$ becomes $z = 40 - 55 = -15$. The solution is $(120, 40, -15)$.

PRACTICE 5 Solve the system.
$$\begin{cases} x + 2y + 4z = 16 \\ x + 2z = -4 \\ y - 3z = 30 \end{cases}$$

4.2 EXERCISE SET

Solve.

1. Multiple Choice. Choose the equation(s) that has $(-1, 3, 1)$ as a solution.
  a. $x + y + z = 3$ **b.** $-x + y + z = 5$
  c. $-x + y + 2z = 0$ **d.** $x + 2y - 3z = 2$

2. Multiple Choice. Choose the equation(s) that has $(2, 1, -4)$ as a solution.
  a. $x + y + z = -1$ **b.** $x - y - z = -3$
  c. $2x - y + z = -1$ **d.** $-x - 3y - z = -1$

3. Use the result of Exercise 1 to determine whether $(-1, 3, 1)$ is a solution of the system below. Explain your answer.
$$\begin{cases} x + y + z = 3 \\ -x + y + z = 5 \\ x + 2y - 3z = 2 \end{cases}$$

4. Use the result of Exercise 2 to determine whether $(2, 1, -4)$ is a solution of the system below. Explain your answer.
$$\begin{cases} x + y + z = -1 \\ x - y - z = -3 \\ 2x - y + z = -1 \end{cases}$$

MIXED PRACTICE

Solve each system. See Examples 1 through 5.

5. $\begin{cases} x - y + z = -4 \\ 3x + 2y - z = 5 \\ -2x + 3y - z = 15 \end{cases}$ **6.** $\begin{cases} x + y - z = -1 \\ -4x - y + 2z = -7 \\ 2x - 2y - 5z = 7 \end{cases}$

7. $\begin{cases} x + y = 3 \\ 2y = 10 \\ 3x + 2y - 3z = 1 \end{cases}$ **8.** $\begin{cases} 5x = 5 \\ 2x + y = 4 \\ 3x + y - 4z = -15 \end{cases}$

9. $\begin{cases} 2x + 2y + z = 1 \\ -x + y + 2z = 3 \\ x + 2y + 4z = 0 \end{cases}$ **10.** $\begin{cases} 2x - 3y + z = 5 \\ x + y + z = 0 \\ 4x + 2y + 4z = 4 \end{cases}$

11. $\begin{cases} x - 2y + z = -5 \\ -3x + 6y - 3z = 15 \\ 2x - 4y + 2z = -10 \end{cases}$ **12.** $\begin{cases} 3x + y - 2z = 2 \\ -6x - 2y + 4z = -2 \\ 9x + 3y - 6z = 6 \end{cases}$

13. $\begin{cases} 4x - y + 2z = 5 \\ 2y + z = 4 \\ 4x + y + 3z = 10 \end{cases}$ **14.** $\begin{cases} 5y - 7z = 14 \\ 2x + y + 4z = 10 \\ 2x + 6y - 3z = 30 \end{cases}$

15. $\begin{cases} x + 5z = 0 \\ 5x + y = 0 \\ y - 3z = 0 \end{cases}$

16. $\begin{cases} x - 5y = 0 \\ x - z = 0 \\ -x + 5z = 0 \end{cases}$

17. $\begin{cases} 6x - 5z = 17 \\ 5x - y + 3z = -1 \\ 2x + y = -41 \end{cases}$

18. $\begin{cases} x + 2y = 6 \\ 7x + 3y + z = -33 \\ x - z = 16 \end{cases}$

19. $\begin{cases} x + y + z = 8 \\ 2x - y - z = 10 \\ x - 2y - 3z = 22 \end{cases}$

20. $\begin{cases} 5x + y + 3z = 1 \\ x - y + 3z = -7 \\ -x + y = 1 \end{cases}$

21. $\begin{cases} x + 2y - z = 5 \\ 6x + y + z = 7 \\ 2x + 4y - 2z = 5 \end{cases}$

22. $\begin{cases} 4x - y + 3z = 10 \\ x + y - z = 5 \\ 8x - 2y + 6z = 10 \end{cases}$

23. $\begin{cases} 2x - 3y + z = 2 \\ x - 5y + 5z = 3 \\ 3x + y - 3z = 5 \end{cases}$

24. $\begin{cases} 4x + y - z = 8 \\ x - y + 2z = 3 \\ 3x - y + z = 6 \end{cases}$

25. $\begin{cases} -2x - 4y + 6z = -8 \\ x + 2y - 3z = 4 \\ 4x + 8y - 12z = 16 \end{cases}$

26. $\begin{cases} -6x + 12y + 3z = -6 \\ 2x - 4y - z = 2 \\ -x + 2y + \dfrac{z}{2} = -1 \end{cases}$

27. $\begin{cases} 2x + 2y - 3z = 1 \\ y + 2z = -14 \\ 3x - 2y = -1 \end{cases}$

28. $\begin{cases} 7x + 4y = 10 \\ x - 4y + 2z = 6 \\ y - 2z = -1 \end{cases}$

29. $\begin{cases} x + 2y - z = 5 \\ -3x - 2y - 3z = 11 \\ 4x + 4y + 5z = -18 \end{cases}$

30. $\begin{cases} 3x - 3y + z = -1 \\ 3x - y - z = 3 \\ -6x + 2y + 2z = -6 \end{cases}$

31. $\begin{cases} \dfrac{3}{4}x - \dfrac{1}{3}y + \dfrac{1}{2}z = 9 \\ \dfrac{1}{6}x + \dfrac{1}{3}y - \dfrac{1}{2}z = 2 \\ \dfrac{1}{2}x - y + \dfrac{1}{2}z = 2 \end{cases}$

32. $\begin{cases} \dfrac{1}{3}x - \dfrac{1}{4}y + z = -9 \\ \dfrac{1}{2}x - \dfrac{1}{3}y - \dfrac{1}{4}z = -6 \\ x - \dfrac{1}{2}y - z = -8 \end{cases}$

REVIEW AND PREVIEW

Solve. See Section 2.2.

33. The sum of two numbers is 45 and one number is twice the other. Find the numbers.

34. The difference between two numbers is 5. Twice the smaller number added to five times the larger number is 53. Find the numbers.

Solve. See Section 2.1.

35. $2(x - 1) - 3x = x - 12$

36. $7(2x - 1) + 4 = 11(3x - 2)$

37. $-y - 5(y + 5) = 3y - 10$

38. $z - 3(z + 7) = 6(2z + 1)$

CONCEPT EXTENSIONS

39. Write a single linear equation in three variables that has $(-1, 2, -4)$ as a solution. (There are many possibilities.) Explain the process you used to write an equation.

40. Write a system of three linear equations in three variables that has $(2, 1, 5)$ as a solution. (There are many possibilities.) Explain the process you used to write an equation.

41. Write a system of linear equations in three variables that has the solution $(-1, 2, -4)$. Explain the process you used to write your system.

42. When solving a system of three equation in three unknowns, explain how to determine that a system has no solution.

43. The fraction $\dfrac{1}{24}$ can be written as the following sum:

$$\dfrac{1}{24} = \dfrac{x}{8} + \dfrac{y}{4} + \dfrac{z}{3}$$

where the numbers x, y, and z are solutions of

$$\begin{cases} x + y + z = 1 \\ 2x - y + z = 0 \\ -x + 2y + 2z = -1 \end{cases}$$

Solve the system and see that the sum of the fractions is $\dfrac{1}{24}$.

44. The fraction $\dfrac{1}{18}$ can be written as the following sum:

$$\dfrac{1}{18} = \dfrac{x}{2} + \dfrac{y}{3} + \dfrac{z}{9}$$

where the numbers x, y, and z are solutions of

$$\begin{cases} x + 3y + z = -3 \\ -x + y + 2z = -14 \\ 3x + 2y - z = 12 \end{cases}$$

Solve the system and see that the sum of the fractions is $\dfrac{1}{18}$.

Solving systems involving more than three variables can be accomplished with methods similar to those encountered in this section. Apply what you already know to solve each system of equations in four variables.

45. $\begin{cases} x + y - w = 0 \\ y + 2z + w = 3 \\ x - z = 1 \\ 2x - y - w = -1 \end{cases}$

46. $\begin{cases} 5x + 4y = 29 \\ y + z - w = -2 \\ 5x + z = 23 \\ y - z + w = 4 \end{cases}$

47. $\begin{cases} x + y + z + w = 5 \\ 2x + y + z + w = 6 \\ x + y + z = 2 \\ x + y = 0 \end{cases}$

48. $\begin{cases} 2x \phantom{{}+y} - z \phantom{{}+w} = -1 \\ y + z + w = 9 \\ y \phantom{{}+z} - 2w = -6 \\ x + y \phantom{{}+z+w} = 3 \end{cases}$

49. Write a system of three linear equations in three variables that are dependent equations.

50. What is the solution to the system in Exercise 49?

4.3 SYSTEMS OF LINEAR EQUATIONS AND PROBLEM SOLVING

OBJECTIVES

1. Solve problems that can be modeled by a system of two linear equations.
2. Solve problems with cost and revenue functions.
3. Solve problems that can be modeled by a system of three linear equations.

OBJECTIVE 1 ▶ Solving problem modeled by systems of two equations. Thus far, we have solved problems by writing one-variable equations and solving for the variable. Some of these problems can be solved, perhaps more easily, by writing a system of equations, as illustrated in this section.

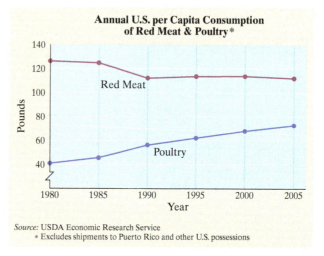

Source: USDA Economic Research Service
* Excludes shipments to Puerto Rico and other U.S. possessions

EXAMPLE 1 Predicting Equal Consumption of Red Meat and Poultry

America's consumption of red meat has decreased most years since 1980 while consumption of poultry has increased. The function $y = -0.59x + 124.6$ approximates the annual pounds of red meat consumed per capita, where x is the number of years since 1980. The function $y = 1.34x + 40.9$ approximates the annual pounds of poultry consumed per capita, where x is also the number of years since 1980. If this trend continues, determine the year in which the annual consumption of red meat and poultry is equal. (*Source:* Based on data from Economic Research Service, U.S. Dept. of Agriculture)

Solution

1. UNDERSTAND. Read and reread the problem and guess a year. Let's guess the year 2020. This year is 40 years since 1980, so $x = 40$. Now let $x = 40$ in each given function.

    Red meat: $y = -0.59x + 124.6 = -0.59(40) + 124.6 = $ 101 pounds
    Poultry: $y = 1.34x + 40.9 = 1.34(40) + 40.9 = $ 94.5 pounds

    Since the projected pounds in 2020 for red meat and poultry are not the same, we guessed incorrectly, but we do have a better understanding of the problem. We also know that the year will be later than 2020 since projected consumption of red meat is still greater than poultry that year.

2. TRANSLATE. We are already given the system of equations.

3. SOLVE. We want to know the year x in which pounds y are the same, so we solve the system:

$$\begin{cases} y = -0.59x + 124.6 \\ y = 1.34x + 40.9 \end{cases}$$

Since both equations are solved for y, one way to solve is to use the substitution method.

$$y = -0.59x + 124.6 \quad \text{First equation}$$

$$1.34x + 40.9 = -0.59x + 124.6 \quad \text{Let } y = 1.34x + 40.9.$$

$$1.93x = 83.7$$

$$x = \frac{83.7}{1.93} \approx 43.37$$

4. INTERPRET. Since we are only asked to give the year, we need only solve for x.

Check: To check, see whether $x \approx 43.37$ gives approximately the same number of pounds of red meat and poultry.

Red meat: $-0.59x + 124.6 = -0.59(43.37) + 124.6 = 99.01$ pounds

Poultry: $\quad 1.34x + 40.9 = 1.34(43.37) + 40.9 = 99.02$ pounds

Since we rounded the number of years, the number of pounds do differ slightly. They differ only by 0.0041, so we can assume that we solved correctly.

State: The consumption of red meat and poultry will be the same about 43.37 years after 1980, or 2023.37. Thus, in the year 2023, we predict the consumption will be the same. □

PRACTICE

1 Read Example 1. If we use the years 1995, 2000, and 2005 only to write functions approximating the consumption of red meat and poultry, we have the following:

Red meat: $y = -0.16x + 113.9$

Poultry: $\quad y = 1.06x + 62.3$

where x is the years since 1995 and y is pounds per year consumed.

a. Assuming this trend continues, predict the year in which the consumption of red meat and poultry will be the same.

b. Does your answer differ from the example? Why or why not?

Note: A similar exercise is found in Section 4.1, Exercise 85. In the example above, the data years used to generate the equations are 1980–2005. In Section 4.1, the data years used are 2000–2005. Note the differing equations and answers.

EXAMPLE 2   Finding Unknown Numbers

A first number is 4 less than a second number. Four times the first number is 6 more than twice the second. Find the numbers.

Solution

1. UNDERSTAND. Read and reread the problem and guess a solution. If a first number is 10 and this is 4 less than a second number, the second number is 14. Four times the first number is 4(10), or 40. This is not equal to 6 more than twice the second number, which is 2(14) + 6 or 34. Although we guessed incorrectly, we now have a better understanding of the problem.

Since we are looking for two numbers, we will let

$$x = \text{first number}$$

$$y = \text{second number}$$

2. TRANSLATE. Since we have assigned two variables to this problem, we will translate the given facts into two equations. For the first statement we have

In words: the first number | is | 4 less than the second number

Translate: $x = y - 4$

Next we translate the second statement into an equation.

In words: four times the first number | is | 6 more than twice the second number

Translate: $4x = 2y + 6$

3. **SOLVE.** Here we solve the system

$$\begin{cases} x = y - 4 \\ 4x = 2y + 6 \end{cases}$$

Since the first equation expresses x in terms of y, we will use substitution. We substitute $y - 4$ for x in the second equation and solve for y.

$4x = 2y + 6$ Second equation

$4(y - 4) = 2y + 6$
$4y - 16 = 2y + 6$ Let $x = y - 4$.
$2y = 22$
$y = 11$

Now we replace y with 11 in the equation $x = y - 4$ and solve for x. Then $x = y - 4$ becomes $x = 11 - 4 = 7$. The ordered pair solution of the system is $(7, 11)$.

4. **INTERPRET.** Since the solution of the system is $(7, 11)$, then the first number we are looking for is 7 and the second number is 11.

Check: Notice that 7 *is* 4 less than 11, and 4 times 7 *is* 6 more than twice 11. The proposed numbers, 7 and 11, are correct.

State: The numbers are 7 and 11.

PRACTICE 2 A first number is 5 more than a second number. Twice the first number is 2 less than 3 times the second number. Find the numbers.

EXAMPLE 3   Finding the Rate of Speed

Two cars leave Indianapolis, one traveling east and the other west. After 3 hours they are 297 miles apart. If one car is traveling 5 mph faster than the other, what is the speed of each?

Solution

1. **UNDERSTAND.** Read and reread the problem. Let's guess a solution and use the formula $d = rt$ (distance = rate · time) to check. Suppose that one car is traveling at a rate of 55 miles per hour. This means that the other car is traveling at a rate of 50 miles per hour since we are told that one car is traveling 5 mph faster than the other. To find the distance apart after 3 hours, we will first find the distance traveled by each car. One car's distance is rate · time = 55(3) = 165 miles. The other car's distance is rate · time = 50(3) = 150 miles. Since one car is traveling east and the other west, their distance apart is the sum of their distances, or 165 miles + 150 miles = 315 miles. Although this distance apart is not the required distance of 297 miles, we now have a better understanding of the problem.

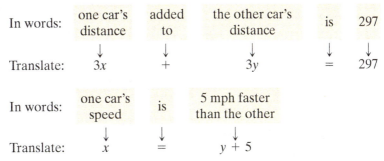

Let's model the problem with a system of equations. We will let

x = speed of one car

y = speed of the other car

We summarize the information on the following chart. Both cars have traveled 3 hours. Since distance = rate · time, their distances are $3x$ and $3y$ miles, respectively.

	Rate	· Time	= Distance
One Car	x	3	$3x$
Other Car	y	3	$3y$

2. **TRANSLATE.** We can now translate the stated conditions into two equations.

In words: one car's distance added to the other car's distance is 297

Translate: $3x + 3y = 297$

In words: one car's speed is 5 mph faster than the other

Translate: $x = y + 5$

3. **SOLVE.** Here we solve the system

$$\begin{cases} 3x + 3y = 297 \\ x = y + 5 \end{cases}$$

Again, the substitution method is appropriate. We replace x with $y + 5$ in the first equation and solve for y.

$3x + 3y = 297$ First equation

$3(y + 5) + 3y = 297$ Let $x = y + 5$.

$3y + 15 + 3y = 297$

$6y = 282$

$y = 47$

To find x, we replace y with 47 in the equation $x = y + 5$. Then $x = 47 + 5 = 52$. The ordered pair solution of the system is (52, 47).

4. **INTERPRET.** The solution (52, 47) means that the cars are traveling at 52 mph and 47 mph, respectively.

Check: Notice that one car is traveling 5 mph faster than the other. Also, if one car travels 52 mph for 3 hours, the distance is 3(52) = 156 miles. The other car traveling for 3 hours at 47 mph travels a distance of 3(47) = 141 miles. The sum of the distances 156 + 141 is 297 miles, the required distance.

State: The cars are traveling at 52 mph and 47 mph.

▶ **Helpful Hint**

Don't forget to attach units, if appropriate.

PRACTICE 3 In 2007, the French train TGV V150 became the fastest conventional rail train in the world. It broke the 1990 record of the next fastest conventional rail train, the French TGV Atlantique. Assume the V150 and the Atlantique left the same station in Paris, with one heading west and one heading east. After 2 hours, they were 2150 kilometers apart. If the V150 is 75 kph faster than the Atlantique, what is the speed of each?

EXAMPLE 4 Mixing Solutions

Lynn Pike, a pharmacist, needs 70 liters of a 50% alcohol solution. She has available a 30% alcohol solution and an 80% alcohol solution. How many liters of each solution should she mix to obtain 70 liters of a 50% alcohol solution?

Solution

1. UNDERSTAND. Read and reread the problem. Next, guess the solution. Suppose that we need 20 liters of the 30% solution. Then we need 70 − 20 = 50 liters of the 80% solution. To see if this gives us 70 liters of a 50% alcohol solution, let's find the amount of pure alcohol in each solution.

number of liters	×	alcohol strength	=	amount of pure alcohol
20 liters	×	0.30	=	6 liters
50 liters	×	0.80	=	40 liters
70 liters	×	0.50	=	35 liters

Since 6 liters + 40 liters = 46 liters and not 35 liters, our guess is incorrect, but we have gained some insight as to how to model and check this problem.

We will let

$$x = \text{amount of 30\% solution, in liters}$$
$$y = \text{amount of 80\% solution, in liters}$$

and use a table to organize the given data.

	Number of Liters	Alcohol Strength	Amount of Pure Alcohol
30% Solution	x	30%	$0.30x$
80% Solution	y	80%	$0.80y$
50% Solution Needed	70	50%	$(0.50)(70)$

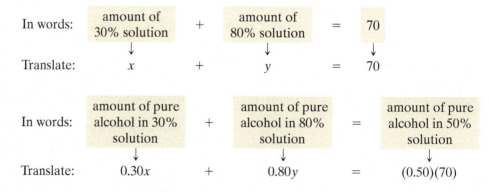

2. TRANSLATE. We translate the stated conditions into two equations.

In words: amount of 30% solution + amount of 80% solution = 70

Translate: $x + y = 70$

In words: amount of pure alcohol in 30% solution + amount of pure alcohol in 80% solution = amount of pure alcohol in 50% solution

Translate: $0.30x + 0.80y = (0.50)(70)$

3. **SOLVE.** Here we solve the system

$$\begin{cases} x + y = 70 \\ 0.30x + 0.80y = (0.50)(70) \end{cases}$$

To solve this system, we use the elimination method. We multiply both sides of the first equation by -3 and both sides of the second equation by 10. Then

$$\begin{cases} -3(x + y) = -3(70) \\ 10(0.30x + 0.80y) = 10(0.50)(70) \end{cases} \begin{array}{c} \text{simplifies} \\ \text{to} \end{array} \begin{cases} -3x - 3y = -210 \\ \underline{3x + 8y = 350} \\ 5y = 140 \\ y = 28 \end{cases}$$

Now we replace y with 28 in the equation $x + y = 70$ and find that $x + 28 = 70$, or $x = 42$.
The ordered pair solution of the system is $(42, 28)$.

4. **INTERPRET.**

Check: Check the solution in the same way that we checked our guess.

State: The pharmacist needs to mix 42 liters of 30% solution and 28 liters of 80% solution to obtain 70 liters of 50% solution. □

PRACTICE

4   Keith Robinson is a chemistry teacher who needs 1 liter of a solution of 5% hydrochloric acid to carry out an experiment. If he only has a stock solution of 99% hydrochloric acid, how much water (0% acid) and how much stock solution (99%) of HCL must he mix to get 1 liter of 5% solution? Round answers to the nearest hundredth of a liter.

Concept Check ✓

Suppose you mix an amount of 25% acid solution with an amount of 60% acid solution. You then calculate the acid strength of the resulting acid mixture. For which of the following results should you suspect an error in your calculation? Why?

a. 14%   **b.** 32%   **c.** 55%

OBJECTIVE 2 ▶ **Solving problems with cost and revenue functions.** Recall that businesses are often computing cost and revenue functions or equations to predict sales, to determine whether prices need to be adjusted, and to see whether the company is making or losing money. Recall also that the value at which revenue equals cost is called the break-even point. When revenue is less than cost, the company is losing money; when revenue is greater than cost, the company is making money.

EXAMPLE 5   **Finding a Break-Even Point**

A manufacturing company recently purchased $3000 worth of new equipment to offer new personalized stationery to its customers. The cost of producing a package of personalized stationery is $3.00, and it is sold for $5.50. Find the number of packages that must be sold for the company to break even.

Answer to Concept Check:
a; answers may vary

Solution

1. **UNDERSTAND.** Read and reread the problem. Notice that the cost to the company will include a one-time cost of $3000 for the equipment and then $3.00 per package produced. The revenue will be $5.50 per package sold.

   To model this problem, we will let

   x = number of packages of personalized stationery
   $C(x)$ = total cost for producing x packages of stationery
   $R(x)$ = total revenue for selling x packages of stationery

2. **TRANSLATE.** The revenue equation is

   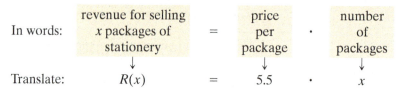

   The cost equation is

   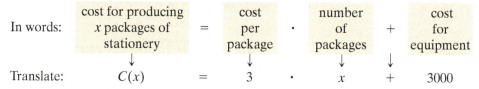

   Since the break-even point is when $R(x) = C(x)$, we solve the equation

   $$5.5x = 3x + 3000$$

3. **SOLVE.**

$5.5x = 3x + 3000$	
$2.5x = 3000$	Subtract $3x$ from both sides.
$x = 1200$	Divide both sides by 2.5.

4. **INTERPRET.**

   Check: To see whether the break-even point occurs when 1200 packages are produced and sold, see if revenue equals cost when $x = 1200$. When $x = 1200$, $R(x) = 5.5x = 5.5(1200) = 6600$ and $C(x) = 3x + 3000 = 3(1200) + 3000 = 6600$. Since $R(1200) = C(1200) = 6600$, the break-even point is 1200.

   State: The company must sell 1200 packages of stationery to break even. The graph of this system is shown.

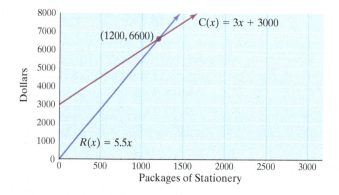

PRACTICE 5 An online-only electronics firm recently purchased $3000 worth of new equipment to create shock-proof packaging for its products. The cost of producing one

shock-proof package is $2.50, and the firm charges the customer $4.50 for the packaging. Find the number of packages that must be sold for the company to break even.

OBJECTIVE 3 ▶ Solving problems modeled by systems of three equations. To introduce problem solving by writing a system of three linear equations in three variables, we solve a problem about triangles.

EXAMPLE 6 Finding Angle Measures

The measure of the largest angle of a triangle is 80° more than the measure of the smallest angle, and the measure of the remaining angle is 10° more than the measure of the smallest angle. Find the measure of each angle.

Solution

1. UNDERSTAND. Read and reread the problem. Recall that the sum of the measures of the angles of a triangle is 180°. Then guess a solution. If the smallest angle measures 20°, the measure of the largest angle is 80° more, or $20° + 80° = 100°$. The measure of the remaining angle is 10° more than the measure of the smallest angle, or $20° + 10° = 30°$. The sum of these three angles is $20° + 100° + 30° = 150°$, not the required 180°. We now know that the measure of the smallest angle is greater than 20°.

   To model this problem we will let

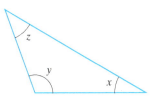

2. TRANSLATE. We translate the given information into three equations.

   In words: ↓   ↓

   Translate: $x + y + z$ =   180

   In words: the largest angle   is   80 more than the smallest angle

   Translate: y = $x + 80$

   In words: the remaining angle   is   10 more than the smallest angle

   Translate: z = $x + 10$

3. SOLVE. We solve the system

$$\begin{cases} x + y + z = 180 \\ y = x + 80 \\ z = x + 10 \end{cases}$$

Since y and z are both expressed in terms of x, we will solve using the substitution method. We substitute $y = x + 80$ and $z = x + 10$ in the first equation. Then

$$x + y + z = 180 \quad \text{First equation}$$
$$x + (x + 80) + (x + 10) = 180 \quad \text{Let } y = x + 80 \text{ and } z = x + 10.$$
$$3x + 90 = 180$$
$$3x = 90$$
$$x = 30$$

Then $y = x + 80 = 30 + 80 = 110$, and $z = x + 10 = 30 + 10 = 40$. The ordered triple solution is $(30, 110, 40)$.

4. **INTERPRET.**

Check: Notice that $30° + 40° + 110° = 180°$. Also, the measure of the largest angle, $110°$, is $80°$ more than the measure of the smallest angle, $30°$. The measure of the remaining angle, $40°$, is $10°$ more than the measure of the smallest angle, $30°$.

PRACTICE 6 The measure of the largest angle of a triangle is $40°$ more than the measure of the smallest angle, and the measure of the remaining angle is $20°$ more than the measure of the smallest angle. Find the measure of each angle.

4.3 EXERCISE SET

MIXED PRACTICE

Solve. See Examples 1 through 4.

1. One number is two more than a second number. Twice the first is 4 less than 3 times the second. Find the numbers.

2. Three times one number minus a second is 8, and the sum of the numbers is 12. Find the numbers.

3. The United States has the world's only "large deck" aircraft carriers which can hold up to 72 aircraft. The Enterprise class carrier is longest in length while the Nimitz class carrier is the second longest. The total length of these two carriers is 2193 feet while the difference of their lengths is only 9 feet. (*Source: U.S.A. Today*)

   a. Find the length of each class carrier.

   b. If a football field has a length of 100 yards, determine the length of the Enterprise class carrier in terms of number of football fields.

4. The rate of growth of participation (age 7 and older) in sports featured in the X-Games has slowed in recent years, but still surpasses that for some older sports such as football. The most popular X-Game sport is inline roller skating, followed by skateboarding. In 2005, the total number of participants in both sports was 25.1 million. If the number of participants in skateboarding was 14.2 million less than twice the number of participants in inline skating, find the number of participants in each sport. (*Source:* National Sporting Goods Association)

5. A B747 aircraft flew 6 hours with the wind. The return trip took 7 hours against the wind. If the speed of the plane in still air is 13 times the speed of the wind, find the wind speed and the speed of the plane in still air.

6. During a multi-day camping trip, Terry Watkins rowed 17 hours downstream. It took 26.5 hours rowing upstream to travel the same distance. If the speed of the current is 6.8 kilometers per hour less than his rowing speed in still water, find his rowing speed and the speed of the current.

7. Find how many quarts of 4% butterfat milk and 1% butterfat milk should be mixed to yield 60 quarts of 2% butterfat milk.

8. A pharmacist needs 500 milliliters of a 20% phenobarbital solution but has only 5% and 25% phenobarbital solutions available. Find how many milliliters of each he should mix to get the desired solution.

9. In 2005, the United Kingdom was the most popular host country in which U.S. students traveling abroad studied. Italy was the second most popular destination. A total of 56,929 students visited one of the two countries. If 7213 more U.S. students studied in the United Kingdom than in Italy, find how many students studied abroad in each country. (*Source:* Institute of International Education, *Open Doors 2006*)

10. Harvard University and Cornell University are each known for their excellent libraries, and each is participating with Google to put their collections into Google's searchable database. In 2005, Harvard libraries contained 266,791 more printed volumes than twice the number of printed volumes in the libraries of Cornell. Together, these two great libraries house 23,199,904 printed volumes. Find the number of printed volumes in each library. (*Source:* Association of Research Libraries)

11. Karen Karlin bought some large frames for $15 each and some small frames for $8 each at a closeout sale. If she bought 22 frames for $239, find how many of each type she bought.

12. Hilton University Drama Club sold 311 tickets for a play. Student tickets cost 50 cents each; nonstudent tickets cost $1.50. If total receipts were $385.50, find how many tickets of each type were sold.

13. One number is two less than a second number. Twice the first is 4 more than 3 times the second. Find the numbers.

14. Twice a first number plus a second number is 42, and the first number minus the second number is −6. Find the numbers.

15. In the United States, the percent of women using the Internet is increasing faster than the percent of men. For the years 2000–2005, the function $y = 5.3x + 39.5$ can be used to estimate the percent of females using the Internet, while the function $y = 4.5x + 45.5$ can be used to estimate the percent of males. For both functions, x is the number of years since 2000. If this trend continues, predict the year in which the percent of females using the Internet equals the percent of males. (*Source:* Pew Internet & American Life Project)

16. The percent of car vehicle sales has been decreasing over a ten-year period while the percent of light truck (pickups, sport-utility vans, and minivans) vehicles has been increasing. For the years 2000–2006, the function $y = -x + 54.2$ can be used to estimate the percent of new car vehicle sales in the United States, while the function $y = x + 45.8$ can be used to estimate the percent of light truck vehicle sales. For both functions, x is the number of years since 2000. (*Source: USA Today*, Environmental Protection Agency, "Light-Duty Automotive Technology and fuel Economy Trends: 1975–2006")

    a. Calculate the year in which the percent of new car sales equaled the percent of light truck sales.

    b. Before the actual 2001 vehicle sales data was published, *USA Today* predicted that light truck sales would likely be greater than car sales in the year 2001. Does your finding in part (a) agree with this statement?

17. An office supply store in San Diego sells 7 writing tablets and 4 pens for $6.40. Also, 2 tablets and 19 pens cost $5.40. Find the price of each.

18. A Candy Barrel shop manager mixes M&M's worth $2.00 per pound with trail mix worth $1.50 per pound. Find how many pounds of each she should use to get 50 pounds of a party mix worth $1.80 per pound.

19. A Piper airplane and a B737 aircraft cross each other (at different altitudes) traveling in opposite directions. The B737 travels 5 times the speed of the Piper. If in 4 hours, they are 2160 miles apart, find the speed of each aircraft.

20. Two cyclists start at the same point and travel in opposite directions. One travels 4 mph faster than the other. In 4 hours they are 112 miles apart. Find how fast each is traveling.

21. While it is said that trains opened up the American West to settlement, U.S. railroad miles have been on the decline for decades. On the other hand, the miles of roads in the U.S. highway system have been increasing. The function $y = -1379.4x + 150,604$ represents the U.S. railroad miles, while the function $y = 478.4x + 157,838$ models the number of U.S. highway miles, where x is the number of years after 1995. For each function, x is the number of years after 1995. (*Source:* Association of American Railroads, Federal Highway Administration)

    a. Explain how the decrease in railroad miles can be verified by their given function while the increase in highway miles can be verified by their given function.

    b. Find the year in which it is estimated that the number of U.S. railroad miles and the number of U.S. highway miles were the same.

22. The annual U.S. per capita consumption of whole milk has decreased since 1980, while the per capita consumption of lower fat milk has increased. For the years 1980–2005, the function $y = -0.40x + 15.9$ approximates the annual U.S. per capita consumption of whole milk in gallons, and the function $y = 0.14x + 11.9$ approximates the annual U.S. per capita consumption of lower fat milk in gallons. Determine the year in which the per capita consumption of whole milk equaled the per capita consumption of lower fat milk. (*Source:* Economic Research Service: U.S.D.A.)

23. The perimeter of a triangle is 93 centimeters. If two sides are equally long and the third side is 9 centimeters longer than the others, find the lengths of the three sides.

24. Jack Reinholt, a car salesman, has a choice of two pay arrangements: a weekly salary of $200 plus 5% commission on sales, or a straight 15% commission. Find the amount of weekly sales for which Jack's earnings are the same regardless of the pay arrangement.

25. Hertz car rental agency charges $25 daily plus 10 cents per mile. Budget charges $20 daily plus 25 cents per mile. Find the daily mileage for which the Budget charge for the day is twice that of the Hertz charge for the day.

26. Carroll Blakemore, a drafting student, bought three templates and a pencil one day for $6.45. Another day he bought two pads of paper and four pencils for $7.50. If the price of a pad of paper is three times the price of a pencil, find the price of each type of item.

27. In the figure, line l and line m are parallel lines cut by transversal t. Find the values of x and y.

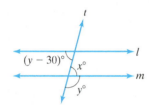

28. Find the values of x and y in the following isosceles triangle.

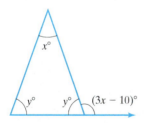

Given the cost function $C(x)$ and the revenue function $R(x)$, find the number of units x that must be sold to break even. See Example 5.

29. $C(x) = 30x + 10,000$ $R(x) = 46x$
30. $C(x) = 12x + 15,000$ $R(x) = 32x$
31. $C(x) = 1.2x + 1500$ $R(x) = 1.7x$
32. $C(x) = 0.8x + 900$ $R(x) = 2x$
33. $C(x) = 75x + 160,000$ $R(x) = 200x$
34. $C(x) = 105x + 70,000$ $R(x) = 245x$

35. **Multiple Steps.** The planning department of Abstract Office Supplies has been asked to determine whether the company should introduce a new computer desk next year. The department estimates that $6000 of new manufacturing equipment will need to be purchased and that the cost of constructing each desk will be $200. The department also estimates that the revenue from each desk will be $450.
    a. Determine the revenue function $R(x)$ from the sale of x desks.
    b. Determine the cost function $C(x)$ for manufacturing x desks.
    c. Find the break-even point.

36. **Multiple Steps.** Baskets, Inc., is planning to introduce a new woven basket. The company estimates that $500 worth of new equipment will be needed to manufacture this new type of basket and that it will cost $15 per basket to manufacture. The company also estimates that the revenue from each basket will be $31.
    a. Determine the revenue function $R(x)$ from the sale of x baskets.
    b. Determine the cost function $C(x)$ for manufacturing x baskets.
    c. Find the break-even point.

Solve. See Example 6.

37. Rabbits in a lab are to be kept on a strict daily diet that includes 30 grams of protein, 16 grams of fat, and 24 grams of carbohydrates. The scientist has only three food mixes available with the following grams of nutrients per unit.

	Protein	Fat	Carbohydrate
Mix A	4	6	3
Mix B	6	1	2
Mix C	4	1	12

Find how many units of each mix are needed daily to meet each rabbit's dietary need.

38. Gerry Gundersen mixes different solutions with concentrations of 25%, 40%, and 50% to get 200 liters of a 32% solution. If he uses twice as much of the 25% solution as of the 40% solution, find how many liters of each kind he uses.

39. The perimeter of a quadrilateral (four-sided polygon) is 29 inches. The longest side is twice as long as the shortest side. The other two sides are equally long and are 2 inches longer than the shortest side. Find the length of all four sides.

40. The measure of the largest angle of a triangle is 90° more than the measure of the smallest angle, and the measure of the remaining angle is 30° more than the measure of the smallest angle. Find the measure of each angle.

41. The sum of three numbers is 40. One number is five more than a second number. It is also twice the third. Find the numbers.

42. The sum of the digits of a three-digit number is 15. The tens-place digit is twice the hundreds-place digit, and the ones-place digit is 1 less than the hundreds-place digit. Find the three-digit number.

43. Diana Taurasi, of the Phoenix Mercury, was the WNBA's top scorer for the 2006 regular season, with a total of 860 points. The number of two-point field goals that Taurasi made was 65 less than double the number of three-point field goals she made. The number of free throws (each worth one point) she made was 34 less than the number of two-point field goals she made. Find how many free throws, two-point field goals, and three-point field goals Diana Taurasi made during the 2006 regular season. (*Source:* Women's National Basketball Association)

44. During the 2006 NBA playoffs, the top scoring player was Dwayne Wade of the Miami Heat. Wade scored a total of 654 points during the playoffs. The number of free throws (each worth one point) he made was three less than the number of two-point field goals he made. He also made 27 fewer three-point field goals than one-fifth the number of two-point field goals. How many free throws, two-point field goals, and three-point field goals did Dwayne Wade make during the 2006 playoffs? (*Source:* National Basketball Association)

△ **45.** Find the values of x, y, and z in the following triangle.

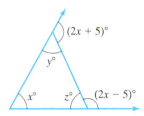

△ **46.** The sum of the measures of the angles of a quadrilateral is $360°$. Find the value of x, y, and z in the following quadrilateral.

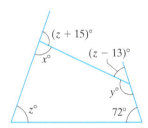

REVIEW AND PREVIEW

Multiply both sides of equation (1) by 2, and add the resulting equation to equation (2). See Section 4.2.

47. $3x - y + z = 2$ (1)
$-x + 2y + 3z = 6$ (2)

48. $2x + y + 3z = 7$ (1)
$-4x + y + 2z = 4$ (2)

Multiply both sides of equation (1) by -3, and add the resulting equation to equation (2). See Section 4.2.

49. $x + 2y - z = 0$ (1)
$3x + y - z = 2$ (2)

50. $2x - 3y + 2z = 5$ (1)
$x - 9y + z = -1$ (2)

CONCEPT EXTENSIONS

51. The number of personal bankruptcy petitions filed in the United States was constantly increasing from the early 1980s until the bankruptcy laws were changed in 2006. In 2006, the number of petitions filed was only 25,765 more than the number of petitions filed in 1996. The total number of personal bankruptcies filed in these two years was 2,144,653. Find the number of personal bankruptcies filed in each year. (*Source:* Based on data from the Administrative Office of the United States Courts)

52. Multiple Steps. In 2006, the median weekly earnings for male postal service mail carriers in the United States was $126 more than the median weekly earnings for female mail postal service carriers. The median weekly earnings for female postal service mail carriers was 0.86 time that of their male counterparts. Also in 2006, the median weekly earnings for female lawyers in the United States was $540 less than the median weekly earnings for male lawyers. The median weekly earnings of male lawyers was 1.4 times that of their female counterparts. (*Source:* Based on data from the Bureau of Labor Statistics)

a. Find the median weekly earnings for female postal service mail carriers in the United States in 2006.

b. Find the median weekly earnings for female lawyers in the United States in 2006.

c. Of the four groups of workers described in the problem, which group makes the greatest weekly earnings? Which group makes the least weekly earnings?

53. Multiple Steps. MySpace and Facebook are both very popular social networking Web sites. The function $f(x) = 0.85x + 41.75$ represents the MySpace minutes (in thousands)/month while the function $f(x) = 1.13x + 10.49$ represents the Facebook minutes (in thousands)/month. In both of these functions $x = 1$ represents Feb. 2007, $x = 2$ represents March 2007 and so on.

a. Solve the system formed by these functions. Round each coordinate to the nearest whole number.

b. Use your answer to part **a** to predict the month and year in which the total pages viewed for MySpace and Facebook are the same.

54. Find the values of a, b, and c such that the equation $y = ax^2 + bx + c$ has ordered pair solutions $(1, 6)$, $(-1, -2)$, and $(0, -1)$. To do so, substitute each ordered pair solution into the equation. Each time, the result is an equation in three unknowns: a, b, and c. Then solve the resulting system of three linear equations in three unknowns, a, b, and c.

55. Find the values of a, b, and c such that the equation $y = ax^2 + bx + c$ has ordered pair solutions $(1, 2)$, $(2, 3)$ and $(-1, 6)$. (*Hint:* See Exercise 54.)

56. Data (x, y) for the total number y (in thousands) of college-bound students who took the ACT assessment in the year x are $(0, 1065)$, $(1, 1070)$ and $(3, 1175)$, where $x = 0$ represents 2000 and $x = 1$ represents 2001. Find the values of a, b, and c such that the equation $y = ax^2 + bx + c$ models this data. According to your model, how many students will take the ACT in 2009? (*Source:* ACT, Inc.)

57. Monthly normal rainfall data (x, y) for Portland, Oregon, are $(4, 2.47)$, $(7, 0.6)$, $(8, 1.1)$, where x represents time in months (with $x = 1$ representing January) and y represents rainfall in inches. Find the values of a, b, and c rounded to 2 decimal places such that the equation $y = ax^2 + bx + c$ models this data. According to your model, how much rain should Portland expect during September? (*Source:* National Climatic Data Center)

INTEGRATED REVIEW SYSTEMS OF LINEAR EQUATIONS

Sections 4.1–4.3

The graphs of various systems of equations are shown. Match each graph with the solution of its corresponding system.

A 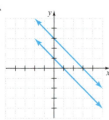 **B** 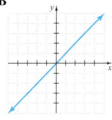 **C** 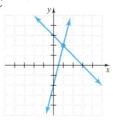 **D**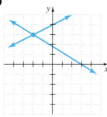

1. Solution: $(1, 2)$
2. Solution: $(-2, 3)$
3. No solution
4. Infinite number of solutions

Solve each system by elimination or substitution.

5. $\begin{cases} x + y = 4 \\ y = 3x \end{cases}$

6. $\begin{cases} x - y = -4 \\ y = 4x \end{cases}$

7. $\begin{cases} x + y = 1 \\ x - 2y = 4 \end{cases}$

8. $\begin{cases} 2x - y = 8 \\ x + 3y = 11 \end{cases}$

9. $\begin{cases} 2x + 5y = 8 \\ 6x + y = 10 \end{cases}$

10. $\begin{cases} \frac{1}{8}x - \frac{1}{2}y = -\frac{5}{8} \\ -3x - 8y = 0 \end{cases}$

11. $\begin{cases} 4x - 7y = 7 \\ 12x - 21y = 24 \end{cases}$

12. $\begin{cases} 2x - 5y = 3 \\ -4x + 10y = -6 \end{cases}$

13. $\begin{cases} y = \frac{1}{3}x \\ 5x - 3y = 4 \end{cases}$

14. $\begin{cases} y = \frac{1}{4}x \\ 2x - 4y = 3 \end{cases}$

15. $\begin{cases} x + y = 2 \\ -3y + z = -7 \\ 2x + y - z = -1 \end{cases}$

16. $\begin{cases} y + 2z = -3 \\ x - 2y = 7 \\ 2x - y + z = 5 \end{cases}$

17. $\begin{cases} 2x + 4y - 6z = 3 \\ -x + y - z = 6 \\ x + 2y - 3z = 1 \end{cases}$

18. $\begin{cases} x - y + 3z = 2 \\ -2x + 2y - 6z = -4 \\ 3x - 3y + 9z = 6 \end{cases}$

19. $\begin{cases} x + y - 4z = 5 \\ x - y + 2z = -2 \\ 3x + 2y + 4z = 18 \end{cases}$

20. $\begin{cases} 2x - y + 3z = 2 \\ x + y - 6z = 0 \\ 3x + 4y - 3z = 6 \end{cases}$

21. A first number is 8 less than a second number. Twice the first number is 11 more than the second number. Find the numbers.

△ 22. The sum of the measures of the angles of a quadrilateral is 360°. The two smallest angles of the quadrilateral have the same measure. The third angle measures 30° more than the measure of one of the smallest angles and the fourth angle measures 50° more than the measure of one of the smallest angles. Find the measure of each angle.

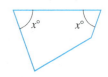

4.4 SOLVING SYSTEMS OF EQUATIONS BY MATRICES

OBJECTIVES

1. Use matrices to solve a system of two equations.
2. Use matrices to solve a system of three equations.

By now, you may have noticed that the solution of a system of equations depends on the coefficients of the equations in the system and not on the variables. In this section, we introduce solving a system of equations by a **matrix**.

OBJECTIVE 1 ▶ Using matrices to solve a system of two equations. A matrix (plural: **matrices**) is a rectangular array of numbers. The following are examples of matrices.

$$\begin{bmatrix} 1 & 0 \\ 0 & 1 \end{bmatrix} \quad \begin{bmatrix} 2 & 1 & 3 & -1 \\ 0 & -1 & 4 & 5 \\ -6 & 2 & 1 & 0 \end{bmatrix} \quad \begin{bmatrix} a & b & c \\ d & e & f \end{bmatrix}$$

The numbers aligned horizontally in a matrix are in the same **row**. The numbers aligned vertically are in the same **column**.

row 1 → $\begin{bmatrix} 2 & 1 & 0 \\ -1 & 6 & 2 \end{bmatrix}$ This matrix has 2 rows and 3 columns. It is called a 2 × 3 (read "two by three") matrix.
row 2 →

column 1, column 2, column 3

To see the relationship between systems of equations and matrices, study the example below.

▶ **Helpful Hint**

Before writing the corresponding matrix associated with a system of equations, make sure that the equations are written in standard form.

System of Equations (in standard form)

$\begin{cases} 2x - 3y = 6 & \text{Equation 1} \\ x + y = 0 & \text{Equation 2} \end{cases}$

Corresponding Matrix

$\begin{bmatrix} 2 & -3 & | & 6 \\ 1 & 1 & | & 0 \end{bmatrix}$ Row 1
Row 2

Notice that the rows of the matrix correspond to the equations in the system. The coefficients of each variable are placed to the left of a vertical dashed line. The constants are placed to the right. Each of these numbers in the matrix is called an **element**.

The method of solving systems by matrices is to write this matrix as an equivalent matrix from which we easily identify the solution. Two matrices are equivalent if they represent systems that have the same solution set. The following **row operations** can be performed on matrices, and the result is an equivalent matrix.

Elementary Row Operations

1. Any two rows in a matrix may be interchanged.
2. The elements of any row may be multiplied (or divided) by the same nonzero number.
3. The elements of any row may be multiplied (or divided) by a nonzero number and added to their corresponding elements in any other row.

▶ **Helpful Hint**

Notice that these *row* operations are the same operations that we can perform on *equations* in a system.

To solve a system of two equations in x and y by matrices, write the corresponding matrix associated with the system. Then use elementary row operations to write equivalent matrices until you have a matrix of the form

$$\begin{bmatrix} 1 & a & | & b \\ 0 & 1 & | & c \end{bmatrix},$$

where a, b, and c are constants. Why? If a matrix associated with a system of equations is in this form, we can easily solve for x and y. For example,

Matrix   **System of Equations**

$\begin{bmatrix} 1 & 2 & | & -3 \\ 0 & 1 & | & 5 \end{bmatrix}$ corresponds to $\begin{cases} 1x + 2y = -3 \\ 0x + 1y = 5 \end{cases}$ or $\begin{cases} x + 2y = -3 \\ y = 5 \end{cases}$

In the second equation, we have $y = 5$. Substituting this in the first equation, we have $x + 2(5) = -3$ or $x = -13$. The solution of the system is the ordered pair $(-13, 5)$.

EXAMPLE 1   Use matrices to solve the system.

$$\begin{cases} x + 3y = 5 \\ 2x - y = -4 \end{cases}$$

Solution   The corresponding matrix is $\begin{bmatrix} 1 & 3 & | & 5 \\ 2 & -1 & | & -4 \end{bmatrix}$. We use elementary row operations to write an equivalent matrix that looks like $\begin{bmatrix} 1 & a & | & b \\ 0 & 1 & | & c \end{bmatrix}$.

For the matrix given, the element in the first row, first column is already 1, as desired. Next we write an equivalent matrix with a 0 below the 1. To do this, we multiply row 1 by -2 and add to row 2. *We will change only row 2.*

$$\begin{bmatrix} 1 & 3 & | & 5 \\ -2(1) + 2 & -2(3) + (-1) & | & -2(5) + (-4) \end{bmatrix} \text{ simplifies to } \begin{bmatrix} 1 & 3 & | & 5 \\ 0 & -7 & | & -14 \end{bmatrix}$$

↑   ↑   ↑   ↑   ↑   ↑
row 1   row 2   row 1   row 2   row 1   row 2
element element element element element element

Now we change the -7 to a 1 by use of an elementary row operation. We divide row 2 by -7, then

$$\begin{bmatrix} 1 & 3 & | & 5 \\ \frac{0}{-7} & \frac{-7}{-7} & | & \frac{-14}{-7} \end{bmatrix} \text{ simplifies to } \begin{bmatrix} 1 & 3 & | & 5 \\ 0 & 1 & | & 2 \end{bmatrix}$$

This last matrix corresponds to the system

$$\begin{cases} x + 3y = 5 \\ y = 2 \end{cases}$$

To find x, we let $y = 2$ in the first equation, $x + 3y = 5$.

$x + 3y = 5$ First equation
$x + 3(2) = 5$ Let $y = 2$.
$x = -1$

The ordered pair solution is $(-1, 2)$. Check to see that this ordered pair satisfies both equations.   □

PRACTICE
1   Use matrices to solve the system.

$$\begin{cases} x + 4y = -2 \\ 3x - y = 7 \end{cases}$$

EXAMPLE 2 Use matrices to solve the system.

$$\begin{cases} 2x - y = 3 \\ 4x - 2y = 5 \end{cases}$$

Solution The corresponding matrix is $\begin{bmatrix} 2 & -1 & | & 3 \\ 4 & -2 & | & 5 \end{bmatrix}$. To get 1 in the row 1, column 1 position, we divide the elements of row 1 by 2.

$$\begin{bmatrix} \frac{2}{2} & -\frac{1}{2} & | & \frac{3}{2} \\ 4 & -2 & | & 5 \end{bmatrix} \quad \text{simplifies to} \quad \begin{bmatrix} 1 & -\frac{1}{2} & | & \frac{3}{2} \\ 4 & -2 & | & 5 \end{bmatrix}$$

To get 0 under the 1, we multiply the elements of row 1 by -4 and add the new elements to the elements of row 2.

$$\begin{bmatrix} 1 & -\frac{1}{2} & | & \frac{3}{2} \\ -4(1) + 4 & -4\left(-\frac{1}{2}\right) - 2 & | & -4\left(\frac{3}{2}\right) + 5 \end{bmatrix} \quad \text{simplifies to} \quad \begin{bmatrix} 1 & -\frac{1}{2} & | & \frac{3}{2} \\ 0 & 0 & | & -1 \end{bmatrix}$$

The corresponding system is $\begin{cases} x - \frac{1}{2}y = \frac{3}{2} \\ 0 = -1 \end{cases}$. The equation $0 = -1$ is false for all y or x values; hence the system is inconsistent and has no solution. □

PRACTICE 2 Use matrices to solve the system.

$$\begin{cases} x - 3y = 3 \\ -2x + 6y = 4 \end{cases}$$

Concept Check ✓

Consider the system

$$\begin{cases} 2x - 3y = 8 \\ x + 5y = -3 \end{cases}$$

What is wrong with its corresponding matrix shown below?

$$\begin{bmatrix} 2 & -3 & | & 8 \\ 0 & 5 & | & -3 \end{bmatrix}$$

OBJECTIVE 2 ▶ Using matrices to solve a system of three equations. To solve a system of three equations in three variables using matrices, we will write the corresponding matrix in the form

$$\begin{bmatrix} 1 & a & b & | & d \\ 0 & 1 & c & | & e \\ 0 & 0 & 1 & | & f \end{bmatrix}$$

Answer to Concept Check:

matrix should be $\begin{bmatrix} 2 & -3 & | & 8 \\ 1 & 5 & | & -3 \end{bmatrix}$

EXAMPLE 3 Use matrices to solve the system.

$$\begin{cases} x + 2y + z = 2 \\ -2x - y + 2z = 5 \\ x + 3y - 2z = -8 \end{cases}$$

Solution The corresponding matrix is $\begin{bmatrix} 1 & 2 & 1 & | & 2 \\ -2 & -1 & 2 & | & 5 \\ 1 & 3 & -2 & | & -8 \end{bmatrix}$. Our goal is to write an equivalent matrix with 1's along the diagonal (see the numbers in red) and 0's below the 1's. The element in row 1, column 1 is already 1. Next we get 0's for each element in the rest of column 1. To do this, first we multiply the elements of row 1 by 2 and add the new elements to row 2. Also, we multiply the elements of row 1 by -1 and add the new elements to the elements of row 3. We *do not change row 1*. Then

$$\begin{bmatrix} 1 & 2 & 1 & | & 2 \\ 2(1)-2 & 2(2)-1 & 2(1)+2 & | & 2(2)+5 \\ -1(1)+1 & -1(2)+3 & -1(1)-2 & | & -1(2)-8 \end{bmatrix} \text{ simplifies to } \begin{bmatrix} 1 & 2 & 1 & | & 2 \\ 0 & 3 & 4 & | & 9 \\ 0 & 1 & -3 & | & -10 \end{bmatrix}$$

We continue down the diagonal and use elementary row operations to get 1 where the element 3 is now. To do this, we interchange rows 2 and 3.

$$\begin{bmatrix} 1 & 2 & 1 & | & 2 \\ 0 & 3 & 4 & | & 9 \\ 0 & 1 & -3 & | & -10 \end{bmatrix} \text{ is equivalent to } \begin{bmatrix} 1 & 2 & 1 & | & 2 \\ 0 & 1 & -3 & | & -10 \\ 0 & 3 & 4 & | & 9 \end{bmatrix}$$

Next we want the new row 3, column 2 element to be 0. We multiply the elements of row 2 by -3 and add the result to the elements of row 3.

$$\begin{bmatrix} 1 & 2 & 1 & | & 2 \\ 0 & 1 & -3 & | & -10 \\ -3(0)+0 & -3(1)+3 & -3(-3)+4 & | & -3(-10)+9 \end{bmatrix} \text{ simplifies to }$$

$$\begin{bmatrix} 1 & 2 & 1 & | & 2 \\ 0 & 1 & -3 & | & -10 \\ 0 & 0 & 13 & | & 39 \end{bmatrix}$$

Finally, we divide the elements of row 3 by 13 so that the final diagonal element is 1.

$$\begin{bmatrix} 1 & 2 & 1 & | & 2 \\ 0 & 1 & -3 & | & -10 \\ \frac{0}{13} & \frac{0}{13} & \frac{13}{13} & | & \frac{39}{13} \end{bmatrix} \text{ simplifies to } \begin{bmatrix} 1 & 2 & 1 & | & 2 \\ 0 & 1 & -3 & | & -10 \\ 0 & 0 & 1 & | & 3 \end{bmatrix}$$

This matrix corresponds to the system

$$\begin{cases} x + 2y + z = 2 \\ y - 3z = -10 \\ z = 3 \end{cases}$$

We identify the z-coordinate of the solution as 3. Next we replace z with 3 in the second equation and solve for y.

$y - 3z = -10$ Second equation
$y - 3(3) = -10$ Let $z = 3$.
$y = -1$

To find x, we let $z = 3$ and $y = -1$ in the first equation.

$$x + 2y + z = 2 \quad \text{First equation}$$
$$x + 2(-1) + 3 = 2 \quad \text{Let } z = 3 \text{ and } y = -1.$$
$$x = 1$$

The ordered triple solution is $(1, -1, 3)$. Check to see that it satisfies all three equations in the original system.

PRACTICE 3 Use matrices to solve the system.
$$\begin{cases} x + 3y - z = 0 \\ 2x + y + 3z = 5 \\ -x - 2y + 4z = 7 \end{cases}$$

VOCABULARY & READINESS CHECK

Word Bank. *Use the choices below to fill in each blank.*

column   element   row   matrix

1. A _____ is a rectangular array of numbers.
2. Each of the numbers in a matrix is called an _____.
3. The numbers aligned horizontally in a matrix are in the same _____.
4. The numbers aligned vertically in a matrix are in the same _____.

True or False. *Answer true or false for each statement about operations within a matrix forming an equivalent matrix.*

5. Any two columns may be interchanged. _____
6. Any two rows may be interchanged. _____
7. The elements in a row may be added to their corresponding elements in another row. _____
8. The elements of a column may be multiplied by any nonzero number. _____

4.4 EXERCISE SET

Solve each system of linear equations using matrices. See Example 1.

1. $\begin{cases} x + y = 1 \\ x - 2y = 4 \end{cases}$

2. $\begin{cases} 2x - y = 8 \\ x + 3y = 11 \end{cases}$

3. $\begin{cases} x + 3y = 2 \\ x + 2y = 0 \end{cases}$

4. $\begin{cases} 4x - y = 5 \\ 3x + 3y = 0 \end{cases}$

Solve each system of linear equations using matrices. See Example 2.

5. $\begin{cases} x - 2y = 4 \\ 2x - 4y = 4 \end{cases}$

6. $\begin{cases} -x + 3y = 6 \\ 3x - 9y = 9 \end{cases}$

7. $\begin{cases} 3x - 3y = 9 \\ 2x - 2y = 6 \end{cases}$

8. $\begin{cases} 9x - 3y = 6 \\ -18x + 6y = -12 \end{cases}$

Solve each system of linear equations using matrices. See Example 3.

9. $\begin{cases} x + y = 3 \\ 2y = 10 \\ 3x + 2y - 4z = 12 \end{cases}$

10. $\begin{cases} 5x = 5 \\ 2x + y = 4 \\ 3x + y - 5z = -15 \end{cases}$

11. $\begin{cases} 2y - z = -7 \\ x + 4y + z = -4 \\ 5x - y + 2z = 13 \end{cases}$

12. $\begin{cases} 4y + 3z = -2 \\ 5x - 4y = 1 \\ -5x + 4y + z = -3 \end{cases}$

MIXED PRACTICE

Solve each system of linear equations using matrices. See Examples 1 through 3.

13. $\begin{cases} x - 4 = 0 \\ x + y = 1 \end{cases}$
14. $\begin{cases} 3y = 6 \\ x + y = 7 \end{cases}$

15. $\begin{cases} x + y + z = 2 \\ 2x - z = 5 \\ 3y + z = 2 \end{cases}$
16. $\begin{cases} x + 2y + z = 5 \\ x - y - z = 3 \\ y + z = 2 \end{cases}$

17. $\begin{cases} 5x - 2y = 27 \\ -3x + 5y = 18 \end{cases}$
18. $\begin{cases} 4x - y = 9 \\ 2x + 3y = -27 \end{cases}$

19. $\begin{cases} 4x - 7y = 7 \\ 12x - 21y = 24 \end{cases}$
20. $\begin{cases} 2x - 5y = 12 \\ -4x + 10y = 20 \end{cases}$

21. $\begin{cases} 4x - y + 2z = 5 \\ 2y + z = 4 \\ 4x + y + 3z = 10 \end{cases}$
22. $\begin{cases} 5y - 7z = 14 \\ 2x + y + 4z = 10 \\ 2x + 6y - 3z = 30 \end{cases}$

23. $\begin{cases} 4x + y + z = 3 \\ -x + y - 2z = -11 \\ x + 2y + 2z = -1 \end{cases}$
24. $\begin{cases} x + y + z = 9 \\ 3x - y + z = -1 \\ -2x + 2y - 3z = -2 \end{cases}$

REVIEW AND PREVIEW

Determine whether each graph is the graph of a function. See Section 3.2.

25.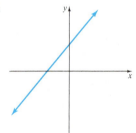
26.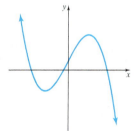

27.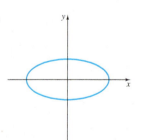
28.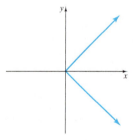

Evaluate. See Section 1.3.

29. $(-1)(-5) - (6)(3)$
30. $(2)(-8) - (-4)(1)$
31. $(4)(-10) - (2)(-2)$
32. $(-7)(3) - (-2)(-6)$
33. $(-3)(-3) - (-1)(-9)$
34. $(5)(6) - (10)(10)$

CONCEPT EXTENSIONS

Solve. See the Concept Check in the section.

35. For the system $\begin{cases} x + z = 7 \\ y + 2z = -6 \\ 3x - y = 0 \end{cases}$, which is the correct corresponding matrix?

   a. $\begin{bmatrix} 1 & 1 & 7 \\ 1 & 2 & -6 \\ 3 & -1 & 0 \end{bmatrix}$
   b. $\begin{bmatrix} 1 & 0 & 1 & 7 \\ 1 & 2 & 0 & -6 \\ 3 & -1 & 0 & 0 \end{bmatrix}$
   c. $\begin{bmatrix} 1 & 0 & 1 & 7 \\ 0 & 1 & 2 & -6 \\ 3 & -1 & 0 & 0 \end{bmatrix}$

36. For the system $\begin{cases} x - 6 = 0 \\ 2x - 3y = 1 \end{cases}$, which is the correct corresponding matrix?

   a. $\begin{bmatrix} 1 & -6 & 0 \\ 2 & -3 & 1 \end{bmatrix}$
   b. $\begin{bmatrix} 1 & 0 & 6 \\ 2 & -3 & 1 \end{bmatrix}$
   c. $\begin{bmatrix} 1 & 0 & -6 \\ 2 & -3 & 1 \end{bmatrix}$

37. **Multiple Steps.** The percent y of U.S. households that owned a black-and-white television set between the years 1980 and 1993 can be modeled by the linear equation $2.3x + y = 52$, where x represents the number of years after 1980. Similarly, the percent y of U.S. households that owned a microwave oven during this same period can be modeled by the linear equation $-5.4x + y = 14$. (*Source:* Based on data from the Energy Information Administration, U.S. Department of Energy)

   a. The data used to form these two models was incomplete. It is impossible to tell from the data the year in which the percent of households owning black-and-white television sets was the same as the percent of households owning microwave ovens. Use matrix methods to estimate the year in which this occurred.

   b. Did more households own black-and-white television sets or microwave ovens in 1980? In 1993? What trends do these models show? Does this seem to make sense? Why or why not?

   c. According to the models, when will the percent of households owning black-and-white television sets reach 0%?

   d. Do you think your answer to part c is accurate? Why or why not?

38. The most popular amusement park in the world currently (according to annual attendance) is Disney World's Magic Kingdom, whose annual attendance in thousands can be approximated by the equation $y = 455x + 14123$, where x is the number of years after 2001. This theme park stole the title from Tokyo Disneyland, which had been in first place for many years. The yearly attendance for Tokyo Disneyland, in thousands, can be represented by the equation $y = -776x + 15985$. Find the last year when attendance at Tokyo Disneyland was greater then attendance at Magic Kingdom. (*Source:* Amusement Business, and TEA Park World)

39. For the system $\begin{cases} 2x - 3y = 8 \\ x + 5y = -3 \end{cases}$, explain what is wrong with writing the corresponding matrix as $\begin{bmatrix} 2 & 3 & | & 8 \\ 0 & 5 & | & -3 \end{bmatrix}$.

4.5 SYSTEMS OF LINEAR INEQUALITIES

OBJECTIVE

1. Graph a system of linear inequalities.

OBJECTIVE 1 ▶ Graphing systems of linear inequalities. In Section 3.7 we solved linear inequalities in two variables as well as their union and intersection. Just as two or more linear equations make a system of linear equations, two or more linear inequalities make a **system of linear inequalities**. Systems of inequalities are very important in a process called linear programming. Many businesses use linear programming to find the most profitable way to use limited resources such as employees, machines, or buildings.

A **solution of a system of linear inequalities** is an ordered pair that satisfies each inequality in the system. The set of all such ordered pairs is the solution set of the system. Graphing this set gives us a picture of the solution set. We can graph a system of inequalities by graphing each inequality in the system and identifying the region of overlap.

> **Graphing the Solutions of a System of Linear Inequalities**
> **STEP 1.** Graph each inequality in the system on the same set of axes.
> **STEP 2.** The solutions of the system are the points common to the graphs of all the inequalities in the system.

EXAMPLE 1 Graph the solutions of the system: $\begin{cases} 3x \geq y \\ x + 2y \leq 8 \end{cases}$

Solution We begin by graphing each inequality on the *same* set of axes. The graph of the solutions of the system is the region contained in the graphs of both inequalities. In other words, it is their intersection.

First let's graph $3x \geq y$. The boundary line is the graph of $3x = y$. We sketch a solid boundary line since the inequality $3x \geq y$ means $3x > y$ or $3x = y$. The test point $(1, 0)$ satisfies the inequality, so we shade the half-plane that includes $(1, 0)$.

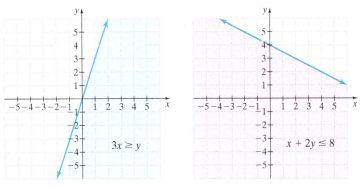

Next we sketch a solid boundary line $x + 2y = 8$ on the same set of axes. The test point $(0, 0)$ satisfies the inequality $x + 2y \leq 8$, so we shade the half-plane that includes $(0, 0)$. (For clarity, the graph of $x + 2y \leq 8$ is shown here on a separate set of axes.) An ordered pair solution of the system must satisfy both inequalities. These solutions are points that lie in both shaded regions. The solution of the system is the darkest shaded region. This solution includes parts of both boundary lines.

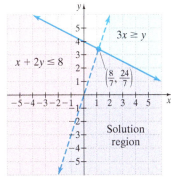

PRACTICE 1 Graph the solutions of the system: $\begin{cases} 4x \geq y \\ x + 3y \geq 6 \end{cases}$.

In linear programming, it is sometimes necessary to find the coordinates of the **corner point:** the point at which the two boundary lines intersect. To find the corner point for the system of Example 1, we solve the related linear system

$$\begin{cases} 3x = y \\ x + 2y = 8 \end{cases}$$

using either the substitution or the elimination method. The lines intersect at $\left(\dfrac{8}{7}, \dfrac{24}{7}\right)$, the corner point of the graph.

EXAMPLE 2 Graph the solutions of the system: $\begin{cases} x - y < 2 \\ x + 2y > -1 \\ y < 2 \end{cases}$

Solution First we graph all three inequalities on the same set of axes. All boundary lines are dashed lines since the inequality symbols are $<$ and $>$. The solution of the system is the region shown by the darkest shading. In this example, the boundary lines are *not* a part of the solution.

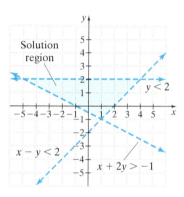

PRACTICE 2 Graph the solutions of the system: $\begin{cases} x - y < 1 \\ y < 4 \\ 3x + y > -3 \end{cases}$.

Concept Check ✓

Describe the solution of the system of inequalities:

$$\begin{cases} x \leq 2 \\ x \geq 2 \end{cases}$$

EXAMPLE 3 Graph the solutions of the system: $\begin{cases} -3x + 4y \leq 12 \\ x \leq 3 \\ x \geq 0 \\ y \geq 0 \end{cases}$

Solution We graph the inequalities on the same set of axes. The intersection of the inequalities is the solution region. It is the only region shaded in this graph and includes the portions of all four boundary lines that border the shaded region.

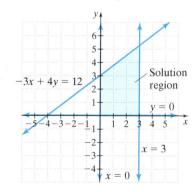

Answer to Concept Check:
the line $x = 2$

Section 4.5 Systems of Linear Inequalities 235

PRACTICE 3 Graph the solutions of the system: $\begin{cases} -2x + 5y \le 10 \\ x \le 4 \\ x \ge 0 \\ y \ge 0 \end{cases}$.

VOCABULARY & READINESS CHECK

Word Bank. *Use the choices below to fill in each blank. Not all choices will be used.*

solution   union   system
corner   intersection

1. Two or more linear inequalities form a _____ of linear inequalities.
2. An ordered pair that satisfies each inequality in a system is a _____ of the system.
3. The point where two boundary lines intersect is a _____ point.
4. The solution region of a system of inequalities consists of the _____ of the solution regions of the inequalities in the system.

4.5 EXERCISE SET

MIXED PRACTICE

Graph the solutions of each system of linear inequalities. See Examples 1 through 3.

1. $\begin{cases} y \ge x + 1 \\ y \ge 3 - x \end{cases}$
2. $\begin{cases} y \ge x - 3 \\ y \ge -1 - x \end{cases}$
3. $\begin{cases} y < 3x - 4 \\ y \le x + 2 \end{cases}$
4. $\begin{cases} y \le 2x + 1 \\ y > x + 2 \end{cases}$
5. $\begin{cases} y < -2x - 2 \\ y > x + 4 \end{cases}$
6. $\begin{cases} y \le 2x + 4 \\ y \ge -x - 5 \end{cases}$
7. $\begin{cases} y > -x + 2 \\ y \le 2x + 5 \end{cases}$
8. $\begin{cases} y \ge x - 5 \\ y \le -3x + 3 \end{cases}$
9. $\begin{cases} x \ge 3y \\ x + 3y \le 6 \end{cases}$
10. $\begin{cases} -2x < y \\ x + 2y < 3 \end{cases}$
11. $\begin{cases} x \le 2 \\ y \ge -3 \end{cases}$
12. $\begin{cases} x \ge -3 \\ y \ge -2 \end{cases}$
13. $\begin{cases} y \ge 1 \\ x < -3 \end{cases}$
14. $\begin{cases} y > 2 \\ x \ge -1 \end{cases}$
15. $\begin{cases} y + 2x \ge 0 \\ 5x - 3y \le 12 \\ y \le 2 \end{cases}$
16. $\begin{cases} y + 2x \le 0 \\ 5x + 3y \ge -2 \\ y \le 4 \end{cases}$
17. $\begin{cases} 3x - 4y \ge -6 \\ 2x + y \le 7 \\ y \ge -3 \end{cases}$
18. $\begin{cases} 4x - y \ge -2 \\ 2x + 3y \le -8 \\ y \ge -5 \end{cases}$
19. $\begin{cases} 2x + y \le 5 \\ x \le 3 \\ x \ge 0 \\ y \ge 0 \end{cases}$
20. $\begin{cases} 3x + y \le 4 \\ x \le 4 \\ x \ge 0 \\ y \ge 0 \end{cases}$

Matching. *Match each system of inequalities to the corresponding graph.*

A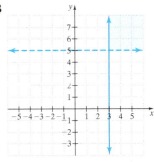

B

C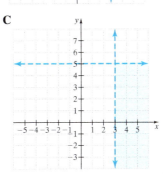

D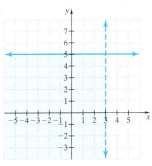

21. $\begin{cases} y < 5 \\ x > 3 \end{cases}$
22. $\begin{cases} y > 5 \\ x < 3 \end{cases}$
23. $\begin{cases} y \le 5 \\ x < 3 \end{cases}$
24. $\begin{cases} y > 5 \\ x \ge 3 \end{cases}$

REVIEW

Evaluate each expression. See Section 1.3.

25. $(-3)^2$ **26.** $(-5)^3$ **27.** $\left(\dfrac{2}{3}\right)^2$ **28.** $\left(\dfrac{3}{4}\right)^3$

Perform each indicated operation. See Section 1.3.

29. $(-2)^2 - (-3) + 2(-1)$ **30.** $5^2 - 11 + 3(-5)$

31. $8^2 + (-13) - 4(-2)$ **32.** $(-12)^2 + (-1)(2) - 6$

CONCEPT EXTENSIONS

Solve. See the Concept Check in this section.

33. Describe the solution of the system: $\begin{cases} y \leq 3 \\ y \geq 3 \end{cases}$.

34. Describe the solution of the system: $\begin{cases} x \leq 5 \\ x \leq 3 \end{cases}$.

35. Explain how to decide which region to shade to show the solution region of the following system.

$$\begin{cases} x \geq 3 \\ y \geq -2 \end{cases}$$

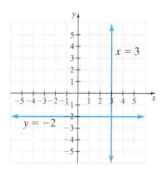

36. Multiple Steps. Tony Noellert budgets his time at work today. Part of the day he can write bills; the rest of the day he can use to write purchase orders. The total time available is at most 8 hours. Less than 3 hours is to be spent writing bills.

   a. Write a system of inequalities to describe the situation. (Let $x =$ hours available for writing bills and $y =$ hours available for writing purchase orders.)

   b. Graph the solutions of the system.

4.6 LINEAR PROGRAMMING

OBJECTIVES

1. Use linear programming to solve problems.
2. Write objective functions and constraints.
3. Use linear programming to solve real-life applications.

In this section, we will look at an important application of systems of linear inequalities. Such systems arise in **linear programming,** a method for solving problems in which a particular quantity that must be maximized or minimized is limited by other factors. These other limiting factors are called **constraints.** In this section, the constraints are given as a system of linear inequalities. The graph of these constraints (system of inequalities) is called the **feasible region.**

Many problems involve quantities that must be optimized (maximized or minimized). **Optimization** is the process of finding the maximum or minimum value of these quantities. For example, businesses are interested in maximizing profit. Also, a relief operation in which bottled water and medical kits are shipped to earthquake survivors needs to maximize the number of survivors helped by this shipment. An **objective function** is an algebraic expression in two or more variables describing a quantity that must be maximized or minimized.

OBJECTIVE 1 ▶ Solving problems with linear programming. To solve a problem by linear programming, you may want to use the following steps. After becoming familiar with this process, we use linear programming to solve applications.

Solving a Linear Programming Problem

Let $z = ax + by$ be an objective function that depends on x and y. Furthermore, z is subject to a number of linear constraints on x and y. If a maximum or minimum value of z exists, it can be determined as follows:

1. Graph the system of inequalities representing the constraints.
2. Find the value of the objective function at each corner, or **vertex,** of the graphed region. The maximum and minimum of the objective function occur at one or more of the corner points.

EXAMPLE 1 Find the maximum value and the minimum value of the objective function

$$z = 2x + y$$

subject to the following constraints:

$$x \geq 0, y \geq 0$$
$$x + 2y \leq 5$$
$$x - y \leq 2.$$

Solution

STEP 1. Graph the system of inequalities representing the constraints. The graph of the inequalities $x \geq 0$ and $y \geq 0$ form Quadrant I, along with the nonnegative x-axis and nonnegative y-axis. (Think of the location of points whose x- and y-coordinates are positive numbers, or 0.) The intersection of this region, along with $x + 2y \leq 5$ and $x - y \leq 2$ form the graph in the margin.

STEP 2. Find the value of the objective function at each corner (vertex) of the graphed region. The maximum and minimum of the objective function occur at one or more of the corner points.

Now we evaluate the objective function at the four vertices of this region.

Objective function: $z = 2x + y$

At $(0, 0)$: $z = 2 \cdot 0 + 0 = 0$ Minimum value of z

At $(2, 0)$: $z = 2 \cdot 2 + 0 = 4$

At $(3, 1)$: $z = 2 \cdot 3 + 1 = 7$ Maximum value of z

At $(0, 2.5)$: $z = 2 \cdot 0 + 2.5 = 2.5$

Thus, the maximum value of z is 7, and this occurs when $x = 3$ and $y = 1$. The minimum value of z is 0, and this occurs when $x = 0$ and $y = 0$.

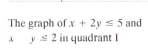

The graph of $x + 2y \leq 5$ and $x - y \leq 2$ in quadrant I

PRACTICE 1 Find the maximum value and the minimum value of the objective function $z = 3x + 5y$ subject to the constraints $x \geq 0, y \geq 0, x + y \geq 1, x + y \leq 6$.

OBJECTIVE 2 ▶ Writing objective functions and constraints. In this objective, we practice writing objective functions and constraints having to do with a real-life application. Then in objective 3, we solve the application.

EXAMPLE 2 Bottled water and medical supplies are to be shipped to survivors of an earthquake by plane. Each container of bottled water will serve 10 people and each medical kit will aid 6 people. If x represents the number of bottles of water to be shipped and y represents the number of medical kits, write the objective function that models the number of people that can be helped.

Solution Because each bottle of water serves 10 people and each medical kit aids 6 people, we have

The number of people helped	is	10 times the number of bottles of water	plus	6 times the number of medical kits.
=		$10x$	+	$6y.$

Using z to represent the number of people helped, the objective function is

$$z = 10x + 6y.$$

Unlike the functions that we have seen so far, the objective function is an equation in three variables. For a value of x and a value of y, there is one and only one value of z. Thus, z is a function of x and y. □

PRACTICE 2 A company manufactures bookshelves and desks for computers. Let x represent the number of bookshelves manufactured daily and y the number of desks manufactured daily. The company's profits are $25 per bookshelf and $55 per desk. Write the objective function that models the company's total daily profit, z, from x bookshelves and y desks. (Practice 3 through 5 are related to this situation, so keep track of your answers.)

Ideally, the number of earthquake survivors helped in Example 2 should increase without restriction so that every survivor receives water and medical supplies. However, the planes that ship these supplies are subject to weight and volume restrictions. In linear programming problems, such restrictions are called **constraints.** Each constraint is expressed as a linear inequality. The list of constraints forms a system of linear inequalities.

EXAMPLE 3 Each plane can carry no more than 80,000 pounds. The bottled water weighs 20 pounds per container and each medical kit weighs 10 pounds. Let x represent the number of bottles of water to be shipped and y the number of medical kits. Write an inequality that models this constraint.

Solution Because each plane can carry no more than 80,000 pounds, we have

The total weight of the water bottles	plus	the total weight of the medical kits	must be less than or equal to	80,000 pounds.
$20x$	+	$10y$	≤	80,000.

↑ Each bottle weighs 20 pounds.   ↑ Each kit weighs 10 pounds.

The plane's weight constraint is modeled by the inequality

$$20x + 10y \leq 80,000.$$

□

PRACTICE 3 To maintain high quality, the company in Practice 2 should not manufacture more than a total of 80 bookshelves and desks per day. Write an inequality that models this constraint.

In addition to a weight constraint on its cargo, each plane has a limited amount of space in which to carry supplies. Example 4 demonstrates how to express this constraint.

EXAMPLE 4 Each plane can carry a total volume of supplies that does not exceed 6000 cubic feet. Each water bottle is 1 cubic foot and each medical kit also has a volume of 1 cubic foot. With x still representing the number of water bottles and y the number of medical kits, write an inequality that models this second constraint.

Solution Because each plane can carry a volume of supplies that does not exceed 6000 cubic feet, we have

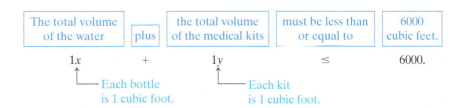

The plane's volume constraint is modeled by the inequality $x + y \leq 6000$. □

In summary, here's what we have described so far in this aid-to-earthquake-survivors situation:

$$z = 10x + 6y$$ This is the objective function modeling the number of people helped with x bottles of water and y medical kits.

$$20x + 10y \leq 80{,}000$$
$$x + y \leq 6000.$$ These are the constraints based on each plane's weight and volume limitations.

PRACTICE 4 To meet customer demand, the company in Practice 2 must manufacture between 30 and 80 bookshelves per day, inclusive. Furthermore, the company must manufacture at least 10 and no more than 30 desks per day. Write an inequality that models each of these sentences. Then summarize what you have described about this company by writing the objective function for its profits and the three constraints.

OBJECTIVE 3 ▶ Solving applications with linear programming. The problem in the earthquake situation described previously is to maximize the number of survivors who can be helped, subject to each plane's weight and volume constraints. We use linear programming to solve this next.

EXAMPLE 5 Determine how many bottles of water and how many medical kits should be sent on each plane to maximize the number of earthquake survivors who can be helped.

Solution We must maximize $z = 10x + 6y$ subject to the following constraints:

$$20x + 10y \leq 80{,}000$$
$$x + y \leq 6000.$$

STEP 1. Graph the system of inequalities representing the constraints. Because x (the number of bottles of water per plane) and y (the number of medical kits per plane) must be nonnegative, we need to graph the system of inequalities in quadrant I and its boundary only.

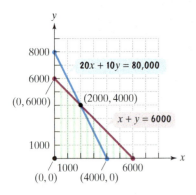

The region in Quadrant I representing the constraints $20x + 10y \leq 80{,}000$ and $x + y \leq 6000$

To graph the inequality $20x + 10y \leq 80{,}000$, we graph the equation $20x + 10y = 80{,}000$ as a solid blue line (see the graph in the margin). Setting $y = 0$, the x-intercept is 4000 and setting $x = 0$, the y-intercept is 8000. Using $(0, 0)$ as a test point, the inequality is satisfied, so we shade below the blue line, as shown in yellow in the margin graph.

Now we graph $x + y \leq 6000$ by first graphing $x + y = 6000$ as a solid red line. Setting $y = 0$, the x-intercept is 6000. Setting $x = 0$, the y-intercept is 6000. Using $(0, 0)$ as a test point, the inequality is satisfied, so we shade below the red line, as shown using green vertical shading.

We use the addition method to find where the lines $20x + 10y = 80{,}000$ and $x + y = 6000$ intersect.

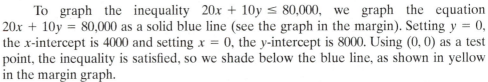

Back-substituting 2000 for x in $x + y = 6000$, we find $y = 4000$, so the intersection point is $(2000, 4000)$.

The system of inequalities representing the constraints is shown by the region in which the yellow shading and the green vertical shading overlap. The graph of the system of inequalities is shown again in the second margin graph. The red and blue line segments are included in the graph.

STEP 2. Find the value of the objective function at each corner of the graphed region. The maximum and minimum of the objective function occur at one or more of the corner points. We must evaluate the objective function, $z = 10x + 6y$, at the four corners, or vertices, of the region.

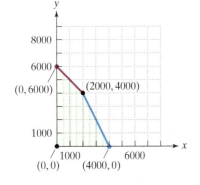

Corner (x, y)	Objective Function $z = 10x + 6y$
$(0, 0)$	$z = 10(0) + 6(0) = 0$
$(4000, 0)$	$z = 10(4000) + 6(0) = 40{,}000$
$(2000, 4000)$	$z = 10(2000) + 6(4000) = 44{,}000$ ← maximum
$(0, 6000)$	$z = 10(0) + 6(6000) = 36{,}000$

Thus, the maximum value of z is 44,000 and this occurs when $x = 2000$ and $y = 4000$. In practical terms, this means that the maximum number of earthquake survivors who can be helped with each plane shipment is 44,000. This can be accomplished by sending 2000 water bottles and 4000 medical kits per plane. □

PRACTICE 5 For the company in Practice 2–4, how many bookshelves and how many desks should be manufactured per day to obtain maximum profit? What is the maximum daily profit?

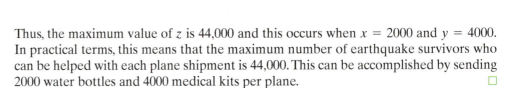

4.6 EXERCISE SET

In Exercises 1–4, find the value of the objective function at each corner of the graphed region. What is the maximum value of the objective function? What is the minimum value of the objective function?

1. Objective Function
$z = 5x + 6y$

2. Objective Function
$z = 3x + 2y$

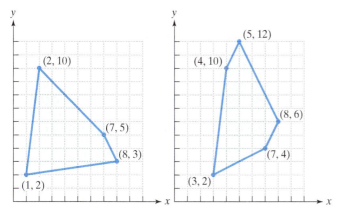

3. Objective Function
$z = 40x + 50y$

4. Objective Function
$z = 30x + 45y$

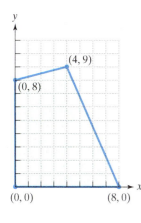 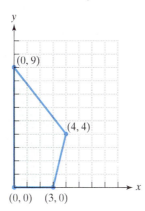

In Exercises 5–14, an objective function and a system of linear inequalities representing constraints are given.

a. Graph the system of inequalities representing the constraints.

b. Find the value of the objective function at each corner of the graphed region.

c. Use the values in part (b) to determine the maximum value of the objective function and the values of x and y for which the maximum occurs.

5. Objective Function $\quad z = 3x + 2y$
Constraints $\quad x \geq 0, y \geq 0$
$\quad 2x + y \leq 8$
$\quad x + y \geq 4$

6. Objective Function $\quad z = 2x + 3y$
Constraints $\quad x \geq 0, y \geq 0$
$\quad 2x + y \leq 8$
$\quad 2x + 3y \leq 12$

7. Objective Function $\quad z = 4x + y$
Constraints $\quad x \geq 0, y \geq 0$
$\quad 2x + 3y \leq 12$
$\quad x + y \geq 3$

8. Objective Function $\quad z = x + 6y$
Constraints $\quad x \geq 0, y \geq 0$
$\quad 2x + y \leq 10$
$\quad x - 2y \geq -10$

9. Objective Function $\quad z = 3x - 2y$
Constraints $\quad 1 \leq x \leq 5$
$\quad y \geq 2$
$\quad x - y \geq -3$

10. Objective Function $\quad z = 5x - 2y$
Constraints $\quad 0 \leq x \leq 5$
$\quad 0 \leq y \leq 3$
$\quad x + y \geq 2$

11. Objective Function $\quad z = 4x + 2y$
Constraints $\quad x \geq 0, y \geq 0$
$\quad 2x + 3y \leq 12$
$\quad 3x + 2y \leq 12$
$\quad x + y \geq 2$

12. Objective Function $\quad z = 2x + 4y$
Constraints $\quad x \geq 0, y \geq 0$
$\quad x + 3y \geq 6$
$\quad x + y \geq 3$
$\quad x + y \leq 9$

13. Objective Function $\quad z = 10x + 12y$
Constraints $\quad x \geq 0, y \geq 0$
$\quad 2x + y \leq 10$
$\quad 2x + 3y \leq 18$

14. Objective Function $\quad z = 5x + 6y$
Constraints $\quad x \geq 0, y \geq 0$
$\quad 2x + y \geq 10$
$\quad x + 2y \geq 10$
$\quad x + y \leq 10$

15. Multiple Steps. A television manufacturer makes rear-projection and plasma televisions. The profit per unit is

$125 for the rear-projection televisions and $200 for the plasma televisions.

a. Let x = the number of rear-projection televisions manufactured in a month and y = the number of plasma televisions manufactured in a month. Write the objective function that models the total monthly profit.

b. The manufacturer is bound by the following constraints:
   - Equipment in the factory allows for making at most 450 rear-projection televisions in one month.
   - Equipment in the factory allows for making at most 200 plasma televisions in one month.
   - The cost to the manufacturer per unit is $600 for the rear-projection televisions and $900 for the plasma televisions. Total monthly costs cannot exceed $360,000.

   Write a system of three inequalities that models these constraints.

c. Graph the system of inequalities in part (b). Use only the first quadrant and its boundary, because x and y must both be nonnegative.

d. Evaluate the objective function for total monthly profit at each of the five vertices of the graphed region. [The vertices should occur at (0, 0), (0, 200), (300, 200), (450, 100), and (450, 0).]

e. Complete the missing portions of this statement: The television manufacturer will make the greatest profit by manufacturing ____ rear-projection televisions each month and ____ plasma televisions each month. The maximum monthly profit is $____.

16. a. **Multiple Steps.** A student earns $10 per hour for tutoring and $7 per hour as a teacher's aid. Let x = the number of hours each week spent tutoring and y = the number of hours each week spent as a teacher's aid. Write the objective function that models total weekly earnings.

    b. The student is bound by the following constraints:
       - To have enough time for studies, the student can work no more than 20 hours a week.
       - The tutoring center requires that each tutor spend at least three hours a week tutoring.
       - The tutoring center requires that each tutor spend no more than eight hours a week tutoring.

       Write a system of three inequalities that models these constraints.

    c. Graph the system of inequalities in part (b). Use only the first quadrant and its boundary, because x and y are nonnegative.

    d. Evaluate the objective function for total weekly earnings at each of the four vertices of the graphed region. [The vertices should occur at (3, 0), (8, 0), (3, 17), and (8, 12).]

    e. Complete the missing portions of this statement: The student can earn the maximum amount per week by tutoring for ____ hours per week and working as a teacher's aid for ____ hours per week. The maximum amount that the student can earn each week is $____.

Use linear programming to solve the problems in Exercises 17–23.

17. A manufacturer produces two models of mountain bicycles. The times (in hours) required for assembling and painting each model are given in the following table:

	Model A	Model B
Assembling	5	4
Painting	2	3

The maximum total weekly hours available in the assembly department and the paint department are 200 hours and 108 hours, respectively. The profits per unit are $25 for model A and $15 for model B. How many of each type should be produced to maximize profit?

18. A large institution is preparing lunch menus containing foods A and B. The specifications for the two foods are given in the following table:

Food	Units of Fat per Ounce	Units of Carbohydrates per Ounce	Units of Protein per Ounce
A	1	2	1
B	1	1	1

Each lunch must provide at least 6 units of fat per serving, no more than 7 units of protein, and at least 10 units of carbohydrates. The institution can purchase food A for $0.12 per ounce and food B for $0.08 per ounce. How many ounces of each food should a serving contain to meet the dietary requirement at the least cost?

19. Food and clothing are shipped to survivors of a hurricane. Each carton of food will feed 12 people, while each carton of clothing will help 5 people. Each 20-cubic-foot box of food weighs 50 pounds and each 10-cubic-foot box of clothing weighs 20 pounds. The commercial carriers transporting food and clothing are bound by the following constraints:
    - The total weight per carrier cannot exceed 19,000 pounds.
    - The total volume must be less than 8000 cubic feet.

    How many cartons of food and how many cartons of clothing should be sent with each plane shipment to maximize the number of people who can be helped?

20. On June 24, 1948, the former Soviet Union blocked all land and water routes through East Germany to Berlin. A gigantic airlift was organized using American and British planes to bring food, clothing, and other supplies to the more than 2 million people in West Berlin. The cargo capacity was 30,000 cubic feet for an American plane and 20,000 cubic feet for a British plane. To break the Soviet blockade, the Western Allies had to maximize cargo capacity, but were subject to the following restrictions:
    - No more than 44 planes could be used.
    - The larger American planes required 16 personnel per flight, double that of the requirement for the British planes. The total number of personnel available could not exceed 512.
    - The cost of an American flight was $9000 and the cost of a British flight was $5000. Total weekly costs could not exceed $300,000.

Find the number of American planes and the number of British planes that were used to maximize cargo capacity.

21. A theater is presenting a program on community service for students and their parents. The proceeds will be donated to a local charity. Admission is $2.00 for parents and $1.00 for students. However, the situation has two constraints: The theater can hold no more than 150 people and every two parents must bring at least one student. How many parents and students should attend to raise the maximum amount of money?

22. You are about to take a test that contains computation problems worth 6 points each and word problems worth 10 points each. You can do a computation problem in 2 minutes and a word problem in 4 minutes. You have 40 minutes to take the test and may answer no more than 12 problems. Assuming you answer all the problems attempted correctly, how many of each type of problem must you do to maximize your score? What is the maximum score?

23. In 1978, a ruling by the Civil Aeronautics Board allowed Federal Express to purchase larger aircraft. Federal Express's options included 20 Boeing 727s that United Airlines was retiring and/or the French-built Dassault Fanjet Falcon 20. To aid in their decision, executives at Federal Express analyzed the following data:

	Boeing 727	Falcon 20
Direct Operating Cost	$1400 per hour	$500 per hour
Payload	42,000 pounds	6000 pounds

Federal Express was faced with the following constraints:
- Hourly operating cost was limited to $35,000.
- Total payload had to be at least 672,000 pounds.
- Only twenty 727s were available.

Given the constraints, how many of each kind of aircraft should Federal Express have purchased to maximize the number of aircraft?

24. What kinds of problems are solved using the linear programming method?

25. What is an objective function in a linear programming problem?

26. What is a constraint in a linear programming problem? How is a constraint represented?

27. In your own words, describe how to solve a linear programming problem.

28. Describe a situation in your life in which you would like to maximize something, but are limited by at least two constraints. Can linear programming be used in this situation? Explain your answer.

CONCEPT EXTENSIONS

Logic. *In Exercises 29–32, determine whether each statement "makes sense" or "does not make sense" and explain your reasoning.*

29. In order to solve a linear programming problem, I use the graph representing the constraints and the graph of the objective function.

30. I use the coordinates of each vertex from my graph representing the constraints to find the values that maximize or minimize an objective function.

31. I need to be able to graph systems of linear inequalities in order to solve linear programming problems.

32. An important application of linear programming for businesses involves maximizing profit.

REVIEW AND PREVIEW

For Exercises 33–35, see Sections 2.3 and 3.2.

33. Solve for x: $y = 3x - 2$

34. Solve for L: $3P = \dfrac{2L - W}{4}$.

35. If $f(x) = x^3 + 2x^2 - 5x + 4$, find $f(-1)$.

In Exercises 36–37, simplify each algebraic expression. See Section 1.4.

36. $-9x^3 + 7x^2 - 5x + 3 + 13x^3 + 2x^2 - 8x - 6$

37. $7x^3 - 8x^2 + 9x - 6 - 2x^3 + 6x^2 + 3x - 9$

38. The figures show the graphs of two functions.

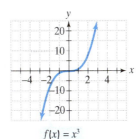
$f(x) = x^3$

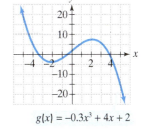
$g(x) = -0.3x^3 + 4x + 2$

a. Which function, f or g, has a graph that rises to the left and falls to the right?

b. Which function, f or g, has a graph that falls to the left and rises to the right?

CHAPTER 4 VOCABULARY CHECK

Fill in each blank with one of the words or phrases listed below.

matrix   consistent   optimization   square   objective function
solution   inconsistent   system of equations   linear programming   feasible region

1. Two or more linear equations in two variables form a _____.
2. A _____ of a system of two equations in two variables is an ordered pair that makes both equations true.
3. A(n) _____ system of equations has at least one solution.
4. If a matrix has the same number of rows and columns, it is called a _____ matrix.
5. A(n) _____ system of equations has no solution.
6. A _____ is a rectangular array of numbers.
7. _____ is the process of finding the maximum or minimum value.
8. The graph of the system of constraints is called the _____.
9. _____ is a method for solving problems in which a particular quantity that must be maximized or minimized is limited by other factors.
10. A(n) _____ describes a quantity that must be maximized or minimized.

CHAPTER 4 REVIEW

(4.1) *Solve each system of equations in two variables by each method: (a) graphing, (b) substitution, and (c) elimination.*

1. $\begin{cases} 3x + 10y = 1 \\ x + 2y = -1 \end{cases}$

2. $\begin{cases} y = \frac{1}{2}x + \frac{2}{3} \\ 4x + 6y = 4 \end{cases}$

3. $\begin{cases} 2x - 4y = 22 \\ 5x - 10y = 15 \end{cases}$

4. $\begin{cases} 3x - 6y = 12 \\ 2y = x - 4 \end{cases}$

5. $\begin{cases} \frac{1}{2}x - \frac{3}{4}y = -\frac{1}{2} \\ \frac{1}{8}x + \frac{3}{4}y = \frac{19}{8} \end{cases}$

6. The revenue equation for a certain style of backpack is $y = 32x$, where x is the number of backpacks sold and y is the income in dollars for selling x backpacks. The cost equation for these units is $y = 15x + 25{,}500$, where x is the number of backpacks manufactured and y is the cost in dollars for manufacturing x backpacks. Find the number of units to be sold for the company to break even. (*Hint:* Solve the system of equations formed by the two given equations.)

(4.2) *Solve each system of equations in three variables.*

7. $\begin{cases} x \phantom{{}-y} + z = 4 \\ 2x - y \phantom{{}+z} = 4 \\ x + y - z = 0 \end{cases}$

8. $\begin{cases} 2x + 5y \phantom{{}+z} = 4 \\ x - 5y + z = -1 \\ 4x \phantom{{}-5y} - z = 11 \end{cases}$

9. $\begin{cases} 4y + 2z = 5 \\ 2x + 8y \phantom{{}+2z} = 5 \\ 6x \phantom{{}+8y} + 4z = 1 \end{cases}$

10. $\begin{cases} 5x + 7y \phantom{{}-z} = 9 \\ \phantom{5x+{}} 14y - z = 28 \\ 4x \phantom{{}+14y} + 2z = -4 \end{cases}$

11. $\begin{cases} 3x - 2y + 2z = 5 \\ -x + 6y + z = 4 \\ 3x + 14y + 7z = 20 \end{cases}$

12. $\begin{cases} x + 2y + 3z = 11 \\ \phantom{x+{}} y + 2z = 3 \\ 2x \phantom{{}+2y} + 2z = 10 \end{cases}$

13. $\begin{cases} 7x - 3y + 2z = 0 \\ 4x - 4y - z = 2 \\ 5x + 2y + 3z = 1 \end{cases}$

14. $\begin{cases} x - 3y - 5z = -5 \\ 4x - 2y + 3z = 13 \\ 5x + 3y + 4z = 22 \end{cases}$

(4.3) *Use systems of equations to solve.*

15. The sum of three numbers is 98. The sum of the first and second is two more than the third number, and the second is four times the first. Find the numbers.

16. One number is three times a second number, and twice the sum of the numbers is 168. Find the numbers.

17. Two cars leave Chicago, one traveling east and the other west. After 4 hours they are 492 miles apart. If one car is traveling 7 mph faster than the other, find the speed of each.

18. The foundation for a rectangular Hardware Warehouse has a length three times the width and is 296 feet around. Find the dimensions of the building.

19. James Callahan has available a 10% alcohol solution and a 60% alcohol solution. Find how many liters of each solution he should mix to make 50 liters of a 40% alcohol solution.

20. An employee at See's Candy Store needs a special mixture of candy. She has creme-filled chocolates that sell for $3.00 per pound, chocolate-covered nuts that sell for $2.70 per pound, and chocolate-covered raisins that sell for $2.25 per pound. She wants to have twice as many raisins as nuts in the mixture. Find how many pounds of each she should use to make 45 pounds worth $2.80 per pound.

21. Chris Kringler has $2.77 in her coin jar—all in pennies, nickels, and dimes. If she has 53 coins in all and four more nickels than dimes, find how many of each type of coin she has.

22. If $10,000 and $4000 are invested such that $1250 in interest is earned in one year, and if the rate of interest on the larger investment is 2% more than that on the smaller investment, find the rates of interest.

23. The perimeter of an isosceles (two sides equal) triangle is 73 centimeters. If the unequal side is 7 centimeters longer than the two equal sides, find the lengths of the three sides.

24. The sum of three numbers is 295. One number is five more than a second and twice the third. Find the numbers.

(4.4) Use matrices to solve each system.

25. $\begin{cases} 3x + 10y = 1 \\ x + 2y = -1 \end{cases}$

26. $\begin{cases} 3x - 6y = 12 \\ 2y = x - 4 \end{cases}$

27. $\begin{cases} 3x - 2y = -8 \\ 6x + 5y = 11 \end{cases}$

28. $\begin{cases} 6x - 6y = -5 \\ 10x - 2y = 1 \end{cases}$

29. $\begin{cases} 3x - 6y = 0 \\ 2x + 4y = 5 \end{cases}$

30. $\begin{cases} 5x - 3y = 10 \\ -2x + y = -1 \end{cases}$

31. $\begin{cases} 0.2x - 0.3y = -0.7 \\ 0.5x + 0.3y = 1.4 \end{cases}$

32. $\begin{cases} 3x + 2y = 8 \\ 3x - y = 5 \end{cases}$

33. $\begin{cases} x + z = 4 \\ 2x - y = 0 \\ x + y - z = 0 \end{cases}$

34. $\begin{cases} 2x + 5y = 4 \\ x - 5y + z = -1 \\ 4x - z = 11 \end{cases}$

35. $\begin{cases} 3x - y = 11 \\ x + 2z = 13 \\ y - z = -7 \end{cases}$

36. $\begin{cases} 5x + 7y + 3z = 9 \\ 14y - z = 28 \\ 4x + 2z = -4 \end{cases}$

37. $\begin{cases} 7x - 3y + 2z = 0 \\ 4x - 4y - z = 2 \\ 5x + 2y + 3z = 1 \end{cases}$

38. $\begin{cases} x + 2y + 3z = 14 \\ y + 2z = 3 \\ 2x - 2z = 10 \end{cases}$

(4.5) Graph the solution of each system of linear inequalities.

39. $\begin{cases} y \geq 2x - 3 \\ y \leq -2x + 1 \end{cases}$

40. $\begin{cases} y \leq -3x - 3 \\ y \leq 2x + 7 \end{cases}$

41. $\begin{cases} x + 2y > 0 \\ x - y \leq 6 \end{cases}$

42. $\begin{cases} x - 2y \geq 7 \\ x + y \leq -5 \end{cases}$

43. $\begin{cases} 3x - 2y \leq 4 \\ 2x + y \geq 5 \\ y \leq 4 \end{cases}$

44. $\begin{cases} 4x - y \leq 0 \\ 3x - 2y \geq -5 \\ y \geq -4 \end{cases}$

45. $\begin{cases} x + 2y \leq 5 \\ x \leq 2 \\ x \geq 0 \\ y \geq 0 \end{cases}$

46. $\begin{cases} x + 3y \leq 7 \\ y \leq 5 \\ x \geq 0 \\ y \geq 0 \end{cases}$

(4.6)

47. Find the value of the objective function $z = 2x + 3y$ at each corner of the graphed region shown. What is the maximum value of the objective function? What is the minimum value of the objective function?

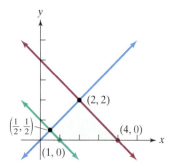

In Exercises 48–50, graph the region determined by the constraints. Then find the maximum value of the given objective function, subject to the constraints.

48. Objective Function $\quad z = 2x + 3y$
Constraints $\quad\quad\quad\; x \geq 0, y \geq 0$
$\quad\quad\quad\quad\quad\quad\quad\; x + y \leq 8$
$\quad\quad\quad\quad\quad\quad\quad\; 3x + 2y \geq 6$

49. Objective Function $\quad z = x + 4y$
Constraints $\quad\quad\quad\; 0 \leq x \leq 5, 0 \leq y \leq 7$
$\quad\quad\quad\quad\quad\quad\quad\; x + y \geq 3$

50. Objective Function $\quad z = 5x + 6y$
Constraints $\quad\quad\quad\; x \geq 0, y \geq 0$
$\quad\quad\quad\quad\quad\quad\quad\; y \leq x$
$\quad\quad\quad\quad\quad\quad\quad\; 2x + y \leq 12$
$\quad\quad\quad\quad\quad\quad\quad\; 2x + 3y \geq 6$

51. A paper manufacturing company converts wood pulp to writing paper and newsprint. The profit on a unit of writing paper is $500 and the profit on a unit of newsprint is $350.

a. Let x represent the number of units of writing paper produced daily. Let y represent the number of units of newsprint produced daily. Write the objective function that models total daily profit.

b. The manufacturer is bound by the following constraints:

- Equipment in the factory allows for making at most 200 units of paper (writing paper and newsprint) in a day.
- Regular customers require at least 10 units of writing paper and at least 80 units of newsprint daily.

Write a system of inequalities that models these constraints.

c. Graph the inequalities in part (b). Use only the first quadrant, because x and y must both be positive. (*Suggestion*: Let each unit along the x- and y-axes represent 20.)

d. Evaluate the objective function at each of the three vertices of the graphed region.

e. Complete the missing portions of this statement: The company will make the greatest profit by producing ___ units of writing paper and ___ units of newsprint each day. The maximum daily profit is $_____

52. A manufacturer of lightweight tents makes two models whose specifications are given in the following table.

	Cutting Time per Tent	Assembly Time per Tent
Model A	0.9 hour	0.8 hour
Model B	1.8 hours	1.2 hours

Each month, the manufacturer has no more than 864 hours of labor available in the cutting department and at most 672 hours in the assembly division. The profits come to $25 per tent for model A and $40 per tent for model B. How many of each should be manufactured monthly to maximize the profit?

MIXED REVIEW

Solve each system.

53. $\begin{cases} y = x - 5 \\ y = -2x + 2 \end{cases}$

54. $\begin{cases} \dfrac{2}{5}x + \dfrac{3}{4}y = 1 \\ x + 3y = -2 \end{cases}$

55. $\begin{cases} 5x - 2y = 10 \\ x = \dfrac{2}{5}y + 2 \end{cases}$

56. $\begin{cases} x - 4y = 4 \\ \dfrac{1}{8}x - \dfrac{1}{2}y = 3 \end{cases}$

57. $\begin{cases} x - 3y + 2z = 0 \\ 9y - z = 22 \\ 5x + 3z = 10 \end{cases}$

58. One number is five less than three times a second number. If the sum of the numbers is 127, find the numbers.

59. The perimeter of a triangle is 126 units. The length of one side is twice the length of the shortest side. The length of the third side is fourteen more than the length of the shortest side. Find the lengths of the sides of the triangles.

60. Graph the solution of the system: $\begin{cases} y \leq 3x - \dfrac{1}{2} \\ 3x + 4y \geq 6 \end{cases}$

61. In the United States, the consumer spending on VCR decks is decreasing while the spending on DVD players is increasing. For the years 1998–2003, the function $y = -443x + 2584$ estimates the millions of dollars spent on purchasing VCR decks while the function $y = 500x + 551$ estimates the millions of dollars spent on purchasing DVD players. For both functions, x is the number of years since 1998. Use these equations to determine the year in which the amount of money spent on VCR decks equals the amount of money spent on DVD players. (*Source:* Consumer Electronics Association)

CHAPTER 4 TEST

Remember to use the Chapter Test Prep Videos to see the fully worked-out solutions to any of the exercises you want to review.

Solve each system of equations graphically and then solve by the elimination method or the substitution method.

1. $\begin{cases} 2x - y = -1 \\ 5x + 4y = 17 \end{cases}$

2. $\begin{cases} 7x - 14y = 5 \\ x = 2y \end{cases}$

Solve each system.

3. $\begin{cases} 4x - 7y = 29 \\ 2x + 5y = -11 \end{cases}$

4. $\begin{cases} 15x + 6y = 15 \\ 10x + 4y = 10 \end{cases}$

5. $\begin{cases} 2x - 3y = 4 \\ 3y + 2z = 2 \\ x - z = -5 \end{cases}$

6. $\begin{cases} 3x - 2y - z = -1 \\ 2x - 2y = 4 \\ 2x - 2z = -12 \end{cases}$

7. $\begin{cases} \dfrac{x}{2} + \dfrac{y}{4} = -\dfrac{3}{4} \\ x + \dfrac{3}{4}y = -4 \end{cases}$

Use matrices to solve each system.

8. $\begin{cases} x - y = -2 \\ 3x - 3y = -6 \end{cases}$

9. $\begin{cases} x + 2y = -1 \\ 2x + 5y = -5 \end{cases}$

10. $\begin{cases} x - y - z = 0 \\ 3x - y - 5z = -2 \\ 2x + 3y = -5 \end{cases}$

11. A motel in New Orleans charges $90 per day for double occupancy and $80 per day for single occupancy. If 80 rooms are occupied for a total of $6930, how many rooms of each kind are occupied?

12. The research department of a company that manufactures children's fruit drinks is experimenting with a new flavor. A 17.5% fructose solution is needed, but only 10% and 20% solutions are available. How many gallons of a 10% fructose solution should be mixed with a 20% fructose solution to obtain 20 gallons of a 17.5% fructose solution?

13. A company that manufactures boxes recently purchased $2000 worth of new equipment to offer gift boxes to its customers. The cost of producing a package of gift boxes is $1.50 and it is sold for $4.00. Find the number of packages that must be sold for the company to break even.

14. The measure of the largest angle of a triangle is 3 less than five times the measure of the smallest angle. The measure of the remaining angle is 1 less than twice the measure of the smallest angle. Find the measure of each angle.

Graph the solutions of each system of linear inequalities.

15. $\begin{cases} 2y - x \geq 1 \\ x + y \geq -4 \\ y \leq 2 \end{cases}$

16. Find the maximum value of the objective function $z = 3x + 5y$ subject to the following constraints: $x \geq 0, y \geq 0, x + y \leq 6, x \geq 2$.

17. A manufacturer makes two types of jet skis, regular and deluxe. The profit on a regular jet ski is $200 and the profit on the deluxe model is $250. To meet customer demand, the company must manufacture at least 50 regular jet skis per week and at least 75 deluxe models. To maintain high quality, the total number of both models of jet skis manufactured by the company should not exceed 150 per week. How many jet skis of each type should be manufactured per week to obtain maximum profit? What is the maximum weekly profit?

CHAPTER 4 STANDARDIZED TEST

Multiple Choice. *Choose the one alternative that best completes the statement or answers the question. Solve the system of equations graphically.*

1. $\begin{cases} 4x - y = -2 \\ x + 2y = 13 \end{cases}$

   a. $(6, -1)$ b. $(6, 1)$ c. $(1, 6)$ d. $(1, -6)$

2. $\begin{cases} 5x + 2y = 16 \\ x = -2y \end{cases}$

   a. $(4, 2)$ b. $(-2, 4)$ c. $(4, -2)$ d. $(-4, -2)$

Solve the system.

3. $\begin{cases} 2x + 4y = -16 \\ 12x + 2y = 80 \end{cases}$

   a. $(8, -8)$ b. $(12, -12)$ c. $(-8, 8)$ d. $(-2, 8)$

4. $\begin{cases} 2x - 7y = -12 \\ -7x - 4y = -15 \end{cases}$

   a. $(-1, 2)$ b. $(-1, -2)$ c. $(1, 2)$ d. $(1, -2)$

5. $\begin{cases} 5x - 2y = 4 \\ 2y + 2z = -2 \\ x + z = -2 \end{cases}$

   a. $(-2, 3, 4)$ b. no solution
   c. $(3, 2, -4)$ d. $(2, 3, -4)$

6. $\begin{cases} y - 2z = 15 \\ 4x + y - 4z = 21 \\ 3x + 4z = -23 \end{cases}$

   a. $(-1, 5, -5)$ b. $(3, -23, -8)$
   c. $(3, 6, -8)$ d. $(-1, 7, -4)$

7. $\begin{cases} \dfrac{x}{3} + \dfrac{y}{6} = 1 \\ \dfrac{x}{2} - \dfrac{y}{4} = 0 \end{cases}$

   a. no solution   b. $\left(\dfrac{3}{2}, 3\right)$
   c. $\left(3, \dfrac{3}{2}\right)$ d. infinite number of solutions

Use matrices to solve the system.

8. $\begin{cases} x + 8y = -24 \\ 5x + 9y = -27 \end{cases}$

   a. $(0, -3)$ b. no solution
   c. $(1, -4)$ d. $(3, 0)$

9. $\begin{cases} x - 4y = 20 \\ 3x - 4y = 36 \end{cases}$

   a. $(-3, 8)$ b. no solution
   c. $(3, 8)$ d. $(8, -3)$

10. $\begin{cases} x - y + 2z = 2 \\ 5x + z = 2 \\ x + 5y + z = 12 \end{cases}$

    a. no solution   b. $(0, 2, 2)$ c. $(2, 2, 0)$ d. $(2, 0, 2)$

Solve the problem.

11. 34,000 people attended a ballgame at a stadium that offers two kinds of seats: general admission and reserved. The day's receipts were $252,000. How many people paid $14.00 for reserved seats, and how many paid $6.00 for general admission?

    a. Reserved: 6000; general admission: 28,000
    b. Reserved: 12,000; general admission: 22,000
    c. Reserved: 28,000; general admission: 6000
    d. Reserved: 22,000; general admission: 12,000

12. A chemist needs 160 milliliters of a 57% solution but has only 21% and 85% solutions available. Find how many milliliters of each should be mixed to get the desired solution.

    a. 75 ml of 21%; 90 ml of 85%
    b. 75 ml of 21%; 85 ml of 85%
    c. 90 ml of 21%; 70 ml of 85%
    d. 70 ml of 21%; 90 ml of 85%

13. A shoe company will make a new type of shoe. The fixed cost for the production will be $24,000. The variable cost will be $34 per pair of shoes. The shoes will sell for $106 for each pair. How many pairs of shoes will have to be sold for the company to break even on this new line of shoes?

    a. 706 pairs   b. 72 pairs
    c. 334 pairs   d. 227 pairs

14. The perimeter of a triangle is 33 centimeters. Twice the length of the longest side minus the length of the shortest side is 30 centimeters. The sum of the length of the longest side and three times the sum of both the other side lengths is 63 centimeters. Find the side lengths.

    a. 5 cm, 9 cm, 19 cm   b. 6 cm, 9 cm, 18 cm
    c. No solution   d. 6 cm, 10 cm, 17 cm

Graph the solution to the system of linear inequalities.

15. $3y - x \leq 9$
$y + 2x \leq 10$
$y \geq 0$

a. **b.**

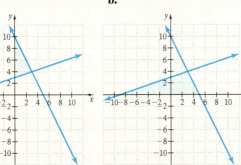

c. **d.**

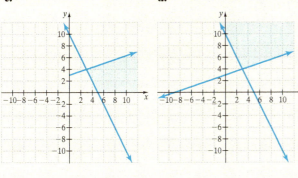

16. Find the maximum value of the objective function $z = 4x + 5y$ subject to the following constraints: $x \geq 0$, $y \geq 0$, $3x + y \leq 6$, $x + y \geq 4$.

a. 20 **b.** 19
c. 8   **d.** 24

17. Bruce is bringing items to sell at a flea market, where he plans to sell televisions at $125 each and DVD players at $100 each. Due to space limitations, he can only store at most 150 items for the day. However, because more people already own televisions, Bruce knows that the number of DVD sales must at least match the number of television sales. How many of each item should Bruce bring to the flea market to maximize his sales?

a. 25 televisions and 75 DVD players

b. 50 televisions and 100 DVD players

c. 100 televisions and 50 DVD players

d. 75 televisions and 75 DVD players

CHAPTER 5

More Work with Matrices

- **5.1** Matrix Operations and Solving Matrix Equations
- **5.2** Multiplying Matrices and Solving Applications

    Integrated Review— Operations on Matrices

- **5.3** Solving Systems of Equations Using Determinants
- **5.4** Multiplicative Inverses of Matrices and Matrix Equations
- **5.5** Using Inverse Matrices to Solve Systems

The images you view on your computer screen are based on matrices. Matrices have applications in numerous fields, including the new technology of digital photography in which pictures are represented by numbers rather than film. In this chapter, we learn matrix algebra and some of its applications.

5.1 MATRIX OPERATIONS AND SOLVING MATRIX EQUATIONS

OBJECTIVES

1. Use matrix notation.
2. Understand what is meant by equal matrices.
3. Add and subtract matrices.
4. Perform scalar multiplication.
5. Solve matrix equations.

OBJECTIVE 1 ▶ Use matrix notation. We have seen that an array of numbers, arranged in rows and columns and placed in brackets, is called a matrix. In Section 4.4, we used matrices to help us solve systems of equations. We can represent a matrix in two different ways.

- A capital letter, such as A, B, or C, can denote a matrix.
- A lowercase letter enclosed in brackets, such as that shown below, can denote a matrix.

$$A = [a_{ij}] \quad \text{Matrix } A \text{ with elements } a_{ij}$$

A general element in matrix A is denoted by a_{ij}. This refers to the element in the ith row and jth column. For example, a_{32} is the element of A located in the third row, second column.

A matrix of **order $m \times n$** has m rows and n columns. If $m = n$, a matrix has the same number of rows as columns and is called a **square matrix**.

EXAMPLE 1 Matrix Notation

Let

$$A = \begin{bmatrix} 3 & 2 & 0 \\ -4 & -5 & -\frac{1}{5} \end{bmatrix}.$$

a. What is the order of A?

b. If $A = [a_{ij}]$, identify a_{23} and a_{12}.

Solution

a. The matrix has 2 rows and 3 columns, so it is of order 2×3.

b. The element a_{23} is in the second row and third column. Thus, $a_{23} = -\frac{1}{5}$. The element a_{12} is in the first row and second column. Consequently, $a_{12} = 2$.

PRACTICE 1 Let

$$A = \begin{bmatrix} 5 & -2 \\ -3 & \pi \\ 1 & 6 \end{bmatrix}.$$

a. What is the order of A? **b.** Identify a_{12} and a_{31}.

OBJECTIVE 2 ▶ Understand what is meant by equal matrices. Two matrices are **equal** if and only if they have the same order and corresponding elements are equal.

> **Definition of Equality of Matrices**
>
> Two matrices A and B are **equal** if and only if they have the same order $m \times n$ and $a_{ij} = b_{ij}$ for $i = 1, 2, \ldots, m$ and $j = 1, 2, \ldots, n$.

For example, if $A = \begin{bmatrix} x & y+1 \\ z & 6 \end{bmatrix}$ and $B = \begin{bmatrix} 1 & 5 \\ 3 & 6 \end{bmatrix}$, then $A = B$ if and only if $x = 1$, $y + 1 = 5$ (so $y = 4$), and $z = 3$.

OBJECTIVE 3 ▶ Add and subtract matrices. The table below shows that matrices of the same order can be added or subtracted by simply adding or subtracting corresponding elements.

Let $A = [a_{ij}]$ and $B = [b_{ij}]$ be matrices of order $m \times n$.

Definition	The Definition in Words	Example
Matrix Addition $A + B = [a_{ij} + b_{ij}]$	Matrices of the same order are added by adding the elements in corresponding positions.	$\begin{bmatrix} 1 & -2 \\ 3 & 5 \end{bmatrix} + \begin{bmatrix} -1 & 6 \\ 0 & 4 \end{bmatrix}$ $= \begin{bmatrix} 1+(-1) & -2+6 \\ 3+0 & 5+4 \end{bmatrix} = \begin{bmatrix} 0 & 4 \\ 3 & 9 \end{bmatrix}$
Matrix Subtraction $A - B = [a_{ij} - b_{ij}]$	Matrices of the same order are subtracted by subtracting the elements in corresponding positions.	$\begin{bmatrix} 1 & -2 \\ 3 & 5 \end{bmatrix} - \begin{bmatrix} -1 & 6 \\ 0 & 4 \end{bmatrix}$ $= \begin{bmatrix} 1-(-1) & -2-6 \\ 3-0 & 5-4 \end{bmatrix} = \begin{bmatrix} 2 & -8 \\ 3 & 1 \end{bmatrix}$

The sum or difference of two matrices of different orders is undefined. For example, consider the matrices

$$A = \begin{bmatrix} 0 & 3 \\ 4 & 3 \end{bmatrix} \text{ and } B = \begin{bmatrix} 1 & 9 \\ 4 & 5 \\ 2 & 3 \end{bmatrix}.$$

The order of A is 2×2; the order of B is 3×2. These matrices are of different orders and cannot be added or subtracted.

TECHNOLOGY NOTE

Graphing utilities can add and subtract matrices. Enter the matrices and name them $[A]$ and $[B]$. Then use a keystroke sequence similar to

Consult your manual and verify the results in Example 2.

EXAMPLE 2 Adding and Subtracting Matrices

Perform the indicated matrix operations:

a. $\begin{bmatrix} 0 & 5 & 3 \\ -2 & 6 & -8 \end{bmatrix} + \begin{bmatrix} -2 & 3 & 5 \\ 7 & -9 & 6 \end{bmatrix}$

b. $\begin{bmatrix} -6 & 7 \\ 2 & -3 \end{bmatrix} - \begin{bmatrix} -5 & 6 \\ 0 & -4 \end{bmatrix}$.

Solution

a. $\begin{bmatrix} 0 & 5 & 3 \\ -2 & 6 & -8 \end{bmatrix} + \begin{bmatrix} -2 & 3 & 5 \\ 7 & -9 & 6 \end{bmatrix}$

$= \begin{bmatrix} 0+(-2) & 5+3 & 3+5 \\ -2+7 & 6+(-9) & -8+6 \end{bmatrix}$ Add the corresponding elements in the 2×3 matrices.

$= \begin{bmatrix} -2 & 8 & 8 \\ 5 & -3 & -2 \end{bmatrix}$ Simplify.

b. $\begin{bmatrix} -6 & 7 \\ 2 & -3 \end{bmatrix} - \begin{bmatrix} -5 & 6 \\ 0 & -4 \end{bmatrix}$

$= \begin{bmatrix} -6 - (-5) & 7 - 6 \\ 2 - 0 & -3 - (-4) \end{bmatrix}$ Subtract the corresponding elements in the 2 × 2 matrices.

$= \begin{bmatrix} -1 & 1 \\ 2 & 1 \end{bmatrix}$ Simplify.

PRACTICE 2 Perform the indicated matrix operations:

a. $\begin{bmatrix} -4 & 3 \\ 7 & -6 \end{bmatrix} + \begin{bmatrix} 6 & -3 \\ 2 & -4 \end{bmatrix}$ **b.** $\begin{bmatrix} 5 & 4 \\ -3 & 7 \\ 0 & 1 \end{bmatrix} - \begin{bmatrix} -4 & 8 \\ 6 & 0 \\ -5 & 3 \end{bmatrix}$.

A matrix whose elements are all equal to 0 is called a **zero matrix.** If A is an $m \times n$ matrix and 0 is the $m \times n$ zero matrix, then $A + 0 = A$. For example,

$$\begin{bmatrix} -5 & 2 \\ 3 & 6 \end{bmatrix} + \begin{bmatrix} 0 & 0 \\ 0 & 0 \end{bmatrix} = \begin{bmatrix} -5 & 2 \\ 3 & 6 \end{bmatrix}.$$

The $m \times n$ zero matrix is called the **additive identity** for $m \times n$ matrices.

For any matrix A, the **additive inverse** of A, written $-A$, is the matrix with the same order as A such that every element of $-A$ is the opposite of the corresponding element of A. Because corresponding elements are added in matrix addition, $A + (-A)$ is a zero matrix. For example,

$$\begin{bmatrix} -5 & 2 \\ 3 & 6 \end{bmatrix} + \begin{bmatrix} 5 & -2 \\ -3 & -6 \end{bmatrix} = \begin{bmatrix} 0 & 0 \\ 0 & 0 \end{bmatrix}.$$

Properties of matrix addition are similar to properties for adding real numbers.

Properties of Matrix Addition

If A, B, and C are $m \times n$ matrices and 0 is the $m \times n$ zero matrix, then the following properties are true.

1. $A + B = B + A$ Commutative property of addition
2. $(A + B) + C = A + (B + C)$ Associative property of addition
3. $A + 0 = 0 + A = A$ Additive identity property
4. $A + (-A) = (-A) + A = 0$ Additive inverse property

OBJECTIVE 4 ▶ Perform scalar multiplication. A matrix of order 1×1, such as $[6]$, contains only one entry. To distinguish this matrix from the number 6, we refer to 6 as a **scalar.** In general, in our work with matrices, we will refer to real numbers as scalars.

To multiply a matrix A by a scalar c, we multiply each entry in A by c. For example,

$$\underset{\text{Scalar}}{4} \underset{\text{Matrix}}{\begin{bmatrix} 2 & 5 \\ -3 & 0 \end{bmatrix}} = \begin{bmatrix} 4(2) & 4(5) \\ 4(-3) & 4(0) \end{bmatrix} = \begin{bmatrix} 8 & 20 \\ -12 & 0 \end{bmatrix}.$$

> **Definition of Scalar Multiplication**
>
> If $A = [a_{ij}]$ is a matrix of order $m \times n$ and c is a scalar, then the matrix cA is the $m \times n$ matrix given by
>
> $$cA = [ca_{ij}].$$
>
> This matrix is obtained by multiplying each element of A by the real number c. We call cA a **scalar multiple** of A.

EXAMPLE 3 Scalar Multiplication

If $A = \begin{bmatrix} -1 & 4 \\ 3 & 0 \end{bmatrix}$ and $B = \begin{bmatrix} 2 & -3 \\ 5 & -6 \end{bmatrix}$, find the following matrices:

a. $-5B$ **b.** $2A + 3B$.

Solution

a. $-5B = -5\begin{bmatrix} 2 & -3 \\ 5 & -6 \end{bmatrix} = \begin{bmatrix} -5(2) & -5(-3) \\ -5(5) & -5(-6) \end{bmatrix} = \begin{bmatrix} -10 & 15 \\ -25 & 30 \end{bmatrix}$

Multiply each element by -5.

b. $2A + 3B = 2\begin{bmatrix} -1 & 4 \\ 3 & 0 \end{bmatrix} + 3\begin{bmatrix} 2 & -3 \\ 5 & -6 \end{bmatrix}$

$= \begin{bmatrix} 2(-1) & 2(4) \\ 2(3) & 2(0) \end{bmatrix} + \begin{bmatrix} 3(2) & 3(-3) \\ 3(5) & 3(-6) \end{bmatrix}$

Multiply each element in A by 2. *Multiply each element in B by 3.*

$= \begin{bmatrix} -2 & 8 \\ 6 & 0 \end{bmatrix} + \begin{bmatrix} 6 & -9 \\ 15 & -18 \end{bmatrix} = \begin{bmatrix} -2+6 & 8+(-9) \\ 6+15 & 0+(-18) \end{bmatrix}$

Perform the addition of these 2×2 matrices by adding corresponding elements.

$= \begin{bmatrix} 4 & -1 \\ 21 & -18 \end{bmatrix}$

TECHNOLOGY NOTE

You can verify the algebraic solution in Example 3(b) by first entering the matrices $[A]$ and $[B]$ into your graphing utility. The screen below shows the required computation.

```
2[A]+3[B]
         [[4   -1 ]
          [21  -18]]
```

PRACTICE 3 If $A = \begin{bmatrix} -4 & 1 \\ 3 & 0 \end{bmatrix}$ and $B = \begin{bmatrix} -1 & -2 \\ 8 & 5 \end{bmatrix}$, find the following matrices:

a. $-6B$ **b.** $3A + 2B$.

Properties of scalar multiplication are similar to properties for multiplying real numbers.

> **Properties of Scalar Multiplication**
>
> If A and B are $m \times n$ matrices, and c and d are scalars, then the following properties are true.
>
> **1.** $(cd)A = c(dA)$
>
> **2.** $1A = A$
>
> **3.** $c(A + B) = cA + cB$
>
> **4.** $(c + d)A = cA + dA$

DISCOVERY

Verify each of the four properties listed in the box using

$A = \begin{bmatrix} 2 & -4 \\ -5 & 3 \end{bmatrix}$,

$B = \begin{bmatrix} 4 & 0 \\ 1 & -6 \end{bmatrix}$,

$c = 4$, and $d = 2$.

OBJECTIVE 5 ▶ **Solve matrix equations.** Have you noticed the many similarities between addition of real numbers and matrix addition, subtraction of real numbers and matrix subtraction, and multiplication of real numbers and scalar multiplication? Example 4 shows how these similarities can be used to solve matrix equations involving matrix addition, matrix subtraction, and scalar multiplication.

EXAMPLE 4   Solving a Matrix Equation

Solve for X in the matrix equation

$$2X + A = B,$$

where $A = \begin{bmatrix} 1 & -5 \\ 0 & 2 \end{bmatrix}$ and $B = \begin{bmatrix} -6 & 5 \\ 9 & 1 \end{bmatrix}$.

Solution   We begin by solving the matrix equation for X.

$2X + A = B$	This is the given matrix equation.
$2X = B - A$	Subtract matrix A from both sides.
$X = \dfrac{1}{2}(B - A)$	Multiply both sides by $\dfrac{1}{2}$ and solve for matrix X.

We multiply both sides by $\frac{1}{2}$ rather than divide both sides by 2. This is in anticipation of performing scalar multiplication.

Now we use the matrices A and B to find the matrix X.

$$X = \frac{1}{2}\left(\begin{bmatrix} -6 & 5 \\ 9 & 1 \end{bmatrix} - \begin{bmatrix} 1 & -5 \\ 0 & 2 \end{bmatrix}\right)$$
Substitute the matrices into $X = \frac{1}{2}(B - A)$.

$$= \frac{1}{2}\begin{bmatrix} -7 & 10 \\ 9 & -1 \end{bmatrix}$$
Subtract matrices by subtracting corresponding elements.

$$= \begin{bmatrix} -\dfrac{7}{2} & 5 \\ \dfrac{9}{2} & -\dfrac{1}{2} \end{bmatrix}$$
Perform the scalar multiplication by multiplying each element by $\frac{1}{2}$.

Take a few minutes to show that this matrix satisfies the given equation $2X + A = B$. Substitute the matrix for X and the given matrices for A and B into the equation. The matrices on each side of the equal sign, $2X + A$ and B, should be equal.   ☐

PRACTICE 4   Solve for X in the matrix equation $3X + A = B$, where

$$A = \begin{bmatrix} 2 & -8 \\ 0 & 4 \end{bmatrix} \quad \text{and} \quad B = \begin{bmatrix} -10 & 1 \\ -9 & 17 \end{bmatrix}.$$

5.1 EXERCISE SET

In Exercises 1–4,

a. Give the order of each matrix.

b. If $A = [a_{ij}]$, identify a_{32} and a_{23}, or explain why identification is not possible.

1. $\begin{bmatrix} 4 & -7 & 5 \\ -6 & 8 & -1 \end{bmatrix}$

2. $\begin{bmatrix} -6 & 4 & -1 \\ -9 & 0 & \frac{1}{2} \end{bmatrix}$

3. $\begin{bmatrix} 1 & -5 & \pi & e \\ 0 & 7 & -6 & -\pi \\ -2 & \frac{1}{2} & 11 & -\frac{1}{5} \end{bmatrix}$

4. $\begin{bmatrix} -4 & 1 & 3 & -5 \\ 2 & -1 & \pi & 0 \\ 1 & 0 & -e & \frac{1}{5} \end{bmatrix}$

In Exercises 5–8, find values for the variables so that the matrices in each exercise are equal.

5. $\begin{bmatrix} x \\ 4 \end{bmatrix} = \begin{bmatrix} 6 \\ y \end{bmatrix}$
6. $\begin{bmatrix} x \\ 7 \end{bmatrix} = \begin{bmatrix} 11 \\ y \end{bmatrix}$
7. $\begin{bmatrix} x & 2y \\ z & 9 \end{bmatrix} = \begin{bmatrix} 4 & 12 \\ 3 & 9 \end{bmatrix}$
8. $\begin{bmatrix} x & y+3 \\ 2z & 8 \end{bmatrix} = \begin{bmatrix} 12 & 5 \\ 6 & 8 \end{bmatrix}$

In Exercises 9–16, find the following matrices:

a. $A + B$ **b.** $A - B$
c. $-4A$ **d.** $3A + 2B$.

9. $A = \begin{bmatrix} 4 & 1 \\ 3 & 2 \end{bmatrix}$, $B = \begin{bmatrix} 5 & 9 \\ 0 & 7 \end{bmatrix}$

10. $A = \begin{bmatrix} -2 & 3 \\ 0 & 1 \end{bmatrix}$, $B = \begin{bmatrix} 8 & 1 \\ 5 & 4 \end{bmatrix}$

11. $A = \begin{bmatrix} 1 & 3 \\ 3 & 4 \\ 5 & 6 \end{bmatrix}$, $B = \begin{bmatrix} 2 & -1 \\ 3 & -2 \\ 0 & 1 \end{bmatrix}$

12. $A = \begin{bmatrix} 3 & 1 & 1 \\ -1 & 2 & 5 \end{bmatrix}$, $B = \begin{bmatrix} 2 & -3 & 6 \\ -3 & 1 & -4 \end{bmatrix}$

13. $A = \begin{bmatrix} 2 \\ -4 \\ 1 \end{bmatrix}$, $B = \begin{bmatrix} -5 \\ 3 \\ -1 \end{bmatrix}$

14. $A = \begin{bmatrix} 6 & 2 & -3 \end{bmatrix}$, $B = \begin{bmatrix} 4 & -2 & 3 \end{bmatrix}$

15. $A = \begin{bmatrix} 2 & -10 & -2 \\ 14 & 12 & 10 \\ 4 & -2 & 2 \end{bmatrix}$, $B = \begin{bmatrix} 6 & 10 & -2 \\ 0 & -12 & -4 \\ -5 & 2 & -2 \end{bmatrix}$

16. $A = \begin{bmatrix} 6 & -3 & 5 \\ 6 & 0 & -2 \\ -4 & 2 & -1 \end{bmatrix}$, $B = \begin{bmatrix} -3 & 5 & 1 \\ -1 & 2 & -6 \\ 2 & 0 & 4 \end{bmatrix}$

In Exercises 17–26, let

$A = \begin{bmatrix} -3 & -7 \\ 2 & -9 \\ 5 & 0 \end{bmatrix}$ and $B = \begin{bmatrix} -5 & -1 \\ 0 & 0 \\ 3 & -4 \end{bmatrix}$.

Solve each matrix equation for X.

17. $X - A = B$
18. $X - B = A$
19. $2X + A = B$
20. $3X + A = B$
21. $3X + 2A = B$
22. $2X + 5A = B$
23. $B - X = 4A$
24. $A - X = 4B$
25. $4A + 3B = -2X$
26. $4B + 3A = -2X$

CONCEPT EXTENSIONS

27. **Multiple Steps.** Completing the transition to adulthood is measured by one or more of the following: leaving home, finishing school, getting married, having a child, or being financially independent. The bar graph shows the percentage of Americans, ages 20 and 30, who had completed the transition to adulthood in 1960 and in 2000.

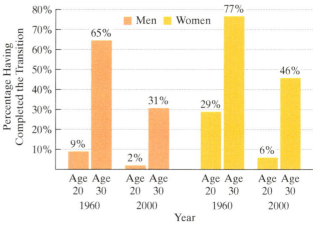

Percentage Having Completed the Transition to Adulthood

Source: James M. Henslin, Sociology, Eighth Edition, Allyn and Bacon, 2007

a. Use a 2×2 matrix to represent the data for 2000. Entries in the matrix should be percents that are organized as follows:

$\begin{array}{c} \\ \text{Age 20} \\ \text{Age 30} \end{array} \begin{bmatrix} \text{Men} & \text{Women} \\ & \\ & \end{bmatrix}$.

Call this matrix A.

b. Use a 2×2 matrix to represent the data for 1960. Call this matrix B.

c. Find $B - A$. What does this matrix represent?

28. **Multiple Steps.** The table gives an estimate of basic caloric needs for different age groups and activity levels.

Age Range	Sedentary		Moderately Active		Active	
	Men	Women	Men	Women	Men	Women
19 – 30	2400	2000	2700	2100	3000	2400
31 – 50	2200	1800	2500	2000	2900	2200
51 +	2000	1600	2300	1800	2600	2100

Source: USA Today

a. Use a 3×3 matrix to represent the daily caloric needs, by age and activity level, for men. Call this matrix M.

b. Use a 3×3 matrix to represent the daily caloric needs, by age and activity level, for women. Call this matrix W.

c. Find $M - W$. What does this matrix represent?

29. What is meant by the order of a matrix? Give an example with your explanation.

30. What does a_{ij} mean?

31. What are equal matrices?

32. How are matrices added?

33. Describe how to subtract matrices.

34. Describe matrices that cannot be added or subtracted.

35. Describe how to perform scalar multiplication. Provide an example with your description.

5.2 MULTIPLYING MATRICES AND SOLVING APPLICATIONS

OBJECTIVES

1. Multiply matrices.
2. Model applied situations with matrix operations.

OBJECTIVE 1 ▶ Multiply matrices. We do not multiply two matrices by multiplying the corresponding entries of the matrices. Instead, we must think of matrix multiplication as *row-by-column multiplication*. To better understand how this works, let's begin with the definition of matrix multiplication for matrices of order 2×2.

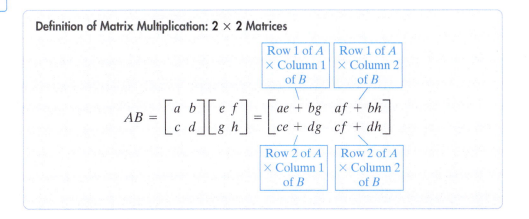

Notice that we obtain the element in the ith row and jth column in AB by performing computations with elements in the ith row of A and the jth column of B. For example, we obtain the element in the first row and first column of AB by performing computations with elements in the first row of A and the first column of B.

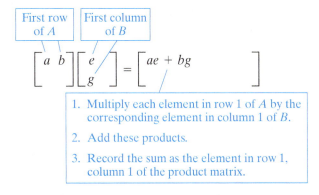

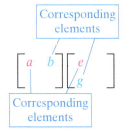

Finding corresponding elements when multiplying matrices

You may wonder how to find the corresponding elements in step 1 in the voice balloon. The element at the far left of row 1 corresponds to the element at the top of column 1. The second element from the left of row 1 corresponds to the second element from the top of column 1. This is illustrated in the margin.

EXAMPLE 1 Multiplying Matrices

Find AB, given

$$A = \begin{bmatrix} 2 & 3 \\ 4 & 7 \end{bmatrix} \text{ and } B = \begin{bmatrix} 0 & 1 \\ 5 & 6 \end{bmatrix}.$$

Solution We will perform a row-by-column computation.

$$AB = \begin{bmatrix} 2 & 3 \\ 4 & 7 \end{bmatrix} \begin{bmatrix} 0 & 1 \\ 5 & 6 \end{bmatrix}$$

$$= \begin{bmatrix} 2(0)+3(5) & 2(1)+3(6) \\ 4(0)+7(5) & 4(1)+7(6) \end{bmatrix} = \begin{bmatrix} 15 & 20 \\ 35 & 46 \end{bmatrix}$$

Row 1 of A × Column 1 of B | Row 1 of A × Column 2 of B
Row 2 of A × Column 1 of B | Row 2 of A × Column 2 of B

PRACTICE 1 Find AB, given $A = \begin{bmatrix} 1 & 3 \\ 2 & 5 \end{bmatrix}$ and $B = \begin{bmatrix} 4 & 6 \\ 1 & 0 \end{bmatrix}$.

We can generalize the process of Example 1 to multiply an $m \times n$ matrix and an $n \times p$ matrix. **For the product of two matrices to be defined, the number of columns of the first matrix must equal the number of rows of the second matrix.**

First Matrix Second Matrix
$m \times n$ $n \times p$

The number of columns in the first matrix must be the same as the number of rows in the second matrix.

> **Helpful Hint**
> The following diagram illustrates the first sentence in the box defining matrix multiplication. The diagram is helpful in determining the order of the product AB.
>
>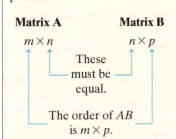

Definition of Matrix Multiplication

The **product** of an $m \times n$ matrix, A, and an $n \times p$ matrix, B, is an $m \times p$ matrix, AB, whose elements are found as follows: The element in the ith row and jth column of AB is found by multiplying each element in the ith row of A by the corresponding element in the jth column of B and adding the products.

To find a product AB, each row of A must have the same number of elements as each column of B. We obtain p_{ij}, the element in the ith row and jth column in AB, by performing computations with elements in the ith row of A and the jth column of B:

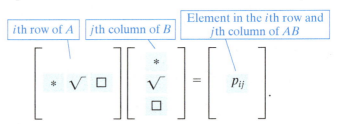

When multiplying corresponding elements, keep in mind that the element at the far left of row i corresponds to the element at the top of column j. The element second from the left in row i corresponds to the element second from the top in column j. Likewise, the element third from the left in row i corresponds to the element third from the top in column j, and so on.

EXAMPLE 2 Multiplying Matrices

Matrices A and B are defined as follows:

$$A = \begin{bmatrix} 1 & 2 & 3 \end{bmatrix} \quad B = \begin{bmatrix} 4 \\ 5 \\ 6 \end{bmatrix}.$$

Find each product: **a.** AB **b.** BA.

Solution

a. Matrix A is a 1×3 matrix and matrix B is a 3×1 matrix. Thus, the product AB is a 1×1 matrix.

Section 5.2 Multiplying Matrices and Solving Applications 259

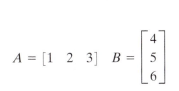

$$A = \begin{bmatrix} 1 & 2 & 3 \end{bmatrix} \quad B = \begin{bmatrix} 4 \\ 5 \\ 6 \end{bmatrix}$$

Matrix A — 1×3
Matrix B — 3×1
These are equal.
The order of AB is 1×1.

$$AB = \begin{bmatrix} 1 & 2 & 3 \end{bmatrix} \begin{bmatrix} 4 \\ 5 \\ 6 \end{bmatrix}$$ We will perform a row-by-column computation.

$$= [(1)(4) + (2)(5) + (3)(6)]$$ Multiply elements in row 1 of A by corresponding elements in column 1 of B and add the products.

$$= [4 + 10 + 18]$$ Perform the multiplications.

$$= [32]$$ Add.

b. Matrix B is a 3×1 matrix and matrix A is a 1×3 matrix. Thus, the product BA is a 3×3 matrix.

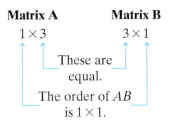

$$A = \begin{bmatrix} 1 & 2 & 3 \end{bmatrix} \quad B = \begin{bmatrix} 4 \\ 5 \\ 6 \end{bmatrix}$$

Matrix B — 3×1
Matrix A — 1×3
These are equal.
The order of BA is 3×3.

$$BA = \begin{bmatrix} 4 \\ 5 \\ 6 \end{bmatrix} \begin{bmatrix} 1 & 2 & 3 \end{bmatrix}$$ We perform a row-by-column computation.

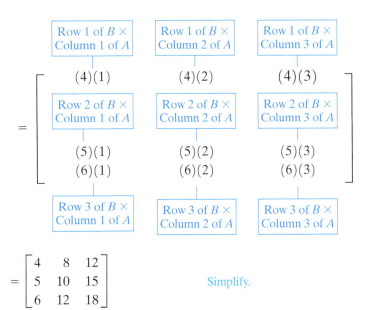

$$= \begin{bmatrix} 4 & 8 & 12 \\ 5 & 10 & 15 \\ 6 & 12 & 18 \end{bmatrix}$$ Simplify.

In Example 2, did you notice that AB and BA are different matrices? For most matrices A and B, $AB \neq BA$. Because **matrix multiplication is not commutative**, be careful about the order in which matrices appear when performing this operation.

PRACTICE 2 If $A = \begin{bmatrix} 2 & 0 & 4 \end{bmatrix}$ and $B = \begin{bmatrix} 1 \\ 3 \\ 7 \end{bmatrix}$, find AB and BA.

TECHNOLOGY NOTE

The screens illustrate the solution of Example 2 using a graphing utility.

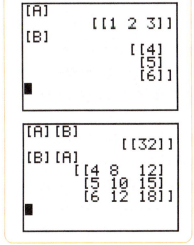

EXAMPLE 3   Multiplying Matrices

Where possible, find each product:

a. $\begin{bmatrix} 4 & 2 \\ 1 & 3 \end{bmatrix} \begin{bmatrix} 1 & 2 & 3 & 4 \\ 0 & 2 & -1 & 6 \end{bmatrix}$ b. $\begin{bmatrix} 1 & 2 & 3 & 4 \\ 0 & 2 & -1 & 6 \end{bmatrix} \begin{bmatrix} 4 & 2 \\ 1 & 3 \end{bmatrix}.$

Solution

a. The first matrix is a 2×2 matrix and the second is a 2×4 matrix. The product will be a 2×4 matrix.

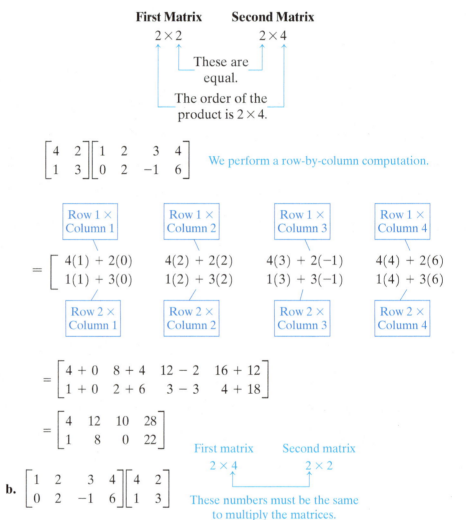

The number of columns in the first matrix does not equal the number of rows in the second matrix. Thus, the product of these two matrices is undefined. □

PRACTICE 3   Where possible, find each product:

a. $\begin{bmatrix} 1 & 3 \\ 0 & 2 \end{bmatrix} \begin{bmatrix} 2 & 3 & -1 & 6 \\ 0 & 5 & 4 & 1 \end{bmatrix}$ b. $\begin{bmatrix} 2 & 3 & -1 & 6 \\ 0 & 5 & 4 & 1 \end{bmatrix} \begin{bmatrix} 1 & 3 \\ 0 & 2 \end{bmatrix}.$

Although matrix multiplication is not commutative, it does obey many of the properties of real numbers.

DISCOVERY

Verify the properties listed in the box using

$A = \begin{bmatrix} 3 & 2 \\ -1 & 4 \end{bmatrix}$,

$B = \begin{bmatrix} 1 & 0 \\ 3 & 2 \end{bmatrix}$,

$C = \begin{bmatrix} 1 & 2 \\ -1 & 1 \end{bmatrix}$,

and $c = 3$.

Properties of Matrix Multiplication

If A, B, and C are matrices and c is a scalar, then the following properties are true. (Assume the order of each matrix is such that all operations in these properties are defined.)

1. $(AB)C = A(BC)$ Associative Property of Matrix Multiplication
2. $A(B + C) = AB + AC$ Distributive Properties of Matrix
   $(A + B)C = AC + BC$ Multiplication
3. $c(AB) = (cA)B$ Associative Property of Scalar Multiplication

OBJECTIVE 2 ▶ Model applied situations with matrix operations. All of the still images that you see on the Web have been created or manipulated on a computer in a digital format—made up of hundreds of thousands, or even millions, of tiny squares called **pixels**. Pixels are created by dividing an image into a grid. The computer can change the brightness of every square or pixel in this grid. A digital camera captures photos in this digital format. Also, you can scan pictures to convert them into digital format. Example 4 illustrates the role that matrices play in this new technology.

EXAMPLE 4   Matrices and Digital Photography

The letter L in the below left figure is shown using 9 pixels in a 3×3 grid. The colors possible in the grid are shown in the below right figure. Each color is represented by a specific number: 0, 1, 2, or 3.

The letter L

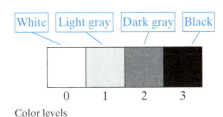

Color levels

a. Find a matrix that represents a digital photograph of this letter L.
b. Increase the contrast of the letter L by changing the dark gray to black and the light gray to white. Use matrix addition to accomplish this.

Solution

a. Look at the L and the background in the above left figure. Because the L is dark gray, color level 2, and the background is light gray, color level 1, a digital photograph of this figure can be represented by the matrix

$$\begin{bmatrix} 2 & 1 & 1 \\ 2 & 1 & 1 \\ 2 & 2 & 1 \end{bmatrix}.$$

b. We can make the L black, color level 3, by increasing each 2 in the above matrix to 3. We can make the background white, color level 0, by decreasing each 1 in the above matrix to 0. This is accomplished using the following matrix addition:

$$\begin{bmatrix} 2 & 1 & 1 \\ 2 & 1 & 1 \\ 2 & 2 & 1 \end{bmatrix} + \begin{bmatrix} 1 & -1 & -1 \\ 1 & -1 & -1 \\ 1 & 1 & -1 \end{bmatrix} = \begin{bmatrix} 3 & 0 & 0 \\ 3 & 0 & 0 \\ 3 & 3 & 0 \end{bmatrix}.$$

The picture corresponding to the matrix sum to the right of the equal sign is shown in the figure in the margin. ☐

Changing contrast: the letter L

PRACTICE 4 Change the contrast of the letter L in the original Example 4 figure on the previous page by making the L light gray and the background black. Use matrix addition to accomplish this.

Images of Space

Photographs sent back from space use matrices with thousands of pixels. Each pixel is assigned a number from 0 to 63 representing its color–0 for pure white and 63 for pure black. In the image of Saturn shown here, matrix operations provide false colors that emphasize the banding of the planet's upper atmosphere.

We have seen how functions can be transformed using translations, reflections, stretching, and shrinking. In a similar way, matrix operations are used to transform and manipulate computer graphics.

EXAMPLE 5 Transformations of an Image

The quadrilateral in the margin can be represented by the matrix

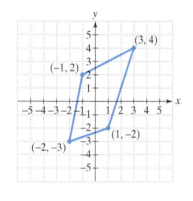

$$A = \begin{bmatrix} -2 & -1 & 3 & 1 \\ -3 & 2 & 4 & -2 \end{bmatrix}$$

(Coordinates of vertices — x-coordinates on top row, y-coordinates on bottom row.)

Each column in the matrix gives the coordinates of a vertex, or corner, of the quadrilateral. Use matrix operations to perfom the following transformations:

a. Move the quadrilateral 4 units to the right and 1 unit down.

b. Shrink the quadrilateral to half its perimeter.

c. Let $B = \begin{bmatrix} -1 & 0 \\ 0 & 1 \end{bmatrix}$. Find BA. What effect does this have on the quadrilateral?

Solution

a. We translate the quadrilateral 4 units right and 1 unit down by adding 4 to each x-coordinate and subtracting 1 from each y-coordinate. This is accomplished using the following matrix addition:

$$\begin{bmatrix} -2 & -1 & 3 & 1 \\ -3 & 2 & 4 & -2 \end{bmatrix} + \begin{bmatrix} 4 & 4 & 4 & 4 \\ -1 & -1 & -1 & -1 \end{bmatrix} = \begin{bmatrix} 2 & 3 & 7 & 5 \\ -4 & 1 & 3 & -3 \end{bmatrix}.$$

(This matrix represents the original quadrilateral. Shift 4 units to the right and 1 unit down. This matrix represents the translated quadrilateral.)

Each column in the matrix on the right gives the coordinates of a vertex of the translated quadrilateral. The original quadrilateral and the translated image are shown in the Solution a figure.

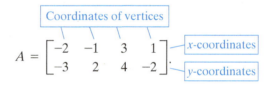

Solution a: Shifting the quadrilateral 4 units right and 1 unit down

b. We shrink the original quadrilateral, shown in blue in the Solution b graph on the next page, to half its perimeter by multiplying each x-coordinate and each y-coordinate by $\frac{1}{2}$. This is accomplished using the following scalar multiplication:

$$\frac{1}{2}\begin{bmatrix} -2 & -1 & 3 & 1 \\ -3 & 2 & 4 & -2 \end{bmatrix} = \begin{bmatrix} -1 & -\frac{1}{2} & \frac{3}{2} & \frac{1}{2} \\ -\frac{3}{2} & 1 & 2 & -1 \end{bmatrix}.$$

(This matrix represents the original quadrilateral. This matrix represents the quadrilateral with half the original perimeter.)

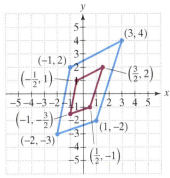

Solution b: Shrinking the quadrilateral to half the original perimeter

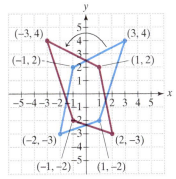

Solution c

Each column in the matrix on the right on the previous page gives the coordinates of a vertex of the reduced quadrilateral. The original quadrilateral and the reduced image are shown in the Solution b figure.

c. We begin by finding BA. Keep in mind that A represents the original quadrilateral, shown in blue in the Solution c figure.

$$BA = \begin{bmatrix} -1 & 0 \\ 0 & 1 \end{bmatrix} \begin{bmatrix} -2 & -1 & 3 & 1 \\ -3 & 2 & 4 & -2 \end{bmatrix}$$

$$= \begin{bmatrix} (-1)(-2) + 0(-3) & (-1)(-1) + 0(2) & (-1)(3) + 0(4) & (-1)(1) + 0(-2) \\ 0(-2) + 1(-3) & 0(-1) + 1(2) & 0(3) + 1(4) & 0(1) + 1(-2) \end{bmatrix}$$

$$= \begin{bmatrix} 2 & 1 & -3 & -1 \\ -3 & 2 & 4 & -2 \end{bmatrix}$$

Each column in the matrix multiplication gives the coordinates of a vertex of the transformed image. The original quadrilateral and this transformed image are shown in the Solution c figure. Notice that each x-coordinate on the original blue image is replaced with its opposite on the transformed red image.

We can conclude that multiplication by $\begin{bmatrix} -1 & 0 \\ 0 & 1 \end{bmatrix}$ reflected the blue quadrilateral about the y-axis. □

PRACTICE 5 Consider the triangle represented by the matrix

$$A = \begin{bmatrix} 0 & 3 & 4 \\ 0 & 5 & 2 \end{bmatrix}.$$

Use matrix operations to perform the following transformations:

a. Move the triangle 3 units to the left and 1 unit down.

b. Enlarge the triangle to twice its original perimeter.

Illustrate your results in parts (a) and (b) by showing the original triangle and the transformed image in a rectangular coordinate system.

c. Let $B = \begin{bmatrix} 1 & 0 \\ 0 & -1 \end{bmatrix}$. Find BA. What effect does this have on the original triangle?

5.2 EXERCISE SET

In Exercises 1–10, find (if possible) the following matrices:

a. AB b. BA.

1. $A = \begin{bmatrix} 1 & 3 \\ 5 & 3 \end{bmatrix}$, $B = \begin{bmatrix} 3 & -2 \\ -1 & 6 \end{bmatrix}$

2. $A = \begin{bmatrix} 3 & -2 \\ 1 & 5 \end{bmatrix}$, $B = \begin{bmatrix} 0 & 0 \\ 5 & -6 \end{bmatrix}$

3. $A = \begin{bmatrix} 1 & 2 & 3 & 4 \end{bmatrix}$, $B = \begin{bmatrix} 1 \\ 2 \\ 3 \\ 4 \end{bmatrix}$

4. $A = \begin{bmatrix} -1 \\ -2 \\ -3 \end{bmatrix}$, $B = \begin{bmatrix} 1 & 2 & 3 \end{bmatrix}$

5. $A = \begin{bmatrix} 1 & -1 & 4 \\ 4 & -1 & 3 \\ 2 & 0 & -2 \end{bmatrix}$, $B = \begin{bmatrix} 1 & 1 & 0 \\ 1 & 2 & 4 \\ 1 & -1 & 3 \end{bmatrix}$

6. $A = \begin{bmatrix} 1 & -1 & 1 \\ 5 & 0 & -2 \\ 3 & -2 & 2 \end{bmatrix}$, $B = \begin{bmatrix} 1 & 1 & 0 \\ 1 & -4 & 5 \\ 3 & -1 & 2 \end{bmatrix}$

7. $A = \begin{bmatrix} 4 & 2 \\ 6 & 1 \\ 3 & 5 \end{bmatrix}$, $B = \begin{bmatrix} 2 & 3 & 4 \\ -1 & -2 & 0 \end{bmatrix}$

8. $A = \begin{bmatrix} 2 & 4 \\ 3 & 1 \\ 4 & 2 \end{bmatrix}$, $B = \begin{bmatrix} 3 & 2 & 0 \\ -1 & -3 & 5 \end{bmatrix}$

9. $A = \begin{bmatrix} 2 & -3 & 1 & -1 \\ 1 & 1 & -2 & 1 \end{bmatrix}$, $B = \begin{bmatrix} 1 & 2 \\ -1 & 1 \\ 5 & 4 \\ 10 & 5 \end{bmatrix}$

10. $A = \begin{bmatrix} 2 & -1 & 3 & 2 \\ 1 & 0 & -2 & 1 \end{bmatrix}$, $B = \begin{bmatrix} -1 & 2 \\ 1 & 1 \\ 3 & -4 \\ 6 & 5 \end{bmatrix}$

In Exercises 11–18, perform the indicated matrix operations given that A, B, and C are defined as follows. If an operation is not defined, state the reason.

$$A = \begin{bmatrix} 4 & 0 \\ -3 & 5 \\ 0 & 1 \end{bmatrix} \quad B = \begin{bmatrix} 5 & 1 \\ -2 & -2 \end{bmatrix} \quad C = \begin{bmatrix} 1 & -1 \\ -1 & 1 \end{bmatrix}$$

11. $4B - 3C$
12. $5C - 2B$
13. $BC + CB$
14. $A(B + C)$
15. $A - C$
16. $B - A$
17. $A(BC)$
18. $A(CB)$

In Exercises 19–24, let

$$A = \begin{bmatrix} 1 & 0 \\ 0 & 1 \end{bmatrix}, \quad B = \begin{bmatrix} 1 & 0 \\ 0 & -1 \end{bmatrix}, \quad C = \begin{bmatrix} -1 & 0 \\ 0 & 1 \end{bmatrix},$$

$$D = \begin{bmatrix} -1 & 0 \\ 0 & -1 \end{bmatrix}.$$

19. Find the product of the sum of A and B and the difference between C and D.

20. Find the product of the difference between A and B and the sum of C and D.

21. Use any three of the matrices to verify a distributive property.

22. Use any three of the matrices to verify an associative property.

In Exercises 23–24, suppose that the vertices of a computer graphic are points, (x, y), represented by the matrix

$$Z = \begin{bmatrix} x \\ y \end{bmatrix}.$$

23. Find BZ and explain why this reflects the graphic about the x-axis.

24. Find CZ and explain why this reflects the graphic about the y-axis.

The + sign in the figure is shown using 9 pixels in a 3 × 3 grid. The color levels are given to the right of the figure. Each color is represented by a specific number: 0, 1, 2, or 3. Use this information to solve Exercises 25–26.

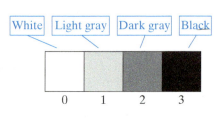

25. a. Find a matrix that represents a digital photograph of the + sign.

  b. Adjust the contrast by changing the black to dark gray and the light gray to white. Use matrix addition to accomplish this.

  c. Adjust the contrast by changing the black to light gray and the light gray to dark gray. Use matrix addition to accomplish this.

26. a. Find a matrix that represents a digital photograph of the + sign.

  b. Adjust the contrast by changing the black to dark gray and the light gray to black. Use matrix addition to accomplish this.

  c. Adjust the contrast by leaving the black alone and changing the light gray to white. Use matrix addition to accomplish this.

The figure shows the letter L in a rectangular coordinate system.

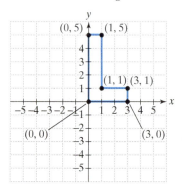

The figure can be represented by the matrix

$$B = \begin{bmatrix} 0 & 3 & 3 & 1 & 1 & 0 \\ 0 & 0 & 1 & 1 & 5 & 5 \end{bmatrix}.$$

Each column in the matrix describes a point on the letter. The order of the columns shows the direction in which a pencil must move to draw the letter. The L is completed by connecting the last point in the matrix, (0, 5), to the starting point, (0, 0). Use these ideas to solve Exercises 27–34.

27. Use matrix operations to move the L 2 units to the left and 3 units down. Then graph the letter and its transformation in a rectangular coordinate system.

28. Use matrix operations to move the L 2 units to the right and 3 units down. Then graph the letter and its transformation in a rectangular coordinate system.

29. Reduce the L to half its perimeter and move the reduced image 1 unit up. Then graph the letter and its transformation.

30. Reduce the L to half its perimeter and move the reduced image 2 units up. Then graph the letter and its transformation.

31. a. If $A = \begin{bmatrix} 1 & 0 \\ 0 & -1 \end{bmatrix}$, find AB.

  b. Graph the object represented by matrix AB. What effect does the matrix multiplication have on the letter L represented by matrix B?

32. a. If $A = \begin{bmatrix} -1 & 0 \\ 0 & 1 \end{bmatrix}$, find AB.

  b. Graph the object represented by matrix AB. What effect does the matrix multiplication have on the letter L represented by matrix B?

33. a. If $A = \begin{bmatrix} 0 & -1 \\ 1 & 0 \end{bmatrix}$, find AB.

  b. Graph the object represented by matrix AB. What effect does the matrix multiplication have on the letter L represented by matrix B?

34. a. If $A = \begin{bmatrix} 2 & 0 \\ 0 & 1 \end{bmatrix}$, find AB.

  b. Graph the object represented by matrix AB. What effect does the matrix multiplication have on the letter L represented by matrix B?

35. Multiple Steps. The final grade in a particular course is determined by grades on the midterm and final. The grades for five students and the two grading systems are modeled by the following matrices. Call the first matrix A and the second B.

	Midterm	Final
Student 1	76	92
Student 2	74	84
Student 3	94	86
Student 4	84	62
Student 5	58	80

	System 1	System 2
Midterm	0.5	0.3
Final	0.5	0.7

  a. Describe the grading system that is represented by matrix B.

  b. Compute the matrix AB and assign each of the five students a final course grade first using system 1 and then using system 2. ($89.5 - 100 = A$, $79.5 - 89.4 = B$, $69.5 - 79.4 = C$, $59.5 - 69.4 = D$, below $59.5 = F$)

36. Multiple Steps. In a certain county, the proportion of voters in each age group registered as Republicans, Democrats, or Independents is given by the following matrix, which we'll call A.

	Age		
	18–30	31–50	Over 50
Republicans	0.40	0.30	0.70
Democrats	0.30	0.60	0.25
Independents	0.30	0.10	0.05

The distribution, by age and gender, of this county's voting population is given by the following matrix, which we'll call B.

		Male	Female
	18–30	6000	8000
Age	31–50	12,000	14,000
	Over 50	14,000	16,000

  a. Calculate the product AB.

  b. How many female Democrats are there?

  c. How many male Republicans are there?

37. Describe how to multiply matrices.

38. Describe when the multiplication of two matrices is not defined.

39. If two matrices can be multiplied, describe how to determine the order of the product.

40. Low-resolution digital photographs use 262,144 pixels in a 512×512 grid. If you enlarge a low-resolution digital photograph enough, describe what will happen.

CRITICAL THINKING EXERCISES

Decision Making. *In Exercises 41–44, determine whether each statement makes sense or does not make sense, and explain your reasoning.*

41. I added matrices of the same order by adding corresponding elements.

42. I multiplied an $m \times n$ matrix and an $n \times p$ matrix by multiplying corresponding elements.

43. I'm working with two matrices that can be added but not multiplied.

44. I'm working with two matrices that can be multiplied but not added.

45. Find two matrices A and B such that $AB = BA$.

46. Consider a square matrix such that each element that is not on the diagonal from upper left to lower right is zero. Experiment with such matrices (call each matrix A) by finding AA. Then write a sentence or two describing a method for multiplying this kind of matrix by itself.

47. If $AB = -BA$, then A and B are said to be anticommutative. Are $A = \begin{bmatrix} 0 & -1 \\ 1 & 0 \end{bmatrix}$ and $B = \begin{bmatrix} 1 & 0 \\ 0 & -1 \end{bmatrix}$ anticommutative?

INTEGRATED REVIEW — OPERATIONS ON MATRICES

Sections 5.1–5.2

In Exercises 1–5, perform the indicated matrix operations or solve the matrix equation for X given that A, B, and C are defined as follows. If an operation is not defined, state the reason.

$$A = \begin{bmatrix} 0 & 2 \\ -1 & 3 \\ 1 & 0 \end{bmatrix} \quad B = \begin{bmatrix} 4 & 1 \\ -6 & -2 \end{bmatrix} \quad C = \begin{bmatrix} -1 & 0 \\ 0 & 1 \end{bmatrix}$$

1. $2C - \frac{1}{2}B$
2. $A(B + C)$
3. $A(BC)$
4. $A + C$
5. $2X - 3C = B$

5.3 SOLVING SYSTEMS OF EQUATIONS USING DETERMINANTS

OBJECTIVES

1. Define and evaluate a 2 × 2 determinant.
2. Use Cramer's rule to solve a system of two linear equations in two variables.
3. Define and evaluate a 3 × 3 determinant.
4. Use Cramer's rule to solve a system of three linear equations in three variables.

We have solved systems of two linear equations in two variables in four different ways: graphically, by substitution, by elimination, and by matrices. Now we analyze another method called **Cramer's rule.**

OBJECTIVE 1 ▶ Evaluating 2 × 2 determinants. Recall that a matrix is a rectangular array of numbers. If a matrix has the same number of rows and columns, it is called a **square matrix.** Examples of square matrices are

$$\begin{bmatrix} 1 & 6 \\ 5 & 2 \end{bmatrix} \quad \begin{bmatrix} 2 & 4 & 1 \\ 0 & 5 & 2 \\ 3 & 6 & 9 \end{bmatrix}$$

A **determinant** is a real number associated with a square matrix. The determinant of a square matrix is denoted by placing vertical bars about the array of numbers. Thus,

The determinant of the square matrix $\begin{bmatrix} 1 & 6 \\ 5 & 2 \end{bmatrix}$ is $\begin{vmatrix} 1 & 6 \\ 5 & 2 \end{vmatrix}$.

The determinant of the square matrix $\begin{bmatrix} 2 & 4 & 1 \\ 0 & 5 & 2 \\ 3 & 6 & 9 \end{bmatrix}$ is $\begin{vmatrix} 2 & 4 & 1 \\ 0 & 5 & 2 \\ 3 & 6 & 9 \end{vmatrix}$.

We define the determinant of a 2 × 2 matrix first. (Recall that 2 × 2 is read "two by two." It means that the matrix has 2 rows and 2 columns.)

Determinant of a 2 × 2 Matrix

$$\begin{vmatrix} a & b \\ c & d \end{vmatrix} = ad - bc$$

EXAMPLE 1 Evaluate each determinant

a. $\begin{vmatrix} -1 & 2 \\ 3 & -4 \end{vmatrix}$

b. $\begin{vmatrix} 2 & 0 \\ 7 & -5 \end{vmatrix}$

Solution First we identify the values of $a, b, c,$ and d. Then we perform the evaluation.

a. Here $a = -1, b = 2, c = 3,$ and $d = -4$.

$$\begin{vmatrix} -1 & 2 \\ 3 & -4 \end{vmatrix} = ad - bc = (-1)(-4) - (2)(3) = -2$$

b. In this example, $a = 2, b = 0, c = 7$, and $d = -5$.

$$\begin{vmatrix} 2 & 0 \\ 7 & -5 \end{vmatrix} = ad - bc = 2(-5) - (0)(7) = -10$$

PRACTICE

1 Evaluate each determinant

a. $\begin{vmatrix} 3 & -5 \\ -1 & 7 \end{vmatrix}$ 　　**b.** $\begin{vmatrix} 0 & 3 \\ 9 & -4 \end{vmatrix}$

OBJECTIVE 2 ▶ Using Cramer's rule to solve a system of two linear equations. To develop Cramer's rule, we solve the system $\begin{cases} ax + by = h \\ cx + dy = k \end{cases}$ using elimination. First, we eliminate y by multiplying both sides of the first equation by d and both sides of the second equation by $-b$ so that the coefficients of y are opposites. The result is that

$\begin{cases} d(ax + by) = d \cdot h \\ -b(cx + dy) = -b \cdot k \end{cases}$　simplifies to　$\begin{cases} adx + bdy = hd \\ -bcx - bdy = -kb \end{cases}$

We now add the two equations and solve for x.

$$\begin{aligned} adx + bdy &= hd \\ \underline{-bcx - bdy} &= \underline{-kb} \\ adx - bcx &= hd - kb \quad \text{Add the equations.} \\ (ad - bc)x &= hd - kb \\ x &= \frac{hd - kb}{ad - bc} \quad \text{Solve for } x. \end{aligned}$$

When we replace x with $\dfrac{hd - kb}{ad - bc}$ in the equation $ax + by = h$ and solve for y, we find that $y = \dfrac{ak - ch}{ad - bc}$.

Notice that the numerator of the value of x is the determinant of

$$\begin{vmatrix} h & b \\ k & d \end{vmatrix} = hd - kb$$

Also, the numerator of the value of y is the determinant of

$$\begin{vmatrix} a & h \\ c & k \end{vmatrix} = ak - hc$$

Finally, the denominators of the values of x and y are the same and are the determinant of

$$\begin{vmatrix} a & b \\ c & d \end{vmatrix} = ad - bc$$

This means that the values of x and y can be written in determinant notation:

$$x = \frac{\begin{vmatrix} h & b \\ k & d \end{vmatrix}}{\begin{vmatrix} a & b \\ c & d \end{vmatrix}} \quad \text{and} \quad y = \frac{\begin{vmatrix} a & h \\ c & k \end{vmatrix}}{\begin{vmatrix} a & b \\ c & d \end{vmatrix}}$$

For convenience, we label the determinants D, D_x, and D_y.

$$\underbrace{\begin{vmatrix} a & b \\ c & d \end{vmatrix}}_{\substack{\text{x-coefficients} \\ \text{y-coefficients}}} = D \qquad \begin{vmatrix} h & b \\ k & d \end{vmatrix} = D_x \qquad \begin{vmatrix} a & h \\ c & k \end{vmatrix} = D_y$$

x-column replaced by constants $\qquad$ y-column replaced by constants

These determinant formulas for the coordinates of the solution of a system are known as **Cramer's rule.**

Cramer's Rule for Two Linear Equations in Two Variables

The solution of the system $\begin{cases} ax + by = h \\ cx + dy = k \end{cases}$ is given by

$$x = \frac{\begin{vmatrix} h & b \\ k & d \end{vmatrix}}{\begin{vmatrix} a & b \\ c & d \end{vmatrix}} = \frac{D_x}{D} \qquad y = \frac{\begin{vmatrix} a & h \\ c & k \end{vmatrix}}{\begin{vmatrix} a & b \\ c & d \end{vmatrix}} = \frac{D_y}{D}$$

as long as $D = ad - bc$ is not 0.

When $D = 0$, the system is either inconsistent or the equations are dependent. When this happens, we need to use another method to see which is the case.

EXAMPLE 2 Use Cramer's rule to solve the system

$$\begin{cases} 3x + 4y = -7 \\ x - 2y = -9 \end{cases}$$

Solution First we find D, D_x, and D_y.

$$\begin{array}{ccc} a & b & h \\ \downarrow & \downarrow & \downarrow \end{array}$$
$$\begin{cases} 3x + 4y = -7 \\ x - 2y = -9 \end{cases}$$
$$\begin{array}{ccc} \uparrow & \uparrow & \uparrow \\ c & d & k \end{array}$$

$$D = \begin{vmatrix} a & b \\ c & d \end{vmatrix} = \begin{vmatrix} 3 & 4 \\ 1 & -2 \end{vmatrix} = 3(-2) - 4(1) = -10$$

$$D_x = \begin{vmatrix} h & b \\ k & d \end{vmatrix} = \begin{vmatrix} -7 & 4 \\ -9 & -2 \end{vmatrix} = (-7)(-2) - 4(-9) = 50$$

$$D_y = \begin{vmatrix} a & h \\ c & d \end{vmatrix} = \begin{vmatrix} 3 & -7 \\ 1 & -9 \end{vmatrix} = 3(-9) - (-7)(1) = -20$$

Then $x = \dfrac{D_x}{D} = \dfrac{50}{-10} = -5$ and $y = \dfrac{D_y}{D} = \dfrac{-20}{-10} = 2$.

The ordered pair solution is $(-5, 2)$.

As always, check the solution in both original equations.

Section 5.3 Solving Systems of Equations Using Determinants 269

PRACTICE 2 Use Cramer's rule to solve the system
$$\begin{cases} 2x + 5y = -7 \\ x + 3y = -5 \end{cases}$$

EXAMPLE 3 Use Cramer's rule to solve the system
$$\begin{cases} 5x + y = 5 \\ -7x - 2y = -7 \end{cases}$$

Solution First we find D, D_x, and D_y.

$$D = \begin{vmatrix} 5 & 1 \\ -7 & -2 \end{vmatrix} = 5(-2) - (-7)(1) = -3$$

$$D_x = \begin{vmatrix} 5 & 1 \\ -7 & -2 \end{vmatrix} = 5(-2) - (-7)(1) = -3$$

$$D_y = \begin{vmatrix} 5 & 5 \\ -7 & -7 \end{vmatrix} = 5(-7) - 5(-7) = 0$$

Then

$$x = \frac{D_x}{D} = \frac{-3}{-3} = 1 \qquad y = \frac{D_y}{D} = \frac{0}{-3} = 0$$

The ordered pair solution is $(1, 0)$.

PRACTICE 3 Use Cramer's rule to solve the system
$$\begin{cases} 7x - y = -3 \\ 4x + 3y = 9 \end{cases}$$

OBJECTIVE 3 ▶ Evaluating 3 × 3 determinants. A 3×3 determinant can be used to solve a system of three equations in three variables. There are many ways to evaluate a 3×3 determinant. We will use the method below.

Determinant of a 3 × 3 Matrix

$$\begin{vmatrix} a & b & c \\ d & e & f \\ g & h & i \end{vmatrix} = \begin{vmatrix} a & b & c & a & b \\ d & e & f & d & e \\ g & h & i & g & h \end{vmatrix} = (aei + bfg + cdh) - (gec + hfa + idb)$$

EXAMPLE 4 Evaluate the determinant.

$$\begin{vmatrix} 0 & 5 & 1 \\ 1 & 3 & -1 \\ -2 & 2 & 4 \end{vmatrix}$$

Solution

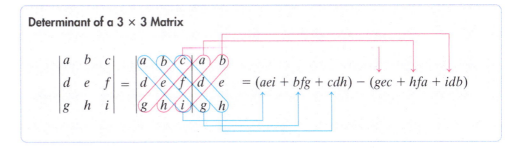

$$= (12) - (14)$$
$$= -2$$

PRACTICE 4 Evaluate the determinant.

$$\begin{vmatrix} 2 & 6 & -1 \\ 0 & 1 & 4 \\ 3 & -2 & 1 \end{vmatrix}$$

OBJECTIVE 4 ▶ **Using Cramer's rule to solve a system of three linear equations.** A system of three equations in three variables may be solved with Cramer's rule also. Using the elimination process to solve a system with unknown constants as coefficients leads to the following.

Cramer's Rule for Three Equations in Three Variables

The solution of the system $\begin{cases} ax + by + cz = k \\ dx + ey + fz = m \\ gx + hy + iz = n \end{cases}$ is given by

$$x = \frac{D_x}{D} \qquad y = \frac{D_y}{D} \qquad \text{and} \qquad z = \frac{D_z}{D}$$

where

$$D = \begin{vmatrix} a & b & c \\ d & e & f \\ g & h & i \end{vmatrix} \qquad D_x = \begin{vmatrix} k & b & c \\ m & e & f \\ n & h & i \end{vmatrix}$$

x-column replaced by constants

$$D_y = \begin{vmatrix} a & k & c \\ d & m & f \\ g & n & i \end{vmatrix} \qquad D_z = \begin{vmatrix} a & b & k \\ d & e & m \\ g & h & n \end{vmatrix}$$

as long as D is not 0. y-column replaced by constants z-column replaced by constants

---

EXAMPLE 5 Use Cramer's rule to solve the system

$$\begin{cases} x - 2y + z = 4 \\ 3x + y - 2z = 3 \\ 5x + 5y + 3z = -8 \end{cases}$$

Solution First we find D, D_x, D_y, and D_z.

$$D = \begin{vmatrix} 1 & -2 & 1 \\ 3 & 1 & -2 \\ 5 & 5 & 3 \end{vmatrix} = (3 + 20 + 15) - (5 + (-10) + (-18)) = 61$$

$$D_x = \begin{vmatrix} 4 & -2 & 1 \\ 3 & 1 & -2 \\ -8 & 5 & 3 \end{vmatrix} = (12 + (-32) + 15) - (-8 + (-40) + (-18)) = 61$$

$$D_y = \begin{vmatrix} 1 & 4 & 1 \\ 3 & 3 & -2 \\ 5 & -8 & 3 \end{vmatrix} = (9 + (-40) + (-24)) - (15 + 16 + 36) = -122$$

$$D_z = \begin{vmatrix} 1 & -2 & 4 \\ 3 & 1 & 3 \\ 5 & 5 & -8 \end{vmatrix} = (-8 + (-30) + 60) - (20 + 15 + 48) = -61$$

From these determinants, we calculate the solution:

$$x = \frac{D_x}{D} = \frac{61}{61} = 1 \quad y = \frac{D_y}{D} = \frac{-122}{61} = -2 \quad z = \frac{D_z}{D} = \frac{-61}{61} = -1$$

The ordered triple solution is $(1, -2, -1)$. Check this solution by verifying that it satisfies each equation of the system.

PRACTICE 5 Use Cramer's rule to solve the system

$$\begin{cases} 3x + y + 5z = 1 \\ x - 4y + z = 1 \\ 2x - 3y - 6z = 10 \end{cases}$$

VOCABULARY & READINESS CHECK

Evaluate each determinant mentally.

1. $\begin{vmatrix} 7 & 2 \\ 0 & 8 \end{vmatrix}$
2. $\begin{vmatrix} 6 & 0 \\ 1 & 2 \end{vmatrix}$
3. $\begin{vmatrix} -4 & 2 \\ 0 & 8 \end{vmatrix}$
4. $\begin{vmatrix} 5 & 0 \\ 3 & -5 \end{vmatrix}$
5. $\begin{vmatrix} -2 & 0 \\ 3 & -10 \end{vmatrix}$
6. $\begin{vmatrix} -1 & 4 \\ 0 & -18 \end{vmatrix}$

5.3 EXERCISE SET

Evaluate each determinant. See Example 1.

1. $\begin{vmatrix} 3 & 5 \\ -1 & 7 \end{vmatrix}$
2. $\begin{vmatrix} -5 & 1 \\ 1 & -4 \end{vmatrix}$
3. $\begin{vmatrix} 9 & -2 \\ 4 & -3 \end{vmatrix}$
4. $\begin{vmatrix} 4 & -1 \\ 9 & 8 \end{vmatrix}$
5. $\begin{vmatrix} -2 & 9 \\ 4 & -18 \end{vmatrix}$
6. $\begin{vmatrix} -40 & 8 \\ 70 & -14 \end{vmatrix}$
7. $\begin{vmatrix} \frac{3}{4} & \frac{5}{2} \\ -\frac{1}{6} & \frac{7}{3} \end{vmatrix}$
8. $\begin{vmatrix} \frac{5}{7} & \frac{1}{3} \\ \frac{6}{7} & \frac{2}{3} \end{vmatrix}$

Use Cramer's rule, if possible, to solve each system of linear equations. See Examples 2 and 3.

9. $\begin{cases} 2y - 4 = 0 \\ x + 2y = 5 \end{cases}$
10. $\begin{cases} 4x - y = 5 \\ 3x - 3 = 0 \end{cases}$
11. $\begin{cases} 3x + y = 1 \\ 2y = 2 - 6x \end{cases}$
12. $\begin{cases} y = 2x - 5 \\ 8x - 4y = 20 \end{cases}$
13. $\begin{cases} 5x - 2y = 27 \\ -3x + 5y = 18 \end{cases}$
14. $\begin{cases} 4x - y = 9 \\ 2x + 3y = -27 \end{cases}$
15. $\begin{cases} 2x - 5y = 4 \\ x + 2y = -7 \end{cases}$
16. $\begin{cases} 3x - y = 2 \\ -5x + 2y = 0 \end{cases}$
17. $\begin{cases} \frac{2}{3}x - \frac{3}{4}y = -1 \\ -\frac{1}{6}x + \frac{3}{4}y = \frac{5}{2} \end{cases}$
18. $\begin{cases} \frac{1}{2}x - \frac{1}{3}y = -3 \\ \frac{1}{8}x + \frac{1}{6}y = 0 \end{cases}$

Evaluate. See Example 4.

19. $\begin{vmatrix} 2 & 1 & 0 \\ 0 & 5 & -3 \\ 4 & 0 & 2 \end{vmatrix}$
20. $\begin{vmatrix} -6 & 4 & 2 \\ 1 & 0 & 5 \\ 0 & 3 & 1 \end{vmatrix}$
21. $\begin{vmatrix} 4 & -6 & 0 \\ -2 & 3 & 0 \\ 4 & -6 & 1 \end{vmatrix}$
22. $\begin{vmatrix} 5 & 2 & 1 \\ 3 & -6 & 0 \\ -2 & 8 & 0 \end{vmatrix}$
23. $\begin{vmatrix} 1 & 0 & 4 \\ 1 & -1 & 2 \\ 3 & 2 & 1 \end{vmatrix}$
24. $\begin{vmatrix} 0 & 1 & 2 \\ 3 & -1 & 2 \\ 3 & 2 & -2 \end{vmatrix}$
25. $\begin{vmatrix} 3 & 6 & -3 \\ -1 & -2 & 3 \\ 4 & -1 & 6 \end{vmatrix}$
26. $\begin{vmatrix} 2 & -2 & 1 \\ 4 & 1 & 3 \\ 3 & 1 & 2 \end{vmatrix}$

Use Cramer's rule, if possible, to solve each system of linear equations. See Example 5.

27. $\begin{cases} 3x + z = -1 \\ -x - 3y + z = 7 \\ 3y + z = 5 \end{cases}$

28. $\begin{cases} 4y - 3z = -2 \\ 8x - 4y = 4 \\ -8x + 4y + z = -2 \end{cases}$

29. $\begin{cases} x + y + z = 8 \\ 2x - y - z = 10 \\ x - 2y + 3z = 22 \end{cases}$

30. $\begin{cases} 5x + y + 3z = 1 \\ x - y - 3z = -7 \\ -x + y = 1 \end{cases}$

31. $\begin{cases} 2x + 2y + z = 1 \\ -x + y + 2z = 3 \\ x + 2y + 4z = 0 \end{cases}$

32. $\begin{cases} 2x - 3y + z = 5 \\ x + y + z = 0 \\ 4x + 2y + 4z = 4 \end{cases}$

33. $\begin{cases} x - 2y + z = -5 \\ 3y + 2z = 4 \\ 3x - y = -2 \end{cases}$

34. $\begin{cases} 4x + 5y = 10 \\ 3y + 2z = -6 \\ x + y + z = 3 \end{cases}$

CONCEPT EXTENSIONS

Find the value of x that will make each a true statement.

35. $\begin{vmatrix} 1 & x \\ 2 & 7 \end{vmatrix} = -3$

36. $\begin{vmatrix} 6 & 1 \\ -2 & x \end{vmatrix} = 26$

37. If all the elements in a single row of a determinant are zero, what is the value of the determinant? Explain your answer.

38. If all the elements in a single column of a determinant are 0, what is the value of the determinant? Explain your answer.

5.4 MULTIPLICATIVE INVERSES OF MATRICES

OBJECTIVES

1 Finding the multiplicative inverse of a square matrix.

For the real numbers, we know that 1 is the multiplicative identity because $a \cdot 1 = 1 \cdot a = a$. Is there a similar property for matrix multiplication? That is, is there a matrix I such that $AI = A$ and $IA = A$? The answer is yes. A square matrix with 1s down the main diagonal from upper left to lower right and 0s elsewhere does not change the elements in a matrix in products with that matrix. In the case of 2×2 matrices,

$$\begin{bmatrix} a_{11} & a_{12} \\ a_{21} & a_{22} \end{bmatrix} \begin{bmatrix} 1 & 0 \\ 0 & 1 \end{bmatrix} = \begin{bmatrix} a_{11} & a_{12} \\ a_{21} & a_{22} \end{bmatrix}$$

The elements in the matrix do not change.

and $\begin{bmatrix} 1 & 0 \\ 0 & 1 \end{bmatrix} \begin{bmatrix} a_{11} & a_{12} \\ a_{21} & a_{22} \end{bmatrix} = \begin{bmatrix} a_{11} & a_{12} \\ a_{21} & a_{22} \end{bmatrix}.$

The elements in the matrix do not change.

The $n \times n$ square matrix with 1s down the main diagonal from upper left to lower right and 0s elsewhere is called the **multiplicative identity matrix of order n.** This matrix is designated by I_n. For example,

$$I_2 = \begin{bmatrix} 1 & 0 \\ 0 & 1 \end{bmatrix}, \quad I_3 = \begin{bmatrix} 1 & 0 & 0 \\ 0 & 1 & 0 \\ 0 & 0 & 1 \end{bmatrix},$$

and so on.

OBJECTIVE 1 ▶ Finding the multiplicative inverse of a square matrix. The multiplicative identity matrix, I_n, will help us to define a new concept: the multiplicative inverse of a matrix. To do so, let's consider a similar concept, the multiplicative inverse of a nonzero number, a. Recall that the multiplicative inverse of a is $\frac{1}{a}$. The multiplicative inverse has the following property:

$$a \cdot \frac{1}{a} = 1 \quad \text{and} \quad \frac{1}{a} \cdot a = 1.$$

We can define the multiplicative inverse of a square matrix in a similar manner.

Definition of the Multiplicative Inverse of a Square Matrix

Let A be an $n \times n$ matrix. If there exists an $n \times n$ matrix A^{-1} (read: "A inverse") such that

$$AA^{-1} = I_n \quad \text{and} \quad A^{-1}A = I_n,$$

then A^{-1} is the **multiplicative inverse** of A.

We have seen that matrix multiplication is not commutative. Thus, to show that a matrix B is the multiplicative inverse of the matrix A, find both AB and BA. If B is the multiplicative inverse of A, both products (AB and BA) will be the multiplicative identity matrix, I_n.

EXAMPLE 1 The Multiplicative Inverse of a Matrix

Show that B is the multiplicative inverse of A, where

$$A = \begin{bmatrix} -1 & 3 \\ 2 & -5 \end{bmatrix} \quad \text{and} \quad B = \begin{bmatrix} 5 & 3 \\ 2 & 1 \end{bmatrix}.$$

Solution To show that B is the multiplicative inverse of A, we must find the products AB and BA. If B is the multiplicative inverse of A, then AB will be the multiplicative identity matrix and BA will be the multiplicative identity matrix. Because A and B are 2×2 matrices, $n = 2$. Thus, we denote the multiplicative identity matrix as I_2; it is also a 2×2 matrix. We must show that

- $AB = I_2 = \begin{bmatrix} 1 & 0 \\ 0 & 1 \end{bmatrix}$ and
- $BA = I_2 = \begin{bmatrix} 1 & 0 \\ 0 & 1 \end{bmatrix}.$

Let's first show $AB = I_2$.

$$AB = \begin{bmatrix} -1 & 3 \\ 2 & -5 \end{bmatrix} \begin{bmatrix} 5 & 3 \\ 2 & 1 \end{bmatrix}$$

$$= \begin{bmatrix} -1(5) + 3(2) & -1(3) + 3(1) \\ 2(5) + (-5)(2) & 2(3) + (-5)(1) \end{bmatrix} = \begin{bmatrix} 1 & 0 \\ 0 & 1 \end{bmatrix}$$

Let's now show $BA = I_2$.

$$BA = \begin{bmatrix} 5 & 3 \\ 2 & 1 \end{bmatrix} \begin{bmatrix} -1 & 3 \\ 2 & -5 \end{bmatrix}$$

$$= \begin{bmatrix} 5(-1) + 3(2) & 5(3) + 3(-5) \\ 2(-1) + 1(2) & 2(3) + 1(-5) \end{bmatrix} = \begin{bmatrix} 1 & 0 \\ 0 & 1 \end{bmatrix}$$

Both products give the multiplicative identity matrix. Thus, B is the multiplicative inverse of A and we can designate B as $A^{-1} = \begin{bmatrix} 5 & 3 \\ 2 & 1 \end{bmatrix}$.

Helpful Hint

To find the matrix that appears as the second factor for the inverse of

$$A = \begin{bmatrix} a & b \\ c & d \end{bmatrix}:$$

- Reverse a and d, the numbers in the diagonal from upper left to lower right.
- Negate b and c, the numbers in the other diagonal.

Helpful Hint

When using the formula to find the multiplicative inverse, start by computing $ad - bc$. If the computed value is 0, there is no need to continue. The given matrix is singular—that is, it does not have a multiplicative inverse.

PRACTICE 1 Show that B is the multiplicative inverse of A, where

$$A = \begin{bmatrix} 2 & 1 \\ 1 & 1 \end{bmatrix} \text{ and } B = \begin{bmatrix} 1 & -1 \\ -1 & 2 \end{bmatrix}.$$

It is important to note that only square matrices of order $n \times n$ have multiplicative inverses, but not every square matrix possesses a multiplicative inverse.

A nonsquare matrix, one with a different number of rows than columns, cannot have a multiplicative inverse. If A is an $m \times n$ matrix and B is an $n \times m$ matrix ($n \neq m$), then the products AB and BA are of different orders. This means that they could not be equal to each other, so that AB and BA could not both equal the multiplicative identity matrix.

If a square matrix has a multiplicative inverse, that inverse is unique. This means that the square matrix has no more than one inverse. If a square matrix has a multiplicative inverse, it is said to be **invertible** or **nonsingular**. If a square matrix has no multiplicative inverse, it is called **singular**.

A Formula for Finding the Multiplicative Inverse of a 2 × 2 Matrix

There is a general form of the multiplicative inverse of a 2 × 2 matrix. The following formula enables us to calculate the multiplicative inverse, if there is one:

Multiplicative Inverse of a 2 × 2 Matrix

If $A = \begin{bmatrix} a & b \\ c & d \end{bmatrix}$, then $A^{-1} = \dfrac{1}{ad - bc}\begin{bmatrix} d & -b \\ -c & a \end{bmatrix}$.

The matrix A is invertible if and only if $ad - bc \neq 0$. If $ad - bc = 0$, then A does not have a multiplicative inverse.

TECHNOLOGY NOTE

You can use a graphing utility to find the inverse of the matrix

$$A = \begin{bmatrix} 2 & 1 \\ 5 & 3 \end{bmatrix}.$$

Enter the matrix and name it A. The screens show A and A^{-1}. Verify that this is correct by showing that

$$AA^{-1} = I_2 \text{ and } A^{-1}A = I_2.$$

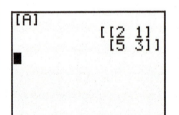

EXAMPLE 2 Using the Quick Method to Find a Multiplicative Inverse

Find the multiplicative inverse of

$$A = \begin{bmatrix} -1 & -2 \\ 3 & 4 \end{bmatrix}.$$

Solution

$$A = \begin{bmatrix} \overset{a}{-1} & \overset{b}{-2} \\ \underset{c}{3} & \underset{d}{4} \end{bmatrix}$$

This is the given matrix. We've designated the elements a, b, c, and d.

$$A^{-1} = \dfrac{1}{ad - bc}\begin{bmatrix} d & -b \\ -c & a \end{bmatrix}$$

This is the formula for the inverse of $\begin{bmatrix} a & b \\ c & d \end{bmatrix}$.

$$= \dfrac{1}{(-1)(4) - (-2)(3)}\begin{bmatrix} 4 & -(-2) \\ -3 & -1 \end{bmatrix}$$

Apply the formula with $a = -1$, $b = -2$, $c = 3$, and $d = 4$.

$$= \dfrac{1}{2}\begin{bmatrix} 4 & 2 \\ -3 & -1 \end{bmatrix}$$

Simplify.

Section 5.4 Multiplicative Inverses of Matrices

$$= \begin{bmatrix} 2 & 1 \\ -\frac{3}{2} & -\frac{1}{2} \end{bmatrix}$$

Perform the scalar multiplication by multiplying each element in the matrix by $\frac{1}{2}$.

The inverse of $A = \begin{bmatrix} -1 & -2 \\ 3 & 4 \end{bmatrix}$ is $A^{-1} = \begin{bmatrix} 2 & 1 \\ -\frac{3}{2} & -\frac{1}{2} \end{bmatrix}$.

We can verify this result by showing that $AA^{-1} = I_2$ and $A^{-1}A = I_2$.

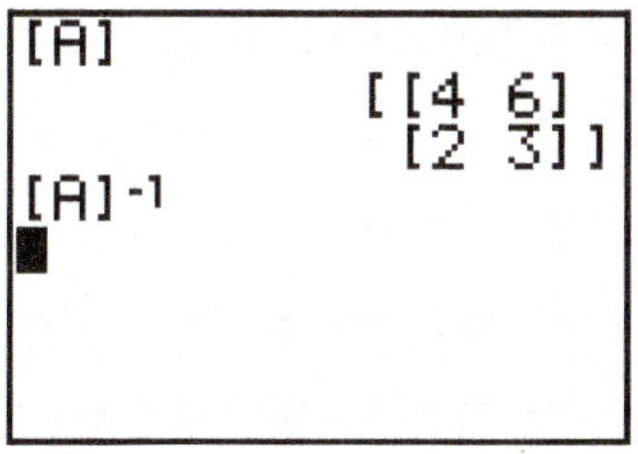

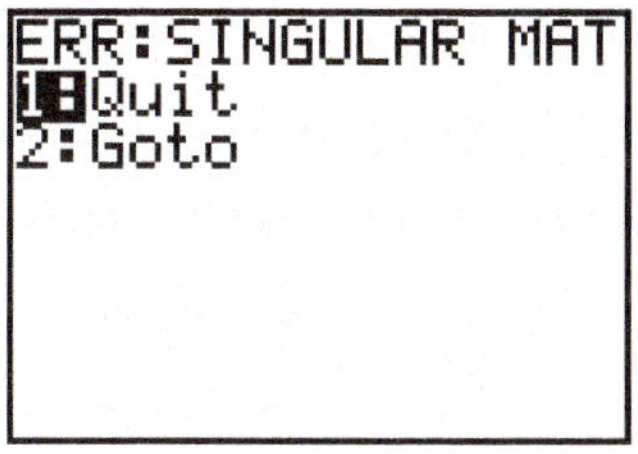

PRACTICE 2 Find the multiplicative inverse of

$$A = \begin{bmatrix} 3 & -2 \\ -1 & 1 \end{bmatrix}.$$

TECHNOLOGY NOTE

The matrix

$$A = \begin{bmatrix} 4 & 6 \\ 2 & 3 \end{bmatrix} = \begin{bmatrix} a & b \\ c & d \end{bmatrix}$$

has no multiplicative inverse because

$ad - bc = 4 \cdot 3 - 6 \cdot 2$
$= 12 - 12 = 0$.

When we try to find the inverse with a graphing utility, an ERROR message occurs, indicating the matrix is singular.

```
[A]
       [[4 6]
        [2 3]]
[A]⁻¹
█
```

```
ERR:SINGULAR MAT
1:Quit
2:Goto
```

In this text, we will use a graphing utility to find multiplicative inverses of $n \times n$ matrices with $n > 2$.

EXAMPLE 3 Finding the Multiplicative Inverse of a 3×3 Matrix

Find the multiplicative inverse of

$$A = \begin{bmatrix} 1 & -1 & 1 \\ 0 & -2 & 1 \\ -2 & -3 & 0 \end{bmatrix}.$$

Solution

We can use a graphing utility to find the inverse matrix. Enter the elements in matrix A and press $\boxed{x^{-1}}$ to display A^{-1}.

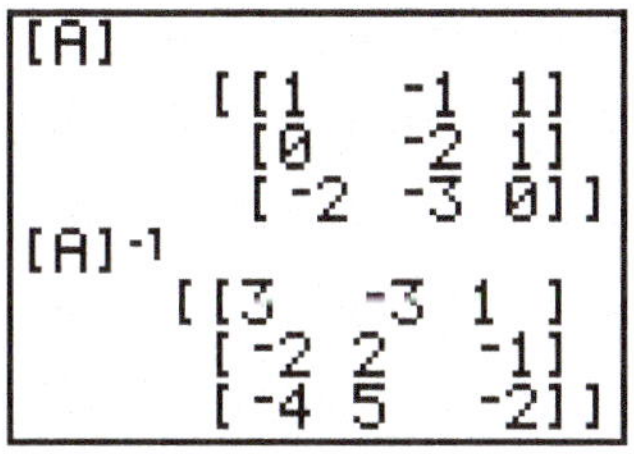

```
[A]
       [[1  -1  1]
        [0  -2  1]
        [-2 -3  0]]
[A]⁻¹
       [[3  -3  1]
        [-2  2  -1]
        [-4  5  -2]]
```

PRACTICE 3 Find the multiplicative inverse of

$$A = \begin{bmatrix} 1 & 0 & 2 \\ -1 & 2 & 3 \\ 1 & -1 & 0 \end{bmatrix}.$$

Summary: Finding Multiplicative Inverses for Invertible Matrices

Use a graphing utility with matrix capabilities, or

a. If the matrix is 2×2: The inverse of $A = \begin{bmatrix} a & b \\ c & d \end{bmatrix}$ is

$$A^{-1} = \frac{1}{ad - bc} \begin{bmatrix} d & -b \\ -c & a \end{bmatrix}.$$

b. If the matrix A is $n \times n$ where $n > 2$: Use a graphing utility.

5.4 EXERCISE SET

In Exercises 1–12, find the products AB and BA to determine whether B is the multiplicative inverse of A.

1. $A = \begin{bmatrix} 4 & -3 \\ -5 & 4 \end{bmatrix}$, $B = \begin{bmatrix} 4 & 3 \\ 5 & 4 \end{bmatrix}$

2. $A = \begin{bmatrix} -2 & -1 \\ -1 & 1 \end{bmatrix}$, $B = \begin{bmatrix} 1 & 1 \\ 1 & 2 \end{bmatrix}$

3. $A = \begin{bmatrix} -4 & 0 \\ 1 & 3 \end{bmatrix}$, $B = \begin{bmatrix} -2 & 4 \\ 0 & 1 \end{bmatrix}$

4. $A = \begin{bmatrix} -2 & 4 \\ 1 & -2 \end{bmatrix}$, $B = \begin{bmatrix} 1 & 2 \\ -1 & -2 \end{bmatrix}$

5. $A = \begin{bmatrix} -2 & 1 \\ \frac{3}{2} & -\frac{1}{2} \end{bmatrix}$, $B = \begin{bmatrix} 1 & 2 \\ 3 & 4 \end{bmatrix}$

6. $A = \begin{bmatrix} 4 & 5 \\ 2 & 3 \end{bmatrix}$, $B = \begin{bmatrix} \frac{3}{2} & -\frac{5}{2} \\ -1 & 2 \end{bmatrix}$

7. $A = \begin{bmatrix} 0 & 1 & 0 \\ 0 & 0 & 1 \\ 1 & 0 & 0 \end{bmatrix}$, $B = \begin{bmatrix} 0 & 0 & 1 \\ 1 & 0 & 0 \\ 0 & 1 & 0 \end{bmatrix}$

8. $A = \begin{bmatrix} -2 & 1 & -1 \\ -5 & 2 & -1 \\ 3 & -1 & 1 \end{bmatrix}$, $B = \begin{bmatrix} 1 & 0 & 1 \\ 2 & 1 & 3 \\ -1 & 1 & 1 \end{bmatrix}$

9. $A = \begin{bmatrix} 1 & 2 & 3 \\ 1 & 3 & 4 \\ 1 & 4 & 3 \end{bmatrix}$, $B = \begin{bmatrix} \frac{7}{2} & -3 & \frac{1}{2} \\ -\frac{1}{2} & 0 & \frac{1}{2} \\ -\frac{1}{2} & 1 & -\frac{1}{2} \end{bmatrix}$

10. $A = \begin{bmatrix} 0 & 2 & 0 \\ 3 & 3 & 2 \\ 2 & 5 & 1 \end{bmatrix}$, $B = \begin{bmatrix} -3.5 & -1 & 2 \\ 0.5 & 0 & 0 \\ 4.5 & 2 & -3 \end{bmatrix}$

11. $A = \begin{bmatrix} 0 & 0 & -2 & 1 \\ -1 & 0 & 1 & 1 \\ 0 & 1 & -1 & 0 \\ 1 & 0 & 0 & -1 \end{bmatrix}$, $B = \begin{bmatrix} 1 & 2 & 0 & 3 \\ 0 & 1 & 1 & 1 \\ 0 & 1 & 0 & 1 \\ 1 & 2 & 0 & 2 \end{bmatrix}$

12. $A = \begin{bmatrix} 1 & -2 & 1 & 0 \\ 0 & 1 & -2 & 1 \\ 0 & 0 & 1 & -2 \\ 0 & 0 & 0 & 1 \end{bmatrix}$, $B = \begin{bmatrix} 1 & 2 & 3 & 4 \\ 0 & 1 & 2 & 3 \\ 0 & 0 & 1 & 2 \\ 0 & 0 & 0 & 1 \end{bmatrix}$

In Exercises 13–18, use the fact that if $A = \begin{bmatrix} a & b \\ c & d \end{bmatrix}$, then

$A^{-1} = \dfrac{1}{ad-bc} \begin{bmatrix} d & -b \\ -c & a \end{bmatrix}$ *to find the inverse of each matrix, if possible. Check that $AA^{-1} = I_2$ and $A^{-1}A = I_2$.*

13. $A = \begin{bmatrix} 2 & 3 \\ -1 & 2 \end{bmatrix}$

14. $A = \begin{bmatrix} 0 & 3 \\ 4 & -2 \end{bmatrix}$

15. $A = \begin{bmatrix} 3 & -1 \\ -4 & 2 \end{bmatrix}$

16. $A = \begin{bmatrix} 2 & -6 \\ 1 & -2 \end{bmatrix}$

17. $A = \begin{bmatrix} 10 & -2 \\ -5 & 1 \end{bmatrix}$

18. $A = \begin{bmatrix} 6 & -3 \\ -2 & 1 \end{bmatrix}$

In Exercises 19–28, use a graphing utility to find A^{-1}.

19. $A = \begin{bmatrix} 2 & 0 & 0 \\ 0 & 4 & 0 \\ 0 & 0 & 6 \end{bmatrix}$

20. $A = \begin{bmatrix} 3 & 0 & 0 \\ 0 & 6 & 0 \\ 0 & 0 & 9 \end{bmatrix}$

21. $A = \begin{bmatrix} 1 & 2 & -1 \\ -2 & 0 & 1 \\ 1 & -1 & 0 \end{bmatrix}$

22. $A = \begin{bmatrix} 1 & -1 & 1 \\ 0 & 2 & -1 \\ 2 & 3 & 0 \end{bmatrix}$

23. $A = \begin{bmatrix} 2 & 2 & -1 \\ 0 & 3 & -1 \\ -1 & -2 & 1 \end{bmatrix}$

24. $A = \begin{bmatrix} 2 & 4 & -4 \\ 1 & 3 & -4 \\ 2 & 4 & -3 \end{bmatrix}$

25. $A = \begin{bmatrix} 5 & 0 & 2 \\ 2 & 2 & 1 \\ -3 & 1 & -1 \end{bmatrix}$

26. $A = \begin{bmatrix} 3 & 2 & 6 \\ 1 & 1 & 2 \\ 2 & 2 & 5 \end{bmatrix}$

27. $A = \begin{bmatrix} 1 & 0 & 0 & 0 \\ 0 & -1 & 0 & 0 \\ 0 & 0 & 3 & 0 \\ 1 & 0 & 0 & 1 \end{bmatrix}$

28. $A = \begin{bmatrix} 2 & 0 & 0 & 1 \\ 0 & 1 & 0 & 0 \\ 0 & 0 & -1 & 0 \\ 0 & 0 & 0 & 2 \end{bmatrix}$

In Exercises 29–30, find $(AB)^{-1}$, $A^{-1}B^{-1}$, and $B^{-1}A^{-1}$. What do you observe?

29. $A = \begin{bmatrix} 2 & 1 \\ 3 & 1 \end{bmatrix}$ $B = \begin{bmatrix} 4 & 7 \\ 1 & 2 \end{bmatrix}$

30. $A = \begin{bmatrix} 2 & -9 \\ 1 & -4 \end{bmatrix}$ $B = \begin{bmatrix} 9 & 5 \\ 7 & 4 \end{bmatrix}$

31. What is the multiplicative identity matrix?

32. If you are given two matrices, A and B, explain how to determine if B is the multiplicative inverse of A.

33. Explain how to find the multiplicative inverse for a 2×2 invertible matrix.

True or False. *In Exercises 34–38, determine whether each statement is true or false. If the statement is false, make the necessary change(s) to produce a true statement.*

34. All square 2×2 matrices have inverses because there is a formula for finding these inverses.

35. $(AB)^{-1} = A^{-1}B^{-1}$, assuming A, B, and AB are invertible.

36. $(A + B)^{-1} = A^{-1} + B^{-1}$, assuming A, B, and $A + B$ are invertible.

37. Two 2×2 invertible matrices can have a matrix sum that is not invertible.

38. $\begin{bmatrix} 1 & -3 \\ -1 & 3 \end{bmatrix}$ is an invertible matrix.

39. Give an example of a 2×2 matrix that is its own inverse.

40. If $A = \begin{bmatrix} 3 & 5 \\ 2 & 4 \end{bmatrix}$, find $(A^{-1})^{-1}$.

41. Find values of a for which the following matrix is not invertible:

$\begin{bmatrix} 1 & a+1 \\ a-2 & 4 \end{bmatrix}$.

REVIEW AND PREVIEW

Simplify the expression in each exercise. (See Section 1.3.)

42. $2(-5) - (-3)(4)$

43. $\dfrac{2(-5) - 1(-4)}{5(-5) - 6(-4)}$

44. $2(-30 - (-3)) - 3(6 - 9) + (-1)(1 - 15)$

5.5 MATRIX EQUATIONS

OBJECTIVES

1. Use inverses to solve matrix equations.
2. Encode and decode messages.

In 1939, Britain's secret service hired top chess players, mathematicians, and other masters of logic to break enemy code. The project, which employed over 10,000 people, broke the code less than a year later.

Messages must often be sent in such a way that the real meaning is hidden from everyone but the sender and the recipient. In this section, we will look at the role that matrices and their inverses play in this process.

This 1941 RCA radiogram shows an encoded message.

Solving Systems of Equations Using Multiplicative Inverses of Matrices

Matrix multiplication can be used to represent a system of linear equations.

Linear System	Matrix Form of the System
$\begin{cases} a_1 x + b_1 y + c_1 z = d_1 \\ a_2 x + b_2 y + c_2 z = d_2 \\ a_3 x + b_3 y + c_3 z = d_3 \end{cases}$	$\begin{bmatrix} a_1 & b_1 & c_1 \\ a_2 & b_2 & c_2 \\ a_3 & b_3 & c_3 \end{bmatrix} \begin{bmatrix} x \\ y \\ z \end{bmatrix} = \begin{bmatrix} d_1 \\ d_2 \\ d_3 \end{bmatrix}$
	The matrix contains the system's coefficients. — The matrix contains the system's variables. — The matrix contains the system's constants.

You can work with the matrix form of the system and obtain the form of the linear system on the left. To do so, perform the matrix multiplication on the left side of the matrix equation. Then equate the corresponding elements.

The matrix equation

$$\underbrace{\begin{bmatrix} a_1 & b_1 & c_1 \\ a_2 & b_2 & c_2 \\ a_3 & b_3 & c_3 \end{bmatrix}}_{A} \underbrace{\begin{bmatrix} x \\ y \\ z \end{bmatrix}}_{X} = \underbrace{\begin{bmatrix} d_1 \\ d_2 \\ d_3 \end{bmatrix}}_{B}$$

is abbreviated as $AX = B$, where A is the **coefficient matrix** of the system, and X and B are matrices containing one column, called **column matrices**. The matrix B is called the **constant matrix.**

Here is a specific example of a linear system and its matrix form:

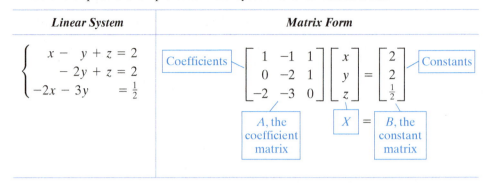

The matrix equation $AX = B$ can be solved using A^{-1} if it exists.

$AX = B$ This is the matrix equation.

$A^{-1}AX = A^{-1}B$ Multiply both sides by A^{-1}. Because matrix multiplication is not commutative, put A^{-1} in the same left position on both sides.

$I_n X = A^{-1}B$ The multiplicative inverse property tells us that $A^{-1}A = I_n$.

$X = A^{-1}B$ Because I_n is the multiplicative identity, $I_n X = X$.

We see that if $AX = B$, then $X = A^{-1}B$.

OBJECTIVE 1 ▶ **Use inverses to solve matrix equations.**

Solving a System Using A^{-1}

If $AX = B$ has a unique solution, then $X = A^{-1}B$. To solve a linear system of equations, multiply A^{-1} and B to find X.

EXAMPLE 1   Using the Inverse of a Matrix to Solve a System

Solve the system by using A^{-1}, the inverse of the coefficient matrix:

$$\begin{cases} x - y + z = 2 \\ - 2y + z = 2 \\ -2x - 3y = \tfrac{1}{2}. \end{cases}$$

Solution   The linear system can be written as

$$\underbrace{\begin{bmatrix} 1 & -1 & 1 \\ 0 & -2 & 1 \\ -2 & -3 & 0 \end{bmatrix}}_{A} \underbrace{\begin{bmatrix} x \\ y \\ z \end{bmatrix}}_{X} = \underbrace{\begin{bmatrix} 2 \\ 2 \\ \tfrac{1}{2} \end{bmatrix}}_{B}.$$

The solution is given by $X = A^{-1}B$. Consequently, we must find A^{-1}. We found the inverse of matrix A in Section 5.4. Using this result,

$$X = A^{-1}B = \begin{bmatrix} 3 & -3 & 1 \\ -2 & 2 & -1 \\ -4 & 5 & -2 \end{bmatrix} \begin{bmatrix} 2 \\ 2 \\ \tfrac{1}{2} \end{bmatrix} = \begin{bmatrix} 3 \cdot 2 + (-3) \cdot 2 + 1 \cdot \tfrac{1}{2} \\ -2 \cdot 2 + 2 \cdot 2 + (-1) \cdot \tfrac{1}{2} \\ -4 \cdot 2 + 5 \cdot 2 + (-2) \cdot \tfrac{1}{2} \end{bmatrix} = \begin{bmatrix} \tfrac{1}{2} \\ -\tfrac{1}{2} \\ 1 \end{bmatrix}.$$

Thus, $x = \tfrac{1}{2}$, $y = -\tfrac{1}{2}$, and $z = 1$. The solution is $\left(\tfrac{1}{2}, -\tfrac{1}{2}, 1\right)$.

TECHNOLOGY NOTE

We can use a graphing utility to solve a linear system with a unique solution by entering the elements in A, the coefficient matrix, and B, the column matrix. Then find the product of A^{-1} and B. The screen below verifies our solution in Example 1.

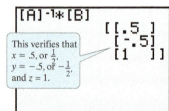

This verifies that $x = .5$, or $\tfrac{1}{2}$, $y = -.5$, or $-\tfrac{1}{2}$, and $z = 1$.

PRACTICE

1 Solve the system by using A^{-1}, the inverse of the coefficient matrix that you found in Practice 3; Section 5.4.

$$\begin{cases} x + 2z = 6 \\ -x + 2y + 3z = -5 \\ x - y = 6. \end{cases}$$

OBJECTIVE 2 ▸ Encode and decode messages. A **cryptogram** is a message written so that no one other than the intended recipient can understand it. To encode a message, we begin by assigning a number to each letter in the alphabet: $A = 1, B = 2, C = 3, \ldots,$ $Z = 26$, and a space $= 0$. For example, the numerical equivalent of the word MATH is 13, 1, 20, 8. The numerical equivalent of the message is then converted into a matrix. Finally, an invertible matrix can be used to convert the message into code. The multiplicative inverse of this matrix can be used to decode the message.

Encoding a Word or Message

1. Express the word or message numerically.
2. List the numbers in step 1 by columns and form a square matrix. If you do not have enough numbers to form a square matrix, put zeros in any remaining spaces in the last column.
3. Select any square invertible matrix, called the **coding matrix,** the same size as the matrix in step 2. Multiply the coding matrix by the square matrix that expresses the message numerically. The resulting matrix is the **coded matrix.**
4. Use the numbers, by columns, from the coded matrix in step 3 to write the encoded message.

EXAMPLE 2 Encoding a Word

Use matrices to encode the word MATH.

Solution

Step 1 Express the word numerically. As shown previously, the numerical equivalent of MATH is 13, 1, 20, 8.

Step 2 List the numbers in step 1 by columns and form a square matrix. The 2×2 matrix for the numerical equivalent of MATH, 13, 1, 20, 8, is

$$\begin{bmatrix} 13 & 20 \\ 1 & 8 \end{bmatrix}.$$

Step 3 Multiply the matrix in step 2 by a square invertible matrix of your choice.

We will use $\begin{bmatrix} -2 & -3 \\ 3 & 4 \end{bmatrix}$ as the coding matrix.

$$\underbrace{\begin{bmatrix} -2 & -3 \\ 3 & 4 \end{bmatrix}}_{\text{Coding matrix}} \underbrace{\begin{bmatrix} 13 & 20 \\ 1 & 8 \end{bmatrix}}_{\substack{\text{Numerical} \\ \text{representation of} \\ \text{MATH}}} = \begin{bmatrix} -2(13) - 3(1) & -2(20) - 3(8) \\ 3(13) + 4(1) & 3(20) + 4(8) \end{bmatrix}$$

$$= \underbrace{\begin{bmatrix} -29 & -64 \\ 43 & 92 \end{bmatrix}}_{\text{Coded matrix}}$$

Step 4 **Use the numbers, by columns, from the coded matrix in step 3 to write the encoded message.** The encoded message is $-29, 43, -64, 92$.

PRACTICE 2 Use the coding matrix in Example 2, $\begin{bmatrix} -2 & -3 \\ 3 & 4 \end{bmatrix}$, to encode the word BASE.

The inverse of a coding matrix can be used to decode a word or message that was encoded.

> **Decoding a Word or Message That Was Encoded**
> 1. Find the multiplicative inverse of the coding matrix.
> 2. Multiply the multiplicative inverse of the coding matrix and the coded matrix.
> 3. Express the numbers, by columns, from the matrix in step 2 as letters.

EXAMPLE 3   Decoding a Word

Decode $-29, 43, -64, 92$ from Example 2.

Solution

Step 1 **Find the inverse of the coding matrix.** The coding matrix in Example 2 was $\begin{bmatrix} -2 & -3 \\ 3 & 4 \end{bmatrix}$. We use the formula for the multiplicative inverse of a 2×2 matrix to find the multiplicative inverse of this matrix. It is $\begin{bmatrix} 4 & 3 \\ -3 & -2 \end{bmatrix}$.

Step 2 **Multiply the multiplicative inverse of the coding matrix and the coded matrix.**

$$\underbrace{\begin{bmatrix} 4 & 3 \\ -3 & -2 \end{bmatrix}}_{\text{Multiplicative inverse of the coding matrix}} \underbrace{\begin{bmatrix} -29 & -64 \\ 43 & 92 \end{bmatrix}}_{\text{Coded matrix}} = \begin{bmatrix} 4(-29) + 3(43) & 4(-64) + 3(92) \\ -3(-29) - 2(43) & -3(-64) - 2(92) \end{bmatrix}$$

$$= \begin{bmatrix} 13 & 20 \\ 1 & 8 \end{bmatrix}$$

Step 3 **Express the numbers, by columns, from the matrix in step 2 as letters.** The numbers are $13, 1, 20$, and 8. Using letters, the decoded message is MATH.

PRACTICE 3 Decode the word that you encoded in Practice 2.

Decoding is simple for an authorized receiver who knows the coding matrix. Because any invertible matrix can be used for the coding matrix, decoding a cryptogram for an unauthorized receiver who does not know this matrix is extremely difficult.

5.5 EXERCISE SET

In Exercises 1–4, write each linear system as a matrix equation in the form $AX = B$, where A is the coefficient matrix and B is the constant matrix.

1. $\begin{cases} 6x + 5y = 13 \\ 5x + 4y = 10 \end{cases}$

2. $\begin{cases} 7x + 5y = 23 \\ 3x + 2y = 10 \end{cases}$

3. $\begin{cases} x + 3y + 4z = -3 \\ x + 2y + 3z = -2 \\ x + 4y + 3z = -6 \end{cases}$

4. $\begin{cases} x + 4y - z = 3 \\ x + 3y - 2z = 5 \\ 2x + 7y - 5z = 12 \end{cases}$

In Exercises 5–8, write each matrix equation as a system of linear equations without matrices.

5. $\begin{bmatrix} 4 & -7 \\ 2 & -3 \end{bmatrix} \begin{bmatrix} x \\ y \end{bmatrix} = \begin{bmatrix} -3 \\ 1 \end{bmatrix}$

6. $\begin{bmatrix} 3 & 0 \\ -3 & 1 \end{bmatrix} \begin{bmatrix} x \\ y \end{bmatrix} = \begin{bmatrix} 6 \\ -7 \end{bmatrix}$

7. $\begin{bmatrix} 2 & 0 & -1 \\ 0 & 3 & 0 \\ 1 & 1 & 0 \end{bmatrix} \begin{bmatrix} x \\ y \\ z \end{bmatrix} = \begin{bmatrix} 6 \\ 9 \\ 5 \end{bmatrix}$

8. $\begin{bmatrix} -1 & 0 & 1 \\ 0 & -1 & 0 \\ 0 & 1 & 1 \end{bmatrix} \begin{bmatrix} x \\ y \\ z \end{bmatrix} = \begin{bmatrix} -4 \\ 2 \\ 4 \end{bmatrix}$

In Exercises 9–14,

   a. *Write each linear system as a matrix equation in the form $AX = B$.*

   b. *Solve the system using the inverse that is given for the coefficient matrix.*

9. $\begin{cases} 2x + 6y + 6z = 8 \\ 2x + 7y + 6z = 10 \\ 2x + 7y + 7z = 9 \end{cases}$ The inverse of $\begin{bmatrix} 2 & 6 & 6 \\ 2 & 7 & 6 \\ 2 & 7 & 7 \end{bmatrix}$ is $\begin{bmatrix} \frac{7}{2} & 0 & -3 \\ -1 & 1 & 0 \\ 0 & -1 & 1 \end{bmatrix}$.

10. $\begin{cases} x + 2y + 5z = 2 \\ 2x + 3y + 8z = 3 \\ -x + y + 2z = 3 \end{cases}$ The inverse of $\begin{bmatrix} 1 & 2 & 5 \\ 2 & 3 & 8 \\ -1 & 1 & 2 \end{bmatrix}$ is $\begin{bmatrix} 2 & -1 & -1 \\ 12 & -7 & -2 \\ -5 & 3 & 1 \end{bmatrix}$.

11. $\begin{cases} x - y + z = 8 \\ 2y - z = -7 \\ 2x + 3y = 1 \end{cases}$ The inverse of $\begin{bmatrix} 1 & -1 & 1 \\ 0 & 2 & -1 \\ 2 & 3 & 0 \end{bmatrix}$ is $\begin{bmatrix} 3 & 3 & -1 \\ -2 & -2 & 1 \\ -4 & -5 & 2 \end{bmatrix}$.

12. $\begin{cases} x - 6y + 3z = 11 \\ 2x - 7y + 3z = 14 \\ 4x - 12y + 5z = 25 \end{cases}$ The inverse of $\begin{bmatrix} 1 & -6 & 3 \\ 2 & -7 & 3 \\ 4 & -12 & 5 \end{bmatrix}$ is $\begin{bmatrix} 1 & -6 & 3 \\ 2 & -7 & 3 \\ 4 & -12 & 5 \end{bmatrix}$.

13. $\begin{cases} w - x + 2y = -3 \\ x - y + z = 4 \\ -w + x - y + 2z = 2 \\ -x + y - 2z = -4 \end{cases}$

The inverse of $\begin{bmatrix} 1 & -1 & 2 & 0 \\ 0 & 1 & -1 & 1 \\ -1 & 1 & -1 & 2 \\ 0 & -1 & 1 & -2 \end{bmatrix}$ is $\begin{bmatrix} 0 & 0 & -1 & -1 \\ 1 & 4 & 1 & 3 \\ 1 & 2 & 1 & 2 \\ 0 & -1 & 0 & -1 \end{bmatrix}$.

14. $\begin{cases} 2w + y + z = 6 \\ 3w + z = 9 \\ -w + x - 2y + z = 4 \\ 4w - x + y = 6 \end{cases}$

The inverse of $\begin{bmatrix} 2 & 0 & 1 & 1 \\ 3 & 0 & 0 & 1 \\ -1 & 1 & -2 & 1 \\ 4 & -1 & 1 & 0 \end{bmatrix}$ is $\begin{bmatrix} -1 & 2 & -1 & -1 \\ -4 & 9 & -5 & -6 \\ 0 & 1 & -1 & -1 \\ 3 & -5 & 3 & 3 \end{bmatrix}$.

In Exercises 15–16, use the coding matrix

$$A = \begin{bmatrix} 4 & -1 \\ -3 & 1 \end{bmatrix} \text{ and its inverse } A^{-1} = \begin{bmatrix} 1 & 1 \\ 3 & 4 \end{bmatrix}$$

to encode and then decode the given message.

15. HELP   **16.** LOVE

In Exercises 17–18, use the coding matrix

$$A = \begin{bmatrix} 1 & -1 & 0 \\ 3 & 0 & 2 \\ -1 & 0 & -1 \end{bmatrix} \text{ and its inverse}$$

$$A^{-1} = \begin{bmatrix} 0 & 1 & 2 \\ -1 & 1 & 2 \\ 0 & -1 & -3 \end{bmatrix} \text{ to write a cryptogram for each}$$

message. Check your result by decoding the cryptogram.

17. S E N D _ C A S H
19 5 14 4 0 3 1 19 8

Use $\begin{bmatrix} 19 & 4 & 1 \\ 5 & 0 & 19 \\ 14 & 3 & 8 \end{bmatrix}$.

18. S T A Y _ W E L L
19 20 1 25 0 23 5 12 12

Use $\begin{bmatrix} 19 & 25 & 5 \\ 20 & 0 & 12 \\ 1 & 23 & 12 \end{bmatrix}$.

19. Explain how to write a linear system of three equations in three variables as a matrix equation.

20. Explain how to solve the matrix equation $AX = B$.

In Exercises 21–26, use a graphing utility to find the multiplicative inverse of each matrix. Check that the displayed inverse is correct.

21. $\begin{bmatrix} 3 & -1 \\ -2 & 1 \end{bmatrix}$ 22. $\begin{bmatrix} -4 & 1 \\ 6 & -2 \end{bmatrix}$

23. $\begin{bmatrix} -2 & 1 & -1 \\ -5 & 2 & -1 \\ 3 & -1 & 1 \end{bmatrix}$ 24. $\begin{bmatrix} 1 & 1 & -1 \\ -3 & 2 & -1 \\ 3 & -3 & 2 \end{bmatrix}$

25. $\begin{bmatrix} 7 & -3 & 0 & 2 \\ -2 & 1 & 0 & -1 \\ 4 & 0 & 1 & -2 \\ -1 & 1 & 0 & -1 \end{bmatrix}$ 26. $\begin{bmatrix} 1 & 2 & 0 & 0 \\ 0 & 0 & 1 & 0 \\ 1 & 3 & 0 & 1 \\ 4 & 0 & 0 & 2 \end{bmatrix}$

In Exercises 27–32, write each system in the form $AX = B$. Then solve the system by entering A and B into your graphing utility and computing $A^{-1}B$.

27. $\begin{cases} x - y + z = -6 \\ 4x + 2y + z = 9 \\ 4x - 2y + z = -3 \end{cases}$ 28. $\begin{cases} y + 2z = 0 \\ -x + y = 1 \\ 2x - y + z = -1 \end{cases}$

29. $\begin{cases} 3x - 2y + z = -2 \\ 4x - 5y + 3z = -9 \\ 2x - y + 5z = -5 \end{cases}$ 30. $\begin{cases} x - y = 1 \\ 6x + y + 20z = 14 \\ y + 3z = 1 \end{cases}$

31. $\begin{cases} v - 3x + z = -3 \\ w + y = -1 \\ x + z = 7 \\ v + w - x + 4y = -8 \\ v + w + x + y + z = 8 \end{cases}$

32. $\begin{cases} w + x + y + z = 4 \\ w + 3x - 2y + 2z = 7 \\ 2w + 2x + y + z = 3 \\ w - x + 2y + 3z = 5 \end{cases}$

In Exercises 33–34, use a coding matrix A of your choice. Use a graphing utility to find the multiplicative inverse of your coding matrix. Write a cryptogram for each message. Check your result by decoding the cryptogram. Use your graphing utility to perform all necessary matrix multiplications.

33. A R R I V E D _ S A F E L Y
    1 18 18 9 22 5 4 0 19 1 6 5 12 25

34. A R T _ E N R I C H E S
    1 18 20 0 5 14 18 9 3 8 5 19

GROUP EXERCISE

35. Each person in the group should work with one partner. Send a coded word or message to each other by giving your partner the coded matrix and the coding matrix that you selected. Once messages are sent, each person should decode the message received.

CHAPTER 5 VOCABULARY CHECK

Fill in each blank with one of the words or phrases below. Not all words or phrases will be used.

nonsingular   cryptogram   square   columns
scalar   rows   Cramer's rule   equal
determinant   singular   invertible   multiplicative inverse
$A^{-1}B$ BA^{-1}

1. To multiply two matrices, the number of columns of the first matrix must equal the number of _____ of the second matrix.
2. If a square matrix has no multiplicative inverse, it is called _____.
3. A matrix with the same number of rows and columns is called a _____ matrix.
4. A _____ is a message written so that no one other than the intended recipient can understand it.
5. A _____ is a real number associated with a square matrix.
6. The notation A^{-1} represents the _____ of A.
7. If a square matrix has a multiplicative inverse, it is called _____ or _____.
8. Two matrices are _____ if they have the same order and corresponding elements are equal.
9. A method for solving systems of equations using determinants is called _____.
10. When working with matrices, we call a number, such as 5, a _____.
11. If $AX = B$, then $X = $ _____.

CHAPTER 5 REVIEW

(5.1 and 5.2) *(Section 5.2 starts with Exercise 9.)*

1. Find values for x, y, and z so that the following matrices are equal:

$$\begin{bmatrix} 2x & y+7 \\ z & 4 \end{bmatrix} = \begin{bmatrix} -10 & 13 \\ 6 & 4 \end{bmatrix}.$$

In Exercises 2–15, perform the indicated matrix operations given that A, B, C, and D are defined as follows. If an operation is not defined, state the reason.

$$A = \begin{bmatrix} 2 & -1 & 2 \\ 5 & 3 & -1 \end{bmatrix} \quad B = \begin{bmatrix} 0 & -2 \\ 3 & 2 \\ 1 & -5 \end{bmatrix}$$

$$C = \begin{bmatrix} 1 & 2 & 3 \\ -1 & 1 & 2 \\ -1 & 2 & 1 \end{bmatrix} \quad D = \begin{bmatrix} -2 & 3 & 1 \\ 3 & -2 & 4 \end{bmatrix}$$

2. $A + D$
3. $2B$
4. $D - A$
5. $B + C$
6. $3A + 2D$
7. $-2A + 4D$
8. $-5(A + D)$
9. AB
10. BA
11. BD
12. DB
13. $AB - BA$
14. $(A - D)C$
15. $B(AC)$

16. Solve for X in the matrix equation

$$3X + A = B,$$

where $A = \begin{bmatrix} 4 & 6 \\ -5 & 0 \end{bmatrix}$ and $B = \begin{bmatrix} -2 & -12 \\ 4 & 1 \end{bmatrix}.$

In Exercises 17–18, use nine pixels in a 3 × 3 grid and the color levels shown.

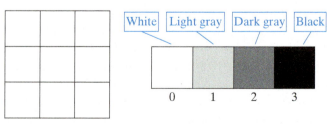

17. Write a 3 × 3 matrix that represents a digital photograph of the letter T in dark gray on a light gray background.

18. Find a matrix B so that $A + B$ increases the contrast of the letter T by changing the dark gray to black and the light gray to white.

The figure shows a right triangle in a rectangular coordinate system.

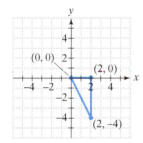

The figure can be represented by the matrix

$$B = \begin{bmatrix} 0 & 2 & 2 \\ 0 & 0 & -4 \end{bmatrix}.$$

Use the triangle and the matrix that represents it to solve Exercises 19–20.

19. Use matrix operations to move the triangle 2 units to the left and 1 unit up. Then graph the triangle and its transformation in a rectangular coordinate system.

20. Use matrix operations to reduce the triangle to half its perimeter and move the reduced image 2 units down. Then graph the triangle and its transformation in a rectangular coordinate system.

In Exercises 21–24, find AB and graph the resulting image. What effect does the multiplication have on the triangle represented by matrix B?

21. $A = \begin{bmatrix} 1 & 0 \\ 0 & -1 \end{bmatrix}$

22. $A = \begin{bmatrix} -1 & 0 \\ 0 & 1 \end{bmatrix}$

23. $A = \begin{bmatrix} 0 & -1 \\ 1 & 0 \end{bmatrix}$

24. $A = \begin{bmatrix} 2 & 0 \\ 0 & 1 \end{bmatrix}$

(5.3) In Exercises 25–28, evaluate each determinant.

25. $\begin{vmatrix} 3 & 2 \\ -1 & 5 \end{vmatrix}$

26. $\begin{vmatrix} -2 & -3 \\ -4 & -8 \end{vmatrix}$

27. $\begin{vmatrix} 2 & 4 & -3 \\ 1 & -1 & 5 \\ -2 & 4 & 0 \end{vmatrix}$

28. $\begin{vmatrix} 4 & 7 & 0 \\ -5 & 6 & 0 \\ 3 & 2 & -4 \end{vmatrix}$

In Exercises 29–32, use Cramer's rule to solve each system.

29. $\begin{cases} x - 2y = 8 \\ 3x + 2y = -1 \end{cases}$

30. $\begin{cases} 7x + 2y = 0 \\ 2x + y = -3 \end{cases}$

31. $\begin{cases} x + 2y + 2z = 5 \\ 2x + 4y + 7z = 19 \\ -2x - 5y - 2z = 8 \end{cases}$

32. $\begin{cases} 2x + y = -4 \\ y - 2z = 0 \\ 3x - 2z = -11 \end{cases}$

(5.4) In Exercises 33–34, find the products AB and BA to determine whether B is the multiplicative inverse of A.

33. $A = \begin{bmatrix} 2 & 7 \\ 1 & 4 \end{bmatrix}$, $B = \begin{bmatrix} 4 & -7 \\ -1 & 3 \end{bmatrix}$

34. $A = \begin{bmatrix} 1 & 0 & 0 \\ 0 & 2 & -7 \\ 0 & -1 & 4 \end{bmatrix}$, $B = \begin{bmatrix} 1 & 0 & 0 \\ 0 & 4 & 7 \\ 0 & 1 & 2 \end{bmatrix}$

In Exercises 35–38, find A^{-1}. Check that $AA^{-1} = I$ and $A^{-1}A = I$.

35. $A = \begin{bmatrix} 1 & -1 \\ -2 & 3 \end{bmatrix}$

36. $A = \begin{bmatrix} 0 & 1 \\ 5 & 3 \end{bmatrix}$

37. $A = \begin{bmatrix} 1 & 0 & -2 \\ 2 & 1 & 0 \\ 1 & 0 & -3 \end{bmatrix}$

38. $A = \begin{bmatrix} 1 & 3 & -2 \\ 4 & 13 & -7 \\ 5 & 16 & -8 \end{bmatrix}$

(5.5) In Exercises 39–40,

  a. *Write each linear system as a matrix equation in the form $AX = B$.*

  b. *Solve the system using the inverse that is given for the coefficient matrix.*

39. $\begin{cases} x + y + 2z = 7 \\ y + 3z = -2 \\ 3x - 2z = 0 \end{cases}$ The inverse of $\begin{bmatrix} 1 & 1 & 2 \\ 0 & 1 & 3 \\ 3 & 0 & -2 \end{bmatrix}$ is $\begin{bmatrix} -2 & 2 & 1 \\ 9 & -8 & -3 \\ -3 & 3 & 1 \end{bmatrix}$.

40. $\begin{cases} x - y + 2z = 12 \\ y - z = -5 \\ x + 2z = 10 \end{cases}$ The inverse of $\begin{bmatrix} 1 & -1 & 2 \\ 0 & 1 & -1 \\ 1 & 0 & 2 \end{bmatrix}$ is $\begin{bmatrix} 2 & 2 & -1 \\ -1 & 0 & 1 \\ -1 & -1 & 1 \end{bmatrix}$.

41. Use the coding matrix $A = \begin{bmatrix} 3 & 2 \\ 4 & 3 \end{bmatrix}$ and its inverse $A^{-1} = \begin{bmatrix} 3 & -2 \\ -4 & 3 \end{bmatrix}$ to encode and then decode the word RULE.

CHAPTER 5 TEST

 Remember to use the Chapter Test Prep Videos to see the fully worked-out solutions to any of the exercises you want to review.

In Exercises 1–4, let

$$A = \begin{bmatrix} 3 & 1 \\ 1 & 0 \\ 2 & 1 \end{bmatrix}, \quad B = \begin{bmatrix} 1 & -1 \\ 2 & 1 \end{bmatrix}, \quad \text{and} \quad C = \begin{bmatrix} 1 & 2 \\ -1 & 3 \end{bmatrix}.$$

Carry out the indicated operations.

1. $2B + 3C$
2. AB
3. C^{-1}
4. $BC - 3B$

5. If $A = \begin{bmatrix} 1 & 2 & 2 \\ 2 & 3 & 3 \\ 1 & -1 & -2 \end{bmatrix}$ and $B = \begin{bmatrix} -3 & 2 & 0 \\ 7 & -4 & 1 \\ -5 & 3 & -1 \end{bmatrix}$, show that B is the inverse of A.

6. Consider the system
$$3x + 5y = 9$$
$$2x - 3y = -13.$$

   a. Express the system in the form $AX = B$, where A, X, and B are appropriate matrices.
   b. Find A^{-1}, the inverse of the coefficient matrix.
   c. Use A^{-1} to solve the given system.

7. Evaluate: $\begin{vmatrix} 8 & 1 \\ 4 & -6 \end{vmatrix}$.

8. Evaluate: $\begin{vmatrix} 4 & -1 & 3 \\ 0 & 5 & -1 \\ 5 & 2 & 4 \end{vmatrix}$.

9. Use Cramer's rule to solve $\begin{cases} x - 5y = 3 \\ 2x + 4y = -8 \end{cases}$

10. Solve for x only using Cramer's rule:
$$\begin{cases} 3x + y - 2z = -3 \\ 2x + 7y + 3z = 9 \\ 4x - 3y - z = 7. \end{cases}$$

CHAPTER 5 STANDARDIZED TEST

Multiple Choice. *Choose the one alternative that best completes the statement or answers the question.*

Perform the indicated operations.

1. Let $A = \begin{bmatrix} 1 & 3 \\ 2 & 4 \end{bmatrix}$ and $B = \begin{bmatrix} 0 & 4 \\ -1 & 6 \end{bmatrix}$. Find $2A + B$.

   a. $\begin{bmatrix} 2 & 10 \\ 3 & 14 \end{bmatrix}$ b. $\begin{bmatrix} 2 & 14 \\ 2 & 20 \end{bmatrix}$
   c. $\begin{bmatrix} 2 & 10 \\ 1 & 10 \end{bmatrix}$ d. $\begin{bmatrix} 2 & 7 \\ 3 & 10 \end{bmatrix}$

2. Let $A = \begin{bmatrix} -1 & 3 \\ 1 & 4 \end{bmatrix}$ and $B = \begin{bmatrix} 0 & -2 & 6 \\ 1 & -3 & 2 \end{bmatrix}$. Find AB.

   a. $\begin{bmatrix} 3 & 4 \\ -7 & -14 \\ 0 & 14 \end{bmatrix}$ b. AB is not defined
   c. $\begin{bmatrix} 3 & -7 & 0 \\ 4 & -14 & 14 \end{bmatrix}$ d. $\begin{bmatrix} 0 & -6 & 18 \\ 1 & -12 & 8 \end{bmatrix}$

3. Let $A = \begin{bmatrix} -6 & 0 \\ -3 & -4 \end{bmatrix}$. Find A^{-1}.

   a. $\begin{bmatrix} -\frac{1}{4} & 0 \\ -\frac{1}{8} & \frac{1}{6} \end{bmatrix}$ b. $\begin{bmatrix} -\frac{1}{6} & 0 \\ \frac{1}{8} & -\frac{1}{4} \end{bmatrix}$
   c. No inverse   d. $\begin{bmatrix} -\frac{1}{6} & 0 \\ -\frac{1}{8} & -\frac{1}{4} \end{bmatrix}$

4. Let $A = \begin{bmatrix} 1 \\ -3 \\ 2 \end{bmatrix}$ and $B = \begin{bmatrix} -1 \\ 3 \\ -2 \end{bmatrix}$. Find $A - 2B$.

   a. $\begin{bmatrix} -1 \\ 3 \\ -2 \end{bmatrix}$ b. $\begin{bmatrix} 3 \\ -9 \\ 6 \end{bmatrix}$
   c. $\begin{bmatrix} -3 \\ 9 \\ -6 \end{bmatrix}$ d. $\begin{bmatrix} 3 \\ -6 \\ 4 \end{bmatrix}$

Find the products AB and BA to determine whether B is the multiplicative inverse of A.

5. $A = \begin{bmatrix} 2 & -1 & 0 \\ -1 & 1 & -2 \\ 1 & 0 & -1 \end{bmatrix}$, $B = \begin{bmatrix} 1 & -1 & 2 \\ -3 & -2 & 4 \\ -1 & 1 & 1 \end{bmatrix}$

   a. $B \neq A^{-1}$ b. $B = A^{-1}$

Write the linear system as a matrix equation in the form $AX = B$, where A is the coefficient matrix and B is the constant matrix.

6. $4x - 2y = 6$
   $7x + 3y = 69$

   a. $\begin{bmatrix} 4 & 7 \\ -2 & 3 \end{bmatrix}\begin{bmatrix} x \\ y \end{bmatrix} = \begin{bmatrix} 6 \\ 69 \end{bmatrix}$ b. $\begin{bmatrix} 6 & -2 \\ 69 & 7 \end{bmatrix}\begin{bmatrix} x \\ y \end{bmatrix} = \begin{bmatrix} 4 \\ 3 \end{bmatrix}$
   c. $\begin{bmatrix} 4 & -2 \\ 7 & 3 \end{bmatrix}\begin{bmatrix} x \\ y \end{bmatrix} = \begin{bmatrix} 6 \\ 69 \end{bmatrix}$ d. $\begin{bmatrix} 4 & -2 \\ 3 & 7 \end{bmatrix}\begin{bmatrix} x \\ y \end{bmatrix} = \begin{bmatrix} 69 \\ 6 \end{bmatrix}$

Solve the system using the inverse that is given for the coefficient matrix.

7. $x + 2y + 3z = -1$
$x + y + z = 10$
$x - 2z = -4$

The inverse of $\begin{bmatrix} 1 & 2 & 3 \\ 1 & 1 & 1 \\ 1 & 0 & -2 \end{bmatrix}$ is $\begin{bmatrix} -2 & 4 & -1 \\ 3 & -5 & 2 \\ -1 & 2 & -1 \end{bmatrix}$.

a. $(46, -61, 25)$ **b.** $(36, -62, 25)$
c. $(-1, 0, 0)$ **d.** $(34, 39, 15)$

Evaluate.

8. $\begin{vmatrix} 2 & 1 \\ 3 & 2 \end{vmatrix}$

a. 1 **b.** 7
c. -1 **d.** -4

9. $\begin{vmatrix} -3 & -4 & 5 \\ 5 & 0 & -2 \\ -1 & 0 & 2 \end{vmatrix}$

a. 48 **b.** -48
c. -32 **d.** 32

Use Cramer's rule to solve each system.

10. $-2x + 5y = -25$
$-5x + 2y = -10$

a. $(0, -5)$ **b.** $(2, -6)$
c. $(-6, -5)$ **d.** $(2, 4)$

11. $3x + 3y - z = 19$
$x - 9y - 6z = -35$
$-6x + y + z = -19$

a. $(3, 2, 3)$ **b.** $(4, 3, 2)$
c. $(4, -3, -2)$ **d.** $(5, 1, 2)$

CHAPTER

Exponents, Polynomials, and Polynomial Functions

- **6.1** Exponents and Scientific Notation
- **6.2** More Work with Exponents and Scientific Notation
- **6.3** Polynomials and Polynomial Functions
- **6.4** Multiplying Polynomials
- **6.5** The Greatest Common Factor and Factoring by Grouping
- **6.6** Factoring Trinomials
- **6.7** Factoring by Special Products

    Integrated Review—Operations on Polynomials and Factoring Strategies

- **6.8** Solving Equations by Factoring and Problem Solving

    Extension: Even and Odd Power Functions and End Behavior

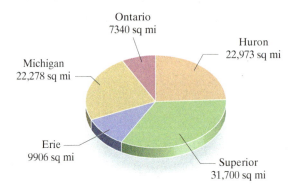

Surface Areas of Great Lakes

To remember the Great Lakes, remember the word "**HOMES.**"

   H = Huron
   O = Ontario
   M = Michigan
   E = Erie
   S = Superior

The Great Lakes are a group of five lakes in North America on or near the United States-Canada border. The total surface area of the Great Lakes is about the size of Texas. In this chapter, we will use our work with scientific notation to explore the mass of the water in Lake Superior.

6.1 EXPONENTS AND SCIENTIFIC NOTATION

OBJECTIVES

1. Use the product rule for exponents.
2. Evaluate expressions raised to the 0 power.
3. Use the quotient rule for exponents.
4. Evaluate expressions raised to the negative nth power.
5. Convert between scientific notation and standard notation.

OBJECTIVE 1 ▶ Using the product rule. Recall that exponents may be used to write repeated factors in a more compact form. As we have seen in the previous chapters, exponents can be used when the repeated factor is a number or a variable. For example,

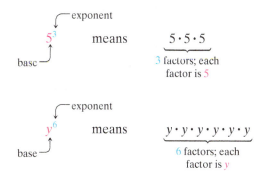

Expressions such as 5^3 and y^6 that contain exponents are called **exponential expressions.**

Exponential expressions can be multiplied, divided, added, subtracted, and themselves raised to powers. In this section, we review operations on exponential expressions.

We review multiplication first. To multiply x^2 by x^3, use the definition of an exponent.

$$x^2 \cdot x^3 = \underbrace{(x \cdot x)(x \cdot x \cdot x)}_{x \text{ is a factor 5 times}}$$
$$= x^5$$

Notice that the result is exactly the same if we add the exponents.

$$x^2 \cdot x^3 = x^{2+3} = x^5$$

This suggests the following.

Product Rule for Exponents

If m and n are positive integers and a is a real number, then

$$a^m \cdot a^n = a^{m+n}$$

In other words, the *product* of exponential expressions with a common base is the common base raised to a power equal to the *sum* of the exponents of the factors.

EXAMPLE 1 Use the product rule to simplify.

a. $2^2 \cdot 2^5$ **b.** $x^7 x^3$ **c.** $y \cdot y^2 \cdot y^4$

Solution

a. $2^2 \cdot 2^5 = 2^{2+5} = 2^7$
b. $x^7 x^3 = x^{7+3} = x^{10}$
c. $y \cdot y^2 \cdot y^4 = (y^1 \cdot y^2) \cdot y^4$
              $= y^3 \cdot y^4$
              $= y^7$

PRACTICE 1 Use the product rule to simplify.

a. $3^4 \cdot 3^2$ **b.** $x^5 \cdot x^2$ **c.** $y \cdot y^3 \cdot y^5$

EXAMPLE 2 Use the product rule to simplify.

a. $(3x^6)(5x)$ **b.** $(-2.4x^3p^2)(4xp^{10})$

Solution Here, we use properties of multiplication to group together like bases.

a. $(3x^6)(5x) = 3(5)x^6x^1 = 15x^7$
b. $(-2.4x^3p^2)(4xp^{10}) = -2.4(4)x^3x^1p^2p^{10} = -9.6x^4p^{12}$

PRACTICE 2 Use the product rule to simplify.

a. $(5z^3)(7z)$ **b.** $(-4.1t^5q^3)(5tq^5)$

OBJECTIVE 2 ▶ Evaluating expressions raised to the 0 power. The definition of a^n does not include the possibility that n might be 0. But if it did, then, by the product rule,

$$\underbrace{a^0 \cdot a^n}_{} = a^{0+n} = a^n = \underbrace{1 \cdot a^n}_{}$$

From this, we reasonably define that $a^0 = 1$, as long as a does not equal 0.

> **Zero Exponent**
> If a does not equal 0, then $a^0 = 1$.

EXAMPLE 3 Evaluate the following.

a. 7^0 **b.** -7^0 **c.** $(2x + 5)^0$ **d.** $2x^0$

Solution

a. $7^0 = 1$
b. Without parentheses, only 7 is raised to the 0 power.
$$-7^0 = -(7^0) = -(1) = -1$$
c. $(2x + 5)^0 = 1$
d. $2x^0 = 2(1) = 2$

PRACTICE 3 Evaluate the following.

a. 5^0 **b.** -5^0 **c.** $(3x - 8)^0$ **d.** $3x^0$

OBJECTIVE 3 ▶ Using the quotient rule. To find quotients of exponential expressions, we again begin with the definition of a^n to simplify $\dfrac{x^9}{x^2}$. For example,

$$\frac{x^9}{x^2} = \frac{x \cdot x \cdot x \cdot x \cdot x \cdot x \cdot x \cdot x \cdot x}{x \cdot x} = x^7$$

(Assume for the next two sections that denominators containing variables are not 0.) Notice that the result is exactly the same if we subtract the exponents.

$$\frac{x^9}{x^2} = x^{9-2} = x^7$$

This suggests the following.

> **Quotient Rule for Exponents**
> If a is a nonzero real number and n and m are integers, then
> $$\frac{a^m}{a^n} = a^{m-n}$$

In other words, the *quotient* of exponential expressions with a common base is the common base raised to a power equal to the *difference* of the exponents.

EXAMPLE 4 Use the quotient rule to simplify.

a. $\dfrac{x^7}{x^4}$ **b.** $\dfrac{5^8}{5^2}$ **c.** $\dfrac{20x^6}{4x^5}$ **d.** $\dfrac{12y^{10}z^7}{14y^8z^7}$

Solution

a. $\dfrac{x^7}{x^4} = x^{7-4} = x^3$

b. $\dfrac{5^8}{5^2} = 5^{8-2} = 5^6$

c. $\dfrac{20x^6}{4x^5} = 5x^{6-5} = 5x^1$, or $5x$

d. $\dfrac{12y^{10}z^7}{14y^8z^7} = \dfrac{6}{7}y^{10-8} \cdot z^{7-7} = \dfrac{6}{7}y^2z^0 = \dfrac{6}{7}y^2$, or $\dfrac{6y^2}{7}$

PRACTICE 4 Use the quotient rule to simplify.

a. $\dfrac{z^8}{z^3}$ **b.** $\dfrac{3^9}{3^3}$ **c.** $\dfrac{45x^7}{5x^3}$ **d.** $\dfrac{24a^{14}b^6}{18a^7b^6}$

OBJECTIVE 4 ▶ Evaluating exponents raised to the negative *n*th power. When the exponent of the denominator is larger than the exponent of the numerator, applying the quotient rule yields a negative exponent. For example,

$$\frac{x^3}{x^5} = x^{3-5} = x^{-2}$$

Using the definition of a^n, though, gives us

$$\frac{x^3}{x^5} = \frac{x \cdot x \cdot x}{x \cdot x \cdot x \cdot x \cdot x} = \frac{1}{x^2}$$

From this, we reasonably define $x^{-2} = \dfrac{1}{x^2}$ or, in general, $a^{-n} = \dfrac{1}{a^n}$.

> **Negative Exponents**
> If a is a real number other than 0 and n is a positive integer, then
> $$a^{-n} = \frac{1}{a^n}$$

EXAMPLE 5 Simplify and write with positive exponents only.

a. 5^{-2} b. $(-4)^{-4}$ c. $2x^{-3}$ d. $(3x)^{-1}$

e. $\dfrac{m^5}{m^{15}}$ f. $\dfrac{3^3}{3^6}$ g. $2^{-1} + 3^{-2}$ h. $\dfrac{1}{t^{-5}}$

Solution

a. $5^{-2} = \dfrac{1}{5^2} = \dfrac{1}{25}$

b. $(-4)^{-4} = \dfrac{1}{(-4)^4} = \dfrac{1}{256}$

c. $2x^{-3} = 2 \cdot \dfrac{1}{x^3} = \dfrac{2}{x^3}$ Without parentheses, only x is raised to the -3 power.

d. $(3x)^{-1} = \dfrac{1}{(3x)^1} = \dfrac{1}{3x}$ With parentheses, both 3 and x are raised to the -1 power.

e. $\dfrac{m^5}{m^{15}} = m^{5-15} = m^{-10} = \dfrac{1}{m^{10}}$

f. $\dfrac{3^3}{3^6} = 3^{3-6} = 3^{-3} = \dfrac{1}{3^3} = \dfrac{1}{27}$

g. $2^{-1} + 3^{-2} = \dfrac{1}{2^1} + \dfrac{1}{3^2} = \dfrac{1}{2} + \dfrac{1}{9} = \dfrac{9}{18} + \dfrac{2}{18} = \dfrac{11}{18}$

h. $\dfrac{1}{t^{-5}} = \dfrac{1}{\frac{1}{t^5}} = 1 \div \dfrac{1}{t^5} = 1 \cdot \dfrac{t^5}{1} = t^5$

PRACTICE 5 Simplify and write with positive exponents only.

a. 6^{-2} b. $(-2)^{-6}$ c. $3x^{-5}$ d. $(5y)^{-1}$ e. $\dfrac{k^4}{k^{11}}$

f. $\dfrac{5^3}{5^5}$ g. $5^{-1} + 2^{-2}$ h. $\dfrac{1}{z^{-8}}$

> **▶ Helpful Hint**
> Notice that when a factor containing an exponent is moved from the numerator to the denominator or from the denominator to the numerator, the sign of its exponent changes.
>
> $x^{-3} = \dfrac{1}{x^3}, \quad 5^{-2} = \dfrac{1}{5^2} = \dfrac{1}{25}$
>
> $\dfrac{1}{y^{-4}} = y^4, \quad \dfrac{1}{2^{-3}} = 2^3 = 8$

EXAMPLE 6 Simplify and write with positive exponents only.

a. $\dfrac{x^{-9}}{x^2}$ b. $\dfrac{5p^4}{p^{-3}}$ c. $\dfrac{2^{-3}}{2^{-1}}$ d. $\dfrac{2x^{-7}y^2}{10xy^{-5}}$ e. $\dfrac{(3x^{-3})(x^2)}{x^6}$

Solution

a. $\dfrac{x^{-9}}{x^2} = x^{-9-2} = x^{-11} = \dfrac{1}{x^{11}}$

b. $\dfrac{5p^4}{p^{-3}} = 5 \cdot p^{4-(-3)} = 5p^7$

c. $\dfrac{2^{-3}}{2^{-1}} = 2^{-3-(-1)} = 2^{-2} = \dfrac{1}{2^2} = \dfrac{1}{4}$

d. $\dfrac{2x^{-7}y^2}{10xy^{-5}} = \dfrac{x^{-7-1} \cdot y^{2-(-5)}}{5} = \dfrac{x^{-8}y^7}{5} = \dfrac{y^7}{5x^8}$

e. Simplify the numerator first.

$$\dfrac{(3x^{-3})(x^2)}{x^6} = \dfrac{3x^{-3+2}}{x^6} = \dfrac{3x^{-1}}{x^6} = 3x^{-1-6} = 3x^{-7} = \dfrac{3}{x^7}$$

PRACTICE 6 Simplify and write with positive exponents only.

a. $\dfrac{z^{-8}}{z^3}$ b. $\dfrac{7t^3}{t^{-5}}$ c. $\dfrac{3^{-2}}{3^{-4}}$ d. $\dfrac{5a^{-5}b^3}{15a^2b^{-4}}$ e. $\dfrac{(2x^{-5})(x^6)}{x^5}$

Concept Check ✓

Find and correct the error in the following:

$$\dfrac{y^{-6}}{y^{-2}} = y^{-6-2} = y^{-8} = \dfrac{1}{y^8}$$

EXAMPLE 7 Simplify. Assume that a and t are nonzero integers and that x is not 0.

a. $x^{2a} \cdot x^3$ b. $\dfrac{x^{2t-1}}{x^{t-5}}$

Solution

a. $x^{2a} \cdot x^3 = x^{2a+3}$ Use the product rule.

b. $\dfrac{x^{2t-1}}{x^{t-5}} = x^{(2t-1)-(t-5)}$ Use the quotient rule.

   $= x^{2t-1-t+5} = x^{t+4}$

PRACTICE 7 Simplify. Assume that a and t are nonzero integers and that x is not 0.

a. $x^{3a} \cdot x^4$ b. $\dfrac{x^{3t-2}}{x^{t-3}}$

OBJECTIVE 5 ▶ Converting between scientific notation and standard notation. Very large and very small numbers occur frequently in nature. For example, the distance between the Earth and the Sun is approximately 150,000,000 kilometers. A helium atom has a diameter of 0.000 000 022 centimeters. It can be tedious to write these very large and very small numbers in standard notation like this. **Scientific notation** is a convenient shorthand notation for writing very large and very small numbers.

Helium atom

0.000 000 022 centimeters

150,000,000 km

Answer to Concept Check:

$\dfrac{y^{-6}}{y^{-2}} = y^{-6-(-2)} = y^{-4} = \dfrac{1}{y^4}$

Scientific Notation

A positive number is written in **scientific notation** if it is written as the product of a number a, where $1 \leq a < 10$ and an integer power r of 10:

$$a \times 10^r$$

The following are examples of numbers written in scientific notation.

diameter of helium atom → 2.2×10^{-8} cm; 1.5×10^8 km ← approximate distance between Earth and Sun

Writing a Number in Scientific Notation

STEP 1. Move the decimal point in the original number until the new number has a value between 1 and 10.

STEP 2. Count the number of decimal places the decimal point was moved in Step 1. If the original number is 10 or greater, the count is positive. If the original number is less than 1, the count is negative.

STEP 3. Write the product of the new number in Step 1 by 10 raised to an exponent equal to the count found in Step 2.

EXAMPLE 8 Write each number in scientific notation.

a. 730,000   b. 0.00000104

Solution

a. **STEP 1.** Move the decimal point until the number is between 1 and 10.

730,000.

STEP 2. The decimal point is moved 5 places and the original number is 10 or greater, so the count is positive 5.

STEP 3. $730,000 = 7.3 \times 10^5$.

b. **STEP 1.** Move the decimal point until the number is between 1 and 10.

0.00000104

STEP 2. The decimal point is moved 6 places and the original number is less than 1, so the count is -6.

STEP 3. $0.00000104 = 1.04 \times 10^{-6}$.

PRACTICE 8 Write each number in scientific notation.

a. 65,000   b. 0.000038

To write a scientific notation number in standard form, we reverse the preceding steps.

Writing a Scientific Notation Number in Standard Notation

Move the decimal point in the number the same number of places as the exponent on 10. If the exponent is positive, move the decimal point to the right. If the exponent is negative, move the decimal point to the left.

Section 6.1 Exponents and Scientific Notation 293

EXAMPLE 9 Write each number in standard notation.
a. 7.7×10^8 **b.** 1.025×10^{-3}

Solution

a. $7.7 \times 10^8 = 770,000,000$ Since the exponent is positive, move the decimal point 8 places to the right. Add zeros as needed.

b. $1.025 \times 10^{-3} = 0.001025$ Since the exponent is negative, move the decimal point 3 places to the left. Add zeros as needed.

PRACTICE 9 Write each number in standard notation.
a. 6.2×10^5 **b.** 3.109×10^{-2}

Concept Check

Which of the following numbers have values that are less than 1?

a. 3.5×10^{-5} **b.** 3.5×10^5 **c.** -3.5×10^5 **d.** -3.5×10^{-5}

Answers to Concept Check:
a, c, d

Scientific Calculator Explorations

Multiply 5,000,000 by 700,000 on your calculator. The display should read $\boxed{3.5 \;\; 12}$ or $\boxed{3.5 \text{ E } 12}$, which is the product written in scientific notation. Both these notations mean 3.5×10^{12}.

To enter a number written in scientific notation on a calculator, find the key marked $\boxed{\text{EE}}$. (On some calculators, this key may be marked $\boxed{\text{EXP}}$.)
To enter 7.26×10^{13}, press the keys

$$\boxed{7.26} \;\; \boxed{\text{EE}} \;\; \boxed{13}$$

The display will read $\boxed{7.26 \;\; 13}$ or $\boxed{7.26 \text{ E } 13}$.

Use your calculator to perform each operation indicated.

1. Multiply 3×10^{11} and 2×10^{32}.
2. Divide 6×10^{14} by 3×10^9.
3. Multiply 5.2×10^{23} and 7.3×10^4.
4. Divide 4.38×10^{41} by 3×10^{17}.

VOCABULARY & READINESS CHECK

State the base of the exponent 5 in each expression.

1. $9x^5$ **2.** yz^5 **3.** -3^5 **4.** $(-3)^5$ **5.** $(y^7)^5$ **6.** $9 \cdot 2^5$

Write each expression with positive exponents.

7. $5x^{-1}y^{-2}$ **8.** $7xy^{-4}$ **9.** $a^2 b^{-1} c^{-5}$ **10.** $a^{-4} b^2 c^{-6}$ **11.** $\dfrac{y^{-2}}{x^{-4}}$ **12.** $\dfrac{x^{-7}}{z^{-3}}$

6.1 EXERCISE SET

Use the product rule to simplify each expression. See Examples 1 and 2.

1. $4^2 \cdot 4^3$
2. $3^3 \cdot 3^5$
3. $x^5 \cdot x^3$
4. $a^2 \cdot a^9$
5. $m \cdot m^7 \cdot m^6$
6. $n \cdot n^{10} \cdot n^{12}$
7. $(4xy)(-5x)$
8. $(-7xy)(7y)$
9. $(-4x^3p^2)(4y^3x^3)$
10. $(-6a^2b^3)(-3ab^3)$

Evaluate each expression. See Example 3.

11. -8^0
12. $(-9)^0$
13. $(4x+5)^0$
14. $(3x-1)^0$
15. $-x^0$
16. $-5x^0$
17. $4x^0 + 5$
18. $8x^0 + 1$

Use the quotient rule to simplify. See Example 4.

19. $\dfrac{a^5}{a^2}$
20. $\dfrac{x^9}{x^4}$
21. $-\dfrac{26z^{11}}{2z^7}$
22. $-\dfrac{16x^5}{8x}$
23. $\dfrac{x^9 y^6}{x^8 y^6}$
24. $\dfrac{a^{12}b^2}{a^9 b}$
25. $\dfrac{12x^4 y^7}{9xy^5}$
26. $\dfrac{24a^{10}b^{11}}{10ab^3}$
27. $\dfrac{-36a^5 b^7 c^{10}}{6ab^3 c^4}$
28. $\dfrac{49a^3 bc^{14}}{-7abc^8}$

Simplify and write using positive exponents only. See Examples 5 and 6.

29. 4^{-2}
30. 2^{-3}
31. $(-3)^{-3}$
32. $(-6)^{-2}$
33. $\dfrac{x^7}{x^{15}}$
34. $\dfrac{z}{z^3}$
35. $5a^{-4}$
36. $10b^{-1}$
37. $\dfrac{x^{-7}}{y^{-2}}$
38. $\dfrac{p^{-13}}{q^{-3}}$
39. $\dfrac{x^{-2}}{x^5}$
40. $\dfrac{z^{-12}}{z^{10}}$
41. $\dfrac{8r^4}{2r^{-4}}$
42. $\dfrac{3s^3}{15s^{-3}}$
43. $\dfrac{x^{-9}x^4}{x^{-5}}$
44. $\dfrac{y^{-7}y}{y^8}$
45. $\dfrac{2a^{-6}b^2}{18ab^{-5}}$
46. $\dfrac{18ab^{-6}}{3a^{-3}b^6}$
47. $\dfrac{(24x^8)(x)}{20x^{-7}}$
48. $\dfrac{(30z^2)(z^5)}{55z^{-4}}$

MIXED PRACTICE

Simplify and write using positive exponents only. See Examples 1 through 6.

49. $-7x^3 \cdot 20x^9$
50. $-3y \cdot -9y^4$
51. $x^7 \cdot x^8 \cdot x$
52. $y^6 \cdot y \cdot y^9$
53. $2x^3 \cdot 5x^7$
54. $-3z^4 \cdot 10z^7$
55. $(5x)^0 + 5x^0$
56. $4y^0 - (4y)^0$
57. $\dfrac{z^{12}}{z^{15}}$
58. $\dfrac{x^{11}}{x^{20}}$
59. $3^0 - 3t^0$
60. $4^0 + 4x^0$
61. $\dfrac{y^{-3}}{y^{-7}}$
62. $\dfrac{y^{-6}}{y^{-9}}$
63. $4^{-1} + 3^{-2}$
64. $1^{-3} - 4^{-2}$
65. $3x^{-1}$
66. $(4x)^{-1}$
67. $\dfrac{r^4}{r^{-4}}$
68. $\dfrac{x^{-5}}{x^3}$
69. $\dfrac{x^{-7}y^{-2}}{x^2 y^2}$
70. $\dfrac{a^{-5}b^7}{a^{-2}b^{-3}}$
71. $(-4x^2 y)(3x^4)(-2xy^5)$
72. $(-6a^4 b)(2b^3)(-3ab^6)$
73. $2^{-4} \cdot x$
74. $5^{-2} \cdot y$
75. $\dfrac{5^{17}}{5^{13}}$
76. $\dfrac{10^{25}}{10^{23}}$
77. $\dfrac{8^{-7}}{8^{-6}}$
78. $\dfrac{13^{-10}}{13^{-9}}$
79. $\dfrac{9^{-5}a^4}{9^{-3}a^{-1}}$
80. $\dfrac{11^{-9}b^3}{11^{-7}b^{-4}}$
81. $\dfrac{14x^{-2}yz^{-4}}{2xyz}$
82. $\dfrac{30x^{-7}yz^{-14}}{3xyz}$

Simplify. Assume that variables in the exponents represent nonzero integers and that x, y, and z are not 0. See Example 7.

83. $x^5 \cdot x^{7a}$
84. $y^{2p} \cdot y^{9p}$
85. $\dfrac{x^{3t-1}}{x^t}$
86. $\dfrac{y^{4p-2}}{y^{3p}}$
87. $x^{4a} \cdot x^7$
88. $x^{9y} \cdot x^{-7y}$
89. $\dfrac{z^{6x}}{z^7}$
90. $\dfrac{y^6}{y^{4z}}$
91. $\dfrac{x^{3t} \cdot x^{4t-1}}{x^t}$
92. $\dfrac{z^{5x} \cdot z^{x-7}}{z^x}$

Write each number in scientific notation. See Example 8.

93. 31,250,000
94. 678,000
95. 0.016
96. 0.007613
97. 67,413
98. 36,800,000

99. 0.0125
100. 0.00084
101. 0.000053
102. 98,700,000,000

Write each number in scientific notation.

103. Total revenues for Wal-Mart in fiscal year ending January 2007 were $344,992,000,000. (*Source:* Wal-Mart Stores, Inc.)

104. The University of Texas system has more than 170,000 students statewide. (*Source:* University of Texas)

105. On a recent day, the Apple iTunes Store featured more than 3,500,000 songs to buy for $0.99 each.

106. In 2006, approximately 61,049,000 passengers passed through the Los Angeles International Airport. (*Source:* Los Angeles International Airport)

107. Lake Mead, created from the Colorado River by the Hoover Dam, has a capacity of 124,000,000,000 cubic feet of water. (*Source:* U.S. Bureau of Reclamation)

108. The temperature of the core of the sun is about 27,000,000°F.

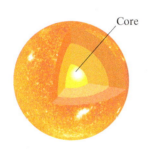

109. A pulsar is a rotating neutron star that gives off sharp, regular pulses of radio waves. For one particular pulsar, the rate of pulses is every 0.001 second.

110. To convert from cubic inches to cubic meters, multiply by 0.0000164.

Write each number in standard notation, without exponents. See Example 9.

111. 3.6×10^{-9}
112. 2.7×10^{-5}
113. 9.3×10^{7}
114. 6.378×10^{8}
115. 1.278×10^{6}
116. 7.6×10^{4}
117. 7.35×10^{12}
118. 1.66×10^{-5}
119. 4.03×10^{-7}
120. 8.007×10^{8}

Write each number in standard notation.

121. The estimated world population in 1 A.D. was 3.0×10^{8}. (*Source:* World Almanac and Book of Facts)

122. There are 3.949×10^{6} miles of highways, roads, and streets in the United States. (*Source:* Bureau of Transportation Statistics)

123. In 2006, teenagers had an estimated spending power of 1.53×10^{11} dollars. (*Source:* A. C. Neilson Research)

124. Each day, an estimated 1.2×10^{9} beverages consumed throughout the world are Coca Cola products. (*Source:* Coca-Cola)

REVIEW AND PREVIEW

Evaluate. See Sections 1.3 and 6.1.

125. $(5 \cdot 2)^2$
126. $5^2 \cdot 2^2$
127. $\left(\dfrac{3}{4}\right)^3$
128. $\dfrac{3^3}{4^3}$
129. $(2^3)^2$
130. $(2^2)^3$

CONCEPT EXTENSIONS

131. Explain how to convert a number from standard notation to scientific notation.

132. Explain how to convert a number from scientific notation to standard notation.

133. Explain why $(-5)^0$ simplifies to 1 but -5^0 simplifies to -1.

134. Explain why both $4x^0 - 3y^0$ and $(4x - 3y)^0$ simplify to 1.

135. Simplify where possible.
   a. $x^a \cdot x^a$
   b. $x^a + x^a$
   c. $\dfrac{x^a}{x^b}$
   d. $x^a \cdot x^b$
   e. $x^a + x^b$

136. Decision Making. Which numbers are equal to 36,000? Of these, which is written in scientific notation?
   a. 36×10^3
   b. 360×10^2
   c. 0.36×10^5
   d. 3.6×10^4

Decision Making. *Without calculating, determine which number is larger.*

137. 7^{11} or 7^{13}
138. 5^{10} or 5^9
139. 7^{-11} or 7^{-13}
140. 5^{-10} or 5^{-9}

6.2 MORE WORK WITH EXPONENTS AND SCIENTIFIC NOTATION

OBJECTIVES

1. Use the power rules for exponents.
2. Use exponent rules and definitions to simplify exponential expressions.
3. Compute, using scientific notation.

OBJECTIVE 1 ▶ Using the power rules. The volume of the cube shown whose side measures x^2 units is $(x^2)^3$ cubic units. To simplify an expression such as $(x^2)^3$, we use the definition of a^n. Then

$$(x^2)^3 = \underbrace{(x^2)(x^2)(x^2)}_{x^2 \text{ is a factor 3 times}} = x^{2+2+2} = x^6$$

Notice that the result is exactly the same if the exponents are multiplied.

$$(x^2)^3 = x^{2 \cdot 3} = x^6$$

This suggests that the power of an exponential expression raised to a power is the product of the exponents. Two additional rules for exponents are given in the following box.

x^2 units

The Power Rule and Power of a Product or Quotient Rules for Exponents

If a and b are real numbers and m and n are integers, then

$$(a^m)^n = a^{m \cdot n} \quad \text{Power rule}$$

$$(ab)^m = a^m b^m \quad \text{Power of a product}$$

$$\left(\frac{a}{b}\right)^n = \frac{a^n}{b^n} \, (b \neq 0) \quad \text{Power of a quotient}$$

EXAMPLE 1 Use the power rule to simplify the following expressions. Use positive exponents to write all results.

a. $(x^5)^7$ **b.** $(2^2)^3$ **c.** $(5^{-1})^2$ **d.** $(y^{-3})^{-4}$

Solution

a. $(x^5)^7 = x^{5 \cdot 7} = x^{35}$ **b.** $(2^2)^3 = 2^{2 \cdot 3} = 2^6 = 64$

c. $(5^{-1})^2 = 5^{-1 \cdot 2} = 5^{-2} = \frac{1}{5^2} = \frac{1}{25}$ **d.** $(y^{-3})^{-4} = y^{-3(-4)} = y^{12}$ □

PRACTICE 1 Use the power rule to simplify the following expressions. Use positive exponents to write all results.

a. $(z^3)^5$ **b.** $(5^2)^2$ **c.** $(3^{-1})^3$ **d.** $(x^{-4})^{-6}$

EXAMPLE 2 Use the power rules to simplify the following. Use positive exponents to write all results.

a. $(5x^2)^3$ **b.** $\left(\frac{2}{3}\right)^3$ **c.** $\left(\frac{3p^4}{q^5}\right)^2$ **d.** $\left(\frac{2^{-3}}{y}\right)^{-2}$ **e.** $(x^{-5}y^2z^{-1})^7$

Solution

a. $(5x^2)^3 = 5^3 \cdot (x^2)^3 = 5^3 \cdot x^{2 \cdot 3} = 125x^6$

b. $\left(\frac{2}{3}\right)^3 = \frac{2^3}{3^3} = \frac{8}{27}$

c. $\left(\frac{3p^4}{q^5}\right)^2 = \frac{(3p^4)^2}{(q^5)^2} = \frac{3^2 \cdot (p^4)^2}{(q^5)^2} = \frac{9p^8}{q^{10}}$

d. $\left(\dfrac{2^{-3}}{y}\right)^{-2} = \dfrac{(2^{-3})^{-2}}{y^{-2}}$

$= \dfrac{2^6}{y^{-2}} = 64y^2$ Use the negative exponent rule.

e. $(x^{-5}y^2z^{-1})^7 = (x^{-5})^7 \cdot (y^2)^7 \cdot (z^{-1})^7$

$= x^{-35}y^{14}z^{-7} = \dfrac{y^{14}}{x^{35}z^7}$

PRACTICE 2 Use the power rules to simplify the following. Use positive exponents to write all results.

a. $(2x^3)^5$ b. $\left(\dfrac{3}{5}\right)^2$ c. $\left(\dfrac{2a^5}{b^7}\right)^4$ d. $\left(\dfrac{3^{-2}}{x}\right)^{-1}$ e. $(a^{-2}b^{-5}c^4)^{-2}$

OBJECTIVE 2 ▶ **Using exponent rules and definitions to simplify.** In the next few examples, we practice the use of several of the rules and definitions for exponents. The following is a summary of these rules and definitions.

Summary of Rules for Exponents
If a and b are real numbers and m and n are integers, then

Product rule	$a^m \cdot a^n = a^{m+n}$	
Zero exponent	$a^0 = 1$	$(a \neq 0)$
Negative exponent	$a^{-n} = \dfrac{1}{a^n}$	$(a \neq 0)$
Quotient rule	$\dfrac{a^m}{a^n} = a^{m-n}$	$(a \neq 0)$
Power rule	$(a^m)^n = a^{m \cdot n}$	
Power of a product	$(ab)^m = a^m \cdot b^m$	
Power of a quotient	$\left(\dfrac{a}{b}\right)^m = \dfrac{a^m}{b^m}$	$(b \neq 0)$

EXAMPLE 3   Simplify each expression. Use positive exponents to write the answers.

a. $(2x^0y^{-3})^{-2}$ b. $\left(\dfrac{x^{-5}}{x^{-2}}\right)^{-3}$ c. $\left(\dfrac{2}{7}\right)^{-2}$ d. $\dfrac{5^{-2}x^{-3}y^{11}}{x^2y^{-5}}$

Solution

a. $(2x^0y^{-3})^{-2} = 2^{-2}(x^0)^{-2}(y^{-3})^{-2}$

$= 2^{-2}x^0y^6$

$= \dfrac{1(y^6)}{2^2}$ Write x^0 as 1.

$= \dfrac{y^6}{4}$

b. $\left(\dfrac{x^{-5}}{x^{-2}}\right)^{-3} = \dfrac{(x^{-5})^{-3}}{(x^{-2})^{-3}} = \dfrac{x^{15}}{x^6} = x^{15-6} = x^9$

c. $\left(\dfrac{2}{7}\right)^{-2} = \dfrac{2^{-2}}{7^{-2}} = \dfrac{7^2}{2^2} = \dfrac{49}{4}$

d. $\dfrac{5^{-2}x^{-3}y^{11}}{x^2 y^{-5}} = (5^{-2})\left(\dfrac{x^{-3}}{x^2}\right)\left(\dfrac{y^{11}}{y^{-5}}\right) = 5^{-2}x^{-3-2}y^{11-(-5)} = 5^{-2}x^{-5}y^{16}$

$= \dfrac{y^{16}}{5^2 x^5} = \dfrac{y^{16}}{25 x^5}$

PRACTICE 3 Simplify each expression. Use positive exponents to write the answer.

a. $(3ab^{-5})^{-3}$
b. $\left(\dfrac{y^{-7}}{y^{-4}}\right)^{-5}$
c. $\left(\dfrac{3}{8}\right)^{-2}$
d. $\dfrac{9^{-2}a^{-4}b^3}{a^2 b^{-5}}$

EXAMPLE 4 Simplify each expression. Use positive exponents to write the answers.

a. $\left(\dfrac{3x^2 y}{y^{-9} z}\right)^{-2}$
b. $\left(\dfrac{3a^2}{2x^{-1}}\right)^3 \left(\dfrac{x^{-3}}{4a^{-2}}\right)^{-1}$

Solution There is often more than one way to simplify exponential expressions. Here, we will simplify inside the parentheses if possible before we apply the power rules for exponents.

a. $\left(\dfrac{3x^2 y}{y^{-9} z}\right)^{-2} = \left(\dfrac{3x^2 y^{10}}{z}\right)^{-2} = \dfrac{3^{-2} x^{-4} y^{-20}}{z^{-2}} = \dfrac{z^2}{3^2 x^4 y^{20}} = \dfrac{z^2}{9 x^4 y^{20}}$

b. $\left(\dfrac{3a^2}{2x^{-1}}\right)^3 \left(\dfrac{x^{-3}}{4a^{-2}}\right)^{-1} = \dfrac{27 a^6}{8 x^{-3}} \cdot \dfrac{x^3}{4^{-1} a^2}$

$= \dfrac{27 \cdot 4 \cdot a^6 x^3 x^3}{8 \cdot a^2} = \dfrac{27 a^4 x^6}{2}$

PRACTICE 4 Simplify each expression. Use positive exponents to write the answers.

a. $\left(\dfrac{5a^4 b}{a^{-8} c}\right)^{-3}$
b. $\left(\dfrac{2x^4}{5y^{-2}}\right)^3 \left(\dfrac{x^{-4}}{10 y^{-2}}\right)^{-1}$

EXAMPLE 5 Simplify each expression. Assume that a and b are integers and that x and y are not 0.

a. $x^{-b}(2x^b)^2$
b. $\dfrac{(y^{3a})^2}{y^{a-6}}$

Solution

a. $x^{-b}(2x^b)^2 = x^{-b} 2^2 x^{2b} = 4 x^{-b+2b} = 4x^b$

b. $\dfrac{(y^{3a})^2}{y^{a-6}} = \dfrac{y^{6a}}{y^{a-6}} = y^{6a-(a-6)} = y^{6a-a+6} = y^{5a+6}$

PRACTICE 5 Simplify each expression. Assume that a and b are integers and that x and y are not 0.

a. $x^{-2a}(3x^a)^3$
b. $\dfrac{(y^{3b})^3}{y^{4b-3}}$

Section 6.2 More Work with Exponents and Scientific Notation **299**

OBJECTIVE 3 ▶ **Computing, using scientific notation.** To perform operations on numbers written in scientific notation, we use properties of exponents.

EXAMPLE 6 Perform the indicated operations. Write each result in scientific notation.

a. $(8.1 \times 10^5)(5 \times 10^{-7})$ **b.** $\dfrac{1.2 \times 10^4}{3 \times 10^{-2}}$

Solution

a. $(8.1 \times 10^5)(5 \times 10^{-7}) = 8.1 \times 5 \times 10^5 \times 10^{-7}$
$= 40.5 \times 10^{-2}$ Not in scientific notation because 40.5 is not between 1 and 10.
$= (4.05 \times 10^1) \times 10^{-2}$
$= 4.05 \times 10^{-1}$

b. $\dfrac{1.2 \times 10^4}{3 \times 10^{-2}} = \left(\dfrac{1.2}{3}\right)\left(\dfrac{10^4}{10^{-2}}\right) = 0.4 \times 10^{4-(-2)}$
$= 0.4 \times 10^6 = (4 \times 10^{-1}) \times 10^6 = 4 \times 10^5$

PRACTICE 6 Perform the indicated operations. Write each result in scientific notation.

a. $(3.4 \times 10^4)(5 \times 10^{-7})$ **b.** $\dfrac{5.6 \times 10^8}{4 \times 10^{-2}}$

EXAMPLE 7 Use scientific notation to simplify $\dfrac{2000 \times 0.000021}{700}$. Write the result in scientific notation.

Solution $\dfrac{2000 \times 0.000021}{700} = \dfrac{(2 \times 10^3)(2.1 \times 10^{-5})}{7 \times 10^2} = \dfrac{2(2.1)}{7} \cdot \dfrac{10^3 \cdot 10^{-5}}{10^2}$
$= 0.6 \times 10^{-4}$
$= (6 \times 10^{-1}) \times 10^{-4}$
$= 6 \times 10^{-5}$

PRACTICE 7 Use scientific notation to simplify $\dfrac{2400 \times 0.0000014}{800}$. Write the result in scientific notation.

VOCABULARY & READINESS CHECK

Simplify. See Examples 1 through 4.

1. $(x^4)^5$ **2.** $(5^6)^2$ **3.** $x^4 \cdot x^5$ **4.** $x^7 \cdot x^8$ **5.** $(y^6)^7$
6. $(x^3)^4$ **7.** $(z^4)^9$ **8.** $(z^3)^7$ **9.** $(z^{-6})^{-3}$ **10.** $(y^{-4})^{-2}$

6.2 EXERCISE SET

Simplify. Write each answer using positive exponents only. See Examples 1 and 2.

1. $(3^{-1})^2$
2. $(2^{-2})^2$
3. $(x^4)^{-9}$
4. $(y^7)^{-3}$
5. $(y)^{-5}$
6. $(z^{-1})^{10}$
7. $(3x^2y^3)^2$
8. $(4x^3yz)^2$
9. $\left(\dfrac{2x^5}{y^{-3}}\right)^4$
10. $\left(\dfrac{3a^{-4}}{b^7}\right)^3$
11. $(a^2bc^{-3})^{-6}$
12. $(6x^{-6}y^7z^0)^{-2}$
13. $\left(\dfrac{x^7y^{-3}}{z^{-4}}\right)^{-5}$
14. $\left(\dfrac{a^{-2}b^{-5}}{c^{-11}}\right)^{-6}$
15. $(5^{-1})^3$

Simplify. Write each answer using positive exponents only. See Examples 3 and 4.

16. $\left(\dfrac{a^{-4}}{a^{-5}}\right)^{-2}$
17. $\left(\dfrac{x^{-9}}{x^{-4}}\right)^{-3}$
18. $\left(\dfrac{2a^{-2}b^5}{4a^2b^7}\right)^{-2}$
19. $\left(\dfrac{5x^7y^4}{10x^3y^{-2}}\right)^{-3}$
20. $\dfrac{4^{-1}x^2yz}{x^{-2}yz^3}$
21. $\dfrac{8^{-2}x^{-3}y^{11}}{x^2y^{-5}}$
22. $\left(\dfrac{6p^6}{p^{12}}\right)^2$
23. $\left(\dfrac{4p^6}{p^9}\right)^3$
24. $(-8y^3xa^{-2})^{-3}$
25. $(-xy^0x^2a^3)^{-3}$
26. $\left(\dfrac{x^{-2}y^{-2}}{a^{-3}}\right)^{-7}$
27. $\left(\dfrac{x^{-1}y^{-2}}{5^{-3}}\right)^{-5}$

MIXED PRACTICE

Simplify. Write each answer using positive exponents.

28. $(8^2)^{-1}$
29. $(x^7)^{-9}$
30. $(y^{-4})^5$
31. $\left(\dfrac{7}{8}\right)^3$
32. $\left(\dfrac{4}{3}\right)^2$
33. $(4x^2)^2$
34. $(-8x^3)^2$
35. $(-2^{-2}y)^3$
36. $(-4^{-6}y^{-6})^{-4}$
37. $\left(\dfrac{4^{-4}}{y^3x}\right)^{-2}$
38. $\left(\dfrac{7^{-3}}{ab^2}\right)^{-2}$
39. $\left(\dfrac{1}{4}\right)^{-3}$
40. $\left(\dfrac{1}{8}\right)^{-2}$
41. $\left(\dfrac{3x^5}{6x^4}\right)^4$
42. $\left(\dfrac{8^{-3}}{y^2}\right)^{-2}$
43. $\dfrac{(y^3)^{-4}}{y^3}$
44. $\dfrac{2(y^3)^{-3}}{y^{-3}}$
45. $\left(\dfrac{2x^{-3}}{y^{-1}}\right)^{-3}$
46. $\left(\dfrac{n^5}{2m^{-2}}\right)^{-4}$
47. $\dfrac{3^{-2}a^{-5}b^6}{4^{-2}a^{-7}b^{-3}}$
48. $\dfrac{2^{-3}m^{-4}n^{-5}}{5^{-2}m^{-5}n}$
49. $(4x^6y^5)^{-2}(6x^4y^3)$
50. $(5xy)^3(z^{-2})^{-3}$
51. $x^6(x^6bc)^{-6}$
52. $2(y^2b)^{-4}$
53. $\dfrac{2^{-3}x^2y^{-5}}{5^{-2}x^7y^{-1}}$
54. $\dfrac{7^{-1}a^{-3}b^5}{a^2b^{-2}}$
55. $\left(\dfrac{2x^2}{y^4}\right)^3\left(\dfrac{2x^5}{y}\right)^{-2}$
56. $\left(\dfrac{3z^{-2}}{y}\right)^2\left(\dfrac{9y^{-4}}{z^{-3}}\right)^{-1}$

Simplify the following. Assume that variables in the exponents represent integers and that all other variables are not 0. See Example 5.

57. $(x^{3a+6})^3$
58. $(x^{2b+7})^2$
59. $\dfrac{x^{4a}(x^{4a})^3}{x^{4a-2}}$
60. $\dfrac{x^{-5y+2}x^{2y}}{x}$
61. $(b^{5x-2})^2$
62. $(c^{2a+3})^3$
63. $\dfrac{(y^{2a})^8}{y^{a-3}}$
64. $\dfrac{(y^{4a})^7}{y^{2a-1}}$
65. $\left(\dfrac{2x^{3t}}{x^{2t-1}}\right)^4$
66. $\left(\dfrac{3y^{5a}}{y^{-a+1}}\right)^2$
67. $\dfrac{25x^{2a+1}y^{a-1}}{5x^{3a+1}y^{2a-3}}$
68. $\dfrac{16x^{-5-3a}y^{-2a-b}}{2x^{-5+3b}y^{-2b-a}}$

Perform each indicated operation. Write each answer in scientific notation. See Examples 6 and 7.

69. $(5 \times 10^{11})(2.9 \times 10^{-3})$
70. $(3.6 \times 10^{-12})(6 \times 10^9)$
71. $(2 \times 10^5)^3$
72. $(3 \times 10^{-7})^3$
73. $\dfrac{3.6 \times 10^{-4}}{9 \times 10^2}$
74. $\dfrac{1.2 \times 10^9}{2 \times 10^{-5}}$
75. $\dfrac{0.0069}{0.023}$
76. $\dfrac{0.00048}{0.0016}$

77. $\dfrac{18{,}200 \times 100}{91{,}000}$

78. $\dfrac{0.0003 \times 0.0024}{0.0006 \times 20}$

79. $\dfrac{6000 \times 0.006}{0.009 \times 400}$

80. $\dfrac{0.00016 \times 300}{0.064 \times 100}$

81. $\dfrac{0.00064 \times 2000}{16{,}000}$

82. $\dfrac{0.00072 \times 0.003}{0.00024}$

83. $\dfrac{66{,}000 \times 0.001}{0.002 \times 0.003}$

84. $\dfrac{0.0007 \times 11{,}000}{0.001 \times 0.0001}$

85. $\dfrac{9.24 \times 10^{15}}{(2.2 \times 10^{-2})(1.2 \times 10^{-5})}$

86. $\dfrac{(2.6 \times 10^{-3})(4.8 \times 10^{-4})}{1.3 \times 10^{-12}}$

Solve.

87. A computer can add two numbers in about 10^{-8} second. Express in scientific notation how long it would take this computer to do this task 200,000 times.

88. To convert from square inches to square meters, multiply by 6.452×10^{-4}. The area of the following square is 4×10^{-2} square inches. Convert this area to square meters.

4×10^{-2} sq in.

89. To convert from cubic inches to cubic meters, multiply by 1.64×10^{-5}. A grain of salt is in the shape of a cube. If an average size of a grain of salt is 3.8×10^{-6} cubic inches, convert this volume to cubic meters.

REVIEW AND PREVIEW

Simplify each expression. See Section 1.4.

90. $-5y + 4y - 18 - y$

91. $12m - 14 - 15m - 1$

92. $-3x - (4r - 2)$

93. $-9y - (5 - 6y)$

94. $3(z - 4) - 2(3z + 1)$

95. $5(x - 3) - 4(2x - 5)$

CONCEPT EXTENSIONS

96. Each side of the cube shown is $\dfrac{2x^{-2}}{y}$ meters. Find its volume.

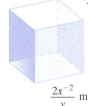

$\dfrac{2x^{-2}}{y}$ m

97. The lot shown is in the shape of a parallelogram with base $\dfrac{3x^{-1}}{y^{-3}}$ feet and height $5x^{-7}$ feet. Find its area.

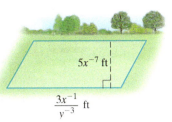

$5x^{-7}$ ft

$\dfrac{3x^{-1}}{y^{-3}}$ ft

98. The density D of an object is equivalent to the quotient of its mass M and volume V. Thus $D = \dfrac{M}{V}$. Express in scientific notation the density of an object whose mass is 500,000 pounds and whose volume is 250 cubic feet.

99. The density of ordinary water is 3.12×10^{-2} tons per cubic foot. The volume of water in the largest of the Great Lakes, Lake Superior, is 4.269×10^{14} cubic feet. Use the formula $D = \dfrac{M}{V}$ (see Exercise 98) to find the mass (in tons) of the water in Lake Superior. Express your answer in scientific notation. (*Source:* National Ocean Service)

100. **Decision Making.** Is there a number a such that $a^{-1} = a^{1}$? If so, give the value of a.

101. **Decision Making.** Is there a number a such that a^{-2} is a negative number? If so, give the value of a.

102. Explain whether 0.4×10^{-5} is written in scientific notation.

103. The estimated population of the United States in 2007 was 3.016×10^{8}. The land area of the United States is 3.536×10^{6} square miles. Find the population density (number of people per square mile) for the United States in 2007. Round to the nearest whole number. (*Source:* U.S. Census Bureau)

104. In 2006, the value of goods imported into the United States was $\$1.855 \times 10^{12}$. The estimated population of the United States in 2006 was 2.98×10^{8}. Find the average value of imports per person in the United States for 2006. Round to the nearest dollar. (*Sources:* U.S. Census Bureau, Bureau of Economic Analysis)

105. The largest subway system in the world (based on passenger volume) is in Tokyo, Japan, with an estimated 2.82×10^9 riders per year. The subway system in Toronto boasts an estimated 4.44×10^8 riders per year. How many times greater is the Tokyo subway volume than the Toronto subway volume? Round to the nearest tenth. (*Source:* Tokyo and Toronto Transit Authorities)

106. Explain whether 0.4×10^{-5} is written in scientific notation.

107. In 2006, the population of Beijing was approximately 15.38×10^6. To prepare for the 2008 Summer Olympic Games, the Chinese put forth a massive effort to increase the numbers of their population who speak a foreign language. By the end of 2006, about 4.87×10^6 people in Beijing could boast that they speak a foreign language. What percent of the residents of Beijing could speak a foreign language at the end of 2006? Round to the nearest tenth of a percent. (*Source: China Daily*)

108. In 2006, downtown office space in downtown New York City was estimated to be 4.21×10^8 sq ft, while office space in downtown Dallas was 4.8×10^7 sq feet. How many times greater is the square footage of office space in New York City than Dallas? Round to the nearest tenth. (*Source:* National Center for Real Estate Research)

6.3 POLYNOMIALS AND POLYNOMIAL FUNCTIONS

OBJECTIVES

1. Identify term, constant, polynomial, monomial, binomial, trinomial, and the degree of a term and of a polynomial.
2. Define polynomial functions.
3. Review combining like terms.
4. Add polynomials.
5. Subtract polynomials.
6. Recognize the graph of a polynomial function from the degree of the polynomial.

OBJECTIVE 1 ▶ Identifing polynomial terms and degrees of terms and polynomials. A **term** is a number or the product of a number and one or more variables raised to powers. The **numerical coefficient,** or simply the **coefficient,** is the numerical factor of a term.

Term	Numerical Coefficient of Term
$-1.2x^5$	-1.2
x^3y	1
$-z$	-1
2	2
$\dfrac{x^9}{7}\left(\text{or } \dfrac{1}{7}x^9\right)$	$\dfrac{1}{7}$

If a term contains only a number, it is called a **constant term,** or simply a **constant.**

A **polynomial** is a finite sum of terms in which all variables are raised to nonnegative integer powers and no variables appear in any denominator.

Polynomials	Not Polynomials	
$4x^5y + 7xz$	$5x^{-3} + 2x$	Negative integer exponent
$-5x^3 + 2x + \dfrac{2}{3}$	$\dfrac{6}{x^2} - 5x + 1$	Variable in denominator

A polynomial that contains only one variable is called a **polynomial in one variable.** For example, $3x^2 - 2x + 7$ is a **polynomial in x.** This polynomial in x is written in *descending order* since the terms are listed in descending order of the variable's exponents. (The term 7 can be thought of as $7x^0$.) The following examples are polynomials in one variable written in **descending order.**

$$4x^3 - 7x^2 + 5 \qquad y^2 - 4 \qquad 8a^4 - 7a^2 + 4a$$

A **monomial** is a polynomial consisting of one term. A **binomial** is a polynomial consisting of two terms. A **trinomial** is a polynomial consisting of three terms.

Monomials	Binomials	Trinomials
ax^2	$x + y$	$x^2 + 4xy + y^2$
$-3x$	$6y^2 - 2$	$-x^4 + 3x^3 + 1$
4	$\frac{5}{7}z^3 - 2z$	$8y^2 - 2y - 10$

By definition, all monomials, binomials, and trinomials are also polynomials.

Each term of a polynomial has a **degree**.

> **Degree of a Term**
> The **degree of a term** is the sum of the exponents on the *variables* contained in the term.

EXAMPLE 1 Find the degree of each term.

a. $3x^2$ **b.** $-2^3 x^5$ **c.** y **d.** $12x^2 yz^3$ **e.** 5.27

Solution

a. The exponent on x is 2, so the degree of the term is 2.
b. The exponent on x is 5, so the degree of the term is 5. (Recall that the degree is the sum of the exponents on only the *variables*.)
c. The degree of y, or y^1, is 1.
d. The degree is the sum of the exponents on the variables, or $2 + 1 + 3 = 6$.
e. The degree of 5.27, which can be written as $5.27x^0$, is 0.

PRACTICE 1 Find the degree of each term.

a. $4x^5$ **b.** $-4^3 y^3$ **c.** z **d.** $65a^3 b^7 c$ **e.** 36

From the preceding example, we can say that the degree of a constant is 0. Also, the term 0 has no degree.

Each polynomial also has a degree.

> **Degree of a Polynomial**
> The **degree of a polynomial** is the largest degree of all its terms.

EXAMPLE 2 Find the degree of each polynomial and indicate whether the polynomial is also a monomial, binomial, or trinomial.

	Polynomial	Degree	Classification
a.	$7x^3 - \frac{3}{4}x + 2$	3	Trinomial
b.	$-xyz$	$1 + 1 + 1 = 3$	Monomial
c.	$x^4 - 16.5$	4	Binomial

PRACTICE 2 Find the degree of each polynomial and indicate whether the polynomial is also a monomial, binomial, or trinomial.

	Polynomial	Degree	Classification
a.	$3x^4 + 2x^2 - 3$		
b.	$9abc^3$		
c.	$8x^5 + 5x^3$		

EXAMPLE 3 Find the degree of the polynomial
$$3xy + x^2y^2 - 5x^2 - 6.7$$

Solution The degree of each term is

$$3xy + x^2y^2 - 5x^2 - 6.7$$
Degree: 2   4   2   0

The largest degree of any term is 4, so the degree of this polynomial is 4.

PRACTICE 3 Find the degree of the polynomial $2x^3y - 3x^3y^2 - 9y^5 + 9.6$.

OBJECTIVE 2 ▶ Defining polynomial functions. At times, it is convenient to use function notation to represent polynomials. For example, we may write $P(x)$ to represent the polynomial $3x^2 - 2x - 5$. In symbols, this is

$$P(x) = 3x^2 - 2x - 5$$

This function is called a **polynomial function** because the expression $3x^2 - 2x - 5$ is a polynomial.

> ▶ **Helpful Hint**
> Recall that the symbol $P(x)$ **does not mean** P times x. It is a special symbol used to denote a function.

EXAMPLE 4 If $P(x) = 3x^2 - 2x - 5$, find the following.

a. $P(1)$ **b.** $P(-2)$

Solution

a. Substitute 1 for x in $P(x) = 3x^2 - 2x - 5$ and simplify.
$$P(x) = 3x^2 - 2x - 5$$
$$P(1) = 3(1)^2 - 2(1) - 5 = -4$$

b. Substitute -2 for x in $P(x) = 3x^2 - 2x - 5$ and simplify.
$$P(x) = 3x^2 - 2x - 5$$
$$P(-2) = 3(-2)^2 - 2(-2) - 5 = 11$$

PRACTICE 4 If $P(x) = -5x^2 + 2x - 8$, find the following.

a. $P(-1)$ **b.** $P(3)$

Many real-world phenomena are modeled by polynomial functions. If the polynomial function model is given, we can often find the solution of a problem by evaluating the function at a certain value.

EXAMPLE 5 Finding the Height of an Object

The world's highest bridge, the Millau Viaduct in France, is 1125 feet above the River Tarn. An object is dropped from the top of this bridge. Neglecting air resistance, the height of the object at time t seconds is given by the polynomial function $P(t) = -16t^2 + 1125$. Find the height of the object when $t = 1$ second and when $t = 8$ seconds.

Solution To find the height of the object at 1 second, we find $P(1)$.

$$P(t) = -16t^2 + 1125$$
$$P(1) = -16(1)^2 + 1125$$
$$P(1) = 1109$$

When $t = 1$ second, the height of the object is 1109 feet.
To find the height of the object at 8 seconds, we find $P(8)$.

$$P(t) = -16t^2 + 1125$$
$$P(8) = -16(8)^2 + 1125$$
$$P(8) = 101$$

When $t = 8$ seconds, the height of the object is 101 feet. Notice that as time t increases, the height of the object decreases.

PRACTICE 5 The largest natural bridge is in the canyons at the base of Navajo Mountain, Utah. From the base to the top of the arch, it measures 290 feet. Neglecting air resistance, the height of an object dropped off the bridge is given by the polynomial function $P(t) = -16t^2 + 290$ at time t seconds. Find the height of the object at time $t = 0$ second and $t = 2$ seconds.

OBJECTIVE 3 ▶ Combining like terms review. Before we add polynomials, recall that terms are considered to be **like terms** if they contain exactly the same variables raised to exactly the same powers.

Like Terms	Unlike Terms
$-5x^2, -x^2$	$4x^2, 3x$
$7xy^3z, -2xzy^3$	$12x^2y^3, -2xy^3$

To simplify a polynomial, **combine like terms** by using the distributive property. For example, by the distributive property,

$$5x + 7x = (5 + 7)x = 12x$$

EXAMPLE 6 Simplify by combining like terms.

a. $-12x^2 + 7x^2 - 6x$ **b.** $3xy - 2x + 5xy - x$

Solution By the distributive property,

a. $-12x^2 + 7x^2 - 6x = (-12 + 7)x^2 - 6x = -5x^2 - 6x$

b. Use the associative and commutative properties to group together like terms; then combine.

$$3xy - 2x + 5xy - x = 3xy + 5xy - 2x - x$$
$$= (3 + 5)xy + (-2 - 1)x$$
$$= 8xy - 3x$$

> **Helpful Hint**
> These two terms are unlike terms. They cannot be combined.

PRACTICE 6 Simplify by combining like terms.

a. $8x^4 - 5x^4 - 5x$ **b.** $4ab - 5b + 3ab + 2b$

OBJECTIVE 4 ▶ **Adding polynomials.** Now we have reviewed the necessary skills to add polynomials.

> **Adding Polynomials**
> To add polynomials, combine all like terms.

EXAMPLE 7 Add.

a. $(7x^3y - xy^3 + 11) + (6x^3y - 4)$ **b.** $(3a^3 - b + 2a - 5) + (a + b + 5)$

Solution

a. To add, remove the parentheses and group like terms.

$$(7x^3y - xy^3 + 11) + (6x^3y - 4)$$
$$= 7x^3y - xy^3 + 11 + 6x^3y - 4$$
$$= 7x^3y + 6x^3y - xy^3 + 11 - 4 \quad \text{Group like terms.}$$
$$= 13x^3y - xy^3 + 7 \quad \text{Combine like terms.}$$

b.
$$(3a^3 - b + 2a - 5) + (a + b + 5)$$
$$= 3a^3 - b + 2a - 5 + a + b + 5$$
$$= 3a^3 - b + b + 2a + a - 5 + 5 \quad \text{Group like terms.}$$
$$= 3a^3 + 3a \quad \text{Combine like terms.}$$

PRACTICE 7 Add.

a. $(3a^4b - 5ab^2 + 7) + (9ab^2 - 12)$ **b.** $(2x^5 - 3y + x - 6) + (4y - 2x - 3)$

EXAMPLE 8 Add $11x^3 - 12x^2 + x - 3$ and $x^3 - 10x + 5$.

Solution
$$(11x^3 - 12x^2 + x - 3) + (x^3 - 10x + 5)$$
$$= 11x^3 + x^3 - 12x^2 + x - 10x - 3 + 5 \quad \text{Group like terms.}$$
$$= 12x^3 - 12x^2 - 9x + 2 \quad \text{Combine like terms.}$$

PRACTICE 8 Add $5x^3 - 3x^2 - 9x - 8$ and $x^3 + 9x^2 + 2x$.

Sometimes it is more convenient to add polynomials vertically. To do this, line up like terms beneath one another and add like terms.

OBJECTIVE 5 ▶ **Subtracting polynomials.** The definition of subtraction of real numbers can be extended to apply to polynomials. To subtract a number, we add its opposite.

$$a - b = a + (-b)$$

Likewise, to subtract a polynomial, we add its opposite. In other words, if P and Q are polynomials, then

$$P - Q = P + (-Q)$$

The polynomial $-Q$ is the **opposite**, or **additive inverse**, of the polynomial Q. We can find $-Q$ by writing the opposite of each term of Q.

> **Subtracting Polynomials**
> To subtract a polynomial, add its opposite.

For example,

To subtract, change the signs; then add.

$$(3x^2 + 4x - 7) - (3x^2 - 2x - 5) = (3x^2 + 4x - 7) + (-3x^2 + 2x + 5)$$
$$= 3x^2 + 4x - 7 - 3x^2 + 2x + 5$$
$$= 6x - 2 \qquad \text{Combine like terms.}$$

Concept Check ✓
Which polynomial is the opposite of $16x^3 - 5x + 7$?

a. $-16x^3 - 5x + 7$ **b.** $-16x^3 + 5x - 7$
c. $16x^3 + 5x + 7$ **d.** $-16x^3 + 5x + 7$

EXAMPLE 9   Subtract: $(12z^5 - 12z^3 + z) - (-3z^4 + z^3 + 12z)$

Solution   To subtract, add the opposite of the second polynomial to the first polynomial.

$(12z^5 - 12z^3 + z) - (-3z^4 + z^3 + 12z)$
$= 12z^5 - 12z^3 + z + 3z^4 - z^3 - 12z)$ Add the opposite of the polynomial being subtracted.
$= 12z^5 + 3z^4 - 12z^3 - z^3 + z - 12z$ Group like terms.
$= 12z^5 + 3z^4 - 13z^3 - 11z$ Combine like terms.

PRACTICE 9   Subtract: $(13a^4 - 7a^3 - 9) - (-2a^4 + 8a^3 - 12)$.

Concept Check ✓
Why is the following subtraction incorrect?

$(7z - 5) - (3z - 4)$
$= 7z - 5 - 3z - 4$
$= 4z - 9$

Answers to Concept Check:
First Concept Check: b
Second Concept Check: With parentheses removed, the expression should be
$7z - 5 - 3z + 4 = 4z - 1$

EXAMPLE 10 Subtract $4x^3y^2 - 3x^2y^2 + 2y^2$ from $10x^3y^2 - 7x^2y^2$.

Solution If we subtract 2 from 8, the difference is $8 - 2 = 6$. Notice the order of the numbers, and then write "Subtract $4x^3y^2 - 3x^2y^2 + 2y^2$ from $10x^3y^2 - 7x^2y^2$" as a mathematical expression.

$$(10x^3y^2 - 7x^2y^2) - (4x^3y^2 - 3x^2y^2 + 2y^2)$$
$$= 10x^3y^2 - 7x^2y^2 - 4x^3y^2 + 3x^2y^2 - 2y^2 \quad \text{Remove parentheses.}$$
$$= 6x^3y^2 - 4x^2y^2 - 2y^2 \quad \text{Combine like terms.}$$

PRACTICE 10 Subtract $5x^2y^2 - 3xy^2 + 5y^3$ from $11x^2y^2 - 7xy^2$.

To add or subtract polynomials vertically, just remember to line up like terms. For example, perform the subtraction $(10x^3y^2 - 7x^2y^2) - (4x^3y^2 - 3x^2y^2 + 2y^2)$ vertically.

Add the opposite of the second polynomial.

$$\begin{array}{r} 10x^3y^2 - 7x^2y^2 \\ -(4x^3y^2 - 3x^2y^2 + 2y^2) \end{array} \quad \text{is equivalent to} \quad \begin{array}{r} 10x^3y^2 - 7x^2y^2 \\ -4x^3y^2 + 3x^2y^2 - 2y^2 \\ \hline 6x^3y^2 - 4x^2y^2 - 2y^2 \end{array}$$

Polynomial functions, like polynomials, can be added, subtracted, multiplied, and divided. For example, if

$$P(x) = x^2 + x + 1$$

then

$$2P(x) = 2(x^2 + x + 1) = 2x^2 + 2x + 2 \quad \text{Use the distributive property.}$$

Also, if $Q(x) = 5x^2 - 1$, then $P(x) + Q(x) = (x^2 + x + 1) + (5x^2 - 1) = 6x^2 + x$.

A useful business and economics application of subtracting polynomial functions is finding the profit function $P(x)$ when given a revenue function $R(x)$ and a cost function $C(x)$. In business, it is true that

$$\text{profit} = \text{revenue} - \text{cost, or}$$
$$P(x) = R(x) - C(x)$$

For example, if the revenue function is $R(x) = 7x$ and the cost function is $C(x) = 2x + 5000$, then the profit function is

$$P(x) = R(x) - C(x)$$

or

$$P(x) = 7x - (2x + 5000) \quad \text{Substitute } R(x) = 7x$$
$$P(x) = 5x - 5000 \quad \text{and } C(x) = 2x + 5000.$$

Problem-solving exercises involving profit are in the exercise set.

OBJECTIVE 6 ▶ Recognizing graphs of polynomial functions from their degree. In this section, we reviewed how to find the degree of a polynomial. Knowing the degree of a polynomial can help us recognize the graph of the related polynomial function. For example, we know from Section 3.1 that the graph of the polynomial function $f(x) = x^2$ is a parabola as shown to the left.

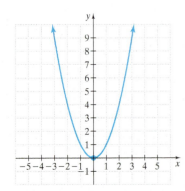

The polynomial x^2 has degree 2. The graphs of all polynomial functions of degree 2 will have this same general shape—opening upward, as shown, or downward. Graphs of polynomial functions of degree 2 or 3 will, in general, resemble one of the graphs shown next.

General Shapes of Graphs of Polynomial Functions
Degree 2

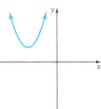
Coefficient of x^2 is a positive number.

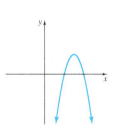
Coefficient of x^2 is a negative number.

Degree 3

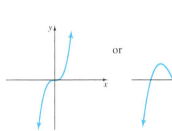 or

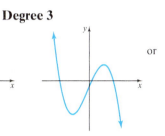 or

Coefficient of x^3 is a positive number.

Coefficient of x^3 is a negative number.

EXAMPLE 11 Determine which of the following graphs most closely resembles the graph of $f(x) = 5x^3 - 6x^2 + 2x + 3$

A 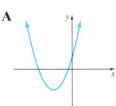 B C D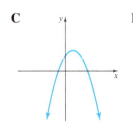

Solution The degree of $f(x)$ is 3, which means that its graph has the shape of B or D. The coefficient of x^3 is 5, a positive number, so the graph has the shape of B.

PRACTICE 11 Determine which of the following graphs most closely resembles the graph of $f(x) = x^3 - 3$.

A 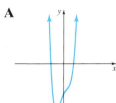 B 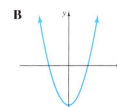 C 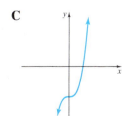 D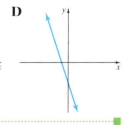

Graphing Calculator Explorations

A graphing calculator may be used to visualize addition and subtraction of polynomials in one variable. For example, to visualize the following polynomial subtraction statement

$$(3x^2 - 6x + 9) - (x^2 - 5x + 6) = 2x^2 - x + 3$$

graph both

$$Y_1 = (3x^2 - 6x + 9) - (x^2 - 5x + 6) \quad \text{Left side of equation}$$

and

$$Y_2 = 2x^2 - x + 3 \quad \text{Right side of equation}$$

on the same screen and see that their graphs coincide. (*Note:* If the graphs do not coincide, we can be sure that a mistake has been made in combining polynomials or in calculator keystrokes. If the graphs appear to coincide, we cannot be sure that our work is correct. This is because it is possible for the graphs to differ so slightly that we do not notice it.)

The graphs of Y_1 and Y_2 are shown. The graphs appear to coincide, so the subtraction statement

$$(3x^2 - 6x + 9) - (x^2 - 5x + 6) = 2x^2 - x + 3$$

appears to be correct.

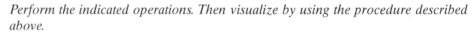

Perform the indicated operations. Then visualize by using the procedure described above.

1. $(2x^2 + 7x + 6) + (x^3 - 6x^2 - 14)$
2. $(-14x^3 - x + 2) + (-x^3 + 3x^2 + 4x)$
3. $(1.8x^2 - 6.8x - 1.7) - (3.9x^2 - 3.6x)$
4. $(-4.8x^2 + 12.5x - 7.8) - (3.1x^2 - 7.8x)$
5. $(1.29x - 5.68) + (7.69x^2 - 2.55x + 10.98)$
6. $(-0.98x^2 - 1.56x + 5.57) + (4.36x - 3.71)$

VOCABULARY & READINESS CHECK

Word Bank. *Use the choices below to fill in each blank. Not all choices will be used.*

monomial	trinomial	like	degree	coefficient
binomial	polynomial	unlike	variables	term

1. The numerical factor of a term is the _____.
2. A _____ is a finite sum of terms in which all variables are raised to nonnegative integer powers and no variables appear in any denominator.
3. A _____ is a polynomial with 2 terms.
4. A _____ is a polynomial with 1 term.
5. A _____ is a polynomial with 3 terms.
6. The degree of a term is the sum of the exponents on the _____ in the term.
7. The _____ of a polynomial is the largest degree of all its terms.
8. _____ terms contain the same variables raised to the same powers.

Add or subtract, if possible.

9. $5x + x$
10. $5x - x$
11. $y + y$
12. $z^2 + z^2$
13. $7xy^2 - y^2$
14. $x^3 - 9x^3$

6.3 EXERCISE SET

Find the degree of each term. See Example 1.

1. 4
2. 7
3. $5x^2$
4. $-z^3$
5. $-3xy^2$
6. $12x^3z$
7. -8^7y^3
8. $-9^{11}y^5$
9. $3.78ab^3c^5$
10. $9.11r^2st^{12}$

Find the degree of each polynomial and indicate whether the polynomial is a monomial, binomial, trinomial, or none of these. See Examples 2 and 3.

11. $6x + 0.3$
12. $7x - 0.8$
13. $3x^2 - 2x + 5$
14. $5x^2 - 3x - 2$
15. -3^4xy^2
16. -7^5abc
17. $x^2y - 4xy^2 + 5x + y^4$
18. $-2x^2y - 3y^2 + 4x + y^5$

If $P(x) = x^2 + x + 1$ and $Q(x) = 5x^2 - 1$, find the following. See Example 4.

19. $P(7)$
20. $Q(4)$
21. $Q(-10)$
22. $P(-4)$
23. $Q\left(\dfrac{1}{4}\right)$
24. $P\left(\dfrac{1}{2}\right)$

Refer to Example 5 for Exercises 25 through 28.

25. Find the height of the object at $t = 2$ seconds.
26. Find the height of the object at $t = 4$ seconds.
27. Find the height of the object at $t = 6$ seconds.
28. Approximate (to the nearest second) how long it takes before the object hits the ground. (*Hint:* The object hits the ground when $P(x) = 0$.)

Simplify by combining like terms. See Example 6.

29. $5y + y$
30. $-x + 3x$
31. $4x + 7x - 3$
32. $-8y + 9y + 4y^2$
33. $4xy + 2x - 3xy - 1$
34. $-8xy^2 + 4x - x + 2xy^2$
35. $7x^2 - 2xy + 5y^2 - x^2 + xy + 11y^2$
36. $-a^2 + 18ab - 2b^2 + 14a^2 - 12ab - b^2$

MIXED PRACTICE

Perform the indicated operations. See Examples 7 through 10.

37. $(9y^2 - 8) + (9y^2 - 9)$
38. $(x^2 + 4x - 7) + (8x^2 + 9x - 7)$
39. Add $(x^2 + xy - y^2)$ and $(2x^2 - 4xy + 7y^2)$.
40. Add $(4x^3 - 6x^2 + 5x + 7)$ and $(2x^2 + 6x - 3)$.

41. $\quad x^2 - 6x + 3$
    $+\;\;(2x + 5)$

42. $\quad -2x^2 + 3x - 9$
    $+\;\;(2x - 3)$

43. $(9y^2 - 7y + 5) - (8y^2 - 7y + 2)$
44. $(2x^2 + 3x + 12) - (5x - 7)$
45. Subtract $(6x^2 - 3x)$ from $(4x^2 + 2x)$.
46. Subtract $(xy + x - y)$ from $(xy + x - 3)$.

47. $\quad 3x^2 - 4x + 8$
    $-\;\;(5x^2 - 7)$

48. $\quad -3x^2 - 4x + 8$
    $-\;\;(5x + 12)$

49. $(5x - 11) + (-x - 2)$
50. $(3x^2 - 2x) + (5x^2 - 9x)$
51. $(7x^2 + x + 1) - (6x^2 + x - 1)$
52. $(4x - 4) - (-x - 4)$
53. $(7x^3 - 4x + 8) + (5x^3 + 4x + 8x)$
54. $(9xyz + 4x - y) + (-9xyz - 3x + y + 2)$
55. $(9x^3 - 2x^2 + 4x - 7) - (2x^3 - 6x^2 - 4x + 3)$
56. $(3x^2 + 6xy + 3y^2) - (8x^2 - 6xy - y^2)$
57. Add $(y^2 + 4yx + 7)$ and $(-19y^2 + 7yx + 7)$.
58. Subtract $(x - 4)$ from $(3x^2 - 4x + 5)$.
59. $(3x^3 - b + 2a - 6) + (-4x^3 + b + 6a - 6)$
60. $(5x^2 - 6) + (2x^2 - 4x + 8)$
61. $(4x^2 - 6x + 2) - (-x^2 + 3x + 5)$
62. $(5x^2 + x + 9) - (2x^2 - 9)$
63. $(-3x + 8) + (-3x^2 + 3x - 5)$
64. $(5y^2 - 2y + 4) + (3y + 7)$
65. $(-3 + 4x^2 + 7xy^2) + (2x^3 - x^2 + xy^2)$
66. $(-3x^2y + 4) - (-7x^2y - 8y)$

67. $\quad 6y^2 - 6y + 4$
    $-(-y^2 - 6y + 7)$

68. $\quad -4x^3 + 4x^2 - 4x$
    $-(2x^3 - 2x^2 + 3x)$

69. $\quad 3x^2 + 15x + 8$
    $+(2x^2 + 7x + 8)$

70. $\quad 9x^2 + 9x - 4$
    $+(7x^2 - 3x - 4)$

71. $\left(\dfrac{1}{2}x^2 - \dfrac{1}{3}x^2y + 2y^3\right) + \left(\dfrac{1}{4}x^2 - \dfrac{8}{3}x^2y - \dfrac{1}{2}y^3\right)$

72. $\left(\frac{2}{5}a^2 - ab + \frac{4}{3}b^2\right) + \left(\frac{1}{5}a^2b - ab + \frac{5}{6}b^2\right)$

73. Find the sum of $(5q^4 - 2q^2 - 3q)$ and $(-6q^4 + 3q^2 + 5)$.

74. Find the sum of $(5y^4 - 7y^2 + x^2 - 3)$ and $(-3y^4 + 2y^2 + 4)$.

75. Subtract $(3x + 7)$ from the sum of $(7x^2 + 4x + 9)$ and $(8x^2 + 7x - 8)$.

76. Subtract $(9x + 8)$ from the sum of $(3x^2 - 2x - x^3 + 2)$ and $(5x^2 - 8x - x^3 + 4)$.

77. Find the sum of $(4x^4 - 7x^2 + 3)$ and $(2 - 3x^4)$.

78. Find the sum of $(8x^4 - 14x^2 + 6)$ and $(-12x^6 - 21x^4 - 9x^2)$.

79. $\left(\frac{2}{3}x^2 - \frac{1}{6}x + \frac{5}{6}\right) - \left(\frac{1}{3}x^2 + \frac{5}{6}x - \frac{1}{6}\right)$

80. $\left(\frac{3}{16}x^2 + \frac{5}{8}x - \frac{1}{4}\right) - \left(\frac{5}{16}x^2 - \frac{3}{8}x + \frac{3}{4}\right)$

Solve. See Example 5.

The surface area of a rectangular box is given by the polynomial function

$$f(x) = 2HL + 2LW + 2HW$$

and is measured in square units. In business, surface area is often calculated to help determine cost of materials.

81. A rectangular box is to be constructed to hold a new camcorder. The box is to have dimensions 5 inches by 4 inches by 9 inches. Find the surface area of the box.

82. Suppose it has been determined that a box of dimensions 4 inches by 4 inches by 8.5 inches can be used to contain the camcorder in Exercise 81. Find the surface area of this box and calculate the square inches of material saved by using this box instead of the box in Exercise 81.

83. Multiple Steps. A projectile is fired upward from the ground with an initial velocity of 300 feet per second. Neglecting air resistance, the height of the projectile at any time t can be described by the polynomial function $P(t) = -16t^2 + 300t$. Find the height of the projectile at each given time.

  a. $t = 1$ second **b.** $t = 2$ seconds
  c. $t = 3$ seconds **d.** $t = 4$ seconds
  e. Explain why the height increases and then decreases as time passes.
  f. Approximate (to the nearest second) how long before the object hits the ground.

84. Multiple Steps. An object is thrown upward with an initial velocity of 25 feet per second from the top of the 984-foot-high Eiffel Tower in Paris, France. The height of the object at any time t can be described by the polynomial function $P(t) = -16t^2 + 25t + 984$. Find the height of the projectile at each given time. (*Source:* Council on Tall Buildings and Urban Habitat, Lehigh University)

  a. $t = 1$ second
  b. $t = 3$ seconds
  c. $t = 5$ seconds
  d. Approximate (to the nearest second) how long before the object hits the ground.

85. The polynomial function $P(x) = 45x - 100,000$ models the relationship between the number of computer briefcases x that a company sells and the profit the company makes, $P(x)$. Find $P(4000)$, the profit from selling 4000 computer briefcases.

86. The total cost (in dollars) for MCD, Inc., Manufacturing Company to produce x blank audiocassette tapes per week is given by the polynomial function $C(x) = 0.8x + 10,000$. Find the total cost of producing 20,000 tapes per week.

87. The total revenues (in dollars) for MCD, Inc., Manufacturing Company to sell x blank audiocassette tapes per week is given by the polynomial function $R(x) = 2x$. Find the total revenue from selling 20,000 tapes per week.

88. In business, profit equals revenue minus cost, or $P(x) = R(x) - C(x)$. Find the profit function for MCD, Inc. by subtracting the given functions in Exercises 86 and 87.

Matching. *Match each equation with its graph. See Example 11.*

89. $f(x) = 3x^2 - 2$

90. $h(x) = 5x^3 - 6x + 2$

91. $g(x) = -2x^3 - 3x^2 + 3x - 2$

92. $F(x) = -2x^2 - 6x + 2$

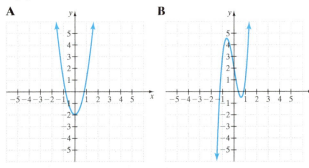

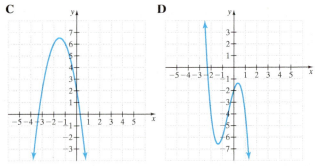

REVIEW AND PREVIEW

Multiply. See Section 1.4.

93. $5(3x - 2)$

94. $-7(2z - 6y)$

95. $-2(x^2 - 5x + 6)$

96. $5(-3y^2 - 2y + 7)$

CONCEPT EXTENSIONS

Solve. See the Concept Checks in this section.

97. Which polynomial(s) is the opposite of $8x - 6$?
  a. $-(8x - 6)$
  b. $8x + 6$
  c. $-8x + 6$
  d. $-8x - 6$

98. Which polynomial(s) is the opposite of $-y^5 + 10y^3 - 2.3$?
  a. $y^5 + 10y^3 + 2.3$
  b. $-y^5 - 10y^3 - 2.3$
  c. $y^5 + 10y^3 - 2.3$
  d. $y^5 - 10y^3 + 2.3$

99. Correct the subtraction.
$$(12x - 1.7) - (15x + 6.2) = 12x - 1.7 - 15x + 6.2$$
$$= -3x + 4.5$$

100. Correct the addition.
$$(12x - 1.7) + (15x + 6.2) = 12x - 1.7 + 15x + 6.2$$
$$= 27x + 7.9$$

101. Write a function, $P(x)$, so that $P(0) = 7$.

102. Write a function, $R(x)$, so that $R(1) = 2$.

103. In your own words, describe how to find the degree of a term.

104. In your own words, describe how to find the degree of a polynomial.

Perform the indicated operations.

105. $(4x^{2a} - 3x^a + 0.5) - (x^{2a} - 5x^a - 0.2)$

106. $(9y^{5a} - 4y^{3a} + 1.5y) - (6y^{5a} - y^{3a} + 4.7y)$

107. $(8x^{2y} - 7x^y + 3) + (-4x^{2y} + 9x^y - 14)$

108. $(14z^{5x} + 3z^{2x} + z) - (2z^{5x} - 10z^{2x} + 3z)$

Find each perimeter.

109.

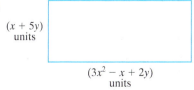

110.

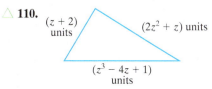

If $P(x) = 3x + 3$, $Q(x) = 4x^2 - 6x + 3$, and $R(x) = 5x^2 - 7$, find the following.

111. $P(x) + Q(x)$

112. $R(x) + P(x)$

113. $Q(x) - R(x)$

114. $P(x) - Q(x)$

115. $2[Q(x)] - R(x)$

116. $-5[P(x)] - Q(x)$

117. $3[R(x)] + 4[P(x)]$

118. $2[Q(x)] + 7[R(x)]$

If $P(x)$ is the polynomial given, find a. $P(a)$, b. $P(-x)$, and c. $P(x + h)$.

119. $P(x) = 2x - 3$

120. $P(x) = 8x + 3$

121. $P(x) = 4x$

122. $P(x) = -4x$

123. $P(x) = 4x - 1$

124. $P(x) = 3x - 2$

125. Read a Graph. The function $f(x) = 0.07x^2 - 0.8x + 3.6$ can be used to approximate the amazing growth of the number of Web logs (Blogs) appearing on the Internet from January 2004 to October 2006, where January, 2004 = 1 for x, February 2004 = 2 for x, and so on, and y is the number of blogs (in millions). Round answers to the nearest tenth of a million. (Note: This is one company's tracking of the cumulative number of blogs. These numbers vary greatly according to source and activity of blog.) (*Source:* Technorati)

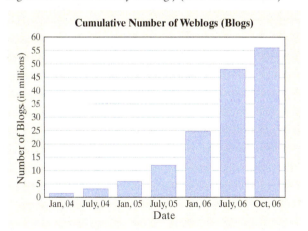

a. Approximate the number of Web logs on the Internet in January 2004.

b. Approximate the number of Web logs on the Internet in October 2006.

c. Use this function to approximate the number of Web logs on the Internet in May 2009. (65 months)

d. From parts (a), (b), and (c), determine whether the number of Web logs on the Internet is increasing at a steady rate. Explain why or why not.

126. The function $f(x) = -61x^2 - 5530x + 585{,}753$ can be used to approximate the number of international students studying in the United States during the academic years 2002 through 2006, where x is the number of years after 2002 and $f(x)$ is the number of international students.

(*Source:* Institute of International Education: *Open Doors 2006*)

a. Approximate the number of international students studying in the United States in 2003.

b. Approximate the number of international students studying in the United States in 2005.

c. Use the function to predict the number of international students studying in the United States in 2008.

127. The function $f(x) = -0.39x^2 + 2.49x + 38.7$ can be used to approximate the number of Americans under age 65 without health insurance during the period 1999–2005, where x is the number of years after 1999 and $f(x)$ is the number in millions of Americans. Round answers to the nearest tenth of a million. (*Source:* National Center for Health Statistics)

a. Approximate the number of Americans under 65 without health insurance in 2003.

b. Use the function to predict the number of Americans under 65 without health insurance in 2008.

128. University libraries need to continue to grow to meet the educational needs of their students. The function $f(x) = -14x^2 + 269.2x + 7414.2$ approximates the number of written volumes (in thousands) to be found in the University of California, Los Angeles, libraries for the years from 2002 to 2005, where x is the number of years after 2002. (*Source:* Association of Research Libraries)

a. Approximate the number of volumes in 2004.

b. Use the function to estimate the number of volumes at UCLA libraries in 2008.

129. Sport utility vehicle (SUV) sales in the United States have increased since 1995. The function $f(x) = -0.005x^2 + 0.377x + 1.71$ can be used to approximate the number of SUV sales during the years 1995–2004, where x is the number of years after 1995 and $f(x)$ is the SUV sales (in millions). Round answers to the nearest tenth of a million. (*Source:* Bureau of Transportation Statistics)

a. Approximate the number of SUVs sold in 2003.

b. Use the function to predict the number of SUVs sold in 2010.

130. The function $f(x) = 873x^2 - 4104x + 40,263$ can be used to approximate the number of AIDS cases diagnosed in the United States from 2001 to 2005, where x is the number of years since 2001. (*Source:* Based on data from the U.S. Centers for Disease Control and Prevention)

a. Approximate the number of AIDS cases diagnosed in the United States in 2001.

b. Approximate the number of AIDS cases diagnosed in the United States in 2003.

c. Approximate the number of AIDS cases diagnosed in the United States in 2005.

d. Describe the trend in the number of AIDS cases diagnosed during the period covered by this model.

6.4 MULTIPLYING POLYNOMIALS

OBJECTIVES

1. Multiply two polynomials.
2. Multiply binomials.
3. Square binomials.
4. Multiply the sum and difference of two terms.
5. Multiply three or more polynomials.
6. Evaluate polynomial functions.

OBJECTIVE 1 ▶ Multiplying two polynomials. Properties of real numbers and exponents are used continually in the process of multiplying polynomials. To multiply monomials, for example, we apply the commutative and associative properties of real numbers and the product rule for *exponents*.

EXAMPLE 1 Multiply.

a. $(2x^3)(5x^6)$
b. $(7y^4z^4)(-xy^{11}z^5)$

Solution Group like bases and apply the product rule for exponents.

a. $(2x^3)(5x^6) = 2(5)(x^3)(x^6) = 10x^9$
b. $(7y^4z^4)(-xy^{11}z^5) = 7(-1)x(y^4y^{11})(z^4z^5) = -7xy^{15}z^9$

PRACTICE 1 Multiply.

a. $(3x^4)(2x^2)$
b. $(-5m^4np^3)(-8mnp^5)$

To multiply a monomial by a polynomial other than a monomial, we use an expanded form of the distributive property.

$$a(b + c + d + \cdots + z) = ab + ac + ad + \cdots + az$$

Notice that the monomial a is multiplied by each term of the polynomial.

▶ **Helpful Hint**

See Sections 6.1 and 6.2 to review exponential expressions further.

Section 6.4 Multiplying Polynomials **315**

EXAMPLE 2 Multiply.

a. $2x(5x - 4)$ **b.** $-3x^2(4x^2 - 6x + 1)$ **c.** $-xy(7x^2y + 3xy - 11)$

Solution Apply the distributive property.

a. $2x(5x - 4) = 2x(5x) + 2x(-4)$ Use the distributive property.
$ = 10x^2 - 8x$ Multiply.

b. $-3x^2(4x^2 - 6x + 1) = -3x^2(4x^2) + (-3x^2)(-6x) + (-3x^2)(1)$
$ = -12x^4 + 18x^3 - 3x^2$

c. $-xy(7x^2y + 3xy - 11) = -xy(7x^2y) + (-xy)(3xy) + (-xy)(-11)$
$ = -7x^3y^2 - 3x^2y^2 + 11xy$

PRACTICE
2 Multiply.

a. $3x(7x - 1)$ **b.** $-5a^2(3a^2 - 6a + 5)$ **c.** $-mn^3(5m^2n^2 + 2mn - 5m)$

To multiply any two polynomials, we can use the following.

Multiplying Two Polynomials
To multiply any two polynomials, use the distributive property and multiply each term of one polynomial by each term of the other polynomial. Then combine any like terms.

Concept Check ✓
Find the error:

$$4x(x - 5) + 2x$$
$$= 4x(x) + 4x(-5) + 4x(2x)$$
$$= 4x^2 - 20x + 8x^2$$
$$= 12x^2 - 20x$$

EXAMPLE 3 Multiply and simplify the product if possible.

a. $(x + 3)(2x + 5)$ **b.** $(2x - 3)(5x^2 - 6x + 7)$

Solution

a. Multiply each term of $(x + 3)$ by $(2x + 5)$.

$(x + 3)(2x + 5) = x(2x + 5) + 3(2x + 5)$ Apply the distributive property.
$ = 2x^2 + 5x + 6x + 15$ Apply the distributive property again.
$ = 2x^2 + 11x + 15$ Combine like terms.

b. Multiply each term of $(2x - 3)$ by each term of $(5x^2 - 6x + 7)$.

$(2x - 3)(5x^2 - 6x + 7) = 2x(5x^2 - 6x + 7) + (-3)(5x^2 - 6x + 7)$
$ = 10x^3 - 12x^2 + 14x - 15x^2 + 18x - 21$
$ = 10x^3 - 27x^2 + 32x - 21$ Combine like terms.

PRACTICE
3 Multiply and simplify the product if possible.

a. $(x + 5)(2x + 3)$ **b.** $(3x - 1)(x^2 - 6x + 2)$

Answer to Concept Check:
$4x(x - 5) + 2x$
$= 4x(x) + 4x(-5) + 2x$
$= 4x^2 - 20x + 2x$
$= 4x^2 - 18x$

Sometimes polynomials are easier to multiply vertically, in the same way we multiply real numbers. When multiplying vertically, we line up like terms in the **partial products** vertically. This makes combining like terms easier.

EXAMPLE 4 Multiply vertically $(4x^2 + 7)(x^2 + 2x + 8)$.

Solution

$$
\begin{array}{r}
x^2 + 2x + 8 \\
4x^2 + 7 \\
\hline
7x^2 + 14x + 56 \\
4x^4 + 8x^3 + 32x^2 \\
\hline
4x^4 + 8x^3 + 39x^2 + 14x + 56
\end{array}
$$

$7(x^2 + 2x + 8)$
$4x^2(x^2 + 2x + 8)$
Combine like terms.

PRACTICE 4 Multiply vertically: $(3x^2 + 2)(x^2 - 4x - 5)$.

OBJECTIVE 2 ▶ Multiplying binomials. When multiplying a binomial by a binomial, we can use a special order of multiplying terms, called the **FOIL** order. The letters of FOIL stand for "**F**irst-**O**uter-**I**nner-**L**ast." To illustrate this method, let's multiply $(2x - 3)$ by $(3x + 1)$.

Multiply the **F**irst terms of each binomial. $(2x - 3)(3x + 1)$ **F** $2x(3x) = 6x^2$

Multiply the **O**uter terms of each binomial. $(2x - 3)(3x + 1)$ **O** $2x(1) = 2x$

Multiply the **I**nner terms of each binomial. $(2x - 3)(3x + 1)$ **I** $-3(3x) = -9x$

Multiply the **L**ast terms of each binomial. $(2x - 3)(3x + 1)$ **L** $-3(1) = -3$
Combine like terms.

$$6x^2 + 2x - 9x - 3 = 6x^2 - 7x - 3$$

EXAMPLE 5 Use the FOIL order to multiply $(x - 1)(x + 2)$.

Solution

$$
\begin{aligned}
(x - 1)(x + 2) &= \overset{\text{First}}{x \cdot x} + \overset{\text{Outer}}{2 \cdot x} + \overset{\text{Inner}}{(-1)x} + \overset{\text{Last}}{(-1)(2)} \\
&= x^2 + 2x - x - 2 \\
&= x^2 + x - 2 \quad \text{Combine like terms.}
\end{aligned}
$$

PRACTICE 5 Use the FOIL order to multiply $(x - 5)(x + 3)$.

EXAMPLE 6 Multiply.

a. $(2x - 7)(3x - 4)$ **b.** $(3x^2 + y)(5x^2 - 2y)$

Solution

$$
\begin{aligned}
\textbf{a. } (2x - 7)(3x - 4) &= \overset{\text{First}}{2x(3x)} + \overset{\text{Outer}}{2x(-4)} + \overset{\text{Inner}}{(-7)(3x)} + \overset{\text{Last}}{(-7)(-4)} \\
&= 6x^2 - 8x - 21x + 28 \\
&= 6x^2 - 29x + 28
\end{aligned}
$$

Section 6.4 Multiplying Polynomials **317**

$$\text{b. } (3x^2 + y)(5x^2 - 2y) \overset{F\ \ O\ \ I\ \ L}{=} 15x^4 - 6x^2y + 5x^2y - 2y^2$$
$$= 15x^4 - x^2y - 2y^2$$

PRACTICE 6 Multiply.

a. $(3x - 5)(2x - 7)$ **b.** $(2x^2 - 3y)(4x^2 + y)$

OBJECTIVE 3 ▶ Squaring binomials. The **square of a binomial** is a special case of the product of two binomials. By the FOIL order for multiplying two binomials, we have

$$(a + b)^2 = (a + b)(a + b)$$
$$\overset{F\ \ O\ \ I\ \ L}{= a^2 + ab + ba + b^2}$$
$$= a^2 + 2ab + b^2$$

This product can be visualized geometrically by analyzing areas.

Area of larger square: $(a + b)^2$

Sum of areas of smaller rectangles: $a^2 + 2ab + b^2$

Thus, $(a + b)^2 = a^2 + 2ab + b^2$

The same pattern occurs for the square of a difference. In general,

---

Square of a Binomial

$$(a + b)^2 = a^2 + 2ab + b^2 \qquad (a - b)^2 = a^2 - 2ab + b^2$$

In other words, a binomial squared is the sum of the first term squared, twice the product of both terms, and the second term squared.

EXAMPLE 7 Multiply.

a. $(x + 5)^2$ **b.** $(x - 9)^2$ **c.** $(3x + 2z)^2$ **d.** $(4m^2 - 3n)^2$

Solution

$$(a + b)^2 = a^2 + 2 \cdot a \cdot b + b^2$$

a. $(x + 5)^2 = x^2 + 2 \cdot x \cdot 5 + 5^2 = x^2 + 10x + 25$
b. $(x - 9)^2 = x^2 - 2 \cdot x \cdot 9 + 9^2 = x^2 - 18x + 81$
c. $(3x + 2z)^2 = (3x)^2 + 2(3x)(2z) + (2z)^2 = 9x^2 + 12xz + 4z^2$
d. $(4m^2 - 3n)^2 = (4m^2)^2 - 2(4m^2)(3n) + (3n)^2 = 16m^4 - 24m^2n + 9n^2$

PRACTICE 7 Multiply.

a. $(x + 6)^2$ **b.** $(x - 2)^2$ **c.** $(3x + 5y)^2$ **d.** $(3x^2 - 8b)^2$

▶ **Helpful Hint**

Note that $(a + b)^2 = a^2 + 2ab + b^2$, **not** $a^2 + b^2$. Also,
$(a - b)^2 = a^2 - 2ab + b^2$, **not** $a^2 - b^2$.

OBJECTIVE 4 ▶ Multiplying the sum and difference of two terms. Another special product applies to the sum and difference of the same two terms. Multiply $(a + b)(a - b)$ to see a pattern.

$$(a + b)(a - b) = a^2 - ab + ba - b^2$$
$$= a^2 - b^2$$

> **Product of the Sum and Difference of Two Terms**
>
> $$(a + b)(a - b) = a^2 - b^2$$

The product of the sum and difference of the same two terms is the difference of the first term squared and the second term squared.

EXAMPLE 8 Multiply.

a. $(x - 3)(x + 3)$

b. $(4y + 1)(4y - 1)$

c. $(x^2 + 2y)(x^2 - 2y)$

d. $\left(3m^2 - \dfrac{1}{2}\right)\left(3m^2 + \dfrac{1}{2}\right)$

Solution

$(a + b)(a - b) = a^2 - b^2$

a. $\;\;\;\downarrow\;\;\downarrow\;\;\;\downarrow\;\;\;\;\downarrow\;\;\;\downarrow$
$(x + 3)(x - 3) = x^2 - 3^2 = x^2 - 9$

b. $(4y + 1)(4y - 1) = (4y)^2 - 1^2 = 16y^2 - 1$

c. $(x^2 + 2y)(x^2 - 2y) = (x^2)^2 - (2y)^2 = x^4 - 4y^2$

d. $\left(3m^2 - \dfrac{1}{2}\right)\left(3m^2 + \dfrac{1}{2}\right) = (3m^2)^2 - \left(\dfrac{1}{2}\right)^2 = 9m^4 - \dfrac{1}{4}$ □

PRACTICE 8 Multiply.

a. $(x - 7)(x + 7)$

b. $(2a + 5)(2a - 5)$

c. $\left(5x^2 + \dfrac{1}{4}\right)\left(5x^2 - \dfrac{1}{4}\right)$

d. $(a^3 - 4b^2)(a^3 + 4b^2)$

EXAMPLE 9 Multiply $[3 + (2a + b)]^2$.

Solution Think of 3 as the first term and $(2a + b)$ as the second term, and apply the method for squaring a binomial.

$[a\;\;+\;\;\;b]^2 = a^2 + 2(a) \cdot b + b^2$
$[3 + \overbrace{(2a + b)}]^2 = 3^2 + 2(3)\overbrace{(2a + b)} + \overbrace{(2a + b)}^2$
$= 9 + 6(2a + b) + (2a + b)^2$
$= 9 + 12a + 6b + (2a)^2 + 2(2a)(b) + b^2 \quad\text{Square }(2a + b).$
$= 9 + 12a + 6b + 4a^2 + 4ab + b^2$ □

PRACTICE 9 Multiply $[2 + (3x - y)]^2$.

Section 6.4 Multiplying Polynomials 319

EXAMPLE 10 Multiply $[(5x - 2y) - 1][(5x - 2y) + 1]$.

Solution Think of $(5x - 2y)$ as the first term and 1 as the second term, and apply the method for the product of the sum and difference of two terms.

$$\overbrace{[(5x - 2y)}^{(a} \overbrace{- 1][}^{- b)} \overbrace{(5x - 2y)}^{(a} \overbrace{+ 1]}^{+ b)} = \overbrace{(5x - 2y)^2}^{a^2} - \overbrace{1^2}^{- b^2}$$

$$= (5x)^2 - 2(5x)(2y) + (2y)^2 - 1 \quad \text{Square } (5x - 2y).$$

$$= 25x^2 - 20xy + 4y^2 - 1$$

PRACTICE 10 Multiply $[(3x - y) - 5][(3x - y) + 5]$.

OBJECTIVE 5 ▶ Multiplying three or more polynomials. To multiply three or more polynomials, more than one method may be needed.

EXAMPLE 11 Multiply: $(x - 3)(x + 3)(x^2 - 9)$

Solution We multiply the first two binomials, the sum and difference of two terms. Then we multiply the resulting two binomials, the square of a binomial.

$$(x - 3)(x + 3)(x^2 - 9) = (x^2 - 9)(x^2 - 9) \quad \text{Multiply } (x - 3)(x + 3).$$
$$= (x^2 - 9)^2$$
$$= x^4 - 18x^2 + 81 \quad \text{Square } (x^2 - 9).$$

PRACTICE 11 Multiply $(x + 4)(x - 4)(x^2 - 16)$.

OBJECTIVE 6 ▶ Evaluating polynomial functions. Our work in multiplying polynomials is often useful in evaluating polynomial functions.

EXAMPLE 12 If $f(x) = x^2 + 5x - 2$, find $f(a + 1)$.

Solution To find $f(a + 1)$, replace x with the expression $a + 1$ in the polynomial function $f(x)$.

$$f(x) = x^2 + 5x - 2$$
$$f(a + 1) = (a + 1)^2 + 5(a + 1) - 2$$
$$= a^2 + 2a + 1 + 5a + 5 - 2$$
$$= a^2 + 7a + 4$$

PRACTICE 12 If $f(x) = x^2 - 3x + 5$, find $f(h + 1)$.

Graphing Calculator Explorations

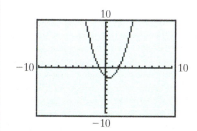

In the previous section, we used a graphing calculator to visualize addition and subtraction of polynomials in one variable. In this section, the same method is used to visualize multiplication of polynomials in one variable. For example, to see that

$$(x - 2)(x + 1) = x^2 - x - 2,$$

graph both $Y_1 = (x - 2)(x + 1)$ and $Y_2 = x^2 - x - 2$ on the same screen and see whether their graphs coincide.

By tracing along both graphs, we see that the graphs of Y_1 and Y_2 appear to coincide, and thus $(x - 2)(x + 1) = x^2 - x - 2$ appears to be correct.

320 CHAPTER 6 Exponents, Polynomials, and Polynomial Functions

Multiply. Then use a graphing calculator to visualize the results.

1. $(x + 4)(x - 4)$
2. $(x + 3)(x + 3)$
3. $(3x - 7)^2$
4. $(5x - 2)^2$
5. $(5x + 1)(x^2 - 3x - 2)$
6. $(7x + 4)(2x^2 + 3x - 5)$

VOCABULARY & READINESS CHECK

Multiple Choice. *Use the choices to fill in each blank.*

1. $(6x^3)\left(\dfrac{1}{2}x^3\right) = $ _____

    a. $3x^3$ b. $3x^6$ c. $10x^6$ d. $\dfrac{13}{2}x^6$

2. $(x + 7)^2 = $ _____

    a. $x^2 + 49$ b. $x^2 - 49$ c. $x^2 + 14x + 49$ d. $x^2 + 7x + 49$

3. $(x + 7)(x - 7) = $ _____

    a. $x^2 + 49$ b. $x^2 - 49$ c. $x^2 + 14x - 49$ d. $x^2 + 7x - 49$

4. The product of $(3x - 1)(4x^2 - 2x + 1)$ is a polynomial of degree _____.

    a. 3   b. 12   c. $12x^3$ d. 2

5. If $f(x) = x^2 + 1$ then $f(a + 1) = $ _____

    a. $(a + 1)^2$ b. $a + 1$ c. $(a + 1)^2 + (a + 1)$ d. $(a + 1)^2 + 1$

6. $[x + (2y + 1)]^2 = $ _____

    a. $[x + (2y + 1)][x - (2y + 1)]$ b. $[x + (2y + 1)][x + (2y + 1)]$ c. $[x + (2y + 1)][x + (2y - 1)]$

6.4 EXERCISE SET

Multiply. See Examples 1 through 4.

1. $(-4x^3)(3x^2)$
2. $(-6a)(4a)$
3. $3x(4x + 7)$
4. $5x(6x - 4)$
5. $-6xy(4x + y)$
6. $-8y(6xy + 4x)$
7. $-4ab(xa^2 + ya^2 - 3)$
8. $-6b^2z(z^2a + baz - 3b)$
9. $(x - 3)(2x + 4)$
10. $(y + 5)(3y - 2)$
11. $(2x + 3)(x^3 - x + 2)$
12. $(a + 2)(3a^2 - a + 5)$
13. $\begin{array}{r} 3x - 2 \\ \times\ 5x + 1 \end{array}$
14. $\begin{array}{r} 2z - 4 \\ \times\ 6z - 2 \end{array}$
15. $\begin{array}{r} 3m^2 + 2m - 1 \\ \times\ \qquad 5m + 2 \end{array}$
16. $\begin{array}{r} 2x^2 - 3x - 4 \\ \times\ \qquad x + 5 \end{array}$

Multiply the binomials. See Examples 5 and 6.

17. $(x - 3)(x + 4)$
18. $(c - 3)(c + 1)$
19. $(5x + 8y)(2x - y)$
20. $(2n - 9m)(n - 7m)$
21. $(3x - 1)(x + 3)$
22. $(5d - 3)(d + 6)$
23. $\left(3x + \dfrac{1}{2}\right)\left(3x - \dfrac{1}{2}\right)$
24. $\left(2x - \dfrac{1}{3}\right)\left(2x + \dfrac{1}{3}\right)$
25. $(5x^2 - 2y^2)(x^2 - 3y^2)$
26. $(4x^2 - 5y^2)(x^2 - 2y^2)$

Multiply, using special product methods. See Examples 7 and 8.

27. $(x + 4)^2$
28. $(x - 5)^2$
29. $(6y - 1)(6y + 1)$
30. $(7x - 9)(7x + 9)$
31. $(3x - y)^2$
32. $(4x - z)^2$
33. $(5b - 6y)(5b + 6y)$
34. $(2x - 4y)(2x + 4y)$

Multiply, using special product methods. See Examples 9 and 10.

35. $[3 + (4b + 1)]^2$
36. $[5 - (3b - 3)]^2$
37. $[(2s - 3) - 1][(2s - 3) + 1]$
38. $[(2y + 5) + 6][(2y + 5) - 6]$
39. $[(xy + 4) - 6]^2$
40. $[(2a^2 + 4a) + 1]^2$

41. Explain when the FOIL method can be used to multiply polynomials.
42. Explain why the product of $(a + b)$ and $(a - b)$ is not a trinomial.

Multiply. See Example 11.

43. $(x + y)(x - y)(x^2 - y^2)$
44. $(z - y)(z + y)(z^2 - y^2)$
45. $(x - 2)^4$
46. $(x - 1)^4$
47. $(x - 5)(x + 5)(x^2 + 25)$
48. $(x + 3)(x - 3)(x^2 + 9)$

MIXED PRACTICE

Multiply.

49. $(3x + 1)(3x + 5)$
50. $(4x - 5)(5x + 6)$
51. $(2x^3 + 5)(5x^2 + 4x + 1)$
52. $(3y^3 - 1)(3y^3 - 6y + 1)$
53. $(7x - 3)(7x + 3)$
54. $(4x + 1)(4x - 1)$
55. $\quad 3x^2 + 4x - 4$
    $\underline{\times \quad\quad 3x + 6}$
56. $\quad 6x^2 + 2x - 1$
    $\underline{\times \quad\quad 3x - 6}$
57. $\left(4x + \dfrac{1}{3}\right)\left(4x - \dfrac{1}{2}\right)$
58. $\left(4y - \dfrac{1}{3}\right)\left(3y - \dfrac{1}{8}\right)$
59. $(6x + 1)^2$
60. $(4x + 7)^2$
61. $(x^2 + 2y)(x^2 - 2y)$
62. $(3x + 2y)(3x - 2y)$
63. $-6a^2b^2[5a^2b^2 - 6a - 6b]$
64. $7x^2y^3(-3ax - 4xy + z)$
65. $(a - 4)(2a - 4)$
66. $(2x - 3)(x + 1)$
67. $(7ab + 3c)(7ab - 3c)$
68. $(3xy - 2b)(3xy + 2b)$
69. $(m - 4)^2$
70. $(x + 2)^2$
71. $(3x + 1)^2$
72. $(4x + 6)^2$
73. $(y - 4)(y - 3)$
74. $(c - 8)(c + 2)$
75. $(x + y)(2x - 1)(x + 1)$
76. $(z + 2)(z - 3)(2z + 1)$
77. $(3x^2 + 2x - 1)^2$
78. $(4x^2 + 4x - 4)^2$
79. $(3x + 1)(4x^2 - 2x + 5)$
80. $(2x - 1)(5x^2 - x - 2)$

If $f(x) = x^2 - 3x$, find the following. See Example 12.

81. $f(a)$
82. $f(c)$
83. $f(a + h)$
84. $f(a + 5)$
85. $f(b - 2)$
86. $f(a - b)$

REVIEW AND PREVIEW

Use the slope-intercept form of a line, $y = mx + b$, to find the slope of each line. See Section 3.4.

87. $y = -2x + 7$
88. $y = \dfrac{3}{2}x - 1$
89. $3x - 5y = 14$
90. $x + 7y = 2$

Use the vertical line test to determine which of the following are graphs of functions. See Section 3.2.

91.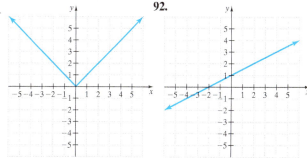
92.

CONCEPT EXTENSIONS

Solve. See the Concept Check in this section.

93. Find the error: $7y(3z - 2) + 1$
    $= 21yz - 14y + 7y$
    $= 21yz - 7y$

322 CHAPTER 6 Exponents, Polynomials, and Polynomial Functions

94. Find the error:
$$2x + 3x(12 - x)$$
$$= 5x(2 - x)$$
$$= 60x - 5x^2$$

95. Explain how to multiply a polynomial by a polynomial.

96. Explain why $(3x + 2)^2$ does not equal $9x^2 + 4$.

97. **Multiple Steps.** If $F(x) = x^2 + 3x + 2$, find
   a. $F(a + h)$
   b. $F(a)$
   c. $F(a + h) - F(a)$

98. **Multiple Steps.** If $g(x) = x^2 + 2x + 1$, find
   a. $g(a + h)$
   b. $g(a)$
   c. $g(a + h) - g(a)$

Multiply. Assume that variables represent positive integers.

99. $5x^2y^n(6y^{n+1} - 2)$
100. $-3yz^n(2y^3z^{2n} - 1)$
101. $(x^a + 5)(x^{2a} - 3)$
102. $(x^a + y^{2b})(x^a - y^{2b})$

For Exercises 103 through 106, write the result as a simplified polynomial.

△ 103. Find the area of the circle. Do not approximate π.

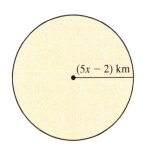
$(5x - 2)$ km

△ 104. Find the volume of the cylinder. Do not approximate π.

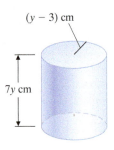
$(y - 3)$ cm
$7y$ cm

Find the area of each shaded region.

△ 105. $(3x - 2)$ in., $(3x - 2)$ in., x, x

△ 106. $x - 7$, $2x$, x

107. **Multiple Steps.** Perform each indicated operation. Explain the difference between the two problems.
   a. $(3x + 5) + (3x + 7)$
   b. $(3x + 5)(3x + 7)$

108. Explain when the FOIL method can be used to multiply polynomials.

If $R(x) = x + 5$, $Q(x) = x^2 - 2$, and $P(x) = 5x$, find the following.

109. $P(x) \cdot R(x)$
110. $P(x) \cdot Q(x)$
111. $[Q(x)]^2$
112. $[R(x)]^2$
113. $R(x) \cdot Q(x)$
114. $P(x) \cdot R(x) \cdot Q(x)$

6.5 THE GREATEST COMMON FACTOR AND FACTORING BY GROUPING

OBJECTIVES
1. Identify the GCF.
2. Factor out the GCF of a polynomial's terms.
3. Factor polynomials by grouping.

OBJECTIVE 1 ▶ Identifying the GCF. **Factoring** is the reverse process of multiplying. It is the process of writing a polynomial as a product.

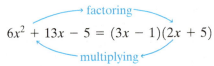
$$6x^2 + 13x - 5 = (3x - 1)(2x + 5)$$
factoring / multiplying

In the next few sections, we review techniques for factoring polynomials. These techniques are used at the end of this chapter to solve polynomial equations.

To factor a polynomial, we first factor out the greatest common factor (GCF) of its terms, using the distributive property. The GCF of a list of terms or monomials is the product of the GCF of the numerical coefficients and each GCF of the powers of a common variable.

Finding the GCF of a List of Monomials

STEP 1. Find the GCF of the numerical coefficients.

STEP 2. Find the GCF of the variable factors.

STEP 3. The product of the factors found in Steps 1 and 2 is the GCF of the monomials.

EXAMPLE 1 Find the GCF of $20x^3y$, $10x^2y^2$, and $35x^3$.

Solution The GCF of the numerical coefficients 20, 10, and 35 is 5, the largest integer that is a factor of each integer. The GCF of the variable factors x^3, x^2, and x^3 is x^2 because x^2 is the largest factor common to all three powers of x. The variable y is not a common factor because it does not appear in all three monomials. The GCF is thus

$$5 \cdot x^2, \text{ or } 5x^2$$

To see this in factored form,

$$20x^3y = 2 \cdot 2 \cdot 5 \cdot x^2 \cdot x \cdot y$$
$$10x^2y^2 = 2 \cdot 5 \cdot x^2 \cdot y$$
$$35x^3 = 3 \cdot 5 \cdot x^2 \cdot x$$
$$\text{GCF} = 5 \cdot x^2$$

PRACTICE 1 Find the GCF of $32x^4y^2$, $48x^3y$, $24y^2$.

OBJECTIVE 2 ▶ Factoring out the GCF of a polynomial's terms. A first step in factoring polynomials is to use the distributive property and write the polynomial as a product of the GCF of its monomial terms and a simpler polynomial. This is called **factoring out the GCF**.

EXAMPLE 2 Factor.

a. $8x^2 + 4$ **b.** $5y - 2z^4$ **c.** $6x^2 - 3x^3 + 12x^4$

Solution

a. The GCF of terms $8x^2$ and 4 is 4.

$$8x^2 + 4 = 4 \cdot 2x^2 + 4 \cdot 1 \quad \text{Factor out 4 from each term.}$$
$$= 4(2x^2 + 1) \quad \text{Apply the distributive property.}$$

The factored form of $8x^2 + 4$ is $4(2x^2 + 1)$. To check, multiply $4(2x^2 + 1)$ to see that the product is $8x^2 + 4$.

b. There is no common factor of the terms $5y$ and $-2z^4$ other than 1 (or -1).

c. The greatest common factor of $6x^2$, $-3x^3$, and $12x^4$ is $3x^2$. Thus,

$$6x^2 - 3x^3 + 12x^4 = 3x^2 \cdot 2 - 3x^2 \cdot x + 3x^2 \cdot 4x^2$$
$$= 3x^2(2 - x + 4x^2)$$

PRACTICE 2 Factor.

a. $6x^2 + 9 + 15x$ **b.** $3x - 8y^3$ **c.** $8a^4 - 2a^3$

> **▶ Helpful Hint**
> To verify that the GCF has been factored out correctly, multiply the factors together and see that their product is the original polynomial.

EXAMPLE 3 Factor $17x^3y^2 - 34x^4y^2$.

Solution The GCF of the two terms is $17x^3y^2$, which we factor out of each term.
$$17x^3y^2 - 34x^4y^2 = 17x^3y^2 \cdot 1 - 17x^3y^2 \cdot 2x$$
$$= 17x^3y^2(1 - 2x)$$

PRACTICE 3 Factor $64x^5y^2 - 8x^3y^2$.

> **Helpful Hint**
> If the GCF happens to be one of the terms in the polynomial, a factor of 1 will remain for this term when the GCF is factored out. For example, in the polynomial $21x^2 + 7x$, the GCF of $21x^2$ and $7x$ is $7x$, so
> $$21x^2 + 7x = 7x \cdot 3x + 7x \cdot 1 = 7x(3x + 1)$$

Concept Check ✓

Which factorization of $12x^2 + 9x - 3$ is correct?

a. $3(4x^2 + 3x + 1)$ **b.** $3(4x^2 + 3x - 1)$ **c.** $3(4x^2 + 3x - 3)$ **d.** $3(4x^2 + 3x)$

EXAMPLE 4 Factor $-3x^3y + 2x^2y - 5xy$.

Solution Two possibilities are shown for factoring this polynomial. First, the common factor xy is factored out.
$$-3x^3y + 2x^2y - 5xy = xy(-3x^2 + 2x - 5)$$

Also, the common factor $-xy$ can be factored out as shown.
$$-3x^3y + 2x^2y - 5xy = -xy(3x^2) + (-xy)(-2x) + (-xy)(5)$$
$$= -xy(3x^2 - 2x + 5)$$

Both of these alternatives are correct.

PRACTICE 4 Factor $-9x^4y^2 + 5x^2y^2 + 7xy^2$.

EXAMPLE 5 Factor $2(x - 5) + 3a(x - 5)$.

Solution The greatest common factor is the binomial factor $(x - 5)$.
$$2(x - 5) + 3a(x - 5) = (x - 5)(2 + 3a)$$

PRACTICE 5 Factor $3(x + 4) + 5b(x + 4)$.

> **Helpful Hint**
> Notice that we wrote $-(x^2 + 5y)$ as $-1(x^2 + 5y)$ to aid in factoring.

EXAMPLE 6 Factor $7x(x^2 + 5y) - (x^2 + 5y)$.

Solution
$$7x(x^2 + 5y) - (x^2 + 5y) = 7x(x^2 + 5y) - 1(x^2 + 5y)$$
$$= (x^2 + 5y)(7x - 1)$$

PRACTICE 6 Factor $8b(a^3 + 2y) - (a^3 + 2y)$.

Answer to Concept Check: b

Section 6.5 The Greatest Common Factor and Factoring by Grouping 325

OBJECTIVE 3 ▶ **Factoring polynomials by grouping.** Sometimes it is possible to factor a polynomial by grouping the terms of the polynomial and looking for common factors in each group. This method of factoring is called **factoring by grouping.**

EXAMPLE 7 Factor $ab - 6a + 2b - 12$.

Solution First look for the GCF of all four terms. The GCF of all four terms is 1. Next group the first two terms and the last two terms and factor out common factors from each group.

$$ab - 6a + 2b - 12 = (ab - 6a) + (2b - 12)$$

Factor a from the first group and 2 from the second group.

$$= a(b - 6) + 2(b - 6)$$

Now we see a GCF of $(b - 6)$. Factor out $(b - 6)$ to get

$$a(b - 6) + 2(b - 6) = (b - 6)(a + 2)$$

Check: To check, multiply $(b - 6)$ and $(a + 2)$ to see that the product is $ab - 6a + 2b - 12$. □

PRACTICE 7 Factor $xy + 2y - 10 - 5x$.

▶ **Helpful Hint**
Notice that the polynomial $a(b - 6) + 2(b - 6)$ is *not* in factored form. It is a *sum*, not a *product*. The factored form is $(b - 6)(a + 2)$.

EXAMPLE 8 Factor $x^3 + 5x^2 + 3x + 15$.

Solution
$x^3 + 5x^2 + 3x + 15 = (x^3 + 5x^2) + (3x + 15)$ Group pairs of terms.
$= x^2(x + 5) + 3(x + 5)$ Factor each binomial.
$= (x + 5)(x^2 + 3)$ Factor out the common factor, $(x + 5)$. □

PRACTICE 8 Factor $a^3 + 2a^2 + 5a + 10$.

EXAMPLE 9 Factor $m^2n^2 + m^2 - 2n^2 - 2$.

Solution
$m^2n^2 + m^2 - 2n^2 - 2 = (m^2n^2 + m^2) + (-2n^2 - 2)$ Group pairs of terms.
$= m^2(n^2 + 1) - 2(n^2 + 1)$ Factor each binomial.
$= (n^2 + 1)(m^2 - 2)$ Factor out the common factor, $(n^2 + 1)$. □

PRACTICE 9 Factor $x^2y^2 + 3y^2 - 5x^2 - 15$.

EXAMPLE 10 Factor $xy + 2x - y - 2$.

Solution
$xy + 2x - y - 2 = (xy + 2x) + (-y - 2)$ Group pairs of terms.
$= x(y + 2) - 1(y + 2)$ Factor each binomial.
$= (y + 2)(x - 1)$ Factor out the common factor $(y + 2)$. □

PRACTICE 10 Factor $pq + 3p - q - 3$.

326 CHAPTER 6 Exponents, Polynomials, and Polynomial Functions

VOCABULARY & READINESS CHECK

Word Bank. *Use the choices below to fill in each blank. Some choices will be used more than once and some not at all.*

  least   greatest   sum   product   factoring x^3 x^7 true   false

1. The reverse process of multiplying is _____.
2. The greatest common factor (GCF) of x^7, x^3, x^5 is ____.
3. In general, the GCF of a list of common variables raised to powers is the _____ exponent in the list.
4. Factoring means writing as a _____.
5. True or false: A factored form of $2xy^3 + 10xy$ is $2xy \cdot y^2 + 2xy \cdot 5$. _____
6. True or false: A factored form of $x^3 - 6x^2 + x$ is $x(x^2 - 6x)$. _____
7. True or false: A factored form of $5x - 5y + x^3 - x^2y$ is $5(x - y) + x^2(x - y)$. _____
8. True or false: A factored form of $5x - 5y + x^3 - x^2y$ is $(x - y)(5 + x^2)$. _____

Find the GCF of each list of monomials.

9. 6, 12   10. 9, 27   11. $15x, 10$ 12. $9x, 12$
13. $13x, 2x$ 14. $4y, 5y$ 15. $7x, 14x$ 16. $8z, 4z$

6.5 EXERCISE SET

Find the GCF of each list of monomials. See Example 1.

1. a^8, a^5, a^3
2. b^9, b^2, b^5
3. $x^2y^3z^3, y^2z^3, xy^2z^2$
4. $xy^2z^3, x^2y^2z^2, x^2y^3$
5. $6x^3y, 9x^2y^2, 12x^2y$
6. $4xy^2, 16xy^3, 8x^2y^2$
7. $10x^3yz^3, 20x^2z^5, 45xz^3$
8. $12y^2z^4, 9xy^3z^4, 15x^2y^2z^3$

Factor out the GCF in each polynomial. See Examples 2 through 6.

9. $18x - 12$
10. $21x + 14$
11. $4y^2 - 16xy^3$
12. $3z - 21xz^4$
13. $6x^5 - 8x^4 + 2x^3$
14. $9x + 3x^2 - 6x^3$
15. $8a^3b^3 - 4a^2b^2 + 4ab + 16ab^2$
16. $12a^3b - 6ab + 18ab^2 - 18a^2b$
17. $6(x + 3) + 5a(x + 3)$
18. $2(x - 4) + 3y(x - 4)$
19. $2x(z + 7) + (z + 7)$
20. $x(y - 2) + (y - 2)$
21. $3x(x^2 + 5) - 2(x^2 + 5)$
22. $4x(2y + 3) - 5(2y + 3)$
23. When $3x^2 - 9x + 3$ is factored, the result is $3(x^2 - 3x + 1)$. Explain why it is necessary to include the term 1 in this factored form.
24. Construct a trinomial whose GCF is $5x^2y^3$.

Factor each polynomial by grouping. See Examples 7 through 10.

25. $ab + 3a + 2b + 6$
26. $ab + 2a + 5b + 10$
27. $ac + 4a - 2c - 8$
28. $bc + 8b - 3c - 24$
29. $2xy - 3x - 4y + 6$
30. $12xy - 18x - 10y + 15$
31. $12xy - 8x - 3y + 2$
32. $20xy - 15x - 4y + 3$

MIXED PRACTICE

Factor each polynomial

33. $6x^3 + 9$
34. $6x^2 - 8$
35. $x^3 + 3x^2$
36. $x^4 - 4x^3$
37. $8a^3 - 4a$
38. $12b^4 + 3b^2$
39. $-20x^2y + 16xy^3$
40. $-18xy^3 + 27x^4y$
41. $10a^2b^3 + 5ab^2 - 15ab^3$
42. $10ef - 20e^2f^3 + 30e^3f$
43. $9abc^2 + 6a^2bc - 6ab + 3bc$
44. $4a^2b^2c - 6ab^2c - 4ac + 8a$
45. $4x(y - 2) - 3(y - 2)$
46. $8y(z + 8) - 3(z + 8)$
47. $6xy + 10x + 9y + 15$
48. $15xy + 20x + 6y + 8$
49. $xy + 3y - 5x - 15$
50. $xy + 4y - 3x - 12$
51. $6ab - 2a - 9b + 3$
52. $16ab - 8a - 6b + 3$

53. $12xy + 18x + 2y + 3$
54. $20xy + 8x + 5y + 2$
55. $2m(n - 8) - (n - 8)$
56. $3a(b - 4) - (b - 4)$
57. $15x^3y^2 - 18x^2y^2$
58. $12x^4y^2 - 16x^3y^3$
59. $2x^2 + 3xy + 4x + 6y$
60. $3x^2 + 12x + 4xy + 16y$
61. $5x^2 + 5xy - 3x - 3y$
62. $4x^2 + 2xy - 10x - 5y$
63. $x^3 + 3x^2 + 4x + 12$
64. $x^3 + 4x^2 + 3x + 12$
65. $x^3 - x^2 - 2x + 2$
66. $x^3 - 2x^2 - 3x + 6$

REVIEW AND PREVIEW

Simplify the following. See Section 6.1.

67. $(5x^2)(11x^5)$
68. $(7y)(-2y^3)$
69. $(5x^2)^3$
70. $(-2y^3)^4$

Find each product by using the FOIL order of multiplying binomials. See Section 6.4.

71. $(x + 2)(x - 5)$
72. $(x - 7)(x - 1)$
73. $(x + 3)(x + 2)$
74. $(x - 4)(x + 2)$
75. $(y - 3)(y - 1)$
76. $(s + 8)(s + 10)$

CONCEPT EXTENSIONS

Multiple Choice. *See the Concept Check in this section.*

77. Which factorization of $10x^2 - 2x - 2$ is correct?
    a. $2(5x^2 - x + 1)$
    b. $2(5x^2 - x)$
    c. $2(5x^2 - x - 2)$
    d. $2(5x^2 - x - 1)$

78. Which factorization of $x^4 + 5x^3 - x^2$ is correct?
    a. $-1(x^4 + 5x^3 + x^2)$
    b. $x^2(x^2 + 5x^3 - x^2)$
    c. $x^2(x^2 + 5x - 1)$
    d. $5x^2(x^2 + 5x - 5)$

Solve.

79. The area of the material needed to manufacture a tin can is given by the polynomial $2\pi r^2 + 2\pi rh$, where the radius is r and height is h. Factor this expression.

80. To estimate the cost of a new product, one expression used by the production department is $4\pi r^2 + \frac{4}{3}\pi r^3$. Write an equivalent expression by factoring $4\pi r^2$ from both terms.

81. At the end of T years, the amount of money A in a savings account earning simple interest from an initial investment of $5600 at rate r is given by the formula $A = 5600 + 5600rt$. Write an equivalent equation by factoring the expression $5600 + 5600rt$.

82. An open-topped box has a square base and a height of 10 inches. If each of the bottom edges of the box has length x inches, find the amount of material needed to construct the box. Write the answer in factored form.

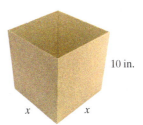

83. Explain why $9(5 - x) + y(5 - x)$ is not a factored form of $45 - 9x + 5y - xy$.

84. Construct a 4-term polynomial whose greatest common factor is $2a^3b^4$.

85. **Decision Making.** A factored polynomial can be in many forms. For example, a factored form of $xy - 3x - 2y + 6$ is $(x - 2)(y - 3)$. Which of the following is not a factored form of $xy - 3x - 2y + 6$?
    a. $(2 - x)(3 - y)$
    b. $(-2 + x)(-3 + y)$
    c. $(y - 3)(x - 2)$
    d. $(-x + 2)(-y + 3)$

86. Consider the following sequence of algebraic steps:
$$x^3 - 6x^2 + 2x - 10 = (x^3 - 6x^2) + (2x - 10)$$
$$= x^2(x - 6) + 2(x - 5)$$

Explain whether the final result is the factored form of the original polynomial.

87. **Decision Making.** Which factorization of $12x^2 + 9x + 3$ is correct?
    a. $3(4x^2 + 3x + 1)$
    b. $3(4x^2 + 3x - 1)$
    c. $3(4x^2 + 3x - 3)$
    d. $3(4x^2 + 3x)$

88. The amount E of voltage in an electrical circuit is given by the formula
$$IR_1 + IR_2 = E$$
Write an equivalent equation by factoring the expression $IR_1 + IR_2$.

89. At the end of T years, the amount of money A in a savings account earning simple interest from an initial investment of P dollars at rate R is given by the formula
$$A = P + PRT$$
Write an equivalent equation by factoring the expression $P + PRT$.

Factor out the greatest common factor. Assume that variables used as exponents represent positive integers.

90. $x^{3n} - 2x^{2n} + 5x^n$
91. $3y^n + 3y^{2n} + 5y^{8n}$
92. $6x^{8a} - 2x^{5a} - 4x^{3a}$

93. $3x^{5a} - 6x^{3a} + 9x^{2a}$

94. **Multiple Steps.** An object is thrown upward from the ground with an initial velocity of 64 feet per second. The height $h(t)$ in feet of the object after t seconds is given by the polynomial function
$$h(t) = -16t^2 + 64t$$

   a. Write an equivalent factored expression for the function $h(t)$ by factoring $-16t^2 + 64t$.

   b. Find $h(1)$ by using
$$h(t) = -16t^2 + 64t$$
   and then by using the factored form of $h(t)$.

   c. Explain why the values found in part (b) are the same.

95. **Multiple Steps.** An object is dropped from the gondola of a hot-air balloon at a height of 224 feet. The height $h(t)$ of the object after t seconds is given by the polynomial function
$$h(t) = -16t^2 + 224$$

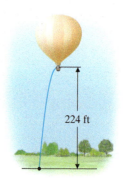
224 ft

   a. Write an equivalent factored expression for the function $h(t)$ by factoring $-16t^2 + 224$.

   b. Find $h(2)$ by using $h(t) = -16t^2 + 224$ and then by using the factored form of the function.

   c. Explain why the values found in part **b** are the same.

6.6 FACTORING TRINOMIALS

OBJECTIVES

1. Factor trinomials of the form $x^2 + bx + c$.
2. Factor trinomials of the form $ax^2 + bx + c$.
   a. Method 1—Trial and Check
   b. Method 2—Grouping
3. Factor by substitution.

OBJECTIVE 1 ▶ Factoring trinomials of the form $x^2 + bx + c$. In the previous section, we used factoring by grouping to factor four-term polynomials. In this section, we present techniques for factoring trinomials. Since $(x - 2)(x + 5) = x^2 + 3x - 10$, we say that $(x - 2)(x + 5)$ is a factored form of $x^2 + 3x - 10$. Taking a close look at how $(x - 2)$ and $(x + 5)$ are multiplied suggests a pattern for factoring trinomials of the form
$$x^2 + bx + c$$

$$(x - 2)(x + 5) = x^2 + 3x - 10$$
$$-2 + 5$$
$$-2 \cdot 5$$

The pattern for factoring is summarized next.

Factoring a Trinomial of the Form $x^2 + bx + c$

Find two numbers whose product is c and whose sum is b. The factored form of $x^2 + bx + c$ is

$$(x + \text{one number})(x + \text{other number})$$

EXAMPLE 1 Factor $x^2 + 10x + 16$.

Solution We look for two integers whose product is 16 and whose sum is 10. Since our integers must have a positive product and a positive sum, we look at only positive factors of 16.

Positive Factors of 16	Sum of Factors
1, 16	$1 + 16 = 17$
4, 4	$4 + 4 = 8$
2, 8	$2 + 8 = 10$ Correct pair

The correct pair of numbers is 2 and 8 because their product is 16 and their sum is 10. Thus,
$$x^2 + 10x + 16 = (x + 2)(x + 8)$$

Check: To check, see that $(x + 2)(x + 8) = x^2 + 10x + 16$.

PRACTICE 1 Factor $x^2 + 5x + 6$.

EXAMPLE 2 Factor $x^2 - 12x + 35$.

Solution We need to find two integers whose product is 35 and whose sum is -12. Since our integers must have a positive product and a negative sum, we consider only negative factors of 35.

Negative Factors of 35	Sum of Factors
$-1, -35$	$-1 + (-35) = -36$
$-5, -7$	$-5 + (-7) = -12$ Correct pair

The numbers are -5 and -7.
$$x^2 - 12x + 35 = [x + (-5)][x + (-7)]$$
$$= (x - 5)(x - 7)$$

Check: To check, see that $(x - 5)(x - 7) = x^2 - 12x + 35$.

PRACTICE 2 Factor $x^2 - 11x + 24$.

EXAMPLE 3 Factor $5x^3 - 30x^2 - 35x$.

Solution First we factor out the greatest common factor, $5x$.
$$5x^3 - 30x^2 - 35x = 5x(x^2 - 6x - 7)$$

Next we try to factor $x^2 - 6x - 7$ by finding two numbers whose product is -7 and whose sum is -6. The numbers are 1 and -7.
$$5x^3 - 30x^2 - 35x = 5x(x^2 - 6x - 7)$$
$$= 5x(x + 1)(x - 7)$$

PRACTICE 3 Factor $3x^3 - 9x^2 - 30x$.

▶ **Helpful Hint**
If the polynomial to be factored contains a common factor that is factored out, don't forget to include that common factor in the final factored form of the original polynomial.

EXAMPLE 4 Factor $2n^2 - 38n + 80$.

Solution The terms of this polynomial have a greatest common factor of 2, which we factor out first.
$$2n^2 - 38n + 80 = 2(n^2 - 19n + 40)$$

Next we factor $n^2 - 19n + 40$ by finding two numbers whose product is 40 and whose sum is -19. Both numbers must be negative since their sum is -19. Possibilities are

-1 and -40, -2 and -20, -4 and -10, -5 and -8

None of the pairs has a sum of -19, so no further factoring with integers is possible. The factored form of $2n^2 - 38n + 80$ is

$$2n^2 - 38n + 80 = 2(n^2 - 19n + 40)$$

PRACTICE 4 Factor $2b^2 - 18b - 22$.

We call a polynomial such as $n^2 - 19n + 40$ that cannot be factored further, a **prime polynomial**.

OBJECTIVE 2 ▶ **Factoring trinomials of the form $ax^2 + bx + c$.** Next, we factor trinomials of the form $ax^2 + bx + c$, where the coefficient a of x^2 is not 1. Don't forget that the first step in factoring any polynomial is to factor out the greatest common factor of its terms. We will review two methods here. The first method we'll call trial and check.

EXAMPLE 5 Method 1—Trial and Check

Factor $2x^2 + 11x + 15$.

Solution Factors of $2x^2$ are $2x$ and x. Let's try these factors as first terms of the binomials.

$$2x^2 + 11x + 15 = (2x +)(x +)$$

Next we try combinations of factors of 15 until the correct middle term, $11x$, is obtained. We will try only positive factors of 15 since the coefficient of the middle term, 11, is positive. Positive factors of 15 are 1 and 15 and 3 and 5.

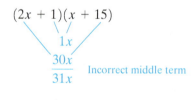
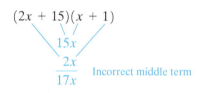
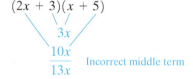
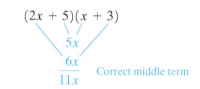

Thus, the factored form of $2x^2 + 11x + 15$ is $(2x + 5)(x + 3)$.

PRACTICE 5 Factor $2x^2 + 13x + 6$.

Factoring a Trinomial of the Form $ax^2 + bx + c$

STEP 1. Write all pairs of factors of ax^2.

STEP 2. Write all pairs of factors of c, the constant term.

STEP 3. Try various combinations of these factors until the correct middle term bx is found.

STEP 4. If no combination exists, the polynomial is **prime**.

EXAMPLE 6 Factor $3x^2 - x - 4$.

Solution Factors of $3x^2$: $3x \cdot x$
Factors of -4: $-1 \cdot 4$, $1 \cdot -4$, $-2 \cdot 2$, $2 \cdot -2$

Let's try possible combinations of these factors.

$(3x - 1)(x + 4)$
$-1x$
$12x$
$11x$ Incorrect middle term

$(3x + 4)(x - 1)$
$4x$
$-3x$
$1x$ Incorrect middle term

$(3x - 4)(x + 1)$
$-4x$
$3x$
$-1x$ Correct middle term

Thus, $3x^2 - x - 4 = (3x - 4)(x + 1)$.

PRACTICE 6 Factor $4x^2 + 5x - 6$.

> **Helpful Hint—Sign Patterns**
> A positive constant in a trinomial tells us to look for two numbers with the same sign. The sign of the coefficient of the middle term tells us whether the signs are both positive or both negative.
>
> both   same
> positive   sign
> ↓   ↓
> $2x^2 + 7x + 3 = (2x + 1)(x + 3)$
>
> both   same
> negative   sign
> ↓   ↓
> $2x^2 - 7x + 3 = (2x - 1)(x - 3)$
>
> A negative constant in a trinomial tells us to look for two numbers with opposite signs.
>
> opposite
> signs
> ↓
> $2x^2 - 5x - 3 = (2x + 1)(x - 3)$
>
> opposite
> signs
> ↓
> $2x^2 + 5x - 3 = (2x - 1)(x + 3)$

EXAMPLE 7 Factor $12x^3y - 22x^2y + 8xy$.

Solution First we factor out the greatest common factor of the terms of this trinomial, $2xy$.

$$12x^3y - 22x^2y + 8xy = 2xy(6x^2 - 11x + 4)$$

Now we try to factor the trinomial $6x^2 - 11x + 4$.
Factors of $6x^2$: $2x \cdot 3x$, $6x \cdot x$

Let's try $2x$ and $3x$.

$$2xy(6x^2 - 11x + 4) = 2xy(2x +)(3x +)$$

The constant term, 4, is positive and the coefficient of the middle term, −11, is negative, so we factor 4 into negative factors only.

Negative factors of 4: −4(−1),   −2(−2)

Let's try −4 and −1.

$$2xy(2x - 4)(3x - 1)$$

$$\begin{array}{r} -12x \\ -2x \\ \hline -14x \end{array}$$ Incorrect middle term

This combination cannot be correct, because one of the factors, $(2x - 4)$, has a common factor of 2. This cannot happen if the polynomial $6x^2 - 11x + 4$ has no common factors.

Now let's try −1 and −4.

$$2xy(2x - 1)(3x - 4)$$

$$\begin{array}{r} -3x \\ -8x \\ \hline -11x \end{array}$$ Correct middle term

Thus,

$$12x^3y - 22x^2y + 8xy = 2xy(2x - 1)(3x - 4)$$

If this combination had not worked, we would have tried −2 and −2 as factors of 4 and then $6x$ and x as factors of $6x^2$.

PRACTICE 7   Factor $18b^4 - 57b^3 + 30b^2$.

> **Helpful Hint**
> If a trinomial has no common factor (other than 1), then none of its binomial factors will contain a common factor (other than 1).

EXAMPLE 8   Factor $16x^2 + 24xy + 9y^2$.

Solution   No greatest common factor can be factored out of this trinomial.

Factors of $16x^2$: $16x \cdot x$, $8x \cdot 2x$, $4x \cdot 4x$

Factors of $9y^2$: $y \cdot 9y$, $3y \cdot 3y$

We try possible combinations until the correct factorization is found.

$$16x^2 + 24xy + 9y^2 = (4x + 3y)(4x + 3y) \quad \text{or} \quad (4x + 3y)^2$$

PRACTICE 8   Factor $25x^2 + 20xy + 4y^2$.

The trinomial $16x^2 + 24xy + 9y^2$ in Example 8 is an example of a **perfect square trinomial** since its factors are two identical binomials. In the next section, we examine a special method for factoring perfect square trinomials.

Method 2—Grouping

There is another method we can use when factoring trinomials of the form $ax^2 + bx + c$: Write the trinomial as a four-term polynomial, and then factor by grouping.

> **Factoring a Trinomial of the Form $ax^2 + bx + c$ by Grouping**
>
> **STEP 1.** Find two numbers whose product is $a \cdot c$ and whose sum is b.
>
> **STEP 2.** Write the term bx as a sum by using the factors found in Step 1.
>
> **STEP 3.** Factor by grouping.

EXAMPLE 9 Factor $6x^2 + 13x + 6$.

Solution In this trinomial, $a = 6$, $b = 13$, and $c = 6$.

STEP 1. Find two numbers whose product is $a \cdot c$, or $6 \cdot 6 = 36$, and whose sum is b, 13. The two numbers are 4 and 9.

STEP 2. Write the middle term, $13x$, as the sum $4x + 9x$.
$$6x^2 + 13x + 6 = 6x^2 + 4x + 9x + 6$$

STEP 3. Factor $6x^2 + 4x + 9x + 6$ by grouping.
$$(6x^2 + 4x) + (9x + 6) = 2x(3x + 2) + 3(3x + 2)$$
$$= (3x + 2)(2x + 3)$$

PRACTICE 9 Factor $20x^2 + 23x + 6$.

Concept Check ✓

Name one way that a factorization can be checked.

EXAMPLE 10 Factor $18x^2 - 9x - 2$.

Solution In this trinomial, $a = 18$, $b = -9$, and $c = -2$.

STEP 1. Find two numbers whose product is $a \cdot c$ or $18(-2) = -36$ and whose sum is b, -9. The two numbers are -12 and 3.

STEP 2. Write the middle term, $-9x$, as the sum $-12x + 3x$.
$$18x^2 - 9x - 2 = 18x^2 - 12x + 3x - 2$$

STEP 3. Factor by grouping.
$$(18x^2 - 12x) + (3x - 2) = 6x(3x - 2) + 1(3x - 2)$$
$$= (3x - 2)(6x + 1).$$

PRACTICE 10 Factor $15x^2 + 4x - 3$.

Answer to Concept Check:
Answers may vary. A sample is: By multiplying the factors to see that the product is the original polynomial.

OBJECTIVE 3 ▶ Factoring by substitution. A complicated looking polynomial may be a simpler trinomial "in disguise." Revealing the simpler trinomial is possible by substitution.

334 CHAPTER 6 Exponents, Polynomials, and Polynomial Functions

EXAMPLE 11 Factor $2(a + 3)^2 - 5(a + 3) - 7$.

Solution The quantity $(a + 3)$ is in two of the terms of this polynomial. **Substitute** x for $(a + 3)$, and the result is the following simpler trinomial.

$$2(a + 3)^2 - 5(a + 3) - 7 \quad \text{Original trinomial.}$$
$$= 2(x)^2 - 5(x) - 7 \quad \text{Substitute } x \text{ for } (a + 3).$$

Now factor $2x^2 - 5x - 7$.

$$2x^2 - 5x - 7 = (2x - 7)(x + 1)$$

But the quantity in the original polynomial was $(a + 3)$, not x. Thus, we need to reverse the substitution and replace x with $(a + 3)$.

$$(2x - 7)(x + 1) \quad \text{Factored expression.}$$
$$= [2(a + 3) - 7][(a + 3) + 1] \quad \text{Substitute } (a + 3) \text{ for } x.$$
$$= (2a + 6 - 7)(a + 3 + 1) \quad \text{Remove inside parentheses.}$$
$$= (2a - 1)(a + 4) \quad \text{Simplify.}$$

Thus, $2(a + 3)^2 - 5(a + 3) - 7 = (2a - 1)(a + 4)$.

PRACTICE 11 Factor $3(x + 1)^2 - 7(x + 1) - 20$.

EXAMPLE 12 Factor $5x^4 + 29x^2 - 42$.

Solution Again, substitution may help us factor this polynomial more easily. Since this polynomial contains the variable x, we will choose a different substitution variable. Let $y = x^2$, so $y^2 = (x^2)^2$, or x^4. Then

$$5x^4 + 29x^2 - 42$$

becomes

$$5y^2 + 29y - 42$$

which factors as

$$5y^2 + 29y - 42 = (5y - 6)(y + 7)$$

Next, replace y with x^2 to get

$$(5x^2 - 6)(x^2 + 7)$$

PRACTICE 12 Factor $6x^4 - 11x^2 - 10$.

VOCABULARY & READINESS CHECK

1. Find two numbers whose product is 10 and whose sum is 7.
2. Find two numbers whose product is 12 and whose sum is 8.
3. Find two numbers whose product is 24 and whose sum is 11.
4. Find two numbers whose product is 30 and whose sum is 13.

6.6 EXERCISE SET

Factor each trinomial. See Examples 1 through 4.

1. $x^2 + 9x + 18$
2. $x^2 + 9x + 20$
3. $x^2 - 12x + 32$
4. $x^2 - 12x + 27$
5. $x^2 + 10x - 24$
6. $x^2 + 3x - 54$
7. $x^2 - 2x - 24$
8. $x^2 - 9x - 36$
9. $3x^2 - 18x + 24$
10. $x^2y^2 + 4xy^2 + 3y^2$
11. $4x^2z + 28xz + 40z$
12. $5x^2 - 45x + 70$
13. $2x^2 - 24x - 64$
14. $3n^2 - 6n - 51$

Factor each trinomial. See Examples 5 through 10.

15. $5x^2 + 16x + 3$
16. $3x^2 + 8x + 4$
17. $2x^2 - 11x + 12$
18. $3x^2 - 19x + 20$
19. $2x^2 + 25x - 20$
20. $6x^2 + 13x + 8$
21. $4x^2 - 12x + 9$
22. $25x^2 - 30x + 9$
23. $12x^2 + 10x - 50$
24. $12y^2 - 48y + 45$
25. $3y^4 - y^3 - 10y^2$
26. $2x^2z + 5xz - 12z$
27. $6x^3 + 8x^2 + 24x$
28. $18y^3 + 12y^2 + 2y$
29. $2x^2 - 5xy - 3y^2$
30. $6x^2 + 11xy + 4y^2$
31. $28y^2 + 22y + 4$
32. $24y^3 - 2y^2 - y$
33. $2x^2 + 15x - 27$
34. $3x^2 + 14x + 15$

Use substitution to factor each polynomial completely. See Examples 11 and 12.

35. $x^4 + x^2 - 6$
36. $x^4 - x^2 - 20$
37. $(5x + 1)^2 + 8(5x + 1) + 7$
38. $(3x - 1)^2 + 5(3x - 1) + 6$
39. $x^6 - 7x^3 + 12$
40. $x^6 - 4x^3 - 12$
41. $(a + 5)^2 - 5(a + 5) - 24$
42. $(3c + 6)^2 + 12(3c + 6) - 28$

MIXED PRACTICE

Factor each polynomial completely. See Examples 1 through 12.

43. $x^2 - 24x - 81$
44. $x^2 - 48x - 100$
45. $x^2 - 15x - 54$
46. $x^2 - 15x + 54$
47. $3x^2 - 6x + 3$
48. $8x^2 - 8x + 2$
49. $3x^2 - 5x - 2$
50. $5x^2 - 14x - 3$
51. $8x^2 - 26x + 15$
52. $12x^2 - 17x + 6$
53. $18x^4 + 21x^3 + 6x^2$
54. $20x^5 + 54x^4 + 10x^3$
55. $x^2 + 8xz + 7z^2$
56. $a^2 - 2ab - 15b^2$
57. $x^2 - x - 12$
58. $x^2 + 4x - 5$
59. $3a^2 + 12ab + 12b^2$
60. $2x^2 + 16xy + 32y^2$
61. $x^2 + 4x + 5$
62. $x^2 + 6x + 8$
63. $2(x + 4)^2 + 3(x + 4) - 5$
64. $3(x + 3)^2 + 2(x + 3) - 5$
65. $6x^2 - 49x + 30$
66. $4x^2 - 39x + 27$
67. $x^4 - 5x^2 - 6$
68. $x^4 - 5x^2 + 6$
69. $6x^3 - x^2 - x$
70. $12x^3 + x^2 - x$
71. $12a^2 - 29ab + 15b^2$
72. $16y^2 + 6yx - 27x^2$

73. $9x^2 + 30x + 25$

74. $4x^2 + 6x + 9$

75. $3x^2y - 11xy + 8y$

76. $5xy^2 - 9xy + 4x$

77. $2x^2 + 2x - 12$

78. $3x^2 + 6x - 45$

79. $(x - 4)^2 + 3(x - 4) - 18$

80. $(x - 3)^2 - 2(x - 3) - 8$

81. $2x^6 + 3x^3 - 9$

82. $3x^6 - 14x^3 + 8$

83. $72xy^4 - 24xy^2z + 2xz^2$

84. $36xy^2 - 48xyz^2 + 16xz^4$

85. $2x^3y + 2x^2y - 12xy$

86. $3x^2y^3 + 6x^2y^2 - 45x^2y$

87. $x^2 + 6xy + 5y^2$

88. $x^2 + 6xy + 8y^2$

REVIEW AND PREVIEW

Multiply. See Section 6.4.

89. $(x - 3)(x + 3)$

90. $(x - 4)(x + 4)$

91. $(2x + 1)^2$

92. $(3x + 5)^2$

93. $(x - 2)(x^2 + 2x + 4)$

94. $(y + 1)(y^2 - y + 1)$

CONCEPT EXTENSIONS

95. Find all positive and negative integers b such that $x^2 + bx + 6$ is factorable.

96. Find all positive and negative integers b such that $x^2 + bx - 10$ is factorable.

97. The volume $V(x)$ of a box in terms of its height x is given by the function $V(x) = x^3 + 2x^2 - 8x$. Factor this expression for $V(x)$.

98. Based on your results from Exercise 97, find the length and width of the box if the height is 5 inches and the dimensions of the box are whole numbers.

99. **Multiple Steps.** Suppose that a movie is being filmed in New York City. An action shot requires an object to be thrown upward with an initial velocity of 80 feet per second off the top of 1 Madison Square Plaza, a height of 576 feet. The height $h(t)$ in feet of the object after t seconds is given by the function $h(t) = -16t^2 + 80t + 576$. (*Source: The World Almanac*)

   a. Find the height of the object at $t = 0$ seconds, $t = 2$ seconds, $t = 4$ seconds, and $t = 6$ seconds.

   b. Explain why the height of the object increases and then decreases as time passes.

   c. Factor the polynomial $-16t^2 + 80t + 576$.

100. **Multiple Steps.** Suppose that an object is thrown upward with an initial velocity of 64 feet per second off the edge of a 960-foot cliff. The height $h(t)$ in feet of the object after t seconds is given by the function
$$h(t) = -16t^2 + 64t + 960$$

   a. Find the height of the object at $t = 0$ seconds, $t = 3$ seconds, $t = 6$ seconds, and $t = 9$ seconds.

   b. Explain why the height of the object increases and then decreases as time passes.

   c. Factor the polynomial $-16t^2 + 64t + 960$.

Factor. Assume that variables used as exponents represent positive integers.

101. $x^{2n} + 10x^n + 16$

102. $x^{2n} - 7x^n + 12$

103. $x^{2n} - 3x^n - 18$

104. $x^{2n} + 7x^n - 18$

105. $2x^{2n} + 11x^n + 5$

106. $3x^{2n} - 8x^n + 4$

107. $4x^{2n} - 12x^n + 9$

108. $9x^{2n} + 24x^n + 16$

Recall that a graphing calculator may be used to check addition, subtraction, and multiplication of polynomials. In the same manner, a graphing calculator may be used to check factoring of polynomials in one variable. For example, to see that
$$2x^3 - 9x^2 - 5x = x(2x + 1)(x - 5)$$

graph $Y_1 = 2x^3 - 9x^2 - 5x$ *and* $Y_2 = x(2x + 1)(x - 5)$. *Then trace along both graphs to see that they coincide. Factor the following and use this method to check your results.*

109. $x^4 + 6x^3 + 5x^2$

110. $x^3 + 6x^2 + 8x$

111. $30x^3 + 9x^2 - 3x$

112. $-6x^4 + 10x^3 - 4x^2$

6.7 FACTORING BY SPECIAL PRODUCTS

OBJECTIVES

1. Factor a perfect square trinomial.
2. Factor the difference of two squares.
3. Factor the sum or difference of two cubes.

OBJECTIVE 1 ▶ Factoring a perfect square trinomial. In the previous section, we considered a variety of ways to factor trinomials of the form $ax^2 + bx + c$. In one particular example, we factored $16x^2 + 24xy + 9y^2$ as

$$16x^2 + 24xy + 9y^2 = (4x + 3y)^2$$

Recall that $16x^2 + 24xy + 9y^2$ is a perfect square trinomial because its factors are two identical binomials. A perfect square trinomial can be factored quickly if you recognize the trinomial as a perfect square.

A trinomial is a perfect square trinomial if it can be written so that its first term is the square of some quantity a, its last term is the square of some quantity b, and its middle term is twice the product of the quantities a and b. The following special formulas can be used to factor perfect square trinomials.

Perfect Square Trinomials
$$a^2 + 2ab + b^2 = (a + b)^2$$
$$a^2 - 2ab + b^2 = (a - b)^2$$

Notice that these formulas above are the same special products from Section 5.4 for the square of a binomial.

From
$$a^2 + 2ab + b^2 = (a + b)^2,$$
we see that
$$16x^2 + 24xy + 9y^2 = (4x)^2 + 2(4x)(3y) + (3y)^2 = (4x + 3y)^2$$

EXAMPLE 1 Factor $m^2 + 10m + 25$.

Solution Notice that the first term is a square: $m^2 = (m)^2$, the last term is a square: $25 = 5^2$; and $10m = 2 \cdot 5 \cdot m$.

Thus,
$$m^2 + 10m + 25 = m^2 + 2(m)(5) + 5^2 = (m + 5)^2$$

PRACTICE 1 Factor $b^2 + 16b + 64$.

EXAMPLE 2 Factor $3a^2x - 12abx + 12b^2x$.

Solution The terms of this trinomial have a GCF of $3x$, which we factor out first.
$$3a^2x - 12abx + 12b^2x = 3x(a^2 - 4ab + 4b^2)$$

Now, the polynomial $a^2 - 4ab + 4b^2$ is a perfect square trinomial. Notice that the first term is a square: $a^2 = (a)^2$; the last term is a square: $4b^2 = (2b)^2$; and $4ab = 2(a)(2b)$. The factoring can now be completed as
$$3x(a^2 - 4ab + 4b^2) = 3x(a - 2b)^2$$

PRACTICE 2 Factor $45x^2b - 30xb + 5b$.

> **Helpful Hint**
> If you recognize a trinomial as a perfect square trinomial, use the special formulas to factor. However, methods for factoring trinomials in general from Section 6.6 will also result in the correct factored form.

OBJECTIVE 2 ▶ **Factoring the difference of two squares.** We now factor special types of binomials, beginning with the **difference of two squares.** The special product pattern presented in Section 6.4 for the product of a sum and a difference of two terms is used again here. However, the emphasis is now on factoring rather than on multiplying.

> **Difference of Two Squares**
> $$a^2 - b^2 = (a + b)(a - b)$$

Notice that a binomial is a difference of two squares when it is the difference of the square of some quantity a and the square of some quantity b.

EXAMPLE 3 Factor the following.

a. $x^2 - 9$ b. $16y^2 - 9$ c. $50 - 8y^2$ d. $x^2 - \dfrac{1}{4}$

Solution

a. $x^2 - 9 = x^2 - 3^2$
$= (x + 3)(x - 3)$

b. $16y^2 - 9 = (4y)^2 - 3^2$
$= (4y + 3)(4y - 3)$

c. First factor out the common factor of 2.
$50 - 8y^2 = 2(25 - 4y^2)$
$= 2(5 + 2y)(5 - 2y)$

d. $x^2 - \dfrac{1}{4} = x^2 - \left(\dfrac{1}{2}\right)^2 = \left(x + \dfrac{1}{2}\right)\left(x - \dfrac{1}{2}\right)$

PRACTICE 3 Factor the following.

a. $x^2 - 16$
b. $25b^2 - 49$
c. $45 - 20x^2$
d. $y^2 - \dfrac{1}{81}$

The binomial $x^2 + 9$ is a **sum of two squares** and cannot be factored by using real numbers. **In general, except for factoring out a GCF, the sum of two squares usually cannot be factored by using real numbers.**

> **Helpful Hint**
> The sum of two squares whose GCF is 1 usually cannot be factored by using real numbers. For example, $x^2 + 9$ is called a prime polynomial.

Section 6.7 Factoring by Special Products 339

EXAMPLE 4 Factor the following.

a. $p^4 - 16$ **b.** $(x + 3)^2 - 36$

Solution

a. $p^4 - 16 = (p^2)^2 - 4^2$
$= (p^2 + 4)(p^2 - 4)$

The binomial factor $p^2 + 4$ cannot be factored by using real numbers, but the binomial factor $p^2 - 4$ is a difference of squares.

$$(p^2 + 4)(p^2 - 4) = (p^2 + 4)(p + 2)(p - 2)$$

b. Factor $(x + 3)^2 - 36$ as the difference of squares.

$(x + 3)^2 - 36 = (x + 3)^2 - 6^2$
$= [(x + 3) + 6][(x + 3) - 6]$ Factor.
$= [x + 3 + 6][x + 3 - 6]$ Remove parentheses.
$= (x + 9)(x - 3)$ Simplify.

PRACTICE 4 Factor the following.

a. $x^4 - 10000$ **b.** $(x + 2)^2 - 49$

Concept Check ✓

Is $(x - 4)(y^2 - 9)$ completely factored? Why or why not?

EXAMPLE 5 Factor $x^2 + 4x + 4 - y^2$.

Solution Factoring by grouping comes to mind since the sum of the first three terms of this polynomial is a perfect square trinomial.

$x^2 + 4x + 4 - y^2 = (x^2 + 4x + 4) - y^2$ Group the first three terms.
$= (x + 2)^2 - y^2$ Factor the perfect square trinomial.

This is not factored yet since we have a *difference*, not a *product*. Since $(x + 2)^2 - y^2$ is a difference of squares, we have

$(x + 2)^2 - y^2 = [(x + 2) + y][(x + 2) - y]$
$= (x + 2 + y)(x + 2 - y)$

PRACTICE 5 Factor $m^2 + 6m + 9 - n^2$.

OBJECTIVE 3 ▶ Factoring the sum or difference of two cubes. Although the sum of two squares usually cannot be factored, the sum of two cubes, as well as the difference of two cubes, can be factored as follows.

Sum and Difference of Two Cubes
$a^3 + b^3 = (a + b)(a^2 - ab + b^2)$
$a^3 - b^3 = (a - b)(a^2 + ab + b^2)$

Answer to Concept Check:
no; $(y^2 - 9)$ can be factored

To check the first pattern, let's find the product of $(a + b)$ and $(a^2 - ab + b^2)$.

$$(a + b)(a^2 - ab + b^2) = a(a^2 - ab + b^2) + b(a^2 - ab + b^2)$$
$$= a^3 - a^2b + ab^2 + a^2b - ab^2 + b^3$$
$$= a^3 + b^3$$

EXAMPLE 6 Factor $x^3 + 8$.

Solution First we write the binomial in the form $a^3 + b^3$. Then we use the formula

$$a^3 + b^3 = (a + b)(a^2 - a \cdot b + b^2), \quad \text{where } a \text{ is } x \text{ and } b \text{ is } 2.$$

$$x^3 + 8 = x^3 + 2^3 = (x + 2)(x^2 - x \cdot 2 + 2^2)$$

Thus, $x^3 + 8 = (x + 2)(x^2 - 2x + 4)$.

PRACTICE 6 Factor $x^3 + 64$.

EXAMPLE 7 Factor $p^3 + 27q^3$.

Solution
$$p^3 + 27q^3 = p^3 + (3q)^3$$
$$= (p + 3q)[p^2 - (p)(3q) + (3q)^2]$$
$$= (p + 3q)(p^2 - 3pq + 9q^2)$$

PRACTICE 7 Factor $a^3 + 8b^3$.

EXAMPLE 8 Factor $y^3 - 64$.

Solution This is a difference of cubes since $y^3 - 64 = y^3 - 4^3$.

From

$$a^3 - b^3 = (a - b)(a^2 + a \cdot b + b^2)$$

$$y^3 - 4^3 = (y - 4)(y^2 + y \cdot 4 + 4^2)$$

$$= (y - 4)(y^2 + 4y + 16)$$

PRACTICE 8 Factor $27 - y^3$.

> **Helpful Hint**
> When factoring sums or differences of cubes, be sure to notice the sign patterns.
>
> Same sign
> $$x^3 + y^3 = (x + y)(x^2 - xy + y^2)$$
> Opposite sign   Always positive
>
> Same sign
> $$x^3 - y^3 = (x - y)(x^2 + xy + y^2)$$
> Opposite sign

Section 6.7 Factoring by Special Products 341

EXAMPLE 9 Factor $125q^2 - n^3q^2$.

Solution First we factor out a common factor of q^2.

$$125q^2 - n^3q^2 = q^2(125 - n^3)$$
$$= q^2(5^3 - n^3)$$
$$= q^2(5 - n)[5^2 + (5)(n) + (n^2)]$$
$$= q^2(5 - n)(25 + 5n + n^2)$$

Opposite sign — Positive

Thus, $125q^2 - n^3q^2 = q^2(5 - n)(25 + 5n + n^2)$. The trinomial $25 + 5n + n^2$ cannot be factored further.

PRACTICE 9 Factor $b^3x^2 - 8x^2$.

VOCABULARY & READINESS CHECK

Write each term as a square. For example $25x^2$ as a square is $(5x)^2$.

1. $81y^2$
2. $4z^2$
3. $64x^6$
4. $49y^6$

Write each number or term as a cube.

5. 125
6. 216
7. $8x^3$
8. $27y^3$
9. $64x^6$
10. x^3y^6

6.7 EXERCISE SET

Factor the following. See Examples 1 and 2.

1. $x^2 + 6x + 9$
2. $x^2 - 10x + 25$
3. $4x^2 - 12x + 9$
4. $25x^2 + 10x + 1$
5. $3x^2 - 24x + 48$
6. $x^3 + 14x^2 + 49x$
7. $9y^2x^2 + 12yx^2 + 4x^2$
8. $32x^2 - 16xy + 2y^2$

Factor the following. See Examples 3 through 5.

9. $x^2 - 25$
10. $y^2 - 100$
11. $9 - 4z^2$
12. $16x^2 - y^2$
13. $(y + 2)^2 - 49$
14. $(x - 1)^2 - z^2$
15. $64x^2 - 100$
16. $4x^2 - 36$

Factor the following. See Examples 6 through 9.

17. $x^3 + 27$
18. $y^3 + 1$
19. $z^3 - 1$
20. $x^3 - 8$
21. $m^3 + n^3$
22. $r^3 + 125$
23. $x^3y^2 - 27y^2$
24. $64 - p^3$
25. $a^3b + 8b^4$
26. $8ab^3 + 27a^4$
27. $125y^3 - 8x^3$
28. $54y^3 - 128$

Factor the following. See Example 5.

29. $x^2 + 6x + 9 - y^2$
30. $x^2 + 12x + 36 - y^2$
31. $x^2 - 10x + 25 - y^2$

32. $x^2 - 18x + 81 - y^2$
33. $4x^2 + 4x + 1 - z^2$
34. $9y^2 + 12y + 4 - x^2$

MIXED PRACTICE

Factor each polynomial completely.

35. $9x^2 - 49$
36. $25x^2 - 4$
37. $x^2 - 12x + 36$
38. $x^2 - 18x + 81$
39. $x^4 - 81$
40. $x^4 - 256$
41. $x^2 + 8x + 16 - 4y^2$
42. $x^2 + 14x + 49 - 9y^2$
43. $(x + 2y)^2 - 9$
44. $(3x + y)^2 - 25$
45. $x^3 - 216$
46. $8 - a^3$
47. $x^3 + 125$
48. $x^3 + 216$
49. $4x^2 + 25$
50. $16x^2 + 25$
51. $4a^2 + 12a + 9$
52. $9a^2 - 30a + 25$
53. $18x^2y - 2y$
54. $12xy^2 - 108x$
55. $8x^3 + y^3$
56. $27x^3 - y^3$
57. $x^6 - y^3$
58. $x^3 - y^6$
59. $x^2 + 16x + 64 - x^4$
60. $x^2 + 20x + 100 - x^4$
61. $3x^6y^2 + 81y^2$
62. $x^2y^9 + x^2y^3$
63. $(x + y)^3 + 125$
64. $(x + y)^3 + 27$
65. $(2x + 3)^3 - 64$
66. $(4x + 2)^3 - 125$

REVIEW AND PREVIEW

Solve the following equations. See Section 2.1.

67. $x - 5 = 0$
68. $x + 7 = 0$
69. $3x + 1 = 0$
70. $5x - 15 = 0$
71. $-2x = 0$
72. $3x = 0$
73. $-5x + 25 = 0$
74. $-4x - 16 = 0$

CONCEPT EXTENSIONS

Determine whether each polynomial is factored completely or not. See the Concept Check in this section.

75. $5x(x^2 - 4)$
76. $x^2y^2(x^3 - y^3)$
77. $7y(a^2 + a + 1)$
78. $9z(x^2 + 4)$

79. A manufacturer of metal washers needs to determine the cross-sectional area of each washer. If the outer radius of the washer is R and the radius of the hole is r, express the area of the washer as a polynomial. Factor this polynomial completely.

80. Express the area of the shaded region as a polynomial. Factor the polynomial completely.

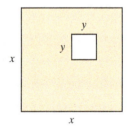

Express the volume of each solid as a polynomial. To do so, subtract the volume of the "hole" from the volume of the larger solid. Then factor the resulting polynomial.

81. 82.

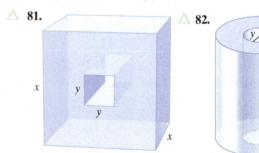

Find the value of c that makes each trinomial a perfect square trinomial.

83. $x^2 + 6x + c$
84. $y^2 + 10y + c$
85. $m^2 - 14m + c$
86. $n^2 - 2n + c$
87. $x^2 + cx + 16$
88. $x^2 + cx + 36$

89. Multiple Steps. Factor $x^6 - 1$ completely, using the following methods from this chapter.

  a. Factor the expression by treating it as the difference of two squares, $(x^3)^2 - 1^2$.
  b. Factor the expression treating it as the difference of two cubes, $(x^2)^3 - 1^3$.
  c. Are the answers to parts **a** and **b** the same? Why or why not?

Factor. Assume that variables used as exponents represent positive integers.

90. $x^{2n} - 25$
91. $x^{2n} - 36$
92. $36x^{2n} - 49$
93. $25x^{2n} - 81$
94. $x^{4n} - 16$
95. $x^{4n} - 625$

INTEGRATED REVIEW — OPERATIONS ON POLYNOMIALS AND FACTORING STRATEGIES

Sections 6.1–6.7

OPERATIONS ON POLYNOMIALS

Perform each indicated operation.

1. $(-y^2 + 6y - 1) + (3y^2 - 4y - 10)$
2. $(5z^4 - 6z^2 + z + 1) - (7z^4 - 2z + 1)$
3. Subtract $(x - 5)$ from $(x^2 - 6x + 2)$.
4. $(2x^2 + 6x - 5) + (5x^2 - 10x)$
5. $(5x - 3)^2$
6. $(5x^2 - 14x - 3) \div (5x + 1)$
7. $(2x^4 - 3x^2 + 5x - 2) \div (x + 2)$
8. $(4x - 1)(x^2 - 3x - 2)$

The rest of the Integrated Review exercises, Exercises 9–57, follow the factoring strategies below. See Examples 1 and 2.

FACTORING STRATEGIES

The key to proficiency in factoring polynomials is to practice until you are comfortable with each technique. A strategy for factoring polynomials completely is given next.

Factoring a Polynomial

STEP 1. Are there any common factors? If so, factor out the greatest common factor.
STEP 2. How many terms are in the polynomial?

  a. If there are *two* terms, decide if one of the following formulas may be applied:
    i. Difference of two squares: $a^2 - b^2 = (a - b)(a + b)$
    ii. Difference of two cubes: $a^3 - b^3 = (a - b)(a^2 + ab + b^2)$
    iii. Sum of two cubes: $a^3 + b^3 = (a + b)(a^2 - ab + b^2)$
  b. If there are *three* terms, try one of the following:
    i. Perfect square trinomial: $a^2 + 2ab + b^2 = (a + b)^2$
    $a^2 - 2ab + b^2 = (a - b)^2$
    ii. If not a perfect square trinomial, factor by using the methods presented in Section 6.6.
  c. If there are *four* or more terms, try factoring by grouping.

STEP 3. See whether any factors in the factored polynomial can be factored further.

A few examples are worked for you below.

EXAMPLE 1 Factor each polynomial completely.

a. $8a^2b - 4ab$ **b.** $36x^2 - 9$ **c.** $2x^2 - 5x - 7$
d. $5p^2 + 5 + qp^2 + q$ **e.** $9x^2 + 24x + 16$ **f.** $y^2 + 25$

Solution

a. STEP 1. The terms have a common factor of $4ab$, which we factor out.

$$8a^2b - 4ab = 4ab(2a - 1)$$

STEP 2. There are two terms, but the binomial $2a - 1$ is not the difference of two squares or the sum or difference of two cubes.

STEP 3. The factor $2a - 1$ cannot be factored further.

b. STEP 1. Factor out a common factor of 9.

$$36x^2 - 9 = 9(4x^2 - 1)$$

STEP 2. The factor $4x^2 - 1$ has two terms, and it is the difference of two squares.

$$9(4x^2 - 1) = 9(2x + 1)(2x - 1)$$

STEP 3. No factor with more than one term can be factored further.

c. STEP 1. The terms of $2x^2 - 5x - 7$ contain no common factor other than 1 or -1.

STEP 2. There are three terms. The trinomial is not a perfect square, so we factor by methods from Section 5.6.

$$2x^2 - 5x - 7 = (2x - 7)(x + 1)$$

STEP 3. No factor with more than one term can be factored further.

d. STEP 1. There is no common factor of all terms of $5p^2 + 5 + qp^2 + q$.

STEP 2. The polynomial has four terms, so try factoring by grouping.

$$5p^2 + 5 + qp^2 + q = (5p^2 + 5) + (qp^2 + q) \quad \text{Group the terms.}$$
$$= 5(p^2 + 1) + q(p^2 + 1)$$
$$= (p^2 + 1)(5 + q)$$

STEP 3. No factor can be factored further.

e. STEP 1. The terms of $9x^2 + 24x + 16$ contain no common factor other than 1 or -1.

STEP 2. The trinomial $9x^2 + 24x + 16$ is a perfect square trinomial, and $9x^2 + 24x + 16 = (3x + 4)^2$.

STEP 3. No factor can be factored further.

f. STEP 1. There is no common factor of $y^2 + 25$ other than 1.

STEP 2. This binomial is the sum of two squares and is prime.

STEP 3. The binomial $y^2 + 25$ cannot be factored further.

PRACTICE 1 Factor each polynomial completely.

a. $12x^2y - 3xy$ **b.** $49x^2 - 4$
c. $5x^2 + 2x - 3$ **d.** $3x^2 + 6 + x^3 + 2x$
e. $4x^2 + 20x + 25$ **f.** $b^2 + 100$

EXAMPLE 2 Factor each completely.

a. $27a^3 - b^3$　　b. $3n^2m^4 - 48m^6$　　c. $2x^2 - 12x + 18 - 2z^2$
d. $8x^4y^2 + 125xy^2$　　e. $(x - 5)^2 - 49y^2$

Solution

a. This binomial is the difference of two cubes.

$$27a^3 - b^3 = (3a)^3 - b^3$$
$$= (3a - b)[(3a)^2 + (3a)(b) + b^2]$$
$$= (3a - b)(9a^2 + 3ab + b^2)$$

b. $3n^2m^4 - 48m^6 = 3m^4(n^2 - 16m^2)$　　Factor out the GCF, $3m^4$.
　　　　　　　　　$= 3m^4(n + 4m)(n - 4m)$　　Factor the difference of squares.

c. $2x^2 - 12x + 18 - 2z^2 = 2(x^2 - 6x + 9 - z^2)$　　The GCF is 2.
　　　　　　　　　　　　$= 2[(x^2 - 6x + 9) - z^2]$　　Group the first three terms together.
　　　　　　　　　　　　$= 2[(x - 3)^2 - z^2]$　　Factor the perfect square trinomial.
　　　　　　　　　　　　$= 2[(x - 3) + z][(x - 3) - z]$　　Factor the difference of squares.
　　　　　　　　　　　　$= 2(x - 3 + z)(x - 3 - z)$

d. $8x^4y^2 + 125xy^2 = xy^2(8x^3 + 125)$　　The GCF is xy^2.
　　　　　　　　　$= xy^2[(2x)^3 + 5^3]$
　　　　　　　　　$= xy^2(2x + 5)[(2x)^2 - (2x)(5) + 5^2]$　　Factor the sum of cubes.
　　　　　　　　　$= xy^2(2x + 5)(4x^2 - 10x + 25)$

e. This binomial is the difference of squares.

$$(x - 5)^2 - 49y^2 = (x - 5)^2 - (7y)^2$$
$$= [(x - 5) + 7y][(x - 5) - 7y]$$
$$= (x - 5 + 7y)(x - 5 - 7y)$$

PRACTICE 2 Factor each polynomial completely.

a. $64x^3 + y^3$
b. $7x^2y^2 - 63y^4$
c. $3x^2 + 12x + 12 - 3b^2$
d. $x^5y^4 + 27x^2y$
e. $(x + 7)^2 - 81y^2$

Factor completely.

9. $x^2 - 8x + 16 - y^2$

10. $12x^2 - 22x - 20$

11. $x^4 - x$

12. $(2x + 1)^2 - 3(2x + 1) + 2$

13. $14x^2y - 2xy$

14. $24ab^2 - 6ab$

15. $4x^2 - 16$

16. $9x^2 - 81$

17. $3x^2 - 8x - 11$

18. $5x^2 - 2x - 3$

19. $4x^2 + 8x - 12$

20. $6x^2 - 6x - 12$

21. $4x^2 + 36x + 81$

22. $25x^2 + 40x + 16$

23. $8x^3 + 125y^3$

24. $27x^3 - 64y^3$

25. $64x^2y^3 - 8x^2$

26. $27x^5y^4 - 216x^2y$

27. $(x + 5)^3 + y^3$

28. $(y - 1)^3 + 27x^3$

29. $(5a - 3)^2 - 6(5a - 3) + 9$

30. $(4r + 1)^2 + 8(4r + 1) + 16$

31. $7x^2 - 63x$

32. $20x^2 + 23x + 6$

33. $ab - 6a + 7b - 42$

34. $20x^2 - 220x + 600$

35. $x^4 - 1$

36. $15x^2 - 20x$

37. $10x^2 - 7x - 33$

38. $45m^3n^3 - 27m^2n^2$

39. $5a^3b^3 - 50a^3b$

40. $x^4 + x$

41. $16x^2 + 25$

42. $20x^3 + 20y^3$

43. $10x^3 - 210x^2 + 1100x$

44. $9y^2 - 42y + 49$

45. $64a^3b^4 - 27a^3b$

46. $y^4 - 16$

47. $2x^3 - 54$

48. $2sr + 10s - r - 5$

49. $3y^5 - 5y^4 + 6y - 10$

50. $64a^2 + b^2$

51. $100z^3 + 100$

52. $250x^4 - 16x$

53. $4b^2 - 36b + 81$

54. $2a^5 - a^4 + 6a - 3$

55. $(y - 6)^2 + 3(y - 6) + 2$

56. $(c + 2)^2 - 6(c + 2) + 5$

△ 57. Express the area of the shaded region as a polynomial. Factor the polynomial completely.

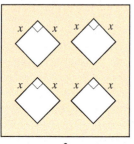

6.8 SOLVING EQUATIONS BY FACTORING AND PROBLEM SOLVING

OBJECTIVES

1. Solve polynomial equations by factoring.
2. Solve problems that can be modeled by polynomial equations.
3. Find the *x*-intercepts of a polynomial function.

OBJECTIVE 1 ▶ Solving polynomial equations by factoring. In this section, your efforts to learn factoring start to pay off. We use factoring to solve polynomial equations, which in turn helps us solve problems that can be modeled by polynomial equations and also helps us sketch the graph of polynomial functions.

A **polynomial equation** is the result of setting two polynomials equal to each other. Examples of polynomial equations are

$$3x^3 - 2x^2 = x^2 + 2x - 1 \qquad 2.6x + 7 = -1.3 \qquad -5x^2 - 5 = -9x^2 - 2x + 1$$

A polynomial equation is in **standard form** if one side of the equation is 0. In standard form the polynomial equations above are

$$3x^3 - 3x^2 - 2x + 1 = 0 \qquad 2.6x + 8.3 = 0 \qquad 4x^2 + 2x - 6 = 0$$

The degree of a simplified polynomial equation in standard form is the same as the highest degree of any of its terms. A polynomial equation of degree 2 is also called a **quadratic equation.**

A solution of a polynomial equation in one variable is a value of the variable that makes the equation true. The method presented in this section for solving polynomial equations is called the **factoring method.** This method is based on the **zero-factor property.**

> **Zero-Factor Property**
> If a and b are real numbers and $a \cdot b = 0$, then $a = 0$ or $b = 0$. This property is true for three or more factors also.

In other words, if the product of two or more real numbers is zero, then at least one number must be zero.

EXAMPLE 1 Solve: $(x + 2)(x - 6) = 0$.

Solution By the zero-factor property, $(x + 2)(x - 6) = 0$ only if $x + 2 = 0$ or $x - 6 = 0$.

$x + 2 = 0 \quad$ or $\quad x - 6 = 0 \quad$ Apply the zero-factor property.
$\qquad x = -2 \quad$ or $\qquad x = 6 \quad$ Solve each linear equation.

To check, let $x = -2$ and then let $x = 6$ in the original equation.

Let $x = -2$.	Let $x = 6$.
Then $(x + 2)(x - 6) = 0$	Then $(x + 2)(x - 6) = 0$
becomes $(-2 + 2)(-2 - 6) \stackrel{?}{=} 0$	becomes $(6 + 2)(6 - 6) \stackrel{?}{=} 0$
$(0)(-8) \stackrel{?}{=} 0$	$(8)(0) \stackrel{?}{=} 0$
$0 = 0 \quad$ True	$0 = 0 \quad$ True

Both -2 and 6 check, so they are both solutions. The solution set is $\{-2, 6\}$. □

PRACTICE 1 Solve: $(x + 8)(x - 5) = 0$.

EXAMPLE 2 Solve: $2x^2 + 9x - 5 = 0$.

Solution To use the zero-factor property, one side of the equation must be 0, and the other side must be in factored form.

$$2x^2 + 9x - 5 = 0$$
$$(2x - 1)(x + 5) = 0 \qquad \text{Factor.}$$
$$2x - 1 = 0 \quad \text{or} \quad x + 5 = 0 \qquad \text{Set each factor equal to zero.}$$
$$2x = 1$$
$$x = \frac{1}{2} \quad \text{or} \quad x = -5 \qquad \text{Solve each linear equation.}$$

The solutions are -5 and $\frac{1}{2}$. To check, let $x = \frac{1}{2}$ in the original equation; then let $x = -5$ in the original equation. The solution set is $\left\{-5, \frac{1}{2}\right\}$. □

PRACTICE 2 Solve: $3x^2 + 10x - 8 = 0$.

Solving Polynomial Equations by Factoring

STEP 1. Write the equation in standard form so that one side of the equation is 0.

STEP 2. Factor the polynomial completely.

STEP 3. Set each factor containing a variable equal to 0.

STEP 4. Solve the resulting equations.

STEP 5. Check each solution in the original equation.

Since it is not always possible to factor a polynomial, not all polynomial equations can be solved by factoring. Other methods of solving polynomial equations are presented in Chapter 9.

EXAMPLE 3 Solve: $x(2x - 7) = 4$.

Solution First, write the equation in standard form; then, factor.

$$x(2x - 7) = 4$$
$$2x^2 - 7x = 4 \qquad \text{Multiply.}$$
$$2x^2 - 7x - 4 = 0 \qquad \text{Write in standard form.}$$
$$(2x + 1)(x - 4) = 0 \qquad \text{Factor.}$$
$$2x + 1 = 0 \quad \text{or} \quad x - 4 = 0 \qquad \text{Set each factor equal to zero.}$$
$$2x = -1 \qquad \text{Solve.}$$
$$x = -\frac{1}{2} \quad \text{or} \quad x = 4$$

The solutions are $-\frac{1}{2}$ and 4. Check both solutions in the original equation. □

PRACTICE 3 Solve: $x(3x + 14) = -8$.

▶ **Helpful Hint**

To apply the zero-factor property, one side of the equation must be 0, and the other side of the equation must be factored. To solve the equation $x(2x - 7) = 4$, for example, you may **not** set each factor equal to 4.

Section 6.8 Solving Equations by Factoring and Problem Solving 349

EXAMPLE 4 Solve: $3(x^2 + 4) + 5 = -6(x^2 + 2x) + 13$.

Solution Rewrite the equation so that one side is 0.

$3(x^2 + 4) + 5 = -6(x^2 + 2x) + 13$.
$3x^2 + 12 + 5 = -6x^2 - 12x + 13$ Apply the distributive property.
$9x^2 + 12x + 4 = 0$ Rewrite the equation so that one side is 0.
$(3x + 2)(3x + 2) = 0$ Factor.
$3x + 2 = 0$ or $3x + 2 = 0$ Set each factor equal to 0.
$3x = -2$ or $3x = -2$
$x = -\dfrac{2}{3}$ or $x = -\dfrac{2}{3}$ Solve each equation.

The solution is $-\dfrac{2}{3}$. Check by substituting $-\dfrac{2}{3}$ into the original equation.   ☐

PRACTICE 4 Solve: $8(x^2 + 3) + 4 = -8x(x + 3) + 19$.

If the equation contains fractions, we clear the equation of fractions as a first step.

EXAMPLE 5 Solve: $2x^2 = \dfrac{17}{3}x + 1$.

Solution

$2x^2 = \dfrac{17}{3}x + 1$

$3(2x^2) = 3\left(\dfrac{17}{3}x + 1\right)$ Clear the equation of fractions.

$6x^2 = 17x + 3$ Apply the distributive property.
$6x^2 - 17x - 3 = 0$ Rewrite the equation in standard form.
$(6x + 1)(x - 3) = 0$ Factor.
$6x + 1 = 0$ or $x - 3 = 0$ Set each factor equal to zero.
$6x = -1$
$x = -\dfrac{1}{6}$ or $x = 3$ Solve each equation.

The solutions are $-\dfrac{1}{6}$ and 3.   ☐

PRACTICE 5 Solve: $4x^2 = \dfrac{15}{2}x + 1$.

EXAMPLE 6 Solve: $x^3 = 4x$.

Solution

$x^3 = 4x$
$x^3 - 4x = 0$ Rewrite the equation so that one side is 0.
$x(x^2 - 4) = 0$ Factor out the GCF, x.
$x(x + 2)(x - 2) = 0$ Factor the difference of squares.
$x = 0$ or $x + 2 = 0$ or $x - 2 = 0$ Set each factor equal to 0.
$x = 0$ or $x = -2$ or $x = 2$ Solve each equation.

The solutions are -2, 0, and 2. Check by substituting into the original equation.   ☐

PRACTICE 6 Solve: $x^3 = 2x^2 + 3x$.

Notice that the *third*-degree equation of Example 6 yielded *three* solutions.

EXAMPLE 7 Solve: $x^3 + 5x^2 = x + 5$.

Solution First, write the equation so that one side is 0.

$$x^3 + 5x^2 - x - 5 = 0$$
$$(x^3 - x) + (5x^2 - 5) = 0 \qquad \text{Factor by grouping.}$$
$$x(x^2 - 1) + 5(x^2 - 1) = 0$$
$$(x^2 - 1)(x + 5) = 0$$
$$(x + 1)(x - 1)(x + 5) = 0 \qquad \text{Factor the difference of squares.}$$
$$x + 1 = 0 \quad \text{or} \quad x - 1 = 0 \quad \text{or} \quad x + 5 = 0 \qquad \text{Set each factor equal to 0.}$$
$$x = -1 \quad \text{or} \quad x = 1 \quad \text{or} \quad x = -5 \qquad \text{Solve each equation.}$$

The solutions are -5, -1, and 1. Check in the original equation. □

PRACTICE 7 Solve: $x^3 - 9x = 18 - 2x^2$.

Concept Check ✓

Which solution strategies are incorrect? Why?

a. Solve $(y - 2)(y + 2) = 4$ by setting each factor equal to 4.
b. Solve $(x + 1)(x + 3) = 0$ by setting each factor equal to 0.
c. Solve $z^2 + 5z + 6 = 0$ by factoring $z^2 + 5z + 6$ and setting each factor equal to 0.
d. Solve $x^2 + 6x + 8 = 10$ by factoring $x^2 + 6x + 8$ and setting each factor equal to 0.

OBJECTIVE 2 ▶ Solving problems modeled by polynomial equations. Some problems may be modeled by polynomial equations. To solve these problems, we use the same problem-solving steps that were introduced in Section 2.2. When solving these problems, keep in mind that a solution of an equation that models a problem is not always a solution to the problem. For example, a person's weight or the length of a side of a geometric figure is always a positive number. Discard solutions that do not make sense as solutions of the problem.

EXAMPLE 8 Finding the Return Time of a Rocket

An Alpha III model rocket is launched from the ground with an A8–3 engine. Without a parachute, the height of the rocket h at time t seconds is approximated by the equation,

$$h = -16t^2 + 144t$$

Find how long it takes the rocket to return to the ground.

Solution

1. UNDERSTAND. Read and reread the problem. The equation $h = -16t^2 + 144t$ models the height of the rocket. Familiarize yourself with this equation by finding a few values.

When $t = 1$ second, the height of the rocket is

$$h = -16(1)^2 + 144(1) = 128 \text{ feet}$$

When $t = 2$ seconds, the height of the rocket is

$$h = -16(2)^2 + 144(2) = 224 \text{ feet}$$

2. TRANSLATE. To find how long it takes the rocket to return to the ground, we want to know what value of t makes the height h equal to 0. That is, we want to solve $h = 0$.

$$-16t^2 + 144t = 0$$

Answer to Concept Check:
a and d; the zero-factor property works only if one side of the equation is 0

3. SOLVE the quadratic equation by factoring.

$$-16t^2 + 144t = 0$$
$$-16t(t - 9) = 0$$
$$-16t = 0 \quad \text{or} \quad t - 9 = 0$$
$$t = 0 \qquad\qquad t = 9$$

4. INTERPRET. The height h is 0 feet at time 0 seconds (when the rocket is launched) and at time 9 seconds.

Check: See that the height of the rocket at 9 seconds equals 0.

$$h = -16(9)^2 + 144(9) = -1296 + 1296 = 0$$

State: The rocket returns to the ground 9 seconds after it is launched. □

PRACTICE 8 A model rocket is launched from the ground. Its height h in feet at time t seconds is approximated by the equation $h = -16t^2 + 96t$. Find how long it takes the rocket to return to the ground.

Some of the exercises at the end of this section make use of the **Pythagorean theorem.** Before we review this theorem, recall that a **right triangle** is a triangle that contains a 90° angle, or right angle. The **hypotenuse** of a right triangle is the side opposite the right angle and is the longest side of the triangle. The **legs** of a right triangle are the other sides of the triangle.

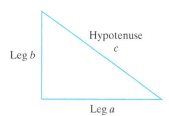

Pythagorean Theorem

In a right triangle, the sum of the squares of the lengths of the two legs is equal to the square of the length of the hypotenuse.

$$(\text{leg})^2 + (\text{leg})^2 = (\text{hypotenuse})^2 \quad \text{or} \quad a^2 + b^2 = c^2$$

⚠ EXAMPLE 9 Using the Pythagorean Theorem

While framing an addition to an existing home, Kim Menzies, a carpenter, used the Pythagorean theorem to determine whether a wall was "square"—that is, whether the wall formed a right angle with the floor. He used a triangle whose sides are three consecutive integers. Find a right triangle whose sides are three consecutive integers.

Solution

1. **UNDERSTAND.** Read and reread the problem.

    Let x, $x + 1$, and $x + 2$ be three consecutive integers. Since these integers represent lengths of the sides of a right triangle, we have

    $$x = \text{one leg}$$
    $$x + 1 = \text{other leg}$$
    $$x + 2 = \text{hypotenuse (longest side)}$$

    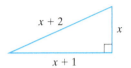

2. **TRANSLATE.** By the Pythagorean theorem, we have

    In words: $(\text{leg})^2 + (\text{leg})^2 = (\text{hypotenuse})^2$

    Translate: $(x)^2 + (x + 1)^2 = (x + 2)^2$

3. **SOLVE** the equation.

    $$x^2 + (x + 1)^2 = (x + 2)^2$$
    $$x^2 + x^2 + 2x + 1 = x^2 + 4x + 4 \quad \text{Multiply.}$$
    $$2x^2 + 2x + 1 = x^2 + 4x + 4$$
    $$x^2 - 2x - 3 = 0 \quad \text{Write in standard form.}$$
    $$(x - 3)(x + 1) = 0$$
    $$x - 3 = 0 \quad \text{or} \quad x + 1 = 0$$
    $$x = 3 \quad\quad\quad\quad x = -1$$

4. **INTERPRET.** Discard $x = -1$ since length cannot be negative. If $x = 3$, then $x + 1 = 4$ and $x + 2 = 5$.

    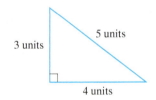

    Check: To check, see that $(\text{leg})^2 + (\text{leg})^2 = (\text{hypotenuse})^2$

    $$3^2 + 4^2 = 5^2$$
    $$9 + 16 = 25 \quad \text{True}$$

    State: The lengths of the sides of the right triangle are 3, 4, and 5 units. Kim used this information, for example, by marking off lengths of 3 and 4 feet on the floor and framing respectively. If the diagonal length between these marks was 5 feet, the wall was "square." If not, adjustments were made.

    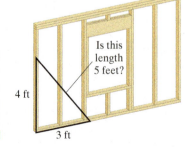

PRACTICE 9 Find a right triangle whose sides are consecutive even integers.

OBJECTIVE 3 ▶ Finding the x-intercepts of polynomial functions. Recall that to find the x-intercepts of the graph of a function, let or and solve for x. This fact gives us a visual interpretation of the results of this section.

From Example 1, we know that the solutions of the equation $(x + 2)(x - 6) = 0$ are -2 and 6. These solutions give us important information about the related polynomial function $p(x) = (x + 2)(x - 6)$. We know that when x is -2 or when x is 6, the value of $p(x)$ is 0.

$$p(x) = (x + 2)(x - 6)$$
$$p(-2) = (-2 + 2)(-2 - 6) = (0)(-8) = 0$$
$$p(6) = (6 + 2)(6 - 6) = (8)(0) = 0$$

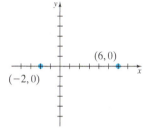

Thus, we know that $(-2, 0)$ and $(6, 0)$ are the x-intercepts of the graph of $p(x)$.

We also know that the graph of $p(x)$ does not cross the x-axis at any other point. For this reason, and the fact that $p(x) = (x + 2)(x - 6) = x^2 - 4x - 12$ has degree 2, we conclude that the graph of p must look something like one of these two graphs:

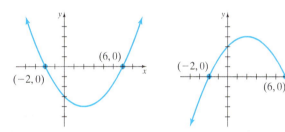

In a later chapter, we explore these graphs more fully. For the moment, know that the solutions of a polynomial equation are the x-intercepts of the graph of the related function and that the x-intercepts of the graph of a polynomial function are the solutions of the related polynomial equation. These values are also called **roots,** or **zeros,** of a polynomial function.

EXAMPLE 10 Match Each Function with Its Graph

$$f(x) = (x - 3)(x + 2) \quad g(x) = x(x + 2)(x - 2) \quad h(x) = (x - 2)(x + 2)(x - 1)$$

A   **B**   **C**

Solution The graph of the function $f(x) = (x - 3)(x + 2)$ has two x-intercepts, $(3, 0)$ and $(-2, 0)$, because the equation $0 = (x - 3)(x + 2)$ has two solutions, 3 and -2.

The graph of $f(x)$ is graph B.

The graph of the function $g(x) = x(x + 2)(x - 2)$ has three x-intercepts $(0, 0)$, $(-2, 0)$, and $(2, 0)$, because the equation $0 = x(x + 2)(x - 2)$ has three solutions, 0, -2, and 2.

The graph of $g(x)$ is graph C.

The graph of the function $h(x) = (x - 2)(x + 2)(x - 1)$ has three x-intercepts, $(-2, 0)$, $(1, 0)$, and $(2, 0)$, because the equation $0 = (x - 2)(x + 2)(x - 1)$ has three solutions, -2, 1, and 2.

The graph of $h(x)$ is graph A.

PRACTICE

10 Match each function with its graph.

$f(x) = (x - 1)(x + 3)$ $g(x) = x(x + 3)(x - 2)$ $h(x) = (x - 3)(x + 2)(x - 2)$

A 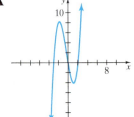   B 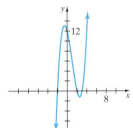   C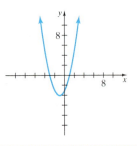

Graphing Calculator Explorations

We can use a graphing calculator to approximate real number solutions of any quadratic equation in standard form, whether the associated polynomial is factorable or not. For example, let's solve the quadratic equation $x^2 - 2x - 4 = 0$. The solutions of this equation will be the x-intercepts of the graph of the function $f(x) = x^2 - 2x - 4$. (Recall that to find x-intercepts, we let $f(x) = 0$, or $y = 0$.) When we use a standard window, the graph of this function looks like this.

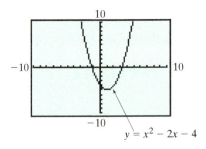

$y = x^2 - 2x - 4$

The graph appears to have one x-intercept between -2 and -1 and one between 3 and 4. To find the x-intercept between 3 and 4 to the nearest hundredth, we can use a zero feature, a Zoom feature, which magnifies a portion of the graph around the cursor, or we can redefine our window. If we redefine our window to

Xmin = 2   Ymin = -1
Xmax = 5   Ymax = 1
Xscl = 1   Yscl = 1

the resulting screen is

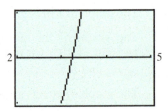

By using the Trace feature, we can now see that one of the intercepts is between 3.21 and 3.25. To approximate to the nearest hundredth, Zoom again or redefine the window to

$$\text{Xmin} = 3.2 \qquad \text{Ymin} = -0.1$$
$$\text{Xmax} = 3.3 \qquad \text{Ymax} = 0.1$$
$$\text{Xscl} = 1 \qquad \text{Yscl} = 1$$

If we use the Trace feature again, we see that, to the nearest hundredth, the x-intercept is 3.24. By repeating this process, we can approximate the other x-intercept to be -1.24.

To check, find $f(3.24)$ and $f(-1.24)$. Both of these values should be close to 0. (They will not be exactly 0 since we approximated these solutions.)

$$f(3.24) = 0.0176 \quad \text{and} \quad f(-1.24) = 0.0176$$

Solve each of these quadratic equations by graphing a related function and approximating the x-intercepts to the nearest thousandth.

1. $x^2 + 3x - 2 = 0$
2. $5x^2 - 7x + 1 = 0$
3. $2.3x^2 - 4.4x - 5.6 = 0$
4. $0.2x^2 + 6.2x + 2.1 = 0$
5. $0.09x^2 - 0.13x - 0.08 = 0$
6. $x^2 + 0.08x - 0.01 = 0$

VOCABULARY & READINESS CHECK

Solve each equation for the variable. See Example 1.

1. $(x - 3)(x + 5) = 0$
2. $(y + 5)(y + 3) = 0$
3. $(z - 3)(z + 7) = 0$
4. $(c - 2)(c - 4) = 0$
5. $x(x - 9) = 0$
6. $w(w + 7) = 0$

6.8 EXERCISE SET

Solve each equation. See Example 1.

1. $(x + 3)(3x - 4) = 0$
2. $(5x + 1)(x - 2) = 0$
3. $3(2x - 5)(4x + 3) = 0$
4. $8(3x - 4)(2x - 7) = 0$

Solve each equation. See Examples 2 through 5.

5. $x^2 + 11x + 24 = 0$
6. $y^2 - 10y + 24 = 0$
7. $12x^2 + 5x - 2 = 0$
8. $3y^2 - y - 14 = 0$
9. $z^2 + 9 = 10z$
10. $n^2 + n = 72$
11. $x(5x + 2) = 3$
12. $n(2n - 3) = 2$
13. $x^2 - 6x = x(8 + x)$
14. $n(3 + n) = n^2 + 4n$
15. $\dfrac{z^2}{6} - \dfrac{z}{2} - 3 = 0$
16. $\dfrac{c^2}{20} - \dfrac{c}{4} + \dfrac{1}{5} = 0$
17. $\dfrac{x^2}{2} + \dfrac{x}{20} = \dfrac{1}{10}$
18. $\dfrac{y^2}{30} = \dfrac{y}{15} + \dfrac{1}{2}$
19. $\dfrac{4t^2}{5} = \dfrac{t}{5} + \dfrac{3}{10}$
20. $\dfrac{5x^2}{6} - \dfrac{7x}{2} + \dfrac{2}{3} = 0$

Solve each equation. See Examples 6 and 7.

21. $(x + 2)(x - 7)(3x - 8) = 0$
22. $(4x + 9)(x - 4)(x + 1) = 0$
23. $y^3 = 9y$
24. $n^3 = 16n$
25. $x^3 - x = 2x^2 - 2$
26. $m^3 = m^2 + 12m$
27. Explain how solving $2(x - 3)(x - 1) = 0$ differs from solving $2x(x - 3)(x - 1) = 0$.
28. Explain why the zero-factor property works for more than two numbers whose product is 0.

MIXED PRACTICE

Solve each equation.

29. $(2x + 7)(x - 10) = 0$
30. $(x + 4)(5x - 1) = 0$
31. $3x(x - 5) = 0$
32. $4x(2x + 3) = 0$

33. $x^2 - 2x - 15 = 0$
34. $x^2 + 6x - 7 = 0$
35. $12x^2 + 2x - 2 = 0$
36. $8x^2 + 13x + 5 = 0$
37. $w^2 - 5w = 36$
38. $x^2 + 32 = 12x$
39. $25x^2 - 40x + 16 = 0$
40. $9n^2 + 30n + 25 = 0$
41. $2r^3 + 6r^2 = 20r$
42. $-2t^3 = 108t - 30t^2$
43. $z(5z - 4)(z + 3) = 0$
44. $2r(r + 3)(5r - 4) = 0$
45. $2z(z + 6) = 2z^2 + 12z - 8$
46. $3c^2 - 8c + 2 = c(3c - 8)$
47. $(x - 1)(x + 4) = 24$
48. $(2x - 1)(x + 2) = -3$
49. $\dfrac{x^2}{4} - \dfrac{5}{2}x + 6 = 0$
50. $\dfrac{x^2}{18} + \dfrac{x}{2} + 1 = 0$
51. $y^2 + \dfrac{1}{4} = -y$
52. $\dfrac{x^2}{10} + \dfrac{5}{2} = x$
53. $y^3 + 4y^2 = 9y + 36$
54. $x^3 + 5x^2 = x + 5$
55. $2x^3 = 50x$
56. $m^5 = 36m^3$
57. $x^2 + (x + 1)^2 = 61$
58. $y^2 + (y + 2)^2 = 34$
59. $m^2(3m - 2) = m$
60. $x^2(5x + 3) = 26x$
61. $3x^2 = -x$
62. $y^2 = -5y$
63. $x(x - 3) = x^2 + 5x + 7$
64. $z^2 - 4z + 10 = z(z - 5)$
65. $3(t - 8) + 2t = 7 + t$
66. $7c - 2(3c + 1) = 5(4 - 2c)$
67. $-3(x - 4) + x = 5(3 - x)$
68. $-4(a + 1) - 3a = -7(2a - 3)$

69. **Decision Making.** Which solution strategies are incorrect? Why?
   a. Solve $(y - 2)(y + 2) = 4$ by setting each factor equal to 4.
   b. Solve $(x + 1)(x + 3) = 0$ by setting each factor equal to 0.
   c. Solve $z^2 + 5z + 6 = 0$ by factoring $z^2 + 5z + 6$ and setting each factor equal to 0.
   d. Solve $x^2 + 6x + 8 = 10$ by factoring $x^2 + 6x + 8$ and setting each factor equal to 0.

70. Describe two ways a linear equation differs from a quadratic equation.

Solve. See Examples 8 and 9.

71. One number exceeds another by five, and their product is 66. Find the numbers.
72. If the sum of two numbers is 4 and their product is $\dfrac{15}{4}$, find the numbers.
73. An electrician needs to run a cable from the top of a 60-foot tower to a transmitter box located 45 feet away from the base of the tower. Find how long he should make the cable.

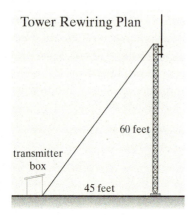

74. A stereo system installer needs to run speaker wire along the two diagonals of a rectangular room whose dimensions are 40 feet by 75 feet. Find how much speaker wire she needs.

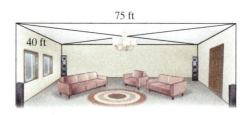

75. If the cost, $C(x)$, for manufacturing x units of a certain product is given by $C(x) = x^2 - 15x + 50$, find the number of units manufactured at a cost of $9500.
76. Determine whether any three consecutive integers represent the lengths of the sides of a right triangle.
77. The shorter leg of a right triangle is 3 centimeters less than the other leg. Find the length of the two legs if the hypotenuse is 15 centimeters.
78. The longer leg of a right triangle is 4 feet longer than the other leg. Find the length of the two legs if the hypotenuse is 20 feet.
79. Marie Mulroney has a rectangular board 12 inches by 16 inches around which she wants to put a uniform border of shells. If she has enough shells for a border whose area is 128 square inches, determine the width of the border.

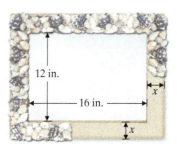

80. A gardener has a rose garden that measures 30 feet by 20 feet. He wants to put a uniform border of pine bark around the outside of the garden. Find how wide the border should be if he has enough pine bark to cover 336 square feet.

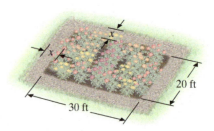

81. While hovering near the top of Ribbon Falls in Yosemite National Park at 1600 feet, a helicopter pilot accidentally drops his sunglasses. The height $h(t)$ of the sunglasses after

t seconds is given by the polynomial function

$$h(t) = -16t^2 + 1600$$

When will the sunglasses hit the ground?

82. After t seconds, the height $h(t)$ of a model rocket launched from the ground into the air is given by the function

$$h(t) = -16t^2 + 80t$$

Find how long it takes the rocket to reach a height of 96 feet.

△ **83.** The floor of a shed has an area of 90 square feet. The floor is in the shape of a rectangle whose length is 3 feet less than twice the width. Find the length and the width of the floor of the shed.

△ **84.** A vegetable garden with an area of 200 square feet is to be fertilized. If the length of the garden is 1 foot less than three times the width, find the dimensions of the garden.

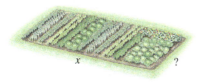

85. The function $W(x) = 0.5x^2$ gives the number of servings of wedding cake that can be obtained from a two-layer x-inch square wedding cake tier. What size square wedding cake tier is needed to serve 50 people? (*Source:* Based on data from the *Wilton 2000 Yearbook of Cake Decorating*)

86. Use the function in Exercise 85 to determine what size square wedding cake tier is needed to serve 200 people.

87. Suppose that a movie is being filmed in New York City. An action shot requires an object to be thrown upward with an initial velocity of 80 feet per second off the top of 1 Madison Square Plaza, a height of 576 feet. The height $h(t)$ in feet of the object after t seconds is given by the function

$$h(t) = -16t^2 + 80t + 576.$$

Determine how long before the object strikes the ground. (See Exercise 99, Section 6.6) (*Source: The World Almanac*)

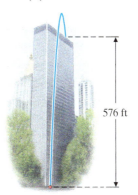

88. Suppose that an object is thrown upward with an initial velocity of 64 feet per second off the edge of a 960-foot-cliff. The height $h(t)$ in feet of the object after t seconds is given by the function

$$h(t) = -16t^2 + 64t + 960$$

Determine how long before the object strikes the ground. (See Exercise 100, Section 6.6)

Matching. *Match each polynomial function with its graph (A–F). See Example 10.*

89. $f(x) = (x - 2)(x + 5)$
90. $g(x) = (x + 1)(x - 6)$
91. $h(x) = x(x + 3)(x - 3)$
92. $F(x) = (x + 1)(x - 2)(x + 5)$
93. $G(x) = 2x^2 + 9x + 4$
94. $H(x) = 2x^2 - 7x - 4$

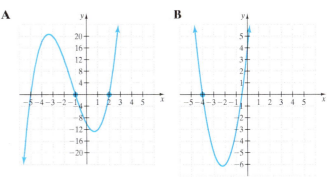

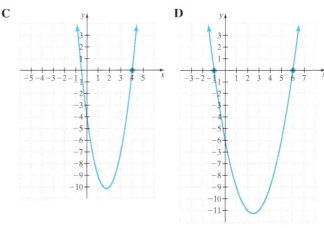

(*Graphs E and F on page 358*)

358 CHAPTER 6 Exponents, Polynomials, and Polynomial Functions

E F

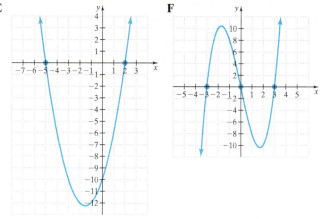

99. Draw a function with intercepts $(-3, 0)$, $(5, 0)$, and $(0, 4)$.

100. Draw a function with intercepts $(-7, 0)$, $\left(-\dfrac{1}{2}, 0\right)$, $(4, 0)$, and $(0, -1)$.

CONCEPT EXTENSIONS

Each exercise contains an error. Find and correct the error. See the Concept Check in the section.

101. $(x - 5)(x + 2) = 0$
  $x - 5 = 0$ or $x + 2 = 0$
  $x = -5$ or $x = -2$

102. $(4x - 5)(x + 7) = 0$
  $4x - 5 = 0$ or $x + 7 = 0$
  $x = \dfrac{4}{5}$ or $x = -7$

103. $y(y - 5) = -6$
  $y = -6$ or $y - 5 = -5$
  $y = -7$ or $y = 0$

104. $3x^2 - 19x = 14$
  $-16x = 14$
  $x = -\dfrac{14}{16}$
  $x = -\dfrac{7}{8}$

Solve.

105. $(x^2 + x - 6)(3x^2 - 14x - 5) = 0$

106. $(x^2 - 9)(x^2 + 8x + 16) = 0$

107. Is the following step correct? Why or why not?
  $x(x - 3) = 5$
  $x = 5$ or $x - 3 = 5$

Write a quadratic equation that has the given numbers as solutions.

108. $5, 3$

109. $6, 7$

110. $-1, 2$

111. $4, -3$

REVIEW AND PREVIEW

Write the x- and y-intercepts for each graph and determine whether the graph is the graph of a function. See Sections 3.1 and 3.2.

95.

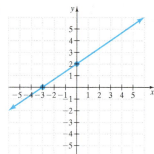

96.

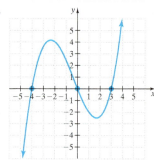

97.

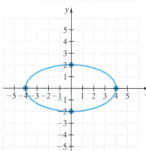

98.

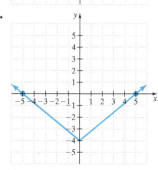

EXTENSION: EVEN AND ODD POWER FUNCTIONS AND END BEHAVIOR

OBJECTIVES

1. Graph even and odd power functions.
2. Describe the end behavior of a polynomial function.

In Section 6.3, we studied general shapes of polynomial functions of degree 2 and degree 3.

OBJECTIVE 1 ▶ Graphing power functions. In this section, we study a special type of polynomial function called a **power function.**

> **Power Function**
> A power function of degree n is of the form
> $$f(x) = ax^n$$
> where a is a real number constant, $a \neq 0$, and n is a positive integer.

Examples of power functions: $f(x) = 3x^2$; $f(x) = -2x^5$; $f(x) = \frac{1}{2}x$. Of course, from Sections 3.6 and 6.3, we already know the shape of the graph of some power functions.

Value of n	Power Function	Description of Graph
$n = 1$	$f(x) = ax$ (Line – think of $y = mx + b$ with $b = 0$)	$a > 0$; $a < 0$
$n = 2$	$f(x) = ax^2$ (parabola)	$a > 0$; $a < 0$
$n = 3$	$f(x) = ax^3$	$a > 0$; $a < 0$

Study the previous table, and we see how the value of a affects these graphs. Let's look at the graph of simple power functions of the form $f(x) = x^n$ (here $a = 1$). From there, we can graph $f(x) = ax^n$ knowing that the value of a with stretch, compress, or reflect the graph of $f(x) = x^n$.

$$f(x) = x^n, \text{ with } n = 2, 4, 6$$

x	$f(x) = x^2$	$f(x) = x^4$	$f(x) = x^6$
0	0	0	0
1	1	1	1
-1	1	1	1
2	4	16	64
-2	4	16	64
$\frac{1}{2}$	$\frac{1}{4}$	$\frac{1}{16}$	$\frac{1}{64}$
$-\frac{1}{2}$	$\frac{1}{4}$	$\frac{1}{16}$	$\frac{1}{64}$

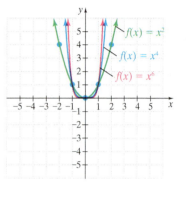

Study the table and graphs and notice the following:
- The domain is all real numbers.
- The range is $y \geq 0$
- All graphs contain the points $(0, 0)$, $(1, 1)$ and $(-1, 1)$.
- As the even powers of n increase, the graph becomes more U–shaped.
- These graphs are each symmetric to the y-axis. (This means that the portion of the graph for negative x-values is the mirror image of the portion for positive x-values.) For every (x, y) point, there is a $(-x, y)$ point and we say these functions are **even**.

$$f(x) = x^n, \text{ with } n = 1, 3, 5$$

x	$f(x) = x$	$f(x) = x^3$	$f(x) = x^5$
0	0	0	0
1	1	1	1
-1	-1	-1	-1
2	2	8	32
-2	-2	-8	-32
$\frac{1}{2}$	$\frac{1}{2}$	$\frac{1}{8}$	$\frac{1}{32}$
$-\frac{1}{2}$	$-\frac{1}{2}$	$-\frac{1}{8}$	$-\frac{1}{32}$

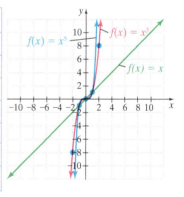

Study the table and graphs and notice the following:
- The domain is all real numbers.
- The range is all real numbers.
- All graphs contain the points $(0, 0)$, $(1, 1)$ and $(-1, -1)$.
- As the odd powers of n increase, the graph gets closer to the x-axis for $-1 \leq x \leq 1$.
- These graphs are each symmetric to the origin. (This means that for every (x, y) point, there is a $(-x, -y)$ point.) We say these functions are **odd**.

EXAMPLE 1 Graph $f(x) = 4x^2$. Determine whether this function is even or odd.

Solution Let's find and plot some ordered-pair solutions, and then recall the general shape of $f(x) = x^2$.

x	y
0	0
1	4
−1	4
2	16
−2	16

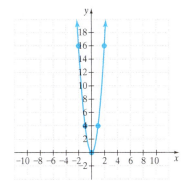

Because the graph is symmetric with respect to the y-axis, this function is odd.

PRACTICE 1 Graph $f(x) = 2x^3$. Determine whether this function is even or odd.

EXAMPLE 2 Graph $f(x) = -3x^5$. Determine whether this function is even or odd.

Solution Let's find and plot some ordered-pair solutions and then recall the general shape of $f(x) = x^5$.

x	y
0	0
1	−3
−1	3
2	−96
−2	96

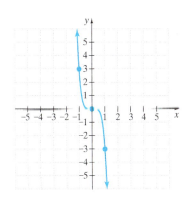

This graph is symmetric with respect to the origin; thus, the function is odd.

PRACTICE 2 Graph $f(x) = -5x^4$. Determine whether this function is even or odd.

OBJECTIVE 2 ▶ Describing end behavior. You may have noticed by now that the end behavior of a power function $f(x) = ax^n$ is determined by not only the power, n, but by the constant, a. To clarify, the **end behavior** of the graph of a function is the behavior of the graph as x approaches positive infinity $(+\infty)$ or negative infinity $(-\infty)$. We will use the notation " $\rightarrow$ " to mean "approaches."

For example, see if you can correctly read these correctly.

▶ **Helpful Hint**
Both $+\infty$ and ∞ both mean positive infinity

Notation	Read as
$x \rightarrow +\infty$	x approaches positive infinity
$f(x) \rightarrow -\infty$	f of x approaches negative infinity

Now, let's review a few graphs from this section and decide upon their end behavior.

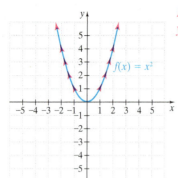

As $x \to -\infty$,
y or $f(x) \to +\infty$

As $x \to +\infty$,
y or $f(x) \to +\infty$

As $x \to -\infty$
y or $f(x) \to -\infty$

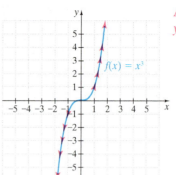

As $x \to +\infty$,
y or $f(x) \to +\infty$

> **Helpful Hint**
>
> For $f(x) = ax^n$, to see the
> - end behavior as $x \to +\infty$, start at $(0, 0)$, follow the graph to the right, and see how y or $f(x)$ behaves.
> - end behavior as $x \to -\infty$, start at $(0, 0)$, follow the graph to the left, and see how y or $f(x)$ behaves.

Remember that for $f(x) = ax^n$, the value of a and the value of n affects the end behavior. This is true in general for polynomial functions.

EXAMPLE 3 Fill in the blanks to describe the end behavior for the given graph.

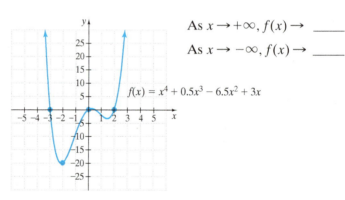

As $x \to +\infty, f(x) \to$ _____

As $x \to -\infty, f(x) \to$ _____

Solution Follow the graph as $x \to +\infty$, then as $x \to -\infty$. We have the following:

As $x \to +\infty, f(x) \to \underline{+\infty}$

As $x \to -\infty, f(x) \to \underline{+\infty}$

PRACTICE 3 Fill in the blanks to describe the end behavior for the given graph.

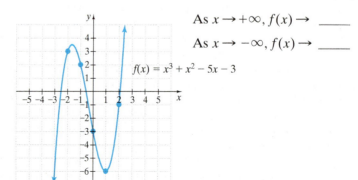

As $x \to +\infty, f(x) \to$ _____

As $x \to -\infty, f(x) \to$ _____

Extension: Even and Odd Power Functions and End Behavior   363

In general, for polynomial functions, we have the following:

End Behavior of Polynomials

$f(x) = (\text{odd} - \text{degree polynomial})$

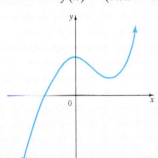

Leading coefficient is positive.
End behavior:
y or $f(x) \to +\infty$ as $x \to +\infty$
y or $f(x) \to -\infty$ as $x \to -\infty$

Leading coefficient is negative.
End behavior:
y or $f(x) \to -\infty$ as $x \to +\infty$
y or $f(x) \to +\infty$ as $x \to -\infty$

$f(x) = (\text{even} - \text{degree polynomial})$

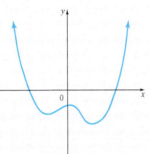

Leading coefficient is positive.
End behavior:
y or $f(x) \to +\infty$ as $x \to +\infty$
y or $f(x) \to +\infty$ as $x \to -\infty$

Leading coefficient is negative.
End behavior:
y or $f(x) \to -\infty$ as $x \to +\infty$
y or $f(x) \to -\infty$ as $x \to -\infty$

CHAPTER 6 EXTENSION | EXERCISE SET

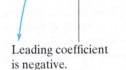

Graph each power function. Use the graph to determine whether each function is even or odd. See Examples 1 and 2.

1. $f(x) = 5x^2$
2. $f(x) = 2x^4$
3. $f(x) = 3x^5$
4. $f(x) = 4x^3$
5. $f(x) = -x^3$
6. $f(x) = -x^5$
7. $f(x) = -x^4$
8. $f(x) = -x^2$
9. $f(x) = \frac{1}{2}x^4$
10. $f(x) = \frac{1}{2}x^6$
11. $f(x) = -\frac{1}{3}x^7$
12. $f(x) = -\frac{1}{3}x^5$

Complete a Table. *Each function below was graphed earlier in this exercise set. Use the graph or what you know about end behavior to complete the table. See Example 3.*

Power Function	As $x \to +\infty$	As $x \to -\infty$
13. $f(x) = 5x^2$		
14. $f(x) = 2x^4$		
15. $f(x) = 3x^5$		
16. $f(x) = 4x^3$		
17. $f(x) = -x^3$		
18. $f(x) = -x^5$		
19. $f(x) = \frac{1}{2}x^4$		
20. $f(x) = \frac{1}{2}x^6$		

Matching. *Use your knowledge of end behavior and graphs of polynomial functions to match the function with the graph it most closely resembles.*

21. $f(x) = x^4 - x^3 - 6x^2 + 3x$
22. $f(x) = 2x^5 + 3x - 1$
23. $f(x) = -x^3 + 2$
24. $f(x) = -3x^4 - 1$

a.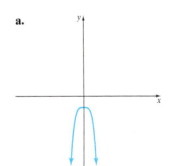

b.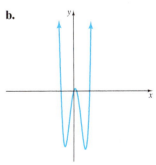

c. 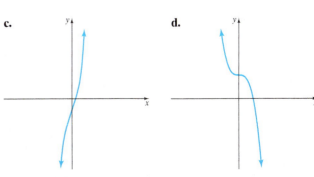   d.

CHAPTER 6 VOCABULARY CHECK

Fill in each blank with one of the words or phrases listed below.

| quadratic equation | scientific notation | polynomial | exponents | 1 | 0 | monomial |
| binomial | trinomial | degree of a polynomial | degree of a term | | | factoring |

1. A _____ is a finite sum of terms in which all variables are raised to nonnegative integer powers and no variables appear in any denominator.
2. _____ is the process of writing a polynomial as a product.
3. _____ are used to write repeated factors in a more compact form.
4. The _____ is the sum of the exponents on the variables contained in the term.
5. A _____ is a polynomial with one term.
6. If a is not 0, $a^0 =$ ____.
7. A _____ is a polynomial with three terms.
8. A polynomial equation of degree 2 is also called a _____.
9. A positive number is written in _____ if it is written as the product of a number a, such that $1 \leq a < 10$ and a power of 10.
10. The _____ is the largest degree of all of its terms.
11. A _____ is a polynomial with two terms.
12. If a and b are real numbers and $a \cdot b =$ ____, then $a = 0$ or $b = 0$.

CHAPTER 6 REVIEW

(6.1) Evaluate.

1. $(-2)^2$
2. $(-3)^4$
3. -2^2
4. -3^4
5. 8^0
6. -9^0
7. -4^{-2}
8. $(-4)^{-2}$

Simplify each expression. Use only positive exponents.

9. $-xy^2 \cdot y^3 \cdot xy^2 z$
10. $(-4xy)(-3xy^2 b)$
11. $a^{-14} \cdot a^5$
12. $\dfrac{a^{16}}{a^{17}}$
13. $\dfrac{x^{-7}}{x^4}$
14. $\dfrac{9a(a^{-3})}{18a^{15}}$
15. $\dfrac{y^{6p-3}}{y^{6p+2}}$

Write in scientific notation.

16. 36,890,000
17. -0.000362

Write each number without exponents.

18. 1.678×10^{-6}
19. 4.1×10^5

(6.2) Simplify. Use only positive exponents.

20. $(8^5)^3$
21. $\left(\dfrac{a}{4}\right)^2$
22. $(3x)^3$
23. $(-4x)^{-2}$
24. $\left(\dfrac{6x}{5}\right)^2$
25. $(8^6)^{-3}$
26. $\left(\dfrac{4}{3}\right)^{-2}$
27. $(-2x^3)^{-3}$
28. $\left(\dfrac{8p^6}{4p^4}\right)^{-2}$
29. $(-3x^{-2}y^2)^3$
30. $\left(\dfrac{x^{-5}y^{-3}}{z^3}\right)^{-5}$
31. $\dfrac{4^{-1}x^3 yz}{x^{-2}yx^4}$
32. $(5xyz)^{-4}(x^{-2})^{-3}$
33. $\dfrac{2(3yz)^{-3}}{y^{-3}}$

Simplify each expression.

34. $x^{4a}(3x^{5a})^3$
35. $\dfrac{4y^{3x-3}}{2y^{2x+4}}$

Use scientific notation to find the quotient. Express each quotient in scientific notation.

36. $\dfrac{(0.00012)(144,000)}{0.0003}$
37. $\dfrac{(-0.00017)(0.00039)}{3000}$

Simplify. Use only positive exponents.

38. $\dfrac{27x^{-5}y^5}{18x^{-6}y^2} \cdot \dfrac{x^4y^{-2}}{x^{-2}y^3}$

39. $\dfrac{3x^5}{y^{-4}} \cdot \dfrac{(3xy^{-3})^{-2}}{(z^{-3})^{-4}}$

40. $\dfrac{(x^w)^2}{(x^{w-4})^{-2}}$

(6.3) Find the degree of each polynomial.

41. $x^2y - 3xy^3z + 5x + 7y$
42. $3x + 2$

Simplify by combining like terms.

43. $4x + 8x - 6x^2 - 6x^2y$
44. $-8xy^3 + 4xy^3 - 3x^3y$

Add or subtract as indicated.

45. $(3x + 7y) + (4x^2 - 3x + 7) + (y - 1)$
46. $(4x^2 - 6xy + 9y^2) - (8x^2 - 6xy - y^2)$
47. $(3x^2 - 4b + 28) + (9x^2 - 30) - (4x^2 - 6b + 20)$
48. Add $(9xy + 4x^2 + 18)$ and $(7xy - 4x^3 - 9x)$.
49. Subtract $(x - 7)$ from the sum of $(3x^2y - 7xy - 4)$ and $(9x^2y + x)$.

50. $\begin{array}{r} x^2 - 5x + 7 \\ -(x + 4) \\ \hline \end{array}$

51. $\begin{array}{r} x^3 + 2xy^2 - y \\ + (x - 4xy^2 -7) \\ \hline \end{array}$

If $P(x) = 9x^2 - 7x + 8$, find the following.

52. $P(6)$
53. $P(-2)$
54. $P(-3)$

If $P(x) = 2x - 1$ and $Q(x) = x^2 + 2x - 5$, find the following.

55. $P(x) + Q(x)$
56. $2[P(x)] - Q(x)$

△ 57. Find the perimeter of the rectangle.

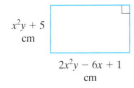

$x^2y + 5$ cm

$2x^2y - 6x + 1$ cm

(6.4) Multiply.

58. $-6x(4x^2 - 6x + 1)$
59. $-4ab^2(3ab^3 + 7ab + 1)$
60. $(x - 4)(2x + 9)$
61. $(-3xa + 4b)^2$
62. $(9x^2 + 4x + 1)(4x - 3)$

63. $(5x - 9y)(3x + 9y)$
64. $\left(x - \dfrac{1}{3}\right)\left(x + \dfrac{2}{3}\right)$
65. $(x^2 + 9x + 1)^2$

Multiply, using special products.

66. $(3x - y)^2$
67. $(4x + 9)^2$
68. $(x + 3y)(x - 3y)$
69. $[4 + (3a - b)][4 - (3a - b)]$
70. If $P(x) = 2x - 1$ and $Q(x) = x^2 + 2x - 5$, find $P(x) \cdot Q(x)$.

△ 71. Find the area of the rectangle.

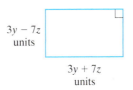

$3y - 7z$ units

$3y + 7z$ units

Multiply. Assume that all variable exponents represent integers.

72. $4a^b(3a^{b+2} - 7)$
73. $(4xy^z - b)^2$
74. $(3x^a - 4)(3x^a + 4)$

(6.5) Factor out the greatest common factor.

75. $16x^3 - 24x^2$
76. $36y - 24y^2$
77. $6ab^2 + 8ab - 4a^2b^2$
78. $14a^2b^2 - 21ab^2 + 7ab$
79. $6a(a + 3b) - 5(a + 3b)$
80. $4x(x - 2y) - 5(x - 2y)$
81. $xy - 6y + 3x - 18$
82. $ab - 8b + 4a - 32$
83. $pq - 3p - 5q + 15$
84. $x^3 - x^2 - 2x + 2$

△ 85. A smaller square is cut from a larger rectangle. Write the area of the shaded region as a factored polynomial.

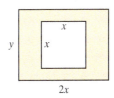

(6.6) Completely factor each polynomial.

86. $x^2 - 14x - 72$
87. $x^2 + 16x - 80$
88. $2x^2 - 18x + 28$

89. $3x^2 + 33x + 54$
90. $2x^3 - 7x^2 - 9x$
91. $3x^2 + 2x - 16$
92. $6x^2 + 17x + 10$
93. $15x^2 - 91x + 6$
94. $4x^2 + 2x - 12$
95. $9x^2 - 12x - 12$
96. $y^2(x+6)^2 - 2y(x+6)^2 - 3(x+6)^2$
97. $(x+5)^2 + 6(x+5) + 8$
98. $x^4 - 6x^2 - 16$
99. $x^4 + 8x^2 - 20$

(6.7) Factor each polynomial completely.

100. $x^2 - 100$
101. $x^2 - 81$
102. $2x^2 - 32$
103. $6x^2 - 54$
104. $81 - x^4$
105. $16 - y^4$
106. $(y+2)^2 - 25$
107. $(x-3)^2 - 16$
108. $x^3 + 216$
109. $y^3 + 512$
110. $8 - 27y^3$
111. $1 - 64y^3$
112. $6x^4y + 48xy$
113. $2x^5 + 16x^2y^3$
114. $x^2 - 2x + 1 - y^2$
115. $x^2 - 6x + 9 - 4y^2$
116. $4x^2 + 12x + 9$
117. $16a^2 - 40ab + 25b^2$
△ 118. The volume of the cylindrical shell is $\pi R^2 h - \pi r^2 h$ cubic units. Write this volume as a factored expression.

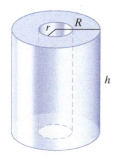

(6.8) Solve each polynomial equation for the variable.

119. $(3x - 1)(x + 7) = 0$
120. $3(x + 5)(8x - 3) = 0$
121. $5x(x - 4)(2x - 9) = 0$
122. $6(x + 3)(x - 4)(5x + 1) = 0$
123. $2x^2 = 12x$
124. $4x^3 - 36x = 0$
125. $(1 - x)(3x + 2) = -4x$
126. $2x(x - 12) = -40$
127. $3x^2 + 2x = 12 - 7x$
△ 128. $2x^2 + 3x = 35$
129. $x^3 - 18x = 3x^2$
130. $19x^2 - 42x = -x^3$
131. $12x = 6x^3 + 6x^2$
132. $8x^3 + 10x^2 = 3x$

133. The sum of a number and twice its square is 105. Find the number.

134. The length of a rectangular piece of carpet is 5 meters less than twice its width. Find the dimensions of the carpet if its area is 33 square meters.

135. A scene from an adventure film calls for a stunt dummy to be dropped from above the second-story platform of the Eiffel Tower, a distance of 400 feet. Its height $h(t)$ at time t seconds is given by

$$h(t) = -16t^2 + 400$$

Determine when the stunt dummy will reach the ground.

MIXED REVIEW

136. The Royal Gorge suspension bridge in Colorado is 1053 feet above the Arkansas River. Neglecting air resistance, the height of an object dropped off the bridge is given by the polynomial function $P(t) = -16t^2 + 1053$ after time t seconds. Find the height of the object when $t = 1$ second and when $t = 8$ seconds.

Perform the indicated operation.

137. $(x + 5)(3x^2 - 2x + 1)$
138. $(3x^2 + 4x - 1.2) - (5x^2 - x + 5.7)$
139. $(3x^2 + 4x - 1.2) + (5x^2 - x + 5.7)$

140. $\left(7ab - \dfrac{1}{2}\right)^2$

145. $6x^2 - 34x - 12$

146. $y^2(4x+3)^2 - 19y(4x+3)^2 - 20(4x+3)^2$

147. $4z^7 - 49z^5$

If $P(x) = -x^2 + x - 4$, find

148. $5x^4 + 4x^2 - 9$

141. $P(5)$ **142.** $P(-2)$

Factor each polynomial completely.

Solve each equation.

143. $12y^5 - 6y^4$

149. $8x^2 = 24x$ **150.** $x(x-11) = 26$

144. $x^2y + 4x^2 - 3y - 12$

CHAPTER 6 TEST

Remember to use the Chapter Test Prep Videos to see the fully worked-out solutions to any of the exercises you want to review.

Simplify. Use positive exponents to write the answers.

1. $(-9x)^{-2}$

2. $-3xy^{-2}(4xy^2)z$

3. $\dfrac{6^{-1}a^2b^{-3}}{3^{-2}a^{-5}b^2}$

4. $\left(\dfrac{-xy^{-5}z}{xy^3}\right)^{-5}$

Write Exercises 5 and 6 in scientific notation.

5. 630,000,000   **6.** 0.01200

7. Write 5×10^{-6} without exponents.

8. Use scientific notation to find the quotient.

$$\dfrac{(0.0024)(0.00012)}{0.00032}$$

Perform the indicated operations.

9. $(4x^3y - 3x - 4) - (9x^3y + 8x + 5)$

10. $-3xy(4x + y)$

11. $(3x + 4)(4x - 7)$

12. $(5a - 2b)(5a + 2b)$

13. $(6m + n)^2$

14. $(2x - 1)(x^2 - 6x + 4)$

Factor each polynomial completely.

15. $16x^3y - 12x^2y^4$

16. $x^2 - 13x - 30$

17. $4y^2 + 20y + 25$

18. $6x^2 - 15x - 9$

19. $4x^2 - 25$

20. $x^3 + 64$

21. $3x^2y - 27y^3$

22. $6x^2 + 24$

23. $16y^3 - 2$

24. $x^2y - 9y - 3x^2 + 27$

Solve the equation for the variable.

25. $3n(7n - 20) = 96$

26. $(x + 2)(x - 2) = 5(x + 4)$

27. $2x^3 + 5x^2 = 8x + 20$

28. Write the area of the shaded region as a factored polynomial.

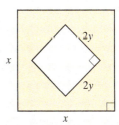

29. A pebble is hurled upward from the top of the Canada Trust Tower, which is 880 feet tall, with an initial velocity of 96 feet per second. Neglecting air resistance, the height $h(t)$ of the pebble after t seconds is given by the polynomial function

$$h(t) = -16t^2 + 96t + 880$$

a. Find the height of the pebble when $t = 1$.

b. Find the height of the pebble when $t = 5.1$.

c. When will the pebble hit the ground?

CHAPTER 6 STANDARDIZED TEST

Multiple Choice. *Choose the one alternative that best completes the statement or answers the question.*

Simplify the expression. All exponents should be positive integers.

1. $(4p)^{-3}$

   a. $\dfrac{1}{-12p^3}$ b. $\dfrac{1}{64p^3}$ c. $\dfrac{1}{12p^{-3}}$ d. $\dfrac{1}{4p^3}$

2. $-4x^{-5}y(7x^5y)z^4$

   a. $-28x^5y^2z^4$ b. $-28y^4z^4$ c. $28y^2z^4$ d. $-28y^2z^4$

3. $\dfrac{3^{-7}x^{-5}y^3}{3^{-4}x^{-8}y^6}$

   a. $\dfrac{3x^3}{y^3}$ b. $\dfrac{27}{x^3y^3}$ c. $\dfrac{1}{27x^8y^3}$ d. $\dfrac{x^3}{27y^3}$

4. $\left[\dfrac{6x^{-3}z^3}{2xz^{-3}}\right]^{-3}$

   a. $\dfrac{3x^{12}}{z^{18}}$ b. $\dfrac{x^{12}z^{18}}{27}$ c. $\dfrac{x^{12}}{27z^{18}}$ d. $\dfrac{x^6}{27z^{18}}$

Write the number in scientific notation.

5. 64,000,000

   a. 6.4×10^{-6} b. 6.4×10^6
   c. 6.4×10^7 d. 6.4×10^{-7}

6. 0.000557

   a. 5.57×10^{-4} b. 5.57×10^{-5}
   c. 5.57×10^4 d. 5.57×10^{-3}

Write without exponents.

7. 6×10^{-4}

   a. $-600,000$ b. 0.0006   c. 0.00006   d. 0.006

Use scientific notation to find the quotient.

8. $\dfrac{(0.0026)(0.00016)}{0.00008}$

   a. 0.52   b. 0.0052   c. 0.052   d. 0.00052

9. $(5x^2 - xy - y^2) + (x^2 + 7xy + 3y^2)$

   a. $6x^2 + 8xy + 4y^2$ b. $4x^2 - 8xy - 4y^2$
   c. $5x^2 + 7xy + 3y^2$ d. $6x^2 + 6xy + 2y^2$

10. $2xy(8x - 5y)$

    a. $16x^2y - 10xy^2$ b. $16x^2 - 10y^2$
    c. $10x^2 - 7y^2$ d. $10x^2y - 7xy^2$

11. $(2x - 9)(3x - 9)$

    a. $5x^2 - 45x + 81$ b. $5x^2 - 45x - 45$
    c. $6x^2 - 45x + 81$ d. $6x^2 - 45x - 45$

12. $(3x + 7y)(3x - 7y)$

    a. $9x^2 - 49y^2$ b. $9x^2 + 42xy - 49y^2$
    c. $9x^2 - 42xy - 49y^2$ d. $9x^2 + 49y^2$

13. $(5x + 6y)^2$

    a. $25x^2 + 60xy + 36y^2$ b. $5x^2 + 36y^2$
    c. $5x^2 + 60xy + 36y^2$ d. $25x^2 + 36y^2$

14. $(7y + 11)(6y^2 - 2y - 3)$

    a. $108y^2 - 36y - 54$ b. $42y^3 + 52y^2 - 43y - 33$
    c. $42y^3 - 14y^2 - 21y + 11$ d. $42y^3 + 80y^2 + 43y + 33$

Factor the polynomial completely.

15. $28x^4y + 36xy^6$

    a. $xy(28x^3 + 36y^5)$ b. $4xy(7x^3 + 9y^5)$
    c. $4x(7x^3y + 9y^6)$ d. $4y(7x^4 + 9xy^5)$

16. $x^2 - 3x + 10$

    a. $(x - 10)(x + 1)$ b. $(x + 5)(x - 2)$
    c. prime   d. $(x - 5)(x + 2)$

17. $9x^2 + 6x + 1$

    a. $(x + 3)^2$ b. $(3x + 1)(3x - 1)$
    c. $(3x + 1)^2$ d. prime

18. $14z^2 - 49z - 28$

    a. $(14z - 7)(z + 4)$ b. $7(2z - 1)(z + 4)$
    c. prime   d. $7(2z + 1)(z - 4)$

19. $9x^2 - 16$

    a. $(3x + 4)^2$ b. $(3x + 4)(3x - 4)$
    c. $(3x - 4)^2$ d. prime

20. $x^3 + 343$

    a. $(x - 343)(x + 1)(x - 1)$ b. $(x - 7)(x^2 + 7x + 49)$
    c. $(x + 7)(x^2 + 49)$ d. $(x + 7)(x^2 - 7x + 49)$

21. $75x^2y - 147y$

    a. $3y(5x + 7)(5x - 7)$ b. prime
    c. $3y(5x + 7)^2$ d. $3y(5x - 7)^2$

22. $5x^2 - 40$
  a. prime
  b. $5(x - 8)^2$
  c. $5(x + 8)(x - 8)$
  d. $5(x^2 - 8)$

23. $128x^3 + 54$
  a. $2(64x^3 + 27)$
  b. $2(4x + 3)(16x^2 - 12x + 9)$
  c. $2(4x + 3)(16x^2 + 9)$
  d. $2(4x - 3)(16x^2 + 12x + 9)$

24. $x^2y - 6x^2 - 16y + 96$
  a. $(y - 6)(x - 4)^2$
  b. $(y - 6)(x + 4)(x - 4)$
  c. $(y + 6)(x + 4)(x - 4)$
  d. prime

Solve the equation.

25. $x(3x + 13) = 10$
  a. $x = \dfrac{3}{2}, 5$
  b. $x = 0, \dfrac{13}{3}$
  c. $x = \dfrac{2}{3}, -5$
  d. $x = 0, -\dfrac{13}{3}$

26. $3x(x + 8) = (2x - 1)(x + 8)$
  a. $x = -8, -1$
  b. $x = 1$
  c. $x = 8, 1$
  d. $x = -1$

27. $2x^3 + 5x^2 = 18x + 45$
  a. $x = -3, 3$
  b. $x = -\dfrac{5}{2}, 3$
  c. $x = -\dfrac{5}{2}, 0$
  d. $x = -3, -\dfrac{5}{2}, 3$

Find an expression, in factored form, for the area of the shaded region.

28. a. $y^2 + 4$
  b. $(y + 2)^2$
  c. $(y + 2)(y - 2)$
  d. $(y - 2)^2$

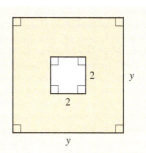

Solve.

29. A pebble is hurled upward from the top of a 256-foot-tall building with an initial velocity of 96 feet per second. Neglecting air resistance, the height $h(t)$ in feet of the pebble after t seconds is given by the polynomial function
$$h(t) = -16t^2 + 96t + 256$$
  a. Find the height of the pebble when $t = 1$.
  b. Find the height of the pebble when $t = 6.8$.
  c. Factor the polynomial $-16t^2 + 96t + 256$.
  d. When will the pebble hit the ground?

  A. a. 336 ft
  b. -1136.64 ft
  c. $-16(t + 8)(t - 2)$
  d. 2 sec

  B. a. 144 ft
  b. -1136.64 ft
  c. $-16(t + 8)(t - 2)$
  d. 2 sec

  C. a. 144 ft
  b. 168.96 ft
  c. $-16(t - 8)(t + 2)$
  d. 8 sec

  D. a. 336 ft
  b. 168.96 ft
  c. $-16(t - 8)(t + 2)$
  d. 8 sec

CHAPTER

7 Rational Expressions

7.1 Rational Functions and Multiplying and Dividing Rational Expressions

7.2 Adding and Subtracting Rational Expressions

7.3 Simplifying Complex Fractions

7.4 Dividing Polynomials: Long Division and Synthetic Division

7.5 Solving Equations Containing Rational Expressions

Integrated Review—Expressions and Equations Containing Rational Expressions

7.6 Rational Equations and Problem Solving

7.7 Variation and Problem Solving

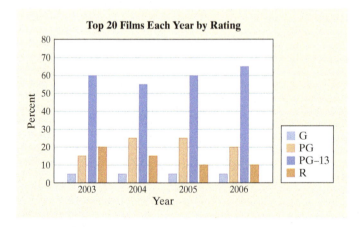

The graph above shows yearly rating changes for top grossing films. In this chapter, we use a new algebraic form, called a rational expression, to help us solve applications about movie ratings and costs to make a movie.

7.1 RATIONAL FUNCTIONS AND MULTIPLYING AND DIVIDING RATIONAL EXPRESSIONS

OBJECTIVES

1. Find the domain of a rational expression.
2. Simplify rational expressions.
3. Multiply rational expressions.
4. Divide rational expressions.
5. Use rational functions in applications.

Recall that a *rational number*, or *fraction*, is a number that can be written as the quotient $\frac{p}{q}$ of two integers p and q as long as q is not 0. A **rational expression** is an expression that can be written as the quotient $\frac{P}{Q}$ of two polynomials P and Q as long as Q is not 0.

Examples of Rational Expressions

$$\frac{3x + 7}{2} \qquad \frac{5x^2 - 3}{x - 1} \qquad \frac{7x - 2}{2x^2 + 7x + 6}$$

Rational expressions are sometimes used to describe functions. For example, we call the function $f(x) = \frac{x^2 + 2}{x - 3}$ a **rational function** since $\frac{x^2 + 2}{x - 3}$ is a rational expression.

OBJECTIVE 1 ▶ Finding the domain of a rational expression. As with fractions, a rational expression is **undefined** if the denominator is 0. If a variable in a rational expression is replaced with a number that makes the denominator 0, we say that the rational expression is **undefined** for this value of the variable. For example, the rational expression $\frac{x^2 + 2}{x - 3}$ is undefined when x is 3, because replacing x with 3 results in a denominator of 0. For this reason, we must exclude 3 from the domain of the function $f(x) = \frac{x^2 + 2}{x - 3}$.

The domain of f is then all real numbers except 3.

In this section, we will use this notation to write domains. Also, unless told otherwise, we assume that the domain of a function described by an equation is the set of all real numbers for which the equation is defined.

Note: It is also possible to write domains using set builder notation, as shown below.

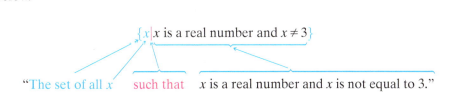

$\{x | x$ is a real number and $x \neq 3\}$

"The set of all x"   such that x is a real number and x is not equal to 3."

EXAMPLE 1   Find the domain of each rational function.

a. $f(x) = \dfrac{8x^3 + 7x^2 + 20}{2}$ **b.** $g(x) = \dfrac{5x^2 - 3}{x - 1}$ **c.** $f(x) = \dfrac{7x - 2}{x^2 - 2x - 15}$

Solution   The domain of each function will contain all real numbers except those values that make the denominator 0.

a. No matter what the value of x, the denominator of $f(x) = \dfrac{8x^3 + 7x^2 + 20}{2}$ is never 0, so the domain of f is all real numbers.

b. To find the values of x that make the denominator of $g(x)$ equal to 0, we solve the equation "denominator = 0":

$$x - 1 = 0, \quad \text{or} \quad x = 1$$

The domain must exclude 1 since the rational expression is undefined when x is 1. The domain of g is all real numbers except 1.

c. We find the domain by setting the denominator equal to 0.

$$x^2 - 2x - 15 = 0 \quad \text{Set the denominator equal to 0 and solve.}$$
$$(x - 5)(x + 3) = 0$$
$$x - 5 = 0 \quad \text{or} \quad x + 3 = 0$$
$$x = 5 \quad \text{or} \quad x = -3$$

If x is replaced with 5 or with -3, the rational expression is undefined.

The domain of f is all real numbers except 5 and -3. □

PRACTICE 1 Find the domain of each rational function.

a. $f(x) = \dfrac{4x^5 - 3x^2 + 2}{-6}$ **b.** $g(x) = \dfrac{6x^2 + 1}{x + 3}$ **c.** $h(x) = \dfrac{8x - 3}{x^2 - 5x + 6}$

Concept Check ✓

For which of these values (if any) is the rational expression $\dfrac{x - 3}{x^2 + 2}$ undefined?

a. 2   **b.** 3   **c.** -2 **d.** 0   **e.** None of these

OBJECTIVE 2 ▶ Simplifying rational expressions. Recall that a fraction is in lowest terms or simplest form if the numerator and denominator have no common factors other than 1 (or -1). For example, $\dfrac{3}{13}$ is in lowest terms since 3 and 13 have no common factors other than 1 (or -1).

To **simplify** a rational expression, or to write it in lowest terms, we use a method similar to simplifying a fraction.

Recall that to simplify a fraction, we essentially "remove factors of 1." Our ability to do this comes from these facts:

- If $c \neq 0$, then $\dfrac{c}{c} = 1$. For example, $\dfrac{7}{7} = 1$ and $\dfrac{-8.65}{-8.65} = 1$.

- $n \cdot 1 = n$. For example, $-5 \cdot 1 = -5$, $126.8 \cdot 1 = 126.8$, and $\dfrac{a}{b} \cdot 1 = \dfrac{a}{b}, b \neq 0$.

In other words, we have the following:

$$\dfrac{a \cdot c}{b \cdot c} = \dfrac{a}{b} \cdot \dfrac{c}{c} = \dfrac{a}{b}$$

Since $\dfrac{a}{b} \cdot 1 = \dfrac{a}{b}$

Let's practice simplifying a fraction by simplifying $\dfrac{15}{65}$.

$$\dfrac{15}{65} = \dfrac{3 \cdot 5}{13 \cdot 5} = \dfrac{3}{13} \cdot \dfrac{5}{5} = \dfrac{3}{13} \cdot 1 = \dfrac{3}{13}$$

Let's use the same technique and simplify the rational expression $\dfrac{(x + 2)^2}{x^2 - 4}$.

$$\dfrac{(x + 2)^2}{x^2 - 4} = \dfrac{(x + 2)(x + 2)}{(x - 2)(x + 2)}$$
$$= \dfrac{(x + 2)}{(x - 2)} \cdot \dfrac{x + 2}{x + 2}$$
$$= \dfrac{x + 2}{x - 2} \cdot 1$$
$$= \dfrac{x + 2}{x - 2}$$

Answer to Concept Check: e

Section 7.1 Rational Functions and Multiplying and Dividing Rational Expressions 373

This means that the rational expression $\dfrac{(x+2)^2}{x^2-4}$ has the same value as the rational expression $\dfrac{x+2}{x-2}$ for all values of x except 2 and -2. (Remember that when x is 2, the denominators of both rational expressions are 0 and that when x is -2, the original rational expression has a denominator of 0.)

As we simplify rational expressions, we will assume that the simplified rational expression is equivalent to the original rational expression for all real numbers except those for which either denominator is 0.

Just as for numerical fractions, we can use a shortcut notation. Remember that as long as exact factors in both the numerator and denominator are divided out, we are "removing a factor of 1." We can use the following notation:

$$\dfrac{(x+2)^2}{x^2-4} = \dfrac{(x+2)\,(x+2)}{(x-2)\,(x+2)} \quad \text{A factor of 1 is identified by the shading.}$$

$$= \dfrac{x+2}{x-2} \quad \text{"Remove" the factor of 1.}$$

This "removing a factor of 1" is stated in the principle below:

Fundamental Principle of Rational Expressions

For any rational expression $\dfrac{P}{Q}$ and any polynomial R, where $R \neq 0$,

$$\dfrac{PR}{QR} = \dfrac{P}{Q} \cdot \dfrac{R}{R} = \dfrac{P}{Q} \cdot 1 = \dfrac{P}{Q}$$

or, simply,

$$\dfrac{PR}{QR} = \dfrac{P}{Q}$$

In general, the following steps may be used to simplify rational expressions or to write a rational expression in lowest terms.

Simplifying or Writing a Rational Expression in Lowest Terms

STEP 1. Completely factor the numerator and denominator of the rational expression.

STEP 2. Divide out factors common to the numerator and denominator. (This is the same as "removing a factor of 1.")

For now, we assume that variables in a rational expression do not represent values that make the denominator 0.

EXAMPLE 2 Simplify each rational expression.

a. $\dfrac{2x^2}{10x^3 - 2x^2}$ **b.** $\dfrac{9x^2 + 13x + 4}{8x^2 + x - 7}$

Solution

a. $\dfrac{2x^2}{10x^3 - 2x^2} = \dfrac{2x^2 \cdot 1}{2x^2\,(5x-1)} = 1 \cdot \dfrac{1}{5x-1} = \dfrac{1}{5x-1}$

b. $\dfrac{9x^2 + 13x + 4}{8x^2 + x - 7} = \dfrac{(9x + 4)(x + 1)}{(8x - 7)(x + 1)}$ Factor the numerator and denominator.

$= \dfrac{9x + 4}{8x - 7} \cdot 1$ Since $\dfrac{x + 1}{x + 1} = 1$

$= \dfrac{9x + 4}{8x - 7}$ Simplest form

PRACTICE 2 Simplify each rational expressions.

a. $\dfrac{5z^4}{10z^5 - 5z^4}$ b. $\dfrac{5x^2 + 13x + 6}{6x^2 + 7x - 10}$

EXAMPLE 3 Simplify each rational expression.

a. $\dfrac{2 + x}{x + 2}$ b. $\dfrac{2 - x}{x - 2}$

Solution

a. $\dfrac{2 + x}{x + 2} = \dfrac{x + 2}{x + 2} = 1$ By the commutative property of addition, $2 + x = x + 2$.

b. $\dfrac{2 - x}{x - 2}$

The terms in the numerator of $\dfrac{2 - x}{x - 2}$ differ by sign from the terms of the denominator, so the polynomials are opposites of each other and the expression simplifies to -1. To see this, we factor out -1 from the numerator or the denominator. If -1 is factored from the numerator, then

$$\dfrac{2 - x}{x - 2} = \dfrac{-1(-2 + x)}{x - 2} = \dfrac{-1(x - 2)}{x - 2} = \dfrac{-1}{1} = -1$$

> **Helpful Hint**
> When the numerator and the denominator of a rational expression are opposites of each other, the expression simplifies to -1.

If -1 is factored from the denominator, the result is the same.

$$\dfrac{2 - x}{x - 2} = \dfrac{2 - x}{-1(-x + 2)} = \dfrac{2 - x}{-1(2 - x)} = \dfrac{1}{-1} = -1$$

PRACTICE 3 Simplify each rational expression.

a. $\dfrac{x + 3}{3 + x}$ b. $\dfrac{3 - x}{x - 3}$

EXAMPLE 4 Simplify $\dfrac{18 - 2x^2}{x^2 - 2x - 3}$.

Solution $\dfrac{18 - 2x^2}{x^2 - 2x - 3} = \dfrac{2(9 - x^2)}{(x + 1)(x - 3)}$ Factor.

$= \dfrac{2(3 + x)(3 - x)}{(x + 1)(x - 3)}$ Factor completely.

$= \dfrac{2(3 + x) \cdot -1(x - 3)}{(x + 1)(x - 3)}$ Notice the opposites $3 - x$ and $x - 3$. Write $3 - x$ as $-1(x - 3)$ and simplify.

$= -\dfrac{2(3 + x)}{x + 1}$

PRACTICE 4 Simplify $\dfrac{20 - 5x^2}{x^2 + x - 6}$.

Section 7.1 Rational Functions and Multiplying and Dividing Rational Expressions **375**

> **Helpful Hint**
> Recall that for a fraction $\frac{a}{b}$,
> $$\frac{a}{-b} = \frac{-a}{b} = -\frac{a}{b}$$
> For example
> $$\frac{-(x+1)}{(x+2)} = \frac{(x+1)}{-(x+2)} = -\frac{x+1}{x+2}$$

Concept Check ✓

Which of the following expressions are equivalent to $\frac{x}{8-x}$?

a. $\frac{-x}{x-8}$ b. $\frac{-x}{8-x}$ c. $\frac{x}{x-8}$ d. $\frac{-x}{-8+x}$

EXAMPLE 5 Simplify each rational expression.

a. $\dfrac{x^3+8}{2+x}$ b. $\dfrac{2y^2+2}{y^3-5y^2+y-5}$

Solution

a. $\dfrac{x^3+8}{2+x} = \dfrac{(x+2)(x^2-2x+4)}{x+2}$ Factor the sum of the two cubes.

$\phantom{\dfrac{x^3+8}{2+x}} = x^2 - 2x + 4$ Divide out common factors.

b. $\dfrac{2y^2+2}{y^3-5y^2+y-5} = \dfrac{2(y^2+1)}{(y^3-5y^2)+(y-5)}$ Factor the numerator.

$\phantom{\dfrac{2y^2+2}{y^3-5y^2+y-5}} = \dfrac{2(y^2+1)}{y^2(y-5)+1(y-5)}$ Factor the denominator by grouping.

$\phantom{\dfrac{2y^2+2}{y^3-5y^2+y-5}} = \dfrac{2(y^2+1)}{(y-5)(y^2+1)}$

$\phantom{\dfrac{2y^2+2}{y^3-5y^2+y-5}} = \dfrac{2}{y-5}$ Divide out common factors.

PRACTICE 5 Simplify each rational expression.

a. $\dfrac{x^3+64}{4+x}$ b. $\dfrac{5z^2+10}{z^3-3z^2+2z-6}$

Concept Check ✓

Does $\dfrac{n}{n+2}$ simplify to $\dfrac{1}{2}$? Why or why not?

Answers to Concept Check:
a and d
no; answers may vary.

OBJECTIVE 3 ▶ **Multiplying rational expressions.** Arithmetic operations on rational expressions are performed in the same way as they are on rational numbers.

> **Multiplying Rational Expressions**
> The rule for multiplying rational expressions is
> $$\frac{P}{Q} \cdot \frac{R}{S} = \frac{PR}{QS} \quad \text{as long as } Q \neq 0 \text{ and } S \neq 0.$$
> To multiply rational expressions, you may use these steps:
> **STEP 1.** Completely factor each numerator and denominator.
> **STEP 2.** Use the rule above and multiply the numerators and the denominators.
> **STEP 3.** Simplify the product by dividing the numerator and denominator by their common factors.

When we multiply rational expressions, notice that we factor each numerator and denominator first. This helps when we apply the fundamental principle to write the product in simplest form.

EXAMPLE 6 Multiply.

a. $\dfrac{1 + 3n}{2n} \cdot \dfrac{2n - 4}{3n^2 - 2n - 1}$

b. $\dfrac{x^3 - 1}{-3x + 3} \cdot \dfrac{15x^2}{x^2 + x + 1}$

Solution

a. $\dfrac{1 + 3n}{2n} \cdot \dfrac{2n - 4}{3n^2 - 2n - 1} = \dfrac{1 + 3n}{2n} \cdot \dfrac{2(n - 2)}{(3n + 1)(n - 1)}$ Factor.

$= \dfrac{(1 + 3n) \cdot 2(n - 2)}{2n(3n + 1)(n - 1)}$ Multiply.

$= \dfrac{n - 2}{n(n - 1)}$ Divide out common factors.

b. $\dfrac{x^3 - 1}{-3x + 3} \cdot \dfrac{15x^2}{x^2 + x + 1} = \dfrac{(x - 1)(x^2 + x + 1)}{-3(x - 1)} \cdot \dfrac{15x^2}{x^2 + x + 1}$ Factor.

$= \dfrac{(x - 1)(x^2 + x + 1) \cdot 3 \cdot 5x^2}{-1 \cdot 3(x - 1)(x^2 + x + 1)}$ Factor.

$= \dfrac{5x^2}{-1} = -5x^2$ Simplest form

PRACTICE 6 Multiply.

a. $\dfrac{2 + 5n}{3n} \cdot \dfrac{6n + 3}{5n^2 - 3n - 2}$

b. $\dfrac{x^3 - 8}{-6x + 12} \cdot \dfrac{6x^2}{x^2 + 2x + 4}$

OBJECTIVE 4 ▶ Dividing rational expressions. Recall that two numbers are reciprocals of each other if their product is 1. Similarly, if $\dfrac{P}{Q}$ is a rational expression, then $\dfrac{Q}{P}$ is its **reciprocal,** since

$$\frac{P}{Q} \cdot \frac{Q}{P} = \frac{P \cdot Q}{Q \cdot P} = 1$$

Section 7.1 Rational Functions and Multiplying and Dividing Rational Expressions 377

The following are examples of expressions and their reciprocals.

Expression	Reciprocal
$\dfrac{3}{x}$	$\dfrac{x}{3}$
$\dfrac{2 + x^2}{4x - 3}$	$\dfrac{4x - 3}{2 + x^2}$
x^3	$\dfrac{1}{x^3}$
0	no reciprocal

Dividing Rational Expressions

The rule for dividing rational expressions is

$$\frac{P}{Q} \div \frac{R}{S} = \frac{P}{Q} \cdot \frac{S}{R} = \frac{PS}{QR} \quad \text{as long as } Q \neq 0, S \neq 0, \text{ and } R \neq 0.$$

To divide by a rational expression, use the rule above and multiply by its reciprocal. Then simplify if possible.

Notice that division of rational expressions is the same as for rational numbers.

EXAMPLE 7 Divide.

a. $\dfrac{8m^2}{3m^2 - 12} \div \dfrac{40}{2 - m}$

b. $\dfrac{18y^2 + 9y - 2}{24y^2 - 10y + 1} \div \dfrac{3y^2 + 17y + 10}{8y^2 + 18y - 5}$

Solution

a. $\dfrac{8m^2}{3m^2 - 12} \div \dfrac{40}{2 - m} = \dfrac{8m^2}{3m^2 - 12} \cdot \dfrac{2 - m}{40}$ Multiply by the reciprocal of the divisor.

$= \dfrac{8m^2(2 - m)}{3(m + 2)(m - 2) \cdot 40}$ Factor and multiply.

$= \dfrac{8m^2 \cdot -1(m - 2)}{3(m + 2)(m - 2) \cdot 8 \cdot 5}$ Write $(2 - m)$ as $-1(m - 2)$.

$= -\dfrac{m^2}{15(m + 2)}$ Simplify.

b. $\dfrac{18y^2 + 9y - 2}{24y^2 - 10y + 1} \div \dfrac{3y^2 + 17y + 10}{8y^2 + 18y - 5}$

$= \dfrac{18y^2 + 9y - 2}{24y^2 - 10y + 1} \cdot \dfrac{8y^2 + 18y - 5}{3y^2 + 17y + 10}$ Multiply by the reciprocal.

$= \dfrac{(6y - 1)(3y + 2)}{(6y - 1)(4y - 1)} \cdot \dfrac{(4y - 1)(2y + 5)}{(3y + 2)(y + 5)}$ Factor.

$= \dfrac{2y + 5}{y + 5}$ Simplest form

PRACTICE 7 Divide.

a. $\dfrac{6y^3}{3y^2 - 27} \div \dfrac{42}{3 - y}$

b. $\dfrac{10x^2 + 23x - 5}{5x^2 - 51x + 10} \div \dfrac{2x^2 + 9x + 10}{7x^2 - 68x - 20}$

> **Helpful Hint**
> When dividing rational expressions, do not divide out common factors until the division problem is rewritten as a multiplication problem.

EXAMPLE 8 Perform each indicated operation.

$$\frac{x^2 - 25}{(x+5)^2} \cdot \frac{3x + 15}{4x} \div \frac{x^2 - 3x - 10}{x}$$

Solution
$$\frac{x^2 - 25}{(x+5)^2} \cdot \frac{3x + 15}{4x} \div \frac{x^2 - 3x - 10}{x}$$

$$= \frac{x^2 - 25}{(x+5)^2} \cdot \frac{3x + 15}{4x} \cdot \frac{x}{x^2 - 3x - 10} \quad \text{To divide, multiply by the reciprocal}$$

$$= \frac{(x+5)(x-5)}{(x+5)(x+5)} \cdot \frac{3(x+5)}{4x} \cdot \frac{x}{(x-5)(x+2)}$$

$$= \frac{3}{4(x+2)}$$

PRACTICE 8 Perform each indicated operation.

$$\frac{x^2 - 16}{(x-4)^2} \cdot \frac{5x - 20}{3x} \div \frac{x^2 + x - 12}{x}$$

OBJECTIVE 5 ▶ Using rational functions in applications. Rational functions occur often in real-life situations.

EXAMPLE 9 Cost for Pressing Compact Discs

For the ICL Production Company, the rational function $C(x) = \dfrac{2.6x + 10{,}000}{x}$ describes the company's cost per disc of pressing x compact discs. Find the cost per disc for pressing:

a. 100 compact discs
b. 1000 compact discs

Solution

a. $C(100) = \dfrac{2.6(100) + 10{,}000}{100} = \dfrac{10{,}260}{100} = 102.6$

The cost per disc for pressing 100 compact discs is $102.60.

b. $C(1000) = \dfrac{2.6(1000) + 10{,}000}{1000} = \dfrac{12{,}600}{1000} = 12.6$

The cost per disc for pressing 1000 compact discs is $12.60. Notice that as more compact discs are produced, the cost per disc decreases.

PRACTICE 9 A company's cost per tee shirt for silk screening x tee shirts is given by the rational function $C(x) = \dfrac{3.2x + 400}{x}$. Find the cost per tee shirt for printing:

a. 100 tee shirts
b. 1000 tee shirts

Graphing Calculator Explorations

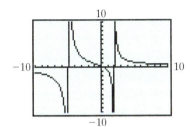

Recall that since the rational expression $\dfrac{7x - 2}{(x - 2)(x + 5)}$ is not defined when $x = 2$ or when $x = -5$, we say that the domain of the rational function $f(x) = \dfrac{7x - 2}{(x - 2)(x + 5)}$ is all real numbers except 2 and -5. This means that the graph of $f(x)$ should not cross the vertical lines $x = 2$ and $x = -5$. The graph of $f(x)$ in *connected* mode is to the left. In connected mode the graphing calculator tries to connect all dots of the graph so that the result is a smooth curve. This is what has happened in the graph. Notice that the graph appears to contain vertical lines at $x = 2$ and at $x = -5$. We know that this cannot happen because the function is not defined at $x = 2$ and at $x = -5$. We also know that this cannot happen because the graph of this function would not pass the vertical line test.

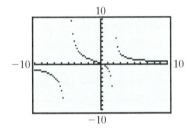

The graph of $f(x)$ in *dot* mode, is to the left. In dot mode the graphing calculator will not connect dots with a smooth curve. Notice that the vertical lines have disappeared, and we have a better picture of the graph. The graph, however, actually appears more like the hand-drawn graph below. By using a Table feature, a Calculate Value feature, or by tracing, we can see that the function is not defined at $x = 2$ and at $x = -5$.

Find the domain of each rational function. Then graph each rational function and use the graph to confirm the domain.

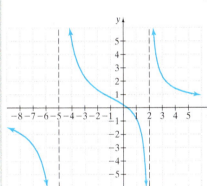

1. $f(x) = \dfrac{x + 1}{x^2 - 4}$

2. $g(x) = \dfrac{5x}{x^2 - 9}$

3. $h(x) = \dfrac{x^2}{2x^2 + 7x - 4}$

4. $f(x) = \dfrac{3x + 2}{4x^2 - 19x - 5}$

VOCABULARY & READINESS CHECK

Word Bank. *Use the choices below to fill in each blank. Some choices may not be used.*

1	true	rational	simplified	$\dfrac{-a}{-b}$	$\dfrac{-a}{b}$	$\dfrac{a}{-b}$
-1	false	domain	0			

1. A _____ expression is an expression that can be written as the quotient $\dfrac{P}{Q}$ of two polynomials P and Q as long as $Q \neq 0$.

2. A rational expression is undefined if the denominator is _____.

3. The _____ of the rational function $f(x) = \dfrac{2}{x}$ is $\{x | x \text{ is a real number and } x \neq 0\}$.

4. A rational expression is _____ if the numerator and denominator have no common factors other than 1 or -1.

5. The expression $\dfrac{x^2 + 2}{2 + x^2}$ simplifies to _____.

6. The expression $\dfrac{y - z}{z - y}$ simplifies to _____.

380 CHAPTER 7 Rational Expressions

7. For a rational expression, $-\dfrac{a}{b} = \underline{\hspace{1cm}} = \underline{\hspace{1cm}}$.

8. **True or False.** $\dfrac{a-6}{a+2} = \dfrac{-(a-6)}{-(a+2)} = \dfrac{-a+6}{-a-2}$. $\underline{\hspace{1cm}}$

Multiply.

9. $\dfrac{x}{5} \cdot \dfrac{y}{2}$
10. $\dfrac{y}{6} \cdot \dfrac{z}{5}$
11. $\dfrac{2}{x} \cdot \dfrac{y}{3}$
12. $\dfrac{a}{5} \cdot \dfrac{7}{b}$
13. $\dfrac{m}{6} \cdot \dfrac{m}{6}$
14. $\dfrac{9}{x} \cdot \dfrac{8}{x}$

7.1 EXERCISE SET   MyMathLab®

Find the domain of each rational expression. See Example 1.

1. $f(x) = \dfrac{5x-7}{4}$
2. $g(x) = \dfrac{4-3x}{2}$
3. $s(t) = \dfrac{t^2+1}{2t}$
4. $v(t) = -\dfrac{5t+t^2}{3t}$
5. $f(x) = \dfrac{3x}{7-x}$
6. $f(x) = \dfrac{-4x}{-2+x}$
7. $f(x) = \dfrac{x}{3x-1}$
8. $g(x) = \dfrac{-2}{2x+5}$
9. $R(x) = \dfrac{3+2x}{x^3+x^2-2x}$
10. $h(x) = \dfrac{5-3x}{2x^2-14x+20}$
11. $C(x) = \dfrac{x+3}{x^2-4}$
12. $R(x) = \dfrac{5}{x^2-7x}$

Simplify each rational expression. See Examples 2 through 5.

13. $\dfrac{8x-16x^2}{8x}$
14. $\dfrac{3x-6x^2}{3x}$
15. $\dfrac{x^2-9}{3+x}$
16. $\dfrac{x^2-25}{5+x}$
17. $\dfrac{9y-18}{7y-14}$
18. $\dfrac{6y-18}{2y-6}$
19. $\dfrac{x^2+6x-40}{x+10}$
20. $\dfrac{x^2-8x+16}{x-4}$
21. $\dfrac{x-9}{9-x}$
22. $\dfrac{x-4}{4-x}$
23. $\dfrac{x^2-49}{7-x}$
24. $\dfrac{x^2-y^2}{y-x}$

25. $\dfrac{2x^2-7x-4}{x^2-5x+4}$
26. $\dfrac{3x^2-11x+10}{x^2-7x+10}$
27. $\dfrac{x^3-125}{2x-10}$
28. $\dfrac{4x+4}{x^3+1}$
29. $\dfrac{3x^2-5x-2}{6x^3+2x^2+3x+1}$
30. $\dfrac{2x^2-x-3}{2x^3-3x^2+2x-3}$
31. $\dfrac{9x^2-15x+25}{27x^3+125}$
32. $\dfrac{8x^3-27}{4x^2+6x+9}$

Multiply and simplify. See Example 6.

33. $\dfrac{2x-4}{15} \cdot \dfrac{6}{2-x}$
34. $\dfrac{10-2x}{7} \cdot \dfrac{14}{5x-25}$
35. $\dfrac{18a-12a^2}{4a^2+4a+1} \cdot \dfrac{4a^2+8a+3}{4a^2-9}$
36. $\dfrac{a-5b}{a^2+ab} \cdot \dfrac{b^2-a^2}{10b-2a}$
37. $\dfrac{9x+9}{4x+8} \cdot \dfrac{2x+4}{3x^2-3}$
38. $\dfrac{2x^2-2}{10x+30} \cdot \dfrac{12x+36}{3x-3}$
39. $\dfrac{2x^3-16}{6x^2+6x-36} \cdot \dfrac{9x+18}{3x^2+6x+12}$
40. $\dfrac{x^2-3x+9}{5x^2-20x-105} \cdot \dfrac{x^2-49}{x^3+27}$
41. $\dfrac{a^3+a^2b+a+b}{5a^3+5a} \cdot \dfrac{6a^2}{2a^2-2b^2}$
42. $\dfrac{4a^2-8a}{ab-2b+3a-6} \cdot \dfrac{8b+24}{3a+6}$
43. $\dfrac{x^2-6x-16}{2x^2-128} \cdot \dfrac{x^2+16x+64}{3x^2+30x+48}$
44. $\dfrac{2x^2+12x-32}{x^2+16x+64} \cdot \dfrac{x^2+10x+16}{x^2-3x-10}$

Divide and simplify. See Example 7.

45. $\dfrac{2x}{5} \div \dfrac{6x+12}{5x+10}$

46. $\dfrac{7}{3x} \div \dfrac{14 - 7x}{18 - 9x}$

47. $\dfrac{a + b}{ab} \div \dfrac{a^2 - b^2}{4a^3b}$

48. $\dfrac{6a^2b^2}{a^2 - 4} \div \dfrac{3ab^2}{a - 2}$

49. $\dfrac{x^2 - 6x + 9}{x^2 - x - 6} \div \dfrac{x^2 - 9}{4}$

50. $\dfrac{x^2 - 4}{3x + 6} \div \dfrac{2x^2 - 8x + 8}{x^2 + 4x + 4}$

51. $\dfrac{x^2 - 6x - 16}{2x^2 - 128} \div \dfrac{x^2 + 10x + 16}{x^2 + 16x + 64}$

52. $\dfrac{a^2 - a - 6}{a^2 - 81} \div \dfrac{a^2 - 7a - 18}{4a + 36}$

53. $\dfrac{3x - x^2}{x^3 - 27} \div \dfrac{x}{x^2 + 3x + 9}$

54. $\dfrac{x^2 - 3x}{x^3 - 27} \div \dfrac{2x}{2x^2 + 6x + 18}$

55. $\dfrac{8b + 24}{3a + 6} \div \dfrac{ab - 2b + 3a - 6}{a^2 - 4a + 4}$

56. $\dfrac{2a^2 - 2b^2}{a^3 + a^2b + a + b} \div \dfrac{6a^2}{a^3 + a}$

MIXED PRACTICE

Perform each indicated operation. See Examples 2 through 8.

57. $\dfrac{x^2 - 9}{4} \cdot \dfrac{x^2 - x - 6}{x^2 - 6x + 9}$

58. $\dfrac{x^2 - 4}{9} \cdot \dfrac{x^2 - 6x + 9}{x^2 - 5x + 6}$

59. $\dfrac{2x^2 - 4x - 30}{5x^2 - 40x - 75} \div \dfrac{x^2 - 8x + 15}{x^2 - 6x + 9}$

60. $\dfrac{4a + 36}{a^2 - 7a - 18} \div \dfrac{a^2 - a - 6}{a^2 - 81}$

61. Simplify: $\dfrac{r^3 + s^3}{r + s}$

62. Simplify: $\dfrac{m^3 - n^3}{m - n}$

63. $\dfrac{4}{x} \div \dfrac{3xy}{x^2} \cdot \dfrac{6x^2}{x^4}$

64. $\dfrac{4}{x} \cdot \dfrac{3xy}{x^2} \div \dfrac{6x^2}{x^4}$

65. $\dfrac{3x^2 - 5x - 2}{y^2 + y - 2} \cdot \dfrac{y^2 + 4y - 5}{12x^2 + 7x + 1} \div \dfrac{5x^2 - 9x - 2}{8x^2 - 2x - 1}$

66. $\dfrac{x^2 + x - 2}{3y^2 - 5y - 2} \cdot \dfrac{12y^2 + y - 1}{x^2 + 4x - 5} \div \dfrac{8y^2 - 6y + 1}{5y^2 - 9y - 2}$

67. $\dfrac{5a^2 - 20}{3a^2 - 12a} \div \dfrac{a^3 + 2a^2}{2a^2 - 8a} \cdot \dfrac{9a^3 + 6a^2}{2a^2 - 4a}$

68. $\dfrac{5a^2 - 20}{3a^2 - 12a} \div \left(\dfrac{a^3 + 2a^2}{2a^2 - 8a} \cdot \dfrac{9a^3 + 6a^2}{2a^2 - 4a}\right)$

69. $\dfrac{5x^4 + 3x^2 - 2}{x - 1} \cdot \dfrac{x + 1}{x^4 - 1}$

70. $\dfrac{3x^4 - 10x^2 - 8}{x - 2} \cdot \dfrac{3x + 6}{15x^2 + 10}$

Find each function value. See Example 9.

71. If $f(x) = \dfrac{x + 8}{2x - 1}$, find $f(2)$, $f(0)$, and $f(-1)$.

72. If $f(x) = \dfrac{x - 2}{-5 + x}$, find $f(-5)$, $f(0)$, and $f(10)$.

73. If $g(x) = \dfrac{x^2 + 8}{x^3 - 25x}$, find $g(3)$, $g(-2)$, and $g(1)$.

74. If $s(t) = \dfrac{t^3 + 1}{t^2 + 1}$, find $s(-1)$, $s(1)$, and $s(2)$.

75. **Multiple Steps.** The total revenue from the sale of a popular book is approximated by the rational function $R(x) = \dfrac{1000x^2}{x^2 + 4}$, where x is the number of years since publication and $R(x)$ is the total revenue in millions of dollars.

   a. Find the total revenue at the end of the first year.
   b. Find the total revenue at the end of the second year.
   c. Find the revenue during the second year only.
   d. Find the domain of function R.

76. **Multiple Steps.** The function $f(x) = \dfrac{100{,}000x}{100 - x}$ models the cost in dollars for removing x percent of the pollutants from a bayou in which a nearby company dumped creosol.

   a. Find the cost of removing 20% of the pollutants from the bayou. [*Hint:* Find $f(20)$.]
   b. Find the cost of removing 60% of the pollutants and then 80% of the pollutants.
   c. Find $f(90)$, then $f(95)$, and then $f(99)$. What happens to the cost as x approaches 100%?
   d. Find the domain of function f.

REVIEW AND PREVIEW

Perform each indicated operation. See Section 1.3.

77. $\dfrac{4}{5} + \dfrac{3}{5}$

78. $\dfrac{4}{10} - \dfrac{7}{10}$

79. $\dfrac{5}{28} - \dfrac{2}{21}$

80. $\dfrac{5}{13} + \dfrac{2}{7}$

81. $\dfrac{3}{8} + \dfrac{1}{2} - \dfrac{3}{16}$

82. $\dfrac{2}{9} - \dfrac{1}{6} + \dfrac{2}{3}$

CONCEPT EXTENSIONS

Solve. For Exercises 83 and 84, see the second Concept Check in this section; for Exercises 85 and 86, see the third Concept Check.

83. **Multiple Choice.** Which of the expressions are equivalent to $\dfrac{x}{5 - x}$?

   a. $\dfrac{-x}{5 - x}$
   b. $\dfrac{-x}{-5 + x}$
   c. $\dfrac{x}{x - 5}$
   d. $\dfrac{-x}{x - 5}$

84. Multiple Choice. Which of the expressions are equivalent to $\dfrac{-2+x}{x}$?

a. $\dfrac{2-x}{-x}$
b. $-\dfrac{2-x}{x}$
c. $\dfrac{x-2}{x}$
d. $\dfrac{x-2}{-x}$

85. Decision Making. Does $\dfrac{x}{x+5}$ simplify to $\dfrac{1}{5}$? Why or why not?

86. Decision Making. Does $\dfrac{x+7}{x}$ simplify to 7? Why or why not?

87. Find the area of the rectangle.

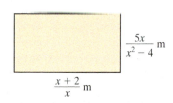

88. Find the area of the triangle.

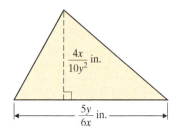

89. A parallelogram has an area of $\dfrac{x^2+x-2}{x^3}$ square feet and a height of $\dfrac{x^2}{x-1}$ feet. Express the length of its base as a rational expression in x. (*Hint:* Since $A = b \cdot h$, then $b = \dfrac{A}{h}$ or $b = A \div h$.)

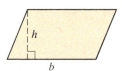

90. A lottery prize of $\dfrac{15x^3}{y^2}$ dollars is to be divided among $5x$ people. Express the amount of money each person is to receive as a rational expression in x and y.

91. In your own words explain how to simplify a rational expression.

92. In your own words, explain the difference between multiplying rational expressions and dividing rational expressions.

93. Decision Making. Decide whether each rational expression equals 1, −1, or neither.

a. $\dfrac{x+5}{5+x}$
b. $\dfrac{x-5}{5-x}$
c. $\dfrac{x+5}{x-5}$
d. $\dfrac{-x-5}{x+5}$
e. $\dfrac{x-5}{-x+5}$
f. $\dfrac{-5+x}{x-5}$

94. In our definition of division for

$$\dfrac{P}{Q} \div \dfrac{R}{S}$$

we stated that $Q \neq 0$, $S \neq 0$, and $R \neq 0$. Explain why R cannot equal 0.

95. Find the polynomial in the second numerator such that the following statement is true.

$$\dfrac{x^2-4}{x^2-7x+10} \cdot \dfrac{?}{2x^2+11x+14} = 1$$

96. In your own words, explain how to find the domain of a rational function.

97. Complete a Table. Graph a portion of the function $f(x) = \dfrac{20x}{100-x}$. To do so, complete the given table, plot the points, and then connect the plotted points with a smooth curve.

x	0	10	30	50	70	90	95	99
y or $f(x)$								

98. Complete a Table. The domain of the function $f(x) = \dfrac{1}{x}$ is all real numbers except 0. This means that the graph of this function will be in two pieces: one piece corresponding to x values less than 0 and one piece corresponding to x values greater than 0. Graph the function by completing the following tables, separately plotting the points, and connecting each set of plotted points with a smooth curve.

x	$\dfrac{1}{4}$	$\dfrac{1}{2}$	1	2	4
y or $f(x)$					

x	−4	−2	−1	$-\dfrac{1}{2}$	$-\dfrac{1}{4}$
y or $f(x)$					

Perform the indicated operation. Write all answers in lowest terms.

99. $\dfrac{x^{2n}-4}{7x} \cdot \dfrac{14x^3}{x^n-2}$

100. $\dfrac{x^{2n}+4x^n+4}{4x-3} \cdot \dfrac{8x^2-6x}{x^n+2}$

101. $\dfrac{y^{2n} + 9}{10y} \cdot \dfrac{y^n - 3}{y^{4n} - 81}$

102. $\dfrac{y^{4n} - 16}{y^{2n} + 4} \cdot \dfrac{6y}{y^n + 2}$

103. $\dfrac{y^{2n} - y^n - 2}{2y^n - 4} \div \dfrac{y^{2n} - 1}{1 + y^n}$

104. $\dfrac{y^{2n} + 7y^n + 10}{10} \div \dfrac{y^{2n} + 4y^n + 4}{5y^n + 25}$

7.2 ADDING AND SUBTRACTING RATIONAL EXPRESSIONS

OBJECTIVES

1. Add or subtract rational expressions with common denominators.
2. Identify the least common denominator of two or more rational expressions.
3. Add or subtract rational expressions with unlike denominators.

OBJECTIVE 1 ▶ **Adding or subtracting rational expressions with common denominators.** Rational expressions, like rational numbers, can be added or subtracted. We add or subtract rational expressions in the same way that we add or subtract rational numbers (fractions).

Adding or Subtracting Rational Expressions with Common Denominators

If $\dfrac{P}{Q}$ and $\dfrac{R}{Q}$ are rational expressions, then

$$\dfrac{P}{Q} + \dfrac{R}{Q} = \dfrac{P + R}{Q} \quad \text{and} \quad \dfrac{P}{Q} - \dfrac{R}{Q} = \dfrac{P - R}{Q}$$

To add or subtract rational expressions with common denominators, add or subtract the numerators and write the sum or difference over the common denominator.

EXAMPLE 1   Add or subtract.

a. $\dfrac{x}{4} + \dfrac{5x}{4}$ b. $\dfrac{5}{7z^2} + \dfrac{x}{7z^2}$ c. $\dfrac{x^2}{x + 7} - \dfrac{49}{x + 7}$ d. $\dfrac{x}{3y^2} - \dfrac{x + 1}{3y^2}$

Solution   The rational expressions have common denominators, so add or subtract their numerators and place the sum or difference over their common denominator.

a. $\dfrac{x}{4} + \dfrac{5x}{4} = \dfrac{x + 5x}{4} = \dfrac{6x}{4} = \dfrac{3x}{2}$ Add the numerators and write the result over the common denominator.

b. $\dfrac{5}{7z^2} + \dfrac{x}{7z^2} = \dfrac{5 + x}{7z^2}$

c. $\dfrac{x^2}{x + 7} - \dfrac{49}{x + 7} = \dfrac{x^2 - 49}{x + 7}$ Subtract the numerators and write the result over the common denominator.

$= \dfrac{(x + 7)(x - 7)}{x + 7}$ Factor the numerator.

$= x - 7$ Simplify.

384 CHAPTER 7 Rational Expressions

> **Helpful Hint**
> **Very Important:** Be sure to insert parentheses here so that the entire numerator is subtracted.

d. $\dfrac{x}{3y^2} - \dfrac{x+1}{3y^2} = \dfrac{x - (x+1)}{3y^2}$ Subtract the numerators.

$= \dfrac{x - x - 1}{3y^2}$ Use the distributive property.

$= -\dfrac{1}{3y^2}$ Simplify.

PRACTICE 1 Add or subtract.

a. $\dfrac{9}{11z^2} + \dfrac{x}{11z^2}$ b. $\dfrac{x}{8} + \dfrac{5x}{8}$ c. $\dfrac{x^2}{x+4} - \dfrac{16}{x+4}$ d. $\dfrac{z}{2a^2} - \dfrac{z+3}{2a^2}$

Concept Check ✓

Find and correct the error.

$$\dfrac{3+2y}{y^2-1} - \dfrac{y+3}{y^2-1} = \dfrac{3+2y-y+3}{y^2-1}$$

$$= \dfrac{y+6}{y^2-1}$$

(marked incorrect)

OBJECTIVE 2 ▶ **Identifying the least common denominator of rational expressions.**
To add or subtract rational expressions with unlike denominators, first write the rational expressions as equivalent rational expressions with common denominators.

The **least common denominator (LCD)** is usually the easiest common denominator to work with. The LCD of a list of rational expressions is a polynomial of least degree whose factors include the denominator factors in the list.

Use the following steps to find the LCD.

> **Finding the Least Common Denominator (LCD)**
> **STEP 1.** Factor each denominator completely.
> **STEP 2.** The LCD is the product of all unique factors each raised to a power equal to the greatest number of times that the factor appears in any factored denominator.

EXAMPLE 2 Find the LCD of the rational expressions in each list.

a. $\dfrac{2}{3x^5y^2}, \dfrac{3z}{5xy^3}$ b. $\dfrac{7}{z+1}, \dfrac{z}{z-1}$

c. $\dfrac{m-1}{m^2-25}, \dfrac{2m}{2m^2-9m-5}, \dfrac{7}{m^2-10m+25}$ d. $\dfrac{x}{x^2-4}, \dfrac{11}{6-3x}$

Solution

a. First we factor each denominator.

$3x^5y^2 = 3 \cdot x^5 \cdot y^2$

$5xy^3 = 5 \cdot x \cdot y^3$

LCD $= 3 \cdot 5 \cdot x^5 \cdot y^3 = 15x^5y^3$

> **Helpful Hint**
> The greatest power of x is 5, so we have a factor of x^5. The greatest power of y is 3, so we have a factor of y^3.

Answer to Concept Check:
$\dfrac{3+2y}{y^2-1} - \dfrac{y+3}{y^2-1}$
$= \dfrac{3+2y-y-3}{y^2-1} = \dfrac{y}{y^2-1}$

Section 7.2 Adding and Subtracting Rational Expressions   385

b. The denominators $z + 1$ and $z - 1$ do not factor further. Thus,
$$LCD = (z + 1)(z - 1)$$

c. We first factor each denominator.
$$m^2 - 25 = (m + 5)(m - 5)$$
$$2m^2 - 9m - 5 = (2m + 1)(m - 5)$$
$$m^2 - 10m + 25 = (m - 5)(m - 5)$$
$$LCD = (m + 5)(2m + 1)(m - 5)^2$$

d. Factor each denominator.
$$x^2 - 4 = (x + 2)(x - 2)$$
$$6 - 3x = 3(2 - x) = 3(-1)(x - 2)$$
$$LCD = 3(-1)(x + 2)(x - 2)$$
$$= -3(x + 2)(x - 2)$$

▶ **Helpful Hint**
$(x - 2)$ and $(2 - x)$ are opposite factors. Notice that -1 was factored from $(2 - x)$ so that the factors are identical.

▶ **Helpful Hint**
If opposite factors occur, do not use both in the LCD. Instead, factor -1 from one of the opposite factors so that the factors are then identical.

PRACTICE
2 Find the LCD of the rational expression in each list.

a. $\dfrac{7}{6x^3y^5}, \dfrac{2}{9x^2y^4}$

b. $\dfrac{11}{x - 2}, \dfrac{x}{x + 3}$

c. $\dfrac{b + 2}{b^2 - 16}, \dfrac{8}{b^2 - 8b + 16}, \dfrac{5b}{2b^2 - 5b - 12}$

d. $\dfrac{y}{y^2 - 9}, \dfrac{3}{12 - 4y}$

OBJECTIVE 3 ▶ **Adding or subtracting rational expressions with unlike denominators.**
To add or subtract rational expressions with unlike denominators, we write each rational expression as an equivalent rational expression so that their denominators are alike.

Adding or Subtracting Rational Expressions with Unlike Denominators
STEP 1. Find the LCD of the rational expressions.
STEP 2. Write each rational expression as an equivalent rational expression whose denominator is the LCD found in Step 1.
STEP 3. Add or subtract numerators, and write the result over the common denominator.
STEP 4. Simplify the resulting rational expression.

EXAMPLE 3 Perform the indicated operation.

a. $\dfrac{2}{x^2y} + \dfrac{5}{3x^3y}$

b. $\dfrac{3}{x + 2} + \dfrac{2x}{x - 2}$

c. $\dfrac{2x - 6}{x - 1} - \dfrac{4}{1 - x}$

Solution

a. The LCD is $3x^3y$. Write each fraction as an equivalent fraction with denominator $3x^3y$. To do this, we multiply both the numerator and denominator of each fraction by the factors needed to obtain the LCD as denominator.

The first fraction is multiplied by $\dfrac{3x}{3x}$ so that the new denominator is the LCD.

$$\dfrac{2}{x^2 y} + \dfrac{5}{3x^3 y} = \dfrac{2 \cdot 3x}{x^2 y \cdot 3x} + \dfrac{5}{3x^3 y}$$ The second expression already has a denominator of $3x^3 y$.

$$= \dfrac{6x}{3x^3 y} + \dfrac{5}{3x^3 y}$$

$$= \dfrac{6x + 5}{3x^3 y}$$ Add the numerators.

b. The LCD is the product of the two denominators: $(x + 2)(x - 2)$.

$$\dfrac{3}{x + 2} + \dfrac{2x}{x - 2} = \dfrac{3 \cdot (x - 2)}{(x + 2) \cdot (x - 2)} + \dfrac{2x \cdot (x + 2)}{(x - 2) \cdot (x + 2)}$$ Write equivalent rational expressions.

$$= \dfrac{3x - 6}{(x + 2)(x - 2)} + \dfrac{2x^2 + 4x}{(x + 2)(x - 2)}$$ Multiply in the numerators.

$$= \dfrac{3x - 6 + 2x^2 + 4x}{(x + 2)(x - 2)}$$ Add the numerators.

$$= \dfrac{2x^2 + 7x - 6}{(x + 2)(x - 2)}$$ Simplify the numerator.

c. The LCD is either $x - 1$ or $1 - x$. To get a common denominator of $x - 1$, we factor -1 from the denominator of the second rational expression.

$$\dfrac{2x - 6}{x - 1} - \dfrac{4}{1 - x} = \dfrac{2x - 6}{x - 1} - \dfrac{4}{-1(x - 1)}$$ Write $1 - x$ as $-1(x - 1)$.

$$= \dfrac{2x - 6}{x - 1} - \dfrac{-1 \cdot 4}{x - 1}$$ Write $\dfrac{4}{-1(x - 1)}$ as $\dfrac{-1 \cdot 4}{x - 1}$.

$$= \dfrac{2x - 6 - (-4)}{x - 1}$$ Combine the numerators.

$$= \dfrac{2x - 6 + 4}{x - 1}$$ Simplify.

$$= \dfrac{2x - 2}{x - 1}$$

$$= \dfrac{2(x - 1)}{x - 1}$$ Factor.

$$= 2$$ Simplest form

PRACTICE 3 Perform the indicated operation.

a. $\dfrac{4}{p^3 q} + \dfrac{3}{5p^4 q}$ **b.** $\dfrac{4}{y + 3} + \dfrac{5y}{y - 3}$ **c.** $\dfrac{3z - 18}{z - 5} - \dfrac{3}{5 - z}$

EXAMPLE 4 Subtract $\dfrac{5k}{k^2 - 4} - \dfrac{2}{k^2 + k - 2}$.

Solution $\dfrac{5k}{k^2 - 4} - \dfrac{2}{k^2 + k - 2} = \dfrac{5k}{(k + 2)(k - 2)} - \dfrac{2}{(k + 2)(k - 1)}$ Factor each denominator to find the LCD.

The LCD is $(k + 2)(k - 2)(k - 1)$. We write equivalent rational expressions with the LCD as denominators.

$$\frac{5k}{(k+2)(k-2)} - \frac{2}{(k+2)(k-1)}$$

$$= \frac{5k \cdot (k-1)}{(k+2)(k-2) \cdot (k-1)} - \frac{2 \cdot (k-2)}{(k+2)(k-1) \cdot (k-2)} \quad \text{Write equivalent rational expressions.}$$

$$= \frac{5k^2 - 5k}{(k+2)(k-2)(k-1)} - \frac{2k - 4}{(k+2)(k-2)(k-1)} \quad \text{Multiply in the numerators.}$$

$$= \frac{5k^2 - 5k - 2k + 4}{(k+2)(k-2)(k-1)} \quad \text{Subtract the numerators.}$$

$$= \frac{5k^2 - 7k + 4}{(k+2)(k-2)(k-1)} \quad \text{Simplify.} \quad \square$$

> **Helpful Hint**
> **Very Important:** Because we are subtracting; notice the sign change on 4.

PRACTICE 4 Subtract $\dfrac{t}{t^2 - 25} - \dfrac{3}{t^2 - 3t - 10}$.

EXAMPLE 5 Add $\dfrac{2x - 1}{2x^2 - 9x - 5} + \dfrac{x + 3}{6x^2 - x - 2}$.

Solution

$$\frac{2x - 1}{2x^2 - 9x - 5} + \frac{x + 3}{6x^2 - x - 2} = \frac{2x - 1}{(2x + 1)(x - 5)} + \frac{x + 3}{(2x + 1)(3x - 2)} \quad \text{Factor the denominators.}$$

The LCD is $(2x + 1)(x - 5)(3x - 2)$.

$$= \frac{(2x - 1) \cdot (3x - 2)}{(2x + 1)(x - 5) \cdot (3x - 2)} + \frac{(x + 3) \cdot (x - 5)}{(2x + 1)(3x - 2) \cdot (x - 5)}$$

$$= \frac{6x^2 - 7x + 2}{(2x + 1)(x - 5)(3x - 2)} + \frac{x^2 - 2x - 15}{(2x + 1)(x - 5)(3x - 2)} \quad \text{Multiply in the numerators.}$$

$$= \frac{6x^2 - 7x + 2 + x^2 - 2x - 15}{(2x + 1)(x - 5)(3x - 2)} \quad \text{Add the numerators.}$$

$$= \frac{7x^2 - 9x - 13}{(2x + 1)(x - 5)(3x - 2)} \quad \text{Simplify.} \quad \square$$

PRACTICE 5 Add $\dfrac{2x + 3}{3x^2 - 5x - 2} + \dfrac{x - 6}{6x^2 - 13x - 5}$.

EXAMPLE 6 Perform each indicated operation.

$$\frac{7}{x - 1} + \frac{10x}{x^2 - 1} - \frac{5}{x + 1}$$

Solution $\dfrac{7}{x - 1} + \dfrac{10x}{x^2 - 1} - \dfrac{5}{x + 1} = \dfrac{7}{x - 1} + \dfrac{10x}{(x - 1)(x + 1)} - \dfrac{5}{x + 1}$ Factor the denominators.

The LCD is $(x-1)(x+1)$.

$$= \frac{7 \cdot (x+1)}{(x-1) \cdot (x+1)} + \frac{10x}{(x-1)(x+1)} - \frac{5 \cdot (x-1)}{(x+1) \cdot (x-1)}$$

$$= \frac{7x+7}{(x-1)(x+1)} + \frac{10x}{(x-1)(x+1)} - \frac{5x-5}{(x+1)(x-1)} \quad \text{Multiply in the numerators.}$$

$$= \frac{7x+7+10x-5x+5}{(x-1)(x+1)} \quad \text{Add and subtract the numerators.}$$

$$= \frac{12x+12}{(x-1)(x+1)} \quad \text{Simplify.}$$

$$= \frac{12(x+1)}{(x-1)(x+1)} \quad \text{Factor the numerator.}$$

$$= \frac{12}{x-1} \quad \text{Divide out common factors.}$$

PRACTICE 6 Perform each indicated operation.

$$\frac{2}{x-2} + \frac{3x}{x^2-x-2} - \frac{1}{x+1}$$

Graphing Calculator Explorations

A graphing calculator can be used to support the results of operations on rational expressions. For example, to verify the result of Example 3b, graph

$$Y_1 = \frac{3}{x+2} + \frac{2x}{x-2} \quad \text{and} \quad Y_2 = \frac{2x^2+7x-6}{(x+2)(x-2)}$$

on the same set of axes. The graphs should be the same. Use a Table feature or a Trace feature to see that this is true.

VOCABULARY & READINESS CHECK

Decision Making. *Name the operation(s) below that make each statement true.*

    a. Addition   **b.** Subtraction   **c.** Multiplication   **d.** Division

1. The denominators must be the same before performing the operation. _____
2. To perform this operation, you multiply the first rational expression by the reciprocal of the second rational expression. _____
3. Numerator times numerator all over denominator times denominator. _____
4. These operations are commutative (order doesn't matter.) _____

For the rational expressions $\frac{5}{y}$ and $\frac{7}{y}$, perform each operation mentally.

5. Addition   **6.** Subtraction   **7.** Multiplication   **8.** Division

Section 7.2 Adding and Subtracting Rational Expressions 389

Be careful when subtracting! For example, $\dfrac{8}{x+1} - \dfrac{x+5}{x+1} = \dfrac{8-(x+5)}{x+1} = \dfrac{3-x}{x+1}$ or $\dfrac{-x+3}{x+1}$.

Use this example to help you perform the subtractions.

9. $\dfrac{5}{2x} - \dfrac{x+1}{2x} =$ _____
10. $\dfrac{9}{5x} - \dfrac{6-x}{5x} =$ _____
11. $\dfrac{y+11}{y-2} - \dfrac{y-5}{y-2} =$ _____
12. $\dfrac{z-1}{z+6} - \dfrac{z+4}{z+6} =$ _____

7.2 EXERCISE SET

Add or subtract as indicated. Simplify each answer. See Example 1.

1. $\dfrac{2}{xz^2} - \dfrac{5}{xz^2}$
2. $\dfrac{4}{x^2y} - \dfrac{2}{x^2y}$
3. $\dfrac{2}{x-2} + \dfrac{x}{x-2}$
4. $\dfrac{x}{5-x} + \dfrac{7}{5-x}$
5. $\dfrac{x^2}{x+2} - \dfrac{4}{x+2}$
6. $\dfrac{x^2}{x+6} - \dfrac{36}{x+6}$
7. $\dfrac{2x-6}{x^2+x-6} + \dfrac{3-3x}{x^2+x-6}$
8. $\dfrac{5x+2}{x^2+2x-8} + \dfrac{2-4x}{x^2+2x-8}$
9. $\dfrac{x-5}{2x} - \dfrac{x+5}{2x}$
10. $\dfrac{x+4}{4x} - \dfrac{x-4}{4x}$

Find the LCD of the rational expressions in each list. See Example 2.

11. $\dfrac{2}{7}, \dfrac{3}{5x}$
12. $\dfrac{4}{5y}, \dfrac{3}{4y^2}$
13. $\dfrac{3}{x}, \dfrac{2}{x+1}$
14. $\dfrac{5}{2x}, \dfrac{7}{2+x}$
15. $\dfrac{12}{x+7}, \dfrac{8}{x-7}$
16. $\dfrac{1}{2x-1}, \dfrac{8}{2x+1}$
17. $\dfrac{5}{3x+6}, \dfrac{2x}{2x-4}$
18. $\dfrac{2}{3a+9}, \dfrac{5}{5a-15}$
19. $\dfrac{2a}{a^2-b^2}, \dfrac{1}{a^2-2ab+b^2}$
20. $\dfrac{2a}{a^2+8a+16}, \dfrac{7a}{a^2+a-12}$
21. $\dfrac{x}{x^2-9}, \dfrac{5}{x}, \dfrac{7}{12-4x}$
22. $\dfrac{9}{x^2-25}, \dfrac{1}{50-10x}, \dfrac{6}{x}$

Add or subtract as indicated. Simplify each answer. See Examples 3a and 3b.

23. $\dfrac{4}{3x} + \dfrac{3}{2x}$
24. $\dfrac{10}{7x} + \dfrac{5}{2x}$
25. $\dfrac{5}{2y^2} - \dfrac{2}{7y}$
26. $\dfrac{4}{11x^4} - \dfrac{1}{4x^2}$
27. $\dfrac{x-3}{x+4} - \dfrac{x+2}{x-4}$
28. $\dfrac{x-1}{x-5} - \dfrac{x+2}{x+5}$

29. $\dfrac{1}{x-5} - \dfrac{19-2x}{(x-5)(x+4)}$
30. $\dfrac{4x-2}{(x-5)(x+4)} - \dfrac{2}{x+4}$

Perform the indicated operation. If possible, simplify your answer. See Example 3c.

31. $\dfrac{1}{a-b} + \dfrac{1}{b-a}$
32. $\dfrac{1}{a-3} - \dfrac{1}{3-a}$
33. $\dfrac{x+1}{1-x} + \dfrac{1}{x-1}$
34. $\dfrac{5}{1-x} - \dfrac{1}{x-1}$
35. $\dfrac{5}{x-2} + \dfrac{x+4}{2-x}$
36. $\dfrac{3}{5-x} + \dfrac{x+2}{x-5}$

Perform each indicated operation. If possible, simplify your answer. See Examples 4 through 6.

37. $\dfrac{y+1}{y^2-6y+8} - \dfrac{3}{y^2-16}$
38. $\dfrac{x+2}{x^2-36} - \dfrac{x}{x^2+9x+18}$
39. $\dfrac{x+4}{3x^2+11x+6} + \dfrac{x}{2x^2+x-15}$
40. $\dfrac{x+3}{5x^2+12x+4} + \dfrac{6}{x^2-x-6}$
41. $\dfrac{7}{x^2-x-2} - \dfrac{x-1}{x^2+4x+3}$
42. $\dfrac{a}{a^2+10a+25} - \dfrac{4-a}{a^2+6a+5}$
43. $\dfrac{x}{x^2-8x+7} - \dfrac{x+2}{2x^2-9x-35}$
44. $\dfrac{x}{x^2-7x+6} - \dfrac{x+4}{3x^2-2x-1}$
45. $\dfrac{2}{a^2+2a+1} + \dfrac{3}{a^2-1}$
46. $\dfrac{9x+2}{3x^2-2x-8} + \dfrac{7}{3x^2+x-4}$

MIXED PRACTICE

Add or subtract as indicated. If possible, simplify your answer. See Examples 1 through 6.

47. $\dfrac{4}{3x^2y^3} + \dfrac{5}{3x^2y^3}$

48. $\dfrac{7}{2xy^4} + \dfrac{1}{2xy^4}$

49. $\dfrac{13x - 5}{2x} - \dfrac{13x + 5}{2x}$

50. $\dfrac{17x + 4}{4x} - \dfrac{17x - 4}{4x}$

51. $\dfrac{3}{2x + 10} + \dfrac{8}{3x + 15}$

52. $\dfrac{10}{3x - 3} + \dfrac{1}{7x - 7}$

53. $\dfrac{-2}{x^2 - 3x} - \dfrac{1}{x^3 - 3x^2}$

54. $\dfrac{-3}{2a + 8} - \dfrac{8}{a^2 + 4a}$

55. $\dfrac{ab}{a^2 - b^2} + \dfrac{b}{a + b}$

56. $\dfrac{x}{25 - x^2} + \dfrac{2}{3x - 15}$

57. $\dfrac{5}{x^2 - 4} - \dfrac{3}{x^2 + 4x + 4}$

58. $\dfrac{3z}{z^2 - 9} - \dfrac{2}{3 - z}$

59. $\dfrac{3x}{2x^2 - 11x + 5} + \dfrac{7}{x^2 - 2x - 15}$

60. $\dfrac{2x}{3x^2 - 13x + 4} + \dfrac{5}{x^2 - 2x - 8}$

61. $\dfrac{2}{x + 1} - \dfrac{3x}{3x + 3} + \dfrac{1}{2x + 2}$

62. $\dfrac{5}{3x - 6} - \dfrac{x}{x - 2} + \dfrac{3 + 2x}{5x - 10}$

63. $\dfrac{3}{x + 3} + \dfrac{5}{x^2 + 6x + 9} - \dfrac{x}{x^2 - 9}$

64. $\dfrac{x + 2}{x^2 - 2x - 3} + \dfrac{x}{x - 3} - \dfrac{x}{x + 1}$

65. $\dfrac{x}{x^2 - 9} + \dfrac{3}{x^2 - 6x + 9} - \dfrac{1}{x + 3}$

66. $\dfrac{3}{x^2 - 9} - \dfrac{x}{x^2 - 6x + 9} + \dfrac{1}{x + 3}$

67. $\left(\dfrac{1}{x} + \dfrac{2}{3}\right) - \left(\dfrac{1}{x} - \dfrac{2}{3}\right)$

68. $\left(\dfrac{1}{2} + \dfrac{2}{x}\right) - \left(\dfrac{1}{2} - \dfrac{1}{x}\right)$

MIXED PRACTICE (SECTIONS 7.1, 7.2)

Perform the indicated operation. If possible, simplify your answer.

69. $\left(\dfrac{2}{3} - \dfrac{1}{x}\right) \cdot \left(\dfrac{3}{x} + \dfrac{1}{2}\right)$

70. $\left(\dfrac{2}{3} - \dfrac{1}{x}\right) \div \left(\dfrac{3}{x} + \dfrac{1}{2}\right)$

71. $\left(\dfrac{2a}{3}\right)^2 \div \left(\dfrac{a^2}{a + 1} - \dfrac{1}{a + 1}\right)$

72. $\left(\dfrac{x + 2}{2x} - \dfrac{x - 2}{2x}\right) \cdot \left(\dfrac{5x}{4}\right)^2$

73. $\left(\dfrac{2x}{3}\right)^2 \div \left(\dfrac{x}{3}\right)^2$

74. $\left(\dfrac{2x}{3}\right)^2 \cdot \left(\dfrac{3}{x}\right)^2$

75. $\left(\dfrac{x}{x + 1} - \dfrac{x}{x - 1}\right) \div \dfrac{x}{2x + 2}$

76. $\dfrac{x}{2x + 2} \div \left(\dfrac{x}{x + 1} + \dfrac{x}{x - 1}\right)$

77. $\dfrac{4}{x} \cdot \left(\dfrac{2}{x + 2} - \dfrac{2}{x - 2}\right)$

78. $\dfrac{1}{x + 1} \cdot \left(\dfrac{5}{x} + \dfrac{2}{x - 3}\right)$

REVIEW AND PREVIEW

Use the distributive property to multiply the following. See Section 1.4.

79. $12\left(\dfrac{2}{3} + \dfrac{1}{6}\right)$

80. $14\left(\dfrac{1}{7} + \dfrac{3}{14}\right)$

81. $x^2\left(\dfrac{4}{x^2} + 1\right)$

82. $5y^2\left(\dfrac{1}{y^2} - \dfrac{1}{5}\right)$

Find each root. See Section 1.3.

83. $\sqrt{100}$

84. $\sqrt{25}$

85. $\sqrt[3]{8}$

86. $\sqrt[3]{27}$

87. $\sqrt[4]{81}$

88. $\sqrt[4]{16}$

Use the Pythagorean theorem to find each unknown length of a right triangle. See Section 6.8.

△ 89.

3 meters

4 meters

△ 90.

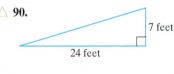

7 feet

24 feet

CONCEPT EXTENSIONS

Find and correct each error. See the Concept Check in this section.

91. $\dfrac{2x - 3}{x^2 + 1} - \dfrac{x - 6}{x^2 + 1} = \dfrac{2x - 3 - x - 6}{x^2 + 1}$

$= \dfrac{x - 9}{x^2 + 1}$

92. $\dfrac{7}{x+7} - \dfrac{x+3}{x+7} = \dfrac{7-x-3}{(x+7)^2}$
    $= \dfrac{-x+4}{(x+7)^2}$

△ 93. Find the perimeter and the area of the square.

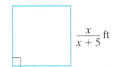

△ 94. Find the perimeter of the quadrilateral.

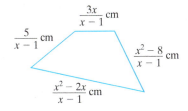

95. When is the LCD of two rational expressions equal to the product of their denominators? $\left(\textit{Hint: } \text{What is the LCD of } \dfrac{1}{x} \text{ and } \dfrac{7}{x+5}?\right)$

96. When is the LCD of two rational expressions with different denominators equal to one of the denominators? $\left(\textit{Hint: } \text{What is the LCD of } \dfrac{3x}{x+2} \text{ and } \dfrac{7x+1}{(x+2)^3}?\right)$

97. In your own words, explain how to add rational expressions with different denominators.

98. In your own words, explain how to multiply rational expressions.

99. In your own words, explain how to divide rational expressions.

100. In your own words, explain how to subtract rational expressions with different denominators.

Perform each indicated operation. (Hint: First write each expression with positive exponents.)

101. $x^{-1} + (2x)^{-1}$
102. $y^{-1} + (4y)^{-1}$
103. $4x^{-2} - 3x^{-1}$
104. $(4x)^{-2} - (3x)^{-1}$

Use a graphing calculator to support the results of each exercise.

105. Exercise 3
106. Exercise 4

7.3 SIMPLIFYING COMPLEX FRACTIONS

OBJECTIVES

1. Simplify complex fractions by simplifying the numerator and denominator and then dividing.
2. Simplify complex fractions by multiplying by a common denominator.
3. Simplify expressions with negative exponents.

OBJECTIVE 1 ▶ Simplifying complex fractions: Method 1. A rational expression whose numerator, denominator, or both contain one or more rational expressions is called a **complex rational expression** or a **complex fraction.**

Complex Fractions

$$\dfrac{\frac{1}{a}}{\frac{b}{2}} \qquad \dfrac{\frac{x}{2y^2}}{\frac{6x-2}{9y}} \qquad \dfrac{x+\frac{1}{y}}{y+1}$$

The parts of a complex fraction are

$$\dfrac{\dfrac{x}{y+2}}{7+\dfrac{1}{y}} \begin{array}{l} \leftarrow \text{Numerator of complex fraction} \\ \leftarrow \text{Main fraction bar} \\ \leftarrow \text{Denominator of complex fraction} \end{array}$$

Our goal in this section is to simplify complex fractions. A complex fraction is simplified when it is in the form $\dfrac{P}{Q}$, where P and Q are polynomials that have no common factors. Two methods of simplifying complex fractions are introduced. The first method evolves from the definition of a fraction as a quotient.

> **Simplifying a Complex Fraction: Method I**
>
> **STEP 1.** Simplify the numerator and the denominator of the complex fraction so that each is a single fraction.
>
> **STEP 2.** Perform the indicated division by multiplying the numerator of the complex fraction by the reciprocal of the denominator of the complex fraction.
>
> **STEP 3.** Simplify if possible.

EXAMPLE 1 Simplify each complex fraction.

a. $\dfrac{\dfrac{2x}{27y^2}}{\dfrac{6x^2}{9}}$ b. $\dfrac{\dfrac{5x}{x+2}}{\dfrac{10}{x-2}}$ c. $\dfrac{\dfrac{x}{y^2}+\dfrac{1}{y}}{\dfrac{y}{x^2}+\dfrac{1}{x}}$

Solution

a. The numerator of the complex fraction is already a single fraction, and so is the denominator. Perform the indicated division by multiplying the numerator, $\dfrac{2x}{27y^2}$, by the reciprocal of the denominator, $\dfrac{6x^2}{9}$. Then simplify.

$$\dfrac{\dfrac{2x}{27y^2}}{\dfrac{6x^2}{9}} = \dfrac{2x}{27y^2} \div \dfrac{6x^2}{9}$$

$$= \dfrac{2x}{27y^2} \cdot \dfrac{9}{6x^2} \qquad \text{Multiply by the reciprocal of } \dfrac{6x^2}{9}.$$

$$= \dfrac{2x \cdot 9}{27y^2 \cdot 6x^2}$$

$$= \dfrac{1}{9xy^2}$$

▶ **Helpful Hint**

Both the numerator and denominator are single fractions, so we perform the indicated division.

b. $\dfrac{\dfrac{5x}{x+2}}{\dfrac{10}{x-2}} = \dfrac{5x}{x+2} \div \dfrac{10}{x-2} = \dfrac{5x}{x+2} \cdot \dfrac{x-2}{10}$ Multiply by the reciprocal of $\dfrac{10}{x-2}$.

$$= \dfrac{5x(x-2)}{2 \cdot 5(x+2)}$$

$$= \dfrac{x(x-2)}{2(x+2)} \qquad \text{Simplify.}$$

c. First simplify the numerator and the denominator of the complex fraction separately so that each is a single fraction. Then perform the indicated division.

$$\frac{\dfrac{x}{y^2}+\dfrac{1}{y}}{\dfrac{y}{x^2}+\dfrac{1}{x}} = \frac{\dfrac{x}{y^2}+\dfrac{1 \cdot y}{y \cdot y}}{\dfrac{y}{x^2}+\dfrac{1 \cdot x}{x \cdot x}}$$ Simplify the numerator. The LCD is y^2.

Simplify the denominator. The LCD is x^2.

$$= \frac{\dfrac{x+y}{y^2}}{\dfrac{y+x}{x^2}}$$ Add.

$$= \frac{x+y}{y^2} \cdot \frac{x^2}{y+x}$$ Multiply by the reciprocal of $\dfrac{y+x}{x^2}$.

$$= \frac{x^2(x+y)}{y^2(y+x)}$$

$$= \frac{x^2}{y^2}$$ Simplify.

PRACTICE

1 Simplify each complex fraction.

a. $\dfrac{\dfrac{5k}{36m}}{\dfrac{15k}{9}}$ **b.** $\dfrac{\dfrac{8x}{x-4}}{\dfrac{3}{x+4}}$ **c.** $\dfrac{\dfrac{5}{a}+\dfrac{b}{a^2}}{\dfrac{5a}{b^2}+\dfrac{1}{b}}$

Concept Check ✓

Which of the following are equivalent to $\dfrac{\dfrac{1}{x}}{\dfrac{3}{y}}$?

a. $\dfrac{1}{x} \div \dfrac{3}{y}$ **b.** $\dfrac{1}{x} \cdot \dfrac{y}{3}$ **c.** $\dfrac{1}{x} \div \dfrac{y}{3}$

OBJECTIVE 2 ▶ Simplifying complex fractions: Method 2. Next we look at another method of simplifying complex fractions. With this method we multiply the numerator and the denominator of the complex fraction by the LCD of all fractions in the complex fraction.

> **Simplifying a Complex Fraction: Method II**
> **STEP 1.** Multiply the numerator and the denominator of the complex fraction by the LCD of the fractions in both the numerator and the denominator.
> **STEP 2.** Simplify.

Answer to Concept Check:
a and b

394 CHAPTER 7 Rational Expressions

EXAMPLE 2 Simplify each complex fraction.

a. $\dfrac{\dfrac{5x}{x+2}}{\dfrac{10}{x-2}}$ b. $\dfrac{\dfrac{x}{y^2}+\dfrac{1}{y}}{\dfrac{y}{x^2}+\dfrac{1}{x}}$

Solution

a. The least common denominator of $\dfrac{5x}{x+2}$ and $\dfrac{10}{x-2}$ is $(x+2)(x-2)$. Multiply both the numerator, $\dfrac{5x}{x+2}$, and the denominator, $\dfrac{10}{x-2}$, by the LCD.

$\dfrac{\dfrac{5x}{x+2}}{\dfrac{10}{x-2}} = \dfrac{\left(\dfrac{5x}{x+2}\right) \cdot (x+2)(x-2)}{\left(\dfrac{10}{x-2}\right) \cdot (x+2)(x-2)}$ Multiply numerator and denominator by the LCD.

$= \dfrac{5x \cdot (x-2)}{2 \cdot 5 \cdot (x+2)}$ Simplify.

$= \dfrac{x(x-2)}{2(x+2)}$ Simplify.

b. The least common denominator of $\dfrac{x}{y^2}, \dfrac{1}{y}, \dfrac{y}{x^2},$ and $\dfrac{1}{x}$ is x^2y^2.

$\dfrac{\dfrac{x}{y^2}+\dfrac{1}{y}}{\dfrac{y}{x^2}+\dfrac{1}{x}} = \dfrac{\left(\dfrac{x}{y^2}+\dfrac{1}{y}\right) \cdot x^2y^2}{\left(\dfrac{y}{x^2}+\dfrac{1}{x}\right) \cdot x^2y^2}$ Multiply the numerator and denominator by the LCD.

$= \dfrac{\dfrac{x}{y^2} \cdot x^2y^2 + \dfrac{1}{y} \cdot x^2y^2}{\dfrac{y}{x^2} \cdot x^2y^2 + \dfrac{1}{x} \cdot x^2y^2}$ Use the distributive property.

$= \dfrac{x^3 + x^2y}{y^3 + xy^2}$ Simplify.

$= \dfrac{x^2(x+y)}{y^2(y+x)}$ Factor.

$= \dfrac{x^2}{y^2}$ Simplify.

PRACTICE 2 Use Method 2 to simplify:

a. $\dfrac{\dfrac{8x}{x-4}}{\dfrac{3}{x+4}}$ b. $\dfrac{\dfrac{b}{a^2}+\dfrac{1}{a}}{\dfrac{a}{b^2}+\dfrac{1}{b}}$

OBJECTIVE 3 ▶ Simplifying expressions with negative exponents. If an expression contains negative exponents, write the expression as an equivalent expression with positive exponents.

EXAMPLE 3 Simplify.

$$\frac{x^{-1} + 2xy^{-1}}{x^{-2} - x^{-2}y^{-1}}$$

Solution This fraction does not appear to be a complex fraction. If we write it by using only positive exponents, however, we see that it is a complex fraction.

$$\frac{x^{-1} + 2xy^{-1}}{x^{-2} - x^{-2}y^{-1}} = \frac{\dfrac{1}{x} + \dfrac{2x}{y}}{\dfrac{1}{x^2} - \dfrac{1}{x^2y}}$$

The LCD of $\dfrac{1}{x}, \dfrac{2x}{y}, \dfrac{1}{x^2},$ and $\dfrac{1}{x^2y}$ is x^2y. Multiply both the numerator and denominator by x^2y.

$$= \frac{\left(\dfrac{1}{x} + \dfrac{2x}{y}\right) \cdot x^2y}{\left(\dfrac{1}{x^2} - \dfrac{1}{x^2y}\right) \cdot x^2y}$$

$$= \frac{\dfrac{1}{x} \cdot x^2y + \dfrac{2x}{y} \cdot x^2y}{\dfrac{1}{x^2} \cdot x^2y - \dfrac{1}{x^2y} \cdot x^2y} \quad \text{Apply the distributive property.}$$

$$= \frac{xy + 2x^3}{y - 1} \quad \text{or} \quad \frac{x(y + 2x^2)}{y - 1} \quad \text{Simplify.}$$

PRACTICE 3 Simplify: $\dfrac{3x^{-1} + x^{-2}y^{-1}}{y^{-2} + xy^{-1}}$.

EXAMPLE 4 Simplify: $\dfrac{(2x)^{-1} + 1}{2x^{-1} - 1}$

> **Helpful Hint**
> Don't forget that $(2x)^{-1} = \dfrac{1}{2x}$, but $2x^{-1} = 2 \cdot \dfrac{1}{x} = \dfrac{2}{x}$.

Solution $\dfrac{(2x)^{-1} + 1}{2x^{-1} - 1} = \dfrac{\dfrac{1}{2x} + 1}{\dfrac{2}{x} - 1}$ Write using positive exponents.

$$= \frac{\left(\dfrac{1}{2x} + 1\right) \cdot 2x}{\left(\dfrac{2}{x} - 1\right) \cdot 2x} \quad \text{The LDC of } \dfrac{1}{2x} \text{ and } \dfrac{2}{x} \text{ is } 2x.$$

$$= \frac{\dfrac{1}{2x} \cdot 2x + 1 \cdot 2x}{\dfrac{2}{x} \cdot 2x - 1 \cdot 2x} \quad \text{Use distributive property.}$$

$$= \frac{1 + 2x}{4 - 2x} \quad \text{or} \quad \frac{1 + 2x}{2(2 - x)} \quad \text{Simplify.}$$

PRACTICE 4 Simplify: $\dfrac{(3x)^{-1} - 2}{5x^{-1} + 2}$.

396 CHAPTER 7 Rational Expressions

VOCABULARY & READINESS CHECK

Fill in the Blank. *Complete the steps by writing the simplified complex fraction.*

1. $\dfrac{\frac{7}{x}}{\frac{1}{x}+\frac{z}{x}} = \dfrac{x\left(\frac{7}{x}\right)}{x\left(\frac{1}{x}\right)+x\left(\frac{z}{x}\right)} =$ _____

2. $\dfrac{\frac{x}{4}}{\frac{x^2}{2}+\frac{1}{4}} = \dfrac{4\left(\frac{x}{4}\right)}{4\left(\frac{x^2}{2}\right)+4\left(\frac{1}{4}\right)} =$ _____

Fill in the Blank. *Write each with positive exponents.*

3. $x^{-2} =$ _____

4. $y^{-3} =$ _____

5. $2x^{-1} =$ _____

6. $(2x)^{-1} =$ _____

7. $(9y)^{-1} =$ _____

8. $9y^{-2} =$ _____

7.3 EXERCISE SET

Simplify each complex fraction. See Examples 1 and 2.

1. $\dfrac{\frac{10}{3x}}{\frac{5}{6x}}$

2. $\dfrac{\frac{15}{2x}}{\frac{5}{6x}}$

3. $\dfrac{1+\frac{2}{5}}{2+\frac{3}{5}}$

4. $\dfrac{2+\frac{1}{7}}{3-\frac{4}{7}}$

5. $\dfrac{\frac{4}{x-1}}{\frac{x}{x-1}}$

6. $\dfrac{\frac{x}{x+2}}{\frac{2}{x+2}}$

7. $\dfrac{1-\frac{2}{x}}{x+\frac{4}{9x}}$

8. $\dfrac{5-\frac{3}{x}}{x+\frac{2}{3x}}$

9. $\dfrac{\frac{4x^2-y^2}{xy}}{\frac{2}{y}-\frac{1}{x}}$

10. $\dfrac{\frac{x^2-9y^2}{xy}}{\frac{1}{y}-\frac{3}{x}}$

11. $\dfrac{\frac{x+1}{3}}{\frac{2x-1}{6}}$

12. $\dfrac{\frac{x+3}{12}}{\frac{4x-5}{15}}$

13. $\dfrac{\frac{2}{x}+\frac{3}{x^2}}{\frac{4}{x^2}-\frac{9}{x}}$

14. $\dfrac{\frac{2}{x^2}+\frac{1}{x}}{\frac{4}{x^2}-\frac{1}{x}}$

15. $\dfrac{\frac{1}{x}+\frac{2}{x^2}}{x+\frac{8}{x^2}}$

16. $\dfrac{\frac{1}{y}+\frac{3}{y^2}}{y+\frac{27}{y^2}}$

17. $\dfrac{\frac{4}{5-x}+\frac{5}{x-5}}{\frac{2}{x}+\frac{3}{x-5}}$

18. $\dfrac{\frac{3}{x-4}-\frac{2}{4-x}}{\frac{2}{x-4}-\frac{2}{x}}$

19. $\dfrac{\frac{x+2}{x}-\frac{2}{x-1}}{\frac{x+1}{x}+\frac{x+1}{x-1}}$

20. $\dfrac{\frac{5}{a+2}-\frac{1}{a-2}}{\frac{3}{2+a}+\frac{6}{2-a}}$

21. $\dfrac{\frac{2}{x}+3}{\frac{4}{x^2}-9}$

22. $\dfrac{2+\frac{1}{x}}{4x-\frac{1}{x}}$

23. $\dfrac{1-\frac{x}{y}}{\frac{x^2}{y^2}-1}$

24. $\dfrac{1-\frac{2}{x}}{x-\frac{4}{x}}$

25. $\dfrac{\frac{-2x}{x-y}}{\frac{y}{x^2}}$

26. $\dfrac{\frac{7y}{x^2+xy}}{\frac{y^2}{x^2}}$

27. $\dfrac{\frac{2}{x}+\frac{1}{x^2}}{\frac{y}{x^2}}$

28. $\dfrac{\frac{5}{x^2}-\frac{2}{x}}{\frac{1}{x}+2}$

29. $\dfrac{\dfrac{x}{9} - \dfrac{1}{x}}{1 + \dfrac{3}{x}}$

30. $\dfrac{\dfrac{x}{4} - \dfrac{4}{x}}{1 - \dfrac{4}{x}}$

31. $\dfrac{\dfrac{x-1}{x^2-4}}{1 + \dfrac{1}{x-2}}$

32. $\dfrac{\dfrac{x+3}{x^2-9}}{1 + \dfrac{1}{x-3}}$

33. $\dfrac{\dfrac{2}{x+5} + \dfrac{4}{x+3}}{\dfrac{3x+13}{x^2+8x+15}}$

34. $\dfrac{\dfrac{2}{x+2} + \dfrac{6}{x+7}}{\dfrac{4x+13}{x^2+9x+14}}$

Simplify. See Examples 3 and 4.

35. $\dfrac{x^{-1}}{x^{-2} + y^{-2}}$

36. $\dfrac{a^{-3} + b^{-1}}{a^{-2}}$

37. $\dfrac{2a^{-1} + 3b^{-2}}{a^{-1} - b^{-1}}$

38. $\dfrac{x^{-1} + y^{-1}}{3x^{-2} + 5y^{-2}}$

39. $\dfrac{1}{x - x^{-1}}$

40. $\dfrac{x^{-2}}{x + 3x^{-1}}$

41. $\dfrac{a^{-1} + 1}{a^{-1} - 1}$

42. $\dfrac{a^{-1} - 4}{4 + a^{-1}}$

43. $\dfrac{3x^{-1} + (2y)^{-1}}{x^{-2}}$

44. $\dfrac{5x^{-2} - 3y^{-1}}{x^{-1} + y^{-1}}$

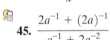
45. $\dfrac{2a^{-1} + (2a)^{-1}}{a^{-1} + 2a^{-2}}$

46. $\dfrac{a^{-1} + 2a^{-2}}{2a^{-1} + (2a)^{-1}}$

47. $\dfrac{5x^{-1} + 2y^{-1}}{x^{-2}y^{-2}}$

48. $\dfrac{x^{-2}y^{-2}}{5x^{-1} + 2y^{-1}}$

49. $\dfrac{5x^{-1} - 2y^{-1}}{25x^{-2} - 4y^{-2}}$

50. $\dfrac{3x^{-1} + 3y^{-1}}{4x^{-2} - 9y^{-2}}$

REVIEW AND PREVIEW

Simplify. See Sections 6.1 and 6.2.

51. $\dfrac{3x^3y^2}{12x}$

52. $\dfrac{-36xb^3}{9xb^2}$

53. $\dfrac{144x^5y^5}{-16x^2y}$

54. $\dfrac{48x^3y^2}{-4xy}$

Solve the following. See Section 2.6.

55. $|x - 5| = 9$

56. $|2y + 1| = 1$

CONCEPT EXTENSIONS

Decision Making. *See the Concept Check in the Section.*

57. Which of the following are equivalent to $\dfrac{\dfrac{x+1}{9}}{\dfrac{y-2}{5}}$?

a. $\dfrac{x+1}{9} \div \dfrac{y-2}{5}$ b. $\dfrac{x+1}{9} \cdot \dfrac{y-2}{5}$ c. $\dfrac{x+1}{9} \cdot \dfrac{5}{y-2}$

58. Which of the following are equivalent to $\dfrac{\dfrac{a}{7}}{\dfrac{b}{13}}$?

a. $\dfrac{a}{7} \cdot \dfrac{b}{13}$ b. $\dfrac{a}{7} \div \dfrac{b}{13}$ c. $\dfrac{a}{7} \div \dfrac{13}{b}$ d. $\dfrac{a}{7} \cdot \dfrac{13}{b}$

59. Which of the following are equivalent to $\dfrac{\dfrac{1}{x}}{\dfrac{3}{y}}$?

a. $\dfrac{1}{x} \div \dfrac{3}{y}$ b. $\dfrac{1}{x} \cdot \dfrac{y}{3}$ c. $\dfrac{1}{x} \div \dfrac{y}{3}$

60. In your own words, explain one method for simplifying a complex fraction.

61. When the source of a sound is traveling toward a listener, the pitch that the listener hears due to the Doppler effect is given by the complex rational compression $\dfrac{a}{1 - \dfrac{s}{770}}$, where a is the actual pitch of the sound and s is the speed of the sound source. Simplify this expression.

62. In baseball, the earned run average (ERA) statistic gives the average number of earned runs scored on a pitcher per game. It is computed with the following expression: $\dfrac{E}{\dfrac{I}{9}}$, where E is the number of earned runs scored on a pitcher and I is the total number of innings pitched by the pitcher. Simplify this expression.

Simplify.

63. $\dfrac{1}{1 + (1+x)^{-1}}$

64. $\dfrac{(x+2)^{-1} + (x-2)^{-1}}{(x^2-4)^{-1}}$

65. $\dfrac{x}{1 - \dfrac{1}{1 + \dfrac{1}{x}}}$

66. $\dfrac{x}{1 - \dfrac{1}{1 - \dfrac{1}{x}}}$

67. $\dfrac{\dfrac{2}{y^2} - \dfrac{5}{xy} - \dfrac{3}{x^2}}{\dfrac{2}{y^2} + \dfrac{7}{xy} + \dfrac{3}{x^2}}$

68. $\dfrac{\dfrac{2}{x^2} - \dfrac{1}{xy} - \dfrac{1}{y^2}}{\dfrac{1}{x^2} - \dfrac{3}{xy} + \dfrac{2}{y^2}}$

69. $\dfrac{3(a+1)^{-1} + 4a^{-2}}{(a^3 + a^2)^{-1}}$

70. $\dfrac{9x^{-1} - 5(x-y)^{-1}}{4(x-y)^{-1}}$

Multiple Steps. *In the study of calculus, the difference quotient $\dfrac{f(a+h) - f(a)}{h}$ is often found and simplified. Find and simplify this quotient for each function f(x) by following steps* **a** *through* **d.**

a. *Find $(a + h)$.*

b. *Find $f(a)$.*

c. *Use steps* **a** *and* **b** *to find* $\dfrac{f(a+h) - f(a)}{h}$

d. *Simplify the result of step* **c.**

71. $f(x) = \dfrac{1}{x}$

72. $f(x) = \dfrac{5}{x}$

73. $\dfrac{3}{x+1}$

74. $\dfrac{2}{x^2}$

7.4 DIVIDING POLYNOMIALS: LONG DIVISION AND SYNTHETIC DIVISION

OBJECTIVES

1. Divide a polynomial by a monomial.
2. Divide by a polynomial.
3. Use synthetic division to divide a polynomial by a binomial.
4. Use the remainder theorem to evaluate polynomials.
5. Use the factor theorem.

OBJECTIVE 1 ▶ Dividing a polynomial by a monomial. Recall that a rational expression is a quotient of polynomials. An equivalent form of a rational expression can be obtained by performing the indicated division. For example, the rational expression $\dfrac{10x^3 - 5x^2 + 20x}{5x}$ can be thought of as the polynomial $10x^3 - 5x^2 + 20x$ divided by the monomial $5x$. To perform this division of a polynomial by a monomial (which we do below) recall the following addition fact for fractions with a common denominator.

$$\dfrac{a}{c} + \dfrac{b}{c} = \dfrac{a+b}{c}$$

If a, b, and c are monomials, we might read this equation from right to left and gain insight into dividing a polynomial by a monomial.

> **Dividing a Polynomial by a Monomial**
> Divide each term in the polynomial by the monomial.
> $$\dfrac{a+b}{c} = \dfrac{a}{c} + \dfrac{b}{c}, \text{ where } c \neq 0$$

EXAMPLE 1 Divide $10x^3 - 5x^2 + 20x$ by $5x$.

Solution We divide each term of $10x^3 - 5x^2 + 20x$ by $5x$ and simplify.

$$\dfrac{10x^3 - 5x^2 + 20x}{5x} = \dfrac{10x^3}{5x} - \dfrac{5x^2}{5x} + \dfrac{20x}{5x} = 2x^2 - x + 4$$

Check: To check, see that (quotient)(divisor) = dividend, or

$$(2x^2 - x + 4)(5x) = 10x^3 - 5x^2 + 20x.$$

PRACTICE 1 Divide $18a^3 - 12a^2 + 30a$ by $6a$.

EXAMPLE 2 Divide: $\dfrac{3x^5y^2 - 15x^3y - x^2y - 6x}{x^2y}$.

Solution We divide each term in the numerator by x^2y.

$$\dfrac{3x^5y^2 - 15x^3y - x^2y - 6x}{x^2y} = \dfrac{3x^5y^2}{x^2y} - \dfrac{15x^3y}{x^2y} - \dfrac{x^2y}{x^2y} - \dfrac{6x}{x^2y}$$

$$= 3x^3y - 15x - 1 - \dfrac{6}{xy}$$

PRACTICE 2 Divide: $\dfrac{5a^3b^4 - 8a^2b^3 + ab^2 - 8b}{ab^2}$.

OBJECTIVE 2 ▸ Dividing by a polynomial. To divide a polynomial by a polynomial other than a monomial, we use **long division**. Polynomial long division is similar to long division of real numbers. We review long division of real numbers by dividing 7 into 296.

$$\begin{array}{r} 42 \\ 7\overline{)296} \\ -28 \\ \hline 16 \\ 14 \\ \hline 2 \end{array}$$

$4(7) = 28.$
Subtract and bring down the next digit in the dividend.
$2(7) = 14.$
Subtract. The remainder is 2.

The quotient is $42\dfrac{2 \text{ (remainder)}}{7 \text{ (divisor)}}$.

Check: To check, notice that

$$42(7) + 2 = 296, \text{ the dividend.}$$

This same division process can be applied to polynomials, as shown next.

EXAMPLE 3 Divide $2x^2 - x - 10$ by $x + 2$.

Solution $2x^2 - x - 10$ is the dividend, and $x + 2$ is the divisor.

STEP 1. Divide $2x^2$ by x.

$$x + 2\overline{)2x^2 - x - 10}^{\,2x} \qquad \dfrac{2x^2}{x} = 2x, \text{ so } 2x \text{ is the first term of the quotient.}$$

STEP 2. Multiply $2x(x + 2)$.

$$\begin{array}{r} 2x \\ x + 2 \overline{)\, 2x^2 - x - 10\,} \\ 2x^2 + 4x \end{array}$$ $2x(x + 2)$
Like terms are lined up vertically.

STEP 3. Subtract $(2x^2 + 4x)$ from $(2x^2 - x - 10)$ by changing the signs of $(2x^2 + 4x)$ and adding.

$$\begin{array}{r} 2x \\ x + 2 \overline{)\, 2x^2 - x - 10\,} \\ \cancel{\mp}2x^2 \cancel{\mp} 4x \\ \hline -5x \end{array}$$

STEP 4. Bring down the next term, -10, and start the process over.

$$\begin{array}{r} 2x \\ x + 2 \overline{)\, 2x^2 - x - 10\,} \\ \cancel{\mp}2x^2 \cancel{\mp} 4x \;\;\downarrow \\ \hline -5x - 10 \end{array}$$

STEP 5. Divide $-5x$ by x.

$$\begin{array}{r} 2x - 5 \\ x + 2 \overline{)\, 2x^2 - x - 10\,} \\ \cancel{\mp}2x^2 \cancel{\mp} 4x \\ \hline -5x - 10 \end{array}$$ $\dfrac{-5x}{x} = -5$, so -5 is the second term of the quotient.

STEP 6. Multiply $-5(x + 2)$.

$$\begin{array}{r} 2x - 5 \\ x + 2 \overline{)\, 2x^2 - x - 10\,} \\ \cancel{\mp}2x^2 \cancel{\mp} 4x \\ \hline -5x - 10 \\ -5x - 10 \end{array}$$ Multiply: $-5(x + 2)$. Like terms are lined up vertically.

STEP 7. Subtract by changing signs of $-5x - 10$ and adding.

$$\begin{array}{r} 2x - 5 \\ x + 2 \overline{)\, 2x^2 - x - 10\,} \\ \cancel{\mp}2x^2 \cancel{\mp} 4x \\ \hline -5x - 10 \\ \cancel{\mp}5x \cancel{\mp} 10 \\ \hline 0 \end{array}$$ Subtract.
Remainder

Then $\dfrac{2x^2 - x - 10}{x + 2} = 2x - 5$. There is no remainder.

Check: Check this result by multiplying $2x - 5$ by $x + 2$. Their product is $(2x - 5)(x + 2) = 2x^2 - x - 10$, the dividend. ☐

PRACTICE
3 Divide $3x^2 + 7x - 6$ by $x + 3$.

EXAMPLE 4 Divide: $(6x^2 - 19x + 12) \div (3x - 5)$

Solution

$$\begin{array}{r} 2x \\ 3x-5{\overline{\smash{\big)}\,6x^2 - 19x + 12}} \\ \underline{6x^2 - 10x} \downarrow \\ -9x + 12 \end{array}$$

Divide $\dfrac{6x^2}{3x} = 2x$.

Multiply $2x(3x - 5)$.

Subtract by adding the opposite. Bring down the next term, $+12$.

$$\begin{array}{r} 2x - 3 \\ 3x-5{\overline{\smash{\big)}\,6x^2 - 19x + 12}} \\ \underline{6x^2 - 10x} \\ -9x + 12 \\ \underline{-9x + 15} \\ -3 \end{array}$$

Divide $\dfrac{-9x}{3x} = -3$.

Multiply $-3(3x - 5)$.

Subtract by adding the opposite.

Check: divisor · quotient + remainder

$(3x - 5) \quad (2x - 3) \quad + 1(-3) = 6x^2 - 19x + 15 - 3$

$ = 6x^2 - 19x + 12$ The dividend

The division checks, so

$$\dfrac{6x^2 - 19x + 12}{3x - 5} = 2x - 3 + \dfrac{-3}{3x - 5}$$

$$\text{or} \quad 2x - 3 - \dfrac{3}{3x - 5}$$

▶ **Helpful Hint**
This fraction is the remainder over the divisor.

PRACTICE 4 Divide $(6x^2 - 7x + 2)$ by $(2x - 1)$.

EXAMPLE 5 Divide: $(7x^3 + 16x^2 + 2x - 1) \div (x + 4)$.

Solution

$$\begin{array}{r} 7x^2 - 12x + 50 \\ x+4{\overline{\smash{\big)}\,7x^3 + 16x^2 + 2x - 1}} \\ \underline{7x^3 + 28x^2} \\ -12x^2 + 2x \\ \underline{-12x^2 - 48x} \\ 50x - 1 \\ \underline{50x + 200} \\ -201 \end{array}$$

Divide $\dfrac{7x^3}{x} = 7x^2$.

$7x^2(x + 4)$

Subtract. Bring down $2x$.

$\dfrac{-12x^2}{x} = -12x$, a term of the quotient.

$-12x(x + 4)$ Subtract. Bring down -1.

$\dfrac{50x}{x} = 50$, a term of the quotient.

$50(x + 4)$.   Subtract.

Thus, $\dfrac{7x^3 + 16x^2 + 2x - 1}{x + 4} = 7x^2 - 12x + 50 + \dfrac{-201}{x + 4}$ or

$$7x^2 - 12x + 50 - \dfrac{201}{x + 4}.$$

PRACTICE 5 Divide $(5x^3 + 9x^2 - 10x + 30) \div (x + 3)$.

EXAMPLE 6 Divide $3x^4 + 2x^3 - 8x + 6$ by $x^2 - 1$.

Solution Before dividing, we represent any "missing powers" by the product of 0 and the variable raised to the missing power. There is no x^2 term in the dividend, so we include $0x^2$ to represent the missing term. Also, there is no x term in the divisor, so we include $0x$ in the divisor.

$$
\begin{array}{r}
3x^2 + 2x + 3 \\
x^2 + 0x - 1 \overline{)3x^4 + 2x^3 + 0x^2 - 8x + 6} \\
\underline{3x^4 \mp 0x^3 \mp 3x^2} \quad \downarrow \\
2x^3 + 3x^2 - 8x \\
\underline{2x^3 \mp 0x^2 \mp 2x} \quad \downarrow \\
3x^2 - 6x + 6 \\
\underline{3x^2 \mp 0x \mp 3} \\
-6x + 9
\end{array}
$$

$\dfrac{3x^4}{x^2} = 3x^2$

$3x^2(x^2 + 0x - 1)$

Subtract. Bring down $-8x$.

$\dfrac{2x^3}{x^2} = 2x$, a term of the quotient.

$2x(x^2 + 0x - 1)$

Subtract. Bring down 6.

$\dfrac{3x^2}{x^2} = 3$, a term of the quotient.

$3(x^2 + 0x - 1)$

Subtract.

The division process is finished when the degree of the remainder polynomial is less than the degree of the divisor. Thus,

$$\frac{3x^4 + 2x^3 - 8x + 6}{x^2 - 1} = 3x^2 + 2x + 3 + \frac{-6x + 9}{x^2 - 1}$$

PRACTICE 6 Divide $2x^4 + 3x^3 - 5x + 2$ by $x^2 + 1$.

EXAMPLE 7 Divide $27x^3 + 8$ by $3x + 2$.

Solution We replace the missing terms in the dividend with $0x^2$ and $0x$.

$$
\begin{array}{r}
9x^2 - 6x + 4 \\
3x + 2 \overline{)27x^3 + 0x^2 + 0x + 8} \\
\underline{27x^3 \mp 18x^2} \quad \downarrow \\
-18x^2 + 0x \\
\underline{\pm 18x^2 \mp 12x} \quad \downarrow \\
12x + 8 \\
\underline{-12x \mp 8}
\end{array}
$$

$9x^2(3x + 2)$

Subtract. Bring down $0x$.

$-6x(3x + 2)$

Subtract. Bring down 8.

$4(3x + 2)$

Thus, $\dfrac{27x^3 + 8}{3x + 2} = 9x^2 - 6x + 4$.

PRACTICE 7 Divide $64x^3 - 125$ by $4x - 5$.

Concept Check ☑

In a division problem, the divisor is $4x^3 - 5$. The division process can be stopped when which of these possible remainder polynomials is reached?

a. $2x^4 + x^2 - 3$ **b.** $x^3 - 5^2$ **c.** $4x^2 + 25$

OBJECTIVE 3 ▶ **Using synthetic division to divide a polynomial by a binomial.** When a polynomial is to be divided by a binomial of the form $x - c$, a shortcut process called **synthetic division** may be used. On the left is an example of long division, and on the

Answer to Concept Check: c

right, the same example showing the coefficients of the variables only.

$$\begin{array}{r} 2x^2 + 5x + 2 \\ x-3\overline{)2x^3 - x^2 - 13x + 1} \\ \underline{2x^3 - 6x^2} \\ 5x^2 - 13x \\ \underline{5x^2 - 15x} \\ 2x + 1 \\ \underline{2x - 6} \\ 7 \end{array} \qquad \begin{array}{r} 2 \quad 5 \quad 2 \\ 1-3\overline{)2 - 1 - 13 + 1} \\ \underline{2 - 6} \\ 5 - 13 \\ \underline{5 - 15} \\ 2 + 1 \\ \underline{2 - 6} \\ 7 \end{array}$$

Notice that as long as we keep coefficients of powers of x in the same column, we can perform division of polynomials by performing algebraic operations on the coefficients only. This shortcut process of dividing with coefficients only in a special format is called synthetic division. To find $(2x^3 - x^2 - 13x + 1) \div (x - 3)$ by synthetic division, follow the next example.

EXAMPLE 8 Use synthetic division to divide $2x^3 - x^2 - 13x + 1$ by $x - 3$.

Solution To use synthetic division, the divisor must be in the form $x - c$. Since we are dividing by $x - 3$, c is 3. Write down 3 and the coefficients of the dividend.

c

$\underline{3|}\ 2\ -1\ -13\ \ 1$

$\overline{}$

2

Next, draw a line and bring down the first coefficient of the dividend.

$\underline{3|}\ 2\ -1\ -13\ \ 1$

6

$\overline{}$

2

Multiply $3 \cdot 2$ and write down the product, 6.

$\underline{3|}\ 2\ -1\ -13\ \ 1$

6

$\overline{}$

$2\ \ \ 5$

Add $-1 + 6$. Write down the sum, 5.

$\underline{3|}\ 2\ -1\ -13\ \ 1$

$6\ \ \ 15$

$2\ \ \ 5\ \ \ 2$

$3 \cdot 5 = 15$.

$-13 + 15 = 2$.

$\underline{3|}\ 2\ -1\ -13\ \ 1$

$6\ \ \ 15\ \ \ 6$

$2\ \ \ 5\ \ \ 2\ \ \ 7$

$3 \cdot 2 = 6$.

$1 + 6 = 7$.

The quotient is found in the bottom row. The numbers 2, 5, and 2 are the coefficients of the quotient polynomial, and the number 7 is the remainder. The degree of the quotient polynomial is one less than the degree of the dividend. In our example, the degree of the dividend is 3, so the degree of the quotient polynomial is 2. As we found when we performed the long division, the quotient is

$$2x^2 + 5x + 2, \quad \text{remainder } 7$$

or

$$2x^2 + 5x + 2 + \frac{7}{x - 3}$$

PRACTICE 8 Use synthetic division to divide $4x^3 - 3x^2 + 6x + 5$ by $x - 1$.

EXAMPLE 9 Use synthetic division to divide $x^4 - 2x^3 - 11x^2 + 5x + 34$ by $x + 2$.

Solution The divisor is $x + 2$, which we write in the form $x - c$ as $x - (-2)$. Thus, c is -2. The dividend coefficients are $1, -2, -11, 5,$ and 34.

$$
\begin{array}{r|rrrrr}
c \\
-2 & 1 & -2 & -11 & 5 & 34 \\
 & & -2 & 8 & 6 & -22 \\
\hline
 & 1 & -4 & -3 & 11 & 12
\end{array}
$$

The dividend is a fourth-degree polynomial, so the quotient polynomial is a third-degree polynomial. The quotient is $x^3 - 4x^2 - 3x + 11$ with a remainder of 12. Thus,

$$\frac{x^4 - 2x^3 - 11x^2 + 5x + 34}{x + 2} = x^3 - 4x^2 - 3x + 11 + \frac{12}{x + 2}$$

PRACTICE 9 Use synthetic division to divide $x^4 + 3x^3 - 5x^2 + 6x + 12$ by $x + 3$.

Concept Check ✓

Which division problems are candidates for the synthetic division process?

a. $(3x^2 + 5) \div (x + 4)$
b. $(x^3 - x^2 + 2) \div (3x^3 - 2)$
c. $(y^4 + y - 3) \div (x^2 + 1)$
d. $x^5 \div (x - 5)$

> **Helpful Hint**
> Before dividing by synthetic division, write the dividend in descending order of variable exponents. Any "missing powers" of the variable should be represented by 0 times the variable raised to the missing power.

EXAMPLE 10 If $P(x) = 2x^3 - 4x^2 + 5$,

a. Find $P(2)$ by substitution.

b. Use synthetic division to find the remainder when $P(x)$ is divided by $x - 2$.

Solution

a. $P(x) = 2x^3 - 4x^2 + 5$
$P(2) = 2(2)^3 - 4(2)^2 + 5$
$\quad\quad = 2(8) - 4(4) + 5 = 16 - 16 + 5 = 5$

Thus, $P(2) = 5$.

b. The coefficients of $P(x)$ are $2, -4, 0,$ and 5. The number 0 is a coefficient of the missing power of x^1. The divisor is $x - 2$, so c is 2.

$$
\begin{array}{r|rrrr}
c \\
2 & 2 & -4 & 0 & 5 \\
 & & 4 & 0 & 0 \\
\hline
 & 2 & 0 & 0 & 5 \text{ remainder}
\end{array}
$$

The remainder when $P(x)$ is divided by $x - 2$ is 5.

PRACTICE 10 If $P(x) = x^3 - 5x - 2$,

a. Find $P(2)$ by substitution.

b. Use synthetic division to find the remainder when $P(x)$ is divided by $x - 2$.

Answer to Concept Check:
a and d

OBJECTIVE 4 ▶ Using the remainder theorem to evaluate polynomials. Notice in the preceding example that $P(2) = 5$ and that the remainder when $P(x)$ is divided by $x - 2$ is 5. This is no accident. This illustrates the **remainder theorem**.

> **Remainder Theorem**
> If a polynomial $P(x)$ is divided by $x - c$, then the remainder is $P(c)$.

EXAMPLE 11 Use the remainder theorem and synthetic division to find $P(4)$ if

$$P(x) = 4x^6 - 25x^5 + 35x^4 + 17x^2.$$

Solution To find $P(4)$ by the remainder theorem, we divide $P(x)$ by $x - 4$. The coefficients of $P(x)$ are $4, -25, 35, 0, 17, 0,$ and 0. Also, c is 4.

```
 c
 ↘4 |  4   -25   35    0    17   0    0
        16   -36   -4   -16   4   16
        ──────────────────────────────
        4    -9    -1   -4    1    4   16  remainder
```

Thus, $P(4) = 16$, the remainder.

PRACTICE 11 Use the remainder theorem and synthetic division to find $P(3)$ if $P(x) = 2x^5 - 18x^4 + 90x^2 + 59x$.

OBJECTIVE 5 ▶ Using the Factor Theorem. Example 11 shows how we can use the Remainder Theorem to evaluate a polynomial function at 4. Rather than substituting 4 for x, we divide the function by $x - 4$. The remainder is $f(4)$.

If the polynomial $f(x)$ is divided by $x - c$ and the remainder is zero, then $f(c) = 0$. This means that c is a solution or zero of the polynomial equation $f(x) = 0$ and $(x - c)$ is a factor of $f(x)$.

> **Factor Theorem**
> A polynomial function $f(x)$ has a factor of $x - c$ if and only if $f(c) = 0$.

> ▶ **Helpful Hint**
> Just remember that if $f(c) = 0$, then $x - c$ is a factor of $f(x)$.

EXAMPLE 12 Given the polynomial equation $2x^3 - 3x^2 - 11x + 6 = 0$,

a. Use the Remainder Theorem to show that 3 is a solution of the equation.
b. Use the Factor Theorem to solve the polynomial equation.

Solution

a. One way to show that 3 is a solution is to substitute 3 for x in the equation and obtain 0. An easier way is to use synthetic division and the Remainder Theorem.

```
Proposed
solution  ↘3 | 2   -3   -11    6
                   6    9    -6
               ──────────────────
               2   3    -2    0
                              ↑
                         Remainder
```

$$\begin{array}{r} 2x^2 + 3x - 2 \\ x - 3 \overline{) 2x^3 - 3x^2 - 11x + 6} \end{array}$$

Equivalently,

$$2x^3 - 3x^2 - 11x + 6 = (x - 3)(2x^2 + 3x - 2).$$

406 CHAPTER 7 Rational Expressions

TECHNOLOGY NOTE

Graphic Connections
Because the solutions of
$$2x^3 - 3x^2 - 11x + 6 = 0$$
are $-2, \frac{1}{2}, 3$, this means that the polynomial function
$$f(x) = 2x^3 - 3x^2 - 11x + 6$$
has x-intercepts at $-2, \frac{1}{2}$, and 3. This is verified by the graph of f.

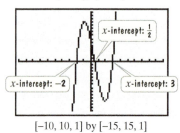

[-10, 10, 1] by [-15, 15, 1]

Because the remainder is 0, the polynomial has a value of 0 when $x = 3$. Thus, 3 is a solution of the given equation.

b. The synthetic division also shows that $x - 3$ divides the polynomial with a zero remainder. Thus, $x - 3$ is a factor of the polynomial, as shown to the right of the synthetic division. The other factor is the quotient found in the last row of the synthetic division. Now we can solve the polynomial equation.

$2x^3 - 3x^2 - 11x + 6 = 0$ This is the given equation.
$(x - 3)(2x^2 + 3x - 2) = 0$ Factor using the result from the synthetic division.
$(x - 3)(2x - 1)(x + 2) = 0$ Factor the trinomial.
$x - 3 = 0$ or $2x - 1 = 0$ or $x + 2 = 0$ Set each factor equal to 0.
$x = 3$ $x = \frac{1}{2}$ $x = -2$ Solve for x.

The solutions are $-2, \frac{1}{2}$, and 3.

PRACTICE 12 **a.** Use synthetic division to show that -1 is a solution of the equation
$$15x^3 + 14x^2 - 3x - 2 = 0.$$

b. Then use the Factor Theorem to solve the polynomial equation.

7.4 EXERCISE SET

Divide. See Examples 1 and 2.

1. $4a^2 + 8a$ by $2a$
2. $6x^4 - 3x^3$ by $3x^2$
3. $\dfrac{12a^5b^2 + 16a^4b}{4a^4b}$
4. $\dfrac{4x^3y + 12x^2y^2 - 4xy^3}{4xy}$
5. $\dfrac{4x^2y^2 + 6xy^2 - 4y^2}{2x^2y}$
6. $\dfrac{6x^5y + 75x^4y - 24x^3y^2}{3x^4y}$

Divide. See Examples 3 through 7.

7. $(x^2 + 3x + 2) \div (x + 2)$
8. $(y^2 + 7y + 10) \div (y + 5)$
9. $(2x^2 - 6x - 8) \div (x + 1)$
10. $(3x^2 + 19x + 20) \div (x + 5)$
11. $2x^2 + 3x - 2$ by $2x + 4$
12. $6x^2 - 17x - 3$ by $3x - 9$
13. $(4x^3 + 7x^2 + 8x + 20) \div (2x + 4)$
14. $(8x^3 + 18x^2 + 16x + 24) \div (4x + 8)$
15. $(2x^2 + 6x^3 - 18x - 6) \div (3x + 1)$
16. $(4x - 15x^2 + 10x^3 - 6) \div (2x - 3)$

17. $(3x^5 - x^3 + 4x^2 - 12x - 8) \div (x^2 - 2)$
18. $(2x^5 - 6x^4 + x^3 - 4x + 3) \div (x^2 - 3)$
19. $\left(2x^4 + \dfrac{1}{2}x^3 + x^2 + x\right) \div (x - 2)$
20. $\left(x^4 - \dfrac{2}{3}x^3 + x\right) \div (x - 3)$

Use synthetic division to divide. See Examples 8 and 9.

21. $\dfrac{x^2 + 3x - 40}{x - 5}$
22. $\dfrac{x^2 - 14x + 24}{x - 2}$
23. $\dfrac{x^2 + 5x - 6}{x + 6}$
24. $\dfrac{x^2 + 12x + 32}{x + 4}$
25. $\dfrac{x^3 - 7x^2 - 13x + 5}{x - 2}$
26. $\dfrac{x^3 + 6x^2 + 4x - 7}{x + 5}$
27. $\dfrac{4x^2 - 9}{x - 2}$
28. $\dfrac{3x^2 - 4}{x - 1}$

MIXED PRACTICE

Divide. See Examples 1–9.

29. $\dfrac{4x^7y^4 + 8xy^2 + 4xy^3}{4xy^3}$
30. $\dfrac{15x^3y - 5x^2y + 10xy^2}{5x^2y}$

31. $(10x^3 - 5x^2 - 12x + 1) \div (2x - 1)$

32. $(20x^3 - 8x^2 + 5x - 5) \div (5x - 2)$

33. $(2x^3 - 6x^2 - 4) \div (x - 4)$

34. $(3x^3 + 4x - 10) \div (x + 2)$

35. $\dfrac{2x^4 - 13x^3 + 16x^2 - 9x + 20}{x - 5}$

36. $\dfrac{3x^4 + 5x^3 - x^2 + x - 2}{x + 2}$

37. $\dfrac{7x^2 - 4x + 12 + 3x^3}{x + 1}$

38. $\dfrac{4x^3 + x^4 - x^2 - 16x - 4}{x - 2}$

39. $\dfrac{3x^3 + 2x^2 - 4x + 1}{x - \frac{1}{3}}$

40. $\dfrac{9y^3 + 9y^2 - y + 2}{y + \frac{2}{3}}$

41. $\dfrac{x^3 - 1}{x - 1}$ **42.** $\dfrac{y^3 - 8}{y - 2}$

43. $(25xy^2 + 75xyz + 125x^2yz) \div (-5x^2y)$

44. $(x^6y^6 - x^3y^3z + 7x^3y) \div (-7yz^2)$

45. $(9x^5 + 6x^4 - 6x^2 - 4x) \div (3x + 2)$

46. $(5x^4 - 5x^2 + 10x^3 - 10x) \div (5x + 10)$

For the given polynomial P(x) and the given c, use the remainder theorem to find P(c). See Examples 10 and 11.

47. $P(x) = x^3 + 3x^2 - 7x + 4; 1$

48. $P(x) = x^3 + 5x^2 - 4x - 6; 2$

49. $P(x) = 3x^3 - 7x^2 - 2x + 5; -3$

50. $P(x) = 4x^3 + 5x^2 - 6x - 4; -2$

51. $P(x) = 4x^4 + x^2 - 2; -1$

52. $P(x) = x^4 - 3x^2 - 2x + 5; -2$

53. $P(x) = 2x^4 - 3x^2 - 2; \dfrac{1}{3}$

54. $P(x) = 4x^4 - 2x^3 + x^2 - x - 4; \dfrac{1}{2}$

55. $P(x) = x^5 + x^4 - x^3 + 3; \dfrac{1}{2}$

56. $P(x) = x^5 - 2x^3 + 4x^2 - 5x + 6; \dfrac{2}{3}$

In Exercises 57–62, use synthetic division to show that the number given to the right of each equation is a solution of the equation. Then solve the polynomial equation. See Example 12.

57. $x^3 - 4x^2 + x + 6 = 0; \quad -1$

58. $x^3 - 2x^2 - x + 2 = 0; \quad -1$

59. $2x^3 - 5x^2 + x + 2 = 0; \quad 2$

60. $2x^3 - 3x^2 - 11x + 6 = 0; \quad -2$

61. $6x^3 + 25x^2 - 24x + 5 = 0; \quad -5$

62. $3x^3 + 7x^2 - 22x - 8 = 0; \quad -4$

In Exercises 63–66, use the graph or the table to determine a solution of each equation. Use synthetic division to verify that this number is a solution of the equation. Then solve the polynomial equation.

63. $x^3 + 2x^2 - 5x - 6 = 0$

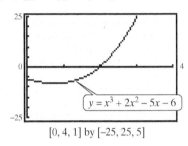

[0, 4, 1] by [–25, 25, 5]

64. $2x^3 + x^2 - 13x + 6 = 0$

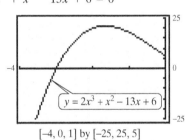

[–4, 0, 1] by [–25, 25, 5]

65. $6x^3 - 11x^2 + 6x - 1 = 0$

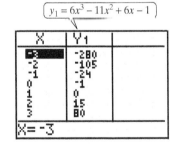

66. $2x^3 + 11x^2 - 7x - 6 = 0$

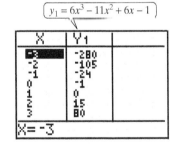

REVIEW AND PREVIEW

Solve each equation for x. See Sections 2.1 and 6.8.

67. $7x + 2 = x - 3$
68. $4 - 2x = 17 - 5x$
69. $x^2 = 4x - 4$
70. $5x^2 + 10x = 15$
71. $\dfrac{x}{3} - 5 = 13$
72. $\dfrac{2x}{9} + 1 = \dfrac{7}{9}$

Factor the following. See Sections 6.5 and 6.7.

73. $x^3 - 1$
74. $8y^3 + 1$
75. $125z^3 + 8$
76. $a^3 - 27$
77. $xy + 2x + 3y + 6$
78. $x^2 - x + xy - y$
79. $x^3 - 9x$
80. $2x^3 - 32x$

CONCEPT EXTENSIONS

Which division problems are candidates for the synthetic division process? See the second Concept Check in this section.

81. $(5x^2 - 3x + 2) \div (x + 2)$
82. $(x^4 - 6) \div (x^3 + 3x - 1)$
83. $(x^7 - 2) \div (x^5 + 1)$
84. $(3x^2 + 7x - 1) \div \left(x - \dfrac{1}{3}\right)$

85. **Multiple Choice.** In a long division exercise, if the divisor is $9x^3 - 2x$, then the division process can be stopped when the degree of the remainder is
    a. 1   b. 3   c. 9   d. 2

86. **Multiple Choice.** In a division exercise, if the divisor is $x - 3$, then the division process can be stopped when the degree of the remainder is
    a. 1   b. 0   c. 2   d. 3

87. A board of length $(3x^4 + 6x^2 - 18)$ meters is to be cut into three pieces of the same length. Find the length of each piece.

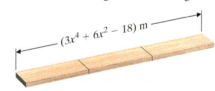

88. The perimeter of a regular hexagon is given to be $(12x^5 - 48x^3 + 3)$ miles. Find the length of each side.

89. If the area of the rectangle is $(15x^2 - 29x - 14)$ square inches, and its length is $(5x + 2)$ inches, find its width.

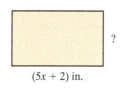

(5x + 2) in.

90. If the area of a parallelogram is $(2x^2 - 17x + 35)$ square centimeters and its base is $(2x - 7)$ centimeters, find its height.

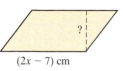

(2x − 7) cm

91. If the area of a parallelogram is $(x^4 - 23x^2 + 9x - 5)$ square centimeters and its base is $(x + 5)$ centimeters, find its height.

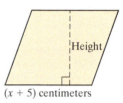

(x + 5) centimeters

92. If the volume of a box is $(x^4 + 6x^3 - 7x^2)$ cubic meters, its height is x^2 meters, and its length is $(x + 7)$ meters, find its width.

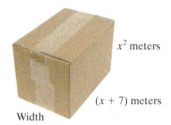

Divide.

93. $\left(x^4 + \dfrac{2}{3}x^3 + x\right) \div (x - 1)$
94. $\left(2x^3 + \dfrac{9}{2}x^2 - 4x - 10\right) \div (x + 2)$
95. $\left(3x^4 - x - x^3 + \dfrac{1}{2}\right) \div (2x - 1)$
96. $\left(2x^4 + \dfrac{1}{2}x^3 - \dfrac{1}{4}x^2 + x\right) \div (2x + 1)$
97. $(5x^4 - 2x^2 + 10x^3 - 4x) \div (5x + 10)$
98. $(9x^5 + 6x^4 - 6x^2 - 4x) \div (3x + 2)$

For each given $f(x)$ and $g(x)$, find $\dfrac{f(x)}{g(x)}$. Also find any x-values that are not in the domain of $\dfrac{f(x)}{g(x)}$. (Note: Since $g(x)$ is in the denominator, $g(x)$ cannot be 0).

99. $f(x) = 25x^2 - 5x + 30; g(x) = 5x$
100. $f(x) = 12x^4 - 9x^3 + 3x - 1; g(x) = 3x$
101. $f(x) = 7x^4 - 3x^2 + 2; g(x) = x - 2$

102. $f(x) = 2x^3 - 4x^2 + 1$; $g(x) = x + 3$

103. Try performing the following division without changing the order of the terms. Describe why this makes the process more complicated. Then perform the division again after putting the terms in the dividend in descending order of exponents.
$$\frac{4x^2 - 12x - 12 + 3x^3}{x - 2}$$

104. Explain how to check polynomial long division.

105. Explain an advantage of using the remainder theorem instead of direct substitution.

106. Explain an advantage of using synthetic division instead of long division.

We say that 2 is a factor of 8 because 2 divides 8 evenly, or with a remainder of 0. In the same manner, the polynomial $x - 2$ is a factor of the polynomial $x^3 - 14x^2 + 24x$ because the remainder is 0 when $x^3 - 14x^2 + 24x$ is divided by $x - 2$. Use this information for Exercises 107 through 109.

107. Use synthetic division to show that $x + 3$ is a factor of $x^3 + 3x^2 + 4x + 12$.

108. Use synthetic division to show that $x - 2$ is a factor of $x^3 - 2x^2 - 3x + 6$.

109. From the remainder theorem, the polynomial $x - c$ is a factor of a polynomial function $P(x)$ if $P(c)$ is what value?

110. If a polynomial is divided by $x - 5$, the quotient is $2x^2 + 5x - 6$ and the remainder is 3. Find the original polynomial.

111. If a polynomial is divided by $x + 3$, the quotient is $x^2 - x + 10$ and the remainder is -2. Find the original polynomial.

112. Multiple Steps. eBay is the leading online auction house. eBay's annual net profit can be modeled by the polynomial function $P(x) = -7x^3 + 94x^2 - 76x + 59$, where $P(x)$ is net profit in millions of dollars and x is the year after 2000. eBay's annual revenue can be modeled by the function $R(x) = 939x - 194$, where $R(x)$ is revenue of millions of dollars and x is years since 2000. (*Source: eBay, Inc.*)

a. Given that
$$\text{Net profit margin} = \frac{\text{net profit}}{\text{revenue}},$$
write a function, $m(x)$, that models eBay's net profit margin.

b. Use part **a** to predict eBay's profit margin in 2010. Round to the nearest hundredth.

7.5 SOLVING EQUATIONS CONTAINING RATIONAL EXPRESSIONS

OBJECTIVE

1. Solve equations containing rational expressions.

OBJECTIVE 1 ▶ Solving equations containing rational expressions. In this section, we solve equations containing rational expressions. Before beginning this section, make sure that you understand the difference between an *equation* and an *expression*. An **equation** contains an equal sign and an **expression** does not.

Equation	*Expression*
$\dfrac{x}{2} + \dfrac{x}{6} = \dfrac{2}{3}$	$\dfrac{x}{2} + \dfrac{x}{6}$

▶ **Helpful Hint**

The method described here is for equations only. It may *not* be used for performing operations on expressions.

Solving Equations Containing Rational Expressions

To solve *equations* containing rational expressions, first clear the equation of fractions by multiplying both sides of the equation by the LCD of all rational expressions. Then solve as usual.

Concept Check ✓

True or false? Clearing fractions is valid when solving an equation and when simplifying rational expressions. Explain.

Answer to Concept Check:
false; answers may vary

EXAMPLE 1 Solve: $\dfrac{4x}{5} + \dfrac{3}{2} = \dfrac{3x}{10}$.

Solution The LCD of $\dfrac{4x}{5}, \dfrac{3}{2},$ and $\dfrac{3x}{10}$ is 10. We multiply both sides of the equation by 10.

$$\frac{4x}{5} + \frac{3}{2} = \frac{3x}{10}$$

$$10\left(\frac{4x}{5} + \frac{3}{2}\right) = 10\left(\frac{3x}{10}\right) \quad \text{Multiply both sides by the LCD.}$$

$$10 \cdot \frac{4x}{5} + 10 \cdot \frac{3}{2} = 10 \cdot \frac{3x}{10} \quad \text{Use the distributive property.}$$

$$8x + 15 = 3x \quad \text{Simplify.}$$

$$15 = -5x \quad \text{Subtract } 8x \text{ from both sides.}$$

$$-3 = x \quad \text{Solve.}$$

Verify this solution by replacing x with -3 in the original equation.

Check:
$$\frac{4x}{5} + \frac{3}{2} = \frac{3x}{10}$$

$$\frac{4(-3)}{5} + \frac{3}{2} \stackrel{?}{=} \frac{3(-3)}{10}$$

$$\frac{-12}{5} + \frac{3}{2} \stackrel{?}{=} \frac{-9}{10}$$

$$-\frac{24}{10} + \frac{15}{10} \stackrel{?}{=} -\frac{9}{10}$$

$$-\frac{9}{10} = -\frac{9}{10} \quad \text{True}$$

The solution is -3 or the solution set is $\{-3\}$. □

PRACTICE 1 Solve: $\dfrac{5x}{4} - \dfrac{3}{2} = \dfrac{7x}{8}$.

The important difference of the equations in this section is that the denominator of a rational expression may contain a variable. Recall that a rational expression is undefined for values of the variable that make the denominator 0. If a proposed solution makes the denominator 0, then it must be rejected as a solution of the original equation. Such proposed solutions are called **extraneous solutions.**

EXAMPLE 2 Solve: $\dfrac{3}{x} - \dfrac{x + 21}{3x} = \dfrac{5}{3}$.

Solution The LCD of the denominators x, $3x$, and 3 is $3x$. We multiply both sides by $3x$.

$$\frac{3}{x} - \frac{x + 21}{3x} = \frac{5}{3}$$

$$3x\left(\frac{3}{x} - \frac{x + 21}{3x}\right) = 3x\left(\frac{5}{3}\right) \quad \text{Multiply both sides by the LCD.}$$

$$3x \cdot \frac{3}{x} - 3x \cdot \frac{x + 21}{3x} = 3x \cdot \frac{5}{3} \quad \text{Use the distributive property.}$$

$$9 - (x + 21) = 5x \quad \text{Simplify.}$$

$$9 - x - 21 = 5x$$

$$-12 = 6x$$

$$-2 = x \quad \text{Solve.}$$

The proposed solution is -2.

Check: Check the proposed solution in the original equation.

$$\frac{3}{x} - \frac{x + 21}{3x} = \frac{5}{3}$$

$$\frac{3}{-2} - \frac{-2+21}{3(-2)} \stackrel{?}{=} \frac{5}{3}$$

$$-\frac{9}{6} + \frac{19}{6} \stackrel{?}{=} \frac{5}{3}$$

$$\frac{10}{6} \stackrel{?}{=} \frac{5}{3} \quad \text{True}$$

The solution is -2 or the solution set is $\{-2\}$.

PRACTICE 2 Solve: $\dfrac{6}{x} - \dfrac{x+9}{5x} = \dfrac{2}{5}$.

The following steps may be used to solve equations containing rational expressions.

Solving an Equation Containing Rational Expressions

STEP 1. Multiply both sides of the equation by the LCD of all rational expressions in the equation.

STEP 2. Simplify both sides.

STEP 3. Determine whether the equation is linear, quadratic, or higher degree and solve accordingly.

STEP 4. Check the solution in the original equation.

EXAMPLE 3 Solve: $\dfrac{x+6}{x-2} = \dfrac{2(x+2)}{x-2}$.

Solution First we multiply both sides of the equation by the LCD, $x - 2$. (Remember, we can only do this if $x \neq 2$ so that we are not multiplying by 0.)

$$\frac{x+6}{x-2} = \frac{2(x+2)}{x-2}$$

$(x-2) \cdot \dfrac{x+6}{x-2} = (x-2) \cdot \dfrac{2(x+2)}{x-2}$ Multiply both sides by $x - 2$.

$x + 6 = 2(x + 2)$ Simplify.

$x + 6 = 2x + 4$ Use the distributive property.

$2 = x$ Solve.

From above, we assumed that $x \neq 2$, so this equation has no solution. This will also show as we attempt to check this proposed solution.

Check: The proposed solution is 2. Notice that 2 makes a denominator 0 in the original equation. This can also be seen in a check. Check the proposed solution 2 in the original equation.

$$\frac{x+6}{x-2} = \frac{2(x+2)}{x-2}$$

$$\frac{2+6}{2-2} = \frac{2(2+2)}{2-2}$$

$$\frac{8}{0} = \frac{2(4)}{0}$$

The denominators are 0, so 2 is not a solution of the original equation. This equation has no solution.

PRACTICE 3 Solve: $\dfrac{x-5}{x+3} = \dfrac{2(x-1)}{x+3}$.

EXAMPLE 4 Solve: $\dfrac{2x}{2x-1} + \dfrac{1}{x} = \dfrac{1}{2x-1}$.

Solution The LCD is $x(2x-1)$. Multiply both sides by $x(2x-1)$. By the distributive property, this is the same as multiplying each term by $x(2x-1)$.

$$x(2x-1) \cdot \dfrac{2x}{2x-1} + x(2x-1) \cdot \dfrac{1}{x} = x(2x-1) \cdot \dfrac{1}{2x-1}$$

$$x(2x) + (2x-1) = x \quad \text{Simplify.}$$
$$2x^2 + 2x - 1 - x = 0$$
$$2x^2 + x - 1 = 0$$
$$(x+1)(2x-1) = 0$$
$$x+1 = 0 \quad \text{or} \quad 2x-1 = 0$$
$$x = -1 \qquad x = \dfrac{1}{2}$$

The number $\dfrac{1}{2}$ makes the denominator $2x-1$ equal 0, so it is not a solution. The solution is -1.

PRACTICE 4 Solve: $\dfrac{5x}{5x-1} + \dfrac{1}{x} = \dfrac{1}{5x-1}$.

EXAMPLE 5 Solve: $\dfrac{2x}{x-3} + \dfrac{6-2x}{x^2-9} = \dfrac{x}{x+3}$.

Solution We factor the second denominator to find that the LCD is $(x+3)(x-3)$. We multiply both sides of the equation by $(x+3)(x-3)$. By the distributive property, this is the same as multiplying each term by $(x+3)(x-3)$.

$$\dfrac{2x}{x-3} + \dfrac{6-2x}{x^2-9} = \dfrac{x}{x+3}$$

$$(x+3)(x-3) \cdot \dfrac{2x}{x-3} + (x+3)(x-3) \cdot \dfrac{6-2x}{(x+3)(x-3)}$$
$$= (x+3)(x-3)\left(\dfrac{x}{x+3}\right)$$

$$2x(x+3) + (6-2x) = x(x-3) \quad \text{Simplify.}$$
$$2x^2 + 6x + 6 - 2x = x^2 - 3x \quad \text{Use the distributive property.}$$

Next we solve this quadratic equation by the factoring method. To do so, we first write the equation so that one side is 0.

$$x^2 + 7x + 6 = 0$$
$$(x+6)(x+1) = 0 \quad \text{Factor.}$$
$$x = -6 \text{ or } x = -1 \quad \text{Set each factor equal to 0.}$$

Neither -6 nor -1 makes any denominator 0 so they are both solutions. The solutions are -6 and -1.

PRACTICE 5 Solve: $\dfrac{2}{x-2} - \dfrac{5+2x}{x^2-4} = \dfrac{x}{x+2}$.

EXAMPLE 6

Solve: $\dfrac{z}{2z^2 + 3z - 2} - \dfrac{1}{2z} = \dfrac{3}{z^2 + 2z}$.

Solution Factor the denominators to find that the LCD is $2z(z + 2)(2z - 1)$. Multiply both sides by the LCD. Remember, by using the distributive property, this is the same as multiplying each term by $2z(z + 2)(2z - 1)$.

$$\dfrac{z}{2z^2 + 3z - 2} - \dfrac{1}{2z} = \dfrac{3}{z^2 + 2z}$$

$$\dfrac{z}{(2z - 1)(z + 2)} - \dfrac{1}{2z} = \dfrac{3}{z(z + 2)}$$

$$2z(z + 2)(2z - 1) \cdot \dfrac{z}{(2z - 1)(z + 2)} - 2z(z + 2)(2z - 1) \cdot \dfrac{1}{2z}$$

$$= 2z(z + 2)(2z - 1) \cdot \dfrac{3}{z(z + 2)} \quad \text{Apply the distributive property.}$$

$$2z(z) - (z + 2)(2z - 1) = 3 \cdot 2(2z - 1) \quad \text{Simplify.}$$
$$2z^2 - (2z^2 + 3z - 2) = 12z - 6$$
$$2z^2 - 2z^2 - 3z + 2 = 12z - 6$$
$$-3z + 2 = 12z - 6$$
$$-15z = -8$$
$$z = \dfrac{8}{15} \quad \text{Solve.}$$

The proposed solution $\dfrac{8}{15}$ does not make any denominator 0; the solution is $\dfrac{8}{15}$.

PRACTICE 6 Solve: $\dfrac{z}{2z^2 - z - 6} - \dfrac{1}{3z} = \dfrac{2}{z^2 - 2z}$.

A graph can be helpful in visualizing solutions of equations. For example, to visualize the solution of the equation $\dfrac{3}{x} - \dfrac{x + 21}{3x} = \dfrac{5}{3}$ in Example 2, the graph of the related rational function $f(x) = \dfrac{3}{x} - \dfrac{x + 21}{3x}$ is shown. A solution of the equation is an x-value that corresponds to a y-value of $\dfrac{5}{3}$.

Notice that an x-value of -2 corresponds to a y-value of $\dfrac{5}{3}$. The solution of the equation is indeed -2 as shown in Example 2.

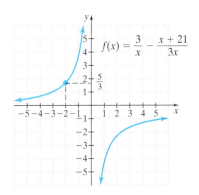

414 CHAPTER 7 Rational Expressions

VOCABULARY & READINESS CHECK

Multiple Choice. *Choose the least common denominator (LCD) for the rational expressions in each equation. Do not solve.*

1. $\dfrac{x}{7} - \dfrac{x}{2} = \dfrac{1}{2}$; LCD = _____
   a. 7   b. 2   c. 14   d. 28

2. $\dfrac{9}{x+1} + \dfrac{5}{(x+1)^2} = \dfrac{x}{x+1}$; LCD = _____
   a. $x+1$ b. $(x+1)^2$ c. $(x+1)^3$

3. $\dfrac{7}{x-4} = \dfrac{x}{x^2-16} + \dfrac{1}{x+4}$; LCD = _____
   a. $(x+4)(x-4)$ b. $x-4$ c. $x+4$ d. $(x^2-16)(x-4)(x+4)$

4. $3 = \dfrac{1}{x-5} - \dfrac{2}{x^2-5x}$; LCD = _____
   a. $x-5$ b. $3(x-5)$ c. $3x(x-5)$ d. $x(x-5)$

7.5 EXERCISE SET

Solve each equation. See Examples 1 and 2.

1. $\dfrac{x}{2} - \dfrac{x}{3} = 12$
2. $x = \dfrac{x}{2} - 4$
3. $\dfrac{x}{3} = \dfrac{1}{6} + \dfrac{x}{4}$
4. $\dfrac{x}{2} = \dfrac{21}{10} - \dfrac{x}{5}$
5. $\dfrac{2}{x} + \dfrac{1}{2} = \dfrac{5}{x}$
6. $\dfrac{5}{3x} + 1 = \dfrac{7}{6}$
7. $\dfrac{x^2+1}{x} = \dfrac{5}{x}$
8. $\dfrac{x^2-14}{2x} = -\dfrac{5}{2x}$

Solve each equation. See Examples 3 through 6.

9. $\dfrac{x+5}{x+3} = \dfrac{2}{x+3}$
10. $\dfrac{x-7}{x-1} = \dfrac{11}{x-1}$
11. $\dfrac{5}{x-2} - \dfrac{2}{x+4} = -\dfrac{4}{x^2+2x-8}$
12. $\dfrac{1}{x-1} + \dfrac{1}{x+1} = \dfrac{2}{x^2-1}$
13. $\dfrac{1}{x-1} = \dfrac{2}{x+1}$
14. $\dfrac{6}{x+3} = \dfrac{4}{x-3}$
15. $\dfrac{x^2-23}{2x^2-5x-3} + \dfrac{2}{x-3} = \dfrac{-1}{2x+1}$
16. $\dfrac{4x^2-24x}{3x^2-x-2} + \dfrac{3}{3x+2} = \dfrac{-4}{x-1}$
17. $\dfrac{1}{x-4} - \dfrac{3x}{x^2-16} = \dfrac{2}{x+4}$
18. $\dfrac{3}{2x+3} - \dfrac{1}{2x-3} = \dfrac{4}{4x^2-9}$

19. $\dfrac{1}{x-4} = \dfrac{8}{x^2-16}$
20. $\dfrac{2}{x^2-4} = \dfrac{1}{2x-4}$
21. $\dfrac{1}{x-2} - \dfrac{2}{x^2-2x} = 1$
22. $\dfrac{12}{3x^2+12x} = 1 - \dfrac{1}{x+4}$

MIXED PRACTICE

Solve each equation. See Examples 1 through 6.

23. $\dfrac{5}{x} = \dfrac{20}{12}$
24. $\dfrac{2}{x} = \dfrac{10}{5}$
25. $1 - \dfrac{4}{a} = 5$
26. $7 + \dfrac{6}{a} = 5$
27. $\dfrac{x^2+5}{x} - 1 = \dfrac{5(x+1)}{x}$
28. $\dfrac{x^2+6}{x} + 5 = \dfrac{2(x+3)}{x}$
29. $\dfrac{1}{2x} - \dfrac{1}{x+1} = \dfrac{1}{3x^2+3x}$
30. $\dfrac{2}{x-5} + \dfrac{1}{2x} = \dfrac{5}{3x^2-15x}$
31. $\dfrac{1}{x} - \dfrac{x}{25} = 0$
32. $\dfrac{x}{4} + \dfrac{5}{x} = 3$
33. $5 - \dfrac{2}{2y-5} = \dfrac{3}{2y-5}$
34. $1 - \dfrac{5}{y+7} = \dfrac{4}{y+7}$
35. $\dfrac{x-1}{x+2} = \dfrac{2}{3}$
36. $\dfrac{6x+7}{2x+9} = \dfrac{5}{3}$
37. $\dfrac{x+3}{x+2} = \dfrac{1}{x+2}$
38. $\dfrac{2x+1}{4-x} = \dfrac{9}{4-x}$

39. $\dfrac{1}{a-3} + \dfrac{2}{a+3} = \dfrac{1}{a^2-9}$

40. $\dfrac{12}{9-a^2} + \dfrac{3}{3+a} = \dfrac{2}{3-a}$

41. $\dfrac{64}{x^2-16} + 1 = \dfrac{2x}{x-4}$

42. $2 + \dfrac{3}{x} = \dfrac{2x}{x+3}$

43. $\dfrac{-15}{4y+1} + 4 = y$

44. $\dfrac{36}{x^2-9} + 1 = \dfrac{2x}{x+3}$

45. $\dfrac{28}{x^2-9} + \dfrac{2x}{x-3} + \dfrac{6}{x+3} = 0$

46. $\dfrac{x^2-20}{x^2-7x+12} = \dfrac{3}{x-3} + \dfrac{5}{x-4}$

47. $\dfrac{x+2}{x^2+7x+10} = \dfrac{1}{3x+6} - \dfrac{1}{x+5}$

48. $\dfrac{3}{2x-5} + \dfrac{2}{2x+3} = 0$

REVIEW AND PREVIEW

Write each sentence as an equation and solve. See Section 2.2.

49. Four more than 3 times a number is 19.

50. The sum of two consecutive integers is 147.

51. The length of a rectangle is 5 inches more than the width. Its perimeter is 50 inches. Find the length and width.

52. The sum of a number and its reciprocal is $\dfrac{5}{2}$.

Read a Graph. *The following graph is from statistics gathered for the National Health and Nutrition Examination Survey. Use this histogram to answer Exercises 53 through 57. (Source: Economic Research Service: USDA). See Section 2.2.*

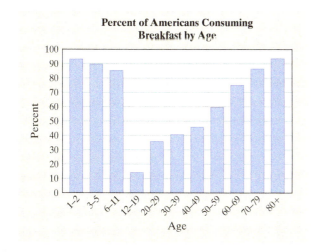

Percent of Americans Consuming Breakfast by Age

53. What percent of Americans ages 20–29 eat breakfast regularly?

54. What percent of Americans over age 80 eat breakfast regularly?

55. What age category shows the smallest percentage of Americans who eat breakfast regularly?

56. What percent of Americans ages 40–49 eat breakfast regularly?

57. According to the New York City Department of Education, there were about 284,000 high schools students at the end of 2006. Approximately how many of these students would you expect to eat breakfast regularly? Round to the nearest ten thousand.

CONCEPT EXTENSIONS

58. In your own words, explain the differences between equations and expressions.

59. In your own words, explain why it is necessary to check solutions to equations containing rational expressions.

60. The average cost of producing x game disks for a computer is given by the function $f(x) = 3.3 + \dfrac{5400}{x}$. Find the number of game disks that must be produced for the average cost to be $5.10.

61. The average cost of producing x electric pencil sharpeners is given by the function $f(x) = 20 + \dfrac{4000}{x}$. Find the number of electric pencil sharpeners that must be produced for the average cost to be $25.

Solve each equation. Begin by writing each equation with positive exponents only.

62. $x^{-2} - 19x^{-1} + 48 = 0$

63. $x^{-2} - 5x^{-1} - 36 = 0$

64. $p^{-2} + 4p^{-1} - 5 = 0$

65. $6p^{-2} - 5p^{-1} + 1 = 0$

Solve each equation. Round solutions to two decimal places.

66. $\dfrac{1.4}{x-2.6} = \dfrac{-3.5}{x+7.1}$

67. $\dfrac{-8.5}{x+1.9} = \dfrac{5.7}{x-3.6}$

68. $\dfrac{10.6}{y} - 14.7 = \dfrac{9.92}{3.2} + 7.6$

69. $\dfrac{12.2}{x} + 17.3 = \dfrac{9.6}{x} - 14.7$

Solve each equation by substitution.

For example, to solve Exercise 70, first let $u = x - 1$. After substituting, we have $u^2 + 3u + 2 = 0$. Solve for u and then substitute back to solve for x.

70. $(x - 1)^2 + 3(x - 1) + 2 = 0$

71. $(4 - x)^2 - 5(4 - x) + 6 = 0$

72. $\left(\dfrac{3}{x - 1}\right)^2 + 2\left(\dfrac{3}{x - 1}\right) + 1 = 0$

73. $\left(\dfrac{5}{2 + x}\right)^2 + \left(\dfrac{5}{2 + x}\right) - 20 = 0$

Use a graphing calculator to verify the solution of each given exercise.

74. Exercise 23 **75.** Exercise 24

76. Exercise 35 **77.** Exercise 36

INTEGRATED REVIEW — EXPRESSIONS AND EQUATIONS CONTAINING RATIONAL EXPRESSIONS

Sections 7.1–7.5

It is very important that you understand the difference between an expression and an equation containing rational expressions. An equation contains an equal sign; an expression does not.

Expression to be Simplified

$$\dfrac{x}{2} + \dfrac{x}{6}$$

Write both rational expressions with the LCD, 6, as the denominator.

$$\dfrac{x}{2} + \dfrac{x}{6} = \dfrac{x \cdot 3}{2 \cdot 3} + \dfrac{x}{6}$$

$$= \dfrac{3x}{6} + \dfrac{x}{6}$$

$$= \dfrac{4x}{6} = \dfrac{2x}{3}$$

Equation to be Solved

$$\dfrac{x}{2} + \dfrac{x}{6} = \dfrac{2}{3}$$

Multiply both sides by the LCD, 6.

$$6\left(\dfrac{1}{2} + \dfrac{x}{6}\right) = 6\left(\dfrac{2}{3}\right)$$

$$3 + x = 4$$

$$x = 1$$

Check to see that the solution set is 1.

> **Helpful Hint**
> Remember: Equations can be cleared of fractions; expressions cannot.

Perform each indicated operation and simplify, or solve the equation for the variable.

1. $\dfrac{x}{2} = \dfrac{1}{8} + \dfrac{x}{4}$

2. $\dfrac{x}{4} = \dfrac{3}{2} + \dfrac{x}{10}$

3. $\dfrac{1}{8} + \dfrac{x}{4}$

4. $\dfrac{3}{2} + \dfrac{x}{10}$

5. $\dfrac{4}{x + 2} - \dfrac{2}{x - 1}$

6. $\dfrac{5}{x - 2} - \dfrac{10}{x + 4}$

7. $\dfrac{4}{x + 2} = \dfrac{2}{x - 1}$

8. $\dfrac{5}{x - 2} = \dfrac{10}{x + 4}$

9. $\dfrac{2}{x^2 - 4} = \dfrac{1}{x + 2} - \dfrac{3}{x - 2}$

10. $\dfrac{3}{x^2 - 25} = \dfrac{1}{x + 5} + \dfrac{2}{x - 5}$

11. $\dfrac{5}{x^2 - 3x} + \dfrac{4}{2x - 6}$

12. $\dfrac{5}{x^2 - 3x} \div \dfrac{4}{2x - 6}$

13. $\dfrac{x - 1}{x + 1} + \dfrac{x + 7}{x - 1} = \dfrac{4}{x^2 - 1}$

14. $\left(1 - \dfrac{y}{x}\right) \div \left(1 - \dfrac{x}{y}\right)$

15. $\dfrac{a^2 - 9}{a - 6} \cdot \dfrac{a^2 - 5a - 6}{a^2 - a - 6}$

16. $\dfrac{2}{a-6} + \dfrac{3a}{a^2-5a-6} - \dfrac{a}{5a+5}$

17. $\dfrac{2x+3}{3x-2} = \dfrac{4x+1}{6x+1}$

18. $\dfrac{5x-3}{2x} = \dfrac{10x+3}{4x+1}$

19. $\dfrac{a}{9a^2-1} + \dfrac{2}{6a-2}$

20. $\dfrac{3}{4a-8} - \dfrac{a+2}{a^2-2a}$

21. $-\dfrac{3}{x^2} - \dfrac{1}{x} + 2 = 0$

22. $\dfrac{x}{2x+6} + \dfrac{5}{x^2-9}$

23. $\dfrac{x-8}{x^2-x-2} + \dfrac{2}{x-2}$

24. $\dfrac{x-8}{x^2-x-2} + \dfrac{2}{x-2} = \dfrac{3}{x+1}$

25. $\dfrac{3}{a} - 5 = \dfrac{7}{a} - 1$

26. $\dfrac{7}{3z-9} + \dfrac{5}{z}$

Use $\dfrac{x}{5} - \dfrac{x}{4} = \dfrac{1}{10}$ and $\dfrac{x}{5} - \dfrac{x}{4} + \dfrac{1}{10}$ for Exercises 27 and 28.

27. a. Which one above is an expression?
   b. Describe the first step to simplify this expression.
   c. Simplify the expression.

28. a. Which one above is an equation?
   b. Describe the first step to solve this equation.
   c. Solve the equation.

For each exercise, choose the correct statement.* *Each figure represents a real number and no denominators are 0.*

29. a. $\dfrac{\triangle + \square}{\triangle} = \square$ **b.** $\dfrac{\triangle + \square}{\triangle} = 1 + \dfrac{\square}{\triangle}$ **c.** $\dfrac{\triangle + \square}{\triangle} = \dfrac{\square}{\triangle}$ **d.** $\dfrac{\triangle + \square}{\triangle} = 1 + \square$ **e.** $\dfrac{\triangle + \square}{\triangle - \square} = -1$

30. a. $\dfrac{\triangle}{\square} + \dfrac{\square}{\triangle} = \dfrac{\triangle + \square}{\square + \triangle} = 1$ **b.** $\dfrac{\triangle}{\square} + \dfrac{\square}{\triangle} = \dfrac{\triangle + \square}{\triangle\square}$ **c.** $\dfrac{\triangle}{\square} + \dfrac{\square}{\triangle} = \triangle\triangle + \square\square$

   d. $\dfrac{\triangle}{\square} + \dfrac{\square}{\triangle} = \dfrac{\triangle\triangle + \square\square}{\square\triangle}$ **e.** $\dfrac{\triangle}{\square} + \dfrac{\square}{\triangle} = \dfrac{\triangle\square}{\square\triangle} = 1$

31. a. $\dfrac{\triangle}{\square} \cdot \dfrac{\bigcirc}{\square} = \dfrac{\triangle\bigcirc}{\square}$ **b.** $\dfrac{\triangle}{\square} \cdot \dfrac{\bigcirc}{\square} = \triangle\bigcirc$ **c.** $\dfrac{\triangle}{\square} \cdot \dfrac{\bigcirc}{\square} = \dfrac{\triangle + \bigcirc}{\square + \square}$ **d.** $\dfrac{\triangle}{\square} \cdot \dfrac{\bigcirc}{\square} = \dfrac{\triangle\bigcirc}{\square\square}$

32. a. $\dfrac{\triangle}{\square} \div \dfrac{\bigcirc}{\triangle} = \dfrac{\triangle\triangle}{\square\bigcirc}$ **b.** $\dfrac{\triangle}{\square} \div \dfrac{\bigcirc}{\triangle} = \dfrac{\bigcirc\square}{\triangle\triangle}$ **c.** $\dfrac{\triangle}{\square} \div \dfrac{\bigcirc}{\triangle} = \dfrac{\bigcirc}{\square}$ **d.** $\dfrac{\triangle}{\square} \div \dfrac{\bigcirc}{\triangle} = \dfrac{\triangle + \triangle}{\square + \bigcirc}$

33. a. $\dfrac{\frac{\triangle + \square}{\bigcirc}}{\frac{\triangle}{\bigcirc}} = \square$ **b.** $\dfrac{\frac{\triangle + \square}{\bigcirc}}{\frac{\triangle}{\bigcirc}} = \dfrac{\triangle\triangle + \triangle\square}{\bigcirc\bigcirc}$ **c.** $\dfrac{\frac{\triangle + \square}{\bigcirc}}{\frac{\triangle}{\bigcirc}} = 1 + \square$ **d.** $\dfrac{\frac{\triangle + \square}{\bigcirc}}{\frac{\triangle}{\bigcirc}} = \dfrac{\triangle + \square}{\triangle}$

**My thanks to Kelly Champagne for permission to use her Exercises for 29 through 33.*

7.6 RATIONAL EQUATIONS AND PROBLEM SOLVING

OBJECTIVES

1. Solve an equation containing rational expressions for a specified variable.
2. Solve problems by writing equations containing rational expressions.

OBJECTIVE 1 ▶ Solving equations with rational expressions for a specified variable.
In Section 2.3 we solved equations for a specified variable. In this section, we continue practicing this skill by solving equations containing rational expressions for a specified variable. The steps given in Section 2.3 for solving equations for a specified variable are repeated here.

Solving Equations for a Specified Variable

STEP 1. Clear the equation of fractions or rational expressions by multiplying each side of the equation by the least common denominator (LCD) of all denominators in the equation.

STEP 2. Use the distributive property to remove grouping symbols such as parentheses.

STEP 3. Combine like terms on each side of the equation.

STEP 4. Use the addition property of equality to rewrite the equation as an equivalent equation with terms containing the specified variable on one side and all other terms on the other side.

STEP 5. Use the distributive property and the multiplication property of equality to get the specified variable alone.

EXAMPLE 1 Solve: $\dfrac{1}{x} + \dfrac{1}{y} = \dfrac{1}{z}$ for x.

Solution To clear this equation of fractions, we multiply both sides of the equation by xyz, the LCD of $\dfrac{1}{x}, \dfrac{1}{y},$ and $\dfrac{1}{z}$.

$$\dfrac{1}{x} + \dfrac{1}{y} = \dfrac{1}{z}$$

$$xyz\left(\dfrac{1}{x} + \dfrac{1}{y}\right) = xyz\left(\dfrac{1}{z}\right) \quad \text{Multiply both sides by } xyz.$$

$$xyz\left(\dfrac{1}{x}\right) + xyz\left(\dfrac{1}{y}\right) = xyz\left(\dfrac{1}{z}\right) \quad \text{Use the distributive property.}$$

$$yz + xz = xy \quad \text{Simplify.}$$

Notice the two terms that contain the specified variable x.

Next, we subtract xz from both sides so that all terms containing the specified variable x are on one side of the equation and all other terms are on the other side.

$$yz = xy - xz$$

Now we use the distributive property to factor x from $xy - xz$ and then the multiplication property of equality to solve for x.

$$yz = x(y - z)$$

$$\dfrac{yz}{y - z} = x \quad \text{or} \quad x = \dfrac{yz}{y - z} \quad \text{Divide both sides by } y - z.$$

PRACTICE 1 Solve: $\dfrac{1}{a} - \dfrac{1}{b} = \dfrac{1}{c}$ for a.

Section 7.6 Rational Equations and Problem Solving

OBJECTIVE 2 ▶ Solving problems modeled by equations with rational expressions.
Problem solving sometimes involves modeling a described situation with an equation containing rational expressions. In Examples 2 through 5, we practice solving such problems and use the problem-solving steps first introduced in Section 2.2.

EXAMPLE 2   Finding an Unknown Number

If a certain number is subtracted from the numerator and added to the denominator of $\frac{9}{19}$, the new fraction is equivalent to $\frac{1}{3}$. Find the number.

Solution

1. UNDERSTAND the problem. Read and reread the problem and try guessing the solution. For example, if the unknown number is 3, we have

$$\frac{9-3}{19+3} = \frac{1}{3}$$

To see if this is a true statement, we simplify the fraction on the left side.

$$\frac{6}{22} = \frac{1}{3} \quad \text{or} \quad \frac{3}{11} = \frac{1}{3} \quad \text{False}$$

Since this is not a true statement, 3 is not the correct number. Remember that the purpose of this step is not to guess the correct solution but to gain an understanding of the problem posed.

We will let n = the number to be subtracted from the numerator and added to the denominator.

2. TRANSLATE the problem.

In words: when the number is subtracted from the numerator and added to the denominator of the fraction $\frac{9}{19}$ | this is equivalent to | $\frac{1}{3}$

Translate: $\frac{9-n}{19+n} = \frac{1}{3}$

3. SOLVE the equation for n.

$$\frac{9-n}{19+n} = \frac{1}{3}$$

To solve for n, we begin by multiplying both sides by the LCD of $3(19+n)$.

$$3(19+n) \cdot \frac{9-n}{19+n} = 3(19+n) \cdot \frac{1}{3} \quad \text{Multiply both sides by the LCD.}$$
$$3(9-n) = 19+n \quad \text{Simplify.}$$
$$27 - 3n = 19 + n$$
$$8 = 4n$$
$$2 = n \quad \text{Solve.}$$

4. INTERPRET the results.

Check: If we subtract 2 from the numerator and add 2 to the denominator of $\frac{9}{19}$, we have $\frac{9-2}{19+2} = \frac{7}{21} = \frac{1}{3}$, and the problem checks.

State: The unknown number is 2. □

PRACTICE 2   Find a number that when added to the numerator and subtracted from the denominator of $\frac{3}{11}$ results in a fraction equivalent to $\frac{5}{2}$.

A **ratio** is the quotient of two number or two quantities. Since rational expressions are quotients of quantities, rational expressions are ratios, also. A **proportion** is a mathematical statement that two ratios are equal.

EXAMPLE 3 Calculating Homes Heated by Electricity

In the United States, 8 out of every 25 homes are heated by electricity. At this rate, how many homes in a community of 36,000 homes would you predict are heated by electricity? (*Source: 2005 American Housing Survey for the United States*)

Solution

1. UNDERSTAND. Read and reread the problem. Try to estimate a reasonable solution. For example, since 8 is less than $\frac{1}{3}$ of 25, we might reason that the solution would be less than $\frac{1}{3}$ of 36,000 or 12,000.

   Let's let $x =$ number of homes in the community heated by electricity.

2. TRANSLATE.

   homes heated by electricity $\rightarrow$ $\quad \dfrac{8}{25} = \dfrac{x}{36{,}000} \quad$ $\leftarrow$ homes heated by electricity
   total homes $\rightarrow$ $\qquad\qquad\qquad\qquad\qquad$ $\leftarrow$ total homes

3. SOLVE. To solve this proportion we can multiply both sides by the LCD, 36,000, or we can set cross products equal. We will set cross products equal.

$$\dfrac{8}{25} = \dfrac{x}{36{,}000}$$

$$25x = 8 \cdot 36{,}000$$
$$x = \dfrac{288{,}000}{25}$$
$$x = 11{,}520$$

4. INTERPRET.

Check: To check, replace x with 11,520 in the proportion and see that a true statement results. Notice that our answer is reasonable since it is less than 12,000 as we stated above.

State: We predict that 11,520 homes are heated by electricity. □

PRACTICE 3 In the United States, 1 out of 12 homes is heated by fuel oil. At this rate, how many homes in a community of 36,000 homes are heated by fuel oil? (*Source: 2005 American Housing Survey for the United States*)

The following work example leads to an equation containing rational expressions.

EXAMPLE 4 Calculating Work Hours

Melissa Scarlatti can clean the house in 4 hours, whereas her husband, Zack, can do the same job in 5 hours. They have agreed to clean together so that they can finish in time to watch a movie on TV that starts in 2 hours. How long will it take them to clean the house together? Can they finish before the movie starts?

Solution

1. UNDERSTAND. Read and reread the problem. The key idea here is the relationship between the *time* (in hours) it takes to complete the job and the *part of the job* completed in 1 unit of time (1 hour). For example, if the *time* it takes Melissa to complete the job is 4 hours, the part of the job she can complete in 1 hour is $\dfrac{1}{4}$. Similarly, Zack can complete $\dfrac{1}{5}$ of the job in 1 hour.

Section 7.6 Rational Equations and Problem Solving 421

We will let $t =$ *the time* in hours it takes Melissa and Zack to clean the house together. Then $\frac{1}{t}$ represents the *part of the job* they complete in 1 hour. We summarize the given information in a chart.

	Hours to Complete the Job	Part of Job Completed in 1 Hour
MELISSA ALONE	4	$\frac{1}{4}$
ZACK ALONE	5	$\frac{1}{5}$
TOGETHER	t	$\frac{1}{t}$

2. TRANSLATE.

In words:	part of job Melissa can complete in 1 hour	added to	part of job Zack can complete in 1 hour	is equal to	part of job they can complete together in 1 hour
Translate:	$\frac{1}{4}$	$+$	$\frac{1}{5}$	$=$	$\frac{1}{t}$

3. SOLVE.

$$\frac{1}{4} + \frac{1}{5} = \frac{1}{t}$$

$$20t\left(\frac{1}{4} + \frac{1}{5}\right) = 20t\left(\frac{1}{t}\right) \quad \text{Multiply both sides by the LCD, } 20t.$$

$$5t + 4t = 20$$
$$9t = 20$$
$$t = \frac{20}{9} \quad \text{or} \quad 2\frac{2}{9} \quad \text{Solve.}$$

4. INTERPRET.

Check: The proposed solution is $2\frac{2}{9}$. That is, Melissa and Zack would take $2\frac{2}{9}$ hours to clean the house together. This proposed solution is reasonable since $2\frac{2}{9}$ hours is more than half of Melissa's time and less than half of Zack's time. Check this solution in the originally stated problem.

State: Melissa and Zack can clean the house together in $2\frac{2}{9}$ hours. They cannot complete the job before the movie starts. □

PRACTICE
4 Elissa Juarez can clean the animal cages at the animal shelter where she volunteers in 3 hours. Bill Stiles can do the same job in 2 hours. How long would it take them to clean the cages if they work together?

EXAMPLE 5   Finding the Speed of a Current

Steve Deitmer takes $1\frac{1}{2}$ times as long to go 72 miles upstream in his boat as he does to return. If the boat cruises at 30 mph in still water, what is the speed of the current?

Solution

1. UNDERSTAND. Read and reread the problem. Guess a solution. Suppose that the current is 4 mph. The speed of the boat upstream is slowed down by the current: $30 - 4$, or 26 mph, and the speed of the boat downstream is speeded up by the current: 30 + 4, or 34 mph. Next let's find out how long it takes to travel 72 miles upstream and 72 miles downstream. To do so, we use the formula $d = rt$, or $\dfrac{d}{r} = t$.

Upstream

$$\dfrac{d}{r} = t$$
$$\dfrac{72}{26} = t$$
$$2\dfrac{10}{13} = t$$

Downstream

$$\dfrac{d}{r} = t$$
$$\dfrac{72}{34} = t$$
$$2\dfrac{2}{17} = t$$

Since the time upstream $\left(2\dfrac{10}{13} \text{ hours}\right)$ is not $1\dfrac{1}{2}$ times the time downstream $\left(2\dfrac{2}{17} \text{ hours}\right)$, our guess is not correct. We do, however, have a better understanding of the problem.

We will let

x = the speed of the current

$30 + x$ = the speed of the boat downstream

$30 - x$ = the speed of the boat upstream

This information is summarized in the following chart, where we use the formula $\dfrac{d}{r} = t$.

	Distance	Rate	Time $\left(\dfrac{d}{r}\right)$
UPSTREAM	72	$30 - x$	$\dfrac{72}{30 - x}$
DOWNSTREAM	72	$30 + x$	$\dfrac{72}{30 + x}$

2. TRANSLATE. Since the time spent traveling upstream is $1\dfrac{1}{2}$ times the time spent traveling downstream, we have

In words: time upstream is $1\dfrac{1}{2}$ times times downstream

Translate: $\dfrac{72}{30 - x} = \dfrac{3}{2} \cdot \dfrac{72}{30 + x}$

3. SOLVE. $\dfrac{72}{30 - x} = \dfrac{3}{2} \cdot \dfrac{72}{30 + x}$

First we multiply both sides by the LCD, $2(30 + x)(30 - x)$.

$$2(30 + x)(30 - x) \cdot \dfrac{72}{30 - x} = 2(30 + x)(30 - x)\left(\dfrac{3}{2} \cdot \dfrac{72}{30 + x}\right)$$

$$72 \cdot 2(30 + x) = 3 \cdot 72 \cdot (30 - x) \quad \text{Simplify.}$$
$$2(30 + x) = 3(30 - x) \quad \text{Divide both sides by 72.}$$
$$60 + 2x = 90 - 3x \quad \text{Use the distributive property.}$$
$$5x = 30$$
$$x = 6 \quad \text{Solve.}$$

4. INTERPRET.

Check: Check the proposed solution of 6 mph in the originally stated problem.

State: The current's speed is 6 mph.

PRACTICE 5 An airplane flying from Los Angeles to Boston at a speed of 450 mph had a tailwind assisting its flight. At the same time, there was another flight doing the same speed, going from Boston to Los Angeles. This second flight encountered a headwind. It took the pilot heading west $1\frac{1}{4}$ times as long to travel from Boston to Los Angeles as it took the pilot flying east from Los Angeles to Boston. What was the speed of the wind?

7.6 EXERCISE SET

Solve each equation for the specified variable. See Example 1.

1. $F = \frac{9}{5}C + 32$ for C (Meteorology)
2. $V = \frac{1}{3}\pi r^2 h$ for h (Volume)
3. $Q = \frac{A - I}{L}$ for I (Finance)
4. $P = 1 - \frac{C}{S}$ for S (Finance)
5. $\frac{1}{R} = \frac{1}{R_1} + \frac{1}{R_2}$ for R (Electronics)
6. $\frac{1}{R} = \frac{1}{R_1} + \frac{1}{R_2}$ for R_1 (Electronics)
7. $S = \frac{n(a + L)}{2}$ for n (Sequences)
8. $S = \frac{n(a + L)}{2}$ for a (Sequences)
9. $A = \frac{h(a + b)}{2}$ for b (Geometry)
10. $A = \frac{h(a + b)}{2}$ for h (Geometry)
11. $\frac{P_1 V_1}{T_1} = \frac{P_2 V_2}{T_2}$ for T_2 (Chemistry)
12. $H = \frac{kA(T_1 - T_2)}{L}$ for T_2 (Physics)
13. $f = \frac{f_1 f_2}{f_1 + f_2}$ for f_2 (Optics)
14. $I = \frac{E}{R + r}$ for r (Electronics)
15. $\lambda = \frac{2L}{n}$ for L (Physics)
16. $S = \frac{a_1 - a_n r}{1 - r}$ for a_1 (Sequences)
17. $\frac{\theta}{\omega} = \frac{2L}{c}$ for c
18. $F = \frac{-GMm}{r^2}$ for M (Physics)

Solve. See Example 2.

19. The sum of a number and 5 times its reciprocal is 6. Find the number(s).
20. The quotient of a number and 9 times its reciprocal is 1. Find the number(s).

21. If a number is added to the numerator of $\frac{12}{41}$ and twice the number is added to the denominator of $\frac{12}{41}$, the resulting fraction is equivalent to $\frac{1}{3}$. Find the number.

22. If a number is subtracted from the numerator of $\frac{13}{8}$ and added to the denominator of $\frac{13}{8}$, the resulting fraction is equivalent to $\frac{2}{5}$. Find the number.

Solve. See Example 3.

23. An Arabian camel can drink 15 gallons of water in 10 minutes. At this rate, how much water can the camel drink in 3 minutes? (*Source:* Grolier, Inc.)

24. An Arabian camel can travel 20 miles in 8 hours, carrying a 300-pound load on its back. At this rate, how far can the camel travel in 10 hours? (*Source:* Grolier, Inc.)

25. In 2005, 5.5 out of every 50 Coast Guard personnel were women. If there are 40,639 total Coast Guard personnel on active duty, estimate the number of women. Round to the nearest whole. (*Source: The World Almanac,* 2007)

26. In 2005, 42.8 out of every 50 Navy personnel were men. If there are 353,496 total Navy personnel on active duty, estimate the number of men. Round to the nearest whole. (*Source: The World Almanac,* 2007)

Solve. See Example 4.

27. An experienced roofer can roof a house in 26 hours. A beginning roofer needs 39 hours to complete the same job. Find how long it takes for the two to do the job together.

28. Alan Cantrell can word process a research paper in 6 hours. With Steve Isaac's help, the paper can be processed in 4 hours. Find how long it takes Steve to word process the paper alone.

29. Three postal workers can sort a stack of mail in 20 minutes, 30 minutes, and 60 minutes, respectively. Find how long it takes them to sort the mail if all three work together.

30. A new printing press can print newspapers twice as fast as the old one can. The old one can print the afternoon edition in 4 hours. Find how long it takes to print the afternoon edition if both printers are operating.

Solve. See Example 5.

31. Mattie Evans drove 150 miles in the same amount of time that it took a turbopropeller plane to travel 600 miles. The speed of the plane was 150 mph faster than the speed of the car. Find the speed of the plane.

32. An F-100 plane and a Toyota truck leave the same town at sunrise and head for a town 450 miles away. The speed of the plane is three times the speed of the truck, and the plane arrives 6 hours ahead of the truck. Find the speed of the truck.

33. The speed of Lazy River's current is 5 mph. If a boat travels 20 miles downstream in the same time that it takes to travel 10 miles upstream, find the speed of the boat in still water.

34. The speed of a boat in still water is 24 mph. If the boat travels 54 miles upstream in the same time that it takes to travel 90 miles downstream, find the speed of the current.

MIXED PRACTICE

Solve.

35. The sum of the reciprocals of two consecutive integers is $-\frac{15}{56}$. Find the two integers.

36. The sum of the reciprocals of two consecutive odd integers is $\frac{20}{99}$. Find the two integers.

37. One hose can fill a goldfish pond in 45 minutes, and two hoses can fill the same pond in 20 minutes. Find how long it takes the second hose alone to fill the pond.

38. If Sarah Clark can do a job in 5 hours and Dick Belli and Sarah working together can do the same job in 2 hours, find how long it takes Dick to do the job alone.

39. Two trains going in opposite directions leave at the same time. One train travels 15 mph faster than the other. In 6 hours the trains are 630 miles apart. Find the speed of each.

40. The speed of a bicyclist is 10 mph faster than the speed of a walker. If the bicyclist travels 26 miles in the same amount of time that the walker travels 6 miles, find the speed of the bicyclist.

41. A giant tortoise can travel 0.17 miles in 1 hour. At this rate, how long would it take the tortoise to travel 1 mile? Round to the nearest tenth of an hour. (*Source: The World Almanac*)

42. A black mamba snake can travel 88 feet in 3 seconds. At this rate, how long does it take to travel 300 feet (the length of a football field)? Round to the nearest tenth of a second. (*Source: The World Almanac*)

43. A local dairy has three machines to fill half-gallon milk cartons. The machines can fill the daily quota in 5 hours, 6 hours, and 7.5 hours, respectively. Find how long it takes to fill the daily quota if all three machines are running.

44. The inlet pipe of an oil tank can fill the tank in 1 hour, 30 minutes. The outlet pipe can empty the tank in 1 hour. Find how long it takes to empty a full tank if both pipes are open.

45. A plane flies 465 miles with the wind and 345 miles against the wind in the same length of time. If the speed of the wind is 20 mph, find the speed of the plane in still air.

46. Two rockets are launched. The first travels at 9000 mph. Fifteen minutes later the second is launched at 10,000 mph. Find the distance at which both rockets are an equal distance from Earth.

47. Two joggers, one averaging 8 mph and one averaging 6 mph, start from a designated initial point. The slower jogger arrives at the end of the run a half-hour after the other jogger. Find the distance of the run.

48. A semi truck travels 300 miles through the flatland in the same amount of time that it travels 180 miles through the Great Smoky Mountains. The rate of the truck is 20 miles per hour slower in the mountains than in the flatland. Find both the flatland rate and mountain rate.

49. The denominator of a fraction is 1 more than the numerator. If both the numerator and the denominator are decreased by 3, the resulting fraction is equivalent to $\frac{4}{5}$. Find the fraction.

50. The numerator of a fraction is 4 less than the denominator. If both the numerator and the denominator are increased by 2, the resulting fraction is equivalent to $\frac{2}{3}$. Find the fraction.

51. In 2 minutes, a conveyor belt can move 300 pounds of recyclable aluminum from the delivery truck to a storage area. A smaller belt can move the same quantity of cans the same distance in 6 minutes. If both belts are used, find how long it takes to move the cans to the storage area.

52. Gary Marcus and Tony Alva work at Lombardo's Pipe and Concrete. Mr. Lombardo is preparing an estimate for a customer. He knows that Gary can lay a slab of concrete in 6 hours. Tony can lay the same size slab in 4 hours. If both work on the job and the cost of labor is $45.00 per hour, determine what the labor estimate should be.

53. Smith Engineering is in the process of reviewing the salaries of their surveyors. During this review, the company found that an experienced surveyor can survey a roadbed in 4 hours. An apprentice surveyor needs 5 hours to survey the same stretch of road. If the two work together, find how long it takes them to complete the job.

54. Mr. Dodson can paint his house by himself in four days. His son will need an additional day to complete the job if he works by himself. If they work together, find how long it takes to paint the house.

55. Cyclist Lance Armstrong of the United States won the Tour de France a record seven times. This inspired an amateur cyclist to train for a local road race. He rode the first 20-mile portion of his workout at a constant rate. For the 16-mile cool-down portion of his workout, he reduced his speed by 2 miles per hour. Each portion of the workout took equal time. Find the cyclist's rate during the first portion and his rate during the cool-down portion.

56. The world record for the largest white bass caught is held by Ronald Sprouse of Virginia. The bass weighed 6 pounds 13 ounces. If Ronald rows to his favorite fishing spot 9 miles downstream in the same amount of time that he rows 3 miles upstream and if the current is 6 mph, find how long it takes him to cover the 12 miles.

57. An experienced bricklayer can construct a small wall in 3 hours. An apprentice can complete the job in 6 hours. Find how long it takes if they work together.

58. Scanner A can scan a document in 3 hours. Scanner B takes 5 hours to do the same job. If both scanners are used, how long will it take for the document to be scanned?

59. A marketing manager travels 1080 miles in a corporate jet and then an additional 240 miles by car. If the car ride takes 1 hour longer, and if the rate of the jet is 6 times the rate of the car, find the time the manager travels by jet and find the time she travels by car.

60. In a recent year, 13 out of 20 top grossing movies were rated PG-13. At this rate, how many movies in a year with 599 new releases would you predict to be rated PG-13? Round to the nearest whole movie. (*Source:* Motion Picture Association)

61. In a recent year, 5 out of 7 movies cost between $50 and $99 million to make. At this rate, how many movies in a year with 599 new releases would you predict to cost between $50 and $99 million to make? Round to the nearest whole movie. (*Source:* Motion Picture Association)

REVIEW AND PREVIEW

Solve each equation for x. See Section 2.1.

62. $\dfrac{x}{5} = \dfrac{x+2}{3}$

63. $\dfrac{x}{4} = \dfrac{x+3}{6}$

64. $\dfrac{x-3}{2} = \dfrac{x-5}{6}$

65. $\dfrac{x-6}{4} = \dfrac{x-2}{5}$

CONCEPT EXTENSIONS

Calculating body-mass index (BMI) is a way to gauge whether a person should lose weight. Doctors recommend that body-mass index values fall between 19 and 25. The formula for body-mass index B is $B = \dfrac{705w}{h^2}$, where w is weight in pounds and h is height in inches. Use this formula to answer Exercises 66 and 67.

66. A patient is 5 ft 8 in. tall. What should his or her weight be to have a body-mass index of 25? Round to the nearest whole pound.

67. A doctor recorded a body-mass index of 47 on a patient's chart. Later, a nurse notices that the doctor recorded the patient's weight as 240 pounds but neglected to record the patient's height. Explain how the nurse can use the information from the chart to find the patient's height. Then find the height.

In physics, when the source of a sound is traveling toward an observer, the relationship between the actual pitch a of the sound and the pitch h that the observer hears due to the Doppler effect is described by the formula $h = \dfrac{a}{1 - \dfrac{s}{770}}$, where s is the speed of the sound source in miles per hour. Use this formula to answer Exercise 68.

68. An emergency vehicle has a single-tone siren with the pitch of the musical note E. As it approaches an observer standing by the road, the vehicle is traveling 50 mph. Is the pitch that the observer hears due to the Doppler effect lower or higher than the actual pitch? To which musical note is the pitch that the observer hears closest?

Pitch of an Octave of Musical Notes in Hertz (Hz)

Note	Pitch
Middle C	261.63
D	293.66
E	329.63
F	349.23
G	392.00
A	440.00
B	493.88

Note: Greater numbers indicate higher pitches (acoustically).
(*Source:* American Standards Association)

In electronics, the relationship among the resistances R_1 and R_2 of two resistors wired in a parallel circuit and their combined resistance R is described by the formula $\dfrac{1}{R} = \dfrac{1}{R_1} + \dfrac{1}{R_2}$. Use this formula to solve Exercises 69 through 71.

69. If the combined resistance is 2 ohms and one of the two resistances is 3 ohms, find the other resistance.

70. Find the combined resistance of two resistors of 12 ohms each when they are wired in a parallel circuit.

71. The relationship among resistance of two resistors wired in a parallel circuit and their combined resistance may be extended to three resistors of resistances R_1, R_2, and R_3. Write an equation you believe may describe the relationship, and use it to find the combined resistance if R_1 is 5, R_2 is 6, and R_3 is 2.

7.7 VARIATION AND PROBLEM SOLVING

OBJECTIVES

1. Solve problems involving direct variation.
2. Solve problems involving inverse variation.
3. Solve problems involving joint variation.
4. Solve problems involving combined variation.

OBJECTIVE 1 ▶ **Solving problems involving direct variation.** A very familiar example of direct variation is the relationship of the circumference C of a circle to its radius r. The formula $C = 2\pi r$ expresses that the circumference is always 2π times the radius. In other words, C is always a constant multiple (2π) of r. Because it is, we say that C **varies directly as** r, that C **varies directly with** r, or that C **is directly proportional to** r.

Direct Variation

y **varies directly as** x, or y **is directly proportional to** x, if there is a nonzero constant k such that

$$y = kx$$

The number k is called the **constant of variation** or the **constant of proportionality.**

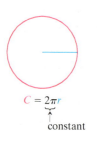

$C = 2\pi r$
constant

In the above definition, the relationship described between x and y is a linear one. In other words, the graph of $y = kx$ is a line. The slope of the line is k, and the line passes through the origin.

For example, the graph of the direct variation equation $C = 2\pi r$ is shown. The horizontal axis represents the radius r, and the vertical axis is the circumference C. From the graph we can read that when the radius is 6 units, the circumference is approximately 38 units. Also, when the circumference is 45 units, the radius is between 7 and 8 units. Notice that as the radius increases, the circumference increases.

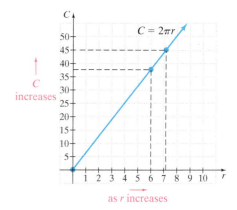

EXAMPLE 1 Suppose that y varies directly as x. If y is 5 when x is 30, find the constant of variation and the direct variation equation.

Solution Since y varies directly as x, we write $y = kx$. If $y = 5$ when $x = 30$, we have that

$$y = kx$$
$$5 = k(30) \quad \text{Replace } y \text{ with 5 and } x \text{ with 30.}$$
$$\frac{1}{6} = k \quad \text{Solve for } k.$$

The constant of variation is $\frac{1}{6}$.

After finding the constant of variation k, the direct variation equation can be written as $y = \frac{1}{6}x$. □

PRACTICE 1 Suppose that y varies directly as x. If y is 20 when x is 15, find the constant of variation and the direct variation equation.

EXAMPLE 2 Using Direct Variation and Hooke's Law

Hooke's law states that the distance a spring stretches is directly proportional to the weight attached to the spring. If a 40-pound weight attached to the spring stretches the spring 5 inches, find the distance that a 65-pound weight attached to the spring stretches the spring.

Solution

1. UNDERSTAND. Read and reread the problem. Notice that we are given that the distance a spring stretches is **directly proportional** to the weight attached. We let

    d = the distance stretched

    w = the weight attached

    The constant of variation is represented by k.

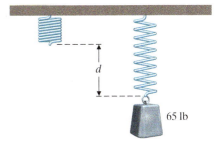

2. TRANSLATE. Because d is directly proportional to w, we write

    $$d = kw$$

3. SOLVE. When a weight of 40 pounds is attached, the spring stretches 5 inches. That is, when $w = 40$, $d = 5$.

    $d = kw$

    $5 = k(40)$ Replace d with 5 and w with 40.

    $\dfrac{1}{8} = k$ Solve for k.

    Now when we replace k with $\dfrac{1}{8}$ in the equation

    $d = kw$, we have

    $$d = \dfrac{1}{8}w$$

    To find the stretch when a weight of 65 pounds is attached, we replace w with 65 to find d.

    $$d = \dfrac{1}{8}(65)$$

    $$= \dfrac{65}{8} = 8\dfrac{1}{8} \quad \text{or} \quad 8.125$$

4. INTERPRET.

Check: Check the proposed solution of 8.125 inches in the original problem.

State: The spring stetches 8.125 inches when a 65-pound weight is attached.

PRACTICE 2 Use Hooke's law as stated in Example 2. If a 36-pound weight attached to a spring stretches the spring 9 inches, find the distance that a 75-pound weight attached to the spring stretches the spring.

OBJECTIVE 2 ▶ Solving problems involving inverse variation. When y is proportional to the **reciprocal** of another variable x, we say that ***y* varies inversely as *x*,** or that ***y* is inversely proportional to *x*.** An example of the inverse variation relationship is the relationship between the pressure that a gas exerts and the volume of its container. As the volume of a container decreases, the pressure of the gas it contains increases.

> **Inverse Variation**
>
> **y varies inversely as x,** or **y is inversely proportional to x,** if there is a nonzero constant k such that
> $$y = \frac{k}{x}$$
>
> The number k is called the **constant of variation** or the **constant of proportionality.**

Notice that $y = \dfrac{k}{x}$ is a rational equation. Its graph for $k > 0$ and $x > 0$ is shown. From the graph, we can see that as x increases, y decreases.

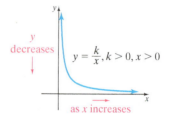

EXAMPLE 3 Suppose that u varies inversely as w. If u is 3 when w is 5, find the constant of variation and the inverse variation equation.

Solution Since u varies inversely as w, we have $u = \dfrac{k}{w}$. We let $u = 3$ and $w = 5$, and we solve for k.

$$u = \frac{k}{w}$$

$$3 = \frac{k}{5} \quad \text{Let } u = 3 \text{ and } w = 5.$$

$$15 = k \quad \text{Multiply both sides by 5.}$$

The constant of variation k is 15. This gives the inverse variation equation

$$u = \frac{15}{w}$$

PRACTICE 3 Suppose that b varies inversely as a. If b is 5 when a is 9, find the constant of variation and the inverse variation equation.

EXAMPLE 4 Using Inverse Variation and Boyle's Law

Boyle's law says that if the temperature stays the same, the pressure P of a gas is inversely proportional to the volume V. If a cylinder in a steam engine has a pressure of 960 kilopascals when the volume is 1.4 cubic meters, find the pressure when the volume increases to 2.5 cubic meters.

Solution

1. UNDERSTAND. Read and reread the problem. Notice that we are given that the pressure of a gas is *inversely proportional* to the volume. We will let P = the pressure and V = the volume. The constant of variation is represented by k.
2. TRANSLATE. Because P is inversely proportional to V, we write

$$P = \frac{k}{V}$$

When $P = 960$ kilopascals, the volume $V = 1.4$ cubic meters. We use this information to find k.

$$960 = \frac{k}{1.4} \quad \text{Let } P = 960 \text{ and } V = 1.4.$$
$$1344 = k \quad \text{Multiply both sides by 1.4.}$$

Thus, the value of k is 1344. Replacing k with 1344 in the variation equation, we have

$$P = \frac{1344}{V}$$

Next we find P when V is 2.5 cubic meters.

3. SOLVE.

$$P = \frac{1344}{2.5} \quad \text{Let } V = 2.5.$$
$$= 537.6$$

4. INTERPRET.

Check: Check the proposed solution in the original problem.

State: When the volume is 2.5 cubic meters, the pressure is 537.6 kilopascals.

PRACTICE 4 Use Boyle's law as stated in Example 4. When $P = 350$ kilopascals and $V = 2.8$ cubic meters, find the pressure when the volume decreases to 1.5 cubic meters.

OBJECTIVE 3 ▶ Solving problems involving joint variation. Sometimes the ratio of a variable to the product of many other variables is constant. For example, the ratio of distance traveled to the product of speed and time traveled is always 1.

$$\frac{d}{rt} = 1 \quad \text{or} \quad d = rt$$

Such a relationship is called **joint variation.**

> **Joint Variation**
>
> If the ratio of a variable y to the product of two or more variables is constant, then y **varies jointly as,** or **is jointly proportional to,** the other variables. If
>
> $$y = kxz$$
>
> then the number k is the **constant of variation** or the **constant of proportionality.**

Concept Check ✓

Which type of variation is represented by the equation $xy = 8$? Explain.

a. Direct variation   b. Inverse variation   c. Joint variation

⚠ EXAMPLE 5   Expressing Surface Area

The lateral surface area of a cylinder varies jointly as its radius and height. Express this surface area S in terms of radius r and height h.

Answer to Concept Check:
b; answers may vary

Solution Because the surface area varies jointly as the radius r and the height h, we equate S to a constant multiple of r and h.

$$S = krh$$

In the equation, $S = krh$, it can be determined that the constant k is 2π, and we then have the formula $S = 2\pi rh$. (The lateral surface area formula does not include the areas of the two circular bases.) □

PRACTICE 5 The area of a regular polygon varies jointly as its apothem and its perimeter. Express the area in terms of the apothem a and the perimeter p.

OBJECTIVE 4 ▶ Solving problems involving combined variation. Some examples of variation involve combinations of direct, inverse, and joint variation. We will call these variations **combined variation.**

EXAMPLE 6 Suppose that y varies directly as the square of x. If y is 24 when x is 2, find the constant of variation and the variation equation.

Solution Since y varies directly as the square of x, we have

$$y = kx^2$$

Now let $y = 24$ and $x = 2$ and solve for k.

$$y = kx^2$$
$$24 = k \cdot 2^2$$
$$24 = 4k$$
$$6 = k$$

The constant of variation is 6, so the variation equation is

$$y = 6x^2$$ □

PRACTICE 6 Suppose that y varies inversely as the cube of x. If y is $\frac{1}{2}$ when x is 2, find the constant of variation and the variation equation.

EXAMPLE 7 Finding Column Weight

The maximum weight that a circular column can support is directly proportional to the fourth power of its diameter and is inversely proportional to the square of its height. A 2-meter-diameter column that is 8 meters in height can support 1 ton. Find the weight that a 1-meter-diameter column that is 4 meters in height can support.

Solution

1. **UNDERSTAND.** Read and reread the problem. Let w = weight, d = diameter, h = height, and k = the constant of variation.

2. **TRANSLATE.** Since w is directly proportional to d^4 and inversely proportional to h^2, we have
$$w = \frac{kd^4}{h^2}$$

3. **SOLVE.** To find k, we are given that a 2-meter-diameter column that is 8 meters in height can support 1 ton. That is, $w = 1$ when $d = 2$ and $h = 8$, or

$$1 = \frac{k \cdot 2^4}{8^2} \qquad \text{Let } w = 1, d = 2, \text{ and } h = 8.$$
$$1 = \frac{k \cdot 16}{64}$$
$$4 = k \qquad \text{Solve for } k.$$

Now replace k with 4 in the equation $w = \frac{kd^4}{h^2}$ and we have
$$w = \frac{4d^4}{h^2}$$

To find weight w for a 1-meter-diameter column that is 4 meters in height, let $d = 1$ and $h = 4$.
$$w = \frac{4 \cdot 1^4}{4^2}$$
$$w = \frac{4}{16} = \frac{1}{4}$$

4. **INTERPRET.**

   Check: Check the proposed solution in the original problem.

   State: The 1-meter-diameter column that is 4 meters in height can hold $\frac{1}{4}$ ton of weight.

PRACTICE 7 Suppose that y varies directly as z and inversely as the cube of x. If y is 15 when $z = 5$ and $x = 3$, find the constant of variation and the variation equation.

VOCABULARY & READINESS CHECK

Decision Making. *State whether each equation represents direct, inverse, or joint variation.*

1. $y = 5x$
2. $y = \dfrac{700}{x}$
3. $y = 5xz$
4. $y = \dfrac{1}{2}abc$
5. $y = \dfrac{9.1}{x}$
6. $y = 2.3x$
7. $y = \dfrac{2}{3}x$
8. $y = 3.1\,st$

7.7 EXERCISE SET

If y varies directly as x, find the constant of variation and the direct variation equation for each situation. See Example 1.

1. $y = 4$ when $x = 20$
2. $y = 5$ when $x = 30$
3. $y = 6$ when $x = 4$
4. $y = 12$ when $x = 8$
5. $y = 7$ when $x = \dfrac{1}{2}$
6. $y = 11$ when $x = \dfrac{1}{3}$
7. $y = 0.2$ when $x = 0.8$
8. $y = 0.4$ when $x = 2.5$

Solve. See Example 2.

9. The weight of a synthetic ball varies directly with the cube of its radius. A ball with a radius of 2 inches weighs 1.20 pounds. Find the weight of a ball of the same material with a 3-inch radius.

10. At sea, the distance to the horizon is directly proportional to the square root of the elevation of the observer. If a person who is 36 feet above the water can see 7.4 miles, find how far a person 64 feet above the water can see. Round to the nearest tenth of a mile.

11. The amount P of pollution varies directly with the population N of people. Kansas City has a population of 442,000 and produces 260,000 tons of pollutants. Find how many tons of pollution we should expect St. Louis to produce, if we know that its population is 348,000. Round to the nearest whole ton. (*Population Source: The World Almanac, 2005*)

12. Charles's law states that if the pressure P stays the same, the volume V of a gas is directly proportional to its temperature T. If a balloon is filled with 20 cubic meters of a gas at a temperature of 300 K, find the new volume if the temperature rises 360 K while the pressure stays the same.

If y varies inversely as x, find the constant of variation and the inverse variation equation for each situation. See Example 3.

13. $y = 6$ when $x = 5$
14. $y = 20$ when $x = 9$
15. $y = 100$ when $x = 7$
16. $y = 63$ when $x = 3$
17. $y = \frac{1}{8}$ when $x = 16$
18. $y = \frac{1}{10}$ when $x = 40$
19. $y = 0.2$ when $x = 0.7$
20. $y = 0.6$ when $x = 0.3$

Solve. See Example 4.

21. Pairs of markings a set distance apart are made on highways so that police can detect drivers exceeding the speed limit. Over a fixed distance, the speed R varies inversely with the time T. In one particular pair of markings, R is 45 mph when T is 6 seconds. Find the speed of a car that travels the given distance in 5 seconds.

22. The weight of an object on or above the surface of Earth varies inversely as the square of the distance between the object and Earth's center. If a person weighs 160 pounds on Earth's surface, find the individual's weight if he moves 200 miles above Earth. Round to the nearest whole pound. (Assume that Earth's radius is 4000 miles.)

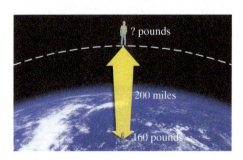

23. If the voltage V in an electric circuit is held constant, the current I is inversely proportional to the resistance R. If the current is 40 amperes when the resistance is 270 ohms, find the current when the resistance is 150 ohms.

24. Because it is more efficient to produce larger numbers of items, the cost of producing Dysan computer disks is inversely proportional to the number produced. If 4000 can be produced at a cost of $1.20 each, find the cost per disk when 6000 are produced.

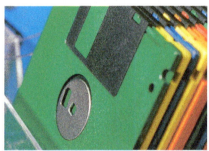

25. The intensity I of light varies inversely as the square of the distance d from the light source. If the distance from the light source is doubled (see the figure), determine what happens to the intensity of light at the new location.

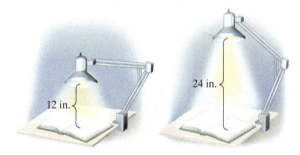

26. The maximum weight that a circular column can hold is inversely proportional to the square of its height. If an 8-foot column can hold 2 tons, find how much weight a 10-foot column can hold.

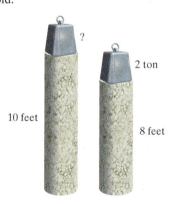

MIXED PRACTICE

Write each statement as an equation. Use k as the constant of variation. See Example 5.

27. x varies jointly as y and z.
28. P varies jointly as R and the square of S.

29. r varies jointly as s and the cube of t.
30. a varies jointly as b and c.

For each statement, find the constant of variation and the variation equation. See Examples 5 and 6.

31. y varies directly as the cube of x; $y = 9$ when $x = 3$
32. y varies directly as the cube of x; $y = 32$ when $x = 4$
33. y varies directly as the square root of x; $y = 0.4$ when $x = 4$
34. y varies directly as the square root of x; $y = 2.1$ when $x = 9$
35. y varies inversely as the square of x; $y = 0.052$ when $x = 5$
36. y varies inversely as the square of x; $y = 0.011$ when $x = 10$
37. y varies jointly as x and the cube of z; $y = 120$ when $x = 5$ and $z = 2$
38. y varies jointly as x and the square of z; $y = 360$ when $x = 4$ and $z = 3$

Solve. See Example 7.

39. The maximum weight that a rectangular beam can support varies jointly as its width and the square of its height and inversely as its length. If a beam $\frac{1}{2}$ foot wide, $\frac{1}{3}$ foot high, and 10 feet long can support 12 tons find how much a similar beam can support if the beam is $\frac{2}{3}$ foot wide, $\frac{1}{2}$ foot high, and 16 feet long.

40. The number of cars manufactured on an assembly line at a General Motors plant varies jointly as the number of workers and the time they work. If 200 workers can produce 60 cars in 2 hours, find how many cars 240 workers should be able to make in 3 hours.

41. The volume of a cone varies jointly as its height and the square of its radius. If the volume of a cone is 32π cubic inches when the radius is 4 inches and the height is 6 inches, find the volume of a cone when the radius is 3 inches and the height is 5 inches.

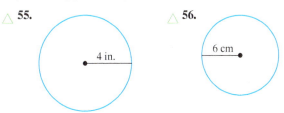

42. When a wind blows perpendicularly against a flat surface, its force is jointly proportional to the surface area and the speed of the wind. A sail whose surface area is 12 square feet experiences a 20-pound force when the wind speed is 10 miles per hour. Find the force on an 8-square-foot sail if the wind speed is 12 miles per hour.

43. The intensity of light (in foot-candles) varies inversely as the square of x, the distance in feet from the light source. The intensity of light 2 feet from the source is 80 foot-candles. How far away is the source if the intensity of light is 5 foot-candles?

44. The horsepower that can be safely transmitted to a shaft varies jointly as the shaft's angular speed of rotation (in revolutions per minute) and the cube of its diameter. A 2-inch shaft making 120 revolutions per minute safely transmits 40 horsepower. Find how much horsepower can be safely transmitted by a 3-inch shaft making 80 revolutions per minute.

MIXED PRACTICE

Write an equation to describe each variation. Use k for the constant of proportionality. See Examples 1 through 7.

45. y varies directly as x
46. p varies directly as q
47. a varies inversely as b
48. y varies inversely as x
49. y varies jointly as x and z
50. y varies jointly as q, r, and t
51. y varies inversely as x^3
52. y varies inversely as a^4
53. y varies directly as x and inversely as p^2
54. y varies directly as a^5 and inversely as b

REVIEW AND PREVIEW

Find the exact circumference and area of each circle. See Appendix A for a list of geometric formulas.

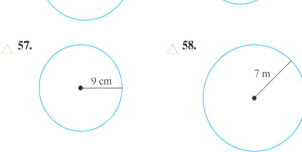

55. (4 in.)
56. (6 cm)
57. (9 cm)
58. (7 m)

Find each square root. See Section 1.3.

59. $\sqrt{81}$
60. $\sqrt{36}$
61. $\sqrt{1}$
62. $\sqrt{4}$
63. $\sqrt{\frac{1}{4}}$
64. $\sqrt{\frac{1}{25}}$
65. $\sqrt{\frac{4}{9}}$
66. $\sqrt{\frac{25}{121}}$

CONCEPT EXTENSIONS

Decision Making. *Solve. See the Concept Check in this section. Choose the type of variation that each equation represents.* **a.** *Direct variation* **b.** *Inverse variation* **c.** *Joint variation*

67. $y = \frac{2}{3}x$
68. $y = \frac{0.6}{x}$
69. $y = 9ab$
70. $xy = \frac{2}{11}$

71. The horsepower to drive a boat varies directly as the cube of the speed of the boat. If the speed of the boat is to double, determine the corresponding increase in horsepower required.

72. The volume of a cylinder varies jointly as the height and the square of the radius. If the height is halved and the radius is doubled, determine what happens to the volume.

73. Suppose that y varies directly as x. If x is doubled, what is the effect on y?

74. Suppose that y varies directly as x^2. If x is doubled, what is the effect on y?

Complete a Table. Complete the following table for the inverse variation $y = \dfrac{k}{x}$ over each given value of k. Plot the points on a rectangular coordinate system.

x	$\dfrac{1}{4}$	$\dfrac{1}{2}$	1	2	4
$y = \dfrac{k}{x}$					

75. $k = 3$ **76.** $k = 1$ **77.** $k = \dfrac{1}{2}$ **78.** $k = 5$

CHAPTER 7 VOCABULARY CHECK

Fill in each blank with one of the words or phrases listed below.

rational expression   equation   complex fraction   opposites   synthetic division
least common denominator   expression   long division   jointly   directly   inversely

1. A rational expression whose numerator, denominator, or both contain one or more rational expressions is called a _____ .
2. To divide a polynomial by a polynomial other than a monomial, we use _____ .
3. In the equation $y = kx$, y varies _____ as x.
4. In the equation $y = \dfrac{k}{x}$, y varies _____ as x.
5. The _____ of a list of rational expressions is a polynomial of least degree whose factors include the denominator factors in the list.
6. When a polynomial is to be divided by a binomial of the form $x - c$, a shortcut process called _____ may be used.
7. In the equation $y = kxz$, y varies, _____ as x and z.
8. The expressions $(x - 5)$ and $(5 - x)$ are called _____ .
9. A _____ is an expression that can be written as the quotient $\dfrac{P}{Q}$ of two polynomials P and Q as long as Q is not 0.
10. Which is an expression and which is an equation? An example of an _____ is $\dfrac{2}{x} + \dfrac{2}{x^2} = 7$ and an example of an _____ is $\dfrac{2}{x} + \dfrac{5}{x^2}$.

CHAPTER 7 REVIEW

(7.1) *Find the domain for each rational function.*

1. $f(x) = \dfrac{3 - 5x}{7}$

2. $g(x) = \dfrac{2x + 4}{11}$

3. $F(x) = \dfrac{-3x^2}{x - 5}$

4. $h(x) = \dfrac{4x}{3x - 12}$

5. $f(x) = \dfrac{x^3 + 2}{x^2 + 8x}$

6. $G(x) = \dfrac{20}{3x^2 - 48}$

Write each rational expression in lowest terms.

7. $\dfrac{x - 12}{12 - x}$

8. $\dfrac{5x - 15}{25x - 75}$

9. $\dfrac{2x}{2x^2 - 2x}$

10. $\dfrac{x + 7}{x^2 - 49}$

11. $\dfrac{2x^2 + 4x - 30}{x^2 + x - 20}$

12. The average cost (per bookcase) of manufacturing x bookcases is given by the rational function.

$$C(x) = \frac{35x + 4200}{x}$$

a. Find the average cost per bookcase of manufacturing 50 bookcases.

b. Find the average cost per bookcase of manufacturing 100 bookcases.

c. As the number of bookcases increases, does the average cost per bookcase increase or decrease? (See parts (a) and (b).)

Perform each indicated operation. Write your answers in lowest terms.

13. $\dfrac{4-x}{5} \cdot \dfrac{15}{2x-8}$

14. $\dfrac{x^2 - 6x + 9}{2x^2 - 18} \cdot \dfrac{4x + 12}{5x - 15}$

15. $\dfrac{a - 4b}{a^2 + ab} \cdot \dfrac{b^2 - a^2}{8b - 2a}$

16. $\dfrac{x^2 - x - 12}{2x^2 - 32} \cdot \dfrac{x^2 + 8x + 16}{3x^2 + 21x + 36}$

17. $\dfrac{4x + 8y}{3} \div \dfrac{5x + 10y}{9}$

18. $\dfrac{x^2 - 25}{3} \div \dfrac{x^2 - 10x + 25}{x^2 - x - 20}$

19. $\dfrac{a - 4b}{a^2 + ab} \div \dfrac{20b - 5a}{b^2 - a^2}$

20. $\dfrac{3x + 3}{x - 1} \div \dfrac{x^2 - 6x - 7}{x^2 - 1}$

21. $\dfrac{2x - x^2}{x^3 - 8} \div \dfrac{x^2}{x^2 + 2x + 4}$

22. $\dfrac{5x - 15}{3 - x} \cdot \dfrac{x + 2}{10x + 20} \cdot \dfrac{x^2 - 9}{x^2 - x - 6}$

(7.2) Find the LCD of the rational expressions in each list.

23. $\dfrac{5}{4x^2y^5}, \dfrac{3}{10x^2y^4}, \dfrac{x}{6y^4}$

24. $\dfrac{5}{2x}, \dfrac{7}{x - 2}$

25. $\dfrac{3}{5x}, \dfrac{2}{x - 5}$

26. $\dfrac{1}{5x^3}, \dfrac{4}{x^2 + 3x - 28}, \dfrac{11}{10x^2 - 30x}$

Perform each indicated operation. Write your answers in lowest terms.

27. $\dfrac{4}{x - 4} + \dfrac{x}{x - 4}$

28. $\dfrac{4}{3x^2} + \dfrac{2}{3x^2}$

29. $\dfrac{1}{x - 2} - \dfrac{1}{4 - 2x}$

30. $\dfrac{1}{10 - x} + \dfrac{x - 1}{x - 10}$

31. $\dfrac{x}{9 - x^2} - \dfrac{2}{5x - 15}$

32. $2x + 1 - \dfrac{1}{x - 3}$

33. $\dfrac{2}{a^2 - 2a + 1} + \dfrac{3}{a^2 - 1}$

34. $\dfrac{x}{9x^2 + 12x + 16} - \dfrac{3x + 4}{27x^3 - 64}$

Perform each indicated operation. Write your answers in lowest terms.

35. $\dfrac{2}{x - 1} - \dfrac{3x}{3x - 3} + \dfrac{1}{2x - 2}$

36. Find the perimeter of the heptagon (a polygon with seven sides).

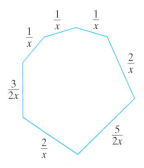

(7.3) Simplify each complex fraction.

37. $\dfrac{1 - \dfrac{3x}{4}}{2 + \dfrac{x}{4}}$

38. $\dfrac{\dfrac{x^2}{15}}{\dfrac{x + 1}{5x}}$

39. $\dfrac{2 - \dfrac{3}{2x}}{x - \dfrac{2}{5x}}$

40. $\dfrac{1 + \dfrac{x}{y}}{\dfrac{x^2}{y^2} - 1}$

41. $\dfrac{\dfrac{5}{x} + \dfrac{1}{xy}}{\dfrac{3}{x^2}}$

42. $\dfrac{\dfrac{x}{3} - \dfrac{3}{x}}{1 + \dfrac{3}{x}}$

43. $\dfrac{\dfrac{1}{x - 1} + 1}{\dfrac{1}{x + 1} - 1}$

44. $\dfrac{\dfrac{x - 3}{x + 3} + \dfrac{x + 3}{x - 3}}{\dfrac{x - 3}{x + 3} - \dfrac{x + 3}{x - 3}}$

If $f(x) = \dfrac{3}{x}, x \neq 0$, find each of the following

45. $f(a + h)$

46. $f(a)$

47. Use Exercises 45 and 46 to find $\dfrac{f(a + h) - f(a)}{h}$.

48. Simplify the results of Exercise 47.

(7.4)

49. $(4xy + 2x^2 - 9) \div 4xy$

50. Divide $12xb^2 + 16xb^4$ by $4xb^3$.

51. $(3x^4 - 25x^2 - 20) \div (x - 3)$

52. $(-x^2 + 2x^4 + 5x - 12) \div (x + 2)$

53. $(2x^3 + 3x^2 - 2x + 2) \div (2x + 3)$

54. $(3x^4 + 5x^3 + 7x^2 + 3x - 2) \div (x^2 + x + 2)$

Use synthetic division to find each quotient.

55. $(3x^3 + 12x - 4) \div (x - 2)$

56. $(x^5 - 1) \div (x + 1)$

57. $(x^3 - 81) \div (x - 3)$

58. $(3x^4 - 2x^2 + 10) \div (x + 2)$

If $P(x) = 3x^5 - 9x + 7$, use the remainder theorem to find the following.

59. $P(4)$

60. $P(-5)$

△ **61.** $P\left(-\dfrac{1}{2}\right)$

62. If the area of the rectangle is $(x^4 - x^3 - 6x^2 - 6x + 18)$ square miles and its width is $(x - 3)$ miles, find the length.

$x^4 - x^3 - 6x^2 - 6x + 18$ square miles ; $x - 3$ miles

In Exercises 63–64, use synthetic division to determine whether or not the number given to the right of each equation is a solution of the equation.

63. $2x^3 - x^2 - 8x + 4 = 0; -2$

64. $x^4 - x^3 - 7x^2 + x + 6 = 0; 4$

65. Use synthetic division to show that $\frac{1}{3}$ is a solution of $3x^3 - 4x^2 - 17x + 6 = 0$. Then solve the polynomial equation.

66. Use synthetic division to show that $\frac{1}{2}$ is a solution of $6x^3 + x^2 - 4x + 1 = 0$. Then solve the polynomial equation.

(7.5) Solve each equation.

67. $\dfrac{3}{x} + \dfrac{1}{3} = \dfrac{5}{x}$

68. $\dfrac{2x + 3}{5x - 9} = \dfrac{3}{2}$

69. $\dfrac{1}{x - 2} - \dfrac{3x}{x^2 - 4} = \dfrac{2}{x + 2}$

70. $\dfrac{7}{x} - \dfrac{x}{7} = 0$

Solve each equation or perform each indicated operation. Simplify.

71. $\dfrac{5}{x^2 - 7x} + \dfrac{4}{2x - 14}$

72. $3 - \dfrac{5}{x} - \dfrac{2}{x^2} = 0$

73. $\dfrac{4}{3 - x} - \dfrac{7}{2x - 6} + \dfrac{5}{x}$

(7.6) Solve each equation for the specified variable.

△ **74.** $A = \dfrac{h(a + b)}{2}$ for a

75. $\dfrac{1}{R} = \dfrac{1}{R_1} + \dfrac{1}{R_2}$ for R_2

76. $I = \dfrac{E}{R + r}$ for R

77. $A = P + Prt$ for r

78. $H = \dfrac{kA(T_1 - T_2)}{L}$ for A

Solve.

79. The sum of a number and twice its reciprocal is 3. Find the number(s).

80. If a number is added to the numerator of $\dfrac{3}{7}$, and twice that number is added to the denominator of $\dfrac{3}{7}$, the result is equivalent to $\dfrac{10}{21}$. Find the number.

81. Three boys can paint a fence in 4 hours, 5 hours, and 6 hours, respectively. Find how long it will take all three boys to paint the fence.

82. If Sue Katz can type a certain number of mailing labels in 6 hours and Tom Neilson and Sue working together can type the same number of mailing labels in 4 hours, find how long it takes Tom alone to type the mailing labels.

83. The speed of a Ranger boat in still water is 32 mph. If the boat travels 72 miles upstream in the same time that it takes to travel 120 miles downstream, find the current of the stream.

84. The speed of a jogger is 3 mph faster than the speed of a walker. If the jogger travels 14 miles in the same amount of time that the walker travels 8 miles, find the speed of the walker.

(7.7) Solve each variation problem.

85. A is directly proportional to B. If $A = 6$ when $B = 14$, find A when $B = 21$.

86. According to Boyle's law, the pressure exerted by a gas is inversely proportional to the volume, as long as the temperature stays the same. If a gas exerts a pressure of 1250 kilopascals when the volume is 2 cubic meters, find the volume when the pressure is 800 kilopascals.

MIXED REVIEW

For expressions, perform the indicated operation and/or simplify. For equations, solve the equation for the unknown variable.

87. $\dfrac{22x + 8}{11x + 4}$

88. $\dfrac{xy - 3x + 2y - 6}{x^2 + 4x + 4}$

89. $\dfrac{2}{5x} \div \dfrac{4 - 18x}{6 - 27x}$

90. $\dfrac{7x + 28}{2x + 4} \div \dfrac{x^2 + 2x - 8}{x^2 - 2x - 8}$

91. $\dfrac{5a^2 - 20}{a^3 + 2a^2 + a + 2} \div \dfrac{7a}{a^3 + a}$

92. $\dfrac{4a + 8}{5a^2 - 20} \cdot \dfrac{3a^2 - 6a}{a + 3} \div \dfrac{2a^2}{5a + 15}$

93. $\dfrac{7}{2x} + \dfrac{5}{6x}$

94. $\dfrac{x - 2}{x + 1} - \dfrac{x - 3}{x - 1}$

95. $\dfrac{2x+1}{x^2+x-6} + \dfrac{2-x}{x^2+x-6}$

96. $\dfrac{2}{x^2-16} - \dfrac{3x}{x^2+8x+16} + \dfrac{3}{x+4}$

97. $\dfrac{\dfrac{1}{x} - \dfrac{2}{3x}}{\dfrac{5}{2x} - \dfrac{1}{3}}$

98. $\dfrac{2}{1 - \dfrac{2}{x}}$

99. $\dfrac{\dfrac{x^2+5x-6}{4x+3}}{\dfrac{(x+6)^2}{8x+6}}$

100. $\dfrac{\dfrac{3}{x-1} - \dfrac{2}{1-x}}{\dfrac{2}{x-1} - \dfrac{2}{x}}$

101. $4 + \dfrac{8}{x} = 8$

102. $\dfrac{x-2}{x^2-7x+10} = \dfrac{1}{5x-10} - \dfrac{1}{x-5}$

103. The denominator of a fraction is 2 more than the numerator. If the numerator is decreased by 3 and the denominator is increased by 5, the resulting fraction is equivalent to $\dfrac{2}{3}$. Find the fraction.

104. The sum of the reciprocals of two consecutive even integers is $-\dfrac{9}{40}$. Find the two integers.

105. The inlet pipe of a water tank can fill the tank in 2 hours and 30 minutes. The outlet pipe can empty the tank in 2 hours. Find how long it takes to empty a full tank if both pipes are open.

106. Timmy Garnica drove 210 miles in the same amount of time that it took a DC-10 jet to travel 1715 miles. The speed of the jet was 430 mph faster than the speed of the car. Find the speed of the jet.

107. Two Amtrak trains traveling on parallel tracks leave Tucson at the same time. In 6 hours the faster train is 382 miles from Tucson and the trains are 112 miles apart. Find how fast each train is traveling.

108. C is inversely proportional to D. If $C = 12$ when $D = 8$, find C when $D = 24$.

109. The surface area of a sphere varies directly as the square of its radius. If the surface area is 36π square inches when the radius is 3 inches, find the surface area when the radius is 4 inches.

110. Divide $(x^3 - x^2 + 3x^4 - 2)$ by $(x - 4)$.

CHAPTER 7 TEST

Remember to use the Chapter Test Prep Videos to see the fully worked-out solutions to any of the exercises you want to review.

Find the domain of each rational function.

1. $f(x) = \dfrac{5x^2}{1-x}$

2. $g(x) = \dfrac{9x^2 - 9}{x^2 + 4x + 3}$

Write each rational expression in lowest terms.

3. $\dfrac{7x - 21}{24 - 8x}$

4. $\dfrac{x^2 - 4x}{x^2 + 5x - 36}$

5. $\dfrac{x^3 - 8}{x - 2}$

Perform the indicated operation. If possible, simplify your answer.

6. $\dfrac{2x^3 + 16}{6x^2 + 12x} \cdot \dfrac{5}{x^2 - 2x + 4}$

7. $\dfrac{5}{4x^3} + \dfrac{7}{4x^3}$

8. $\dfrac{3x^2 - 12}{x^2 + 2x - 8} \div \dfrac{6x + 18}{x + 4}$

9. $\dfrac{4x - 12}{2x - 9} \div \dfrac{3 - x}{4x^2 - 81} \cdot \dfrac{x + 3}{5x + 15}$

10. $\dfrac{3 + 2x}{10 - x} + \dfrac{13 + x}{x - 10}$

11. $\dfrac{2x^2 + 7}{2x^4 - 18x^3} - \dfrac{6x + 7}{2x^4 - 18x^2}$

12. $\dfrac{3}{x^2 - x - 6} + \dfrac{2}{x^2 - 5x + 6}$

13. $\dfrac{5}{x - 7} - \dfrac{2x}{3x - 21} + \dfrac{x}{2x - 14}$

14. $\dfrac{3x}{5} \cdot \left(\dfrac{5}{x} - \dfrac{5}{2x}\right)$

Simplify each complex fraction.

15. $\dfrac{\dfrac{5}{x} - \dfrac{7}{3x}}{\dfrac{9}{8x} - \dfrac{1}{x}}$

16. $\dfrac{\dfrac{x^2 - 5x + 6}{x + 3}}{\dfrac{x^2 - 4x + 4}{x^2 - 9}}$

Divide.

17. $(4x^2y + 9x + 3xz) \div 3xz$

18. $(4x^3 - 5x) \div (2x + 1)$

19. Use synthetic division to divide $(4x^4 - 3x^3 - x - 1)$ by $(x + 3)$.

20. If $P(x) = 4x^4 + 7x^2 - 2x - 5$, use the remainder theorem to find $P(-2)$.

Solve each equation for x.

21. $\dfrac{x}{x-4} = 3 - \dfrac{4}{x-4}$

22. $\dfrac{3}{x+2} - \dfrac{1}{5x} = \dfrac{2}{5x^2+10x}$

23. $\dfrac{x^2+8}{x} - 1 = \dfrac{2(x+4)}{x}$

24. Solve for x: $\dfrac{x+b}{a} = \dfrac{4x-7a}{b}$

25. The product of one more than a number and twice the reciprocal of the number is $\dfrac{12}{5}$. Find the number.

26. If Jan can weed the garden in 2 hours and her husband can weed it in 1 hour and 30 minutes, find how long it takes them to weed the garden together.

27. Suppose that W is inversely proportional to V. If $W = 20$ when $V = 12$, find W when $V = 15$.

28. Suppose that Q is jointly proportional to R and the square of S. If $Q = 24$ when $R = 3$ and $S = 4$, find Q when $R = 2$ and $S = 3$.

29. When an anvil is dropped into a gorge, the speed with which it strikes the ground is directly proportional to the square root of the distance it falls. An anvil that falls 400 feet hits the ground at a speed of 160 feet per second. Find the height of a cliff over the gorge if a dropped anvil hits the ground at a speed of 128 feet per second.

30. Use synthetic division to show that -2 is a solution of $2x^3 - 3x^2 - 11x + 6 = 0$. Then solve the polynomial equation.

CHAPTER 7 STANDARDIZED TEST

Multiple Choice. *Choose the one alternative the best completes the statment or answers the question.*

Find the domain of the rational function.

1. $f(x) = \dfrac{3x^2}{9-x}$
   a. all real numbers except -9
   b. all real numbers except 9
   c. all real numbers except 0 and -9
   d. all real numbers except 0

2. $g(x) = \dfrac{x^2-4}{x^2-8x+12}$
   a. all real numbers except 2 and 6
   b. all real numbers except -2 and 2
   c. all real numbers except 0
   d. all real numbers except -2 and -6

Write the rational expression in lowest terms.

3. $\dfrac{5x-30}{24-4x}$
   a. 6   b. $\dfrac{5}{4}$ c. -6 d. $-\dfrac{5}{4}$

4. $\dfrac{x^2-2x}{x^2+4x-12}$
   a. $\dfrac{x}{x-2}$ b. $\dfrac{x}{x-6}$ c. $\dfrac{x}{x+6}$ d. $\dfrac{x}{x+2}$

5. $\dfrac{x^3-343}{x-7}$
   a. x^2-49 b. $\dfrac{x^3-343}{x-7}$ c. $x^2+7x+49$ d. $\dfrac{1}{x-7}$

Perform the indicated operation. If possible, simplify your answer.

6. $\dfrac{x^3+1}{x^3-x^2+x} \cdot \dfrac{10x}{-40x-40}$
   a. $-\dfrac{1}{4}$ b. $\dfrac{x+1}{4(-x-1)}$ c. $-\dfrac{x^2+1}{4}$ d. $-\dfrac{x^3+1}{4(x+1)}$

7. $\dfrac{7}{5x^2} - \dfrac{4}{5x^2}$
   a. $\dfrac{5}{3x^2}$ b. $\dfrac{3}{10x^4}$ c. $\dfrac{3}{5x^2}$ d. 3

8. $\dfrac{x^2+9x+14}{x^2+14x+49} \div \dfrac{x^2+2x}{x^2+9x+14}$
   a. $\dfrac{x}{x^2+14x+49}$ b. $\dfrac{x+2}{x^2+7x}$ c. $\dfrac{x+2}{x}$ d. $x+2$

9. $\dfrac{x^2-2x}{x^2-7x+12} \cdot \dfrac{x-4}{x^2+4x} \div \dfrac{5x}{x^2-7x+12}$
   a. $\dfrac{(x-2)(x-4)}{x+4}$ b. $\dfrac{(x-3)(x-4)}{5x(x-2)}$ c. $\dfrac{(x-2)}{5x}$ d. $\dfrac{(x-2)(x-4)}{5x(x+4)}$

10. $\dfrac{4-x}{x-8} - \dfrac{2x-2}{8-x}$

   a. $\dfrac{x+2}{x-8}$ b. $-\dfrac{x+6}{x-8}$ c. $-\dfrac{x+2}{x-8}$ d. $\dfrac{x+6}{x-8}$

11. $\dfrac{3x-1}{x^2-2x-8} + \dfrac{3-2x}{x^2-2x-8}$

   a. $\dfrac{1}{x^2-2x-8}$ b. $\dfrac{1}{x-4}$ c. $\dfrac{1}{x+2}$ d. $\dfrac{x-2}{x^2-2x-8}$

12. $\dfrac{2}{y^2-3y+2} + \dfrac{7}{y^2-1}$

   a. $\dfrac{12y-9}{(y-1)(y+1)(y-2)}$ b. $\dfrac{28y-12}{(y-1)(y+1)(y-2)}$

   c. $\dfrac{9y-12}{(y-1)(y-2)}$ d. $\dfrac{9y-12}{(y-1)(y+1)(y-2)}$

13. $\dfrac{3}{x+5} - \dfrac{3x}{5x+25} + \dfrac{5}{2x+10}$

   a. $\dfrac{55+6x}{10(x+5)}$ b. $\dfrac{55-6x}{10(x+5)}$ c. $\dfrac{5+6x}{5(x+5)}$ d. $\dfrac{8-3x}{10(x+5)}$

14. $\dfrac{4x}{5} \cdot \left(\dfrac{5}{x} - \dfrac{5}{2x} \right)$

   a. $-\dfrac{4}{5}$ b. 0   c. 2   d. 6

Simplify the complex fraction.

15. $\dfrac{\dfrac{5}{x} - \dfrac{4}{7x}}{\dfrac{6}{7x} - \dfrac{1}{x}}$

   a. $\dfrac{241}{35}$ b. $\dfrac{1}{5}$ c. $-\dfrac{1}{31}$ d. -31

16. $\dfrac{\dfrac{x^2+5x+6}{x^2+8x+15}}{\dfrac{x^2+2x}{x^2+9x+20}}$

   a. $\dfrac{x+4}{x}$ b. $\dfrac{x}{x^2+8x+15}$ c. $\dfrac{x+4}{x^2+5x}$ d. $x+4$

Divide.

17. $(6x^3y^6 + 24xyz^2 - x^2y^2z) \div 6xy$

   a. $x^2y^5 + 4z^2 - \dfrac{xyz}{6}$ b. $x^2y^5 + 4z^2 - xyz$

   c. $6x^2y^5 + 4z^2 - \dfrac{x^2y^2z}{6}$ d. $x^2y^5 + 24z^2 - \dfrac{xyz}{6}$

18. $(36x^3 - 31x) \div (6x - 1)$

   a. $6x^2 + x + 36$ b. $6x^2 + x - 5 - \dfrac{5}{6x-1}$

   c. $6x^2 + x + 36 + \dfrac{36}{6x-1}$ d. $6x^2 + x - 36$

Solve the problem.

19. Use synthetic division to divide $(5x^4 - 2x^3 + x - 4)$ by $(x - 3)$.

   a. $5x^3 + 13x^2 + 39x + 118 + \dfrac{350}{x-3}$

   b. $5x^3 + 13x^2 + 39x + 118 + \dfrac{351}{x-3}$

   c. $5x^3 + 15x^2 + 42x + 130 + \dfrac{350}{x-3}$

   d. $5x^3 - 13x^2 - 39x - 118 - \dfrac{350}{x-3}$

20. If $R(x) = x^5 + 8x^4 + 2x^3 - 2$, use the remainder theorem to find $R(-3)$.

   a. 37   b. 349   c. -349 d. 592

Solve the equation for x.

21. $\dfrac{x}{x-5} = 5 + \dfrac{5}{x-5}$

   a. no solution   b. $-\dfrac{5}{4}$ c. 5   d. -5

22. $\dfrac{6}{5x} - \dfrac{1}{x+1} = \dfrac{1}{2x^2+2x}$

   a. $-\dfrac{7}{10}$ b. $-\dfrac{7}{2}$ c. no solution   d. -7

23. $\dfrac{x^2+3}{x} + 5 = \dfrac{3(x+1)}{x}$

   a. 0, 2   b. 2   c. -2 d. 0, -2

Solve the problem.

24. Solve for x: $\dfrac{x+z}{y} = \dfrac{6x+3y}{z}$

   a. $x = \dfrac{6y-z}{z^2-3y^2}$ b. $x = \dfrac{3y^2+z^2}{6y+z}$

   c. $x = \dfrac{z-3y^2}{6-z}$ d. $x = \dfrac{z^2-3y^2}{6y-z}$

25. Five divided by the sum of a number and 11, minus the quotient of 3 and the difference of the number and 11 is equal to 6 times the reciprocal of the difference of the number squared and 121.

   a. -41 b. $-\dfrac{41}{4}$ c. 14   d. 47

26. A painter can finish painting a house in 5 hours. Her assistant takes 7 hours to finish the same job. How long would it take for them to complete the job if they were working together?

   a. 4 hr   b. $2\dfrac{11}{12}$ hr   c. $\dfrac{12}{35}$ hr   d. 6 hr

27. Suppose that X is inversely proportional to V. If $X = 6$ when $V = 8$, find X when $V = 16$.

   a. 3   b. 64   c. 2   d. 24

28. Suppose that F is jointly proportional to the square of Q and H. If $F = 36$ when $Q = 3$ and $H = 2$, find F when $Q = 2$ and $H = 5$.

    a. 40   **b.** 10   **c.** 20   **d.** 8

29. The distance an object falls when it is dropped is directly proportional to the square of the amount of time since it was dropped. An object falls 88.2 meters in 3 seconds. Find the distance the object falls in 5 seconds.

    a. 15 m   **b.** 49 m   **c.** 147 m   **d.** 245 m

30. The number $\frac{1}{4}$ is a solution of $4x^3 - x^2 - 36x + 9 = 0$. Use the Remainder Theorem to show this and then find all solutions of this polynomial equation.

    a. $\frac{1}{4}, 9$ **b.** $\frac{1}{4}, 3$ **c.** $\frac{1}{4}, 3, -3$ **d.** $\frac{1}{4}, 9, -9$

CHAPTER 8
Rational Exponents, Radicals, and Complex Numbers

- **8.1** Radicals and Radical Functions
- **8.2** Rational Exponents
- **8.3** Simplifying Radical Expressions
- **8.4** Adding, Subtracting, and Multiplying Radical Expressions
- **8.5** Rationalizing Denominators and Numerators of Radical Expressions

  Integrated Review—Radicals and Rational Exponents

- **8.6** Radical Equations and Problem Solving
- **8.7** Complex Numbers
- **8.8** Standard Deviation

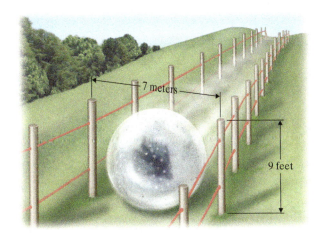

A zorb is a large inflated ball within a ball, and zorbing is a recreational activity which may involve rolling down a hill while strapped in a zorb.

An example of a course is shown in the diagram above. In this chapter, we will use our knowledge of radicals to calculate the outer radius of a zorb, which would certainly be closely associated with the cost of production.

8.1 RADICALS AND RADICAL FUNCTIONS

OBJECTIVES

1. Find square roots.
2. Approximate roots.
3. Find cube roots.
4. Find nth roots.
5. Find $\sqrt[n]{a^n}$ where a is a real number.
6. Graph square and cube root functions.

OBJECTIVE 1 ▶ Finding square roots. Recall from Section 1.3 that to find a **square root** of a number a, we find a number that was squared to get a.

Thus, because
$$5^2 = 25 \quad \text{and} \quad (-5)^2 = 25, \text{ then}$$
both 5 and -5 are square roots of 25.

Recall that we denote the **nonnegative**, or **principal, square root** with the **radical sign**.
$$\sqrt{25} = 5$$

We denote the **negative square root** with the **negative radical sign**.
$$-\sqrt{25} = -5$$

An expression containing a radical sign is called a **radical expression**. An expression within, or "under," a radical sign is called a **radicand**.

radical expression:

Principal and Negative Square Roots

If a is a nonnegative number, then

$\sqrt{a}$ is the **principal**, or **nonnegative square root** of a

$-\sqrt{a}$ is the **negative square root** of a

EXAMPLE 1 Simplify. Assume that all variables represent positive numbers.

a. $\sqrt{36}$ b. $\sqrt{0}$ c. $\sqrt{\dfrac{4}{49}}$ d. $\sqrt{0.25}$

e. $\sqrt{x^6}$ f. $\sqrt{9x^{12}}$ g. $-\sqrt{81}$ h. $\sqrt{-81}$

Solution

a. $\sqrt{36} = 6$ because $6^2 = 36$ and 6 is not negative.
b. $\sqrt{0} = 0$ because $0^2 = 0$ and 0 is not negative.
c. $\sqrt{\dfrac{4}{49}} = \dfrac{2}{7}$ because $\left(\dfrac{2}{7}\right)^2 = \dfrac{4}{49}$ and $\dfrac{2}{7}$ is not negative.
d. $\sqrt{0.25} = 0.5$ because $(0.5)^2 = 0.25$.
e. $\sqrt{x^6} = x^3$ because $(x^3)^2 = x^6$.
f. $\sqrt{9x^{12}} = 3x^6$ because $(3x^6)^2 = 9x^{12}$.
g. $-\sqrt{81} = -9$. The negative in front of the radical indicates the negative square root of 81.
h. $\sqrt{-81}$ is not a real number. □

PRACTICE 1 Simplify. Assume that all variables represent positive numbers.

a. $\sqrt{49}$ b. $\sqrt{\dfrac{0}{1}}$ c. $\sqrt{\dfrac{16}{81}}$ d. $\sqrt{0.64}$

e. $\sqrt{z^8}$ f. $\sqrt{16b^4}$ g. $-\sqrt{36}$ h. $\sqrt{-36}$

Recall from Section 1.3 our discussion of the square root of a negative number. For example, can we simplify $\sqrt{-4}$? That is, can we find a real number whose square is -4? No, there is no real number whose square is -4, and we say that $\sqrt{-4}$ is not a real number. In general:

The square root of a negative number is not a real number.

> **Helpful Hint**
> - Remember: $\sqrt{0} = 0$
> - Don't forget, the square root of a negative number, such as $\sqrt{-9}$, is not a real number. In Section 8.7, we will see what kind of a number $\sqrt{-9}$ is.

OBJECTIVE 2 ▶ Approximating roots. Recall that numbers such as 1, 4, 9, and 25 are called **perfect squares**, since $1 = 1^2, 4 = 2^2, 9 = 3^2$, and $25 = 5^2$. Square roots of perfect square radicands simplify to rational numbers. What happens when we try to simplify a root such as $\sqrt{3}$? Since there is no rational number whose square is 3, then $\sqrt{3}$ is not a rational number. It is called an **irrational number,** and we can find a decimal **approximation** of it. To find decimal approximations, use a calculator. For example, an approximation for $\sqrt{3}$ is

$$\sqrt{3} \approx 1.732$$

↑ approximation symbol

To see if the approximation is reasonable, notice that since

$$1 < 3 < 4, \text{ then}$$
$$\sqrt{1} < \sqrt{3} < \sqrt{4}, \text{ or}$$
$$1 < \sqrt{3} < 2.$$

We found $\sqrt{3} \approx 1.732$, a number between 1 and 2, so our result is reasonable.

EXAMPLE 2 Use a calculator to approximate $\sqrt{20}$. Round the approximation to 3 decimal places and check to see that your approximation is reasonable.

$$\sqrt{20} \approx 4.472$$

Solution Is this reasonable? Since $16 < 20 < 25$, then $\sqrt{16} < \sqrt{20} < \sqrt{25}$, or $4 < \sqrt{20} < 5$. The approximation is between 4 and 5 and thus is reasonable. ☐

PRACTICE 2 Use a calculator to approximate $\sqrt{45}$. Round the approximation to three decimal places and check to see that your approximation is reasonable.

OBJECTIVE 3 ▶ Finding cube roots. Finding roots can be extended to other roots such as cube roots. For example, since $2^3 = 8$, we call 2 the **cube root** of 8. In symbols, we write

$$\sqrt[3]{8} = 2$$

> **Cube Root**
> The **cube root** of a real number a is written as $\sqrt[3]{a}$, and
> $$\sqrt[3]{a} = b \text{ only if } b^3 = a$$

From this definition, we have

$$\sqrt[3]{64} = 4 \text{ since } 4^3 = 64$$
$$\sqrt[3]{-27} = -3 \text{ since } (-3)^3 = -27$$
$$\sqrt[3]{x^3} = x \text{ since } x^3 = x^3$$

Notice that, unlike with square roots, *it is possible to have a negative radicand when finding a cube root*. This is so because the *cube* of a negative number is a negative number. Therefore, the *cube root* of a negative number is a negative number.

EXAMPLE 3 Find the cube roots.

a. $\sqrt[3]{1}$ b. $\sqrt[3]{-64}$ c. $\sqrt[3]{\dfrac{8}{125}}$ d. $\sqrt[3]{x^6}$ e. $\sqrt[3]{-27x^9}$

Solution

a. $\sqrt[3]{1} = 1$ because $1^3 = 1$.
b. $\sqrt[3]{-64} = -4$ because $(-4)^3 = -64$.
c. $\sqrt[3]{\dfrac{8}{125}} = \dfrac{2}{5}$ because $\left(\dfrac{2}{5}\right)^3 = \dfrac{8}{125}$.
d. $\sqrt[3]{x^6} = x^2$ because $(x^2)^3 = x^6$.
e. $\sqrt[3]{-27x^9} = -3x^3$ because $(-3x^3)^3 = -27x^9$.

PRACTICE 3 Find the cube roots.

a. $\sqrt[3]{-1}$ b. $\sqrt[3]{27}$ c. $\sqrt[3]{\dfrac{27}{64}}$ d. $\sqrt[3]{x^{12}}$ e. $\sqrt[3]{-8x^3}$

OBJECTIVE 4 ▶ Finding *n*th roots. Just as we can raise a real number to powers other than 2 or 3, we can find roots other than square roots and cube roots. In fact, we can find the ***n*th root** of a number, where *n* is any natural number. In symbols, the *n*th root of *a* is written as $\sqrt[n]{a}$, where *n* is called the **index.** The index 2 is usually omitted for square roots.

> ▶ **Helpful Hint**
> If the index is even, such as $\sqrt{}, \sqrt[4]{}, \sqrt[6]{}$, and so on, the radicand must be non-negative for the root to be a real number. For example,
>
> $\sqrt[4]{16} = 2$, but $\sqrt[4]{-16}$ is not a real number.
> $\sqrt[6]{64} = 2$, but $\sqrt[6]{-64}$ is not a real number.
>
> If the index is odd, such as $\sqrt[3]{}, \sqrt[5]{}$, and so on, the radicand may be any real number. For example,
>
> $\sqrt[3]{64} = 4$ and $\sqrt[3]{-64} = -4$
> $\sqrt[5]{32} = 2$ and $\sqrt[5]{-32} = -2$

Concept Check ✓

Which one is not a real number?

a. $\sqrt[3]{-15}$ b. $\sqrt[4]{-15}$ c. $\sqrt[5]{-15}$ d. $\sqrt{(-15)^2}$

EXAMPLE 4 Simplify the following expressions.

a. $\sqrt[4]{81}$ b. $\sqrt[5]{-243}$ c. $-\sqrt{25}$ d. $\sqrt[4]{-81}$ e. $\sqrt[3]{64x^3}$

Solution

a. $\sqrt[4]{81} = 3$ because $3^4 = 81$ and 3 is positive.
b. $\sqrt[5]{-243} = -3$ because $(-3)^5 = -243$.
c. $-\sqrt{25} = -5$ because -5 is the opposite of $\sqrt{25}$.

Answer to Concept Check: b

d. $\sqrt[4]{-81}$ is not a real number. There is no real number that, when raised to the fourth power, is -81.

e. $\sqrt[3]{64x^3} = 4x$ because $(4x)^3 = 64x^3$.

PRACTICE 4 Simplify the following expressions.

a. $\sqrt[4]{10000}$ b. $\sqrt[5]{-1}$ c. $-\sqrt{81}$ d. $\sqrt[4]{-625}$ e. $\sqrt[3]{27x^9}$

OBJECTIVE 5 ▶ **Finding $\sqrt[n]{a^n}$ where a is a real number.** Recall that the notation $\sqrt{a^2}$ indicates the positive square root of a^2 only. For example,

$$\sqrt{(-5)^2} = \sqrt{25} = 5$$

When variables are present in the radicand and it is unclear whether the variable represents a positive number or a negative number, absolute value bars are sometimes needed to ensure that the result is a positive number. For example,

$$\sqrt{x^2} = |x|$$

This ensures that the result is positive. This same situation may occur when the index is any *even* positive integer. When the index is any *odd* positive integer, absolute value bars are not necessary.

> **Finding $\sqrt[n]{a^n}$**
> If n is an *even* positive integer, then $\sqrt[n]{a^n} = |a|$.
> If n is an *odd* positive integer, then $\sqrt[n]{a^n} = a$.

EXAMPLE 5   Simplify.

a. $\sqrt{(-3)^2}$ b. $\sqrt{x^2}$ c. $\sqrt[4]{(x-2)^4}$ d. $\sqrt[3]{(-5)^3}$

e. $\sqrt[5]{(2x-7)^5}$ f. $\sqrt{25x^2}$ g. $\sqrt{x^2 + 2x + 1}$

Solution

a. $\sqrt{(-3)^2} = |-3| = 3$ When the index is even, the absolute value bars ensure us that our result is not negative.

b. $\sqrt{x^2} = |x|$

c. $\sqrt[4]{(x-2)^4} = |x-2|$

d. $\sqrt[3]{(-5)^3} = -5$

e. $\sqrt[5]{(2x-7)^5} = 2x - 7$ Absolute value bars are not needed when the index is odd.

f. $\sqrt{25x^2} = 5|x|$

g. $\sqrt{x^2 + 2x + 1} = \sqrt{(x+1)^2} = |x+1|$

PRACTICE 5   Simplify.

a. $\sqrt{(-4)^2}$ b. $\sqrt{x^{14}}$ c. $\sqrt[4]{(x+7)^4}$ d. $\sqrt[3]{(-7)^3}$

e. $\sqrt[5]{(3x-5)^5}$ f. $\sqrt{49x^2}$ g. $\sqrt{x^2 + 4x + 4}$

OBJECTIVE 6 ▶ **Graphing square and cube root functions.** Recall that an equation in x and y describes a function if each x-value is paired with exactly one y-value. With this in mind, does the equation

$$y = \sqrt{x}$$

describe a function? First, notice that replacement values for x must be nonnegative real numbers, since $\sqrt{x}$ is not a real number if $x < 0$. The notation $\sqrt{x}$ denotes the principal square root of x, so for every nonnegative number x, there is exactly one number, $\sqrt{x}$. Therefore, $y = \sqrt{x}$ describes a function, and we may write it as

$$f(x) = \sqrt{x}$$

In general, radical functions are functions of the form

$$f(x) = \sqrt[n]{x}.$$

Recall that the domain of a function in x is the set of all possible replacement values of x. This means that if n is even, the domain consists of all nonnegative numbers, or $x \geq 0$. If n is odd, the domain is all real numbers. Keep this in mind as we find function values.

EXAMPLE 6 If $f(x) = \sqrt{x - 4}$ and $g(x) = \sqrt[3]{x + 2}$, find each function value.

a. $f(8)$ **b.** $f(6)$ **c.** $g(-1)$ **d.** $g(1)$

Solution

a. $f(8) = \sqrt{8 - 4} = \sqrt{4} = 2$ **b.** $f(6) = \sqrt{6 - 4} = \sqrt{2}$
c. $g(-1) = \sqrt[3]{-1 + 2} = \sqrt[3]{1} = 1$ **d.** $g(1) = \sqrt[3]{1 + 2} = \sqrt[3]{3}$

PRACTICE 6 If $f(x) = \sqrt{x + 5}$ and $g(x) = \sqrt[3]{x - 3}$, find each function value.

a. $f(11)$ **b.** $f(-1)$ **c.** $g(11)$ **d.** $g(-5)$

> **▶ Helpful Hint**
> Notice that for the function $f(x) = \sqrt{x - 4}$, the domain includes all real numbers that make the radicand ≥ 0. To see what numbers these are, solve $x - 4 \geq 0$ and find that $x \geq 4$. The domain is $x \geq 4$.
> The domain of the cube root function $g(x) = \sqrt[3]{x + 2}$ is all real numbers.

EXAMPLE 7 Graph the square root function $f(x) = \sqrt{x}$.

Solution To graph, we identify the domain, evaluate the function for several values of x, plot the resulting points, and connect the points with a smooth curve. Since $\sqrt{x}$ represents the nonnegative square root of x, the domain of this function is all nonnegative numbers, $x \geq 0$. We have approximated $\sqrt{3}$ below to help us locate the point corresponding to $(3, \sqrt{3})$.

x	$f(x) = \sqrt{x}$
0	0
1	1
3	$\sqrt{3} \approx 1.7$
4	2
9	3

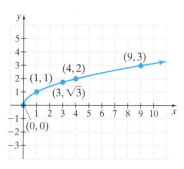

Notice that the graph of this function passes the vertical line test, as expected.

PRACTICE 7 Graph the square root function $h(x) = \sqrt{x + 2}$.

The equation $f(x) = \sqrt[3]{x}$ also describes a function. Here x may be any real number, so the domain of this function is all real numbers. A few function values are given next.

$$f(0) = \sqrt[3]{0} = 0$$
$$f(1) = \sqrt[3]{1} = 1$$
$$f(-1) = \sqrt[3]{-1} = -1$$
$$f(6) = \sqrt[3]{6}$$
$$f(-6) = \sqrt[3]{-6}$$

} Here, there is no rational number whose cube is 6. Thus, the radicals do not simplify to rational numbers.

$$f(8) = \sqrt[3]{8} = 2$$
$$f(-8) = \sqrt[3]{-8} = -2$$

EXAMPLE 8 Graph the function $f(x) = \sqrt[3]{x}$.

Solution To graph, we identify the domain, plot points, and connect the points with a smooth curve. The domain of this function is all real numbers. The table comes from the function values obtained earlier. We have approximated $\sqrt[3]{6}$ and $\sqrt[3]{-6}$ for graphing purposes.

x	$f(x) = \sqrt[3]{x}$
0	0
1	1
-1	-1
6	$\sqrt[3]{6} \approx 1.8$
-6	$\sqrt[3]{-6} \approx -1.8$
8	2
-8	-2

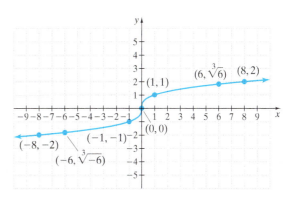

The graph of this function passes the vertical line test, as expected.

PRACTICE 8 Graph the function $f(x) = \sqrt[3]{x} - 4$.

VOCABULARY & READINESS CHECK

Word Bank. *Use the choices below to fill in each blank. Not all choices will be used.*

| is | cubes | $-\sqrt{a}$ | radical sign | index |
| is not | squares | $\sqrt{-a}$ | radicand | |

1. In the expression $\sqrt[n]{a}$, the n is called the _____, the $\sqrt{}$ is called the _____, and a is called the _____.
2. If $\sqrt{a}$ is the positive square root of a, $a \neq 0$, then _____ is the negative square root of a.
3. The square root of a negative number _____ a real number.
4. Numbers such as 1, 4, 9, and 25 are called perfect _____ where numbers such as 1, 8, 27, and 125 are called perfect _____.

Fill in the Blank.

5. The domain of the function $f(x) = \sqrt{x}$ is _____.
6. The domain of the function $f(x) = \sqrt[3]{x}$ is _____.
7. If $f(16) = 4$, the corresponding ordered pair is _____.
8. If $g(-8) = -2$, the corresponding ordered pair is _____.

448 CHAPTER 8 Rational Exponents, Radicals, and Complex Numbers

Multiple Choice. *Choose the correct letter or letters. No pencil is needed, just think your way through these.*

9. Which radical is not a real number?
   a. $\sqrt{3}$ b. $-\sqrt{11}$ c. $\sqrt[3]{-10}$ d. $\sqrt{-10}$

10. Which radical(s) simplify to 3?
    a. $\sqrt{9}$ b. $\sqrt{-9}$ c. $\sqrt[3]{27}$ d. $\sqrt[3]{-27}$

11. Which radical(s) simplify to -3?
    a. $\sqrt{9}$ b. $\sqrt{-9}$ c. $\sqrt[3]{27}$ d. $\sqrt[3]{-27}$

12. Which radical does not simplify to a whole number?
    a. $\sqrt{64}$ b. $\sqrt[3]{64}$ c. $\sqrt{8}$ d. $\sqrt[3]{8}$

8.1 EXERCISE SET

Simplify. Assume that variables represent positive real numbers. See Example 1.

1. $\sqrt{100}$
2. $\sqrt{400}$
3. $\sqrt{\dfrac{1}{4}}$
4. $\sqrt{\dfrac{9}{25}}$
5. $\sqrt{0.0001}$
6. $\sqrt{0.04}$
7. $-\sqrt{36}$
8. $-\sqrt{9}$
9. $\sqrt{x^{10}}$
10. $\sqrt{x^{16}}$
11. $\sqrt{16y^6}$
12. $\sqrt{64y^{20}}$

Use a calculator to approximate each square root to 3 decimal places. Check to see that each approximation is reasonable. See Example 2.

13. $\sqrt{7}$
14. $\sqrt{11}$
15. $\sqrt{38}$
16. $\sqrt{56}$
17. $\sqrt{200}$
18. $\sqrt{300}$

Find each cube root. See Example 3.

19. $\sqrt[3]{64}$
20. $\sqrt[3]{27}$
21. $\sqrt[3]{\dfrac{1}{8}}$
22. $\sqrt[3]{\dfrac{27}{64}}$
23. $\sqrt[3]{-1}$
24. $\sqrt[3]{-125}$
25. $\sqrt[3]{x^{12}}$
26. $\sqrt[3]{x^{15}}$
27. $\sqrt[3]{-27x^9}$
28. $\sqrt[3]{-64x^6}$

Find each root. Assume that all variables represent nonnegative real numbers. See Example 4.

29. $-\sqrt[4]{16}$
30. $\sqrt[5]{-243}$
31. $\sqrt[4]{-16}$
32. $\sqrt{-16}$
33. $\sqrt[5]{-32}$
34. $\sqrt[5]{-1}$
35. $\sqrt[5]{x^{20}}$
36. $\sqrt[4]{x^{20}}$
37. $\sqrt[6]{64x^{12}}$
38. $\sqrt[5]{-32x^{15}}$
39. $\sqrt{81x^4}$
40. $\sqrt[4]{81x^4}$
41. $\sqrt[4]{256x^8}$
42. $\sqrt{256x^8}$

Simplify. Assume that the variables represent any real number. See Example 5.

43. $\sqrt{(-8)^2}$
44. $\sqrt{(-7)^2}$
45. $\sqrt[3]{(-8)^3}$
46. $\sqrt[5]{(-7)^5}$
47. $\sqrt{4x^2}$
48. $\sqrt[4]{16x^4}$
49. $\sqrt[3]{x^3}$
50. $\sqrt[5]{x^5}$
51. $\sqrt{(x-5)^2}$
52. $\sqrt{(y-6)^2}$
53. $\sqrt{x^2 + 4x + 4}$
    (*Hint:* Factor the polynomial first.)
54. $\sqrt{x^2 - 8x + 16}$
    (*Hint:* Factor the polynomial first.)

MIXED PRACTICE

Simplify each radical. Assume that all variables represent positive real numbers.

55. $-\sqrt{121}$
56. $-\sqrt[3]{125}$
57. $\sqrt[3]{8x^3}$
58. $\sqrt{16x^8}$
59. $\sqrt{y^{12}}$
60. $\sqrt[3]{y^{12}}$
61. $\sqrt{25a^2b^{20}}$
62. $\sqrt{9x^4y^6}$
63. $\sqrt[3]{-27x^{12}y^9}$
64. $\sqrt[3]{-8a^{21}b^6}$
65. $\sqrt[4]{a^{16}b^4}$
66. $\sqrt[4]{x^8y^{12}}$
67. $\sqrt[5]{-32x^{10}y^5}$
68. $\sqrt[5]{-243z^{15}}$
69. $\sqrt{\dfrac{25}{49}}$
70. $\sqrt{\dfrac{4}{81}}$
71. $\sqrt{\dfrac{x^2}{4y^2}}$
72. $\sqrt{\dfrac{y^{10}}{9x^6}}$
73. $-\sqrt[3]{\dfrac{z^{21}}{27x^3}}$
74. $-\sqrt[3]{\dfrac{64a^3}{b^9}}$
75. $\sqrt[4]{\dfrac{x^4}{16}}$
76. $\sqrt[4]{\dfrac{y^4}{81x^4}}$

If $f(x) = \sqrt{2x + 3}$ and $g(x) = \sqrt[3]{x - 8}$, find the following function values. See Example 6.

77. $f(0)$
78. $g(0)$
79. $g(7)$
80. $f(-1)$

Section 8.1 Radicals and Radical Functions 449

81. $g(-19)$ **82.** $f(3)$
83. $f(2)$ **84.** $g(1)$

Identify the domain and then graph each function. See Example 7.

85. $f(x) = \sqrt{x} + 2$
86. $f(x) = \sqrt{x} - 2$
87. $f(x) = \sqrt{x - 3}$; use the following table.

x	$f(x)$
3	
4	
7	
12	

88. $f(x) = \sqrt{x + 1}$; use the following table.

x	$f(x)$
-1	
0	
3	
8	

Identify the domain and then graph each function. See Example 8.

89. $f(x) = \sqrt[3]{x} + 1$
90. $f(x) = \sqrt[3]{x} - 2$
91. $g(x) = \sqrt[3]{x - 1}$; use the following table.

x	$g(x)$
1	
2	
0	
9	
-7	

92. $g(x) = \sqrt[3]{x + 1}$; use the following table.

x	$g(x)$
-1	
0	
-2	
7	
-9	

REVIEW AND PREVIEW

Simplify each exponential expression. See Sections 6.1 and 6.2.

93. $(-2x^3y^2)^5$
94. $(4y^6z^7)^3$
95. $(-3x^2y^3z^5)(20x^5y^7)$
96. $(-14a^5bc^2)(2abc^4)$

97. $\dfrac{7x^{-1}y}{14(x^5y^2)^{-2}}$
98. $\dfrac{(2a^{-1}b^2)^3}{(8a^2b)^{-2}}$

CONCEPT EXTENSIONS

Which of the following are not real numbers? See the Concept Check in this section.

99. $\sqrt{-17}$ **100.** $\sqrt[3]{-17}$
101. $\sqrt[10]{-17}$ **102.** $\sqrt[15]{-17}$

103. Explain why $\sqrt{-64}$ is not a real number.
104. Explain why $\sqrt[3]{-64}$ is a real number.

Multiple Choice. *For Exercises 105 through 108, do not use a calculator.*

105. $\sqrt{160}$ is closest to
  a. 10 **b.** 13 **c.** 20 **d.** 40

106. $\sqrt{1000}$ is closest to
  a. 10 **b.** 30 **c.** 100 **d.** 500

107. The perimeter of the triangle is closest to
  a. 12 **b.** 18
  c. 66 **d.** 132

108. The length of the bent wire is closest to
  a. 5 **b.** $\sqrt{28}$
  c. 7 **d.** 14

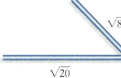

The Mosteller formula for calculating adult body surface area is $B = \sqrt{\dfrac{hw}{3131}}$, *where B is an individual's body surface area in square meters, h is the individual's height in inches, and w is the individual's weight in pounds. Use this information to answer Exercises 109 and 110. Round answers to 2 decimal places.*

109. Find the body surface area of an individual who is 66 inches tall and who weighs 135 pounds.

110. Find the body surface area of an individual who is 74 inches tall and who weighs 225 pounds.

111. Suppose that a friend tells you that $\sqrt{13} \approx 5.7$. Without a calculator, how can you convince your friend that he or she must have made an error?

112. Escape velocity is the minimum speed that an object must reach to escape a planet's pull of gravity. Escape velocity v is given by the equation $v = \sqrt{\dfrac{2Gm}{r}}$, where m is the mass of the planet, r is its radius, and G is the universal gravitational constant, which has a value of $G = 6.67 \times 10^{-11}$ m³/kg·sec². The mass of Earth is 5.97×10^{24} kg and its radius is 6.37×10^6 m. Use this information to find the escape velocity for Earth. Round to the nearest whole number. (Source: National Space Science Data Center)

Use a graphing calculator to verify the domain of each function and its graph.

113. Exercise 85 **114.** Exercise 86
115. Exercise 89 **116.** Exercise 90

8.2 RATIONAL EXPONENTS

OBJECTIVES

1. Understand the meaning of $a^{1/n}$.
2. Understand the meaning of $a^{m/n}$.
3. Understand the meaning of $a^{-m/n}$.
4. Use rules for exponents to simplify expressions that contain rational exponents.
5. Use rational exponents to simplify radical expressions.

OBJECTIVE 1 ▶ Understanding the meaning of $a^{1/n}$. So far in this text, we have not defined expressions with rational exponents such as $3^{1/2}$, $x^{2/3}$, and $-9^{-1/4}$. We will define these expressions so that the rules for exponents will apply to these rational exponents as well.

Suppose that $x = 5^{1/3}$. Then

$$x^3 = (5^{1/3})^3 = 5^{1/3 \cdot 3} = 5^1 \text{ or } 5$$

using rules for exponents

Since $x^3 = 5$, then x is the number whose cube is 5, or $x = \sqrt[3]{5}$. Notice that we also know that $x = 5^{1/3}$. This means

$$5^{1/3} = \sqrt[3]{5}$$

Definition of $a^{1/n}$

If n is a positive integer greater than 1 and $\sqrt[n]{a}$ is a real number, then

$$a^{1/n} = \sqrt[n]{a}$$

Notice that the denominator of the rational exponent corresponds to the index of the radical.

EXAMPLE 1 Use radical notation to write the following. Simplify if possible.

a. $4^{1/2}$ **b.** $64^{1/3}$ **c.** $x^{1/4}$ **d.** $0^{1/6}$ **e.** $-9^{1/2}$ **f.** $(81x^8)^{1/4}$ **g.** $(5y)^{1/3}$

Solution

a. $4^{1/2} = \sqrt{4} = 2$
b. $64^{1/3} = \sqrt[3]{64} = 4$
c. $x^{1/4} = \sqrt[4]{x}$
d. $0^{1/6} = \sqrt[6]{0} = 0$
e. $-9^{1/2} = -\sqrt{9} = -3$
f. $(81x^8)^{1/4} = \sqrt[4]{81x^8} = 3x^2$
g. $(5y)^{1/3} = \sqrt[3]{5y}$

PRACTICE 1 Use radical notation to write the following. Simplify if possible.

a. $36^{1/2}$ **b.** $1000^{1/3}$ **c.** $x^{1/5}$ **d.** $1^{1/4}$ **e.** $-64^{1/2}$
f. $(125x^9)^{1/3}$ **g.** $(3x)^{1/4}$

OBJECTIVE 2 ▶ Understanding the meaning of $a^{m/n}$. As we expand our use of exponents to include $\dfrac{m}{n}$, we define their meaning so that rules for exponents still hold true. For example, by properties of exponents,

$$8^{2/3} = (8^{1/3})^2 = (\sqrt[3]{8})^2 \quad \text{or}$$
$$8^{2/3} = (8^2)^{1/3} = \sqrt[3]{8^2}$$

Section 8.2 Rational Exponents 451

Definition of $a^{m/n}$
If m and n are positive integers greater than 1 with $\dfrac{m}{n}$ in lowest terms, then
$$a^{m/n} = \sqrt[n]{a^m} = \left(\sqrt[n]{a}\right)^m$$
as long as $\sqrt[n]{a}$ is a real number.

Notice that the denominator n of the rational exponent corresponds to the index of the radical. The numerator m of the rational exponent indicates that the base is to be raised to the mth power. This means
$$8^{2/3} = \sqrt[3]{8^2} = \sqrt[3]{64} = 4 \quad \text{or}$$
$$8^{2/3} = \left(\sqrt[3]{8}\right)^2 = 2^2 = 4$$

From simplifying $8^{2/3}$, can you see that it doesn't matter whether you raise to a power first and then take the nth root or you take the nth root first and then raise to a power?

▶ **Helpful Hint**
Most of the time, $\left(\sqrt[n]{a}\right)^m$ will be easier to calculate than $\sqrt[n]{a^m}$.

EXAMPLE 2 Use radical notation to write the following. Then simplify if possible.
a. $4^{3/2}$
b. $-16^{3/4}$
c. $(-27)^{2/3}$
d. $\left(\dfrac{1}{9}\right)^{3/2}$
e. $(4x-1)^{3/5}$

Solution
a. $4^{3/2} = \left(\sqrt{4}\right)^3 = 2^3 = 8$
b. $-16^{3/4} = -\left(\sqrt[4]{16}\right)^3 = -(2)^3 = -8$
c. $(-27)^{2/3} = \left(\sqrt[3]{-27}\right)^2 = (-3)^2 = 9$
d. $\left(\dfrac{1}{9}\right)^{3/2} = \left(\sqrt{\dfrac{1}{9}}\right)^3 = \left(\dfrac{1}{3}\right)^3 = \dfrac{1}{27}$
e. $(4x-1)^{3/5} = \sqrt[5]{(4x-1)^3}$

PRACTICE 2 Use radical notation to write the following. Simplify if possible.
a. $16^{3/2}$
b. $-1^{3/5}$
c. $-(81)^{3/4}$
d. $\left(\dfrac{1}{25}\right)^{3/2}$
e. $(3x+2)^{5/9}$

▶ **Helpful Hint**
The *denominator* of a rational exponent is the index of the corresponding radical. For example, $x^{1/5} = \sqrt[5]{x}$ and $z^{2/3} = \sqrt[3]{z^2}$, or $z^{2/3} = \left(\sqrt[3]{z}\right)^2$.

452 CHAPTER 8 Rational Exponents, Radicals, and Complex Numbers

OBJECTIVE 3 ▶ **Understanding the meaning of $a^{-m/n}$.** The rational exponents we have given meaning to exclude negative rational numbers. To complete the set of definitions, we define $a^{-m/n}$.

> **Definition of $a^{-m/n}$**
>
> $$a^{-m/n} = \frac{1}{a^{m/n}}$$
>
> as long as $a^{m/n}$ is a nonzero real number.

EXAMPLE 3   Write each expression with a positive exponent, and then simplify.

a. $16^{-3/4}$ **b.** $(-27)^{-2/3}$

Solution

a. $16^{-3/4} = \dfrac{1}{16^{3/4}} = \dfrac{1}{(\sqrt[4]{16})^3} = \dfrac{1}{2^3} = \dfrac{1}{8}$

b. $(-27)^{-2/3} = \dfrac{1}{(-27)^{2/3}} = \dfrac{1}{(\sqrt[3]{-27})^2} = \dfrac{1}{(-3)^2} = \dfrac{1}{9}$

PRACTICE 3   Write each expression with a positive exponent; then simplify.

a. $9^{-3/2}$ **b.** $(-64)^{-2/3}$

> ▶ **Helpful Hint**
>
> If an expression contains a negative rational exponent, such as $9^{-3/2}$, you may want to first write the expression with a positive exponent and then interpret the rational exponent. Notice that the sign of the base is not affected by the sign of its exponent. For example,
>
> $$9^{-3/2} = \frac{1}{9^{3/2}} = \frac{1}{(\sqrt{9})^3} = \frac{1}{27}$$
>
> Also,
>
> $$(-27)^{-1/3} = \frac{1}{(-27)^{1/3}} = -\frac{1}{3}$$

Concept Check ✓

Which one is correct?

a. $-8^{2/3} = \dfrac{1}{4}$ **b.** $8^{-2/3} = -\dfrac{1}{4}$ **c.** $8^{-2/3} = -4$ **d.** $-8^{-2/3} = -\dfrac{1}{4}$

OBJECTIVE 4 ▶ **Using rules for exponents to simplify expressions.** It can be shown that the properties of integer exponents hold for rational exponents. By using these properties and definitions, we can now simplify expressions that contain rational exponents.

These rules are repeated here for review.

Note: For the remainder of this chapter, we will assume that variables represent positive real numbers. Since this is so, we need not insert absolute value bars when we simplify even roots.

Answer to Concept Check: d

Section 8.2 Rational Exponents 453

Summary of Exponent Rules

If m and n are rational numbers, and a, b, and c are numbers for which the expressions below exist, then

Product rule for exponents: $\quad a^m \cdot a^n = a^{m+n}$

Power rule for exponents: $\quad (a^m)^n = a^{m \cdot n}$

Power rules for products and quotients: $\quad (ab)^n = a^n b^n \quad$ and

$$\left(\frac{a}{c}\right)^n = \frac{a^n}{c^n}, c \neq 0$$

Quotient rule for exponents: $\quad \dfrac{a^m}{a^n} = a^{m-n}, a \neq 0$

Zero exponent: $\quad a^0 = 1, a \neq 0$

Negative exponent: $\quad a^{-n} = \dfrac{1}{a^n}, a \neq 0$

EXAMPLE 4 Use properties of exponents to simplify. Write results with only positive exponents.

a. $b^{1/3} \cdot b^{5/3}$ **b.** $x^{1/2} x^{1/3}$ **c.** $\dfrac{7^{1/3}}{7^{4/3}}$

d. $y^{-4/7} \cdot y^{6/7}$ **e.** $\dfrac{(2x^{2/5} y^{-1/3})^5}{x^2 y}$

Solution

a. $b^{1/3} \cdot b^{5/3} = b^{(1/3 + 5/3)} = b^{6/3} = b^2$

b. $x^{1/2} x^{1/3} = x^{(1/2 + 1/3)} = x^{3/6 + 2/6} = x^{5/6} \quad$ Use the product rule.

c. $\dfrac{7^{1/3}}{7^{4/3}} = 7^{1/3 - 4/3} = 7^{-3/3} = 7^{-1} = \dfrac{1}{7} \quad$ Use the quotient rule.

d. $y^{-4/7} \cdot y^{6/7} = y^{-4/7 + 6/7} = y^{2/7} \quad$ Use the product rule.

e. We begin by using the power rule $(ab)^m = a^m b^m$ to simplify the numerator.

$$\frac{(2x^{2/5} y^{-1/3})^5}{x^2 y} = \frac{2^5 (x^{2/5})^5 (y^{-1/3})^5}{x^2 y} = \frac{32 x^2 y^{-5/3}}{x^2 y} \quad \text{Use the power rule and simplify}$$

$$= 32 x^{2-2} y^{-5/3 - 3/3} \quad \text{Apply the quotient rule.}$$

$$= 32 x^0 y^{-8/3}$$

$$= \frac{32}{y^{8/3}}$$

PRACTICE 4 Use properties of exponents to simplify.

a. $y^{2/3} \cdot y^{8/3}$ **b.** $x^{3/5} \cdot x^{1/4}$ **c.** $\dfrac{9^{2/7}}{9^{9/7}}$

d. $b^{4/9} \cdot b^{-2/9}$ **e.** $\dfrac{(3x^{1/4} y^{-2/3})^4}{x^4 y}$

EXAMPLE 5 Multiply.

a. $z^{2/3}(z^{1/3} - z^5)$ **b.** $(x^{1/3} - 5)(x^{1/3} + 2)$

Solution

a. $z^{2/3}(z^{1/3} - z^5) = z^{2/3}z^{1/3} - z^{2/3}z^5$ Apply the distributive property.
$= z^{(2/3+1/3)} - z^{(2/3+5)}$ Use the product rule.
$= z^{3/3} - z^{(2/3+15/3)}$
$= z - z^{17/3}$

b. $(x^{1/3} - 5)(x^{1/3} + 2) = x^{2/3} + 2x^{1/3} - 5x^{1/3} - 10$ Think of $(x^{1/3} - 5)$ and $(x^{1/3} + 2)$ as 2 binomials, and FOIL.
$= x^{2/3} - 3x^{1/3} - 10$

PRACTICE 5 Multiply.

a. $x^{3/5}(x^{1/3} - x^2)$ **b.** $(x^{1/2} + 6)(x^{1/2} - 2)$

EXAMPLE 6 Factor $x^{-1/2}$ from the expression $3x^{-1/2} - 7x^{5/2}$. Assume that all variables represent positive numbers.

Solution

$3x^{-1/2} - 7x^{5/2} = (x^{-1/2})(3) - (x^{-1/2})(7x^{6/2})$
$= x^{-1/2}(3 - 7x^3)$

To check, multiply $x^{-1/2}(3 - 7x^3)$ to see that the product is $3x^{-1/2} - 7x^{5/2}$.

PRACTICE 6 Factor $x^{-1/5}$ from the expression $2x^{-1/5} - 7x^{4/5}$.

OBJECTIVE 5 ▶ Using rational exponents to simplify radical expressions. Some radical expressions are easier to simplify when we first write them with rational exponents. We can simplify some radical expressions by first writing the expression with rational exponents. Use properties of exponents to simplify, and then convert back to radical notation.

EXAMPLE 7 Use rational exponents to simplify. Assume that variables represent positive numbers.

a. $\sqrt[8]{x^4}$ **b.** $\sqrt[6]{25}$ **c.** $\sqrt[4]{r^2s^6}$

Solution

a. $\sqrt[8]{x^4} = x^{4/8} = x^{1/2} = \sqrt{x}$
b. $\sqrt[6]{25} = 25^{1/6} = (5^2)^{1/6} = 5^{2/6} = 5^{1/3} = \sqrt[3]{5}$
c. $\sqrt[4]{r^2s^6} = (r^2s^6)^{1/4} = r^{2/4}s^{6/4} = r^{1/2}s^{3/2} = (rs^3)^{1/2} = \sqrt{rs^3}$

PRACTICE 7 Use rational exponents to simplify. Assume that the variables represent positive numbers.

a. $\sqrt[9]{x^3}$ **b.** $\sqrt[4]{36}$ **c.** $\sqrt[8]{a^4b^2}$

EXAMPLE 8 Use rational exponents to write as a single radical.

a. $\sqrt{x} \cdot \sqrt[4]{x}$ **b.** $\dfrac{\sqrt{x}}{\sqrt[3]{x}}$ **c.** $\sqrt[3]{3} \cdot \sqrt{2}$

Solution

a. $\sqrt{x} \cdot \sqrt[4]{x} = x^{1/2} \cdot x^{1/4} = x^{1/2+1/4}$
$= x^{3/4} = \sqrt[4]{x^3}$

b. $\dfrac{\sqrt{x}}{\sqrt[3]{x}} = \dfrac{x^{1/2}}{x^{1/3}} = x^{1/2-1/3} = x^{3/6-2/6}$
$= x^{1/6} = \sqrt[6]{x}$

c. $\sqrt[3]{3} \cdot \sqrt{2} = 3^{1/3} \cdot 2^{1/2}$ Write with rational exponents.
$= 3^{2/6} \cdot 2^{3/6}$ Write the exponents so that they have the same denominator.
$= (3^2 \cdot 2^3)^{1/6}$ Use $a^n b^n = (ab)^n$
$= \sqrt[6]{3^2 \cdot 2^3}$ Write with radical notation.
$= \sqrt[6]{72}$ Multiply $3^2 \cdot 2^3$.

PRACTICE 8 Use rational expressions to write each of the following as a single radical.

a. $\sqrt[3]{x} \cdot \sqrt[4]{x}$ b. $\dfrac{\sqrt[3]{y}}{\sqrt[5]{y}}$ c. $\sqrt[3]{5} \cdot \sqrt{3}$

VOCABULARY & READINESS CHECK

True or False. *Answer each true or false.*

1. $9^{-1/2}$ is a positive number. _____
2. $9^{-1/2}$ is a whole number. _____
3. $\dfrac{1}{a^{-m/n}} = a^{m/n}$ (where $a^{m/n}$ is a nonzero real number). _____

Multiple Choice. *Fill in the blank with the correct choice.*

4. To simplify $x^{2/3} \cdot x^{1/5}$, _____ the exponents.
   a. add   b. subtract   c. multiply   d. divide
5. To simplify $(x^{2/3})^{1/5}$, _____ the exponents.
   a. add   b. subtract   c. multiply   d. divide
6. To simplify $\dfrac{x^{2/3}}{x^{1/5}}$, _____ the exponents.
   a. add   b. subtract   c. multiply   d. divide

Multiple Choice. *Choose the correct letter for each exercise. Letters will be used more than once. No pencil is needed. Just think about the meaning of each expression.*

A = 2, B = −2, C = not a real number

7. $4^{1/2}$ ___   8. $-4^{1/2}$ ___   9. $(-4)^{1/2}$ ___   10. $8^{1/3}$ ___   11. $-8^{1/3}$ ___   12. $(-8)^{1/3}$ ___

8.2 EXERCISE SET

Use radical notation to write each expression. Simplify if possible. See Example 1.

1. $49^{1/2}$
2. $64^{1/3}$
3. $27^{1/3}$
4. $8^{1/3}$
5. $\left(\dfrac{1}{16}\right)^{1/4}$
6. $\left(\dfrac{1}{64}\right)^{1/2}$
7. $169^{1/2}$
8. $81^{1/4}$
9. $2m^{1/3}$
10. $(2m)^{1/3}$

11. $(9x^4)^{1/2}$
12. $(16x^8)^{1/2}$
13. $(-27)^{1/3}$
14. $-64^{1/2}$
15. $-16^{1/4}$
16. $(-32)^{1/5}$

Use radical notation to write each expression. Simplify if possible. See Example 2.

17. $16^{3/4}$
18. $4^{5/2}$
19. $(-64)^{2/3}$
20. $(-8)^{4/3}$
21. $(-16)^{3/4}$
22. $(-9)^{3/2}$
23. $(2x)^{3/5}$
24. $2x^{3/5}$
25. $(7x+2)^{2/3}$
26. $(x-4)^{3/4}$
27. $\left(\dfrac{16}{9}\right)^{3/2}$
28. $\left(\dfrac{49}{25}\right)^{3/2}$

Write with positive exponents. Simplify if possible. See Example 3.

29. $8^{-4/3}$
30. $64^{-2/3}$
31. $(-64)^{-2/3}$
32. $(-8)^{-4/3}$
33. $(-4)^{-3/2}$
34. $(-16)^{-5/4}$
35. $x^{-1/4}$
36. $y^{-1/6}$
37. $\dfrac{1}{a^{-2/3}}$
38. $\dfrac{1}{n^{-8/9}}$
39. $\dfrac{5}{7x^{-3/4}}$
40. $\dfrac{2}{3y^{-5/7}}$

Use the properties of exponents to simplify each expression. Write with positive exponents. See Example 4.

41. $a^{2/3} a^{5/3}$
42. $b^{9/5} b^{8/5}$
43. $x^{-2/5} \cdot x^{7/5}$
44. $y^{4/3} \cdot y^{-1/3}$
45. $3^{1/4} \cdot 3^{3/8}$
46. $5^{1/2} \cdot 5^{1/6}$
47. $\dfrac{y^{1/3}}{y^{1/6}}$
48. $\dfrac{x^{3/4}}{x^{1/8}}$
49. $(4u^2)^{3/2}$
50. $(32^{1/5} x^{2/3})^3$
51. $\dfrac{b^{1/2} b^{3/4}}{-b^{1/4}}$
52. $\dfrac{a^{1/4} a^{-1/2}}{a^{2/3}}$
53. $\dfrac{(x^3)^{1/2}}{x^{7/2}}$
54. $\dfrac{y^{11/3}}{(y^5)^{1/3}}$
55. $\dfrac{(3x^{1/4})^3}{x^{1/12}}$
56. $\dfrac{(2x^{1/5})^4}{x^{3/10}}$
57. $\dfrac{(y^3 z)^{1/6}}{y^{-1/2} z^{1/3}}$
58. $\dfrac{(m^2 n)^{1/4}}{m^{-1/2} n^{5/8}}$
59. $\dfrac{(x^3 y^2)^{1/4}}{(x^{-5} y^{-1})^{-1/2}}$
60. $\dfrac{(a^{-2} b)^{1/8}}{(a^{-3} b)^{-1/4}}$

Multiply. See Example 5.

61. $y^{1/2}(y^{1/2} - y^{2/3})$
62. $x^{1/2}(x^{1/2} + x^{3/2})$
63. $x^{2/3}(x - 2)$
64. $3x^{1/2}(x + y)$
65. $(2x^{1/3} + 3)(2x^{1/3} - 3)$
66. $(y^{1/2} + 5)(y^{1/2} + 5)$

Factor the common factor from the given expression. See Example 6.

67. $x^{8/3}$; $x^{8/3} + x^{10/3}$
68. $x^{3/2}$; $x^{5/2} - x^{3/2}$
69. $x^{1/5}$; $x^{2/5} - 3x^{1/5}$
70. $x^{2/7}$; $x^{3/7} - 2x^{2/7}$
71. $x^{-1/3}$; $5x^{-1/3} + x^{2/3}$
72. $x^{-3/4}$; $x^{-3/4} + 3x^{1/4}$

Use rational exponents to simplify each radical. Assume that all variables represent positive numbers. See Example 7.

73. $\sqrt[6]{x^3}$
74. $\sqrt[9]{a^3}$
75. $\sqrt[6]{4}$
76. $\sqrt[4]{36}$
77. $\sqrt[4]{16x^2}$
78. $\sqrt[8]{4y^2}$
79. $\sqrt[8]{x^4 y^4}$
80. $\sqrt[9]{y^6 z^3}$
81. $\sqrt[12]{a^8 b^4}$
82. $\sqrt[10]{a^5 b^5}$
83. $\sqrt[4]{(x+3)^2}$
84. $\sqrt[8]{(y+1)^4}$

Use rational expressions to write as a single radical expression. See Example 8.

85. $\sqrt[3]{y} \cdot \sqrt[5]{y^2}$
86. $\sqrt[3]{y^2} \cdot \sqrt[6]{y}$
87. $\dfrac{\sqrt[3]{b^2}}{\sqrt[4]{b}}$
88. $\dfrac{\sqrt[4]{a}}{\sqrt[5]{a}}$
89. $\sqrt[3]{x} \cdot \sqrt[4]{x} \cdot \sqrt[8]{x^3}$
90. $\sqrt[6]{y} \cdot \sqrt[3]{y} \cdot \sqrt[5]{y^2}$
91. $\dfrac{\sqrt[3]{a^2}}{\sqrt[6]{a}}$
92. $\dfrac{\sqrt[5]{b^2}}{\sqrt[10]{b^3}}$
93. $\sqrt{3} \cdot \sqrt[3]{4}$
94. $\sqrt[3]{5} \cdot \sqrt{2}$
95. $\sqrt[5]{7} \cdot \sqrt[3]{y}$
96. $\sqrt[4]{5} \cdot \sqrt[3]{x}$
97. $\sqrt{5r} \cdot \sqrt[3]{s}$
98. $\sqrt[3]{b} \cdot \sqrt[5]{4a}$

REVIEW AND PREVIEW

Write each integer as a product of two integers such that one of the factors is a perfect square. For example, write 18 as $9 \cdot 2$, because 9 is a perfect square.

99. 75
100. 20
101. 48
102. 45

Write each integer as a product of two integers such that one of the factors is a perfect cube. For example, write 24 as $8 \cdot 3$, because 8 is a perfect cube.

103. 16
104. 56
105. 54
106. 80

CONCEPT EXTENSIONS

Basal metabolic rate (BMR) is the number of calories per day a person needs to maintain life. A person's basal metabolic rate $B(w)$ in calories per day can be estimated with the function $B(w) = 70w^{3/4}$, where w is the person's weight in kilograms. Use this information to answer Exercises 107 and 108.

107. Estimate the BMR for a person who weighs 60 kilograms. Round to the nearest calorie. (*Note:* 60 kilograms is approximately 132 pounds.)

108. Estimate the BMR for a person who weighs 90 kilograms. Round to the nearest calorie. (*Note:* 90 kilograms is approximately 198 pounds.)

The number of cellular telephone subscriptions in the United States from 1996 through 2006 can be modeled by the function $f(x) = 33.3x^{4/5}$, where y is the number of cellular telephone subscriptions in millions, x years after 1996. (Source: Based on data from the Cellular Telecommunications & Internet Association, 1994–2000.) Use this information to answer Exercises 109 and 110.

109. Use this model to estimate the number of cellular telephone subscriptions in the United States in 2006. Round to the nearest tenth of a million.

110. Predict the number of cellular telephone subscriptions in the United States in 2010. Round to the nearest tenth of a million.

Fill in the Blank. *Fill in each box with the correct expression.*

111. $\square \cdot a^{2/3} = a^{3/3}$, or a

112. $\square \cdot x^{1/8} = x^{4/8}$, or $x^{1/2}$

113. $\dfrac{\square}{x^{-2/5}} = x^{3/5}$

114. $\dfrac{\square}{y^{-3/4}} = y^{4/4}$, or y

Use a calculator to write a four-decimal-place approximation of each number.

115. $8^{1/4}$ **116.** $20^{1/5}$

117. $18^{3/5}$ **118.** $76^{5/7}$

119. In physics, the speed of a wave traveling over a stretched string with tension t and density u is given by the expression $\dfrac{\sqrt{t}}{\sqrt{u}}$. Write this expression with rational exponents.

120. In electronics, the angular frequency of oscillations in a certain type of circuit is given by the expression $(LC)^{-1/2}$. Use radical notation to write this expression.

8.3 SIMPLIFYING RADICAL EXPRESSIONS

OBJECTIVES

1. Use the product rule for radicals.
2. Use the quotient rule for radicals.
3. Simplify radicals.
4. Use the distance and midpoint formula.

OBJECTIVE 1 ▶ Using the product rule. It is possible to simplify some radicals that do not evaluate to rational numbers. To do so, we use a product rule and a quotient rule for radicals. To discover the product rule, notice the following pattern.

$$\sqrt{9} \cdot \sqrt{4} = 3 \cdot 2 = 6$$
$$\sqrt{9 \cdot 4} = \sqrt{36} = 6$$

Since both expressions simplify to 6, it is true that

$$\sqrt{9} \cdot \sqrt{4} = \sqrt{9 \cdot 4}$$

This pattern suggests the following product rule for radicals.

Product Rule for Radicals

If $\sqrt[n]{a}$ and $\sqrt[n]{b}$ are real numbers, then

$$\sqrt[n]{a} \cdot \sqrt[n]{b} = \sqrt[n]{ab}$$

Notice that the product rule is the relationship $a^{1/n} \cdot b^{1/n} = (ab)^{1/n}$ stated in radical notation.

EXAMPLE 1 Multiply.

a. $\sqrt{3} \cdot \sqrt{5}$
b. $\sqrt{21} \cdot \sqrt{x}$
c. $\sqrt[3]{4} \cdot \sqrt[3]{2}$
d. $\sqrt[4]{5y^2} \cdot \sqrt[4]{2x^3}$
e. $\sqrt{\dfrac{2}{a}} \cdot \sqrt{\dfrac{b}{3}}$

Solution

a. $\sqrt{3} \cdot \sqrt{5} = \sqrt{3 \cdot 5} = \sqrt{15}$
b. $\sqrt{21} \cdot \sqrt{x} = \sqrt{21x}$
c. $\sqrt[3]{4} \cdot \sqrt[3]{2} = \sqrt[3]{4 \cdot 2} = \sqrt[3]{8} = 2$
d. $\sqrt[4]{5y^2} \cdot \sqrt[4]{2x^3} = \sqrt[4]{5y^2 \cdot 2x^3} = \sqrt[4]{10y^2x^3}$
e. $\sqrt{\dfrac{2}{a}} \cdot \sqrt{\dfrac{b}{3}} = \sqrt{\dfrac{2}{a} \cdot \dfrac{b}{3}} = \sqrt{\dfrac{2b}{3a}}$

PRACTICE 1 Multiply.

a. $\sqrt{5} \cdot \sqrt{7}$
b. $\sqrt{13} \cdot \sqrt{z}$
c. $\sqrt[4]{125} \cdot \sqrt[4]{5}$
d. $\sqrt[3]{5y} \cdot \sqrt[3]{3x^2}$
e. $\sqrt{\dfrac{5}{m}} \cdot \sqrt{\dfrac{t}{2}}$

OBJECTIVE 2 ▶ Using the quotient rule. To discover a quotient rule for radicals, notice the following pattern.

$$\sqrt{\dfrac{4}{9}} = \dfrac{2}{3}$$

$$\dfrac{\sqrt{4}}{\sqrt{9}} = \dfrac{2}{3}$$

Since both expressions simplify to $\dfrac{2}{3}$, it is true that

$$\sqrt{\dfrac{4}{9}} = \dfrac{\sqrt{4}}{\sqrt{9}}$$

This pattern suggests the following quotient rule for radicals.

Quotient Rule for Radicals

If $\sqrt[n]{a}$ and $\sqrt[n]{b}$ are real numbers and $\sqrt[n]{b}$ is not zero, then

$$\sqrt[n]{\dfrac{a}{b}} = \dfrac{\sqrt[n]{a}}{\sqrt[n]{b}}$$

Notice that the quotient rule is the relationship $\left(\dfrac{a}{b}\right)^{1/n} = \dfrac{a^{1/n}}{b^{1/n}}$ stated in radical notation. We can use the quotient rule to simplify radical expressions by reading the rule from left to right, or to divide radicals by reading the rule from right to left.

Section 8.3 Simplifying Radical Expressions   459

For example,

$$\sqrt{\frac{x}{16}} = \frac{\sqrt{x}}{\sqrt{16}} = \frac{\sqrt{x}}{4} \quad \text{Using } \sqrt[n]{\frac{a}{b}} = \frac{\sqrt[n]{a}}{\sqrt[n]{b}}$$

$$\frac{\sqrt{75}}{\sqrt{3}} = \sqrt{\frac{75}{3}} = \sqrt{25} = 5 \quad \text{Using } \frac{\sqrt[n]{a}}{\sqrt[n]{b}} = \sqrt[n]{\frac{a}{b}}$$

Note: Recall that from Section 8.2 on, we assume that variables represent positive real numbers. Since this is so, we need not insert absolute value bars when we simplify even roots.

EXAMPLE 2   Use the quotient rule to simplify.

a. $\sqrt{\dfrac{25}{49}}$ b. $\sqrt{\dfrac{x}{9}}$ c. $\sqrt[3]{\dfrac{8}{27}}$ d. $\sqrt[4]{\dfrac{3}{16y^4}}$

Solution

a. $\sqrt{\dfrac{25}{49}} = \dfrac{\sqrt{25}}{\sqrt{49}} = \dfrac{5}{7}$ b. $\sqrt{\dfrac{x}{9}} = \dfrac{\sqrt{x}}{\sqrt{9}} = \dfrac{\sqrt{x}}{3}$

c. $\sqrt[3]{\dfrac{8}{27}} = \dfrac{\sqrt[3]{8}}{\sqrt[3]{27}} = \dfrac{2}{3}$ d. $\sqrt[4]{\dfrac{3}{16y^4}} = \dfrac{\sqrt[4]{3}}{\sqrt[4]{16y^4}} = \dfrac{\sqrt[4]{3}}{2y}$

PRACTICE 2   Use the quotient rule to simplify.

a. $\sqrt{\dfrac{36}{49}}$ b. $\sqrt{\dfrac{z}{16}}$ c. $\sqrt[3]{\dfrac{125}{8}}$ d. $\sqrt[4]{\dfrac{5}{81x^8}}$

OBJECTIVE 3 ▶ Simplifying radicals. Both the product and quotient rules can be used to simplify a radical. If the product rule is read from right to left, we have that

$$\sqrt[n]{ab} = \sqrt[n]{a} \cdot \sqrt[n]{b}.$$

This is used to simplify the following radicals.

EXAMPLE 3   Simplify the following.

a. $\sqrt{50}$ b. $\sqrt[3]{24}$ c. $\sqrt{26}$ d. $\sqrt[4]{32}$

Solution

a. Factor 50 such that one factor is the largest perfect square that divides 50. The largest perfect square factor of 50 is 25, so we write 50 as $25 \cdot 2$ and use the product rule for radicals to simplify.

$$\sqrt{50} = \sqrt{25 \cdot 2} = \sqrt{25} \cdot \sqrt{2} = 5\sqrt{2}$$
↑ The largest perfect square factor of 50

▶ **Helpful Hint**
Don't forget that, for example, $5\sqrt{2}$ means $5 \cdot \sqrt{2}$.

b. $\sqrt[3]{24} = \sqrt[3]{8 \cdot 3} = \sqrt[3]{8} \cdot \sqrt[3]{3} = 2\sqrt[3]{3}$
   ↑ The largest perfect cube factor of 24

c. $\sqrt{26}$ The largest perfect square factor of 26 is 1, so $\sqrt{26}$ cannot be simplified further.

d. $\sqrt[4]{32} = \sqrt[4]{16 \cdot 2} = \sqrt[4]{16} \cdot \sqrt[4]{2} = 2\sqrt[4]{2}$
   ↑ The largest fourth power factor of 32

PRACTICE 3   Simplify the following.

a. $\sqrt{98}$ b. $\sqrt[3]{54}$ c. $\sqrt{35}$ d. $\sqrt[4]{243}$

After simplifying a radical such as a square root, always check the radicand to see that it contains no other perfect square factors. It may, if the largest perfect square factor of the radicand was not originally recognized. For example,

$$\sqrt{200} = \sqrt{4 \cdot 50} = \sqrt{4} \cdot \sqrt{50} = 2\sqrt{50}$$

Notice that the radicand 50 still contains the perfect square factor 25. This is because 4 is not the largest perfect square factor of 200. We continue as follows.

$$2\sqrt{50} = 2\sqrt{25 \cdot 2} = 2 \cdot \sqrt{25} \cdot \sqrt{2} = 2 \cdot 5 \cdot \sqrt{2} = 10\sqrt{2}$$

The radical is now simplified since 2 contains no perfect square factors (other than 1).

> **Helpful Hint**
> To help you recognize largest perfect power factors of a radicand, it will help if you are familiar with some perfect powers. A few are listed below.
> Perfect Squares   1,   4,   9,   16, 25, 36, 49, 64, 81, 100, 121, 144
> 1^2 2^2 3^2 4^2 5^2 6^2 7^2 8^2 9^2 10^2 11^2 12^2
> Perfect Cubes   1,   8,   27, 64, 125
> 1^3 2^3 3^3 4^3 5^3
> Perfect Fourth   1,   16, 81, 256
> Powers 1^4 2^4 3^4 4^4

In general, we say that a radicand of the form $\sqrt[n]{a}$ is simplified when the radicand a contains no factors that are perfect nth powers (other than 1 or -1).

EXAMPLE 4 Use the product rule to simplify.

a. $\sqrt{25x^3}$ b. $\sqrt[3]{54x^6y^8}$ c. $\sqrt[4]{81z^{11}}$

Solution

a. $\sqrt{25x^3} = \sqrt{25x^2 \cdot x}$ Find the largest perfect square factor.
   $= \sqrt{25x^2} \cdot \sqrt{x}$ Apply the product rule.
   $= 5x\sqrt{x}$ Simplify.

b. $\sqrt[3]{54x^6y^8} = \sqrt[3]{27 \cdot 2 \cdot x^6 \cdot y^6 \cdot y^2}$ Factor the radicand and identify perfect cube factors.
   $= \sqrt[3]{27x^6y^6 \cdot 2y^2}$
   $= \sqrt[3]{27x^6y^6} \cdot \sqrt[3]{2y^2}$ Apply the product rule.
   $= 3x^2y^2\sqrt[3]{2y^2}$ Simplify.

c. $\sqrt[4]{81z^{11}} = \sqrt[4]{81 \cdot z^8 \cdot z^3}$ Factor the radicand and identify perfect fourth power factors.
   $= \sqrt[4]{81z^8} \cdot \sqrt[4]{z^3}$ Apply the product rule.
   $= 3z^2\sqrt[4]{z^3}$ Simplify.

PRACTICE 4 Use the product rule to simplify.

a. $\sqrt{36z^7}$ b. $\sqrt[3]{32p^4q^7}$ c. $\sqrt[4]{16x^{15}}$

Section 8.3 Simplifying Radical Expressions **461**

EXAMPLE 5 Use the quotient rule to divide, and simplify if possible.

a. $\dfrac{\sqrt{20}}{\sqrt{5}}$ b. $\dfrac{\sqrt{50x}}{2\sqrt{2}}$ c. $\dfrac{7\sqrt[3]{48x^4y^8}}{\sqrt[3]{6y^2}}$ d. $\dfrac{2\sqrt[4]{32a^8b^6}}{\sqrt[4]{a^{-1}b^2}}$

Solution

a. $\dfrac{\sqrt{20}}{\sqrt{5}} = \sqrt{\dfrac{20}{5}}$ Apply the quotient rule.

$\phantom{\dfrac{\sqrt{20}}{\sqrt{5}}} = \sqrt{4}$ Simplify.

$\phantom{\dfrac{\sqrt{20}}{\sqrt{5}}} = 2$ Simplify.

b. $\dfrac{\sqrt{50x}}{2\sqrt{2}} = \dfrac{1}{2} \cdot \sqrt{\dfrac{50x}{2}}$ Apply the quotient rule.

$\phantom{\dfrac{\sqrt{50x}}{2\sqrt{2}}} = \dfrac{1}{2} \cdot \sqrt{25x}$ Simplify.

$\phantom{\dfrac{\sqrt{50x}}{2\sqrt{2}}} = \dfrac{1}{2} \cdot \sqrt{25} \cdot \sqrt{x}$ Factor $25x$.

$\phantom{\dfrac{\sqrt{50x}}{2\sqrt{2}}} = \dfrac{1}{2} \cdot 5 \cdot \sqrt{x}$ Simplify.

$\phantom{\dfrac{\sqrt{50x}}{2\sqrt{2}}} = \dfrac{5}{2}\sqrt{x}$

c. $\dfrac{7\sqrt[3]{48x^4y^8}}{\sqrt[3]{6y^2}} = 7 \cdot \sqrt[3]{\dfrac{48x^4y^8}{6y^2}}$ Apply the quotient rule.

$\phantom{\dfrac{7\sqrt[3]{48x^4y^8}}{\sqrt[3]{6y^2}}} = 7 \cdot \sqrt[3]{8x^4y^6}$ Simplify.

$\phantom{\dfrac{7\sqrt[3]{48x^4y^8}}{\sqrt[3]{6y^2}}} = 7\sqrt[3]{8x^3y^6 \cdot x}$ Factor.

$\phantom{\dfrac{7\sqrt[3]{48x^4y^8}}{\sqrt[3]{6y^2}}} = 7 \cdot \sqrt[3]{8x^3y^6} \cdot \sqrt[3]{x}$ Apply the product rule.

$\phantom{\dfrac{7\sqrt[3]{48x^4y^8}}{\sqrt[3]{6y^2}}} = 7 \cdot 2xy^2 \cdot \sqrt[3]{x}$ Simplify.

$\phantom{\dfrac{7\sqrt[3]{48x^4y^8}}{\sqrt[3]{6y^2}}} = 14xy^2\sqrt[3]{x}$

d. $\dfrac{2\sqrt[4]{32a^8b^6}}{\sqrt[4]{a^{-1}b^2}} = 2\sqrt[4]{\dfrac{32a^8b^6}{a^{-1}b^2}} = 2\sqrt[4]{32a^9b^4} = 2\sqrt[4]{16 \cdot a^8 \cdot b^4 \cdot 2 \cdot a}$

$\phantom{\dfrac{2\sqrt[4]{32a^8b^6}}{\sqrt[4]{a^{-1}b^2}}} = 2\sqrt[4]{16a^8b^4} \cdot \sqrt[4]{2a} = 2 \cdot 2a^2b \cdot \sqrt[4]{2a} = 4a^2b\sqrt[4]{2a}$

PRACTICE 5 Use the quotient rule to divide and simplify.

a. $\dfrac{\sqrt{80}}{\sqrt{5}}$ b. $\dfrac{\sqrt{98z}}{3\sqrt{2}}$ c. $\dfrac{5\sqrt[3]{40x^5y^7}}{\sqrt[3]{5y}}$ d. $\dfrac{3\sqrt[5]{64x^9y^8}}{\sqrt[5]{x^{-1}y^2}}$

Concept Check ✓

Find and correct the error:

$$\dfrac{\sqrt[3]{27}}{\sqrt{9}} = \sqrt[3]{\dfrac{27}{9}} = \sqrt[3]{3}$$

Answer to Concept Check:

$\dfrac{\sqrt[3]{27}}{\sqrt{9}} = \dfrac{3}{3} = 1$

OBJECTIVE 4 ▶ Using the distance and midpoint formulas. Now that we know how to simplify radicals, we can derive and use the distance formula. The midpoint formula is often confused with the distance formula, so to clarify both, we will also review the midpoint formula.

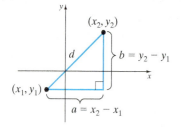

The Cartesian coordinate system helps us visualize a distance between points. To find the distance between two points, we use the distance formula, which is derived from the Pythagorean theorem.

To find the distance d between two points (x_1, y_1) and (x_2, y_2) as shown to the left, notice that the length of leg a is $x_2 - x_1$ and that the length of leg b is $y_2 - y_1$.

Thus, the Pythagorean theorem tells us that

$$d^2 = a^2 + b^2$$

or

$$d^2 = (x_2 - x_1)^2 + (y_2 - y_1)^2$$

or

$$d = \sqrt{(x_2 - x_1)^2 + (y_2 - y_1)^2}$$

This formula gives us the distance between any two points on the real plane.

Distance Formula

The distance d between two points (x_1, y_1) and (x_2, y_2) is given by

$$d = \sqrt{(x_2 - x_1)^2 + (y_2 - y_1)^2}$$

EXAMPLE 6 Find the distance between $(2, -5)$ and $(1, -4)$. Give an exact distance and a three-decimal-place approximation.

Solution To use the distance formula, it makes no difference which point we call (x_1, y_1) and which point we call (x_2, y_2). We will let $(x_1, y_1) = (2, -5)$ and $(x_2, y_2) = (1, -4)$.

$$\begin{aligned} d &= \sqrt{(x_2 - x_1)^2 + (y_2 - y_1)^2} \\ &= \sqrt{(1 - 2)^2 + [-4 - (-5)]^2} \\ &= \sqrt{(-1)^2 + (1)^2} \\ &= \sqrt{1 + 1} \\ &= \sqrt{2} \approx 1.414 \end{aligned}$$

The distance between the two points is exactly $\sqrt{2}$ units, or approximately 1.414 units.

PRACTICE

6 Find the distance between $P(-3, 7)$ and $Q(-2, 3)$. Give an exact distance and a three-decimal-place approximation.

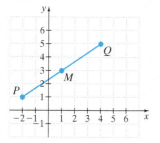

The **midpoint** of a line segment is the **point** located exactly halfway between the two endpoints of the line segment. On the graph to the left, the point M is the midpoint of line segment PQ. Thus, the distance between M and P equals the distance between M and Q.

Note: We usually need no knowledge of roots to calculate the midpoint of a line segment. We review midpoint here only because it is often confused with the distance between two points.

The x-coordinate of M is at half the distance between the x-coordinates of P and Q, and the y-coordinate of M is at half the distance between the y-coordinates of P and Q. That is, the x-coordinate of M is the average of the x-coordinates of P and Q; the y-coordinate of M is the average of the y-coordinates of P and Q.

Section 8.3 Simplifying Radical Expressions 463

> **Midpoint Formula**
> The midpoint of the line segment whose endpoints are (x_1, y_1) and (x_2, y_2) is the point with coordinates
> $$\left(\frac{x_1 + x_2}{2}, \frac{y_1 + y_2}{2}\right)$$

EXAMPLE 7 Find the midpoint of the line segment that joins points $P(-3, 3)$ and $Q(1, 0)$.

Solution Use the midpoint formula. It makes no difference which point we call (x_1, y_1) or which point we call (x_2, y_2). Let $(x_1, y_1) = (-3, 3)$ and $(x_2, y_2) = (1, 0)$.

$$\text{midpoint} = \left(\frac{x_1 + x_2}{2}, \frac{y_1 + y_2}{2}\right)$$
$$= \left(\frac{-3 + 1}{2}, \frac{3 + 0}{2}\right)$$
$$= \left(\frac{-2}{2}, \frac{3}{2}\right)$$
$$= \left(-1, \frac{3}{2}\right)$$

The midpoint of the segment is $\left(-1, \frac{3}{2}\right)$.

PRACTICE 7 Find the midpoint of the line segment that joins points $P(5, -2)$ and $Q(8, -6)$.

> **Helpful Hint**
> The distance between two points is a distance. The midpoint of a line segment is the point halfway between the endpoints of the segment.
>
> distance—measured in units
>
> midpoint—it is a point

VOCABULARY & READINESS CHECK

Word Bank. *Use the choices below to fill in each blank. Some choices may be used more than once.*

    distance   midpoint   point

1. The _____ of a line segment is a _____ exactly halfway between the two endpoints of the line segment.

2. The _____ formula is $d = \sqrt{(x_2 - x_1)^2 + (y_2 - y_1)^2}$.

3. The _____ formula is $\left(\frac{x_1 + x_2}{2}, \frac{y_1 + y_2}{2}\right)$.

464 CHAPTER 8 Rational Exponents, Radicals, and Complex Numbers

True or False. *Answer true or false. Assume all radicals represent nonzero real numbers.*

4. $\sqrt[n]{a} \cdot \sqrt[n]{b} = \sqrt[n]{ab}$ _____
5. $\sqrt[3]{7} \cdot \sqrt[3]{11} = \sqrt[3]{18}$ _____
6. $\sqrt[3]{7} \cdot \sqrt{11} = \sqrt{77}$ _____
7. $\sqrt{x^7 y^8} = \sqrt{x^7} \cdot \sqrt{y^8}$ _____
8. $\dfrac{\sqrt[n]{a}}{\sqrt[n]{b}} = \sqrt[n]{\dfrac{a}{b}}$ _____
9. $\dfrac{\sqrt[3]{12}}{\sqrt[3]{4}} = \sqrt[3]{8}$ _____
10. $\dfrac{\sqrt[n]{x^7}}{\sqrt[n]{x}} = \sqrt[n]{x^6}$ _____

8.3 EXERCISE SET

Use the product rule to multiply. See Example 1.

1. $\sqrt{7} \cdot \sqrt{2}$
2. $\sqrt{11} \cdot \sqrt{10}$
3. $\sqrt[4]{8} \cdot \sqrt[4]{2}$
4. $\sqrt[4]{27} \cdot \sqrt[4]{3}$
5. $\sqrt[3]{4} \cdot \sqrt[3]{9}$
6. $\sqrt[3]{10} \cdot \sqrt[3]{5}$
7. $\sqrt{2} \cdot \sqrt{3x}$
8. $\sqrt{3y} \cdot \sqrt{5x}$
9. $\sqrt{\dfrac{7}{x}} \cdot \sqrt{\dfrac{2}{y}}$
10. $\sqrt{\dfrac{6}{m}} \cdot \sqrt{\dfrac{n}{5}}$
11. $\sqrt[4]{4x^3} \cdot \sqrt[4]{5}$
12. $\sqrt[4]{ab^2} \cdot \sqrt[4]{27ab}$

Use the quotient rule to simplify. See Examples 2 and 3.

13. $\sqrt{\dfrac{6}{49}}$
14. $\sqrt{\dfrac{8}{81}}$
15. $\sqrt{\dfrac{2}{49}}$
16. $\sqrt{\dfrac{5}{121}}$
17. $\sqrt[4]{\dfrac{x^3}{16}}$
18. $\sqrt[4]{\dfrac{y}{81x^4}}$
19. $\sqrt[3]{\dfrac{4}{27}}$
20. $\sqrt[3]{\dfrac{3}{64}}$
21. $\sqrt[4]{\dfrac{8}{x^8}}$
22. $\sqrt[4]{\dfrac{a^3}{81}}$
23. $\sqrt[3]{\dfrac{2x}{81y^{12}}}$
24. $\sqrt[3]{\dfrac{3}{8x^6}}$
25. $\sqrt{\dfrac{x^2 y}{100}}$
26. $\sqrt{\dfrac{y^2 z}{36}}$
27. $\sqrt{\dfrac{5x^2}{4y^2}}$
28. $\sqrt{\dfrac{y^{10}}{9x^6}}$
29. $-\sqrt[3]{\dfrac{z^7}{27x^3}}$
30. $-\sqrt[3]{\dfrac{64a}{b^9}}$

Simplify. See Examples 3 and 4.

31. $\sqrt{32}$
32. $\sqrt{27}$
33. $\sqrt[3]{192}$
34. $\sqrt[3]{108}$
35. $5\sqrt{75}$
36. $3\sqrt{8}$
37. $\sqrt{24}$
38. $\sqrt{20}$
39. $\sqrt{100x^5}$
40. $\sqrt{64y^9}$
41. $\sqrt[3]{16y^7}$
42. $\sqrt[3]{64y^9}$
43. $\sqrt[4]{a^8 b^7}$
44. $\sqrt[5]{32z^{12}}$
45. $\sqrt{y^5}$
46. $\sqrt[3]{y^5}$
47. $\sqrt{25a^2 b^3}$
48. $\sqrt{9x^5 y^7}$
49. $\sqrt[5]{-32x^{10}y}$
50. $\sqrt[5]{-243z^9}$
51. $\sqrt[3]{50x^{14}}$
52. $\sqrt[3]{40y^{10}}$
53. $-\sqrt{32a^8 b^7}$
54. $-\sqrt{20ab^6}$
55. $\sqrt{9x^7 y^9}$
56. $\sqrt{12r^9 s^{12}}$
57. $\sqrt[3]{125r^9 s^{12}}$
58. $\sqrt[3]{8a^6 b^9}$

Use the quotient rule to divide. Then simplify if possible. See Example 5.

59. $\dfrac{\sqrt{14}}{\sqrt{7}}$
60. $\dfrac{\sqrt{45}}{\sqrt{9}}$
61. $\dfrac{\sqrt[3]{24}}{\sqrt[3]{3}}$
62. $\dfrac{\sqrt[3]{10}}{\sqrt[3]{2}}$
63. $\dfrac{5\sqrt[4]{48}}{\sqrt[4]{3}}$
64. $\dfrac{7\sqrt[4]{162}}{\sqrt[4]{2}}$
65. $\dfrac{\sqrt{x^5 y^3}}{\sqrt{xy}}$
66. $\dfrac{\sqrt{a^7 b^6}}{\sqrt{a^3 b^2}}$
67. $\dfrac{8\sqrt[3]{54m^7}}{\sqrt[3]{2m}}$
68. $\dfrac{\sqrt[3]{128x^3}}{-3\sqrt[3]{2x}}$
69. $\dfrac{3\sqrt{100x^2}}{2\sqrt{2x^{-1}}}$
70. $\dfrac{\sqrt{270y^2}}{5\sqrt{3y^{-4}}}$
71. $\dfrac{\sqrt[4]{96a^{10}b^3}}{\sqrt[4]{3a^2 b^3}}$
72. $\dfrac{\sqrt[5]{64x^{10}y^3}}{\sqrt[5]{2x^3 y^{-7}}}$

Find the distance between each pair of points. Give an exact distance and a three-decimal-place approximation. See Example 6.

73. (5, 1) and (8, 5)
74. (2, 3) and (14, 8)

75. $(-3, 2)$ and $(1, -3)$
76. $(3, -2)$ and $(-4, 1)$
77. $(-9, 4)$ and $(-8, 1)$
78. $(-5, -2)$ and $(-6, -6)$
79. $(0, -\sqrt{2})$ and $(\sqrt{3}, 0)$
80. $(-\sqrt{5}, 0)$ and $(0, \sqrt{7})$
81. $(1.7, -3.6)$ and $(-8.6, 5.7)$
82. $(9.6, 2.5)$ and $(-1.9, -3.7)$

Find the midpoint of the line segment whose endpoints are given. See Example 7.

83. $(6, -8), (2, 4)$
84. $(3, 9), (7, 11)$
85. $(-2, -1), (-8, 6)$
86. $(-3, -4), (6, -8)$
87. $(7, 3), (-1, -3)$
88. $(-2, 5), (-1, 6)$
89. $\left(\frac{1}{2}, \frac{3}{8}\right), \left(-\frac{3}{2}, \frac{5}{8}\right)$
90. $\left(-\frac{2}{5}, \frac{7}{15}\right), \left(-\frac{2}{5}, -\frac{4}{15}\right)$
91. $(\sqrt{2}, 3\sqrt{5}), (\sqrt{2}, -2\sqrt{5})$
92. $(\sqrt{8}, -\sqrt{12}), (3\sqrt{2}, 7\sqrt{3})$
93. $(4.6, -3.5), (7.8, -9.8)$
94. $(-4.6, 2.1), (-6.7, 1.9)$

REVIEW AND PREVIEW

Perform each indicated operation. See Sections 1.4 and 6.4.

95. $6x + 8x$
96. $(6x)(8x)$
97. $(2x + 3)(x - 5)$
98. $(2x + 3) + (x - 5)$
99. $9y^2 - 8y^2$
100. $(9y^2)(-8y^2)$
101. $-3(x + 5)$
102. $-3 + x + 5$
103. $(x - 4)^2$
104. $(2x + 1)^2$

CONCEPT EXTENSIONS

Find and correct the error. See a Concept Check in this section.

105. $\dfrac{\sqrt[3]{64}}{\sqrt{64}} = \sqrt[3]{\dfrac{64}{64}} = \sqrt[3]{1} = 1$

106. $\dfrac{\sqrt[4]{16}}{\sqrt{4}} = \sqrt[4]{\dfrac{16}{4}} = \sqrt[4]{4}$

Simplify. See a Concept Check in this section. Assume variables represent positive numbers.

107. $\sqrt[5]{x^{35}}$
108. $\sqrt[6]{y^{48}}$
109. $\sqrt[4]{a^{12}b^4c^{20}}$
110. $\sqrt[3]{a^9b^{21}c^3}$
111. $\sqrt[3]{z^{32}}$
112. $\sqrt[5]{x^{49}}$
113. $\sqrt[7]{q^{17}r^{40}s^7}$
114. $\sqrt[4]{p^{11}q^4r^{45}}$

115. The formula for the radius r of a sphere with surface area A is given by $r = \sqrt{\dfrac{A}{4\pi}}$. Calculate the radius of a standard zorb whose outside surface area is 32.17 sq m. Round to the nearest tenth. (See the chapter opener, page 412. *Source:* Zorb, Ltd.)

116. The formula for the surface area A of a cone with height h and radius r is given by
$$A = \pi r \sqrt{r^2 + h^2}$$

   a. Find the surface area of a cone whose height is 3 centimeters and whose radius is 4 centimeters.

   b. Approximate to two decimal places the surface area of a cone whose height is 7.2 feet and whose radius is 6.8 feet.

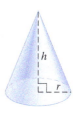

117. The owner of Knightime Video has determined that the demand equation for renting older releases is given by the equation $F(x) = 0.6\sqrt{49 - x^2}$, where x is the price in dollars per two-day rental and $F(x)$ is the number of times the video is demanded per week.

   a. Approximate to one decimal place the demand per week of an older release if the rental price is $3 per two-day rental.

   b. Approximate to one decimal place the demand per week of an older release if the rental price is $5 per two-day rental.

   c. Explain how the owner of the video store can use this equation to predict the number of copies of each tape that should be in stock.

118. Before Mount Vesuvius, a volcano in Italy, erupted violently in 79 A.D., its height was 4190 feet. Vesuvius was roughly cone-shaped, and its base had a radius of approximately 25,200 feet. Use the formula for the surface area of a cone, given in Exercise 116, to approximate the surface area this volcano had before it erupted. (*Source:* Global Volcanism Network)

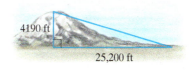

8.4 ADDING, SUBTRACTING, AND MULTIPLYING RADICAL EXPRESSIONS

OBJECTIVES

1. Add or subtract radical expressions.
2. Multiply radical expressions.

OBJECTIVE 1 ▶ Adding or subtracting radical expressions. We have learned that sums or differences of like terms can be simplified. To simplify these sums or differences, we use the distributive property. For example,

$$2x + 3x = (2 + 3)x = 5x \quad \text{and} \quad 7x^2y - 4x^2y = (7 - 4)x^2y = 3x^2y$$

The distributive property can also be used to add **like radicals**.

> **Like Radicals**
> Radicals with the same index and the same radicand are like radicals.

For example, $2\sqrt{7} + 3\sqrt{7} = (2 + 3)\sqrt{7} = 5\sqrt{7}$. Also,

$$\underbrace{5\sqrt{3x} - 7\sqrt{3x}}_{\text{Like radicals}} = (5 - 7)\sqrt{3x} = -2\sqrt{3x}$$

The expression $2\sqrt{7} + 2\sqrt[3]{7}$ cannot be simplified further since $2\sqrt{7}$ and $2\sqrt[3]{7}$ are not like radicals.

Unlike radicals

EXAMPLE 1 Add or subtract as indicated. Assume all variables represent positive real numbers.

a. $4\sqrt{11} + 8\sqrt{11}$ **b.** $5\sqrt[3]{3x} - 7\sqrt[3]{3x}$ **c.** $2\sqrt{7} + 2\sqrt[3]{7}$

Solution

a. $4\sqrt{11} + 8\sqrt{11} = (4 + 8)\sqrt{11} = 12\sqrt{11}$
b. $5\sqrt[3]{3x} - 7\sqrt[3]{3x} = (5 - 7)\sqrt[3]{3x} = -2\sqrt[3]{3x}$
c. $2\sqrt{7} + 2\sqrt[3]{7}$

This expression cannot be simplified since $2\sqrt{7}$ and $2\sqrt[3]{7}$ do not contain like radicals.

PRACTICE 1 Add or subtract as indicated.

a. $3\sqrt{17} + 5\sqrt{17}$ **b.** $7\sqrt[3]{5z} - 12\sqrt[3]{5z}$ **c.** $3\sqrt{2} + 5\sqrt[3]{2}$

When adding or subtracting radicals, always check first to see whether any radicals can be simplified.

Concept Check ✓
True or false?

$$\sqrt{a} + \sqrt{b} = \sqrt{a + b}$$

Explain.

Answer to Concept Check:
false; answers may vary

Section 8.4 Adding, Subtracting, and Multiplying Radical Expressions **467**

EXAMPLE 2 Add or subtract. Assume that variables represent positive real numbers.

a. $\sqrt{20} + 2\sqrt{45}$ **b.** $\sqrt[3]{54} - 5\sqrt[3]{16} + \sqrt[3]{2}$ **c.** $\sqrt{27x} - 2\sqrt{9x} + \sqrt{72x}$
d. $\sqrt[3]{98} + \sqrt{98}$ **e.** $\sqrt[3]{48y^4} + \sqrt[3]{6y^4}$

Solution First, simplify each radical. Then add or subtract any like radicals.

a. $\sqrt{20} + 2\sqrt{45} = \sqrt{4 \cdot 5} + 2\sqrt{9 \cdot 5}$ Factor 20 and 45.
$= \sqrt{4} \cdot \sqrt{5} + 2 \cdot \sqrt{9} \cdot \sqrt{5}$ Use the product rule.
$= 2 \cdot \sqrt{5} + 2 \cdot 3 \cdot \sqrt{5}$ Simplify $\sqrt{4}$ and $\sqrt{9}$.
$= 2\sqrt{5} + 6\sqrt{5}$ Add like radicals.
$= 8\sqrt{5}$

b. $\sqrt[3]{54} - 5\sqrt[3]{16} + \sqrt[3]{2}$
$= \sqrt[3]{27} \cdot \sqrt[3]{2} - 5 \cdot \sqrt[3]{8} \cdot \sqrt[3]{2} + \sqrt[3]{2}$ Factor and use the product rule.
$= 3 \cdot \sqrt[3]{2} - 5 \cdot 2 \cdot \sqrt[3]{2} + \sqrt[3]{2}$ Simplify $\sqrt[3]{27}$ and $\sqrt[3]{8}$.
$= 3\sqrt[3]{2} - 10\sqrt[3]{2} + \sqrt[3]{2}$ Write $5 \cdot 2$ as 10.
$= -6\sqrt[3]{2}$ Combine like radicals.

c. $\sqrt{27x} - 2\sqrt{9x} + \sqrt{72x}$
$= \sqrt{9} \cdot \sqrt{3x} - 2 \cdot \sqrt{9} \cdot \sqrt{x} + \sqrt{36} \cdot \sqrt{2x}$ Factor and use the product rule.
$= 3 \cdot \sqrt{3x} - 2 \cdot 3 \cdot \sqrt{x} + 6 \cdot \sqrt{2x}$ Simplify $\sqrt{9}$ and $\sqrt{36}$.
$= 3\sqrt{3x} - 6\sqrt{x} + 6\sqrt{2x}$ Write $2 \cdot 3$ as 6.

> **Helpful Hint**
> None of these terms contain like radicals. We can simplify no further.

d. $\sqrt[3]{98} + \sqrt{98} = \sqrt[3]{98} + \sqrt{49} \cdot \sqrt{2}$ Factor and use the product rule.
$= \sqrt[3]{98} + 7\sqrt{2}$ No further simplification is possible.

e. $\sqrt[3]{48y^4} + \sqrt[3]{6y^4} = \sqrt[3]{8y^3} \cdot \sqrt[3]{6y} + \sqrt[3]{y^3} \cdot \sqrt[3]{6y}$ Factor and use the product rule.
$= 2y\sqrt[3]{6y} + y\sqrt[3]{6y}$ Simplify $\sqrt[3]{8y^3}$ and $\sqrt[3]{y^3}$.
$= 3y\sqrt[3]{6y}$ Combine like radicals.

PRACTICE 2 Add or subtract.

a. $\sqrt{24} + 3\sqrt{54}$ **b.** $\sqrt[3]{24} - 4\sqrt[3]{81} + \sqrt[3]{3}$ **c.** $\sqrt{75x} - 3\sqrt{27x} + \sqrt{12x}$
d. $\sqrt{40} + \sqrt[3]{40}$ **e.** $\sqrt[3]{81x^4} + \sqrt[3]{3x^4}$

Let's continue to assume that variables represent positive real numbers.

EXAMPLE 3 Add or subtract as indicated.

a. $\dfrac{\sqrt{45}}{4} - \dfrac{\sqrt{5}}{3}$ **b.** $\sqrt[3]{\dfrac{7x}{8}} + 2\sqrt[3]{7x}$

Solution

a. $\dfrac{\sqrt{45}}{4} - \dfrac{\sqrt{5}}{3} = \dfrac{3\sqrt{5}}{4} - \dfrac{\sqrt{5}}{3}$ To subtract, notice that the LCD is 12.

$= \dfrac{3\sqrt{5} \cdot 3}{4 \cdot 3} - \dfrac{\sqrt{5} \cdot 4}{3 \cdot 4}$ Write each expression as an equivalent expression with a denominator of 12.

$= \dfrac{9\sqrt{5}}{12} - \dfrac{4\sqrt{5}}{12}$ Multiply factors in the numerator and the denominator.

$= \dfrac{5\sqrt{5}}{12}$ Subtract.

b. $\sqrt[3]{\dfrac{7x}{8}} + 2\sqrt[3]{7x} = \dfrac{\sqrt[3]{7x}}{\sqrt[3]{8}} + 2\sqrt[3]{7x}$ Apply the quotient rule for radicals.

$= \dfrac{\sqrt[3]{7x}}{2} + 2\sqrt[3]{7x}$ Simplify.

$= \dfrac{\sqrt[3]{7x}}{2} + \dfrac{2\sqrt[3]{7x} \cdot 2}{2}$ Write each expression as an equivalent expression with a denominator of 2.

$= \dfrac{\sqrt[3]{7x}}{2} + \dfrac{4\sqrt[3]{7x}}{2}$

$= \dfrac{5\sqrt[3]{7x}}{2}$ Add.

PRACTICE 3   Add or subtract as indicated.

a. $\dfrac{\sqrt{28}}{3} - \dfrac{\sqrt{7}}{4}$ **b.** $\sqrt[3]{\dfrac{6y}{64}} + 3\sqrt[3]{6y}$

OBJECTIVE 2 ▶ Multiplying radical expressions. We can multiply radical expressions by using many of the same properties used to multiply polynomial expressions. For instance, to multiply $\sqrt{2}(\sqrt{6} - 3\sqrt{2})$, we use the distributive property and multiply $\sqrt{2}$ by each term inside the parentheses.

$\sqrt{2}(\sqrt{6} - 3\sqrt{2}) = \sqrt{2}(\sqrt{6}) - \sqrt{2}(3\sqrt{2})$ Use the distributive property.
$= \sqrt{2 \cdot 6} - 3\sqrt{2 \cdot 2}$
$= \sqrt{2 \cdot 2 \cdot 3} - 3 \cdot 2$ Use the product rule for radicals.
$= 2\sqrt{3} - 6$

EXAMPLE 4   Multiply.

a. $\sqrt{3}(5 + \sqrt{30})$ **b.** $(\sqrt{5} - \sqrt{6})(\sqrt{7} + 1)$ **c.** $(7\sqrt{x} + 5)(3\sqrt{x} - \sqrt{5})$
d. $(4\sqrt{3} - 1)^2$ **e.** $(\sqrt{2x} - 5)(\sqrt{2x} + 5)$ **f.** $(\sqrt{x-3} + 5)^2$

Solution

a. $\sqrt{3}(5 + \sqrt{30}) = \sqrt{3}(5) + \sqrt{3}(\sqrt{30})$
$= 5\sqrt{3} + \sqrt{3 \cdot 30}$
$= 5\sqrt{3} + \sqrt{3 \cdot 3 \cdot 10}$
$= 5\sqrt{3} + 3\sqrt{10}$

b. To multiply, we can use the FOIL method.

$\phantom{(\sqrt{5} - \sqrt{6})(\sqrt{7} + 1) = }$ First   Outer   Inner   Last
$(\sqrt{5} - \sqrt{6})(\sqrt{7} + 1) = \sqrt{5} \cdot \sqrt{7} + \sqrt{5} \cdot 1 - \sqrt{6} \cdot \sqrt{7} - \sqrt{6} \cdot 1$
$= \sqrt{35} + \sqrt{5} - \sqrt{42} - \sqrt{6}$

c. $(7\sqrt{x} + 5)(3\sqrt{x} - \sqrt{5}) = 7\sqrt{x}(3\sqrt{x}) - 7\sqrt{x}(\sqrt{5}) + 5(3\sqrt{x}) - 5(\sqrt{5})$
$= 21x - 7\sqrt{5x} + 15\sqrt{x} - 5\sqrt{5}$

d. $(4\sqrt{3} - 1)^2 = (4\sqrt{3} - 1)(4\sqrt{3} - 1)$
$= 4\sqrt{3}(4\sqrt{3}) - 4\sqrt{3}(1) - 1(4\sqrt{3}) - 1(-1)$
$= 16 \cdot 3 - 4\sqrt{3} - 4\sqrt{3} + 1$
$= 48 - 8\sqrt{3} + 1$
$= 49 - 8\sqrt{3}$

Section 8.4 Adding, Subtracting, and Multiplying Radical Expressions 469

e. $(\sqrt{2x} - 5)(\sqrt{2x} + 5) = \sqrt{2x} \cdot \sqrt{2x} + 5\sqrt{2x} - 5\sqrt{2x} - 5 \cdot 5$
$= 2x - 25$

f. $(\sqrt{x-3} + 5)^2 = (\sqrt{x-3})^2 + 2 \cdot \sqrt{x-3} \cdot 5 + 5^2$

$\quad\quad\quad\quad a \quad\quad b \quad\quad\quad a^2 \quad + 2 \cdot\ a\ \cdot b + b^2$

$= x - 3 + 10\sqrt{x-3} + 25 \quad\quad$ Simplify.
$= x + 22 + 10\sqrt{x-3} \quad\quad$ Combine like terms.

PRACTICE 4 Multiply.

a. $\sqrt{5}(2 + \sqrt{15})$
b. $(\sqrt{2} - \sqrt{5})(\sqrt{6} + 2)$
c. $(3\sqrt{z} - 4)(2\sqrt{z} + 3)$
d. $(\sqrt{6} - 3)^2$
e. $(\sqrt{5x} + 3)(\sqrt{5x} - 3)$
f. $(\sqrt{x+2} + 3)^2$

VOCABULARY & READINESS CHECK

Complete a Table. *Complete the table with "Like" or "Unlike."*

	Terms	Like or Unlike Radical Terms?
1.	$\sqrt{7}, \sqrt[3]{7}$	
2.	$\sqrt[3]{x^2y}, \sqrt[3]{yx^2}$	
3.	$\sqrt[3]{abc}, \sqrt[3]{cba}$	
4.	$2x\sqrt{5}, 2x\sqrt{10}$	

Fill in the Blank. *Simplify. Assume that all variables represent positive real numbers.*

5. $2\sqrt{3} + 4\sqrt{3} =$ _____
6. $5\sqrt{7} + 3\sqrt{7} =$ _____
7. $8\sqrt{x} - \sqrt{x} =$ _____
8. $3\sqrt{y} - \sqrt{y} =$ _____
9. $7\sqrt[3]{x} + \sqrt[3]{x} =$ _____
10. $8\sqrt[3]{z} + \sqrt[3]{z} =$ _____

Fill in the Blank. *Add or subtract if possible.*

11. $\sqrt{11} + \sqrt[3]{11} =$ _____
12. $9\sqrt{13} - \sqrt[4]{13} =$ _____
13. $8\sqrt[3]{2x} + 3\sqrt[3]{2x} - \sqrt[3]{2x} =$ _____
14. $8\sqrt[3]{2x} + 3\sqrt[3]{2x^2} - \sqrt[3]{2x} =$ _____

8.4 EXERCISE SET

Add or subtract. See Examples 1 through 3.

1. $\sqrt{8} - \sqrt{32}$
2. $\sqrt{27} - \sqrt{75}$
3. $2\sqrt{2x^3} + 4x\sqrt{8x}$
4. $3\sqrt{45x^3} + x\sqrt{5x}$
5. $2\sqrt{50} - 3\sqrt{125} + \sqrt{98}$
6. $4\sqrt{32} - \sqrt{18} + 2\sqrt{128}$
7. $\sqrt[3]{16x} - \sqrt[3]{54x}$
8. $2\sqrt[3]{3a^4} - 3a\sqrt[3]{81a}$
9. $\sqrt{9b^3} - \sqrt{25b^3} + \sqrt{49b^3}$

10. $\sqrt{4x^7} + 9x^2\sqrt{x^3} - 5x\sqrt{x^5}$
11. $\dfrac{5\sqrt{2}}{3} + \dfrac{2\sqrt{2}}{5}$
12. $\dfrac{\sqrt{3}}{2} + \dfrac{4\sqrt{3}}{3}$
13. $\sqrt[3]{\dfrac{11}{8}} - \dfrac{\sqrt[3]{11}}{6}$
14. $\dfrac{2\sqrt[3]{4}}{7} - \dfrac{\sqrt[3]{4}}{14}$
15. $\dfrac{\sqrt{20x}}{9} + \sqrt{\dfrac{5x}{9}}$

16. $\dfrac{3x\sqrt{7}}{5} + \sqrt{\dfrac{7x^2}{100}}$

17. $7\sqrt{9} - 7 + \sqrt{3}$

18. $\sqrt{16} - 5\sqrt{10} + 7$

19. $2 + 3\sqrt{y^2} - 6\sqrt{y^2} + 5$

20. $3\sqrt{7} - \sqrt[3]{x} + 4\sqrt{7} - 3\sqrt[3]{x}$

21. $3\sqrt{108} - 2\sqrt{18} - 3\sqrt{48}$

22. $-\sqrt{75} + \sqrt{12} - 3\sqrt{3}$

23. $-5\sqrt[3]{625} + \sqrt[3]{40}$

24. $-2\sqrt[3]{108} - \sqrt[3]{32}$

25. $\sqrt{9b^3} - \sqrt{25b^3} + \sqrt{16b^3}$

26. $\sqrt{4x^7y^5} + 9x^2\sqrt{x^3y^5} - 5xy\sqrt{x^5y^3}$

27. $5y\sqrt{8y} + 2\sqrt{50y^3}$

28. $3\sqrt{8x^2y^3} - 2x\sqrt{32y^3}$

29. $\sqrt[3]{54xy^3} - 5\sqrt[3]{2xy^3} + y\sqrt[3]{128x}$

30. $2\sqrt[3]{24x^3y^4} + 4x\sqrt[3]{81y^4}$

31. $6\sqrt[3]{11} + 8\sqrt{11} - 12\sqrt{11}$

32. $3\sqrt[3]{5} + 4\sqrt{5}$

33. $-2\sqrt[4]{x^7} + 3\sqrt[4]{16x^7}$

34. $6\sqrt[3]{24x^3} - 2\sqrt[3]{81x^3} - x\sqrt[3]{3}$

35. $\dfrac{4\sqrt{3}}{3} - \dfrac{\sqrt{12}}{3}$

36. $\dfrac{\sqrt{45}}{10} + \dfrac{7\sqrt{5}}{10}$

37. $\dfrac{\sqrt[3]{8x^4}}{7} + \dfrac{3x\sqrt[3]{x}}{7}$

38. $\dfrac{\sqrt[4]{48}}{5x} - \dfrac{2\sqrt[4]{3}}{10x}$

39. $\sqrt{\dfrac{28}{x^2}} + \sqrt{\dfrac{7}{4x^2}}$

40. $\dfrac{\sqrt{99}}{5x} - \sqrt{\dfrac{44}{x^2}}$

41. $\sqrt[3]{\dfrac{16}{27}} - \dfrac{\sqrt[3]{54}}{6}$

42. $\dfrac{\sqrt[3]{3}}{10} + \sqrt[3]{\dfrac{24}{125}}$

43. $-\dfrac{\sqrt[3]{2x^4}}{9} + \sqrt[3]{\dfrac{250x^4}{27}}$

44. $\dfrac{\sqrt[3]{y^5}}{8} + \dfrac{5y\sqrt[3]{y^2}}{4}$

△ 45. Find the perimeter of the trapezoid.

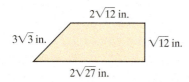

△ 46. Find the perimeter of the triangle.

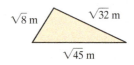

Multiply, and then simplify if possible. See Example 4.

47. $\sqrt{7}(\sqrt{5} + \sqrt{3})$

48. $\sqrt{5}(\sqrt{15} - \sqrt{35})$

49. $(\sqrt{5} - \sqrt{2})^2$

50. $(3x - \sqrt{2})(3x - \sqrt{2})$

51. $\sqrt{3x}(\sqrt{3} - \sqrt{x})$

52. $\sqrt{5y}(\sqrt{y} + \sqrt{5})$

53. $(2\sqrt{x} - 5)(3\sqrt{x} + 1)$

54. $(8\sqrt{y} + z)(4\sqrt{y} - 1)$

55. $(\sqrt[3]{a} - 4)(\sqrt[3]{a} + 5)$

56. $(\sqrt[3]{a} + 2)(\sqrt[3]{a} + 7)$

57. $6(\sqrt{2} - 2)$

58. $\sqrt{5}(6 - \sqrt{5})$

59. $\sqrt{2}(\sqrt{2} + x\sqrt{6})$

60. $\sqrt{3}(\sqrt{3} - 2\sqrt{5x})$

61. $(2\sqrt{7} + 3\sqrt{5})(\sqrt{7} - 2\sqrt{5})$

62. $(\sqrt{6} - 4\sqrt{2})(3\sqrt{6} + \sqrt{2})$

63. $(\sqrt{x} - y)(\sqrt{x} + y)$

64. $(\sqrt{3x} + 2)(\sqrt{3x} - 2)$

65. $(\sqrt{3} + x)^2$

66. $(\sqrt{y} - 3x)^2$

67. $(\sqrt{5x} - 2\sqrt{3x})(\sqrt{5x} - 3\sqrt{3x})$

68. $(5\sqrt{7x} - \sqrt{2x})(4\sqrt{7x} + 6\sqrt{2x})$

69. $(\sqrt[3]{4} + 2)(\sqrt[3]{2} - 1)$

70. $(\sqrt[3]{3} + \sqrt[3]{2})(\sqrt[3]{9} - \sqrt[3]{4})$

71. $(\sqrt[3]{x} + 1)(\sqrt[3]{x^2} - \sqrt[3]{x} + 1)$

72. $(\sqrt[3]{3x} + 2)(\sqrt[3]{9x^2} - 2\sqrt[3]{3x} + 4)$

73. $(\sqrt{x - 1} + 5)^2$

74. $(\sqrt{3x + 1} + 2)^2$

75. $(\sqrt{2x + 5} - 1)^2$

76. $(\sqrt{x - 6} - 7)^2$

REVIEW AND PREVIEW

Factor each numerator and denominator. Then simplify if possible. See Section 7.1.

77. $\dfrac{2x - 14}{2}$

78. $\dfrac{8x - 24y}{4}$

79. $\dfrac{7x - 7y}{x^2 - y^2}$

80. $\dfrac{x^3 - 8}{4x - 8}$

81. $\dfrac{6a^2b - 9ab}{3ab}$

82. $\dfrac{14r - 28r^2s^2}{7rs}$

83. $\dfrac{-4 + 2\sqrt{3}}{6}$

84. $\dfrac{-5 + 10\sqrt{7}}{5}$

87. **Multiple Steps. a.** Add: $\sqrt{3} + \sqrt{3}$.
    b. Multiply: $\sqrt{3} \cdot \sqrt{3}$.
    c. Describe the differences in parts **a** and **b**.

88. Multiply: $(\sqrt{2} + \sqrt{3} - 1)^2$.

89. Explain how simplifying $2x + 3x$ is similar to simplifying $2\sqrt{x} + 3\sqrt{x}$.

90. Explain how multiplying $(x - 2)(x + 3)$ is similar to multiplying $(\sqrt{x} - \sqrt{2})(\sqrt{x} + 3)$.

CONCEPT EXTENSIONS

△ 85. Find the perimeter and area of the rectangle.

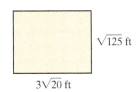

△ 86. Find the area and perimeter of the trapezoid. (*Hint:* The area of a trapezoid is the product of half the height $6\sqrt{3}$ meters and the sum of the bases $2\sqrt{63}$ and $7\sqrt{7}$ meters.)

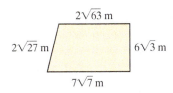

8.5 RATIONALIZING DENOMINATORS AND NUMERATORS OF RADICAL EXPRESSIONS

OBJECTIVES

1. Rationalize denominators.
2. Rationalize denominators having two terms.
3. Rationalize numerators.

OBJECTIVE 1 ▶ Rationalizing denominators of radical expressions. Often in mathematics, it is helpful to write a radical expression such as $\dfrac{\sqrt{3}}{\sqrt{2}}$ either without a radical in the denominator or without a radical in the numerator. The process of writing this expression as an equivalent expression but without a radical in the denominator is called **rationalizing the denominator.** To rationalize the denominator of $\dfrac{\sqrt{3}}{\sqrt{2}}$, we use the fundamental principle of fractions and multiply the numerator and the denominator by $\sqrt{2}$. Recall that this is the same as multiplying by $\dfrac{\sqrt{2}}{\sqrt{2}}$, which simplifies to 1.

$$\dfrac{\sqrt{3}}{\sqrt{2}} = \dfrac{\sqrt{3} \cdot \sqrt{2}}{\sqrt{2} \cdot \sqrt{2}} = \dfrac{\sqrt{6}}{\sqrt{4}} = \dfrac{\sqrt{6}}{2}$$

In this section, we continue to assume that variables represent positive real numbers.

EXAMPLE 1 Rationalize the denominator of each expression.

a. $\dfrac{2}{\sqrt{5}}$ **b.** $\dfrac{2\sqrt{16}}{\sqrt{9x}}$ **c.** $\sqrt[3]{\dfrac{1}{2}}$

Solution

a. To rationalize the denominator, we multiply the numerator and denominator by a factor that makes the radicand in the denominator a perfect square.

$$\frac{2}{\sqrt{5}} = \frac{2 \cdot \sqrt{5}}{\sqrt{5} \cdot \sqrt{5}} = \frac{2\sqrt{5}}{5} \quad \text{The denominator is now rationalized.}$$

b. First, we simplify the radicals and then rationalize the denominator.

$$\frac{2\sqrt{16}}{\sqrt{9x}} = \frac{2(4)}{3\sqrt{x}} = \frac{8}{3\sqrt{x}}$$

To rationalize the denominator, multiply the numerator and denominator by $\sqrt{x}$. Then

$$\frac{8}{3\sqrt{x}} = \frac{8 \cdot \sqrt{x}}{3\sqrt{x} \cdot \sqrt{x}} = \frac{8\sqrt{x}}{3x}$$

c. $\sqrt[3]{\frac{1}{2}} = \frac{\sqrt[3]{1}}{\sqrt[3]{2}} = \frac{1}{\sqrt[3]{2}}$. Now we rationalize the denominator. Since $\sqrt[3]{2}$ is a cube root, we want to multiply by a value that will make the radicand 2 a perfect cube. If we multiply $\sqrt[3]{2}$ by $\sqrt[3]{2^2}$, we get $\sqrt[3]{2^3} = \sqrt[3]{8} = 2$.

$$\frac{1 \cdot \sqrt[3]{2^2}}{\sqrt[3]{2} \cdot \sqrt[3]{2^2}} = \frac{\sqrt[3]{4}}{\sqrt[3]{2^3}} = \frac{\sqrt[3]{4}}{2} \quad \text{Multiply the numerator and denominator by } \sqrt[3]{2^2} \text{ and then simplify.}$$

PRACTICE 1 Rationalize the denominator of each expression.

a. $\dfrac{5}{\sqrt{3}}$ **b.** $\dfrac{3\sqrt{25}}{\sqrt{4x}}$ **c.** $\sqrt[3]{\dfrac{2}{9}}$

Concept Check ✓

Determine by which number both the numerator and denominator can be multiplied to rationalize the denominator of the radical expression.

a. $\dfrac{1}{\sqrt[3]{7}}$ **b.** $\dfrac{1}{\sqrt[4]{8}}$

EXAMPLE 2 Rationalize the denominator of $\sqrt{\dfrac{7x}{3y}}$.

Solution

$$\sqrt{\frac{7x}{3y}} = \frac{\sqrt{7x}}{\sqrt{3y}} \quad \text{Use the quotient rule. No radical may be simplified further.}$$

$$= \frac{\sqrt{7x} \cdot \sqrt{3y}}{\sqrt{3y} \cdot \sqrt{3y}} \quad \text{Multiply numerator and denominator by } \sqrt{3y} \text{ so that the radicand in the denominator is a perfect square.}$$

$$= \frac{\sqrt{21xy}}{3y} \quad \text{Use the product rule in the numerator and denominator. Remember that } \sqrt{3y} \cdot \sqrt{3y} = 3y.$$

Answer to Concept Check:
a. $\sqrt[3]{7^2}$ or $\sqrt[3]{49}$ **b.** $\sqrt[4]{2}$

PRACTICE 2 Rationalize the denominator of $\sqrt{\dfrac{3z}{5y}}$.

Section 8.5 Rationalizing Denominators and Numerators of Radical Expressions 473

EXAMPLE 3 Rationalize the denominator of $\dfrac{\sqrt[4]{x}}{\sqrt[4]{81y^5}}$.

Solution First, simplify each radical if possible.

$\dfrac{\sqrt[4]{x}}{\sqrt[4]{81y^5}} = \dfrac{\sqrt[4]{x}}{\sqrt[4]{81y^4} \cdot \sqrt[4]{y}}$ Use the product rule in the denominator.

$= \dfrac{\sqrt[4]{x}}{3y\sqrt[4]{y}}$ Write $\sqrt[4]{81y^4}$ as $3y$.

$= \dfrac{\sqrt[4]{x} \cdot \sqrt[4]{y^3}}{3y\sqrt[4]{y} \cdot \sqrt[4]{y^3}}$ Multiply numerator and denominator by $\sqrt[4]{y^3}$ so that the radicand in the denominator is a perfect fourth power.

$= \dfrac{\sqrt[4]{xy^3}}{3y\sqrt[4]{y^4}}$ Use the product rule in the numerator and denominator.

$= \dfrac{\sqrt[4]{xy^3}}{3y^2}$ In the denominator, $\sqrt[4]{y^4} = y$ and $3y \cdot y = 3y^2$. □

PRACTICE 3 Rationalize the denominator of $\dfrac{\sqrt[3]{z^2}}{\sqrt[3]{27x^4}}$.

OBJECTIVE 2 ▶ Rationalizing denominators having two terms. Remember the product of the sum and difference of two terms?

$$(a + b)(a - b) = a^2 - b^2$$

These two expressions are called **conjugates** of each other.

To rationalize a numerator or denominator that is a sum or difference of two terms, we use conjugates. To see how and why this works, let's rationalize the denominator of the expression $\dfrac{5}{\sqrt{3} - 2}$. To do so, we multiply both the numerator and the denominator by $\sqrt{3} + 2$, the **conjugate** of the denominator $\sqrt{3} - 2$, and see what happens.

$\dfrac{5}{\sqrt{3} - 2} = \dfrac{5(\sqrt{3} + 2)}{(\sqrt{3} - 2)(\sqrt{3} + 2)}$

$= \dfrac{5(\sqrt{3} + 2)}{(\sqrt{3})^2 - 2^2}$ Multiply the sum and difference of two terms: $(a + b)(a - b) = a^2 - b^2$.

$= \dfrac{5(\sqrt{3} + 2)}{3 - 4}$

$= \dfrac{5(\sqrt{3} + 2)}{-1}$

$= -5(\sqrt{3} + 2)$ or $-5\sqrt{3} - 10$

Notice in the denominator that the product of $(\sqrt{3} - 2)$ and its conjugate, $(\sqrt{3} + 2)$, is -1. In general, the product of an expression and its conjugate will contain no radical terms. This is why, when rationalizing a denominator or a numerator containing two terms, we multiply by its conjugate. Examples of conjugates are

$$\sqrt{a} - \sqrt{b} \quad \text{and} \quad \sqrt{a} + \sqrt{b}$$
$$x + \sqrt{y} \quad \text{and} \quad x - \sqrt{y}$$

EXAMPLE 4 Rationalize each denominator.

a. $\dfrac{2}{3\sqrt{2} + 4}$ b. $\dfrac{\sqrt{6} + 2}{\sqrt{5} - \sqrt{3}}$ c. $\dfrac{2\sqrt{m}}{3\sqrt{x} + \sqrt{m}}$

Solution

a. Multiply the numerator and denominator by the conjugate of the denominator, $3\sqrt{2} + 4$.

$$\dfrac{2}{3\sqrt{2} + 4} = \dfrac{2(3\sqrt{2} - 4)}{(3\sqrt{2} + 4)(3\sqrt{2} - 4)}$$

$$= \dfrac{2(3\sqrt{2} - 4)}{(3\sqrt{2})^2 - 4^2}$$

$$= \dfrac{2(3\sqrt{2} - 4)}{18 - 16}$$

$$= \dfrac{2(3\sqrt{2} - 4)}{2}, \quad \text{or} \quad 3\sqrt{2} - 4$$

It is often useful to leave a numerator in factored form to help determine whether the expression can be simplified.

b. Multiply the numerator and denominator by the conjugate of $\sqrt{5} - \sqrt{3}$.

$$\dfrac{\sqrt{6} + 2}{\sqrt{5} - \sqrt{3}} = \dfrac{(\sqrt{6} + 2)(\sqrt{5} + \sqrt{3})}{(\sqrt{5} - \sqrt{3})(\sqrt{5} + \sqrt{3})}$$

$$= \dfrac{\sqrt{6}\sqrt{5} + \sqrt{6}\sqrt{3} + 2\sqrt{5} + 2\sqrt{3}}{(\sqrt{5})^2 - (\sqrt{3})^2}$$

$$= \dfrac{\sqrt{30} + \sqrt{18} + 2\sqrt{5} + 2\sqrt{3}}{5 - 3}$$

$$= \dfrac{\sqrt{30} + 3\sqrt{2} + 2\sqrt{5} + 2\sqrt{3}}{2}$$

c. Multiply by the conjugate of $3\sqrt{x} + \sqrt{m}$ to eliminate the radicals from the denominator.

$$\dfrac{2\sqrt{m}}{3\sqrt{x} + \sqrt{m}} = \dfrac{2\sqrt{m}(3\sqrt{x} - \sqrt{m})}{(3\sqrt{x} + \sqrt{m})(3\sqrt{x} - \sqrt{m})} = \dfrac{6\sqrt{mx} - 2m}{(3\sqrt{x})^2 - (\sqrt{m})^2}$$

$$= \dfrac{6\sqrt{mx} - 2m}{9x - m}$$

Section 8.5 Rationalizing Denominators and Numerators of Radical Expressions

PRACTICE 4 Rationalize the denominator.

a. $\dfrac{5}{3\sqrt{5}+2}$ b. $\dfrac{\sqrt{2}+5}{\sqrt{3}-\sqrt{5}}$ c. $\dfrac{3\sqrt{x}}{2\sqrt{x}+\sqrt{y}}$

OBJECTIVE 3 ▶ Rationalizing numerators. As mentioned earlier, it is also often helpful to write an expression such as $\dfrac{\sqrt{3}}{\sqrt{2}}$ as an equivalent expression without a radical in the numerator. This process is called **rationalizing the numerator.** To rationalize the numerator of $\dfrac{\sqrt{3}}{\sqrt{2}}$, we multiply the numerator and the denominator by $\sqrt{3}$.

$$\dfrac{\sqrt{3}}{\sqrt{2}} = \dfrac{\sqrt{3} \cdot \sqrt{3}}{\sqrt{2} \cdot \sqrt{3}} = \dfrac{\sqrt{9}}{\sqrt{6}} = \dfrac{3}{\sqrt{6}}$$

EXAMPLE 5 Rationalize the numerator of $\dfrac{\sqrt{7}}{\sqrt{45}}$.

Solution First we simplify $\sqrt{45}$.

$$\dfrac{\sqrt{7}}{\sqrt{45}} = \dfrac{\sqrt{7}}{\sqrt{9 \cdot 5}} = \dfrac{\sqrt{7}}{3\sqrt{5}}$$

Next we rationalize the numerator by multiplying the numerator and the denominator by $\sqrt{7}$.

$$\dfrac{\sqrt{7}}{3\sqrt{5}} = \dfrac{\sqrt{7} \cdot \sqrt{7}}{3\sqrt{5} \cdot \sqrt{7}} = \dfrac{7}{3\sqrt{5 \cdot 7}} = \dfrac{7}{3\sqrt{35}}$$

PRACTICE 5 Rationalize the numerator of $\dfrac{\sqrt{32}}{\sqrt{80}}$.

EXAMPLE 6 Rationalize the numerator of $\dfrac{\sqrt[3]{2x^2}}{\sqrt[3]{5y}}$.

Solution The numerator and the denominator of this expression are already simplified. To rationalize the numerator, $\sqrt[3]{2x^2}$, we multiply the numerator and denominator by a factor that will make the radicand a perfect cube. If we multiply $\sqrt[3]{2x^2}$ by $\sqrt[3]{4x}$, we get $\sqrt[3]{8x^3} = 2x$.

$$\dfrac{\sqrt[3]{2x^2}}{\sqrt[3]{5y}} = \dfrac{\sqrt[3]{2x^2} \cdot \sqrt[3]{4x}}{\sqrt[3]{5y} \cdot \sqrt[3]{4x}} = \dfrac{\sqrt[3]{8x^3}}{\sqrt[3]{20xy}} = \dfrac{2x}{\sqrt[3]{20xy}}$$

PRACTICE 6 Rationalize the numerator of $\dfrac{\sqrt[3]{5b}}{\sqrt[3]{2a}}$.

476 CHAPTER 8 Rational Exponents, Radicals, and Complex Numbers

EXAMPLE 7 Rationalize the numerator of $\dfrac{\sqrt{x}+2}{5}$.

Solution We multiply the numerator and the denominator by the conjugate of the numerator, $\sqrt{x}+2$.

$$\frac{\sqrt{x}+2}{5} = \frac{(\sqrt{x}+2)(\sqrt{x}-2)}{5(\sqrt{x}-2)} \quad \text{Multiply by } \sqrt{x}-2, \text{ the conjugate of } \sqrt{x}+2.$$

$$= \frac{(\sqrt{x})^2 - 2^2}{5(\sqrt{x}-2)} \quad (a+b)(a-b) = a^2 - b^2$$

$$= \frac{x-4}{5(\sqrt{x}-2)}$$

PRACTICE 7 Rationalize the numerator of $\dfrac{\sqrt{x}-3}{4}$.

VOCABULARY & READINESS CHECK

Word Bank. *Use the choices below to fill in each blank. Not all choices will be used.*

rationalizing the numerator   conjugate $\dfrac{\sqrt{3}}{\sqrt{3}}$

rationalizing the denominator $\dfrac{5}{5}$

1. The _____ of $a + b$ is $a - b$.
2. The process of writing an equivalent expression, but without a radical in the denominator is called _____.
3. The process of writing an equivalent expression, but without a radical in the numerator is called _____.
4. To rationalize the denominator of $\dfrac{5}{\sqrt{3}}$, we multiply by _____.

Find the conjugate of each expression.

5. $\sqrt{2} + x$ 6. $\sqrt{3} + y$ 7. $5 - \sqrt{a}$ 8. $6 - \sqrt{b}$
9. $-7\sqrt{5} + 8\sqrt{x}$ 10. $-9\sqrt{2} - 6\sqrt{y}$

8.5 EXERCISE SET

Rationalize each denominator. See Examples 1 through 3.

1. $\dfrac{\sqrt{2}}{\sqrt{7}}$ 2. $\dfrac{\sqrt{3}}{\sqrt{2}}$ 7. $\dfrac{4}{\sqrt[3]{3}}$ 8. $\dfrac{6}{\sqrt[3]{9}}$

3. $\sqrt{\dfrac{1}{5}}$ 4. $\sqrt{\dfrac{1}{2}}$ 9. $\dfrac{3}{\sqrt{8x}}$ 10. $\dfrac{5}{\sqrt{27a}}$

5. $\sqrt{\dfrac{4}{x}}$ 6. $\sqrt{\dfrac{25}{y}}$ 11. $\dfrac{3}{\sqrt[3]{4x^2}}$ 12. $\dfrac{5}{\sqrt[3]{3y}}$

Section 8.5 Rationalizing Denominators and Numerators of Radical Expressions 477

13. $\dfrac{9}{\sqrt{3a}}$
14. $\dfrac{x}{\sqrt{5}}$
15. $\dfrac{3}{\sqrt[3]{2}}$
16. $\dfrac{5}{\sqrt[3]{9}}$
17. $\dfrac{2\sqrt{3}}{\sqrt{7}}$
18. $\dfrac{-5\sqrt{2}}{\sqrt{11}}$
19. $\sqrt{\dfrac{2x}{5y}}$
20. $\sqrt{\dfrac{13a}{2b}}$
21. $\sqrt[3]{\dfrac{3}{5}}$
22. $\sqrt[3]{\dfrac{7}{10}}$
23. $\sqrt{\dfrac{3x}{50}}$
24. $\sqrt{\dfrac{11y}{45}}$
25. $\dfrac{1}{\sqrt{12z}}$
26. $\dfrac{1}{\sqrt{32x}}$
27. $\dfrac{\sqrt[3]{2y^2}}{\sqrt[3]{9x^2}}$
28. $\dfrac{\sqrt[3]{3x}}{\sqrt[3]{4y^4}}$
29. $\sqrt[4]{\dfrac{81}{8}}$
30. $\sqrt[4]{\dfrac{1}{9}}$
31. $\sqrt[4]{\dfrac{16}{9x^7}}$
32. $\sqrt[5]{\dfrac{32}{m^6 n^{13}}}$
33. $\dfrac{5a}{\sqrt[5]{8a^9 b^{11}}}$
34. $\dfrac{9y}{\sqrt[4]{4y^9}}$

53. $\dfrac{\sqrt{4x}}{7}$
54. $\dfrac{\sqrt{3x^5}}{6}$
55. $\dfrac{\sqrt[3]{5y^2}}{\sqrt[3]{4x}}$
56. $\dfrac{\sqrt[3]{4x}}{\sqrt[3]{z^4}}$
57. $\sqrt{\dfrac{2}{5}}$
58. $\sqrt{\dfrac{3}{7}}$
59. $\dfrac{\sqrt{2x}}{11}$
60. $\dfrac{\sqrt{y}}{7}$
61. $\sqrt[3]{\dfrac{7}{8}}$
62. $\sqrt[3]{\dfrac{25}{2}}$
63. $\dfrac{\sqrt[3]{3x^5}}{10}$
64. $\sqrt[3]{\dfrac{9y}{7}}$
65. $\sqrt{\dfrac{18x^4 y^6}{3z}}$
66. $\sqrt{\dfrac{8x^5 y}{2z}}$

67. When rationalizing the denominator of $\dfrac{\sqrt{5}}{\sqrt{7}}$, explain why both the numerator and the denominator must be multiplied by $\sqrt{7}$.

68. When rationalizing the numerator of $\dfrac{\sqrt{5}}{\sqrt{7}}$, explain why both the numerator and the denominator must be multiplied by $\sqrt{5}$.

Rationalize each denominator. See Example 4.

35. $\dfrac{6}{2-\sqrt{7}}$
36. $\dfrac{3}{\sqrt{7}-4}$
37. $\dfrac{-7}{\sqrt{x}-3}$
38. $\dfrac{-8}{\sqrt{y}+4}$
39. $\dfrac{\sqrt{2}-\sqrt{3}}{\sqrt{2}+\sqrt{3}}$
40. $\dfrac{\sqrt{3}+\sqrt{4}}{\sqrt{2}-\sqrt{3}}$
41. $\dfrac{\sqrt{a}+1}{2\sqrt{a}-\sqrt{b}}$
42. $\dfrac{2\sqrt{a}-3}{2\sqrt{a}+\sqrt{b}}$
43. $\dfrac{8}{1+\sqrt{10}}$
44. $\dfrac{-3}{\sqrt{6}-2}$
45. $\dfrac{\sqrt{x}}{\sqrt{x}+\sqrt{y}}$
46. $\dfrac{2\sqrt{a}}{2\sqrt{x}-\sqrt{y}}$
47. $\dfrac{2\sqrt{3}+\sqrt{6}}{4\sqrt{3}-\sqrt{6}}$
48. $\dfrac{4\sqrt{5}+\sqrt{2}}{2\sqrt{5}-\sqrt{2}}$

Rationalize each numerator. See Example 7.

69. $\dfrac{2-\sqrt{11}}{6}$
70. $\dfrac{\sqrt{15}+1}{2}$
71. $\dfrac{2-\sqrt{7}}{-5}$
72. $\dfrac{\sqrt{5}+2}{\sqrt{2}}$
73. $\dfrac{\sqrt{x}+3}{\sqrt{x}}$
74. $\dfrac{5+\sqrt{2}}{\sqrt{2x}}$
75. $\dfrac{\sqrt{2}-1}{\sqrt{2}+1}$
76. $\dfrac{\sqrt{8}-\sqrt{3}}{\sqrt{2}+\sqrt{3}}$
77. $\dfrac{\sqrt{x}+1}{\sqrt{x}-1}$
78. $\dfrac{\sqrt{x}+\sqrt{y}}{\sqrt{x}-\sqrt{y}}$

REVIEW AND PREVIEW

Solve each equation. See Sections 2.1 and 6.8.

79. $2x - 7 = 3(x - 4)$
80. $9x - 4 = 7(x - 2)$
81. $(x - 6)(2x + 1) = 0$
82. $(y + 2)(5y + 4) = 0$
83. $x^2 - 8x = -12$
84. $x^3 = x$

CONCEPTS EXTENSIONS

Determine the smallest number both the numerator and denominator should be multiplied by to rationalize the denominator of the radical expression. See the Concept Check in this section.

85. $\dfrac{9}{\sqrt[3]{5}}$
86. $\dfrac{5}{\sqrt{27}}$

Rationalize each numerator. See Examples 5 and 6.

49. $\sqrt{\dfrac{5}{3}}$
50. $\sqrt{\dfrac{3}{2}}$
51. $\sqrt{\dfrac{18}{5}}$
52. $\sqrt{\dfrac{12}{7}}$

87. The formula of the radius r of a sphere with surface area A is

$$r = \sqrt{\dfrac{A}{4\pi}}$$

Rationalize the denominator of the radical expression in this formula.

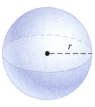

88. The formula for the radius r of a cone with height 7 centimeters and volume V is

$$r = \sqrt{\dfrac{3V}{7\pi}}$$

Rationalize the numerator of the radical expression in this formula.

89. Explain why rationalizing the denominator does not change the value of the original expression.

90. Explain why rationalizing the numerator does not change the value of the original expression.

INTEGRATED REVIEW RADICALS AND RATIONAL EXPONENTS

Sections 8.1–8.5

Find each root. Throughout this review, assume that all variables represent positive real numbers.

1. $\sqrt{81}$
2. $\sqrt[3]{-8}$
3. $\sqrt[4]{\dfrac{1}{16}}$
4. $\sqrt{x^6}$
5. $\sqrt[3]{y^9}$
6. $\sqrt{4y^{10}}$
7. $\sqrt[5]{-32y^5}$
8. $\sqrt[4]{81b^{12}}$

Use radical notation to rewrite each expression. Simplify if possible.

9. $36^{1/2}$
10. $(3y)^{1/4}$
11. $64^{-2/3}$
12. $(x+1)^{3/5}$

Use the properties of exponents to simplify each expression. Write with positive exponents.

13. $y^{-1/6} \cdot y^{7/6}$
14. $\dfrac{(2x^{1/3})^4}{x^{5/6}}$
15. $\dfrac{x^{1/4} x^{3/4}}{x^{-1/4}}$
16. $4^{1/3} \cdot 4^{2/5}$

Use rational exponents to simplify each radical.

17. $\sqrt[3]{8x^6}$
18. $\sqrt[12]{a^9 b^6}$

Use rational exponents to write each as a single radical expression.

19. $\sqrt[4]{x} \cdot \sqrt{x}$
20. $\sqrt{5} \cdot \sqrt[3]{2}$

Simplify.

21. $\sqrt{40}$
22. $\sqrt[4]{16x^7 y^{10}}$
23. $\sqrt[3]{54x^4}$
24. $\sqrt[5]{-64b^{10}}$

Multiply or divide. Then simplify if possible.

25. $\sqrt{5} \cdot \sqrt{x}$
26. $\sqrt[3]{8x} \cdot \sqrt[3]{8x^2}$
27. $\dfrac{\sqrt{98y^6}}{\sqrt{2y}}$
28. $\dfrac{\sqrt[4]{48a^9 b^3}}{\sqrt[4]{ab^3}}$

Perform each indicated operation.

29. $\sqrt{20} - \sqrt{75} + 5\sqrt{7}$
30. $\sqrt[3]{54y^4} - y\sqrt[3]{16y}$
31. $\sqrt{3}\left(\sqrt{5} - \sqrt{2}\right)$
32. $\left(\sqrt{7} + \sqrt{3}\right)^2$
33. $(2x - \sqrt{5})(2x + \sqrt{5})$
34. $\left(\sqrt{x+1} - 1\right)^2$

Rationalize each denominator.

35. $\sqrt{\dfrac{7}{3}}$

36. $\dfrac{5}{\sqrt[3]{2x^2}}$

37. $\dfrac{\sqrt{3} - \sqrt{7}}{2\sqrt{3} + \sqrt{7}}$

Rationalize each numerator.

38. $\sqrt{\dfrac{7}{3}}$

39. $\sqrt[3]{\dfrac{9y}{11}}$

40. $\dfrac{\sqrt{x} - 2}{\sqrt{x}}$

8.6 RADICAL EQUATIONS AND PROBLEM SOLVING

OBJECTIVES

1. Solve equations that contain radical expressions.
2. Use the Pythagorean theorem to model problems.

OBJECTIVE 1 ▶ Solving equations that contain radical expressions. In this section, we present techniques to solve equations containing radical expressions such as

$$\sqrt{2x - 3} = 9$$

We use the power rule to help us solve these radical equations.

> **Power Rule**
>
> If both sides of an equation are raised to the same power, **all** solutions of the original equation are **among** the solutions of the new equation.

This property *does not* say that raising both sides of an equation to a power yields an equivalent equation. A solution of the new equation *may or may not* be a solution of the original equation. For example, $(-2)^2 = 2^2$, but $-2 \neq 2$. Thus, *each solution of the new equation must be checked* to make sure it is a solution of the original equation. Recall that a proposed solution that is not a solution of the original equation is called an **extraneous solution.**

EXAMPLE 1 Solve: $\sqrt{2x - 3} = 9$.

Solution We use the power rule to square both sides of the equation to eliminate the radical.

$$\sqrt{2x - 3} = 9$$
$$(\sqrt{2x - 3})^2 = 9^2$$
$$2x - 3 = 81$$
$$2x = 84$$
$$x = 42$$

Now we, check the solution in the original equation.

Check:

$$\sqrt{2x - 3} = 9$$
$$\sqrt{2(42) - 3} \stackrel{?}{=} 9 \quad \text{Let } x = 42.$$
$$\sqrt{84 - 3} \stackrel{?}{=} 9$$

$$\sqrt{81} \stackrel{?}{=} 9$$
$$9 = 9 \quad \text{True}$$

The solution checks, so we conclude that the solution is 42 or the solution set is {42}.

PRACTICE 1 Solve: $\sqrt{3x - 5} = 7$.

To solve a radical equation, first isolate a radical on one side of the equation.

EXAMPLE 2 Solve: $\sqrt{-10x - 1} + 3x = 0$.

Solution First, isolate the radical on one side of the equation. To do this, we subtract $3x$ from both sides.

$$\sqrt{-10x - 1} + 3x = 0$$
$$\sqrt{-10x - 1} + 3x - 3x = 0 - 3x$$
$$\sqrt{-10x - 1} = -3x$$

Next we use the power rule to eliminate the radical.

$$\left(\sqrt{-10x - 1}\right)^2 = (-3x)^2$$
$$-10x - 1 = 9x^2$$

Since this is a quadratic equation, we can set the equation equal to 0 and try to solve by factoring.

$$9x^2 + 10x + 1 = 0$$
$$(9x + 1)(x + 1) = 0 \quad \text{Factor.}$$
$$9x + 1 = 0 \quad \text{or} \quad x + 1 = 0 \quad \text{Set each factor equal to 0.}$$
$$x = -\frac{1}{9} \quad \text{or} \quad x = -1$$

Check: Let $x = -\frac{1}{9}$.

$$\sqrt{-10x - 1} + 3x = 0$$
$$\sqrt{-10\left(-\frac{1}{9}\right) - 1} + 3\left(-\frac{1}{9}\right) \stackrel{?}{=} 0$$
$$\sqrt{\frac{10}{9} - \frac{9}{9}} - \frac{3}{9} \stackrel{?}{=} 0$$
$$\sqrt{\frac{1}{9}} - \frac{1}{3} \stackrel{?}{=} 0$$
$$\frac{1}{3} - \frac{1}{3} = 0 \quad \text{True}$$

Let $x = -1$.

$$\sqrt{-10x - 1} + 3x = 0$$
$$\sqrt{-10(-1) - 1} + 3(-1) \stackrel{?}{=} 0$$
$$\sqrt{10 - 1} - 3 \stackrel{?}{=} 0$$
$$\sqrt{9} - 3 \stackrel{?}{=} 0$$
$$3 - 3 = 0 \quad \text{True}$$

Both solutions check. The solutions are $-\frac{1}{9}$ and -1.

PRACTICE 2 Solve: $\sqrt{3 - 2x} - 4x = 0$.

Section 8.6 Radical Equations and Problem Solving   481

The following steps may be used to solve a radical equation.

> **Solving a Radical Equation**
> **STEP 1.** Isolate one radical on one side of the equation.
> **STEP 2.** Raise each side of the equation to a power equal to the index of the radical and simplify.
> **STEP 3.** If the equation still contains a radical term, repeat Steps 1 and 2. If not, solve the equation.
> **STEP 4.** Check all proposed solutions in the original equation.

EXAMPLE 3   Solve: $\sqrt[3]{x+1} + 5 = 3$.

Solution   First we isolate the radical by subtracting 5 from both sides of the equation.
$$\sqrt[3]{x+1} + 5 = 3$$
$$\sqrt[3]{x+1} = -2$$

Next we raise both sides of the equation to the third power to eliminate the radical.
$$\left(\sqrt[3]{x+1}\right)^3 = (-2)^3$$
$$x + 1 = -8$$
$$x = -9$$

The solution checks in the original equation, so the solution is -9.

PRACTICE 3   Solve: $\sqrt[3]{x-2} + 1 = 3$.

EXAMPLE 4   Solve: $\sqrt{4-x} = x - 2$.

Solution
$$\sqrt{4-x} = x - 2$$
$$\left(\sqrt{4-x}\right)^2 = (x-2)^2$$
$$4 - x = x^2 - 4x + 4$$
$$x^2 - 3x = 0 \qquad \text{Write the quadratic equation in standard form.}$$
$$x(x-3) = 0 \qquad \text{Factor.}$$
$$x = 0 \quad \text{or} \quad x - 3 = 0 \qquad \text{Set each factor equal to 0.}$$
$$x = 3$$

Check: $\sqrt{4-x} = x - 2$ $\qquad\qquad$ $\sqrt{4-x} = x - 2$
$\sqrt{4-0} \stackrel{?}{=} 0 - 2$ Let $x = 0$. $\qquad$ $\sqrt{4-3} \stackrel{?}{=} 3 - 2$ Let $x = 3$.
$2 = -2$ False $\qquad\qquad\qquad$ $1 = 1$ True

The proposed solution 3 checks, but 0 does not. Since 0 is an extraneous solution, the only solution is 3.

PRACTICE 4   Solve: $\sqrt{16+x} = x - 4$.

> ▶ **Helpful Hint**
> In Example 4, notice that $(x - 2)^2 = x^2 - 4x + 4$. Make sure binomials are squared correctly.

Concept Check ✓

How can you immediately tell that the equation $\sqrt{2y+3} = -4$ has no real solution?

EXAMPLE 5 Solve: $\sqrt{2x+5} + \sqrt{2x} = 3$.

Solution We get one radical alone by subtracting $\sqrt{2x}$ from both sides.

$$\sqrt{2x+5} + \sqrt{2x} = 3$$
$$\sqrt{2x+5} = 3 - \sqrt{2x}$$

Now we use the power rule to begin eliminating the radicals. First we square both sides.

$$(\sqrt{2x+5})^2 = (3 - \sqrt{2x})^2$$
$$2x + 5 = 9 - 6\sqrt{2x} + 2x \quad \text{Multiply } (3 - \sqrt{2x})(3 - \sqrt{2x}).$$

There is still a radical in the equation, so we get a radical alone again. Then we square both sides.

$$2x + 5 = 9 - 6\sqrt{2x} + 2x \quad \text{Get the radical alone.}$$
$$6\sqrt{2x} = 4$$
$$36(2x) = 16 \quad \text{Square both sides of the equation to eliminate the radical.}$$
$$72x = 16 \quad \text{Multiply.}$$
$$x = \frac{16}{72} \quad \text{Solve.}$$
$$x = \frac{2}{9} \quad \text{Simplify.}$$

The proposed solution, $\frac{2}{9}$, checks in the original equation. The solution is $\frac{2}{9}$.

PRACTICE 5 Solve: $\sqrt{8x+1} + \sqrt{3x} = 2$.

▶ **Helpful Hint**

Make sure expressions are squared correctly. In Example 5, we squared $(3 - \sqrt{2x})$ as

$$(3 - \sqrt{2x})^2 = (3 - \sqrt{2x})(3 - \sqrt{2x})$$
$$= 3 \cdot 3 - 3\sqrt{2x} - 3\sqrt{2x} + \sqrt{2x} \cdot \sqrt{2x}$$
$$= 9 - 6\sqrt{2x} + 2x$$

Concept Check ✓

What is wrong with the following solution?

$$\sqrt{2x+5} + \sqrt{4-x} = 8$$
$$(\sqrt{2x+5} + \sqrt{4-x})^2 = 8^2$$
$$(2x+5) + (4-x) = 64$$
$$x + 9 = 64$$
$$x = 55$$

Answers to Concept Check:
First Concept Check: answers may vary
Second Concept Check: $(\sqrt{2x+5} + \sqrt{4-x})^2$ is not $(2x+5) + (4-x)$.

OBJECTIVE 2 ▶ **Using the Pythagorean theorem.** Recall that the Pythagorean theorem states that in a right triangle, the length of the hypotenuse squared equals the sum of the lengths of each of the legs squared.

Section 8.6 Radical Equations and Problem Solving 483

Pythagorean Theorem

If a and b are the lengths of the legs of a right triangle and c is the length of the hypotenuse, then $a^2 + b^2 = c^2$.

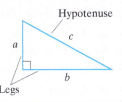

EXAMPLE 6 Find the length of the unknown leg of the right triangle.

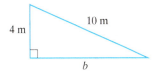

Solution In the formula $a^2 + b^2 = c^2$, c is the hypotenuse. Here, $c = 10$, the length of the hypotenuse, and $a = 4$. We solve for b. Then $a^2 + b^2 = c^2$ becomes

$$4^2 + b^2 = 10^2$$
$$16 + b^2 = 100$$
$$b^2 = 84 \quad \text{Subtract 16 from both sides.}$$
$$b = \pm\sqrt{84} = \pm\sqrt{4 \cdot 21} = \pm 2\sqrt{21}$$

Since b is a length and thus is positive, we will use the positive value only. The unknown leg of the triangle is $2\sqrt{21}$ meters long.

PRACTICE 6 Find the length of the unknown leg of the right triangle.

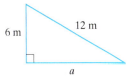

EXAMPLE 7 Calculating Placement of a Wire

A 50-foot supporting wire is to be attached to a 75-foot antenna. Because of surrounding buildings, sidewalks, and roadways, the wire must be anchored exactly 20 feet from the base of the antenna.

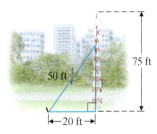

a. How high from the base of the antenna is the wire attached?
b. Local regulations require that a supporting wire be attached at a height no less than $\dfrac{3}{5}$ of the total height of the antenna. From part **a**, have local regulations been met?

Solution

1. **UNDERSTAND.** Read and reread the problem. From the diagram we notice that a right triangle is formed with hypotenuse 50 feet and one leg 20 feet. Let x be the height from the base of the antenna to the attached wire.

2. **TRANSLATE.** Use the Pythagorean theorem.

$$a^2 + b^2 = c^2$$
$$20^2 + x^2 = 50^2 \quad a = 20, c = 50$$

3. **SOLVE.**

$$20^2 + x^2 = 50^2$$
$$400 + x^2 = 2500$$
$$x^2 = 2100 \quad \text{Subtract 400 from both sides.}$$
$$x = \pm\sqrt{2100}$$
$$= \pm 10\sqrt{21}$$

4. **INTERPRET.** *Check* the work and *state* the solution.

Check: We will use only the positive value, $x = 10\sqrt{21}$ because x represents length. The wire is attached exactly $10\sqrt{21}$ feet from the base of the pole, or approximately 45.8 feet.

State: The supporting wire must be attached at a height no less than $\frac{3}{5}$ of the total height of the antenna. This height is $\frac{3}{5}$(75 feet), or 45 feet. Since we know from part **a** that the wire is to be attached at a height of approximately 45.8 feet, local regulations have been met. ◻

PRACTICE

7 Keith Robinson bought two Siamese fighting fish, but when he got home he found he only had one rectangular tank that was 12 in. long, 7 in. wide, and 5 in. deep. Since the fish must be kept separated, he needed to insert a plastic divider in the diagonal of the tank. He already has a piece that is 5 in. in one dimension, but how long must it be to fit corner to corner in the tank?

Graphing Calculator Explorations

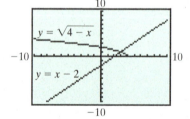

We can use a graphing calculator to solve radical equations. For example, to use a graphing calculator to approximate the solutions of the equation solved in Example 4, we graph the following.

$$Y_1 = \sqrt{4 - x} \quad \text{and} \quad Y_2 = x - 2$$

The *x*-value of the point of intersection is the solution. Use the Intersect feature or the Zoom and Trace features of your graphing calculator to see that the solution is 3.

Use a graphing calculator to solve each radical equation. Round all solutions to the nearest hundredth.

1. $\sqrt{x + 7} = x$
2. $\sqrt{3x + 5} = 2x$
3. $\sqrt{2x + 1} = \sqrt{2x + 2}$
4. $\sqrt{10x - 1} = \sqrt{-10x + 10} - 1$
5. $1.2x = \sqrt{3.1x + 5}$
6. $\sqrt{1.9x^2 - 2.2} = -0.8x + 3$

VOCABULARY & READINESS CHECK

Word Bank. *Use the choices below to fill in each blank. Not all choices will be used.*

hypotenuse	right	$x^2 + 25$	$16 - 8\sqrt{7x} + 7x$
extraneous solution	legs	$x^2 - 10x + 25$	$16 + 7x$

1. A proposed solution that is not a solution of the original equation is called an _____.
2. The Pythagorean theorem states that $a^2 + b^2 = c^2$ where a and b are the lengths of the _____ of a _____ triangle and c is the length of the _____.
3. The square of $x - 5$, or $(x - 5)^2 = $ _____.
4. The square of $4 - \sqrt{7x}$, or $(4 - \sqrt{7x})^2 = $ _____.

8.6 EXERCISE SET

Solve. See Examples 1 and 2.

1. $\sqrt{2x} = 4$
2. $\sqrt{3x} = 3$
3. $\sqrt{x - 3} = 2$
4. $\sqrt{x + 1} = 5$
5. $\sqrt{2x} = -4$
6. $\sqrt{5x} = -5$
7. $\sqrt{4x - 3} - 5 = 0$
8. $\sqrt{x - 3} - 1 = 0$
9. $\sqrt{2x - 3} - 2 = 1$
10. $\sqrt{3x + 3} - 4 = 8$

Solve. See Example 3.

11. $\sqrt[3]{6x} = -3$
12. $\sqrt[3]{4x} = -2$
13. $\sqrt[3]{x - 2} - 3 = 0$
14. $\sqrt[3]{2x - 6} - 4 = 0$

Solve. See Examples 4 and 5.

15. $\sqrt{13 - x} = x - 1$
16. $\sqrt{2x - 3} = 3 - x$
17. $x - \sqrt{4 - 3x} = -8$
18. $2x + \sqrt{x + 1} = 8$
19. $\sqrt{y + 5} = 2 - \sqrt{y - 4}$
20. $\sqrt{x + 3} + \sqrt{x - 5} = 3$
21. $\sqrt{x - 3} + \sqrt{x + 2} = 5$
22. $\sqrt{2x - 4} - \sqrt{3x + 4} = -2$

MIXED PRACTICE

Solve. See Examples 1 through 5.

23. $\sqrt{3x - 2} = 5$
24. $\sqrt{5x - 4} = 9$
25. $-\sqrt{2x} + 4 = -6$
26. $-\sqrt{3x + 9} = -12$
27. $\sqrt{3x + 1} + 2 = 0$
28. $\sqrt{3x + 1} - 2 = 0$
29. $\sqrt[4]{4x + 1} - 2 = 0$
30. $\sqrt[4]{2x - 9} - 3 = 0$
31. $\sqrt{4x - 3} = 7$
32. $\sqrt{3x + 9} = 6$
33. $\sqrt[3]{6x - 3} - 3 = 0$
34. $\sqrt[3]{3x + 4} = 7$
35. $\sqrt[3]{2x - 3} - 2 = -5$
36. $\sqrt[3]{x - 4} - 5 = -7$
37. $\sqrt{x + 4} = \sqrt{2x - 5}$
38. $\sqrt[3]{3y + 6} = \sqrt[3]{7y - 6}$
39. $x - \sqrt{1 - x} = -5$
40. $x - \sqrt{x - 2} = 4$
41. $\sqrt[3]{-6x - 1} = \sqrt[3]{-2x - 5}$
42. $\sqrt[3]{-4x - 3} = \sqrt[3]{-x - 15}$

43. $\sqrt{5x - 1} - \sqrt{x + 2} = 3$
44. $\sqrt{2x - 1} - 4 = -\sqrt{x - 4}$
45. $\sqrt{2x - 1} = \sqrt{1 - 2x}$
46. $\sqrt{7x - 4} = \sqrt{4 - 7x}$
47. $\sqrt{3x + 4} - 1 = \sqrt{2x + 1}$
48. $\sqrt{x - 2} + 3 = \sqrt{4x + 1}$
49. $\sqrt{y + 3} - \sqrt{y - 3} = 1$
50. $\sqrt{x + 1} - \sqrt{x - 1} = 2$

Find the length of the unknown side of each triangle. See Example 6.

51. 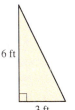 (6 ft, 3 ft)

52. 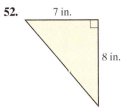 (7 in., 8 in.)

53. 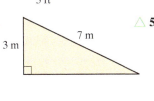 (3 m, 7 m)

54. 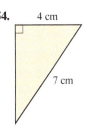 (4 cm, 7 cm)

Find the length of the unknown side of each triangle. Give the exact length and a one-decimal-place approximation. See Example 6.

55. 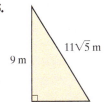 (9 m, $11\sqrt{5}$ m)

56. 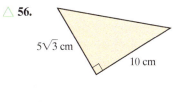 ($5\sqrt{3}$ cm, 10 cm)

57.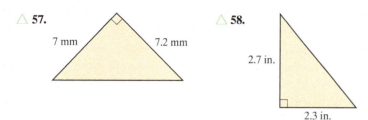

58.

Solve. See Example 7. Give exact answers and two-decimal-place approximations where appropriate.

59. A wire is needed to support a vertical pole 15 feet high. The cable will be anchored to a stake 8 feet from the base of the pole. How much cable is needed?

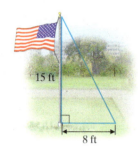

60. The tallest structure in the United States is a TV tower in Blanchard, North Dakota. Its height is 2063 feet. A 2382-foot length of wire is to be used as a guy wire attached to the top of the tower. Approximate to the nearest foot how far from the base of the tower the guy wire must be anchored. (*Source:* U.S. Geological Survey)

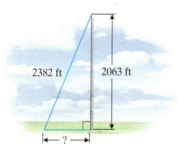

61. A spotlight is mounted on the eaves of a house 12 feet above the ground. A flower bed runs between the house and the sidewalk, so the closest the ladder can be placed to the house is 5 feet. How long a ladder is needed so that an electrician can reach the place where the light is mounted?

62. A wire is to be attached to support a telephone pole. Because of surrounding buildings, sidewalks, and roadways, the wire must be anchored exactly 15 feet from the base of the pole. Telephone company workers have only 30 feet of cable, and 2 feet of that must be used to attach the cable to the pole and to the stake on the ground. How high from the base of the pole can the wire be attached?

63. The radius of the Moon is 1080 miles. Use the formula for the radius r of a sphere given its surface area A,

$$r = \sqrt{\frac{A}{4\pi}}$$

to find the surface area of the Moon. Round to the nearest square mile. (*Source:* National Space Science Data Center)

64. Police departments find it very useful to be able to approximate the speed of a car when they are given the distance that the car skidded before it came to a stop. If the road surface is wet concrete, the function $S(x) = \sqrt{10.5x}$ is used, where $S(x)$ is the speed of the car in miles per hour and x is the distance skidded in feet. Find how fast a car was moving if it skidded 280 feet on wet concrete.

65. The formula $v = \sqrt{2gh}$ gives the velocity v, in feet per second, of an object when it falls h feet accelerated by gravity g, in feet per second squared. If g is approximately 32 feet per second squared, find how far an object has fallen if its velocity is 80 feet per second.

66. Two tractors are pulling a tree stump from a field. If two forces A and B pull at right angles (90°) to each other, the size of the resulting force R is given by the formula $R = \sqrt{A^2 + B^2}$. If tractor A is exerting 600 pounds of force and the resulting force is 850 pounds, find how much force tractor B is exerting.

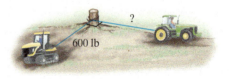

In psychology, it has been suggested that the number S of nonsense syllables that a person can repeat consecutively depends on his or her IQ score I according to the equation $S = 2\sqrt{I} - 9$.

67. Use this relationship to estimate the IQ of a person who can repeat 11 nonsense syllables consecutively.

68. Use this relationship to estimate the IQ of a person who can repeat 15 nonsense syllables consecutively.

*The **period** of a pendulum is the time it takes for the pendulum to make one full back-and-forth swing. The period of a pendulum depends on the length of the pendulum. The formula for the period P, in seconds, is $P = 2\pi\sqrt{\dfrac{l}{32}}$, where l is the length of the pendulum in feet. Use this formula for Exercises 69 through 74.*

69. Find the period of a pendulum whose length is 2 feet. Give an exact answer and a two-decimal-place approximation.

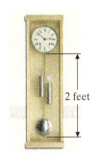

70. Klockit sells a 43-inch lyre pendulum. Find the period of this pendulum. Round your answer to 2 decimal places. (*Hint:* First convert inches to feet.)

71. Find the length of a pendulum whose period is 4 seconds. Round your answer to 2 decimal places.

72. Find the length of a pendulum whose period is 3 seconds. Round your answer to 2 decimal places.

73. Study the relationship between period and pendulum length in Exercises 69 through 72 and make a conjecture about this relationship.

74. Galileo experimented with pendulums. He supposedly made conjectures about pendulums of equal length with different bob weights. Try this experiment. Make two pendulums 3 feet long. Attach a heavy weight (lead) to one and a light weight (a cork) to the other. Pull both pendulums back the same angle measure and release. Make a conjecture from your observations. (There is more about pendulums in the Chapter 7 Group Activity.)

If the three lengths of the sides of a triangle are known, Heron's formula can be used to find its area. If a, b, and c are the three lengths of the sides, Heron's formula for area is

$$A = \sqrt{s(s-a)(s-b)(s-c)}$$

where s is half the perimeter of the triangle, or $s = \dfrac{1}{2}(a + b + c)$.

Use this formula to find the area of each triangle. Give an exact answer and then a two-decimal place approximation.

75.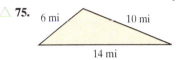

76.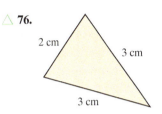

77. Describe when Heron's formula might be useful.

78. In your own words, explain why you think *s* in Heron's formula is called the *semiperimeter*.

The maximum distance D(h) in kilometers that a person can see from a height h kilometers above the ground is given by the function $D(h) = 111.7\sqrt{h}$. Use this function for Exercises 79 and 80. Round your answers to two decimal places.

79. Find the height that would allow a person to see 80 kilometers.

80. Find the height that would allow a person to see 40 kilometers.

REVIEW AND PREVIEW

Use the vertical line test to determine whether each graph represents the graph of a function. See Section 3.2.

81. **82.**

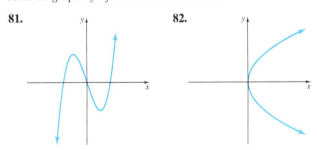

83. **84.**

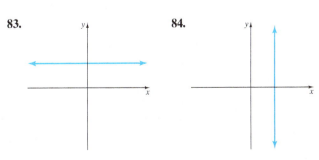

85. 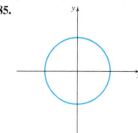 **86.**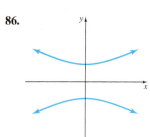

Simplify. See Section 7.3.

87. $\dfrac{\dfrac{x}{6}}{\dfrac{2x}{3} + \dfrac{1}{2}}$

88. $\dfrac{\dfrac{1}{y} + \dfrac{4}{5}}{\dfrac{-3}{20}}$

89. $\dfrac{\dfrac{z}{5} + \dfrac{1}{10}}{\dfrac{z}{20} - \dfrac{z}{5}}$

90. $\dfrac{\dfrac{1}{y} + \dfrac{1}{x}}{\dfrac{1}{y} - \dfrac{1}{x}}$

CONCEPT EXTENSIONS

91. Find the error in the following solution and correct. See the second Concept Check in this section.

$$\sqrt{5x - 1} + 4 = 7$$
$$(\sqrt{5x - 1} + 4)^2 = 7^2$$
$$5x - 1 + 16 = 49$$
$$5x = 34$$
$$x = \dfrac{34}{5}$$

92. Explain why proposed solutions of radical equations must be checked.

93. Solve: $\sqrt{\sqrt{x + 3} + \sqrt{x}} = \sqrt{3}$

94. The cost $C(x)$ in dollars per day to operate a small delivery service is given by $C(x) = 80\sqrt[3]{x} + 500$, where x is the number of deliveries per day. In July, the manager decides that it is necessary to keep delivery costs below $1620.00. Find the greatest number of deliveries this company can make per day and still keep overhead below $1620.00.

95. Multiple Steps. Consider the equations $\sqrt{2x} = 4$ and $\sqrt[3]{2x} = 4$.
  a. Explain the difference in solving these equations.
  b. Explain the similarity in solving these equations.

Example
For Exercises 96 through 99, see the example below.
Solve $(t^2 - 3t) - 2\sqrt{t^2 - 3t} = 0$.

Solution

Substitution can be used to make this problem somewhat simpler. Since $t^2 - 3t$ occurs more than once, let $x = t^2 - 3t$.

$$(t^2 - 3t) - 2\sqrt{t^2 - 3t} = 0$$
$$x - 2\sqrt{x} = 0$$
$$x = 2\sqrt{x}$$
$$x^2 = (2\sqrt{x})^2$$
$$x^2 = 4x$$
$$x^2 - 4x = 0$$
$$x(x - 4) = 0$$
$$x = 0 \quad \text{or} \quad x - 4 = 0$$
$$x = 4$$

Now we "undo" the substitution.
$x = 0$ Replace x with $t^2 - 3t$.
$$t^2 - 3t = 0$$
$$t(t - 3) = 0$$
$$t = 0 \quad \text{or} \quad t - 3 = 0$$
$$t = 3$$

$x = 4$ Replace x with $t^2 - 3t$.
$$t^2 - 3t = 4$$
$$t^2 - 3t - 4 = 0$$
$$(t - 4)(t + 1) = 0$$
$$t - 4 = 0 \quad \text{or} \quad t + 1 = 0$$
$$t = 4 \qquad\qquad t = -1$$

In this problem, we have four possible solutions: 0, 3, 4, and -1. All four solutions check in the original equation, so the solutions are $-1, 0, 3, 4$.

Solve. See the preceding example.

96. $3\sqrt{x^2 - 8x} = x^2 - 8x$

97. $\sqrt{(x^2 - x) + 7} = 2(x^2 - x) - 1$

98. $7 - (x^2 - 3x) = \sqrt{(x^2 - 3x) + 5}$

99. $x^2 + 6x = 4\sqrt{x^2 + 6x}$

8.7 COMPLEX NUMBERS

OBJECTIVES

1. Write square roots of negative numbers in the form bi.
2. Graph complex numbers on the complex plane.
3. Add or subtract complex numbers.
4. Multiply complex numbers.
5. Divide complex numbers.
6. Raise i to powers.

OBJECTIVE 1 ▸ Writing numbers in the form bi. Our work with radical expressions has excluded expressions such as $\sqrt{-16}$ because $\sqrt{-16}$ is not a real number; there is no real number whose square is -16. In this section, we discuss a number system that includes roots of negative numbers. This number system is the **complex number system**, and it includes the set of real numbers as a subset. The complex number system allows us to solve equations such as $x^2 + 1 = 0$ that have no real number solutions. The set of complex numbers includes the **imaginary unit.**

> **Imaginary Unit**
>
> The imaginary unit, written i, is the number whose square is -1. That is,
>
> $$i^2 = -1 \quad \text{and} \quad i = \sqrt{-1}$$

To write the square root of a negative number in terms of i, use the property that if a is a positive number, then

$$\sqrt{-a} = \sqrt{-1} \cdot \sqrt{a}$$
$$= i \cdot \sqrt{a}$$

Using i, we can write $\sqrt{-16}$ as

$$\sqrt{-16} = \sqrt{-1 \cdot 16} = \sqrt{-1} \cdot \sqrt{16} = i \cdot 4, \text{ or } 4i$$

EXAMPLE 1 Write with i notation.

a. $\sqrt{-36}$ b. $\sqrt{-5}$ c. $-\sqrt{-20}$

Solution

a. $\sqrt{-36} = \sqrt{-1 \cdot 36} = \sqrt{-1} \cdot \sqrt{36} = i \cdot 6$, or $6i$
b. $\sqrt{-5} = \sqrt{-1(5)} = \sqrt{-1} \cdot \sqrt{5} = i\sqrt{5}$.
c. $-\sqrt{-20} = -\sqrt{-1 \cdot 20} = -\sqrt{-1} \cdot \sqrt{4 \cdot 5} = -i \cdot 2\sqrt{5} = -2i\sqrt{5}$

> **▸ Helpful Hint**
> Since $\sqrt{5}i$ can easily be confused with $\sqrt{5i}$, we write $\sqrt{5}i$ as $i\sqrt{5}$.

PRACTICE 1 Write with i notation.

a. $\sqrt{-4}$ b. $\sqrt{-7}$ c. $-\sqrt{-18}$

The product rule for radicals does not necessarily hold true for imaginary numbers. *To multiply square roots of negative numbers, first we write each number in terms of the imaginary unit i.* For example, to multiply $\sqrt{-4}$ and $\sqrt{-9}$, we first write each number in the form bi.

$$\sqrt{-4}\sqrt{-9} = 2i(3i) = 6i^2 = 6(-1) = -6 \quad \text{Correct}$$

We will also use this method to simplify quotients of square roots of negative numbers. Why? The product rule does not work for this example. In other words,

$$\sqrt{-4} \cdot \sqrt{-9} = \sqrt{(-4)(-9)} = \sqrt{36} = 6 \quad \text{Incorrect}$$

EXAMPLE 2 Multiply or divide as indicated.

a. $\sqrt{-3} \cdot \sqrt{-5}$ b. $\sqrt{-36} \cdot \sqrt{-1}$ c. $\sqrt{8} \cdot \sqrt{-2}$ d. $\dfrac{\sqrt{-125}}{\sqrt{5}}$

Solution

a. $\sqrt{-3} \cdot \sqrt{-5} = i\sqrt{3}(i\sqrt{5}) = i^2\sqrt{15} = -1\sqrt{15} = -\sqrt{15}$

b. $\sqrt{-36} \cdot \sqrt{-1} = 6i(i) = 6i^2 = 6(-1) = -6$

c. $\sqrt{8} \cdot \sqrt{-2} = 2\sqrt{2}(i\sqrt{2}) = 2i(\sqrt{2}\sqrt{2}) = 2i(2) = 4i$

d. $\dfrac{\sqrt{-125}}{\sqrt{5}} = \dfrac{i\sqrt{125}}{\sqrt{5}} = i\sqrt{25} = 5i$

PRACTICE 2 Multiply or divide as indicated.

a. $\sqrt{-5} \cdot \sqrt{-6}$ b. $\sqrt{-9} \cdot \sqrt{-1}$ c. $\sqrt{125} \cdot \sqrt{-5}$ d. $\dfrac{\sqrt{-27}}{\sqrt{3}}$

Now that we have practiced working with the imaginary unit, we define complex numbers.

> **Complex Numbers**
> A **complex number** is a number that can be written in the form $a + bi$, where a and b are real numbers.

Notice that the set of real numbers is a subset of the complex numbers since any real number can be written in the form of a complex number. For example,

$$16 = 16 + 0i$$

In general, a complex number $a + bi$ is a real number if $b = 0$. Also, a complex number is called a **pure imaginary number** if $a = 0$ and $b \neq 0$. For example,

$$3i = 0 + 3i \quad \text{and} \quad i\sqrt{7} = 0 + i\sqrt{7}$$

are pure imaginary numbers.

The following diagram shows the relationship between complex numbers and their subsets.

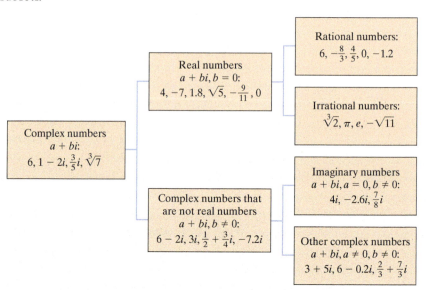

Concept Check ✓

True or false? Every complex number is also a real number.

Answer to Concept Check:
false

OBJECTIVE 2 ▶ Graphing complex numbers. Recall that the graph of a real number is a point on a real number line. In the same manner, the graph of a complex number is a point in the **complex plane.** The complex plane will remind you of the rectangular coordinate system except that the horizontal axis is called the **real axis** and the vertical axis is called the **imaginary axis.**

EXAMPLE 3 Graph the complex numbers in the complex plane.

a. $2 + 3i$ **b.** $-5 + 4i$ **c.** $-3i$ **d.** 5

Solution To plot complex numbers, $a + bi$, on the complex plane, simply form ordered pairs of the form (a, b), then graph just as you would on the rectangular coordinate system.

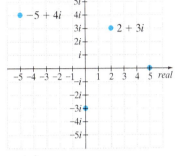

a. To graph $2 + 3i$, think of graphing $(2, 3)$. Start at the origin, move 2 units right and from there, 3 units up.

b. To graph $-5 + 4i$, think of how you graph $(-5, 4)$.

c. To graph $-3i$, remember how to graph $(0, -3)$. (Notice this imaginary number lies on the imaginary axis.)

d. To graph the real number 5, or $5 + 0i$, graph $(5, 0)$. (Notice this real number lies on the real axis.)

PRACTICE 3 Graph the complex numbers in the complex plane.

a. $4 + i$ **b.** $2 - 2i$ **c.** $3i$ **d.** -4

OBJECTIVE 3 ▶ Adding or subtracting complex numbers. Two complex numbers $a + bi$ and $c + di$ are equal if and only if $a = c$ and $b = d$. Complex numbers can be added or subtracted by adding or subtracting their real parts and then adding or subtracting their imaginary parts.

Sum or Difference of Complex Numbers

If $a + bi$ and $c + di$ are complex numbers, then their sum is

$$(a + bi) + (c + di) = (a + c) + (b + d)i$$

Their difference is

$$(a + bi) - (c + di) = a + bi - c - di = (a - c) + (b - d)i$$

EXAMPLE 4 Add or subtract the complex numbers. Write the sum or difference in the form $a + bi$.

a. $(2 + 3i) + (-3 + 2i)$ **b.** $5i - (1 - i)$ **c.** $(-3 - 7i) - (-6)$

Solution

a. $(2 + 3i) + (-3 + 2i) = (2 - 3) + (3 + 2)i = -1 + 5i$

b. $5i - (1 - i) = 5i - 1 + i$

$\qquad\qquad\;\; = -1 + (5 + 1)i$

$\qquad\qquad\;\; = -1 + 6i$

c. $(-3 - 7i) - (-6) = -3 - 7i + 6$
$= (-3 + 6) - 7i$
$= 3 - 7i$

PRACTICE 4 Add or subtract the complex numbers. Write the sum or difference in the form $a + bi$.

a. $(3 - 5i) + (-4 + i)$ **b.** $4i - (3 - i)$ **c.** $(-5 - 2i) - (-8)$

OBJECTIVE 4 ▶ Multiplying complex numbers. To multiply two complex numbers of the form $a + bi$, we multiply as though they are binomials. Then we use the relationship $i^2 = -1$ to simplify.

EXAMPLE 5 Multiply the complex numbers. Write the product in the form $a + bi$.

a. $-7i \cdot 3i$ **b.** $3i(2 - i)$ **c.** $(2 - 5i)(4 + i)$
d. $(2 - i)^2$ **e.** $(7 + 3i)(7 - 3i)$

Solution

a. $-7i \cdot 3i = -21i^2$
$= -21(-1)$ Replace i^2 with -1.
$= 21$

b. $3i(2 - i) = 3i \cdot 2 - 3i \cdot i$ Use the distributive property.
$= 6i - 3i^2$ Multiply.
$= 6i - 3(-1)$ Replace i^2 with -1.
$= 6i + 3$
$= 3 + 6i$

Use the FOIL order below. (First, Outer, Inner, Last)

c. $(2 - 5i)(4 + i) = 2(4) + 2(i) - 5i(4) - 5i(i)$
 F O I L
$= 8 + 2i - 20i - 5i^2$
$= 8 - 18i - 5(-1)$ $i^2 = -1$
$= 8 - 18i + 5$
$= 13 - 18i$

d. $(2 - i)^2 = (2 - i)(2 - i)$
$= 2(2) - 2(i) - 2(i) + i^2$
$= 4 - 4i + (-1)$ $i^2 = -1$
$= 3 - 4i$

e. $(7 + 3i)(7 - 3i) = 7(7) - 7(3i) + 3i(7) - 3i(3i)$
$= 49 - 21i + 21i - 9i^2$
$= 49 - 9(-1)$ $i^2 = -1$
$= 49 + 9$
$= 58$

PRACTICE 5 Multiply the complex numbers. Write the product in the form $a + bi$.

a. $-4i \cdot 5i$ **b.** $5i(2 + i)$ **c.** $(2 + 3i)(6 - i)$
d. $(3 - i)^2$ **e.** $(9 + 2i)(9 - 2i)$

Notice that if you add, subtract, or multiply two complex numbers, just like real numbers, the result is a complex number.

OBJECTIVE 5 ▶ **Dividing complex numbers.** From Example 5e, notice that the product of $7 + 3i$ and $7 - 3i$ is a real number. These two complex numbers are called **complex conjugates** of one another. In general, we have the following definition.

> **Complex Conjugates**
> The complex numbers $(a + bi)$ and $(a - bi)$ are called **complex conjugates** of each other, and $(a + bi)(a - bi) = a^2 + b^2$.

To see that the product of a complex number $a + bi$ and its conjugate $a - bi$ is the real number $a^2 + b^2$, we multiply.

$$(a + bi)(a - bi) = a^2 - abi + abi - b^2i^2$$
$$= a^2 - b^2(-1)$$
$$= a^2 + b^2$$

We use complex conjugates to divide by a complex number.

EXAMPLE 6 Divide. Write in the form $a + bi$.

a. $\dfrac{2 + i}{1 - i}$ **b.** $\dfrac{7}{3i}$

Solution

a. Multiply the numerator and denominator by the complex conjugate of $1 - i$ to eliminate the imaginary number in the denominator.

$$\frac{2 + i}{1 - i} = \frac{(2 + i)(1 + i)}{(1 - i)(1 + i)}$$
$$= \frac{2(1) + 2(i) + 1(i) + i^2}{1^2 - i^2}$$
$$= \frac{2 + 3i - 1}{1 + 1} \qquad \text{Here, } i^2 = -1.$$
$$= \frac{1 + 3i}{2} \quad \text{or} \quad \frac{1}{2} + \frac{3}{2}i$$

b. Multiply the numerator and denominator by the conjugate of $3i$. Note that $3i = 0 + 3i$, so its conjugate is $0 - 3i$ or $-3i$.

$$\frac{7}{3i} = \frac{7(-3i)}{(3i)(-3i)} = \frac{-21i}{-9i^2} = \frac{-21i}{-9(-1)} = \frac{-21i}{9} = \frac{-7i}{3} \quad \text{or} \quad 0 - \frac{7}{3}i \qquad \square$$

PRACTICE 6 Divide. Write in the form $a + bi$.

a. $\dfrac{4 - i}{3 + i}$ **b.** $\dfrac{5}{2i}$

> ▶ **Helpful Hint**
> Recall that division can be checked by multiplication.
> To check that $\dfrac{2 + i}{1 - i} = \dfrac{1}{2} + \dfrac{3}{2}i$, in Example 6a, multiply $\left(\dfrac{1}{2} + \dfrac{3}{2}i\right)(1 - i)$ to verify that the product is $2 + i$.

OBJECTIVE 6 ▶ **Finding powers of i.** We can use the fact that $i^2 = -1$ to find higher powers of i. To find i^3, we rewrite it as the product of i^2 and i.

$$i^3 = i^2 \cdot i = (-1)i = -i$$
$$i^4 = i^2 \cdot i^2 = (-1) \cdot (-1) = 1$$

We continue this process and use the fact that $i^4 = 1$ and $i^2 = -1$ to simplify i^5 and i^6.

$$i^5 = i^4 \cdot i = 1 \cdot i = i$$
$$i^6 = i^4 \cdot i^2 = 1 \cdot (-1) = -1$$

If we continue finding powers of i, we generate the following pattern. Notice that the values i, -1, $-i$, and 1 repeat as i is raised to higher and higher powers.

$$i^1 = i \qquad i^5 = i \qquad i^9 = i$$
$$i^2 = -1 \qquad i^6 = -1 \qquad i^{10} = -1$$
$$i^3 = -i \qquad i^7 = -i \qquad i^{11} = -i$$
$$i^4 = 1 \qquad i^8 = 1 \qquad i^{12} = 1$$

This pattern allows us to find other powers of i. To do so, we will use the fact that $i^4 = 1$ and rewrite a power of i in terms of i^4. For example,

$$i^{22} = i^{20} \cdot i^2 = (i^4)^5 \cdot i^2 = 1^5 \cdot (-1) = 1 \cdot (-1) = -1.$$

EXAMPLE 7 Find the following powers of i.

a. i^7 **b.** i^{20} **c.** i^{46} **d.** i^{-12}

Solution

a. $i^7 = i^4 \cdot i^3 = 1(-i) = -i$
b. $i^{20} = (i^4)^5 = 1^5 = 1$
c. $i^{46} = i^{44} \cdot i^2 = (i^4)^{11} \cdot i^2 = 1^{11}(-1) = -1$
d. $i^{-12} = \dfrac{1}{i^{12}} = \dfrac{1}{(i^4)^3} = \dfrac{1}{(1)^3} = \dfrac{1}{1} = 1$

PRACTICE 7 Find the following powers of i.

a. i^9 **b.** i^{16} **c.** i^{34} **d.** i^{-24}

VOCABULARY & READINESS CHECK

Word Bank. *Use the choices below to fill in each blank. Not all choices will be used.*

-1 $\qquad$ $\sqrt{-1}$ $\qquad$ real $\qquad$ imaginary unit
1 $\qquad$ $\sqrt{1}$ $\qquad$ complex $\qquad$ pure imaginary

1. A _____ number is one that can be written in the form $a + bi$ where a and b are real numbers.
2. In the complex number system, i denotes the _____.
3. $i^2 =$ _____
4. $i =$ _____
5. A complex number, $a + bi$, is a _____ number if $b = 0$.
6. A complex number, $a + bi$, is a _____ number if $a = 0$ and $b \neq 0$.

Simplify. See Example 1.

7. $\sqrt{-81}$ $\qquad$ 8. $\sqrt{-49}$ $\qquad$ 9. $\sqrt{-7}$ $\qquad$ 10. $\sqrt{-3}$
11. $-\sqrt{16}$ $\qquad$ 12. $-\sqrt{4}$ $\qquad$ 13. $\sqrt{-64}$ $\qquad$ 14. $\sqrt{-100}$

8.7 EXERCISE SET

Write in terms of i. See Example 1.

1. $\sqrt{-24}$
2. $\sqrt{-32}$
3. $-\sqrt{-36}$
4. $-\sqrt{-121}$
5. $8\sqrt{-63}$
6. $4\sqrt{-20}$
7. $-\sqrt{54}$
8. $\sqrt{-63}$

Multiply or divide. See Example 2.

9. $\sqrt{-2} \cdot \sqrt{-7}$
10. $\sqrt{-11} \cdot \sqrt{-3}$
11. $\sqrt{-5} \cdot \sqrt{-10}$
12. $\sqrt{-2} \cdot \sqrt{-6}$
13. $\sqrt{16} \cdot \sqrt{-1}$
14. $\sqrt{3} \cdot \sqrt{-27}$
15. $\dfrac{\sqrt{-9}}{\sqrt{3}}$
16. $\dfrac{\sqrt{49}}{\sqrt{-10}}$
17. $\dfrac{\sqrt{-80}}{\sqrt{-10}}$
18. $\dfrac{\sqrt{-40}}{\sqrt{-8}}$

Graph each complex number in a single complex plane. See Example 3.

19. $6 + 3i$
20. $2 + i$
21. $-4 - i$
22. $-3 - 2i$
23. $5i$
24. $-5i$
25. -2
26. 2

Add or subtract. Write the sum or difference in the form a + bi. See Example 4.

27. $(4 - 7i) + (2 + 3i)$
28. $(2 - 4i) - (2 - i)$
29. $(6 + 5i) - (8 - i)$
30. $(8 - 3i) + (-8 + 3i)$
31. $6 - (8 + 4i)$
32. $(9 - 4i) - 9$

Multiply. Write the product in the form a + bi. See Example 5.

33. $-10i \cdot -4i$
34. $-2i \cdot -11i$
35. $6i(2 - 3i)$
36. $5i(4 - 7i)$
37. $(\sqrt{3} + 2i)(\sqrt{3} - 2i)$
38. $(\sqrt{5} - 5i)(\sqrt{5} + 5i)$
39. $(4 - 2i)^2$
40. $(6 - 3i)^2$

Write each quotient in the form a + bi. See Example 6.

41. $\dfrac{4}{i}$
42. $\dfrac{5}{6i}$
43. $\dfrac{7}{4 + 3i}$
44. $\dfrac{9}{1 - 2i}$
45. $\dfrac{3 + 5i}{1 + i}$
46. $\dfrac{6 + 2i}{4 - 3i}$
47. $\dfrac{5 - i}{3 - 2i}$
48. $\dfrac{6 - i}{2 + i}$

MIXED PRACTICE

Perform each indicated operation. Write the result in the form a + bi.

49. $(7i)(-9i)$
50. $(-6i)(-4i)$
51. $(6 - 3i) - (4 - 2i)$
52. $(-2 - 4i) - (6 - 8i)$
53. $-3i(-1 + 9i)$
54. $-5i(-2 + i)$
55. $\dfrac{4 - 5i}{2i}$
56. $\dfrac{6 + 8i}{3i}$
57. $(4 + i)(5 + 2i)$
58. $(3 + i)(2 + 4i)$
59. $(6 - 2i)(3 + i)$
60. $(2 - 4i)(2 - i)$
61. $(8 - 3i) + (2 + 3i)$
62. $(7 + 4i) + (4 - 4i)$
63. $(1 - i)(1 + i)$
64. $(6 + 2i)(6 - 2i)$
65. $\dfrac{16 + 15i}{-3i}$
66. $\dfrac{2 - 3i}{-7i}$
67. $(9 + 8i)^2$
68. $(4 - 7i)^2$
69. $\dfrac{2}{3 + i}$
70. $\dfrac{5}{3 - 2i}$
71. $(5 - 6i) - 4i$
72. $(6 - 2i) + 7i$
73. $\dfrac{2 - 3i}{2 + i}$
74. $\dfrac{6 + 5i}{6 - 5i}$
75. $(2 + 4i) + (6 - 5i)$
76. $(5 - 3i) + (7 - 8i)$
77. $(\sqrt{3} + 2i)(\sqrt{3} - 2i)$
78. $(\sqrt{5} - 5i)(\sqrt{5} + 5i)$
79. $(4 - 2i)^2$
80. $(6 - 3i)^2$

Find each power of i. See Example 7.

81. i^8
82. i^{10}
83. i^{21}
84. i^{15}
85. i^{11}
86. i^{40}
87. i^{-6}
88. i^{-9}
89. $(2i)^6$
90. $(5i)^4$
91. $(-3i)^5$
92. $(-2i)^7$

REVIEW AND PREVIEW

Recall that the sum of the measures of the angles of a triangle is 180°. Find the unknown angle in each triangle.

93.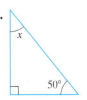

94.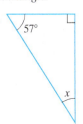

Use synthetic division to divide the following. See Section 7.4.

95. $(x^3 - 6x^2 + 3x - 4) \div (x - 1)$

96. $(5x^4 - 3x^2 + 2) \div (x + 2)$

Thirty people were recently polled about their average monthly balance in their checking accounts. The results of this poll are shown in the following histogram. Use this graph to answer Exercises 97 through 102. See Section 1.2.

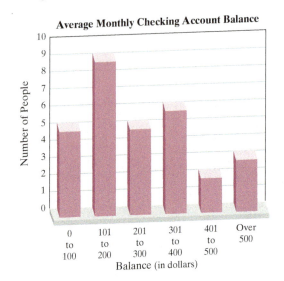

Average Monthly Checking Account Balance

97. How many people polled reported an average checking balance of $201 to $300?

98. How many people polled reported an average checking balance of $0 to $100?

99. How many people polled reported an average checking balance of $200 or less?

100. How many people polled reported an average checking balance of $301 or more?

101. What percent of people polled reported an average checking balance of $201 to $300?

102. What percent of people polled reported an average checking balance of $0 to $100?

CONCEPT EXTENSIONS

Write in the form $a + bi$.

103. $i^3 - i^4$

104. $i^8 - i^7$

105. $i^6 + i^8$

106. $i^4 + i^{12}$

107. $2 + \sqrt{-9}$

108. $5 - \sqrt{-16}$

109. $\dfrac{6 + \sqrt{-18}}{3}$

110. $\dfrac{4 - \sqrt{-8}}{2}$

111. $\dfrac{5 - \sqrt{-75}}{10}$

112. Describe how to find the conjugate of a complex number.

113. Explain why the product of a complex number and its complex conjugate is a real number.

Simplify.

114. $(8 - \sqrt{-3}) - (2 + \sqrt{-12})$

115. $(8 - \sqrt{-4}) - (2 + \sqrt{-16})$

116. Determine whether $2i$ is a solution of $x^2 + 4 = 0$.

117. Determine whether $-1 + i$ is a solution of $x^2 + 2x = -2$.

8.8 STANDARD DEVIATION

OBJECTIVES

1. Review mean, median, and mode.
2. Determine the range for a data set.
3. Determine the standard deviation for a data set.

OBJECTIVE 1 ▶ Reviewing mean, median, and mode. Recall that it is sometimes desirable to be able to describe a set of data, or a set of numbers, by a single "middle" number. Three such **measures of central tendency** are the mean, the median, and the mode.

By far the most commonly used measure of central tendency is the *mean*. The **mean** is obtained by adding all the data items and then dividing the sum by the number of items. The Greek letter sigma, Σ, called a **symbol of summation,** is used to indicate the sum of data items. The notation Σx, read "the sum of x," means to add all the data items in a given data set. We can use this symbol to give a formula for calculating the mean.

> The **mean** is the sum of the data items divided by the number of items
>
> $$\text{Mean} = \frac{\Sigma x}{n},$$
>
> where Σx represents the sum of all the data items and n represents the number of items.

EXAMPLE 1 Seven students in a psychology class conducted an experiment on mazes. Each student was given a pencil and asked to successfully complete the same maze. The timed results are below.

Student	Ann	Thanh	Carlos	Jesse	Melinda	Ramzi	Dayni
Time (Seconds)	13.2	11.8	10.7	16.2	15.9	13.8	18.5

a. Who completed the maze in the shortest time? Who completed the maze in the longest time?
b. Find the mean.
c. How many students look longer than the mean time? How many students took shorter than the mean time?

Solution

a. Carlos completed the maze in 10.7 seconds, the shortest time. Dayni complete the maze in 18.5 seconds, the longest time.
b. To find the mean, find the sum of the data items and divide by 7, the number of items.

$$\text{Mean} = \frac{\Sigma x}{n} = \frac{13.2 + 11.8 + 10.7 + 16.2 + 15.9 + 13.8 + 18.5}{7}$$
$$= \frac{100.1}{7} = 14.3$$

c. Three students, Jesse, Melinda, and Dayni, had times longer than the mean time. Four students, Ann, Thanh, Carlos, and Ramzi, had times shorter than the mean time.

PRACTICE 1 Find the mean for the data: 42, 37, 45, 12, 45, 17.

Two other measures of central tendency are the median and the mode.

> The **median** of an ordered set of numbers is the middle number. If the number of items is even, the median is the mean of the two middle numbers. The **mode** of a set of numbers is the number that occurs most often. It is possible for a data set to have no mode or more than one mode.

EXAMPLE 2 Find the median and the mode of the following list of numbers. These numbers were high temperatures for fourteen consecutive days in a city in Montana.

$$76, 80, 85, 86, 89, 87, 82, 77, 76, 79, 82, 89, 89, 92$$

Solution First, write the numbers in order.

$$76, 76, 77, 79, 80, 82, 82, 85, 86, 87, 89, 89, 89, 92$$

two middle numbers   mode

Since there is an even number of items, the median is the mean of the two middle numbers.

$$\text{median} = \frac{82 + 85}{2} = 83.5$$

The mode is 89, since 89 occurs most often.

PRACTICE 2 Find the median and the mode for the data set: 42, 37, 45, 12, 45, 17.

When you think of Houston, Texas and Honolulu, Hawaii, do balmy temperatures come to mind? Both cities have a mean temperature of 75°. However, the mean temperature does not tell the whole story. The temperature in Houston differs seasonally from a low of about 40° in January to a high of close to 100° in July and August. By contrast, Honolulu's temperature varies less throughout the year, usually ranging between 60° and 90°.

Measures of dispersion are used to describe the spread of data items in a data set. Two of the most common measures of dispersion, the *range* and the *standard deviation*, are discussed here.

OBJECTIVE 2 ▶ The range. A quick but rough measure of dispersion is the **range**, the difference between the highest and lowest data values in a data set. For example, if Houston's hottest annual temperature is 103° and its coldest annual temperature is 33°, the range in temperature is

$$103° - 33°, \quad \text{or} \quad 70°.$$

If Honolulu's hottest day is 89° and its coldest day 61°, the range in temperature is

$$89° - 61°, \quad \text{or} \quad 28°.$$

The Range

The **range**, the difference between the highest and lowest data values in a data set, indicates the total spread of the data.

$$\text{Range} = \text{highest data value} - \text{lowest data value}$$

Section 8.8 Standard Deviation

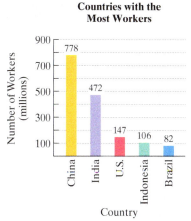

Countries with the Most Workers

Source: Central Intelligence Agency

EXAMPLE 3 Computing the Range

The figure in the margin shows the number of workers, in millions, for the five countries with the largest labor forces. Find the range of workers, in millions, for these five countries.

Solution

$$\text{Range} = \text{highest data value} - \text{lowest data value}$$
$$= 778 - 82 = 696$$

The range is 696 million workers.

PRACTICE 3 Find the range for the following group of data items:

$$4, 2, 11, 7.$$

OBJECTIVE 3 ▶ Determine the standard deviation for a data set. A second measure of dispersion, and one that is dependent on *all* of the data items, is called the **standard deviation.** The standard deviation is found by determining how much each data item differs from the mean.

In order to compute the standard deviation, it is necessary to find by how much each data item deviates from the mean. First compute the mean. Then subtract the mean from each data item. Example 4 shows how this is done. In Example 5, we will use this skill to actually find the standard deviation.

EXAMPLE 4 Preparing to Find the Standard Deviation; Finding Deviations from the Mean

Find the deviations from the mean for the five data items 778, 472, 147, 106, and 82, shown in the figure in the margin above.

Solution First, calculate the mean.

$$\text{Mean} = \frac{\Sigma x}{n} = \frac{778 + 472 + 147 + 106 + 82}{5} = \frac{1585}{5} = 317$$

The mean for the five countries with the largest labor forces is 317 million workers. Now, let's find by how much each of the five data items differs from 317, the mean. For China, with 778 million workers, the computation is shown as follows:

$$\text{Deviation from mean} = \text{data item} - \text{mean}$$
$$= 778 - 317 = 461.$$

This indicates that the labor force in China exceeds the mean by 461 million workers.

The computation for the United States, with 147 million workers, is given by

$$\text{Deviation from mean} = \text{data item} - \text{mean}$$
$$= 147 - 317 = -170.$$

This indicates that the labor force in the United States is 170 million workers below the mean.

The deviations from the mean for each of the five given data items are shown in the table in the margin.

Deviations from the Mean

Data item	Deviation: data item − mean
778	778 − 317 = 461
472	472 − 317 = 155
147	147 − 317 = −170
106	106 − 317 = −211
82	82 − 317 = −235

PRACTICE 4 Compute the mean for the following group of data items:

$$2, 4, 7, 11.$$

Then find the deviations from the mean for the four data items. Organize your work in table form. Keep track of these computations. You will be using them in Practice 5.

The sum of the deviations for a set of data is always zero. For the deviations shown in the table on the previous page,

$$461 + 155 + (-170) + (-211) + (-235) = 616 + (-616) = 0.$$

This shows that we cannot find a measure of dispersion by finding the mean of the deviations, because this value is always zero. However, a kind of average of the deviations from the mean, called the **standard deviation,** can be computed. We do so by squaring each deviation and later introducing a square root in the computation. Here are the details on how to find the standard deviation for a set of data:

Computing the Standard Deviation for a Data Set

STEP 1. Find the mean of the data items.

STEP 2. Find the deviation of each data item from the mean:

$$\text{data item} - \text{mean}.$$

STEP 3. Square each deviation:

$$(\text{data item} - \text{mean})^2.$$

STEP 4. Sum the squared deviations:

$$\Sigma(\text{data item} - \text{mean})^2.$$

STEP 5. Divide the sum in step 4 by $n - 1$, where n represents the number of data items:

$$\frac{\Sigma(\text{data item} - \text{mean})^2}{n - 1}.$$

STEP 6. Take the square root of the quotient in step 5. This value is the standard deviation for the data set.

$$\text{Standard deviation} = \sqrt{\frac{\Sigma(\text{data item} - \text{mean})^2}{n - 1}}$$

The computation of the standard deviation can be organized using a table with three columns:

Data item	Deviation: Data item − mean	(Deviation)^2: (Data item − mean)^2

In Example 4, we worked out the first two columns of such a table. Let's continue working with the data for the countries with the most workers and compute the standard deviation.

EXAMPLE 5 Computing the Standard Deviation

The bar graph showed earlier displayed the number of workers, in millions, for the five countries with the largest labor forces. Find the standard deviation, in millions, for these five countries.

Solution

STEP 1. Find the mean. From our work in Example 4, the mean is 317.

STEP 2. Find the deviation of each data item from the mean: data item − mean. This, too, was done in Example 4 for each of the five data items.

STEP 3. Square each deviation: (data item − mean)². We square each of the numbers in the (data item − mean) column, shown below. Notice that squaring the difference always results in a positive number.

Computing the Standard Deviation

Data item	Deviation: data item − mean	(Deviation)²: (data item − mean)²
778	778 − 317 = 461	$461^2 = 461 \cdot 461 = 212{,}521$
472	472 − 317 = 155	$155^2 = 155 \cdot 155 = 24{,}025$
147	147 − 317 = −170	$(-170)^2 = (-170)(-170) = 28{,}900$
106	106 − 317 = −211	$(-211)^2 = (-211)(-211) = 44{,}521$
82	82 − 317 = −235	$(-235)^2 = (-235)(-235) = 55{,}225$
Totals:	0	365,192

The sum of the deviations for a set of data is always zero.

Adding the five numbers in the third column gives the sum of the squared deviations: $\Sigma(\text{data item} - \text{mean})^2$.

STEP 4. Sum the squared deviations: $\Sigma(\text{data item} - \text{mean})^2$. This step is shown in the table above. The squares in the third column were added, resulting in a sum of 365,192.

STEP 5. Divide the sum in step 4 by $n - 1$, where n represents the number of data items. The number of data items is 5 so we divide by 4.

$$\frac{\Sigma(\text{data item} - \text{mean})^2}{n-1} = \frac{365{,}192}{5-1} = \frac{365{,}192}{4} = 91{,}298$$

STEP 6. The standard deviation is the square root of the quotient in step 5.

$$\text{Standard deviation} = \sqrt{\frac{\Sigma(\text{data item} - \text{mean})^2}{n-1}} = \sqrt{91{,}298} \approx 302.16$$

The standard deviation for the five countries with the largest labor forces is approximately 302.16 million workers.

TECHNOLOGY NOTE

Almost all scientific and graphing calculators compute the standard deviation of a set of data. Using the data items in Example 5,

778, 472, 147, 106, 82,

the keystrokes for obtaining the standard deviation on many scientific calculators are as follows:

778 $\Sigma+$ 472 $\Sigma+$ 147 $\Sigma+$ 106 $\Sigma+$ 82 $\Sigma+$ 2nd $\sigma n - 1$.

Graphing calculators require that you specify if data items are from an entire population or a sample of the population.

PRACTICE 5 Find the standard deviation for the group of data items listed earlier in Practice 4. Round to two decimal places.

Example 6 illustrates that as the spread of data items increases, the standard deviation gets larger.

EXAMPLE 6   Computing the Standard Deviation

Find the standard deviation of the data items in each of the samples shown below.

Sample A	Sample B
17, 18, 19, 20, 21, 22, 23	5, 10, 15, 20, 25, 30, 35

Solution Begin by finding the mean for each sample.

Sample A:

$$\text{Mean} = \frac{17 + 18 + 19 + 20 + 21 + 22 + 23}{7} = \frac{140}{7} = 20$$

Sample B:

$$\text{Mean} = \frac{5 + 10 + 15 + 20 + 25 + 30 + 35}{7} = \frac{140}{7} = 20$$

Although both samples have the same mean, the data items in sample B are more spread out. Thus, we would expect sample B to have the greater standard deviation. The computation of the standard deviation requires that we find $\Sigma(\text{data item} - \text{mean})^2$, shown below.

Computing Standard Deviations for Two Samples

	Sample A			Sample B	
Data item	Deviation: data item − mean	(Deviation)²: (data item − mean)²	Data item	Deviation: data item − mean	(Deviation)²: (data item − mean)²
17	17 − 20 = −3	(−3)² = 9	5	5 − 20 = −15	(−15)² = 225
18	18 − 20 = −2	(−2)² = 4	10	10 − 20 = −10	(−10)² = 100
19	19 − 20 = −1	(−1)² = 1	15	15 − 20 = −5	(−5)² = 25
20	20 − 20 = 0	0² = 0	20	20 − 20 = 0	0² = 0
21	21 − 20 = 1	1² = 1	25	25 − 20 = 5	5² = 25
22	22 − 20 = 2	2² = 4	30	30 − 20 = 10	10² = 100
23	23 − 20 = 3	3² = 9	35	35 − 20 = 15	15² = 225
Totals:		$\Sigma(\text{data item} - \text{mean})^2 = 28$			$\Sigma(\text{data item} - \text{mean})^2 = 700$

Each sample contains seven data items, so we compute the standard deviation by dividing the sums in the previous table, 28 and 700, by 7 − 1, or 6. Then we take the square root of each quotient.

$$\text{Standard deviation} = \sqrt{\frac{\Sigma(\text{data item} - \text{mean})^2}{n - 1}}$$

Sample A:

$$\text{Standard deviation} = \sqrt{\frac{28}{6}} \approx 2.16$$

Sample B:

$$\text{Standard deviation} = \sqrt{\frac{700}{6}} \approx 10.80$$

Sample A has a standard deviation of approximately 2.16 and sample B has a standard deviation of approximately 10.80. The scores in sample B are more spread out than those in sample A. □

PRACTICE 6 Find the standard deviation of the data items in each of the samples shown below. Round to two decimal places.

Sample A: 73, 75, 77, 79, 81, 83

Sample B: 40, 44, 92, 94, 98, 100

The figure on the next page illustrates four sets of data items organized in histograms. From left to right, the data items are

Figure (a): 4, 4, 4, 4, 4, 4, 4
Figure (b): 3, 3, 4, 4, 4, 5, 5
Figure (c): 3, 3, 3, 4, 5, 5, 5
Figure (d): 1, 1, 1, 4, 7, 7, 7.

Each data set has a mean of 4. However, as the spread of data items increases, the standard deviation gets larger. Observe that when all the data items are the same, the standard deviation is 0.

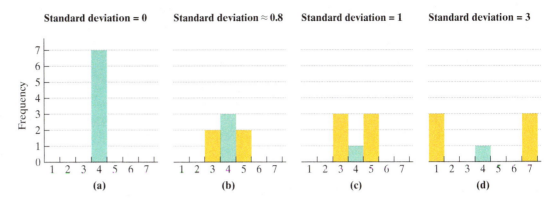

The standard deviation gets larger with increased dispersion among data items. In each case, the mean is 4.

EXAMPLE 7 Interpreting Standard Deviation

Two fifth-grade classes have nearly identical mean scores on an aptitude test, but one class has a standard deviation three times that of the other. All other factors being equal, which class is easier to teach, and why?

Solution The class with the smaller standard deviation is easier to teach because there is less variation among student aptitudes. Course work can be aimed at the average student without too much concern that the work will be too easy for some or too difficult for others. By contrast, the class with greater dispersion poses a greater challenge. By teaching to the average student, the students whose scores are significantly above the mean will be bored; students whose scores are significantly below the mean will be confused.

PRACTICE 7 Shown below are the means and standard deviations of the yearly returns on two investments from 1926 through 2004.

Investment	Mean Yearly Interest	Standard Deviation
Small-Company Stocks	17.5%	33.3%
Large-Company Stocks	12.4%	20.4%

Source: *Summary Statistics of Annual Total Returns 1926 to 2004 Yearbook,* Ibbotson Associates, Chicago

a. Use the means to determine which investment provided the greater yearly return.

b. Use the standard deviations to determine which investment had the greater risk. Explain your answer.

8.8 EXERCISE SET

For each of the following data sets, find the mean, the median, and the mode. If necessary, round the mean to one decimal place. See Examples 1 and 2.

1. 21, 28, 16, 42, 38

2. 42, 35, 36, 40, 50

3. 7.6, 8.2, 8.2, 9.6, 5.7, 9.1

4. 4.9, 7.1, 6.8, 6.8, 5.3, 4.9

5. 0.2, 0.3, 0.5, 0.6, 0.6, 0.9, 0.2, 0.7, 1.1

504 CHAPTER 8 Rational Exponents, Radicals, and Complex Numbers

6. 0.6, 0.6, 0.8, 0.4, 0.5, 0.3, 0.7, 0.8, 0.1

7. 231, 543, 601, 293, 588, 109, 334, 268

8. 451, 356, 478, 776, 892, 500, 467, 780

The following pulse rates were recorded for a group of fifteen students: 78, 80, 66, 68, 71, 64, 82, 71, 70, 65, 70, 75, 77, 86, 72.

9. Find the mean.
10. Find the median.
11. Find the mode.
12. How many rates were higher than the mean?
13. How many rates were lower than the mean?
14. Have each student in your algebra class take his/her pulse rate. Record the data and find the mean, the median, and the mode.

In Exercises 15–20, find the range for each group of data items. See Example 3.

15. 1, 2, 3, 4, 5
16. 16, 17, 18, 19, 20
17. 7, 9, 9, 15
18. 11, 13, 14, 15, 17
19. 3, 3, 4, 4, 5, 5
20. 3, 3, 3, 4, 5, 5, 5

Multiple Steps. *In Exercises 21–24, a group of data items and their mean are given.*

  a. *Find the deviation from the mean for each of the data items.*
  b. *Find the sum of the deviations in part (a).*

21. 3, 5, 7, 12, 18, 27; Mean = 12
22. 84, 88, 90, 95, 98; Mean = 91
23. 29, 38, 48, 49, 53, 77; Mean = 49
24. 60, 60, 62, 65, 65, 65, 66, 67, 70, 70; Mean = 65

Multiple Steps. *In Exercises 25–30, find* **a.** *the mean;* **b.** *the deviation from the mean for each data item; and* **c.** *the sum of the deviations in part (b).*

25. 85, 95, 90, 85, 100
26. 94, 62, 88, 85, 91
27. 146, 153, 155, 160, 161
28. 150, 132, 144, 122
29. 2.25, 3.50, 2.75, 3.10, 1.90
30. 0.35, 0.37, 0.41, 0.39, 0.43

In Exercises 31–40 find the standard deviation for each group of data items. Round answers to two decimal places. See Examples 4 through 6.

31. 1, 2, 3, 4, 5
32. 16, 17, 18, 19, 20
33. 7, 9, 9, 15
34. 11, 13, 14, 15, 17
35. 3, 3, 4, 4, 5, 5
36. 3, 3, 3, 4, 5, 5, 5
37. 1, 1, 1, 4, 7, 7, 7
38. 6, 6, 6, 6, 7, 7, 7, 4, 8, 3
39. 9, 5, 9, 5, 9, 5, 9, 5
40. 6, 10, 6, 10, 6, 10, 6, 10

In Exercises 41–42, compute the mean, range, and standard deviation for the data items in each of the three samples. Then describe one way in which the samples are alike and one way in which they are different.

41. Sample A: 6, 8, 10, 12, 14, 16, 18
Sample B: 6, 7, 8, 12, 16, 17, 18
Sample C: 6, 6, 6, 12, 18, 18, 18

42. Sample A: 8, 10, 12, 14, 16, 18, 20
Sample B: 8, 9, 10, 14, 18, 19, 20
Sample C: 8, 8, 8, 14, 20, 20, 20

Read a Graph. *In Exercises 43–46, use each display of data items to find the standard deviation. Where necessary, round answers to two decimal places.*

43.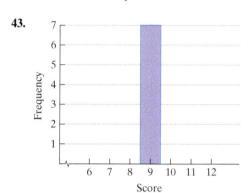

44.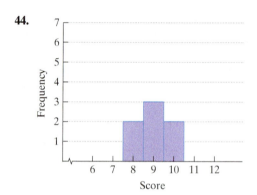

45.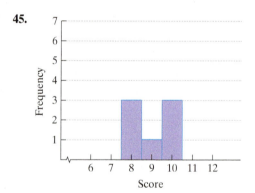

46.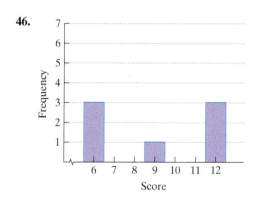

47. Multiple Steps. The data sets give the ages of Oscar winners from 1999 through 2005 at the time of the award.

Year	Best Actor	Age
1999	Kevin Spacey	40
2000	Russell Crowe	36
2001	Denzel Washington	47
2002	Adrien Brody	29
2003	Sean Penn	43
2004	Jamie Foxx	37
2005	Philip Seymour Hoffman	38

Year	Best Actress	Age
1999	Hilary Swank	25
2000	Julia Roberts	33
2001	Halle Berry	35
2002	Nicole Kidman	35
2003	Charlize Theron	28
2004	Hilary Swank	30
2005	Reese Witherspoon	29

Source: www.oscars.org

a. Without calculating, which data set has the greater mean age? Explain your answer.

b. Verify your conjecture from part (a) by calculating the mean age for each data set. Round answers to two decimal places.

c. Without calculating, which data set has the greater standard deviation? Explain your answer.

d. Verify your conjecture from part (c) by calculating the standard deviation for each data set. Round answers to two decimal places.

48. Multiple Steps. The data sets give the ages of the first six U.S. presidents and the last six U.S. presidents (through G. W. Bush).

Age of First Six U.S. Presidents at Inauguration

President	Age
Washington	57
J. Adams	61
Jefferson	57
Madison	57
Monroe	58
J. Q. Adams	57

Age of Last Six U.S. Presidents at Inauguration

President	Age
Ford	61
Carter	52
Reagan	69
G. H. W. Bush	64
Clinton	46
G. W. Bush	54

Source: Time Almanac

a. Without calculating, which set has the greater standard deviation? Explain your answer.

b. Verify your conjecture from part (b) by calculating the standard deviation for each data set. Round answers to two decimal places.

Find the missing numbers in each list of numbers. (These numbers are not necessarily in numerical order.)

49. __, __, 16, 18, __
The mode is 21.   The mean is 20.

50. __, __, __, __, 40
The mode is 35.   The median is 37.   The mean is 38.

51. Describe how to find the range of a data set.

52. Describe why the range might not be the best measure of dispersion.

53. Describe how the standard deviation is computed.

54. Describe what the standard deviation reveals about a data set.

55. If a set of test scores has a standard deviation of zero, what does this mean about the scores?

56. Two classes took a statistics test. Both classes had a mean score of 73. The scores of class A had a standard deviation of 5 and those of class B had a standard deviation of 10. Discuss the difference between the two classes' performance on the test.

57. Decision Making. Which one of the following is true?

a. If the same number is added to each data item in a set of data, the standard deviation does not change.

b. If each number in a data set is multiplied by 4, the standard deviation is doubled.

c. It is possible for a set of scores to have a negative standard deviation.

d. Data sets with different means cannot have the same standard deviation.

58. Describe a situation in which a relatively large standard deviation is desirable.

59. If a set of test scores has a large range but a small standard deviation, describe what this means about students' performance on the test.

60. Multiple Choice. Use the data 1, 2, 3, 5, 6, 7. Without actually computing the standard deviation, which of the following best approximates the standard deviation?

a. 2   b. 6   c. 10   d. 20

61. Use the data 0, 1, 3, 4, 4, 6. Add 2 to each of the numbers. How does this affect the mean? How does this affect the standard deviation?

GROUP EXERCISES

62. Group members should consult a current almanac or the Internet and select intriguing data. The group's function is to use statistics to tell a story. Once "intriguing" data are identified, as a group

a. Summarize the data. Use words, frequency distributions, and graphic displays.

b. Compute measures of central tendency and dispersion, using these statistics to discuss the data.

CHAPTER 8 VOCABULARY CHECK

Fill in each blank with one of the words or phrases listed below.

standard deviation	rationalizing	radicand	mean	mode	range
index	like radicals	principal square root	cube root	midpoint	median
complex number	conjugate	imaginary unit	distance		

1. The _____ of $\sqrt{3} + 2$ is $\sqrt{3} - 2$.
2. The _____ of a nonnegative number a is written as $\sqrt{a}$.
3. The process of writing a radical expression as an equivalent expression but without a radical in the denominator is called _____ the denominator.
4. The _____ written i, is the number whose square is -1.
5. The _____ of a number is written as $\sqrt[3]{a}$.
6. In the notation $\sqrt[n]{a}$, n is called the _____ and a is called the _____.
7. Radicals with the same index and the same radicand are called _____.
8. A _____ is a number that can be written in the form $a + bi$, where a and b are real numbers.
9. The _____ formula is $d = \sqrt{(x_2 - x_1)^2 + (y_2 - y_1)^2}$.
10. The _____ formula is $\left(\dfrac{x_1 + x_2}{2}, \dfrac{y_1 + y_2}{2}\right)$.
11. The _____ of a set of numbers is the number that occurs most often.
12. The _____ is the sum of the data items divided by the number of data items.
13. The _____ is the difference between the highest and lowest data values.
14. The _____ of an ordered set of numbers is the middle number.
15. The _____ is found by determining how much each data item differs from the mean.

CHAPTER 8 REVIEW

(8.1) Find the root. Assume that all variables represent positive numbers.

1. $\sqrt{81}$
2. $\sqrt[4]{81}$
3. $\sqrt[3]{-8}$
4. $\sqrt[4]{-16}$
5. $-\sqrt{\dfrac{1}{49}}$
6. $\sqrt{x^{64}}$
7. $-\sqrt{36}$
8. $\sqrt[3]{64}$
9. $\sqrt[3]{-a^6b^9}$
10. $\sqrt{16a^4b^{12}}$
11. $\sqrt[5]{32a^5b^{10}}$
12. $\sqrt[5]{-32x^{15}y^{20}}$
13. $\sqrt{\dfrac{x^{12}}{36y^2}}$
14. $\sqrt[3]{\dfrac{27y^3}{z^{12}}}$

Simplify. Use absolute value bars when necessary.

15. $\sqrt{(-x)^2}$
16. $\sqrt[4]{(x^2-4)^4}$
17. $\sqrt[3]{(-27)^3}$
18. $\sqrt[5]{(-5)^5}$
19. $-\sqrt[5]{x^5}$
20. $\sqrt[4]{16(2y+z)^{12}}$
21. $\sqrt{25(x-y)^{10}}$
22. $\sqrt[5]{-y^5}$
23. $\sqrt[9]{-x^9}$

Identify the domain and then graph each function.

24. $f(x) = \sqrt{x} + 3$
25. $g(x) = \sqrt[3]{x-3}$; use the accompanying table.

x	-5	2	3	4	11
$g(x)$					

(8.2) Evaluate the following.

26. $\left(\dfrac{1}{81}\right)^{1/4}$
27. $\left(-\dfrac{1}{27}\right)^{1/3}$
28. $(-27)^{-1/3}$
29. $(-64)^{-1/3}$
30. $-9^{3/2}$
31. $64^{-1/3}$
32. $(-25)^{5/2}$
33. $\left(\dfrac{25}{49}\right)^{-3/2}$
34. $\left(\dfrac{8}{27}\right)^{-2/3}$
35. $\left(-\dfrac{1}{36}\right)^{-1/4}$

Write with rational exponents.

36. $\sqrt[3]{x^2}$
37. $\sqrt[5]{5x^2y^3}$

Write with radical notation.

38. $y^{4/5}$

39. $5(xy^2z^5)^{1/3}$

40. $(x+2y)^{-1/2}$

Simplify each expression. Assume that all variables represent positive numbers. Write with only positive exponents.

41. $a^{1/3}a^{4/3}a^{1/2}$

42. $\dfrac{b^{1/3}}{b^{4/3}}$

43. $(a^{1/2}a^{-2})^3$

44. $(x^{-3}y^6)^{1/3}$

45. $\left(\dfrac{b^{3/4}}{a^{-1/2}}\right)^8$

46. $\dfrac{x^{1/4}x^{-1/2}}{x^{2/3}}$

47. $\left(\dfrac{49c^{5/3}}{a^{-1/4}b^{5/6}}\right)^{-1}$

48. $a^{-1/4}(a^{5/4}-a^{9/4})$

Use a calculator and write a three-decimal-place approximation.

49. $\sqrt{20}$

50. $\sqrt[3]{-39}$

51. $\sqrt[4]{726}$

52. $56^{1/3}$

53. $-78^{3/4}$

54. $105^{-2/3}$

Use rational exponents to write each radical with the same index. Then multiply.

55. $\sqrt[3]{2}\cdot\sqrt{7}$

56. $\sqrt[3]{3}\cdot\sqrt[4]{x}$

(8.3) Perform the indicated operations and then simplify if possible. For the remainder of this review, assume that variables represent positive numbers only.

57. $\sqrt{3}\cdot\sqrt{8}$

58. $\sqrt[3]{7y}\cdot\sqrt[3]{x^2z}$

59. $\dfrac{\sqrt{44x^3}}{\sqrt{11x}}$

60. $\dfrac{\sqrt[4]{a^6b^{13}}}{\sqrt[4]{a^2b}}$

Simplify.

61. $\sqrt{60}$

62. $-\sqrt{75}$

63. $\sqrt[3]{162}$

64. $\sqrt[3]{-32}$

65. $\sqrt{36x^7}$

66. $\sqrt[3]{24a^5b^7}$

67. $\sqrt{\dfrac{p^{17}}{121}}$

68. $\sqrt[3]{\dfrac{y^5}{27x^6}}$

69. $\sqrt[4]{\dfrac{xy^6}{81}}$

70. $\sqrt{\dfrac{2x^3}{49y^4}}$

△ **71.** The formula for the radius r of a circle of area A is

$$r=\sqrt{\dfrac{A}{\pi}}$$

   a. Find the exact radius of a circle whose area is 25 square meters.

   b. Approximate to two decimal places the radius of a circle whose area is 104 square inches.

Find the distance between each pair of points. Give an exact value and a three-decimal-place approximation.

72. $(-6,3)$ and $(8,4)$

73. $(-4,-6)$ and $(-1,5)$

74. $(-1,5)$ and $(2,-3)$

75. $(-\sqrt{2},0)$ and $(0,-4\sqrt{6})$

76. $(-\sqrt{5},-\sqrt{11})$ and $(-\sqrt{5},-3\sqrt{11})$

77. $(7.4,-8.6)$ and $(-1.2,5.6)$

Find the midpoint of each line segment whose endpoints are given.

78. $(2,6);(-12,4)$

79. $(-6,-5);(-9,7)$

80. $(4,-6);(-15,2)$

81. $\left(0,-\dfrac{3}{8}\right);\left(\dfrac{1}{10},0\right)$

82. $\left(\dfrac{3}{4},-\dfrac{1}{7}\right);\left(-\dfrac{1}{4},-\dfrac{3}{7}\right)$

83. $(\sqrt{3},-2\sqrt{6})$ and $(\sqrt{3},-4\sqrt{6})$

(8.4) Perform the indicated operation.

84. $2\sqrt{50}-3\sqrt{125}+\sqrt{98}$

85. $x\sqrt{75xy}-\sqrt{27x^3y}$

86. $\sqrt[3]{128}+\sqrt[3]{250}$

87. $3\sqrt[4]{32a^5}-a\sqrt[4]{162a}$

88. $\dfrac{5}{\sqrt{4}}+\dfrac{\sqrt{3}}{3}$

89. $\sqrt{\dfrac{8}{x^2}}-\sqrt{\dfrac{50}{16x^2}}$

90. $2\sqrt{32x^2y^3}-xy\sqrt{98y}$

91. $2a\sqrt[4]{32b^5}-3b\sqrt[4]{162a^4b}+\sqrt[4]{2a^4b^5}$

Multiply and then simplify if possible.

92. $\sqrt{3}(\sqrt{27}-\sqrt{3})$

93. $(\sqrt{x}-3)^2$

94. $(\sqrt{5}-5)(2\sqrt{5}+2)$

95. $(2\sqrt{x}-3\sqrt{y})(2\sqrt{x}+3\sqrt{y})$

96. $(\sqrt{a}+3)(\sqrt{a}-3)$

97. $(\sqrt[3]{a}+2)^2$

98. $(\sqrt[3]{5x}+9)(\sqrt[3]{5x}-9)$

99. $(\sqrt[3]{a}+4)(\sqrt[3]{a^2}-4\sqrt[3]{a}+16)$

(8.5) Rationalize each denominator.

100. $\dfrac{3}{\sqrt{7}}$
101. $\sqrt{\dfrac{x}{12}}$
102. $\dfrac{5}{\sqrt[3]{4}}$
103. $\sqrt{\dfrac{24x^5}{3y^2}}$
104. $\sqrt[3]{\dfrac{15x^6y^7}{z^2}}$
105. $\dfrac{5}{2-\sqrt{7}}$
106. $\dfrac{3}{\sqrt{y}-2}$
107. $\dfrac{\sqrt{2}-\sqrt{3}}{\sqrt{2}+\sqrt{3}}$

Rationalize each numerator.

108. $\dfrac{\sqrt{11}}{3}$
109. $\sqrt{\dfrac{18}{y}}$
110. $\dfrac{\sqrt[3]{9}}{7}$
111. $\sqrt{\dfrac{24x^5}{3y^2}}$
112. $\sqrt[3]{\dfrac{xy^2}{10z}}$
113. $\dfrac{\sqrt{x}+5}{-3}$

(8.6) Solve each equation for the variable.

114. $\sqrt{y-7}=5$
115. $\sqrt{2x}+10=4$
116. $\sqrt[3]{2x-6}=4$
117. $\sqrt{x+6}=\sqrt{x+2}$
118. $2x-5\sqrt{x}=3$
119. $\sqrt{x+9}=2+\sqrt{x-7}$

Find each unknown length.

120.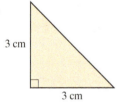

3 cm, 3 cm

121.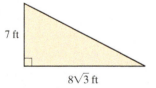

7 ft, $8\sqrt{3}$ ft

122. Beverly Hillis wants to determine the distance x across a pond on her property. She is able to measure the distances shown on the following diagram. Find how wide the lake is at the crossing point, indicated by the triangle, to the nearest tenth of a foot.

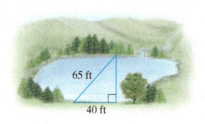

65 ft, 40 ft

123. A pipe fitter needs to connect two underground pipelines that are offset by 3 feet, as pictured in the diagram. Neglecting the joints needed to join the pipes, find the length of the shortest possible connecting pipe rounded to the nearest hundredth of a foot.

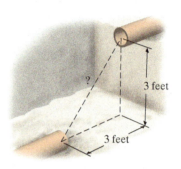

(8.7) Perform the indicated operation and simplify. Write the result in the form $a+bi$.

124. $\sqrt{-8}$
125. $-\sqrt{-6}$
126. $\sqrt{-4}+\sqrt{-16}$
127. $\sqrt{-2}\cdot\sqrt{-5}$
128. $(12-6i)+(3+2i)$
129. $(-8-7i)-(5-4i)$
130. $(2i)^6$
131. $-3i(6-4i)$
132. $(3+2i)(1+i)$
133. $(2-3i)^2$
134. $(\sqrt{6}-9i)(\sqrt{6}+9i)$
135. $\dfrac{2+3i}{2i}$
136. $\dfrac{1+i}{-3i}$

Graph the complex numbers in a complex plane.

137. $4-2i$
138. $-1+i$

(8.8) In Exercises 139–140, find the mean, median, mode, and range for each group of data items.

139. 28, 34, 16, 22, 28
140. 312, 783, 219, 312, 426, 219
141. The mean for the data items 29, 9, 8, 22, 46, 51, 48, 42, 53, 42 is 35. Find **a.** the deviation from the mean for each data item and **b.** the sum of the deviations in part (a).
142. Use the data items 36, 26, 24, 90, and 74 to find **a.** the mean, **b.** the deviation from the mean for each data item, and **c.** the sum of the deviations in part (b).

In Exercises 143–144, find the standard deviation for each group of data items.

143. 3, 3, 5, 8, 10, 13
144. 20, 27, 23, 26, 28, 32, 33, 35
145. A test measuring anxiety levels is administered to a sample of ten college students with the following results. (High scores indicate high anxiety.)

    10, 30, 37, 40, 43, 44, 45, 69, 86, 86

    Find the mean, range, and standard deviation for the data.
146. Compute the mean and the standard deviation for each of the following data sets. Then, write a brief description of similarities and differences between the two sets based on each of your computations.

    Set A: 80, 80, 80, 80   Set B: 70, 70, 90, 90

MIXED REVIEW

Simplify. Use absolute value bars when necessary.

147. $\sqrt[3]{x^3}$ **148.** $\sqrt{(x+2)^2}$

Simplify. Assume that all variables represent positive real numbers. If necessary, write answers with positive exponents only.

149. $-\sqrt{100}$ **150.** $\sqrt[3]{-x^{12}y^3}$

151. $\sqrt[4]{\dfrac{y^{20}}{16x^{12}}}$ **152.** $9^{1/2}$

153. $64^{-1/2}$ **154.** $\left(\dfrac{27}{64}\right)^{-2/3}$

155. $\dfrac{(x^{2/3}x^{-3})^3}{x^{-1/2}}$ **156.** $\sqrt{200x^9}$

157. $\sqrt{\dfrac{3n^3}{121m^{10}}}$ **158.** $3\sqrt{20} - 7x\sqrt[3]{40} + 3\sqrt[3]{5x^3}$

159. $(2\sqrt{x} - 5)^2$

160. Find the distance between $(-3, 5)$ and $(-8, 9)$.

161. Find the midpoint of the line segment joining $(-3, 8)$ and $(11, 24)$.

Rationalize each denominator.

162. $\dfrac{7}{\sqrt{13}}$ **163.** $\dfrac{2}{\sqrt{x}+3}$

Solve.

164. $\sqrt{x+2} = x$

CHAPTER 8 TEST

Remember to use the Chapter Test Prep Videos to see the fully worked-out solutions to any of the exercises you want to review.

Raise to the power or find the root. Assume that all variables represent positive numbers. Write with only positive exponents.

1. $\sqrt{216}$ **2.** $-\sqrt[4]{x^{64}}$

3. $\left(\dfrac{1}{125}\right)^{1/3}$ **4.** $\left(\dfrac{1}{125}\right)^{-1/3}$

5. $\left(\dfrac{8x^3}{27}\right)^{2/3}$ **6.** $\sqrt[3]{-a^{18}b^9}$

7. $\left(\dfrac{64c^{4/3}}{a^{-2/3}b^{5/6}}\right)^{1/2}$ **8.** $a^{-2/3}(a^{5/4} - a^3)$

Find the root. Use absolute value bars when necessary.

9. $\sqrt[4]{(4xy)^4}$ **10.** $\sqrt[3]{(-27)^3}$

Rationalize the denominator. Assume that all variables represent positive numbers.

11. $\sqrt{\dfrac{9}{y}}$ **12.** $\dfrac{4-\sqrt{x}}{4+2\sqrt{x}}$

13. $\dfrac{\sqrt[3]{ab}}{\sqrt[3]{ab^2}}$

14. Rationalize the numerator of $\dfrac{\sqrt{6}+x}{8}$ and simplify.

Perform the indicated operations. Assume that all variables represent positive numbers.

15. $\sqrt{125x^3} - 3\sqrt{20x^3}$

16. $\sqrt{3}(\sqrt{16} - \sqrt{2})$

17. $(\sqrt{x}+1)^2$

18. $(\sqrt{2}-4)(\sqrt{3}+1)$

19. $(\sqrt{5}+5)(\sqrt{5}-5)$

Use a calculator to approximate each to three decimal places.

20. $\sqrt{561}$ **21.** $386^{-2/3}$

Solve.

22. $x = \sqrt{x-2} + 2$ **23.** $\sqrt{x^2-7} + 3 = 0$

24. $\sqrt[3]{x+5} = \sqrt[3]{2x-1}$

Perform the indicated operation and simplify. Write the result in the form $a + bi$.

25. $-\sqrt{-8}$ **26.** $(12 - 6i) - (12 - 3i)$

27. $(6 - 2i)(6 + 2i)$ **28.** $(4 + 3i)^2$

29. $\dfrac{1+4i}{1-i}$

30. Graph the complex numbers on a single complex plane.
  a. $3 - 2i$ **b.** -5 **c.** $4i$

31. Find x.

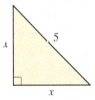

32. Identify the domain of $g(x)$. Then complete the accompanying table and graph $g(x)$.

$$g(x) = \sqrt{x+2}$$

x	-2	-1	2	7
$g(x)$				

33. Find the distance between the points $(-6, 3)$ and $(-8, -7)$.

34. Find the distance between the points $(-2\sqrt{5}, \sqrt{10})$ and $(-\sqrt{5}, 4\sqrt{10})$.

35. Find the midpoint of the line segment whose endpoints are $(-2, -5)$ and $(-6, 12)$.

36. Find the midpoint of the line segment whose endpoints are $\left(-\dfrac{2}{3}, -\dfrac{1}{5}\right)$ and $\left(-\dfrac{1}{3}, \dfrac{4}{5}\right)$.

Solve.

37. The function $V(r) = \sqrt{2.5r}$ can be used to estimate the maximum safe velocity V in miles per hour at which a car can travel if it is driven along a curved road with a *radius of curvature r* in feet. To the nearest whole number, find the maximum safe speed if a cloverleaf exit on an expressway has a radius of curvature of 300 feet.

38. Use the formula from Exercise 37 to find the radius of curvature if the safe velocity is 30 mph.

Use the six data items listed below to solve Exercises 39–42. If needed, round answers to two decimal places.

$$3, 6, 2, 1, 7, 3$$

39. Find the mean.
40. Find the median.
41. Find the mode.
42. Find the standard deviation.

CHAPTER 8 STANDARDIZED TEST

Multiple Choice. *Choose the one alternative that best completes the statement or answers the question.*

Raise to the power or find the root. Assume that all variables represent positive numbers. Write with only positive exponents.

1. $\sqrt{289}$
   a. 144
   b. not a real number
   c. 17
   d. 18

2. $-\sqrt[5]{x^{30}}$
   a. $-6x$
   b. $-x^5$
   c. $-x^7$
   d. $-x^6$

3. $\left(\dfrac{1}{32}\right)^{1/5}$
   a. 2
   b. -2
   c. $-\dfrac{1}{2}$
   d. $\dfrac{1}{2}$

4. $\left(\dfrac{1}{9}\right)^{-1/2}$
   a. 3
   b. $\dfrac{1}{3}$
   c. -3
   d. $\dfrac{-1}{3}$

5. $\left(\dfrac{64x^3}{125}\right)^{4/3}$
   a. $\dfrac{4x}{5}$
   b. $\dfrac{64x^{13/3}}{125}$
   c. $\dfrac{256x^4}{625}$
   d. $\dfrac{64x^4}{125}$

6. $\sqrt[3]{-8a^6b^3}$
   a. $2a^2b$
   b. $-2a^2b$
   c. $8a^2b$
   d. $2a^9b^6$

7. $\left(\dfrac{2^2 x^{1/4} y^7}{x^{1/4}}\right)^{1/2}$
   a. $2y^{2/7}$
   b. $2y^{7/2}$
   c. $2y^7$
   d. $y^{7/2}$

8. $3x^{-1/3}(3x^3 - x^{1/3})$
   a. $9x^{8/3} - x$
   b. $9x^{8/3} - 3$
   c. $9x^{8/3} - 1$
   d. $9x^{8/3} - 3x$

Find the root. Use absolute value bars when necessary.

9. $\sqrt[4]{(4xz)^4}$
   a. not a real number
   b. $16|xz|$
   c. $4xz$
   d. $4|xz|$

10. $\sqrt{(-5)^7}$
    a. $|-5|$
    b. -5
    c. 5
    d. $(-5)^7$

Rationalize the denominator. Assume that all variables represent positive numbers.

11. $\sqrt{\dfrac{121}{x}}$
    a. $\dfrac{11\sqrt{x}}{x}$
    b. $\dfrac{121\sqrt{11x}}{x}$
    c. $\dfrac{11}{x}$
    d. $\dfrac{11\sqrt{x}}{x^2}$

12. $\dfrac{\sqrt{x} - 10}{\sqrt{x} + 10}$
    a. $-20\sqrt{x}$
    b. $\dfrac{x + 100}{x - 100}$
    c. $\dfrac{x - 20\sqrt{x} + 100}{x - 100}$
    d. -1

13. $\dfrac{\sqrt[3]{3x}}{\sqrt[3]{4y}}$
    a. $\dfrac{\sqrt[3]{48xy^2}}{4y}$
    b. $\dfrac{48x}{4y}$
    c. $\dfrac{\sqrt[3]{192xy^2}}{4y}$
    d. $\dfrac{\sqrt[3]{48xy}}{4y}$

Solve the problem.

14. Rationalize the numerator of $\dfrac{\sqrt{2}+x}{5}$ and simplify.

  a. $5(\sqrt{2}+x)$
  b. $\dfrac{2+x^2}{5(\sqrt{2}+x)}$
  c. $\dfrac{2-x^2}{\sqrt{10}-5x}$
  d. $\dfrac{2-x^2}{5(\sqrt{2}-x)}$

Perform the indicated operations. Assume that all variables represent positive numbers.

15. $\sqrt{45x^3} - 10\sqrt{125x^3}$

  a. $53x\sqrt{5x}$
  b. $-47x\sqrt{5x}$
  c. $-10\sqrt{-80x^3}$
  d. $-47\sqrt{5x^3}$

16. $\sqrt{7}(\sqrt{175}+\sqrt{35})$

  a. $35 + 49\sqrt{5}$
  b. $1225 + 7\sqrt{5}$
  c. $35 + 7\sqrt{5}$
  d. 70

17. $(\sqrt{x}-19)^2$

  a. $x - 361$
  b. $x + 361$
  c. $x - 38\sqrt{x} + 361$
  d. $x + 38\sqrt{x} + 361$

18. $(\sqrt{5}+7)(\sqrt{6}+2)$

  a. $\sqrt{30} + 2\sqrt{5} + 7\sqrt{6} + 14$
  b. $\sqrt{30} + 9\sqrt{6} + 14$
  c. $10\sqrt{30} + 14$
  d. $\sqrt{30} + 14$

19. $(\sqrt{10}+3)(\sqrt{10}-3)$

  a. 1
  b. 7
  c. 19
  d. $10 - 2\sqrt{3}$

Use a calculator to approximate the number to three decimal places.

20. $\sqrt{879}$

  a. 29.648
  b. 29.645
  c. 879.000
  d. 29.653

21. $458^{-2/3}$

  a. 0.014
  b. 0.019
  c. 0.017
  d. 0.016

Solve.

22. $x = \sqrt{12x - 12} - 2$

  a. -3
  b. 4
  c. 3
  d. -4

23. $\sqrt{x^2 - 13} + 6 = 0$

  a. $8, -8$
  b. no solution
  c. 7
  d. $7, -7$

24. $\sqrt[5]{5x-7} = \sqrt[3]{x+12}$

  a. $\dfrac{19}{4}$
  b. $\dfrac{5}{6}$
  c. $\dfrac{5}{4}$
  d. $\dfrac{19}{5}$

Perform the indicated operation and simplify. Write the result in the form $a + bi$.

25. $\sqrt{-169}$

  a. $13i$
  b. $-i\sqrt{13}$
  c. ± 13
  d. $-13i$

26. $(5 - 8i) - (5 - i)$

  a. $-9i$
  b. $-7i$
  c. $10 - 7i$
  d. $10 - 9i$

27. $(5 + 3i)(5 - 3i)$

  a. $25 - 9i^2$
  b. 34
  c. $25 - 9i$
  d. 16

28. $(4 + 2i)^2$

  a. $12 + 16i$
  b. $16 + 16i + 4i^2$
  c. $20 + 16i$
  d. 12

29. $\dfrac{8 + 4i}{7 - 9i}$

  a. $-\dfrac{1}{16} + \dfrac{5}{16}i$
  b. $\dfrac{2}{13} + \dfrac{10}{13}i$
  c. $\dfrac{92}{13} + \dfrac{44}{13}i$
  d. $-\dfrac{23}{8} + \dfrac{5}{16}i$

30. Graph the complex numbers below on the complex plane.
  A $-4 + i$ B $-4i$ C 2

a.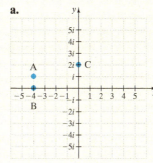
b.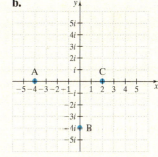
c.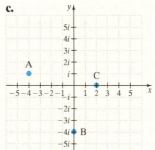
d.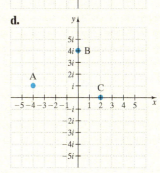

Solve the problem.

31. Find x.

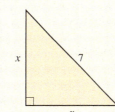

  a. $7\sqrt{2}$ units
  b. 7 units
  c. $\dfrac{\sqrt{14}}{2}$ units
  d. $\dfrac{7\sqrt{2}}{2}$ units

Identify the domain of $f(x)$. Then graph $f(x)$.

32. $f(x) = \sqrt{x+3}$

a. $x \geq 0$

b. $x \geq 0$

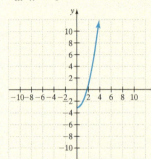
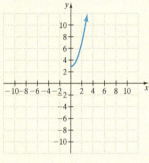

c. $x \geq 3$

d. $x \geq -3$

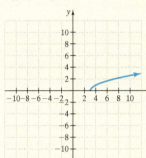
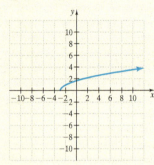

Solve the problem.

33. Find the distance between the points $(7,-6)$ and $(-1,-2)$.

a. $4\sqrt{5}$ units b. 12 units
c. 48 units d. $48\sqrt{3}$ units

34. Find the distance between the points $(2\sqrt{5}, 3)$ and $(6\sqrt{5}, 4)$.

a. 8 units b. 9 units
c. 81 units d. 3 units

35. Find the midpoint of the line segment whose endpoints are $(-2, 3), (6, -6)$.

a. $\left(2, -\dfrac{3}{2}\right)$ b. $(-8, 9)$
c. $\left(-4, \dfrac{9}{2}\right)$ d. $(4, -3)$

36. Find the midpoint of the line segment whose endpoints are $\left(-\dfrac{3}{5}, -\dfrac{7}{2}\right), \left(\dfrac{9}{5}, \dfrac{5}{2}\right)$.

a. $\left(\dfrac{3}{5}, -\dfrac{1}{2}\right)$ b. $\left(\dfrac{6}{5}, -1\right)$
c. $\left(\dfrac{6}{5}, 3\right)$ d. $\left(-\dfrac{6}{5}, -3\right)$

37. Police use the formula $s = \sqrt{30fd}$ to estimate the speed s of a car in miles per hour, where d is the distance in feet that the car skidded and f is the coefficient of friction. If the coefficient of friction on a certain dry road is 0.82 and a car was traveling on it at a rate of 70 mph, how far will the car skid? (Round to the nearest foot.)

a. 41 ft b. 199 ft
c. 1205 ft d. 163 ft

38. The maximum distance d in kilometers that you can see from a height h in meters is given by the formula $d = 3.5\sqrt{h}$. How high above the ground must you be to see 65 kilometers? (Round to the nearest tenth of a meter.)

a. 344.9 m b. 18.6 m
c. 28.2 m d. 1207.1 m

Find the mean for the group of data items. Round to the nearest hundredth, if necessary.

39. 20, 20, 28, 82, 45, 20

a. 43 b. 35.83
c. 32.5 d. 39

Find the median for the group of data items.

40. 10, 9, 4, 0, 1, 1, 1, 0, 0

a. 4 b. 0
c. 5 d. 1

Find the mode for the group of data items. If there is no mode, so state.

41. 10, 6, 5, 0, 1, 1, 1

a. 6 b. 10
c. 1 d. no mode

Find the standard deviation for the group of data items (to the nearest hundredth).

42. 11, 12, 13, 14, 15

a. 1.58 b. 2.5
c. 1.25 d. 0

CHAPTER

Quadratic and Higher Degree Equations and Functions

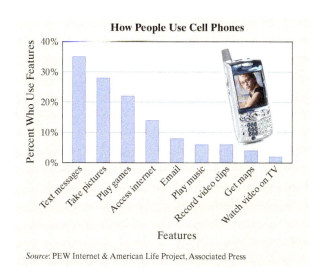

9.1	Solving Quadratic Equations by Completing the Square
9.2	Solving Quadratic Equations by the Quadratic Formula
9.3	Solving Equations by Using Quadratic Methods
	Integrated Review— Summary on Solving Quadratic Equations
9.4	Zeros of Polynomial Function
9.5	The Fundamental Theorem of Algebra
9.6	Nonlinear Inequalities in One Variable

The growth of cell phones can be approximated by a quadratic function. More interesting information is probably given on the graph above. As shown, the cell phone is certainly no longer just a phone.

In this chapter, we continue the work begun in Chapter 6, when we solved polynomial equations in one variable by factoring. Two additional methods of solving quadratic equations are analyzed, as well as methods of solving nonlinear inequalities in one variable.

514   CHAPTER 9   Quadratic and Higher Degree Equations and Functions

9.1 SOLVING QUADRATIC EQUATIONS BY COMPLETING THE SQUARE

OBJECTIVES

1. Use the square root property to solve quadratic equations.
2. Solve quadratic equations by completing the square.
3. Use quadratic equations to solve problems.

OBJECTIVE 1 ▶ **Using the square root property.** In Chapter 6, we solved quadratic equations by factoring. Recall that a **quadratic**, or **second-degree, equation** is an equation that can be written in the form $ax^2 + bx + c = 0$, where a, b, and c are real numbers and a is not 0. To solve a quadratic equation such as $x^2 = 9$ by factoring, we use the zero-factor theorem. To use the zero-factor theorem, the equation must first be written in standard form, $ax^2 + bx + c = 0$.

$$x^2 = 9$$
$$x^2 - 9 = 0 \quad \text{Subtract 9 from both sides.}$$
$$(x + 3)(x - 3) = 0 \quad \text{Factor.}$$
$$x + 3 = 0 \quad \text{or} \quad x - 3 = 0 \quad \text{Set each factor equal to 0.}$$
$$x = -3 \quad \quad x = 3 \quad \text{Solve.}$$

The solutions are -3, 3, the positive and negative square roots of 9. Not all quadratic equations can be solved by factoring, so we need to explore other methods. Notice that the solutions of the equation $x^2 = 9$ are two numbers whose square is 9.

$$3^2 = 9 \quad \text{and} \quad (-3)^2 = 9$$

Thus, we can solve the equation $x^2 = 9$ by taking the square root of both sides. Be sure to include both $\sqrt{9}$ and $-\sqrt{9}$ as solutions since both $\sqrt{9}$ and $-\sqrt{9}$ are numbers whose square is 9.

$$x^2 = 9$$
$$\sqrt{x^2} = \pm\sqrt{9} \quad \text{The notation } \pm\sqrt{9} \text{ (read as "plus or minus } \sqrt{9}\text{")}$$
$$x = \pm 3 \quad \text{indicates the pair of numbers } +\sqrt{9} \text{ and } -\sqrt{9}.$$

This illustrates the square root property.

▶ **Helpful Hint**
The notation ± 3, for example, is read as "plus or minus 3." It is a shorthand notation for the pair of numbers $+3$ and -3.

Square Root Property
If b is a real number and if $a^2 = b$, then $a = \pm\sqrt{b}$.

EXAMPLE 1   Use the square root property to solve $x^2 = 50$.

Solution
$$x^2 = 50$$
$$x = \pm\sqrt{50} \quad \text{Use the square root property.}$$
$$x = \pm 5\sqrt{2} \quad \text{Simplify the radical.}$$

Check: Let $x = 5\sqrt{2}$.   Let $x = -5\sqrt{2}$.

$$x^2 = 50 \quad\quad\quad\quad\quad\quad x^2 = 50$$
$$(5\sqrt{2})^2 \stackrel{?}{=} 50 \quad\quad\quad (-5\sqrt{2})^2 \stackrel{?}{=} 50$$
$$25 \cdot 2 \stackrel{?}{=} 50 \quad\quad\quad\quad 25 \cdot 2 \stackrel{?}{=} 50$$
$$50 = 50 \quad \text{True} \quad\quad 50 = 50 \quad \text{True}$$

The solutions are $5\sqrt{2}$ and $-5\sqrt{2}$, or the solution set is $\{-5\sqrt{2}, 5\sqrt{2}\}$.

PRACTICE
1   Use the square root property to solve $x^2 = 18$.

EXAMPLE 2
Use the square root property to solve $2x^2 - 14 = 0$.

Solution First we get the squared variable alone on one side of the equation.

$$2x^2 - 14 = 0$$
$$2x^2 = 14 \quad \text{Add 14 to both sides.}$$
$$x^2 = 7 \quad \text{Divide both sides by 2.}$$
$$x = \pm\sqrt{7} \quad \text{Use the square root property.}$$

Check to see that the solutions are $\sqrt{7}$ and $-\sqrt{7}$, or the solution set is $\{-\sqrt{7}, \sqrt{7}\}$. □

PRACTICE 2 Use the square root property to solve $3x^2 - 30 = 0$.

EXAMPLE 3
Use the square root property to solve $(x + 1)^2 = 12$.

Solution
$$(x + 1)^2 = 12$$
$$x + 1 = \pm\sqrt{12} \quad \text{Use the square root property.}$$
$$x + 1 = \pm 2\sqrt{3} \quad \text{Simplify the radical.}$$
$$x = -1 \pm 2\sqrt{3} \quad \text{Subtract 1 from both sides.}$$

Check: Below is a check for $-1 + 2\sqrt{3}$. The check for $-1 - 2\sqrt{3}$ is almost the same and is left for you to do on your own.

$$(x + 1)^2 = 12$$
$$\left(-1 + 2\sqrt{3} + 1\right)^2 \stackrel{?}{=} 12$$
$$\left(2\sqrt{3}\right)^2 \stackrel{?}{=} 12$$
$$4 \cdot 3 \stackrel{?}{=} 12$$
$$12 = 12 \quad \text{True}$$

The solutions are $-1 + 2\sqrt{3}$ and $-1 - 2\sqrt{3}$. □

PRACTICE 3 Use the square root property to solve $(x + 3)^2 = 20$.

EXAMPLE 4
Use the square root property to solve $(2x - 5)^2 = -16$.

Solution
$$(2x - 5)^2 = -16$$
$$2x - 5 = \pm\sqrt{-16} \quad \text{Use the square root property.}$$
$$2x - 5 = \pm 4i \quad \text{Simplify the radical.}$$
$$2x = 5 \pm 4i \quad \text{Add 5 to both sides.}$$
$$x = \frac{5 \pm 4i}{2} \quad \text{Divide both sides by 2.}$$

The solutions are $\frac{5 + 4i}{2}$ and $\frac{5 - 4i}{2}$. □

PRACTICE 4 Use the square root property to solve $(5x - 2)^2 = -9$.

Concept Check ✓
How do you know just by looking that $(x - 2)^2 = -4$ has complex, but not real solutions?

Answer to Concept Check: answers may vary

OBJECTIVE 2 ▶ **Solving by completing the square.** Notice from Examples 3 and 4 that, if we write a quadratic equation so that one side is the square of a binomial, we can solve by using the square root property. To write the square of a binomial, we write perfect square trinomials. Recall that a perfect square trinomial is a trinomial that can be factored into two identical binomial factors.

Perfect Square Trinomials	*Factored Form*
$x^2 + 8x + 16$	$(x + 4)^2$
$x^2 - 6x + 9$	$(x - 3)^2$
$x^2 + 3x + \dfrac{9}{4}$	$\left(x + \dfrac{3}{2}\right)^2$

Notice that for each perfect square trinomial, **the constant term of the trinomial is the square of half the coefficient of the x-term.** For example,

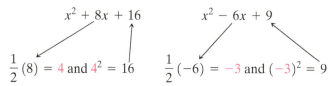

$$\frac{1}{2}(8) = 4 \text{ and } 4^2 = 16 \qquad \frac{1}{2}(-6) = -3 \text{ and } (-3)^2 = 9$$

The process of writing a quadratic equation so that one side is a perfect square trinomial is called **completing the square.**

EXAMPLE 5 Solve $p^2 + 2p = 4$ by completing the square.

Solution First, add the square of half the coefficient of p to both sides so that the resulting trinomial will be a perfect square trinomial. The coefficient of p is 2.

$$\frac{1}{2}(2) = 1 \quad \text{and} \quad 1^2 = 1$$

Add 1 to both sides of the original equation.

$$p^2 + 2p = 4$$
$$p^2 + 2p + 1 = 4 + 1 \quad \text{Add 1 to both sides.}$$
$$(p + 1)^2 = 5 \quad \text{Factor the trinomial; simplify the right side.}$$

We may now use the square root property and solve for p.

$$p + 1 = \pm\sqrt{5} \quad \text{Use the square root property.}$$
$$p = -1 \pm \sqrt{5} \quad \text{Subtract 1 from both sides.}$$

Notice that there are two solutions: $-1 + \sqrt{5}$ and $-1 - \sqrt{5}$. ☐

PRACTICE 5 Solve $b^2 + 4b = 3$ by completing the square.

EXAMPLE 6 Solve $m^2 - 7m - 1 = 0$ for m by completing the square.

Solution First, add 1 to both sides of the equation so that the left side has no constant term.

$$m^2 - 7m - 1 = 0$$
$$m^2 - 7m = 1$$

Now find the constant term that makes the left side a perfect square trinomial by squaring half the coefficient of m. Add this constant to both sides of the equation.

$$\frac{1}{2}(-7) = -\frac{7}{2} \quad \text{and} \quad \left(-\frac{7}{2}\right)^2 = \frac{49}{4}$$

$$m^2 - 7m + \frac{49}{4} = 1 + \frac{49}{4} \qquad \text{Add } \frac{49}{4} \text{ to both sides of the equation.}$$

Section 9.1 Solving Quadratic Equations by Completing the Square **517**

$$\left(m - \frac{7}{2}\right)^2 = \frac{53}{4} \quad \text{Factor the perfect square trinomial and simplify the right side.}$$

$$m - \frac{7}{2} = \pm\sqrt{\frac{53}{4}} \quad \text{Apply the square root property.}$$

$$m = \frac{7}{2} \pm \frac{\sqrt{53}}{2} \quad \text{Add } \frac{7}{2} \text{ to both sides and simplify } \sqrt{\frac{53}{4}}.$$

$$m = \frac{7 \pm \sqrt{53}}{2} \quad \text{Simplify.}$$

The solutions are $\dfrac{7 + \sqrt{53}}{2}$ and $\dfrac{7 - \sqrt{53}}{2}$.

PRACTICE
6 Solve $p^2 - 3p + 1 = 0$ by completing the square.

EXAMPLE 7 Solve: $2x^2 - 8x + 3 = 0$.

Solution Our procedure for finding the constant term to complete the square works only if the coefficient of the squared variable term is 1. Therefore, to solve this equation, the first step is to divide both sides by 2, the coefficient of x^2.

$$2x^2 - 8x + 3 = 0$$

$$x^2 - 4x + \frac{3}{2} = 0 \quad \text{Divide both sides by 2.}$$

$$x^2 - 4x = -\frac{3}{2} \quad \text{Subtract } \frac{3}{2} \text{ from both sides.}$$

Next find the square of half of -4.

$$\frac{1}{2}(-4) = -2 \quad \text{and} \quad (-2)^2 = 4$$

Add 4 to both sides of the equation to complete the square.

$$x^2 - 4x + 4 = -\frac{3}{2} + 4$$

$$(x - 2)^2 = \frac{5}{2} \quad \text{Factor the perfect square and simplify the right side.}$$

$$x - 2 = \pm\sqrt{\frac{5}{2}} \quad \text{Apply the square root property.}$$

$$x - 2 = \pm\frac{\sqrt{10}}{2} \quad \text{Rationalize the denominator.}$$

$$x = 2 \pm \frac{\sqrt{10}}{2} \quad \text{Add 2 to both sides.}$$

$$= \frac{4}{2} \pm \frac{\sqrt{10}}{2} \quad \text{Find the common denominator.}$$

$$= \frac{4 \pm \sqrt{10}}{2} \quad \text{Simplify.}$$

The solutions are $\dfrac{4 + \sqrt{10}}{2}$ and $\dfrac{4 - \sqrt{10}}{2}$.

PRACTICE
7 Solve: $3x^2 - 12x + 1 = 0$.

The following steps may be used to solve a quadratic equation such as $ax^2 + bx + c = 0$ by completing the square. This method may be used whether or not the polynomial $ax^2 + bx + c$ is factorable.

> **Solving a Quadratic Equation in x by Completing the Square**
>
> **STEP 1.** If the coefficient of x^2 is 1, go to Step 2. Otherwise, divide both sides of the equation by the coefficient of x^2.
>
> **STEP 2.** Isolate all variable terms on one side of the equation.
>
> **STEP 3.** Complete the square for the resulting binomial by adding the square of half of the coefficient of x to both sides of the equation.
>
> **STEP 4.** Factor the resulting perfect square trinomial and write it as the square of a binomial.
>
> **STEP 5.** Use the square root property to solve for x.

EXAMPLE 8 Solve $3x^2 - 9x + 8 = 0$ by completing the square.

Solution $3x^2 - 9x + 8 = 0$

STEP 1. $x^2 - 3x + \dfrac{8}{3} = 0$ Divide both sides of the equation by 3.

STEP 2. $x^2 - 3x = -\dfrac{8}{3}$ Subtract $\dfrac{8}{3}$ from both sides.

Since $\dfrac{1}{2}(-3) = -\dfrac{3}{2}$ and $\left(-\dfrac{3}{2}\right)^2 = \dfrac{9}{4}$, we add $\dfrac{9}{4}$ to both sides of the equation.

STEP 3. $x^2 - 3x + \dfrac{9}{4} = -\dfrac{8}{3} + \dfrac{9}{4}$

STEP 4. $\left(x - \dfrac{3}{2}\right)^2 = -\dfrac{5}{12}$ Factor the perfect square trinomial.

STEP 5. $x - \dfrac{3}{2} = \pm\sqrt{-\dfrac{5}{12}}$ Apply the square root property.

$x - \dfrac{3}{2} = \pm\dfrac{i\sqrt{5}}{2\sqrt{3}}$ Simplify the radical.

$x - \dfrac{3}{2} = \pm\dfrac{i\sqrt{15}}{6}$ Rationalize the denominator.

$x = \dfrac{3}{2} \pm \dfrac{i\sqrt{15}}{6}$ Add $\dfrac{3}{2}$ to both sides.

$= \dfrac{9}{6} \pm \dfrac{i\sqrt{15}}{6}$ Find a common denominator.

$= \dfrac{9 \pm i\sqrt{15}}{6}$ Simplify.

The solutions are $\dfrac{9 + i\sqrt{15}}{6}$ and $\dfrac{9 - i\sqrt{15}}{6}$.

PRACTICE 8 Solve $2x^2 - 5x + 7 = 0$ by completing the square.

OBJECTIVE 3 ▶ Solving problems modeled by quadratic equations. Recall the **simple interest** formula $I = Prt$, where I is the interest earned, P is the principal, r is the rate of interest, and t is time in years. If $100 is invested at a simple interest rate of 5% annually, at the end of 3 years the total interest I earned is

$$I = P \cdot r \cdot t$$

or

$$I = 100 \cdot 0.05 \cdot 3 = \$15$$

and the new principal is

$$\$100 + \$15 = \$115$$

Most of the time, the interest computed on money borrowed or money deposited is **compound interest.** Compound interest, unlike simple interest, is computed on original principal *and* on interest already earned. To see the difference between simple interest and compound interest, suppose that $100 is invested at a rate of 5% compounded annually. To find the total amount of money at the end of 3 years, we calculate as follows.

$$I = P \cdot r \cdot t$$

First year: Interest = $100 · 0.05 · 1 = $5.00
               New principal = $100.00 + $5.00 = $105.00

Second year: Interest = $105.00 · 0.05 · 1 = $5.25
               New principal = $105.00 + $5.25 = $110.25

Third year: Interest = $110.25 · 0.05 · 1 ≈ $5.51
               New principal = $110.25 + $5.51 = $115.76

At the end of the third year, the total compound interest earned is $115.76, whereas the total simple interest earned is $15.

It is tedious to calculate compound interest as we did above, so we use a compound interest formula. The formula for calculating the total amount of money when interest is compounded annually is

$$A = P(1 + r)^t$$

where P is the original investment, r is the interest rate per compounding period, and t is the number of periods. For example, the amount of money A at the end of 3 years if $100 is invested at 5% compounded annually is

$$A = \$100(1 + 0.05)^3 \approx \$100(1.1576) = \$115.76$$

as we previously calculated.

EXAMPLE 9   Finding Interest Rates

Use the formula $A = P(1 + r)^t$ to find the interest rate r if $2000 compounded annually grows to $2420 in 2 years.

Solution

1. UNDERSTAND the problem. Since the $2000 is compounded annually, we use the compound interest formula. For this example, make sure that you understand the formula for compounding interest annually.

2. TRANSLATE. We substitute the given values into the formula.

$$A = P(1 + r)^t$$
$$2420 = 2000(1 + r)^2 \quad \text{Let } A = 2420, P = 2000, \text{ and } t = 2.$$

3. SOLVE. Solve the equation for r.

$$2420 = 2000(1 + r)^2$$

$$\frac{2420}{2000} = (1 + r)^2 \quad \text{Divide both sides by 2000.}$$

$$\frac{121}{100} = (1 + r)^2 \quad \text{Simplify the fraction.}$$

$$\pm\sqrt{\frac{121}{100}} = 1 + r \quad \text{Use the square root property.}$$

$$\pm \frac{11}{10} = 1 + r \qquad \text{Simplify.}$$

$$-1 \pm \frac{11}{10} = r$$

$$-\frac{10}{10} \pm \frac{11}{10} = r$$

$$\frac{1}{10} = r \quad \text{or} \quad -\frac{21}{10} = r$$

4. INTERPRET. The rate cannot be negative, so we reject $-\frac{21}{10}$.

Check: $\frac{1}{10} = 0.10 = 10\%$ per year. If we invest \$2000 at 10% compounded annually, in 2 years the amount in the account would be $2000(1 + 0.10)^2 = 2420$ dollars, the desired amount.

State: The interest rate is 10% compounded annually.

PRACTICE

9 Use the formula from Example 9 to find the interest rate r if \$5000 compounded annually grows to \$5618 in 2 years.

Graphing Calculator Explorations

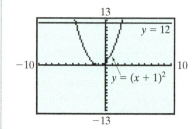

In Section 6.8, we showed how we can use a grapher to approximate real number solutions of a quadratic equation written in standard form. We can also use a grapher to solve a quadratic equation when it is not written in standard form. For example, to solve $(x + 1)^2 = 12$, the quadratic equation in Example 3, we graph the following on the same set of axes. Use Xmin $= -10$, Xmax $= 10$, Ymin $= -13$, and Ymax $= 13$.

$$Y_1 = (x + 1)^2 \quad \text{and} \quad Y_2 = 12$$

Use the Intersect feature or the Zoom and Trace features to locate the points of intersection of the graphs. (See your manuals for specific instructions.) The x-values of these points are the solutions of $(x + 1)^2 = 12$. The solutions, rounded to two decimal places, are 2.46 and -4.46.

Check to see that these numbers are approximations of the exact solutions $-1 \pm 2\sqrt{3}$.

Use a graphing calculator to solve each quadratic equation. Round all solutions to the nearest hundredth.

1. $x(x - 5) = 8$
2. $x(x + 2) = 5$
3. $x^2 + 0.5x = 0.3x + 1$
4. $x^2 - 2.6x = -2.2x + 3$
5. Use a graphing calculator and solve $(2x - 5)^2 = -16$, Example 4 in this section, using the window

$$\text{Xmin} = -20$$
$$\text{Xmax} = 20$$
$$\text{Xscl} = 1$$
$$\text{Ymin} = -20$$
$$\text{Ymax} = 20$$
$$\text{Yscl} = 1$$

Explain the results. Compare your results with the solution found in Example 4.

6. What are the advantages and disadvantages of using a graphing calculator to solve quadratic equations?

VOCABULARY & READINESS CHECK

Word Bank. *Use the choices below to fill in each blank. Not all choices will be used.*

binomial	$\sqrt{b}$	$\pm\sqrt{b}$	b^2	9	25	completing the square
quadratic	$-\sqrt{b}$	$\dfrac{b}{2}$	$\left(\dfrac{b}{2}\right)^2$	3	5	

1. By the square root property, if b is a real number, and $a^2 = b$, then $a =$ _____.

2. A _____ equation can be written in the form $ax^2 + bx + c = 0, a \neq 0$.

3. The process of writing a quadratic equation so that one side is a perfect square trinomial is called _____.

4. A perfect square trinomial is one that can be factored as a _____ squared.

5. To solve $x^2 + 6x = 10$ by completing the square, add _____ to both sides.

6. To solve $x^2 + bx = c$ by completing the square, add _____ to both sides.

Fill in the Blank. *Fill in the blank with the number needed to make the expression a perfect square trinomial.*

7. $m^2 + 2m +$ _____
8. $m^2 - 2m +$ _____
9. $y^2 - 14y +$ _____
10. $z^2 + z +$ _____

9.1 EXERCISE SET

Use the square root property to solve each equation. These equations have real-number solutions. See Examples 1 through 3.

1. $x^2 = 16$
2. $x^2 = 49$
3. $x^2 - 7 = 0$
4. $x^2 - 11 = 0$
5. $x^2 = 18$
6. $y^2 = 20$
7. $3z^2 - 30 = 0$
8. $2x^2 - 4 = 0$
9. $(x + 5)^2 = 9$
10. $(y - 3)^2 = 4$
11. $(z - 6)^2 = 18$
12. $(y + 4)^2 = 27$
13. $(2x - 3)^2 = 8$
14. $(4x + 9)^2 = 6$

Use the square root property to solve each equation. See Examples 1 through 4.

15. $x^2 + 9 = 0$
16. $x^2 + 4 = 0$
17. $x^2 - 6 = 0$
18. $y^2 - 10 = 0$
19. $2z^2 + 16 = 0$
20. $3p^2 + 36 = 0$
21. $(x - 1)^2 = -16$
22. $(y + 2)^2 = -25$
23. $(z + 7)^2 = 5$
24. $(x + 10)^2 = 11$
25. $(x + 3)^2 = -8$
26. $(y - 4)^2 = -18$

Fill in the Blank. *Add the proper constant to each binomial so that the resulting trinomial is a perfect square trinomial. Then factor the trinomial.*

27. $x^2 + 16x +$ _____
28. $y^2 + 2y +$ _____
29. $z^2 - 12z +$ _____
30. $x^2 - 8x +$ _____
31. $p^2 + 9p +$ _____
32. $n^2 + 5n +$ _____
33. $x^2 + x +$ _____
34. $y^2 - y +$ _____

MIXED PRACTICE

Solve each equation by completing the square. These equations have real number solutions. See Examples 5 through 7.

35. $x^2 + 8x = -15$
36. $y^2 + 6y = -8$
37. $x^2 + 6x + 2 = 0$
38. $x^2 - 2x - 2 = 0$
39. $x^2 + x - 1 = 0$
40. $x^2 + 3x - 2 = 0$
41. $x^2 + 2x - 5 = 0$
42. $y^2 + y - 7 = 0$
43. $3p^2 - 12p + 2 = 0$

44. $2x^2 + 14x - 1 = 0$

45. $4y^2 - 12y - 2 = 0$

46. $6x^2 - 3 = 6x$

47. $2x^2 + 7x = 4$

48. $3x^2 - 4x = 4$

49. $x^2 - 4x - 5 = 0$

50. $y^2 + 6y - 8 = 0$

51. $x^2 + 8x + 1 = 0$

52. $x^2 - 10x + 2 = 0$

53. $3y^2 + 6y - 4 = 0$

54. $2y^2 + 12y + 3 = 0$

55. $2x^2 - 3x - 5 = 0$

56. $5x^2 + 3x - 2 = 0$

Solve each equation by completing the square. See Examples 5 through 8.

57. $y^2 + 2y + 2 = 0$

58. $x^2 + 4x + 6 = 0$

59. $x^2 - 6x + 3 = 0$

60. $x^2 - 7x - 1 = 0$

61. $2a^2 + 8a = -12$

62. $3x^2 + 12x = -14$

63. $5x^2 + 15x - 1 = 0$

64. $16y^2 + 16y - 1 = 0$

65. $2x^2 - x + 6 = 0$

66. $4x^2 - 2x + 5 = 0$

67. $x^2 + 10x + 28 = 0$

68. $y^2 + 8y + 18 = 0$

69. $z^2 + 3z - 4 = 0$

70. $y^2 + y - 2 = 0$

71. $2x^2 - 4x = -3$

72. $9x^2 - 36x = -40$

73. $3x^2 + 3x = 5$

74. $5y^2 - 15y = 1$

Use the formula $A = P(1 + r)^t$ to solve Exercises 75 through 78. See Example 9.

75. Find the rate r at which $3000 compounded annually grows to $4320 in 2 years.

76. Find the rate r at which $800 compounded annually grows to $882 in 2 years.

77. Find the rate at which $15,000 compounded annually grows to $16,224 in 2 years.

78. Find the rate at which $2000 compounded annually grows to $2880 in 2 years.

79. In your own words, what is the difference between simple interest and compound interest?

Neglecting air resistance, the distance s(t) in feet traveled by a freely falling object is given by the function $s(t) = 16t^2$, where t is time in seconds. Use this formula to solve Exercises 80 through 83. Round answers to two decimal places.

80. The Petronas Towers in Kuala Lumpur, built in 1997, are the tallest buildings in Malaysia. Each tower is 1483 feet tall. How long would it take an object to fall to the ground from the top of one of the towers? (*Source:* Council on Tall Buildings and Urban Habitat, Lehigh University)

81. The height of the Chicago Beach Tower Hotel, built in 1998 in Dubai, United Arab Emirates, is 1053 feet. How long would it take an object to fall to the ground from the top of the building? (*Source:* Council on Tall Buildings and Urban Habitat, Lehigh University)

82. The height of the Nurek Dam in Tajikistan (part of the former USSR that borders Afghanistan) is 984 feet. How long would it take an object to fall from the top to the base of the dam? (*Source:* U.S. Committee on Large Dams of the International Commission on Large Dams)

83. The Hoover Dam, located on the Colorado River on the border of Nevada and Arizona near Las Vegas, is 725 feet tall. How long would it take an object to fall from the top to the base of the dam? (*Source:* U.S. Committee on Large Dams of the International Commission on Large Dams)

84. If you are depositing money in an account that pays 4%, would you prefer the interest to be simple or compound? Explain why.

85. If you are borrowing money at a rate of 10%, would you prefer the interest to be simple or compound? Explain why.

REVIEW AND PREVIEW

Simplify each expression. See Section 8.1.

86. $\dfrac{3}{4} - \sqrt{\dfrac{25}{16}}$

87. $\dfrac{3}{5} + \sqrt{\dfrac{16}{25}}$

88. $\dfrac{1}{2} - \sqrt{\dfrac{9}{4}}$

89. $\dfrac{9}{10} - \sqrt{\dfrac{49}{100}}$

Simplify each expression. See Section 8.5.

90. $\dfrac{6 + 4\sqrt{5}}{2}$

91. $\dfrac{10 - 20\sqrt{3}}{2}$

92. $\dfrac{3 - 9\sqrt{2}}{6}$

93. $\dfrac{12 - 8\sqrt{7}}{16}$

Evaluate $\sqrt{b^2 - 4ac}$ for each set of values. See Section 8.3.

94. $a = 2, b = 4, c = -1$

95. $a = 1, b = 6, c = 2$

96. $a = 3, b = -1, c = -2$

97. $a = 1, b = -3, c = -1$

CONCEPT EXTENSIONS

Without solving, determine whether the solutions of each equation are real numbers or complex, but not real numbers. See the Concept Check in this section.

98. $(x + 1)^2 = -1$

99. $(y - 5)^2 = -9$

100. $3z^2 = 10$

101. $4x^2 = 17$

102. $(2y - 5)^2 + 7 = 3$

103. $(3m + 2)^2 + 4 = 1$

Fill in the Blank. *Find two possible missing terms so that each is a perfect square trinomial.*

104. $x^2 + \underline{} + 16$

105. $y^2 + \underline{} + 9$

106. $z^2 + \underline{} + \dfrac{25}{4}$

107. $x^2 + \underline{} + \dfrac{1}{4}$

Solve.

 108. The area of a square room is 225 square feet. Find the dimensions of the room.

△ 109. The area of a circle is 36π square inches. Find the radius of the circle.

△ 110. An isosceles right triangle has legs of equal length. If the hypotenuse is 20 centimeters long, find the length of each leg.

△ 111. A 27-inch TV is advertised in the *Daily Sentry* newspaper. If 27 inches is the measure of the diagonal of the picture tube, find the measure of each side of the picture tube.

A common equation used in business is a demand equation. It expresses the relationship between the unit price of some commodity and the quantity demanded. For Exercises 112 and 113, p represents the unit price and x represents the quantity demanded in thousands.

112. A manufacturing company has found that the demand equation for a certain type of scissors is given by the equation $p = -x^2 + 47$. Find the demand for the scissors if the price is $11 per pair.

113. Acme, Inc., sells desk lamps and has found that the demand equation for a certain style of desk lamp is given by the equation $p = -x^2 + 15$. Find the demand for the desk lamp if the price is $7 per lamp.

9.2 SOLVING QUADRATIC EQUATIONS BY THE QUADRATIC FORMULA

OBJECTIVES

1. Solve quadratic equations by using the quadratic formula.
2. Determine the number and type of solutions of a quadratic equation by using the discriminant.
3. Solve geometric problems modeled by quadratic equations.

OBJECTIVE 1 ▶ **Solving quadratic equations by using the quadratic formula.** Any quadratic equation can be solved by completing the square. Since the same sequence of steps is repeated each time we complete the square, let's complete the square for a general quadratic equation, $ax^2 + bx + c = 0, a \neq 0$. By doing so, we find a pattern for the solutions of a quadratic equation known as the **quadratic formula.**

Recall that to complete the square for an equation such as $ax^2 + bx + c = 0$, we first divide both sides by the coefficient of x^2.

$$ax^2 + bx + c = 0$$

$$x^2 + \dfrac{b}{a}x + \dfrac{c}{a} = 0 \quad \text{Divide both sides by } a, \text{ the coefficient of } x^2.$$

$$x^2 + \dfrac{b}{a}x = -\dfrac{c}{a} \quad \text{Subtract the constant } \dfrac{c}{a} \text{ from both sides.}$$

Next, find the square of half $\frac{b}{a}$, the coefficient of x.

$$\frac{1}{2}\left(\frac{b}{a}\right) = \frac{b}{2a} \quad \text{and} \quad \left(\frac{b}{2a}\right)^2 = \frac{b^2}{4a^2}$$

Add this result to both sides of the equation.

$$x^2 + \frac{b}{a}x + \frac{b^2}{4a^2} = -\frac{c}{a} + \frac{b^2}{4a^2} \qquad \text{Add } \frac{b^2}{4a^2} \text{ to both sides.}$$

$$x^2 + \frac{b}{a}x + \frac{b^2}{4a^2} = \frac{-c \cdot 4a}{a \cdot 4a} + \frac{b^2}{4a^2} \qquad \text{Find a common denominator on the right side.}$$

$$x^2 + \frac{b}{a}x + \frac{b^2}{4a^2} = \frac{b^2 - 4ac}{4a^2} \qquad \text{Simplify the right side.}$$

$$\left(x + \frac{b}{2a}\right)^2 = \frac{b^2 - 4ac}{4a^2} \qquad \text{Factor the perfect square trinomial on the left side.}$$

$$x + \frac{b}{2a} = \pm\sqrt{\frac{b^2 - 4ac}{4a^2}} \qquad \text{Apply the square root property.}$$

$$x + \frac{b}{2a} = \pm\frac{\sqrt{b^2 - 4ac}}{2a} \qquad \text{Simplify the radical.}$$

$$x = -\frac{b}{2a} \pm \frac{\sqrt{b^2 - 4ac}}{2a} \qquad \text{Subtract } \frac{b}{2a} \text{ from both sides.}$$

$$x = \frac{-b \pm \sqrt{b^2 - 4ac}}{2a} \qquad \text{Simplify.}$$

This equation identifies the solutions of the general quadratic equation in standard form and is called the quadratic formula. It can be used to solve any equation written in standard form $ax^2 + bx + c = 0$ as long as a is not 0.

Quadratic Formula

A quadratic equation written in the form $ax^2 + bx + c = 0$ has the solutions

$$x = \frac{-b \pm \sqrt{b^2 - 4ac}}{2a}$$

EXAMPLE 1 Solve $3x^2 + 16x + 5 = 0$ for x.

Solution This equation is in standard form, so $a = 3$, $b = 16$, and $c = 5$. Substitute these values into the quadratic formula.

$$x = \frac{-b \pm \sqrt{b^2 - 4ac}}{2a} \qquad \text{Quadratic formula}$$

$$= \frac{-16 \pm \sqrt{16^2 - 4(3)(5)}}{2 \cdot 3} \qquad \text{Use } a = 3, b = 16, \text{ and } c = 5.$$

$$= \frac{-16 \pm \sqrt{256 - 60}}{6}$$

$$= \frac{-16 \pm \sqrt{196}}{6} = \frac{-16 \pm 14}{6}$$

$$x = \frac{-16 + 14}{6} = -\frac{1}{3} \quad \text{or} \quad x = \frac{-16 - 14}{6} = -\frac{30}{6} = -5$$

The solutions are $-\frac{1}{3}$ and -5, or the solution set is $\left\{-\frac{1}{3}, -5\right\}$.

PRACTICE

1 Solve $3x^2 - 5x - 2 = 0$ for x.

Section 9.2 Solving Quadratic Equations by the Quadratic Formula 525

> **Helpful Hint**
> To replace a, b, and c correctly in the quadratic formula, write the quadratic equation in standard form $ax^2 + bx + c = 0$.

EXAMPLE 2 Solve: $2x^2 - 4x = 3$.

Solution First write the equation in standard form by subtracting 3 from both sides.

$$2x^2 - 4x - 3 = 0$$

Now $a = 2$, $b = -4$, and $c = -3$. Substitute these values into the quadratic formula.

$$x = \frac{-b \pm \sqrt{b^2 - 4ac}}{2a}$$

$$= \frac{-(-4) \pm \sqrt{(-4)^2 - 4(2)(-3)}}{2 \cdot 2}$$

$$= \frac{4 \pm \sqrt{16 + 24}}{4}$$

$$= \frac{4 \pm \sqrt{40}}{4} = \frac{4 \pm 2\sqrt{10}}{4}$$

$$= \frac{2(2 \pm \sqrt{10})}{2 \cdot 2} = \frac{2 \pm \sqrt{10}}{2}$$

The solutions are $\frac{2 + \sqrt{10}}{2}$ and $\frac{2 - \sqrt{10}}{2}$, or the solution set is $\left\{\frac{2 - \sqrt{10}}{2}, \frac{2 + \sqrt{10}}{2}\right\}$.

PRACTICE 2 Solve: $3x^2 - 8x = 2$.

> **Helpful Hint**
> To simplify the expression $\frac{4 \pm 2\sqrt{10}}{4}$ in the preceding example, note that 2 is factored out of both terms of the numerator *before* simplifying.
>
> $$\frac{4 \pm 2\sqrt{10}}{4} = \frac{2(2 \pm \sqrt{10})}{2 \cdot 2} = \frac{2 \pm \sqrt{10}}{2}$$

Concept Check ✓

For the quadratic equation $x^2 = 7$, which substitution is correct?

a. $a = 1$, $b = 0$, and $c = -7$
b. $a = 1$, $b = 0$, and $c = 7$
c. $a = 0$, $b = 0$, and $c = 7$
d. $a = 1$, $b = 1$, and $c = -7$

EXAMPLE 3 Solve: $\frac{1}{4}m^2 - m + \frac{1}{2} = 0$.

Solution We could use the quadratic formula with $a = \frac{1}{4}$, $b = -1$, and $c = \frac{1}{2}$. Instead, we find a simpler, equivalent standard form equation whose coefficients are not fractions. Multiply both sides of the equation by the LCD 4 to clear fractions.

$$4\left(\frac{1}{4}m^2 - m + \frac{1}{2}\right) = 4 \cdot 0$$

$$m^2 - 4m + 2 = 0 \quad \text{Simplify.}$$

Answer to Concept Check: a

Substitute $a = 1$, $b = -4$, and $c = 2$ into the quadratic formula and simplify.

$$m = \frac{-(-4) \pm \sqrt{(-4)^2 - 4(1)(2)}}{2 \cdot 1} = \frac{4 \pm \sqrt{16 - 8}}{2}$$

$$= \frac{4 \pm \sqrt{8}}{2} = \frac{4 \pm 2\sqrt{2}}{2} = \frac{2(2 \pm \sqrt{2})}{2}$$

$$= 2 \pm \sqrt{2}$$

The solutions are $2 + \sqrt{2}$ and $2 - \sqrt{2}$.

PRACTICE 3 Solve: $\frac{1}{8}x^2 - \frac{1}{4}x - 2 = 0$.

EXAMPLE 4 Solve: $x = -3x^2 - 3$.

Solution The equation in standard form is $3x^2 + x + 3 = 0$. Thus, let $a = 3$, $b = 1$, and $c = 3$ in the quadratic formula.

$$x = \frac{-1 \pm \sqrt{1^2 - 4(3)(3)}}{2 \cdot 3} = \frac{-1 \pm \sqrt{1 - 36}}{6} = \frac{-1 \pm \sqrt{-35}}{6} = \frac{-1 \pm i\sqrt{35}}{6}$$

The solutions are $\frac{-1 + i\sqrt{35}}{6}$ and $\frac{-1 - i\sqrt{35}}{6}$.

PRACTICE 4 Solve: $x = -2x^2 - 2$.

▶ **Helpful Hint**

See how the x-intercepts of the graph of $f(x)$ relate to the roots of $f(x) = 0$.

$f(x) = 3x^2 + 16x + 5$

2 x-intercepts: $(-5, 0), \left(-\frac{1}{3}, 0\right)$

$3x^2 + 16x + 5 = 0$

2 roots: $-5, -\frac{1}{3}$

$f(x) = 3x^2 + x + 3$

no x-intercepts

$3x^2 + x + 3 = 0$

no real roots

Concept Check ✓

What is the first step in solving $-3x^2 = 5x - 4$ using the quadratic formula?

In Example 1, the equation $3x^2 + 16x + 5 = 0$ had 2 real roots, $-\frac{1}{3}$ and -5. In Example 4, the equation $3x^2 + x + 3 = 0$ (written in standard form) had no real roots. How do their related graphs compare? Recall that the x-intercepts of $f(x) = 3x^2 + 16x + 5$ occur where $f(x) = 0$ or where $3x^2 + 16x + 5 = 0$. Since this equation has 2 real roots, the graph has 2 x-intercepts. Similarly, since the equation $3x^2 + x + 3 = 0$ has no real roots, the graph of $f(x) = 3x^2 + x + 3$ has no x-intercepts.

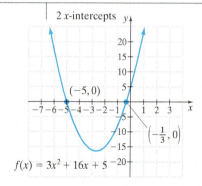

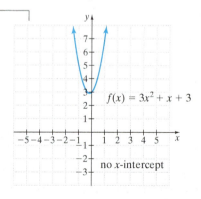

OBJECTIVE 2 ▶ **Using the discriminant.** In the quadratic formula, $x = \frac{-b \pm \sqrt{b^2 - 4ac}}{2a}$, the radicand $b^2 - 4ac$ is called the **discriminant** because, by knowing its value, we can **discriminate** among the possible number and type of solutions of a quadratic equation. Possible values of the discriminant and their meanings are summarized next.

Answer to Concept Check:
Write the equation in standard form.

Section 9.2 Solving Quadratic Equations by the Quadratic Formula   527

Discriminant

The following table corresponds the discriminant $b^2 - 4ac$ of a quadratic equation of the form $ax^2 + bx + c = 0$ with the number and type of solutions of the equation.

$b^2 - 4ac$	Number and Type of Solutions
Positive	Two real solutions
Zero	One real solution
Negative	Two complex but not real solutions

EXAMPLE 5 Use the discriminant to determine the number and type of solutions of each quadratic equation.

a. $x^2 + 2x + 1 = 0$ **b.** $3x^2 + 2 = 0$ **c.** $2x^2 - 7x - 4 = 0$

Solution

a. In $x^2 + 2x + 1 = 0$, $a = 1$, $b = 2$, and $c = 1$. Thus,
$$b^2 - 4ac = 2^2 - 4(1)(1) = 0$$
Since $b^2 - 4ac = 0$, this quadratic equation has one real solution.

b. In this equation, $a = 3$, $b = 0$, $c = 2$. Then $b^2 - 4ac = 0 - 4(3)(2) = -24$. Since $b^2 - 4ac$ is negative, the quadratic equation has two complex but not real solutions.

c. In this equation, $a = 2$, $b = -7$, and $c = -4$. Then
$$b^2 - 4ac = (-7)^2 - 4(2)(-4) = 81$$
Since $b^2 - 4ac$ is positive, the quadratic equation has two real solutions.

PRACTICE 5 Use the discriminant to determine the number and type of solutions of each quadratic equation.

a. $x^2 - 6x + 9 = 0$ **b.** $x^2 - 3x - 1 = 0$ **c.** $7x^2 + 11 = 0$

The discriminant helps us determine the number and type of solutions of a quadratic equation, $ax^2 + bx + c = 0$. Recall that the solutions of this equation are the same as the x-intercepts of its related graph $f(x) = ax^2 + bx + c$. This means that the discriminant of $ax^2 + bx + c = 0$ also tells us the number of x-intercepts for the graph of $f(x) = ax^2 + bx + c$, or equivalently $y = ax^2 + bx + c$.

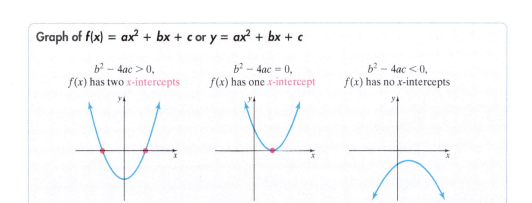

Graph of $f(x) = ax^2 + bx + c$ or $y = ax^2 + bx + c$

$b^2 - 4ac > 0$, $f(x)$ has two x-intercepts

$b^2 - 4ac = 0$, $f(x)$ has one x-intercept

$b^2 - 4ac < 0$, $f(x)$ has no x-intercepts

OBJECTIVE 3 ▶ **Solving problems modeled by quadratic equations.** The quadratic formula is useful in solving problems that are modeled by quadratic equations.

EXAMPLE 6 Calculating Distance Saved

At a local university, students often leave the sidewalk and cut across the lawn to save walking distance. Given the diagram below of a favorite place to cut across the lawn, approximate how many feet of walking distance a student saves by cutting across the lawn instead of walking on the sidewalk.

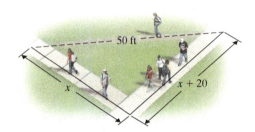

Solution

1. **UNDERSTAND.** Read and reread the problem. In the diagram, notice that a triangle is formed. Since the corner of the block forms a right angle, we use the Pythagorean theorem for right triangles. You may want to review this theorem.

2. **TRANSLATE.** By the Pythagorean theorem, we have

   In words: $(\text{leg})^2 + (\text{leg})^2 = (\text{hypotenuse})^2$
   Translate: $x^2 + (x + 20)^2 = 50^2$

3. **SOLVE.** Use the quadratic formula to solve.

   $x^2 + x^2 + 40x + 400 = 2500$ — Square $(x + 20)$ and 50.
   $2x^2 + 40x - 2100 = 0$ — Set the equation equal to 0.
   $x^2 + 20x - 1050 = 0$ — Divide by 2.

   Here, $a = 1, b = 20, c = -1050$. By the quadratic formula,

   $$x = \frac{-20 \pm \sqrt{20^2 - 4(1)(-1050)}}{2 \cdot 1}$$
   $$= \frac{-20 \pm \sqrt{400 + 4200}}{2} = \frac{-20 \pm \sqrt{4600}}{2}$$
   $$= \frac{-20 \pm \sqrt{100 \cdot 46}}{2} = \frac{-20 \pm 10\sqrt{46}}{2}$$
   $$= -10 \pm 5\sqrt{46} \quad \text{Simplify.}$$

4. **INTERPRET.**

   Check: Your calculations in the quadratic formula. The length of a side of a triangle can't be negative, so we reject $-10 - 5\sqrt{46}$. Since $-10 + 5\sqrt{46} \approx 24$ feet, the walking distance along the sidewalk is

   $$x + (x + 20) \approx 24 + (24 + 20) = 68 \text{ feet.}$$

   State: A student saves about $68 - 50$ or 18 feet of walking distance by cutting across the lawn.

PRACTICE
6 Given the diagram, approximate to the nearest foot how many feet of walking distance a person can save by cutting across the lawn instead of walking on the sidewalk.

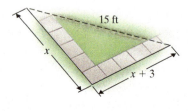

EXAMPLE 7 Calculating Landing Time

An object is thrown upward from the top of a 200-foot cliff with a velocity of 12 feet per second. The height h in feet of the object after t seconds is

$$h = -16t^2 + 12t + 200$$

How long after the object is thrown will it strike the ground? Round to the nearest tenth of a second.

Solution

1. UNDERSTAND. Read and reread the problem.
2. TRANSLATE. Since we want to know when the object strikes the ground, we want to know when the height $h = 0$, or

$$0 = -16t^2 + 12t + 200$$

3. SOLVE. First we divide both sides of the equation by -4.

$$0 = 4t^2 - 3t - 50 \quad \text{Divide both sides by } -4.$$

Here, $a = 4$, $b = -3$, and $c = -50$. By the quadratic formula,

$$t = \frac{-(-3) \pm \sqrt{(-3)^2 - 4(4)(-50)}}{2 \cdot 4}$$

$$= \frac{3 \pm \sqrt{9 + 800}}{8}$$

$$= \frac{3 \pm \sqrt{809}}{8}$$

4. INTERPRET.

Check: We check our calculations from the quadratic formula. Since the time won't be negative, we reject the proposed solution

$$\frac{3 - \sqrt{809}}{8}.$$

State: The time it takes for the object to strike the ground is exactly

$$\frac{3 + \sqrt{809}}{8} \text{ seconds} \approx 3.9 \text{ seconds}.$$

PRACTICE 7

A toy rocket is shot upward at the edge of a building, 45 feet high, with an initial velocity of 20 feet per second. The height h in feet of the rocket after t seconds is

$$h = -16t^2 + 20t + 45$$

How long after the rocket is launched will it strike the ground? Round to the nearest tenth of a second.

VOCABULARY & READINESS CHECK

Fill in the Blank. *Fill in each blank.*

1. The quadratic formula is _____ .
2. For $2x^2 + x + 1 = 0$, if $a = 2$, then $b = $ ____ and $c = $ ____ .
3. For $5x^2 - 5x - 7 = 0$, if $a = 5$, then $b = $ ____ and $c = $ ____ .
4. For $7x^2 - 4 = 0$, if $a = 7$, then $b = $ ____ and $c = $ ____ .
5. For $x^2 + 9 = 0$, if $c = 9$, then $a = $ ____ and $b = $ ____ .
6. **Multiple Choice.** The correct simplified form of $\dfrac{5 \pm 10\sqrt{2}}{5}$ is _____ .
   a. $1 \pm 10\sqrt{2}$ b. $2\sqrt{2}$ c. $1 \pm 2\sqrt{2}$ d. $\pm 5\sqrt{2}$

9.2 EXERCISE SET

Use the quadratic formula to solve each equation. These equations have real number solutions only. See Examples 1 through 3.

1. $m^2 + 5m - 6 = 0$
2. $p^2 + 11p - 12 = 0$
3. $2y = 5y^2 - 3$
4. $5x^2 - 3 = 14x$
5. $x^2 - 6x + 9 = 0$
6. $y^2 + 10y + 25 = 0$
7. $x^2 + 7x + 4 = 0$
8. $y^2 + 5y + 3 = 0$
9. $8m^2 - 2m = 7$
10. $11n^2 - 9n = 1$
11. $3m^2 - 7m = 3$
12. $x^2 - 13 = 5x$
13. $\dfrac{1}{2}x^2 - x - 1 = 0$
14. $\dfrac{1}{6}x^2 + x + \dfrac{1}{3} = 0$
15. $\dfrac{2}{5}y^2 + \dfrac{1}{5}y = \dfrac{3}{5}$
16. $\dfrac{1}{8}x^2 + x = \dfrac{5}{2}$
17. $\dfrac{1}{3}y^2 = y + \dfrac{1}{6}$
18. $\dfrac{1}{2}y^2 = y + \dfrac{1}{2}$
19. $x^2 + 5x = -2$
20. $y^2 - 8 = 4y$
21. $(m + 2)(2m - 6) = 5(m - 1) - 12$
22. $7p(p - 2) + 2(p + 4) = 3$

MIXED PRACTICE

Use the quadratic formula to solve each equation. These equations have real solutions and complex, but not real, solutions. See Examples 1 through 4.

23. $x^2 + 6x + 13 = 0$
24. $x^2 + 2x + 2 = 0$
25. $(x + 5)(x - 1) = 2$
26. $x(x + 6) = 2$
27. $6 = -4x^2 + 3x$
28. $2 = -9x^2 - x$
29. $\dfrac{x^2}{3} - x = \dfrac{5}{3}$
30. $\dfrac{x^2}{2} - 3 = -\dfrac{9}{2}x$
31. $10y^2 + 10y + 3 = 0$
32. $3y^2 + 6y + 5 = 0$
33. $x(6x + 2) = 3$
34. $x(7x + 1) = 2$
35. $\dfrac{2}{5}y^2 + \dfrac{1}{5}y + \dfrac{3}{5} = 0$
36. $\dfrac{1}{8}x^2 + x + \dfrac{5}{2} = 0$
37. $\dfrac{1}{2}y^2 = y - \dfrac{1}{2}$
38. $\dfrac{2}{3}x^2 - \dfrac{20}{3}x = -\dfrac{100}{6}$

39. $(n-2)^2 = 2n$

40. $\left(p - \dfrac{1}{2}\right)^2 = \dfrac{p}{2}$

Use the discriminant to determine the number and types of solutions of each equation. See Example 5.

41. $x^2 - 5 = 0$

42. $x^2 - 7 = 0$

43. $4x^2 + 12x = -9$

44. $9x^2 + 1 = 6x$

45. $3x = -2x^2 + 7$

46. $3x^2 = 5 - 7x$

47. $6 = 4x - 5x^2$

48. $8x = 3 - 9x^2$

49. $9x - 2x^2 + 5 = 0$

50. $5 - 4x + 12x^2 = 0$

Solve. See Examples 6 and 7.

51. Nancy, Thelma, and John Varner live on a corner lot. Often, neighborhood children cut across their lot to save walking distance. Given the diagram below, approximate to the nearest foot how many feet of walking distance is saved by cutting across their property instead of walking around the lot.

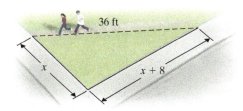

52. Given the diagram below, approximate to the nearest foot how many feet of walking distance a person saves by cutting across the lawn instead of walking on the sidewalk.

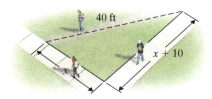

53. The hypotenuse of an isosceles right triangle is 2 centimeters longer than either of its legs. Find the exact length of each side. (*Hint:* An isosceles right triangle is a right triangle whose legs are the same length.)

54. The hypotenuse of an isosceles right triangle is one meter longer than either of its legs. Find the length of each side.

55. Bailey's rectangular dog pen for his Irish setter must have an area of 400 square feet. Also, the length must be 10 feet longer than the width. Find the dimensions of the pen.

56. An entry in the Peach Festival Poster Contest must be rectangular and have an area of 1200 square inches. Furthermore, its length must be 20 inches longer than its width. Find the dimensions each entry must have.

57. **Multiple Steps.** A holding pen for cattle must be square and have a diagonal length of 100 meters.

a. Find the length of a side of the pen.

b. Find the area of the pen.

58. **Multiple Steps.** A rectangle is three times longer than it is wide. It has a diagonal of length 50 centimeters.

a. Find the dimensions of the rectangle.

b. Find the perimeter of the rectangle.

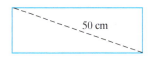

59. The heaviest reported door in the world is the 708.6 ton radiation shield door in the National Institute for Fusion Science at Toki, Japan. If the height of the door is 1.1 feet longer than its width, and its front area (neglecting depth) is 1439.9 square feet, find its width and height [Interesting note: the door is 6.6 feet thick.] (*Source: Guiness World Records*)

60. Christi and Robbie Wegmann are constructing a rectangular stained glass window whose length is 7.3 inches longer than its width. If the area of the window is 569.9 square inches, find its width and length.

61. The base of a triangle is four more than twice its height. If the area of the triangle is 42 square centimeters, find its base and height.

62. If a point B divides a line segment such that the smaller portion is to the larger portion as the larger is to the whole, the whole is the length of the *golden ratio*.

The golden ratio was thought by the Greeks to be the most pleasing to the eye, and many of their buildings contained numerous examples of the golden ratio. The value of the golden ratio is the positive solution of

(smaller) $\dfrac{x-1}{1} = \dfrac{1}{x}$ (larger)
(larger)   (whole)

Find this value.

The Wollomombi Falls in Australia have a height of 1100 feet. A pebble is thrown upward from the top of the falls with an initial velocity of 20 feet per second. The height of the pebble h after t seconds is given by the equation $h = -16t^2 + 20t + 1100$. Use this equation for Exercises 63 and 64.

63. How long after the pebble is thrown will it hit the ground? Round to the nearest tenth of a second.

64. How long after the pebble is thrown will it be 550 feet from the ground? Round to the nearest tenth of a second.

A ball is thrown downward from the top of a 180-foot building with an initial velocity of 20 feet per second. The height of the ball h after t seconds is given by the equation $h = -16t^2 - 20t + 180$. Use this equation to answer Exercises 65 and 66.

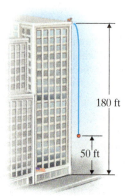

65. How long after the ball is thrown will it strike the ground? Round the result to the nearest tenth of a second.

66. How long after the ball is thrown will it be 50 feet from the ground? Round the result to the nearest tenth of a second.

REVIEW AND PREVIEW

Solve each equation. See Sections 7.6 and 8.6.

67. $\sqrt{5x - 2} = 3$

68. $\sqrt{y + 2} + 7 = 12$

69. $\dfrac{1}{x} + \dfrac{2}{5} = \dfrac{7}{x}$

70. $\dfrac{10}{z} = \dfrac{5}{z} - \dfrac{1}{3}$

Factor. See Section 6.7.

71. $x^4 + x^2 - 20$

72. $2y^4 + 11y^2 - 6$

73. $z^4 - 13z^2 + 36$

74. $x^4 - 1$

CONCEPT EXTENSIONS

Multiple Choice. *For each quadratic equation, choose the correct substitution for a, b, and c in the standard form $ax^2 + bx + c = 0$.*

75. $x^2 = -10$
 a. $a = 1, b = 0, c = -10$
 b. $a = 1, b = 0, c = 10$
 c. $a = 0, b = 1, c = -10$
 d. $a = 1, b = 1, c = 10$

76. $x^2 + 5 = -x$
 a. $a = 1, b = 5, c = -1$
 b. $a = 1, b = -1, c = 5$
 c. $a = 1, b = 5, c = 1$
 d. $a = 1, b = 1, c = 5$

77. Solve Exercise 1 by factoring. Explain the result.

78. Solve Exercise 2 by factoring. Explain the result.

Use the quadratic formula and a calculator to approximate each solution to the nearest tenth.

79. $2x^2 - 6x + 3 = 0$

80. $3.6x^2 + 1.8x - 4.3 = 0$

The accompanying graph shows the daily low temperatures for one week in New Orleans, Louisiana.

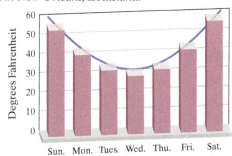

81. Which day of the week shows the greatest decrease in low temperature?
82. Which day of the week shows the greatest increase in low temperature?
83. Which day of the week had the lowest low temperature?
84. Use the graph to estimate the low temperature on Thursday.

Notice that the shape of the temperature graph is similar to the curve drawn. In fact, this graph can be modeled by the quadratic function $f(x) = 3x^2 - 18x + 56$, where $f(x)$ is the temperature in degrees Fahrenheit and x is the number of days from Sunday. (This graph is shown in blue.) Use this function to answer Exercises 85 and 86.

85. Use the quadratic function given to approximate the temperature on Thursday. Does your answer agree with the graph?
86. Use the function given and the quadratic formula to find when the temperature was 35° F. [*Hint:* Let $f(x) = 35$ and solve for x.] Round your answer to one decimal place and interpret your result. Does your answer agree with the graph?
87. The number of Starbucks stores can be modeled by the quadratic function $f(x) = 115x^2 + 711x + 3946$, where $f(x)$ is the number of Starbucks and x is the number of years after 2000. (*Source: Starbuck's Annual Report 2006*)
    a. Find the number of Starbucks in 2004.
    b. If the trend described by the model continues, predict the years after 2000 in which the number of Starbucks will be 25,000. Round to the nearest whole year.
88. The number of visitors to U.S. theme parks can be modeled by the quadratic equation $v(x) = 0.25x^2 + 2.6x + 315.6$, where $v(x)$ is the number of visitors (in millions) and x is the number of years after 2000. (*Source:* Price Waterhouse Coopers)
    a. Find the number of visitors to U.S. theme parks in 2005. Round to the nearest million.
    b. Find the projected number of visitors to U.S. theme parks in 2010. Round to the nearest million.

The solutions of the quadratic equation $ax^2 + bx + c = 0$ are $\dfrac{-b + \sqrt{b^2 - 4ac}}{2a}$ and $\dfrac{-b - \sqrt{b^2 - 4ac}}{2a}$.

89. Show that the sum of these solutions is $\dfrac{-b}{a}$.
90. Show that the product of these solutions is $\dfrac{c}{a}$.

Use the quadratic formula to solve each quadratic equation.

91. $3x^2 - \sqrt{12}x + 1 = 0$,
    (*Hint:* $a = 3, b = -\sqrt{12}, c = 1$)
92. $5x^2 + \sqrt{20}x + 1 = 0$
93. $x^2 + \sqrt{2}x + 1 = 0$
94. $x^2 - \sqrt{2}x + 1 = 0$
95. $2x^2 - \sqrt{3}x - 1 = 0$
96. $7x^2 + \sqrt{7}x - 2 = 0$
97. Use a graphing calculator to solve Exercises 63 and 65.
98. Use a graphing calculator to solve Exercises 64 and 66.

Recall that the discriminant also tells us the number of x-intercepts of the related function.

99. Check the results of Exercise 49 by graphing $y = 9x - 2x^2 + 5$.
100. Check the results of Exercise 50 by graphing $y = 5 - 4x + 12x^2$.

9.3 SOLVING EQUATIONS BY USING QUADRATIC METHODS

OBJECTIVES

1. Solve various equations that are quadratic in form.
2. Solve problems that lead to quadratic equations.

OBJECTIVE 1 ▶ Solving equations that are quadratic in form. In this section, we discuss various types of equations that can be solved in part by using the methods for solving quadratic equations.

Once each equation is simplified, you may want to use these steps when deciding what method to use to solve the quadratic equation.

Solving a Quadratic Equation

STEP 1. If the equation is in the form $(ax + b)^2 = c$, use the square root property and solve. If not, go to Step 2.

STEP 2. Write the equation in standard form: $ax^2 + bx + c = 0$.

STEP 3. Try to solve the equation by the factoring method. If not possible, go to Step 4.

STEP 4. Solve the equation by the quadratic formula.

The first example is a radical equation that becomes a quadratic equation once we square both sides.

EXAMPLE 1 Solve: $x - \sqrt{x} - 6 = 0$.

Solution Recall that to solve a radical equation, first get the radical alone on one side of the equation. Then square both sides.

$$x - 6 = \sqrt{x} \quad \text{Add } \sqrt{x} \text{ to both sides.}$$
$$(x - 6)^2 = (\sqrt{x})^2 \quad \text{Square both sides.}$$
$$x^2 - 12x + 36 = x$$
$$x^2 - 13x + 36 = 0 \quad \text{Set the equation equal to 0.}$$
$$(x - 9)(x - 4) = 0$$
$$x - 9 = 0 \quad \text{or} \quad x - 4 = 0$$
$$x = 9 \qquad\qquad x = 4$$

Check:

Let $x = 9$
$$x - \sqrt{x} - 6 = 0$$
$$9 - \sqrt{9} - 6 \stackrel{?}{=} 0$$
$$9 - 3 - 6 \stackrel{?}{=} 0$$
$$0 = 0 \quad \text{True}$$

Let $x = 4$
$$x - \sqrt{x} - 6 = 0$$
$$4 - \sqrt{4} - 6 \stackrel{?}{=} 0$$
$$4 - 2 - 6 \stackrel{?}{=} 0$$
$$-4 = 0 \quad \text{False}$$

The solution is 9 or the solution set is {9}. □

PRACTICE 1 Solve: $x - \sqrt{x + 1} - 5 = 0$.

EXAMPLE 2 Solve: $\dfrac{3x}{x - 2} - \dfrac{x + 1}{x} = \dfrac{6}{x(x - 2)}$.

Solution In this equation, x cannot be either 2 or 0, because these values cause denominators to equal zero. To solve for x, we first multiply both sides of the equation by $x(x - 2)$ to clear the fractions. By the distributive property, this means that we multiply each term by $x(x - 2)$.

$$x(x-2)\left(\frac{3x}{x-2}\right) - x(x-2)\left(\frac{x+1}{x}\right) = x(x-2)\left[\frac{6}{x(x-2)}\right]$$
$$3x^2 - (x-2)(x+1) = 6 \quad \text{Simplify.}$$
$$3x^2 - (x^2 - x - 2) = 6 \quad \text{Multiply.}$$
$$3x^2 - x^2 + x + 2 = 6$$
$$2x^2 + x - 4 = 0 \quad \text{Simplify.}$$

This equation cannot be factored using integers, so we solve by the quadratic formula.

$$x = \frac{-1 \pm \sqrt{1^2 - 4(2)(-4)}}{2 \cdot 2} \quad \text{Use } a = 2, b = 1, \text{ and } c = -4 \text{ in the quadratic formula.}$$
$$= \frac{-1 \pm \sqrt{1 + 32}}{4} \quad \text{Simplify.}$$
$$= \frac{-1 \pm \sqrt{33}}{4}$$

Neither proposed solution will make the denominators 0.

The solutions are $\dfrac{-1 + \sqrt{33}}{4}$ and $\dfrac{-1 - \sqrt{33}}{4}$ or the solution set is $\left\{\dfrac{-1 + \sqrt{33}}{4}, \dfrac{-1 - \sqrt{33}}{4}\right\}$.

PRACTICE 2 Solve: $\dfrac{5x}{x + 1} - \dfrac{x + 4}{x} = \dfrac{3}{x(x + 1)}$.

EXAMPLE 3 Solve: $p^4 - 3p^2 - 4 = 0$.

Solution First we factor the trinomial.

$$p^4 - 3p^2 - 4 = 0$$
$$(p^2 - 4)(p^2 + 1) = 0 \qquad \text{Factor.}$$
$$(p - 2)(p + 2)(p^2 + 1) = 0 \qquad \text{Factor further.}$$
$$p - 2 = 0 \quad \text{or} \quad p + 2 = 0 \quad \text{or} \quad p^2 + 1 = 0 \qquad \text{Set each factor equal to 0 and solve.}$$
$$p = 2 \qquad\qquad p = -2 \qquad\qquad p^2 = -1$$
$$p = \pm\sqrt{-1} = \pm i$$

The solutions are $2, -2, i$ and $-i$.

PRACTICE 3 Solve: $p^4 - 7p^2 - 144 = 0$.

> **Helpful Hint**
> Example 3 can be solved using substitution also. Think of $p^4 - 3p^2 - 4 = 0$ as
> $$(p^2)^2 - 3p^2 - 4 = 0 \qquad \text{Then let } x = p^2, \text{ and solve and substitute back.}$$
> $$x^2 - 3x - 4 = 0 \qquad \text{The solutions will be the same.}$$

Concept Check

a. True or false? The maximum number of solutions that a quadratic equation can have is 2.

b. True or false? The maximum number of solutions that an equation in quadratic form can have is 2.

EXAMPLE 4 Solve: $(x - 3)^2 - 3(x - 3) - 4 = 0$.

Solution Notice that the quantity $(x - 3)$ is repeated in this equation. Sometimes it is helpful to substitute a variable (in this case other than x) for the repeated quantity. We will let $y = x - 3$. Then

becomes
$$(x - 3)^2 - 3(x - 3) - 4 = 0$$
$$y^2 - 3y - 4 = 0 \qquad \text{Let } x - 3 = y.$$
$$(y - 4)(y + 1) = 0 \qquad \text{Factor.}$$

To solve, we use the zero factor property.

$$y - 4 = 0 \quad \text{or} \quad y + 1 = 0 \qquad \text{Set each factor equal to 0.}$$
$$y = 4 \qquad\qquad y = -1 \qquad \text{Solve.}$$

To find values of x, we substitute back. That is, we substitute $x - 3$ for y.

$$x - 3 = 4 \quad \text{or} \quad x - 3 = -1$$
$$x = 7 \qquad\qquad x = 2$$

Answer to Concept Check:
a. true **b.** false

> **Helpful Hint**
> When using substitution, don't forget to substitute back to the original variable.

Both 2 and 7 check. The solutions are 2 and 7.

PRACTICE 4 Solve: $(x + 2)^2 - 2(x + 2) - 3 = 0$.

EXAMPLE 5 Solve: $x^{2/3} - 5x^{1/3} + 6 = 0$.

Solution The key to solving this equation is recognizing that $x^{2/3} = (x^{1/3})^2$. We replace $x^{1/3}$ with m so that

$$(x^{1/3})^2 - 5x^{1/3} + 6 = 0$$

becomes

$$m^2 - 5m + 6 = 0$$

Now we solve by factoring.

$$m^2 - 5m + 6 = 0$$
$$(m - 3)(m - 2) = 0 \quad \text{Factor.}$$
$$m - 3 = 0 \quad \text{or} \quad m - 2 = 0 \quad \text{Set each factor equal to 0.}$$
$$m = 3 \qquad\qquad m = 2$$

Since $m = x^{1/3}$, we have

$$x^{1/3} = 3 \quad \text{or} \quad x^{1/3} = 2$$
$$x = 3^3 = 27 \quad \text{or} \quad x = 2^3 = 8$$

Both 8 and 27 check. The solutions are 8 and 27.

PRACTICE 5 Solve: $x^{2/3} - 5x^{1/3} + 4 = 0$.

OBJECTIVE 2 ▶ Solving problems that lead to quadratic equations. The next example is a work problem. This problem is modeled by a rational equation that simplifies to a quadratic equation.

EXAMPLE 6 Finding Work Time

Together, an experienced word processor and an apprentice word processor can create a word document in 6 hours. Alone, the experienced word processor can create the document 2 hours faster than the apprentice word processor can. Find the time in which each person can create the word document alone.

Solution

1. UNDERSTAND. Read and reread the problem. The key idea here is the relationship between the *time* (hours) it takes to complete the job and the *part of the job* completed in one unit of time (hour). For example, because they can complete the job together in 6 hours, the *part of the job* they can complete in 1 hour is $\frac{1}{6}$.

   Let

   $x =$ the *time* in hours it takes the apprentice word processor to complete the job alone

   $x - 2 =$ the *time* in hours it takes the experienced word processor to complete the job alone

   We can summarize in a chart the information discussed

	Total Hours to Complete Job	Part of Job Completed in 1 Hour
Apprentice Word Processor	x	$\dfrac{1}{x}$
Experienced Word Processor	$x-2$	$\dfrac{1}{x-2}$
Together	6	$\dfrac{1}{6}$

2. TRANSLATE.

In words:	part of job completed by apprentice word processor in 1 hour	added to	part of job completed by experienced word processor in 1 hour	is equal to	part of job completed together in 1 hour
	↓	↓	↓	↓	↓
Translate:	$\dfrac{1}{x}$	$+$	$\dfrac{1}{x-2}$	$=$	$\dfrac{1}{6}$

3. SOLVE.

$$\frac{1}{x} + \frac{1}{x-2} = \frac{1}{6}$$

$$6x(x-2)\left(\frac{1}{x} + \frac{1}{x-2}\right) = 6x(x-2) \cdot \frac{1}{6} \quad \text{Multiply both sides by the LCD } 6x(x-2).$$

$$6x(x-2) \cdot \frac{1}{x} + 6x(x-2) \cdot \frac{1}{x-2} = 6x(x-2) \cdot \frac{1}{6} \quad \text{Use the distributive property.}$$

$$6(x-2) + 6x = x(x-2)$$
$$6x - 12 + 6x = x^2 - 2x$$
$$0 = x^2 - 14x + 12$$

Now we can substitute $a = 1$, $b = -14$, and $c = 12$ into the quadratic formula and simplify.

$$x = \frac{-(-14) \pm \sqrt{(-14)^2 - 4(1)(12)}}{2 \cdot 1} = \frac{14 \pm \sqrt{148}}{2}^*$$

(*This expression can be simplified further, but this will suffice as we are approximating.)

Using a calculator or a square root table, we see that $\sqrt{148} \approx 12.2$ rounded to one decimal place. Thus,

$$x \approx \frac{14 \pm 12.2}{2}$$

$$x \approx \frac{14 + 12.2}{2} = 13.1 \quad \text{or} \quad x \approx \frac{14 - 12.2}{2} = 0.9$$

4. INTERPRET.

Check: If the apprentice word processor completes the job alone in 0.9 hours, the experienced word processor completes the job alone in $x - 2 = 0.9 - 2 = -1.1$ hours. Since this is not possible, we reject the solution of 0.9. The approximate solution thus is 13.1 hours.

State: The apprentice word processor can complete the job alone in approximately 13.1 hours, and the experienced word processor can complete the job alone in approximately

$$x - 2 = 13.1 - 2 = 11.1 \text{ hours.}$$

538 CHAPTER 9 Quadratic and Higher Degree Equations and Functions

> **PRACTICE**
> **6** Together, Katy and Steve can groom all the dogs at the Barkin' Doggie Day Care in 4 hours. Alone, Katy can groom the dogs 1 hour faster than Steve can groom the dogs alone. Find the time in which each of them can groom the dogs alone.

EXAMPLE 7 Finding Driving Speeds

Beach and Fargo are about 400 miles apart. A salesperson travels from Fargo to Beach one day at a certain speed. She returns to Fargo the next day and drives 10 mph faster. Her total travel time was $14\frac{2}{3}$ hours. Find her speed to Beach and the return speed to Fargo.

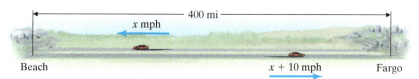

Solution

1. UNDERSTAND. Read and reread the problem. Let

$$x = \text{the speed to Beach, so}$$
$$x + 10 = \text{the return speed to Fargo.}$$

Then organize the given information in a table.

> **Helpful Hint**
> Since $d = rt$, then $t = \dfrac{d}{r}$. The time column was completed using $\dfrac{d}{r}$.

	distance	=	rate	·	time	
To Beach	400		x		$\dfrac{400}{x}$	← distance ← rate
Return to Fargo	400		$x + 10$		$\dfrac{400}{x+10}$	← distance ← rate

2. TRANSLATE.

In words: time to Beach + return time to Fargo = $14\frac{2}{3}$ hours

Translate: $\dfrac{400}{x} + \dfrac{400}{x+10} = \dfrac{44}{3}$

3. SOLVE.

$$\dfrac{400}{x} + \dfrac{400}{x+10} = \dfrac{44}{3}$$

$$\dfrac{100}{x} + \dfrac{100}{x+10} = \dfrac{11}{3} \qquad \text{Divide both sides by 4.}$$

$$3x(x+10)\left(\dfrac{100}{x} + \dfrac{100}{x+10}\right) = 3x(x+10) \cdot \dfrac{11}{3} \qquad \text{Multiply both sides by the LCD } 3x(x+10).$$

$$3x(x+10) \cdot \dfrac{100}{x} + 3x(x+10) \cdot \dfrac{100}{x+10} = 3x(x+10) \cdot \dfrac{11}{3} \qquad \text{Use the distributive property.}$$

$$3(x+10) \cdot 100 + 3x \cdot 100 = x(x+10) \cdot 11$$

$$300x + 3000 + 300x = 11x^2 + 110x$$

Section 9.3 Solving Equations by using Quadratic Methods 539

$$0 = 11x^2 - 490x - 3000 \quad \text{Set equation equal to 0.}$$
$$0 = (11x + 60)(x - 50) \quad \text{Factor.}$$
$$11x + 60 = 0 \quad \text{or} \quad x - 50 = 0 \quad \text{Set each factor equal to 0.}$$
$$x = -\frac{60}{11} \text{ or } -5\frac{5}{11}; \quad x = 50$$

4. INTERPRET.

Check: The speed is not negative, so it's not $-5\frac{5}{11}$. The number 50 does check.

State: The speed to Beach was 50 mph and her return speed to Fargo was 60 mph.

PRACTICE 7 The 36-km S-shaped Hangzhou Bay Bridge is the longest cross-sea bridge in the world, linking Ningbo and Shanghai, China. A merchant drives over the bridge one morning from Ningbo to Shanghai in very heavy traffic and returns home that night driving 50 km per hour faster. The total travel time was 1.3 hours. Find the speed to Shanghai and the return speed to Ningbo.

9.3 EXERCISE SET

Solve. See Example 1.

1. $2x = \sqrt{10 + 3x}$
2. $3x = \sqrt{8x + 1}$
3. $x - 2\sqrt{x} = 8$
4. $x - \sqrt{2x} = 4$
5. $\sqrt{9x} = x + 2$
6. $\sqrt{16x} = x + 3$

Solve. See Example 2.

7. $\dfrac{2}{x} + \dfrac{3}{x - 1} = 1$
8. $\dfrac{6}{x^2} = \dfrac{3}{x + 1}$
9. $\dfrac{3}{x} + \dfrac{4}{x + 2} = 2$
10. $\dfrac{5}{x - 2} + \dfrac{4}{x + 2} = 1$
11. $\dfrac{7}{x^2 - 5x + 6} = \dfrac{2x}{x - 3} - \dfrac{x}{x - 2}$
12. $\dfrac{11}{2x^2 + x - 15} = \dfrac{5}{2x - 5} - \dfrac{x}{x + 3}$

Solve. See Example 3.

13. $p^4 - 16 = 0$
14. $x^4 + 2x^2 - 3 = 0$
15. $4x^4 + 11x^2 = 3$
16. $z^4 = 81$
17. $z^4 - 13z^2 + 36 = 0$
18. $9x^4 + 5x^2 - 4 = 0$

Solve. See Examples 4 and 5.

19. $x^{2/3} - 3x^{1/3} - 10 = 0$
20. $x^{2/3} + 2x^{1/3} + 1 = 0$
21. $(5n + 1)^2 + 2(5n + 1) - 3 = 0$
22. $(m - 6)^2 + 5(m - 6) + 4 = 0$
23. $2x^{2/3} - 5x^{1/3} = 3$
24. $3x^{2/3} + 11x^{1/3} = 4$
25. $1 + \dfrac{2}{3t - 2} = \dfrac{8}{(3t - 2)^2}$
26. $2 - \dfrac{7}{x + 6} = \dfrac{15}{(x + 6)^2}$
27. $20x^{2/3} - 6x^{1/3} - 2 = 0$
28. $4x^{2/3} + 16x^{1/3} = -15$

MIXED PRACTICE

Solve. See Examples 1 through 5.

29. $a^4 - 5a^2 + 6 = 0$
30. $x^4 - 12x^2 + 11 = 0$
31. $\dfrac{2x}{x - 2} + \dfrac{x}{x + 3} = -\dfrac{5}{x + 3}$
32. $\dfrac{5}{x - 3} + \dfrac{x}{x + 3} = \dfrac{19}{x^2 - 9}$
33. $(p + 2)^2 = 9(p + 2) - 20$
34. $2(4m - 3)^2 - 9(4m - 3) = 5$
35. $2x = \sqrt{11x + 3}$
36. $4x = \sqrt{2x + 3}$
37. $x^{2/3} - 8x^{1/3} + 15 = 0$
38. $x^{2/3} - 2x^{1/3} - 8 = 0$
39. $y^3 + 9y - y^2 - 9 = 0$
40. $x^3 + x - 3x^2 - 3 = 0$
41. $2x^{2/3} + 3x^{1/3} - 2 = 0$

42. $6x^{2/3} - 25x^{1/3} - 25 = 0$
43. $x^{-2} - x^{-1} - 6 = 0$
44. $y^{-2} - 8y^{-1} + 7 = 0$
45. $x - \sqrt{x} = 2$
46. $x - \sqrt{3x} = 6$
47. $\dfrac{x}{x-1} + \dfrac{1}{x+1} = \dfrac{2}{x^2-1}$
48. $\dfrac{x}{x-5} + \dfrac{5}{x+5} = -\dfrac{1}{x^2-25}$
49. $p^4 - p^2 - 20 = 0$
50. $x^4 - 10x^2 + 9 = 0$
51. $(x+3)(x^2 - 3x + 9) = 0$
52. $(x-6)(x^2 + 6x + 36) = 0$
53. $1 = \dfrac{4}{x-7} + \dfrac{5}{(x-7)^2}$
54. $3 + \dfrac{1}{2p+4} = \dfrac{10}{(2p+4)^2}$
55. $27y^4 + 15y^2 = 2$
56. $8z^4 + 14z^2 = -5$

Solve. See Examples 6 and 7.

57. A jogger ran 3 miles, decreased her speed by 1 mile per hour, and then ran another 4 miles. If her total time jogging was $1\dfrac{3}{5}$ hours, find her speed for each part of her run.

58. Mark Keaton's workout consists of jogging for 3 miles, and then riding his bike for 5 miles at a speed 4 miles per hour faster than he jogs. If his total workout time is 1 hour, find his jogging speed and his biking speed.

59. A Chinese restaurant in Mandeville, Louisiana, has a large goldfish pond around the restaurant. Suppose that an inlet pipe and a hose together can fill the pond in 8 hours. The inlet pipe alone can complete the job in one hour less time than the hose alone. Find the time that the hose can complete the job alone and the time that the inlet pipe can complete the job alone. Round each to the nearest tenth of an hour.

60. A water tank on a farm in Flatonia, Texas, can be filled with a large inlet pipe and a small inlet pipe in 3 hours. The large inlet pipe alone can fill the tank in 2 hours less time than the small inlet pipe alone. Find the time to the nearest tenth of an hour each pipe can fill the tank alone.

61. Roma Sherry drove 330 miles from her hometown to Tucson. During her return trip, she was able to increase her speed by 11 mph. If her return trip took 1 hour less time, find her original speed and her speed returning home.

62. A salesperson drove to Portland, a distance of 300 miles. During the last 80 miles of his trip, heavy rainfall forced him to decrease his speed by 15 mph. If his total driving time was 6 hours, find his original speed and his speed during the rainfall.

63. Bill Shaughnessy and his son Billy can clean the house together in 4 hours. When the son works alone, it takes him an hour longer to clean than it takes his dad alone. Find how long to the nearest tenth of an hour it takes the son to clean alone.

64. Together, Noodles and Freckles eat a 50-pound bag of dog food in 30 days. Noodles by himself eats a 50-pound bag in 2 weeks less time than Freckles does by himself. How many days to the nearest whole day would a 50-pound bag of dog food last Freckles?

65. The product of a number and 4 less than the number is 96. Find the number.

66. A whole number increased by its square is two more than twice itself. Find the number.

67. Suppose that an open box is to be made from a square sheet of cardboard by cutting out squares from each corner as shown and then folding along the dotted lines. If the box is to have a volume of 300 cubic centimeters, find the original dimensions of the sheet of cardboard.

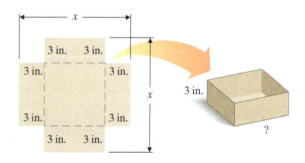

a. The ? in the drawing above will be the length (and also the width) of the box as shown. Represent this length in terms of x.

b. Use the formula for volume of a box, $V = l \cdot w \cdot h$, to write an equation in x.

c. Solve the equation for x and give the dimensions of the sheet of cardboard. Check your solution.

68. Suppose that an open box is to be made from a square sheet of cardboard by cutting out squares from each corner as shown and then folding along the dotted lines. If the box is to have a volume of 128 cubic inches, find the original dimensions of the sheet of cardboard.

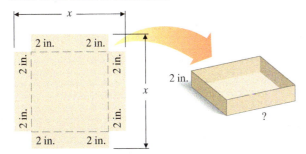

a. The ? in the drawing above will be the length (and also the width) of the box as shown. Represent this length in terms of x.

b. Use the formula for volume of a box, $V = l \cdot w \cdot h$, to write an equation in x.

c. Solve the equation for x and give the dimensions of the sheet of cardboard. Check your solution.

69. A sprinkler that sprays water in a circular motion is to be used to water a square garden. If the area of the garden is 920 square feet, find the smallest whole number *radius* that the sprinkler can be adjusted to so that the entire garden is watered.

70. Suppose that a square field has an area of 6270 square feet. See Exercise 69 and find a new sprinkler radius.

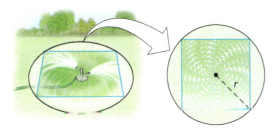

REVIEW AND PREVIEW

Solve each inequality. See Section 2.4.

71. $\dfrac{5x}{3} + 2 \le 7$

72. $\dfrac{2x}{3} + \dfrac{1}{6} \ge 2$

73. $\dfrac{y-1}{15} > -\dfrac{2}{5}$

74. $\dfrac{z-2}{12} < \dfrac{1}{4}$

Find the domain and range of each graphed relation. Decide which relations are also functions. See Section 3.2.

75.

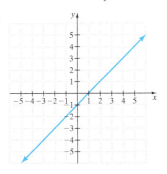

76.

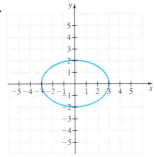

77.

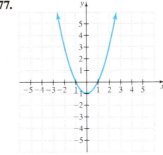

78.

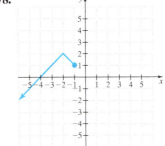

CONCEPT EXTENSIONS

Solve.

79. $y^3 + 9y - y^2 - 9 = 0$

80. $x^3 + x - 3x^2 - 3 = 0$

81. $x^{-2} - x^{-1} - 6 = 0$

82. $y^{-2} - 8y^{-1} + 7 = 0$

83. $2x^3 = -54$

84. $y^3 - 216 = 0$

85. Write a polynomial equation that has three solutions: 2, 5, and -7.

86. Write a polynomial equation that has three solutions: 0, $2i$, and $-2i$.

87. Multiple Steps. At the 2007 Grand Prix of Long Beach auto race, Simon Pagenaud posted the fastest lap speed, but Sebastian Bourdais won the race. One lap through the streets of Long Beach is 10,391 feet (1.968 miles) long. Pagenaud's fastest lap speed was 0.55 foot per second faster than Bourdais's fastest lap speed. Traveling at these fastest speeds, Bourdais would have taken 0.25 second longer than Pagenaud to complete a lap. (*Source:* Championship Auto Racing Teams, Inc.)

a. Find Sebastian Bourdais's fastest lap speed during the race. Round to two decimal places.
b. Find Simon Pagenaud's fastest last speed during the race. Round to two decimal places.
c. Convert each speed to miles per hour. Round to one decimal place.

 88. Use a graphing calculator to solve Exercise 29. Compare the solution with the solution from Exercise 29. Explain any differences.

INTEGRATED REVIEW SUMMARY ON SOLVING QUADRATIC EQUATIONS

Sections 9.1–9.3

Use the square root property to solve each equation.

1. $x^2 - 10 = 0$
2. $x^2 - 14 = 0$
3. $(x - 1)^2 = 8$
4. $(x + 5)^2 = 12$

Solve each equation by completing the square.

5. $x^2 + 2x - 12 = 0$
6. $x^2 - 12x + 11 = 0$
7. $3x^2 + 3x = 5$
8. $16y^2 + 16y = 1$

Use the quadratic formula to solve each equation.

9. $2x^2 - 4x + 1 = 0$
10. $\frac{1}{2}x^2 + 3x + 2 = 0$
11. $x^2 + 4x = -7$
12. $x^2 + x = -3$

Solve each equation. Use a method of your choice.

13. $x^2 + 3x + 6 = 0$
14. $2x^2 + 18 = 0$
15. $x^2 + 17x = 0$
16. $4x^2 - 2x - 3 = 0$
17. $(x - 2)^2 = 27$
18. $\frac{1}{2}x^2 - 2x + \frac{1}{2} = 0$
19. $3x^2 + 2x = 8$
20. $2x^2 = -5x - 1$
21. $x(x - 2) = 5$
22. $x^2 - 31 = 0$
23. $5x^2 - 55 = 0$
24. $5x^2 + 55 = 0$
25. $x(x + 5) = 66$
26. $5x^2 + 6x - 2 = 0$
27. $2x^2 + 3x = 1$

△ 28. The diagonal of a square room measures 20 feet. Find the exact length of a side of the room. Then approximate the length to the nearest tenth of a foot.

29. Together, Jack and Lucy Hoag can prepare a crawfish boil for a large party in 4 hours. Lucy alone can complete the job in 2 hours less time than Jack alone. Find the time that each person can prepare the crawfish boil alone. Round each time to the nearest tenth of an hour.

30. Diane Gray exercises at Total Body Gym. On the treadmill, she runs 5 miles, then increases her speed by 1 mile per hour and runs an additional 2 miles. If her total time on the tread mill is $1\frac{1}{3}$ hours, find her speed during each part of her run.

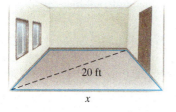

9.4 ZEROS OF POLYNOMIAL FUNCTIONS

OBJECTIVES

1. Use the Rational Zero Theorem to find possible rational zeros.
2. Find zeros of a polynomial function.

Now that we can solve quadratic equations, in this section, we study methods for finding zeros of polynomial functions with degree greater than 2. We begin with a theorem that plays an important role in this process.

> **Helpful Hint**
> Be sure you are familiar with the various kinds of zeros of polynomial functions. Here's a quick example:
> $$f(x) = (x + 3)(2x - 1)(x + \sqrt{2})(x - \sqrt{2})(x - 4 + 5i)(x - 4 - 5i).$$
> **Zeros:** $\;-3,\; \dfrac{1}{2},\; -\sqrt{2},\; \sqrt{2},\; 4 - 5i,\; 4 + 5i$
>
> $-3, \dfrac{1}{2}$ → Rational zeros
> $-\sqrt{2}, \sqrt{2}$ → Irrational zeros
> $4 - 5i, 4 + 5i$ → Complex imaginary zeros
> Rational zeros and Irrational zeros → Real zeros
> Complex imaginary zeros → Nonreal zeros

> **Helpful Hint**
> Recall from Section 6.8 that a zero of a polynomial function is a solution of the related polynomial equation.

OBJECTIVE 1 ▶ **The Rational Zero Theorem.** *The Rational Zero Theorem* provides us with a tool that we can use to make a list of all possible rational zeros of a polynomial function. Equivalently, the theorem gives all possible rational roots of a polynomial equation. Not every number in the list will be a zero of the function, but every rational zero of the polynomial function will appear somewhere in the list.

> **The Rational Zero Theorem**
> If $f(x) = a_n x^n + a_{n-1} x^{n-1} + \cdots + a_1 x + a_0$ has *integer* coefficients and $\dfrac{p}{q}$ (where $\dfrac{p}{q}$ is reduced to lowest terms) is a rational zero of f, then p is a factor of the constant term, a_0, and q is a factor of the leading coefficient, a_n.
>
> Let's see if we can figure out what the theorem tells us about possible rational zeros. To use the theorem, list all the integers that are factors of the constant term, a_0. Then list all the integers that are factors of the leading coefficient, a_n. Finally, list all possible rational zeros:
>
> $$\text{Possible rational zeros} = \dfrac{\text{Factors of the constant term}}{\text{Factors of the leading coefficient}}.$$

EXAMPLE 1 Using the Rational Zero Theorem

List all possible rational zeros of $f(x) = -x^4 + 3x^2 + 4$.

Solution The constant term is 4. We list all of its factors: $\pm 1, \pm 2, \pm 4$. The leading coefficient is -1. Its factors are ± 1.

$$\text{Factors of the constant term, } 4: \quad \pm 1,\; \pm 2,\; \pm 4$$
$$\text{Factors of the leading coefficient, } -1: \quad \pm 1$$

Because

$$\text{Possible rational zeros} = \dfrac{\text{Factors of the constant term}}{\text{Factors of the leading coefficient}},$$

we must take each number in the first row, $\pm 1, \pm 2, \pm 4$, and divide by each number in the second row, ± 1.

$$\text{Possible rational zeros} = \dfrac{\text{Factors of 4}}{\text{Factors of } -1} = \dfrac{\pm 1, \pm 2, \pm 4}{\pm 1} = \pm 1,\; \pm 2,\; \pm 4$$

(Divide ± 1 by ± 1. Divide ± 2 by ± 1. Divide ± 4 by ± 1.)

> **Helpful Hint**
> Always keep in mind the relationship among zeros, roots, and x-intercepts. The zeros of a function f are the roots, or solutions, of the equation $f(x) = 0$. Furthermore, the real zeros, or real roots, are the x-intercepts of the graph of f.

There are six possible rational zeros. The graph of $f(x) = -x^4 + 3x^2 + 4$ is shown and the x-intercepts are -2 and 2. Thus, -2 and 2 are the actual rational zeros.

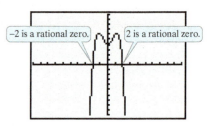

The graph of $f(x) = -x^4 + 3x^2 + 4$ shows that -2 and 2 are rational zeros.

PRACTICE 1 List all possible rational zeros of
$$f(x) = x^3 + 2x^2 - 5x - 6.$$

EXAMPLE 2   Using the Rational Zero Theorem

List all possible rational zeros of $f(x) = 15x^3 + 14x^2 - 3x - 2$.

Solution   The constant term is -2 and the leading coefficient is 15.

$$\text{Possible rational zeros} = \frac{\text{Factors of the constant term, } -2}{\text{Factors of the leading coefficient, } 15} = \frac{\pm 1, \pm 2}{\pm 1, \pm 3, \pm 5, \pm 15}$$

$$= \pm 1, \ \pm 2, \ \pm\tfrac{1}{3}, \ \pm\tfrac{2}{3}, \ \pm\tfrac{1}{5}, \ \pm\tfrac{2}{5}, \ \pm\tfrac{1}{15}, \ \pm\tfrac{2}{15}$$

- Divide ± 1 and ± 2 by ± 1.
- Divide ± 1 and ± 2 by ± 3.
- Divide ± 1 and ± 2 by ± 5.
- Divide ± 1 and ± 2 by ± 15.

There are 16 possible rational zeros. The actual solutions of
$$15x^3 + 14x^2 - 3x - 2 = 0$$
are $-1, -\tfrac{1}{3}, \tfrac{2}{5}$, which are three of the 16 possible zeros.

PRACTICE 2 List all possible rational zeros of
$$f(x) = 4x^5 + 12x^4 - x - 3.$$

OBJECTIVE 2 ▶ **Finding zeros of a polynomial function.** How do we determine which (if any) of the possible rational zeros are rational zeros of the polynomial function? To find the first rational zero, we can use a trial-and-error process involving synthetic division: If $f(x)$ is divided by $x - c$ and the remainder is zero, then c is a zero of f. After we identify the first rational zero, we use the result of the synthetic division to factor the original polynomial. Then we set each factor equal to zero to identify any additional rational zeros.

EXAMPLE 3   Finding Zeros of a Polynomial Function

Find all zeros of $f(x) = x^3 + 2x^2 - 5x - 6$.

Solution   We begin by listing all possible rational zeros.

Possible rational zeros
$$= \frac{\text{Factors of the constant term, } -6}{\text{Factors of the leading coefficient, } 1} = \frac{\pm 1, \pm 2, \pm 3, \pm 6}{\pm 1} = \pm 1, \pm 2, \pm 3, \pm 6$$

Divide the eight numbers in the numerator by ± 1.

Now we will use synthetic division to see if we can find a rational zero among the possible rational zeros ±1, ±2, ±3, ±6. Keep in mind that if $f(x)$ is divided by $x - c$ and the remainder is zero, then c is a zero of f. Let's start by testing 1. If 1 is not a rational zero, then we will test other possible rational zeros.

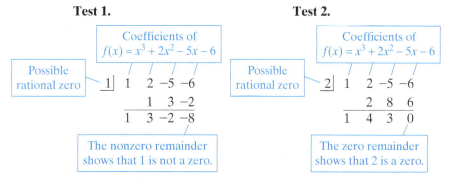

The zero remainder tells us that 2 is a zero of the polynomial function $f(x) = x^3 + 2x^2 - 5x - 6$. Equivalently, 2 is a solution, or root, of the polynomial equation $x^3 + 2x^2 - 5x - 6 = 0$. Thus, $x - 2$ is a factor of the polynomial. The first three numbers in the bottom row of the synthetic division on the right, 1, 4, and 3, give the coefficients of the other factor. This factor is $x^2 + 4x + 3$.

$$x^3 + 2x^2 - 5x - 6 = 0 \qquad \text{Finding the zeros of } f(x) = x^3 + 2x^2 - 5x - 6$$
is the same as finding the roots of this equation.

$$(x - 2)(x^2 + 4x + 3) = 0 \qquad \text{Factor using the result from the synthetic division.}$$

$$(x - 2)(x + 3)(x + 1) = 0 \qquad \text{Factor completely.}$$

$x - 2 = 0$ or $x + 3 = 0$ or $x + 1 = 0$ Set each factor equal to zero.

$x = 2$ $x = -3$ $x = -1$ Solve for x.

The solutions are -3, -1, and 2. The zeros of f are -3, -1, and 2. □

PRACTICE 3   Find all zeros of

$$f(x) = x^3 + 8x^2 + 11x - 20.$$

Our work in Example 3 involved finding zeros of a third-degree polynomial function. The Rational Zero Theorem is a tool that allows us to rewrite such functions as products of two factors, one linear and one quadratic. Zeros of the quadratic factor are found by factoring, the quadratic formula, or the square root property.

EXAMPLE 4   Finding Zeros of a Polynomial Function

Find all zeros of $f(x) = x^3 + 7x^2 + 11x - 3$.

Solution   We begin by listing all possible rational zeros.

$$\text{Possible rational zeros} = \frac{\text{Factors of the constant term, } -3}{\text{Factors of the leading coefficient, } 1} = \frac{\pm 1, \pm 3}{\pm 1} = \pm 1, \pm 3$$

Now we will use synthetic division to see if we can find a rational zero among the four possible rational zeros.

Test 1.	Test −1.	Test 3.	Test −3.
1⌋ 1 7 11 −3	−1⌋ 1 7 11 −3	3⌋ 1 7 11 −3	−3⌋ 1 7 11 −3
1 8 19	−1 −6 −5	3 30 123	−3 −12 3
1 8 19 16	1 6 5 −8	1 10 41 120	1 4 −1 0

546 CHAPTER 9 Quadratic and Higher Degree Equations and Functions

Test −3. (repeated)

$$\begin{array}{r|rrrr} -3 & 1 & 7 & 11 & -3 \\ & & -3 & -12 & 3 \\ \hline & 1 & 4 & -1 & 0 \end{array}$$

The zero remainder when testing −3, repeated in the margin, tells us that −3 is a zero of the polynomial function $f(x) = x^3 + 7x^2 + 11x - 3$. To find all zeros of f, we proceed as follows:

$x^3 + 7x^2 + 11x - 3 = 0$ Finding the zeros of f is the same thing as finding the roots of $f(x) = 0$.

$(x + 3)(x^2 + 4x - 1) = 0$ This result is from the last synthetic division, repeated in the margin. The first three numbers in the bottom row, 1, 4, and −1, give the coefficients of the second factor.

$x + 3 = 0$ or $x^2 + 4x - 1 = 0$ Set each factor equal to 0.
$x = -3$.   Solve the linear equation.

We can use the quadratic formula to solve $x^2 + 4x - 1 = 0$.

$$x = \frac{-b \pm \sqrt{b^2 - 4ac}}{2a}$$ We use the quadratic formula because $x^2 + 4x - 1$ cannot be factored.

$$= \frac{-4 \pm \sqrt{4^2 - 4(1)(-1)}}{2(1)}$$ Let $a = 1$, $b = 4$, and $c = -1$.

$$= \frac{-4 \pm \sqrt{20}}{2}$$ Multiply and subtract under the radical: $4^2 - 4(1)(-1) = 16 - (-4) = 16 + 4 = 20$.

$$= \frac{-4 \pm 2\sqrt{5}}{2}$$ $\sqrt{20} = \sqrt{4 \cdot 5} = 2\sqrt{5}$

$$= -2 \pm \sqrt{5}$$ Divide the numerator and the denominator by 2.

The solutions are $-3, -2 - \sqrt{5}$, and $-2 + \sqrt{5}$. The zeros of $f(x) = x^3 + 7x^3 + 11x - 3$ are $-3, -2 - \sqrt{5}$, and $-2 + \sqrt{5}$. Among these three real zeros, one zero is rational and two are irrational. □

PRACTICE 4   Find all zeros of $f(x) = x^3 + x^2 - 5x - 2$.

9.4 EXERCISE SET

Use the Rational Zero Theorem to list all possible rational zeros for each given function.

1. $f(x) = x^3 + x^2 - 4x - 4$
2. $f(x) = x^3 + 3x^2 - 6x - 8$
3. $f(x) = 3x^4 - 11x^3 - x^2 + 19x + 6$
4. $f(x) = 2x^4 + 3x^3 - 11x^2 - 9x + 15$
5. $f(x) = 4x^4 - x^3 + 5x^2 - 2x - 6$
6. $f(x) = 3x^4 - 11x^3 - 3x^2 - 6x + 8$
7. $f(x) = x^5 - x^4 - 7x^3 + 7x^2 - 12x - 12$
8. $f(x) = 4x^5 - 8x^4 - x + 2$

Multiple Steps. *In Exercises 9–16,*
  a. List all possible rational zeros.
  b. Use synthetic division to test the possible rational zeros and find an actual zero.
  c. Use the quotient from part (b) to find the remaining zeros of the polynomial function.

9. $f(x) = x^3 + x^2 - 4x - 4$
10. $f(x) = x^3 - 2x^2 - 11x + 12$
11. $f(x) = 2x^3 - 3x^2 - 11x + 6$
12. $f(x) = 2x^3 - 5x^2 + x + 2$
13. $f(x) = x^3 + 4x^2 - 3x - 6$
14. $f(x) = 2x^3 + x^2 - 3x + 1$
 15. $f(x) = 2x^3 + 6x^2 + 5x + 2$
16. $f(x) = x^3 - 4x^2 + 8x - 5$

In Exercises 17–22, find all zeros of the polynomial function.

17. $f(x) = x^3 - 4x^2 - 7x + 10$
18. $f(x) = x^3 + 12x^2 + 21x + 10$
19. $f(x) = x^4 - 2x^3 + x^2 + 12x + 8$

20. $f(x) = x^4 - 4x^3 - x^2 + 14x + 10$

21. $f(x) = 3x^4 - 11x^3 - x^2 + 19x + 6$

22. $f(x) = 2x^4 + 3x^3 - 11x^2 - 9x + 15$

Exercises 23–30 show incomplete graphs of given polynomial functions.

   a. *Find all the zeros of each function.*

   b. *Without using a graphing utility, draw a complete graph of the function.*

23. $f(x) = -x^3 + x^2 + 16x - 16$

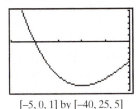

[−5, 0, 1] by [−40, 25, 5]

24. $f(x) = -x^3 + 3x^2 - 4$

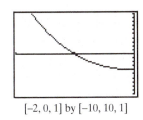

[−2, 0, 1] by [−10, 10, 1]

25. $f(x) = 4x^3 - 8x^2 - 3x + 9$

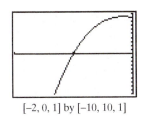

[−2, 0, 1] by [−10, 10, 1]

26. $f(x) = 3x^3 + 2x^2 + 2x - 1$

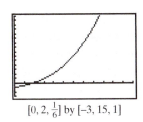

[0, 2, $\frac{1}{6}$] by [−3, 15, 1]

27. $f(x) = 2x^4 - 3x^3 - 7x^2 - 8x + 6$

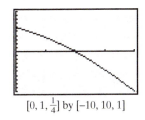

[0, 1, $\frac{1}{4}$] by [−10, 10, 1]

28. $f(x) = 2x^4 + 2x^3 - 22x^2 - 18x + 36$

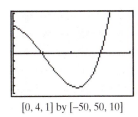

[0, 4, 1] by [−50, 50, 10]

29. $f(x) = 3x^5 + 2x^4 - 15x^3 - 10x^2 + 12x + 8$

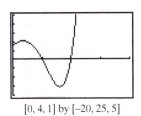

[0, 4, 1] by [−20, 25, 5]

30. $f(x) = -5x^4 + 4x^3 - 19x^2 + 16x + 4$

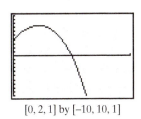

[0, 2, 1] by [−10, 10, 1]

REVIEW AND PREVIEW

Solve each quadratic equation. (Try to solve by factoring. If the quadratic does not factor, use the quadratic formula.) See Sections 6.8 and 9.2.

31. $3x^2 + 14x - 5 = 0$

32. $2x^2 + 13x - 7 = 0$

33. $2x^2 + 7x + 1 = 0$

34. $3x^2 + 9x + 1 = 0$

CONCEPT EXTENSIONS

A popular model of carry-on luggage has a length that is 10 inches greater than its depth. Airline regulations require that the sum of the length, width, and depth cannot exceed 40 inches. These conditions, with the assumption that this sum is 40 inches, can be modeled by a function that gives the volume of the luggage, V, in cubic inches, in terms of its depth, x, in inches.

Volume = depth · length · width: 40 − (depth + length)

$V(x) = x \cdot (x + 10) \cdot [40 - (x + x + 10)]$

$V(x) = x(x + 10)(30 - 2x)$

548 CHAPTER 9 Quadratic and Higher Degree Equations and Functions

Use function V to solve Exercises 35–36.

35. If the volume of the carry-on luggage is 2000 cubic inches, determine two possibilities for its depth. Where necessary, round to the nearest tenth of an inch.

36. If the volume of the carry-on luggage is 1500 cubic inches, determine two possibilities for its depth. Where necessary, round to the nearest tenth of an inch.

Read a Graph. *Use the graph of the function modeling the volume of the carry-on luggage to solve Exercises 37–38.*

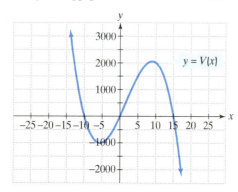

37. a. Identify your answers from Exercise 35 as points on the graph.
   b. Use the graph to describe a realistic domain, x, for the volume function, where x represents the depth of the carry-on luggage.

38. a. Identify your answers from Exercise 36 as points on the graph.
   b. Use the graph to describe a realistic domain, x, for the volume function, where x represents the depth of the carry-on luggage.

39. Describe how to find the possible rational zeros of a polynomial function.

40. Write equations for several polynomial functions of odd degree and graph each function. Is it possible for the graph to have no real zeros? Explain. Try doing the same thing for polynomial functions of even degree. Now is it possible to have no real zeros?

9.5 THE FUNDAMENTAL THEOREM OF ALGEBRA

OBJECTIVES

1. Solve polynomial equations.
2. Find polynomials with given zeros.

OBJECTIVE 1 ▶ Solve polynomial equations. If the degree of a polynomial function or equation is 4 or higher, it is often necessary to find more than one linear factor by synthetic division.

One way to speed up the process of finding the first zero is to graph the function. Any x-intercept is a zero.

EXAMPLE 1 Solving a Polynomial Equation

Solve: $x^4 - 6x^2 - 8x + 24 = 0$.

Solution Recall that we refer to the *zeros* of a polynomial function and the *roots* of a polynomial equation. Because we are given an equation, we will use the word "roots," rather than "zeros," in the solution process. We begin by listing all possible rational roots.

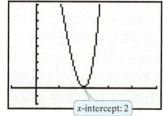

The graph of $f(x) = x^4 - 6x^2 - 8x + 24$ in a $[-1, 5, 1]$ by $[-2, 10, 1]$ viewing rectangle

$$\text{Possible rational roots} = \frac{\text{Factors of the constant term, 24}}{\text{Factors of the leading coefficient, 1}}$$
$$= \frac{\pm 1, \pm 2, \pm 3, \pm 4, \pm 6, \pm 8, \pm 12, \pm 24}{\pm 1}$$
$$= \pm 1, \pm 2, \pm 3, \pm 4, \pm 6, \pm 8, \pm 12, \pm 24$$

Part of the graph of $f(x) = x^4 - 6x^2 - 8x + 24$ is shown in the margin. Because the x-intercept is 2, we will test 2 by synthetic division and show that it is a root of the given equation. Without the graph, the procedure would be to start the trial-and-error synthetic division with 1 and proceed until a zero remainder is found.

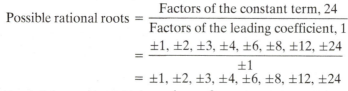

Now we can rewrite the given equation in factored form.

$$x^4 - 6x^2 - 8x + 24 = 0 \quad \text{This is the given equation.}$$

$$(x - 2)(x^3 + 2x^2 - 2x - 12) = 0 \quad \text{This is the result obtained from the synthetic division. The first four numbers in the bottom row, 1, 2, } -2, \text{ and } -12, \text{ give the coefficients of the second factor.}$$

$$x - 2 = 0 \quad \text{or} \quad x^3 + 2x^2 - 2x - 12 = 0 \quad \text{Set each factor equal to 0.}$$

We can use the same approach to look for rational roots of the polynomial equation $x^3 + 2x^2 - 2x - 12 = 0$, listing all possible rational roots. Without the graph on the previous page, the procedure would be to start testing possible rational roots by trial-and-error synthetic division. However, take a second look at this graph. Because the graph turns around at 2, this means that 2 is a root of even multiplicity. Thus, 2 must also be a root of $x^3 + 2x^2 - 2x - 12 = 0$, confirmed by the following synthetic division.

$$\underline{2|}\ \begin{array}{rrrr} 1 & 2 & -2 & -12 \\ & 2 & 8 & 12 \\ \hline 1 & 4 & 6 & 0 \end{array}$$

These are the coefficients of $x^3 + 2x^2 - 2x - 12 = 0$.

The zero remainder indicates that 2 is a root of $x^3 + 2x^2 - 2x - 12 = 0$.

Now we can solve the original equation as follows:

$$x^4 - 6x^2 - 8x + 24 = 0 \quad \text{This is the given equation.}$$

$$(x - 2)(x^3 + 2x^2 - 2x - 12) = 0 \quad \text{This factorization was obtained from the first synthetic division.}$$

$$(x - 2)(x - 2)(x^2 + 4x + 6) = 0 \quad \text{This factorization was obtained from the second synthetic division. The first three numbers in the bottom row, 1, 4, and 6, give the coefficients of the third factor.}$$

$$x - 2 = 0 \quad \text{or} \quad x - 2 = 0 \quad \text{or} \quad x^2 + 4x + 6 = 0 \quad \text{Set each factor equal to 0.}$$

$$x = 2 \qquad\qquad x = 2. \qquad\qquad\qquad\qquad\qquad \text{Solve the linear equations.}$$

We can use the quadratic formula to solve $x^2 + 4x + 6 = 0$.

$$x = \frac{-b \pm \sqrt{b^2 - 4ac}}{2a} \quad \text{We use the quadratic formula because } x^2 + 4x + 6 \text{ cannot be factored.}$$

$$= \frac{-4 \pm \sqrt{4^2 - 4(1)(6)}}{2(1)} \quad \text{Let } a = 1, b = 4, \text{ and } c = 6.$$

$$= \frac{-4 \pm \sqrt{-8}}{2} \quad \text{Multiply and subtract under the radical: } 4^2 - 4(1)(6) = 16 - 24 = -8.$$

$$= \frac{-4 \pm 2i\sqrt{2}}{2} \quad \sqrt{-8} = \sqrt{4(2)(-1)} = 2i\sqrt{2}$$

$$= -2 \pm i\sqrt{2} \quad \text{Simplify.}$$

The solutions of the original equation, $x^4 - 6x^2 - 8x + 24 = 0$, are 2, $-2 - i\sqrt{2}$, and $-2 + i\sqrt{2}$. A graphing utility does not reveal the two imaginary roots.

PRACTICE 1 Solve: $x^4 - 6x^3 + 22x^2 - 30x + 13 = 0$.

In Example 1, 2 is a repeated root of the equation with multiplicity 2. Counting this multiple root separately, the fourth-degree equation $x^4 - 6x^2 - 8x + 24 = 0$ has four roots: 2, 2, $-2 + i\sqrt{2}$, and $-2 - i\sqrt{2}$. The equation and its roots illustrate two general properties:

Properties of Roots of Polynomial Equations

1. If a polynomial equation is of degree n, then counting multiple roots separately, the equation has n roots.
2. If $a + bi$ is a root of a polynomial equation with real coefficients ($b \neq 0$), then the imaginary number $a - bi$ is also a root. Imaginary roots, if they exist, occur in conjugate pairs.

The Fundamental Theorem of Algebra The fact that a polynomial equation of degree n has n roots is a consequence of a theorem proved in 1799 by a 22-year-old student named Carl Friedrich Gauss in his doctoral dissertation. His result is called the **Fundamental Theorem of Algebra.**

> **The Fundamental Theorem of Algebra**
>
> If $f(x)$ is a polynomial of degree n, where $n \geq 1$, then the equation $f(x) = 0$ has at least one complex root.

> **Helpful Hint**
>
> As you read the Fundamental Theorem of Algebra, don't confuse *complex root* with *imaginary root* and conclude that every polynomial equation has at least one imaginary root. Recall that complex numbers, $a + bi$, include both real numbers ($b = 0$) and imaginary numbers ($b \neq 0$).

The following statement is a result of the Fundamental Theorem of Algebra, and we will use it often. If $f(x)$ is a polynomial of degree n, where $n \geq 1$, then $f(x) = 0$ has exactly n roots, where roots are counted according to their multiplicity.

OBJECTIVE 2 ▶ **Find Polynomials with given Zeros.** In Example 1, we found that $x^4 - 6x^2 - 8x + 24 = 0$ has 2 and $-2 \pm i\sqrt{2}$ as solutions where 2 is a repeated root with multiplicity 2. The polynomial can be factored over the complex nonreal numbers as follows:

$$f(x) = x^4 - 6x^2 - 8x + 24$$
$$= [x - (-2 + i\sqrt{2})][x - (-2 - i\sqrt{2})](x - 2)(x - 2).$$

These are the four zeros. These are the linear factors.

This fourth-degree polynomial has four linear factors. Just as an nth-degree polynomial equation has n roots, an nth-degree polynomial has n linear factors. This is formally stated as the **Linear Factorization Theorem.**

The Linear Factorization Theorem If $f(x) = a_n x^n + a_{n-1} x^{n-1} + \cdots + a_1 x + a_0$, where $n \geq 1$ and $a_n \neq 0$, then

$$f(x) = a_n(x - c_1)(x - c_2) \cdots (x - c_n),$$

where $c_1, c_2, \ldots, c_n$ are complex numbers (possibly real and not necessarily distinct). In words: An nth-degree polynomial can be expressed as the product of a nonzero constant and n linear factors, where each linear factor has a leading coefficient of 1.

Many of our problems involving polynomial functions and polynomial equations dealt with the process of finding zeros and roots. The Linear Factorization Theorem enables us to reverse this process, finding a polynomial function when the zeros are given.

EXAMPLE 2 Finding a Polynomial Function with Given Zeros

Find a fourth-degree polynomial function $f(x)$ with real coefficients, a leading coefficient of 1, and has -2, 2, and i as zeros.

Solution Because i is a zero and the polynomial has real coefficients, the conjugate, $-i$, must also be a zero. We can now use the Linear Factorization Theorem.

$f(x) = (x - (-2))(x - 2)(x - i)(x - (-i))$ This is the linear factorization for a fourth-degree polynomial.

$f(x) = (x + 2)(x - 2)(x - i)(x + i)$ Simplify.

$ = (x^2 - 4)(x^2 + 1)$ Multiply: $(x - i)(x + i) = x^2 - i^2 = x^2 - (-1) = x^2 + 1$.

$f(x) = x^4 - 3x^2 - 4$ Complete the multiplication.

Thus, $f(x) = x^4 - 3x^2 - 4$.

PRACTICE 2 Find a third-degree polynomial function $f(x)$ with real coefficients, a leading coefficient of 1, and has -3 and i as zeros.

9.5 EXERCISE SET

In Exercises 1–8,

a. List all possible rational roots.
b. Use synthetic division to test the possible rational roots and find an actual root.
c. Use the quotient from part (b) to find the remaining roots and solve the equation.

1. $x^3 - 2x^2 - 11x + 12 = 0$
2. $x^3 - 2x^2 - 7x - 4 = 0$
3. $x^3 - 10x - 12 = 0$
4. $x^3 - 5x^2 + 17x - 13 = 0$
5. $6x^3 + 25x^2 - 24x + 5 = 0$
6. $2x^3 - 5x^2 - 6x + 4 = 0$
7. $x^4 - 2x^3 - 5x^2 + 8x + 4 = 0$
8. $x^4 - 2x^2 - 16x - 15 = 0$

Find an nth-degree polynomial function with real coefficients, a leading coefficient, of 1, satisfying the given conditions. See Example 2.

9. $n = 3$; 1 and $5i$ are zeros
10. $n = 3$; 4 and $2i$ are zeros
11. $n = 3$; -5 and $4 + 3i$ are zeros
12. $n = 3$; 6 and $-5 + 2i$ are zeros
13. $n = 4$; i and $3i$ are zeros
14. $n = 4$; $-2, -\frac{1}{2}$, and i are zeros
15. $n = 4$; $-2, 5$, and $3 + 2i$ are zeros
16. $n = 4$; $-4, \frac{1}{3}$, and $2 + 3i$ are zeros

In Exercises 17–24, solve the given polynomial equation.

17. $2x^3 - x^2 - 9x - 4 = 0$
18. $3x^3 - 8x^2 - 8x + 8 = 0$
19. $x^4 - 3x^3 - 20x^2 - 24x - 8 = 0$
20. $x^4 - x^3 + 2x^2 - 4x - 8 = 0$
21. $4x^4 - x^3 + 5x^2 - 2x - 6 = 0$
22. $3x^4 - 11x^3 - 3x^2 - 6x + 8 = 0$
23. $2x^5 + 7x^4 - 18x^2 - 8x + 8 = 0$
24. $4x^5 + 12x^4 - 41x^3 - 99x^2 + 10x + 24 = 0$
25. How does the linear factorization of $f(x)$, that is,
$$f(x) = a_n(x - c_1)(x - c_2) \cdots (x - c_n),$$
show that a polynomial equation of degree n has n roots?
26. Explain why the equation $x^4 + 6x^2 + 2 = 0$ has no rational roots.

REVIEW AND PREVIEW

Use the graph of function f to solve each exercise. See Sections 3.2 and 7.1.

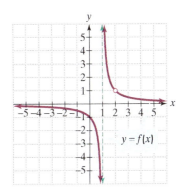

27. For what value(s) of x is the function undefined?
28. What value(s) of y are not in the range of the function?
29. Write the equation of the vertical asymptote, or the vertical line that the graph of f approaches but does not touch.
30. Write the equation of the horizontal asymptote, or the horizontal line that the graph of f approaches but does not touch.

552 CHAPTER 9 Quadratic and Higher Degree Equations and Functions

CONCEPT EXTENSIONS

31. If the volume of the solid shown in the figure is 208 cubic inches, find the value of x.

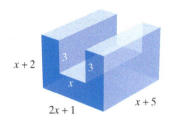

True or False. *Determine whether each statement is true or false. If the statement is false, make the necessary change(s) to produce a true statement.*

32. The equation $x^3 + 5x^2 + 6x + 1 = 0$ has one positive real root.

33. Every polynomial equation of degree 3 with integer coefficients has at least one rational root.

34. Every polynomial equation of degree n has n distinct solutions.

Logic. *In Exercises 35–36, determine whether each statement makes sense or does not make sense, and explain your reasoning.*

35. By using the quadratic formula, I do not need to bother with synthetic division when solving polynomial equations of degree 3 or higher.

36. I'm working with the polynomial function $f(x) = x^4 + 3x^2 + 2$ that has four possible rational zeros but no actual rational zeros.

The equations below have real roots that are rational. Use the Rational Zero Theorem to list all possible rational roots. Then graph the polynomial function in the given viewing rectangle to determine which possible rational roots are actual roots of the equation.

37. $2x^3 - 15x^2 + 22x + 15 = 0; [-1, 6, 1]$ by $[-50, 50, 10]$

38. $6x^3 - 19x^2 + 16x - 4 = 0; [0, 2, 1]$ by $[-3, 2, 1]$

39. $2x^4 + 7x^3 - 4x^2 - 27x - 18 = 0; [-4, 3, 1]$ by $[-45, 45, 15]$

40. $4x^4 + 4x^3 + 7x^2 - x - 2 = 0; [-2, 2, 1]$ by $[-5, 5, 1]$

Use a graphing utility to obtain a complete graph for each polynomial function. Then determine the number of real zeros and the number of imaginary zeros for each function.

41. $f(x) = x^3 - 6x - 9$

42. $f(x) = 3x^5 - 2x^4 + 6x^3 - 4x^2 - 24x + 16$

43. $f(x) = 3x^4 + 4x^3 - 7x^2 - 2x - 3$

44. $f(x) = x^6 - 64$

9.6 NONLINEAR INEQUALITIES IN ONE VARIABLE

OBJECTIVES

1. Solve polynomial inequalities of degree 2 or greater.
2. Solve inequalities that contain rational expressions with variables in the denominator.

OBJECTIVE 1 ▶ Solving polynomial inequalities. Just as we can solve linear inequalities in one variable, so can we also solve quadratic inequalities in one variable. A **quadratic inequality** is an inequality that can be written so that one side is a quadratic expression and the other side is 0. Here are examples of quadratic inequalities in one variable. Each is written in **standard form.**

$$x^2 - 10x + 7 \leq 0 \qquad 3x^2 + 2x - 6 > 0$$
$$2x^2 + 9x - 2 < 0 \qquad x^2 - 3x + 11 \geq 0$$

A solution of a quadratic inequality in one variable is a value of the variable that makes the inequality a true statement.

The value of an expression such as $x^2 - 3x - 10$ will sometimes be positive, sometimes negative, and sometimes 0, depending on the value substituted for x. To solve the inequality $x^2 - 3x - 10 < 0$, we are looking for all values of x that make the expression $x^2 - 3x - 10$ **less than 0,** or **negative.** To understand how we find these values, we'll study the graph of the quadratic function $y = x^2 - 3x - 10$.

Notice that the x-values for which y is positive are separated from the x values for which y is negative by the x-intercepts. (Recall that the x-intercepts correspond to values of x for which $y = 0$.) Thus, the solutions of $x^2 - 3x - 10 < 0$ consist of all real numbers from -2 to 5, or $-2 < x < 5$.

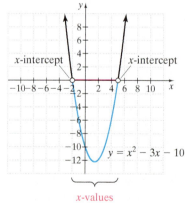

It is not necessary to graph $y = x^2 - 3x - 10$ to solve the related inequality $x^2 - 3x - 10 < 0$. Instead, we can draw a number line representing the x-axis and keep the following in mind: *A region on the number line for which the value of $x^2 - 3x - 10$ is positive is separated from a region on the number line for which the value of $x^2 - 3x - 10$ is negative by a value for which the expression is 0.*

Let's find these values for which the expression is 0 by solving the related equation:

$$x^2 - 3x - 10 = 0$$
$$(x - 5)(x + 2) = 0 \qquad \text{Factor.}$$
$$x - 5 = 0 \quad \text{or} \quad x + 2 = 0 \qquad \text{Set each factor equal to 0.}$$
$$x = 5 \quad x = -2 \qquad \text{Solve.}$$

▶ **Helpful Hint**
Use a graphing calculator to check solutions in this section.

These two numbers -2 and 5, divide the number line into three regions. We will call the regions A, B, and C. These regions are important because, if the value of $x^2 - 3x - 10$ is negative when a number from a region is substituted for x, then $x^2 - 3x - 10$ is negative when any number in that region is substituted for x. The same is true if the value of $x^2 - 3x - 10$ is positive for a particular value of x in a region.

To see whether the inequality $x^2 - 3x - 10 < 0$ is true or false in each region, we choose a test point from each region and substitute its value for x in the inequality $x^2 - 3x - 10 < 0$. If the resulting inequality is true, the region containing the test point is a solution region.

Region	Test Point Value	$(x-5)(x+2) < 0$	Result
A	-3	$(-8)(-1) < 0$	False
B	0	$(-5)(2) < 0$	True
C	6	$(1)(8) < 0$	False

The values in region B satisfy the inequality. The numbers -2 and 5 are not included in the solution set since the inequality symbol is $<$. The solutions are $-2 < x < 5$, and the graph is shown.

EXAMPLE 1 Solve: $(x+3)(x-3) > 0$.

Solution First we solve the related equation, $(x+3)(x-3) = 0$.

$$(x+3)(x-3) = 0$$
$$x + 3 = 0 \quad \text{or} \quad x - 3 = 0$$
$$x = -3 \qquad \qquad x = 3$$

The two numbers -3 and 3 separate the number line into three regions, A, B, and C.

Now we substitute the value of a test point from each region. If the test value satisfies the inequality, every value in the region containing the test value is a solution.

Region	Test Point Value	$(x+3)(x-3) > 0$	Result
A	-4	$(-1)(-7) > 0$	True
B	0	$(3)(-3) > 0$	False
C	4	$(7)(1) > 0$	True

The points in regions A and C satisfy the inequality. The numbers -3 and 3 are not included in the solution since the inequality symbol is $>$. The solutions are $x < -3$ or $x > 3$, and the graph is shown.

PRACTICE 1 Solve: $(x-4)(x+3) > 0$.

The following steps may be used to solve a polynomial inequality.

> **Solving a Polynomial Inequality**
> **STEP 1.** Write the inequality in standard form and then solve the related equation.
> **STEP 2.** Separate the number line into regions with the solutions from Step 1.
> **STEP 3.** For each region, choose a test point and determine whether its value satisfies the *original inequality*.
> **STEP 4.** The solution includes the regions whose test point value is a solution. If the inequality symbol is $\leq$ or $\geq$, the values from Step 1 are solutions; if $<$ or $>$, they are not.

Concept Check ✓

When choosing a test point in Step 4, why would the solutions from Step 2 not make good choices for test points?

EXAMPLE 2 Solve: $x^2 - 4x \leq 0$.

Solution First we solve the related equation, $x^2 - 4x = 0$.

$$x^2 - 4x = 0$$
$$x(x - 4) = 0$$
$$x = 0 \quad \text{or} \quad x = 4$$

The numbers 0 and 4 separate the number line into three regions, A, B, and C.

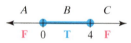

We check a test value in each region in the original inequality. Values in region B satisfy the inequality. The numbers 0 and 4 are included in the solution since the inequality symbol is $\leq$. The solutions are $0 \leq x \leq 4$, and the graph is shown.

PRACTICE 2 Solve: $x^2 - 8x \leq 0$.

EXAMPLE 3 Solve: $(x + 2)(x - 1)(x - 5) \leq 0$.

Solution First we solve $(x + 2)(x - 1)(x - 5) = 0$. By inspection, we see that the solutions are $-2, 1,$ and 5. They separate the number line into four regions, $A, B, C,$ and D. Next we check test points from each region.

Region	Test Point Value	$(x + 2)(x - 1)(x - 5) \leq 0$	Result
A	-3	$(-1)(-4)(-8) \leq 0$	True
B	0	$(2)(-1)(-5) \leq 0$	False
C	2	$(4)(1)(-3) \leq 0$	True
D	6	$(8)(5)(1) \leq 0$	False

Answer to Concept Check:
The solutions found in Step 2 have a value of 0 in the original inequality.

The solution is $x \leq -2$ or $1 \leq x \leq 5$, and the graph is shown. We include the numbers $-2, 1,$ and 5 because the inequality symbol is $\leq$.

```
        A   B   C   D
    ←———●———●———●———→
      T -2 F 1 T 5 F
```

PRACTICE 3 Solve: $(x + 3)(x - 2)(x + 1) \leq 0$.

OBJECTIVE 2 ▶ Solving rational inequalities. Inequalities containing rational expressions with variables in the denominator are solved by using a similar procedure.

EXAMPLE 4 Solve: $\dfrac{x + 2}{x - 3} \leq 0$.

Solution First we find all values that make the denominator equal to 0. To do this, we solve $x - 3 = 0$ and find that $x = 3$.

Next, we solve the related equation $\dfrac{x + 2}{x - 3} = 0$.

$$\dfrac{x + 2}{x - 3} = 0$$

$$x + 2 = 0 \quad \text{Multiply both sides by the LCD, } x - 3.$$

$$x = -2$$

Now we place these numbers on a number line and proceed as before, checking test point values in the original inequality.

```
        A        B       C
    ←———+————————+————→
        -2       3
```

Choose -3 from region A.   *Choose 0 from region B.*   *Choose 4 from region C.*

$\dfrac{x + 2}{x - 3} \leq 0$ $\dfrac{x + 2}{x - 3} \leq 0$ $\dfrac{x + 2}{x - 3} \leq 0$

$\dfrac{-3 + 2}{-3 - 3} \leq 0$ $\dfrac{0 + 2}{0 - 3} \leq 0$ $\dfrac{4 + 2}{4 - 3} \leq 0$

$\dfrac{-1}{-6} \leq 0$ $-\dfrac{2}{3} \leq 0$ True $6 \leq 0$ False

$\dfrac{1}{6} \leq 0$ False

The solution is $(-2 \leq x < 3)$. This inequality includes -2 because -2 satisfies the original inequality. This interval does not include 3, because 3 would make the denominator 0.

```
        A        B       C
    ←———●————————○————→
      F -2       T 3     F
```

PRACTICE 4 Solve: $\dfrac{x - 5}{x + 4} \leq 0$.

The following steps may be used to solve a rational inequality with variables in the denominator.

> **Solving a Rational Inequality**
> **STEP 1.** Solve for values that make all denominators 0.
> **STEP 2.** Solve the related equation.
> **STEP 3.** Separate the number line into regions with the solutions from Steps 1 and 2.
> **STEP 4.** For each region, choose a test point and determine whether its value satisfies the *original inequality*.
> **STEP 5.** The solution includes the regions whose test point value is a solution. Check whether to include values from Step 2. Be sure *not* to include values that make any denominator 0.

EXAMPLE 5 Solve: $\dfrac{5}{x+1} < -2$.

Solution First we find values for x that make the denominator equal to 0.
$$x + 1 = 0$$
$$x = -1$$

Next we solve $\dfrac{5}{x+1} = -2$.

$$(x+1) \cdot \dfrac{5}{x+1} = (x+1) \cdot -2 \quad \text{Multiply both sides by the LCD, } x+1.$$
$$5 = -2x - 2 \quad \text{Simplify.}$$
$$7 = -2x$$
$$-\dfrac{7}{2} = x$$

We use these two solutions to divide a number line into three regions and choose test points. Only a test point value from region B satisfies the *original inequality*. The solutions are $-\dfrac{7}{2} < x < -1$, and the graph is shown.

PRACTICE 5 Solve: $\dfrac{7}{x+3} < 5$.

VOCABULARY & READINESS CHECK

Fill in the Blank. *Write the graphed solutions. Use the variable x in each inequality.*

1.

2.

3.

4.

5.

6.

9.6 EXERCISE SET

Solve each quadratic inequality. See Examples 1 through 3.

1. $(x + 1)(x + 5) > 0$
2. $(x + 1)(x + 5) \leq 0$
3. $(x - 3)(x + 4) \leq 0$
4. $(x + 4)(x - 1) > 0$
5. $x^2 - 7x + 10 \leq 0$
6. $x^2 + 8x + 15 \geq 0$
7. $3x^2 + 16x < -5$
8. $2x^2 - 5x < 7$
9. $(x - 6)(x - 4)(x - 2) > 0$
10. $(x - 6)(x - 4)(x - 2) \leq 0$
11. $x(x - 1)(x + 4) \leq 0$
12. $x(x - 6)(x + 2) > 0$
13. $(x^2 - 9)(x^2 - 4) > 0$
14. $(x^2 - 16)(x^2 - 1) \leq 0$

Solve each inequality. See Example 4.

15. $\dfrac{x + 7}{x - 2} < 0$
16. $\dfrac{x - 5}{x - 6} > 0$
17. $\dfrac{5}{x + 1} > 0$
18. $\dfrac{3}{y - 5} < 0$
19. $\dfrac{x + 1}{x - 4} \geq 0$
20. $\dfrac{x + 1}{x - 4} \leq 0$

Solve each inequality. See Example 5.

21. $\dfrac{3}{x - 2} < 4$
22. $\dfrac{-2}{y + 3} > 2$
23. $\dfrac{x^2 + 6}{5x} \geq 1$
24. $\dfrac{y^2 + 15}{8y} \leq 1$

MIXED PRACTICE

Solve each inequality.

25. $(x - 8)(x + 7) > 0$
26. $(x - 5)(x + 1) < 0$
27. $(2x - 3)(4x + 5) \leq 0$
28. $(6x + 7)(7x - 12) > 0$
29. $x^2 > x$
30. $x^2 < 25$
31. $(2x - 8)(x + 4)(x - 6) \leq 0$
32. $(3x - 12)(x + 5)(2x - 3) \geq 0$
33. $6x^2 - 5x \geq 6$
34. $12x^2 + 11x \leq 15$
35. $4x^3 + 16x^2 - 9x - 36 > 0$
36. $x^3 + 2x^2 - 4x - 8 < 0$
37. $x^4 - 26x^2 + 25 \geq 0$
38. $16x^4 - 40x^2 + 9 \leq 0$
39. $(2x - 7)(3x + 5) > 0$
40. $(4x - 9)(2x + 5) < 0$
41. $\dfrac{x}{x - 10} < 0$
42. $\dfrac{x + 10}{x - 10} > 0$
43. $\dfrac{x - 5}{x + 4} \geq 0$
44. $\dfrac{x - 3}{x + 2} \leq 0$
45. $\dfrac{x(x + 6)}{(x - 7)(x + 1)} \geq 0$
46. $\dfrac{(x - 2)(x + 2)}{(x + 1)(x - 4)} \leq 0$
47. $\dfrac{-1}{x - 1} > -1$
48. $\dfrac{4}{y + 2} < -2$
49. $\dfrac{x}{x + 4} \leq 2$
50. $\dfrac{4x}{x - 3} \geq 5$
51. $\dfrac{z}{z - 5} \geq 2z$
52. $\dfrac{p}{p + 4} \leq 3p$
53. $\dfrac{(x + 1)^2}{5x} > 0$
54. $\dfrac{(2x - 3)^2}{x} < 0$

REVIEW AND PREVIEW

Read a Graph. *Recall that the graph of $f(x) + K$ is the same as the graph of $f(x)$ shifted K units upward if $K > 0$ and $|K|$ units downward if $K < 0$. Use the graph of $f(x) = |x|$ on the following page to sketch the graph of each function. See Section 3.6.*

55. $g(x) = |x| + 2$
56. $H(x) = |x| - 2$
57. $F(x) = |x| - 1$
58. $h(x) = |x| + 5$

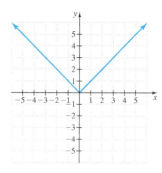

Read a Graph. *Use the graph of $f(x) = x^2$ below to sketch the graph of each function.*

59. $F(x) = x^2 - 3$
60. $h(x) = x^2 - 4$
61. $H(x) = x^2 + 1$
62. $g(x) = x^2 + 3$

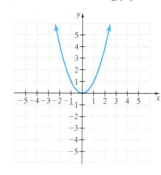

64. Explain why $\dfrac{x+2}{x-3} \geq 0$ and $(x+2)(x-3) \geq 0$ do not have the same solutions.

Find all numbers that satisfy each of the following.

65. A number minus its reciprocal is less than zero. Find the numbers.
66. Twice a number added to its reciprocal is nonnegative. Find the numbers.
67. The total profit function $P(x)$ for a company producing x thousand units is given by
$$P(x) = -2x^2 + 26x - 44$$
Find the values of x for which the company makes a profit. [*Hint:* The company makes a profit when $P(x) > 0$.]
68. A projectile is fired straight up from the ground with an initial velocity of 80 feet per second. Its height $s(t)$ in feet at any time t is given by the function
$$s(t) = -16t^2 + 80t$$
Find the interval of time for which the height of the projectile is greater than 96 feet.

Use a graphing calculator to check each exercise.

69. Exercise 25
70. Exercise 26
71. Exercise 37
72. Exercise 38

CONCEPT EXTENSIONS

63. Explain why $\dfrac{x+2}{x-3} > 0$ and $(x+2)(x-3) > 0$ have the same solutions.

CHAPTER 9 VOCABULARY CHECK

Fill in each blank with one of the words or phrases listed below.

| quadratic formula | quadratic | discriminant | $\pm\sqrt{b}$ |
| completing the square | quadratic inequality | n | $a - bi$ |

1. The _____ helps us find the number and type of solutions of a quadratic equation.
2. If $a^2 = b$, then $a = $ _____
3. A(n) _____ is an inequality that can be written so that one side is a quadratic expression and the other side is 0.
4. The process of writing a quadratic equation so that one side is a perfect square trinomial is called _____.
5. The formula $x = \dfrac{-b \pm \sqrt{b^2 - 4ac}}{2a}$ is called the _____.
6. A(n) _____ equation is one that can be written in the form $ax^2 + bx + c = 0$ where $a, b,$ and c are real numbers and a is not 0.
7. If $a + bi$ is a root of a polynomial equation with real coefficients, then _____ is also a root.
8. A polynomial of degree n has _____ roots if we count multiple roots separately.

CHAPTER 9 REVIEW

(9.1) *Solve by factoring.*

1. $x^2 - 15x + 14 = 0$
2. $7a^2 = 29a + 30$

Solve by using the square root property.

3. $4m^2 = 196$
4. $(5x - 2)^2 = 2$

Solve by completing the square.

5. $z^2 + 3z + 1 = 0$
6. $(2x + 1)^2 = x$

7. If P dollars are originally invested, the formula $A = P(1 + r)^2$ gives the amount A in an account paying interest rate r compounded annually after 2 years. Find the interest rate r such that $2500 increases to $2717 in 2 years. Round the result to the nearest hundredth of a percent.

8. Two ships leave a port at the same time and travel at the same speed. One ship is traveling due north and the other due east. In a few hours, the ships are 150 miles apart. How many miles has each ship traveled? Give an exact answer and a one-decimal-place approximation.

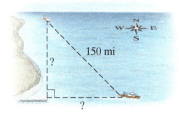

(9.2) *If the discriminant of a quadratic equation has the given value, determine the number and type of solutions of the equation.*

9. -8
10. 48
11. 100
12. 0

Solve by using the quadratic formula.

13. $x^2 - 16x + 64 = 0$
14. $x^2 + 5x = 0$
15. $2x^2 + 3x = 5$
16. $9a^2 + 4 = 2a$
17. $6x^2 + 7 = 5x$
18. $(2x - 3)^2 = x$

19. Cadets graduating from military school usually toss their hats high into the air at the end of the ceremony. One cadet threw his hat so that its distance $d(t)$ in feet above the ground t seconds after it was thrown was $d(t) = -16t^2 + 30t + 6$.
    a. Find the distance above the ground of the hat 1 second after it was thrown.
    b. Find the time it takes the hat to hit the ground. Give an exact time and a one-decimal-place approximation.

20. The hypotenuse of an isosceles right triangle is 6 centimeters longer than either of the legs. Find the length of the legs.

(9.3) *Solve each equation for the variable.*

21. $x^3 = 27$
22. $y^3 = -64$
23. $\dfrac{5}{x} + \dfrac{6}{x - 2} = 3$
24. $x^4 - 21x^2 - 100 = 0$
25. $x^{2/3} - 6x^{1/3} + 5 = 0$
26. $5(x + 3)^2 - 19(x + 3) = 4$
27. $a^6 - a^2 = a^4 - 1$
28. $y^{-2} + y^{-1} = 20$

29. Two postal workers, Jerome Grant and Tim Bozik, can sort a stack of mail in 5 hours. Working alone, Tim can sort the mail in 1 hour less time than Jerome can. Find the time that each postal worker can sort the mail alone. Round the result to one decimal place.

30. A negative number decreased by its reciprocal is $-\dfrac{24}{5}$. Find the number.

(9.4) *Use the Rational Zero Theorem to list all possible rational zeros for each given function.*

31. $f(r) = r^4 - 6r^3 + 14r^2 - 14r + 5$
32. $f(x) = 3x^5 - 2x^4 - 15x^3 + 10x^2 + 12x - 8$

(9.4 and 9.5) *For Exercises 33–38,*
   a. List all possible rational roots or rational zeros.
   b. Use synthetic division to test the possible rational roots or zeros and find an actual root or zero.
   c. Use the quotient from part (b) to find all the remaining roots or zeros.

33. $f(x) = 6x^3 + x^2 - 4x + 1$
34. $f(x) = x^3 + 3x^2 - 4$
35. $2x^3 + 9x^2 - 7x + 1 = 0$
36. $8x^3 - 36x^2 + 46x - 15 = 0$
37. $4x^4 + 7x^2 - 2 = 0$
38. $x^4 - x^3 - 7x^2 + x + 6 = 0$

(9.5) *Find an nth-degree polynomial function with real coefficients, whose leading coefficient is 1, satisfying the given conditions.*

39. $n = 3$; 2 and $2 - 3i$ are zeros
40. $n = 4$; i is a zero; -3 is a zero of multiplicity 2

Find all the zeros of each polynomial function and write the polynomial as a product of linear factors.

41. $f(x) = 2x^4 + 3x^3 + 3x - 2$
42. $g(x) = x^4 - 6x^3 + x^2 + 24x + 16$

In Exercises 43–46, graphs of fifth-degree polynomial functions are shown. In each case, specify the number of real zeros and the number of imaginary zeros. Indicate whether there are any real zeros with multiplicity other than 1.

43.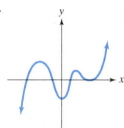

44.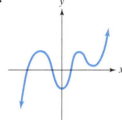

45.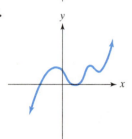

46.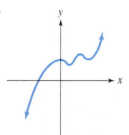

(9.6) Solve each inequality for x.

47. $2x^2 - 50 \leq 0$

48. $\dfrac{1}{4}x^2 < \dfrac{1}{16}$

49. $\dfrac{x-5}{x-6} < 0$

50. $(x^2 - 16)(x^2 - 1) > 0$

51. $\dfrac{(4x+3)(x-5)}{x(x+6)} > 0$

52. $(x+5)(x-6)(x+2) \leq 0$

53. $x^3 + 3x^2 - 25x - 75 > 0$

54. $\dfrac{x^2 + 4}{3x} \leq 1$

55. $\dfrac{(5x+6)(x-3)}{x(6x-5)} < 0$

56. $\dfrac{3}{x-2} > 2$

MIXED REVIEW

Solve each equation or inequality.

57. $x^2 - x - 30 = 0$

58. $10x^2 = 3x + 4$

59. $9y^2 = 36$

60. $(9n + 1)^2 = 9$

61. $x^2 + x + 7 = 0$

62. $(3x - 4)^2 = 10x$

63. $x^2 + 11 = 0$

64. $(5a - 2)^2 - a = 0$

65. $\dfrac{7}{8} = \dfrac{8}{x^2}$

66. $x^{2/3} - 6x^{1/3} = -8$

67. $(2x - 3)(4x + 5) \geq 0$

68. $\dfrac{x(x+5)}{4x-3} \geq 0$

69. $\dfrac{3}{x-2} > 2$

 70. The total amount of passenger traffic at Phoenix Sky Harbor International Airport in Phoenix, Arizona, during the period 1980 through 2005 can be modeled by the equation $y = 6.46x^2 + 1236.5x + 7289$, where y is the number of passengers enplaned and deplaned in thousands and x is the number of years after 1980. (*Source*: Based on data from The City of Phoenix Aviation Department, 1980–2005)

a. Estimate the passenger traffic at Phoenix Sky Harbor International Airport in 2000.

b. According to this model, in what year will passenger traffic at Phoenix Sky Harbor International Airport reach 60,000,000 passengers?

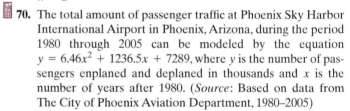

Remember to use the Chapter Test Prep Videos to see the fully worked-out solutions to any of the exercises you want to review.

Solve each equation for the variable.

1. $5x^2 - 2x = 7$

2. $(x + 1)^2 = 10$

3. $m^2 - m + 8 = 0$

4. $u^2 - 6u + 2 = 0$

5. $7x^2 + 8x + 1 = 0$

6. $y^2 - 3y = 5$

7. $\dfrac{4}{x+2} + \dfrac{2x}{x-2} = \dfrac{6}{x^2 - 4}$

8. $x^5 + 3x^4 = x + 3$

9. $x^6 + 1 = x^4 + x^2$

10. $(x + 1)^2 - 15(x + 1) + 56 = 0$

Solve the equation for the variable by completing the square.

11. $x^2 - 6x = -2$

12. $2a^2 + 5 = 4a$

Solve each inequality for x.

13. $2x^2 - 7x > 15$

14. $(x^2 - 16)(x^2 - 25) \geq 0$

15. $\dfrac{5}{x+3} < 1$

16. $\dfrac{7x - 14}{x^2 - 9} \leq 0$

17. The graph of $f(x) = 6x^3 - 19x^2 + 16x - 4$ is shown in the figure.

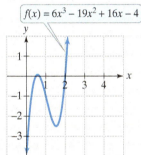

   a. Based on the graph of f, find the root of the equation $6x^3 - 19x^2 + 16x - 4 = 0$ that is an integer.
   b. Use synthetic division to find the other two roots of $6x^3 - 19x^2 + 16x - 4 = 0$.

18. Solve: $x^3 + 9x^2 + 16x - 6 = 0$.

19. Consider the function whose equation is given by $f(x) = 2x^4 - x^3 - 13x^2 + 5x + 15$.
   a. List all possible rational zeros.
   b. Use the graph of f in the figure shown and synthetic division to find all zeros of the function.

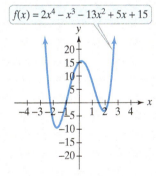

20. Use the graph of $f(x) = x^3 + 3x^2 - 4$ in the figure shown to factor $x^3 + 3x^2 - 4$.

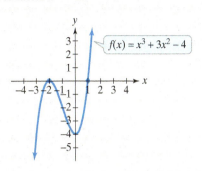

21. Find a fourth-degree polynomial function $f(x)$ with real coefficients, leading coefficient of 1, that has -1, 1, and i as zeros.

22. Dave and Sandy Hartranft can paint a room together in 4 hours. Working alone, Dave can paint the room in 2 hours less time than Sandy can. Find how long it takes Sandy to paint the room alone.

23. Given the diagram shown, approximate to the nearest foot how many feet of walking distance a person saves by cutting across the lawn instead of walking on the sidewalk.

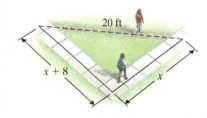

CHAPTER 9 STANDARDIZED TEST

Multiple Choice. *Choose the one alternative that best completes the statement or answers the question.*

Solve the equation.

1. $4x^2 - 3x = 7$
   a. $\frac{7}{4}, 1$ b. $\frac{4}{7}, -1$ c. $\frac{4}{7}, 1$ d. $\frac{7}{4}, -1$

2. $(x + 5)^2 = 11$
   a. 6
   b. $-5 - \sqrt{11}, -5 + \sqrt{11}$
   c. $-\sqrt{11}, \sqrt{11}$
   d. $5 - \sqrt{11}, 5 + \sqrt{11}$

3. $m^2 + m + 6 = 0$
   a. $\frac{-1 - \sqrt{23}}{2}, \frac{-1 + \sqrt{23}}{2}$
   b. $\frac{1 - i\sqrt{23}}{2}, \frac{1 + i\sqrt{23}}{2}$
   c. $\frac{1 - \sqrt{23}}{2}, \frac{1 + \sqrt{23}}{2}$
   d. $\frac{-1 - i\sqrt{23}}{2}, \frac{-1 + i\sqrt{23}}{2}$

4. $u^2 + 12u + 26 = 0$
   a. $6 - \sqrt{26}, 6 + \sqrt{26}$ b. $-12 + \sqrt{26}$
   c. $-6 - \sqrt{10}, -6 + \sqrt{10}$ d. $6 + \sqrt{10}$

5. $6x^2 + 7x + 1 = 0$
   a. $-\frac{1}{6}, 1$ b. $\frac{1}{6}, -1$ c. $-\frac{1}{6}, -1$ d. $\frac{1}{6}, 1$

6. $y^2 - 5y = 3$
   a. $\frac{-5 + \sqrt{37}}{2}, \frac{-5 - \sqrt{37}}{2}$ b. $\frac{5 + i\sqrt{37}}{2}, \frac{5 - i\sqrt{37}}{2}$
   c. $\frac{5 + \sqrt{37}}{2}, \frac{5 - \sqrt{37}}{2}$ d. no solution

7. $\frac{9}{x - 1} + \frac{x}{x + 1} = \frac{17}{x^2 - 1}$
   a. $4 - 2\sqrt{6}, 4 + 2\sqrt{6}$ b. $-4 - 2\sqrt{6}, -4 + 2\sqrt{6}$
   c. $4 - 2\sqrt{2}, 4 + 2\sqrt{2}$ d. $-4 - 2\sqrt{2}, -4 + 2\sqrt{2}$

8. $x^5 + 6x^4 = x + 6$
   a. $-1, 1, -6$ b. no solution
   c. $-1, 1, -i, i, -6$ d. $1, i, -6$

9. $x^6 + 64 = 64x^4 + x^2$
   a. $-8, 8, -1, 1, -8i, 8i$ b. $-8, 8, -i, i$
   c. $-8, 8, -1, 1, -i, i$ d. $-8, 8, -1, 1$

10. $(x + 1)^2 - 3(x + 1) - 4 = 0$
    a. $-2, 3$ b. $-3, 2$ c. $-5, 0$ d. $0, 5$

Solve the equation by completing the square.

11. $x^2 + 12x = -21$
    a. $-12 + \sqrt{21}$ b. $6 + \sqrt{15}$
    c. $-6 - \sqrt{15}, -6 + \sqrt{15}$ d. $6 - \sqrt{21}, 6 + \sqrt{21}$

12. $8a^2 + 1 = 3a$
    a. $\frac{3 - i\sqrt{23}}{16}, \frac{-3 + i\sqrt{23}}{16}$ b. $\frac{-3 - i\sqrt{23}}{16}, \frac{3 + i\sqrt{23}}{16}$
    c. $\frac{-3 - i\sqrt{23}}{16}, \frac{-3 + i\sqrt{23}}{16}$ d. $\frac{3 - i\sqrt{23}}{16}, \frac{3 + i\sqrt{23}}{16}$

Solve the inequality.

13. $x^2 + 3x \geq 4$
    a. $-4 \leq x \leq 1$ b. $x \leq -4$ or $x \geq 1$
    c. $x \geq 1$ d. $x \leq -4$

14. $(x^2 - 49)(x^2 - 9) > 0$
    a. $-7 < x < -3$ or $3 < x < 7$
    b. $x < -7$ or $-3 < x < 3$ or $x > 7$
    c. $x \leq -7$ or $-3 \leq x \leq 3$ or $x \geq 7$
    d. $-7 \leq x \leq -3$ or $3 \leq x \leq 7$

15. $\frac{7}{x - 1} < 1$
    a. $x < 1$ b. $x \leq 1$ or $x \geq 8$
    c. $1 < x < 8$ d. $x < 1$ or $x > 8$

16. $\frac{2x - 12}{x^2 - 4} \geq 0$
    a. $-2 < x < 2$ or $x \geq 6$ b. $-2 < x \leq 6$
    c. $x < 2$ or $x \geq 6$ d. $-2 \leq x \leq 2$ or $x \geq 6$

Use the Rational Zero Theorem to list all possible rational zeros for the given function.

17. $f(x) = -2x^3 + 2x^2 - 3x + 8$
    a. $\pm\frac{1}{2}, \pm 1, \pm 2, \pm 4$
    b. $\pm\frac{1}{4}, \pm\frac{1}{2}, \pm 1, \pm 2, \pm 4, \pm 8$
    c. $\pm\frac{1}{8}, \pm\frac{1}{4}, \pm\frac{1}{2}, \pm 1, \pm 2, \pm 4, \pm 8$
    d. $\pm\frac{1}{2}, \pm 1, \pm 2, \pm 4, \pm 8$

Find a rational zero of the polynomial function and use it to find all the zeros of the function.

18. $f(x) = x^3 + 2x^2 - 5x - 6$
    a. $-3, -1, 2$ b. $-2, 1, 3$ c. -3 d. -1

Solve the polynomial equation.

19. Use synthetic division and the Rational Zero Theorem to find the first two roots.
    $2x^4 + 11x^3 - 4x^2 + 11x - 6 = 0$

    a. $-6, \frac{1}{2}$ b. $-6, \frac{1}{2}$ c. $6, -\frac{1}{2}$ d. $-6, -\frac{1}{2}$

Find a 3rd degree polynomial function with real coefficients satisfying the given conditions.

20. 2 and $-3 + 3i$ are zeros; leading coefficients is 1

    a. $f(x) = x^3 + 4x^2 + 15x - 36$
    b. $f(x) = x^3 - 4x^2 + 6x - 36$
    c. $f(x) = x^3 + 4x^2 + 6x - 36$
    d. $f(x) = x^3 + 5x^2 + 6x - 14$

Solve.

21. Shelly can cut a lawn with a riding mower in 4 hours less time than it takes William to cut the lawn with a push mower. If they can cut the lawn in 4 hours working together find how long to the nearest tenth of an hour it takes for William to cut the lawn alone.

    a. 10.6 hr   b. 10.5 hr   c. 6.6 hr   d. 6.5 hr

22. A rocket is launched from the top of a cliff that is 112 feet high with an initial velocity of 224 feet per second. The height, $h(t)$, of the rocket after t seconds is given by the equation $h(t) = -16t^2 + 224t + 112$. How long after the rocket is launced will it strike the ground? Round to the nearest tenth of a second, if necessary.

    a. 14.5 sec   b. 15.1 sec   c. 16.1 sec   d. 15.7 sec

23. Because of the increase in traffic between Springfield and Orangeville, a new road was built to connect the two towns. The old road goes south x miles from Springfield to Freeport and then goes east $x + 3$ miles from Freeport to Orangeville. The new road is 7 miles long and goes straight from Springfield to Orangeville. Find the number of miles that a person saves by driving the new road over the old one.

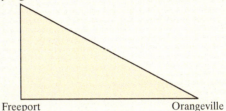

    a. $\frac{3}{2} + \frac{\sqrt{89}}{2}$ miles   b. $\sqrt{89} + 7$ miles
    c. $-\frac{3}{2} + \frac{\sqrt{89}}{2}$ miles   d. $\sqrt{89} - 7$ miles

CHAPTER

10 Exponential and Logarithmic Functions

10.1 The Algebra of Functions; Composite Functions

10.2 Inverse Functions

10.3 Exponential Functions

10.4 Logarithmic Functions

10.5 Properties of Logarithms

Integrated Review—Functions and Properties of Logarithms

10.6 Common Logarithms, Natural Logarithms, and Change of Base

10.7 Exponential and Logarithmic Equations and Applications

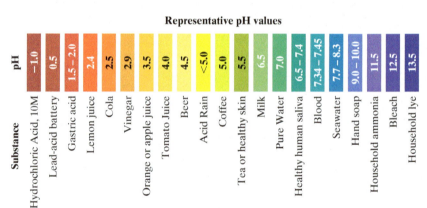

pH (Potential of Hydrogen) is a measure of the acidity or alkalinity of a solution. Solutions with a pH less than 7 are considered acidic, those with a pH greater than 7 are considered basic (alkaline) and those equal to 7 are defined as "neutral." The pH scale is logarithmic and some examples are in the table above.

In this chapter, we will use our knowledge of logarithms to calculate the pH for lemonade.

10.1 THE ALGEBRA OF FUNCTIONS; COMPOSITE FUNCTIONS

OBJECTIVES

1. Add, subtract, multiply, and divide functions.
2. Construct composite functions.

OBJECTIVE 1 ▶ Adding, subtracting, multiplying, and dividing functions. As we have seen in earlier chapters, it is possible to add, subtract, multiply, and divide functions. Although we have not stated it as such, the sums, differences, products, and quotients of functions are themselves functions. For example, if $f(x) = 3x$ and $g(x) = x + 1$, their product, $f(x) \cdot g(x) = 3x(x + 1) = 3x^2 + 3x$, is a new function. We can use the notation $(f \cdot g)(x)$ to denote this new function. Finding the sum, difference, product, and quotient of functions to generate new functions is called the **algebra of functions.**

Algebra of Functions

Let f and g be functions. New functions from f and g are defined as follows.

Sum $\qquad (f + g)(x) = f(x) + g(x)$

Difference $\qquad (f - g)(x) = f(x) - g(x)$

Product $\qquad (f \cdot g)(x) = f(x) \cdot g(x)$

Quotient $\qquad \left(\dfrac{f}{g}\right)(x) = \dfrac{f(x)}{g(x)}, \quad g(x) \neq 0$

EXAMPLE 1 If $f(x) = x - 1$ and $g(x) = 2x - 3$, find

a. $(f + g)(x)$ **b.** $(f - g)(x)$ **c.** $(f \cdot g)(x)$ **d.** $\left(\dfrac{f}{g}\right)(x)$

Solution Use the algebra of functions and replace $f(x)$ by $x - 1$ and $g(x)$ by $2x - 3$. Then we simplify.

a. $(f + g)(x) = f(x) + g(x)$
$\qquad\qquad\quad = (x - 1) + (2x - 3)$
$\qquad\qquad\quad = 3x - 4$

b. $(f - g)(x) = f(x) - g(x)$
$\qquad\qquad\quad = (x - 1) - (2x - 3)$
$\qquad\qquad\quad = x - 1 - 2x + 3$
$\qquad\qquad\quad = -x + 2$

c. $(f \cdot g)(x) = f(x) \cdot g(x)$
$\qquad\qquad\quad = (x - 1)(2x - 3)$
$\qquad\qquad\quad = 2x^2 - 5x + 3$

d. $\left(\dfrac{f}{g}\right)(x) = \dfrac{f(x)}{g(x)} = \dfrac{x - 1}{2x - 3}$, where $x \neq \dfrac{3}{2}$

PRACTICE 1 If $f(x) = x + 2$ and $g(x) = 3x + 5$, find

a. $(f + g)(x)$ **b.** $(f - g)(x)$ **c.** $(f \cdot g)(x)$ **d.** $\left(\dfrac{f}{g}\right)(x)$

There is an interesting but not surprising relationship between the graphs of functions and the graphs of their sum, difference, product, and quotient. For example, the graph of $(f + g)(x)$ can be found by adding the graph of $f(x)$ to the graph of $g(x)$. We add two graphs by adding y-values of corresponding x-values.

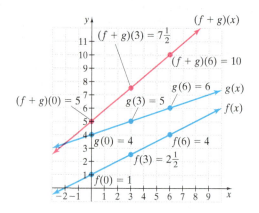

OBJECTIVE 2 ▶ Constructing composite functions. Another way to combine functions is called **function composition.** To understand this new way of combining functions, study the diagrams below. The left diagram shows degrees Celsius $f(x)$ as a function of degrees Fahrenheit x. The right diagram shows kelvins $g(x)$ as a function of degrees Celsius x. (The kelvin scale is a temperature scale devised by Lord kelvin in 1848.) The function represented by the first diagram we will call f, and the second function we will call g.

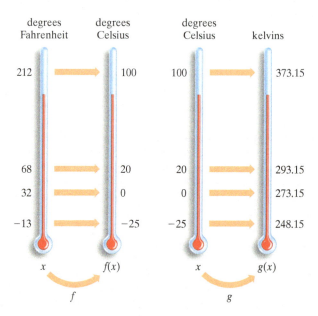

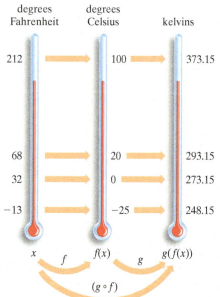

Suppose that we want a function that shows a direct conversion from degrees Fahrenheit to kelvins. In other words, suppose that a function is needed that shows kelvins as a function of degrees Fahrenheit. This can easily be done because the output of the first function $f(x)$ is the same as the input of the second function. If we use $f(x)$ to represent this, then we get the left diagram.

For example $g(f(-13)) = 248.15$, and so on.

Since the output of the first function is used as the input of the second function, we write the new function as $g(f(x))$. The new function is formed from the composition of the other two functions. The mathematical symbol for this composition is $(g \circ f)(x)$. Thus, $(g \circ f)(x) = g(f(x))$.

It is possible to find an equation for the composition of the two functions f and g. In other words, we can find a function that converts degrees Fahrenheit directly to kelvins. The function $f(x) = \frac{5}{9}(x - 32)$ converts degrees Fahrenheit to degrees Celsius, and the function $g(x) = x + 273.15$ converts degrees Celsius to kelvins. Thus,

$$(g \circ f)(x) = g(f(x)) = g\left(\frac{5}{9}(x - 32)\right) = \frac{5}{9}(x - 32) + 273.15$$

In general, the notation $g(f(x))$ means "g composed with f" and can be written as $(g \circ f)(x)$. Also $f(g(x))$, or $(f \circ g)(x)$, means "f composed with g."

Composition of Functions
The composition of functions f and g is
$$(f \circ g)(x) = f(g(x))$$

▶ **Helpful Hint**
$(f \circ g)(x)$ does not mean the same as $(f \cdot g)(x)$.

$(f \circ g)(x) = f(g(x))$ while $(f \cdot g)(x) = f(x) \cdot g(x)$
↑ ↑
Composition of functions   Multiplication of functions

EXAMPLE 2 If $f(x) = x^2$ and $g(x) = x + 3$, find each composition.

a. $(f \circ g)(2)$ and $(g \circ f)(2)$ **b.** $(f \circ g)(x)$ and $(g \circ f)(x)$

Solution

a. $(f \circ g)(2) = f(g(2))$
$ = f(5)$ Replace $g(2)$ with 5. [Since $g(x) = x + 3$, then $g(2) = 2 + 3 = 5$.]
$ = 5^2 = 25$

$(g \circ f)(2) = g(f(2))$
$ = g(4)$ Since $f(x) = x^2$, then $f(2) = 2^2 = 4$.
$ = 4 + 3 = 7$

b. $(f \circ g)(x) = f(g(x))$
$ = f(x + 3)$ Replace $g(x)$ with $x + 3$.
$ = (x + 3)^2$ $f(x + 3) = (x + 3)^2$
$ = x^2 + 6x + 9$ Square $(x + 3)$.

$(g \circ f)(x) = g(f(x))$
$ = g(x^2)$ Replace $f(x)$ with x^2.
$ = x^2 + 3$ $g(x^2) = x^2 + 3$

PRACTICE 2 If $f(x) = x^2 + 1$ and $g(x) = 3x - 5$, find

a. $(f \circ g)(4)$ **b.** $(f \circ g)(x)$
$(g \circ f)(4)$ $(g \circ f)(x)$

EXAMPLE 3 If $f(x) = |x|$ and $g(x) = x - 2$, find each composition.

a. $(f \circ g)(x)$ b. $(g \circ f)(x)$

Solution

a. $(f \circ g)(x) = f(g(x)) = f(x - 2) = |x - 2|$
b. $(g \circ f)(x) = g(f(x)) = g(|x|) = |x| - 2$

> **Helpful Hint**
> In Examples 2 and 3, notice that $(g \circ f)(x) \neq (f \circ g)(x)$. In general, $(g \circ f)(x)$ *may* or *may not* equal $(f \circ g)(x)$.

PRACTICE 3 If $f(x) = x^2 + 5$ and $g(x) = x + 3$, find each composition.

a. $(f \circ g)(x)$ b. $(g \circ f)(x)$

EXAMPLE 4 If $f(x) = 5x$, $g(x) = x - 2$, and $h(x) = \sqrt{x}$, write each function as a composition using two of the given functions.

a. $F(x) = \sqrt{x - 2}$ b. $G(x) = 5x - 2$

Solution

a. Notice the order in which the function F operates on an input value x. First, 2 is subtracted from x. This is the function $g(x) = x - 2$. Then the square root *of that result* is taken. The square root function is $h(x) = \sqrt{x}$. This means that $F = h \circ g$. To check, we find $h \circ g$.

$$F(x) = (h \circ g)(x) = h(g(x)) = h(x - 2) = \sqrt{x - 2}$$

b. Notice the order in which the function G operates on an input value x. First, x is multiplied by 5, and then 2 is subtracted from the result. This means that $G = g \circ f$. To check, we find $g \circ f$.

$$G(x) = (g \circ f)(x) = g(f(x)) = g(5x) = 5x - 2$$

PRACTICE 4 If $f(x) = 3x$, $g(x) = x - 4$, and $h(x) = |x|$, write each function as a composition using two of the given functions.

a. $F(x) = |x - 4|$ b. $G(x) = 3x - 4$

Graphing Calculator Explorations

If $f(x) = \frac{1}{2}x + 2$ and $g(x) = \frac{1}{3}x^2 + 4$, then

$$(f + g)(x) = f(x) + g(x)$$
$$= \left(\frac{1}{2}x + 2\right) + \left(\frac{1}{3}x^2 + 4\right)$$
$$= \frac{1}{3}x^2 + \frac{1}{2}x + 6.$$

To visualize this addition of functions with a graphing calculator, graph

$$Y_1 = \frac{1}{2}x + 2, \quad Y_2 = \frac{1}{3}x^2 + 4, \quad Y_3 = \frac{1}{3}x^2 + \frac{1}{2}x + 6$$

Use a TABLE feature to verify that for a given x value, $Y_1 + Y_2 = Y_3$. For example, verify that when $x = 0$, $Y_1 = 2$, $Y_2 = 4$, and $Y_3 = 2 + 4 = 6$.

Section 10.1 The Algebra of Functions; Composite Functions

VOCABULARY & READINESS CHECK

Matching. Match each function with its definition.

1. $(f \circ g)(x)$
2. $(f \cdot g)(x)$
3. $(f - g)(x)$
4. $(g \circ f)(x)$
5. $\left(\dfrac{f}{g}\right)(x)$
6. $(f + g)(x)$

A. $g(f(x))$
B. $f(x) + g(x)$
C. $f(g(x))$
D. $\dfrac{f(x)}{g(x)}, g(x) \neq 0$
E. $f(x) \cdot g(x)$
F. $f(x) - g(x)$

10.1 EXERCISE SET

For the functions f and g, find **a.** $(f + g)(x)$, **b.** $(f - g)(x)$, **c.** $(f \cdot g)(x)$, and **d.** $\left(\dfrac{f}{g}\right)(x)$. *See Example 1.*

1. $f(x) = x - 7, g(x) = 2x + 1$
2. $f(x) = x + 4, g(x) = 5x - 2$
3. $f(x) = x^2 + 1, g(x) = 5x$
4. $f(x) = x^2 - 2, g(x) = 3x$
5. $f(x) = \sqrt{x}, g(x) = x + 5$
6. $f(x) = \sqrt[3]{x}, g(x) = x - 3$
7. $f(x) = -3x, g(x) = 5x^2$
8. $f(x) = 4x^3, g(x) = -6x$

If $f(x) = x^2 - 6x + 2, g(x) = -2x$, and $h(x) = \sqrt{x}$, find each composition. See Example 2.

9. $(f \circ g)(2)$
10. $(h \circ f)(-2)$
11. $(g \circ f)(-1)$
12. $(f \circ h)(1)$
13. $(g \circ h)(0)$
14. $(h \circ g)(0)$

Find $(f \circ g)(x)$ and $(g \circ f)(x)$. See Examples 2 and 3.

15. $f(x) = x^2 + 1, g(x) = 5x$
16. $f(x) = x - 3, g(x) = x^2$
17. $f(x) = 2x - 3, g(x) = x + 7$
18. $f(x) = x + 10, g(x) = 3x + 1$
19. $f(x) = x^3 + x - 2, g(x) = -2x$
20. $f(x) = -4x, g(x) = x^3 + x^2 - 6$
21. $f(x) = |x|; g(x) = 10x - 3$
22. $f(x) = |x|; g(x) = 14x - 8$
23. $f(x) = \sqrt{x}, g(x) = -5x + 2$
24. $f(x) = 7x - 1, g(x) = \sqrt[3]{x}$

If $f(x) = 3x, g(x) = \sqrt{x}$, and $h(x) = x^2 + 2$, write each function as a composition using two of the given functions. See Example 4.

25. $H(x) = \sqrt{x^2 + 2}$
26. $G(x) = \sqrt{3x}$
27. $F(x) = 9x^2 + 2$
28. $H(x) = 3x^2 + 6$
29. $G(x) = 3\sqrt{x}$
30. $F(x) = x + 2$

Find f(x) and g(x) so that the given function $h(x) = (f \circ g)(x)$.

31. $h(x) = (x + 2)^2$
32. $h(x) = |x - 1|$
33. $h(x) = \sqrt{x + 5} + 2$
34. $h(x) = (3x + 4)^2 + 3$
35. $h(x) = \dfrac{1}{2x - 3}$
36. $h(x) = \dfrac{1}{x + 10}$

REVIEW AND PREVIEW

Solve each equation for y. See Section 2.3.

37. $x = y + 2$
38. $x = y - 5$
39. $x = 3y$
40. $x = -6y$
41. $x = -2y - 7$
42. $x = 4y + 7$

CONCEPT EXTENSIONS

Given that $f(-1) = 4 \quad g(-1) = -4$
$f(0) = 5 \quad g(0) = -3$
$f(2) = 7 \quad g(2) = -1$
$f(7) = 1 \quad g(7) = 4$

Find each function value.

43. $(f + g)(2)$
44. $(f - g)(7)$
45. $(f \circ g)(2)$
46. $(g \circ f)(2)$
47. $(f \cdot g)(7)$
48. $(f \cdot g)(0)$
49. $\left(\dfrac{f}{g}\right)(-1)$
50. $\left(\dfrac{g}{f}\right)(-1)$

51. If you are given $f(x)$ and $g(x)$, explain in your own words how to find $(f \circ g)(x)$, and then how to find $(g \circ f)(x)$.
52. Given $f(x)$ and $g(x)$, describe in your own words the difference between $(f \circ g)(x)$ and $(f \cdot g)(x)$.

Solve.

53. Business people are concerned with cost functions, revenue functions, and profit functions. Recall that the profit $P(x)$ obtained from x units of a product is equal to the revenue $R(x)$ from selling the x units minus the cost $C(x)$ of manufacturing the x units. Write an equation expressing this relationship among $C(x)$, $R(x)$, and $P(x)$.
54. Suppose the revenue $R(x)$ for x units of a product can be described by $R(x) = 25x$, and the cost $C(x)$ can be described by $C(x) = 50 + x^2 + 4x$. Find the profit $P(x)$ for x units. (See Exercise 53.)

10.2 INVERSE FUNCTIONS

OBJECTIVES

1. Determine whether a function is a one-to-one function.
2. Use the horizontal line test to decide whether a function is a one-to-one function.
3. Find the inverse of a function.
4. Find the equation of the inverse of a function.
5. Graph functions and their inverses.
6. Determine whether two functions are inverses of each other.

OBJECTIVE 1 ▶ Determining whether a function is one-to-one. In the next section, we begin a study of two new functions: exponential and logarithmic functions. As we learn more about these functions, we will discover that they share a special relation to each other: They are inverses of each other.

Before we study these functions, we need to learn about inverses. We begin by defining one-to-one functions.

Study the following diagram.

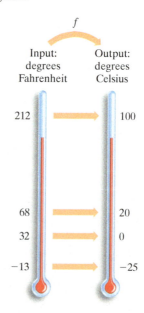

Recall that since each degrees Fahrenheit (input) corresponds to exactly one degrees Celsius (output), this pairing of inputs and outputs does describe a function. Also notice that each output corresponds to exactly one input. This type of function is given a special name—a one-to-one function.

Does the set $f = \{(0, 1), (2, 2), (-3, 5), (7, 6)\}$ describe a one-to-one function? It is a function since each *x*-value corresponds to a unique *y*-value. For this particular function *f*, each *y*-value also corresponds to a unique *x*-value. Thus, this function is also a **one-to-one function.**

> **One-to-One Function**
> For a **one-to-one function,** each *x*-value (input) corresponds to only one *y*-value (output), and each *y*-value (output) corresponds to only one *x*-value (input).

EXAMPLE 1 Determine whether each function described is one-to-one.

a. $f = \{(6, 2), (5, 4), (-1, 0), (7, 3)\}$
b. $g = \{(3, 9), (-4, 2), (-3, 9), (0, 0)\}$
c. $h = \{(1, 1), (2, 2), (10, 10), (-5, -5)\}$

d.

Mineral (Input)	Talc	Gypsum	Diamond	Topaz	Stibnite
Hardness on the Mohs Scale (Output)	1	2	10	8	2

e.

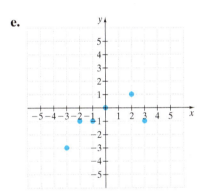

f.

Cities	Percent of Cell Phone Subscribers
Atlanta (highest)	75
Buffalo	53
Austin	72
Washington, D.C.	
Charleston (lowest)	47
Detroit	74

Solution

a. *f* is one-to-one since each *y*-value corresponds to only one *x*-value.
b. *g* is not one-to-one because the *y*-value 9 in (3, 9) and (−3, 9) corresponds to two different *x*-values.
c. *h* is a one-to-one function since each *y*-value corresponds to only one *x*-value.
d. This table does not describe a one-to-one function since the output 2 corresponds to two different inputs, gypsum and stibnite.
e. This graph does not describe a one-to-one function since the *y*-value −1 corresponds to three different *x*-values, −2, −1, and 3.
f. The mapping is not one-to-one since 72% corresponds to Austin and Washington, D.C.

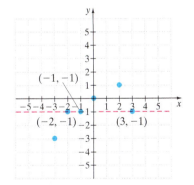

PRACTICE

1 Determine whether each function described is one-to-one.

a. $f = \{(4, -3), (3, -4), (2, 7), (5, 0)\}$
b. $g = \{(8, 4), (-2, 0), (6, 4), (2, 6)\}$
c. $h = \{(2, 4), (1, 3), (4, 6), (-2, 4)\}$

d.

Year	1950	1963	1968	1975	1997	2002
Federal Minimum Wage	$0.75	$1.25	$1.60	$2.10	$5.15	$5.15

e.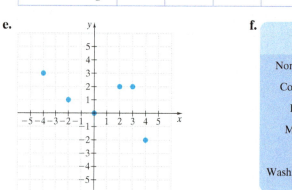

f.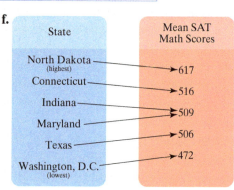

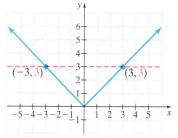

Not a one-to-one function.

OBJECTIVE 2 ▶ Using the horizontal line test. Recall that we recognize the graph of a function when it passes the vertical line test. Since every x-value of the function corresponds to exactly one y-value, each vertical line intersects the function's graph at most once. The graph shown (left), for instance, is the graph of a function.

Is this function a *one-to-one* function? The answer is no. To see why not, notice that the y-value of the ordered pair $(-3, 3)$, for example, is the same as the y-value of the ordered pair $(3, 3)$. In other words, the y-value 3 corresponds to two x-values, -3 and 3. This function is therefore not one-to-one.

To test whether a graph is the graph of a one-to-one function, apply the vertical line test to see if it is a function, and then apply a similar **horizontal line test** to see if it is a one-to-one function.

Horizontal Line Test

If every horizontal line intersects the graph of a function at most once, then the function is a one-to-one function.

EXAMPLE 2 Determine whether each graph is the graph of a one-to-one function.

a.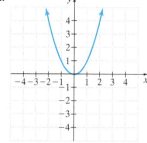

b.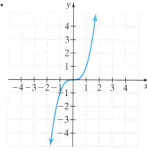

c.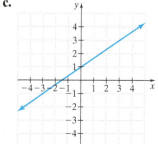

d.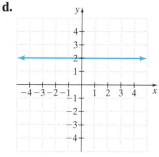

e.

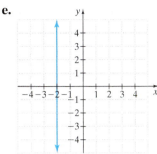

Solution Graphs **a, b, c,** and **d** all pass the vertical line test, so only these graphs are graphs of functions. But, of these, only **b** and **c** pass the horizontal line test, so only **b** and **c** are graphs of one-to-one functions. □

PRACTICE 2 Determine whether each graph is the graph of a one-to-one function.

a.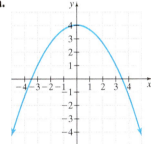

b.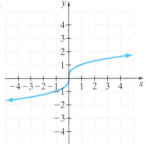

c.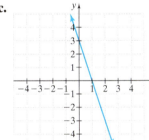

d.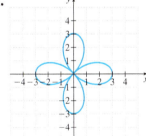

e.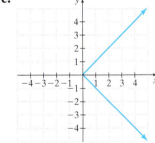

> **Helpful Hint**
> All linear equations are one-to-one functions except those whose graphs are horizontal or vertical lines. A vertical line does not pass the vertical line test and hence is not the graph of a function. A horizontal line is the graph of a function but does not pass the horizontal line test and hence is not the graph of a one-to-one function.

not a function   function, but not one-to-one

574 CHAPTER 10 Exponential and Logarithmic Functions

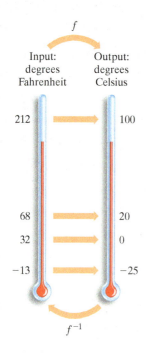

OBJECTIVE 3 ▶ **Finding the inverse of a function.** One-to-one functions are special in that their graphs pass both the vertical and horizontal line tests. They are special, too, in another sense: For each one-to-one function, we can find its **inverse function** by switching the coordinates of the ordered pairs of the function, or the inputs and the outputs. For example, the inverse of the one-to-one function $f = \{(2, -3), (5, 10), (9, 1)\}$ is $\{(-3, 2), (10, 5), (1, 9)\}$.

For a function f, we use the notation f^{-1}, read "f inverse," to denote its inverse function. Notice that since the coordinates of each ordered pair have been switched, the domain (set of inputs) of f is the range (set of outputs) of f^{-1}, and the range of f is the domain of f^{-1}.

The diagram to the left shows the inverse of the one-to-one function f with ordered pairs of the form (degrees Fahrenheit, degrees Celsuis) is the function f^{-1} with ordered pairs of the form (degrees Celsuis, degrees Fahrenheit). Notice that the ordered pair $(-13, -25)$ of the function, for example, becomes the ordered pair $(-25, -13)$ of its inverse.

> **Inverse Function**
>
> The inverse of a one-to-one function f is the one-to-one function f^{-1} that consists of the set of all ordered pairs (y, x) where (x, y) belongs to f.

> ▶ **Helpful Hint**
>
> If a function is not one-to-one, it does not have an inverse function.

EXAMPLE 3   Find the inverse of the one-to-one function.
$$f = \{(0, 1), (-2, 7), (3, -6), (4, 4)\}$$

Solution $f^{-1} = \{(1, 0), (7, -2), (-6, 3), (4, 4)\}$
          ↑   ↑   ↑   ↑ Switch coordinates of each ordered pair.

PRACTICE 3   Find the inverse of the one-to-one function.
$$f(x) = \{(3, 4), (-2, 0), (2, 8), (6, 6)\}$$

> ▶ **Helpful Hint**
>
> The symbol f^{-1} is the single symbol used to denote the inverse of the function f.
> It is read as "f inverse." This symbol *does not mean* $\frac{1}{f}$.

Concept Check ✓

Suppose that f is a one-to-one function and that $f(1) = 5$.

a. Write the corresponding ordered pair.

b. Write one point that we know must belong to the inverse function f^{-1}.

Answer to Concept Check:
a. $(1, 5)$, **b.** $(5, 1)$

OBJECTIVE 4 ▶ **Finding the equation of the inverse of a function.** If a one-to-one function f is defined as a set of ordered pairs, we can find f^{-1} by interchanging the x- and y-coordinates of the ordered pairs. If a one-to-one function f is given in the form of an equation, we can find f^{-1} by using a similar procedure.

Finding the Inverse of a One-to-One Function f(x)

STEP 1. Replace $f(x)$ with y.

STEP 2. Interchange x and y.

STEP 3. Solve the equation for y.

STEP 4. Replace y with the notation $f^{-1}(x)$.

EXAMPLE 4 Find an equation of the inverse of $f(x) = x + 3$.

Solution $f(x) = x + 3$

STEP 1. $y = x + 3$ Replace $f(x)$ with y.

STEP 2. $x = y + 3$ Interchange x and y.

STEP 3. $x - 3 = y$ Solve for y.

STEP 4. $f^{-1}(x) = x - 3$ Replace y with $f^{-1}(x)$.

The inverse of $f(x) = x + 3$ is $f^{-1}(x) = x - 3$. Notice that, for example,

$$f(1) = 1 + 3 = 4 \quad \text{and} \quad f^{-1}(4) = 4 - 3 = 1$$

Ordered pair: $(1, 4)$ Ordered pair: $(4, 1)$

The coordinates are switched, as expected.

PRACTICE 4 Find the equation of the inverse of $f(x) = 6 - x$.

EXAMPLE 5 Find the equation of the inverse of $f(x) = 3x - 5$. Graph f and f^{-1} on the same set of axes.

Solution $f(x) = 3x - 5$

STEP 1. $y = 3x - 5$ Replace $f(x)$ with y.

STEP 2. $x = 3y - 5$ Interchange x and y.

STEP 3. $3y = x + 5$ Solve for y.

$$y = \frac{x + 5}{3}$$

STEP 4. $f^{-1}(x) = \dfrac{x + 5}{3}$ Replace y with $f^{-1}(x)$.

576 CHAPTER 10 Exponential and Logarithmic Functions

Now we graph $f(x)$ and $f^{-1}(x)$ on the same set of axes. Both $f(x) = 3x - 5$ and $f^{-1}(x) = \dfrac{x+5}{3}$ are linear functions, so each graph is a line.

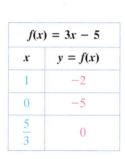
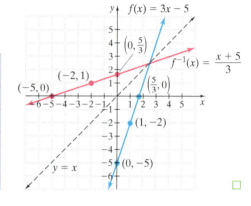

PRACTICE 5 Find the equation of the inverse of $f(x) = 5x + 2$. Graph f and f^{-1} on the same set of axes.

OBJECTIVE 5 ▶ Graphing inverse functions. Notice that the graphs of f and f^{-1} in Example 5 are mirror images of each other, and the "mirror" is the dashed line $y = x$. This is true for every function and its inverse. For this reason, we say that *the graphs of f and f^{-1} are symmetric about the line $y = x$.*

To see why this happens, study the graph of a few ordered pairs and their switched coordinates in the diagram to the right.

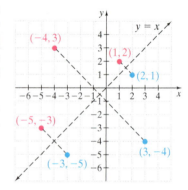

EXAMPLE 6 Graph the inverse of each function.

Solution The function is graphed in blue and the inverse is graphed in red.

a.
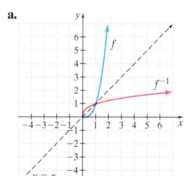

b.
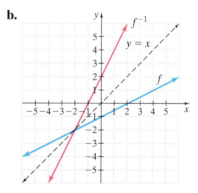

PRACTICE
6 Graph the inverse of each function.

a.
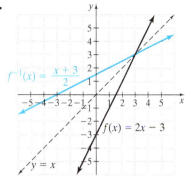

b.
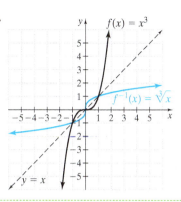

OBJECTIVE 6 ▶ Determining whether functions are inverses of each other. Notice in the table of values in Example 5 that $f(0) = -5$ and $f^{-1}(-5) = 0$, as expected. Also, for example, $f(1) = -2$ and $f^{-1}(-2) = 1$. In words, we say that for some input x, the function f^{-1} takes the output of x, called $f(x)$, back to x.

$$x \rightarrow f(x) \quad \text{and} \quad f^{-1}(f(x)) \rightarrow x$$
$$\downarrow \quad \downarrow \qquad\qquad \downarrow \quad \downarrow$$
$$f(0) = -5 \quad \text{and} \quad f^{-1}(-5) = 0$$
$$f(1) = -2 \quad \text{and} \quad f^{-1}(-2) = 1$$

In general,

> If f is a one-to-one function, then the inverse of f is the function f^{-1} such that
> $$(f^{-1} \circ f)(x) = x \quad \text{and} \quad (f \circ f^{-1})(x) = x$$

EXAMPLE 7 Show that if $f(x) = 3x + 2$, then $f^{-1}(x) = \dfrac{x-2}{3}$.

Solution See that $(f^{-1} \circ f)(x) = x$ and $(f \circ f^{-1})(x) = x$.

$$(f^{-1} \circ f)(x) = f^{-1}(f(x))$$
$$= f^{-1}(3x + 2) \qquad \text{Replace } f(x) \text{ with } 3x + 2.$$
$$= \frac{3x + 2 - 2}{3}$$
$$= \frac{3x}{3}$$
$$= x$$

$$(f \circ f^{-1})(x) = f(f^{-1}(x))$$
$$= f\left(\frac{x-2}{3}\right) \qquad \text{Replace } f^{-1}(x) \text{ with } \frac{x-2}{3}.$$

$$= 3\left(\frac{x-2}{3}\right) + 2$$
$$= x - 2 + 2$$
$$= x$$

PRACTICE 7 Show that if $f(x) = 4x - 1$, then $f^{-1}(x) = \dfrac{x+1}{4}$.

Graphing Calculator Explorations

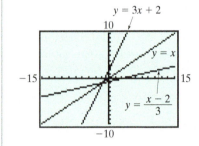

A graphing calculator can be used to visualize the results of Example 7. Recall that the graph of a function f and its inverse f^{-1} are mirror images of each other across the line $y = x$. To see this for the function from Example 7, use a square window and graph

the given function: $Y_1 = 3x + 2$

its inverse: $Y_2 = \dfrac{x-2}{3}$

and the line: $Y_3 = x$

Exercises follow in Exercise Set 10.2.

VOCABULARY & READINESS CHECK

Word Bank. *Use the choices below to fill in each blank. Some choices will not be used and some will be used more than once.*

| vertical | (3, 7) | (11, 2) | $y = x$ | x |
| horizontal | (7, 3) | (2, 11) | $\dfrac{1}{f}$ | the inverse of f |

1. If $f(2) = 11$, the corresponding ordered pair is _____.
2. The symbol f^{-1} means _____.
3. If $(7, 3)$ is an ordered pair solution of $f(x)$, and $f(x)$ has an inverse, then an ordered pair solution of $f^{-1}(x)$ is _____.
4. To tell whether a graph is the graph of a function, use the _____ line test.
5. To tell whether the graph of a function is also a one-to-one function, use the _____ line test.
6. The graphs of f and f^{-1} are symmetric about the _____ line.
7. Two functions are inverse of each other if $(f \circ f^{-1})(x) =$ ____ and $(f^{-1} \circ f)(x) =$ ____.

10.2 EXERCISE SET

Determine whether each function is a one-to-one function. If it is one-to-one, list the inverse function by switching coordinates, or inputs and outputs. See Examples 1 and 3.

1. $f = \{(-1, -1), (1, 1), (0, 2), (2, 0)\}$
2. $g = \{(8, 6), (9, 6), (3, 4), (-4, 4)\}$
3. $h = \{(10, 10)\}$
4. $r = \{(1, 2), (3, 4), (5, 6), (6, 7)\}$

5. $f = \{(11, 12), (4, 3), (3, 4), (6, 6)\}$

6. $g = \{(0, 3), (3, 7), (6, 7), (-2, -2)\}$

7.
Month of 2007 (Input)	January	February	March	April
Unemployment Rate in Percent	4.6	4.6	4.4	4.4

(*Source:* Bureau of Labor Statistics, U.S. Department of Housing and Urban Development)

8.
State (Input)	Wisconsin	Ohio	Georgia	Colorado	California	Arizona
Electoral Votes (Output)	10	20	15	9	55	10

9.
State (Input)	California	Maryland	Nevada	Florida	North Dakota
Rank in Population (Output)	1	19	35	4	48

(*Source:* U.S. Bureau of the Census)

10.
Shape (Input)	Triangle	Pentagon	Quadrilateral	Hexagon	Decagon
Number of Sides (Output)	3	5	4	6	10

(*Source:* U.S. Bureau of the Census)

Given the one-to-one function $f(x) = x^3 + 2$, *find the following.*
[*Hint: You do not need to find the equation for* $f^{-1}(x)$.]

11. a. $f(1)$ 12. a. $f(0)$
    b. $f^{-1}(3)$ b. $f^{-1}(2)$

13. a. $f(-1)$ 14. a. $f(-2)$
    b. $f^{-1}(1)$ b. $f^{-1}(-6)$

Determine whether the graph of each function is the graph of a one-to-one function. See Example 2.

17.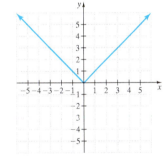

18.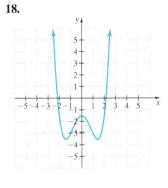

15.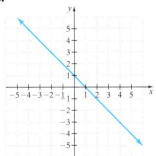

16.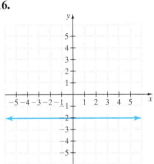

19.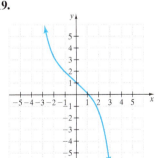

20.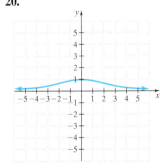

580 CHAPTER 10 Exponential and Logarithmic Functions

21. **22.**

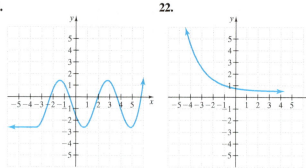

43. **44.**

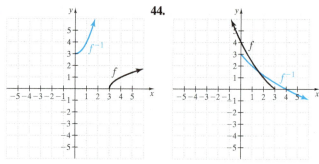

MIXED PRACTICE

Each of the following functions is one-to-one. Find the inverse of each function and graph the function and its inverse on the same set of axes. See Examples 4 and 5.

23. $f(x) = x + 4$
24. $f(x) = x - 5$
25. $f(x) = 2x - 3$
26. $f(x) = 4x + 9$
27. $f(x) = \frac{1}{2}x - 1$
28. $f(x) = -\frac{1}{2}x + 2$
29. $f(x) = x^3$
30. $f(x) = x^3 - 1$

Find the inverse of each one-to-one function. See Examples 4 and 5.

31. $f(x) = 5x + 2$
32. $f(x) = 6x - 1$
33. $f(x) = \frac{x - 2}{5}$
34. $f(x) = \frac{4x - 3}{2}$
35. $f(x) = \sqrt[3]{x}$
36. $f(x) = \sqrt[3]{x + 1}$
37. $f(x) = \frac{5}{3x + 1}$
38. $f(x) = \frac{7}{2x + 4}$
39. $f(x) = (x + 2)^3$
40. $f(x) = (x - 5)^3$

Graph the inverse of each function on the same set of axes. See Example 6.

41. **42.**

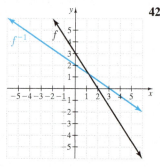
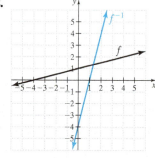

45. **46.**

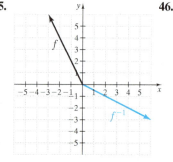
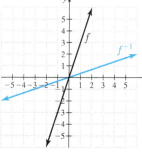

Solve. See Example 7.

47. If $f(x) = 2x + 1$, show that $f^{-1}(x) = \frac{x - 1}{2}$.

48. If $f(x) = 3x - 10$, show that $f^{-1}(x) = \frac{x + 10}{3}$.

49. If $f(x) = x^3 + 6$, show that $f^{-1}(x) = \sqrt[3]{x - 6}$.

50. If $f(x) = x^3 - 5$, show that $f^{-1}(x) = \sqrt[3]{x + 5}$.

REVIEW AND PREVIEW

Evaluate each of the following. See Section 8.2.

51. $25^{1/2}$
52. $49^{1/2}$
53. $16^{3/4}$
54. $27^{2/3}$
55. $9^{-3/2}$
56. $81^{-3/4}$

If $f(x) = 3^x$, find the following. In Exercises 59 and 60, give an exact answer and a two-decimal-place approximation. See Sections 3.2, 6.1, and 8.2.

57. $f(2)$
58. $f(0)$
59. $f\left(\frac{1}{2}\right)$
60. $f\left(\frac{2}{3}\right)$

CONCEPT EXTENSIONS

Solve. See the Concept Check in this section.

61. Suppose that f is a one-to-one function and that $f(2) = 9$.
  a. Write the corresponding ordered pair.
  b. Name one ordered-pair that we know is a solution of the inverse of f, or f^{-1}.

62. Suppose that F is a one-to-one function and that $F\left(\dfrac{1}{2}\right) = -0.7$.

   a. Write the corresponding ordered pair.

   b. Name one ordered pair that we know is a solution of the inverse of F, or F^{-1}.

Multiple Steps. *For Exercises 63 and 64,*

a. *Write the ordered pairs for $f(x)$ whose points are highlighted. (Include the points whose coordinates are given.)*

b. *Write the corresponding ordered pairs for the inverse of f, f^{-1}.*

c. *Graph the ordered pairs for f^{-1} found in part* **b.**

d. *Graph $f^{-1}(x)$ by drawing a smooth curve through the plotted points.*

63.

64.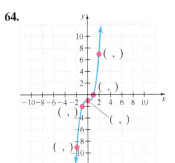

65. If you are given the graph of a function, describe how you can tell from the graph whether a function has an inverse.

66. Describe the appearance of the graphs of a function and its inverse.

Find the inverse of each given one-to-one function. Then use a graphing calculator to graph the function and its inverse on a square window.

67. $f(x) = 3x + 1$

68. $f(x) = -2x - 6$

69. $f(x) = \sqrt[3]{x + 1}$

70. $f(x) = x^3 - 3$

10.3   EXPONENTIAL FUNCTIONS

OBJECTIVES

1. Graph exponential functions.
2. Solve equations of the form $b^x = b^y$.
3. Solve problems modeled by exponential equations.

OBJECTIVE 1 ▶ Graphing exponential functions. In earlier chapters, we gave meaning to exponential expressions such as 2^x, where x is a rational number. For example,

$$2^3 = 2 \cdot 2 \cdot 2 \quad \text{Three factors; each factor is 2}$$
$$2^{3/2} = (2^{1/2})^3 = \sqrt{2} \cdot \sqrt{2} \cdot \sqrt{2} \quad \text{Three factors; each factor is } \sqrt{2}$$

When x is an irrational number (for example, $\sqrt{3}$), what meaning can we give to $2^{\sqrt{3}}$?

It is beyond the scope of this book to give precise meaning to 2^x if x is irrational. We can confirm your intuition and say that $2^{\sqrt{3}}$ is a real number, and since $1 \leq \sqrt{3} < 2$, then $2^1 < 2^{\sqrt{3}} < 2^2$. We can also use a calculator and approximate $2^{\sqrt{3}}$: $2^{\sqrt{3}} \approx 3.321997$. In fact, as long as the base b is positive, b^x is a real number for all real numbers x. Finally, the rules of exponents apply whether x is rational or irrational, as long as b is positive. In this section, we are interested in functions of the form $f(x) = b^x$, where $b > 0$. A function of this form is called an **exponential function.**

> **Exponential Function**
>
> A function of the form
>
> $$f(x) = b^x$$
>
> is called an **exponential function** if $b > 0$, b is not 1, and x is a real number.

Next, we practice graphing exponential functions.

EXAMPLE 1 Graph the exponential functions defined by $f(x) = 2^x$ and $g(x) = 3^x$ on the same set of axes.

Solution Graph each function by plotting points. Set up a table of values for each of the two functions.

If each set of points is plotted and connected with a smooth curve, the following graphs result.

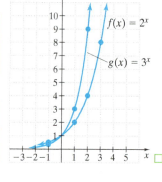

$f(x) = 2^x$	x	0	1	2	3	-1	-2
	$f(x)$	1	2	4	8	$\frac{1}{2}$	$\frac{1}{4}$

$g(x) = 3^x$	x	0	1	2	3	-1	-2
	$g(x)$	1	3	9	27	$\frac{1}{3}$	$\frac{1}{9}$

PRACTICE 1 Graph the exponential functions defined by $f(x) = 2^x$ and $g(x) = 7^x$ on the same set of axes.

A number of things should be noted about the two graphs of exponential functions in Example 1. First, the graphs show that $f(x) = 2^x$ and $g(x) = 3^x$ are one-to-one functions since each graph passes the vertical and horizontal line tests. The y-intercept of each graph is $(0, 1)$, but neither graph has an x-intercept. From the graph, we can also see that the domain of each function is all real numbers and that the range is $(y > 0)$. We can also see that as x-values are increasing, y-values are increasing also.

EXAMPLE 2 Graph the exponential functions $y = \left(\frac{1}{2}\right)^x$ and $y = \left(\frac{1}{3}\right)^x$ on the same set of axes.

Solution As before, plot points and connect them with a smooth curve.

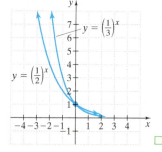

$y = \left(\frac{1}{2}\right)^x$	x	0	1	2	3	-1	-2
	y	1	$\frac{1}{2}$	$\frac{1}{4}$	$\frac{1}{8}$	2	4

$y = \left(\frac{1}{3}\right)^x$	x	0	1	2	3	-1	-2
	y	1	$\frac{1}{3}$	$\frac{1}{9}$	$\frac{1}{27}$	3	9

PRACTICE 2 Graph the exponential functions $f(x) = \left(\frac{1}{3}\right)^x$ and $g(x) = \left(\frac{1}{5}\right)^x$ on the same set of axes.

Each function in Example 2 again is a one-to-one function. The y-intercept of both is $(0, 1)$. The domain is all real numbers, and the range is $y > 0$.

Notice the difference between the graphs of Example 1 and the graphs of Example 2. An exponential function is always increasing if the base is greater than 1.

When the base is between 0 and 1, the graph is always decreasing. The following figures summarize these characteristics of exponential functions.

Section 10.3 Exponential Functions 583

$f(x) = b^x, \quad b > 0, \quad b \neq 1$

- one-to-one function
- y-intercept $(0, 1)$
- no x-intercept
- domain: all real numbers
- range: $y > 0$

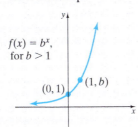

EXAMPLE 3 Graph the exponential function $f(x) = 3^{x+2}$.

Solution As before, we find and plot a few ordered pair solutions. Then we connect the points with a smooth curve.

$y = 3^{x+2}$	
x	y
0	9
-1	3
-2	1
-3	$\frac{1}{3}$
-4	$\frac{1}{9}$

PRACTICE 3 Graph the exponential function $f(x) = 2^{x+3}$.

Concept Check ✓

Which functions are exponential functions?

a. $f(x) = x^3$ b. $g(x) = \left(\frac{2}{3}\right)^x$ c. $h(x) = 5^{x-2}$ d. $w(x) = (2x)^2$

OBJECTIVE 2 ▶ **Solving equations of the form $b^x = b^y$.** We have seen that an exponential function $y = b^x$ is a one-to-one function. Another way of stating this fact is a property that we can use to solve exponential equations.

Uniqueness of b^x

Let $b > 0$ and $b \neq 1$. Then $b^x = b^y$ is equivalent to $x = y$.

EXAMPLE 4 Solve each equation for x.

a. $2^x = 16$ b. $9^x = 27$ c. $4^{x+3} = 8^x$

Solution

a. We write 16 as a power of 2 and then use the uniqueness of b^x to solve.

$$2^x = 16$$
$$2^x = 2^4$$

Answer to Concept Check:
b, c

Since the bases are the same and are nonnegative, by the uniqueness of b^x, we then have that the exponents are equal. Thus,

$$x = 4$$

The solution is 4, or the solution set is $\{4\}$.

b. Notice that both 9 and 27 are powers of 3.

$$9^x = 27$$
$$(3^2)^x = 3^3 \quad \text{Write 9 and 27 as powers of 3.}$$
$$3^{2x} = 3^3$$
$$2x = 3 \quad \text{Apply the uniqueness of } b^x.$$
$$x = \frac{3}{2} \quad \text{Divide by 2.}$$

To check, replace x with $\frac{3}{2}$ in the original expression, $9^x = 27$. The solution is $\frac{3}{2}$.

c. Write both 4 and 8 as powers of 2.

$$4^{x+3} = 8^x$$
$$(2^2)^{x+3} = (2^3)^x$$
$$2^{2x+6} = 2^{3x}$$
$$2x + 6 = 3x \quad \text{Apply the uniqueness of } b^x.$$
$$6 = x \quad \text{Subtract } 2x \text{ from both sides.}$$

The solution is 6.

PRACTICE 4 Solve each equation for x.

a. $3^x = 9$ **b.** $8^x = 16$ **c.** $125^x = 25^{x-2}$

There is one major problem with the preceding technique. Often the two sides of an equation cannot easily be written as powers of a common base. We explore how to solve an equation such as $4 = 3^x$ with the help of **logarithms** later.

OBJECTIVE 3 ▶ Solving problems modeled by exponential equations. The bar graph below shows the increase in the number of cellular phone users. Notice that the graph of the exponential function $y = 110.6(1.132)^x$ approximates the heights of the bars.

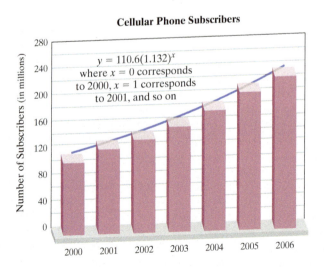

Source: Cellular Telecommunications & Internet Association

The graph on the previous page shows just one example of how the world abounds with patterns that can be modeled by exponential functions. To make these applications realistic, we use numbers that warrant a calculator. Another application of an exponential function has to do with interest rates on loans.

The exponential function defined by $A = P\left(1 + \dfrac{r}{n}\right)^{nt}$ models the dollars A accrued (or owed) after P dollars are invested (or loaned) at an annual rate of interest r compounded n times each year for t years. This function is known as the compound interest formula.

EXAMPLE 5 Using the Compound Interest Formula

Find the amount owed at the end of 5 years if $1600 is loaned at a rate of 9% compounded monthly.

Solution We use the formula $A = P\left(1 + \dfrac{r}{n}\right)^{nt}$, with the following values.

$P = \$1600$ (the amount of the loan)
$r = 9\% = 0.09$ (the annual rate of interest)
$n = 12$ (the number of times interest is compounded each year)
$t = 5$ (the duration of the loan, in years)

$$A = P\left(1 + \dfrac{r}{n}\right)^{nt} \quad \text{Compound interest formula}$$

$$= 1600\left(1 + \dfrac{0.09}{12}\right)^{12(5)} \quad \text{Substitute known values.}$$

$$= 1600(1.0075)^{60}$$

To approximate A, use the $\boxed{y^x}$ or $\boxed{\wedge}$ key on your calculator.

$$\boxed{2505.0896}$$

Thus, the amount A owed is approximately $2505.09.

PRACTICE

5 Find the amount owed at the end of 4 years if $3000 is loaned at a rate of 7% compounded semiannually (twice a year).

EXAMPLE 6 Estimating Percent of Radioactive Material

As a result of the Chernobyl nuclear accident, radioactive debris was carried through the atmosphere. One immediate concern was the impact that the debris had on the milk supply. The percent y of radioactive material in raw milk after t days is estimated by $y = 100(2.7)^{-0.1t}$. Estimate the expected percent of radioactive material in the milk after 30 days.

Solution Replace t with 30 in the given equation.

$$y = 100(2.7)^{-0.1t}$$
$$= 100(2.7)^{-0.1(30)} \quad \text{Let } t = 30.$$
$$= 100(2.7)^{-3}$$

To approximate the percent y, the following keystrokes may be used on a scientific calculator.

| 2.7 | y^x | 3 | +/− | = | × | 100 | = |

The display should read

| 5.0805263 |

Thus, approximately 5% of the radioactive material still remained in the milk supply after 30 days.

PRACTICE

6 If a single sheet of glass prevents 5% of the incoming light from passing through it, then the percent p of light that passes through n successive sheets of glass is given approximately by the function $p(n) = 100(2.7)^{-0.05n}$. Estimate the expected percent of light that will pass through 10 sheets of glass. Round to the nearest hundredth of a percent.

Graphing Calculator Explorations

We can use a graphing calculator and its TRACE feature to solve Example 6 graphically.

To estimate the expected percent of radioactive material in the milk after 30 days, enter $Y_1 = 100(2.7)^{-0.1x}$. (The variable t in Example 6 is changed to x here to better accomodate our work on the graphing calculator.) The graph does not appear on a standard viewing window, so we need to determine an appropriate viewing window. Because it doesn't make sense to look at radioactivity *before* the Chernobyl nuclear accident, we use Xmin = 0. We are interested in finding the percent of radioactive material in the milk when $x = 30$, so we choose Xmax = 35 to leave enough space to see the graph at $x = 30$. Because the values of y are percents, it seems appropriate that $0 \leq y \leq 100$. (We also use Xscl = 1 and Yscl = 10.) Now we graph the function.

We can use the TRACE feature to obtain an approximation of the expected percent of radioactive material in the milk when $x = 30$. (A TABLE feature may also be used to approximate the percent.) To obtain a better approximation, let's use the ZOOM feature several times to zoom in near $x = 30$.

The percent of radioactive material in the milk 30 days after the Chernobyl accident was 5.08%, accurate to two decimal places.

Use a graphing calculator to find each percent. Approximate your solutions so that they are accurate to two decimal places.

1. Estimate the expected percent of radioactive material in the milk 2 days after the Chernobyl nuclear accident.

2. Estimate the expected percent of radioactive material in the milk 10 days after the Chernobyl nuclear accident.

3. Estimate the expected percent of radioactive material in the milk 15 days after the Chernobyl nuclear accident.

4. Estimate the expected percent of radioactive material in the milk 25 days after the Chernobyl nuclear accident.

VOCABULARY & READINESS CHECK

Multiple Choice. *Use the choices to fill in each blank.*

1. A function such as $f(x) = 2^x$ is a(n) _____ function.
   - **A.** linear
   - **B.** quadratic
   - **C.** exponential
2. If $7^x = 7^y$, then _____.
   - **A.** $x = 7^y$
   - **B.** $x = y$
   - **C.** $y = 7^x$
   - **D.** $7 = 7^y$

Read a Graph. *Answer the questions about the graph of $y = 2^x$, shown to the right.*

3. Is this a one-to-one function? _____
4. Is there an *x*-intercept? _____ If so, name the coordinates. _____
5. Is there a *y*-intercept? _____ If so, name the coordinates. _____
6. The domain of this function, in interval notation, is _____.
7. The range of this function, in interval notation, is _____.

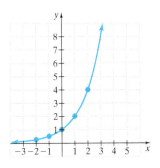

10.3 EXERCISE SET

Graph each exponential function. See Examples 1 through 3.

1. $y = 4^x$
2. $y = 5^x$
3. $y = 2^x + 1$
4. $y = 3^x - 1$
5. $y = \left(\dfrac{1}{4}\right)^x$
6. $y = \left(\dfrac{1}{5}\right)^x$
7. $y = \left(\dfrac{1}{2}\right)^x - 2$
8. $y = \left(\dfrac{1}{3}\right)^x + 2$
9. $y = -2^x$
10. $y = -3^x$
11. $y = -\left(\dfrac{1}{4}\right)^x$
12. $y = -\left(\dfrac{1}{5}\right)^x$
13. $f(x) = 2^{x+1}$
14. $f(x) = 3^{x-1}$
15. $f(x) = 4^{x-2}$
16. $f(x) = 2^{x+3}$

Matching. *Match each exponential equation with its graph below or in the next column. See Examples 1 through 3.*

17. $f(x) = \left(\dfrac{1}{2}\right)^x$
18. $f(x) = \left(\dfrac{1}{4}\right)^x$
19. $f(x) = 2^x$
20. $f(x) = 3^x$

A.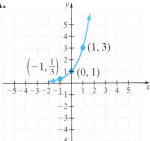

B.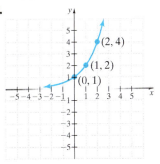

C.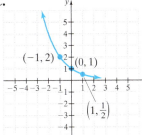

D.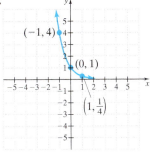

Solve each equation for x. See Example 4.

21. $3^x = 27$
22. $6^x = 36$
23. $16^x = 8$
24. $64^x = 16$
25. $32^{2x-3} = 2$
26. $9^{2x+1} = 81$
27. $\dfrac{1}{4} = 2^{3x}$
28. $\dfrac{1}{27} = 3^{2x}$
29. $5^x = 625$
30. $2^x = 64$
31. $4^x = 8$
32. $32^x = 4$
33. $27^{x+1} = 9$
34. $125^{x-2} = 25$
35. $81^{x-1} = 27^{2x}$
36. $4^{3x-7} = 32^{2x}$

Solve. Unless otherwise indicated, round results to one decimal place. See Example 6.

37. One type of uranium has a daily radioactive decay rate of 0.4%. If 30 pounds of this uranium is available today, find how much will still remain after 50 days. Use $y = 30(2.7)^{-0.004t}$, and let t be 50.

38. The nuclear waste from an atomic energy plant decays at a rate of 3% each century. If 150 pounds of nuclear waste is

disposed of, find how much of it will still remain after 10 centuries. Use $y = 150(2.7)^{-0.03t}$, and let t be 10.

39. National Park Service personnel are trying to increase the size of the bison population of Theodore Roosevelt National Park. If 260 bison currently live in the park, and if the population's rate of growth is 2.5% annually, find how many bison (rounded to the nearest whole) there should be in 10 years. Use $y = 260(2.7)^{0.025t}$.

40. The size of the rat population of a wharf area grows at a rate of 8% monthly. If there are 200 rats in January, find how many rats (rounded to the nearest whole) should be expected by next January. Use $y = 200(2.7)^{0.08t}$.

41. A rare isotope of a nuclear material is very unstable, decaying at a rate of 15% each second. Find how much isotope remains 10 seconds after 5 grams of the isotope is created. Use $y = 5(2.7)^{-0.15t}$.

42. An accidental spill of 75 grams of radioactive material in a local stream has led to the presence of radioactive debris decaying at a rate of 4% each day. Find how much debris still remains after 14 days. Use $y = 75(2.7)^{-0.04t}$.

43. The atmospheric pressure p, in pascals, on a weather balloon decreases with increasing height. This pressure, measured in millimeters of mercury, is related to the number of kilometers h above sea level by the function $p(h) = 760(2.7)^{-0.145h}$. Round to the nearest tenth of a pascal.

   a. Find the atmospheric pressure at a height of 1 kilometer.

   b. Find the atmospheric pressure at a height of 10 kilometers.

44. An unusually wet spring has caused the size of the Cape Cod mosquito population to increase by 8% each day. If an estimated 200,000 mosquitoes are on Cape Cod on May 12, find how many mosquitoes will inhabit the Cape on May 25. Use $y = 200,000(2.7)^{0.08t}$. Round to the nearest thousand.

45. The equation $y = 84,949(1.096)^x$ models the number of American college students who study abroad each year from 1995 through 2006. In the equation, y is the number of American students studying abroad and x represents the number of years after 1995. Round answers to the nearest whole. (*Source:* Based on data from Institute of International Education, Open Doors 2006)

   a. Estimate the number of American students studying abroad in 2000.

   b. Assuming this equation continues to be valid in the future, use this equation to predict the number of American students studying abroad in 2020.

46. Carbon dioxide (CO_2) is a greenhouse gas that contributes to global warming. Partially due to the combustion of fossil fuels, the amount of CO_2 in Earth's atmosphere has been increasing by 0.4% annually over the past century. In 2000, the concentration of CO_2 in the atmosphere was 369.4 parts per million by volume. To make the following predictions, use $y = 369.4(1.004)^t$ where y is the concentration of CO_2 in parts per million and t is the number of years after 2000. Round answers to the nearest tenth. (*Sources:* Based on data from the United Nations Environment Programme and the Carbon Dioxide Information Analysis Center)

   a. Predict the concentration of CO_2 in the atmosphere in the year 2006.

   b. Predict the concentration of CO_2 in the atmosphere in the year 2030.

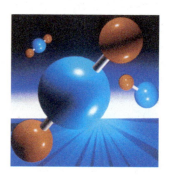

Solve. Use $A = P\left(1 + \dfrac{r}{n}\right)^{nt}$. *Round answers to two decimal places. See Example 5.*

47. Find the amount Erica owes at the end of 3 years if $6000 is loaned to her at a rate of 8% compounded monthly.

48. Find the amount owed at the end of 5 years if $3000 is loaned at a rate of 10% compounded quarterly.

49. Find the total amount Janina has in a college savings account if $2000 was invested and earned 6% compounded semiannually for 12 years.

50. Find the amount accrued if $500 is invested and earns 7% compounded monthly for 4 years.

The formula $y = 18(1.24)^x$ *gives the number of cellular phone users y (in millions) in the United States for the years 1994 through 2006. In this formula, $x = 0$ corresponds to 1994, $x = 1$ corresponds to 1995, and so on. Use this formula to solve Exercises 51 and 52. Round results to the nearest whole million.*

51. Use this model to predict the number of cellular phone users in the year 2010.

52. Use this model to predict the number of cellular phone users in the year 2014.

REVIEW AND PREVIEW

Solve each equation. See Sections 2.1 and 6.8.

53. $5x - 2 = 18$
54. $3x - 7 = 11$
55. $3x - 4 = 3(x + 1)$
56. $2 - 6x = 6(1 - x)$
57. $x^2 + 6 = 5x$
58. $18 = 11x - x^2$

By inspection, find the value for x that makes each statement true. See Section 6.1.

59. $2^x = 8$
60. $3^x = 9$
61. $5^x = \dfrac{1}{5}$
62. $4^x = 1$

CONCEPT EXTENSIONS

63. Explain why the graph of an exponential function $y = b^x$ contains the point $(1, b)$.
64. Explain why an exponential function $y = b^x$ has a y-intercept of $(0, 1)$.

Graph.

65. $y = |3^x|$
66. $y = \left|\left(\dfrac{1}{3}\right)^x\right|$
67. $y = 3^{|x|}$
68. $y = \left(\dfrac{1}{3}\right)^{|x|}$

69. Graph $y = 2^x$ and $y = \left(\dfrac{1}{2}\right)^{-x}$ on the same set of axes. Describe what you see and why.

70. Graph $y = 2^x$ and $x = 2^y$ on the same set of axes. Describe what you see.

Use a graphing calculator to solve. Estimate each result to two decimal places.

71. Verify the results of Exercise 37.
72. From Exercise 37, estimate the number of pounds of uranium that will be available after 100 days.
73. From Exercise 37, estimate the number of pounds of uranium that will be available after 120 days.
74. Verify the results of Exercise 42.
75. From Exercise 42, estimate the amount of debris that remains after 10 days.
76. From Exercise 42, estimate the amount of debris that remains after 20 days.

10.4 LOGARITHMIC FUNCTIONS

OBJECTIVES

1. Write exponential equations with logarithmic notation and write logarithmic equations with exponential notation.
2. Solve logarithmic equations by using exponential notation.
3. Identify and graph logarithmic functions.

OBJECTIVE 1 ▶ Using logarithmic notation. Since the exponential function $f(x) = 2^x$ is a one-to-one function, it has an inverse.

We can create a table of values for f^{-1} by switching the coordinates in the accompanying table of values for $f(x) = 2^x$.

$$f(x) = 2^x$$

x	$y = f(x)$	x	$y = f^{-1}(x)$
-3	$\dfrac{1}{8}$	$\dfrac{1}{8}$	-3
-2	$\dfrac{1}{4}$	$\dfrac{1}{4}$	-2
-1	$\dfrac{1}{2}$	$\dfrac{1}{2}$	-1
0	1	1	0
1	2	2	1
2	4	4	2
3	8	8	3

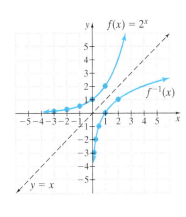

The graphs of $f(x)$ and its inverse are shown above. Notice that the graphs of f and f^{-1} are symmetric about the line $y = x$, as expected.

Now we would like to be able to write an equation for f^{-1}. To do so, we follow the steps for finding an inverse.

$$f(x) = 2^x$$

STEP 1. Replace $f(x)$ by y. $y = 2^x$

STEP 2. Interchange x and y. $x = 2^y$

STEP 3. Solve for y.

At this point, we are stuck. To solve this equation for y, a new notation, the **logarithmic notation,** is needed. The symbol $\log_b x$ means "the power to which b is raised in order to produce a result of x."

$$\log_b x = y \quad \text{means} \quad b^y = x$$

We say that $\log_b x$ is "the logarithm of x to the base b" or "the log of x to the base b."

> **Logarithmic Definition**
> If $b > 0$ and $b \neq 1$, then
> $$y = \log_b x \text{ means } x = b^y$$
> for every $x > 0$ and every real number y.

Before returning to the function $x = 2^y$ and solving it for y in terms of x, let's practice using the new notation $\log_b x$.

It is important to be able to write exponential equations from logarithmic notation, and vice versa. The following table shows examples of both forms.

▶ **Helpful Hint**

Notice that a *logarithm* is an *exponent*. In other words, $\log_3 9$ is the *power* that we raise 3 to in order to get 9.

Logarithmic Equation	Corresponding Exponential Equation
$\log_3 9 = 2$	$3^2 = 9$
$\log_6 1 = 0$	$6^0 = 1$
$\log_2 8 = 3$	$2^3 = 8$
$\log_4 \dfrac{1}{16} = -2$	$4^{-2} = \dfrac{1}{16}$
$\log_8 2 = \dfrac{1}{3}$	$8^{1/3} = 2$

EXAMPLE 1 Write as an exponential equation.

a. $\log_5 25 = 2$ **b.** $\log_6 \dfrac{1}{6} = -1$ **c.** $\log_2 \sqrt{2} = \dfrac{1}{2}$ **d.** $\log_7 x = 5$

Solution

a. $\log_5 25 = 2$ means $5^2 = 25$

b. $\log_6 \dfrac{1}{6} = -1$ means $6^{-1} = \dfrac{1}{6}$

c. $\log_2 \sqrt{2} = \dfrac{1}{2}$ means $2^{1/2} = \sqrt{2}$

d. $\log_7 x = 5$ means $7^5 = x$

PRACTICE 1 Write as an exponential equation.

a. $\log_3 81 = 4$ **b.** $\log_5 \dfrac{1}{5} = -1$ **c.** $\log_7 \sqrt{7} = \dfrac{1}{2}$ **d.** $\log_{13} y = 4$

EXAMPLE 2 Write as a logarithmic equation.

a. $9^3 = 729$ **b.** $6^{-2} = \dfrac{1}{36}$ **c.** $5^{1/3} = \sqrt[3]{5}$ **d.** $\pi^4 = x$

Solution

a. $9^3 = 729$ means $\log_9 729 = 3$

b. $6^{-2} = \dfrac{1}{36}$ means $\log_6 \dfrac{1}{36} = -2$

Section 10.4 Logarithmic Functions 591

c. $5^{1/3} = \sqrt[3]{5}$ means $\log_5 \sqrt[3]{5} = \frac{1}{3}$

d. $\pi^4 = x$ means $\log_\pi x = 4$

PRACTICE 2 Write as a logarithmic equation.

a. $4^3 = 64$ b. $6^{1/3} = \sqrt[3]{6}$ c. $5^{-3} = \frac{1}{125}$ d. $\pi^7 = z$

EXAMPLE 3 Find the value of each logarithmic expression.

a. $\log_4 16$ b. $\log_{10} \frac{1}{10}$ c. $\log_9 3$

Solution

a. $\log_4 16 = 2$ because $4^2 = 16$

b. $\log_{10} \frac{1}{10} = -1$ because $10^{-1} = \frac{1}{10}$

c. $\log_9 3 = \frac{1}{2}$ because $9^{1/2} = \sqrt{9} = 3$

PRACTICE 3 Find the value of each logarithmic expression.

a. $\log_3 9$ b. $\log_2 \frac{1}{8}$ c. $\log_{49} 7$

▶ **Helpful Hint**

Another method for evaluating logarithms such as those in Example 3 is to set the expression equal to x and then write them in exponential form to find x. For example:

a. $\log_4 16 = x$ means $4^x = 16$. Since $4^2 = 16$, $x = 2$ or $\log_4 16 = 2$.

b. $\log_{10} \frac{1}{10} = x$ means $10^x = \frac{1}{10}$. Since $10^{-1} = \frac{1}{10}$, $x = -1$ or $\log_{10} \frac{1}{10} = -1$.

c. $\log_9 3 = x$ means $9^x = 3$. Since $9^{1/2} = 3$, $x = \frac{1}{2}$ or $\log_9 3 = \frac{1}{2}$.

OBJECTIVE 2 ▶ **Solving logarithmic equations.** The ability to interchange the logarithmic and exponential forms of a statement is often the key to solving logarithmic equations.

EXAMPLE 4 Solve each equation for x.

a. $\log_4 \frac{1}{4} = x$ b. $\log_5 x = 3$ c. $\log_x 25 = 2$ d. $\log_3 1 = x$ e. $\log_b 1 = x$

Solution

a. $\log_4 \frac{1}{4} = x$ means $4^x = \frac{1}{4}$. Solve $4^x = \frac{1}{4}$ for x.

$$4^x = \frac{1}{4}$$

$$4^x = 4^{-1}$$

Since the bases are the same, by the uniqueness of b^x, we have that
$$x = -1$$
The solution is -1. To check, see that $\log_4 \frac{1}{4} = -1$, since $4^{-1} = \frac{1}{4}$.

b. $\log_5 x = 3$

$5^3 = x$ Write as an exponential equation.

$125 = x$

The solution is 125.

c. $\log_x 25 = 2$

$x^2 = 25$ Write as an exponential equation. Here $x > 0$, $x \neq 1$.

$x = 5$

Even though $(-5)^2 = 25$, the base b of a logarithm must be positive. The solution is 5.

d. $\log_3 1 = x$

$3^x = 1$ Write as an exponential equation.

$3^x = 3^0$ Write 1 as 3^0.

$x = 0$ Use the uniqueness of b^x.

The solution is 0.

e. $\log_b 1 = x$

$b^x = 1$ Write as an exponential equation. Here, $b > 0$ and $b \neq 1$.

$b^x = b^0$ Write 1 as b^0.

$x = 0$ Apply the uniqueness of b^x.

The solution is 0.

PRACTICE 4 Solve each equation for x.

a. $\log_5 \frac{1}{25} = x$ **b.** $\log_x 8 = 3$ **c.** $\log_6 x = 2$

d. $\log_{13} 1 = x$ **e.** $\log_h 1 = x$

In Example 4e we proved an important property of logarithms. That is, $\log_b 1$ is always 0. This property as well as two important others are given next.

> **Properties of Logarithms**
> If b is a real number, $b > 0$, and $b \neq 1$, then
>
> 1. $\log_b 1 = 0$
> 2. $\log_b b^x = x$
> 3. $b^{\log_b x} = x$

To see that **2.** $\log_b b^x = x$, change the logarithmic form to exponential form. Then, $\log_b b^x = x$ means $b^x = b^x$. In exponential form, the statement is true, so in logarithmic form, the statement is also true. To understand **3.** $b^{\log_b x} = x$, write this exponential equation as an equivalent logarithm.

EXAMPLE 5 Simplify.

a. $\log_3 3^2$ **b.** $\log_7 7^{-1}$ **c.** $5^{\log_5 3}$ **d.** $2^{\log_2 6}$

Solution

a. From Property 2, $\log_3 3^2 = 2$.
b. From Property 2, $\log_7 7^{-1} = -1$.
c. From Property 3, $5^{\log_5 3} = 3$.
d. From Property 3, $2^{\log_2 6} = 6$.

PRACTICE 5 Simplify.

a. $\log_5 5^4$ **b.** $\log_9 9^{-2}$ **c.** $6^{\log_6 5}$ **d.** $7^{\log_7 4}$

OBJECTIVE 3 ▶ Graphing logarithmic functions. Let us now return to the function $f(x) = 2^x$ and write an equation for its inverse, $f^{-1}(x)$. Recall our earlier work.

$$f(x) = 2^x$$

STEP 1. Replace $f(x)$ by y. $\qquad y = 2^x$

STEP 2. Interchange x and y. $\qquad x = 2^y$

Having gained proficiency with the notation $\log_b x$, we can now complete the steps for writing the inverse equation by writing $x = 2^y$ as an equivalent logarithm.

STEP 1. Solve for y. $\qquad y = \log_2 x$

STEP 2. Replace y with $f^{-1}(x)$. $\qquad f^{-1}(x) = \log_2 x$

Thus, $f^{-1}(x) = \log_2 x$ defines a function that is the inverse function of the function $f(x) = 2^x$. The function $f^{-1}(x)$ or $y = \log_2 x$ is called a **logarithmic function.**

> **Logarithmic Function**
>
> If x is a positive real number, b is a constant positive real number, and b is not 1, then a **logarithmic function** is a function that can be defined by
>
> $$f(x) = \log_b x$$
>
> The domain of f is the set of positive real numbers, and the range of f is the set of real numbers.

Concept Check ✓

Let $f(x) = \log_3 x$ and $g(x) = 3^x$. These two functions are inverses of each other. Since $(2, 9)$ is an ordered pair solution of $g(x)$ or $g(2) = 9$, what ordered pair do we know to be a solution of $f(x)$? Also, find $f(9)$. Explain why.

We can explore logarithmic functions by graphing them.

EXAMPLE 6 Graph the logarithmic function $y = \log_2 x$.

Solution First we write the equation with exponential notation as $2^y = x$. Then we find some ordered pair solutions that satisfy this equation. Finally, we plot the points and connect them with a smooth curve. The domain of this function is $x > 0$, and the range is all real numbers.

Answer to Concept Check:
$(9, 2); f(9) = 2$; answers may vary

Since $x = 2^y$ is solved for x, we choose y-values and compute corresponding x-values.

If $y = 0$, $x = 2^0 = 1$
If $y = 1$, $x = 2^1 = 2$
If $y = 2$, $x = 2^2 = 4$
If $y = -1$, $x = 2^{-1} = \dfrac{1}{2}$

$x = 2^y$	y
1	0
2	1
4	2
$\dfrac{1}{2}$	-1

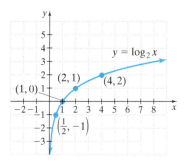

Notice that the x-intercept is $(1, 0)$ and there is no y-intercept.

PRACTICE 6 Graph the logarithmic function $y = \log_7 x$.

EXAMPLE 7 Graph the logarithmic function $f(x) = \log_{1/3} x$.

Solution Replace $f(x)$ with y, and write the result with exponential notation.

$$f(x) = \log_{1/3} x$$
$$y = \log_{1/3} x \quad \text{Replace } f(x) \text{ with } y.$$
$$\left(\dfrac{1}{3}\right)^y = x \quad \text{Write in exponential form.}$$

Now we can find ordered pair solutions that satisfy $\left(\dfrac{1}{3}\right)^y = x$, plot these points, and connect them with a smooth curve.

If $y = 0$, $x = \left(\dfrac{1}{3}\right)^0 = 1$

If $y = 1$, $x = \left(\dfrac{1}{3}\right)^1 = \dfrac{1}{3}$

If $y = -1$, $x = \left(\dfrac{1}{3}\right)^{-1} = 3$

If $y = -2$, $x = \left(\dfrac{1}{3}\right)^{-2} = 9$

$x = \left(\dfrac{1}{3}\right)^y$	y
1	0
$\dfrac{1}{3}$	1
3	-1
9	-2

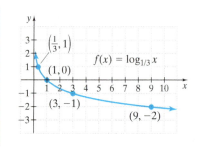

The domain of this function is $x > 0$, and the range is all real numbers. The x-intercept is $(1, 0)$ and there is no y-intercept.

PRACTICE 7 Graph the logarithmic function $y = \log_{1/4} x$.

The following figures summarize characteristics of logarithmic functions.

$$f(x) = \log_b x, \, b > 0, \, b \neq 1$$

- one-to-one function
- x-intercept $(1, 0)$
- no y-intercept
- domain: $x > 0$
- range: all real numbers

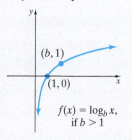

$f(x) = \log_b x$, if $b > 1$

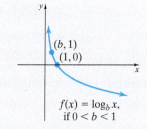

$f(x) = \log_b x$, if $0 < b < 1$

VOCABULARY & READINESS CHECK

Multiple Choice. *Use the choices to fill in each blank.*

1. A function, such as $y = \log_2 x$ is a(n) _____ function.
   a. linear   **b.** logarithmic   **c.** quadratic   **d.** exponential
2. If $y = \log_2 x$, then _____.
   a. $x = y$ **b.** $2^x = y$ **c.** $2^y = x$ **d.** $2y = x$

Read a Graph. *Answer the questions about the graph of $y = \log_2 x$, shown to the left.*

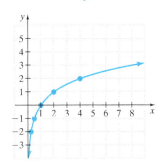

3. Is this a one-to-one function? _____
4. Is there an x-intercept? _____ If so, name the coordinates. _____
5. Is there a y-intercept? _____ If so, name the coordinates. _____
6. The domain of this function, in interval notation, is _____.
7. The range of this function, in interval notation, is _____.

10.4 EXERCISE SET

Write each as an exponential equation. See Example 1.

1. $\log_6 36 = 2$
2. $\log_2 32 = 5$
3. $\log_3 \dfrac{1}{27} = -3$
4. $\log_5 \dfrac{1}{25} = -2$
5. $\log_{10} 1000 = 3$
6. $\log_{10} 10 = 1$
7. $\log_9 x = 4$
8. $\log_8 y = 7$
9. $\log_\pi \dfrac{1}{\pi^2} = -2$
10. $\log_e \dfrac{1}{e} = -1$
11. $\log_7 \sqrt{7} = \dfrac{1}{2}$
12. $\log_{11} \sqrt[4]{11} = \dfrac{1}{4}$
13. $\log_{0.7} 0.343 = 3$
14. $\log_{1.2} 1.44 = 2$
15. $\log_3 \dfrac{1}{81} = -4$
16. $\log_{1/4} 16 = -2$

Write each as a logarithmic equation. See Example 2.

17. $2^4 = 16$
18. $5^3 = 125$
19. $10^2 = 100$
20. $10^4 = 10{,}000$
21. $\pi^3 = x$
22. $\pi^5 = y$
23. $10^{-1} = \dfrac{1}{10}$
24. $10^{-2} = \dfrac{1}{100}$
25. $4^{-2} = \dfrac{1}{16}$
26. $3^{-4} = \dfrac{1}{81}$
27. $5^{1/2} = \sqrt{5}$
28. $4^{1/3} = \sqrt[3]{4}$

Find the value of each logarithmic expression. See Examples 3 and 5.

29. $\log_2 8$
30. $\log_3 9$
31. $\log_3 \dfrac{1}{9}$
32. $\log_2 \dfrac{1}{32}$
33. $\log_{25} 5$
34. $\log_8 \dfrac{1}{2}$
35. $\log_{1/2} 2$
36. $\log_{2/3} \dfrac{4}{9}$
37. $\log_6 1$
38. $\log_9 9$
39. $\log_{10} 100$
40. $\log_{10} \dfrac{1}{10}$
41. $\log_3 81$
42. $\log_2 16$
43. $\log_4 \dfrac{1}{64}$
44. $\log_3 \dfrac{1}{9}$

Solve. See Example 4.

45. $\log_3 9 = x$
46. $\log_2 8 = x$
47. $\log_3 x = 4$
48. $\log_2 x = 3$
49. $\log_x 49 = 2$
50. $\log_x 8 = 3$
51. $\log_2 \dfrac{1}{8} = x$
52. $\log_3 \dfrac{1}{81} = x$

53. $\log_3 \dfrac{1}{27} = x$

54. $\log_5 \dfrac{1}{125} = x$

55. $\log_8 x = \dfrac{1}{3}$

56. $\log_9 x = \dfrac{1}{2}$

57. $\log_4 16 = x$

58. $\log_2 16 = x$

59. $\log_{3/4} x = 3$

60. $\log_{2/3} x = 2$

61. $\log_x 100 = 2$

62. $\log_x 27 = 3$

63. $\log_2 2^4 = x$

64. $\log_6 6^{-2} = x$

65. $3^{\log_3 5} = x$

66. $5^{\log_5 7} = x$

67. $\log_x \dfrac{1}{7} = \dfrac{1}{2}$

68. $\log_x 2 = -\dfrac{1}{3}$

Simplify. See Example 5.

69. $\log_5 5^3$

70. $\log_6 6^2$

71. $2^{\log_2 3}$

72. $7^{\log_7 4}$

73. $\log_9 9$

74. $\log_8(8)^{-1}$

Graph each logarithmic function. Label any intercepts. See Examples 6 and 7.

75. $y = \log_3 x$

76. $y = \log_8 x$

77. $f(x) = \log_{1/4} x$

78. $f(x) = \log_{1/2} x$

79. $f(x) = \log_5 x$

80. $f(x) = \log_6 x$

81. $f(x) = \log_{1/6} x$

82. $f(x) = \log_{1/5} x$

REVIEW AND PREVIEW

Simplify each rational expression. See Section 7.1.

83. $\dfrac{x+3}{3+x}$

84. $\dfrac{x-5}{5-x}$

85. $\dfrac{x^2 - 8x + 16}{2x - 8}$

86. $\dfrac{x^2 - 3x - 10}{2 + x}$

Add or subtract as indicated. See Section 7.2.

87. $\dfrac{2}{x} + \dfrac{3}{x^2}$

88. $\dfrac{3x}{x+3} + \dfrac{9}{x+3}$

89. $\dfrac{m^2}{m+1} - \dfrac{1}{m+1}$

90. $\dfrac{5}{y+1} - \dfrac{4}{y-1}$

CONCEPT EXTENSIONS

Multiple Steps. *Solve. See the Concept Check in this section.*

91. Let $f(x) = \log_5 x$. Then $g(x) = 5^x$ is the inverse of $f(x)$. The ordered pair $(2, 25)$ is a solution of the function $g(x)$.

    a. Write this solution using function notation.
    b. Write an ordered pair that we know to be a solution of $f(x)$.
    c. Use the answer to part b and write the solution using function notation.

92. Let $f(x) = \log_{0.3} x$. Then $g(x) = 0.3^x$ is the inverse of $f(x)$. The ordered pair $(3, 0.027)$ is a solution of the function $g(x)$.

    a. Write this solution using function notation.
    b. Write an ordered pair that we know to be a solution of $f(x)$.
    c. Use the answer to part b and write the solution using function notation.

93. Explain why negative numbers are not included as logarithmic bases.

94. Explain why 1 is not included as a logarithmic base.

Solve by first writing as an exponential.

95. $\log_7(5x - 2) = 1$

96. $\log_3(2x + 4) = 2$

97. Simplify: $\log_3(\log_5 125)$

98. Simplify: $\log_7(\log_4(\log_2 16))$

Graph each function and its inverse function on the same set of axes. Label any intercepts.

99. $y = 4^x$; $y = \log_4 x$

100. $y = 3^x$; $y = \log_3 x$

101. $y = \left(\dfrac{1}{3}\right)^x$; $y = \log_{1/3} x$

102. $y = \left(\dfrac{1}{2}\right)^x$; $y = \log_{1/2} x$

103. Explain why the graph of the function $y = \log_b x$ contains the point $(1, 0)$ no matter what b is.

104. $\log_3 10$ is between which two integers? Explain your answer.

105. The formula $\log_{10}(1 - k) = \dfrac{-0.3}{H}$ models the relationship between the half-life H of a radioactive material and its rate of decay k. Find the rate of decay of the iodine isotope I-131 if its half-life is 8 days. Round to four decimal places.

106. The formula $pH = -\log_{10}(H^+)$ provides the pH for a liquid, where H^+ stands for the concentration of hydronium ions. Find the pH of lemonade, whose concentration of hydronium ions is 0.0050 moles/liter.

10.5 PROPERTIES OF LOGARITHMS

OBJECTIVES

1. Use the product property of logarithms.
2. Use the quotient property of logarithms.
3. Use the power property of logarithms.
4. Use the properties of logarithms together.

In the previous section we explored some basic properties of logarithms. We now introduce and explore additional properties. Because a logarithm is an exponent, logarithmic properties are just restatements of exponential properties.

OBJECTIVE 1 ▶ Using the product property. The first of these properties is called the **product property of logarithms,** because it deals with the logarithm of a product.

> **Product Property of Logarithms**
> If x, y, and b are positive real numbers and $b \neq 1$, then
> $$\log_b xy = \log_b x + \log_b y$$

To prove this, let $\log_b x = M$ and $\log_b y = N$. Now write each logarithm with exponential notation.

$$\log_b x = M \quad \text{is equivalent to} \quad b^M = x$$
$$\log_b y = N \quad \text{is equivalent to} \quad b^N = y$$

Multiply the left sides and the right sides of the exponential equations, and we have that

$$xy = (b^M)(b^N) = b^{M+N}$$

If we write the equation $xy = b^{M+N}$ in equivalent logarithmic form, we have

$$\log_b xy = M + N$$

But since $M = \log_b x$ and $N = \log_b y$, we can write

$$\log_b xy = \log_b x + \log_b y \quad \text{Let } M = \log_b x \text{ and } N = \log_b y.$$

In other words, the logarithm of a product is the sum of the logarithms of the factors. This property is sometimes used to simplify logarithmic expressions.

In the examples that follow, assume that variables represent positive numbers.

EXAMPLE 1 Write each sum as a single logarithm.

a. $\log_{11} 10 + \log_{11} 3$ **b.** $\log_3 \frac{1}{2} + \log_3 12$ **c.** $\log_2(x + 2) + \log_2 x$

Solution

In each case, both terms have a common logarithmic base.

a. $\log_{11} 10 + \log_{11} 3 = \log_{11}(10 \cdot 3)$ Apply the product property.
$= \log_{11} 30$

b. $\log_3 \frac{1}{2} + \log_3 12 = \log_3 \left(\frac{1}{2} \cdot 12\right) = \log_3 6$

c. $\log_2(x + 2) + \log_2 x = \log_2[(x + 2) \cdot x] = \log_2(x^2 + 2x)$

▶ **Helpful Hint**
Check your logarithm properties. Make sure you understand that $\log_2(x + 2)$ *is not* $\log_2 x + \log_2 2$.

PRACTICE 1 Write each sum as a single logarithm.

a. $\log_8 5 + \log_8 3$
b. $\log_2 \frac{1}{3} + \log_2 18$
c. $\log_5(x - 1) + \log_5(x + 1)$

OBJECTIVE 2 ▶ **Using the quotient property.** The second property is the **quotient property of logarithms.**

> **Quotient Property of Logarithms**
> If x, y, and b are positive real numbers and $b \neq 1$, then
> $$\log_b \frac{x}{y} = \log_b x - \log_b y$$

The proof of the quotient property of logarithms is similar to the proof of the product property. Notice that the quotient property says that the logarithm of a quotient is the difference of the logarithms of the dividend and divisor.

Concept Check ✓

Which of the following is the correct way to rewrite $\log_5 \frac{7}{2}$?

a. $\log_5 7 - \log_5 2$ **b.** $\log_5(7-2)$ **c.** $\frac{\log_5 7}{\log_5 2}$ **d.** $\log_5 14$

EXAMPLE 2 Write each difference as a single logarithm.

a. $\log_{10} 27 - \log_{10} 3$ **b.** $\log_5 8 - \log_5 x$ **c.** $\log_3(x^2 + 5) - \log_3(x^2 + 1)$

Solution All terms have a common logarithmic base.

a. $\log_{10} 27 - \log_{10} 3 = \log_{10} \frac{27}{3} = \log_{10} 9$

b. $\log_5 8 - \log_5 x = \log_5 \frac{8}{x}$

c. $\log_3(x^2 + 5) - \log_3(x^2 + 1) = \log_3 \frac{x^2 + 5}{x^2 + 1}$ Apply the quotient property.

PRACTICE 2 Write each difference as a single logarithm.

a. $\log_5 18 - \log_5 6$ **b.** $\log_6 x - \log_6 3$ **c.** $\log_4(x^2 + 1) - \log_4(x^2 + 3)$

OBJECTIVE 3 ▶ **Using the power property.** The third and final property we introduce is the **power property of logarithms.**

> **Power Property of Logarithms**
> If x and b are positive real numbers, $b \neq 1$, and r is a real number, then
> $$\log_b x^r = r \log_b x$$

EXAMPLE 3 Use the power property to rewrite each expression.

a. $\log_5 x^3$ **b.** $\log_4 \sqrt{2}$

Solution

a. $\log_5 x^3 = 3 \log_5 x$ **b.** $\log_4 \sqrt{2} = \log_4 2^{1/2} = \frac{1}{2} \log_4 2$

PRACTICE 3 Use the power property to rewrite each expression.

a. $\log_7 x^8$ **b.** $\log_5 \sqrt[4]{7}$

Answer to Concept Check: a

OBJECTIVE 4 ▶ **Using the properties together.** Many times we must use more than one property of logarithms to simplify a logarithmic expression.

EXAMPLE 4 Write as a single logarithm.

a. $2 \log_5 3 + 3 \log_5 2$ **b.** $3 \log_9 x - \log_9(x + 1)$ **c.** $\log_4 25 + \log_4 3 - \log_4 5$

Solution In each case, all terms have a common logarithmic base.

a. $2 \log_5 3 + 3 \log_5 2 = \log_5 3^2 + \log_5 2^3$ Apply the power property.
$\qquad = \log_5 9 + \log_5 8$
$\qquad = \log_5(9 \cdot 8)$ Apply the product property.
$\qquad = \log_5 72$

b. $3 \log_9 x - \log_9(x + 1) = \log_9 x^3 - \log_9(x + 1)$ Apply the power property.
$\qquad = \log_9 \dfrac{x^3}{x + 1}$ Apply the quotient property.

c. Use both the product and quotient properties.

$\log_4 25 + \log_4 3 - \log_4 5 = \log_4(25 \cdot 3) - \log_4 5$ Apply the product property.
$\qquad = \log_4 75 - \log_4 5$ Simplify.
$\qquad = \log_4 \dfrac{75}{5}$ Apply the quotient property.
$\qquad = \log_4 15$ Simplify.

PRACTICE 4 Write as a single logarithm.

a. $2 \log_5 4 + 5 \log_5 2$ **b.** $2 \log_8 x - \log_8(x + 3)$ **c.** $\log_7 12 + \log_7 5 - \log_7 4$

EXAMPLE 5 Write each expression as sums or differences of multiples of logarithms.

a. $\log_3 \dfrac{5 \cdot 7}{4}$ **b.** $\log_2 \dfrac{x^5}{y^2}$

Solution

a. $\log_3 \dfrac{5 \cdot 7}{4} = \log_3(5 \cdot 7) - \log_3 4$ Apply the quotient property.
$\qquad = \log_3 5 + \log_3 7 - \log_3 4$ Apply the product property.

b. $\log_2 \dfrac{x^5}{y^2} = \log_2(x^5) - \log_2(y^2)$ Apply the quotient property.
$\qquad = 5 \log_2 x - 2 \log_2 y$ Apply the power property.

PRACTICE 5 Write each expression as sums or differences of multiples of logarithms.

a. $\log_5 \dfrac{4 \cdot 3}{7}$ **b.** $\log_4 \dfrac{a^2}{b^5}$

▶ **Helpful Hint**
Notice that we are not able to simplify further a logarithmic expression such as $\log_5(2x - 1)$. None of the basic properties gives a way to write the logarithm of a difference in some equivalent form.

Concept Check ✓

What is wrong with the following?

$$\log_{10}(x^2 + 5) = \log_{10} x^2 + \log_{10} 5$$
$$= 2 \log_{10} x + \log_{10} 5$$

Use a numerical example to demonstrate that the result is incorrect.

EXAMPLE 6 If $\log_b 2 = 0.43$ and $\log_b 3 = 0.68$, use the properties of logarithms to evaluate.

a. $\log_b 6$ **b.** $\log_b 9$ **c.** $\log_b \sqrt{2}$

Solution

a. $\log_b 6 = \log_b(2 \cdot 3)$ Write 6 as $2 \cdot 3$.
$ = \log_b 2 + \log_b 3$ Apply the product property.
$ = 0.43 + 0.68$ Substitute given values.
$ = 1.11$ Simplify.

b. $\log_b 9 = \log_b 3^2$ Write 9 as 3^2.
$ = 2 \log_b 3$
$ = 2(0.68)$ Substitute 0.68 for $\log_b 3$.
$ = 1.36$ Simplify.

c. First, recall that $\sqrt{2} = 2^{1/2}$. Then

$\log_b \sqrt{2} = \log_b 2^{1/2}$ Write $\sqrt{2}$ as $2^{1/2}$.
$\phantom{\log_b \sqrt{2}} = \frac{1}{2} \log_b 2$ Apply the power property.
$\phantom{\log_b \sqrt{2}} = \frac{1}{2}(0.43)$ Substitute the given value.
$\phantom{\log_b \sqrt{2}} = 0.215$ Simplify.

PRACTICE 6 If $\log_b 5 = 0.83$ and $\log_b 3 = 0.56$, use the properties of logarithms to evaluate.

a. $\log_b 15$ **b.** $\log_b 25$ **c.** $\log_b \sqrt{3}$

A summary of the basic properties of logarithms that we have developed so far is given next.

Properties of Logarithms

If x, y, and b are positive real numbers, $b \neq 1$, and r is a real number, then

1. $\log_b 1 = 0$
2. $\log_b b^x = x$
3. $b^{\log_b x} = x$
4. $\log_b xy = \log_b x + \log_b y$ Product property.
5. $\log_b \frac{x}{y} = \log_b x - \log_b y$ Quotient property.
6. $\log_b x^r = r \log_b x$ Power property.

Answer to Concept Check:
The properties do not give any way to simplify the logarithm of a sum; answers may vary.

VOCABULARY & READINESS CHECK

Multiple Choice. *Select the correct choice.*

1. $\log_b 12 + \log_b 3 = \log_b$ ____
  a. 36 **b.** 15 **c.** 4 **d.** 9

2. $\log_b 12 - \log_b 3 = \log_b$ ____
  a. 36 **b.** 15 **c.** 4 **d.** 9

3. $7 \log_b 2 =$ _____
  a. $\log_b 14$ **b.** $\log_b 2^7$ **c.** $\log_b 7^2$ **d.** $(\log_b 2)^7$

4. $\log_b 1 =$ ____
  a. b **b.** 1 **c.** 0 **d.** no answer

5. $b^{\log_b x} =$ ____
  a. x **b.** b **c.** 1 **d.** 0

6. $\log_5 5^2 =$ ____
  a. 25 **b.** 2 **c.** 5^{5^2} **d.** 32

10.5 EXERCISE SET

Write each sum as a single logarithm. Assume that variables represent positive numbers. See Example 1.

1. $\log_5 2 + \log_5 7$
2. $\log_3 8 + \log_3 4$
3. $\log_4 9 + \log_4 x$
4. $\log_2 x + \log_2 y$
5. $\log_6 x + \log_6 (x+1)$
6. $\log_5 y^3 + \log_5 (y-7)$
7. $\log_{10} 5 + \log_{10} 2 + \log_{10} (x^2 + 2)$
8. $\log_6 3 + \log_6 (x+4) + \log_6 5$

Write each difference as a single logarithm. Assume that variables represent positive numbers. See Examples 2 and 4.

9. $\log_5 12 - \log_5 4$
10. $\log_7 20 - \log_7 4$
11. $\log_3 8 - \log_3 2$
12. $\log_5 12 - \log_5 3$
13. $\log_2 x - \log_2 y$
14. $\log_3 12 - \log_3 z$
15. $\log_2 (x^2 + 6) - \log_2 (x^2 + 1)$
16. $\log_7 (x+9) - \log_7 (x^2 + 10)$

Use the power property to rewrite each expression. See Example 3.

17. $\log_3 x^2$
18. $\log_2 x^5$
19. $\log_4 5^{-1}$
20. $\log_6 7^{-2}$
21. $\log_5 \sqrt{y}$
22. $\log_5 \sqrt[3]{x}$

MIXED PRACTICE

Write each as a single logarithm. Assume that variables represent positive numbers. See Example 4.

23. $\log_2 5 + \log_2 x^3$
24. $\log_5 2 + \log_5 y^2$
25. $3\log_4 2 + \log_4 6$
26. $2\log_3 5 + \log_3 2$
27. $3\log_5 x + 6\log_5 z$
28. $2\log_7 y + 6\log_7 z$
29. $\log_4 2 + \log_4 10 - \log_4 5$
30. $\log_6 18 + \log_6 2 - \log_6 9$
31. $\log_7 6 + \log_7 3 - \log_7 4$
32. $\log_8 5 + \log_8 15 - \log_8 20$
33. $\log_{10} x - \log_{10}(x+1) + \log_{10}(x^2 - 2)$
34. $\log_9(4x) - \log_9(x-3) + \log_9(x^3 + 1)$
35. $3\log_2 x + \frac{1}{2}\log_2 x - 2\log_2(x+1)$
36. $2\log_5 x + \frac{1}{3}\log_5 x - 3\log_5(x+5)$
37. $2\log_8 x - \frac{2}{3}\log_8 x + 4\log_8 x$
38. $5\log_6 x - \frac{3}{4}\log_6 x + 3\log_6 x$

MIXED PRACTICE

Write each expression as a sum or difference of logarithms. Assume that variables represent positive numbers. See Example 5.

39. $\log_3 \frac{4y}{5}$
40. $\log_7 \frac{5x}{4}$
41. $\log_4 \frac{2}{9z}$
42. $\log_9 \frac{7}{8y}$
43. $\log_2 \frac{x^3}{y}$
44. $\log_5 \frac{x}{y^4}$
45. $\log_b \sqrt{7x}$
46. $\log_b \sqrt{\frac{3}{y}}$
47. $\log_6 x^4 y^5$
48. $\log_2 y^3 z$
49. $\log_5 x^3(x+1)$
50. $\log_3 x^2(x-9)$
51. $\log_6 \frac{x^2}{x+3}$
52. $\log_3 \frac{(x+5)^2}{x}$

If $\log_b 3 = 0.5$ and $\log_b 5 = 0.7$, evaluate each expression. See Example 6.

53. $\log_b 15$
54. $\log_b 25$
55. $\log_b \frac{5}{3}$
56. $\log_b \frac{3}{5}$
57. $\log_b \sqrt{5}$
58. $\log_b \sqrt[4]{3}$

If $\log_b 2 = 0.43$ and $\log_b 3 = 0.68$, evaluate each expression. See Example 6.

59. $\log_b 8$
60. $\log_b 81$
61. $\log_b \frac{3}{9}$
62. $\log_b \frac{4}{32}$
63. $\log_b \sqrt{\frac{2}{3}}$
64. $\log_b \sqrt{\frac{3}{2}}$

REVIEW AND PREVIEW

65. Graph the functions $y = 10^x$ and $y = \log_{10} x$ on the same set of axes. See Section 10.4.

Evaluate each expression. See Section 10.4.

66. $\log_{10} 100$
67. $\log_{10} \frac{1}{10}$
68. $\log_7 7^2$
69. $\log_7 \sqrt{7}$

CONCEPT EXTENSIONS

Multiple Choice. *Solve. See the Concept Checks in this section.*

70. Which of the following is the correct way to rewrite $\log_3 \frac{14}{11}$?
    a. $\frac{\log_3 14}{\log_3 11}$
    b. $\log_3 14 - \log_3 11$
    c. $\log_3(14 - 11)$
    d. $\log_3 154$

71. Which of the following is the correct way to rewrite $\log_9 \frac{21}{3}$?
    a. $\log_9 7$
    b. $\log_9(21 - 3)$
    c. $\frac{\log_9 21}{\log_9 3}$
    d. $\log_9 21 - \log_9 3$

True or False. *Answer the following true or false. Study your logarithm properties carefully before answering.*

72. $\log_2 x^3 = 3 \log_2 x$

73. $\log_3(x + y) = \log_3 x + \log_3 y$

74. $\dfrac{\log_7 10}{\log_7 5} = \log_7 2$

75. $\log_7 \dfrac{14}{8} = \log_7 14 - \log_7 8$

76. $\dfrac{\log_7 x}{\log_7 y} = (\log_7 x) - (\log_7 y)$

77. $(\log_3 6) \cdot (\log_3 4) = \log_3 24$

78. It is true that $\log 8 = \log(8 \cdot 1) = \log 8 + \log 1$. Explain how $\log 8$ can equal $\log 8 + \log 1$.

INTEGRATED REVIEW — FUNCTIONS AND PROPERTIES OF LOGARITHMS
Sections 10.1–10.5

If $f(x) = x - 6$ and $g(x) = x^2 + 1$, find each value.

1. $(f + g)(x)$
2. $(f - g)(x)$
3. $(f \cdot g)(x)$
4. $\left(\dfrac{f}{g}\right)(x)$

If $f(x) = \sqrt{x}$ and $g(x) = 3x - 1$, find each function.

5. $(f \circ g)(x)$
6. $(g \circ f)(x)$

Determine whether each is a one-to-one function. If it is, find its inverse.

7. $f = \{(-2, 6), (4, 8), (2, -6), (3, 3)\}$
8. $g = \{(4, 2), (-1, 3), (5, 3), (7, 1)\}$

Determine whether the graph of each function is one-to-one.

9.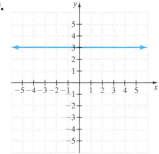

10.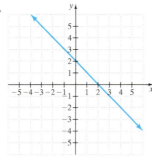

11.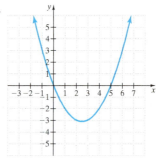

Each function listed is one-to-one. Find the inverse of each function.

12. $f(x) = 3x$
13. $f(x) = x + 4$
14. $f(x) = 5x - 1$
15. $f(x) = 3x + 2$

Graph each function.

16. $y = \left(\dfrac{1}{2}\right)^x$
17. $y = 2^x + 1$
18. $y = \log_3 x$
19. $y = \log_{1/3} x$

Solve.

20. $2^x = 8$
21. $9 = 3^{x-5}$
22. $4^{x-1} = 8^{x+2}$
23. $25^x = 125^{x-1}$
24. $\log_4 16 = x$
25. $\log_{49} 7 = x$
26. $\log_2 x = 5$
27. $\log_x 64 = 3$
28. $\log_x \dfrac{1}{125} = -3$
29. $\log_3 x = -2$

Write each as a single logarithm.

30. $5 \log_2 x$ **31.** $x \log_2 5$ **32.** $3 \log_5 x - 5 \log_5 y$ **33.** $9 \log_5 x + 3 \log_5 y$

34. $\log_2 x + \log_2(x - 3) - \log_2(x^2 + 4)$ **35.** $\log_3 y - \log_3(y + 2) + \log_3(y^3 + 11)$

Write each expression as sums or differences of multiples of logarithms.

36. $\log_7 \dfrac{9x^2}{y}$ **37.** $\log_6 \dfrac{5y}{z^2}$

10.6 COMMON LOGARITHMS, NATURAL LOGARITHMS, AND CHANGE OF BASE

OBJECTIVES

1. Identify common logarithms and approximate them by calculator.
2. Evaluate common logarithms of powers of 10.
3. Identify natural logarithms and approximate them by calculator.
4. Evaluate natural logarithms of powers of e.
5. Use the change of base formula.

In this section we look closely at two particular logarithmic bases. These two logarithmic bases are used so frequently that logarithms to their bases are given special names. **Common logarithms** are logarithms to base 10. **Natural logarithms** are logarithms to base e, which we introduce in this section. The work in this section is based on the use of the calculator, which has both the common "log" $\boxed{\text{LOG}}$ and the natural "log" $\boxed{\text{LN}}$ keys.

OBJECTIVE 1 ▶ Approximating common logarithms. Logarithms to base 10, common logarithms, are used frequently because our number system is a base 10 decimal system. The notation $\log x$ means the same as $\log_{10} x$.

> **Common Logarithms**
>
> $\log x$ means $\log_{10} x$

EXAMPLE 1   Use a calculator to approximate $\log 7$ to four decimal places.

Solution   Press the following sequence of keys.

$\boxed{7}\ \boxed{\text{LOG}}$ or $\boxed{\text{LOG}}\ \boxed{7}\ \boxed{\text{ENTER}}$

To four decimal places,

$$\log 7 \approx 0.8451$$

PRACTICE 1   Use a calculator to approximate $\log 15$ to four decimal places.

OBJECTIVE 2 ▶ Evaluating common logarithms of powers of 10. To evaluate the common log of a power of 10, a calculator is not needed. According to the property of logarithms,

$$\log_b b^x = x$$

It follows that if b is replaced with 10, we have

$$\log 10^x = x$$

> ▶ **Helpful Hint**
> Remember that $\log 10^x$ means $\log_{10} 10^x = x$.

EXAMPLE 2 Find the exact value of each logarithm.

a. $\log 10$ **b.** $\log 1000$ **c.** $\log \dfrac{1}{10}$ **d.** $\log \sqrt{10}$

Solution

a. $\log 10 = \log 10^1 = 1$ **b.** $\log 1000 = \log 10^3 = 3$

c. $\log \dfrac{1}{10} = \log 10^{-1} = -1$ **d.** $\log \sqrt{10} = \log 10^{1/2} = \dfrac{1}{2}$

PRACTICE 2 Find the exact value of each logarithm.

a. $\log \dfrac{1}{100}$ **b.** $\log 100{,}000$ **c.** $\log \sqrt[5]{10}$ **d.** $\log 0.001$

As we will soon see, equations containing common logs are useful models of many natural phenomena.

EXAMPLE 3 Solve $\log x = 1.2$ for x. Give an exact solution, and then approximate the solution to four decimal places.

Solution Remember that the base of a common log is understood to be 10.

$$\log x = 1.2$$
$$10^{1.2} = x \quad \text{Write with exponential notation.}$$

> **Helpful Hint**
> The understood base is 10.

The exact solution is $10^{1.2}$. To four decimal places, $x \approx 15.8489$.

PRACTICE 3 Solve $\log x = 3.4$ for x. Give an exact solution, and then approximate the solution to four decimal places.

The Richter scale measures the intensity, or magnitude, of an earthquake. The formula for the magnitude R of an earthquake is $R = \log\left(\dfrac{a}{T}\right) + B$, where a is the amplitude in micrometers of the vertical motion of the ground at the recording station, T is the number of seconds between successive seismic waves, and B is an adjustment factor that takes into account the weakening of the seismic wave as the distance increases from the epicenter of the earthquake.

EXAMPLE 4 Finding the Magnitude of an Earthquake

Find an earthquake's magnitude on the Richter scale if a recording station measures an amplitude of 300 micrometers and 2.5 seconds between waves. Assume that B is 4.2. Approximate the solution to the nearest tenth.

Solution Substitute the known values into the formula for earthquake intensity.

$$R = \log\left(\dfrac{a}{T}\right) + B \quad \text{Richter scale formula}$$
$$= \log\left(\dfrac{300}{2.5}\right) + 4.2 \quad \text{Let } a = 300, T = 2.5, \text{ and } B = 4.2.$$
$$= \log(120) + 4.2$$
$$\approx 2.1 + 4.2 \quad \text{Approximate } \log 120 \text{ by } 2.1.$$
$$= 6.3$$

This earthquake had a magnitude of 6.3 on the Richter scale.

Section 10.6 Common Logarithms, Natural Logarithms, and Change of Base

PRACTICE 4 Find an earthquake's magnitude on the Richter scale if a recording station measures an amplitude of 450 micrometers and 4.2 seconds between waves with $B = 3.6$. Approximate the solution to the nearest tenth.

OBJECTIVE 3 ▶ **Approximating natural logarithms.** **Natural logarithms** are also frequently used, especially to describe natural events; hence the label "natural logarithm." Natural logarithms are logarithms to the base e, which is a constant approximately equal to 2.7183. The number e is an irrational number, as is π. The notation $\log_e x$ is usually abbreviated to $\ln x$. (The abbreviation ln is read "el en.")

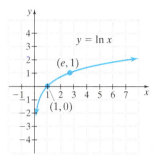

Natural Logarithms

$\ln x$ means $\log_e x$

The graph of $y = \ln x$ is shown to the left.

EXAMPLE 5 Use a calculator to approximate $\ln 8$ to four decimal places.

Solution Press the following sequence of keys.

$$\boxed{8}\ \boxed{\text{LN}} \quad \text{or} \quad \boxed{\text{LN}}\ \boxed{8}\ \boxed{\text{ENTER}}$$

To four decimal places,

$$\ln 8 \approx 2.0794$$

PRACTICE 5 Use a calculator to approximate $\ln 13$ to four decimal places.

OBJECTIVE 4 ▶ **Evaluating natural logarithms of powers of e.** As a result of the property $\log_b b^x = x$, we know that $\log_e e^x = x$, or **ln e^x = x.**
Since $\ln e^x = x$, then $\ln e^5 = 5$, $\ln e^{22} = 22$ and so on. Also,

$$\ln e^1 = 1 \text{ or simply } \ln e = 1.$$

That is why the graph of $y = \ln x$ shown on the previous page passes through $(e, 1)$.
If $x = e$, then $y = \ln e = 1$, thus the ordered pair is $(e, 1)$.

EXAMPLE 6 Find the exact value of each natural logarithm.

a. $\ln e^3$ **b.** $\ln \sqrt[5]{e}$

Solution

a. $\ln e^3 = 3$ **b.** $\ln \sqrt[5]{e} = \ln e^{1/5} = \dfrac{1}{5}$

PRACTICE 6 Find the exact value of each natural logarithm.

a. $\ln e^4$ **b.** $\ln \sqrt[3]{e}$

EXAMPLE 7 Solve $\ln 3x = 5$. Give an exact solution, and then approximate the solution to four decimal places.

Solution Remember that the base of a natural logarithm is understood to be e.

$$\ln 3x = 5$$

$$e^5 = 3x \quad \text{Write with exponential notation.}$$

$$\dfrac{e^5}{3} = x \quad \text{Solve for } x.$$

▶ **Helpful Hint**
The understood base is e.

The exact solution is $\frac{e^5}{3}$. To four decimal places,
$$x \approx 49.4711.$$

PRACTICE 7 Solve $\ln 5x = 8$. Give an exact solution, and then approximate the solution to four decimal places.

Recall from Section 10.3 the formula $A = P\left(1 + \frac{r}{n}\right)^{nt}$ for compound interest, where n represents the number of compoundings per year. When interest is compounded continuously, the formula $A = Pe^{rt}$ is used, where r is the annual interest rate and interest is compounded continuously for t years.

EXAMPLE 8 Finding Final Loan Payment

Find the amount owed at the end of 5 years if $1600 is loaned at a rate of 9% compounded continuously.

Solution Use the formula $A = Pe^{rt}$, where

$P = \$1600$ (the size of the loan)
$r = 9\% = 0.09$ (the rate of interest)
$t = 5$ (the 5-year duration of the loan)
$A = Pe^{rt}$
$= 1600e^{0.09(5)}$ Substitute in known values.
$= 1600e^{0.45}$

Now we can use a calculator to approximate the solution.
$$A \approx 2509.30$$
The total amount of money owed is $2509.30.

PRACTICE 8 Find the amount owed at the end of 4 years if $2400 is borrowed at a rate of 6% compounded continuously.

OBJECTIVE 5 ▶ Using the change of base formula. Calculators are handy tools for approximating natural and common logarithms. Unfortunately, some calculators cannot be used to approximate logarithms to bases other than e or 10—at least not directly. In such cases, we use the change of base formula.

Change of Base
If a, b, and c are positive real numbers and neither b nor c is 1, then
$$\log_b a = \frac{\log_c a}{\log_c b}$$

EXAMPLE 9 Approximate $\log_5 3$ to four decimal places.

Solution Use the change of base property to write $\log_5 3$ as a quotient of logarithms to base 10.

$\log_5 3 = \frac{\log 3}{\log 5}$ Use the change of base property. In the change of base property, we let $a = 3$, $b = 5$, and $c = 10$.

$\approx \frac{0.4771213}{0.69897}$ Approximate logarithms by calculator.

≈ 0.6826062 Simplify by calculator.

To four decimal places, $\log_5 3 \approx 0.6826$.

PRACTICE 9 Approximate $\log_8 5$ to four decimal places.

Answer to Concept Check:
$f(x) = \dfrac{\log x}{\log 5}$

Concept Check ✓
If a graphing calculator cannot directly evaluate logarithms to base 5, describe how you could use the graphing calculator to graph the function $f(x) = \log_5 x$.

VOCABULARY & READINESS CHECK

Multiple Choice. *Use the choices to fill in each blank.*

1. The base of log 7 is ___.
   a. e b. 7   c. 10   d. no answer

2. The base of ln 7 is ___.
   a. e b. 7   c. 10   d. no answer

3. $\log_{10} 10^7 = $ ___.
   a. e b. 7   c. 10   d. no answer

4. $\log_7 1 = $ ___.
   a. e b. 7   c. 10   d. 0

5. $\log_e e^5 = $ ___.
   a. e b. 5   c. 0   d. 1

6. Study exercise 5 to the left. Then answer: $\ln e^5 = $ ___.
   a. e b. 5   c. 0   d. 1

7. $\log_2 7 = $ _____ (There may be more than one answer.)

   a. $\dfrac{\log 7}{\log 2}$ b. $\dfrac{\ln 7}{\ln 2}$ c. $\dfrac{\log 2}{\log 7}$ d. $\log \dfrac{7}{2}$

10.6 EXERCISE SET

MIXED PRACTICE

Use a calculator to approximate each logarithm to four decimal places. See Examples 1 and 5.

1. log 8
2. log 6
3. log 2.31
4. log 4.86
5. ln 2
6. ln 3
7. ln 0.0716
8. ln 0.0032
9. log 12.6
10. log 25.9
11. ln 5
12. ln 7
13. log 41.5
14. ln 41.5
15. Use a calculator and try to approximate log 0. Describe what happens and explain why.
16. Use a calculator and try to approximate ln 0. Describe what happens and explain why.

MIXED PRACTICE

Find the exact value. See Examples 2 and 6.

17. log 100
18. log 10,000
19. $\log\left(\dfrac{1}{1000}\right)$
20. $\log\left(\dfrac{1}{100}\right)$
21. $\ln e^2$
22. $\ln e^4$
23. $\ln \sqrt[4]{e}$
24. $\ln \sqrt[5]{e}$
25. $\log 10^3$
26. $\log 10^7$
27. $\ln e^{-7}$
28. $\ln e^{-5}$
29. log 0.0001
30. log 0.001
31. $\ln \sqrt{e}$
32. $\log \sqrt{10}$

Solve each equation for x. Give an exact solution and a four-decimal-place approximation. See Examples 3 and 7.

33. $\ln 2x = 7$
34. $\ln 5x = 9$
35. $\log x = 1.3$
36. $\log x = 2.1$
37. $\log 2x = 1.1$
38. $\log 3x = 1.3$
39. $\ln x = 1.4$
40. $\ln x = 2.1$
41. $\ln(3x - 4) = 2.3$
42. $\ln(2x + 5) = 3.4$
43. $\log x = 2.3$
44. $\log x = 3.1$
45. $\ln x = -2.3$
46. $\ln x = -3.7$
47. $\log(2x + 1) = -0.5$
48. $\log(3x - 2) = -0.8$
49. $\ln 4x = 0.18$
50. $\ln 3x = 0.76$

Approximate each logarithm to four decimal places. See Example 9.

51. $\log_2 3$ **52.** $\log_3 2$

53. $\log_{1/2} 5$ **54.** $\log_{1/3} 2$

55. $\log_4 9$ **56.** $\log_9 4$

57. $\log_3 \frac{1}{6}$ **58.** $\log_6 \frac{2}{3}$

59. $\log_8 6$ **60.** $\log_6 8$

Use the formula $R = \log\left(\dfrac{a}{T}\right) + B$ to find the intensity R on the Richter scale of the earthquakes that fit the descriptions given. Round answers to one decimal place. See Example 4.

61. Amplitude a is 200 micrometers, time T between waves is 1.6 seconds, and B is 2.1.

62. Amplitude a is 150 micrometers, time T between waves is 3.6 seconds, and B is 1.9.

63. Amplitude a is 400 micrometers, time T between waves is 2.6 seconds, and B is 3.1.

64. Amplitude a is 450 micrometers, time T between waves is 4.2 seconds, and B is 2.7.

Use the formula $A = Pe^{rt}$ to solve. See Example 8.

65. Find how much money Dana Jones has after 12 years if $1400 is invested at 8% interest compounded continuously.

66. Determine the size of an account in which $3500 earns 6% interest compounded continuously for 1 year.

67. Find the amount of money Barbara Mack owes at the end of 4 years if 6% interest is compounded continuously on her $2000 debt.

68. Find the amount of money for which a $2500 certificate of deposit is redeemable if it has been paying 10% interest compounded continuously for 3 years.

REVIEW AND PREVIEW

Solve each equation for x. See Sections 2.1, 2.3, and 6.8.

69. $6x - 3(2 - 5x) = 6$ **70.** $2x + 3 = 5 - 2(3x - 1)$

71. $2x + 3y = 6x$ **72.** $4x - 8y = 10x$

73. $x^2 + 7x = -6$ **74.** $x^2 + 4x = 12$

Solve each system of equations. See Section 4.1.

75. $\begin{cases} x + 2y = -4 \\ 3x - y = 9 \end{cases}$ **76.** $\begin{cases} 5x + y = 5 \\ -3x - 2y = -10 \end{cases}$

CONCEPT EXTENSIONS

77. Without using a calculator, explain which of log 50 or ln 50 must be larger and why.

78. Without using a calculator, explain which of $\log 50^{-1}$ or $\ln 50^{-1}$ must be larger and why.

Graph each function by finding ordered pair solutions, plotting the solutions, and then drawing a smooth curve through the plotted points.

79. $f(x) = e^x$ **80.** $f(x) = e^{2x}$

81. $f(x) = e^{-3x}$ **82.** $f(x) = e^{-x}$

83. $f(x) = e^x + 2$ **84.** $f(x) = e^x - 3$

85. $f(x) = e^{x-1}$ **86.** $f(x) = e^{x+4}$

87. $f(x) = 3e^x$ **88.** $f(x) = -2e^x$

89. $f(x) = \ln x$ **90.** $f(x) = \log x$

91. $f(x) = -2 \log x$ **92.** $f(x) = 3 \ln x$

93. $f(x) = \log(x + 2)$ **94.** $f(x) = \log(x - 2)$

95. $f(x) = \ln x - 3$ **96.** $f(x) = \ln x + 3$

97. Graph $f(x) = e^x$ (Exercise 79), $f(x) = e^x + 2$ (Exercise 83), and $f(x) = e^x - 3$ (Exercise 84) on the same screen. Discuss any trends shown on the graphs.

98. Graph $f(x) = \ln x$ (Exercise 89), $f(x) = \ln x - 3$ (Exercise 95), and $f(x) = \ln x + 3$ (Exercise 96). Discuss any trends shown on the graphs.

10.7 EXPONENTIAL AND LOGARITHMIC EQUATIONS AND APPLICATIONS

OBJECTIVES

1. Solve exponential equations.
2. Solve logarithmic equations.
3. Solve problems that can be modeled by exponential and logarithmic equations.

OBJECTIVE 1 ▶ Solving exponential equations. In Section 10.3 we solved exponential equations such as $2^x = 16$ by writing 16 as a power of 2 and applying the uniqueness of b^x.

$$2^x = 16$$
$$2^x = 2^4 \quad \text{Write 16 as } 2^4.$$
$$x = 4 \quad \text{Use the uniqueness of } b^x.$$

Solving the equation in this manner is possible since 16 is a power of 2. If solving an equation such as $2^x = a\ number$, where the number is not a power of 2, we use logarithms. For example, to solve an equation such as $3^x = 7$, we use the fact that $f(x) = \log_b x$ is a one-to-one function. Another way of stating this fact is as a property of equality.

Section 10.7 Exponential and Logarithmic Equations and Applications

> **Logarithm Property of Equality**
> Let a, b, and c be real numbers such that $\log_b a$ and $\log_b c$ are real numbers and b is not 1. Then
> $$\log_b a = \log_b c \text{ is equivalent to } a = c$$

EXAMPLE 1   Solve: $3^x = 7$.

Solution   To solve, we use the logarithm property of equality and take the logarithm of both sides. For this example, we use the common logarithm.

$$3^x = 7$$
$$\log 3^x = \log 7 \quad \text{Take the common log of both sides.}$$
$$x \log 3 = \log 7 \quad \text{Apply the power property of logarithms.}$$
$$x = \frac{\log 7}{\log 3} \quad \text{Divide both sides by log 3.}$$

The exact solution is $\frac{\log 7}{\log 3}$. If a decimal approximation is preferred,

$$\frac{\log 7}{\log 3} \approx \frac{0.845098}{0.4771213} \approx 1.7712 \text{ to four decimal places.}$$

The solution is $\frac{\log 7}{\log 3}$, or *approximately* 1.7712.

PRACTICE 1   Solve: $5^x = 9$.

OBJECTIVE 2 ▶ **Solving logarithmic equations.** By applying the appropriate properties of logarithms, we can solve a broad variety of logarithmic equations.

EXAMPLE 2   Solve: $\log_4(x - 2) = 2$.

Solution   Notice that $x - 2$ must be positive, so x must be greater than 2. With this in mind, we first write the equation with exponential notation.

$$\log_4(x - 2) = 2$$
$$4^2 = x - 2$$
$$16 = x - 2$$
$$18 = x \quad \text{Add 2 to both sides.}$$

Check: To check, we replace x with 18 in the original equation.

$$\log_4(x - 2) = 2$$
$$\log_4(18 - 2) \stackrel{?}{=} 2 \quad \text{Let } x = 18.$$
$$\log_4 16 \stackrel{?}{=} 2$$
$$4^2 = 16 \quad \text{True}$$

The solution is 18.

PRACTICE 2   Solve: $\log_2(x - 1) = 5$.

EXAMPLE 3 Solve: $\log_2 x + \log_2(x - 1) = 1$.

Solution Notice that $x - 1$ must be positive, so x must be greater than 1. We use the product property on the left side of the equation.

$$\log_2 x + \log_2(x - 1) = 1$$
$$\log_2 x(x - 1) = 1 \quad \text{Apply the product property.}$$
$$\log_2(x^2 - x) = 1$$

Next we write the equation with exponential notation and solve for x.

$$2^1 = x^2 - x$$
$$0 = x^2 - x - 2 \quad \text{Subtract 2 from both sides.}$$
$$0 = (x - 2)(x + 1) \quad \text{Factor.}$$
$$0 = x - 2 \quad \text{or} \quad 0 = x + 1 \quad \text{Set each factor equal to 0.}$$
$$2 = x \quad \quad -1 = x$$

Recall that -1 cannot be a solution because x must be greater than 1. If we forgot this, we would still reject -1 after checking. To see this, we replace x with -1 in the original equation.

$$\log_2 x + \log_2(x - 1) = 1$$
$$\log_2(-1) + \log_2(-1 - 1) \stackrel{?}{=} 1 \quad \text{Let } x = -1.$$

Because the logarithm of a negative number is undefined, -1 is rejected. Check to see that the solution is 2.

PRACTICE 3 Solve: $\log_5 x + \log_5(x + 4) = 1$.

EXAMPLE 4 Solve: $\log(x + 2) - \log x = 2$.

We use the quotient property of logarithms on the left side of the equation.

Solution $\log(x + 2) - \log x = 2$

$$\log \frac{x + 2}{x} = 2 \quad \text{Apply the quotient property.}$$
$$10^2 = \frac{x + 2}{x} \quad \text{Write using exponential notation.}$$
$$100 = \frac{x + 2}{x} \quad \text{Simplify.}$$
$$100x = x + 2 \quad \text{Multiply both sides by } x.$$
$$99x = 2 \quad \text{Subtract } x \text{ from both sides.}$$
$$x = \frac{2}{99} \quad \text{Divide both sides by 99.}$$

Verify that the solution is $\frac{2}{99}$.

PRACTICE 4 Solve: $\log(x + 3) - \log x = 1$.

OBJECTIVE 3 ▶ **Solving problems modeled by exponential and logarithmic equations.**
Logarithmic and exponential functions are used in a variety of scientific, technical, and business settings. A few examples follow.

Section 10.7 Exponential and Logarithmic Equations and Applications   611

EXAMPLE 5   Estimating Population Size

The population size y of a community of lemmings varies according to the relationship $y = y_0 e^{0.15t}$. In this formula, t is time in months, and y_0 is the initial population at time 0. Estimate the population after 6 months if there were originally 5000 lemmings.

Solution   We substitute 5000 for y_0 and 6 for t.

$$y = y_0 e^{0.15t}$$
$$= 5000 e^{0.15(6)} \quad \text{Let } t = 6 \text{ and } y_0 = 5000.$$
$$= 5000 e^{0.9} \quad \text{Multiply.}$$

Using a calculator, we find that $y \approx 12{,}298.016$. In 6 months the population will be approximately 12,300 lemmings.   □

PRACTICE 5   The population size y of a group of rabbits varies according to the relationship $y = y_0 e^{0.916t}$. In this formula, t is time in years and y_0 is the initial population at time $t = 0$. Estimate the population in three years if there were originally 60 rabbits.

EXAMPLE 6   Doubling an Investment

How long does it take an investment of $2000 to double if it is invested at 5% interest compounded quarterly? The necessary formula is $A = P\left(1 + \dfrac{r}{n}\right)^{nt}$, where A is the accrued (or owed) amount, P is the principal invested, r is the annual rate of interest, n is the number of compounding periods per year, and t is the number of years.

Solution   We are given that $P = \$2000$ and $r = 5\% = 0.05$. Compounding quarterly means 4 times a year, so $n = 4$. The investment is to double, so A must be $4000. Substitute these values and solve for t.

$$A = P\left(1 + \frac{r}{n}\right)^{nt}$$
$$4000 = 2000\left(1 + \frac{0.05}{4}\right)^{4t} \quad \text{Substitute in known values.}$$
$$4000 = 2000(1.0125)^{4t} \quad \text{Simplify } 1 + \frac{0.05}{4}.$$
$$2 = (1.0125)^{4t} \quad \text{Divide both sides by 2000.}$$
$$\log 2 = \log 1.0125^{4t} \quad \text{Take the logarithm of both sides.}$$
$$\log 2 = 4t(\log 1.0125) \quad \text{Apply the power property.}$$
$$\frac{\log 2}{4 \log 1.0125} = t \quad \text{Divide both sides by } 4 \log 1.0125.$$
$$13.949408 \approx t \quad \text{Approximate by calculator.}$$

Thus, it takes nearly 14 years for the money to double in value.   □

PRACTICE 6   How long does it take for an investment of $3000 to double if it is invested at 7% interest compounded monthly? Round to the nearest whole year.

Graphing Calculator Explorations

Use a graphing calculator to find how long it takes an investment of $1500 to triple if it is invested at 8% interest compounded monthly.

First, let $P = \$1500$, $r = 0.08$, and $n = 12$ (for 12 months) in the formula

$$A = P\left(1 + \frac{r}{n}\right)^{nt}$$

Notice that when the investment has tripled, the accrued amount A is $4500. Thus,

$$4500 = 1500\left(1 + \frac{0.08}{12}\right)^{12t}$$

Determine an appropriate viewing window and enter and graph the equations

$$Y_1 = 1500\left(1 + \frac{0.08}{12}\right)^{12x}$$

and

$$Y_2 = 4500$$

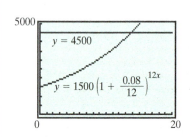

The point of intersection of the two curves is the solution. The x-coordinate tells how long it takes for the investment to triple.

Use a TRACE feature or an INTERSECT feature to approximate the coordinates of the point of intersection of the two curves. It takes approximately 13.78 years, or 13 years and 9 months, for the investment to triple in value to $4500.

Use this graphical solution method to solve each problem. Round each answer to the nearest hundredth.

1. Find how long it takes an investment of $5000 to grow to $6000 if it is invested at 5% interest compounded quarterly.

2. Find how long it takes an investment of $1000 to double if it is invested at 4.5% interest compounded daily. (Use 365 days in a year.)

3. Find how long it takes an investment of $10,000 to quadruple if it is invested at 6% interest compounded monthly.

4. Find how long it takes $500 to grow to $800 if it is invested at 4% interest compounded semiannually.

10.7 EXERCISE SET

Solve each equation. Give an exact solution, and also approximate the solution to four decimal places. See Example 1.

1. $3^x = 6$
2. $4^x = 7$
3. $3^{2x} = 3.8$
4. $5^{3x} = 5.6$
5. $2^{x-3} = 5$
6. $8^{x-2} = 12$
7. $9^x = 5$
8. $3^x = 11$
9. $4^{x+7} = 3$
10. $6^{x+3} = 2$

MIXED PRACTICE

Solve each equation. See Examples 1 through 4.

11. $7^{3x-4} = 11$
12. $5^{2x-6} = 12$
13. $e^{6x} = 5$
14. $e^{2x} = 8$
15. $\log_2(x + 5) = 4$
16. $\log_6(x^2 - x) = 1$
17. $\log_3 x^2 = 4$
18. $\log_2 x^2 = 6$
19. $\log_4 2 + \log_4 x = 0$
20. $\log_3 5 + \log_3 x = 1$
21. $\log_2 6 - \log_2 x = 3$
22. $\log_4 10 - \log_4 x = 2$
23. $\log_4 x + \log_4(x + 6) = 2$
24. $\log_3 x + \log_3(x + 6) = 3$
25. $\log_5(x + 3) - \log_5 x = 2$
26. $\log_6(x + 2) - \log_6 x = 2$
27. $\log_3(x - 2) = 2$
28. $\log_2(x - 5) = 3$
29. $\log_4(x^2 - 3x) = 1$
30. $\log_8(x^2 - 2x) = 1$
31. $\ln 5 + \ln x = 0$
32. $\ln 3 + \ln(x - 1) = 0$
33. $3 \log x - \log x^2 = 2$
34. $2 \log x - \log x = 3$

35. $\log_2 x + \log_2(x + 5) = 1$
36. $\log_4 x + \log_4(x + 7) = 1$
37. $\log_4 x - \log_4(2x - 3) = 3$
38. $\log_2 x - \log_2(3x + 5) = 4$
39. $\log_2 x + \log_2(3x + 1) = 1$
40. $\log_3 x + \log_3(x - 8) = 2$

Solve. See Example 5.

41. The size of the wolf population at Isle Royale National Park increases at a rate of 4.3% per year. If the size of the current population is 83 wolves, find how many there should be in 5 years. Use $y = y_0 e^{0.043t}$ and round to the nearest whole.

42. The number of victims of a flu epidemic is increasing at a rate of 7.5% per week. If 20,000 persons are currently infected, find in how many days we can expect 45,000 to have the flu. Use $y = y_0 e^{0.075t}$ and round to the nearest whole. (*Hint:* Don't forget to convert your answer to days.)

43. The size of the population of Belize is increasing at a rate of 2.3% per year. If 294,380 people lived in Belize in 2007, find how many inhabitants there will be by 2015. Round to the nearest thousand. Use $y = y_0 e^{0.023t}$. (*Source: CIA 2007 World Factbook*)

44. In 2007, 1730 million people were citizens of India. Find how long it will take India's population to reach a size of 2000 million (that is, 2 billion) if the population size is growing at a rate of 1.6% per year. Use $y = y_0 e^{0.016t}$ and round to the nearest tenth. (*Source: U.S. Bureau of the Census, International Data Base*)

45. In 2007, Germany had a population of 82,400 thousand. At that time, Germany's population was declining at a rate of 0.033% per year. If this continues, how long will it take Germany's population to reach 82,000 thousand? Use $y = y_0 e^{-0.00033t}$ and round to the nearest tenth. (*Source: CIA 2007 World Factbook*)

46. The population of the United States has been increasing at a rate of 0.894% per year. If there were 301,140,000 people living in the United States in 2007, how many inhabitants will there be by 2020? Use $y = y_0 e^{0.00894t}$ and round to the nearest ten-thousand. (*Source: CIA 2007 World Factbook*)

Use the formula $A = P\left(1 + \dfrac{r}{n}\right)^{nt}$ to solve these compound interest problems. Round to the nearest tenth. See Example 6.

47. Find how long it takes $600 to double if it is invested at 7% interest compounded monthly.

48. Find how long it takes $600 to double if it is invested at 12% interest compounded monthly.

49. Find how long it takes a $1200 investment to earn $200 interest if it is invested at 9% interest compounded quarterly.

614 CHAPTER 10 Exponential and Logarithmic Functions

50. Find how long it takes a $1500 investment to earn $200 interest if it is invested at 10% compounded semiannually.

51. Find how long it takes $1000 to double if it is invested at 8% interest compounded semiannually.

52. Find how long it takes $1000 to double if it is invested at 8% interest compounded monthly.

The formula $w = 0.00185h^{2.67}$ is used to estimate the normal weight w of a boy h inches tall. Use this formula to solve the height-weight problems. Round to the nearest tenth.

53. Find the expected weight of a boy who is 35 inches tall.

54. Find the expected weight of a boy who is 43 inches tall.

55. Find the expected height of a boy who weighs 85 pounds.

56. Find the expected height of a boy who weighs 140 pounds.

The formula $P = 14.7e^{-0.21x}$ gives the average atmospheric pressure P, in pounds per square inch, at an altitude x, in miles above sea level. Use this formula to solve these pressure problems. Round answers to the nearest tenth.

57. Find the average atmospheric pressure of Denver, which is 1 mile above sea level.

58. Find the average atmospheric pressure of Pikes Peak, which is 2.7 miles above sea level.

59. Find the elevation of a Delta jet if the atmospheric pressure outside the jet is 7.5 lb/in.^{2}.

60. Find the elevation of a remote Himalayan peak if the atmospheric pressure atop the peak is 6.5 lb/in.^{2}.

Psychologists call the graph of the formula $t = \dfrac{1}{c}\ln\left(\dfrac{A}{A-N}\right)$ the learning curve, since the formula relates time t passed, in weeks, to a measure N of learning achieved, to a measure A of maximum learning possible, and to a measure c of an individual's learning style. Round to the nearest week.

61. Norman is learning to type. If he wants to type at a rate of 50 words per minute (N is 50) and his expected maximum rate is 75 words per minute (A is 75), find how many weeks it should take him to achieve his goal. Assume that c is 0.09.

62. An experiment with teaching chimpanzees sign language shows that a typical chimp can master a maximum of 65 signs. Find how many weeks it should take a chimpanzee to master 30 signs if c is 0.03.

63. Janine is working on her dictation skills. She wants to take dictation at a rate of 150 words per minute and believes that the maximum rate she can hope for is 210 words per minute. Find how many weeks it should take her to achieve the 150 words per minute level if c is 0.07.

64. A psychologist is measuring human capability to memorize nonsense syllables. Find how many weeks it should take a subject to learn 15 nonsense syllables if the maximum possible to learn is 24 syllables and c is 0.17.

REVIEW AND PREVIEW

If $x = -2$, $y = 0$, and $z = 3$, find the value of each expression. See Section 1.3.

65. $\dfrac{x^2 - y + 2z}{3x}$

66. $\dfrac{x^3 - 2y + z}{2z}$

67. $\dfrac{3z - 4x + y}{x + 2z}$

68. $\dfrac{4y - 3x + z}{2x + y}$

Find the inverse function of each one-to-one function. See Section 10.2.

69. $f(x) = 5x + 2$

70. $f(x) = \dfrac{x - 3}{4}$

CONCEPT EXTENSIONS

The formula $y = y_0 e^{kt}$ gives the population size y of a population that experiences an annual rate of population growth k (given as a decimal). In this formula, t is time in years and y_0 is the initial population at time 0. Use this formula to solve Exercises 71 and 72.

71. In 2000, the population of Arizona was 5,130,632. By 2006, the population had grown to 6,123,106. Find the annual rate of population growth over this period. Round your answer to the nearest tenth of a percent. (*Source:* State of Arizona)

72. In 2000, the population of Nevada was 2,018,456. By 2006, the population had grown to 2,495,529. Find the annual rate of population growth over this period. Round your answer to the nearest tenth of a percent. (*Source:* State of Nevada)

73. When solving a logarithmic equation, explain why you must check possible solutions in the original equation.

74. Solve $5^x = 9$ by taking the common logarithm of both sides of the equation. Next, solve this equation by taking the natural logarithm of both sides. Compare your solutions. Are they the same? Why or why not?

Use a graphing calculator to solve each equation. For example, to solve Exercise 75, let $Y_1 = e^{0.3x}$ and $Y_2 = 8$, and graph the equations. The x-value of the point of intersection is the solution. Round all solutions to two decimal places.

75. $e^{0.3x} = 8$

76. $10^{0.5x} = 7$

77. $2\log(-5.6x + 1.3) + x + 1 = 0$

78. $\ln(1.3x - 2.1) + 3.5x - 5 = 0$

79. Check Exercise 11. Graph $7^{3x-4} - 11 = 0$

80. Check Exercise 12. Graph $5^{2x-6} - 12 = 0$

81. Check Exercise 31.

82. Check Exercise 32.

CHAPTER 10 VOCABULARY CHECK

Fill in each blank with one of the words or phrases listed below.

inverse   common   composition   symmetric   exponential
vertical   logarithmic   natural   horizontal

1. For each one-to-one function, we can find its _____ function by switching the coordinates of the ordered pairs of the function.
2. The _____ of functions f and g is $(f \circ g)(x) = f(g(x))$.
3. A function of the form $f(x) = b^x$ is called an _____ function if $b > 0$, b is not 1, and x is a real number.
4. The graphs of f and f^{-1} are _____ about the line $y = x$.
5. _____ logarithms are logarithms to base e.
6. _____ logarithms are logarithms to base 10.
7. To see whether a graph is the graph of a one-to-one function, apply the _____ line test to see if it is a function, and then apply the _____ line test to see if it is a one-to-one function.
8. A _____ function is a function that can be defined by $f(x) = \log_b x$ where x is a positive real number, b is a constant positive real number, and b is not 1.

CHAPTER 10 REVIEW

(10.1) If $f(x) = x - 5$ and $g(x) = 2x + 1$, find

1. $(f + g)(x)$
2. $(f - g)(x)$
3. $(f \cdot g)(x)$
4. $\left(\dfrac{g}{f}\right)(x)$

If $f(x) = x^2 - 2$, $g(x) = x + 1$, and $h(x) = x^3 - x^2$, find each composition.

5. $(f \circ g)(x)$
6. $(g \circ f)(x)$
7. $(h \circ g)(2)$
8. $(f \circ f)(x)$
9. $(f \circ g)(-1)$
10. $(h \circ h)(2)$

(10.2) Determine whether each function is a one-to-one function. If it is one-to-one, list the elements of its inverse.

11. $h = \{(-9, 14), (6, 8), (-11, 12), (15, 15)\}$

12. $f = \{(-5, 5), (0, 4), (13, 5), (11, -6)\}$

13.

U.S. Region (Input)	West	Midwest	South	Northeast
Rank in Automobile Thefts (Output)	2	4	1	3

 14.

Shape (Input)	Square	Triangle	Parallelogram	Rectangle
Number of Sides (Output)	4	3	4	4

Given that $f(x) = \sqrt{x + 2}$ is a one-to-one function, find the following.

15. a. $f(7)$ b. $f^{-1}(3)$
16. a. $f(-1)$ b. $f^{-1}(1)$

Determine whether each function is a one-to-one function.

17.
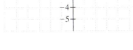

18.
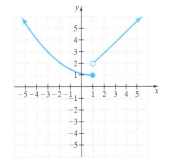

19.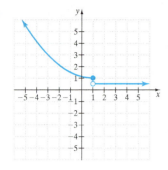

20.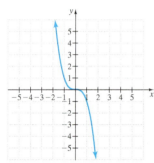

Find an equation defining the inverse function of the given one-to-one function.

21. $f(x) = x - 9$
22. $f(x) = x + 8$
23. $f(x) = 6x + 11$
24. $f(x) = 12x$
25. $f(x) = x^3 - 5$
26. $f(x) = \sqrt[3]{x + 2}$
27. $g(x) = \dfrac{12x - 7}{6}$
28. $r(x) = \dfrac{13}{2}x - 4$

On the same set of axes, graph the given one-to-one function and its inverse.

29. $g(x) = \sqrt{x}$
30. $h(x) = 5x - 5$

31. Find the inverse of the one-to-one function $f(x) = 2x - 3$. Then graph both $f(x)$ and $f^{-1}(x)$ with a square window.

(10.3) Solve each equation for x.

32. $4^x = 64$
33. $3^x = \dfrac{1}{9}$
34. $2^{3x} = \dfrac{1}{16}$
35. $5^{2x} = 125$
36. $9^{x+1} = 243$
37. $8^{3x-2} = 4$

Graph each exponential function.

38. $y = 3^x$
39. $y = \left(\dfrac{1}{3}\right)^x$
40. $y = 4 \cdot 2^x$
41. $y = 2^x + 4$

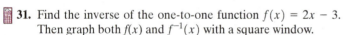

Use the formula $A = P\left(1 + \dfrac{r}{n}\right)^{nt}$ to solve the interest problems. In this formula,

A = amount accrued (or owed)
P = principal invested (or loaned)
r = rate of interest
n = number of compounding periods per year
t = time in years

42. Find the amount accrued if $1600 is invested at 9% interest compounded semiannually for 7 years.

43. A total of $800 is invested in a 7% certificate of deposit for which interest is compounded quarterly. Find the value that this certificate will have at the end of 5 years.

44. Use a graphing calculator to verify the results of Exercise 40.

(10.4) Write each equation with logarithmic notation.

45. $49 = 7^2$
46. $2^{-4} = \dfrac{1}{16}$

Write each logarithmic equation with exponential notation.

47. $\log_{1/2} 16 = -4$
48. $\log_{0.4} 0.064 = 3$

Solve for x.

49. $\log_4 x = -3$
50. $\log_3 x = 2$
51. $\log_3 1 = x$
52. $\log_4 64 = x$
53. $\log_x 64 = 2$
54. $\log_x 81 = 4$
55. $\log_4 4^5 = x$
56. $\log_7 7^{-2} = x$
57. $5^{\log_5 4} = x$
58. $2^{\log_2 9} = x$
59. $\log_2(3x - 1) = 4$
60. $\log_3(2x + 5) = 2$
61. $\log_4(x^2 - 3x) = 1$
62. $\log_8(x^2 + 7x) = 1$

Graph each pair of equations on the same coordinate system.

63. $y = 2^x$ and $y = \log_2 x$
64. $y = \left(\dfrac{1}{2}\right)^x$ and $y = \log_{1/2} x$

(10.5) Write each of the following as single logarithms.

65. $\log_3 8 + \log_3 4$
66. $\log_2 6 + \log_2 3$
67. $\log_7 15 - \log_7 20$
68. $\log 18 - \log 12$
69. $\log_{11} 8 + \log_{11} 3 - \log_{11} 6$
70. $\log_5 14 + \log_5 3 - \log_5 21$
71. $2 \log_5 x - 2 \log_5(x + 1) + \log_5 x$
72. $4 \log_3 x - \log_3 x + \log_3(x + 2)$

Use properties of logarithms to write each expression as a sum or difference of multiples of logarithms.

73. $\log_3 \dfrac{x^3}{x + 2}$
74. $\log_4 \dfrac{x + 5}{x^2}$
75. $\log_2 \dfrac{3x^2 y}{z}$

76. $\log_7 \dfrac{yz^3}{x}$

If $\log_b 2 = 0.36$ and $\log_b 5 = 0.83$, find the following.

77. $\log_b 50$ **78.** $\log_b \dfrac{4}{5}$

(10.6) Use a calculator to approximate the logarithm to four decimal places.

79. $\log 3.6$ **80.** $\log 0.15$

81. $\ln 1.25$ **82.** $\ln 4.63$

Find the exact value.

83. $\log 1000$ **84.** $\log \dfrac{1}{10}$

85. $\ln \dfrac{1}{e}$ **86.** $\ln e^4$

Solve each equation for x.

87. $\ln(2x) = 2$ **88.** $\ln(3x) = 1.6$

89. $\ln(2x - 3) = -1$ **90.** $\ln(3x + 1) = 2$

Use the formula $\ln \dfrac{I}{I_0} = -kx$ to solve radiation problems. In this formula,

x = depth in millimeters
I = intensity of radiation
I_0 = initial intensity
k = a constant measure dependent on the material

Round answers to two decimal places.

91. Find the depth at which the intensity of the radiation passing through a lead shield is reduced to 3% of the original intensity if the value of k is 2.1.

92. If k is 3.2, find the depth at which 2% of the original radiation will penetrate.

Approximate the logarithm to four decimal places.

93. $\log_5 1.6$ **94.** $\log_3 4$

Use the formula $A = Pe^{rt}$ to solve the interest problems in which interest is compounded continuously. In this formula,

A = amount accrued (or owed)
P = principal invested (or loaned)
r = rate of interest
t = time in years

95. Bank of New York offers a 5-year, 6% continuously compounded investment option. Find the amount accrued if $1450 is invested.

96. Find the amount to which a $940 investment grows if it is invested at 11% compounded continuously for 3 years.

(10.7) Solve each exponential equation for x. Give an exact solution and also approximate the solution to four decimal places.

97. $3^{2x} = 7$

98. $6^{3x} = 5$

99. $3^{2x+1} = 6$

100. $4^{3x+2} = 9$

101. $5^{3x-5} = 4$

102. $8^{4x-2} = 3$

103. $2 \cdot 5^{x-1} = 1$

104. $3 \cdot 4^{x+5} = 2$

Solve the equation for x.

105. $\log_5 2 + \log_5 x = 2$

106. $\log_3 x + \log_3 10 = 2$

107. $\log(5x) - \log(x + 1) = 4$

108. $\ln(3x) - \ln(x - 3) = 2$

109. $\log_2 x + \log_2 2x - 3 = 1$

110. $-\log_6(4x + 7) + \log_6 x = 1$

Use the formula $y = y_0 e^{kt}$ to solve the population growth problems. In this formula,

y = size of population
y_0 = initial count of population
k = rate of growth written as a decimal
t = time

Round each answer to the nearest whole.

111. The population of mallard ducks in Nova Scotia is expected to grow at a rate of 6% per week during the spring migration. If 155,000 ducks are already in Nova Scotia, find how many are expected by the end of 4 weeks.

112. The population of Armenia is declining at a rate of 0.129% per year. If the population in 2007 was 2,971,650, find the expected population by the year 2015. (*Source:* U.S. Bureau of the Census, International Data Base)

113. China is experiencing an annual growth rate of 0.606%. In 2007, the population of China was 1,321,851,888. How long will it take for the population to be 1,500,000,000? Round to the nearest tenth. (*Source: CIA 2007 World Factbook*)

114. In 2007, Canada had a population of 33,390,141. How long will it take for Canada to double its population if the growth rate is 0.9% annually? Round to the nearest tenth. (*Source: CIA 2007 World Factbook*)

115. Malaysia's population is increasing at a rate of 1.8% per year. How long will it take the 2007 population of 24,821,286 to double in size? Round to the nearest tenth. (*Source: CIA 2007 World Factbook*)

Use the compound interest equation $A = P\left(1 + \dfrac{r}{n}\right)^{nt}$ to solve the following. (See the directions for Exercises 42 and 43 for an explanation of this formula. Round answers to the nearest tenth.)

116. Find how long it will take a $5000 investment to grow to $10,000 if it is invested at 8% interest compounded quarterly.

117. An investment of $6000 has grown to $10,000 while the money was invested at 6% interest compounded monthly. Find how long it was invested.

Use a graphing calculator to solve each equation. Round all solutions to two decimal places.

118. $e^x = 2$

119. $10^{0.3x} = 7$

MIXED REVIEW

Solve each equation.

120. $3^x = \dfrac{1}{81}$

121. $7^{4x} = 49$

122. $8^{3x-2} = 32$

123. $\log_4 4 = x$

124. $\log_3 x = 4$

125. $\log_5(x^2 - 4x) = 1$

126. $\log_4(3x - 1) = 2$

127. $\ln x = -3.2$

128. $\log_5 x + \log_5 10 = 2$

129. $\ln x - \ln 2 = 1$

130. $\log_6 x - \log_6(4x + 7) = 1$

CHAPTER 10 TEST

Remember to use the Chapter Test Prep Videos to see the fully worked-out solutions to any of the exercises you want to review.

If $f(x) = x$ and $g(x) = 2x - 3$, find the following.

1. $(f \cdot g)(x)$
2. $(f - g)(x)$

If $f(x) = x$, $g(x) = x - 7$, and $h(x) = x^2 - 6x + 5$, find the following.

3. $(f \circ h)(0)$
4. $(g \circ f)(x)$
5. $(g \circ h)(x)$

On the same set of axes, graph the given one-to-one function and its inverse.

6. $f(x) = 7x - 14$

Determine whether the given graph is the graph of a one-to-one function.

7.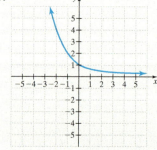
8.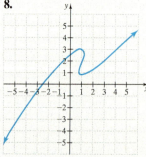

Determine whether each function is one-to-one. If it is one-to-one, find an equation or a set of ordered pairs that defines the inverse function of the given function.

9. $f(x) = 6 - 2x$
10. $f = \{(0, 0), (2, 3), (-1, 5)\}$

11.

Word (Input)	Dog	Cat	House	Desk	Circle
First Letter of Word (Output)	d	c	h	d	c

Use the properties of logarithms to write each expression as a single logarithm.

12. $\log_3 6 + \log_3 4$

13. $\log_5 x + 3 \log_5 x - \log_5(x + 1)$

14. Write the expression $\log_6 \dfrac{2x}{y^3}$ as the sum or difference of multiples of logarithms.

15. If $\log_b 3 = 0.79$ and $\log_b 5 = 1.16$, find the value of $\log_b \dfrac{3}{25}$.

16. Approximate $\log_7 8$ to four decimal places.

17. Solve $8^{x-1} = \dfrac{1}{64}$ for x. Give an exact solution.

18. Solve $3^{2x+5} = 4$ for x. Give an exact solution, and also approximate the solution to four decimal places.

Solve each logarithmic equation for x. Give an exact solution.

19. $\log_3 x = -2$

20. $\ln \sqrt{e} = x$

21. $\log_8(3x - 2) = 2$

22. $\log_5 x + \log_5 3 = 2$

23. $\log_4(x+1) - \log_4(x-2) = 3$

24. Solve $\ln(3x+7) = 1.31$ accurate to four decimal places.

25. Graph $y = \left(\dfrac{1}{2}\right)^x + 1$.

26. Graph the functions $y = 3^x$ and $y = \log_3 x$ on the same coordinate system.

Use the formula $A = P\left(1 + \dfrac{r}{n}\right)^{nt}$ to solve Exercises 27 and 28.

27. Find the amount in the account if $4000 is invested for 3 years at 9% interest compounded monthly.

28. Find how long it will take $2000 to grow to $3000 if the money is invested at 7% interest compounded semiannually. Round to the nearest whole.

Use the population growth formula $y = y_0 e^{kt}$ to solve Exercises 29 and 30.

29. The prairie dog population of the Grand Rapids area now stands at 57,000 animals. If the population is growing at a rate of 2.6% annually, find how many prairie dogs there will be in that area 5 years from now.

30. In an attempt to save an endangered species of wood duck, naturalists would like to increase the wood duck population from 400 to 1000 ducks. If the annual population growth rate is 6.2%, find how long it will take the naturalists to reach their goal. Round to the nearest whole year.

31. The formula $\log(1+k) = \dfrac{0.3}{D}$ relates the doubling time D, in days, and the growth rate k for a population of mice. Find the rate at which the population is increasing if the doubling time is 56 days. Round to the nearest tenth of a percent.

CHAPTER 10 STANDARDIZED TEST

Multiple Choice. *Choose the one alternative that best completes the statement or answers the question.*

For the given functions f and g, find the requested function.

1. $f(x) = 3x + 2;\ g(x) = 2x + 5$
   Find $(f \cdot g)(x)$.
   a. $(f \cdot g)(x) = 6x^2 + 9x + 10$
   b. $(f \cdot g)(x) = 5x^2 + 19x + 7$
   c. $(f \cdot g)(x) = 6x^2 + 19x + 10$
   d. $(f \cdot g)(x) = 6x^2 + 10$

2. $f(x) = 9x - 7;\ g(x) = 2x - 4$
   Find $(f - g)(x)$.
   a. $(f - g)(x) = -7x + 3$
   b. $(f - g)(x) = 11x - 11$
   c. $(f - g)(x) = 7x - 11$
   d. $(f - g)(x) = 7x - 3$

For the given functions f and g, find the indicated composition.

3. $f(x) = x^2 + 4x;\ g(x) = x + 2$
   Find $(g \circ f)(4)$.
   a. 34   b. 192
   c. 60   d. 36

4. $f(x) = 6x + 11,\ g(x) = 3x - 1$
   Find $(f \circ g)(x)$.
   a. $18x + 10$ b. $18x + 32$
   c. $18x + 17$ d. $18x + 5$

5. $f(x) = 4x^2 + 4x + 6,\ g(x) = 4x - 3$
   Find $(g \circ f)(x)$.
   a. $16x^2 + 16x + 27$ b. $4x^2 + 16x + 21$
   c. $4x^2 + 4x + 3$ d. $16x^2 + 16x + 21$

On the same set of axes, graph the given one-to-one function and its inverse.

6. $f(x) = 2x - 2$

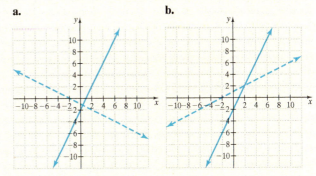

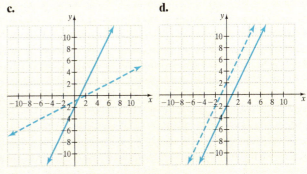

Determine whether the given graph is the graph of a one-to-one function.

7.

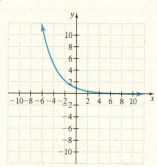

a. yes   b. no

8.

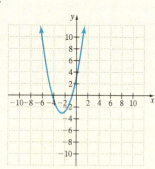

a. yes   b. no

Determine whether the function is one-to-one. If it is one-to-one, find an equation or a set of ordered pairs that defines the inverse function of the given function.

9. $y = 6x + 4$

a. one-to-one; $f^{-1}(x) = \dfrac{x-4}{6}$

b. one-to-one; $f^{-1}(x) = -\dfrac{x+6}{4}$

c. one-to-one; $f^{-1}(x) = \dfrac{x+4}{6}$

d. not one-to-one

10. $f = \{(-14, 4), (-1, -8), (-4, 15)\}$

a. one-to-one; $f^{-1} = \{(4, -14), (-4, -1), (15, -8)\}$

b. one-to-one; $f^{-1} = \{(-14, -8), (-14, -1), (15, -4)\}$

c. one-to-one; $f^{-1} = \{(4, -14), (-8, -1), (15, -4)\}$

d. not one-to-one

11.

Weekdays (input)	Mon.	Tue.	Wed.	Thu.	Fri.
Student: Avg. Minutes of Study (output)	389	322	187	322	127

a. one-to-one

Student: Avg. Minutes of Study(input)	127	322	187	322	389
Weekdays (output)	Mon.	Tue.	Wed.	Thu.	Fri.

b. one-to-one

Student: Avg. Minutes of Study (input)	389	322	187	322	127
Weekdays (output)	Mon.	Tue.	Wed.	Thu.	Fri.

c. one-to-one

Weekdays (input)	Mon.	Tue.	Wed.	Thu.	Fri.
Student: Avg. Minutes of Study (output)	389	322	187	322	127

d. not one-to-one

Use the properties of logarithms to write the expression as a single logarithm.

12. $\log_5 7 + \log_5 9$

a. $\log_{10} 16$ b. $\log_5 63$ c. $\log_{10} 63$ d. $\log_5 16$

13. $\log_2 x + 5\log_2 x - \log_2 (x+7)$

a. $\log_2 \dfrac{x^4}{x+7}$ b. $\log_2[x^6(x+7)]$

c. $\log_2 \dfrac{x^6}{x+7}$ d. $\log_2 \dfrac{x+7}{x^4}$

Choose an appropriate response.

14. Write the expression $\log_2 \dfrac{3x^8}{y^6}$ as a sum or difference of multiples of logarithms.

a. $\log_2 3 + 8\log_2 x - 6\log_2 y$

b. $(\log_2 3)(8\log_2 x) - 6\log_2 y$

c. $\log_2 3 + 8\log_2 x + 6\log_2 y$

d. $\log_2 3 - 8\log_2 x - 6\log_2 y$

15. If $\log_{10} 2 = 0.3010$ and $\log_{10} 3 = 0.4771$, find the value of $\log_{10} \dfrac{9}{8}$.

a. 0.0512   b. 2.0333
c. 0.8293   d. 0.1992

16. Approximate $\log_5 3$ to four decimal places.

a. 0.6826   b. 1.1761
c. 1.4650   d. -0.2218

17. Solve $3^{6+3x} = \dfrac{1}{27}$ for x. Give an exact solution.

a. -3 b. $\dfrac{1}{9}$
c. 3   d. 9

18. Solve $4^{x+6} = 7$ for x. Give an exact solution.

a. $\log 7 - \log 4 - \log 6$ b. $\dfrac{\log 4}{\log 7} + \log 6$

c. $\dfrac{\log 4}{\log 7} + 6$ d. $\dfrac{\log 7}{\log 4} - 6$

19. Solve $5^{x+6} = 4$ for x. Approximate the solution to four decimal places.

a. -5.1386 b. 7.1610
c. -0.8751 d. 1.9391

Solve the logarithmic equation for x. Give an exact solution.

20. $\log_5 x = -3$
   a. $\frac{1}{125}$ b. 2
   c. -15 d. $\frac{1}{243}$

21. $\ln \sqrt[4]{e} = x$
   a. $4e$ b. $\frac{1}{4}$
   c. $\frac{e}{4}$ d. 4

22. $\log_6 (x - 7) = 4$
   a. 17 b. 1289
   c. 1303 d. 31

23. $\log_3 4 + \log_3 x = 1$
   a. $\sqrt[4]{3}$ b. $\frac{4}{3}$
   c. $\frac{1}{4}$ d. $\frac{3}{4}$

24. $\log_6 (x + 2) - \log_6 x = 2$
   a. $\frac{1}{18}$ b. $\frac{35}{2}$
   c. 6 d. $\frac{2}{35}$

Provide an appropriate response.

25. Solve $\ln (9x - 7) = 1.31$ accurate to four decimal places.
   a. 1.1896 b. -0.3660
   c. 2.5177 d. 451.5903

26. Graph $y = \left(\frac{1}{3}\right)^x - 2$.

a.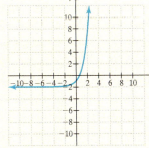
b.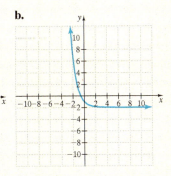

c.
d.

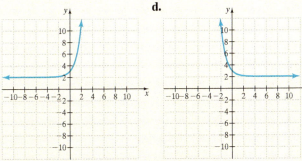

27. Graph the functions $y = 2^x$ and $y = \log_2 x$ on the same coordinate system.

a.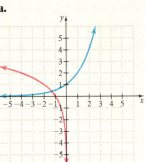
b.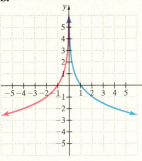
c.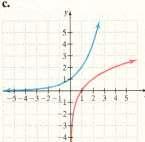
d.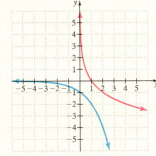

Use the formula $A = P\left(1 + \frac{r}{n}\right)^{nt}$ to solve.

28. Find the amount of money in an account after 8 years if $4800 is deposited at 7% annual interest compounded monthly.
   a. $8389.57 b. $8362.62
   c. $8323.13 d. $8247.29

29. $7500 is invested at 8% compounded quarterly. In how many years will the account have grown to $12,500? Round to the nearest tenth of a year.
   a. 1.1 years b. 6.6 years
   c. 6.4 years d. 13.2 years

Use the population growth formula $y = y_0 e^{kt}$ to solve.

30. The size of the raccoon population at a national park increases according to the growth formula $y = y_0 e^{(0.046t)}$ where t is in years. If the size of the current population is 167, find how many raccoons there should be in 3 years.
   a. 192 b. 196
   c. 194 d. 190

31. A certain bird population grows according to the growth formulas $y = y_0 e^{(0.005t)}$ where t is in years. If the annual population growth rate is 5.5%, find how long will it take a population of birds to increase from 600 birds to 1100. Round to the nearest whole year.
   a. 3 b. 127
   c. 95 d. 11

Solve the problem.

32. The formula $\log (1 + k) = \frac{0.5}{D}$ relates the doubling time D, in days, and the growth rate k for a population of rodents. Find the rate at which the population is increasing if the doubling time is 59 days. Round to the nearest tenth of a percent.
   a. 0.9% b. 0.5%
   c. 0.8% d. 2.0%

CHAPTER

11 Graphing Quadratic Functions, Rational Functions, and Conic Sections

11.1 Quadratic Functions and Their Graphs
11.2 Further Graphing of Quadratic Functions
11.3 Graphing Rational Functions by Translations
11.4 Further Graphing of Rational Functions
11.5 The Parabola and the Circle
11.6 The Ellipse and the Hyperbola

Integrated Review—Graphing Conic Sections

11.7 Solving Nonlinear Systems of Equations
11.8 Nonlinear Inequalities and Systems of Inequalities

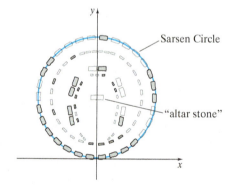

When the sun rises above the horizon on June 21 or 22, thousands of people gather to witness and celebrate summer solstice at Stonehenge. Stonehenge is a megalithic ruin located on the Salisbury Plain in Wiltshire, England. It is a series of earth, timber and stone structures that were constructed, revised, and reconstructed over a period of 1400 years or so. In this chapter, we explore the dimensions of the outer stone circle, known as the Sarsen circle, or Stonehenge. (*Source:* The Discovery Channel)

622

11.1 QUADRATIC FUNCTIONS AND THEIR GRAPHS

OBJECTIVES

1. Graph quadratic functions of the form $f(x) = x^2 + k$.
2. Graph quadratic functions of the form $f(x) = (x - h)^2$.
3. Graph quadratic functions of the form $f(x) = (x - h)^2 + k$.
4. Graph quadratic functions of the form $f(x) = ax^2$.
5. Graph quadratic functions of the form $f(x) = a(x - h)^2 + k$.

OBJECTIVE 1 ▶ **Graphing $f(x) = x^2 + k$.** We first graphed the quadratic equation $y = x^2$ in Section 3.1. In Section 3.2, we learned that this graph defines a function, and we wrote $y = x^2$ as $f(x) = x^2$. In these sections, we discovered that the graph of a quadratic function is a parabola opening upward or downward. In this section, we continue our study of quadratic functions and their graphs. (Much of the contents of this section is a review of shifting and reflecting techniques from Section 3.6.)

First, let's recall the definition of a quadratic function.

> **Quadratic Function**
>
> A quadratic function is a function that can be written in the form $f(x) = ax^2 + bx + c$, where $a, b,$ and c are real numbers and $a \neq 0$.

Notice that equations of the form $y = ax^2 + bx + c$, where $a \neq 0$, define quadratic functions, since y is a function of x or $y = f(x)$.

Recall that if $a > 0$, the parabola opens upward and if $a < 0$, the parabola opens downward. Also, the vertex of a parabola is the lowest point if the parabola opens upward and the highest point if the parabola opens downward. The axis of symmetry is the vertical line that passes through the vertex.

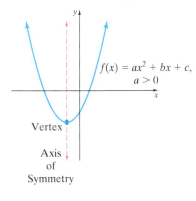
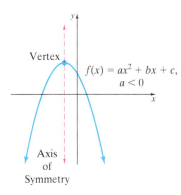

EXAMPLE 1 Graph $f(x) = x^2$ and $g(x) = x^2 + 6$ on the same set of axes.

Solution First we construct a table of values for $f(x)$ and plot the points. Notice that for each x-value, the corresponding value of $g(x)$ must be 6 more than the corresponding value of $f(x)$ since $f(x) = x^2$ and $g(x) = x^2 + 6$. In other words, the graph of $g(x) = x^2 + 6$ is the same as the graph of $f(x) = x^2$ shifted upward 6 units. The axis of symmetry for both graphs is the y-axis.

x	$f(x) = x^2$	$g(x) = x^2 + 6$
-2	4	10
-1	1	7
0	0	6
1	1	7
2	4	10

Each y-value is increased by 6.

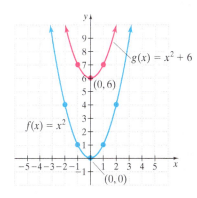

PRACTICE 1 Graph $f(x) = x^2$ and $g(x) = x^2 - 4$ on the same set of axes.

In general, we have the following properties.

> **Graphing the Parabola Defined by f(x) = x² + k**
> If k is positive, the graph of $f(x) = x^2 + k$ is the graph of $y = x^2$ shifted upward k units.
> If k is negative, the graph of $f(x) = x^2 + k$ is the graph of $y = x^2$ shifted downward $|k|$ units.
> The vertex is $(0, k)$, and the axis of symmetry is the y-axis.

EXAMPLE 2 Graph each function.

a. $F(x) = x^2 + 2$ **b.** $g(x) = x^2 - 3$

Solution

a. $F(x) = x^2 + 2$

The graph of $F(x) = x^2 + 2$ is obtained by shifting the graph of $y = x^2$ upward 2 units.

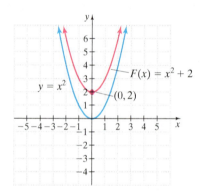

b. $g(x) = x^2 - 3$

The graph of $g(x) = x^2 - 3$ is obtained by shifting the graph of $y = x^2$ downward 3 units.

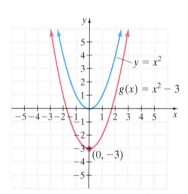

PRACTICE 2 Graph each function.

a. $f(x) = x^2 - 5$ **b.** $g(x) = x^2 + 3$

OBJECTIVE 2 ▶ Graphing $f(x) = (x - h)^2$. Now we will graph functions of the form $f(x) = (x - h)^2$.

EXAMPLE 3 Graph $f(x) = x^2$ and $g(x) = (x - 2)^2$ on the same set of axes.

Solution By plotting points, we see that for each x-value, the corresponding value of $g(x)$ is the same as the value of $f(x)$ when the x-value is increased by 2. Thus, the graph of $g(x) = (x - 2)^2$ is the graph of $f(x) = x^2$ shifted to the right 2 units. The axis of symmetry for the graph of $g(x) = (x - 2)^2$ is also shifted 2 units to the right and is the line $x = 2$.

x	$f(x) = x^2$	x	$g(x) = (x - 2)^2$
−2	4	0	4
−1	1	1	1
0	0	2	0
1	1	3	1
2	4	4	4

Each x-value increased by 2 corresponds to same y-value.

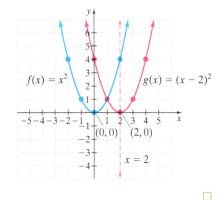

PRACTICE 3 Graph $f(x) = x^2$ and $g(x) = (x + 6)^2$ on the same set of axes.

In general, we have the following properties.

> **Graphing the Parabola Defined by $f(x) = (x - h)^2$**
> If h is positive, the graph of $f(x) = (x - h)^2$ is the graph of $y = x^2$ shifted to the right h units.
> If h is negative, the graph of $f(x) = (x - h)^2$ is the graph of $y = x^2$ shifted to the left $|h|$ units.
> The vertex is $(h, 0)$, and the axis of symmetry is the vertical line $x = h$.

EXAMPLE 4 Graph each function.

a. $G(x) = (x - 3)^2$ **b.** $F(x) = (x + 1)^2$

Solution

a. The graph of $G(x) = (x - 3)^2$ is obtained by shifting the graph of $y = x^2$ to the right 3 units. The graph of $G(x)$ is below on the left.

b. The equation $F(x) = (x + 1)^2$ can be written as $F(x) = [x - (-1)]^2$. The graph of $F(x) = [x - (-1)]^2$ is obtained by shifting the graph of $y = x^2$ to the left 1 unit. The graph of $F(x)$ is below on the right.

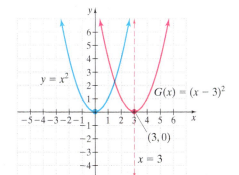 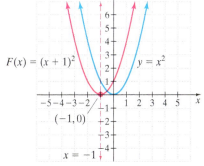

626 CHAPTER 11 Graphing Quadratic Functions, Rational Functions, and Conic Sections

PRACTICE 4 Graph each function.

a. $G(x) = (x + 4)^2$ **b.** $H(x) = (x - 7)^2$

OBJECTIVE 3 ▶ Graphing $f(x) = (x - h)^2 + k$. As we will see in graphing functions of the form $f(x) = (x - h)^2 + k$, it is possible to combine vertical and horizontal shifts.

> **Graphing the Parabola Defined by $f(x) = (x - h)^2 + k$**
> The parabola has the same shape as $y = x^2$.
> The vertex is (h, k), and the axis of symmetry is the vertical line $x = h$.

EXAMPLE 5 Graph $F(x) = (x - 3)^2 + 1$.

Solution The graph of $F(x) = (x - 3)^2 + 1$ is the graph of $y = x^2$ shifted 3 units to the right and 1 unit up. The vertex is then $(3, 1)$, and the axis of symmetry is $x = 3$. A few ordered pair solutions are plotted to aid in graphing.

x	$F(x) = (x - 3)^2 + 1$
1	5
2	2
4	2
5	5

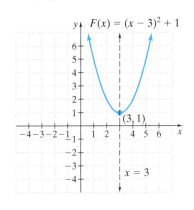

PRACTICE 5 Graph $f(x) = (x + 2)^2 + 2$.

OBJECTIVE 4 ▶ Graphing $f(x) = ax^2$. Next, we discover the change in the shape of the graph when the coefficient of x^2 is not 1.

EXAMPLE 6 Graph $f(x) = x^2$, $g(x) = 3x^2$, and $h(x) = \frac{1}{2}x^2$ on the same set of axes.

Solution Comparing the tables of values, we see that for each x-value, the corresponding value of $g(x)$ is triple the corresponding value of $f(x)$. Similarly, the value of $h(x)$ is half the value of $f(x)$.

x	$f(x) = x^2$
-2	4
-1	1
0	0
1	1
2	4

x	$g(x) = 3x^2$
-2	12
-1	3
0	0
1	3
2	12

x	$h(x) = \frac{1}{2}x^2$
-2	2
-1	$\frac{1}{2}$
0	0
1	$\frac{1}{2}$
2	2

The result is that the graph of $g(x) = 3x^2$ is narrower than the graph of $f(x) = x^2$ and the graph of $h(x) = \frac{1}{2}x^2$ is wider. The vertex for each graph is $(0, 0)$, and the axis of symmetry is the y-axis.

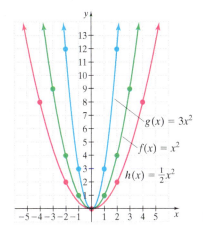

PRACTICE 6 Graph $f(x) = x^2$, $g(x) = 4x^2$, and $h(x) = \frac{1}{4}x^2$ on the same set of axes.

Graphing the Parabola Defined by f(x) = ax²

If a is positive, the parabola opens upward, and if a is negative, the parabola opens downward.
If $|a| > 1$, the graph of the parabola is narrower than the graph of $y = x^2$.
If $|a| < 1$, the graph of the parabola is wider than the graph of $y = x^2$.

EXAMPLE 7 Graph $f(x) = -2x^2$.

Solution Because $a = -2$, a negative value, this parabola opens downward. Since $|-2| = 2$ and $2 > 1$, the parabola is narrower than the graph of $y = x^2$. The vertex is $(0, 0)$, and the axis of symmetry is the y-axis. We verify this by plotting a few points.

x	$f(x) = -2x^2$
-2	-8
-1	-2
0	0
1	-2
2	-8

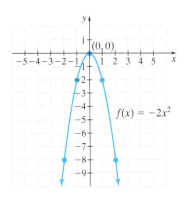

PRACTICE 7 Graph $f(x) = -\frac{1}{2}x^2$.

OBJECTIVE 5 ▶ **Graphing $f(x) = a(x - h)^2 + k$.** Now we will see the shape of the graph of a quadratic function of the form $f(x) = a(x - h)^2 + k$.

EXAMPLE 8 Graph $g(x) = \frac{1}{2}(x+2)^2 + 5$. Find the vertex and the axis of symmetry.

Solution The function $g(x) = \frac{1}{2}(x+2)^2 + 5$ may be written as $g(x) = \frac{1}{2}[x-(-2)]^2 + 5$. Thus, this graph is the same as the graph of $y = x^2$ shifted 2 units to the left and 5 units up, and it is wider because a is $\frac{1}{2}$. The vertex is $(-2, 5)$, and the axis of symmetry is $x = -2$. We plot a few points to verify.

x	$g(x) = \frac{1}{2}(x+2)^2 + 5$
-4	7
-3	$5\frac{1}{2}$
-2	5
-1	$5\frac{1}{2}$
0	7

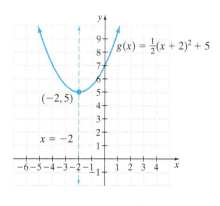

PRACTICE 8 Graph $h(x) = \frac{1}{3}(x-4)^2 - 3$.

In general, the following holds.

Graph of a Quadratic Function

The graph of a quadratic function written in the form $f(x) = a(x - h)^2 + k$ is a parabola with vertex (h, k). If $a > 0$, the parabola opens upward, and if $a < 0$, the parabola opens downward. The axis of symmetry is the line whose equation is $x = h$.

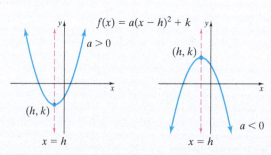

Concept Check ✓

Which description of the graph of $f(x) = -0.35(x+3)^2 - 4$ is correct?

a. The graph opens downward and has its vertex at $(-3, 4)$.
b. The graph opens upward and has its vertex at $(-3, 4)$.
c. The graph opens downward and has its vertex at $(-3, -4)$.
d. The graph is narrower than the graph of $y = x^2$.

Answer to Concept Check: c

Section 11.1 Quadratic Functions and Their Graphs 629

Graphing Calculator Explorations

Use a graphing calculator to graph the first function of each pair that follows. Then use its graph to predict the graph of the second function. Check your prediction by graphing both on the same set of axes.

1. $F(x) = \sqrt{x}; G(x) = \sqrt{x} + 1$
2. $g(x) = x^3; H(x) = x^3 - 2$
3. $H(x) = |x|; f(x) = |x - 5|$
4. $h(x) = x^3 + 2; g(x) = (x - 3)^3 + 2$
5. $f(x) = |x + 4|; F(x) = |x + 4| + 3$
6. $G(x) = \sqrt{x} - 2; g(x) = \sqrt{x - 4} - 2$

VOCABULARY & READINESS CHECK

Word Bank. *Use the choices below to fill in each blank. Some choices will be used more than once.*

 upward highest parabola downward lowest quadratic

1. A _____ function is one that can be written in the form $f(x) = ax^2 + bx + c, a \neq 0$.
2. The graph of a quadratic function is a _____ opening _____ or _____.
3. If $a > 0$, the graph of the quadratic function opens _____.
4. If $a < 0$, the graph of the quadratic function opens _____.
5. The vertex of a parabola is the _____ point if $a > 0$.
6. The vertex of a parabola is the _____ point if $a < 0$.

State the vertex of the graph of each quadratic function.

7. $f(x) = x^2$
8. $f(x) = -5x^2$
9. $g(x) = (x - 2)^2$
10. $g(x) = (x + 5)^2$
11. $f(x) = 2x^2 + 3$
12. $h(x) = x^2 - 1$
13. $g(x) = (x + 1)^2 + 5$
14. $h(x) = (x - 10)^2 - 7$

11.1 EXERCISE SET

MIXED PRACTICE

Sketch the graph of each quadratic function. Label the vertex, and sketch and label the axis of symmetry. See Examples 1 through 5.

1. $f(x) = x^2 - 1$
2. $g(x) = x^2 + 3$
3. $h(x) = x^2 + 5$
4. $h(x) = x^2 - 4$
5. $g(x) = x^2 + 7$
6. $f(x) = x^2 - 2$
7. $f(x) = (x - 5)^2$
8. $g(x) = (x + 5)^2$
9. $h(x) = (x + 2)^2$
10. $H(x) = (x - 1)^2$
11. $G(x) = (x + 3)^2$
12. $f(x) = (x - 6)^2$
13. $f(x) = (x - 2)^2 + 5$
14. $g(x) = (x - 6)^2 + 1$
15. $h(x) = (x + 1)^2 + 4$
16. $G(x) = (x + 3)^2 + 3$
17. $g(x) = (x + 2)^2 - 5$
18. $h(x) = (x + 4)^2 - 6$

Sketch the graph of each quadratic function. Label the vertex, and sketch and label the axis of symmetry. See Examples 6 and 7.

19. $g(x) = -x^2$
20. $f(x) = 5x^2$
21. $h(x) = \dfrac{1}{3}x^2$
22. $f(x) = -\dfrac{1}{4}x^2$
23. $H(x) = 2x^2$
24. $g(x) = -3x^2$

Sketch the graph of each quadratic function. Label the vertex, and sketch and label the axis of symmetry. See Example 8.

25. $f(x) = 2(x - 1)^2 + 3$
26. $g(x) = 4(x - 4)^2 + 2$
27. $h(x) = -3(x + 3)^2 + 1$
28. $f(x) = -(x - 2)^2 - 6$
29. $H(x) = \frac{1}{2}(x - 6)^2 - 3$
30. $G(x) = \frac{1}{5}(x + 4)^2 + 3$

MIXED PRACTICE

Sketch the graph of each quadratic function. Label the vertex, and sketch and label the axis of symmetry.

31. $f(x) = -(x - 2)^2$
32. $g(x) = -(x + 6)^2$
33. $F(x) = -x^2 + 4$
34. $H(x) = -x^2 + 10$
35. $F(x) = 2x^2 - 5$
36. $g(x) = \frac{1}{2}x^2 - 2$
37. $h(x) = (x - 6)^2 + 4$
38. $f(x) = (x - 5)^2 + 2$
39. $F(x) = \left(x + \frac{1}{2}\right)^2 - 2$
40. $H(x) = \left(x + \frac{1}{2}\right)^2 - 3$
41. $F(x) = \frac{3}{2}(x + 7)^2 + 1$
42. $g(x) = -\frac{3}{2}(x - 1)^2 - 5$
43. $f(x) = \frac{1}{4}x^2 - 9$
44. $H(x) = \frac{3}{4}x^2 - 2$
45. $G(x) = 5\left(x + \frac{1}{2}\right)^2$
46. $F(x) = 3\left(x - \frac{3}{2}\right)^2$
47. $h(x) = -(x - 1)^2 - 1$
48. $f(x) = -3(x + 2)^2 + 2$
49. $g(x) = \sqrt{3}(x + 5)^2 + \frac{3}{4}$
50. $G(x) = \sqrt{5}(x - 7)^2 - \frac{1}{2}$
51. $h(x) = 10(x + 4)^2 - 6$
52. $h(x) = 8(x + 1)^2 + 9$
53. $f(x) = -2(x - 4)^2 + 5$
54. $G(x) = -4(x + 9)^2 - 1$

REVIEW AND PREVIEW

Add the proper constant to each binomial so that the resulting trinomial is a perfect square trinomial. See Section 9.1.

55. $x^2 + 8x$
56. $y^2 + 4y$
57. $z^2 - 16z$
58. $x^2 - 10x$
59. $y^2 + y$
60. $z^2 - 3z$

Solve by completing the square. See Section 9.1.

61. $x^2 + 4x = 12$
62. $y^2 + 6y = -5$
63. $z^2 + 10z - 1 = 0$
64. $x^2 + 14x + 20 = 0$
65. $z^2 - 8z = 2$
66. $y^2 - 10y = 3$

CONCEPT EXTENSIONS

Multiple Choice. *See the Concept Check in this section.*

67. Which description of $f(x) = -213(x - 0.1)^2 + 3.6$ is correct?

Graph Opens	Vertex
a. upward	$(0.1, 3.6)$
b. upward	$(-213, 3.6)$
c. downward	$(0.1, 3.6)$
d. downward	$(-0.1, 3.6)$

68. Which description of $f(x) = 5\left(x + \frac{1}{2}\right)^2 + \frac{1}{2}$ is correct?

Graph Opens	Vertex
a. upward	$\left(\frac{1}{2}, \frac{1}{2}\right)$
b. upward	$\left(-\frac{1}{2}, \frac{1}{2}\right)$
c. downward	$\left(\frac{1}{2}, -\frac{1}{2}\right)$
d. downward	$\left(-\frac{1}{2}, -\frac{1}{2}\right)$

Write the equation of the parabola that has the same shape as $f(x) = 5x^2$ but with the following vertex.

69. $(2, 3)$
70. $(1, 6)$
71. $(-3, 6)$
72. $(4, -1)$

Read a Graph. *The shifting properties covered in this section apply to the graphs of all functions. Given the accompanying graph of $y = f(x)$, sketch the graph of each of the following.*

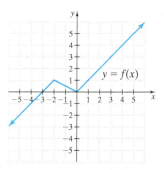

73. $y = f(x) + 1$
74. $y = f(x) - 2$
75. $y = f(x - 3)$
76. $y = f(x + 3)$
77. $y = f(x + 2) + 2$
78. $y = f(x - 1) + 1$

79. The quadratic function $f(x) = 668.7x^2 - 2990.7x + 938$ approximates the U.S. growth of cell phone subscribers between 1985 and 2005 where x is the number of years past 1985 and $f(x)$ is the number of subscribers in thousands.

   a. Use this function to approximate the number of subscribers in 2004.

   b. Use this function to predict the number of subscribers in 2007.

80. **Multiple Steps.** Use the function in Exercise 79.

   a. Predict the number of cell phone subscribers in 2010.

   b. Look up the current population of the U.S.

   c. Based on your answers for parts **a.** and **b.**, discuss some limitations of using this quadratic function to predict data.

11.2 FURTHER GRAPHING OF QUADRATIC FUNCTIONS

OBJECTIVES

1. Write quadratic functions in the form $y = a(x - h)^2 + k$.
2. Derive a formula for finding the vertex of a parabola.
3. Find the minimum or maximum value of a quadratic function.

OBJECTIVE 1 ▶ **Writing quadratic functions in the form** $y = a(x - h)^2 + k$. We know that the graph of a quadratic function is a parabola. If a quadratic function is written in the form

$$f(x) = a(x - h)^2 + k$$

we can easily find the vertex (h, k) and graph the parabola. To write a quadratic function in this form, complete the square. (See Section 9.1 for a review of completing the square.)

EXAMPLE 1 Graph $f(x) = x^2 - 4x - 12$. Find the vertex and any intercepts.

Solution The graph of this quadratic function is a parabola. To find the vertex of the parabola, we will write the function in the form $y = (x - h)^2 + k$. To do this, we complete the square on the binomial $x^2 - 4x$. To simplify our work, we let $f(x) = y$.

$$y = x^2 - 4x - 12 \quad \text{Let } f(x) = y.$$
$$y + 12 = x^2 - 4x \quad \text{Add 12 to both sides to get the } x\text{-variable terms alone.}$$

Now we add the square of half of -4 to both sides.

$$\frac{1}{2}(-4) = -2 \quad \text{and} \quad (-2)^2 = 4$$

$$y + 12 + 4 = x^2 - 4x + 4 \quad \text{Add 4 to both sides.}$$
$$y + 16 = (x - 2)^2 \quad \text{Factor the trinomial.}$$
$$y = (x - 2)^2 - 16 \quad \text{Subtract 16 from both sides.}$$
$$f(x) = (x - 2)^2 - 16 \quad \text{Replace } y \text{ with } f(x).$$

From this equation, we can see that the vertex of the parabola is $(2, -16)$, a point in quadrant IV, and the axis of symmetry is the line $x = 2$.

Notice that $a = 1$. Since $a > 0$, the parabola opens upward. This parabola opening upward with vertex $(2, -16)$ will have two x-intercepts and one y-intercept. (See the Helpful Hint after this example.)

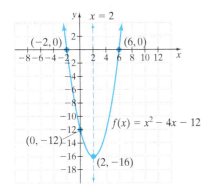

x-intercepts: let y or $f(x) = 0$

$f(x) = x^2 - 4x - 12$
$0 = x^2 - 4x - 12$
$0 = (x - 6)(x + 2)$
$0 = x - 6 \quad \text{or} \quad 0 = x + 2$
$6 = x \qquad\qquad -2 = x$

y-intercept: let $x = 0$

$f(x) = x^2 - 4x - 12$
$f(0) = 0^2 - 4 \cdot 0 - 12$
$\quad = -12$

The two x-intercepts are $(6, 0)$ and $(-2, 0)$. The y-intercept is $(0, -12)$. The sketch of $f(x) = x^2 - 4x - 12$ is shown.

Notice that the axis of symmetry is always halfway between the x-intercepts. For the example above, halfway between -2 and 6 is $\dfrac{-2 + 6}{2} = 2$, and the axis of symmetry is $x = 2$. □

PRACTICE

1 Graph $g(x) = x^2 - 2x - 3$. Find the vertex and any intercepts.

632 CHAPTER 11 Graphing Quadratic Functions, Rational Functions, and Conic Sections

> **▶ Helpful Hint**
> Parabola Opens Upward
> Vertex in I or II: no x-intercept
> Vertex in III or IV: 2 x-intercepts
>
> Parabola Opens Downward
> Vertex in I or II: 2 x-intercepts
> Vertex in III or IV: no x-intercept.

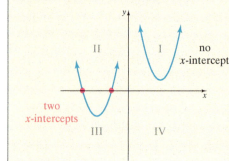
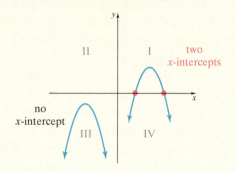

EXAMPLE 2 Graph $f(x) = 3x^2 + 3x + 1$. Find the vertex and any intercepts.

Solution Replace $f(x)$ with y and complete the square on x to write the equation in the form $y = a(x - h)^2 + k$.

$$y = 3x^2 + 3x + 1 \quad \text{Replace } f(x) \text{ with } y.$$
$$y - 1 = 3x^2 + 3x \quad \text{Isolate } x\text{-variable terms.}$$

Factor 3 from the terms $3x^2 + 3x$ so that the coefficient of x^2 is 1.

$$y - 1 = 3(x^2 + x) \quad \text{Factor out 3.}$$

The coefficient of x in the parentheses above is 1. Then $\frac{1}{2}(1) = \frac{1}{2}$ and $\left(\frac{1}{2}\right)^2 = \frac{1}{4}$.

Since we are adding $\frac{1}{4}$ inside the parentheses, we are really adding $3\left(\frac{1}{4}\right)$, so we *must* add $3\left(\frac{1}{4}\right)$ to the left side.

$$y - 1 + 3\left(\frac{1}{4}\right) = 3\left(x^2 + x + \frac{1}{4}\right)$$
$$y - \frac{1}{4} = 3\left(x + \frac{1}{2}\right)^2 \quad \text{Simplify the left side and factor the right side.}$$
$$y = 3\left(x + \frac{1}{2}\right)^2 + \frac{1}{4} \quad \text{Add } \frac{1}{4} \text{ to both sides.}$$
$$f(x) = 3\left(x + \frac{1}{2}\right)^2 + \frac{1}{4} \quad \text{Replace } y \text{ with } f(x).$$

Then $a = 3$, $h = -\frac{1}{2}$, and $k = \frac{1}{4}$. This means that the parabola opens upward with vertex $\left(-\frac{1}{2}, \frac{1}{4}\right)$ and that the axis of symmetry is the line $x = -\frac{1}{2}$.

To find the y-intercept, let $x = 0$. Then

$$f(0) = 3(0)^2 + 3(0) + 1 = 1$$

Thus the y-intercept is $(0, 1)$.

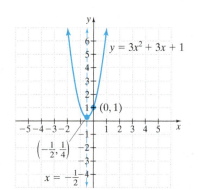

This parabola has no x-intercepts since the vertex is in the second quadrant and opens upward. Use the vertex, axis of symmetry, and y-intercept to sketch the parabola. □

PRACTICE 2 Graph $g(x) = 4x^2 + 4x + 3$. Find the vertex and any intercepts.

EXAMPLE 3 Graph $f(x) = -x^2 - 2x + 3$. Find the vertex and any intercepts.

Solution We write $f(x)$ in the form $a(x - h)^2 + k$ by completing the square. First we replace $f(x)$ with y.

$$f(x) = -x^2 - 2x + 3$$
$$y = -x^2 - 2x + 3$$
$$y - 3 = -x^2 - 2x \quad \text{Subtract 3 from both sides to get the } x\text{-variable terms alone.}$$
$$y - 3 = -1(x^2 + 2x) \quad \text{Factor } -1 \text{ from the terms } -x^2 - 2x.$$

The coefficient of x is 2. Then $\frac{1}{2}(2) = 1$ and $1^2 = 1$. We add 1 to the right side inside the parentheses and add $-1(1)$ to the left side.

$$y - 3 - 1(1) = -1(x^2 + 2x + 1)$$
$$y - 4 = -1(x + 1)^2 \quad \text{Simplify the left side and factor the right side.}$$
$$y = -1(x + 1)^2 + 4 \quad \text{Add 4 to both sides.}$$
$$f(x) = -1(x + 1)^2 + 4 \quad \text{Replace } y \text{ with } f(x).$$

> **Helpful Hint**
> This can be written as $f(x) = -1[x - (-1)]^2 + 4$. Notice that the vertex is $(-1, 4)$.

Since $a = -1$, the parabola opens downward with vertex $(-1, 4)$ and axis of symmetry $x = -1$.

To find the y-intercept, we let $x = 0$ and solve for y. Then
$$f(0) = -0^2 - 2(0) + 3 = 3$$

Thus, $(0, 3)$ is the y-intercept.

To find the x-intercepts, we let y or $f(x) = 0$ and solve for x.
$$f(x) = -x^2 - 2x + 3$$
$$0 = -x^2 - 2x + 3 \quad \text{Let } f(x) = 0.$$

Now we divide both sides by -1 so that the coefficient of x^2 is 1.

$$\frac{0}{-1} = \frac{-x^2}{-1} - \frac{2x}{-1} + \frac{3}{-1} \quad \text{Divide both sides by } -1.$$
$$0 = x^2 + 2x - 3 \quad \text{Simplify.}$$
$$0 = (x + 3)(x - 1) \quad \text{Factor.}$$
$$x + 3 = 0 \quad \text{or} \quad x - 1 = 0 \quad \text{Set each factor equal to 0.}$$
$$x = -3 \quad\quad\quad x = 1 \quad \text{Solve.}$$

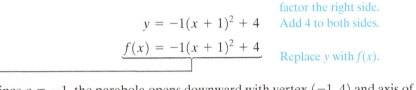

The x-intercepts are $(-3, 0)$ and $(1, 0)$. Use these points to sketch the parabola.

PRACTICE 3 Graph $g(x) = -x^2 + 5x + 6$. Find the vertex and any intercepts.

OBJECTIVE 2 ▶ Deriving a formula for finding the vertex. There is also a formula that may be used to find the vertex of a parabola. Now that we have practiced completing the square, we will show that the x-coordinate of the vertex of the graph of $f(x)$ or $y = ax^2 + bx + c$ can be found by the formula $x = \frac{-b}{2a}$. To do so, we complete the square on x and write the equation in the form $y = a(x - h)^2 + k$.

First, isolate the x-variable terms by subtracting c from both sides.

$$y = ax^2 + bx + c$$
$$y - c = ax^2 + bx$$

634 CHAPTER 11 Graphing Quadratic Functions, Rational Functions, and Conic Sections

Next, factor a from the terms $ax^2 + bx$.

$$y - c = a\left(x^2 + \frac{b}{a}x\right)$$

Next, add the square of half of $\frac{b}{a}$, or $\left(\frac{b}{2a}\right)^2 = \frac{b^2}{4a^2}$, to the right side inside the parentheses. Because of the factor a, what we really added was $a\left(\frac{b^2}{4a^2}\right)$ and this must be added to the left side.

$$y - c + a\left(\frac{b^2}{4a^2}\right) = a\left(x^2 + \frac{b}{a}x + \frac{b^2}{4a^2}\right)$$

$$y - c + \frac{b^2}{4a} = a\left(x + \frac{b}{2a}\right)^2 \qquad \text{Simplify the left side and factor the right side.}$$

$$y = a\left(x + \frac{b}{2a}\right)^2 + c - \frac{b^2}{4a} \qquad \text{Add } c \text{ to both sides and subtract } \frac{b^2}{4a} \text{ from both sides.}$$

Compare this form with $f(x)$ or $y = a(x - h)^2 + k$ and see that h is $\frac{-b}{2a}$, which means that the x-coordinate of the vertex of the graph of $f(x) = ax^2 + bx + c$ is $\frac{-b}{2a}$.

Vertex Formula

The graph of $f(x) = ax^2 + bx + c$, when $a \neq 0$, is a parabola with vertex

$$\left(\frac{-b}{2a}, f\left(\frac{-b}{2a}\right)\right)$$

Let's use this formula to find the vertex of the parabola we graphed in Example 1.

EXAMPLE 4 Find the vertex of the graph of $f(x) = x^2 - 4x - 12$.

Solution In the quadratic function $f(x) = x^2 - 4x - 12$, notice that $a = 1$, $b = -4$, and $c = -12$. Then

$$\frac{-b}{2a} = \frac{-(-4)}{2(1)} = 2$$

The x-value of the vertex is 2. To find the corresponding $f(x)$ or y-value, find $f(2)$. Then

$$f(2) = 2^2 - 4(2) - 12 = 4 - 8 - 12 = -16$$

The vertex is $(2, -16)$. These results agree with our findings in Example 1. □

PRACTICE 4 Find the vertex of the graph of $g(x) = x^2 - 2x - 3$.

OBJECTIVE 3 ▶ Finding minimum and maximum values. The vertex of a parabola gives us some important information about its corresponding quadratic function. The quadratic function whose graph is a parabola that opens upward has a minimum value, and the quadratic function whose graph is a parabola that opens downward has a maximum value. The $f(x)$ or y-value of the vertex is the minimum or maximum value of the function.

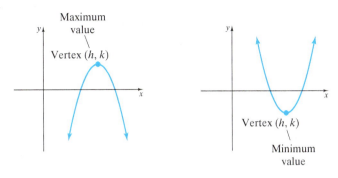

Concept Check ✓

Without making any calculations, tell whether the graph of $f(x) = 7 - x - 0.3x^2$ has a maximum value or a minimum value. Explain your reasoning.

EXAMPLE 5 Finding Maximum Height

A rock is thrown upward from the ground. Its height in feet above ground after t seconds is given by the function $f(t) = -16t^2 + 20t$. Find the maximum height of the rock and the number of seconds it took for the rock to reach its maximum height.

Solution

1. UNDERSTAND. The maximum height of the rock is the largest value of $f(t)$. Since the function $f(t) = -16t^2 + 20t$ is a quadratic function, its graph is a parabola. It opens downward since $-16 < 0$. Thus, the maximum value of $f(t)$ is the $f(t)$ or y-value of the vertex of its graph.

2. TRANSLATE. To find the vertex (h, k), notice that for $f(t) = -16t^2 + 20t$, $a = -16$, $b = 20$, and $c = 0$. We will use these values and the vertex formula

$$\left(\frac{-b}{2a}, f\left(\frac{-b}{2a}\right)\right)$$

3. SOLVE.

$$h = \frac{-b}{2a} = \frac{-20}{-32} = \frac{5}{8}$$

$$f\left(\frac{5}{8}\right) = -16\left(\frac{5}{8}\right)^2 + 20\left(\frac{5}{8}\right)$$

$$= -16\left(\frac{25}{64}\right) + \frac{25}{2}$$

$$= -\frac{25}{4} + \frac{50}{4} = \frac{25}{4}$$

4. INTERPRET. The graph of $f(t)$ is a parabola opening downward with vertex $\left(\frac{5}{8}, \frac{25}{4}\right)$. This means that the rock's maximum height is $\frac{25}{4}$ feet, or $6\frac{1}{4}$ feet, which was reached in $\frac{5}{8}$ second. □

PRACTICE

5 A ball is tossed upward from the ground. Its height in feet above ground after t seconds is given by the function $h(t) = -16t^2 + 24t$. Find the maximum height of the ball and the number of seconds it took for the ball to reach the maximum height.

Answer to Concept Check:
$f(x)$ has a maximum value since it opens downward.

VOCABULARY & READINESS CHECK

Fill in the blank.

1. If a quadratic function is in the form $f(x) = a(x - h)^2 + k$, the vertex of its graph is _____.

2. The graph of $f(x) = ax^2 + bx + c, a \neq 0$ is a parabola whose vertex has an x-value of _____.

Complete a Table.

	Parabola Opens	Vertex Location	Number of x-intercept(s)	Number of y-intercept(s)
3.	up	Q I		
4.	up	Q III		
5.	down	Q II		
6.	down	Q IV		
7.	up	x-axis		
8.	down	x-axis		
9.		Q III	0	
10.		Q I	2	
11.		Q IV	2	
12.		Q II	0	

11.2 EXERCISE SET

Find the vertex of the graph of each quadratic function. See Examples 1 through 4.

1. $f(x) = x^2 + 8x + 7$
2. $f(x) = x^2 + 6x + 5$
3. $f(x) = -x^2 + 10x + 5$
4. $f(x) = -x^2 - 8x + 2$
5. $f(x) = 5x^2 - 10x + 3$
6. $f(x) = -3x^2 + 6x + 4$
7. $f(x) = -x^2 + x + 1$
8. $f(x) = x^2 - 9x + 8$

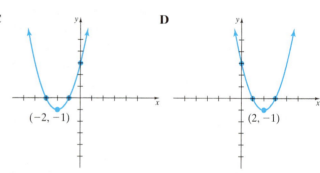
C (−2, −1)   D (2, −1)

9. $f(x) = x^2 - 4x + 3$
10. $f(x) = x^2 + 2x - 3$
11. $f(x) = x^2 - 2x - 3$
12. $f(x) = x^2 + 4x + 3$

Match each function with its graph. See Examples 1 through 4.

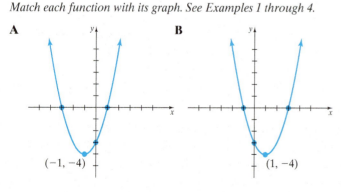
A (−1, −4)   B (1, −4)

MIXED PRACTICE

Find the vertex of the graph of each quadratic function. Determine whether the graph opens upward or downward, find any intercepts, and sketch the graph. See Examples 1 through 4.

13. $f(x) = x^2 + 4x - 5$
14. $f(x) = x^2 + 2x - 3$
15. $f(x) = -x^2 + 2x - 1$
16. $f(x) = -x^2 + 4x - 4$
17. $f(x) = x^2 - 4$
18. $f(x) = x^2 - 1$
19. $f(x) = 4x^2 + 4x - 3$
20. $f(x) = 2x^2 - x - 3$
21. $f(x) = x^2 + 8x + 15$
22. $f(x) = x^2 + 10x + 9$

23. $f(x) = x^2 - 6x + 5$
24. $f(x) = x^2 - 4x + 3$
25. $f(x) = x^2 - 4x + 5$
26. $f(x) = x^2 - 6x + 11$
27. $f(x) = 2x^2 + 4x + 5$
28. $f(x) = 3x^2 + 12x + 16$
29. $f(x) = -2x^2 + 12x$
30. $f(x) = -4x^2 + 8x$
31. $f(x) = x^2 + 1$
32. $f(x) = x^2 + 4$
33. $f(x) = x^2 - 2x - 15$
34. $f(x) = x^2 - x - 12$
35. $f(x) = -5x^2 + 5x$
36. $f(x) = 3x^2 - 12x$
37. $f(x) = -x^2 + 2x - 12$
38. $f(x) = -x^2 + 8x - 17$
39. $f(x) = 3x^2 - 12x + 15$
40. $f(x) = 2x^2 - 8x + 11$
41. $f(x) = x^2 + x - 6$
42. $f(x) = x^2 + 3x - 18$
43. $f(x) = -2x^2 - 3x + 35$
44. $f(x) = 3x^2 - 13x - 10$

Solve. See Example 5.

45. If a projectile is fired straight upward from the ground with an initial speed of 96 feet per second, then its height h in feet after t seconds is given by the equation
$$h(t) = -16t^2 + 96t$$
Find the maximum height of the projectile.

46. If Rheam Gaspar throws a ball upward with an initial speed of 32 feet per second, then its height h in feet after t seconds is given by the equation
$$h(t) = -16t^2 + 32t$$
Find the maximum height of the ball.

47. **Multiple Steps.** The cost C in dollars of manufacturing x bicycles at Holladay's Production Plant is given by the function
$$C(x) = 2x^2 - 800x + 92{,}000.$$

   a. Find the number of bicycles that must be manufactured to minimize the cost.
   b. Find the minimum cost.

48. **Multiple Steps.** The Utah Ski Club sells calendars to raise money. The profit P, in cents, from selling x calendars is given by the equation $P(x) = 360x - x^2$.
   a. Find how many calendars must be sold to maximize profit.
   b. Find the maximum profit.

49. **Multiple Steps.** Find two numbers whose sum is 60 and whose product is as large as possible. [*Hint:* Let x and $60 - x$ be the two positive numbers. Their product can be described by the function $f(x) = x(60 - x)$.]

50. Find two numbers whose sum is 11 and whose product is as large as possible. (Use the hint for Exercise 49.)

51. Find two numbers whose difference is 10 and whose product is as small as possible. (Use the hint for Exercise 49.)

52. Find two numbers whose difference is 8 and whose product is as small as possible.

53. The length and width of a rectangle must have a sum of 40. Find the dimensions of the rectangle that will have the maximum area. (Use the hint for Exercise 49.)

54. The length and width of a rectangle must have a sum of 50. Find the dimensions of the rectangle that will have maximum area.

REVIEW AND PREVIEW

Sketch the graph of each function. See Section 11.1.

55. $f(x) = x^2 + 2$
56. $f(x) = (x - 3)^2$
57. $g(x) = x + 2$
58. $h(x) = x - 3$
59. $f(x) = (x + 5)^2 + 2$
60. $f(x) = 2(x - 3)^2 + 2$
61. $f(x) = 3(x - 4)^2 + 1$
62. $f(x) = (x + 1)^2 + 4$
63. $f(x) = -(x - 4)^2 + \frac{3}{2}$
64. $f(x) = -2(x + 7)^2 + \frac{1}{2}$

CONCEPT EXTENSIONS

Without calculating, tell whether each graph has a minimum value or a maximum value. See the Concept Check in the section.

65. $f(x) = 2x^2 - 5$
66. $g(x) = -7x^2 + x + 1$
67. $F(x) = 3 - \frac{1}{2}x^2$
68. $G(x) = 3 - \frac{1}{2}x + 0.8x^2$

Find the vertex of the graph of each quadratic function. Determine whether the graph opens upward or downward, find the y-intercept, approximate the x-intercepts to one decimal place, and sketch the graph.

69. $f(x) = x^2 + 10x + 15$
70. $f(x) = x^2 - 6x + 4$
71. $f(x) = 3x^2 - 6x + 7$
72. $f(x) = 2x^2 + 4x - 1$

Find the maximum or minimum value of each function. Approximate to two decimal places.

73. $f(x) = 2.3x^2 - 6.1x + 3.2$
74. $f(x) = 7.6x^2 + 9.8x - 2.1$
75. $f(x) = -1.9x^2 + 5.6x - 2.7$
76. $f(x) = -5.2x^2 - 3.8x + 5.1$

77. **Multiple Steps.** The number of McDonald's restaurants worldwide can be modeled by the quadratic equation $f(x) = -96x^2 + 1018x + 28{,}824$, where $f(x)$ is the number of McDonald's restaurants and x is the number of years after 2000. (*Source:* Based on data from McDonald's Corporation)
   a. Will this function have a maximum or minimum? How can you tell?
   b. According to this model, in what year will the number of McDonald's restaurants be at its maximum/minimum?
   c. What is the maximum/minimum number of McDonald's restaurants predicted?

78. Multiple Steps. Methane is a gas produced by landfills, natural gas systems, and coal mining that contributes to the greenhouse effect and global warming. Projected methane emissions in the United States can be modeled by the quadratic function

$$f(x) = -0.072x^2 + 1.93x + 173.9$$

where $f(x)$ is the amount of methane produced in million metric tons and x is the number of years after 2000. (*Source:* Based on data from the U.S. Environmental Protection Agency, 2000–2020)

a. According to this model, what will U.S. emissions of methane be in 2009? (Round to 2 decimal places.)

b. Will this function have a maximum or a minimum? How can you tell?

c. In what year will methane emissions in the United States be at their maximum/minimum? Round to the nearest whole year.

d. What is the level of methane emissions for that year? (Use your rounded answer from part c.) (Round this answer to 2 decimals places.)

Use a graphing calculator to check each exercise.

79. Exercise 27   **80.** Exercise 28
81. Exercise 37   **82.** Exercise 38

11.3 GRAPHING RATIONAL FUNCTIONS BY TRANSFORMATIONS

OBJECTIVES

1. Find the domains of rational functions.
2. Graph $f(x) = \dfrac{1}{x}$ and $f(x) = \dfrac{1}{x^2}$.
3. Identify vertical asymptotes.
4. Identify horizontal asymptotes.
5. Use transformations to graph rational functions.

OBJECTIVE 1 ▶ Finding domains of rational functions. **Rational functions** are quotients of polynomial functions. This means that rational functions can be expressed as

$$f(x) = \frac{p(x)}{q(x)},$$

where p and q are polynomial functions and $q(x) \neq 0$. The **domain** of a rational function consists of all real numbers except the x-values that make the denominator zero. For example, the domain of the rational function

$$f(x) = \frac{x^2 + 7x + 9}{x(x - 2)(x + 5)} \quad \begin{array}{l}\text{This is } p(x).\\ \text{This is } q(x).\end{array}$$

consists of all real numbers except 0, 2, and −5.

EXAMPLE 1 Finding the Domain of a Rational Function

Find the domain of each rational function:

a. $f(x) = \dfrac{x^2 - 9}{x - 3}$ b. $g(x) = \dfrac{x}{x^2 - 9}$ c. $h(x) = \dfrac{x + 3}{x^2 + 9}$.

Solution Rational functions contain division. Because division by 0 is undefined, we must exclude from the domain of each function values of x that cause the polynomial function in the denominator to be 0.

a. The denominator of $f(x) = \dfrac{x^2 - 9}{x - 3}$ is 0 if $x = 3$. Thus, x cannot equal 3.

The domain of f consists of all real numbers except 3.

> **Helpful Hint**
> Because the domain of a rational function is the set of all real numbers except those for which the denominator is 0, you can identify such numbers by setting the denominator equal to 0 and solving for x. Exclude the resulting real values of x from the domain.

b. The denominator of $g(x) = \dfrac{x}{x^2 - 9}$ is 0 if $x = -3$ or $x = 3$. Thus, the domain of g consists of all real numbers except -3 and 3.

c. No real numbers cause the denominator of $h(x) = \dfrac{x + 3}{x^2 + 9}$ to equal 0. The domain of h consists of all real numbers. □

PRACTICE 1 Find the domain of each rational function:

a. $f(x) = \dfrac{x^2 - 25}{x - 5}$ **b.** $g(x) = \dfrac{x}{x^2 - 25}$ **c.** $h(x) = \dfrac{x + 5}{x^2 + 25}$.

OBJECTIVE 2 ▶ **Graphing $f(x) = \dfrac{1}{x}$ and $f(x) = \dfrac{1}{x^2}$.** The most basic rational function is the **reciprocal function,** defined by $f(x) = \dfrac{1}{x}$. The denominator of the reciprocal function is zero when $x = 0$, so the domain of f is the set of all real numbers except 0.

Let's take our time as we graph $f(x) = \dfrac{1}{x}$ and find many ordered-pair solutions so that we can clearly understand the graph.

x	-1	-0.5	-0.1	-0.01	-0.001
$f(x) = \dfrac{1}{x}$	-1	-2	-10	-100	-1000

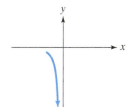

From the table and the accompanying graph, it appears that as x approaches 0 from the left, the function values, $f(x)$, decrease without bound. We say that "$f(x)$ approaches negative infinity."

Let's continue finding ordered-pair solutions for $f(x) = \dfrac{1}{x}$.

x	0.001	0.01	0.1	0.5	1
$f(x) = \dfrac{1}{x}$	1000	100	10	2	1

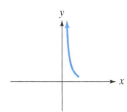

From the table and the accompanying graph, it appears that as x approaches 0 from the right, the function values, $f(x)$, increase without bound. We say that "$f(x)$ approaches infinity."

Now let's see what happens to the function values of $f(x) = \dfrac{1}{x}$ as x gets farther away from the origin. The following tables suggest what happens to $f(x)$ as x increases or decreases without bound.

x increases without bound:					**x decreases without bound:**			
x	1	10	100	1000	x	-1	-10	-100	-1000
$f(x) = \dfrac{1}{x}$	1	0.1	0.01	0.001	$f(x) = \dfrac{1}{x}$	-1	-0.1	-0.01	-0.001

It appears that as x increases or decreases without bound, the function values, $f(x)$, are getting progressively closer to 0.

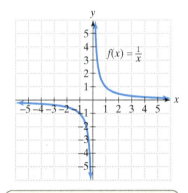

$f(x)$ approaches 0 as x increases or decreases without bound.

The end behavior of $f(x) = \frac{1}{x}$ as x increases or decreases without bound is shown in the first graph in the margin. The graph shows that the function values, $f(x)$, are approaching 0. This means that as x increases or decreases without bound, the graph of f is approaching the horizontal line $y = 0$ (that is, the x-axis).

As $x \to \infty$, $f(x) \to 0$ and as $x \to -\infty$, $f(x) \to 0$.

As x approaches infinity (that is, increases without bound), $f(x)$ approaches 0.

As x approaches negative infinity (that is, decreases without bound), $f(x)$ approaches 0.

The graph of the reciprocal function $f(x) = \frac{1}{x}$ is shown in the second graph in the margin. Unlike the graph of a polynomial function, the graph of the reciprocal function has a break and is composed of two distinct branches.

Another basic rational function is $f(x) = \frac{1}{x^2}$. The graph of this even function, with y-axis symmetry and positive function values, is shown in below. Like the reciprocal function, the graph has a break and is composed of two distinct branches.

> **Helpful Hint**
> If x is far from 0, then $\frac{1}{x}$ is close to 0.
> By contrast, if x is close to 0, then $\frac{1}{x}$ is far from 0.

x	1	-1	2	-2	3	-3	$\frac{1}{2}$	$-\frac{1}{2}$
y or $f(x) = \frac{1}{x^2}$	1	1	$\frac{1}{4}$	$\frac{1}{4}$	$\frac{1}{9}$	$\frac{1}{9}$	4	4

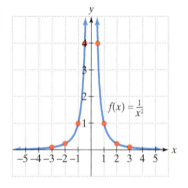

OBJECTIVE 3 ▶ **Vertical asymptotes of rational functions.** Look again at the graph of $f(x) = \frac{1}{x^2}$ above. The curve approaches, but does not touch, the y-axis. The y-axis, or $x = 0$, is said to be a *vertical asymptote* of the graph. A rational function may have no vertical asymptotes, one vertical asymptote, or several vertical asymptotes. The graph of a rational function never intersects a vertical asymptote. We will use dashed lines to show asymptotes.

If the graph of a rational function has vertical asymptotes, they can be located using the following theorem:

Locating Vertical Asymptotes

Let $f(x) = \frac{p(x)}{q(x)}$ be a rational function in which $p(x)$ and $q(x)$ have no common factors.

If a is a zero of $q(x)$, the denominator, then $x = a$ is a vertical asymptote of the graph of f.

EXAMPLE 2 Finding the Vertical Asymptotes of a Rational Function

Find the vertical asymptotes, if any, of the graph of each rational function:

a. $f(x) = \dfrac{x+1}{x-5}$ **b.** $f(x) = \dfrac{x}{x^2-9}$ **c.** $h(x) = \dfrac{x+3}{x^2+9}$.

Solution

a. $f(x) = \dfrac{x+1}{x-5}$

The only zero of the denominator of $f(x)$ is 5. Thus, the line $x = 5$ is the only vertical asymptote of the graph.

b. If possible, factoring is usually helpful in identifying zeros of denominators and any common factors in the numerators and denominators.

$$f(x) = \frac{x}{x^2 - 9} = \frac{x}{(x+3)(x-3)}$$

This factor is 0 if $x = -3$. This factor is 0 if $x = 3$.

There are no common factors in the numerator and the denominator. The zeros of the denominator are -3 and 3. Thus, the lines $x = -3$ and $x = 3$ are the vertical asymptotes for the graph.

c. We cannot factor the denominator of $h(x)$ over the real numbers.

$$h(x) = \frac{x+3}{x^2 + 9}$$

No real numbers make this denominator 0.

The denominator has no real zeros. Thus, the graph has no vertical asymptotes.

PRACTICE 2 Find the vertical asymptotes, if any, of the graph of each rational function:

a. $f(x) = \dfrac{x+7}{x-3}$ **b.** $f(x) = \dfrac{x}{x^2 - 1}$ **c.** $h(x) = \dfrac{x-1}{x^2 + 1}$

OBJECTIVE 4 ▶ Horizontal asymptotes of rational functions. The graph of the reciprocal function $f(x) = \dfrac{1}{x}$ is shown again in the margin. As $x \to \infty$ and as $x \to -\infty$, the function values are approaching 0: $f(x) \to 0$. The line $y = 0$ (that is, the x-axis) is a *horizontal asymptote* of the graph. Many, but not all, rational functions have horizontal asymptotes.

The graph of $f(x) = \dfrac{1}{x}$

> **▶ Helpful Hint**
> Unlike identifying possible vertical asymptotes, we do not use factoring to determine a possible horizontal asymptote.

Locating Horizontal Asymptotes

Let f be the rational function given by

$$f(x) = \frac{a_n x^n + a_{n-1} x^{n-1} + \cdots + a_1 x + a_0}{b_m x^m + b_{m-1} x^{m-1} + \cdots + b_1 x + b_0}, \quad a_n \neq 0, b_m \neq 0.$$

The degree of the numerator is n. The degree of the denominator is m.

1. If $n < m$, the x-axis, or $y = 0$, is the horizontal asymptote of the graph of f.
2. If $n = m$, the line $y = \dfrac{a_n}{b_m}$ is the horizontal asymptote of the graph of f.
3. If $n > m$, the graph of f has no horizontal asymptote.

EXAMPLE 3 Finding the Horizontal Asymptote of a Rational Function

Find the horizontal asymptote, if any, of the graph of each rational function:

a. $f(x) = \dfrac{4x}{2x^2 + 1}$ **b.** $g(x) = \dfrac{4x^2}{2x^2 + 1}$ **c.** $h(x) = \dfrac{4x^3}{2x^2 + 1}$

Solution

a. $f(x) = \dfrac{4x}{2x^2 + 1}$

The degree of the numerator, 1, is less than the degree of the denominator, 2. Thus, the graph of f has the x-axis as a horizontal asymptote. The equation of the horizontal asymptote is $y = 0$.

b. $g(x) = \dfrac{4x^2}{2x^2 + 1}$

The degree of the numerator, 2, is equal to the degree of the denominator, 2. The leading coefficients of the numerator and denominator, 4 and 2, are used to obtain the equation of the horizontal asymptote. The equation of the horizontal asymptote is $y = \dfrac{4}{2}$ or $y = 2$.

c. $h(x) = \dfrac{4x^3}{2x^2 + 1}$

The degree of the numerator, 3, is greater than the degree of the denominator, 2. Thus, the graph of h has no horizontal asymptote. □

PRACTICE 3 Find the horizontal asymptote, if any, of the graph of each rational function:

a. $f(x) = \dfrac{9x^2}{3x^2 + 1}$ **b.** $g(x) = \dfrac{9x}{3x^2 + 1}$ **c.** $h(x) = \dfrac{9x^3}{3x^2 + 1}$.

OBJECTIVE 5 ▶ Using transformations to graph rational functions. Below, we show the graphs of two rational functions, $f(x) = \dfrac{1}{x}$ and $f(x) = \dfrac{1}{x^2}$. The dashed green lines indicate the asymptotes.

Graphs of Common Rational Functions

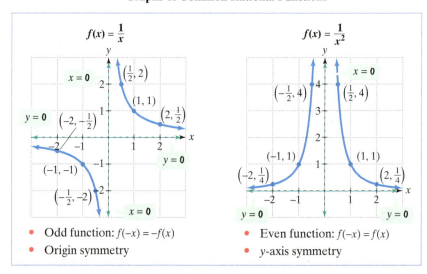

- Odd function: $f(-x) = -f(x)$
- Origin symmetry

- Even function: $f(-x) = f(x)$
- y-axis symmetry

Some rational functions can be graphed using transformations (horizontal shifting, stretching or shrinking, reflecting, vertical shifting) of these two common graphs. (See Sections 3.6 and 11.1 for a review.)

EXAMPLE 4 Using Transformations to Graph a Rational Function

Use the graph of $f(x) = \dfrac{1}{x^2}$ to graph $g(x) = \dfrac{1}{(x-2)^2} + 1$.

Section 11.3 Graphing Rational Functions by Transformations   643

Solution

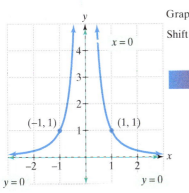

Begin with $f(x) = \frac{1}{x^2}$.
We've identified two points and the asymptotes.

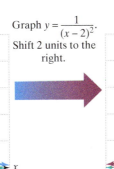

Graph $y = \frac{1}{(x-2)^2}$.
Shift 2 units to the right.

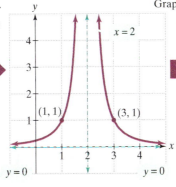

The graph of $y = \frac{1}{(x-2)^2}$ showing two points and the asymptotes

Graph $g(x) = \frac{1}{(x-2)^2} + 1$.
Shift 1 unit up.

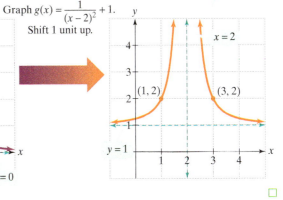

The graph of $g(x) = \frac{1}{(x-2)^2} + 1$ showing two points and the asymptotes

PRACTICE 4 Use the graph of $f(x) = \frac{1}{x}$ to graph $g(x) = \frac{1}{x+2} - 1$.

TECHNOLOGY NOTE

The graph of the rational function $f(x) = \frac{x}{x^2 - 9}$, is graphed below in a $[-5, 5, 1]$ by $[-4, 4, 1]$ viewing rectangle. The graph is shown in connected mode and in dot mode. In connected mode, the graphing utility plots many points and connects the points with curves. In dot mode, the utility plots the same points, but does not connect them.

Connected Mode

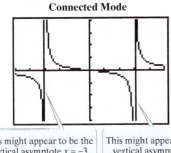

This might appear to be the vertical asymptote $x = -3$, but it is neither vertical nor an asymptote.

This might appear to be the vertical asymptote $x = 3$, but it is neither vertical nor an asymptote.

Dot Mode

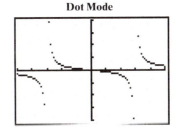

The steep lines in connected mode that are "almost" the vertical asymptotes $x = -3$ and $x = 3$ are not part of the graph and do not represent the vertical asymptotes. The graphing utility has incorrectly connected the last point to the left of $x = -3$ with the first point to the right of $x = -3$. It has also incorrectly connected the last point to the left of $x = 3$ with the first point to the right of $x = 3$. The effect is to create two near-vertical segments that look like asymptotes. This erroneous effect does not appear using dot mode.

11.3 EXERCISE SET

Find the domain of each rational function.

1. $f(x) = \dfrac{5x}{x - 4}$

2. $f(x) = \dfrac{7x}{x - 8}$

3. $g(x) = \dfrac{3x^2}{(x - 5)(x + 4)}$

4. $g(x) = \dfrac{2x^2}{(x - 2)(x + 6)}$

5. $h(x) = \dfrac{x + 7}{x^2 - 49}$

6. $h(x) = \dfrac{x + 8}{x^2 - 64}$

7. $f(x) = \dfrac{x + 7}{x^2 + 49}$

8. $f(x) = \dfrac{x + 8}{x^2 + 64}$

Find the vertical asymptotes, if any, of the graph of each rational function.

9. $f(x) = \dfrac{x}{x+4}$
10. $f(x) = \dfrac{x}{x-3}$
11. $g(x) = \dfrac{x+3}{x(x+4)}$
12. $g(x) = \dfrac{x+3}{x(x-3)}$
13. $h(x) = \dfrac{x}{x(x+4)}$
14. $h(x) = \dfrac{x}{x(x-3)}$
15. $r(x) = \dfrac{x}{x^2+4}$
16. $r(x) = \dfrac{x}{x^2+3}$

Find the horizontal asymptote, if any, of the graph of each rational function.

17. $f(x) = \dfrac{12x}{3x^2+1}$
18. $f(x) = \dfrac{15x}{3x^2+1}$
19. $g(x) = \dfrac{12x^2}{3x^2+1}$
20. $g(x) = \dfrac{15x^2}{3x^2+1}$
21. $h(x) = \dfrac{12x^3}{3x^2+1}$
22. $h(x) = \dfrac{15x^3}{3x^2+1}$
23. $f(x) = \dfrac{-2x+1}{3x+5}$
24. $f(x) = \dfrac{-3x+7}{5x-2}$

Use transformations of $f(x) = \dfrac{1}{x}$ or $f(x) = \dfrac{1}{x^2}$ to graph each rational function.

25. $g(x) = \dfrac{1}{x-1}$
26. $g(x) = \dfrac{1}{x-2}$
27. $h(x) = \dfrac{1}{x} + 2$
28. $h(x) = \dfrac{1}{x} + 1$
29. $g(x) = \dfrac{1}{x+1} - 2$
30. $g(x) = \dfrac{1}{x+2} - 2$
31. $g(x) = \dfrac{1}{(x+2)^2}$
32. $g(x) = \dfrac{1}{(x+1)^2}$
33. $h(x) = \dfrac{1}{x^2} - 4$
34. $h(x) = \dfrac{1}{x^2} - 3$
35. $h(x) = \dfrac{1}{(x-3)^2} + 1$
36. $h(x) = \dfrac{1}{(x-3)^2} + 2$

37. What is a rational function?
38. If you are given the equation of a rational function, explain how to find the vertical asymptotes, if any, of the function's graph.
39. If you are given the equation of a rational function, explain how to find the horizontal asymptote, if any, of the function's graph.
40. Is every rational function a polynomial function? Why or why not? Does a true statement result if the two adjectives *rational* and *polynomial* are reversed? Explain.
41. Use a graphing utility to verify any five of your hand-drawn graphs in Exercises 25–36.
42. Use a graphing utility to graph $y = \dfrac{1}{x}$, $y = \dfrac{1}{x^3}$, and $\dfrac{1}{x^5}$ in the same viewing rectangle. For odd values of n, how does changing n affect the graph of $y = \dfrac{1}{x^n}$?
43. Use a graphing utility to graph $y = \dfrac{1}{x^2}$, $y = \dfrac{1}{x^4}$, and $y = \dfrac{1}{x^6}$ in the same viewing rectangle. For even values of n, how does changing n affect the graph of $y = \dfrac{1}{x^n}$?

True or False. *Determine whether each statement is true or false. If the statement is false, make the necessary change(s) to produce a true statement.*

44. The graph of a rational function cannot have both a vertical asymptote and a horizontal asymptote.
45. It is possible to have a rational function whose graph has no y-intercept.
46. The graph of a rational function can have three vertical asymptotes.

REVIEW AND PREVIEW

Solve. See Sections 6.8 and 9.2.

47. $2x^2 + x = 15$.
48. $x^3 + x^2 = 4x + 4$.
49. $x^2 - 6x + 4 = 0$.
50. $9x^2 - 6x = 4$.

11.4 FURTHER GRAPHING OF RATIONAL FUNCTIONS

OBJECTIVES

1. Graph rational functions.
2. Identify slant asymptotes.
3. Solve applied problems involving rational functions.

Japanese researchers have developed the robotic exoskeleton shown on the next page to help the elderly and disabled walk and even lift heavy objects like the three 22-pound bags of rice in the photo. It's called the Hybrid Assistive Limb, or HAL. HAL's brain is a computer housed in a back-pack that learns to mimic the wearer's gait and posture. Bioelectric sensors pick up signals transmitted from the brain to the muscles, so it can anticipate movements the moment the wearer thinks of them. A commercial version is available at a hefty cost ranging between $14,000 and $20,000. (*Source*: sanlab.kz.tsukuba.ac.jp)

The cost of manufacturing robotic exoskeletons can be modeled by rational functions. In this section, you will see that high production levels of HAL can eventually

Section 11.4 Further Graphing of Rational Functions 645

make this amazing invention more affordable for the elderly and people with disabilities.

OBJECTIVE 1 ▶ **Graphing rational functions.** Rational functions that are not transformations of $f(x) = \dfrac{1}{x}$ or $f(x) = \dfrac{1}{x^2}$ can be graphed using the following procedure:

Strategy for Graphing a Rational Function

The following strategy can be used to graph

$$f(x) = \frac{p(x)}{q(x)},$$

where p and q are polynomial functions with no common factors.

1. Find the y-intercept (if there is one) by evaluating $f(0)$.
2. Find the x-intercepts (if there are any) by solving the equation $p(x) = 0$.
3. Find any vertical asymptote(s) by solving the equation $q(x) = 0$.
4. Find the horizontal asymptote (if there is one) using the rule for determining the horizontal asymptote of a rational function.
5. Plot at least one point between and beyond each x-intercept and vertical asymptote.
6. Use the information obtained previously to graph the function between and beyond the vertical asymptotes.

EXAMPLE 1 Graphing a Rational Function

Graph: $f(x) = \dfrac{2x - 1}{x - 1}$.

Solution

Step 1 Find the y-intercept. Evaluate $f(0)$.

$$f(0) = \frac{2 \cdot 0 - 1}{0 - 1} = \frac{-1}{-1} = 1$$

The y-intercept is $(0, 1)$.

Step 2 Find x-intercept(s). This is done by solving $p(x) = 0$, where $p(x)$ is the numerator of $f(x)$.

$2x - 1 = 0$ Set the numerator equal to 0.
$2x = 1$ Add 1 to both sides.
$x = \dfrac{1}{2}$ Divide both sides by 2.

The x-intercept is $\left(\dfrac{1}{2}, 0\right)$.

Step 3 Find the vertical asymptote(s). Solve $q(x) = 0$, where $q(x)$ is the denominator of $f(x)$, thereby finding zeros of the denominator.

$x - 1 = 0$ Set the denominator equal to 0.
$x = 1$ Add 1 to both sides.

The equation of the vertical asymptote is $x = 1$.

Step 4 Find the horizontal asymptote. Because the numerator and denominator of $f(x) = \dfrac{2x - 1}{x - 1}$ have the same degree, 1, the leading coefficients of the numerator and denominator, 2 and 1, respectively, are used to obtain the equation of the horizontal asymptote. The equation is

$$y = \frac{2}{1} = 2.$$

The equation of the horizontal asymptote is $y = 2$.

Step 5 Plot points between and beyond each x-intercept and vertical asymptote. With an x-intercept at $\frac{1}{2}$ and a vertical asymptote at $x = 1$, we evaluate the function at $-2, -1, \frac{3}{4}, 2,$ and 4.

x	-2	-1	$\frac{3}{4}$	2	4
$f(x) = \dfrac{2x-1}{x-1}$	$\frac{5}{3}$	$\frac{3}{2}$	-2	3	$\frac{7}{3}$

Graph these points, the y-intercept, the x-intercept, and the asymptotes.

Step 6 Graph the function. The graph of $f(x) = \dfrac{2x-1}{x-1}$ is shown next.

TECHNOLOGY NOTE

The graph of $y = \dfrac{2x-1}{x-1}$, obtained using the dot mode in a $[-6, 6, 1]$ by $[-6, 6, 1]$ viewing rectangle, verifies that our hand-drawn graph is correct.

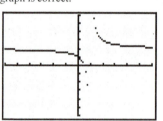

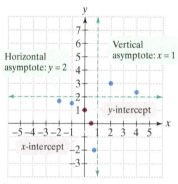

Step 5 Preparing to graph the rational function $f(x) = \dfrac{2x-1}{x-1}$

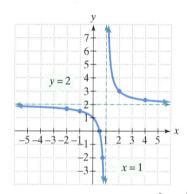

Step 6 The graph of $f(x) = \dfrac{2x-1}{x-1}$

PRACTICE 1 Graph: $f(x) = \dfrac{3x-3}{x-2}$.

EXAMPLE 2 Graphing a Rational Function

Graph: $f(x) = \dfrac{3x^2}{x^2 - 4}$.

Solution

Step 1 Find the y-intercept. $f(0) = \dfrac{3 \cdot 0^2}{0^2 - 4} = \dfrac{0}{-4} = 0$: The y-intercept is $(0, 0)$.

Step 2 Find the x-intercept(s). $3x^2 = 0$, so $x = 0$: The x-intercept is $(0, 0)$, verifying that the graph passes through the origin.

Step 3 Find the vertical asymptote(s). Set $q(x) = 0$. (Note that the numerator and denominator of $f(x) = \dfrac{3x^2}{x^2 - 4}$ have no common factors.)

$$x^2 - 4 = 0 \quad \text{Set the denominator equal to 0.}$$
$$x^2 = 4 \quad \text{Add 4 to both sides.}$$
$$x = \pm 2 \quad \text{Use the square root property.}$$

The vertical asymptotes are $x = -2$ and $x = 2$.

Step 4 Find the horizontal asymptote. Because the numerator and denominator of $f(x) = \dfrac{3x^2}{x^2 - 4}$ have the same degree, 2, their leading coefficients, 3 and 1, are used to determine the equation of the horizontal asymptote. The equation is $y = \dfrac{3}{1} = 3$.

Step 5 Plot points between and beyond each x-intercept and vertical asymptote. With an x-intercept at 0 and vertical asymptotes at $x = -2$ and $x = 2$, we evaluate the function at $-3, -1, 1, 3,$ and 4.

x	-3	-1	1	3	4
$f(x) = \dfrac{3x^2}{x^2 - 4}$	$\dfrac{27}{5}$	-1	-1	$\dfrac{27}{5}$	4

The figure below on the left shows the points $\left(-3, \dfrac{27}{5}\right), (-1, -1), (1, -1), \left(3, \dfrac{27}{5}\right)$, and $(4, 4)$, the y-intercept, the x-intercept, and the asymptotes.

Step 6 Graph the function. The graph of $f(x) = \dfrac{3x^2}{x^2 - 4}$ is shown below on the right.

TECHNOLOGY NOTE

The graph of $y = \dfrac{3x^2}{x^2 - 4}$, generated by a graphing utility, verifies that our hand-drawn graph is correct.

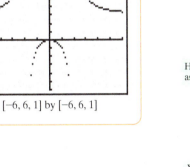

$[-6, 6, 1]$ by $[-6, 6, 1]$

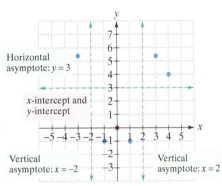

Step 5 Preparing to graph $f(x) = \dfrac{3x^2}{x^2 - 4}$

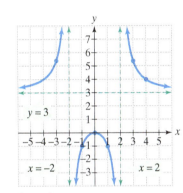

Step 6 The graph of $f(x) = \dfrac{3x^2}{x^2 - 4}$

PRACTICE 2 Graph: $f(x) = \dfrac{2x^2}{x^2 - 9}$.

Example 3 illustrates that not every rational function has vertical and horizontal asymptotes.

EXAMPLE 3 Graphing a Rational Function

Graph: $f(x) = \dfrac{x^4}{x^2 + 1}$.

Solution

Step 1 Find the y-intercept. $f(0) = \dfrac{0^4}{0^2 + 1} = \dfrac{0}{1} = 0$: The y-intercept is $(0, 0)$.

Step 2 Find the x-intercept(s). $x^4 = 0$, so $x = 0$: The x-intercept is $(0, 0)$.

Step 3 Find the vertical asymptote. Set $q(x) = 0$.

$$x^2 + 1 = 0 \quad \text{Set the denominator equal to 0.}$$
$$x^2 = -1 \quad \text{Subtract 1 from both sides.}$$

Although this equation has imaginary roots ($x = \pm i$), there are no real roots. Thus, the graph of f has no vertical asymptotes.

Step 4 Find the horizontal asymptote. Because the degree of the numerator, 4, is greater than the degree of the denominator, 2, there is no horizontal asymptote.

Step 5 Plot points between and beyond each x-intercept and vertical asymptote. With an x-intercept at 0 and no vertical asymptotes, let's look at function values at $-2, -1, 1,$ and 2.

x	-2	-1	1	2
$f(x) = \dfrac{x^4}{x^2 + 1}$	$\dfrac{16}{5}$	$\dfrac{1}{2}$	$\dfrac{1}{2}$	$\dfrac{16}{5}$

Step 6 Graph the function. The graph in the margin shows the graph of f using the points obtained from the table and y-axis symmetry. □

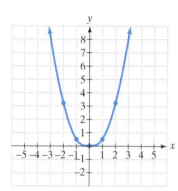

Step 6 The graph of $f(x) = \dfrac{x^4}{x^2 + 1}$

PRACTICE 3 Graph: $f(x) = \dfrac{x^4}{x^2 + 2}$.

OBJECTIVE 2 ▶ Slant asymptotes. Examine the graph of

$$f(x) = \dfrac{x^2 + 1}{x - 1},$$

shown in the margin. Note that the degree of the numerator, 2, is greater than the degree of the denominator, 1. Thus, the graph of this function has no horizontal asymptote. However, the graph has a **slant asymptote,** $y = x + 1$.

The graph of a rational function has a slant asymptote if the degree of the numerator is one more than the degree of the denominator. The equation of the slant asymptote can be found by division. For example, to find the slant asymptote for the graph of $f(x) = \dfrac{x^2 + 1}{x - 1}$, divide $x - 1$ into $x^2 + 1$:

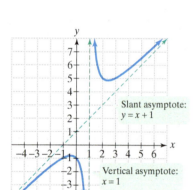

The graph of $f(x) = \dfrac{x^2 + 1}{x - 1}$ with a slant asymptote

$$\begin{array}{r} \underline{1|\ 1\ \ 0\ \ 1} \\ 1\ \ 1 \\ \overline{1\ \ 1\ \ 2} \end{array}$$

Remainder

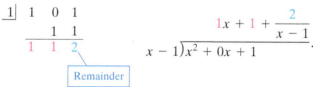

Observe that

$$f(x) = \dfrac{x^2 + 1}{x - 1} = \underbrace{x + 1}_{} + \dfrac{2}{x - 1}.$$

The equation of the slant asymptote is $y = x + 1$.

As $x \to +\infty$ and $x \to -\infty$, the graph of $f(x)$ approaches the line $y = x + 1$. Thus, the line $y = x + 1$ is a slant asymptote of the graph.

In general, if $f(x) = \dfrac{p(x)}{q(x)}$, p and q have no common factors, and the degree of p is one greater than the degree of q, find the slant asymptote by dividing $q(x)$ into $p(x)$. The division will take the form

$$\dfrac{p(x)}{q(x)} = \underbrace{mx + b}_{} + \dfrac{\text{remainder}}{q(x)}.$$

Slant asymptote: $y = mx + b$

The equation of the slant asymptote is obtained by dropping the term with the remainder. Thus, the equation of the slant asymptote is $y = mx + b$.

EXAMPLE 4 Finding the Slant Asymptote of a Rational Function

Find the slant asymptote of $f(x) = \dfrac{x^2 - 4x - 5}{x - 3}$.

Solution Because the degree of the numerator, 2, is exactly one more than the degree of the denominator, 1, and $x - 3$ is not a factor of $x^2 - 4x - 5$, the graph of f has a slant asymptote. To find the equation of the slant asymptote, divide $x - 3$ into $x^2 - 4x - 5$:

$$\begin{array}{r|rrr} 3 & 1 & -4 & -5 \\ & & 3 & -3 \\ \hline & 1 & -1 & -8 \end{array}$$

Remainder

$$x - 3 \overline{\smash{\big)}\, x^2 - 4x - 5} \quad \to \quad 1x - 1 - \dfrac{8}{x - 3}$$

Drop the remainder term and you'll have the equation of the slant asymptote.

The equation of the slant asymptote is $y = x - 1$. Using our strategy for graphing rational functions, the graph of $f(x) = \dfrac{x^2 - 4x - 5}{x - 3}$ is shown in the margin.

Slant asymptote: $y = x - 1$

Vertical asymptote: $x = 3$

The graph of $f(x) = \dfrac{x^2 - 4x - 5}{x - 3}$

PRACTICE 4 Find the slant asymptote of $f(x) = \dfrac{2x^2 - 5x + 7}{x - 2}$.

OBJECTIVE 3 ▶ Solve applied problems involving rational functions. There are numerous examples of asymptotic behavior in functions that model real-world phenomena. Let's consider an example from the business world. The **cost function**, C, for a business is the sum of its fixed and variable costs:

$$C(x) = (\text{fixed cost}) + cx.$$

Cost per unit times the number of units produced, x

The **average cost** per unit for a company to produce x units is the sum of its fixed and variable costs divided by the number of units produced. The **average cost function** is a rational function that is denoted by $\overline{C}$. Thus,

Cost of producing x units: fixed plus variable costs

$$\overline{C}(x) = \dfrac{(\text{fixed cost}) + cx}{x}.$$

Number of units produced

EXAMPLE 5 Average Cost for a Business

We return to the robotic exoskeleton described in the section opener. Suppose a company that manufactures this invention has a fixed monthly cost of $1,000,000 and that it costs $5000 to produce each robotic system.

    a. Write the cost function, C, of producing x robotic systems.

    b. Write the average cost function, $\overline{C}$, of producing x robotic systems.

    c. Find and interpret $\overline{C}(1000)$, $\overline{C}(10,000)$, and $\overline{C}(100,000)$.

d. What is the horizontal asymptote for the graph of the average cost function, $\overline{C}$? Describe what this represents for the company.

Solution

a. The cost function, C, is the sum of the fixed cost and the variable costs.

$$C(x) = \underbrace{1{,}000{,}000}_{\text{Fixed cost is \$1,000,000.}} + \underbrace{5000x}_{\text{Variable cost: \$5000 for each robotic system produced}}$$

b. The average cost function, $\overline{C}$, is the sum of fixed and variable costs divided by the number of robotic systems produced.

$$\overline{C}(x) = \frac{1{,}000{,}000 + 5000x}{x} \quad \text{or} \quad \overline{C}(x) = \frac{5000x + 1{,}000{,}000}{x}$$

c. We evaluate $\overline{C}$ at 1000, 10,000, and 100,000, interpreting the results.

$$\overline{C}(1000) = \frac{5000(1000) + 1{,}000{,}000}{1000} = 6000$$

The average cost per robotic system of producing 1000 systems per month is $6000.

$$\overline{C}(10{,}000) = \frac{5000(10{,}000) + 1{,}000{,}000}{10{,}000} = 5100$$

The average cost per robotic system of producing 10,000 systems per month is $5100.

$$\overline{C}(100{,}000) = \frac{5000(100{,}000) + 1{,}000{,}000}{100{,}000} = 5010$$

The average cost per robotic system of producing 100,000 systems per month is $5010. Notice that with higher production levels, the cost of producing each robotic exoskeleton decreases.

d. We developed the average cost function

$$\overline{C}(x) = \frac{5000x + 1{,}000{,}000}{x}$$

in which the degree of the numerator, 1, is equal to the degree of the denominator, 1. The leading coefficients of the numerator and denominator, 5000 and 1, are used to obtain the equation of the horizontal asymptote. The equation of the horizontal asymptote is

$$y = \frac{5000}{1} \quad \text{or} \quad y = 5000.$$

The horizontal asymptote is shown in the margin. This means that the more robotic systems produced each month, the closer the average cost per system for the company comes to $5000. The least possible cost per robotic exoskeleton is approaching $5000. Competitively low prices take place with high production levels, posing a major problem for small businesses. □

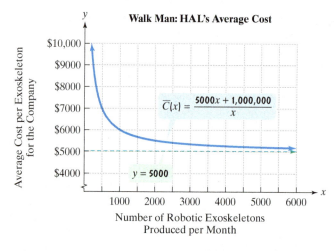

Walk Man: HAL's Average Cost

$\overline{C}(x) = \dfrac{5000x + 1{,}000{,}000}{x}$

$y = 5000$

Number of Robotic Exoskeletons Produced per Month

Average Cost per Exoskeleton for the Company

PRACTICE 5 A company is planning to manufacture wheelchairs that are light, fast, and beautiful. The fixed monthly cost will be $500,000 and it will cost $400 to produce each radically innovative chair.

a. Write the cost function, C, of producing x wheelchairs.

b. Write the average cost function, $\overline{C}$, of producing x wheelchairs.

c. Find and interpret $\overline{C}(1000), \overline{C}(10{,}000),$ and $\overline{C}(100{,}000)$.

d. What is the horizontal asymptote for the graph of the average cost function, $\overline{C}$? Describe what this represents for the company.

11.4 EXERCISE SET

Follow the six steps to graph each rational function. See Examples 1–4.

1. $f(x) = \dfrac{4x}{x-2}$
2. $f(x) = \dfrac{3x}{x-1}$
3. $f(x) = \dfrac{2x}{x^2-4}$
4. $f(x) = \dfrac{4x}{x^2-1}$
5. $f(x) = \dfrac{2x^2}{x^2-1}$
6. $f(x) = \dfrac{4x^2}{x^2-9}$
7. $f(x) = \dfrac{-x}{x+1}$
8. $f(x) = \dfrac{-3x}{x+2}$
9. $f(x) = -\dfrac{1}{x^2-4}$
10. $f(x) = -\dfrac{2}{x^2-1}$
11. $f(x) = \dfrac{2}{x^2+x-2}$
12. $f(x) = \dfrac{-2}{x^2-x-2}$
13. $f(x) = \dfrac{2x^2}{x^2+4}$
14. $f(x) = \dfrac{4x^2}{x^2+1}$
15. $f(x) = \dfrac{x+2}{x^2+x-6}$
16. $f(x) = \dfrac{x-4}{x^2-x-6}$
17. $f(x) = \dfrac{x^4}{x^2+2}$
18. $f(x) = \dfrac{2x^4}{x^2+1}$
19. $f(x) = \dfrac{x^2+x-12}{x^2-4}$
20. $f(x) = \dfrac{x^2}{x^2+x-6}$
21. $f(x) = \dfrac{3x^2+x-4}{2x^2-5x}$
22. $f(x) = \dfrac{x^2-4x+3}{(x+1)^2}$

In Exercises 23–30, **a.** *Find the slant asymptote of the graph of each rational function and* **b.** *Follow the six-step strategy and use the slant asymptote to graph each rational function. See Example 4.*

23. $f(x) = \dfrac{x^2-1}{x}$
24. $f(x) = \dfrac{x^2-4}{x}$
25. $f(x) = \dfrac{x^2+1}{x}$
26. $f(x) = \dfrac{x^2+4}{x}$
27. $f(x) = \dfrac{x^2+x-6}{x-3}$
28. $f(x) = \dfrac{x^2-x+1}{x-1}$
29. $f(x) = \dfrac{x^3+1}{x^2+2x}$
30. $f(x) = \dfrac{x^3-1}{x^2-9}$

Solve. *See Example 5.*

31. A company is planning to manufacture mountain bikes. The fixed monthly cost will be $100,000 and it will cost $100 to produce each bicycle.
    a. Write the cost function, C, of producing x mountain bikes.
    b. Write the average cost function, $\overline{C}$, of producing x mountain bikes.
    c. Find and interpret $\overline{C}(500), \overline{C}(1000), \overline{C}(2000),$ and $\overline{C}(4000)$.
    d. What is the horizontal asymptote for the graph of the average cost function, $\overline{C}$? Describe what this means in practical terms.

32. A company that manufactures running shoes has a fixed monthly cost of $300,000. It costs $30 to produce each pair of shoes.
    a. Write the cost function, C, of producing x pairs of shoes.
    b. Write the average cost function, $\overline{C}$, of producing x pairs of shoes.
    c. Find and interpret $\overline{C}(1000), \overline{C}(10,000),$ and $\overline{C}(100,000)$.
    d. What is the horizontal asymptote for the graph of the average cost function, $\overline{C}$? Describe what this represents for the company.

33. The function
$$f(x) = \dfrac{6.5x^2 - 20.4x + 234}{x^2 + 36}$$
models the pH level, $f(x)$, of the human mouth x minutes after a person eats food containing sugar. The graph of this function is shown in the figure.

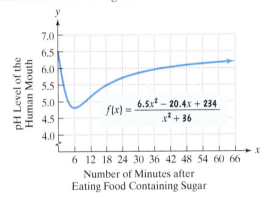

a. Use the graph to obtain a reasonable estimate, to the nearest tenth, of the pH level of the human mouth 42 minutes after a person eats food containing sugar.
b. After eating sugar, when is the pH level the lowest? Use the function's equation to determine the pH level, to the nearest tenth, at this time.
c. According to the graph, what is the normal pH level of the human mouth?
d. What is the equation of the horizontal asymptote associated with this function? Describe what this means in terms of the mouth's pH level over time.
e. Use the graph to describe what happens to the pH level during the first hour.

34. A drug is injected into a patient and the concentration of the drug in the bloodstream is monitored. The drug's concentration, $C(t)$, in milligrams per liter, after t hours is modeled by
$$C(t) = \dfrac{5t}{t^2+1}.$$
The graph of this rational function, obtained with a graphing utility, is shown in the figure.

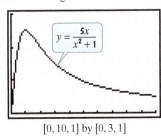

[0, 10, 1] by [0, 3, 1]

a. Use the graph at the bottom of the previous page to obtain a reasonable estimate of the drug's concentration after 3 hours.
b. Use the function's equation displayed in the voice balloon by the graph to determine the drug's concentration after 3 hours.
c. Use the function's equation to find the horizontal asymptote for the graph. Describe what this means about the drug's concentration in the patient's bloodstream as time increases.

*Among all deaths from a particular disease, the percentage that are smoking related (21–39 cigarettes per day) is a function of the disease's **incidence ratio**. The incidence ratio describes the number of times more likely smokers are than nonsmokers to die from the disease. The following table shows the incidence ratios for heart disease and lung cancer for two age groups.*

Incidence Ratios

	Heart Disease	Lung Cancer
Ages 55–64	1.9	10
Ages 65–74	1.7	9

Source: Alexander M. Walker, *Observations and Inference*, Epidemiology Resources Inc., 1991.

For example, the incidence ratio of 9 in the table means that smokers between the ages of 65 and 74 are 9 times more likely than nonsmokers in the same age group to die from lung cancer. The rational function

$$P(x) = \frac{100(x-1)}{x}$$

models the percentage of smoking-related deaths among all deaths from a disease, $P(x)$, in terms of the disease's incidence ratio, x. The graph of the rational function is shown. Use this function to solve Exercises 35–38.

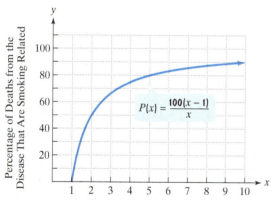

The Disease's Incidence Ratio:
The number of times more likely smokers are than nonsmokers to die from the disease

35. Find $P(10)$. Describe what this means in terms of the incidence ratio, 10, given in the table. Identify your solution as a point on the graph.

36. Find $P(9)$. Round to the nearest percent. Describe what this means in terms of the incidence ratio, 9, given in the table. Identify your solution as a point on the graph.

37. What is the horizontal asymptote of the graph? Describe what this means about the percentage of deaths caused by smoking with increasing incidence ratios.

38. According to the model and its graph, is there a disease for which all deaths are caused by smoking? Explain your answer.

39. Describe how to graph a rational function.

40. If you are given the equation of a rational function, how can you tell if the graph has a slant asymptote? If it does, how do you find its equation?

41. Use a graphing utility to graph

$$f(x) = \frac{x^2 - 4x + 3}{x - 2} \quad \text{and} \quad g(x) = \frac{x^2 - 5x + 6}{x - 2}.$$

What differences do you observe between the graph of f and the graph of g? How do you account for these differences?

42. The rational function

$$f(x) = \frac{27,725(x - 14)}{x^2 + 9} - 5x$$

models the number of arrests, $f(x)$, per 100,000 drivers, for driving under the influence of alcohol, as a function of a driver's age, x.

a. Graph the function in a [0, 70, 5] by [0, 400, 20] viewing rectangle.
b. Describe the trend shown by the graph.
c. Use the ZOOM and TRACE features or the maximum function feature of your graphing utility to find the age that corresponds to the greatest number of arrests. How many arrests, per 100,000 drivers, are there for this age group?

Decision Making. *Determine whether Exercise 43 makes sense or does not make sense, and explain your reasoning.*

43. I've graphed a rational function that has two vertical asymptotes and two horizontal asymptotes.

44. True or False. The graph of a rational function can never cross a vertical asymptote.

In Exercises 45–48, write the equation of a rational function $f(x) = \dfrac{p(x)}{q(x)}$ having the indicated properties, in which the degrees of p and q are as small as possible. More than one correct function may be possible. Graph your function using a graphing utility to verify that it has the required properties.

45. f has a vertical asymptote given by $x = 3$, a horizontal asymptote $y = 0$, y-intercept at -1, and no x-intercept.

46. f has vertical asymptotes given by $x = -2$ and $x = 2$, a horizontal asymptote $y = 2$, y-intercept at $\frac{9}{2}$, x-intercepts at -3 and 3, and y-axis symmetry.

47. f has a vertical asymptote given by $x = 1$, a slant asymptote whose equation is $y = x$, y-intercept at 2, and x-intercepts at -1 and 2.

48. f has no vertical, horizontal, or slant asymptotes, and no x-intercepts.

REVIEW AND PREVIEW

Simplify each expression. See Section 7.2.

49. $\dfrac{x+1}{x+3} - 2.$

50. $\dfrac{x+2}{2x-3} - \dfrac{4}{x+3}$

11.5 THE PARABOLA AND THE CIRCLE

OBJECTIVES

1. Graph parabolas of the form $x = a(y - k)^2 + h$ and $y = a(x - h)^2 + k$.
2. Graph circles of the form $(x - h)^2 + (y - k)^2 = r^2$.
3. Write the equation of a circle, given its center and radius.
4. Find the center and the radius of a circle, given its equation.

Conic sections derive their name because each conic section is the intersection of a right circular cone and a plane. The circle, parabola, ellipse, and hyperbola are the conic sections.

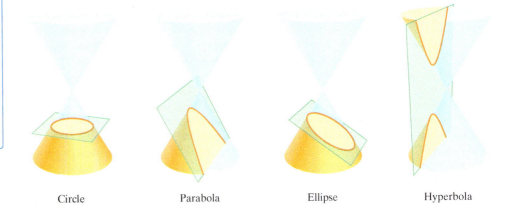

Circle Parabola Ellipse Hyperbola

OBJECTIVE 1 ▶ Graphing parabolas in standard form. Thus far, we have seen that $f(x)$ or $y = a(x - h)^2 + k$ is the equation of a parabola that opens upward if $a > 0$ or downward if $a < 0$. Parabolas can also open left or right, or even on a slant. Equations of these parabolas are not functions of x, of course, since a parabola opening any way other than upward or downward fails the vertical line test. In this section, we introduce parabolas that open to the left and to the right. Parabolas opening on a slant will not be developed in this book.

Just as $y = a(x - h)^2 + k$ is the equation of a parabola that opens upward or downward, $x = a(y - k)^2 + h$ is the equation of a parabola that opens to the right or to the left. The parabola opens to the right if $a > 0$ and to the left if $a < 0$. The parabola has vertex (h, k), and its axis of symmetry is the line $y = k$.

Parabolas

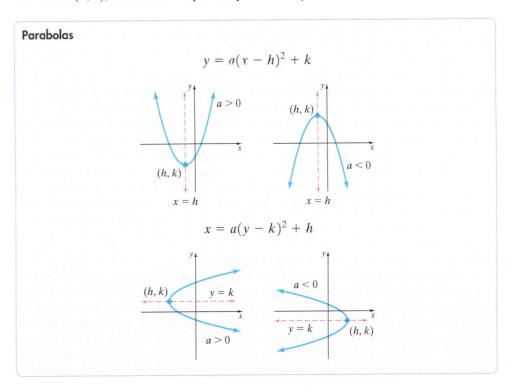

The equations $y = a(x - h)^2 + k$ and $x = a(y - k)^2 + h$ are called **standard forms**.

654 CHAPTER 11 Graphing Quadratic Functions, Rational Functions, and Conic Sections

Concept Check ✓

Does the graph of the parabola given by the equation $x = -3y^2$ open to the left, to the right, upward, or downward?

EXAMPLE 1 Graph the parabola $x = 2y^2$.

Solution Written in standard form, the equation $x = 2y^2$ is $x = 2(y - 0)^2 + 0$ with $a = 2, h = 0$, and $k = 0$. Its graph is a parabola with vertex $(0, 0)$, and its axis of symmetry is the line $y = 0$. Since $a > 0$, this parabola opens to the right. The table shows a few more ordered pair solutions of $x = 2y^2$. Its graph is also shown.

x	y
8	-2
2	-1
0	0
2	1
8	2

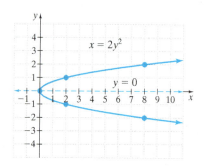

PRACTICE 1 Graph the parabola $x = \frac{1}{2}y^2$.

EXAMPLE 2 Graph the parabola $x = -3(y - 1)^2 + 2$.

Solution The equation $x = -3(y - 1)^2 + 2$ is in the form $x = a(y - k)^2 + h$ with $a = -3, k = 1$, and $h = 2$. Since $a < 0$, the parabola opens to the left. The vertex (h, k) is $(2, 1)$, and the axis of symmetry is the line $y = 1$. When $y = 0, x = -1$, so the x-intercept is $(-1, 0)$. Again, we obtain a few ordered pair solutions and then graph the parabola.

x	y
2	1
-1	0
-1	2
-10	3
-10	-1

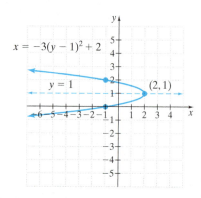

PRACTICE 2 Graph the parabola $x = -2(y + 4)^2 - 1$.

EXAMPLE 3 Graph $y = -x^2 - 2x + 15$.

Solution Complete the square on x to write the equation in standard form.

$y - 15 = -x^2 - 2x$ Subtract 15 from both sides.

$y - 15 = -1(x^2 + 2x)$ Factor -1 from the terms $-x^2 - 2x$.

Answer to Concept Check: to the left

The coefficient of x is 2. Find the square of half of 2.

$$\frac{1}{2}(2) = 1 \quad \text{and} \quad 1^2 = 1$$

$y - 15 - 1(1) = -1(x^2 + 2x + 1)$ Add $-1(1)$ to both sides.

$y - 16 = -1(x + 1)^2$ Simplify the left side and factor the right side.

$y = -(x + 1)^2 + 16$ Add 16 to both sides.

The equation is now in standard form $y = a(x - h)^2 + k$ with $a = -1, h = -1$, and $k = 16$.

The vertex is then (h, k), or $(-1, 16)$.

A second method for finding the vertex is by using the formula $\frac{-b}{2a}$.

$$x = \frac{-(-2)}{2(-1)} = \frac{2}{-2} = -1$$

$$y = -(-1)^2 - 2(-1) + 15 = -1 + 2 + 15 = 16$$

Again, we see that the vertex is $(-1, 16)$, and the axis of symmetry is the vertical line $x = -1$. The y-intercept is $(0, 15)$. Now we can use a few more ordered pair solutions to graph the parabola.

x	y
-1	16
0	15
-2	15
1	12
-3	12
3	0
-5	0

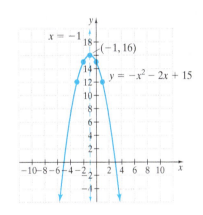

PRACTICE 3 Graph $y = -x^2 + 4x + 6$.

EXAMPLE 4 Graph $x = 2y^2 + 4y + 5$.

Solution Notice that this equation is quadratic in y, so its graph is a parabola that opens to the left or the right. We can complete the square on y or we can use the formula $\frac{-b}{2a}$ to find the vertex.

Since the equation is quadratic in y, the formula gives us the y-value of the vertex.

$$y = \frac{-4}{2 \cdot 2} = \frac{-4}{4} = -1$$

$$x = 2(-1)^2 + 4(-1) + 5 = 2 \cdot 1 - 4 + 5 = 3$$

The vertex is $(3, -1)$, and the axis of symmetry is the line $y = -1$. The parabola opens to the right since $a > 0$. The x-intercept is $(5, 0)$.

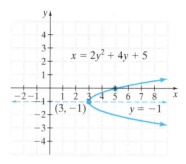

PRACTICE 4 Graph $x = 3y^2 + 6y + 4$.

OBJECTIVE 2 ▶ Graphing circles in standard form. Another conic section is the **circle**. A circle is the set of all points in a plane that are the same distance from a fixed point called the **center**. The distance is called the **radius** of the circle. To find a standard equation for a circle, let (h, k) represent the center of the circle, and let (x, y) represent any point on the circle. The distance between (h, k) and (x, y) is defined to be the circle's radius, r units. We can find this distance r by using the distance formula.

$$r = \sqrt{(x - h)^2 + (y - k)^2}$$

$$r^2 = (x - h)^2 + (y - k)^2 \qquad \text{Square both sides.}$$

Circle
The graph of $(x - h)^2 + (y - k)^2 = r^2$ is a circle with center (h, k) and radius r.

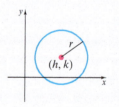

The equation $(x - h)^2 + (y - k)^2 = r^2$ is called **standard form**.

If an equation can be written in the standard form

$$(x - h)^2 + (y - k)^2 = r^2$$

then its graph is a circle, which we can draw by graphing the center (h, k) and using the radius r.

▶ **Helpful Hint**
Notice that the radius is the *distance* from the center of the circle to any point of the circle. Also notice that the *midpoint* of a diameter of a circle is the center of the circle.

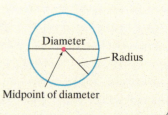

EXAMPLE 5 Graph $x^2 + y^2 = 4$.

Solution The equation can be written in standard form as

$$(x - 0)^2 + (y - 0)^2 = 2^2$$

The center of the circle is $(0, 0)$, and the radius is 2. Its graph is shown.

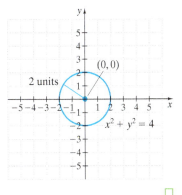

PRACTICE 5 Graph $x^2 + y^2 = 25$.

> **Helpful Hint**
> Notice the difference between the equation of a circle and the equation of a parabola. The equation of a circle contains both x^2 and y^2 terms on the same side of the equation with equal coefficients. The equation of a parabola has either an x^2 term or a y^2 term but not both.

EXAMPLE 6 Graph $(x + 1)^2 + y^2 = 8$.

Solution The equation can be written as $(x + 1)^2 + (y - 0)^2 = 8$ with $h = -1$, $k = 0$, and $r = \sqrt{8}$. The center is $(-1, 0)$, and the radius is $\sqrt{8} = 2\sqrt{2} \approx 2.8$.

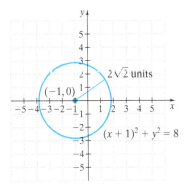

PRACTICE 6 Graph $(x - 3)^2 + (y + 2)^2 = 4$.

Concept Check ✓

In the graph of the equation $(x - 3)^2 + (y - 2)^2 = 5$, what is the distance between the center of the circle and any point on the circle?

Answer to Concept Check:
$\sqrt{5}$ units

OBJECTIVE 3 ▶ Writing equations of circles. Since a circle is determined entirely by its center and radius, this information is all we need to write the equation of a circle.

EXAMPLE 7   Find an equation of the circle with center $(-7, 3)$ and radius 10.

Solution   Using the given values $h = -7$, $k = 3$, and $r = 10$, we write the equation

$$(x - h)^2 + (y - k)^2 = r^2$$

or

$$[x - (-7)]^2 + (y - 3)^2 = 10^2 \quad \text{Substitute the given values.}$$

or

$$(x + 7)^2 + (y - 3)^2 = 100$$

PRACTICE 7   Find the equation of a circle with center $(-2, -5)$ and radius 9.

OBJECTIVE 4 ▶ Finding the center and the radius of a circle. To find the center and the radius of a circle from its equation, write the equation in standard form. To write the equation of a circle in standard form, we complete the square on both x and y.

EXAMPLE 8   Graph $x^2 + y^2 + 4x - 8y = 16$.

Solution   Since this equation contains x^2 and y^2 terms on the same side of the equation with equal coefficients, its graph is a circle. To write the equation in standard form, group the terms involving x and the terms involving y, and then complete the square on each variable.

$$(x^2 + 4x) + (y^2 - 8y) = 16$$

Thus, $\frac{1}{2}(4) = 2$ and $2^2 = 4$. Also, $\frac{1}{2}(-8) = -4$ and $(-4)^2 = 16$. Add 4 and then 16 to both sides.

$$(x^2 + 4x + 4) + (y^2 - 8y + 16) = 16 + 4 + 16$$
$$(x + 2)^2 + (y - 4)^2 = 36 \quad \text{Factor.}$$

This circle has the center $(-2, 4)$ and radius 6, as shown.

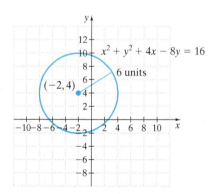

PRACTICE 8   Graph $x^2 + y^2 + 6x - 2y = 6$.

Graphing Calculator Explorations

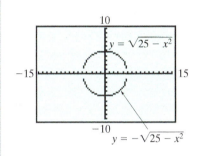

To graph an equation such as $x^2 + y^2 = 25$ with a graphing calculator, we first solve the equation for y.

$$x^2 + y^2 = 25$$
$$y^2 = 25 - x^2$$
$$y = \pm\sqrt{25 - x^2}$$

The graph of $y = \sqrt{25 - x^2}$ will be the top half of the circle, and the graph of $y = -\sqrt{25 - x^2}$ will be the bottom half of the circle.

To graph, press $\boxed{Y=}$ and enter $Y_1 = \sqrt{25 - x^2}$ and $Y_2 = -\sqrt{25 - x^2}$. Insert parentheses around $25 - x^2$ so that $\sqrt{25 - x^2}$ and not $\sqrt{25} - x^2$ is graphed.

The top graph to the left does not appear to be a circle because we are currently using a standard window and the screen is rectangular. This causes the tick marks on the x-axis to be farther apart than the tick marks on the y-axis and, thus, creates the distorted circle. If we want the graph to appear circular, we must define a square window by using a feature of the graphing calculator or by redefining the window to show the x-axis from -15 to 15 and the y-axis from -10 to 10. Using a square window, the graph appears as shown on the bottom to the left.

Use a graphing calculator to graph each circle.

1. $x^2 + y^2 = 55$
2. $x^2 + y^2 = 20$
3. $5x^2 + 5y^2 = 50$
4. $6x^2 + 6y^2 = 105$
5. $2x^2 + 2y^2 - 34 = 0$
6. $4x^2 + 4y^2 - 48 = 0$
7. $7x^2 + 7y^2 - 89 = 0$
8. $3x^2 + 3y^2 - 35 = 0$

VOCABULARY & READINESS CHECK

Word Bank. *Use the choices below to fill in each blank. Some choices may be used more than once.*

  radius   center   vertex
  diameter   circle   conic sections

1. The circle, parabola, ellipse, and hyperbola are called the _____.
2. For a parabola that opens upward the lowest point is the _____.
3. A _____ is the set of all points in a plane that are the same distance from a fixed point. The fixed point is called the _____.
4. The midpoint of a diameter of a circle is the _____.
5. The distance from the center of a circle to any point of the circle is called the _____.
6. Twice a circle's radius is its _____.

Decision Making. *The graph of each equation is a parabola. Determine whether the parabola opens upward, downward, to the left, or to the right.*

7. $y = x^2 - 7x + 5$
8. $y = -x^2 + 16$
9. $x = -y^2 - y + 2$
10. $x = 3y^2 + 2y - 5$
11. $y = -x^2 + 2x + 1$
12. $x = -y^2 + 2y - 6$

11.5 EXERCISE SET

The graph of each equation is a parabola. Find the vertex of the parabola and sketch its graph. See Examples 1 through 4.

1. $x = 3y^2$
2. $x = -2y^2$
3. $x = (y - 2)^2 + 3$
4. $x = (y - 4)^2 - 1$
5. $y = 3(x - 1)^2 + 5$
6. $x = -4(y - 2)^2 + 2$
7. $x = y^2 + 6y + 8$
8. $x = y^2 - 6y + 6$
9. $y = x^2 + 10x + 20$
10. $y = x^2 + 4x - 5$
11. $x = -2y^2 + 4y + 6$
12. $x = 3y^2 + 6y + 7$

The graph of each equation is a circle. Find the center and the radius, and then sketch. See Examples 5, 6, and 8.

13. $x^2 + y^2 = 9$
14. $x^2 + y^2 = 100$
15. $x^2 + (y - 2)^2 = 1$
16. $(x - 3)^2 + y^2 = 9$
17. $(x - 5)^2 + (y + 2)^2 = 1$
18. $(x + 3)^2 + (y + 3)^2 = 4$
19. $x^2 + y^2 + 6y = 0$
20. $x^2 + 10x + y^2 = 0$
21. $x^2 + y^2 + 2x - 4y = 4$
22. $x^2 + 6x - 4y + y^2 = 3$
23. $x^2 + y^2 - 4x - 8y - 2 = 0$
24. $x^2 + y^2 - 2x - 6y - 5 = 0$

Write an equation of the circle with the given center and radius. See Example 7.

25. $(2, 3); 6$
26. $(-7, 6); 2$
27. $(0, 0); \sqrt{3}$
28. $(0, -6); \sqrt{2}$
29. $(-5, 4); 3\sqrt{5}$
30. the origin; $4\sqrt{7}$

31. Explain the error in the statement: The graph of $x^2 + (y + 3)^2 = 10$ is a circle with center $(0, -3)$ and radius 5.

MIXED PRACTICE

Sketch the graph of each equation. If the graph is a parabola, find its vertex. If the graph is a circle, find its center and radius.

32. $x = y^2 + 2$
33. $x = y^2 - 3$
34. $y = (x + 3)^2 + 3$
35. $y = (x - 2)^2 - 2$
36. $x^2 + y^2 = 49$
37. $x^2 + y^2 = 1$
38. $x = (y - 1)^2 + 4$
39. $x = (y + 3)^2 - 1$
40. $(x + 3)^2 + (y - 1)^2 = 9$
41. $(x - 2)^2 + (y - 2)^2 = 16$
42. $x = -2(y + 5)^2$
43. $x = -(y - 1)^2$
44. $x^2 + (y + 5)^2 = 5$
45. $(x - 4)^2 + y^2 = 7$
46. $y = 3(x - 4)^2 + 2$
47. $y = 5(x + 5)^2 + 3$
48. $2x^2 + 2y^2 = \frac{1}{2}$
49. $\frac{x^2}{8} + \frac{y^2}{8} = 2$
50. $y = x^2 - 2x - 15$
51. $y = x^2 + 7x + 6$
52. $x^2 + y^2 + 6x + 10y - 2 = 0$
53. $x^2 + y^2 + 2x + 12y - 12 = 0$
54. $x = y^2 + 6y + 2$
55. $x = y^2 + 8y - 4$
56. $x^2 + y^2 - 8y + 5 = 0$
57. $x^2 - 10y + y^2 + 4 = 0$
58. $x = -2y^2 - 4y$
59. $x = -3y^2 + 30y$

60. $\dfrac{x^2}{3} + \dfrac{y^2}{3} = 2$
61. $5x^2 + 5y^2 = 25$
62. $y = 4x^2 - 40x + 105$
63. $y = 5x^2 - 20x + 16$

REVIEW AND PREVIEW

Graph each equation. See Section 3.3.

64. $y = 2x + 5$
65. $y = -3x + 3$
66. $y = 3$
67. $x = -2$

Rationalize each denominator and simplify, if possible. See Section 8.5.

68. $\dfrac{1}{\sqrt{3}}$
69. $\dfrac{\sqrt{5}}{\sqrt{8}}$
70. $\dfrac{4\sqrt{7}}{\sqrt{6}}$
71. $\dfrac{10}{\sqrt{5}}$

CONCEPT EXTENSIONS

72. **Multiple Steps.** **The Sarsen Circle:** The first image that comes to mind when one thinks of Stonehenge is the very large sandstone blocks with sandstone lintels across the top. The Sarsen Circle of Stonehenge is the outer circle of the sandstone blocks, each of which weighs up to 50 tons. There were originally 30 of these monolithic blocks, but only 17 remain upright to this day. The "altar stone" lies at the center of this circle, which has a diameter of 33 meters.

   a. What is the radius of the Sarsen circle?
   b. What is the circumference of the Sarsen circle? Round your result to 2 decimal places.
   c. Since there were originally 30 Sarsen stones located on the circumference, how far apart would the centers of the stones have been? Round to the nearest tenth of a meter.
   d. Using the axes in the drawing, what are the coordinates of the center of the circle?
   e. Use parts **a** and **d** to write the equation of the Sarsen circle.

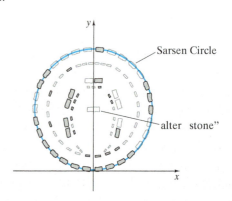

73. **Multiple Steps.** Opened in 2000 to honor the millennium, the British Airways London Eye is the world's biggest observation wheel. Each of the 32 enclosed capsules, which each hold 25 passengers, completes a full rotation every 30 minutes.

Its diameter is 135 meters, and it is constructed on London's South Bank, to allow passengers to enter the Eye at ground level. (*Source: Guinness Book of World Records*)

a. What is the radius of the London Eye?

b. How close is the wheel to the ground?

c. How high is the center of the wheel from the ground?

d. Using the axes in the drawing, what are the coordinates of the center of the wheel?

e. Use parts **a** and **d** to write the equation of the Eye.

74. **Multiple Steps.** In 1893, Pittsburgh bridge builder George Ferris designed and built a gigantic revolving steel wheel whose height was 264 feet and diameter was 250 feet. This Ferris wheel opened at the 1893 exposition in Chicago. It had 36 wooden cars, each capable of holding 60 passengers. (*Source: The Handy Science Answer Book*)

a. What was the radius of this Ferris wheel?

b. How close is the wheel to the ground?

c. How high is the center of the wheel from the ground?

d. Using the axes in the drawing, what are the coordinates of the center of the wheel?

e. Use parts **a** and **d** to write the equation of the wheel.

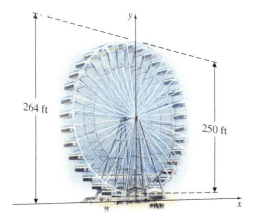

75. **Multiple Steps.** As of this writing, the world's largest-diameter Ferris wheel currently in operation is the Star of Nanchung in Jiangxi Province, China. It has 60 compartments, each of which carries eight people. It is 160 meters tall, and the diameter of the wheel is 153 meters. (*Source:* China News Agency)

a. What is the radius of this Ferris wheel?

b. How close is the wheel to the ground?

c. How high is the center of the wheel from the ground?

d. Using the axes in the drawing, what are the coordinates of the center of the wheel?

e. Use parts **a** and **d** to write the equation of the wheel.

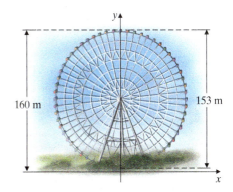

76. If you are given a list of equations of circles and parabolas and none are in standard form, explain how you would determine which is an equation of a circle and which is an equation of a parabola. Explain also how you would distinguish the upward or downward parabolas from the left-opening or right-opening parabolas.

77. **Multiple Steps.** Cindy Brown, an architect, is drawing plans on grid paper for a circular pool with a fountain in the middle. The paper is marked off in centimeters, and each centimeter represents 1 foot. On the paper, the diameter of the "pool" is 20 centimeters, and "fountain" is the point $(0, 0)$.

a. Sketch the architect's drawing. Be sure to label the axes.

b. Write an equation that describes the circular pool.

c. Cindy plans to place a circle of lights around the fountain such that each light is 5 feet from the fountain. Write an equation for the circle of lights and sketch the circle on your drawing.

78. A bridge constructed over a bayou has a supporting arch in the shape of a parabola. Find an equation of the parabolic arch if the length of the road over the arch is 100 meters and the maximum height of the arch is 40 meters.

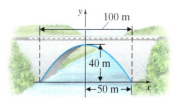

Use a graphing calculator to verify each exercise. Use a square viewing window.

79. Exercise 61.

80. Exercise 60.

81. Exercise 63.

82. Exercise 62.

662 CHAPTER 11 Graphing Quadratic Functions, Rational Functions, and Conic Sections

11.6 THE ELLIPSE AND THE HYPERBOLA

OBJECTIVES

1. Define and graph an ellipse.
2. Define and graph a hyperbola.

OBJECTIVE 1 ▶ Graphing ellipses. An **ellipse** can be thought of as the set of points in a plane such that the sum of the distances of those points from two fixed points is constant. Each of the two fixed points is called a **focus.** (The plural of focus is **foci.**) The point midway between the foci is called the **center.**

An ellipse may be drawn by hand by using two thumbtacks, a piece of string, and a pencil. Secure the two thumbtacks in a piece of cardboard, for example, and tie each end of the string to a tack. Use your pencil to pull the string tight and draw the ellipse. The two thumbtacks are the foci of the drawn ellipse.

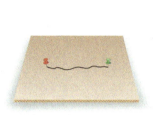 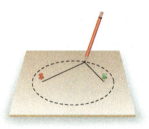 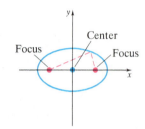

Ellipse with Center (0, 0)

The graph of an equation of the form $\dfrac{x^2}{a^2} + \dfrac{y^2}{b^2} = 1$ is an ellipse with center $(0, 0)$.

The x-intercepts are $(a, 0)$ and $(-a, 0)$, and the y-intercepts are $(0, b)$, and $(0, -b)$.

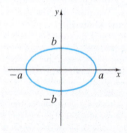

The **standard form** of an ellipse with center $(0, 0)$ is $\dfrac{x^2}{a^2} + \dfrac{y^2}{b^2} = 1$.

EXAMPLE 1 Graph $\dfrac{x^2}{9} + \dfrac{y^2}{16} = 1$.

Solution The equation is of the form $\dfrac{x^2}{a^2} + \dfrac{y^2}{b^2} = 1$, with $a = 3$ and $b = 4$, so its graph is an ellipse with center $(0, 0)$, x-intercepts $(3, 0)$ and $(-3, 0)$, and y-intercepts $(0, 4)$ and $(0, -4)$.

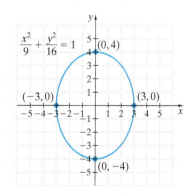

PRACTICE 1 Graph $\dfrac{x^2}{25} + \dfrac{y^2}{4} = 1$.

Section 11.6 The Ellipse and the Hyperbola 663

EXAMPLE 2 Graph $4x^2 + 16y^2 = 64$.

Solution Although this equation contains a sum of squared terms in x and y on the same side of an equation, this is not the equation of a circle since the coefficients of x^2 and y^2 are not the same. The graph of this equation is an ellipse. Since the standard form of the equation of an ellipse has 1 on one side, divide both sides of this equation by 64.

$$4x^2 + 16y^2 = 64$$

$$\frac{4x^2}{64} + \frac{16y^2}{64} = \frac{64}{64} \quad \text{Divide both sides by 64.}$$

$$\frac{x^2}{16} + \frac{y^2}{4} = 1 \quad \text{Simplify.}$$

We now recognize the equation of an ellipse with $a = 4$ and $b = 2$. This ellipse has center $(0, 0)$, x-intercepts $(4, 0)$ and $(-4, 0)$, and y-intercepts $(0, 2)$ and $(0, -2)$.

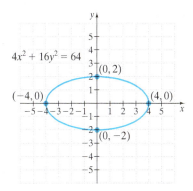

PRACTICE
2 Graph $9x^2 + 4y^2 = 36$.

The center of an ellipse is not always $(0, 0)$, as shown in the next example.

EXAMPLE 3 Graph $\dfrac{(x + 3)^2}{25} + \dfrac{(y - 2)^2}{36} = 1$.

Solution The center of this ellipse is found in a way that is similar to finding the center of a circle. This ellipse has center $(-3, 2)$. Notice that $a = 5$ and $b = 6$. To find four points on the graph of the ellipse, first graph the center, $(-3, 2)$. Since $a = 5$, count 5 units right and then 5 units left of the point with coordinates $(-3, 2)$. Next, since $b = 6$, start at $(-3, 2)$ and count 6 units up and then 6 units down to find two more points on the ellipse.

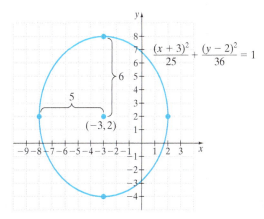

PRACTICE
3 Graph $\dfrac{(x - 4)^2}{49} + \dfrac{(y + 1)^2}{81} = 1$.

Concept Check ✓

In the graph of the equation $\dfrac{x^2}{64} + \dfrac{y^2}{36} = 1$, which distance is longer: the distance between the x-intercepts or the distance between the y-intercepts? How much longer? Explain.

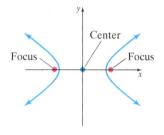

OBJECTIVE 2 ▶ Graphing hyperbolas. The final conic section is the **hyperbola**. A hyperbola is the set of points in a plane such that the absolute value of the difference of the distances from two fixed points is constant. Each of the two fixed points is called a **focus**. The point midway between the foci is called the **center**.

Using the distance formula, we can show that the graph of $\dfrac{x^2}{a^2} - \dfrac{y^2}{b^2} = 1$ is a hyperbola with center $(0, 0)$ and x-intercepts $(a, 0)$ and $(-a, 0)$. Also, the graph of $\dfrac{y^2}{b^2} - \dfrac{x^2}{a^2} = 1$ is a hyperbola with center $(0, 0)$ and y-intercepts $(0, b)$ and $(0, -b)$.

Hyperbola with Center (0, 0)

The graph of an equation of the form $\dfrac{x^2}{a^2} - \dfrac{y^2}{b^2} = 1$ is a hyperbola with center $(0, 0)$ and x-intercepts $(a, 0)$ and $(-a, 0)$.

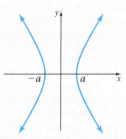

The graph of an equation of the form $\dfrac{y^2}{b^2} - \dfrac{x^2}{a^2} = 1$ is a hyperbola with center $(0, 0)$ and y-intercepts $(0, b)$ and $(0, -b)$.

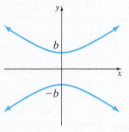

The equations $\dfrac{x^2}{a^2} - \dfrac{y^2}{b^2} = 1$ and $\dfrac{y^2}{b^2} - \dfrac{x^2}{a^2} = 1$ are the **standard forms** for the equation of a hyperbola.

▶ **Helpful Hint**

Notice the difference between the equation of an ellipse and a hyperbola. The equation of the ellipse contains x^2 and y^2 terms on the same side of the equation with same-sign coefficients. For a hyperbola, the coefficients on the same side of the equation have different signs.

Answer to Concept Check:
x-intercepts, by 4 units

Graphing a hyperbola such as $\dfrac{y^2}{b^2} - \dfrac{x^2}{a^2} = 1$ is made easier by recognizing one of its important characteristics. Examining the figure to the left, notice how the sides of the branches of the hyperbola extend indefinitely and seem to approach the dashed lines in the figure. These dashed lines are the **asymptotes** of the hyperbola.

To sketch these lines, or asymptotes, draw a rectangle with vertices (a, b), $(-a, b)$, $(a, -b)$, and $(-a, -b)$. The asymptotes of the hyperbola are the extended diagonals of this rectangle.

EXAMPLE 4 Graph $\dfrac{x^2}{16} - \dfrac{y^2}{25} = 1$.

Solution This equation has the form $\dfrac{x^2}{a^2} - \dfrac{y^2}{b^2} = 1$, with $a = 4$ and $b = 5$. Thus, its graph is a hyperbola that opens to the left and right. It has center $(0, 0)$ and x-intercepts $(4, 0)$ and $(-4, 0)$. To aid in graphing the hyperbola, we first sketch its asymptotes. The extended diagonals of the rectangle with corners $(4, 5)$, $(4, -5)$, $(-4, 5)$, and $(-4, -5)$ are the asymptotes of the hyperbola. Then we use the asymptotes to aid in sketching the hyperbola.

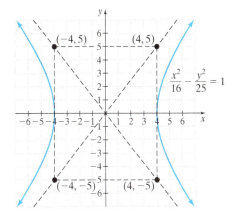

PRACTICE 4 Graph $\dfrac{x^2}{9} - \dfrac{y^2}{16} = 1$.

EXAMPLE 5 Graph $4y^2 - 9x^2 = 36$.

Solution Since this is a difference of squared terms in x and y on the same side of the equation, its graph is a hyperbola, as opposed to an ellipse or a circle. The standard form of the equation of a hyperbola has a 1 on one side, so divide both sides of the equation by 36.

$$4y^2 - 9x^2 = 36$$

$$\dfrac{4y^2}{36} - \dfrac{9x^2}{36} = \dfrac{36}{36} \quad \text{Divide both sides by 36.}$$

$$\dfrac{y^2}{9} - \dfrac{x^2}{4} = 1 \quad \text{Simplify.}$$

The equation is of the form $\dfrac{y^2}{b^2} - \dfrac{x^2}{a^2} = 1$, with $a = 2$ and $b = 3$, so the hyperbola is centered at $(0, 0)$ with y-intercepts $(0, 3)$ and $(0, -3)$. The sketch of the hyperbola is shown.

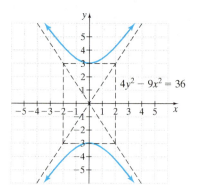

PRACTICE 5 Graph $9y^2 - 25x^2 = 225$.

Graphing Calculator Explorations

To find the graph of an ellipse by using a graphing calculator, use the same procedure as for graphing a circle. For example, to graph $x^2 + 3y^2 = 22$, first solve for y.

$$3y^2 = 22 - x^2$$

$$y^2 = \dfrac{22 - x^2}{3}$$

$$y = \pm\sqrt{\dfrac{22 - x^2}{3}}$$

Next press the $\boxed{Y=}$ key and enter $Y_1 = \sqrt{\dfrac{22 - x^2}{3}}$ and $Y_2 = -\sqrt{\dfrac{22 - x^2}{3}}$.

(Insert two sets of parentheses in the radicand as $\sqrt{((22 - x^2)/3)}$ so that the desired graph is obtained.) The graph appears as follows.

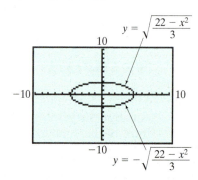

Use a graphing calculator to graph each ellipse.

1. $10x^2 + y^2 = 32$
2. $x^2 + 6y^2 = 35$
3. $20x^2 + 5y^2 = 100$
4. $4y^2 + 12x^2 = 48$
5. $7.3x^2 + 15.5y^2 = 95.2$
6. $18.8x^2 + 36.1y^2 = 205.8$

VOCABULARY & READINESS CHECK

Word Bank. *Use the choices below to fill in each blank. Some choices will be used more than once and some not at all.*

ellipse	(0, 0)	focus	(a, 0) and (−a, 0)	(0, a) and (0, −a)
hyperbola	center	x	(b, 0) and (−b, 0)	(0, b) and (0, −b)
		y		

1. A(n) _____ is the set of points in a plane such that the absolute value of the differences of their distances from two fixed points is constant.

2. A(n) _____ is the set of points in a plane such that the sum of their distances from two fixed points is constant.

For exercises 1 and 2 above,

3. The two fixed points are each called a _____.

4. The point midway between the foci is called the _____.

5. The graph of $\dfrac{x^2}{a^2} - \dfrac{y^2}{b^2} = 1$ is a(n) _____ with center _____ and _____-intercepts of _____.

6. The graph of $\dfrac{x^2}{b^2} + \dfrac{y^2}{a^2} = 1$ is a(n) _____ with center _____ and x-intercepts of _____.

Decision Making. *Identify the graph of each equation as an ellipse or a hyperbola.*

7. $\dfrac{x^2}{16} + \dfrac{y^2}{4} = 1$

8. $\dfrac{x^2}{16} - \dfrac{y^2}{4} = 1$

9. $x^2 - 5y^2 = 3$

10. $-x^2 + 5y^2 = 3$

11. $-\dfrac{y^2}{25} + \dfrac{x^2}{36} = 1$

12. $\dfrac{y^2}{25} + \dfrac{x^2}{36} = 1$

11.6 EXERCISE SET

Sketch the graph of each equation. See Examples 1 and 2.

1. $\dfrac{x^2}{4} + \dfrac{y^2}{25} = 1$

2. $\dfrac{x^2}{16} + \dfrac{y^2}{9} = 1$

3. $\dfrac{x^2}{9} + y^2 = 1$

4. $x^2 + \dfrac{y^2}{4} = 1$

5. $9x^2 + y^2 = 36$

6. $x^2 + 4y^2 = 16$

7. $4x^2 + 25y^2 = 100$

8. $36x^2 + y^2 = 36$

Sketch the graph of each equation. See Example 3.

9. $\dfrac{(x+1)^2}{36} + \dfrac{(y-2)^2}{49} = 1$

10. $\dfrac{(x-3)^2}{9} + \dfrac{(y+3)^2}{16} = 1$

11. $\dfrac{(x-1)^2}{4} + \dfrac{(y-1)^2}{25} = 1$

12. $\dfrac{(x+3)^2}{16} + \dfrac{(y+2)^2}{4} = 1$

Sketch the graph of each equation. See Examples 4 and 5.

13. $\dfrac{x^2}{4} - \dfrac{y^2}{9} = 1$

14. $\dfrac{x^2}{36} - \dfrac{y^2}{36} = 1$

15. $\dfrac{y^2}{25} - \dfrac{x^2}{16} = 1$

16. $\dfrac{y^2}{25} - \dfrac{x^2}{49} = 1$

17. $x^2 - 4y^2 = 16$

18. $4x^2 - y^2 = 36$

19. $16y^2 - x^2 = 16$

20. $4y^2 - 25x^2 = 100$

21. If you are given a list of equations of circles, parabolas, ellipses, and hyperbolas, explain how you could distinguish the different conic sections from their equations.

MIXED PRACTICE

Decision Making. *Identify whether each equation, when graphed, will be a parabola, circle, ellipse, or hyperbola. Sketch the graph of each equation.*

22. $(x-7)^2 + (y-2)^2 = 4$

23. $y = x^2 + 4$

24. $y = x^2 + 12x + 36$

25. $\dfrac{x^2}{4} + \dfrac{y^2}{9} = 1$

26. $\dfrac{y^2}{9} - \dfrac{x^2}{9} = 1$

27. $\dfrac{x^2}{16} - \dfrac{y^2}{4} = 1$

28. $\dfrac{x^2}{16} + \dfrac{y^2}{4} = 1$

29. $x^2 + y^2 = 16$

30. $x = y^2 + 4y - 1$

31. $x = -y^2 + 6y$

32. $9x^2 - 4y^2 = 36$

33. $9x^2 + 4y^2 = 36$

34. $\dfrac{(x-1)^2}{49} + \dfrac{(y+2)^2}{25} = 1$

35. $y^2 = x^2 + 16$

36. $\left(x + \dfrac{1}{2}\right)^2 + \left(y - \dfrac{1}{2}\right)^2 = 1$

37. $y = -2x^2 + 4x - 3$

REVIEW AND PREVIEW

Solve each inequality. See Section 2.5.

38. $x < 5$ and $x < 1$
39. $x < 5$ or $x < 1$
40. $2x - 1 \geq 7$ or $-3x \leq -6$
41. $2x - 1 \geq 7$ and $-3x \leq -6$

Perform the indicated operations. See Sections 6.1 and 6.3.

42. $(2x^3)(-4x^2)$
43. $2x^3 - 4x^3$
44. $-5x^2 + x^2$
45. $(-5x^2)(x^2)$

CONCEPT EXTENSIONS

The graph of each equation is an ellipse. Determine which distance is longer. The distance between the x-intercepts or the distance between the y-intercepts. How much longer? See the Concept Check in this section.

46. $\dfrac{x^2}{16} + \dfrac{y^2}{25} = 1$
47. $\dfrac{x^2}{100} + \dfrac{y^2}{49} = 1$
48. $4x^2 + y^2 = 16$
49. $x^2 + 4y^2 = 36$

50. We know that $x^2 + y^2 = 25$ is the equation of a circle. Rewrite the equation so that the right side is equal to 1. Which type of conic section does this equation form resemble? In fact, the circle is a special case of this type of conic section. Describe the conditions under which this type of conic section is a circle.

The orbits of stars, planets, comets, asteroids, and satellites all have the shape of one of the conic sections. Astronomers use a measure called eccentricity to describe the shape and elongation of an orbital path. For the circle and ellipse, eccentricity e is calculated with the formula $e = \dfrac{c}{d}$, where $c^2 = |a^2 - b^2|$ and d is the larger value of a or b. For a hyperbola, eccentricity e is calculated with the formula $e = \dfrac{c}{d}$, where $c^2 = a^2 + b^2$ and the value of d is equal to a if the hyperbola has x-intercepts or equal to b if the hyperbola has y-intercepts. Use equations A–H to answer Exercises 51–60.

A. $\dfrac{x^2}{36} - \dfrac{y^2}{13} = 1$
B. $\dfrac{x^2}{4} + \dfrac{y^2}{4} = 1$
C. $\dfrac{x^2}{25} + \dfrac{y^2}{16} = 1$
D. $\dfrac{y^2}{25} - \dfrac{x^2}{39} = 1$
E. $\dfrac{x^2}{17} + \dfrac{y^2}{81} = 1$
F. $\dfrac{x^2}{36} + \dfrac{y^2}{36} = 1$
G. $\dfrac{x^2}{16} - \dfrac{y^2}{65} = 1$
H. $\dfrac{x^2}{144} + \dfrac{y^2}{140} = 1$

51. Identify the type of conic section represented by each of the equations A–H.
52. For each of the equations A–H, identify the values of a^2 and b^2.
53. For each of the equations A–H, calculate the value of c^2 and c.
54. For each of the equations A–H, find the value of d.
55. For each of the equations A–H, calculate the eccentricity e.
56. What do you notice about the values of e for the equations you identified as ellipses?
57. What do you notice about the values of e for the equations you identified as circles?
58. What do you notice about the values of e for the equations you identified as hyperbolas?
59. The eccentricity of a parabola is exactly 1. Use this information and the observations you made in Exercises 31, 32, and 33 to describe a way that could be used to identify the type of conic section based on its eccentricity value.
60. Graph each of the conic sections given in equations A–H. What do you notice about the shape of the ellipses for increasing values of eccentricity? Which is the most elliptical? Which is the least elliptical, that is, the most circular?
61. A planet's orbit about the Sun can be described as an ellipse. Consider the Sun as the origin of a rectangular coordinate system. Suppose that the x-intercepts of the elliptical path of the planet are $\pm 130,000,000$ and that the y-intercepts are $\pm 125,000,000$. Write the equation of the elliptical path of the planet.
62. Comets orbit the Sun in elongated ellipses. Consider the Sun as the origin of a rectangular coordinate system. Suppose that the equation of the path of the comet is

$$\dfrac{(x - 1{,}782{,}000{,}000)^2}{3.42 \cdot 10^{23}} + \dfrac{(y - 356{,}400{,}000)^2}{1.368 \cdot 10^{22}} = 1$$

Find the center of the path of the comet.

63. Use a graphing calculator to verify Exercise 33.
64. Use a graphing calculator to verify Exercise 6.

For Exercises 65 through 70, see the example below.

Example

Sketch the graph of $\dfrac{(x - 2)^2}{25} - \dfrac{(y - 1)^2}{9} = 1$.

Solution

This hyperbola has center $(2, 1)$. Notice that $a = 5$ and $b = 3$.

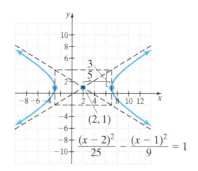

$\dfrac{(x - 2)^2}{25} - \dfrac{(x - 1)^2}{9} = 1$

Sketch the graph of each equation.

65. $\dfrac{(x - 1)^2}{4} - \dfrac{(y + 1)^2}{25} = 1$
66. $\dfrac{(x + 2)^2}{9} - \dfrac{(y - 1)^2}{4} = 1$
67. $\dfrac{y^2}{16} - \dfrac{(x + 3)^2}{9} = 1$
68. $\dfrac{(y + 4)^2}{4} - \dfrac{x^2}{25} = 1$
69. $\dfrac{(x + 5)^2}{16} - \dfrac{(y + 2)^2}{25} = 1$
70. $\dfrac{(x - 3)^2}{9} - \dfrac{(y - 2)^2}{4} = 1$

INTEGRATED REVIEW — REVIEW OF CONIC SECTIONS ONLY

Following is a summary of conic sections.

Conic Sections

	Standard Form	Graph
Parabola	$y = a(x - h)^2 + k$	
Parabola	$x = a(y - k)^2 + h$	
Circle	$(x - h)^2 + (y - k)^2 = r^2$	
Ellipse center $(0, 0)$	$\dfrac{x^2}{a^2} + \dfrac{y^2}{b^2} = 1$	
Hyperbola center $(0, 0)$	$\dfrac{x^2}{a^2} - \dfrac{y^2}{b^2} = 1$	
Hyperbola center $(0, 0)$	$\dfrac{y^2}{b^2} - \dfrac{x^2}{a^2} = 1$	

Identify whether each equation, when graphed, will be a parabola, circle, ellipse, or hyperbola. Then graph each equation.

1. $(x - 7)^2 + (y - 2)^2 = 4$
2. $y = x^2 + 4$
3. $y = x^2 + 12x + 36$
4. $\dfrac{x^2}{4} + \dfrac{y^2}{9} = 1$
5. $\dfrac{y^2}{9} - \dfrac{x^2}{9} = 1$
6. $\dfrac{x^2}{16} - \dfrac{y^2}{4} = 1$
7. $\dfrac{x^2}{16} + \dfrac{y^2}{4} = 1$
8. $x^2 + y^2 = 16$
9. $x = y^2 + 4y - 1$
10. $x = -y^2 + 6y$
11. $9x^2 - 4y^2 = 36$
12. $9x^2 + 4y^2 = 36$
13. $\dfrac{(x - 1)^2}{49} + \dfrac{(y + 2)^2}{25} = 1$
14. $y^2 = x^2 + 16$
15. $\left(x + \dfrac{1}{2}\right)^2 + \left(y - \dfrac{1}{2}\right)^2 = 1$

11.7 SOLVING NONLINEAR SYSTEMS OF EQUATIONS

OBJECTIVES

1. Solve a nonlinear system by substitution.
2. Solve a nonlinear system by elimination.

In Section 4.1, we used graphing, substitution, and elimination methods to find solutions of systems of linear equations in two variables. We now apply these same methods to nonlinear systems of equations in two variables. A **nonlinear system of equations** is a system of equations at least one of which is not linear. Since we will be graphing the equations in each system, we are interested in real number solutions only.

OBJECTIVE 1 ▶ Solving nonlinear systems by substitution. First, nonlinear systems are solved by the substitution method.

EXAMPLE 1   Solve the system

$$\begin{cases} x^2 - 3y = 1 \\ x - y = 1 \end{cases}$$

Solution   We can solve this system by substitution if we solve one equation for one of the variables. Solving the first equation for x is not the best choice since doing so introduces a radical. Also, solving for y in the first equation introduces a fraction. We solve the second equation for y.

$x - y = 1$ Second equation
$x - 1 = y$ Solve for y.

Replace y with $x - 1$ in the first equation, and then solve for x.

$x^2 - 3y = 1$ First equation
$x^2 - 3(x - 1) = 1$ Replace y with $x - 1$.
$x^2 - 3x + 3 = 1$
$x^2 - 3x + 2 = 0$
$(x - 2)(x - 1) = 0$
$x = 2$ or $x = 1$

Let $x = 2$ and then let $x = 1$ in the equation $y = x - 1$ to find corresponding y-values.

Let $x = 2$.   Let $x = 1$.
$y = x - 1$ $y = x - 1$
$y = 2 - 1 = 1$ $y = 1 - 1 = 0$

The solutions are $(2, 1)$ and $(1, 0)$ or the solution set is $\{(2, 1), (1, 0)\}$. Check both solutions in both equations. Both solutions satisfy both equations, so both are solutions of the system. The graph of each equation in the system is shown next. Intersections of the graphs are at $(2, 1)$ and $(1, 0)$.

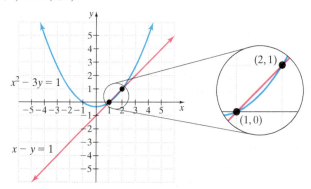

PRACTICE 1   Solve the system $\begin{cases} x^2 - 4y = 4 \\ x + y = -1 \end{cases}$.

Section 11.7 Solving Nonlinear Systems of Equations   671

EXAMPLE 2 Solve the system
$$\begin{cases} y = \sqrt{x} \\ x^2 + y^2 = 6 \end{cases}$$

Solution This system is ideal for substitution since y is expressed in terms of x in the first equation. Notice that if $y = \sqrt{x}$, then both x and y must be nonnegative if they are real numbers. Substitute $\sqrt{x}$ for y in the second equation, and solve for x.

$$x^2 + y^2 = 6$$
$$x^2 + (\sqrt{x})^2 = 6 \quad \text{Let } y = \sqrt{x}$$
$$x^2 + x = 6$$
$$x^2 + x - 6 = 0$$
$$(x + 3)(x - 2) = 0$$
$$x = -3 \quad \text{or} \quad x = 2$$

The solution -3 is discarded because we have noted that x must be nonnegative. To see this, let $x = -3$ in the first equation. Then let $x = 2$ in the first equation to find a corresponding y-value.

Let $x = -3$.   Let $x = 2$.
$y = \sqrt{x}$ $y = \sqrt{x}$
$y = \sqrt{-3}$ Not a real number $y = \sqrt{2}$

Since we are interested only in real number solutions, the only solution is $(2, \sqrt{2})$. Check to see that this solution satisfies both equations. The graph of each equation in the system is shown next.

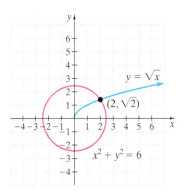

PRACTICE 2 Solve the system $\begin{cases} y = -\sqrt{x} \\ x^2 + y^2 = 20 \end{cases}$.

EXAMPLE 3 Solve the system
$$\begin{cases} x^2 + y^2 = 4 \\ x + y = 3 \end{cases}$$

Solution We use the substitution method and solve the second equation for x.

$$x + y = 3 \quad \text{Second equation}$$
$$x = 3 - y$$

Now we let $x = 3 - y$ in the first equation.

$$x^2 + y^2 = 4 \quad \text{First equation}$$
$$(3 - y)^2 + y^2 = 4 \quad \text{Let } x = 3 - y.$$
$$9 - 6y + y^2 + y^2 = 4$$
$$2y^2 - 6y + 5 = 0$$

By the quadratic formula, where $a = 2$, $b = -6$, and $c = 5$, we have

$$y = \frac{6 \pm \sqrt{(-6)^2 - 4 \cdot 2 \cdot 5}}{2 \cdot 2} = \frac{6 \pm \sqrt{-4}}{4}$$

Since $\sqrt{-4}$ is not a real number, there is no real solution. Graphically, the circle and the line do not intersect, as shown below.

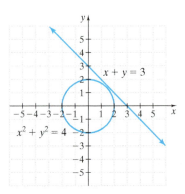

PRACTICE 3 Solve the system $\begin{cases} x^2 + y^2 = 9 \\ x - y = 5 \end{cases}$.

Concept Check ✓

Without solving, how can you tell that $x^2 + y^2 = 9$ and $x^2 + y^2 = 16$ do not have any points of intersection?

OBJECTIVE 2 ▶ Solving nonlinear systems by elimination. Some nonlinear systems may be solved by the elimination method.

EXAMPLE 4 Solve the system

$$\begin{cases} x^2 + 2y^2 = 10 \\ x^2 - y^2 = 1 \end{cases}$$

Solution We will use the elimination, or addition, method to solve this system. To eliminate x^2 when we add the two equations, multiply both sides of the second equation by -1. Then

$$\begin{cases} x^2 + 2y^2 = 10 \\ (-1)(x^2 - y^2) = -1 \cdot 1 \end{cases} \text{ is equivalent to } \begin{cases} x^2 + 2y^2 = 10 \\ -x^2 + y^2 = -1 \end{cases}$$

$$\begin{aligned} 3y^2 &= 9 & \text{Add.} \\ y^2 &= 3 & \text{Divide both sides by 3.} \\ y &= \pm\sqrt{3} \end{aligned}$$

To find the corresponding x-values, we let $y = \sqrt{3}$ and $y = -\sqrt{3}$ in either original equation. We choose the second equation.

Let $y = \sqrt{3}$.
$x^2 - y^2 = 1$
$x^2 - (\sqrt{3})^2 = 1$
$x^2 - 3 = 1$
$x^2 = 4$
$x = \pm\sqrt{4} = \pm 2$

Let $y = -\sqrt{3}$.
$x^2 - y^2 = 1$
$x^2 - (-\sqrt{3})^2 = 1$
$x^2 - 3 = 1$
$x^2 = 4$
$x = \pm\sqrt{4} = \pm 2$

Answer to Concept Check:
$x^2 + y^2 = 9$ is a circle inside the circle $x^2 + y^2 = 16$, therefore they do not have any points of intersection.

The solutions are $(2, \sqrt{3}), (-2, \sqrt{3}), (2, -\sqrt{3})$, and $(-2, -\sqrt{3})$. Check all four ordered pairs in both equations of the system. The graph of each equation in this system is shown.

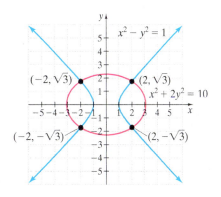

PRACTICE 4 Solve the system $\begin{cases} x^2 + 4y^2 = 16 \\ x^2 - y^2 = 1 \end{cases}$.

11.7 EXERCISE SET

MIXED PRACTICE

Solve each nonlinear system of equations for real solutions. See Examples 1 through 4.

1. $\begin{cases} x^2 + y^2 = 25 \\ 4x + 3y = 0 \end{cases}$

2. $\begin{cases} x^2 + y^2 = 25 \\ 3x + 4y = 0 \end{cases}$

3. $\begin{cases} x^2 + 4y^2 = 10 \\ y = x \end{cases}$

4. $\begin{cases} 4x^2 + y^2 = 10 \\ y = x \end{cases}$

5. $\begin{cases} y^2 = 4 - x \\ x - 2y = 4 \end{cases}$

6. $\begin{cases} x^2 + y^2 = 4 \\ x + y = -2 \end{cases}$

7. $\begin{cases} x^2 + y^2 = 9 \\ 16x^2 - 4y^2 = 64 \end{cases}$

8. $\begin{cases} 4x^2 + 3y^2 = 35 \\ 5x^2 + 2y^2 = 42 \end{cases}$

9. $\begin{cases} x^2 + 2y^2 = 2 \\ x - y = 2 \end{cases}$

10. $\begin{cases} x^2 + 2y^2 = 2 \\ x^2 - 2y^2 = 6 \end{cases}$

11. $\begin{cases} y = x^2 - 3 \\ 4x - y = 6 \end{cases}$

12. $\begin{cases} y = x + 1 \\ x^2 - y^2 = 1 \end{cases}$

13. $\begin{cases} y = x^2 \\ 3x + y = 10 \end{cases}$

14. $\begin{cases} 6x - y = 5 \\ xy = 1 \end{cases}$

15. $\begin{cases} y = 2x^2 + 1 \\ x + y = -1 \end{cases}$

16. $\begin{cases} x^2 + y^2 = 9 \\ x + y = 5 \end{cases}$

17. $\begin{cases} y = x^2 - 4 \\ y = x^2 - 4x \end{cases}$

18. $\begin{cases} x = y^2 - 3 \\ x = y^2 - 3y \end{cases}$

19. $\begin{cases} 2x^2 + 3y^2 = 14 \\ -x^2 + y^2 = 3 \end{cases}$

20. $\begin{cases} 4x^2 - 2y^2 = 2 \\ -x^2 + y^2 = 2 \end{cases}$

21. $\begin{cases} x^2 + y^2 = 1 \\ x^2 + (y + 3)^2 = 4 \end{cases}$

22. $\begin{cases} x^2 + 2y^2 = 4 \\ x^2 - y^2 = 4 \end{cases}$

23. $\begin{cases} y = x^2 + 2 \\ y = -x^2 + 4 \end{cases}$

24. $\begin{cases} x = -y^2 - 3 \\ x = y^2 - 5 \end{cases}$

25. $\begin{cases} 3x^2 + y^2 = 9 \\ 3x^2 - y^2 = 9 \end{cases}$

26. $\begin{cases} x^2 + y^2 = 25 \\ x = y^2 - 5 \end{cases}$

27. $\begin{cases} x^2 + 3y^2 = 6 \\ x^2 - 3y^2 = 10 \end{cases}$

28. $\begin{cases} x^2 + y^2 = 1 \\ y = x^2 - 9 \end{cases}$

29. $\begin{cases} x^2 + y^2 = 36 \\ y = \frac{1}{6}x^2 - 6 \end{cases}$

30. $\begin{cases} x^2 + y^2 = 16 \\ y = -\frac{1}{4}x^2 + 4 \end{cases}$

REVIEW AND PREVIEW

Graph each inequality in two variables. See Section 3.7.

31. $x > -3$
32. $y \leq 1$
33. $y < 2x - 1$
34. $3x - y \leq 4$

Find the perimeter of each geometric figure. See Section 6.3.

35.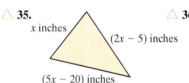

36.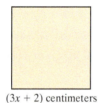

37.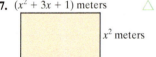

38.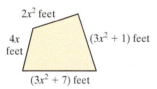

CONCEPT EXTENSIONS

For the exercises below, see the Concept Check in this section.

39. Without graphing, how can you tell that the graph of $x^2 + y^2 = 1$ and $x^2 + y^2 = 4$ do not have any points of intersection?

40. Without solving, how can you tell that the graphs of $y = 2x + 3$ and $y = 2x + 7$ do not have any points of intersection?

41. How many real solutions are possible for a system of equations whose graphs are a circle and a parabola? Draw diagrams to illustrate each possibility.

42. How many real solutions are possible for a system of equations whose graphs are an ellipse and a line? Draw diagrams to illustrate each possibility.

Solve.

43. The sum of the squares of two numbers is 130. The difference of the squares of the two numbers is 32. Find the two numbers.

44. The sum of the squares of two numbers is 20. Their product is 8. Find the two numbers.

45. During the development stage of a new rectangular keypad for a security system, it was decided that the area of the rectangle should be 285 square centimeters and the perimeter should be 68 centimeters. Find the dimensions of the keypad.

46. A rectangular holding pen for cattle is to be designed so that its perimeter is 92 feet and its area is 525 feet. Find the dimensions of the holding pen.

Recall that in business, a demand function expresses the quantity of a commodity demanded as a function of the commodity's unit price. A supply function expresses the quantity of a commodity supplied as a function of the commodity's unit price. When the quantity produced and supplied is equal to the quantity demanded, then we have what is called **market equilibrium.**

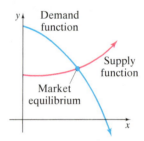

47. The demand function for a certain compact disc is given by the function

$$p = -0.01x^2 - 0.2x + 9$$

and the corresponding supply function is given by

$$p = 0.01x^2 - 0.1x + 3$$

where p is in dollars and x is in thousands of units. Find the equilibrium quantity and the corresponding price by solving the system consisting of the two given equations.

48. The demand function for a certain style of picture frame is given by the function

$$p = -2x^2 + 90$$

and the corresponding supply function is given by

$$p = 9x + 34$$

where p is in dollars and x is in thousands of units. Find the equilibrium quantity and the corresponding price by solving the system consisting of the two given equations.

Use a graphing calculator to verify the results of each exercise.

49. Exercise 3.
50. Exercise 4.
51. Exercise 23.
52. Exercise 24.

11.8 NONLINEAR INEQUALITIES AND SYSTEMS OF INEQUALITIES

OBJECTIVES

1. Graph a nonlinear inequality.
2. Graph a system of nonlinear inequalities.

OBJECTIVE 1 ▶ Graphing nonlinear inequalities. We can graph a nonlinear inequality in two variables such as $\frac{x^2}{9} + \frac{y^2}{16} \leq 1$ in a way similar to the way we graphed a linear inequality in two variables in Section 3.7. First, we graph the related equation $\frac{x^2}{9} + \frac{y^2}{16} = 1$. The graph of the equation is our boundary. Then, using test points, we determine and shade the region whose points satisfy the inequality.

EXAMPLE 1 Graph $\frac{x^2}{9} + \frac{y^2}{16} \leq 1$.

Solution First, graph the equation $\frac{x^2}{9} + \frac{y^2}{16} = 1$. Sketch a solid curve since the graph of $\frac{x^2}{9} + \frac{y^2}{16} \leq 1$ includes the graph of $\frac{x^2}{9} + \frac{y^2}{16} = 1$. The graph is an ellipse, and it divides the plane into two regions, the "inside" and the "outside" of the ellipse. To determine which region contains the solutions, select a test point in either region and determine whether the coordinates of the point satisfy the inequality. We choose $(0, 0)$ as the test point.

$$\frac{x^2}{9} + \frac{y^2}{16} \leq 1$$

$$\frac{0^2}{9} + \frac{0^2}{16} \leq 1 \quad \text{Let } x = 0 \text{ and } y = 0.$$

$$0 \leq 1 \quad \text{True}$$

Since this statement is true, the solution set is the region containing $(0, 0)$. The graph of the solution set includes the points on and inside the ellipse, as shaded in the figure.

PRACTICE 1 Graph $\frac{x^2}{36} + \frac{y^2}{16} \geq 1$.

EXAMPLE 2 Graph $4y^2 > x^2 + 16$.

Solution The related equation is $4y^2 = x^2 + 16$. Subtract x^2 from both sides and divide both sides by 16, and we have $\frac{y^2}{4} - \frac{x^2}{16} = 1$, which is a hyperbola. Graph the hyperbola as a dashed curve since the graph of $4y^2 > x^2 + 16$ does *not* include the graph of $4y^2 = x^2 + 16$. The hyperbola divides the plane into three regions. Select a test point in each region—not on a boundary line—to determine whether that region contains solutions of the inequality.

Test Region A with $(0, 4)$	*Test Region B with* $(0, 0)$	*Test Region C with* $(0, -4)$
$4y^2 > x^2 + 16$	$4y^2 > x^2 + 16$	$4y^2 > x^2 + 16$
$4(4)^2 > 0^2 + 16$	$4(0)^2 > 0^2 + 16$	$4(-4)^2 > 0^2 + 16$
$64 > 16$ True	$0 > 16$ False	$64 > 16$ True

The graph of the solution set includes the shaded regions A and C only, not the boundary.

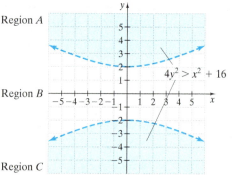

PRACTICE 2 Graph $16y^2 > 9x^2 + 144$.

OBJECTIVE 2 ▶ Graphing systems of nonlinear inequalities. In Section 4.5 we graphed systems of linear inequalities. Recall that the graph of a system of inequalities is the intersection of the graphs of the inequalities.

EXAMPLE 3 Graph the system
$$\begin{cases} x \leq 1 - 2y \\ y \leq x^2 \end{cases}$$

Solution We graph each inequality on the same set of axes. The intersection is shown in the third graph below. It is the darkest shaded (appears purple) region along with its boundary lines. The coordinates of the points of intersection can be found by solving the related system.

$$\begin{cases} x = 1 - 2y \\ y = x^2 \end{cases}$$

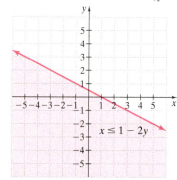 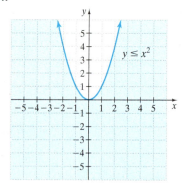

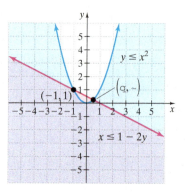

PRACTICE 3 Graph the system $\begin{cases} y \geq x^2 \\ y \leq -3x + 2 \end{cases}$.

Section 11.8 Nonlinear Inequalities and Systems of Inequalities 677

EXAMPLE 4 Graph the system

$$\begin{cases} x^2 + y^2 < 25 \\ \dfrac{x^2}{9} - \dfrac{y^2}{25} < 1 \\ y < x + 3 \end{cases}$$

Solution We graph each inequality. The graph of $x^2 + y^2 < 25$ contains points "inside" the circle that has center $(0, 0)$ and radius 5. The graph of $\dfrac{x^2}{9} - \dfrac{y^2}{25} < 1$ is the region between the two branches of the hyperbola with x-intercepts -3 and 3 and center $(0, 0)$. The graph of $y < x + 3$ is the region "below" the line with slope 1 and y-intercept $(0, 3)$. The graph of the solution set of the system is the intersection of all the graphs, the darkest shaded region shown. The boundary of this region is not part of the solution.

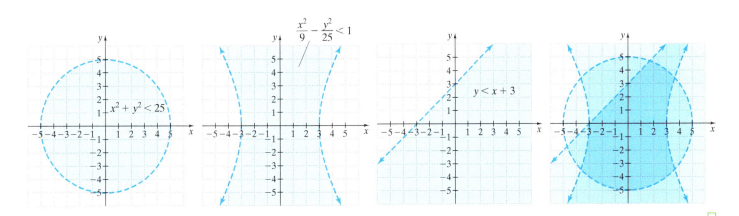

PRACTICE 4 Graph the system $\begin{cases} x^2 + y^2 < 16 \\ \dfrac{x^2}{4} - \dfrac{y^2}{9} < 1 \\ y < x + 3 \end{cases}$.

11.8 EXERCISE SET

Graph each inequality. See Examples 1 and 2.

1. $y < x^2$
2. $y < -x^2$
3. $x^2 + y^2 \geq 16$
4. $x^2 + y^2 < 36$
5. $\dfrac{x^2}{4} - y^2 < 1$
6. $x^2 - \dfrac{y^2}{9} \geq 1$
7. $y > (x - 1)^2 - 3$
8. $y > (x + 3)^2 + 2$
9. $x^2 + y^2 \leq 9$
10. $x^2 + y^2 > 4$
11. $y > -x^2 + 5$
12. $y < -x^2 + 5$
13. $\dfrac{x^2}{4} + \dfrac{y^2}{9} \leq 1$
14. $\dfrac{x^2}{25} + \dfrac{y^2}{4} \geq 1$
15. $\dfrac{y^2}{4} - x^2 \leq 1$
16. $\dfrac{y^2}{16} - \dfrac{x^2}{9} > 1$
17. $y < (x - 2)^2 + 1$
18. $y > (x - 2)^2 + 1$
19. $y \leq x^2 + x - 2$
20. $y > x^2 + x - 2$

Graph each system. See Examples 3 and 4.

21. $\begin{cases} 4x + 3y \geq 12 \\ x^2 + y^2 < 16 \end{cases}$
22. $\begin{cases} 3x - 4y \leq 12 \\ x^2 + y^2 < 16 \end{cases}$
23. $\begin{cases} x^2 + y^2 \leq 9 \\ x^2 + y^2 \geq 1 \end{cases}$
24. $\begin{cases} x^2 + y^2 \geq 9 \\ x^2 + y^2 \geq 16 \end{cases}$

678 CHAPTER 11 Graphing Quadratic Functions, Rational Functions, and Conic Sections

25. $\begin{cases} y > x^2 \\ y \geq 2x + 1 \end{cases}$

26. $\begin{cases} y \leq -x^2 + 3 \\ y \leq 2x - 1 \end{cases}$

27. $\begin{cases} x^2 + y^2 > 9 \\ y > x^2 \end{cases}$

28. $\begin{cases} x^2 + y^2 \leq 9 \\ y < x^2 \end{cases}$

29. $\begin{cases} \dfrac{x^2}{4} + \dfrac{y^2}{9} \geq 1 \\ x^2 + y^2 \geq 4 \end{cases}$

30. $\begin{cases} x^2 + (y - 2)^2 \geq 9 \\ \dfrac{x^2}{4} + \dfrac{y^2}{25} < 1 \end{cases}$

31. $\begin{cases} x^2 - y^2 \geq 1 \\ y \geq 0 \end{cases}$

32. $\begin{cases} x^2 - y^2 \geq 1 \\ x \geq 0 \end{cases}$

33. $\begin{cases} x + y \geq 1 \\ 2x + 3y < 1 \\ x > -3 \end{cases}$

34. $\begin{cases} x - y < -1 \\ 4x - 3y > 0 \\ y > 0 \end{cases}$

35. $\begin{cases} x^2 - y^2 < 1 \\ \dfrac{x^2}{16} + y^2 \leq 1 \\ x \geq -2 \end{cases}$

36. $\begin{cases} x^2 - y^2 \geq 1 \\ \dfrac{x^2}{16} + \dfrac{y^2}{4} \leq 1 \\ y \geq 1 \end{cases}$

REVIEW AND PREVIEW

Determine which graph is the graph of a function. See Section 3.2.

37.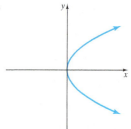

38.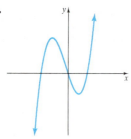

39.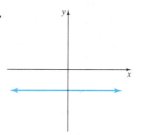

40.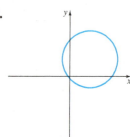

Find each function value if $f(x) = 3x^2 - 2$. See Section 3.2.

41. $f(-1)$
42. $f(-3)$
43. $f(a)$
44. $f(b)$

CONCEPT EXTENSIONS

45. Discuss how graphing a linear inequality such as $x + y < 9$ is similar to graphing a nonlinear inequality such as $x^2 + y^2 < 9$.

46. Discuss how graphing a linear inequality such as $x + y < 9$ is different from graphing a nonlinear inequality such as $x^2 + y^2 < 9$.

47. Graph the system $\begin{cases} y \leq x^2 \\ y \geq x + 2 \\ x \geq 0 \\ y \geq 0 \end{cases}$.

CHAPTER 11 VOCABULARY CHECK

Fill in each blank with one of the words or phrases listed below.

quadratic formula	quadratic	discriminant	$\pm\sqrt{b}$	circle	nonlinear system of equations
completing the square	quadratic inequality	(h, k)	$(0, k)$	radius	hyperbola
$(h, 0)$	$\dfrac{-b}{2a}$	center		ellipse	rational

1. The _____ helps us find the number and type of solutions of a quadratic equation.

2. If $a^2 = b$, then $a =$ _____

3. The graph of $f(x) = ax^2 + bx + c$ where a is not 0 is a parabola whose vertex has x-value of _____.

4. A(n) _____ is an inequality that can be written so that one side is a quadratic expression and the other side is 0.

5. The process of writing a quadratic equation so that one side is a perfect square trinomial is called _____.

6. The graph of $f(x) = x^2 + k$ has vertex _____.

7. The graph of $f(x) = (x - h)^2$ has vertex _____.

8. The graph of $f(x) = (x - h)^2 + k$ has vertex _____.

9. The formula $x = \dfrac{-b \pm \sqrt{b^2 - 4ac}}{2a}$ is called the _____.

10. A _____ equation is one that can be written in the form $ax^2 + bx + c = 0$ where $a, b,$ and c are real numbers and a is not 0.

11. _____ functions are quotients of polynomial functions.

12. A(n) _____ is the set of all points in a plane that are the same distance from a fixed point, called the _____.

13. A _____ is a system of equations at least one of which is not linear.

14. A(n) _____ is the set of points on a plane such that the sum of the distances of those points from two fixed points is a constant.

15. In a circle, the distance from the center to a point of the circle is called its _____.

16. A(n) _____ is the set of points in a plane such that the absolute value of the difference of the distance from two fixed points is constant.

CHAPTER 11 REVIEW

(11.1) Sketch the graph of each function. Label the vertex and the axis of symmetry.

1. $f(x) = x^2 - 4$
2. $g(x) = x^2 + 7$
3. $H(x) = 2x^2$
4. $h(x) = -\frac{1}{3}x^2$
5. $F(x) = (x - 1)^2$
6. $G(x) = (x + 5)^2$
7. $f(x) = (x - 4)^2 - 2$
8. $f(x) = -3(x - 1)^2 + 1$

(11.2) Sketch the graph of each function. Find the vertex and the intercepts.

9. $f(x) = x^2 + 10x + 25$
10. $f(x) = -x^2 + 6x - 9$
11. $f(x) = 4x^2 - 1$
12. $f(x) = -5x^2 + 5$
13. Find the vertex of the graph of $f(x) = -3x^2 - 5x + 4$. Determine whether the graph opens upward or downward, find the y-intercept, approximate the x-intercepts to one decimal place, and sketch the graph.
14. The function $h(t) = -16t^2 + 120t + 300$ gives the height in feet of a projectile fired from the top of a building in t seconds.
    a. When will the object reach a height of 350 feet? Round your answer to one decimal place.
    b. Explain why part **a** has two answers.
15. Find two numbers whose product is as large as possible, given that their sum is 420.
16. Write an equation of a quadratic function whose graph is a parabola that has vertex $(-3, 7)$ and that passes through the origin.

(11.3) Use transformations of $f(x) = \frac{1}{x}$ or $f(x) = \frac{1}{x^2}$ to graph each rational function.

17. $g(x) = \frac{1}{(x + 2)^2} - 1$
18. $h(x) = \frac{1}{x - 1} + 3$

(11.3 and 11.4) Find the vertical asymptotes, if any, the horizontal asymptote, if one exists, and the slant asymptote, if there is one, of the graph of each rational function. Then graph the rational function.

19. $f(x) = \frac{2x}{x^2 - 9}$
20. $g(x) = \frac{2x - 4}{x + 3}$
21. $h(x) = \frac{x^2 - 3x - 4}{x^2 - x - 6}$
22. $r(x) = \frac{x^2 + 4x + 3}{(x + 2)^2}$
23. $y = \frac{x^2}{x + 1}$
24. $y = \frac{x^2 + 2x - 3}{x - 3}$
25. $f(x) = \frac{-2x^3}{x^2 + 1}$
26. $g(x) = \frac{4x^2 - 16x + 16}{2x - 3}$

27. A company is planning to manufacture affordable graphing calculators. The fixed monthly cost will be $50,000 and it will cost $25 to produce each calculator.
    a. Write the cost function, C, of producing x graphing calculators.
    b. Write the average cost function, $\overline{C}$, of producing x graphing calculators.
    c. Find and interpret $\overline{C}(50), \overline{C}(100), \overline{C}(1000),$ and $\overline{C}(100,000)$.
    d. What is the horizontal asymptote for the graph of this function and what does it represent?

28. Find the horizontal asymptote for $f(x) = \frac{150x + 120}{0.05x + 10}$.

(11.5) Write an equation of the circle with the given center and radius.

29. center $(-4, 4)$, radius 3
30. center $(5, 0)$, radius 5
31. center $(-7, -9)$, radius $\sqrt{11}$
32. center $(0, 0)$, radius $\frac{7}{2}$

Sketch the graph of the equation. If the graph is a circle, find its center. If the graph is a parabola, find its vertex.

33. $x^2 + y^2 = 7$
34. $x = 2(y - 5)^2 + 4$
35. $x = -(y + 2)^2 + 3$
36. $(x - 1)^2 + (y - 2)^2 = 4$
37. $y = -x^2 + 4x + 10$
38. $x = -y^2 - 4y + 6$
39. $x = \frac{1}{2}y^2 + 2y + 1$
40. $y = -3x^2 + \frac{1}{2}x + 4$
41. $x^2 + y^2 + 2x + y = \frac{3}{4}$
42. $x^2 + y^2 - 3y = \frac{7}{4}$
43. $4x^2 + 4y^2 + 16x + 8y = 1$

(11.6) *Sketch the graph of each equation.*

44. $x^2 + \frac{y^2}{4} = 1$
45. $x^2 - \frac{y^2}{4} = 1$
46. $\frac{x^2}{5} + \frac{y^2}{5} = 1$
47. $\frac{x^2}{5} - \frac{y^2}{5} = 1$
48. $-5x^2 + 25y^2 = 125$
49. $4y^2 + 9x^2 = 36$
50. $x^2 - y^2 = 1$
51. $\frac{(x + 3)^2}{9} + \frac{(y - 4)^2}{25} = 1$
52. $y^2 = x^2 + 9$
53. $x^2 = 4y^2 - 16$
54. $100 - 25x^2 = 4y^2$

(11.7) *Solve each system of equations.*

55. $\begin{cases} y = 2x - 4 \\ y^2 = 4x \end{cases}$
56. $\begin{cases} x^2 + y^2 = 4 \\ x - y = 4 \end{cases}$
57. $\begin{cases} y = x + 2 \\ y = x^2 \end{cases}$
58. $\begin{cases} x^2 + 4y^2 = 16 \\ x^2 + y^2 = 4 \end{cases}$
59. $\begin{cases} 4x - y^2 = 0 \\ 2x^2 + y^2 = 16 \end{cases}$
60. $\begin{cases} x^2 + 2y = 9 \\ 5x - 2y = 5 \end{cases}$
61. $\begin{cases} y = 3x^2 + 5x - 4 \\ y = 3x^2 - x + 2 \end{cases}$
62. $\begin{cases} x^2 - 3y^2 = 1 \\ 4x^2 + 5y^2 = 21 \end{cases}$

63. Find the length and the width of a room whose area is 150 square feet and whose perimeter is 50 feet.

64. What is the greatest number of real solutions possible for a system of two equations whose graphs are an ellipse and a hyperbola?

(11.8) *Graph the inequality or system of inequalities.*

65. $y \leq -x^2 + 3$
66. $x^2 + y^2 < 9$
67. $\begin{cases} 2x \leq 4 \\ x + y \geq 1 \end{cases}$
68. $\frac{x^2}{4} + \frac{y^2}{9} \geq 1$
69. $\begin{cases} x^2 + y^2 < 4 \\ x^2 - y^2 \leq 1 \end{cases}$
70. $\begin{cases} x^2 + y^2 \leq 16 \\ x^2 + y^2 \geq 4 \end{cases}$

MIXED REVIEW

Solve each equation.

71. $x^2 - x - 30 = 0$
72. $10x^2 = 3x + 4$
73. $9y^2 = 36$
74. $(9n + 1)^2 = 9$
75. $x^2 + x + 7 = 0$
76. $(3x - 4)^2 = 10x$
77. $x^2 + 11 = 0$
78. $(5a - 2)^2 - a = 0$
79. $\frac{7}{8} = \frac{8}{x^2}$
80. $x^{2/3} - 6x^{1/3} = -8$
81. $(2x - 3)(4x + 5) \geq 0$
82. $\frac{x(x + 5)}{4x - 3} \geq 0$
83. $\frac{3}{x - 2} > 2$

84. The total amount of passenger traffic at Phoenix Sky Harbor International Airport in Phoenix, Arizona, during the period 1980 through 2005 can be modeled by the equation $y = 6.46x^2 + 1236.5x + 7289$, where y is the number of passengers enplaned and deplaned in thousands and x is the number of years after 1980. (*Source*: Based on data from The City of Phoenix Aviation Department, 1980–2005)

   a. Estimate the passenger traffic at Phoenix Sky Harbor International Airport in 2000.

   b. According to this model, in what year will passenger traffic at Phoenix Sky Harbor International Airport reach 60,000,000 passengers?

MIXED REVIEW

85. Write an equation of the circle with center $(-7, 8)$ and radius 5.

Graph each equation.

86. $3x^2 + 6x + 3y^2 = 9$
87. $y = x^2 + 6x + 9$
88. $x = y^2 + 6y + 9$
89. $\frac{y^2}{4} - \frac{x^2}{16} = 1$

90. $\dfrac{y^2}{4} + \dfrac{x^2}{16} = 1$

91. $\dfrac{(x-2)^2}{4} + (y-1)^2 = 1$

92. $y^2 = x^2 + 6$

93. $y^2 + x^2 = 4x + 6$

94. $x^2 + y^2 - 8y = 0$

95. $6(x-2)^2 + 9(y+5)^2 = 36$

96. $\dfrac{x^2}{16} - \dfrac{y^2}{25} = 1$

97. $f(x) = \dfrac{1}{x-2} + 3$

98. $f(x) = \dfrac{x+2}{x^2-9}$

Solve each system of equations.

99. $\begin{cases} y = x^2 - 5x + 1 \\ y = -x + 6 \end{cases}$

100. $\begin{cases} x^2 + y^2 = 10 \\ 9x^2 + y^2 = 18 \end{cases}$

Graph each inequality or system of inequalities.

101. $x^2 - y^2 < 1$

102. $\begin{cases} y > x^2 \\ x + y \geq 3 \end{cases}$

CHAPTER 11 TEST

Remember to use the Chapter Test Prep Videos to see the fully worked-out solutions to any of the exercises you want to review.

Graph each function. Label the vertex.

1. $f(x) = 3x^2$
2. $G(x) = -2(x-1)^2 + 5$

Graph each function. Find and label the vertex, y-intercept, and x-intercepts (if any).

3. $h(x) = x^2 - 4x + 4$
4. $F(x) = 2x^2 - 8x + 9$
5. A stone is thrown upward from a bridge. The stone's height in feet, $s(t)$, above the water t seconds after the stone is thrown is a function given by the equation $s(t) = -16t^2 + 32t + 256$.
   a. Find the maximum height of the stone.
   b. Find the time it takes the stone to hit the water. Round the answer to two decimal places.

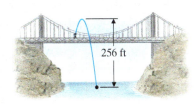

Find the domain of each rational function and graph the function.

6. $f(x) = \dfrac{1}{(x+3)^2}$
7. $f(x) = \dfrac{1}{x-1} + 2$
8. $f(x) = \dfrac{x^2-9}{x-2}$
9. $f(x) = \dfrac{x+1}{x^2+2x-3}$
10. $f(x) = \dfrac{4x^2}{x^2+3}$
11. A company is planning to manufacture portable satellite radio players. The fixed monthly cost will be $300,000 and it will cost $10 to produce each player.

   a. Write the average cost function, $\overline{C}$, of producing x players.
   b. What is the horizontal asymptote for the graph of this function and what does it represent?

Sketch the graph of each equation.

12. $x^2 + y^2 = 36$
13. $x^2 - y^2 = 36$
14. $16x^2 + 9y^2 = 144$
15. $x^2 + y^2 + 6x = 16$
16. $x = y^2 + 8y - 3$
17. $\dfrac{(x-4)^2}{16} + \dfrac{(y-3)^2}{9} = 1$

Solve each system.

18. $\begin{cases} x^2 + y^2 = 26 \\ x^2 - 2y^2 = 23 \end{cases}$

19. $\begin{cases} y = x^2 - 5x + 6 \\ y = 2x \end{cases}$

Graph the solution of each system.

20. $\begin{cases} 2x + 5y \geq 10 \\ y \geq x^2 + 1 \end{cases}$

21. $\begin{cases} \dfrac{x^2}{4} + y^2 \leq 1 \\ x + y > 1 \end{cases}$

22. A bridge has an arch in the shape of a half-ellipse. If the equation of the ellipse, measured in feet, is $100x^2 + 225y^2 = 22{,}500$, find the height of the arch from the road and the width of the arch.

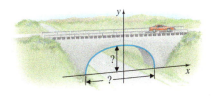

CHAPTER 11 STANDARDIZED TEST

Graph the function. Find the vertex.

1. $f(x) = 5x^2$

   a. vertex: $(0, 0)$
   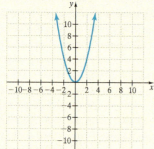

   b. vertex: $(0, 5)$
   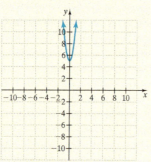

   c. vertex: $(0, 0)$
   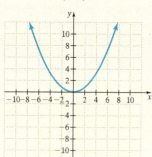

   d. vertex: $(0, 0)$
   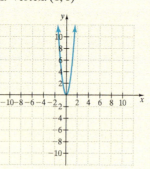

2. $G(x) = -2(x - 5)^2 + 6$

   a. vertex: $(5, 6)$
   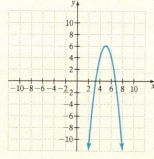

   b. vertex: $(-6, -5)$
   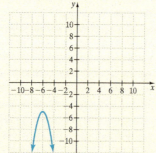

   c. vertex: $(6, 5)$
   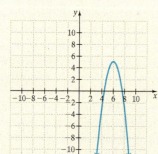

   d. vertex: $(-5, 6)$
   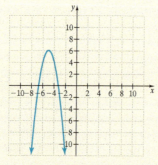

Graph the function. Find the vertex, y-intercept, and x-intercepts (if any).

3. $h(x) = x^2 - 2x + 1$

   a. vertex: $(1, 0)$
      x-intercept: $(1, 0)$,
      y-intercept: $(0, -1)$
   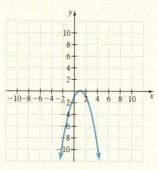

   b. vertex: $(0, 1)$
      x-intercept: $(1, 0)$,
      y-intercept: $(0, 1)$
   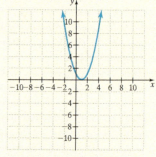

   c. vertex: $(1, 0)$
      x-intercept: $(1, 0)$,
      y-intercept: $(0, 1)$
   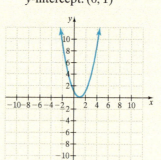

   d. vertex: $(-1, 0)$
      x-intercept: $(1, 0)$,
      y-intercept: $(0, 1)$
   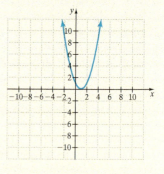

4. $F(x) = 2x^2 - 4x + 5$

   a. vertex: $(1, 3)$
      x-intercept: none,
      y-intercept: $(0, 5)$
   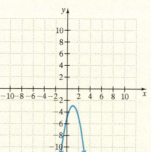

   b. vertex: $(1, 3)$
      x-intercept: $(5, 0)$,
      y-intercept: none
   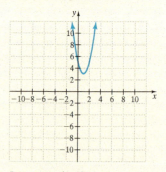

   c. vertex: $(1, 3)$
      x-intercept: none,
      y-intercept: $(0, 5)$
   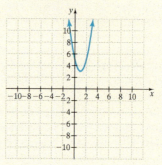

   d. vertex: $(1, 3)$
      x-intercept: $(0, 0)$,
      y-intercept: $(0, 5)$
   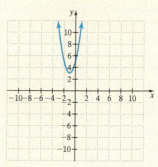

5. A stone is thrown upward from the edge of a cliff. The stone's height in feet, $s(t)$, above the ground t seconds after the stone is thrown is a function given by the equation $s(t) = -16t^2 + 32t + 320$. Find the maximum height of the stone.

   a. 1 ft
   b. 320 ft
   c. 336 ft
   d. 32 ft

Multiple Choice. *Choose the one alternative that best completes the statement or answers the question. Sketch the graph of the equation.*

6. $x^2 + y^2 = 36$

   a.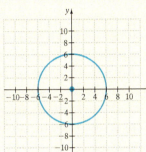
   b.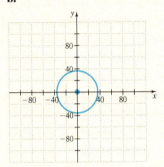
   c.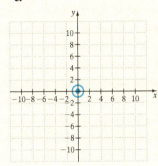
   d.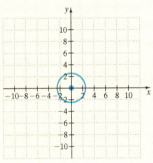

7. $x^2 - y^2 = 16$

   a.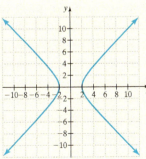
   b.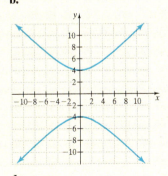
   c.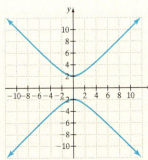
   d.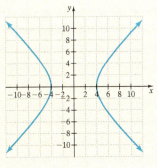

8. $9x^2 + 16y^2 = 144$

   a.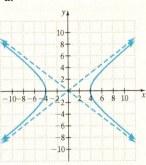
   b.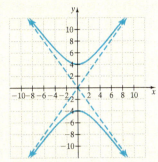
   c.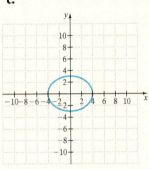
   d.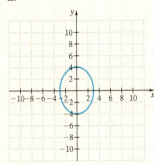

9. $x^2 + y^2 + 8y = 0$

   a.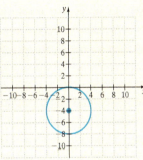
   b.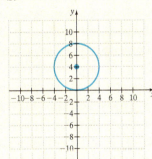
   c.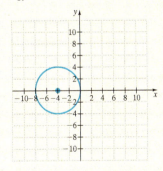
   d.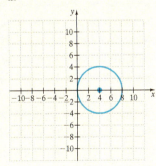

10. $x = y^2 + 8y + 11$

a.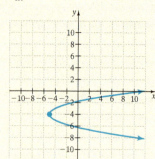
b.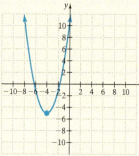
c.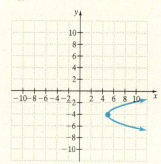
d.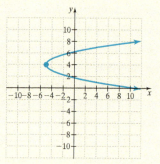

11. $\dfrac{(x+2)^2}{4} + \dfrac{(y+1)^2}{16} = 1$

a.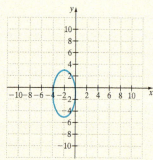
b.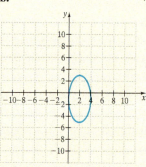
c.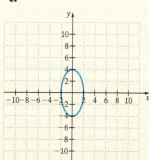
d.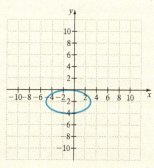

12. $y^2 - x^2 = 9$

a.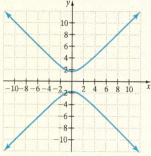
b.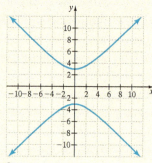
c.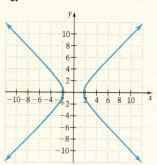
d.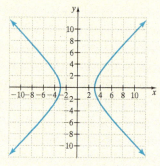

Solve the system.

13. $\begin{cases} x^2 + y^2 = 89 \\ x^2 - y^2 = -39 \end{cases}$

a. $(5, 8), (-5, 8), (5, -8), (-5, -8)$
b. $(-5, -8), (-8, -5)$
c. $(5, 8), (8, 5), (-5, -8), (-8, -5)$
d. $(5, -8), (5, 8)$

14. $\begin{cases} y = x^2 - 12x + 36 \\ y = -x + 8 \end{cases}$

a. $(7, 1), (4, 4)$
b. $(6, 2)$
c. $(-7, 15), (-4, 12)$
d. $(7, 15), (4, 4)$

Graph the solution of the system.

15. $\begin{cases} y > x^2 \\ 6x + 2y \leq 12 \end{cases}$

a.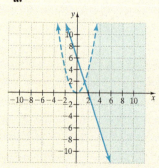
b.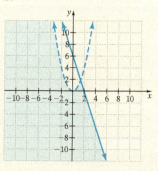

c.
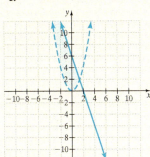

d.
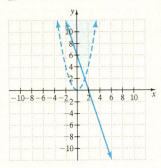

16. $\begin{cases} \dfrac{x^2}{36} + y^2 < 1 \\ x + y \geq 1 \end{cases}$

a.
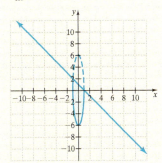

b.
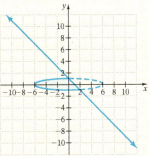

c.
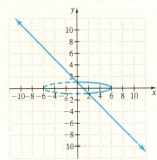

d.
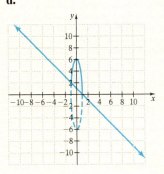

Solve the problem.

17. A bridge has an arch in the shape of a half-ellipse. If the equation of the ellipse, measured in feet, is $81x^2 + 225y^2 = 18{,}225$, find the height of the arch from the road and the width of the arch.

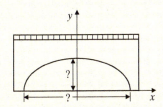

a. height, 9 ft; width 30 ft
b. height, 18 ft; width 30 ft
c. height, 15 ft; width 18 ft
d. height, 9 ft; width 15 ft

For Exercises 18–22, graph each rational function.

18. $f(x) = \dfrac{1}{x-2}$

a.
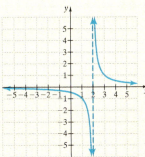

b.
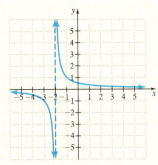

c.
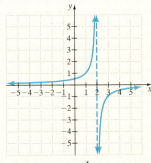

d.
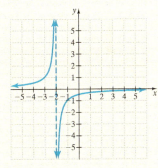

19. $f(x) = \dfrac{1}{(x+1)^2} - 2$

a.
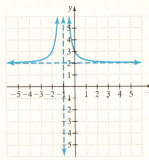

b.
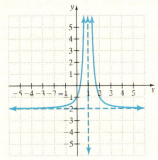

c.
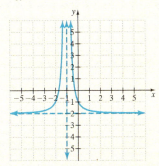

d.
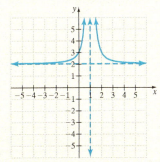

20. $f(x) = \dfrac{3x^2}{x^2 + 1}$

a.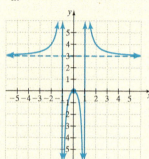

b.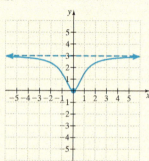

c.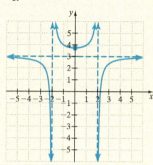

d.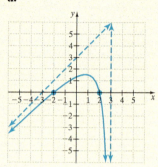

c.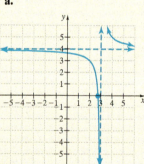

d.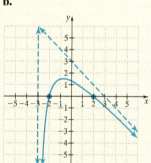

21. $f(x) = \dfrac{x^2 - 4}{x - 3}$

22. $f(x) = \dfrac{x - 2}{x^2 - 2x - 3}$

a.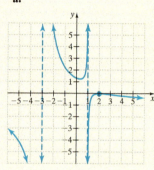

b.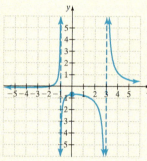

c.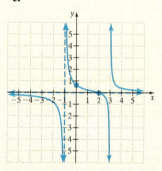

d.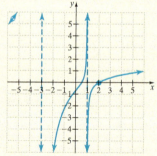

CHAPTER

12 Sequences, Series, and the Binomial Theorem

A tiling with squares whose sides are successive Fibonacci numbers in length

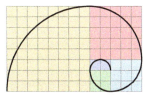

A Fibonacci spiral, created by drawing arcs connecting the opposite corners of squares in the Fibonacci tiling

12.1 Sequences

12.2 Arithmetic and Geometric Sequences

12.3 Series

Integrated Review— Sequences and Series

12.4 Partial Sums of Arithmetic and Geometric Sequences

12.5 The Binomial Theorem

Extension: Inductive and Deductive Reasoning

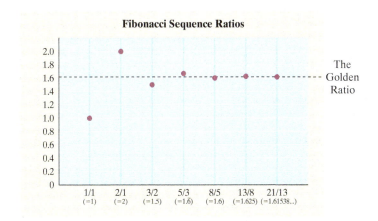

The Fibonacci Sequence is a special sequence in which the first two terms are 1 and each term thereafter is the sum of the two previous terms:

$$1, 1, 2, 3, 5, 8, 13, 21, \ldots$$

The Fibonacci numbers are named after Leonardo of Pisa, known as Fibonacci.

There are numerous interesting facts about this sequence, and some are shown on the diagrams on this page.

The ratio of successive numbers in the Fibonacci Sequence approaches a number called the golden ratio or golden number, which is approximately 1.618034.

In this chapter, we study this sequence as well as others.

12.1 SEQUENCES

OBJECTIVES

1. Write the terms of a sequence given its general term.
2. Find the general term of a sequence.
3. Solve applications that involve sequences.

Suppose that a town's present population of 100,000 is growing by 5% each year. After the first year, the town's population will be

$$100{,}000 + 0.05(100{,}000) = 105{,}000$$

After the second year, the town's population will be

$$105{,}000 + 0.05(105{,}000) = 110{,}250$$

After the third year, the town's population will be

$$110{,}250 + 0.05(110{,}250) \approx 115{,}763$$

If we continue to calculate, the town's yearly population can be written as the **infinite sequence** of numbers

$$105{,}000, 110{,}250, 115{,}763, \ldots$$

If we decide to stop calculating after a certain year (say, the fourth year), we obtain the **finite sequence**

$$105{,}000, \ 110{,}250, \ 115{,}763, \ 121{,}551$$

> **Sequences**
> An infinite sequence is a function whose domain is the set of natural numbers $\{1, 2, 3, 4, \ldots\}$.
> A finite sequence is a function whose domain is the set of natural numbers $\{1, 2, 3, 4, \ldots, n\}$, where n is some natural number.

OBJECTIVE 1 ▶ Writing the terms of a sequence. Given the sequence $2, 4, 8, 16, \ldots$, we say that each number is a **term** of the sequence. Because a sequence is a function, we could describe it by writing $f(n) = 2^n$, where n is a natural number. Instead, we use the notation

$$a_n = 2^n$$

Some function values are

$$a_1 = 2^1 = 2 \quad \text{First term of the sequence}$$
$$a_2 = 2^2 = 4 \quad \text{Second term}$$
$$a_3 = 2^3 = 8 \quad \text{Third term}$$
$$a_4 = 2^4 = 16 \quad \text{Fourth term}$$
$$a_{10} = 2^{10} = 1024 \quad \text{Tenth term}$$

The nth term of the sequence a_n is called the **general term.**

> **▶ Helpful Hint**
> If it helps, think of a sequence as simply a list of values in which a position is assigned. For the sequence directly above,
> Value: 2,   4,   8,   16, …, 1024
>   ↑ ↑ ↑ ↑   ↑
> Position   1st 2nd 3rd 4th   10th

EXAMPLE 1   Write the first five terms of the sequence whose general term is given by

$$a_n = n^2 - 1$$

Solution   Evaluate a_n, where n is 1, 2, 3, 4, and 5.

$$a_n = n^2 - 1$$
$$a_1 = 1^2 - 1 = 0 \quad \text{Replace } n \text{ with 1.}$$

$a_2 = 2^2 - 1 = 3$ Replace n with 2.
$a_3 = 3^2 - 1 = 8$ Replace n with 3.
$a_4 = 4^2 - 1 = 15$ Replace n with 4.
$a_5 = 5^2 - 1 = 24$ Replace n with 5.

Thus, the first five terms of the sequence $a_n = n^2 - 1$ are 0, 3, 8, 15, and 24.

PRACTICE

1   Write the first five terms of the sequence whose general term is given by $a_n = 5 + n^2$.

EXAMPLE 2   If the general term of a sequence is given by $a_n = \dfrac{(-1)^n}{3n}$, find

a. the first term of the sequence   **b.** a_8

c. the one-hundredth term of the sequence   **d.** a_{15}

Solution

a. $a_1 = \dfrac{(-1)^1}{3(1)} = -\dfrac{1}{3}$ Replace n with 1.

b. $a_8 = \dfrac{(-1)^8}{3(8)} = \dfrac{1}{24}$ Replace n with 8.

c. $a_{100} = \dfrac{(-1)^{100}}{3(100)} = \dfrac{1}{300}$ Replace n with 100.

d. $a_{15} = \dfrac{(-1)^{15}}{3(15)} = -\dfrac{1}{45}$ Replace n with 15.

PRACTICE

2   If the general term of a sequence is given by $a_n = \dfrac{(-1)^n}{5n}$, find

a. the first term of the sequence   **b.** a_4

c. The thirtieth term of the sequence   **d.** a_{19}

OBJECTIVE 2 ▶ Finding the general term of a sequence. Suppose we know the first few terms of a sequence and want to find a general term that fits the pattern of the first few terms.

EXAMPLE 3   Find a general term a_n of the sequence whose first few terms are given.

a. $1, 4, 9, 16, \ldots$ **b.** $\dfrac{1}{1}, \dfrac{1}{2}, \dfrac{1}{3}, \dfrac{1}{4}, \dfrac{1}{5}, \ldots$

c. $-3, -6, -9, -12, \ldots$ **d.** $\dfrac{1}{2}, \dfrac{1}{4}, \dfrac{1}{8}, \dfrac{1}{16}, \ldots$

Solution

a. These numbers are the squares of the first four natural numbers, so a general term might be $a_n = n^2$.

b. These numbers are the reciprocals of the first five natural numbers, so a general term might be $a_n = \dfrac{1}{n}$.

c. These numbers are the product of -3 and the first four natural numbers, so a general term might be $a_n = -3n$.

d. Notice that the denominators double each time.

$$\frac{1}{2}, \frac{1}{2\cdot 2}, \frac{1}{2(2\cdot 2)}, \frac{1}{2(2\cdot 2\cdot 2)}$$

or

$$\frac{1}{2^1}, \frac{1}{2^2}, \frac{1}{2^3}, \frac{1}{2^4}$$

We might then suppose that the general term is $a_n = \dfrac{1}{2^n}$.

PRACTICE 3 Find the general term a_n of the sequence whose first few terms are given.

a. $1, 3, 5, 7, \ldots$ **b.** $3, 9, 27, 81, \ldots$

c. $\dfrac{1}{2}, \dfrac{2}{3}, \dfrac{3}{4}, \dfrac{4}{5}, \ldots$ **d.** $-\dfrac{1}{2}, -\dfrac{1}{3}, -\dfrac{1}{4}, -\dfrac{1}{5}, \ldots$

OBJECTIVE 3 ▶ **Solving applications modeled by sequences.** Sequences model many phenomena of the physical world, as illustrated by the following example.

EXAMPLE 4 Finding a Puppy's Weight Gain

The amount of weight, in pounds, a puppy gains in each month of its first year is modeled by a sequence whose general term is $a_n = n + 4$, where n is the number of the month. Write the first five terms of the sequence, and find how much weight the puppy should gain in its fifth month.

Solution Evaluate $a_n = n + 4$ when n is 1, 2, 3, 4, and 5.

$$a_1 = 1 + 4 = 5$$
$$a_2 = 2 + 4 = 6$$
$$a_3 = 3 + 4 = 7$$
$$a_4 = 4 + 4 = 8$$
$$a_5 = 5 + 4 = 9$$

The puppy should gain 9 pounds in its fifth month.

PRACTICE 4 The value v, in dollars, of an office copier depreciates according to the sequence $v_n = 3950(0.8)^n$, where n is the time in years. Find the value of the copier after three years.

VOCABULARY & READINESS CHECK

Word Bank. *Use the choices below to fill in each blank.*

    infinite   finite   general

1. The *n*th term of the sequence a_n is called the _____ term.
2. A(n) _____ sequence is a function whose domain is $\{1, 2, 3, 4, \ldots, n\}$ where n is some natural number.
3. A(n) _____ sequence is a function whose domain is $\{1, 2, 3, 4, \ldots\}$.

Fill in the Blank. *Write the first term of each sequence.*

4. $a_n = 7^n; a_1 = $ _____.   **5.** $a_n = \dfrac{(-1)^n}{n}; a_1 = $ _____.   **6.** $a_n = (-1)^n \cdot n^4; a_1 = $ _____.

12.1 EXERCISE SET

Write the first five terms of each sequence whose general term is given. See Example 1.

1. $a_n = n + 4$
2. $a_n = 5 - n$
3. $a_n = (-1)^n$
4. $a_n = (-2)^n$
5. $a_n = \dfrac{1}{n + 3}$
6. $a_n = \dfrac{1}{7 - n}$
7. $a_n = 2n$
8. $a_n = -6n$
9. $a_n = -n^2$
10. $a_n = n^2 + 2$
11. $a_n = 2^n$
12. $a_n = 3^{n-2}$
13. $a_n = 2n + 5$
14. $a_n = 1 - 3n$
15. $a_n = (-1)^n n^2$
16. $a_n = (-1)^{n+1}(n - 1)$

Find the indicated term for each sequence whose general term is given. See Example 2.

17. $a_n = 3n^2; a_5$
18. $a_n = -n^2; a_{15}$
19. $a_n = 6n - 2; a_{20}$
20. $a_n = 100 - 7n; a_{50}$
21. $a_n = \dfrac{n + 3}{n}; a_{15}$
22. $a_n = \dfrac{n}{n + 4}; a_{24}$
23. $a_n = (-3)^n; a_6$
24. $a_n = 5^{n+1}; a_3$
25. $a_n = \dfrac{n - 2}{n + 1}; a_6$
26. $a_n = \dfrac{n + 3}{n + 4}; a_8$
27. $a_n = \dfrac{(-1)^n}{n}; a_8$
28. $a_n = \dfrac{(-1)^n}{2n}; a_{100}$
29. $a_n = -n^2 + 5; a_{10}$
30. $a_n = 8 - n^2; a_{20}$
31. $a_n = \dfrac{(-1)^n}{n + 6}; a_{19}$
32. $a_n = \dfrac{n - 4}{(-2)^n}; a_6$

Find a general term a_n for each sequence whose first four terms are given. See Example 3.

33. $3, 7, 11, 15$
34. $2, 7, 12, 17$
35. $-2, -4, -8, -16$
36. $-4, 16, -64, 256$
37. $\dfrac{1}{3}, \dfrac{1}{9}, \dfrac{1}{27}, \dfrac{1}{81}$
38. $\dfrac{2}{5}, \dfrac{2}{25}, \dfrac{2}{125}, \dfrac{2}{625}$

Solve. See Example 4.

39. The distance, in feet, that a Thermos dropped from a cliff falls in each consecutive second is modeled by a sequence whose general term is $a_n = 32n - 16$, where n is the number of seconds. Find the distance the Thermos falls in the second, third, and fourth seconds.

40. The population size of a culture of bacteria triples every hour such that its size is modeled by the sequence $a_n = 50(3)^{n-1}$, where n is the number of the hour just beginning. Find the size of the culture at the beginning of the fourth hour and the size of the culture at the beginning of the first hour.

41. Mrs. Laser agrees to give her son Mark an allowance of $0.10 on the first day of his 14-day vacation, $0.20 on the second day, $0.40 on the third day, and so on. Write an equation of a sequence whose terms correspond to Mark's allowance. Find the allowance Mark will receive on the last day of his vacation.

42. A small theater has 10 rows with 12 seats in the first row, 15 seats in the second row, 18 seats in the third row, and so on. Write an equation of a sequence whose terms correspond to the seats in each row. Find the number of seats in the eighth row.

43. The number of cases of a new infectious disease is doubling every year such that the number of cases is modeled by a sequence whose general term is $a_n = 75(2)^{n-1}$, where n is the number of the year just beginning. Find how many cases there will be at the beginning of the sixth year. Find how many cases there were at the beginning of the first year.

44. A new college had an initial enrollment of 2700 students in 2000, and each year the enrollment increases by 150 students. Find the enrollment for each of 5 years, beginning with 2000.

45. An endangered species of sparrow had an estimated population of 800 in 2000, and scientists predict that its population will decrease by half each year. Estimate the population in 2004. Estimate the year the sparrow will be extinct.

46. A **Fibonacci sequence** is a special type of sequence in which the first two terms are 1, and each term thereafter is the sum of the two previous terms: 1, 1, 2, 3, 5, 8, etc. The formula for the nth Fibonacci term is $a_n = \dfrac{1}{\sqrt{5}}\left[\left(\dfrac{1 + \sqrt{5}}{2}\right)^n - \left(\dfrac{1 - \sqrt{5}}{2}\right)^n\right]$.

Verify that the first two terms of the Fibonacci sequence are each 1.

REVIEW AND PREVIEW

Sketch the graph of each quadratic function. See Section 11.1.

47. $f(x) = (x - 1)^2 + 3$
48. $f(x) = (x - 2)^2 + 1$
49. $f(x) = 2(x + 4)^2 + 2$
50. $f(x) = 3(x - 3)^2 + 4$

Find the distance between each pair of points. See Section 8.3.

51. $(-4, -1)$ and $(-7, -3)$
52. $(-2, -1)$ and $(-1, 5)$
53. $(2, -7)$ and $(-3, -3)$
54. $(10, -14)$ and $(5, -11)$

CONCEPT EXTENSIONS

Find the first five terms of each sequence. Round each term after the first to four decimal places.

55. $a_n = \dfrac{1}{\sqrt{n}}$
56. $\dfrac{\sqrt{n}}{\sqrt{n} + 1}$
57. $a_n = \left(1 + \dfrac{1}{n}\right)^n$
58. $a_n = \left(1 + \dfrac{0.05}{n}\right)^n$

12.2 ARITHMETIC AND GEOMETRIC SEQUENCES

OBJECTIVES

1. Identify arithmetic sequences and their common differences.
2. Identify geometric sequences and their common ratios.

OBJECTIVE 1 ▶ Identifying arithmetic sequences. Find the first four terms of the sequence whose general term is $a_n = 5 + (n - 1)3$.

$a_1 = 5 + (1 - 1)3 = 5$ Replace n with 1.
$a_2 = 5 + (2 - 1)3 = 8$ Replace n with 2.
$a_3 = 5 + (3 - 1)3 = 11$ Replace n with 3.
$a_4 = 5 + (4 - 1)3 = 14$ Replace n with 4.

The first four terms are 5, 8, 11, and 14. Notice that the difference of any two successive terms is 3.

$$8 - 5 = 3$$
$$11 - 8 = 3$$
$$14 - 11 = 3$$
$$\vdots$$
$$a_n - a_{n-1} = 3$$

$\uparrow$ $\quad$ $\uparrow$
nth $\quad$ previous
term $\quad$ term

Because the difference of any two successive terms is a constant, we call the sequence an **arithmetic sequence,** or an **arithmetic progression.** The constant difference d in successive terms is called the **common difference.** In this example, d is 3.

> **Arithmetic Sequence and Common Difference**
> An **arithmetic sequence** is a sequence in which each term (after the first) differs from the preceding term by a constant amount d. The constant d is called the **common difference** of the sequence.

The sequence 2, 6, 10, 14, 18, ... is an arithmetic sequence. Its common difference is 4. Given the first term a_1 and the common difference d of an arithmetic sequence, we can find any term of the sequence.

EXAMPLE 1 Write the first five terms of the arithmetic sequence whose first term is 7 and whose common difference is 2.

Solution
$a_1 = 7$
$a_2 = 7 + 2 = 9$
$a_3 = 9 + 2 = 11$
$a_4 = 11 + 2 = 13$
$a_5 = 13 + 2 = 15$

The first five terms are 7, 9, 11, 13, 15.

PRACTICE

1 Write the first five terms of the arithmetic sequence whose first term is 4 and whose common difference is 5.

Notice the general pattern of the terms in Example 1.

$a_1 = 7$
$a_2 = 7 + 2 = 9$ or $a_2 = a_1 + d$
$a_3 = 9 + 2 = 11$ or $a_3 = a_2 + d = (a_1 + d) + d = a_1 + 2d$
$a_4 = 11 + 2 = 13$ or $a_4 = a_3 + d = (a_1 + 2d) + d = a_1 + 3d$
$a_5 = 13 + 2 = 15$ or $a_5 = a_4 + d = (a_1 + 3d) + d = a_1 + 4d$

$\longrightarrow$ (subscript $- 1$) is multiplier $\longrightarrow$

The pattern on the right suggests that the general term a_n of an arithmetic sequence is given by

$$a_n = a_1 + (n - 1)d$$

> **General Term of an Arithmetic Sequence**
> The general term a_n of an arithmetic sequence is given by
> $$a_n = a_1 + (n - 1)d$$
> where a_1 is the first term and d is the common difference.

EXAMPLE 2 Consider the arithmetic sequence whose first term is 3 and common difference is -5.

a. Write an expression for the general term a_n.
b. Find the twentieth term of this sequence.

Solution

a. Since this is an arithmetic sequence, the general term a_n is given by $a_n = a_1 + (n - 1)d$. Here, $a_1 = 3$ and $d = -5$, so

$$\begin{align} a_n &= 3 + (n - 1)(-5) && \text{Let } a_1 = 3 \text{ and } d = -5. \\ &= 3 - 5n + 5 && \text{Multiply.} \\ &= 8 - 5n && \text{Simplify.} \end{align}$$

b. $a_n = 8 - 5n$
$a_{20} = 8 - 5 \cdot 20$ Let $n = 20$.
$\quad\ = 8 - 100 = -92$

PRACTICE 2 Consider the arithmetic sequence whose first term is 2 and whose common difference is -3.

a. Write an expression for the general term a_n.
b. Find the twelfth term of the sequence.

EXAMPLE 3 Find the eleventh term of the arithmetic sequence whose first three terms are 2, 9, and 16.

Solution Since the sequence is arithmetic, the eleventh term is

$$a_{11} = a_1 + (11 - 1)d = a_1 + 10d$$

We know a_1 is the first term of the sequence, so $a_1 = 2$. Also, d is the constant difference of terms, so $d = a_2 - a_1 = 9 - 2 = 7$. Thus,

$$\begin{align} a_{11} &= a_1 + 10d \\ &= 2 + 10 \cdot 7 && \text{Let } a_1 = 2 \text{ and } d = 7. \\ &= 72 \end{align}$$

PRACTICE 3 Find the ninth term of the arithmetic sequence whose first three terms are 3, 9, and 15.

EXAMPLE 4 If the third term of an arithmetic sequence is 12 and the eighth term is 27, find the fifth term.

Solution We need to find a_1 and d to write the general term, which then enables us to find a_5, the fifth term. The given facts about terms a_3 and a_8 lead to a system of linear equations.

$$\begin{cases} a_3 = a_1 + (3-1)d \\ a_8 = a_1 + (8-1)d \end{cases} \text{ or } \begin{cases} 12 = a_1 + 2d \\ 27 = a_1 + 7d \end{cases}$$

Next, we solve the system $\begin{cases} 12 = a_1 + 2d \\ 27 = a_1 + 7d \end{cases}$ by elimination. Multiply both sides of the second equation by -1 so that

$$\begin{cases} 12 = a_1 + 2d \\ -1(27) = -1(a_1 + 7d) \end{cases} \text{ simplifies to } \begin{cases} 12 = a_1 + 2d \\ -27 = -a_1 - 7d \end{cases}$$
$$-15 = -5d \quad \text{Add the equations.}$$
$$3 = d \quad \text{Divide both sides by } -5.$$

To find a_1, let $d = 3$ in $12 = a_1 + 2d$. Then

$$12 = a_1 + 2(3)$$
$$12 = a_1 + 6$$
$$6 = a_1$$

Thus, $a_1 = 6$ and $d = 3$, so

$$a_n = 6 + (n-1)(3)$$
$$= 6 + 3n - 3$$
$$= 3 + 3n$$

and

$$a_5 = 3 + 3 \cdot 5 = 18$$

PRACTICE 4 If the third term of an arithmetic sequence is 23 and the eighth term is 63, find the sixth term.

EXAMPLE 5 Finding Salary

Donna Theime has an offer for a job starting at $40,000 per year and guaranteeing her a raise of $1600 per year for the next 5 years. Write the general term for the arithmetic sequence that models Donna's potential annual salaries, and find her salary for the fourth year.

Solution The first term, a_1, is 40,000, and d is 1600. So

$$a_n = 40,000 + (n-1)(1600) = 38,400 + 1600n$$
$$a_4 = 38,400 + 1600 \cdot 4 = 44,800$$

Her salary for the fourth year will be $44,800.

PRACTICE 5 A starting salary for a consulting company is $57,000 per year, with guaranteed annual increases of $2200 for the next 4 years. Write the general term for the arithmetic sequence that models the potential annual salaries, and find the salary for the third year.

OBJECTIVE 2 ▶ Identifying geometric sequences. We now investigate a **geometric sequence**, also called a **geometric progression**. In the sequence 5, 15, 45, 135, ..., each term after the first is the *product* of 3 and the preceding term. This pattern of multiplying by a constant to get the next term defines a geometric sequence. The constant is called the **common ratio** because it is the ratio of any term (after the first) to its preceding term.

$$\frac{15}{5} = 3$$

$$\frac{45}{15} = 3$$

$$\frac{135}{45} = 3$$

$$\vdots$$

nth term $\longrightarrow$ $\dfrac{a_n}{a_{n-1}} = 3$
previous term $\longrightarrow$

> **Geometric Sequence and Common Ratio**
> A **geometric sequence** is a sequence in which each term (after the first) is obtained by multiplying the preceding term by a constant r. The constant r is called the **common ratio** of the sequence.

The sequence $12, 6, 3, \dfrac{3}{2}, \ldots$ is geometric since each term after the first is the product of the previous term and $\dfrac{1}{2}$.

EXAMPLE 6 Write the first five terms of a geometric sequence whose first term is 7 and whose common ratio is 2.

Solution
$a_1 = 7$
$a_2 = 7(2) = 14$
$a_3 = 14(2) = 28$
$a_4 = 28(2) = 56$
$a_5 = 56(2) = 112$

The first five terms are 7, 14, 28, 56, and 112.

PRACTICE
6 Write the first four terms of a geometric sequence whose first term is 8 and whose common ratio is -3.

Notice the general pattern of the terms in Example 6.

$a_1 = 7$
$a_2 = 7(2) = 14$ or $a_2 = a_1(r)$
$a_3 = 14(2) = 28$ or $a_3 = a_2(r) = (a_1 \cdot r) \cdot r = a_1 r^2$
$a_4 = 28(2) = 56$ or $a_4 = a_3(r) = (a_1 \cdot r^2) \cdot r = a_1 r^3$
$a_5 = 56(2) = 112$ or $a_5 = a_4(r) = (a_1 \cdot r^3) \cdot r = a_1 r^4$
$\longrightarrow$ (subscript -1) is power $\longleftarrow$

The pattern on the right above suggests that the general term of a geometric sequence is given by $a_n = a_1 r^{n-1}$.

> **General Term of a Geometric Sequence**
> The general term a_n of a geometric sequence is given by
> $$a_n = a_1 r^{n-1}$$
> where a_1 is the first term and r is the common ratio.

EXAMPLE 7 Find the eighth term of the geometric sequence whose first term is 12 and whose common ratio is $\frac{1}{2}$.

Solution Since this is a geometric sequence, the general term a_n is given by
$$a_n = a_1 r^{n-1}$$
Here $a_1 = 12$ and $r = \frac{1}{2}$, so $a_n = 12\left(\frac{1}{2}\right)^{n-1}$. Evaluate a_n for $n = 8$.
$$a_8 = 12\left(\frac{1}{2}\right)^{8-1} = 12\left(\frac{1}{2}\right)^7 = 12\left(\frac{1}{128}\right) = \frac{3}{32}$$

PRACTICE 7 Find the seventh term of the geometric sequence whose first term is 64 and whose common ratio is $\frac{1}{4}$.

EXAMPLE 8 Find the fifth term of the geometric sequence whose first three terms are 2, −6, and 18.

Solution Since the sequence is geometric and $a_1 = 2$, the fifth term must be $a_1 r^{5-1}$, or $2r^4$. We know that r is the common ratio of terms, so r must be $\frac{-6}{2}$, or −3. Thus,
$$a_5 = 2r^4$$
$$a_5 = 2(-3)^4 = 162$$

PRACTICE 8 Find the seventh term of the geometric sequence whose first three terms are −3, 6, and −12.

EXAMPLE 9 If the second term of a geometric sequence is $\frac{5}{4}$ and the third term is $\frac{5}{16}$, find the first term and the common ratio.

Solution Notice that $\frac{5}{16} \div \frac{5}{4} = \frac{1}{4}$, so $r = \frac{1}{4}$. Then
$$a_2 = a_1\left(\frac{1}{4}\right)^{2-1}$$
$$\frac{5}{4} = a_1\left(\frac{1}{4}\right)^1, \quad \text{or} \quad a_1 = 5 \quad \text{Replace } a_2 \text{ with } \frac{5}{4}.$$

The first term is 5.

PRACTICE 9 If the second term of a geometric sequence is $\frac{9}{2}$ and the third term is $\frac{27}{4}$, find the first term and the common ratio.

EXAMPLE 10 Predicting Population of a Bacterial Culture

The population size of a bacterial culture growing under controlled conditions is doubling each day. Predict how large the culture will be at the beginning of day 7 if it measures 10 units at the beginning of day 1.

Solution Since the culture doubles in size each day, the population sizes are modeled by a geometric sequence. Here $a_1 = 10$ and $r = 2$. Thus,
$$a_n = a_1 r^{n-1} = 10(2)^{n-1} \quad \text{and} \quad a_7 = 10(2)^{7-1} = 640$$

The bacterial culture should measure 640 units at the beginning of day 7.

PRACTICE

10 After applying a test antibiotic, the population of a bacterial culture is reduced by one-half every day. Predict how large the culture will be at the start of day 7 if it measures 4800 units at the beginning of day 1.

VOCABULARY & READINESS CHECK

Word Bank. *Use the choices below to fill in each blank. Some choices may be used more than once and some not at all.*

first   arithmetic   difference
last   geometric   ratio

1. A(n) _____ sequence is one in which each term (after the first) is obtained by multiplying the preceding term by a constant r. The constant r is called the common _____.
2. A(n) _____ sequence is one in which each term (after the first) differs from the preceding term by a constant amount d. The constant d is called the common _____.
3. The general term of an arithmetic sequence is $a_n = a_1 + (n - 1)d$ where a_1 is the _____ term and d is the common _____.
4. The general term of a geometric sequence is $a_n = a_1 r^{n-1}$ where a_1 is the _____ term and r is the common _____.

12.2 EXERCISE SET

Write the first five terms of the arithmetic or geometric sequence whose first term, a_1, and common difference, d, or common ratio, r, are given. See Examples 1 and 6.

1. $a_1 = 4; d = 2$
2. $a_1 = 3; d = 10$
3. $a_1 = 6; d = -2$
4. $a_1 = -20; d = 3$
5. $a_1 = 1; r = 3$
6. $a_1 = -2; r = 2$
7. $a_1 = 48; r = \frac{1}{2}$
8. $a_1 = 1; r = \frac{1}{3}$

Find the indicated term of each sequence. See Examples 2 and 7.

9. The eighth term of the arithmetic sequence whose first term is 12 and whose common difference is 3
10. The twelfth term of the arithmetic sequence whose first term is 32 and whose common difference is -4
11. The fourth term of the geometric sequence whose first term is 7 and whose common ratio is -5
12. The fifth term of the geometric sequence whose first term is 3 and whose common ratio is 3
13. The fifteenth term of the arithmetic sequence whose first term is -4 and whose common difference is -4
14. The sixth term of the geometric sequence whose first term is 5 and whose common ratio is -4

Find the indicated term of each sequence. See Examples 3 and 8.

15. The ninth term of the arithmetic sequence $0, 12, 24, \ldots$
16. The thirteenth term of the arithmetic sequence $-3, 0, 3, \ldots$
17. The twenty-fifth term of the arithmetic sequence $20, 18, 16, \ldots$
18. The ninth term of the geometric sequence $5, 10, 20, \ldots$
19. The fifth term of the geometric sequence $2, -10, 50, \ldots$
20. The sixth term of the geometric sequence $\frac{1}{2}, \frac{3}{2}, \frac{9}{2}, \ldots$

Find the indicated term of each sequence. See Examples 4 and 9.

21. The eighth term of the arithmetic sequence whose fourth term is 19 and whose fifteenth term is 52
22. If the second term of an arithmetic sequence is 6 and the tenth term is 30, find the twenty-fifth term.
23. If the second term of an arithmetic progression is -1 and the fourth term is 5, find the ninth term.
24. If the second term of a geometric progression is 15 and the third term is 3, find a_1 and r.
25. If the second term of a geometric progression is $-\frac{4}{3}$ and the third term is $\frac{8}{3}$, find a_1 and r.
26. If the third term of a geometric sequence is 4 and the fourth term is -12, find a_1 and r.
27. Explain why 14, 10, and 6 may be the first three terms of an arithmetic sequence when it appears we are subtracting instead of adding to get the next term.

28. Explain why 80, 20, and 5 may be the first three terms of a geometric sequence when it appears we are dividing instead of multiplying to get the next term.

MIXED PRACTICE

Decision Making. *Given are the first three terms of a sequence that is either arithmetic or geometric. If the sequence is arithmetic, find a_1 and d. If a sequence is geometric, find a_1 and r.*

29. $2, 4, 6$
30. $8, 16, 24$
31. $5, 10, 20$
32. $2, 6, 18$
33. $\frac{1}{2}, \frac{1}{10}, \frac{1}{50}$
34. $\frac{2}{3}, \frac{4}{3}, 2$
35. $x, 5x, 25x$
36. $y, -3y, 9y$
37. $p, p+4, p+8$
38. $t, t-1, t-2$

Find the indicated term of each sequence.

39. The twenty-first term of the arithmetic sequence whose first term is 14 and whose common difference is $\frac{1}{4}$

40. The fifth term of the geometric sequence whose first term is 8 and whose common ratio is -3

41. The fourth term of the geometric sequence whose first term is 3 and whose common ratio is $-\frac{2}{3}$

42. The fourth term of the arithmetic sequence whose first term is 9 and whose common difference is 5

43. The fifteenth term of the arithmetic sequence $\frac{3}{2}, 2, \frac{5}{2}, \ldots$

44. The eleventh term of the arithmetic sequence $2, \frac{5}{3}, \frac{4}{3}, \ldots$

45. The sixth term of the geometric sequence $24, 8, \frac{8}{3}, \ldots$

46. The eighteenth term of the arithmetic sequence $5, 2, -1, \ldots$

47. If the third term of an arithmetic sequence is 2 and the seventeenth term is -40, find the tenth term.

48. If the third term of a geometric sequence is -28 and the fourth term is -56, find a_1 and r.

Solve. See Examples 5 and 10.

49. An auditorium has 54 seats in the first row, 58 seats in the second row, 62 seats in the third row, and so on. Find the general term of this arithmetic sequence and the number of seats in the twentieth row.

50. A triangular display of cans in a grocery store has 20 cans in the first row, 17 cans in the next row, and so on, in an arithmetic sequence. Find the general term and the number of cans in the fifth row. Find how many rows there are in the display and how many cans are in the top row.

51. The initial size of a virus culture is 6 units, and it triples its size every day. Find the general term of the geometric sequence that models the culture's size.

52. A real estate investment broker predicts that a certain property will increase in value 15% each year. Thus, the yearly property values can be modeled by a geometric sequence whose common ratio r is 1.15. If the initial property value was $500,000, write the first four terms of the sequence and predict the value at the end of the third year.

53. A rubber ball is dropped from a height of 486 feet, and it continues to bounce one-third the height from which it last fell. Write out the first five terms of this geometric sequence and find the general term. Find how many bounces it takes for the ball to rebound less than 1 foot.

54. On the first swing, the length of the arc through which a pendulum swings is 50 inches. The length of each successive swing is 80% of the preceding swing. Determine whether this sequence is arithmetic or geometric. Find the length of the fourth swing.

55. Jose takes a job that offers a monthly starting salary of $4000 and guarantees him a monthly raise of $125 during his first year of training. Find the general term of this arithmetic sequence and his monthly salary at the end of his training.

56. At the beginning of Claudia Schaffer's exercise program, she rides 15 minutes on the Lifecycle. Each week she increases her riding time by 5 minutes. Write the general term of this arithmetic sequence, and find her riding time after 7 weeks. Find how many weeks it takes her to reach a riding time of 1 hour.

57. If a radioactive element has a half-life of 3 hours, then x grams of the element dwindles to $\frac{x}{2}$ grams after 3 hours. If a nuclear reactor has 400 grams of that radioactive element, find the amount of radioactive material after 12 hours.

REVIEW AND PREVIEW

Evaluate. See Section 1.3.

58. $5(1) + 5(2) + 5(3) + 5(4)$
59. $\frac{1}{3(1)} + \frac{1}{3(2)} + \frac{1}{3(3)}$
60. $2(2-4) + 3(3-4) + 4(4-4)$
61. $3^0 + 3^1 + 3^2 + 3^3$
62. $\frac{1}{4(1)} + \frac{1}{4(2)} + \frac{1}{4(3)}$
63. $\frac{8-1}{8+1} + \frac{8-2}{8+2} + \frac{8-3}{8+3}$

CONCEPT EXTENSIONS

Write the first four terms of the arithmetic or geometric sequence whose first term, a_1, and common difference, d, or common ratio, r, are given.

64. $a_1 = \$3720, d = -\$268.50$

65. $a_1 = \$11,782.40, r = 0.5$

66. $a_1 = 26.8, r = 2.5$

67. $a_1 = 19.652; d = -0.034$

68. Describe a situation in your life that can be modeled by a geometric sequence. Write an equation for the sequence.

69. Describe a situation in your life that can be modeled by an arithmetic sequence. Write an equation for the sequence.

12.3 SERIES

OBJECTIVES

1. Identify finite and infinite series and use summation notation.
2. Find partial sums.

OBJECTIVE 1 ▶ Identifying finite and infinite series and using summation notation. A person who conscientiously saves money by saving first $100 and then saving $10 more each month than he saved the preceding month is saving money according to the arithmetic sequence

$$a_n = 100 + 10(n - 1)$$

Following this sequence, he can predict how much money he should save for any particular month. But if he also wants to know how much money *in total* he has saved, say, by the fifth month, he must find the *sum* of the first five terms of the sequence

$$\underbrace{100}_{a_1} + \underbrace{100 + 10}_{a_2} + \underbrace{100 + 20}_{a_3} + \underbrace{100 + 30}_{a_4} + \underbrace{100 + 40}_{a_5}$$

A sum of the terms of a sequence is called a **series** (the plural is also "series"). As our example here suggests, series are frequently used to model financial and natural phenomena.

A series is a **finite series** if it is the sum of a finite number of terms. A series is an **infinite series** if it is the sum of all the terms of an infinite sequence. For example,

Sequence	*Series*	
$5, 9, 13$	$5 + 9 + 13$	Finite; sum of 3 terms
$5, 9, 13, \ldots$	$5 + 9 + 13 + \cdots$	Infinite
$4, -2, 1, -\frac{1}{2}, \frac{1}{4}$	$4 + (-2) + 1 + \left(-\frac{1}{2}\right) + \left(\frac{1}{4}\right)$	Finite; sum of 5 terms
$4, -2, 1, \ldots$	$4 + (-2) + 1 + \cdots$	Infinite
$3, 6, \ldots, 99$	$3 + 6 + \cdots + 99$	Finite; sum of 33 terms

Recall from Section 8.8 that a shorthand notation for denoting a series when the general term of the sequence is known is called **summation notation.** The Greek uppercase letter **sigma**, Σ, is used to mean "sum." The expression $\sum_{n=1}^{5}(3n + 1)$ is read "the sum of $3n + 1$ as n goes from 1 to 5"; this expression means the sum of the first five terms of the sequence whose general term is $a_n = 3n + 1$. Often, the variable i is used instead of n in summation notation: $\sum_{i=1}^{5}(3i + 1)$. Whether we use $n, i, k,$ or some other variable, the variable is called the **index of summation.** The notation $i = 1$ below the symbol Σ indicates the beginning value of i, and the number 5 above the symbol Σ indicates the ending value of i. Thus, the terms of the sequence are found by successively replacing i with the natural numbers 1, 2, 3, 4, 5. To find the sum, we write out the terms and then add.

$$\sum_{i=1}^{5}(3i + 1) = (3 \cdot 1 + 1) + (3 \cdot 2 + 1) + (3 \cdot 3 + 1) + (3 \cdot 4 + 1) + (3 \cdot 5 + 1)$$
$$= 4 + 7 + 10 + 13 + 16 = 50$$

EXAMPLE 1 Evaluate.

a. $\sum_{i=0}^{6} \frac{i-2}{2}$

b. $\sum_{i=3}^{5} 2^i$

Solution

a. $\sum_{i=0}^{6} \dfrac{i-2}{2} = \dfrac{0-2}{2} + \dfrac{1-2}{2} + \dfrac{2-2}{2} + \dfrac{3-2}{2} + \dfrac{4-2}{2} + \dfrac{5-2}{2} + \dfrac{6-2}{2}$

$= (-1) + \left(-\dfrac{1}{2}\right) + 0 + \dfrac{1}{2} + 1 + \dfrac{3}{2} + 2$

$= \dfrac{7}{2}, \text{ or } 3\dfrac{1}{2}$

b. $\sum_{i=3}^{5} 2^i = 2^3 + 2^4 + 2^5$

$= 8 + 16 + 32$

$= 56$

PRACTICE 1 Evaluate.

a. $\sum_{i=0}^{4} \dfrac{i-3}{4}$ b. $\sum_{i=2}^{5} 3^i$

EXAMPLE 2 Write each series with summation notation.

a. $3 + 6 + 9 + 12 + 15$ b. $\dfrac{1}{2} + \dfrac{1}{4} + \dfrac{1}{8} + \dfrac{1}{16}$

Solution

a. Since the *difference* of each term and the preceding term is 3, the terms correspond to the first five terms of the arithmetic sequence $a_n = a_1 + (n-1)d$ with $a_1 = 3$ and $d = 3$. So $a_n = 3 + (n-1)3 = 3n$, when simplified. Thus, in summation notation,

$$3 + 6 + 9 + 12 + 15 = \sum_{i=1}^{5} 3i.$$

b. Since each term is the *product* of the preceding term and $\dfrac{1}{2}$, these terms correspond to the first four terms of the geometric sequence $a_n = a_1 r^{n-1}$. Here $a_1 = \dfrac{1}{2}$ and $r = \dfrac{1}{2}$, so $a_n = \left(\dfrac{1}{2}\right)\left(\dfrac{1}{2}\right)^{n-1} = \left(\dfrac{1}{2}\right)^{1+(n-1)} = \left(\dfrac{1}{2}\right)^n$. In summation notation,

$$\dfrac{1}{2} + \dfrac{1}{4} + \dfrac{1}{8} + \dfrac{1}{16} = \sum_{i=1}^{4} \left(\dfrac{1}{2}\right)^i$$

PRACTICE 2 Write each series with summation notation.

a. $5 + 10 + 15 + 20 + 25 + 30$ b. $\dfrac{1}{5} + \dfrac{1}{25} + \dfrac{1}{125} + \dfrac{1}{625}$

OBJECTIVE 2 ▶ **Finding partial sums.** The sum of the first n terms of a sequence is a finite series known as a **partial sum**, S_n. Thus, for the sequence $a_1, a_2, \ldots, a_n$, the first three partial sums are

$$S_1 = a_1$$
$$S_2 = a_1 + a_2$$
$$S_3 = a_1 + a_2 + a_3$$

In general, S_n is the sum of the first n terms of a sequence.

$$S_n = \sum_{i=1}^{n} a_n$$

EXAMPLE 3 Find the sum of the first three terms of the sequence whose general term is $a_n = \dfrac{n+3}{2n}$.

Solution

$$S_3 = \sum_{i=1}^{3} \dfrac{i+3}{2i} = \dfrac{1+3}{2 \cdot 1} + \dfrac{2+3}{2 \cdot 2} + \dfrac{3+3}{2 \cdot 3}$$

$$= 2 + \dfrac{5}{4} + 1 = 4\dfrac{1}{4}$$

PRACTICE 3 Find the sum of the first four terms of the sequence whose general term is $a_n = \dfrac{2+3n}{n^2}$.

The next example illustrates how these sums model real-life phenomena.

EXAMPLE 4 Number of Baby Gorillas Born

The number of baby gorillas born at the San Diego Zoo is a sequence defined by $a_n = n(n-1)$, where n is the number of years the zoo has owned gorillas. Find the *total* number of baby gorillas born in the *first 4 years*.

Solution To solve, find the sum

$$S_4 = \sum_{i=1}^{4} i(i-1)$$

$$= 1(1-1) + 2(2-1) + 3(3-1) + 4(4-1)$$

$$= 0 + 2 + 6 + 12 = 20$$

There were 20 gorillas born in the first 4 years.

PRACTICE 4 The number of strawberry plants growing in a garden is a sequence defined by $a_n = n(2n-1)$, where n is the number of years after planting a strawberry plant. Find the total number of strawberry plants after 5 years.

VOCABULARY & READINESS CHECK

Word Bank. *Use the choices below to fill in each blank. Not all choices may be used.*

index of summation	infinite	sigma	1	7
partial sum	finite	summation	5	

1. A series is a(n) _____ series if it is the sum of all the terms of the sequence.
2. A series is a(n) _____ series if it is the sum of a finite number of terms.
3. A shorthand notation for denoting a series when the general term of the sequence is known is called _____ notation.
4. In the notation $\sum_{i=1}^{7}(5i-2)$, the Σ is the Greek uppercase letter _____ and the i is called the _____.
5. The sum of the first n terms of a sequence is a finite series known as a _____.
6. For the notation in Exercise 4 above, the beginning value of i is ____ and the ending value of i is ____.

12.3 EXERCISE SET

Evaluate. See Example 1.

1. $\sum_{i=1}^{4}(i-3)$
2. $\sum_{i=1}^{5}(i+6)$
3. $\sum_{i=4}^{7}(2i+4)$
4. $\sum_{i=2}^{3}(5i-1)$
5. $\sum_{i=2}^{4}(i^2-3)$
6. $\sum_{i=3}^{5}i^3$
7. $\sum_{i=1}^{3}\left(\frac{1}{i+5}\right)$
8. $\sum_{i=2}^{4}\left(\frac{2}{i+3}\right)$
9. $\sum_{i=1}^{3}\frac{1}{6i}$
10. $\sum_{i=1}^{3}\frac{1}{3i}$
11. $\sum_{i=2}^{6}3i$
12. $\sum_{i=3}^{6}-4i$
13. $\sum_{i=3}^{5}i(i+2)$
14. $\sum_{i=2}^{4}i(i-3)$
15. $\sum_{i=1}^{5}2^i$
16. $\sum_{i=1}^{4}3^{i-1}$
17. $\sum_{i=1}^{4}\frac{4i}{i+3}$
18. $\sum_{i=2}^{5}\frac{6-i}{6+i}$

Write each series with summation notation. See Example 2.

19. $1 + 3 + 5 + 7 + 9$
20. $4 + 7 + 10 + 13$
21. $4 + 12 + 36 + 108$
22. $5 + 10 + 20 + 40 + 80 + 160$
23. $12 + 9 + 6 + 3 + 0 + (-3)$
24. $5 + 1 + (-3) + (-7)$
25. $12 + 4 + \frac{4}{3} + \frac{4}{9}$
26. $80 + 20 + 5 + \frac{5}{4} + \frac{5}{16}$
27. $1 + 4 + 9 + 16 + 25 + 36 + 49$
28. $1 + (-4) + 9 + (-16)$

Find each partial sum. See Example 3.

29. Find the sum of the first two terms of the sequence whose general term is $a_n = (n+2)(n-5)$.
30. Find the sum of the first two terms of the sequence whose general term is $a_n = n(n-6)$.
31. Find the sum of the first six terms of the sequence whose general term is $a_n = (-1)^n$.
32. Find the sum of the first seven terms of the sequence whose general term is $a_n = (-1)^{n-1}$.
33. Find the sum of the first four terms of the sequence whose general term is $a_n = (n+3)(n+1)$.
34. Find the sum of the first five terms of the sequence whose general term is $a_n = \frac{(-1)^n}{2n}$.
35. Find the sum of the first four terms of the sequence whose general term is $a_n = -2n$.
36. Find the sum of the first five terms of the sequence whose general term is $a_n = (n-1)^2$.
37. Find the sum of the first three terms of the sequence whose general term is $a_n = -\frac{n}{3}$.
38. Find the sum of the first three terms of the sequence whose general term is $a_n = (n+4)^2$.

Solve. See Example 4.

39. A gardener is making a triangular planting with 1 tree in the first row, 2 trees in the second row, 3 trees in the third row, and so on for 10 rows. Write the sequence that describes the number of trees in each row. Find the total number of trees planted.

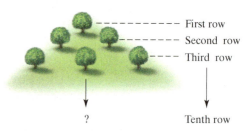

40. Some surfers at the beach form a human pyramid with 2 surfers in the top row, 3 surfers in the second row, 4 surfers in the third row, and so on. If there are 6 rows in the pyramid, write the sequence that describes the number of surfers in each row of the pyramid. Find the total number of surfers.

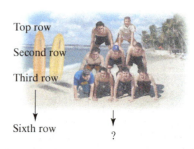

41. A culture of fungus starts with 6 units and doubles every day. Write the general term of the sequence that describes the growth of this fungus. Find the number of fungus units there will be at the beginning of the fifth day.
42. A bacterial colony begins with 100 bacteria and doubles every 6 hours. Write the general term of the sequence describing the growth of the bacteria. Find the number of bacteria there will be after 24 hours.

43. A bacterial colony begins with 50 bacteria and doubles every 12 hours. Write the sequence that describes the growth of the bacteria. Find the number of bacteria there will be after 48 hours.

44. The number of otters born each year in a new aquarium forms a sequence whose general term is $a_n = (n-1)(n+3)$. Find the number of otters born in the third year, and find the total number of otters born in the first three years.

45. The number of opossums killed each month on a new highway forms the sequence whose general term is $a_n = (n+1)(n+2)$, where n is the number of the months. Find the number of opossums killed in the fourth month, and find the total number killed in the first four months.

46. In 2007, the population of the Northern Spotted Owl continued to decline, and the owl remained on the endangered species list, as old-growth Northwest forests were logged. The size of the decrease in the population in a given year can be estimated by $200 - 6n$ pairs of birds. Find the decrease in population in 2010 if year 1 is 2007. Find the estimated total decrease in the spotted owl population for the years 2007 through 2010. (*Source:* United States Forest Service)

47. The amount of decay in pounds of a radioactive isotope each year is given by the sequence whose general term is $a_n = 100(0.5)^n$, where n is the number of the year. Find the amount of decay in the fourth year, and find the total amount of decay in the first four years.

48. Susan has a choice between two job offers. Job A has an annual starting salary of $20,000 with guaranteed annual raises of $1200 for the next four years, whereas job B has an annual starting salary of $18,000 with guaranteed annual raises of $2500 for the next four years. Compare the fifth partial sums for each sequence to determine which job would pay Susan more money over the next 5 years.

49. A pendulum swings a length of 40 inches on its first swing. Each successive swing is $\frac{4}{5}$ of the preceding swing. Find the length of the fifth swing and the total length swung during the first five swings. (Round to the nearest tenth of an inch.)

50. Explain the difference between a sequence and a series.

REVIEW AND PREVIEW

Evaluate. See Section 1.3.

51. $\dfrac{5}{1 - \dfrac{1}{2}}$

52. $\dfrac{-3}{1 - \dfrac{1}{7}}$

53. $\dfrac{\dfrac{1}{3}}{1 - \dfrac{1}{10}}$

54. $\dfrac{\dfrac{6}{11}}{1 - \dfrac{1}{10}}$

55. $\dfrac{3(1 - 2^4)}{1 - 2}$

56. $\dfrac{2(1 - 5^3)}{1 - 5}$

57. $\dfrac{10}{2}(3 + 15)$

58. $\dfrac{12}{2}(2 + 19)$

CONCEPT EXTENSIONS

59. Multiple Steps. a. Write the sum $\sum_{i=1}^{7}(i + i^2)$ without summation notation.

b. Write the sum $\sum_{i=1}^{7} i + \sum_{i=1}^{7} i^2$ without summation notation.

c. Compare the results of parts **a** and **b**.

d. Do you think the following is true or false? Explain your answer.

$$\sum_{i=1}^{n}(a_n + b_n) = \sum_{i=1}^{n} a_n + \sum_{i=1}^{n} b_n$$

60. Multiple Steps. a. Write the sum $\sum_{i=1}^{6} 5i^3$ without summation notation.

b. Write the expression $5 \cdot \sum_{i=1}^{6} i^3$ without summation notation.

c. Compare the results of parts **a** and **b**.

d. Do you think the following is true or false? Explain your answer.

$$\sum_{i=1}^{n} c \cdot a_n = c \cdot \sum_{i=1}^{n} a_n, \text{ where } c \text{ is a constant}$$

INTEGRATED REVIEW SEQUENCES AND SERIES

Sections 12.1–12.3

Write the first five terms of each sequence whose general term is given.

1. $a_n = n - 3$

2. $a_n = \dfrac{7}{1 + n}$

3. $a_n = 3^{n-1}$

4. $a_n = n^2 - 5$

Find the indicated term for each sequence.

5. $(-2)^n$; a_6

6. $-n^2 + 2$; a_4

7. $\dfrac{(-1)^n}{n}$; a_{40}

8. $\dfrac{(-1)^n}{2n}$; a_{41}

Write the first five terms of the arithmetic or geometric sequence whose first term is a_1, and common difference, d, or common ratio, r, are given.

9. $a_1 = 7; d = -3$

10. $a_1 = -3; r = 5$

11. $a_1 = 45; r = \dfrac{1}{3}$

12. $a_1 = -12; d = 10$

Find the indicated term of each sequence.

13. The tenth term of the arithmetic sequence whose first term is 20 and whose common difference is 9.

14. The sixth term of the geometric sequence whose first term is 64 and whose common ratio is $\dfrac{3}{4}$.

15. The seventh term of the geometric sequence $6, -12, 24, \ldots$

16. The twentieth term of the arithmetic sequence $-100, -85, -70, \ldots$

17. The fifth term of the arithmetic sequence whose fourth term is -5 and whose tenth term is -35.

18. The fifth term of the geometric sequence whose fourth term is 1 and whose seventh term is $\dfrac{1}{125}$.

Evaluate.

19. $\sum_{i=1}^{4} 5i$

20. $\sum_{i=1}^{7} (3i + 2)$

21. $\sum_{i=3}^{7} 2^{i-4}$

22. $\sum_{i=2}^{5} \dfrac{i}{i+1}$

Find each partial sum.

23. Find the sum of the first three terms of the sequence whose general term is $a_n = n(n-4)$.

24. Find the sum of the first ten terms of the sequence whose general term is $a_n = (-1)^n(n+1)$.

12.4 PARTIAL SUMS OF ARITHMETIC AND GEOMETRIC SEQUENCES

OBJECTIVES

1. Find the partial sum of an arithmetic sequence.
2. Find the partial sum of a geometric sequence.
3. Find the sum of the terms of an infinite geometric sequence.

OBJECTIVE 1 ▶ Finding partial sums of arithmetic sequences. Partial sums S_n are relatively easy to find when n is small—that is, when the number of terms to add is small. But when n is large, finding S_n can be tedious. For a large n, S_n is still relatively easy to find if the addends are terms of an arithmetic sequence or a geometric sequence.

For an arithmetic sequence, $a_n = a_1 + (n-1)d$ for some first term a_1 and some common difference d. So S_n, the sum of the first n terms, is

$$S_n = a_1 + (a_1 + d) + (a_1 + 2d) + \cdots + (a_1 + (n-1)d)$$

We might also find S_n by "working backward" from the nth term a_n, finding the preceding term a_{n-1}, by subtracting d each time.

$$S_n = a_n + (a_n - d) + (a_n - 2d) + \cdots + (a_n - (n-1)d)$$

Now add the left sides of these two equations and add the right sides.

$$2S_n = (a_1 + a_n) + (a_1 + a_n) + (a_1 + a_n) + \cdots + (a_1 + a_n)$$

The d terms subtract out, leaving n sums of the first term, a_1, and last term, a_n. Thus, we write

$$2S_n = n(a_1 + a_n)$$

or

$$S_n = \dfrac{n}{2}(a_1 + a_n)$$

Partial Sum S_n of an Arithmetic Sequence

The partial sum S_n of the first n terms of an arithmetic sequence is given by

$$S_n = \frac{n}{2}(a_1 + a_n)$$

where a_1 is the first term of the sequence and a_n is the nth term.

EXAMPLE 1 Use the partial sum formula to find the sum of the first six terms of the arithmetic sequence 2, 5, 8, 11, 14, 17, ...

Solution Use the formula for S_n of an arithmetic sequence, replacing n with 6, a_1 with 2, and a_n with 17.

$$S_n = \frac{n}{2}(a_1 + a_n)$$

$$S_6 = \frac{6}{2}(2 + 17) = 3(19) = 57$$

PRACTICE 1 Use the partial sum formula to find the sum of the first five terms of the arithmetic sequence 2, 9, 16, 23, 30.

EXAMPLE 2 Find the sum of the first 30 positive integers.

Solution Because 1, 2, 3, ..., 30 is an arithmetic sequence, use the formula for S_n with $n = 30$, $a_1 = 1$, and $a_n = 30$. Thus,

$$S_n = \frac{n}{2}(a_1 + a_n)$$

$$S_{30} = \frac{30}{2}(1 + 30) = 15(31) = 465$$

PRACTICE 2 Find the sum of the first 50 positive integers.

EXAMPLE 3 Stacking Rolls of Carpet

Rolls of carpet are stacked in 20 rows with 3 rolls in the top row, 4 rolls in the next row, and so on, forming an arithmetic sequence. Find the total number of carpet rolls if there are 22 rolls in the bottom row.

- 3 rolls
- 4 rolls
- 5 rolls

Solution The list 3, 4, 5, ..., 22 is the first 20 terms of an arithmetic sequence. Use the formula for S_n with $a_1 = 3$, $a_n = 22$, and $n = 20$ terms. Thus,

$$S_{20} = \frac{20}{2}(3 + 22) = 10(25) = 250$$

There are a total of 250 rolls of carpet.

PRACTICE 3 An ice sculptor is creating a gigantic castle-facade ice sculpture for First Night festivities in Boston. To get the volume of ice necessary, large blocks of ice were stacked atop each other. The topmost row was comprised of 6 blocks of ice, the next row of 7 blocks of ice, and so on, forming an arithmetic sequence. Find the total number of ice blocks needed if there were 15 blocks in the bottom row.

OBJECTIVE 2 ▶ **Finding partial sums of geometric sequences.** We can also derive a formula for the partial sum S_n of the first n terms of a geometric series. If $a_n = a_1 r^{n-1}$, then

$$S_n = \underset{\text{1st term}}{a_1} + \underset{\text{2nd term}}{a_1 r} + \underset{\text{3rd term}}{a_1 r^2} + \cdots + \underset{n\text{th term}}{a_1 r^{n-1}}$$

Multiply each side of the equation by $-r$.

$$-rS_n = -a_1 r - a_1 r^2 - a_1 r^3 - \cdots - a_1 r^n$$

Add the two equations.

$$S_n - rS_n = a_1 + (a_1 r - a_1 r) + (a_1 r^2 - a_1 r^2) + (a_1 r^3 - a_1 r^3) + \cdots - a_1 r^n$$
$$S_n - rS_n = a_1 - a_1 r^n$$

Now factor each side.

$$S_n(1 - r) = a_1(1 - r^n)$$

Solve for S_n by dividing both sides by $1 - r$. Thus,

$$S_n = \frac{a_1(1 - r^n)}{1 - r}$$

as long as r is not 1.

Partial Sum S_n of a Geometric Sequence

The partial sum S_n of the first n terms of a geometric sequence is given by

$$S_n = \frac{a_1(1 - r^n)}{1 - r}$$

where a_1 is the first term of the sequence, r is the common ratio, and $r \neq 1$.

EXAMPLE 4 Find the sum of the first six terms of the geometric sequence 5, 10, 20, 40, 80, 160.

Solution Use the formula for the partial sum S_n of the terms of a geometric sequence. Here, $n = 6$, the first term $a_1 = 5$, and the common ratio $r = 2$.

$$S_n = \frac{a_1(1 - r^n)}{1 - r}$$

$$S_6 = \frac{5(1 - 2^6)}{1 - 2} = \frac{5(-63)}{-1} = 315 \qquad \square$$

PRACTICE 4 Find the sum of the first five terms of the geometric sequence $32, 8, 2, \frac{1}{2}, \frac{1}{8}$.

EXAMPLE 5 Finding Amount of Donation

A grant from an alumnus to a university specified that the university was to receive $800,000 during the first year and 75% of the preceding year's donation during each of the following 5 years. Find the total amount donated during the 6 years.

Solution The donations are modeled by the first six terms of a geometric sequence. Evaluate S_n when $n = 6$, $a_1 = 800{,}000$, and $r = 0.75$.

$$S_6 = \frac{800{,}000[1 - (0.75)^6]}{1 - 0.75}$$

$$= \$2{,}630{,}468.75$$

The total amount donated during the 6 years is $2,630,468.75. □

PRACTICE

5 A new youth center is being established in a downtown urban area. A philanthropic charity has agreed to help it get off the ground. The charity has pledged to donate $250,000 in the first year, with 80% of the preceding year's donation for each of the following 6 years. Find the total amount donated during the 7 years.

OBJECTIVE 3 ▶ Finding sums of terms of infinite geometric sequences. Is it possible to find the sum of all the terms of an infinite sequence? Examine the partial sums of the geometric sequence $\frac{1}{2}, \frac{1}{4}, \frac{1}{8}, \ldots$.

$$S_1 = \frac{1}{2}$$

$$S_2 = \frac{1}{2} + \frac{1}{4} = \frac{3}{4}$$

$$S_3 = \frac{1}{2} + \frac{1}{4} + \frac{1}{8} = \frac{7}{8}$$

$$S_4 = \frac{1}{2} + \frac{1}{4} + \frac{1}{8} + \frac{1}{16} = \frac{15}{16}$$

$$S_5 = \frac{1}{2} + \frac{1}{4} + \frac{1}{8} + \frac{1}{16} + \frac{1}{32} = \frac{31}{32}$$

$$\vdots$$

$$S_{10} = \frac{1}{2} + \frac{1}{4} + \frac{1}{8} + \cdots + \frac{1}{2^{10}} = \frac{1023}{1024}$$

Even though each partial sum is larger than the preceding partial sum, we see that each partial sum is closer to 1 than the preceding partial sum. If n gets larger and larger, then S_n gets closer and closer to 1. We say that 1 is the **limit** of S_n and also that 1 is the sum of the terms of this infinite sequence. In general, if $|r| < 1$, the following formula gives the sum of the terms of an infinite geometric sequence.

Sum of the Terms of an Infinite Geometric Sequence

The sum S_∞ of the terms of an infinite geometric sequence is given by

$$S_\infty = \frac{a_1}{1 - r}$$

where a_1 is the first term of the sequence, r is the common ratio, and $|r| < 1$. If $|r| \geq 1$, S_∞ does not exist.

What happens for other values of r? For example, in the following geometric sequence, $r = 3$.

$$6, 18, 54, 162, \ldots$$

Here, as n increases, the sum S_n increases also. This time, though, S_n does not get closer and closer to a fixed number but instead increases without bound.

EXAMPLE 6 Find the sum of the terms of the geometric sequence $2, \frac{2}{3}, \frac{2}{9}, \frac{2}{27}, \ldots$.

Solution For this geometric sequence, $r = \frac{1}{3}$. Since $|r| < 1$, we may use the formula for S_∞ of a geometric sequence with $a_1 = 2$ and $r = \frac{1}{3}$.

$$S_\infty = \frac{a_1}{1-r} = \frac{2}{1 - \frac{1}{3}} = \frac{2}{\frac{2}{3}} = 3$$

The formula for the sum of the terms of an infinite geometric sequence can be used to write a repeating decimal as a fraction. For example,

$$0.33\overline{3} = \frac{3}{10} + \frac{3}{100} + \frac{3}{1000} + \cdots$$

This sum is the sum of the terms of an infinite geometric sequence whose first term a_1 is $\frac{3}{10}$ and whose common ratio r is $\frac{1}{10}$. Using the formula for S_∞,

$$S_\infty = \frac{a_1}{1-r} = \frac{\frac{3}{10}}{1 - \frac{1}{10}} = \frac{1}{3}$$

So, $0.33\overline{3} = \frac{1}{3}$.

PRACTICE 6 Find the sum of the terms of the geometric sequence $7, \frac{7}{4}, \frac{7}{16}, \frac{7}{64}, \ldots$.

EXAMPLE 7 **Distance Traveled by a Pendulum**

On its first pass, a pendulum swings through an arc whose length is 24 inches. On each pass thereafter, the arc length is 75% of the arc length on the preceding pass. Find the total distance the pendulum travels before it comes to rest.

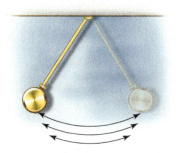

Solution We must find the sum of the terms of an infinite geometric sequence whose first term, a_1, is 24 and whose common ratio, r, is 0.75. Since $|r| < 1$, we may use the formula for S_∞.

$$S_\infty = \frac{a_1}{1-r} = \frac{24}{1 - 0.75} = \frac{24}{0.25} = 96$$

The pendulum travels a total distance of 96 inches before it comes to rest.

PRACTICE 7 The manufacturers of the "perpetual bouncing ball" claim that the ball rises to 96% of its dropped height on each bounce of the ball. Find the total distance the ball travels before it comes to rest, if it is dropped from a height of 36 inches.

VOCABULARY & READINESS CHECK

Decision Making. *Decide whether each sequence is geometric or arithmetic.*

1. $5, 10, 15, 20, 25, \ldots$; _____
2. $5, 10, 20, 40, 80, \ldots$; _____
3. $-1, 3, -9, 27, -81 \ldots$; _____
4. $-1, 1, 3, 5, 7, \ldots$; _____
5. $-7, 0, 7, 14, 21, \ldots$; _____
6. $-7, 7, -7, 7, -7, \ldots$; _____

12.4 EXERCISE SET

Use the partial sum formula to find the partial sum of the given arithmetic or geometric sequence. See Examples 1 and 4.

1. Find the sum of the first six terms of the arithmetic sequence $1, 3, 5, 7, \ldots$.
2. Find the sum of the first seven terms of the arithmetic sequence $-7, -11, -15, \ldots$.
3. Find the sum of the first five terms of the geometric sequence $4, 12, 36, \ldots$.
4. Find the sum of the first eight terms of the geometric sequence $-1, 2, -4, \ldots$.
5. Find the sum of the first six terms of the arithmetic sequence $3, 6, 9, \ldots$.
6. Find the sum of the first four terms of the arithmetic sequence $-4, -8, -12, \ldots$.
7. Find the sum of the first four terms of the geometric sequence $2, \frac{2}{5}, \frac{2}{25}, \ldots$.
8. Find the sum of the first five terms of the geometric sequence $\frac{1}{3}, -\frac{2}{3}, \frac{4}{3}, \ldots$.

Solve. See Example 2.

9. Find the sum of the first ten positive integers.
10. Find the sum of the first eight negative integers.
11. Find the sum of the first four positive odd integers.
12. Find the sum of the first five negative odd integers.

Find the sum of the terms of each infinite geometric sequence. See Example 6.

13. $12, 6, 3, \ldots$
14. $45, 15, 5, \ldots$
15. $\frac{1}{10}, \frac{1}{100}, \frac{1}{1000}, \ldots$
16. $\frac{3}{5}, \frac{3}{20}, \frac{3}{80}, \ldots$
17. $-10, -5, -\frac{5}{2}, \ldots$
18. $-16, -4, -1, \ldots$
19. $2, -\frac{1}{4}, \frac{1}{32}, \ldots$
20. $-3, \frac{3}{5}, -\frac{3}{25}, \ldots$
21. $\frac{2}{3}, -\frac{1}{3}, \frac{1}{6}, \ldots$
22. $6, -4, \frac{8}{3}, \ldots$

MIXED PRACTICE

Solve.

23. Find the sum of the first ten terms of the sequence $-4, 1, 6, \ldots, 41$ where 41 is the tenth term.
24. Find the sum of the first twelve terms of the sequence $-3, -13, -23, \ldots, -113$ where -113 is the twelfth term.
25. Find the sum of the first seven terms of the sequence $3, \frac{3}{2}, \frac{3}{4}, \ldots$.
26. Find the sum of the first five terms of the sequence $-2, -6, -18, \ldots$.
27. Find the sum of the first five terms of the sequence $-12, 6, -3, \ldots$.
28. Find the sum of the first four terms of the sequence $-\frac{1}{4}, -\frac{3}{4}, -\frac{9}{4}, \ldots$.
29. Find the sum of the first twenty terms of the sequence $\frac{1}{2}, \frac{1}{4}, 0, \ldots, -\frac{17}{4}$ where $-\frac{17}{4}$ is the twentieth term.
30. Find the sum of the first fifteen terms of the sequence $-5, -9, -13, \ldots, -61$ where -61 is the fifteenth term.
31. If a_1 is 8 and r is $-\frac{2}{3}$, find S_3.
32. If a_1 is 10, a_{18} is $\frac{3}{2}$, and d is $-\frac{1}{2}$, find S_{18}.

Solve. See Example 3.

33. Modern Car Company has come out with a new car model. Market analysts predict that 4000 cars will be sold in the first month and that sales will drop by 50 cars per month after that during the first year. Write out the first five terms of the sequence, and find the number of sold cars predicted for the twelfth month. Find the total predicted number of sold cars for the first year.
34. A company that sends faxes charges $3 for the first page sent and $0.10 less than the preceding page for each additional page sent. The cost per page forms an arithmetic sequence. Write the first five terms of this sequence, and use a partial sum to find the cost of sending a nine-page document.
35. Sal has two job offers: Firm A starts at $22,000 per year and guarantees raises of $1000 per year, whereas Firm B starts

at $20,000 and guarantees raises of $1200 per year. Over a 10-year period, determine the more profitable offer.

36. The game of pool uses 15 balls numbered 1 to 15. In the variety called rotation, a player who sinks a ball receives as many points as the number on the ball. Use an arithmetic series to find the score of a player who sinks all 15 balls.

Solve. See Example 5.

37. A woman made $30,000 during the first year she owned her business and made an additional 10% over the previous year in each subsequent year. Find how much she made during her fourth year of business. Find her total earnings during the first four years.

38. In free fall, a parachutist falls 16 feet during the first second, 48 feet during the second second, 80 feet during the third second, and so on. Find how far she falls during the eighth second. Find the total distance she falls during the first 8 seconds.

39. A trainee in a computer company takes 0.9 times as long to assemble each computer as he took to assemble the preceding computer. If it took him 30 minutes to assemble the first computer, find how long it takes him to assemble the fifth computer. Find the total time he takes to assemble the first five computers (round to the nearest minute).

40. On a gambling trip to Reno, Carol doubled her bet each time she lost. If her first losing bet was $5 and she lost six consecutive bets, find how much she lost on the sixth bet. Find the total amount lost on these six bets.

Solve. See Example 7.

41. A ball is dropped from a height of 20 feet and repeatedly rebounds to a height that is $\frac{4}{5}$ of its previous height. Find the total distance the ball covers before it comes to rest.

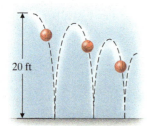

42. A rotating flywheel coming to rest makes 300 revolutions in the first minute and in each minute thereafter makes $\frac{2}{5}$ as many revolutions as in the preceding minute. Find how many revolutions the wheel makes before it comes to rest.

MIXED PRACTICE

Solve.

43. In the pool game of rotation, player *A* sinks balls numbered 1 to 9, and player *B* sinks the rest of the balls. Use arithmetic series to find each player's score (see Exercise 36).

44. A godfather deposited $250 in a savings account on the day his godchild was born. On each subsequent birthday he deposited $50 more than he deposited the previous year. Find how much money he deposited on his godchild's twenty-first birthday. Find the total amount deposited over the 21 years.

45. During the holiday rush a business can rent a computer system for $200 the first day, with the rental fee decreasing $5 for each additional day. Find the fee paid for 20 days during the holiday rush.

46. The spraying of a field with insecticide killed 6400 weevils the first day, 1600 the second day, 400 the third day, and so on. Find the total number of weevils killed during the first 5 days.

47. A college student humorously asks his parents to charge him room and board according to this geometric sequence: $0.01 for the first day of the month, $0.02 for the second day, $0.04 for the third day, and so on. Find the total room and board he would pay for 30 days.

48. Following its television advertising campaign, a bank attracted 80 new customers the first day, 120 the second day, 160 the third day, and so on, in an arithmetic sequence. Find how many new customers were attracted during the first 5 days following its television campaign.

REVIEW AND PREVIEW

Evaluate. See Section 1.3.

49. $6 \cdot 5 \cdot 4 \cdot 3 \cdot 2 \cdot 1$
50. $8 \cdot 7 \cdot 6 \cdot 5 \cdot 4 \cdot 3 \cdot 2 \cdot 1$
51. $\dfrac{3 \cdot 2 \cdot 1}{2 \cdot 1}$
52. $\dfrac{5 \cdot 4 \cdot 3 \cdot 2 \cdot 1}{3 \cdot 2 \cdot 1}$

Multiply. See Section 6.4.

53. $(x + 5)^2$
54. $(x - 2)^2$
55. $(2x - 1)^3$
56. $(3x + 2)^3$

CONCEPT EXTENSIONS

57. Write $0.88\overline{8}$ as an infinite geometric series and use the formula for S_∞ to write it as a rational number.

58. Write $0.54\overline{54}$ as an infinite geometric series and use the formula S_∞ to write it as a rational number.

59. Explain whether the sequence $5, 5, 5, \ldots$ is arithmetic, geometric, neither, or both.

60. Describe a situation in everyday life that can be modeled by an infinite geometric series.

12.5 THE BINOMIAL THEOREM

OBJECTIVES

1. Use Pascal's triangle to expand binomials.
2. Evaluate factorials.
3. Use the binomial theorem to expand binomials.
4. Find the nth term in the expansion of a binomial raised to a positive power.

In this section, we learn how to **expand** binomials of the form $(a + b)^n$ easily. Expanding a binomial such as $(a + b)^n$ means to write the factored form as a sum. First, we review the patterns in the expansions of $(a + b)^n$.

$(a + b)^0 = 1$ 1 term
$(a + b)^1 = a + b$ 2 terms
$(a + b)^2 = a^2 + 2ab + b^2$ 3 terms
$(a + b)^3 = a^3 + 3a^2b + 3ab^2 + b^3$ 4 terms
$(a + b)^4 = a^4 + 4a^3b + 6a^2b^2 + 4ab^3 + b^4$ 5 terms
$(a + b)^5 = a^5 + 5a^4b + 10a^3b^2 + 10a^2b^3 + 5ab^4 + b^5$ 6 terms

Notice the following patterns.

1. The expansion of $(a + b)^n$ contains $n + 1$ terms. For example, for $(a + b)^3$, $n = 3$, and the expansion contains $3 + 1$ terms, or 4 terms.
2. The first term of the expansion of $(a + b)^n$ is a^n, and the last term is b^n.
3. The powers of a decrease by 1 for each term, whereas the powers of b increase by 1 for each term.
4. For each term of the expansion of $(a + b)^n$, the sum of the exponents of a and b is n. (For example, the sum of the exponents of $5a^4b$ is $4 + 1$, or 5, and the sum of the exponents of $10a^3b^2$ is $3 + 2$, or 5.)

OBJECTIVE 1 ▶ Using Pascal's triangle. There are patterns in the coefficients of the terms as well. Written in a triangular array, the coefficients are called **Pascal's triangle.**

$(a + b)^0$:   1 $n = 0$
$(a + b)^1$:   1   1 $n = 1$
$(a + b)^2$:   1   2   1 $n = 2$
$(a + b)^3$:   1   3   3   1 $n = 3$
$(a + b)^4$:   1   4   6   4   1 $n = 4$
$(a + b)^5$: 1   5   10   10   5   1 $n = 5$

Each row in Pascal's triangle begins and ends with 1. Any other number in a row is the sum of the two closest numbers above it. Using this pattern, we can write the next row, for $n = 6$, by first writing the number 1. Then we can add the consecutive numbers in the row for $n = 5$ and write each sum "between and below" the pair. We complete the row by writing a 1.

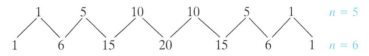

We can use Pascal's triangle and the patterns noted to expand $(a + b)^n$ without actually multiplying any terms.

EXAMPLE 1   Expand $(a + b)^6$.

Solution   Using the $n = 6$ row of Pascal's triangle as the coefficients and following the patterns noted, $(a + b)^6$ can be expanded as

$$a^6 + 6a^5b + 15a^4b^2 + 20a^3b^3 + 15a^2b^4 + 6ab^5 + b^6$$

PRACTICE 1   Expand $(p + r)^7$.

OBJECTIVE 2 ▶ Evaluating factorials. For a large n, the use of Pascal's triangle to find coefficients for $(a + b)^n$ can be tedious. An alternative method for determining these coefficients is based on the concept of a **factorial.**

The **factorial of n**, written $n!$ (read "n factorial"), is the product of the first n consecutive natural numbers.

> **Factorial of n: $n!$**
> If n is a natural number, then $n! = n(n - 1)(n - 2)(n - 3) \cdots 3 \cdot 2 \cdot 1$. The factorial of 0, written $0!$, is defined to be 1.

For example, $3! = 3 \cdot 2 \cdot 1 = 6$, $5! = 5 \cdot 4 \cdot 3 \cdot 2 \cdot 1 = 120$, and $0! = 1$.

EXAMPLE 2 Evaluate each expression.

a. $\dfrac{5!}{6!}$ **b.** $\dfrac{10!}{7!3!}$ **c.** $\dfrac{3!}{2!1!}$ **d.** $\dfrac{7!}{7!0!}$

Solution

a. $\dfrac{5!}{6!} = \dfrac{5 \cdot 4 \cdot 3 \cdot 2 \cdot 1}{6 \cdot 5 \cdot 4 \cdot 3 \cdot 2 \cdot 1} = \dfrac{1}{6}$

b. $\dfrac{10!}{7!3!} = \dfrac{10 \cdot 9 \cdot 8 \cdot 7!}{7! \cdot 3 \cdot 2 \cdot 1} = \dfrac{10 \cdot 9 \cdot 8}{3 \cdot 2 \cdot 1} = 10 \cdot 3 \cdot 4 = 120$

c. $\dfrac{3!}{2!1!} = \dfrac{3 \cdot 2 \cdot 1}{2 \cdot 1 \cdot 1} = 3$

d. $\dfrac{7!}{7!0!} = \dfrac{7!}{7! \cdot 1} = 1$

PRACTICE 2 Evaluate each expression.

a. $\dfrac{6!}{7!}$ **b.** $\dfrac{8!}{4!2!}$ **c.** $\dfrac{5!}{4!1!}$ **d.** $\dfrac{9!}{9!0!}$

> ▶ **Helpful Hint**
> We can use a calculator with a factorial key to evaluate a factorial. A calculator uses scientific notation for large results.

OBJECTIVE 3 ▶ Using the binomial theorem. It can be proved, although we won't do so here, that the coefficients of terms in the expansion of $(a + b)^n$ can be expressed in terms of factorials. Following patterns 1 through 4 given earlier and using the factorial expressions of the coefficients, we have what is known as the **binomial theorem.**

> **Binomial Theorem**
> If n is a positive integer, then
> $$(a + b)^n = a^n + \frac{n}{1!}a^{n-1}b^1 + \frac{n(n-1)}{2!}a^{n-2}b^2$$
> $$+ \frac{n(n-1)(n-2)}{3!}a^{n-3}b^3 + \cdots + b^n$$

We call the formula for $(a + b)^n$ given by the binomial theorem the **binomial formula.**

EXAMPLE 3   Use the binomial theorem to expand $(x + y)^{10}$.

Solution   Let $a = x$, $b = y$, and $n = 10$ in the binomial formula.

$$(x + y)^{10} = x^{10} + \frac{10}{1!}x^9 y + \frac{10 \cdot 9}{2!}x^8 y^2 + \frac{10 \cdot 9 \cdot 8}{3!}x^7 y^3 + \frac{10 \cdot 9 \cdot 8 \cdot 7}{4!}x^6 y^4$$
$$+ \frac{10 \cdot 9 \cdot 8 \cdot 7 \cdot 6}{5!}x^5 y^5 + \frac{10 \cdot 9 \cdot 8 \cdot 7 \cdot 6 \cdot 5}{6!}x^4 y^6$$
$$+ \frac{10 \cdot 9 \cdot 8 \cdot 7 \cdot 6 \cdot 5 \cdot 4}{7!}x^3 y^7$$
$$+ \frac{10 \cdot 9 \cdot 8 \cdot 7 \cdot 6 \cdot 5 \cdot 4 \cdot 3}{8!}x^2 y^8$$
$$+ \frac{10 \cdot 9 \cdot 8 \cdot 7 \cdot 6 \cdot 5 \cdot 4 \cdot 3 \cdot 2}{9!}xy^9 + y^{10}$$
$$= x^{10} + 10x^9 y + 45x^8 y^2 + 120x^7 y^3 + 210x^6 y^4 + 252x^5 y^5 + 210x^4 y^6$$
$$+ 120x^3 y^7 + 45x^2 y^8 + 10xy^9 + y^{10}$$

PRACTICE 3   Use the binomial theorem to expand $(a + b)^9$.

EXAMPLE 4   Use the binomial theorem to expand $(x + 2y)^5$.

Solution   Let $a = x$ and $b = 2y$ in the binomial formula.

$$(x + 2y)^5 = x^5 + \frac{5}{1!}x^4(2y) + \frac{5 \cdot 4}{2!}x^3(2y)^2 + \frac{5 \cdot 4 \cdot 3}{3!}x^2(2y)^3$$
$$+ \frac{5 \cdot 4 \cdot 3 \cdot 2}{4!}x(2y)^4 + (2y)^5$$
$$= x^5 + 10x^4 y + 40x^3 y^2 + 80x^2 y^3 + 80xy^4 + 32y^5$$

PRACTICE 4   Use the binomial theorem to expand $(a + 5b)^3$.

EXAMPLE 5   Use the binomial theorem to expand $(3m - n)^4$.

Solution   Let $a = 3m$ and $b = -n$ in the binomial formula.

$$(3m - n)^4 = (3m)^4 + \frac{4}{1!}(3m)^3(-n) + \frac{4 \cdot 3}{2!}(3m)^2(-n)^2$$
$$+ \frac{4 \cdot 3 \cdot 2}{3!}(3m)(-n)^3 + (-n)^4$$
$$= 81m^4 - 108m^3 n + 54m^2 n^2 - 12mn^3 + n^4$$

PRACTICE 5   Use the binomial theorem to expand $(3x - 2y)^3$.

OBJECTIVE 4 ▶ **Finding the rth term of a binomial expansion.** Sometimes it is convenient to find a specific term of a binomial expansion without writing out the entire expansion. By studying the expansion of binomials, a pattern forms for each term. This pattern is most easily stated for the $(r + 1)$st term.

$(r + 1)$st Term in a Binomial Expansion

The $(r + 1)$st term of the expansion of $(a + b)^n$ is $\dfrac{n!}{r!(n - r)!} a^{n-r} b^r$.

EXAMPLE 6 Find the eighth term in the expansion of $(2x - y)^{10}$.

Solution Use the formula, with $n = 10$, $a = 2x$, $b = -y$, and $r + 1 = 8$. Notice that, since $r + 1 = 8$, $r = 7$.

$$\frac{n!}{r!(n-r)!}a^{n-r}b^r = \frac{10!}{7!3!}(2x)^3(-y)^7$$
$$= 120(8x^3)(-y^7)$$
$$= -960x^3y^7$$

PRACTICE 6 Find the seventh term in the expansion of $(x - 4y)^{11}$.

VOCABULARY & READINESS CHECK

Fill in the Blank. *Fill in each blank.*

1. $0! =$ _____
2. $1! =$ _____
3. $4! =$ _____
4. $2! =$ _____
5. $3!0! =$ _____
6. $0!2! =$ _____

12.5 EXERCISE SET

Use Pascal's triangle to expand the binomial. See Example 1.

1. $(m + n)^3$
2. $(x + y)^4$
3. $(c + d)^5$
4. $(a + b)^6$
5. $(y - x)^5$
6. $(q - r)^7$
7. Explain how to generate a row of Pascal's triangle.
8. Write the $n = 8$ row of Pascal's triangle.

Evaluate each expression. See Example 2.

9. $\dfrac{8!}{7!}$
10. $\dfrac{6!}{0!}$
11. $\dfrac{7!}{5!}$
12. $\dfrac{8!}{5!}$
13. $\dfrac{10!}{7!2!}$
14. $\dfrac{9!}{5!3!}$
15. $\dfrac{8!}{6!0!}$
16. $\dfrac{10!}{4!6!}$

MIXED PRACTICE

Use the binomial formula to expand each binomial. See Examples 3 through 5.

17. $(a + b)^7$
18. $(x + y)^8$
19. $(a + 2b)^5$
20. $(x + 3y)^6$
21. $(q + r)^9$
22. $(b + c)^6$
23. $(4a + b)^5$
24. $(3m + n)^4$
25. $(5a - 2b)^4$
26. $(m - 4)^6$
27. $(2a + 3b)^3$
28. $(4 - 3x)^5$
29. $(x + 2)^5$
30. $(3 + 2a)^4$

Find the indicated term. See Example 6.

31. The fifth term of the expansion of $(c - d)^5$
32. The fourth term of the expansion of $(x - y)^6$
33. The eighth term of the expansion of $(2c + d)^7$
34. The tenth term of the expansion of $(5x - y)^9$
35. The fourth term of the expansion of $(2r - s)^5$
36. The first term of the expansion of $(3q - 7r)^6$
37. The third term of the expansion of $(x + y)^4$
38. The fourth term of the expansion of $(a + b)^8$
39. The second term of the expansion of $(a + 3b)^{10}$
40. The third term of the expansion of $(m + 5n)^7$

REVIEW AND PREVIEW

Sketch the graph of each function. Decide whether each function is one-to-one. See Sections 3.2 and 3.6.

41. $f(x) = |x|$
42. $g(x) = 3(x-1)^2$
43. $H(x) = 2x + 3$
44. $F(x) = -2$
45. $f(x) = x^2 + 3$
46. $h(x) = -(x+1)^2 - 4$

CONCEPT EXTENSIONS

47. Expand the expression $(\sqrt{x} + \sqrt{3})^5$.

48. Find the term containing x^2 in the expansion of $(\sqrt{x} - \sqrt{5})^6$.

Evaluate the following.

The notation $\binom{n}{r}$ means $\dfrac{n!}{r!(n-r)!}$. For example,

$$\binom{5}{3} = \frac{5!}{3!(5-3)!} = \frac{5!}{3!2!} = \frac{5 \cdot 4 \cdot 3 \cdot 2 \cdot 1}{(3 \cdot 2 \cdot 1) \cdot (2 \cdot 1)} = 10.$$

49. $\binom{9}{5}$
50. $\binom{4}{3}$
51. $\binom{8}{2}$
52. $\binom{12}{11}$

53. Show that $\binom{n}{n} = 1$ for any whole number n.

EXTENSION: INDUCTIVE AND DEDUCTIVE REASONING

OBJECTIVES

1. Understand and use inductive reasoning.
2. Understand and use deductive reasoning.

OBJECTIVE 1 ▶ Inductive reasoning. Mathematics involves the study of patterns. In everyday life, we frequently rely on patterns and routines to draw conclusions. Here is an example:

> The last six times I went to the beach, the traffic was light on Wednesdays and heavy on Sundays. My conclusion is that weekdays have lighter traffic than weekends.

This type of reasoning process is referred to as *inductive reasoning*, or *induction*.

> **Inductive Reasoning**
>
> **Inductive reasoning** is the process of arriving at a general conclusion based on observations of specific examples.

Although inductive reasoning is a powerful method of drawing conclusions, we can never be absolutely certain that these conclusions are true. For this reason, the conclusions are called **conjectures, hypotheses,** or educated guesses. A strong inductive argument does not guarantee the truth of the conclusion, but rather provides strong support for the conclusion. If there is just one case for which the conjecture does not hold, then the conjecture is false. Such a case is called a **counterexample.**

Inductive reasoning is extremely important to mathematicians. Discovery in mathematics often begins with an examination of individual cases to reveal patterns about numbers.

EXAMPLE 1 Using Inductive Reasoning

Identify a pattern in each list of numbers. Then use this pattern to find the next number.

a. 3, 12, 21, 30, 39, _____
b. 3, 12, 48, 192, 768, _____
c. 3, 4, 6, 9, 13, 18, _____
d. 3, 6, 18, 36, 108, 216, _____

Solution

a. Because 3, 12, 21, 30, 39, _____ is increasing relatively slowly, let's use addition as the basis for our individual observations.

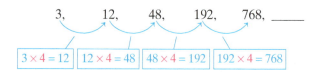

Generalizing from these observations, we conclude that each number after the first is obtained by adding 9 to the previous number. Using this pattern, the next number is 39 + 9, or 48.

b. Because 3, 12, 48, 192, 768, _____ is increasing relatively rapidly, let's use multiplication as the basis for our individual observations.

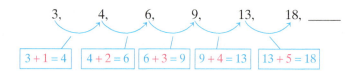

Generalizing from these observations, we conclude that each number after the first is obtained by multiplying the previous number by 4. Using this pattern, the next number is 768 × 4, or 3072.

c. Because 3, 4, 6, 9, 13, 18, _____ is increasing relatively slowly, let's use addition as the basis for our individual observations.

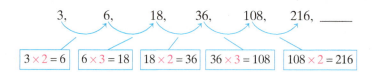

Generalizing from these observations, we conclude that each number after the first is obtained by adding a counting number to the previous number. The additions begin with 1 and continue through each successive counting number. Using this pattern, the next number is 18 + 6, or 24.

c. Because 3, 6, 18, 36, 108, 216, _____ is increasing relatively rapidly, let's use multiplication as the basis for our individual observations.

$$3, \quad 6, \quad 18, \quad 36, \quad 108, \quad 216, \quad \_\_\_\_$$

$$\boxed{3 \times 2 = 6} \quad \boxed{6 \times 3 = 18} \quad \boxed{18 \times 2 = 36} \quad \boxed{36 \times 3 = 108} \quad \boxed{108 \times 2 = 216}$$

Generalizing from these observations, we conclude that each number after the first is obtained by multiplying the previous number by 2 or by 3. The multiplications begin with 2 and then alternate, multiplying by 2, then 3, then 2, then 3, and so on. Using this pattern, the next number is 216 × 3, or 648.

PRACTICE

1 Identify a pattern in each list of numbers. Then use this pattern to find the next number.

a. 3, 9, 15, 21, 27, _____   **b.** 2, 10, 50, 250, _____
c. 3, 6, 18, 72, 144, 432, 1728, _____   **d.** 1, 9, 17, 3, 11, 19, 5, 13, 21, _____

Helpful Hint

The illusion in Figure 1.1 is an ambiguous figure containing two patterns, where it is not clear which pattern should predominate. Do you see a wine goblet or two faces looking at each other? Like this ambiguous figure, some lists of numbers can display more than one pattern, particularly if only a few numbers are given. Inductive reasoning can result in more than one probable next number in a list.

Example: 1, 2, 4, _____

Pattern: Each number after the first is obtained by multiplying the previous number by 2. The missing number is 4×2, or 8.

Pattern: Each number after the first is obtained by adding successive counting numbers, starting with 1, to the previous number. The second number is $1 + 1$, or 2. The third number is $2 + 2$, or 4. The missing number is $4 + 3$, or 7.

Inductive reasoning can also result in different patterns that produce the same probable next number in a list.

Example: 1, 4, 9, 16, 25, _____

Pattern: Start by adding 3 to the first number. Then add successive odd numbers, 5, 7, 9, and so on. The missing number is $25 + 11$, or 36.

Pattern: Each number is obtained by squaring its position in the list: The first number is $1^2 = 1 \times 1 = 1$, the second number is $2^2 = 2 \times 2 = 4$, the third number is $3^2 = 3 \times 3 = 9$, and so on. The missing sixth number is $6^2 = 6 \times 6$, or 36.

The numbers that we found in Example 1 are probable numbers. Perhaps you found patterns other than the ones we pointed out that might have resulted in different answers.

FIGURE 1.1

In our next example, the patterns are a bit more complex than the additions and multiplications we encountered in Example 1.

EXAMPLE 2 Using Inductive Reasoning

Identify a pattern in each list of numbers. Then use this pattern to find the next number.

a. 1, 1, 2, 3, 5, 8, 13, 21, _____   **b.** 23, 54, 95, 146, 117, 98, _____

Solution

a. Starting with the third number in the list, let's form our observations by comparing each number with the two numbers that immediately precede it.

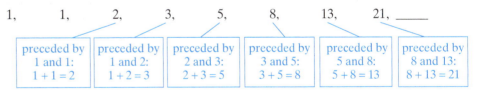

1,   1,   2,   3,   5,   8,   13,   21, _____

preceded by 1 and 1: $1 + 1 = 2$
preceded by 1 and 2: $1 + 2 = 3$
preceded by 2 and 3: $2 + 3 = 5$
preceded by 3 and 5: $3 + 5 = 8$
preceded by 5 and 8: $5 + 8 = 13$
preceded by 8 and 13: $8 + 13 = 21$

Generalizing from these observations, we conclude that the first two numbers are 1. Each number thereafter is the sum of the two preceding numbers. Using this pattern, the next number is $13 + 21$, or 34. (The numbers 1, 1, 2, 3, 5, 8, 13, 21, and 34 are the first nine terms of the *Fibonacci sequence*, discussed in the opening page of this chapter.)

b. Let's use the digits that form each number as the basis for our individual observations. Focus on the sum of the digits, as well as the final digit increased by 1.

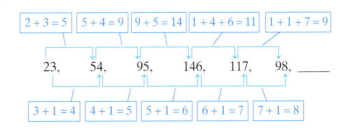

$2+3=5$ $5+4=9$ $9+5=14$ $1+4+6=11$ $1+1+7=9$

23,   54,   95,   146,   117,   98, _____

$3+1=4$ $4+1=5$ $5+1=6$ $6+1=7$ $7+1=8$

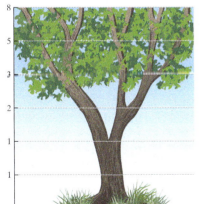

As this tree branches, the number of branches forms the Fibonacci sequence.

Generalizing from these observations, we conclude that for each number after the first, we obtain the first digit or the first two digits by adding the digits of the previous number. We obtain the last digit by adding 1 to the final digit of the preceding number. Applying this pattern to the number that follows 98, the first two digits are 9 + 8, or 17. The last digit is 8 + 1, or 9. Thus, the next number in the list is 179.

PRACTICE 2 Identify a pattern in each list of numbers. Then use this pattern to find the next number.
a. 1, 3, 4, 7, 11, 18, 29, 47, _____ **b.** 2, 3, 5, 9, 17, 33, 65, 129, _____

Mathematics is more than recognizing number patterns. It is about the patterns that arise in the world around us. For example, by describing patterns formed by various kinds of knots, mathematicians are helping scientists investigate the knotty shapes and patterns of viruses. One of the weapons used against viruses is based on recognizing visual patterns in the possible ways that knots can be tied.

Our next example deals with recognizing visual patterns.

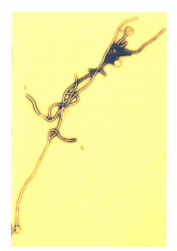

This electron microscope photograph shows the knotty shape of the Ebola virus.

EXAMPLE 3 Finding the Next Figure in a Visual Sequence

Describe two patterns in this sequence of figures. Use the patterns to draw the next figure in the sequence.

 , , , , _____

Solution

The more obvious pattern is that the figures alternate between circles and squares. We conclude that the next figure will be a circle. We can identify the second pattern in the four regions containing no dots, one dot, two dots, and three dots. The dots are placed in order (no dots, one dot, two dots, three dots) in a clockwise direction. However, the entire pattern of the dots rotates counterclockwise as we follow the figures from left to right.

This means that the next figure should be a circle with a single dot in the right-hand region, two dots in the bottom region, three dots in the left-hand region, and no dots in the top region. This figure is drawn to the right.

PRACTICE 3 Describe two patterns in this sequence of figures. Use the patterns to draw the next figure in the sequence.

 , , , , _____

OBJECTIVE 2 ▶ Deductive reasoning. We use inductive reasoning in everyday life. Many of the conjectures that come from this kind of thinking seem highly likely, although we can never be absolutely certain that they are true. Another method of reasoning, called *deductive reasoning*, or *deduction*, can be used to prove that some conjectures are true.

> **Deductive Reasoning**
>
> **Deductive reasoning** is the process of proving a specific conclusion from one or more general statements. A conclusion that is proved true by deductive reasoning is called a **theorem**.

Deductive reasoning allows us to draw a specific conclusion from one or more general statements. Here is an example of deductive reasoning. Notice that in this situation, the general statement from which the conclusion is drawn is implied rather than directly stated.

Situation	Deductive Reasoning
One player to another in a Scrabble game: "You have to remove those five letters. You can't use TEXAS as a word."	• All proper names are prohibited in Scrabble. [general statement] TEXAS is a proper name. Therefore, TEXAS is [conclusion] prohibited in Scrabble.

Our next example illustrates the difference between inductive and deductive reasoning. The first part of the example involves reasoning that moves from specific examples to a general statement, illustrating inductive reasoning. The second part of the example begins with the general case rather than specific examples, and illustrates deductive reasoning.

EXAMPLE 4 Using Inductive and Deductive Reasoning

Consider the following procedure:
Select a number. Multiply the number by 6. Add 8 to the product. Divide this sum by 2. Subtract 4 from the quotient.

a. Repeat this procedure for at least four different numbers. Write a conjecture that relates the result of this process to the original number selected.
b. Represent the original number by the variable n and use deductive reasoning to prove the conjecture in part (a).

Solution

a. First, let us pick our starting numbers. We will use 4, 7, 11, and 100, but we could pick any four numbers. Next we will apply the procedure given in this example to 4, 7, 11, and 100, four individual cases.

Applying a Procedure to Four Individual Cases				
Select a number.	4	7	11	100
Multiply the number by 6.	$4 \times 6 = 24$	$7 \times 6 = 42$	$11 \times 6 = 66$	$100 \times 6 = 600$
Add 8 to the product.	$24 + 8 = 32$	$42 + 8 = 50$	$66 + 8 = 74$	$600 + 8 = 608$
Divide this sum by 2.	$\frac{32}{2} = 16$	$\frac{50}{2} = 25$	$\frac{74}{2} = 37$	$\frac{608}{2} = 304$
Subtract 4 from the quotient.	$16 - 4 = 12$	$25 - 4 = 21$	$37 - 4 = 33$	$304 - 4 = 300$

Because we are asked to write a conjecture that relates the result of this process to the original number selected, let us focus on the result of each case.

Original number selected	4	7	11	100
Result of the process	12	21	33	300

Do you see a pattern? Our conjecture is that the result of the process is three times the original number selected. We have used inductive reasoning.

b. Now we begin with the general case rather than specific examples. We use the variable n to represent any number.

Select a number. — n

Multiply the number by 6. — $6n$ (This means 6 times n.)

Add 8 to the product. — $6n + 8$

Divide this sum by 2. — $\dfrac{6n + 8}{2} = \dfrac{6n}{2} + \dfrac{8}{2} = 3n + 4$

Subtract 4 from the quotient. — $3n + 4 - 4 = 3n$

Using the variable n to represent any number, the result is $3n$, or three times the number n. This proves that the result of the procedure is three times the original number selected for any number. We have used deductive reasoning.

PRACTICE 4 Consider the following procedure:

Select a number. Multiply the number by 4. Add 6 to the product. Divide this sum by 2. Subtract 3 from the quotient.

a. Repeat this procedure for at least four different numbers. Write a conjecture that relates the result of this process to the original number selected.

b. Represent the original number by the variable n and use deductive reasoning to prove the conjecture in part (a).

CHAPTER 12 EXTENSION EXERCISE SET

Identify a pattern in each list of numbers. Then use this pattern to find the next number. (More than one pattern might exist, so it is possible that there is more than one correct answer.)

1. 8, 12, 16, 20, 24, ____
2. 19, 24, 29, 34, 39, ____
3. 37, 32, 27, 22, 17, ____
4. 33, 29, 25, 21, 17, ____
5. 3, 9, 27, 81, 243, ____
6. 2, 8, 32, 128, 512, ____
7. 1, 2, 4, 8, 16, ____
8. 1, 5, 25, 125, ____
9. 1, 4, 1, 8, 1, 16, 1, ____
10. 1, 4, 1, 7, 1, 10, 1, ____
11. 4, 2, 0, −2, −4, ____
12. 6, 3, 0, −3, −6, ____
13. $\frac{1}{2}, \frac{1}{6}, \frac{1}{10}, \frac{1}{14}, \frac{1}{18}$, ____
14. $1, \frac{1}{2}, \frac{1}{3}, \frac{1}{4}, \frac{1}{5}$, ____
15. $1, \frac{1}{3}, \frac{1}{9}, \frac{1}{27}$, ____
16. $1, \frac{1}{2}, \frac{1}{4}, \frac{1}{8}$, ____
17. 3, 7, 12, 18, 25, 33, ____
18. 2, 5, 9, 14, 20, 27, ____
19. 3, 6, 11, 18, 27, 38, ____
20. 2, 5, 10, 17, 26, 37, ____
21. 3, 7, 10, 17, 27, 44, ____
22. 2, 5, 7, 12, 19, 31, ____
23. 2, 7, 12, 5, 10, 15, 8, 13, ____
24. 3, 9, 15, 5, 11, 17, 7, 13, ____
25. 3, 6, 5, 10, 9, 18, 17, 34, ____
26. 2, 6, 5, 15, 14, 42, 41, 123, ____
27. 64, −16, 4, −1, ____
28. 125, −25, 5, −1, ____
29. $(6, 2), (0, -4), \left(7\frac{1}{2}, 3\frac{1}{2}\right), (2, -2), (3, \underline{\quad})$
30. $\left(\frac{2}{3}, \frac{4}{9}\right), \left(\frac{1}{5}, \frac{1}{25}\right), (7, 49), \left(-\frac{5}{6}, \frac{25}{36}\right), \left(-\frac{4}{7}, \underline{\quad}\right)$

Identify a pattern in each sequence of figures. Then use the pattern to find the next figure in the sequence.

31. , , , , ,

32.

33.

34.

Exercises 35–38 describe procedures that are to be applied to numbers. In each exercise,

a. Repeat the procedure for four numbers of your choice. Write a conjecture that relates the result of the process to the original number selected.

b. Represent the original number by the variable n and use deductive reasoning to prove the conjecture in part (a).

35. Select a number. Multiply the number by 4. Add 8 to the product. Divide this sum by 2. Subtract 4 from the quotient.

36. Select a number. Multiply the number by 3. Add 6 to the product. Divide this sum by 3. Subtract the original selected number from the quotient.

37. Select a number. Add 5. Double the result. Subtract 4. Divide by 2. Subtract the original selected number.

38. Select a number. Add 3. Double the result. Add 4. Divide by 2. Subtract the original selected number.

In Exercises 39–44, use inductive reasoning to predict the next line in each sequence of computations. Then use a calculator or perform the arithmetic by hand to determine whether your conjecture is correct.

39.
$$1 + 2 = \frac{2 \times 3}{2}$$
$$1 + 2 + 3 = \frac{3 \times 4}{2}$$
$$1 + 2 + 3 + 4 = \frac{4 \times 5}{2}$$
$$1 + 2 + 3 + 4 + 5 = \frac{5 \times 6}{2}$$

40.
$$3 + 6 = \frac{6 \times 3}{2}$$
$$3 + 6 + 9 = \frac{9 \times 4}{2}$$
$$3 + 6 + 9 + 12 = \frac{12 \times 5}{2}$$
$$3 + 6 + 9 + 12 + 15 = \frac{15 \times 6}{2}$$

41.
$$1 + 3 = 2 \times 2$$
$$1 + 3 + 5 = 3 \times 3$$
$$1 + 3 + 5 + 7 = 4 \times 4$$
$$1 + 3 + 5 + 7 + 9 = 5 \times 5$$

42.
$$\frac{1}{1 \times 2} + \frac{1}{2 \times 3} = \frac{2}{3}$$
$$\frac{1}{1 \times 2} + \frac{1}{2 \times 3} + \frac{1}{3 \times 4} = \frac{3}{4}$$
$$\frac{1}{1 \times 2} + \frac{1}{2 \times 3} + \frac{1}{3 \times 4} + \frac{1}{4 \times 5} = \frac{4}{5}$$

43.
$$9 \times 9 + 7 = 88$$
$$98 \times 9 + 6 = 888$$
$$987 \times 9 + 5 = 8888$$
$$9876 \times 9 + 4 = 88{,}888$$

44.
$$1 \times 9 - 1 = 8$$
$$21 \times 9 - 1 = 188$$
$$321 \times 9 - 1 = 2888$$
$$4321 \times 9 - 1 = 38{,}888$$

In Exercises 45–46, use inductive reasoning to predict the next line in each sequence of computations. Then use a calculator or perform the arithmetic by hand to determine whether your conjecture is correct.

45.
$$33 \times 3367 = 111{,}111$$
$$66 \times 3367 = 222{,}222$$
$$99 \times 3367 = 333{,}333$$
$$132 \times 3367 = 444{,}444$$

46.
$$1 \times 8 + 1 = 9$$
$$12 \times 8 + 2 = 98$$
$$123 \times 8 + 3 = 987$$
$$1234 \times 8 + 4 = 9876$$
$$12{,}345 \times 8 + 5 = 98{,}765$$

47. **Multiple Choice.** Study the pattern in these examples:
$$a^2 \# a^4 = a^{10} \quad a^3 \# a^2 = a^7 \quad a^5 \# a^3 = a^{11}.$$
Select the equation that describes the pattern.

a. $a^x \# a^y = a^{2x+y}$
b. $a^x \# a^y = a^{x+2y}$
c. $a^x \# a^y = a^{x+y+4}$
d. $a^x \# a^y = a^{xy+2}$

48. **Multiple Choice.** Study the pattern in these examples:
$$a^5 * a^3 * a^2 = a^5 \quad a^3 * a^7 * a^2 = a^6 \quad a^2 * a^4 * a^8 = a^7.$$
Select the equation that describes the pattern.

a. $a^x * a^y * a^z = a^{x+y+z}$
b. $a^x * a^y * a^z = a^{\frac{xyz}{2}}$
c. $a^x * a^y * a^z = a^{\frac{x+y+z}{2}}$
d. $a^x * a^y * a^z = a^{\frac{xy}{2}+z}$

49. **Multiple Choice.** Study the pattern, or trend, shown by the data in the bar graph. Then select the expression that *best* describes the number of movie tickets sold, in billions, n years after 2002.

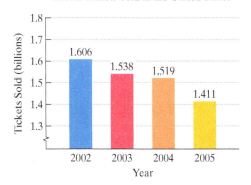

Source: Entertainment Weekly

a. $1.6 + 0.06n$
b. $1.6 + 1.06n$
c. $1.6 - 0.06n$
d. $1.6 - 1.06n$

50. Multiple Choice. The data displayed by the graph indicate that watching movies at home is becoming more popular. Study the pattern, or trend, shown by the data. Then select the expression that *best* describes the number of hours Americans watched prerecorded movies at home n years after 2004.

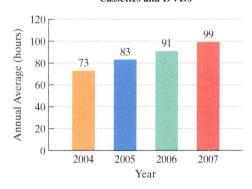

Number of Hours Americans Age 12 and Older Watch Prerecorded Video Cassettes and DVDs

Source: U.S. Census Bureau

a. $73.6 + 12.5n$
b. $73.6 + 8.6n$
c. $73.6 - 12.5n$
d. $73.6 - 8.6n$

In Exercises 51–54, identify the reasoning process, induction or deduction, in each example. Explain your answer.

51. It can be shown that
$$1 + 2 + 3 + \cdots + n = \frac{n(n+1)}{2}.$$
I can use this formula to conclude that the sum of the first one hundred counting numbers, $1 + 2 + 3 + \cdots + 100$, is
$$\frac{100(100+1)}{2} = \frac{100(101)}{2} = 50(101), \text{ or } 5050.$$

52. The course policy states that work turned in late will be marked down a grade. I turned in my report a day late, so it was marked down from B to C.

53. Multiple Steps. The ancient Greeks studied **figurate numbers,** so named because of their representations as geometric arrangements of points.

Triangular Numbers

1 3 6 10 15 21

Square Numbers

1 4 9 16 25

Pentagonal Numbers

1 5 12 22

a. Use inductive reasoning to write the five triangular numbers that follow 21.

b. Use inductive reasoning to write the five square numbers that follow 25.

c. Use inductive reasoning to write the five pentagonal numbers that follow 22.

d. Use inductive reasoning to complete this statement: If a triangular number is multiplied by 8 and then 1 is added to the product, a _____ number is obtained.

54. The triangular arrangement of numbers shown below is known as **Pascal's triangle,** credited to French mathematician Blaise Pascal (1623–1662). Use inductive reasoning to find the six numbers designated by question marks.

```
        1
       1 1
      1 2 1
     1 3 3 1
    1 4 6 4 1
   ? ? ? ? ? ?
```

55. The word *induce* comes from a Latin term meaning to lead. Explain what leading has to do with inductive reasoning.

56. Describe what is meant by deductive reasoning. Give an example.

57. Give an example of a decision that you made recently in which the method of reasoning you used to reach the decision was induction. Describe your reasoning process.

58. If $(6 - 2)^2 = 36 - 24 + 4$ and $(8 - 5)^2 = 64 - 80 + 25$, use inductive reasoning to write a compatible expression for $(11 - 7)^2$.

59. Study the first three figures. Then use inductive reasoning to determine the area of the same type of figure with a radius of 9 and a height of 10.

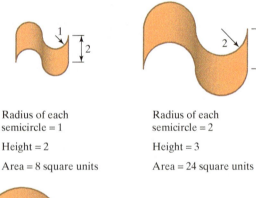

Radius of each semicircle = 1
Height = 2
Area = 8 square units

Radius of each semicircle = 2
Height = 3
Area = 24 square units

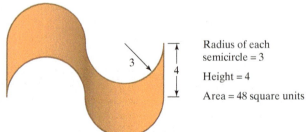

Radius of each semicircle = 3
Height = 4
Area = 48 square units

60. Write a list of numbers that has two patterns so that the next number in the list can be 15 or 20.

61. Multiple Steps. a. Repeat the following procedure with at least five people. Write a conjecture that relates the result of the procedure to each person's birthday.

Take the number of the month of your birthday (January = 1, February = 2,..., December = 12), multiply by 5, add 6, multiply this sum by 4, add 9, multiply this new sum by 5, and add the number of the day on which you were born. Finally, subtract 165.

b. Let M represent the month number and let D represent the day number of any person's birthday. Use deductive reasoning to prove your conjecture in part (a).

62. **Multiple Steps. a.** Use a calculator to find 6×6, 66×66, 666×666, and 6666×6666.

b. Describe a pattern in the numbers being multiplied and the resulting products.

c. Use the pattern to write the next two multiplications and their products. Then use your calculator to verify these results.

d. Is this process an example of inductive or deductive reasoning? Explain your answer.

63. **Multiple Steps. a.** Use a calculator to find 3367×3, 3367×6, 3367×9, and 3367×12.

b. Describe a pattern in the numbers being multiplied and the resulting products.

c. Use the pattern to write the next two multiplications and their products. Then use your calculator to verify these results.

d. Is this process an example of inductive or deductive reasoning? Explain your answer.

CHAPTER 12 VOCABULARY CHECK

Fill in each blank with one of the words or phrases listed below.

| general term | common difference | finite sequence | common ratio | Pascal's triangle |
| infinite sequence | factorial of n | arithmetic sequence | geometric sequence | series |

1. A(n) _____ is a function whose domain is the set of natural numbers $\{1, 2, 3, \ldots, n\}$, where n is some natural number.

2. The _____, written $n!$, is the product of the first n consecutive natural numbers.

3. A(n) _____ is a function whose domain is the set of natural numbers.

4. A(n) _____ is a sequence in which each term (after the first) is obtained by multiplying the preceding term by a constant amount r. The constant r is called the _____ of the sequence.

5. The sum of the terms of a sequence is called a _____.

6. The nth term of the sequence a_n is called the _____.

7. A(n) _____ is a sequence in which each term (after the first) differs from the preceding term by a constant amount d. The constant d is called the _____ of the sequence.

8. A(n) triangle array of the coefficients of the terms of the expansions of $(a + b)^n$ is called _____.

CHAPTER 12 REVIEW

(12.1) Find the indicated term(s) of the given sequence.

1. The first five terms of the sequence $a_n = -3n^2$

2. The first five terms of the sequence $a_n = n^2 + 2n$

3. The one-hundredth term of the sequence $a_n = \dfrac{(-1)^n}{100}$

4. The fiftieth term of the sequence $a_n = \dfrac{2n}{(-1)^2}$

5. The general term a_n of the sequence $\dfrac{1}{6}, \dfrac{1}{12}, \dfrac{1}{18}, \ldots$

6. The general term a_n of the sequence $-1, 4, -9, 16, \ldots$

Solve the following applications.

7. The distance in feet that an olive falling from rest in a vacuum will travel during each second is given by an arithmetic sequence whose general term is $a_n = 32n - 16$, where n is the number of the second. Find the distance the olive will fall during the fifth, sixth, and seventh seconds.

8. A culture of yeast doubles every day in a geometric progression whose general term is $a_n = 100(2)^{n-1}$, where n is the number of the day just ending. Find how many days it takes the yeast culture to measure at least 10,000. Find the original measure of the yeast culture.

9. The Colorado Forest Service reported that western pine beetle infestation, which kills trees, affected approximately 660,000 acres of lodgepole forests in Colorado in 2006. The forest service predicts that during the next 5 years, the beetles will infest twice the number of acres per year as the year before. Write out the first 5 terms of this geometric sequence, and predict the number of acres of infested trees there will be in 2010.

10. The first row of an amphitheater contains 50 seats, and each row thereafter contains 8 additional seats. Write the first ten terms

of this arithmetic progression, and find the number of seats in the tenth row.

(12.2)

11. Find the first five terms of the geometric sequence whose first term is -2 and whose common ratio is $\frac{2}{3}$.

12. Find the first five terms of the arithmetic sequence whose first term is 12 and whose common difference is -1.5.

13. Find the thirtieth term of the arithmetic sequence whose first term is -5 and whose common difference is 4.

14. Find the eleventh term of the arithmetic sequence whose first term is 2 and whose common difference is $\frac{3}{4}$.

15. Find the twentieth term of the arithmetic sequence whose first three terms are 12, 7, and 2.

16. Find the sixth term of the geometric sequence whose first three terms are 4, 6, and 9.

17. If the fourth term of an arithmetic sequence is 18 and the twentieth term is 98, find the first term and the common difference.

18. If the third term of a geometric sequence is -48 and the fourth term is 192, find the first term and the common ratio.

19. Find the general term of the sequence $\frac{3}{10}, \frac{3}{100}, \frac{3}{1000}, \ldots$.

20. Find a general term that satisfies the terms shown for the sequence $50, 58, 66, \ldots$.

Determine whether each of the following sequences is arithmetic, geometric, or neither. If a sequence is arithmetic, find a_1 and d. If a sequence is geometric, find a_1 and r.

21. $\frac{8}{3}, 4, 6, \ldots$

22. $-10.5, -6.1, -1.7$

23. $7x, -14x, 28x$

24. $3x^2, 9x^4, 81x^8, \ldots$

Solve the following applications.

25. To test the bounce of a racquetball, the ball is dropped from a height of 8 feet. The ball is judged "good" if it rebounds at least 75% of its previous height with each bounce. Write out the first six terms of this geometric sequence (round to the nearest tenth). Determine if a ball is "good" that rebounds to a height of 2.5 feet after the fifth bounce.

26. A display of oil cans in an auto parts store has 25 cans in the bottom row, 21 cans in the next row, and so on, in an arithmetic progression. Find the general term and the number of cans in the top row.

27. Suppose that you save $1 the first day of a month, $2 the second day, $4 the third day, continuing to double your savings each day. Write the general term of this geometric sequence and find the amount you will save on the tenth day. Estimate the amount you will save on the thirtieth day of the month, and check your estimate with a calculator.

28. On the first swing, the length of an arc through which a pendulum swings is 30 inches. The length of the arc for each successive swing is 70% of the preceding swing. Find the length of the arc for the fifth swing.

29. Rosa takes a job that has a monthly starting salary of $900 and guarantees her a monthly raise of $150 during her 6-month training period. Find the general term of this sequence and her salary at the end of her training.

30. A sheet of paper is $\frac{1}{512}$-inch thick. By folding the sheet in half, the total thickness will be $\frac{1}{256}$ inch. A second fold produces a total thickness of $\frac{1}{128}$ inch. Estimate the thickness of the stack after 15 folds, and then check your estimate with a calculator.

(12.3) *Write out the terms and find the sum for each of the following.*

31. $\sum_{i=1}^{5}(2i-1)$

32. $\sum_{i=1}^{5}i(i+2)$

33. $\sum_{i=2}^{4}\frac{(-1)^i}{2i}$

34. $\sum_{i=3}^{5}5(-1)^{i-1}$

Find the partial sum of the given sequence.

35. S_4 of the sequence $a_n = (n-3)(n+2)$

36. S_6 of the sequence $a_n = n^2$

37. S_5 of the sequence $a_n = -8 + (n-1)3$

38. S_3 of the sequence $a_n = 5(4)^{n-1}$

Write the sum with Σ notation.

39. $1 + 3 + 9 + 27 + 81 + 243$

40. $6 + 2 + (-2) + (-6) + (-10) + (-14) + (-18)$

41. $\frac{1}{4} + \frac{1}{16} + \frac{1}{64} + \frac{1}{256}$

42. $1 + \left(-\frac{3}{2}\right) + \frac{9}{4}$

Solve.

43. A yeast colony begins with 20 yeast and doubles every 8 hours. Write the sequence that describes the growth of the yeast, and find the total yeast after 48 hours.

44. The number of cranes born each year in a new aviary forms a sequence whose general term is $a_n = n^2 + 2n - 1$. Find the

number of cranes born in the fourth year and the total number of cranes born in the first four years.

45. Harold has a choice between two job offers. Job A has an annual starting salary of $39,500 with guaranteed annual raises of $2200 for the next four years, whereas job B has an annual starting salary of $41,000 with guaranteed annual raises of $1400 for the next four years. Compare the salaries for the fifth year under each job offer.

46. A sample of radioactive waste is decaying such that the amount decaying in kilograms during year n is $a_n = 200(0.5)^n$. Find the amount of decay in the third year, and the total amount of decay in the first three years.

(12.4) Find the partial sum of the given sequence.

47. The sixth partial sum of the sequence 15, 19, 23, ...

48. The ninth partial sum of the sequence 5, −10, 20, ...

49. The sum of the first 30 odd positive integers

50. The sum of the first 20 positive multiples of 7

51. The sum of the first 20 terms of the sequence 8, 5, 2, ...

52. The sum of the first eight terms of the sequence $\frac{3}{4}, \frac{9}{4}, \frac{27}{4}, \ldots$

53. S_4 if $a_1 = 6$ and $r = 5$

54. S_{100} if $a_1 = -3$ and $d = -6$

Find the sum of each infinite geometric sequence.

55. $5, \frac{5}{2}, \frac{5}{4}, \ldots$

56. $18, -2, \frac{2}{9}, \ldots$

57. $-20, -4, -\frac{4}{5}, \ldots$

58. $0.2, 0.02, 0.002, \ldots$

Solve.

59. A frozen yogurt store owner cleared $20,000 the first year he owned his business and made an additional 15% over the previous year in each subsequent year. Find how much he made during his fourth year of business. Find his total earnings during the first 4 years (round to the nearest dollar).

60. On his first morning in a television assembly factory, a trainee takes 0.8 times as long to assemble each television as he took to assemble the one before. If it took him 40 minutes to assemble the first television, find how long it takes him to assemble the fourth television. Find the total time he takes to assemble the first four televisions (round to the nearest minute).

61. During the harvest season a farmer can rent a combine machine for $100 the first day, with the rental fee decreasing $7 for each additional day. Find how much the farmer pays for the rental on the seventh day. Find how much total rent the farmer pays for 7 days.

62. A rubber ball is dropped from a height of 15 feet and rebounds 80% of its previous height after each bounce. Find the total distance the ball travels before it comes to rest.

63. After a pond was sprayed once with insecticide, 1800 mosquitoes were killed the first day, 600 the second day, 200 the third day, and so on. Find the total number of mosquitoes killed during the first 6 days after the spraying (round to the nearest unit).

64. See Exercise 63. Find the day on which the insecticide is no longer effective, and find the total number of mosquitoes killed (round to the nearest mosquito).

65. Use the formula S_∞ to write $0.5\overline{55}$ as a fraction.

66. A movie theater has 27 seats in the first row, 30 seats in the second row, 33 seats in the third row, and so on. Find the total number of seats in the theater if there are 20 rows.

(12.5) Use Pascal's triangle to expand each binomial.

67. $(x + z)^5$

68. $(y - r)^6$

69. $(2x + y)^4$

70. $(3y - z)^4$

Use the binomial formula to expand the following.

71. $(b + c)^8$

72. $(x - w)^7$

73. $(4m - n)^4$

74. $(p - 2r)^5$

Find the indicated term.

75. The fourth term of the expansion of $(a + b)^7$

76. The eleventh term of the expansion of $(y + 2z)^{10}$

MIXED REVIEW

77. Evaluate: $\sum_{i=1}^{4} i^2(i + 1)$

78. Find the fifteenth term of the arithmetic sequence whose first three terms are 14, 8, and 2.

79. Find the sum of the infinite geometric sequence 27, 9, 3, 1, ...

80. Expand: $(2x - 3)^4$

CHAPTER 12 TEST

Find the indicated term(s) of the given sequence.

1. The first five terms of the sequence $a_n = \dfrac{(-1)^n}{n+4}$

2. The eightieth term of the sequence $a_n = 10 + 3(n-1)$

3. The general term of the sequence $\dfrac{2}{5}, \dfrac{2}{25}, \dfrac{2}{125}, \ldots$

4. The general term of the sequence $-9, 18, -27, 36, \ldots$

Find the partial sum of the given sequence.

5. S_5 of the sequence $a_n = 5(2)^{n-1}$

6. S_{30} of the sequence $a_n = 18 + (n-1)(-2)$

7. S_∞ of the sequence $a_1 = 24$ and $r = \dfrac{1}{6}$

8. S_∞ of the sequence $\dfrac{3}{2}, -\dfrac{3}{4}, \dfrac{3}{8}, \ldots$

9. $\displaystyle\sum_{i=1}^{4} i(i-2)$

10. $\displaystyle\sum_{i=2}^{4} 5(2)^i (-1)^{i-1}$

Expand each binomial.

11. $(a-b)^6$

12. $(2x+y)^5$

Solve the following applications.

13. The population of a small town is growing yearly according to the sequence defined by $a_n = 250 + 75(n-1)$, where n is the number of the year just beginning. Predict the population at the beginning of the tenth year. Find the town's initial population.

14. A gardener is making a triangular planting with one shrub in the first row, three shrubs in the second row, five shrubs in the third row, and so on, for eight rows. Write the finite series of this sequence, and find the total number of shrubs planted.

15. A pendulum swings through an arc of length 80 centimeters on its first swing. On each successive swing, the length of the arc is $\dfrac{3}{4}$ the length of the arc on the preceding swing. Find the length of the arc on the fourth swing, and find the total arc length for the first four swings.

16. See Exercise 15. Find the total arc length before the pendulum comes to rest.

17. A parachutist in free-fall falls 16 feet during the first second, 48 feet during the second second, 80 feet during the third second, and so on. Find how far he falls during the tenth second. Find the total distance he falls during the first 10 seconds.

18. Use the formula S_∞ to write $0.4\overline{242}$ as a fraction.

CHAPTER 12 STANDARDIZED TEST

Multiple Choice. *Choose the one alternative that best completes the statement or answers the question. Find the indicated term(s) of the given sequence.*

1. The first five terms of the sequence $a_n = \dfrac{(-1)^n}{n^2 + 2}$

   a. $-\dfrac{1}{3}, \dfrac{1}{6}, -\dfrac{1}{11}, \dfrac{1}{18}, -\dfrac{1}{27}$

   b. $\dfrac{1}{3}, -\dfrac{1}{6}, \dfrac{1}{11}, -\dfrac{1}{18}, \dfrac{1}{27}$

   c. $\dfrac{1}{2}, -\dfrac{1}{3}, \dfrac{1}{6}, -\dfrac{1}{11}, \dfrac{1}{18}$

   d. $-\dfrac{1}{3}, \dfrac{1}{6}, -\dfrac{1}{11}, \dfrac{1}{18}, \dfrac{1}{27}$

2. The eighth term of the sequence $a_n = -3 - 4(n-1)$

   a. -31 b. 29 c. 25 d. -35

3. The general term of the sequence $3, \dfrac{3}{5}, \dfrac{3}{25}, \dfrac{3}{125}, \dfrac{3}{625}, \ldots$

   a. $a_n = 3\left(\dfrac{1}{25}\right)^{n-1}$ b. $a_n = 3\left(\dfrac{1}{5}\right)^n$

   c. $a_n = 3\left(\dfrac{1}{5}\right)^{n-1}$ d. $a_n = 3\left(\dfrac{1}{5}\right)^{n+1}$

4. The general term of the sequence $-6, 36, -216, 1296, \ldots$

   a. $a_n = (-1)^{n+1} 6^{n+1}$ b. $a_n = (-1)^n 6^n$

   c. $a_n = 6^{n+1}$ d. $a_n = 6^n$

Find the partial sum of the given sequence.

5. S_5 of the sequence $a_n = 2(4)^{n-1}$
   a. 41   b. 42   c. 341   d. 682

6. S_{45} of the sequence $a_n = -14 + 8(n-1)$
   a. 6640   b. 7290   c. 7128   d. 7470

7. S_∞ of the sequence $a_1 = 13, r = \dfrac{1}{5}$
   a. $\dfrac{65}{4}$ b. $\dfrac{65}{6}$ c. $\dfrac{13}{6}$ d. $\dfrac{13}{4}$

8. S_∞ of the sequence $5, -\dfrac{5}{4}, \dfrac{5}{16}, \ldots$
   a. $\dfrac{15}{4}$ b. $-\dfrac{5}{4}$ c. 4   d. 5

9. $\displaystyle\sum_{i=2}^{4} i(i+3)$
   a. 56   b. 60   c. 27   d. 38

10. $\displaystyle\sum_{i=3}^{5} 9(3)^i(-1)^{i-1}$
    a. -1215 b. 1647   c. 3159   d. 1701

Expand the binomial.

11. $(w - s)^6$
    a. $w^6 - 6w^5s + 15w^4s^2 - 20w^3s^3 + 15w^2s^4 - 6ws^5 + s^6$
    b. $w^6 - 6w^5s - 30w^4s^2 + 120w^3s^3 + 360w^2s^4 - 720ws^5 - 720s^6$
    c. $w^6 - 8w^5s + 17w^4s^2 - 22w^3s^3 + 17w^2s^4 - 8ws^5 + s^6$
    d. $w^6 - s^6$

12. $(3x - 3y)^3$
    a. $27x^3 - 81x^2y + 81xy^2 - 27y^3$
    b. $9x^3y - 9x^2y^2 + 9xy^3$
    c. $27x^3 - 27x^2y + 27xy^2 - 27y^3$
    d. $9x^3y - 18x^2y^2 + 9xy^3$

Solve the problem.

13. The population of a small town is growing yearly according to the sequence defined by $a_n = 300 + 65(n-1)$, where n is the number of the year just beginning. Predict the population at the beginning of the eighth year. Find the town's initial population.
    a. 755 people; 300 people initially
    b. 755 people; 365 people initially
    c. 820 people; 365 people initially
    d. 820 people; 300 people initially

14. A stocker at a grocery store has created a display of stacked cans such that the top row contains 4 cans, the second row contains 7 cans, the third row contains 10 cans, and so on for six rows. Write the finite series of this sequence, and find the total number of cans in the display.
    a. $7 + 10 + 13 + 16 + 19 + 22$; 87 cans
    b. $4 + 7 + 10 + 13 + 16 + 19$; 49 cans
    c. $4 + 7 + 10 + 13 + 16 + 19$; 69 cans
    d. $7 + 10 + 13 + 16 + 19 + 22$; 67 cans

15. A pendulum swings through an arc of length 50 inches on its first swing. On each successive swing, the length of the arc is $\dfrac{5}{6}$ the length of the arc on the preceding swing. Find the length of the arc on the fifth swing, and find the total arc length for the first five swings. Round to two decimal places.
    a. 20.09 in.; 179.44 in.
    b. 24.11 in.; 155.32 in.
    c. 20.09 in.; 155.32 in.
    d. 24.11 in.; 179.44 in.

16. A pendulum swings through an arc 40 inches long on its first swing. Each swing thereafter, it swings only $\dfrac{3}{5}$ as far as on the previous swing. How far will it swing altogether before coming to a complete stop? If necessary, round to the nearest inch.
    a. 133 in.   b. 50 in.   c. 100 in.   d. 67 in.

17. A gambler has a specific betting system where the first bet made is $16, the second bet made is $32, the third bet is $64, and so on. Find how much the gambler bets on the seventh bet. Find the total amount of money the gambler has bet over the first seven bets.
    a. $224; 688
    b. $192; 912
    c. $224; 912
    d. $192; 688

18. Use the formula S_∞ to write $0.4\overline{040}$ as a fraction.
    a. $\dfrac{4000}{99}$ b. $\dfrac{2}{5}$ c. $\dfrac{1}{25}$ d. $\dfrac{40}{99}$

CHAPTER

13 Counting Methods and Probability Theory

- **13.1** The Fundamental Counting Principle
- **13.2** Permutations
- **13.3** Combinations
- **13.4** Fundamentals of Probability

  Integrated Review
- **13.5** Probability with the Fundamental Counting Principle, Permutations, and Combinations
- **13.6** Events Involving *NOT* AND *OR*; ODDS
- **13.7** Events Involving *AND*; Conditional Probability
- **13.8** The Normal Distribution
- **Extension** Expected Value

The Saffir/Simpson Hurricane Scale

Category	Winds (Miles per Hour)
1	74–95
2	96–110
3	111–130
4	131–155
5	>155

The Saffir/Simpson scale assigns numbers 1 through 5 to measure the disaster potential of a hurricane's winds.

In this chapter, we study counting and probability. In one particular application, we calculate the probability that South Florida will be hit by a hurricane at least once in the next ten years.

13.1 THE FUNDAMENTAL COUNTING PRINCIPLE

OBJECTIVE

1. Use the Fundamental Counting Principle to determine the number of possible outcomes in a given situation.

OBJECTIVE 1 ▶ Use the Fundamental Counting Principle. Let's suppose this morning you are selecting the clothes you will wear today. You have two pairs of jeans to choose from (one blue, one black) and three T-shirts to choose from (one beige, one yellow, and one blue). Your morning decision is illustrated in the figure below.

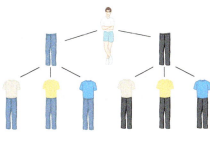

FIGURE 13.1 Selecting a wardrobe

The **tree diagram,** so named because of its branches, shows that you can form six different outfits from your two pairs of jeans and three T-shirts. Each pair of jeans can be combined with one of three T-shirts. Notice that the total number of outfits can be obtained by multiplying the number of choices for the jeans, 2, by the number of choices for the T-shirts, 3:

$$2 \cdot 3 = 6.$$

We can generalize this idea to any two groups of items—not just jeans and T-shirts—with the **Fundamental Counting Principle.**

The Fundamental Counting Principle

If you can choose one item from a group of M items and a second item from a group of N items, then the total number of two-item choices is $M \cdot N$.

EXAMPLE 1 Applying the Fundamental Counting Principle

A restaurant offers 6 appetizers and 14 main courses. In how many ways can a person order a two-course meal?

Solution Choosing from one of 6 appetizers and one of 14 main courses, the total number of two-course meals is

$$6 \cdot 14 = 84.$$

A person can order a two-course meal in 84 different ways.

PRACTICE 1 Another restaurant offers 10 appetizers and 15 main courses. In how many ways can you order a two-course meal?

The Fundamental Counting Principle with More Than Two Groups of Items

Let's continue our earlier clothing decision by now including a decision of shoes. You have two pairs of sneakers to choose from—one black and one red. Your possible outfits, including sneakers, are shown on the next page.

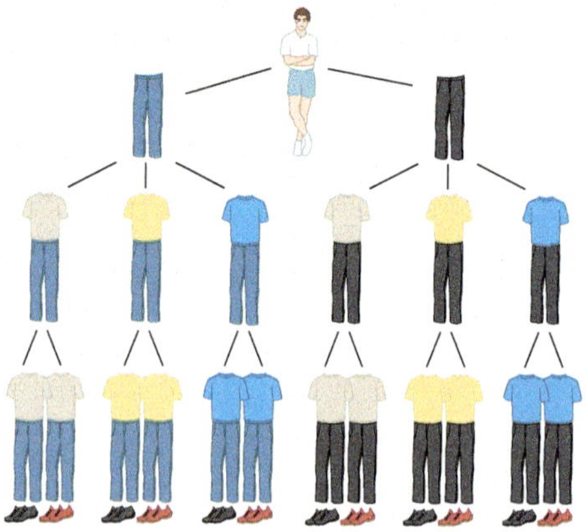

FIGURE 13.2 Increasing wardrobe selections

The tree diagram shows that you can form 12 outfits from your two pairs of jeans, three T-shirts, and two pairs of sneakers. Notice that the number of outfits can be obtained by multiplying the number of choices for jeans, 2, the number of choices for T-shirts, 3, and the number of choices for sneakers, 2:

$$2 \cdot 3 \cdot 2 = 12.$$

Unlike your earlier decision, you are now dealing with *three* groups of items. The Fundamental Counting Principle can be extended to determine the number of possible outcomes in situations in which there are three or more groups of items.

The Fundamental Counting Principle

The number of ways in which a series of successive things can occur is found by multiplying the number of ways in which each thing can occur.

For example, if you own 30 pairs of jeans, 20 T-shirts, and 12 pairs of sneakers, you have

$$30 \cdot 20 \cdot 12 = 7200$$

choices for your wardrobe.

EXAMPLE 2 Options in Planning a Course Schedule

Next year you are planning to take three courses in college—math, English, and humanities. Based on time blocks and highly recommended professors, there are 8 sections of math, 5 of English, and 4 of humanities that you find suitable. Assuming no scheduling conflicts, how many different three-course schedules are possible?

Solution This situation involves making choices with three groups of items.

$$\underbrace{\boxed{\text{Math}}}_{\text{8 choices}} \quad \underbrace{\boxed{\text{English}}}_{\text{5 choices}} \quad \underbrace{\boxed{\text{Humanities}}}_{\text{4 choices}}$$

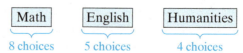

We use the Fundamental Counting Principle to find the number of three-course schedules. Multiply the number of choices for each of the three groups.

$$8 \cdot 5 \cdot 4 = 160$$

Thus, there are 160 different three-course schedules. □

PRACTICE 2 A pizza can be ordered with two choices of size (medium or large), three choices of crust (thin, thick, or regular), and five choices of toppings (ground beef, sausage, pepperoni, bacon, or mushrooms). How many different one-topping pizzas can be ordered?

EXAMPLE 3 Car of the Future

Car manufacturers are now experimenting with lightweight three-wheel cars, designed for one person, and considered ideal for city driving. Intrigued? Suppose you could order such a car with a choice of 9 possible colors, with or without air conditioning, electric or gas powered, and with or without an onboard computer. In how many ways can this car be ordered with regard to these options?

Solution This situation involves making choices with four groups of items.

We use the Fundamental Counting Principle to find the number of ordering options. Multiply the number of choices for each of the four groups.

$$9 \cdot 2 \cdot 2 \cdot 2 = 72$$

Thus, the car can be ordered in 72 different ways.

PRACTICE 3 The car in Example 3 is now available in 10 possible colors. The options involving air conditioning, power, and an onboard computer still apply. Furthermore, the car is available with or without a global positioning system (for pinpointing your location at every moment). In how many ways can this car be ordered in terms of these options?

EXAMPLE 4 A Multiple-Choice Test

You are taking a multiple-choice test that has ten questions. Each of the questions has four answer choices, with one correct answer per question. If you select one of these four choices for each question and leave nothing blank, in how many ways can you answer the questions?

Solution This situation involves making choices with ten questions.

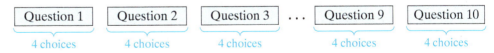

We use the Fundamental Counting Principle to determine the number of ways that you can answer the questions on the test. Multiply the number of choices, 4, for each of the ten questions.

$$4 \cdot 4 \cdot 4 \cdot 4 \cdot 4 \cdot 4 \cdot 4 \cdot 4 \cdot 4 \cdot 4 = 4^{10} = 1,048,576 \quad \text{Use a calculator: } 4 \boxed{y^x} 10 \boxed{=}.$$

Thus, you can answer the questions in 1,048,576 different ways.

Are you surprised that there are over one million ways of answering a ten-question multiple-choice test? Of course, there is only one way to answer the test and receive a perfect score. The probability of guessing your way into a perfect score involves calculating the chance of getting a perfect score, just one way, from all 1,048,576 possible outcomes. In short, prepare for the test and do not rely on guessing!

PRACTICE 4 You are taking a multiple-choice test that has six questions. Each of the questions has three answer choices, with one correct answer per question. If you select one of these three choices for each question and leave nothing blank, in how many ways can you answer the questions?

EXAMPLE 5 Telephone Numbers in the United States

Telephone numbers in the United States begin with three-digit area codes followed by seven-digit local telephone numbers. Area codes and local telephone numbers cannot begin with 0 or 1. How many different telephone numbers are possible?

Solution This situation involves making choices with ten groups of items.

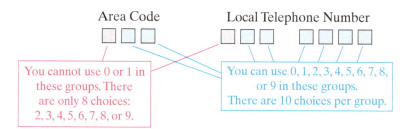

Here are the choices for each of the ten groups of items:

Area Code |8|10|10| **Local Telephone Number** |8|10|10| |10|10|10|10|.

We use the Fundamental Counting Principle to determine the number of different telephone numbers that are possible. The total number of telephone numbers possible is

$$8 \cdot 10 \cdot 10 \cdot 8 \cdot 10 \cdot 10 \cdot 10 \cdot 10 \cdot 10 \cdot 10 = 6{,}400{,}000{,}000.$$

There are six billion four hundred million different telephone numbers that are possible.

PRACTICE 5 An electronic gate can be opened by entering five digits on a keypad containing the digits 0, 1, 2, 3, ..., 8, 9. How many different keypad sequences are possible if the digit 0 cannot be used as the first digit?

13.1 EXERCISE SET

PRACTICE AND APPLICATION EXERCISES

Solve Exercises 1–6 using the Fundamental Counting Principle with two groups of items.

1. A restaurant offers 8 appetizers and 10 main courses. In how many ways can a person order a two-course meal?

2. The model of the car you are thinking of buying is available in nine different colors and three different styles (hatchback, sedan, or station wagon). In how many ways can you order the car?

3. A popular brand of pen is available in three colors (red, green, or blue) and four writing tips (bold, medium, fine, or micro). How many different choices of pens do you have with this brand?

4. In how many ways can a casting director choose a female lead and a male lead from five female actors and six male actors?

5. A student is planning a two-part trip. The first leg of the trip is from San Francisco to New York, and the second leg is from New York to Paris. From San Francisco to New York, travel options include airplane, train, or bus. From New York to Paris, the options are limited to airplane or ship. In how many ways can the two-part trip be made?

6. For a temporary job between semesters, you are painting the parking spaces for a new shopping mall with a letter of the alphabet and a single digit from 1 to 9. The first parking space is A1 and the last parking space is Z9. How many parking spaces can you paint with distinct labels?

Solve Exercises 7–22 using the Fundamental Counting Principle with three or more groups of items.

7. An ice cream store sells two drinks (sodas or milk shakes), in four sizes (small, medium, large, or jumbo), and five flavors (vanilla, strawberry, chocolate, coffee, or pistachio). In how many ways can a customer order a drink?

8. A pizza can be ordered with three choices of size (small, medium, or large), four choices of crust (thin, thick, crispy, or regular), and six choices of toppings (ground beef, sausage, pepperoni, bacon, mushrooms, or onions). How many one-topping pizzas can be ordered?

9. A restaurant offers the following limited lunch menu.

Main Course	Vegetables	Beverages	Desserts
Ham	Potatoes	Coffee	Cake
Chicken	Peas	Tea	Pie
Fish	Green beans	Milk	Ice cream
Beef		Soda	

If one item is selected from each of the four groups, in how many ways can a meal be ordered? Describe two such orders.

10. An apartment complex offers apartments with four different options, designated by A through D.

A	B	C	D
one bedroom	one bathroom	first floor	lake view
two bedrooms	two bathrooms	second floor	golf course view
three bedrooms			no special view

How many apartment options are available? Describe two such options.

11. Shoppers in a large shopping mall are categorized as male or female, over 30 or 30 and under, and cash or credit card shoppers. In how many ways can the shoppers be categorized?

12. There are three highways from city A to city B, two highways from city B to city C, and four highways from city C to city D. How many different highway routes are there from city A to city D?

13. A person can order a new car with a choice of six possible colors, with or without air conditioning, with or without automatic transmission, with or without power windows, and with or without a CD player. In how many different ways can a new car be ordered with regard to these options?

14. A car model comes in nine colors, with or without air conditioning, with or without a sun roof, with or without automatic transmission, and with or without antilock brakes. In how many ways can the car be ordered with regard to these options?

15. You are taking a multiple-choice test that has five questions. Each of the questions has three answer choices, with one correct answer per question. If you select one of these three choices for each question and leave nothing blank, in how many ways can you answer the questions?

16. You are taking a multiple-choice test that has eight questions. Each of the questions has three answer choices, with one correct answer per question. If you select one of these three choices for each question and leave nothing blank, in how many ways can you answer the questions?

17. In the original plan for area codes in 1945, the first digit could be any number from 2 through 9, the second digit was either 0 or 1, and the third digit could be any number except 0. With this plan, how many different area codes are possible?

18. The local seven-digit telephone numbers in Inverness, California, have 669 as the first three digits. How many different telephone numbers are possible in Inverness?

19. License plates in a particular state display two letters followed by three numbers, such as AT-887 or BB-013. How many different license plates can be manufactured for this state?

20. How many different four-letter radio station call letters can be formed if the first letter must be W or K?

21. A stock can go up, go down, or stay unchanged. How many possibilities are there if you own seven stocks?

22. A social security number contains nine digits, such as 074-66-7795. How many different social security numbers can be formed?

WRITING IN MATHEMATICS

23. Explain the Fundamental Counting Principle.

24. Figure 13.2 shows that a tree diagram can be used to find the total number of outfits. Describe one advantage of using the Fundamental Counting Principle rather than a tree diagram.

25. Write an original problem that can be solved using the Fundamental Counting Principle. Then solve the problem.

CRITICAL THINKING EXERCISES

26. How many four-digit odd numbers are there? Assume that the digit on the left cannot be 0.

27. In order to develop a more appealing hamburger, a franchise used taste tests with 12 different buns, 30 sauces, 4 types of lettuce, and 3 types of tomatoes. If the taste test was done at one restaurant by one tester who took 10 minutes to eat each hamburger, approximately how long would it take the tester to eat all possible hamburgers?

GROUP EXERCISE

28. The group should select real-world situations where the Fundamental Counting Principle can be applied. These can involve the number of possible student ID numbers on your campus, the number of possible phone numbers in your community, the number of meal options at a local restaurant, and the number of ways a person in the group can select outfits for class. Once situations have been selected, group members should determine in how many ways each part of the task can be done. Group members will need to obtain menus, find out about telephone-digit requirements in the community, count shirts, pants, shoes in closets, and so on. Once the group reassembles, apply the Fundamental Counting Principle to determine the number of available options in each situation. Because these numbers may be quite large, use a calculator.

13.2 PERMUTATIONS

OBJECTIVES

1. Use the Fundamental Counting Principle to count permutations.
2. Evaluate factorial expressions.
3. Use the permutations formula.
4. Find the number of permutations of duplicate items.

OBJECTIVE 1 ▶ **Use the Fundamental Counting Principle to count permutations.**

Suppose you are in charge of scheduling the order of 4 musical groups playing in a concert. You can choose any of the four groups as the first performer. Once you've chosen the first group, you'll have three groups left to choose from for the second performer. You'll then have two groups left to choose from for the third performance. After the first three performers are determined, you'll have only one group left for the final appearance in the concert. This situation can be shown as follows:

We use the Fundamental Counting Principle to find the number of ways you can put together the concert. Multiply the choices:

$$4 \cdot 3 \cdot 2 \cdot 1 = 24.$$

Thus, there are 24 different ways to arrange the concert. Such an ordered arrangement is called a *permutation* of the four groups.

A **permutation** is an ordered arrangement of items that occurs when

- No item is used more than once. (Each group performs exactly once.)
- The order of arrangement makes a difference. (It will make a difference in terms of how the concert is received if a musical group is the first or the last to perform.)

EXAMPLE 1 Counting Permutations

Based on their long-standing contribution to music, you decide that musical Group B should be the last group to perform at the four-group concert. Given this decision, in how many ways can you put together the concert?

Solution You can now choose any one of the three groups, A, C, or D as the opening act. Once you've chosen the first group, you'll have two groups left to choose from for the second performance. You'll then have just one group left to choose for the third performance. There is also just one choice for the closing act—musical group B. This situation can be shown as follows:

We use the Fundamental Counting Principle to find the number of ways you can put together the concert. Multiply the choices:

$$3 \cdot 2 \cdot 1 \cdot 1 = 6.$$

Thus, there are six different ways to arrange the concert if Group B is the final group to perform.

PRACTICE 1 For the concert in Example 1, suppose that Group C is to be the opening act and that Group B is to be the last group to perform. In how many ways can you put together the concert?

EXAMPLE 2 Counting Permutations

You need to arrange seven of your favorite books along a small shelf. How many different ways can you arrange the books, assuming that the order of the books makes a difference to you?

Solution You may choose any of the seven books for the first position on the shelf. This leaves six choices for second position. After the first two positions are filled, there are five books to choose from for third position, four choices left for the fourth position, three choices left for the fifth position, then two choices for the sixth position, and only one choice for the last position. This situation can be shown as follows:

We use the Fundamental Counting Principle to find the number of ways you can arrange the seven books along the shelf. Multiply the choices:

$$7 \cdot 6 \cdot 5 \cdot 4 \cdot 3 \cdot 2 \cdot 1 = 5040.$$

Thus, you can arrange the books in 5040 ways. There are 5040 different possible permutations.

PRACTICE 2 In how many ways can you arrange five books along a shelf, assuming that the order of the books makes a difference?

OBJECTIVE 2 ▶ Factorial notation. Recall from Section 12.5 that the product in Example 2,

$$7 \cdot 6 \cdot 5 \cdot 4 \cdot 3 \cdot 2 \cdot 1$$

is given a special name and symbol. It is called 7 **factorial,** and written 7!. Thus,

$$7! = 7 \cdot 6 \cdot 5 \cdot 4 \cdot 3 \cdot 2 \cdot 1.$$

To review, if n is a positive integer, then $n!$ (n *factorial*) is the product of all positive integers from n down through 1. For example,

$$1! = 1$$
$$2! = 2 \cdot 1 = 2$$
$$3! = 3 \cdot 2 \cdot 1 = 6$$
$$4! = 4 \cdot 3 \cdot 2 \cdot 1 = 24$$
$$5! = 5 \cdot 4 \cdot 3 \cdot 2 \cdot 1 = 120$$
$$6! = 6 \cdot 5 \cdot 4 \cdot 3 \cdot 2 \cdot 1 = 720.$$

Factorials From 0 Through 20

0!	1
1!	1
2!	2
3!	6
4!	24
5!	120
6!	720
7!	5040
8!	40,320
9!	362,880
10!	3,628,800
11!	39,916,800
12!	479,001,600
13!	6,227,020,800
14!	87,178,291,200
15!	1,307,674,368,000
16!	20,922,789,888,000
17!	355,687,428,096,000
18!	6,402,373,705,728,000
19!	121,645,100,408,832,000
20!	2,432,902,008,176,640,000

As n increases, $n!$ grows very rapidly. Factorial growth is more explosive than exponential growth discussed in Chapter 10.

Factorial Notation

If n is a positive integer, the notation $n!$ (read "n factorial") is the product of all positive integers from n down through 1.

$$n! = n(n-1)(n-2) \cdots (3)(2)(1)$$

0! (zero factorial), by definition, is 1.

$$0! = 1$$

736 CHAPTER 13 Counting Methods and Probability Theory

> **EXAMPLE 3** Using Factorial Notation
>
> Evaluate the following factorial expressions without using the factorial key on your calculator:
>
> **a.** $\dfrac{8!}{5!}$ **b.** $\dfrac{26!}{21!}$ **c.** $\dfrac{500!}{499!}$.

TECHNOLOGY NOTE

Most calculators have a key or menu item for calculating factorials. Here are the keystrokes for finding 9!:

MANY SCIENTIFIC CALCULATORS:

9 $\boxed{x!}$ $\boxed{=}$

MANY GRAPHING CALCULATORS:

9 $\boxed{!}$ $\boxed{\text{ENTER}}$.

Because *n!* becomes quite large as *n* increases, your calculator will display these larger values in scientific notation.

Solution

a. We can evaluate the numerator and the denominator of $\frac{8!}{5!}$. However, it is easier to use the following simplification:

$$\frac{8!}{5!} = \frac{8 \cdot 7 \cdot 6 \cdot \boxed{5 \cdot 4 \cdot 3 \cdot 2 \cdot 1}}{\boxed{5 \cdot 4 \cdot 3 \cdot 2 \cdot 1}} = \frac{8 \cdot 7 \cdot 6 \cdot \boxed{5!}}{\boxed{5!}} = \frac{8 \cdot 7 \cdot 6 \cdot \cancel{5!}}{\cancel{5!}} = 8 \cdot 7 \cdot 6 = 336.$$

b. Rather than write out 26!, the numerator of $\frac{26!}{21!}$, as the product of all integers from 26 down to 1, we can express 26! as

$$26! = 26 \cdot 25 \cdot 24 \cdot 23 \cdot 22 \cdot 21!.$$

In this way, we can cancel 21! in the numerator and the denominator of the given expression.

$$\frac{26!}{21!} = \frac{26 \cdot 25 \cdot 24 \cdot 23 \cdot 22 \cdot 21!}{21!} = \frac{26 \cdot 25 \cdot 24 \cdot 23 \cdot 22 \cdot \cancel{21!}}{\cancel{21!}}$$
$$= 26 \cdot 25 \cdot 24 \cdot 23 \cdot 22 = 7{,}893{,}600$$

c. In order to cancel identical factorials in the numerator and the denominator of $\frac{500!}{499!}$, we can express 500! as $500 \cdot 499!$.

$$\frac{500!}{499!} = \frac{500 \cdot 499!}{499!} = \frac{500 \cdot \cancel{499!}}{\cancel{499!}} = 500$$

PRACTICE 3 Evaluate without using a calculator's factorial key:

a. $\dfrac{9!}{6!}$ **b.** $\dfrac{16!}{11!}$ **c.** $\dfrac{100!}{99!}$.

OBJECTIVE 3 ▶ A formula for permutations. You are the coach of a little league baseball team. There are 13 players on the team. You need to choose a batting order having 9 players. The order makes a difference, because, for instance, if bases are loaded and your best hitter is fourth or fifth at bat, his possible home run will drive in three additional runs. How many batting orders can you form?

You can choose any of 13 players for the first person at bat. Then you will have 12 players from which to choose the second batter, then 11 from which to choose the third batter, and so on. The situation can be shown as follows:

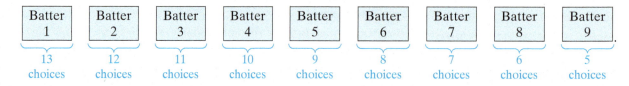

The total number of batting orders is

$$13 \cdot 12 \cdot 11 \cdot 10 \cdot 9 \cdot 8 \cdot 7 \cdot 6 \cdot 5 = 259{,}459{,}200.$$

Nearly 260 million batting orders are possible for your 13-player little league team. Each batting order is a permutation because the order of the batters makes a difference. The number of permutations of 13 players taken 9 at a time is 259,459,200.

We can obtain a formula for finding the number of permutations by rewriting our computation:

$$13 \cdot 12 \cdot 11 \cdot 10 \cdot 9 \cdot 8 \cdot 7 \cdot 6 \cdot 5$$

$$= \frac{13 \cdot 12 \cdot 11 \cdot 10 \cdot 9 \cdot 8 \cdot 7 \cdot 6 \cdot 5 \cdot \boxed{4 \cdot 3 \cdot 2 \cdot 1}}{\boxed{4 \cdot 3 \cdot 2 \cdot 1}} = \frac{13!}{4!} = \frac{13!}{(13-9)!}.$$

Thus, the number of permutations of 13 things taken 9 at a time is $\frac{13!}{(13-9)!}$. The special notation $_{13}P_9$ is used to replace the phrase "the number of permutations of 13 things taken 9 at a time." Using this new notation, we can write

$$_{13}P_9 = \frac{13!}{(13-9)!}.$$

The numerator of this expression is the factorial of the number of items, 13 team members: 13!. The denominator is also a factorial. It is the factorial of the difference between the number of items, 13, and the number of items in each permutation, 9 batters: $(13-9)!$.

The notation $_nP_r$ means the **number of permutations of n things taken r at a time**. We can generalize from the situation in which 9 batters were taken from 13 players. By generalizing, we obtain the following formula for the number of permutations if r items are taken from n items:

> **Permutations of n Things Taken r at a Time**
>
> The number of possible permutations if r items are taken from n items is
>
> $$_nP_r = \frac{n!}{(n-r)!}.$$

▶ **Helpful Hint**

Because all permutation problems are also Fundamental Counting problems, they can be solved using the formula for $_nP_r$ or using the Fundamental Counting Principle.

TECHNOLOGY NOTE

Graphing calculators have a menu item for calculating permutations, usually labeled $\boxed{_nP_r}$. For example, to find $_{20}P_3$, the keystrokes are

20 $\boxed{_nP_r}$ 3 $\boxed{\text{ENTER}}$.

```
20 nPr 3
              6840
```

If you are using a scientific calculator, check your manual for the location of the menu item for calculating permutations and the required keystrokes.

EXAMPLE 4 Using the Formula for Permutations

You and 19 of your friends have decided to form an Internet marketing consulting firm. The group needs to choose three officers—a CEO, an operating manager, and a treasurer. In how many ways can those offices be filled?

Solution Your group is choosing $r = 3$ officers from a group of $n = 20$ people (you and 19 friends). The order in which the officers are chosen matters because the CEO, the operating manager, and the treasurer each have different responsibilities. Thus, we are looking for the number of permutations of 20 things taken 3 at a time. We use the formula

$$_nP_r = \frac{n!}{(n-r)!}$$

with $n = 20$ and $r = 3$.

$$_{20}P_3 = \frac{20!}{(20-3)!} = \frac{20!}{17!} = \frac{20 \cdot 19 \cdot 18 \cdot 17!}{17!} = \frac{20 \cdot 19 \cdot 18 \cdot \cancel{17!}}{\cancel{17!}} = 20 \cdot 19 \cdot 18 = 6840$$

Thus, there are 6840 different ways of filling the three offices.

PRACTICE 4 A corporation has seven members on its board of directors. In how many different ways can it elect a president, vice-president, secretary, and treasurer?

738 CHAPTER 13 Counting Methods and Probability Theory

EXAMPLE 5 Using the Formula for Permutations

You are working for The Sitcom Television Network. Your assignment is to help set up the television schedule for Monday evenings between 7 and 10 P.M. You need to schedule a show in each of six 30-minute time blocks, beginning with 7 to 7:30 and ending with 9:30 to 10:00. You can select from among the following situation comedies: *Home Improvement, Seinfeld, Mad About You, Cheers, Friends, Frasier, All in the Family, I Love Lucy, M*A*S*H, The Larry Sanders Show, The Jeffersons, Married with Children,* and *Happy Days*. How many different programming schedules can be arranged?

Solution You are choosing $r = 6$ situation comedies from a collection of $n = 13$ classic sitcoms. The order in which the programs are aired matters. Family-oriented comedies have higher ratings when aired in earlier time blocks, such as 7 to 7:30. By contrast, comedies with adult themes do better in later time blocks. In short, we are looking for the number of permutations of 13 things taken 6 at a time. We use the formula

$$_nP_r = \frac{n!}{(n-r)!}$$

with $n = 13$ and $r = 6$.

$$_{13}P_6 = \frac{13!}{(13-6)!} = \frac{13!}{7!} = \frac{13 \cdot 12 \cdot 11 \cdot 10 \cdot 9 \cdot 8 \cdot 7!}{7!} = 13 \cdot 12 \cdot 11 \cdot 10 \cdot 9 \cdot 8 = 1{,}235{,}520$$

There are 1,235,520 different programming schedules that can be arranged. □

PRACTICE 5 How many different programming schedules can be arranged by choosing 5 situation comedies from a collection of 9 classic sitcoms?

OBJECTIVE 4 ▶ Permutations of duplicate items. The number of permutations of the letters in the word SET is 3!, or 6. The six permutations are

SET,   STE,   EST,   ETS,   TES,   TSE.

Are there also six permutations of the letters in the name ANA? The answer is no. Unlike SET, with three distinct letters, ANA contains three letters, of which the two As are duplicates. If we rearrange the letters just as we did with SET, we obtain

ANA,   AAN,   NAA,   NAA,   ANA,   AAN.

Without the use of color to distinguish between the two As, there are only three distinct permutations: ANA, AAN, NAA.

There is a formula for finding the number of distinct permutations when duplicate items exist:

> **Permutations of Duplicate Items**
>
> The number of permutations of n items, where p items are identical, q items are identical, r items are identical, and so on, is given by
>
> $$\frac{n!}{p!\,q!\,r!\ldots}.$$

For example, ANA contains three letters ($n = 3$), where two of the letters are identical ($p = 2$). The number of distinct permutations is

$$\frac{n!}{p!} = \frac{3!}{2!} = \frac{3 \cdot 2!}{2!} = 3.$$

We saw that the three distinct permutations are ANA, AAN, and NAA.

TECHNOLOGY NOTE

Parentheses are necessary to enclose the factorials in the denominator when using a calculator to find

$$\frac{11!}{4!\,4!\,2!}.$$

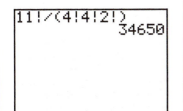

EXAMPLE 6 Using the Formula for Permutations of Duplicate Items

In how many distinct ways can the letters of the word MISSISSIPPI be arranged?

Solution The word contains 11 letters ($n = 11$), where four Is are identical ($p = 4$), four Ss are identical ($q = 4$), and 2 Ps are identical ($r = 2$). The number of distinct permutations is

$$\frac{n!}{p!\,q!\,r!} = \frac{11!}{4!\,4!\,2!} = \frac{11 \cdot 10 \cdot 9 \cdot 8 \cdot 7 \cdot 6 \cdot 5 \cdot 4!}{4!\,4 \cdot 3 \cdot 2 \cdot 1 \cdot 2 \cdot 1} = 34{,}650$$

There are 34,650 distinct ways the letters in the word MISSISSIPPI can be arranged. □

PRACTICE 6 In how many ways can the letters of the word OSMOSIS be arranged?

13.2 EXERCISE SET

PRACTICE AND APPLICATION EXERCISES

Use the Fundamental Counting Principle to solve Exercises 1–12.

1. Six performers are to present their comedy acts on a weekend evening at a comedy club. How many different ways are there to schedule their appearances?

2. Five singers are to perform on a weekend evening at a night club. How many different ways are there to schedule their appearances?

3. In the *Cambridge Encyclopedia of Language* (Cambridge University Press, 1987), author David Crystal presents five sentences that make a reasonable paragraph regardless of their order. The sentences are as follows:

    Mark had told him about the foxes.
    John looked out of the window.
    Could it be a fox?
    However, nobody had seen one for months.
    He thought he saw a shape in the bushes.

    In how many different orders can the five sentences be arranged?

4. In how many different ways can a police department arrange eight suspects in a police lineup if each lineup contains all eight people?

5. As in Exercise 1, six performers are to present their comedy acts on a weekend evening at a comedy club. One of the performers insists on being the last stand-up comic of the evening. If this performer's request is granted, how many different ways are there to schedule the appearances?

6. As in Exercise 2, five singers are to perform at a night club. One of the singers insists on being the last performer of the evening. If this singer's request is granted, how many different ways are there to schedule the appearances?

7. You need to arrange nine of your favorite books along a small shelf. How many different ways can you arrange the books, assuming that the order of the books makes a difference to you?

8. You need to arrange ten of your favorite photographs on the mantel above a fireplace. How many ways can you arrange the photographs, assuming that the order of the pictures makes a difference to you?

In Exercises 9–10, use the five sentences that are given in Exercise 3.

9. How many different five-sentence paragraphs can be formed if the paragraph begins with "He thought he saw a shape in the bushes" and ends with "John looked out of the window"?

10. How many different five-sentence paragraphs can be formed if the paragraph begins with "He thought he saw a shape in the bushes" followed by "Mark had told him about the foxes"?

11. A television programmer is arranging the order that five movies will be seen between the hours of 6 P.M. and 4 A.M. Two of the movies have a G rating, and they are to be shown in the first two time blocks. One of the movies is rated NC-17, and it is to be shown in the last of the time blocks, from 2 A.M. until 4 A.M. Given these restrictions, in how many ways can the five movies be arranged during the indicated time blocks?

12. A camp counselor and six campers are to be seated along a picnic bench. In how many ways can this be done if the counselor must be seated in the middle and a camper who has a tendency to engage in food fights must sit to the counselor's immediate left?

In Exercises 13–32, evaluate each factorial expression.

13. $\dfrac{9!}{6!}$
14. $\dfrac{12!}{10!}$
15. $\dfrac{29!}{25!}$

16. $\dfrac{31!}{28!}$
17. $\dfrac{19!}{11!}$
18. $\dfrac{17!}{9!}$

19. $\dfrac{600!}{599!}$
20. $\dfrac{700!}{699!}$
21. $\dfrac{104!}{102!}$

22. $\dfrac{106!}{104!}$
23. $7! - 3!$
24. $6! - 3!$

25. $(7 - 3)!$
26. $(6 - 3)!$
27. $\left(\dfrac{12}{4}\right)!$

28. $\left(\dfrac{45}{9}\right)!$
29. $\dfrac{7!}{(7 - 2)!}$
30. $\dfrac{8!}{(8 - 5)!}$

31. $\dfrac{13!}{(13 - 3)!}$
32. $\dfrac{17!}{(17 - 3)!}$

In Exercises 33–40, use the formula for $_nP_r$ to evaluate each expression.

33. $_9P_4$
34. $_7P_3$
35. $_8P_5$
36. $_{10}P_4$
37. $_6P_6$
38. $_9P_9$
39. $_8P_0$
40. $_6P_0$

Use the formula for $_nP_r$ to solve Exercises 41–48.

41. A club with ten members is to choose three officers—president, vice-president, and secretary-treasurer. If each office is to be held by one person and no person can hold more than one office, in how many ways can those offices be filled?

42. A corporation has seven members on its board of directors. In how many different ways can it elect a president, vice-president, secretary, and treasurer?

43. For a segment of a radio show, a disc jockey can play 7 records. If there are 13 records to select from, in how many ways can the program for this segment be arranged?

44. Suppose you are asked to list, in order of preference, the three best movies you have seen this year. If you saw 20 movies during the year, in how many ways can the three best be chosen and ranked?

45. In a race in which six automobiles are entered and there are no ties, in how many ways can the first three finishers come in?

46. In a production of *West Side Story*, eight actors are considered for the male roles of Tony, Riff, and Bernardo. In how many ways can the director cast the male roles?

47. Nine bands have volunteered to perform at a benefit concert, but there is only enough time for five of the bands to play. How many lineups are possible?

48. How many arrangements can be made using four of the letters of the word COMBINE if no letter is to be used more than once?

Use the formula for the number of permutations of duplicate items to solve Exercises 49–56.

49. In how many distinct ways can the letters of the word DALLAS be arranged?

50. In how many distinct ways can the letters of the word SCIENCE be arranged?

51. How many distinct permutations can be formed using the letters of the word TALLAHASSEE?

52. How many distinct permutations can be formed using the letters of the word TENNESSEE?

53. In how many ways can the digits in the number 5,446,666 be arranged?

54. In how many ways can the digits in the number 5,432,435 be arranged?

In Exercises 55–56, a signal can be formed by running different colored flags up a pole, one above the other.

55. Find the number of different signals consisting of eight flags that can be made using three white flags, four red flags, and one blue flag.

56. Find the number of different signals consisting of nine flags that can be made using three white flags, five red flags, and one blue flag.

WRITING IN MATHEMATICS

57. What is a permutation?
58. Explain how to find $n!$, where n is a positive integer.
59. Explain the best way to evaluate $\frac{900!}{899!}$ without a calculator.
60. Describe what $_nP_r$ represents.
61. Write a word problem that can be solved by evaluating $5!$.
62. Write a word problem that can be solved by evaluating $_7P_3$.
63. If 24 permutations can be formed using the letters in the word BAKE, why can't 24 permutations also be formed using the letters in the word BABE? How is the number of permutations in BABE determined?

CRITICAL THINKING EXERCISES

64. Ten people board an airplane that has 12 aisle seats. In how many ways can they be seated if they all select aisle seats?

65. Six horses are entered in a race. If two horses are tied for first place, and there are no ties among the other four horses, in how many ways can the six horses cross the finish line?

66. Performing at a concert are eight rock bands and eight jazz groups. How many ways can the program be arranged if the first, third, and eighth performers are jazz groups?

67. Five men and five women line up at a checkout counter in a store. In how many ways can they line up if the first person in line is a woman, and the people in line alternate woman, man, woman, man, and so on?

68. How many four-digit odd numbers less than 6000 can be formed using the digits 2, 4, 6, 7, 8, and 9?

69. Express $_nP_{n-2}$ without using factorials.

13.3 COMBINATIONS

OBJECTIVES

1. Distinguish between permutation and combination problems.
2. Solve problems involving combinations using the combinations formula.

Suppose you survey your friends and ask each the same question: "Of these five colors—red, blue, yellow, green, purple—which three are your favorite?"

OBJECTIVE 1 ▶ Distinguish between permutation and combination problems. One friend answers, "yellow, blue, and purple." Another responds, "purple, blue, and yellow." These two people have the same colors in their group of selections, even if they are named in a different order. We are interested *in which colors are named, not* *the order in which they are named.* Because the colors are taken without regard to order, this is not a permutation problem. No ranking of any sort is involved.

Later on, you ask your roommate which three colors she would select for your survey. She names red, green, and purple. Her selection is different from those of your two other friends because different colors are cited.

Mathematicians describe the group of colors given by your roommate as a *combination*. A **combination** of items occurs when

- The items are selected from the same group (the five colors).
- No item is used more than once. (You may adore red, but your three selections cannot be red, red, and red.)
- The order of items makes no difference. (Yellow, blue, and purple is the same group as purple, blue, and yellow.)

Do you see the difference between a permutation and a combination? A permutation is an ordered arrangement of a given group of items. A combination is a group of items taken without regard to their order. **Permutation** problems involve situations in which **order matters. Combination** problems involve situations in which the **order** of items **makes no difference.**

EXAMPLE 1   Distinguishing between Permutations and Combinations

For each of the following problems, determine whether the problem is one involving permutations or combinations. (It is not necessary to solve the problem.)

a. Six students are running for student government president, vice-president, and treasurer. The student with the greatest number of votes becomes the president, the second highest vote-getter becomes vice-president, and the student who gets the third largest number of votes will be treasurer. How many different outcomes are possible for these three positions?

b. Six people are on the board of supervisors for your neighborhood park. A three-person committee is needed to study the possibility of expanding the park. How many different committees could be formed from the six people?

c. Baskin-Robbins offers 31 different flavors of ice cream. One of their items is a bowl consisting of three scoops of ice cream, each a different flavor. How many such bowls are possible?

Solution

a. Students are choosing three student government officers from six candidates. The order in which the officers are chosen makes a difference because each of the offices (president, vice-president, treasurer) is different. Order matters. This is a problem involving permutations.

b. A three-person committee is to be formed from the six-person board of supervisors. The order in which the three people are selected does not matter because they are not filling different roles on the committee. Because order makes no difference, this is a problem involving combinations.

c. A three-scoop bowl of three different flavors is to be formed from Baskin-Robbin's 31 flavors. The order in which the three scoops of ice cream are put into the bowl is irrelevant. A bowl with chocolate, vanilla, and strawberry is exactly the same as a bowl with vanilla, strawberry, and chocolate. Different orderings do not change things, and so this is a problem involving combinations.

PRACTICE

1 For each of the following problems, determine whether the problem is one involving permutations or combinations. (It is not necessary to solve the problem.)

a. How many ways can you select 6 free DVDs from a list of 200 DVDs?

b. In a race in which there are 50 runners and no ties, in how many ways can the first three finishers come in?

OBJECTIVE 2 ▶ A formula for combinations. We have seen that the notation $_nP_r$ means the number of permutations of n things taken r at a time. Similarly, the notation $_nC_r$ **means the number of combinations of n things taken r at a time.**

We can develop a formula for $_nC_r$ by comparing permutations and combinations. Consider the letters A, B, C, and D. The number of permutations of these four letters taken three at a time is

$$_4P_3 = \frac{4!}{(4-3)!} = \frac{4!}{1!} = \frac{4 \cdot 3 \cdot 2 \cdot 1}{1} = 24.$$

Here are the 24 permutations:

ABC,	ABD,	ACD,	BCD,
ACB,	ADB,	ADC,	BDC,
BAC,	BAD,	CAD,	CBD,
BCA,	BDA,	CDA,	CDB,
CAB,	DAB,	DAC,	DBC,
CBA,	DBA,	DCA,	DCB.

This column contains only one combination, ABC.
This column contains only one combination, ABD.
This column contains only one combination, ACD.
This column contains only one combination, BCD.

Because the order of items makes no difference in determining combinations, each column of six permutations represents one combination. There are a total of four combinations:

ABC, ABD, ACD, BCD.

Thus, $_4C_3 = 4$: The number of combinations of 4 things taken 3 at a time is 4. With 24 permutations and only four combinations, there are 6, or 3!, times as many permutations as there are combinations.

In general, there are $r!$ times as many permutations of n things taken r at a time as there are combinations of n things taken r at a time. Thus, we find the number of combinations of n things taken r at a time by dividing the number of permutations of n things taken r at a time by $r!$.

$$_nC_r = \frac{_nP_r}{r!} = \frac{\frac{n!}{(n-r)!}}{r!} = \frac{n!}{(n-r)!\,r!}$$

▶ **Helpful Hint**

The number of combinations if r items are taken from n items cannot be found using the Fundamental Counting Principle and requires the use of the formula shown on the right.

Combinations of n Things Taken r at a Time

The number of possible combinations if r items are taken from n items is

$$_nC_r = \frac{n!}{(n-r)!\,r!}.$$

EXAMPLE 2 Using the Formula for Combinations

A three-person committee is needed to study ways of improving public transportation. How many committees could be formed from the eight people on the board of supervisors?

Solution The order in which the three people are selected does not matter. This is a problem of selecting $r = 3$ people from a group of $n = 8$ people. We are looking for the number of combinations of eight things taken three at a time. We use the formula

$$_nC_r = \frac{n!}{(n-r)!\,r!}$$

Section 13.3 Combinations

with $n = 8$ and $r = 3$.

$$_8C_3 = \frac{8!}{(8-3)!\,3!} = \frac{8!}{5!\,3!} = \frac{8 \cdot 7 \cdot 6 \cdot 5!}{5! \cdot 3 \cdot 2 \cdot 1} = \frac{8 \cdot 7 \cdot 6 \cdot \cancel{5!}}{\cancel{5!} \cdot 3 \cdot 2 \cdot 1} = 56$$

Thus, 56 committees of three people each can be formed from the eight people on the board of supervisors.

TECHNOLOGY NOTE

Graphing calculators have a menu item for calculating combinations, usually labeled $_nC_r$. For example, to find $_8C_3$, the keystrokes on most graphing calculators are

8 $_nC_r$ 3 ENTER.

If you are using a scientific calculator, check your manual to see whether there is a menu item for calculating combinations.

If you use your calculator's factorial key to find $\frac{8!}{5!\,3!}$, be sure to enclose the factorials in the denominator with parentheses

8 ! ÷ (5 ! × 3 !)

pressing = or ENTER to obtain the answer.

PRACTICE 2 You volunteer to pet-sit for your friend who has seven different animals. How many different pet combinations are possible if you take three of the seven pets?

EXAMPLE 3 Using the Formula for Combinations

In poker, a person is dealt 5 cards from a standard 52-card deck. The order in which you are dealt the 5 cards does not matter. How many different 5-card poker hands are possible?

Solution Because the order in which the 5 cards are dealt does not matter, this is a problem involving combinations. We are looking for the number of combinations of $n = 52$ cards drawn $r = 5$ at a time. We use the formula

$$_nC_r = \frac{n!}{(n-r)!\,r!}$$

with $n = 52$ and $r = 5$.

$$_{52}C_5 = \frac{52!}{(52-5)!\,5!} = \frac{52!}{47!\,5!} = \frac{52 \cdot 51 \cdot 50 \cdot 49 \cdot 48 \cdot \cancel{47!}}{\cancel{47!} \cdot 5 \cdot 4 \cdot 3 \cdot 2 \cdot 1} = 2{,}598{,}960$$

Thus, there are 2,598,960 different 5-card poker hands possible. It surprises many people that more than 2.5 million 5-card hands can be dealt from a mere 52 cards.

If you are a card player, it does not get any better than to be dealt the 5-card poker hand shown in Figure 13.3. This hand is called a *royal flush*. It consists of an ace, king, queen, jack, and 10, all of the same suit: all hearts, all diamonds, all clubs, or all spades. The probability of being dealt a royal flush involves calculating the number of ways of being dealt such a hand: just 4 of all 2,598,960 possible hands. In the next section, we move from counting possibilities to computing probabilities.

FIGURE 13.3 A royal flush

PRACTICE 3 How many different 4-card hands can be dealt from a deck that has 16 different cards?

There are situations in which both the formula for combinations and the Fundamental Counting Principle are used together. Let's say that the U.S. Senate, with 100 members, consists of 54 Republicans and 46 Democrats. We want to form a committee of 3 Republicans and 2 Democrats.

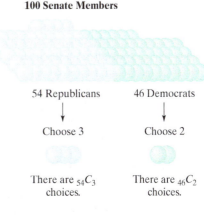

100 Senate Members

54 Republicans → Choose 3 → There are $_{54}C_3$ choices.

46 Democrats → Choose 2 → There are $_{46}C_2$ choices.

By the Fundamental Counting Principle, the number of ways of choosing 3 Republicans and 2 Democrats is given by

$$_{54}C_3 \cdot {}_{46}C_2.$$

In Example 4, we develop these ideas in more detail.

EXAMPLE 4 Using the Formula for Combinations and the Fundamental Counting Principle

The U.S. Senate of the 104th Congress consisted of 54 Republicans and 46 Democrats. How many committees can be formed if each committee must have 3 Republicans and 2 Democrats?

Solution The order in which the members are selected does not matter. Thus, this is a problem involving combinations.

We begin with the number of ways of selecting 3 Republicans out of 54 Republicans without regard to order. We are looking for the number of combinations of $n = 54$ people taken $r = 3$ people at a time. We use the formula

$$_nC_r = \frac{n!}{(n-r)!\,r!}$$

with $n = 54$ and $r = 3$.

$$_{54}C_3 = \frac{54!}{(54-3)!\,3!} = \frac{54!}{51!\,3!} = \frac{54 \cdot 53 \cdot 52 \cdot \cancel{51!}}{\cancel{51!} \cdot 3 \cdot 2 \cdot 1} = \frac{54 \cdot 53 \cdot 52}{3 \cdot 2 \cdot 1} = 24{,}804$$

There are 24,804 choices for forming 3-member Republican committees.

Next, we find the number of ways of selecting 2 Democrats out of 46 Democrats without regard to order. We are looking for the number of combinations of $n = 46$ people taken $r = 2$ people at a time. Once again, we use the formula

$$_nC_r = \frac{n!}{(n-r)!\,r!}.$$

This time, $n = 46$ and $r = 2$.

$$_{46}C_2 = \frac{46!}{(46-2)!\,2!} = \frac{46!}{44!\,2!} = \frac{46 \cdot 45 \cdot \cancel{44!}}{\cancel{44!} \cdot 2 \cdot 1} = 1035$$

There are 1035 choices for forming 2-member Democratic committees.

We use the Fundamental Counting Principle to find the number of committees that can be formed:

$$_{54}C_3 \cdot {}_{46}C_2 = 24{,}804 \cdot 1035 = 25{,}672{,}140.$$

Thus, 25,672,140 committees can be formed.

PRACTICE 4 The U.S. Senate of the 107th Congress consisted of 50 Democrats, 49 Republicans, and one Independent. How many committees can be formed if each committee must have 3 Democrats and 2 Republicans?

13.3 EXERCISE SET

PRACTICE EXERCISES

In Exercises 1–4, does the problem involve permutations or combinations? Explain your answer. (It is not necessary to solve the problem.)

1. A medical researcher needs 6 people to test the effectiveness of an experimental drug. If 13 people have volunteered for the test, in how many ways can 6 people be selected?
2. Fifty people purchase raffle tickets. Three winning tickets are selected at random. If first prize is $1000, second prize is $500, and third prize is $100, in how many different ways can the prizes be awarded?
3. How many different four-letter passwords can be formed from the letters A, B, C, D, E, F, and G if no repetition of letters is allowed?
4. Fifty people purchase raffle tickets. Three winning tickets are selected at random. If each prize is $500, in how many different ways can the prizes be awarded?

In Exercises 5–20, use the formula for $_nC_r$ to evaluate each expression.

5. $_6C_5$
6. $_8C_7$
7. $_9C_5$
8. $_{10}C_6$
9. $_{11}C_4$
10. $_{12}C_5$
11. $_8C_1$
12. $_7C_1$
13. $_7C_7$
14. $_4C_4$
15. $_{30}C_3$
16. $_{25}C_4$
17. $_5C_0$
18. $_6C_0$
19. $\dfrac{_7C_3}{_5C_4}$
20. $\dfrac{_{10}C_3}{_6C_4}$

PRACTICE PLUS

In Exercises 21–28, evaluate each expression.

21. $\dfrac{_7P_3}{3!} - {_7C_3}$
22. $\dfrac{_{20}P_2}{2!} - {_{20}C_2}$
23. $1 - \dfrac{_3P_2}{_4P_3}$
24. $1 - \dfrac{_5P_3}{_{10}P_4}$
25. $\dfrac{_7C_3}{_5C_4} - \dfrac{98!}{96!}$
26. $\dfrac{_{10}C_3}{_6C_4} - \dfrac{46!}{44!}$
27. $\dfrac{_4C_2 \cdot {_6C_1}}{_{18}C_3}$
28. $\dfrac{_5C_1 \cdot {_7C_2}}{_{12}C_3}$

APPLICATION EXERCISES

Use the formula for $_nC_r$ to solve Exercises 29–36.

29. An election ballot asks voters to select three city commissioners from a group of six candidates. In how many ways can this be done?
30. A four-person committee is to be elected from an organization's membership of 11 people. How many different committees are possible?
31. Of 12 possible books, you plan to take 4 with you on vacation. How many different collections of 4 books can you take?
32. There are 14 standbys who hope to get seats on a flight, but only 6 seats are available on the plane. How many different ways can the 6 people be selected?
33. You volunteer to help drive children at a charity event to the zoo, but you can fit only 8 of the 17 children present in your van. How many different groups of 8 children can you drive?
34. Of the 100 people in the U.S. Senate, 18 serve on the Foreign Relations Committee. How many ways are there to select Senate members for this committee (assuming party affiliation is not a factor in the selection)?
35. To win at LOTTO in the state of Florida, one must correctly select 6 numbers from a collection of 53 numbers (1 through 53). The order in which the selection is made does not matter. How many different selections are possible?
36. To win in the New York State lottery, one must correctly select 6 numbers from 59 numbers. The order in which the selection is made does not matter. How many different selections are possible?

In Exercises 37–46, solve by the method of your choice.

37. In a race in which six automobiles are entered and there are no ties, in how many ways can the first four finishers come in?
38. A book club offers a choice of 8 books from a list of 40. In how many ways can a member make a selection?
39. A medical researcher needs 6 people to test the effectiveness of an experimental drug. If 13 people have volunteered for the test, in how many ways can 6 people be selected?
40. Fifty people purchase raffle tickets. Three winning tickets are selected at random. If first prize is $1000, second prize is $500, and third prize is $100, in how many different ways can the prizes be awarded?
41. From a club of 20 people, in how many ways can a group of three members be selected to attend a conference?
42. Fifty people purchase raffle tickets. Three winning tickets are selected at random. If each prize is $500, in how many different ways can the prizes be awarded?
43. How many different four-letter passwords can be formed from the letters A, B, C, D, E, F, and G if no repetition of letters is allowed?
44. Nine comedy acts will perform over two evenings. Five of the acts will perform on the first evening. How many ways can the schedule for the first evening be made?
45. Using 15 flavors of ice cream, how many cones with three different flavors can you create if it is important to you which flavor goes on the top, middle, and bottom?
46. Baskin-Robbins offers 31 different flavors of ice cream. One of its items is a bowl consisting of three scoops of ice cream, each a different flavor. How many such bowls are possible?

Use the formula for $_nC_r$ and the Fundamental Counting Principle to solve Exercises 47–50.

47. In how many ways can a committee of four men and five women be formed from a group of seven men and seven women?
48. How many different committees can be formed from 5 professors and 15 students if each committee is made up of 2 professors and 10 students?
49. The U.S. Senate of the 109th Congress consisted of 55 Republicans, 44 Democrats, and 1 Independent. How many committees can be formed if each committee must have 4 Republicans and 3 Democrats?
50. A mathematics exam consists of 10 multiple-choice questions and 5 open-ended problems in which all work must be

shown. If an examinee must answer 8 of the multiple-choice questions and 3 of the open-ended problems, in how many ways can the questions and problems be chosen?

WRITING IN MATHEMATICS

51. What is a combination?
52. Explain how to distinguish between permutation and combination problems.
53. Write a word problem that can be solved by evaluating $_7C_3$.

CRITICAL THINKING EXERCISES

54. Write a word problem that can be solved by evaluating $_{10}C_3 \cdot {}_7C_2$.
55. A 6/53 lottery involves choosing 6 of the numbers from 1 through 53 and a 5/36 lottery involves choosing 5 of the numbers from 1 through 36. The order in which the numbers are chosen does not matter. Which lottery is easier to win? Explain your answer.
56. If the number of permutations of n objects taken r at a time is six times the number of combinations of n objects taken r at a time, determine the value of r. Is there enough information to determine the value of n? Why or why not?
57. In a group of 20 people, how long will it take each person to shake hands with each of the other persons in the group, assuming that it takes three seconds for each shake and only 2 people can shake hands at a time? What if the group is increased to 40 people?
58. A sample of 4 telephones is selected from a shipment of 20 phones. There are 5 defective telephones in the shipment. How many of the samples of 4 phones do not include any of the defective ones?

13.4 FUNDAMENTALS OF PROBABILITY

OBJECTIVES

1. Compute theoretical probability.
2. Compute empirical probability.

TABLE 13.1 The Hours of Sleep Americans Get on a Typical Night

Hours of Sleep	Number of Americans, in millions
4 or less	12
5	27
6	75
7	90
8	81
9	9
10 or more	6

Total: 300

Source: Discovery Health Media

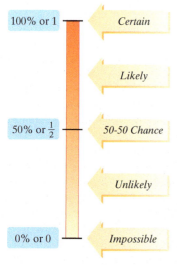

Possible Values for Probabilities

How many hours of sleep do you typically get each night? Table 13.1 indicates that 75 million out of 300 million Americans are getting six hours of sleep on a typical night. The *probability* of an American getting six hours of sleep on a typical night is $\frac{75}{300}$. This fraction can be reduced to $\frac{1}{4}$, or expressed as 0.25, or 25%. Thus, 25% of Americans get six hours of sleep each night.

We find a probability by dividing one number by another. Probabilities are assigned to an *event*, such as getting six hours of sleep on a typical night. Events that are certain to occur are assigned probabilities of 1, or 100%. For example, the probability that a given individual will eventually die is 1. By contrast, if an event cannot occur, its probability is 0.

Probabilities of events are expressed as numbers ranging from 0 to 1, or 0% to 100%. The closer the probability of a given event is to 1, the more likely it is that the event will occur. The closer the probability of a given event is to 0, the less likely it is that the event will occur.

OBJECTIVE 1 ▶ **Compute theoretical probability.** You toss a coin. Although it is equally likely to land either heads up, denoted by H, or tails up, denoted by T, the actual outcome is uncertain. Any occurrence for which the outcome is uncertain is called an **experiment.** Thus, tossing a coin is an example of an experiment. The set of all possible outcomes of an experiment is the **sample space** of the experiment, denoted by S. The sample space for the coin-tossing experiment is

$$S = \{H, T\}.$$

- H: Lands heads up
- T: Lands tails up

An **event,** denoted by E, is any subset of a sample space. For example, the subset $E = \{T\}$ is the event of landing tails up when a coin is tossed.

Theoretical probability applies to situations like this, in which the sample space only contains equally likely outcomes, all of which are known. To calculate the theoretical probability of an event, we divide the number of outcomes resulting in the event by the total number of outcomes in the sample space.

Computing Theoretical Probability

If an event E has $n(E)$ equally likely outcomes and its sample space S has $n(S)$ equally likely outcomes, the **theoretical probability** of event E, denoted by $P(E)$, is

$$P(E) = \frac{\text{number of outcomes in event } E}{\text{total number of possible outcomes}} = \frac{n(E)}{n(S)}.$$

How can we use this formula to compute the probability of a coin landing tails up? We use the following sets:

$$E = \{T\} \qquad S = \{H, T\}.$$

- $E = \{T\}$: This is the event of landing tails up.
- $S = \{H, T\}$: This is the sample space with all equally likely outcomes.

The probability of a coin landing tails up is

$$P(E) = \frac{\text{number of outcomes that result in tails up}}{\text{total number of possible outcomes}} = \frac{n(E)}{n(S)} = \frac{1}{2}.$$

Theoretical probability applies to many games of chance, including dice rolling, lotteries, card games, and roulette. We begin with rolling a die. Figure 13.4 illustrates that when a die is rolled, there are six equally likely possible outcomes. The sample space can be shown as

$$S = \{1, 2, 3, 4, 5, 6\}.$$

FIGURE 13.4 Outcomes when a die is rolled

EXAMPLE 1 Computing Theoretical Probability

A die is rolled once. Find the probability of rolling

a. a 3. **b.** an even number. **c.** a number less than 5.
d. a number less than 10. **e.** a number greater than 6.

Solution The sample space is $S = \{1, 2, 3, 4, 5, 6\}$ with $n(S) = 6$. We will use 6, the total number of possible outcomes, in the denominator of each probability fraction.

a. The phrase "rolling a 3" describes the event $E = \{3\}$. This event can occur in one way: $n(E) = 1$.

$$P(3) = \frac{\text{number of outcomes that result in 3}}{\text{total number of possible outcomes}} = \frac{n(E)}{n(S)} = \frac{1}{6}$$

The probability of rolling a 3 is $\frac{1}{6}$.

b. The phrase "rolling an even number" describes the event $E = \{2, 4, 6\}$. This event can occur in three ways: $n(E) = 3$.

$$P(\text{even number}) = \frac{\text{number of outcomes that result in an even number}}{\text{total number of possible outcomes}} = \frac{n(E)}{n(S)} = \frac{3}{6} = \frac{1}{2}$$

The probability of rolling an even number is $\frac{1}{2}$.

c. The phrase "rolling a number less than 5" describes the event $E = \{1, 2, 3, 4\}$. This event can occur in four ways: $n(E) = 4$.

$$P(\text{less than 5}) = \frac{\text{number of outcomes that are less than 5}}{\text{total number of possible outcomes}} = \frac{n(E)}{n(S)} = \frac{4}{6} = \frac{2}{3}$$

The probability of rolling a number less than 5 is $\frac{2}{3}$.

d. The phrase "rolling a number less than 10" describes the event $E = \{1, 2, 3, 4, 5, 6\}$. This event can occur in six ways: $n(E) = 6$. Can you see that all of the possible outcomes are less than 10? This event is certain to occur.

$$P(\text{less than 10}) = \frac{\text{number of outcomes that are less than 10}}{\text{total number of possible outcomes}} = \frac{n(E)}{n(S)} = \frac{6}{6} = 1$$

The probability of any certain event is 1.

e. The phrase "rolling a number greater than 6" describes an event that cannot occur, or the empty set. Thus, $E = \emptyset$ and $n(E) = 0$.

$$P(\text{greater than 6}) = \frac{\text{number of outcomes that are greater than 6}}{\text{total number of possible outcomes}} = \frac{n(E)}{n(S)} = \frac{0}{6} = 0$$

The probability of an event that cannot occur is 0.

In Example 1, there are six possible outcomes, each with a probability of $\frac{1}{6}$:

$$P(1) = \frac{1}{6} \quad P(2) = \frac{1}{6} \quad P(3) = \frac{1}{6} \quad P(4) = \frac{1}{6} \quad P(5) = \frac{1}{6} \quad P(6) = \frac{1}{6}.$$

The sum of these probabilities is 1: $\frac{1}{6} + \frac{1}{6} + \frac{1}{6} + \frac{1}{6} + \frac{1}{6} + \frac{1}{6} = 1$. In general, **the sum of the theoretical probabilities of all possible outcomes in the sample space is 1.**

PRACTICE 1 A die is rolled once. Find the probability of rolling

a. a 2.
b. a number less than 4.
c. a number greater than 7.
d. a number less than 7.

Our next example involves a standard 52-card bridge deck, illustrated in Figure 13.5. The deck has four suits: Hearts and diamonds are red, and clubs and spades are black. Each suit has 13 different face values—A(ace), 2, 3, 4, 5, 6, 7, 8, 9, 10, J(jack), Q(queen), and K(king). Jacks, queens, and kings are called **picture cards** or **face cards.**

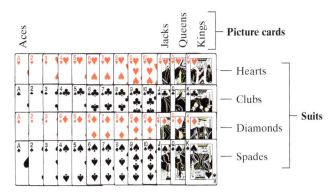

FIGURE 13.5 A standard 52-card bridge deck

EXAMPLE 2 Probability and a Deck of 52 Cards

You are dealt one card from a standard 52-card deck. Find the probability of being dealt

a. a king. **b.** a heart. **c.** the king of hearts.

Solution Because there are 52 cards in the deck, the total number of possible ways of being dealt a single card is 52. The number of outcomes in the sample space is 52: $n(S) = 52$. We use 52 as the denominator of each probability fraction.

a. Let E be the event of being dealt a king. Because there are four kings in the deck, this event can occur in four ways: $n(E) = 4$.

$$P(\text{king}) = \frac{\text{number of outcomes that result in a king}}{\text{total number of possible outcomes}} = \frac{n(E)}{n(S)} = \frac{4}{52} = \frac{1}{13}$$

The probability of being dealt a king is $\frac{1}{13}$.

b. Let E be the event of being dealt a heart. Because there are 13 hearts in the deck, this event can occur in 13 ways: $n(E) = 13$.

$$P(\text{heart}) = \frac{\text{number of outcomes that result in a heart}}{\text{total number of possible outcomes}} = \frac{n(E)}{n(S)} = \frac{13}{52} = \frac{1}{4}$$

The probability of being dealt a heart is $\frac{1}{4}$.

c. Let E be the event of being dealt the king of hearts. Because there is only one card in the deck that is the king of hearts, this event can occur in just one way: $n(E) = 1$.

$$P(\text{king of hearts}) = \frac{\text{number of outcomes that result in the king of hearts}}{\text{total number of possible outcomes}} = \frac{n(E)}{n(S)} = \frac{1}{52}$$

The probability of being dealt the king of hearts is $\frac{1}{52}$.

PRACTICE 2 You are dealt one card from a standard 52-card deck. Find the probability of being dealt

a. an ace. **b.** a red card. **c.** a red king.

Probabilities play a valuable role in the science of genetics. Example 3 deals with cystic fibrosis, an inherited lung disease occurring in about 1 out of every 2000 births among Caucasians and in about 1 out of every 250,000 births among non-Caucasians.

EXAMPLE 3 Probabilities in Genetics

Each person carries two genes that are related to the absence or presence of the disease cystic fibrosis. Most Americans have two normal genes for this trait and are unaffected by cystic fibrosis. However, 1 in 25 Americans carries one normal gene and one defective gene. If we use c to represent a defective gene and C a normal gene, such a carrier can be designated as Cc. Thus, CC is a person who neither carries nor has cystic fibrosis, Cc is a carrier who is not actually sick, and cc is a person sick with the disease. Table 13.2 shows the four equally likely outcomes for a child's genetic inheritance from two parents who are both carrying one cystic fibrosis gene. One copy of each gene is passed on to the child from the parents.

TABLE 13.2 Cystic Fibrosis and Genetic Inheritance

		Second Parent	
		C	c
First Parent	C	CC	Cc
	c	cC	cc

Shown in the table are the four possibilities for a child whose parents each carry one cystic fibrosis gene.

If each parent carries one cystic fibrosis gene, what is the probability that their child will have cystic fibrosis?

Solution Table 13.2 shows that there are four equally likely outcomes. The sample space is $S = \{CC, Cc, cC, cc\}$ and $n(S) = 4$. The phrase "will have cystic fibrosis" describes only the cc child. Thus, $E = \{cc\}$ and $n(E) = 1$.

$$P(\text{cystic fibrosis}) = \frac{\text{number of outcomes that result in cystic fibrosis}}{\text{total number of possible outcomes}} = \frac{n(E)}{n(S)} = \frac{1}{4}$$

If each parent carries one cystic fibrosis gene, the probability that their child will have cystic fibrosis is $\frac{1}{4}$.

PRACTICE 3 Use the table in Example 3 to solve this exercise. If each parent carries one cystic fibrosis gene, find the probability that their child will be a carrier of the disease who is not actually sick.

OBJECTIVE 2 ▶ Compute empirical probability. Theoretical probability is based on a set of equally likely outcomes and the number of elements in the set. By contrast, *empirical probability* applies to situations in which we observe how frequently an event occurs. We use the following formula to compute the empirical probability of an event:

Computing Empirical Probability

The empirical probability of event E is

$$P(E) = \frac{\text{observed number of times } E \text{ occurs}}{\text{total number of observed occurrences}}.$$

Genetic engineering offers some hope for cystic fibrosis patients. Geneticists can now isolate the c gene, the gene responsible for the disease. It is hoped that it will soon be possible to replace the defective c gene with a normal C gene.

EXAMPLE 4 Computing Empirical Probability

The table below shows the distribution, by marital status and gender, of the 212.5 million Americans ages 18 or older.

TABLE 13.3 Marital Status of the U.S. Population, Ages 18 or Older, in Millions

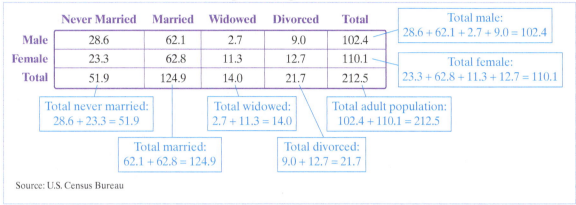

	Never Married	Married	Widowed	Divorced	Total
Male	28.6	62.1	2.7	9.0	102.4
Female	23.3	62.8	11.3	12.7	110.1
Total	51.9	124.9	14.0	21.7	212.5

Source: U.S. Census Bureau

> **Helpful Hint**
>
> Our selection from the U.S. adult population is *random*. This means that every person in the population has an equal chance of being chosen.

If one person is randomly selected from the population described in the table, find the probability, to the nearest hundreth, that the person

a. is divorced.   **b.** is female.

Solution

a. The probability of selecting a divorced person is the observed number of divorced people, 21.7 (million), divided by the total number of U.S. adults, 212.5 (million).

P(selecting a divorced person from the U.S. adult population)

$$= \frac{\text{number of divorced people}}{\text{total number of U.S. adults}} = \frac{21.7}{212.5} \approx 0.10$$

The empirical probability of selecting a divorced person from the U.S. adult population is approximately 0.10.

b. Be sure to refer to Table 13.3. The probability of selecting a female is the observed number of females, 110.1 (million), divided by the total number of U.S. adults, 212.5 (million).

P(selecting a female from the U.S. adult population)

$$= \frac{\text{number of females}}{\text{total number of U.S. adults}} = \frac{110.1}{212.5} \approx 0.52$$

The empirical probability of selecting a female from the U.S. adult population is approximately 0.52.

PRACTICE 4 If one person is randomly selected from the population described in Table 13.3, find the probability, expressed as a decimal rounded to the nearest hundredth, that the person

a. has never been married.   **b.** is male.

In certain situations, we can establish a relationship between the two kinds of probability. Consider, for example, a coin that is equally likely to land heads or tails. Such a coin is called a **fair coin**. Empirical probability can be used to determine whether a coin is fair. Suppose we toss a coin 10, 50, 100, 1000, 10,000, and 100,000 times. We record the number of heads observed, shown in the table below. For each of the six cases in the table, the empirical probability of heads is determined by dividing the number of heads observed by the number of tosses.

TABLE 13.4 Empirical Probabilities of Heads as the Number of Tosses Increases

Number of Tosses	Number of Heads Observed	Empirical Probability of Heads, or P(H)
10	4	$P(H) = \frac{4}{10} = 0.4$
50	27	$P(H) = \frac{27}{50} = 0.54$
100	44	$P(H) = \frac{44}{100} = 0.44$
1000	530	$P(H) = \frac{530}{1000} = 0.53$
10,000	4851	$P(H) = \frac{4851}{10,000} = 0.4851$
100,000	49,880	$P(H) = \frac{49,880}{100,000} = 0.4988$

A pattern is exhibited by the empirical probabilities in the right-hand column of the table. As the number of tosses increases, the empirical probabilities tend to get closer to 0.5, the theoretical probability. These results give us no reason to suspect that the coin is not fair.

This table illustrates an important principle when observing uncertain outcomes such as the event of a coin landing on heads. As an experiment is repeated more and more times, the empirical probability of an event tends to get closer to the theoretical probability of that event. This principle is known as the **law of large numbers.**

13.4 EXERCISE SET

PRACTICE AND APPLICATION EXERCISES

Exercises 1–48 involve theoretical probability. Use the theoretical probability formula to solve each exercise. Express each probability as a fraction reduced to lowest terms.

In Exercises 1–10, a die is rolled. The set of equally likely outcomes is {1, 2, 3, 4, 5, 6}. Find the probability of rolling

1. a 4.
2. a 5.
3. an odd number.
4. a number greater than 3.
5. a number less than 3.
6. a number greater than 4.
7. a number less than 7.
8. a number less than 8.
9. a number greater than 7.
10. a number greater than 8.

In Exercises 11–20, you are dealt one card from a standard 52-card deck. Find the probability of being dealt

11. a queen.
12. a jack.
13. a club.
14. a diamond.
15. a picture card.
16. a card greater than 3 and less than 7.
17. the queen of spades.
18. the ace of clubs.
19. a diamond and a spade.
20. a card with a green heart.

In Exercises 21–26, a fair coin is tossed two times in succession. The set of equally likely outcomes is {HH, HT, TH, TT}. Find the probability of getting

21. two heads.
22. two tails.
23. the same outcome on each toss.
24. different outcomes on each toss.
25. a head on the second toss.
26. at least one head.

In Exercises 27–34, you select a family with three children. If M represents a male child and F a female child, the set of equally likely outcomes for the children's genders is {MMM, MMF,

$MFM, MFF, FMM, FMF, FFM, FFF\}$. Find the probability of selecting a family with

27. exactly one female child.
28. exactly one male child.
29. exactly two male children.
30. exactly two female children.
31. at least one male child.
32. at least two female children.
33. four male children.
34. fewer than four female children.

In Exercises 35–40, a single die is rolled twice. The 36 equally likely outcomes are shown as follows:

	Second Roll					
	⚀	⚁	⚂	⚃	⚄	⚅
⚀	(1,1)	(1,2)	(1,3)	(1,4)	(1,5)	(1,6)
⚁	(2,1)	(2,2)	(2,3)	(2,4)	(2,5)	(2,6)
⚂	(3,1)	(3,2)	(3,3)	(3,4)	(3,5)	(3,6)
⚃	(4,1)	(4,2)	(4,3)	(4,4)	(4,5)	(4,6)
⚄	(5,1)	(5,2)	(5,3)	(5,4)	(5,5)	(5,6)
⚅	(6,1)	(6,2)	(6,3)	(6,4)	(6,5)	(6,6)

Find the probability of getting

35. two even numbers.
36. two odd numbers.
37. two numbers whose sum is 5.
38. two numbers whose sum is 6.
39. two numbers whose sum exceeds 12.
40. two numbers whose sum is less than 13.

Use the spinner shown to answer Exercises 41–48. Assume that it is equally probable that the pointer will land on any one of the ten colored regions. If the pointer lands on a borderline, spin again.

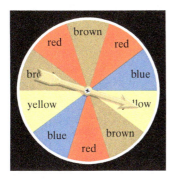

Find the probability that the spinner lands in

41. a red region.
42. a yellow region.
43. a blue region.
44. a brown region.
45. a region that is red or blue.
46. a region that is yellow or brown.
47. a region that is red and blue.
48. a region that is yellow and brown

Number of People in the United States Living alone, in Millions

	Ages 15–24	Ages 25–34	Ages 35–44	Ages 45–64	Ages 65–74	Ages ≥75	Total
Male	0.7	2.2	2.6	4.3	1.3	1.4	12.5
Female	0.8	1.6	1.6	5.0	2.9	4.9	16.8
Total	1.5	3.8	4.2	9.3	4.2	6.3	29.3

Source: U.S. Census Bureau

Find the probability, expressed as a decimal rounded to the nearest hundredth, that a randomly selected American living alone is

49. male.
50. female.
51. in the 25–34 age range.
52. in the 35–44 age range.
53. a woman in the 15–24 age range.
54. a man in the 45–64 age range.

The table shows the number of Americans who moved in 2004, categorized by where they moved and whether they were an owner or a renter. Use the data in the table, expressed in millions, to solve Exercises 55–60.

Number of People in the United States who Moved in 2004, in Millions

	Moved to Same State	Moved to Different State	Moved to Different Country
Owner	11.7	2.8	0.3
Renter	18.7	4.5	1.0

Source: U.S. Census Bureau

Find the probability, expressed as a decimal rounded to the nearest hundredth, that a randomly selected American who moved in 2004 was

55. an owner.
56. a renter.
57. a person who moved within the same state.
58. a person who moved to a different country.
59. a renter who moved to a different state.
60. an owner who moved to a different state.

WRITING IN MATHEMATICS

61. What is the sample space of an experiment? What is an event?
62. How is the theoretical probability of an event computed?
63. Describe the difference between theoretical probability and empirical probability.
64. Give an example of an event whose probability must be determined empirically rather than theoretically.
65. Use the definition of theoretical probability to explain why the probability of an event that cannot occur is 0.

754 CHAPTER 13 Counting Methods and Probability Theory

66. Use the definition of theoretical probability to explain why the probability of an event that is certain to occur is 1.

67. Write a probability word problem whose answer is one of the following fractions: $\frac{1}{6}$ or $\frac{1}{4}$ or $\frac{1}{3}$.

CRITICAL THINKING EXERCISES

68. Some three-digit numbers, such as 101 and 313, read the same forward and backward. If you select a number from all three-digit numbers, find the probability that it will read the same forward and backward.

69. The target in the figure shown in the next column contains four squares. If a dart thrown at random hits the target, find the probability that it will land in an orange region.

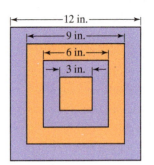

INTEGRATED REVIEW
Sections 13.1–13.4

Multiple Choice. *Choose the one alternative that best completes the statement or answers the question.*

1. A restaurant offers 10 entrees and 6 desserts. In how many ways can a person order a two-course meal?
   a. 16   b. 60   c. 18   d. 120

2. How many different four-letter secret codes can be formed if the first letter must be an S or a T?
   a. 421,824   b. 456,976   c. 35,152   d. 72

3. A person can order a new car with a choice of 9 possible colors, with or without air conditioning, with or without heated seats, with or without anti-lock brakes, with or without power windows, and with or without a CD player. In how many different ways can a new car be ordered in terms of these options?
   a. 18   b. 144   c. 576   d. 288

Solve.

4. Jamie is joining a music club. As part of her 4-CD introductory package, she can choose from 12 rock selections, 10 alternative selections, 7 country selections, and 5 classical selections. If Jamie chooses one selection from each category, how many ways can she choose her introductory package?

Multiple Choice. *Choose the one alternative that best completes the statement or answers the question.*

5. $\dfrac{700!}{699!} =$
   a. 1   b. 489,300   c. 700   d. 699

6. $(9 - 4)! =$
   a. 362,856   b. 5   c. 120   d. 362,876

7. A teacher and 10 students are to be seated along a bench in the bleachers at a basketball game. One of the students is the yearbook's sports photographer. In how many ways can this be done if the teacher must be seated in the middle and the student photographer must sit to the teacher's immediate left?
   a. 20   b. 40,320   c. 362,880   d. 3,628,800

8. How many arrangements can be made using 4 letters of the word HYPERBOLAS if no letter is to be used more than once?
   a. 210   b. 5040   c. 302,400   d. 151,200

9. From 8 names on a ballot, a committee of 3 will be elected to attend a political national convention. How many different committees are possible?
   a. 56   b. 168   c. 6720   d. 336

Section 13.5 Probability with the Fundamental Counting Principle, Permutations, and Combinations 755

For exercises 10 and 11, does the problem involve permutations or combinations? It is not necessary to solve the problem.

10. How many different user IDs can be formed from the letters W, X, Y, Z if no repetition of letters is allowed?
   a. Permutations, because the order of the letters matters.
   b. Combinations, because the order of the letters does not matter.

11. One hundred people purchase raffle tickets. Three winning tickets will be selected at random. If first prize is $100, second prize is $50, and third prize is $25, in how many different ways can the prizes be awarded?
   a. Combinations, because the order of the prizes awarded does not matter.
   a. Permutations, because the order of the prizes awarded matters.

12. A die is rolled. The set of equally likely outcomes is {1, 2, 3, 4, 5, 6}. Find the probability of getting a 7.
   a. 1 **b.** 7 **c.** $\frac{7}{6}$ **d.** 0

13. Use the spinner below to answer the question. Assume that it is equally probable that the pointer will land on any one of the five numbered spaces. If the pointer lands on a borderline, spin again.

Find the probability that the arrow will land on an odd number.
   a. 0 **b.** $\frac{3}{5}$ **c.** 1 **d.** $\frac{2}{5}$

14. You are dealt one card from a standard 52-card deck. Find the probability of being dealt an ace or a 9.
   a. $\frac{2}{13}$ **b.** $\frac{5}{13}$ **c.** 10 **d.** $\frac{13}{2}$

13.5 PROBABILITY WITH THE FUNDAMENTAL COUNTING PRINCIPLE, PERMUTATIONS, AND COMBINATIONS

OBJECTIVES

1 Compute probabilities with permutations.
2 Compute probabilities with combinations.

OBJECTIVE 1 ▶ Compute probability with permutations. We return to our musical concert from Section 13.2, but now with five musical groups. In which order should the five groups in the concert perform? Because order makes a difference, this is a permutation situation. Example 1 is based on this scenario, and uses permutations to solve a probability problem.

EXAMPLE 1 Probability and Permutations

The five groups in the tour, Groups A, B, C, D, and E, agree to determine the order of performance based on a random selection. Each band's name is written on one of five cards. The cards are placed in a hat and then five cards are drawn, one at a time. The order in which the cards are drawn determines the order in which the bands perform. What is the probability of Group A performing fourth and Group C last?

Solution We begin by applying the definition of probability to this situation.

P(Group A fourth, Group C last)

$$= \frac{\text{number of permutations with Group A fourth, Group C last}}{\text{total number of possible permutations}}$$

We can use the Fundamental Counting Principle to find the total number of possible permutations. This represents the number of ways you can put together the concert.

There are $5 \cdot 4 \cdot 3 \cdot 2 \cdot 1$, or 120, possible permutations. Equivalently, the five groups can perform in 120 different orders.

We can also use the Fundamental Counting Principle to find the number of permutations with Group A performing fourth and Group C performing last. You can choose any one of the three groups, Groups B, D, or E as the opening act. This leaves two choices for the second group to perform, and only one choice for the third group to perform. There is only one choice for the fourth group—Group A, and one choice for the closing act—Group C:

Thus, there are $3 \cdot 2 \cdot 1 \cdot 1 \cdot 1$, or 6 possible permutations. Equivalently, there are 6 lineups with Group A performing fourth and Group C last.

Now we can return to our probability fraction.

P(Group A fourth, Group C last)

$$= \frac{\text{number of permutations with Group A fourth, Group C last}}{\text{total number of possible permutations}}$$

$$= \frac{6}{120} = \frac{1}{20}$$

The probability of the Group A performing fourth and Group C last is $\frac{1}{20}$.

PRACTICE 1 Use the information given in Example 1 to find the probability of Group B performing first, Group A performing fourth, and Group C last.

OBJECTIVE 2 ▶ Compute probabilities with combinations. In 2006, 41 states and Washington, D.C., had lotteries, and several states were considering selling lottery tickets on the Internet. If your state has a lottery drawing each week, the probability that someone will win the top prize is relatively high. If there is no winner this week, it is virtually certain that eventually someone will be graced with millions of dollars. So, why are you so unlucky compared to this undisclosed someone? In Example 2, we provide an answer to this question.

EXAMPLE 2 Probability and Combinations: Winning the Lottery

Florida's lottery game, LOTTO, is set up so that each player chooses six different numbers from 1 to 53. If the six numbers chosen match the six numbers drawn randomly, the player wins (or shares) the top cash prize. (As of this writing, the top cash prize has ranged from $7 million to $106.5 million.) With one LOTTO ticket, what is the probability of winning this prize?

Solution Because the order of the six numbers does not matter, this is a situation involving combinations. We begin with the formula for probability.

$$P(\text{winning}) = \frac{\text{number of ways of winning}}{\text{total number of possible combinations}}$$

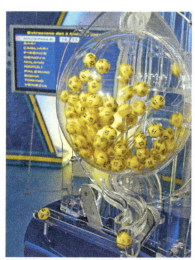

In 2004, Americans spent $49.4 billion on lotteries set up by revenue-hungry states. Once prizes and administrative costs were paid, $15.1 billion was left in revenue for the states. Throughout the United States, 64% of lottery profits go to education funding.
Source: North American Association of State and Provincial Lotteries

We can use the combinations formula

$$_nC_r = \frac{n!}{(n-r)!\,r!}$$

to find the total number of possible combinations. We are selecting $r = 6$ numbers from a collection of $n = 53$ numbers.

$$_{53}C_6 = \frac{53!}{(53-6)!\,6!} = \frac{53!}{47!\,6!} = \frac{53 \cdot 52 \cdot 51 \cdot 50 \cdot 49 \cdot 48 \cdot 47!}{47! \cdot 6 \cdot 5 \cdot 4 \cdot 3 \cdot 2 \cdot 1} = 22{,}957{,}480$$

There are nearly 23 million number combinations possible in LOTTO. If a person buys one LOTTO ticket, that person has selected only one combination of the six numbers. With one LOTTO ticket, there is only one way of winning.

Now we can return to our probability fraction.

$$P(\text{winning}) = \frac{\text{number of ways of winning}}{\text{total number of possible combinations}} = \frac{1}{22{,}957{,}480} \approx 0.0000000436$$

The probability of winning the top prize with one LOTTO ticket is $\frac{1}{22{,}957{,}480}$, or about 1 in 23 million.

Suppose that a person buys 5000 different tickets in Florida's LOTTO. Because that person has selected 5000 different combinations of the six numbers, the probability of winning is

$$\frac{5000}{22{,}957{,}480} \approx 0.000218.$$

The chances of winning top prize are about 218 in a million. At $1 per LOTTO ticket, it is highly probable that our LOTTO player will be $5000 poorer. Knowing a little probability helps a lotto.

PRACTICE 2 People lose interest when they do not win at games of chance, including Florida's LOTTO. With drawings twice weekly instead of once, the game described in Example 2 was brought in to bring back lost players and increase ticket sales. The original LOTTO was set up so that each player chose six different numbers from 1 to 49, rather than from 1 to 53, with a lottery drawing only once a week. With one LOTTO ticket, what was the probability of winning the top cash prize in Florida's original LOTTO? Express the answer as a fraction and as a decimal correct to ten places.

EXAMPLE 3   Probability and Combinations

A club consists of five men and seven women. Three members are selected at random to attend a conference. Find the probability that the selected group consists of

a. three men.

b. one man and two women.

Solution The order in which the three people are selected does not matter, so this is a problem involving combinations.

12 Club Members

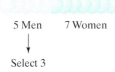

5 Men   7 Women
↓
Select 3

a. We begin with the probability of selecting three men.

$$P(3 \text{ men}) = \frac{\text{number of ways of selecting 3 men}}{\text{total number of possible combinations}}$$

First, we consider the denominator of the probability fraction. We are selecting $r = 3$ people from a total group of $n = 12$ people (five men and seven women). The total number of possible combinations is

$$_{12}C_3 = \frac{12!}{(12-3)!\,3!} = \frac{12!}{9!\,3!} = \frac{12 \cdot 11 \cdot 10 \cdot 9!}{9! \cdot 3 \cdot 2 \cdot 1} = 220.$$

Thus, there are 220 possible three-person selections.

Next, we consider the numerator of the probability fraction. We are interested in the number of ways of selecting three men from five men. We are selecting $r = 3$ men from a total group of $n = 5$ men. The number of possible combinations of three men is

$$_5C_3 = \frac{5!}{(5-3)!\,3!} = \frac{5!}{2!\,3!} = \frac{5 \cdot 4 \cdot 3!}{2 \cdot 1 \cdot 3!} = 10.$$

Thus, there are 10 ways of selecting three men from five men. Now we can fill in the numbers in the numerator and the denominator of our probability fraction.

$$P(3 \text{ men}) = \frac{\text{number of ways of selecting 3 men}}{\text{total number of possible combinations}} = \frac{10}{220} = \frac{1}{22}$$

The probability that the group selected to attend the conference consists of three men is $\frac{1}{22}$.

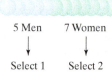

12 Club Members

5 Men   7 Women

Select 1   Select 2

b. We set up the fraction for the probability that the selected group consists of one man and two women.

$$P(1 \text{ man, 2 women}) = \frac{\text{number of ways of selecting 1 man and 2 women}}{\text{total number of possible combinations}}$$

The denominator of this fraction is the same as the denominator in part (a). The total number of possible combinations is found by selecting $r = 3$ people from $n = 12$ people: $_{12}C_3 = 220$.

Next, we move to the numerator of the probability fraction. The number of ways of selecting $r = 1$ man from $n = 5$ men is

$$_5C_1 = \frac{5!}{(5-1)!\,1!} = \frac{5!}{4!\,1!} = \frac{5 \cdot 4!}{4! \cdot 1} = 5.$$

The number of ways of selecting $r = 2$ women from $n = 7$ women is

$$_7C_2 = \frac{7!}{(7-2)!\,2!} = \frac{7!}{5!\,2!} = \frac{7 \cdot 6 \cdot 5!}{5! \cdot 2 \cdot 1} = 21.$$

By the Fundamental Counting Principle, the number of ways of selecting 1 man and 2 women is

$$_5C_1 \cdot {}_7C_2 = 5 \cdot 21 = 105.$$

Now we can fill in the numbers in the numerator and the denominator of our probability fraction.

$$P(1 \text{ man, 2 women}) = \frac{\text{number of ways of selecting 1 man and 2 women}}{\text{total number of possible combinations}} = \frac{{}_5C_1 \cdot {}_7C_2}{{}_{12}C_3} = \frac{105}{220} = \frac{21}{44}$$

The probability that the group selected to attend the conference consists of one man and two women is $\frac{21}{44}$. □

PRACTICE 3 A club consists of six men and four women. Three members are selected at random to attend a conference. Find the probability that the selected group consists of

a. three men.

b. two men and one woman.

13.5 EXERCISE SET

PRACTICE AND APPLICATION EXERCISES

1. Martha, Lee, Nancy, Paul, and Armando have all been invited to a dinner party. They arrive randomly and each person arrives at a different time.
   a. In how many ways can they arrive?
   b. In how many ways can Martha arrive first and Armando last?
   c. Find the probability that Martha will arrive first and Armando last.

2. Three men and three women line up at a checkout counter in a store.
   a. In how many ways can they line up?
   b. In how many ways can they line up if the first person in line is a woman, and then the line alternates by gender— that is a woman, a man, a woman, a man, and so on?
   c. Find the probability that the first person in line is a woman and the line alternates by gender.

3. Six stand-up comics, A, B, C, D, E, and F, are to perform on a single evening at a comedy club. The order of performance is determined by random selection. Find the probability that
   a. Comic E will perform first.
   b. Comic C will perform fifth and comic B will perform last.
   c. The comedians will perform in the following order: D, E, C, A, B, F.
   d. Comic A or comic B will perform first.

4. Seven performers, A, B, C, D, E, F, and G, are to appear in a fund raiser. The order of performance is determined by random selection. Find the probability that
   a. D will perform first.
   b. E will perform sixth and B will perform last.
   c. They will perform in the following order: C, D, B, A, G, F, E.
   d. F or G will perform first.

5. A group consists of four men and five women. Three people are selected to attend a conference.
   a. In how many ways can three people be selected from this group of nine?
   b. In how many ways can three women be selected from the five women?
   c. Find the probability that the selected group will consist of all women.

6. A political discussion group consists of five Democrats and six Republicans. Four people are selected to attend a conference.
   a. In how many ways can four people be selected from this group of eleven?
   b. In how many ways can four Republicans be selected from the six Republicans?
   c. Find the probability that the selected group will consist of all Republicans.

7. To play the California lottery, a person has to correctly select 6 out of 51 numbers, paying $1 for each six-number selection. If the six numbers picked are the same as the ones drawn by the lottery, mountains of money are bestowed. What is the probability that a person with one combination of six numbers will win? What is the probability of winning if 100 different lottery tickets are purchased?

8. A state lottery is designed so that a player chooses five numbers from 1 to 30 on one lottery ticket. What is the probability that a player with one lottery ticket will win? What is the probability of winning if 100 different lottery tickets are purchased?

9. A box contains 25 transistors, 6 of which are defective. If 6 are selected at random, find the probability that
   a. all are defective.
   b. none are defective.

10. A committee of five people is to be formed from six lawyers and seven teachers. Find the probability that
    a. all are lawyers.
    b. none are lawyers.

11. A city council consists of six Democrats and four Republicans. If a committee of three people is selected, find the probability of selecting one Democrat and two Republicans.

12. A parent-teacher committee consisting of four people is to be selected from fifteen parents and five teachers. Find the probability of selecting two parents and two teachers.

Exercises 13–18 involve a deck of 52 cards. If necessary, refer to the picture of a deck of cards, Figure 13.5.

13. A poker hand consists of five cards.
    a. Find the total number of possible five-card poker hands.
    b. A diamond flush is a five-card hand consisting of all diamonds. Find the number of possible diamond flushes.
    c. Find the probability of being dealt a diamond flush.

14. A poker hand consists of five cards.
    a. Find the total number of possible five-card poker hands.
    b. Find the number of ways in which four aces can be selected.
    c. Find the number of ways in which one king can be selected.
    d. Use the Fundamental Counting Principle and your answers from parts (b) and (c) to find the number of ways of getting four aces and one king.
    e. Find the probability of getting a poker hand consisting of four aces and one king.

15. If you are dealt 3 cards from a shuffled deck of 52 cards, find the probability that all 3 cards are picture cards.

16. If you are dealt 4 cards from a shuffled deck of 52 cards, find the probability that all 4 are hearts.

17. If you are dealt 4 cards from a shuffled deck of 52 cards, find the probability of getting two queens and two kings.

18. If you are dealt 4 cards from a shuffled deck of 52 cards, find the probability of getting three jacks and one queen.

WRITING IN MATHEMATICS

19. If people understood the mathematics involving probabilities and lotteries, as you now do, do you think they would continue to spend hundreds of dollars per year on lottery tickets? Explain your answer.
20. Write and solve an original problem involving probability and permutations.
21. Write and solve an original problem involving probability and combinations whose solution requires $\frac{_{14}C_{10}}{_{20}C_{10}}$.

CRITICAL THINKING EXERCISES

22. An apartment complex offers apartments with four different options, designated by A through D. There are an equal number of apartments with each combination of options.

A	B	C	D
one bedroom two bedrooms three bedrooms	one bathroom two bathrooms	first floor second floor	lake view golf course view no special view

If there is only one apartment left, what is the probability that it is precisely what a person is looking for, namely two bedrooms, two bathrooms, first floor, and a lake or golf course view?

23. Reread Exercise 7. How much must a person spend so that the probability of winning the California lottery is $\frac{1}{2}$?
24. Suppose that it is a week in which the cash prize in Florida's LOTTO is promised to exceed $50 million. If a person purchases 22,957,480 tickets in LOTTO at $1 per ticket (all possible combinations), isn't this a guarantee of winning the lottery? Because the probability in this situation is 1, what's wrong with doing this?
25. The digits 1, 2, 3, 4, and 5 are randomly arranged to form a three-digit number. (Digits are not repeated.) Find the probability that the number is even and greater than 500.
26. In a five-card poker hand, what is the probability of being dealt exactly one ace and no picture cards?

13.6 EVENTS INVOLVING *NOT* AND *OR*; ODDS

OBJECTIVES

1. Find the probability that an event will not occur.
2. Find the probability of one event or a second event occurring.
3. Understand and use odds.

There are several ways to express the likelihood of an event. For example, we can discuss the probability of an event. We can also discuss *odds against* an event and *odds in favor* of an event. In this section, we expand our knowledge of probability and explain the meaning of odds.

OBJECTIVE 1 ▶ Find the probability that an event will not occur. If we know $P(E)$, the probability of an event E, we can determine the probability that the event will not occur, denoted by $P(\text{not } E)$. The event *not E* is the **complement** of E because it is the set of all outcomes in the sample space S that are not outcomes in the event E. In any experiment, an event must occur or its complement must occur. Thus, the sum of the probability that an event will occur and the probability that it will not occur is 1:

$$P(E) + P(\text{not } E) = 1.$$

Solving for $P(E)$ or for $P(\text{not } E)$, we obtain the following formulas:

> **Complement Rules of Probability**
>
> - The probability that an event E will not occur is equal to 1 minus the probability that it will occur.
>
> $$P(\text{not } E) = 1 - P(E)$$
>
> - The probability that an event E will occur is equal to 1 minus the probability that it will not occur.
>
> $$P(E) = 1 - P(\text{not } E)$$
>
> Using set notation, if E' is the complement of E, then $P(E') = 1 - P(E)$ and $P(E) = 1 - P(E')$.

Section 13.6 Events Involving *Not* and *Or;* Odds   **761**

EXAMPLE 1   The Probability of an Event not Occurring

If you are dealt one card from a standard 52-card deck, find the probability that you are not dealt a queen.

Solution   Because

$$P(\text{not } E) = 1 - P(E)$$

then

$$P(\text{not a queen}) = 1 - P(\text{queen}).$$

There are four queens in a deck of 52 cards. The probability of being dealt a queen is $\frac{4}{52} = \frac{1}{13}$. Thus,

$$P(\text{not a queen}) = 1 - P(\text{queen}) = 1 - \frac{1}{13} = \frac{13}{13} - \frac{1}{13} = \frac{12}{13}.$$

The probability that you are not dealt a queen is $\frac{12}{13}$.   □

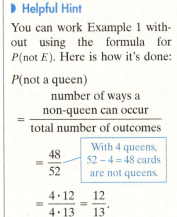

> **Helpful Hint**
>
> You can work Example 1 without using the formula for $P(\text{not } E)$. Here is how it's done:
>
> $P(\text{not a queen})$
>
> $= \dfrac{\text{number of ways a non-queen can occur}}{\text{total number of outcomes}}$
>
> $= \dfrac{48}{52}$ ⟵ With 4 queens, 52 − 4 = 48 cards are not queens.
>
> $= \dfrac{4 \cdot 12}{4 \cdot 13} = \dfrac{12}{13}.$

PRACTICE 1   If you are dealt one card from a standard 52-card deck, find the probability that you are not dealt a diamond.

EXAMPLE 2   Using the Complement Rules

The circle graph below shows the distribution, by age group, of the 191 million car drivers in the United States, with all numbers rounded to the nearest million. If one driver is randomly selected from this population, find the probability that the person

a. is not in the 20–29 age group.

b. is less than 80 years old.

Express probabilities as simplified fractions.

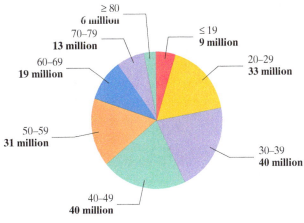

FIGURE 13.6
Source: U.S. Census Bureau

Solution

a. We begin with the probability that a randomly selected driver is not in the 20–29 age group.

$P(\text{not in 20–29 age group})$

$= 1 - P(\text{in 20–29 age group})$

$= 1 - \dfrac{33}{191}$ *The graph shows 33 million drivers in the 20–29 age group.*

This number, 191 million drivers, was given, but can be obtained by adding the numbers in the eight sectors.

$= \dfrac{191}{191} - \dfrac{33}{191} = \dfrac{158}{191}$

The probability that a randomly selected driver is not in the 20–29 age group is $\dfrac{158}{191}$.

b. We could compute the probability that a randomly selected driver is less than 80 years old by adding the numbers in each of the seven sectors representing drivers less than 80 and dividing this sum by 191 (million). However, it is easier to use complements. The complement of selecting a driver less than 80 years old is selecting a driver 80 or older.

$P(\text{less than 80 years old})$

$= 1 - P(80 \text{ or older})$

$= 1 - \dfrac{6}{191}$ *The graph shows 6 million drivers 80 or older.*

$= \dfrac{191}{191} - \dfrac{6}{191} = \dfrac{185}{191}$

The probability that a randomly selected driver is less than 80 years old is $\dfrac{185}{191}$.

PRACTICE 2   If one driver is randomly selected from the population represented in Figure 13.6, find the probability, expressed as a simplified fraction, that the person

a. is not in the 50–59 age group.
b. is at least 20 years old.

OBJECTIVE 2 ▶ Find the probability of one event or a second event occurring.

Suppose that you randomly select one card from a deck of 52 cards. Let A be the event of selecting a king and B be the event of selecting a queen. Only one card is selected, so it is impossible to get both a king and a queen. The events of selecting a king and a queen cannot occur simultaneously. They are called *mutually exclusive events*.

> **Mutually Exclusive Events**
> If it is impossible for events A and B to occur simultaneously, the events are said to be **mutually exclusive.**

In general, if A and B are mutually exclusive events, the probability that either A or B will occur is determined by adding their individual probabilities.

> **Or Probabilities with Mutually Exclusive Events**
> If A and B are mutually exclusive events, then
> $$P(A \text{ or } B) = P(A) + P(B).$$
> Using set notation, $P(A \cup B) = P(A) + P(B)$.

EXAMPLE 3 The Probability of Either of Two Mutually Exclusive Events Occurring

If one card is randomly selected from a deck of cards, what is the probability of selecting a king or a queen?

Solution We find the probability that either of these mutually exclusive events will occur by adding their individual probabilities.

$$P(\text{king or queen}) = P(\text{king}) + P(\text{queen}) = \frac{4}{52} + \frac{4}{52} = \frac{8}{52} = \frac{2}{13}$$

The probability of selecting a king or a queen is $\frac{2}{13}$.

PRACTICE 3 If you roll a single, six-sided die, what is the probability of getting either a 4 or a 5?

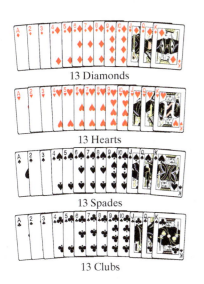

FIGURE 13.7 A deck of 52 cards

Consider the deck of 52 cards shown in the margin. Suppose that these cards are shuffled and you randomly select one card from the deck. What is the probability of selecting a diamond or a picture card (jack, queen, king)? Begin by adding their individual probabilities.

$$P(\text{diamond}) + P(\text{picture card}) = \frac{13}{52} + \frac{12}{52}$$

There are 13 diamonds in the deck of 52 cards.
There are 12 picture cards in the deck of 52 cards.

However, this sum is not the probability of selecting a diamond or a picture card. The problem is that there are three cards that are *simultaneously* diamonds and picture cards, shown to the right. The events of selecting a diamond and selecting a picture card are not mutually exclusive. It is possible to select a card that is both a diamond and a picture card.

The situation is illustrated in the Venn diagram in Figure 13.9. Why can't we find the probability of selecting a diamond or a picture card by adding their individual probabilities? The Venn diagram shows that three of the cards, the three diamonds that are picture cards, get counted twice when we add the individual probabilities. First the three cards get counted as diamonds, and then they get counted as picture cards. In order to avoid the error of counting the three cards twice, we need to subtract the probability of getting a diamond and a picture card, $\frac{3}{52}$, as follows:

FIGURE 13.8 Three diamonds are picture cards.

$P(\text{diamond or picture card})$

$$= P(\text{diamond}) + P(\text{picture card}) - P(\text{diamond and picture card})$$

$$= \frac{13}{52} + \frac{12}{52} - \frac{3}{52} = \frac{13 + 12 - 3}{52} = \frac{22}{52} = \frac{11}{26}.$$

Thus, the probability of selecting a diamond or a picture card is $\frac{11}{26}$.

In general, if A and B are events that are not mutually exclusive, the probability that A or B will occur is determined by adding their individual probabilities and then subtracting the probability that A and B occur simultaneously.

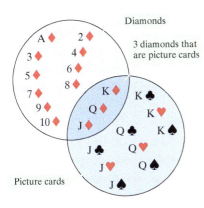

FIGURE 13.9

> **Or Probabilities with Events That Are Not Mutually Exclusive**
> If A and B are not mutually exclusive events, then
> $$P(A \text{ or } B) = P(A) + P(B) - P(A \text{ and } B).$$
> Using set notation,
> $$P(A \cup B) = P(A) + P(B) - P(A \cap B).$$

EXAMPLE 4 An *or* Probability with Events That Are Not Mutually Exclusive

In a group of 25 baboons, 18 enjoy grooming their neighbors, 16 enjoy screeching wildly, while 10 enjoy grooming their neighbors and screeching wildly. If one baboon is selected at random from the group, find the probability that it enjoys grooming its neighbors or screeching wildly.

Solution It is possible for a baboon in the group to enjoy both grooming its neighbors and screeching wildly. Ten of the baboons are given to engage in both activities. These events are not mutually exclusive.

$$P\binom{\text{grooming}}{\text{or screeching}} = P(\text{grooming}) + P(\text{screeching}) - P\binom{\text{grooming}}{\text{and screeching}}$$

$$= \frac{18}{25} + \frac{16}{25} - \frac{10}{25}$$

- 18 of the 25 baboons enjoy grooming.
- 16 of the 25 baboons enjoy screeching.
- 10 of the 25 baboons enjoy both.

$$= \frac{18 + 16 - 10}{25} = \frac{24}{25}$$

The probability that a baboon in the group enjoys grooming its neighbors or screeching wildly is $\frac{24}{25}$.

PRACTICE 4 In a group of 50 students, 23 take math, 11 take psychology, and 7 take both math and psychology. If one student is selected at random, find the probability that the student takes math or psychology.

EXAMPLE 5 An *Or* Probability with Events That Are Not Mutually Exclusive

For the spinner in the margin, suppose it is equally probable that the pointer will land on any one of the eight regions, numbered 1 through 8. If the pointer lands on a borderline, spin again. Find the probability that the pointer will stop on an even number or on a number greater than 5.

FIGURE 13.10 It is equally probable that the pointer will land on any one of the eight regions.

Solution It is possible for the pointer to land on a number that is both even and greater than 5. Two of the numbers, 6 and 8, are even and greater than 5. These events are not mutually exclusive. The probability of landing on a number that is even or greater than 5 is calculated as follows:

Section 13.6 Events Involving *Not* and *Or*; Odds 765

$$P\binom{\text{even or}}{\text{greater than 5}} = P(\text{even}) + P(\text{greater than 5}) - P\binom{\text{even and}}{\text{greater than 5}}$$

$$= \frac{4}{8} + \frac{3}{8} - \frac{2}{8}$$

- Four of the eight numbers, 2, 4, 6, and 8, are even.
- Three of the eight numbers, 6, 7, and 8, are greater than 5.
- Two of the eight numbers, 6 and 8, are even and greater than 5.

$$= \frac{4 + 3 - 2}{8} = \frac{5}{8}.$$

The probability that the pointer will stop on an even number or a number greater than 5 is $\frac{5}{8}$.

PRACTICE 5   Use the spinner from Example 5 to find the probability that the pointer will stop on an odd number or a number less than 5.

OBJECTIVE 3 ▶ Understand and use odds. If we know the probability of an event E, we can also speak of the *odds in favor*, or the *odds against*, the event. The following definitions link together the concepts of odds and probabilities:

Probability to Odds

If $P(E)$ is the probability of an event E occurring, then

1. The **odds in favor of E** are found by taking the probability that E will occur and dividing by the probability that E will not occur.

$$\text{Odds in favor of } E = \frac{P(E)}{P(\text{not } E)}$$

2. The **odds against E** are found by taking the probability that E will not occur and dividing by the probability that E will occur.

$$\text{Odds against } E = \frac{P(\text{not } E)}{P(E)}$$

The odds against E can also be found by reversing the ratio representing the odds in favor of E.

EXAMPLE 6   From Probability to Odds

You roll a single, six-sided die.

a. Find the odds in favor of rolling a 2.
b. Find the odds against rolling a 2.

Solution   Let E represent the event of rolling a 2. In order to determine odds, we must first find the probability of E occurring and the probability of E not occurring. With $S = \{1, 2, 3, 4, 5, 6\}$ and $E = \{2\}$, we see that

$$P(E) = \frac{1}{6}$$

and $P(\text{not } E) = 1 - \frac{1}{6} = \frac{6}{6} - \frac{1}{6} = \frac{5}{6}.$

▶ **Helpful Hint**
When computing odds, the denominators of the two probabilities will always divide out.

Now we are ready to construct the ratios for the odds in favor of E and the odds against E.

a. $\quad$ Odds in favor of $E(\text{rolling a 2}) = \dfrac{P(E)}{P(\text{not } E)} = \dfrac{\frac{1}{6}}{\frac{5}{6}} = \dfrac{1}{6} \cdot \dfrac{6}{5} = \dfrac{1}{5}$

The odds in favor of rolling a 2 are $\frac{1}{5}$. The ratio $\frac{1}{5}$ is usually written 1:5 and is read "1 to 5." Thus, the odds in favor of rolling a 2 are 1 to 5.

b. Now that we have the odds in favor of rolling a 2, namely $\frac{1}{5}$ or 1:5, we can find the odds against rolling a 2 by reversing this ratio. Thus,

$$\text{Odds against } E(\text{rolling a 2}) = \dfrac{5}{1} \quad \text{or} \quad 5:1.$$

The odds against rolling a 2 are 5 to 1.

PRACTICE 6 You are dealt one card from a 52-card deck.

a. Find the odds in favor of getting a red queen.
b. Find the odds against getting a red queen.

EXAMPLE 7 From Probability to Odds

The winner of a raffle will receive a new sports utility vehicle. If 500 raffle tickets were sold and you purchased ten tickets, what are the odds against your winning the car?

Solution Let E represent the event of winning the SUV. Because you purchased ten tickets and 500 tickets were sold,

$$P(E) = \dfrac{10}{500} = \dfrac{1}{50} \quad \text{and} \quad P(\text{not } E) = 1 - \dfrac{1}{50} = \dfrac{50}{50} - \dfrac{1}{50} = \dfrac{49}{50}.$$

Now we are ready to construct the ratio for the odds against E (winning the SUV).

$$\text{Odds against } E = \dfrac{P(\text{not } E)}{P(E)} = \dfrac{\frac{49}{50}}{\frac{1}{50}} = \dfrac{49}{50} \cdot \dfrac{50}{1} = \dfrac{49}{1}$$

The odds against winning the SUV are 49 to 1, written 49:1.

PRACTICE 7 The winner of a raffle will receive a two-year scholarship to the college of his or her choice. If 1000 raffle tickets were sold and you purchased five tickets, what are the odds against your winning the scholarship?

Odds enable us to play and bet fairly on games. For example, we have seen that the odds in favor of getting 2 when you roll a die are 1 to 5. Suppose this is a gaming situation and you bet $1 on a 2 turning up. In terms of your bet, there is one favorable outcome, rolling 2, and five unfavorable outcomes, rolling 1, 3, 4, 5, or 6. The odds in favor of getting 2, 1 to 5, compares the number of favorable outcomes, one, to the number of unfavorable outcomes, five.

Using odds in a gaming situation where money is waged, we can determine if the game is *fair*. If the odds in favor of an event E are a to b, the **game is fair** if a bet of $\$a$ is lost if event E does not occur, but a win of $\$b$ (as well as returning the bet of $\$a$) is realized if event E does occur. For example, the odds in favor of getting 2 on a die roll are 1 to 5. If you bet $1 on a 2 turning up and the game is fair, you should win $5 (and have your bet of $1 returned) if a 2 turns up.

Now that we know how to convert from probability to odds, let's see how to convert from odds to probability. Suppose that the odds in favor of event E occurring are a to b. This means that

$$\frac{P(E)}{P(\text{not } E)} = \frac{a}{b} \quad \text{or} \quad \frac{P(E)}{1 - P(E)} = \frac{a}{b}.$$

By solving the equation on the right for $P(E)$, we obtain the following formula for converting from odds to probability:

> **Odds to Probability**
> If the odds in favor of event E are a to b, then the probability of the event is given by
> $$P(E) = \frac{a}{a + b}.$$

EXAMPLE 8 From Odds to Probability

The odds in favor of a particular horse winning a race are 2 to 5. What is the probability that this horse will win the race?

Solution Because odds in favor, a to b, means a probability of $\frac{a}{a+b}$, then odds in favor, 2 to 5, means a probability of

$$\frac{2}{2 + 5} = \frac{2}{7}.$$

The probability that this horse will win the race is $\frac{2}{7}$.

PRACTICE 8 The odds against a particular horse winning a race are 15 to 1. Find the odds in favor of the horse winning the race and the probability of the horse winning the race.

13.6 EXERCISE SET

PRACTICE AND APPLICATION EXERCISES

In Exercises 1–6, you are dealt one card from a 52-card deck. Find the probability that you are not dealt

1. an ace.   **2.** a 3.   **3.** a heart.   **4.** a club.   **5.** a picture card.   **6.** a red picture card.

In 5-card poker, played with a standard 52-card deck, $_{52}C_5$, or 2,598,960, different hands are possible. The probability of being dealt various hands is the number of different ways they can occur divided by 2,598,960. Shown in Exercises 7–10 are various types of poker hands and their probabilities. In each exercise, find the probability of not being dealt this type of hand.

Type of Hand	Illustration	Number of Ways the Hand Can Occur	Probability
7. Straight flush: 5 cards with consecutive numbers, all in the same suit (excluding royal flush)		36	$\dfrac{36}{2{,}598{,}960}$
8. Four of a kind: 4 cards with the same number, plus 1 additional card		624	$\dfrac{624}{2{,}598{,}960}$

9. Full house: 3 cards of one number and 2 cards of a second number		3744	$\dfrac{3744}{2{,}598{,}960}$
10. Flush: 5 cards of the same suit (excluding royal flush and straight flush)		5108	$\dfrac{5108}{2{,}598{,}960}$

The graph shows the probability of cardiovascular disease, by age and gender. Use the information in the graph to solve Exercises 11–12. Express all probabilities as decimals, estimated to two decimal places.

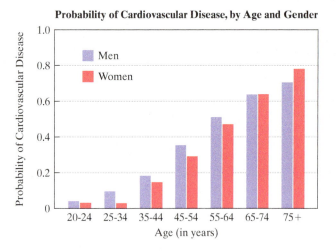

Probability of Cardiovascular Disease, by Age and Gender

Source: American Heart Association

11. a. What is the probability that a randomly selected man between the ages of 25 and 34 has cardiovascular disease?

b. What is the probability that a randomly selected man between the ages of 25 and 34 does not have cardiovascular disease?

12. a. What is the probability that a randomly selected woman, 75 or older, has cardiovascular disease?

b. What is the probability that a randomly selected woman, 75 or older, does not have cardiovascular disease?

The table shows the distribution, by annual income, of the 112 million households in the United States in 2003, with all numbers rounded to the nearest million. Use this distribution to solve Exercises 13–16.

Income Distribution of U.S. Households, in Millions

Annual Income	Number	Annual Income	Number
Less than $10,000	10	$35,000–$49,999	17
$10,000–$14,999	8	$50,000–$74,999	20
$15,000–$24,999	15	$75,000–$99,999	12
$25,000–$34,999	13	$100,000 or more	17

Source: U.S. Census Bureau

If one household is randomly selected from this population, find the probability, expressed as a simplified fraction, that

13. the household income is not in the $50,000–$74,999 range.

14. the household income is not in the $15,000–$24,999 range.

15. the household income is less than $100,000.

16. the household income is at least $10,000.

In Exercises 17–22, you randomly select one card from a 52-card deck. Find the probability of selecting

17. a 2 or a 3. **18.** a 7 or an 8.

19. a red 2 or a black 3. **20.** a red 7 or a black 8.

21. the 2 of hearts or the 3 of spades.

22. the 7 of hearts or the 8 of spades.

23. The mathematics faculty at a college consists of 8 professors, 12 associate professors, 14 assistant professors, and 10 instructors. If one faculty member is randomly selected, find the probability of choosing a professor or an instructor.

24. A political discussion group consists of 30 Republicans, 25 Democrats, 8 Independents, and 4 members of the Green party. If one person is randomly selected from the group, find the probability of choosing an Independent or a Green.

In Exercises 25–26, a single die is rolled. Find the probability of rolling

25. an even number or a number less than 5.

26. an odd number or a number less than 4.

In Exercises 27–30, you are dealt one card from a 52-card deck. Find the probability that you are dealt

27. a 7 or a red card.

28. a 5 or a black card.

29. a heart or a picture card.

30. a card greater than 2 and less than 7, or a diamond.

In Exercises 31–34, it is equally probable that the pointer on the spinner shown will land on any one of the eight regions, numbered 1 through 8. If the pointer lands on a borderline, spin again.

Find the probability that the pointer will stop on

31. an odd number or a number less than 6.
32. an odd number or a number greater than 3.
33. an even number or a number greater than 5.
34. an even number or a number less than 4.

Use this information to solve Exercises 35–38. The mathematics department of a college has 8 male professors, 11 female professors, 14 male teaching assistants, and 7 female teaching assistants. If a person is selected at random from the group, find the probability that the selected person is

35. a professor or a male.
36. a professor or a female.
37. a teaching assistant or a female.
38. a teaching assistant or a male.
39. In a class of 50 students, 29 are Democrats, 11 are business majors, and 5 of the business majors are Democrats. If one student is randomly selected from the class, find the probability of choosing a Democrat or a business major.
40. A student is selected at random from a group of 200 students in which 135 take math, 85 take English, and 65 take both math and English. Find the probability that the selected student takes math or English.

The table shows the educational attainment of the U.S. population, ages 25 and over, in 2004. Use the data in the table, expressed in millions, to solve Exercises 41–48.

Educational Attainment of the U.S. Population, Ages 25 and Over, in Millions

	Less Than 4 Years High School	4 Years High School Only	Some College (Less than 4 years)	4 Years College (or More)	Total
Male	14	28	22	26	90
Female	14	32	26	25	97
Total	28	60	48	51	187

Source: U.S. Census Bureau

Find the probability, expressed as a simplified fraction, that a randomly selected American, aged 25 or over,

41. has not completed four years (or more) of college.
42. has not completed four years of high school.
43. has completed four years of high school only or less than four years of college.
44. has completed less than four years of high school or four years of high school only.
45. has completed four years of high school only or is a man.
46. has completed four years of high school only or is a woman.

Find the odds in favor and the odds against a randomly selected American, aged 25 and over, with

47. four years (or more) of college.
48. less than four years of high school.

The graph shows the distribution, by branch and gender, of the 1.43 million, or 1430 thousand, active-duty personnel in the U.S. military in 2003. Numbers are given in thousands and rounded to the nearest ten thousand. Use the data to solve Exercises 49–60.

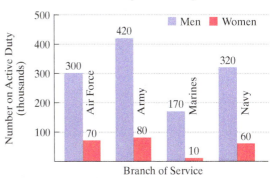

Source: U.S. Defense Department

If one person is randomly selected from the population represented in the bar graph in the previous column, find the probability, expressed as a simplified fraction, that the person

49. is not in the Army.
50. is not in the Marines.
51. is in the Navy or is a man.
52. is in the Army or is a woman.
53. is in the Air Force or the Marines.
54. is in the Army or the Navy.

Find the odds in favor and the odds against a randomly selected person from the population represented in the bar graph in the previous column being

55. in the Navy.
56. in the Army.
57. a woman in the Marines.
58. a woman in the Air Force.
59. a man.
60. a woman.

In Exercises 61–64, a single die is rolled. Find the odds

61. in favor of rolling a number greater than 2.
62. in favor of rolling a number less than 5.
63. against rolling a number greater than 2.
64. against rolling a number less than 5.

The circle graphs show the percentage of children in the United States whose parents are college graduates in one-parent households and two-parent households. Use the information shown to solve Exercises 65–66.

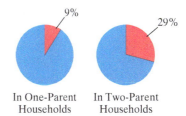

Source: U.S. Census Bureau

65. a. What are the odds in favor of a child in a one-parent household having a parent who is a college graduate?
    b. What are the odds against a child in a one-parent household having a parent who is a college graduate?
66. a. What are the odds in favor of a child in a two-parent household having parents who are college graduates?
    b. What are the odds against a child in a two-parent household having parents who are college graduates?

In Exercises 67–76, one card is randomly selected from a deck of cards. Find the odds

67. in favor of drawing a heart.
68. in favor of drawing a picture card.
69. in favor of drawing a red card.
70. in favor of drawing a black card.
71. against drawing a 9.
72. against drawing a 5.
73. against drawing a black king.
74. against drawing a red jack.
75. against drawing a spade greater than 3 and less than 9.
76. against drawing a club greater than 4 and less than 10.
77. The winner of a raffle will receive a 21-foot outboard boat. If 1000 raffle tickets were sold and you purchased 20 tickets, what are the odds against your winning the boat?
78. The winner of a raffle will receive a 30-day all-expense-paid trip throughout Europe. If 5000 raffle tickets were sold and you purchased 30 tickets, what are the odds against your winning the trip?

Of the 38 plays attributed to Shakespeare, 18 are comedies, 10 are tragedies, and 10 are histories. In Exercises 79–86, one play is randomly selected from Shakespeare's 38 plays. Find the odds

79. in favor of selecting a comedy.
80. in favor of selecting a tragedy.
81. against selecting a history.
82. against selecting a comedy.
83. in favor of selecting a comedy or a tragedy.
84. in favor of selecting a tragedy or a history.
85. against selecting a tragedy or a history.
86. against selecting a comedy or a history.
87. If you are given odds of 3 to 4 in favor of winning a bet, what is the probability of winning the bet?
88. If you are given odds of 3 to 7 in favor of winning a bet, what is the probability of winning the bet?
89. Based on his skills in basketball, it was computed that when Michael Jordan shot a free throw, the odds in favor of his making it were 21 to 4. Find the probability that when Michael Jordan shot a free throw, he missed it. Out of every 100 free throws he attempted, on the average how many did he make?
90. The odds in favor of a person who is alive at age 20 still being alive at age 70 are 193 to 270. Find the probability that a person who is alive at age 20 will still be alive at age 70.

Exercises 91–92 give the odds against various flight risks. (Source: Men's Health, August 2005) Use these odds to determine the probability of the underlined event for those in flight.

91. odds against <u>contracting an airborne disease</u>: 999 to 1
92. odds against <u>deep-vein thrombosis</u> (blood clot in the leg): 28 to 1

WRITING IN MATHEMATICS

93. Explain how to find the probability of an event not occurring. Give an example.
94. What are mutually exclusive events? Give an example of two events that are mutually exclusive.
95. Explain how to find *or* probabilities with mutually exclusive events. Give an example.
96. Give an example of two events that are not mutually exclusive.
97. Explain how to find *or* probabilities with events that are not mutually exclusive. Give an example.
98. Explain how to find the odds in favor of an event if you know the probability that the event will occur.
99. Explain how to find the probability of an event if you know the odds in favor of that event.

CRITICAL THINKING EXERCISES

100. In Exercise 39, find the probability of choosing **a.** a Democrat who is not a business major; **b.** a student who is neither a Democrat nor a business major.

13.7 EVENTS INVOLVING *AND*; CONDITIONAL PROBABILITY

OBJECTIVES

1 Find the probability of one event and a second event occurring.
2 Compute conditional probabilities.

OBJECTIVE 1 ▶ *And* probabilities with independent events. Consider tossing a fair coin two times in succession. The outcome of the first toss, heads or tails, does not affect what happens when you toss the coin a second time. For example, the occurrence of tails on the first toss does not make tails more likely or less likely to occur on the second toss. The repeated toss of a coin produces *independent events* because the outcome of one toss does not affect the outcome of others.

Helpful Hint

Do not confuse *independent events* and *mutually exclusive events*. Mutually exclusive events cannot occur at the same time. Independent events occur at different times, although they have no effect on each other.

> **Independent Events**
>
> Two events are **independent events** if the occurrence of either of them has no effect on the probability of the other.

When a fair coin is tossed two times in succession, the set of equally likely outcomes is

{heads heads, heads tails, tails heads, tails tails}.

We can use this set to find the probability of getting heads on the first toss and heads on the second toss:

$$P(\text{heads and heads}) = \frac{\text{number of ways two heads can occur}}{\text{total number of possible outcomes}} = \frac{1}{4}.$$

We can also determine the probability of two heads, $\frac{1}{4}$, without having to list all the equally likely outcomes. The probability of heads on the first toss is $\frac{1}{2}$. The probability of heads on the second toss is also $\frac{1}{2}$. The product of these probabilities, $\frac{1}{2} \cdot \frac{1}{2}$, results in the probability of two heads, namely $\frac{1}{4}$. Thus,

$$P(\text{heads and heads}) = P(\text{heads}) \cdot P(\text{heads}).$$

In general, if two events are independent, we can calculate the probability of the first occurring and the second occurring by multiplying their probabilities.

> **And Probabilities with Independent Events**
>
> If A and B are independent events, then
>
> $$P(A \text{ and } B) = P(A) \cdot P(B).$$

EXAMPLE 1 Independent Events on a Roulette Wheel

The figure in the margin shows a U.S. roulette wheel that has 38 numbered slots (1 through 36, 0, and 00). Of the 38 compartments, 18 are black, 18 are red, and 2 are green. A play has the dealer spin the wheel and a small ball in opposite directions. As the ball slows to a stop, it can land with equal probability on any one of the 38 numbered slots. Find the probability of red occurring on two consecutive plays.

Solution The wheel has 38 equally likely outcomes and 18 are red. Thus, the probability of red occurring on a play is $\frac{18}{38}$, or $\frac{9}{19}$. The result that occurs on each play is independent of all previous results. Thus,

$$P(\text{red and red}) = P(\text{red}) \cdot P(\text{red}) = \frac{9}{19} \cdot \frac{9}{19} = \frac{81}{361} \approx 0.224.$$

The probability of red occurring on two consecutive plays is $\frac{81}{361}$.

Some roulette players incorrectly believe that if red occurs on two consecutive plays, then another color is "due." Because the events are independent, the outcomes of previous spins have no effect on any other spins.

FIGURE 13.11 A U.S. roulette wheel

PRACTICE 1 Find the probability of green occurring on two consecutive plays on a roulette wheel.

The *and* rule for independent events can be extended to cover three or more events. Thus, if A, B, and C are independent events, then

$$P(A \text{ and } B \text{ and } C) = P(A) \cdot P(B) \cdot P(C).$$

EXAMPLE 2   Independent Events in a Family

The picture in the margin shows a family that had nine girls in a row. Find the probability of this occurrence.

Solution   If two or more events are independent, we can find the probability of them all occurring by multiplying their probabilities. The probability of a baby girl is $\frac{1}{2}$, so the probability of nine girls in a row is $\frac{1}{2}$ used as a factor nine times.

$$P(\text{nine girls in a row}) = \frac{1}{2} \cdot \frac{1}{2} \cdot \frac{1}{2} \cdot \frac{1}{2} \cdot \frac{1}{2} \cdot \frac{1}{2} \cdot \frac{1}{2} \cdot \frac{1}{2} \cdot \frac{1}{2}$$

$$= \left(\frac{1}{2}\right)^9 = \frac{1}{512}$$

The probability of a run of nine girls in a row is $\frac{1}{512}$. (If another child is born into the family, this event is independent of the other nine and the probability of a girl is still $\frac{1}{2}$.)

PRACTICE 2   Find the probability of a family having four boys in a row.

Now let us return to the hurricane problem that opened this chapter. The Saffir/Simpson scale assigns numbers 1 through 5 to measure the disaster potential of a hurricane's winds. The table in the margin describes the scale. According to the National Hurricane Center, the probability that South Florida will be hit by a category 1 hurricane or higher in any single year is $\frac{5}{19}$, or approximately 0.26. In Example 3, we explore the risks of living in "Hurricane Alley."

TABLE 13.5   The Saffir/Simpson Hurricane Scale

Category	Winds (Miles per Hour)
1	74–95
2	96–110
3	111–130
4	131–155
5	>155

EXAMPLE 3   Hurricanes and Probabilities

If the probability that South Florida will be hit by a hurricane in any single year is $\frac{5}{19}$,

a. What is the probability that South Florida will be hit by a hurricane in three consecutive years?

b. What is the probability that South Florida will not be hit by a hurricane in the next ten years?

Solution

a. The probability that South Florida will be hit by a hurricane in three consecutive years is

$$P(\text{hurricane and hurricane and hurricane})$$
$$= P(\text{hurricane}) \cdot P(\text{hurricane}) \cdot P(\text{hurricane}) = \frac{5}{19} \cdot \frac{5}{19} \cdot \frac{5}{19} = \frac{125}{6859} \approx 0.018.$$

b. We will first find the probability that South Florida will not be hit by a hurricane in any single year.

$$P(\text{no hurricane}) = 1 - P(\text{hurricane}) = 1 - \frac{5}{19} = \frac{14}{19} \approx 0.737$$

The probability of not being hit by a hurricane in a single year is $\frac{14}{19}$. Therefore, the probability of not being hit by a hurricane ten years in a row is $\frac{14}{19}$ used as a factor ten times.

> **Helpful Hint**
>
> When solving probability problems, begin by deciding whether to use the *or* formulas or the *and* formulas.
>
> - *Or* problems usually have the word *or* in the statement of the problem. These problems involve only one selection.
>
> Example:
>
> > If one person is selected, find the probability of selecting a man or a Canadian.
>
> - *And* problems often do not have the word *and* in the statement of the problem. These problems involve more than one selection.
>
> Example:
>
> > If two people are selected, find the probability that both are men.

$P(\text{no hurricanes for ten years})$

$$= P\binom{\text{no hurricane}}{\text{for year 1}} \cdot P\binom{\text{no hurricane}}{\text{for year 2}} \cdot P\binom{\text{no hurricane}}{\text{for year 3}} \cdot \ldots \cdot P\binom{\text{no hurricane}}{\text{for year 10}}$$

$$= \frac{14}{19} \cdot \frac{14}{19} \cdot \frac{14}{19} \cdot \ldots \cdot \frac{14}{19}$$

$$= \left(\frac{14}{19}\right)^{10} \approx (0.737)^{10} \approx 0.047$$

The probability that South Florida will not be hit by a hurricane in the next ten years is approximately 0.047.

Now we are ready to answer your question:

What is the probability that South Florida will be hit by a hurricane at least once in the next ten years?

Because $P(\text{not } E) = 1 - P(E)$,

$P(\text{no hurricane for ten years}) = 1 - P(\text{at least one hurricane in ten years}).$

> The negation of "at least one" is "no."

Equivalently,

$P(\text{at least one hurricane in ten years}) = 1 - P(\text{no hurricane for ten years})$
$= 1 - 0.047 = 0.953.$

With a probability of 0.953, it is nearly certain that South Florida will be hit by a hurricane at least once in the next ten years.

> **The Probability of an Event Happening at Least Once**
>
> $P(\text{event happening at least once}) = 1 - P(\text{event does not happen})$

PRACTICE 3 If the probability that South Florida will be hit by a hurricane in any single year is $\frac{5}{19}$,

a. What is the probability that South Florida will be hit by a hurricane in four consecutive years?

b. What is the probability that South Florida will not be hit by a hurricane in the next four years?

c. What is the probability that South Florida will be hit by a hurricane at least once in the next four years?

Express all probabilities as fractions and as decimals rounded to three places.

And Probabilities with Dependent Events

The candy box in the margin contains 20 assorted chocolates. We do know that there are exactly 5 chocolate-covered cherries, and it's impossible to tell what is inside each piece.

Suppose you want to know what your chances are of selecting 2 chocolate-covered cherries? Five of the 20 pieces are chocolate-covered cherries, so the probability of getting one of them on your first selection is $\frac{5}{20}$, or $\frac{1}{4}$. Now, suppose that you did choose a chocolate-covered cherry on your first pick. There are now only 19 pieces of chocolate left. Only 4 are chocolate-covered cherries. The probability of getting a chocolate-covered cherry on your second try is 4 out of 19, or $\frac{4}{19}$. This is a different probability

5 chocolate-covered cherries lie within the 20 pieces.

Once a chocolate-covered cherry is selected, only 4 chocolate-covered cherries lie within the remaining 19 pieces.

than the $\frac{1}{4}$ probability on your first selection. Selecting a chocolate-covered cherry the first time changes what is in the candy box. The probability of what you select the second time *is* affected by the outcome of the first event. For this reason, we say that these are *dependent events*.

> **Dependent Events**
> Two events are **dependent events** if the occurrence of one of them has an effect on the probability of the other.

The probability of selecting two chocolate-covered cherries in a row can be found by multiplying the $\frac{1}{4}$ probability on the first selection by the $\frac{4}{19}$ probability on the second selection:

P(chocolate-covered cherry and chocolate-covered cherry)

$$= P(\text{chocolate-covered cherry}) \cdot P\begin{pmatrix} \text{chocolate-covered cherry} \\ \text{given that one was selected} \end{pmatrix}$$

$$= \frac{1}{4} \cdot \frac{4}{19} = \frac{1}{19}.$$

The probability of selecting two chocolate-covered cherries in a row is $\frac{1}{19}$. This is a special case of finding the probability that each of two dependent events occurs.

> **And Probabilities with Dependent Events**
> If A and B are dependent events, then
> $$P(A \text{ and } B) = P(A) \cdot P(B \text{ given that } A \text{ has occurred}).$$

EXAMPLE 4 An *And* Probability with Dependent Events

Good news: You won a free trip to Madrid and can take two people with you, all expenses paid. Bad news: Ten of your cousins have appeared out of nowhere and are begging you to take them. You write each cousin's name on a card, place the cards in a hat, and select one name. Then you select a second name without replacing the first card. If three of your ten cousins speak Spanish, find the probability of selecting two Spanish-speaking cousins.

Solution Because $P(A \text{ and } B) = P(A) \cdot P(B \text{ given that } A \text{ has occurred})$, then P(two Spanish-speaking cousins)

$$= P(\text{speaks Spanish and speaks Spanish})$$

$$= P(\text{speaks Spanish}) \cdot P\begin{pmatrix} \text{speaks Spanish given that a Spanish-speaking} \\ \text{cousin was selected first} \end{pmatrix}$$

$$= \underbrace{\frac{3}{10}}_{\substack{\text{There are ten cousins,} \\ \text{three of whom speak Spanish.}}} \cdot \underbrace{\frac{2}{9}}_{\substack{\text{After picking a Spanish-speaking} \\ \text{cousin, there are nine cousins left,} \\ \text{two of whom speak Spanish.}}}$$

$$= \frac{6}{90} = \frac{1}{15} \approx 0.067.$$

> **Helpful Hint**
> Example 4 can also be solved using the combinations formula.
>
> P(two Spanish speakers)
>
> $= \dfrac{\text{number of ways of selecting 2 Spanish-speaking cousins}}{\text{number of ways of selecting 2 cousins}}$
>
> $= \dfrac{{}_3C_2}{{}_{10}C_2}$
>
> ({}_3C_2: 2 Spanish speakers selected from 3 Spanish-speaking cousins)
> ({}_{10}C_2: 2 cousins selected from 10 cousins)
>
> $= \dfrac{3}{45} = \dfrac{1}{15}$

The probability of selecting two Spanish-speaking cousins is $\frac{1}{15}$.

PRACTICE 4 You are dealt two cards from a 52-card deck. Find the probability of getting two kings.

The multiplication rule for dependent events can be extended to cover three or more dependent events. For example, in the case of three such events,

$P(A \text{ and } B \text{ and } C)$
$= P(A) \cdot P(B \text{ given that } A \text{ occurred}) \cdot P(C \text{ given that } A \text{ and } B \text{ occurred}).$

EXAMPLE 5 An *And* Probability with Three Dependent Events

Three people are randomly selected, one person at a time, from five freshmen, two sophomores, and four juniors. Find the probability that the first two people selected are freshmen and the third is a junior.

Solution

5 freshmen
2 sophomores
4 juniors

The given numbers (repeated)

$P(\text{first two are freshmen and the third is a junior})$

$= P(\text{freshman}) \cdot P\binom{\text{freshman given that a}}{\text{freshman was selected first}} \cdot P\binom{\text{junior given that a freshman was}}{\text{selected first and a freshman was}}_{\text{selected second}}$

$= \dfrac{5}{11} \cdot \dfrac{4}{10} \cdot \dfrac{4}{9}$

- There are 11 people, five of whom are freshmen.
- After picking a freshman, there are 10 people left, four of whom are freshmen.
- After the first two selections, 9 people are left, four of whom are juniors.

$= \dfrac{8}{99}$

The probability that the first two people selected are freshmen and the third is a junior is $\frac{8}{99}$.

PRACTICE 5 You are dealt three cards from a 52-card deck. Find the probability of getting three hearts.

OBJECTIVE 2 ▶ **Compute conditional probability.** We have seen that for any two dependent events A and B,

$P(A \text{ and } B) = P(A) \cdot P(B \text{ given that } A \text{ occurs}).$

The probability of B given that A occurs is called *conditional probability*, denoted by $P(B|A)$.

> **Conditional Probability**
>
> The probability of event B, assuming that the event A has already occurred, is called the **conditional probability** of B, given A. This probability is denoted by $P(B|A)$.

It is helpful to think of the conditional probability $P(B|A)$ as the **probability that event B occurs if the sample space is restricted to the outcomes associated with event A.**

EXAMPLE 6 Finding Conditional Probability

A letter is randomly selected from the letters of the English alphabet. Find the probability of selecting a vowel, given that the outcome is a letter that precedes h.

Solution We are looking for
$$P(\text{vowel}|\text{letter precedes h}).$$
This is the probability of a vowel if the sample space is restricted to the set of letters that precede h. Thus, the sample space is given by
$$S = \{a, b, c, d, e, f, g\}.$$
There are seven possible outcomes in the sample space. We can select a vowel from this set in one of two ways: a or e. Therefore, the probability of selecting a vowel, given that the outcome is a letter that precedes h, is $\frac{2}{7}$.
$$P(\text{vowel}|\text{letter precedes h}) = \tfrac{2}{7}$$

PRACTICE 6 You are dealt one card from a 52-card deck. Find the probability of getting a heart, given that the card you were dealt is a red card.

We have seen that $P(B|A)$ is the probability that event B occurs if the sample space is restricted to event A. Thus,

$$P(B|A) = \frac{\text{number of outcomes of } B \text{ that are in the restricted sample space } A}{\text{number of outcomes in the restricted sample space } A}.$$

This can be stated in terms of the following formula:

A Formula for Conditional Probability
$$P(B|A) = \frac{n(B \cap A)}{n(A)} = \frac{\text{number of outcomes common to } B \text{ and } A}{\text{number of outcomes in } A}$$

13.7 EXERCISE SET

PRACTICE AND APPLICATION EXERCISES

Exercises 1–26 involve probabilities with independent events.

Use the spinner shown to solve Exercises 1–10. It is equally probable that the pointer will land on any one of the six regions. If the pointer lands on a borderline, spin again. If the pointer is spun twice, find the probability it will land on

1. green and then red.
2. yellow and then green.
3. yellow and then yellow.
4. red and then red.
5. a color other than red each time.
6. a color other than green each time.

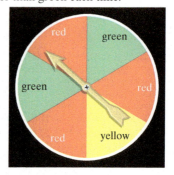

If the pointer is spun three times, find the probability it will land on

7. green and then red and then yellow.
8. red and then red and then green.
9. red every time.
10. green every time.

In Exercises 11–14, a single die is rolled twice. Find the probability of rolling

11. a 2 the first time and a 3 the second time.
12. a 5 the first time and a 1 the second time.
13. an even number the first time and a number greater than 2 the second time.
14. an odd number the first time and a number less than 3 the second time.

In Exercises 15–20, you draw one card from a 52-card deck. Then the card is replaced in the deck, the deck is shuffled, and you draw again. Find the probability of drawing

15. a picture card the first time and a heart the second time.
16. a jack the first time and a club the second time.
17. a king each time.
18. a 3 each time.
19. a red card each time.
20. a black card each time.
21. If you toss a fair coin six times, what is the probability of getting all heads?
22. If you toss a fair coin seven times, what is the probability of getting all tails?

In Exercises 23–24, a coin is tossed and a die is rolled. Find the probability of getting

23. a head and a number greater than 4.
24. a tail and a number less than 5.

25. **Multiple Steps.** The probability that South Florida will be hit by a major hurricane (category 4 or 5) in any single year is $\frac{1}{16}$.
    (*Source:* National Hurricane Center)
    a. What is the probability that South Florida will be hit by a major hurricane two years in a row?
    b. What is the probability that South Florida will be hit by a major hurricane in three consecutive years?
    c. What is the probability that South Florida will not be hit by a major hurricane in the next ten years?
    d. What is the probability that South Florida will be hit by a major hurricane at least once in the next ten years?

26. **Multiple Steps.** The probability that a region prone to flooding will flood in any single year is $\frac{1}{10}$.
    a. What is the probability of a flood two years in a row?
    b. What is the probability of flooding in three consecutive years?
    c. What is the probability of no flooding for ten consecutive years?
    d. What is the probability of flooding at least once in the next ten years?

The graph shows that U.S. adults dependent on tobacco have a greater probability of suffering from some ailments than the general adult population. When making two or more selections from populations with large numbers, such as the U.S. adult population or the population dependent on tobacco, we assume that each selection is independent of every other selection. In Exercises 27–32, assume that the selections are independent events.

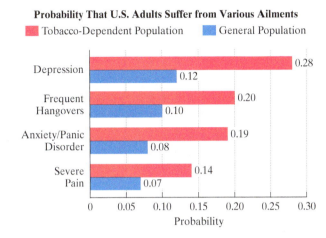

Source: MARS 2005 OTC/DTC

27. If two adults are randomly selected from the general population, what is the probability that they both suffer from depression?
28. If two adults are randomly selected from the population of cigarette smokers, what is the probability that they both suffer from depression?
29. If three adults are randomly selected from the population of cigarette smokers, what is the probability that they all suffer from frequent hangovers?
30. If three adults are randomly selected from the general population, what is the probability that they all suffer from frequent hangovers?
31. If three adults are randomly selected from the population of cigarette smokers, what is the probability, expressed as a decimal correct to four places, that at least one person suffers from anxiety/panic disorder?
32. If three adults are randomly selected from the population of cigarette smokers, what is the probability, expressed as a decimal correct to four places, that at least one person suffers from severe pain?

Exercises 33–48 involve probabilities with dependent events.

In Exercises 33–36, we return to our box of chocolates. There are 30 chocolates in the box, all identically shaped. Five are filled with coconut, 10 with caramel, and 15 are solid chocolate. You randomly select one piece, eat it, and then select a second piece. Find the probability of selecting

33. two solid chocolates in a row.
34. two caramel-filled chocolates in a row.
35. a coconut-filled chocolate followed by a caramel-filled chocolate.
36. a coconut-filled chocolate followed by a solid chocolate.

In Exercises 37–42, consider a political discussion group consisting of 5 Democrats, 6 Republicans, and 4 Independents. Suppose that two group members are randomly selected, in succession, to attend a political convention. Find the probability of selecting

37. two Democrats.
38. two Republicans.
39. an Independent and then a Republican.
40. an Independent and then a Democrat.
41. no Independents.
42. no Democrats.

In Exercises 43–48, an ice chest contains six cans of apple juice, eight cans of grape juice, four cans of orange juice, and two cans of mango juice. Suppose that you reach into the container and randomly select three cans in succession. Find the probability of selecting

43. three cans of apple juice.
44. three cans of grape juice.
45. a can of grape juice, then a can of orange juice, then a can of mango juice.
46. a can of apple juice, then a can of grape juice, then a can of orange juice.
47. no grape juice.
48. no apple juice.

In Exercises 49–56, the numbered disks shown are placed in a box and one disk is selected at random.

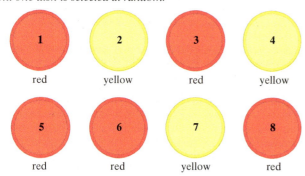

Find the probability of selecting

49. a 3, given that a red disk is selected.
50. a 7, given that a yellow disk is selected.
51. an even number, given that a yellow disk is selected.
52. an odd number, given that a red disk is selected.
53. a red disk, given that an odd number is selected.
54. a yellow disk, given that an odd number is selected.
55. a red disk, given that the number selected is at least 5.
56. a yellow disk, given that the number selected is at most 3.

WRITING IN MATHEMATICS

57. Explain how to find *and* probabilities with independent events. Give an example.
58. Explain how to find *and* probabilities with dependent events. Give an example.
59. What does $P(B|A)$ mean? Give an example.

In Exercises 60–64, write a probability problem involving the word "and" whose solution results in the probability fractions shown.

60. $\frac{1}{2} \cdot \frac{1}{2}$
61. $\frac{1}{6} \cdot \frac{1}{6} \cdot \frac{1}{6}$
62. $\frac{1}{2} \cdot \frac{1}{6}$
63. $\frac{13}{52} \cdot \frac{12}{51}$
64. $\frac{1}{4} \cdot \frac{3}{5}$

CRITICAL THINKING EXERCISES

65. If the probability of being hospitalized during a year is 0.1, find the probability that no one in a family of five will be hospitalized in a year.
66. If a single die is rolled five times, what is the probability it lands on 2 on the first, third, and fourth rolls, but not on any of the other rolls?
67. **Multiple Steps.** Probabilities and Coincidence of Shared Birthdays
    a. If two people are selected at random, the probability that they do not have the same birthday (day and month) is $\frac{365}{365} \cdot \frac{364}{365}$. Explain why this is so. (Ignore leap years and assume 365 days in a year.)
    b. If three people are selected at random, find the probability that they all have different birthdays.
    c. If three people are selected at random, find the probability that at least two of them have the same birthday.
    d. If 20 people are selected at random, find the probability that at least 2 of them have the same birthday.
    e. How large a group is needed to give a 0.5 chance of at least two people having the same birthday?
68. Nine cards numbered from 1 through 9 are placed into a box and two cards are selected without replacement. Find the probability that both numbers selected are odd, given that their sum is even.

GROUP EXERCISES

69. Do you live in an area prone to catastrophes, such as earthquakes, fires, tornados, hurricanes, or floods? If so, research the probability of this catastrophe occurring in a single year. Group members should then use this probability to write and solve a problem similar to Exercise 25 in this exercise set.

13.8 THE NORMAL DISTRIBUTION

OBJECTIVES

1. Recognize characteristics of normal distributions.
2. Understand the 68-95-99.7 Rule.
3. Find scores at a specified standard deviation from the mean.
4. Use the 68-95-99.7 Rule.

Our heights are on the rise! Because of improved diets and medical care, the mean height for men is now 5 feet 10 inches and for women it is 5 feet 5 inches. Mean adult heights are expected to plateau by 2050.

Mean Adult Heights

5'2" 5'7"
1900

5'5" 5'10"
2000

5'7" 6'0"
2050

Source: National Center for Health Statistics

OBJECTIVE 1 ▶ Recognize the characteristics of the normal distribution.

Suppose that a researcher selects a random sample of 100 adult men, measures their heights, and constructs a histogram. The graph is shown in Figure 13.12. Parts (a), (b), and (c) illustrate what happens as the sample size increases. In Part (c), if you were to fold the graph down the middle, the left side would fit the right side. As we move out from the middle, the heights of the bars are the same to the left and right. Such a histogram is called **symmetric.** As the sample size increases, so does the graph's symmetry. If it were possible to measure the heights of all adult males, the entire population, the histogram would approach what is called the **normal distribution,** shown in Figure 13.12(d). This distribution is also called the **bell curve** or the **Gaussian distribution,** named for the German mathematician Carl Friedrich Gauss (1777–1855).

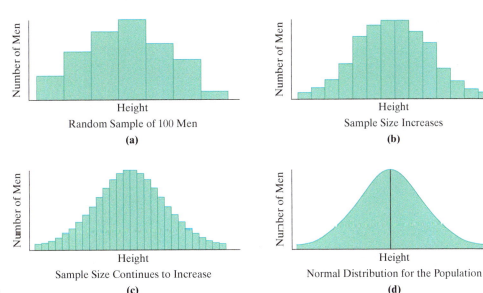

FIGURE 13.12 Heights of adult males

Part (d) of the figure above illustrates that the normal distribution is bell shaped and symmetric about a vertical line through its center. Furthermore, **the mean, median, and mode** of a normal distribution **are all equal** and located at the center of the distribution.

The shape of the normal distribution depends on the mean and the standard deviation. The figure below illustrates three normal distributions with the same mean, but different standard deviations. As the standard deviation increases, the distribution becomes more dispersed, or spread out, but retains its symmetric bell shape.

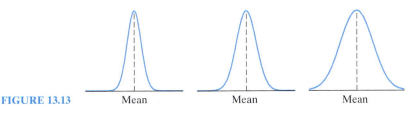

FIGURE 13.13

The normal distribution provides a wonderful model for all kinds of phenomena because many sets of data items closely resemble this population distribution. Examples include heights and weights of adult males, intelligence quotients, SAT scores, prices paid for a new car model, and life spans of light bulbs. In these distributions, the data items tend to cluster around the mean. The more an item differs from the mean, the less likely it is to occur.

The normal distribution is used to make predictions about an entire population using data from a sample. In this section, we focus on the characteristics and applications of the normal distribution.

OBJECTIVE 2 ▶ The standard deviation in normal distributions. The standard deviation plays a crucial role in the normal distribution, summarized by the **68–95–99.7 Rule.** This rule is illustrated below.

The 68–95–99.7 Rule for the Normal Distribution

1. Approximately 68% of the data items fall within 1 standard deviation of the mean (in both directions).
2. Approximately 95% of the data items fall within 2 standard deviations of the mean.
3. Approximately 99.7% of the data items fall within 3 standard deviations of the mean.

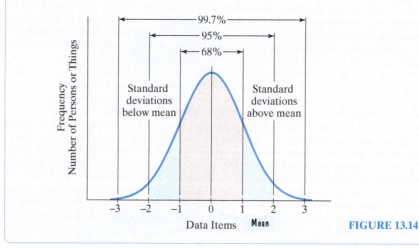

FIGURE 13.14

The figure above illustrates that a very small percentage of the data in a normal distribution lies more than 3 standard deviations above or below the mean. As we move from the mean, the curve falls rapidly, and then more and more gradually, toward the horizontal axis. The tails of the curve approach, but never touch, the horizontal axis, although they are quite close to the axis at 3 standard deviations from the mean. The range of the normal distribution is infinite. No matter how far out from the mean we move, there is always the probability (although very small) of a data item occurring even farther out.

OBJECTIVE 3 ▶ Find scores at a specified standard deviation from the mean.

EXAMPLE 1 Finding Scores at a Specified Standard Deviation from the Mean

Male adult heights in North America are approximately normally distributed with a mean of 70 inches and a standard deviation of 4 inches. Find the height that is

a. 2 standard deviations above the mean.

b. 3 standard deviations below the mean.

Solution

a. First, let us find the height that is 2 standard deviations above the mean.

$$\text{Height} = \text{mean} + 2 \cdot \text{standard deviation}$$
$$= 70 + 2 \cdot 4 = 70 + 8 = 78$$

A height of 78 inches is 2 standard deviations above the mean.

b. Next, let us find the height that is 3 standard deviations below the mean.

$$\text{Height} = \text{mean} - 3 \cdot \text{standard deviation}$$
$$= 70 - 3 \cdot 4 = 70 - 12 = 58$$

A height of 58 inches is 3 standard deviations below the mean.

The distribution of male adult heights in North America is illustrated as a normal distribution in Figure 13.15.

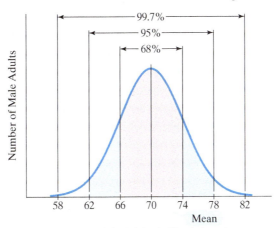

Normal Distribution of Male Adult Heights

Male Adult Heights in North America   **FIGURE 13.15**

PRACTICE 1 Female adult heights in North America are approximately normally distributed with a mean of 65 inches and a standard deviation of 3.5 inches. Find the height that is

a. 3 standard deviations above the mean.

b. 2 standard deviations below the mean.

OBJECTIVE 4 ▶ Use the 68–95–99.7 Rule.

EXAMPLE 2 Using the 68–95–99.7 Rule

Use the distribution of male adult heights in Example 1 to find the percentage of men in North America with heights

a. between 66 inches and 74 inches.   **b.** between 70 inches and 74 inches.

c. above 78 inches.

Solution

a. The 68–95–99.7 Rule states that approximately 68% of the data items fall within 1 standard deviation, 4, of the mean, 70.

$$\text{mean} - 1 \cdot \text{standard deviation} = 70 - 1 \cdot 4 = 70 - 4 = 66$$
$$\text{mean} + 1 \cdot \text{standard deviation} = 70 + 1 \cdot 4 = 70 + 4 = 74$$

The figure in Example 1 shows that 68% of male adults have heights between 66 inches and 74 inches.

b. The percentage of men with heights between 70 inches and 74 inches is not given directly in the figures. Because of the distribution's symmetry, the percentage with heights between 66 inches and 70 inches is the same as the percentage with heights between 70 and 74 inches. The figure to the right indicates that 68% have heights between 66 inches and 74 inches. Thus, half of 68%, or 34%, of men have heights between 70 inches and 74 inches.

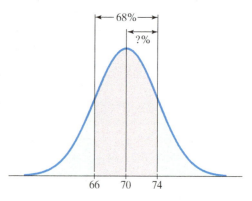

FIGURE 13.16 What percentage have heights between 70 inches and 74 inches?

c. A height of 78 inches is 2 standard deviations, 2 · 4, or 8 inches, above the mean, 70 inches. The 68–95–99.7 Rule states that approximately 95% of the data items fall within 2 standard deviations of the mean. Thus, approximately 100% − 95%, or 5%, of the data items are farther than 2 standard deviations from the mean. The 5% of the data items are represented by the two shaded green regions in the figure below. Because of the distribution's symmetry, half of 5%, or 2.5%, of the data items are more than 2 standard deviations above the mean. This means that 2.5% of men have heights above 78 inches.

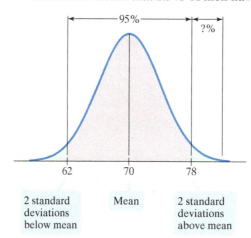

FIGURE 13.17 What percentage have heights above 78 inches?

PRACTICE 2 Use the distribution of male adult heights in North America in Example 1 to find the percentage of men with heights
a. between 62 inches and 78 inches.
b. between 70 inches and 78 inches.
c. above 74 inches.

13.8 EXERCISE SET

PRACTICE AND APPLICATION EXERCISES

The scores on a test are normally distributed with a mean of 100 and a standard deviation of 20. In Exercises 1–10, find the score that is

1. 1 standard deviation above the mean.
2. 2 standard deviations above the mean.
3. 3 standard deviations above the mean.
4. $1\frac{1}{2}$ standard deviations above the mean.
5. $2\frac{1}{2}$ standard deviations above the mean.
6. 1 standard deviation below the mean.
7. 2 standard deviations below the mean.
8. 3 standard deviations below the mean.
9. one-half a standard deviation below the mean.
10. $2\frac{1}{2}$ standard deviations below the mean.

Not everyone pays the same price for the same model of a car. The figure illustrates a normal distribution for the prices paid for a particular model of a new car. The mean is $17,000 and the standard deviation is $500.

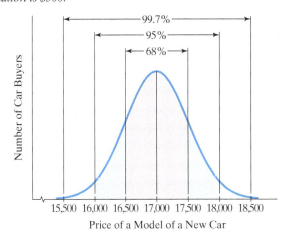

In Exercises 11–22, use the 68–95–99.7 Rule, illustrated in the figure to the left, to find the percentage of buyers who paid

11. between $16,500 and $17,500.
12. between $16,000 and $18,000.
13. between $17,000 and $17,500.
14. between $17,000 and $18,000.
15. between $16,000 and $17,000.
16. between $16,500 and $17,000.
17. between $15,500 and $17,000.
18. between $17,000 and $18,500.
19. more than $17,500.
20. more than $18,000.
21. less than $16,000.
22. less than $16,500.

Intelligence quotients (IQs) on the Stanford-Binet intelligence test are normally distributed with a mean of 100 and a standard deviation of 16. In Exercises 23–32, use the 68–95–99.7 Rule to find the percentage of people with IQs

23. between 68 and 132.
24. between 84 and 116.
25. between 68 and 100.
26. between 84 and 100.
27. above 116.
28. above 132.
29. below 68.
30. below 84.
31. above 148.
32. below 52.

WRITING IN MATHEMATICS

33. What is a symmetric histogram?
34. Describe the normal distribution and discuss some of its properties.
35. Describe the 68–95–99.7 Rule.

EXTENSION EXPECTED VALUE

OBJECTIVES

1. Compute expected value.
2. Use expected value to solve applied problems.

OBJECTIVE 1 ▶ Compute expected value. Expected value is a mathematical way to use probabilities to determine what to expect in various situations over the long run. Expected value is used to determine premiums on insurance policies, weigh the risks versus the benefits of alternatives in business ventures, and indicate to a player of any game of chance what will happen if the game is played repeatedly.

The standard way to find expected value is to multiply each possible outcome by its probability, and then add these products. We use the letter E to represent expected value.

EXAMPLE 1 Computing Expected Value

Find the expected value for the outcome of the roll of a fair die.

Solution The outcomes are 1, 2, 3, 4, 5, and 6, each with a probability of $\frac{1}{6}$. The expected value, E, is computed by multiplying each outcome by its probability and then adding these products.

$$E = 1 \cdot \frac{1}{6} + 2 \cdot \frac{1}{6} + 3 \cdot \frac{1}{6} + 4 \cdot \frac{1}{6} + 5 \cdot \frac{1}{6} + 6 \cdot \frac{1}{6}$$
$$= \frac{1 + 2 + 3 + 4 + 5 + 6}{6} = \frac{21}{6} = 3.5$$

The expected value of the roll of a fair die is 3.5. This means that if the die is rolled repeatedly, there are an average of 3.5 dots per roll over the long run. This expected value cannot occur on a single roll of the die. However, it is a long-run average of the various outcomes that can occur when a fair die is rolled.

PRACTICE 1 It is equally probable that a pointer will land on any one of four regions, numbered 1 through 4. Find the expected value for where the pointer will stop.

TABLE 13.6 Outcomes and Probabilities for the Number of Girls in a Three-Child Family

Outcome: Number of Girls	Probability
0	$\frac{1}{8}$
1	$\frac{3}{8}$
2	$\frac{3}{8}$
3	$\frac{1}{8}$

EXAMPLE 2 Computing Expected Value

Find the expected value for the number of girls for a family with three children.

Solution A family with three children can have 0, 1, 2, or 3 girls. There are eight ways these outcomes can occur.

No girls : Boy Boy Boy — One way
One girl : Girl Boy Boy, Boy Girl Boy, Boy Boy Girl — Three ways
Two girls : Girl Girl Boy, Girl Boy Girl, Boy Girl Girl — Three ways
Three girls : Girl Girl Girl — One way

The table in the margin shows the probabilities for 0, 1, 2, and 3 girls.

The expected value, E, is computed by multiplying each outcome by its probability and then adding these products.

$$E = 0 \cdot \frac{1}{8} + 1 \cdot \frac{3}{8} + 2 \cdot \frac{3}{8} + 3 \cdot \frac{1}{8} = \frac{0 + 3 + 6 + 3}{8} = \frac{12}{8} = \frac{3}{2} = 1.5$$

The expected value is 1.5. This means that if we record the number of girls in many different three-child families, the average number of girls for all these families will be 1.5. In a three-child family, half the children are expected to be girls, so the expected value of 1.5 is consistent with this observation.

TABLE 13.7

Number of Heads	Probability
0	$\frac{1}{16}$
1	$\frac{4}{16}$
2	$\frac{6}{16}$
3	$\frac{4}{16}$
4	$\frac{1}{16}$

PRACTICE 2 A fair coin is tossed four times in succession. The table in the margin shows the probabilities for the different number of heads that can arise. Find the expected value for the number of heads.

OBJECTIVE 2 ▶ **Applications of expected value.** Empirical probabilities can be determined in many situations by examining what has occurred in the past. For example, an insurance company can tally various claim amounts over many years. If 15% of these amounts are for a $2000 claim, then the probability of this claim amount is 0.15. By studying sales of similar houses in a particular area, a realtor can determine the probability that he or she will sell a listed house, another agent will sell the house, or the listed house will remain unsold. Once probabilities have been assigned to all possible outcomes, expected value can indicate what is expected to happen in the long run. These ideas are illustrated in Examples 3 and 4.

TABLE 13.8 Probabilities for Auto Claims

Amount of Claim (to the nearest $2000)	Probability
$0	0.70
$2000	0.15
$4000	0.08
$6000	0.05
$8000	0.01
$10,000	0.01

EXAMPLE 3   Determining an Insurance Premium

An automobile insurance company has determined the probabilities for various claim amounts for drivers ages 16 through 21, shown in the table in the margin.

a. Calculate the expected value and describe what this means in practical terms.

b. How much should the company charge as an average premium so that it does not lose or gain money on its claim costs?

Solution

a. The expected value, E, is computed by multiplying each outcome by its probability, and then adding these products.

$$\begin{aligned} E &= \$0(0.70) + \$2000(0.15) + \$4000(0.08) + \$6000(0.05) \\ &\quad + \$8000(0.01) + \$10,000(0.01) \\ &= \$0 + \$300 + \$320 + \$300 + \$80 + \$100 \\ &= \$1100 \end{aligned}$$

The expected value is $1100. This means that in the long run the average cost of a claim is $1100. The insurance company should expect to pay $1100 per car insured to people in the 16–21 age group.

b. At the very least, the amount that the company should charge as an average premium for each person in the 16–21 group is $1100. In this way, it will not lose or gain money on its claims costs. It's quite probable that the company will charge more, moving from break-even to profit. □

PRACTICE 3   Work Example 3 again if the probabilities for claims of $0 and $10,000 are reversed. Thus, the probability of a $0 claim is 0.01 and the probability of a $10,000 claim is 0.70.

Business decisions are interpreted in terms of dollars and cents. In these situations, **expected value is calculated by multiplying the gain or loss for each possible outcome by its probability. The sum of these products is the expected value.**

The Realtor's Summary Sheet

My Cost:	$5000
My Possible Income:	
I sell house:	$30,000
Another agent sells house:	$15,000
House unsold after 4 months:	$0
The Probabilities:	
I sell house:	0.3
Another agent sells house:	0.2
House unsold after 4 months:	0.5
My Bottom Line:	
I take the listing only if I anticipate earning at least $6000.	

EXAMPLE 4   Expectation in a Business Decision

You are a realtor considering listing a $500,000 house. The cost of advertising and providing food for other realtors during open showings is anticipated to cost you $5000. If you are given a four-month listing and the house is unsold after four months, you lose the listing and receive nothing. You anticipate that the probability you sell your own listed house is 0.3, the probability that another agent sells your listing is 0.2, and the probability that the house is unsold after 4 months is 0.5. If you sell your own listed house, the commission is a hefty $30,000. If another realtor sells your listing, the commission is $15,000. The bottom line: You will not take the listing unless you anticipate earning at least $6000. Should you list the house?

Solution
Shown in the margin is a summary of the amounts of money and probabilities that will determine your decision. The expected value in this situation is the sum of each income possibility times its probability. The expected value represents the amount you can anticipate earning if you take the listing. If the expected value is not at least $6000, you should not list the house.

The possible incomes listed in the margin, $30,000, $15,000, and $0, do not take into account your $5000 costs. Because of these costs, each amount needs to be reduced by $5000. Thus, you can gain $30,000 − $5000, or $25,000, or you can gain $15,000 − $5000,

The Realtor's Summary Sheet (repeated)	
My Cost:	$5000
My Possible Income:	
I sell house:	$30,000
Another agent sells house:	$15,000
House unsold after 4 months:	$0
The Probabilities:	
I sell house:	0.3
Another agent sells house:	0.2
House unsold after 4 months:	0.5
My Bottom Line:	
I take the listing only if I anticipate earning at least $6000.	

or $10,000. Because $0 − $5000 = −$5000, you can also lose $5000. The table below summarizes possible outcomes if you take the listing, and their respective probabilities.

TABLE 13.9 Gains, Losses, and Probabilities for Listing a $500,000 House

Outcome	Gain or Loss	Probability
Sells house	$25,000	0.3
Another agent sells house	$10,000	0.2
House doesn't sell	−$5000	0.5

The expected value, E, is computed by multiplying each gain or loss in Table 13.9 by its probability, and then adding these results.

$$E = \$25{,}000(0.3) + \$10{,}000(0.2) + (-\$5000)(0.5)$$
$$= \$7500 + \$2000 + (-\$2500) = \$7000$$

You can expect to earn $7000 by listing the house. Because the expected value exceeds $6000, you should list the house.

PRACTICE 4

The SAT is a multiple-choice test. Each question has five possible answers. The test taker must select one answer for each question or not answer the question. One point is awarded for each correct response and $\frac{1}{4}$ point is subtracted for each wrong answer. No points are added or subtracted for answers left blank. The table below summarizes the information for the outcomes of a random guess on an SAT question. Find the expected point value of a random guess. Is there anything to gain or lose on average by guessing? Explain your answer.

TABLE 13.10 Gains and Losses for Guessing on the SAT

Outcome	Gain or Loss	Probability
Guess correctly	1	$\frac{1}{5}$
Guess incorrectly	$-\frac{1}{4}$	$\frac{4}{5}$

CHAPTER 13 EXTENSION | EXERCISE SET

PRACTICE AND APPLICATION EXERCISES

In Exercises 1–2, the numbers that each pointer can land on and their respective probabilities are shown. Compute the expected value for the number on which each pointer lands.

1.

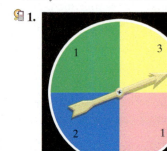

Outcome	Probability
1	$\frac{1}{2}$
2	$\frac{1}{4}$
3	$\frac{1}{4}$

2.

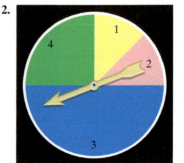

Outcome	Probability
1	$\frac{1}{8}$
2	$\frac{1}{8}$
3	$\frac{1}{2}$
4	$\frac{1}{4}$

The tables in Exercises 3–4 show claims and their probabilities for an insurance company.

a. Calculate the expected value and describe what this means in practical terms.

b. How much should the company charge as an average premium so that it breaks even on its claim costs?

c. How much should the company charge to make a profit of $50 per policy?

3. **Probabilities for Homeowners' Insurance Claims**

Amount of Claim (to the nearest $50,000)	Probability
$0	0.65
$50,000	0.20
$100,000	0.10
$150,000	0.03
$200,000	0.01
$250,000	0.01

4. **Probabilities for Medical Insurance Claims**

Amount of Claim (to the nearest $20,000)	Probability
$0	0.70
$20,000	0.20
$40,000	0.06
$60,000	0.02
$80,000	0.01
$100,000	0.01

5. An architect is considering bidding for the design of a new museum. The cost of drawing plans and submitting a model is $10,000. The probability of being awarded the bid is 0.1, and anticipated profits are $100,000, resulting in a possible gain of this amount minus the $10,000 cost for plans and a model. What is the expected value in this situation? Describe what this value means.

6. A construction company is planning to bid on a building contract. The bid costs the company $1500. The probability that the bid is accepted is $\frac{1}{5}$. If the bid is accepted, the company will make $40,000 minus the cost of the bid. Find the expected value in this situation. Describe what this value means.

7. It is estimated that there are 27 deaths for every 10 million people who use airplanes. A company that sells flight insurance provides $100,000 in case of death in a plane crash. A policy can be purchased for $1. Calculate the expected value and thereby determine how much the insurance company can make over the long run for each policy that it sells.

8. A 25-year-old can purchase a one-year life insurance policy for $10,000 at a cost of $100. Past history indicates that the probability of a person dying at age 25 is 0.002. Determine the company's expected gain per policy.

Exercises 9–10 are related to the SAT, described in Practice 4.

9. Suppose that you can eliminate one of the possible five answers. Modify the two probabilities shown in the final column in Table 13.10 by finding the probabilities of guessing correctly and guessing incorrectly under these circumstances. What is the expected point value of a random guess? Is it advantageous to guess under these circumstances?

10. Suppose that you can eliminate two of the possible five answers. Modify the two probabilities shown in the final column in Table 13.10 by finding the probabilities of guessing correctly and guessing incorrectly under these circumstances. What is the expected point value of a random guess? Is it advantageous to guess under these circumstances?

11. A store specializing in mountain bikes is to open in one of two malls. If the first mall is selected, the store anticipates a yearly profit of $300,000 if successful and a yearly loss of $100,000 otherwise. The probability of success is $\frac{1}{2}$. If the second mall is selected, it is estimated that the yearly profit will be $200,000 if successful; otherwise, the annual loss will be $60,000. The probability of success at the second mall is $\frac{3}{4}$. Which mall should be chosen in order to maximize the expected profit?

12. An oil company is considering two sites on which to drill, described as follows:

   Site A: Profit if oil is found: $80 million
   Loss if no oil is found: $10 million
   Probability of finding oil: 0.2

   Site B: Profit if oil is found: $120 million
   Loss if no oil is found: $18 million
   Probability of finding oil: 0.1

   Which site has the larger expected profit? By how much?

13. In a product liability case, a company can settle out of court for a loss of $350,000, or go to trial, losing $700,000 if found guilty and nothing if found not guilty. Lawyers for the company estimate the probability of a not-guilty verdict to be 0.8.

   a. Find the expected value of the amount the company can lose by taking the case to court.

   b. Should the company settle out of court?

14. A service that repairs air conditioners sells maintenance agreements for $80 a year. The average cost for repairing an air conditioner is $350 and 1 in every 100 people who purchase maintenance agreements have air conditioners that require repair. Find the service's expected profit per maintenance agreement.

WRITING IN MATHEMATICS

15. What does the expected value for the outcome of the roll of a fair die represent?

16. Explain how to find the expected value for the number of girls for a family with two children. What is the expected value?

17. How do insurance companies use expected value to determine what to charge for a policy?

18. Describe a situation in which a business can use expected value.

19. The expected value for purchasing a ticket in a raffle is −$0.75. Describe what this means. Will a person who purchases a ticket lose $0.75?

CRITICAL THINKING EXERCISES

20. A popular state lottery is the 5/35 lottery, played in Arizona, Connecticut, Illinois, Iowa, Kentucky, Maine, Massachusetts, New Hampshire, South Dakota, and Vermont. In Arizona's version of the game, prizes are set: First prize is $50,000, second prize is $500, and third prize is $5. To win first prize, you must select all five of the winning numbers, numbered from 1 to 35. Second prize is awarded to players who select any four of the five winning numbers, and third prize is awarded to players who select any three of the winning numbers. The cost to purchase a lottery ticket is $1. Find the expected value of Arizona's "Fantasy Five" game, and describe what this means in terms of buying a lottery ticket over the long run.

CHAPTER 13 REVIEW

13.1

1. A restaurant offers 20 appetizers and 40 main courses. In how many ways can a person order a two-course meal?
2. A popular brand of pen comes in red, green, blue, or black ink. The writing tip can be chosen from extra bold, bold, regular, fine, or micro. How many different choices of pens do you have with this brand?
3. In how many ways can first and second prize be awarded in a contest with 100 people, assuming that each prize is awarded to a different person?
4. You are answering three multiple-choice questions. Each question has five answer choices, with one correct answer per question. If you select one of these five choices for each question and leave nothing blank, in how many ways can you answer the questions?
5. A stock can go up, go down, or stay unchanged. How many possibilities are there if you own five stocks?
6. A person can purchase a condominium with a choice of five kinds of carpeting, with or without a pool, with or without a porch, and with one, two, or three bedrooms. How many different options are there for the condominium?

13.2

7. Six acts are scheduled to perform in a variety show. How many different ways are there to schedule their appearances?
8. In how many ways can five airplanes line up for departure on a runway?
9. You need to arrange seven of your favorite books along a small shelf. Although you are not arranging the books by height, the tallest of the books is to be placed at the left end and the shortest of the books at the right end. How many different ways can you arrange the books?

In Exercises 10–13, evaluate each factorial expression.

10. $\dfrac{16!}{14!}$
11. $\dfrac{800!}{799!}$
12. $5! - 3!$
13. $\dfrac{11!}{(11-3)!}$

In Exercises 14–15, use the formula for $_nP_r$ to evaluate each expression.

14. $_{10}P_6$
15. $_{100}P_2$

Use the formula for $_nP_r$ to solve Exercises 16–17.

16. A club with 15 members is to choose four officers—president, vice-president, secretary, and treasurer. In how many ways can these offices be filled?
17. Suppose you are asked to list, in order of preference, the five favorite CDs you purchased in the past 12 months. If you bought 20 CDs over this time period, in how many ways can the five favorite be ranked?

Use the formula for the number of permutations with duplicate items to solve Exercises 18–19.

18. In how many distinct ways can the letters of the word TORONTO be arranged?
19. In how many ways can the digits in the number 335,557 be arranged?

13.3

In Exercises 20–22, does the problem involve permutations or combinations? Explain your answer. (It is not necessary to solve the problem.)

20. How many different 4-card hands can be dealt from a 52-card deck?
21. How many different ways can a director select from 20 male actors to cast the roles of Mark, Roger, Angel, and Collins in the musical *Rent*?
22. How many different ways can a director select 4 actors from a group of 20 actors to attend a workshop on performing in rock musicals?

In Exercises 23–24, use the formula for $_nC_r$ to evaluate each expression.

23. $_{11}C_7$
24. $_{14}C_5$

Use the formula for $_nC_r$ to solve Exercises 25–28.

25. An election ballot asks voters to select four city commissioners from a group of ten candidates. In how many ways can this be done?
26. How many different 5-card hands can be dealt from a deck that has only hearts (13 different cards)?
27. From the 20 CDs that you've bought during the past year, you plan to take 3 with you on vacation. How many different sets of three CDs can you take?
28. A political discussion group consists of 12 Republicans and 8 Democrats. In how many ways can 5 Republicans and 4 Democrats be selected to attend a conference on politics and social issues?

13.4

In Exercises 29–32, a die is rolled. Find the probability of rolling

29. a 6.
30. a number less than 5.
31. a number less than 7.
32. a number greater than 6.

In Exercises 33–37, you are dealt one card from a 52-card deck. Find the probability of being dealt

33. a 5.
34. a picture card.
35. a card greater than 4 and less than 8.
36. a 4 of diamonds.
37. a red ace.

In Exercises 38–40, suppose that you reach into a bag and randomly select one piece of candy from 15 chocolates, 10 caramels, and 5 peppermints. Find the probability of selecting

38. a chocolate.
39. a caramel.
40. a peppermint.
41. Tay-Sachs disease occurs in 1 of every 3600 births among Jews from central and eastern Europe, and in 1 in 600,000 births in other populations. The disease causes abnormal accumulation of certain fat compounds in the spinal cord and brain, resulting in paralysis, blindness, and mental impairment. Death generally occurs before the age of five. If we use t to represent a Tay-Sachs gene and T a healthy gene, the table below shows the four possibilities for the children of one healthy, TT, parent, and one parent who carries the disease, Tt, but is not sick.
    a. Find the probability that a child of these parents will be a carrier without the disease.
    b. Find the probability that a child of these parents will have the disease.

		Second Parent	
		T	t
First Parent	T	TT	Tt
	T	TT	Tt

The table below shows the employment status of the U.S. civilian labor force in 2004, by gender. Use the data in the table, expressed in millions, to solve Exercises 42–44.

Employment Status of the U.S. Labor Force, in Millions, in 2004

	Employed	Unemployed	Total
Male	74.5	33.2	107.7
Female	64.7	51.0	115.7
Total	139.2	84.2	223.4

Source: U.S. Bureau of Labor Statistics

Find the probability, expressed as a decimal rounded to three places, that a randomly selected person from the civilian labor force represented in the table

42. is employed.
43. is female.
44. is an unemployed male.

13.5

45. If cities A, B, C, and D are visited in random order, each city visited once, find the probability that city D will be visited first, city B second, city A third, and city C last.

In Exercises 46–49, suppose that six singers are being lined up to perform at a charity. Call the singers A, B, C, D, E, and F. The order of performance is determined by writing each singer's name on one of six cards, placing the cards in a hat, and then drawing one card at a time. The order in which the cards are drawn determines the order in which the singers perform. Find the probability that

46. singer C will perform last.
47. singer B will perform first and singer A will perform last.
48. the singers will perform in the following order: F, E, A, D, C, B.
49. the performance will begin with singer A or C.
50. A lottery game is set up so that each player chooses five different numbers from 1 to 20. If the five numbers match the five numbers drawn in the lottery, the player wins (or shares) the top cash prize. What is the probability of winning the prize
    a. with one lottery ticket?
    b. with 100 different lottery tickets?
51. A committee of four people is to be selected from six Democrats and four Republicans. Find the probability that
    a. all are Democrats.
    b. two are Democrats and two are Republicans.
52. If you are dealt 3 cards from a shuffled deck of red cards (26 different cards), find the probability of getting exactly 2 picture cards.

13.6

In Exercises 53–57, a die is rolled. Find the probability of

53. not rolling a 5.
54. not rolling a number less than 4.
55. rolling a 3 or a 5.
56. rolling a number less than 3 or greater than 4.
57. rolling a number less than 5 or greater than 2.

In Exercises 58–63, you draw one card from a 52-card deck. Find the probability of

58. not drawing a picture card.
59. not drawing a diamond.
60. drawing an ace or a king.
61. drawing a black 6 or a red 7.
62. drawing a queen or a red card.
63. drawing a club or a picture card.

In Exercises 64–69, it is equally probable that the pointer on the spinner shown will land on any one of the six regions, numbered 1 through 6, and colored as shown. If the pointer lands on a borderline, spin again. Find the probability of

64. not stopping on 4.
65. not stopping on yellow.
66. not stopping on red.
67. stopping on red or yellow.
68. stopping on red or an even number.
69. stopping on red or a number greater than 3.

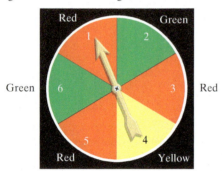

Use this information to solve Exercises 70–71. At a workshop on police work and the African-American community, there are 50 African-American male police officers, 20 African-American female police officers, 90 white male police officers, and 40 white female police officers. If one police officer is selected at random from the people at the workshop, find the probability that the selected person is

70. African American or male.
71. female or white.

Suppose that a survey of 350 college students is taken. Each student is asked the type of college attended (public or private) and the family's income level (low, middle, high). Use the data in the table to solve Exercises 72–75. Express probabilities as simplified fractions.

	Public	Private	Total
Low	120	20	140
Middle	110	50	160
High	22	28	50
Total	252	98	350

Find the probability that a randomly selected student in the survey

72. attends a public college.
73. is not from a high-income family.
74. is from a middle-income or a high-income family.
75. attends a private college or is from a high-income family.
76. One card is randomly selected from a deck of 52 cards. Find the odds in favor and the odds against getting a queen.
77. The winner of a raffle will receive a two-year scholarship to any college of the winner's choice. If 2000 raffle tickets were sold and you purchased 20 tickets, what are the odds against your winning the scholarship?
78. The odds in favor of a candidate winning an election are given at 3 to 1. What is the probability that this candidate will win the election?

13.7

Use the spinner shown to solve Exercises 79–83. It is equally likely that the pointer will land on any one of the six regions, numbered 1 through 6, and colored as shown. If the pointer lands on a borderline, spin again. If the pointer is spun twice, find the probability it will land on

79. yellow and then red.
80. 1 and then 3.
81. yellow both times.

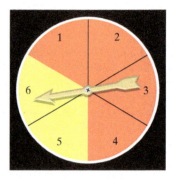

If the pointer is spun three times, find the probability it will land on

82. yellow and then 4 and then an odd number.
83. red every time.
84. What is the probability of a family having five boys born in a row?
85. The probability of a flood in any given year in a region prone to flooding is 0.2.
    a. What is the probability of a flood two years in a row?
    b. What is the probability of a flood for three consecutive years?
    c. What is the probability of no flooding for four consecutive years?
    d. What is the probability of a flood at least once in the next four years?

In Exercises 86–87, two students are selected from a group of four psychology majors, three business majors, and two music majors. The two students are to meet with the campus cafeteria manager to voice the group's concerns about food prices and quality. One student is randomly selected and leaves for the cafeteria manager's office. Then, a second student is selected. Find the probability of selecting

86. a music major and then a psychology major.
87. two business majors.
88. A final visit to the box of chocolates: It's now grown to a box of 50, of which 30 are solid chocolate, 15 are filled with jelly, and 5 are filled with cherries. The story is still the same: They all look alike. You select a piece, eat it, select a second piece,

eat it, and help yourself to a final sugar rush. Find the probability of selecting a solid chocolate followed by two cherry-filled chocolates.

89. A single die is tossed. Find the probability that the tossed die shows 5, given that the outcome is an odd number.

90. A letter is randomly selected from the letters of the English alphabet. Find the probability of selecting a vowel, given that the outcome is a letter that precedes k.

91. The numbers shown below are each written on a colored chip. The chips are placed into a bag and one chip is selected at random. Find the probability of selecting

   a. an odd number, given that a red chip is selected.

   b. a yellow chip, given that the number selected is at least 3.

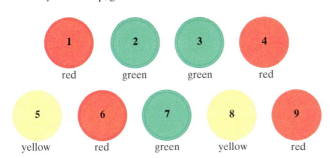

The data in the table are based on 145 Americans tested for tuberculosis. Use the data to solve Exercises 92–99. Express probabilities as simplified fractions.

	TB	*No TB*
Positive Screening Test	9	11
Negative Screening Test	1	124

Source: Deborah J. Bennett, *Randomness*, Harvard University Press, 1998

Find the probability that a randomly selected person from this group

92. does not have TB.
93. tests positive.
94. does not have TB or tests positive.
95. does not have TB, given a positive test.
96. has a positive test, given no TB.
97. has TB, given a negative test.

Suppose that two people are randomly selected, in succession, from this group. Find the probability of selecting

98. two people with TB.
99. two people with positive screening tests.

13.8

The scores on a test are normally distributed with a mean of 70 and a standard deviation of 8. In Exercises 100–102, find the score that is

100. 2 standard deviations above the mean.
101. $3\frac{1}{2}$ standard deviations above the mean.
102. $1\frac{1}{4}$ standard deviations below the mean.

The ages of people living in a retirement community are normally distributed with a mean age of 68 years and a standard deviation of 4 years. In Exercises 103–109, use the 68–95–99.7 Rule to find the percentage of people in the community whose ages

103. are between 64 and 72.
104. are between 60 and 76.
105. are between 68 and 72.
106. are between 56 and 80.
107. exceed 72.
108. are less than 72.
109. exceed 76.

CHAPTER 13 TEST

Remember to use the Chapter Test Prep Videos to see the fully worked-out solutions to any of the exercises you want to review.

1. A person can purchase a particular model of a new car with a choice of ten colors, with or without automatic transmission, with or without four-wheel drive, with or without air conditioning, and with two, three, or four radio-CD speakers. How many different options are there for this model of the car?

2. In how many ways can seven airplanes line up for a departure on a runway if the plane with the greatest number of passengers must depart first?

3. A human resource manager has 11 applicants to fill three different positions. Assuming that all applicants are equally qualified for any of the three positions, in how many ways can this be done?

4. From the ten books that you've recently bought but not read, you plan to take four with you on vacation. How many different sets of four books can you take?

5. In how many distinct ways can the letters of the word ATLANTA be arranged?

In Exercises 6–8, one student is selected at random from a group of 12 freshmen, 16 sophomores, 20 juniors, and 2 seniors. Find the probability that the person selected is

6. a freshman.
7. not a sophomore.
8. a junior or a senior.

9. One card is randomly selected from a deck of 52 cards. Find the probability of selecting a black card or a picture card.

10. A box contains five red balls, six green balls, and nine yellow balls. Suppose you select one ball at random from the box and do not replace it. Then you randomly select a second ball. Find the probability that both balls selected are red.

11. A quiz consisting of four multiple-choice questions has four available options (a, b, c, or d) for each question. If a person guesses at every question, what is the probability of answering *all* questions correctly?

12. The odds against a candidate winning an election are given at 1 to 4.

a. What are the odds in favor of the candidate winning?
b. What is the probability that the candidate will win the election?

A class is collecting data on eye color and gender. They organize the data they collected into the table shown. Numbers in the table represent the number of students from the class that belong to each of the categories. Use the data to solve Exercises 13–14. Express probabilities as simplified fractions.

	Brown	Blue	Green
Male	22	18	10
Female	18	20	12

Find the probability that a randomly selected student from this class

13. is female or has green eyes.
14. is male, given the student has blue eyes.

According to the American Freshman, *the number of hours that college freshmen spend studying each week is normally distributed with a mean of 7 hours and a standard deviation of 5.3 hours. In Exercises 15–16, use the 68–95–99.7 Rule to find the percentage of college freshmen who study*

15. between 7 and 12.3 hours each week.
16. more than 17.6 hours each week.

CHAPTER 13 STANDARDIZED TEST

Multiple Choice. *Choose the one alternative that best completes the statement or answers the question.*

Solve.

1. A person can order a new car with a choice of 11 possible colors, with or without air conditioning, with or without heated seats, with or without anti-lock brakes, with or without power windows, and with or without a CD player. In how many different ways can a new car be ordered in terms of these options?
   a. 176   b. 352   c. 704   d. 22

2. There are 9 performers who are to present their acts at a variety show. One of them insists on being the first act of the evening. If this request is granted, how many different ways are there to schedule the appearances?
   a. 40,320   b. 81   c. 72   d. 362,880

3. A club elects a president, vice-president, and secretary-treasurer. How many sets of officers are possible if there are 13 members and any member can be elected to each position? No person can hold more than one office.
   a. 858   b. 572   c. 17,160   d. 1716

4. From 8 names on a ballot, a committee of 3 will be elected to attend a political national convention. How many different committees are possible?
   a. 6720   b. 168   c. 336   d. 56

5. In how many distinct ways can the letters in ENGINEERING be arranged?
   a. 277,200   b. 25,200   c. 39,916,800   d. 554,400

6. In a class of 50 students, 31 are Democrats, 13 are business majors, and 3 of the business majors are Democrats. If one student is randomly selected from the class, find the probability of choosing a Democrat or a business major.
   a. $\frac{22}{25}$ b. $\frac{41}{50}$ c. $\frac{47}{50}$ d. $\frac{1}{5}$

7. Amy, Jean, Keith, Tom, Susan, and Dave have all been invited to a birthday party. They arrive randomly and each person arrives at a different time. In how many ways can they arrive? In how many ways can Jean arrive first and Keith last? Find the probability that Jean will arrive first and Keith will arrive last.
   a. 120; 6; $\frac{1}{20}$ b. 120; 10; $\frac{1}{12}$
   c. 720; 24; $\frac{1}{30}$ d. 720; 15; $\frac{1}{48}$

8. Based on his skills in basketball, it was computed that when Joe Sureshot threw a free throw, the odds in favor of his making it were 3 to 21. Find the probability that when Joe shot a free throw, he made it. Out of every 100 free throws he attempted on the average how many did he miss?
   a. $\frac{7}{8}$; 87   b. $\frac{1}{8}$; 12
   c. $\frac{1}{8}$; 87   d. $\frac{7}{8}$; 12

9. There are 37 chocolates in a box, all identically shaped. There are 10 filled with nuts, 12 with caramel, and 15 are solid chocolate. You randomly select one piece, eat it, and then select a second piece. Find the probability of selecting 2 solid chocolates in a row.
   a. $\frac{5}{444}$ b. $\frac{225}{1369}$ c. $\frac{35}{222}$ d. $\frac{210}{1369}$

A single die is rolled. Find the odds:

10. in favor of getting a number less than 3.
    a. 1:2   b. 2:1   c. 1:1   d. 1:3

11. against getting a number less than 4.
    a. 2:1   b. 1:1   c. 1:2   d. 3:2

Use the theoretical probability formula to solve the problem. Express the probability as a fraction reduced to lowest terms.

12. This problem deals with eye color, an inherited trait. For purposes of this problem, assume that only two eye colors are possible, brown and blue. We use b to represent a blue eye gene and B a brown eye gene. If any B genes are present, the person will have brown eyes. The table shows the four possibilities for the children of two Bb (brown-eyed) parents, where each parent has one of each eye color gene.

		Second Parent	
		B	b
First	**B**	BB	Bb
Parent	**b**	Bb	bb

Find the probability that these parents give birth to a child who has blue eyes.

a. $\frac{1}{4}$ **b.** 0   **c.** $\frac{1}{2}$ **d.** 1

Suppose that prices of a certain model of new homes are normally distributed with a mean of $150,000. Use the 68–95–99.7 Rule to find the percent of buyers who paid:

13. between $150,000 and $153,600 if the standard deviation is $1800.

a. 68%   **b.** 99.7%   **c.** 34%   **d.** 47.5%

Suppose that prices of a certain model of new homes are normally distributed with a mean of $150,000. Use the 68–95–99.7 Rule to find the percentage of buyers who paid:

14. less than $147,000 if the standard deviation is $1500.

a. 2.5%   **b.** 97.5%   **c.** 34%   **d.** 47.5%

CHAPTER

14 Trigonometric Functions

- **14.1** Angles and Radian Measure
- **14.2** Right Triangle Trigonometry
- **14.3** Trigonometric Functions of Any Angle
- **14.4** Trigonometric Functions of Real Numbers; Periodic Functions

  Integrated Review—Angles and Right Triangles

- **14.5** Graphs of Sine and Cosine Function
- **14.6** Graph of the Tangent Function
- **14.7** Inverse Trigonometric Functions
- **14.8** Applications of Trigonometric Functions

The San Francisco Museum of Modern Art was constructed in 1995 to illustrate how art and architecture can enrich one another.

Angles play a critical role in creating modern architecture. They are also fundamental in trigonometry. In this chapter, we begin our study of trigonometry by looking at angles and methods for measuring them.

14.1 ANGLES AND RADIAN MEASURE

OBJECTIVES

1. Recognize and use the vocabulary of angles.
2. Use degree measure.
3. Use radian measure.
4. Convert between degrees and radians.
5. Draw angles in standard position.
6. Find coterminal angles.
7. Find the length of a circular arc.
8. Use linear and angular speed to describe motion on a circular path.

OBJECTIVE 1 ▶ Recognize and use the vocabulary of angles. The hour hand of a clock suggests a **ray,** a part of a line that has only one endpoint and extends forever in the opposite direction. An **angle** is formed by two rays that have a common endpoint. One ray is called the **initial side** and the other the **terminal side.**

A rotating ray is often a useful way to think about angles. The ray in Figure 14.1 rotates from 12 to 2. The ray pointing to 12 is the **initial side** and the ray pointing to 2 is the **terminal side.** The common endpoint of an angle's initial side and terminal side is the **vertex** of the angle.

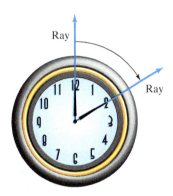

FIGURE 14.1 Clock with hands forming an angle

Figure 14.2 shows an angle. The arrow near the vertex shows the direction and the amount of rotation from the initial side to the terminal side. Several methods can be used to name an angle. Lowercase Greek letters, such as α (alpha), β (beta), γ (gamma), and θ (theta), are often used.

An angle is in **standard position** if

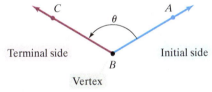

FIGURE 14.2 An angle; two rays with a common endpoint

- its vertex is at the origin of a rectangular coordinate system and
- its initial side lies along the positive x-axis.

The angles in Figure 14.3 are both in standard position.

When we see an initial side and a terminal side in place, there are two kinds of rotations that could have generated the angle. The arrow in Figure 14.3(a) indicates that the rotation from the initial side to the terminal side is in the counterclockwise direction. **Positive angles** are generated by counterclockwise rotation. Thus, angle α is positive. By contrast, the arrow in Figure 14.3(b) shows that the rotation from the initial side to the terminal side is in the clockwise direction. **Negative angles** are generated by clockwise rotation. Thus, angle θ is negative.

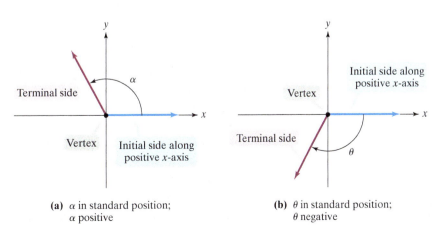

(a) α in standard position; α positive

(b) θ in standard position; θ negative

FIGURE 14.3 Two angles in standard position

796 CHAPTER 14 Trigonometric Functions

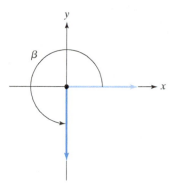

FIGURE 14.4 β is a quadrantal angle.

A complete 360° rotation

TECHNOLOGY NOTE

Fractional parts of degrees are measured in minutes and seconds.

One minute, written $1'$, is $\frac{1}{60}$ degree: $1' = \frac{1}{60}°$.

One second, written $1''$, is $\frac{1}{3600}$ degree: $1'' = \frac{1}{3600}°$.

For example,

$$31°47'12'' = \left(31 + \frac{47}{60} + \frac{12}{3600}\right)°$$

$$\approx 31.787°.$$

Many calculators have keys for changing an angle from degree-minute-second notation (D°M'S") to a decimal form and vice versa.

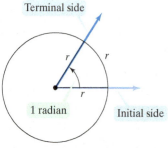

FIGURE 14.6 For a 1-radian angle, the intercepted arc and the radius are equal.

When an angle is in standard position, its terminal side can lie in a quadrant. We say that the angle **lies in that quadrant.** For example, in Figure 14.3(a), the terminal side of angle α lies in quadrant II. Thus, angle α lies in quadrant II. By contrast, in Figure 14.3(b), the terminal side of angle θ lies in quadrant III. Thus, angle θ lies in quadrant III.

Must all angles in standard position lie in a quadrant? The answer is no. The terminal side can lie on the x-axis or the y-axis. For example, angle β in Figure 14.4 has a terminal side that lies on the negative y-axis. An angle is called a **quadrantal angle** if its terminal side lies on the x-axis or on the y-axis. Angle β in Figure 14.4 is an example of a quadrantal angle.

OBJECTIVE 2 ▶ **Measuring angles using degrees.** Angles are measured by determining the amount of rotation from the initial side to the terminal side. One way to measure angles is in **degrees,** symbolized by a small, raised circle °. Think of the hour hand of a clock. From 12 noon to 12 midnight, the hour hand moves around in a complete circle. By definition, the ray has rotated through 360 degrees, or 360°. Using 360° as the amount of rotation of a ray back onto itself, a degree, 1°, is $\frac{1}{360}$ of a complete rotation.

Figure 14.5 shows that certain angles have special names. An **acute angle** measures less than 90° [see Figure 14.5(a)]. A **right angle,** one quarter of a complete rotation, measures 90° [Figure 14.5(b)]. Examine the right angle—do you see a small square at the vertex? This symbol is used to indicate a right angle. An **obtuse angle** measures more than 90°, but less than 180° [Figure 14.5(c)]. Finally, a **straight angle,** one-half a complete rotation, measures 180° [Figure 14.5(d)].

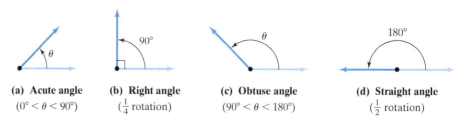

(a) **Acute angle** ($0° < θ < 90°$)

(b) **Right angle** ($\frac{1}{4}$ rotation)

(c) **Obtuse angle** ($90° < θ < 180°$)

(d) **Straight angle** ($\frac{1}{2}$ rotation)

FIGURE 14.5 Classifying angles by their degree measurement

We will be using notation such as $θ = 60°$ to refer to an angle θ whose measure is 60°. We also use the phrases *an angle of* 60° or a 60° *angle*.

OBJECTIVE 3 ▶ **Measuring angles using radians.** Another way to measure angles is in *radians*. Let's first define an angle measuring **1 radian.** We use a circle of radius r. In Figure 14.6, we've constructed an angle whose vertex is at the center of the circle. Such an angle is called a **central angle.** Notice that this central angle intercepts an arc along the circle measuring r units. The radius of the circle is also r units. The measure of such an angle is 1 radian.

> **Definition of a Radian**
>
> **One radian** is the measure of the central angle of a circle that intercepts an arc equal in length to the radius of the circle.

The **radian measure** of any central angle is the length of the intercepted arc divided by the circle's radius. In Figure 14.7(a), the length of the arc intercepted by angle β is double the radius, r. We find the measure of angle β in radians by dividing the length of the intercepted arc by the radius.

$$β = \frac{\text{length of the intercepted arc}}{\text{radius}} = \frac{2r}{r} = 2$$

Thus, angle β measures 2 radians.

Section 14.1 Angles and Radian Measure 797

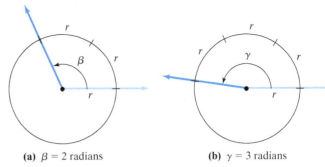

(a) $\beta = 2$ radians (b) $\gamma = 3$ radians

FIGURE 14.7 Two central angles measured in radians

In Figure 14.7(b), the length of the intercepted arc is triple the radius, r. Let us find the measure of angle γ:

$$\gamma = \frac{\text{length of the intercepted arc}}{\text{radius}} = \frac{3r}{r} = 3.$$

Thus, angle γ measures 3 radians.

Radian Measure

Consider an arc of length s on a circle of radius r. The measure of the central angle, θ, that intercepts the arc is

$$\theta = \frac{s}{r} \text{ radians.}$$

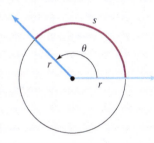

EXAMPLE 1 Computing Radian Measure

A central angle, θ, in a circle of radius 6 inches intercepts an arc of length 15 inches. What is the radian measure of θ?

Solution Angle θ is shown in Figure 14.8. The radian measure of a central angle is the length of the intercepted arc, s, divided by the circle's radius, r. The length of the intercepted arc is 15 inches: $s = 15$ inches. The circle's radius is 6 inches: $r = 6$ inches. Now we use the formula for radian measure to find the radian measure of θ.

$$\theta = \frac{s}{r} = \frac{15 \text{ inches}}{6 \text{ inches}} = 2.5$$

Thus, the radian measure of θ is 2.5.

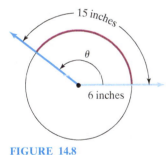

FIGURE 14.8

> **Helpful Hint**
> Before applying the formula for radian measure, be sure that the same unit of length is used for the intercepted arc, s, and the radius, r.

> **Helpful Hint**
> Degree units are always written. For example, $\theta = 36°$.
> Radian units may or may not be written. For example, $\theta = 2.5$ or $\theta = 2.5$ radians mean the same.
> (If no units are written with angle measure, the angle measure is radians.)

PRACTICE

1 A central angle, θ, in a circle of radius 12 feet intercepts an arc of length 42 feet. What is the radian measure of θ?

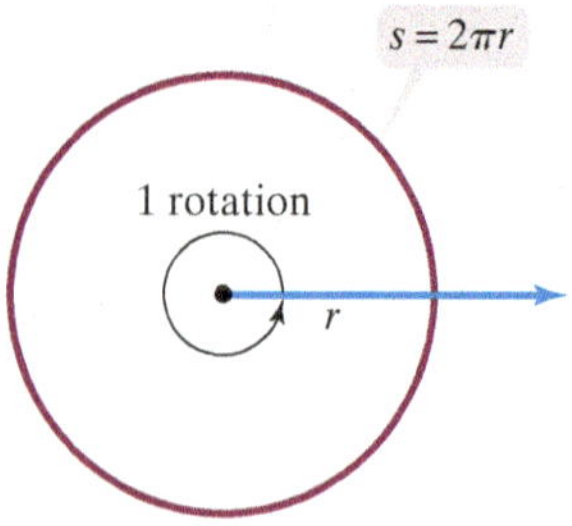

CHAPTER 14 Trigonometric Functions

FIGURE 14.9 A complete rotation

OBJECTIVE 4 ▶ Convert between degrees and radians. How can we obtain a relationship between degrees and radians? We compare the number of degrees and the number of radians in one complete rotation, shown in Figure 14.9. We know that 360° is the amount of rotation of a ray back onto itself. The length of the intercepted arc is equal to the circumference of the circle. Thus, the radian measure of this central angle is the circumference of the circle divided by the circle's radius, r. The circumference of a circle of radius r is $2\pi r$. We use the formula for radian measure to find the radian measure of the 360° angle.

$$\theta = \frac{s}{r} = \frac{\text{the circle's circumference}}{r} = \frac{2\pi r}{r} = 2\pi$$

Because one complete rotation measures 360° and 2π radians,

$$360° = 2\pi \text{ radians}.$$

Dividing both sides by 2, we have

$$180° = \pi \text{ radians}.$$

Dividing this last equation by 180° or π gives the conversion rules in the following box.

> **▶ Helpful Hint**
> The unit you are converting *to* appears in the *numerator* of the conversion factor.

Conversion Between Degrees and Radians

Using the basic relationship π radians $= 180°$,

To convert degrees to radians, multiply degrees by $\dfrac{\pi \text{ radians}}{180°}$.

To convert radians to degrees, multiply radians by $\dfrac{180°}{\pi \text{ radians}}$.

Angles that are fractions of a complete rotation are usually expressed in radian measure as fractional multiples of π, rather than as decimal approximations. For example, we write $\theta = \dfrac{\pi}{2}$ rather than using the decimal approximation $\theta \approx 1.57$.

EXAMPLE 2   Converting from Degrees to Radians

Convert each angle in degrees to radians:

a. 30°   **b.** 90°   **c.** −135°.

Solution To convert degrees to radians, multiply by $\dfrac{\pi \text{ radians}}{180°}$. Observe how the degree units cancel.

a. $30° = 30° \cdot \dfrac{\pi \text{ radians}}{180°} = \dfrac{30\pi}{180} \text{ radians} = \dfrac{\pi}{6} \text{ radians}$

b. $90° = 90° \cdot \dfrac{\pi \text{ radians}}{180°} = \dfrac{90\pi}{180} \text{ radians} = \dfrac{\pi}{2} \text{ radians}$

c. $-135° = -135° \cdot \dfrac{\pi \text{ radians}}{180°} = -\dfrac{135\pi}{180} \text{ radians} = -\dfrac{3\pi}{4} \text{ radians}$

Divide the numerator and denominator by 45.

PRACTICE 2 Convert each angle in degrees to radians:

a. 60°   **b.** 270°   **c.** −300°.

EXAMPLE 3   Converting from Radians to Degrees

Convert each angle in radians to degrees:

a. $\dfrac{\pi}{3}$ radians   **b.** $-\dfrac{5\pi}{3}$ radians   **c.** 1 radian.

Solution   To convert radians to degrees, multiply by $\dfrac{180°}{\pi \text{ radians}}$. Observe how the radian units cancel.

a. $\dfrac{\pi}{3}$ radians $= \dfrac{\pi \text{ radians}}{3} \cdot \dfrac{180°}{\pi \text{ radians}} = \dfrac{180°}{3} = 60°$

b. $-\dfrac{5\pi}{3}$ radians $= -\dfrac{5\pi \text{ radians}}{3} \cdot \dfrac{180°}{\pi \text{ radians}} = -\dfrac{5 \cdot 180°}{3} = -300°$

c. 1 radian $= 1 \text{ radian} \cdot \dfrac{180°}{\pi \text{ radians}} = \dfrac{180°}{\pi} \approx 57.3°$

> **Helpful Hint**
> In Example 3(c), we see that 1 radian is approximately 57°. Keep in mind that a radian is much larger than a degree.

PRACTICE 3 Convert each angle in radians to degrees:

a. $\dfrac{\pi}{4}$ radians   **b.** $-\dfrac{4\pi}{3}$ radians   **c.** 6 radians.

OBJECTIVE 5 ▶ Drawing angles in standard position. Although we can convert angles in radians to degrees, it is helpful to "think in radians" without having to make this conversion. To help, we draw angles in standard position. An angle is in **standard position** if its vertex is at the origin and its initial side lies along the positive x-axis.

Figure 14.10 is a starting point for learning to think in radians. The figure illustrates that when the terminal side makes one full revolution, it forms an angle whose radian measure is 2π. The figure shows the quadrantal angles formed by $\frac{3}{4}$ of a revolution, $\frac{1}{2}$ of a revolution, and $\frac{1}{4}$ of a revolution.

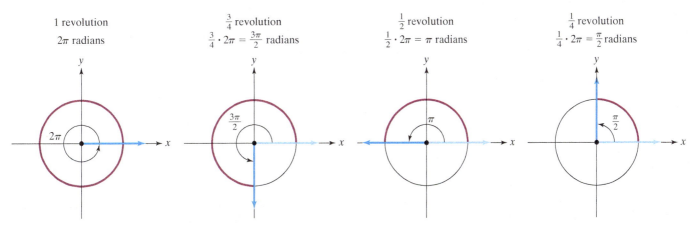

FIGURE 14.10   Angles formed by revolutions of terminal sides

EXAMPLE 4 Drawing Angles in Standard Position

Draw and label each angle in standard position:

a. $\theta = \dfrac{\pi}{4}$ [theta] **b.** $\alpha = \dfrac{5\pi}{4}$ [alpha] **c.** $\beta = -\dfrac{3\pi}{4}$ [beta] **d.** $\gamma = \dfrac{9\pi}{4}$ [gamma].

Solution Because we are drawing angles in standard position, each vertex is at the origin and each initial side lies along the positive x-axis.

a. An angle of $\dfrac{\pi}{4}$ radians is a positive angle. It is obtained by rotating the terminal side counterclockwise. Because 2π is a full-circle revolution, we can express $\dfrac{\pi}{4}$ as a fractional part of 2π to determine the necessary rotation:

$$\dfrac{\pi}{4} = \dfrac{1}{8} \cdot 2\pi.$$

[$\dfrac{\pi}{4}$ is $\dfrac{1}{8}$ of a complete revolution of 2π radians.]

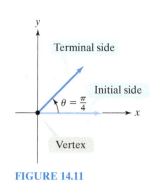

FIGURE 14.11

We see that $\theta = \dfrac{\pi}{4}$ is obtained by rotating the terminal side counterclockwise for $\dfrac{1}{8}$ of a revolution. The angle lies in quadrant I and is shown in Figure 14.11.

b. An angle of $\dfrac{5\pi}{4}$ radians is a positive angle. It is obtained by rotating the terminal side counterclockwise. Here are two ways to determine the necessary rotation:

Method 1

$$\dfrac{5\pi}{4} = \dfrac{5}{8} \cdot 2\pi$$

[$\dfrac{5\pi}{4}$ is $\dfrac{5}{8}$ of a complete revolution of 2π radians.]

Method 2

$$\dfrac{5\pi}{4} = \pi + \dfrac{\pi}{4}.$$

[π is a half-circle revolution.] [$\dfrac{\pi}{4}$ is $\dfrac{1}{8}$ of a complete revolution.]

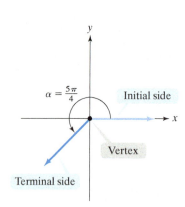

FIGURE 14.12

Method 1 shows that $\alpha = \dfrac{5\pi}{4}$ is obtained by rotating the terminal side counterclockwise for $\dfrac{5}{8}$ of a revolution. Method 2 shows that $\alpha = \dfrac{5\pi}{4}$ is obtained by rotating the terminal side counterclockwise for half of a revolution followed by a counterclockwise rotation of $\dfrac{1}{8}$ of a revolution. The angle lies in quadrant III and is shown in Figure 14.12.

c. An angle of $-\dfrac{3\pi}{4}$ is a negative angle. It is obtained by rotating the terminal side clockwise. We use $\left|-\dfrac{3\pi}{4}\right|$, or $\dfrac{3\pi}{4}$, to determine the necessary rotation.

Method 1

$$\dfrac{3\pi}{4} = \dfrac{3}{8} \cdot 2\pi$$

[$\dfrac{3\pi}{4}$ is $\dfrac{3}{8}$ of a complete revolution of 2π radians.]

Method 2

$$\dfrac{3\pi}{4} = \dfrac{2\pi}{4} + \dfrac{\pi}{4} = \dfrac{\pi}{2} + \dfrac{\pi}{4}$$

[$\dfrac{\pi}{2}$ is a quarter-circle revolution.] [$\dfrac{\pi}{4}$ is $\dfrac{1}{8}$ of a complete revolution.]

Section 14.1 Angles and Radian Measure   801

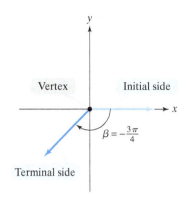

FIGURE 14.13

Method 1 shows that $\beta = -\dfrac{3\pi}{4}$ is obtained by rotating the terminal side clockwise for $\dfrac{3}{8}$ of a revolution. Method 2 shows that $\beta = -\dfrac{3\pi}{4}$ is obtained rotating by the terminal side clockwise for $\dfrac{1}{4}$ of a revolution followed by a clockwise rotation of $\dfrac{1}{8}$ of a revolution. The angle lies in quadrant III and is shown in Figure 14.13.

d. An angle of $\dfrac{9\pi}{4}$ radians is a positive angle. It is obtained by rotating the terminal side counterclockwise. Here are two methods to determine the necessary rotation:

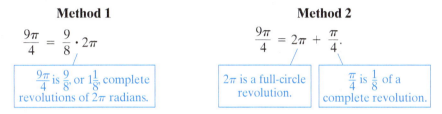

Method 1 shows that $\gamma = \dfrac{9\pi}{4}$ is obtained by rotating the terminal side counterclockwise for $1\dfrac{1}{8}$ revolutions. Method 2 shows that $\gamma = \dfrac{9\pi}{4}$ is obtained by rotating the terminal side counterclockwise for a full-circle revolution followed by a counterclockwise rotation of $\dfrac{1}{8}$ of a revolution. The angle lies in quadrant I and is shown in Figure 14.14.

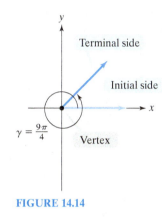

FIGURE 14.14

PRACTICE 4 Draw and label each angle in standard position:

a. $\theta = -\dfrac{\pi}{4}$ **b.** $\alpha = \dfrac{3\pi}{4}$ **c.** $\beta = -\dfrac{7\pi}{4}$ **d.** $\gamma = \dfrac{13\pi}{4}$.

Figure 14.15 illustrates the degree and radian measures of angles that you will commonly see in trigonometry. Each angle is in standard position, so that the initial side lies along the positive x-axis. We will be using both degree and radian measure for these angles.

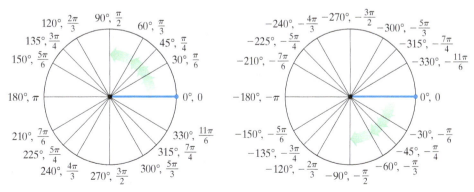

FIGURE 14.15 Degree and radian measures of selected positive and negative angles

Table 14.1 describes some of the positive angles in Figure 14.15 in terms of revolutions of the angle's terminal side around the origin.

802 CHAPTER 14 Trigonometric Functions

▶ **Helpful Hint**

When drawing the angles in Table 14.1 and Figure 14.15, it is helpful to first divide the rectangular coordinate system into eight equal sectors:

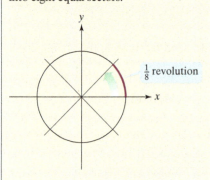

or 12 equal sectors:

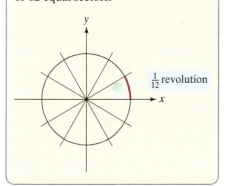

TABLE 14.1

Terminal Side	Radian Measure of Angle	Degree Measure of Angle
$\frac{1}{12}$ revolution	$\frac{1}{12} \cdot 2\pi = \frac{\pi}{6}$	$\frac{1}{12} \cdot 360° = 30°$
$\frac{1}{8}$ revolution	$\frac{1}{8} \cdot 2\pi = \frac{\pi}{4}$	$\frac{1}{8} \cdot 360° = 45°$
$\frac{1}{6}$ revolution	$\frac{1}{6} \cdot 2\pi = \frac{\pi}{3}$	$\frac{1}{6} \cdot 360° = 60°$
$\frac{1}{4}$ revolution	$\frac{1}{4} \cdot 2\pi = \frac{\pi}{2}$	$\frac{1}{4} \cdot 360° = 90°$
$\frac{1}{3}$ revolution	$\frac{1}{3} \cdot 2\pi = \frac{2\pi}{3}$	$\frac{1}{3} \cdot 360° = 120°$
$\frac{1}{2}$ revolution	$\frac{1}{2} \cdot 2\pi = \pi$	$\frac{1}{2} \cdot 360° = 180°$
$\frac{2}{3}$ revolution	$\frac{2}{3} \cdot 2\pi = \frac{4\pi}{3}$	$\frac{2}{3} \cdot 360° = 240°$
$\frac{3}{4}$ revolution	$\frac{3}{4} \cdot 2\pi = \frac{3\pi}{2}$	$\frac{3}{4} \cdot 360° = 270°$
$\frac{7}{8}$ revolution	$\frac{7}{8} \cdot 2\pi = \frac{7\pi}{4}$	$\frac{7}{8} \cdot 360° = 315°$
1 revolution	$1 \cdot 2\pi = 2\pi$	$1 \cdot 360° = 360°$

OBJECTIVE 6 ▶ **Find coterminal angles.** Two angles with the same initial and terminal sides but possibly different rotations are called **coterminal angles.**

Every angle has infinitely many coterminal angles. Why? Think of an angle in standard position. If the rotation of the angle is extended by one or more complete rotations of 360° or 2π, clockwise or counterclockwise, the result is an angle with the same initial and terminal sides as the original angle.

Coterminal Angles

Increasing or decreasing the degree measure of an angle in standard position by an integer multiple of 360° results in a coterminal angle. Thus, an angle of $\theta°$ is coterminal with angles of $\theta° \pm 360°k$, where k is an integer.

Increasing or decreasing the radian measure of an angle by an integer multiple of 2π results in a coterminal angle. Thus, an angle of θ radians is coterminal with angles of $\theta \pm 2\pi k$, where k is an integer.

Two coterminal angles for an angle of $\theta°$ can be found by adding 360° to $\theta°$ and subtracting 360° from $\theta°$.

EXAMPLE 5 Finding Coterminal Angles

Assume the following angles are in standard position. Find a positive angle less than 360° that is coterminal with each of the following:

a. a 420° angle   **b.** a −120° angle.

Solution We obtain the coterminal angle by adding or subtracting 360°. The requirement to obtain a positive angle less than 360° determines whether we should add or subtract.

a. For a 420° angle, subtract 360° to find a positive coterminal angle.

$$420° - 360° = 60°$$

A 60° angle is coterminal with a 420° angle. Figure 14.16(a) illustrates that these angles have the same initial and terminal sides.

b. For a −120° angle, add 360° to find a positive coterminal angle.

$$-120° + 360° = 240°$$

A 240° angle is coterminal with a −120° angle. Figure 14.16(b) illustrates that these angles have the same initial and terminal sides.

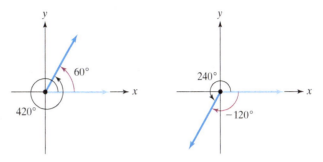

(a) Angles of 420° and 60° are coterminal.

(b) Angles of −120° and 240° are coterminal.

FIGURE 14.16 Pairs of coterminal angles

PRACTICE

5 Find a positive angle less than 360° that is coterminal with each of the following:

a. a 400° angle   **b.** a −135° angle.

Two coterminal angles for an angle of θ radians can be found by adding 2π to θ and subtracting 2π from θ.

EXAMPLE 6   Finding Coterminal Angles

Assume the following angles are in standard position. Find a positive angle less than 2π that is coterminal with each of the following:

a. a $\dfrac{17\pi}{6}$ angle   **b.** a $-\dfrac{\pi}{12}$ angle.

Solution We obtain the coterminal angle by adding or subtracting 2π. The requirement to obtain a positive angle less than 2π determines whether we should add or subtract.

a. For a $\dfrac{17\pi}{6}$, or $2\dfrac{5}{6}\pi$, angle, subtract 2π to find a positive coterminal angle.

$$\frac{17\pi}{6} - 2\pi = \frac{17\pi}{6} - \frac{12\pi}{6} = \frac{5\pi}{6}$$

A $\dfrac{5\pi}{6}$ angle is coterminal with a $\dfrac{17\pi}{6}$ angle. Figure 14.17(a) illustrates that these angles have the same initial and terminal sides.

b. For a $-\dfrac{\pi}{12}$ angle, add 2π to find a positive coterminal angle.

$$-\frac{\pi}{12} + 2\pi = -\frac{\pi}{12} + \frac{24\pi}{12} = \frac{23\pi}{12}$$

A $\frac{23\pi}{12}$ angle is coterminal with a $-\frac{\pi}{12}$ angle. Figure 14.17(b) illustrates that these angles have the same initial and terminal sides.

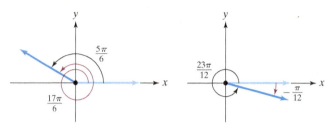

(a) Angles of $\frac{17\pi}{6}$ and $\frac{5\pi}{6}$ are coterminal.

(b) Angles of $-\frac{\pi}{12}$ and $\frac{23\pi}{12}$ are coterminal.

FIGURE 14.17 Pairs of coterminal angles

PRACTICE 6 Find a positive angle less than 2π that is coterminal with each of the following:

a. a $\frac{13\pi}{5}$ angle   **b.** a $-\frac{\pi}{15}$ angle.

To find a positive coterminal angle less than 360° or 2π, it is sometimes necessary to add or subtract more than one multiple of 360° or 2π.

EXAMPLE 7 Finding Coterminal Angles

Find a positive angle less than 360° or 2π that is coterminal with each of the following:

a. a 750° angle   **b.** a $\frac{22\pi}{3}$ angle   **c.** a $-\frac{17\pi}{6}$ angle.

Solution

a. For a 750° angle, subtract two multiples of 360°, or 720°, to find a positive coterminal angle less than 360°.

$$750° - 360° \cdot 2 = 750° - 720° = 30°$$

A 30° angle is coterminal with a 750° angle.

b. For a $\frac{22\pi}{3}$, or $7\frac{1}{3}\pi$, angle, subtract three multiples of 2π, or 6π, to find a positive coterminal angle less than 2π.

$$\frac{22\pi}{3} - 2\pi \cdot 3 = \frac{22\pi}{3} - 6\pi = \frac{22\pi}{3} - \frac{18\pi}{3} = \frac{4\pi}{3}$$

A $\frac{4\pi}{3}$ angle is coterminal with a $\frac{22\pi}{3}$ angle.

c. For a $-\frac{17\pi}{6}$, or $-2\frac{5}{6}\pi$ angle, add two multiples of 2π, or 4π, to find a positive coterminal angle less than 2π.

$$-\frac{17\pi}{6} + 2\pi \cdot 2 = -\frac{17\pi}{6} + 4\pi = -\frac{17\pi}{6} + \frac{24\pi}{6} = \frac{7\pi}{6}$$

A $\frac{7\pi}{6}$ angle is coterminal with a $-\frac{17\pi}{6}$ angle.

PRACTICE 7 Find a positive angle less than 360° or 2π that is coterminal with each of the following:

a. an 855° angle **b.** a $\dfrac{17\pi}{3}$ angle **c.** a $-\dfrac{25\pi}{6}$ angle.

OBJECTIVE 7 ▶ Find the length of a circular arc. We can use the radian measure formula, $\theta = \dfrac{s}{r}$, to find the length of the arc of a circle. How do we do this? Remember that s represents the length of the arc intercepted by the central angle θ. Thus, by solving the formula for s, we have an equation for arc length.

The Length of a Circular Arc

Let r be the radius of a circle and θ the nonnegative radian measure of a central angle of the circle. The length of the arc intercepted by the central angle is

$$s = r\theta.$$

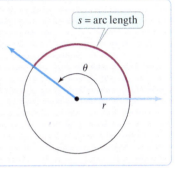

EXAMPLE 8 Finding the Length of a Circular Arc

A circle has a radius of 10 inches. Find the length of the arc intercepted by a central angle of 120°.

Solution The formula $s = r\theta$ can be used only when θ is expressed in radians. Thus, we begin by converting 120° to radians. Multiply by $\dfrac{\pi \text{ radians}}{180°}$.

$$120° = 120° \cdot \dfrac{\pi \text{ radians}}{180°} = \dfrac{120\pi}{180} \text{ radians} = \dfrac{2\pi}{3} \text{ radians}$$

Now we can use the formula $s = r\theta$ to find the length of the arc. The circle's radius is 10 inches: $r = 10$ inches. The measure of the central angle, in radians, is $\dfrac{2\pi}{3}$: $\theta = \dfrac{2\pi}{3}$. The length of the arc intercepted by this central angle is

$$s = r\theta = (10 \text{ inches})\left(\dfrac{2\pi}{3}\right) = \dfrac{20\pi}{3} \text{ inches} \approx 20.94 \text{ inches.}$$

▶ **Helpful Hint**
The unit used to describe the length of a circular arc is the same unit that is given in the circle's radius.

PRACTICE 8 A circle has a radius of 6 inches. Find the length of the arc intercepted by a central angle of 45°. Express arc length in terms of π. Then round your answer to two decimal places.

OBJECTIVE 8 ▶ Linear and angular speed. A carousel contains four circular rows of animals. As the carousel revolves, the animals in the outer row travel a greater distance per unit of time than those in the inner rows. These animals have a greater *linear speed* than those in the inner rows. By contrast, all animals, regardless of the row, complete the same number of revolutions per unit of time. All animals in the four circular rows travel at the same *angular speed*.

Using v for linear speed and ω (omega) for angular speed, we define these two kinds of speeds along a circular path as follows:

> **Definitions of Linear and Angular Speed**
>
> If a point is in motion on a circle of radius r through an angle of θ radians in time t, then its **linear speed** is
>
> $$v = \frac{s}{t},$$
>
> where s is the arc length given by $s = r\theta$, and its **angular speed** is
>
> $$\omega = \frac{\theta}{t}.$$

The hard drive in a computer rotates at 3600 revolutions per minute. This angular speed, expressed in revolutions per minute, can also be expressed in revolutions per second, radians per minute, and radians per second. Using 2π radians = 1 revolution, we express the angular speed of a hard drive in radians per minute as follows:

3600 revolutions per minute

$$= \frac{3600 \text{ revolutions}}{1 \text{ minute}} \cdot \frac{2\pi \text{ radians}}{1 \text{ revolution}} = \frac{7200\pi \text{ radians}}{1 \text{ minute}}$$

$= 7200\pi$ radians per minute.

We can establish a relationship between the two kinds of speed by dividing both sides of the arc length formula, $s = r\theta$, by t:

$$\frac{s}{t} = \frac{r\theta}{t} = r\frac{\theta}{t}.$$

| This expression defines linear speed. | This expression defines angular speed. |

Thus, linear speed is the product of the radius and the angular speed.

> **Linear Speed in Terms of Angular Speed**
>
> The linear speed, v, of a point a distance r from the center of rotation is given by
>
> $$v = r\omega,$$
>
> where ω is the angular speed in radians per unit of time.

EXAMPLE 9 Finding Linear Speed

A wind machine used to generate electricity has blades that are 10 feet in length (see Figure 14.18). The propeller is rotating at four revolutions per second. Find the linear speed, in feet per second, of the tips of the blades.

Solution We are given ω, the angular speed.

$\omega = 4$ revolutions per second

FIGURE 14.18

We use the formula $v = r\omega$ to find v, the linear speed. Before applying the formula, we must express ω in radians per second.

$$\omega = \frac{4 \text{ revolutions}}{1 \text{ second}} \cdot \frac{2\pi \text{ radians}}{1 \text{ revolution}} = \frac{8\pi \text{ radians}}{1 \text{ second}} \text{ or } \frac{8\pi}{1 \text{ second}}$$

The angular speed of the propeller is 8π radians per second. The linear speed is

$$v = r\omega = 10 \text{ feet} \cdot \frac{8\pi}{1 \text{ second}} = \frac{80\pi \text{ feet}}{\text{second}}.$$

The linear speed of the tips of the blades is 80π feet per second, which is approximately 251 feet per second.

PRACTICE 9 Long before iPods that hold thousands of songs and play them with superb audio quality, individual songs were delivered on 75-rpm and 45-rpm circular records. A 45-rpm record has an angular speed of 45 revolutions per minute. Find the linear speed, in inches per minute, at the point where the needle is 1.5 inches from the record's center.

14.1 EXERCISE SET

PRACTICE EXERCISES

In Exercises 1–6, the measure of an angle is given. Classify the angle as acute, right, obtuse, or straight.

1. 135°   **2.** 177°
3. 83.135°   **4.** 87.177°
5. π **6.** $\frac{\pi}{2}$

Read a Table. *In Exercises 7–12, find the radian measure of the central angle of a circle of radius r that intercepts an arc of length s.*

Radius, r	Arc Length, s
7. 10 inches	40 inches
8. 5 feet	30 feet
9. 6 yards	8 yards
10. 8 yards	18 yards
11. 1 meter	400 centimeters
12. 1 meter	600 centimeters

In Exercises 13–20, convert each angle in degrees to radians. Express your answer as a multiple of π.

13. 45°   **14.** 18°   **15.** 135°
16. 150°   **17.** 300°   **18.** 330°
19. −225°   **20.** −270°

In Exercises 21–28, convert each angle in radians to degrees.

21. $\frac{\pi}{2}$ **22.** $\frac{\pi}{9}$ **23.** $\frac{2\pi}{3}$
24. $\frac{3\pi}{4}$ **25.** $\frac{7\pi}{6}$ **26.** $\frac{11\pi}{6}$
27. -3π **28.** -4π

In Exercises 29–34, convert each angle in degrees to radians. Round to two decimal places.

29. 18°   **30.** 76°   **31.** −40°
32. −50°   **33.** 200°   **34.** 250°

In Exercises 35–40, convert each angle in radians to degrees. Round to two decimal places.

35. 2 radians   **36.** 3 radians
37. $\frac{\pi}{13}$ radians   **38.** $\frac{\pi}{17}$ radians
39. −4.8 radians   **40.** −5.2 radians

In Exercises 41–56, use the circle shown in the rectangular coordinate system to draw each angle in standard position. State the quadrant in which the angle lies. When an angle's measure is given in radians, work the exercise without converting to degrees.

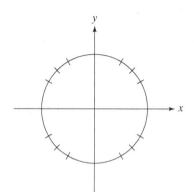

PRACTICE PLUS

Use the circle shown in the rectangular coordinate system to solve Exercises 77–82. Find two angles, in radians, between -2π and 2π such that each angle's terminal side passes through the origin and the given point.

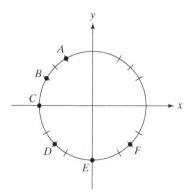

41. $\dfrac{7\pi}{6}$ **42.** $\dfrac{4\pi}{3}$ **43.** $\dfrac{3\pi}{4}$

44. $\dfrac{7\pi}{4}$ **45.** $-\dfrac{2\pi}{3}$ **46.** $-\dfrac{5\pi}{6}$

47. $-\dfrac{5\pi}{4}$ **48.** $-\dfrac{7\pi}{4}$ **49.** $\dfrac{16\pi}{3}$

50. $\dfrac{14\pi}{3}$ **51.** 120° **52.** 150°

53. −210° **54.** −240° **55.** 420°

56. 405°

77. A **78.** B
79. D **80.** F
81. E **82.** C

In Exercises 83–86, find the positive radian measure of the angle that the second hand of a clock moves through in the given time.

83. 55 seconds **84.** 35 seconds

85. 3 minutes and 40 seconds

86. 4 minutes and 25 seconds

In Exercises 57–70, find a positive angle less than 360° or 2π that is coterminal with the given angle.

57. 395° **58.** 415° **59.** −150°

60. −160° **61.** −765° **62.** −760°

63. $\dfrac{19\pi}{6}$ **64.** $\dfrac{17\pi}{5}$ **65.** $\dfrac{23\pi}{5}$

66. $\dfrac{25\pi}{6}$ **67.** $-\dfrac{\pi}{50}$ **68.** $-\dfrac{\pi}{40}$

69. $-\dfrac{31\pi}{7}$ **70.** $-\dfrac{38\pi}{9}$

APPLICATION EXERCISES

87. The minute hand of a clock moves from 12 to 2 o'clock, or $\frac{1}{6}$ of a complete revolution. Through how many degrees does it move? Through how many radians does it move?

88. The minute hand of a clock moves from 12 to 4 o'clock, or $\frac{1}{3}$ of a complete revolution. Through how many degrees does it move? Through how many radians does it move?

89. The minute hand of a clock is 8 inches long and moves from 12 to 2 o'clock. How far does the tip of the minute hand move? Express your answer in terms of π and then round to two decimal places.

90. The minute hand of a clock is 6 inches long and moves from 12 to 4 o'clock. How far does the tip of the minute hand move? Express your answer in terms of π and then round to two decimal places.

91. The figure shows a highway sign that warns of a railway crossing. The lines that form the cross pass through the circle's center and intersect at right angles. If the radius of the circle is 24 inches, find the length of each of the four arcs formed by the cross. Express your answer in terms of π and then round to two decimal places.

Read a Table. In Exercises 71–74, find the length of the arc on a circle of radius r intercepted by a central angle θ. Express arc length in terms of π. Then round your answer to two decimal places.

Radius, r	Central Angle, θ
71. 12 inches	$\theta = 45°$
72. 16 inches	$\theta = 60°$
73. 8 feet	$\theta = 225°$
74. 9 yards	$\theta = 315°$

In Exercises 75–76, express each angular speed in radians per second.

75. 6 revolutions per second

76. 20 revolutions per second

92. The radius of a wheel rolling on the ground is 80 centimeters. If the wheel rotates through an angle of 60°, how many centimeters does it move? Express your answer in terms of π and then round to two decimal places.

How do we measure the distance between two points, A and B, on Earth? We measure along a circle with a center, C, at the center of Earth. The radius of the circle is equal to the distance from C to the surface. Use the fact that Earth is a sphere of radius equal to approximately 4000 miles to solve Exercises 93–96.

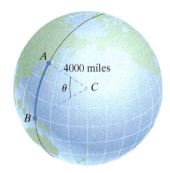

93. If two points, A and B, are 8000 miles apart, express angle θ in radians and in degrees.

94. If two points, A and B, are 10,000 miles apart, express angle θ in radians and in degrees.

95. If $\theta = 30°$, find the distance between A and B to the nearest mile.

96. If $\theta = 10°$, find the distance between A and B to the nearest mile.

97. The angular speed of a point on Earth is $\frac{\pi}{12}$ radian per hour. The Equator lies on a circle of radius approximately 4000 miles. Find the linear velocity, in miles per hour, of a point on the Equator.

98. A Ferris wheel has a radius of 25 feet. The wheel is rotating at two revolutions per minute. Find the linear speed, in feet per minute, of a seat on this Ferris wheel.

99. A water wheel has a radius of 12 feet. The wheel is rotating at 20 revolutions per minute. Find the linear speed, in feet per minute, of the water.

100. On a carousel, the outer row of animals is 20 feet from the center. The inner row of animals is 10 feet from the center. The carousel is rotating at 2.5 revolutions per minute. What is the difference, in feet per minute, in the linear speeds of the animals in the outer and inner rows? Round to the nearest foot per minute.

WRITING IN MATHEMATICS

101. What is an angle?
102. What determines the size of an angle?
103. Describe an angle in standard position.
104. Explain the difference between positive and negative angles. What are coterminal angles?
105. Explain what is meant by one radian.
106. Explain how to find the radian measure of a central angle.
107. Describe how to convert an angle in degrees to radians.
108. Explain how to convert an angle in radians to degrees.
109. Explain how to find the length of a circular arc.
110. If a carousel is rotating at 2.5 revolutions per minute, explain how to find the linear speed of a child seated on one of the animals.
111. The angular velocity of a point on Earth is $\frac{\pi}{12}$ radian per hour. Describe what happens every 24 hours.
112. Have you ever noticed that we use the vocabulary of angles in everyday speech? Here is an example:

    My opinion about art museums took a 180° turn after visiting the San Francisco Museum of Modern Art.

    Explain what this means. Then give another example of the vocabulary of angles in everyday use.

TECHNOLOGY EXERCISES

In Exercises 113–116, use the keys on your calculator or graphing utility for converting an angle in degrees, minutes, and seconds ($D°M'S''$) into decimal form, and vice versa.

In Exercises 113–114, convert each angle to a decimal in degrees. Round your answer to two decimal places.

113. $30°15'10''$
114. $65°45'20''$

In Exercises 115–116, convert each angle to $D°M'S''$ form. Round your answer to the nearest second.

115. $30.42°$
116. $50.42°$

CRITICAL THINKING EXERCISES

Make Sense? *In Exercises 117–120, determine whether each statement makes sense or does not make sense, and explain your reasoning.*

117. I made an error because the angle I drew in standard position exceeded a straight angle.
118. When an angle's measure is given in terms of π, I know that it's measured using radians.
119. When I convert degrees to radians, I multiply by 1, choosing $\frac{\pi}{180°}$ for 1.
120. Using radian measure, I can always find a positive angle less than 2π coterminal with a given angle by adding or subtracting 2π.
121. If $\theta = \frac{3}{2}$, is this angle larger or smaller than a right angle?
122. A railroad curve is laid out on a circle. What radius should be used if the track is to change direction by 20° in a distance of 100 miles? Round your answer to the nearest mile.
123. Assuming Earth to be a sphere of radius 4000 miles, how many miles north of the Equator is Miami, Florida, if it is 26° north from the Equator? Round your answer to the nearest mile.

810 CHAPTER 14 Trigonometric Functions

REVIEW AND PREVIEW EXERCISES

Exercises 124–126 will help you prepare for the material covered in the next section. In each exercise, let θ be an acute angle in a right triangle, as shown in the figure. These exercises require the use of the Pythagorean Theorem.

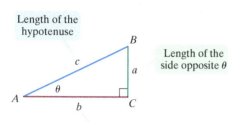

124. If $a = 5$ and $b = 12$, find the ratio of the length of the side opposite θ to the length of the hypotenuse.

125. If $a = 1$ and $b = 1$, find the ratio of the length of the side opposite θ to the length of the hypotenuse. Simplify the ratio by rationalizing the denominator.

126. Simplify: $\left(\dfrac{a}{c}\right)^2 + \left(\dfrac{b}{c}\right)^2$.

14.2 RIGHT TRIANGLE TRIGONOMETRY

OBJECTIVES

1. Use right triangles to evaluate trigonometric functions.
2. Find function values for $30° \left(\dfrac{\pi}{6}\right)$, $45° \left(\dfrac{\pi}{4}\right)$, and $60° \left(\dfrac{\pi}{3}\right)$.
3. Recognize and use fundamental identities.
4. Use equal cofunctions of complements.
5. Evaluate trigonometric functions with a calculator.
6. Use right triangle trigonometry to solve applied problems.

The word "trigonometry" means "*measurement of triangles.*" Trigonometry is used in navigation, building, and engineering. Today, trigonometry is used to study the structure of DNA, the master molecule that determines how we grow from a single cell to a complex, fully developed adult.

OBJECTIVE 1 ▶ **The six trigonometric functions.** We begin the study of trigonometry by defining six functions, the six *trigonometric functions*. The inputs for these functions are measures of acute angles in right triangles. The outputs are the ratios of the lengths of the sides of right triangles.

Figure 14.19 shows a right triangle with one of its acute angles labeled θ. The side opposite the right angle is known as the **hypotenuse.** The other sides of the triangle are described by their position relative to the acute angle θ. One side is opposite θ and one is adjacent to θ.

The trigonometric functions have names that are words, rather than single letters such as f, g, and h. For example, the **sine of θ** is the length of the side opposite θ divided by the length of the hypotenuse:

$$\sin \theta = \frac{\text{length of side opposite } \theta}{\text{length of hypotenuse}}.$$

Input is the measure of an acute angle. Output is the ratio of the lengths of the sides.

FIGURE 14.19 Naming a right triangle's sides from the point of view of an acute angle θ

The ratio of lengths depends on angle θ and thus is a function of θ. The expression $\sin \theta$ really means $\sin(\theta)$, where sine is the name of the function and θ, the measure of an acute angle, is the input.

Here are the names of the six trigonometric functions, along with their abbreviations:

Name	Abbreviation	Name	Abbreviation
sine	sin	cosecant	csc
cosine	cos	secant	sec
tangent	tan	cotangent	cot

Now, let θ be an acute angle in a right triangle, as shown in Figure 14.20. The length of the side opposite θ is a, the length of the side adjacent to θ is b, and the length of the hypotenuse is c.

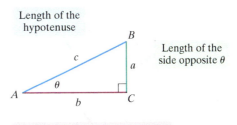

FIGURE 14.20

Right Triangle Definitions of Trigonometric Functions

See Figure 14.20. The six **trigonometric functions of the acute angle θ** are defined as follows:

$$\sin \theta = \frac{\text{length of side opposite angle } \theta}{\text{length of hypotenuse}} = \frac{a}{c} \qquad \csc \theta = \frac{\text{length of hypotenuse}}{\text{length of side opposite angle } \theta} = \frac{c}{a}$$

$$\cos \theta = \frac{\text{length of side adjacent to angle } \theta}{\text{length of hypotenuse}} = \frac{b}{c} \qquad \sec \theta = \frac{\text{length of hypotenuse}}{\text{length of side adjacent to angle } \theta} = \frac{c}{b}$$

$$\tan \theta = \frac{\text{length of side opposite angle } \theta}{\text{length of side adjacent to angle } \theta} = \frac{a}{b} \qquad \cot \theta = \frac{\text{length of side adjacent to angle } \theta}{\text{length of side opposite angle } \theta} = \frac{b}{a}.$$

Each of the trigonometric functions of the acute angle θ is positive. Observe that the ratios in the second column in the box are the reciprocals of the corresponding ratios in the first column.

> **Helpful Hint**
>
> The word
>
> SOHCAHTOA (pronounced: so-cah-tow-ah)
>
> is a way to remember the right triangle definitions of the three basic trigonometric functions, sine, cosine, and tangent.
>
>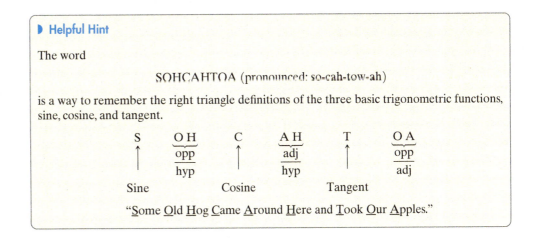
>
> "Some Old Hog Came Around Here and Took Our Apples."

Figure 14.21 shows four right triangles of varying sizes. In each of the triangles, θ is the same acute angle, measuring approximately 56.3°. All four of these similar triangles have the same shape and the lengths of corresponding sides are in the same ratio. In each triangle, the tangent function has the same value for the angle θ: $\tan \theta = \frac{3}{2}$.

In general, **the trigonometric function values of θ depend only on the size of angle θ and not on the size of the triangle.**

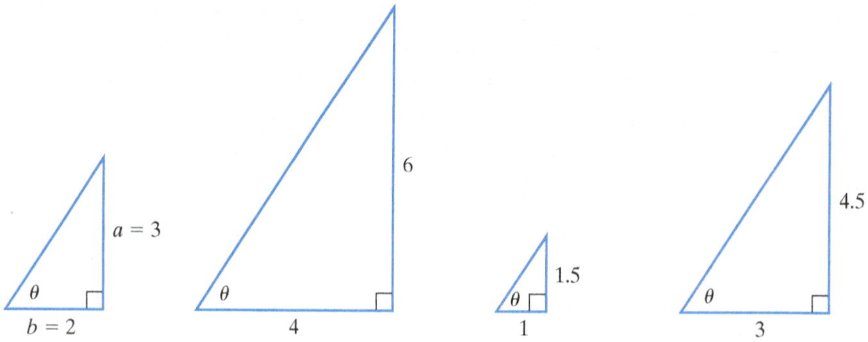

812 CHAPTER 14 Trigonometric Functions

FIGURE 14.21 A particular acute angle always gives the same ratio of opposite to adjacent sides.

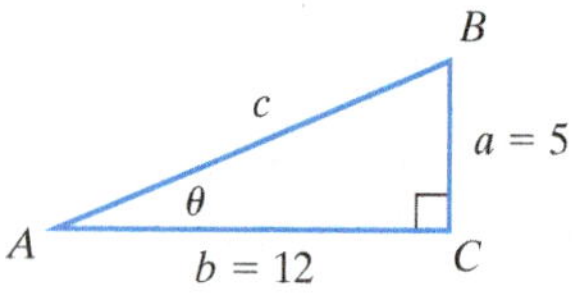

$\tan \theta = \frac{a}{b} = \frac{3}{2}$ $\tan \theta = \frac{6}{4} = \frac{3}{2}$ $\tan \theta = \frac{1.5}{1} = \frac{3}{2}$ $\tan \theta = \frac{4.5}{3} = \frac{3}{2}$

EXAMPLE 1   Evaluating Trigonometric Functions

Find the value of each of the six trigonometric functions of θ in Figure 14.22.

Solution   We need to find the values of the six trigonometric functions of θ. However, we must know the lengths of all three sides of the triangle (a, b, and c) to evaluate all six functions. The values of a and b are given. We can use the Pythagorean Theorem, $c^2 = a^2 + b^2$, to find c.

FIGURE 14.22

$$c^2 = a^2 + b^2 = 5^2 + 12^2 = 25 + 144 = 169$$
$$c = \sqrt{169} = 13$$

Now that we know the lengths of the three sides of the triangle, we apply the definitions of the six trigonometric functions of θ. Referring to these lengths as opposite, adjacent, and hypotenuse, we have

> **Helpful Hint**
> The function values in the second column are reciprocals of those in the first column. You can obtain each of these values by exchanging the numerator and denominator of the corresponding ratio in the first column.

$\sin \theta = \dfrac{\text{opposite}}{\text{hypotenuse}} = \dfrac{5}{13}$ $\csc \theta = \dfrac{\text{hypotenuse}}{\text{opposite}} = \dfrac{13}{5}$

$\cos \theta = \dfrac{\text{adjacent}}{\text{hypotenuse}} = \dfrac{12}{13}$ $\sec \theta = \dfrac{\text{hypotenuse}}{\text{adjacent}} = \dfrac{13}{12}$

$\tan \theta = \dfrac{\text{opposite}}{\text{adjacent}} = \dfrac{5}{12}$ $\cot \theta = \dfrac{\text{adjacent}}{\text{opposite}} = \dfrac{12}{5}$.

PRACTICE 1   Find the value of each of the six trigonometric functions of θ in the figure.

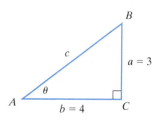

EXAMPLE 2   Evaluating Trigonometric Functions

Find the value of each of the six trigonometric functions of θ in Figure 14.23.

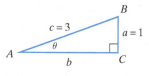

FIGURE 14.23

Solution   We begin by finding b.

$a^2 + b^2 = c^2$ Use the Pythagorean Theorem.

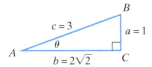

FIGURE 14.23 (repeated, showing $b = 2\sqrt{2}$)

$$1^2 + b^2 = 3^2 \quad \text{Figure 14.23 shows that } a = 1 \text{ and } c = 3.$$
$$1 + b^2 = 9 \quad \text{$1^2 = 1$ and $3^2 = 9$.}$$
$$b^2 = 8 \quad \text{Subtract 1 from both sides.}$$
$$b = \sqrt{8} = 2\sqrt{2} \quad \text{Take the principal square root and simplify:}$$
$$\sqrt{8} = \sqrt{4 \cdot 2} = \sqrt{4}\sqrt{2} = 2\sqrt{2}.$$

Now that we know the lengths of the three sides of the triangle, we apply the definitions of the six trigonometric functions of θ.

$$\sin\theta = \frac{\text{opposite}}{\text{hypotenuse}} = \frac{1}{3} \qquad \csc\theta = \frac{\text{hypotenuse}}{\text{opposite}} = \frac{3}{1} = 3$$

$$\cos\theta = \frac{\text{adjacent}}{\text{hypotenuse}} = \frac{2\sqrt{2}}{3} \qquad \sec\theta = \frac{\text{hypotenuse}}{\text{adjacent}} = \frac{3}{2\sqrt{2}}$$

$$\tan\theta = \frac{\text{opposite}}{\text{adjacent}} = \frac{1}{2\sqrt{2}} \qquad \cot\theta = \frac{\text{adjacent}}{\text{opposite}} = \frac{2\sqrt{2}}{1} = 2\sqrt{2}$$

Because fractional expressions are usually written without radicals in the denominators, we simplify the values of $\tan\theta$ and $\sec\theta$ by rationalizing the denominators:

$$\tan\theta = \frac{1}{2\sqrt{2}} = \frac{1}{2\sqrt{2}} \cdot \frac{\sqrt{2}}{\sqrt{2}} = \frac{\sqrt{2}}{2 \cdot 2} = \frac{\sqrt{2}}{4} \qquad \sec\theta = \frac{3}{2\sqrt{2}} = \frac{3}{2\sqrt{2}} \cdot \frac{\sqrt{2}}{\sqrt{2}} = \frac{3\sqrt{2}}{2 \cdot 2} = \frac{3\sqrt{2}}{4}.$$

We are multiplying by 1 and not changing the value of $\frac{1}{2\sqrt{2}}$.

We are multiplying by 1 and not changing the value of $\frac{3}{2\sqrt{2}}$.

PRACTICE 2 Find the value of each of the six trigonometric functions of θ in the figure. Express each value in simplified form.

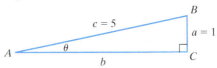

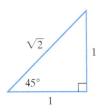

FIGURE 14.24 An isosceles right triangle

OBJECTIVE 2 ▶ Function values for some special angles. A 45°, or $\frac{\pi}{4}$ radian, angle occurs frequently in trigonometry. How do we find the values of the trigonometric functions of 45°? We construct a right triangle with a 45° angle, as shown in Figure 14.24. The triangle actually has two 45° angles. Thus, the triangle is isosceles—that is, it has two sides of the same length. Assume that each leg of the triangle has a length equal to 1. We can find the length of the hypotenuse using the Pythagorean Theorem.

$$(\text{length of hypotenuse})^2 = 1^2 + 1^2 = 2$$
$$\text{length of hypotenuse} = \sqrt{2}$$

With Figure 14.24, we can determine the trigonometric function values for 45°.

EXAMPLE 3 **Evaluating Trigonometric Functions of 45°**

Use Figure 14.24 to find sin 45°, cos 45°, and tan 45°.

Solution We apply the definitions of these three trigonometric functions. Where appropriate, we simplify by rationalizing denominators.

$$\sin 45° = \frac{\text{length of side opposite 45°}}{\text{length of hypotenuse}} = \frac{1}{\sqrt{2}} = \frac{1}{\sqrt{2}} \cdot \frac{\sqrt{2}}{\sqrt{2}} = \frac{\sqrt{2}}{2}$$

Rationalize denominators

$$\cos 45° = \frac{\text{length of side adjacent to 45°}}{\text{length of hypotenuse}} = \frac{1}{\sqrt{2}} = \frac{1}{\sqrt{2}} \cdot \frac{\sqrt{2}}{\sqrt{2}} = \frac{\sqrt{2}}{2}$$

$$\tan 45° = \frac{\text{length of side opposite 45°}}{\text{length of side adjacent to 45°}} = \frac{1}{1} = 1$$

PRACTICE 3 Use Figure 14.24 to find csc 45°, sec 45°, and cot 45°.

When you worked Practice 3, did you actually use Figure 14.24 or did you use reciprocals to find the values?

$$\csc 45° = \sqrt{2} \qquad \sec 45° = \sqrt{2} \qquad \cot 45° = 1$$

Take the reciprocal of $\sin 45° = \frac{1}{\sqrt{2}}$. Take the reciprocal of $\cos 45° = \frac{1}{\sqrt{2}}$. Take the reciprocal of $\tan 45° = \frac{1}{1}$.

Notice that if you use reciprocals, you should take the reciprocal of a function value before the denominator is rationalized. In this way, the reciprocal value will not contain a radical in the denominator.

Two other angles that occur frequently in trigonometry are 30°, or $\frac{\pi}{6}$ radian, and 60°, or $\frac{\pi}{3}$ radian, angles. We can find the values of the trigonometric functions of 30° and 60° by using a right triangle. To form this right triangle, draw an equilateral triangle—that is, a triangle with all sides the same length. Assume that each side has a length equal to 2. Now take half of the equilateral triangle. We obtain the right triangle in Figure 14.25. This right triangle has a hypotenuse of length 2 and a leg of length 1. The other leg has length a, which can be found using the Pythagorean Theorem.

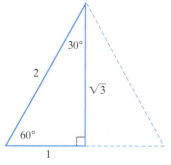

FIGURE 14.25 30°–60°–90° triangle

$$a^2 + 1^2 = 2^2$$
$$a^2 + 1 = 4$$
$$a^2 = 3$$
$$a = \sqrt{3}$$

With the right triangle in Figure 14.25, we can determine the trigonometric functions for 30° and 60°.

EXAMPLE 4 Evaluating Trigonometric Functions of 30° and 60°

Use Figure 14.25 to find sin 60°, cos 60°, sin 30°, and cos 30°.

Solution We begin with 60°. Use the angle on the lower left in Figure 14.25.

$$\sin 60° = \frac{\text{length of side opposite 60°}}{\text{length of hypotenuse}} = \frac{\sqrt{3}}{2}$$

$$\cos 60° = \frac{\text{length of side adjacent to 60°}}{\text{length of hypotenuse}} = \frac{1}{2}$$

To find sin 30° and cos 30°, use the angle on the upper right in Figure 14.25.

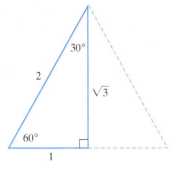

FIGURE 14.25 (repeated)

$$\sin 30° = \frac{\text{length of side opposite } 30°}{\text{length of hypotenuse}} = \frac{1}{2}$$

$$\cos 30° = \frac{\text{length of side adjacent to } 30°}{\text{length of hypotenuse}} = \frac{\sqrt{3}}{2}$$

PRACTICE 4 Use Figure 14.25 to find tan 60° and tan 30°. If a radical appears in a denominator, rationalize the denominator.

Because we will often use the function values of 30°, 45°, and 60°, you should learn to construct the right triangles in Figures 14.24 and 14.25, shown previously. With sufficient practice, you will memorize the values in Table 14.2.

TABLE 14.2 Trigonometric Functions of Special Angles

θ	$30° = \frac{\pi}{6}$	$45° = \frac{\pi}{4}$	$60° = \frac{\pi}{3}$
$\sin \theta$	$\frac{1}{2}$	$\frac{\sqrt{2}}{2}$	$\frac{\sqrt{3}}{2}$
$\cos \theta$	$\frac{\sqrt{3}}{2}$	$\frac{\sqrt{2}}{2}$	$\frac{1}{2}$
$\tan \theta$	$\frac{\sqrt{3}}{3}$	1	$\sqrt{3}$

OBJECTIVE 3 ▶ Fundamental identities. Many relationships exist among the six trigonometric functions. These relationships are described using **trigonometric identities.** For example, csc θ is defined as the reciprocal of sin θ. This relationship can be expressed by the identity

$$\csc \theta = \frac{1}{\sin \theta}.$$

This identity is one of six **reciprocal identities.**

Reciprocal Identities

$$\sin \theta = \frac{1}{\csc \theta} \qquad \csc \theta = \frac{1}{\sin \theta}$$

$$\cos \theta = \frac{1}{\sec \theta} \qquad \sec \theta = \frac{1}{\cos \theta}$$

$$\tan \theta = \frac{1}{\cot \theta} \qquad \cot \theta = \frac{1}{\tan \theta}$$

Two other relationships that follow from the definitions of the trigonometric functions are called the **quotient identities.**

Quotient Identities

$$\tan \theta = \frac{\sin \theta}{\cos \theta} \qquad \cot \theta = \frac{\cos \theta}{\sin \theta}$$

If sin θ and cos θ are known, a quotient identity and three reciprocal identities make it possible to find the value of each of the four remaining trigonometric functions.

EXAMPLE 5 Using Quotient and Reciprocal Identities

Given $\sin \theta = \dfrac{2}{5}$ and $\cos \theta = \dfrac{\sqrt{21}}{5}$, find the value of each of the four remaining trigonometric functions.

Solution We can find $\tan \theta$ by using the quotient identity that describes $\tan \theta$ as the quotient of $\sin \theta$ and $\cos \theta$.

$$\tan \theta = \dfrac{\sin \theta}{\cos \theta} = \dfrac{\dfrac{2}{5}}{\dfrac{\sqrt{21}}{5}} = \dfrac{2}{5} \cdot \dfrac{5}{\sqrt{21}} = \dfrac{2}{\sqrt{21}} = \dfrac{2}{\sqrt{21}} \cdot \dfrac{\sqrt{21}}{\sqrt{21}} = \dfrac{2\sqrt{21}}{21}$$

Rationalize the denominator.

We use the reciprocal identities to find the value of each of the remaining three functions.

$$\csc \theta = \dfrac{1}{\sin \theta} = \dfrac{1}{\dfrac{2}{5}} = \dfrac{5}{2}$$

$$\sec \theta = \dfrac{1}{\cos \theta} = \dfrac{1}{\dfrac{\sqrt{21}}{5}} = \dfrac{5}{\sqrt{21}} = \dfrac{5}{\sqrt{21}} \cdot \dfrac{\sqrt{21}}{\sqrt{21}} = \dfrac{5\sqrt{21}}{21}$$

Rationalize the denominator.

$$\cot \theta = \dfrac{1}{\tan \theta} = \dfrac{1}{\dfrac{2}{\sqrt{21}}} = \dfrac{\sqrt{21}}{2}$$

We found $\tan \theta = \dfrac{2}{\sqrt{21}}$. We could use $\tan \theta = \dfrac{2\sqrt{21}}{21}$, but then we would have to rationalize the denominator.

PRACTICE 5 Given $\sin \theta = \dfrac{2}{3}$ and $\cos \theta = \dfrac{\sqrt{5}}{3}$, find the value of each of the four remaining trigonometric functions.

Other relationships among trigonometric functions follow from the Pythagorean Theorem. Using Figure 14.26, the Pythagorean Theorem states that

$$a^2 + b^2 = c^2.$$

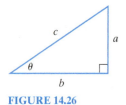

FIGURE 14.26

To obtain ratios that correspond to trigonometric functions, divide both sides of this equation by c^2.

$$\dfrac{a^2}{c^2} + \dfrac{b^2}{c^2} = 1 \quad \text{or} \quad \left(\dfrac{a}{c}\right)^2 + \left(\dfrac{b}{c}\right)^2 = 1$$

In **Figure 14.26**, $\sin \theta = \dfrac{a}{c}$, so this is $(\sin \theta)^2$.

In **Figure 14.26**, $\cos \theta = \dfrac{b}{c}$, so this is $(\cos \theta)^2$.

Based on the observations above, we see that

$$(\sin \theta)^2 + (\cos \theta)^2 = 1.$$

We will use the notation $\sin^2 \theta$ for $(\sin \theta)^2$ and $\cos^2 \theta$ for $(\cos \theta)^2$. With this notation, we can write the identity as

$$\sin^2 \theta + \cos^2 \theta = 1.$$

Two additional identities can be obtained from $a^2 + b^2 = c^2$ by dividing both sides by b^2 and a^2, respectively. The three identities are called the **Pythagorean identities**.

Section 14.2 Right Triangle Trigonometry 817

Pythagorean Identities

$$\sin^2\theta + \cos^2\theta = 1 \quad 1 + \tan^2\theta = \sec^2\theta \quad 1 + \cot^2\theta = \csc^2\theta$$

EXAMPLE 6 Using a Pythagorean Identity

Given that $\sin\theta = \frac{3}{5}$ and θ is an acute angle, find the value of $\cos\theta$ using a trigonometric identity.

Solution We can find the value of $\cos\theta$ by using the Pythagorean identity

$$\sin^2\theta + \cos^2\theta = 1.$$

$\left(\dfrac{3}{5}\right)^2 + \cos^2\theta = 1$ We are given that $\sin\theta = \dfrac{3}{5}$.

$\dfrac{9}{25} + \cos^2\theta = 1$ Square $\dfrac{3}{5}$: $\left(\dfrac{3}{5}\right)^2 = \dfrac{3^2}{5^2} = \dfrac{9}{25}$.

$\cos^2\theta = 1 - \dfrac{9}{25}$ Subtract $\dfrac{9}{25}$ from both sides.

$\cos^2\theta = \dfrac{16}{25}$ Simplify: $1 - \dfrac{9}{25} = \dfrac{25}{25} - \dfrac{9}{25} = \dfrac{16}{25}$.

$\cos\theta = \sqrt{\dfrac{16}{25}} = \dfrac{4}{5}$ Because θ is an acute angle, $\cos\theta$ is positive.

Thus, $\cos\theta = \dfrac{4}{5}$.

PRACTICE 6 Given that $\sin\theta = \frac{1}{2}$ and θ is an acute angle, find the value of $\cos\theta$ using a trigonometric identity.

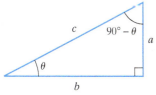

FIGURE 14.27

OBJECTIVE 4 ▶ Trigonometric functions and complements. Two positive angles are **complements** if their sum is 90° or $\dfrac{\pi}{2}$. For example, angles of 70° and 20° are complements because 70° + 20° = 90°.

Another relationship among trigonometric functions is based on angles that are complements. Refer to Figure 14.27. Because the sum of the angles of any triangle is 180°, in a right triangle the sum of the acute angles is 90°. Thus, the acute angles are complements. If the degree measure of one acute angle is θ, then the degree measure of the other acute angle is (90° − θ). This angle is shown on the upper right in Figure 14.27.

Let's use Figure 14.27 to compare $\sin\theta$ and $\cos(90° - \theta)$.

$$\sin\theta = \frac{\text{length of side opposite } \theta}{\text{length of hypotenuse}} = \frac{a}{c}$$

$$\cos(90° - \theta) = \frac{\text{length of side adjacent to } (90° - \theta)}{\text{length of hypotenuse}} = \frac{a}{c}$$

Thus, $\sin\theta = \cos(90° - \theta)$. If two angles are complements, the sine of one equals the cosine of the other. Because of this relationship, the sine and cosine are called *cofunctions* of each other. Using Figure 14.27, we can show that the tangent and cotangent are also cofunctions of each other.

Cofunction Identities

The value of a trigonometric function of θ is equal to the cofunction of the complement of θ. Cofunctions of complementary angles are equal.

$$\sin\theta = \cos(90° - \theta) \qquad \cos\theta = \sin(90° - \theta)$$
$$\tan\theta = \cot(90° - \theta) \qquad \cot\theta = \tan(90° - \theta)$$
$$\sec\theta = \csc(90° - \theta) \qquad \csc\theta = \sec(90° - \theta)$$

If θ is in radians, replace 90° with $\dfrac{\pi}{2}$.

EXAMPLE 7 Using Cofunction Identities

Find a cofunction with the same value as the given expression: $\sin 72°$

Solution Because the value of a trigonometric function of θ is equal to the cofunction of the complement of θ, we need to find the complement of each angle. We do this by subtracting the angle's measure from 90° or its radian equivalent, $\dfrac{\pi}{2}$.

$$\sin 72° = \cos(90° - 72°) = \cos 18°$$

We have a function and its cofunction.

PRACTICE 7 Find a cofunction with the same value as the given expression: $\sin 46°$

OBJECTIVE 5 ▶ Using a calculator to evaluate trigonometric functions. The values of the trigonometric functions obtained with the special triangles are exact values. For most acute angles other than 30°, 45°, and 60°, we approximate the value of each of the trigonometric functions using a calculator. The first step is to set the calculator to the correct *mode*, degrees or radians, depending on how the acute angle is measured.

Most calculators have keys marked $\boxed{\text{SIN}}$, $\boxed{\text{COS}}$, and $\boxed{\text{TAN}}$. For example, to find the value of sin 30°, set the calculator to the degree mode and enter 30 $\boxed{\text{SIN}}$ on most scientific calculators and $\boxed{\text{SIN}}$ 30 $\boxed{\text{ENTER}}$ on most graphing calculators. Consult the manual for your calculator.

To evaluate the cosecant, secant, and cotangent functions, use the key for the respective reciprocal function, $\boxed{\text{SIN}}$, $\boxed{\text{COS}}$, or $\boxed{\text{TAN}}$, and then use the reciprocal key. The reciprocal key is $\boxed{1/x}$ on many scientific calculators and $\boxed{x^{-1}}$ on many graphing calculators. For example, we can evaluate $\sec\dfrac{\pi}{12}$ using the following reciprocal relationship:

$$\sec\dfrac{\pi}{12} = \dfrac{1}{\cos\dfrac{\pi}{12}}.$$

Using the radian mode, enter one of the following keystroke sequences:

Many Scientific Calculators

$\boxed{\pi}\ \boxed{\div}\ 12\ \boxed{=}\ \boxed{\text{COS}}\ \boxed{1/x}$

Many Graphing Calculators

$\boxed{(}\ \boxed{\text{COS}}\ \boxed{(}\ \boxed{\pi}\ \boxed{\div}\ 12\ \boxed{)}\ \boxed{)}\ \boxed{x^{-1}}\ \boxed{\text{ENTER}}$

Rounding the display to four decimal places, we obtain $\sec\dfrac{\pi}{12} \approx 1.0353$.

Section 14.2 Right Triangle Trigonometry 819

EXAMPLE 8 Evaluating Trigonometric Functions with a Calculator

Use a calculator to find the value to four decimal places:

a. cos 48.2°   **b.** cot 1.2.

Solution

Scientific Calculator Solution

Function	Mode	Keystrokes	Display, Rounded to Four Decimal Places
a. cos 48.2°	Degree	48.2 [COS]	0.6665
b. cot 1.2	Radian	1.2 [TAN] [1/x]	0.3888

Graphing Calculator Solution

Function	Mode	Keystrokes	Display, Rounded to Four Decimal Places
a. cos 48.2°	Degree	[COS] 48.2 [ENTER]	0.6665
b. cot 1.2	Radian	[(] [TAN] 1.2 [)] [x^{-1}] [ENTER]	0.3888

PRACTICE 8 Use a calculator to find the value to four decimal places:

a. sin 72.8°   **b.** csc 1.5.

OBJECTIVE 6 ▶ Applications. Many applications of right triangle trigonometry involve the angle made with an imaginary horizontal line. As shown in Figure 14.28, an angle formed by a horizontal line and the line of sight to an object that is above the horizontal line is called the **angle of elevation.** The angle formed by a horizontal line and the line of sight to an object that is below the horizontal line is called the **angle of depression.** Transits and sextants are instruments used to measure such angles.

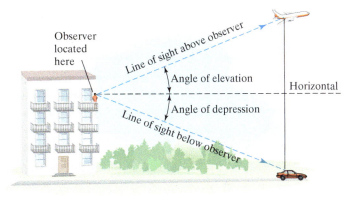

FIGURE 14.28

EXAMPLE 9 Problem Solving Using an Angle of Elevation

Sighting the top of a building, a surveyor measured the angle of elevation to be 22°. The transit is 5 feet above the ground and 300 feet from the building. Find the building's height.

Solution The situation is illustrated in Figure 14.29. Let a be the height of the portion of the building that lies above the transit. The height of the building is the transit's height, 5 feet, plus *a*. Thus, we need to identify a trigonometric function that will make it possible to find *a*. In terms of the 22° angle, we are looking for the side opposite the angle. The transit is 300 feet from the building, so the side adjacent to the 22° angle is 300 feet. Because we have a known angle, an unknown opposite side, and a known adjacent side, we select the tangent function.

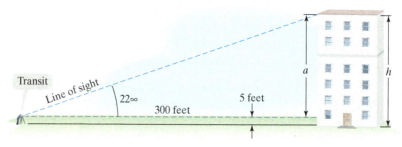

FIGURE 14.29

$$\tan 22° = \frac{a}{300}$$ ⟵ Length of side opposite the 22° angle
⟵ Length of side adjacent to the 22° angle

$a = 300 \tan 22°$ Multiply both sides of the equation by 300.
$a \approx 121$ Use a calculator in the degree mode.

The height of the part of the building above the transit is approximately 121 feet. Thus, the height of the building is determined by adding the transit's height, 5 feet, to 121 feet.

$$h \approx 5 + 121 = 126$$

The building's height is approximately 126 feet.   □

PRACTICE 9 The irregular blue shape in Figure 14.30 represents a lake. The distance across the lake, *a*, is unknown. To find this distance, a surveyor took the measurements shown in the figure. What is the distance across the lake?

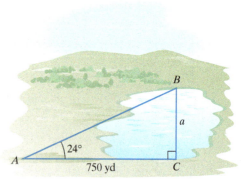

FIGURE 14.30

If two sides of a right triangle are known, an appropriate trigonometric function can be used to find an acute angle θ in the triangle. You will also need to use an inverse trigonometric key on a calculator. These keys use a function value to display the acute angle θ. For example, suppose that $\sin \theta = 0.866$. We can find θ in the degree mode by using the secondary *inverse sine* key, usually labeled $\boxed{\text{SIN}^{-1}}$. The key $\boxed{\text{SIN}^{-1}}$ is not a button you will actually press. It is the secondary function for the button labeled $\boxed{\text{SIN}}$.

Many Scientific Calculators:

.866 [2nd] [SIN]

Pressing [2nd] [SIN] accesses the inverse sine key, [SIN⁻¹].

Many Graphing Calculators:

[2nd] [SIN] .866 [ENTER]

The display should show approximately 59.99, which can be rounded to 60. Thus, if $\sin \theta = 0.866$, then $\theta \approx 60°$.

EXAMPLE 10   Determining the Angle of Elevation

A building that is 21 meters tall casts a shadow 25 meters long. Find the angle of elevation of the sun to the nearest degree.

Solution   The situation is illustrated in Figure 14.31. We are asked to find θ.

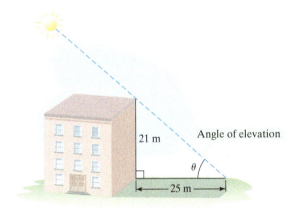

FIGURE 14.31

We begin with the tangent function.

$$\tan \theta = \frac{\text{side opposite } \theta}{\text{side adjacent to } \theta} = \frac{21}{25}$$

We use a calculator in the degree mode to find θ.

Many Scientific Calculators:

[(] 21 [÷] 25 [)] [2nd] [TAN]

Pressing [2nd] [TAN] accesses the inverse sine key, [TAN⁻¹].

Many Graphing Calculators:

[2nd] [TAN] [(] 21 [÷] 25 [)] [ENTER]

The display should show approximately 40. Thus, the angle of elevation of the sun is approximately 40°.   □

PRACTICE 10   A flagpole that is 14 meters tall casts a shadow 10 meters long. Find the angle of elevation of the sun to the nearest degree.

14.2 EXERCISE SET

PRACTICE EXERCISES

In Exercises 1–8, use the Pythagorean Theorem to find the length of the missing side of each right triangle. Then find the value of each of the six trigonometric functions of θ.

1.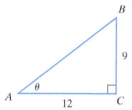

2.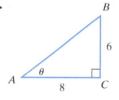

3.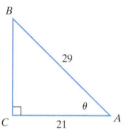

4.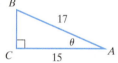

5.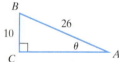

6.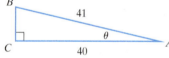

7.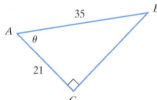

8.

In Exercises 9–16, use the given triangles to evaluate each expression. If necessary, express the value without a square root in the denominator by rationalizing the denominator.

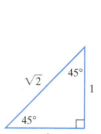 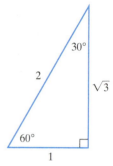

9. $\cos 30°$
10. $\tan 30°$
11. $\sec 45°$
12. $\csc 45°$
13. $\tan \dfrac{\pi}{3}$
14. $\cot \dfrac{\pi}{3}$
15. $\sin \dfrac{\pi}{4} - \cos \dfrac{\pi}{4}$
16. $\tan \dfrac{\pi}{4} + \csc \dfrac{\pi}{6}$

In Exercises 17–20, θ is an acute angle and sin θ and cos θ are given. Use identities to find tan θ, csc θ, sec θ, and cot θ. Where necessary, rationalize denominators.

17. $\sin \theta = \dfrac{8}{17}, \quad \cos \theta = \dfrac{15}{17}$
18. $\sin \theta = \dfrac{3}{5}, \quad \cos \theta = \dfrac{4}{5}$
19. $\sin \theta = \dfrac{1}{3}, \quad \cos \theta = \dfrac{2\sqrt{2}}{3}$
20. $\sin \theta = \dfrac{6}{7}, \quad \cos \theta = \dfrac{\sqrt{13}}{7}$

In Exercises 21–24, θ is an acute angle and sin θ is given. Use the Pythagorean identity $\sin^2 \theta + \cos^2 \theta = 1$ to find cos θ.

21. $\sin \theta = \dfrac{6}{7}$
22. $\sin \theta = \dfrac{7}{8}$
23. $\sin \theta = \dfrac{\sqrt{39}}{8}$
24. $\sin \theta = \dfrac{\sqrt{21}}{5}$

In Exercises 25–30, use an identity to find the value of each expression. Do not use a calculator.

25. $\sin 37° \csc 37°$
26. $\cos 53° \sec 53°$
27. $\sin^2 \dfrac{\pi}{9} + \cos^2 \dfrac{\pi}{9}$
28. $\sin^2 \dfrac{\pi}{10} + \cos^2 \dfrac{\pi}{10}$
29. $\sec^2 23° - \tan^2 23°$
30. $\csc^2 63° - \cot^2 63°$

In Exercises 31–38, find a cofunction with the same value as the given expression.

31. $\sin 7°$
32. $\sin 19°$
33. $\cos 25°$
34. $\sin 35°$
35. $\tan \dfrac{\pi}{9}$
36. $\tan \dfrac{\pi}{7}$

37. $\cos \dfrac{2\pi}{5}$

38. $\cos \dfrac{3\pi}{8}$

In Exercises 39–48, use a calculator to find the value of the trigonometric function to four decimal places.

39. $\sin 38°$

40. $\cos 21°$

41. $\tan 32.7°$

42. $\tan 52.6°$

43. $\csc 17°$

44. $\sec 55°$

45. $\cos \dfrac{\pi}{10}$

46. $\sin \dfrac{3\pi}{10}$

47. $\cot \dfrac{\pi}{12}$

48. $\cot \dfrac{\pi}{18}$

In Exercises 49–54, find the measure of the side of the right triangle whose length is designated by a lowercase letter. Round answers to the nearest whole number.

49.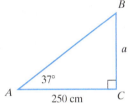

50.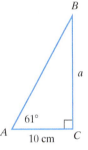

51.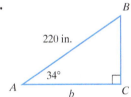

52.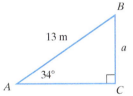

53.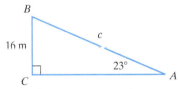

54.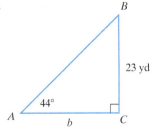

In Exercises 55–58, use a calculator to find the value of the acute angle θ to the nearest degree.

55. $\sin \theta = 0.2974$

56. $\cos \theta = 0.8771$

57. $\tan \theta = 4.6252$

58. $\tan \theta = 26.0307$

In Exercises 59–62, use a calculator to find the value of the acute angle θ in radians, rounded to three decimal places.

59. $\cos \theta = 0.4112$

60. $\sin \theta = 0.9499$

61. $\tan \theta = 0.4169$

62. $\tan \theta = 0.5117$

PRACTICE PLUS

In Exercises 63–68, find the exact value of each expression. Do not use a calculator.

63. $\dfrac{\tan \dfrac{\pi}{3}}{2} - \dfrac{1}{\sec \dfrac{\pi}{6}}$

64. $\dfrac{1}{\cot \dfrac{\pi}{4}} - \dfrac{2}{\csc \dfrac{\pi}{6}}$

65. $1 + \sin^2 40° + \sin^2 50°$

66. $1 - \tan^2 10° + \csc^2 80°$

67. $\csc 37° \sec 53° - \tan 53° \cot 37°$

68. $\cos 12° \sin 78° + \cos 78° \sin 12°$

In Exercises 69–70, express the exact value of each function as a single fraction. Do not use a calculator.

69. If $f(\theta) = 2\cos\theta - \cos 2\theta$, find $f\left(\dfrac{\pi}{6}\right)$.

70. If $f(\theta) = 2\sin\theta - \sin\dfrac{\theta}{2}$, find $f\left(\dfrac{\pi}{3}\right)$.

71. If θ is an acute angle and $\cot\theta = \dfrac{1}{4}$, find $\tan\left(\dfrac{\pi}{2} - \theta\right)$.

72. If θ is an acute angle and $\cos\theta = \dfrac{1}{3}$, find $\csc\left(\dfrac{\pi}{2} - \theta\right)$.

APPLICATION EXERCISES

73. To find the distance across a lake, a surveyor took the measurements shown in the figure. Use these measurements to determine how far it is across the lake. Round to the nearest yard.

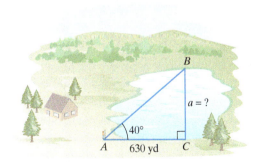

74. At a certain time of day, the angle of elevation of the sun is 40°. To the nearest foot, find the height of a tree whose shadow is 35 feet long.

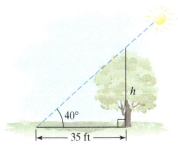

75. A tower that is 125 feet tall casts a shadow 172 feet long. Find the angle of elevation of the sun to the nearest degree.

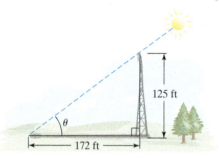

76. The Washington Monument is 555 feet high. If you are standing one quarter of a mile, or 1320 feet, from the base of the monument and looking to the top, find the angle of elevation to the nearest degree.

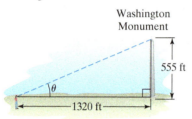

77. A plane rises from take-off and flies at an angle of 10° with the horizontal runway. When it has gained 500 feet, find the distance, to the nearest foot, the plane has flown.

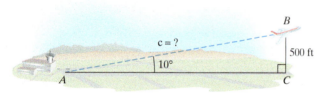

78. A road is inclined at an angle of 5°. After driving 5000 feet along this road, find the driver's increase in altitude. Round to the nearest foot.

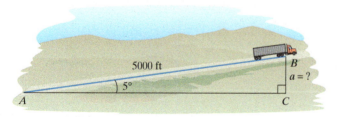

79. A telephone pole is 60 feet tall. A guy wire 75 feet long is attached from the ground to the top of the pole. Find the angle between the wire and the pole to the nearest degree.

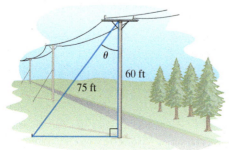

80. A telephone pole is 55 feet tall. A guy wire 80 feet long is attached from the ground to the top of the pole. Find the angle between the wire and the pole to the nearest degree.

WRITING IN MATHEMATICS

81. If you are given the lengths of the sides of a right triangle, describe how to find the sine of either acute angle.

82. Describe one similarity and one difference between the definitions of $\sin \theta$ and $\cos \theta$, where θ is an acute angle of a right triangle.

83. Describe the triangle used to find the trigonometric functions of 45°.

84. Describe the triangle used to find the trigonometric functions of 30° and 60°.

85. What is a trigonometric identity?

86. Use words (not an equation) to describe one of the reciprocal identities.

87. Use words (not an equation) to describe one of the quotient identities.

88. Use words (not an equation) to describe one of the Pythagorean identities.

89. Describe a relationship among trigonometric functions that is based on angles that are complements.

90. Describe what is meant by an angle of elevation and an angle of depression.

91. Stonehenge, the famous "stone circle" in England, was built between 2750 B.C. and 1300 B.C. using solid stone blocks weighing over 99,000 pounds each. It required 550 people to pull a single stone up a ramp inclined at a 9° angle. Describe how right triangle trigonometry can be used to determine the distance the 550 workers had to drag a stone in order to raise it to a height of 30 feet.

TECHNOLOGY EXERCISES

92. **Complete a Table.** Use a calculator in the radian mode to fill in the values in the following table. Then draw a conclusion about $\dfrac{\sin \theta}{\theta}$ as θ approaches 0.

θ	0.4	0.3	0.2	0.1	0.01	0.001	0.0001	0.00001
$\sin \theta$								
$\dfrac{\sin \theta}{\theta}$								

93. Use a calculator in the radian mode to fill in the values in the following table. Then draw a conclusion about $\dfrac{\cos \theta - 1}{\theta}$ as θ approaches 0.

θ	0.4	0.3	0.2	0.1	0.01	0.001	0.0001	0.00001
$\cos \theta$								
$\dfrac{\cos \theta - 1}{\theta}$								

CRITICAL THINKING EXERCISES

Make Sense? *In Exercises 94–97, determine whether each statement makes sense or does not make sense, and explain your reasoning.*

94. For a given angle θ, I found a slight increase in $\sin \theta$ as the size of the triangle increased.

95. Although I can use an isosceles right triangle to determine the exact value of $\sin \frac{\pi}{4}$, I can also use my calculator to obtain this value.

96. I can rewrite $\tan \theta$ as $\frac{1}{\cot \theta}$, as well as $\frac{\sin \theta}{\cos \theta}$.

97. Standing under this arch, I can determine its height by measuring the angle of elevation to the top of the arch and my distance to a point directly under the arch.

Delicate Arch in Arches National Park, Utah

In Exercises 98–101, determine whether each statement is true or false. If the statement is false, make the necessary change(s) to produce a true statement.

98. $\dfrac{\tan 45°}{\tan 15°} = \tan 3°$

99. $\tan^2 15° - \sec^2 15° = -1$

100. $\sin 45° + \cos 45° = 1$

101. $\tan^2 5° = \tan 25°$

102. Explain why the sine or cosine of an acute angle cannot be greater than or equal to 1.

103. Describe what happens to the tangent of an acute angle as the angle gets close to 90°. What happens at 90°?

104. From the top of a 250-foot lighthouse, a plane is sighted overhead and a ship is observed directly below the plane. The angle of elevation of the plane is 22° and the angle of depression of the ship is 35°. Find **a.** the distance of the ship from the lighthouse; **b.** the plane's height above the water. Round to the nearest foot.

PREVIEW EXERCISES

Exercises 105–107 will help you prepare for the material covered in the next section. Use these figures to solve Exercises 105–106.

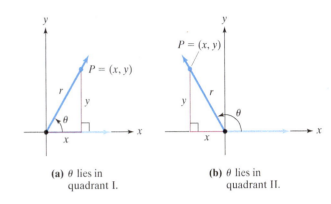

(a) θ lies in quadrant I.

(b) θ lies in quadrant II.

105. **Multiple Steps. a.** Write a ratio that expresses $\sin \theta$ for the right triangle in Figure (a).

  b. Determine the ratio that you wrote in part (a) for Figure (b) with $x = -3$ and $y = 4$. Is this ratio positive or negative?

106. **Multiple Steps. a.** Write a ratio that expresses $\cos \theta$ for the right triangle in Figure (a).

  b. Determine the ratio that you wrote in part (a) for Figure (b) with $x = -3$ and $y = 5$. Is this ratio positive or negative?

107. Find the positive angle θ' formed by the terminal side of θ and the x-axis.

  a.

  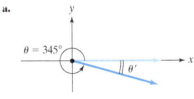

  b.

  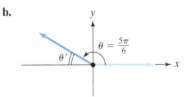

14.3 TRIGONOMETRIC FUNCTIONS OF ANY ANGLE

OBJECTIVES

1. Use the definitions of trigonometric functions of any angle.
2. Use the signs of the trigonometric functions.
3. Find reference angles.
4. Use reference angles to evaluate trigonometric functions.

OBJECTIVE 1 ▶ **Use the definitions of trigonometric functions of any angle.** In the last section, we evaluated trigonometric functions of acute angles, such as that shown in Figure 14.32(a). Note that this angle is in standard position. The point $P = (x, y)$ is a point r units from the origin on the terminal side of θ. A right triangle is formed by drawing a line segment from $P = (x, y)$ perpendicular to the x-axis. Note that y is the length of the side opposite θ and x is the length of the side adjacent to θ.

Figures 14.32(b), (c), and (d) show angles in standard position, but they are not acute. We can extend our definitions of the six trigonometric functions to include such angles, as well as quadrantal angles. (Recall that a quadrantal angle has its terminal side on the x-axis or y-axis; such angles are *not* shown in Figure 14.32.) The point $P = (x, y)$ may be any point on the terminal side of the angle θ other than the origin, $(0, 0)$.

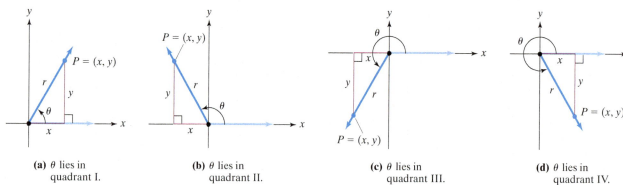

(a) θ lies in quadrant I.   (b) θ lies in quadrant II.   (c) θ lies in quadrant III.   (d) θ lies in quadrant IV.

FIGURE 14.32

▶ **Helpful Hint**

If θ is acute, we have the right triangle shown in Figure 14.32(a). In this situation, the definitions in the box are the right triangle definitions of the trigonometric functions. This should make it easier for you to remember the six definitions.

Definitions of Trigonometric Functions of Any Angle

Let θ be any angle in standard position and let $P = (x, y)$ be a point on the terminal side of θ. If $r = \sqrt{x^2 + y^2}$ is the distance from $(0, 0)$ to (x, y), as shown in Figure 14.32, the **six trigonometric functions of θ** are defined by the following ratios:

$$\sin \theta = \frac{y}{r} \qquad \csc \theta = \frac{r}{y}, y \neq 0$$

$$\cos \theta = \frac{x}{r} \qquad \sec \theta = \frac{r}{x}, x \neq 0$$

$$\tan \theta = \frac{y}{x}, x \neq 0 \qquad \cot \theta = \frac{x}{y}, y \neq 0.$$

The ratios in the second column are the reciprocals of the corresponding ratios in the first column.

Because the point $P = (x, y)$ is any point on the terminal side of θ other than the origin, $(0, 0)$, $r = \sqrt{x^2 + y^2}$ cannot be zero. Examine the six trigonometric functions defined above. Note that the denominator of the sine and cosine functions is r. Because $r \neq 0$, the sine and cosine functions are defined for any angle θ. This is not true for the other four trigonometric functions. Note that the denominator of the tangent and secant functions is x: $\tan \theta = \frac{y}{x}$ and $\sec \theta = \frac{r}{x}$. These functions are not defined if $x = 0$. If the point $P = (x, y)$ is on the y-axis, then $x = 0$. Thus, the tangent and secant functions are undefined for all quadrantal angles with terminal sides on the positive or negative y-axis. Likewise, if $P = (x, y)$ is on the x-axis, then $y = 0$, and the cotangent and cosecant functions are undefined: $\cot\theta = \dfrac{x}{y}$ and $\csc\theta = \dfrac{r}{y}$. The cotangent and cosecant functions are undefined for all quadrantal angles with terminal sides on the positive or negative x-axis.

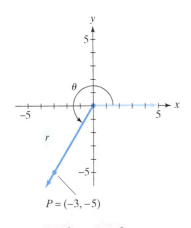

FIGURE 14.33

EXAMPLE 1 Evaluating Trigonometric Functions

Let $P = (-3, -5)$ be a point on the terminal side of θ. Find each of the six trigonometric functions of θ.

Solution The situation is shown in Figure 14.33. We need values for x, y, and r to evaluate all six trigonometric functions. We are given the values of x and y. Because $P = (-3, -5)$ is a point on the terminal side of θ, $x = -3$ and $y = -5$. Furthermore,

$$r = \sqrt{x^2 + y^2} = \sqrt{(-3)^2 + (-5)^2} = \sqrt{9 + 25} = \sqrt{34}.$$

Now that we know x, y, and r, we can find the six trigonometric functions of θ. Where appropriate, we will rationalize denominators.

$$\sin\theta = \frac{y}{r} = \frac{-5}{\sqrt{34}} = -\frac{5}{\sqrt{34}} \cdot \frac{\sqrt{34}}{\sqrt{34}} = -\frac{5\sqrt{34}}{34} \qquad \csc\theta = \frac{r}{y} = \frac{\sqrt{34}}{-5} = -\frac{\sqrt{34}}{5}$$

$$\cos\theta = \frac{x}{r} = \frac{-3}{\sqrt{34}} = -\frac{3}{\sqrt{34}} \cdot \frac{\sqrt{34}}{\sqrt{34}} = -\frac{3\sqrt{34}}{34} \qquad \sec\theta = \frac{r}{x} = \frac{\sqrt{34}}{-3} = -\frac{\sqrt{34}}{3}$$

$$\tan\theta = \frac{y}{x} = \frac{-5}{-3} = \frac{5}{3} \qquad\qquad \cot\theta = \frac{x}{y} = \frac{-3}{-5} = \frac{3}{5}$$

PRACTICE 1 Let $P = (1, -3)$ be a point on the terminal side of θ. Find each of the six trigonometric functions of θ.

How do we find the values of the trigonometric functions for a quadrantal angle? First, draw the angle in standard position. Second, choose a point P on the angle's terminal side. The trigonometric function values of θ depend only on the size of θ and not on the distance of point P from the origin. Thus, we will choose a point that is 1 unit from the origin. Finally, apply the definitions of the appropriate trigonometric functions.

EXAMPLE 2 Trigonometric Functions of Quadrantal Angles

Evaluate, if possible, the sine function and the tangent function at the following four quadrantal angles:

a. $\theta = 0° = 0$ **b.** $\theta = 90° = \dfrac{\pi}{2}$ **c.** $\theta = 180° = \pi$ **d.** $\theta = 270° = \dfrac{3\pi}{2}$.

Solution

a. If $\theta = 0° = 0$ radians, then the terminal side of the angle is on the positive x-axis. Let us select the point $P = (1, 0)$ with $x = 1$ and $y = 0$. This point is 1 unit from the origin, so $r = 1$. Figure 14.34 shows values of x, y, and r corresponding to $\theta = 0°$ or 0 radians. Now that we know x, y, and r, we can apply the definitions of the sine and tangent functions.

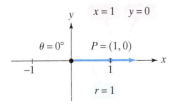

FIGURE 14.34

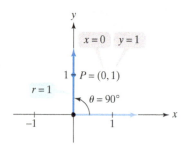

FIGURE 14.35

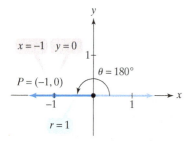

FIGURE 14.36

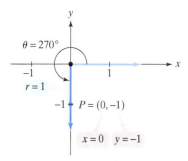

FIGURE 14.37

$$\sin 0° = \sin 0 = \frac{y}{r} = \frac{0}{1} = 0$$

$$\tan 0° = \tan 0 = \frac{y}{x} = \frac{0}{1} = 0$$

b. If $\theta = 90° = \frac{\pi}{2}$ radians, then the terminal side of the angle is on the positive y-axis. Let us select the point $P = (0, 1)$ with $x = 0$ and $y = 1$. This point is 1 unit from the origin, so $r = 1$. Figure 14.35 shows values of x, y, and r corresponding to $\theta = 90°$ or $\frac{\pi}{2}$. Now that we know x, y, and r, we can apply the definitions of the sine and tangent functions.

$$\sin 90° = \sin \frac{\pi}{2} = \frac{y}{r} = \frac{1}{1} = 1$$

$$\tan 90° = \tan \frac{\pi}{2} = \frac{y}{x} = \frac{1}{0}$$

Because division by 0 is undefined, tan 90° is undefined.

c. If $\theta = 180° = \pi$ radians, then the terminal side of the angle is on the negative x-axis. Let us select the point $P = (-1, 0)$ with $x = -1$ and $y = 0$. This point is 1 unit from the origin, so $r = 1$. Figure 14.36 shows values of x, y, and r corresponding to $\theta = 180°$ or π. Now that we know x, y, and r, we can apply the definitions of the sine and tangent functions.

$$\sin 180° = \sin \pi = \frac{y}{r} = \frac{0}{1} = 0$$

$$\tan 180° = \tan \pi = \frac{y}{x} = \frac{0}{-1} = 0$$

d. If $\theta = 270° = \frac{3\pi}{2}$ radians, then the terminal side of the angle is on the negative y-axis. Let us select the point $P = (0, -1)$ with $x = 0$ and $y = -1$. This point is 1 unit from the origin, so $r = 1$. Figure 14.37 shows values of x, y, and r corresponding to $\theta = 270°$ or $\frac{3\pi}{2}$. Now that we know x, y, and r, we can apply the definitions of the sine and tangent functions.

$$\sin 270° = \sin \frac{3\pi}{2} = \frac{y}{r} = \frac{-1}{1} = -1$$

$$\tan 270° = \tan \frac{3\pi}{2} = \frac{y}{x} = \frac{-1}{0}$$

Because division by 0 is undefined, tan 270° is undefined. □

PRACTICE 2 Evaluate, if possible, the cosine function and the cosecant function at the following four quadrantal angles:

a. $\theta = 0° = 0$ **b.** $\theta = 90° = \frac{\pi}{2}$ **c.** $\theta = 180° = \pi$ **d.** $\theta = 270° = \frac{3\pi}{2}$.

OBJECTIVE 2 ▶ The signs of the trigonometric functions. In Example 2, we evaluated trigonometric functions of quadrantal angles. However, we will now return to the trigonometric functions of nonquadrantal angles. **If θ is not a quadrantal angle, the sign of a trigonometric function depends on the quadrant in which θ lies.** In all four quadrants, r is positive. However, x and y can be positive or negative. For example, if θ lies in quadrant II, x is negative and y is positive. Thus, the only positive ratios in this quadrant are $\frac{y}{r}$ and its reciprocal, $\frac{r}{y}$. These ratios are the function values for the sine and cosecant, respectively. In short, if θ lies in quadrant II, $\sin \theta$ and $\csc \theta$ are positive. The other four trigonometric functions are negative.

Figure 14.38 summarizes the signs of the trigonometric functions. If θ lies in quadrant I, all six functions are positive. If θ lies in quadrant II, only $\sin\theta$ and $\csc\theta$ are positive. If θ lies in quadrant III, only $\tan\theta$ and $\cot\theta$ are positive. Finally, if θ lies in quadrant IV, only $\cos\theta$ and $\sec\theta$ are positive. Observe that the positive functions in each quadrant occur in reciprocal pairs.

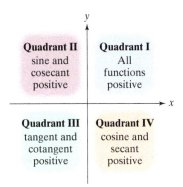

FIGURE 14.38 The signs of the trigonometric functions

> **Helpful Hint**
> Here's a phrase to help you remember the signs of the trig functions:

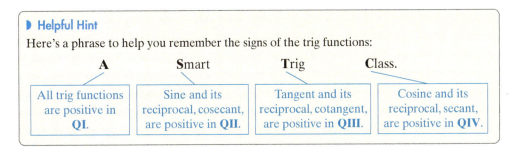

EXAMPLE 3 Finding the Quadrant in Which an Angle Lies

If $\tan\theta < 0$ and $\cos\theta > 0$, name the quadrant in which angle θ lies.

Solution When $\tan\theta < 0$, θ lies in quadrant II or IV. When $\cos\theta > 0$, θ lies in quadrant I or IV. When both conditions are met ($\tan\theta < 0$ and $\cos\theta > 0$), θ must lie in quadrant IV. □

PRACTICE 3 If $\sin\theta < 0$ and $\cos\theta < 0$, name the quadrant in which angle θ lies.

EXAMPLE 4 Evaluating Trigonometric Functions

Given $\tan\theta = -\frac{2}{3}$ and $\cos\theta > 0$, find $\cos\theta$ and $\csc\theta$.

Solution Because the tangent is negative and the cosine is positive, θ lies in quadrant IV. This will help us to determine whether the negative sign in $\tan\theta = -\frac{2}{3}$ should be associated with the numerator or the denominator. Keep in mind that in quadrant IV, x is positive and y is negative. Thus,

$$\tan\theta = -\frac{2}{3} = \frac{y}{x} = \frac{-2}{3}.$$

(In quadrant IV, y is negative.)

(See Figure 14.39.) Thus, $x = 3$ and $y = -2$. Furthermore,

$$r = \sqrt{x^2 + y^2} = \sqrt{3^2 + (-2)^2} = \sqrt{9 + 4} = \sqrt{13}.$$

FIGURE 14.39 $\tan\theta = -\frac{2}{3}$ and $\cos\theta > 0$

Now that we know x, y, and r, we can find $\cos\theta$ and $\csc\theta$.

$$\cos\theta = \frac{x}{r} = \frac{3}{\sqrt{13}} = \frac{3}{\sqrt{13}} \cdot \frac{\sqrt{13}}{\sqrt{13}} = \frac{3\sqrt{13}}{13} \qquad \csc\theta = \frac{r}{y} = \frac{\sqrt{13}}{-2} = -\frac{\sqrt{13}}{2} \quad □$$

PRACTICE 4 Given $\tan\theta = -\frac{1}{3}$ and $\cos\theta < 0$, find $\sin\theta$ and $\sec\theta$.

In Example 4, we used the quadrant in which θ lies to determine whether a negative sign should be associated with the numerator or the denominator. Here's a situation, similar to Example 4, where negative signs should be associated with *both* the numerator and the denominator:

$$\tan\theta = \frac{3}{5} \quad \text{and} \quad \cos\theta < 0.$$

Because the tangent is positive and the cosine is negative, θ lies in quadrant III. In quadrant III, x is negative and y is negative. Thus,

$$\tan \theta = \frac{3}{5} = \frac{y}{x} = \frac{-3}{-5}. \quad \text{We see that } x = -5 \text{ and } y = -3.$$

OBJECTIVE 3 ▶ Reference angles. We will often evaluate trigonometric functions of positive angles greater than 90° and all negative angles by making use of a positive acute angle. This positive acute angle is called a *reference angle*.

> **Definition of a Reference Angle**
> Let θ be a nonacute angle in standard position that lies in a quadrant. Its **reference angle** is the positive acute angle θ' formed by the terminal side of θ and the x-axis.

Figure 14.40 shows the reference angle for θ lying in quadrants II, III, and IV. Notice that the formula used to find θ', the reference angle, varies according to the quadrant in which θ lies. You may find it easier to find the reference angle for a given angle by making a figure that shows the angle in standard position. The acute angle formed by the terminal side of this angle and the x-axis is the reference angle.

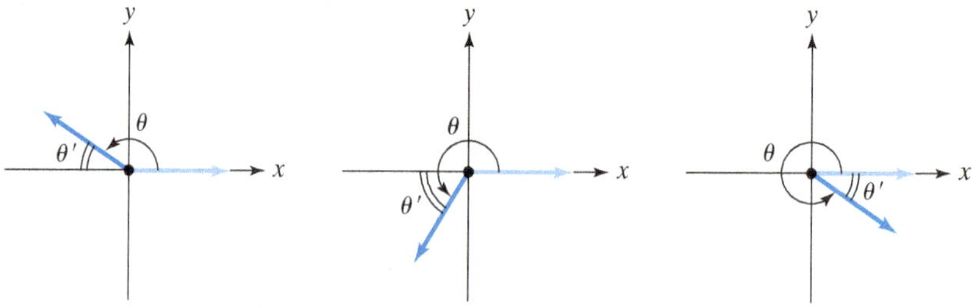

If $90° < \theta < 180°$, then $\theta' = 180° - \theta$.

If $180° < \theta < 270°$, then $\theta' = \theta - 180°$.

If $270° < \theta < 360°$, then $\theta' = 360° - \theta$.

FIGURE 14.40 Reference angles, θ', for positive angles, θ, in quadrants II, III, and IV

EXAMPLE 5 Finding Reference Angles

Find the reference angle, θ', for each of the following angles:

a. $\theta = 345°$ **b.** $\theta = \frac{5\pi}{6}$ **c.** $\theta = -135°$ **d.** $\theta = 2.5$.

Solution

a. A 345° angle in standard position is shown in Figure 14.41. Because 345° lies in quadrant IV, the reference angle is

$$\theta' = 360° - 345° = 15°.$$

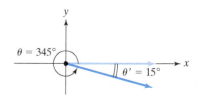

FIGURE 14.41

b. Because $\frac{5\pi}{6}$ lies between $\frac{\pi}{2} = \frac{3\pi}{6}$ and $\pi = \frac{6\pi}{6}, \theta = \frac{5\pi}{6}$ lies in quadrant II. The angle is shown in Figure 5.42. The reference angle is

$$\theta' = \pi - \frac{5\pi}{6} = \frac{6\pi}{6} - \frac{5\pi}{6} = \frac{\pi}{6}.$$

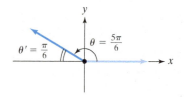

FIGURE 14.42

---**DISCOVERY**---

Solve part (c) by first finding a positive coterminal angle for $-135°$ less than 360°. Use the positive coterminal angle to find the reference angle.

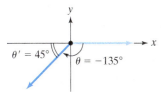

FIGURE 14.43

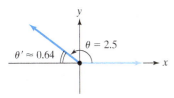

FIGURE 14.44

c. A −135° angle in standard position is shown in Figure 14.43. The figure indicates that the positive acute angle formed by the terminal side of θ and the x-axis is 45°. The reference angle is

$$\theta' = 45°.$$

d. The angle θ = 2.5 lies between $\frac{\pi}{2} \approx 1.57$ and $\pi \approx 3.14$. This means that θ = 2.5 is in quadrant II, shown in Figure 14.44. The reference angle is

$$\theta' = \pi - 2.5 \approx 0.64.$$

PRACTICE 5 Find the reference angle, θ', for each of the following angles:

a. θ = 210°   b. θ = $\frac{7\pi}{4}$ c. θ = −240°   d. θ = 3.6.

Finding reference angles for angles that are greater than 360° (2π) or less than −360° (−2π) involves using coterminal angles. We have seen that coterminal angles have the same initial and terminal sides. Recall that coterminal angles can be obtained by increasing or decreasing an angle's measure by an integer multiple of 360° or 2π.

Finding Reference Angles for Angles Greater Than 360°(2π) or Less Than −360°(−2π)

STEP 1. Find a positive angle α less than 360° or 2π that is coterminal with the given angle.

STEP 2. Draw α in standard position.

STEP 3. Use the drawing to find the reference angle for the given angle. The positive acute angle formed by the terminal side of α and the x-axis is the reference angle.

EXAMPLE 6 Finding Reference Angles

Find the reference angle for each of the following angles:

a. θ = 580°   b. θ = $\frac{8\pi}{3}$ c. θ = $-\frac{13\pi}{6}$.

Solution

a. For a 580° angle, subtract 360° to find a positive coterminal angle less than 360°.

$$580° - 360° = 220°$$

Figure 14.45 shows α = 220° in standard position. Because 220° lies in quadrant III, the reference angle is

$$\alpha' = 220° - 180° = 40°.$$

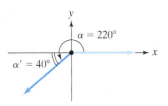

FIGURE 14.45

b. For an $\frac{8\pi}{3}$, or $2\frac{2}{3}\pi$, angle, subtract 2π to find a positive coterminal angle less than 2π.

$$\frac{8\pi}{3} - 2\pi = \frac{8\pi}{3} - \frac{6\pi}{3} = \frac{2\pi}{3}$$

Figure 14.46 shows α = $\frac{2\pi}{3}$ in standard position.

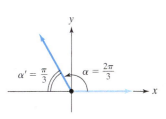

FIGURE 14.46

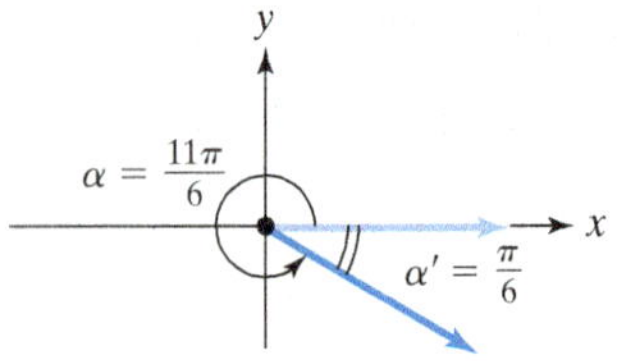

FIGURE 14.47

Because $\dfrac{2\pi}{3}$ lies in quadrant II, the reference angle is

$$\alpha' = \pi - \dfrac{2\pi}{3} = \dfrac{3\pi}{3} - \dfrac{2\pi}{3} = \dfrac{\pi}{3}.$$

c. For a $-\dfrac{13\pi}{6}$, or $-2\dfrac{1}{6}\pi$, angle, add 4π to find a positive coterminal angle less than 2π.

$$-\dfrac{13\pi}{6} + 4\pi = -\dfrac{13\pi}{6} + \dfrac{24\pi}{6} = \dfrac{11\pi}{6}$$

Figure 14.47 shows $\alpha = \dfrac{11\pi}{6}$ in standard position. Because $\dfrac{11\pi}{6}$ lies in quadrant IV, the reference angle is

$$\alpha' = 2\pi - \dfrac{11\pi}{6} = \dfrac{12\pi}{6} - \dfrac{11\pi}{6} = \dfrac{\pi}{6}.$$

PRACTICE 6 Find the reference angle for each of the following angles:

a. $\theta = 665°$ b. $\theta = \dfrac{15\pi}{4}$ c. $\theta = -\dfrac{11\pi}{3}$.

OBJECTIVE 4 ▶ Evaluating trigonometric functions using reference angles. The way that reference angles are defined makes them useful in evaluating trigonometric functions.

> **Using Reference Angles to Evaluate Trigonometric Functions**
> The values of the trigonometric functions of a given angle, θ, are the same as the values of the trigonometric functions of the reference angle, θ', except possibly for the sign. A function value of the acute reference angle, θ', is always positive. However, the same function value for θ may be positive or negative.

For example, we can use a reference angle, θ', to obtain an exact value for $\tan 120°$. The reference angle for $\theta = 120°$ is $\theta' = 180° - 120° = 60°$. We know the exact value of the tangent function of the reference angle: $\tan 60° = \sqrt{3}$. We also know that the value of a trigonometric function of a given angle, θ, is the same as that of its reference angle, θ', except possibly for the sign. Thus, we can conclude that $\tan 120°$ equals $-\sqrt{3}$ or $\sqrt{3}$.

What sign should we attach to $\sqrt{3}$? A $120°$ angle lies in quadrant II, where only the sine and cosecant are positive. Thus, the tangent function is negative for a $120°$ angle. Therefore,

$$\tan 120° = -\tan 60° = -\sqrt{3}.$$

Prefix by a negative sign to show tangent is negative in quadrant II.

The reference angle for $120°$ is $60°$.

In the previous section, we used two right triangles to find exact trigonometric values of $30°$, $45°$, and $60°$. Using a procedure similar to finding $\tan 120°$, we can now find the exact function values of all angles for which $30°$, $45°$, or $60°$ are reference angles.

A Procedure for Using Reference Angles to Evaluate Trigonometric Functions

The value of a trigonometric function of any angle θ is found as follows:

STEP 1. Find the associated reference angle, θ', and the function value for θ'.

STEP 2. Use the quadrant in which θ lies to prefix the appropriate sign to the function value in step 1.

EXAMPLE 7   Using Reference Angles to Evaluate Trigonometric Functions

Use reference angles to find the exact value of each of the following trigonometric functions:

a. $\sin 135°$ **b.** $\cos \dfrac{4\pi}{3}$ **c.** $\cot\left(-\dfrac{\pi}{3}\right)$.

Solution

a. We use our two-step procedure to find $\sin 135°$.

Step 1   **Find the reference angle, θ', and $\sin \theta'$.** Figure 14.48 shows $135°$ lies in quadrant II. The reference angle is

$$\theta' = 180° - 135° = 45°.$$

The function value for the reference angle is $\sin 45° = \dfrac{\sqrt{2}}{2}$.

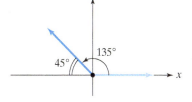

FIGURE 14.48 Reference angle for $135°$

Step 2   **Use the quadrant in which θ lies to prefix the appropriate sign to the function value in step 1.** The angle $\theta = 135°$ lies in quadrant II. Because the sine is positive in quadrant II, we put a $+$ sign before the function value of the reference angle. Thus,

$$\sin 135° = +\sin 45° = \dfrac{\sqrt{2}}{2}.$$

     ↑ The sine is positive in quadrant II.
     ↓ The reference angle for $135°$ is $45°$.

b. We use our two-step procedure to find $\cos \dfrac{4\pi}{3}$.

Step 1   **Find the reference angle, θ', and $\cos \theta'$.** Figure 14.49 shows that $\theta = \dfrac{4\pi}{3}$ lies in quadrant III. The reference angle is

$$\theta' = \dfrac{4\pi}{3} - \pi = \dfrac{4\pi}{3} - \dfrac{3\pi}{3} = \dfrac{\pi}{3}.$$

The function value for the reference angle is

$$\cos \dfrac{\pi}{3} = \dfrac{1}{2}.$$

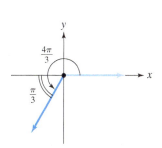

FIGURE 14.49 Reference angle for $\dfrac{4\pi}{3}$

Step 2   **Use the quadrant in which θ lies to prefix the appropriate sign to the function value in step 1.** The angle $\theta = \dfrac{4\pi}{3}$ lies in quadrant III. Because only the tangent and cotangent are positive in quadrant III, the cosine is negative in this quadrant. We put a $-$ sign before the function value of the reference angle. Thus,

The cosine is negative in quadrant III.

$$\cos\frac{4\pi}{3} = -\cos\frac{\pi}{3} = -\frac{1}{2}.$$

The reference angle for $\frac{4\pi}{3}$ is $\frac{\pi}{3}$.

c. We use our two-step procedure to find $\cot\left(-\frac{\pi}{3}\right)$.

Step 1 Find the reference angle, θ', and $\cot\theta'$. Figure 14.50 shows that $\theta = -\frac{\pi}{3}$ lies in quadrant IV. The reference angle is $\theta' = \frac{\pi}{3}$. The function value for the reference angle is $\cot\frac{\pi}{3} = \frac{\sqrt{3}}{3}$.

Step 2 Use the quadrant in which θ lies to prefix the appropriate sign to the function value in step 1. The angle $\theta = -\frac{\pi}{3}$ lies in quadrant IV. Because only the cosine and secant are positive in quadrant IV, the cotangent is negative in this quadrant. We put a $-$ sign before the function value of the reference angle. Thus,

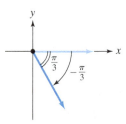

FIGURE 14.50 Reference angle for $-\frac{\pi}{3}$

The cotangent is negative in quadrant IV.

$$\cot\left(-\frac{\pi}{3}\right) = -\cot\frac{\pi}{3} = -\frac{\sqrt{3}}{3}.$$

The reference angle for $-\frac{\pi}{3}$ is $\frac{\pi}{3}$.

PRACTICE 7 Use reference angles to find the exact value of the following trigonometric functions:

a. $\sin 300°$ b. $\tan\frac{5\pi}{4}$ c. $\sec\left(-\frac{\pi}{6}\right)$.

In our final example, we use positive coterminal angles less than 2π to find the reference angles.

EXAMPLE 8 Using Reference Angles to Evaluate Trigonometric Functions

Use reference angles to find the exact value of each of the following trigonometric functions:

a. $\tan\frac{14\pi}{3}$ b. $\sec\left(-\frac{17\pi}{4}\right)$.

Solution

a. We use our two-step procedure to find $\tan\frac{14\pi}{3}$.

Step 1 Find the reference angle, θ', and $\tan\theta'$. Because the given angle, $\frac{14\pi}{3}$ or $4\frac{2}{3}\pi$, exceeds 2π, subtract 4π to find a positive coterminal angle less than 2π.

$$\theta = \frac{14\pi}{3} - 4\pi = \frac{14\pi}{3} - \frac{12\pi}{3} = \frac{2\pi}{3}$$

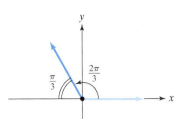

FIGURE 14.51 Reference angle for $\dfrac{2\pi}{3}$

Figure 14.51 shows $\theta = \dfrac{2\pi}{3}$ in standard position. The angle lies in quadrant II. The reference angle is

$$\theta' = \pi - \dfrac{2\pi}{3} = \dfrac{3\pi}{3} - \dfrac{2\pi}{3} = \dfrac{\pi}{3}.$$

The function value for the reference angle is $\tan \dfrac{\pi}{3} = \sqrt{3}$.

Step 2 Use the quadrant in which θ lies to prefix the appropriate sign to the function value in step 1. The coterminal angle $\theta = \dfrac{2\pi}{3}$ lies in quadrant II. Because the tangent is negative in quadrant II, we put a $-$ sign before the function value of the reference angle. Thus,

$$\tan \dfrac{14\pi}{3} = \tan \dfrac{2\pi}{3} = -\tan \dfrac{\pi}{3} = -\sqrt{3}.$$

(The tangent is negative in quadrant II. The reference angle for $\dfrac{2\pi}{3}$ is $\dfrac{\pi}{3}$.)

b. We use our two-step procedure to find $\sec\left(-\dfrac{17\pi}{4}\right)$.

Step 1 Find the reference angle, θ', and $\sec \theta'$. Because the given angle, $-\dfrac{17\pi}{4}$ or $-4\dfrac{1}{4}\pi$, is less than -2π, add 6π (three multiples of 2π) to find a positive coterminal angle less than 2π.

$$\theta = -\dfrac{17\pi}{4} + 6\pi = -\dfrac{17\pi}{4} + \dfrac{24\pi}{4} = \dfrac{7\pi}{4}$$

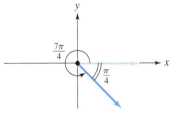

FIGURE 14.52 Reference angle for $\dfrac{7\pi}{4}$

Figure 14.52 shows $\theta = \dfrac{7\pi}{4}$ in standard position. The angle lies in quadrant IV. The reference angle is

$$\theta' = 2\pi - \dfrac{7\pi}{4} = \dfrac{8\pi}{4} - \dfrac{7\pi}{4} = \dfrac{\pi}{4}.$$

The function value for the reference angle is $\sec \dfrac{\pi}{4} = \sqrt{2}$.

Step 2 Use the quadrant in which θ lies to prefix the appropriate sign to the function value in step 1. The coterminal angle $\theta = \dfrac{7\pi}{4}$ lies in quadrant IV. Because the secant is positive in quadrant IV, we put a $+$ sign before the function value of the reference angle. Thus,

$$\sec\left(-\dfrac{17\pi}{4}\right) = \sec \dfrac{7\pi}{4} = +\sec \dfrac{\pi}{4} = \sqrt{2}.$$

(The secant is positive in quadrant IV. The reference angle for $\dfrac{7\pi}{4}$ is $\dfrac{\pi}{4}$.)

PRACTICE

8 Use reference angles to find the exact value of each of the following trigonometric functions:

a. $\cos \dfrac{17\pi}{6}$ b. $\sin\left(-\dfrac{22\pi}{3}\right)$.

> **Helpful Hint**
> Evaluating trigonometric functions like those in Example 8 and Practice 8 involves using a number of concepts, including finding coterminal angles and reference angles, locating special angles, determining the signs of trigonometric functions in specific quadrants, and finding the trigonometric functions of special angles $\left(30° = \dfrac{\pi}{6}, 45° = \dfrac{\pi}{4}, \text{ and } 60° = \dfrac{\pi}{3}\right)$. To be successful in trigonometry, it is often necessary to connect concepts. Here's an early reference sheet showing some of the concepts you should have at your fingertips (or memorized).

Degree and Radian Measures of Special and Quadrantal Angles

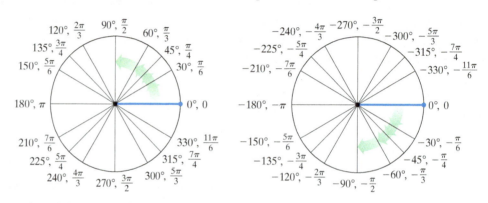

Signs of the Trigonometric Functions

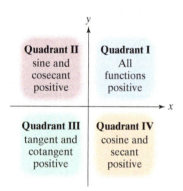

Using Reference Angles to Evaluate Trigonometric Functions

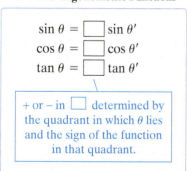

Special Right Triangles and Trigonometric Functions of Special Angles

θ	$30° = \dfrac{\pi}{6}$	$45° = \dfrac{\pi}{4}$	$60° = \dfrac{\pi}{3}$
$\sin\theta$	$\dfrac{1}{2}$	$\dfrac{\sqrt{2}}{2}$	$\dfrac{\sqrt{3}}{2}$
$\cos\theta$	$\dfrac{\sqrt{3}}{2}$	$\dfrac{\sqrt{2}}{2}$	$\dfrac{1}{2}$
$\tan\theta$	$\dfrac{\sqrt{3}}{3}$	1	$\sqrt{3}$

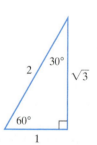

Trigonometric Functions of Quadrantal Angles

θ	$0° = 0$	$90° = \dfrac{\pi}{2}$	$180° = \pi$	$270° = \dfrac{3\pi}{2}$
$\sin\theta$	0	1	0	-1
$\cos\theta$	1	0	-1	0
$\tan\theta$	0	undefined	0	undefined

14.3 EXERCISE SET

PRACTICE EXERCISES

In Exercises 1–8, a point on the terminal side of angle θ is given. Find the exact value of each of the six trigonometric functions of θ.

1. $(-4, 3)$
2. $(-12, 5)$
3. $(2, 3)$
4. $(3, 7)$
5. $(3, -3)$
6. $(5, -5)$
7. $(-2, -5)$
8. $(-1, -3)$

In Exercises 9–16, evaluate the trigonometric function at the quadrantal angle, or state that the expression is undefined.

9. $\cos \pi$
10. $\tan \pi$
11. $\sec \pi$
12. $\csc \pi$
13. $\tan \dfrac{3\pi}{2}$
14. $\cos \dfrac{3\pi}{2}$
15. $\cot \dfrac{\pi}{2}$
16. $\tan \dfrac{\pi}{2}$

In Exercises 17–22, let θ be an angle in standard position. Name the quadrant in which θ lies.

17. $\sin \theta > 0$, $\cos \theta > 0$
18. $\sin \theta < 0$, $\cos \theta > 0$
19. $\sin \theta < 0$, $\cos \theta < 0$
20. $\tan \theta < 0$, $\sin \theta < 0$
21. $\tan \theta < 0$, $\cos \theta < 0$
22. $\cot \theta > 0$, $\sec \theta < 0$

In Exercises 23–34, find the exact value of each of the remaining trigonometric functions of θ.

23. $\cos \theta = -\tfrac{3}{5}$, θ in quadrant III
24. $\sin \theta = -\tfrac{12}{13}$, θ in quadrant III
25. $\sin \theta = \tfrac{5}{13}$, θ in quadrant II
26. $\cos \theta = \tfrac{4}{5}$, θ in quadrant IV
27. $\cos \theta = \tfrac{8}{17}$, $270° < \theta < 360°$
28. $\cos \theta = \tfrac{1}{3}$, $270° < \theta < 360°$
29. $\tan \theta = -\tfrac{2}{3}$, $\sin \theta > 0$
30. $\tan \theta = -\tfrac{1}{3}$, $\sin \theta > 0$
31. $\tan \theta = \tfrac{4}{3}$, $\cos \theta < 0$
32. $\tan \theta = \tfrac{5}{12}$, $\cos \theta < 0$
33. $\sec \theta = -3$, $\tan \theta > 0$
34. $\csc \theta = -4$, $\tan \theta > 0$

In Exercises 35–60, find the reference angle for each angle.

35. $160°$
36. $170°$
37. $205°$
38. $210°$
39. $355°$
40. $351°$
41. $\dfrac{7\pi}{4}$
42. $\dfrac{5\pi}{4}$
43. $\dfrac{5\pi}{6}$
44. $\dfrac{5\pi}{7}$
45. $-150°$
46. $-250°$
47. $-335°$
48. $-359°$
49. 4.7
50. 5.5
51. $565°$
52. $553°$
53. $\dfrac{17\pi}{6}$
54. $\dfrac{11\pi}{4}$
55. $\dfrac{23\pi}{4}$
56. $\dfrac{17\pi}{3}$
57. $-\dfrac{11\pi}{4}$
58. $-\dfrac{17\pi}{6}$
59. $-\dfrac{25\pi}{6}$
60. $-\dfrac{13\pi}{3}$

In Exercises 61–86, use reference angles to find the exact value of each expression. Do not use a calculator.

61. $\cos 225°$
62. $\sin 300°$
63. $\tan 210°$
64. $\sec 240°$
65. $\tan 420°$
66. $\tan 405°$
67. $\sin \dfrac{2\pi}{3}$
68. $\cos \dfrac{3\pi}{4}$
69. $\csc \dfrac{7\pi}{6}$
70. $\cot \dfrac{7\pi}{4}$
71. $\tan \dfrac{9\pi}{4}$
72. $\tan \dfrac{9\pi}{2}$
73. $\sin(-240°)$
74. $\sin(-225°)$
75. $\tan\left(-\dfrac{\pi}{4}\right)$
76. $\tan\left(-\dfrac{\pi}{6}\right)$
77. $\sec 495°$
78. $\sec 510°$
79. $\cot \dfrac{19\pi}{6}$
80. $\cot \dfrac{13\pi}{3}$
81. $\cos \dfrac{23\pi}{4}$
82. $\cos \dfrac{35\pi}{6}$
83. $\tan\left(-\dfrac{17\pi}{6}\right)$
84. $\tan\left(-\dfrac{11\pi}{4}\right)$
85. $\sin\left(-\dfrac{17\pi}{3}\right)$
86. $\sin\left(-\dfrac{35\pi}{6}\right)$

PRACTICE PLUS

In Exercises 87–92, find the exact value of each expression. Write the answer as a single fraction. Do not use a calculator.

87. $\sin \dfrac{\pi}{3} \cos \pi - \cos \dfrac{\pi}{3} \sin \dfrac{3\pi}{2}$
88. $\sin \dfrac{\pi}{4} \cos 0 - \sin \dfrac{\pi}{6} \cos \pi$
89. $\sin \dfrac{11\pi}{4} \cos \dfrac{5\pi}{6} + \cos \dfrac{11\pi}{4} \sin \dfrac{5\pi}{6}$
90. $\sin \dfrac{17\pi}{3} \cos \dfrac{5\pi}{4} + \cos \dfrac{17\pi}{3} \sin \dfrac{5\pi}{4}$
91. $\sin \dfrac{3\pi}{2} \tan\left(-\dfrac{15\pi}{4}\right) - \cos\left(-\dfrac{5\pi}{3}\right)$
92. $\sin \dfrac{3\pi}{2} \tan\left(-\dfrac{8\pi}{3}\right) + \cos\left(-\dfrac{5\pi}{6}\right)$

In Exercises 93–98, let
$$f(x) = \sin x, \; g(x) = \cos x, \text{ and } h(x) = 2x.$$
Find the exact value of each expression. Do not use a calculator.

93. $f\left(\dfrac{4\pi}{3} + \dfrac{\pi}{6}\right) + f\left(\dfrac{4\pi}{3}\right) + f\left(\dfrac{\pi}{6}\right)$
94. $g\left(\dfrac{5\pi}{6} + \dfrac{\pi}{6}\right) + g\left(\dfrac{5\pi}{6}\right) + g\left(\dfrac{\pi}{6}\right)$
95. $(h \circ g)\left(\dfrac{17\pi}{3}\right)$
96. $(h \circ f)\left(\dfrac{11\pi}{4}\right)$
97. the average rate of change of f from $x_1 = \dfrac{5\pi}{4}$ to $x_2 = \dfrac{3\pi}{2}$
98. the average rate of change of g from $x_1 = \dfrac{3\pi}{4}$ to $x_2 = \pi$

In Exercises 99–104, find two values of θ, $0 \le \theta < 2\pi$, that satisfy each equation.

99. $\sin \theta = \dfrac{\sqrt{2}}{2}$
100. $\cos \theta = \dfrac{1}{2}$
101. $\sin \theta = -\dfrac{\sqrt{2}}{2}$
102. $\cos \theta = -\dfrac{1}{2}$
103. $\tan \theta = -\sqrt{3}$
104. $\tan \theta = -\dfrac{\sqrt{3}}{3}$

WRITING IN MATHEMATICS

105. If you are given a point on the terminal side of angle θ, explain how to find $\sin \theta$.
106. Explain why $\tan 90°$ is undefined.
107. If $\cos \theta > 0$ and $\tan \theta < 0$, explain how to find the quadrant in which θ lies.
108. What is a reference angle? Give an example with your description.
109. Explain how reference angles are used to evaluate trigonometric functions. Give an example with your description.

CRITICAL THINKING EXERCISES

Make Sense? *In Exercises 110–113, determine whether each statement makes sense or does not make sense, and explain your reasoning.*

110. I'm working with a quadrantal angle θ for which $\sin \theta$ is undefined.
111. This angle θ is in a quadrant in which $\sin \theta < 0$ and $\csc \theta > 0$.
112. I am given that $\tan \theta = \frac{3}{5}$, so I can conclude that $y = 3$ and $x = 5$.
113. When I found the exact value of $\cos \frac{14\pi}{3}$, I used a number of concepts, including coterminal angles, reference angles, finding the cosine of a special angle, and knowing the cosine's sign in various quadrants.

REVIEW AND PREVIEW

Exercises 114–116 will help you prepare for the material covered in the next section.

114. Graph: $x^2 + y^2 = 1$. Then locate the point $\left(-\frac{1}{2}, \frac{\sqrt{3}}{2}\right)$ on the graph.
115. Use your graph of $x^2 + y^2 = 1$ from Exercise 114 to determine the relation's domain and range.
116. **a.** Find the exact value of $\sin\left(\frac{\pi}{4}\right)$, $\sin\left(-\frac{\pi}{4}\right)$, $\sin\left(\frac{\pi}{3}\right)$, and $\sin\left(-\frac{\pi}{3}\right)$. Based on your results, can the sine function be an even function? Explain your answer.
    b. Find the exact value of $\cos\left(\frac{\pi}{4}\right)$, $\cos\left(-\frac{\pi}{4}\right)$, $\cos\left(\frac{\pi}{3}\right)$, and $\cos\left(-\frac{\pi}{3}\right)$. Based on your results, can the cosine function be an odd function? Explain your answer.

14.4 TRIGONOMETRIC FUNCTIONS OF REAL NUMBERS; PERIODIC FUNCTIONS

OBJECTIVES

1. Use a unit circle to define trigonometric functions of real numbers.
2. Recognize the domain and range of sine and cosine functions.
3. Use even and odd trigonometric functions.
4. Use periodic properties.

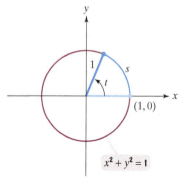

FIGURE 14.53 Unit circle with a central angle measuring t radians

Cycles govern many aspects of life—heartbeats, sleep patterns, seasons, and tides all follow regular, predictable cycles. In this section, we will see why trigonometric functions are used to model phenomena that occur in cycles. To do this, we need to move beyond angles and consider trigonometric functions of real numbers.

OBJECTIVE 1 ▶ **Trigonometric functions of real numbers.** Thus far, we have considered trigonometric functions of angles measured in degrees or radians. To define trigonometric functions of real numbers, rather than angles, we use a unit circle. A **unit circle** is a circle of radius 1, with its center at the origin of a rectangular coordinate system. The equation of this unit circle is $x^2 + y^2 = 1$. Figure 14.53 shows a unit circle in which the central angle measures t radians. We can use the formula for the length of a circular arc, $s = r\theta$, to find the length of the intercepted arc.

$$s = r\theta = 1 \cdot t = t$$

The radius of a unit circle is 1. The radian measure of the central angle is t.

Thus, the length of the intercepted arc is t. This is also the radian measure of the central angle. Thus, **in a unit circle, the radian measure of the central angle is equal to the length of the intercepted arc.** Both are given by the same *real number t*.

In Figure 14.54, the radian measure of the angle and the length of the intercepted arc are both shown by t. Let $P = (x, y)$ denote the point on the unit circle that has arc length t from $(1, 0)$. Figure 14.54(a) shows that if t is positive, point P is reached by moving counterclockwise along the unit circle from $(1, 0)$. Figure 14.54(b) shows that if t is negative, point P is reached by moving clockwise along the unit circle from $(1, 0)$. For each real number t, there corresponds a point $P = (x, y)$ on the unit circle.

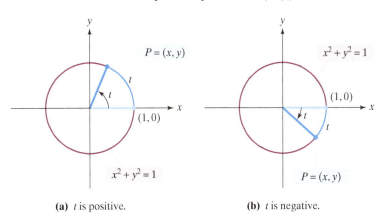

(a) t is positive. **(b)** t is negative.

FIGURE 14.54

Using Figure 14.54, we define the cosine function at t as the x-coordinate of P and the sine function at t as the y-coordinate of P. Thus,

$$x = \cos t \quad \text{and} \quad y = \sin t.$$

For example, a point $P = (x, y)$ on the unit circle corresponding to a real number t is shown in Figure 14.55 for $\pi < t < \dfrac{3\pi}{2}$. We see that the coordinates of $P = (x, y)$ are $x = -\tfrac{3}{5}$ and $y = -\tfrac{4}{5}$. Because the cosine function is the x-coordinate of P and the sine function is the y-coordinate of P, the values of these trigonometric functions at the real number t are

$$\cos t = -\frac{3}{5} \quad \text{and} \quad \sin t = -\frac{4}{5}.$$

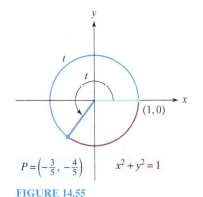

FIGURE 14.55

Definitions of the Trigonometric Functions in Terms of a Unit Circle

If t is a real number and $P = (x, y)$ is a point on the unit circle that corresponds to t, then

$$\sin t = y \qquad \csc t = \frac{1}{y}, \, y \neq 0$$

$$\cos t = x \qquad \sec t = \frac{1}{x}, \, x \neq 0$$

$$\tan t = \frac{y}{x}, \, x \neq 0 \qquad \cot t = \frac{x}{y}, \, y \neq 0.$$

Because this definition expresses function values in terms of coordinates of a point on a unit circle, the trigonometric functions are sometimes called the **circular functions.**

840 CHAPTER 14 Trigonometric Functions

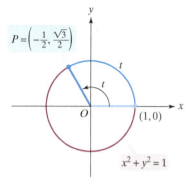

FIGURE 14.56

EXAMPLE 1 Finding Values of the Trigonometric Functions

In Figure 14.56, t is a real number equal to the length of the intercepted arc of an that measures t radians and $P = \left(-\frac{1}{2}, \frac{\sqrt{3}}{2}\right)$ is a point on the unit circle that corresponds to t. Use the figure to find the values of the trigonometric functions at t.

Solution The point P on the unit circle that corresponds to t has coordinates $\left(-\frac{1}{2}, \frac{\sqrt{3}}{2}\right)$. We use $x = -\frac{1}{2}$ and $y = \frac{\sqrt{3}}{2}$ to find the values of the trigonometric functions.

$$\sin t = y = \frac{\sqrt{3}}{2} \qquad \csc t = \frac{1}{y} = \frac{1}{\frac{\sqrt{3}}{2}} = \frac{2}{\sqrt{3}} = \frac{2}{\sqrt{3}} \cdot \frac{\sqrt{3}}{\sqrt{3}} = \frac{2\sqrt{3}}{3}$$

$$\cos t = x = -\frac{1}{2} \qquad \sec t = \frac{1}{x} = \frac{1}{-\frac{1}{2}} = -2$$

$$\tan t = \frac{y}{x} = \frac{\frac{\sqrt{3}}{2}}{-\frac{1}{2}} = -\sqrt{3} \qquad \cot t = \frac{x}{y} = \frac{-\frac{1}{2}}{\frac{\sqrt{3}}{2}} = -\frac{1}{\sqrt{3}} = -\frac{1}{\sqrt{3}} \cdot \frac{\sqrt{3}}{\sqrt{3}} = -\frac{\sqrt{3}}{3} \qquad \square$$

PRACTICE 1 Use the figure on the right to find the values of the trigonometric functions at t.

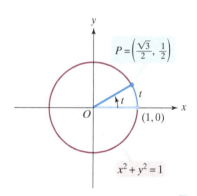

EXAMPLE 2 Finding Values of the Trigonometric Functions

Use Figure 14.57 to find the values of the trigonometric functions at $t = \frac{\pi}{2}$.

Solution The point P on the unit circle that corresponds to $t = \frac{\pi}{2}$ has coordinates $(0, 1)$. We use $x = 0$ and $y = 1$ to find the values of the trigonometric functions at $\frac{\pi}{2}$.

$$\sin \frac{\pi}{2} = y = 1 \qquad \csc \frac{\pi}{2} = \frac{1}{y} = \frac{1}{1} = 1$$

$$\cos \frac{\pi}{2} = x = 0 \qquad \sec \frac{\pi}{2} = \frac{1}{x} = \frac{1}{0}$$

$$\tan \frac{\pi}{2} = \frac{y}{x} = \frac{1}{0} \qquad \cot \frac{\pi}{2} = \frac{x}{y} = \frac{0}{1} = 0 \qquad \square$$

sec $\frac{\pi}{2}$ and tan $\frac{\pi}{2}$ are undefined.

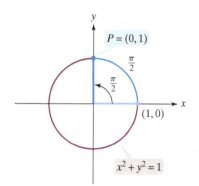

FIGURE 14.57

PRACTICE 2 Use the figure on the right to find the values of the trigonometric functions at $t = \pi$.

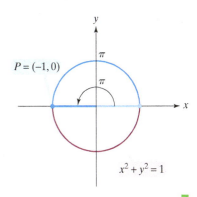

OBJECTIVE 2 ▶ Domain and range of sine and cosine functions. The value of a trigonometric function at the real number t is its value at an angle of t radians. However, using real number domains, we can observe properties of trigonometric functions that are not as apparent using the angle approach. For example, the domain and range of each trigonometric function can be found from the unit circle definition. At this point, let's look only at the sine and cosine functions,

$$\sin t = y \quad \text{and} \quad \cos t = x.$$

Figure 14.58 shows the sine function at t as the y-coordinate of a point along the unit circle:

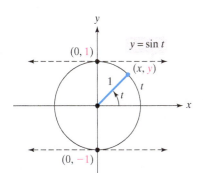

FIGURE 14.58

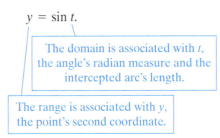

Because t can be any real number, the domain of the sine function is all real numbers. The radius of the unit circle is 1 and the dashed horizontal lines in Figure 14.58 show that y cannot be less than -1 or greater than 1. Thus, the range of the sine function is $-1 \le y \le 1$.

Figure 14.59 shows the cosine function at t as the x-coordinate of a point along the unit circle:

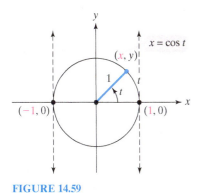

FIGURE 14.59

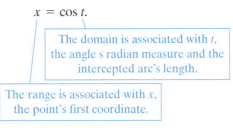

Because t can be any real number, the domain of the cosine function is all real numbers. The radius of the unit circle is 1 and the dashed vertical lines in Figure 14.59 show that x cannot be less than -1 or greater than 1. Thus, the range of the cosine function is $-1 \le y \le 1$.

> **The Domain and Range of the Sine and Cosine Functions**
>
> The domain of the sine function and the cosine function is all real numbers. The range of these functions is $-1 \le y \le 1$.

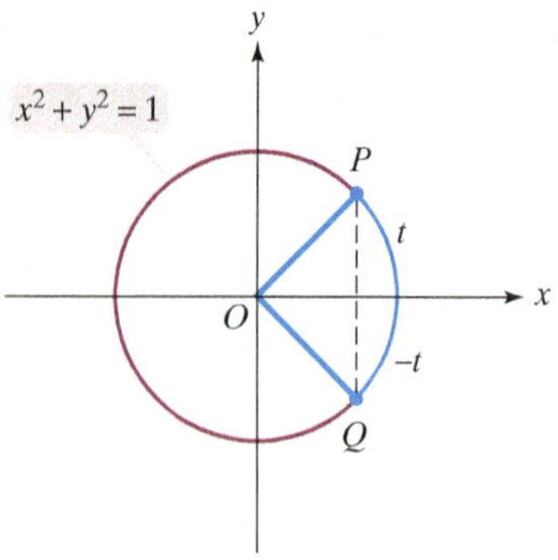

FIGURE 14.60

OBJECTIVE 3 ▶ **Even and odd trigonometric functions.** By definition, the coordinates of the points P and Q in Figure 14.60 are as follows:

$$P: (\cos t, \sin t)$$
$$Q: (\cos(-t), \sin(-t)).$$

In Figure 14.60, the x-coordinates of P and Q are the same. Thus,

$$\cos(-t) = \cos t.$$

By contrast, the y-coordinates of P and Q are negatives of each other. Thus,

$$\sin(-t) = -\sin t.$$

> **Even and Odd Trigonometric Functions**
> $$\cos(-t) = \cos t$$
> $$\sin(-t) = -\sin t$$
> $$\tan(-t) = -\tan t$$

From the above, we know that $y = \cos x$ is an even function. Also, $y = \sin x$ and $y = \tan x$ are odd functions.

EXAMPLE 3 Using Even and Odd Functions to Find Exact Values

Find the exact value of each trigonometric function:

a. $\cos(-45°)$ **b.** $\tan\left(-\dfrac{\pi}{3}\right)$.

Solution

a. $\cos(-45°) = \cos 45° = \dfrac{\sqrt{2}}{2}$

b. $\tan\left(-\dfrac{\pi}{3}\right) = -\tan\dfrac{\pi}{3} = -\sqrt{3}$

PRACTICE 3 Find the exact value of each trigonometric function:

a. $\cos(-60°)$ **b.** $\tan\left(-\dfrac{\pi}{6}\right)$.

OBJECTIVE 4 ▶ **Periodic functions.** If we begin at any point P on the unit circle and travel a distance of 2π units along the perimeter, we will return to the same point P. Because the trigonometric functions are defined in terms of the coordinates of that point P, we obtain the following results:

> **Periodic Properties of the Sine and Cosine Functions**
> $$\sin(t + 2\pi) = \sin t \quad \text{and} \quad \cos(t + 2\pi) = \cos t$$
> The sine and cosine functions are periodic functions and have period 2π.

EXAMPLE 4 Using Periodic Properties to Find Exact Values

Find the exact value of each trigonometric function:

a. $\cos 420°$ **b.** $\sin\dfrac{9\pi}{4}$.

Solution

a. $\cos 420° = \cos(60° + 360°) = \cos 60° = \dfrac{1}{2}$

b. $\sin\dfrac{9\pi}{4} = \sin\left(\dfrac{\pi}{4} + 2\pi\right) = \sin\dfrac{\pi}{4} = \dfrac{\sqrt{2}}{2}$

Section 14.4 Trigonometric Functions of Real Numbers; Periodic Functions 843

PRACTICE 4 Find the exact value of each trigonometric function:

a. $\cos 405°$ b. $\sin \dfrac{7\pi}{3}$.

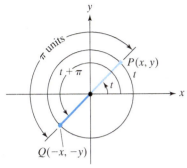

FIGURE 14.61 tangent at P = tangent at Q

The tangent function has a smaller period. Figure 14.61 shows that if we begin at any point $P(x, y)$ on the unit circle and travel a distance of π units along the perimeter, we arrive at the point $Q(-x, -y)$. The tangent function, defined in terms of the coordinates of a point, is the same at (x, y) and $(-x, -y)$.

$$\underset{\text{at }(x,y)}{\text{Tangent function}} \quad \dfrac{y}{x} = \dfrac{-y}{-x} \quad \underset{\pi \text{ radians later}}{\text{Tangent function}}$$

We see that $\tan(t + \pi) = \tan t$.

Periodic Properties of the Tangent Function

$$\tan(t + \pi) = \tan t$$

The tangent function has a period of π.

14.4 EXERCISE SET

PRACTICE EXERCISES

In Exercises 1–4, a point $P(x, y)$ is shown on the unit circle corresponding to a real number t. Find the values of the trigonometric functions at t.

1.

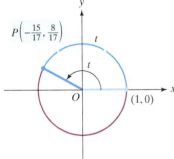

2.

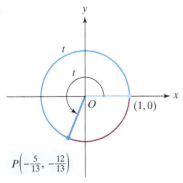

3.

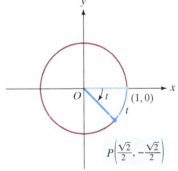

4.

In Exercises 5–18, the unit circle has been divided into twelve equal arcs, corresponding to t-values of

$$0, \dfrac{\pi}{6}, \dfrac{\pi}{3}, \dfrac{\pi}{2}, \dfrac{2\pi}{3}, \dfrac{5\pi}{6}, \pi, \dfrac{7\pi}{6}, \dfrac{4\pi}{3}, \dfrac{3\pi}{2}, \dfrac{5\pi}{3}, \dfrac{11\pi}{6}, \text{ and } 2\pi.$$

Use the (x, y) coordinates in the figure to find the value of each trigonometric function at the indicated real number, t, or state that the expression is undefined.

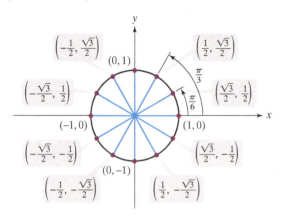

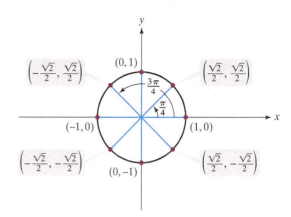

5. $\sin \dfrac{\pi}{6}$ 6. $\sin \dfrac{\pi}{3}$ 7. $\cos \dfrac{5\pi}{6}$

8. $\cos \dfrac{2\pi}{3}$ 9. $\tan \pi$ 10. $\tan 0$

11. $\csc \dfrac{7\pi}{6}$ 12. $\csc \dfrac{4\pi}{3}$ 13. $\sec \dfrac{11\pi}{6}$

14. $\sec \dfrac{5\pi}{3}$ 15. $\sin \dfrac{3\pi}{2}$ 16. $\cos \dfrac{3\pi}{2}$

17. $\sec \dfrac{3\pi}{2}$ 18. $\tan \dfrac{3\pi}{2}$

Multiple Steps. *In Exercises 19–24,*
  a. Use the unit circle shown for Exercises 5–18 to find the value of the trigonometric function.
  b. Use even and odd properties of trigonometric functions and your answer from part (a) to find the value of the same trigonometric function at the indicated real number.

19. a. $\cos \dfrac{\pi}{6}$
    b. $\cos\left(-\dfrac{\pi}{6}\right)$

20. a. $\cos \dfrac{\pi}{3}$
    b. $\cos\left(-\dfrac{\pi}{3}\right)$

21. a. $\sin \dfrac{5\pi}{6}$
    b. $\sin\left(-\dfrac{5\pi}{6}\right)$

22. a. $\sin \dfrac{2\pi}{3}$
    b. $\sin\left(-\dfrac{2\pi}{3}\right)$

23. a. $\tan \dfrac{5\pi}{3}$
    b. $\tan\left(-\dfrac{5\pi}{3}\right)$

24. a. $\tan \dfrac{11\pi}{6}$
    b. $\tan\left(-\dfrac{11\pi}{6}\right)$

Multiple Steps. *In Exercises 25–32, the unit circle has been divided into eight equal arcs, corresponding to t-values of*
$$0, \dfrac{\pi}{4}, \dfrac{\pi}{2}, \dfrac{3\pi}{4}, \pi, \dfrac{5\pi}{4}, \dfrac{3\pi}{2}, \dfrac{7\pi}{4}, \text{ and } 2\pi.$$
  a. Use the (x, y) coordinates in the figure to find the value of the trigonometric function.
  b. Use periodic properties and your answer from part (a) to find the value of the same trigonometric function at the indicated real number.

25. a. $\sin \dfrac{3\pi}{4}$
    b. $\sin \dfrac{11\pi}{4}$

26. a. $\cos \dfrac{3\pi}{4}$
    b. $\cos \dfrac{11\pi}{4}$

27. a. $\cos \dfrac{\pi}{2}$
    b. $\cos \dfrac{9\pi}{2}$

28. a. $\sin \dfrac{\pi}{2}$
    b. $\sin \dfrac{9\pi}{2}$

29. a. $\tan \pi$
    b. $\tan 17\pi$

30. a. $\cot \dfrac{\pi}{2}$
    b. $\cot \dfrac{15\pi}{2}$

31. a. $\sin \dfrac{7\pi}{4}$
    b. $\sin \dfrac{47\pi}{4}$

32. a. $\cos \dfrac{7\pi}{4}$
    b. $\cos \dfrac{47\pi}{4}$

PRACTICE PLUS

In Exercises 33–42, let
$$\sin t = a, \cos t = b, \text{ and } \tan t = c.$$
Write each expression in terms of a, b, and c.

33. $\sin(-t) - \sin t$
34. $\tan(-t) - \tan t$
35. $4\cos(-t) - \cos t$
36. $3\cos(-t) - \cos t$
37. $\sin(t + 2\pi) - \cos(t + 4\pi) + \tan(t + \pi)$
38. $\sin(t + 2\pi) + \cos(t + 4\pi) - \tan(t + \pi)$
39. $\sin(-t - 2\pi) - \cos(-t - 4\pi) - \tan(-t - \pi)$
40. $\sin(-t - 2\pi) + \cos(-t - 4\pi) - \tan(-t - \pi)$
41. $\cos t + \cos(t + 1000\pi) - \tan t - \tan(t + 999\pi) - \sin t + 4\sin(t - 1000\pi)$
42. $-\cos t + 7\cos(t + 1000\pi) + \tan t + \tan(t + 999\pi) + \sin t + \sin(t - 1000\pi)$

APPLICATION EXERCISES

43. The number of hours of daylight, H, on day t of any given year (on January 1, $t = 1$) in Fairbanks, Alaska, can be modeled by the function
$$H(t) = 12 + 8.3 \sin\left[\dfrac{2\pi}{365}(t - 80)\right].$$
  a. March 21, the 80th day of the year, is the spring equinox. Find the number of hours of daylight in Fairbanks on this day.

b. June 21, the 172nd day of the year, is the summer solstice, the day with the maximum number of hours of daylight. To the nearest tenth of an hour, find the number of hours of daylight in Fairbanks on this day.

c. December 21, the 355th day of the year, is the winter solstice, the day with the minimum number of hours of daylight. Find, to the nearest tenth of an hour, the number of hours of daylight in Fairbanks on this day.

44. The number of hours of daylight, H, on day t of any given year (on January 1, $t = 1$) in San Diego, California, can be modeled by the function

$$H(t) = 12 + 2.4 \sin\left[\frac{2\pi}{365}(t - 80)\right].$$

a. March 21, the 80th day of the year, is the spring equinox. Find the number of hours of daylight in San Diego on this day.

b. June 21, the 172nd day of the year, is the summer solstice, the day with the maximum number of hours of daylight. Find, to the nearest tenth of an hour, the number of hours of daylight in San Diego on this day.

c. December 21, the 355th day of the year, is the winter solstice, the day with the minimum number of hours of daylight. To the nearest tenth of an hour, find the number of hours of daylight in San Diego on this day.

45. People who believe in biorhythms claim that there are three cycles that rule our behavior—the physical, emotional, and mental. Each is a sine function of a certain period. The function for our emotional fluctuations is

$$E = \sin\frac{\pi}{14}t,$$

where t is measured in days starting at birth. Emotional fluctuations, E, are measured from -1 to 1, inclusive, with 1 representing peak emotional well-being, -1 representing the low for emotional well-being, and 0 representing feeling neither emotionally high nor low.

a. Find E corresponding to $t = 7, 14, 21, 28$, and 35. Describe what you observe.

b. What is the period of the emotional cycle?

46. The height of the water, H, in feet, at a boat dock t hours after 6 A.M. is given by

$$H = 10 + 4\sin\frac{\pi}{6}t.$$

a. Find the height of the water at the dock at 6 A.M., 9 A.M., noon, 6 P.M., midnight, and 3 A.M.

b. When is low tide and when is high tide?

c. What is the period of this function and what does this mean about the tides?

WRITING IN MATHEMATICS

47. Why are the trigonometric functions sometimes called circular functions?

48. What is the range of the sine function? Use the unit circle to explain where this range comes from.

49. What do we mean by even trigonometric functions? Which of the six functions fall into this category?

50. What is a periodic function? Why are the sine and cosine functions periodic?

51. Explain how you can use the function for emotional fluctuations in Exercise 45 to determine good days for having dinner with your boss.

52. Describe a phenomenon that repeats infinitely. What is its period?

CRITICAL THINKING EXERCISES

Make Sense? *In Exercises 53–56, determine whether each statement makes sense or does not make sense, and explain your reasoning.*

53. Assuming that the innermost circle on this Navajo sand painting is a unit circle, as A moves around the circle, its coordinates define the cosine and sine functions, respectively.

54. I'm using a value for t and a point on the unit circle corresponding to t for which $\sin t = -\frac{\sqrt{10}}{2}$.

55. Because $\cos\frac{\pi}{6} = \frac{\sqrt{3}}{2}$, I can conclude that $\cos\left(-\frac{\pi}{6}\right) = -\frac{\sqrt{3}}{2}$.

56. I can find the exact value of $\sin\frac{7\pi}{3}$ using periodic properties of the sine function, or using a coterminal angle and a reference angle.

57. Find the exact value of
$$\cos 0° + \cos 1° + \cos 2° + \cos 3° + \cdots + \cos 179° + \cos 180°.$$

58. If $f(x) = \sin x$ and $f(a) = \frac{1}{4}$, find the value of
$$f(a) + f(a + 2\pi) + f(a + 4\pi) + f(a + 6\pi).$$

59. If $f(x) = \sin x$ and $f(a) = \frac{1}{4}$, find the value of $f(a) + 2f(-a)$.

60. The seats of a Ferris wheel are 40 feet from the wheel's center. When you get on the ride, your seat is 5 feet above the ground. How far above the ground are you after rotating through an angle of 765°? Round to the nearest foot.

REVIEW AND PREVIEW

Exercises 61–63 will help you prepare for the material covered in the next section. In each exercise, complete the table of coordinates. Do not use a calculator.

61. $y = \frac{1}{2}\cos(4x + \pi)$

x	$-\frac{\pi}{4}$	$-\frac{\pi}{8}$	0	$\frac{\pi}{8}$	$\frac{\pi}{4}$
y					

62. $y = 4 \sin\left(2x - \frac{2\pi}{3}\right)$

x	$\frac{\pi}{3}$	$\frac{7\pi}{12}$	$\frac{5\pi}{6}$	$\frac{13\pi}{12}$	$\frac{4\pi}{3}$
y					

x	0	$\frac{1}{3}$	1	$\frac{5}{3}$	2	$\frac{7}{3}$	3	$\frac{11}{3}$	4
y									

After completing this table of coordinates, plot the nine ordered pairs as points in a rectangular coordinate system. Then connect the points with a smooth curve.

63. $y = 3 \sin \frac{\pi}{2} x$

INTEGRATED REVIEW ANGLES AND RIGHT TRIANGLES

Sections 14.1–14.4

In Exercises 1–2, convert each angle in degrees to radians. Express your answer as a multiple of π.

1. 10° **2.** −105°

In Exercises 3–4, convert each angle in radians to degrees.

3. $\frac{5\pi}{12}$ **4.** $-\frac{13\pi}{20}$

In Exercises 5–7,
  a. *Find a positive angle less than 360° or 2π that is coterminal with the given angle.*
  b. *Draw the given angle in standard position.*
  c. *Find the reference angle for the given angle.*

5. $\frac{11\pi}{3}$ **6.** $-\frac{19\pi}{4}$ **7.** 510°

8. Use the triangle to find each of the six trigonometric functions of θ.

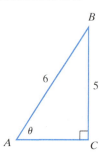

9. Use the point on the terminal side of θ to find each of the six trigonometric functions of θ.

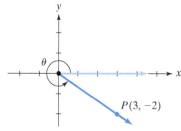

10. Use the point shown on the unit circle to find each of the six trigonometric functions at t.

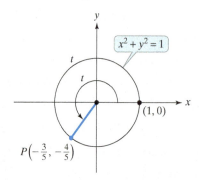

In Exercises 11–12, find the exact value of the remaining trigonometric functions of θ.

11. $\tan \theta = -\dfrac{3}{4}, \cos \theta < 0$ **12.** $\cos \theta = \dfrac{3}{7}, \sin \theta < 0$

In Exercises 13–14, find the measure of the side of the right triangle whose length is designated by a lowercase letter. Round the answer to the nearest whole number.

13. 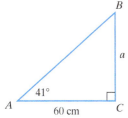   **14.**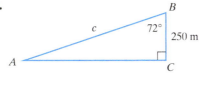

15. If $\cos \theta = \dfrac{1}{6}$ and θ is acute, find $\cot\left(\dfrac{\pi}{2} - \theta\right)$.

In Exercises 16–26, find the exact value of each expression. Do not use a calculator.

16. $\tan 30°$ **17.** $\cot 120°$ **18.** $\cos 240°$ **19.** $\sec \dfrac{11\pi}{6}$ **20.** $\sin^2 \dfrac{\pi}{7} + \cos^2 \dfrac{\pi}{7}$

21. $\sin\left(-\dfrac{2\pi}{3}\right)$ **22.** $\csc\left(\dfrac{22\pi}{3}\right)$ **23.** $\cos 495°$ **24.** $\tan\left(-\dfrac{17\pi}{6}\right)$

25. $\sin^2 \dfrac{\pi}{2} - \cos \pi$ **26.** $\cos\left(\dfrac{5\pi}{6} + 2\pi n\right) + \tan\left(\dfrac{5\pi}{6} + n\pi\right)$, n is an integer.

27. A circle has a radius of 40 centimeters. Find the length of the arc intercepted by a central angle of 36°. Express the answer in terms of π. Then round to two decimal places.

28. A merry-go-round makes 8 revolutions per minute. Find the linear speed, in feet per minute, of a horse 10 feet from the center. Express the answer in terms of π. Then round to one decimal place.

29. A plane takes off at an angle of 6°. After traveling for one mile, or 5280 feet, along this flight path, find the plane's height, to the nearest tenth of a foot, above the ground.

30. A tree that is 50 feet tall casts a shadow that is 60 feet long. Find the angle of elevation, to the nearest degree, of the sun.

14.5 GRAPHS OF SINE AND COSINE FUNCTIONS

OBJECTIVES

1. Understand the graph of $y = \sin x$.
2. Graph variations of $y = \sin x$.
3. Understand the graph of $y = \cos x$.
4. Graph variations of $y = \cos x$.
5. Use vertical shifts of sine and cosine curves.
6. Model periodic behavior.

In this section, we use graphs of sine and cosine functions to visualize their properties. We use the traditional symbol x, rather than θ or t, to represent the independent variable. We use the symbol y for the dependent variable, or the function's value at x. Thus, we will be graphing $y = \sin x$ and $y = \cos x$ in rectangular coordinates. In all graphs of trigonometric functions, x, is measured in radians.

OBJECTIVE 1 ▶ The graph of $y = \sin x$. The trigonometric functions can be graphed in a rectangular coordinate system by plotting points whose coordinates satisfy the function. Thus, we graph $y = \sin x$ by listing some points on the graph. Because the period of the sine function is 2π, we will graph the function on $0 \leq x \leq 2\pi$. The rest of the graph is made up of repetitions of this portion.

Table 14.3 lists some values of (x, y) on the graph of $y = \sin x$, $0 \leq x \leq 2\pi$.

TABLE 14.3 Values of (x, y) on the graph of $y = \sin x$

x	0	$\frac{\pi}{6}$	$\frac{\pi}{3}$	$\frac{\pi}{2}$	$\frac{2\pi}{3}$	$\frac{5\pi}{6}$	π	$\frac{7\pi}{6}$	$\frac{4\pi}{3}$	$\frac{3\pi}{2}$	$\frac{5\pi}{3}$	$\frac{11\pi}{6}$	2π
$y = \sin x$	0	$\frac{1}{2}$	$\frac{\sqrt{3}}{2}$	1	$\frac{\sqrt{3}}{2}$	$\frac{1}{2}$	0	$-\frac{1}{2}$	$-\frac{\sqrt{3}}{2}$	-1	$-\frac{\sqrt{3}}{2}$	$-\frac{1}{2}$	0

As x increases from 0 to $\frac{\pi}{2}$, y increases from 0 to 1.

As x increases from $\frac{\pi}{2}$ to π, y decreases from 1 to 0.

As x increases from π to $\frac{3\pi}{2}$, y decreases from 0 to -1.

As x increases from $\frac{3\pi}{2}$ to 2π, y increases from -1 to 0.

In plotting the points obtained in Table 14.3, we will use the approximation $\frac{\sqrt{3}}{2} \approx 0.87$. If we connect these points with a smooth curve, we obtain the graph of $y = \sin x$.

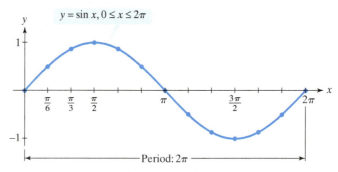

FIGURE 14.62 One period of the graph of $y = \sin x$

We can obtain a more complete graph of $y = \sin x$ by continuing the portion shown in Figure 14.62 to the left and to the right. The graph of the sine function, called a **sine curve,** is shown in Figure 14.63. Any part of the graph that corresponds to one period (2π) is one cycle of the graph of $y = \sin x$.

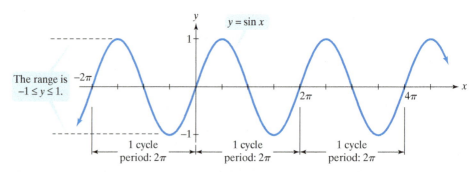

FIGURE 14.63 The graph of $y = \sin x$

The graph of $y = \sin x$ allows us to viualize some of the properties of the sine function.

- The domain is all real numbers.
- The range is $-1 \leq y \leq 1$. The graph never rises above 1 or falls below -1.
- The period is 2π. The graph's pattern repeats in every interval of length 2π.

OBJECTIVE 2 ▶ Graphing variations of $y = \sin x$.

To graph variations of $y = \sin x$ by hand, it is helpful to find x-intercepts, maximum points, and minimum points. One complete cycle of the sine curve includes three x-intercepts, one maximum point, and one minimum point. The graph of $y = \sin x$ has x-intercepts at the beginning, middle, and end of its full period, shown in Figure 14.64. The curve reaches its maximum point $\frac{1}{4}$ of the way through the period. It reaches its minimum point $\frac{3}{4}$ of the way through the period. Thus, key points in graphing sine functions are obtained by dividing the period into four equal parts. The x-coordinates of the five key points are as follows:

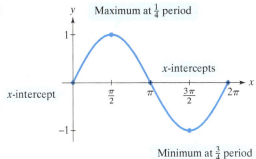

FIGURE 14.64 Key points in graphing the sine function

$$x_1 = \text{value of } x \text{ where the cycle begins}$$

$$x_2 = x_1 + \frac{\text{period}}{4}$$

$$x_3 = x_2 + \frac{\text{period}}{4}$$

$$x_4 = x_3 + \frac{\text{period}}{4}$$

$$x_5 = x_4 + \frac{\text{period}}{4}.$$

Add "quarter-periods" to find successive values of x.

The y-coordinates of the five key points are obtained by evaluating the given function at each of these values of x.

The graph of $y = \sin x$ forms the basis for graphing functions of the form

$$y = A \sin x.$$

For example, consider $y = 2 \sin x$, in which $A = 2$. We can obtain the graph of $y = 2 \sin x$ from that of $y = \sin x$ if we multiply each y-coordinate on the graph of $y = \sin x$ by 2. Figure 14.65 shows the graphs. The basic sine curve is *stretched* and ranges between -2 and 2, rather than between -1 and 1. However, both $y = \sin x$ and $y = 2 \sin x$ have a period of 2π.

In general, the graph of $y = A \sin x$ ranges between $-|A|$ and $|A|$. Thus, the range of the function is $-|A| \leq y \leq |A|$. If $|A| > 1$, the basic sine curve is *stretched*, as in Figure 14.65. If $|A| < 1$, the basic sine curve is *shrunk*. We call $|A|$ the **amplitude** of $y = A \sin x$. The maximum value of y on the graph of $y = A \sin x$ is $|A|$, the amplitude.

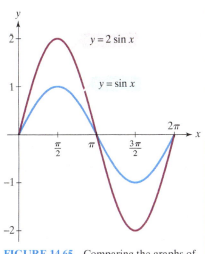

FIGURE 14.65 Comparing the graphs of $y = \sin x$ and $y = 2 \sin x$

Graphing Variations of $y = \sin x$

STEP 1. Identify the amplitude and the period.

STEP 2. Find the values of x for the five key points—the three x-intercepts, the maximum point, and the minimum point. Start with the value of x where the cycle begins and add quarter-periods—that is, $\frac{\text{period}}{4}$—to find successive values of x.

STEP 3. Find the values of y for the five key points by evaluating the function at each value of x from step 2.

STEP 4. Connect the five key points with a smooth curve and graph one complete cycle of the given function.

STEP 5. Extend the graph in step 4 to the left or right as desired.

EXAMPLE 1 Graphing a Variation of $y = \sin x$

Determine the amplitude of $y = \frac{1}{2}\sin x$. Then graph $y = \sin x$ and $y = \frac{1}{2}\sin x$ for $0 \leq x \leq 2\pi$.

Solution

Step 1 Identify the amplitude and the period. The equation $y = \frac{1}{2}\sin x$ is of the form $y = A\sin x$ with $A = \frac{1}{2}$. Thus, the amplitude is $|A| = \frac{1}{2}$. This means that the maximum value of y is $\frac{1}{2}$ and the minimum value of y is $-\frac{1}{2}$. The period for both $y = \frac{1}{2}\sin x$ and $y = \sin x$ is 2π.

Step 2 Find the values of x for the five key points. We need to find the three x-intercepts, the maximum point, and the minimum point for $0 \leq x \leq 2\pi$. To do so, we begin by dividing the period, 2π, by 4.

$$\frac{\text{period}}{4} = \frac{2\pi}{4} = \frac{\pi}{2}$$

We start with the value of x where the cycle begins: $x_1 = 0$. Now we add quarter-periods, $\frac{\pi}{2}$, to generate x-values for each of the key points. The five x-values are

$$x_1 = 0, \quad x_2 = 0 + \frac{\pi}{2} = \frac{\pi}{2}, \quad x_3 = \frac{\pi}{2} + \frac{\pi}{2} = \pi,$$

$$x_4 = \pi + \frac{\pi}{2} = \frac{3\pi}{2}, \quad x_5 = \frac{3\pi}{2} + \frac{\pi}{2} = 2\pi.$$

Step 3 Find the values of y for the five key points. We evaluate the function at each value of x from step 2.

Value of x	Value of y: $y = \frac{1}{2}\sin x$	Coordinates of key point
0	$y = \frac{1}{2}\sin 0 = \frac{1}{2}\cdot 0 = 0$	$(0, 0)$
$\frac{\pi}{2}$	$y = \frac{1}{2}\sin\frac{\pi}{2} = \frac{1}{2}\cdot 1 = \frac{1}{2}$	$\left(\frac{\pi}{2}, \frac{1}{2}\right)$ — maximum point
π	$y = \frac{1}{2}\sin\pi = \frac{1}{2}\cdot 0 = 0$	$(\pi, 0)$
$\frac{3\pi}{2}$	$y = \frac{1}{2}\sin\frac{3\pi}{2} = \frac{1}{2}(-1) = -\frac{1}{2}$	$\left(\frac{3\pi}{2}, -\frac{1}{2}\right)$ — minimum point
2π	$y = \frac{1}{2}\sin 2\pi = \frac{1}{2}\cdot 0 = 0$	$(2\pi, 0)$

There are x-intercepts at 0, π, and 2π. The maximum and minimum points are indicated by the voice balloons.

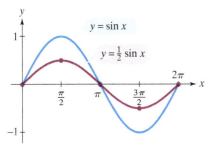

FIGURE 14.66 The graphs of $y = \sin x$ and $y = \frac{1}{2}\sin x, 0 \le x \le 2\pi$

Step 4 Connect the five key points with a smooth curve and graph one complete cycle of the given function. The five key points for $y = \frac{1}{2}\sin x$ are shown in Figure 14.66. By connecting the points with a smooth curve, the figure shows one complete cycle of $y = \frac{1}{2}\sin x$. Also shown is the graph of $y = \sin x$. The graph of $y = \frac{1}{2}\sin x$ is the graph of $y = \sin x$ vertically shrunk by a factor of $\frac{1}{2}$. ☐

PRACTICE 1 Determine the amplitude of $y = 3\sin x$. Then graph $y = \sin x$ and $y = 3\sin x$ for $0 \le x \le 2\pi$.

EXAMPLE 2 Graphing a Variation of $y = \sin x$

Determine the amplitude of $y = -2\sin x$. Then graph $y = \sin x$ and $y = -2\sin x$ for $-\pi \le x \le 3\pi$.

Solution

Step 1 Identify the amplitude and the period. The equation $y = -2\sin x$ is of the form $y = A\sin x$ with $A = -2$. Thus, the amplitude is $|A| = |-2| = 2$. This means that the maximum value of y is 2 and the minimum value of y is -2. Both $y = \sin x$ and $y = -2\sin x$ have a period of 2π.

Step 2 Find the x-values for the five key points. Begin by dividing the period, 2π, by 4.

$$\frac{\text{period}}{4} = \frac{2\pi}{4} = \frac{\pi}{2}$$

Start with the value of x where the cycle begins: $x_1 = 0$. Adding quarter-periods, $\frac{\pi}{2}$, the five x-values for the key points are

$$x_1 = 0, \quad x_2 = 0 + \frac{\pi}{2} = \frac{\pi}{2}, \quad x_3 = \frac{\pi}{2} + \frac{\pi}{2} = \pi,$$

$$x_4 = \pi + \frac{\pi}{2} = \frac{3\pi}{2}, \quad x_5 = \frac{3\pi}{2} + \frac{\pi}{2} = 2\pi.$$

Although we will be graphing for $-\pi \le x \le 3\pi$, we select $x_1 = 0$ rather than $x_1 = -\pi$. Knowing the graph's shape for $0 \le x \le 2\pi$ will enable us to continue the pattern and extend it to the left to $-\pi$ and to the right to 3π.

Step 3 Find the values of y for the five key points. We evaluate the function at each value of x from step 2.

Value of x	Value of y: $y = -2\sin x$	Coordinates of key point	
0	$y = -2\sin 0 = -2 \cdot 0 = 0$	$(0, 0)$	
$\frac{\pi}{2}$	$y = -2\sin\frac{\pi}{2} = -2 \cdot 1 = -2$	$\left(\frac{\pi}{2}, -2\right)$	minimum point
π	$y = -2\sin\pi = -2 \cdot 0 = 0$	$(\pi, 0)$	
$\frac{3\pi}{2}$	$y = -2\sin\frac{3\pi}{2} = -2(-1) = 2$	$\left(\frac{3\pi}{2}, 2\right)$	maximum point
2π	$y = -2\sin 2\pi = -2 \cdot 0 = 0$	$(2\pi, 0)$	

There are x-intercepts at $0, \pi,$ and 2π. The minimum and maximum points are indicated by the voice balloons.

Step 4 Connect the five key points with a smooth curve and graph one complete cycle of the given function. The five key points for $y = -2 \sin x$ are shown in Figure 14.67. By connecting the points with a smooth curve, the dark red portion shows one complete cycle of $y = -2 \sin x$. Also shown in dark blue is one complete cycle of the graph of $y = \sin x$. The graph of $y = -2 \sin x$ is the graph of $y = \sin x$ reflected about the x-axis and vertically stretched by a factor of 2.

Step 5 Extend the graph in step 4 to the left or right as desired. The dark red and dark blue portions of the graphs in Figure 14.67 are from 0 to 2π. In order to graph for $-\pi \leq x \leq 3\pi$, continue the pattern of each graph to the left and to the right. These extensions are shown by the lighter colors in Figure 14.68. ☐

FIGURE 14.67 The graphs of $y = \sin x$ and $y = -2 \sin x$, $0 \leq x \leq 2\pi$

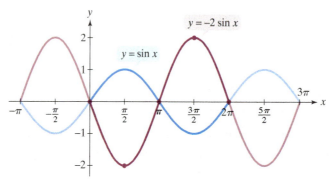

FIGURE 14.68 The graphs of $y = \sin x$ and $y = -2 \sin x$, $-\pi \leq x \leq 3\pi$

PRACTICE 2 Determine the amplitude of $y = -\frac{1}{2}\sin x$. Then graph $y = \sin x$ and $y = -\frac{1}{2}\sin x$ for $-\pi \leq x \leq 3\pi$.

▶ **Helpful Hint**

If $B < 0$ in $y = A \sin Bx$, use $\sin(-\theta) = -\sin \theta$ to rewrite the equation before obtaining its graph.

Now let us examine the graphs of functions of the form $y = A \sin Bx$, where B is the coefficient of x and $B > 0$. How do such graphs compare to those of functions of the form $y = A \sin x$? We know that $y = A \sin x$ completes one cycle from $x = 0$ to $x = 2\pi$. Thus, $y = A \sin Bx$ completes one cycle as Bx increases from 0 to 2π. Set up an inequality to represent this and solve for x to determine the values of x for which $y = \sin Bx$ completes one cycle.

$0 \leq Bx \leq 2\pi$ $y = \sin Bx$ completes one cycle as Bx increases from 0 to 2π.

$0 \leq x \leq \dfrac{2\pi}{B}$ Divide by B, where $B > 0$, and solve for x.

The inequality $0 \leq x \leq \dfrac{2\pi}{B}$ means that $y = A \sin Bx$ completes one cycle from 0 to $\dfrac{2\pi}{B}$. The period is $\dfrac{2\pi}{B}$. The graph of $y = A \sin Bx$ is the graph of $y = A \sin x$ horizontally shrunk by a factor of $\dfrac{1}{B}$ if $B > 1$ and horizontally stretched by a factor of $\dfrac{1}{B}$ if $0 < B < 1$.

Amplitudes and Periods

The graph of $y = A \sin Bx$ has

$$\text{amplitude} = |A|$$

$$\text{period} = \dfrac{2\pi}{B}.$$

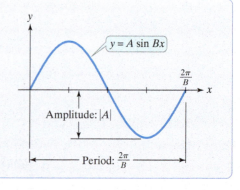

EXAMPLE 3 Graphing a Function of the Form $y = A \sin Bx$

Determine the amplitude and period of $y = 3 \sin 2x$. Then graph the function for $0 \le x \le 2\pi$.

Solution

Step 1 Identify the amplitude and the period. The equation $y = 3 \sin 2x$ is of the form $y = A \sin Bx$ with $A = 3$ and $B = 2$.

$$\text{amplitude:} \quad |A| = |3| = 3$$

$$\text{period:} \quad \frac{2\pi}{B} = \frac{2\pi}{2} = \pi$$

The amplitude, 3, tells us that the maximum value of y is 3 and the minimum value of y is -3. The period, π, tells us that the graph completes one cycle from 0 to π.

Step 2 Find the x-values for the five key points. Begin by dividing the period of $y = 3 \sin 2x$, π, by 4.

$$\frac{\text{period}}{4} = \frac{\pi}{4}$$

Start with the value of x where the cycle begins: $x_1 = 0$. Adding quarter-periods, $\frac{\pi}{4}$, the five x-values for the key points are

$$x_1 = 0, \quad x_2 = 0 + \frac{\pi}{4} = \frac{\pi}{4}, \quad x_3 = \frac{\pi}{4} + \frac{\pi}{4} = \frac{\pi}{2},$$

$$x_4 = \frac{\pi}{2} + \frac{\pi}{4} = \frac{3\pi}{4}, \quad x_5 = \frac{3\pi}{4} + \frac{\pi}{4} = \pi.$$

Step 3 Find the values of y for the five key points. We evaluate the function at each value of x from step 2.

Value of x	Value of y: $y = 3 \sin 2x$	Coordinates of key point	
0	$y = 3 \sin (2 \cdot 0)$ $= 3 \sin 0 = 3 \cdot 0 = 0$	$(0, 0)$	
$\frac{\pi}{4}$	$y = 3 \sin \left(2 \cdot \frac{\pi}{4}\right)$ $= 3 \sin \frac{\pi}{2} = 3 \cdot 1 = 3$	$\left(\frac{\pi}{4}, 3\right)$	maximum point
$\frac{\pi}{2}$	$y = 3 \sin \left(2 \cdot \frac{\pi}{2}\right)$ $= 3 \sin \pi = 3 \cdot 0 = 0$	$\left(\frac{\pi}{2}, 0\right)$	
$\frac{3\pi}{4}$	$y = 3 \sin \left(2 \cdot \frac{3\pi}{4}\right)$ $= 3 \sin \frac{3\pi}{2} = 3(-1) = -3$	$\left(\frac{3\pi}{4}, -3\right)$	minimum point
π	$y = 3 \sin (2 \cdot \pi)$ $= 3 \sin 2\pi = 3 \cdot 0 = 0$	$(\pi, 0)$	

For $0 \le x \le \pi$, there are x-intercepts at $0, \frac{\pi}{2}$, and π. The maximum and minimum points are indicated by notes to the right.

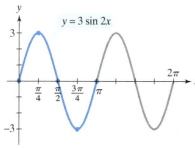

FIGURE 14.69 The graph of $y = 3 \sin 2x$, $0 \le x \le \pi$

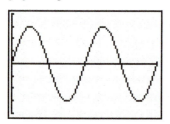

FIGURE 14.70

TECHNOLOGY NOTE

The graph of $y = 3 \sin 2x$ in a $\left[0, 2\pi, \dfrac{\pi}{2}\right]$ by $[-4, 4, 1]$ viewing rectangle verifies our hand-drawn graph in Figure 14.70.

Step 4 Connect the five key points with a smooth curve and graph one complete cycle of the given function. The five key points for $y = 3 \sin 2x$ are shown in Figure 14.69. By connecting the points with a smooth curve, the blue portion shows one complete cycle of $y = 3 \sin 2x$ from 0 to π. The graph of $y = 3 \sin 2x$ is the graph of $y = \sin x$ vertically stretched by a factor of 3 and horizontally shrunk by a factor of $\dfrac{1}{2}$.

Step 5 Extend the graph in step 4 to the left or right as desired. The blue portion of the graph in Figure 14.69 is from 0 to π. In order to graph for $0 \le x \le 2\pi$, we continue this portion and extend the graph another full period to the right. This extension is shown in gray in Figure 14.70. □

PRACTICE 3 Determine the amplitude and period of $y = 2 \sin \tfrac{1}{2}x$. Then graph the function for $0 \le x \le 8\pi$.

Now let us examine the graphs of functions of the form $y = A \sin(Bx - C)$, where $B > 0$. How do such graphs compare to those of functions of the form $y = A \sin Bx$? In both cases, the amplitude is $|A|$ and the period is $\dfrac{2\pi}{B}$. One complete cycle occurs if $Bx - C$ increases from 0 to 2π. This means that we can find an interval containing one cycle by solving the following inequality:

$0 \le Bx - C \le 2\pi$. $y = A \sin(Bx - C)$ completes one cycle as $Bx - C$ increases from 0 to 2π.

$C \le Bx \le C + 2\pi$ Add C to all three parts.

$\dfrac{C}{B} \le x \le \dfrac{C}{B} + \dfrac{2\pi}{B}$ Divide by B, where $B > 0$, and solve for x.

This is the x-coordinate on the left where the cycle begins.

This is the x-coordinate on the right where the cycle ends. $\dfrac{2\pi}{B}$ is the period.

The note above on the left indicates that the graph of $y = A \sin(Bx - C)$ is the graph of $y = A \sin Bx$ shifted horizontally by $\dfrac{C}{B}$. Thus, the number $\dfrac{C}{B}$ is the **phase shift** associated with the graph.

The Graph of $y = A \sin(Bx - C)$

The graph of $y = A \sin(Bx - C)$ is obtained by horizontally shifting the graph of $y = A \sin Bx$ so that the starting point of the cycle is shifted from $x = 0$ to $x = \dfrac{C}{B}$.

If $\dfrac{C}{B} > 0$, the shift is to the right. If $\dfrac{C}{B} < 0$, the shift is to the left. The number $\dfrac{C}{B}$ is called the **phase shift**.

$$\text{amplitude} = |A|$$

$$\text{period} = \dfrac{2\pi}{B}$$

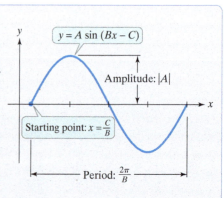

Section 14.5 Graphs of Sine and Cosine Functions 855

EXAMPLE 4 Graphing a Function of the Form $y = A \sin(Bx - C)$

Determine the amplitude, period, and phase shift of $y = 4\sin\left(2x - \dfrac{2\pi}{3}\right)$. Then graph one period of the function.

Solution

Step 1 Identify the amplitude, the period, and the phase shift. We must first identify values for A, B, and C.

The equation is of the form $y = A\sin(Bx - C)$.

$$y = 4\sin\left(2x - \dfrac{2\pi}{3}\right)$$

Using the voice balloon, we see that $A = 4$, $B = 2$, and $C = \dfrac{2\pi}{3}$.

amplitude: $|A| = |4| = 4$ — The maximum y is 4 and the minimum is -4.

period: $\dfrac{2\pi}{B} = \dfrac{2\pi}{2} = \pi$ — Each cycle is of length π.

phase shift: $\dfrac{C}{B} = \dfrac{\frac{2\pi}{3}}{2} = \dfrac{2\pi}{3} \cdot \dfrac{1}{2} = \dfrac{\pi}{3}$ — A cycle starts at $x = \dfrac{\pi}{3}$.

Step 2 Find the x-values for the five key points. Begin by dividing the period, π, by 4.

$$\dfrac{\text{period}}{4} = \dfrac{\pi}{4}$$

Start with the value of x where the cycle begins: $x_1 = \dfrac{\pi}{3}$. Adding quarter-periods, $\dfrac{\pi}{4}$, the five x-values for the key points are

$$x_1 = \dfrac{\pi}{3}, \quad x_2 = \dfrac{\pi}{3} + \dfrac{\pi}{4} = \dfrac{4\pi}{12} + \dfrac{3\pi}{12} = \dfrac{7\pi}{12},$$

$$x_3 = \dfrac{7\pi}{12} + \dfrac{\pi}{4} = \dfrac{7\pi}{12} + \dfrac{3\pi}{12} = \dfrac{10\pi}{12} = \dfrac{5\pi}{6},$$

$$x_4 = \dfrac{5\pi}{6} + \dfrac{\pi}{4} = \dfrac{10\pi}{12} + \dfrac{3\pi}{12} = \dfrac{13\pi}{12},$$

$$x_5 = \dfrac{13\pi}{12} + \dfrac{\pi}{4} = \dfrac{13\pi}{12} + \dfrac{3\pi}{12} = \dfrac{16\pi}{12} = \dfrac{4\pi}{3}.$$

> **Helpful Hint**
> You can speed up the additions on the right by first writing the starting point, $\dfrac{\pi}{3}$, and the quarter-period, $\dfrac{\pi}{4}$, with a common denominator, 12.
>
> starting point $= \dfrac{\pi}{3} = \dfrac{4\pi}{12}$
>
> quarter-period $= \dfrac{\pi}{4} = \dfrac{3\pi}{12}$

> **Helpful Hint**
> You can check your computations for the x-values for the five key points. The difference between x_5 and x_1, or $x_5 - x_1$, should equal the period.
>
> $$x_5 - x_1 = \dfrac{4\pi}{3} - \dfrac{\pi}{3} = \dfrac{3\pi}{3} = \pi$$
>
> Because the period is π, this verifies that our five x-values are correct.

Step 3 Find the values of y for the five key points. We evaluate the function at each value of x from step 2.

856 CHAPTER 14 Trigonometric Functions

Value of x	Value of y: $y = 4\sin\left(2x - \frac{2\pi}{3}\right)$	Coordinates of key point
$\frac{\pi}{3}$	$y = 4\sin\left(2 \cdot \frac{\pi}{3} - \frac{2\pi}{3}\right)$ $= 4\sin 0 = 4 \cdot 0 = 0$	$\left(\frac{\pi}{3}, 0\right)$
$\frac{7\pi}{12}$	$y = 4\sin\left(2 \cdot \frac{7\pi}{12} - \frac{2\pi}{3}\right)$ $= 4\sin\left(\frac{7\pi}{6} - \frac{2\pi}{3}\right)$ $= 4\sin\frac{3\pi}{6} = 4\sin\frac{\pi}{2} = 4 \cdot 1 = 4$	$\left(\frac{7\pi}{12}, 4\right)$ — maximum point
$\frac{5\pi}{6}$	$y = 4\sin\left(2 \cdot \frac{5\pi}{6} - \frac{2\pi}{3}\right)$ $= 4\sin\left(\frac{5\pi}{3} - \frac{2\pi}{3}\right)$ $= 4\sin\frac{3\pi}{3} = 4\sin\pi = 4 \cdot 0 = 0$	$\left(\frac{5\pi}{6}, 0\right)$
$\frac{13\pi}{12}$	$y = 4\sin\left(2 \cdot \frac{13\pi}{12} - \frac{2\pi}{3}\right)$ $= 4\sin\left(\frac{13\pi}{6} - \frac{4\pi}{6}\right)$ $= 4\sin\frac{9\pi}{6} = 4\sin\frac{3\pi}{2} = 4(-1) = -4$	$\left(\frac{13\pi}{12}, -4\right)$ — minimum point
$\frac{4\pi}{3}$	$y = 4\sin\left(2 \cdot \frac{4\pi}{3} - \frac{2\pi}{3}\right)$ $= 4\sin\frac{6\pi}{3} = 4\sin 2\pi = 4 \cdot 0 = 0$	$\left(\frac{4\pi}{3}, 0\right)$

For $\frac{\pi}{3} \leq x \leq \frac{4\pi}{3}$, there are x-intercepts at $\frac{\pi}{3}$, $\frac{5\pi}{6}$, and $\frac{4\pi}{3}$. The maximum and minimum points are indicated by the voice balloons.

Step 4 Connect the five key points with a smooth curve and graph one complete cycle of the given function. The five key points, repeated in the margin, are shown on the graph of $y = 4\sin\left(2x - \frac{2\pi}{3}\right)$ in Figure 14.71.

Value of x	Coordinates of Key Point
$\frac{\pi}{3}$	$\left(\frac{\pi}{3}, 0\right)$
$\frac{7\pi}{12}$	$\left(\frac{7\pi}{12}, 4\right)$
$\frac{5\pi}{6}$	$\left(\frac{5\pi}{6}, 0\right)$
$\frac{13\pi}{12}$	$\left(\frac{13\pi}{12}, -4\right)$
$\frac{4\pi}{3}$	$\left(\frac{4\pi}{3}, 0\right)$

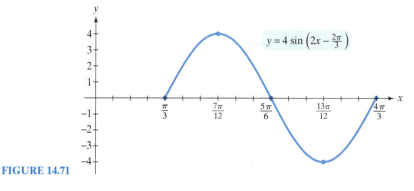

FIGURE 14.71

PRACTICE 4 Determine the amplitude, period, and phase shift of $y = 3\sin\left(2x - \frac{\pi}{3}\right)$. Then graph one period of the function.

OBJECTIVE 3 ▶ **The graph of y = cos x.** We graph $y = \cos x$ by listing some points on the graph. Because the period of the cosine function is 2π, we will concentrate on the graph of the basic cosine curve on $0 \leq x \leq 2\pi$. The rest of the graph is made up of repetitions of this portion. Table 14.4 lists some values of (x, y) on the graph of $y = \cos x$.

TABLE 14.4 Values of (x, y) on the graph of y = cos x

x	0	$\frac{\pi}{6}$	$\frac{\pi}{3}$	$\frac{\pi}{2}$	$\frac{2\pi}{3}$	$\frac{5\pi}{6}$	π	$\frac{7\pi}{6}$	$\frac{4\pi}{3}$	$\frac{3\pi}{2}$	$\frac{5\pi}{3}$	$\frac{11\pi}{6}$	2π
$y = \cos x$	1	$\frac{\sqrt{3}}{2}$	$\frac{1}{2}$	0	$-\frac{1}{2}$	$-\frac{\sqrt{3}}{2}$	-1	$-\frac{\sqrt{3}}{2}$	$-\frac{1}{2}$	0	$\frac{1}{2}$	$\frac{\sqrt{3}}{2}$	1

As x increases from 0 to $\frac{\pi}{2}$, y decreases from 1 to 0.

As x increases from $\frac{\pi}{2}$ to π, y decreases from 0 to -1.

As x increases from π to $\frac{3\pi}{2}$, y increases from -1 to 0.

As x increases from $\frac{3\pi}{2}$ to 2π, y increases from 0 to 1.

Plotting the points in Table 14.4 and connecting them with a smooth curve, we obtain the graph shown in Figure 14.72. The portion of the graph in dark blue shows one complete period. We can obtain a more complete graph of $y = \cos x$ by extending this dark blue portion to the left and to the right.

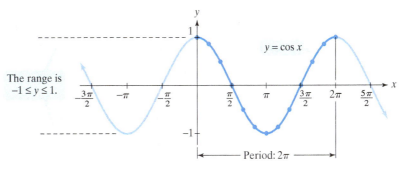

The range is $-1 \leq y \leq 1$.

FIGURE 14.72 The graph of $y = \cos x$

The graph of $y = \cos x$ allows us to visualize some of the properties of the cosine function.

- The domain is all real numbers.
- The range is $-1 \leq y \leq 1$. The graph never rises above 1 or falls below -1.
- The period is 2π. The graph's pattern repeats in every interval of length 2π.

Take a second look at Figure 14.72. Can you see that the graph of $y = \cos x$ is the graph of $y = \sin x$ with a phase shift of $-\frac{\pi}{2}$?

OBJECTIVE 4 ▶ **Graphing variations of y = cos x.** We use the same steps to graph variations of $y = \cos x$ as we did for graphing variations of $y = \sin x$. We will continue finding key points by dividing the period into four equal parts. Amplitudes, periods, and phase shifts play an important role when graphing by hand.

▶ **Helpful Hint**

If $B < 0$ in $y = A \cos Bx$, use $\cos(-\theta) = \cos \theta$ to rewrite the equation before obtaining its graph.

The Graph of y = A cos Bx

The graph of $y = A \cos Bx$ has

$$\text{amplitude} = |A|$$

$$\text{period} = \frac{2\pi}{B}.$$

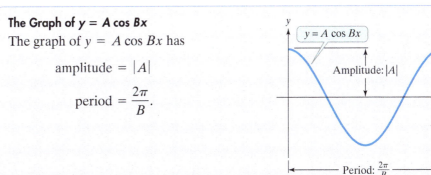

EXAMPLE 5 Graphing a Function of the Form $y = A \cos Bx$

Determine the amplitude and period of $y = -3 \cos \frac{\pi}{2} x$. Then graph the function for $-4 \leq x \leq 4$.

Solution

Step 1 Identify the amplitude and the period. The equation $y = -3 \cos \frac{\pi}{2} x$ is of the form $y = A \cos Bx$ with $A = -3$ and $B = \frac{\pi}{2}$.

amplitude: $|A| = |-3| = 3$ — The maximum y is 3 and the minimum is -3.

period: $\frac{2\pi}{B} = \frac{2\pi}{\frac{\pi}{2}} = 2\pi \cdot \frac{2}{\pi} = 4$ — Each cycle is of length 4.

Step 2 Find the x-values for the five key points. Begin by dividing the period, 4, by 4.

$$\frac{\text{period}}{4} = \frac{4}{4} = 1$$

Start with the value of x where the cycle begins: $x_1 = 0$. Adding quarter-periods, 1, the five x-values for the key points are

$$x_1 = 0, \quad x_2 = 0 + 1 = 1, \quad x_3 = 1 + 1 = 2, \quad x_4 = 2 + 1 = 3, \quad x_5 = 3 + 1 = 4.$$

Step 3 Find the values of y for the five key points. We evaluate the function at each value of x from step 2.

Value of x	Value of y: $y = -3 \cos \frac{\pi}{2} x$	Coordinates of key point	
0	$y = -3 \cos\left(\frac{\pi}{2} \cdot 0\right)$ $= -3 \cos 0 = -3 \cdot 1 = -3$	$(0, -3)$	minimum point
1	$y = -3 \cos\left(\frac{\pi}{2} \cdot 1\right)$ $= -3 \cos \frac{\pi}{2} = -3 \cdot 0 = 0$	$(1, 0)$	
2	$y = -3 \cos\left(\frac{\pi}{2} \cdot 2\right)$ $= -3 \cos \pi = -3(-1) = 3$	$(2, 3)$	maximum point
3	$y = -3 \cos\left(\frac{\pi}{2} \cdot 3\right)$ $= -3 \cos \frac{3\pi}{2} = -3 \cdot 0 = 0$	$(3, 0)$	
4	$y = -3 \cos\left(\frac{\pi}{2} \cdot 4\right)$ $= -3 \cos 2\pi = -3 \cdot 1 = -3$	$(4, -3)$	minimum point

TECHNOLOGY NOTE

The graph of $y = -3 \cos \frac{\pi}{2} x$ in a $[-4, 4, 1]$ by $[-4, 4, 1]$ viewing rectangle verifies our hand-drawn graph in Figure 14.73.

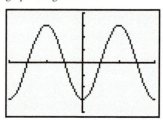

For $0 \leq x \leq 4$, there are x-intercepts at 1 and 3. The minimum and maximum points are indicated by the voice balloons.

Step 4 Connect the five key points with a smooth curve and graph one complete cycle of the given function. The five key points for $y = -3 \cos \frac{\pi}{2} x$ are shown in Figure 14.73.

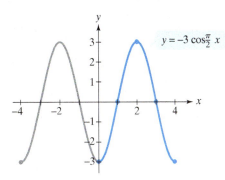

FIGURE 14.73

By connecting the points with a smooth curve, the blue portion shows one complete cycle of $y = -3 \cos \frac{\pi}{2} x$ from 0 to 4.

Step 5 Extend the graph in step 4 to the left or right as desired. The blue portion of the graph in Figure 14.73 is for x from 0 to 4. In order to graph for $-4 \leq x \leq 4$, we continue this portion and extend the graph another full period to the left. This extension is shown in gray in Figure 14.73. □

PRACTICE

5 Determine the amplitude and period of $y = -4 \cos \pi x$. Then graph the function for $-2 \leq x \leq 2$.

Finally, let us examine the graphs of functions of the form $y = A \cos(Bx - C)$. Graphs of these functions shift the graph of $y = A \cos Bx$ horizontally by $\frac{C}{B}$.

The Graph of $y = A \cos(Bx - C)$

The graph of $y = A \cos(Bx - C)$ is obtained by horizontally shifting the graph of $y = A \cos Bx$ so that the starting point of the cycle is shifted from $x = 0$ to $x = \frac{C}{B}$. If $\frac{C}{B} > 0$, the shift is to the right. If $\frac{C}{B} < 0$, the shift is to the left. The number $\frac{C}{B}$ is called the **phase shift.**

$$\text{amplitude} = |A|$$

$$\text{period} = \frac{2\pi}{B}$$

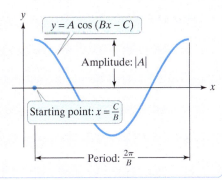

EXAMPLE 6 Graphing a Function of the Form $y = A \cos(Bx - C)$

Determine the amplitude, period, and phase shift of $y = \frac{1}{2} \cos(4x + \pi)$. Then graph one period of the function.

Solution

Step 1 Identify the amplitude, the period, and the phase shift. We must first identify values for A, B, and C. To do this, we need to express the equation in the form $y = A \cos(Bx - C)$. Thus, we write $y = \frac{1}{2} \cos(4x + \pi)$ as $y = \frac{1}{2} \cos[4x - (-\pi)]$. Now we can identify values for A, B, and C.

$$y = \frac{1}{2}\cos[4x - (-\pi)]$$

The equation is of the form $y = A\cos(Bx - C)$.

Using the voice balloon, we see that $A = \frac{1}{2}$, $B = 4$, and $C = -\pi$.

amplitude: $|A| = \left|\frac{1}{2}\right| = \frac{1}{2}$ The maximum y is $\frac{1}{2}$ and the minimum is $-\frac{1}{2}$.

period: $\frac{2\pi}{B} = \frac{2\pi}{4} = \frac{\pi}{2}$ Each cycle is of length $\frac{\pi}{2}$.

phase shift: $\frac{C}{B} = -\frac{\pi}{4}$ A cycle starts at $x = -\frac{\pi}{4}$.

Step 2 Find the x-values for the five key points. Begin by dividing the period, $\frac{\pi}{2}$, by 4.

$$\frac{\text{period}}{4} = \frac{\frac{\pi}{2}}{4} = \frac{\pi}{8}$$

Start with the value of x where the cycle begins: $x_1 = -\frac{\pi}{4}$. Adding quarter-periods, $\frac{\pi}{8}$, the five x-values for the key points are

$$x_1 = -\frac{\pi}{4}, \quad x_2 = -\frac{\pi}{4} + \frac{\pi}{8} = -\frac{2\pi}{8} + \frac{\pi}{8} = -\frac{\pi}{8}, \quad x_3 = -\frac{\pi}{8} + \frac{\pi}{8} = 0,$$

$$x_4 = 0 + \frac{\pi}{8} = \frac{\pi}{8}, \quad x_5 = \frac{\pi}{8} + \frac{\pi}{8} = \frac{2\pi}{8} = \frac{\pi}{4}.$$

Step 3 Find the values of y for the five key points. Take a few minutes and use your calculator to evaluate the function at each value of x from step 2. Show that the key points are

$$\left(-\frac{\pi}{4}, \frac{1}{2}\right), \quad \left(-\frac{\pi}{8}, 0\right), \quad \left(0, -\frac{1}{2}\right), \quad \left(\frac{\pi}{8}, 0\right), \text{ and } \left(\frac{\pi}{4}, \frac{1}{2}\right).$$

maximum point | x-intercept at $-\frac{\pi}{8}$ | minimum point | x-intercept at $\frac{\pi}{8}$ | maximum point

Step 4 Connect the five key points with a smooth curve and graph one complete cycle of the given function. The key points and the graph of $y = \frac{1}{2}\cos(4x + \pi)$ are shown in Figure 14.74.

TECHNOLOGY NOTE

The graph of

$$y = \frac{1}{2}\cos(4x + \pi)$$

in a $\left[-\frac{\pi}{4}, \frac{\pi}{4}, \frac{\pi}{8}\right]$ by $[-1, 1, 1]$ viewing rectangle verifies our hand-drawn graph in Figure 14.74.

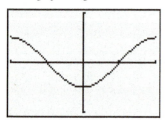

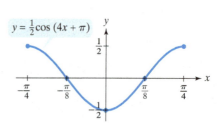

FIGURE 14.74

PRACTICE 6 Determine the amplitude, period, and phase shift of $y = \frac{3}{2}\cos(2x + \pi)$. Then graph one period of the function.

OBJECTIVE 5 ▶ Vertical shifts of sinusoidal graphs. We now look at graphs of

$$y = A\sin(Bx - C) + D \quad \text{and} \quad y = A\cos(Bx - C) + D.$$

The constant D causes vertical shifts in the graphs of $y = A\sin(Bx - C)$ and $y = A\cos(Bx - C)$. If D is positive, the shift is D units upward. If D is negative, the shift is $|D|$ units downward. These vertical shifts result in these graphs oscillating about the horizontal line $y = D$ rather than about the x-axis. Thus, the maximum y is $D + |A|$ and the minimum y is $D - |A|$.

EXAMPLE 7 A Vertical Shift

Graph one period of the function $y = \frac{1}{2}\cos x - 1$.

Solution The graph of $y = \frac{1}{2}\cos x - 1$ is the graph of $y = \frac{1}{2}\cos x$ shifted one unit downward. The period of $y = \frac{1}{2}\cos x$ is 2π, which is also the period for the vertically shifted graph. The key points for $0 \le x \le 2\pi$ for $y = \frac{1}{2}\cos x - 1$ are found by first determining their x-coordinates. The quarter-period is $\frac{2\pi}{4}$, or $\frac{\pi}{2}$. The cycle begins at $x = 0$. As always, we add quarter-periods to generate x-values for each of the key points. The five x-values are

$$x_1 = 0, \quad x_2 = 0 + \frac{\pi}{2} = \frac{\pi}{2}, \quad x_3 = \frac{\pi}{2} + \frac{\pi}{2} = \pi,$$

$$x_4 = \pi + \frac{\pi}{2} = \frac{3\pi}{2}, \quad x_5 = \frac{3\pi}{2} + \frac{\pi}{2} = 2\pi.$$

The values of y for the five key points and their coordinates are determined as follows.

Value of x	Value of y: $y = \frac{1}{2}\cos x - 1$	Coordinates of Key Point
0	$y = \frac{1}{2}\cos 0 - 1$ $= \frac{1}{2}\cdot 1 - 1 = -\frac{1}{2}$	$\left(0, -\frac{1}{2}\right)$
$\frac{\pi}{2}$	$y = \frac{1}{2}\cos\frac{\pi}{2} - 1$ $= \frac{1}{2}\cdot 0 - 1 = -1$	$\left(\frac{\pi}{2}, -1\right)$
π	$y = \frac{1}{2}\cos \pi - 1$ $= \frac{1}{2}(-1) - 1 = -\frac{3}{2}$	$\left(\pi, -\frac{3}{2}\right)$
$\frac{3\pi}{2}$	$y = \frac{1}{2}\cos\frac{3\pi}{2} - 1$ $= \frac{1}{2}\cdot 0 - 1 = -1$	$\left(\frac{3\pi}{2}, -1\right)$
2π	$y = \frac{1}{2}\cos 2\pi - 1$ $= \frac{1}{2}\cdot 1 - 1 = -\frac{1}{2}$	$\left(2\pi, -\frac{1}{2}\right)$

The five key points for $y = \frac{1}{2} \cos x - 1$ are shown in Figure 14.75. By connecting the points with a smooth curve, we obtain one period of the graph.

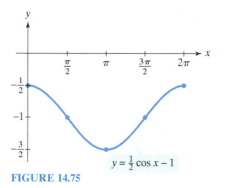

FIGURE 14.75

PRACTICE 7 Graph one period of the function $y = 2 \cos x + 1$.

OBJECTIVE 6 ▶ Modeling periodic behavior. Our breathing consists of alternating periods of inhaling and exhaling. Each complete pumping cycle of the human heart can be described using a sine function. Our brain waves during deep sleep are sinusoidal.

Some graphing utilities have a SINe REGression feature. This feature gives the sine function in the form $y = A \sin(Bx + C) + D$ of best fit for wavelike data. At least four data points must be used. However, it is not always necessary to use technology. In our next example, we use our understanding of the sine and cosine graphs to model the process of breathing.

EXAMPLE 8 A Trigonometric Breath of Life

The graph in Figure 14.76 shows one complete normal breathing cycle. The cycle consists of inhaling and exhaling. It takes place every 5 seconds. Velocity of air flow is positive when we inhale and negative when we exhale. It is measured in liters per second. If y represents velocity of air flow after x seconds, find a function of the form $y = A \sin Bx$ that models air flow in a normal breathing cycle.

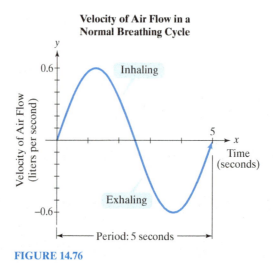

FIGURE 14.76

Solution We need to determine values for A and B in the equation $y = A \sin Bx$. The amplitude, A, is the maximum value of y. Figure 14.76 shows that this maximum value is 0.6. Thus, $A = 0.6$.

The value of B in $y = A \sin Bx$ can be found using the formula for the period: period $= \dfrac{2\pi}{B}$. The period of our breathing cycle is 5 seconds. Thus,

$$5 = \dfrac{2\pi}{B} \quad \text{Our goal is to solve this equation for } B.$$

$$5B = 2\pi \quad \text{Multiply both sides of the equation by } B.$$

$$B = \dfrac{2\pi}{5}. \quad \text{Divide both sides of the equation by 5.}$$

We see that $A = 0.6$ and $B = \dfrac{2\pi}{5}$. Substitute these values into $y = A \sin Bx$. The breathing cycle is modeled by

$$y = 0.6 \sin \dfrac{2\pi}{5} x.$$

PRACTICE

8 Find an equation of the form $y = A \sin Bx$ that produces the graph shown in the figure on the right.

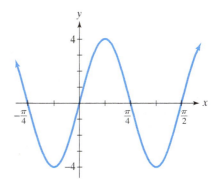

EXAMPLE 9 Modeling a Tidal Cycle

Figure 14.77 shows that the depth of water at a boat dock varies with the tides. The depth is 5 feet at low tide and 13 feet at high tide. On a certain day, low tide occurs at 4 A.M. and high tide at 10 A.M. If y represents the depth of the water, in feet, x hours after midnight, use a sine function of the form $y = A \sin(Bx - C) + D$ to model the water's depth.

Solution We need to determine values for $A, B, C,$ and D in the equation $y = A \sin(Bx - C) + D$. We can find these values using Figure 14.77. We begin with D.

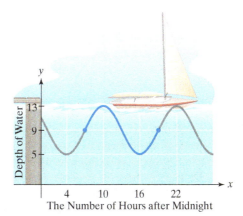

FIGURE 14.77

To find D, we use the vertical shift. Because the water's depth ranges from a minimum of 5 feet to a maximum of 13 feet, the curve oscillates about the middle value, 9 feet. Thus, $D = 9$, which is the vertical shift.

At maximum depth, the water is 4 feet above 9 feet. Thus, A, the amplitude, is 4: $A = 4$.

To find B, we use the period. The blue portion of the graph shows that one complete tidal cycle occurs in $19 - 7$, or 12 hours. The period is 12. Thus,

$$12 = \frac{2\pi}{B} \quad \text{Our goal is to solve this equation for } B.$$

$$12B = 2\pi \quad \text{Multiply both sides by } B.$$

$$B = \frac{2\pi}{12} = \frac{\pi}{6}. \quad \text{Divide both sides by 12.}$$

To find C, we use the phase shift. The blue portion of the graph shows that the starting point of the cycle is shifted from 0 to 7. The phase shift, $\frac{C}{B}$, is 7.

$$7 = \frac{C}{B} \quad \text{The phase shift of } y = A \sin(Bx - C) \text{ is } \frac{C}{B}.$$

$$7 = \frac{C}{\frac{\pi}{6}} \quad \text{From above, we have } B = \frac{\pi}{6}.$$

$$\frac{7\pi}{6} = C \quad \text{Multiply both sides of the equation by } \frac{\pi}{6}.$$

We see that $A = 4$, $B = \frac{\pi}{6}$, $C = \frac{7\pi}{6}$, and $D = 9$. Substitute these values into $y = A \sin(Bx - C) + D$. The water's depth, in feet, x hours after midnight is modeled by

$$y = 4 \sin\left(\frac{\pi}{6}x - \frac{7\pi}{6}\right) + 9.$$

TECHNOLOGY NOTE

Graphic Connections

We can use a graphing utility to verify that the model in Example 9,

$$y = 4 \sin\left(\frac{\pi}{6}x - \frac{7\pi}{6}\right) + 9,$$

is correct. The graph of the function is shown in a $[0, 28, 4]$ by $[0, 15, 5]$ viewing rectangle.

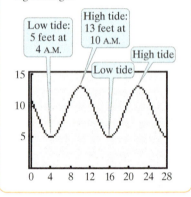

PRACTICE 9
A region that is 30° north of the Equator averages a minimum of 10 hours of daylight in December. Hours of daylight are at a maximum of 14 hours in June. Let x represent the month of the year, with 1 for January, 2 for February, 3 for March, and 12 for December. If y represents the number of hours of daylight in month x, use a sine function of the form $y = A \sin(Bx - C) + D$ to model the hours of daylight.

14.5 EXERCISE SET

PRACTICE EXERCISES

In Exercises 1–6, determine the amplitude of each function. Then graph the function and $y = \sin x$ in the same rectangular coordinate system for $0 \leq x \leq 2\pi$.

1. $y = 4 \sin x$
2. $y = 5 \sin x$
3. $y = \frac{1}{3} \sin x$
4. $y = \frac{1}{4} \sin x$
5. $y = -3 \sin x$
6. $y = -4 \sin x$

In Exercises 7–16, determine the amplitude and period of each function. Then graph one period of the function.

7. $y = \sin 2x$
8. $y = \sin 4x$
9. $y = 3 \sin \frac{1}{2} x$
10. $y = 2 \sin \frac{1}{4} x$
11. $y = 4 \sin \pi x$
12. $y = 3 \sin 2\pi x$
13. $y = -3 \sin 2\pi x$
14. $y = -2 \sin \pi x$
15. $y = -\sin \frac{2}{3} x$
16. $y = -\sin \frac{4}{3} x$

In Exercises 17–30, determine the amplitude, period, and phase shift of each function. Then graph one period of the function.

17. $y = \sin(x - \pi)$
18. $y = \sin\left(x - \frac{\pi}{2}\right)$
19. $y = \sin(2x - \pi)$
20. $y = \sin\left(2x - \frac{\pi}{2}\right)$
21. $y = 3 \sin(2x - \pi)$
22. $y = 3 \sin\left(2x - \frac{\pi}{2}\right)$

23. $y = \frac{1}{2}\sin\left(x + \frac{\pi}{2}\right)$
24. $y = \frac{1}{2}\sin(x + \pi)$
25. $y = -2\sin\left(2x + \frac{\pi}{2}\right)$
26. $y = -3\sin\left(2x + \frac{\pi}{2}\right)$
27. $y = 3\sin(\pi x + 2)$
28. $y = 3\sin(2\pi x + 4)$
29. $y = -2\sin(2\pi x + 4\pi)$
30. $y = -3\sin(2\pi x + 4\pi)$

In Exercises 31–34, determine the amplitude of each function. Then graph the function and $y = \cos x$ in the same rectangular coordinate system for $0 \le x \le 2\pi$.

31. $y = 2\cos x$
32. $y = 3\cos x$
33. $y = -2\cos x$
34. $y = -3\cos x$

In Exercises 35–42, determine the amplitude and period of each function. Then graph one period of the function.

35. $y = \cos 2x$
36. $y = \cos 4x$
37. $y = 4\cos 2\pi x$
38. $y = 5\cos 2\pi x$
39. $y = -4\cos \frac{1}{2}x$
40. $y = -3\cos \frac{1}{3}x$
41. $y = -\frac{1}{2}\cos \frac{\pi}{3}x$
42. $y = -\frac{1}{2}\cos \frac{\pi}{4}x$

In Exercises 43–52, determine the amplitude, period, and phase shift of each function. Then graph one period of the function.

43. $y = \cos\left(x - \frac{\pi}{2}\right)$
44. $y = \cos\left(x + \frac{\pi}{2}\right)$
45. $y = 3\cos(2x - \pi)$
46. $y = 4\cos(2x - \pi)$
47. $y = \frac{1}{2}\cos\left(3x + \frac{\pi}{2}\right)$
48. $y = \frac{1}{2}\cos(2x + \pi)$
49. $y = -3\cos\left(2x - \frac{\pi}{2}\right)$
50. $y = -4\cos\left(2x - \frac{\pi}{2}\right)$
51. $y = 2\cos(2\pi x + 8\pi)$
52. $y = 3\cos(2\pi x + 4\pi)$

In Exercises 53–60, use a vertical shift to graph one period of the function.

53. $y = \sin x + 2$
54. $y = \sin x - 2$
55. $y = \cos x - 3$
56. $y = \cos x + 3$
57. $y = 2\sin \frac{1}{2}x + 1$
58. $y = 2\cos \frac{1}{2}x + 1$
59. $y = -3\cos 2\pi x + 2$
60. $y = -3\sin 2\pi x + 2$

PRACTICE PLUS

In Exercises 61–66, find an equation for each graph.

61.
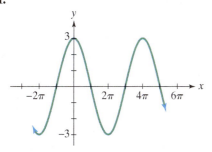

62.
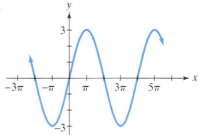

63.
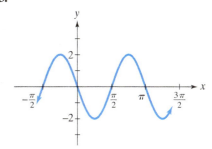

64.
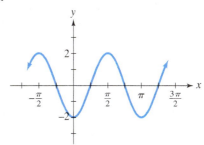

65.
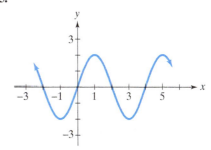

66.
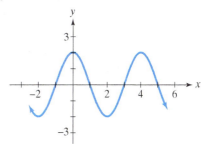

In Exercises 67–70, graph one period of each function.

67. $y = \left|2\cos \frac{x}{2}\right|$
68. $y = \left|3\cos \frac{2x}{3}\right|$
69. $y = -|3\sin \pi x|$
70. $y = -\left|2\sin \frac{\pi x}{2}\right|$

In Exercises 71–74, graph f, g, and h in the same rectangular coordinate system for $0 \leq x \leq 2\pi$. Obtain the graph of h by adding or subtracting the corresponding y-coordinates on the graphs of f and g.

71. $f(x) = -2 \sin x, g(x) = \sin 2x, h(x) = (f + g)(x)$
72. $f(x) = 2 \cos x, g(x) = \cos 2x, h(x) = (f + g)(x)$
73. $f(x) = \sin x, g(x) = \cos 2x, h(x) = (f - g)(x)$
74. $f(x) = \cos x, g(x) = \sin 2x, h(x) = (f - g)(x)$

APPLICATION EXERCISES

75. Rounded to the nearest hour, Los Angeles averages 14 hours of daylight in June, 10 hours in December, and 12 hours in March and September. Let x represent the number of months after June and let y represent the number of hours of daylight in month x. Make a graph that displays the information from June of one year to June of the following year.

76. A clock with an hour hand that is 15 inches long is hanging on a wall. At noon, the distance between the tip of the hour hand and the ceiling is 23 inches. At 3 P.M., the distance is 38 inches; at 6 P.M., 53 inches; at 9 P.M., 38 inches; and at midnight the distance is again 23 inches. If y represents the distance between the tip of the hour hand and the ceiling x hours after noon, make a graph that displays the information for $0 \leq x \leq 24$.

77. The number of hours of daylight in Boston is given by

$$y = 3 \sin \frac{2\pi}{365}(x - 79) + 12,$$

where x is the number of days after January 1.
   a. What is the amplitude of this function?
   b. What is the period of this function?
   c. How many hours of daylight are there on the longest day of the year?
   d. How many hours of daylight are there on the shortest day of the year?
   e. Graph the function for one period, starting on January 1.

78. The average monthly temperature, y, in degrees Fahrenheit, for Juneau, Alaska, can be modeled by $y = 16 \sin\left(\frac{\pi}{6}x - \frac{2\pi}{3}\right) + 40$, where x is the month of the year (January = 1, February = 2, ... December = 12). Graph the function for $1 \leq x \leq 12$. What is the highest average monthly temperature? In which month does this occur?

79. The figure shows the depth of water at the end of a boat dock. The depth is 6 feet at low tide and 12 feet at high tide. On a

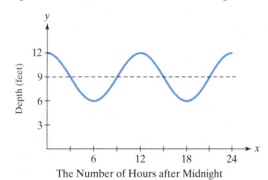

certain day, low tide occurs at 6 A.M. and high tide at noon. If y represents the depth of the water x hours after midnight, use a cosine function of the form $y = A \cos Bx + D$ to model the water's depth.

80. The figure in the next column shows the depth of water at the end of a boat dock. The depth is 5 feet at high tide and 3 feet at low tide. On a certain day, high tide occurs at noon and low tide at 6 P.M. If y represents the depth of the water x hours after noon, use a cosine function of the form $y = A \cos Bx + D$ to model the water's depth.

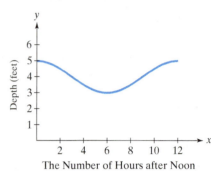

WRITING IN MATHEMATICS

81. Without drawing a graph, describe the behavior of the basic sine curve.
82. What is the amplitude of the sine function? What does this tell you about the graph?
83. If you are given the equation of a sine function, how do you determine the period?
84. Describe a general procedure for obtaining the graph of $y = A \sin(Bx - C)$.
85. Without drawing a graph, describe the behavior of the basic cosine curve.
86. Describe a relationship between the graphs of $y = \sin x$ and $y = \cos x$.
87. Describe the relationship between the graphs of $y = A \cos(Bx - C)$ and $y = A \cos(Bx - C) + D$.

TECHNOLOGY EXERCISES

88. Use a graphing utility to verify any five of the sine curves that you drew by hand in Exercises 7–30. The amplitude, period, and phase shift should help you to determine appropriate viewing rectangle settings.
89. Use a graphing utility to verify any five of the cosine curves that you drew by hand in Exercises 35–52.
90. Use a graphing utility to verify any two of the curves with vertical shifts that you drew in Exercises 53–60.

In Exercises 91–94, use a graphing utility to graph two periods of the function.

91. $y = 3 \sin(2x + \pi)$
92. $y = -2 \cos\left(2\pi x - \frac{\pi}{2}\right)$
93. $y = 0.2 \sin\left(\frac{\pi}{10}x + \pi\right)$
94. $y = 3 \sin(2x - \pi) + 5$

95. Use a graphing utility to graph $y = \sin x$ and $y = x - \frac{x^3}{6} + \frac{x^5}{120}$ in a $\left[-\pi, \pi, \frac{\pi}{2}\right]$ by $[-2, 2, 1]$ viewing rectangle. How do the graphs compare?

96. Use a graphing utility to graph $y = \cos x$ and $y = 1 - \dfrac{x^2}{2} + \dfrac{x^4}{24}$ in a $\left[-\pi, \pi, \dfrac{\pi}{2}\right]$ by $[-2, 2, 1]$ viewing rectangle. How do the graphs compare?

97. Use a graphing utility to graph
$$y = \sin x + \frac{\sin 2x}{2} + \frac{\sin 3x}{3} + \frac{\sin 4x}{4}$$
in a $\left[-2\pi, 2\pi, \dfrac{\pi}{2}\right]$ by $[-2, 2, 1]$ viewing rectangle. How do these waves compare to the smooth rolling waves of the basic sine curve?

98. Use a graphing utility to graph
$$y = \sin x - \frac{\sin 3x}{9} + \frac{\sin 5x}{25}$$
in a $\left[-2\pi, 2\pi, \dfrac{\pi}{2}\right]$ by $[-2, 2, 1]$ viewing rectangle. How do these waves compare to the smooth rolling waves of the basic sine curve?

99. Read a Table. The data show the average monthly temperatures for Washington, D.C.

x (Month)	Average Monthly Temperature, °F
1 (January)	34.6
2 (February)	37.5
3 (March)	47.2
4 (April)	56.5
5 (May)	66.4
6 (June)	75.6
7 (July)	80.0
8 (August)	78.5
9 (September)	71.3
10 (October)	59.7
11 (November)	49.8
12 (December)	39.4

Source: U.S. National Oceanic and Atmospheric Administration

a. Use your graphing utility to draw a scatter plot of the data from $x = 1$ through $x = 12$.

b. Use the SINe REGression feature to find the sinusoidal function of the form $y = A \sin(Bx + C) + D$ that best fits the data.

c. Use your graphing utility to draw the sine or cosine function of best fit on the scatter plot.

100. Repeat Exercise 99 for data of your choice. The data can involve the average monthly temperatures for the region where you live or any data whose scatter plot takes the form of a sinusoidal function.

CRITICAL THINKING EXERCISES

Make Sense? *In Exercises 101–104, determine whether each statement makes sense or does not make sense, and explain your reasoning.*

101. When graphing one complete cycle of $y = A \sin(Bx - C)$, I find it easiest to begin my graph on the x-axis.

102. When graphing one complete cycle of $y = A \cos(Bx - C)$, I find it easiest to begin my graph on the x-axis.

103. Using the equation $y = A \sin Bx$, if I replace either A or B with its opposite, the graph of the resulting equation is a reflection of the graph of the original equation about the x-axis.

104. A ride on a circular Ferris wheel is like riding sine or cosine graphs.

105. Determine the range of each of the following functions. Then give a viewing rectangle, or window, that shows two periods of the function's graph.

a. $f(x) = 3 \sin\left(x + \dfrac{\pi}{6}\right) - 2$

b. $g(x) = \sin 3\left(x + \dfrac{\pi}{6}\right) - 2$

106. Write the equation for a cosine function with amplitude π, period 1, and phase shift -2.

REVIEW AND PREVIEW

Exercises 107–108 will help you prepare for the material covered in the next section.

107. Solve: $-\dfrac{\pi}{2} < x + \dfrac{\pi}{4} < \dfrac{\pi}{2}$.

108. Simplify: $\dfrac{-\dfrac{3\pi}{4} + \dfrac{\pi}{4}}{2}$.

14.6 GRAPH OF THE TANGENT FUNCTION

OBJECTIVES

1. Understand the graph of $y = \tan x$.
2. Graph variations of $y = \tan x$.

OBJECTIVE 1 ▶ The graph of $y = \tan x$. The properties of the tangent function discussed in Section 14.4 will help us determine its graph.

- The period is π. It is only necessary to graph $y = \tan x$ over an interval of length π. The remainder of the graph consists of repetitions of that graph at intervals of π.
- $\tan(-x) = -\tan x$. The graph is symmetric with respect to the origin.
- The tangent function is undefined at $\dfrac{\pi}{2}$. The graph of $y = \tan x$ has a vertical asymptote at $x = \dfrac{\pi}{2}$.

We obtain the graph of $y = \tan x$ using some points on the graph and origin symmetry. Table 14.5 lists some values of (x, y) on the graph of $y = \tan x$ on $0 \leq x < \frac{\pi}{2}$.

TABLE 14.5 Values of (x, y) on the graph of $y = \tan x$

x	0	$\frac{\pi}{6}$	$\frac{\pi}{4}$	$\frac{\pi}{3}$	$\frac{5\pi}{12}$ (75°)	$\frac{17\pi}{36}$ (85°)	$\frac{89\pi}{180}$ (89°)	1.57	$\frac{\pi}{2}$
$y = \tan x$	0	$\frac{\sqrt{3}}{3} \approx 0.6$	1	$\sqrt{3} \approx 1.7$	3.7	11.4	57.3	1255.8	undefined

As x increases from 0 toward $\frac{\pi}{2}$, y increases slowly at first, then more and more rapidly.

The graph in Figure 14.78(a) is based on our observation that as x increases from 0 toward $\frac{\pi}{2}$, y increases slowly at first, then more and more rapidly. Notice that y increases without bound as x approaches $\frac{\pi}{2}$. As the figure shows, the graph of $y = \tan x$ has a vertical asymptote at $x = \frac{\pi}{2}$.

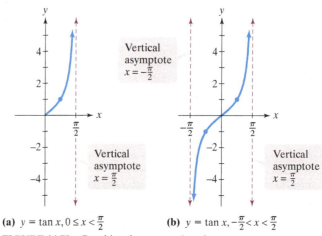

(a) $y = \tan x, 0 \leq x < \frac{\pi}{2}$
(b) $y = \tan x, -\frac{\pi}{2} < x < \frac{\pi}{2}$

FIGURE 14.78 Graphing the tangent function

The graph of $y = \tan x$ can be completed on $-\frac{\pi}{2} < x < \frac{\pi}{2}$ by using origin symmetry. Figure 14.78(b) shows the result of reflecting the graph in Figure 14.78(a) about the origin. The graph of $y = \tan x$ has another vertical asymptote at $x = -\frac{\pi}{2}$. Notice that y decreases without bound as x approaches $-\frac{\pi}{2}$.

Because the period of the tangent function is π, the graph in Figure 14.78(b) shows one complete period of $y = \tan x$. We obtain the complete graph of $y = \tan x$ by repeating the graph in Figure 14.78(b) to the left and right over intervals of π. The resulting graph and its main characteristics are shown in the following box:

The Tangent Curve: The Graph of $y = \tan x$ and Its Characteristics

Characteristics

- **Period:** π
- **Domain:** All real numbers except odd multiples of $\frac{\pi}{2}$
- **Range:** All real numbers

- **Vertical asymptotes** at odd multiples of $\frac{\pi}{2}$.
- **An x-intercept** occurs midway between each pair of consecutive asymptotes.
- Points on the graph $\frac{1}{4}$ and $\frac{3}{4}$ of the way between consecutive asymptotes have y-coordinates of -1 and 1, respectively.

OBJECTIVE 2 ▶ Graphing variations of $y = \tan x$. We use the characteristics of the tangent curve to graph tangent functions of the form $y = A \tan(Bx - C)$.

Graphing $y = A \tan(Bx - C)$

STEP 1. Find two consecutive asymptotes by finding an interval containing one period:

$$-\frac{\pi}{2} < Bx - C < \frac{\pi}{2}.$$

A pair of consecutive asymptotes occur at

$$Bx - C = -\frac{\pi}{2} \text{ and } Bx - C = \frac{\pi}{2}.$$

STEP 2. Identify an x-intercept, midway between the consecutive asymptotes.

STEP 3. Find the points on the graph $\frac{1}{4}$ and $\frac{3}{4}$ of the way between the consecutive asymptotes. These points have y-coordinates of $-A$ and A, respectively.

STEP 4. Use steps 1–3 to graph one full period of the function. Add additional cycles to the left or right as needed.

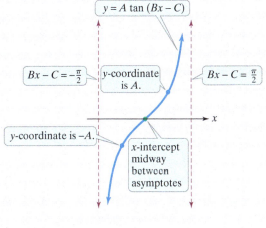

EXAMPLE 1   **Graphing a Tangent Function**

Graph $y = 2 \tan \dfrac{x}{2}$ for $-\pi < x < 3\pi$.

Solution   Refer to Figure 14.79 as you read each step.

Step 1   **Find two consecutive asymptotes.** We do this by finding an interval containing one period.

$$-\frac{\pi}{2} < \frac{x}{2} < \frac{\pi}{2} \quad \text{Set up the inequality } -\frac{\pi}{2} < \text{variable expression in tangent} < \frac{\pi}{2}.$$

$$-\pi < x < \pi \quad \text{Multiply all parts by 2 and solve for } x.$$

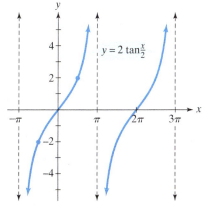

FIGURE 14.79   The graph is shown for two full periods.

An interval containing one period is $-\pi < x < \pi$. Thus, two consecutive asymptotes occur at $x = -\pi$ and $x = \pi$.

Step 2   Identify an x-intercept, midway between the consecutive asymptotes. Midway between $x = -\pi$ and $x = \pi$ is $x = 0$. An x-intercept is 0 and the graph passes through $(0, 0)$.

Step 3   Find points on the graph $\frac{1}{4}$ and $\frac{3}{4}$ of the way between the consecutive asymptotes. These points have y-coordinates of $-A$ and A. Because A, the coefficient of the tangent in $y = 2 \tan \frac{x}{2}$ is 2, these points have y-coordinates of -2 and 2. The graph passes through $\left(-\frac{\pi}{2}, -2\right)$ and $\left(\frac{\pi}{2}, 2\right)$.

Step 4   Use steps 1–3 to graph one full period of the function. We use the two consecutive asymptotes, $x = -\pi$ and $x = \pi$, an x-intercept of 0, and points midway between the x-intercept and asymptotes with y-coordinates of -2 and 2. We graph one period of $y = 2 \tan \frac{x}{2}$ from $-\pi$ to π. In order to graph for $-\pi < x < 3\pi$, we continue the pattern and extend the graph another full period to the right. The graph is shown in Figure 14.79. □

PRACTICE 1   Graph $y = 3 \tan 2x$ for $-\frac{\pi}{4} < x < \frac{3\pi}{4}$.

EXAMPLE 2   Graphing a Tangent Function

Graph two full periods of $y = \tan\left(x + \frac{\pi}{4}\right)$.

Solution   The graph of $y = \tan\left(x + \frac{\pi}{4}\right)$ is the graph of $y = \tan x$ shifted horizontally to the left $\frac{\pi}{4}$ units. Refer to Figure 14.80 as you read each step.

Step 1   Find two consecutive asymptotes. We do this by finding an interval containing one period.

$-\frac{\pi}{2} < x + \frac{\pi}{4} < \frac{\pi}{2}$ Set up the inequality $-\frac{\pi}{2} <$ variable expression in tangent $< \frac{\pi}{2}$.

$-\frac{\pi}{2} - \frac{\pi}{4} < x < \frac{\pi}{2} - \frac{\pi}{4}$ Subtract $\frac{\pi}{4}$ from all parts and solve for x.

$-\frac{3\pi}{4} < x < \frac{\pi}{4}$ Simplify: $-\frac{\pi}{2} - \frac{\pi}{4} = -\frac{2\pi}{4} - \frac{\pi}{4} = -\frac{3\pi}{4}$

and $\frac{\pi}{2} - \frac{\pi}{4} = \frac{2\pi}{4} - \frac{\pi}{4} = \frac{\pi}{4}$.

An interval containing one period is $\left(-\frac{3\pi}{4}, \frac{\pi}{4}\right)$. Thus, two consecutive asymptotes occur at $x = -\frac{3\pi}{4}$ and $x = \frac{\pi}{4}$.

Step 2   Identify an x-intercept, midway between the consecutive asymptotes.

$$x\text{-intercept} = \frac{-\frac{3\pi}{4} + \frac{\pi}{4}}{2} = \frac{-\frac{2\pi}{4}}{2} = -\frac{2\pi}{8} = -\frac{\pi}{4}$$

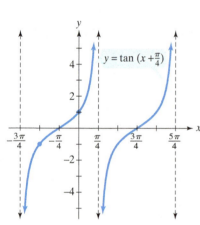

FIGURE 14.80   The graph is shown for two full periods.

An x-intercept is $-\frac{\pi}{4}$ and the graph passes through $\left(-\frac{\pi}{4}, 0\right)$.

Step 3 Find points on the graph $\frac{1}{4}$ and $\frac{3}{4}$ of the way between the consecutive asymptotes. These points have y-coordinates of $-A$ and A. Because A, the coefficient of the tangent in $y = \tan\left(x + \frac{\pi}{4}\right)$ is 1, these points have y-coordinates of -1 and 1. They are shown as blue dots in Figure 14.80.

Step 4 Use steps 1–3 to graph one full period of the function. We use the two consecutive asymptotes, $x = -\frac{3\pi}{4}$ and $x = \frac{\pi}{4}$, to graph one full period of $y = \tan\left(x + \frac{\pi}{4}\right)$ from $-\frac{3\pi}{4}$ to $\frac{\pi}{4}$. We graph two full periods by continuing the pattern and extending the graph another full period to the right. The graph is shown in Figure 14.80. □

PRACTICE 2 Graph two full periods of $y = \tan\left(x - \frac{\pi}{2}\right)$.

Three Curves of Trigonometry Table 14.6 summarizes the graphs of three trigonometric functions. Below each of the graphs is a description of the domain, range, and period of the function.

TABLE 14.6 Graphs of Three Trigonometric Functions

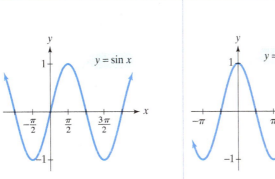
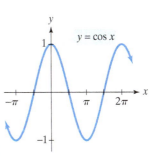
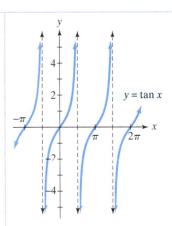

$y = \sin x$	$y = \cos x$	$y = \tan x$
Domain: all real numbers	**Domain:** all real numbers	**Domain:** all real numbers except odd multiples of $\frac{\pi}{2}$
Range: $-1 \leq y \leq 1$	**Range:** $-1 \leq y \leq 1$	**Range:** all real numbers
Period: 2π	**Period:** 2π	**Period:** π

14.6 EXERCISE SET

PRACTICE EXERCISES

In Exercises 1–4, the graph of a tangent function is given. Select the equation for each graph from the following options:

$$y = \tan\left(x + \frac{\pi}{2}\right), \quad y = \tan(x + \pi),$$

$$y = -\tan x, \quad y = -\tan\left(x - \frac{\pi}{2}\right).$$

1.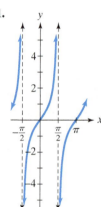

2.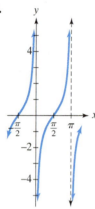

3.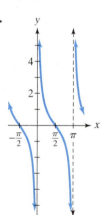

4.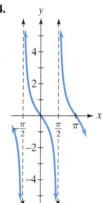

In Exercises 5–12, graph two periods of the given tangent function.

5. $y = 3 \tan \dfrac{x}{4}$

6. $y = 2 \tan \dfrac{x}{4}$

7. $y = \dfrac{1}{2} \tan 2x$

8. $y = 2 \tan 2x$

9. $y = -2 \tan \dfrac{1}{2}x$

10. $y = -3 \tan \dfrac{1}{2}x$

11. $y = \tan(x - \pi)$

12. $y = \tan\left(x - \dfrac{\pi}{4}\right)$

APPLICATION EXERCISES

13. Multiple Steps. An ambulance with a rotating beam of light is parked 12 feet from a building. The function

$$d = 12 \tan 2\pi t$$

describes the distance, d, in feet, of the rotating beam of light from point C after t seconds.

a. Graph the function on $0 \leq x \leq 2$.

b. For what values of t in $0 \leq x \leq 2$ is the function undefined? What does this mean in terms of the rotating beam of light in the figure shown?

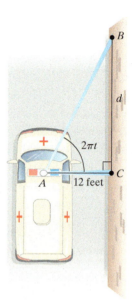

WRITING IN MATHEMATICS

14. Without drawing a graph, describe the behavior of the basic tangent curve.

15. If you are given the equation of a tangent function, how do you find a pair of consecutive asymptotes?

16. If you are given the equation of a tangent function, how do you identify an x-intercept?

TECHNOLOGY EXERCISES

In working Exercise 17, describe what happens at the asymptotes on the graphing utility. Compare the graphs in the connected and dot modes.

17. Use a graphing utility to verify any two of the tangent curves that you drew by hand in Exercises 5–12.

In Exercises 18–21, use a graphing utility to graph each function. Use a range setting so that the graph is shown for at least two periods.

18. $y = \tan \dfrac{x}{4}$

19. $y = \tan 4x$

20. $y = \dfrac{1}{2} \tan \pi x$

21. $y = \dfrac{1}{2} \tan(\pi x + 1)$

In Exercises 22–23 write an equation for each blue graph.

22.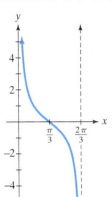

23.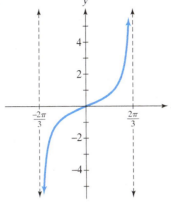

PREVIEW EXERCISES

Exercises 24–26 will help you prepare for the material covered in the next section.

24. **a.** Graph $y = \sin x$ for $-\dfrac{\pi}{2} \leq x \leq \dfrac{\pi}{2}$.

    b. Based on your graph in part (a), does $y = \sin x$ have an inverse function if the domain is restricted to $-\dfrac{\pi}{2} \leq x \leq \dfrac{\pi}{2}$? Explain your answer.

    c. Determine the angle in $-\dfrac{\pi}{2} \leq x \leq \dfrac{\pi}{2}$ whose sine is $-\dfrac{1}{2}$. Identify this information as a point on your graph in part (a).

25. **a.** Graph $y = \cos x$ for $0 \leq x \leq \pi$.

    b. Based on your graph in part (a), does $y = \cos x$ have an inverse function if the domain is restricted to $0 \leq x \leq \pi$? Explain your answer.

    c. Determine the angle in $0 \leq x \leq \pi$ whose cosine is $-\dfrac{\sqrt{3}}{2}$. Identify this information as a point on your graph in part (a).

26. **a.** Graph $y = \tan x$ for $-\dfrac{\pi}{2} < x < \dfrac{\pi}{2}$.

    b. Based on your graph in part (a), does $y = \tan x$ have an inverse function if the domain is restricted to $-\dfrac{\pi}{2} < x < \dfrac{\pi}{2}$? Explain your answer.

    c. Determine the angle in $-\dfrac{\pi}{2} < x < \dfrac{\pi}{2}$ whose tangent is $-\sqrt{3}$. Identify this information as a point on your graph in part (a).

14.7 INVERSE TRIGONOMETRIC FUNCTIONS

OBJECTIVES

1. Understand and use the inverse sine function.
2. Understand and use the inverse cosine function.
3. Understand and use the inverse tangent function.
4. Use a calculator to evaluate inverse trigonometric functions.
5. Find exact values of composite functions with inverse trigonometric functions.

▶ **Helpful Hint**

Here are some helpful things to remember from our earlier discussion of inverse functions.

- If no horizontal line intersects the graph of a function more than once, the function is one-to-one and has an inverse function.
- If the point (a, b) is on the graph of f, then the point (b, a) is on the graph of the inverse function, denoted f^{-1}. The graph of f^{-1} is a reflection of the graph of f about the line $y = x$.

OBJECTIVE 1 ▶ **The inverse sine function.** Figure 14.86 shows the graph of $y = \sin x$. Can you see that by the horizontal line test, many horizontal lines can be drawn between -1 and 1 that intersect the graph infinitely many times? Thus, the sine function is not one-to-one and has no inverse function.

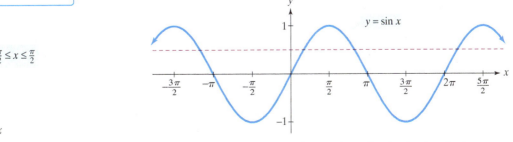

FIGURE 14.86 The horizontal line test shows that the sine function is not one-to-one and has no inverse function.

In Figure 14.87, we have taken a portion of the sine curve, restricting the domain of the sine function to $-\dfrac{\pi}{2} \leq x \leq \dfrac{\pi}{2}$. With this restricted domain, every horizontal line that can be drawn between -1 and 1 intersects the graph exactly once. Thus, the restricted function passes the horizontal line test and is one-to-one.

FIGURE 14.87 The restricted sine function passes the horizontal line test. It is one-to-one and has an inverse function.

874 CHAPTER 14 Trigonometric Functions

On the restricted domain $-\frac{\pi}{2} \leq x \leq \frac{\pi}{2}$, $y = \sin x$ has an inverse function. The inverse of the restricted sine function is called the **inverse sine function.** Two notations are commonly used to denote the inverse sine function:

$$y = \sin^{-1} x \quad \text{or} \quad y = \arcsin x.$$

In this book, we will use $y = \sin^{-1} x$.

> **The Inverse Sine Function**
>
> The **inverse sine function,** denoted by $\sin^{-1}$, is the inverse of the restricted sine function $y = \sin x$, $-\frac{\pi}{2} \leq x \leq \frac{\pi}{2}$. Thus,
>
> $$y = \sin^{-1} x \quad \text{means} \quad \sin y = x,$$
>
> where $-\frac{\pi}{2} \leq y \leq \frac{\pi}{2}$ and $-1 \leq x \leq 1$. We read $y = \sin^{-1} x$ as "y equals the inverse sine at x."

> ▸ **Helpful Hint**
>
> The notation $y = \sin^{-1} x$ does not mean $y = \dfrac{1}{\sin x}$. See the difference below.
>
> Inverse sine function: $y = \sin^{-1} x$
>
> Reciprocal of sine function: $y = (\sin x)^{-1} = \dfrac{1}{\sin x} = \csc x$

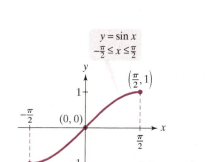

FIGURE 14.88 The restricted sine function

One way to graph $y = \sin^{-1} x$ is to take points on the graph of the restricted sine function and reverse the order of the coordinates. For example, Figure 14.88 shows that $\left(-\frac{\pi}{2}, -1\right)$, $(0, 0)$, and $\left(\frac{\pi}{2}, 1\right)$ are on the graph of the restricted sine function. Reversing the order of the coordinates gives $\left(-1, -\frac{\pi}{2}\right)$, $(0, 0)$, and $\left(1, \frac{\pi}{2}\right)$. We now use these three points to sketch the inverse sine function. The graph of $y = \sin^{-1} x$ is shown in Figure 14.89.

Another way to obtain the graph of $y = \sin^{-1} x$ is to reflect the graph of the restricted sine function about the line $y = x$, shown in Figure 14.90. The red graph is the restricted sine function and the blue graph is the graph of $y = \sin^{-1} x$.

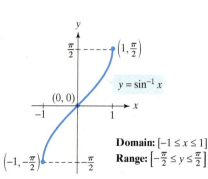

FIGURE 14.89 The graph of the inverse sine function

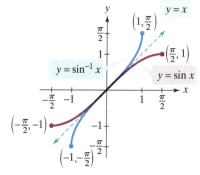

FIGURE 14.90 Using a reflection to obtain the graph of the inverse sine function

Exact values of $\sin^{-1} x$ can be found by thinking of **$\sin^{-1} x$ as the angle in the interval $-\dfrac{\pi}{2} \le y \le \dfrac{\pi}{2}$ whose sine is x.** For example, we can use the two points on the blue graph of the inverse sine function in Figure 14.90 to write

$$\sin^{-1}(-1) = -\frac{\pi}{2} \quad \text{and} \quad \sin^{-1} 1 = \frac{\pi}{2}.$$

> The angle whose sine is −1 is $-\dfrac{\pi}{2}$.

> The angle whose sine is 1 is $\dfrac{\pi}{2}$.

Because we are thinking of $\sin^{-1} x$ in terms of an angle, we will represent such an angle by θ.

Finding Exact Values of $\sin^{-1} x$

STEP 1. Let $\theta = \sin^{-1} x$.

STEP 2. Rewrite $\theta = \sin^{-1} x$ as $\sin \theta = x$, where $-\dfrac{\pi}{2} \le \theta \le \dfrac{\pi}{2}$.

STEP 3. Use the exact values in Table 14.7 to find the value of θ in $-\dfrac{\pi}{2} \le \theta \le \dfrac{\pi}{2}$ that satisfies $\sin \theta = x$.

TABLE 14.7 Exact Values for $\sin \theta$, $-\dfrac{\pi}{2} \le \theta \le \dfrac{\pi}{2}$

θ	$-\dfrac{\pi}{2}$	$-\dfrac{\pi}{3}$	$-\dfrac{\pi}{4}$	$-\dfrac{\pi}{6}$	0	$\dfrac{\pi}{6}$	$\dfrac{\pi}{4}$	$\dfrac{\pi}{3}$	$\dfrac{\pi}{2}$
$\sin \theta$	-1	$-\dfrac{\sqrt{3}}{2}$	$-\dfrac{\sqrt{2}}{2}$	$-\dfrac{1}{2}$	0	$\dfrac{1}{2}$	$\dfrac{\sqrt{2}}{2}$	$\dfrac{\sqrt{3}}{2}$	1

EXAMPLE 1 Finding the Exact Value of an Inverse Sine Function

Find the exact value of $\sin^{-1} \dfrac{\sqrt{2}}{2}$.

Solution

Step 1 Let $\theta = \sin^{-1} x$. Thus,

$$\theta = \sin^{-1} \frac{\sqrt{2}}{2}.$$

We must find the angle θ, $-\dfrac{\pi}{2} \le \theta \le \dfrac{\pi}{2}$, whose sine equals $\dfrac{\sqrt{2}}{2}$.

Step 2 Rewrite $\theta = \sin^{-1} x$ as $\sin \theta = x$, where $-\dfrac{\pi}{2} \le \theta \le \dfrac{\pi}{2}$. Using the definition of the inverse sine function, we rewrite $\theta = \sin^{-1} \dfrac{\sqrt{2}}{2}$ as

$$\sin \theta = \frac{\sqrt{2}}{2}, \text{ where } -\frac{\pi}{2} \le \theta \le \frac{\pi}{2}.$$

Step 3 Use the exact values in Table 14.7 to find the value of θ in $-\dfrac{\pi}{2} \le \theta \le \dfrac{\pi}{2}$ that satisfies $\sin \theta = x$. Table 14.7 shows that the only angle in the interval $-\dfrac{\pi}{2} \le \theta \le \dfrac{\pi}{2}$ that satisfies $\sin \theta = \dfrac{\sqrt{2}}{2}$ is $\dfrac{\pi}{4}$. Thus, $\theta = \dfrac{\pi}{4}$. Because θ, in step 1, represents $\sin^{-1} \dfrac{\sqrt{2}}{2}$, we conclude that

$$\sin^{-1} \frac{\sqrt{2}}{2} = \frac{\pi}{4}. \quad \text{The angle in } -\frac{\pi}{2} \le \theta \le \frac{\pi}{2} \text{ whose sine is } \frac{\sqrt{2}}{2} \text{ is } \frac{\pi}{4}. \quad \square$$

PRACTICE 1 Find the exact value of $\sin^{-1}\dfrac{\sqrt{3}}{2}$.

EXAMPLE 2 Finding the Exact Value of an Inverse Sine Function

Find the exact value of $\sin^{-1}\left(-\dfrac{1}{2}\right)$.

Solution

Step 1 Let $\theta = \sin^{-1} x$. Thus,

$$\theta = \sin^{-1}\left(-\dfrac{1}{2}\right).$$

We must find the angle θ, $-\dfrac{\pi}{2} \leq \theta \leq \dfrac{\pi}{2}$, whose sine equals $-\dfrac{1}{2}$.

Step 2 Rewrite $\theta = \sin^{-1} x$ as $\sin \theta = x$, where $-\dfrac{\pi}{2} \leq \theta \leq \dfrac{\pi}{2}$. We rewrite $\theta = \sin^{-1}\left(-\dfrac{1}{2}\right)$ and obtain

$$\sin \theta = -\dfrac{1}{2}, \text{ where } -\dfrac{\pi}{2} \leq \theta \leq \dfrac{\pi}{2}.$$

Step 3 Use the exact values in Table 14.7 to find the value of θ in $-\dfrac{\pi}{2} \leq \theta \leq \dfrac{\pi}{2}$ that satisfies $\sin \theta = x$. Table 14.7 shows that the only angle in the interval $-\dfrac{\pi}{2} \leq \theta \leq \dfrac{\pi}{2}$ that satisfies $\sin \theta = -\dfrac{1}{2}$ is $-\dfrac{\pi}{6}$. Thus,

$$\sin^{-1}\left(-\dfrac{1}{2}\right) = -\dfrac{\pi}{6}.$$

PRACTICE 2 Find the exact value of $\sin^{-1}\left(-\dfrac{\sqrt{2}}{2}\right)$.

Some inverse sine expressions cannot be evaluated. Because the domain of the inverse sine function is $-1 \leq x \leq 1$, it is only possible to evaluate $\sin^{-1} x$ for values of x in this domain. Thus, $\sin^{-1} 3$ cannot be evaluated. There is no angle whose sine is 3.

OBJECTIVE 2 ▶ The inverse cosine function. Figure 14.91 shows how we restrict the domain of the cosine function so that it becomes one-to-one and has an inverse function. Restrict the domain to the interval $0 \leq x \leq \pi$, shown by the dark blue graph. Over this interval, the restricted cosine function passes the horizontal line test and has an inverse function.

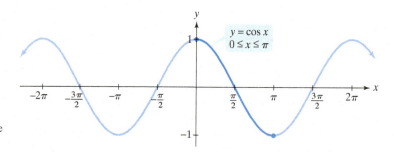

FIGURE 14.91 $y = \cos x$ is one-to-one on the interval $[0, \pi]$.

The Inverse Cosine Function

The **inverse cosine function,** denoted by $\cos^{-1}$, is the inverse of the restricted cosine function $y = \cos x$, $0 \leq x \leq \pi$. Thus,

$$y = \cos^{-1} x \quad \text{means} \quad \cos y = x,$$

where $0 \leq y \leq \pi$ and $-1 \leq x \leq 1$.

One way to graph $y = \cos^{-1} x$ is to take points on the graph of the restricted cosine function and reverse the order of the coordinates. For example, Figure 14.92 shows that $(0, 1)$, $\left(\dfrac{\pi}{2}, 0\right)$, and $(\pi, -1)$ are on the graph of the restricted cosine function. Reversing the order of the coordinates gives $(1, 0)$, $\left(0, \dfrac{\pi}{2}\right)$, and $(-1, \pi)$.

We now use these three points to sketch the inverse cosine function. The graph of $y = \cos^{-1} x$ is shown in Figure 14.93. You can also obtain this graph by reflecting the graph of the restricted cosine function about the line $y = x$.

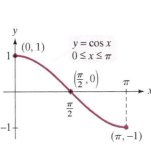

Domain: $[0 \leq x \leq \pi]$
Range: $[-1 \leq y \leq 1]$

FIGURE 14.92 The restricted cosine function

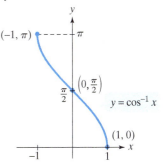

Domain: $[-1 \leq x \leq 1]$
Range: $[0 \leq y \leq \pi]$

FIGURE 14.93 The graph of the inverse cosine function

Exact values of $\cos^{-1} x$ can be found by thinking of $\cos^{-1} x$ **as the angle in the interval** $0 \leq y \leq \pi$ **whose cosine is** x.

Finding Exact Values of $\cos^{-1} x$

STEP 1. Let $\theta = \cos^{-1} x$.

STEP 2. Rewrite $\theta = \cos^{-1} x$ as $\cos \theta = x$, where $0 \leq \theta \leq \pi$.

STEP 3. Use the exact values in Table 14.8 to find the value of θ in $0 \leq \theta \leq \pi$ that satisfies $\cos \theta = x$.

TABLE 14.8 Exact Values for $\cos \theta$, $0 \leq \theta \leq \pi$

θ	0	$\dfrac{\pi}{6}$	$\dfrac{\pi}{4}$	$\dfrac{\pi}{3}$	$\dfrac{\pi}{2}$	$\dfrac{2\pi}{3}$	$\dfrac{3\pi}{4}$	$\dfrac{5\pi}{6}$	π
$\cos \theta$	1	$\dfrac{\sqrt{3}}{2}$	$\dfrac{\sqrt{2}}{2}$	$\dfrac{1}{2}$	0	$-\dfrac{1}{2}$	$-\dfrac{\sqrt{2}}{2}$	$-\dfrac{\sqrt{3}}{2}$	-1

EXAMPLE 3 Finding the Exact Value of an Inverse Cosine Function

Find the exact value of $\cos^{-1}\left(-\dfrac{\sqrt{3}}{2}\right)$.

Solution

Step 1 Let $\theta = \cos^{-1} x$. Thus,

$$\theta = \cos^{-1}\left(-\dfrac{\sqrt{3}}{2}\right).$$

We must find the angle θ, $0 \le \theta \le \pi$, whose cosine equals $-\dfrac{\sqrt{3}}{2}$.

Step 2 Rewrite $\theta = \cos^{-1} x$ as $\cos\theta = x$, where $0 \le \theta \le \pi$. We obtain

$$\cos\theta = -\frac{\sqrt{3}}{2}, \text{ where } 0 \le \theta \le \pi.$$

Step 3 Use the exact values in Table 14.8 to find the value of θ in $0 \le \theta \le \pi$ that satisfies $\cos\theta = x$. The table on the previous page shows that the only angle in the interval $0 \le \theta \le \pi$ that satisfies $\cos\theta = -\dfrac{\sqrt{3}}{2}$ is $\dfrac{5\pi}{6}$. Thus, $\theta = \dfrac{5\pi}{6}$ and

$$\cos^{-1}\left(-\frac{\sqrt{3}}{2}\right) = \frac{5\pi}{6}. \quad \text{The angle in } [0, \pi] \text{ whose cosine is } -\frac{\sqrt{3}}{2} \text{ is } \frac{5\pi}{6}.$$

PRACTICE 3 Find the exact value of $\cos^{-1}\left(-\dfrac{1}{2}\right)$.

OBJECTIVE 3 ▶ The inverse tangent function. Figure 14.94 shows how we restrict the domain of the tangent function so that it becomes one-to-one and has an inverse function. Restrict the domain to the interval $-\dfrac{\pi}{2} < x < \dfrac{\pi}{2}$, shown by the solid blue graph. Over this interval, the restricted tangent function passes the horizontal line test and has an inverse function.

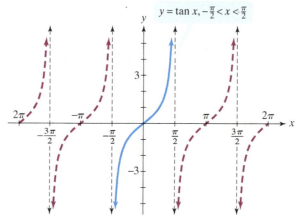

FIGURE 14.94 $y = \tan x$ is one-to-one on $-\dfrac{\pi}{2} < x < \dfrac{\pi}{2}$.

The Inverse Tangent Function
The **inverse tangent function**, denoted by $\tan^{-1}$, is the inverse of the restricted tangent function $y = \tan x$, $-\dfrac{\pi}{2} < x < \dfrac{\pi}{2}$. Thus,

$$y = \tan^{-1} x \quad \text{means} \quad \tan y = x,$$

where $-\dfrac{\pi}{2} < y < \dfrac{\pi}{2}$ and $-\infty < x < \infty$.

We graph $y = \tan^{-1} x$ by taking points on the graph of the restricted function and reversing the order of the coordinates. Figure 14.95 shows that $\left(-\dfrac{\pi}{4}, -1\right)$, $(0, 0)$, and

$\left(\frac{\pi}{4}, 1\right)$ are on the graph of the restricted tangent function. Reversing the order gives $\left(-1, -\frac{\pi}{4}\right)$, $(0, 0)$, and $\left(1, \frac{\pi}{4}\right)$. We now use these three points to graph the inverse tangent function. The graph of $y = \tan^{-1} x$ is shown in Figure 14.96. Notice that the vertical asymptotes become horizontal asymptotes for the graph of the inverse function.

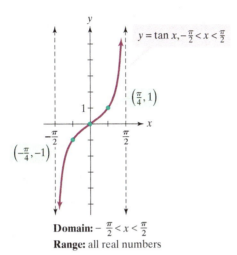

FIGURE 14.95 The restricted tangent function

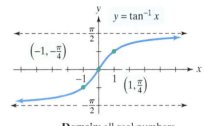

FIGURE 14.96 The graph of the inverse tangent function

Exact values of $\tan^{-1} x$ can be found by thinking of **$\tan^{-1} x$ as the angle in the interval $-\frac{\pi}{2} < y < \frac{\pi}{2}$ whose tangent is x.**

Finding Exact Values of $\tan^{-1} x$

STEP 1. Let $\theta = \tan^{-1} x$.

STEP 2. Rewrite $\theta = \tan^{-1} x$ as $\tan \theta = x$, where $-\frac{\pi}{2} < \theta < \frac{\pi}{2}$.

STEP 3. Use the exact values in Table 14.9 to find the value of θ in $-\frac{\pi}{2} < \theta < \frac{\pi}{2}$ that satisfies $\tan \theta = x$.

TABLE 14.9 Exact Values for $\tan \theta$, $-\frac{\pi}{2} < \theta < \frac{\pi}{2}$

θ	$-\frac{\pi}{3}$	$-\frac{\pi}{4}$	$-\frac{\pi}{6}$	0	$\frac{\pi}{6}$	$\frac{\pi}{4}$	$\frac{\pi}{3}$
$\tan \theta$	$-\sqrt{3}$	-1	$-\frac{\sqrt{3}}{3}$	0	$\frac{\sqrt{3}}{3}$	1	$\sqrt{3}$

EXAMPLE 4 Finding the Exact Value of an Inverse Tangent Function

Find the exact value of $\tan^{-1} \sqrt{3}$.

Solution

Step 1 Let $\theta = \tan^{-1} x$. Thus,
$$\theta = \tan^{-1} \sqrt{3}.$$

We must find the angle θ, $-\frac{\pi}{2} < \theta < \frac{\pi}{2}$, whose tangent equals $\sqrt{3}$.

Step 2 Rewrite $\theta = \tan^{-1} x$ as $\tan \theta = x$, where $-\dfrac{\pi}{2} < \theta < \dfrac{\pi}{2}$. We obtain

$$\tan \theta = \sqrt{3}, \text{ where } -\dfrac{\pi}{2} < \theta < \dfrac{\pi}{2}.$$

Step 3 Use the exact values in Table 14.9 to find the value of θ in $-\dfrac{\pi}{2} < \theta < \dfrac{\pi}{2}$ that satisfies $\tan \theta = x$. The table on the previous page shows that the only angle in the interval $-\dfrac{\pi}{2} < \theta < \dfrac{\pi}{2}$ that satisfies $\tan \theta = \sqrt{3}$ is $\dfrac{\pi}{3}$. Thus, $\theta = \dfrac{\pi}{3}$ and

$$\tan^{-1} \sqrt{3} = \dfrac{\pi}{3}. \quad \text{The angle in } \left(-\dfrac{\pi}{2}, \dfrac{\pi}{2}\right) \text{ whose tangent is } \sqrt{3} \text{ is } \dfrac{\pi}{3}.$$

PRACTICE 4 Find the exact value of $\tan^{-1}(-1)$.

OBJECTIVE 4 ▶ **Using a calculator to evaluate inverse trigonometric functions.** Calculators give approximate values of inverse trigonometric functions. Use the secondary keys marked $\boxed{\text{SIN}^{-1}}$, $\boxed{\text{COS}^{-1}}$, and $\boxed{\text{TAN}^{-1}}$. These keys are not buttons that you actually press. They are the secondary functions for the buttons labeled $\boxed{\text{SIN}}$, $\boxed{\text{COS}}$, and $\boxed{\text{TAN}}$, respectively. Consult your manual for the location of this feature.

EXAMPLE 5 Calculators and Inverse Trigonometric Functions

Use a calculator to find the value to four decimal places of each function:

a. $\sin^{-1} \dfrac{1}{4}$ **b.** $\tan^{-1}(-9.65)$.

Solution

Scientific Calculator Solution

Function	Mode	Keystrokes	Display, Rounded to Four Places
a. $\sin^{-1} \dfrac{1}{4}$	Radian	1 $\boxed{\div}$ 4 $\boxed{=}$ $\boxed{\text{2nd}}$ $\boxed{\text{SIN}}$	0.2527
b. $\tan^{-1}(-9.65)$	Radian	9.65 $\boxed{+/-}$ $\boxed{\text{2nd}}$ $\boxed{\text{TAN}}$	-1.4675

Graphing Calculator Solution

Function	Mode	Keystrokes	Display, Rounded to Four Places
a. $\sin^{-1} \dfrac{1}{4}$	Radian	$\boxed{\text{2nd}}$ $\boxed{\text{SIN}}$ $\boxed{(}$ 1 $\boxed{\div}$ 4 $\boxed{)}$ $\boxed{\text{ENTER}}$	0.2527
b. $\tan^{-1}(-9.65)$	Radian	$\boxed{\text{2nd}}$ $\boxed{\text{TAN}}$ $\boxed{(-)}$ 9.65 $\boxed{\text{ENTER}}$	-1.4675

PRACTICE 5 Use a calculator to find the value to four decimal places of each function:

a. $\cos^{-1} \dfrac{1}{3}$ **b.** $\tan^{-1}(-35.85)$.

What happens if you attempt to evaluate an inverse trigomometric function at a value that is not in its domain? In real number mode, most calculators will display an error message. For example, an error message can result if you attempt to approximate

$\cos^{-1} 3$. There is no angle whose cosine is 3. The domain of the inverse cosine function is $-1 \leq x \leq 1$ and 3 does not belong to this domain.

OBJECTIVE 5 ▶ **Composition of functions involving inverse trigonometric functions.**
In our earlier discussion of functions and their inverses, we saw that

$$f(f^{-1}(x)) = x \quad \text{and} \quad f^{-1}(f(x)) = x.$$

- x must be in the domain of f^{-1}.
- x must be in the domain of f.

We apply these properties to the sine, cosine, tangent, and their inverse functions to obtain the following properties:

Inverse Properties

The Sine Function and Its Inverse

$$\sin(\sin^{-1} x) = x \quad \text{for } -1 \leq x \leq 1$$

$$\sin^{-1}(\sin x) = x \quad \text{for } -\frac{\pi}{2} \leq x \leq \frac{\pi}{2}$$

The Cosine Function and Its Inverse

$$\cos(\cos^{-1} x) = x \quad \text{for } -1 \leq x \leq 1$$

$$\cos^{-1}(\cos x) = x \quad \text{for } 0 \leq x \leq \pi$$

The Tangent Function and Its Inverse

$$\tan(\tan^{-1} x) = x \quad \text{for every real number } x$$

$$\tan^{-1}(\tan x) = x \quad \text{for } -\frac{\pi}{2} < x < \frac{\pi}{2}$$

The restrictions on x in the inverse properties are a bit tricky. For example,

$$\sin^{-1}\left(\sin \frac{\pi}{4}\right) = \frac{\pi}{4}.$$

$\sin^{-1}(\sin x) = x$ for $\left[-\frac{\pi}{2} \leq x \leq \frac{\pi}{2}\right]$.
Observe that $\frac{\pi}{4}$ is in this interval.

Can we use $\sin^{-1}(\sin x) = x$ to find the exact value of $\sin^{-1}\left(\sin \frac{5\pi}{4}\right)$? Is $\frac{5\pi}{4}$ in the interval $-\frac{\pi}{2} \leq x \leq \frac{\pi}{2}$? No. Thus, to evaluate $\sin^{-1}\left(\sin \frac{5\pi}{4}\right)$, we must first find $\sin \frac{5\pi}{4}$.

$\frac{5\pi}{4}$ is in quadrant III, where the sine is negative.

$$\sin \frac{5\pi}{4} = -\sin \frac{\pi}{4} = -\frac{\sqrt{2}}{2}$$

The reference angle for $\frac{5\pi}{4}$ is $\frac{\pi}{4}$.

We evaluate $\sin^{-1}\left(\sin\frac{5\pi}{4}\right)$ as follows:

$$\sin^{-1}\left(\sin\frac{5\pi}{4}\right) = \sin^{-1}\left(-\frac{\sqrt{2}}{2}\right) = -\frac{\pi}{4}.$$ If necessary, see Table 14.7 on page 875.

To determine how to evaluate the composition of functions involving inverse trigonometric functions, first examine the value of x. You can use the inverse properties in the box only if x is in the specified interval.

EXAMPLE 6 Evaluating Compositions of Functions and Their Inverses

Find the exact value, if possible:

a. $\cos(\cos^{-1} 0.6)$ **b.** $\sin^{-1}\left(\sin\frac{3\pi}{2}\right)$ **c.** $\cos(\cos^{-1} 1.5)$.

Solution

a. The inverse property $\cos(\cos^{-1} x) = x$ applies for $-1 \le x \le 1$. To evaluate $\cos(\cos^{-1} 0.6)$, observe that $x = 0.6$. This value of x lies in $-1 \le x \le 1$, which is the domain of the inverse cosine function. This means that we can use the inverse property $\cos(\cos^{-1} x) = x$. Thus,

$$\cos(\cos^{-1} 0.6) = 0.6.$$

b. The inverse property $\sin^{-1}(\sin x) = x$ applies for $-\frac{\pi}{2} \le x \le \frac{\pi}{2}$. To evaluate $\sin^{-1}\left(\sin\frac{3\pi}{2}\right)$, observe that $x = \frac{3\pi}{2}$. This value of x does not lie in $-\frac{\pi}{2} \le x \le \frac{\pi}{2}$.

To evaluate this expression, we first find $\sin\frac{3\pi}{2}$.

$$\sin^{-1}\left(\sin\frac{3\pi}{2}\right) = \sin^{-1}(-1) = -\frac{\pi}{2} \quad \text{The angle in } \left[-\frac{\pi}{2}, \frac{\pi}{2}\right] \text{ whose sine is } -1 \text{ is } -\frac{\pi}{2}.$$

c. The inverse property $\cos(\cos^{-1} x) = x$ applies for $-1 \le x \le 1$. To attempt to evaluate $\cos(\cos^{-1} 1.5)$, observe that $x = 1.5$. This value of x does not lie in $-1 \le x \le 1$, which is the domain of the inverse cosine function. Thus, the expression $\cos(\cos^{-1} 1.5)$ is not defined because $\cos^{-1} 1.5$ is not defined. □

PRACTICE 6 Find the exact value, if possible:

a. $\cos(\cos^{-1} 0.7)$ **b.** $\sin^{-1}(\sin \pi)$ **c.** $\cos[\cos^{-1}(-1.2)]$.

We can use points on terminal sides of angles in standard position to find exact values of expressions involving the composition of a function and a different inverse function. Here are two examples:

$$\cos\left(\tan^{-1}\frac{5}{12}\right) \qquad \cot\left[\sin^{-1}\left(-\frac{1}{3}\right)\right].$$

Inner part involves the angle in $\left(-\frac{\pi}{2}, \frac{\pi}{2}\right)$ whose tangent is $\frac{5}{12}$.

Inner part involves the angle in $\left[-\frac{\pi}{2}, \frac{\pi}{2}\right]$ whose sine is $-\frac{1}{3}$.

The inner part of each expression involves an angle. To evaluate such expressions, we represent such angles by θ. Then we use a sketch that illustrates our representation. Examples 7 and 8 show how to carry out such evaluations.

EXAMPLE 7 Evaluating a Composite Trigonometric Expression

Find the exact value of $\cos\left(\tan^{-1}\dfrac{5}{12}\right)$.

Solution We let θ represent the angle in $-\dfrac{\pi}{2} < \theta < \dfrac{\pi}{2}$ whose tangent is $\dfrac{5}{12}$. Thus,

$$\theta = \tan^{-1}\dfrac{5}{12}.$$

We are looking for the exact value of $\cos\left(\tan^{-1}\dfrac{5}{12}\right)$, with $\theta = \tan^{-1}\dfrac{5}{12}$. Using the definition of the inverse tangent function, we can rewrite $\theta = \tan^{-1}\dfrac{5}{12}$ as

$$\tan\theta = \dfrac{5}{12}, \quad \text{where} \quad -\dfrac{\pi}{2} < \theta < \dfrac{\pi}{2}.$$

Because $\tan\theta$ is positive, θ must be an angle in $0 < \theta < \dfrac{\pi}{2}$. Thus, θ is a first-quadrant angle. Figure 14.97 shows a right triangle in quadrant I with

$$\tan\theta = \dfrac{5}{12}. \quad \text{\small Side opposite } \theta \text{, or } y \;/\; \text{Side adjacent to } \theta \text{, or } x$$

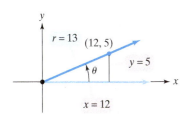

FIGURE 14.97 Representing $\tan\theta = \dfrac{5}{12}$

The hypotenuse of the triangle, r, or the distance from the origin to $(12, 5)$, is found using $r = \sqrt{x^2 + y^2}$.

$$r = \sqrt{x^2 + y^2} = \sqrt{12^2 + 5^2} = \sqrt{144 + 25} = \sqrt{169} = 13$$

We use the values for x and r to find the exact value of $\cos\left(\tan^{-1}\dfrac{5}{12}\right)$.

$$\cos\left(\tan^{-1}\dfrac{5}{12}\right) = \cos\theta = \dfrac{\text{side adjacent to } \theta, \text{ or } x}{\text{hypotenuse, or } r} = \dfrac{12}{13} \quad \blacksquare$$

PRACTICE 7 Find the exact value of $\sin\left(\tan^{-1}\dfrac{3}{4}\right)$.

EXAMPLE 8 Evaluating a Composite Trigonometric Expression

Find the exact value of $\cot\left[\sin^{-1}\left(-\dfrac{1}{3}\right)\right]$.

Solution We let θ represent the angle in $-\dfrac{\pi}{2} \leq \theta \leq \dfrac{\pi}{2}$ whose sine is $-\dfrac{1}{3}$. Thus,

$$\theta = \sin^{-1}\left(-\dfrac{1}{3}\right) \quad \text{and} \quad \sin\theta = -\dfrac{1}{3}, \quad \text{where} \quad -\dfrac{\pi}{2} \leq \theta \leq \dfrac{\pi}{2}.$$

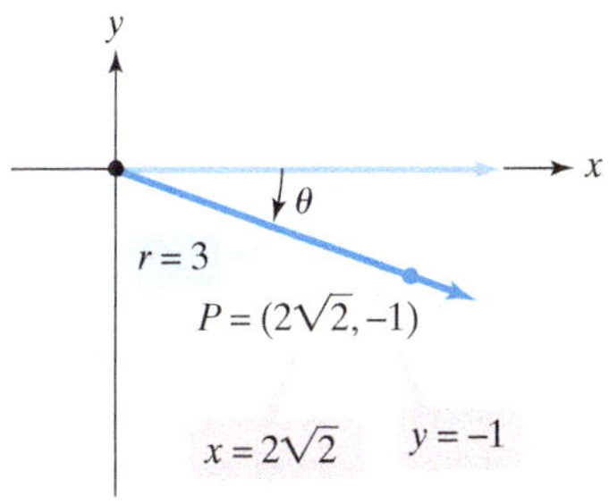

Because $\sin\theta$ is negative in $\sin\theta = -\dfrac{1}{3}$, θ must be an angle in $-\dfrac{\pi}{2} \leq \theta < 0$. Thus, θ is a negative angle that lies in quadrant IV. Figure 14.98 shows angle θ in quadrant IV with

$$\sin\theta = -\dfrac{1}{3} = \dfrac{y}{r} = \dfrac{-1}{3}. \quad \text{\small In quadrant IV, } y \text{ is negative.}$$

FIGURE 14.98 Representing $\sin\theta = -\dfrac{1}{3}$

Thus, $y = -1$ and $r = 3$. The value of x can be found using $r = \sqrt{x^2 + y^2}$ or $x^2 + y^2 = r^2$.

$$x^2 + (-1)^2 = 3^2 \qquad \text{Use } x^2 + y^2 = r^2 \text{ with } y = -1 \text{ and } r = 3.$$
$$x^2 + 1 = 9 \qquad \text{Square } -1 \text{ and square } 3.$$
$$x^2 = 8 \qquad \text{Subtract 1 from both sides.}$$
$$x = \sqrt{8} = \sqrt{4 \cdot 2} = 2\sqrt{2} \qquad \text{Use the square root property. Remember that } x \text{ is positive in quadrant IV.}$$

We use values for x and y to find the exact value of $\cot\left[\sin^{-1}\left(-\frac{1}{3}\right)\right]$.

$$\cot\left[\sin^{-1}\left(-\frac{1}{3}\right)\right] = \cot\theta = \frac{x}{y} = \frac{2\sqrt{2}}{-1} = -2\sqrt{2}$$

PRACTICE 8 Find the exact value of $\cos\left[\sin^{-1}\left(-\frac{1}{2}\right)\right]$.

Some composite functions with inverse trigonometric functions can be simplified to algebraic expressions. To simplify such an expression, we represent the inverse trigonometric function in the expression by θ. Then we use a right triangle.

EXAMPLE 9 Simplifying an Expression Involving $\sin^{-1} x$

If $0 < x \leq 1$, write $\cos(\sin^{-1} x)$ as an algebraic expression in x.

Solution We let θ represent the angle in $-\frac{\pi}{2} \leq \theta \leq \frac{\pi}{2}$ whose sine is x. Thus,

$$\theta = \sin^{-1} x \quad \text{and} \quad \sin\theta = x, \quad \text{where} \quad -\frac{\pi}{2} \leq \theta \leq \frac{\pi}{2}.$$

Because $0 < x \leq 1$, $\sin\theta$ is positive. Thus, θ is a first-quadrant angle and can be represented as an acute angle of a right triangle. Figure 14.99 shows a right triangle with

$$\sin\theta = x = \frac{x}{1}. \quad \begin{array}{l}\text{Side opposite }\theta\\ \text{Hypotenuse}\end{array}$$

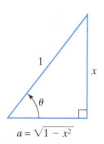

FIGURE 14.99 Representing $\sin\theta = x$

The third side, a in Figure 14.99, can be found using the Pythagorean Theorem.

$$a^2 + x^2 = 1^2 \qquad \text{Apply the Pythagorean Theorem to the right triangle in Figure 14.99.}$$
$$a^2 = 1 - x^2 \qquad \text{Subtract } x^2 \text{ from both sides.}$$
$$a = \sqrt{1 - x^2} \qquad \text{Use the square root property and solve for } a. \text{ Remember that side } a \text{ is positive.}$$

We use the right triangle in Figure 14.99 to write $\cos(\sin^{-1} x)$ as an algebraic expression.

$$\cos(\sin^{-1} x) = \cos\theta = \frac{\text{side adjacent to }\theta}{\text{hypotenuse}} = \frac{\sqrt{1 - x^2}}{1} = \sqrt{1 - x^2}$$

PRACTICE 9 If $x > 0$, write $\sec(\tan^{-1} x)$ as an algebraic expression in x.

14.7 EXERCISE SET

PRACTICE EXERCISES

In Exercises 1–18, find the exact value of each expression.

1. $\sin^{-1}\frac{1}{2}$
2. $\sin^{-1} 0$
3. $\sin^{-1}\frac{\sqrt{2}}{2}$
4. $\sin^{-1}\frac{\sqrt{3}}{2}$
5. $\sin^{-1}\left(-\frac{1}{2}\right)$
6. $\sin^{-1}\left(-\frac{\sqrt{3}}{2}\right)$
7. $\cos^{-1}\frac{\sqrt{3}}{2}$
8. $\cos^{-1}\frac{\sqrt{2}}{2}$
9. $\cos^{-1}\left(-\frac{\sqrt{2}}{2}\right)$
10. $\cos^{-1}\left(-\frac{\sqrt{3}}{2}\right)$
11. $\cos^{-1} 0$
12. $\cos^{-1} 1$
13. $\tan^{-1}\frac{\sqrt{3}}{3}$
14. $\tan^{-1} 1$
15. $\tan^{-1} 0$
16. $\tan^{-1}(-1)$
17. $\tan^{-1}(-\sqrt{3})$
18. $\tan^{-1}\left(-\frac{\sqrt{3}}{3}\right)$

In Exercises 19–30, use a calculator to find the value of each expression rounded to two decimal places.

19. $\sin^{-1} 0.3$
20. $\sin^{-1} 0.47$
21. $\sin^{-1}(-0.32)$
22. $\sin^{-1}(-0.625)$
23. $\cos^{-1}\frac{3}{8}$
24. $\cos^{-1}\frac{4}{9}$
25. $\cos^{-1}\frac{\sqrt{5}}{7}$
26. $\cos^{-1}\frac{\sqrt{7}}{10}$
27. $\tan^{-1}(-20)$
28. $\tan^{-1}(-30)$
29. $\tan^{-1}(-\sqrt{473})$
30. $\tan^{-1}(-\sqrt{5061})$

In Exercises 31–46, find the exact value of each expression, if possible. Do not use a calculator.

31. $\sin(\sin^{-1} 0.9)$
32. $\cos(\cos^{-1} 0.57)$
33. $\sin^{-1}\left(\sin\frac{\pi}{3}\right)$
34. $\cos^{-1}\left(\cos\frac{2\pi}{3}\right)$
35. $\sin^{-1}\left(\sin\frac{5\pi}{6}\right)$
36. $\cos^{-1}\left(\cos\frac{4\pi}{3}\right)$
37. $\tan(\tan^{-1} 125)$
38. $\tan(\tan^{-1} 380)$
39. $\tan^{-1}\left[\tan\left(-\frac{\pi}{6}\right)\right]$
40. $\tan^{-1}\left[\tan\left(-\frac{\pi}{3}\right)\right]$
41. $\tan^{-1}\left(\tan\frac{2\pi}{3}\right)$
42. $\tan^{-1}\left(\tan\frac{3\pi}{4}\right)$
43. $\sin^{-1}(\sin \pi)$
44. $\cos^{-1}(\cos 2\pi)$
45. $\sin(\sin^{-1} \pi)$
46. $\cos^{-1}(\cos^{-1} 3\pi)$

In Exercises 47–62, use a sketch to find the exact value of each expression.

47. $\cos\left(\sin^{-1}\frac{4}{5}\right)$
48. $\sin\left(\tan^{-1}\frac{7}{24}\right)$
49. $\tan\left(\cos^{-1}\frac{5}{13}\right)$
50. $\cot\left(\sin^{-1}\frac{5}{13}\right)$
51. $\tan\left[\sin^{-1}\left(-\frac{3}{5}\right)\right]$
52. $\cos\left[\sin^{-1}\left(-\frac{4}{5}\right)\right]$
53. $\sin\left(\cos^{-1}\frac{\sqrt{2}}{2}\right)$
54. $\cos\left(\sin^{-1}\frac{1}{2}\right)$
55. $\sec\left[\sin^{-1}\left(-\frac{1}{4}\right)\right]$
56. $\sec\left[\sin^{-1}\left(-\frac{1}{2}\right)\right]$
57. $\tan\left[\cos^{-1}\left(-\frac{1}{3}\right)\right]$
58. $\tan\left[\cos^{-1}\left(-\frac{1}{4}\right)\right]$
59. $\csc\left[\cos^{-1}\left(-\frac{\sqrt{3}}{2}\right)\right]$
60. $\sec\left[\sin^{-1}\left(-\frac{\sqrt{2}}{2}\right)\right]$
61. $\cos\left[\tan^{-1}\left(-\frac{2}{3}\right)\right]$
62. $\sin\left[\tan^{-1}\left(-\frac{3}{4}\right)\right]$

In Exercises 63–72, use a right triangle to write each expression as an algebraic expression. Assume that x is positive and that the given inverse trigonometric function is defined for the expression in x.

63. $\tan(\cos^{-1} x)$
64. $\sin(\tan^{-1} x)$
65. $\cos(\sin^{-1} 2x)$
66. $\sin(\cos^{-1} 2x)$
67. $\cos\left(\sin^{-1}\frac{1}{x}\right)$
68. $\sec\left(\cos^{-1}\frac{1}{x}\right)$
69. $\cot\left(\tan^{-1}\frac{x}{\sqrt{3}}\right)$
70. $\cot\left(\tan^{-1}\frac{x}{\sqrt{2}}\right)$
71. $\sec\left(\sin^{-1}\frac{x}{\sqrt{x^2+4}}\right)$
72. $\cot\left(\sin^{-1}\frac{\sqrt{x^2-9}}{x}\right)$

PRACTICE PLUS

In Exercises 73–80, determine the domain and the range of each function.

73. $f(x) = \sin(\sin^{-1} x)$
74. $f(x) = \cos(\cos^{-1} x)$
75. $f(x) = \cos^{-1}(\cos x)$
76. $f(x) = \sin^{-1}(\sin x)$
77. $f(x) = \sin^{-1}(\cos x)$
78. $f(x) = \cos^{-1}(\sin x)$
79. $f(x) = \sin^{-1} x + \cos^{-1} x$
80. $f(x) = \cos^{-1} x - \sin^{-1} x$

APPLICATION EXERCISES

81. Your neighborhood movie theater has a 25-foot-high screen located 8 feet above your eye level. If you sit too close to the screen, your viewing angle is too small, resulting in a distorted picture. By contrast, if you sit too far back, the image is quite small, diminishing the movie's visual impact. If you sit x feet back from the screen, your viewing angle, θ, is given by

$$\theta = \tan^{-1}\frac{33}{x} - \tan^{-1}\frac{8}{x}.$$

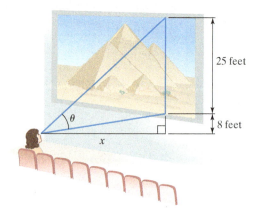

Find the viewing angle, in radians, at distances of 5 feet, 10 feet, 15 feet, 20 feet, and 25 feet.

82. The function $\theta = \tan^{-1}\dfrac{33}{x} - \tan^{-1}\dfrac{8}{x}$, described in Exercise 81, is graphed below in a $[0, 50, 10]$ by $[0, 1, 0.1]$ viewing rectangle. Use the graph to describe what happens to your viewing angle as you move farther back from the screen. How far back from the screen, to the nearest foot, should you sit to maximize your viewing angle? Verify this observation by finding the viewing angle one foot closer to the screen and one foot farther from the screen for this ideal viewing distance.

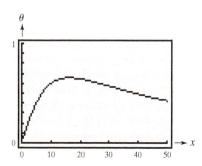

The formula
$$\theta = 2\tan^{-1}\dfrac{21.634}{x}$$
gives the viewing angle, θ, in radians, for a camera whose lens is x millimeters wide. Use this formula to solve Exercises 83–84.

83. Find the viewing angle, in radians and in degrees (to the nearest tenth of a degree), of a 28-millimeter lens.
84. Find the viewing angle, in radians and in degrees (to the nearest tenth of a degree), of a 300-millimeter telephoto lens.

For years, mathematicians were challenged by the following problem: What is the area of a region under a curve between two values of x? The problem was solved in the seventeenth century with the development of integral calculus. Using calculus, the area of the region under $y = \dfrac{1}{x^2 + 1}$, above the x-axis, and between $x = a$ and $x = b$ is $\tan^{-1} b - \tan^{-1} a$. Use this result, shown in the figure, to find the area of the region under $y = \dfrac{1}{x^2 + 1}$, above the x-axis, and between the values of a and b given in Exercises 85–86.

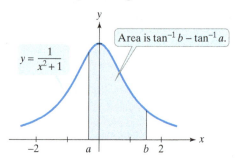

85. $a = 0$ and $b = 2$
86. $a = -2$ and $b = 1$

WRITING IN MATHEMATICS

87. Explain why, without restrictions, no trigonometric function has an inverse function.
88. Describe the restriction on the sine function so that it has an inverse function.
89. How can the graph of $y = \sin^{-1} x$ be obtained from the graph of the restricted sine function?
90. Without drawing a graph, describe the behavior of the graph of $y = \sin^{-1} x$. Mention the function's domain and range in your description.
91. Describe the restriction on the cosine function so that it has an inverse function.
92. Without drawing a graph, describe the behavior of the graph of $y = \cos^{-1} x$. Mention the function's domain and range in your description.
93. Describe the restriction on the tangent function so that it has an inverse function.
94. Without drawing a graph, describe the behavior of the graph of $y = \tan^{-1} x$. Mention the function's domain and range in your description.
95. If $\sin^{-1}\left(\sin\dfrac{\pi}{3}\right) = \dfrac{\pi}{3}$, is $\sin^{-1}\left(\sin\dfrac{5\pi}{6}\right) = \dfrac{5\pi}{6}$? Explain your answer.
96. Explain how a right triangle can be used to find the exact value of $\sec\left(\sin^{-1}\dfrac{4}{5}\right)$.
97. Find the height of the screen and the number of feet that it is located above eye level in your favorite movie theater. Modify the formula given in Exercise 81 so that it applies to your theater. Then describe where in the theater you should sit so that a movie creates the greatest visual impact.

TECHNOLOGY EXERCISES

In Exercises 98–101, graph each pair of functions in the same viewing rectangle. Use your knowledge of the domain and range for the inverse trigonometric function to select an appropriate viewing rectangle. How is the graph of the second equation in each exercise related to the graph of the first equation?

98. $y = \sin^{-1} x$ and $y = \sin^{-1} x + 2$

99. $y = \cos^{-1} x$ and $y = \cos^{-1}(x - 1)$

100. $y = \tan^{-1} x$ and $y = -2 \tan^{-1} x$

101. $y = \sin^{-1} x$ and $y = \sin^{-1}(x + 2) + 1$

102. Graph $y = \tan^{-1} x$ and its two horizontal asymptotes in a $[-3, 3, 1]$ by $\left[-\pi, \pi, \dfrac{\pi}{2}\right]$ viewing rectangle. Then change the viewing rectangle to $[-50, 50, 5]$ by $\left[-\pi, \pi, \dfrac{\pi}{2}\right]$. What do you observe?

103. Graph $y = \sin^{-1} x + \cos^{-1} x$ in a $[-2, 2, 1]$ by $[0, 3, 1]$ viewing rectangle. What appears to be true about the sum of the inverse sine and inverse cosine for values between -1 and 1, inclusive?

CRITICAL THINKING EXERCISES

Make Sense? *In Exercises 104–107, determine whether each statement makes sense or does not make sense, and explain your reasoning.*

104. Because $y = \sin x$ has an inverse function if x is restricted to $-\dfrac{\pi}{2} \leq x \leq \dfrac{\pi}{2}$, they should make restrictions easier to remember by also using $-\dfrac{\pi}{2} \leq x \leq \dfrac{\pi}{2}$ as the restriction for $y = \cos x$.

105. Because $y = \sin x$ has an inverse function if x is restricted to $-\dfrac{\pi}{2} \leq x \leq \dfrac{\pi}{2}$, they should make restrictions easier to remember by also using $-\dfrac{\pi}{2} \leq x \leq \dfrac{\pi}{2}$ as the restriction for $y = \tan x$.

106. Although $\sin^{-1}\left(-\dfrac{1}{2}\right)$ is negative, $\cos^{-1}\left(-\dfrac{1}{2}\right)$ is positive.

107. I used $f^{-1}(f(x)) = x$ and concluded that $\sin^{-1}\left(\sin \dfrac{5\pi}{4}\right) = \dfrac{5\pi}{4}$.

108. Solve $y = 2 \sin^{-1}(x - 5)$ for x in terms of y.

109. Solve for x: $2 \sin^{-1} x = \dfrac{\pi}{4}$.

110. Prove that if $x > 0$, $\tan^{-1} x + \tan^{-1} \dfrac{1}{x} = \dfrac{\pi}{2}$.

111. Derive the formula for θ, your viewing angle at the movie theater, in Exercise 93. *Hint:* Use the figure shown and represent the acute angle on the left in the smaller right triangle by α. Find expressions for $\tan \alpha$ and $\tan(\alpha + \theta)$.

REVIEW AND PREVIEW

Exercises 112–114 will help you prepare for the material covered in the next section.

112. Use trigonometric functions to find a and c to two decimal places.

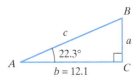

113. Find θ to the nearest tenth of a degree.

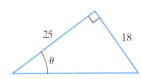

114. Determine the amplitude and period of $y = 10 \cos \dfrac{\pi}{6} x$.

14.8 APPLICATIONS OF TRIGONOMETRIC FUNCTIONS

OBJECTIVES

1. Solve a right triangle.
2. Solve problems involving bearings.
3. Model simple harmonic motion.

In the late 1960s, popular musicians were searching for new sounds. Film composers were looking for ways to create unique sounds as well. From these efforts, synthesizers that electronically reproduce musical sounds were born. From providing the backbone of today's most popular music to providing the strange sounds for the most

888 CHAPTER 14 Trigonometric Functions

experimental music, synthesizing programs now available on computers are at the forefront of music technology.

If we did not understand the periodic nature of sine and cosine functions, the synthesizing programs used in almost all forms of music would not exist. In this section, we look at applications of trigonometric functions in solving right triangles and in modeling periodic phenomena such as sound.

OBJECTIVE 1 ▶ Solving right triangles. **Solving a right triangle** means finding the missing lengths of its sides and the measurements of its angles. We will label right triangles so that side a is opposite angle A, side b is opposite angle B, and side c, the hypotenuse, is opposite right angle C. Figure 14.100 illustrates this labeling.

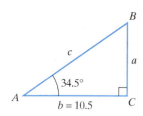

FIGURE 14.100 Labeling right triangles

When solving a right triangle, we will use the sine, cosine, and tangent functions, rather than their reciprocals. Example 1 shows how to solve a right triangle when we know the length of a side and the measure of an acute angle.

EXAMPLE 1   Solving a Right Triangle

Solve the right triangle shown in Figure 14.101, rounding lengths to two decimal places.

Solution We begin by finding the measure of angle B. We do not need a trigonometric function to do so. Because $C = 90°$ and the sum of a triangle's angles is $180°$, we see that $A + B = 90°$. Thus,

$$B = 90° - A = 90° - 34.5° = 55.5°.$$

Now we need to find a. Because we have a known angle, an unknown opposite side, and a known adjacent side, we use the tangent function.

$$\tan 34.5° = \frac{a}{10.5} \quad \begin{array}{l}\text{Side opposite the 34.5° angle}\\ \text{Side adjacent to the 34.5° angle}\end{array}$$

FIGURE 14.101 Find B, a, and c.

Now we multiply both sides of this equation by 10.5 and solve for a.

$$a = 10.5 \tan 34.5° \approx 7.22$$

Finally, we need to find c. Because we have a known angle, a known adjacent side, and an unknown hypotenuse, we use the cosine function.

$$\cos 34.5° = \frac{10.5}{c} \quad \begin{array}{l}\text{Side adjacent to the 34.5° angle}\\ \text{Hypotenuse}\end{array}$$

Now we multiply both sides of $\cos 34.5° = \dfrac{10.5}{c}$ by c and then solve for c.

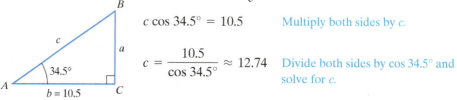

$c \cos 34.5° = 10.5$ Multiply both sides by c.

$c = \dfrac{10.5}{\cos 34.5°} \approx 12.74$ Divide both sides by $\cos 34.5°$ and solve for c.

FIGURE 14.101 (repeated)

---DISCOVERY---

There is often more than one correct way to solve a right triangle. In Example 1, find a using angle $B = 55.5°$. Find c using the Pythagorean Theorem.

In summary, $B = 55.5°$, $a \approx 7.22$, and $c \approx 12.74$.

PRACTICE 1 In Figure 14.100 on the previous page, let $A = 62.7°$ and $a = 8.4$. Solve the right triangle, rounding lengths to two decimal places.

Trigonometry was first developed to measure heights and distances that were inconvenient or impossible to measure directly. In solving application problems, begin by making a sketch involving a right triangle that illustrates the problem's conditions. Then put your knowledge of solving right triangles to work and find the required distance or height.

EXAMPLE 2 Finding a Side of a Right Triangle

From a point on level ground 125 feet from the base of a tower, the angle of elevation is 57.2°. Approximate the height of the tower to the nearest foot.

Solution A sketch is shown in Figure 14.102, where a represents the height of the tower. In the right triangle, we have a known angle, an unknown opposite side, and a known adjacent side. Therefore, we use the tangent function.

$$\tan 57.2° = \frac{a}{125}$$

- Side opposite the 57.2° angle
- Side adjacent to the 57.2° angle

Now we multiply both sides of this equation by 125 and solve for a.

$$a = 125 \tan 57.2° \approx 194$$

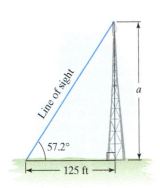

FIGURE 14.102 Determining height without using direct measurement

The tower is approximately 194 feet high.

PRACTICE 2 From a point on level ground 80 feet from the base of the Eiffel Tower, the angle of elevation is 85.4°. Approximate the height of the Eiffel Tower to the nearest foot.

Example 3 illustrates how to find the measure of an acute angle of a right triangle if the lengths of two sides are known.

EXAMPLE 3 Finding an Angle of a Right Triangle

A kite flies at a height of 30 feet when 65 feet of string is out. If the string is in a straight line, find the angle that it makes with the ground. Round to the nearest tenth of a degree.

Solution A sketch is shown in Figure 14.103, where A represents the angle the string makes with the ground. In the right triangle, we have an unknown angle, a known opposite side, and a known hypotenuse. Therefore, we use the sine function.

$$\sin A = \frac{30}{65}$$

- Side opposite A
- Hypotenuse

$$A = \sin^{-1} \frac{30}{65} \approx 27.5°$$

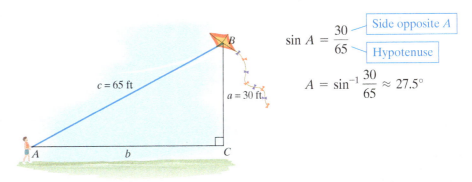

FIGURE 14.103 Flying a kite

The string makes an angle of approximately 27.5° with the ground.

PRACTICE 3 A guy wire is 13.8 yards long and is attached from the ground to a pole 6.7 yards above the ground. Find the angle, to the nearest tenth of a degree, that the wire makes with the ground.

EXAMPLE 4 Using Two Right Triangles to Solve a Problem

You are taking your first hot-air balloon ride. Your friend is standing on level ground, 100 feet away from your point of launch, making a video of your ascent. How rapidly? At one instant, the angle of elevation from the video camera to your face is 31.7°. One minute later, the angle of elevation is 76.2°. How far did you travel, to the nearest tenth of a foot, during that minute?

Solution A sketch that illustrates the problem is shown in Figure 14.104. We need to determine $b - a$, the distance traveled during the one-minute period. We find a using the small right triangle. Because we have a known angle, an unknown opposite side, and a known adjacent side, we use the tangent function.

$$\tan 31.7° = \frac{a}{100}$$

Side opposite the 31.7° angle
Side adjacent to the 31.7° angle

$$a = 100 \tan 31.7° \approx 61.8$$

We find b using the tangent function in the large right triangle.

$$\tan 76.2° = \frac{b}{100}$$

Side opposite the 76.2° angle
Side adjacent to the 76.2° angle

$$b = 100 \tan 76.2° \approx 407.1$$

The balloon traveled $407.1 - 61.8$, or approximately 345.3 feet, during the minute. □

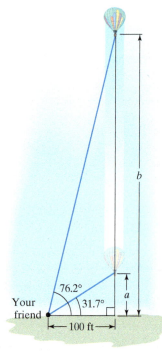

FIGURE 14.104 Ascending in a hot-air balloon

PRACTICE 4 You are standing on level ground 800 feet from Mt. Rushmore, looking at the sculpture of Abraham Lincoln's face. The angle of elevation to the bottom of the sculpture is 32° and the angle of elevation to the top is 35°. Find the height of the sculpture of Lincoln's face to the nearest tenth of a foot.

OBJECTIVE 2 ▶ Trigonometry and bearings. In navigation and surveying problems, the term *bearing* is used to specify the location of one point relative to another. The **bearing** from point O to point P is the acute angle, measured in degrees, between ray OP and a north-south line. Figure 14.105 illustrates some examples of bearings. The north-south line and the east-west line intersect at right angles.

▶ **Helpful Hint**

The bearing from O to P can also be described using the phrase "the bearing of P from O."

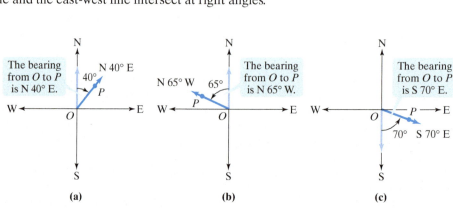

FIGURE 14.105 An illustration of three bearings

Each bearing has three parts: a letter (N or S), the measure of an acute angle, and a letter (E or W). Here's how we write a bearing:

- If the acute angle is measured from the *north side* of the north-south line, then we write N first. [See Figure 14.105(a).] If the acute angle is measured from the *south side* of the north-south line, then we write S first. [See Figure 14.105(c).]
- Second, we write the measure of the acute angle.
- If the acute angle is measured on the *east side* of the north-south line, then we write E last. [See Figure 14.105(a)]. If the acute angle is measured on the *west side* of the north-south line, then we write W last. [See Figure 14.105(b).]

EXAMPLE 5   Understanding Bearings

Use Figure 14.106 to find each of the following:

a. the bearing from O to B

b. the bearing from O to A.

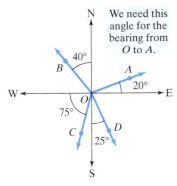

FIGURE 14.106 Finding bearings

Solution

a. To find the bearing from O to B, we need the acute angle between the ray OB and the north-south line through O. The measurement of this angle is given to be 40°. Figure 14.106 shows that the angle is measured from the north side of the north-south line and lies west of the north-south line. Thus, the bearing from O to B is N 40° W.

b. To find the bearing from O to A, we need the acute angle between the ray OA and the north-south line through O. This angle is specified by the voice balloon in Figure 14.106. Because of the given 20° angle, this angle measures 90° − 20°, or 70°. This angle is measured from the north side of the north-south line. This angle is also east of the north-south line. Thus, the bearing from O to A is N 70° E.

PRACTICE 5   Use Figure 14.106 to find each of the following:

a. the bearing from O to D

b. the bearing from O to C.

EXAMPLE 6   Finding the Bearing of a Boat

A boat leaves the entrance to a harbor and travels 25 miles on a bearing of N 42° E. Figure 14.107 shows that the captain then turns the boat 90° clockwise and travels 18 miles on a bearing of S 48° E. At that time:

a. How far is the boat, to the nearest tenth of a mile, from the harbor entrance?

b. What is the bearing, to the nearest tenth of a degree, of the boat from the harbor entrance?

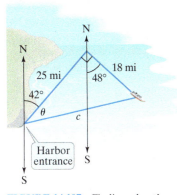

FIGURE 14.107 Finding a boat's bearing from the harbor entrance

Solution

a. The boat's distance from the harbor entrance is represented by c in Figure 14.107. Because we know the length of two sides of the right triangle, we find c using the Pythagorean Theorem. We have
$$c^2 = a^2 + b^2 = 25^2 + 18^2 = 949$$
$$c = \sqrt{949} \approx 30.8.$$

The boat is approximately 30.8 miles from the harbor entrance.

b. The bearing of the boat from the harbor entrance means the bearing from the harbor entrance to the boat. Look at the north-south line passing through the harbor entrance on the left in Figure 14.107. The acute angle from this line to the ray on which the boat lies is 42° + θ. Because we are measuring the angle from the north side of the line and the boat is east of the harbor, its bearing from the harbor entrance is N(42° + θ)E. To find θ, we use the right triangle shown in Figure 14.107 and the tangent function.

$$\tan \theta = \frac{\text{side opposite } \theta}{\text{side adjacent to } \theta} = \frac{18}{25}$$

$$\theta = \tan^{-1} \frac{18}{25}$$

We can use a calculator in degree mode to find the value of θ: θ ≈ 35.8°. Thus, 42° + θ = 42° + 35.8° = 77.8°. The bearing of the boat from the harbor entrance is N 77.8° E. □

> **Helpful Hint**
> When making a diagram showing bearings, draw a north-south line through each point at which a change in course occurs. The north side of the line lies above each point. The south side of the line lies below each point.

PRACTICE 6 You leave the entrance to a system of hiking trails and hike 2.3 miles on a bearing of S 31° W. Then the trail turns 90° clockwise and you hike 3.5 miles on a bearing of N 59° W. At that time:

a. How far are you, to the nearest tenth of a mile, from the entrance to the trail system?
b. What is your bearing, to the nearest tenth of a degree, from the entrance to the trail system?

OBJECTIVE 3 ▶ Simple harmonic motion. Because of their periodic nature, trigonometric functions are used to model phenomena that occur again and again. This includes vibratory or oscillatory motion, such as the motion of a vibrating guitar string, the swinging of a pendulum, or the bobbing of an object attached to a spring. Trigonometric functions are also used to describe radio waves from your favorite FM station, television waves from your not-to-be-missed weekly sitcom, and sound waves from your most-prized CDs.

To see how trigonometric functions are used to model vibratory motion, consider this: A ball is attached to a spring hung from the ceiling. You pull the ball down 4 inches and then release it. If we neglect the effects of friction and air resistance, the ball will continue bobbing up and down on the end of the spring. These up-and-down oscillations are called **simple harmonic motion.**

To better understand this motion, we use a *d*-axis, where *d* represents distance. This axis is shown in Figure 14.108. On this axis, the position of the ball before you pull it down is *d* = 0. This rest position is called the **equilibrium position.** Now you pull the ball down 4 inches to *d* = −4 and release it. Figure 14.109 shows a sequence of "photographs" taken at one-second time intervals illustrating the distance of the ball from its rest position, *d*.

The curve in Figure 14.109 shows how the ball's distance from its rest position changes over time. The curve is sinusoidal and the motion can be described using a cosine or a sine function.

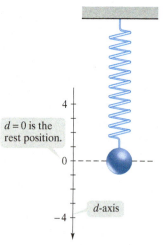

FIGURE 14.108 Using a *d*-axis to describe a ball's distance from its rest position

> **Simple Harmonic Motion**
> An object that moves on a coordinate axis is in **simple harmonic motion** if its distance from the origin, *d*, at time *t* is given by either
>
> $$d = a \cos \omega t \quad \text{or} \quad d = a \sin \omega t.$$
>
> The motion has **amplitude** |*a*|, the maximum displacement of the object from its rest position. The **period** of the motion is $\frac{2\pi}{\omega}$, where ω > 0. The period gives the time it takes for the motion to go through one complete cycle.

In describing simple harmonic motion, the equation with the cosine function, *d* = *a* cos ω*t*, is used if the object is at its greatest distance from rest position, the origin,

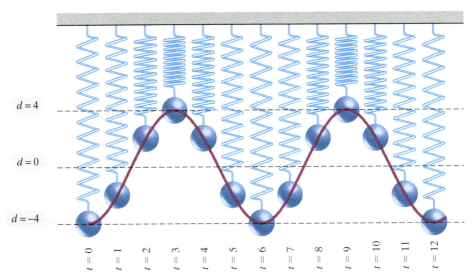

FIGURE 14.109 A sequence of "photographs" showing the bobbing ball's distance from the rest position, taken at one-second intervals

Diminishing Motion with Increasing Time

Due to friction and other resistive forces, the motion of an oscillating object decreases over time. The function

$$d = 3e^{-0.1t} \cos 2t$$

models this type of motion. The graph of the function is shown in a $t = [0, 10, 1]$ by $d = [-3, 3, 1]$ viewing rectangle. Notice how the amplitude is decreasing with time as the moving object loses energy.

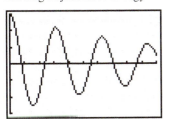

at $t = 0$. By contrast, the equation with the sine function, $d = a \sin \omega t$, is used if the object is at its rest position, the origin, at $t = 0$.

EXAMPLE 7 Finding an Equation for an Object in Simple Harmonic Motion

A ball on a spring is pulled 4 inches below its rest position and then released. The period of the motion is 6 seconds. Write the equation for the ball's simple harmonic motion.

Solution We need to write an equation that describes d, the distance of the ball from its rest position, after t seconds. (The motion is illustrated by the "photo" sequence in Figure 14.109.) When the object is released ($t = 0$), the ball's distance from its rest position is 4 inches down. Because it is *down* 4 inches, d is negative: When $t = 0, d = -4$. Notice that the greatest distance from rest position occurs at $t = 0$. Thus, we will use the equation with the cosine function,

$$d = a \cos \omega t,$$

to model the ball's simple harmonic motion.

Now we determine values for a and ω. Recall that $|a|$ is the maximum displacement. Because the ball is initially below rest position, $a = -4$.

The value of ω in $d = a \cos \omega t$ can be found using the formula for the period.

$$\text{period} = \frac{2\pi}{\omega} = 6 \qquad \text{We are given that the period of the motion is 6 seconds.}$$

$$2\pi = 6\omega \qquad \text{Multiply both sides by } \omega.$$

$$\omega = \frac{2\pi}{6} = \frac{\pi}{3} \qquad \text{Divide both sides by 6 and solve for } \omega.$$

We see that $a = -4$ and $\omega = \frac{\pi}{3}$. Substitute these values into $d = a \cos \omega t$. The equation for the ball's simple harmonic motion is

$$d = -4 \cos \frac{\pi}{3} t.$$

PRACTICE 7 A ball on a spring is pulled 6 inches below its rest position and then released. The period for the motion is 4 seconds. Write the equation for the ball's simple harmonic motion.

Modeling Music

Sounds are caused by vibrating objects that result in variations in pressure in the surrounding air. Areas of high and low pressure moving through the air are modeled by the harmonic motion formulas. When these vibrations reach our eardrums, the eardrums' vibrations send signals to our brains which create the sensation of hearing.

French mathematician John Fourier (1768–1830) proved that all musical sounds—instrumental and vocal—could be modeled by sums involving sine functions. Modeling musical sounds with sinusoidal functions is used by synthesizing programs available on computers to electronically produce sounds unobtainable from ordinary musical instruments.

The period of the harmonic motion in Example 7 was 6 seconds. It takes 6 seconds for the moving object to complete one cycle. Thus, $\frac{1}{6}$ of a cycle is completed every second. We call $\frac{1}{6}$ the *frequency* of the moving object. **Frequency** describes the number of complete cycles per unit time and is the reciprocal of the period.

> **Frequency of an Object in Simple Harmonic Motion**
> An object in simple harmonic motion given by
> $$d = a \cos \omega t \quad \text{or} \quad d = a \sin \omega t$$
> has **frequency** f given by
> $$f = \frac{\omega}{2\pi}, \omega > 0.$$
> Equivalently,
> $$f = \frac{1}{\text{period}}.$$

EXAMPLE 8   Analyzing Simple Harmonic Motion

Figure 14.110 shows a mass on a smooth surface attached to a spring. The mass moves in simple harmonic motion described by

$$d = 10 \cos \frac{\pi}{6} t,$$

with t measured in seconds and d in centimeters. Find:

a. the maximum displacement
b. the frequency
c. the time required for one cycle.

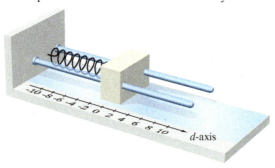

FIGURE 14.110   A mass attached to a spring, moving in simple harmonic motion

Solution   We begin by identifying values for a and ω.

$$d = 10 \cos \frac{\pi}{6} t$$

The form of this equation is $d = a \cos \omega t$ with $a = 10$ and $\omega = \frac{\pi}{6}$.

a. The maximum displacement from the rest position is the amplitude. Because $a = 10$, the maximum displacement is 10 centimeters.

b. The frequency, f, is

$$f = \frac{\omega}{2\pi} = \frac{\frac{\pi}{6}}{2\pi} = \frac{\pi}{6} \cdot \frac{1}{2\pi} = \frac{1}{12}.$$

The frequency is $\frac{1}{12}$ cycle (or oscillation) per second.

c. The time required for one cycle is the period.

$$\text{period} = \frac{2\pi}{\omega} = \frac{2\pi}{\frac{\pi}{6}} = 2\pi \cdot \frac{6}{\pi} = 12$$

The time required for one cycle is 12 seconds. This value can also be obtained by taking the reciprocal of the frequency in part (b). ∎

PRACTICE 8 An object moves in simple harmonic motion described by $d = 12 \cos \frac{\pi}{4} t$, where t is measured in seconds and d in centimeters. Find **a.** the maximum displacement, **b.** the frequency, and **c.** the time required for one cycle.

Resisting Damage of Simple Harmonic Motion

Simple harmonic motion from an earthquake caused this highway in Oakland, California, to collapse. By studying the harmonic motion of the soil under the highway, engineers learn to build structures that can resist damage.

14.8 EXERCISE SET

PRACTICE EXERCISES

In Exercises 1–12, solve the right triangle shown in the figure. Round lengths to two decimal places and express angles to the nearest tenth of a degree.

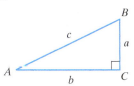

1. $A = 23.5°, b = 10$
2. $A = 41.5°, b = 20$
3. $A = 52.6°, c = 54$
4. $A = 54.8°, c = 80$
5. $B = 16.8°, b = 30.5$
6. $B = 23.8°, b = 40.5$
7. $a = 30.4, c = 50.2$
8. $a = 11.2, c = 65.8$
9. $a = 10.8, b = 24.7$
10. $a = 15.3, b = 17.6$
11. $b = 2, c = 7$
12. $b = 4, c = 9$

Use the figure shown to solve Exercises 13–16.

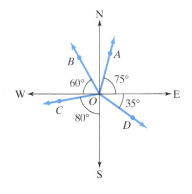

13. Find the bearing from O to A.
14. Find the bearing from O to B.
15. Find the bearing from O to C.
16. Find the bearing from O to D.

In Exercises 17–20, an object is attached to a coiled spring. In Exercises 17–18, the object is pulled down (negative direction from the rest position) and then released. In Exercises 19–20, the object is propelled downward from its rest position at time $t = 0$. Write an equation for the distance of the object from its rest position after t seconds.

Distance from Rest Position at $t = 0$	Amplitude	Period
17. 6 centimeters	6 centimeters	4 seconds
18. 8 inches	8 inches	2 seconds
19. 0 inches	3 inches	1.5 seconds
20. 0 centimeters	5 centimeters	2.5 seconds

In Exercises 21–28, an object moves in simple harmonic motion described by the given equation, where t is measured in seconds and d in inches. In each exercise, find the following:

a. the maximum displacement
b. the frequency
c. the time required for one cycle.

21. $d = 5 \cos \frac{\pi}{2} t$
22. $d = 10 \cos 2\pi t$
23. $d = -6 \cos 2\pi t$
24. $d = -8 \cos \frac{\pi}{2} t$
25. $d = \frac{1}{2} \sin 2t$
26. $d = \frac{1}{3} \sin 2t$

27. $d = -5 \sin \dfrac{2\pi}{3} t$ **28.** $d = -4 \sin \dfrac{3\pi}{2} t$

PRACTICE PLUS

In Exercises 29–36, find the length x to the nearest whole number.

29.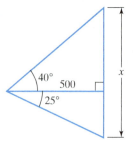

30.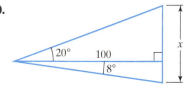

31.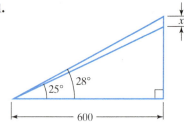

32.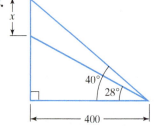

33.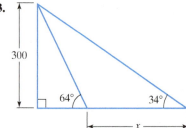

34.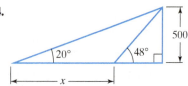

35.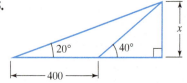

36.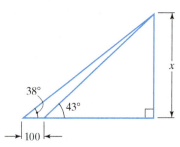

In Exercises 37–40, an object moves in simple harmonic motion described by the given equation, where t is measured in seconds and d in inches. In each exercise, graph one period of the equation. Then find the following:

  a. *the maximum displacement*
  b. *the frequency*
  c. *the time required for one cycle*
  d. *the phase shift of the motion.*

Describe how (a) through (d) are illustrated by your graph.

37. $d = 4 \cos\left(\pi t - \dfrac{\pi}{2}\right)$ **38.** $d = 3 \cos\left(\pi t + \dfrac{\pi}{2}\right)$

39. $d = -2 \sin\left(\dfrac{\pi t}{4} + \dfrac{\pi}{2}\right)$ **40.** $d = -\dfrac{1}{2} \sin\left(\dfrac{\pi t}{4} - \dfrac{\pi}{2}\right)$

APPLICATION EXERCISES

41. The tallest television transmitting tower in the world is in North Dakota. From a point on level ground 5280 feet (one mile) from the base of the tower, the angle of elevation is 21.3°. Approximate the height of the tower to the nearest foot.

42. From a point on level ground 30 yards from the base of a building, the angle of elevation is 38.7°. Approximate the height of the building to the nearest foot.

43. The Statue of Liberty is approximately 305 feet tall. If the angle of elevation from a ship to the top of the statue is 23.7°, how far, to the nearest foot, is the ship from the statue's base?

44. A 200-foot cliff drops vertically into the ocean. If the angle of elevation from a ship to the top of the cliff is 22.3°, how far off shore, to the nearest foot, is the ship?

45. A helicopter hovers 1000 feet above a small island. The figure shows that the angle of depression from the helicopter to point *P* on the coast is 36°. How far off the coast, to the nearest foot, is the island?

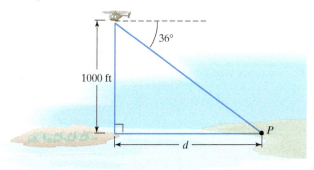

46. A police helicopter is flying at 800 feet. A stolen car is sighted at an angle of depression of 72°. Find the distance of the stolen car, to the nearest foot, from a point directly below the helicopter.

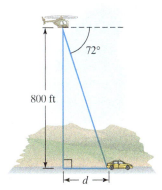

47. A wheelchair ramp is to be built beside the steps to the campus library. Find the angle of elevation of the 23-foot ramp, to the nearest tenth of a degree, if its final height is 6 feet.

48. A building that is 250 feet high casts a shadow 40 feet long. Find the angle of elevation, to the nearest tenth of a degree, of the sun at this time.

49. A hot-air balloon is rising vertically. From a point on level ground 125 feet from the point directly under the passenger compartment, the angle of elevation to the ballon changes from 19.2° to 31.7°. How far, to the nearest tenth of a foot, does the balloon rise during this period?

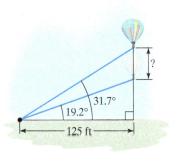

50. A flagpole is situated on top of a building. The angle of elevation from a point on level ground 330 feet from the building to the top of the flagpole is 63°. The angle of elevation from the same point to the bottom of the flagpole is 53°. Find the height of the flagpole to the nearest tenth of a foot.

51. A boat leaves the entrance to a harbor and travels 150 miles on a bearing of N53°E. How many miles north and how many miles east from the harbor has the boat traveled?

52. A boat leaves the entrance to a harbor and travels 40 miles on a bearing of S64°E. How many miles south and how many miles east from the harbor has the boat traveled?

53. A forest ranger sights a fire directly to the south. A second ranger, 7 miles east of the first ranger, also sights the fire. The bearing from the second ranger to the fire is S 28° W. How far, to the nearest tenth of a mile, is the first ranger from the fire?

54. A ship sights a lighthouse directly to the south. A second ship, 9 miles east of the first ship, also sights the lighthouse. The bearing from the second ship to the lighthouse is S 34° W. How far, to the nearest tenth of a mile, is the first ship from the lighthouse?

55. You leave your house and run 2 miles due west followed by 1.5 miles due north. At that time, what is your bearing from your house?

56. A ship is 9 miles east and 6 miles south of a harbor. What bearing should be taken to sail directly to the harbor?

57. A jet leaves a runway whose bearing is N 35° E from the control tower. After flying 5 miles, the jet turns 90° and files on a bearing of S 55° E for 7 miles. At that time, what is the bearing of the jet from the control tower?

58. A ship leaves port with a bearing of S 40° W. After traveling 7 miles, the ship turns 90° and travels on a bearing of N 50° W for 11 miles. At that time, what is the bearing of the ship from port?

59. An object in simple harmonic motion has a frequency of $\frac{1}{2}$ oscillation per minute and an amplitude of 6 feet. Write an equation in the form $d = a \sin \omega t$ for the object's simple harmonic motion.

60. An object in simple harmonic motion has a frequency of $\frac{1}{4}$ oscillation per minute and an amplitude of 8 feet. Write an equation in the form $d = a \sin \omega t$ for the object's simple harmonic motion.

61. A piano tuner uses a tuning fork. If middle C has a frequency of 264 vibrations per second, write an equation in the form $d = \sin \omega t$ for the simple harmonic motion.

62. A radio station, 98.1 on the FM dial, has radio waves with a frequency of 98.1 million cycles per second. Write an equation in the form $d = \sin \omega t$ for the simple harmonic motion of the radio waves.

WRITING IN MATHEMATICS

63. What does it mean to solve a right triangle?

64. Explain how to find one of the acute angles of a right triangle if two sides are known.

65. Describe a situation in which a right triangle and a trigonometric function are used to measure a height or distance that would otherwise be inconvenient or impossible to measure.

66. What is meant by the bearing from point O to point P? Give an example with your description.

67. What is simple harmonic motion? Give an example with your description.

68. Explain the period and the frequency of simple harmonic motion. How are they related?

69. Explain how the photograph of the damaged highway at the end of the section illustrates simple harmonic motion.

TECHNOLOGY EXERCISES

The functions in Exercises 70–71 model motion in which the amplitude decreases with time due to friction or other resistive forces. Graph each function in the given viewing rectangle. How many complete oscillations occur on the time interval $0 \leq x \leq 10$?

70. $y = 4e^{-0.1x} \cos 2x$; $[0, 10, 1]$ by $[-4, 4, 1]$

71. $y = -6e^{-0.09x} \cos 2\pi x$; $[0, 10, 1]$ by $[-6, 6, 1]$

CRITICAL THINKING EXERCISES

Make Sense? *In Exercises 72–75, determine whether each statement makes sense or does not make sense, and explain your reasoning.*

72. A wheelchair ramp must be constructed so that the slope is not more than 1 inch of rise for every 1 foot of run, so I used the tangent function to determine the maximum angle that the ramp can make with the ground.

73. The bearing from O to A is N 103° W.

74. The bearing from O to B is E 70° S.

75. I analyzed simple harmonic motion in which the period was 10 seconds and the frequency was 0.2 oscillation per second.

76. The figure shows a satellite circling 112 miles above Earth. When the satellite is directly above point B, angle A measures 76.6°. Find Earth's radius to the nearest mile.

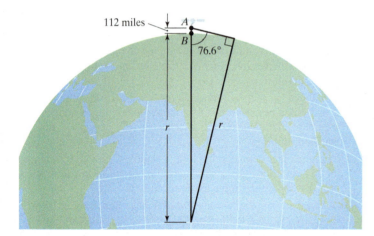

77. The angle of elevation to the top of a building changes from 20° to 40° as an observer advances 75 feet toward the building. Find the height of the building to the nearest foot.

GROUP EXERCISE

78. Music and mathematics have been linked over the centuries. Group members should research and present a seminar to the class on music and mathematics. Be sure to include the role of trigonometric functions in the music-mathematics link.

REVIEW AND PREVIEW

Exercises 79–81 will help you prepare for the material covered in the first section of the next chapter. The exercises use identities, introduced in Section 14.2, that enable you to rewrite trigonometric expressions so that they contain only sines and cosines:

$$\csc x = \frac{1}{\sin x} \qquad \sec x = \frac{1}{\cos x}$$
$$\tan x = \frac{\sin x}{\cos x} \qquad \cot x = \frac{\cos x}{\sin x}.$$

In Exercises 79–81, rewrite each expression by changing to sines and cosines. Then simplify the resulting expression.

79. $\sec x \cot x$

80. $\tan x \csc x \cos x$

81. $\sec x + \tan x$

> **▶ Helpful Hint**
>
> Much of the essential information in this chapter can be found in three places:
>
> - Study Tip in Section 14.3, showing special angles and how to obtain exact values of trigonometric functions at these angles
> - Table 14.6 in Section 14.6, showing the graphs of three trigonometric functions, with their domains, ranges, and periods
>
> Make copies of these pages and mount them on cardstock. Use this reference sheet as you work the review exercises until you have all the information on the reference sheet memorized for the chapter test.

CHAPTER 14 REVIEW

14.1

1. Find the radian measure of the central angle of a circle of radius 6 centimeters that intercepts an arc of length 27 centimeters.

In Exercises 2–4, convert each angle in degrees to radians. Express your answer as a multiple of π.

2. 15°   **3.** 120°   **4.** 315°

In Exercises 5–7, convert each angle in radians to degrees.

5. $\dfrac{5\pi}{3}$ **6.** $\dfrac{7\pi}{5}$ **7.** $-\dfrac{5\pi}{6}$

In Exercises 8–12, draw each angle in standard position.

8. $\dfrac{5\pi}{6}$ **9.** $-\dfrac{2\pi}{3}$ **10.** $\dfrac{8\pi}{3}$

11. 190°   **12.** −135°

In Exercises 13–17, find a positive angle less than 360° or 2π that is coterminal with the given angle.

13. 400°   **14.** −445°   **15.** $\dfrac{13\pi}{4}$

16. $\dfrac{31\pi}{6}$ **17.** $-\dfrac{8\pi}{3}$

18. Find the length of the arc on a circle of radius 10 feet intercepted by a 135° central angle. Express arc length in terms of π. Then round your answer to two decimal places.

19. The angular speed of a propeller on a wind generator is 10.3 revolutions per minute. Express this angular speed in radians per minute.

20. The propeller of an airplane has a radius of 3 feet. The propeller is rotating at 2250 revolutions per minute. Find the linear speed, in feet per minute, of the tip of the propeller.

14.2

21. Use the triangle to find each of the six trigonometric functions of θ.

In Exercises 22–25, find the exact value of each expression. Do not use a calculator.

22. $\sin\dfrac{\pi}{6} + \tan^2\dfrac{\pi}{3}$

23. $\cos^2\dfrac{\pi}{4} - \tan^2\dfrac{\pi}{4}$

24. $\sec^2\dfrac{\pi}{5} - \tan^2\dfrac{\pi}{5}$

25. $\cos\dfrac{2\pi}{9}\sec\dfrac{2\pi}{9}$

26. If θ is an acute angle and $\sin\theta = \dfrac{2\sqrt{7}}{7}$, use the identity $\sin^2\theta + \cos^2\theta = 1$ to find $\cos\theta$.

In Exercises 27–28, find a cofunction with the same value as the given expression.

27. $\sin 70°$

28. $\cos\dfrac{\pi}{2}$

In Exercises 29–31, find the measure of the side of the right triangle whose length is designated by a lowercase letter. Round answers to the nearest whole number.

29.
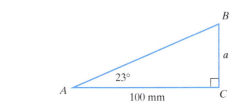

30.
31.
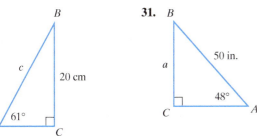

32. If $\sin\theta = \dfrac{1}{4}$ and θ is acute, find $\tan\left(\dfrac{\pi}{2} - \theta\right)$.

33. A hiker climbs for a half mile up a slope whose inclination is 17°. How many feet of altitude, to the nearest foot, does the hiker gain?

34. To find the distance across a lake, a surveyor took the measurements in the figure shown. What is the distance across the lake? Round to the nearest meter.

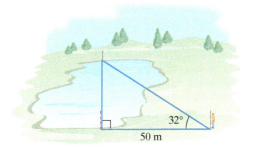

35. When a six-foot pole casts a four-foot shadow, what is the angle of elevation of the sun? Round to the nearest whole degree.

14.3 and 14.4

In Exercises 36–37, a point on the terminal side of angle θ is given. Find the exact value of each of the six trigonometric functions of θ, or state that the function is undefined.

36. $(-1, -5)$

37. $(0, -1)$

In Exercises 38–39, let θ be an angle in standard position. Name the quadrant in which θ lies.

38. $\tan\theta > 0$ and $\sec\theta > 0$

39. $\tan\theta > 0$ and $\cos\theta < 0$

In Exercises 40–42, find the exact value of each of the remaining trigonometric functions of θ.

40. $\cos\theta = \frac{2}{5}$, $\sin\theta < 0$

41. $\tan\theta = -\frac{1}{3}$, $\sin\theta > 0$

42. $\cot\theta = 3$, $\cos\theta < 0$

In Exercises 43–47, find the reference angle for each angle.

43. $265°$

44. $\dfrac{5\pi}{8}$

45. $-410°$

46. $\dfrac{17\pi}{6}$

47. $-\dfrac{11\pi}{3}$

In Exercises 48–58, find the exact value of each expression. Do not use a calculator.

48. $\sin 240°$

49. $\tan 120°$

50. $\sec\dfrac{7\pi}{4}$

51. $\cos\dfrac{11\pi}{6}$

52. $\cot(-210°)$

53. $\csc\left(-\dfrac{2\pi}{3}\right)$

54. $\sin\left(-\dfrac{\pi}{3}\right)$

55. $\sin 495°$

56. $\tan\dfrac{13\pi}{4}$

57. $\sin\dfrac{22\pi}{3}$

58. $\cos\left(-\dfrac{35\pi}{6}\right)$

14.5

In Exercises 59–64, determine the amplitude and period of each function. Then graph one period of the function.

59. $y = 3\sin 4x$

60. $y = -2\cos 2x$

61. $y = 2\cos\dfrac{1}{2}x$

62. $y = \dfrac{1}{2}\sin\dfrac{\pi}{3}x$

63. $y = -\sin\pi x$

64. $y = 3\cos\dfrac{x}{3}$

In Exercises 65–69, determine the amplitude, period, and phase shift of each function. Then graph one period of the function.

65. $y = 2\sin(x - \pi)$

66. $y = 3\cos(x + \pi)$

67. $y = \dfrac{3}{2}\cos\left(2x + \dfrac{\pi}{4}\right)$

68. $y = \dfrac{5}{2}\sin\left(2x + \dfrac{\pi}{2}\right)$

69. $y = -3\sin\left(\dfrac{\pi}{3}x - 3\pi\right)$

In Exercises 70–71, use a vertical shift to graph one period of the function.

70. $y = \sin 2x + 1$

71. $y = 2\cos\frac{1}{3}x - 2$

72. Light waves can be modeled by sine functions. The graphs show waves of red and blue light. Write an equation in the form $y = A\sin Bx$ that models each of these light waves.

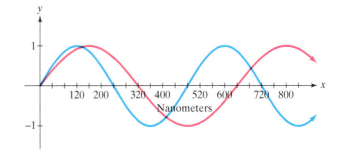

14.6

In Exercises 73–76, graph two full periods of the given tangent or cotangent function.

73. $y = 4 \tan 2x$

74. $y = -2 \tan \dfrac{\pi}{4} x$

75. $y = \tan(x + \pi)$

76. $y = -\tan\left(x - \dfrac{\pi}{4}\right)$

14.7

In Exercises 81–99, find the exact value of each expression. Do not use a calculator.

77. $\sin^{-1} 1$

78. $\cos^{-1} 1$

79. $\tan^{-1} 1$

80. $\sin^{-1}\left(-\dfrac{\sqrt{3}}{2}\right)$

81. $\cos^{-1}\left(-\dfrac{1}{2}\right)$

82. $\tan^{-1}\left(-\dfrac{\sqrt{3}}{3}\right)$

83. $\cos\left(\sin^{-1} \dfrac{\sqrt{2}}{2}\right)$

84. $\sin(\cos^{-1} 0)$

85. $\tan\left[\sin^{-1}\left(-\dfrac{1}{2}\right)\right]$

86. $\tan\left[\cos^{-1}\left(-\dfrac{\sqrt{3}}{2}\right)\right]$

87. $\csc\left(\tan^{-1} \dfrac{\sqrt{3}}{3}\right)$

88. $\cos\left(\tan^{-1} \dfrac{3}{4}\right)$

89. $\sin\left(\cos^{-1} \dfrac{3}{5}\right)$

90. $\tan\left[\sin^{-1}\left(-\dfrac{3}{5}\right)\right]$

91. $\tan\left[\cos^{-1}\left(-\dfrac{4}{5}\right)\right]$

92. $\sin\left[\tan^{-1}\left(-\dfrac{1}{3}\right)\right]$

93. $\sin^{-1}\left(\sin \dfrac{\pi}{3}\right)$

94. $\sin^{-1}\left(\sin \dfrac{2\pi}{3}\right)$

95. $\sin^{-1}\left(\cos \dfrac{2\pi}{3}\right)$

In Exercises 96–97, use a right triangle to write each expression as an algebraic expression. Assume that x is positive and that the given inverse trigonometric function is defined for the expression in x.

96. $\cos\left(\tan^{-1} \dfrac{x}{2}\right)$

97. $\sec\left(\sin^{-1} \dfrac{1}{x}\right)$

14.8

In Exercises 106–109, solve the right triangle shown in the figure. Round lengths to two decimal places and express angles to the nearest tenth of a degree.

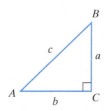

98. $A = 22.3°, c = 10$

99. $B = 37.4°, b = 6$

100. $a = 2, c = 7$

101. $a = 1.4, b = 3.6$

102. From a point on level ground 80 feet from the base of a building, the angle of elevation is 25.6°. Approximate the height of the building to the nearest foot.

103. Two buildings with flat roofs are 60 yards apart. The height of the shorter building is 40 yards. From its roof, the angle of elevation to the edge of the roof of the taller building is 40°. Find the height of the taller building to the nearest yard.

104. You want to measure the height of an antenna on the top of a 125-foot building. From a point in front of the building, you measure the angle of elevation to the top of the building to be 68° and the angle of elevation to the top of the antenna to be 71°. How tall is the antenna, to the nearest tenth of a foot?

In Exercises 105–106, use the figures shown to find the bearing from O to A.

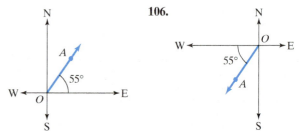

107. A ship is due west of a lighthouse. A second ship is 12 miles south of the first ship. The bearing from the second ship to the lighthouse is N 64° E. How far, to the nearest tenth of a mile, is the first ship from the lighthouse?

108. From city A to city B, a plane flies 850 miles at a bearing of N 58° E. From city B to city C, the plane flies 960 miles at a bearing of S 32° E.

   a. Find, to the nearest tenth of a mile, the distance from city A to city C.

   b. What is the bearing from city A to city C?

In Exercises 109–110, an object moves in simple harmonic motion described by the given equation, where t is measured in seconds and d in centimeters. In each exercise, find:

   a. the maximum displacement

   b. the frequency

   c. the time required for one cycle.

109. $d = 20 \cos \dfrac{\pi}{4} t$

110. $d = \dfrac{1}{2} \sin 4t$

In Exercises 111–112, an object is attached to a coiled spring. In Exercise 111, the object is pulled down (negative direction from the rest position) and then released. In Exercise 112, the object is initially at its rest position. After that, it is pulled down and then released. Write an equation for the distance of the object from its rest position after t seconds

Distance from Rest Position at $t = 0$	Amplitude	Period
111. 30 inches	30 inches	2 seconds
112. 0 inches	$\dfrac{1}{4}$ inch	5 seconds

CHAPTER 14 TEST

Remember to use the Chapter Test Prep Videos to see the fully worked-out solutions to any of the exercises you want to review.

1. Convert 135° to an exact radian measure.
2. Find the length of the arc on a circle of radius 20 feet intercepted by a 75° central angle. Express arc length in terms of π. Then round your answer to two decimal places.
3. a. Find a positive angle less than 2π that is coterminal with $\frac{16\pi}{3}$.
   b. Find the reference angle for $\frac{16\pi}{3}$.
4. If $(-2, 5)$ is a point on the terminal side of angle θ, find the exact value of each of the six trigonometric functions of θ.
5. If $\cos \theta = \frac{1}{3}$ and $\tan \theta < 0$, find the exact value of each of the remaining trigonometric functions of θ.

In Exercises 6–10, find the exact value of each expression. Do not use a calculator.

6. $\tan \frac{\pi}{6} \cos \frac{\pi}{3} - \cos \frac{\pi}{2}$
7. $\tan 300°$
8. $\sin \frac{7\pi}{4}$
9. $\sec \frac{22\pi}{3}$
10. $\cot \left(-\frac{8\pi}{3}\right)$

In Exercises 11–13, graph one period of each function.

11. $y = 3 \sin 2x$
12. $y = -2 \cos\left(x - \frac{\pi}{2}\right)$
13. $y = 2 \tan \frac{x}{2}$
14. Find the exact value of $\tan\left[\cos^{-1}\left(-\frac{1}{2}\right)\right]$.
15. Solve the right triangle in the figure shown. Round lengths to one decimal place.

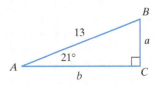

16. The angle of elevation to the top of a building from a point on the ground 30 yards from its base is 37°. Find the height of the building to the nearest yard.
17. A 73-foot rope from the top of a circus tent pole is anchored to the flat ground 43 feet from the bottom of the pole. Find the angle, to the nearest tenth of a degree, that the rope makes with the pole.

CHAPTER 14 STANDARDIZED TEST

Multiple Choice. *Choose the one alternative that best completes the statement or answers the question.*

Convert the angle in degrees to radians. Express answer as a multiple of π.

1. 150°
   a. $\frac{6\pi}{7}$ radians
   b. $\frac{4\pi}{5}$ radians
   c. $\frac{5\pi}{6}$ radians
   d. $\frac{2}{3}\pi$ radians

Convert the angle in radians to degrees.

2. $\frac{7\pi}{4}$
   a. 45°
   b. $\frac{\pi}{4}$
   c. 315°
   d. $\frac{7}{4}°$

Find the length of the arc on a circle of radius r intercepted by a central angle θ. Round answer to two decimal places.

3. $r = 2$ yards, $\theta = 55°$
   a. 1.73 yards
   b. 1.92 yards
   c. 1.54 yards
   d. 2.11 yards

Find a positive angle less than 360° or 2π that is coterminal with the given angle.

4. $\frac{12\pi}{5}$
   a. $-\frac{12\pi}{5}$
   b. $\frac{7\pi}{5}$
   c. $\frac{2\pi}{5}$
   d. $\frac{8\pi}{5}$

5. $-150°$
   a. 210°
   b. $-30°$
   c. 150°
   d. 30°

Find the reference angle for the given angle.

6. $\frac{11\pi}{12}$
   a. $\frac{13\pi}{12}$
   b. $\frac{\pi}{24}$
   c. $\frac{11\pi}{12}$
   d. $\frac{\pi}{12}$

7. $-150°$
   a. 210°
   b. $-30°$
   c. 150°
   d. 30°

A point on the terminal side of angle θ is given. Find the exact value of the indicated trigonometric function of θ.

8. $(-20, 48)$ Find $\sin \theta$.
   a. $-\frac{5}{13}$
   b. $-\frac{12}{13}$
   c. $\frac{12}{13}$
   d. $\frac{5}{13}$

Find the exact value of the indicated trigonometric function of θ.

9. $\cos\theta = \frac{2}{3}$, $\tan\theta < 0$ Find $\sin\theta$.

   a. $-\frac{\sqrt{5}}{3}$ b. $-\sqrt{5}$

   c. $-\frac{3}{2}$ d. $-\frac{\sqrt{5}}{2}$

Find the exact value of the expression. Do not use a calculator.

10. $\sin\frac{3\pi}{2}$

    a. 0   b. 1

    c. −1   d. undefined

11. $\tan 930°$

    a. $-\sqrt{3}$ b. $\sqrt{3}$

    c. $\frac{\sqrt{3}}{3}$ d. $\frac{\sqrt{3}}{2}$

12. $\cot\frac{-53\pi}{6}$

    a. $-\sqrt{3}$ b. $\frac{\sqrt{3}}{3}$

    c. $\sqrt{3}$ d. $-\frac{\sqrt{3}}{3}$

13. $\cos 90°$

    a. undefined   b. 1

    c. $\frac{\pi}{2}$ d. 0

Graph the function.

14. $y = 3\sin 2x$

    a.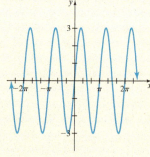

    b. (graph)

    c.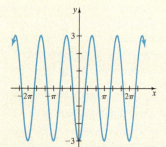

    d.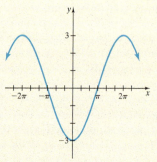

15. $y = -\frac{1}{2}\cos\left[2x - \frac{\pi}{4}\right]$

    a.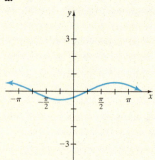

    b.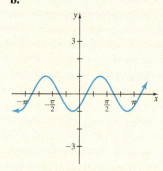

    c.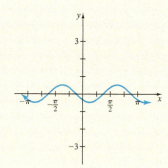

    d.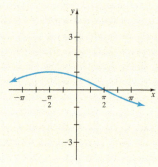

16. $y = 3\tan\frac{x}{2}$

    a.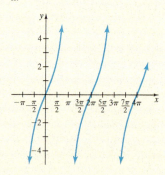

    b.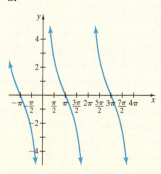

    c.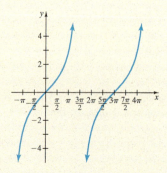

    d.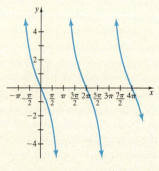

Find the exact value of the expression.

17. $\tan^{-1}(-\sqrt{3})$

   a. $-\dfrac{\pi}{3}$ **b.** $-\dfrac{\pi}{6}$

   c. $\dfrac{\pi}{6}$ **d.** $\dfrac{\pi}{3}$

18. $\tan\left(\cos^{-1}\dfrac{3}{5}\right)$

   a. $\dfrac{4}{5}$ **b.** $\dfrac{3}{4}$

   c. $\dfrac{4}{3}$ **d.** $\dfrac{5}{3}$

Solve the right triangle shown in the figure. Round lengths to one decimal place and express angles to the nearest tenth of a degree.

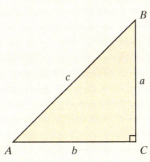

19. $A = 44°, b = 56.1$

   a. $B = 46°, a = 58.1, c = 80.8$

   b. $B = 44°, a = 58.1, c = 40.4$

   c. $B = 46°, a = 54.2, c = 78$

   d. $B = 44°, a = 40.4, c = 54.2$

Solve the problem.

20. From a boat on the lake, the angle of elevation to the top of a cliff is 24°38′. If the base of the cliff is 1594 feet from the boat, how high is the cliff (to the nearest foot)?

   a. 741 feet   **b.** 734 feet

   c. 744 feet   **d.** 731 feet

21. A building 170 feet tall casts a 50 foot long shadow. If a person looks down from the top of the building, what is the measure of the angle between the end of the shadow and the vertical side of the building (to the nearest degree)? (Assume the person's eyes are level with the top of the building.)

   a. 73°   **b.** 74°

   c. 16°   **d.** 17°

CHAPTER

15 Trigonometric Identities, Equations, and Applications

15.1 Verifying Trigonometric Identities
15.2 Sum and Difference Formulas
15.3 Double-Angle and Half-Angle Formulas
Integrated Review
15.4 Trigonometric Equations
15.5 The Law of Sines
15.6 The Law of Cosines

Listen to the same note played on a piano and a violin. The notes have a different quality or "tone." Tone depends on the way an instrument vibrates.

When a note is played, it vibrates at a specific fundamental frequency and has a particular amplitude. Two sounds from tuning forks can be modeled by $p = 3 \sin 2t$ and $p = 2 \sin(2t + \pi)$. Notice that the second equation contains the sine of the sum of two angles. In this chapter, we will be developing identities, including the sums or differences of two angles.

15.1 VERIFYING TRIGONOMETRIC IDENTITIES

OBJECTIVE

1. Use the fundamental trigonometric identities to verify identities.

The Fundamental Identities. In Chapter 14, we used right triangles to establish relationships among the trigonometric functions. Although we limited domains to acute angles, the fundamental identities listed in the following box are true for all values of x for which the expressions are defined.

> **Fundamental Trigonometric Identities**
> **Reciprocal Identities**
> $$\sin x = \frac{1}{\csc x} \quad \cos x = \frac{1}{\sec x} \quad \tan x = \frac{1}{\cot x}$$
> $$\csc x = \frac{1}{\sin x} \quad \sec x = \frac{1}{\cos x} \quad \cot x = \frac{1}{\tan x}$$
>
> **Quotient Identities**
> $$\tan x = \frac{\sin x}{\cos x} \quad \cot x = \frac{\cos x}{\sin x}$$
>
> **Pythagorean Identities**
> $$\sin^2 x + \cos^2 x = 1 \quad 1 + \tan^2 x = \sec^2 x \quad 1 + \cot^2 x = \csc^2 x$$
>
> **Even-Odd Identities**
> $$\sin(-x) = -\sin x \quad \cos(-x) = \cos x \quad \tan(-x) = -\tan x$$
> $$\csc(-x) = -\csc x \quad \sec(-x) = \sec x \quad \cot(-x) = -\cot x$$

> **Helpful Hint**
>
> Memorize the identities in the box. You may need to use variations of these fundamental identities. For example, instead of
> $$\sin^2 x + \cos^2 x = 1$$
> you might want to use
> $$\sin^2 x = 1 - \cos^2 x$$
> or
> $$\cos^2 x = 1 - \sin^2 x.$$
> Therefore, it is important to know each relationship well so that mental algebraic manipulation is possible.

OBJECTIVE 1 ▶ **Using fundamental identities to verify other identities.** The fundamental trigonometric identities are used to establish other relationships among trigonometric functions. To **verify an identity,** we show that one side of the identity can be simplified so that it is identical to the other side. Each side of the equation is manipulated independently of the other side of the equation. You may want to start with the side containing the more complicated expression. If you substitute one or more fundamental identities on the more complicated side, you will often be able to rewrite it in a form identical to that of the other side.

No one method or technique can be used to verify every identity. Some identities can be verified by rewriting the more complicated side so that it contains only sines and cosines.

EXAMPLE 1 Changing to Sines and Cosines to Verify an Identity

Verify the identity: $\sec x \cot x = \csc x$.

Solution The left side of the equation contains the more complicated expression. Thus, we work with the left side. Let us express this side of the identity in terms of sines and cosines. Perhaps this strategy will enable us to transform the left side into $\csc x$, the expression on the right.

$$\sec x \cot x = \frac{1}{\cos x} \cdot \frac{\cos x}{\sin x}$$

Apply a reciprocal identity: $\sec x = \frac{1}{\cos x}$ and a quotient identity: $\cot x = \frac{\cos x}{\sin x}$.

$$= \frac{1}{\cancel{\cos x}} \cdot \frac{\cancel{\cos x}}{\sin x}$$

Divide both the numerator and the denominator by $\cos x$, the common factor.

$$= \frac{1}{\sin x}$$ Multiply the remaining factors in the numerator and denominator.

$$= \csc x$$ Apply a reciprocal identity: $\csc x = \frac{1}{\sin x}$.

By working with the left side and simplifying it so that it is identical to the right side, we have verified the given identity. ∎

TECHNOLOGY NOTE

Numeric and Graphic Connections

You can use a graphing utility to provide evidence of an identity. Enter each side of the identity separately under y_1 and y_2. Then use the TABLE feature or the graphs. The table should show that the function values are the same except for those values of x for which y_1, y_2, or both, are undefined. The graphs should appear to be identical.

Let's check the identity in Example 1:

$$\sec x \cot x = \csc x.$$

$y_1 = \sec x \cot x$
Enter $\sec x$ as $\frac{1}{\cos x}$
and $\cot x$ as $\frac{1}{\tan x}$.

$y_2 = \csc x$
Enter $\csc x$ as $\frac{1}{\sin x}$.

Numeric Check

Display a table for y_1 and y_2. We started our table at $-\pi$ and used $\Delta Tbl = \frac{\pi}{8}$.

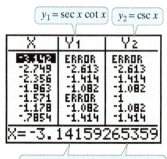

Function values are the same except for values of x for which y_1, y_2, or both, are undefined.

Graphic Check

Display graphs for y_1 and y_2.

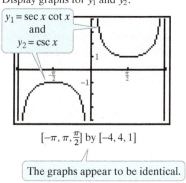

$y_1 = \sec x \cot x$ and $y_2 = \csc x$

$[-\pi, \pi, \frac{\pi}{2}]$ by $[-4, 4, 1]$

The graphs appear to be identical.

PRACTICE 1 Verify the identity: $\csc x \tan x = \sec x$.

In verifying an identity, stay focused on your goal. When manipulating one side of the equation, continue to look at the other side to keep the desired form of the result in mind.

> **Helpful Hint**
>
> Verifying that an equation is an identity is different from solving an equation. You do not verify an identity by adding, subtracting, multiplying, or dividing each side by the same expression. If you do this, you have already assumed that the given statement is true. You do not know that it is true until after you have verified it.

EXAMPLE 2 Changing to Sines and Cosines to Verify an Identity

Verify the identity: $\sin x \tan x + \cos x = \sec x$.

Solution The left side is more complicated, so we start with it. Notice that the left side contains the sum of two terms, but the right side contains only one term. This means

> **Helpful Hint**
>
> When proving identities, be sure to write the variable associated with each trigonometric function. Do not write
>
> $$\sin \tan + \cos$$
>
> for
>
> $$\sin x \tan x + \cos x$$
>
> because sin, tan, and cos are meaningless without specified variables.

that somewhere during the verification process, the two terms on the left side must be added to form one term.

Let's begin by expressing the left side of the identity so that it contains only sines and cosines. Thus, we apply a quotient identity and replace $\tan x$ by $\dfrac{\sin x}{\cos x}$. Perhaps this strategy will enable us to transform the left side into $\sec x$, the expression on the right.

$$\sin x \tan x + \cos x = \sin x \left(\dfrac{\sin x}{\cos x}\right) + \cos x \quad \text{Apply a quotient identity: } \tan x = \dfrac{\sin x}{\cos x}.$$

$$= \dfrac{\sin^2 x}{\cos x} + \cos x \quad \text{Multiply.}$$

$$= \dfrac{\sin^2 x}{\cos x} + \cos x \cdot \dfrac{\cos x}{\cos x} \quad \text{The least common denominator is } \cos x. \text{ Write the second expression with a denominator of } \cos x.$$

$$= \dfrac{\sin^2 x}{\cos x} + \dfrac{\cos^2 x}{\cos x} \quad \text{Multiply.}$$

$$= \dfrac{\sin^2 x + \cos^2 x}{\cos x} \quad \text{Add numerators and place this sum over the least common denominator.}$$

$$= \dfrac{1}{\cos x} \quad \text{Apply a Pythagorean identity: } \sin^2 x + \cos^2 x = 1.$$

$$= \sec x \quad \text{Apply a reciprocal identity: } \sec x = \dfrac{1}{\cos x}.$$

By working with the left side and arriving at the right side, the identity is verified.

PRACTICE 2 Verify the identity: $\cos x \cot x + \sin x = \csc x$.

Some identities are verified using factoring to simplify a trigonometric expression.

EXAMPLE 3   Using Factoring to Verify an Identity

Verify the identity: $\cos x - \cos x \sin^2 x = \cos^3 x$.

Solution We start with the more complicated side, the left side. Factor out the greatest common factor, $\cos x$, from each of the two terms.

$$\cos x - \cos x \sin^2 x = \cos x (1 - \sin^2 x) \quad \text{Factor } \cos x \text{ from the two terms.}$$

$$= \cos x \cdot \cos^2 x \quad \text{Use a variation of } \sin^2 x + \cos^2 x = 1. \text{ Solving for } \cos^2 x, \text{ we obtain } \cos^2 x = 1 - \sin^2 x.$$

$$= \cos^3 x \quad \text{Multiply.}$$

We worked with the left side and arrived at the right side. Thus, the identity is verified.

PRACTICE 3 Verify the identity: $\sin x - \sin x \cos^2 x = \sin^3 x$.

Trigonometric Identities, Equations, and Applications

There is often more than one technique that can be used to verify an identity.

EXAMPLE 4 Using Two Techniques to Verify an Identity

Verify the identity: $\dfrac{1 + \sin \theta}{\cos \theta} = \sec \theta + \tan \theta$.

Solution

Method 1. Separating a Single-Term Quotient into Two Terms

Let's separate the quotient on the left side into two terms using

$$\frac{a + b}{c} = \frac{a}{c} + \frac{b}{c}.$$

Perhaps this strategy will enable us to transform the left side into $\sec \theta + \tan \theta$, the sum on the right.

$$\frac{1 + \sin \theta}{\cos \theta} = \frac{1}{\cos \theta} + \frac{\sin \theta}{\cos \theta} \quad \text{Divide each term in the numerator by } \cos \theta.$$

$$= \sec \theta + \tan \theta \quad \text{Apply a reciprocal identity and a quotient identity:}$$
$$\sec \theta = \frac{1}{\cos \theta} \text{ and } \tan \theta = \frac{\sin \theta}{\cos \theta}.$$

We worked with the left side and arrived at the right side. Thus, the identity is verified.

Method 2. Changing to Sines and Cosines

Let's work with the right side of the identity and express it so that it contains only sines and cosines.

$$\sec \theta + \tan \theta = \frac{1}{\cos \theta} + \frac{\sin \theta}{\cos \theta} \quad \text{Apply a reciprocal identity and a quotient identity:}$$
$$\sec \theta = \frac{1}{\cos \theta} \text{ and } \tan \theta = \frac{\sin \theta}{\cos \theta}.$$

$$= \frac{1 + \sin \theta}{\cos \theta} \quad \text{Add numerators. Put this sum over the common denominator.}$$

We worked with the right side and arrived at the left side. Thus, the identity is verified.

PRACTICE 4 Verify the identity: $\dfrac{1 + \cos \theta}{\sin \theta} = \csc \theta + \cot \theta$.

How do we verify identities in which sums or differences of fractions with trigonometric functions appear on one side? Use the least common denominator and combine the fractions. This technique is especially useful when the other side of the identity contains only one term.

EXAMPLE 5 Combining Fractional Expressions to Verify an Identity

Verify the identity: $\dfrac{\cos x}{1 + \sin x} + \dfrac{1 + \sin x}{\cos x} = 2 \sec x$.

Solution We start with the more complicated side, the left side. The least common denominator of the fractions is $(1 + \sin x)(\cos x)$. We express each fraction in terms of this least common denominator by multiplying the numerator and denominator by the extra factor needed to form $(1 + \sin x)(\cos x)$.

$$\frac{\cos x}{1 + \sin x} + \frac{1 + \sin x}{\cos x} \quad \text{The least common denominator is } (1 + \sin x)(\cos x).$$

$$= \frac{\cos x (\cos x)}{(1 + \sin x)(\cos x)} + \frac{(1 + \sin x)(1 + \sin x)}{(1 + \sin x)(\cos x)} \quad \text{Rewrite each fraction with the least common denominator.}$$

$$= \frac{\cos^2 x}{(1 + \sin x)(\cos x)} + \frac{1 + 2 \sin x + \sin^2 x}{(1 + \sin x)(\cos x)} \quad \text{Use the FOIL method to multiply } (1 + \sin x)(1 + \sin x).$$

$$= \frac{\cos^2 x + 1 + 2\sin x + \sin^2 x}{(1 + \sin x)(\cos x)}$$
Add numerators. Put this sum over the least common denominator.

$$= \frac{(\sin^2 x + \cos^2 x) + 1 + 2\sin x}{(1 + \sin x)(\cos x)}$$
Regroup terms to apply a Pythagorean identity.

$$= \frac{1 + 1 + 2\sin x}{(1 + \sin x)(\cos x)}$$
Apply a Pythagorean identity: $\sin^2 x + \cos^2 x = 1$.

$$= \frac{2 + 2\sin x}{(1 + \sin x)(\cos x)}$$
Add constant terms in the numerator: $1 + 1 = 2$.

$$= \frac{2\cancel{(1 + \sin x)}}{\cancel{(1 + \sin x)}(\cos x)}$$
Factor and simplify.

$$= \frac{2}{\cos x}$$

$$= 2\sec x$$
Apply a reciprocal identity: $\sec x = \dfrac{1}{\cos x}$.

We worked with the left side and arrived at the right side. Thus, the identity is verified.

PRACTICE 5 Verify the identity: $\dfrac{\sin x}{1 + \cos x} + \dfrac{1 + \cos x}{\sin x} = 2\csc x$.

Some identities are verified using a technique that may remind you of rationalizing a denominator.

EXAMPLE 6 Multiplying the Numerator and Denominator by the Same Factor to Verify an Identity

Verify the identity: $\dfrac{\sin x}{1 + \cos x} = \dfrac{1 - \cos x}{\sin x}$.

Solution The suggestions given in the previous examples do not apply here. Everything is already expressed in terms of sines and cosines. Furthermore, there are no fractions to combine and neither side looks more complicated than the other. Let's solve the puzzle by working with the left side and making it look like the expression on the right. The expression on the right contains $1 - \cos x$ in the numerator. This suggests multiplying the numerator and denominator of the left side by $1 - \cos x$. By doing this, we obtain a factor of $1 - \cos x$ in the numerator, as in the numerator on the right.

$$\frac{\sin x}{1 + \cos x} = \frac{\sin x}{1 + \cos x} \cdot \frac{1 - \cos x}{1 - \cos x}$$
Multiply numerator and denominator by $1 - \cos x$.

$$= \frac{\sin x(1 - \cos x)}{1 - \cos^2 x}$$
Multiply. Use $(A + B)(A - B) = A^2 - B^2$, with $A = 1$ and $B = \cos x$, to multiply denominators.

$$= \frac{\sin x(1 - \cos x)}{\sin^2 x}$$
Use a variation of $\sin^2 x + \cos^2 x = 1$. Solving for $\sin^2 x$, we obtain $\sin^2 x = 1 - \cos^2 x$.

$$= \frac{1 - \cos x}{\sin x}$$
Simplify: $\dfrac{\sin x}{\sin^2 x} = \dfrac{\cancel{\sin x}}{\cancel{\sin x} \cdot \sin x} = \dfrac{1}{\sin x}$.

We worked with the left side and arrived at the right side. Thus, the identity is verified.

PRACTICE 6 Verify the identity: $\dfrac{\cos x}{1 + \sin x} = \dfrac{1 - \sin x}{\cos x}$.

910 CHAPTER 15 Trigonometric Identities, Equations, and Applications

EXAMPLE 7   Changing to Sines and Cosines to Verify an Identity

Verify the identity: $\dfrac{\tan x - \sin(-x)}{1 + \cos x} = \tan x$.

Solution   We begin with the left side. Our goal is to obtain $\tan x$, the expression on the right.

> **DISCOVERY**
>
> Try simplifying
>
> $$\dfrac{\dfrac{\sin x}{\cos x} + \sin x}{1 + \cos x}$$
>
> by multiplying the two terms in the numerator and the two terms in the denominator by $\cos x$. This method for simplifying the complex fraction involves multiplying the numerator and the denominator by the least common denominator of all fractions in the expression. Do you prefer this simplification procedure over the method used on the right?

$\dfrac{\tan x - \sin(-x)}{1 + \cos x} = \dfrac{\tan x - (-\sin x)}{1 + \cos x}$ The sine function is odd: $\sin(-x) = -\sin x$.

$= \dfrac{\tan x + \sin x}{1 + \cos x}$ Simplify.

$= \dfrac{\dfrac{\sin x}{\cos x} + \sin x}{1 + \cos x}$ Apply a quotient identity: $\tan x = \dfrac{\sin x}{\cos x}$.

$= \dfrac{\dfrac{\sin x}{\cos x} + \dfrac{\sin x \cos x}{\cos x}}{1 + \cos x}$ Express the terms in the numerator with the least common denominator, $\cos x$.

$= \dfrac{\dfrac{\sin x + \sin x \cos x}{\cos x}}{1 + \cos x}$ Add in the numerator.

$= \dfrac{\sin x + \sin x \cos x}{\cos x} \div \dfrac{1 + \cos x}{1}$ Rewrite the main fraction bar as $\div$.

$= \dfrac{\sin x + \sin x \cos x}{\cos x} \cdot \dfrac{1}{1 + \cos x}$ Invert the divisor and multiply.

$= \dfrac{\sin x \cancel{(1 + \cos x)}}{\cos x} \cdot \dfrac{1}{\cancel{1 + \cos x}}$ Factor and simplify.

$= \dfrac{\sin x}{\cos x}$ Multiply the remaining factors in the numerator and in the denominator.

$= \tan x$ Apply a quotient identity.

The left side simplifies to $\tan x$, the right side. Thus, the identity is verified. ∎

PRACTICE 7   Verify the identity: $\dfrac{\sec x + \csc(-x)}{\sec x \csc x} = \sin x - \cos x$.

Is every identity verified by working with only one side? No. You can sometimes work with each side separately and show that both sides are equal to the same trigonometric expression. This is illustrated in Example 8.

EXAMPLE 8   Working with Both Sides Separately to Verify an Identity

Verify the identity: $\dfrac{1}{1 + \cos \theta} + \dfrac{1}{1 - \cos \theta} = 2 + 2\cot^2 \theta$.

Solution   We begin by working with the left side.

$\dfrac{1}{1 + \cos \theta} + \dfrac{1}{1 - \cos \theta}$ The least common denominator is $(1 + \cos \theta)(1 - \cos \theta)$.

$= \dfrac{1(1 - \cos \theta)}{(1 + \cos \theta)(1 - \cos \theta)} + \dfrac{1(1 + \cos \theta)}{(1 + \cos \theta)(1 - \cos \theta)}$ Rewrite each fraction with the least common denominator.

$$= \frac{1 - \cos\theta + 1 + \cos\theta}{(1 + \cos\theta)(1 - \cos\theta)}$$ Add numerators. Put this sum over the least common denominator.

$$= \frac{2}{(1 + \cos\theta)(1 - \cos\theta)}$$ Simplify the numerator: $-\cos\theta + \cos\theta = 0$ and $1 + 1 = 2$.

$$= \frac{2}{1 - \cos^2\theta}$$ Multiply the factors in the denominator.

Now we work with the right side. Our goal is to transform this side into the simplified form attained for the left side, $\frac{2}{1 - \cos^2\theta}$.

$$2 + 2\cot^2\theta = 2 + 2\left(\frac{\cos^2\theta}{\sin^2\theta}\right)$$ Use a quotient identity: $\cot\theta = \frac{\cos\theta}{\sin\theta}$.

$$= \frac{2\sin^2\theta}{\sin^2\theta} + \frac{2\cos^2\theta}{\sin^2\theta}$$ Rewrite each term with the least common denominator, $\sin^2\theta$.

$$= \frac{2\sin^2\theta + 2\cos^2\theta}{\sin^2\theta}$$ Add numerators. Put this sum over the least common denominator.

$$= \frac{2(\sin^2\theta + \cos^2\theta)}{\sin^2\theta}$$ Factor out the greatest common factor, 2.

$$= \frac{2}{\sin^2\theta}$$ Apply a Pythagorean identity: $\sin^2\theta + \cos^2\theta = 1$.

$$= \frac{2}{1 - \cos^2\theta}$$ Use a variation of $\sin^2\theta + \cos^2\theta = 1$, and solve for $\sin^2\theta$: $\sin^2\theta = 1 - \cos^2\theta$.
$\sin^2\theta + \cos^2\theta = 1$

The identity is verified because both sides are equal to $\frac{2}{1 - \cos^2\theta}$.   □

PRACTICE 8 Verify the identity: $\dfrac{1}{1 + \sin\theta} + \dfrac{1}{1 - \sin\theta} = 2 + 2\tan^2\theta$.

Guidelines for Verifying Trigonometric Identities There is often more than one correct way to solve a puzzle, although one method may be shorter and more efficient than another. The same is true for verifying an identity. For example, how would you verify

$$\frac{\csc^2 x - 1}{\csc^2 x} = \cos^2 x?$$

One approach is to use a Pythagorean identity, $1 + \cot^2 x = \csc^2 x$, on the left side. Then change the resulting expression to sines and cosines.

$$\frac{\csc^2 x - 1}{\csc^2 x} = \frac{(1 + \cot^2 x) - 1}{\csc^2 x} = \frac{\cot^2 x}{\csc^2 x} = \frac{\dfrac{\cos^2 x}{\sin^2 x}}{\dfrac{1}{\sin^2 x}} = \frac{\cos^2 x}{\sin^2 x} \cdot \frac{\sin^2 x}{1} = \cos^2 x$$

Apply a Pythagorean identity: $1 + \cot^2 x = \csc^2 x$.

Use $\cot x = \dfrac{\cos x}{\sin x}$ and $\csc x = \dfrac{1}{\sin x}$ to change to sines and cosines.

Invert the divisor and multiply.

A more efficient strategy for verifying this identity may not be apparent at first glance. Work with the left side and divide each term in the numerator by the denominator, $\csc^2 x$.

$$\frac{\csc^2 x - 1}{\csc^2 x} = \frac{\csc^2 x}{\csc^2 x} - \frac{1}{\csc^2 x} = 1 - \sin^2 x = \cos^2 x$$

Apply a reciprocal identity: $\sin x = \frac{1}{\csc x}$.

Use $\sin^2 x + \cos^2 x = 1$ and solve for $\cos^2 x$.

With this strategy, we again obtain $\cos^2 x$, the expression on the right side, and it takes fewer steps than the first approach.

An even longer strategy, but one that works, is to replace each of the two occurrences of $\csc^2 x$ on the left side by $\frac{1}{\sin^2 x}$. This may be the approach that you first consider, particularly if you become accustomed to rewriting the more complicated side in terms of sines and cosines. The selection of an appropriate fundamental identity to solve the puzzle most efficiently is learned through lots of practice.

The more identities you prove, the more confident and efficient you will become. Although practice is the only way to learn how to verify identities, there are some guidelines developed throughout the section that should help you get started.

Guidelines for Verifying Trigonometric Identities

- Work with each side of the equation independently of the other side. Start with the more complicated side and transform it in a step-by-step fashion until it looks exactly like the other side.
- Analyze the identity and look for opportunities to apply the fundamental identities.
- Try using one or more of the following techniques:
  1. Rewrite the more complicated side in terms of sines and cosines.
  2. Factor out the greatest common factor.
  3. Separate a single-term quotient into two terms:

  $$\frac{a+b}{c} = \frac{a}{c} + \frac{b}{c} \quad \text{and} \quad \frac{a-b}{c} = \frac{a}{c} - \frac{b}{c}.$$

  4. Combine fractional expressions using the least common denominator.
  5. Multiply the numerator and the denominator by a binomial factor that appears on the other side of the identity.
- Don't be afraid to stop and start over again if you are not getting anywhere. Creative puzzle solvers know that strategies leading to dead ends often provide good problem-solving ideas.

15.1 EXERCISE SET

PRACTICE EXERCISES

In Exercises 1–60, verify each identity.

1. $\sin x \sec x = \tan x$
2. $\cos x \csc x = \cot x$
3. $\tan(-x) \cos x = -\sin x$
4. $\cot(-x) \sin x = -\cos x$
5. $\tan x \csc x \cos x = 1$
6. $\cot x \sec x \sin x = 1$
7. $\sec x - \sec x \sin^2 x = \cos x$
8. $\csc x - \csc x \cos^2 x = \sin x$
9. $\cos^2 x - \sin^2 x = 1 - 2\sin^2 x$
10. $\cos^2 x - \sin^2 x = 2\cos^2 x - 1$
11. $\csc \theta - \sin \theta = \cot \theta \cos \theta$
12. $\tan \theta + \cot \theta = \sec \theta \csc \theta$
13. $\dfrac{\tan \theta \cot \theta}{\csc \theta} = \sin \theta$
14. $\dfrac{\cos \theta \sec \theta}{\cot \theta} = \tan \theta$
15. $\sin^2 \theta (1 + \cot^2 \theta) = 1$
16. $\cos^2 \theta (1 + \tan^2 \theta) = 1$

17. $\sin t \tan t = \dfrac{1 - \cos^2 t}{\cos t}$

18. $\cos t \cot t = \dfrac{1 - \sin^2 t}{\sin t}$

19. $\dfrac{\csc^2 t}{\cot t} = \csc t \sec t$

20. $\dfrac{\sec^2 t}{\tan t} = \sec t \csc t$

21. $\dfrac{\tan^2 t}{\sec t} = \sec t - \cos t$

22. $\dfrac{\cot^2 t}{\csc t} = \csc t - \sin t$

23. $\dfrac{1 - \cos \theta}{\sin \theta} = \csc \theta - \cot \theta$

24. $\dfrac{1 - \sin \theta}{\cos \theta} = \sec \theta - \tan \theta$

25. $\dfrac{\sin t}{\csc t} + \dfrac{\cos t}{\sec t} = 1$

26. $\dfrac{\sin t}{\tan t} + \dfrac{\cos t}{\cot t} = \sin t + \cos t$

27. $\tan t + \dfrac{\cos t}{1 + \sin t} = \sec t$

28. $\cot t + \dfrac{\sin t}{1 + \cos t} = \csc t$

29. $1 - \dfrac{\sin^2 x}{1 + \cos x} = \cos x$

30. $1 - \dfrac{\cos^2 x}{1 + \sin x} = \sin x$

31. $\dfrac{\cos x}{1 - \sin x} + \dfrac{1 - \sin x}{\cos x} = 2 \sec x$

32. $\dfrac{\sin x}{\cos x + 1} + \dfrac{\cos x - 1}{\sin x} = 0$

33. $\sec^2 x \csc^2 x = \sec^2 x + \csc^2 x$

34. $\csc^2 x \sec x = \sec x + \csc x \cot x$

35. $\dfrac{\sec x - \csc x}{\sec x + \csc x} = \dfrac{\tan x - 1}{\tan x + 1}$

36. $\dfrac{\csc x - \sec x}{\csc x + \sec x} = \dfrac{\cot x - 1}{\cot x + 1}$

37. $\dfrac{\sin^2 x - \cos^2 x}{\sin x + \cos x} = \sin x - \cos x$

38. $\dfrac{\tan^2 x - \cot^2 x}{\tan x + \cot x} = \tan x - \cot x$

39. $\tan^2 2x + \sin^2 2x + \cos^2 2x = \sec^2 2x$

40. $\cot^2 2x + \cos^2 2x + \sin^2 2x = \csc^2 2x$

41. $\dfrac{\tan 2\theta + \cot 2\theta}{\csc 2\theta} = \sec 2\theta$

42. $\dfrac{\tan 2\theta + \cot 2\theta}{\sec 2\theta} = \csc 2\theta$

43. $\dfrac{\tan x + \tan y}{1 - \tan x \tan y} = \dfrac{\sin x \cos y + \cos x \sin y}{\cos x \cos y - \sin x \sin y}$

44. $\dfrac{\cot x + \cot y}{1 - \cot x \cot y} = \dfrac{\cos x \sin y + \sin x \cos y}{\sin x \sin y - \cos x \cos y}$

45. $(\sec x - \tan x)^2 = \dfrac{1 - \sin x}{1 + \sin x}$

46. $(\csc x - \cot x)^2 = \dfrac{1 - \cos x}{1 + \cos x}$

47. $\dfrac{\sec t + 1}{\tan t} = \dfrac{\tan t}{\sec t - 1}$

48. $\dfrac{\csc t - 1}{\cot t} = \dfrac{\cot t}{\csc t + 1}$

49. $\dfrac{1 + \cos t}{1 - \cos t} = (\csc t + \cot t)^2$

50. $\dfrac{\cos^2 t + 4 \cos t + 4}{\cos t + 2} = \dfrac{2 \sec t + 1}{\sec t}$

51. $\cos^4 t - \sin^4 t = 1 - 2 \sin^2 t$

52. $\sin^4 t - \cos^4 t = 1 - 2 \cos^2 t$

53. $\dfrac{\sin \theta - \cos \theta}{\sin \theta} + \dfrac{\cos \theta - \sin \theta}{\cos \theta} = 2 - \sec \theta \csc \theta$

54. $\dfrac{\sin \theta}{1 - \cot \theta} - \dfrac{\cos \theta}{\tan \theta - 1} = \sin \theta + \cos \theta$

55. $(\tan^2 \theta + 1)(\cos^2 \theta + 1) = \tan^2 \theta + 2$

56. $(\cot^2 \theta + 1)(\sin^2 \theta + 1) = \cot^2 \theta + 2$

57. $(\cos \theta - \sin \theta)^2 + (\cos \theta + \sin \theta)^2 = 2$

58. $(3 \cos \theta - 4 \sin \theta)^2 + (4 \cos \theta + 3 \sin \theta)^2 = 25$

59. $\dfrac{\cos^2 x - \sin^2 x}{1 - \tan^2 x} = \cos^2 x$

60. $\dfrac{\sin x + \cos x}{\sin x} - \dfrac{\cos x - \sin x}{\cos x} = \sec x \csc x$

PRACTICE PLUS

In Exercises 61–66, half of an identity and the graph of this half are given. Use the graph to make a conjecture as to what the right side of the identity should be. Then prove your conjecture.

61. $\dfrac{(\sec x + \tan x)(\sec x - \tan x)}{\sec x} = \;?$

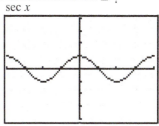

$[-2\pi, 2\pi, \tfrac{\pi}{2}]$ by $[-4, 4, 1]$

62. $\dfrac{\sec^2 x \csc x}{\sec^2 x + \csc^2 x} = \;?$

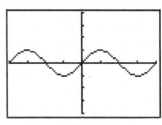

$[-2\pi, 2\pi, \tfrac{\pi}{2}]$ by $[-4, 4, 1]$

63. $\dfrac{\cos x + \cot x \sin x}{\cot x} = \;?$

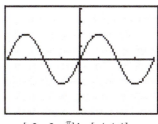

$[-2\pi, 2\pi, \tfrac{\pi}{2}]$ by $[-4, 4, 1]$

64. $\dfrac{\cos x \tan x - \tan x + 2\cos x - 2}{\tan x + 2} = ?$

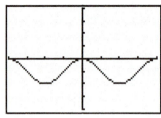

$[-2\pi, 2\pi, \tfrac{\pi}{2}]$ by $[-4, 4, 1]$

65. $\dfrac{1}{\sec x + \tan x} + \dfrac{1}{\sec x - \tan x} = ?$

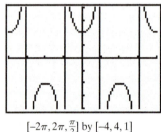

$[-2\pi, 2\pi, \tfrac{\pi}{2}]$ by $[-4, 4, 1]$

66. $\dfrac{1 + \cos x}{\sin x} + \dfrac{\sin x}{1 + \cos x} = ?$

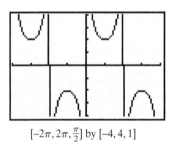

$[-2\pi, 2\pi, \tfrac{\pi}{2}]$ by $[-4, 4, 1]$

In Exercises 67–74, rewrite each expression in terms of the given function or functions.

67. $\dfrac{\tan x + \cot x}{\csc x}$; $\cos x$

68. $\dfrac{\sec x + \csc x}{1 + \tan x}$; $\sin x$

69. $\dfrac{\cos x}{1 + \sin x} + \tan x$; $\cos x$

70. $\dfrac{1}{\sin x \cos x} - \cot x$; $\cot x$

71. $\dfrac{1}{1 - \cos x} - \dfrac{\cos x}{1 + \cos x}$; $\csc x$

72. $(\sec x + \csc x)(\sin x + \cos x) - 2 - \cot x$; $\tan x$

73. $\dfrac{1}{\csc x - \sin x}$; $\sec x$ and $\tan x$

74. $\dfrac{1 - \sin x}{1 + \sin x} - \dfrac{1 + \sin x}{1 - \sin x}$; $\sec x$ and $\tan x$

WRITING IN MATHEMATICS

75. Explain how to verify an identity.

76. Describe two strategies that can be used to verify identities.

77. Describe how you feel when you successfully verify a difficult identity.

78. A 10-point question on a quiz asks students to verify the identity

$$\dfrac{\sin^2 x - \cos^2 x}{\sin x + \cos x} = \sin x - \cos x.$$

One student begins with the left side and obtains the right side as follows:

$$\dfrac{\sin^2 x - \cos^2 x}{\sin x + \cos x} = \dfrac{\sin^2 x}{\sin x} - \dfrac{\cos^2 x}{\cos x} = \sin x - \cos x.$$

How many points (out of 10) would you give this student? Explain your answer.

TECHNOLOGY EXERCISES

In Exercises 79–87, graph each side of the equation in the same viewing rectangle. If the graphs appear to coincide, verify that the equation is an identity. If the graphs do not appear to coincide, this indicates the equation is not an identity. In these exercises, find a value of x for which both sides are defined but not equal.

79. $\tan x = \sec x (\sin x - \cos x) + 1$

80. $\sin x = -\cos x \tan(-x)$

81. $\sin\left(x + \dfrac{\pi}{4}\right) = \sin x + \sin \dfrac{\pi}{4}$

82. $\cos\left(x + \dfrac{\pi}{4}\right) = \cos x + \cos \dfrac{\pi}{4}$

83. $\cos(x + \pi) = \cos x$

84. $\sin(x + \pi) = \sin x$

85. $\dfrac{\sin x}{1 - \cos^2 x} = \csc x$

86. $\sin x - \sin x \cos^2 x = \sin^3 x$

87. $\sqrt{\sin^2 x + \cos^2 x} = \sin x + \cos x$

CRITICAL THINKING EXERCISES

Make Sense? *In Exercises 88–91, determine whether each statement makes sense or does not make sense, and explain your reasoning.*

88. The word *identity* is used in different ways in additive identity, multiplicative identity, and trigonometric identity.

89. To prove a trigonometric identity, I select one side of the equation and transform it until it is the other side of the equation, or I manipulate both sides to a common trigonometric expression.

90. In order to simplify $\dfrac{\cos x}{1 - \sin x} - \dfrac{\sin x}{\cos x}$, I need to know how to subtract rational expressions with unlike denominators.

91. The most efficient way that I can simplify $\dfrac{(\sec x + 1)(\sec x - 1)}{\sin^2 x}$ is to immediately rewrite the expression in terms of cosines and sines.

In Exercises 92–95, verify each identity.

92. $\dfrac{\sin^3 x - \cos^3 x}{\sin x - \cos x} = 1 + \sin x \cos x$

93. $\dfrac{\sin x - \cos x + 1}{\sin x + \cos x - 1} = \dfrac{\sin x + 1}{\cos x}$

94. $\ln|\sec x| = -\ln|\cos x|$ 95. $\ln e^{\tan^2 x - \sec^2 x} = -1$

96. Use one of the fundamental identities in the box at the beginning of the section to create an original identity.

GROUP EXERCISE

97. Group members are to write a helpful list of items for a pamphlet called "The Underground Guide to Verifying Identities." List easy ways to remember the fundamental identities. What helpful guidelines can you offer from the perspective of a student? If you have your own strategies that work particularly well, include them in the pamphlet.

PREVIEW EXERCISES

Exercises 98–100 will help you prepare for the material covered in the next section.

98. Give exact values for cos 30°, sin 30°, cos 60°, sin 60°, cos 90°, and sin 90°.

99. Use the appropriate values from Exercise 98 to answer each of the following.
    a. Is cos (30° + 60°), or cos 90°, equal to cos 30° + cos 60°?
    b. Is cos (30° + 60°), or cos 90°, equal to cos 30° cos 60° − sin 30° sin 60°?

100. Use the appropriate values from Exercise 98 to answer each of the following.
    a. Is sin (30° + 60°), or sin 90°, equal to sin 30° + sin 60°?
    b. Is sin (30° + 60°), or sin 90°, equal to sin 30° cos 60° + cos 30° sin 60°?

15.2 SUM AND DIFFERENCE FORMULAS

OBJECTIVES

1. Use the formula for the cosine of the difference of two angles.
2. Use sum and difference formulas for cosines and sines.
3. Use sum and difference formulas for tangents.

OBJECTIVE 1 ▶ The cosine of the difference of two angles

> **The Cosine of the Difference of Two Angles**
>
> $$\cos(\alpha - \beta) = \cos\alpha \cos\beta + \sin\alpha \sin\beta$$
>
> The cosine of the difference of two angles equals the cosine of the first angle times the cosine of the second angle plus the sine of the first angle times the sine of the second angle.

We use Figure 15.1 to prove the identity in the box. The graph in Figure 15.1(a) shows a unit circle, $x^2 + y^2 = 1$. The figure uses the definitions of the cosine and sine functions as the x- and y-coordinates of points along the unit circle. For example, point P corresponds to angle β. By definition, the x-coordinate of P is $\cos\beta$ and the y-coordinate is $\sin\beta$. Similarly, point Q corresponds to angle α. By definition, the x-coordinate of Q is $\cos\alpha$ and the y-coordinate is $\sin\alpha$.

Note that if we draw a line segment between points P and Q, a triangle is formed. Angle $\alpha - \beta$ is one of the angles of this triangle. What happens if we rotate this triangle so that point P falls on the x-axis at $(1, 0)$? The result is shown in Figure 15.1(b). This rotation changes the coordinates of points P and Q. However, it has no effect on the length of line segment PQ.

We can use the distance formula, $d = \sqrt{(x_2 - x_1)^2 + (y_2 - y_1)^2}$, to find an expression for PQ in Figure 15.1(a) and in Figure 15.1(b). By equating the two expressions for PQ, we will obtain the identity for the cosine of the difference of two angles, $\alpha - \beta$. We first apply the distance formula in Figure 15.1(a).

$PQ = \sqrt{(\cos\alpha - \cos\beta)^2 + (\sin\alpha - \sin\beta)^2}$ Apply the distance formula, $d = \sqrt{(x_2 - x_1)^2 + (y_2 - y_1)^2}$, to find the distance between $(\cos\beta, \sin\beta)$ and $(\cos\alpha, \sin\alpha)$.

$= \sqrt{\cos^2\alpha - 2\cos\alpha\cos\beta + \cos^2\beta + \sin^2\alpha - 2\sin\alpha\sin\beta + \sin^2\beta}$ Square each expression using $(A - B)^2 = A^2 - 2AB + B^2$.

$$= \sqrt{(\sin^2 \alpha + \cos^2 \alpha) + (\sin^2 \beta + \cos^2 \beta) - 2\cos\alpha\cos\beta - 2\sin\alpha\sin\beta}$$ Regroup terms to apply a Pythagorean identity.

$$= \sqrt{1 + 1 - 2\cos\alpha\cos\beta - 2\sin\alpha\sin\beta}$$ Because $\sin^2 x + \cos^2 x = 1$, each expression in parentheses equals 1.

$$= \sqrt{2 - 2\cos\alpha\cos\beta - 2\sin\alpha\sin\beta}$$ Simplify.

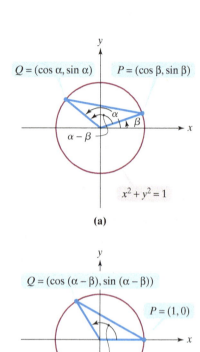

FIGURE 15.1 Using the unit circle and PQ to develop a formula for $\cos(\alpha - \beta)$

Next, we apply the distance formula in Figure 15.1(b) to obtain a second expression for PQ. We let $(x_1, y_1) = (1, 0)$ and $(x_2, y_2) = (\cos(\alpha - \beta), \sin(\alpha - \beta))$.

$$PQ = \sqrt{[\cos(\alpha - \beta) - 1]^2 + [\sin(\alpha - \beta) - 0]^2}$$ Apply the distance formula to find the distance between $(1, 0)$ and $(\cos(\alpha - \beta), \sin(\alpha - \beta))$.

$$= \sqrt{\cos^2(\alpha - \beta) - 2\cos(\alpha - \beta) + 1 + \sin^2(\alpha - \beta)}$$ Square each expression.

$$= \sqrt{\cos^2(\alpha - \beta) - 2\cos(\alpha - \beta) + 1 + \sin^2(\alpha - \beta)}$$

Using a Pythagorean identity, $\sin^2(\alpha - \beta) + \cos^2(\alpha - \beta) = 1$.

$$= \sqrt{1 - 2\cos(\alpha - \beta) + 1}$$ Use a Pythagorean identity.

$$= \sqrt{2 - 2\cos(\alpha - \beta)}$$ Simplify.

Now we equate the two expressions for PQ.

$$\sqrt{2 - 2\cos(\alpha - \beta)} = \sqrt{2 - 2\cos\alpha\cos\beta - 2\sin\alpha\sin\beta}$$ The rotation does not change the length of PQ.

$$2 - 2\cos(\alpha - \beta) = 2 - 2\cos\alpha\cos\beta - 2\sin\alpha\sin\beta$$ Square both sides to eliminate radicals.

$$-2\cos(\alpha - \beta) = -2\cos\alpha\cos\beta - 2\sin\alpha\sin\beta$$ Subtract 2 from both sides of the equation.

$$\cos(\alpha - \beta) = \cos\alpha\cos\beta + \sin\alpha\sin\beta$$ Divide both sides of the equation by -2.

This proves the identity for the cosine of the difference of two angles.

Now that we see where the identity for the cosine of the difference of two angles comes from, let's look at some applications of this result.

EXAMPLE 1 Using the Difference Formula for Cosines to Find an Exact Value

Find the exact value of $\cos 15°$.

Solution We know exact values for trigonometric functions of $60°$ and $45°$. Thus, we write $15°$ as $60° - 45°$ and use the difference formula for cosines.

$$\cos 15° = \cos(60° - 45°)$$

$$= \cos 60° \cos 45° + \sin 60° \sin 45°$$ $\cos(\alpha - \beta) = \cos\alpha\cos\beta + \sin\alpha\sin\beta$

$$= \frac{1}{2} \cdot \frac{\sqrt{2}}{2} + \frac{\sqrt{3}}{2} \cdot \frac{\sqrt{2}}{2}$$ Substitute exact values from memory or use special right triangles.

$$= \frac{\sqrt{2}}{4} + \frac{\sqrt{6}}{4}$$ Multiply.

$$= \frac{\sqrt{2} + \sqrt{6}}{4}$$ Add.

PRACTICE 1

We know that $\cos 30° = \dfrac{\sqrt{3}}{2}$. Obtain this exact value using $\cos 30° = \cos(90° - 60°)$ and the difference formula for cosines.

EXAMPLE 2 Using the Difference Formula for Cosines to Find an Exact Value

Find the exact value of $\cos 80° \cos 20° + \sin 80° \sin 20°$.

Solution The given expression is the right side of the formula for $\cos(\alpha - \beta)$ with $\alpha = 80°$ and $\beta = 20°$.

$$\cos(\alpha - \beta) = \cos\alpha\cos\beta + \sin\alpha\sin\beta$$

$$\cos 80° \cos 20° + \sin 80° \sin 20° = \cos(80° - 20°) = \cos 60° = \dfrac{1}{2}$$

PRACTICE 2

Find the exact value of

$$\cos 70° \cos 40° + \sin 70° \sin 40°.$$

EXAMPLE 3 Verifying an Identity

Verify the identity: $\dfrac{\cos(\alpha - \beta)}{\sin\alpha\cos\beta} = \cot\alpha + \tan\beta$.

Solution We work with the left side.

$$\dfrac{\cos(\alpha - \beta)}{\sin\alpha\cos\beta} = \dfrac{\cos\alpha\cos\beta + \sin\alpha\sin\beta}{\sin\alpha\cos\beta} \qquad \text{Use the formula for } \cos(\alpha - \beta).$$

$$= \dfrac{\cos\alpha\cos\beta}{\sin\alpha\cos\beta} + \dfrac{\sin\alpha\sin\beta}{\sin\alpha\cos\beta} \qquad \text{Divide each term in the numerator by } \sin\alpha\cos\beta.$$

$$= \dfrac{\cos\alpha}{\sin\alpha} \cdot \dfrac{\cos\beta}{\cos\beta} + \dfrac{\sin\alpha}{\sin\alpha} \cdot \dfrac{\sin\beta}{\cos\beta} \qquad \text{This step can be done mentally. We wanted you to see the substitutions that follow.}$$

$$= \cot\alpha \cdot 1 + 1 \cdot \tan\beta \qquad \text{Use quotient identities.}$$

$$= \cot\alpha + \tan\beta \qquad \text{Simplify.}$$

We worked with the left side and arrived at the right side. Thus, the identity is verified.

TECHNOLOGY NOTE

Graphic Connections

The graphs of

$$y = \cos\left(\dfrac{\pi}{2} - x\right)$$

and

$$y = \sin x$$

are shown in the same viewing rectangle. The graphs are the same. The displayed math on the right with the voice balloon on top shows the equivalence algebraically.

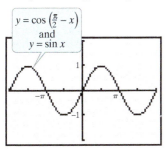

PRACTICE 3

Verify the identity: $\dfrac{\cos(\alpha - \beta)}{\cos\alpha\cos\beta} = 1 + \tan\alpha\tan\beta$.

The difference formula for cosines is used to establish other identities. For example, in our work with right triangles, we noted that cofunctions of complements are equal. Thus, because $\dfrac{\pi}{2} - \theta$ and θ are complements,

$$\cos\left(\dfrac{\pi}{2} - \theta\right) = \sin\theta.$$

We can use the formula for $\cos(\alpha - \beta)$ to prove this cofunction identity for all angles.

$$\cos\left(\frac{\pi}{2} - \theta\right) = \cos\frac{\pi}{2}\cos\theta + \sin\frac{\pi}{2}\sin\theta$$

Apply $\cos(\alpha - \beta)$ with $\alpha = \frac{\pi}{2}$ and $\beta = \theta$.
$\cos(\alpha - \beta) = \cos\alpha\cos\beta + \sin\alpha\sin\beta$

$$= 0 \cdot \cos\theta + 1 \cdot \sin\theta$$
$$= \sin\theta$$

OBJECTIVE 2 ▶ Sum and difference formulas for cosines and sines. Our formula for $\cos(\alpha - \beta)$ can be used to verify an identity for a sum involving cosines, as well as identities for a sum and a difference for sines.

Sum and Difference Formulas for Cosines and Sines

1. $\cos(\alpha + \beta) = \cos\alpha\cos\beta - \sin\alpha\sin\beta$
2. $\cos(\alpha - \beta) = \cos\alpha\cos\beta + \sin\alpha\sin\beta$
3. $\sin(\alpha + \beta) = \sin\alpha\cos\beta + \cos\alpha\sin\beta$
4. $\sin(\alpha - \beta) = \sin\alpha\cos\beta - \cos\alpha\sin\beta$

Up to now, we have concentrated on the second formula in the box on the previous page, $\cos(\alpha - \beta) = \cos\alpha\cos\beta + \sin\alpha\sin\beta$. The first identity gives a formula for the cosine of the sum of two angles. It is proved as follows:

$\cos(\alpha + \beta) = \cos[\alpha - (-\beta)]$ — Express addition as subtraction of an additive inverse.

$= \cos\alpha\cos(-\beta) + \sin\alpha\sin(-\beta)$ — Use the difference formula for cosines.

$= \cos\alpha\cos\beta + \sin\alpha(-\sin\beta)$ — Cosine is even: $\cos(-\beta) = \cos\beta$. Sine is odd: $\sin(-\beta) = -\sin\beta$.

$= \cos\alpha\cos\beta - \sin\alpha\sin\beta$. — Simplify.

Thus, the cosine of the sum of two angles equals the cosine of the first angle times the cosine of the second angle minus the sine of the first angle times the sine of the second angle.

The third identity in the box gives a formula for $\sin(\alpha + \beta)$, the sine of the sum of two angles. It is proved as follows:

$\sin(\alpha + \beta) = \cos\left[\frac{\pi}{2} - (\alpha + \beta)\right]$ — Use a cofunction identity: $\sin\theta = \cos\left(\frac{\pi}{2} - \theta\right)$.

$= \cos\left[\left(\frac{\pi}{2} - \alpha\right) - \beta\right]$ — Regroup.

$= \cos\left(\frac{\pi}{2} - \alpha\right)\cos\beta + \sin\left(\frac{\pi}{2} - \alpha\right)\sin\beta$ — Use the difference formula for cosines.

$= \sin\alpha\cos\beta + \cos\alpha\sin\beta$. — Use cofunction identities.

Thus, the sine of the sum of two angles equals the sine of the first angle times the cosine of the second angle plus the cosine of the first angle times the sine of the second angle.

The final identity in the box, $\sin(\alpha - \beta) = \sin\alpha\cos\beta - \cos\alpha\sin\beta$, gives a formula for $\sin(\alpha - \beta)$, the sine of the difference of two angles. It is proved by writing $\sin(\alpha - \beta)$ as $\sin[\alpha + (-\beta)]$ and then using the formula for the sine of a sum.

EXAMPLE 4 Using the Sine of a Sum to Find an Exact Value

Find the exact value of $\sin \dfrac{7\pi}{12}$ using the fact that $\dfrac{7\pi}{12} = \dfrac{\pi}{3} + \dfrac{\pi}{4}$.

Solution We apply the formula for the sine of a sum.

$$\sin \frac{7\pi}{12} = \sin\left(\frac{\pi}{3} + \frac{\pi}{4}\right)$$

$$= \sin\frac{\pi}{3}\cos\frac{\pi}{4} + \cos\frac{\pi}{3}\sin\frac{\pi}{4} \qquad \sin(\alpha + \beta) = \sin\alpha\cos\beta + \cos\alpha\sin\beta$$

$$= \frac{\sqrt{3}}{2}\cdot\frac{\sqrt{2}}{2} + \frac{1}{2}\cdot\frac{\sqrt{2}}{2} \qquad \text{Substitute exact values.}$$

$$= \frac{\sqrt{6} + \sqrt{2}}{4} \qquad \text{Simplify.}$$

PRACTICE 4 Find the exact value of $\sin \dfrac{5\pi}{12}$ using the fact that

$$\frac{5\pi}{12} = \frac{\pi}{6} + \frac{\pi}{4}.$$

EXAMPLE 5 Finding Exact Values

Suppose that $\sin \alpha = \frac{12}{13}$ for a quadrant II angle α and $\sin \beta = \frac{3}{5}$ for a quadrant I angle β. Find the exact value of each of the following:

a. $\cos \alpha$ **b.** $\cos \beta$ **c.** $\cos(\alpha + \beta)$ **d.** $\sin(\alpha + \beta)$.

Solution

a. We find $\cos \alpha$ using a sketch that illustrates

$$\sin \alpha = \frac{12}{13} = \frac{y}{r}.$$

Figure 15.2 shows a quadrant II angle α with $\sin \alpha = \frac{12}{13}$. We find x using $x^2 + y^2 = r^2$. Because α lies in quadrant II, x is negative.

$$x^2 + 12^2 = 13^2 \qquad x^2 + y^2 = r^2$$
$$x^2 + 144 = 169 \qquad \text{Square 12 and 13, respectively.}$$
$$x^2 = 25 \qquad \text{Subtract 144 from both sides.}$$
$$x = -\sqrt{25} = -5 \qquad \text{If } x^2 = 25, \text{ then } x = \pm\sqrt{25} = \pm 5.$$
$$\phantom{x = -\sqrt{25} = -5} \qquad \text{Choose } x = -\sqrt{25} \text{ because in quadrant II,}$$
$$\phantom{x = -\sqrt{25} = -5} \qquad x \text{ is negative.}$$

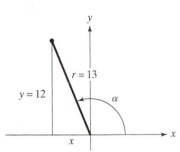

FIGURE 15.2 $\sin \alpha = \frac{12}{13}$; α lies in quadrant II.

Thus,

$$\cos \alpha = \frac{x}{r} = \frac{-5}{13} = -\frac{5}{13}.$$

b. We find $\cos \beta$ using a sketch that illustrates

$$\sin \beta = \frac{3}{5} = \frac{y}{r}.$$

Figure 15.3 shows a quadrant I angle β with $\sin \beta = \frac{3}{5}$. We find x using $x^2 + y^2 = r^2$.

$$x^2 + 3^2 = 5^2 \qquad x^2 + y^2 = r^2$$
$$x^2 + 9 = 25 \qquad \text{Square 3 and 5, respectively.}$$
$$x^2 = 16 \qquad \text{Subtract 9 from both sides.}$$

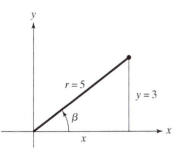

FIGURE 15.3 $\sin \beta = \frac{3}{5}$; β lies in quadrant I.

$$x = \sqrt{16} = 4 \qquad \text{If } x^2 = 16, \text{ then } x = \pm\sqrt{16} = \pm 4.$$
$$\text{Choose } x = \sqrt{16} \text{ because in quadrant 1,}$$
$$x \text{ is positive.}$$

Thus,
$$\cos\beta = \frac{x}{r} = \frac{4}{5}.$$

We use the given values and the exact values that we determined to find exact values for $\cos(\alpha + \beta)$ and $\sin(\alpha + \beta)$.

$$\underbrace{\sin\alpha = \frac{12}{13},\ \sin\beta = \frac{3}{5}}_{\text{These values are given.}} \qquad \underbrace{\cos\alpha = -\frac{5}{13},\ \cos\beta = \frac{4}{5}}_{\text{These are the values we found.}}$$

c. We use the formula for the cosine of a sum.

$$\cos(\alpha + \beta) = \cos\alpha\cos\beta - \sin\alpha\sin\beta$$
$$= \left(-\frac{5}{13}\right)\left(\frac{4}{5}\right) - \frac{12}{13}\left(\frac{3}{5}\right) = -\frac{56}{65}$$

d. We use the formula for the sine of a sum.

$$\underbrace{\sin\alpha = \frac{12}{13},\ \sin\beta = \frac{3}{5}}_{\text{These values are given.}} \quad \underbrace{\cos\alpha = -\frac{5}{13},\ \cos\beta = \frac{4}{5}}_{\text{These are the values we found.}} \quad \sin(\alpha + \beta) = \sin\alpha\cos\beta + \cos\alpha\sin\beta$$
$$= \frac{12}{13}\cdot\frac{4}{5} + \left(-\frac{5}{13}\right)\cdot\frac{3}{5} = \frac{33}{65} \qquad \square$$

PRACTICE 5 Suppose that $\sin\alpha = \frac{4}{5}$ for a quadrant II angle α and $\sin\beta = \frac{1}{2}$ for a quadrant I angle β. Find the exact value of each of the following:

a. $\cos\alpha$ **b.** $\cos\beta$ **c.** $\cos(\alpha + \beta)$ **d.** $\sin(\alpha + \beta)$.

EXAMPLE 6 Verifying Observations on a Graphing Utility

Figure 15.4 shows the graph of $y = \sin\left(x - \frac{3\pi}{2}\right)$ in a $\left[0, 2\pi, \frac{\pi}{2}\right]$ by $[-2, 2, 1]$ viewing rectangle.

a. Describe the graph using another equation.
b. Verify that the two equations are equivalent.

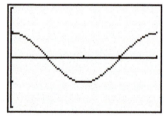

FIGURE 15.4 The graph of $y = \sin\left(x - \frac{3\pi}{2}\right)$ in a $\left[0, 2\pi, \frac{\pi}{2}\right]$ by $[-2, 2, 1]$ viewing rectangle

Solution

a. The graph appears to be the cosine curve $y = \cos x$. It cycles through maximum, intercept, minimum, intercept, and back to maximum. Thus, $y = \cos x$ also describes the graph.

b. We must show that
$$\sin\left(x - \frac{3\pi}{2}\right) = \cos x.$$

We apply the formula for the sine of a difference on the left side.

$$\sin\left(x - \frac{3\pi}{2}\right) = \sin x \cos\frac{3\pi}{2} - \cos x \sin\frac{3\pi}{2} \qquad \begin{array}{l} \sin(\alpha - \beta) = \\ \sin\alpha\cos\beta - \cos\alpha\sin\beta \end{array}$$

$$= \sin x \cdot 0 - \cos x(-1) \qquad \cos\frac{3\pi}{2} = 0 \text{ and } \sin\frac{3\pi}{2} = -1$$

$$= \cos x \qquad \text{Simplify.}$$

This verifies our observation that $y = \sin\left(x - \frac{3\pi}{2}\right)$ and $y = \cos x$ describe the same graph. □

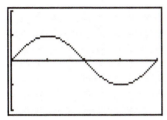

FIGURE 15.5

PRACTICE 6 Figure 15.5 shows the graph of $y = \cos\left(x + \frac{3\pi}{2}\right)$ in a $\left[0, 2\pi, \frac{\pi}{2}\right]$ by $[-2, 2, 1]$ viewing rectangle.

a. Describe the graph using another equation.
b. Verify that the two equations are equivalent.

OBJECTIVE 3 ▶ Sum and difference formulas for tangents. By writing $\tan(\alpha + \beta)$ as the quotient of $\sin(\alpha + \beta)$ and $\cos(\alpha + \beta)$, we can develop a formula for the tangent of a sum. Writing subtraction as addition of an inverse leads to a formula for the tangent of a difference.

Sum and Difference Formulas for Tangents

$$\tan(\alpha + \beta) = \frac{\tan \alpha + \tan \beta}{1 - \tan \alpha \tan \beta}$$

The tangent of the sum of two angles equals the tangent of the first angle plus the tangent of the second angle divided by 1 minus their product.

$$\tan(\alpha - \beta) = \frac{\tan \alpha - \tan \beta}{1 + \tan \alpha \tan \beta}$$

The tangent of the difference of two angles equals the tangent of the first angle minus the tangent of the second angle divided by 1 plus their product.

EXAMPLE 7 Verifying an Identity

Verify the identity: $\tan\left(x - \frac{\pi}{4}\right) = \frac{\tan x - 1}{\tan x + 1}$.

Solution We work with the left side.

$$\tan\left(x - \frac{\pi}{4}\right) = \frac{\tan x - \tan\frac{\pi}{4}}{1 + \tan x \tan\frac{\pi}{4}} \qquad \tan(\alpha - \beta) = \frac{\tan \alpha - \tan \beta}{1 + \tan \alpha \tan \beta}$$

$$= \frac{\tan x - 1}{1 + \tan x \cdot 1} \qquad \tan\frac{\pi}{4} = 1$$

$$= \frac{\tan x - 1}{\tan x + 1} \qquad □$$

PRACTICE 7 Verify the identity: $\tan(x + \pi) = \tan x$.

15.2 EXERCISE SET

PRACTICE EXERCISES

Use the formula for the cosine of the difference of two angles to solve Exercises 1–12.

In Exercises 1–4, find the exact value of each expression.

1. $\cos(45° - 30°)$
2. $\cos(120° - 45°)$
3. $\cos\left(\dfrac{3\pi}{4} - \dfrac{\pi}{6}\right)$
4. $\cos\left(\dfrac{2\pi}{3} - \dfrac{\pi}{6}\right)$

In Exercises 5–8, each expression is the right side of the formula for $\cos(\alpha - \beta)$ with particular values for α and β.

a. Identify α and β in each expression.
b. Write the expression as the cosine of an angle.
c. Find the exact value of the expression.

5. $\cos 50° \cos 20° + \sin 50° \sin 20°$
6. $\cos 50° \cos 5° + \sin 50° \sin 5°$
7. $\cos\dfrac{5\pi}{12}\cos\dfrac{\pi}{12} + \sin\dfrac{5\pi}{12}\sin\dfrac{\pi}{12}$
8. $\cos\dfrac{5\pi}{18}\cos\dfrac{\pi}{9} + \sin\dfrac{5\pi}{18}\sin\dfrac{\pi}{9}$

In Exercises 9–12, verify each identity.

9. $\dfrac{\cos(\alpha - \beta)}{\cos \alpha \sin \beta} = \tan \alpha + \cot \beta$
10. $\dfrac{\cos(\alpha - \beta)}{\sin \alpha \sin \beta} = \cot \alpha \cot \beta + 1$
11. $\cos\left(x - \dfrac{\pi}{4}\right) = \dfrac{\sqrt{2}}{2}(\cos x + \sin x)$
12. $\cos\left(x - \dfrac{5\pi}{4}\right) = -\dfrac{\sqrt{2}}{2}(\cos x + \sin x)$

Use one or more of the six sum and difference identities to solve Exercises 13–54.
In Exercises 13–24, find the exact value of each expression.

13. $\sin(45° - 30°)$
14. $\sin(60° - 45°)$
15. $\sin 105°$
16. $\sin 75°$
17. $\cos(135° + 30°)$
18. $\cos(240° + 45°)$
19. $\cos 75°$
20. $\cos 105°$
21. $\tan\left(\dfrac{\pi}{6} + \dfrac{\pi}{4}\right)$
22. $\tan\left(\dfrac{\pi}{3} + \dfrac{\pi}{4}\right)$
23. $\tan\left(\dfrac{4\pi}{3} - \dfrac{\pi}{4}\right)$
24. $\tan\left(\dfrac{5\pi}{3} - \dfrac{\pi}{4}\right)$

In Exercises 25–32, write each expression as the sine, cosine, or tangent of an angle. Then find the exact value of the expression.

25. $\sin 25° \cos 5° + \cos 25° \sin 5°$
26. $\sin 40° \cos 20° + \cos 40° \sin 20°$
27. $\dfrac{\tan 10° + \tan 35°}{1 - \tan 10° \tan 35°}$
28. $\dfrac{\tan 50° - \tan 20°}{1 + \tan 50° \tan 20°}$
29. $\sin\dfrac{5\pi}{12}\cos\dfrac{\pi}{4} - \cos\dfrac{5\pi}{12}\sin\dfrac{\pi}{4}$
30. $\sin\dfrac{7\pi}{12}\cos\dfrac{\pi}{12} - \cos\dfrac{7\pi}{12}\sin\dfrac{\pi}{12}$
31. $\dfrac{\tan\dfrac{\pi}{5} - \tan\dfrac{\pi}{30}}{1 + \tan\dfrac{\pi}{5}\tan\dfrac{\pi}{30}}$
32. $\dfrac{\tan\dfrac{\pi}{5} + \tan\dfrac{4\pi}{5}}{1 - \tan\dfrac{\pi}{5}\tan\dfrac{4\pi}{5}}$

In Exercises 33–54, verify each identity.

33. $\sin\left(x + \dfrac{\pi}{2}\right) = \cos x$
34. $\sin\left(x + \dfrac{3\pi}{2}\right) = -\cos x$
35. $\cos\left(x - \dfrac{\pi}{2}\right) = \sin x$
36. $\cos(\pi - x) = -\cos x$
37. $\tan(2\pi - x) = -\tan x$
38. $\tan(\pi - x) = -\tan x$
39. $\sin(\alpha + \beta) + \sin(\alpha - \beta) = 2 \sin \alpha \cos \beta$
40. $\cos(\alpha + \beta) + \cos(\alpha - \beta) = 2 \cos \alpha \cos \beta$
41. $\dfrac{\sin(\alpha - \beta)}{\cos \alpha \cos \beta} = \tan \alpha - \tan \beta$
42. $\dfrac{\sin(\alpha + \beta)}{\cos \alpha \cos \beta} = \tan \alpha + \tan \beta$
43. $\tan\left(\theta + \dfrac{\pi}{4}\right) = \dfrac{\cos \theta + \sin \theta}{\cos \theta - \sin \theta}$
44. $\tan\left(\dfrac{\pi}{4} - \theta\right) = \dfrac{\cos \theta - \sin \theta}{\cos \theta + \sin \theta}$
45. $\cos(\alpha + \beta) \cos(\alpha - \beta) = \cos^2 \beta - \sin^2 \alpha$
46. $\sin(\alpha + \beta) \sin(\alpha - \beta) = \cos^2 \beta - \cos^2 \alpha$
47. $\dfrac{\sin(\alpha + \beta)}{\sin(\alpha - \beta)} = \dfrac{\tan \alpha + \tan \beta}{\tan \alpha - \tan \beta}$
48. $\dfrac{\cos(\alpha + \beta)}{\cos(\alpha - \beta)} = \dfrac{1 - \tan \alpha \tan \beta}{1 + \tan \alpha \tan \beta}$
49. $\dfrac{\cos(x + h) - \cos x}{h} = \cos x \cdot \dfrac{\cos h - 1}{h} - \sin x \cdot \dfrac{\sin h}{h}$
50. $\dfrac{\sin(x + h) - \sin x}{h} = \cos x \cdot \dfrac{\sin h}{h} + \sin x \cdot \dfrac{\cos h - 1}{h}$
51. $\sin 2\alpha = 2 \sin \alpha \cos \alpha$

Hint: Write $\sin 2\alpha$ as $\sin(\alpha + \alpha)$.

52. $\cos 2\alpha = \cos^2 \alpha - \sin^2 \alpha$

Hint: Write $\cos 2\alpha$ as $\cos(\alpha + \alpha)$.

53. $\tan 2\alpha = \dfrac{2 \tan \alpha}{1 - \tan^2 \alpha}$

Hint: Write $\tan 2\alpha$ as $\tan(\alpha + \alpha)$.

54. $\tan\left(\dfrac{\pi}{4} + \alpha\right) - \tan\left(\dfrac{\pi}{4} - \alpha\right) = 2\tan 2\alpha$

Hint: Use the result in Exercise 53.

55. Derive the identity for $\tan(\alpha + \beta)$ using

$$\tan(\alpha + \beta) = \dfrac{\sin(\alpha + \beta)}{\cos(\alpha + \beta)}.$$

After applying the formulas for sums of sines and cosines, divide the numerator and denominator by $\cos\alpha\cos\beta$.

56. Derive the identity for $\tan(\alpha - \beta)$ using

$$\tan(\alpha - \beta) = \tan[\alpha + (-\beta)].$$

After applying the formula for the tangent of the sum of two angles, use the fact that the tangent is an odd function.

In Exercises 57–64, find the exact value of the following under the given conditions:

   a. $\cos(\alpha + \beta)$ **b.** $\sin(\alpha + \beta)$ **c.** $\tan(\alpha + \beta)$.

57. $\sin\alpha = \dfrac{3}{5}$, α lies in quadrant I, and $\sin\beta = \dfrac{5}{13}$, β lies in quadrant II.

58. $\sin\alpha = \dfrac{4}{5}$, α lies in quadrant I, and $\sin\beta = \dfrac{7}{25}$, β lies in quadrant II.

59. $\tan\alpha = -\dfrac{3}{4}$, α lies in quadrant II, and $\cos\beta = \dfrac{1}{3}$, β lies in quadrant I.

60. $\tan\alpha = -\dfrac{4}{3}$, α lies in quadrant II, and $\cos\beta = \dfrac{2}{3}$, β lies in quadrant I.

61. $\cos\alpha = \dfrac{8}{17}$, α lies in quadrant IV, and $\sin\beta = -\dfrac{1}{2}$, β lies in quadrant III.

62. $\cos\alpha = \dfrac{1}{2}$, α lies in quadrant IV, and $\sin\beta = -\dfrac{1}{3}$, β lies in quadrant III.

63. $\tan\alpha = \dfrac{3}{4}$, $\pi < \alpha < \dfrac{3\pi}{2}$, and $\cos\beta = \dfrac{1}{4}$, $\dfrac{3\pi}{2} < \beta < 2\pi$.

64. $\sin\alpha = \dfrac{5}{6}$, $\dfrac{\pi}{2} < \alpha < \pi$, and $\tan\beta = \dfrac{3}{7}$, $\pi < \beta < \dfrac{3\pi}{2}$.

In Exercises 65–68, the graph with the given equation is shown in a $\left[0, 2\pi, \dfrac{\pi}{2}\right]$ by $[-2, 2, 1]$ viewing rectangle.

   a. Describe the graph using another equation.

   b. Verify that the two equations are equivalent.

65. $y = \sin(\pi - x)$

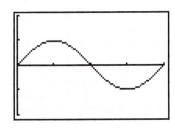

66. $y = \cos(x - 2\pi)$

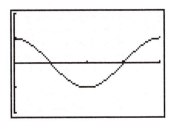

67. $y = \sin\left(x + \dfrac{\pi}{2}\right) + \sin\left(\dfrac{\pi}{2} - x\right)$

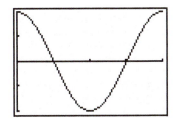

68. $y = \cos\left(x - \dfrac{\pi}{2}\right) - \cos\left(x + \dfrac{\pi}{2}\right)$

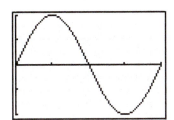

PRACTICE PLUS

In Exercises 69–74, rewrite each expression as a simplified expression containing one term.

69. $\cos(\alpha + \beta)\cos\beta + \sin(\alpha + \beta)\sin\beta$

70. $\sin(\alpha - \beta)\cos\beta + \cos(\alpha - \beta)\sin\beta$

71. $\dfrac{\sin(\alpha + \beta) - \sin(\alpha - \beta)}{\cos(\alpha + \beta) + \cos(\alpha - \beta)}$

72. $\dfrac{\cos(\alpha - \beta) + \cos(\alpha + \beta)}{-\sin(\alpha - \beta) + \sin(\alpha + \beta)}$

73. $\cos\left(\dfrac{\pi}{6} + \alpha\right)\cos\left(\dfrac{\pi}{6} - \alpha\right) - \sin\left(\dfrac{\pi}{6} + \alpha\right)\sin\left(\dfrac{\pi}{6} - \alpha\right)$

(Do not use four different identities to solve this exercise.)

74. $\sin\left(\dfrac{\pi}{3} - \alpha\right)\cos\left(\dfrac{\pi}{3} + \alpha\right) + \cos\left(\dfrac{\pi}{3} - \alpha\right)\sin\left(\dfrac{\pi}{3} + \alpha\right)$

(Do not use four different identities to solve this exercise.)

In Exercises 75–78, half of an identity and the graph of this half are given. Use the graph to make a conjecture as to what the right side of the identity should be. Then prove your conjecture.

75. $\cos 2x \cos 5x + \sin 2x \sin 5x = ?$

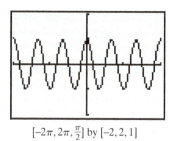

$[-2\pi, 2\pi, \frac{\pi}{2}]$ by $[-2, 2, 1]$

76. $\sin 5x \cos 2x - \cos 5x \sin 2x = ?$

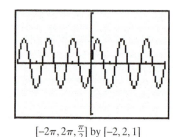

$[-2\pi, 2\pi, \frac{\pi}{2}]$ by $[-2, 2, 1]$

77. $\sin\frac{5x}{2}\cos 2x - \cos\frac{5x}{2}\sin 2x = ?$

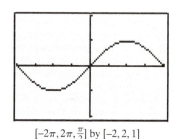

$[-2\pi, 2\pi, \frac{\pi}{2}]$ by $[-2, 2, 1]$

78. $\cos\frac{5x}{2}\cos 2x + \sin\frac{5x}{2}\sin 2x = ?$

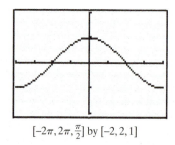

$[-2\pi, 2\pi, \frac{\pi}{2}]$ by $[-2, 2, 1]$

APPLICATION EXERCISES

79. A ball attached to a spring is raised 2 feet and released with an initial vertical velocity of 3 feet per second. The distance of the ball from its rest position after t seconds is given by $d = 2 \cos t + 3 \sin t$. Show that

$$2 \cos t + 3 \sin t = \sqrt{13} \cos(t - \theta),$$

where θ lies in quadrant I and $\tan \theta = \frac{3}{2}$. Use the identity to find the amplitude and the period of the ball's motion.

80. A tuning fork is held a certain distance from your ears and struck. Your eardrums' vibrations after t seconds are given by $p = 3 \sin 2t$. When a second tuning fork is struck, the formula $p = 2 \sin(2t + \pi)$ describes the effects of the sound on the eardrums' vibrations. The total vibrations are given by $p = 3 \sin 2t + 2 \sin(2t + \pi)$.

   a. Simplify p to a single term containing the sine.

   b. If the amplitude of p is zero, no sound is heard. Based on your equation in part (a), does this occur with the two tuning forks in this exercise? Explain your answer.

WRITING IN MATHEMATICS

In Exercises 81–86, use words to describe the formula for each of the following:

81. the cosine of the difference of two angles.

82. the cosine of the sum of two angles.

83. the sine of the sum of two angles.

84. the sine of the difference of two angles.

85. the tangent of the difference of two angles.

86. the tangent of the sum of two angles.

87. The distance formula and the definitions for cosine and sine are used to prove the formula for the cosine of the difference of two angles. This formula logically leads the way to the other sum and difference identities. Using this development of ideas and formulas, describe a characteristic of mathematical logic.

TECHNOLOGY EXERCISES

In Exercises 88–93, graph each side of the equation in the same viewing rectangle. If the graphs appear to coincide, verify that the equation is an identity. If the graphs do not appear to coincide, this indicates that the equation is not an identity. In these exercises, find a value of x for which both sides are defined but not equal.

88. $\cos\left(\frac{3\pi}{2} - x\right) = -\sin x$

89. $\tan(\pi - x) = -\tan x$

90. $\sin\left(x + \frac{\pi}{2}\right) = \sin x + \sin\frac{\pi}{2}$

91. $\cos\left(x + \frac{\pi}{2}\right) = \cos x + \cos\frac{\pi}{2}$

92. $\cos 1.2x \cos 0.8x - \sin 1.2x \sin 0.8x = \cos 2x$

93. $\sin 1.2x \cos 0.8x + \cos 1.2x \sin 0.8x = \sin 2x$

CRITICAL THINKING EXERCISES

Make Sense? *In Exercises 94–97, determine whether each statement makes sense or does not make sense, and explain your reasoning.*

94. I've noticed that for sine, cosine, and tangent, the trig function for the sum of two angles is not equal to that trig function of the first angle plus that trig function of the second angle.

95. After using an identity to determine the exact value of sin 105°, I verified the result with a calculator.

96. Using sum and difference formulas, I can find exact values for sine, cosine, and tangent at any angle.

97. After the difference formula for cosines is verified, I noticed that the other sum and difference formulas are verified relatively quickly.

98. Verify the identity:

$$\frac{\sin(x-y)}{\cos x \cos y} + \frac{\sin(y-z)}{\cos y \cos z} + \frac{\sin(z-x)}{\cos z \cos x} = 0.$$

In Exercises 99–102, find the exact value of each expression. Do not use a calculator.

99. $\sin\left(\cos^{-1}\frac{1}{2} + \sin^{-1}\frac{3}{5}\right)$

100. $\sin\left[\sin^{-1}\frac{3}{5} - \cos^{-1}\left(-\frac{4}{5}\right)\right]$

101. $\cos\left(\tan^{-1}\frac{4}{3} + \cos^{-1}\frac{5}{13}\right)$

102. $\cos\left[\cos^{-1}\left(-\frac{\sqrt{3}}{2}\right) - \sin^{-1}\left(-\frac{1}{2}\right)\right]$

In Exercises 103–105, write each trigonometric expression as an algebraic expression (that is, without any trigonometric functions). Assume that x and y are positive and in the domain of the given inverse trigonometric function.

103. $\cos(\sin^{-1} x - \cos^{-1} y)$

104. $\sin(\tan^{-1} x - \sin^{-1} y)$

105. $\tan(\sin^{-1} x + \cos^{-1} y)$

GROUP EXERCISE

106. Remembering the six sum and difference identities can be difficult. Did you have problems with some exercises because the identity you were using in your head turned out to be an incorrect formula? Are there easy ways to remember the six new identities presented in this section? Group members should address this question, considering one identity at a time. For each formula, list ways to make it easier to remember.

PREVIEW EXERCISES

Exercises 107–109 will help you prepare for the material covered in the next section.

107. Give exact values for sin 30°, cos 30°, sin 60°, and cos 60°.

108. Use the appropriate values from Exercise 107 to answer each of the following.
    a. Is sin 2·30°, or sin 60°, equal to 2 sin 30°?
    b. Is sin 2·30°, or sin 60°, equal to 2 sin 30° cos 30°?

109. Use appropriate values from Exercise 107 to answer each of the following.
    a. Is cos (2·30°), or cos 60°, equal to 2 cos 30°?
    b. Is cos (2·30°), or cos 60°, equal to $\cos^2 30° - \sin^2 30°$?

15.3 DOUBLE-ANGLE AND HALF-ANGLE FORMULAS

OBJECTIVES

1. Use the double-angle formulas.
2. Use the half-angle formulas.

In this section, we develop other important classes of identities, called the double-angle, power-reducing, and half-angle formulas. We will see how one of these formulas can be used by athletes to increase throwing distance.

OBJECTIVE 1 ▶ Double-angle formulas. A number of basic identities follow from the sum formulas for sine, cosine, and tangent. The first category of identities involves **double-angle formulas.**

Double-Angle Formulas

$$\sin 2\theta = 2 \sin \theta \cos \theta$$

$$\cos 2\theta = \cos^2 \theta - \sin^2 \theta$$

$$\tan 2\theta = \frac{2 \tan \theta}{1 - \tan^2 \theta}$$

926 CHAPTER 15 Trigonometric Identities, Equations, and Applications

> **Helpful Hint**
>
> The 2 that appears in each of the double-angle expressions cannot be pulled to the front and written as a coefficient.
>
> **Incorrect!**
>
> $\sin 2\theta = 2 \sin \theta$
> $\cos 2\theta = 2 \cos \theta$
> $\tan 2\theta = 2 \tan \theta$
>
> The figure shows that the graphs of
>
> $$y = \sin 2x$$
>
> and
>
> $$y = 2 \sin x$$
>
> do not coincide: $\sin 2x \neq 2 \sin x$.
>
>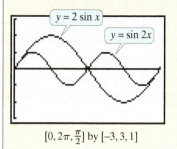
>
> $[0, 2\pi, \frac{\pi}{2}]$ by $[-3, 3, 1]$

To prove each of these formulas, we replace α and β by θ in the sum formulas for $\sin(\alpha + \beta)$, $\cos(\alpha + \beta)$, and $\tan(\alpha + \beta)$.

- $\sin 2\theta = \sin(\theta + \theta) = \sin \theta \cos \theta + \cos \theta \sin \theta = 2 \sin \theta \cos \theta$

  We use $\sin(\alpha + \beta) = \sin \alpha \cos \beta + \cos \alpha \sin \beta$.

- $\cos 2\theta = \cos(\theta + \theta) = \cos \theta \cos \theta - \sin \theta \sin \theta = \cos^2 \theta - \sin^2 \theta$

  We use $\cos(\alpha + \beta) = \cos \alpha \cos \beta - \sin \alpha \sin \beta$.

- $\tan 2\theta = \tan(\theta + \theta) = \dfrac{\tan \theta + \tan \theta}{1 - \tan \theta \tan \theta} = \dfrac{2 \tan \theta}{1 - \tan^2 \theta}$

  We use $\tan(\alpha + \beta) = \dfrac{\tan \alpha + \tan \beta}{1 - \tan \alpha \tan \beta}$.

EXAMPLE 1 Using Double-Angle Formulas to Find Exact Values

If $\sin \theta = \frac{5}{13}$ and θ lies in quadrant II, find the exact value of each of the following:

a. $\sin 2\theta$ **b.** $\cos 2\theta$ **c.** $\tan 2\theta$.

Solution We begin with a sketch that illustrates

$$\sin \theta = \frac{5}{13} = \frac{y}{r}.$$

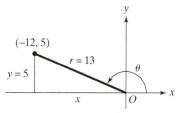

FIGURE 15.6 $\sin \theta = \frac{5}{13}$ and θ lies in quadrant II.

Figure 15.6 shows a quadrant II angle θ for which $\sin \theta = \frac{5}{13}$. We find x using $x^2 + y^2 = r^2$. Because θ lies in quadrant II, x is negative.

$x^2 + 5^2 = 13^2$ $x^2 + y^2 = r^2$

$x^2 + 25 = 169$ Square 5 and 13, respectively.

$x^2 = 144$ Subtract 25 from both sides.

$x = -\sqrt{144} = -12$ If $x^2 = 144$, then $x = \pm\sqrt{144} = \pm 12$. Choose $x = -\sqrt{144}$ because in quadrant II, x is negative.

Now we can use values for x, y, and r to find the required values. We will use $\cos \theta = \dfrac{x}{r} = -\dfrac{12}{13}$ and $\tan \theta = \dfrac{y}{x} = -\dfrac{5}{12}$. We were given $\sin \theta = \dfrac{5}{13}$.

a. $\sin 2\theta = 2 \sin \theta \cos \theta = 2\left(\dfrac{5}{13}\right)\left(-\dfrac{12}{13}\right) = -\dfrac{120}{169}$

b. $\cos 2\theta = \cos^2 \theta - \sin^2 \theta = \left(-\dfrac{12}{13}\right)^2 - \left(\dfrac{5}{13}\right)^2 = \dfrac{144}{169} - \dfrac{25}{169} = \dfrac{119}{169}$

c. $\tan 2\theta = \dfrac{2 \tan \theta}{1 - \tan^2 \theta} = \dfrac{2\left(-\dfrac{5}{12}\right)}{1 - \left(-\dfrac{5}{12}\right)^2} = \dfrac{-\dfrac{5}{6}}{1 - \dfrac{25}{144}} = \dfrac{-\dfrac{5}{6}}{\dfrac{119}{144}}$

$= \left(-\dfrac{5}{6}\right)\left(\dfrac{144}{119}\right) = -\dfrac{120}{119}$

PRACTICE 1 If $\sin\theta = \frac{4}{5}$ and θ lies in quadrant II, find the exact value of each of the following:

a. $\sin 2\theta$ **b.** $\cos 2\theta$ **c.** $\tan 2\theta$.

EXAMPLE 2 Using the Double-Angle Formula for Tangent to Find an Exact Value

Find the exact value of $\dfrac{2\tan 15°}{1 - \tan^2 15°}$.

Solution The given expression is the right side of the formula for $\tan 2\theta$ with $\theta = 15°$.

$$\tan 2\theta = \frac{2\tan\theta}{1-\tan^2\theta}$$

$$\frac{2\tan 15°}{1 - \tan^2 15°} = \tan(2 \cdot 15°) = \tan 30° = \frac{\sqrt{3}}{3}$$

PRACTICE 2 Find the exact value of $\cos^2 15° - \sin^2 15°$.

There are three forms of the double-angle formula for $\cos 2\theta$. The form we have seen involves both the cosine and the sine:

$$\cos 2\theta = \cos^2\theta - \sin^2\theta.$$

There are situations where it is more efficient to express $\cos 2\theta$ in terms of just one trigonometric function. Using the Pythagorean identity $\sin^2\theta + \cos^2\theta = 1$, we can write $\cos 2\theta = \cos^2\theta - \sin^2\theta$ in terms of the cosine only. We substitute $1 - \cos^2\theta$ for $\sin^2\theta$.

$$\cos 2\theta = \cos^2\theta - \sin^2\theta = \cos^2\theta - (1 - \cos^2\theta)$$
$$= \cos^2\theta - 1 + \cos^2\theta = 2\cos^2\theta - 1$$

We can also use a Pythagorean identity to write $\cos 2\theta$ in terms of sine only. We substitute $1 - \sin^2\theta$ for $\cos^2\theta$.

$$\cos 2\theta = \cos^2\theta - \sin^2\theta = 1 - \sin^2\theta - \sin^2\theta = 1 - 2\sin^2\theta$$

Three Forms of the Double-Angle Formula for $\cos 2\theta$

$$\cos 2\theta = \cos^2\theta - \sin^2\theta$$
$$\cos 2\theta = 2\cos^2\theta - 1$$
$$\cos 2\theta = 1 - 2\sin^2\theta$$

EXAMPLE 3 Verifying an Identity

Verify the identity: $\cos 3\theta = 4\cos^3\theta - 3\cos\theta$.

Solution We begin by working with the left side. In order to obtain an expression for $\cos 3\theta$, we use the sum formula and write 3θ as $2\theta + \theta$.

$\cos 3\theta = \cos(2\theta + \theta)$ Write 3θ as $2\theta + \theta$.
$ = \underbrace{\cos 2\theta}_{2\cos^2\theta - 1} \cos\theta - \underbrace{\sin 2\theta}_{2\sin\theta\cos\theta} \sin\theta$ $\cos(\alpha + \beta)$
$ = \cos\alpha\cos\beta - \sin\alpha\sin\beta$

$$= (2\cos^2\theta - 1)\cos\theta - 2\sin\theta\cos\theta\sin\theta \quad \text{Substitute double-angle formulas.}$$

Because the right side of the given equation involves cosines only, use this form for $\cos 2\theta$.

$$= 2\cos^3\theta - \cos\theta - 2\underbrace{\sin^2\theta}_{1-\cos^2\theta}\cos\theta \quad \text{Multiply.}$$

$$\cos 3\theta = 2\cos^3\theta - \cos\theta - 2\sin^2\theta\cos\theta \quad \text{We've repeated the last step from the previous page.}$$

$$= 2\cos^3\theta - \cos\theta - 2(1 - \cos^2\theta)\cos\theta \quad \text{To get cosines only, use } \sin^2\theta + \cos^2\theta = 1 \text{ and substitute } 1 - \cos^2\theta \text{ for } \sin^2\theta.$$

$$= 2\cos^3\theta - \cos\theta - 2\cos\theta + 2\cos^3\theta \quad \text{Multiply.}$$

$$= 4\cos^3\theta - 3\cos\theta \quad \text{Simplify:}$$

$2\cos^3\theta + 2\cos^3\theta = 4\cos^3\theta$ and $-\cos\theta - 2\cos\theta = -3\cos\theta$.

We were required to verify $\cos 3\theta = 4\cos^3\theta - 3\cos\theta$. By working with the left side, $\cos 3\theta$, and expressing it in a form identical to the right side, we have verified the identity.

▶ **Helpful Hint**

The $\frac{1}{2}$ that appears in each of the half-angle formulas cannot be pulled to the front and written as a coefficient.

Incorrect!

$\sin\dfrac{\theta}{2} \overset{\times}{=} \dfrac{1}{2}\sin\theta$

$\cos\dfrac{\theta}{2} \overset{\times}{=} \dfrac{1}{2}\cos\theta$

$\tan\dfrac{\theta}{2} \overset{\times}{=} \dfrac{1}{2}\tan\theta$

The figure shows that the graphs of $y = \sin\dfrac{x}{2}$ and $y = \dfrac{1}{2}\sin x$ do not coincide:

$\sin\dfrac{x}{2} \neq \dfrac{1}{2}\sin x.$

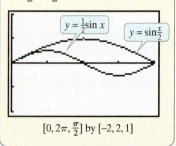

$[0, 2\pi, \frac{\pi}{2}]$ by $[-2, 2, 1]$

PRACTICE 3 Verify the identity: $\sin 3\theta = 3\sin\theta - 4\sin^3\theta$.

OBJECTIVE 2 ▶ **Half-angle formulas.** Useful **half-angle formulas** can be obtained from other formulas. These formulas are listed below.

Half-Angle Formulas

$$\sin\frac{\alpha}{2} = \pm\sqrt{\frac{1 - \cos\alpha}{2}} \qquad \tan\frac{\alpha}{2} = \frac{1 - \cos\alpha}{\sin\alpha}$$

$$\cos\frac{\alpha}{2} = \pm\sqrt{\frac{1 + \cos\alpha}{2}} \qquad \tan\frac{\alpha}{2} = \frac{\sin\alpha}{1 + \cos\alpha}$$

The $\pm$ symbol in each formula does not mean that there are two possible values for each function. Instead, the $\pm$ indicates that you must determine the sign of the trigonometric function, $+$ or $-$, based on the quadrant in which the half-angle $\dfrac{\alpha}{2}$ lies.

If we know the exact value for the cosine of an angle, we can use the half-angle formulas to find exact values of sine, cosine, and tangent for half of that angle. For example, we know that $\cos 225° = -\dfrac{\sqrt{2}}{2}$. In the next example, we find the exact value of the cosine of half of $225°$, or $\cos 112.5°$.

EXAMPLE 4 Using a Half-Angle Formula to Find an Exact Value

Find the exact value of cos 112.5°.

Solution Because $112.5° = \dfrac{225°}{2}$, we use the half-angle formula for $\cos\dfrac{\alpha}{2}$ with $\alpha = 225°$. What sign should we use when we apply the formula? Because 112.5° lies in quadrant II, where only the sine and cosecant are positive, cos 112.5° < 0. Thus, we use the − sign in the half-angle formula.

$$\cos 112.5° = \cos\dfrac{225°}{2}$$

$$= -\sqrt{\dfrac{1 + \cos 225°}{2}} \qquad \text{Use } \cos\dfrac{\alpha}{2} = -\sqrt{\dfrac{1 + \cos \alpha}{2}} \text{ with } \alpha = 225°.$$

$$= -\sqrt{\dfrac{1 + \left(-\dfrac{\sqrt{2}}{2}\right)}{2}} \qquad \cos 225° = -\dfrac{\sqrt{2}}{2}$$

$$= -\sqrt{\dfrac{2 - \sqrt{2}}{4}} \qquad \text{Multiply the radicand by } \tfrac{2}{2}:$$

$$\dfrac{1 + \left(-\dfrac{\sqrt{2}}{2}\right)}{2} \cdot \dfrac{2}{2} = \dfrac{2 - \sqrt{2}}{4}.$$

$$= -\dfrac{\sqrt{2 - \sqrt{2}}}{2} \qquad \text{Simplify: } \sqrt{4} = 2.$$

DISCOVERY

Use your calculator to find approximations for

$$-\dfrac{\sqrt{2 - \sqrt{2}}}{2}$$

and cos 112.5°. What do you observe?

▶ **Helpful Hint**

Keep in mind as you work with the half-angle formulas that the sign *outside* the radical is determined by the half angle $\dfrac{\alpha}{2}$. By contrast, the sign of cos α, which appears *under* the radical, is determined by the full angle α.

$$\sin\dfrac{\alpha}{2} = \pm\sqrt{\dfrac{1 - \cos \alpha}{2}}$$

The sign is determined by the quadrant of $\dfrac{\alpha}{2}$.

The sign of cos α is determined by the quadrant of α.

PRACTICE 4 Use $\cos 210° = -\dfrac{\sqrt{3}}{2}$ to find the exact value of cos 105°.

EXAMPLE 5 Verifying an Identity

Verify the identity: $\tan\dfrac{\alpha}{2} = \csc \alpha - \cot \alpha$.

Solution We begin with the right side.

$$\csc\alpha - \cot\alpha = \frac{1}{\sin\alpha} - \frac{\cos\alpha}{\sin\alpha} = \frac{1-\cos\alpha}{\sin\alpha} = \tan\frac{\alpha}{2}$$

Express functions in terms of sines and cosines.

This is the first of the two half-angle formulas in the preceding box.

We worked with the right side and arrived at the left side. Thus, the identity is verified.

PRACTICE 5 Verify the identity: $\tan\dfrac{\alpha}{2} = \dfrac{\sec\alpha}{\sec\alpha\csc\alpha + \csc\alpha}$.

We conclude with a summary of the principal trigonometric identities developed in this section and the previous section. The fundamental identities can be found in the box at the beginning of section 15.1.

Principal Trigonometric Identities

Sum and Difference Formulas

$$\sin(\alpha + \beta) = \sin\alpha\cos\beta + \cos\alpha\sin\beta \qquad \sin(\alpha - \beta) = \sin\alpha\cos\beta - \cos\alpha\sin\beta$$

$$\cos(\alpha + \beta) = \cos\alpha\cos\beta - \sin\alpha\sin\beta \qquad \cos(\alpha - \beta) = \cos\alpha\cos\beta + \sin\alpha\sin\beta$$

$$\tan(\alpha + \beta) = \frac{\tan\alpha + \tan\beta}{1 - \tan\alpha\tan\beta} \qquad \tan(\alpha - \beta) = \frac{\tan\alpha - \tan\beta}{1 + \tan\alpha\tan\beta}$$

Double-Angle Formulas

$$\sin 2\theta = 2\sin\theta\cos\theta$$

$$\cos 2\theta = \cos^2\theta - \sin^2\theta = 2\cos^2\theta - 1 = 1 - 2\sin^2\theta$$

$$\tan 2\theta = \frac{2\tan\theta}{1 - \tan^2\theta}$$

Half-Angle Formulas

$$\sin\frac{\alpha}{2} = \pm\sqrt{\frac{1-\cos\alpha}{2}} \qquad \cos\frac{\alpha}{2} = \pm\sqrt{\frac{1+\cos\alpha}{2}}$$

$$\tan\frac{\alpha}{2} = \frac{1-\cos\alpha}{\sin\alpha} = \frac{\sin\alpha}{1+\cos\alpha}$$

15.3 EXERCISE SET

PRACTICE EXERCISES

In Exercises 1–6, use the figures to find the exact value of each trigonometric function.

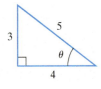
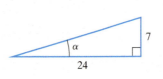

1. $\sin 2\theta$
2. $\cos 2\theta$
3. $\tan 2\theta$
4. $\sin 2\alpha$
5. $\cos 2\alpha$
6. $\tan 2\alpha$

In Exercises 7–14, use the given information to find the exact value of each of the following:

    a. $\sin 2\theta$ **b.** $\cos 2\theta$ **c.** $\tan 2\theta$.

7. $\sin\theta = \frac{15}{17}$, θ lies in quadrant II.
8. $\sin\theta = \frac{12}{13}$, θ lies in quadrant II.

9. $\cos\theta = \frac{24}{25}$, θ lies in quadrant IV.
10. $\cos\theta = \frac{40}{41}$, θ lies in quadrant IV.
11. $\cot\theta = 2$, θ lies in quadrant III.
12. $\cot\theta = 3$, θ lies in quadrant III.
13. $\sin\theta = -\frac{9}{41}$, θ lies in quadrant III.
14. $\sin\theta = -\frac{2}{3}$, θ lies in quadrant III.

In Exercises 15–22, write each expression as the sine, cosine, or tangent of a double angle. Then find the exact value of the expression.

15. $2\sin 15°\cos 15°$
16. $2\sin 22.5°\cos 22.5°$
17. $\cos^2 75° - \sin^2 75°$
18. $\cos^2 105° - \sin^2 105°$
19. $2\cos^2\frac{\pi}{8} - 1$
20. $1 - 2\sin^2\frac{\pi}{12}$
21. $\dfrac{2\tan\frac{\pi}{12}}{1 - \tan^2\frac{\pi}{12}}$
22. $\dfrac{2\tan\frac{\pi}{8}}{1 - \tan^2\frac{\pi}{8}}$

In Exercises 23–34, verify each identity.

23. $\sin 2\theta = \dfrac{2\tan\theta}{1 + \tan^2\theta}$
24. $\sin 2\theta = \dfrac{2\cot\theta}{1 + \cot^2\theta}$
25. $(\sin\theta + \cos\theta)^2 = 1 + \sin 2\theta$
26. $(\sin\theta - \cos\theta)^2 = 1 - \sin 2\theta$
27. $\sin^2 x + \cos 2x = \cos^2 x$
28. $1 - \tan^2 x = \dfrac{\cos 2x}{\cos^2 x}$
29. $\cot x = \dfrac{\sin 2x}{1 - \cos 2x}$
30. $\cot x = \dfrac{1 + \cos 2x}{\sin 2x}$
31. $\sin 2t - \tan t = \tan t\cos 2t$
32. $\sin 2t - \cot t = -\cot t\cos 2t$
33. $\sin 4t = 4\sin t\cos^3 t - 4\sin^3 t\cos t$
34. $\cos 4t = 8\cos^4 t - 8\cos^2 t + 1$

In Exercises 35–42, use a half-angle formula to find the exact value of each expression.

35. $\sin 15°$
36. $\cos 22.5°$
37. $\cos 157.5°$
38. $\sin 105°$
39. $\tan 75°$
40. $\tan 112.5°$
41. $\tan\dfrac{7\pi}{8}$
42. $\tan\dfrac{3\pi}{8}$

In Exercises 43–50, use the figures to find the exact value of each trigonometric function.

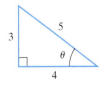
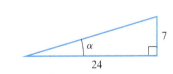

43. $\sin\dfrac{\theta}{2}$
44. $\cos\dfrac{\theta}{2}$
45. $\tan\dfrac{\theta}{2}$
46. $\sin\dfrac{\alpha}{2}$
47. $\cos\dfrac{\alpha}{2}$
48. $\tan\dfrac{\alpha}{2}$

49. $2\sin\dfrac{\theta}{2}\cos\dfrac{\theta}{2}$
50. $2\sin\dfrac{\alpha}{2}\cos\dfrac{\alpha}{2}$

In Exercises 51–54, use the given information to find the exact value of each of the following:

 a. $\sin\dfrac{\alpha}{2}$ b. $\cos\dfrac{\alpha}{2}$ c. $\tan\dfrac{\alpha}{2}$.

51. $\tan\alpha = \frac{4}{3}$, $180° < \alpha < 270°$
52. $\tan\alpha = \frac{8}{15}$, $180° < \alpha < 270°$
53. $\sec\alpha = -\frac{13}{5}$, $\frac{\pi}{2} < \alpha < \pi$
54. $\sec\alpha = -3$, $\frac{\pi}{2} < \alpha < \pi$

In Exercises 55–60, verify each identity.

55. $\sin^2\dfrac{\theta}{2} = \dfrac{\sec\theta - 1}{2\sec\theta}$
56. $\sin^2\dfrac{\theta}{2} = \dfrac{\csc\theta - \cot\theta}{2\csc\theta}$
57. $\cos^2\dfrac{\theta}{2} = \dfrac{\sin\theta + \tan\theta}{2\tan\theta}$
58. $\cos^2\dfrac{\theta}{2} = \dfrac{\sec\theta + 1}{2\sec\theta}$
59. $\tan\dfrac{\alpha}{2} = \dfrac{\tan\alpha}{\sec\alpha + 1}$
60. $2\tan\dfrac{\alpha}{2} = \dfrac{\sin^2\alpha + 1 - \cos^2\alpha}{\sin\alpha(1 + \cos\alpha)}$

PRACTICE PLUS

In Exercises 61–66, half of an identity and the graph of this half are given. Use the graph to make a conjecture as to what the right side of the identity should be. Then prove your conjecture.

61. $\dfrac{\cot x - \tan x}{\cot x + \tan x} = ?$

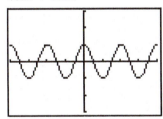

$[-2\pi, 2\pi, \frac{\pi}{2}]$ by $[-3, 3, 1]$

62. $\dfrac{2(\tan x - \cot x)}{\tan^2 x - \cot^2 x} = ?$

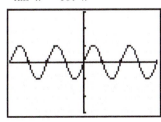

$[-2\pi, 2\pi, \frac{\pi}{2}]$ by $[-3, 3, 1]$

63. $\left(\sin\dfrac{x}{2} + \cos\dfrac{x}{2}\right)^2 = ?$

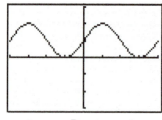

$[-2\pi, 2\pi, \frac{\pi}{2}]$ by $[-3, 3, 1]$

64. $\sin^2\dfrac{x}{2} - \cos^2\dfrac{x}{2} = ?$

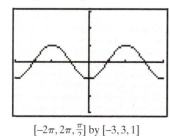

$[-2\pi, 2\pi, \frac{\pi}{2}]$ by $[-3, 3, 1]$

65. $\sin x(4\cos^2 x - 1) = ?$

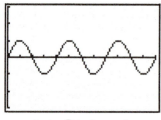

$[0, 2\pi, \frac{\pi}{6}]$ by $[-3, 3, 1]$

66. $1 - 8\sin^2 x \cos^2 x = ?$

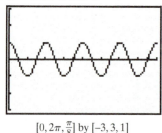

$[0, 2\pi, \frac{\pi}{8}]$ by $[-3, 3, 1]$

APPLICATION EXERCISES

67. **Multiple Steps.** Throwing events in track and field include the shot put, the discus throw, the hammer throw, and the javelin throw. The distance that the athlete can achieve depends on the initial speed of the object thrown and the angle above the horizontal at which the object leaves the hand. This angle is represented by θ in the figure shown. The distance, d, in feet, that the athlete throws is modeled by the formula

$$d = \dfrac{v_0^2}{16}\sin\theta\cos\theta,$$

in which v_0 is the initial speed of the object thrown, in feet per second, and θ is the angle, in degrees, at which the object leaves the hand.

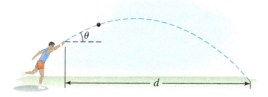

a. Use an identity to express the formula so that it contains the sine function only.

b. Use your formula from part (a) to find the angle, θ, that produces the maximum distance, d, for a given initial speed, v_0.

Use this information to solve Exercises 68–69: The speed of a supersonic aircraft is usually represented by a Mach number, named after Austrian physicist Ernst Mach (1838–1916). A Mach number is the speed of the aircraft, in miles per hour, divided by the speed of sound, approximately 740 miles per hour. Thus, a plane flying at twice the speed of sound has a speed, M, of Mach 2.

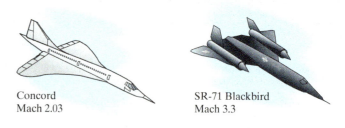

If an aircraft has a speed greater than Mach 1, a sonic boom is heard, created by sound waves that form a cone with a vertex angle θ, shown in the figure.

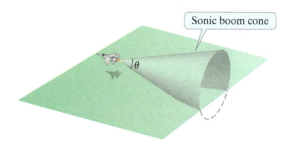

The relationship between the cone's vertex angle, θ, and the Mach speed, M, of an aircraft that is flying faster than the speed of sound is given by

$$\sin\dfrac{\theta}{2} = \dfrac{1}{M}.$$

68. If $\theta = \dfrac{\pi}{6}$, determine the Mach speed, M, of the aircraft.

Express the speed as an exact value and as a decimal to the nearest tenth.

69. If $\theta = \dfrac{\pi}{4}$, determine the Mach speed, M, of the aircraft.

Express the speed as an exact value and as a decimal to the nearest tenth.

WRITING IN MATHEMATICS

In Exercises 70–76, use words to describe the formula for:

70. the sine of double an angle.
71. the cosine of double an angle. (Describe one of the three formulas.)
72. the tangent of double an angle.
73. the sine of half an angle.
74. the cosine of half an angle.
75. the tangent of half an angle. (Describe one of the two formulas that does not involve a square root.)
76. How can there be three forms of the double-angle formula for $\cos 2\theta$?

TECHNOLOGY EXERCISES

In Exercises 77–80, graph each side of the equation in the same viewing rectangle. If the graphs appear to coincide, verify that the equation is an identity. If the graphs do not appear to coincide, find a value of x for which both sides are defined but not equal.

77. $3 - 6\sin^2 x = 3\cos 2x$
78. $4\cos^2\frac{x}{2} = 2 + 2\cos x$
79. $\sin\frac{x}{2} = \frac{1}{2}\sin x$
80. $\cos\frac{x}{2} = \frac{1}{2}\cos x$

*In Exercises 81–83, graph each equation in a $\left[-2\pi, 2\pi, \frac{\pi}{2}\right]$ by $[-3, 3, 1]$ viewing rectangle. Then **a.** Describe the graph using another equation, and **b.** Verify that the two equations are equivalent.*

81. $y = \dfrac{1 - 2\cos 2x}{2\sin x - 1}$
82. $y = \dfrac{2\tan\dfrac{x}{2}}{1 + \tan^2\dfrac{x}{2}}$
83. $y = \csc x - \cot x$

CRITICAL THINKING EXERCISES

Make Sense? *In Exercises 84–86, determine whether each statement makes sense or does not make sense, and explain your reasoning.*

84. The double-angle identities are derived from the sum identities by adding an angle to itself.
85. I simplified a double-angle trigonometric expression by pulling 2 to the front and treating it as a coefficient.
86. I used a half-angle formula to find the exact value of $\cos 100°$.

In Exercises 87–88, find the exact value of each expression. Do not use a calculator.

87. $\sin\left(2\sin^{-1}\dfrac{\sqrt{3}}{2}\right)$
88. $\cos\left[2\tan^{-1}\left(-\dfrac{4}{3}\right)\right]$

REVIEW AND PREVIEW

Exercises 89–91 will help you prepare for the material covered in the next section.

89. Solve: $2(1 - u^2) + 3u = 0$.
90. Solve: $u^3 - 3u = 0$.
91. Solve: $u^2 - u - 1 = 0$.

INTEGRATED REVIEW WHAT YOU KNOW

Verifying an identity means showing that the expressions on each side are identical. Like solving puzzles, the process can be intriguing because there are sometimes several "best" ways to proceed. We presented some guidelines to help you get started in Section 15.1. We used fundamental trigonometric identities, as well as sum and difference formulas, double-angle formulas, and half-angle formulas to verify identities. We also used these formulas to find exact values of trigonometric functions.

> **Helpful Hint**
> Make copies of the boxes in Sections 15.1 and 15.3 that contain the essential trigonometric identities. Mount these boxes on cardstock and add this reference sheet to the one you prepared for Chapter 14. (If you didn't prepare a reference sheet for Chapter 14, it's not too late.)

In Exercises 1–18, verify each identity.

1. $\cos x(\tan x + \cot x) = \csc x$
2. $\dfrac{\sin(x + \pi)}{\cos\left(x + \dfrac{3\pi}{2}\right)} = \tan^2 x - \sec^2 x$
3. $(\sin\theta + \cos\theta)^2 + (\sin\theta - \cos\theta)^2 = 2$
4. $\dfrac{\sin t - 1}{\cos t} = \dfrac{\cos t - \cot t}{\cos t \cot t}$
5. $\dfrac{1 - \cos 2x}{\sin 2x} = \tan x$
6. $\sin\theta\cos\theta + \cos^2\theta = \dfrac{\cos\theta(1 + \cot\theta)}{\csc\theta}$
7. $\dfrac{\sin x}{\tan x} + \dfrac{\cos x}{\cot x} = \sin x + \cos x$
8. $\sin^2\dfrac{t}{2} = \dfrac{\tan t - \sin t}{2\tan t}$
9. $\sin\alpha\cos\beta = \dfrac{1}{2}[\sin(\alpha + \beta) + \sin(\alpha - \beta)]$
10. $\dfrac{1 + \csc x}{\sec x} - \cot x = \cos x$
11. $\dfrac{\cot x - 1}{\cot x + 1} = \dfrac{1 - \tan x}{1 + \tan x}$
12. $2\sin^3\theta\cos\theta + 2\sin\theta\cos^3\theta = \sin 2\theta$
13. $\dfrac{\sin t + \cos t}{\sec t + \csc t} = \dfrac{\sin t}{\sec t}$

14. $\sec 2x = \dfrac{\sec^2 x}{2 - \sec^2 x}$

15. $\tan(\alpha + \beta)\tan(\alpha - \beta) = \dfrac{\tan^2 \alpha - \tan^2 \beta}{1 - \tan^2 \alpha \tan^2 \beta}$

16. $\csc \theta + \cot \theta = \dfrac{\sin \theta}{1 - \cos \theta}$

17. $\dfrac{1}{\csc 2x} = \dfrac{2 \tan x}{1 + \tan^2 x}$

18. $\dfrac{\sec t - 1}{t \sec t} = \dfrac{1 - \cos t}{t}$

Use the following conditions to solve Exercises 19–22:

$$\sin \alpha = \dfrac{3}{5}, \quad \dfrac{\pi}{2} < \alpha < \pi$$

$$\cos \beta = -\dfrac{12}{13}, \quad \pi < \beta < \dfrac{3\pi}{2}.$$

Find the exact value of each of the following.

19. $\cos(\alpha - \beta)$
20. $\tan(\alpha + \beta)$
21. $\sin 2\alpha$
22. $\cos \dfrac{\beta}{2}$

In Exercises 23–26, find the exact value of each expression. Do not use a calculator.

23. $\sin\left(\dfrac{3\pi}{4} + \dfrac{5\pi}{6}\right)$
24. $\cos^2 15° - \sin^2 15°$
25. $\cos\dfrac{5\pi}{12}\cos\dfrac{\pi}{12} + \sin\dfrac{5\pi}{12}\sin\dfrac{\pi}{12}$
26. $\tan 22.5°$

15.4 TRIGONOMETRIC EQUATIONS

OBJECTIVES

1. Find all solutions of a trigonometric equation.
2. Solve equations with multiple angles.
3. Solve trigonometric equations quadratic in form.
4. Use factoring to separate different functions in trigonometric equations.
5. Use identities to solve trigonometric equations.
6. Use a calculator to solve trigonometric equations.

Exponential functions display the manic energies of uncontrolled growth. By contrast, trigonometric functions repeat their behavior. The cycles of periodic phenomena provide events that we can comfortably count on. When will the moon look just as it does at this moment? When can I count on 13.5 hours of daylight? When will my breathing be exactly as it is right now? Models with trigonometric functions embrace the periodic rhythms of our world. Equations containing trigonometric functions are used to answer questions about these models.

OBJECTIVE 1 ▶ **Trigonometric equations and their solutions.** A **trigonometric equation** is an equation that contains a trigonometric expression with a variable, such as sin *x*. We have seen that some trigonometric equations are identities, such as $\sin^2 x + \cos^2 x = 1$. These equations are true for every value of the variable for which the expressions are defined. In this section, we consider trigonometric equations that are true for only some values of the variable. The values that satisfy such an equation are its **solutions.** (There are trigonometric equations that have no solution.)

An example of a trigonometric equation is

$$\sin x = \tfrac{1}{2}.$$

A solution of this equation is $\tfrac{\pi}{6}$ because $\sin \tfrac{\pi}{6} = \tfrac{1}{2}$. By contrast, π is not a solution because $\sin \pi = 0 \neq \tfrac{1}{2}$.

Is $\tfrac{\pi}{6}$ the only solution of $\sin x = \tfrac{1}{2}$? The answer is no. Because of the periodic nature of the sine function, there are infinitely many values of *x* for which $\sin x = \tfrac{1}{2}$. Figure 15.7 shows five of the solutions, including $\tfrac{\pi}{6}$, for $-\tfrac{3\pi}{2} \le x \le \tfrac{7\pi}{2}$. Notice that the *x*-coordinates of the points where the graph of $y = \sin x$ intersects the line $y = \tfrac{1}{2}$ are the solutions of the equation $\sin x = \tfrac{1}{2}$.

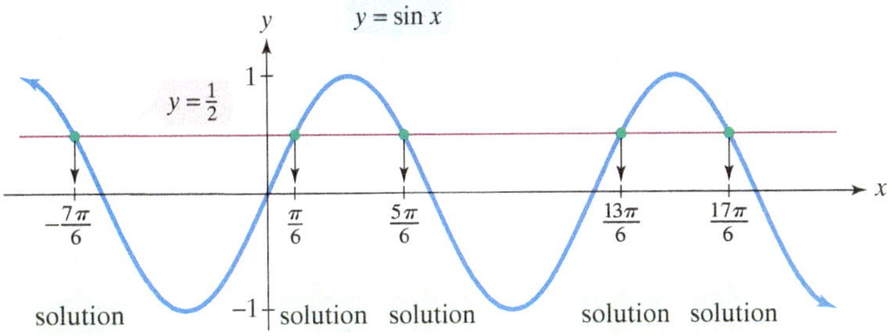

FIGURE 15.7 The equation $\sin x = \frac{1}{2}$ has five solutions when x is restricted to the interval $-\frac{3\pi}{2} \le x \le \frac{7\pi}{2}$.

How do we represent all solutions of $\sin x = \frac{1}{2}$? Because the period of the sine function is 2π, first find all solutions in $0 \le x < 2\pi$. The solutions are

$$x = \frac{\pi}{6} \quad \text{and} \quad x = \pi - \frac{\pi}{6} = \frac{5\pi}{6}.$$

The sine is positive in quadrants I and II.

Any multiple of 2π can be added to these values and the sine is still $\frac{1}{2}$. Thus, all solutions of $\sin x = \frac{1}{2}$ are given by

$$x = \frac{\pi}{6} + 2n\pi \quad \text{or} \quad x = \frac{5\pi}{6} + 2n\pi,$$

where n is any integer. By choosing any two integers, such as $n = 0$ and $n = 1$, we can find some solutions of $\sin x = \frac{1}{2}$. Thus, four of the solutions are determined as follows:

Let $n = 0$.

$$x = \frac{\pi}{6} + 2 \cdot 0\pi \quad x = \frac{5\pi}{6} + 2 \cdot 0\pi$$

$$= \frac{\pi}{6} \qquad\qquad = \frac{5\pi}{6}$$

Let $n = 1$.

$$x = \frac{\pi}{6} + 2 \cdot 1\pi \qquad x = \frac{5\pi}{6} + 2 \cdot 1\pi$$

$$= \frac{\pi}{6} + 2\pi \qquad\qquad = \frac{5\pi}{6} + 2\pi$$

$$= \frac{\pi}{6} + \frac{12\pi}{6} = \frac{13\pi}{6} \qquad = \frac{5\pi}{6} + \frac{12\pi}{6} = \frac{17\pi}{6}.$$

These four solutions are shown among the five solutions in Figure 15.7.

Equations Involving a Single Trigonometric Function
To solve an equation containing a single trigonometric function:

- Isolate the function on one side of the equation.
- Solve for the variable.

EXAMPLE 1 **Finding All Solutions of a Trigonometric Equation** Solve the equation: $3 \sin x - 2 = 5 \sin x - 1$.

Solution The equation contains a single trigonometric function, $\sin x$.

Step 1 Isolate the function on one side of the equation. We can solve for $\sin x$ by collecting terms with $\sin x$ on the left side and constant terms on the right side.

$3 \sin x - 2 = 5 \sin x - 1$	This is the given equation.
$3 \sin x - 5 \sin x - 2 = 5 \sin x - 5 \sin x - 1$	Subtract $5 \sin x$ from both sides.
$-2 \sin x - 2 = -1$	Simplify.
$-2 \sin x = 1$	Add 2 to both sides.

$$\sin x = -\tfrac{1}{2} \quad \text{Divide both sides by } -2 \text{ and solve for } \sin x.$$

Step 2 Solve for the variable. We must solve for x in $\sin x = -\tfrac{1}{2}$. Because $\sin \tfrac{\pi}{6} = \tfrac{1}{2}$, the solutions of $\sin x = -\tfrac{1}{2}$ in $0 \le x < 2\pi$ are

$$x = \pi + \frac{\pi}{6} = \frac{6\pi}{6} + \frac{\pi}{6} = \frac{7\pi}{6} \qquad x = 2\pi - \frac{\pi}{6} = \frac{12\pi}{6} - \frac{\pi}{6} = \frac{11\pi}{6}.$$

The sine is negative in quadrant III.   The sine is negative in quadrant IV.

Because the period of the sine function is 2π, the solutions of the equation are given by

$$x = \frac{7\pi}{6} + 2n\pi \quad \text{and} \quad x = \frac{11\pi}{6} + 2n\pi,$$

where n is any integer.

PRACTICE 1 Solve the equation: $5 \sin x = 3 \sin x + \sqrt{3}$.

Now we will concentrate on finding solutions of trigonometric equations for $0 \le x < 2\pi$. You can use a graphing utility to check the solutions of these equations. Graph the left side and graph the right side. The solutions are the x-coordinates of the points where the graphs intersect.

OBJECTIVE 2 ▶ Equations involving multiple angles. Here are examples of two equations that include multiple angles:

$$\tan 3x = 1 \qquad \sin \frac{x}{2} = \frac{\sqrt{3}}{2}.$$

The angle is a multiple of 3.   The angle is a multiple of $\tfrac{1}{2}$.

We will solve each equation for $0 \le x < 2\pi$. The period of the function plays an important role in ensuring that we do not leave out any solutions.

EXAMPLE 2 Solving an Equation with a Multiple Angle

Solve the equation: $\tan 3x = 1$, $0 \le x < 2\pi$.

Solution The period of the tangent function is π. In the interval $[0, \pi)$, the only value for which the tangent function is 1 is $\tfrac{\pi}{4}$. This means that $3x = \tfrac{\pi}{4}$. Because the period is π, all the solutions to $\tan 3x = 1$ are given by

$$3x = \frac{\pi}{4} + n\pi. \qquad n \text{ is any integer.}$$

$$x = \frac{\pi}{12} + \frac{n\pi}{3} \qquad \text{Divide both sides by 3 and solve for } x.$$

In the interval $0 \le x < 2\pi$ we obtain the solutions of $\tan 3x = 1$ as follows:

Let $n = 0$.
$$x = \frac{\pi}{12} + \frac{0\pi}{3}$$
$$= \frac{\pi}{12}$$

Let $n = 1$.
$$x = \frac{\pi}{12} + \frac{1\pi}{3}$$
$$= \frac{\pi}{12} + \frac{4\pi}{12} = \frac{5\pi}{12}$$

Let $n = 2$.
$$x = \frac{\pi}{12} + \frac{2\pi}{3}$$
$$= \frac{\pi}{12} + \frac{8\pi}{12} = \frac{9\pi}{12} = \frac{3\pi}{4}$$

TECHNOLOGY NOTE

Graphic Connections

Shown below are the graphs of

$$y = \tan 3x$$

and

$$y = 1$$

in a $\left[0, 2\pi, \tfrac{\pi}{2}\right]$ by $[-3, 3, 1]$ viewing rectangle. The solutions of

$$\tan 3x = 1$$

in $[0, 2\pi)$ are shown by the x-coordinates of the six intersection points.

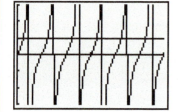

Let $n = 3.$

$$x = \frac{\pi}{12} + \frac{3\pi}{3}$$
$$= \frac{\pi}{12} + \frac{12\pi}{12} = \frac{13\pi}{12}$$

Let $n = 4.$

$$x = \frac{\pi}{12} + \frac{4\pi}{3}$$
$$= \frac{\pi}{12} + \frac{16\pi}{12} = \frac{17\pi}{12}$$

Let $n = 5.$

$$x = \frac{\pi}{12} + \frac{5\pi}{3}$$
$$= \frac{\pi}{12} + \frac{20\pi}{12} = \frac{21\pi}{12} = \frac{7\pi}{4}.$$

If you let $n = 6$, you will obtain $x = \frac{25\pi}{12}$. This value exceeds 2π. In the interval $0 \le x < 2\pi$ the solutions of $\tan 3x = 1$ are $\frac{\pi}{12}, \frac{5\pi}{12}, \frac{3\pi}{4}, \frac{13\pi}{12}, \frac{17\pi}{12}$, and $\frac{7\pi}{4}$. These solutions are illustrated by the six intersection points in the technology box. □

PRACTICE 2 Solve the equation: $\tan 2x = \sqrt{3}, 0 \le x < 2\pi.$

EXAMPLE 3 Solving an Equation with a Multiple Angle

Solve the equation: $\sin \frac{x}{2} = \frac{\sqrt{3}}{2}, 0 \le x < 2\pi.$

Solution The period of the sine function is 2π. In the interval $0 \le x < 2\pi$, there are two values at which the sine function is $\frac{\sqrt{3}}{2}$. One of these values is $\frac{\pi}{3}$. The sine is positive in quadrant II; thus, the other value is $\pi - \frac{\pi}{3}$, or $\frac{2\pi}{3}$. This means that $\frac{x}{2} = \frac{\pi}{3}$ or $\frac{x}{2} = \frac{2\pi}{3}$. Because the period is 2π, all the solutions of $\sin \frac{x}{2} = \frac{\sqrt{3}}{2}$ are given by

$$\frac{x}{2} = \frac{\pi}{3} + 2n\pi \quad \text{or} \quad \frac{x}{2} = \frac{2\pi}{3} + 2n\pi \quad n \text{ is any integer.}$$

$$x = \frac{2\pi}{3} + 4n\pi \qquad x = \frac{4\pi}{3} + 4n\pi. \quad \text{Multiply both sides by 2 and solve for } x.$$

We see that $x = \frac{2\pi}{3} + 4n\pi$ or $x = \frac{4\pi}{3} + 4n\pi$. If $n = 0$, we obtain $x = \frac{2\pi}{3}$ from the first equation and $x = \frac{4\pi}{3}$ from the second equation. If we let $n = 1$, we are adding $4 \cdot 1 \cdot \pi$, or 4π, to $\frac{2\pi}{3}$ and $\frac{4\pi}{3}$. These values of x exceed 2π. Thus, in the interval $0 \le x < 2\pi$, the only solutions of $\sin \frac{x}{2} = \frac{\sqrt{3}}{2}$ are $\frac{2\pi}{3}$ and $\frac{4\pi}{3}$. □

PRACTICE 3 Solve the equation: $\sin \frac{x}{3} = \frac{1}{2}, 0 \le x < 2\pi.$

OBJECTIVE 3 ▶ Trigonometric equations quadratic in form. Some trigonometric equations are in the form of a quadratic equation $au^2 + bu + c = 0$, where u is a trigonometric function and $a \ne 0$. Here are two examples of trigonometric equations that are quadratic in form:

$$2 \cos^2 x + \cos x - 1 = 0 \qquad 2 \sin^2 x - 3 \sin x + 1 = 0.$$

The form of this equation is $2u^2 + u - 1 = 0$ with $u = \cos x$.

The form of this equation is $2u^2 - 3u + 1 = 0$ with $u = \sin x$.

To solve this kind of equation, try using factoring. If the trigonometric expression does not factor, use another method, such as the quadratic formula or the square root property.

TECHNOLOGY NOTE

Graphic Connections

The graph of

$$y = 2\cos^2 x + \cos x - 1$$

is shown in a

$$\left[0, 2\pi, \frac{\pi}{2}\right] \text{ by } [-3, 3, 1]$$

viewing rectangle. The x-intercepts, $\frac{\pi}{3}, \pi,$ and $\frac{5\pi}{3}$, verify the three solutions of

$$2\cos^2 x + \cos x - 1 = 0$$

in $[0, 2\pi)$.

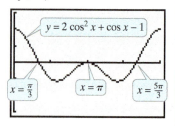

EXAMPLE 4 Solving a Trigonometric Equation Quadratic in Form

Solve the equation: $2\cos^2 x + \cos x - 1 = 0, \ 0 \leq x < 2\pi$.

Solution The given equation is in quadratic form $2u^2 + u - 1 = 0$ with $u = \cos x$. Let us attempt to solve the equation by factoring.

$2\cos^2 x + \cos x - 1 = 0$	This is the given equation.
$(2\cos x - 1)(\cos x + 1) = 0$	Factor: Notice that $2u^2 + u - 1$ factors as $(2u - 1)(u + 1)$.
$2\cos x - 1 = 0 \quad \text{or} \quad \cos x + 1 = 0$	Set each factor equal to 0.
$2\cos x = 1 \quad\quad\quad\quad \cos x = -1$	Solve for $\cos x$.
$\cos x = \frac{1}{2}$	
$x = \frac{\pi}{3} \quad x = 2\pi - \frac{\pi}{3} = \frac{5\pi}{3} \quad\quad x = \pi$	Solve each equation for x, $0 \leq x < 2\pi$.

The cosine is positive in quadrants I and IV.

The solutions in the interval $0 \leq x < 2\pi$, are $\frac{\pi}{3}, \pi,$ and $\frac{5\pi}{3}$. ☐

PRACTICE 4 Solve the equation: $2\sin^2 x - 3\sin x + 1 = 0, \ 0 \leq x < 2\pi$.

EXAMPLE 5 Solving a Trigonometric Equation Quadratic in Form

Solve the equation: $4\sin^2 x - 1 = 0, \ 0 \leq x < 2\pi$.

Solution The given equation is in quadratic form $4u^2 - 1 = 0$ with $u = \sin x$. We can solve this equation by the square root property: If $u^2 = c$, then $u = \pm\sqrt{c}$.

$4\sin^2 x - 1 = 0$	This is the given equation.
$4\sin^2 x = 1$	Add 1 to both sides.
$\sin^2 x = \frac{1}{4}$	Divide both sides by 4 and solve for $\sin^2 x$.
$\sin x = \sqrt{\frac{1}{4}} = \frac{1}{2} \quad \text{or} \quad \sin x = -\sqrt{\frac{1}{4}} = -\frac{1}{2}$	Apply the square root property: If $u^2 = c$, then $u = \sqrt{c}$ or $u = -\sqrt{c}$.

$$x = \frac{\pi}{6} \quad x = \pi - \frac{\pi}{6} = \frac{5\pi}{6} \quad x = \pi + \frac{\pi}{6} = \frac{7\pi}{6} \quad x = 2\pi - \frac{\pi}{6} = \frac{11\pi}{6}$$

Solve each equation for x, $0 \leq x < 2\pi$.

The sine is positive in quadrants I and II.

The sine is negative in quadrants III and IV.

The solutions in the interval $0 \leq x < 2\pi$ are $\frac{\pi}{6}, \frac{5\pi}{6}, \frac{7\pi}{6},$ and $\frac{11\pi}{6}$. ☐

TECHNOLOGY NOTE

Numeric Connections

You can use a graphing utility's TABLE feature to verify that the solutions of $4\sin^2 x - 1 = 0$ in $0 \le x < 2\pi$ are $\dfrac{\pi}{6}, \dfrac{5\pi}{6}, \dfrac{7\pi}{6}$, and $\dfrac{11\pi}{6}$. The table for $y = 4\sin^2 x - 1$, shown on the right, verifies that $\dfrac{\pi}{6}$ and $\dfrac{5\pi}{6}$ are solutions. Scroll through the table to verify the other two solutions.

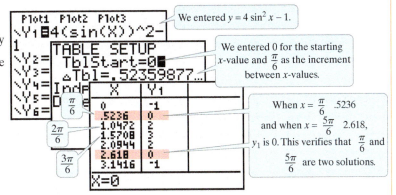

PRACTICE 5 Solve the equation: $4\cos^2 x - 3 = 0$, $0 \le x < 2\pi$.

OBJECTIVE 4 ▶ Using factoring to separate two different trigonometric functions in an equation. We have seen that factoring is used to solve some trigonometric equations that are quadratic in form. Factoring can also be used to solve some trigonometric equations that contain two different functions such as

$$\tan x \sin^2 x = 3 \tan x.$$

In such a case, move all terms to one side and obtain zero on the other side. Then try to use factoring to separate the different functions. Example 6 shows how this is done.

EXAMPLE 6 Using Factoring to Separate Different Functions

Solve the equation: $\tan x \sin^2 x = 3 \tan x$, $0 \le x < 2\pi$.

Solution Move all terms to one side and obtain zero on the other side.

$\tan x \sin^2 x = 3 \tan x$ This is the given equation.

$\tan x \sin^2 x - 3 \tan x = 0$ Subtract $3 \tan x$ from both sides.

We now have $\tan x \sin^2 x - 3 \tan x = 0$, which contains both tangent and sine functions. Use factoring to separate the two functions.

$\tan x (\sin^2 x - 3) = 0$ Factor out $\tan x$ from the two terms on the left side.

$\tan x = 0$ or $\sin^2 x - 3 = 0$ Set each factor equal to 0.

$x = 0 \quad x = \pi \qquad \sin^2 x = 3$ Solve for x.

$\sin x = \pm\sqrt{3}$

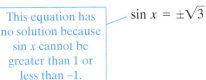

The solutions in the interval $0 \le x < 2\pi$ are 0 and π.

PRACTICE 6 Solve the equation: $\sin x \tan x = \sin x$, $0 \le x < 2\pi$.

> **Helpful Hint**
> In solving
> $$\tan x \sin^2 x = 3 \tan x,$$
> do not begin by dividing both sides by $\tan x$. Division by zero is undefined. If you divide by $\tan x$, you lose the two solutions for which $\tan x = 0$, namely 0 and π.

OBJECTIVE 5 ▶ Using identities to solve trigonometric equations. Some trigonometric equations contain more than one function on the same side and these functions cannot be separated by factoring. For example, consider the equation

$$2\cos^2 x + 3\sin x = 0.$$

How can we obtain an equivalent equation that has only one trigonometric function? We use the identity $\sin^2 x + \cos^2 x = 1$ and substitute $1 - \sin^2 x$ for $\cos^2 x$. This forms the basis of our next example.

EXAMPLE 7   Using an Identity to Solve a Trigonometric Equation

Solve the equation: $2 \cos^2 x + 3 \sin x = 0, \quad 0 \leq x < 2\pi$.

Solution

$2 \cos^2 x + 3 \sin x = 0$	This is the given equation.
$2(1 - \sin^2 x) + 3 \sin x = 0$	$\cos^2 x = 1 - \sin^2 x$
$2 - 2 \sin^2 x + 3 \sin x = 0$	Use the distributive property.
$-2 \sin^2 x + 3 \sin x + 2 = 0$	Write the equation in descending powers of $\sin x$.
$2 \sin^2 x - 3 \sin x - 2 = 0$	Multiply both sides by -1. The equation is in quadratic form $2u^2 - 3u - 2 = 0$ with $u = \sin x$.
$(2 \sin x + 1)(\sin x - 2) = 0$	Factor. Notice that $2u^2 - 3u - 2$ factors as $(2u + 1)(u - 2)$.
$2 \sin x + 1 = 0 \quad \text{or} \quad \sin x - 2 = 0$	Set each factor equal to 0. Solve $2 \sin x + 1 = 0$ and $\sin x - 2 = 0$ for $\sin x$.
$2 \sin x = -1$	
$\sin x = -\dfrac{1}{2} \qquad \sin x = 2$	

It's easier to factor with a positive leading coefficient.

This equation has no solution because $\sin x$ cannot be greater than 1.

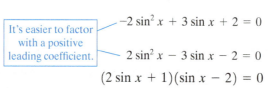

$$x = \pi + \frac{\pi}{6} = \frac{7\pi}{6} \qquad x = 2\pi - \frac{\pi}{6} = \frac{11\pi}{6} \qquad \text{Solve for } x.$$

$\sin \dfrac{\pi}{6} = \dfrac{1}{2}$. The sine is negative in quadrants III and IV.

The solutions of $2 \cos^2 x + 3 \sin x = 0$ in the interval $0 \leq x < 2\pi$ are $\dfrac{7\pi}{6}$ and $\dfrac{11\pi}{6}$. ☐

PRACTICE 7   Solve the equation: $2 \sin^2 x - 3 \cos x = 0, \quad 0 \leq x < 2\pi$.

EXAMPLE 8   Using an Identity to Solve a Trigonometric Equation

Solve the equation: $\cos 2x + 3 \sin x - 2 = 0, \quad 0 \leq x < 2\pi$.

Solution The given equation contains a cosine function and a sine function. The cosine is a function of $2x$ and the sine is a function of x. We want one trigonometric function of the same angle. This can be accomplished by using the double-angle identity $\cos 2x = 1 - 2 \sin^2 x$ to obtain an equivalent equation involving $\sin x$ only.

$\cos 2x + 3 \sin x - 2 = 0$	This is the given equation.
$1 - 2 \sin^2 x + 3 \sin x - 2 = 0$	$\cos 2x = 1 - 2 \sin^2 x$
$-2 \sin^2 x + 3 \sin x - 1 = 0$	Combine like terms.
$2 \sin^2 x - 3 \sin x + 1 = 0$	Multiply both sides by -1. The equation is in quadratic form $2u^2 - 3u + 1 = 0$ with $u = \sin x$.
$(2 \sin x - 1)(\sin x - 1) = 0$	Factor. Notice that $2u^2 - 3u + 1$ factors as $(2u - 1)(u - 1)$.
$2 \sin x - 1 = 0 \quad \text{or} \quad \sin x - 1 = 0$	Set each factor equal to 0.

$$\sin x = \tfrac{1}{2} \qquad \sin x = 1 \quad \text{Solve for } \sin x.$$

$$x = \frac{\pi}{6} \qquad x = \pi - \frac{\pi}{6} = \frac{5\pi}{6} \qquad x = \frac{\pi}{2} \quad \text{Solve each equation for } x, 0 \le x < 2\pi.$$

The sine is positive in quadrants I and II.

The solutions in the interval $0 \le x < 2\pi$ are $\dfrac{\pi}{6}, \dfrac{\pi}{2}$, and $\dfrac{5\pi}{6}$. ☐

PRACTICE 8 Solve the equation: $\cos 2x + \sin x = 0, \ 0 \le x < 2\pi$.

Sometimes it is necessary to do something to both sides of a trigonometric equation before using an identity. For example, consider the equation

$$\sin x \cos x = \tfrac{1}{2}.$$

This equation contains both a sine and a cosine function. How can we obtain a single function? Multiply both sides by 2. In this way, we can use the double-angle identity $\sin 2x = 2 \sin x \cos x$ and obtain $\sin 2x$, a single function, on the left side.

EXAMPLE 9   Using an Identity to Solve a Trigonometric Equation

Solve the equation: $\sin x \cos x = \tfrac{1}{2}, \ 0 \le x < 2\pi$.

Solution

$$\sin x \cos x = \tfrac{1}{2} \quad \text{This is the given equation.}$$
$$2 \sin x \cos x = 1 \quad \text{Multiply both sides by 2 in anticipation of using } \sin 2x = 2 \sin x \cos x.$$
$$\sin 2x = 1 \quad \text{Use a double-angle identity.}$$

Notice that we have an equation, $\sin 2x = 1$, with $2x$, a multiple angle. The period of the sine function is 2π. In the interval $0 \le x < 2\pi$, the only value for which the sine function is 1 is $\dfrac{\pi}{2}$. This means that $2x = \dfrac{\pi}{2}$. Because the period is 2π, all the solutions of $\sin 2x = 1$ are given by

$$2x = \frac{\pi}{2} + 2n\pi \quad n \text{ is any integer.}$$
$$x = \frac{\pi}{4} + n\pi \quad \text{Divide both sides by 2 and solve for } x.$$

The solutions of $\sin x \cos x = \dfrac{1}{2}$ in the interval $0 \le x < 2\pi$ are obtained by letting $n = 0$ and $n = 1$. The solutions are $\dfrac{\pi}{4}$ and $\dfrac{5\pi}{4}$. ☐

PRACTICE 9 Solve the equation: $\sin x \cos x = -\tfrac{1}{2}, \ 0 \le x < 2\pi$.

Let's look at another equation that contains two different functions, $\sin x - \cos x = 1$. Can you think of an identity that can be used to produce only one function? Perhaps $\sin^2 x + \cos^2 x = 1$ might be helpful. The next example shows how we can use this identity after squaring both sides of the given equation. Remember that if we raise both sides of an equation to an even power, we have the possibility of introducing extraneous solutions. Thus, we must check each proposed solution in the given equation. Alternatively, we can use a graphing utility to verify actual solutions.

TECHNOLOGY NOTE

Graphic Connections

Shown below are the graphs of
$$y = \sin x \cos x$$
and
$$y = \tfrac{1}{2}$$
in a $\left[0, 2\pi, \dfrac{\pi}{2}\right]$ by $[-1, 1, 1]$ viewing rectangle.
The solutions of
$$\sin x \cos x = \tfrac{1}{2}$$
are shown by the x-coordinates of the two intersection points.

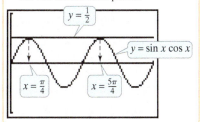

TECHNOLOGY NOTE

Graphic Connections

A graphing utility can be used instead of an algebraic check. Shown are the graphs of
$$y = \sin x - \cos x$$
and
$$y = 1$$
in a $\left[0, 2\pi, \dfrac{\pi}{2}\right]$ by $[-2, 2, 1]$ viewing rectangle. The actual solutions of
$$\sin x - \cos x = 1$$
are shown by the x-coordinates of the two intersection points, $\dfrac{\pi}{2}$ and π.

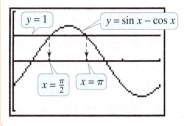

EXAMPLE 10 Using an Identity to Solve a Trigonometric Equation

Solve the equation: $\sin x - \cos x = 1$, $0 \leq x < 2\pi$.

Solution We square both sides of the equation in anticipation of using $\sin^2 x + \cos^2 x = 1$.

$\sin x - \cos x = 1$	This is the given equation.
$(\sin x - \cos x)^2 = 1^2$	Square both sides.
$\sin^2 x - 2 \sin x \cos x + \cos^2 x = 1$	Square the left side using $(A - B)^2 = A^2 - 2AB + B^2$.
$\sin^2 x + \cos^2 x - 2 \sin x \cos x = 1$	Rearrange terms.
$1 - 2 \sin x \cos x = 1$	Apply a Pythagorean identity: $\sin^2 x + \cos^2 x = 1$.
$-2 \sin x \cos x = 0$	Subtract 1 from both sides of the equation.
$\sin x \cos x = 0$	Divide both sides of the equation by -2.
$\sin x = 0$ or $\cos x = 0$	Set each factor equal to 0.
$x = 0$ $x = \pi$ $x = \dfrac{\pi}{2}$ $x = \dfrac{3\pi}{2}$	Solve for x in $0 \leq x < 2\pi$.

We check these proposed solutions to see if any are extraneous.

Check 0:

$\sin x - \cos x = 1$

$\sin 0 - \cos 0 \stackrel{?}{=} 1$

$0 - 1 \stackrel{?}{=} 1$

$-1 = 1$, false

0 is extraneous.

Check $\dfrac{\pi}{2}$:

$\sin x - \cos x = 1$

$\sin \dfrac{\pi}{2} - \cos \dfrac{\pi}{2} \stackrel{?}{=} 1$

$1 - 0 \stackrel{?}{=} 1$

$1 = 1$, true

Check π:

$\sin x - \cos x = 1$

$\sin \pi - \cos \pi \stackrel{?}{=} 1$

$0 - (-1) \stackrel{?}{=} 1$

$1 = 1$, true

Check $\dfrac{3\pi}{2}$:

$\sin x - \cos x = 1$

$\sin \dfrac{3\pi}{2} - \cos \dfrac{3\pi}{2} \stackrel{?}{=} 1$

$-1 - 0 \stackrel{?}{=} 1$

$-1 = 1$, false

$\dfrac{3\pi}{2}$ is extraneous.

The actual solutions of $\sin x - \cos x = 1$ in the interval $0 \leq x < 2\pi$ are $\dfrac{\pi}{2}$ and π.

PRACTICE 10 Solve the equation: $\cos x - \sin x = -1$, $0 \leq x < 2\pi$.

OBJECTIVE 6 ▶ Using a calculator to solve trigonometric equations. In all our previous examples, the equations had solutions that were found by knowing the exact values of trigonometric functions of special angles, such as $\dfrac{\pi}{6}$, $\dfrac{\pi}{4}$, and $\dfrac{\pi}{3}$. However, not all trigonometric equations involve these special angles. For those that do not, we will use the secondary keys marked $\boxed{\text{SIN}^{-1}}$, $\boxed{\text{COS}^{-1}}$, and $\boxed{\text{TAN}^{-1}}$ on a calculator. Recall that on most calculators, the inverse trigonometric function keys are the secondary functions for the buttons labeled $\boxed{\text{SIN}}$, $\boxed{\text{COS}}$, and $\boxed{\text{TAN}}$, respectively.

EXAMPLE 11 Solving Trigonometric Equations with a Calculator

Solve each equation, correct to four decimal places, for $0 \leq x < 2\pi$:

a. $\tan x = 12.8044$ **b.** $\cos x = -0.4317$.

Solution We begin by using a calculator to find θ, $0 \le \theta < \frac{\pi}{2}$ satisfying the following equations:

$$\tan \theta = 12.8044 \qquad \cos \theta = 0.4317.$$

> These numbers are the absolute values of the given range values.

Once θ is determined, we use our knowledge of the signs of the trigonometric functions to find x in $0 \le x < 2\pi$ satisfying $\tan x = 12.8044$ and $\cos x = -0.4317$.

a. $\tan x = 12.8044$ This is the given equation.

$\tan \theta = 12.8044$ Use a calculator to solve this equation for θ, $0 \le \theta < \frac{\pi}{2}$.

$\theta = \tan^{-1}(12.8044) \approx 1.4929$ 12.8044 [2nd] [TAN] or [2nd] [TAN] 12.8044 [ENTER]

$\tan x = 12.8044$ Return to the given equation. Because the tangent is positive, x lies in quadrant I or III.

$x \approx 1.4929$ $x \approx \pi + 1.4929 \approx 4.6345$ Solve for x, $0 \le x < 2\pi$.

> The tangent is positive in quadrant I.
> The tangent is positive in quadrant III.

> **Helpful Hint**
>
> To find solutions for x in $0 \le x < 2\pi$ your calculator must be in radian mode. Most scientific calculators revert to degree mode every time they are cleared.

Correct to four decimal places, the solutions of $\tan x = 12.8044$ in the interval $0 \le x < 2\pi$ are 1.4929 and 4.6345.

b. $\cos x = -0.4317$ This is the given equation.

$\cos \theta = 0.4317$ Use a calculator to solve this equation for θ, $0 \le \theta < \frac{\pi}{2}$.

$\theta = \cos^{-1}(0.4317) \approx 1.1244$ .4317 [2nd] [COS] or [2nd] [COS] .4317 [ENTER]

$\cos x = -0.4317$ Return to the given equation. Because the cosine is negative, x lies in quadrant II or III.

$x \approx \pi - 1.1244 \approx 2.0172$ $x \approx \pi + 1.1244 \approx 4.2660$ Solve for x, $0 \le x < 2\pi$.

> The cosine is negative in quadrant II.
> The cosine is negative in quadrant III.

Correct to four decimal places, the solutions of $\cos x = -0.4317$ in the interval $0 \le x < 2\pi$ are 2.0172 and 4.2660. ☐

PRACTICE 11 Solve each equation, correct to four decimal places, for $0 \le x < 2\pi$:

a. $\tan x = 3.1044$ **b.** $\sin x = -0.2315$.

EXAMPLE 12   Solving a trigonometric equation using the quadratic formula and a calculator

Solve the equation, correct to four decimal places, for $0 \le x < 2\pi$:

$$\sin^2 x - \sin x - 1 = 0.$$

Solution The given equation is in quadratic form $u^2 - u - 1 = 0$ with $u = \sin x$. We use the quadratic formula to solve for $\sin x$ because $u^2 - u - 1$ cannot be factored. Begin by identifying the values for a, b, and c.

$$\sin^2 x - \sin x - 1 = 0$$

$a = 1$ $b = -1$ $c = -1$

Substituting these values into the quadratic formula and simplifying gives the values for sin x. Once we obtain these values, we will solve for x.

$$\sin x = \frac{-b \pm \sqrt{b^2 - 4ac}}{2a} = \frac{-(-1) \pm \sqrt{(-1)^2 - 4(1)(-1)}}{2(1)} = \frac{1 \pm \sqrt{1-(-4)}}{2} = \frac{1 \pm \sqrt{5}}{2}$$

$$\sin x = \frac{1 + \sqrt{5}}{2} \approx 1.6180$$

This equation has no solution because sin x cannot be greater than 1.

or

$$\sin x = \frac{1 - \sqrt{5}}{2} \approx -0.6180$$

The sine is negative in quadrants III and IV. Use a calculator to solve $\sin \theta = 0.6180, 0 \leq \theta < \frac{\pi}{2}$.

Using a calculator to solve $\sin \theta = 0.6180$, we have

$$\theta = \sin^{-1}(0.6180) \approx 0.6662.$$

We use 0.6662 to solve $\sin x = -0.6180$, $0 \leq x < 2\pi$.

$$x \approx \pi + 0.6662 \approx 3.8078 \qquad x \approx 2\pi - 0.6662 \approx 5.6170$$

The sine is negative in quadrant III.   The sine is negative in quadrant IV.

Correct to four decimal places, the solutions of $\sin^2 x - \sin x - 1 = 0$ in the interval $0 \leq x < 2\pi$ are 3.8078 and 5.6170.

PRACTICE 12 Solve the equation, correct to four decimal places, for $0 \leq x < 2\pi$:

$$\cos^2 x + 5 \cos x + 3 = 0.$$

15.4 EXERCISE SET

PRACTICE EXERCISES

In Exercises 1–10, use substitution to determine whether the given x-value is a solution of the equation.

1. $\cos x = \frac{\sqrt{2}}{2}$, $x = \frac{\pi}{4}$
2. $\tan x = \sqrt{3}$, $x = \frac{\pi}{3}$
3. $\sin x = \frac{\sqrt{3}}{2}$, $x = \frac{\pi}{6}$
4. $\sin x = \frac{\sqrt{2}}{2}$, $x = \frac{\pi}{3}$
5. $\cos x = -\frac{1}{2}$, $x = \frac{2\pi}{3}$
6. $\cos x = -\frac{1}{2}$, $x = \frac{4\pi}{3}$
7. $\tan 2x = -\frac{\sqrt{3}}{3}$, $x = \frac{5\pi}{12}$
8. $\cos \frac{2x}{3} = -\frac{1}{2}$, $x = \pi$
9. $\cos x = \sin 2x$, $x = \frac{\pi}{3}$
10. $\cos x + 2 = \sqrt{3} \sin x$, $x = \frac{\pi}{6}$

In Exercises 11–24, find all solutions of each equation.

11. $\sin x = \frac{\sqrt{3}}{2}$
12. $\cos x = \frac{\sqrt{3}}{2}$
13. $\tan x = 1$
14. $\tan x = \sqrt{3}$
15. $\cos x = -\frac{1}{2}$
16. $\sin x = -\frac{\sqrt{2}}{2}$
17. $\tan x = 0$
18. $\sin x = 0$
19. $2 \cos x + \sqrt{3} = 0$
20. $2 \sin x + \sqrt{3} = 0$
21. $4 \sin \theta - 1 = 2 \sin \theta$
22. $5 \sin \theta + 1 = 3 \sin \theta$
23. $3 \sin \theta + 5 = -2 \sin \theta$
24. $7 \cos \theta + 9 = -2 \cos \theta$

Exercises 25–38 involve equations with multiple angles. Solve each equation on the interval $0 \leq x < 2\pi$.

25. $\sin 2x = \frac{\sqrt{3}}{2}$
26. $\cos 2x = \frac{\sqrt{2}}{2}$
27. $\cos 4x = -\frac{\sqrt{3}}{2}$
28. $\sin 4x = -\frac{\sqrt{2}}{2}$
29. $\tan 3x = \frac{\sqrt{3}}{3}$
30. $\tan 3x = \sqrt{3}$
31. $\tan \frac{x}{2} = \sqrt{3}$
32. $\tan \frac{x}{2} = \frac{\sqrt{3}}{3}$
33. $\sin \frac{2\theta}{3} = -1$
34. $\cos \frac{2\theta}{3} = -1$

35. $\sec\dfrac{3\theta}{2} = -2$

36. $\cot\dfrac{3\theta}{2} = -\sqrt{3}$

37. $\sin\left(2x + \dfrac{\pi}{6}\right) = \dfrac{1}{2}$

38. $\sin\left(2x - \dfrac{\pi}{4}\right) = \dfrac{\sqrt{2}}{2}$

Exercises 39–52 involve trigonometric equations quadratic in form. Solve each equation on the interval $0 \le x < 2\pi$.

39. $2\sin^2 x - \sin x - 1 = 0$

40. $2\sin^2 x + \sin x - 1 = 0$

41. $2\cos^2 x + 3\cos x + 1 = 0$

42. $\cos^2 x + 2\cos x - 3 = 0$

43. $2\sin^2 x = \sin x + 3$

44. $2\sin^2 x = 4\sin x + 6$

45. $\sin^2 \theta - 1 = 0$

46. $\cos^2 \theta - 1 = 0$

47. $4\cos^2 x - 1 = 0$

48. $4\sin^2 x - 3 = 0$

49. $9\tan^2 x - 3 = 0$

50. $3\tan^2 x - 9 = 0$

51. $\sec^2 x - 2 = 0$

52. $4\sec^2 x - 2 = 0$

In Exercises 53–62, solve each equation on the interval $0 \le x < 2\pi$.

53. $(\tan x - 1)(\cos x + 1) = 0$

54. $(\tan x + 1)(\sin x - 1) = 0$

55. $(2\cos x + \sqrt{3})(2\sin x + 1) = 0$

56. $(2\cos x - \sqrt{3})(2\sin x - 1) = 0$

57. $\cot x(\tan x - 1) = 0$

58. $\cot x(\tan x + 1) = 0$

59. $\sin x + 2\sin x \cos x = 0$

60. $\cos x - 2\sin x \cos x = 0$

61. $\tan^2 x \cos x = \tan^2 x$

62. $\cot^2 x \sin x = \cot^2 x$

In Exercises 63–84, use an identity to solve each equation on the interval $0 \le x < 2\pi$.

63. $2\cos^2 x + \sin x - 1 = 0$

64. $2\cos^2 x - \sin x - 1 = 0$

65. $\sin^2 x - 2\cos x - 2 = 0$

66. $4\sin^2 x + 4\cos x - 5 = 0$

67. $4\cos^2 x = 5 - 4\sin x$

68. $3\cos^2 x = \sin^2 x$

69. $\sin 2x = \cos x$

70. $\sin 2x = \sin x$

71. $\cos 2x = \cos x$

72. $\cos 2x = \sin x$

73. $\cos 2x + 5\cos x + 3 = 0$

74. $\cos 2x + \cos x + 1 = 0$

75. $\sin x \cos x = \dfrac{\sqrt{2}}{4}$

76. $\sin x \cos x = \dfrac{\sqrt{3}}{4}$

77. $\sin x + \cos x = 1$

78. $\sin x + \cos x = -1$

79. $\sin\left(x + \dfrac{\pi}{4}\right) + \sin\left(x - \dfrac{\pi}{4}\right) = 1$

80. $\sin\left(x + \dfrac{\pi}{3}\right) + \sin\left(x - \dfrac{\pi}{3}\right) = 1$

81. $\sin 2x \cos x + \cos 2x \sin x = \dfrac{\sqrt{2}}{2}$

82. $\sin 3x \cos 2x + \cos 3x \sin 2x = 1$

83. $\tan x + \sec x = 1$

84. $\tan x - \sec x = 1$

In Exercises 85–96, use a calculator to solve each equation, correct to four decimal places, on the interval $0 \le x < 2\pi$.

85. $\sin x = 0.8246$

86. $\sin x = 0.7392$

87. $\cos x = -\dfrac{2}{5}$

88. $\cos x = -\dfrac{4}{7}$

89. $\tan x = -3$

90. $\tan x = -5$

91. $\cos^2 x - \cos x - 1 = 0$

92. $3\cos^2 x - 8\cos x - 3 = 0$

93. $4\tan^2 x - 8\tan x + 3 = 0$

94. $\tan^2 x - 3\tan x + 1 = 0$

95. $7\sin^2 x - 1 = 0$

96. $5\sin^2 x - 1 = 0$

In Exercises 97–116, use the most appropriate method to solve each equation on the interval $0 \le x < 2\pi$. Use exact values where possible or give approximate solutions correct to four decimal places.

97. $2\cos 2x + 1 = 0$

98. $2\sin 3x + \sqrt{3} = 0$

99. $\sin 2x + \sin x = 0$

100. $\sin 2x + \cos x = 0$

101. $3\cos x - 6\sqrt{3} = \cos x - 5\sqrt{3}$

102. $\cos x - 5 = 3\cos x + 6$

103. $\tan x = -4.7143$

104. $\tan x = -6.2154$

105. $2\sin^2 x = 3 - \sin x$

106. $2\sin^2 x = 2 - 3\sin x$

107. $\cos x \csc x = 2\cos x$

108. $\tan x \sec x = 2\tan x$

109. $5\cot^2 x - 15 = 0$

110. $5\sec^2 x - 10 = 0$

111. $\cos^2 x + 2\cos x - 2 = 0$

112. $\cos^2 x + 5\cos x - 1 = 0$

113. $5\sin x = 2\cos^2 x - 4$

114. $7\cos x = 4 - 2\sin^2 x$

115. $2\tan^2 x + 5\tan x + 3 = 0$

116. $3\tan^2 x - \tan x - 2 = 0$

PRACTICE PLUS

In Exercises 117–120, graph f and g in the same rectangular coordinate system for $0 \le x \le 2\pi$. Then solve a trigonometric equation to determine points of intersection and identify these points on your graphs.

117. $f(x) = 3\cos x,\ g(x) = \cos x - 1$

118. $f(x) = 3\sin x,\ g(x) = \sin x - 1$

119. $f(x) = \cos 2x,\ g(x) = -2\sin x$

120. $f(x) = \cos 2x,\ g(x) = 1 - \sin x$

In Exercises 121–126, solve each equation on the interval $0 \le x < 2\pi$.

121. $|\cos x| = \dfrac{\sqrt{3}}{2}$

122. $|\sin x| = \dfrac{1}{2}$

123. $10 \cos^2 x + 3 \sin x - 9 = 0$

124. $3 \cos^2 x - \sin x = \cos^2 x$

125. $2 \cos^3 x + \cos^2 x - 2 \cos x - 1 = 0$ (*Hint:* Use factoring by grouping.)

126. $2 \sin^3 x - \sin^2 x - 2 \sin x + 1 = 0$ (*Hint:* Use factoring by grouping.)

In Exercises 127–128, find the x-intercepts, correct to four decimal places, of the graph of each function. Then use the x-intercepts to match the function with its graph. The graphs are labeled (a) and (b).

127. $f(x) = \tan^2 x - 3 \tan x + 1$

128. $g(x) = 4 \tan^2 x - 8 \tan x + 3$

a.
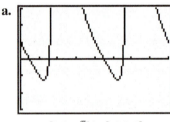
$[0, 2\pi, \tfrac{\pi}{4}]$ by $[-3, 3, 1]$

b.
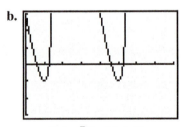
$[0, 2\pi, \tfrac{\pi}{4}]$ by $[-3, 3, 1]$

APPLICATION EXERCISES

Use this information to solve Exercises 129–130. Our cycle of normal breathing takes place every 5 seconds. Velocity of air flow, y, measured in liters per second, after x seconds is modeled by

$$y = 0.6 \sin \dfrac{2\pi}{5} x.$$

Velocity of air flow is positive when we inhale and negative when we exhale.

129. Within each breathing cycle, when are we inhaling at a rate of 0.3 liter per second? Round to the nearest tenth of a second.

130. Within each breathing cycle, when are we exhaling at a rate of 0.3 liter per second? Round to the nearest tenth of a second.

Use this information to solve Exercises 131–132. The number of hours of daylight in Boston is given by

$$y = 3 \sin\left[\dfrac{2\pi}{365}(x - 79)\right] + 12,$$

where x is the number of days after January 1.

131. Within a year, when does Boston have 10.5 hours of daylight? Give your answer in days after January 1 and round to the nearest day.

132. Within a year, when does Boston have 13.5 hours of daylight? Give your answer in days after January 1 and round to the nearest day.

Use this information to solve Exercises 133–134. A ball on a spring is pulled 4 inches below its rest position and then released. After t seconds, the ball's distance, d, in inches from its rest position is given by

$$d = -4 \cos \dfrac{\pi}{3} t.$$

133. Find all values of t for which the ball is 2 inches above its rest position.

134. Find all values of t for which the ball is 2 inches below its rest position.

Use this information to solve Exercises 135–136. When throwing an object, the distance achieved depends on its initial velocity, v_0, and the angle above the horizontal at which the object is thrown, θ. The distance, d, in feet, that describes the range covered is given by

$$d = \dfrac{v_0^2}{16} \sin \theta \cos \theta,$$

where v_0 is measured in feet per second.

135. You and your friend are throwing a baseball back and forth. If you throw the ball with an initial velocity of $v_0 = 90$ feet per second, at what angle of elevation, θ, to the nearest degree, should you direct your throw so that it can be easily caught by your friend located 170 feet away?

136. In Exercise 135, you increase the distance between you and your friend to 200 feet. With this increase, at what angle of elevation, θ, to the nearest degree, should you direct your throw?

WRITING IN MATHEMATICS

137. What are the solutions of a trigonometric equation?

138. Describe the difference between verifying a trigonometric identity and solving a trigonometric equation.

139. Without actually solving the equation, describe how to solve

$$3 \tan x - 2 = 5 \tan x - 1.$$

140. In the interval $0 \le x < 2\pi$ the solutions of $\sin x = \cos 2x$ are $\dfrac{\pi}{6}, \dfrac{5\pi}{6}$, and $\dfrac{3\pi}{2}$. Explain how to use graphs generated by a graphing utility to check these solutions.

141. Suppose you are solving equations in the interval $0 \le x < 2\pi$. Without actually solving equations, what is the difference between the number of solutions of $\sin x = \tfrac{1}{2}$ and $\sin 2x = \tfrac{1}{2}$? How do you account for this difference?

In Exercises 142–143, describe a general strategy for solving each equation. Do not solve the equation.

142. $2 \sin^2 x + 5 \sin x + 3 = 0$

143. $\sin 2x = \sin x$

144. Describe a natural periodic phenomenon. Give an example of a question that can be answered by a trigonometric equation in the study of this phenomenon.

145. A city's tall buildings and narrow streets reduce the amount of sunlight. If h is the average height of the buildings and w is the width of the street, the angle of elevation from the street to the top of the buildings is given by the trigonometric equation
$$\tan \theta = \frac{h}{w}.$$
A value of $\theta = 63°$ can result in an 85% loss of illumination. Some people experience depression with loss of sunlight. Determine whether such a person should live on a city street that is 80 feet wide with buildings whose heights average 400 feet. Explain your answer and include θ, to the nearest degree, in your argument.

TECHNOLOGY EXERCISES

146. Use a graphing utility to verify the solutions of any five equations that you solved in Exercises 63–84.

In Exercises 147–151, use a graphing utility to approximate the solutions of each equation in the interval $0 \leq x < 2\pi$. Round to the nearest hundredth of a radian.

147. $15 \cos^2 x + 7 \cos x - 2 = 0$ 148. $\cos x = x$
149. $2 \sin^2 x = 1 - 2 \sin x$ 150. $\sin 2x = 2 - x^2$
151. $\sin x + \sin 2x + \sin 3x = 0$

CRITICAL THINKING EXERCISES

Decision Making. *In Exercises 152–155, determine whether each statement makes sense or does not make sense, and explain your reasoning.*

152. I solved $4 \cos^2 x = 5 - 4 \sin x$ by working independently with the left side, applying a Pythagorean identity, and transforming the left side into $5 - 4 \sin x$.

153. There are similarities and differences between solving $4x + 1 = 3$ and $4 \sin \theta + 1 = 3$: In the first equation, I need to isolate x to get the solution. In the trigonometric equation, I need to first isolate $\sin \theta$, but then I must continue to solve for θ.

154. I solved $\cos\left(x - \frac{\pi}{3}\right) = -1$ by first applying the formula for the cosine of the difference of two angles.

155. Using the equation for simple harmonic motion described in Exercises 133–134, I need to solve a trigonometric equation to determine the ball's distance from its rest position after 2 seconds.

In Exercises 156–159, determine whether each statement is true or false. If the statement is false, make the necessary change(s) to produce a true statement.

156. The equation $(\sin x - 3)(\cos x + 2) = 0$ has no solution.

157. The equation $\tan x = \frac{\pi}{2}$ has no solution.

158. A trigonometric equation with an infinite number of solutions is an identity.

159. The equations $\sin 2x = 1$ and $\sin 2x = \frac{1}{2}$ have the same number of solutions on the interval $0 \leq x < 2\pi$.

In Exercises 160–162, solve each equation on the interval $0 \leq x < 2\pi$. Do not use a calculator.

160. $2 \cos x - 1 + 3 \sec x = 0$ 161. $\sin 3x + \sin x + \cos x = 0$
162. $\sin x + 2 \sin \frac{x}{2} = \cos \frac{x}{2} + 1$

REVIEW AND PREVIEW

Solve each equation by using the cross-products principle to clear fractions from the proportion:

$$\text{If } \frac{a}{b} = \frac{c}{d}, \text{ then } ad = bc. \ (b \neq 0 \text{ and } d \neq 0)$$

Round to the nearest tenth.

163. Solve for a: $\dfrac{a}{\sin 46°} = \dfrac{56}{\sin 63°}$.

164. Solve for B, $0 < B < 180°$: $\dfrac{81}{\sin 43°} = \dfrac{62}{\sin B}$.

165. Solve for B: $\dfrac{51}{\sin 75°} = \dfrac{71}{\sin B}$.

15.5 THE LAW OF SINES

OBJECTIVES

1. Use the Law of Sines to solve oblique triangles.
2. Use the Law of Sines to solve, if possible, the triangle or triangles in the ambiguous case.
3. Find the area of an oblique triangle using the sine function.
4. Solve applied problems using the Law of Sines.

Point Reyes National Seashore, 40 miles north of San Francisco, consists of 75,000 acres with miles of pristine surf-pummeled beaches, forested ridges, and bays flanked by white cliffs. In 1995, a fire in the park burned 12,350 acres and destroyed 45 homes.

Fire is a necessary part of the life cycle in many wilderness areas. It is also an ongoing threat to those who choose to live surrounded by nature's unspoiled beauty. In this section, we see how trigonometry can be used to locate small wilderness fires before they become raging infernos. To do this, we begin by considering triangles other than right triangles.

The Law of Sines and Its Derivation An **oblique triangle** is a triangle that does not contain a right angle. Figure 15.8 shows that an oblique triangle has either three acute angles or two acute angles and one obtuse angle. Notice that the angles are labeled $A, B,$ and C. The sides opposite each angle are labeled as $a, b,$ and $c,$ respectively.

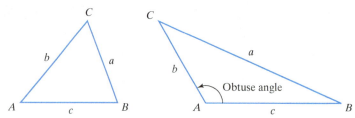

FIGURE 15.8 Oblique triangles

> **Helpful Hint**
> Up until now, our work with triangles has involved right triangles. **Do not apply relationships that are valid for right triangles to oblique triangles.** Avoid the error of using the Pythagorean Theorem, $a^2 + b^2 = c^2$, to find a missing side of an oblique triangle. This relationship among the three sides applies only to right triangles.

The relationships among the sides and angles of right triangles defined by the trigonometric functions are not valid for oblique triangles. Thus, we must observe and develop new relationships in order to work with oblique triangles.

Many relationships exist among the sides and angles in oblique triangles. One such relationship is called the **Law of Sines.**

> **Helpful Hint**
> The Law of Sines can be expressed with the sines in the numerator:
> $$\frac{\sin A}{a} = \frac{\sin B}{b} = \frac{\sin C}{c}.$$

The Law of Sines

If $A, B,$ and C are the measures of the angles of a triangle, and $a, b,$ and c are the lengths of the sides opposite these angles, then

$$\frac{a}{\sin A} = \frac{b}{\sin B} = \frac{c}{\sin C}.$$

The ratio of the length of the side of any triangle to the sine of the angle opposite that side is the same for all three sides of the triangle.

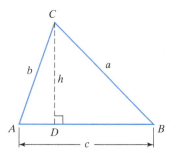

FIGURE 15.9 Drawing an altitude to prove the Law of Sines

To prove the Law of Sines, we draw an altitude of length h from one of the vertices of the triangle. In Figure 15.9, the altitude is drawn from vertex C. Two smaller triangles are formed, triangles ACD and BCD. Note that both are right triangles. Thus, we can use the definition of the sine of an angle of a right triangle.

$$\sin B = \frac{h}{a} \qquad \sin A = \frac{h}{b} \qquad \sin \theta = \frac{\text{opposite}}{\text{hypotenuse}}$$

$$h = a \sin B \qquad h = b \sin A \qquad \text{Solve each equation for } h.$$

Because we have found two expressions for h, we can set these expressions equal to each other.

$$a \sin B = b \sin A \qquad \text{Equate the expressions for } h.$$

$$\frac{a \sin B}{\sin A \sin B} = \frac{b \sin A}{\sin A \sin B} \qquad \text{Divide both sides by } \sin A \sin B.$$

$$\frac{a}{\sin A} = \frac{b}{\sin B} \qquad \text{Simplify.}$$

This proves part of the Law of Sines. If we use the same process and draw an altitude of length h from vertex A, we obtain the following result:

$$\frac{b}{\sin B} = \frac{c}{\sin C}.$$

When this equation is combined with the previous equation, we obtain the Law of Sines. Because the sine of an angle is equal to the sine of 180° minus that angle, the Law of Sines is derived in a similar manner if the oblique triangle contains an obtuse angle.

OBJECTIVE 1 ▶ Solving oblique triangles. Solving an oblique triangle means finding the lengths of its sides and the measurements of its angles. The Law of Sines can be used to solve a triangle in which one side and two angles are known. The three known measurements can be abbreviated using SAA (a side and two angles are known) or ASA (two angles and the side between them are known).

EXAMPLE 1 Solving an SAA Triangle Using the Law of Sines

Solve the triangle shown in Figure 15.10 with $A = 46°$, $C = 63°$, and $c = 56$ inches. Round lengths of sides to the nearest tenth.

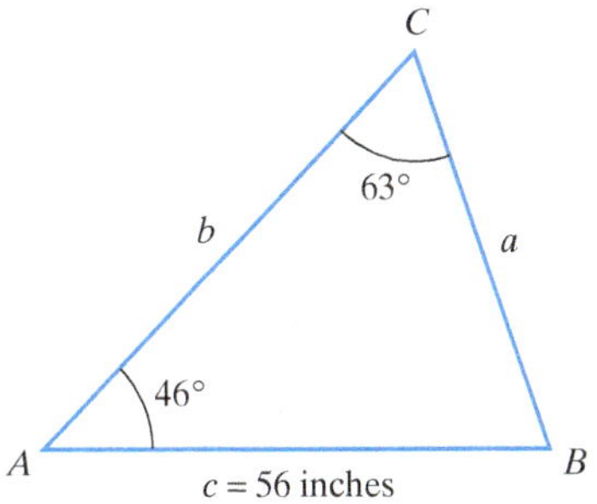

Solution We begin by finding B, the third angle of the triangle. We do not need the Law of Sines to do this. Instead, we use the fact that the sum of the measures of the interior angles of a triangle is $180°$.

$$A + B + C = 180°$$
$$46° + B + 63° = 180° \quad \text{Substitute the given values:}$$
$$\qquad\qquad\qquad\qquad\qquad A = 46° \text{ and } C = 63°.$$
$$109° + B = 180° \quad \text{Add.}$$
$$B = 71° \quad \text{Subtract } 109° \text{ from both sides.}$$

FIGURE 15.10 Solving an oblique SAA triangle

When we use the Law of Sines, we must be given one of the three ratios. In this example, we are given c and C: $c = 56$ and $C = 63°$. Thus, we use the ratio $\dfrac{c}{\sin C}$, or $\dfrac{56}{\sin 63°}$, to find the other two sides. Use the Law of Sines to find a.

$$\dfrac{a}{\sin A} = \dfrac{c}{\sin C} \quad \text{The ratio of any side to the sine of its opposite angle equals the ratio of any other side to the sine of its opposite angle.}$$

$$\dfrac{a}{\sin 46°} = \dfrac{56}{\sin 63°} \quad A = 46°, c = 56, \text{ and } C = 63°.$$

$$a = \dfrac{56 \sin 46°}{\sin 63°} \quad \text{Multiply both sides by } \sin 46° \text{ and solve for } a.$$

$$a \approx 45.2 \text{ inches} \quad \text{Use a calculator.}$$

Use the Law of Sines again, this time to find b.

$$\dfrac{b}{\sin B} = \dfrac{c}{\sin C} \quad \text{We use the given ratio, } \dfrac{c}{\sin C}, \text{ to find } b.$$

$$\dfrac{b}{\sin 71°} = \dfrac{56}{\sin 63°} \quad \text{We found that } B = 71°. \text{ We are given } c = 56 \text{ and } C = 63°.$$

$$b = \dfrac{56 \sin 71°}{\sin 63°} \quad \text{Multiply both sides by } \sin 71° \text{ and solve for } b.$$

$$b \approx 59.4 \text{ inches} \quad \text{Use a calculator.}$$

The solution is $B = 71°$, $a \approx 45.2$ inches, and $b \approx 59.4$ inches.

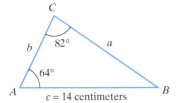

FIGURE 15.11

PRACTICE

1 Solve the triangle shown in Figure 15.11 with $A = 64°$, $C = 82°$, and $c = 14$ centimeters. Round as in Example 1.

EXAMPLE 2 Solving an ASA Triangle Using the Law of Sines

Solve triangle ABC if $A = 50°$, $C = 33.5°$, and $b = 76$. Round measures to the nearest tenth.

Solution We begin by drawing a picture of triangle ABC and labeling it with the given information. Figure 15.12 shows the triangle that we must solve. We begin by finding B.

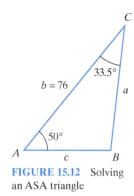

FIGURE 15.12 Solving an ASA triangle

$A + B + C = 180°$ The sum of the measures of a triangle's interior angles is 180°.
$50° + B + 33.5° = 180°$ $A = 50°$ and $C = 33.5°$.
$83.5° + B = 180°$ Add.
$B = 96.5°$ Subtract 83.5° from both sides.

Keep in mind that we must be given one of the three ratios to apply the Law of Sines.

In this example, we are given that $b = 76$ and we found that $B = 96.5°$. Thus, we use the ratio $\dfrac{b}{\sin B}$, or $\dfrac{76}{\sin 96.5°}$, to find the other two sides. Use the Law of Sines to find a and c.

Find a:

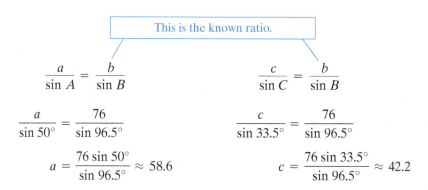

$\dfrac{a}{\sin A} = \dfrac{b}{\sin B}$

$\dfrac{a}{\sin 50°} = \dfrac{76}{\sin 96.5°}$

$a = \dfrac{76 \sin 50°}{\sin 96.5°} \approx 58.6$

Find c:

$\dfrac{c}{\sin C} = \dfrac{b}{\sin B}$

$\dfrac{c}{\sin 33.5°} = \dfrac{76}{\sin 96.5°}$

$c = \dfrac{76 \sin 33.5°}{\sin 96.5°} \approx 42.2$

The solution is $B = 96.5°$, $a \approx 58.6$, and $c \approx 42.2$.

PRACTICE 2 Solve triangle ABC if $A = 40°$, $C = 22.5°$, and $b = 12$. Round as in Example 2.

OBJECTIVE 2 ▶ The ambiguous case (SSA). If we are given two sides and an angle opposite one of them (SSA), does this determine a unique triangle? Can we solve this case using the Law of Sines? Such a case is called the **ambiguous case** because the given information may result in one triangle, two triangles, or no triangle at all. For example, in Figure 15.13, we are given a, b, and A. Because a is shorter than h, it is not long enough to form a triangle. The number of possible triangles, if any, that can be formed in the SSA case depends on h, the length of the altitude, where $h = b \sin A$.

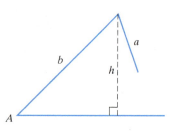

FIGURE 15.13 Given SSA, no triangle may result.

The Ambiguous Case (SSA)

Consider a triangle in which a, b, and A are given. This information may result in

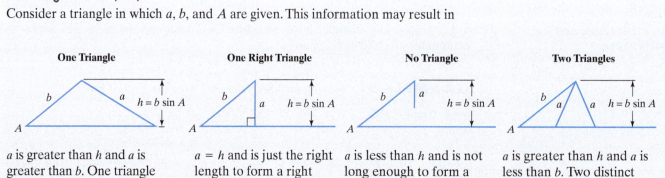

One Triangle

a is greater than h and a is greater than b. One triangle is formed.

One Right Triangle

$a = h$ and is just the right length to form a right triangle.

No Triangle

a is less than h and is not long enough to form a triangle.

Two Triangles

a is greater than h and a is less than b. Two distinct triangles are formed.

In an SSA situation, it is not necessary to draw an accurate sketch like those shown in the box. The Law of Sines determines the number of triangles, if any, and gives the solution for each triangle.

EXAMPLE 3 Solving an SSA Triangle Using the Law of Sines (One Solution)

Solve triangle ABC if $A = 43°$, $a = 81$, and $b = 62$. Round lengths of sides to the nearest tenth and angle measures to the nearest degree.

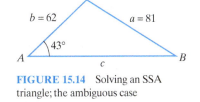

FIGURE 15.14 Solving an SSA triangle; the ambiguous case

Solution We begin with the sketch in Figure 15.14. The known ratio is $\dfrac{a}{\sin A}$, or $\dfrac{81}{\sin 43°}$. Because side b is given, we use the Law of Sines to find angle B.

$\dfrac{a}{\sin A} = \dfrac{b}{\sin B}$ Apply the Law of Sines.

$\dfrac{81}{\sin 43°} = \dfrac{62}{\sin B}$ $a = 81, b = 62,$ and $A = 43°.$

$81 \sin B = 62 \sin 43°$ Cross multiply: If $\dfrac{a}{b} = \dfrac{c}{d}$, then $ad = bc.$

$\sin B = \dfrac{62 \sin 43°}{81}$ Divide both sides by 81 and solve for $\sin B$.

$\sin B \approx 0.5220$ Use a calculator.

There are two angles B between $0°$ and $180°$ for which $\sin B \approx 0.5220$.

$B_1 \approx 31°$ $B_2 \approx 180° - 31° = 149°$

Obtain the acute angle with your calculator in degree mode: $\sin^{-1} 0.5220$.   The sine is positive in quadrant II.

Look at Figure 15.14. Given that $A = 43°$, can you see that $B_2 \approx 149°$ is impossible? By adding $149°$ to the given angle, $43°$, we exceed a $180°$ sum:

$43° + 149° = 192°.$

Thus, the only possibility is that $B_1 \approx 31°$. We find C using this approximation for B_1 and the measure that was given for A: $A = 43°$.

$C = 180° - B_1 - A \approx 180° - 31° - 43° = 106°$

Side c that lies opposite this $106°$ angle can now be found using the Law of Sines.

$\dfrac{c}{\sin C} = \dfrac{a}{\sin A}$ Apply the Law of Sines.

$\dfrac{c}{\sin 106°} = \dfrac{81}{\sin 43°}$ $a = 81, C \approx 106°,$ and $A = 43°.$

$c = \dfrac{81 \sin 106°}{\sin 43°} \approx 114.2$ Multiply both sides by $\sin 106°$ and solve for c.

There is one triangle and the solution is B_1 (or B) $\approx 31°$, $C \approx 106°$, and $c \approx 114.2$.

PRACTICE 3 Solve triangle ABC if $A = 57°$, $a = 33$, and $b = 26$. Round as in Example 3.

EXAMPLE 4 Solving an SSA Triangle Using the Law of Sines (No Solution)

Solve triangle ABC if $A = 75°$, $a = 51$, and $b = 71$.

Solution The known ratio is $\dfrac{a}{\sin A}$, or $\dfrac{51}{\sin 75°}$. Because side b is given, we use the Law of Sines to find angle B.

$$\dfrac{a}{\sin A} = \dfrac{b}{\sin B} \quad \text{Use the Law of Sines.}$$

$$\dfrac{51}{\sin 75°} = \dfrac{71}{\sin B} \quad \text{Substitute the given values.}$$

$$51 \sin B = 71 \sin 75° \quad \text{Cross multiply: If } \dfrac{a}{b} = \dfrac{c}{d}, \text{ then } ad = bc.$$

$$\sin B = \dfrac{71 \sin 75°}{51} \approx 1.34 \quad \text{Divide by 51 and solve for } \sin B.$$

Because the sine can never exceed 1, there is no angle B for which $\sin B \approx 1.34$. There is no triangle with the given measurements, as illustrated in Figure 15.15.

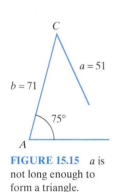

FIGURE 15.15 a is not long enough to form a triangle.

PRACTICE 4 Solve triangle ABC if $A = 50°$, $a = 10$, and $b = 20$.

EXAMPLE 5 Solving an SSA Triangle Using the Law of Sines (Two Solutions)

Solve triangle ABC if $A = 40°$, $a = 54$, and $b = 62$. Round lengths of sides to the nearest tenth and angle measures to the nearest degree.

Solution The known ratio is $\dfrac{a}{\sin A}$, or $\dfrac{54}{\sin 40°}$. We use the Law of Sines to find angle B.

$$\dfrac{a}{\sin A} = \dfrac{b}{\sin B} \quad \text{Use the Law of Sines.}$$

$$\dfrac{54}{\sin 40°} = \dfrac{62}{\sin B} \quad \text{Substitute the given values.}$$

$$54 \sin B = 62 \sin 40° \quad \text{Cross multiply: If } \dfrac{a}{b} = \dfrac{c}{d}, \text{ then } ad = bc.$$

$$\sin B = \dfrac{62 \sin 40°}{54} \approx 0.7380 \quad \text{Divide by 54 and solve for } \sin B.$$

There are two angles B between $0°$ and $180°$ for which $\sin B \approx 0.7380$.

$$B_1 \approx 48° \qquad B_2 \approx 180° - 48° = 132°$$

> Find $\sin^{-1} 0.7380$ with your calculator.   The sine is positive in quadrant II.

If you add either angle to the given angle, $40°$, the sum does not exceed $180°$. Thus, there are two triangles with the given conditions, shown in Figure 15.16(a). The triangles, AB_1C_1 and AB_2C_2, are shown separately in Figure 15.16(b) and Figure 15.16(c).

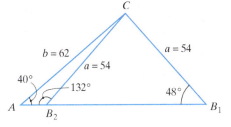

(a) Two triangles are possible with $A = 40°$, $a = 54$, and $b = 62$.

(b) In one possible triangle, $B_1 = 48°$.

(c) In the second possible triangle, $B_2 = 132°$.

FIGURE 15.16

> **Helpful Hint**
>
> The two triangles shown in Figure 15.16 are helpful in organizing the solutions. However, if you keep track of the two triangles, one with the given information and $B_1 = 48°$, and the other with the given information and $B_2 = 132°$, you do not have to draw the figure to solve the triangles.

We find angles C_1 and C_2 using a 180° angle sum in each of the two triangles.

$$C_1 = 180° - A - B_1 \qquad\qquad C_2 = 180° - A - B_2$$
$$\approx 180° - 40° - 48° \qquad\quad \approx 180° - 40° - 132°$$
$$= 92° \qquad\qquad\qquad\qquad = 8°$$

We use the Law of Sines to find c_1 and c_2.

$$\frac{c_1}{\sin C_1} = \frac{a}{\sin A} \qquad\qquad \frac{c_2}{\sin C_2} = \frac{a}{\sin A}$$

$$\frac{c_1}{\sin 92°} = \frac{54}{\sin 40°} \qquad\qquad \frac{c_2}{\sin 8°} = \frac{54}{\sin 40°}$$

$$c_1 = \frac{54 \sin 92°}{\sin 40°} \approx 84.0 \qquad c_2 = \frac{54 \sin 8°}{\sin 40°} \approx 11.7$$

There are two triangles. In one triangle, the solution is $B_1 \approx 48°$, $C_1 \approx 92°$, and $c_1 \approx 84.0$. In the other triangle, $B_2 \approx 132°$, $C_2 \approx 8°$, and $c_2 \approx 11.7$. □

PRACTICE 5 Solve triangle ABC if $A = 35°$, $a = 12$, and $b = 16$. Round as in Example 5.

OBJECTIVE 3 ▶ The area of an oblique triangle. A formula for the area of an oblique triangle can be obtained using the procedure for proving the Law of Sines. We draw an altitude of length h from one of the vertices of the triangle, as shown in Figure 15.17. We apply the definition of the sine of angle A, $\dfrac{\text{opposite}}{\text{hypotenuse}}$, in right triangle ACD:

$$\sin A = \frac{h}{b}, \quad \text{so} \quad h = b \sin A.$$

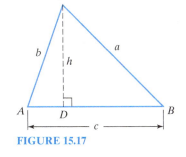

FIGURE 15.17

The area of a triangle is $\frac{1}{2}$ the product of any side and the altitude drawn to that side. Using the altitude h in Figure 15.17, we have

$$\text{Area} = \frac{1}{2} ch = \frac{1}{2} cb \sin A.$$

Use the result from above: $h = b \sin A$.

This result, Area $= \frac{1}{2} cb \sin A$, or $\frac{1}{2} bc \sin A$, indicates that the area of the triangle is one-half the product of b and c times the sine of their included angle. If we draw altitudes from the other two vertices, we see that we can use any two sides to compute the area.

> **Area of an Oblique Triangle**
>
> The area of a triangle equals one-half the product of the lengths of two sides times the sine of their included angle. In Figure 15.17 this wording can be epressed by the formulas
>
> $$\text{Area} = \tfrac{1}{2} bc \sin A = \tfrac{1}{2} ab \sin C = \tfrac{1}{2} ac \sin B$$

EXAMPLE 6   Finding the Area of an Oblique Triangle

Find the area of a triangle having two sides of lengths 24 meters and 10 meters and an included angle of 62°. Round to the nearest square meter.

Solution   The triangle is shown in Figure 15.18. Its area is half the product of the lengths of the two sides times the sine of the included angle.

$$\text{Area} = \tfrac{1}{2}(24)(10)(\sin 62°) \approx 106$$

The area of the triangle is approximately 106 square meters.

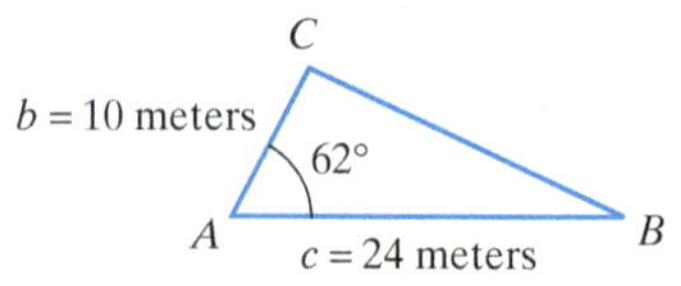

FIGURE 15.18 Finding the area of an SAS triangle

PRACTICE 6   Find the area of a triangle having two sides of lengths 8 meters and 12 meters and an included angle of 135°. Round to the nearest square meter.

OBJECTIVE 4 ▶ Applications of the Law of Sines. We have seen how the trigonometry of right triangles can be used to solve many different kinds of applied problems. The Law of Sines enables us to work with triangles that are not right triangles. As a result, this law can be used to solve problems involving surveying, engineering, astronomy, navigation, and the environment. Example 7 illustrates the use of the Law of Sines in detecting potentially devastating fires.

EXAMPLE 7   An Application of the Law of Sines

Two fire-lookout stations are 20 miles apart, with station B directly east of station A. Both stations spot a fire on a mountain to the north. The bearing from station A to the fire is N50°E (50° east of north). The bearing from station B to the fire is N36°W (36° west of north). How far, to the nearest tenth of a mile, is the fire from station A?

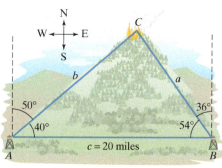

FIGURE 15.19

Solution   Figure 15.19 shows the information given in the problem. The distance from station A to the fire is represented by b. Notice that the angles describing the bearing from each station to the fire, 50° and 36°, are not interior angles of triangle ABC. Using a north-south line, the interior angles are found as follows:

$$A = 90° - 50° = 40° \qquad B = 90° - 36° = 54°.$$

To find b using the Law of Sines, we need a known side and an angle opposite that side. Because $c = 20$ miles, we find angle C using a 180° angle sum in the triangle. Thus,

$$C = 180° - A - B = 180° - 40° - 54° = 86°.$$

The ratio $\dfrac{c}{\sin C}$ or $\dfrac{20}{\sin 86°}$ is now known. We use this ratio and the Law of Sines to find b.

$$\dfrac{b}{\sin B} = \dfrac{c}{\sin C} \qquad \text{Use the Law of Sines.}$$

$$\dfrac{b}{\sin 54°} = \dfrac{20}{\sin 86°} \qquad c = 20, B = 54°, \text{ and } C = 86°.$$

$$b = \dfrac{20 \sin 54°}{\sin 86°} \approx 16.2 \qquad \text{Multiply both sides by } \sin 54° \text{ and solve for } b.$$

The fire is approximately 16.2 miles from station A.

PRACTICE 7 Two fire-lookout stations are 13 miles apart, with station B directly east of station A. Both stations spot a fire. The bearing of the fire from station A is N35°E and the bearing of the fire from station B is N49°W. How far, to the nearest tenth of a mile, is the fire from station B?

15.5 EXERCISE SET

PRACTICE EXERCISES

In Exercises 1–8, solve each triangle. Round lengths of sides to the nearest tenth and angle measures to the nearest degree.

1.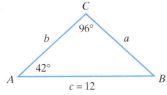

2.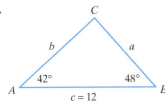

3.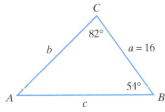

4.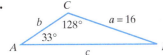

5.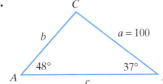

6.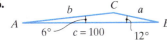

7.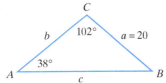

8.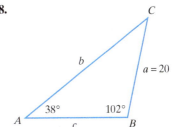

In Exercises 9–16, solve each triangle. Round lengths to the nearest tenth and angle measures to the nearest degree.

9. $A = 44°, B = 25°, a = 12$

10. $A = 56°, C = 24°, a = 22$

11. $B = 85°, C = 15°, b = 40$

12. $A = 85°, B = 35°, c = 30$

13. $A = 115°, C = 35°, c = 200$

14. $B = 5°, C = 125°, b = 200$

15. $A = 65°, B = 65°, c = 6$

16. $B = 80°, C = 10°, a = 8$

In Exercises 17–32, two sides and an angle (SSA) of a triangle are given. Determine whether the given measurements produce one triangle, two triangles, or no triangle at all. Solve each triangle that results. Round to the nearest tenth and the nearest degree for sides and angles, respectively.

17. $a = 20, b = 15, A = 40°$

18. $a = 30, b = 20, A = 50°$

19. $a = 10, c = 8.9, A = 63°$

20. $a = 57.5, c = 49.8, A = 136°$

21. $a = 42.1, c = 37, A = 112°$

22. $a = 6.1, b = 4, A = 162°$
23. $a = 10, b = 40, A = 30°$
24. $a = 10, b = 30, A = 150°$
25. $a = 16, b = 18, A = 60°$
26. $a = 30, b = 40, A = 20°$
27. $a = 12, b = 16.1, A = 37°$
28. $a = 7, b = 28, A = 12°$
29. $a = 22, c = 24.1, A = 58°$
30. $a = 95, c = 125, A = 49°$
31. $a = 9.3, b = 41, A = 18°$
32. $a = 1.4, b = 2.9, A = 142°$

In Exercises 33–38, find the area of the triangle having the given measurements. Round to the nearest square unit.

33. $A = 48°, b = 20$ feet, $c = 40$ feet
34. $A = 22°, b = 20$ feet, $c = 50$ feet
35. $B = 36°, a = 3$ yards, $c = 6$ yards
36. $B = 125°, a = 8$ yards, $c = 5$ yards
37. $C = 124°, a = 4$ meters, $b = 6$ meters
38. $C = 102°, a = 16$ meters, $b = 20$ meters

PRACTICE PLUS

In Exercises 39–40, find h to the nearest tenth.

39.

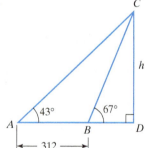

40.

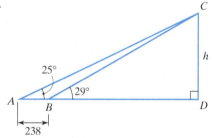

In Exercises 41–42, find a to the nearest tenth.

41.

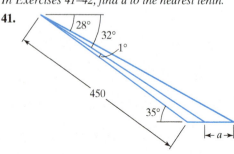

42.

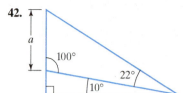

In Exercises 43–44, use the given measurements to solve the following triangle. Round lengths of sides to the nearest tenth and angle measures to the nearest degree.

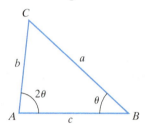

43. $a = 300, b = 200$
44. $a = 400, b = 300$

In Exercises 45–46, find the area of the triangle with the given vertices. Round to the nearest square unit.

45. $(-3, -2), (2, -2), (1, 2)$
46. $(-2, -3), (-2, 2), (2, 1)$

APPLICATION EXERCISES

47. Two fire-lookout stations are 10 miles apart, with station B directly east of station A. Both stations spot a fire. The bearing of the fire from station A is N25°E and the bearing of the fire from station B is N56°W. How far, to the nearest tenth of a mile, is the fire from each lookout station?

48. The Federal Communications Commission is attempting to locate an illegal radio station. It sets up two monitoring stations, A and B, with station B 40 miles east of station A. Station A measures the illegal signal from the radio station as coming from a direction of 48° east of north. Station B measures the signal as coming from a point 34° west of north. How far is the illegal radio station from monitoring stations A and B? Round to the nearest tenth of a mile.

49. The figure shows a 1200-yard-long sand beach and an oil platform in the ocean. The angle made with the platform from one end of the beach is 85° and from the other end is 76°. Find the distance of the oil platform, to the nearest tenth of a yard, from each end of the beach.

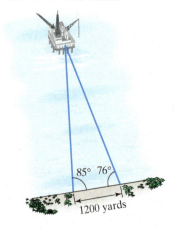

50. A surveyor needs to determine the distance between two points that lie on opposite banks of a river. The figure shows that 300 yards are measured along one bank. The angles from each end of this line segment to a point on the opposite bank are 62° and 53°. Find the distance between A and B to the nearest tenth of a yard.

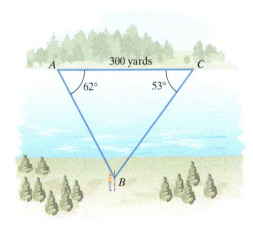

51. The Leaning Tower of Pisa in Italy leans at an angle of about 84.7°. The figure shows that 171 feet from the base of the tower, the angle of elevation to the top is 50°. Find the distance, to the nearest tenth of a foot, from the base to the top of the tower.

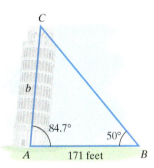

52. A pine tree growing on a hillside makes a 75° angle with the hill. From a point 80 feet up the hill, the angle of elevation to the top of the tree is 62° and the angle of depression to the bottom is 23°. Find, to the nearest tenth of a foot, the height of the tree.

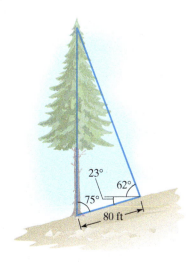

53. The figure shows a shot-put ring. The shot is tossed from A and lands at B. Using modern electronic equipment, the distance of the toss can be measured without the use of measuring tapes. When the shot lands at B, an electronic transmitter placed at B sends a signal to a device in the official's booth above the track. The device determines the angles at B and C. At a track meet, the distance from the official's booth to the shot-put ring is 562 feet. If $B = 85.3°$ and $C = 5.7°$, determine the length of the toss to the nearest tenth of a foot.

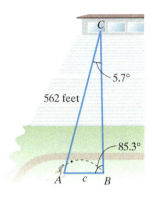

54. A pier forms an 85° angle with a straight shore. At a distance of 100 feet from the pier, the line of sight to the tip forms a 37° angle. Find the length of the pier to the nearest tenth of a foot.

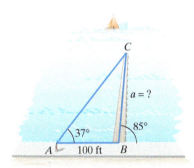

55. When the angle of elevation of the sun is 62°, a telephone pole that is tilted at an angle of 8° directly away from the sun casts a shadow 20 feet long. Determine the length of the pole to the nearest tenth of a foot.

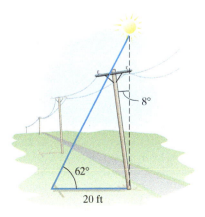

56. A leaning wall is inclined 6° from the vertical. At a distance of 40 feet from the wall, the angle of elevation to the top is 22°. Find the height of the wall to the nearest tenth of a foot.

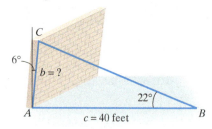

57. Redwood trees in California's Redwood National Park are hundreds of feet tall. The height of one of these trees is represented by *h* in the figure shown.

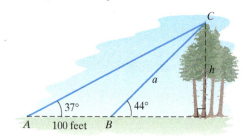

  a. Use the measurements shown to find *a*, to the nearest tenth of a foot, in oblique triangle *ABC*.

  b. Use the right triangle shown to find the height, to the nearest tenth of a foot, of a typical redwood tree in the park.

58. The figure at the top of the next page shows a cable car that carries passengers from *A* to *C*. Point *A* is 1.6 miles from the base of the mountain. The angles of elevation from *A* and *B* to the mountain's peak are 22° and 66°, respectively.

  a. Determine, to the nearest tenth of a foot, the distance covered by the cable car.

  b. Find *a*, to the nearest tenth of a foot, in oblique triangle *ABC*.

  c. Use the right triangle to find the height of the mountain to the nearest tenth of a foot.

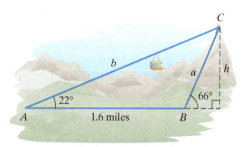

59. Lighthouse *B* is 7 miles west of lighthouse *A*. A boat leaves *A* and sails 5 miles. At this time, it is sighted from *B*. If the bearing of the boat from *B* is N62°E, how far from *B* is the boat? Round to the nearest tenth of a mile.

60. After a wind storm, you notice that your 16-foot flagpole may be leaning, but you are not sure. From a point on the ground 15 feet from the base of the flagpole, you find that the angle of elevation to the top is 48°. Is the flagpole leaning? If so, find the acute angle, to the nearest degree, that the flagpole makes with the ground.

WRITING IN MATHEMATICS

61. What is an oblique triangle?

62. Without using symbols, state the Law of Sines in your own words.

63. Briefly describe how the Law of Sines is proved.

64. What does it mean to solve an oblique triangle?

65. What do the abbreviations SAA and ASA mean?

66. Why is SSA called the ambiguous case?

67. How is the sine function used to find the area of an oblique triangle?

68. Write an original problem that can be solved using the Law of Sines. Then solve the problem.

69. Use Exercise 53 to describe how the Law of Sines is used for throwing events at track and field meets. Why aren't tape measures used to determine tossing distance?

70. You are cruising in your boat parallel to the coast, looking at a lighthouse. Explain how you can use your boat's speed and a device for measuring angles to determine the distance at any instant from your boat to the lighthouse.

CRITICAL THINKING EXERCISES

Decision Making. *In Exercises 71–74, determine whether each statement makes sense or does not make sense, and explain your reasoning.*

71. I began using the Law of Sines to solve an oblique triangle in which the measures of two sides and the angle between them were known.

72. If I know the measures of the sides and angles of an oblique triangle, I have three ways of determining the triangle's area.

73. When solving an SSA triangle using the Law of Sines, my calculator gave me both the acute and obtuse angles *B* for which $\sin B = 0.5833$.

74. Under certain conditions, a fire can be located by superimposing a triangle onto the situation and applying the Law of Sines.

75. If you are given two sides of a triangle and their included angle, you can find the triangle's area. Can the Law of Sines be used to solve the triangle with this given information? Explain your answer.

76. Two buildings of equal height are 800 feet apart. An observer on the street between the buildings measures the angles of elevation to the tops of the buildings as 27° and 41°, respectively. How high, to the nearest foot, are the buildings?

77. The figure shows the design for the top of the wing of a jet fighter. The fuselage is 5 feet wide. Find the wing span *CC'* to the nearest tenth of a foot.

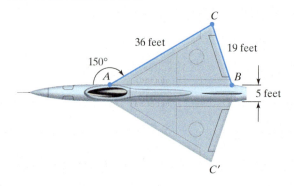

REVIEW AND PREVIEW

Exercises 78–80 will help you prepare for the material covered in the next section.

78. Find the obtuse angle B, rounded to the nearest degree, satisfying

$$\cos B = \frac{6^2 + 4^2 - 9^2}{2 \cdot 6 \cdot 4}.$$

79. Simplify and round to the nearest whole number:

$$\sqrt{26(26 - 12)(26 - 16)(26 - 24)}.$$

80. Two airplanes leave an airport at the same time on different runways. The first plane, flying on a bearing of N66°W, travels 650 miles after two hours. The second plane, flying on a bearing of S26°W, travels 600 miles after two hours. Illustrate the situation with an oblique triangle that shows how far apart the airplanes will be after two hours.

15.6 THE LAW OF COSINES

OBJECTIVES

1. Use the Law of Cosines to solve oblique triangles.
2. Solve applied problems using the Law of Cosines.
3. Use Heron's formula to find the area of a triangle.

Paleontologists use trigonometry to study the movements made by dinosaurs millions of years ago. Figure 15.20, based on data collected at Dinosaur Valley State Park in Glen Rose, Texas, shows footprints made by a two-footed carnivorous (meat-eating) dinosaur and the hindfeet of a herbivorous (plant-eating) dinosaur.

For each dinosaur, the figure indicates the *pace* and the *stride*. The pace is the distance from the left footprint to the right footprint, and vice versa. The stride is the distance from the left footprint to the next left footprint or from the right footprint to the next right footprint. Also shown in Figure 15.20 is the pace angle, designated by θ. Notice that neither dinosaur moves with a pace angle of 180°, meaning that the footprints are directly in line. The footprints show a "zig-zig" pattern that is numerically described by the pace angle. A dinosaur that is an efficient walker has a pace angle close to 180°, minimizing zig-zag motion and maximizing forward motion.

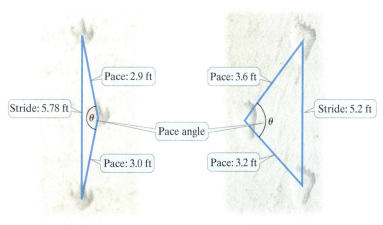

FIGURE 15.20 Dinosaur Footprints
Source: Glen J. Kuban, *An Overview of Dinosaur Tracking*

How can we determine the pace angles for the carnivore and the herbivore in Figure 15.20? Problems such as this, in which we know the measures of three sides of a triangle and we need to find the measurement of a missing angle, cannot be solved by the Law of Sines. To numerically describe which dinosaur in Figure 15.20 made more forward progress with each step, we turn to the Law of Cosines.

The Law of Cosines and Its Derivation We now look at another relationship that exists among the sides and angles in an oblique triangle. **The Law of Cosines** is used to solve triangles in which two sides and the included angle (SAS) are known, or those in which three sides (SSS) are known.

---DISCOVERY---

What happens to the Law of Cosines

$$c^2 = a^2 + b^2 - 2ab \cos C$$

if $C = 90°$? What familiar theorem do you obtain?

The Law of Cosines

If A, B, and C are the measures of the angles of a triangle, and a, b, and c are the lengths of the sides opposite these angles, then

$$a^2 = b^2 + c^2 - 2bc \cos A$$
$$b^2 = a^2 + c^2 - 2ac \cos B$$
$$c^2 = a^2 + b^2 - 2ab \cos C.$$

The square of a side of a triangle equals the sum of the squares of the other two sides minus twice their product times the cosine of their included angle.

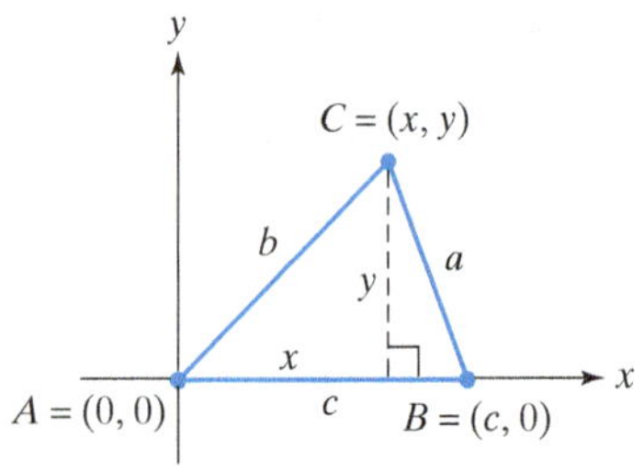

To prove the Law of Cosines, we place triangle ABC in a rectangular coordinate system. Figure 15.21 shows a triangle with three acute angles. The vertex A is at the origin and side c lies along the positive x-axis. The coordinates of C are (x, y). Using the right triangle that contains angle A, we apply the definitions of the cosine and the sine.

$$\cos A = \frac{x}{b} \qquad \sin A = \frac{y}{b}$$
$$x = b \cos A \qquad y = b \sin A$$

Multiply both sides of each equation by b and solve for x and y, respectively.

FIGURE 15.21

Thus, the coordinates of C are $(x, y) = (b \cos A, b \sin A)$. Although triangle ABC in Figure 15.21 shows angle A as an acute angle, if A were obtuse, the coordinates of C would still be $(b \cos A, b \sin A)$. This means that our proof applies to both kinds of oblique triangles.

We now apply the distance formula to the side of the triangle with length a. Notice that a is the distance from (x, y) to $(c, 0)$.

$$a = \sqrt{(x - c)^2 + (y - 0)^2} \quad \text{Use the distance formula.}$$
$$a^2 = (x - c)^2 + y^2 \quad \text{Square both sides of the equation.}$$
$$a^2 = (b \cos A - c)^2 + (b \sin A)^2 \quad x = b \cos A \text{ and } y = b \sin A.$$
$$a^2 = b^2 \cos^2 A - 2bc \cos A + c^2 + b^2 \sin^2 A \quad \text{Square the two expressions.}$$
$$a^2 = b^2 \sin^2 A + b^2 \cos^2 A + c^2 - 2bc \cos A \quad \text{Rearrange terms.}$$
$$a^2 = b^2(\sin^2 A + \cos^2 A) + c^2 - 2bc \cos A \quad \text{Factor } b^2 \text{ from the first two terms.}$$
$$a^2 = b^2 + c^2 - 2bc \cos A \quad \sin^2 A + \cos^2 A = 1$$

The resulting equation is one of the three formulas for the Law of Cosines. The other two formulas are derived in a similar manner.

OBJECTIVE 1 ▶ Solving oblique triangles. If you are given two sides and an included angle (SAS) of an oblique triangle, none of the three ratios in the Law of Sines is known. This means that we do not begin solving the triangle using the Law of Sines. Instead, we apply the Law of Cosines and the following procedure:

Section 15.6 The Law of Cosines 961

Solving an SAS Triangle
STEP 1. Use the Law of Cosines to find the side opposite the given angle.
STEP 2. Use the Law of Sines to find the angle opposite the shorter of the two given sides. This angle is always acute.
STEP 3. Find the third angle by subtracting the measure of the given angle and the angle found in step 2 from 180°.

EXAMPLE 1   Solving an SAS Triangle

Solve the triangle in Figure 15.22 with $A = 60°$, $b = 20$, and $c = 30$. Round lengths of sides to the nearest tenth and angle measures to the nearest degree.

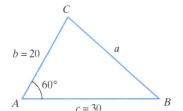

FIGURE 15.22 Solving an SAS triangle

Solution   We are given two sides and an included angle. Therefore, we apply the three-step procedure for solving an SAS triangle.

Step 1   Use the Law of Cosines to find the side opposite the given angle. Thus, we will find a.

$$a^2 = b^2 + c^2 - 2bc \cos A \quad \text{Apply the Law of Cosines to find } a.$$
$$a^2 = 20^2 + 30^2 - 2(20)(30) \cos 60° \quad b = 20, c = 30, \text{ and } A = 60°.$$
$$= 400 + 900 - 1200(0.5) \quad \text{Perform the indicated operations.}$$
$$= 700$$
$$a = \sqrt{700} \approx 26.5 \quad \text{Take the square root of both sides and solve for } a.$$

Step 2   Use the Law of Sines to find the angle opposite the shorter of the two given sides. This angle is always acute. The shorter of the two given sides is $b = 20$. Thus, we will find acute angle B.

$$\frac{b}{\sin B} = \frac{a}{\sin A} \quad \text{Apply the Law of Sines.}$$
$$\frac{20}{\sin B} = \frac{\sqrt{700}}{\sin 60°} \quad \text{We are given } b = 20 \text{ and } A = 60°. \text{ Use the exact value of } a, \sqrt{700}, \text{ from step 1.}$$
$$\sqrt{700} \sin B = 20 \sin 60° \quad \text{Cross multiply: If } \frac{a}{b} = \frac{c}{d}, \text{ then } ad = bc.$$
$$\sin B = \frac{20 \sin 60°}{\sqrt{700}} \approx 0.6547 \quad \text{Divide by } \sqrt{700} \text{ and solve for } \sin B.$$
$$B \approx 41° \quad \text{Find } \sin^{-1} 0.6547 \text{ using a calculator.}$$

Step 3   Find the third angle. Subtract the measure of the given angle and the angle found in step 2 from 180°.

$$C = 180° - A - B \approx 180° - 60° - 41° = 79°$$

The solution is $a \approx 26.5$, $B \approx 41°$, and $C \approx 79°$. ☐

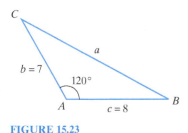

FIGURE 15.23

PRACTICE
1   Solve the triangle shown in Figure 15.23 with $A = 120°$, $b = 7$, and $c = 8$. Round as in Example 1.

If you are given three sides of a triangle (SSS), solving the triangle involves finding the three angles. We use the following procedure:

> **Solving an SSS Triangle**
>
> **STEP 1.** Use the Law of Cosines to find the angle opposite the longest side.
>
> **STEP 2.** Use the Law of Sines to find either of the two remaining acute angles.
>
> **STEP 3.** Find the third angle by subtracting the measures of the angles found in steps 1 and 2 from 180°.

EXAMPLE 2   Solving an SSS Triangle

Solve triangle ABC if $a = 6$, $b = 9$, and $c = 4$. Round angle measures to the nearest degree.

Solution   We are given three sides. Therefore, we apply the three-step procedure for solving an SSS triangle. The triangle is shown in Figure 15.24.

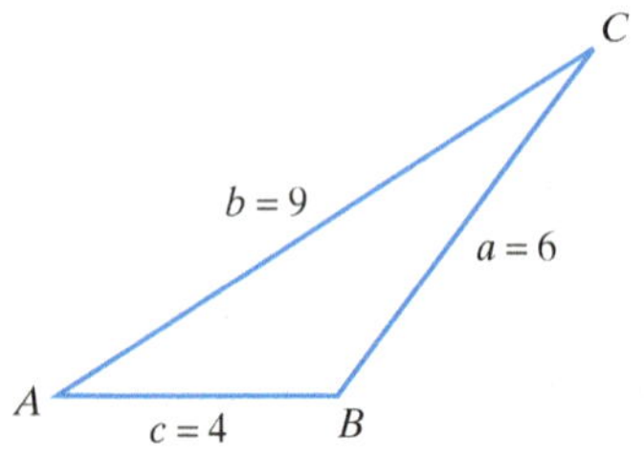

FIGURE 15.24   Solving an SSS triangle

Step 1   **Use the Law of Cosines to find the angle opposite the longest side.** The longest side is $b = 9$. Thus, we will find angle B.

$$b^2 = a^2 + c^2 - 2ac \cos B \qquad \text{Apply the Law of Cosines to find } B.$$
$$2ac \cos B = a^2 + c^2 - b^2 \qquad \text{Solve for } \cos B.$$
$$\cos B = \frac{a^2 + c^2 - b^2}{2ac}$$

$$\cos B = \frac{6^2 + 4^2 - 9^2}{2 \cdot 6 \cdot 4} = -\frac{29}{48} \qquad a = 6, b = 9, \text{ and } c = 4.$$

Using a calculator, $\cos^{-1}\left(\frac{29}{48}\right) \approx 53°$. Because $\cos B$ is negative, B is an obtuse angle. Thus,

$$B \approx 180° - 53° = 127°. \qquad \begin{array}{l}\text{Because the domain of } y = \cos^{-1}x \text{ is } [0, \pi], \\ \text{you can use a calculator to find} \\ \cos^{-1}\left(-\frac{29}{48}\right) \approx 127°.\end{array}$$

Step 2   **Use the Law of Sines to find either of the two remaining acute angles.** We will find angle A.

$$\frac{a}{\sin A} = \frac{b}{\sin B} \qquad \text{Apply the Law of Sines.}$$
$$\frac{6}{\sin A} = \frac{9}{\sin 127°} \qquad \text{We are given } a = 6 \text{ and } b = 9. \text{ We found that } B \approx 127°.$$
$$9 \sin A = 6 \sin 127° \qquad \text{Cross multiply.}$$
$$\sin A = \frac{6 \sin 127°}{9} \approx 0.5324 \qquad \text{Divide by 9 and solve for } \sin A.$$
$$A \approx 32° \qquad \text{Find } \sin^{-1} 0.5324 \text{ using a calculator.}$$

Step 3   **Find the third angle. Subtract the measures of the angles found in steps 1 and 2 from 180°.**

$$C = 180° - B - A \approx 180° - 127° - 32° = 21°$$

The solution is $B \approx 127°$, $A \approx 32°$, and $C \approx 21°$.

> ▶ **Helpful Hint**
>
> You can use the Law of Cosines in step 2 to find either of the remaining angles. However, it is simpler to use the Law of Sines. Because the largest angle has been found, the remaining angles must be acute. Thus, there is no need to be concerned about two possible triangles or an ambiguous case.

PRACTICE 2   Solve triangle ABC if $a = 8$, $b = 10$, and $c = 5$. Round angle measures to the nearest degree.

OBJECTIVE 2 ▶ **Applications of the law of cosines.**   Applied problems involving SAS and SSS triangles can be solved using the Law of Cosines.

Section 15.6 The Law of Cosines 963

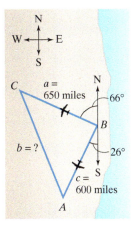

FIGURE 15.25

EXAMPLE 3 An Application of the Law of Cosines

Two airplanes leave an airport at the same time on different runways. One flies on a bearing of N66°W at 325 miles per hour. The other airplane flies on a bearing of S26°W at 300 miles per hour. How far apart will the airplanes be after two hours?

Solution After two hours, the plane flying at 325 miles per hour travels $325 \cdot 2$ miles, or 650 miles. Similarly, the plane flying at 300 miles per hour travels 600 miles. The situation is illustrated in Figure 15.25.

Let b = the distance between the planes after two hours. We can use a north-south line to find angle B in triangle ABC. Thus,

$$B = 180° - 66° - 26° = 88°.$$

We now have $a = 650$, $c = 600$, and $B = 88°$. We use the Law of Cosines to find b in this SAS situation.

$b^2 = a^2 + c^2 - 2ac \cos B$ Apply the Law of Cosines.
$b^2 = 650^2 + 600^2 - 2(650)(600) \cos 88°$ Substitute: $a = 650$, $c = 600$, and $B = 88°$.
$ \approx 755{,}278$ Use a calculator.
$b \approx \sqrt{755{,}278} \approx 869$ Take the square root and solve for b.

After two hours, the planes are approximately 869 miles apart. □

PRACTICE 3 Two airplanes leave an airport at the same time on different runways. One flies directly north at 400 miles per hour. The other airplane flies on a bearing of N75°E at 350 miles per hour. How far apart will the airplanes be after two hours?

OBJECTIVE 3 ▶ Heron's Formula. Approximately 2000 years ago, the Greek mathematician Heron of Alexandria derived a formula for the area of a triangle in terms of the lengths of its sides. A more modern derivation uses the Law of Cosines and can be found in the appendix.

> **Heron's Formula for the Area of a Triangle**
> The area of a triangle with sides a, b, and c is
> $$\text{Area} = \sqrt{s(s-a)(s-b)(s-c)},$$
> where s is one-half its perimeter: $s = \tfrac{1}{2}(a + b + c)$.

EXAMPLE 4 Using Heron's Formula
Find the area of the triangle with $a = 12$ yards, $b = 16$ yards, and $c = 24$ yards. Round to the nearest square yard.

Solution Begin by calculating one-half the perimeter:

$$s = \tfrac{1}{2}(a + b + c) = \tfrac{1}{2}(12 + 16 + 24) = 26.$$

Use Heron's formula to find the area:

$$\text{Area} = \sqrt{s(s-a)(s-b)(s-c)}$$

$$= \sqrt{26(26-12)(26-16)(26-24)}$$
$$= \sqrt{7280} \approx 85.$$

The area of the triangle is approximately 85 square yards.

PRACTICE 4 Find the area of the triangle with $a = 6$ meters, $b = 16$ meters, and $c = 18$ meters. Round to the nearest square meter.

15.6 EXERCISE SET

PRACTICE EXERCISES

In Exercises 1–8, solve each triangle. Round lengths of sides to the nearest tenth and angle measures to the nearest degree.

1.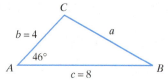

2.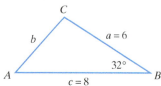

3.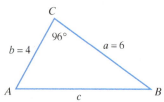

4.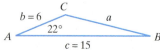

5.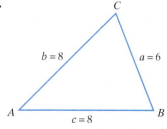

6.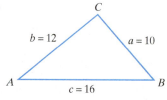

7.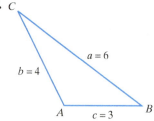

8.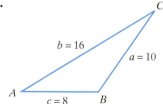

In Exercises 9–24, solve each triangle. Round lengths to the nearest tenth and angle measures to the nearest degree.

9. $a = 5, b = 7, C = 42°$
10. $a = 10, b = 3, C = 15°$
11. $b = 5, c = 3, A = 102°$
12. $b = 4, c = 1, A = 100°$
13. $a = 6, c = 5, B = 50°$
14. $a = 4, c = 7, B = 55°$
15. $a = 5, c = 2, B = 90°$
16. $a = 7, c = 3, B = 90°$
17. $a = 5, b = 7, c = 10$
18. $a = 4, b = 6, c = 9$
19. $a = 3, b = 9, c = 8$
20. $a = 4, b = 7, c = 6$
21. $a = 3, b = 3, c = 3$
22. $a = 5, b = 5, c = 5$

23. $a = 63, b = 22, c = 50$

24. $a = 66, b = 25, c = 45$

In Exercises 25–30, use Heron's formula to find the area of each triangle. Round to the nearest square unit.

25. $a = 4$ feet, $b = 4$ feet, $c = 2$ feet

26. $a = 5$ feet, $b = 5$ feet, $c = 4$ feet

27. $a = 14$ meters, $b = 12$ meters, $c = 4$ meters

28. $a = 16$ meters, $b = 10$ meters, $c = 8$ meters

29. $a = 11$ yards, $b = 9$ yards, $c = 7$ yards

30. $a = 13$ yards, $b = 9$ yards, $c = 5$ yards

PRACTICE PLUS

In Exercises 31–32, solve each triangle. Round lengths of sides to the nearest tenth and angle measures to the nearest degree.

31.
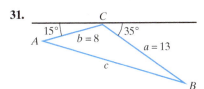

32.
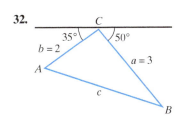

In Exercises 33–34, the three circles are arranged so that they touch each other, as shown in the figure. Use the given radii for the circles with centers A, B, and C, respectively, to solve triangle ABC. Round angle measures to the nearest degree.

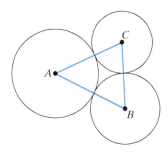

33. 5.0, 4.0, 3.5   **34.** 7.5, 4.3, 3.0

In Exercises 35–36, the three given points are the vertices of a triangle. Solve each triangle, rounding lengths of sides to the nearest tenth and angle measures to the nearest degree.

35. $A(0, 0), B(-3, 4), C(3, -1)$

36. $A(0, 0), B(4, -3), C(1, -5)$

APPLICATION EXERCISES

37. Use Figure 15.20 to find the pace angle, to the nearest degree, for the carnivore. Does the angle indicate that this dinosaur was an efficient walker? Describe your answer.

38. Use Figure 15.20 to find the pace angle, to the nearest degree, for the herbivore. Does the angle indicate that this dinosaur was an efficient walker? Describe your answer.

39. Two ships leave a harbor at the same time. One ship travels on a bearing of S12°W at 14 miles per hour. The other ship travels on a bearing of N75°E at 10 miles per hour. How far apart will the ships be after three hours? Round to the nearest tenth of a mile.

40. A plane leaves airport A and travels 580 miles to airport B on a bearing of N34°E. The plane later leaves airport B and travels to airport C 400 miles away on a bearing of S74°E. Find the distance from airport A to airport C to the nearest tenth of a mile.

41. Find the distance across the lake from A to C, to the nearest yard, using the measurements shown in the figure.

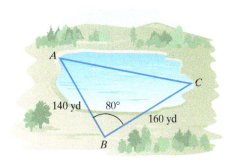

42. To find the distance across a protected cove at a lake, a surveyor makes the measurements shown in the figure. Use these measurements to find the distance from A to B to the nearest yard.

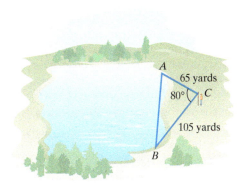

The diagram shows three islands in Florida Bay. You rent a boat and plan to visit each of these remote islands. Use the diagram to solve Exercises 43–44.

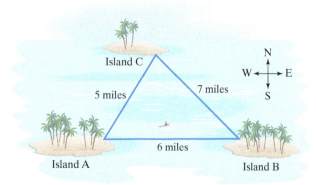

43. If you are on island A, on what bearing should you navigate to go to island C?

44. If you are on island B, on what bearing should you navigate to go to island C?

45. You are on a fishing boat that leaves its pier and heads east. After traveling for 25 miles, there is a report warning of rough seas directly south. The captain turns the boat and follows a bearing of S40°W for 13.5 miles.
   a. At this time, how far are you from the boat's pier? Round to the nearest tenth of a mile.
   b. What bearing could the boat have originally taken to arrive at this spot?

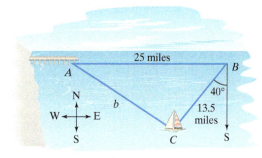

46. You are on a fishing boat that leaves its pier and heads east. After traveling for 30 miles, there is a report warning of rough seas directly south. The captain turns the boat and follows a bearing of S45°W for 12 miles.
   a. At this time, how far are you from the boat's pier? Round to the nearest tenth of a mile.
   b. What bearing could the boat have originally taken to arrive at this spot?

47. The figure shows a 400-foot tower on the side of a hill that forms a 7° angle with the horizontal. Find the length of each of the two guy wires that are anchored 80 feet uphill and downhill from the tower's base and extend to the top of the tower. Round to the nearest tenth of a foot.

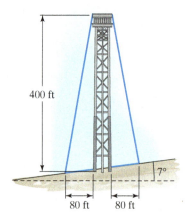

48. The figure shows a 200-foot tower on the side of a hill that forms a 5° angle with the horizontal. Find the length of each of the two guy wires that are anchored 150 feet uphill and downhill from the tower's base and extend to the top of the tower. Round to the nearest tenth of a foot.

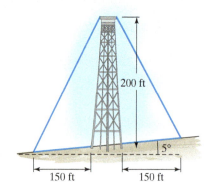

49. A Major League baseball diamond has four bases forming a square whose sides measure 90 feet each. The pitcher's mound is 60.5 feet from home plate on a line joining home plate and second base. Find the distance from the pitcher's mound to first base. Round to the nearest tenth of a foot.

50. A Little League baseball diamond has four bases forming a square whose sides measure 60 feet each. The pitcher's mound is 46 feet from home plate on a line joining home plate and second base. Find the distance from the pitcher's mound to third base. Round to the nearest tenth of a foot.

51. A piece of commercial real estate is priced at $3.50 per square foot. Find the cost, to the nearest dollar, of a triangular lot measuring 240 feet by 300 feet by 420 feet.

52. A piece of commercial real estate is priced at $4.50 per square foot. Find the cost, to the nearest dollar, of a triangular lot measuring 320 feet by 510 feet by 410 feet.

WRITING IN MATHEMATICS

53. Without using symbols, state the Law of Cosines in your own words.

54. Why can't the Law of Sines be used in the first step to solve an SAS triangle?
55. Describe a strategy for solving an SAS triangle.
56. Describe a strategy for solving an SSS triangle.
57. Under what conditions would you use Heron's formula to find the area of a triangle?
58. Describe an applied problem that can be solved using the Law of Cosines, but not the Law of Sines.
59. The pitcher on a Little League team is studying angles in geometry and has a question. "Coach, suppose I'm on the pitcher's mound facing home plate. I catch a fly ball hit in my direction. If I turn to face first base and throw the ball, through how many degrees should I turn for a direct throw?" Use the information given in Exercise 50 and write an answer to the pitcher's question. Without getting too technical, describe to the pitcher how you obtained this angle.

CRITICAL THINKING EXERCISES

Decision Making. *In Exercises 60–63, determine whether each statement makes sense or does not make sense, and explain your reasoning.*

60. The Law of Cosines is similar to the Law of Sines, with all the sines replaced with cosines.
61. If I know the measures of all three angles of an oblique triangle, neither the Law of Sines nor the Law of Cosines can be used to find the length of a side.
62. I noticed that for a right triangle, the Law of Cosines reduces to the Pythagorean Theorem.
63. Solving an SSS triangle, I do not have to be concerned about the ambiguous case when using the Law of Sines.
64. The lengths of the diagonals of a parallelogram are 20 inches and 30 inches. The diagonals intersect at an angle of 35°. Find the lengths of the parallelogram's sides. (*Hint:* Diagonals of a parallelogram bisect one another.)

65. Use the figure to solve triangle ABC. Round lengths of sides to the nearest tenth and angle measures to the nearest degree.

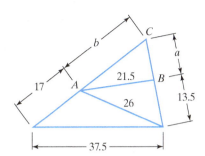

66. The minute hand and the hour hand of a clock have lengths m inches and h inches, respectively. Determine the distance between the tips of the hands at 10:00 in terms of m and h.

GROUP EXERCISES

67. The group should design five original problems that can be solved using the Laws of Sines and Cosines. At least two problems should be solved using the Law of Sines, one should be the ambiguous case, and at least two problems should be solved using the Law of Cosines. At least one problem should be an application problem using the Law of Sines and at least one problem should involve an application using the Law of Cosines. The group should turn in both the problems and their solutions.

REVIEW AND PREVIEW

68. Graph: $y = 3$.
69. Graph: $x^2 + (y - 1)^2 = 1$.
70. Complete the square and write the equation in standard form: $x^2 + 6x + y^2 = 0$. Then give the center and radius of the circle, and graph the equation.

CHAPTER 15 REVIEW

15.1 *In Exercises 1–13, verify each identity.*

1. $\sec x - \cos x = \tan x \sin x$
2. $\cos x + \sin x \tan x = \sec x$
3. $\sin^2 \theta (1 + \cot^2 \theta) = 1$
4. $(\sec \theta - 1)(\sec \theta + 1) = \tan^2 \theta$
5. $\dfrac{1 - \tan x}{\sin x} = \csc x - \sec x$
6. $\dfrac{1}{\sin t - 1} + \dfrac{1}{\sin t + 1} = -2 \tan t \sec t$
7. $\dfrac{1 + \sin t}{\cos^2 t} = \tan^2 t + 1 + \tan t \sec t$
8. $\dfrac{\cos x}{1 - \sin x} = \dfrac{1 + \sin x}{\cos x}$
9. $1 - \dfrac{\sin^2 x}{1 + \cos x} = \cos x$
10. $(\tan \theta + \cot \theta)^2 = \sec^2 \theta + \csc^2 \theta$
11. $\dfrac{1}{\sin \theta + \cos \theta} + \dfrac{1}{\sin \theta - \cos \theta} = \dfrac{2 \sin \theta}{\sin^4 \theta - \cos^4 \theta}$
12. $\dfrac{\cos t}{\cot t - 5 \cos t} = \dfrac{1}{\csc t - 5}$
13. $\dfrac{1 - \cos t}{1 + \cos t} = (\csc t - \cot t)^2$

15.2 and 15.3 *In Exercises 14–19, use a sum or difference formula to find the exact value of each expression.*

14. $\cos(45° + 30°)$
15. $\sin 195°$

16. $\tan\left(\dfrac{4\pi}{3} - \dfrac{\pi}{4}\right)$ 17. $\tan\dfrac{5\pi}{12}$

18. $\cos 65°\cos 5° + \sin 65°\sin 5°$

19. $\sin 80°\cos 50° - \cos 80°\sin 50°$

In Exercises 20–31, verify each identity.

20. $\sin\left(x + \dfrac{\pi}{6}\right) - \cos\left(x + \dfrac{\pi}{3}\right) = \sqrt{3}\sin x$

21. $\tan\left(x + \dfrac{3\pi}{4}\right) = \dfrac{\tan x - 1}{1 + \tan x}$

22. $\sec(\alpha + \beta) = \dfrac{\sec\alpha\sec\beta}{1 - \tan\alpha\tan\beta}$

23. $\dfrac{\cos(\alpha - \beta)}{\cos\alpha\cos\beta} = 1 + \tan\alpha\tan\beta$

24. $\cos^4 t - \sin^4 t = \cos 2t$

25. $\sin t - \cos 2t = (2\sin t - 1)(\sin t + 1)$

26. $\dfrac{\sin 2\theta - \sin\theta}{\cos 2\theta + \cos\theta} = \dfrac{1 - \cos\theta}{\sin\theta}$

27. $\tan\dfrac{x}{2} = \dfrac{\sec x - 1}{\tan x}$

28. $\tan\dfrac{x}{2}(1 + \cos x) = \sin x$

In Exercises 29–30, the graph with the given equation is shown in a $\left[0, 2\pi, \dfrac{\pi}{2}\right]$ by $[-2, 2, 1]$ viewing rectangle.

 a. Describe the graph using another equation.

 b. Verify that the two equations are equivalent.

29. $y = \cos\left(x + \dfrac{\pi}{2}\right)$

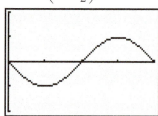

30. $y = \sin\left(x - \dfrac{3\pi}{2}\right)$

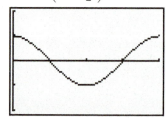

In Exercises 31–34, find the exact value of the following under the given conditions:

 a. $\sin(\alpha + \beta)$
 b. $\cos(\alpha - \beta)$
 c. $\tan(\alpha + \beta)$
 d. $\sin 2\alpha$
 e. $\cos\dfrac{\beta}{2}$

31. $\sin\alpha = \dfrac{3}{5}, 0 < \alpha < \dfrac{\pi}{2}$, and $\sin\beta = \dfrac{12}{13}, \dfrac{\pi}{2} < \beta < \pi$.

32. $\tan\alpha = \dfrac{4}{3}, \pi < \alpha < \dfrac{3\pi}{2}$, and $\tan\beta = \dfrac{5}{12}, 0 < \beta < \dfrac{\pi}{2}$.

33. $\tan\alpha = -3, \dfrac{\pi}{2} < \alpha < \pi$, and $\cot\beta = -3, \dfrac{3\pi}{2} < \beta < 2\pi$.

34. $\sin\alpha = -\dfrac{1}{3}, \pi < \alpha < \dfrac{3\pi}{2}$, and $\cos\beta = -\dfrac{1}{3}, \pi < \beta < \dfrac{3\pi}{2}$.

In Exercises 35–38, use double- and half-angle formulas to find the exact value of each expression.

35. $\cos^2 15° - \sin^2 15°$

36. $\dfrac{2\tan\dfrac{5\pi}{12}}{1 - \tan^2\dfrac{5\pi}{12}}$

37. $\sin 22.5°$

38. $\tan\dfrac{\pi}{12}$

15.4 *In Exercises 39–42, find all solutions of each equation.*

39. $\sin x = \dfrac{\sqrt{2}}{2}$ 40. $\cos x = -\dfrac{1}{2}$

41. $\sqrt{3}\tan x - 1 = 0$ 42. $2\sin x + 1 = 0$

In Exercises 43–56, solve each equation on the interval $0 \le x < 2\pi$. Use exact values where possible or give approximate solutions correct to four decimal places.

43. $\sin 3x = 1$ 44. $\cos 2x = -1$

45. $\tan x = 2\cos x \tan x$ 46. $\tan\dfrac{x}{2} = -1$

47. $2\cos^2 x - \sin x = 1$ 48. $\cos^2 x - 2\cos x = 3$

49. $\cos 2x - \sin x = 1$ 50. $4\sin^2 x = 1$

51. $\sin x = \tan x$ 52. $\sin 2x = \sqrt{3}\sin x$

53. $5\cos^2 x - 3 = 0$ 54. $\sin x = -0.6031$

55. $2\sin^2 x + \sin x - 2 = 0$ 56. $\sec^2 x = 4\tan x - 2$

57. You are playing catch with a friend located 100 feet away. If you throw the ball with an initial velocity of $v_0 = 90$ feet per second, at what angle of elevation, θ, to the nearest degree should you direct your throw so that it can be caught easily? Use the formula
$$d = \dfrac{v_0^2}{16}\sin\theta\cos\theta.$$

58. A ball on a spring is pulled 6 inches below its rest position and then released. After t seconds, the ball's distance, d, in inches from its rest position is given by
$$d = -6\cos\dfrac{\pi}{2}t.$$
Find all values of t for which the ball is 3 inches below its rest position.

REVIEW EXERCISES

15.5 and 15.6 *In Exercises 59–70, solve each triangle. Round lengths to the nearest tenth and angle measures to the nearest degree. If no triangle exists, state "no triangle." If two triangles exist, solve each triangle.*

59. $A = 70°, B = 55°, a = 12$ 60. $B = 107°, C = 30°, c = 126$

61. $B = 66°, a = 17, c = 12$ 62. $a = 117, b = 66, c = 142$

63. $A = 35°, B = 25°, c = 68$ 64. $A = 39°, a = 20, b = 26$

65. $C = 50°, a = 3, c = 1$

66. $A = 162°, b = 11.2, c = 48.2$
67. $a = 26.1, b = 40.2, c = 36.5$
68. $A = 40°, a = 6, b = 4$ 69. $B = 37°, a = 12.4, b = 8.7$
70. $A = 23°, a = 54.3, b = 22.1$

In Exercises 71–74, find the area of the triangle having the given measurements. Round to the nearest square unit.

71. $C = 42°, a = 4$ feet, $b = 6$ feet
72. $A = 22°, b = 4$ feet, $c = 5$ feet
73. $a = 2$ meters, $b = 4$ meters, $c = 5$ meters
74. $a = 2$ meters, $b = 2$ meters, $c = 2$ meters

75. The A-frame cabin shown below is 35 feet wide. The roof of the cabin makes a 60° angle with the cabin's base. Find the length of one side of the roof from its ground level to the peak. Round to the nearest tenth of a foot.

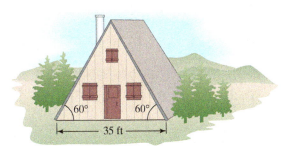

76. Two cars leave a city at the same time and travel along straight highways that differ in direction by 80°. One car averages 60 miles per hour and the other averages 50 miles per hour. How far apart will the cars be after 30 minutes? Round to the nearest tenth of a mile.

77. Two airplanes leave an airport at the same time on different runways. One flies on a bearing of N66.5°W at 325 miles per hour. The other airplane flies on a bearing of S26.5°W at 300 miles per hour. How far apart will the airplanes be after two hours?

78. The figure shows three roads that intersect to bound a triangular piece of land. Find the lengths of the other two sides of the land to the nearest foot.

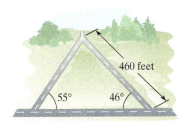

79. A commercial piece of real estate is priced at $5.25 per square foot. Find the cost, to the nearest dollar, of a triangular lot measuring 260 feet by 320 feet by 450 feet.

CHAPTER 15 TEST

Remember to use the Chapter Test Prep Videos to see the fully worked-out solutions to any of the exercises you want to review.

Use the following conditions to solve Exercises 1–4:

$$\sin \alpha = \tfrac{4}{5}, \tfrac{\pi}{2} < \alpha < \pi$$
$$\cos \beta = \tfrac{5}{13}, 0 < \beta < \tfrac{\pi}{2}$$

Find the exact value of each of the following.

1. $\sin 2\alpha$
2. $\cos \dfrac{\beta}{2}$
3. $\tan(\alpha - \beta)$
4. Use $105° = 135° - 30°$ to find the exact value of $\sin 105°$.

In Exercises 5–8, verify each identity.

5. $\cos x \csc x = \cot x$
6. $\dfrac{\sec x}{\cot x + \tan x} = \sin x$
7. $\cos\left(\theta + \dfrac{\pi}{2}\right) = -\sin \theta$
8. $\sin t \cos t (\tan t + \cot t) = 1$

In Exercises 9–12, solve each equation on the interval $[0, 2\pi)$. Use exact values where possible or give approximate solutions correct to four decimal places.

9. $\sin 3x = -\tfrac{1}{2}$
10. $\sin 2x + \cos x = 0$
11. $2 \sin^2 x + \cos x = 1$
12. $\tan x \sec x = 3 \tan x$
13. In oblique triangle ABC, $A = 34°$, $B = 68°$, and $a = 4.8$. Find b to the nearest tenth.
14. In oblique triangle ABC, $C = 68°$, $a = 5$, and $b = 6$. Find c to the nearest tenth.
15. A small fire is sighted from ranger stations A and B. Station B is 1.6 miles due east of station A. The bearing of the fire from station A is N40°E and the bearing of the fire from station B is N50°W. How far, to the nearest tenth of a mile, is the fire from station A?

CHAPTER 15 STANDARDIZED TEST

Multiple Choice. *Choose the one alternative that best completes the statement or answers the question.*

Use the given information to find the exact value of the expression.

1. $\sin \alpha = \dfrac{8}{17}$, α lies in quadrant I, and $\cos \beta = \dfrac{21}{29}$, β lies in quadrant I   Find $\cos(\alpha + \beta)$.
   a. $\dfrac{155}{493}$
   b. $\dfrac{475}{493}$
   c. $\dfrac{468}{493}$
   d. $-\dfrac{132}{493}$

2. $\sin \alpha = \dfrac{21}{29}$, α lies in quadrant II, and $\cos \beta = \dfrac{3}{5}$, β lies in quadrant I   Find $\sin(\alpha - \beta)$.
   a. $-\dfrac{17}{145}$
   b. $-\dfrac{24}{145}$
   c. $\dfrac{143}{145}$
   d. $\dfrac{144}{145}$

3. $\tan \alpha = \dfrac{5}{12}$, α lies in quadrant III   Find $\sin 2\alpha$.
   a. $-\dfrac{120}{169}$
   b. $\dfrac{120}{169}$
   c. $\dfrac{10}{13}$
   d. $\dfrac{-10}{13}$

4. $\cos \alpha = \dfrac{2}{5}$, α lies in quadrant I   Find $\cos \dfrac{\alpha}{2}$.
   a. $\dfrac{1}{5}$
   b. $\dfrac{\sqrt{70}}{10}$
   c. $\dfrac{3}{10}$
   d. $-\sqrt{\dfrac{7}{10}}$

5. $\sin \alpha = \dfrac{21}{29}, 0 < \alpha < \dfrac{\pi}{2}$; $\cos \beta = \dfrac{4}{5}, 0 < \beta < \dfrac{\pi}{2}$ Find $\tan(\alpha + \beta)$.
   a. $\dfrac{144}{145}$
   b. $\dfrac{144}{17}$
   c. $\dfrac{17}{145}$
   d. $\dfrac{143}{145}$

Write the word or phrase that best completes each statement or answers the question.

Verify the identity.

6. $\cos\left[\dfrac{3\pi}{2} - \theta\right] = -\sin\theta$

7. $\sin(\alpha - \beta)\cos(\alpha + \beta) = \sin\alpha\cos\alpha - \sin\beta\cos\beta$

Choose the one alternative that best completes the statement or answers the question.

Find all solutions of the equation.

8. $2\sin x - 1 = 0$
   a. $x = \dfrac{7\pi}{6} + 2n\pi$ or $x = \dfrac{11\pi}{6} + 2n\pi$
   b. $x = \dfrac{\pi}{6} + n\pi$ or $x = \dfrac{5\pi}{6} + n\pi$
   c. $x = \dfrac{7\pi}{6} + n\pi$ or $x = \dfrac{11\pi}{6} + n\pi$
   d. $x = \dfrac{\pi}{6} + 2n\pi$ or $x = \dfrac{5\pi}{6} + 2n\pi$

9. $\cot x \sec x = 2 \cot x$
   a. $x = \dfrac{2\pi}{3} + 2n\pi$ or $x = \dfrac{4\pi}{3} + 2n\pi$ or $x = \dfrac{\pi}{2} + n\pi$
   b. $x = \dfrac{2\pi}{3} + n\pi$ or $x = \dfrac{4\pi}{3} + n\pi$ or $x = \dfrac{\pi}{2} + n\pi$
   c. $x = \dfrac{\pi}{3} + n\pi$ or $x = \dfrac{5\pi}{3} + n\pi$ or $x = \dfrac{\pi}{2} + n\pi$
   d. $x = \dfrac{\pi}{3} + 2n\pi$ or $x = \dfrac{5\pi}{3} + 2n\pi$ or $x = \dfrac{\pi}{2} + n\pi$

Solve the equation on the interval $[0, 2\pi]$.

10. $\sin 4x = \dfrac{\sqrt{3}}{2}$
    a. $0, \dfrac{\pi}{4}, \pi$
    b. 0
    c. $\dfrac{\pi}{12}, \dfrac{\pi}{6}, \dfrac{2\pi}{3}, \dfrac{7\pi}{12}, \dfrac{7\pi}{6}, \dfrac{13\pi}{12}, \dfrac{5\pi}{3}, \dfrac{19\pi}{12}$
    d. $\dfrac{\pi}{4}, \dfrac{5\pi}{4}$

11. $\cos 2x = \dfrac{\sqrt{2}}{2}$
    a. $\dfrac{\pi}{4}, \dfrac{3\pi}{4}, \dfrac{5\pi}{4}, \dfrac{7\pi}{4}$
    b. $\dfrac{\pi}{8}, \dfrac{7\pi}{8}, \dfrac{9\pi}{8}, \dfrac{15\pi}{8}$
    c. $0, \dfrac{2\pi}{3}, \pi, \dfrac{4\pi}{3}$
    d. no solution

12. $2\sin^2 x = \sin x$
    a. $0, \pi, \dfrac{\pi}{6}, \dfrac{5\pi}{6}$
    b. $\dfrac{\pi}{6}, \dfrac{5\pi}{6}$
    c. $\dfrac{\pi}{2}, \dfrac{3\pi}{2}, \dfrac{\pi}{3}, \dfrac{2\pi}{3}$
    d. $\dfrac{\pi}{3}, \dfrac{2\pi}{3}$

13. $\sin^2 x - \cos^2 x = 0$
    a. $\dfrac{\pi}{4}, \dfrac{\pi}{3}$
    b. $\dfrac{\pi}{4}, \dfrac{3\pi}{4}, \dfrac{5\pi}{4}, \dfrac{7\pi}{4}$
    c. $\dfrac{\pi}{4}$
    d. $\dfrac{\pi}{4}, \dfrac{\pi}{6}$

14. $\tan x + \sec x = 1$
    a. no solution
    b. 0
    c. $\dfrac{5\pi}{4}$
    d. $\dfrac{\pi}{4}$

Solve the triangle. Round lengths to the nearest tenth and angle measures to the nearest degree.

15. $A = 47°$
    $B = 33°$
    $a = 37.4$
    a. $C = 101°, b = 27.9, c = 50.4$
    b. $C = 101°, b = 50.4, c = 27.9$
    c. $C = 100°, b = 50.4, c = 27.9$
    d. $C = 100°, b = 27.9, c = 50.4$

16. $a = 20$
    $b = 48$
    $c = 58$
    a. $A = 19°, B = 51°, C = 110°$
    b. $A = 17°, B = 93°, C = 70°$
    c. $A = 19°, B = 91°, C = 70°$
    d. $A = 161°$, so no triangle is formed.

Solve the problem.

17. Two tracking stations are on the equator 140 miles apart. A weather balloon is located on a bearing of N41°E from the western station and on a bearing of N15°W from the eastern station. How far is the ballon from the western station? Round to the nearest mile.

    a. 172 miles b. 118 miles
    c. 163 miles d. 127 miles

Appendix A

A.1 GEOMETRIC FIGURES AND FORMULAS

Rectangle

Perimeter: $P = 2l + 2w$
Area: $A = lw$

Square

Perimeter: $P = 4s$
Area: $A = s^2$

Triangle

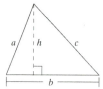

Perimeter: $P = a + b + c$
Area: $A = \frac{1}{2}bh$

Sum of Angles of Triangle

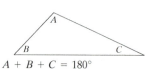

$A + B + C = 180°$
The sum of the measures of the three angles is 180°.

Right Triangles

Perimeter: $P = a + b + c$
Area: $A = \frac{1}{2}ab$
One 90° (right) angle

Pythagorean Theorem (for right triangles)

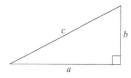

$a^2 + b^2 = c^2$

Isosceles Triangle

Triangle has:
two equal sides and two equal angles.

Equilateral Triangle

Triangle has:
three equal sides and three equal angles.
Measure of each angle is 60°.

Trapezoid

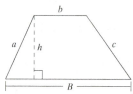

Perimeter: $P = a + b + c + B$
Area: $A = \frac{1}{2}h(B + b)$

Parallelogram

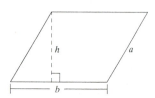

Perimeter: $P = 2a + 2b$
Area: $A = bh$

Circle

Circumference: $C = \pi d$
 $C = 2\pi r$
Area: $A = \pi r^2$

Rectangular Solid

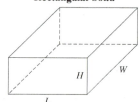

Volume: $V = LWH$
Surface Area:
$S = 2LW + 2HL + 2HW$

Cube

Volume: $V = s^3$
Surface Area: $S = 6s^2$

Cone

Volume: $V = \frac{1}{3}\pi r^2 h$

Right Circular Cylinder

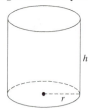

Volume: $V = \pi r^2 h$
Surface Area: $S = 2\pi r^2 + 2\pi r h$

Sphere

Volume: $V = \frac{4}{3}\pi r^3$
Surface Area: $S = 4\pi r^2$

Other Formulas

Distance: $d = rt$ (r = rate, t = time)
Percent: $p = br$ (p = percentage, b = base, r = rate)
Temperature: $F = \frac{9}{5}C + 32$ $C = \frac{5}{9}(F - 32)$
Simple Interest: $I = Prt$
(P = principal, r = annual interest rate, t = time in years)

A.2 TRIGONOMETRIC FORMULAS
RIGHT TRIANGLE DEFINITIONS OF TRIGONOMETRIC FUNCTIONS

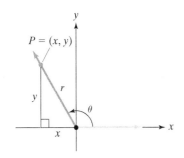

$$\sin \theta = \frac{\text{opp.}}{\text{hyp.}} = \frac{a}{c} \qquad \csc \theta = \frac{\text{hyp.}}{\text{opp.}} = \frac{c}{a}$$

$$\cos \theta = \frac{\text{adj.}}{\text{hyp.}} = \frac{b}{c} \qquad \sec \theta = \frac{\text{hyp.}}{\text{adj.}} = \frac{c}{b}$$

$$\tan \theta = \frac{\text{opp.}}{\text{adj.}} = \frac{a}{b} \qquad \cot \theta = \frac{\text{adj.}}{\text{opp.}} = \frac{b}{a}$$

TRIGONOMETRIC FUNCTIONS OF ANY ANGLE

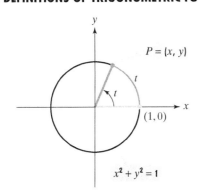

$$\sin \theta = \frac{y}{r} \qquad \csc \theta = \frac{r}{y}, \quad y \neq 0$$

$$\cos \theta = \frac{x}{r} \qquad \sec \theta = \frac{r}{x}, \quad x \neq 0$$

$$\tan \theta = \frac{y}{x}, \quad x \neq 0 \qquad \cot \theta = \frac{x}{y}, \quad y \neq 0$$

UNIT CIRCLE DEFINITIONS OF TRIGONOMETRIC FUNCTIONS

$$\sin t = y \qquad \csc t = \frac{1}{y}, \quad y \neq 0$$

$$\cos t = x \qquad \sec t = \frac{1}{x}, \quad x \neq 0$$

$$\tan t = \frac{y}{x}, \quad x \neq 0 \qquad \cot t = \frac{x}{y}, \quad y \neq 0$$

GRAPHS OF TRIGONOMETRIC FUNCTIONS

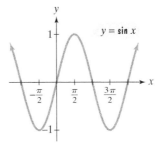

Domain: all real numbers
Range: $-1 \leq y \leq 1$
Period: 2π

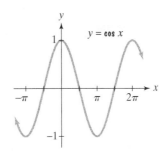

Domain: all real numbers
Range: $-1 \leq y \leq 1$
Period: 2π

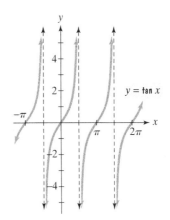

Domain: all real numbers except odd multiples of $\dfrac{\pi}{2}$
Range: all real numbers
Period: π

FUNDAMENTAL TRIGONOMETRIC IDENTITIES

Reciprocal Identities

$$\sin x = \frac{1}{\csc x} \qquad \csc x = \frac{1}{\sin x}$$
$$\cos x = \frac{1}{\sec x} \qquad \sec x = \frac{1}{\cos x}$$
$$\tan x = \frac{1}{\cot x} \qquad \cot x = \frac{1}{\tan x}$$

Quotient Identities

$$\tan x = \frac{\sin x}{\cos x} \qquad \cot x = \frac{\cos x}{\sin x}$$

Pythagorean Identities

$$\sin^2 x + \cos^2 x = 1$$
$$1 + \tan^2 x = \sec^2 x$$
$$1 + \cot^2 x = \csc^2 x$$

Even-Odd Identities

$$\sin(-x) = -\sin x \qquad \cos(-x) = \cos x \qquad \tan(-x) = -\tan x$$

OTHER TRIGONOMETRIC IDENTITIES

Sum and Difference Formulas

$$\sin(\alpha + \beta) = \sin\alpha \cos\beta + \cos\alpha \sin\beta$$
$$\sin(\alpha - \beta) = \sin\alpha \cos\beta - \cos\alpha \sin\beta$$
$$\cos(\alpha + \beta) = \cos\alpha \cos\beta - \sin\alpha \sin\beta$$
$$\cos(\alpha - \beta) = \cos\alpha \cos\beta + \sin\alpha \sin\beta$$
$$\tan(\alpha + \beta) = \frac{\tan\alpha + \tan\beta}{1 - \tan\alpha \tan\beta}$$
$$\tan(\alpha - \beta) = \frac{\tan\alpha - \tan\beta}{1 + \tan\alpha \tan\beta}$$

Double-Angle Formulas

$$\sin 2\theta = 2\sin\theta \cos\theta$$
$$\cos 2\theta = \cos^2\theta - \sin^2\theta = 2\cos^2\theta - 1 = 1 - 2\sin^2\theta$$
$$\tan 2\theta = \frac{2\tan\theta}{1 - \tan^2\theta}$$

Half-Angle Formulas

$$\sin\frac{\alpha}{2} = \pm\sqrt{\frac{1 - \cos\alpha}{2}}$$
$$\cos\frac{\alpha}{2} = \pm\sqrt{\frac{1 + \cos\alpha}{2}}$$
$$\tan\frac{\alpha}{2} = \pm\sqrt{\frac{1 - \cos\alpha}{1 + \cos\alpha}} = \frac{1 - \cos\alpha}{\sin\alpha} = \frac{\sin\alpha}{1 + \cos\alpha}$$

OBLIQUE TRIANGLES

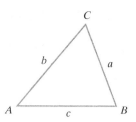

Law of Sines

$$\frac{a}{\sin A} = \frac{b}{\sin B} = \frac{c}{\sin C}$$

Law of Cosines

$$a^2 = b^2 + c^2 - 2bc \cos A$$
$$b^2 = a^2 + c^2 - 2ac \cos B$$
$$c^2 = a^2 + b^2 - 2ab \cos C$$

A.3 TABLE OF PERCENT, DECIMAL, AND FRACTION EQUIVALENTS

Percent, Decimal, and Fraction Equivalents		
Percent	Decimal	Fraction
1%	0.01	$\frac{1}{100}$
5%	0.05	$\frac{1}{20}$
10%	0.1	$\frac{1}{10}$
12.5% or $12\frac{1}{2}$%	0.125	$\frac{1}{8}$
$16.\overline{6}$% or $16\frac{2}{3}$%	$0.1\overline{6}$	$\frac{1}{6}$
20%	0.2	$\frac{1}{5}$
25%	0.25	$\frac{1}{4}$
30%	0.3	$\frac{3}{10}$
$33.\overline{3}$% or $33\frac{1}{3}$%	$0.\overline{3}$	$\frac{1}{3}$
37.5% or $37\frac{1}{2}$%	0.375	$\frac{3}{8}$
40%	0.4	$\frac{2}{5}$
50%	0.5	$\frac{1}{2}$
60%	0.6	$\frac{3}{5}$
62.5% or $62\frac{1}{2}$%	0.625	$\frac{5}{8}$
$66.\overline{6}$% or $66\frac{2}{3}$%	$0.\overline{6}$	$\frac{2}{3}$
70%	0.7	$\frac{7}{10}$
75%	0.75	$\frac{3}{4}$
80%	0.8	$\frac{4}{5}$
$83.\overline{3}$% or $83\frac{1}{3}$%	$0.8\overline{3}$	$\frac{5}{6}$
87.5% or $87\frac{1}{2}$%	0.875	$\frac{7}{8}$
90%	0.9	$\frac{9}{10}$
100%	1.0	1
110%	1.1	$1\frac{1}{10}$
125%	1.25	$1\frac{1}{4}$
$133.\overline{3}$% or $133\frac{1}{3}$%	$1.\overline{3}$	$1\frac{1}{3}$
150%	1.5	$1\frac{1}{2}$
$166.\overline{6}$% or $166\frac{2}{3}$%	$1.\overline{6}$	$1\frac{2}{3}$
175%	1.75	$1\frac{3}{4}$
200%	2.0	2

Appendix B

Surveys and Margins of Error

When you were between the ages of 6 and 14, how would you have responded to this question:

What is bad about being a kid?

In a random sample of 1172 children ages 6 through 14, 17% of the children responded, "Getting bossed around." The problem is that this is a single random sample. Do 17% of kids in the entire population of children ages 6 through 14 think that getting bossed around is a bad thing?

Statisticians use properties of the normal distribution to estimate the probability that a result obtained from a single sample reflects what is truly happening in the population. If you look at the results of a poll like the one shown in the margin, you will observe that a *margin of error* is reported. Surveys and opinion polls often give a margin of error. Let's use our understanding of the normal distribution to see how to calculate and interpret margins of error.

Suppose that $p\%$ of the population of children ages 6 through 14 hold the opinion that getting bossed around is a bad thing about being a kid. Instead of taking only one random sample of 1172 children, we repeat the process of selecting a random sample of 1172 children hundreds of times. Then, we calculate the percentage of children for each sample who think being bossed around is bad. With random sampling, we expect to find the percentage in many of the samples close to $p\%$, with relatively few samples having percentages far from $p\%$. The next figure shows that the percentages of children from the hundreds of samples can be modeled by a normal distribution. The mean of this distribution is the actual population percent, $p\%$, and is the most frequent result from the samples.

What Is Bad about Being a Kid?

Kids Say	
Getting bossed around	17%
School, homework	15%
Can't do everything I want	11%
Chores	9%
Being grounded	9%

Source: Penn, Schoen, and Berland using 1172 interviews with children ages 6 to 14 from May 14 to June 1, 1999, Margin of error: ±2.9%

Note the margin of error.

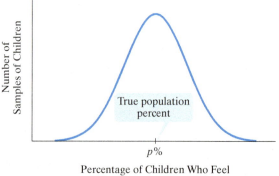

Percentage of children who feel being bossed around is bad

Mathematicians have shown that the standard deviation of a normal distribution of samples like the one above is approximately $\dfrac{1}{2\sqrt{n}}$, where n is the sample size. Using the 68–95–99.7 Rule, approximately 95% of the samples have a percentage within 2 standard deviations of the true population percentage, $p\%$:

$$2 \text{ standard deviations} = 2 \cdot \dfrac{1}{2\sqrt{n}} = \dfrac{1}{\sqrt{n}}.$$

If we use a sample of size n, there is a 95% probability that the percent obtained will lie within two standard deviations, or $\frac{1}{\sqrt{n}}$, of the true population percent. We can be 95% confident that the true population percent lies between

$$\text{the sample percent} - \frac{1}{\sqrt{n}}$$

and

$$\text{the sample percent} + \frac{1}{\sqrt{n}}.$$

We call $\pm\frac{1}{\sqrt{n}}$ the **margin of error**.

> **Margin of Error in a Survey**
>
> If a statistic is obtained from a random sample of size n, there is a 95% probability that it lies within $\frac{1}{\sqrt{n}}$ of the true population statistic, where $\pm\frac{1}{\sqrt{n}}$ is called the **margin of error**.

EXAMPLE 1 Using and Interpreting Margin of Error

In a random sample of 1172 children ages 6 through 14, 17% of the children said getting bossed around is a bad thing about being a kid.

What Is Bad about Being a Kid?

Kids Say	
Getting bossed around	17%
School, homework	15%
Can't do everything I want	11%
Chores	9%
Being grounded	9%

Source: Penn, Schoen, and Berland using 1172 interviews with children ages 6 to 14 from May 14 to June 1, 1999, Margin of error: ±2.9%

a. Verify the margin of error that was given for this survey.
b. Write a statement about the percentage of children in the population who feel that getting bossed around is a bad thing about being a kid.

Solution

a. The sample size is $n = 1172$. The margin of error is

$$\pm\frac{1}{\sqrt{n}} = \pm\frac{1}{\sqrt{1172}} \approx \pm 0.029 = \pm 2.9\%.$$

b. There is a 95% probability that the true population percentage lies between

$$\text{the sample percent} - \frac{1}{\sqrt{n}} = 17\% - 2.9\% = 14.1\%$$

and

$$\text{the sample percent} + \frac{1}{\sqrt{n}} = 17\% + 2.9\% = 19.9\%.$$

We can be 95% confident that between 14.1% and 19.9% of all children feel that getting bossed around is a bad thing about being a kid.

PRACTICE

1 The circle graph shows the question and results of a *USA Today*, CNN/Gallup poll of 485 randomly selected American adults on physician-assisted suicide.

a. Find the margin of error for this survey. Round to the nearest tenth of a percent.
b. Write a statement about the percentage of American adults in the population who support physician-assisted suicide.
c. Based on your answer to part (b), explain how the title given with the circle graph is misleading.

Majority Supports Assisted Suicide

Should a doctor be allowed to help a terminally ill patient end his or her life with an overdose of medication if the patient is mentally competent and requests it?

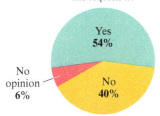

Yes 54%
No 40%
No opinion 6%

Source: USA Today, CNN/Gallup Poll

APPENDIX B | EXERCISE SET

1. In a survey of 2500 students, 87% preferred school starting at 9 AM.
   a. Find the margin of error for this survey.
   b. Write a statement about students preferring that school start at 9 AM.

2. In a survey of 1600 students, 72% chose pizza as their favorite meal.
   a. Find the margin of error for this survey.
   b. Write a statement about students preferring a meal of pizza.

3. Suppose the survey of Example 1 was increased to a total of 1430 interviews.
   a. Calculate the new margin of error to the nearest tenth of a percent.
   b. If 9% of the children still list "doing chores" as a bad thing about being a kid, write a statement about this percent and margin of error.

4. Now suppose that the survey of Example 1 was decreased to 600 interviews.
   a. Calculate the new margin of error to the nearest tenth of a percent.
   b. If 9% of the children still list "being grounded" as a bad thing about being a kid, write a statement about this percent and margin of error.

For a survey with each sample size below, calculate the margin of error. Round each answer to the nearest tenth of a percent.

5. 12,000
6. 15,000
7. 450
8. 590

9. Using a random sample of 2272 American adults with children, a Harris survey asked respondents to name their dream job for their child or children. The top five responses and the percentage of parents who named each of these jobs are shown in the bar graph below.

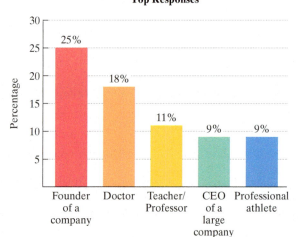

What is Your Dream Job for Your Child/Children? Top Responses

Founder of a company: 25%
Doctor: 18%
Teacher/Professor: 11%
CEO of a large company: 9%
Professional athlete: 9%

a. Find the margin of error, to the nearest tenth of a percent, for this survey.
b. Write a statement about the percentage of parents in the population who consider a doctor as the dream job for their child.

10. Using a random sample of 2297 American adults, an NBC *Today Show* poll asked respondents if they got enough sleep at night. The responses are shown in the circle graph.

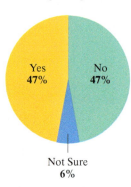

Do You Get Enough Sleep at Night?

Yes 47%
No 47%
Not Sure 6%

a. Find the margin of error, to the nearest tenth of a percent, for this survey.
b. Write a statement about the percentage of American adults in the population who do not get enough sleep at night.

11. Using a random sample of 4000 TV households, Nielsen Media Research found that 60.2% watched the final episode of *M*A*S*H*.
    a. Find the margin of error in this percent.
    b. Write a statement about the percentage of TV households in the population who tuned in to the final episode of *M*A*S*H*.

12. Using a random sample of 4000 TV households, Nielsen Media Research found that 51.1% watched *Roots, Part 8*.
    a. Find the margin of error in this percent.
    b. Write a statement about the percentage of TV households in the population who tuned in to *Roots, Part 8*.

13. In 1997, Nielsen Media Research increased its random sample to 5000 TV households. By how much, to the nearest tenth of a percent, did this improve the margin of error over that in Exercises 11 and 12?

14. If Nielsen Media Research were to increase its random sample from 5000 to 10,000 TV households, by how much, to the nearest tenth of a percent, would this improve the margin of error?

GROUP EXERCISE

15. For this activity, group members will conduct interviews with a random sample of students on campus. Each student is to be asked. "What is the worst thing about being a student?" One response should be recorded for each student.

(continued next page)

a. Each member should interview enough students so that there are at least 50 randomly selected students in the sample.
b. After all responses have been recorded, the group should organize the four most common answers. For each answer, compute the percentage of students in the sample who felt that this is the worst thing about being a student.
c. Find the margin of error for your survey.
d. For each of the four most common answers, write a statement about the percentage of all students on your campus who feel that this is the worst thing about being a student.

Appendix C

PRACTICE FINAL EXAM

Simplify. If needed, write answers with positive exponents only.

1. $\sqrt{216}$
2. $\dfrac{(4 - \sqrt{16}) - (-7 - 20)}{-2(1 - 4)^2}$
3. $\left(\dfrac{1}{125}\right)^{-1/3}$
4. $(-9x)^{-2}$
5. $\dfrac{\dfrac{5}{x} - \dfrac{7}{3x}}{\dfrac{9}{8x} - \dfrac{1}{x}}$
6. $\dfrac{6^{-1}a^2b^{-3}}{3^{-2}a^{-5}b^2}$
7. $\left(\dfrac{64c^{4/3}}{a^{-2/3}b^{5/6}}\right)^{1/2}$

Factor completely.

8. $16y^3 - 2$
9. $x^2y - 9y - 3x^2 + 27$

Perform the indicated operations and simplify if possible.

10. $(4x^3y - 3x - 4) - (9x^3y + 8x + 5)$
11. $(6m + n)^2$
12. $(2x - 1)(x^2 - 6x + 4)$
13. $\dfrac{3x^2 - 12}{x^2 + 2x - 8} \div \dfrac{6x + 18}{x + 4}$
14. $\dfrac{2x^2 + 7}{2x^4 - 18x^2} - \dfrac{6x + 7}{2x^4 - 18x^2}$
15. $\dfrac{3}{x^2 - x - 6} + \dfrac{2}{x^2 - 5x + 6}$
16. $\sqrt{125x^3} - 3\sqrt{20x^3}$
17. $(\sqrt{5} + 5)(\sqrt{5} - 5)$
18. $(4x^3 - 5x) \div (2x + 1)$ [Use long division.]

Solve each equation or inequality.

19. $9(x + 2) = 5[11 - 2(2 - x) + 3]$
20. $|6x - 5| - 3 = -2$
21. $3n(7n - 20) = 96$
22. $-3 < 2(x - 3) \leq 4$
23. $|3x + 1| > 5$
24. $\dfrac{x^2 + 8}{x} - 1 = \dfrac{2(x + 4)}{x}$
25. $y^2 - 3y = 5$
26. $x = \sqrt{x - 2} + 2$
27. $2x^2 - 7x > 15$
28. Use the Rational Zero Theorem to solve: $x^3 + 9x^2 + 16x - 6 = 0$
29. Solve the system: $\begin{cases} \dfrac{x}{2} + \dfrac{y}{4} = -\dfrac{3}{4} \\ x + \dfrac{3}{4}y = -4 \end{cases}$

Graph the following.

30. $4x + 6y = 7$
31. $2x - y > 5$
32. $y = -3$
33. $g(x) = -|x + 2| - 1$. Also, find the domain and range of this function.
34. $h(x) = x^2 - 4x + 4$. Label the vertex and any intercepts.
35. $f(x) = \begin{cases} -\dfrac{1}{2}x & \text{if } x \leq 0 \\ 2x - 3 & \text{if } x > 0 \end{cases}$. Also, find the domain and range of this function.

Write equations of the following lines. Write each equation using function notation.

36. through $(4, -2)$ and $(6, -3)$
37. through $(-1, 2)$ and perpendicular to $3x - y = 4$

Find the distance or midpoint.

38. Find the distance between the points $(-6, 3)$ and $(-8, -7)$.
39. Find the midpoint of the line segment whose endpoints are $(-2, -5)$ and $(-6, 12)$.

Find the domain of each rational function and graph the function.

40. $f(x) = \dfrac{1}{(x + 3)^2}$
41. $f(x) = \dfrac{x + 1}{x^2 + 2x - 3}$

Rationalize each denominator. Assume that variables represent positive numbers.

42. $\sqrt{\dfrac{9}{y}}$
43. $\dfrac{4 - \sqrt{x}}{4 + 2\sqrt{x}}$

Solve.

44. The most populous city in the United States is New York, although it is only the third most populous city in the world. Tokyo is the most populous city in the world. Second place is held by Seoul, Korea. Seoul's population is 1.3 million more than New York's and Tokyo's is 10.2 million less than twice the population of New York. If the sum of the populations of these three cities is 78.3 million, find the population of each city.

45. Write the area of the shaded region as a factored polynomial.

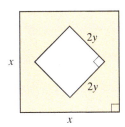

46. The product of one more than a number and twice the reciprocal of the number is $\frac{12}{5}$. Find the number.

47. Suppose that W is inversely proportional to V. If $W = 20$ when $V = 12$, find W when $V = 15$.

48. Given the diagram shown, approximate to the nearest foot how many feet of walking distance a person saves by cutting across the lawn instead of walking on the sidewalk.

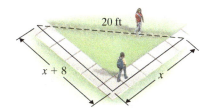

49. A stone is thrown upward from a bridge. The stone's height in feet, $s(t)$, above the water t seconds after the stone is thrown is a function given by the equation

$$s(t) = -16t^2 + 32t + 256$$

  a. Find the maximum height of the stone.
  b. Find the time it takes the stone to hit the water. Round the answer to two decimal places.

50. The research department of a company that manufactures children's fruit drinks is experimenting with a new flavor. A 17.5% fructose solution is needed, but only 10% and 20% solutions are available. How many gallons of a 10% fructose solution should be mixed with a 20% fructose solution to obtain 20 gallons of a 17.5% fructose solution?

Matrices: Chapter 5

In Exercises 51 and 52

$$A = \begin{bmatrix} 3 & 1 \\ 1 & 0 \\ 2 & 1 \end{bmatrix}, B = \begin{bmatrix} 1 & -1 \\ 2 & 1 \end{bmatrix}, C = \begin{bmatrix} 1 & 2 \\ -1 & 3 \end{bmatrix}.$$

Carry out the indicated operations.

51. AB **52.** $BC - 3B$

53. Consider the system
$$3x + 5y = 9$$
$$2x - 3y = -13$$

  a. Express the system in the form $AX = B$, where A, X, and B are appropriate matrices.
  b. Find A^{-1}, the inverse of the coefficient matrix.
  c. Use A^{-1} to solve the given system.

54. Evaluate: $\begin{vmatrix} 4 & -1 & 3 \\ 0 & 5 & -1 \\ 5 & 2 & 4 \end{vmatrix}$

Complex Numbers: Chapter 8

Perform the indicated operation and simplify. Write the result in the form $a + bi$.

55. $-\sqrt{-8}$ **56.** $(12 - 6i) - (12 - 3i)$

57. $(4 + 3i)^2$ **58.** $\dfrac{1 + 4i}{1 - i}$

Inverse, Exponential, and Logarithmic Functions: Chapter 10

59. If $g(x) = x - 7$ and $h(x) = x^2 - 6x + 5$, find $(g \circ h)(x)$.

60. Decide whether $f(x) = 6 - 2x$ is a one-to-one function. If it is, find its inverse.

61. Use properties of logarithms to write the expression as a single logarithm.

$$\log_5 x + 3\log_5 x - \log_5(x + 1)$$

Solve. Give exact solutions.

62. $8^{x-1} = \dfrac{1}{64}$

63. $3^{2x+5} = 4$ Give an exact solution and a 4 decimal place approximation.

64. $\log_8(3x - 2) = 2$

65. $\log_4(x + 1) - \log_4(x - 2) = 3$

66. $\ln \sqrt{e} = x$

67. Graph $y = \left(\dfrac{1}{2}\right)^x + 1$

68. The prairie dog population of the Grand Rapids area now stands at 57,000 animals. If the population is growing at a rate of 2.6% annually, use the formula $y = y_0 e^{kt}$ to find how many prairie dogs there will be in that area 5 years from now.

Conic Sections: Chapter 11

Sketch the graph of each equation.

69. $x^2 - y^2 = 36$

70. $16x^2 + 9y^2 = 144$

71. $x^2 + y^2 + 6x = 16$

72. Solve the system:
$$\begin{cases} x^2 + y^2 = 26 \\ x^2 - 2y^2 = 23 \end{cases}$$

Sequences, Series, and the Binomial Theorem: Chapter 12

73. Find the first five terms of the sequence $a_n = \dfrac{(-1)^n}{n+4}$.

74. Find the partial sum, S_5, of the sequence $a_n = 5(2)^{n-1}$.

75. Find S_∞ of the sequence $\dfrac{3}{2}, -\dfrac{3}{4}, \dfrac{3}{8}, \ldots$

76. Find $\sum_{i=1}^{4} i(i-2)$

77. Expand: $(2x + y)^5$

Counting Methods and Probability: Chapter 13

78. In how many ways can seven airplanes line up for a departure on a runway if the plane with the greatest number of passengers must depart first?

79. A human resource manager has 11 applicants to fill three different positions. Assuming that all applicants are equally qualified for any of the three positions, in how many ways can this be done?

80. In how many distinct ways can the letters of the word ATLANTA be arranged?

81. One card is randomly selected from a deck of 52 cards. Find the probability of selecting a black card or a picture card.

82. A box contains five red balls, six green balls, and nine yellow balls. Suppose you select one ball at random from the box and do not replace it. Then you randomly select a second ball. Find the probability that both balls selected are red.

According to the American Freshman, *the number of hours that college freshman spend studying each, week is normally distributed with a mean of 7 hours and a standard deviation of 5.3 hours. In Exercise 83 use the 68–95–99.7 Rule to find the percentage of college freshmen who study*

83. more than 17.6 hours each week.

Trigonometry: Chapters 14 and 15

Find the exact value.

84. $\tan 300°$ 85. $\sin \dfrac{7\pi}{4}$

86. Find the length of the arc on a circle of radius 20 feet intercepted by a 75° central angle. Express arc length in terms of π. Then round your answer to two decimal places.

87. If $\cos \theta = \dfrac{1}{3}$ and $\tan \theta < 0$, find the exact value of each of the remaining trigonometric functions of θ.

88. Graph one period of the function $y = -2 \cos\left(x - \dfrac{\pi}{2}\right)$.

89. Find the exact value of $\tan\left[\cos^{-1}\left(-\dfrac{1}{2}\right)\right]$.

90. Solve the right triangle in the figure shown. Round lengths to one decimal place.

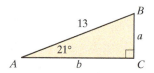

91. The angle of elevation to the top of a building from a point on the ground 30 yards from its base is 37°. Find the height of the building to the nearest yard.

92. *Use the following conditions to find* $\sin 2\alpha$.
$$\sin \alpha = \dfrac{4}{5}, \dfrac{\pi}{2} < \alpha < \pi$$

93. Verify the identity:
$$\dfrac{\sec x}{\cot x + \tan x} = \sin x$$

94. Use $105° = 135° - 30°$ to find the exact value of $\sin 105°$.

95. *Solve the equation on the interval $0 \le x < 2\pi$. Use exact values where possible or give approximate solutions correct to four decimal places.*
$$2 \sin^2 x + \cos x = 1$$

96. In oblique triangle ABC, $A = 34°$, $B = 68°$, and $a = 4.8$. Find b to the nearest tenth.

97. In oblique triangle ABC, $C = 68°$, $a = 5$, and $b = 6$. Find c to the nearest tenth.

Answers to Selected Exercises

CHAPTER 1 REAL NUMBERS AND ALGEBRAIC EXPRESSIONS

Section 1.2
Practice Exercises
1. 14 sq cm   **2.** 31   **3. a.** {6, 7, 8, 9}   **b.** {41, 42, 43, …}   **4. a.** true   **b.** true   **5. a.** true   **b.** false   **c.** true   **d.** false
6. a. 4   **b.** $\frac{1}{2}$ **c.** 1   **d.** -6.8 **e.** -4 **7. a.** -5.4 **b.** $\frac{3}{5}$ **c.** -18 **8. a.** $3x$ **b.** $2x - 5$ **c.** $3\frac{5}{8} + x$ **d.** $\frac{x}{2}$ **e.** $x - 14$ **f.** $5(x + 10)$

Vocabulary and Readiness Check 1.2
1. variables   **3.** absolute value   **5.** natural numbers   **7.** integers   **9.** rational number

Exercise Set 1.2
1. 35   **3.** 30.38   **5.** $\frac{3}{8}$ **7.** 22   **9.** 2000 mi   **11.** 20.4 sq. ft   **13.** $10,612.80   **15.** {1, 2, 3, 4, 5}   **17.** {11, 12, 13, 14, 15, 16}   **19.** {0}
21. {0, 2, 4, 6, 8}   **23.** [number line with points at 0, 2, 4, 6]   **25.** [number line with points at 0, 1]   **27.** [number line with points at −10, −6, −2]
29. answers may vary   **31.** $\{3, 0, \sqrt{36}\}$ **33.** $\{3, \sqrt{36}\}$ **35.** $\{\sqrt{7}\}$ **37.** $\in$ **39.** $\notin$ **41.** $\notin$ **43.** $\notin$ **45.** true   **47.** true
49. false   **51.** false   **53.** true   **55.** false   **57.** answers may vary   **59.** -2 **61.** 4   **63.** 0   **65.** -3 **67.** answers may vary   **69.** 6.2
71. $-\frac{4}{7}$ **73.** $\frac{2}{3}$ **75.** 0   **77.** $2x$ **79.** $2x + 5$ **81.** $x - 10$ **83.** $x + 2$ **85.** $\frac{x}{11}$ **87.** $12 - 3x$ **89.** $x + 2.3$ or $x + 2\frac{3}{10}$ **91.** $1\frac{1}{3} - x$
93. $\frac{5}{4 - x}$ **95.** $2(x + 3)$ **97.** 137   **99.** 69   **101.** answers may vary

Section 1.3
Practice Exercises
1. a. -8 **b.** -3 **c.** 5   **d.** -8.1 **e.** $\frac{1}{15}$ **2. a.** -8 **b.** -3 **c.** -12 **d.** 7.7   **e.** $\frac{8}{21}$ **f.** 1.8   **g.** -7 **3. a.** 12   **b.** -4
4. a. -15 **b.** $\frac{1}{2}$ **c.** -10.2 **d.** 0   **e.** $-\frac{2}{13}$ **f.** 36   **g.** -11.5 **5. a.** -2 **b.** 5   **c.** $-\frac{1}{6}$ **d.** -6 **e.** $\frac{1}{9}$ **f.** 0   **6. a.** 8   **b.** $\frac{1}{9}$
c. -36 **d.** 36   **e.** -64 **f.** -64 **7. a.** 7   **b.** $\frac{1}{4}$ **c.** -8 **d.** not a real number   **e.** 10   **8. a.** 4   **b.** -1 **c.** 10   **9. a.** 2
b. 27   **c.** -29 **10.** 19   **11.** $-\frac{17}{44}$ **12. a.** 67   **b.** -100 **c.** $-\frac{39}{80}$ **13.** 23; 50; 77

Vocabulary and Readiness Check 1.3
1. b, c   **3.** b, d   **5.** b   **7.** 0   **9.** reciprocal   **11.** exponent   **13.** square root

Exercise Set 1.3
1. 5   **3.** -24 **5.** -11 **7.** -4 **9.** $\frac{4}{3}$ **11.** -2 **13.** $-\frac{1}{2}$ **15.** -6 **17.** -60 **19.** 0   **21.** 0   **23.** -3 **25.** 3   **27.** $-\frac{1}{6}$ **29.** 0.56
31. -7 **33.** -8 **35.** -49 **37.** 36   **39.** -8 **41.** $-\frac{1}{27}$ **43.** 7   **45.** $-\frac{2}{3}$ **47.** 4   **49.** 3   **51.** not a real number   **53.** 48   **55.** -1
57. -9 **59.** 17   **61.** -4 **63.** -2 **65.** 11   **67.** $-\frac{3}{4}$ **69.** 7   **71.** -11 **73.** -2.1 **75.** $-\frac{1}{3}$ **77.** $-\frac{79}{15}$ **79.** $-\frac{4}{5}$ **81.** -81
83. $-\frac{20}{33}$ **85.** 93   **87.** -12 **89.** $-\frac{23}{18}$ **91.** 5   **93.** $-\frac{3}{19}$ **95.** 18; 22; 28; 208   **97.** 600; 150; 105   **99.** $\frac{5}{2}$ **101.** $\frac{13}{35}$ **103.** True
105. False; Counter Example: $7(-1) + 11$ simplifies to a positive number, 4   **107.** False; Counter Example: $(3)^2 < (-7)^2$ **109.** 4205 m
111. $(2 + 7) \cdot (1 + 3)$ **113.** answers may vary   **115.** 3.1623   **117.** 2.8107

Integrated Review
1. 16   **2.** -16 **3.** 0   **4.** -11 **5.** -5 **6.** $-\frac{1}{60}$ **7.** undefined   **8.** -2.97 **9.** 4   **10.** -50 **11.** 35   **12.** 92   **13.** $-15 - 2x$
14. $3x + 5$ **15.** 0   **16.** true

A2 Answers to Selected Exercises

Section 1.4
Practice Exercises
1. $-4x = 20$ **2.** $3(z-3) = 9$ **3.** $x + 5 = 2x - 3$ **4.** $y + 2 = 4 + \frac{z}{8}$ **5. a.** $<$ **b.** $=$ **c.** $>$ **d.** $>$ **6. a.** $x - 3 \leq 5$ **b.** $y \neq -4$ **c.** $2 < 4 + \frac{1}{2}z$ **7. a.** 7 **b.** -4.7 **c.** $\frac{3}{8}$ **8. a.** $-\frac{3}{5}$ **b.** $\frac{1}{14}$ **c.** $-\frac{1}{2}$ **9.** $13x + 8$ **10.** $(3 \cdot 11)b = 33b$ **11. a.** $4x + 20y$ **b.** $-3 + 2z$ **c.** $0.3xy - 0.9x$ **12. a.** $0.10x$ **b.** $26y$ **c.** $1.75z$ **d.** $0.15t$ **13. a.** $16 - x$ **b.** $180 - x$ **c.** $x + 2$ **d.** $x + 9$ **14. a.** $5ab$ **b.** $10x - 5$ **c.** $17p - 9$ **15. a.** $-pq + 7$ **b.** $x^2 + 19$ **c.** $5.8x + 3.8$ **d.** $-c - 8d + \frac{1}{4}$

Vocabulary and Readiness Check 1.4
1. $<$ **3.** $\neq$ **5.** $\geq$ **7.** $-a$ **9.** commutative **11.** distributive **13.** terms

Exercise Set 1.4
1. $10 + x = -12$ **3.** $2x + 5 = -14$ **5.** $\frac{n}{5} = 4n$ **7.** $z - \frac{1}{2} = \frac{1}{2}z$ **9.** $7x \leq -21$ **11.** $2(x - 6) > \frac{1}{11}$ **13.** $2(x - 6) = -27$ **15.** $>$ **17.** $=$ **19.** $<$ **21.** $<$ **23.** $<$ **25.** $-5; \frac{1}{5}$ **27.** $-8; -\frac{1}{8}$ **29.** $\frac{1}{7}; -7$ **31.** 0; undefined **33.** $\frac{7}{8}; -\frac{7}{8}$ **35.** Zero. For every real number $x, 0 \cdot x \neq 1$, so 0 has no reciprocal. It is the only real number that has no reciprocal because if $x \neq 0$, then $x \cdot \frac{1}{x} = 1$ by definition. **37.** $y + 7x$ **39.** $w \cdot z$ **41.** $\frac{x}{5} \cdot \frac{1}{3}$ **43.** no; answers may vary **45.** $(5 \cdot 7)x$ **47.** $x + (1.2 + y)$ **49.** $14(z \cdot y)$ **51.** 10 and 4. Subtraction is not associative. **53.** $3x + 15$ **55.** $-2a - b$ **57.** $12x + 10y + 4z$ **59.** $-4x + 8y - 28$ **61.** $3xy - 1.5x$ **63.** $6 + 3x$ **65.** 0 **67.** 7 **69.** $(10 \cdot 2)y$ **71.** $a(b + c) = ab + ac$ **73.** $0.1d$ **75.** $112 - x$ **77.** $90 - 5x$ **79.** $\$35.61y$ **81.** $2x + 2$ **83.** $-8y - 14$ **85.** $-9c - 4$ **87.** $4 - 8y$ **89.** $y^2 - 11yz - 11$ **91.** $3t - 14$ **93.** 0 **95.** $13n - 20$ **97.** $8.5y - 20.8$ **99.** $\frac{3}{8}a - \frac{1}{12}$ **101.** $20y + 48$ **103.** $-5x + \frac{5}{6}y - 1$ **105.** $-x - 6y - \frac{11}{24}$ **107.** $(5 \cdot 7)y$ **109.** $6.5y - 7.92x + 25.47$ **111.** b **113.** no **115.** 80 million **117.** 35 million **119.** 20.25%

Chapter 1 Vocabulary Check
1. algebraic expression **2.** opposite **3.** distributive **4.** absolute value **5.** exponent **6.** variable **7.** inequality **8.** reciprocals **9.** commutative **10.** associative **11.** whole **12.** real

Chapter 1 Review
1. 21 **3.** 324,000 **5.** $\{-2, 0, 2, 4, 6\}$ **7.** $\emptyset$ **9.** $\{\ldots, -1, 0, 1, 2\}$ **11.** false **13.** true **15.** true **17.** true **19.** true **21.** true **23.** true **25.** true **27.** true **29.** $\{5, \frac{8}{2}, \sqrt{9}\}$ **31.** $\{\sqrt{7}, \pi\}$ **33.** $\{5, \frac{8}{2}, \sqrt{9}, -1\}$ **35.** -0.6 **37.** -1 **39.** $\frac{1}{0.6}$ **41.** 1 **43.** -35 **45.** 0.31 **47.** 13.3 **49.** 0 **51.** 0 **53.** -5 **55.** 4 **57.** 9 **59.** 3 **61.** $-\frac{32}{135}$ **63.** $-\frac{5}{4}$ **65.** $\frac{5}{8}$ **67.** -1 **69.** 1 **71.** -4 **73.** $\frac{5}{7}$ **75.** $\frac{1}{5}$ **77.** -5 **79.** 5 **81. a.** 6.28; 62.8; 628 **b.** increase **83.** $-5x - 9$ **85.** $-15x^2 + 6$ **87.** $5.7x + 1.1$ **89.** $n + 2n = -15$ **91.** $6(t - 5) = 4$ **93.** $9x - 10 = 5$ **95.** $-4 < 7y$ **97.** $t + 6 \leq -12$ **99.** distributive property **101.** commutative property of addition **103.** multiplicative inverse property **105.** associative property of multiplication **107.** multiplicative identity property **109.** $(3 + x) + (7 + y)$ **111.** $2 \cdot \frac{1}{2}$, for example **113.** $7 + 0$ **115.** $>$ **117.** $=$ **119.** $>$ **121.** $5; \frac{1}{5}$ **123.** 9 **125.** 15 **127.** $\frac{1}{11}$ **129.** 1.8, 1.0, 0.4, 0.7, 0.2, 0.7, 1.0

Chapter 1 Test
1. true **2.** false **3.** false **4.** false **5.** true **6.** false **7.** -3 **8.** -56 **9.** -225 **10.** 3 **11.** 1 **12.** $-\frac{3}{2}$ **13.** 12 **14.** 1 **15. a.** 5.75; 17.25; 57.50; 115.00 **b.** increase **16.** $2(x + 5) = 30$ **17.** $\frac{(6-y)^2}{7} < -2$ **18.** $\frac{9z}{|-12|} \neq 10$ **19.** $3\left(\frac{n}{5}\right) = -n$ **20.** $20 = 2x - 6$ **21.** $-2 = \frac{x}{x+5}$ **22.** distributive property **23.** associative property of addition **24.** additive inverse property **25.** multiplication property of zero **26.** $0.05n + 0.1d$ **27.** $-6x - 14$ **28.** $\frac{1}{2}a - \frac{9}{8}$ **29.** $2y - 10$ **30.** $-1.3x + 1.9$

Chapter 1 Standardized Test
1. a **2.** a **3.** b **4.** a **5.** a **6.** b **7.** b **8.** b **9.** a **10.** d **11.** b **12.** c **13.** b **14.** c **15.** c **16.** c **17.** a **18.** a **19.** a **20.** b **21.** b **22.** a **23.** b **24.** d **25.** a **26.** a **27.** a **28.** c **29.** b **30.** c

CHAPTER 2 EQUATIONS, INEQUALITIES, AND PROBLEM SOLVING

Section 2.1
Practice Exercises
1. 5 **2.** 0.2 **3.** -5 **4.** -4 **5.** $\frac{5}{6}$ **6.** $\frac{5}{4}$ **7.** -3 **8.** no solution **9.** all real numbers or $\mathbb{R}$

Vocabulary and Readiness Check 2.1
1. equivalent **3.** addition **5.** expression **7.** equation **9.** all real numbers **11.** no solution

Exercise Set 2.1
1. 6 **3.** -22 **5.** 4.7 **7.** 10 **9.** -1.1 **11.** -5 **13.** -2 **15.** 0 **17.** 2 **19.** -9 **21.** $-\frac{10}{7}$ **23.** $\frac{9}{10}$ **25.** 4 **27.** 1 **29.** 5 **31.** $\frac{40}{3}$ **33.** 17 **35.** all real numbers **37.** no solution **39.** all real numbers **41.** no solution **43.** $\frac{1}{8}$ **45.** 0 **47.** all real numbers **49.** 4 **51.** $\frac{4}{5}$ **53.** 8 **55.** no solution **57.** -8 **59.** $-\frac{5}{4}$ **61.** -2 **63.** 23 **65.** $-\frac{2}{9}$ **67.** $\frac{8}{x}$ **69.** $8x$ **71.** $2x - 5$ **73.** subtract 19 instead of adding; -3 **75.** $0.4 - 1.6 = -1.2$, not 1.2; -0.24 **77. a.** $4x + 5$ **b.** -3 **c.** answers may vary **79.** answers may vary **81.** $K = -11$ **83.** $K = -23$ **85.** answers may vary **87.** 1 **89.** 3 **91.** 4.86 **93.** 1.53

Section 2.2
Practice Exercises
1. a. $3x + 6$ **b.** $6x - 1$ **2.** $3x + 17.3$ **3.** 14, 34, 70 **4.** $450 **5.** width: 32 in.; length: 48 in. **6.** 25, 27, 29

Vocabulary and Readiness Check 2.2
1. > **3.** = **5.** 31, 32, 33, 34 **7.** 18, 20, 22 **9.** $y, y + 1, y + 2$ **11.** $p, p + 1, p + 2, p + 3$

Exercise Set 2.2
1. $4y$ **3.** $3z + 3$ **5.** $(65x + 30)$ cents **7.** $10x + 3$ **9.** $2x + 14$ **11.** -5 **13.** 45, 145, 225 **15.** approximately 1612.41 million acres **17.** 2344 earthquakes **19.** 1275 shoppers **21.** 22% **23.** 417 employees **25.** 29.98 million **27.** 29°, 35°, 116° **29.** 28 m, 36 m, 38 m **31.** 18 in., 18 in., 27 in., 36 in. **33.** 75, 76, 77 **35.** Fallon's zip code is 89406; Fernley's zip code is 89408; Gardnerville Ranchos' zip code is 89410 **37.** 317 thousand; 279 thousand; 184 thousand **39.** medical assistant: 215 thousand; postsecondary teacher jobs: 603 thousand; registered nurses: 623 thousand **41.** 757-200: 190 seats; 737-200: 113 seats; 737-300: 134 seats **43.** $430.00 **45.** 41.7 million **47.** 40°, 140° **49.** 64°, 32°, 84° **51.** square: 18 cm; triangle: 24 cm **53.** 76, 78, 80 **55.** 40.5 ft; 202.5 ft; 240 ft **57.** Los Angeles: 61.0 million, Atlanta: 74.3 million, Chicago: 62.3 million **59.** incandescent: 1500 bulb hours; fluorescent: 100,000 bulb hours; halogen: 4000 bulb hours **61.** height: 48 in.; width: 108 in. **63. a.** $4.9 billion **b.** $1.23 billion **65.** Russia: 5.6%; China: 19.3%; U.S.: 9.9% **67.** 309 pages **69.** Germany: 11; U.S.: 9; Canada: 7 **71.** -54 **73.** 155 **75.** 557.424 **77.** answers may vary **79.** 50° **81. a.** 2032 **b.** 1015.8 **c.** 3 cigarettes per day; answers may vary **83.** 500 boards; $30,000 **85.** company makes a profit

Section 2.3
Practice Exercises
1. $t = \frac{I}{Pr}$ **2.** $y = \frac{7}{2}x - \frac{5}{2}$ **3.** $r = \frac{A - P}{Pt}$ **4.** $10,134.16 **5.** 25.6 hr; 25 hr 36 min

Exercise Set 2.3
1. $t = \frac{D}{r}$ **3.** $R = \frac{I}{PT}$ **5.** $y = \frac{9x - 16}{4}$ **7.** $W = \frac{P - 2L}{2}$ **9.** $A = \frac{J + 3}{C}$ **11.** $g = \frac{W}{h - 3t^2}$ **13.** $B = \frac{T - 2C}{AC}$ **15.** $r = \frac{C}{2\pi}$ **17.** $r = \frac{E - IR}{I}$ **19.** $L = \frac{2s - an}{n}$ **21.** $v = \frac{3st^4 - N}{5s}$ **23.** $H = \frac{S - 2LW}{2L + 2W}$ **25.** $4703.71; $4713.99; $4719.22; $4722.74; $4724.45 **27. a.** $7313.97 **b.** $7321.14 **c.** $7325.98 **29.** 40°C **31.** 3.6 hr, or 3 hr and 36 min **33.** 171 packages **35.** 9 ft **37.** 2 gal **39. a.** 1174.86 cu. m **b.** 310.34 cu. m **c.** 1485.20 cu. m **41.** 128.3 mph **43.** 0.42 ft **45.** 41.125π ft ≈ 129.1325 ft **47.** $1831.96 **49.** $f = \frac{C - 4h - 4p}{9}$ **51.** 178 cal **53.** 1.5 g **55.** $-3, -2, -1$ **57.** $-3, -2, -1, 0, 1$ **59.** answers may vary **61.** 0.388; 0.723; 1.00; 1.523; 5.202; 9.538; 19.193; 30.065; 39.505 **63.** $6.80 per person **65.** 4 times a year; answers may vary **67.** 0.25 sec **69.** $\frac{1}{4}$ **71.** $\frac{3}{8}$ **73.** $\frac{3}{8}$ **75.** $\frac{3}{4}$ **77.** 1 **79.** 1

Section 2.4
Practice Exercises

1. a. [number line: open circle at 3.5] b. [number line: closed circle at −3, arrow right] c. [number line: closed circle at −1, open circle at 4] 2. $x > 4$ [number line: open circle at 4, arrow right]
3. $x \leq -4$ [number line: closed circle at −4, arrow left] 4. a. $x \geq \frac{2}{3}$ [number line: closed circle at 2/3, arrow right] b. $x > -4$ [number line: open circle at −4, arrow right] 5. $x \geq -\frac{3}{2}$ [number line: closed circle at −3/2, arrow right]
6. $x \leq 13$ [number line: closed circle at 13, arrow left] 7. all real numbers [number line with arrows both ways through 0] 8. Sales must be $\geq \$10{,}000$ per month. 9. the entire year 2021 and after

Vocabulary and Readiness Check 2.4
1. d 3. b 5. no 9. yes

Exercise Set 2.4

1. [open circle at −3, arrow left] 3. [closed circle at 0.3, arrow right] 5. [closed circle at −7, arrow left] 7. [open circles at −2 and 5]
9. [open circle at −1, closed circle at 5] 11. $x \geq -2$ [closed circle at −2, arrow right] 13. $x < 1$ [open circle at 1, arrow left] 15. $x \leq 2$ [closed circle at 2, arrow left]
17. $x \geq 8$ [closed circle at 8, arrow right] 19. $x < -4.7$ [open circle at −4.7, arrow left] 21. $x \leq -3$ [closed circle at −3, arrow left] 23. $x \leq -1$ 25. $x \leq 11$ 27. $x > 0$
29. $x > -13$ 31. $x \geq -\frac{79}{3}$ 33. $x < -\frac{35}{6}$ 35. $x < -6$ 37. $x > 4$ 39. $x \geq -0.5$ 41. $x \leq 7$ 43. $x \geq 0$ 45. $x \leq -29$
47. $x \geq 3$ 49. $x \leq -1$ 51. $x \geq -31$ 53. $x \leq -2$ 55. $x < -15$ 57. $x \geq -\frac{37}{3}$ 59. $x < 5$ 61. $x < 9$ 63. $x \leq -\frac{11}{2}$
65. all real numbers 67. no solution 69. a. $x \geq 81$ b. A final exam grade of 81 or higher will result in an average of 77 or higher.
71. a. $x \leq 1040$ b. The luggage and cargo must weight 1040 pounds or less. 73. a. $x \leq 20$
b. She can move at most 20 whole boxes at one time. 75. a. $x > 200$ b. If you make more than 200 calls, plan 1 is more economical.
77. $F \geq 932°$ 79. a. 2011 b. answers may vary 81. decreasing; answers may vary 83. 5.7 gal 85. during 2008
87. answers may vary 89. 2, 3, 4 91. 2, 3, 4, ... 93. 5 95. $\frac{13}{6}$ 97. $x \geq 2$ 99. [open circle at 0, arrow left]
101. [open circle at −2, closed circle at 1.5] 103. 4 105. $x > 4$ 107. answers may vary 109. answers may vary 111. answers may vary

Integrated Review

1. −5 2. $x > -5$ 3. $x > \frac{8}{3}$ 4. $x \geq -1$ 5. 0 6. $x \geq -\frac{1}{10}$ 7. $x \leq -\frac{1}{6}$ 8. 0 9. no solution 10. $x \geq -\frac{3}{5}$ 11. 4.2 12. 6
13. −8 14. $x < -16$ 15. $\frac{20}{11}$ 16. 1 17. $x > 38$ 18. −5.5 19. $\frac{3}{5}$ 20. all real numbers 21. 29 22. all real numbers
23. $x < 1$ 24. $\frac{9}{13}$ 25. $x > 23$ 26. $x \leq 6$ 27. $x \leq \frac{3}{5}$ 28. $x \leq -\frac{19}{32}$

Section 2.5
Practice Exercises

1. $\{1, 3\}$ 2. $x < 2$ 3. no solution 4. $-4 < x < 2$ 5. $-6 \leq x \leq 8$ 6. $\{1, 2, 3, 4, 5, 6, 7, 9\}$ 7. $x \leq \frac{3}{8}$ or $x \geq 3$ 8. all real numbers

Vocabulary and Readiness Check 2.5
1. compound 3. or 5. ∪ 7. and

Exercise Set 2.5

1. $\{2, 3, 4, 5, 6, 7\}$ 3. $\{4, 6\}$ 5. $\{\ldots, -2, -1, 0, 1, \ldots\}$ 7. $\{5, 7\}$ 9. $\{x \mid x \text{ is an odd integer or } x = 2 \text{ or } x = 4\}$ 11. $\{2, 4\}$
13. [open circles at −3 and 1] $-3 < x < 1$ 15. [closed circle at 0] no solution 17. [open circle at −1, arrow left] $x < -1$ 19. $x \geq 6$ 21. $x \leq -3$ 23. $4 < x < 10$
25. $11 < x < 17$ 27. $1 \leq x \leq 4$ 29. $-3 \leq x \leq \frac{3}{2}$ 31. $-\frac{7}{3} \leq x \leq 7$ 33. [open circle at 5, arrow left] $x < 5$ 35. [closed circles at −4 and 1] $x \leq -4$ or $x \geq 1$
37. [arrows both ways through 0] all real numbers 39. $x \geq 2$ 41. $x < -4$ or $x > -2$ 43. all real numbers 45. $-\frac{1}{2} < x < \frac{2}{3}$ 47. all real numbers
49. $\frac{3}{2} \leq x \leq 6$ 51. $\frac{5}{4} < x < \frac{11}{4}$ 53. no solution 55. $x < -\frac{56}{5}$ or $x \geq \frac{5}{3}$ 57. $-5 < x < \frac{5}{2}$ 59. $0 < x \leq \frac{14}{3}$ 61. $x \leq -3$
63. $x \leq 1$ or $x > \frac{29}{7}$ 65. no solution 67. $-\frac{1}{2} \leq x < \frac{3}{2}$ 69. $-\frac{4}{3} < x < \frac{7}{3}$ 71. $6 < x < 12$ 73. −12 75. −4 77. −7, 7 79. 0
81. 2003, 2004, 2005 83. $-20.2° \leq F \leq 95°$ 85. $67 \leq \text{final score} \leq 94$ 87. $x > 6$ 89. $3 \leq x \leq 7$ 91. $x < -1$

Section 2.6
Practice Exercises
1. $-7, 7$ 2. $-1, 4$ 3. $-80, 70$ 4. $-2, 2$ 5. 0 6. no solution 7. no solution 8. $-\frac{3}{5}, 5$ 9. 5

Vocabulary and Readiness Check 2.6
1. C 3. B 5. D

Exercise Set 2.6
1. $7, -7$ 3. $4.2, -4.2$ 5. $7, -2$ 7. $8, 4$ 9. $5, -5$ 11. $3, -3$ 13. 0 15. no solution 17. $\frac{1}{5}$ 19. $|x| = 5$ 21. $9, -\frac{1}{2}$ 23. $-\frac{5}{2}$
25. answers may vary 27. $4, -4$ 29. 0 31. no solution 33. $0, \frac{14}{3}$ 35. $2, -2$ 37. no solution 39. $7, -1$ 41. no solution
43. no solution 45. $-\frac{1}{8}$ 47. $\frac{1}{2}, -\frac{5}{6}$ 49. $2, -\frac{12}{5}$ 51. $3, -2$ 53. $-8, \frac{2}{3}$ 55. no solution 57. 4 59. $13, -8$ 61. $3, -3$ 63. $8, -7$
65. $2, 3$ 67. $2, -\frac{10}{3}$ 69. $\frac{3}{2}$ 71. no solution 73. answers may vary 75. 34% 77. 39.6 lb 79. answers may vary 81. no solution
83. $|x - 7| = 2$ 85. $|2x - 1| = 4$ 87. a. $c = 0$ b. c is a negative number c. c is a positive number

Section 2.7
Practice Exercises
1. $-2 < x < 2$; 2. $-4 < b < 2$; 3. $-\frac{2}{3} \leq x \leq 2$; 4. no solution
5. $y \leq -10$ or $y \geq 2$; 6. all real numbers 7. $x < 0$ or $x > 12$; 8. 2

Vocabulary and Readiness Check 2.7
1. D 3. C 5. A

Exercise Set 2.7
1. $-4 \leq x \leq 4$; 3. $1 < x < 5$; 5. $-5 < x < -1$; 7. $-10 \leq x \leq 3$;
9. $-5 \leq x \leq 5$; 11. no solution; 13. $0 \leq x \leq 12$; 15. $x < -3$ or $x > 3$;
17. $x \leq -24$ or $x \geq 4$; 19. $x < -4$ or $x > 4$; 21. all real numbers;
23. $x < \frac{2}{3}$ or $x > 2$; 25. 0; 27. $x < -\frac{3}{8}$ or $x > -\frac{3}{8}$; 29. $-2 \leq x \leq 2$;
31. $y < -1$ or $y > 1$; 33. $-5 < x < 11$; 35. $x < 4$ or $x > 6$; 37. no solution;
39. all real numbers; 41. $-2 \leq x \leq 9$; 43. $x \leq -11$ or $x \geq 1$;
45. $x < 0$ or $x > 0$; 47. all real numbers; 49. $-\frac{1}{2} \leq x \leq 1$;
51. $x < -3$ or $x > 0$; 53. no solution; 55. $\frac{3}{8}$; 57. $-\frac{2}{3} < x < 0$;
59. $x < -12$ or $x > 0$; 61. $-1 \leq x \leq 8$; 63. $-\frac{23}{8} \leq x \leq \frac{17}{8}$;
65. $-2 < x < 5$ 67. $5, -2$ 69. $x \leq -7$ or $x \geq 17$ 71. $-\frac{9}{4}$ 73. $-2 < x < 1$ 75. $2, \frac{4}{3}$ 77. no solution 79. $\frac{19}{2}, -\frac{17}{2}$ 81. $x < -\frac{25}{3}$ or $x > \frac{35}{3}$
83. $\frac{1}{6}$ 85. 0 87. $\frac{1}{3}$ 89. -1.5 91. 0 93. $|x| < 7$ 95. $|x| \leq 5$ 97. answers may vary 99. $3.45 < x < 3.55$

Chapter 2 Vocabulary Check
1. compound inequality 2. contradiction 3. intersection 4. union 5. identity 6. formula 7. absolute value 8. solution
9. consecutive integers 10. linear inequality in one variable 11. linear equation in one variable

Chapter 2 Review

1. 3   **3.** $-\dfrac{45}{14}$ **5.** 0   **7.** 6   **9.** all real numbers   **11.** no solution   **13.** -3 **15.** $\dfrac{96}{5}$ **17.** 32   **19.** 8   **21.** no solution   **23.** -7 **25.** 52   **27.** 940.5 million   **29.** no such integers exist   **31.** 258 mi   **33.** $W = \dfrac{V}{LH}$ **35.** $y = \dfrac{5x + 12}{4}$ **37.** $m = \dfrac{y - y_1}{x - x_1}$ **39.** $r = \dfrac{E - IR}{I}$ **41.** $g = \dfrac{T}{r + vt}$ **43. a.** $3695.27   **b.** $3700.81   **45.** length: 10 in.; width: 8 in.   **47.** $x > 3$ **49.** $x > -4$ **51.** $x \le 7$ **53.** $x < 1$ **55.** more economical to use housekeeper for more than 35 pounds per week   **57.** 9.6   **59.** $2 \le x \le \dfrac{5}{2}$ **61.** $\dfrac{1}{8} < x < 2$ **63.** $\dfrac{7}{8} < x \le \dfrac{27}{20}$ **65.** $x > \dfrac{11}{3}$ **67.** 5, 11   **69.** $-1, \dfrac{11}{3}$ **71.** $-\dfrac{1}{6}$ **73.** no solution   **75.** $5, -\dfrac{1}{3}$ **77.** $-\dfrac{8}{5} < x < 2$;   **79.** $x < -3$ or $x > 3$;   **81.** no solution;   **83.** $x < -27$ or $x > -9$;   **85.** 2   **87.** China: 137 million; USA: 102 million; France: 93 million   **89.** $h = \dfrac{3V}{\pi r^2}$ **91.** 58 mph   **93.** $x > 2$ **95.** all real numbers   **97.** 3, -3 **99.** $-10, -\dfrac{4}{3}$ **101.** $-\dfrac{1}{2} < x < 2$

Chapter 2 Test

1. 10   **2.** -32 **3.** no solution   **4.** all real numbers   **5.** $-\dfrac{80}{29}$ **6.** $\dfrac{29}{4}$ **7.** $1, \dfrac{2}{3}$ **8.** no solution   **9.** $-4, -\dfrac{1}{3}$ **10.** $\dfrac{3}{2}$ **11.** $y = \dfrac{3x - 8}{4}$ **12.** $g = \dfrac{S}{t^2 + vt}$ **13.** $C = \dfrac{5}{9}(F - 32)$ **14.** $x > 5$ **15.** $x \le -\dfrac{11}{3}$ **16.** $\dfrac{3}{2} < x \le 5$ **17.** $x < -2$ or $x > \dfrac{4}{3}$ **18.** $3 < x < 7$ **19.** $x \ge 5$ **20.** $x \ge 4$ **21.** $1 \le x < \dfrac{11}{2}$ **22.** all real numbers   **23.** 9.6   **24.** 230,323 people   **25.** approximately 8 hunting dogs   **26.** more than 850 sunglasses   **27.** $3542.27   **28.** New York: 21.8 million; Seoul: 23.1 million; Tokyo: 33.4 million

Chapter 2 Standardized Test

1. c   **2.** d   **3.** b   **4.** c   **5.** d   **6.** c   **7.** b   **8.** d   **9.** c   **10.** b   **11.** d   **12.** d   **13.** a   **14.** c   **15.** b   **16.** b   **17.** a   **18.** d   **19.** d   **20.** a   **21.** b   **22.** c   **23.** c   **24.** d   **25.** a   **26.** a   **27.** a   **28.** a

CHAPTER 3 GRAPHS AND FUNCTIONS

Section 3.1
Practice Exercises

1.
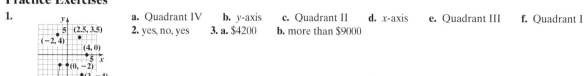

a. Quadrant IV   **b.** y-axis   **c.** Quadrant II   **d.** x-axis   **e.** Quadrant III   **f.** Quadrant I

2. yes, no, yes   **3. a.** $4200   **b.** more than $9000

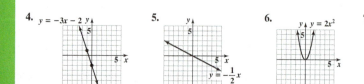

Graphing Calculator Explorations 3.1

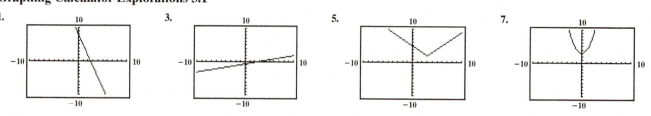

Vocabulary and Readiness Check 3.1
1. (5, 2) **3.** (3, 0) **5.** (−5, −2) **7.** (−1, 0) **9.** QI **11.** QII **13.** QIII **15.** y-axis **17.** QIII **19.** x-axis

Exercise Set 3.1
1. Quadrant I **3.** Quadrant II **5.** Quadrant IV **7.** y-axis **9.** Quadrant III

11. Quadrant IV **13.** x-axis **15.** Quadrant III **17.** no; yes **19.** yes; yes **21.** yes; yes **23.** yes; no **25.** yes; yes
27. linear **29.** linear **31.** linear **33.** not linear **35.** linear **37.** not linear

39. not linear **41.** linear **43.** linear **45.** not linear **47.** not linear **49.** not linear

 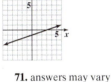

51. linear **53.** linear **55.** −5 **57.** $-\dfrac{1}{10}$ **59.** $x \leq -5$ **61.** $x < -4$ **63.** b **65.** b **67.** c

 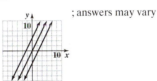

69. 1991 **71.** answers may vary **73.** **75. a.** **b.** 14 in. **77.** $7000 **79.** $500

81. Depreciation is the same from year to year. **83.** ; answers may vary **85.** answers may vary

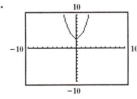 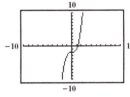

87. $y = -3 - 2x$; **89.** $y = 5 - x^2$; **91.** **93.**

Section 3.2
Practice Exercises
1. a. Domain: {4, 5}; Range: {1, −3, −2, 6}   **b.** Domain: {3}; Range: {−4, −3, −2, −1, 0, 1, 2, 3, 4}   **c.** Domain: {Administrative Secretary, Game Developer, Engineer, Restaurant Manager, Marketing}; Range: {27, 50, 73, 35}   **2. a.** yes, a function   **b.** not a function   **c.** yes, a function
3. yes, a function   **4.** yes, a function   **5. a.** yes, a function   **b.** yes, a function   **c.** no, not a function   **d.** yes, a function   **e.** no, not a function
6. a. Domain: $-1 \leq x \leq 2$; Range: $-2 \leq y \leq 9$; yes, a function   **b.** Domain: $-1 \leq x \leq 1$; Range: $-4 \leq y \leq 4$; not a function
c. Domain: all real numbers; Range: $(-\infty, 4]$; yes, a function   **d.** Domain: all real numbers; Range: all real numbers; yes, a function
7. a. 1   **b.** 6   **c.** −2   **d.** 15   **8. a.** −3   **b.** −2   **c.** 3   **d.** 1   **e.** −1 and 3   **f.** −3   **9.** $35 billion   **10.** $57.224 billion

Graphing Calculator Explorations 3.2

1. 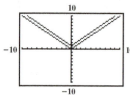 3. 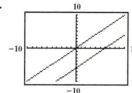 5.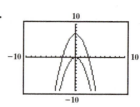

Vocabulary and Readiness Check 3.2

1. origin **3.** x; y **5.** V-shaped **7.** relation **9.** domain **11.** vertical

Exercise Set 3.2

1. domain: $\{-1, 0, -2, 5\}$; range: $\{7, 6, 2\}$; function **3.** domain: $\{-2, 6, -7\}$; range: $\{4, -3, -8\}$; not a function
5. domain: $\{1\}$; range: $\{1, 2, 3, 4\}$; not a function **7.** domain: $\left\{\frac{3}{2}, 0\right\}$; range: $\left\{\frac{1}{2}, -7, \frac{4}{5}\right\}$; not a function
9. domain: $\{-3, 0, 3\}$; range: $\{-3, 0, 3\}$; function **11.** domain: $\{-1, 1, 2, 3\}$; range: $\{2, 1\}$; function **13.** domain: {Iowa, Alaska, Delaware, Illinois, Connecticut, New York}; range: $\{5, 1, 19, 29\}$; function **15.** domain: $\{32°, 104°, 212°, 50°\}$; range: $\{0°, 40°, 10°, 100°\}$; function
17. domain: $\{0\}$; range: $\{2, -1, 5, 100\}$; not a function **19.** function **21.** not a function **23.** function **25.** not a function **27.** function
29. domain: $x \geq 0$; range: all real numbers; not a function **31.** domain: $-1 \leq x \leq 1$; range: all real numbers; not a function **33.** domain: all real numbers; range: $y \leq -3$ or $y \geq 3$; not a function **35.** domain: $2 \leq x \leq 7$; range: $1 \leq y \leq 6$; not a function **37.** domain: $\{-2\}$; range: all real numbers; not a function **39.** domain: all real numbers; range: $y \leq 3$; function **41.** answers may vary **43.** yes **45.** no **47.** yes **49.** yes
51. yes **53.** no **55.** 15 **57.** 38 **59.** 7 **61.** 3 **63. a.** 0 **b.** 1 **c.** -1 **65. a.** 246 **b.** 6 **c.** $\frac{9}{2}$ **67. a.** -5 **b.** -5 **c.** -5
69. a. 5.1 **b.** 15.5 **c.** 9.533 **71.** $(1, -10)$ **73.** $(4, 56)$ **75.** $f(-1) = -2$ **77.** $g(2) = 0$ **79.** $-4, 0$ **81.** 3 **83.** infinite number
85. a. $17 billion **b.** $15.592 billion **87.** $15.54 billion **89.** $f(x) = x + 7$ **91.** 25π sq cm **93.** 2744 cu in. **95.** 166.38 cm
97. 163.2 mg **99. a.** 106.26; per capita consumption of poultry was 106.26 lb in 2006. **b.** 108.54 lb **101.** 5, -5, 6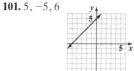

103. $2, \frac{8}{7}, \frac{12}{7}$ **105.** 0, 0, -6 **107.** yes; 170 m **109.** false **111.** true **113. a.** $-3s + 12$ **b.** $-3r + 12$
115. a. 132 **b.** $a^2 - 12$ **117.** answers may vary

Section 3.3
Practice Exercises

1. 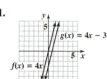 **2.** 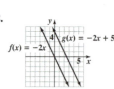 **3. a.** $\left(0, -\frac{2}{5}\right)$ **b.** $(0, 4.1)$ **4.** 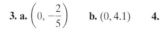 **5.** $y = -3x$

6. $x = -4$ **7.**

Graphing Calculator Explorations 3.3

1. $y = \dfrac{x}{3.5}$ 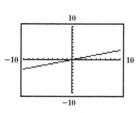 **3.** $y = -\dfrac{5.78}{2.31}x + \dfrac{10.98}{2.31}$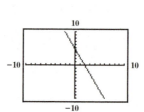

5. $y = |x| + 3.78$ 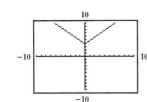 **7.** $y = 5.6x^2 + 7.7x + 1.5$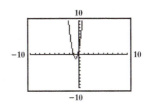

Vocabulary and Readiness Check 3.3
1. linear   **3.** vertical; $(c, 0)$ **5.** y; $f(x)$; x

Exercise Set 3.3
1. 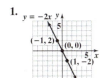   **3.** 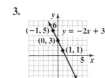   **5.** 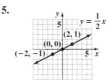   **7.** 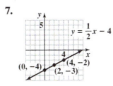   **9.** C   **11.** D   **13.**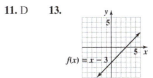

15. 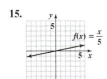   **17.** 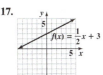   **19.**   **21.** answers may vary   **23.**   **25.**

27. 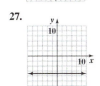   **29.** C   **31.** A   **33.** The vertical line $x = 0$ has y-intercepts.   **35.**   **37.**

39. 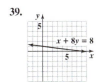   **41.** 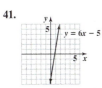   **43.** 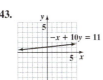   **45.**   **47.**

49. $x = -3$ 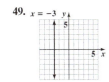   **51.**   **53.**   **55.** 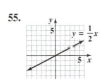   **57.** 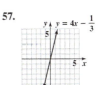   **59.** $x = -3$

61. 9, −3   **63.** $x < -4$ or $x > -1$ **65.** $\frac{2}{3} \leq x \leq 2$ **67.** $\frac{3}{2}$ **69.** 6   **71.** $-\frac{6}{5}$

73. a. $(0, 500)$; if no tables are produced, 500 chairs can be produced   **b.** $(750, 0)$; if no chairs are produced, 750 tables can be produced   **c.** 466 chairs
75. a. $64   **b.** 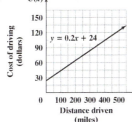   **c.** The line moves upward from left to right.   **77. a.** $2855.12   **b.** 2012   **c.** answers may vary
79. 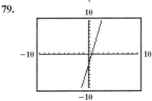   **81.**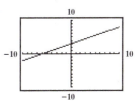

83. a. a line parallel to $y = -4x$ but with y-intercept $(0, 2)$ **b.** a line parallel to $y = -4x$ but with y-intercept $(0, -5)$ **85.** b   **87.** a

Section 3.4
Practice Exercises

1. $m = -\dfrac{1}{2}$; 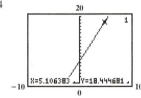 2. $m = \dfrac{3}{5}$; 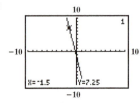 3. $m = -4$ 4. $m = \dfrac{2}{3}$; y-intercept: $(0, -3)$ 5. $81.84 6. undefined 7. $m = 0$ 8. a. perpendicular b. parallel

Graphing Calculator Explorations 3.4

1. 18.4   3. -1.5 5. 14.0; 4.2, -9.4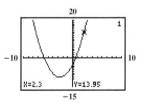

Vocabulary and Readiness Check 3.4

1. slope   3. $m; (0, b)$ 5. horizontal   7. -1 9. upward   11. horizontal

Exercise Set 3.4

1. $\dfrac{9}{5}$ 3. $-\dfrac{7}{2}$ 5. $-\dfrac{5}{6}$ 7. $\dfrac{1}{3}$ 9. $-\dfrac{4}{3}$ 11. 0   13. undefined   15. 2   17. -1 19. l_2 21. l_2 23. l_2 25. $m = 5; (0, -2)$
27. $m = -2; (0, 7)$ 29. $m = \dfrac{2}{3}; \left(0, -\dfrac{10}{3}\right)$ 31. $m = \dfrac{1}{2}; (0, 0)$ 33. A   35. B   37. undefined   39. 0   41. undefined
43. answers may vary   45. $m = -1; (0, 5)$ 47. $m = \dfrac{6}{5}; (0, 6)$ 49. $m = 3; (0, 9)$ 51. $m = 0; (0, 4)$ 53. $m = 7; (0, 0)$
55. $m = 0; (0, -6)$ 57. slope is undefined, no y-intercept   59. neither   61. parallel   63. perpendicular   65. answers may vary
67. $\dfrac{3}{2}$ 69. $-\dfrac{1}{2}$ 71. $\dfrac{2}{3}$ 73. approximately -0.12 75. a. $50,139   b. $m = 694.9$; The annual income increases $694.90 every year.
c. y-intercept: $(0, 43,884.9)$; At year $x = 0$, or 2000, the annual average income was $43,884.90.   77. a. $m = 33$; y-intercept: $(0, 42)$
b. The number of WiFi hotspots increases by 33 thousand for every 1 year.   c. There were 42 thousand WiFi hotspots in 2003.
79. a. The yearly cost of tuition increases $291.50 every 1 year.   b. The yearly cost of tuition in 2000 was $2944.05.   81. $y = 5x + 32$
83. $y = 2x - 1$ 85. $m = -\dfrac{20}{9}$ 87. $-\dfrac{5}{3}$ 89. $-\dfrac{7}{2}$ 91. $\dfrac{2}{7}$ 93. $\dfrac{5}{2}$ 95. $-\dfrac{2}{5}$
97. a. $(6, 20)$ b. $(10, 13)$ c. $-\dfrac{7}{4}$ or -1.75 yd per sec   d. $\dfrac{3}{2}$ or 1.5 yd per sec   99.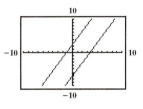
101. a. 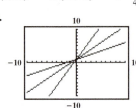   b. 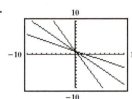   c. true

Section 3.5
Practice Exercises

1. $y = -\dfrac{3}{4}x + 4$ 2.   3.   4. $y = -4x - 3$ 5. $f(x) = -\dfrac{2}{3}x + \dfrac{4}{3}$ 6. $2x + 3y = 5$ 7. 12,568 house sales
8. $y = -2$ 9. $x = 6$ 10. $3x + 4y = 12$ 11. $f(x) = \dfrac{4}{3}x - \dfrac{41}{3}$

Vocabulary and Readiness Check 3.5

1. $m = -4$, y-intercept: $(0, 12)$ 3. $m = 5$, y-intercept: $(0, 0)$ 5. $m = \dfrac{1}{2}$, y-intercept: $(0, 6)$ 7. parallel   9. neither

Answers to Selected Exercises A11

Exercise Set 3.5

1. $y = -x + 1$ **3.** $y = 2x + \frac{3}{4}$ **5.** $y = \frac{2}{7}x$ **7.** 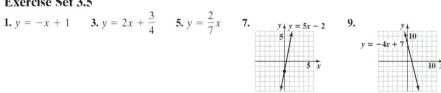   **9.**   **11.**   **13.** $y = 3x - 1$

15. $y = -2x - 1$ **17.** $y = \frac{1}{2}x + 5$ **19.** $y = -\frac{9}{10}x - \frac{27}{10}$ **21.** $f(x) = 3x - 6$ **23.** $f(x) = -2x + 1$ **25.** $f(x) = -\frac{1}{2}x - 5$
27. $f(x) = \frac{1}{3}x - 7$ **29.** $f(x) = -\frac{3}{8}x + \frac{5}{8}$ **31.** $2x + y = 3$ **33.** $2x - 3y = -7$ **35.** -2 **37.** 2
39. -2 **41.** $y = -4$ **43.** $x = 4$ **45.** $y = 5$ **47.** $f(x) = 4x - 4$ **49.** $f(x) = -3x + 1$ **51.** $f(x) = -\frac{3}{2}x - 6$ **53.** $2x - y = -7$
55. $f(x) = -x + 7$ **57.** $x + 2y = 22$ **59.** $2x + 7y = -42$ **61.** $4x + 3y = -20$ **63.** $x = -2$ **65.** $x + 2y = 2$ **67.** $y = 12$
69. $8x - y = 47$ **71.** $x = 5$ **73.** $f(x) = -\frac{3}{8}x - \frac{29}{4}$ **75. a.** $P(x) = 12{,}000x + 18{,}000$ **b.** $102,000   **c.** end of the ninth yr
77. a. $y = -1000x + 13{,}000$ **b.** 9500 Fun Noodles   **79. a.** $y = 14{,}220x + 150{,}900$ **b.** $278,880   **c.** every year, the median price of a home increases by $14,220.   **81. a.** $y = 20.2x + 387$ **b.** 568.8 thousand people   **83.** $x \le 14$ **85.** $x \ge \frac{7}{2}$ **87.** $x < -\frac{1}{4}$ **89.** true
91. $-4x + y = 4$ **93.** $2x + y = -23$ **95.** $3x - 2y = -13$ **97.** answers may vary   **99.**
101.   **103.**

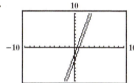
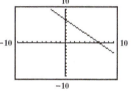

Integrated Review

1. **2.** **3.** **4.**   **5.** 0   **6.** $-\frac{3}{5}$ **7.** $m = 3; (0, -5)$ **8.** $m = \frac{5}{2}; \left(0, -\frac{7}{2}\right)$

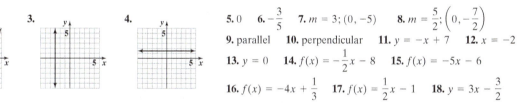

9. parallel   **10.** perpendicular   **11.** $y = -x + 7$ **12.** $x = -2$
13. $y = 0$ **14.** $f(x) = -\frac{1}{2}x - 8$ **15.** $f(x) = -5x - 6$
16. $f(x) = -4x + \frac{1}{3}$ **17.** $f(x) = \frac{1}{2}x - 1$ **18.** $y = 3x - \frac{3}{2}$
19. $y = 3x - 2$ **20.** $y = -\frac{5}{4}x + 4$ **21.** $y = \frac{1}{4}x - \frac{7}{2}$ **22.** $y = -\frac{5}{2}x - \frac{5}{2}$ **23.** $x = -1$ **24.** $y = 3$

Section 3.6
Practice Exercises

1. $f(4) = 5; f(-2) = 6; f(0) = -2$ **2.**   **3.**   **4.**   **5.**

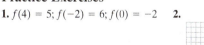

6. 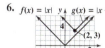   **7.**

Vocabulary and Readiness Check 3.6
1. C   **3.** D

A12 Answers to Selected Exercises

Exercise Set 3.6

1. 3. 5. 7. 9. domain: all real numbers; range: $y \geq 0$

11. domain: all real numbers; range: $y < 5$ 13. domain: all real numbers; range: $y \leq 6$ 15. domain: $x \leq 0$ or $x \geq 1$; range: $\{-4, -2\}$

17. 19. 21. 23. 25. 27.

29. 31. 33. 35. 37. 39.

41. 43. 45. 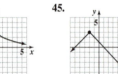 47. 49. A 51. D 53. answers may vary
55. 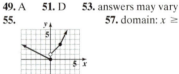 57. domain: $x \geq 2$; range: $y \geq 3$

59. domain: all real numbers; range: $y \leq 3$ 61. $x \geq 20$ 63. all real numbers 65. $x \geq -103$

67. domain: all real numbers; range: $y \geq 0$ 69. domain: all real numbers; range: $y \leq 0$ or $y > 2$

Section 3.7
Practice Exercises

1. 2. 3. 4.

Exercise Set 3.7

1. $x < 2$ 3. 5. 7. 9. 11. 13. answers may vary

15. **17.** **19.** **21.** **23.** **25.**

27. **29.** **31.** **33.** **35.** 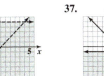 **37.**

39. **41.** **43.** **45.**

47. D   **49.** A   **51.** $x \geq 2$ **53.** $y \leq -3$ **55.** $y > 4$
57. $x < 1$ **59.** 8   **61.** -25 **63.** 16   **65.** $\dfrac{27}{125}$
67. domain: $1 \leq x \leq 5$; range: $1 \leq y \leq 3$; no

69. $x \leq 20$ and $y \geq 10$.   **71.**

Chapter 3 Extension
Practice Exercises
1. **2.** **3.** $y = 3|x + 1| - 2$

Extension Exercise Set
1. **3.** **5.** **7.** **9.**

11. **13.** **15.**   **17.** $y = 3|x|$ **19.** $y = -\dfrac{1}{2}|x| + 2$ **21.** $y = -|x - 2| + 1$
23. $y = 4|x + 3| - 4$

Chapter 3 Vocabulary Check
1. relation   **3.** linear inequality   **5.** range   **7.** slope-intercept   **9.** slope   **11.** y   **13.** linear function   **15.** point-slope

Chapter 3 Review
1.   **3.** no, yes   **5.** yes, yes   **7.** linear   **9.** linear   **11.** nonlinear

13. linear 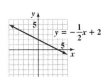   **15.** linear   **17.** linear $y = -1.36x$

19. domain: $\left\{-\frac{1}{2}, 6, 0, 25\right\}$; range: $\left\{\frac{3}{4} \text{ or } 0.75, -12, 25\right\}$; function **21.** domain: $\{2, 4, 6, 8\}$; range: $\{2, 4, 5, 6\}$; not a function
23. domain: all real numbers; range: $y \leq -1$ or $y \geq 1$; not a function **25.** domain: all real numbers; range: $\{4\}$; function **27.** -3 **29.** 18
31. -3 **33.** 381 lb **35.** 0 **37.** $-2, 4$ **39.**   **41.**   **43.** A **45.** D **47.**

49.   **51.**   **53.**   **55.** -3 **57.** $\frac{5}{2}$ **59.** $m = \frac{2}{5}, b = -\frac{4}{3}$ **61.** 0 **63.** l_2 **65.** l_2

67. a. $m = 0.3$; The cost increases by \$0.30 for each additional mile driven.
b. $b = 42$; The cost for 0 miles driven is \$42. **69.** parallel

71.   **73.**   **75.** $x = -2$ **77.** $y = 5$ **79.** $2x - y = 12$ **81.** $11x + y = -52$ **83.** $y = -5$
85. $f(x) = -x - 2$ **87.** $f(x) = -\frac{3}{2}x - 8$ **89.** $f(x) = -\frac{3}{2}x - 1$
91. a. $y = \frac{17}{22}x + 43$ **b.** 52 million

93.   **95.**   **97.**   **99.**   **101.**

103.   **105.**   **107.**   **109.** $x = -7$
111. $y = \frac{3}{4}x + 2$ **113.** $y = -\frac{3}{2}x - 8$
115.   **117.**

Chapter 3 Test

1. A: quadrant IV B: x-axis C: quadrant II **2.**   **3.** 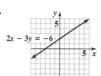 **4.**

5.   **6.** $-\frac{3}{2}$ **7.** $m = -\frac{1}{4}, b = \frac{2}{3}$ **8.**   **9.**   **10.** $y = -8$
11. $x = -4$
12. $y = -2$
13. $3x + y = 11$

14. $5x - y = 2$ **15.** $f(x) = -\frac{1}{2}x$ **16.** $f(x) = -\frac{1}{3}x + \frac{5}{3}$ **17.** $f(x) = -\frac{1}{2}x - \frac{1}{2}$ **18.** neither

19. **20.** **21.** **22.** domain: all real numbers; range: $\{5\}$; function
23. domain: $\{-2\}$; range: all real numbers; not a function
24. domain: all real numbers; range: $y \geq 0$; function
25. domain: all real numbers; range: all real numbers; function
26. a. \$25,193 **b.** \$32,410 **c.** 2015 **d.** The average yearly earnings for high school graduates increases \$1031 per year. **e.** The average yearly earnings for a high school graduate in 2000 was \$25,193.

27. domain: all real numbers; range: $y > -3$ **28.**   **29.** domain: all real numbers; range: $y \le -1$ **30.**

Chapter 3 Standardized Test
1. b **2.** c **3.** c **4.** c **5.** c **6.** c **7.** b **8.** c **9.** d **10.** c **11.** d **12.** a **13.** c **14.** d **15.** d **16.** a **17.** a **18.** c
19. d **20.** c **21.** c **22.** b **23.** c **24.** a **25.** a **26.** c **27.** d **28.** c **29.** b **30.** a **31.** d **32.** b **33.** b

CHAPTER 4 SYSTEMS OF EQUATIONS
Section 4.1
Practice Exercises
1. a. yes **b.** no **2. a.** infinite number of solutions

2. b. solution: $(1, 5)$ **c.** no solution 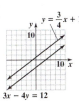 **3.** $\left(-\dfrac{1}{2}, 5\right)$ **4.** $\left(-\dfrac{9}{5}, -\dfrac{2}{5}\right)$ **5.** $(2, 1)$ **6.** $(-2, 0)$

7. no solution **8.** infinite number of solutions

Graphing Calculator Explorations 4.1
1. $(2.11, 0.17)$ **3.** $(0.57, -1.97)$

Vocabulary and Readiness Check 4.1
1. B **3.** A

Exercise Set 4.1
1. yes **3.** no **5.** no **7.** $(2, -1)$ 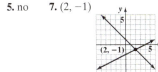 **9.** $(1, 2)$ **11.** no solution   **13.** No; answers may vary

15. $(2, 8)$ **17.** $(0, -9)$ **19.** $(1, -1)$ **21.** $(-5, 3)$ **23.** $\left(\dfrac{5}{2}, \dfrac{5}{4}\right)$ **25.** $(1, -2)$ **27.** $(8, 2)$ **29.** $(7, 2)$ **31.** no solution

33. infinite number of solutions **35.** $\left(\dfrac{3}{2}, 1\right)$ **37.** $(2, -1)$ **39.** $(-5, 3)$ **41.** infinite number of solutions **43.** no solution **45.** $\left(\dfrac{1}{2}, \dfrac{1}{5}\right)$

47. $(9, 9)$ **49.** infinite number of solutions **51.** $\left(-\dfrac{1}{4}, \dfrac{1}{2}\right)$ **53.** $(3, 2)$ **55.** $(7, -3)$ **57.** no solution **59.** $(3, 4)$ **61.** $(-2, 1)$ **63.** $(1.2, -3.6)$

65. true **67.** false **69.** $6y - 4z = 25$ **71.** $x + 10y = 2$ **73.** 5000 DVDs; $21 **75.** supply greater than demand **77.** $(1875, 4687.5)$

79. makes money **81.** for x-values greater than 1875 **83.** answers may vary; One possibility: $\begin{cases} -2x + y = 1 \\ x - 2y = -8 \end{cases}$ **85. a.** Consumption of red

meat is decreasing while consumption of poultry is increasing. **b.** $(35, 103)$ **c.** In the year 2035, red meat and poultry consumption will each be

about 103 pounds per person. **87.** $\left(\dfrac{1}{4}, 8\right)$ **89.** $\left(\dfrac{1}{3}, \dfrac{1}{2}\right)$ **91.** $\left(\dfrac{1}{4}, -\dfrac{1}{3}\right)$ **93.** no solution

Section 4.2
Practice Exercises
1. $(-1, 2, 1)$ **2.** no solution   **3.** $\left(\dfrac{2}{3}, -\dfrac{1}{2}, 0\right)$ **4.** infinite number of solutions   **5.** $(6, 15, -5)$

Exercise Set 4.2
1. a, b, d   **3.** Yes; answers may vary   **5.** $(-1, 5, 2)$ **7.** $(-2, 5, 1)$ **9.** $(-2, 3, -1)$ **11.** infinite number of solutions   **13.** no solution
15. $(0, 0, 0)$ **17.** $(-3, -35, -7)$ **19.** $(6, 22, -20)$ **21.** no solution   **23.** $(3, 2, 2)$ **25.** infinite number of solutions   **27.** $(-3, -4, -5)$
29. $\left(0, \dfrac{1}{2}, -4\right)$ **31.** $(12, 6, 4)$ **33.** 15 and 30   **35.** 5   **37.** $-\dfrac{5}{3}$ **39.** answers may vary   **41.** answers may vary   **43.** $(1, 1, -1)$
45. $(1, 1, 0, 2)$ **47.** $(1, -1, 2, 3)$ **49.** answers may vary

Section 4.3
Practice Exercises
1. a. 2037   **b.** yes; answers may vary   **2.** 12 and 17   **3.** Atlantique: 500 kph; V150: 575 kph   **4.** 0.95 liter of water; 0.05 liter of 99% HCL
5. 1500 packages   **6.** 40°, 60°, 80°

Exercise Set 4.3
1. 10 and 8   **3. a.** Enterprise class: 1101 ft; Nimitz class: 1092 ft   **b.** 3.67 foot ball fields   **5.** plane: 520 mph; wind: 40 mph   **7.** 20 qt of 4%; 40 qt of 1%   **9.** United Kingdom: 32,071 students; Italy: 24,858 students   **11.** 9 large frames; 13 small frames   **13.** -10 and -8 **15.** 2007
17. tablets: $0.80; pens: $0.20   **19.** B737: 450 mph; Piper: 90 mph   **21. a.** answers may vary but notice the slope of each function   **b.** 1991
23. 28 cm; 28 cm; 37 cm   **25.** 600 mi   **27.** $x = 75; y = 105$ **29.** 625 units   **31.** 3000 units   **33.** 1280 units   **35. a.** $R(x) = 450x$
b. $C(x) = 200x + 6000$ **c.** 24 desks   **37.** 2 units of Mix A; 3 units of Mix B; 1 unit of Mix C   **39.** 5 in.; 7 in.; 10 in.   **41.** 18, 13, and 9
43. 143 free throws; 177 two-point field goals; 121 three-point field goals   **45.** $x = 60; y = 55; z = 65$ **47.** $5x + 5z = 10$ **49.** $-5y + 2z = 2$
51. 1996: 1,059,444; 2006: 1,085,209   **53. a.** $(112, 137)$ **b.** June 2016   **55.** $a = 1, b = -2, c = 3$
57. $a = 0.28, b = -3.71, c = 12.83; 2.12$ in. in Sept.

Integrated Review
1. C   **2.** D   **3.** A   **4.** B   **5.** $(1, 3)$ **6.** $\left(\dfrac{4}{3}, \dfrac{16}{3}\right)$ **7.** $(2, -1)$ **8.** $(5, 2)$ **9.** $\left(\dfrac{3}{2}, 1\right)$ **10.** $\left(-2, \dfrac{3}{4}\right)$ **11.** no solution
12. infinite number of solutions   **13.** $\left(1, \dfrac{1}{3}\right)$ **14.** $\left(3, \dfrac{3}{4}\right)$ **15.** $(-1, 3, 2)$ **16.** $(1, -3, 0)$ **17.** no solution   **18.** infinite number of solutions
19. $\left(2, 5, \dfrac{1}{2}\right)$ **20.** $\left(1, 1, \dfrac{1}{3}\right)$ **21.** 19 and 27   **22.** 70°; 70°; 100°; 120°

Section 4.4
Practice Exercises
1. $(2, -1)$ **2.** no solution   **3.** $(-1, 1, 2)$

Vocabulary and Readiness Check 4.4
1. matrix   **3.** row   **5.** false   **7.** true

Exercise Set 4.4
1. $(2, -1)$ **3.** $(-4, 2)$ **5.** no solution   **7.** infinite number of solutions   **9.** $(-2, 5, -2)$ **11.** $(1, -2, 3)$ **13.** $(4, -3)$ **15.** $(2, 1, -1)$
17. $(9, 9)$ **19.** no solution   **21.** no solution   **23.** $(1, -4, 3)$ **25.** function   **27.** not a function   **29.** -13 **31.** -36 **33.** 0   **35.** c
37. a. end of 1984   **b.** black-and-white sets; microwave ovens; The percent of households owning black-and-white television sets is decreasing and the percent of households owning microwave ovens is increasing; answers may vary   **c.** in 2002   **d.** no; answers may vary   **39.** answers may vary

Section 4.5
Practice Exercises

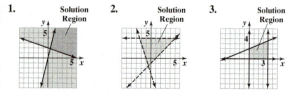

Vocabulary and Readiness Check 4.5
1. system   **3.** corner

Exercise Set 4.5

1.
3.
5.
7.
9.
11.

13.
15.
17.
19.
21. C   23. D   25. 9   27. $\frac{4}{9}$ 29. 5   31. 59
33. the line $y = 3$ 35. answers may vary

Section 4.6
Practice Exercises
1. maximum: 30; minimum: 3   2. $z = 25x + 55y$ 3. $x + y \leq 80$
4. $30 \leq x \leq 80, 10 \leq y \leq 30$; $z = 25x + 55y, x + y \leq 80, 30 \leq x \leq 80, 10 \leq y \leq 30$ 5. 50 bookshelves and 30 desks; $2900

Exercise Set 4.6
1. (1, 2): 17; (2, 10): 70; (7, 5): 65; (8, 3): 58; maximum: 70; minimum: 17   3. (0, 0): 0; (0, 8): 400; (4, 9): 610; (8, 0): 320; maximum: 610; minimum: 0

5. a.
7. a.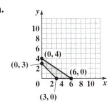
9. a.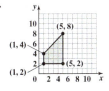

b. (0, 4): 8; (0, 8): 16; (4, 0): 12
c. maximum: 16; at (0, 8)

b. (0, 3): 3; (0, 4): 4; (6, 0): 24; (3, 0): 12
c. maximum: 24; at (6, 0)

b. (1, 2): −1; (1, 4): −5; (5, 8): −1; (5, 2): 11
c. maximum: 11; at (5, 2)

11. a.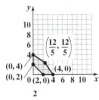
13. a.
15. a. $z = 125x + 200y$
b. $x \leq 450; y \leq 200; 600x + 900y \leq 360{,}000$
c.

b. (0, 2): 4; (0, 4): 8; $\left(\frac{12}{5}, \frac{12}{5}\right): \frac{72}{5} = 14.4$; (4, 0): 16; (2, 0): 8
c. maximum: 16; at (4, 0)

b. (0, 0): 0; (0, 6): 72; (3, 4): 78; (5, 0): 50
c. maximum: 78; at (3, 4)

d. 0; 40,000; 77,500; 76,250; 56,250
e. 300; 200; 77,500

17. 40 of model A and 0 of model B   19. 300 boxes of food and 200 boxes of clothing   21. 100 parents and 50 students
23. 10 Boeing 727s and 42 Falcon 20s   29. does not make sense   31. makes sense   33. $x = \frac{y+2}{3}$ 35. 10   37. $5x^3 - 2x^2 + 12x - 15$

Chapter 4 Vocabulary Check
1. system of equations   3. consistent   5. inconsistent   7. optimization   9. linear programming

Chapter 4 Review
1. (−3, 1)   2. $\left(0, \frac{2}{3}\right)$ 3. no solution   4. infinite number of solutions   5. $\left(3, \frac{8}{3}\right)$ 6. 1500 backpacks   7. (2, 0, 2)   8. (2, 0, −3)
9. $\left(-\frac{1}{2}, \frac{3}{4}, 1\right)$ 10. (−1, 2, 0)   11. no solution   12. (5, 3, 0)   13. (1, 1, −2)   14. (3, 1, 1)   15. 10, 40, and 48   16. 63 and 21
17. 58 mph; 65 mph   18. width: 37 ft; length: 111 ft   19. 20 L of 10% solution; 30 L of 60% solution   20. 30 lb of creme-filled; 5 lb of chocolate-covered nuts; 10 lb of chocolate-covered raisins   21. 17 pennies; 20 nickels; 16 dimes   22. larger investment: 9.5%; smaller investment: 7.5%
23. two sides: 22 cm each; third side; 29 cm   24. 120, 115, and 60   25. (−3, 1)   26. infinite number of solutions   27. $\left(-\frac{2}{3}, 3\right)$

28. $\left(\dfrac{1}{3}, \dfrac{7}{6}\right)$ **29.** $\left(\dfrac{5}{4}, \dfrac{5}{8}\right)$ **30.** $(-7, -15)$ **31.** $(1, 3)$ **32.** $(2, 1)$ **33.** $(1, 2, 3)$ **34.** $(2, 0, -3)$ **35.** $(3, -2, 5)$ **36.** $(-1, 2, 0)$
37. $(1, 1, -2)$ **38.** no solution   **39.**    **40.**   **41.**   **42.**   **43.**

44.   **45.** 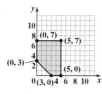   **46.** 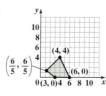   **47.** $\left(\dfrac{1}{2}, \dfrac{1}{2}\right): \dfrac{5}{2}$; $(2, 2): 10$; $(4, 0): 8$; $(1, 0): 2$; maximum: 10; minimum: 2

48.

maximum: 24

49.

maximum: 33

50.

maximum: 44

51. a. $z = 500x + 350y$
c.

b. $x + y \le 200$; $x \ge 10$; $y \ge 80$
d. $(10, 80): 33{,}000$; $(10, 190): 71{,}500$; $(120, 80): 88{,}000$
e. 120; 80; 88,000

52. 480 of model A and 240 of model B
53. $\left(\dfrac{7}{3}, -\dfrac{8}{3}\right)$ **54.** $(10, -4)$
55. infinite number of solutions
56. no solution

57. $(-1, 3, 5)$ **58.** 33 and 94   **59.** 28 units, 42 units, 56 units   **60.**   **61.** 2000

Chapter 4 Test

1. $(1, 3)$ **2.** ∅   **3.** $(2, -3)$ **4.** $\{(x, y) \mid 10x + 4y = 10\}$ **5.** $(-1, -2, 4)$ **6.** ∅   **7.** $\left(\dfrac{7}{2}, -10\right)$

8. $\{(x, y) \mid x - y = -2\}$ **9.** $(5, -3)$ **10.** $(-1, -1, 0)$ **11.** 53 double rooms; 27 single rooms   **12.** 5 gal of 10%; 15 gal of 20%
13. 800 packages   **14.** 23°, 45°, 112°   **15.**   **16.** maximum: 26   **17.** 50 regular and 100 deluxe; $35,000

Chapter 4 Standardized Test
1. c   **2.** c   **3.** a   **4.** c   **5.** d   **6.** a   **7.** b   **8.** a   **9.** d   **10.** b   **11.** a   **12.** d   **13.** c   **14.** b   **15.** b   **16.** a   **17.** d

CHAPTER 5 MORE WORK WITH MATRICES

Section 5.1
Practice Exercises

1. a. 3×2 **b.** $a_{12} = -2$; $a_{31} = 1$ **2. a.** $\begin{bmatrix} 2 & 0 \\ 9 & -10 \end{bmatrix}$ **b.** $\begin{bmatrix} 9 & -4 \\ -9 & 7 \\ 5 & -2 \end{bmatrix}$ **3. a.** $\begin{bmatrix} 6 & 12 \\ -48 & -30 \end{bmatrix}$ **b.** $\begin{bmatrix} -14 & -1 \\ 25 & 10 \end{bmatrix}$ **4.** $\begin{bmatrix} -4 & 3 \\ -3 & \frac{13}{3} \end{bmatrix}$

Exercise Set 5.1

1. a. 2×3 **b.** a_{32} does not exist; $a_{23} = -1$ **3. a.** 3×4 **b.** $a_{32} = \frac{1}{2}$; $a_{23} = -6$ **5.** $x = 6$; $y = 4$ **7.** $x = 4$; $y = 6$; $z = 3$

9. a. $\begin{bmatrix} 9 & 10 \\ 3 & 9 \end{bmatrix}$ **b.** $\begin{bmatrix} -1 & -8 \\ 3 & -5 \end{bmatrix}$ **c.** $\begin{bmatrix} -16 & -4 \\ -12 & -8 \end{bmatrix}$ **d.** $\begin{bmatrix} 22 & 21 \\ 9 & 20 \end{bmatrix}$ **11. a.** $\begin{bmatrix} 3 & 2 \\ 6 & 2 \\ 5 & 7 \end{bmatrix}$ **b.** $\begin{bmatrix} -1 & 4 \\ 0 & 6 \\ 5 & 5 \end{bmatrix}$

c. $\begin{bmatrix} -4 & -12 \\ -12 & -16 \\ -20 & -24 \end{bmatrix}$ **d.** $\begin{bmatrix} 7 & 7 \\ 15 & 8 \\ 15 & 20 \end{bmatrix}$ **13. a.** $\begin{bmatrix} -3 \\ -1 \\ 0 \end{bmatrix}$ **b.** $\begin{bmatrix} 7 \\ -7 \\ 2 \end{bmatrix}$ **c.** $\begin{bmatrix} -8 \\ 16 \\ -4 \end{bmatrix}$ **d.** $\begin{bmatrix} -4 \\ -6 \\ 1 \end{bmatrix}$

15. a. $\begin{bmatrix} 8 & 0 & -4 \\ 14 & 0 & 6 \\ -1 & 0 & 0 \end{bmatrix}$ **b.** $\begin{bmatrix} -4 & -20 & 0 \\ 14 & 24 & 14 \\ 9 & -4 & 4 \end{bmatrix}$ **c.** $\begin{bmatrix} -8 & 40 & 8 \\ -56 & -48 & -40 \\ -16 & 8 & -8 \end{bmatrix}$ **d.** $\begin{bmatrix} 18 & -10 & -10 \\ 42 & 12 & 22 \\ 2 & -2 & 2 \end{bmatrix}$ **17.** $\begin{bmatrix} -8 & -8 \\ 2 & -9 \\ 8 & -4 \end{bmatrix}$ **19.** $\begin{bmatrix} -1 & 3 \\ -1 & \frac{9}{2} \\ -1 & -2 \end{bmatrix}$

21. $\begin{bmatrix} \frac{1}{3} & \frac{13}{3} \\ -\frac{4}{3} & 6 \\ -\frac{7}{3} & -\frac{4}{3} \end{bmatrix}$ **23.** $\begin{bmatrix} 7 & 27 \\ -8 & 36 \\ -17 & -4 \end{bmatrix}$ **25.** $\begin{bmatrix} \frac{27}{2} & \frac{31}{2} \\ -4 & 18 \\ -\frac{29}{2} & 6 \end{bmatrix}$ **27. a.** $A = \begin{bmatrix} 2 & 6 \\ 31 & 46 \end{bmatrix}$ **b.** $B = \begin{bmatrix} 9 & 29 \\ 65 & 77 \end{bmatrix}$ **c.** $B - A = \begin{bmatrix} 7 & 23 \\ 34 & 31 \end{bmatrix}$

The difference between the percentage of people completing the transition to adulthood in 1960 and 2000 by age and gender.

29, 31, 33, 35, answers may vary

Section 5.2
Practice Exercises

1. $\begin{bmatrix} 7 & 6 \\ 13 & 12 \end{bmatrix}$ **2.** $[30]$; $\begin{bmatrix} 2 & 0 & 4 \\ 6 & 0 & 12 \\ 14 & 0 & 28 \end{bmatrix}$ **3. a.** $\begin{bmatrix} 2 & 18 & 11 & 9 \\ 0 & 10 & 8 & 2 \end{bmatrix}$ **b.** The product is undefined.

4. $\begin{bmatrix} 2 & 1 & 1 \\ 2 & 1 & 1 \\ 2 & 2 & 1 \end{bmatrix} + \begin{bmatrix} -1 & 2 & 2 \\ -1 & 2 & 2 \\ -1 & -1 & 2 \end{bmatrix} = \begin{bmatrix} 1 & 3 & 3 \\ 1 & 3 & 3 \\ 1 & 1 & 3 \end{bmatrix}$

5. a. $\begin{bmatrix} 0 & 3 & 4 \\ 0 & 5 & 2 \end{bmatrix} + \begin{bmatrix} -3 & -3 & -3 \\ -1 & -1 & -1 \end{bmatrix} = \begin{bmatrix} -3 & 0 & 1 \\ -1 & 4 & 1 \end{bmatrix}$ **b.** $2\begin{bmatrix} 0 & 3 & 4 \\ 0 & 5 & 2 \end{bmatrix} = \begin{bmatrix} 0 & 6 & 8 \\ 0 & 10 & 4 \end{bmatrix}$

c. $\begin{bmatrix} 0 & 3 & 4 \\ 0 & -5 & -2 \end{bmatrix}$; Multiplying by B reflects the triangle over the x-axis.

Exercise Set 5.2

1. a. $\begin{bmatrix} 0 & 16 \\ 12 & 8 \end{bmatrix}$ **b.** $\begin{bmatrix} -7 & 3 \\ 29 & 15 \end{bmatrix}$ **3. a.** $[30]$ **b.** $\begin{bmatrix} 1 & 2 & 3 & 4 \\ 2 & 4 & 6 & 8 \\ 3 & 6 & 9 & 12 \\ 4 & 8 & 12 & 16 \end{bmatrix}$ **5. a.** $\begin{bmatrix} 4 & -5 & 8 \\ 6 & -1 & 5 \\ 0 & 4 & -6 \end{bmatrix}$ **b.** $\begin{bmatrix} 5 & -2 & 7 \\ 17 & -3 & 2 \\ 3 & 0 & -5 \end{bmatrix}$

7. a. $\begin{bmatrix} 6 & 8 & 16 \\ 11 & 16 & 24 \\ 1 & -1 & 12 \end{bmatrix}$ **b.** $\begin{bmatrix} 38 & 27 \\ -16 & -4 \end{bmatrix}$ **9. a.** $\begin{bmatrix} 0 & 0 \\ 0 & 0 \end{bmatrix}$ **b.** $\begin{bmatrix} 4 & -1 & -3 & 1 \\ -1 & 4 & -3 & 2 \\ 14 & -11 & -3 & -1 \\ 25 & -25 & 0 & -5 \end{bmatrix}$ **11.** $\begin{bmatrix} 17 & 7 \\ -5 & -11 \end{bmatrix}$ **13.** $\begin{bmatrix} 11 & -1 \\ -7 & -3 \end{bmatrix}$

15. $A - C$ is not defined because A is 3×2 and C is 2×2.

17. $\begin{bmatrix} 16 & -16 \\ -12 & 12 \\ 0 & 0 \end{bmatrix}$ **19.** $\begin{bmatrix} 0 & 0 \\ 0 & 0 \end{bmatrix}$

21. Answers will vary; Example:

$A(B+C) = \begin{bmatrix} 1 & 0 \\ 0 & 1 \end{bmatrix} \left(\begin{bmatrix} 1 & 0 \\ 0 & -1 \end{bmatrix} + \begin{bmatrix} -1 & 0 \\ 0 & 1 \end{bmatrix} \right) = \begin{bmatrix} 1 & 0 \\ 0 & 1 \end{bmatrix} \begin{bmatrix} 0 & 0 \\ 0 & 0 \end{bmatrix} = \begin{bmatrix} 0 & 0 \\ 0 & 0 \end{bmatrix}$

$AB + AC = \begin{bmatrix} 1 & 0 \\ 0 & 1 \end{bmatrix} \begin{bmatrix} 1 & 0 \\ 0 & -1 \end{bmatrix} + \begin{bmatrix} 1 & 0 \\ 0 & 1 \end{bmatrix} \begin{bmatrix} -1 & 0 \\ 0 & 1 \end{bmatrix} = \begin{bmatrix} 1 & 0 \\ 0 & -1 \end{bmatrix} + \begin{bmatrix} -1 & 0 \\ 0 & 1 \end{bmatrix} = \begin{bmatrix} 0 & 0 \\ 0 & 0 \end{bmatrix}$

So, $A(B+C) = AB + AC$.

23. $\begin{bmatrix} x \\ -y \end{bmatrix}$; It changes the sign of the y-coordinate.

25. a. $\begin{bmatrix} 1 & 3 & 1 \\ 3 & 3 & 3 \\ 1 & 3 & 1 \end{bmatrix}$ **b.** $\begin{bmatrix} 1 & 3 & 1 \\ 3 & 3 & 3 \\ 1 & 3 & 1 \end{bmatrix} + \begin{bmatrix} -1 & -1 & -1 \\ -1 & -1 & -1 \\ -1 & -1 & -1 \end{bmatrix} = \begin{bmatrix} 0 & 2 & 0 \\ 2 & 2 & 2 \\ 0 & 2 & 0 \end{bmatrix}$ **c.** $\begin{bmatrix} 1 & 3 & 1 \\ 3 & 3 & 3 \\ 1 & 3 & 1 \end{bmatrix} + \begin{bmatrix} 1 & -2 & 1 \\ -2 & -2 & -2 \\ 1 & -2 & 1 \end{bmatrix} = \begin{bmatrix} 2 & 1 & 2 \\ 1 & 1 & 1 \\ 2 & 1 & 2 \end{bmatrix}$

27. $\begin{bmatrix} -2 & 1 & 1 & -1 & -1 & -2 \\ -3 & -3 & -2 & -2 & 2 & 2 \end{bmatrix}$ **29.** $\begin{bmatrix} 0 & \frac{3}{2} & \frac{3}{2} & \frac{1}{2} & \frac{1}{2} & 0 \\ 1 & 1 & \frac{3}{2} & \frac{3}{2} & \frac{7}{2} & \frac{7}{2} \end{bmatrix}$

31. a. $\begin{bmatrix} 0 & 3 & 3 & 1 & 1 & 0 \\ 0 & 0 & -1 & -1 & -5 & -5 \end{bmatrix}$ **33. a.** $\begin{bmatrix} 0 & 0 & -1 & -1 & -5 & -5 \\ 0 & 3 & 3 & 1 & 1 & 0 \end{bmatrix}$

b. The effect is a reflection across the x-axis. **b.** The effect is a 90° counterclockwise rotation about the origin.

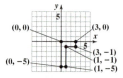 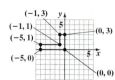

35. a. System 1: The midterm and final both count for 50% of the course grade. System 2: The midterm counts for 30% of the course grade and the final counts for 70%.

b. $\begin{bmatrix} 84 & 87.2 \\ 79 & 81 \\ 90 & 88.4 \\ 73 & 68.6 \\ 69 & 73.4 \end{bmatrix}$ System 1 grades are listed first (if different). Student 1: B; Student 2: C or B; Student 3: A or B; Student 4: C or D; Student 5: D or C

37, 39 answers may vary

41. makes sense   **43.** makes sense   **45.** answers may vary   **47.** $AB = -BA$ so they are anticommutative.

Integrated Review

1. $\begin{bmatrix} -4 & \frac{1}{2} \\ 3 & 3 \end{bmatrix}$ **2.** $\begin{bmatrix} -12 & -2 \\ -21 & -4 \\ 3 & 1 \end{bmatrix}$ **3.** $\begin{bmatrix} 12 & -4 \\ 22 & -7 \\ -4 & 1 \end{bmatrix}$

4. $A + C$ does not exist because A is 3×2 and C is 2×2. **5.** $\begin{bmatrix} \frac{1}{2} & \frac{1}{2} \\ -3 & \frac{1}{2} \end{bmatrix}$

Section 5.3
Practice Exercises
1. a. 16 **b.** -27 **2.** $(4, -3)$ **3.** $(0, 3)$ **4.** 93 **5.** $(2, 0, -1)$

Vocabulary and Readiness Check
1. 56 **3.** -32 **5.** 20

Exercise Set 5.3
1. 26 **3.** -19 **5.** 0 **7.** $\frac{13}{6}$ **9.** $(1, 2)$ **11.** $\{(x, y) | 3x + y = 1\}$ **13.** $(9, 9)$ **15.** $(-3, -2)$ **17.** $(3, 4)$ **19.** 8 **21.** 0 **23.** 15
25. 54 **27.** $(-2, 0, 5)$ **29.** $(6, -2, 4)$ **31.** $(-2, 3, -1)$ **33.** $(0, 2, -1)$ **35.** 5 **37.** 0; answers may vary

Section 5.4
Practice Exercises
1. $AB = I_2; BA = I_2$ **2.** $\begin{bmatrix} 1 & 2 \\ 1 & 3 \end{bmatrix}$ **3.** $\begin{bmatrix} 3 & -2 & -4 \\ 3 & -2 & -5 \\ -1 & 1 & 2 \end{bmatrix}$

Exercise Set 5.4
1. $AB = I_2; BA = I_2; B = A^{-1}$ **3.** $AB = \begin{bmatrix} 8 & -16 \\ -2 & 7 \end{bmatrix}; BA = \begin{bmatrix} 12 & 12 \\ 1 & 3 \end{bmatrix}; B \neq A^{-1}$ **5.** $AB = I_2; BA = I_2; B = A^{-1}$

7. $AB = I_3; BA = I_3; B = A^{-1}$ **9.** $AB = I_3; BA = I_3; B = A^{-1}$ **11.** $AB = I_4; BA = I_4; B = A^{-1}$

13. $\begin{bmatrix} \frac{2}{7} & -\frac{3}{7} \\ \frac{1}{7} & \frac{2}{7} \end{bmatrix}$ **15.** $\begin{bmatrix} 1 & \frac{1}{2} \\ 2 & \frac{3}{2} \end{bmatrix}$ **17.** A does not have an inverse. **19.** $\begin{bmatrix} \frac{1}{2} & 0 & 0 \\ 0 & \frac{1}{4} & 0 \\ 0 & 0 & \frac{1}{6} \end{bmatrix}$ **21.** $\begin{bmatrix} 1 & 1 & 2 \\ 1 & 1 & 1 \\ 2 & 3 & 4 \end{bmatrix}$ **23.** $\begin{bmatrix} 1 & 0 & 1 \\ 1 & 1 & 2 \\ 3 & 2 & 6 \end{bmatrix}$

25. $\begin{bmatrix} -3 & 2 & -4 \\ -1 & 1 & -1 \\ 8 & -5 & 10 \end{bmatrix}$ **27.** $\begin{bmatrix} 1 & 0 & 0 & 0 \\ 0 & -1 & 0 & 0 \\ 0 & 0 & \frac{1}{3} & 0 \\ -1 & 0 & 0 & 1 \end{bmatrix}$

29. $(AB)^{-1} = \begin{bmatrix} -23 & 16 \\ 13 & -9 \end{bmatrix}; A^{-1}B^{-1} = \begin{bmatrix} -3 & 11 \\ 8 & -29 \end{bmatrix}; B^{-1}A^{-1} = \begin{bmatrix} -23 & 16 \\ 13 & -9 \end{bmatrix}; (AB)^{-1} = B^{-1}A^{-1}$

31, 33 answers may vary
35. false **37.** true **39.** answers may vary **41.** $a = 3$ or $a = -2$ **43.** 6

Section 5.5
Practice Exercises
1. $(4, -2, 1)$ **2.** The encoded message is $-7, 10, -53, 77$. **3.** The decoded message is 2, 1, 19, 5 or BASE.

Exercise Set 5.5

1. $\begin{bmatrix} 6 & 5 \\ 5 & 4 \end{bmatrix} \begin{bmatrix} x \\ y \end{bmatrix} = \begin{bmatrix} 13 \\ 10 \end{bmatrix}$ **3.** $\begin{bmatrix} 1 & 3 & 4 \\ 1 & 2 & 3 \\ 1 & 4 & 3 \end{bmatrix} \begin{bmatrix} x \\ y \\ z \end{bmatrix} = \begin{bmatrix} -3 \\ -2 \\ -6 \end{bmatrix}$ **5.** $4x - 7y = -3$; $2x - 3y = 1$ **7.** $2x - z = 6$; $3y = 9$; $x + y = 5$ **9. a.** $\begin{bmatrix} 2 & 6 & 6 \\ 2 & 7 & 6 \\ 2 & 7 & 7 \end{bmatrix} \begin{bmatrix} x \\ y \\ z \end{bmatrix} = \begin{bmatrix} 8 \\ 10 \\ 9 \end{bmatrix}$ **b.** $\{(1, 2, -1)\}$

11. a. $\begin{bmatrix} 1 & -1 & 1 \\ 0 & 2 & -1 \\ 2 & 3 & 0 \end{bmatrix} \begin{bmatrix} x \\ y \\ z \end{bmatrix} = \begin{bmatrix} 8 \\ -7 \\ 1 \end{bmatrix}$ **b.** $\{(2, -1, 5)\}$ **13. a.** $\begin{bmatrix} 1 & -1 & 2 & 0 \\ 0 & 1 & -1 & 1 \\ -1 & 1 & -1 & 2 \\ 0 & -1 & 1 & -2 \end{bmatrix} \begin{bmatrix} w \\ x \\ y \\ z \end{bmatrix} = \begin{bmatrix} -3 \\ 4 \\ 2 \\ -4 \end{bmatrix}$ **b.** $\{(2, 3, -1, 0)\}$

15. The encoded message is $27, -19, 32, -20$; The decoded message is 8, 5, 12, 16 or HELP.

17. The encoded message is $14, 85, -33, 4, 18, -7, -18, 19, -9$.

19. answers may vary

21. $\begin{bmatrix} 1 & 1 \\ 2 & 3 \end{bmatrix}$ **23.** $\begin{bmatrix} 1 & 0 & 1 \\ 2 & 1 & 3 \\ -1 & 1 & 1 \end{bmatrix}$ **25.** $\begin{bmatrix} 0 & -1 & 0 & 1 \\ -1 & -5 & 0 & 3 \\ -2 & -4 & 1 & -2 \\ -1 & -4 & 0 & 1 \end{bmatrix}$

27. $\{(2, 3, -5)\}$,   **29.** $\{(1, 2, -1)\}$ **31.** $\{(2, 1, 3, -2, 4)\}$

Chapter 5 Vocabulary Check

1. rows   **2.** singular   **3.** square   **4.** cryptogram   **5.** determinant   **6.** multiplicative inverse   **7.** invertible; nonsingular   **8.** equal   **9.** Cramers's Rule   **10.** scalar   **11.** $A^{-1}B$

Chapter 5 Review Exercises

1. $x = -5; y = 6; z = 6$ **2.** $\begin{bmatrix} 0 & 2 & 3 \\ 8 & 1 & 3 \end{bmatrix}$ **3.** $\begin{bmatrix} 0 & -4 \\ 6 & 4 \\ 2 & -10 \end{bmatrix}$ **4.** $\begin{bmatrix} -4 & 4 & -1 \\ -2 & -5 & 5 \end{bmatrix}$ **5.** Not possible since B is 3×2 and C is 3×3.

6. $\begin{bmatrix} 2 & 3 & 8 \\ 21 & 5 & 5 \end{bmatrix}$ **7.** $\begin{bmatrix} -12 & 14 & 0 \\ 2 & -14 & 18 \end{bmatrix}$ **8.** $\begin{bmatrix} 0 & -10 & -15 \\ -40 & -5 & -15 \end{bmatrix}$ **9.** $\begin{bmatrix} -1 & -16 \\ 8 & 1 \end{bmatrix}$ **10.** $\begin{bmatrix} -10 & -6 & 2 \\ 16 & 3 & 4 \\ -23 & -16 & 7 \end{bmatrix}$ **11.** $\begin{bmatrix} -6 & 4 & -8 \\ 0 & 5 & 11 \\ -17 & 13 & -19 \end{bmatrix}$

12. $\begin{bmatrix} 10 & 5 \\ -2 & -30 \end{bmatrix}$ **13.** Not possible since AB is 2×2 and BA is 3×3.   **14.** $\begin{bmatrix} 7 & 6 & 5 \\ 2 & -1 & 11 \end{bmatrix}$ **15.** $\begin{bmatrix} -6 & -22 & -40 \\ 9 & 43 & 58 \\ -14 & -48 & -94 \end{bmatrix}$

16. $\begin{bmatrix} -2 & -6 \\ 3 & \frac{1}{3} \end{bmatrix}$ **17.** $\begin{bmatrix} 2 & 2 & 2 \\ 1 & 2 & 1 \\ 1 & 2 & 1 \end{bmatrix}$ **18.** $\begin{bmatrix} 1 & 1 & 1 \\ -1 & 1 & -1 \\ -1 & 1 & -1 \end{bmatrix}$

19. $\begin{bmatrix} -2 & 0 & 0 \\ 1 & 1 & -3 \end{bmatrix}$ **20.** $\begin{bmatrix} 0 & 1 & 1 \\ -2 & -2 & -4 \end{bmatrix}$ **21.** $\begin{bmatrix} 0 & 2 & 2 \\ 0 & 0 & 4 \end{bmatrix}$

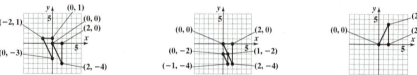

The effect is a reflection over the x-axis

22. $\begin{bmatrix} 0 & -2 & -2 \\ 0 & 0 & -4 \end{bmatrix}$ **23.** $\begin{bmatrix} 0 & 0 & 4 \\ 0 & 2 & 2 \end{bmatrix}$ **24.** $\begin{bmatrix} 0 & 4 & 4 \\ 0 & 0 & -4 \end{bmatrix}$

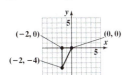
The effect is a reflection over the y-axis.

The effect is a 90° counter-clockwise rotation about the origin.

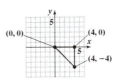
The effect is a horizontal stretch by a factor of 2.

25. 17 **26.** 4 **27.** -86 **28.** -236 **29.** $\left(\dfrac{7}{4}, -\dfrac{25}{8}\right)$ **30.** $(2, -7)$ **31.** $(23, -12, 3)$ **32.** $(-3, 2, 1)$

33. $AB = \begin{bmatrix} 1 & 7 \\ 0 & 5 \end{bmatrix}$; $BA = \begin{bmatrix} 1 & 0 \\ 1 & 5 \end{bmatrix}$; $B \neq A^{-1}$ **34.** $AB = I_3$; $BA = I_3$; $B = A^{-1}$ **35.** $\begin{bmatrix} 3 & 1 \\ 2 & 1 \end{bmatrix}$ **36.** $\begin{bmatrix} -\dfrac{3}{5} & \dfrac{1}{5} \\ 1 & 0 \end{bmatrix}$

37. $\begin{bmatrix} 3 & 0 & -2 \\ -6 & 1 & 4 \\ 1 & 0 & -1 \end{bmatrix}$ **38.** $\begin{bmatrix} 8 & -8 & 5 \\ -3 & 2 & -1 \\ -1 & -1 & 1 \end{bmatrix}$ **39. a.** $\begin{bmatrix} 1 & 1 & 2 \\ 0 & 1 & 3 \\ 3 & 0 & -2 \end{bmatrix}\begin{bmatrix} x \\ y \\ z \end{bmatrix} = \begin{bmatrix} 7 \\ -2 \\ 0 \end{bmatrix}$ **b.** $\{(-18, 79, -27)\}$

40. a. $\begin{bmatrix} 1 & -1 & 2 \\ 0 & 1 & -1 \\ 1 & 0 & 2 \end{bmatrix}\begin{bmatrix} x \\ y \\ z \end{bmatrix} = \begin{bmatrix} 12 \\ -5 \\ 10 \end{bmatrix}$ **b.** $\{(4, -2, 3)\}$ **41.** The encoded message is 96, 135, 46, 63; The decoded message is 18, 21, 12, 5 or RULE.

Chapter 5 Test

1. $\begin{bmatrix} 5 & 4 \\ 1 & 11 \end{bmatrix}$ **2.** $\begin{bmatrix} 5 & -2 \\ 1 & -1 \\ 4 & -1 \end{bmatrix}$ **3.** $\begin{bmatrix} \dfrac{3}{5} & -\dfrac{2}{5} \\ \dfrac{1}{5} & \dfrac{1}{5} \end{bmatrix}$ **4.** $\begin{bmatrix} -1 & 2 \\ -5 & 4 \end{bmatrix}$ **5.** $AB = I_3$; $BA = I_3$

6. a. $\begin{bmatrix} 3 & 5 \\ 2 & -3 \end{bmatrix}\begin{bmatrix} x \\ y \end{bmatrix} = \begin{bmatrix} 9 \\ -13 \end{bmatrix}$ **b.** $\begin{bmatrix} \dfrac{3}{19} & \dfrac{5}{19} \\ \dfrac{2}{19} & \dfrac{3}{19} \end{bmatrix}$ **c.** $\{(-2, 3)\}$ **7.** -52 **8.** 18 **9.** $(-2, -1)$ **10.** $x = 2$

Chapter 5 Standardized Test
1. a **2.** c **3.** d **4.** b **5.** a **6.** c **7.** a **8.** a **9.** d **10.** a **11.** b

CHAPTER 6 EXPONENTS, POLYNOMIALS, AND POLYNOMIAL FUNCTIONS

Section 6.1
Practice Exercises
1. a. 3^6 **b.** x^7 **c.** y^9 **2. a.** $35z^4$ **b.** $-20.5t^6q^8$ **3. a.** 1 **b.** -1 **c.** 1 **d.** 3 **4. a.** z^5 **b.** 3^6 **c.** $9x^4$ **d.** $\dfrac{4a^7}{3}$ or $\dfrac{4}{3}a^7$
5. a. $\dfrac{1}{36}$ **b.** $\dfrac{1}{64}$ **c.** $\dfrac{3}{x^5}$ **d.** $\dfrac{1}{5y}$ **e.** $\dfrac{1}{k^7}$ **f.** $\dfrac{1}{25}$ **g.** $\dfrac{9}{20}$ **h.** z^8 **6. a.** $\dfrac{1}{z^{11}}$ **b.** $7t^8$ **c.** 9 **d.** $\dfrac{b^7}{3a^7}$ **e.** $\dfrac{2}{x^4}$ **7. a.** x^{3a+4} **b.** x^{2t+1}
8. a. 6.5×10^4 **b.** 3.8×10^{-5} **9. a.** 620,000 **b.** 0.03109

Graphing Calculator Explorations 6.1
1. 6×10^{43} **3.** 3.796×10^{28}

Vocabulary and Readiness Check 6.1
1. x **3.** 3 **5.** y^7 **7.** $\dfrac{5}{xy^2}$ **9.** $\dfrac{a^2}{bc^5}$ **11.** $\dfrac{x^4}{y^2}$

Exercise Set 6.1
1. 4^5 **3.** x^8 **5.** m^{14} **7.** $-20x^2y$ **9.** $-16x^6y^3p^2$ **11.** -1 **13.** 1 **15.** -1 **17.** 9 **19.** a^3 **21.** $-13z^4$ **23.** x **25.** $\dfrac{4}{3}x^3y^2$
27. $-6a^4b^4c^6$ **29.** $\dfrac{1}{16}$ **31.** $-\dfrac{1}{27}$ **33.** $\dfrac{1}{x^8}$ **35.** $\dfrac{5}{a^4}$ **37.** $\dfrac{y^2}{x^7}$ **39.** $\dfrac{1}{x^7}$ **41.** $4r^8$ **43.** 1 **45.** $\dfrac{b^7}{9a^7}$ **47.** $\dfrac{6x^{16}}{5}$ **49.** $-140x^{12}$

51. x^{16} **53.** $10x^{10}$ **55.** 6 **57.** $\frac{1}{z^3}$ **59.** -2 **61.** y^4 **63.** $\frac{13}{36}$ **65.** $\frac{3}{x}$ **67.** r^8 **69.** $\frac{1}{x^9 y^4}$ **71.** $24x^7 y^6$ **73.** $\frac{x}{16}$ **75.** 625
77. $\frac{1}{8}$ **79.** $\frac{a^5}{81}$ **81.** $\frac{7}{x^3 z^5}$ **83.** x^{7a+5} **85.** x^{2t-1} **87.** x^{4a+7} **89.** z^{6x-7} **91.** x^{6t-1} **93.** 3.125×10^7 **95.** 1.6×10^{-2} **97.** 6.7413×10^4
99. 1.25×10^{-2} **101.** 5.3×10^{-5} **103.** 3.44992×10^{11} **105.** 3.5×10^6 **107.** 1.24×10^{11} **109.** 1.0×10^{-3} **111.** 0.0000000036
113. 93,000,000 **115.** 1,278,000 **117.** 7,350,000,000,000 **119.** 0.000000403 **121.** 300,000,000 **123.** \$153,000,000,000 **125.** 100 **127.** $\frac{27}{64}$
129. 64 **131.** answers may vary **133.** answers may vary **135. a.** x^{2a} **b.** $2x^a$ **c.** x^{a-b} **d.** x^{a+b} **e.** $x^a + x^b$ **137.** 7^{13} **139.** 7^{-11}

Section 6.2
Practice Exercises
1. a. z^{15} **b.** 625 **c.** $\frac{1}{27}$ **d.** x^{24} **2. a.** $32x^{15}$ **b.** $\frac{9}{25}$ **c.** $\frac{16a^{20}}{b^{28}}$ **d.** $9x$ **e.** $\frac{a^4 b^{10}}{c^8}$ **3. a.** $\frac{b^{15}}{27a^3}$ **b.** y^{15} **c.** $\frac{64}{9}$ **d.** $\frac{b^8}{81a^6}$
4. a. $\frac{c^3}{125 a^{36} b^3}$ **b.** $\frac{16 x^{16} y^4}{25}$ **5. a.** $27x^a$ **b.** y^{5b+3} **6. a.** 1.7×10^{-2} **b.** 1.4×10^{10} **7.** 4.2×10^{-6}

Vocabulary and Readiness Check 6.2
1. x^{20} **3.** x^9 **5.** y^{42} **7.** z^{36} **9.** z^{18}

Exercise Set 6.2
1. $\frac{1}{9}$ **3.** $\frac{1}{x^{36}}$ **5.** $\frac{1}{y^5}$ **7.** $9x^4 y^6$ **9.** $16x^{20} y^{12}$ **11.** $\frac{c^{18}}{a^{12} b^6}$ **13.** $\frac{y^{15}}{x^{35} z^{20}}$ **15.** $\frac{1}{125}$ **17.** x^{15} **19.** $\frac{8}{x^{12} y^{18}}$ **21.** $\frac{y^{16}}{64 x^5}$ **23.** $\frac{64}{p^9}$
25. $-\frac{1}{x^9 a^9}$ **27.** $\frac{x^5 y^{10}}{5^{15}}$ **29.** $\frac{1}{x^{63}}$ **31.** $\frac{343}{512}$ **33.** $16x^4$ **35.** $-\frac{y^3}{64}$ **37.** $4^8 x^2 y^6$ **39.** 64 **41.** $\frac{x^4}{16}$ **43.** $\frac{1}{y^{15}}$ **45.** $\frac{x^9}{8y^3}$
47. $\frac{16a^2 b^9}{9}$ **49.** $\frac{3}{8x^8 y^7}$ **51.** $\frac{1}{x^{30} b^6 c^6}$ **53.** $\frac{25}{8x^5 y^4}$ **55.** $\frac{2}{x^4 y^{10}}$ **57.** x^{9a+18} **59.** x^{12a+2} **61.** b^{10x-4} **63.** y^{15a+3} **65.** $16x^{4t+4}$
67. $5x^{-a} y^{-a+2}$ **69.** 1.45×10^9 **71.** 8×10^{15} **73.** 4×10^{-7} **75.** 3×10^{-1} **77.** 2×10^1 **79.** 1×10^1 **81.** 8×10^{-5} **83.** 1.1×10^7
85. 3.5×10^{22} **87.** 2×10^{-3} sec **89.** 6.232×10^{-11} cu m **91.** $-3m - 15$ **93.** $-3y - 5$ **95.** $-3x + 5$ **97.** $\frac{15y^3}{x^8}$ sq ft **99.** 1.331928×10^{13}
101. no **103.** 85 people per sq mi **105.** 6.4 times **107.** 31.7%

Section 6.3
Practice Exercises
1. a. 5 **b.** 3 **c.** 1 **d.** 11 **e.** 0 **2. a.** degree 4; trinomial **b.** degree 5; monomial **c.** degree 5; binomial **3.** 5
4. a. -15 **b.** -47 **5.** 290 feet; 226 feet **6. a.** $3x^4 - 5x$ **b.** $7ab - 3b$ **7. a.** $3a^4 b + 4ab^2 - 5$ **b.** $2x^5 + y - x - 9$
8. $6x^3 + 6x^2 - 7x - 8$ **9.** $15a^4 - 15a^3 + 3$ **10.** $6x^2 y^2 - 4xy^2 - 5y^3$ **11.** C

Graphing Calculator Explorations 6.3
1. $x^3 - 4x^2 + 7x - 8$ **3.** $-2.1x^2 - 3.2x - 1.7$ **5.** $7.69x^2 - 1.26x + 5.3$

Vocabulary and Readiness Check 6.3
1. coefficient **3.** binomial **5.** trinomial **7.** degree **9.** $6x$ **11.** $2y$ **13.** $7xy^2 - y^2$

Exercise Set 6.3
1. 0 **3.** 2 **5.** 3 **7.** 3 **9.** 9 **11.** degree 1; binomial **13.** degree 2; trinomial **15.** degree 3; monomial **17.** degree 4; none of these
19. 57 **21.** 499 **23.** $-\frac{11}{16}$ **25.** 1061 ft **27.** 549 ft **29.** $6y$ **31.** $11x - 3$ **33.** $xy + 2x - 1$ **35.** $6x^2 - xy + 16y^2$ **37.** $18y^2 - 17$
39. $3x^2 - 3xy + 6y^2$ **41.** $x^2 - 4x + 8$ **43.** $y^2 + 3$ **45.** $-2x^2 + 5x$ **47.** $-2x^2 - 4x + 15$ **49.** $4x - 13$ **51.** $x^2 + 2$ **53.** $12x^3 + 8x + 8$
55. $7x^3 + 4x^2 + 8x - 10$ **57.** $-18y^2 + 11yx + 14$ **59.** $-x^3 + 8a - 12$ **61.** $5x^2 - 9x - 3$ **63.** $-3x^2 + 3$ **65.** $8xy^2 + 2x^3 + 3x^2 - 3$
67. $7y^2 - 3$ **69.** $5x^2 + 22x + 16$ **71.** $\frac{3}{4}x^2 - \frac{1}{3}x^2 y - \frac{8}{3}x^2 y^2 + \frac{3}{2}y^3$ **73.** $-q^4 + q^2 - 3q + 5$ **75.** $15x^2 + 8x - 6$ **77.** $x^4 - 7x^2 + 5$
79. $\frac{1}{3}x^2 - x + 1$ **81.** 202 sq in. **83. a.** 284 ft **b.** 536 ft **c.** 756 ft **d.** 944 ft **e.** answers may vary **f.** 19 sec **85.** \$80,000
87. \$40,000 **89.** A **91.** D **93.** $15x - 10$ **95.** $-2x^2 + 10x - 12$ **97.** a and c
99. $(12x - 1.7) - (15x + 6.2) = 12x - 1.7 - 15x - 6.2 = -3x - 7.9$ **101.** answers may vary **103.** answers may vary
105. $3x^{2a} + 2x^a + 0.7$ **107.** $4x^{2y} + 2x^y - 11$ **109.** $(6x^2 + 14y)$ units **111.** $4x^2 - 3x + 6$ **113.** $-x^2 - 6x + 10$ **115.** $3x^2 - 12x + 13$
117. $15x^2 + 12x - 9$ **119. a.** $2a - 3$ **b.** $-2x - 3$ **c.** $2x + 2h - 3$ **121. a.** $4a$ **b.** $-4x$ **c.** $4x + 4h$
123. a. $4a - 1$ **b.** $-4x - 1$ **c.** $4x + 4h - 1$ **125. a.** 2.9 million **b.** 57.3 million **c.** 247.4 million **d.** answers may vary
127. a. 42.4 million **b.** 29.5 million **129. a.** 4.4 million **b.** 6.2 million

Section 6.4
Practice Exercises
1. a. $6x^6$ **b.** $40m^5n^2p^8$ **2. a.** $21x^2 - 3x$ **b.** $-15a^4 + 30a^3 - 25a^2$ **c.** $-5m^3n^5 - 2m^2n^4 + 5m^2n^3$
3. a. $2x^2 + 13x + 15$ **b.** $3x^3 - 19x^2 + 12x - 2$ **4.** $3x^4 - 12x^3 - 13x^2 - 8x - 10$ **5.** $x^2 - 2x - 15$
6. a. $6x^2 - 31x + 35$ **b.** $8x^4 - 10x^2y - 3y^2$ **7. a.** $x^2 + 12x + 36$ **b.** $x^2 - 4x + 4$ **c.** $9x^2 + 30xy + 25y^2$ **d.** $9x^4 - 48x^2b + 64b^2$
8. a. $x^2 - 49$ **b.** $4a^2 - 25$ **c.** $25x^4 - \dfrac{1}{16}$ **d.** $a^6 - 16b^4$ **9.** $4 + 12x - 4y + 9x^2 - 6xy + y^2$ **10.** $9x^2 - 6xy + y^2 - 25$
11. $x^4 - 32x^2 + 256$ **12.** $h^2 - h + 3$

Graphing Calculator Explorations 6.4
1. $x^2 - 16$ **3.** $9x^2 - 42x + 49$ **5.** $5x^3 - 14x^2 - 13x - 2$

Vocabulary and Readiness Check 6.4
1. b **3.** b **5.** d

Exercise Set 6.4
1. $-12x^5$ **3.** $12x^2 + 21x$ **5.** $-24x^2y - 6xy^2$ **7.** $-4a^3bx - 4a^3by + 12ab$ **9.** $2x^2 - 2x - 12$ **11.** $2x^4 + 3x^3 - 2x^2 + x + 6$
13. $15x^2 - 7x - 2$ **15.** $15m^3 + 16m^2 - m - 2$ **17.** $x^2 + x - 12$ **19.** $10x^2 + 11xy - 8y^2$ **21.** $3x^2 + 8x - 3$
23. $9x^2 - \dfrac{1}{4}$ **25.** $5x^4 - 17x^2y^2 + 6y^4$ **27.** $x^2 + 8x + 16$ **29.** $36y^2 - 1$ **31.** $9x^2 - 6xy + y^2$ **33.** $25b^2 - 36y^2$ **35.** $16b^2 + 32b + 16$
37. $4s^2 - 12s + 8$ **39.** $x^2y^2 - 4xy + 4$ **41.** answers may vary **43.** $x^4 - 2x^2y^2 + y^4$ **45.** $x^4 - 8x^3 + 24x^2 - 32x + 16$ **47.** $x^4 - 625$
49. $9x^2 + 18x + 5$ **51.** $10x^5 + 8x^4 + 2x^3 + 25x^2 + 20x + 5$ **53.** $49x^2 - 9$ **55.** $9x^3 + 30x^2 + 12x - 24$ **57.** $16x^2 - \dfrac{2}{3}x - \dfrac{1}{6}$
59. $36x^2 + 12x + 1$ **61.** $x^4 - 4y^2$ **63.** $-30a^4b^4 + 36a^3b^2 + 36a^2b^3$ **65.** $2a^2 - 12a + 16$ **67.** $49a^2b^2 - 9c^2$ **69.** $m^2 - 8m + 16$
71. $9x^2 + 6x + 1$ **73.** $y^2 - 7y + 12$ **75.** $2x^3 + 2x^2y + x^2 + xy - x - y$ **77.** $9x^4 + 12x^3 - 2x^2 - 4x + 1$ **79.** $12x^3 - 2x^2 + 13x + 5$
81. $a^2 - 3a$ **83.** $a^2 + 2ah + h^2 - 3a - 3h$ **85.** $b^2 - 7b + 10$ **87.** -2 **89.** $\dfrac{3}{5}$ **91.** function **93.** $7y(3z - 2) + 1 = 21yz - 14y + 1$
95. answers may vary **97. a.** $a^2 + 2ah + h^2 + 3a + 3h + 2$ **b.** $a^2 + 3a + 2$ **c.** $2ah + h^2 + 3h$ **99.** $30x^2y^{2n+1} - 10x^2y^n$
101. $x^{3a} + 5x^{2a} - 3x^a - 15$ **103.** $\pi(25x^2 - 20x + 4)$ sq km **105.** $(8x^2 - 12x + 4)$ sq in. **107. a.** $6x + 12$
b. $9x^2 + 36x + 35$; one operation is addition, the other is multiplication. **109.** $5x^2 + 25x$ **111.** $x^4 - 4x^2 + 4$ **113.** $x^3 + 5x^2 - 2x - 10$

Section 6.5
Practice Exercises
1. $8y$ **2. a.** $3(2x^2 + 3 + 5x)$ **b.** $3x - 8y^3$ **c.** $2a^3(4a - 1)$ **3.** $8x^3y^2(8x^2 - 1)$ **4.** $-xy^2(9x^3 - 5x - 7)$ **5.** $(3 + 5b)(x + 4)$
6. $(8b - 1)(a^3 + 2y)$ **7.** $(x + 2)(y - 5)$ **8.** $(a + 2)(a^2 + 5)$ **9.** $(x^2 + 3)(y^2 - 5)$ **10.** $(q + 3)(p - 1)$

Vocabulary and Readiness Check 6.5
1. factoring **3.** least **5.** false **7.** false **9.** 6 **11.** 5 **13.** x **15.** $7x$

Exercise Set 6.5
1. a^3 **3.** y^2z^2 **5.** $3x^2y$ **7.** $5xz^3$ **9.** $6(3x - 2)$ **11.** $4y^2(1 - 4xy)$ **13.** $2x^3(3x^2 - 4x + 1)$ **15.** $4ab(2a^2b^2 - ab + 1 + 4b)$
17. $(x + 3)(6 + 5a)$ **19.** $(z + 7)(2x + 1)$ **21.** $(x^2 + 5)(3x - 2)$ **23.** answers may vary **25.** $(a + 2)(b + 3)$
27. $(a - 2)(c + 4)$ **29.** $(x - 2)(2y - 3)$ **31.** $(4x - 1)(3y - 2)$ **33.** $3(2x^3 + 3)$ **35.** $x^2(x + 3)$ **37.** $4a(2a^2 - 1)$
39. $-4xy(5x - 4y^2)$ or $4xy(-5x + 4y^2)$ **41.** $5ab^2(2ab + 1 - 3b)$ **43.** $3b(3ac^2 + 2a^2c - 2a + c)$ **45.** $(y - 2)(4x - 3)$
47. $(2x + 3)(3y + 5)$ **49.** $(x + 3)(y - 5)$ **51.** $(2a - 3)(3b - 1)$ **53.** $(6x + 1)(2y + 3)$ **55.** $(n - 8)(2m - 1)$ **57.** $3x^2y^2(5x - 6)$
59. $(2x + 3y)(x + 2)$ **61.** $(5x - 3)(x + y)$ **63.** $(x^2 + 4)(x + 3)$ **65.** $(x^2 - 2)(x - 1)$ **67.** $55x^7$ **69.** $125x^6$ **71.** $x^2 - 3x - 10$
73. $x^2 + 5x + 6$ **75.** $y^2 - 4y + 3$ **77.** d **79.** $2\pi r(r + h)$ **81.** $A = 5600(1 + rt)$ **83.** answers may vary **85.** none **87.** a
89. $A = P(1 + RT)$ **91.** $y^n(3 + 3y^n + 5y^{7n})$ **93.** $3x^{2a}(x^{3a} - 2x^a + 3)$ **95. a.** $h(t) = -16(t^2 - 14)$ **b.** 160 **c.** answers may vary

Section 6.6
Practice Exercises
1. $(x + 3)(x + 2)$ **2.** $(x - 3)(x - 8)$ **3.** $3x(x - 5)(x + 2)$ **4.** $2(b^2 - 9b - 11)$ **5.** $(2x + 1)(x + 6)$ **6.** $(4x - 3)(x + 2)$
7. $3b^2(2b - 5)(3b - 2)$ **8.** $(5x + 2y)^2$ **9.** $(5x + 2)(4x + 3)$ **10.** $(5x + 3)(3x - 1)$ **11.** $(x - 3)(3x + 8)$ **12.** $(3x^2 + 2)(2x^2 - 5)$

Vocabulary and Readiness Check 6.6
1. 5 and 2 **3.** 8 and 3

Exercise Set 6.6
1. $(x + 3)(x + 6)$ **3.** $(x - 8)(x - 4)$ **5.** $(x + 12)(x - 2)$ **7.** $(x - 6)(x + 4)$ **9.** $3(x - 2)(x - 4)$ **11.** $4z(x + 2)(x + 5)$
13. $2(x^2 - 12x - 32)$ **15.** $(5x + 1)(x + 3)$ **17.** $(2x - 3)(x - 4)$ **19.** prime polynomial **21.** $(2x - 3)^2$ **23.** $2(3x - 5)(2x + 5)$

25. $y^2(3y + 5)(y - 2)$ **27.** $2x(3x^2 + 4x + 12)$ **29.** $(2x + y)(x - 3y)$ **31.** $2(7y + 2)(2y + 1)$ **33.** $(2x - 3)(x + 9)$
35. $(x^2 + 3)(x^2 - 2)$ **37.** $(5x + 8)(5x + 2)$ **39.** $(x^3 - 4)(x^3 - 3)$ **41.** $(a - 3)(a + 8)$ **43.** $(x - 27)(x + 3)$ **45.** $(x - 18)(x + 3)$
47. $3(x - 1)^2$ **49.** $(3x + 1)(x - 2)$ **51.** $(4x - 3)(2x - 5)$ **53.** $3x^2(2x + 1)(3x + 2)$ **55.** $(x + 7z)(x + z)$ **57.** $(x - 4)(x + 3)$
59. $3(a + 2b)^2$ **61.** prime polynomial **63.** $(2x + 13)(x + 3)$ **65.** $(3x - 2)(2x - 15)$ **67.** $(x^2 - 6)(x^2 + 1)$ **69.** $x(3x + 1)(2x - 1)$
71. $(4a - 3b)(3a - 5b)$ **73.** $(3x + 5)^2$ **75.** $y(3x - 8)(x - 1)$ **77.** $2(x + 3)(x - 2)$ **79.** $(x + 2)(x - 7)$ **81.** $(2x^3 - 3)(x^3 + 3)$
83. $2x(6y^2 - z)^2$ **85.** $2xy(x + 3)(x - 2)$ **87.** $(x + 5y)(x + y)$ **89.** $x^2 - 9$ **91.** $4x^2 + 4x + 1$ **93.** $x^3 - 8$ **95.** $\pm 5, \pm 7$
97. $x(x + 4)(x - 2)$ **99. a.** 576 ft; 672 ft; 640 ft; 480 ft **b.** answers may vary **c.** $-16(t + 4)(t - 9)$ **101.** $(x^n + 2)(x^n + 8)$
103. $(x^n - 6)(x^n + 3)$ **105.** $(2x^n + 1)(x^n + 5)$ **107.** $(2x^n - 3)^2$ **109.** $x^2(x + 5)(x + 1)$ **111.** $3x(5x - 1)(2x + 1)$

Section 6.7

Practice Exercises

1. $(b + 8)^2$ **2.** $5b(3x - 1)^2$ **3. a.** $(x + 4)(x - 4)$ **b.** $(5b - 7)(5b + 7)$ **c.** $5(3 - 2x)(3 + 2x)$ **d.** $\left(y - \dfrac{1}{9}\right)\left(y + \dfrac{1}{9}\right)$
4. a. $(x^2 + 100)(x + 10)(x - 10)$ **b.** $(x + 9)(x - 5)$ **5.** $(m + 3 + n)(m + 3 - n)$ **6.** $(x + 4)(x^2 - 4x + 16)$
7. $(a + 2b)(a^2 - 2ab + 4b^2)$ **8.** $(3 - y)(9 + 3y + y^2)$ **9.** $x^2(b - 2)(b^2 + 2b + 4)$

Vocabulary and Readiness Check 6.7

1. $(9y)^2$ **3.** $(8x^3)^2$ **5.** 5^3 **7.** $(2x)^3$ **9.** $(4x^2)^3$

Exercise Set 6.7

1. $(x + 3)^2$ **3.** $(2x - 3)^2$ **5.** $3(x - 4)^2$ **7.** $x^2(3y + 2)^2$ **9.** $(x + 5)(x - 5)$ **11.** $(3 + 2z)(3 - 2z)$ **13.** $(y + 9)(y - 5)$
15. $4(4x + 5)(4x - 5)$ **17.** $(x + 3)(x^2 - 3x + 9)$ **19.** $(z - 1)(z^2 + z + 1)$ **21.** $(m + n)(m^2 - mn + n^2)$ **23.** $y^2(x - 3)(x^2 + 3x + 9)$
25. $b(a + 2b)(a^2 - 2ab + 4b^2)$ **27.** $(5y - 2x)(25y^2 + 10yx + 4x^2)$ **29.** $(x + 3 + y)(x + 3 - y)$ **31.** $(x - 5 + y)(x - 5 - y)$
33. $(2x + 1 + z)(2x + 1 - z)$ **35.** $(3x + 7)(3x - 7)$ **37.** $(x - 6)^2$ **39.** $(x^2 + 9)(x + 3)(x - 3)$ **41.** $(x + 4 + 2y)(x + 4 - 2y)$
43. $(x + 2y + 3)(x + 2y - 3)$ **45.** $(x - 6)(x^2 + 6x + 36)$ **47.** $(x + 5)(x^2 - 5x + 25)$ **49.** prime polynomial **51.** $(2a + 3)^2$
53. $2y(3x + 1)(3x - 1)$ **55.** $(2x + y)(4x^2 - 2xy + y^2)$ **57.** $(x^2 - y)(x^4 + x^2y + y^2)$ **59.** $(x + 8 + x^2)(x + 8 - x^2)$
61. $3y^2(x^2 + 3)(x^4 - 3x^2 + 9)$ **63.** $(x + y + 5)(x^2 + 2xy + y^2 - 5x - 5y + 25)$ **65.** $(2x - 1)(4x^2 + 20x + 37)$ **67.** 5 **69.** $-\dfrac{1}{3}$ **71.** 0
73. 5 **75.** no; $x^2 - 4$ can be factored further **77.** yes **79.** $\pi R^2 - \pi r^2 = \pi(R + r)(R - r)$ **81.** $x^3 - y^2x; x(x + y)(x - y)$ **83.** $c = 9$
85. $c = 49$ **87.** $c = \pm 8$ **89. a.** $(x + 1)(x^2 - x + 1)(x - 1)(x^2 + x + 1)$ **b.** $(x + 1)(x - 1)(x^4 + x^2 + 1)$ **c.** answers may vary
91. $(x^n + 6)(x^n - 6)$ **93.** $(5x^n + 9)(5x^n - 9)$ **95.** $(x^{2n} + 25)(x^n + 5)(x^n - 5)$

Integrated Review Practice Exercises

1. a. $3xy(4x - 1)$ **b.** $(7x + 2)(7x - 2)$ **c.** $(5x - 3)(x + 1)$ **d.** $(3 + x)(x^2 + 2)$ **e.** $(2x + 5)^2$ **f.** cannot be factored
2. a. $(4x + y)(16x^2 - 4xy + y^2)$ **b.** $7y^2(x - 3y)(x + 3y)$ **c.** $3(x + 2 + b)(x + 2 - b)$ **d.** $x^2y(xy + 3)(x^2y^2 - 3xy + 9)$
e. $(x + 7 + 9y)(x + 7 - 9y)$

Integrated Review

1. $2y^2 + 2y - 11$ **2.** $-2z^4 - 6z^2 + 3z$ **3.** $x^2 - 7x + 7$ **4.** $7x^2 - 4x - 5$ **5.** $25x^2 - 30x + 9$ **6.** $x - 3$
7. $2x^3 - 4x^2 + 5x - 5 + \dfrac{8}{x + 2}$ **8.** $4x^3 - 13x^2 - 5x + 2$ **9.** $(x - 4 + y)(x - 4 - y)$ **10.** $2(3x + 2)(2x - 5)$ **11.** $x(x - 1)(x^2 + x + 1)$
12. $2x(2x - 1)$ **13.** $2xy(7x - 1)$ **14.** $6ab(4b - 1)$ **15.** $4(x + 2)(x - 2)$ **16.** $9(x + 3)(x - 3)$ **17.** $(3x - 11)(x + 1)$
18. $(5x + 3)(x - 1)$ **19.** $4(x + 3)(x - 1)$ **20.** $6(x + 1)(x - 2)$ **21.** $(2x + 9)^2$ **22.** $(5x + 4)^2$ **23.** $(2x + 5y)(4x^2 - 10xy + 25y^2)$
24. $(3x - 4y)(9x^2 + 12xy + 16y^2)$ **25.** $8x^2(2y - 1)(4y^2 + 2y + 1)$ **26.** $27x^2y(xy - 2)(x^2y^2 + 2xy + 4)$
27. $(x + 5 + y)(x^2 + 10x - xy - 5y + y^2 + 25)$ **28.** $(y - 1 + 3x)(y^2 - 2y + 1 - 3xy + 3x + 9x^2)$ **29.** $(5a - 6)^2$ **30.** $(4r + 5)^2$
31. $7x(x - 9)$ **32.** $(4x + 3)(5x + 2)$ **33.** $(a + 7)(b - 6)$ **34.** $20(x - 6)(x - 5)$ **35.** $(x^2 + 1)(x - 1)(x + 1)$ **36.** $5x(3x - 4)$
37. $(5x - 11)(2x + 3)$ **38.** $9m^2n^2(5mn - 3)$ **39.** $5a^3b(b^2 - 10)$ **40.** $x(x + 1)(x^2 - x + 1)$ **41.** prime **42.** $20(x + y)(x^2 - xy + y^2)$
43. $10x(x - 10)(x - 11)$ **44.** $(3y - 7)^2$ **45.** $a^3b(4b - 3)(16b^2 + 12b + 9)$ **46.** $(y^2 + 4)(y + 2)(y - 2)$ **47.** $2(x - 3)(x^2 + 3x + 9)$
48. $(2s - 1)(r + 5)$ **49.** $(y^4 + 2)(3y - 5)$ **50.** prime **51.** $100(z + 1)(z^2 - z + 1)$ **52.** $2x(5x - 2)(25x^2 + 10x + 4)$ **53.** $(2b - 9)^2$
54. $(a^4 + 3)(2a - 1)$ **55.** $(y - 4)(y - 5)$ **56.** $(c - 3)(c + 1)$ **57.** $A = 9 - 4x^2 = (3 + 2x)(3 - 2x)$

Section 6.8

Practice Exercises

1. $-8, 5$ **2.** $-4, \dfrac{2}{3}$ **3.** $-4, -\dfrac{2}{3}$ **4.** $-\dfrac{3}{4}$ **5.** $-\dfrac{1}{8}, 2$ **6.** $0, 3, -1$ **7.** $3, -3, -2$ **8.** 6 seconds **9.** 6, 8, 10 units **10.** $f(x)$: C; $g(x)$: A; $h(x)$: B

Graphing Calculator Explorations 6.8

1. $-3.562, 0.562$ **3.** $-0.874, 2.787$ **5.** $-0.465, 1.910$

Vocabulary and Readiness Check 6.8

1. $3, -5$ **3.** $3, -7$ **5.** $0, 9$

Exercise Set 6.8

1. $-3, \frac{4}{3}$ **3.** $\frac{5}{2}, -\frac{3}{4}$ **5.** $-3, -8$ **7.** $\frac{1}{4}, -\frac{2}{3}$ **9.** $1, 9$ **11.** $\frac{3}{5}, -1$ **13.** 0 **15.** $6, -3$ **17.** $\frac{2}{5}, -\frac{1}{2}$ **19.** $\frac{3}{4}, -\frac{1}{2}$ **21.** $-2, 7, \frac{8}{3}$
23. $0, 3, -3$ **25.** $2, 1, -1$ **27.** answers may vary **29.** $-\frac{7}{2}, 10$ **31.** $0, 5$ **33.** $-3, 5$ **35.** $-\frac{1}{2}, \frac{1}{3}$ **37.** $-4, 9$ **39.** $\frac{4}{5}$ **41.** $-5, 0, 2$
43. $-3, 0, \frac{4}{5}$ **45.** $\emptyset$ **47.** $-7, 4$ **49.** $4, 6$ **51.** $-\frac{1}{2}$ **53.** $-4, -3, 3$ **55.** $-5, 0, 5$ **57.** $-6, 5$ **59.** $-\frac{1}{3}, 0, 1$ **61.** $-\frac{1}{3}, 0$ **63.** $-\frac{7}{8}$
65. $\frac{31}{4}$ **67.** 1 **69. a.** incorrect **b.** correct **c.** correct **d.** incorrect **71.** -11 and -6 or 6 and 11 **73.** 75 ft **75.** 105 units
77. 12 cm and 9 cm **79.** 2 in. **81.** 10 sec **83.** width: $7\frac{1}{2}$ ft; length: 12 ft **85.** 10 in. sq tier **87.** 9 sec **89.** E **91.** F **93.** B
95. $(-3, 0), (0, 2)$; function **97.** $(-4, 0), (0, 2), (4, 0), (0, -2)$; not a function **99.** answers may vary
101. $x - 5 = 0$ or $x + 2 = 0$ **103.** $y(y - 5) = -6$ **105.** $-3, -\frac{1}{3}, 2, 5$ **107.** no; answers may vary **109.** answers may vary
$x = 5$ or $x = -2$ $y^2 - 5y + 6 = 0$ **111.** answers may vary
$(y - 2)(y - 3) = 0$
$y - 2 = 0$ or $y - 3 = 0$
$y = 2$ or $y = 3$

Chapter 6 Extension Practices

1. odd **2.** even **3.** $+\infty; -\infty$

Chapter 6 Extension Exercises

1. even **3.** odd **5.** odd **7.** even **9.** even **11.** odd

  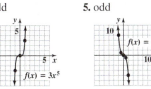 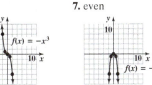 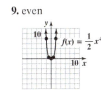 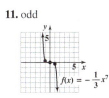

13. $+\infty; +\infty$ **15.** $+\infty; -\infty$ **17.** $-\infty; +\infty$ **19.** $+\infty; +\infty$ **21.** B **23.** D

Chapter 6 Vocabulary Check

1. polynomial **2.** factoring **3.** exponents **4.** degree of a term **5.** monomial **6.** 1 **7.** trinomial
8. quadratic equation **9.** scientific notation **10.** degree of a polynomial **11.** binomial **12.** 0

Chapter 6 Review

1. 4 **3.** -4 **5.** 1 **7.** $-\frac{1}{16}$ **9.** $-x^2 y^7 z$ **11.** $\frac{1}{a^9}$ **13.** $\frac{1}{x^{11}}$ **15.** $\frac{1}{y^5}$ **17.** -3.62×10^{-4} **19.** $410{,}000$ **21.** $\frac{a^2}{16}$ **23.** $\frac{1}{16x^2}$
25. $\frac{1}{8^{18}}$ **27.** $-\frac{1}{8x^9}$ **29.** $\frac{-27y^6}{x^6}$ **31.** $\frac{xz}{4}$ **33.** $\frac{2}{27z^3}$ **35.** $2y^{x-7}$ **37.** -2.21×10^{-11} **39.** $\frac{x^3 y^{10}}{3z^{12}}$ **41.** 5 **43.** $12x - 6x^2 - 6x^2 y$
45. $4x^2 + 8y + 6$ **47.** $8x^2 + 2b - 22$ **49.** $12x^2 y - 7xy + 3$ **51.** $x^3 + x - 2xy^2 - y - 7$ **53.** 58 **55.** $x^2 + 4x - 6$
57. $(6x^2 y - 12x + 12)$ cm **59.** $-12a^2 b^5 - 28a^2 b^3 - 4ab^2$ **61.** $9x^2 a^2 - 24xab + 16b^2$ **63.** $15x^2 + 18xy - 81y^2$
65. $x^4 + 18x^3 + 83x^2 + 18x + 1$ **67.** $16x^2 + 72x + 81$ **69.** $16 - 9a^2 + 6ab - b^2$ **71.** $(9y^2 - 49z^2)$ sq units
73. $16x^2 y^2 z - 8xy^2 b + b^2$ **75.** $8x^2(2x - 3)$ **77.** $2ab(3b + 4 - 2ab)$ **79.** $(a + 3b)(6a - 5)$ **81.** $(x - 6)(y + 3)$ **83.** $(p - 5)(q - 3)$
85. $x(2y - x)$ **87.** $(x - 4)(x + 20)$ **89.** $3(x + 2)(x + 9)$ **91.** $(3x + 8)(x - 2)$ **93.** $(15x - 1)(x - 6)$ **95.** $3(x - 2)(3x + 2)$
97. $(x + 7)(x + 9)$ **99.** $(x^2 - 2)(x^2 + 10)$ **101.** $(x + 9)(x - 9)$ **103.** $6(x + 3)(x - 3)$ **105.** $(4 + y^2)(2 + y)(2 - y)$ **107.** $(x - 7)(x + 1)$
109. $(y + 8)(y^2 - 8y + 64)$ **111.** $(1 - 4y)(1 + 4y + 16y^2)$ **113.** $2x^2(x + 2y)(x^2 - 2xy + 4y^2)$ **115.** $(x - 3 - 2y)(x - 3 + 2y)$
117. $(4a - 5b)^2$ **119.** $\frac{1}{3}, -7$ **121.** $0, 4, \frac{9}{2}$ **123.** $0, 6$ **125.** $-\frac{1}{3}, 2$ **127.** $-4, 1$ **129.** $0, 6, -3$ **131.** $0, -2, 1$ **133.** $-\frac{15}{2}, 7$ **135.** 5 sec
137. $3x^3 + 13x^2 - 9x + 5$ **139.** $8x^2 + 3x + 4.5$ **141.** -24 **143.** $6y^4(2y - 1)$ **145.** $2(3x + 1)(x - 6)$ **147.** $z^5(2z + 7)(2z - 7)$ **149.** $0, 3$

Chapter 6 Test

1. $\frac{1}{81x^2}$ **2.** $-12x^2 z$ **3.** $\frac{3a^7}{2b^5}$ **4.** $-\frac{y^{40}}{z^5}$ **5.** 6.3×10^8 **6.** 1.2×10^{-2} **7.** 0.000005 **8.** 0.0009 **9.** $-5x^3 y - 11x - 9$
10. $-12x^2 y - 3xy^2$ **11.** $12x^2 - 5x - 28$ **12.** $25a^2 - 4b^2$ **13.** $36m^2 + 12mn + n^2$ **14.** $2x^3 - 13x^2 + 14x - 4$ **15.** $4x^2 y(4x - 3y^3)$
16. $(x - 15)(x + 2)$ **17.** $(2y + 5)^2$ **18.** $3(2x + 1)(x - 3)$ **19.** $(2x + 5)(2x - 5)$ **20.** $(x + 4)(x^2 - 4x + 16)$

21. $3y(x + 3y)(x - 3y)$ **22.** $6(x^2 + 4)$ **23.** $2(2y - 1)(4y^2 + 2y + 1)$ **24.** $(x + 3)(x - 3)(y - 3)$ **25.** $4, -\frac{8}{7}$ **26.** $-3, 8$
27. $-\frac{5}{2}, -2, 2$ **28.** $(x + 2y)(x - 2y)$ **29. a.** 960 ft **b.** 953.44 ft **c.** 11 sec

Chapter 6 Standardized Test
1. b **2.** d **3.** d **4.** c **5.** c **6.** a **7.** b **8.** b **9.** d **10.** a **11.** c **12.** a **13.** a **14.** b **15.** b **16.** d
17. c **18.** d **19.** b **20.** d **21.** a **22.** d **23.** b **24.** b **25.** c **26.** a **27.** d **28.** c **29.** d

CHAPTER 7 RATIONAL EXPRESSIONS

Section 7.1
Practice Exercises
1. a. all real numbers **b.** all real numbers except -3 **c.** all real numbers except 2 and 3
2. a. $\frac{1}{2z - 1}$ **b.** $\frac{5x + 3}{6x - 5}$ **3. a.** 1 **b.** -1 **4.** $-\frac{5(2 + x)}{x + 3}$ **5. a.** $x^2 - 4x + 16$ **b.** $\frac{5}{z - 3}$ **6. a.** $\frac{2n + 1}{n(n - 1)}$ **b.** $-x^2$
7. a. $\frac{-y^3}{21(y + 3)}$ **b.** $\frac{7x + 2}{x + 2}$ **8.** $\frac{5}{3(x - 3)}$ **9. a.** \$7.20 **b.** \$3.60

Graphing Calculator Explorations 7.1
1. all real numbers except -2 and 2 **3.** all real numbers except -4 and $\frac{1}{2}$

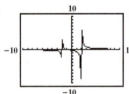 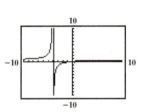

Vocabulary and Readiness Check 7.1
1. rational **3.** domain **5.** 1 **7.** $\frac{-a}{b}; \frac{a}{-b}$ **9.** $\frac{xy}{10}$ **11.** $\frac{2y}{3x}$ **13.** $\frac{m^2}{36}$

Exercise Set 7.1
1. all real numbers **3.** all real numbers except 0 **5.** all real numbers except 7
7. all real numbers except $\frac{1}{3}$ **9.** all real numbers except $-2, 0,$ and 1 **11.** all real numbers except -2 and 2
13. $1 - 2x$ **15.** $x - 3$ **17.** $\frac{9}{7}$ **19.** $x - 4$ **21.** -1 **23.** $-(x + 7)$ **25.** $\frac{2x + 1}{x - 1}$ **27.** $\frac{x^2 + 5x + 25}{2}$ **29.** $\frac{x - 2}{2x^2 + 1}$
31. $\frac{1}{3x + 5}$ **33.** $-\frac{4}{5}$ **35.** $-\frac{6a}{2a + 1}$ **37.** $\frac{3}{2(x - 1)}$ **39.** $\frac{x + 2}{x + 3}$ **41.** $\frac{3a}{5(a - b)}$ **43.** $\frac{1}{6}$ **45.** $\frac{x}{3}$ **47.** $\frac{4a^2}{a - b}$
49. $\frac{4}{(x + 2)(x + 3)}$ **51.** $\frac{1}{2}$ **53.** -1 **55.** $\frac{8(a - 2)}{3(a + 2)}$ **57.** $\frac{(x + 2)(x + 3)}{4}$ **59.** $\frac{2(x + 3)(x - 3)}{5(x^2 - 8x - 15)}$ **61.** $r^2 - rs + s^2$
63. $\frac{8}{x^2 y}$ **65.** $\frac{(y + 5)(2x - 1)}{(y + 2)(5x + 1)}$ **67.** $\frac{5(3a + 2)}{a}$ **69.** $\frac{5x^2 - 2}{(x - 1)^2}$ **71.** $\frac{10}{3}, -8, -\frac{7}{3}$ **73.** $-\frac{17}{48}, \frac{2}{7}, -\frac{3}{8}$
75. a. \$200 million **b.** \$500 million **c.** \$300 million **d.** all real numbers **77.** $\frac{7}{5}$ **79.** $\frac{1}{12}$ **81.** $\frac{11}{16}$
83. b and d **85.** no; answers may vary **87.** $\frac{5}{x - 2}$ sq m **89.** $\frac{(x + 2)(x - 1)^2}{x^5}$ ft **91.** answers may vary
93. a. 1 **b.** -1 **c.** neither **d.** -1 **e.** -1 **f.** 1 **95.** $(x - 5)(2x + 7)$ **97.** $0, \frac{20}{9}, \frac{60}{7}, 20, \frac{140}{3}, 180, 380, 1980;$
99. $2x^2(x^n + 2)$ **101.** $\frac{1}{10y(y^n + 3)}$ **103.** $\frac{y^n + 1}{2(y^n - 1)}$

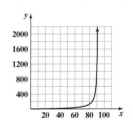

Section 7.2
Practice Exercises
1. a. $\frac{9 + x}{11z^2}$ **b.** $\frac{3x}{4}$ **c.** $x - 4$ **d.** $\frac{-3}{2a^2}$ **2. a.** $18x^3 y^5$ **b.** $(x - 2)(x + 3)$ **c.** $(b - 4)^2 (b + 4)(2b + 3)$ **d.** $-4(y - 3)(y + 3)$

3. a. $\dfrac{20p+3}{5p^4q}$ **b.** $\dfrac{5y^2+19y-12}{(y+3)(y-3)}$ **c.** 3   **4.** $\dfrac{t^2-t-15}{(t+5)(t-5)(t+2)}$ **5.** $\dfrac{5x^2-12x-3}{(3x+1)(x-2)(2x-5)}$ **6.** $\dfrac{4}{x-2}$

Vocabulary and Readiness Check 7.2

1. a, b   **3.** c   **5.** $\dfrac{12}{y}$ **7.** $\dfrac{35}{y^2}$ **9.** $\dfrac{-x+4}{2x}$ **11.** $\dfrac{16}{y-2}$

Exercise Set 7.2

1. $-\dfrac{3}{xz^2}$ **3.** $\dfrac{x+2}{x-2}$ **5.** $x-2$ **7.** $\dfrac{-1}{x-2}$ or $\dfrac{1}{2-x}$ **9.** $-\dfrac{5}{x}$ **11.** $35x$ **13.** $x(x+1)$ **15.** $(x+7)(x-7)$ **17.** $6(x+2)(x-2)$
19. $(a+b)(a-b)^2$ **21.** $-4x(x+3)(x-3)$ **23.** $\dfrac{17}{6x}$ **25.** $\dfrac{35-4y}{14y^2}$ **27.** $\dfrac{-13x+4}{(x+4)(x-4)}$ **29.** $\dfrac{3}{x+4}$ **31.** 0   **33.** $-\dfrac{x}{x-1}$
35. $\dfrac{-x+1}{x-2}$ **37.** $\dfrac{y^2+2y+10}{(y+4)(y-4)(y-2)}$ **39.** $\dfrac{5(x^2+x-4)}{(3x+2)(x+3)(2x-5)}$ **41.** $\dfrac{-x^2+10x+19}{(x-2)(x+1)(x+3)}$ **43.** $\dfrac{x^2+4x+2}{(2x+5)(x-7)(x-1)}$
45. $\dfrac{5a+1}{(a+1)^2(a-1)}$ **47.** $\dfrac{3}{x^2y^3}$ **49.** $-\dfrac{5}{x}$ **51.** $\dfrac{25}{6(x+5)}$ **53.** $\dfrac{-2x-1}{x^2(x-3)}$ **55.** $\dfrac{b(2a-b)}{(a+b)(a-b)}$ **57.** $\dfrac{2(x+8)}{(x+2)^2(x-2)}$
59. $\dfrac{3x^2+23x-7}{(2x-1)(x-5)(x+3)}$ **61.** $\dfrac{5-2x}{2(x+1)}$ **63.** $\dfrac{2(x^2+x-21)}{(x+3)^2(x-3)}$ **65.** $\dfrac{6x}{(x+3)(x-3)^2}$ **67.** $\dfrac{4}{3}$ **69.** $\dfrac{2x^2+9x-18}{6x^2}$ or $\dfrac{(x+6)(2x-3)}{6x^2}$
71. $\dfrac{4a^2}{9(a-1)}$ **73.** 4   **75.** $-\dfrac{4}{x-1}$ **77.** $-\dfrac{32}{x(x+2)(x-2)}$ **79.** 10   **81.** $4+x^2$ **83.** 10   **85.** 2   **87.** 3   **89.** 5 m
91. $\dfrac{2x-3}{x^2+1}-\dfrac{x-6}{x^2+1}=\dfrac{2x-3-x+6}{x^2+1}=\dfrac{x+3}{x^2+1}$ **93.** $\dfrac{4x}{x+5}$ ft; $\dfrac{x^2}{(x+5)^2}$ sq ft   **95.** answers may vary   **97.** answers may vary
99. answers may vary   **101.** $\dfrac{3}{2x}$ **103.** $\dfrac{4-3x}{x^2}$ **105.**

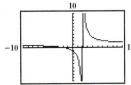

Section 7.3

Practice Exercises

1. a. $\dfrac{1}{12m}$ **b.** $\dfrac{8x(x+4)}{3(x-4)}$ **c.** $\dfrac{b^2}{a^2}$ **2. a.** $\dfrac{8x(x+4)}{3(x-4)}$ **b.** $\dfrac{b^2}{a^2}$ **3.** $\dfrac{y(3xy+1)}{x^2(1+xy)}$ **4.** $\dfrac{1-6x}{15+6x}$

Vocabulary and Readiness Check 7.3

1. $\dfrac{7}{1+z}$ **3.** $\dfrac{1}{x^2}$ **5.** $\dfrac{2}{x}$ **7.** $\dfrac{1}{9y}$

Exercise Set 7.3

1. 4   **3.** $\dfrac{7}{13}$ **5.** $\dfrac{4}{x}$ **7.** $\dfrac{9(x-2)}{9x^2+4}$ **9.** $2x+y$ **11.** $\dfrac{2(x+1)}{2x-1}$ **13.** $\dfrac{2x+3}{4-9x}$ **15.** $\dfrac{1}{x^2-2x+4}$ **17.** $\dfrac{x}{5(x-2)}$
19. $\dfrac{x-2}{2x-1}$ **21.** $\dfrac{x}{2-3x}$ **23.** $-\dfrac{y}{x+y}$ **25.** $-\dfrac{2x^3}{y(x-y)}$ **27.** $\dfrac{2x+1}{y}$ **29.** $\dfrac{x-3}{9}$ **31.** $\dfrac{1}{x+2}$ **33.** 2
35. $\dfrac{xy^2}{x^2+y^2}$ **37.** $\dfrac{2b^2+3a}{b(b-a)}$ **39.** $\dfrac{x}{(x+1)(x-1)}$ **41.** $\dfrac{1+a}{1-a}$ **43.** $\dfrac{x(x+6y)}{2y}$ **45.** $\dfrac{5a}{2(a+2)}$ **47.** $xy(5y+2x)$
49. $\dfrac{xy}{2x+5y}$ **51.** $\dfrac{x^2y^2}{4}$ **53.** $-9x^3y^4$ **55.** $-4, 14$ **57.** a and c   **59.** a, b   **61.** $\dfrac{770a}{770-s}$ **63.** $\dfrac{1+x}{2+x}$ **65.** $x(x+1)$
67. $\dfrac{x-3y}{x+3y}$ **69.** $3a^2+4a+4$ **71. a.** $\dfrac{1}{a+h}$ **b.** $\dfrac{1}{a}$ **c.** $\dfrac{\dfrac{1}{a+h}-\dfrac{1}{a}}{h}$ **d.** $\dfrac{-1}{a(a+h)}$ **73. a.** $\dfrac{3}{a+h+1}$
b. $\dfrac{3}{a+1}$ **c.** $\dfrac{\dfrac{3}{a+h+1}-\dfrac{3}{a+1}}{h}$ **d.** $\dfrac{-3}{(a+h+1)(a+1)}$

Section 7.4
Practice Exercises

1. $3a^2 - 2a + 5$ 2. $5a^2b^2 - 8ab + 1 - \dfrac{8}{ab}$ 3. $3x - 2$ 4. $3x - 2$ 5. $5x^2 - 6x + 8 + \dfrac{6}{x+3}$ 6. $2x^2 + 3x - 2 + \dfrac{-8x+4}{x^2+1}$

7. $16x^2 + 20x + 25$ 8. $4x^2 + x + 7 + \dfrac{12}{x-1}$ 9. $x^3 - 5x + 21 - \dfrac{51}{x+3}$ 10. a. -4 b. -4 11. 15 12. a. yes b. $-1, -\dfrac{1}{3}, \dfrac{2}{5}$

Exercise Set 7.4

1. $2a + 4$ 3. $3ab + 4$ 5. $2y + \dfrac{3y}{x} - \dfrac{2y}{x^2}$ 7. $x + 1$ 9. $2x - 8$ 11. $x - \dfrac{1}{2}$ 13. $2x^2 - \dfrac{1}{2}x + 5$ 15. $2x^2 - 6$

17. $3x^3 + 5x + 4 - \dfrac{2x}{x^2-2}$ 19. $2x^3 + \dfrac{9}{2}x^2 + 10x + 21 + \dfrac{42}{x-2}$ 21. $x + 8$ 23. $x - 1$ 25. $x^2 - 5x - 23 - \dfrac{41}{x-2}$

27. $4x + 8 + \dfrac{7}{x-2}$ 29. $x^6y + \dfrac{2}{y} + 1$ 31. $5x^2 - 6 - \dfrac{5}{2x-1}$ 33. $2x^2 + 2x + 8 + \dfrac{28}{x-4}$ 35. $2x^3 - 3x^2 + x - 4$

37. $3x^2 + 4x - 8 + \dfrac{20}{x+1}$ 39. $3x^2 + 3x - 3$ 41. $x^2 + x + 1$ 43. $-\dfrac{5y}{x} - \dfrac{15z}{x} - 25z$ 45. $3x^4 - 2x$ 47. 1 49. -133

51. 3 53. $-\dfrac{187}{81}$ 55. $\dfrac{95}{32}$ 57. The remainder is 0.; solutions: $-1, 2, 3$ 59. The remainder is 0.; solutions: $-\dfrac{1}{2}, 1, 2$

61. The remainder is 0.; solutions: $-5, \dfrac{1}{3}, \dfrac{1}{2}$ 63. 2; The remainder is zero.; solutions: $-3, -1,$ and 2

65. 1; The remainder is zero.; solutions: $\dfrac{1}{3}, \dfrac{1}{2},$ and 1 67. $-\dfrac{5}{6}$ 69. 2 71. 54 73. $(x-1)(x^2+x+1)$ 75. $(5z+2)(25z^2-10z+4)$

77. $(y+2)(x+3)$ 79. $x(x+3)(x-3)$ 81. yes 83. no 85. a or d 87. $(x^4 + 2x^2 - 6)$ m 89. $(3x - 7)$ in.

91. $(x^3 - 5x^2 + 2x - 1)$ cm 93. $x^3 + \dfrac{5}{3}x^2 + \dfrac{5}{3}x + \dfrac{8}{3} + \dfrac{8}{3(x-1)}$ 95. $\dfrac{3}{2}x^3 + \dfrac{1}{4}x^2 + \dfrac{1}{8}x - \dfrac{7}{16} + \dfrac{1}{16(2x-1)}$ 97. $x^3 - \dfrac{2}{5}x$

99. $5x - 1 + \dfrac{6}{x}; x \neq 0$ 101. $7x^3 + 14x^2 + 25x + 50 + \dfrac{102}{x-2}; x \neq 2$ 103. answers may vary 105. answers may vary

107. $(x+3)(x^2+4) = x^3 + 3x^2 + 4x + 12$ 109. 0 111. $x^3 + 2x^2 + 7x + 28$

Section 7.5
Practice Exercises

1. 4 2. 7 3. no solution 4. -1 5. 1 6. $12, -1$

Vocabulary and Readiness Check 7.5

1. c 3. a

Exercise Set 7.5

1. 72 3. 2 5. 6 7. $2, -2$ 9. no solution 11. $-\dfrac{28}{3}$ 13. 3 15. -8 17. 3 19. no solution 21. 1 23. 3 25. -1 27. 6

29. $\dfrac{1}{3}$ 31. $-5, 5$ 33. 3 35. 7 37. no solution 39. $\dfrac{4}{3}$ 41. -12 43. $1, \dfrac{11}{4}$ 45. $-5, -1$ 47. $-\dfrac{7}{5}$ 49. 5

51. length, 15 in.; width, 10 in. 53. 36% 55. 12–19 57. 40,000 students 59. answers may vary 61. 800 pencil sharpeners

63. $\dfrac{1}{9}, -\dfrac{1}{4}$ 65. $3, 2$ 67. 1.39 69. -0.08 71. $1, 2$ 73. $-3, -\dfrac{3}{4}$ 75. 77.

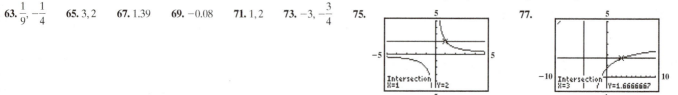

Integrated Review

1. $\dfrac{1}{2}$ 2. 10 3. $\dfrac{1+2x}{8}$ 4. $\dfrac{15+x}{10}$ 5. $\dfrac{2(x-4)}{(x+2)(x-1)}$ 6. $-\dfrac{5(x-8)}{(x-2)(x+4)}$ 7. 4 8. 8 9. -5 10. $-\dfrac{2}{3}$ 11. $\dfrac{2x+5}{x(x-3)}$

12. $\dfrac{5}{2x}$ 13. -2 14. $-\dfrac{y}{x}$ 15. $\dfrac{(a+3)(a+1)}{a+2}$ 16. $\dfrac{-a^2+31a+10}{5(a-6)(a+1)}$ 17. $-\dfrac{1}{5}$ 18. $-\dfrac{3}{13}$ 19. $\dfrac{4a+1}{(3a+1)(3a-1)}$

20. $\dfrac{-a-8}{4a(a-2)}$ or $-\dfrac{a+8}{4a(a-2)}$ 21. $-1, \dfrac{3}{2}$ 22. $\dfrac{x^2-3x+10}{2(x+3)(x-3)}$ 23. $\dfrac{3}{x+1}$ 24. all real numbers except 2 and -1 25. -1

26. $\dfrac{22z-45}{3z(z-3)}$ 27. a. $\dfrac{x}{5} - \dfrac{x}{4} + \dfrac{1}{10}$ b. Write each rational expression term so that the denominator is the LCD, 20. c. $\dfrac{-x+2}{20}$

28. a. $\dfrac{x}{5} - \dfrac{x}{4} = \dfrac{1}{10}$ b. Clear the equation of fractions by multiplying each term by the LCD, 20. c. -2 29. b 30. d 31. d 32. a 33. d

Section 7.6
Practice Exercises
1. $a = \dfrac{bc}{b+c}$ **2.** 7 **3.** 3000 **4.** $1\dfrac{1}{5}$ hr **5.** 50 mph

Exercise Set 7.6
1. $C = \dfrac{5}{9}(F-32)$ **3.** $I = A - QL$ **5.** $R = \dfrac{R_1 R_2}{R_1 + R_2}$ **7.** $n = \dfrac{2S}{a+L}$ **9.** $b = \dfrac{2A-ah}{h}$ **11.** $T_2 = \dfrac{P_2 V_2 T_1}{P_1 V_1}$ **13.** $f_2 = \dfrac{f_1 f}{f_1 - f}$
15. $L = \dfrac{n\lambda}{2}$ **17.** $c = \dfrac{2L\omega}{\theta}$ **19.** 1 and 5 **21.** 5 **23.** 4.5 gal **25.** 4470 women **27.** 15.6 hr **29.** 10 min **31.** 200 mph
33. 15 mph **35.** -8 and -7 **37.** 36 min **39.** 45 mph; 60 mph **41.** 5.9 hr **43.** 2 hr **45.** 135 mph **47.** 12 mi **49.** $\dfrac{7}{8}$
51. $1\dfrac{1}{2}$ min **53.** $2\dfrac{2}{9}$ hr **55.** 10 mph; 8 mph **57.** 2 hr **59.** by jet: 3 hr; by car: 4 hr **61.** 428 movies **63.** 6
65. 22 **67.** answers may vary; 60 in. or 5 ft **69.** 6 ohms **71.** $\dfrac{1}{R} = \dfrac{1}{R_1} + \dfrac{1}{R_2} + \dfrac{1}{R_3}; R = \dfrac{15}{13}$ ohms

Section 7.7
Practice Exercises
1. $k = \dfrac{4}{3}; y = \dfrac{4}{3}x$ **2.** $18\dfrac{3}{4}$ inches **3.** $k = 45; b = \dfrac{45}{a}$ **4.** $P = 653\dfrac{1}{3}$ kilopascals **5.** $A = $ kpa **6.** $k = 4; y = \dfrac{4}{x^3}$ **7.** $k = 81; y = \dfrac{81z}{x^3}$

Vocabulary and Readiness Check 7.7
1. direct **3.** joint **5.** inverse **7.** direct

Exercise Set 7.7
1. $k = \dfrac{1}{5}; y = \dfrac{1}{5}x$ **3.** $k = \dfrac{3}{2}; y = \dfrac{3}{2}x$ **5.** $k = 14; y = 14x$ **7.** $k = 0.25; y = 0.25x$ **9.** 4.05 lb **11.** 204,706 tons **13.** $k = 30; y = \dfrac{30}{x}$
15. $k = 700; y = \dfrac{700}{x}$ **17.** $k = 2; y = \dfrac{2}{x}$ **19.** $k = 0.14; y = \dfrac{0.14}{x}$ **21.** 54 mph **23.** 72 amps **25.** divided by 4 **27.** $x = kyz$
29. $r = kst^3$ **31.** $k = \dfrac{1}{3}; y = \dfrac{1}{3}x^3$ **33.** $k = 0.2; y = 0.2\sqrt{x}$ **35.** $k = 1.3; y = \dfrac{1.3}{x^2}$ **37.** $k = 3; y = 3xz^3$ **39.** 22.5 tons
41. 15π cu in. **43.** 8 ft **45.** $y = kx$ **47.** $a = \dfrac{k}{b}$ **49.** $y = kxz$ **51.** $y = \dfrac{k}{x^3}$ **53.** $y = \dfrac{kx}{p^2}$ **55.** $C = 8\pi$ in.; $A = 16\pi$ sq in.
57. $C = 18\pi$ cm; $A = 81\pi$ sq cm **59.** 9 **61.** 1 **63.** $\dfrac{1}{2}$ **65.** $\dfrac{2}{3}$ **67.** a **69.** c **71.** multiplied by 8 **73.** multiplied by 2

75. **77.**

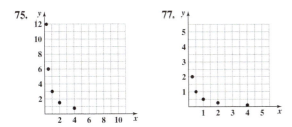

Chapter 7 Vocabulary Check
1. complex fraction **2.** long division **3.** directly **4.** inversely **5.** least common denominator
6. synthetic division **7.** jointly **8.** opposites **9.** rational expression **10.** equation, expression

Chapter 7 Review
1. all real numbers **3.** all real numbers except 5 **5.** all real numbers except 0 and -8 **7.** -1 **9.** $\dfrac{1}{x-1}$
11. $\dfrac{2(x-3)}{x-4}$ **13.** $-\dfrac{3}{2}$ **15.** $\dfrac{a-b}{2a}$ **17.** $\dfrac{12}{5}$ **19.** $\dfrac{a-b}{5a}$ **21.** $-\dfrac{1}{x}$ **23.** $60x^2 y^5$ **25.** $5x(x-5)$ **27.** $\dfrac{4+x}{x-4}$
29. $\dfrac{3}{2(x-2)}$ **31.** $\dfrac{-7x-6}{5(x-3)(x+3)}$ **33.** $\dfrac{5a-1}{(a-1)^2(a+1)}$ **35.** $\dfrac{5-2x}{2(x-1)}$ **37.** $\dfrac{4-3x}{8+x}$ **39.** $\dfrac{5(4x-3)}{2(5x^2-2)}$ **41.** $\dfrac{x(5y+1)}{3y}$

A32 Answers to Selected Exercises

43. $\dfrac{1+x}{1-x}$ **45.** $\dfrac{3}{a+h}$ **47.** $\dfrac{\frac{3}{a+h}-\frac{3}{a}}{h}$ **49.** $1+\dfrac{x}{2y}-\dfrac{9}{4xy}$ **51.** $3x^3+9x^2+2x+6-\dfrac{2}{x-3}$ **53.** $x^2-1+\dfrac{5}{2x+3}$
55. $3x^2+6x+24+\dfrac{44}{x-2}$ **57.** $x^2+3x+9-\dfrac{54}{x-3}$ **59.** 3043 **61.** $\dfrac{365}{32}$ **63.** solution **65.** solution; $-2, \dfrac{1}{3}, 3$ **67.** 6 **69.** $\dfrac{3}{2}$
71. $\dfrac{2x+5}{x(x-7)}$ **73.** $\dfrac{-5(x+6)}{2x(x-3)}$ **75.** $R_2=\dfrac{RR_1}{R_1-R}$ **77.** $r=\dfrac{A-P}{Pt}$ **79.** 1, 2 **81.** $1\dfrac{23}{37}$ hr **83.** 8 mph **85.** 9 **87.** 2 **89.** $\dfrac{3}{5x}$
91. $\dfrac{5(a-2)}{7}$ **93.** $\dfrac{13}{3x}$ **95.** $\dfrac{1}{x-2}$ **97.** $\dfrac{2}{15-2x}$ **99.** $\dfrac{2(x-1)}{x+6}$ **101.** 2 **103.** $\dfrac{23}{25}$ **105.** 10 hr **107.** $63\dfrac{2}{3}$ mph; 45 mph **109.** 64π sq in.

Chapter 7 Test
1. all real numbers except 1 **2.** all real numbers except -3 and -1 **3.** $-\dfrac{7}{8}$ **4.** $\dfrac{x}{x+9}$ **5.** x^2+2x+4
6. $\dfrac{5}{3x}$ **7.** $\dfrac{3}{x^3}$ **8.** $\dfrac{x+2}{2(x+3)}$ **9.** $-\dfrac{4(2x+9)}{5}$ **10.** -1 **11.** $\dfrac{1}{x(x+3)}$ **12.** $\dfrac{5x-2}{(x-3)(x+2)(x-2)}$ **13.** $\dfrac{-x+30}{6(x-7)}$
14. $\dfrac{3}{2}$ **15.** $\dfrac{64}{3}$ **16.** $\dfrac{(x-3)^2}{x-2}$ **17.** $\dfrac{4xy}{3z}+\dfrac{3}{z}+1$ **18.** $2x^2-x-2+\dfrac{2}{2x+1}$ **19.** $4x^3-15x^2+45x-136+\dfrac{407}{x+3}$
20. 91 **21.** 8 **22.** $\dfrac{2}{7}$ **23.** 3 **24.** $x=\dfrac{7a^2+b^2}{4a-b}$ **25.** 5 **26.** $\dfrac{6}{7}$ hr **27.** 16 **28.** 9 **29.** 256 ft **30.** solution; $-2, \dfrac{1}{2}, 3$

Chapter 7 Standardized Test
1. b **2.** a **3.** d **4.** c **5.** c **6.** a **7.** c **8.** c **9.** d **10.** a **11.** b **12.** d **13.** b **14.** c **15.** d **16.** a **17.** a **18.** b
19. a **20.** b **21.** a **22.** b **23.** c **24.** d **25.** d **26.** b **27.** a **28.** a **29.** d **30.** c

CHAPTER 8 RATIONAL EXPONENTS, RADICALS, AND COMPLEX NUMBERS

Section 8.1
Practice Exercises
1. a. 7 **b.** 0 **c.** $\dfrac{4}{9}$ **d.** 0.8 **e.** z^4 **f.** $4b^2$ **g.** -6 **h.** not a real number **2.** 6.708 **3. a.** -1 **b.** 3 **c.** $\dfrac{3}{4}$ **d.** x^4 **e.** $-2x$
4. a. 10 **b.** -1 **c.** -9 **d.** not a real number **e.** $3x^3$ **5. a.** 4 **b.** $|x^7|$ **c.** $|x+7|$ **d.** -7 **e.** $3x-5$ **f.** $7|x|$ **g.** $|x+2|$
6. a. 4 **b.** 2 **c.** 2 **d.** -2 **7.** [graph with (0,−2), (2,2), (7,3)] **8.** [graph with (−8,−6), (−1,−5), (0,−4), (1,−3), (8,−2)]

Vocabulary and Readiness Check 8.1
1. index; radical sign; radicand **3.** is not **5.** $x \geq 0$ **7.** (16, 4) **9.** d **11.** d

Exercise Set 8.1
1. 10 **3.** $\dfrac{1}{2}$ **5.** 0.01 **7.** -6 **9.** x^5 **11.** $4y^3$ **13.** 2.646 **15.** 6.164 **17.** 14.142 **19.** 4 **21.** $\dfrac{1}{2}$
23. -1 **25.** x^4 **27.** $-3x^3$ **29.** -2 **31.** not a real number **33.** -2 **35.** x^4 **37.** $2x^2$ **39.** $9x^2$ **41.** $4x^2$
43. 8 **45.** -8 **47.** $2|x|$ **49.** x **51.** $|x-5|$ **53.** $|x+2|$ **55.** -11 **57.** $2x$ **59.** y^6 **61.** $5ab^{10}$
63. $-3x^4y^3$ **65.** a^4b **67.** $-2x^2y$ **69.** $\dfrac{5}{7}$ **71.** $\dfrac{x}{2y}$ **73.** $-\dfrac{z^7}{3x}$ **75.** $\dfrac{x}{2}$ **77.** $\sqrt{3}$ **79.** -1 **81.** -3 **83.** $\sqrt{7}$
85. $x \geq 0$; **87.** $x \geq 3$; 0, 1, 2, 3 **89.** all real numbers; **91.** all real numbers; 0, 1, -1, 2, -2

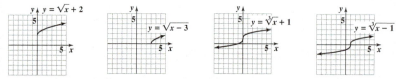

93. $-32x^{15}y^{10}$ **95.** $-60x^7y^{10}z^5$ **97.** $\dfrac{x^9y^5}{2}$ **99.** not a real number   **101.** not a real number   **103.** answers may vary   **105.** 13; b   **107.** 18; b
109. 1.69 sq m   **111.** answers may vary   **113.** 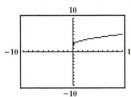   **115.**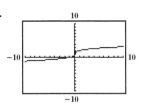

Section 8.2
Practice Exercises
1. a. 6   **b.** 10   **c.** $\sqrt[5]{x}$ **d.** 1   **e.** -8 **f.** $5x^3$ **g.** $\sqrt[4]{3x}$ **2. a.** 64   **b.** -1 **c.** -27 **d.** $\dfrac{1}{125}$ **e.** $\sqrt[9]{(3x+2)^5}$
3. a. $\dfrac{1}{27}$ **b.** $\dfrac{1}{16}$ **4. a.** $y^{10/3}$ **b.** $x^{17/20}$ **c.** $\dfrac{1}{9}$ **d.** $b^{2/9}$ **e.** $\dfrac{81}{x^3y^{11/3}}$ **5. a.** $x^{14/15} - x^{13/5}$ **b.** $x + 4x^{1/2} - 12$ **6.** $x^{-1/5}(2 - 7x)$
7. a. $\sqrt[3]{x}$ **b.** $\sqrt{6}$ **c.** $\sqrt[4]{a^2b}$ **8. a.** $\sqrt[12]{x^7}$ **b.** $\sqrt[15]{y^2}$ **c.** $\sqrt[6]{675}$

Vocabulary and Readiness Check 8.2
1. true   **3.** true   **5.** multiply; c   **7.** A   **9.** C   **11.** B

Exercise Set 8.2
1. 7   **3.** 3   **5.** $\dfrac{1}{2}$ **7.** 13   **9.** $2\sqrt[3]{m}$ **11.** $3x^2$ **13.** -3 **15.** -2 **17.** 8   **19.** 16   **21.** not a real number   **23.** $\sqrt[5]{(2x)^3}$
25. $\sqrt[3]{(7x+2)^2}$ **27.** $\dfrac{64}{27}$ **29.** $\dfrac{1}{16}$ **31.** $\dfrac{1}{16}$ **33.** not a real number   **35.** $\dfrac{1}{x^{1/4}}$ **37.** $a^{2/3}$ **39.** $\dfrac{5x^{3/4}}{7}$ **41.** $a^{7/3}$ **43.** x **45.** $3^{5/8}$
47. $y^{1/6}$ **49.** $8u^3$ **51.** $-b$ **53.** $\dfrac{1}{x^2}$ **55.** $27x^{2/3}$ **57.** $\dfrac{y}{z^{1/6}}$ **59.** $\dfrac{1}{x^{7/4}}$ **61.** $y - y^{7/6}$ **63.** $x^{5/3} - 2x^{2/3}$ **65.** $4x^{2/3} - 9$ **67.** $x^{8/3}(1 + x^{2/3})$
69. $x^{1/5}(x^{1/5} - 3)$ **71.** $x^{-1/3}(5 + x)$ **73.** $\sqrt{x}$ **75.** $\sqrt[3]{2}$ **77.** $2\sqrt{x}$ **79.** $\sqrt{xy}$ **81.** $\sqrt[3]{a^2b}$ **83.** $\sqrt{x+3}$ **85.** $\sqrt[15]{y^{11}}$
87. $\sqrt[12]{b^5}$ **89.** $\sqrt[24]{x^{23}}$ **91.** $\sqrt{a}$ **93.** $\sqrt[6]{432}$ **95.** $\sqrt[15]{343y^5}$ **97.** $\sqrt[6]{125r^3s^2}$ **99.** $25 \cdot 3$ **101.** $16 \cdot 3$ or $4 \cdot 12$ **103.** $8 \cdot 2$ **105.** $27 \cdot 2$
107. 1509 calories   **109.** 210.1 million   **111.** $a^{1/3}$ **113.** $x^{1/5}$ **115.** 1.6818   **117.** 5.6645   **119.** $\dfrac{t^{1/2}}{u^{1/2}}$

Section 8.3
Practice Exercises
1. a. $\sqrt{35}$ **b.** $\sqrt{13z}$ **c.** 5   **d.** $\sqrt[3]{15x^2y}$ **e.** $\sqrt{\dfrac{5t}{2m}}$ **2. a.** $\dfrac{6}{7}$ **b.** $\dfrac{\sqrt{z}}{4}$ **c.** $\dfrac{5}{2}$ **d.** $\dfrac{\sqrt[4]{5}}{3r^2}$ **3. a.** $7\sqrt{2}$ **b.** $3\sqrt[3]{2}$ **c.** $\sqrt{35}$ **d.** $3\sqrt[4]{3}$
4. a. $6z^3\sqrt{z}$ **b.** $2pq^2\sqrt[3]{4pq}$ **c.** $2x^3\sqrt[4]{x^3}$ **5. a.** 4   **b.** $\dfrac{7}{3}\sqrt{z}$ **c.** $10xy^2\sqrt[3]{x^2}$ **d.** $6x^2y\sqrt[5]{2y}$ **6.** $\sqrt{17} \approx 4.123$ **7.** $\left(\dfrac{13}{2}, -4\right)$

Vocabulary and Readiness Check 8.3
1. midpoint; point   **3.** midpoint   **5.** false   **7.** true   **9.** false

Exercise Set 8.3
1. $\sqrt{14}$ **3.** 2   **5.** $\sqrt[3]{36}$ **7.** $\sqrt{6x}$ **9.** $\sqrt{\dfrac{14}{xy}}$ **11.** $\sqrt[4]{20x^3}$ **13.** $\dfrac{\sqrt{6}}{7}$ **15.** $\dfrac{\sqrt{2}}{7}$ **17.** $\dfrac{\sqrt[4]{x^3}}{2}$ **19.** $\dfrac{\sqrt[3]{4}}{3}$ **21.** $\dfrac{\sqrt[4]{8}}{x^2}$ **23.** $\dfrac{\sqrt[3]{2x}}{3y^4\sqrt[3]{3}}$
25. $\dfrac{x\sqrt{y}}{10}$ **27.** $\dfrac{x\sqrt{5}}{2y}$ **29.** $-\dfrac{z^2\sqrt[3]{z}}{3x}$ **31.** $4\sqrt{2}$ **33.** $4\sqrt[3]{3}$ **35.** $25\sqrt{3}$ **37.** $2\sqrt{6}$ **39.** $10x^2\sqrt{x}$ **41.** $2y^2\sqrt[3]{2y}$ **43.** $a^2b\sqrt[4]{b^3}$
45. $y^2\sqrt{y}$ **47.** $5ab\sqrt{b}$ **49.** $-2x^2\sqrt[5]{y}$ **51.** $x^4\sqrt[3]{50x^2}$ **53.** $-4a^4b^3\sqrt{2b}$ **55.** $3x^3y^4\sqrt[4]{xy}$ **57.** $5r^3s^4$ **59.** $\sqrt{2}$ **61.** 2   **63.** 10
65. x^2y **67.** $24m^2$ **69.** $\dfrac{15x\sqrt{2x}}{2}$ or $\dfrac{15x}{2}\sqrt{2x}$ **71.** $2a^2\sqrt{2}$ **73.** 5 units   **75.** $\sqrt{41}$ units ≈ 6.403 **77.** $\sqrt{10}$ units ≈ 3.162
79. $\sqrt{5}$ units ≈ 2.236 **81.** $\sqrt{192.58}$ units ≈ 13.877 **83.** $(4, -2)$ **85.** $\left(-5, \dfrac{5}{2}\right)$ **87.** $(3, 0)$ **89.** $\left(-\dfrac{1}{2}, \dfrac{1}{2}\right)$ **91.** $\left(\sqrt{2}, \dfrac{\sqrt{5}}{2}\right)$
93. $(6.2, -6.65)$ **95.** $14x$ **97.** $2x^2 - 7x - 15$ **99.** y^2 **101.** $-3x - 15$ **103.** $x^2 - 8x + 16$ **105.** $\dfrac{\sqrt[3]{64}}{\sqrt{64}} = \dfrac{4}{8} = \dfrac{1}{2}$ **107.** x^7 **109.** a^3bc^5
111. $z^{10}\sqrt[3]{z^2}$ **113.** $q^2r^5s\sqrt[4]{q^3r^5}$ **115.** $r = 1.6$ meters   **117. a.** 3.8 times   **b.** 2.9 times   **c.** answers may vary

Section 8.4
Practice Exercises
1. a. $8\sqrt{17}$ b. $-5\sqrt[3]{5z}$ c. $3\sqrt{2} + 5\sqrt[3]{2}$ 2. a. $11\sqrt{6}$ b. $-9\sqrt[3]{3}$ c. $-2\sqrt{3x}$ d. $2\sqrt{10} + 2\sqrt[3]{5}$ e. $4x\sqrt[3]{3x}$ 3. a. $\dfrac{5\sqrt{7}}{12}$
b. $\dfrac{13\sqrt[3]{6y}}{4}$ 4. a. $2\sqrt{5} + 5\sqrt{3}$ b. $2\sqrt{3} + 2\sqrt{2} - \sqrt{30} - 2\sqrt{5}$ c. $6z + \sqrt{z} - 12$ d. $-6\sqrt{6} + 15$ e. $5x - 9$ f. $6\sqrt{x+2} + x + 11$

Vocabulary and Readiness Check 8.4
1. Unlike   3. Like   5. $6\sqrt{3}$ 7. $7\sqrt{x}$ 9. $8\sqrt[3]{x}$ 11. $\sqrt{11} + \sqrt[3]{11}$ 13. $10\sqrt[3]{2x}$

Exercise Set 8.4
1. $-2\sqrt{2}$ 3. $10x\sqrt{2x}$ 5. $17\sqrt{2} - 15\sqrt{5}$ 7. $-\sqrt[3]{2x}$ 9. $5b\sqrt{b}$ 11. $\dfrac{31\sqrt{2}}{15}$ 13. $\dfrac{\sqrt[3]{11}}{3}$ 15. $\dfrac{5\sqrt{5x}}{9}$ 17. $14 + \sqrt{3}$ 19. $7 - 3y$
21. $6\sqrt{3} - 6\sqrt{2}$ 23. $-23\sqrt[3]{5}$ 25. $2b\sqrt{b}$ 27. $20y\sqrt{2y}$ 29. $2y\sqrt[3]{2x}$ 31. $6\sqrt[3]{11} - 4\sqrt{11}$ 33. $4x\sqrt[4]{x^3}$ 35. $\dfrac{2\sqrt{3}}{3}$ 37. $\dfrac{5x\sqrt[3]{x}}{7}$
39. $\dfrac{5\sqrt{7}}{2x}$ 41. $\dfrac{\sqrt[3]{2}}{6}$ 43. $\dfrac{14x\sqrt[3]{2x}}{9}$ 45. $15\sqrt{3}$ in.   47. $\sqrt{35} + \sqrt{21}$ 49. $7 - 2\sqrt{10}$ 51. $3\sqrt{x} - x\sqrt{3}$ 53. $6x - 13\sqrt{x} - 5$
55. $\sqrt[3]{a^2} + \sqrt[3]{a} - 20$ 57. $6\sqrt{2} - 12$ 59. $2 + 2x\sqrt{3}$ 61. $-16 - \sqrt{35}$ 63. $x - y^2$ 65. $3 + 2x\sqrt{3} + x^2$ 67. $23x - 5x\sqrt{15}$
69. $2\sqrt[3]{2} - \sqrt[3]{4}$ 71. $x + 1$ 73. $x + 24 + 10\sqrt{x-1}$ 75. $2x + 6 - 2\sqrt{2x+5}$ 77. $x - 7$ 79. $\dfrac{7}{x+y}$ 81. $2a - 3$ 83. $\dfrac{-2 + \sqrt{3}}{3}$
85. $22\sqrt{5}$ ft; 150 sq ft   87. a. $2\sqrt{3}$ b. 3 c. answers may vary   89. answers may vary

Section 8.5
Practice Exercises
1. a. $\dfrac{5\sqrt{3}}{3}$ b. $\dfrac{15\sqrt{x}}{2x}$ c. $\dfrac{\sqrt[3]{6}}{3}$ 2. $\dfrac{\sqrt{15yz}}{5y}$ 3. $\dfrac{\sqrt[3]{z^2x^2}}{3x^2}$ 4. a. $\dfrac{5(3\sqrt{5} - 2)}{41}$ b. $\dfrac{\sqrt{6} + 5\sqrt{3} + \sqrt{10} + 5\sqrt{5}}{-2}$ c. $\dfrac{6x - 3\sqrt{xy}}{4x - y}$
5. $\dfrac{2}{\sqrt{10}}$ 6. $\dfrac{5b}{\sqrt[3]{50ab^2}}$ 7. $\dfrac{x - 9}{4(\sqrt{x} + 3)}$

Vocabulary and Readiness Check 8.5
1. conjugate   3. rationalizing the numerator   5. $\sqrt{2} - x$ 7. $5 + \sqrt{a}$ 9. $-7\sqrt{5} - 8\sqrt{x}$

Exercise Set 8.5
1. $\dfrac{\sqrt{14}}{7}$ 3. $\dfrac{\sqrt{5}}{5}$ 5. $\dfrac{2\sqrt{x}}{x}$ 7. $\dfrac{4\sqrt[3]{9}}{3}$ 9. $\dfrac{3\sqrt{2x}}{4x}$ 11. $\dfrac{3\sqrt[3]{2x}}{2x}$ 13. $\dfrac{3\sqrt{3a}}{a}$ 15. $\dfrac{3\sqrt[3]{4}}{2}$ 17. $\dfrac{2\sqrt{21}}{7}$ 19. $\dfrac{\sqrt{10xy}}{5y}$ 21. $\dfrac{\sqrt[3]{75}}{5}$
23. $\dfrac{\sqrt{6x}}{10}$ 25. $\dfrac{\sqrt{3z}}{6z}$ 27. $\dfrac{\sqrt[3]{6xy^2}}{3x}$ 29. $\dfrac{3\sqrt[4]{2}}{2}$ 31. $\dfrac{2\sqrt[4]{9x}}{3x^2}$ 33. $\dfrac{5a\sqrt[5]{4ab^4}}{2a^2b^3}$ 35. $-2(2 + \sqrt{7})$ 37. $\dfrac{7(3 + \sqrt{x})}{9 - x}$ 39. $-5 + 2\sqrt{6}$
41. $\dfrac{2a + 2\sqrt{a} + \sqrt{ab} + \sqrt{b}}{4a - b}$ 43. $-\dfrac{8(1 - \sqrt{10})}{9}$ 45. $\dfrac{x - \sqrt{xy}}{x - y}$ 47. $\dfrac{5 + 3\sqrt{2}}{7}$ 49. $\dfrac{5}{\sqrt{15}}$ 51. $\dfrac{6}{\sqrt{10}}$ 53. $\dfrac{2x}{7\sqrt{x}}$ 55. $\dfrac{5y}{\sqrt[3]{100xy}}$
57. $\dfrac{2}{\sqrt{10}}$ 59. $\dfrac{2x}{11\sqrt{2x}}$ 61. $\dfrac{7}{2\sqrt[3]{49}}$ 63. $\dfrac{3x^2}{10\sqrt[3]{9x}}$ 65. $\dfrac{6x^2y^3}{\sqrt{6z}}$ 67. answers may vary   69. $\dfrac{-7}{12 + 6\sqrt{11}}$ 71. $\dfrac{3}{10 + 5\sqrt{7}}$
73. $\dfrac{x - 9}{x - 3\sqrt{x}}$ 75. $\dfrac{1}{3 + 2\sqrt{2}}$ 77. $\dfrac{x - 1}{x - 2\sqrt{x} + 1}$ 79. 5   81. $-\dfrac{1}{2}, 6$ 83. 2, 6   85. $\sqrt[3]{25}$ 87. $r = \dfrac{\sqrt{A\pi}}{2\pi}$ 89. answers may vary

Integrated Review
1. 9   2. -2 3. $\dfrac{1}{2}$ 4. x^3 5. y^3 6. $2y^5$ 7. $-2y$ 8. $3b^3$ 9. 6   10. $\sqrt[4]{3y}$ 11. $\dfrac{1}{16}$ 12. $\sqrt[5]{(x+1)^3}$ 13. y 14. $16x^{1/2}$
15. $x^{5/4}$ 16. $4^{11/15}$ 17. $2x^2$ 18. $\sqrt[4]{a^3b^2}$ 19. $\sqrt[4]{x^3}$ 20. $\sqrt[6]{500}$ 21. $2\sqrt{10}$ 22. $2xy^2\sqrt[4]{x^3y^2}$ 23. $3x\sqrt[3]{2x}$ 24. $-2b^2\sqrt[5]{2}$
25. $\sqrt{5x}$ 26. $4x$ 27. $7y^2\sqrt{y}$ 28. $2a^2\sqrt[3]{3}$ 29. $2\sqrt{5} - 5\sqrt{3} + 5\sqrt{7}$ 30. $y\sqrt[3]{2y}$ 31. $\sqrt{15} - \sqrt{6}$ 32. $10 + 2\sqrt{21}$
33. $4x^2 - 5$ 34. $x + 2 - 2\sqrt{x+1}$ 35. $\dfrac{\sqrt{21}}{3}$ 36. $\dfrac{5\sqrt[3]{4x}}{2x}$ 37. $\dfrac{13 - 3\sqrt{21}}{5}$ 38. $\dfrac{7}{\sqrt{21}}$ 39. $\dfrac{3y}{\sqrt[3]{33y^2}}$ 40. $\dfrac{x - 4}{x + 2\sqrt{x}}$

Section 8.6
Practice Exercises
1. 18 **2.** $\frac{3}{8}, -\frac{1}{2}$ **3.** 10 **4.** 9 **5.** $\frac{3}{25}$ **6.** $6\sqrt{3}$ meters **7.** $\sqrt{193}$ in. $\approx$ 13.89 in.

Graphing Calculator Explorations 8.6
1. 3.19 **3.** no solution **5.** 3.23

Vocabulary and Readiness Check 8.6
1. extraneous solution **3.** $x^2 - 10x + 25$

Exercise Set 8.6
1. 8 **3.** 7 **5.** no solution **7.** 7 **9.** 6 **11.** $-\frac{9}{2}$ **13.** 29 **15.** 4 **17.** -4 **19.** no solution **21.** 7 **23.** 9 **25.** 50 **27.** no solution
29. $\frac{15}{4}$ **31.** 13 **33.** 5 **35.** -12 **37.** 9 **39.** -3 **41.** 1 **43.** 1 **45.** $\frac{1}{2}$ **47.** 0, 4 **49.** $\frac{37}{4}$ **51.** $3\sqrt{5}$ ft **53.** $2\sqrt{10}$ m
55. $2\sqrt{131}$ m $\approx$ 22.9 m **57.** $\sqrt{100.84}$ mm $\approx$ 10.0 mm **59.** 17 ft **61.** 13 ft **63.** 14,657,415 sq mi **65.** 100 ft **67.** 100
69. $\frac{\pi}{2}$ sec $\approx$ 1.57 sec **71.** 12.97 ft **73.** answers may vary **75.** $15\sqrt{3}$ sq mi $\approx$ 25.98 sq mi **77.** answers may vary **79.** 0.51 km
81. function **83.** function **85.** not a function **87.** $\frac{x}{4x+3}$ **89.** $-\frac{4z+2}{3z}$
91. $\sqrt{5x-1} + 4 = 7$ **93.** 1 **95. a.–b.** answers may vary **97.** $-1, 2$ **99.** $-8, -6, 0, 2$
$\sqrt{5x-1} = 3$
$(\sqrt{5x-1})^2 = 3^2$
$5x - 1 = 9$
$5x = 10$
$x = 2$

Section 8.7
Practice Exercises
1. a. $2i$ **b.** $i\sqrt{7}$ **c.** $-3i\sqrt{2}$ **2. a.** $-\sqrt{30}$ **b.** -3 **c.** $25i$ **d.** $3i$ **3.** imaginary **4. a.** $-1 - 4i$ **b.** $-3 + 5i$
c. $3 - 2i$ **5. a.** 20 **b.** $-5 + 10i$
c. $15 + 16i$ **d.** $8 - 6i$ **e.** 85 **6. a.** $\frac{11}{10} - \frac{7i}{10}$ **b.** $0 - \frac{5i}{2}$
7. a. i **b.** 1 **c.** -1 **d.** 1

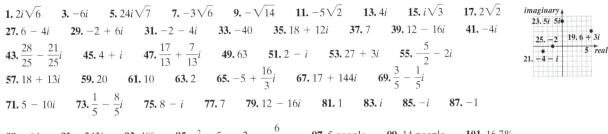

Vocabulary and Readiness Check 8.7
1. complex **3.** -1 **5.** real **7.** $9i$ **9.** $i\sqrt{7}$ **11.** -4 **13.** $8i$

Exercise Set 8.7
1. $2i\sqrt{6}$ **3.** $-6i$ **5.** $24i\sqrt{7}$ **7.** $-3\sqrt{6}$ **9.** $-\sqrt{14}$ **11.** $-5\sqrt{2}$ **13.** $4i$ **15.** $i\sqrt{3}$ **17.** $2\sqrt{2}$
27. $6 - 4i$ **29.** $-2 + 6i$ **31.** $-2 - 4i$ **33.** -40 **35.** $18 + 12i$ **37.** 7 **39.** $12 - 16i$ **41.** $-4i$
43. $\frac{28}{25} - \frac{21}{25}i$ **45.** $4 + i$ **47.** $\frac{17}{13} + \frac{7}{13}i$ **49.** 63 **51.** $2 - i$ **53.** $27 + 3i$ **55.** $-\frac{5}{2} - 2i$
57. $18 + 13i$ **59.** 20 **61.** 10 **63.** 2 **65.** $-5 + \frac{16}{3}i$ **67.** $17 + 144i$ **69.** $\frac{3}{5} - \frac{1}{5}i$
71. $5 - 10i$ **73.** $\frac{1}{5} - \frac{8}{5}i$ **75.** $8 - i$ **77.** 7 **79.** $12 - 16i$ **81.** 1 **83.** i **85.** $-i$ **87.** -1
89. -64 **91.** $-243i$ **93.** $40°$ **95.** $x^2 - 5x - 2 - \frac{6}{x-1}$ **97.** 5 people **99.** 14 people **101.** 16.7%
103. $-1 - i$ **105.** 0 **107.** $2 + 3i$ **109.** $2 + i\sqrt{2}$ **111.** $\frac{1}{2} - \frac{\sqrt{3}}{2}i$
113. answers may vary **115.** $6 - 6i$ **117.** yes

Section 8.8
Practice Exercises
1. 33 **2.** median: 39.5; mode: 45 **3.** 9 **4.** mean: 6;

Data item	Deviation
2	−4
4	−2
7	1
11	5

5. ≈ 3.92 **6.** sample A: 3.74; sample B: 28.06 **7. a.** Small-Company Stocks **b.** Small-Company Stocks; answers may vary

Exercise Set 8.8
1. mean: 29, median: 28, no mode **3.** mean: 8.1, median: 8.2, mode: 8.2 **5.** mean: 0.6, median: 0.6, mode: 0.2 and 0.6
7. mean: 370.9, median: 313.5, no mode **9.** 73 **11.** 70 and 71 **13.** 9 **15.** 4 **17.** 8 **19.** 2
21. a.

Data item	Deviation
3	−9
5	−7
7	−5
12	0
18	6
27	15

b. 0

23. a.

Data item	Deviation
29	−20
38	−11
48	−1
49	0
53	4
77	28

b. 0

25. a. 91 **b.**

Data item	Deviation
85	−6
95	4
90	−1
85	−6
100	9

c. 0

27. a. 155 **b.**

Data item	Deviation
146	−9
153	−2
155	0
160	5
161	6

c. 0

29. a. 2.70 **b.**

Data item	Deviation
2.25	−0.45
3.50	0.80
2.75	0.05
3.10	0.40
1.90	−0.80

c. 0

31. ≈ 1.58 **33.** ≈ 3.46 **35.** ≈ 0.89 **37.** 3 **39.** ≈ 2.14
41. Sample A: mean: 12; range: 12; standard deviation: ≈ 4.32
Sample B: mean: 12; range: 12; standard deviation: ≈ 5.07
Sample C: mean: 12; range: 12; standard deviation: 6
The samples have the same mean and range, but different standard deviations.
43. 0 **45.** 1 **47. a.** Best Actor; Most of the ages for Best Actor are in the upper 30s and lower 40s while all of the ages for Best Actress are in the upper 20s and lower 30s. **b.** Best Actor: 38.57; Best Actress: 30.71 **c.** Best Actor; There is greater spread in the ages for Best Actor, since one age, 29, is much lower than the other ages. **d.** Best Actor: 5.68; Best Actress: 3.77 **49.** 21, 21, 24 **51., 53., 55.** answers may vary **57.** a **59.** answers may vary **61.** The mean is increased by 2; The standard deviation is unaffected.

Chapter 8 Vocabulary Check
1. conjugate **2.** principal square root **3.** rationalizing **4.** imaginary unit **5.** cube root **6.** index, radicand **7.** like radicals **8.** complex number **9.** distance **10.** midpoint **11.** mode **12.** mean **13.** range **14.** median **15.** standard deviation

Chapter 8 Review
1. 9 **3.** −2 **5.** $-\frac{1}{7}$ **7.** −6 **9.** $-a^2b^3$ **11.** $2ab^2$ **13.** $\frac{x^6}{6y}$ **15.** $|x|$ **17.** −27 **19.** $-x$ **21.** $5|(x-y)^5|$ **23.** $-x$
25. all real numbers; −2, −1, 0, 1, 2 **27.** $-\frac{1}{3}$ **29.** $-\frac{1}{4}$ **31.** $\frac{1}{4}$ **33.** $\frac{343}{125}$ **35.** not a real number **37.** $5^{1/5}x^{2/5}y^{3/5}$ **39.** $5\sqrt[3]{xy^2z^5}$

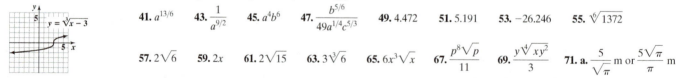

41. $a^{13/6}$ **43.** $\frac{1}{a^{9/2}}$ **45.** a^4b^6 **47.** $\frac{b^{5/6}}{49a^{1/4}c^{5/3}}$ **49.** 4.472 **51.** 5.191 **53.** −26.246 **55.** $\sqrt[6]{1372}$
57. $2\sqrt{6}$ **59.** $2x$ **61.** $2\sqrt{15}$ **63.** $3\sqrt[3]{6}$ **65.** $6x^3\sqrt{x}$ **67.** $\frac{p^8\sqrt{p}}{11}$ **69.** $\frac{y\sqrt[4]{xy^2}}{3}$ **71. a.** $\frac{5}{\sqrt{\pi}}$ m or $\frac{5\sqrt{\pi}}{\pi}$ m
b. 5.75 in. **73.** $\sqrt{130}$ units ≈ 11.402 **75.** $7\sqrt{2}$ units ≈ 9.899 **77.** $\sqrt{275.6}$ units ≈ 16.601 **79.** $\left(-\frac{15}{2}, 1\right)$ **81.** $\left(\frac{1}{20}, -\frac{3}{16}\right)$
83. $(\sqrt{3}, -3\sqrt{6})$ **85.** $2x\sqrt{3xy}$ **87.** $3a\sqrt[4]{2a}$ **89.** $\frac{3\sqrt{2}}{4x}$ **91.** $-4ab\sqrt[4]{2b}$ **93.** $x - 6\sqrt{x} + 9$ **95.** $4x - 9y$ **97.** $\sqrt[3]{a^2} + 4\sqrt[3]{a} + 4$
99. $a + 64$ **101.** $\frac{\sqrt{3x}}{6}$ **103.** $\frac{2x^2\sqrt{2x}}{y}$ **105.** $-\frac{10 + 5\sqrt{7}}{3}$ **107.** $-5 + 2\sqrt{6}$ **109.** $\frac{6}{\sqrt{2y}}$ **111.** $\frac{4x^3}{y\sqrt{2x}}$ **113.** $\frac{x - 25}{-3\sqrt{x} + 15}$
115. no solution **117.** no solution **119.** 16 **121.** $\sqrt{241}$ **123.** 4.24 ft **125.** $-i\sqrt{6}$ **127.** $-\sqrt{10}$ **129.** $-13 - 3i$ **131.** $-12 - 18i$

133. $-5 - 12i$ **135.** $\frac{3}{2} - i$ **137.**   **139.** mean: 25.6, median: 28, mode: 28   **141. a.**

Data item	Deviation
29	−6
9	−26
8	−27
22	−13
46	11
51	16
48	13
42	7
53	18
42	7

b. 0

143. ≈ 4.05 **145.** mean: 49, range: 76; standard deviation: ≈ 24.32 **147.** x **149.** -10 **151.** $\frac{y^5}{2x^3}$ **153.** $\frac{1}{8}$ **155.** $\frac{1}{x^{13/2}}$ **157.** $\frac{n\sqrt{3n}}{11m^5}$
159. $4x - 20\sqrt{x} + 25$ **161.** (4, 16)   **163.** $\frac{2\sqrt{x} - 6}{x - 9}$

Chapter 8 Test
1. $6\sqrt{6}$ **2.** $-x^{16}$ **3.** $\frac{1}{5}$ **4.** 5   **5.** $\frac{4x^2}{9}$ **6.** $-a^6b^3$ **7.** $\frac{8a^{1/3}c^{2/3}}{b^{5/12}}$ **8.** $a^{7/12} - a^{7/3}$ **9.** $|4xy|$ or $4|xy|$ **10.** -27 **11.** $\frac{3\sqrt{y}}{y}$
12. $\frac{8 - 6\sqrt{x} + x}{8 - 2x}$ **13.** $\frac{\sqrt[3]{b^2}}{b}$ **14.** $\frac{6 - x^2}{8(\sqrt{6} - x)}$ **15.** $-x\sqrt{5x}$ **16.** $4\sqrt{3} - \sqrt{6}$ **17.** $x + 2\sqrt{x} + 1$ **18.** $\sqrt{6} - 4\sqrt{3} + \sqrt{2} - 4$
19. -20 **20.** 23.685   **21.** 0.019   **22.** 2, 3   **23.** no solution   **24.** 6   **25.** $-2i\sqrt{2}$ **26.** $-3i$ **27.** 40   **28.** $7 + 24i$ **29.** $-\frac{3}{2} + \frac{5}{2}i$
30. 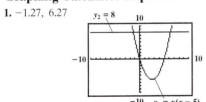   **31.** $\frac{5\sqrt{2}}{2}$ **32.** $x \geq -2$ 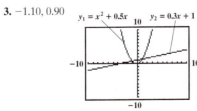; 0, 1, 2, 3   **33.** $2\sqrt{26}$ units   **34.** $\sqrt{95}$ units   **35.** $\left(-4, \frac{7}{2}\right)$ **36.** $\left(-\frac{1}{2}, \frac{3}{10}\right)$
37. 27 mph   **38.** 360 ft   **39.** 3.67   **40.** 3   **41.** 3   **42.** 2.34

Chapter 8 Standardized Test
1. c   **2.** d   **3.** d   **4.** a   **5.** c   **6.** b   **7.** b   **8.** b   **9.** d   **10.** b   **11.** a   **12.** c   **13.** a   **14.** d   **15.** b   **16.** c   **17.** c
18. a   **19.** a   **20.** a   **21.** c   **22.** b   **23.** b   **24.** a   **25.** a   **26.** b   **27.** b   **28.** a   **29.** b   **30.** c   **31.** d   **32.** d
33. a   **34.** b   **35.** a   **36.** a   **37.** b   **38.** a   **39.** b   **40.** d   **41.** c   **42.** a

CHAPTER 9 QUADRATIC AND HIGHER EQUATIONS AND FUNCTIONS
Section 9.1
Practice Exercises
1. $-3\sqrt{2}, 3\sqrt{2}$ **2.** $\pm\sqrt{10}$ **3.** $-3 \pm 2\sqrt{5}$ **4.** $\frac{2 + 3i}{5}, \frac{2 - 3i}{5}$ **5.** $-2 \pm \sqrt{7}$ **6.** $\frac{3 \pm \sqrt{5}}{2}$ **7.** $\frac{6 \pm \sqrt{33}}{3}$ **8.** $\frac{5 \pm i\sqrt{31}}{4}$ **9.** 6%

Graphing Calculator Explorations 9.1
1. $-1.27, 6.27$ **3.** $-1.10, 0.90$ **5.** no real solutions

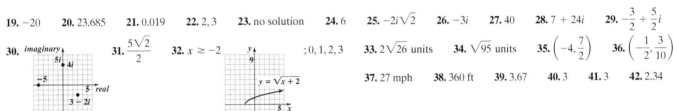

Vocabulary and Readiness Check 9.1
1. $\pm\sqrt{b}$ **3.** completing the square   **5.** 9   **7.** 1   **9.** 49

Exercise Set 9.1

1. $-4, 4$ 3. $-\sqrt{7}, \sqrt{7}$ 5. $-3\sqrt{2}, 3\sqrt{2}$ 7. $-\sqrt{10}, \sqrt{10}$ 9. $-8, -2$ 11. $6 - 3\sqrt{2}, 6 + 3\sqrt{2}$ 13. $\dfrac{3 - 2\sqrt{2}}{2}, \dfrac{3 + 2\sqrt{2}}{2}$
15. $-3i, 3i$ 17. $-\sqrt{6}, \sqrt{6}$ 19. $-2i\sqrt{2}, 2i\sqrt{2}$ 21. $1 - 4i, 1 + 4i$ 23. $-7 - \sqrt{5}, -7 + \sqrt{5}$ 25. $-3 - 2i\sqrt{2}, -3 + 2i\sqrt{2}$
27. $x^2 + 16x + 64 = (x + 8)^2$ 29. $z^2 - 12z + 36 = (z - 6)^2$ 31. $p^2 + 9p + \dfrac{81}{4} = \left(p + \dfrac{9}{2}\right)^2$ 33. $x^2 + x + \dfrac{1}{4} = \left(x + \dfrac{1}{2}\right)^2$ 35. $-5, -3$
37. $-3 - \sqrt{7}, -3 + \sqrt{7}$ 39. $\dfrac{-1 - \sqrt{5}}{2}, \dfrac{-1 + \sqrt{5}}{2}$ 41. $-1 - \sqrt{6}, -1 + \sqrt{6}$ 43. $\dfrac{6 - \sqrt{30}}{3}, \dfrac{6 + \sqrt{30}}{3}$ 45. $\dfrac{3 - \sqrt{11}}{2}, \dfrac{3 + \sqrt{11}}{2}$
47. $-4, \dfrac{1}{2}$ 49. $-1, 5$ 51. $-4 - \sqrt{15}, -4 + \sqrt{15}$ 53. $\dfrac{-3 - \sqrt{21}}{3}, \dfrac{-3 + \sqrt{21}}{3}$ 55. $-1, \dfrac{5}{2}$ 57. $-1 - i, -1 + i$ 59. $3 - \sqrt{6}, 3 + \sqrt{6}$
61. $-2 - i\sqrt{2}, -2 + i\sqrt{2}$ 63. $\dfrac{-15 - 7\sqrt{5}}{10}, \dfrac{-15 + 7\sqrt{5}}{10}$ 65. $\dfrac{1 - i\sqrt{47}}{4}, \dfrac{1 + i\sqrt{47}}{4}$ 67. $-5 - i\sqrt{3}, -5 + i\sqrt{3}$ 69. $-4, 1$
71. $\dfrac{2 - i\sqrt{2}}{2}, \dfrac{2 + i\sqrt{2}}{2}$ 73. $\dfrac{-3 - \sqrt{69}}{6}, \dfrac{-3 + \sqrt{69}}{6}$ 75. 20% 77. 4% 79. answers may vary 81. 8.11 sec 83. 6.73 sec
85. simple; answers may vary 87. $\dfrac{7}{5}$ 89. $\dfrac{1}{5}$ 91. $5 - 10\sqrt{3}$ 93. $\dfrac{3 - 2\sqrt{7}}{4}$ 95. $2\sqrt{7}$ 97. $\sqrt{13}$ 99. complex, but not real numbers
101. real solutions 103. complex, but not real numbers 105. $-6y, 6y$ 107. $-x, x$ 109. 6 in. 111. 16.2 in. $\times$ 21.6 in.
113. 2.828 thousand units or 2828 units

Section 9.2
Practice Exercises

1. $2, -\dfrac{1}{3}$ 2. $\dfrac{4 \pm \sqrt{22}}{3}$ 3. $1 \pm \sqrt{17}$ 4. $\dfrac{-1 \pm i\sqrt{15}}{4}$ 5. a. one real solution b. two real solutions c. two complex, but not real
solutions 6. 6 ft 7. 2.4 sec

Vocabulary and Readiness Check 9.2

1. $x = \dfrac{-b \pm \sqrt{b^2 - 4ac}}{2a}$ 3. $-5; -7$ 5. $1; 0$

Exercise Set 9.2

1. $-6, 1$ 3. $-\dfrac{3}{5}, 1$ 5. 3 7. $\dfrac{-7 - \sqrt{33}}{2}, \dfrac{-7 + \sqrt{33}}{2}$ 9. $\dfrac{1 - \sqrt{57}}{8}, \dfrac{1 + \sqrt{57}}{8}$ 11. $\dfrac{7 - \sqrt{85}}{6}, \dfrac{7 + \sqrt{85}}{6}$ 13. $1 - \sqrt{3}, 1 + \sqrt{3}$
15. $-\dfrac{3}{2}, 1$ 17. $\dfrac{3 - \sqrt{11}}{2}, \dfrac{3 + \sqrt{11}}{2}$ 19. $\dfrac{-5 - \sqrt{17}}{2}, \dfrac{-5 + \sqrt{17}}{2}$ 21. $\dfrac{5}{2}, 1$ 23. $-3 - 2i, -3 + 2i$ 25. $-2 - \sqrt{11}, -2 + \sqrt{11}$
27. $\dfrac{3 - i\sqrt{87}}{8}, \dfrac{3 + i\sqrt{87}}{8}$ 29. $\dfrac{3 - \sqrt{29}}{2}, \dfrac{3 + \sqrt{29}}{2}$ 31. $\dfrac{-5 - i\sqrt{5}}{10}, \dfrac{-5 + i\sqrt{5}}{10}$ 33. $\dfrac{-1 - \sqrt{19}}{6}, \dfrac{-1 + \sqrt{19}}{6}$
35. $\dfrac{-1 - i\sqrt{23}}{4}, \dfrac{-1 + i\sqrt{23}}{4}$ 37. 1 39. $3 + \sqrt{5}, 3 - \sqrt{5}$ 41. two real solutions 43. one real solution 45. two real solutions
47. two complex but not real solutions 49. two real solutions 51. 14 ft 53. $2 + 2\sqrt{2}$ cm, $2 + 2\sqrt{2}$ cm, $4 + 2\sqrt{2}$ cm
55. width: $-5 + 5\sqrt{17}$ ft; length: $5 + 5\sqrt{17}$ ft 57. a. $50\sqrt{2}$ m b. 5000 sq m 59. 37.4 ft by 38.5 ft 61. base, $2 + 2\sqrt{43}$ cm;
height, $-1 + \sqrt{43}$ cm 63. 8.9 sec 65. 2.8 sec 67. $\dfrac{11}{5}$ 69. 15 71. $(x^2 + 5)(x + 2)(x - 2)$ 73. $(z + 3)(z - 3)(z + 2)(z - 2)$
75. b 77. answers may vary 79. 0.6, 2.4 81. Sunday to Monday 83. Wednesday 85. 32; yes 87. a. 8630 stores b. 2011
89. answers may vary 91. $\dfrac{\sqrt{3}}{3}$ 93. $\dfrac{-\sqrt{2} - i\sqrt{2}}{2}, \dfrac{-\sqrt{2} + i\sqrt{2}}{2}$ 95. $\dfrac{\sqrt{3} - \sqrt{11}}{4}, \dfrac{\sqrt{3} + \sqrt{11}}{4}$
97. 8.9 sec: 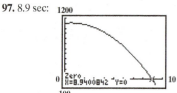 2.8 sec: 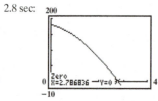 99. two real solutions

Section 9.3
Practice Exercises

1. 8 2. $\dfrac{5 \pm \sqrt{137}}{8}$ 3. $4, -4, 3i, -3i$ 4. $1, -3$ 5. $1, 64$ 6. Katy: $\dfrac{7 + \sqrt{65}}{2} \approx 7.5$ hr; Steve: $\dfrac{9 + \sqrt{65}}{2} \approx 8.5$ hr
7. to Shanghai: 40 km/hr; to Ningbo: 90 km/hr

Exercise Set 9.3

1. 2 **3.** 16 **5.** 1, 4 **7.** $3 - \sqrt{7}, 3 + \sqrt{7}$ **9.** $\dfrac{3-\sqrt{57}}{4}, \dfrac{3+\sqrt{57}}{4}$ **11.** $\dfrac{1-\sqrt{29}}{2}, \dfrac{1+\sqrt{29}}{2}$ **13.** $-2, 2, -2i, 2i$

15. $-\dfrac{1}{2}, \dfrac{1}{2}, -i\sqrt{3}, i\sqrt{3}$ **17.** $-3, 3, -2, 2$ **19.** $125, -8$ **21.** $-\dfrac{4}{5}, 0$ **23.** $-\dfrac{1}{8}, 27$ **25.** $-\dfrac{2}{3}, \dfrac{4}{3}$ **27.** $-\dfrac{1}{125}, \dfrac{1}{8}$ **29.** $-\sqrt{2}, \sqrt{2}, -\sqrt{3}, \sqrt{3}$

31. $\dfrac{-9-\sqrt{201}}{6}, \dfrac{-9+\sqrt{201}}{6}$ **33.** 2, 3 **35.** 3 **37.** 27, 125 **39.** $1, -3i, 3i$ **41.** $\dfrac{1}{8}, -8$ **43.** $-\dfrac{1}{2}, \dfrac{1}{3}$ **45.** 4

47. -3 **49.** $-\sqrt{5}, \sqrt{5}, -2i, 2i$ **51.** $-3, \dfrac{3-3i\sqrt{3}}{2}, \dfrac{3+3i\sqrt{3}}{2}$ **53.** 6, 12 **55.** $-\dfrac{1}{3}, \dfrac{1}{3}, -\dfrac{i\sqrt{6}}{3}, \dfrac{i\sqrt{6}}{3}$ **57.** 5 mph, then 4 mph

59. inlet pipe: 15.5 hr; hose: 16.5 hr **61.** 55 mph, 66 mph **63.** 8.5 hr **65.** 12 or -8 **67. a.** $(x-6)$ in. **b.** $300 = (x-6) \cdot (x-6) \cdot 3$

c. 16 cm by 16 cm **69.** 22 feet **71.** $x \leq 3$ **73.** $y > -5$ **75.** domain: all real numbers; range: all real numbers; function

77. domain: all real numbers; range: $y \geq -1$; function **79.** $1, -3i, 3i$ **81.** $-\dfrac{1}{2}, \dfrac{1}{3}$ **83.** $-3, \dfrac{3-3i\sqrt{3}}{2}, \dfrac{3+3i\sqrt{3}}{2}$ **85.** answers may vary

87. a. 150.94 ft/sec **b.** 151.49 ft/sec **c.** Bourdais: 102.9 mph; Pagenaud: 103.3 mph

Integrated Review

1. $-\sqrt{10}, \sqrt{10}$ **2.** $-\sqrt{14}, \sqrt{14}$ **3.** $1 - 2\sqrt{2}, 1 + 2\sqrt{2}$ **4.** $-5 - 2\sqrt{3}, -5 + 2\sqrt{3}$ **5.** $-1 - \sqrt{13}, -1 + \sqrt{13}$

6. 1, 11 **7.** $\dfrac{-3-\sqrt{69}}{6}, \dfrac{-3+\sqrt{69}}{6}$ **8.** $\dfrac{-2-\sqrt{5}}{4}, \dfrac{-2+\sqrt{5}}{4}$ **9.** $\dfrac{2-\sqrt{2}}{2}, \dfrac{2+\sqrt{2}}{2}$ **10.** $-3 - \sqrt{5}, -3 + \sqrt{5}$

11. $-2 + i\sqrt{3}, -2 - i\sqrt{3}$ **12.** $\dfrac{-1-i\sqrt{11}}{2}, \dfrac{-1+i\sqrt{11}}{2}$ **13.** $\dfrac{-3+i\sqrt{15}}{2}, \dfrac{-3-i\sqrt{15}}{2}$ **14.** $3i, -3i$ **15.** $0, -17$

16. $\dfrac{1+\sqrt{13}}{4}, \dfrac{1-\sqrt{13}}{4}$ **17.** $2 + 3\sqrt{3}, 2 - 3\sqrt{3}$ **18.** $2 + \sqrt{3}, 2 - \sqrt{3}$ **19.** $-2, \dfrac{4}{3}$ **20.** $\dfrac{-5+\sqrt{17}}{4}, \dfrac{-5-\sqrt{17}}{4}$ **21.** $1 - \sqrt{6}, 1 + \sqrt{6}$

22. $-\sqrt{31}, \sqrt{31}$ **23.** $-\sqrt{11}, \sqrt{11}$ **24.** $-i\sqrt{11}, i\sqrt{11}$ **25.** $-11, 6$ **26.** $\dfrac{-3+\sqrt{19}}{5}, \dfrac{-3-\sqrt{19}}{5}$ **27.** $\dfrac{-3+\sqrt{17}}{4}, \dfrac{-3-\sqrt{17}}{4}$

28. $10\sqrt{2}$ ft ≈ 14.1 ft **29.** Jack: 9.1 hr; Lucy: 7.1 hr **30.** 5 mph during the first part, then 6 mph

Section 9.4
Practice Exercises

1. $\pm 1, \pm 2, \pm 3, \pm 6$ **2.** $\pm 1, \pm 3, \pm\dfrac{1}{2}, \pm\dfrac{1}{4}, \pm\dfrac{3}{2}, \pm\dfrac{3}{4}$ **3.** $-5, -4, 1$ **4.** $2, \dfrac{-3-\sqrt{5}}{2}, \dfrac{-3+\sqrt{5}}{2}$

Exercise Set 9.4

1. $\pm 1, \pm 2, \pm 4$ **3.** $\pm 1, \pm 2, \pm 3, \pm 6, \pm\dfrac{1}{3}, \pm\dfrac{2}{3}$ **5.** $\pm 1, \pm 2, \pm 3, \pm 6, \pm\dfrac{1}{2}, \pm\dfrac{1}{4}, \pm\dfrac{3}{2}, \pm\dfrac{3}{4}$ **7.** $\pm 1, \pm 2, \pm 3, \pm 4, \pm 6, \pm 12$ **9. a.** $\pm 1, \pm 2, \pm 4$

b. $-2, -1,$ or 2 **c.** $-2, -1, 2$ **11. a.** $\pm 1, \pm 2, \pm 3, \pm 6, \pm\dfrac{1}{2}, \pm\dfrac{3}{2}$ **b.** $-2, \dfrac{1}{2},$ or 3 **c.** $-2, \dfrac{1}{2}, 3$ **13. a.** $\pm 1, \pm 2, \pm 3, \pm 6$

b. -1 **c.** $-1, \dfrac{-3-\sqrt{33}}{2}, \dfrac{-3+\sqrt{33}}{2}$ **15. a.** $\pm 1, \pm\dfrac{1}{2}, \pm 2$ **b.** -2 **c.** $-2, \dfrac{-1+i}{2}, \dfrac{-1-i}{2}$ **17.** $x = -2, x = 5, x = 1$

19. $-1, 2 + 2i,$ and $2 - 2i$ **21.** $x = -1, x = 2, x = -\dfrac{1}{3}, x = 3$

23. a. $-4, 1,$ and 4 **25. a.** -1 and $\dfrac{3}{2}$ **27. a.** $\dfrac{1}{2}, 3, -1 \pm i$ **29. a.** $-2, -1, -\dfrac{2}{3}, 1,$ and 2

b.

$f(x) = -x^3 + x^2 + 16x - 16$	$f(x) = 4x^3 - 8x^2 - 3x + 9$	$f(x) = 2x^4 - 3x^3 - 7x^2 - 8x + 6$	$f(x) = 3x^5 + 2x^4 - 15x^3 - 10x^2 + 12x + 8$

31. $\dfrac{1}{3}, -5$ **33.** $\dfrac{-7+\sqrt{41}}{4}, \dfrac{-7-\sqrt{41}}{4}$ **35.** 7.8 in., 10 in. **37. a.** $(7.8, 2000), (10, 2000)$ **b.** $0 < x < 15$ **39.** answers may vary

Section 9.5
Practice Exercises

1. $1, 2 - 3i, 2 + 3i$ **2.** $f(x) = x^3 + 3x^2 + x + 3$

Exercise Set 9.5

1. a. $\pm 1, \pm 2, \pm 3, \pm 4, \pm 6, \pm 12$ **b.** $-3, 1,$ or 4 **c.** $-3, 1, 4$ **3. a.** $\pm 1, \pm 2, \pm 3, \pm 4, \pm 6, \pm 12$ **b.** -2 **c.** $-2, 1 + \sqrt{7}, 1 - \sqrt{7}$
5. a. $\pm 1, \pm 5, \pm\frac{1}{2}, \pm\frac{5}{2}, \pm\frac{1}{3}, \pm\frac{5}{3}, \pm\frac{1}{6}, \pm\frac{5}{6}$ **b.** $-5, \frac{1}{3},$ or $\frac{1}{2}$ **c.** $-5, \frac{1}{3}, \frac{1}{2}$ **7. a.** $\pm 1, \pm 2, \pm 4$ **b.** -2 or 2 **c.** $-2, 2, 1 + \sqrt{2}, 1 - \sqrt{2}$
9. $f(x) = x^3 - x^2 + 25x - 25$ **11.** $f(x) = x^3 - 3x^2 - 15x + 125$ **13.** $f(x) = x^4 + 10x^2 + 9$ **15.** $f(x) = x^4 - 9x^3 + 21x^2 + 21x - 130$
17. $-\frac{1}{2}, \frac{1 + \sqrt{17}}{2}, \frac{1 - \sqrt{17}}{2}$ **19.** $-1, -2, 3 + \sqrt{13}, 3 - \sqrt{13}$ **21.** $1, -\frac{3}{4}, i\sqrt{2}, -i\sqrt{2}$ **23.** $-2, \frac{1}{2}, \sqrt{2}, -\sqrt{2}$ **25.** answers may vary
27. $x = 1$ and $x = 2$ **29.** $x = 1$ **31.** 3 in. **33.** true **35.** does not make sense **37.** $-\frac{1}{2}, 3, 5$ **39.** $-3, -\frac{3}{2}, -1, 2$

41.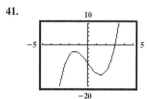
1 real zero, 2 nonreal complex zeros

43.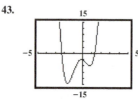
2 real zeros, 2 nonreal complex zeros

Section 9.6
Practice Exercises
1. $x < -3$ or $x > 4$ **2.** $0 \le x \le 8$ **3.** $x \le -3$ or $-1 \le x \le 2$ **4.** $-4 < x \le 5$ **5.** $x < -3$ or $x > -\frac{8}{5}$

Vocabulary and Readiness Check 9.6
1. $-7 \le x < 3$ **3.** $x \le 0$ **5.** $x < -12$ or $x \ge -10$

Exercise Set 9.6
1. $x < -5$ or $x > -1$ **3.** $-4 \le x \le 3$ **5.** $2 \le x \le 5$ **7.** $-5 < x < -\frac{1}{3}$ **9.** $2 < x < 4$ or $x > 6$ **11.** $x \le -4$ or $0 \le x \le 1$
13. $x < -3$ or $-2 < x < 2$ or $x > 3$ **15.** $-7 < x < 2$ **17.** $x > -1$ **19.** $x \le -1$ or $x > 4$ **21.** $x < 2$ or $x > \frac{11}{4}$ **23.** $0 < x \le 2$ or $x \ge 3$
25. $x < -7$ or $x > 8$ **27.** $-\frac{5}{4} \le x \le \frac{3}{2}$ **29.** $x < 0$ or $x > 1$ **31.** $x \le -4$ or $4 \le x \le 6$ **33.** $x \le -\frac{2}{3}$ or $x \ge \frac{3}{2}$
35. $-4 < x < -\frac{3}{2}$ or $x > \frac{3}{2}$ **37.** $x \le -5$ or $-1 \le x \le 1$ or $x \ge 5$ **39.** $x < -\frac{5}{3}$ or $x > \frac{7}{2}$ **41.** $0 < x < 10$ **43.** $x < -4$ or $x > 5$
45. $x \le -6$ or $-1 < x \le 0$ or $x > 7$ **47.** $x < 1$ or $x > 2$ **49.** $x \le -8$ or $x > -4$ **51.** $x \le 0$ or $5 < x \le \frac{11}{2}$ **53.** $x > 0$

55. **57.** 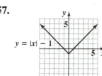 **59.** **61.** **63.** answers may vary

65. any number less than -1 or between 0 and 1 **67.** x is between 2 and 11 **69.** [graph] **71.** [graph]

Chapter 9 Vocabulary Check
1. discriminant **2.** $\pm\sqrt{b}$ **3.** quadratic inequality **4.** completing the square **5.** quadratic formula **6.** quadratic **7.** $a - bi$ **8.** n

Chapter 9 Review
1. $14, 1$ **3.** $-7, 7$ **5.** $\frac{-3 - \sqrt{5}}{2}, \frac{-3 + \sqrt{5}}{2}$ **7.** 4.25% **9.** two complex but not real solutions **11.** two real solutions **13.** 8 **15.** $-\frac{5}{2}, 1$
17. $\frac{5 - i\sqrt{143}}{12}, \frac{5 + i\sqrt{143}}{12}$ **19. a.** 20 ft **b.** $\frac{15 + \sqrt{321}}{16}$ sec; 2.1 sec **21.** $3, \frac{-3 + 3i\sqrt{3}}{2}, \frac{-3 - 3i\sqrt{3}}{2}$ **23.** $\frac{2}{3}, 5$ **25.** $1, 125$ **27.** $-1, 1, -i, i$

29. Jerome: 10.5 hr; Tim: 9.5 hr   **31.** $+1, +5$ **33. a.** $\pm 1, \pm\frac{1}{2}, \pm\frac{1}{3}, \pm\frac{1}{6}$ **b.** $-1, \frac{1}{3},$ or $\frac{1}{2}$ **c.** $-1, \frac{1}{3}, \frac{1}{2}$ **35. a.** $\pm 1, \pm\frac{1}{2}$ **b.** $\frac{1}{2}$
c. $\frac{1}{2}, \frac{-5-\sqrt{29}}{2}, \frac{-5+\sqrt{29}}{2}$ **37. a.** $\pm 1, \pm 2, \pm\frac{1}{2}, \pm\frac{1}{4}$ **b.** $-\frac{1}{2}$ or $\frac{1}{2}$ **c.** $-\frac{1}{2}, \frac{1}{2}, i\sqrt{2}, -i\sqrt{2}$ **39.** $f(x) = x^3 - 6x^2 + 21x - 26$
41. $-2, \frac{1}{2}, \pm i; f(x) = (x-i)(x+i)(x+2)(2x-1)$

43. 4 real zeros, one with multiplicity two   **45.** 2 real zeros, one with multiplicity two; 2 nonreal complex zeros

47. $-5 \leq x \leq 5$ **49.** $5 < x < 6$ **51.** $x < -6$ or $-\frac{3}{4} < x < 0$ or $x > 5$ **53.** $-5 < x < -3$ or $x > 5$ **55.** $-\frac{6}{5} < x < 0$ or $\frac{5}{6} < x < 3$
57. $-5, 6$ **59.** $-2, 2$ **61.** $\frac{-1 - 3i\sqrt{3}}{2}, \frac{-1 + 3i\sqrt{3}}{2}$ **63.** $-i\sqrt{11}, i\sqrt{11}$ **65.** $-\frac{8\sqrt{7}}{7}, \frac{8\sqrt{7}}{7}$ **67.** $x \leq -\frac{5}{4}$ or $x \geq \frac{3}{2}$ **69.** $2 < x < \frac{7}{2}$

Chapter 9 Test
1. $\frac{7}{5}, -1$ **2.** $-1 - \sqrt{10}, -1 + \sqrt{10}$ **3.** $\frac{1 + i\sqrt{31}}{2}, \frac{1 - i\sqrt{31}}{2}$ **4.** $3 - \sqrt{7}, 3 + \sqrt{7}$ **5.** $-\frac{1}{7}, -1$ **6.** $\frac{3 + \sqrt{29}}{2}, \frac{3 - \sqrt{29}}{2}$
7. $-2 - \sqrt{11}, -2 + \sqrt{11}$ **8.** $-1, 1, -i, i, -3$ **9.** $-1, 1, -i, i$ **10.** $6, 7$ **11.** $3 - \sqrt{7}, 3 + \sqrt{7}$ **12.** $\frac{2 - i\sqrt{6}}{2}, \frac{2 + i\sqrt{6}}{2}$
13. $x < -\frac{3}{2}$ or $x > 5$ **14.** $x \leq -5$ or $-4 \leq x \leq 4$ or $x \geq 5$ **15.** $x < -3$ or $x > 2$ **16.** $x < -3$ or $2 \leq x < 3$ **17. a.** 2   **b.** $\frac{1}{2}, \frac{2}{3}$
18. $-3, -3 - \sqrt{11}, -3 + \sqrt{11}$ **19. a.** $\pm 1, \pm 3, \pm 5 \pm 15, \pm\frac{1}{2}, \pm\frac{3}{2}, \pm\frac{5}{2} \pm\frac{15}{2}$ **b.** $-\sqrt{5}, -1, \frac{3}{2},$ and $\sqrt{5}$ **20.** $(x-1)(x+2)^2$

21. $f(x) = x^4 - 1$ **22.** $(5 + \sqrt{17})$ hr ≈ 9.12 hr   **23.** 7 ft

Chapter 9 Standardized Test
1. d   **2.** b   **3.** d   **4.** c   **5.** c   **6.** c   **7.** b   **8.** c   **9.** c   **10.** a   **11.** c   **12.** d   **13.** b   **14.** b   **15.** d   **16.** a   **17.** d   **18.** a
19. b   **20.** c   **21.** b   **22.** a   **23.** d

CHAPTER 10 EXPONENTIAL AND LOGARITHMIC FUNCTIONS
Section 10.1
Practice Exercises
1. a. $4x + 7$ **b.** $-2x - 3$ **c.** $3x^2 + 11x + 10$ **d.** $\frac{x + 2}{3x + 5}$, where $x \neq -\frac{5}{3}$ **2. a.** $50; 46$ **b.** $9x^2 - 30x + 26; 3x^2 - 2$
3. a. $x^2 + 6x + 14$ **b.** $x^2 + 8$ **4. a.** $(h \circ g)(x)$ **b.** $(g \circ f)(x)$

Vocabulary and Readiness Check 10.1
1. C   **3.** F   **5.** D

Exercise Set 10.1
1. a. $3x - 6$ **b.** $-x - 8$ **c.** $2x^2 - 13x - 7$ **d.** $\frac{x - 7}{2x + 1}$, where $x \neq -\frac{1}{2}$ **3. a.** $x^2 + 5x + 1$ **b.** $x^2 - 5x + 1$ **c.** $5x^3 + 5x$
d. $\frac{x^2 + 1}{5x}$, where $x \neq 0$ **5. a.** $\sqrt{x} + x + 5$ **b.** $\sqrt{x} - x - 5$ **c.** $x\sqrt{x} + 5\sqrt{x}$ **d.** $\frac{\sqrt{x}}{x + 5}$, where $x \neq -5$
7. a. $5x^2 - 3x$ **b.** $-5x^2 - 3x$ **c.** $-15x^3$ **d.** $-\frac{3}{5x}$, where $x \neq 0$ **9.** 42   **11.** -18 **13.** 0
15. $(f \circ g)(x) = 25x^2 + 1; (g \circ f)(x) = 5x^2 + 5$ **17.** $(f \circ g)(x) = 2x + 11; (g \circ f)(x) = 2x + 4$
19. $(f \circ g)(x) = -8x^3 - 2x - 2; (g \circ f)(x) = -2x^3 - 2x + 4$ **21.** $(f \circ g)(x) = |10x - 3|; (g \circ f)(x) = 10|x| - 3$
23. $(f \circ g)(x) = \sqrt{-5x + 2}; (g \circ f)(x) = -5\sqrt{x} + 2$ **25.** $H(x) = (g \circ h)(x)$ **27.** $F(x) = (h \circ f)(x)$ **29.** $G(x) = (f \circ g)(x)$
31. answers may vary; for example $g(x) = x + 2$ and $f(x) = x^2$ **33.** answers may vary; for example, $g(x) = x + 5$ and $f(x) = \sqrt{x} + 2$
35. answers may vary; for example, $g(x) = 2x - 3$ and $f(x) = \frac{1}{x}$ **37.** $y = x - 2$ **39.** $y = \frac{x}{3}$ **41.** $y = -\frac{x + 7}{2}$ **43.** 6   **45.** 4   **47.** 4
49. -1 **51.** answers may vary   **53.** $P(x) = R(x) - C(x)$

Section 10.2
Practice Exercises
1. a. one-to-one **b.** not one-to-one **c.** not one-to-one **d.** not one-to-one **e.** not one-to-one **f.** not one-to-one
2. a. no, not one-to-one **b.** yes **c.** yes **d.** no, not a function **e.** no, not a function
3. $f^{-1}(x) = \{(4,3),(0,-2),(8,2),(6,6)\}$ **4.** $f^{-1}(x) = 6 - x$

5. 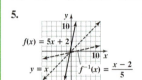 **6. a.** 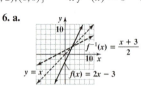 **b.**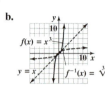

7. $f(f^{-1}(x)) = f\left(\dfrac{x+1}{4}\right) = 4\left(\dfrac{x+1}{4}\right) - 1 = x + 1 - 1 = x$

$f^{-1}(f(x)) = f^{-1}(4x - 1) = \dfrac{(4x-1)+1}{4} = \dfrac{4x}{4} = x$

Vocabulary and Readiness Check 10.2
1. (2, 11) **3.** (3, 7) **5.** horizontal **7.** $x; x$

Exercise Set 10.2
1. one-to-one; $f^{-1} = \{(-1,-1),(1,1),(2,0),(0,2)\}$ **3.** one-to-one; $h^{-1} = \{(10,10)\}$ **5.** one-to-one; $f^{-1} = \{(12,11),(3,4),(4,3),(6,6)\}$
7. not one-to-one **9.** one-to-one;

Rank in Population (Input)	1	19	35	4	48
State (Output)	CA	MD	NV	FL	ND

11. a. 3 **b.** 1 **13. a.** 1 **b.** −1
15. one-to-one **17.** not one-to-one
19. one-to-one **21.** not one-to-one
23. $f^{-1}(x) = x - 4$ **25.** $f^{-1}(x) = \dfrac{x+3}{2}$ **27.** $f^{-1}(x) = 2x + 2$ **29.** $f^{-1}(x) = \sqrt[3]{x}$

31. $f^{-1}(x) = \dfrac{x-2}{5}$ **33.** $f^{-1}(x) = 5x + 2$ **35.** $f^{-1}(x) = x^3$ **37.** $f^{-1}(x) = \dfrac{5-x}{3x}$ **39.** $f^{-1}(x) = \sqrt[3]{x} - 2$
41.   **43.**   **45.**   **47.** $(f \circ f^{-1})(x) = x; (f^{-1} \circ f)(x) = x$

49. $(f \circ f^{-1})(x) = x; (f^{-1} \circ f)(x) = x$ **51.** 5 **53.** 8 **55.** $\dfrac{1}{27}$ **57.** 9 **59.** $3^{1/2} \approx 1.73$ **61. a.** (2, 9) **b.** (9, 2)
63. a. $\left(-2, \dfrac{1}{4}\right), \left(-1, \dfrac{1}{2}\right), (0, 1), (1, 2), (2, 5)$ **b.** $\left(\dfrac{1}{4}, -2\right), \left(\dfrac{1}{2}, -1\right), (1, 0), (2, 1), (5, 2)$

c. 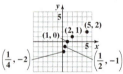 **d.**   **65.** answers may vary **67.** $f^{-1}(x) = \dfrac{x-1}{3}$; 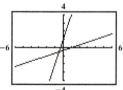 **69.** $f^{-1}(x) = x^3 - 1$;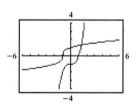

Section 10.3
Practice Exercises
1.   **2.** 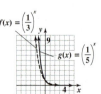 **3.**   **4. a.** 2; **b.** $\dfrac{4}{3}$; **c.** −4 **5.** $3950.43 **6.** 60.86%

Graphing Calculator Explorations 10.3

1. 81.98%; 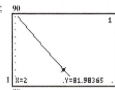   **3.** 22.54%;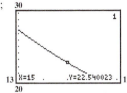

Vocabulary and Readiness Check 10.3

1. exponential   **3.** yes   **5.** yes; (0, 1)   **7.** $(0, \infty)$

Exercise Set 10.3

1.   **3.**   **5.**   **7.** 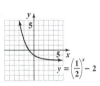   **9.**

11.   **13.**   **15.**   **17.** C   **19.** B   **21.** 3   **23.** $\dfrac{3}{4}$ **25.** $\dfrac{8}{5}$ **27.** $-\dfrac{2}{3}$ **29.** 4   **31.** $\dfrac{3}{2}$

33. $-\dfrac{1}{3}$ **35.** -2 **37.** 24.6 lb   **39.** 333 bison   **41.** 1.1 g   **43. a.** 658.1 pascals   **b.** 180.0 pascals   **45. a.** 134,342 students   **b.** 840,276 students   **47.** $7621.42   **49.** $4065.59   **51.** 562 million cell phone users   **53.** 4   **55.** no solution   **57.** 2, 3   **59.** 3   **61.** -1 **63.** answers may vary

65.   **67.**   **69.** The graphs are the same since $\left(\dfrac{1}{2}\right)^{-x} = 2^x$.   **71.** 24.60 lb;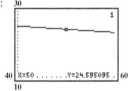

73. 18.62 lb; 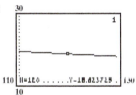   **75.** 50.41 g;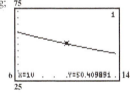

Section 10.4
Practice Exercises

1. a. $3^4 = 81$ **b.** $5^{-1} = \dfrac{1}{5}$ **c.** $7^{1/2} = \sqrt{7}$ **d.** $13^4 = y$ **2. a.** $\log_4 64 = 3$ **b.** $\log_6 \sqrt[3]{6} = \dfrac{1}{3}$ **c.** $\log_5 \dfrac{1}{125} = -3$ **d.** $\log_\pi z = 7$

3. a. 2   **b.** -3 **c.** $\dfrac{1}{2}$ **4. a.** -2 **b.** 2   **c.** 36   **d.** 0   **e.** 0   **5. a.** 4   **b.** -2 **c.** 5   **d.** 4

6.   **7.**

Vocabulary and Readiness Check 10.4

1. logarithmic   **3.** yes   **5.** no; none   **7.** $(-\infty, \infty)$

Exercise Set 10.4

1. $6^2 = 36$ **3.** $3^{-3} = \dfrac{1}{27}$ **5.** $10^3 = 1000$ **7.** $9^4 = x$ **9.** $\pi^{-2} = \dfrac{1}{\pi^2}$ **11.** $7^{1/2} = \sqrt{7}$ **13.** $0.7^3 = 0.343$
15. $3^{-4} = \dfrac{1}{81}$ **17.** $\log_2 16 = 4$ **19.** $\log_{10} 100 = 2$ **21.** $\log_\pi x = 3$ **23.** $\log_{10} \dfrac{1}{10} = -1$ **25.** $\log_4 \dfrac{1}{16} = -2$

27. $\log_5\sqrt{5} = \frac{1}{2}$ **29.** 3 **31.** -2 **33.** $\frac{1}{2}$ **35.** -1 **37.** 0 **39.** 2 **41.** 4 **43.** -3 **45.** 2 **47.** 81
49. 7 **51.** -3 **53.** -3 **55.** 2 **57.** 2 **59.** $\frac{27}{64}$ **61.** 10 **63.** 4 **65.** 5 **67.** $\frac{1}{49}$ **69.** 3 **71.** 3 **73.** 1
75.   **77.**   **79.**   **81.**   **83.** 1

85. $\frac{x-4}{2}$ **87.** $\frac{2x+3}{x^2}$ **89.** $m-1$ **91. a.** $g(2)=25$ **b.** $(25, 2)$ **c.** $f(25)=2$ **93.** answers may vary **95.** $\frac{9}{5}$ **97.** 1
99.   **101.**   **103.** answers may vary **105.** 0.0827

Section 10.5
Practice Exercises
1. a. $\log_8 15$ **b.** $\log_2 6$ **c.** $\log_5(x^2-1)$ **2. a.** $\log_5 3$ **b.** $\log_6 \frac{x}{3}$ **c.** $\log_4 \frac{x^2+1}{x^2+3}$ **3. a.** $8\log_7 x$ **b.** $\frac{1}{4}\log_5 7$
4. a. $\log_5 512$ **b.** $\log_8 \frac{x^2}{x+3}$ **c.** $\log_7 15$ **5. a.** $\log_5 4 + \log_5 3 - \log_5 7$ **b.** $2\log_4 a - 5\log_4 b$ **6. a.** 1.39 **b.** 1.66 **c.** 0.28

Vocabulary and Readiness Check 10.5
1. 36 **3.** $\log_b 2^7$ **5.** x

Exercise Set 10.5
1. $\log_5 14$ **3.** $\log_4 9x$ **5.** $\log_6(x^2+x)$ **7.** $\log_{10}(10x^2+20)$ **9.** $\log_5 3$ **11.** $\log_3 4$ **13.** $\log_2 \frac{x}{y}$ **15.** $\log_2 \frac{x^2+6}{x^2+1}$ **17.** $2\log_3 x$
19. $-1\log_4 5 = -\log_4 5$ **21.** $\frac{1}{2}\log_5 y$ **23.** $\log_2 5x^3$ **25.** $\log_4 48$ **27.** $\log_5 x^3 z^6$ **29.** $\log_4 4$, or 1 **31.** $\log_7 \frac{9}{2}$ **33.** $\log_{10} \frac{x^3-2x}{x+1}$
35. $\log_2 \frac{x^{7/2}}{(x+1)^2}$ **37.** $\log_8 x^{16/3}$ **39.** $\log_3 4 + \log_3 y - \log_3 5$ **41.** $\log_4 2 - \log_4 9 - \log_4 z$ **43.** $3\log_2 x - \log_2 y$ **45.** $\frac{1}{2}\log_b 7 + \frac{1}{2}\log_b x$
47. $4\log_6 x + 5\log_6 y$ **49.** $3\log_5 x + \log_5(x+1)$ **51.** $2\log_6 x - \log_6(x+3)$ **53.** 1.2 **55.** 0.2 **57.** 0.35 **59.** 1.29 **61.** -0.68
63. -0.125 **65.**   **67.** -1 **69.** $\frac{1}{2}$ **71.** a and d **73.** false **75.** true **77.** false

Integrated Review
1. x^2+x-5 **2.** $-x^2+x-7$ **3.** x^3-6x^2+x-6 **4.** $\frac{x-6}{x^2+1}$ **5.** $\sqrt{3x-1}$ **6.** $3\sqrt{x}-1$
7. one-to-one; $\{(6,-2),(8,4),(-6,2),(3,3)\}$ **8.** not one-to-one **9.** not one-to-one **10.** one-to-one
11. not one-to-one **12.** $f^{-1}(x) = \frac{x}{3}$ **13.** $f^{-1}(x) = x-4$ **14.** $f^{-1}(x) = \frac{x+1}{5}$ **15.** $f^{-1}(x) = \frac{x-2}{3}$
16. 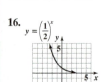 **17.**   **18.**   **19.**   **20.** 3

21. 7 **22.** -8 **23.** 3 **24.** 2 **25.** $\frac{1}{2}$ **26.** 32 **27.** 4 **28.** 5 **29.** $\frac{1}{9}$ **30.** $\log_2 x^5$ **31.** $\log_2 5^x$ **32.** $\log_5 \frac{x^3}{y^5}$
33. $\log_5 x^9 y^3$ **34.** $\log_2 \frac{x^2-3x}{x^2+4}$ **35.** $\log_3 \frac{y^4+11y}{y+2}$ **36.** $\log_7 9 + 2\log_7 x - \log_7 y$ **37.** $\log_6 5 + \log_6 y - 2\log_6 z$

Section 10.6
Practice Exercises
1. 1.1761 **2. a.** -2 **b.** 5 **c.** $\frac{1}{5}$ **d.** -3 **3.** $10^{3.4} \approx 2511.8864$ **4.** 5.6 **5.** 2.5649 **6. a.** 4 **b.** $\frac{1}{3}$

7. $\frac{e^8}{5} \approx 596.1916$ **8.** $3051 **9.** 0.7740

Vocabulary and Readiness Check 10.6
1. 10 **3.** 7 **5.** 5 **7.** $\frac{\log 7}{\log 2}$ or $\frac{\ln 7}{\ln 2}$

Exercise Set 10.6
1. 0.9031 **3.** 0.3636 **5.** 0.6931 **7.** -2.6367 **9.** 1.1004 **11.** 1.6094 **13.** 1.6180 **15.** answers may vary **17.** 2 **19.** -3 **21.** 2
23. $\frac{1}{4}$ **25.** 3 **27.** -7 **29.** -4 **31.** $\frac{1}{2}$ **33.** $\frac{e^7}{2} \approx 548.3166$ **35.** $10^{1.3} \approx 19.9526$ **37.** $\frac{10^{1.1}}{2} \approx 6.2946$ **39.** $e^{1.4} \approx 4.0552$
41. $\frac{4 + e^{2.3}}{3} \approx 4.6581$ **43.** $10^{2.3} \approx 199.5262$ **45.** $e^{-2.3} \approx 0.1003$ **47.** $\frac{10^{-0.5} - 1}{2} \approx -0.3419$ **49.** $\frac{e^{0.18}}{4} \approx 0.2993$ **51.** 1.5850 **53.** -2.3219
55. 1.5850 **57.** -1.6309 **59.** 0.8617 **61.** 4.2 **63.** 5.3 **65.** $3656.38 **67.** $2542.50 **69.** $\frac{4}{7}$ **71.** $x = \frac{3y}{4}$ **73.** $-6, -1$ **75.** $(2, -3)$
77. ln 50; answers may vary

79. $f(x) = e^x$ 81. $f(x) = e^{-3x}$ 83. $f(x) = e^x + 2$ 85. $f(x) = e^{x-1}$ 87. $f(x) = 3e^x$

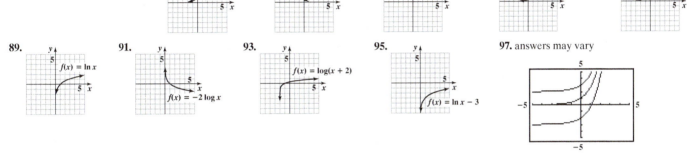

89. $f(x) = \ln x$ 91. $f(x) = -2 \log x$ 93. $f(x) = \log(x + 2)$ 95. $f(x) = \ln x - 3$ **97.** answers may vary

Section 10.7
Practice Exercises
1. $\frac{\log 9}{\log 5} \approx 1.3652$ **2.** 33 **3.** 1 **4.** $\frac{1}{3}$ **5.** 937 rabbits **6.** 10 years

Graphing Calculator Explorations 10.7
1. 3.67 years, or 3 years and 8 months **3.** 23.16 years, or 23 years and 2 months

Exercise Set 10.7
1. $\frac{\log 6}{\log 3}$; 1.6309 **3.** $\frac{\log 3.8}{2 \log 3}$; 0.6076 **5.** $3 + \frac{\log 5}{\log 2}$; 5.3219 **7.** $\frac{\log 5}{\log 9}$; 0.7325 **9.** $\frac{\log 3}{\log 4} - 7$; -6.2075 **11.** $\frac{1}{3}\left(4 + \frac{\log 11}{\log 7}\right)$; 1.7441
13. $\frac{\ln 5}{6}$; 0.2682 **15.** 11 **17.** $9, -9$ **19.** $\frac{1}{2}$ **21.** $\frac{3}{4}$ **23.** 2 **25.** $\frac{1}{8}$ **27.** 11 **29.** $4, -1$ **31.** $\frac{1}{5}$ **33.** 100 **35.** $\frac{-5 + \sqrt{33}}{2}$
37. $\frac{192}{127}$ **39.** $\frac{2}{3}$ **41.** 103 wolves **43.** 354,000 inhabitants **45.** 14.7 yr **47.** 9.9 yr **49.** 1.7 yr **51.** 8.8 yr **53.** 24.5 lb **55.** 55.7 in.
57. 11.9 lb/sq in. **59.** 3.2 mi **61.** 12 weeks **63.** 18 weeks **65.** $-\frac{5}{3}$ **67.** $\frac{17}{4}$ **69.** $f^{-1}(x) = \frac{x - 2}{5}$ **71.** 2.9% **73.** answers may vary
75. 6.93 **77.** -3.68 **79.** 1.74 **81.** 0.2

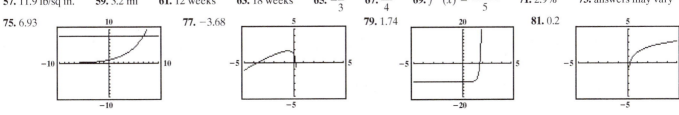

Chapter 10 Vocabulary Check
1. inverse **2.** composition **3.** exponential **4.** symmetric **5.** Natural **6.** Common **7.** vertical; horizontal **8.** logarithmic

Chapter 10 Review
1. $3x - 4$ **3.** $2x^2 - 9x - 5$ **5.** $x^2 + 2x - 1$ **7.** 18 **9.** -2 **11.** one-to-one; $h^{-1} = \{(14, -9), (8, 6), (12, -11), (15, 15)\}$ **13.** one-to-one;

Rank in Automobile Thefts (Input)	2	4	1	3
US Region (Output)	W	Midwest	S	NE

15. a. 3 **b.** 7 **17.** not one-to-one **19.** not one-to-one **21.** $f^{-1}(x) = x + 9$ **23.** $f^{-1}(x) = \dfrac{x - 11}{6}$ **25.** $f^{-1}(x) = \sqrt[3]{x + 5}$ **27.** $g^{-1}(x) = \dfrac{6x + 7}{12}$ **29.**   **31.** $f^{-1}(x) = \dfrac{x + 3}{2}$; 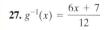 **33.** -2 **35.** $\dfrac{3}{2}$ **37.** $\dfrac{8}{9}$ **39.**   **41.**

43. $1131.82 **45.** $\log_7 49 = 2$ **47.** $\left(\dfrac{1}{2}\right)^{-4} = 16$ **49.** $\dfrac{1}{64}$ **51.** 0 **53.** 8 **55.** 5 **57.** 4 **59.** $\dfrac{17}{3}$ **61.** $-1, 4$ **63.**
65. $\log_3 32$ **67.** $\log_7 \dfrac{3}{4}$ **69.** $\log_{11} 4$ **71.** $\log_5 \dfrac{x^3}{(x+1)^2}$ **73.** $3 \log_3 x - \log_3 (x + 2)$ **75.** $\log_2 3 + 2 \log_2 x + \log_2 y - \log_2 z$
77. 2.02 **79.** 0.5563 **81.** 0.2231 **83.** 3 **85.** -1 **87.** $\dfrac{e^2}{2}$ **89.** $\dfrac{e^{-1} + 3}{2}$ **91.** 1.67 mm **93.** 0.2920 **95.** $1957.30
97. $\dfrac{\log 7}{2 \log 3}$; 0.8856 **99.** $\dfrac{1}{2}\left(\dfrac{\log 6}{\log 3} - 1\right)$; 0.3155 **101.** $\dfrac{1}{3}\left(\dfrac{\log 4}{\log 5} + 5\right)$; 1.9538 **103.** $-\dfrac{\log 2}{\log 5} + 1$; 0.5693 **105.** $\dfrac{25}{2}$ **107.** no solution **109.** $2\sqrt{2}$
111. 197,044 ducks **113.** 20.9 yr **115.** 38.5 yr **117.** 8.5 yr **119.** 2.82 **121.** $\dfrac{1}{2}$ **123.** 1 **125.** $-1, 5$ **127.** $e^{-3.2}$ **129.** $2e$

Chapter 10 Test
1. $2x^2 - 3x$ **2.** $3 - x$ **3.** 5 **4.** $x - 7$ **5.** $x^2 - 6x - 2$ **6.** **7.** one-to-one **8.** not one-to-one **9.** one-to-one; $f^{-1}(x) = \dfrac{-x + 6}{2}$ **10.** one-to-one; $f^{-1} = \{(0, 0), (3, 2)(5, -1)\}$
11. not one-to-one **12.** $\log_3 24$ **13.** $\log_5 \dfrac{x^4}{x + 1}$ **14.** $\log_6 2 + \log_6 x - 3 \log_6 y$ **15.** -1.53 **16.** 1.0686 **17.** -1
18. $\dfrac{1}{2}\left(\dfrac{\log 4}{\log 3} - 5\right)$; -1.8691 **19.** $\dfrac{1}{9}$ **20.** $\dfrac{1}{2}$ **21.** 22 **22.** $\dfrac{25}{3}$ **23.** $\dfrac{43}{21}$ **24.** -1.0979
25. **26.** **27.** $5234.58 **28.** 6 yr **29.** 64,913 prairie dogs **30.** 15 yr **31.** 1.2%

Chapter 10 Standardized Test
1. c **2.** d **3.** a **4.** d **5.** d **6.** b **7.** a **8.** b **9.** a **10.** c **11.** d **12.** b **13.** c **14.** a **15.** a **16.** a **17.** a **18.** d
19. a **20.** a **21.** b **22.** c **23.** d **24.** d **25.** a **26.** b **27.** c **28.** a **29.** c **30.** a **31.** d **32.** d

CHAPTER 11 GRAPHING QUADRATIC FUNCTIONS, RATIONAL FUNCTIONS, AND CONIC SECTIONS
Section 11.1
Practice Exercises
1. 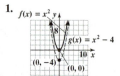 **2.**   **3.** 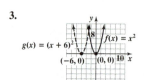 **4.**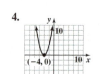

5. 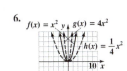 **6.**   **7.** 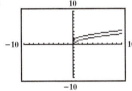 **8.**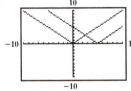

Graphing Calculator Explorations 11.1

1. 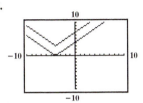 **3.**   **5.**

Vocabulary and Readiness Check 11.1

1. quadratic **3.** upward **5.** lowest **7.** $(0, 0)$ **9.** $(2, 0)$ **11.** $(0, 3)$ **13.** $(-1, 5)$

Exercise Set 11.1

1.   **3.**   **5.**   **7.**   **9.**   **11.**

13.   **15.**   **17.**   **19.**   **21.**   **23.**

25.   **27.**   **29.**   **31.**   **33.** 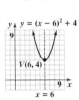 **35.**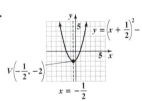

37. 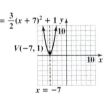 **39.** 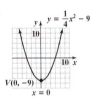 **41.** 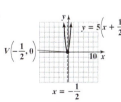 **43.**

45. 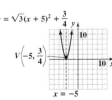 **47.** 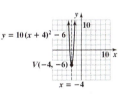 **49.**   **51.**

53.   **55.** $x^2 + 8x + 16$ **57.** $z^2 - 16z + 64$ **59.** $y^2 + y + \dfrac{1}{4}$ **61.** $-6, 2$ **63.** $-5 - \sqrt{26}, -5 + \sqrt{26}$ **65.** $4 - 3\sqrt{2}, 4 + 3\sqrt{2}$ **67.** c **69.** $f(x) = 5(x - 2)^2 + 3$ **71.** $f(x) = 5(x + 3)^2 + 6$

73. **75.** **77.** **79. a.** 185,515 thousand **b.** 258,793 thousand

Section 11.2
Practice Exercises
1. **2.** **3.** **4.** $(1, -4)$ **5.** Maximum height 9 feet in $\frac{3}{4}$ second

Vocabulary and Readiness Check 11.2
1. (h, k) **3.** 0; 1 **5.** 2; 1 **7.** 1; 1 **9.** down **11.** up

Exercise Set 11.2
1. $(-4, -9)$ **3.** $(5, 30)$ **5.** $(1, -2)$ **7.** $\left(\frac{1}{2}, \frac{5}{4}\right)$ **9.** D **11.** B

13. **15.** **17.** 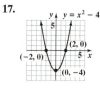 **19.** 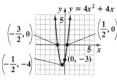 **21.**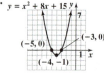

23. **25.** **27.** **29.** **31.**

33. **35.** 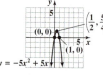 **37.** **39.**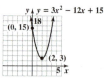

41. 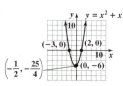 **43.** **45.** 144 ft **47. a.** 200 bicycles **b.** $12,000 **49.** 30 and 30 **51.** 5, -5
53. length, 20 units; width, 20 units

55. **57.** **59.** 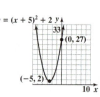 **61.** 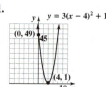 **63.**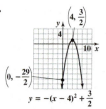

65. minimum value **67.** maximum value **69.** 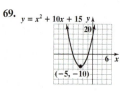 **71.** **73.** -0.84 **75.** 1.43

77. a. maximum; answers may vary   **b.** 2005   **c.** 31,523   **79.** 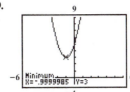   **81.**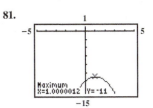

Section 11.3
Practice Exercises
1. a. all real numbers except 5   **b.** all real numbers except -5 and 5   **c.** all real numbers   **2. a.** $x = 3$ **b.** $x = 1, x = -1$ **c.** none
3. a. $y = 3$ **b.** $y = 0$ **c.** none   **4.**

Exercise Set 11.3
1. all real numbers except 4   **3.** all real numbers except -4 and 5   **5.** all real numbers except -7 and 7   **7.** all real numbers   **9.** $x = -4$
11. $x = 0, x = -4$ **13.** $x = -4$ **15.** no vertical asymptotes   **17.** $y = 0$ **19.** $y = 4$ **21.** no horizontal asymptote   **23.** $y = -\dfrac{2}{3}$
25.   **27.** 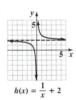   **29.**   **31.**
33. 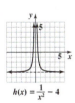   **35.** 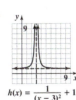   **37, 39, 41.** answers may vary   **43.**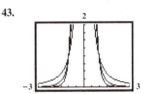

The graph approaches the horizontal asymptote faster and the vertical asymptote slower as n increases.

45. true   **47.** $-3, \dfrac{5}{2}$ **49.** $3 + \sqrt{5}, 3 - \sqrt{5}$

Section 11.4
Practice Exercises
1.   **2.**   **3.**

4. $y = 2x - 1$ **5. a.** $C(x) = 500{,}000 + 400x$ **b.** $\overline{C}(x) = \dfrac{500{,}000 + 400x}{x}$ **c.** $\overline{C}(1000) = 900$: The average cost per wheelchair of producing 1000 wheelchairs per month is $900.; $\overline{C}(10{,}000) = 450$: The average cost per wheelchair of producing 10,000 wheelchairs per month is $450.; $\overline{C}(100{,}000) = 405$: The average cost per wheelchair of producing 100,000 wheelchairs per month is $405.   **d.** $y = 400$; The cost per wheelchair approaches $400 as more wheelchairs are produced.

Exercise Set 11.4

1.
$f(x) = \dfrac{4x}{x-2}$

3.
$f(x) = \dfrac{2x}{x^2-4}$

5.
$f(x) = \dfrac{2x^2}{x^2-1}$

7.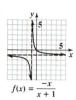
$f(x) = \dfrac{-x}{x+1}$

9.
$f(x) = -\dfrac{1}{x^2-4}$

11.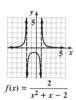
$f(x) = \dfrac{2}{x^2+x-2}$

13.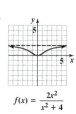
$f(x) = \dfrac{2x^2}{x^2+4}$

15.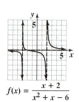
$f(x) = \dfrac{x+2}{x^2+x-6}$

17.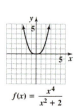
$f(x) = \dfrac{x^4}{x^2+2}$

19.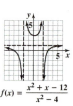
$f(x) = \dfrac{x^2+x-12}{x^2-4}$

21.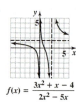
$f(x) = \dfrac{3x^2+x-4}{2x^2-5x}$

23. **a.** Slant asymptote: $y = x$
b.
$f(x) = \dfrac{x^2-1}{x}$

25. **a.** Slant asymptote: $y = x$
b.
$f(x) = \dfrac{x^2+1}{x}$

27. **a.** Slant asymptote: $y = x + 4$
b.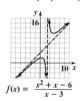
$f(x) = \dfrac{x^2+x-6}{x-3}$

29. **a.** Slant asymptote: $y = x - 2$
b.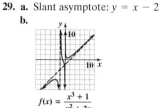
$f(x) = \dfrac{x^3+1}{x^2+2x}$

31. **a.** $C(x) = 100x + 100{,}000$ **b.** $\overline{C}(x) = \dfrac{100x + 100{,}000}{x}$

c. $\overline{C}(500) = 300$, when 500 bicycles are produced, it costs \$300 to produce each bicycle; $\overline{C}(1000) = 200$, when 1000 bicycles are produced, it costs \$200 to produce each bicycle; $\overline{C}(2000) = 150$, when 2000 bicycles are produced, it costs \$150 to produce each bicycle; $\overline{C}(4000) = 125$, when 4000 bicycles are produced, it costs \$125 to produce each bicycle.

d. $y = 100$; The cost per bicycle approaches \$100 as more bicycles are produced

33. **a.** 6.0 **b.** after 6 minutes; about 4.8 **c.** 6.5 **d.** $y = 6.5$; Over time, the pH level rises back to normal. **e.** It quickly drops below normal and then slowly begins to approach the normal level.

35. 90; An incidence ratio of 10 means 90% of the deaths are smoking related. 37. $y = 100$; The percentage of deaths cannot exceed 100% as the incidence ratios increase. 39. answers may vary

41.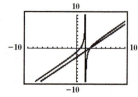

43. does not make sense 45, 47. answers may vary 49. $\dfrac{-x-5}{x+3}$ or $-\dfrac{x+5}{x+3}$

$g(x)$ is the graph of a line whereas $f(x)$ is the graph of a rational function with a slant asymptote; In $g(x)$, $x - 2$ is a factor of $x^2 - 5x + 6$.

Section 11.5
Practice Exercises

1. $x = \frac{1}{2}y^2$
2. $x = -2(y+4)^2 - 1$
3. $y = -x^2 + 4x + 6$
4. $x = 3y^2 + 6y + 4$
5. $x^2 + y^2 = 25$
6. $(x-3)^2 + (y+2)^2 = 4$
7. $(x+2)^2 + (y+5)^2 = 81$
8. $x^2 + y^2 + 6x - 2y = 6$

Graphing Calculator Explorations 11.5

1.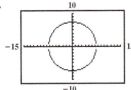
3.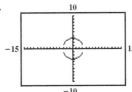
5.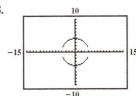
7.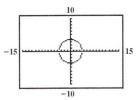

Vocabulary and Readiness Check 11.5

1. conic sections   3. circle, center   5. radius   7. upward   9. to the left   11. downward

Exercise Set 11.5

1.
3.
5.
7.
9.

11.
13.
15.
17.
19.

21.
23.
25. $(x-2)^2 + (y-3)^2 = 36$
27. $x^2 + y^2 = 3$
29. $(x+5)^2 + (y-4)^2 = 45$

31. The radius is $\sqrt{10}$.
33.
35.
37.
39.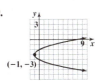

41. **43.** **45.** **47.** **49.**

51. 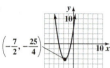 **53.** **55.** **57.** **59.**

61. **63.** **65.** **67.** **69.** $\dfrac{\sqrt{10}}{4}$ **71.** $2\sqrt{5}$

73. a. 67.5 meters **b.** ground level or 0 m **c.** 67.5 meters **d.** $(0, 67.5)$ **e.** $x^2 + (y - 67.5)^2 = (67.5)^2$
75. a. 76.5 m **b.** 7 m **c.** 83.5 m **d.** $(0, 83.5)$ **e.** $x^2 + (y - 83.5)^2 = (76.5)^2$
77. a. **b.** $x^2 + y^2 = 100$ **c.** $x^2 + y^2 = 25$ **79.** 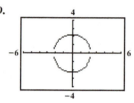 **81.**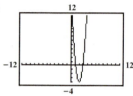

Section 11.6
Practice Exercises

1. $\dfrac{x^2}{25} + \dfrac{y^2}{4} = 1$ **2.** $9x^2 + 4y^2 = 36$ **3.** $\dfrac{(x-4)^2}{49} + \dfrac{(y+1)^2}{81} = 1$

4. $\dfrac{x^2}{9} - \dfrac{y^2}{16} = 1$ **5.** (image) $9y^2 - 25x^2 = 225$

Graphing Calculator Explorations 11.6

1. 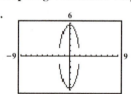 **3.** 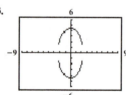 **5.**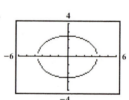

Vocabulary and Readiness Check 11.6

1. hyperbola **3.** focus **5.** hyperbola; $(0, 0)$; x; $(a, 0)$ and $(-a, 0)$ **7.** ellipse **9.** hyperbola **11.** hyperbola

Exercise Set 11.6

1. **3.** **5.** **7.** **9.**

11. 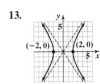 **13.**   **15.**   **17.**   **19.**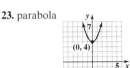

21. answers may vary **23.** parabola   **25.** ellipse   **27.** hyperbola

29. circle   **31.** parabola   **33.** ellipse **35.** hyperbola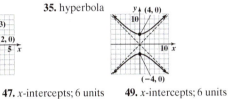

37. parabola   **39.** $x < 5$ **41.** $x \geq 4$ **43.** $-2x^3$ **45.** $-5x^4$ **47.** x-intercepts; 6 units **49.** x-intercepts; 6 units

51. ellipses: C, E, H; circles: B, F; hyperbolas: A, D, G   **53.** A: 49, 7; B: 0, 0; C: 9, 3; D: 64, 8; E: 64, 8; F: 0, 0; G: 81, 9; H: 4, 2

55. A: $\frac{7}{6}$; B: 0; C: $\frac{3}{5}$; D: $\frac{8}{5}$; E: $\frac{8}{9}$; F: 0; G: $\frac{9}{4}$; H: $\frac{1}{6}$ **57.** equal to zero   **59.** answers may vary   **61.** $\frac{x^2}{1.69 \cdot 10^{16}} + \frac{y^2}{1.5625 \cdot 10^{16}} = 1$

63. $9x^2 + 4y^2 = 36$ 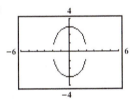 **65.**   **67.**   **69.**

Integrated Review

1.   **2.**   **3.**   **4.**   **5.**

6. **7.** 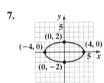 **8.**   **9.**   **10.**

11. 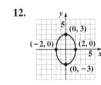 **12.**   **13.**   **14.** **15.**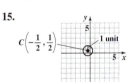

Section 11.7
Practice Exercises
1. $(-4, 3)(0, -1)$ **2.** $(4, -2)$ **3.** no solution   **4.** $(2, \sqrt{3}); (2, -\sqrt{3}); (-2, \sqrt{3}); (-2, -\sqrt{3})$

Exercise Set 11.7
1. $(3, -4), (-3, 4)$ **3.** $(\sqrt{2}, \sqrt{2}), (-\sqrt{2}, -\sqrt{2})$ **5.** $(4, 0), (0, -2)$ **7.** $(-\sqrt{5}, -2), (-\sqrt{5}, 2), (\sqrt{5}, -2), (\sqrt{5}, 2)$ **9.** no solution
11. $(1, -2), (3, 6)$ **13.** $(2, 4), (-5, 25)$ **15.** no solution   **17.** $(1, -3)$ **19.** $(-1, -2), (-1, 2), (1, -2), (1, 2)$ **21.** $(0, -1)$ **23.** $(-1, 3), (1, 3)$

25. $(\sqrt{3}, 0), (-\sqrt{3}, 0)$ **27.** no solution **29.** $(-6, 0), (6, 0), (0, -6)$ **31.**   **33.** 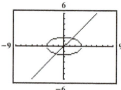 **35.** $(8x - 25)$ in.

37. $(4x^2 + 6x + 2)$ m **39.** answers may vary **41.** 0, 1, 2, 3, or 4; answers may vary **43.** 9 and 7; 9 and -7; -9 and 7; -9 and -7
45. 15 cm by 19 cm **47.** 15 thousand compact discs price: $3.75 **49.**   **51.**

Section 11.8
Practice Exercises

1. $\dfrac{x^2}{36} + \dfrac{y^2}{16} \geq 1$ **2.** $16y^2 > 9x^2 + 144$ **3.** $\begin{cases} y \geq x^2 \\ y \leq -3x + 2 \end{cases}$ **4.** 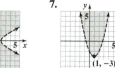 $\begin{cases} x^2 + y^2 < 16 \\ \dfrac{x^2}{4} - \dfrac{y^2}{9} < 1 \\ y < x + 3 \end{cases}$

Exercise Set 11.8

1.   **3.**   **5.**   **7.** 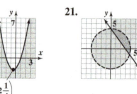 **9.** 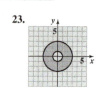 **11.**

13.   **15.**   **17.**   **19.**   **21.** **23.**

25. **27.** **29.** **31.** **33.** **35.**

37. not a function **39.** function **41.** 1 **43.** $3a^2 - 2$ **45.** answers may vary **47.**

Chapter 11 Vocabulary Check

1. discriminant **2.** $\pm \sqrt{b}$ **3.** $\dfrac{-b}{2a}$ **4.** quadratic inequality **5.** completing the square **6.** $(0, k)$ **7.** $(h, 0)$ **8.** (h, k)
9. quadratic formula **10.** quadratic **11.** rational **12.** circle; center **13.** nonlinear system of equations **14.** ellipse **15.** radius
16. hyperbola

Chapter 11 Review

1.
3.
5.
7.
9.
11.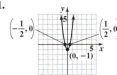

13.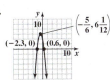
15. The numbers are both 210.
17.
19. Vertical asymptote: $x = 3$ and $x = -3$
    horizontal asymptote: $y = 0$
    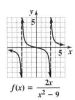

21. Vertical asymptotes: $x = 3, -2$
    horizontal asymptote: $y = 1$
    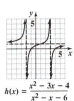

23. Vertical asymptote: $x = -1$
    no horizontal asymptote
    slant asymptote: $y = x - 1$
    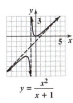

25. No vertical asymptote
    no horizontal asymptote
    slant asymptote: $y = -2x$

27. a. $C(x) = 25x + 50{,}000$
    b. $\overline{C}(x) = \dfrac{25x + 50{,}000}{x}$
    c. $\overline{C}(50) = 1025$, when 50 calculators are manufactured, it costs $1025 to manufacture each;
    $\overline{C}(100) = 525$, when 100 calculators are manufactured, it costs $525 to manufacture each;
    $\overline{C}(1000) = 75$, when 1000 calculators are manufactured, it costs $75 to manufacture each;
    $\overline{C}(100{,}000) = 25.5$, when 100,000 calculators are manufactured, it costs $25.50 to manufacture each.
    d. $y = 25$; costs will approach $25.

29. $(x + 4)^2 + (y - 4)^2 = 9$
31. $(x + 7)^2 + (y + 9)^2 = 11$
33.
35.
37.

39.
41.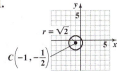
43.
45.
47.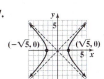

49.
51.
53.
55. $(1, -2), (4, 4)$
57. $(-1, 1), (2, 4)$
59. $(2, 2\sqrt{2}), (2, -2\sqrt{2})$

61. $(1, 4)$ **63.** 15 ft by 10 ft **65.**   **67.**   **69.**   **71.** $-5, 6$ **73.** $-2, 2$

75. $\dfrac{-1 - 3i\sqrt{3}}{2}, \dfrac{-1 + 3i\sqrt{3}}{2}$ **77.** $-i\sqrt{11}, i\sqrt{11}$ **79.** $-\dfrac{8\sqrt{7}}{7}, \dfrac{8\sqrt{7}}{7}$ **81.** $x \leq -\dfrac{5}{4}$ or $x \geq \dfrac{3}{2}$ **83.** $2 < x < \dfrac{7}{2}$

85. $(x + 7)^2 + (y - 8)^2 = 25$ **87.**   **89.**   **91.**   **93.**

95.   **97.**   **99.** $(5, 1), (-1, 7)$ **101.**

Chapter 11 Test

1.   **2.**   **3.** 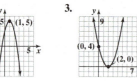 **4.**   **5. a.** 272 ft **b.** 5.12 sec

6. all real numbers except -3 **7.** all real numbers except 1 **8.** all real numbers except 2 **9.** all real numbers except 3 and -1

$f(x) = \dfrac{1}{(x+3)^2}$ $f(x) = \dfrac{1}{x-1} + 2$ $f(x) = \dfrac{x^2 - 9}{x - 2}$ $f(x) = \dfrac{x + 1}{x^2 + 2x - 3}$

10. all real numbers **11. a.** $\overline{C}(x) = \dfrac{300{,}000 + 10x}{x}$ **b.** $y = 10$; As the number of satellite radio players increases, the average cost approaches \$10.

$f(x) = \dfrac{4x^2}{x^2 + 3}$

12.   **13.**   **14.**   **15.**   **16.**

17.   **18.** $(-5, -1), (-5, 1), (5, -1), (5, 1)$ **19.** $(6, 12), (1, 2)$ **20.**

21.   **22.** height, 10 ft; width, 30 ft

Chapter 11 Standardized Test
1. d **2.** a **3.** c **4.** c **5.** c **6.** a **7.** d **8.** c **9.** a **10.** a **11.** a **12.** b **13.** a **14.** a **15.** c **16.** c **17.** a
18. a **19.** c **20.** b **21.** d **22.** c

CHAPTER 12 SEQUENCES, SERIES, AND THE BINOMIAL THEOREM

Section 12.1
Practice Exercises
1. 6, 9, 14, 21, 30 **2. a.** $-\dfrac{1}{5}$ **b.** $\dfrac{1}{20}$ **c.** $\dfrac{1}{150}$ **d.** $-\dfrac{1}{95}$ **3. a.** $a_n = (2n - 1)$ **b.** $a_n = 3^n$ **c.** $a_n = \dfrac{n}{n+1}$ **d.** $a_n = -\dfrac{1}{n+1}$ **4.** $2022.40

Vocabulary and Readiness Check 12.1
1. general **3.** infinite **5.** -1

Exercise Set 12.1
1. 5, 6, 7, 8, 9 **3.** $-1, 1, -1, 1, -1$ **5.** $\dfrac{1}{4}, \dfrac{1}{5}, \dfrac{1}{6}, \dfrac{1}{7}, \dfrac{1}{8}$ **7.** 2, 4, 6, 8, 10 **9.** $-1, -4, -9, -16, -25$ **11.** 2, 4, 8, 16, 32 **13.** 7, 9, 11, 13, 15
15. $-1, 4, -9, 16, -25$ **17.** 75 **19.** 118 **21.** $\dfrac{6}{5}$ **23.** 729 **25.** $\dfrac{4}{7}$ **27.** $\dfrac{1}{8}$ **29.** -95 **31.** $-\dfrac{1}{25}$ **33.** $a_n = 4n - 1$ **35.** $a_n = -2^n$
37. $a_n = \dfrac{1}{3^n}$ **39.** 48 ft, 80 ft, and 112 ft **41.** $a_n = 0.10(2)^{n-1}$; $819.20 **43.** 2400 cases; 75 cases **45.** 50 sparrows in 2004; extinct in 2010
47. 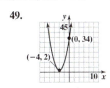 **49.**   **51.** $\sqrt{13}$ units **53.** $\sqrt{41}$ units **55.** 1, 0.7071, 0.5774, 0.5, 0.4472
57. 2, 2.25, 2.3704, 2.4414, 2.4883

Section 12.2
Practice Exercises
1. 4, 9, 14, 19, 24 **2. a.** $a_n = 5 - 3n$ **b.** -31 **3.** 51 **4.** 47 **5.** $a_n = 54{,}800 + 2200n$; $61,400 **6.** 8, -24, 72, -216 **7.** $\dfrac{1}{64}$ **8.** -192
9. $a_1 = 3; r = \dfrac{3}{2}$ **10.** 75 units

Vocabulary and Readiness Check 12.2
1. geometric; ratio **3.** first; difference

Exercise Set 12.2
1. 4, 6, 8, 10, 12 **3.** 6, 4, 2, 0, -2 **5.** 1, 3, 9, 27, 81 **7.** 48, 24, 12, 6, 3 **9.** 33 **11.** -875 **13.** -60 **15.** 96 **17.** -28 **19.** 1250
21. 31 **23.** 20 **25.** $a_1 = \dfrac{2}{3}; r = -2$ **27.** answers may vary **29.** $a_1 = 2; d = 2$ **31.** $a_1 = 5; r = 2$ **33.** $a_1 = \dfrac{1}{2}; r = \dfrac{1}{5}$ **35.** $a_1 = x; r = 5$
37. $a_1 = p; d = 4$ **39.** 19 **41.** $-\dfrac{8}{9}$ **43.** $\dfrac{17}{2}$ **45.** $\dfrac{8}{81}$ **47.** -19 **49.** $a_n = 4n + 50$; 130 seats **51.** $a_n = 6(3)^{n-1}$
53. 486, 162, 54, 18, 6; $a_n = \dfrac{486}{3^{n-1}}$; 6 bounces **55.** $a_n = 4000 + 125(n - 1)$ or $a_n = 3875 + 125n$; $5375 **57.** 25 g **59.** $\dfrac{11}{18}$ **61.** 40 **63.** $\dfrac{907}{495}$
65. $11,782.40, $5891.20, $2945.60, $1472.80 **67.** 19.652, 19.618, 19.584, 19.55 **69.** answers may vary

Section 12.3
Practice Exercises
1. a. $-\dfrac{5}{4}$ **b.** 360 **2. a.** $\displaystyle\sum_{i=1}^{6} 5i$ **b.** $\displaystyle\sum_{i=1}^{4}\left(\dfrac{1}{5}\right)^i$ **3.** $\dfrac{655}{72}$ **4.** 95 plants

Vocabulary and Readiness Check 12.3
1. infinite **3.** summation **5.** partial sum

Exercise Set 12.3

1. -2 **3.** 60 **5.** 20 **7.** $\frac{73}{168}$ **9.** $\frac{11}{36}$ **11.** 60 **13.** 74 **15.** 62 **17.** $\frac{241}{35}$ **19.** $\sum_{i=1}^{5}(2i-1)$ **21.** $\sum_{i=1}^{4}4(3)^{i-1}$
23. $\sum_{i=1}^{6}(-3i+15)$ **25.** $\sum_{i=1}^{4}\frac{4}{3^{i-2}}$ **27.** $\sum_{i=1}^{7}i^2$ **29.** -24 **31.** 0 **33.** 82 **35.** -20 **37.** -2 **39.** $1, 2, 3, \ldots, 10$; 55 trees
41. $a_n = 6(2)^{n-1}$; 96 units **43.** $a_n = 50(2)^n$; n represents the number of 12-hour periods; 800 bacteria **45.** 30 opossums; 68 opossums
47. 6.25 lb; 93.75 lb **49.** 16.4 in.; 134.5 in. **51.** 10 **53.** $\frac{10}{27}$ **55.** 45 **57.** 90 **59. a.** $2+6+12+20+30+42+56$
b. $1+2+3+4+5+6+7+1+4+9+16+25+36+49$ **c.** answers may vary **d.** true; answers may vary

Integrated Review

1. $-2, -1, 0, 1, 2$ **2.** $\frac{7}{2}, \frac{7}{3}, \frac{7}{4}, \frac{7}{5}, \frac{7}{6}$ **3.** $1, 3, 9, 27, 81$ **4.** $-4, -1, 4, 11, 20$ **5.** 64 **6.** -14 **7.** $\frac{1}{40}$ **8.** $-\frac{1}{82}$ **9.** $7, 4, 1, -2, -5$
10. $-3, -15, -75, -375, -1875$ **11.** $45, 15, 5, \frac{5}{3}, \frac{5}{9}$ **12.** $-12, -2, 8, 18, 28$ **13.** 101 **14.** $\frac{243}{16}$ **15.** 384 **16.** 185 **17.** -10 **18.** $\frac{1}{5}$
19. 50 **20.** 98 **21.** $\frac{31}{2}$ **22.** $\frac{61}{20}$ **23.** -10 **24.** 5

Section 12.4
Practice Exercises

1. 80 **2.** 1275 **3.** 105 blocks of ice **4.** $42\frac{5}{8}$ **5.** $987,856 **6.** $9\frac{1}{3}$ **7.** 900 in.

Vocabulary and Readiness Check 12.4
1. arithmetic **3.** geometric **5.** arithmetic

Exercise Set 12.4

1. 36 **3.** 484 **5.** 63 **7.** 2.496 **9.** 55 **11.** 16 **13.** 24 **15.** $\frac{1}{9}$ **17.** -20 **19.** $\frac{16}{9}$ **21.** $\frac{4}{9}$ **23.** 185 **25.** $\frac{381}{64}$
27. $-\frac{33}{4}$, or -8.25 **29.** $-\frac{75}{2}$ **31.** $\frac{56}{9}$ **33.** 4000, 3950, 3900, 3850, 3800; 3450 cars; 44,700 cars **35.** Firm A (Firm A, $265,000; Firm B, $254,000)
37. $39,930; $139,230 **39.** 20 min; 123 min **41.** 180 ft **43.** Player A, 45 points; Player B, 75 points **45.** $3050 **47.** $10,737,418.23
49. 720 **51.** 3 **53.** $x^2 + 10x + 25$ **55.** $8x^3 - 12x^2 + 6x - 1$ **57.** $\frac{8}{10} + \frac{8}{100} + \frac{8}{1000} + \cdots; \frac{8}{9}$ **59.** answers may vary

Section 12.5
Practice Exercises

1. $p^7 + 7p^6r + 21p^5r^2 + 35p^4r^3 + 35p^3r^4 + 21p^2r^5 + 7pr^6 + r^7$ **2. a.** $\frac{1}{7}$ **b.** 840 **c.** 5 **d.** 1
3. $a^9 + 9a^8b + 36a^7b^2 + 84a^6b^3 + 126a^5b^4 + 126a^4b^5 + 84a^3b^6 + 36a^2b^7 + 9ab^8 + b^9$ **4.** $a^3 + 15a^2b + 75ab^2 + 125b^3$
5. $27x^3 - 54x^2y + 36xy^2 - 8y^3$ **6.** $1,892,352x^5y^6$

Vocabulary and Readiness Check 12.5
1. 1 **3.** 24 **5.** 6

Exercise Set 12.5

1. $m^3 + 3m^2n + 3mn^2 + n^3$ **3.** $c^5 + 5c^4d + 10c^3d^2 + 10c^2d^3 + 5cd^4 + d^5$ **5.** $y^5 - 5y^4x + 10y^3x^2 - 10y^2x^3 + 5yx^4 - x^5$
7. answers may vary **9.** 8 **11.** 42 **13.** 360 **15.** 56 **17.** $a^7 + 7a^6b + 21a^5b^2 + 35a^4b^3 + 35a^3b^4 + 21a^2b^5 + 7ab^6 + b^7$
19. $a^5 + 10a^4b + 40a^3b^2 + 80a^2b^3 + 80ab^4 + 32b^5$ **21.** $q^9 + 9q^8r + 36q^7r^2 + 84q^6r^3 + 126q^5r^4 + 126q^4r^5 + 84q^3r^6 + 36q^2r^7 + 9qr^8 + r^9$
23. $1024a^5 + 1280a^4b + 640a^3b^2 + 160a^2b^3 + 20ab^4 + b^5$ **25.** $625a^4 - 1000a^3b + 600a^2b^2 - 160ab^3 + 16b^4$ **27.** $8a^3 + 36a^2b + 54ab^2 + 27b^3$
29. $x^5 + 10x^4 + 40x^3 + 80x^2 + 80x + 32$ **31.** $5cd^4$ **33.** d^7 **35.** $-40r^2s^3$ **37.** $6x^2y^2$ **39.** $30a^9b$
41. 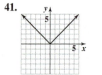 **43.** 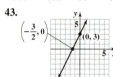 **45.**   **47.** $x^2\sqrt{x} + 5\sqrt{3}x^2 + 30x\sqrt{x} + 30\sqrt{3}x + 45\sqrt{x} + 9\sqrt{3}$
49. 126 **51.** 28 **53.** answers may vary

Chapter 12 Extension
Practice Exercises

1. a. Each number in the list is obtained by adding 6 to the previous number.; 33 **b.** Each number in the list is obtained by multiplying the previous number by 5.; 1250 **c.** To get the second number, multiply the previous number by 2. Then multiply by 3 and then by 4. Then multiply by 2, then by 3, and then by 4, repeatedly.; 3456 **d.** To get the second number, add 8 to the previous number. Then add 8 and then subtract 14. Then add 8, then add 8, and then subtract 14, repeatedly.; 7 **2. a.** Starting with the third number, each number is the sum of the previous two

numbers.; 76   **b.** Starting with the second number, each number is one less than twice the previous number.; 257
3. The figures alternate between rectangles and triangles, and the number of appendages follows the pattern: one, two, three, one, two, three, etc.;
4. a. The result of the process is two times the original number selected.
  b. Representing the original number as *n*, we have

Select a number:	n
Multiply the number by 4:	$4n$
Add 6 to the product:	$4n + 6$
Divide this sum by 2:	$\frac{4n+6}{2} = 2n + 3$
Subtract 3 from the quotient:	$2n + 3 - 3 = 2n.$

Chapter 12 Extension
Exercise Set

1. Each number in the list is obtained by adding 4 to the previous number.; 28
3. Each number in the list is obtained by subtracting 5 from the previous number.; 12
5. Each number in the list is obtained by multiplying the previous number by 3.; 729
7. Each number in the list is obtained by multiplying the previous number by 2.; 32
9. The numbers in the list alternate between 1 and numbers obtained by multiplying the number prior to the previous number by 2.; 32
11. Each number in the list is obtained by subtracting 2 from the previous number.; −6
13. Each number in the list is obtained by adding 4 to the denominator of the previous fraction.; $\frac{1}{22}$
15. Each number in the list is obtained by multiplying the previous number by $\frac{1}{3}$.; $\frac{1}{81}$
17. The second number is obtained by adding 4 to the first number. The third number is obtained by adding 5 to the second number. The number being added to the previous number increases by 1 each time.; 42   **19.** The second number is obtained by adding 3 to the first number. The third number is obtained by adding 5 to the second number. The number being added to the previous number increases by 2 each time.; 51   **21.** Starting with the third number, each number is the sum of the previous two numbers.; 71   **23.** To get the second number, add 5 to the previous number. Then add 5 and then subtract 7. Then add 5, then add 5, and then subtract 7, repeatedly.; 18   **25.** The second number is obtained by multiplying the first number by 2. The third number is obtained by subtracting 1 from the second number. Then multiply by 2 and then subtract 1, repeatedly.; 33
27. Each number in the list is obtained by multiplying the previous number by $-\frac{1}{4}$; $\frac{1}{4}$ **29.** For each pair in the list, the second number is obtained by subtracting 4 from the first number.; −1

31. The pattern is: square, triangle, circle, square, triangle, circle, etc.;

33. Each figure contains the letter of the alphabet following the letter in the previous figure with one more occurrence than in the previous figure.;

35. a. The result of the process is two times the original number selected.
  b. Representing the original number as *n*, we have

select a number:	n
Multiply the number by 4:	$4n$
Add 8 to the product:	$4n + 8$
Divide this sum by 2:	$\frac{4n+8}{2} = 2n + 4$
Subtract 4 from the quotient:	$2n + 4 - 4 = 2n.$

37. a. The result of the process is 3.
  b. Representing the original number as *n*, we have

Select a number:	n
Add 5:	$n + 5$
Double the result:	$2(n + 5) = 2n + 10$
Subtract 4:	$2n + 10 - 4 = 2n + 6$
Divide by 2:	$\frac{2n+6}{2} = n + 3$
Subtract *n*:	$n + 3 - n = 3.$

39. $1 + 2 + 3 + 4 + 5 + 6 = \frac{6 \times 7}{2}; 21 = 21$ **41.** $1 + 3 + 5 + 7 + 9 + 11 = 6 \times 6; 36 = 36$ **43.** $98,765 \times 9 + 3 = 888,888$; correct
45. $165 \times 3367 = 555,555$; correct   **47.** b   **49.** c   **51.** deductive reasoning; Answers will vary.   **53. a.** 28, 36, 45, 55, 66   **b.** 36, 49, 64, 81, 100   **c.** 35, 51, 70, 92, 117   **d.** square   **55, 57.** answers may vary   **59.** 360 square units   **61. a.** The result is a three- or four-digit number in which the thousands and hundreds places represent the month of the birthday and the tens and ones places represent the day of the birthday.
b. $5[4(5M + 6) + 9] + D - 165 = 100M + D$ **63. a.** 10,101; 20,202; 30,303; 40,404   **b.** In the multiplications, the first factor is always 3367, and the second factors are consecutive multiples of 3, beginning with $3 \times 1 = 3$.; The second and fourth digits of the products are always 0; the first, third, and last digits are the same within each product; this digit is 1 in the first product and increases by 1 in each subsequent product.
c. $3367 \times 15 = 50,505; 3367 \times 18 = 60,606$ **d.** inductive reasoning; Answers will vary.

Chapter 12 Vocabulary Check
1. finite sequence   2. factorial of n 3. infinite sequence   4. geometric sequence, common ratio   5. series   6. general term
7. arithmetic sequence, common difference   8. Pascal's triangle

Chapter 12 Review
1. $-3, -12, -27, -48, -75$ 3. $\dfrac{1}{100}$ 5. $a_n = \dfrac{1}{6n}$ 7. 144 ft, 176 ft, 208 ft   9. 660,000; 1,320,000; 2,640,000; 5,280,000; 10,560,000; 2010: 10,560,000 infested acres   11. $-2, -\dfrac{4}{3}, -\dfrac{8}{9}, -\dfrac{16}{27}, -\dfrac{32}{81}$ 13. 111   15. -83 17. $a_1 = 3; d = 5$ 19. $a_n = \dfrac{3}{10^n}$ 21. $a_1 = \dfrac{8}{3}, r = \dfrac{3}{2}$
23. $a_1 = 7x, r = -2$ 25. 8, 6, 4.5, 3.4, 2.5, 1.9; good   27. $a_n = 2^{n-1}$, $512, $536,870,912   29. $a_n = 900 + (n-1)150$ or $a_n = 150n + 750$; $1650/month   31. $1 + 3 + 5 + 7 + 9 = 25$ 33. $\dfrac{1}{4} - \dfrac{1}{6} + \dfrac{1}{8} = \dfrac{5}{24}$ 35. -4 37. -10 39. $\sum_{i=1}^{6} 3^{i-1}$ 41. $\sum_{i=1}^{4} \dfrac{1}{4^i}$ 43. $a_n = 20(2)^n$; n represents the number of 8-hour periods; 1280 yeast   45. Job A, $48,300; Job B, $46,600   47. 150   49. 900   51. -410 53. 936   55. 10
57. -25 59. $30,418; $99,868   61. $58; $553   63. 2696 mosquitoes   65. $\dfrac{5}{9}$ 67. $x^5 + 5x^4z + 10x^3z^2 + 10x^2z^3 + 5xz^4 + z^5$
69. $16x^4 + 32x^3y + 24x^2y^2 + 8xy^3 + y^4$ 71. $b^8 + 8b^7c + 28b^6c^2 + 56b^5c^3 + 70b^4c^4 + 56b^3c^5 + 28b^2c^6 + 8bc^7 + c^8$
73. $256m^4 - 256m^3n + 96m^2n^2 - 16mn^3 + n^4$ 75. $35a^4b^3$ 77. 130   79. 40.5

Chapter 12 Test
1. $-\dfrac{1}{5}, \dfrac{1}{6}, -\dfrac{1}{7}, \dfrac{1}{8}, -\dfrac{1}{9}$ 2. 247   3. $a_n = \dfrac{2}{5}\left(\dfrac{1}{5}\right)^{n-1}$ 4. $a_n = (-1)^n 9n$ 5. 155   6. -330 7. $\dfrac{144}{5}$ 8. 1   9. 10   10. -60
11. $a^6 - 6a^5b + 15a^4b^2 - 20a^3b^3 + 15a^2b^4 - 6ab^5 + b^6$ 12. $32x^5 + 80x^4y + 80x^3y^2 + 40x^2y^3 + 10xy^4 + y^5$ 13. 925 people; 250 people initially
14. $1 + 3 + 5 + 7 + 9 + 11 + 13 + 15$; 64 shrubs   15. 33.75 cm, 218.75 cm   16. 320 cm   17. 304 ft; 1600 ft   18. $\dfrac{14}{33}$

Chapter 12 Standardized Test
1. a   2. a   3. c   4. b   5. d   6. b   7. a   8. c   9. a   10. d   11. a   12. a   13. a   14. c   15. d   16. c   17. d   18. d

CHAPTER 13 COUNTING METHODS AND PROBABILITY THEORY

Section 13.1
Exercises
1. 150   2. 30   3. 160   4. 729   5. 90,000

Exercise Set 13.1
1. 80   3. 12   5. 6   7. 40   9. 144; Answers will vary.   11. 8   13. 96   15. 243   17. 144   19. 676,000   21. 2187
23, 25. answers may vary   27. 720 hr

Section 13.2
Practice Exercises
1. 2   2. 120   3. a. 504   b. 524,160   c. 100   4. 840   5. 15,120   6. 420

Exercise Set 13.2
1. 720   3. 120   5. 120   7. 362,880   9. 6   11. 4   13. 504   15. 570,024   17. 3,047,466,240   19. 600   21. 10,712   23. 5034
25. 24   27. 6   29. 42   31. 1716   33. 3024   35. 6720   37. 720   39. 1   41. 720   43. 8,648,640   45. 120   47. 15,120
49. 180   51. 831,600   53. 105   55. 280   57, 59, 61, 63. answers may vary   65. 360   67. 14,400   69. $\dfrac{n(n-1)\cdots 3 \cdot 2 \cdot 1}{2} = n(n-1)\cdots 3$

Section 13.3
Practice Exercises
1. a. combinations   b. permutations   2. 35   3. 1820   4. 23,049,600

Exercise Set 13.3
1. combinations   3. permutations   5. 6   7. 126   9. 330   11. 8   13. 1   15. 4060   17. 1   19. 7   21. 0   23. $\dfrac{3}{4}$
25. -9499 27. $\dfrac{3}{68}$ 29. 20   31. 495   33. 24,310   35. 22,957,480   37. 360 ways   39. 1716 ways   41. 1140 ways
43. 840 passwords   45. 2730 cones   47. 735   49. 4,516,932,420   51, 53. answers may vary   55. The 5/36 lottery is easier to win.; Answers will vary.   57. 570 sec or 9.5 min; 2340 sec or 39 min

Section 13.4
Practice Exercises
1. a. $\frac{1}{6}$ **b.** $\frac{1}{2}$ **c.** 0 **d.** 1 **2. a.** $\frac{1}{13}$ **b.** $\frac{1}{2}$ **c.** $\frac{1}{26}$ **3.** $\frac{1}{2}$ **4. a.** 0.24 **b.** 0.48

Exercise Set 13.4
1. $\frac{1}{6}$ **3.** $\frac{1}{2}$ **5.** $\frac{1}{3}$ **7.** 1 **9.** 0 **11.** $\frac{1}{13}$ **13.** $\frac{1}{4}$ **15.** $\frac{3}{13}$ **17.** $\frac{1}{52}$ **19.** 0 **21.** $\frac{1}{4}$ **23.** $\frac{1}{2}$ **25.** $\frac{1}{2}$ **27.** $\frac{3}{8}$ **29.** $\frac{3}{8}$
31. $\frac{7}{8}$ **33.** 0 **35.** $\frac{1}{4}$ **37.** $\frac{1}{9}$ **39.** 0 **41.** $\frac{3}{10}$ **43.** $\frac{1}{5}$ **45.** $\frac{1}{2}$ **47.** 0 **49.** 0.43 **51.** 0.13 **53.** 0.03 **55.** 0.38 **57.** 0.78
59. 0.12 **61, 63, 67.** answers may vary **69.** $\frac{3}{8} = 0.375$

Integrated Review
1. b **2.** c **3.** d **4.** 4200 **5.** c **6.** c **7.** c **8.** b **9.** a **10.** a **11.** b **12.** d **13.** b **14.** a

Section 13.5
Practice Exercises
1. $\frac{1}{60}$ **2.** $\frac{1}{13,983,816} \approx 0.0000000715$ **3. a.** $\frac{1}{6}$ **b.** $\frac{1}{2}$

Exercise Set 13.5
1. a. 120 **b.** 6 **c.** $\frac{1}{20}$ **3. a.** $\frac{1}{6}$ **b.** $\frac{1}{30}$ **c.** $\frac{1}{720}$ **d.** $\frac{1}{3}$ **5. a.** 84 **b.** 10 **c.** $\frac{5}{42}$
7. $\frac{1}{18,009,460} \approx 0.0000000555$; $\frac{100}{18,009,460} \approx 0.00000555$ **9. a.** $\frac{1}{177,100} \approx 0.00000565$ **b.** $\frac{27,132}{177,100} \approx 0.153$
11. $\frac{3}{10} = 0.3$ **13. a.** 2,598,960 **b.** 1287 **c.** $\frac{1287}{2,598,960} \approx 0.000495$ **15.** $\frac{11}{1105} \approx 0.00995$ **17.** $\frac{36}{270,725} \approx 0.000133$
19, 21. answers may vary **23.** $9,004,730 **25.** $\frac{1}{10}$

Section 13.6
Practice Exercises
1. $\frac{3}{4}$ **2. a.** $\frac{160}{191}$ **b.** $\frac{182}{191}$ **3.** $\frac{1}{3}$ **4.** $\frac{27}{50}$ **5.** $\frac{3}{4}$ **6. a.** 2:50 or 1:25 **b.** 50:2 or 25:1 **7.** 199:1 **8.** 1:15; $\frac{1}{16}$

Exercise Set 13.6
1. $\frac{12}{13}$ **3.** $\frac{3}{4}$ **5.** $\frac{10}{13}$ **7.** $\frac{2,598,924}{2,598,960} \approx 0.999986$ **9.** $\frac{2,595,216}{2,598,960} \approx 0.998559$ **11. a.** 0.10 **b.** 0.90 **13.** $\frac{23}{28}$ **15.** $\frac{95}{112}$ **17.** $\frac{2}{13}$
19. $\frac{1}{13}$ **21.** $\frac{1}{26}$ **23.** $\frac{9}{22}$ **25.** $\frac{5}{6}$ **27.** $\frac{7}{13}$ **29.** $\frac{11}{26}$ **31.** $\frac{3}{4}$ **33.** $\frac{5}{8}$ **35.** $\frac{33}{40}$ **37.** $\frac{4}{5}$ **39.** $\frac{7}{10}$ **41.** $\frac{8}{11}$ **43.** $\frac{108}{187}$
45. $\frac{122}{187}$ **47.** 3:8; 8:3 **49.** $\frac{93}{143}$ **51.** $\frac{127}{143}$ **53.** $\frac{5}{13}$ **55.** 38:105; 105:38 **57.** 1:142; 142:1 **59.** 11:2; 2:11 **61.** 2:1 **63.** 1:2
65. a. 9:91 **b.** 91:9 **67.** 1:3 **69.** 1:1 **71.** 12:1 **73.** 25:1 **75.** 47:5 **77.** 49:1 **79.** 9:10 **81.** 14:5 **83.** 14:5 **85.** 9:10
87. $\frac{3}{7}$ **89.** $\frac{4}{25}$; 84 **91.** $\frac{1}{1000}$ **93, 95, 97, 99.** answers may vary

Section 13.7
Practice Exercises
1. $\frac{1}{361} \approx 0.00277$ **2.** $\frac{1}{16}$ **3. a.** $\frac{625}{130,321} \approx 0.005$ **b.** $\frac{38,416}{130,321} \approx 0.295$ **c.** $\frac{91,905}{130,321} \approx 0.705$ **4.** $\frac{1}{221} \approx 0.00452$
5. $\frac{11}{850} \approx 0.0129$ **6.** $\frac{1}{2}$

Exercise Set 13.7
1. $\frac{1}{6}$ **3.** $\frac{1}{36}$ **5.** $\frac{1}{4}$ **7.** $\frac{1}{36}$ **9.** $\frac{1}{8}$ **11.** $\frac{1}{36}$ **13.** $\frac{1}{3}$ **15.** $\frac{3}{52}$ **17.** $\frac{1}{169}$ **19.** $\frac{1}{4}$ **21.** $\frac{1}{64}$ **23.** $\frac{1}{6}$
25. a. $\frac{1}{256} \approx 0.00391$ **b.** $\frac{1}{4096} \approx 0.000244$ **c.** ≈ 0.524 **d.** ≈ 0.476 **27.** 0.0144 **29.** 0.008 **31.** 0.4686 **33.** $\frac{7}{29}$ **35.** $\frac{5}{87}$
37. $\frac{2}{21}$ **39.** $\frac{4}{35}$ **41.** $\frac{11}{21}$ **43.** $\frac{1}{57}$ **45.** $\frac{8}{855}$ **47.** $\frac{11}{57}$ **49.** $\frac{1}{5}$ **51.** $\frac{2}{3}$ **53.** $\frac{3}{4}$ **55.** $\frac{3}{4}$ **57, 59, 61, 63.** answers may vary
65. 0.59049 **67. a.** Answers will vary. **b.** $\frac{365}{365} \cdot \frac{364}{365} \cdot \frac{363}{365} \approx 0.992$ **c.** ≈ 0.008 **d.** 0.411 **e.** 23 people

Section 13.8
Practice Exercises
1. a. 75.5 in. **b.** 58 in. **2. a.** 95% **b.** 47.5% **c.** 16%

Exercise Set 13.8
1. 120 **3.** 160 **5.** 150 **7.** 60 **9.** 90 **11.** 68% **13.** 34% **15.** 47.5% **17.** 49.85% **19.** 16% **21.** 2.5% **23.** 95% **25.** 47.5% **27.** 16% **29.** 2.5% **31.** 0.15% **33, 35.** answers may vary

Extension Exercises
Practice Exercises
1. 2.5 **2.** 2 **3. a.** $8000; In the long run, the average cost of a claim is $8000. **b.** $8000 **4.** 0; no; Answers will vary.

Extension Exercise Set
1. 1.75 **3. a.** $29,000; In the long run, the average cost of a claim is $29,000. **b.** $29,000 **c.** $29,050 **5.** $0; Answers will vary. **7.** $0.73 **9.** $\frac{1}{16} = 0.0625$; yes **11.** the second mall **13. a.** $140,000 **b.** no **15, 17, 19.** answers may vary

Chapter 13 Review Exercises
1. 800 **3.** 9900 **5.** 243 **7.** 720 **9.** 120 **11.** 800 **13.** 990 **15.** 9900 **17.** 1,860,480 **19.** 60 **21.** permutations **23.** 330 **25.** 210 **27.** 1140 **29.** $\frac{1}{6}$ **31.** 1 **33.** $\frac{1}{13}$ **35.** $\frac{3}{13}$ **37.** $\frac{1}{26}$ **39.** $\frac{1}{3}$ **41. a.** $\frac{1}{2}$ **b.** 0 **43.** 0.518 **45.** $\frac{1}{24}$ **47.** $\frac{1}{30}$ **49.** $\frac{1}{3}$ **51. a.** $\frac{1}{14}$ **b.** $\frac{3}{7}$ **53.** $\frac{5}{6}$ **55.** $\frac{1}{3}$ **57.** 1 **59.** $\frac{3}{4}$ **61.** $\frac{1}{13}$ **63.** $\frac{11}{26}$ **65.** $\frac{5}{6}$ **67.** $\frac{2}{3}$ **69.** $\frac{5}{6}$ **71.** $\frac{3}{4}$ **73.** $\frac{6}{7}$ **75.** $\frac{12}{35}$ **77.** 99:1 **79.** $\frac{2}{9}$ **81.** $\frac{1}{9}$ **83.** $\frac{8}{27}$ **85. a.** 0.04 **b.** 0.008 **c.** 0.4096 **d.** 0.5904 **87.** $\frac{1}{12}$ **89.** $\frac{1}{3}$ **91. a.** $\frac{1}{2}$ **b.** $\frac{2}{7}$ **93.** $\frac{4}{29}$ **95.** $\frac{11}{20}$ **97.** $\frac{1}{125}$ **99.** $\frac{19}{1044}$ **101.** 98 **103.** 68% **105.** 34% **107.** 16% **109.** 2.5%

Chapter 13 Test
1. 240 **2.** 720 **3.** 990 **4.** 210 **5.** 420 **6.** $\frac{6}{25}$ **7.** $\frac{17}{25}$ **8.** $\frac{11}{25}$ **9.** $\frac{8}{13}$ **10.** $\frac{1}{19}$ **11.** $\frac{1}{256}$ **12. a.** 4:1 **b.** $\frac{4}{5}$ **13.** $\frac{3}{5}$ **14.** $\frac{9}{19}$ **15.** 34% **16.** 2.5%

Chapter 13 Standardized Test
1. b **2.** a **3.** d **4.** d **5.** a **6.** b **7.** c **8.** c **9.** c **10.** a **11.** b **12.** a **13.** d **14.** a

CHAPTER 14 TRIGONOMETRIC FUNCTIONS
Section 14.1
Practice Exercises
1. 3.5 radians **2. a.** $\frac{\pi}{3}$ radians **b.** $\frac{3\pi}{2}$ radians **c.** $-\frac{5\pi}{3}$ radians **3. a.** 45° **b.** −240° **c.** 343.8°

4. a. 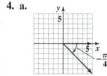 **b.**   **c.**   **d.**

5. a. 40° **b.** 225° **6. a.** $\frac{3\pi}{5}$ **b.** $\frac{29\pi}{15}$ **7. a.** 135° **b.** $\frac{5\pi}{3}$ **c.** $\frac{11\pi}{6}$ **8.** $\frac{3\pi}{2}$ in. ≈ 4.71 in. **9.** 135π in./min ≈ 424 in./min

Exercise Set 14.1
1. obtuse **3.** acute **5.** straight **7.** 4 radians **9.** $\frac{4}{3}$ radians **11.** 4 radians **13.** $\frac{\pi}{4}$ radians **15.** $\frac{3\pi}{4}$ radians **17.** $\frac{5\pi}{3}$ radians **19.** $-\frac{5\pi}{4}$ radians **21.** 90° **23.** 120° **25.** 210° **27.** −540° **29.** 0.31 radians **31.** −0.70 radians **33.** 3.49 radians **35.** 114.59° **37.** 13.85° **39.** −275.02°

41. quadrant III **43.** quadrant II **45.** quadrant III

47. quadrant II **49.** 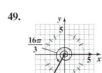 quadrant III **51.** quadrant II

53. quadrant II **55.** quadrant I **57.** 35° **59.** 210° **61.** 315° **63.** $\dfrac{7\pi}{6}$ **65.** $\dfrac{3\pi}{5}$

67. $\dfrac{99\pi}{50}$ **69.** $\dfrac{11\pi}{7}$ **71.** 3π in. ≈ 9.42 in. **73.** 10π ft ≈ 31.42 ft **75.** $\dfrac{12\pi \text{ radians}}{\text{second}}$ **77.** $-\dfrac{4\pi}{3}$ and $\dfrac{2\pi}{3}$ **79.** $-\dfrac{3\pi}{4}$ and $\dfrac{5\pi}{4}$
81. $-\dfrac{\pi}{2}$ and $\dfrac{3\pi}{2}$ **83.** $\dfrac{11\pi}{6}$ **85.** $\dfrac{22\pi}{3}$ **87.** 60°; $\dfrac{\pi}{3}$ radians **89.** $\dfrac{8\pi}{3}$ in. ≈ 8.38 in. **91.** 12π in. ≈ 37.70 in.
93. 2 radians; 114.59° **95.** 2094 mi **97.** 1047 mph **99.** 1508 ft/min **101, 103, 105, 107, 109, 111.** answers may vary **113.** 30.25°
115. 30°25′12″ **117.** does not make sense **119.** makes sense **121.** smaller than a right angle **123.** 1815 mi **125.** $\dfrac{\sqrt{2}}{2}$

Section 14.2
Practice Exercises
1. $\sin\theta = \dfrac{3}{5}; \cos\theta = \dfrac{4}{5}; \tan\theta = \dfrac{3}{4}; \csc\theta = \dfrac{5}{3}; \sec\theta = \dfrac{5}{4}; \cot\theta = \dfrac{4}{3}$ **2.** $\sin\theta = \dfrac{1}{5}; \cos\theta = \dfrac{2\sqrt{6}}{5}; \tan\theta = \dfrac{\sqrt{6}}{12}; \csc\theta = 5; \sec\theta = \dfrac{5\sqrt{6}}{12}; \cot\theta = 2\sqrt{6}$
3. $\sqrt{2}; \sqrt{2}; 1$ **4.** $\sqrt{3}; \dfrac{\sqrt{3}}{3}$ **5.** $\tan\theta = \dfrac{2\sqrt{5}}{5}; \csc\theta = \dfrac{3}{2}; \sec\theta = \dfrac{3\sqrt{5}}{5}; \cot\theta = \dfrac{\sqrt{5}}{2}$ **6.** $\dfrac{\sqrt{3}}{2}$ **7.** cos 44° **8. a.** 0.9553
b. 1.0025 **9.** 333.9 yd **10.** 54°

Exercise Set 14.2
1. 15; $\sin\theta = \dfrac{3}{5}; \cos\theta = \dfrac{4}{5}; \tan\theta = \dfrac{3}{4}; \csc\theta = \dfrac{5}{3}; \sec\theta = \dfrac{5}{4}; \cot\theta = \dfrac{4}{3}$ **3.** 20; $\sin\theta = \dfrac{20}{29}; \cos\theta = \dfrac{21}{29}; \tan\theta = \dfrac{20}{21}; \csc\theta = \dfrac{29}{20}; \sec\theta = \dfrac{29}{21}; \cot\theta = \dfrac{21}{20}$
5. 24; $\sin\theta = \dfrac{5}{13}; \cos\theta = \dfrac{12}{13}; \tan\theta = \dfrac{5}{12}; \csc\theta = \dfrac{13}{5}; \sec\theta = \dfrac{13}{12}; \cot\theta = \dfrac{12}{5}$ **7.** 28; $\sin\theta = \dfrac{4}{5}; \cos\theta = \dfrac{3}{5}; \tan\theta = \dfrac{4}{3}; \csc\theta = \dfrac{5}{4}; \sec\theta = \dfrac{5}{3}; \cot\theta = \dfrac{3}{4}$
9. $\dfrac{\sqrt{3}}{2}$ **11.** $\sqrt{2}$ **13.** $\sqrt{3}$ **15.** 0 **17.** $\tan\theta = \dfrac{8}{15}; \csc\theta = \dfrac{17}{8}; \sec\theta = \dfrac{17}{15}; \cot\theta = \dfrac{15}{8}$ **19.** $\tan\theta = \dfrac{\sqrt{2}}{4}; \csc\theta = 3;$
$\sec\theta = \dfrac{3\sqrt{2}}{4}; \cot\theta = 2\sqrt{2}$ **21.** $\dfrac{\sqrt{13}}{7}$ **23.** $\dfrac{5}{8}$ **25.** 1 **27.** 1 **29.** 1 **31.** cos 83° **33.** sin 65° **35.** cot $\dfrac{7\pi}{18}$
37. $\sin\dfrac{\pi}{10}$ **39.** 0.6157 **41.** 0.6420 **43.** 3.4203 **45.** 0.9511 **47.** 3.7321 **49.** 188 cm **51.** 182 in. **53.** 41 m
55. 17° **57.** 78° **59.** 1.147 radians **61.** 0.395 radians **63.** 0 **65.** 2 **67.** 1 **69.** $\dfrac{2\sqrt{3}-1}{2}$ **71.** $\dfrac{1}{4}$ **73.** 529 yd **75.** 36°
77. 2879 ft **79.** 37° 81, 83, 85, 87, 87, 91, answers may vary. **93.** 0.92106, −0.19735; 0.95534, −0.148878; 0.98007, −0.099667; 0.99500,
−0.04996; 0.99995, −0.005; 0.9999995, −0.0005; 0.999999995, −0.00005; 0.99999999995, −0.000005; $\dfrac{\cos\theta - 1}{\theta}$ approaches 0 as θ approaches 0.
95. does not make sense **97.** makes sense **99.** true **101.** false; $\tan^2 5° = (\tan 5°)^2$ **103.** As θ approaches 90°, tan θ increases without bound.
At 90°, tan θ is undefined. **105. a.** $\dfrac{y}{r}$ **b.** $\dfrac{4}{5}$; positive **106. a.** $\dfrac{x}{r}$ **b.** $-\dfrac{3\sqrt{34}}{34}$; negative **107. a.** 15° **b.** $\dfrac{\pi}{6}$

Section 14.3
Practice Exercises
1. $\sin\theta = -\dfrac{3\sqrt{10}}{10}; \cos\theta = \dfrac{\sqrt{10}}{10}; \tan\theta = -3; \csc\theta = -\dfrac{\sqrt{10}}{3}; \sec\theta = \sqrt{10}; \cot\theta = -\dfrac{1}{3}$ **2. a.** 1; undefined **b.** 0; 1 **c.** −1; undefined
d. 0; −1 **3.** quadrant III **4.** $\dfrac{\sqrt{10}}{10}; -\dfrac{\sqrt{10}}{3}$ **5. a.** 30° **b.** $\dfrac{\pi}{4}$ **c.** 60° **d.** 0.46 **6. a.** 55° **b.** $\dfrac{\pi}{4}$ **c.** $\dfrac{\pi}{3}$
7. a. $-\dfrac{\sqrt{3}}{2}$ **b.** 1 **c.** $\dfrac{2\sqrt{3}}{3}$ **8. a.** $-\dfrac{\sqrt{3}}{2}$ **b.** $\dfrac{\sqrt{3}}{2}$

Exercise Set 14.3

1. $\sin\theta = \frac{3}{5}$; $\cos\theta = -\frac{4}{5}$; $\tan\theta = -\frac{3}{4}$; $\csc\theta = \frac{5}{3}$; $\sec\theta = -\frac{5}{4}$; $\cot\theta = -\frac{4}{3}$ 3. $\sin\theta = \frac{3\sqrt{13}}{13}$; $\cos\theta = \frac{2\sqrt{13}}{13}$; $\tan\theta = \frac{3}{2}$; $\csc\theta = \frac{\sqrt{13}}{3}$; $\sec\theta = \frac{\sqrt{13}}{2}$; $\cot\theta = \frac{2}{3}$ 5. $\sin\theta = -\frac{\sqrt{2}}{2}$; $\cos\theta = \frac{\sqrt{2}}{2}$; $\tan\theta = -1$; $\csc\theta = -\sqrt{2}$; $\sec\theta = \sqrt{2}$; $\cot\theta = -1$ 7. $\sin\theta = -\frac{\sqrt{}}{}$; $\cos\theta = -\frac{2\sqrt{29}}{29}$; $\tan\theta = \frac{5}{2}$; $\csc\theta = -\frac{\sqrt{29}}{5}$; $\sec\theta = -\frac{\sqrt{29}}{2}$; $\cot\theta = \frac{2}{5}$ 9. -1 11. -1 13. undefined   15. 0 17. quadrant I   19. quadrant III   21. quadrant II   23. $\sin\theta = -\frac{4}{5}$; $\tan\theta = \frac{4}{3}$; $\csc\theta = -\frac{5}{4}$; $\sec\theta = -\frac{5}{3}$; $\cot\theta = \frac{3}{4}$ 25. $\cos\theta = -\frac{12}{13}$; $\tan\theta = -\frac{5}{12}$; $\csc\theta = \frac{13}{5}$; $\sec\theta = -\frac{13}{12}$; $\cot\theta = -\frac{12}{5}$ 27. $\sin\theta = -\frac{15}{17}$; $\tan\theta = -\frac{15}{8}$; $\csc\theta = -\frac{17}{15}$; $\sec\theta = \frac{17}{8}$; $\cot\theta = -\frac{8}{15}$ 29. $\sin\theta = \frac{2\sqrt{13}}{13}$; $\cos\theta = -\frac{3\sqrt{13}}{13}$; $\csc\theta = \frac{\sqrt{13}}{2}$; $\sec\theta = -\frac{\sqrt{13}}{3}$; $\cot\theta = -\frac{3}{2}$ 31. $\sin\theta = -\frac{4}{5}$; $\cos\theta = -\frac{3}{5}$; $\csc\theta = -\frac{5}{4}$; $\sec\theta = -\frac{5}{3}$; $\cot\theta = \frac{3}{4}$ 33. $\sin\theta = -\frac{2\sqrt{2}}{3}$; $\cos\theta = -\frac{1}{3}$; $\tan\theta = 2\sqrt{2}$; $\csc\theta = -\frac{3\sqrt{2}}{4}$; $\cot\theta = \frac{\sqrt{2}}{4}$ 35. $20°$ 37. $25°$ 39. $5°$ 41. $\frac{\pi}{4}$ 43. $\frac{\pi}{6}$ 45. $30°$ 47. $25°$ 49. 1.56 51. $25°$ 53. $\frac{\pi}{6}$ 55. $\frac{\pi}{4}$ 57. $\frac{\pi}{4}$ 59. $\frac{\pi}{6}$ 61. $-\frac{\sqrt{2}}{2}$ 63. $\frac{\sqrt{3}}{3}$ 65. $\sqrt{3}$ 67. $\frac{\sqrt{3}}{2}$ 69. -2 71. 1 73. $\frac{\sqrt{3}}{2}$ 75. -1 77. $-\sqrt{2}$ 79. $\sqrt{3}$ 81. $\frac{\sqrt{2}}{2}$ 83. $\frac{\sqrt{3}}{3}$ 85. $\frac{\sqrt{3}}{2}$ 87. $\frac{1-\sqrt{3}}{2}$ 89. $\frac{-\sqrt{6}-\sqrt{2}}{4}$ or $-\frac{\sqrt{6}+\sqrt{2}}{4}$ 91. $-\frac{3}{2}$ 93. $\frac{-1-\sqrt{3}}{2}$ or $-\frac{1+\sqrt{3}}{2}$ 95. 1 97. $\frac{2\sqrt{2}-4}{\pi}$ 99. $\frac{\pi}{4}$ and $\frac{3\pi}{4}$ 101. $\frac{5\pi}{4}$ and $\frac{7\pi}{4}$ 103. $\frac{2\pi}{3}$ and $\frac{5\pi}{3}$ 105, 107, 109. answers may vary   111. does not make sense   113. makes sense   115. domain: $-1 \le x \le 1$ range: $-1 \le y \le 1$

Section 14.4
Practice Exercises

1. $\sin t = \frac{1}{2}$; $\cos t = \frac{\sqrt{3}}{2}$; $\tan t = \frac{\sqrt{3}}{3}$; $\csc t = 2$; $\sec t = \frac{2\sqrt{3}}{3}$; $\cot t = \sqrt{3}$ 2. $\sin\pi = 0$; $\cos\pi = -1$; $\tan\pi = 0$; $\csc\pi$ is undefined; $\sec\pi = -1$; $\cot\pi$ is undefined   3. a. $\frac{1}{2}$ b. $-\frac{\sqrt{3}}{3}$ 4. a. $\frac{\sqrt{2}}{2}$ b. $\frac{\sqrt{3}}{2}$

Exercise Set 14.4

1. $\sin t = \frac{8}{17}$; $\cos t = -\frac{15}{17}$; $\tan t = -\frac{8}{15}$; $\csc t = \frac{17}{8}$; $\sec t = -\frac{17}{15}$; $\cot t = -\frac{15}{8}$ 3. $\sin t = -\frac{\sqrt{2}}{2}$; $\cos t = \frac{\sqrt{2}}{2}$; $\tan t = -1$; $\csc t = -\sqrt{2}$; $\sec t = \sqrt{2}$; $\cot t = -1$ 5. $\frac{1}{2}$ 7. $-\frac{\sqrt{3}}{2}$ 9. 0 11. -2 13. $\frac{2\sqrt{3}}{3}$ 15. -1 17. undefined   19. a. $\frac{\sqrt{3}}{2}$ b. $\frac{\sqrt{3}}{2}$ 21. a. $\frac{1}{2}$ b. $-\frac{1}{2}$ 23. a. $-\sqrt{3}$ b. $\sqrt{3}$ 25. a. $\frac{\sqrt{2}}{2}$ b. $\frac{\sqrt{2}}{2}$ 27. a. 0 b. 0 29. a. 0 b. 0 31. a. $-\frac{\sqrt{2}}{2}$ b. $-\frac{\sqrt{2}}{2}$ 33. $-2a$ 35. $3b$ 37. $a - b + c$ 39. $-a - b + c$ 41. $3a + 2b - 2c$ 43. a. 12 hr   b. 20.3 hr   c. 3.7 hr   45. a. $1; 0; -1; 0; 1$ b. 28 days   47. answers may vary   49. answers may vary   51. answers may vary   53. makes sense   55. does not make sense   57. 0 59. $-\frac{1}{4}$ 61. $\frac{1}{2}; 0; -\frac{1}{2}; 0; \frac{1}{2}$ 63. $0; \frac{3}{2}; 3; \frac{3}{2}; 0; -\frac{3}{2}; -3; -\frac{3}{2}; 0$

Integrated Review

1. $\frac{\pi}{18}$ 2. $-\frac{7\pi}{12}$ 3. $75°$ 4. $-117°$

5. a. $\frac{5\pi}{3}$ b. [graph showing $\frac{11\pi}{3}$]   c. $\frac{\pi}{3}$

6. a. $\frac{5\pi}{4}$ b. [graph showing $-\frac{19\pi}{4}$]   c. $\frac{\pi}{4}$

7. a. $150°$ b. [graph showing $510°$]   c. $30°$

8. $\sin\theta = \frac{5}{6}$; $\cos\theta = \frac{\sqrt{11}}{6}$; $\tan\theta = \frac{5\sqrt{11}}{11}$; $\csc\theta = \frac{6}{5}$; $\sec\theta = \frac{6\sqrt{11}}{11}$; $\cot\theta = \frac{\sqrt{11}}{5}$ 9. $\sin\theta = -\frac{2\sqrt{13}}{13}$; $\cos\theta = \frac{3\sqrt{13}}{13}$; $\tan\theta = -\frac{2}{3}$; $\csc\theta = -\frac{\sqrt{13}}{2}$;

Answers to Selected Exercises A65

$\sec\theta = \dfrac{\sqrt{13}}{3}$; $\cot\theta = -\dfrac{3}{2}$ **10.** $\sin t = -\dfrac{4}{5}$; $\cos t = -\dfrac{3}{5}$; $\tan t = \dfrac{4}{3}$; $\csc t = -\dfrac{5}{4}$; $\sec t = -\dfrac{5}{3}$; $\cot t = \dfrac{3}{4}$ **11.** $\sin\theta = \dfrac{3}{5}$; $\cos\theta = -\dfrac{4}{5}$; $\csc\theta = \dfrac{5}{3}$; $\sec\theta = -\dfrac{5}{4}$; $\cot\theta = -\dfrac{4}{3}$ **12.** $\sin\theta = -\dfrac{2\sqrt{10}}{7}$; $\tan\theta = -\dfrac{2\sqrt{10}}{3}$; $\csc\theta = -\dfrac{7\sqrt{10}}{20}$; $\sec\theta = \dfrac{7}{3}$; $\cot\theta = -\dfrac{3\sqrt{10}}{20}$ **13.** 52 cm   **14.** 809 m
15. $\sqrt{35}$ **16.** $\dfrac{\sqrt{3}}{3}$ **17.** $-\dfrac{\sqrt{3}}{3}$ **18.** $-\dfrac{1}{2}$ **19.** $\dfrac{2\sqrt{3}}{3}$ **20.** 1   **21.** $-\dfrac{\sqrt{3}}{2}$ **22.** $-\dfrac{2\sqrt{3}}{3}$ **23.** $-\dfrac{\sqrt{2}}{2}$ **24.** $\dfrac{\sqrt{3}}{3}$ **25.** 2
26. $-\dfrac{5\sqrt{3}}{6}$ **27.** 8π cm $\approx$ 25.13 cm   **28.** 160π ft/min $\approx$ 502 ft/min   **29.** 551.9 ft   **30.** 40°

Section 14.5
Practice Exercises
1. 3   **2.** $\dfrac{1}{2}$ **3.** 2; 4π **4.** 3; π; $\dfrac{\pi}{6}$

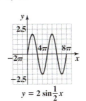
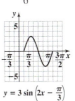

5. 4; 2   **6.** $\dfrac{3}{2}$; π; $-\dfrac{\pi}{2}$ **7.**   **8.** $y = 4\sin 4x$
9. $y = 2\sin\left(\dfrac{\pi}{6}x - \dfrac{\pi}{2}\right) + 12$

Exercise Set 14.5
1. 4   **3.** $\dfrac{1}{3}$ **5.** 3   **7.** 1; π

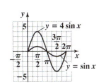

9. 3; 4π **11.** 4; 2   **13.** 3; 1   **15.** 1; 3π

17. 1; 2π; π **19.** 1; π; $\dfrac{\pi}{2}$ **21.** 3; π; $\dfrac{\pi}{2}$ **23.** $\dfrac{1}{2}$; 2π; $-\dfrac{\pi}{2}$

25. 2; π; $-\dfrac{\pi}{4}$ **27.** 3; 2; $-\dfrac{2}{\pi}$ **29.** 2; 1; -2 **31.** 2

A66 Answers to Selected Exercises

33. 2

35. 1; π

37. 4; 1

39. 4; 4π

41. $\dfrac{1}{2}$; 6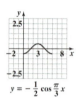

43. 1; 2π, $\dfrac{\pi}{2}$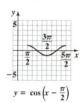

45. 3; π; $\dfrac{\pi}{2}$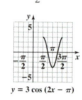

47. $\dfrac{1}{2}$; $\dfrac{2\pi}{3}$; $-\dfrac{\pi}{6}$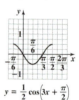

49. 3; π; $\dfrac{\pi}{4}$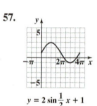

51. 2; 1; −4

53.

55.

57.

59.

61. One possibility: $y = 3\cos\left(\dfrac{1}{2}x\right)$

63. One possibility: $y = -2\sin(2x)$

65. One possibility: $y = 2\sin\left(\dfrac{\pi}{2}x\right)$

67.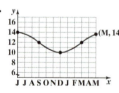

69.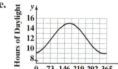

71.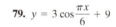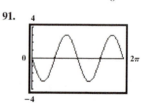

73.

75.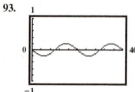

77. a. 3 b. 365 days c. 15 hours of daylight d. 9 hours of daylight e.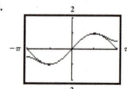

79. $y = 3\cos\dfrac{\pi x}{6} + 9$

81, 83, 85, 87. answers may vary.

91.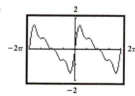

93.

95.

97.

The graph is similar to $y = \sin x$, except the amplitude is greater and the curve is less smooth.

Answers to Selected Exercises **A67**

99. a.   **b.** $y = 22.61 \sin(0.50x - 2.04) + 57.17$ **101.** makes sense **103.** makes sense

c.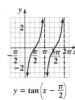

105. a. range: $-5 \leq y \leq 1$; $\left[-\dfrac{\pi}{6}, \dfrac{23\pi}{6}, \dfrac{\pi}{6}\right]$ by $[-5, 1, 1]$

b. range: $-3 \leq y \leq 1$; $\left[-\dfrac{\pi}{6}, \dfrac{7\pi}{6}, \dfrac{\pi}{6}\right]$ by $[-3, -1, 1]$

107. $-\dfrac{3\pi}{4} < x < \dfrac{\pi}{4}$

Section 14.6
Practice Exercises

1.   **2.**

Exercise Set 14.6

1. $y = \tan(x + \pi)$ **3.** $y = -\tan\left(x - \dfrac{\pi}{2}\right)$ **5.**   **7.**   **9.**   **11.**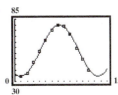

13. a. 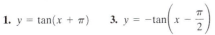   **b.** 0.25, 0.75, 1.25, 1.75; The beam of light is shining parallel to the wall at these times.   **15.** answers may vary   **19.** 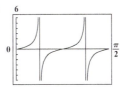   **21.**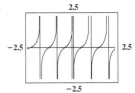

23. $y = \tan\dfrac{3}{4}x$ **25. a.**   **b.** yes   **c.** $\dfrac{5\pi}{6}$; $\left(\dfrac{5\pi}{6}, -\dfrac{\sqrt{3}}{2}\right)$

Section 14.7
Practice Exercises

1. $\dfrac{\pi}{3}$ **2.** $-\dfrac{\pi}{4}$ **3.** $\dfrac{2\pi}{3}$ **4.** $-\dfrac{\pi}{4}$ **5. a.** 1.2310   **b.** -1.5429 **6. a.** 0.7   **b.** 0   **c.** not defined   **7.** $\dfrac{3}{5}$ **8.** $\dfrac{\sqrt{3}}{2}$ **9.** $\sqrt{x^2 + 1}$

Exercise Set 14.7

1. $\dfrac{\pi}{6}$ **3.** $\dfrac{\pi}{4}$ **5.** $-\dfrac{\pi}{6}$ **7.** $\dfrac{\pi}{6}$ **9.** $\dfrac{3\pi}{4}$ **11.** $\dfrac{\pi}{2}$ **13.** $\dfrac{\pi}{6}$ **15.** 0   **17.** $-\dfrac{\pi}{3}$ **19.** 0.30   **21.** -0.33 **23.** 1.19   **25.** 1.25
27. -1.52 **29.** -1.52 **31.** 0.9   **33.** $\dfrac{\pi}{3}$ **35.** $\dfrac{\pi}{6}$ **37.** 125   **39.** $-\dfrac{\pi}{6}$ **41.** $-\dfrac{\pi}{3}$ **43.** 0   **45.** not defined   **47.** $\dfrac{3}{5}$ **49.** $\dfrac{12}{5}$
51. $-\dfrac{3}{4}$ **53.** $\dfrac{\sqrt{2}}{2}$ **55.** $\dfrac{4\sqrt{15}}{15}$ **57.** $-2\sqrt{2}$ **59.** 2   **61.** $\dfrac{3\sqrt{13}}{13}$ **63.** $\dfrac{\sqrt{1-x^2}}{x}$ **65.** $\sqrt{1-4x^2}$ **67.** $\dfrac{\sqrt{x^2-1}}{x}$ **69.** $\dfrac{\sqrt{3}}{x}$
71. $\dfrac{\sqrt{x^2+4}}{2}$ **73.** domain: $-1 \leq x \leq 1$; range: $-1 \leq y \leq 1$ **75.** domain: all real numbers; range: $0 \leq y \leq \pi$ **77.** domain: all real numbers; range: $-\dfrac{\pi}{2} \leq y \leq \dfrac{\pi}{2}$ **79.** domain: $-1 \leq x \leq 1$; range: $\left\{\dfrac{\pi}{2}\right\}$ **81.** 0.408 radians; 0.602 radians; 0.654 radians; 0.645 radians; 0.613 radians
83. 1.3157 radians or 75.4°   **85.** 1.1071 sq units   **87, 89, 91 93, 95, 97.** answers may vary

99.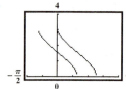

101.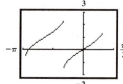
Shifted left 2 units and up 1 unit

103.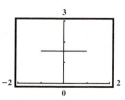
It seems
$\sin^{-1} x + \cos^{-1} x = \frac{\pi}{2}$ for $-1 \le x \le 1$.

105. does not make sense   **107.** does not make sense   **109.** $x = \sin\frac{\pi}{8}$ **111.** $\tan \alpha = \frac{8}{x}$, so $\tan^{-1}\frac{8}{x} = \alpha$.
$\tan(\alpha + \theta) = \frac{33}{x}$, so $\tan^{-1}\frac{33}{x} = \alpha + \theta$. $\theta = \alpha + \theta - \alpha = \tan^{-1}\frac{33}{x} - \tan^{-1}\frac{8}{x}$.   **113.** 35.8°

Section 14.8
Practice Exercises
1. $B = 27.3°$; $b \approx 4.34$; $c \approx 9.45$ **2.** 994 ft   **3.** 29.0°   **4.** 60.3 ft   **5. a.** S 25°E   **b.** S 15°W   **6. a.** 4.2 miles   **b.** S87.7°W
7. $d = -6\cos\frac{\pi}{2}t$ **8. a.** 12 cm   **b.** $\frac{1}{8}$ cycle (oscillation) per sec   **c.** 8 sec

Exercise Set 14.8
1. $B = 66.5°$; $a \approx 4.35$; $c \approx 10.90$ **3.** $B = 37.4°$; $a \approx 42.90$; $b \approx 32.80$ **5.** $A = 73.2°$; $a \approx 101.02$; $c \approx 105.52$
7. $b \approx 39.95$; $A \approx 37.3°$; $B \approx 52.7°$ **9.** $c \approx 26.96$; $A \approx 23.6°$; $B \approx 66.4°$ **11.** $a \approx 6.71$; $B \approx 16.6°$; $A \approx 73.4°$ **13.** N 15° E
15. S 80° W   **17.** $d = -6\cos\frac{\pi}{2}t$ **19.** $d = -3\sin\frac{4\pi}{3}t$ **21. a.** 5 in.   **b.** $\frac{1}{4}$ cycle (oscillation) per sec   **c.** 4 sec
23. a. 6 in.   **b.** 1 cycle (oscillation) per sec   **c.** 1 sec   **25. a.** $\frac{1}{2}$ in.   **b.** 0.32 cycle (oscillation) per sec   **c.** 3.14 sec
27. a. 5 in.   **b.** $\frac{1}{3}$ cycle (oscillation) per sec   **c.** 3 sec   **29.** 653 units   **31.** 39 units   **33.** 298 units   **35.** 257 units

37.
$d = 4\cos\left(\pi t - \frac{\pi}{2}\right)$
a. 4 in.   **b.** $\frac{1}{2}$ cycle (oscillation) per sec
c. 2 sec   **d.** $\frac{1}{2}$

39.
$d = -2\sin\left(\frac{\pi}{4}t + \frac{\pi}{2}\right)$
a. 2 in.   **b.** $\frac{1}{8}$ cycle (oscillation) per sec
c. 8 sec   **d.** -2

41. 2059 ft   **43.** 695 ft   **45.** 1376 ft   **47.** 15.1°   **49.** 33.7 ft
51. 90 mi north and 120 mi east   **53.** 13.2 mi   **55.** N 53° W
57. N 89.5° E   **59.** $d = 6\sin \pi t$ **61.** $d = \sin 528\pi t$
63, 65, 67, 69. answers may vary

71.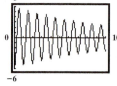
10 complete oscillations

73. does not make sense
75. does not make sense
77. 48 ft
79. $\csc x$
80. 1
81. $\dfrac{1 + \sin x}{\cos x}$

Chapter 14 Review Exercises
1. 4.5 radians   **2.** $\dfrac{\pi}{12}$ radians   **3.** $\dfrac{2\pi}{3}$ radians   **4.** $\dfrac{7\pi}{4}$ radians   **5.** 300°   **6.** 252°   **7.** $-150°$

8.   **9.**   **10.**   **11.**   **12.**

13. 40°   **14.** 275°   **15.** $\dfrac{5\pi}{4}$ **16.** $\dfrac{7\pi}{6}$ **17.** $\dfrac{4\pi}{3}$ **18.** $\dfrac{15\pi}{2}$ ft ≈ 23.56 ft   **19.** 20.6π radians per min   **20.** 42,412 ft per min

21. $\sin\theta = \dfrac{5\sqrt{89}}{89}$; $\cos\theta = \dfrac{3\sqrt{89}}{89}$; $\tan\theta = \dfrac{5}{3}$; $\csc\theta = \dfrac{\sqrt{89}}{5}$; $\sec\theta = \dfrac{\sqrt{89}}{8}$; $\cot\theta = \dfrac{3}{5}$ **22.** $\dfrac{7}{2}$ **23.** $-\dfrac{1}{2}$ **24.** 1 **25.** 1 **26.** $\dfrac{\sqrt{21}}{7}$
27. $\cos 20°$ **28.** $\sin 0$ **29.** 42 mm **30.** 23 cm **31.** 37 in. **32.** $\sqrt{15}$ **33.** 772 ft **34.** 31 m **35.** 56°
36. $\sin\theta = -\dfrac{5\sqrt{26}}{26}$; $\cos\theta = -\dfrac{\sqrt{26}}{26}$; $\tan\theta = 5$; $\csc\theta = -\dfrac{\sqrt{26}}{5}$; $\sec\theta = -\sqrt{26}$; $\cot\theta = \dfrac{1}{5}$ **37.** $\sin\theta = -1$; $\cos\theta = 0$; $\tan\theta$ is undefined; $\csc\theta = -1$; $\sec\theta$ is undefined; $\cot\theta = 0$ **38.** quadrant I **39.** quadrant III
40. $\sin\theta = -\dfrac{\sqrt{21}}{5}$; $\tan\theta = -\dfrac{\sqrt{21}}{2}$; $\csc\theta = -\dfrac{5\sqrt{21}}{21}$; $\sec\theta = \dfrac{5}{2}$; $\cot\theta = -\dfrac{2\sqrt{21}}{21}$ **41.** $\sin\theta = \dfrac{\sqrt{10}}{10}$; $\cos\theta = -\dfrac{3\sqrt{10}}{10}$; $\csc\theta = \sqrt{10}$; $\sec\theta = -\dfrac{\sqrt{10}}{3}$; $\cot\theta = -3$ **42.** $\sin\theta = -\dfrac{\sqrt{10}}{10}$; $\cos\theta = -\dfrac{3\sqrt{10}}{10}$; $\tan\theta = \dfrac{1}{3}$; $\csc\theta = -\sqrt{10}$; $\sec\theta = -\dfrac{\sqrt{10}}{3}$
43. 85° **44.** $\dfrac{3\pi}{8}$ **45.** 50° **46.** $\dfrac{\pi}{6}$ **47.** $\dfrac{\pi}{3}$ **48.** $-\dfrac{\sqrt{3}}{2}$ **49.** $-\sqrt{3}$ **50.** $\sqrt{2}$ **51.** $\dfrac{\sqrt{3}}{2}$ **52.** $-\sqrt{3}$
53. $-\dfrac{2\sqrt{3}}{3}$ **54.** $-\dfrac{\sqrt{3}}{2}$ **55.** $\dfrac{\sqrt{2}}{2}$ **56.** 1 **57.** $-\dfrac{\sqrt{3}}{2}$ **58.** $\dfrac{\sqrt{3}}{2}$

59.–70. [graphs]

71. [graph] $y = 2\cos\dfrac{1}{3}x - 2$ **72.** blue: $y = \sin\dfrac{\pi}{240}x$; red: $y = \sin\dfrac{\pi}{320}x$ **73.** 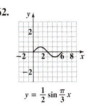 $y = 4\tan 2x$ **74.** $y = -2\tan\dfrac{\pi}{4}x$

75. 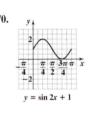 $y = \tan(x+\pi)$ **76.** $y = -\tan\left(x-\dfrac{\pi}{4}\right)$ **77.** $\dfrac{\pi}{2}$ **78.** 0   **79.** $\dfrac{\pi}{4}$ **80.** $-\dfrac{\pi}{3}$ **81.** $\dfrac{2\pi}{3}$ **82.** $-\dfrac{\pi}{6}$

83. $\dfrac{\sqrt{2}}{2}$ **84.** 1   **85.** $-\dfrac{\sqrt{3}}{3}$ **86.** $-\dfrac{\sqrt{3}}{3}$ **87.** 2   **88.** $\dfrac{4}{5}$ **89.** $\dfrac{4}{5}$ **90.** $-\dfrac{3}{4}$ **91.** $-\dfrac{3}{4}$ **92.** $-\dfrac{\sqrt{10}}{10}$ **93.** $\dfrac{\pi}{3}$
94. $\dfrac{\pi}{3}$ **95.** $-\dfrac{\pi}{6}$ **96.** $\dfrac{2\sqrt{x^2+4}}{x^2+4}$ **97.** $\dfrac{x\sqrt{x^2-1}}{x^2-1}$ **98.** $B \approx 67.7°$; $a \approx 37.9$; $b \approx 9.25$
99. $A \approx 52.6°$; $a \approx 7.85$; $c \approx 9.88$ **100.** $A \approx 16.6°$; $B \approx 73.4°$; $b \approx 6.71$ **101.** $A \approx 21.3°$; $B \approx 68.7°$; $c \approx 3.86$ **107.** 38 ft
103. 90 yd   **104.** 21.7 ft   **105.** N 35° E   **106.** S 35° W   **107.** 24.6 mi   **108. a.** 1282.2 mi   **b.** S 74° E

A70 Answers to Selected Exercises

109. a. 20 cm   **b.** $\frac{1}{8}$ cycle (oscillation) per sec   **c.** 8 sec   **110. a.** $\frac{1}{2}$ cm   **b.** 0.64 cycle (oscillation) per sec   **c.** 1.57 sec
111. $d = -30 \cos \pi t$ **112.** $d = \frac{1}{4} \sin \frac{2\pi}{5} t$

Chapter 14 Test

1. $\frac{3\pi}{4}$ radians   **2.** $\frac{25\pi}{3}$ ft ≈ 26.18 ft   **3. a.** $\frac{4\pi}{3}$ **b.** $\frac{\pi}{3}$
4. $\sin \theta = \frac{5\sqrt{29}}{29}$; $\cos \theta = -\frac{2\sqrt{29}}{29}$; $\tan \theta = -\frac{5}{2}$; $\csc \theta = \frac{\sqrt{29}}{5}$; $\sec \theta = -\frac{\sqrt{29}}{2}$; $\cot \theta = -\frac{2}{5}$
5. $\sin \theta = -\frac{2\sqrt{2}}{3}$; $\tan \theta = -2\sqrt{2}$; $\csc \theta = -\frac{3\sqrt{2}}{4}$; $\sec \theta = 3$; $\cot \theta = -\frac{\sqrt{2}}{4}$ **6.** $\frac{\sqrt{3}}{6}$ **7.** $-\sqrt{3}$ **8.** $-\frac{\sqrt{2}}{2}$ **9.** -2 **10.** $\frac{\sqrt{3}}{3}$
11. $y = 3 \sin 2x$
12. $y = -2 \cos\left(x - \frac{\pi}{2}\right)$
13. 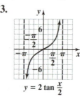 $y = 2 \tan \frac{x}{2}$
14. $-\sqrt{3}$

15. $B = 69°$; $a = 4.7$; $b = 12.1$ **16.** 23 yd   **17.** 36.1°

Chapter 14 Standardized Test

1. c   **2.** c   **3.** b   **4.** c   **5.** a   **6.** d   **7.** d   **8.** c   **9.** a   **10.** c   **11.** c   **12.** c   **13.** d   **14.** b   **15.** c   **16.** a   **17.** a
18. c   **19.** c   **20.** d   **21.** c

CHAPTER 15 TRIGONOMETRIC IDENTITIES, EQUATIONS, AND APPLICATIONS

Section 15.1
Practice Exercises

1. $\csc x \tan x = \frac{1}{\sin x} \cdot \frac{\sin x}{\cos x} = \frac{1}{\cos x} = \sec x$

2. $\cos x \cot x + \sin x = \cos x \cdot \frac{\cos x}{\sin x} + \sin x = \frac{\cos^2 x}{\sin x} + \sin x \cdot \frac{\sin x}{\sin x} = \frac{\cos^2 x + \sin^2 x}{\sin x} = \frac{1}{\sin x} = \csc x$

3. $\sin x - \sin x \cos^2 x = \sin x(1 - \cos^2 x) = \sin x \cdot \sin^2 x = \sin^3 x$ **4.** $\frac{1 + \cos \theta}{\sin \theta} = \frac{1}{\sin \theta} + \frac{\cos \theta}{\sin \theta} = \csc \theta + \cot \theta$

5. $\frac{\sin x}{1 + \cos x} + \frac{1 + \cos x}{\sin x} = \frac{\sin x(\sin x)}{(1 + \cos x)(\sin x)} + \frac{(1 + \cos x)(1 + \cos x)}{(\sin x)(1 + \cos x)} = \frac{\sin^2 x + 1 + 2\cos x + \cos^2 x}{(1 + \cos x)(\sin x)}$
$= \frac{\sin^2 x + \cos^2 x + 1 + 2\cos x}{(1 + \cos x)(\sin x)} = \frac{1 + 1 + 2\cos x}{(1 + \cos x)(\sin x)} = \frac{2 + 2\cos x}{(1 + \cos x)(\sin x)} = \frac{2(1 + \cos x)}{(1 + \cos x)(\sin x)} = \frac{2}{\sin x} = 2\csc x$

6. $\frac{\cos x}{1 + \sin x} = \frac{\cos x(1 - \sin x)}{(1 + \sin x)(1 - \sin x)} = \frac{\cos x(1 - \sin x)}{1 - \sin^2 x} = \frac{\cos x(1 - \sin x)}{\cos^2 x} = \frac{1 - \sin x}{\cos x}$ **7.** $\frac{\sec x + \csc(-x)}{\sec x \csc x} = \frac{\sec x - \csc x}{\sec x \csc x}$

$= \frac{\frac{1}{\cos x} - \frac{1}{\sin x}}{\frac{1}{\cos x} \cdot \frac{1}{\sin x}} = \frac{\frac{\sin x}{\cos x \cdot \sin x} - \frac{\cos x}{\cos x \cdot \sin x}}{\frac{1}{\cos x \cdot \sin x}} = \frac{\frac{\sin x - \cos x}{\cos x \cdot \sin x}}{\frac{1}{\cos x \cdot \sin x}} = \frac{\sin x - \cos x}{\cos x \cdot \sin x} \cdot \frac{\cos x \cdot \sin x}{1} = \sin x - \cos x$

8. Left side: $\frac{1}{1 + \sin \theta} + \frac{1}{1 - \sin \theta} = \frac{1(1 - \sin \theta)}{(1 + \sin \theta)(1 - \sin \theta)} + \frac{1(1 + \sin \theta)}{(1 - \sin \theta)(1 + \sin \theta)} = \frac{1 - \sin \theta + 1 + \sin \theta}{(1 + \sin \theta)(1 - \sin \theta)} = \frac{2}{1 - \sin^2 \theta}$;

Right side: $2 + 2\tan^2 \theta = 2 + 2\left(\frac{\sin^2 \theta}{\cos^2 \theta}\right) = \frac{2\cos^2 \theta}{\cos^2 \theta} + \frac{2\sin^2 \theta}{\cos^2 \theta} = \frac{2\cos^2 \theta + 2\sin^2 \theta}{\cos^2 \theta} = \frac{2(\cos^2 \theta + \sin^2 \theta)}{\cos^2 \theta} = \frac{2}{\cos^2 \theta} = \frac{2}{1 - \sin^2 \theta}$

Exercise Set 15.1

For Exercises 1–60, proofs may vary.
61. $\cos x$; Proofs may vary.   **63.** $2 \sin x$; Proofs may vary.   **65.** $2 \sec x$; Proofs may vary.
67. $\frac{1}{\cos x}$ **69.** $\frac{1}{\cos x}$ **71.** $2\csc^2 x - 1$ **73.** $\sec x \tan x$

79.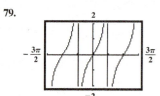
Proofs may vary.

81.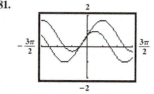
Values for x may vary.

83.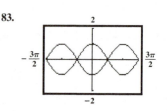
Values for x may vary.

85.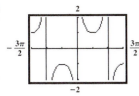
Proofs may vary.

87.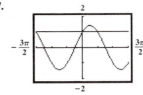
Values for x may vary.

89. makes sense
91. does not make sense
For Exercises 92–95, proofs may vary.
99. a. no   **b.** yes

Section 15.2
Practice Exercises
1. $\dfrac{\sqrt{3}}{2}$ **2.** $\dfrac{\sqrt{3}}{2}$ **3.** $\dfrac{\cos(\alpha - \beta)}{\cos \alpha \cos \beta} = \dfrac{\cos \alpha \cos \beta + \sin \alpha \sin \beta}{\cos \alpha \cos \beta} = \dfrac{\cos \alpha}{\cos \alpha} \cdot \dfrac{\cos \beta}{\cos \beta} + \dfrac{\sin \alpha}{\cos \alpha} \cdot \dfrac{\sin \beta}{\cos \beta} = 1 + \tan \alpha \tan \beta$

4. $\dfrac{\sqrt{2} + \sqrt{6}}{4}$ **5. a.** $\cos \alpha = -\dfrac{3}{5}$ **b.** $\cos \beta = \dfrac{\sqrt{3}}{2}$ **c.** $\dfrac{-3\sqrt{3} - 4}{10}$ **d.** $\dfrac{4\sqrt{3} - 3}{10}$

6. a. $y = \sin x$ **b.** $\cos\left(x + \dfrac{3\pi}{2}\right) = \cos x \cos \dfrac{3\pi}{2} - \sin x \sin \dfrac{3\pi}{2} = \cos x \cdot 0 - \sin x \cdot (-1) = \sin x$

7. $\tan(x + \pi) = \dfrac{\tan x + \tan \pi}{1 - \tan x \tan \pi} = \dfrac{\tan x + 0}{1 - \tan x \cdot 0} = \dfrac{\tan x}{1} = \tan x$

Exercise Set 15.2
1. $\dfrac{\sqrt{6} + \sqrt{2}}{4}$ **3.** $\dfrac{\sqrt{2} - \sqrt{6}}{4}$ **5. a.** $\alpha = 50°, \beta = 20°$ **b.** $\cos 30°$ **c.** $\dfrac{\sqrt{3}}{2}$ **7. a.** $\alpha = \dfrac{5\pi}{12}, \beta = \dfrac{\pi}{12}$ **b.** $\cos \dfrac{\pi}{3}$ **c.** $\dfrac{1}{2}$

For Exercises 9–12, proofs may vary.   **13.** $\dfrac{\sqrt{6} - \sqrt{2}}{4}$ **15.** $\dfrac{\sqrt{6} + \sqrt{2}}{4}$ **17.** $-\dfrac{\sqrt{6} + \sqrt{2}}{4}$ **19.** $\dfrac{\sqrt{6} - \sqrt{2}}{4}$ **21.** $\dfrac{\sqrt{3} + 1}{\sqrt{3} - 1}$ **23.** $\dfrac{\sqrt{3} - 1}{\sqrt{3} + 1}$

25. $\sin 30°; \dfrac{1}{2}$ **27.** $\tan 45°; 1$ **29.** $\sin \dfrac{\pi}{6}; \dfrac{1}{2}$ **31.** $\tan \dfrac{\pi}{6}; \dfrac{\sqrt{3}}{3}$ For Exercises 33–56, proofs may vary.

57. a. $-\dfrac{63}{65}$ **b.** $-\dfrac{16}{65}$ **c.** $\dfrac{16}{63}$ **59. a.** $-\dfrac{4 + 6\sqrt{2}}{15}$ **b.** $\dfrac{3 - 8\sqrt{2}}{15}$ **c.** $\dfrac{54 - 25\sqrt{2}}{28}$ **61. a.** $-\dfrac{8\sqrt{3} + 15}{34}$ **b.** $\dfrac{15\sqrt{3} - 8}{34}$

c. $\dfrac{480 - 289\sqrt{3}}{33}$ **63. a.** $-\dfrac{4 + 3\sqrt{15}}{20}$ **b.** $\dfrac{-3 + 4\sqrt{15}}{20}$ **c.** $\dfrac{3 - 4\sqrt{15}}{4 + 3\sqrt{15}}$ **65. a.** $y = \sin x$

b. $\sin(\pi - x) = \sin \pi \cos x - \cos \pi \sin x = 0 \cdot \cos x - (-1) \sin x = \sin x$ **67. a.** $y = 2 \cos x$

b. $\sin\left(x + \dfrac{\pi}{2}\right) + \sin\left(\dfrac{\pi}{2} - x\right) = \sin x \cos \dfrac{\pi}{2} + \cos x \sin \dfrac{\pi}{2} + \sin \dfrac{\pi}{2} \cos x - \cos \dfrac{\pi}{2} \sin x = \sin x \cdot 0 + \cos x \cdot 1 + 1 \cdot \cos x - 0 \cdot \sin x$
$= \cos x + \cos x = 2 \cos x$ **69.** $\cos \alpha$ **71.** $\tan \beta$ **73.** $\cos \dfrac{\pi}{3} = \dfrac{1}{2}$ **75.** $\cos 3x$; Proofs may vary.   **77.** $\sin \dfrac{x}{2}$; Proofs may vary.

79. Proofs may vary.; amplitude is $\sqrt{13}$; period is 2π

89.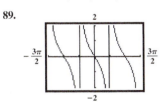
Proofs may vary.

91.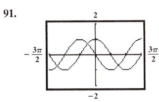
Values for x may vary.

93.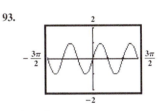
Proofs may vary.

95. makes sense   **97.** makes sense.   **99.** $\dfrac{4\sqrt{3} + 3}{10}$ **101.** $-\dfrac{33}{65}$ **103.** $y\sqrt{1 - x^2} + x\sqrt{1 - y^2}$ **105.** $\dfrac{xy + \left(\sqrt{1 - x^2}\right)\left(\sqrt{1 - y^2}\right)}{y\sqrt{1 - x^2} - x\sqrt{1 - y^2}}$

107. $\dfrac{\sqrt{3}}{2}; \dfrac{1}{2}; \dfrac{1}{2}; \dfrac{\sqrt{3}}{2}$ **109. a.** no   **b.** yes

Section 15.3
Practice Exercises
1. a. $-\dfrac{24}{25}$ **b.** $-\dfrac{7}{25}$ **c.** $\dfrac{24}{7}$ **2.** $\dfrac{\sqrt{3}}{2}$ **3.** $\sin 3\theta = \sin(2\theta + \theta) = \sin 2\theta \cos \theta + \cos 2\theta \sin \theta = 2 \sin \theta \cos \theta \cos \theta$
$+ (2\cos^2 \theta - 1)\sin \theta = 2 \sin \theta \cos^2 \theta + 2 \sin \theta \cos^2 \theta - \sin \theta = 4 \sin \theta \cos^2 \theta - \sin \theta = 4 \sin \theta(1 - \sin^2 \theta) - \sin \theta$
$= 4 \sin \theta - 4 \sin^3 \theta - \sin \theta = 3 \sin \theta - 4 \sin^3 \theta$ **4.** $-\dfrac{\sqrt{2 - \sqrt{3}}}{2}$

A72 Answers to Selected Exercises

5. $\dfrac{\sec \alpha}{\sec \alpha \csc \alpha + \csc \alpha} = \dfrac{\frac{1}{\cos \alpha}}{\frac{1}{\cos \alpha} \cdot \frac{1}{\sin \alpha} + \frac{1}{\sin \alpha}} = \dfrac{\frac{1}{\cos \alpha}}{\frac{1}{\cos \alpha \sin \alpha} + \frac{\cos \alpha}{\cos \alpha \sin \alpha}} = \dfrac{\frac{1}{\cos \alpha}}{\frac{1 + \cos \alpha}{\cos \alpha \sin \alpha}} = \dfrac{1}{\cos \alpha} \cdot \dfrac{\cos \alpha \sin \alpha}{1 + \cos \alpha} = \dfrac{\sin \alpha}{1 + \cos \alpha} = \tan\dfrac{\alpha}{2}$

Exercise Set 15.3

1. $\dfrac{24}{25}$ **3.** $\dfrac{24}{7}$ **5.** $\dfrac{527}{625}$ **7. a.** $-\dfrac{240}{289}$ **b.** $-\dfrac{161}{289}$ **c.** $\dfrac{240}{161}$ **9. a.** $-\dfrac{336}{625}$ **b.** $\dfrac{527}{625}$ **c.** $-\dfrac{336}{527}$ **11. a.** $\dfrac{4}{5}$ **b.** $\dfrac{3}{5}$ **c.** $\dfrac{4}{3}$
13. a. $\dfrac{720}{1681}$ **b.** $\dfrac{1519}{1681}$ **c.** $\dfrac{720}{1519}$ **15.** $\dfrac{1}{2}$ **17.** $-\dfrac{\sqrt{3}}{2}$ **19.** $\dfrac{\sqrt{2}}{2}$ **21.** $\dfrac{\sqrt{3}}{3}$ For Exercises 23–34, proofs may vary.
35. $\dfrac{\sqrt{2} - \sqrt{3}}{2}$ **37.** $-\dfrac{\sqrt{2 + \sqrt{2}}}{2}$ **39.** $2 + \sqrt{3}$ **41.** $-\sqrt{2} + 1$ **43.** $\dfrac{\sqrt{10}}{10}$ **45.** $\dfrac{1}{3}$ **47.** $\dfrac{7\sqrt{2}}{10}$
49. $\dfrac{3}{5}$ **51. a.** $\dfrac{2\sqrt{5}}{5}$ **b.** $-\dfrac{\sqrt{5}}{5}$ **c.** -2 **53. a.** $\dfrac{3\sqrt{13}}{13}$ **b.** $\dfrac{2\sqrt{13}}{13}$ **c.** $\dfrac{3}{2}$ For Exercises 55–60, proofs may vary.
61. $\cos 2x$; Proofs may vary. **63.** $1 + \sin x$; Proofs may vary. **65.** $\sin 3x$; Proofs may vary. **67. a.** $\dfrac{v_0^2}{32} \cdot \sin 2\theta$ **b.** $\theta = \dfrac{\pi}{4}$
69. $\sqrt{2 - \sqrt{2}} \cdot (2 + \sqrt{2}) \approx 2.6$ **71, 73, 75.** answers may vary **77.** 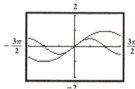 **79.**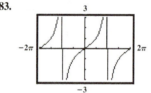

Proofs may vary. Values for x may vary.

81.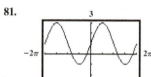
a. $y = 1 + 2 \sin x$
b. Proofs may vary.

83.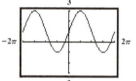
a. $y = \tan\dfrac{x}{2}$
b. Proofs may vary.

85. does not make sense **87.** $\dfrac{\sqrt{3}}{2}$ **89.** $-\dfrac{1}{2}, 2$ **91.** $\dfrac{1 - \sqrt{5}}{2}, \dfrac{1 + \sqrt{5}}{2}$

Chapter 15 Integrated Review

For Exercises 1–18, proofs may vary.
19. $\dfrac{33}{65}$ **20.** $-\dfrac{16}{63}$ **21.** $-\dfrac{24}{25}$ **22.** $-\dfrac{\sqrt{26}}{26}$ **23.** $-\dfrac{\sqrt{6} + \sqrt{2}}{4}$ **24.** $\dfrac{\sqrt{3}}{2}$ **25.** $\dfrac{1}{2}$ **26.** $\sqrt{\dfrac{\sqrt{2} - 1}{\sqrt{2} + 1}}$

Section 15.4

Practice Exercises

1. $x = \dfrac{\pi}{3} + 2n\pi$ or $x = \dfrac{2\pi}{3} + 2n\pi$, where n is any integer. **2.** $\dfrac{\pi}{6}, \dfrac{2\pi}{3}, \dfrac{7\pi}{6}, \dfrac{5\pi}{3}$ **3.** $\dfrac{\pi}{2}$ **4.** $\dfrac{\pi}{6}, \dfrac{\pi}{2}, \dfrac{5\pi}{6}$ **5.** $\dfrac{\pi}{6}, \dfrac{5\pi}{6}, \dfrac{7\pi}{6}, \dfrac{11\pi}{6}$ **6.** $0, \dfrac{\pi}{4}, \pi, \dfrac{5\pi}{4}$
7. $\dfrac{\pi}{3}, \dfrac{5\pi}{3}$ **8.** $\dfrac{\pi}{2}, \dfrac{7\pi}{6}, \dfrac{11\pi}{6}$ **9.** $\dfrac{3\pi}{4}, \dfrac{7\pi}{4}$ **10.** $\dfrac{\pi}{2}, \pi$ **11. a.** 1.2592, 4.4008 **b.** 3.3752, 6.0496 **12.** 2.3423, 3.9409

Exercise Set 15.4

1. Solution **3.** Not a solution **5.** Solution **7.** Solution **9.** Not a solution **11.** $x = \dfrac{\pi}{3} + 2n\pi$ or $x = \dfrac{2\pi}{3} + 2n\pi$, where n is any integer.
13. $x = \dfrac{\pi}{4} + n\pi$, where n is any integer. **15.** $x = \dfrac{2\pi}{3} + 2n\pi$ or $x = \dfrac{4\pi}{3} + 2n\pi$, where n is any integer. **17.** $x = n\pi$, where n is any integer.
19. $x = \dfrac{5\pi}{6} + 2n\pi$ or $x = \dfrac{7\pi}{6} + 2n\pi$, where n is any integer. **21.** $\theta = \dfrac{\pi}{6} + 2n\pi$ or $\theta = \dfrac{5\pi}{6} + 2n\pi$, where n is any integer.
23. $\theta = \dfrac{3\pi}{2} + 2n\pi$, where n is any integer. **25.** $\dfrac{\pi}{6}, \dfrac{\pi}{3}, \dfrac{7\pi}{6}, \dfrac{4\pi}{3}$ **27.** $\dfrac{5\pi}{24}, \dfrac{7\pi}{24}, \dfrac{17\pi}{24}, \dfrac{19\pi}{24}, \dfrac{29\pi}{24}, \dfrac{31\pi}{24}, \dfrac{41\pi}{24}, \dfrac{43\pi}{24}$ **29.** $\dfrac{\pi}{18}, \dfrac{7\pi}{18}, \dfrac{13\pi}{18}, \dfrac{19\pi}{18}, \dfrac{25\pi}{18}, \dfrac{31\pi}{18}$
31. 0 **33.** no solution **35.** $\dfrac{4\pi}{9}, \dfrac{8\pi}{9}, \dfrac{16\pi}{9}$ **37.** $0, \dfrac{\pi}{3}, \pi, \dfrac{4\pi}{3}$ **39.** $\dfrac{\pi}{2}, \dfrac{7\pi}{6}, \dfrac{11\pi}{6}$ **41.** $\dfrac{2\pi}{3}, \pi, \dfrac{4\pi}{3}$ **43.** $\dfrac{3\pi}{2}$ **45.** $\dfrac{\pi}{2}, \dfrac{3\pi}{2}$
47. $\dfrac{\pi}{3}, \dfrac{2\pi}{3}, \dfrac{4\pi}{3}, \dfrac{5\pi}{3}$ **49.** $\dfrac{\pi}{6}, \dfrac{5\pi}{6}, \dfrac{7\pi}{6}, \dfrac{11\pi}{6}$ **51.** $\dfrac{\pi}{4}, \dfrac{3\pi}{4}, \dfrac{5\pi}{4}, \dfrac{7\pi}{4}$ **53.** $\dfrac{\pi}{4}, \pi, \dfrac{5\pi}{4}$ **55.** $\dfrac{5\pi}{6}, \dfrac{7\pi}{6}, \dfrac{11\pi}{6}$ **57.** $\dfrac{\pi}{4}, \dfrac{5\pi}{4}$ **59.** $0, \dfrac{2\pi}{3}, \pi, \dfrac{4\pi}{3}$
61. $0, \pi$ **63.** $\dfrac{\pi}{2}, \dfrac{7\pi}{6}, \dfrac{11\pi}{6}$ **65.** π **67.** $\dfrac{\pi}{6}, \dfrac{5\pi}{6}$ **69.** $\dfrac{\pi}{6}, \dfrac{\pi}{2}, \dfrac{5\pi}{6}, \dfrac{3\pi}{2}$ **71.** $0, \dfrac{2\pi}{3}, \dfrac{4\pi}{3}$ **73.** $\dfrac{2\pi}{3}, \dfrac{4\pi}{3}$ **75.** $\dfrac{\pi}{8}, \dfrac{3\pi}{8}, \dfrac{9\pi}{8}, \dfrac{11\pi}{8}$ **77.** $0, \dfrac{\pi}{2}$

79. $\frac{\pi}{4}, \frac{3\pi}{4}$ **81.** $\frac{\pi}{12}, \frac{\pi}{4}, \frac{3\pi}{4}, \frac{11\pi}{12}, \frac{17\pi}{12}, \frac{19\pi}{12}$ **83.** 0 **85.** 0.9695, 2.1721 **87.** 1.9823, 4.3009 **89.** 1.8925, 5.0341 **91.** 2.2370, 4.0461 **93.** 0.4636, 0.9828, 3.6052, 4.1244 **95.** 0.3876, 2.7540, 3.5292, 5.8956 **97.** $\frac{\pi}{3}, \frac{2\pi}{3}, \frac{4\pi}{3}, \frac{5\pi}{3}$ **99.** $0, \frac{2\pi}{3}, \pi, \frac{4\pi}{3}$ **101.** $\frac{\pi}{6}, \frac{11\pi}{6}$ **103.** 1.7798, 4.9214 **105.** $\frac{\pi}{2}$ **107.** $\frac{\pi}{6}, \frac{\pi}{2}, \frac{5\pi}{6}, \frac{3\pi}{2}$ **109.** $\frac{\pi}{6}, \frac{5\pi}{6}, \frac{7\pi}{6}, \frac{11\pi}{6}$ **111.** 0.7495, 5.5337 **113.** $\frac{7\pi}{6}, \frac{11\pi}{6}$

115. 2.1588, $\frac{3\pi}{4}$, 5.3004, $\frac{7\pi}{4}$ **117.** $\left(\frac{2\pi}{3}, -\frac{3}{2}\right), \left(\frac{4\pi}{3}, -\frac{3}{2}\right)$ **119.** (3.5163, 0.7321), (5.9085, 0.7321) **121.** $\frac{\pi}{6}, \frac{5\pi}{6}, \frac{7\pi}{6}, \frac{11\pi}{6}$

123. $\frac{\pi}{6}, \frac{5\pi}{6}$, 3.3430, 6.0818

125. $0, \frac{2\pi}{3}, \pi, \frac{4\pi}{3}$

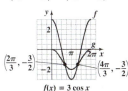

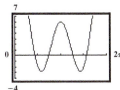 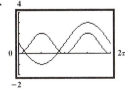

127. 0.3649, 1.2059, 3.5064, 4.3475; a

129. 0.4 sec and 2.1 sec   **131.** 49 days and 292 days   **133.** $t = 2 + 6n$ or $t = 4 + 6n$ where n is any nonnegative integer.   **135.** 21° or 69°.

137. answers may vary   **139.** answers may vary   **141.** answers may vary   **143.** answers may vary   **145.** answers may vary

147. 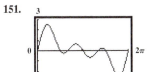 **149.** **151.**

$x = 1.37, x = 2.30, x = 3.98,$ or $x = 4.91$ $x = 0.37$ or $x = 2.77$ $x = 0, x = 1.57, x = 2.09, x = 3.14, x = 4.19,$ or $x = 4.71$

153. makes sense   **155.** does not make sense   **157.** false   **159.** false   **161.** $\frac{\pi}{2}, \frac{3\pi}{2}, \frac{7\pi}{12}, \frac{11\pi}{12}, \frac{19\pi}{12}, \frac{23\pi}{12}$ **163.** $a \approx 45.2$

165. no solution or $\varnothing$

Section 15.5
Practice Exercises
1. $B = 34°, a \approx 12.7$ cm, $b \approx 7.4$ cm   **2.** $B = 117.5°, a \approx 8.7, c \approx 5.2$ **3.** $B \approx 41°, C \approx 82°, c \approx 39.0$ **4.** no triangle
5. two triangles; $B_1 \approx 50°, C_1 \approx 95°, c_1 = 20.8; B_2 \approx 130°, C_2 \approx 15°, c_2 \approx 5.4$ **6.** approximately 34 sq m   **7.** approximately 11 mi

Exercise Set 15.5
1. $B = 42°, a \approx 8.1, b \approx 8.1$ **3.** $A = 44°, b \approx 18.6, c \approx 22.8$ **5.** $C = 95°, b \approx 81.0, c \approx 134.1$ **7.** $B = 40°, b \approx 20.9, c \approx 31.8$
9. $C = 111°, b \approx 7.3, c \approx 16.1$ **11.** $A = 80°, a \approx 39.5, c \approx 10.4$ **13.** $B = 30°, a \approx 316.0, b \approx 174.3$ **15.** $C = 50°, a \approx 7.1, b \approx 7.1$
17. one triangle; $B \approx 29°, c \approx 111°, c \approx 29.0$ **19.** one triangle; $C \approx 52°, B \approx 65°, b \approx 10.2$ **21.** one triangle; $C \approx 55°, B \approx 13°, b \approx 10.2$
23. no triangle   **25.** two triangles; $B_1 \approx 77°, C_1 \approx 43°, c_1 \approx 12.6; B_2 \approx 103°, C_2 \approx 17°, c_2 \approx 5.4$
27. two triangles; $B_1 \approx 54°, C_1 \approx 89°, c_1 \approx 19.9; B_2 \approx 126°, C_2 \approx 17°, c_2 \approx 5.8$
29. two triangles; $C_1 \approx 68°, B_1 \approx 54°, b_1 \approx 21.0; C_2 \approx 112°, B_2 \approx 10°, b_2 \approx 4.5$ **31.** no triangle   **33.** 297 sq ft
35. 5 sq yd   **37.** 10 sq m   **39.** 481.6   **41.** 64.4   **43.** $A \approx 82°, B \approx 41°, C \approx 57°, c \approx 255.7$ **45.** 10
47. Station A is about 6 miles from the fire, station B is about 9 miles from the fire.   **49.** The platform is about 3672 yards from one end of the beach and 3576 yards from the other.   **51.** about 184 ft   **53.** about 56 ft   **55.** about 30 ft   **57. a.** $a \approx 494$ ft   **b.** about 343 ft
59. either 9.9 mi or 2.4 mi   **61.** answers may vary   **63.** answers may vary   **65.** answers may vary   **67.** answers may vary
69. answers may vary   **71.** does not make sense   **73.** does not make sense   **75.** no   **77.** 41 ft   **79.** $\sqrt{7280} = 4\sqrt{455} \approx 85$

Section 15.6
Practice Exercises
1. $a = 13, B \approx 28°, C \approx 32°$ **2.** $A \approx 52°, B \approx 98°, C \approx 30°$ **3.** approximately 917 mi apart   **4.** approximately 47 sq m

Exercise Set 15.6
1. $a \approx 6.0, B \approx 29°, C \approx 105°$ **3.** $c \approx 7.6, A \approx 52°, B \approx 32°$ **5.** $A \approx 44°, B \approx 68°, C \approx 68°$ **7.** $A \approx 117°, B \approx 36°, C \approx 27°$
9. $c \approx 4.7, A \approx 46°, B \approx 92°$ **11.** $a \approx 6.3, C \approx 28°, B \approx 50°$ **13.** $b \approx 4.7, C \approx 54°, A \approx 76°$ **15.** $b \approx 5.4, C \approx 22°, A \approx 68°$
17. $C \approx 112°, A \approx 28°, B \approx 40°$ **19.** $B \approx 100°, A \approx 19°, C \approx 61°$ **21.** $A = 60°, B = 60°, C = 60°$ **23.** $A \approx 117°, B \approx 18°, C \approx 45°$
25. 4 sq ft   **27.** 22 sq m   **29.** 31 sq yd   **31.** $A \approx 31°, B \approx 19°, C = 130°, c \approx 19.1$

33. $A \approx 51°, B \approx 61°, C \approx 68°, AB = 9, AC = 8.5, BC = 7.5$ **35.** $A \approx 145°, B \approx 13°, C \approx 22°, a = \sqrt{61} \approx 7.8, b = \sqrt{10} \approx 3.2, c = 5$
37. $157°$ **39.** about 61.7 mi apart **41.** about 193 yd **43.** N12°E **45. a.** about 19.3 mi **b.** S58°E
47. The guy wire anchored downhill is about 417.4 feet. The one anchored uphill is about 398.2 feet. **49.** about 63.7 ft **51.** $123,454
53. answers may vary **55.** answers may vary **57.** answers may vary **59.** answers may vary **61.** makes sense
63. makes sense **65.** $A \approx 29°, B \approx 87°, C \approx 64°, a \approx 11.6, b \approx 23.9$ **67.** answers may vary **69.**

Chapter 15 Review Exercises

For Exercises 1–13, proofs may vary.

14. $\dfrac{\sqrt{6} - \sqrt{2}}{4}$ **15.** $\dfrac{\sqrt{2} - \sqrt{6}}{4}$ **16.** $2 - \sqrt{3}$ **17.** $\sqrt{3} + 2$ **18.** $\dfrac{1}{2}$ **19.** $\dfrac{1}{2}$ For Exercises 20–28, proofs may vary.

29. a. $y = -\sin x$ **b.** $\cos\left(x + \dfrac{\pi}{2}\right) = \cos x \cos \dfrac{\pi}{2} - \sin x \sin \dfrac{\pi}{2} = \cos x \cdot 0 - \sin x \cdot 1 = -\sin x$

30. a. $y = \cos x$ **b.** $\sin\left(x - \dfrac{3\pi}{2}\right) = \sin x \cos \dfrac{3\pi}{2} - \cos x \sin \dfrac{3\pi}{2} = \sin x \cdot 0 - \cos x \cdot -1 = \cos x$

31. a. $\dfrac{33}{65}$ **b.** $\dfrac{16}{65}$ **c.** $-\dfrac{33}{56}$ **d.** $\dfrac{24}{25}$ **e.** $\dfrac{2\sqrt{13}}{13}$ **32. a.** $-\dfrac{63}{65}$ **b.** $-\dfrac{56}{65}$ **c.** $\dfrac{63}{16}$ **d.** $\dfrac{24}{25}$ **e.** $\dfrac{5\sqrt{26}}{26}$
33. a. 1 **b.** $-\dfrac{3}{5}$ **c.** undefined **d.** $-\dfrac{3}{5}$ **e.** $\dfrac{\sqrt{10} + 3\sqrt{10}}{2\sqrt{5}}$ **34. a.** 1 **b.** $\dfrac{4\sqrt{2}}{9}$ **c.** undefined **d.** $\dfrac{4\sqrt{2}}{9}$ **e.** $-\dfrac{\sqrt{3}}{3}$
35. $\dfrac{\sqrt{3}}{2}$ **36.** $-\dfrac{\sqrt{3}}{3}$ **37.** $\dfrac{\sqrt{2} - \sqrt{2}}{2}$ **38.** $2 - \sqrt{3}$ **39.** $x = \dfrac{\pi}{4} + 2n\pi$ or $x = \dfrac{3\pi}{4} + 2n\pi$, where n is any integer.
40. $x = \dfrac{2\pi}{3} + 2n\pi$ or $x = \dfrac{4\pi}{3} + 2n\pi$, where n is any integer. **41.** $x = \dfrac{\pi}{6} + n\pi$, where n is any integer.
42. $x = \dfrac{7\pi}{6} + 2n\pi$ or $x = \dfrac{11\pi}{6} + 2n\pi$, where n is any integer **43.** $\dfrac{\pi}{6}, \dfrac{5\pi}{6}, \dfrac{9\pi}{6}$ **44.** $\dfrac{\pi}{2}, \dfrac{3\pi}{2}$ **45.** $0, \dfrac{\pi}{3}, \pi, \dfrac{5\pi}{3}$ **46.** $\dfrac{3\pi}{2}$ **47.** $\dfrac{\pi}{6}, \dfrac{5\pi}{6}, \dfrac{3\pi}{2}$
48. π **49.** $0, \pi, \dfrac{7\pi}{6}, \dfrac{11\pi}{6}$ **50.** $\dfrac{\pi}{6}, \dfrac{5\pi}{6}, \dfrac{7\pi}{6}, \dfrac{11\pi}{6}$ **51.** $0, \pi$ **52.** $0, \dfrac{\pi}{6}, \pi, \dfrac{11\pi}{6}$ **53.** 0.6847, 2.4569, 3.8263, 5.5985
54. 3.7890, 5.6358 **55.** 0.8959, 2.2457 **56.** $\dfrac{\pi}{4}, 1.2490, \dfrac{5\pi}{4}, 4.3906$ **57.** 12° or 78° **58.** $t = \dfrac{2}{3} + 4n$ or $t = \dfrac{10}{3} + 4n$, where n is any integer.
59. $C = 55°, b \approx 10.5,$ and $c \approx 10.5$ **60.** $A = 43°, a \approx 171.9,$ and $b \approx 241.0$ **61.** $b \approx 16.3, A \approx 72°,$ and $C \approx 42°$
62. $C \approx 98°, A \approx 55°,$ and $B \approx 27°$ **63.** $C = 120°, a \approx 45.0,$ and $b \approx 33.2$ **64.** two triangles; $B_1 \approx 55°, C_1 \approx 86°,$ and $c_1 \approx 31.7$;
$B_2 \approx 125°, C_2 \approx 16°,$ and $c_2 \approx 8.8$ **65.** no triangle **66.** $a \approx 59.0, B \approx 3°,$ and $C \approx 15°$ **67.** $B \approx 78°, A \approx 39°,$ and $C \approx 63°$
68. $B \approx 25°, C \approx 115°,$ and $c \approx 8.5$ **69.** two triangles; $A_1 \approx 59°, C_1 \approx 84°, c_1 \approx 14.4; A_2 \approx 121°, C_2 \approx 22°, c_2 \approx 5.4$
70. $B \approx 9°, C \approx 148°,$ and $c \approx 73.6$ **71.** 8 sq ft **72.** 4 sq ft **73.** 4 sq m **74.** 2 sq m **75.** 35 ft **76.** 35.6 mi
77. 861 mi **78.** 404 ft; 551 ft **79.** $214,194

Chapter 15 Test

1. $-\dfrac{24}{25}$ **2.** $\dfrac{3\sqrt{13}}{13}$ **3.** $\dfrac{56}{33}$ **4.** $\dfrac{\sqrt{6} + \sqrt{2}}{4}$ **5.** $\cos x \csc x = \cos x \cdot \dfrac{1}{\sin x} = \dfrac{\cos x}{\sin x} = \cot x$

6. $\dfrac{\sec x}{\cot x + \tan x} = \dfrac{\dfrac{1}{\cos x}}{\dfrac{\cos x}{\sin x} + \dfrac{\sin x}{\cos x}} = \dfrac{\dfrac{1}{\cos x}}{\dfrac{\cos^2 x + \sin^2 x}{\sin x \cos x}} = \dfrac{1}{\cos x} \cdot \dfrac{\sin x \cos x}{1} = \sin x$

7. $\cos\left(\theta + \dfrac{\pi}{2}\right) = \cos \theta \cos \dfrac{\pi}{2} - \sin \theta \sin \dfrac{\pi}{2} = \cos \theta \cdot 0 - \sin \theta \cdot 1 = -\sin \theta$

8. $\sin t \cos t (\tan t + \cot t) = \sin t \cos t \left(\dfrac{\sin t}{\cos t} + \dfrac{\cos t}{\sin t}\right) = \sin^2 t + \cos^2 t = 1$ **9.** $\dfrac{7\pi}{18}, \dfrac{11\pi}{18}, \dfrac{19\pi}{18}, \dfrac{23\pi}{18}, \dfrac{31\pi}{18},$ and $\dfrac{35\pi}{18}$

10. $\dfrac{\pi}{2}, \dfrac{7\pi}{6}, \dfrac{3\pi}{2}, \dfrac{11\pi}{6}$ **11.** $0, \dfrac{2\pi}{3}, \dfrac{4\pi}{3}$ **12.** $1.2340, \dfrac{\pi}{2}, \dfrac{3\pi}{2}, 5.0522$ **13.** 8.0 **14.** 6.2 **15.** 1 mile

Chapter 15 Standardized Test

1. a **2.** c **3.** b **4.** b **5.** b **6.** $\cos\left[\dfrac{3\pi}{2}-\theta\right] = \cos\dfrac{3\pi}{2}\cos\theta + \sin\dfrac{3\pi}{2}\sin\theta = 0\cdot\cos\theta - 1\cdot\sin\theta = -\sin\theta$

7. $\sin(\alpha-\beta)\cos(\alpha+\beta) = (\sin\alpha\cos\beta - \cos\alpha\sin\beta)(\cos\alpha\cos\beta - \sin\alpha\sin\beta)$
$= \sin\alpha\cos\alpha\cos^2\beta - \sin^2\alpha\cos\beta\sin\beta - \cos^2\alpha\sin\beta\cos\beta + \cos\alpha\sin\alpha\sin^2\beta$
$= \sin\alpha\cos\alpha(\cos^2\beta + \sin^2\beta) - \sin\beta\cos\beta(\sin^2\alpha + \cos^2\alpha) = \sin\alpha\cos\alpha - \sin\beta\cos\beta$

8. d **9.** d **10.** c **11.** b **12.** a **13.** b **14.** b **15.** d **16.** a **17.** c

APPENDIX B SURVEYS AND MARGINS OF ERROR

Practice Exercises

1. a. ±4.5 **b.** We can be 95% confident that between 49.5% and 58.5% of American adults support physician-assisted suicide. **c.** The percentage of American adults who support physician-assisted suicide may be less than 50%.

Appendix B Exercise Set

1. a. ±2% **b.** We can be 95% confident that between 85% and 89% of students prefer school starting at 9 AM. **3. a.** ±2.6%
b. We can be 95% confident that between 6.4% and 11.6% of all children feel that doing chores is a bad thing about being a kid. **5.** ±0.9%
7. ±4.7% **9. a.** ±2.1% **b.** We can be 95% confident that between 15.9% and 20.1% of parents in the population consider a doctor as the dream job for their child. **11. a.** ±1.6% **b.** We can be 95% confident that between 58.6% and 61.8% of all TV households watched the final episode of "M*A*S*H". **13.** 0.2% **15.** answers may vary

APPENDIX C PRACTICE FINAL EXAM

1. $6\sqrt{6}$ **2.** $-\dfrac{3}{2}$ **3.** 5 **4.** $\dfrac{1}{81x^2}$ **5.** $\dfrac{64}{3}$ **6.** $\dfrac{3a^7}{2b^5}$ **7.** $\dfrac{8a^{1/3}c^{2/3}}{b^{5/12}}$ **8.** $2(2y-1)(4y^2+2y+1)$ **9.** $(x+3)(x-3)(y-3)$
10. $-5x^3y - 11x - 9$ **11.** $36m^2 + 12mn + n^2$ **12.** $2x^3 - 13x^2 + 14x - 4$ **13.** $\dfrac{x+2}{2(x+3)}$ **14.** $\dfrac{1}{x(x+3)}$ **15.** $\dfrac{5x-2}{(x-3)(x+2)(x-2)}$
16. $-x\sqrt{5x}$ **17.** -20 **18.** $2x^2 - x - 2 + \dfrac{2}{2x+1}$ **19.** -32 **20.** $1, \dfrac{2}{3}$ **21.** $4, -\dfrac{8}{7}$ **22.** $\dfrac{3}{2} < x \le 5$ **23.** $x < -2$ or $x > \dfrac{4}{3}$
24. 3 **25.** $\dfrac{3 \pm \sqrt{29}}{2}$ **26.** 2, 3 **27.** $x < -\dfrac{3}{2}$ or $x > 5$ **28.** $-3, -3-\sqrt{11}, -3+\sqrt{11}$ **29.** $\left(\dfrac{7}{2}, -10\right)$

30. 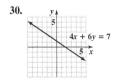 **31.**  **32.**   **33.**   **34.**   **35.**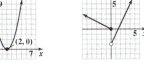

Domain: all real numbers
Range: $y \le -1$

Domain: all real numbers
Range: $y > -3$

36. $f(x) = -\dfrac{1}{2}x$ **37.** $f(x) = -\dfrac{1}{3}x + \dfrac{5}{3}$ **38.** $2\sqrt{26}$ units **39.** $\left(-4, \dfrac{7}{2}\right)$ **40.** all real numbers except -3 **41.** all real numbers except -3 and 1

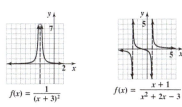

$f(x) = \dfrac{1}{(x+3)^2}$ $f(x) = \dfrac{x+1}{x^2+2x-3}$

42. $\dfrac{3\sqrt{y}}{y}$ **43.** $\dfrac{8 - 6\sqrt{x} + x}{8 - 2x}$ **44.** New York: 21.8 million; Seoul: 23.1 million; Tokyo: 33.4 million **45.** $(x+2y)(x-2y)$ **46.** 5
47. 16 **48.** 7 ft **49. a.** 272 ft **b.** 5.12 sec **50.** 5 gal of 10%: 15 gal of 20% **51.** $\begin{bmatrix} 5 & -2 \\ 1 & -1 \\ 4 & -1 \end{bmatrix}$ **52.** $\begin{bmatrix} -1 & 2 \\ -5 & 4 \end{bmatrix}$

53. a. $\begin{bmatrix} 3 & 5 \\ 2 & -3 \end{bmatrix} \begin{bmatrix} x \\ y \end{bmatrix} = \begin{bmatrix} 9 \\ -13 \end{bmatrix}$ **b.** $\begin{bmatrix} \frac{3}{19} & \frac{5}{19} \\ \frac{2}{19} & -\frac{3}{19} \end{bmatrix}$ **c.** $(-2, 3)$ **54.** 18   **55.** $-2i\sqrt{2}$ **56.** $-3i$ **57.** $7 + 24i$ **58.** $-\frac{3}{2} + \frac{5}{2}i$

59. $(g \circ h)(x) = x^2 - 6x - 2$ **60.** $f^{-1}(x) = \frac{-x+6}{2}$ **61.** $\log_5 \frac{x^4}{x+1}$ **62.** -1 **63.** $\frac{1}{2}\left(\frac{\log 4}{\log 3} - 5\right); -1.8691$ **64.** 22

65. $\frac{43}{21}$ **66.** $\frac{1}{2}$ **67.**   **68.** 64,913 prairie dogs   **69.**   **70.**   **71.**

72. $(-5, -1)(-5, 1), (5, -1), (5, 1)$ **73.** $-\frac{1}{5}, \frac{1}{6}, -\frac{1}{7}, \frac{1}{8}, -\frac{1}{9}$ **74.** 155   **75.** 1   **76.** 10   **77.** $32x^5 + 80x^4y + 80x^3y^2 + 40x^2y^3 + 10xy^4 + y^5$

78. 720   **79.** 990   **80.** 420   **81.** $\frac{8}{13}$ **82.** $\frac{1}{19}$ **83.** 2.5%   **84.** $-\sqrt{3}$ **85.** $-\frac{\sqrt{2}}{2}$ **86.** $\frac{25\pi}{3}$ ft ≈ 26.18 ft

87. $\sin\theta = -\frac{2\sqrt{2}}{3}$; $\tan\theta = -2\sqrt{2}$; $\csc\theta = -\frac{3\sqrt{2}}{4}$; $\sec\theta = 3$; $\cot\theta = -\frac{\sqrt{2}}{4}$ **88.**   **89.** $-\sqrt{3}$

90. $B = 69°; a = 4.7; b = 12.1$ **91.** 23 yd   **92.** $-\frac{24}{25}$ **93.** $\frac{\sec x}{\cot x + \tan x} = \frac{\frac{1}{\cos x}}{\frac{\cos x}{\sin x} + \frac{\sin x}{\cos x}} = \frac{\frac{1}{\cos x}}{\frac{\cos^2 x + \sin^2 x}{\sin x \cos x}} = \frac{1}{\cos x} \cdot \frac{\sin x \cos x}{1} = \sin x$

94. $\frac{\sqrt{6} + \sqrt{2}}{4}$ **95.** $0, \frac{2\pi}{3}, \frac{4\pi}{3}$ **96.** 8.0   **97.** 6.2

Index

A
Abscissa, 109
Absolute error, 102
Absolute value, 12–13, 98
Absolute value bars, 92, 93
Absolute value equations
   explanation of, 92
   method to solve, 92–95, 101
Absolute value functions, 181–183
Absolute value inequalities
   explanation of, 97
   methods to solve, 97–101
   solution set of, 97
Acute angles, 796
Addition
   associative property of, 33
   commutative property of, 33
   of complex numbers, 491–492
   of functions, 565, 566
   of matrices, 252–253
   of polynomials, 306
   of radical expressions, 466–468
   of rational expressions, 383–388
   of real numbers, 17–18
Addition method. *See* Elimination method
Addition property of equality, 48
Addition property of inequality, 76–79
Additive identity, 32, 253
Additive inverse, 253, 307. *See also* Opposites
Algebra
   of functions, 565–566
   Fundamental Theorem of, 550–551
Algebraic expressions
   evaluation of, 7–9, 25–26, 70
   explanation of, 7
   method to simplify, 8, 36–37, 55–57
   method to write, 34–36, 55–56
   writing phrases as, 14–15
Ambiguous case (SSA), 950–953
$a^{m/n}$, 450–451
$a^{-m/n}$, 452
Amplitude
   simple harmonic motion and, 892
   sine function and, 852–853, 855
$a^{1/n}$, 450
Angle of elevation, 819–821
Angles
   acute, 796
   central, 796
   complementary, 64, 817, 818
   coterminal, 802–805
   degrees to measure, 796–799
   explanation of, 795
   finding measures of, 221–222
   negative, 795
   obtuse, 796
   positive, 795
   quadrantal, 796, 826
   radians to measure, 796–799
   reference, 830–836
   right, 796
   standard position of, 795–796, 799–802
   straight, 796
   supplementary, 64
   trigonometric functions of special, 813–815
Angular speed, 805–807
Approximation
   of common logarithms, 603
   decimal, 443
   of natural logarithms, 605
   of square roots, 443
Arc, circular, 805
Arithmetic operations. *See* Division; Multiplication; Order of operations; Subtraction
Arithmetic progression. *See* Arithmetic sequences
Arithmetic sequences
   explanation of, 692
   general term of, 693–694
   partial sums of, 704–705
Associative property of addition, 33
Associative property of multiplication, 33

Asymptotes
    horizontal, 621–642
    of rational functions, 640–642, 648–649
    slant, 648–649
    vertical, 640–641
Axis of symmetry, 623, 624, 628

B

Base, of exponents, 21
Bearings, 890–892
Binomial formula, 712
Binomials. *See also* Polynomials
    division of polynomials by, 402–404
    expansion of, 711, 713–714
    explanation of, 303
    square of, 317
Binomial Theorem, 712–713
Boundary equation, 176
Boundary line, 177
Boyle's law, 428–429
Braces, 24
Brackets, 24
Break-even point, 196, 219–220

C

Calculators. *See* Graphing calculators
Calculus, integral, 886
Cartesian coordinate system. *See*
        Rectangular coordinate system
Center
    of circle, 656
    of ellipse, 662, 663
    of hyperbola, 664
Central angles, 796
Change of base formula, 606–607
Circles
    center and radius of, 656
    eccentricity of, 668
    equation of, 656–659
    explanation of, 656
    formulas for, 972
    on graphing calculator, 659
    graphs of, 63, 656–659
    unit, 838–839
Circular arc, length of, 805

Circular functions, 839. *See also* Trigonometric
        functions
Coded matrix, 279, 280
Coding matrix, 279
Coefficient matrix, 277
Coefficients, 302
Cofunction identities, 817, 818
Cofunctions, 817, 818
Column matrix, 277
Combinations
    computing probability with, 756–758
    explanation of, 741
    formula for, 742–744
    permutations vs., 740–741
Combined variation, 430–431
Combining like terms, 36, 49
Common denominators, adding and
        subtracting rational expressions with,
        383–384. *See also* Denominators
Common difference, of sequence, 692
Common logarithms
    approximation of, 603
    change of base formula and, 606–607
    explanation of, 603
    of power of 10, 603–604
Commutative property of addition, 33
Commutative property of multiplication, 33
Complementary angles
    explanation of, 64
    trigonometric functions and, 817, 818
Completing the square
    explanation of, 516
    to solve quadratic equations, 516–518
Complex conjugates, 493
Complex fractions. *See also* Rational
        expressions
    explanation of, 391
    method to simplify, 391–395
Complex numbers
    division of, 493
    explanation of, 490
    form bi and, 489–490
    graphs of, 491–492
    multiplication of, 492–493
    powers of i and, 494

Complex number system, 489
Complex plane, 491
Composite functions, 566–568
Composition of functions
   explanation of, 566–568
   involving trigonometric functions, 881–882
Compound inequalities
   containing the word *and,* 86–88
   containing the word *or,* 88–89
   explanation of, 75, 85
   intersection of sets and, 85
   solution set of, 85
   union of sets and, 88
Compound interest
   applications of, 519–520, 585, 611
   explanation of, 519–520
   on graphing calculator, 612
Compound interest formula, 586, 606
Conditional equations, 52
Conditional probability, 775–776
Conditional probability formula, 776
Cones
   formulas for, 972
   radius of, 478
Conic sections, 653. *See also* Circles; Ellipses; Geometric figures; Hyperbolas; Parabolas
Conjectures, 715
Conjugates
   complex, 493
   explanation of, 473
   rationalizing denominators using, 473–475
Consecutive integers
   explanation of, 55–56
   method to find, 60–61
Consistent systems of linear equations
   in three variables, 207
   in two variables, 197, 199
Constant matrix, 277
Constant of variation, 426, 428, 429
Constant term, 302
Constraints
   explanation of, 236
   problem solving with objective functions and, 237–240

Contradictions, 52
Coordinate plane. *See* Rectangular coordinate system
Corner point, 234
Cosine function. *See also* Trigonometric functions
   domain and range of, 841
   explanation of, 810
   graph of, 857–862
   inverse, 876–878
   periodic properties of, 842–843
Cosines
   difference formula for, 916–917
   of difference of two angles, 915–918
   explanation of, 810
   Law of, 960–964, 974
   sum and difference formulas for, 918–921
Cost function, 219–221, 649–650
Cotangent, 810
Coterminal angles, 802–805
Counterexamples, 715
Cramer's rule
   explanation of, 268
   to solve system of three linear equations, 270–271
   to solve system of two linear equations, 267–269
Cryptograms, 279–280
Cube root functions, graphs of, 445–446
Cube roots
   explanation of, 23, 443
   method to find, 443–444
Cubes
   formulas for, 972
   sum or difference of two, 339–341
Cylinder, right circular, 972

D

Decimal, percent, and fraction equivalent table, 975
Decimal approximation, 443
Decimals, 51–52
Deductive reasoning
   explanation of, 718–719
   use of, 719–720

Degrees
    converting between radians and, 798–799
    measurement of angles in, 796
    of polynomial, 303–304
Demand equations, 206
Denominators. *See also* Least common denominator (LCD)
    of rational exponents, 451
    of rational expressions, 383–388, 410
    rationalizing the, 471–473
Dependent equations, 198, 199, 208
Dependent events, 773–775
Dependent variables, 127
Depreciation, straight-line, 119
Descartes, René, 109
Determinants
    Cramer's rule and, 267–271
    evaluation of 2×2, 266–267
    evaluation of 3×3, 269
    explanation of, 266
Difference formula, 916–917
Difference of two squares, 338–339
Diminishing motion, 893
Direct variation, 426–427
Discriminant, 526–527
Distance, 463
Distance formula, 461, 462, 915–917
Distributive property, 34, 52, 53, 69
Division
    of functions, 565, 566
    long, 399–403
    of polynomials, 398–406
    of rational expressions, 376–378
    of real numbers, 20–21
    synthetic, 402–404
Domain
    of functions, 125–126
    of rational expressions, 371–372
    of rational functions, 371–372, 638–639
    of relation, 120
Double-angle formulas, 925–928, 930, 974

E

Eccentricity, 668
Elementary row operations, 227–228
Elements, of set, 9, 10

Elimination method
    explanation of, 201
    to solve nonlinear system of equations, 672–673
    to solve systems of linear equations, 201–203, 208–210
Ellipses
    eccentricity of, 668
    equation of, 662–664
    explanation of, 9, 662
    focus of, 662
    on graphing calculator, 666
    graphs of, 662–664
Empirical probability, 750–752
Empty set, 9
End behavior, of polynomial functions, 361–363
Equality
    addition property of, 48
    logarithm property of, 609
    of matrices, 251–252
    multiplication property of, 48
Equality symbols, 30–31
Equations. *See also* Linear equations in one variable; Linear equations in three variables; Linear equations in two variables; Nonlinear systems of equations; Quadratic equations; Systems of linear equations in three variables; Systems of linear equations in two variables; *specific types of equations*
    absolute value, 92–95, 101
    boundary, 176
    of circle, 656–659
    conditional, 52
    demand, 206
    dependent, 198, 199, 208
    of ellipse, 662–664
    equivalent, 48
    explanation of, 47, 409
    exponential, 584–586, 608–611
    expressions vs., 409, 416
    on graphing calculator, 116–117, 130–131, 141
    graphs of linear, 111–115
    graphs of nonlinear, 115–116
    of horizontal lines, 162

independent, 198, 199
of lines, 157–163
logarithmic, 590–592, 609–611
matrix, 255, 277–280
ordered pair as solution to, 111
of parabola, 653–656
of parallel and perpendicular lines, 163
point-slope form of, 159–160
polynomial, 347–352, 548–550
in quadratic form, 533–536
with radical expressions, 479–482
with rational expressions, 409–413, 418–422
revenue, 206
solution of, 47, 413
trigonometric, 934–944
of unit circles, 838–839
of vertical lines, 162
Equilateral triangles, 972
Equilibrium, market, 674
Equilibrium point, 206
Equilibrium position, 892
Equivalent equations, 48
Even-odd identities, 905
Events
complement of, 760
dependent, 773–775
independent, 770–773
mutually exclusive, 762–763
odds against, 760–762
odds in favor of, 762–765
probability of, 73–74, 746–747
probability of odds and, 765–767
Exams. *See* Mathematics class
Expected value
applications of, 784–786
explanation of, 783
method to compute, 784
Exponential equations
method to solve, 608–609
problem solving with, 584–586
Exponential expressions, 287, 288
Exponential functions
explanation of, 581
on graphing calculator, 586
graphs of, 582–583
method to solve, 583–584

Exponents
evaluating expressions containing, 21–22
explanation of, 21–22
negative, 289–291, 394–395
power of product rule for, 296
power rule for, 296–297
product rule for, 287–288
quotient rule for, 288–289
raised to negative nth power, 289–291
scientific notation and, 299
simplifying expressions using rules for, 452–454
summary of rules for, 297, 453
Expressions. *See also* Algebraic expressions; Radical expressions; Rational expressions
equations vs., 416
evaluation of, 8, 25
explanation of, 409
Extraneous solutions, 410, 479

F
Factorial notation, 735–736
Factorials, 712, 735
Factors/factoring. *See also* Polynomials
difference of two squares, 338–339
explanation of, 21, 322
greatest common, 322–325
by grouping, 325, 333, 339
perfect square trinomials, 332–333, 337–338
to separate different trigonometric functions, 939
to solve polynomials equations, 347–352
strategy for, 343–345
by substitution, 333–334
sum or difference of two cubes, 339–341
trinomials of form $ax^2 + bx + c$, 330–333
trinomials of form $x^2 + bx + c$, 328–330
to verify identities, 907
Factor Theorem, 406
Feasible region, 236
Fibonacci (Leonardo of Pisa), 687
Fibonacci sequence, 687, 691
Figurate numbers, 722
Finite sequences, 688
Finite series, 699–700

First-degree equations. *See* Linear equations in one variable
First-degree equations in two variables. *See* Linear equations in two variables
First-degree polynomial equations. *See* Linear equations in one variable
Focus
   of ellipse, 662
   of hyperbola, 664
FOIL method, 316, 317
Formulas. *See also specific formulas*
   explanation of, 67
   geometric, 972
   solved for specified variables, 67–69
   trigonometric, 973
   used to solve problems, 69–71
Fraction bar, 24
Fractions. *See also* Ratios
   explanation of, 371
   solving linear equations containing, 50–52
Frequency, 894
Function notation, 127–130, 139
Functions. *See also* Polynomial functions; *specific types of functions*
   absolute value, 181–183
   algebra of, 565–566
   composition of, 566–568, 881–882
   domain of, 125–126
   end behavior of graphs of, 361–362
   explanation of, 122
   exponential, 581–584
   on graphing calculators, 458, 578
   graphs of linear, 136–141
   inverse, 574–578
   linear, 136–141
   logarithmic, 593–594
   one-to-one, 570–578
   piecewise-defined, 168–169
   quadratic, 623–629, 631–635
   range of, 125–126
   rational, 378, 379, 638–650
   reciprocal, 639–640
   vertical line test for, 123–125
Fundamental Counting Principle
   combinations formula and, 745
   counting permutations using, 734–735, 756
   explanation of, 729
   with more than two groups of items, 729–732
Fundamental Principle of Rational Expressions, 373
Fundamental Theorem of Algebra, 550–551

G

General term
   of arithmetic sequence, 693–694
   of geometric sequence, 695–696
   of sequence, 688–690
Geometric figures, 972. *See also specific figures*
Geometric formulas, 972
Geometric progression. *See* Geometric sequences
Geometric sequences
   explanation of, 694–696
   partial sums of, 706–708
Golden ratio, 687
Graphing calculators
   circles on, 659
   compound interest on, 612
   evaluating expressions on, 70
   exponential functions on, 586
   functions on, 458, 578
   graphing equations on, 116–117, 130–131, 141
   INTERSECT feature on, 612
   inverse functions on, 578
   inverse trigonometric functions on, 880–881
   polynomials on, 310, 319–320, 406
   quadratic equations on, 354–355, 520
   quadratic functions on, 629
   radical equations on, 484
   rational expressions on, 379, 388
   rational functions on, 379, 643, 646, 647
   scientific notation on, 293
   systems of linear equations on, 204
   TRACE feature on, 153, 586, 612
   trigonometric equations on, 942–944
   trigonometric functions on, 818–819
   trigonometric identities on, 818–819
   windows and window settings on, 116–117

Graphs
  on calculators, 117–118
  of circles, 63, 656–659
  of complex numbers, 491–492
  of cosine function, 857–862
  of ellipses, 662–664
  of horizontal lines, 140–141
  of hyperbolas, 664–666
  of inverse functions, 576–577
  of linear equations, 111–115
  of linear functions, 136–141, 169
  of linear inequalities, 74–75, 176–179
  of logarithmic functions, 593–594
  of nonlinear equations, 115–116
  of nonlinear functions, 170
  of nonlinear inequalities, 675–676
  of parabolas, 623–629, 631–635, 653–656
  plotting ordered pairs on, 109–111
  of polynomial functions, 308–309, 353–354
  of power functions, 359–363
  of quadratic functions, 623–629, 631–635
  of rational functions, 639–650
  reflecting, 173–174
  review of common, 169–172
  of sine function, 847–856
  sinusoidal, 861–862
  of slope-intercept form, 149
  of square root function, 170–171
  of square root functions, 170–171, 445–447
  of systems of linear equations, 197–199
  of systems of linear inequalities, 233–235
  of systems of nonlinear inequalities, 676–677
  of tangent function, 867–871
  of trigonometric functions, 973
  of vertical lines, 140–141
Greatest common factor (GCF)
  explanation of, 322–323
  factoring out, 323–324
Grouping, factoring by, 325, 333, 339
Grouping symbols, 24. *See also* Brackets; Parentheses

H

Half-angle formulas, 928–930, 974
Half-planes, 176

Heron's formula, 487, 963–964
Histograms, 779
Hooke's law, 427
Horizontal asymptotes, of rational functions, 621–642
Horizontal lines
  equations of, 162
  graphs of, 140–141
  slope of, 163.149–151
Horizontal line test, 572–573
Horizontal shifts, 171–173
Hyperbolas
  eccentricity of, 668
  equation of, 664–666
  explanation of, 664
  focus of, 664
  graphs of, 664–666
Hypotenuse, 351, 810
Hypotheses, 715

I

Identities. *See also* Trigonometric identities
  cofunction, 817, 818
  even-odd, 905
  explanation of, 32, 52
  identification of, 32–33, 52–53
  Pythagorean, 816–817, 905, 911, 974
  quotient, 815, 816, 905, 974
  reciprocal, 815, 816, 905, 974
Imaginary axis, 491
Imaginary numbers, 489, 490
Imaginary unit *(i)*, 494, 499
Incidence ratio, 652
Inconsistent systems of linear equations
  in three variables, 207, 209
  in two variables, 198, 199
Independent equations, 198, 199
Independent events, 770–773
Independent variables, 127
Index, 444
Index of summation, 699
Inductive reasoning
  explanation of, 715
  patterns and, 717
  use of, 715–718

Inequalities. *See also specific types of inequalities*
  absolute value, 97–101
  addition property of, 76–79
  compound, 75, 85–89
  graphs of, 74–75
  linear, 74–81, 176–179
  multiplication property of, 76–79
  nonlinear, 552–556
  polynomial, 552–555
  rational, 555–556
  solutions of, 74–75, 97, 233
  solving problems modeled by, 80–81
Inequality symbols, 30–31, 74, 77, 97
Infinite sequences, 688
Infinite series, 699
Initial side, of ray, 795
Integers
  consecutive, 55–56, 60–61
  explanation of, 9, 11
  as rational numbers, 11, 12
Integral calculus, 886
Intercepts, 137–139
Interest
  compound, 519–520, 585, 586, 606, 611, 612
  simple, 518–519
Intersections
  of linear inequalities, 178–179
  of solution sets of inequalities, 85
Intersection symbol, 85
Interval notation, compound inequalities and, 519–520, 585
Inverse functions
  explanation of, 574
  on graphing calculator, 578
  graphs of, 576–577
  one-to-one, 574–575
Inverse of functions
  equation for, 575–576
  method to find, 577–578
Inverse trigonometric functions
  calculators to evaluate, 880–881
  composition of functions involving, 881–884
  cosine, 876–878
  sine, 873–876
  tangent, 878–880
Inverse variation, 427–429
Invertible matrix, 274
Irrational numbers, 10, 11, 443
Isosceles triangles, 972

J
Joint variation, 429–430

L
Law of Cosines
  applications of, 962–963
  derivation of, 960
  explanation of, 960, 974
  Heron's formula and, 963–964
  oblique triangles and, 960–962
Law of Large Numbers, 752
Law of Sines
  ambiguous case and, 950–953
  applications of, 954–955
  derivation of, 947–948
  explanation of, 947, 974
  oblique triangles and, 948–950, 953–954, 960
Learning curve formula, 614
Least common denominator (LCD), 50, 384–385. *See also* Denominators
Least squares method, 130, 148
Legs, of right triangle, 351, 352
Leonardo of Pisa (Fibonacci), 687
Like radicals, 466
Like terms, 36, 37, 49, 305–306
Linear equations in one variable. *See also* Equations
  combining like terms to solve, 49–50
  containing fractions or decimals, 50
  explanation of, 47
  with no solution, 52
  properties of equality to solve, 47–49
  steps to solve, 51–52
Linear equations in three variables, 207
Linear equations in two variables. *See also* Equations
  explanation of, 112
  forms of, 163, 167

graphs of, 111–115
in point-slope form, 163
in slope-intercept form, 163
standard form of, 112, 163
Linear Factorization Theorem, 550
Linear functions
explanation of, 137
graphs of, 136–141, 169
Linear inequalities. *See also* Inequalities
addition property to solve, 76–79
explanation of, 74
graphs of, 74–75, 176–179
intersections or unions of, 178–179
multiplication property of inequality to solve, 76–79
in one variable, 74–79
solving problems modeled by, 80–81
systems of, 233–235
Linear programming
applications of, 239–240
explanation of, 236
problem solving with, 236–240
writing objective functions and constraints and, 237–239
Linear speed, 805–807
Lines
equations of, 157–163
horizontal, 140–141, 149–151, 162
parallel, 151–153, 162–163
perpendicular, 151–153, 163
point-slope form of, 159–160
slope-intercept form of, 148–149, 157
slope of, 145–148
vertical, 140–141, 149–151, 162
Logarithmic equations
method to solve, 591–592, 609–610
method to write, 590–591
Logarithmic functions, 593–594
Logarithmic notation, 589–591
Logarithm property of equality, 609
Logarithms
change of base formula and, 606–607
common, 603–605
explanation of, 590
natural, 603, 605–606
power property of, 598–600

product property of, 597–600
properties of, 592–593, 597–600
quotient property of, 598
Long division, 399–403
Lowest terms, of rational expressions, 372–373

M

Mach speed, 932
Margin of error, 976–977
Market equilibrium, 674
Mathematics class
exams for, 5
getting help with, 5
practice final exam for, 980–982
resources for, 3–4
time management for, 6, 7
tips for success in, 2–6
Matrices
addition and subtraction of, 252–253
coded, 279, 280
coding, 279
coefficient, 277
column, 277
constant, 277
equality of, 251–252
explanation of, 227
multiplication with, 253–254, 257–261
multiplicative inverses of, 273–275
problem solving with, 261–263
to solve systems of linear equations, 227–231
square, 251, 274
3×3, 269, 275
2×2, 266–267, 274–275
zero, 253
Matrix equations
inverses to solve, 277–278
method to solve, 255
Matrix notation, 251
Maximum value, in graphs of parabolas, 634–635
Mean
explanation of, 496–497
finding scores at specified standard deviation from, 780–782

Mean (*continued*)
   of normal distribution, 779
   standard deviation from, 499–500
Measures of central tendency
   explanation of, 496
   mean as, 496–497
   median as, 497–498
   mode as, 497–498
Measures of dispersion, 498
Median, 497–498
   of normal distribution, 779
Midpoint, 462, 463
Midpoint formula, 462, 463
Minimum value, in graphs of parabolas, 634–635
Mixture problems, 218–219
Mode, 497–498, 779
Monomials. *See also* Polynomials
   dividing polynomials by, 398–399
   explanation of, 303
Mosteller formula, 449
Multiplication. *See also* Products
   associative property of, 33, 34
   commutative property of, 33
   of complex numbers, 492–493
   distributive property of, 34
   of functions, 565, 566
   matrix, 253–254, 257–261
   of polynomials, 314–319
   of radical expressions, 468–469
   of rational expressions, 375–376
   of real numbers, 19–20
   scalar, 253–254
Multiplication property of equality, 48
Multiplication property of inequality, 76–79
Multiplicative identity
   explanation of, 32, 33
   of matrices, 272
Multiplicative inverse
   of matrices, 273–275
   to solve matrix equations, 277–278
Musical sounds, 894
Mutually exclusive events, 762–763

N

Natural logarithms
   approximation of, 605
   change of base formula and, 606–607
   explanation of, 603, 605
   of powers of e, 605–606
Natural numbers, 9
Negative angles, 795
Negative exponents
   explanation of, 289–291
   simplifying expressions with, 394–395
Negative numbers, 9
Negative square root, 442
Nonlinear equations, graphs of, 115–116
Nonlinear functions, graphs of, 170
Nonlinear inequalities
   graphs of, 675–676
   in one variable, 552–556
   systems of, 676–677
Nonlinear systems of equations
   elimination method to solve, 672–673
   explanation of, 670
   substitution method to solve, 670–672
Nonsingular matrix, 274
Normal distribution
   characteristics of, 779–780
   explanation of, 779
   specified standard deviation from mean and, 780–782
   standard deviation in, 780, 976–977
Notation. *See* Symbols/notation
nth power, evaluating exponents raised to negative, 289–291
nth roots, 444–445
Null set, 9
Number lines
   absolute value on, 92
   explanation of, 9
   integers on, 9
   natural numbers on, 9
   rational and irrational numbers on, 11
   whole numbers on, 9
Numbers. *See also* Complex numbers; Integers; Real numbers
   figurate, 722
   finding absolute value of, 12–14
   finding opposite of, 13–14
   finding unknown, 57–58, 215–216, 419

identifying common sets of, 9–12
irrational, 10, 11, 443
natural, 9
negative, 9
positive, 9
rational, 10, 11
whole, 9
Numerators, rationalizing the, 475–476

O

Oblique triangles
ambiguous case and, 950–953
area of, 953–954
explanation of, 947–948, 974
method to solve, 948–950, 960–962
Obtuse angles, 796
One-to-one functions
explanation of, 570–571
exponential functions as, 582, 583
graphs of, 576–577
horizontal line test to determine, 572–573
inverse of, 574–578
Opposites, 13–14. *See also* Additive inverse
Ordered pairs
explanation of, 109
plotting, 109–110
relation as set of, 120
as solution to equations, 111, 139
as solution to system of linear equations, 196–197
Ordered triples, 207
Order of operations, 23–25
Ordinate, 109
Origin, 9, 109

P

Parabolas. *See also* Quadratic functions
axis of symmetry of, 623, 624, 628
equation of, 653–656
explanation of, 170
graphs of, 623–629, 631–635, 653–656
vertex of, 623, 624, 628, 633–634
Parallel lines
equations of, 162–163
explanation of, 151, 163
slope of, 151–153

Parallelograms, formulas for, 972
Parentheses
distributive property to remove, 52, 53, 69
use of, 24
Partial sums
of arithmetic sequences, 704–705
explanation of, 700–701
of geometric sequences, 706–708
Pascal's triangle, 711, 712, 722
Patterns, inductive reasoning and, 717–718
Pendulums, 487
Pentagonal numbers, 722
Percent, decimal and fraction equivalent table, 975
Perfect squares factor, 459–460
Perfect square trinomials
completing the square for, 516–518
explanation of, 332
factoring, 337–338
Period, of simple harmonic motion, 892–894
Periodic behavior, 862–864
Periodic functions, 842–843
Permutations
combinations vs., 740–741
computing probability with, 755–756
of duplicate items, 738–739
explanation of, 734–735, 741
formula for, 736–738
Perpendicular lines
equations of, 163
explanation of, 151, 152, 163
slope of, 151–153
Phase shift, 854, 855
pH level, 564, 651
Piecewise-defined functions, 168–169
Plotting points, 109–111
Point-slope form
equations of lines in, 159–160
explanation of, 159, 163
problem solving with, 160–161
Polynomial equations. *See also* Quadratic equations
explanation of, 347
factoring to solve, 347–350
Fundamental Theorem of Algebra and, 550–551

Polynomial equations (*continued*)
  process to solve, 548–550
  roots of, 548–550
  solving problems modeled by, 350–352
  in standard form, 347
Polynomial functions
  end behavior of, 361–363
  evaluation of, 319
  explanation of, 304–305
  finding x-intercepts of, 353–354
  on graphing calculator, 406
  graphs of, 308–309, 353–354
  operations with, 308
  rational functions as quotients of, 638
  zeros of, 353, 543–546, 548, 550–551
Polynomial inequalities, 552–555
Polynomials. *See also* Binomials; Factors/
    factoring; Monomials; Trinomials
  addition of, 306
  degree of, 303–304
  in descending order, 302
  division of, 398–406
  explanation of, 302
  Factor Theorem to evaluate, 406
  on graphing calculator, 310, 319–320
  multiplication of, 314–319
  in one variable, 302
  prime, 330
  Remainder Theorem to evaluate, 406
  subtraction of, 307–308
  use of Remainder Theorem to
    evaluate, 405
Positive angles, 795
Positive numbers, 9
Positive square root. *See* Principal
    square root
Power functions
  explanation of, 359
  graphs of, 359–363
Power of product rule for exponents, 296
Power of quotient rule, 297
Power property of logarithms, 598–600
Power rules
  for exponents, 296–297
  to solve radical equations, 479
Powers of 10, 603–604

Powers of e, 605–606
Practice final exam, 980–982
Prime polynomials, 330
Principal square root, 22, 442
Probability
  applications for, 749–750
  combinations to compute, 756–758
  complementary rules of, 760–762
  conditional, 775–776
  with dependent events, 773–775
  empirical, 750–752
  of event, 73–74, 746–747
  expected value and, 783–786
  with independent events, 770–773
  normal distribution and, 779–782
  overview of, 746
  permutations to compute, 755–756
  that event will not occur, 760–762
  that event will occur, 762–765
  theoretical, 747–749
  use of odds in, 765–767
Problem solving
  with expected value, 784–786
  with exponential equations, 584–586,
    610–611
  with formulas, 69–71
  with Fundamental Counting Principle,
    729–732
  general strategy for, 57–61
  with Law of Cosines, 962–963
  with Law of Sines, 954–955
  with linear inequalities, 80–81
  with linear programming, 236–240
  with logarithmic equations, 610–611
  with matrices, 261–263
  with point-slope form, 160–161
  with polynomial equations, 350–352
  with quadratic equations, 518–520,
    528–529, 536–539
  with rational expressions, 419–422
  with rational functions, 378, 649–650
  with sequences, 690, 696, 701, 705–708
  with systems of linear equations in three
    variables, 221–222
  with systems of linear equations in two
    variables, 196, 214–221

with trigonometry, 819–821, 887–895
with variation, 426–431
Product property, of logarithms, 597
Product rule
   for exponents, 287–288
   power of, 296
   for radicals, 457–458, 460
Products. *See also* Multiplication
   factoring by special, 337–341
   matrix, 258
   of sum and difference of two terms, 318–319
Proportions, 420. *See also* Ratios
Pure imaginary numbers, 490
Pythagorean identities, 816–817, 905, 911, 974
Pythagorean Theorem
   applications of, 351–352, 482–484
   distance formula and, 462
   explanation of, 351, 816, 972

Q

Quadrantal angles
   explanation of, 796
   terminal side of, 826
   trigonometric functions of, 827–828
Quadrants, 9, 109
Quadratic equations. *See also* Polynomial equations
   completing the square to solve, 516–518
   explanation of, 347, 514
   on graphing calculator, 354–355, 520
   problem solving with, 518–520, 528–529, 536–539
   square root property to solve, 514–515
   standard form of, 520, 524, 526
   steps to solve, 533–536
   zero-factor property to solve, 347–350, 514
Quadratic formula
   explanation of, 523–524
   to solve quadratic equations, 524–526
   use of, 546, 943–944
Quadratic functions
   explanation of, 623
   of form $f(x) = ax^2$, 626–627
   of form $f(x) = a(x - h)^2 + k$, 627–628
   of form $f(x) = (x - h)^2$, 624–626

of form $f(x) = (x - h)^2 + k$, 626
of form $f(x) = x^2 + k$, 623–624
formula to find vertex in graphs of, 633–634
of form $y = a(x - h)^2 + k$, 631–633
on graphing calculator, 629
graphs of, 623–629, 631–635
minimum and maximum values in graphs of, 634–635
Quadratic in form
   equations, 533–536
   trigonometric equations, 937–938
Quotient identities, 815, 816, 905, 974
Quotient property of logarithms, 598–600
Quotient rule
   for exponents, 288–289
   power of, 297
   for radicals, 458–459, 461

R

Radian measure
   converting between degrees and, 798–799
   explanation of, 796–797
   method to compute, 797
   table of, 802
   in unit circle, 839
Radians, 796
Radical equations
   on graphing calculator, 484
   method to solve, 479–482
Radical expressions
   addition and subtraction of, 466–468
   explanation of, 442
   midpoint and distance formulas and, 461–463
   multiplication of, 468–469
   product rule to simplify, 457–459
   quotient rule to simplify, 458–459
   rationalizing denominators of, 471–475
   solving equations that contain, 479–482
   use of rational exponents to simplify, 454–455
Radicals. *See also* Roots; Square roots
   like, 466
   method to simplify, 459–461
   product rule for, 457–458, 460
   quotient rule for, 458–459, 461

Radical sign, 22, 442
Radicand
　explanation of, 442
　perfect square factors in, 460
　variables in, 445
Radioactive material, 585–586
Radius
　of circle, 656, 658
　of cone, 478
　of sphere, 465, 478
Range
　of functions, 125–126
　as measure of dispersion, 499
　of relation, 120, 121, 125–126
Rate of change, 145
Rational exponents
　$a^{m/n}$, 450–451
　$a^{-m/n}$, 452
　$a^{1/n}$, 450
　to simplify radical expressions, 454–455
Rational expressions. *See also* Fractions
　addition and subtraction of, 383–388
　complex, 391–395
　division of, 376–378
　domain of, 371–372
　equations containing, 409–413, 418–422
　examples of, 371
　explanation of, 371
　fundamental principle of, 373
　on graphing calculator, 379, 388
　identifying least common denominator of, 384–385
　lowest terms of, 372–373
　method to simplify, 372–375
　multiplication of, 375–376
Rational functions
　asymptotes of, 640–642, 648–649
　domain of, 371–372, 638–639
　explanation of, 638
　on graphing calculator, 379, 643, 646, 647
　graphs of, 639–650
　problem solving with, 378, 649–650
　transformations to graph, 642–643
Rational inequalities, 555–556
Rationalizing the denominator, 471–475
Rationalizing the numerator, 475–476

Rational numbers, 10, 11. *See also* Fractions
Rational Zero Theorem, 543–545
Ratios, 420, 652
Rays, 795
Real numbers
　addition of, 17–18
　division of, 20–21
　explanation of, 10, 11
　multiplication of, 19–20
　set of, 12
　subtraction of, 18–19
　trigonometric functions of, 838–842
Reasoning
　deductive, 718–720
　inductive, 715–720
Reciprocal functions, 639–640
Reciprocal identities, 815, 816, 905, 974
Reciprocals, 20
Rectangles, formulas for, 972
Rectangular coordinate system, 109–111
Rectangular solids, 972
Reference angles
　evaluating trigonometric functions using, 832–836
　explanation of, 830
　method to find, 830–832
Reflecting graphs, 173–174
Relations
　domain of, 120, 125–126
　explanation of, 120–121, 123
　functions as type of, 122
　range of, 120, 121, 125–126
Remainder Theorem, 405
Resistance formula, 425
Revenue equations, 206
Revenue functions, 219–221
Richter scale, 604
Right angles, 796
Right circular cylinder, 972
Right triangles
　explanation of, 351, 972
　method to solve, 888–890
　Pythagorean Theorem and, 351–352, 482–484
Roots. *See also* Radicals; Square roots
　cube, 23, 443–444

method to find, 22–23
nth, 444–445
of polynomial equations, 548–550
Roster form, 9

S
Scalar multiplication, 253–254
Scientific calculators. *See also* Graphing calculators
  inverse trigonometric functions on, 880–881
  trigonometric functions on, 818, 819
Scientific notation
  on calculator, 293
  conversions between standard notation and, 291–293
  explanation of, 291–292
  operations with, 299
  writing numbers in, 292
Secant, 810
Second-degree equations. *See* Quadratic equations
Sequences
  arithmetic, 692–694, 704–705
  explanation of, 688
  Fibonacci, 687, 691
  finite, 688
  geometric, 694–696, 706–708
  infinite, 688
  problem solving with, 690, 696, 701, 705–708
  terms of, 688–690, 693–696
  visual, 718
Series
  explanation of, 699
  finite, 699–700
  infinite, 699
  partial sum, 700–701
  summation notation and, 699, 700
Set builder notation, 9
Sets
  of complex numbers, 489
  elements of, 9, 10
  empty or null, 9–10
  intersection of two, 85
  union of two, 88
Sigma (Σ), 496

Simple harmonic motion and, 892–895
Simple interest formula, 518–519
Simplification
  of algebraic expressions, 8, 36–37, 55–57
  of complex fractions, 391–395
  of radical expressions, 454–459
  of rational expressions, 372–375
Sine curve, 848, 873
Sine function. *See also* Trigonometric functions
  domain and range of, 841
  graph of, 847–856
  inverse, 873–876
  periodic properties of, 842–843
Sines
  explanation of, 810
  Law of, 947–955
  sum and difference formulas for, 918–921
Sinusoidal graphs, 861–862
68-95-99.7 Rule, 780–782
Slope
  explanation of, 145
  graphs of line using y-intercept and, 157–158
  of horizontal and vertical lines, 149–151
  method to find from two points, 147
  method to find given equation, 147
  of parallel and perpendicular lines, 151–153
  as rate of change, 145
Slope-intercept form
  explanation of, 148, 163
  interpreting, 148–149
  shifting and, 171
  to write equations of lines, 157
Solution region, 176
Solutions
  of equations, 47
  extraneous, 410, 479
  of inequalities, 74–75, 97, 233
  of trigonometric equations, 934–935
Solution set
  of compound inequalities, 85
  of equations, 47–48
  of inequalities, 74
Special products, factoring by, 337–341

Speed, linear and angular, 805–807
Sphere, radius of, 465, 478
Spheres, formulas for, 972
Square matrix, 251, 274
Square numbers, 722
Square root functions, 170–171, 445–447
Square root property, 514–515
Square roots. *See also* Radicals
   approximation of, 443
   explanation of, 9, 11, 442
   imaginary unit and, 489
   negative, 442
   positive or principal, 22, 442
   symbol for, 22
Squares. *See also* Completing the square
   of binomials, 317
   difference of two, 338–339
   formulas for, 972
   perfect, 459–460
Standard deviation
   explanation of, 499
   interpretation of, 503
   from mean, 780–782
   method to compute, 500–502
   in normal distribution, 780, 976–977
Standard form
   of equation of circle, 656–659
   of equation of ellipse, 662–664
   of equation of hyperbola, 664, 665
   of equation of parabola, 653–656
   graphs of parabolas in, 653–656
   of linear equations, 112, 163
   polynomial equations in, 347
   of quadratic equations, 520, 524, 526
   of quadratic inequalities, 552
   of system of equations, 227
Standard position, of angles, 795–796, 799–802
Straight angles, 796
Straight-line depreciation, 119
Subscripts, 25
Substitution method
   explanation of, 199
   factoring by, 333–334
   to solve nonlinear system of equations, 670–672
   to solve systems of linear equations, 199–201, 208, 211–212
Subtraction
   of complex numbers, 491–492
   of functions, 565, 566
   of matrices, 252–253
   of polynomials, 307–308
   of radical expressions, 466–468
   of rational expressions, 383–388
   of real numbers, 18–19
Sum and difference formulas
   for cosines and sines, 918–921
   review of, 930, 974
   for tangents, 921
Summation notation, 699, 700
Supplementary angles, 64
Surveys, 976–977
Symbols/notation
   absolute value, 92, 93
   element of, 10
   empty or null set, 9
   equality, 30–31
   factorial, 735–736
   fraction bar, 24
   function, 127–130, 139
   grouping, 24
   inequality, 30–31, 74, 77, 97
   intersection of sets, 85
   logarithmic, 589–591
   matrix, 251
   radical, 22, 442
   scientific notation, 291–293
   set builder, 9
   sigma (Σ), 496
   writing mathematical sentences using, 30–32
Synthetic division, 402–404
Systems of linear equations in three variables
   consistent, 207
   Cramer's rule to solve, 270–271
   elimination method to solve, 208–210
   explanation of, 207–208
   inconsistent, 207, 209
   inverses of matrices to solve, 277–278
   matrices to solve, 229–231
   methods to solve, 208–212

problem solving with, 221–222
substitution method to solve, 208, 211–212
3 × 3 determinants to solve, 269
Systems of linear equations in two variables
consistent, 197, 199
Cramer's rule to solve, 266–269
determinants to solve, 267–269
elimination method to solve, 201–203
explanation of, 195
on graphing calculator, 204
graphs to solve, 197–199
inconsistent, 198, 199
matrices to solve, 227–229
ordered pair as solution to, 196–197
solution of, 196
substitution method to solve, 199–201
Systems of linear inequalities, 233–235
Systems of nonlinear equations. *See* Nonlinear systems of equations
Systems of nonlinear inequalities, 676–677

T

Tangent function. *See also* Trigonometric functions
graph of, 867–871
inverse, 878–880
periodic property of, 843
Tangents, 810, 921
Temperature conversions, 26, 91
Terminal side
of ray, 795
rotation of, 799–802
Terms
constant, 302
explanation of, 36
like, 36, 37, 49, 305–306
of sequence, 688–690, 693–696
Theoretical probability, 747–750
Three-part inequalities. *See* Compound inequalities
Transformations
with matrices, 262–263
reflection as, 173–174
shifting as, 169–173

used to graph rational functions, 642–643
Tree diagram, 720
Triangles
equilateral, 972
finding of side of, 59–60, 889
formulas for, 972
isosceles, 972
oblique, 947–955, 960–962, 974
Pascal's, 711, 712, 722
right, 351–352, 482–484, 888–890, 972
sum of angles of, 972
Triangular numbers, 722
Trigonometric equations
explanation of, 934
factoring and, 939
on graphing calculator, 938, 942–944
identities to solve, 939–942
involving multiple angles, 936–937
solutions of, 934–936
that are quadratic in form, 937–938
Trigonometric formulas, 973
Trigonometric functions. *See also specific trigonometric function*
of any angle, 826–828
on calculator, 818–819
complements and, 817–818
curves of, 871
description of, 810–811
domain and range of sine and cosine functions and, 841
equations involving single, 935–936
evaluation of, 812–815, 818–819, 829–830, 832–836
even and off, 842
finding values of, 840–841
inverse, 873–884
periodic, 842–843
periodic behavior and, 862–864
problem solving with, 887–895
of quadrantal angles, 827–828
of real numbers, 838–840
reference angles and, 830–836
review of, 973
right triangle definitions of, 811
signs of, 828–829
of special angles, 813–815

Trigonometric identities
  on calculator, 818–819
  description of, 815–817
  double-angle formulas and, 925–928
  fundamental, 905
  guidelines to verifying, 911–912
  half-angle formulas and, 928–930
  review of, 974
  review of principal, 930
  to solve trigonometric equations, 939–942
  sum and difference formulas and, 915–921
  to verify other identities, 905–911
Trigonometry
  applications for, 887–895, 959–960
  bearings and, 890–892
  connecting concepts in, 836
  explanation of, 810
  problem solving with, 819–821
  right triangle, 810–821
  simple harmonic motion and, 892–895
Trinomials. *See also* Polynomials
  explanation of, 303
  factoring, 328–334
  of form $ax^2 + bx + c$, 330–333
  of form $x^2 + bx + c$, 328–330
  perfect square, 332, 337–338, 516
  positive and negative constant in, 331

U
Union
  of linear inequalities, 178–179
  of sets, 88
Unit circle, 838–839
Unit distance, 9

V
Value of expression, 25
Variables
  dependent and independent, 127
  in radicand, 445
Variation
  combined, 430–431
  constant of, 426, 428, 429
  direct, 426–427
  inverse, 427–429
  joint, 429–430
Vertex, of parabola, 623, 624, 628
Vertex formula, 633–634
Vertical asymptotes, of rational functions, 640–641
Vertical lines
  equations of, 162
  graphs of, 140–141
  slope of, 149–151, 163
Vertical line test, 123–125, 136
Vertical shifts
  explanation of, 171–173
  in sinusoidal graphs, 861–862
Visual patterns, 717

W
Whole numbers, 9
Work problems, 536–538

X
x-axis, 109
x-coordinates, 110, 462
x-intercepts
  explanation of, 114
  method to find, 114, 138
  of polynomial functions, 353–354

Y
y-axis, 109
y-coordinates, 110, 462
y-intercepts
  explanation of, 114
  graphing line using slope and, 157–158
  method to find, 114, 138
  slope-intercept form and, 149

Z
Zero-factor property
  explanation of, 347
  to solve quadratic equations, 347–350, 514
Zero matrix, 253
Zeros, of polynomial functions, 353, 543–546, 548, 550–551

Photo Credits

Chapter 1

Page 1 Mira.com

Page 2 Sepp Seitz/Woodfin Camp & Associates

Page 8 © The Boeing Company

Chapter 2

Page 46 Annette Brieger/Goldpitt/Pearson Education/PH College

Page 59 Richard B. Levine/Newscom

Page 61 Jeremy Woodhouse/Getty Images

Page 64 Jeff Robbins/AP Wide World Photos

Page 70 Georgia, Fredrica/Photo Researchers

Chapter 3

Page 108 Private Collection/Boltin Picture Library/Bridgeman Art Library

Page 113 Bonn Sequenz/Imapress/The Image Works

Page 129 Mark Richards/PhotoEdit

Page 135 Corbis

Page 135 Royalty-free/AGE Fotostock America

Page 161 Royalty Free/CORBIS

Page 166 Michael Newman/Photo Edit

Page 187 David Young Wolff/Photo Edit

Chapter 4

Page 195 David Young Wolff/Photo Edit

Page 196 Lon C. Diehl/PhotoEdit

Page 222 SuperStock

Page 223 Visions of America, LLC/Alamy Images Royalty Free

Page 238 Pascal Parrot/Sygma-Corbis

Chapter 5

Page 250 Colin Anderson/Jupiter Images/Brand X/Alamy Images Royalty Free

Page 262 NASA/Tim Furniss/Genesis Space Photo Library

Page 277 RCA Communications

Chapter 6

Page 295 © F. Hall

Page 301 Animals Animals/John Lemker

Page 305 REUTERS/Jean-Philippe Arles/Landov Media

Page 357 PhotoDisc/Getty Images

Chapter 7

Page 370 John Eder/G.D.T./Stone/Getty Images

Page 397 Pictor Images/ImageState Media Partners Limited

Page 415 Spike Mafford/Getty Images

Page 420 Rob Melnychuk/Getty Images

Page 421 Amy C. Etra/PhotoEdit

Page 424 Michael Gadomski/Photo Researchers

Page 428 Richard A. Cooke III/Getty Images Inc.—Stone Allstock

Page 432 Ken Welsh/AGE Fotostock America

Chapter 8

Page 441 William West/Agence France Presse/Getty Images

Page 457 Susan Findlay/Masterfile

Page 486 Tom Carter/PhotoEdit

Page 498 Photodisc/Royalty Free/Getty Images

Chapter 9

Page 519 Tony Freeman/PhotoEdit

Page 522 David Parker/Science Photo Library/Photo Researchers

Page 531 Dr. Chikaraishi/National Institute for Fusion Science

Page 532 Shane Pedersen/Wildlight Photo

Page 537 Zefa Collection/CORBIS—NY

Page 540 Tim Flach/Getty Images Inc.—Stone Allstock

Page 540 Arthur S. Aubry Photography/Getty Images

Page 559 AP Wide World Photos

Chapter 10

Page 564 Andrew McClenaghan/Photo Researchers

Page 588 Alfred Pasieka/Peter Arnold

Page 611 Weiss/Sunset/Animals Animals

Chapter 11

Page 622 Peter Adams/Getty Images

Page 638 Robert Harding/Robert Harding Images

Page 645 Yuriko Nakao-Reuters/Corbis

Page 661 Steve Vidler/ImageState Media Partners Limited

Chapter 12

Page 718 LSHTM/Getty Images

Chapter 13

Page 728 Jerry Driendl/Getty Images

Page 746 Larry Kolvoord/The Image Works

Page 750 Paul S. Howell

Page 756 Corrado Giambalvo/AP Wide World Photos

Page 764 Manoj Shah/Getty Images

Page 772 Bettman/Corbis

Chapter 14

Page 794 San Francisco MOMA/Olivier Laude Photography

Page 825 Wesley Hitt/Photographer's Choice/Getty Images

Page 838 nagelestock.com/Alamy Images

Page 845 Dale O'Dell Photography

Page 887 Scott Kleinman/Stone/Getty Images

Page 895 Paul Sakuma/AP Photos

Chapter 15

Page 902 Idamini/Alamy Images

Page 932 Dia Max/Getty Images

Page 945 Frank Clarkson

Page 957 Tom Bean/CORBIS